Easy to read
Bible
Simple English Version

First edition 2016

Published by CIS
© As Told in the Bible

All rights reserved

Royalties from the © As Told in the Bible collection, support young Christians to undertake mission trips around the world.

Designed and typeset by CIS

The authors and publisher are grateful to the following for permission to reproduce material in this book:

© Wycliffe Associates (UK)

Every effort has been made to contact the copyright holders and we apologise if any have been overlooked. Should copyright have been unwittingly infringed in this book, the owners should contact the publishers, who will make correction at reprint.

Welcome to As Told in the Bible – a collection of Bibles translated into clear, understandable, simple, modern English

As told in the Bible is a collection of easy-to-read Bibles which aims to give today's reader's maximum understanding of the original bible text. They do not follow the traditional vocabulary and style found in the historic English Bible versions. Instead they attempt to present the biblical content and message of the bible in everyday, simple, modern English.

These easy to read bibles are suitable for all ages and can be read alongside your traditional bible.

Our mission is to help people to read, understand, and apply the "Word of God" to their lives by providing Bible Translations, Bible Commentaries, and Bible Studies in simple modern English.

This Bible edition concentrates on the translation of all chapters and verses of both the Old and New Testaments. It also includes a list of where you will find passages on well-known Bible events, key people as well as passages to use for help and guidance.

Books of the Old Testament:

Genesis Page: 21

Genesis is the first book in the Old Testament section of the Bible.

The Book of Genesis explains that God created a beautiful world (Genesis 1). But the first people did not obey God (Genesis 3). Everyone suffers because of this.

Genesis is a history book. It tells the life stories of many important people. For example: Adam and Eve; Cain and Abel; Noah; Abraham and Sarah; Isaac and Ishmael; Jacob; and Joseph and his brothers.

Jesus was born 1600 years after the events at the end of Genesis. But even in the book of Genesis, God promised that Jesus would come. See Genesis 3:15, Galatians 3:6-20, Hebrews 7 and Hebrews 11:1-22.

Exodus Page: 45

Exodus is a history book in the Bible's Old Testament. And Exodus is also a law book.

The people called Hebrews were slaves in Egypt. God sent Moses to free them (Exodus 3). The people in Egypt did not want to free these slaves. But God caused many terrible troubles in Egypt. These troubles forced the people in Egypt to free their Hebrew slaves. So, the Hebrew people left Egypt.

God promised the land called Israel to the Hebrew people. But the journey to Israel was through a desert. God did many wonderful things to help the people through the desert. God provided water (Exodus 17) and food (Exodus 16).

Moses met God at a mountain called Sinai (Exodus 19). There, God gave the law to Moses (Exodus chapters 20-30). Moses made a special tent where the priests would serve God (Exodus chapters 35-40).

Leviticus Page: 69

The Book of Leviticus is about the law of God. The law teaches us that God is holy. The Book of Leviticus contains many rules for the Hebrew people.

But we do not obey all the rules in Leviticus today, because we trust Jesus (see Galatians 3:23-25).

The Book of Leviticus also describes the duties of priests during the time of the Old Testament. And, in Leviticus 23, there is a list of special holidays, when the Hebrew people praised God together.

God also told the people that they must kill animals. And, they gave these animals to God. The people did this so that God would forgive their evil deeds (Leviticus chapters 1-7). This teaches us why Jesus had to die. Jesus died so that today, God forgives our evil deeds. We must confess our evil deeds to God. And we must invite God into our lives.

The Book of Leviticus is in the Old Testament part of the Bible.

Numbers Page: 83

The Book of Numbers is a law book in the Old Testament section of the Bible. But the Book of Numbers is also a history book. It is the story of the people whom Moses led through the desert. Moses counted the people in Numbers 1 and Numbers 26.

The people did not always obey God. They complained about the food in the desert (Numbers 11 and Numbers 21). They refused to enter the land that God had promised to them (Numbers 13). They even wanted to return to Egypt (Numbers 14). This is why they were in the desert for 40 years.

The Book of Numbers also tells the story of Balaam. Balaam was a foreign prophet (holy man). Balaam intended to announce an evil fate for the people.

But instead, Balaam saw that God was with them. Balaam spoke only the words that God wanted him to say. So, Balaam blessed the people (Numbers chapters 22-24).

Deuteronomy Page: 103

Deuteronomy is the last book about Moses. It is in the Old Testament part of the Bible.

The Book of Deuteronomy contains the instructions that Moses gave to the people, just before his death. He reminded them about the things that happened in the desert. He taught them God's law. He encouraged them to obey God. Then, God would help them; and good things would happen. But if they did not obey God, they would suffer (Deuteronomy 28).

Moses was the greatest prophet (holy man) in the Old Testament. But God did not allow Moses to lead the people into Israel. Moses appointed Joshua to lead the people after Moses' death.

Joshua Page: 124

Joshua led God's people after Moses died. Joshua brought the people into the land that God had promised to them. And he commanded their army in many battles against evil nations. God helped Joshua to win these battles. Joshua's first battle was the battle of Jericho (Joshua 6).

Joshua also directed the people to obey God's law (Joshua 5, Joshua 7 and Joshua 24). The Book of Joshua also contains records about the division of land (Joshua chapters 13-21).

The Book of Joshua is a history book from the Bible's Old Testament.

Judges Page: 136

The Book of Judges is a history book in the Old Testament of the Bible. But it does not only contain history. It also teaches us to trust God more.

The Book of Judges contains the history of about 300 years when Israel had no king. Instead, God appointed special people, called 'judges' to lead the people. These 'judges' were not like judges today. They were holy men (and one woman), whom God called. They led the people in battles. And they helped the people to serve God.

When there was a judge, the people obeyed God. And God helped the people in their battles against their enemies. But, when there was no judge, the people forgot God. And God allowed their enemies to be strong. So, the people asked God to help. And then, God appointed another judge. (Judges 2:16-19).
Some of the famous judges were Deborah (Judges Chapters 4-5), Gideon (Judges Chapters 6-8) and Samson (Judges Chapters 13-16).

Ruth Page: 147

The Book of Ruth is a beautiful story. It is in the Old Testament part of the Bible.

The Book of Ruth is about a young widow, Ruth. Ruth was a foreigner. But she came to Israel to help Naomi. (Naomi was Ruth's husband's mother.)

Ruth left her own gods, to serve the real God. Naomi and Ruth were very poor. But Ruth could collect any grain that remained after the harvest. This was God's law. And one man who respected this law was called Boaz. So, Ruth came to Boaz's field to collect grain. Boaz saw Ruth and he loved her.

He agreed to pay her family's debts, so that he could marry Ruth.

Ruth was just a poor foreigner. But her family became Israel's royal family. Both King David and Jesus belonged to this family.

1 Samuel Page: 149

1 Samuel is a history book in the Old Testament of the Bible. This book teaches us that we must always obey God.

1 Samuel tells the story of the first king of Israel. For many centuries, Israel had no kings. The people did whatever they wanted to do. But God appointed special judges to lead the people.

The last of these special judges was Samuel (1 Samuel 7:15). Samuel was a very holy man.

When Samuel was old, the people asked Samuel to appoint a king (1 Samuel 8). God told Samuel to appoint Saul. Saul sometimes obeyed God. But sometimes, Saul was evil.

So, God chose David to be king instead of Saul (1 Samuel 16). David trusted God. We see this when David fought Goliath (1 Samuel 17). And David loved God. But David did not become king immediately. Saul was still the king. David respected Saul. David even refused to attack Saul. The book of 1 Samuel ends with the story of Saul's death.

2 Samuel Page: 167

2 Samuel is in the Old Testament of the Bible. It is a history book. We can learn many lessons for our own lives from the events in this book.

The book of 2 Samuel is about King David. The book discusses the events while David was king. David's soldiers fought many wars. They obtained the city of Jerusalem in a successful battle (2 Samuel 5). Jerusalem became their capital city.

David loved God. David was a good king, but he made some terrible errors. He had sex with a married woman called Bathsheba (2 Samuel 11). And David ordered the death of Bathsheba's husband. Later, David confessed his evil deed to God (Psalm 51).

Afterwards, David's own son, Absalom, fought against David (2 Samuel 18).

But God saved David from all his enemies (2 Samuel 22).

1 Kings Page: 186

1 Kings is a book about the history of the people called Israelites. It is in the Old Testament, in the Bible. The Books of Kings continue the story that began in the Books of Samuel. In these history books, the Bible contains many examples which teach how we should live (2 Timothy 3:16).

1 Kings begins with the story of Solomon. Solomon was a wise king at first (1 Kings 3). Then he became rich (1 Kings 10:14-29). He built a temple (house of God) in Jerusalem (1 Kings 6). But then Solomon took many wives. When he was old, they encouraged him to serve evil gods (1 Kings 11).

After Solomon died, there was a revolution. The country called Israel became two countries. The south was called Judah. Rehoboam was the first king of Judah. The north was still called Israel. Here Jeroboam became king (1 Kings 12).

The writer wants to teach a lesson. When the kings obeyed God, the people were at peace. When the kings did not obey God, but served other gods, bad things happened. When the people of Israel stopped serving God, he sent a prophet (a holy man). He was Elijah. He did wonderful things. He told the people to serve God again.

2 Kings Page: 203

2 Kings continues the story of the nations of Israel and Judah. It is a history book, from the Old Testament of the Bible. In these history books, the Bible contains many important lessons for us today (2 Timothy 3:16).

2 Kings describes how the kings of these nations refused to obey God's law. The kings and their people did not respect God. Instead, they served evil gods. And the behaviour of the people was very wicked. However, there were a few people who truly served God. And God sent his servants (called "the prophets") to warn the evil people.

But the nations of Israel and Judah would not obey the words of the prophets. God allowed enemy nations to attack. These nations destroyed Israel and (later) Judah. And the soldiers took the inhabitants of Israel and Judah to distant countries. But God still cared about the people from Israel and Judah.

God promised that, in the future, these people (or their children or grandchildren) would return home.

2 Kings begins with the end of the story of Elijah. Elijah was a great prophet of God. And God did not allow Elijah to die. Instead, Elijah went up to heaven. Elijah's companion was a man named Elisha. Elisha saw Elijah rise to heaven, in a vehicle of fire (2 Kings 2).

1 Chronicles Page: 220

Chronicles is a history book in the Bible's Old Testament. The Books of Chronicles contain the same story as the Books of Samuel and Kings. But the

Books of Chronicles also contain many official records and lists of people.

1 Chronicles contains the story of King David. Especially, the book describes his plans for the temple (the house of God in Jerusalem). David gave careful instructions to the priests. He wanted everyone to serve God properly.

2 Chronicles Page: 239

2 Chronicles contains the story of the kings of Israel. It discusses the 400 years after King David. It is in the Old Testament of the Bible.

2 Chronicles describes the great temple (house of God) that Solomon built in Jerusalem. This building was a great work for God. The temple was a very beautiful building. And the priests and people came to the temple to pray. After Solomon died, his country divided into two countries. 2 Chronicles describes the kings of both these countries and their work. Some of these kings were good kings, who served God. But most of these kings were very evil. They did not obey God's law. They served false gods. And these kings were cruel to the people. So, God allowed the enemies of these two countries to attack. And the enemies destroyed both countries.

Ezra Page: 260

God's special people, the Jews, did not obey God. So he punished them. He allowed the king of Babylon and his army to defeat them. The king of Babylon ordered most Jews to live in Babylon. Babylon was a long way from their own country, called Judah.

Many years later, the army from Persia defeated the army from Babylon. The book of Ezra in the Bible tells us that the king of Persia allowed the Jews to return to their own land. Not all the Jews returned to Judah, but some did return.

The Jews started to build a temple (house of God) in Jerusalem. But the people who lived near them did not want the Jews back in the land. They opposed the Jews so that the Jews did not continue to build the temple. Many years later, God helped the Jews and they finished the building.

Many years after that, Ezra led another group of Jews who returned to Judah. Ezra was a teacher who taught the people from God's word. God sent Ezra to teach the people so that they would become God's special people again. Often the people did not obey God's word, but Ezra continued to teach them. He told them how to live in a way that would please God.

Nehemiah Page: 268

God's special people, the Jews, did not obey God. So he punished them. He allowed the king of Babylon and his army to defeat them. The king of Babylon ordered most Jews to live in Babylon. Babylon was a long way from their country, called Judah.

Many years later, the army from Persia defeated the army from Babylon. The king of Persia allowed the Jews to return to their own land. Only some of the Jews returned to Judah.

Many years later a man called Hanani left Judah to visit his brother, Nehemiah. Nehemiah was an important servant of the king of Persia. Nehemiah asked Hanani for news about Jerusalem, which was the chief city in Judah. Hanani told Nehemiah that the walls of Jerusalem were only heaps of stones. Fire had burned the gates of the city. This news made Nehemiah very sad. So Nehemiah asked the king to send him to Jerusalem to build the walls of the city again.

The book of Nehemiah in the Bible tells the story of how Nehemiah and the people built the walls of Jerusalem again. The people who lived near Jerusalem did not want the Jews to build the city again. They opposed the Jews and tried to stop the work. But God helped them and they finished the work in 52 days.

God wanted the Jews to become his special people again. So Nehemiah, with the help of Ezra, helped the people to obey God. But often the people did not obey God's word. They had forgotten that God had punished the people many years earlier. He did that because they did not obey him. God had allowed a foreign king to defeat the Jews. That was why the city of Jerusalem needed these repairs.

Esther Page: 275

Esther belonged to God's special people, the Jews. Esther and many other Jews lived in the land called Persia. Persia was a long way from their own land.

The king of Persia was angry with the queen and he sent her away. Then he searched for another wife who would be the new queen. He chose Esther.

One of the king's chief officials, called Haman, hated the Jews and he plotted to destroy them. But Esther's uncle Mordecai asked Esther to speak to the king to save the Jews. Although Esther was the queen, Mordecai was asking her to do a dangerous thing. People could not go to see the king if he had not invited them. But Esther did what Mordecai asked. The king was pleased with her and listened to her. The king gave to the evil Haman the punishment that Haman had wanted to give to the Jews.

The book of Esther does not mention the name of God. This is strange for a book that is in the Bible. Sometimes God seems to be silent. We might even think that he does not care about us. The writer of the book of Esther probably wanted his readers to realise that God is always in control. Although we cannot see God, he is always doing things in the world. Nobody can stop his plans. The events in the book of Esther show us that God is in control.

Job Page: 279

The Book of Job (in the Bible's Old Testament) is a long poem. The Book of Job discusses why innocent people suffer. God cares about people who suffer troubles. And God will help them, although sometimes they must be patient.

Job was a good man. But Job lost all his possessions. Job's children died. Job became so ill that he wanted to die. But Job refused to insult God.

Job's friends supposed that Job was ill because of his evil deeds. But Job was innocent. Then, a wise man named Elihu explained the truth to Job and his friends. And God proved to them that God is great. God also showed them that he cares. Finally, God wanted Job to pray for his friends. In the end,

God made Job successful again.

Psalms Page: 318

The Book of Psalms is a collection of 150 ancient songs. King David wrote many Psalms (that is, songs).

There are many different subjects. Many Psalms are glad songs which praise God (for example, Psalms 103 and 150). Other Psalms are sad prayers (Psalm 74). Some Psalms explain that God will rescue us from our troubles (Psalms 40 and 41). And some Psalms are about the history of Israel (Psalms 74 and 78). Psalm 119 is about the Bible. In Psalm 51, David confesses an evil deed. Psalm 22 describes how Jesus would suffer. Psalm 2 tells us that God will rule the world. Psalm 1 teaches that we must love God.

The Psalms are a very special part of the Bible. We can learn many things about God from their beautiful words. They are in the Bible's Old Testament.

Proverbs Page: 370

The Book of Proverbs is a collection of articles about wisdom. It is in the Old Testament part of the Bible. Its main author was King Solomon.

The Book of Proverbs teaches that we must respect God. This is the most important lesson about wisdom.

The Book of Proverbs begins with Solomon's advice to his son. In Proverbs chapters 1-9, Solomon explains the choice between wise behaviour and foolish behaviour. Good people are wise because they respect God. But evil people are fools. God will punish evil people. So, Solomon advised his son to study wisdom.

In Proverbs chapters 10-22, there are 375 proverbs (wise words). These proverbs teach us how to be wise in many different situations. Then, there are 30 wise lessons (Proverbs chapters 22-24), many more proverbs (Proverbs chapters 25-29), two hard puzzles, and a poem (Proverbs chapters 30-31).

Ecclesiastes Page: 392

The Book of Ecclesiastes is in the Bible's Old Testament. We do not know who wrote Ecclesiastes. Many people think that the author of Ecclesiastes was King Solomon. However, in the book, the author simply calls himself 'The Teacher'.

Solomon was very wise. But he did not know the purpose of his own life. He discovered that pleasure achieved nothing. He realised that even a wise man would die like a fool. And he did not know the purpose of work (Ecclesiastes 2). He even saw that money has no real value (Ecclesiastes 5).

Solomon did know that rulers should be fair (Ecclesiastes 8). And everybody must respect God ((Ecclesiastes 5). And he believed that wisdom is good (Ecclesiastes 9:13-18).

Solomon warned that everybody will die (Ecclesiastes 12). So, we must respect God now. We should not delay.

Song of Solomon Page: 400

The Song of Solomon is also called the Song of Songs. This book is a beautiful love poem. It is in the Bible's Old Testament.

The Song of Solomon is the story of the king and the woman that he loves. So, he asks her to marry him. But she hesitates. And he encourages her.

In the end, they marry. They are glad to be together. They love each other deeply.

The Song of Solomon teaches us that God loves his people. Elsewhere, the Bible describes Christians as 'the bride of Christ' (2 Corinthians 11:2).

Isaiah Page: 410

Isaiah was a prophet (holy man). God appointed Isaiah to warn the people in Judah. The people were evil. So, they should ask God to forgive them.
Isaiah lived before Ezekiel and Jeremiah.

Isaiah described the future of many countries (Isaiah chapters 13-24). But especially, he warned his own people in Judah and Israel (Isaiah chapters 28-31).

But this book also contains many happy words. Isaiah wrote about a child who would have no human father (Isaiah 7:14). This child would become king (Isaiah 9:6). He would rule fairly (Isaiah 32). And the people would be glad (Isaiah 35). So, God will comfort his people (Isaiah 40). This child would be God's servant (Isaiah 42). But people would not accept him. God's servant would die so that God will forgive us. Then, God's servant would live again (Isaiah 53). Everyone must trust him (Isaiah 55). God will forgive the people who confess their evil deeds to God (Isaiah 59). So, God himself will rescue his people (Isaiah 63).

We now know that Isaiah wrote these words about Jesus.

The Book of Isaiah is in the Old Testament section of the Bible.

Jeremiah Page: 453

Jeremiah was a prophet (holy man). God chose Jeremiah as a prophet when Jeremiah was a young man (Jeremiah 1). Jeremiah lived at the same time as the last kings of Judah. Jeremiah warned the people that God would punish them (Jeremiah 4). They must return to God. Otherwise, they would suffer terrible troubles (Jeremiah chapters 14-16).

God wanted the people to trust him. But they refused (Jeremiah 18). So, God told Jeremiah that the people must serve their enemies for 70 years (Jeremiah 25). But then, people from Israel would return to their land (Jeremiah chapters 30-33).

Jeremiah also wrote about the future of other nations (Jeremiah chapters 46-51). And Jeremiah knew that God would send Jesus (Jeremiah 23:1-8, Jeremiah 31:31-37, and Jeremiah 33).

This Book is in the Old Testament section of the Bible.

Lamentations Page: 509

Lamentations is a book of very sad poems. Lamentations is in the Old Testament of the Bible.

Jeremiah wrote the Book of Lamentations after soldiers from Babylon destroyed Jerusalem.

Jerusalem had been a beautiful city. The temple (house of God) was in Jerusalem. But the soldiers destroyed the buildings. They killed many people (Lamentations 2:21). They led the young men away to Babylon. The soldiers even forced the young women to have sex with them (Lamentations 5:11-13).

Jeremiah saw these terrible events. And he knew why these things happened. They happened because the people in Jerusalem had not obeyed God's law. The people prayed to evil gods. And the people were very evil. God sent his servants to warn the people. But the people did not change their behaviour. So, God punished them (2 Chronicles 36:14-17).

Jeremiah was very sad when he wrote Lamentations. But he still had hope. Between his sad words, he wrote about God's love. Jeremiah knew that God cares (Lamentations 3:22-33).

Jeremiah wanted the people to trust God again (Lamentations 3:40-42). And Jeremiah knew that God would not always punish his people (Lamentations 4:22). Jeremiah prayed that the people could return to Jerusalem (Lamentations 5:21).

Ezekiel Page: 518

Ezekiel was a prophet (holy man) who lived at the same time as the last kings of Judah. God showed Ezekiel events that would happen in the future.

God told Ezekiel that Ezekiel must warn the people about these events (Ezekiel 33).

God would punish Judah because its people did not obey God's law. Their enemies would surround Jerusalem, which was Judah's capital city (Ezekiel chapters 4-5). God would leave his temple (the house of God in Jerusalem) - Ezekiel 10. This was because the leaders of Judah served false gods (Ezekiel 8). And the soldiers from Babylon would destroy Jerusalem (Ezekiel 21). God would also punish other evil nations (Ezekiel chapters 25-32).

But God still cared about his people (Ezekiel 37). God would send someone from David's family to be their leader (Ezekiel 37:24-28). We now know that this person was Jesus.

God also showed Ezekiel a picture of a new temple in the future (Ezekiel chapters 40-48). God himself would return to this temple (Ezekiel 43).
The Book of Ezekiel is in the Old Testament section of the Bible.

Daniel Page: 545

God's special people, the Jews, did not obey God. So God punished them. He allowed the king of Babylon and his army to defeat them. The king of Babylon forced most Jews to live in Babylon. Babylon was a long way from their own country.

A young man called Daniel was among the people who went to live in Babylon.

The first part of the book of Daniel in the Bible tells some stories from the life of Daniel and his friends. Many times the people of Babylon tried to make them forget the real God and to serve false gods. The people of Babylon even tried to kill Daniel and his friends because they would not serve the false gods. But Daniel and his friends were loyal to the real God. Daniel became a very important man in the government of Babylon.
The second part of the book of Daniel tells about Daniel's dreams. These were strange dreams. Sometimes Daniel was awake when he had his dreams.
These were special dreams that God sent to Daniel to tell him what would happen in the future. Some things that Daniel saw in his dreams have now happened. Other things that God told Daniel in his dreams have not happened yet. But God is in control of the future. God will do what he has promised.

Hosea Page: 555

Hosea was a prophet (holy man). The Book of Hosea is in the Bible (Old Testament).

God told Hosea to marry a wife who was not loyal (Hosea 1). Hosea loved his wife. He tried to persuade his wife to remain with him. His wife was not loyal to him. But Hosea still loved her. And he still wanted her to be his wife (Hosea 3).

Hosea's troubles with his wife were like God's troubles with Israel. The people in Israel were not loyal to God. God loved them. But they were very evil.

So, God would punish them for their evil deeds. But afterwards, the people from Israel would trust in God again. They would confess their evil deeds to God. God would forgive them. And he would love them again (Hosea 14).

Joel Page: 566

Joel was a prophet (holy man). The Book of Joel is in the Old Testament part of the Bible.

The Book of Joel describes some terrible events. Joel called these events 'the Day of God'. A terrible army would attack Jerusalem. They would destroy everything. Nobody could escape from this army.

So, the people must confess their evil deeds to God. Even when these terrible things happen, they must ask God to save them (Joel 2:12-17).

Then, God will be kind to his people. He will hear their prayers. He will cause this terrible army to leave. He will provide food for his people. And he will send his Spirit on all people (Joel 2:28-32).

God will also punish the nations that attack Jerusalem (Joel 3:1-16). But God will protect his own people always (Joel 3:17-21).

Amos Page: 571

Amos was a not a prophet (holy man). Amos looked after sheep. But God sent Amos with a message to his nation (Amos 7:14-15).

Amos knew that many nations were evil. Because of these evil deeds, God would punish the nations (Amos chapters 1-2).

But Amos's own nation, Israel, was also evil. They were cruel to poor people. The judges were not fair in court. And they served evil gods. Amos warned his people that they must confess their evil deeds to God. And they must learn to do the right things (Amos 5). Otherwise, God would allow Israel's enemies to attack (Amos chapters 6-9). And these enemies would destroy the nation.

But God would not always punish the people from Israel. After these terrible punishments, God would allow some of the people to return to their own land (Amos 9:11-15).

The Book of Amos is in the Bible (Old Testament).

Obadiah Page: 575

Obadiah was a prophet (holy man). The Book of Obadiah is in the Bible (Old Testament).

The Book of Obadiah contains a short message about the country called Edom. The people from Edom were relatives of the people from Israel. But the inhabitants of Edom refused to help when the people from Israel suffered. So, God would punish the people from Edom for this evil deed. God would destroy their country.

In the future, people who trust God will live in Edom.

Jonah Page: 577

God sent Jonah to Ninevah. Nineveh was an enemy of Jonah's country, Israel. So, Jonah did not want to go to Nineveh.

Jonah tried to escape God. He tried to travel elsewhere, by ship. But there was a terrible storm. Jonah knew that God had caused the storm. So, he asked the sailors to throw him into the sea. But Jonah did not drown, because God sent a whale (large fish) to swallow Jonah. Then, Jonah prayed to God again. He thanked God, who had rescued him (Jonah 2). And God caused the fish to return Jonah to the dry land.

So, Jonah went to Nineveh. He warned the people that they must confess their evil deeds to God. Otherwise, God would destroy their nation. The people obeyed Jonah. So, God forgave the people in Nineveh. God did not destroy Nineveh at this time.

But Jonah was sad, because Nineveh was his enemy. Jonah wanted God to destroy Nineveh. But God told Jonah that God cares about the people from every nation.

The Book of Jonah is in the Bible (Old Testament).

Micah Page: 578

Micah was a prophet (holy man). The Book of Micah is in the Old Testament part of the Bible.

Micah warned the people in Israel and Judah (Micah 1). God would punish them for their evil deeds. The people had cruel schemes. They were thieves. And they listened to false prophets (false holy men) whose words were lies (Micah 2).

God did not want terrible things to happen. God wants to teach people. And he wants the nations to be at peace (chapter 4). God promised to send a leader for Israel. This leader would be from Bethlehem. We now know that this leader was Jesus (Micah 5:1-5).

So, God accused the people (Micah 6). God did not want their gifts (Micah 6:6). God wanted them to be humble and to do the right things (Micah 6:8).

But they refused to obey God. They were proud, and they did many evil deeds. This is why God would punish them (Micah 6:9-16).

But afterwards, when the people served God, Israel would become a great nation again (Micah 7:7-20).

Nahum Page: 587

Nahum was a prophet (holy man). He wrote about a country which was an enemy of Israel, called Nineveh. The people in Nineveh were very evil (Nahum 3:1).

The people from Nineveh were also cruel to the people in other countries. But God cares about the people who trust him (Nahum 1:7). So, God would send the enemies of Nineveh to destroy Nineveh.

God would end Nineveh's cruelty. But God would help his own people, Israel. And Israel would become a great nation again (Nahum 1:15).

The Book of Nahum is in the Bible (Old Testament).

Habakkuk Page: 588

Habakkuk wrote a book in the Old Testament part of the Bible. Habakkuk was a prophet (holy man). In his book, Habakkuk complained twice to God.

Habakkuk asked God why good people must suffer. And, Habakkuk asks why cruel people seem to succeed.

Firstly, Habakkuk complained that the rulers of his country were wicked. God replied that soldiers from Babylon would attack these wicked rulers (Habakkuk 1:2-11).

But Habakkuk complained to God again. Habakkuk said that God allows cruel people to attack good people (Habakkuk 1:12 to Habakkuk 2:1). God replied that he would punish cruel people. But this does not always happen immediately. But God told Habakkuk to write this down, because God will definitely punish evil people. (Habakkuk 2:2-20).

So, good people must trust God (Habakkuk 2:4). The time will come when God will rule the whole world (Habakkuk 2:14).

The Book of Habakkuk ends with a Psalm (song) - Habakkuk 3. This song says that God will rescue his people.

Zephaniah Page: 591

Zephaniah was a prophet (holy man). The Book of Zephaniah is in the Bible (Old Testament).

Zephaniah explained that God would punish many countries because of their evil deeds (Zephaniah chapters 1-2). God would also punish the evil people in Jerusalem (Zephaniah 3:1-5).

So, the people should pray to God (Zephaniah 2:1-3). They must confess their evil deeds to God. And they must be humble.

When these terrible punishments happen, God will protect the people who trust him (Zephaniah 3:9-13). God will rescue them. He loves them. And he will make them glad (Zephaniah 3:14-20).

Haggai Page: 595

Haggai was a prophet (holy man). He lived at the same time as Zechariah. Then, some people from Israel had returned from Babylon. They rebuilt their own houses in Jerusalem. Haggai explained why they were poor. He said that God was not blessing them.

Haggai told them that they should also rebuild God's temple (the house of God) - Haggai 1.

The new temple was small. But God told Haggai that it would be greater than the old temple (Haggai 2). And now, God would bless the people because they had rebuilt the temple.

Zechariah Page: 596

Zechariah was a prophet (holy man). The Book of Zechariah is in the Old Testament part of the Bible.

Zechariah lived at the same time as Haggai. God showed Zechariah many strange pictures to encourage the people in Jerusalem. These pictures explained good things that God would do in the future. Zechariah wrote about some things that would happen during his own life. And we now know that Zechariah wrote some things about Jesus. Jesus is both a priest and a king (Zechariah 6:12-13). Zechariah describes Jesus' death in Zechariah 12:10.

Some things that Zechariah described have not happened yet (Zechariah 14). These things will happen in the future.

Malachi Page: 603

Malachi was a prophet (holy man). The Book of Malachi is the last book in the Bible's Old Testament.

Malachi said that God accused the people. They were doing many wrong things. They did not give the best gifts to God (Malachi 1:6-14). The priests did not teach well (Malachi 2:1-9). The men divorced their wives without a proper reason (Malachi 2:13-16).

But God himself would come to his temple (the house of God) (Malachi 3:1-5). But before this, God would send his special servant. This servant would teach the correct way to serve God. Then, the people would be ready for God's arrival. This was good news for the people who respected God. But this was terrible news for the people who refused to obey God (Malachi 4).

Malachi's book was written after all the other books in the Old Testament. 400 years later, Jesus came. But before Jesus began his work, a special servant of God taught near the river Jordan. This servant of God was called John the Baptist. John taught the people that they must confess their evil deeds to God. He taught that they must prepare themselves for the arrival of the Christ. (The 'Christ' means God's king. Many Old Testament prophets taught that the Christ would save us from the punishment for our evil deeds.)

Books of the New Testament

Matthew Page: 605

Matthew's Gospel (good news) is in the Bible's New Testament.

Matthew knew well the Bible's Old Testament. In the past, God appointed people (called 'prophets') to write about the future. Many prophets described Jesus' life and work. The things that the prophets wrote actually happened during Jesus' life on earth. Matthew explained this to prove that Jesus is the Christ. (The 'Christ' means God's king. The prophets said that the Christ would save us from the punishment for our evil deeds.)

Matthew's Gospel is a book about Jesus' life. Matthew wrote about the things that Jesus taught. His book includes a speech by Jesus, in Matthew chapters 5-7. This speech is called 'The Sermon on the Mount'.

Matthew's Gospel also explains that Jesus cured many ill people. Jesus caused blind people to see again (Matthew 20:29-34). He caused deaf people to hear again (Matthew 11:5). He freed people who had evil spirits (Matthew 8:28).

But some important people hated Jesus. They killed Jesus on the cross. But Jesus knew that this would happen (Matthew 16:21). The prophets had written that the Christ would die (Isaiah 53; Matthew 12:40). When Jesus died, he suffered the punishment for our evil deeds (Matthew 20:28, Matthew 26:28).

But Jesus did not remain dead. God caused Jesus to live again (Matthew 28). And Jesus is alive today, in heaven.

Mark Page: 636

The Gospel of Mark is the second book in the New Testament part of the Bible. Mark was the first person to write a Gospel. A Gospel is a book that describes the life and death of Jesus. The Gospels also explain how Jesus came back to life again.
People think that Mark got his information from Peter. Peter was a friend of Jesus.

Mark's Gospel is the shortest life story of Jesus. It is an exciting book. Jesus did many wonderful things. He cured ill people. He spoke wise words about God. And he warned about future events. The people were excited about Jesus. They followed Jesus. They listened to him. But they did not realise why God sent Jesus. They thought that Jesus would become their king. But Jesus knew the real reason why God sent him.

The rulers hated Jesus. They thought that Jesus would destroy their country. They did not care whether God had sent Jesus. They decided to kill Jesus. Jesus knew about this. But Jesus allowed these things to happen, because this was God's plan.

When Jesus was dying, the people were very afraid. Even Jesus' friend, Peter, denied that he knew Jesus. Even the priests insulted Jesus. Jesus' death was a terrible death (Mark chapters 14-15).

But some important people believed Jesus, even when he died. An important soldier said, 'This man (Jesus) was God's son.' And Joseph from Arimathea was bold, and he buried Jesus' body in his own grave. But, two days later, an angel (servant of God from heaven) announced that Jesus was alive again. Later, Jesus himself met his friends. They saw that he was alive. And he told them to take God's message to people from all nations.

Mark wrote his gospel for everyone. He did not only write it for his own people. People from all nations can become Christians.

Luke Page: 653

Luke's Gospel (good news) is a record, in order, of the main events in Jesus' life. Its author was Luke, who was a doctor. Luke was a friend of Paul.

Luke probably did not belong to the Jewish people. His book shows that Jesus cared about everyone. Jesus cured many ill people. Jesus cared about women (for example, Luke 7:11-17). Jesus allowed children to come to him (Luke 18:15-17). And Jesus cared about poor people (Luke 21:1-4).

Jesus taught many lessons to the people. Often, he told parables (stories with a meaning) to teach the people about God. Jesus wanted everybody to confess their evil deeds and to trust in God.

Some evil leaders opposed Jesus. They plotted that Jesus would die. Jesus knew about their plans (Luke 18:31-34). But Jesus also knew that God wanted him to die (Luke 22:20-22, Luke 22:42). And, after Jesus' death, God would cause Jesus to live again.

Luke describes these events. The Bible taught that these things would happen (Luke 24:25-27, Luke 24:44-49).

Luke explained these events further in his other book, called Acts (Acts chapters 2-3). When Jesus died, he suffered the punishment for our evil deeds. So, we must confess our evil deeds to God. And we must invite God into our lives.

John Page: 684

John was a close friend of Jesus. For three years, John lived with Jesus. John saw how Jesus behaved. And John believed that Jesus is God (John 1:1-18). John wrote his Gospel (good news) so that other people would believe this too (John 20:31).

John saw that Jesus did many wonderful things (John 21:25). Jesus cured ill people (John 4:43-54). Jesus walked on water (John 6:14-24). He provided food for 5000 men (John 6:1-15). Jesus was alive again after his own death (John 20). John describes these events in the same way as the other Gospels.

But the main part of John's Gospel is not about these wonderful deeds. Instead, many chapters contain Jesus' words. For example, John 13-17 contain Jesus' words on the night before he died. John thought that Jesus' words were wonderful (John 3:34). And we must accept Jesus' words. If we believe Jesus' words, then we will live with God in heaven always. But if we do not obey Jesus, God will punish us (John 3:36).

Jesus died so that we can live with God in heaven (John 3:16). This is why we must confess our evil deeds to God. And this is why we must invite Jesus into our lives. Then, we will become the children of God (John 1:12).

Acts Page: 701

The Book of Acts (in the New Testament of the Bible) is also called 'Acts of the Apostles'. The author of Acts was Luke, who also wrote the Gospel of Luke.

Acts tells the story of the first Christians. After Jesus went up to heaven, they waited in Jerusalem. Then, God sent his Holy Spirit (Acts 2). The Holy Spirit gave power to the first Christians. So, they told the people about Jesus. The Christians explained that the people must confess their evil deeds to God. Then, they must invite God into their lives.

The first Christians did wonderful things by God's power. Peter cured a man who could not walk by God's power (Acts 3:1-10). God even cured ill people when Peter's shadow went over them (Acts 5:15-16).

Many people opposed the first Christians. A Christian called Stephen did many wonderful things (Acts 6:8). But the rulers opposed him. They did not want him to speak about Jesus. So, the rulers killed Stephen. But Stephen was not afraid. He knew that he was going to heaven. Like Jesus, Stephen prayed for the people who were killing him (Acts 7:60).

But the number of Christians continued to increase. And new churches began in many areas, for example Samaria and Antioch. Soon, God taught Peter and the other Christians that God's good news is for everyone, from every nation (Acts 10). So, they began to speak to people who were not from Israel.

Saul was a religious leader who opposed the first Christians. Saul even helped to kill Stephen (Acts 8:1). But God spoke to Saul on the road to Damascus. And Saul became a Christian (Acts 9). He travelled to many places, to tell everyone about Jesus (Acts chapters 13-28). Later, Saul changed his name to Paul. Paul wrote many books in the New Testament of the Bible.

The first Christians had many dangers and many troubles. But they trusted God. And they told people about Jesus in each place where they went. God was with them. God did wonderful things wherever they went. And boldly, they taught the message of the Bible.

Romans Page: 729

The Book of Romans is a letter from Paul to the Christians in Rome. Rome was probably the largest city in the world. Paul wrote the letter about the year 57. He probably wrote it while he was living in Corinth.

The Book of Romans shows us how God can save us from the punishment for our evil deeds. And the Book of Romans also teaches how we should live. Some of the important things we can learn from this book are:

- Everyone has done wrong things against God.
- God is angry about our evil deeds.
- God saves people who trust him.
- We cannot save ourselves by our own good works.
- When Jesus died, he died for us.
- God's Spirit helps us to do what is right.
- God always loves us.
- God shows us how to live.

The Book of Romans is in the New Testament part of the Bible.

1 Corinthians Page: 743

Paul wrote this long letter to the Christians who lived in the city of Corinth. He had set up the church in Corinth when he himself lived there for 18 months (Acts 18). After he left the city, evil things happened in the church. So Paul wrote this letter to the Christians in Corinth, to help them.

Corinth was a city in the country of Greece. The people in Greece were proud of their clever minds. But Paul explained that God considers human wisdom to be foolish. So, Christians must recognise that Jesus Christ is their Lord. He has God's wisdom; and Christians must obey him always (1 Corinthians chapters 1-2).

Then they will be able to live holy lives. They will not quarrel with each other. They will be loyal to their husbands or wives. They will not try to understand the Bible by their own clever ideas. Instead, they will be true servants of Christ (1 Corinthians chapters 5-6).

Paul wanted to teach the Christians in Corinth how to praise God together. He taught them that they should share bread and wine to remember Jesus' death (1 Corinthians 11). God's Holy Spirit would help them to work together (1 Corinthians chapters 12 and 14). And God's greatest gift is love (1 Corinthians 13).

Paul also taught about life after death. After Jesus died, God caused Jesus to live again. Many people saw that Jesus was alive again (1 Corinthians 15:1-8). In the same way, God will cause us to live again after our deaths. God is even greater than death (1 Corinthians 15).

2 Corinthians Page: 754

This letter is in the Bible's New Testament. Paul wrote this letter to Christians in Corinth because there were false teachers in the church. They spoke badly about Paul. They said he kept changing his mind. This was because he did not visit Corinth. They also said he was not a genuine apostle*. Unlike the false teachers, Paul was not a great speaker. Also unlike them, Paul did not ask the church for money.

Paul explained why he had not visited them. He also explained why he had been so severe towards the Christians in Corinth. But he was happy that they had confessed their evil deeds to God. And now, they accepted Paul as a friend again. He was not a powerful person like the false teachers.

But because he was weak, people saw God's power through him. He had not come to talk about himself. He had come to tell them about Jesus. By the death of Jesus, God had changed them from enemies into friends. Then he asked them for a generous gift for the poor Christians in Judea.

Finally he gave reasons why he was a genuine apostle*. God chose him to be an apostle*. And he had suffered many troubles because he taught God's message. But Paul was glad to work for God. This was his answer to those who spoke badly about him.
*Apostle: a person whom God sent to teach the Christian message to the world.

Galatians Page: 761

Galatians is a book in the New Testament part of the Bible.

The Book of Galatians is a letter. Paul wrote it. It might be the first letter that Paul wrote to a Christian church. At that time, many people who were not Jews were becoming Christians. Some people said that the new Christians also needed to become Jews. These people said that the new Christians must obey all the laws and traditions of the Jews.

Paul said that a person became a Christian by believing in Jesus Christ. Jesus died to take the punishment for their evil deeds. They did not need to obey the laws and traditions of the Jews.

Many people today do not obey the traditions of the Jews. But these people have their own traditions and ideas. But traditions cannot be more important than God. So, these people must trust Jesus.

Paul also wrote about how Christians should live. They should show love and joy. They should be calm. Christians should be patient, kind and good.

And Christians should be loyal, gentle and show discipline. (Galatians 5:22-23.) Christians do good deeds to please God. But they are Christians because they trust in Jesus. So, their good deeds do not make them Christians.

Ephesians Page: 765

The Book of Ephesians is in the Bible's New Testament. Paul wrote this letter to the church at Ephesus, which he had led for over two years (Acts 19:10).

When Paul wrote the Book of Ephesians, Paul was in prison. But the letter is not a sad letter. Paul was excited about God's good gifts (Ephesians 1:3). Paul was pleased that the Christians in Ephesus continued to serve God. Paul wanted to encourage them. And he told them about his prayers for them (Ephesians 1:15-22, Ephesians 3:14-21).

Paul reminded the Christians in Ephesus that previously they were enemies of God. But God sent Jesus to die for them. Because of Jesus' death, they became friends of God (Ephesians 2:11-22). So, they should live lives that please God (Ephesians 4:17-32, Ephesians 5). And, they should trust God more. God had appointed teachers to help the Christians. And the Christians would learn to be more like Jesus. Troubles would come, so they needed

God's protection (Ephesians 6:10-18).

Philippians Page: 768

The Book of Philippians is in the Bible's New Testament. Paul wrote this letter to the church at Philippi, which he had established (Acts 16:11-40).

Paul was a prisoner when he wrote the book of Philippians. But he used his time in prison well. He even told his guards about Jesus (Philippians 1:13).
And he was glad that people were speaking about Jesus (Philippians 1:12-30).

Paul encouraged the Christians in Philippi to work together (Philippians 1:27). They should love each other (Philippians 2:1-4). So, they should be humble. Paul reminded them that Jesus was very humble. (Philippians 2:5-11). But now, God gives great honour to Jesus.
Paul warned the Christians about some people who did not know Jesus (Philippians 3:1-4, Philippians 3:17-19). He wanted the Christians to trust God more. Even Paul himself wanted to know God better (Philippians 3:10-11).

Paul did not pretend that he was already perfect (Philippians 3:12). But he knew that God will change us totally (Philippians 3:21). So, we should be glad (Philippians 4:4). We should do the right things (Philippians 4:8-9). And we should trust God to provide whatever we need (Philippians 4:10-19).

Colossians Page: 772

The Book of Colossians is Paul's letter to the Christians at Colosse. Paul had not visited Colosse. But he often prayed for the Christians there (Colossians 1:3-14).

Paul reminded the Christians about the importance of Jesus. Jesus is God, and he created everything. Then, Jesus became a man, so that he could die for us. Because Jesus died, God will forgive us. If we invite Jesus into our lives, we will become friends of God (Colossians 1:15-23).

Then, Paul warned the Christians about some people (Colossians 2). These people wanted the Christians to obey the ancient rules of the Hebrew nation. And these people said that real Christians must obey all such rules. Paul did not agree. He wrote that these rules were human traditions (Colossians 2:8). Christians ought to obey Christ, instead of tradition. Traditions might seem wise, but they cannot help us to live good lives (Colossians 2:23).

Paul reminded the Christians how they should live. They should think about the things in heaven (Colossians 3:2), because they belong with Christ (Colossians 3:3-4). They should not do evil deeds (Colossians 3:5-11). Instead, they should love other people (Colossians 3:12-14). And they should serve God (Colossians 3:15-17).

1 Thessalonians Page: 774

This is a letter in the Bible's New Testament. Paul wrote this letter to Christians in Thessalonica. He thanked God for their faith, love and hope. They had turned from idols (false gods) to serve God. They were waiting for the return of Jesus. They trusted God in spite of great difficulties. Paul told them to please God by the way that they lived. They should be holy. They should work hard. And they should love each other. Then he answered their questions about the return of Jesus. He told them not to worry about those who had died. They would not miss Jesus' return. They would meet him before those who were still alive. The return of Jesus will be sudden. Therefore the Christians in Thessalonica must be ready for this. They must continue to work quietly.

2 Thessalonians Page: 777

This is a letter in the Bible's New Testament. Paul wrote it to Christians in Thessalonica not long after his first letter to them. People were behaving in a cruel way towards the Christians there. Paul told them have confidence in God. When Jesus returned God would punish those wicked people. He would also punish everybody who did not accept the good news about Jesus. Some Christians in Thessalonica thought that Jesus had already returned. Paul said that the Wicked One would come first. He would oppose Jesus. So, Christians should trust God, even when they suffer. Other Christians in

Thessalonica thought that Jesus was coming back very soon. So, they refused to work. Paul reminded them that he himself worked hard in

Thessalonica. And they all must work too.

1 Timothy Page: 779

This letter is in the Bible's New Testament. Paul wrote it to Timothy. He was a young follower of Paul who was looking after the church in Ephesus. Paul warned him about false teachers. In 1 Timothy 1, he wrote about false teachers of the law. These men gave long speeches about God's law. But they did not know the purpose of the law. And they did not know that they must love other people. In 1 Timothy 4, Paul writes about some more evil teachers.

He warns Timothy not to listen to them. Instead, Timothy should teach people to trust God (1 Timothy 4:9-11).

He then told Timothy about meetings in church. He described how they should pray. He told him how women should behave. He described the qualities that church leaders must have. Paul then told him how to care for different groups in the church. These included slaves, widows, and church leaders. He told Timothy to be content. And, Timothy should not love money. But he should learn to improve his character while he serves God.

2 Timothy Page: 782

This is the second letter that Paul wrote to Timothy in the Bible's New Testament. Paul wrote this letter from prison. Timothy was one of Paul's followers. He was looking after a church. Paul wanted Timothy to visit him. Timothy was rather nervous. Paul told Timothy to suffer difficulties like a soldier, a runner or a farmer.

He warned Timothy not to allow foolish arguments to upset him. Timothy must refuse to do evil deeds. And he must be a good and patient teacher. Paul warned him also that things would get worse and worse. False teachers would lead weak people away from the truth. Timothy must teach the truths that he learned from the Bible. Paul knew he would die soon. Paul reminded Timothy about Paul's own faith and great difficulties. But Paul knew that God would reward him in heaven.

Titus Page: 785

Paul wrote the Book of Titus to his friend, called Titus. Titus was working on an island called Crete. There were many churches on Crete, but these churches did not have leaders. So, Paul told Titus to appoint a leader for the church in each town. But Titus must choose the leaders carefully. Each leader must be a good man, who is kind, holy and honest. And the leaders must teach God's message accurately (Titus 1:5-9).

This was an important task. Some people were trying to convince the Christians to obey their traditions. These people pretended to know God. But their actions proved that they denied God (Titus 1:10-16). Paul advised Titus not to argue with people who taught the wrong things. He told Titus to warn them on two occasions only. Then, Titus should leave that person (Titus 3:9-11).

Philemon Page: 787

The book of Philemon is a short, personal letter. It is in the New Testament part of the Bible.

Paul wrote some encouraging words to Philemon. Then, Paul appealed to Philemon on behalf of Philemon's slave. The slave was called Onesimus. Onesimus had escaped from Philemon. Later, Onesimus became a Christian. He helped Paul. But Philemon still owned Onesimus, because Onesimus was a slave.

Paul decided to return Onesimus to Philemon. Paul asked Philemon to accept Onesimus as his Christian brother, instead of a slave.

Hebrews Page: 788

Hebrews is a Bible book, in the New Testament.

The Book of Hebrews teaches many things about Jesus. We do not know the author of Hebrews. Some people think that Paul wrote Hebrews.

The Book of Hebrews is an important book that teaches many lessons about the Bible. The Book of Hebrews teaches that Jesus was not an angel (a servant of God from heaven) (Hebrews 1). Jesus is God. But Jesus became a man. Jesus is our priest (Hebrews chapters 5-9). And Jesus is the perfect priest (Hebrews 7:25-28). In the Old Testament, priests killed animals so that God would forgive the people. But Jesus died himself, to suffer the punishment for our evil deeds. God accepted Jesus's blood (that is, his death - Hebrews 9). So, God will forgive us when we trust Jesus.

In the Bible's Old Testament, many people trusted God (Hebrews 11). They believed that God would send Jesus. So, they were not afraid, although they had great troubles. So, we too should trust God when we have troubles (Hebrews 12:1-2).

James Page: 798

The book of James is a letter in the New Testament of the Bible. People think that the writer was James the brother of Jesus. He became a leader of the church in Jerusalem (Galatians1:19).

James tells his readers about different things:

We may suffer because we follow Jesus. But we must be patient (James 5:7-11). This will make us better people (James 1:2-4)

He speaks against rich people who do wrong things to poor people (James 2:1-4, James 5:1-7). God will say that they are wrong. If poor people trust God, this is better than wealth (James 2:5-7)

God will give wisdom to those who ask for it (James 1:5). This is because true wisdom comes from God (James 1:16-18). God's wisdom teaches us the right behaviour (James 3:13-16).

If we trust in God, we will show it in our actions (James 2:14-26).

James warns us to be careful about our words (James 3:1-12).

He tells us that we should pray sincerely (James 5:13-16).

James is a favourite book for many people.

1 Peter Page: 801

1 Peter is a letter in the Bible's New Testament. The author of the letter is Peter. Peter was a disciple (student) of Jesus. And Peter became a leader in the first Christian church, in Jerusalem.

Peter wrote his letter to Christians who were suffering great troubles. Peter wanted them to trust God more. Their troubles would test them. But they were joyful, even when they suffered. They were joyful, because they trusted God's promises. And they were joyful, because Jesus died for them.

So, Peter encouraged them to be holy. Their troubles would last for a short time. But God's word lasts always. And they will always live with God in heaven. There, they will not suffer.

God chose them to be his people (1 Peter 2:10). So, they were special people. They did not belong to this world (1 Peter 2:11). They belonged in heaven.

Jesus suffered many terrible things, too. But he did not reply when people insulted him. He did not complain. He trusted God. And when Jesus died, he suffered the punishment for our evil deeds. This was how he made us into the people of God (1 Peter 2:21-25).

We should copy Jesus, even when we suffer. We should respect our husbands and wives (1 Peter 3:1-7). We should respect our employers (1 Peter 2:18-21). And we should even respect rulers and governments (1 Peter 2:13-17). They might be evil. But we should still be good. We should tell them gently about Jesus (1 Peter 3:15).

We might suffer because we are Christians. But even if this happens, we should be glad. And we should praise God that we are Christians (1 Peter 4:12-19).

Peter advised these Christians to love each other (1 Peter 4:8). And, he had special advice for the church leaders (1 Peter 5:1-4).

Peter Page: 805

The second letter from Peter is found in the New Testament of the Bible. Peter was a leader of the church. He sent this letter to all believers.

Peter told the Christians how they could grow as Christians. He explained that God himself directed the authors of the Bible (2 Peter 1:20-21). Peter warned the Christians about evil teachers. These teachers were teaching false ideas. And their behaviour was very evil. God will punish such teachers.

And he will also punish the people who follow them.

Peter also explained about Jesus' return to this earth. Some people might suppose that Jesus will never return. But Peter explained that they are wrong.

God made the earth.

And God will also destroy the earth. God is not slow; but God is patient. And, because God is patient, we have the opportunity to trust God now. Then, we will enjoy the things that God promises. a new heaven, and a new earth.

1 John Page: 808

John was one of the first men to follow Jesus. He knew Jesus well. But John also understood that Jesus is God (1 John 1:1-3).

John wrote this letter to all Christians. John wanted Christians to be certain that God loves them (1 John 3:1). Because God loves us, we too must love other Christians (1 John 3:17; 1 John 4:19-21). This has always been the law of God (1 John 2:8). We must love other people.

John also wanted to remind Christians about some important facts:

- Christians are God's children and they can enjoy friendship with him. (1 John 3:1 and 2:3)
- They do not need to do wrong things. But God will forgive them if they confess their evil deed to God (1 John 2:1).
- The Holy Spirit is with them to warn them about false ideas. (1 John 2:18-27)
- They can be joyful and have true friendship with other Christians. (1 John 1:4 and 7)

2 John Page: 810

2 John is a short letter, in the Bible (New Testament). The author was John, who also wrote John's Gospel, Revelation, and two other letters.

The book of 2 John teaches that we should love other Christians. God orders us to love each other (2 John 5-6).

We must not accept people who teach wrong things about Jesus (2 John 7-11). Jesus is God. But he became a man so that he could die for us. When he died, he suffered the punishment for our evil deeds. This is the true Christian message.

3 John Page: 810

3 John is a personal letter from John to Gaius. It is in the New Testament of the Bible.

John was glad to hear that Gaius taught the true Christian message. John was also glad that Gaius looked after other Christians. These Christians were travelling to teach God's message elsewhere. And Gaius helped them.

There were some problems in Gaius's church. John wanted to come so that he could help Gaius.

Jude Page: 811

The Book of Jude is a short letter in the Bible (New Testament). The author, Jude, was a brother of Jesus. Jude wrote his letter to warn the church about some men. These men lived evil lives. And they denied that Jesus is God. Jude explained that God would punish these men. And Jude encouraged the people in that church to continue to trust God.

Revelation Page: 812

The Book of Revelation is a book about the future. It is the last book in the Bible's New Testament. Its author was John, who was a disciple (student) of Jesus.

The Book of Revelation uses picture stories to describe future events. These stories are often difficult to explain. But the book contains some clear lessons about the future:

- Good people will not always suffer. God has prepared a home in heaven for everyone who trusts Jesus. Nobody will be sad there. Heaven will be a wonderful place.
- There will not always be evil rulers. Their cruelty will end. Their power will end. God will punish them.
- Jesus will return to this earth. Then everyone will know that Jesus is God. And he will be the judge of everyone.
- The devil will not always be powerful. God will punish the devil. And the devil will lose his evil powers.
- We must invite God into our lives now. Terrible things will happen before Jesus returns. But God will protect us if we trust him.

In the Beginning

Genesis

Genesis is the first book in the Bible. The word 'Genesis' means 'beginning'.

Genesis is a book about things that happened a long time ago. It tells us about the lives of many important people. It tells us about Adam and Eve; Cain, Abel and Noah. It also tells us about Abraham and Sarah; Isaac and Ishmael; Jacob; and Joseph and his brothers. Can learn from those people's lives.

The Book of Genesis also teaches us many important things that we need to know. It teaches us about the world, about ourselves, and about God.

It explains that God made the world. It tells us that God filled the world with beautiful plants and animals. It tells us that he made men and women like him. And everything was very good.

It explains how the first man and woman refused to obey God. And it explains that everyone has trouble and pain because of this.

It also tells us about God's promise to forgive people and to bless them. And it tells us that God decided to send Jesus to the world.

Chapter 1

God makes the earth

1 In the beginning, God began to make the earth and the heavens and everything in them. 2 The earth was without shape. Nothing was alive on it. Deep water covered the earth. There was no light. Everywhere was dark. The Spirit of God moved above the water.

3 God said 'I want light to appear.' And there was light. 4 God looked at the light. And he saw that it was good. He separated the light from the dark. 5 God called the light 'day'. He called the dark 'night'. Evening passed and morning came. This was the first (1st) day.

6 Then God said 'A wide space will appear between the waters. So the waters will separate. Some of the water will stay above the space. The rest of the water will stay below the space.' 7 So God made a wide space. He separated the water under the space from the water above it. And what God said happened. 8 God called the wide space 'sky'. Evening passed and then it was morning. This was the second (2nd) day. 9 God said 'The water under the sky will gather in one place. And dry ground will appear.' And what God said happened. 10 God called the dry ground 'land'. He called the water (that he put in one place) 'sea'. God looked at what he had made. And he saw that it was good. 11 God said 'Plants will grow in the land. They will make seeds. And fruit trees will grow, with seeds inside the fruit. Then they can make more plants and trees. These plants and trees will be the same as the plants and trees that they have come from.' And it was like that. 12 So plants and trees began to grow in the ground. The plants and trees made seeds, so that more of the same plants and trees could grow. God looked at what he had made. And he saw that it was good. 13 Evening passed, and then it was morning. This was the third (3rd) day.

14 God said 'There will be lights in the sky. They will separate the day from the night. They will show the seasons, days and years. 15 The lights in the sky will give light to the earth.' And this happened. 16 God made two great lights. The brightest light ruled over the day. The less bright light ruled over the night. God also made the stars. 17 God put the lights and stars in the sky to give light on the earth. 18 They were to rule over the day and night. And they separated the light from dark. God looked at what he had made. And he saw that it was good. 19 Evening passed, and then it was morning. This was the fourth (4th) day.

20 God said 'The waters will be filled with fish and other living things. And birds will appear and fly in the sky, above the earth.'

21 So God made big animals to live in the sea. He made every different living thing that filled the sea. God made every different bird and flying thing in the sky. God looked at what he made. And he saw that it was good. 22 God blessed them. He said 'Have many young ones, and grow in number. Fill the water in the seas. And let the birds also have many young ones so that they will grow in number on the earth.' 23 Evening passed and then it was morning. This was the fifth (5th) day.

24 God said 'I will make different animals come up from the ground. I will make livestock and wild animals. There will be other small animals to move along the ground. I will make many different animals to live on the earth.' And what God said happened. 25 So God made the different wild animals and the different livestock. He made all the different animals that move along the ground. God looked at what he had made. And he saw that it was good.

26 God said 'We will make man. Men and women will be like us. They will rule over the fish of the sea and over the birds of the sky. They will rule over the livestock. And they will rule over the earth. They will rule over the animals that move along the ground.'

27 So God made man. He made man to be like God. God made them. He made some males, and some females.

28 God blessed them. He said, 'Grow in number. Fill the earth and rule over it. Rule over the fish of the seas and over the birds of the sky. Rule over every different living animal that moves on the ground.' 29 Then God said, 'Look! I give you every plant on the earth that has seeds in it. I give you every tree that has fruit with a seed in it. They are yours. The seeds and fruits will be food for you. 30 And they will be food for all the animals on the earth. They will be food for all the birds in the sky and for all the animals that move along the ground. Everything that has life can eat every green plant.' And what God said happened.

31 God looked at everything that he had made. And he saw that it was very good. Evening passed. And then it was morning. This was the sixth (6th) day.

Chapter 2

1 So God finished making the earth and everything in it. He made the whole world.

2 The seventh (7th) day came. And God stopped working, because he had finished making the earth. God rested on the 7th day. 3 God blessed the 7th day. He made it a special day, because he had finished making the earth. God did not work on that day.

God makes a man and a woman

4 This is what happened when God made the earth and everything in it.

When the Lord God made the heavens and the earth, 5 there were no plants or trees growing on it. That was because God had not sent any rain. And there was no man to work and care for the ground. There was no man to care for things that grow from the ground. 6 But streams came up from the earth. And they made all the top of the ground wet. 7 Then the Lord God made a man from the ground. He gave life to the man. He put air from himself into the nose of the man. And the man became alive.

8 The Lord God planted a garden. This was east of Israel. It was in a place called Eden. And he put the man that he made in the garden. 9 And the Lord God made different trees grow from the ground. These trees were good to look at. The fruit from the trees was good to eat. In the middle of the garden were two trees. One was the tree that lets you live forever. And the other was the tree of knowledge of good and evil.

10 A river began in Eden. It went through Eden. And it gave water for the ground. It separated into four smaller rivers. 11 The name of the first river is the Piston. It goes through the whole of the land of Havildar. There is gold in this land. 12 The gold there is good. Bdellium and onyx stone are also in Havildar.

13 The name of the second river is the Gihon. It goes through the whole of the land of Cush. 14 The name of the third river is the Tigris. It goes along the east side of the Ashur. The name of the fourth river is the Euphrates.

15 The Lord God put the man into the Garden of Eden. The man was to work on the ground and work in the garden. 16 Then the Lord God told the man, 'You can eat the fruit from any tree in the garden. 17 But you must not eat the fruit from the tree of knowledge of good and evil. The day when you eat this fruit you will die.'

18 Then the Lord God said, 'The man should not be alone. I will make a helper for him.

19 The Lord God had made all the animals and birds. He made them from the ground. And he brought them to the man to hear what names the man would give them. Whatever the man called each living thing would be its name. 20 So the man gave names to the livestock, the birds of the air, and all the other animals.

But the man did not find a helper. 21 So the Lord God made the man go to sleep. While the man was sleeping, the Lord God took a rib from the man. Then he closed up the place that he took the rib from. He closed up that part of the man's body with skin. 22 Then the Lord God made a woman.

23 Then the man said to God, 'At last, this is one like me. She has bones taken from my bones. And her body is from my body. I will call her 'woman' because God took her out of a man.' 24 Because of this, a man will leave his father and mother to be with his wife. And the two people will become like one person.

25 The man and his wife did not wear any clothes. But they did not feel ashamed.

Chapter 3

The man and woman turn away from God

1 God made many wild animals. But the snake was the most cunning (clever and evil) of them all. The snake asked the woman, 'Did God really say, "Both of you must not eat from any tree in the garden"?'

2 The woman replied, 'We can eat fruit from the trees in the garden. 3 But God said, "You must not eat fruit from the tree that is in the middle of the garden and you must not touch it. You will die if you touch that fruit." '

4 But the snake said to the woman, 'You will not die. 5 God knows that when you eat the fruit from this tree you will be like him. You will understand. And you will know good and evil.'

6 The woman looked at the fruit. She saw that it was good to eat. And she thought that it would be good to know about good and evil. So, she took some fruit and ate it. She gave some to her husband who was with her. And he ate it. 7 Then they saw that they had no clothes. And they felt ashamed. So, they joined leaves from fig trees together to cover their bodies.

8 In the evening the man and the woman heard the sound of the Lord God walking in the garden. They hid behind the trees. They hid because they did not want the Lord God to see them. 9 The Lord God called out to the man. He asked 'Where are you?'

10 The man replied, 'I heard you in the garden. I was afraid because I had no clothes. So I hid from you.'

11 The Lord God said, 'Who told you that you had no clothes? Have you eaten from the tree that I told you not to eat from?'

12 The man said, 'The woman that you put here – she gave me some fruit from the tree. So I ate it.'

13 The Lord God asked the woman, 'What have you done?' The woman replied, 'The snake told me that I would not die if I ate the fruit. So I ate the fruit.'

14 The Lord God said to the snake, 'Because you have done this, out of all the livestock and wild animals I will only curse you. I tell you that you will move across the ground on your stomach. And you will eat dust. You will do this for the whole of your life.

15 I will make you and the woman enemies. Your descendant and her descendant will always be enemies. He will hit your head and you will hurt his foot.' 16 The Lord God said to the woman, 'I will make it more painful for you while you are pregnant. And I will make it very painful for you when you give birth. You will still want to be with your husband. He will rule over you and be like a master.'

17 The Lord God said to Adam, 'You listened to your wife. You ate the fruit from the tree after I said, "You must not eat from this tree." Because you did this, I will curse the ground. You will have to work for a long time before any food plants grow from it. It will be like this for the whole of your life. 18 Thistles and thorns will grow out of the ground. You will eat the plants that grow in the fields. 19 But you will have to work for a long time before you have any food to eat. You will do this until you return to the ground. This is where you came from. I made you from the ground. And you will return to the ground.'

20 Adam gave the woman a name. He called her Eve. This was because she would be the mother of all people.

21 The Lord God made clothes for Adam and Eve to wear. He made them from animal skins.

22 The Lord God said, 'The man has now become like one of us. He understands good and evil. He must not eat the fruit from the tree that lets him live forever. If he does, he will live forever. He will not die.' 23So, the Lord God sent Adam and Eve out of the Garden of Eden. Adam had to work on the ground that he came from. They could not return to the garden. 24 Then God put cherubim and a sword of fire at the east of the garden. The sword went from side to side. So, no one could go near to the tree that lets him live forever.

Chapter 4

Cain and Abel

1 Adam had sex with his wife Eve. And she became pregnant. Some time passed and she gave birth to Cain. She said, 'With the help of the Lord I have given birth to a son.'

2 After some time had passed, Eve gave birth to Cain's brother. She called him Abel. When they had grown, Abel kept sheep. And Cain worked on the land.

3 Some time passed. Then one day Cain brought to God some of the fruit that he had grown. The fruits were an offering to the Lord God. 4 But Abel brought fat pieces from some of the first young ones of the animals that he kept. The Lord God was happy with Abel and his offering. 5 But the Lord God was not happy with Cain and his offering. Cain was very angry. His face looked sad.

6 Then God said to Cain, 'Why are you angry? Why do you look sad? 7 If you do what is right, I will be happy with you. But if you do wrong things, sin will be like a wild animal at your door. It will be like an animal that wants to eat you. But you must be its master.

Cain kills Abel

8 One day Cain said to his brother Abel, 'Let us go out to the field.' While they were in the field, Cain attacked his brother Abel. And he killed him.

9 Some time passed and God said to Cain, 'Where is Abel, your brother?' Cain replied, 'I do not know. Must I always keep my brother safe?'

10 Then the Lord God said, 'What have you done? Listen! The blood of your brother is like a dead person calling out to me from the ground.'

11 Then God said, 'I have cursed you. I will not let you grow food in the ground. This is because it is wet with your brother's blood. This is because you killed your brother.

12 When you work on the land, no plants will grow in it. There will be no plants that you can eat. You will travel from place to place. You will not live in one place.'

13 Cain said to the Lord, 'What you are doing to me is too much. 14 From today, you will not let me work on the land. You will not be with me. I will be like a traveller without a home. If someone sees me, they will kill me.'

15 But God said to Cain, 'I will not let anyone kill you. If anyone kills Cain, I will hurt that person 7 times more.' Then the Lord God put a mark on Cain. This was to let other people know that they must not kill Cain. 16 Cain went away from God. He went to live in the land of Nod, which is East of Eden.

17 Cain had sex with his wife. After some time she gave birth to Enoch. Cain was building a city. He called the city Enoch because it was his son's name. 18 Enoch was the father of Iran. Iran was the father of Mehujael. Mehujael was the father of Methushael. Methushael was the father of Lamech.

19 Lamech married 2 women. One was called Adah and one was called Zillah. 20 Adah gave birth to Jabal. Jabal was the father of the people who live in tents and keep livestock.

21 Jabal had a brother called Jubal. Jubal was the father of the people who play the harp and flute.

22 A son was born to Zillah. His name was Tubal-Cain. He made tools out of bronze and iron. Tubal-Cain had a sister. Her name was Naamah.

23 Lamech said to his wives, 'Adah and Zillah, listen to me; wives of Lamech hear my words. A man hurt me, so I killed him. I killed a young man because he hurt me. 24 If a man kills Cain, then God will hurt him 7 times more. So I will hurt the man who hurts me 77 times more.'

25 Adam had sex with Eve. And she gave birth to a son. She called him Seth. Eve said, 'God has given me another child because Cain killed Abel.' 26 Seth became the father of Enosh.

At this time, men began to worship and to praise the name of God.

Chapter 5

The descendants of Adam and Eve

1 This is a report of Adam's family. When God made man, he made him like God. 2 God made both male and female. He blessed them. When God made them, he called them 'man'.

3 When Adam was 130 years old, he had a son. The son was like Adam. Adam called him Seth. 4 After Seth was born, Adam was alive for 800 years. During this time, he had other sons and daughters. 5 Adam was 930 years old when he died.

6 When Seth was 105 years old, he had a son. He called him Enosh. 7 After Seth became the father of Enosh, Seth was alive for 807 years. During this time, he had other sons and daughters. 8 Seth was 912 years old when he died.

9 When Enosh was 90 years old, he had a son. He called him Kenan. 10 Enosh was alive for 815 years. During this time, he had other sons and daughters. 11 Enosh was 905 years old when he died.

12 When Kenan was 70 years old, he had a son. He called him Mahalalel. 13 After Kenan became the father of Mahalalel, Kenan was alive for 840 years. During this time, he had other sons and daughters. 14 Kenan was 910 years old when he died.

15 When Mahalalel was 65 years old, he had a son. He called him Jared. 16 After he became the father of Jared, Mahalalel was alive for 830 years. During this time, he had other sons and daughters. 17 Mahalalel was 895 years old when he died.

18 When Jared was 162 years old, he had a son. He called him Enoch. 19 After Jared became the father of Enoch, Jared was alive for 800 years. During this time, he had other sons and daughters. 20 Jared was 962 years old when he died.

21 When Enoch was 65 years old, he had a son. He called him Methuselah. 22 After that, Enoch did as God wanted for 300 years. During this time, he had other sons and daughters. 23 Enoch lived on earth for 365 years. 24 Enoch did as God wanted for all this time; then Enoch was no more. God took Enoch to be with him.

25 When Methuselah was 187 years old, he had a son. He called him Lamech.

26 After Methuselah became the father of Lamech, Methuselah was alive for 782 years. During this time, he had other sons and daughters. 27 Methuselah was 969 years old when he died.

28 When Lamech was 182 years old, he had a son. 29 He called his son Noah. Lamech said 'He will help us in our difficult work on the land. Our hands hurt when we work the land. That is because the Lord God cursed it.' 30 After Noah was born, Lamech was alive for 595 years. During this time, he had other sons and daughters. 31 Lamech was 777 years old when he died.

32 When Noah was 500 years old, he became the father of Shem, Ham and Japheth.

Chapter 6

1 People began to grow in number all over the earth. And daughters were born to them. 2 The sons of God saw the daughters. They thought that the daughters of men were beautiful to look at. They took the daughters of men as their wives. They took anyone that they wanted.

3 The Lord said, 'I will not let men and women live forever. One day they will die. I will not let them live for more than 120 years. Then they will die.

4 The Nephilim lived on the earth at that time. (They also lived on the earth after this time.) This is when the sons of God had children with the daughters of men. People thought that the Nephilim were great men and leaders.

5 The Lord God saw how bad men and women had become. God saw that they thought only of evil things.6 He was sad that he had made men and women. And he was sad that he had put them on the earth. 7 So the Lord God said, 'I made men and women, but I will take them off the earth. I will take men and animals off the earth. I will take animals that move across the ground and the birds in the air off the earth. Because I am very sad that I made them.' 8 But God was happy with Noah.

God saves Noah

9 This is a report of Noah. Noah was a good man. He was the only man at that time who obeyed God. The people who lived near him could not find anything wrong with what he did. 10 Noah was the father of Shem, Ham and Japheth.

11 God saw that everything on the earth was bad. People began to hurt and kill each other. And they did everything that was wrong. 12 God saw how bad the earth had become. All the people were doing bad things. 13 He said to Noah, 'I am going to destroy all the people. The earth is bad because of them. I am going to destroy the people and the earth. 14 Make yourself a boat. Use wood from cypress trees. Make rooms in the boat. Cover the inside and outside of the boat with pitch.'

15 'This is how you will build the boat. The boat must be 150 metres long, 25 metres wide and 15 metres high.

16 Make a roof for the boat and put windows 45 centimetres high along the top of it. Put a door in the side of the boat. Make 3 floors on top of each other (lower, middle and top floor).

17 I am going to cover the earth with water. I will destroy all life under the heavens. Everything that has my life in it will die. 18 But I will make a covenant with you (Noah). You will go into the boat. You and your sons will go into the boat. And their wives and your wife will go with you.

19 You must bring 2 of all the different animals into the boat. They must be male and female. They will stay alive with you.

20 Bring 2 of every different bird. And bring 2 of every different animal and 2 of every different animal that moves along the ground. All these will come to you, and they will stay alive with you. 21 You must take every different food on the earth. Store this for food for you and the animals.'

22 Noah did everything that God had told him.

Chapter 7

God Destroys his Creatures

1 Then the Lord said to Noah, 'Go into the ark (large boat) with your wife and family. I have found you to be righteous in these times.'

2 God said 'Take 7 of every different clean animal. Take a male and a female together. Take 2 of every different unclean animal. Take a male and a female together. 3 Take 7 of every kind of bird. Take males and females. Do this so that they will have young ones again. Then the different animals and birds will not die.

4 In 7 days, I will send rain down to the earth. It will rain for 40 days and 40 nights. I will destroy every living thing that I have made on the earth.'

5 Noah did everything that God told him.

6 Noah was 600 years old when God sent the rain to cover the earth with water. 7 Noah and his wife went into the boat. And his sons and their wives went into it. They all went into the boat to be safe from the water that would cover the earth. 8 Pairs of clean and unclean animals came to Noah. Also, pairs of birds and pairs of all the animals that move across the ground came to him. 9 Both males and females came to Noah and went into the ark. Everything happened as God had told Noah. 10 After 7 days had passed; God sent the waters to cover the earth.

11 On the 17th day of the 2nd month all the water below the earth came up and covered the earth. All the water in the heavens came down on the earth. At that time, Noah was 600 years old. 12 Rain fell on the earth for 40 days and 40 nights.

13 On the day that the rains began, Noah and his sons went into the boat with their wives. (Noah's sons are Shem, Ham and Japheth.) 14 With them was every different wild animal and every different livestock animal. They also had with them every kind of animal that moves along the ground, and every different kind of bird and flying thing. 15 Pairs of every animal alive came to Noah and went into the boat.

16 The animals were male and female of every different animal. This happened as God told Noah. Then Noah went into the boat and God shut the door.

17 For 40 days, the waters came on the earth. More water came and lifted the boat high above the ground.

18 The waters rose and covered the earth. The boat was safe on top of the water. 19 More water came and covered every high mountain on the earth. 20 And even more water came. It covered all the mountains. The water was more than 20 feet higher than the top of the mountains. 21 Everything still living on the earth died. Birds, livestock and wild animals died. Every animal that moved across the ground died. All the people living on the earth died. 22 Everything that was alive on the dry land died. 23 Every living thing on the earth died. Men and animals died. The animals that move across the ground and the birds of the air died. God destroyed all of them. Only Noah and his family, and the animals that were in the boat stayed alive.

24 The waters covered the earth for 150 days.

Chapter 8

The water goes away

1 Then God thought of Noah, and all the animals in the boat. He sent a wind to blow over the whole world. And the waters began to go down. 2 Water stopped coming up from below the earth. And water stopped coming down from heaven. The rain stopped falling from the sky.

3 The waters went down, and at the end of 150 days the water had almost gone. 4 On the 17th day of the 7th month, the boat settled on the mountains of Ararat. 5 The water continued to go down until the 10th month. On the 1st day of the 10th month the tops of the mountains appeared.

6 After 40 more days, Noah opened the window in the boat. 7 He sent out a raven. The raven flew back to the boat. Then it flew away from it again. It did this several times until the earth was dry. 8 Noah also sent out a dove. He sent the dove to see if the water had gone from the top of the ground. 9 But the dove could not find anywhere to stand. This was because still there was water over all of the ground. So it returned to Noah in the boat. Noah put out his hand and took the dove back into the boat. 10 He waited for 7 days. Then he sent the dove out again. 11 The dove returned to him in the evening. It carried a fresh olive leaf in its mouth. Then Noah knew that the waters had gone down. 12 He waited for 7 more days. Then he sent the dove out again. This time, it did not return to Noah.

13 It was the 1st day of the first month. Noah was now 601 years old. The water that covered the earth was gone. The earth was dry. Noah removed the top of the ark. He saw that the top of the ground was dry. 14 Some time passed. On the 27th day of the 2nd month, the earth was completely dry.

15 God said to Noah, 16 'Come out of the boat. Bring your wife, your sons and their wives with you. 17 Bring every different living animal out of the boat. Bring out the birds and the animals. And bring out those animals that move across the ground. Bring them out so that they may have young ones. Then they can grow in number on the earth.'

18 Noah came out of the boat. His wife, and his sons and their wives came too. 19 All the animals came out of the boat. Those that moved across the ground and the birds came too. Every different animal came out of the boat.

God makes a promise to Noah

20 Then Noah built an altar to the Lord. He took some of the clean animals and birds. And he sacrificed a burnt offering on the altar.

21 The Lord smelled the sacrifice and was happy with it. He said (in his heart) 'I will never again curse the ground because of men and women. I will never curse it even when they think of doing wrong. They think of doing wrong from the time that they are children. But still I will never destroy all the living animals again, as I have done.

22 As long as the earth is here, the time for planting will come each year. The time for getting the plants out of the ground will come each year. Cold and heat, and summer and winter will always come. They will never stop. Day and night will never stop.'

Chapter 9

1 God blessed Noah and his sons. He said 'Have many children and fill the earth with them. 2 Every animal will be afraid of you. All the birds will be afraid of you. And every animal that moves across the ground will be afraid of you. All the fish in the sea will be afraid of you. You will have authority over all of them. 3 All living animals will be food for you. Before, I gave you the green plants to eat. Now I give you everything.

4 But you must not eat meat that still has the blood of life in it.

5 Men must not kill other men. Animals must not kill men. If an animal kills a man, kill the animal. If a man kills another man, kill the man.

6 God made men like himself. So, if anyone kills a man or a woman, a man must kill him. 7 You must have many children, so that the number of people on the earth will grow.'

8 God said to Noah and his sons that were with him, 9 'I will make my promise with you, and with all your descendants,

10 and with all the animals on the earth. 11 This is my promise. I will never destroy all life on the earth again. I will never cover the earth with water again.'

12 God said, 'I will show you that I have made a promise with you, and every living animal. It is a promise for all that live on the earth, now and as long as the earth is here. 13 I have put my rainbow in the sky. It will show you the promise between me and everything on the earth. 14 When I bring clouds over the earth, a rainbow will appear. 15 Then I will remember my promise. Never again will the waters destroy all life. 16 When I see a rainbow in the clouds, I will remember my promise to you. It is for all time. It is a promise between God and everything that lives on the earth.' 17 God said to Noah, 'This will show you the promise that I have made. My promise is between me and all life on earth.'

18 The names of Noah's sons were Shem, Ham and Japheth. Ham had a son called Canaan. They all came out of the ark with Noah. 19 All the people who are on the earth are descendants of Noah's three sons.

20 Noah worked on the ground. He planted a vineyard.

21 He drank some of the wine that he made. And he became drunk. He lay inside his tent and fell asleep. He was not wearing any clothes. 22 Ham, Canaan's father, saw that Noah was not wearing any clothes. He went outside. He told his two brothers what he had seen. 23 Shem and Japheth took some clothes and put them across their shoulders. They walked into Noah's tent. They kept their backs to Noah, so that they could not see him. Then they covered their father with the clothes. They did not look at their father's body because there were no clothes on it.

24 Noah woke up from his sleep. He found out what his youngest son (Ham) had done. 25 He said 'Cursed be Canaan! He will be a slave to his brothers.' 26 Noah also said, 'Blessings to the Lord, the God of Shem! Let Canaan be the slave of Shem. 27 Let God make the land of Japheth grow. Let Japheth receive the good things of Shem. Let Canaan be his slave.'

28 Noah was alive for 350 years after God covered the earth with water. 29 Noah's whole life lasted for 950 years. Then he died.

Chapter 10

1 This is the story of Shem, Ham and Japheth. They are Noah's sons. After God covered the earth with water, they had sons.

The Japhethites

2 These are the sons of Japheth: Gomer, Magog, Madai, Javan, Tubal, Meshech and Tiras. 3 These are the sons of Gomer: Ashkenaz, Riphath and Togarmah. 4 These are the sons of Javan: Elishah, Tarshish, the Kittim and the Rodanim.

5 These people lived by the sea. They lived in groups. Each group went to live in a different place. Each group spoke its own language.

The Hamites

6 These are the sons of Ham: Cush, Mizraim, Put and Canaan. 7 These are the sons of Cush: Seba, Havildar, Sabtah, Raamah and Sabteca. 8 These are the sons of Raamah: Sheba and Dedan. 9 Cush was the father of Nimrod. Nimrod grew into a great soldier on the earth. Nimrod was a great hunter in front of the Lord. That is why people say 'Like Nimrod, a great hunter in front of the Lord'.

10 The first of Nimrod's lands were Babylon, Erech, Akkad and Calneh, in Shinar. 11 From that land he went to Assyria. This is where he built Nineveh, Rehoboth-Ir and Calah. 12 He also built Resen. Resen is between Nineveh and Calah, which is a large city. 13 Mizraim was the father of the Ludites, Anamites, Lehabites, Naphtuhites, 14 Pathrusites, Casluhites (this is where Philistines came from) and Caphtorites.

15 Canaan was the father of Sidon, who was born first. Canaan was also the father of the Hittites, 16 Jebusites, Amorites, Girgashites, 17 Hivites, Arkites, Sinites, 18 Arvadites, Zemarites and Hamathites. After some time had passed, the Canaanite families separated, 19 and the land of Canaan went from Sidon to Gerar, as far as Gaza. It went to Sodom, Gomorrah, Admah and Zeboiim, as far as Lasha. 20 These are all descendants of Ham. They lived in groups in their own parts of the land. Each group spoke their own language.

The Semites

21 Shem also had sons. Shem's older brother was Japheth. All the sons of Eber are descendants of Shem. 22 These are the sons of Shem: Elam, Ashur, Arphaxad, Lud and Aram. 23 These are the sons of Aram: Uz, Hul, Gether and Meshech. 24 Arphaxad was the father of Shelah. Shelah was the father of Eber. 25 Eber had 2 sons. He called one Peleg. When he was alive, people began to live in different places on the earth. So he called him Peleg. He called the other son Joktan.

26 Joktan was the father of Almodad, Sheleph, Hazarmaveth, Jerah, 27 Hadoram, Uzal, Diklah, 28 Obal, Abimael, Sheba, 29 Ophir, Havildar and Jobab. All these were the sons of Joktan. 30 The land where they lived went from Mesha to Sephar. This is in the land with hills in the east. 31 These are the descendants of Shem. They lived in groups in their own parts of the land. Each group spoke their own language.

32 All these people (verses 2-13) are descendants of Noah, through many years. They went to live in different parts of the earth. This happened after God covered the earth with water.

Chapter 11

1 At this time, everyone who lived on the earth spoke one language. 2 People moved to the East. They reached a large flat piece of land called Shinar. They stayed and lived there. 3 They said to each other, 'Let us build a city with a tower. We will first make bricks and heat them until they are hard. They used brick instead of stone. They used tar to hold the bricks together.

4 They said, 'Let us build a city with a tower. The tower will go up into the heavens. Then people will remember us. If we build a tower then we will not have to go and live in different places.'

5 But the Lord came down. He came down to see the city and the tower that the men were building. 6 The Lord said, 'Because they all speak the same language, they can build this tower. What will they do after this? 7 Let us go down. Let us make them speak in different languages. Then they will not understand each other.' 8 So God separated the people, and they went to live in different lands. They stopped building the city. 9 That is why people called the city Babel. It was because the Lord gave the people different languages. They could not understand each other. From that time, the Lord separated the people. They lived in different countries all over the earth.

10 This is the report of the descendants of Shem. Two years after the earth was dry, Shem was 100 years old. He became the father of Arphaxad. 11 After he became the father of Arphaxad, Shem was alive for 500 years. He had other sons and daughters.

12 When Arphaxad was 35 years old, he became the father of Shelah. 13 After he became the father of Shelah, Arphaxad was alive for 403 years. He had other sons and daughters.

14 When Shelah was 30 years old, he became the father of Eber. 15 After he became the father of Eber, Shelah was alive for 403 years. He had other sons and daughters.

16 When Eber was 34 years old, he became the father of Peleg. 17 After he became the father of Peleg, Eber was alive for 430 years. He had other sons and daughters.

18 When Peleg was 30 years old, he became the father of Rue. 19 After he became the father of Rue, Peleg was alive for 209 years. He had other sons and daughters.

20 When Rue was 32 years old, he became the father of Serum. 21 After he became the father of Serum, Rue was alive for 207 years. He had other sons and daughters.

22 When Serum was 30 years old, he became the father of Anchor. 23 After he became the father of Anchor, Serum was alive for 200 years. He had other sons and daughters.

24 When Anchor was 29 years old, he became the father of Tear. 25 After he became the father of Tear, Anchor was alive for 119 years. He had other sons and daughters.

26 When Tear was 70 years old, he became the father of Abram, Anchor and Haran.

27 This is the report of the descendants of Tear. Tear became the father of Abram, Anchor and Haran. Haran became the father of Lot. 28 While Tear was alive, Haran died. Haran died in Ur, the land of the Chaldeans. This was where Haran was born. 29 Abram married Sarai. Anchor married Micah. Micah was Haran's daughter. Haran was the father of Micah and Iscah. 30 Sarai could not give birth to children. She did not have any children.

31 Tear took his son Abram, and Abram's wife, Sarai. Tear took his grandson Lot. (Lot is the son of Haran.) They all left Ur, the land of the Chaldeans. They began to go to Canaan. But when they came to Haran, they stayed there. 32 Tear was alive for 205 years. He died in Haran.

Chapter 12

1 The Lord had said to Abram, 'Leave your land and your people. Leave your father's house. Go to the land that I will show you.'

2 (The Lord said), 'I will make you the father of many children. I will bless you. Everyone will know your name. You will be a blessing to other people.' 3 'I will bless people who bless you. I will curse people who curse you. I will bless all the people on the earth through you.'

4 Abram left Haran as the Lord told him. Lot went with him. Abram was 75 years old when he left Haran. 5Abram took his wife Sarai, and his nephew Lot. Abram took everything that was theirs. He took their slaves and the servants that he had in Haran. They all left to go to the land of Canaan. And they arrived there.

6 Abram walked through the land. He went as far as the big tree of Moreh at Shechem. At that time, Canaanites lived in this land. 7 The Lord appeared to Abram. The Lord said 'I will give this land to your children.' So Abram built an altar to the Lord because the Lord had appeared to him.

8 Abram left Shechem. He went to the hills. The hills are east of Bethel. This is where he put his tent. Bethel was to the west of his tent. Ai was to the east of his tent. Abram built an altar there to worship the Lord and he prayed to the Lord. 9 Then Abram took his tent and left that place. He began to go to the Negev.

10 There was a famine in the land. So Abram went to live in Egypt for a while. He went there because the famine was very bad.

11 When Abram was going into Egypt, he said to his wife Sarai, 'I know that you are a very beautiful woman. 12 When the people of Egypt see you they will say, "This is his wife." They will kill me. But they will not kill you. 13 Tell them that you are my sister. Then they will do good things for me because of you. They will not kill me. Because they will think that you are my sister.'

14 When Abram came to Egypt, the people saw that Sarai was a very beautiful woman. 15 Pharaoh's officers saw her. They said good things about her to Pharaoh. They took Sarai to Pharaoh's palace. (Pharaoh is the name for all the kings of Egypt.)

16 Pharaoh did good things for Abram because of Sarai. He gave him sheep and cows. He also gave Abram male and female donkeys. And he gave him camels and male servants and female servants.

17 But the Lord made Pharaoh and the people in the palace very ill. The Lord did this because of Abram's wife Sarai. 18 So Pharaoh called Abram to come before him. Pharaoh said, 'You have done this to me. You did not tell me that she was your wife! 19 You told me "She is my sister", so I took her to be my wife. Now, here is your wife. Take her and go!' 20 Pharaoh told his men what to do with Abram. They sent Abram away with his wife and everything that they had.

Chapter 13

1 Abram went from Egypt to the Negev. He took his wife and everything that he had. Lot went with him.

2 Abram had many valuable things. He had cows, silver and gold.

3 Abram left the Negev. He went from place to place until he came to Bethel. He came to the place between Bethel and Ai. This is where he had put his tent before. 4 This is where Abram had built an altar to worship God. There, Abram called out to the Lord.

5 Lot was moving from place to place with Abram. Lot also had cows, sheep and tents. 6 The ground could not grow enough food for all the animals to eat. The ground could not grow enough food for Abram's animals and for Lot's animals. Abram and Lot could not stay together. They had too many animals and people with them. 7 Abram's herdsmen and Lot's herdsmen began to quarrel. At that time, Canaanites and Perizzites also lived in the land.

8 Abram said to Lot, 'We must not quarrel with each other. Your herdsmen and my herdsmen must not quarrel with each other. There must be no more quarrelling because we belong to the same family.'

9 'The whole land is in front of you. We must separate. If you go to the left, I will go to the right. If you go to the right, I will go to the left.'

10 Lot looked up. He saw the flat land of Jordan. He saw that it had water. It was like the garden of the Lord. It was like the land of Egypt, towards Zoar. (This was before the Lord destroyed Sodom and Gomorrah.) 11 So Lot chose the flat land of Jordan. He went towards the East.

12 Abram lived in the land of Canaan. Lot lived in the cities of the land that he had chosen. Lot put his tents near Sodom. 13 The men of Sodom were very bad. They sinned against the Lord.

14 After Lot had gone, the Lord said to Abram, 'Look up from where you are. Look to the north and south. Look to the east and west. 15 I will give you all the land that you can see. I will give it to you and your descendants for all time. 16 I will make your descendants like the dust of the ground. If anyone can count the pieces of dust, they can count your descendants.'

17 The Lord said, 'Go and walk through all this land. Because I am giving it to you.' 18 Abram moved his tents. He went to live near the big trees of Mamre. This is at Hebron. Abram built an altar here. This was so that he could worship the Lord.

Chapter 14

1-4 Now there were many kings living in that land, at that time. They fought against each other. One fight was when Kedorlaomer had ruled over the other kings for 12 years. And in the next year, 5 kings made one group like that and fought against him. Kedorlaomer joined with 3 other kings. So, it was 4 kings against 5 other kings.

The 4 kings were Amraphel king of Shinar, Arioch king of Ellasar, Kedorlaomer king of Elam and Tidal king of Goiim. And these fought a war against Bera king of Sodom, Birsha king of Gomorrah, Shinab king of Admah, Shemeber king of Zeboiim and the king of Bela. Bela is another name for the town Zoar. They fought in the Valley of Siddim. (That is the Salt Sea.) 5 In the 14th year, Kedorlaomer and the kings with him beat the Rephaites. This was in Ashteroth Karnaim. They beat the Zuzites in Ham. They beat the Emites in Shaveh Kiriathaim. 6 And they beat the Horites in the country of Seir. This was as far as El Paran near the land of dry sand. 7 They then went back. They went to En Mishpat. (That is Kadesh.) They took the whole land of the Amalekites. They also took the land of the Amorites who were living in Hazezon Tamar. 8 Then, the king of Sodom, the king of Gomorrah, the king of Admah, the king of Zeboiim and the king of Bela (that is Zoar) went to fight. This was in the Valley of Siddim. 9 They fought against Kedorlaomer king of Elam, Tidal king of Goiim, Amraphel king of Shinar and Arioch king of Ellasar. There were 4 kings fighting against 5 kings. 10 The Valley of Siddim had many holes in the ground. The holes were filled with tar. The kings of Sodom and Gomorrah ran away. And some of their men fell into the tar. The rest of the men ran away to the hills. 11 The 4 kings took everything in Sodom and Gomorrah. And they took all the food. Then they went away. 12 They also took Abram's nephew. This is Lot. They took everything that Lot had. That was because Lot lived in Sodom.

13 A man ran away from the kings. He told Abram the Hebrew everything that had happened. Abram lived near the big trees of Mamre the Amorite. Mamre was a brother of Eshcol and Aner. These men would fight with Abram. 14 Abram heard that the kings caught his nephew. He called 318 men. These men knew how to fight. They were born into Abram's household. Abram and the men went after the men who took Lot. They went as

15 During the night, Abram separated his men into 2 groups. Then they attacked the men who took Lot. Abram followed them as far as Hobah. Hobah is North of Damascus. 16 Abram took back everything that the men took from Sodom. He brought back his nephew Lot. Abram also brought back the women and other people.

17 Abram beat Kedorlaomer and the kings with him. He returned, and the king of Sodom came out to meet Abram. This was in the Valley of Shaveh. (That is the Kings' valley.) 18 Melchizedek was the king of Salem. He brought out bread and wine. Melchizedek was a priest of God Most High. 19 He blessed Abram. He said 'Abram is blessed by God Most High who made heaven and earth. 20 Blessed is God Most High. He gave your enemies to you.' Abram gave King Melchizedek a 10th of everything.

21 The king of Sodom said to Abram, 'Give me the people. Keep everything else.' 22 But Abram said 'I have raised my hand to the Lord God Most High. He made heaven and earth. And I have made a promise to him. 23 I promised not to take anything from you. I will not take even a part of your shoe. So you can never say "I made Abram rich." 24 The men who went with me may take their part. They may take their part of anything that we took. They are Aner, Eshcol and Mamre. Let them have their part.'

Chapter 15

1 After this, Abram had a dream. God spoke to Abram in this dream. God said, 'Do not be afraid Abram. I will keep you safe. And I will give you many good things.'

2 But Abram said, 'Lord, I have no children. I want you to give me a son. You have not given me a son. So Eliezer of Damascus will inherit everything that I have.'

.3 Abram said 'You have not given me any children. So a servant in my house will inherit everything that I have.' 4 Then the Lord said to him, 'Eliezer will not inherit everything that you have. You will have your own son. He will inherit everything that you have.' 5 Then the Lord took Abram outside. The Lord said, 'Look up at the heavens. Count the stars. You cannot count them because there are too many.' Then the Lord said, 'This is how many descendants you will have.' 6 Abram believed the Lord. And God said that Abram was righteous. God said this because Abram believed.

7 The Lord also said to Abram, 'I am the Lord. I brought you out of Ur of the Chaldeans. I did this to give you this land. It will be yours to take.' 8 But Abram said, 'My Lord, how will I know that I can take this land?' 9 The Lord said to Abram, 'Bring me a young cow, a goat and a male sheep. Each animal must be 3 years old. Also bring a dove and a young pigeon.'

10 Abram brought all the animals and birds to God. Abram cut each one in half. He put the halves opposite each other. But he did not cut the birds in half. 11 Some other birds came. These birds liked to eat dead animals. But Abram sent them away.

12 The sun went down. Abram fell asleep. It was very dark. He felt afraid. 13 Then the Lord said to Abram, 'Be sure of this. Your descendants will live in a country which is not their own. They will be strangers there. They will be slaves. People will do bad things to them. This will go on for 400 years. 14 But I will judge the people who made them slaves. After this, your descendants will leave that land. They will take many valuable things. 15 And yet, you will have a long life. You will have a long, good and quiet life. Then you will die very happy. 16 After 4 generations, your descendants will come back here. The Amorites sin against me. But I will not do anything against them. I will not do anything until the 4th generation (of your people).'

17 The sun went down. It became dark. Abram saw a smoking pot of fire. He also saw a light made of fire. Both of these passed between the halves of the animals.

18 On that day, the Lord made a covenant with Abram. The Lord said, 'I give this land to your descendants. I give them the land from the river of Egypt to the River Euphrates. 19 This is the land where these people live: Kenites, Kenizzites, Kadmonites, 20 Hittites, Perizzites, Rephaites, 21 Amorites, Canaanites, Girgashites and Jebusites.'

Chapter 16

1 Abram's wife was Sarai. She did not have any children. She had a servant from Egypt. The servant's name was Hagar. 2 Sarai said to Abram, 'The Lord has stopped me having children. Go and sleep with my servant. Her children will be mine.' Abram agreed to do this.

3 Abram had been living in Canaan for 10 years. Sarai took Hagar. She gave Hagar to Abram to be his wife.

4 Abram had sex with Hagar. And Hagar became pregnant. Hagar knew that she was pregnant. Because of this, she would not respect Sarai.

5 Sarai said to Abram, 'It is because of you that this has happened. What Hagar is doing is wrong. I gave her to you. And now she is pregnant. So now she does not respect me. The Lord will say who is right, you or me.' 6 Abram said to Sarai, 'Do whatever you think is right. Do what you want to do with Hagar.' Then Sarai did bad things to Hagar. So Hagar ran away.

7 The angel of the Lord found Hagar. She was by some water in the land of dry sand. The water was by the road to Shur. 8 The angel said, 'Hagar, servant of Sarai, where have you come from? Where are you going?' Hagar replied, 'I am running away from Sarai. I am her servant.'

9 The angel of the Lord told Hagar, 'Go back to Sarai. You are her servant. Do whatever she tells you to.'

10 The angel also said, 'I will make the number of your descendants grow. They will be too many to count.' 11 The angel of the Lord said,

'You will have a child.

You will have a son.

You must name him Ishmael.

Because the Lord has heard how sad you are.

12 He will be a wild man.

He will be like a donkey.

He will fight against everyone.

And everyone will fight against him.

He will think that everyone is his enemy.

He will think that his brothers are his enemies.'

13 Hagar said to the Lord 'You are the God who sees me.' And she said 'I have seen the One who sees me. And he has let me live.' 14 That is why they called the well 'Beer Lahai Roi'. The well is between Kadesh and Bered.

15 Some time passed. Hagar had a son. Abram was his father. Abram gave Hagar's son a name. The name of Hagar's son was Ishmael. 16 Abram was 86 years old when Hagar gave birth to Ishmael.

Chapter 17

1 Abram was 99 years old. The Lord appeared to him. The Lord said 'I am God Almighty. Walk before me. And do nothing wrong.

2 'I will fix my covenant. My covenant will be between me and you. I will make the number of your descendants grow.

3 Abram fell to the ground. He put his face to the ground. God said to him,

4 'This is what I will do. This is my covenant to you. You will be the father of many people.'

5 'Your name is not Abram any longer. Now your name is Abraham. This is because you are the father of many people. I will make this happen. 6 I will give you many descendants. These will make many different groups of people. Some of your descendants will be kings.

7 My covenant will be for all time. It is between me and you. And it will be between me and your descendants and their sons. (It will be for all time.) I will be your God. I will also be the God of all your descendants. 8 You are a foreign person here. This is the land of Canaan. I will give you all of Canaan. I give it to you and all your descendants. And I will be their God.

9 This is what you must do. You must do as I tell you. Then you will keep my covenant. You, and all your descendants must keep it. 10 This is my covenant with you and with all your descendants. This is what you must do to keep my covenant. This is for every male who lives with you. You must circumcise them. 11 You must be circumcised too. This will show that the covenant is between you and me. 12 You must circumcise every generation of males. Do this when they are 8 days old. This is for every male that lives with you. Circumcise servants and slaves bought with money. This includes males that are not your children. 13They may be born in your household. Or you may have bought them with your money. Circumcise all males. This is my covenant in your body. It will be for all time.

14 'Circumcise every male. If you do not circumcise someone, I will separate him from his people. Because my covenant is broken.'

15 God also said to Abraham, 'As for your wife Sarai, you must not call her Sarai. Her name will be Sarah.16 I will bless her. I will give you a son through her. I will bless her. And she will be the mother of many descendants. Some of her descendants will be kings.' 17 Abraham fell to the ground. He put his face to the ground. Abraham laughed. He said to himself, 'I am 100 years old. That is too old to have a son. Sarah is 90 years old. That is too old to have a child.' 18 Abraham said to God, 'If only Ishmael may have your blessing.' 19 God said to Abraham, 'No, your wife Sarah will have a child. You must call him Isaac. I will make my covenant with him. It will be for all time. My covenant will be for him and all his descendants.'

20 God said, 'I have heard what you want for Ishmael. I will bless him. He will have many descendants. 12 rulers will come from his descendants. His descendants will be great people. 21 But I will make my covenant with Isaac. Isaac will be Sarah's child. He will be born before one year has passed.'

22 God had finished speaking to Abraham. So God left Abraham.

23 On that day, Abraham went to Ishmael. He also went to all the males born into his household. Also, he went to every male that he had bought with money. Abraham went to every male in his household. He circumcised them. He did this because God had told him to do it. 24 Abraham's circumcision happened when he was 99 years old. 25 Ishmael's circumcision happened when he was 13 years old. 26 Abraham and his son Ishmael were circumcised on the same day. 27 Abraham circumcised every male living in his household. This included males bought with money. It also included foreign males living in Abraham's household. He circumcised them all on that day.

Chapter 18

1 The Lord appeared to Abraham. This happened near the big trees of Mamre. Abraham was sitting by the door of his tent. 2 Abraham looked up. He saw 3 men. He hurried to meet them. He bowed to the ground.

3 Abraham said to them, 'If it makes you happy, my lords, do not go past me.

4 'Let us bring some water for you. Then you can all wash your feet. Then you can rest under this tree.' 5Abraham said, 'Let me get you some bread. Then you will be ready to continue with your journey. I will do this now because you have come to me.' The men replied, 'Very well, do as you have said.' 6 Abraham hurried to the tent. This is where Sarah was. He said to her, 'Quick, get some good flour. Make bread with it.' 7 Then Abraham ran to his cows. He chose a baby cow. He gave it to a servant. The servant quickly prepared it for the men to eat. 8 Then Abraham brought some butter, milk and the meat from the cow. He put all these in front of the men. The men ate the food. And Abraham stood near them. He stood under a tree.

9 The men asked Abraham 'Where is Sarah, your wife?' Abraham replied, 'She is in the tent.' 10 Then the Lord said, 'I will return to you at this time, after one year has passed. And you and Sarah your wife will have a son.' Sarah was in the tent. She heard what the Lord said. She heard it because the tent was behind him. 11 Abraham and Sarah were very old. Sarah was past the age of giving birth to a child. 12 So Sarah laughed to herself. She thought 'I am too old. And my husband is too old. I cannot have this baby now.' 13The Lord said to Abraham, 'Sarah laughed. She said, "I am too old to have a child." ' 14 The Lord said, 'Nothing is too difficult for the Lord. At this time next year, I will return to you. I will return to you and Sarah will have a son.' 15 Sarah was afraid. So she did not say what was true. She said, 'I did not laugh.' But the Lord said, 'Yes, you did laugh.'

16 The men got up. They were leaving. They looked down in the direction of Sodom. Abraham walked with them. He walked with them for part of their journey. 17 Then the Lord said, 'Will I tell Abraham my plan?'18 'Abraham's descendants will be great people. They will be very powerful. Because of him, everyone on the earth will receive my blessing.'

19 'I chose him. Then he will teach his children and everyone in his household. He will teach them to know me. He will teach them to do what is right. Then I will keep the promise that I made to him.' 20 The Lord said to Abraham, 'The outcry against Sodom and Gomorrah is great. The people who live there are evil.'

21 'I will go down to Sodom and Gomorrah. I will see what they have done. I will see if it is as bad as the outcry against them. Then I will know how badly they have sinned.'

22 The men turned away. They went towards Sodom. But Abraham remained with the Lord.

23 Then Abraham went near to the Lord. Abraham asked, 'Will you kill your people with the evil people? 24There might be 50 people who know you in the city. Will you still destroy the city? Or will you let the people live, because of the 50 people who know you? 25 The ruler of all the earth will do what is right! So, you will not kill the people who know you. You will not kill them along with the evil people. You will not do the same thing to the people who know you, as you do to the evil people. I know that you would not do such a thing!'

26 The Lord said, 'Because of 50 people who know me in the city of Sodom, I will not destroy that place and everybody in it.' 27 Then Abraham spoke again. 'I have been brave enough to speak to the Lord. I know that I am nothing but dust and ashes.'

28 Then Abraham asked, 'What if there are 45 people in the city who know you. Will you destroy the city, because there are only 45 good people there?' The Lord said, 'Because of 45 people who know me in the city, I will not destroy it.' 29 Abraham spoke to God again. 'What will you do if only 40 good people are there?' The Lord said, 'Because of 40 good people I will not destroy the city.' 30 Then Abraham said 'Please do not be angry. Let me speak. What if there are only 30 people who know you there?' The Lord answered, 'I will not destroy the city if I find 30 good people in the city.' 31 Abraham said 'I have been brave. I have spoken to the Lord. What if only 20 good people are there?' The Lord said, 'Because of 20 good people I will not destroy the city.' 32 Abraham said, 'Please do not be angry. Let me speak once more. What if only 10 good people live there?' The Lord answered, 'Because of 10 good people I will not destroy the city.' 33 The Lord had finished speaking with Abraham. So the Lord left him. And Abraham returned home.

Chapter 19

1 The 2 angels arrived at Sodom. It was evening. Lot was sitting at the city gate. Lot saw the angels. He got up to meet them. He bowed down. He put his face to the ground.

2 Lot said 'My lords, please come to my house. You can wash your feet and stay the night there. You can continue your journey early in the morning.' The angels replied, 'No, we will stay the night in the square.'

3 But Lot asked them to stay with him again. So they went with Lot. The angels went to Lot's house. Lot prepared a meal for them. He made special bread. The angels ate the food.

4 They had not yet gone to bed. All the men from every part of Sodom came to the house. Old and young men came. They were all outside the house. 5 The men said 'Where are the men who are staying with you tonight? Bring them out to us so that we can have sex with them' 6 Lot went outside to the men. He shut the door of his house. 7 Lot said, 'No, my friends. Do not do this bad thing. 8 I have 2 daughters. They have never had sex with a man. Let me bring them out to you. You can do whatever you want with them. But do not do anything to these men. They are staying at my house. I cannot let anyone hurt them.' 9 The men from the city said 'Get out of our way. You are a foreign person in this city. Now you are telling us what to do! We will do worse things to you.' They pushed Lot. They began to break the door of his house. 10 The 2 men inside the house pulled Lot. They pulled him back into his house. They shut the door. 11 Then they made the men outside blind. They made the young men blind. They also made the old men blind. This was so that they could not find the door to the house.

12 The 2 men spoke to Lot. They said, 'Do you have any people belonging to you here? Do you have men who are going to marry your daughters? Do you have sons or daughters? Do you have any people belonging to you in the city? If you do, get them out of here. 13 We are going to destroy this city. The outcry against this city is great. God has sent us to destroy it.' 14 Lot went out. He spoke to the men who were going to marry his daughters. Lot said to them, 'Hurry! Leave this place because the Lord is going to destroy this city.' But the men laughed.

15 At dawn, the angels said to Lot, 'Hurry! Take your wife. And take your 2 daughters that are here. If not, you will all be killed when the city is destroyed.' 16 Lot did not go with the angels at once. So the angels held on to Lot's hand. And they held the hands of his wife and his 2 daughters. The angels led them away from the city, because the Lord was merciful to them.

17 As soon as the angel brought them out he said, 'Run! Your life is in danger. Do not look back. Do not stop anywhere on this land. Run to the mountains or you will die.' 18 But Lot said, 'No! Please, my lords. 19 You are happy with me, your servant. You have been very kind to me. You have saved my life. But I cannot run to the mountains. This evil will over take me. Then I will die.'

20 Lot said, 'Look! Here is a town. It is near. I can run to it. And the town is small. Let me run to it. The town is very small. Then I will stay alive.' 21 The angel said to Lot, 'Very well, I will let you do what you have asked. I will not destroy the town of which you speak. 22 But run to the town quickly. I cannot do anything until you get to the town.' (The name of the town was Zoar.) 23 The sun had risen in the sky. Then Lot reached Zoar.

24 Then the Lord made it rain. He made it rain burning sulphur on Sodom and Gomorrah. The burning sulphur came from the Lord. It came out of the heavens.

25 So the Lord destroyed those cities. He killed everyone who lived in those cities. And he killed all the plants that grew on that land.

26 But Lot's wife looked back at the city. And she changed into a large piece of salt.

27 Early the next morning, Abraham returned to where he had stood before God. 28 He looked down towards Sodom and Gomorrah. And he looked down towards all the land near the cities. He saw thick smoke. It was rising from the land. It was the smoke from a big fire.

29 God destroyed the cities of that land. And Lot lived in these cities. But God had remembered Abraham. God brought Lot out of the cities, before he destroyed them.

30 Lot was afraid to live in Zoar. So, he and his 2 daughters stayed in the mountains.

Lot and his 2 daughters lived in the rocks in the side of the mountain. 31 The oldest daughter said to the youngest daughter, 'Our father is old. And there is no other man here. So, we will not have any man to marry us. Then we will not have children. Everyone on the earth wants to have children. 32 Let us cause our father to drink wine. Then we will have sex with him. Then our family will continue.'

33 That night they gave their father wine to drink. And the oldest daughter had sex with him. Lot did not know when she came to him. And he did not know when she left him. 34 The next day the oldest daughter said to the youngest daughter, 'Last night I had sex with my father. Let us make him drink wine tonight. Then you can have sex with him. Then our family line will continue through him.' 35 So that night, they gave their father wine to drink. And the youngest daughter had sex with her father. He did not know when she came to him. And he did not know when she left him. 36 Both of Lot's daughters would give birth to a baby. This was because they had both had sex with their father. 37 The oldest daughter had a son. She called him Moab. All the Moabites of today are his descendants. 38 The youngest daughter also had a son. She called him Ben-Ammi. All the Ammonites of today are his descendants.

Chapter 20

1 Abraham moved on to the land of Negev. He lived between Kadesh and Shur. For a time he stayed in Gerar. 2 While he was there, he told people that Sarah was his sister. Because of this, Abimelech sent for Sarah. Abimelech is the king of Gerar. He wanted Sarah to be his wife.

3 But God spoke to Abimelech in a dream. God said, 'You are a dead man. This is because of the woman that you have taken. She is a married woman.' 4 But Abimelech had not gone near Sarah. He said, 'Will you destroy people who have not done anything wrong? 5 Abraham said to me "I am her brother." Sarah said to me "I am his sister." I did not know that I was doing anything wrong.' 6 God spoke to Abimelech in a dream. God said, 'You did not know that you were doing wrong. I knew that. So I kept you from sinning against me. I did not let you touch her. 7 Give her back to her husband. He is a prophet. He will pray for you. Then you will live. If you do not give her back, be sure of this. You and your household will die.'

8 Early the next morning, Abimelech called together his officers. He told them what had happened. They were very afraid. 9 Then Abimelech called Abraham to him. Abimelech said, 'What have you done to us? What have I done against you? Why have you brought this bad sin on me? You should not have done this to me.' 10 Abimelech asked Abraham, 'Why did you do this?' 11 Abraham said, 'Because I thought that the people here were not afraid of God. They will kill me because of my wife.'

12 Abraham said, 'But she is my sister. She is the daughter of my father. But she is not the daughter of my mother. And she became my wife. 13 God caused me to leave my father's household. Then I said to her, "This is how you can show your love for me. Everywhere we go, say to people, 'He is my brother'." '

14 Abimelech brought sheep and cows. He also brought male and female slaves. He gave them to Abraham. He gave Sarah, Abraham's wife back to him. 15 Abimelech said, 'Here is my land. Live anywhere you want to live.' 16 He said to Sarah, 'I have given your brother 1000 pieces of silver. This is to show everyone that you did nothing wrong.' 17 Then Abraham prayed to God. And God made Abimelech well again. He also made his wife and his female slaves well again. So, they could have children again. 18 God had made them unable to have children. God had done this because of Abraham's wife, Sarah.

Chapter 21

1 The Lord was good to Sarah. He kept his promise to her. 2 Sarah became pregnant. She gave birth to a son. Abraham was his father. Abraham was old. This happened at the time that God said it would.

3 Abraham called his son Isaac. This is the son that Sarah gave birth to. 4 Isaac was 8 days old. Abraham circumcised him. This is what God had told him to do.

5 Abraham was 100 years old when Isaac was born. 6 Sarah said, 'God has made me laugh. Everyone who hears about my son will be happy with me.' 7 She also said, 'Who would think that I would have a child? But I have given Abraham a son, even when he is old.'

8 The child grew, and his mother weaned him. On that day, Abraham gave a big feast.

9 Sarah saw that Ishmael was laughing at Isaac. Ishmael was Hagar's son. Hagar was the slave from Egypt. 10 Sarah said to Abraham, 'Send that slave woman and her son away. He must never have a part in the inheritance. He will not have a part with my son Isaac.'

11 This made Abraham very sad, because it was about his son Ishmael.

12 God said to Abraham, 'Do not be sad about the boy Ishmael and your female servant. Listen to Sarah. Do whatever she tells you, because I will continue my promise through Isaac. 13 I will also make many people from the descendants of Ishmael, too. I will do that because he is your son.'

14 Abraham was awake early the next morning. He took some food. And he took a bottle that someone had made out of animal skin. He filled it with water. He put the food and water on Hagar's shoulders. Then he sent Hagar and her son Ishmael away. She went to the desert of Beersheba.

15 After they had drunk the water, Hagar put her son under a bush. 16 She thought, 'I cannot watch the boy die.' As she sat near the boy, she began to cry. Then she went away from him. She sat down. She was not very far away from him. 17 God heard the boy crying. The angel of God spoke to Hagar from heaven. He said 'What is the matter Hagar? Do not be afraid. God has heard the boy crying, while the boy is lying there. 18 Lift the boy up. Take him by the hand. I will make him into a great people.'

19 Then God opened Hagar's eyes. She saw a well of water. Hagar filled the bottle with water. And she gave the boy a drink. 20 God was with the boy while he grew up. The boy lived in the desert. He became an archer.

21 The boy lived in the desert of Paran. And his mother found a wife for him. The wife was from Egypt.

22 At that time Abimelech and Phicol, his officer, said to Abraham, 'God is with you in everything that you do. 23 Tell me that you will not do things in a false way. You will not do anything false with me or with my children or with my descendants. Do this before God. You live here as a foreign person. Be kind to me, as I was to you.' 24 Abraham said 'I will do as you say.'

25 Then Abraham told Abimelech about a well of water. Abimelech's servants had said that the well belonged to them and not to Abraham. 26 Abimelech said 'I do not know who has done this. You did not tell me before. I only heard about it today.' 27 Abraham brought sheep and cows. He gave them to Abimelech. The two men made a promise. 28 Abraham separated 7 young female sheep from the other sheep. 29 Abimelech asked Abraham 'Why have you separated 7 young female sheep? What does this mean?' 30 Abraham replied 'Take these 7 young female sheep from my hand. You know that I dug this well. This shows that you know it.' 31 So he called that place Beersheba. He called it that because the 2 men made a promise there.

32 So they made a promise at Beersheba. Abimelech and Phicol, his officer, returned to the land of the Philistines.

33 Abraham planted a tamarisk tree in Beersheba. He called on the name of the Lord who is for ever. That is the Lord who never changes.

34 Abraham stayed in the land of the Philistines for a long time.

Chapter 22

1 Some time passed. God wanted to see how faithful Abraham was. God said to him, 'Abraham!' Abraham replied, 'Here I am.' 2 God said 'Take your son. Take your only son Isaac, whom you love. Go to the place of Moriah. Sacrifice your son there, as a burnt offering. Do this on a mountain. I will tell you which mountain.'

3 Abraham got up early the next morning. He put a blanket on his donkey. He took 2 servants, and his son Isaac. He cut wood for the fire for the burnt offering. He started to go to the place that God had told him. He took the wood with him. 4 On the 3rd day, Abraham looked up. He saw the place. It was not too far away. 5 Abraham spoke to his servants. He said 'Stay here with the donkey. The boy and I will go over there. We will worship God. Then we will come back to you.'

6 Abraham took the wood for the burnt offering. He gave it to Isaac to carry. Abraham carried the fire and the knife. And the 2 of them went on together. 7 Isaac spoke to Abraham. He said 'Father?' Abraham replied 'Yes my son?' Isaac said, 'The fire and the wood are here. But where is the lamb, the lamb for the burnt offering?'

8 Abraham replied, 'God will give himself the lamb for the burnt offering, my son.' And the 2 of them went on together.

9 They came to the place that God told them. Abraham built an altar. He put the wood on it. He tied his son Isaac. And he put him on top of the wood on the altar. 10 Then Abraham took the knife in his hand to kill his son.

11 But the angel of the Lord called out to him. He said 'Abraham! Abraham!' Abraham replied 'Here I Am.' 12 The angel of the Lord said, 'Do not put a hand on the boy. Do not do anything to him. Now I know that you fear God. I know this because you have not kept your son from me. And he is your only son.'

13 Abraham looked up. He saw a ram, caught in a bush. He took the ram. Abraham sacrificed it as a burnt offering. He sacrificed the ram instead of his son.

14 Abraham called that place 'The Lord will provide.' And it is still said 'On the mountain of the Lord it will be provided'.

15 The angel of the Lord called to Abraham again. He called from heaven. 16 The angel said, 'I tell you this, says the Lord. You did not keep your son from me. And he was your only son. 17 Because you have done this, I will bless you. I will make your descendants as many as the stars. They will be as many as the stars that are in the sky. They will be as many as the pieces of sand by the sea. Your descendants will take the cities of their enemies. 18 I will bless everyone on the earth through your descendants. I will do this because you obeyed me.' 19 Abraham returned to his servants. Together they left for Beersheba.

20 Some time passed. Someone told Abraham 'Milcah is also a mother. She has given birth to sons through your brother Nahor. 21 They are: Uz, the first born, his brother Buz, Kemuel, (who is the father of Aram), 22 Kesed, Hazo, Pildash, Jidlaph and Bethuel. 23 Bethuel became the father of Rebekah. Milcah gave birth to these 8 sons. Nahor was the father of these 8 sons. Nahor was Abraham's brother. 24 Nahor had a slave wife. Her name was Reumah. She also had sons. They were Tebah, Gaham, Tahash and Maacah.

Chapter 23

1 Sarah lived for 127 years. 2 She died in Kiriath Arba (that is Hebron) in the land of Canaan. Abraham was very sad because Sarah had died. He sat by her body and cried. He cried because she was dead.

3 Then Abraham got up and said, 4 'I am a foreign person among you. Sell me some land for a burial place here so that I can bury my dead.' 5 The Hittites replied, 6 'My lord, you are a powerful person among us. Bury your dead in any burial place that you choose. No one will refuse what you ask. You may have a burial place belonging to any of us. Then you can bury your dead.' 7 Abraham got up. He bowed down before the people of the land, in front of the Hittites.

8 He said to the Hittites 'As you will let me bury my dead, listen to me. Speak with Ephron son of Zohar for me. 9 Speak to him so that he will sell me the burial place in Machpelah. This belongs to him. It is at the end of the field. Ask Ephron to sell it to me. I will pay the full price. It will be a place to bury my dead among you.' 10 Ephron the Hittite was sitting with his people. He spoke so that all the Hittites could hear him. They were at the city gate. 11 Ephron said 'No my lord. Listen to me. I give you the field. And I give you the burial place that is in the field. I give it to you now. I give it to you in front of all my people. Bury your dead.' 12 Abraham bowed down to the Hittites again. 13 He said to Ephron, 'Listen to me. I will pay you the price of the field. Accept the price from me. Then I can bury my dead there.' Abraham said this so that everyone could hear him. 14 Ephron replied to Abraham, 15 'Listen to me, my lord. The land is worth 400 shekels of silver. But that is nothing between you and me. Bury your dead there.'

16 Abraham agreed to this price. He weighed the amount of silver that Ephron had asked for.

All the Hittites heard that this amount was 400 shekels of silver. Abraham used the weights that the people who sell things use.

17 Ephron's field in Machpelah, near Mamre, now belonged to Abraham. The field, the burial place in it and all the trees in the field now belonged to Abraham. They recorded the field as belonging to Abraham. 18 It now belonged to Abraham. They did this in front of all the Hittites at the city gate. 19 After this, Abraham buried Sarah his wife. He did this in the burial place in the field of Machpelah. This is near Mamre. (Mamre is at Hebron.) This is in the land of Canaan. 20 They recorded the field and the burial place as belonging to Abraham. The Hittites sold it to him. They sold it as a burial place to bury his family.

Chapter 24

1 Abraham was now very old. He had been alive for many years. The Lord had blessed him in every way. 2 Abraham had a servant. This servant had authority over everything in Abraham's household. Abraham said to him 'Put your hand under my thigh.'

3 Abraham said 'I live among the Canaanites. But I want you to make a promise to me. Make a promise to me in front of the Lord who is the God of heaven. He is also the God of earth. Say that you will not get a Canaanite wife for my son. 4 You must go to my country. Go to my relatives and get a wife for my son Isaac.' 5 The servant asked Abraham 'What if the woman will not come back with me to this land? Must I take your son to the country that you came from?' 6 Abraham replied 'You must not take my son back there. 7 The Lord, who is the God of heaven, brought me from there. He brought me out of my father's household. That was in the land where I was born. The Lord spoke to me. He made a promise to me. He said "I will give this land to your descendants." Because of this, the Lord will send His angel to go before you. He will send him so that you can get a wife for my son. Get the wife from the land that I was born in. 8 Perhaps the woman will not come back. Then you do not have to do as I have told you. But do not take my son back to that land.' 9 The servant put his hand under Abraham's thigh. The servant said that he would do everything that Abraham had said.

10 The servant took 10 of his master's camels. He left. He took many good things with him. These were from his master. He started to go to Aram Naharaim. He made his way to the town of Nahor.

11 The servant was outside the town. He made the camels go down on their knees. They were near the well. It was almost evening. At this time, women came to the well to get water. 12 The servant prayed to God. He prayed 'Lord, God of my master, Abraham. Help me to do what I promised. And be kind to my master Abraham. 13 See, I am standing by this well. The daughters of the people who live in the town are coming out. They are coming to get water from the well. 14 May this happen. I will say to a girl "Please put your water pot down the well so that I may have a drink." She may say, "Drink and I will give water to your camels". Then let her be the wife that you have chosen for your servant Isaac. I want you to do this. Then I know that you have been kind to my master Abraham.'

15 The servant was still praying when Rebekah came out. She had her pot on her shoulder. She was the daughter of Bethuel. Bethuel was the son of Milcah. Milcah was the wife of Abraham's brother, Nahor. 16 The girl was very beautiful. She had not had sex with a man. No man had slept with her. She went down to the well. She filled her pot with water. And she came up again. 17 The servant hurried to meet the girl. He said 'Please give me some water from your pot.' 18 The girl replied 'Drink my lord. She quickly took the pot from her shoulders. She held the pot in her hands and gave him a drink. 19 After she had done this, she said 'I will get water for your camels too. I will do this until they have finished drinking.' 20 So Rebekah quickly emptied her pot. She emptied the water into the place where animals drank. She ran back to the well. She took more water from the well. She took enough for all the camels. 21 The servant did not say anything. But he watched the girl. He wanted to see if the Lord had shown him a wife for Isaac.

22 The camels finished drinking. The servant took out a gold nose ring. It weighed a beka. He also took out two gold bracelets. They weighed 10 shekels.

23 The servant asked 'Whose daughter are you? Please tell me. Is there room in your father's house for me and my men to spend the night there?' 24 She replied 'I am the daughter of Bethuel. He is the son of Milcah (his mother) and Nahor (his father).'

25 She said 'We have plenty of dry grass and food for the camels. And we have room for you. You can stay the night with us.'

26 Then the man bowed down. He worshipped the Lord. 27 He said 'Praise to the Lord, the God of my master Abraham. He is kind and faithful to my master. And the Lord has been kind to me. He has led me on a journey to my master's relatives.'

28 The girl ran on before the servant. She told her mother's household about what had happened.

29 Rebekah had a brother. His name was Laban. 30 Laban saw the nose ring and the bracelets. The bracelets were on his sister's arms. He heard Rebekah tell what the man said to her. So Laban went out to the servant. He found him standing by the camels, near the well. 31 Laban said 'You are blessed by the Lord. Why are you standing out here? Come, I have prepared the house for you and a place for your camels.' 32 So the servant went to the house. He took everything off the camels. Someone brought dried grass and food for the camels. And they brought water so that he could wash his feet. And the men with him could wash their feet.

33 They gave him food. But the servant said 'I will not eat. Not until I tell you why I have come here.' Laban said, 'Then tell us.'

34 The servant said 'I am Abraham's servant. 35 The Lord has given my master many blessings. My master is very rich. The Lord has given him sheep and cows, and silver and gold. He has also given him male and female servants, and camels and donkeys. 36 Sarah was my master's wife. She gave him a son even when she was very old. My master has given his son everything that belongs to him. 37 My master made me make a promise. He said, "You must not get a Canaanite woman to be a wife for my son. I live in the land of the Canaanites. 38 Go to my father's family and to my own relatives. And get a wife for my son." 39 I asked my master "What if the woman will not return with me?" 40 My master said "The Lord will send His angel with you. You will find what you want on your journey. You will get a wife for my son. Get a wife from my own relatives. 41 Go to my relatives' house. If they will not let you take her, you will be free from your promise."

42 I came to the well today. I prayed to the Lord. I prayed "Lord, God of my master Abraham. If you will, let me find a wife for my master's son. This is why I have travelled. 43 Look. I am standing by a well. If a girl comes to get water, I will say to her, 'Please let me drink some water from your jar.' 44 She may say to me, 'Drink and I will get some water for your camels too.' Then I will know that she is the wife for my master's son. She will be the wife that the Lord has chosen."

45 While I was still praying, Rebekah came out. She carried her pot on her shoulder. She went down to the well, and got some water. I said to her "Please give me a drink." 46 She quickly took her pot off her shoulder. She said, "Drink. And I will get water for your camels too." So I drank. And she gave water to the camels. 47 I asked her "Whose daughter are you?" She said, "I am the daughter of Bethuel. He is the son of Nahor. Milcah is Bethuel's mother." I put the ring in her nose. I put the bracelets on her arms. 48 And I bowed down. I worshipped the Lord. I praised the Lord, the God of my master, Abraham. The Lord led me to this girl. She is the granddaughter of my master's brother. The Lord led me to her, for my master's son. 49 If you want to say, "No" then tell me. Or if you want to say, "Yes" then tell me. Then I will know what to do.'

50 Laban and Bethuel replied 'These things are from the Lord. We cannot go against the Lord. 51 Here is Rebekah. Take her and go. She will become the wife of your master's son. This is as the Lord has said.'

52 Abraham's servant heard what they said. He bowed to the ground in front of the Lord. 53 Then the servant brought out things made from gold and silver. He brought out special clothes. He gave them to Rebekah. He also gave valuable things to her brother and to her mother.

54 Then the servant ate and drank. And the men with him ate and drank. They stayed the night there. The next morning they woke up. The servant said, 'Let me go back to my master.'

55 Rebekah's brother and mother replied 'Let her stay with us for 10 days or so. Then you can go.'

56 The servant said 'Do not stop me. The Lord has given me what I need. Let me go now. Then I can go to my master.'

57 The brother and mother said 'Let us call the girl. Let us ask her what she wants to do.' 58 So they called out to Rebekah. They asked her 'Will you go with this man?' Rebekah said 'I will go.' 59 So they sent their sister Rebekah away. And her nurse went with her. They went with Abraham's servant, and his men. 60 And her brother and mother blessed Rebekah. They said 'Our sister may you be the mother of thousands, and the mother of ten thousands. May your descendants take the gates of their enemies?'

61 Rebekah and her female servants left. They rode on camels. And they went back with the servant. The servant took Rebekah and left.

62 Isaac came from Beer Lahai Roi because he was living in the Negev.

63 It was evening. And Isaac went out to the field to meditate. He looked up. And he saw camels coming near.

64 Rebekah looked up. She saw Isaac. She got down from her camel. 65 She asked the servant 'Who is that man in the field? Who is that man coming to meet us?' The servant replied 'He is my master'. Rebekah covered herself with her veil.

66 The servant told Isaac everything that happened. 67 Isaac brought Rebekah into his mother's tent. Isaac married Rebekah. Rebekah became his wife. And Isaac loved Rebekah. So, Isaac was happy again, after the death of his mother.

Chapter 25

1 Abraham took another wife. Her name was Keturah. 2 She gave birth to Zimran, Jokshan, Medan, Midian, Ishbak and Shuah. 3 Jokshan became the father of Sheba and Dedan. The descendants of Dedan were the Asshurites, the Letushites and the Leummites. 4 Midian became the father of Ephah, Epher, Hanoch, Abida and Eldaah. All these were descendants of Keturah. 5 When he died, Abraham left everything that was his to Isaac. 6 When he was still alive, he gave gifts to the sons of the other wives. He sent these sons away from Isaac. He sent them to the land of the east.

7 Abraham's whole life was 175 years. 8 And he died when he was very old. He joined his people who had died before him. 9 Isaac and Ishmael buried him. They were his sons. They buried Abraham in the burial place of Machpelah. This is near Mamre. It is in the field of Ephron, the son of Zohar. He is a Hittite. 10 Abraham bought this field. He bought it from the Hittites. They buried Abraham there with his wife, Sarah.

11 After the death of Abraham, God blessed Isaac. Isaac is Abraham's son. Isaac then lived near Beer Lahai Roi.

12 This is a report of Ishmael. Ishmael is Abraham's son. Sarah's female servant gave birth to Ishmael. Her name was Hagar. She was from Egypt. 13 These are the names of Ishmael's sons. The list starts from the first-born son and ends with the last born son. Nebaioth was the first born son of Ishmael. Then there were Kedar, Adbeel, Mibsam, 14 Mishma, Dumah, Massa, 15 Hadad, Tema, Jetur, Naphish and Kedmah. 16 These were all Ishmael's sons. And these were the names of the 12 groups of people. They separated and lived in their own land. They ruled over the 12 groups of people. 17 Ishmael was alive for 137 years. He took his last breath and died. He joined his people who had died before him. 18 Ishmael's descendants lived in the lands from Havilah to Shur. These are near Egypt, towards Asshur. And they were always at war with each other.

19 This is a report of what happened to Isaac. He was Abraham's son. Abraham became the father of Isaac. 20 When Isaac was 40 years old, he married Rebekah. Rebekah was the daughter of Bethuel. Bethuel was an Aramean from Paddan Aram. She was the sister of Laban the Aramean. 21 Rebekah could not have children. So Isaac prayed to the Lord for Rebekah. The Lord did as Isaac asked. And Isaac's wife, Rebekah became pregnant. 22 The babies inside her were fighting with each other. Rebekah said 'Why is this happening to me?' So Rebekah went to ask the Lord. 23 The Lord said to Rebekah, 'The two who are in your body will separate. And they will be two groups of people. Two groups of people will separate from your body. One group will be stronger than the other. And the older will be like servants to the younger.'

24 The time came for Rebekah to give birth. There were two babies inside her. 25 The first baby to come out was red. Hair covered the whole of his body. They called him Esau.

26 After this, his brother came out. His hand was holding the back of Esau's foot. They called him Jacob. Isaac was 166 years old when Rebekah gave birth to them.

27 Time passed and the boys grew. Esau became a good hunter. He liked being in the country. Jacob was a quiet man. He stayed among the tents. 28 Isaac liked to eat the meat from the animals that Esau killed. So he loved Esau. But Rebekah loved Jacob.

29 One day, Jacob was cooking a meal. Esau came back from the country. He was very hungry. 30 He said to Jacob 'Quick let me have some of that red food! I am very hungry.' (That is also why he was called Edom.) 31 Jacob said, 'You must first sell me your birthright.'

32 Esau said 'Look I am going to die now. What good is my birthright to me?'

33 Jacob said 'First, say a promise to me.' So Esau said a promise to Jacob. He promised to sell his birthright to Jacob. 34 Then Jacob gave Esau some bread and the meal made from seeds. Esau ate and drank. Then he got up and left. So Esau showed that he did not care about his birthright (he did not think that it was important).

Chapter 26

1 There was a famine in the land. This had happened before, when Abraham was alive. Isaac went to Gerar to visit Abimelech. He was the king of the Philistines. 2 The Lord appeared to Isaac. He said 'Do not go to Egypt. Live in the land that I tell you to live in. 3 Stay in this land for a time. And I will be with you. And I will bless you. I will give these lands to you and your descendants. I will say again the promise that I told your father Abraham. 4 I will give you many descendants. They will be as many as the stars in the sky. And I will give these lands to them. Through your descendant, I will bless everyone on the earth. 5 This will happen because of Abraham. He kept all my laws and obeyed me.

6 So Isaac stayed in Gerar.

7 The men of Gerar asked Isaac about his wife. He said, 'She is my sister.' He was afraid to say 'She is my wife.' He thought 'The men of Gerar may kill me. They may kill me because of Rebekah. They may kill me because she is beautiful.'

8 Isaac stayed in Gerar for a long time. One day Abimelech, the king of the Philistines, looked down from his window. Abimelech saw Isaac touching his wife, Rebekah.

9 Abimelech called Isaac to come to him. Abimelech said 'She is your wife! Why did you say, "She is my sister"?' Isaac replied 'I thought that someone might kill me because of her.' 10 Abimelech said 'What have you done to us? One of my men might have had sex with your wife. Then we would have done wrong.' 11 Abimelech told his people, 'I will kill anyone who hurts this man.'

12 Isaac planted crops in the land. They grew well. They grew to 100 times the amount that he planted. This was because the Lord blessed him.

13 Isaac became rich. His riches continued to grow. Then Isaac became very rich. 14 Isaac had many sheep, goats and cows. He also had many servants. He had so many that the Philistines became angry with him. They thought that he had more than they had. And they wanted what he had. That is why they were angry. 15 When Abraham was alive; his servants had dug many wells. Now, the Philistines filled them in again. They did this because they did not want Isaac to get rich. 16 Abimelech said to Isaac 'You have become too powerful for us. Go and live away from us.'

17 So Isaac moved away from that place. He put his tents in the Valley of Gerar. And he stayed there. 18 Isaac dug the wells again. They were the wells that Abraham had dug. But the Philistines filled them with the ground. This happened when Abraham died. Isaac opened them. He gave them the same names as his father had given them. 19 Isaac's servants dug in the valley. They found a well there. It was full of fresh water. 20 But the herdsmen of Gerar quarrelled with Isaac's herdsmen. They said 'The water belongs to us!' So Isaac called the well Esek. He called it that because they quarrelled with him.

21 So Isaac's men dug another well. But the herdsmen of Gerar quarrelled about that one. Isaac called that well Sitnah.

22 Isaac moved on from Sitnah. He dug another well. No one quarrelled with him about this well. He called it Rehoboth. He said 'Now the Lord has given us space. We will have good things in this land.'

23 From that place, Isaac went to Beersheba. 24 That night the Lord appeared to him. The Lord said 'I am the God of your father Abraham. Do not be afraid, because I am with you. I will bless you. I will give you many descendants because of my servant Abraham.'

25 Isaac built an altar. He called out to the Lord. He put his tent there. And his servants dug a well.

26 During that time, Abimelech came to Isaac. He came from Gerar. He came with Ahuzzath his officer and with Phicol the officer of his army.

27 Isaac asked them 'Why have you come to me? You were like an enemy. And you sent me away.' 28 They replied 'We saw that the Lord is with you. So we said to one another, "There should be a promise between us and you." So, let us make a promise with you. 29 Promise that you will not hurt us. We did not hurt you. We did only good to you. And we sent you away as friends. And now the Lord is blessing you.' 30 Then Isaac made a large meal for them. And they all ate and drank.

31 Early the next morning, they made a promise to each other. And Isaac sent them away. They left without fighting. 32 The same day, Isaac's servants came to him. They told him about a well that they had dug. They said, 'We have found water!' 33 Isaac called the well Shibah. And the name of the town is Beersheba.

34 When Esau was 40 years old, he got married. He married Judith. She was the daughter of Beer the Hittite. He also married Basemath. She was the daughter of Elon the Hittite. 35 This made Isaac and Rebekah very sad.

Chapter 27

1 Isaac became old. He could not see anything. He could not see because his eyes were weak. He called for Esau. Esau was his oldest son. Isaac said, 'My son.' Esau replied, 'Yes'. 2 Isaac said 'I am an old man. I do not know when I will die. 3 Now get your bow and arrows. Go out into the country. Kill some wild animals for me.'

4 Isaac said, 'Prepare the food that I like to eat. And bring it to me. Bring it to me so that I can eat it. Then I can give you my blessing before I die.'

5 Rebekah listened to what Isaac said to Esau. Esau went out into the country. He went to kill an animal and bring back the meat.

6 Rebekah said to Jacob 'I heard your father say this to Esau. 7 "Bring me some meat. And prepare the food that I like to eat. Bring it to me. Then I can give you my blessing. I will bless you in front of the Lord. I will do this before I die." ' 8 Rebekah said 'Now my son, listen carefully. And do as I tell you. 9 Go out to the animals. Bring me two nice looking goats. Bring me two young goats. Then I will prepare some food that your father likes to eat. It will be prepared how he likes it. 10 Then take the food to your father to eat. Then he will give you his blessing before he dies.' 11 Jacob said 'Hair covers my brother's skin. But my skin does not have any hair. 12 My father may touch me. Then he will know that I am telling him lies (words that are not true). Then he will not bless me. He will curse me.' 13 Jacob's mother said, 'My son. Let the curse fall on me. Do what I say. Go and get the things that I told you.' 14 Jacob went and got the goats. He brought them to his mother. She prepared some food. She prepared the food that Isaac liked to eat. 15 Then Rebekah took some of Esau's clothes. They were his best clothes. Rebekah had them in her house. She put them on Jacob, her younger son. 16 She covered Jacob's hands with the skin from the goats. She also covered the part of his neck that had no hair.

17 Then she gave Jacob (her son) the food that Isaac liked to eat. And she gave him some bread that she had made.

18 Jacob went to his father. He said 'My father.' Isaac replied 'Yes, my son. Who is it?'

19 Jacob said 'I am Esau. I am your first born son. I have done as you told me. Please sit up and eat some of my meat. Then you can give me your blessing.' 20 Isaac asked his son 'My son. How did you find it so quickly?' Jacob replied, 'The Lord your God helped me find it.'

21 Isaac said to Jacob 'Come near to me so that I can touch you. Then I will know if you really are my son Esau.' 22 Jacob went close to his father. Isaac touched him. He said 'The voice is that of Jacob. But the hands are those of Esau.' 23 Isaac did not know that it was Jacob. He did not know because he could feel the hair on Jacob's hands. They felt like Esau's hands. So Isaac blessed Jacob. 24 Isaac asked 'Are you really my son Esau?' Jacob replied 'I am.' 25 Isaac said 'My son, bring me some of your meat. I will eat it. Then I can give you my blessing.' So Jacob brought the food to him. Isaac ate it. Then Jacob brought some wine. And Isaac drank it. 26 Then Isaac said 'Come here my son. And kiss me.' 27 So Jacob went to Isaac and kissed him. Isaac smelled the clothes that Jacob wore. Then Isaac blessed him. He said, 'The smell of my son is like the smell of a field. It is like a field that God has blessed. 28 May God give you rain for your crops. Then may he give you a good harvest of crops, and grapes for wine.

29 May you be the master of many peoples living in many countries? And may they bow down to you. Be master over your brothers. May the sons of your mother bow down to you. May people who curse you receive curses? And may people who bless you receive blessings.'

30 Isaac finished blessing Jacob. And Jacob left him. Then Esau came in from the country. He had killed an animal. 31 Esau prepared the food that Isaac liked to eat. Then he took the food to Isaac. Esau said 'My father. Sit up and eat some of my meat. Then you can give me your blessing.'

32 His father Isaac asked 'Who are you?' Esau replied 'I am your son. I am your first born son Esau.' 33 Isaac shook and trembled. He said 'Who was it who killed the animal? Who brought it to me? I ate it, just before you came. And I blessed him. And he will get the blessing!'

34 Esau understood what his father had said. And he cried aloud. He said 'Bless me. Bless me as well my father!' 35 But Isaac said 'Your brother came to me. He deceived me. And he took your blessing.' 36 Esau said 'Jacob is the right name for him. He has deceived me two times. He took my birthright. And now he has taken my blessing!' Then Esau asked 'Do you have any blessing left for me?'

37 Isaac replied 'I have made him master over you. And I have made all his relatives his servants. I have given him crops and wine. So what can I do for you my son?'

38 Esau said 'My father! Do you have only one blessing? My father! Bless me as well!' Then Esau wept aloud.

39 Isaac replied 'You will not grow rich from the earth. You will not have rain to make your crops grow. 40 You will have to fight for everything. And your brother will rule over you. But after a time, you will break away from him, and from his descendants.'

41 Esau did not forget what Jacob had done. He hated Jacob because of the blessing that Isaac gave him. Esau said, 'My father will die soon. Then I will kill my brother.' 42 Someone told Rebekah what Esau had said. She sent for Jacob. She said to him 'Your brother Esau wants to kill you. When he thinks about killing you, it helps him to feel better. 43 Now my son, do what I tell you. Go to my brother Laban. He lives in Haran. 44 Stay with him for a time. Stay there until your brother is not angry with you. 45 When Esau is not angry with you, I will send someone to tell you. When he forgets what you did to him, you can come back from Haran. I do not want to lose both of you in one day.'

46 Rebekah said to Isaac 'I do not like living with Esau's wives. I do not like it because they are Hittites. My life will be worse if Jacob marries a Hittite woman (a woman from the people of this land).'

Chapter 28

1 Isaac called for Jacob. Isaac blessed him. He told him 'Do not marry a Canaanite woman. 2 Go now to Paddan Aram. Go to the house of Bethuel. He is your mother's father. Take a wife from there. Take a wife from the daughters of Laban. He is your mother's brother.

3 May God Almighty bless you? May he make you rich? And may he give you many descendants so that your descendants become a group of people. 4May God give to you the blessing that he gave to Abraham. And may he give it to your descendants. Then you can take the land in which you live as a foreign person. This is the land that God gave to Abraham.' 5Isaac sent Jacob on his journey. Jacob went to Paddan Aram. He went to Laban, who was the son of Bethuel the Aramean. Laban was the brother of Rebekah. Rebekah was the mother of Jacob and Esau.

6 Esau heard that Isaac blessed Jacob. He knew that Isaac sent Jacob to Paddan Aram. And he knew that Isaac told Jacob to take a wife from Paddan Aram. Esau knew that Isaac told Jacob 'Do not marry a Canaanite woman.' 7 Esau knew that Jacob obeyed his father and mother. And that Jacob went to Paddan Aram. 8 Esau knew that Isaac did not like the Canaanite women. 9 So Esau went to Ishmael. He married Mahalath, the sister of Nebaioth. Mahalath is also the daughter of Ishmael. Ishmael is the son of Abraham. Esau married Mahalath. And he kept his other wives.

10 Jacob left Beersheba. He went towards Haran. 11 He came to a place. And he stayed there for the night. He stayed there because the sun had gone down. He took a stone. He put it under his head. And he lay down and went to sleep. 12 He had a dream. In the dream, he saw some steps. The steps went from the earth, into heaven. The angels of God went up and down the steps. 13 The Lord stood above the steps. He said 'I am the Lord. I am the God of your father Abraham. And I am the God of Isaac. I will give you the land that you lie on. I will give it to you and to your descendants. 14 Your descendants will be as many as the dust of the earth. They will go to the west and to the east. They will go to the north and to the south. I will bless the people of the earth because of one of your descendants.

15 I am with you. And I will watch over you everywhere you go. I will bring you back to this land. I will not leave you. Not until I have done what I have promised you.'

16 Jacob woke from his sleep. He thought 'The Lord is in this place. And I did not know.' 17 Jacob was afraid. He said 'How great this place is! This must be the house of God. This is the gate of heaven.'

18 In the morning Jacob took the stone that he had put under his head. He made it stand up straight in the ground. He poured oil on top of it.

19 Jacob called that place Bethel. The name of the place was Luz. But Jacob called it Bethel.

20 Then Jacob made a promise. He said 'I want God to be with me and to watch over me, while I am on this journey. I want him to give me food to eat and clothes to wear. 21 I want to return to my father's house. If God does all these things, then the Lord will be my God. 22 This stone that I have put here will be God's house. And from everything that God gives me, I will give God one tenth.'

Chapter 29

1 Jacob continued on his journey. He came to the land where the people from the east live. 2 He saw a well in a field. Three groups of sheep lay by the well. They lay there because the sheep had water from that well. A large stone covered the top of the well. 3 Shepherds waited until all the sheep were there. Then they removed the stone from the well. And they gave their sheep water to drink. After this, they put the stone back on the top of the well.

4 Jacob asked the shepherds 'My brothers, where are you from?' The shepherds replied, 'We are from Haran.' 5 Jacob said 'Do you know Laban? He is Nahor's grandson.' The shepherds replied 'Yes, we know him.' 6 Jacob asked them 'Is he in good health?' They replied 'Yes he is. Here comes his daughter with the sheep. Her name is Rachel.' 7 Jacob said 'Look. The sun is high in the sky. It is not the right time to bring all the sheep together. Give the sheep water. And take them back to the fields.' 8 The shepherds said 'We cannot do that. We have to wait until all the sheep are here. Then we can remove the stone and give the sheep water.'

9 When Jacob was speaking, Rachel came. She brought her father's sheep with her. She was a shepherdess.

10 Jacob saw Rachel. She was the daughter of Laban. Laban was Jacob's mother's brother. Jacob saw Laban's sheep.

So Jacob went to the stone on the well. He removed it from the well. Then he gave water to Laban's sheep. 11 Then Jacob kissed Rachel. He began to cry aloud...

12 Jacob told Rachel that he was a relative of Laban. He told him that he was a son of Rebekah. And Rachel ran in front of Jacob. She told her father.

13 Laban heard what Rachel said. He hurried to meet Jacob. Jacob was the son of Laban's sister. He put his arms round Jacob. And he kissed him. Laban brought Jacob to his home. And Jacob told Laban why he had come to him. 14 Then Laban said 'You are my own relative.' Jacob stayed with Laban for a whole month.

15 Then Laban said to Jacob 'You should not work for me for nothing because you are my relative. Tell me what I should pay you.' 16 Laban had 2 daughters. The name of the older daughter was Leah. The name of the younger daughter was Rachel. 17 Leah had weak eyes. But Rachel was beautiful. 18 Jacob loved Rachel. He said 'I will work for you for 7 years. In return, I want your daughter Rachel.' 19 Laban said 'It is better to give her to you than to another man. Stay here with me.' 20 Jacob worked for 7 years to have Rachel. But the years passed quickly. They seemed like a few days to Jacob because he loved Rachel very much.

21 After 7 years, Jacob said to Laban, 'Give me my wife. My time is finished. And I want to marry her.' 22Laban called all the people in that place together. He gave a feast. 23 Evening came. But Laban took his daughter Leah. And he gave her to Jacob. And Jacob married her. 24 Laban gave his female servant to Leah. Her name was Zilpah. Zilpah was now Leah's servant. 25 When morning came, Jacob saw Leah! Jacob said to Laban, 'What have you done to me? I worked for you to have Rachel. Why have you deceived me?' 26 Laban replied 'In this land, we do not give the younger daughter first. We do not give her before the older daughter. 27 Finish Leah's marriage week. Then we will give you the younger daughter also. And you must work for another 7 years.

28 So Jacob did this. He finished the week with Leah. 29 Then Laban gave Rachel to Jacob to be his wife. Laban give his female servant Bilhah to Rachel. Bilhah was now one of Rachel's servants. 30 Jacob married Rachel also. He loved Rachel more than he loved Leah. Jacob worked for Laban. He worked for 7 more years.

31 The Lord saw that Jacob did not love Leah. So he let her give birth to children. But the Lord did not let Rachel give birth to children. 32 Leah became pregnant. She gave birth to a son. She called him Reuben. She said 'It is because the Lord has heard. He has heard how sad I am. My husband will love me now because I have given birth to a son.' 33 Leah became pregnant again. She gave birth to another son. She said 'The Lord gave me another son. Because he knows that I am not loved.' She called this son Simeon. 34Leah became pregnant again. And again she gave birth to a son. She said 'I have given my husband 3 sons. So now he will want to stay with me.' She called this son Levi. 35 Leah became pregnant again. She gave birth to a son. She said 'This time I will praise the Lord.' She called this son Judah. Then she stopped having children.

Chapter 30

1 Rachel now knew that she could not have any children. She knew that she could not give Jacob any children. So, she did not like her sister because her sister had children. Rachel said to Jacob, 'Give me children, or I will die.'

2 Jacob became angry with Rachel. He said 'Am I God? God has stopped you from giving birth to children!' 3 Rachel said 'Here is Bilhah. She is my female servant. Have sex with her so that she can have children for me. Through her, I can build a family.'

4 So Rachel gave her servant Bilhah to Jacob. Jacob took her as a wife. 5 She became pregnant. And she gave Jacob a son. 6 Rachel said 'God has done what is right to me. He has listened to me. And he has given me a son.' Because of this, she called the baby Dan. 7 Rachel's servant Bilhah became pregnant again. She gave Jacob another son. 8 Rachel said 'I have fought with my sister. And I have won.' She called this baby Naphtali.

9 Leah saw that she had stopped having children. So she took her female servant. Her name was Zilpah. She gave her to Jacob as a wife. 10 Zilpah became pregnant. And she gave Jacob a son.

11 Leah said 'This is very good.' And she called the baby Gad. 12 Leah's servant gave Jacob another son. 13 Leah said 'I am very happy! Women will call me happy.' So she called this baby Asher.

14 It was the time to get the wheat in from the fields. Reuben went out into the fields. He found some mandrake plants. He brought them to Leah, his mother. Rachel said to Leah, 'Please give me some of the mandrake plants that your son gave to you.'

15 But Leah said to Rachel 'You took my husband. Was not that enough? Now you want my son's mandrakes too!' Rachel said, 'You must give me some of your son's mandrakes. Then Jacob can sleep with you tonight.' 16 In the evening, Jacob came in from the fields. Leah went out to meet him. She said 'You must sleep with me tonight. I have bought you with my son's mandrakes.' So Jacob slept with Leah that night. 17 God listened to Leah. And she became pregnant. She gave Jacob a 5th son. 18 Leah said 'God has paid me because I gave my servant to Jacob.' She called her son Issachar. 19 Leah became pregnant again. And she gave Jacob a 6th son. 20 Leah said 'God has given me this valuable gift. Now my husband will want to stay with me because I have given him 6 sons.' She called this son Zebulun. 21 Some time passed. And Leah became pregnant again. She gave birth to a daughter. She called her daughter Dinah. 22 Then God remembered Rachel. He listened to her. And he let her give birth to children. 23 She became pregnant. She gave birth to a son. Rachel said, 'I am not ashamed any more because God has given me a son.' 24 Rachel called her son Joseph. She said 'May the Lord give me another son.'

25 After Rachel gave birth to Joseph, Jacob spoke to Laban. He said 'Let me go on my way. Let me go so that I can go back to my own land. 26 Give me my wives. Give me my children. I have worked for you to have them. Then I will go on my journey. You know how much I have worked for you.' 27 Laban said to Jacob 'If you are happy with me then please stay. I know that the Lord has blessed me. That is because you are here.' 28 Laban continued, 'Say what you want. And I will pay it.' 29 Jacob said 'You know how much I have worked for you. And you know how many more animals you have. 30 You had a small number of sheep and goats before I came. Now the number of them is much bigger. And anywhere that I have been, the Lord has blessed you. But now I want to give my family what they need. 31 Laban asked 'What must I give you?' Jacob replied, 'Do not give me anything. But do one thing for me. Then I will still care for your animals. And I will see that nothing bad happens to them. 32 Let me go among all your animals today. And let me remove any animal that has a mark on it. Let me remove any animal that has more than one colour on its skin. I will take them from your sheep and from your goats. These animals will be what I receive from you. 33 And this will show that I am honest. You can check on my animals when you want to. I may have a sheep or a goat that does not have more than one colour on its skin. Then you can say that I have taken it from you.' 34 Laban said 'I agree to this. It will be as you have said.' 35 On that same day, Laban went to his animals. He quickly removed any animal that had more than one colour on its skin. And he gave them to his sons to care for. 36 Then Laban went away. It would take Jacob 3 days to reach Laban. While this was happening, Jacob cared for the rest of Laban's animals.

37 Jacob took branches cut from trees. He took them from the poplar tree, the almond tree and the plane tree. He made white lines on them. He did this by taking the outside part of the wood from some of the branch. Then he could see the white part of the branch. 38 Then he put the branches in the place where the animals drank. They were in front of the animals when they came to drink. Sometimes it was the right time when the animals came to drink. 39 They would have sex and become pregnant. They did this in front of the branches. And they gave birth to young ones that had more than one colour on their skin. 40 Jacob kept the animals separate from Laban's animals. Then he separated Laban's animals. He separated the female animals from the male animals. And he would only let the female animals have sex with his own black male sheep. 41 Jacob waited until the time was right for the stronger female animals. Then he put the branches in front of them, when they had sex with his own black male animals. 42 But if the female animals were weak, he did not put the branches in front of the animals. So Jacob put the weak animals with Laban's animals. But Jacob kept the strong animals. 43 By doing this, Jacob became very rich. He had many animals, female servants and male servants and camels and donkeys.

Chapter 31

1 Jacob heard Laban's sons saying, 'Jacob has taken everything that our father had. He has got rich from things belonging to our father.' 2 And Jacob saw that Laban was not as nice to him as he had been before.

3 Then the Lord said to Jacob 'Go back to the land where your fathers lived. Go back to your relatives. I will be with you.'

4 Jacob sent someone to go to Rachel and Leah. Jacob said that they must come to the field where he was. He was with his animals. 5 Jacob said to Rachel and Leah, 'Your father is not as nice to me now, as he was before. I have seen that he is not so nice. But the God of my father has been with me. 6 You know how I have worked for your father. I have worked as well as I can. 7 But your father has changed what I receive in return for working. He changed it many times. But God has not let him hurt me. 8 Sometimes Laban said, "The animals with different colours on their skin will be your payment." Then the animals gave birth to young ones with different colours on their skins. Sometimes he said, "The animals with marks on them will be your payment." Then the animals gave birth to young ones with marks on them. 9 In this way God took your father's animals, and gave them to me. 10 I had a dream. It was at the time when the animals became pregnant. I looked up. I saw that the male animals had different colours on their skin. 11 The angel of God spoke to me in the dream. He said "Jacob." I replied, "Yes." 12 And the angel said, "Look up. See all the male animals have different colours on their skin. I have seen the bad things that Laban has done to you. 13 I am the God who appeared to you at Bethel. This is where you poured oil on the stone. And this is where you made a promise to me. Now leave this land. Go back to the land where your father lived." ' 14 Then Rachel and Leah replied, 'We no longer have any part of our father's inheritance. 15 He thinks of us as foreign people. He sold us. Then he used what he received for us on himself.'

16 They said, 'Everything that God took from our father belongs to us, and to our children. So you must do what God tells you.'

17 So Jacob put his children and wives on camels. 18 He took all his animals, and everything that he had got in Paddan Aram. He left to go to his father Isaac. He left to go to the land of Canaan. 19 Before they left, Laban went to cut wool from his sheep. While he was gone, Rachel took his household gods.

20 Jacob did not tell Laban the Aramean that he was going away. 21 So Jacob ran away. He took everything that he had. He went across the river. He went towards the hill country of Gilead.

22 After 3 days, someone told Laban that Jacob had run away with his family. 23 Laban took his relatives and followed Jacob. He followed him for 7 days, and then he found him. He found him in the hill country of Gilead. 24 Then God came to Laban the Aramean. He appeared to him in a dream at night. God said to Laban, 'Be careful what you say to Jacob. Do not say that you will do anything to him.'

25 Jacob had put up his tent in the hill country of Gilead. And Laban found him. So Laban and his relatives also put up their tents in this place. 26 Laban said to Jacob, 'What have you done? You have deceived me. And you have taken my daughters as if you caught them in a war. 27 Why did you keep it a secret that you were leaving? You deceived me. Why did you not tell me that you were leaving? I would have sent you away with joy and singing to music. 28 You did not even let me kiss my grandchildren goodbye. Or let me kiss my daughters goodbye. What you have done is not right. 29 I have the power to hurt you. But last night the God of your father came to me. He said, "Be careful what you say to Jacob. Do not say that you will do anything to him." 30 I know that you want to return to your father's house. But why did you take my gods?' 31 Jacob replied, 'I was afraid. I thought that you would try to stop me. And I thought that you would try to take your daughters away from me. 32 But if you find your gods with anyone here, that person will die. While our relatives watch, you may look for anything that belongs to you. If you find anything then take it.' Jacob did not know that Rachel had taken her father's gods.

33 So Laban went into Jacob's tent. Then he went into Leah's tent. He also went into the female servants' tent. But he did not find anything. When he left Leah's tent, he went into Rachel's tent. 34 Rachel had taken the household gods. She put them inside the seat that she sat on to ride her camel. Then she sat on them. Laban looked through everything in the tent. But he did not find the gods. 35 When he went into Rachel's tent, she said, 'Do not be angry with me my lord. I cannot stand up in front of you. It is the time of my monthly blood loss.' So, Laban looked for the gods, but he did not find them.

36 Then Jacob became angry with Laban. He asked him 'What have I done wrong? What have I done against you? Why have you followed me? 37 Now you have looked through everything that I have. And what have you found that belongs to you? If you have found anything, put it in front of your relatives and mine. Let them say which one of us is right. 38 I have worked for you for 20 years. Your animals have all given birth to young ones. I have not eaten any of your male animals. 39 I did not bring you animals killed by wild animals. I paid you for them. You said that I must pay for any animals that someone took in the day or night.'

40 Jacob said, 'This is what it was like to work for you: I could not get away from the heat of the sun in the day. It felt like it was eating me. And the night-time was so cold that I could not sleep. 41 It was like this for 20 years. That is the time that I have been working for you, in your household. I worked for 14 years to pay you for your daughters. Then I worked for 6 years for your animals. And you changed what I received from you many times. 42 The God of my father, the God of Abraham and the Fear of Isaac was with me. If he were not, then you would have sent me away with nothing. But God has seen what you have done to me. He has seen how I have worked for you. And last night he told you that he knew what you had done.'

43 Laban replied 'These women are my daughters. Their children are my children. The animals are my animals. But what can I do today about my daughters or about their children? 44 Let us make a promise between you and me. And let it show what has happened between us.' 45 So Jacob took a large stone and made it stand up. 46 He said to his relatives, 'Go and get some stones.' So they went and got some stones. They put them together on the ground. Then they all ate a meal together, near the heap of stones.

47 Laban called the place Jegar Sahadutha. Jacob called it Galeed.

48 Laban said 'These stones show that we made a promise today.' That is why Jacob called that place Galeed. 49 That place also had the name 'Mizpah'. That was because Laban said 'May the Lord watch you and me when we are away from each other. 50 Remember that God is watching you. If you do wrong to my daughters, God will see it. And if you marry any other women, remember this. God is watching you. Even if no one else is with you, God will know.'

51 Laban also said 'I have set this stone up. And I have set the heap of stones by it. They are between you and me. 52 I will not go past the stones to your side to hurt you. And you must not go past them to my side to hurt me. The stones will show where we can go. 53 Let the God of Abraham, the God of Nahor, the God of their father say who is right between us.' So Jacob made a promise in the name of God. 54 He offered a sacrifice to God in the hill country. He asked his relatives to eat a meal with him. After they had eaten, they stayed the night there.

55 Early the next morning, Laban woke. He kissed his grandchildren. And he kissed his daughters. He blessed them. Then he left and went back to his home.

Chapter 32

1 Jacob continued to go to his father's house. And the angels of God met him.

2 Jacob saw them and said, 'This is where God's army is!' So he called that place Mahanaim.

3 Jacob sent men with messages in front of him. He sent them to his brother Esau. He was in the land of Seir, the country of Edom. 4 Jacob told his men, 'This is what you must say to my master Esau: Your servant Jacob says, "I have been staying with Laban. I have stayed there until now. 5 I have cows and donkeys, sheep and goats. And I have male and female servants. Now I am sending this message to my lord so that you will be happy with me." '

6 When the men returned, they said to Jacob, 'We went to your brother Esau. And now he is coming to meet you. And he has 400 men with him.' 7 Jacob was very frightened and worried. So he separated his people into 2 groups. He also separated the animals. 8 He thought 'If Esau attacks one group, the other group may be safe.'

9 Then Jacob prayed, 'God of Abraham and God of my father Isaac, Lord, you said to me "Go back to your country. And go to your relatives and I will do good things for you." 10 I am not worth all the kind things that you have done for me. You have stayed with me. And I am not worth this. When I crossed the River Jordan, I only had my stick. But now I can make 2 groups of good things from what I have. 11 I pray that you will save me from my brother Esau. Because I am afraid that he will come and attack me. He may also attack my family. 12 But you have said, "I will give you many good things. I will make your descendants as many as the pieces of sand by the sea. They are so many that they cannot be counted." '.

13 Jacob stayed the night in that place. He chose a gift for Esau from everything that he had.

14 He chose 200 female goats, 200 female sheep and 20 male sheep. 15 Also he chose 30 female camels, with their young ones, 40 cows and 10 male cows and 20 female donkeys and 10 male donkeys. 16 He told his servants to care for them. He separated each group of animals from the other groups. Jacob said to his servants 'Go before me. Keep some space between each group of animals.' 17 He told the servant at the front, 'When my brother Esau meets you and asks, "Who do you belong to? Where are you going? Who do all these animals belong to?" 18 You must say, "They belong to your servant Jacob. They are a gift that he has sent to my lord Esau. And Jacob is coming behind us." ' 19 Jacob also told the other servants who followed a group of animals 'You are to say the same thing to Esau, when you meet him. 20 And you must say "Your servant Jacob is coming behind us." ' Jacob thought 'Esau will be pleased with my gifts. Then he will not hurt me.' 21 So Jacob's gifts went on before him. But he spent the night with his people.

22 That night Jacob took his 2 wives, 11 sons and 2 female servants. And he sent them over the part of the River Jabbok that was not very deep. 23 After he had sent his people across, he sent everything that was his over the stream. 24 Jacob was alone. And a man came and fought with him. The man fought with Jacob until it was day.

25 The man saw that he was not beating Jacob. So, he touched Jacob's hip. And Jacob's hip broke as he fought with the man. 26 Then the man said 'Let me go because now it is day.' But Jacob said, 'I will not let you go until you bless me.'

27 The man asked Jacob 'What is your name?' Jacob replied 'Jacob'. 28 Then the man said 'Your name will not be Jacob any more. Your name will be Israel. This is because you have fought with God. And you have fought with men. And you have shown that you are strong.'

29 Jacob said 'Please tell me your name.' But the man said 'Why do you ask my name?' Then he blessed Jacob there. 30 So Jacob called that place Peniel. He said 'I saw God face to face. And I did not die.'

31 The sun rose in the sky as Jacob passed through Peniel. And Jacob could not walk very well because of his hip.

32 Even today, the Israelites do not eat the part of an animal joined to the hip. This is because God touched Jacob's hip.

Chapter 33

1 Jacob looked up. He saw Esau with 400 men coming towards him. So, he separated his children into groups. Some went with Leah, some with his 2 female servants and Joseph went with Rachel. 2 He put his female servants and their children at the front of the group. Then came Leah and her children. But Jacob put Rachel and Joseph at the back of the group. 3 Jacob went in front of the group. He bowed down to the ground. He did this 7 times as he came close to his brother Esau.

4 But Esau ran to meet Jacob. And he hugged him. He hugged Jacob's neck. And Esau kissed him. And they both wept.

5 Then Esau looked up. He saw the women and children. He asked 'Who are these people with you?' Jacob replied, 'They are the children that God has given to me.' 6 Then the female servants and their children came to Esau. As they came close to him, they bowed down. 7 Then Leah and her children came and bowed down in front of Esau. Last of all, Joseph and Rachel came and bowed down to Esau. 8 Esau asked 'Why did you send all those animals in front of you?' Jacob replied, 'So that you would be happy to see me, my lord.' 9 But Esau said 'Keep your animals for yourself my brother. I have enough of my own.' 10 But Jacob replied 'No! If you are happy to see me, accept these as a gift from me. I was afraid to see you. I was as afraid as if I could see the face of God. But I have seen you. And I did not die. 11 Please accept the gift that I brought to you. Accept it because God has given me many good things. And I have everything that I need.' So, Esau accepted the gifts because Jacob wanted him to.

12 Then Esau said 'Let us go on our way. I will go with you.' 13 But Jacob said, 'My lord, the children are young. And many of the animals have young ones. If we go too far in a day, then the animals will die. 14 So my lord should go in front of me. I will move along slowly with the animals and children. I will come to you my lord, in Seir.'

15 Esau said 'Then let me leave some of my men with you.' But Jacob replied 'You do not have to do that. All I want is for you to be happy with me.' 16 So Esau began his journey back to Seir. 17 But Jacob went to Succoth. He built a hut for himself. And he made places for his animals to sleep. That is why they called the place Succoth.

18 After Jacob left Paddan Aram he arrived at the city of Shechem. This is in Canaan. He put up his tent near the city. 19 He bought the piece of ground where he put up his tents. He bought it from the sons of Hamor, the father of Shechem. He paid 400 pieces of silver for the land. 20 Jacob built an altar there. And he called the altar El Elohe Israel.

Chapter 34

1 Dinah was the daughter of Leah and Jacob. One day she went out to visit the women who lived in the land. 2 Shechem was the son of Hamor the Hivite. Hamor was the ruler of the land. When Shechem saw Dinah, he took her. And he had sex with her. Dinah did not want this to happen. 3 He liked Dinah, Jacob's daughter, very much. And he loved her. He spoke kind words to her. 4 And Shechem said to Hamor his father 'Get me this girl. I want her for my wife.' 5 Jacob heard what had happened to his daughter. But his sons were out in the fields with his animals. So, Jacob did not do anything until his sons came home. And he did not say anything.

6 Shechem's father Hamor went to talk to Jacob. 7 Now Jacob's sons heard what had happened. And they came in from the fields at once. They were very angry. They were angry because Shechem had done a very bad thing by having sex with Dinah. It was so bad that the whole of Jacob's family were ashamed because of it. Shechem should not have done this.

8 Hamor said to them, 'My son Shechem loves your daughter. Please give her to him so that she can be his wife. 9 And make marriages with our people. Give your daughter to us. And take our daughters for wives for your people. 10 You can live among us. You can live anywhere you want to in this land. Live here. And buy and sell things here. Buy land and houses here.

11 Then Shechem said to Dinah's father and brothers 'Perhaps what I say will make you happy. Then I will give you whatever you ask. 12 Tell me what you want me to pay for your daughter. Tell me the gift that I should bring. It can be as large as you want it to be. I will pay whatever you ask me. But give me the girl as my wife.'

13 Because of what Shechem did to Dinah, Jacob's sons planned to deceive Shechem. And they deceived his father Hamor too. 14 They said 'We cannot do what you want. We cannot give our sister to an uncircumcised man. We would be ashamed to do this. 15 You must do one thing. Then we will agree to what you want. You must circumcise all your males. 16 Then we will give you our daughters so that your people can marry them. And we will marry your daughters. We will live among you. And we will be like one people with you. 17 But you must agree to circumcision. Or we will take our sister and leave this place.'

18 What Jacob's sons suggested seemed good to Hamor and his son Shechem. 19 Shechem's people liked him very much. So, he and his father agreed at once to do what Jacob's sons told them. Shechem agreed with them because he loved Dinah. 20 So Hamor and his son Shechem went to the city gate. And they spoke to their people. 21 They said 'These men are our friends. Let them live in our land. And they can sell things to us, and buy things from us. This land is big enough for them. We can marry their daughters. And they can marry our daughters. 22 But we must do what the men say. If we do not, then they will not agree to live among us. They say that we have to circumcise all our males. This is because their men are circumcised. 23 If they live among us, their things and animals will become ours. So let us agree to be circumcised. And then they will live among us.' 24 All the men who were at the city gate agreed with Hamor and Shechem. And they circumcised every male in the city.

25 And 3 days after the men were circumcised; they were still all in a lot of pain. And at this time, 2 of Jacob's sons, Dinah's brothers, attacked the men with their swords. The 2 brothers were Simeon and Levi. And they killed every male in the city.

26 Simeon and Levi killed Hamor and his son Shechem with their swords. And they took Dinah from Shechem's house and left. 27 All Jacob's sons saw that the men of the city were dead. So they took everything from the city. It was the city where Shechem had sex with their sister.

28 They took all the animals and everything in the city. And they took everything that was out in the fields. 29 They carried away everything valuable. And they took all the women and children, and everything from the houses in the city. 30 When they returned to Jacob, he said, 'You have brought trouble on me. You have made me like a bad smell to the Canaanites and Perizzites, by what you have done. These people also live in this land. We do not have many men. If the Perizzites and Canaanites attack, they will destroy us all.' 31 But Levi and Simeon replied 'Shechem should not have used our sister as if she were a prostitute.'

Chapter 35

1 After these things had happened, God said to Jacob, 'Go to Bethel. Live there. Build an altar to worship the God who appeared to you. He appeared to you when you were running from Esau.' 2 So Jacob told his household. He told everyone who was with him, 'Throw out all the foreign gods that you have with you. Wash your body. And change your clothes.' 3 'Then we will go to Bethel. There I will build an altar to worship God. We will worship the God who answered me. He answered me when I was in trouble. And he has been with me everywhere that I went.' 4 So the people gave all their foreign gods to Jacob. And they gave him the rings from their ears. And Jacob buried them under the oak tree at the place called Shechem.

5 Then they began their journey. And the fear of God fell on all the towns near to them. So, no one attacked or followed them.

6 Jacob and everyone with him arrived at Luz. (That is Bethel.) This is in the land of Canaan. 7 And he built an altar there. And he called the place El Bethel. Because that was where God appeared to him. He appeared to him when he was running from his brother Esau.

8 Deborah was Rebekah's nurse. (She was travelling with Jacob.) Deborah died. Jacob buried her under the oak tree below Bethel. That is why they call the place Allon Bacuth.

9 After Jacob returned from Paddan Aram, God appeared to him again. And God blessed Jacob. 10 God said to Jacob 'Your name is Jacob. But your name will no longer be Jacob your name will be Israel.' So God called Jacob Israel.

11 And God said to Jacob, 'I am Almighty God. You will have many descendants. Your descendants will be a great people. Some of your descendants will be kings. 12 I give you the land that I gave to Abraham and Isaac. Yes, I will give this land to your descendants that come after you.'

13 Then God went from Jacob. He went from that place. It was the place where he spoke with Jacob. 14 Jacob set up a stone. This was at the place where God spoke to him. He poured a drink offering on the stone. He also poured oil on it. 15 Jacob called the place where God talked to him Bethel.

16 Then they left Bethel. When they were still several miles from Ephrath, Rachel began to give birth. She had a lot of difficulty. 17 As she was having so much difficulty, the woman helping her said, 'Do not be afraid. You have another son.' 18 Rachel was dying. And with her last breath, she gave a name to her son. The name was Ben-Oni. But Jacob, his father, called him Benjamin.

19 Rachel died. They buried her on the way to Ephrath. 20 Jacob set up a stone over the place where he buried her. This stone shows where Jacob buried Rachel.

21 Israel moved on again. He put up his tents beyond Migdal Eder.

22 Israel stayed in that place. And Reuben went to Bilhah and had sex with her. Bilhah was his father's concubine. And Israel heard what had happened.

Jacob had 12 sons:

23 The sons of Leah were Reuben, who was the first of her sons, Simeon, Levi, Judah, Issachar and Zebulun. 24 The sons of Rachel were Joseph and Benjamin. 25 The sons of Rachel's female servant, Bilhah were Dan and Naphtali. 26 The sons of Leah's female servant, Zilpah were Gad and Asher. These were the sons of Jacob, who were born to him in Paddan Aram.

27 Jacob arrived home. He arrived at his father Isaac's home. This is in Mamre near Kiriath Arba (that is Hebron.) This is where Abraham and Isaac had stayed. 28 Isaac was alive for 180 years. 29 Then he died. And he joined his people who had died before him. He was an old man when he died. And his sons, Esau and Jacob buried him.

Chapter 36

1 This is a list of the descendants of Esau. (Esau is also called Edom.) 2 Esau took women from Canaan to be his wives. They were: Adah daughter of Elon the Hittite and Oholibamah, the daughter of Anah and granddaughter of Zibeon the Hivite 3 and Basemath, the daughter of Ishmael and sister of Nebaioth. 4Adah had a son called Eliphaz. Basemath had a son called Reuel. 5 Oholibamah had 3 sons: Jeush, Jalam and Korah.

6 Esau took his wives, sons and daughters and everyone in his household. Also, he took his animals and everything that he had got in Canaan. And he went to a land some miles from his brother Jacob. 7 They both owned too much to stay together in the same place. There was not enough land for all their animals. 8So Esau (that is Edom) lived in the land of Seir.

9 This is a list of the descendants of Esau. They lived in the hill country of Seir. All the Edomites were his descendants. 10 These are the names of Esau's sons: Eliphaz, the son of Adah who was Esau's wife. Reuel, the son of Basemath, who was Esau's wife. 11 The sons of Eliphaz were Teman, Omar, Zepho, Gatam and Kenaz. 12 Esau's son Eliphaz also had a concubine. Her name was Timna. She had a son called Amalek. These were the grandsons of Esau's wife Adah. 13 The sons of Reuel were: Nahath, Zerah, Shammah and Mizzah. These were grandsons of Esau's wife Basemath. 14 Esau's wife Oholibamah was the daughter of Anah. And she was the granddaughter of Zibeon. Her sons were: Jeush, Jalam and Korah.

15 These were his descendants who were head of their tribes: The sons of Eliphaz (who was the first born son of Esau): Teman, Omar, Zepho, Kenaz, 16 Korah, Gatam and Amalek. These were the heads of their tribes who were descendants of Eliphaz in Edom. They were grandsons of Adah. 17 The sons of Esau's son Reuel were Nahath, Zerah, Shammah and Mizzah. These were the heads of their tribes who were descendants of Reuel in Edom. They were grandsons of Esau's wife Basemath. 18 The sons of Esau's wife Oholibamah were Jeush, Jalam and Korah. These were the leaders of their tribes who were descendants of Esau's wife Oholibamah. She was the daughter of Anah. 19 These were the sons of Esau (that is Edom) and these were their leaders of their tribes.

20 These were the sons of Seir the Horite. They lived in that place. They were Lotan, Shobal, Zibeon, Anah, 21 Dishon, Ezer and Dishan. These sons of Seir in Edom were leaders of the Horite tribes. 22 The sons of Lotan were Hori and Homam. Timna was Lotan's sister. 23 The sons of Shobal were Alvan, Manahath, Ebal, Shepho and Onam. 24 The sons of Zibeon were Aiah and Anah. This was the same Anah, who found the hot water in the desert. He found it when he took his father's donkey to eat grass. His father's name was Zibeon. 25 The children of Anah were Dishon and Oholibamah daughter of Anah. 26 The sons of Dishon were Hemdan, Eshban, Ithran and Keran. 27 The sons of Ezer were Bilhan, Zaavan and Akan. 28The sons of Dishan were Uz and Aran. 29 These were the leaders of the Horite tribes: Lotan, Shobal, Zibeon, Anah, 30 Dishon, Ezer and Dishan. These were the leaders of the Horite tribes in the land of Seir.

31 These kings ruled in Edom. This was before any Israelite king ruled in this land: 32 Bela the son of Beor became king of Edom. He ruled a city called Dinhabah. 33 When Bela died, Jobab, son of Zerah became king after him. 34 When Jobab died, Husham from the land of the Temanites became king after him. 35When Husham died, Hadad, son of Bedad became king after him. Bedad beat Midian in the country of Moab. He ruled a city called Avith. 36 When Hadad died, Samlah from Masrekah became king after him. 37When Samlah died, Shaul from Rehoboth on the river, became king after him. 38 When Shaul died, Baal-Hanan son of Acbor became king after him. 39 When Baal-Hanan son of Acbor died, Hadar became king after him. He ruled over a city called Pau. His wife's name was Mehetabel daughter of Matred, the daughter of Me-Zahab.

40 These were the leaders of their tribes. They were descendants of Esau: Timna, Alvah, Jetheth, and 41Oholibamah, Elah, Pinon, 42 Kenaz, Teman, Mibzar, 43 Magdiel and Iram. These were the leaders of the tribes of Edom. They lived in different places in the land. These are the descendants of Esau. All the Edomites were his descendants.

Chapter 37

1 Israel (Jacob) lived in Canaan. This is where his father had lived.

2 This is what happened to Jacob's family:

Joseph was Jacob's son. He was 17 years old. He kept the sheep safe with his brothers. These were the sons of Bilhah and the sons of Zilpah. Bilhah and Zilpah were his father's wives. Now Joseph told Jacob bad things about his brothers. 3 Israel (Jacob) loved Joseph. He loved him more than he loved any of his other sons. This was because Joseph was born when Jacob was old. And Jacob made a special coat for him. 4 Joseph's brothers knew that Jacob loved him more than them. And they hated Joseph. They could not say anything nice to him.

5 Joseph had a dream. And he told his brothers about it. And his brothers hated Joseph even more than they did before. 6 Joseph said to his brothers, 'Listen to what happened in my dream: 7 We were out in the field tying the crops into bundles. And my bundle stood up. And your bundles each stood in a circle with mine in the middle. And all your bundles bowed down to my bundle.' 8 Joseph's brothers said to him 'Do you think that you will be like a king to us? Will you rule over us?' And they hated him even more. They hated him because of what Joseph told them about his dream. 9 Then Joseph had another dream. And he told his brothers about it. He said 'Listen to me. I have had another dream. This is what happened. The sun and moon and 11 stars bowed down to me.' 10 Joseph told his father and his brothers about the dream. His father was angry with him. Jacob said, 'What is this dream that you had? Do you think that your mother and me, and your brothers will come and bow down in front of you? Do you really think that this will happen?' 11 Joseph's brothers felt very angry with him. But Jacob thought about what Joseph had said.

12 Some time passed. Joseph's brothers had taken their father's sheep to eat grass. This was near the place called Shechem. 13 And Israel (Jacob) said to Joseph 'You know that your brothers have taken my sheep to eat grass. They are near Shechem. I want you to go to them.' Joseph replied 'Very well.' 14 So Israel said to Joseph 'Go and see your brothers. Come back and tell me how everything is with them. And tell me if the sheep are all right.' Then Israel sent Joseph off from the Valley of Hebron. And Joseph arrived at Shechem. 15 A man found Joseph walking in the fields. He asked Joseph 'What are you looking for?' 16Joseph replied 'I am looking for my brothers. They have taken the sheep to eat grass. Can you tell me where they are?' 17 The man said 'They have moved away from here. I heard them say, "Let us go to Dothan."' So Joseph followed his brothers. And he found them near the place called Dothan. 18 But his brothers recognised Joseph, while he was still far away. And before he had arrived at the place, they planned to kill him. 19 They said to each other 'Here comes the man who dreams! 20 We will kill him. And we will throw him down this dry well. We will that say a wild animal ate him. Then he will not dream again!' 21 When Reuben heard this, he tried to save Joseph. He said 'We should not kill him. 22 Do not have his blood on your hands. Throw him into this dry well in the desert. But do not attack him.' Reuben said this to save Joseph from his brothers. Then later Reuben would save Joseph and take him back to his father.

23 So Joseph arrived at where his brothers were. He was wearing his special coat. They took his coat off him. 24 And they took Joseph. And they threw him into the dry well.

25 Then the brothers sat down to eat their meal. They looked up and saw a group of Ishmaelites coming towards them. They came from the place called Gilead. The Ishmaelites had camels that carried spices, balm and myrrh. They were on their way to Egypt. There they would sell them.

26 Judah said to his brothers, 'We could kill our brother. We could then say that we did not kill him. But then we will not get anything. 27 Let us sell him to the Ishmaelites. Then we will not have to kill him. After all, he is our brother. He is our own relative.' His brothers agreed to what Judah said. 28 When the Midianite merchants (men who buy and sell things) came to them, Joseph's brothers pulled him out of the dry well. And they sold Joseph for 20 pieces of silver. They sold him to the Ishmaelites. And the Ishmaelites took Joseph to Egypt.

29 Reuben returned to the dry well. And he saw that Joseph was not there. He tore his clothes because he was very worried. 30 Reuben went back to his brothers. He said 'The boy is not there! Where can I go now?'

31 Then the brothers got Joseph's special coat. They killed a goat. And they put the blood from the goat on to Joseph's coat. 32 They took the special coat back to their father. They told him 'We found this. Look at it. Tell us if it is your son's coat.'

33 Israel (that is Jacob) saw that it was Joseph's coat. He said 'It is my son's coat! A wild animal has eaten him. The animal has torn Joseph to pieces.' 34 Then Jacob tore his own clothes. He did this because he was very sad. He put on clothes made from sackcloth because he was very sad. He wore sackcloth for many days.

35 All Jacob's sons and daughters came to him. They tried to make Jacob feel less sad. But Jacob was very sad. Jacob said 'I will be sad until I die. I will be sad because my son is dead.' And he wept because Joseph was dead. 36 While this was happening, the Midianites sold Joseph in Egypt. They sold Joseph to Potiphar, one of Pharaoh's officers. Potiphar had authority over all of Pharaoh's guards.

Chapter 38

1 At that time, Judah left his brothers. He went to stay with a man from the town of Adullam. His name was Hirah. 2 Then Judah met the daughter of Shua, a Canaanite man. Judah married her. 3 She became pregnant, and gave birth to a son. She called him Er. 4 She became pregnant again, and gave birth to another son. She called him Onan. 5 She gave birth to another son. She called him Shelah. She gave birth to Shelah at the place called Kezib. 6 Judah got a wife for his oldest son, Er. Her name was Tamar. 7 But God saw that Er, the first born son of Judah, was bad. So the Lord made him die. 8 Then Judah said to Onan 'Marry your dead brother's wife. You must do this because you are her dead husband's brother. You must have a son for your dead brother.

9 But Onan did not want Tamar to have his child. He knew that a child like that would not belong to him. So when he had sex with his brother's wife Tamar, he made his semen go on to the ground. So Tamar could not become pregnant. He would not give Tamar a child for his dead brother.

10 What Onan did was wrong. So God made him die also. 11 So Judah said to Tamar 'Go to your father's house. And live there as a widow. Live there until my son Shelah is older.' Judah thought 'Shelah may also die, because his brothers died.' So Tamar went to live in her father's house.

12 A long time passed. And Judah's wife, the daughter of Shua died. When Judah had stopped being sad because of her, he went to the place called Timnah. He went to some men who were cutting the wool from his sheep. And Judah's friend, Hirah the Adullamite went with him. 13 Someone told Tamar 'Your husband's father is going to Timnah to get the wool off his sheep.'

14 So Tamar took off her widow's clothes. And she covered herself with a veil. She did not want anyone to know who she was. That is why she did this. Then she sat at the place called Enaim. This is on the road going to Timnah. Tamar knew that Jacob's son Shelah had grown into a man. And he had not married her. That is why she did this. 15 Judah saw her. And he thought that she was a prostitute. He thought that because she had covered her face. 16 He did not know that she was his son's widow. And he went over to her while she was at the side of the road. He said 'Let me sleep with you.' Tamar asked, 'If I sleep with you, what will you give me?' 17 Judah replied 'I will send a young goat from my animals.' Tamar said, 'You will have to give me something to show that you will do as you say.' 18 Judah asked 'What should I give you?' Tamar replied 'Give me your seal and the cord that holds it. And give me the staff in your hand.' So Judah gave them to her. And he slept with her. And she became pregnant.

19 After this, Tamar left Judah. And she took off her veil. And she put her widow's clothes on again.

20 Judah sent his friend, the Adullamite with a young goat back to where the woman had been. Judah wanted to get his seal, cord and staff back from the woman that he had slept with. But the Adullamite could not find the woman. 21 The Adullamite asked some men who live there 'Where is the shrine-prostitute? Where is the woman who was by the road at Enaim?' But the men said, 'There has not been any shrine-prostitute here.'

22 So Judah's friend went back to Judah. He said 'I did not find her. The men who lived there said, "There has not been any shrine-prostitute here."' 23 so Judah said 'Let her keep the things that I gave to her. People will laugh at me if you go back there again. I sent a young goat for her. But you could not find her.'

24 Then, 3 months later, someone told Judah 'Your dead son's wife, Tamar, is pregnant. She has been a prostitute.' Judah said 'Bring her out. And burn her to death!'

25 So they brought Tamar out. They were going to kill her. But she sent a message to her dead husband's father. She said 'The man who owns these things has made me pregnant. Look at them. See if you know who the seal and cord and staff belong to.' 26 Judah saw that the things belonged to him. He said 'She is more righteous than I am. That is because I would not give her to Shelah my son. Judah did not sleep with Tamar again. And he did not marry her.

27 The time came for Tamar to give birth. And she had two babies. 28 As she was giving birth, one baby put out his hand. So, the woman who was helping Tamar tied something red to that baby's arm. She said 'This baby came out first.' 29 But the baby put his hand back inside Tamar. And his brother came out. And the woman said 'So you have come out!' And Tamar called him Perez. 30 Then his brother came out. He had something red on his arm. And Tamar called him Zerah.

Chapter 39

1 Now the Ishmaelites took Joseph to Egypt. And they sold Joseph as a slave. Potiphar was one of Pharaoh's officers. He had authority over all the guards. And Potiphar bought Joseph from the Ishmaelites. 2 The Lord was with Joseph. And the Lord made good things happen to him. And Joseph lived in Potiphar's house. Potiphar was Joseph's Egyptian master. 3 Potiphar saw that the Lord was with Joseph. And everything that Joseph did was good. Potiphar saw that too. 4 So Potiphar was happy with Joseph. And Joseph became Potiphar's special servant. Potiphar gave Joseph authority over his household. And Joseph kept safe everything that belonged to Potiphar. 5 Potiphar gave Joseph authority over everything that belonged to him. Then God blessed that household, because of Joseph.

6 So Joseph kept safe everything that belonged to Potiphar. Potiphar did not think about anything in his household. The only thing that Potiphar thought about was the food that he ate. Now, Joseph was a handsome man.

7 And after some time had passed, Potiphar's wife saw that Joseph was handsome. She said 'Come to bed with me!' 8 But Joseph would not do as she asked. He said 'I care for my master's household. And my master does not think about anything in the house. I keep safe everything that belongs to him. 9 No one has more authority in this house than I do. My master keeps nothing from me except you. That is because you are his wife. I could not do such a bad thing. And I will not sin against God.' 10 Potiphar's wife spoke to Joseph every day. But he still would not go to bed with her. He would not even be with her. 11 One day Joseph went into the house to work. And there were no other servants there. 12 Potiphar's wife took hold of Joseph's coat. She said 'Come to bed with me!' but Joseph left his coat in her hand. And he ran out of the house.

13 Potiphar's wife saw that he left his coat in her hand. She saw that he had run out of the house. 14 So she called her household servants. She said to them 'Look, the Hebrew that Potiphar brought to us has no respect for us! He came in here to sleep with me. But I screamed. 15 When he heard me scream he ran out of the house. But he left his coat next to me.' 16 Potiphar's wife kept the coat next to her until Joseph's master, Potiphar came home. 17 Then she told him this story: 'That Hebrew slave you brought us came to me. He wanted to sleep with me. 18 But I screamed for help. And he left his coat next to me. And he ran out of the house.'

19 Joseph's master heard the story that his wife told him. She said 'This is what your slave did to me.' And Potiphar was very angry. 20 Joseph's master took Joseph, and put him in prison. He put Joseph in the king's prison. 21 The Lord was with Joseph while he was in prison. He was kind to Joseph, and the keeper of the prison liked Joseph. 22 So this man gave Joseph authority over all the people in prison. And Joseph cared for everything that was in the prison. 23 The keeper did not think about anything that Joseph had authority over. For the Lord was with Joseph. And everything that Joseph did went well.

Chapter 40

1 Some time later, 2 workers made the king of Egypt angry. He had many workers. He had a cupbearer and a baker. They did something to make him angry.

2 Pharaoh was angry with his two officers. He was angry with the cupbearer and the baker. 3 And Pharaoh put them in the same prison that Joseph was in. 4 The man who had authority in the prison put Joseph over them. And Joseph was over them. And they were there for some time. 5 And each of them - the cupbearer and the baker - had a dream. Both had a dream on the same night. And each dream had a different meaning.

6 Joseph came to them the next day. And he saw that they were worried. 7 So Joseph asked them both 'Why are you sad today?' 8 They replied 'We both had dreams, but there is no one to tell us what they mean.' Joseph said 'Only God knows the meaning of dreams. But tell me your dreams.'

9 So the cupbearer told Joseph his dream. He told Joseph, 'In my dream I saw a fruit plant in front of me. 10 And there were 3 branches on the plant. As soon as new leaves came, flowers came. And they became fruit. 11 Pharaoh's cup was in my hand. And I took the fruit. And I put the juice into Pharaoh's cup. Then I put the cup in his hand.'

12 Joseph said 'This is what your dream means. The 3 branches are 3 days. 13 In 3 days, Pharaoh will lift up your head. Then he will let you come out of this prison. And you will be Pharaoh's cupbearer again. You will put Pharaoh's cup into his hand. You did that when you were his cupbearer. 14 But when these things happen, remember me. And be kind to me. Tell Pharaoh about me. Then I will get out of this prison. 15 Truly, men took me from the land of the Hebrews. I did not want to leave there. And even here, I have not done anything wrong. I should not be in this prison.'

16 The baker heard that Joseph had given a good meaning to the cupbearer's dream. So he said, 'I also had a dream: I had 3 baskets of bread on my head.

17 The top basket contained many different cooked things for Pharaoh. But birds were eating them out of the basket on my head.'

18 Joseph said 'This is what your dream means. The 3 baskets are 3 days. 19 In 3 days, Pharaoh will lift off your head. And he will hang you on a tree. And the birds will eat your body.' 20 Now on the 3rd day it was Pharaoh's birthday. He gave a feast for all his officers. He lifted up the heads of the baker and the cupbearer. He did this in front of all his officers.

21 He let the cupbearer be his own cupbearer again. So, the cupbearer put the cup into Pharaoh's hand again.

22 But Pharaoh hanged the baker. This is what Joseph said would happen. He had told the baker what his dream meant.

23 But the cupbearer did not remember Joseph. The cupbearer forgot about Joseph.

Chapter 41

1 Then 2 years passed and Pharaoh had a dream. In his dream, he was standing by the River Nile. 2 And 7 cows walked out of the river. They were fat and good to look at. They ate the plants at the side of the river. 3 After them, 7 other cows came out of the river. They were thin. And their bones were close to their skin. They stood next to the cows already on the side of the river. 4 And the thin cows ate the 7 fat cows. Then Pharaoh woke up. 5 He went to sleep again. And he had another dream. He dreamed that 7 food plants were growing on one branch. They were fat and good to look at. 6 After them, 7 other food plants grew. They seemed thin and burned by the east wind. 7 Then the thin food plants ate the 7 fat plants. Then Pharaoh woke up. It was a dream. 8 In the morning, Pharaoh was worried. So, he sent for all the men who could tell the meaning of dreams. He also sent for all the wise men in Egypt. Pharaoh told them about his dreams. But no one could tell Pharaoh what his dreams meant.

9 Then the cupbearer said to Pharaoh, 'Now I remember the wrong that I have done! 10 Two (2) years ago, Pharaoh was angry with his servants. He put the baker and me in prison. 11 One night we both had a dream And each of our dreams had a different meaning. 12 A young Hebrew man was there with us. He was a servant of the man with authority over all the men who watched the people in prison. We told the Hebrew our dreams. And then he told each of us the meaning of our dream. 13 And everything happened as he had told us. You gave me my job as cupbearer again. And you hanged the baker.'

14 So Pharaoh sent for Joseph. And they quickly brought him from the prison. Joseph washed himself. He removed the hair that grew on his face. And he put on clean clothes. Then he stood in front of Pharaoh.

15 Pharaoh spoke to Joseph. He said, 'I had a dream. And no one can tell me what it means. But I have heard people saying that you can tell the meaning of dreams.'

16 Joseph replied, 'I cannot do this. But God will give Pharaoh the answer that he is looking for.' 17 Then Pharaoh said, 'In my dream, I stood at the side of the River Nile. 18 Then 7 cows came out of the river. They were fat, and good to look at. And they ate the plants at the side of the river. 19 After them, 7 more cows came out of the river. They were thin and they were not good to look at. I have not seen cows as bad looking as these in Egypt before. 20 The thin bad looking cows ate the fat cows that came out of the river first. 21 They ate the 7 fat cows. But you could not see that they had eaten them. They looked thin before they ate the fat cows. They still looked as thin after they ate them. Then I woke up. 22 In my dream, I also saw 7 food plants. They grew from one branch. They were fat and good to look at. 23 After them, 7 other plants grew. They seemed thin and burned by the east wind. 24 The thin plants ate the fat plants. I told those dreams to my men who can tell the meaning of dreams. But they could not tell me the meaning of my dreams.'

25 Then Joseph said to Pharaoh, 'Pharaoh's dreams both have the same meaning. God has shown Pharaoh what God is going to do. 26 The 7 fat cows are 7 years. And the 7 good food plants are 7 years. Both dreams have the same meaning. 27 The 7 thin cows that came out of the river mean 7 years. And the 7 bad plants mean 7 years. Both dreams mean 7 years of famine. 28 This is what your dreams mean. God has shown Pharaoh what he is going to do. 29 There will be plenty of food for 7 years. All through the land of Egypt, there will be food. 30 But 7 years of famine will follow. People will forget the 7 years of plenty. And famine will destroy the land of Egypt. 31 No one will remember the first 7 years, when there was plenty of food. They will not remember them because the famine will be so bad. 32 God gave you 2 dreams with the same meaning. This is because God has decided what he will do. And he will do it soon. 33 Now Pharaoh should look for a clever man. He should look for a man who knows what is right and wrong. Tell him to rule over the land of Egypt. 34 Pharaoh should choose some officers. They must take 1/5th (20%) of the food grown in Egypt, in the 7 years of plenty. 35 They must store all the food from these good years. Pharaoh will have authority over what happens to the food. 36 This food should be stored. So the people in Egypt will have enough food, when the 7 years of famine come.'

37 Pharaoh thought that Joseph's plan was good. And he told it to all his servants. 38 Pharaoh said to them, 'This man has the Spirit of God in him. Can we find anyone else like him?' 39 Then Pharaoh said to Joseph, 'God has made these things known to you. There is no one more clever than you. 40 You will have authority in my palace. All my people will do whatever things you tell them. Only I will be greater than you because I am the king.' 41 And Pharaoh said to Joseph, 'I give you authority in the whole land of Egypt.' 42 Then Pharaoh took his king's ring from his finger. And he put it on Joseph's finger. He dressed Joseph in clothes of good material. And he put gold on Joseph's neck. 43 Joseph rode in a chariot. All the people knew that only Pharaoh had more authority in Egypt. Men shouted, "Bow down!" So, Joseph had authority over everything in the land of Egypt.

44 Then Pharaoh said to Joseph, 'I am Pharaoh. But nobody in Egypt will do anything, unless you tell them to.' 45 Pharaoh gave Joseph the name Zaphenath-Paneah. He also gave him a wife. She was called Asenath, the daughter of Potiphera. He was priest of On. So Asenath became Joseph's wife. Everyone knew that Joseph had authority in all the land of Egypt.

46 Joseph was 30 years old when he became Pharaoh's special servant. And Joseph started to work at once. And he travelled all over Egypt. 47 During the 7 years of plenty, lots of food grew in the land. 48 Joseph got all this food. He got all the food that they grew in the 7 years of plenty. He stored it in cities in Egypt. He stored the food near the fields where it grew. 49 Joseph stored large quantities of food. It was like the sand by the sea. Joseph stopped keeping records of the food. He stopped because there was too much food to measure.

50 Before the years of famine came, Joseph became a father. Asenath, daughter of Potiphera, priest of On, gave birth to 2 sons. 51 Joseph called his first born son Manasseh. That was because Joseph said 'God made me forget all my trouble. And he made me forget all the people who live with my father.' 52 Joseph called his second son Ephraim. That was because Joseph said, 'God has made me have children. I have had them in the land where bad things happened to me.'

53 Then the 7 good years, when there was plenty of food in Egypt, ended. 54 And the 7 years of famine began. This is what Joseph said would happen. There was a famine in all the other countries. But there was food for all the people in Egypt.

55 The people of Egypt began to go hungry. And they cried out to Pharaoh for food. Then Pharaoh told all the Egyptians, 'Go to Joseph. And do as he tells you.'

56 The famine was over the whole country. Then Joseph opened the places where he had stored the food. And he sold it to the Egyptians because the famine was very bad in all of Egypt. 57 And people from other countries came to Egypt. They came to buy food from Joseph. They came because the famine was very bad all over the world.

Chapter 42.

1 Jacob heard that there was food in Egypt. So he said to his sons, 'Why do you keep looking at each other? 2 I have heard that there is food in Egypt. Go there and buy some for us. Buy it so that we do not die.'

3 Then 10 of Joseph's brothers went to Egypt. They went to buy food. 4 But Israel (Jacob) did not send Benjamin. Jacob was afraid that something bad might happen to him. That is why he did not send him. He was Joseph's brother. 5 Jacob's sons were among the people who went to Egypt, to buy food. They went to Egypt because there was famine in Canaan.

6 Now Joseph was the man who had authority in the land. He was the man who sold food to all the people. Joseph's brothers arrived in Egypt. And they bowed down to him. They put their faces to the ground.

7 As soon as Joseph saw the men, he knew that they were his brothers. But he did not tell them who he was. And he spoke words to them that were not kind. He asked them, 'Where do you come from?' They replied 'From the land of Canaan. We have come to buy food.' 8 Joseph knew that they were his brothers. But they did not recognise Joseph. He spoke to his brothers through a man who could speak Hebrew. That is why they did not recognise him.

9 Then Joseph remembered his dream about his brothers. He said to them, 'You have come to see where you can attack our land.' 10 They replied 'No my lord! Your servants have come to buy food. 11 We are all the sons of one man. We are honest men. We are not enemies.' 12 But Joseph said 'No! You have come to see where you can attack us.' 13 And Joseph's brothers replied 'We were 12 brothers, the sons of one man. He lives in Canaan. The youngest brother is with our father. And one brother is not with us any more.' 14 Joseph said 'It is as I told you. You have come to see where you can attack us. You are enemies! 15 I will see if what you say is true. This is how I will see it. As Pharaoh lives, you will not leave this place. You will not leave until your youngest brother comes here. 16 Send one of you to get your brother. I will keep the other brothers in prison. Then I will know if what you said is true. If you are not saying what is true, then as surely as Pharaoh lives, you are enemies!'

17 And Joseph put his brothers in prison for 3 days.

18 On the 3rd day Joseph said to them 'Do what I say. Then you will stay alive, because I believe in God.'

19 Joseph said 'If you are honest men, let one of your brothers stay in prison. The other brothers can go back to Canaan. And take food back with you, because your families are hungry. 20 But you must return to Egypt. And you must bring your youngest brother to me. Then I will know that what you say is true. And you will not die.' And the brothers said, 'Yes, we will do what you say.'

21 They said to each other, 'This is happening because of what we did to Joseph. He asked us not to kill him. We saw how sad he was. But we would not listen. That is why we are in this trouble.' 22 Reuben said, 'I told you not to do wrong to the boy. But you would not listen! Now we will have bad things done to us.' 23 Joseph had a man who could speak Hebrew. Jooeph spoke to this servant in the Egyptian language. The servant then spoke to the brothers in Hebrew. Joseph understood what the brothers said. But they did not know that.

24 Joseph turned away from his brothers. And he began to weep. But then he turned to face them again. And he spoke to them again. Then Joseph had Simeon taken from them. And the servants tied Simeon's hands. This happened in front of the other brothers. 25 Then Joseph told servants to fill the brothers' bags with food. And he told them to put each man's silver back into his bag. And he told them to give the brothers food for their journey. And the servants did what Joseph told them.

26 Then the brothers put their food on to their donkeys. And they left. 27 They travelled until it was night. Then they stopped. One of the brothers opened his bag to get food for his donkey. And he saw his silver inside his bag.

28 He said to his brothers, 'They have given back my silver. Here it is in my bag.' All the men were surprised. And they were very frightened. They said, 'What has God done to us?'

29 Some time passed. And they arrived at Canaan. They went to their father Jacob. And they told Jacob everything that had happened to them. 30 They said, 'There is a man who is lord over the land. He spoke words to us that were not kind. And he said that we were enemies. He said that we were looking for a place to attack Egypt. 31 But we said to him "We are honest men. We are not enemies. 32 We are 12 brothers, all the sons of one father. One brother is not with us any more. And the youngest brother is with our father in Canaan." 33 Then the man who is lord over the land said, "I want to know if you are honest men. Leave one of your brothers here, with me. Then take food for your hungry families and leave. 34 But you must bring your youngest brother to me. So, I will know that you are not enemies. And I will know that you are honest men. Then I will give your brother back to you. And you can buy and sell things in the land." '

35 The brothers emptied their bags. And in their bags, they found each man's silver! The brothers and their father saw the bags of silver. And they were frightened. 36 Their father Jacob said to them 'You have taken my children away from me. Joseph is not here any more. And Simeon is not here any more. And now you want to take Benjamin. Everything is against me!' 37 Then Reuben said to Jacob, 'I will bring Benjamin back to you. If I do not, then you can kill both of my sons. Trust me with Benjamin. I will bring him back.' 38 But Jacob said, 'My son will not go with you. He will not go with you because his brother is dead. He is the only one left. Something bad may happen on your journey. I am an old man. If something bad happened to him, I would die. I would die because I would be so sad.'

Chapter 43

1 Time passed. And the famine was still bad in the land. 2 Jacob and his household ate all the food from Egypt. So Jacob said, 'Go back to Egypt, and buy some more food.' 3 But Judah said, 'The man told us many times, "Unless your brother is with you, you will not see my face again." 4 You must send Benjamin with us. Then we will go and buy food for you. 5 But if you do not send Benjamin, we will not go. Because the man said to us, "Unless your brother is with you, you will not see my face again." 6 Israel (that is Jacob) asked, 'Why did you bring this trouble on me? You should not have told the man that you had another brother.' 7 The brothers replied, 'The man asked us many questions about our family. He asked, "Is your father still alive? Do you have another brother?" We only answered his questions. We did not know that he would say, "Bring your brother here." 8 Then Judah said to Israel (that is Jacob), 'Send the boy with me. And we will go at once. Then we, and you, and our children will not die.

9 Judah said, 'I will make you a promise. I will keep Benjamin safe. He will be with me. I will bring him back to you. If I do not, then you can say that it was because of me. And you can say this for all of my life. 10 now say what you want to do. We have wasted much time, talking about this. We could have gone to Egypt and returned twice.'

11 Then their father Israel (Jacob) said to them, 'If you must take Benjamin, do what I tell you. Put some of the best things from the land in your bags. And take them to the man as a gift. Take some balm, some honey and some spices. Also take some myrrh, and pistachio nuts and almond nuts.

12 Jacob said, 'Take 2 times the amount of silver with you. This is because you must give back the silver that they put back into your bags. It may have been a mistake. 13 Also take your brother Benjamin. And go back to the man at once. 14 I pray that God Almighty will help you. I pray this; When you go to the man, may he show you mercy. And may he let your older brother and Benjamin return with you. As for me, if I lose my sons, then I lose them.'

15 So the brothers took the gifts. And they took twice as much silver. They also took Benjamin and they hurried to Egypt. When they arrived there, they went to Joseph.

16 Joseph saw that Benjamin was with them. He said to a servant who worked in his house, 'Take these men to my house. Kill an animal and prepare it for a meal. These men will eat with me at noon.' 17 The servant did as Joseph told him. He took the men to Joseph's house.

18 The brothers were frightened when the servant took them to Joseph's house. They thought, 'He has brought us here because of the silver that was in our bags. Someone put it back in when we came here the first time. He wants to attack us. And he will take us to be slaves. And he will take our donkeys.' 19 So the brothers went to Joseph's servant. And they spoke to him at the door to Joseph's house. 20 They said, 'Please sir. The first time we came here, we came to buy food. 21 But on our journey back, we stopped because it was night. We opened our bags. And each of us found the same amount of silver that he brought to Egypt. We brought it to pay for the food. It was in our bags. So we have brought the silver back with us. 22 We have also brought more silver. We have brought it so that we can buy food. We do not know who put the silver back into our bags.' 23 The servant replied, 'Do not worry. Everything is all right. Do not be afraid. Your God, the God of your fathers put the silver there. I received your silver.' Then the servant brought Simeon out to his brothers. 24 The servant took the men into Joseph's house. He gave them water to wash their feet. And he gave them food for their donkeys. 25 The brothers prepared their gifts. They made them ready for when Joseph would come at noon. They had heard that they were to eat there.

26 Joseph arrived. And they gave him the gifts that they had brought into his house. And they bowed down before him. They bowed down to the ground. 27 Joseph asked them if they were all right. Then he said 'How is your old father whom you told me about? Is he still alive?' 28 The brothers replied, 'Your servant, our father is still alive. And he is well.' And they bowed down low to Joseph. 29 Joseph looked about. And he saw his brother Benjamin, who was his mother's son. Joseph asked, 'Is this your youngest brother? Is this the one that you told me about?' And Joseph said to Benjamin, 'God be kind to you, my son'. 30Joseph loved his brother very much and he hurried away. He hurried away because he wanted to weep. He went into his own room. And he wept there. 31 When he had finished weeping, he washed his face. And he returned to his brothers. He said, 'Give them the food.' 32Joseph sat away from his brothers. And he ate there. The brothers sat together. And the Egyptians, who ate there, sat together. The Egyptians could not eat with Hebrews, because that would make the Egyptians ashamed. 33 The brothers sat in front of Joseph. The servants told them to sit in special places, from the oldest to the youngest. And the brothers were surprised.

34 The servants gave the brothers food from Joseph's table. And they gave Benjamin 5 times more food than his brothers. So the brothers ate and drank wine with Joseph.

Chapter 44

1 Joseph told his servant, 'Fill the men's bags. Give them as much food as their animals can carry. And put each man's silver in the top of the bag. 2 Then take my silver cup. And put it in the top of the youngest man's bag. Put it with the silver that he brought to pay for his food.' And the servant did as Joseph said. 3Morning came, and the men went on their journey with their donkeys. 4 They had not gone very far away from the city. Then Joseph said to his servant, 'Go after those men. Go now. And when you find them, say to them. "Why have you done bad things? We did only good things for you. 5 You have taken my master's own cup. It is the cup that he drinks from. And he uses it to know what will happen. What you did is wrong." '

6 So Joseph's servant went after the men. He found them. And he said the words that Joseph had told him. 7 But the men said to him, 'Why do you say these things my lord? Your servants would not do a thing like that!' 8 We even gave back the silver that we found in our bags. We found it when we returned to Canaan. But we gave it back. So why would we take silver or gold from your master's house? 9 If any one of us has this cup, they will die. And the rest of us will become my lord's slaves.' 10 The servant said, 'Very well. It will be as you say. Whoever has the cup, will become my slave. The rest of you will go free.' 11 Each man quickly put his bag on the ground and opened it. 12 Then the servant began to look in the bags. He began with the oldest man's bag. And he finished with the youngest man's bag. And he found the cup in Benjamin's bag. 13 When this happened they tore their clothes. They tore them because they were very upset. Then they put their bags back on their donkeys. And they returned to the city.

14 Joseph was still in his house. And Judah and his brothers arrived. And they threw themselves on the ground in front of Joseph. 15 Joseph said, 'What have you done? Do you not know about a man like me? I can find out what people do.' 16 Judah said, 'I do not know what to say to you, my lord. There is nothing that we can do. We cannot show you that we did not do this. God knows that we have done wrong. We are your slaves. We are all your slaves. One man owns the bag where you found your cup. He is your slave too.' 17 But Joseph said, 'I would not do a thing like that! Only the man whose bag contained the cup will be my slave. The rest of you can return to your father. You may go as friends.'

18 Then Judah went up to Joseph. He said, 'Please my lord. Let me speak to you. You are like Pharaoh, but please do not be angry with me. 19 My lord asked us "Do you have a father? Or a brother?" 20 And we replied, "We have a father. He is old. And he has a young son. This son was born when our father was old. His brother is dead. And he is the only remaining son of his mother. And his father loves him." 21 Then you said, "Bring him to me so that I can see him." 22 And we said, "The boy cannot leave his father. If he leaves his father, his father will die." 23 But you said to us "Your youngest brother must come with you. If he does not come, you will not see my face again." 24 We returned to our father. And we told him what you said. 25 Some time passed. And our father said, "Go back and buy some more food." 26 But we said, "We cannot go. We can only go if our youngest brother comes with us. Unless our youngest brother is with us, we cannot see the man's face again." 27 My father said to us, "My wife gave birth to 2 sons. 28 One of them went away from me. And I said, 'He has been eaten by a wild animal.' And I have not seen him after that.29 If you take my youngest son from me, something bad may happen to him. Then I will die, because I will be so sad." ' 30 Judah said, 'I could go back to my father. But my father lives because of this boy. And if the boy is not with us, then my father will die. He will die because he is so sad. He will die because we did not bring the boy back. 31 He will see that the boy is not with us. And he will die. Because we did not bring the boy back to him, he will be so sad. 32 I promised my father that I would keep the boy safe. I said, "I will bring the boy back. If I do not, then you can say that it was because of me. You can say this for the rest of my life!" 33 Please let me stay here. Let me stay as your slave instead of the boy. And let the boy return with his brothers. 34 I cannot go back to my father. Not if the boy is not with me. No! Do not let me see how sad my father will be.'

Chapter 45

1 After Judah said this, Joseph could not stop himself from crying. In front of all his servants he shouted, 'Make everyone leave me!' So there was no one with Joseph except his brothers. And he told his brothers who he was. 2 And Joseph wept loudly. And the Egyptians heard him. And Pharaoh's household knew about it. 3 Joseph said to his brothers, 'I am Joseph! Is my father still alive?' But his brothers did not answer him. They did not answer him because they were too frightened. They were frightened because Joseph was with them.

4 Then Joseph said to his brothers, 'Come close to me.' When they did this he said, 'I am your brother Joseph. I am the one that you sold into Egypt. 5 Now, do not worry. And do not be angry with yourselves because you sold me. Do not be angry with yourselves because God sent me! He sent me in front of you. He sent me so that I could save people from dying. 6 There has been a famine for 2 years, in this land. And no food will grow for another 5 years. 7 But God sent me in front of you, so that you would stay alive. And to make sure that your descendants live. 8 So you did not send me here. God sent me here. He made me an officer to Pharaoh. I have more authority than any other officer. I have authority over all of Egypt. And I rule all Egypt.'

9 'Now hurry back to my father. Say to him, "This is what your son Joseph says. 'God has made me lord over all Egypt. Come to me. Come now. 10 You can live in the place called Goshen. You and your children can live there. And your grandchildren can live there. And all your animals and everything that you have can live there. And you will be near me. 11 I will give you everything that you need. Because there are still 5 years of famine to come. If you do not come, you and your household will have nothing.' 12 You can all see that I am Joseph. And so can my brother Benjamin. 13 Tell my father how much authority I have in Egypt. And tell him about everything that you saw here. And bring my father here quickly.' 14 Then he hugged his brother Benjamin. And he wept. And Benjamin hugged Joseph. And Benjamin wept. 15 Then Joseph kissed all of his brothers. And he wept over them. After this, his brothers talked to him.

16 Pharaoh heard that Joseph's brothers were in Egypt. And Pharaoh and his officers were happy. 17Pharaoh said to Joseph, 'Tell your brothers, "Do this. Put food on your donkeys' backs. And return to Canaan. 18 And bring your father. And bring your families. Bring them back to me. I will give you the best land in Egypt. And you will have everything that Egypt can give you." ' 19 Pharaoh said, 'You must also tell them, "Do this. Take some carts from Egypt. They are for your wives and children. And get your father. Then come here."

20 "Do not worry. You do not have to bring everything from your own country. The best of everything in Egypt will be yours." '

21 So the sons of Israel (that is Jacob) did this. Joseph gave them carts as Pharaoh told him. He also gave them food for their journey. 22 Joseph gave each brother new clothes. But he gave Benjamin 300 pieces of silver and 5 sets of clothes. 23 And Joseph sent these things to his father:

10 donkeys carrying the best things from Egypt

10 female donkeys carrying food and bread and other food for the journey.

24 Then Joseph sent his brothers on their journey. As they left he said, 'Do not argue on the way!'

25 So the brothers left Egypt. And then they arrived in Canaan, where their father Jacob was. 26 They told him, 'Joseph is still alive!' He rules over all of Egypt.' Jacob was surprised. And he did not believe what they said. 27 So the brothers told Jacob everything that Joseph had said to them. And Jacob saw the carts that Joseph sent to carry him back to Egypt. So Jacob began to be happy. 28 And Israel (that is Jacob) said, 'I am sure! My son Joseph is still alive! I will go and see him before I die.'

Chapter 46

1 So Israel (Jacob) left Canaan. He took everything that was his. When he came to Beersheba, he offered sacrifices to God, the God of his father Isaac. 2 And God spoke to Israel in a dream at night. He said, 'Jacob! Jacob!' And Jacob replied, 'Yes.' 3 God said, 'I am God. I am the God of your father. Do not be afraid to go to Egypt. I will make you have many descendants there. 4 I will go to Egypt with you. And I will bring you back again. And you will be with Joseph when you die.'

5 Then Jacob left Beersheba. And Israel's sons took their father Jacob and their wives and children. They all sat on the carts that Pharaoh sent to take them to Egypt. 6 They also took all their animals and everything that they had got in Canaan. And Jacob and all his family went to Egypt. 7 He took his sons and grandsons, and his daughters and granddaughters. He took all his family to Egypt.

8 These are the names of the sons of Israel, (that is, the descendants of Jacob). Reuben was the first-born of Jacob. 9 The sons of Reuben: Hanoch, Pallu, Hezron and Carmi. 10 The sons of Simeon: Jemuel, Jamin, Ohad, Jachin, Zohar and Shaul the son of a Canaanite woman. 11 The sons of Levi: Gershon, Kohath and Merari. 12 The sons of Judah: Er, Onan, Shelah, Perez and Zerah, (but Er and Onan died in the land of Canaan). The sons of Perez: Hezron and Hamul. 13 The sons of Issachar: Tola, Puah, Jashub and Shimron.14 The sons of Zebulun: Sered, Elon and Jahleel. 15 These were the sons that Leah gave birth to in Paddan Aram. Jacob was their father. Leah also gave birth to a daughter, Dinah. These sons and daughters of Jacob's were 33 in all. 16 The sons of Gad: Zephon, Haggi, Shuni, Ezbon, Eri, Arodi and Areli. 17 The sons of Asher: Imnah, Ishvah, Ishvi and Beriah. Their sister was Serah. The sons of Beriah: Heber and Malkiel.18 These were the children that Zilpah gave birth to. Jacob was their father. Leah gave Zilpah to Jacob as a wife. There were 16 children in all. 19 The sons of Jacob's wife Rachel: Joseph and Benjamin. 20 In Egypt, Manasseh and Ephraim were born to Joseph. Their mother was Asenath daughter of Potiphera, priest of On. 21 The sons of Benjamin were Bela, Becher, Ashbel, Gera, Naaman, Ehi, Rosh, Muppim, Huppim and Ard. 22 These were the sons of Rachel, born to Jacob. There were 14 in all. 23 The son of Dan: Hushim. 24The sons of Naphtali: Jahziel, Guni, Jezer and Shillem. 25 These were the sons born to Jacob. Their mother was Bilhah. Rachel gave her to Jacob as a wife. There were 7 in all. 26 Jacob's descendants (not counting his son's wives) were 66. All these people went with him to Egypt. 27 Jacob's family came to 70 people. This included Joseph's 2 sons. They were born in Egypt. All these were in Egypt with Jacob.

28 Now Jacob sent Judah in front of him. He sent him to Joseph, to learn how to get to Goshen. 29 Joseph had his chariot prepared. And he went to Goshen to meet his father Israel. Joseph saw Jacob. And Joseph hugged his father and wept for a long time.

30 Israel said to Joseph, 'Now I am ready to die. Because I have seen for myself that you are still alive.' 31Then Joseph spoke to his brother and to his father's household. He said, 'I will go and speak to Pharaoh. I will say to him, "My brothers and my father's household have come to me. They were living in Canaan. 32The men are shepherds. They keep animals safe. And they have brought their animals and everything that they have." 33 Pharaoh will call you to him and ask, "What is your job?" 34 Then you should answer, "We are herdsmen. This is what we have always done. And our ancestors were herdsmen." Then Pharaoh will let you stay in the place called Goshen. Say this because Egyptians hate shepherds and herdsmen. And the Egyptians do not want to live near them.'

Chapter 47

1 Joseph went to Pharaoh. He told him, 'My father and brothers, and all their animals are now in Goshen.

They have come from Canaan. And they have brought everything that belongs to them.' 2 Joseph chose 5 of his brothers. And he took them to Pharaoh. 3 Pharaoh asked the brothers, 'What is your job?' The brothers replied, 'We are shepherds. And our ancestors were shepherds.' 4 They said to Pharaoh, 'We have come here because the famine is very bad in Canaan. We would like to stay here for a while because our animals do not have any grass to eat. Now, please let us, who are your servants, stay in Goshen.' 5 Pharaoh said to Joseph, 'Your father and your brothers have come to you. 6 The land of Egypt is here for them. Your fathers and brothers can stay in the best part of the land. They can live in Goshen. You may know some of them who are good at what they do. If you do, then they can keep my own animals safe.'

7 Then Joseph brought his father Jacob in to Pharaoh. Jacob blessed Pharaoh. 8 Then Pharaoh asked Jacob, 'How old are you?' 9 Jacob replied, 'I have been alive for 130 years. My years have been few, and difficult. And I am not as old as my ancestors were.'

10 Then Jacob blessed Pharaoh and left him. 11 So Joseph's father and brothers stayed in Egypt. And Joseph gave them houses in the best part of the land. This was in the place called Rameses. Joseph did as Pharaoh had told him to.

12 Joseph also gave food to his father, his brothers and all his father's household. He gave them enough food for themselves and all their children.

13 But, because the famine was bad, no food grew in all of Egypt. Everyone in Egypt and Canaan was hungry and thin. This was because they had no food to eat. 14 Joseph had all the money in Egypt. He received it from the people in return for food. And Joseph brought all the money to Pharaoh's palace. 15Soon the people did not have any more money. Everyone came to Joseph and said, 'Give us food. Do not let us die. We do not have any more money.' 16 And Joseph replied, 'Then bring me your animals. Because you do not have any more money, I will give you food. But you must give me your animals in return. 17 So the people brought their animals to Joseph. And he sold them food in return for their animals. They brought horses, sheep, goats, cows and donkeys. And Joseph sold them enough food for the year. They used their animals to buy the food. 18 The year ended. And the people came to Joseph again and said, 'You know that we do not have any money. And our animals now belong to you. We have nothing left to sell. We only have our land and ourselves. 19 Do not let us die! And do not let our fields stay empty because we do not have seed to plant. Give us food. And we will be Pharaoh's slaves. And our land will belong to Pharaoh. Give us seed to plant. Give it to us so that we will not die. And then our fields will not be empty.'

20 So Joseph bought all the land in Egypt for Pharaoh. Because the famine was very bad, all the Egyptians sold their fields for food. So Pharaoh owned all the land. 21 And all the people in Egypt worked for Pharaoh. They were like slaves. 22 But Joseph did not buy the land belonging to the tribe of the priests. He did not buy it because Pharaoh gave the priests enough food. So the priests did not sell their land. 23Joseph said to the people, 'I have bought you and your land for Pharaoh. Now I will give you some seed to plant in the fields. 24 But when the plants are ready to eat, you must give 1/5th to Pharaoh. You may keep the other 4/5th. You may keep it for seed to plant again. And for food for you, your households and your children.' 25 The people said, 'You have not let us die. So we agree to be slaves of the king.' 26 So Joseph made a law about the land of Egypt. The law was that 1/5th (or 20%) of all food grown, belonged to Pharaoh. Only the land belonging to the priests did not belong to Pharaoh. And this law is still obeyed today.

27 For all of that time, the Israelites stayed in Goshen. They had property there. And they had many children. 28 Jacob lived in Egypt for 17 years. And he lived for 147 years in all.

29 The time came for Israel (that is Jacob) to die. So he called for his son Joseph. Jacob said to him, 'If you agree, put your hand under my thigh. And promise that you will be kind to me. And promise that you will do as I ask. Do not bury me in Egypt.'

30 Jacob said, 'When I die, carry my body out of Egypt. And bury me where my ancestors are buried. Joseph said, 'I will do as you say.' 31 Jacob said 'Promise me.' Then Joseph made a promise to him. And Israel rested on the top of his staff and worshipped there.

Chapter 48

1 Some time passed. And someone told Joseph, 'Your father is ill.'

So, Joseph took his 2 sons, Manasseh and Ephraim with him. 2 Someone told Jacob, 'Your son Joseph has come to you.' So Israel made himself as strong as he could. And he sat up on the bed. 3 Jacob said to Joseph, 'God Almighty appeared to me at Luz. That is in Canaan. And he blessed me there. 4 He said to me, "I am going to make good things happen to you, and give you many descendants. I will make you into a great group of people. And I will give you this land. And your descendants will have this land when you die." 5 Now you have 2 sons. They were born before I came to Egypt. They will be like my own sons. People will think of Ephraim and Manasseh as my sons, as they think of Reuben and Simeon as my sons. 6 Any children born to you after them will be your own children. They will inherit the land of their brothers. 7 Rachel died on our journey from Paddan. I was very sad. She died a few miles from Ephrath. So I buried her there, next to the road to Ephrath (that is Bethlehem).'

8 Joseph brought Ephraim and Manasseh to Jacob. And Jacob asked, 'Who are these?' 9 Joseph replied, 'They are my sons. God gave them to me in Egypt.' Then Israel said, 'Bring them to me so that I can bless them.' 10 Now Israel could not see very well. He could not see because he was old. So Joseph brought his sons close to Israel. And his father kissed them and hugged them. 11 Israel said to Joseph, 'I never thought that I would see your face again. And now God has let me see your children too.' 12 Then Joseph removed his sons from Jacob's knees. And he bowed down. And put his face to the ground. 13 And Joseph took his 2 sons. He put Ephraim by Israel's left hand. And he put Manasseh by Israel's right hand. Then he brought his sons close to Israel.

14 But Israel put out his right hand. And he put it on Ephraim's head. But Ephraim was the youngest son. Israel crossed his arms. And he put his left hand on Manasseh's head. But Manasseh was the oldest son. 15 Then Israel blessed Joseph. He said, 'May God bless these boys. He is the God in front of whom my ancestors Abraham and Isaac walked. He is the God who has been my shepherd all my life, until this day. 16 He is the Angel who kept me safe. May he bless these boys. May they be called by my name, and the names of my ancestors Abraham and Isaac? And may they have many descendants and fill the earth.'

17 Joseph saw that his father put his right hand on Ephraim's head. And Joseph thought that this was wrong. So he took hold of his father's hand. And he moved it from Ephraim's head. And he put it on Manasseh's head. 18 And Joseph said to Jacob, 'No my father. This son is the oldest. Put your right hand on his head.' 19 But Jacob put his right hand on Ephraim's head. And he said, 'I know, my son, I know. Manasseh will also have many descendants. And he will become famous. But Ephraim his younger brother will be better known than he. And Ephraim's descendants will become many tribes.' 20 That day Jacob blessed them. He said, 'In your name Israel will give this blessing. "May God be good to you, as he was to Ephraim and Manasseh." '
And Israel put Ephraim before Manasseh.

21 Then Israel said to Joseph, 'I will die soon. But God will be with you. And he will take you back to the land where your ancestors lived. 22 And you are over your brothers. So, I give you the part of the land that I took from the Amorites. It is the land that I fought for.

Chapter 49

1 Then Jacob called for his sons. He said, 'Come here to me. Then I can tell you what will happen to you, in future years.

2 Sons of Jacob come together and listen. Listen to your father, Israel.'

3 Jacob said, 'Reuben you are my oldest son. You were my first child after I became a man. Of all my sons, you think yourself most important. And you are the strongest.

4 Yet you are as wild as the sea. People will no longer know you as the most important son (or first-born son) because you went to your father's bed. And you slept with my concubine. This was a wrong thing to do. You made me ashamed.

5 Simeon and Levi are brothers. They use their swords only to hurt people.

6 I will not take part in their plans. They kill men when they are angry. And they hurt animals only because they want to. So, I will not meet with them.

7 May they be cursed because they are angry? This is because they are so cruel. And I will make your descendants live with other people. They will not have their own land. They will live all over the country of Israel.

8 Judah, your brothers will praise you. You will kill your enemies. Your father's sons will bow down to you.

9 Judah is like a wild animal that has eaten its meal. He rests after eating. Nobody would want to wake a wild animal.

10 The royal sceptre will not leave him. And the staff of rulers will stay with him. It will stay with him until one man comes. That will be the man that it belongs to. And everyone will obey that man.'

11 'Judah will tie his donkey to a vine. He will tie his horse to the best branch. He will wash his clothes in red wine.'

12 'His eyes are red from drinking lots of wine. And his teeth are white from drinking milk.'

13 'Zebulun will live by the sea. And his town will be a safe place for ships to stay. His land will go as far as Sidon.

14 Issachar is like a donkey. The donkey is lying down between 2 saddlebags.

15 He saw how good his resting-place was. And he saw how nice the country was. So he stayed there. And he worked like a slave for other people.'

16 'Dan will be a ruler for his people. His descendants will be like other tribes of Israel. They are a small tribe. But they will still be like the other tribes.

17 He will be as dangerous as a snake on the road. He will be like a snake that bites the feet of horses. Then the person falls off the horse.

18 I look to you to keep me safe Lord.'

19 'People will attack Gad, but he will attack them.

20 Asher will have good food. It will be good enough for kings to eat.'

21 'Naphtali is like a wild animal. He runs free and has many young ones.

22 Joseph is like a vine that has lots of fruit. It grows by a well and the branches go over a wall.'

23 'His enemies hated him. And they attacked him.

24 But he stayed strong and beat them. That was because the hand of the Mighty One of Jacob (the Shepherd, the Rock of Israel) helped him.'.

25 'The Almighty (the God of Jacob) blesses you. So he gives you the blessings of the heaven above and the blessings of the deep that lies below. And he gives you the blessings of the breasts and womb.'

26 'The blessings of your father are greater than the blessing of my ancestors. They go up to the top of the mountains that last for ever. They are for Joseph, who was separate from his brothers.

27 Benjamin is like a hungry wild animal. He kills an animal and eats it in the morning. In the evening, he gives what remains to his people.'

28 All these are the 12 tribes of Israel. And this is what their father told them. He told them when he blessed them. He told each son what would happen to his descendants.

29 Then Jacob said to his 12 sons, 'I am about to die. So take my body from here. Take my body to Canaan. Bury me with my ancestors, in the grave in the field that belonged to Ephron the Hittite. 30 The grave is in the field of Machpelah. That is near Mamre in Canaan. Abraham bought this as a place to bury people. He bought it from Ephron the Hittite. Abraham bought the grave with the field. 31 That is where they buried Abraham and his wife Sarah. And it is where they buried Isaac and his wife Rebekah. 32 Abraham bought the field and the grave from the Hittites.' 33 Jacob finished telling his sons what he wanted them to do. And he lay on his bed. He died. And he went to be with his ancestors who had died before him.

Chapter 50

1 Joseph hugged his father's body. And he wept over him. And he kissed him. 2 Then Joseph spoke to his servants who were doctors. He told them to put special oil and material on Jacob's body. They did this so that it would stay whole. And it would not smell. So, Joseph's servants did as he said. 3 The servants did this for 40 days. Because that is how long it takes to put the special oil and material on a body. And the Egyptians were sad for 70 days because Jacob died.

4 The days of showing that they were sad ended. And Joseph said to Pharaoh's officers, 'If you agree, speak to Pharaoh for me. Tell him: 5 "My father made me make a promise. He said, 'I am going to die soon. Bury me in the grave that I dug myself. This is in Canaan.' Now let me go and bury my father. Then I will return." ' 6 Pharaoh said, 'Go and bury your father. Because he made you promise that you would.'

7 So Joseph went to bury his father. All Pharaoh's officers went with him. These were the important people who lived in Pharaoh's palace. And the important people who lived in Egypt went with Joseph. 8And every one in Joseph's household went to bury Jacob. All his brothers and everyone in his brothers' households went. They did not take their children or their animals. They left these in Goshen. 9 Chariots and men on horses went with them. Very many people went with Joseph to bury Jacob. 10 They came to Atad, near the River Jordan. They stopped at the place where people separated food plants. (They separated the good to eat parts from the parts that they could not eat.) And they stayed there for 7 days. And they showed that they were very sad. They were sad because Jacob died. 11 The people were showing that they were sad. The Canaanites saw this at Atad. And they said, 'The Egyptians are showing that they are sad. This is because someone died.' And they called that place Abel Mizraim. 12 So Jacob's sons did what he had told them. 13 They carried his body to Canaan. And they buried him in the grave. That was in the field of Machpelah, near Mamre. Abraham had bought the grave from Ephron the Hittite. He had bought it with the field. 14 So Joseph buried his father. Then he returned to Egypt together with his brothers. And everyone who went with him returned too.

15 So Jacob was dead. And Joseph's brothers were frightened. They said to each other, 'We did a bad thing to Joseph. Perhaps he now wants to do something bad to us.' 16 So they sent a message to Joseph. It said, 'Your father said this to us before he died: 17 "This is what you are to say to Joseph: I, Jacob ask you to forgive your brothers the wrong that they did against you." Now, please forgive our sins. Forgive the sins of the servants of the God of your father.' When Joseph received their message, he wept. 18 Then his brothers came. And they bowed down to the ground in front of Joseph. They said, 'We are your slaves.' 19But Joseph said to them, 'Do not be frightened. Only God judges. I will not. 20 'You wanted to hurt me. But God wanted what you did for his good plan. God is saving many lives because I am here. 21 So do not be frightened. I will give you what you need for you, and your children.' And Joseph spoke kind words to them. So, they knew that he would not hurt them.

22 Joseph stayed in Egypt with all his father's family. He lived for 110 years. 23 And he saw the 3rd descendants of Ephraim. And Makir, son of Manasseh put his children on Joseph's knees.

24 Then Joseph said to his brothers, 'I am about to die. But God will come and help you. And he will take you out of Egypt. He will take you to the land that he promised to Abraham and Isaac and Jacob.' 25 And Joseph made the sons of Israel make a promise. He said, 'God will come and help you. When this happens, you must carry my bones away from this place.' 26 So Joseph died when he was 110 years old. And they put special oil and materials on his body. And they put his body in a special box.

How God Made the Slaves Free

Exodus

About Exodus

The book of Exodus is the second book in the Bible. The book of Genesis is the first book.

In Genesis we read about Joseph, one of the 12 sons of Jacob. Joseph's brothers sold him as a slave, to work in the country called Egypt. Later, there was a famine and all of Jacob's family came to live in Egypt.
Joseph forgave his brothers for what they had done to him.

God gave Jacob another name, Israel.

Exodus continues the story of Jacob's family in Egypt. It tells us these things:

How God brought the Israelites out of Egypt.

Chapter 1

1 The sons of Israel went to Egypt with Jacob. Each one went with his family. Here are their names:

2 Reuben, Simeon, Levi and Judah, 3 Issachar, Zebulun and Benjamin, 4 Dan, Naphtali, Gad and Asher. Joseph was already in Egypt. 5 There were 70 people in Jacob's family.

6 After some time, Joseph died and his brothers also died. All the people who had lived during Joseph's life died. 7 But the Israelites had lots of children and they grew into a very large family. There were so many of them that they filled the country.

8 After some more time had passed, a new king began to rule in Egypt. He did not know anything about Joseph. 9 He said to his people, 'Look! The Israelites have become too many for us. 10 We must be very careful. If we do nothing, even more of them will be born. Then, if there is a war they will join our enemies. The enemies and the Israelites will fight against us and then the Israelites will leave the country.'

11 So the Egyptians made the Israelites work as slaves. Their masters made life difficult for the Israelites. They made the Israelites work for Pharaoh, to build cities. The names of the cities were Pithom and Rameses. They were cities in which the Egyptians stored food.

12 The Egyptians made life more difficult for the Israelites but the Israelites became more in number. They had many children and they lived in every part of the country. Because of this, the Egyptians began to be afraid of them. 13 So the Egyptians made the Israelites work without any rest. 14 The Egyptians made the lives of the Israelites very sad because of their work. The Israelites worked with bricks and mortar. They also did many different jobs in the fields. The Egyptians were cruel. They made the Israelites do all this difficult work.

15 There were two Israelite women who helped the other Israelite women at the birth of their children. These two women were called Shiphrah and Puah. The King of Egypt spoke to them. He said: 16 'When you help the Israelite women at the birth of their children, do this:

If they have a baby boy, kill him.

If they have a baby girl, let her live.'

17 But the two women did not obey the king of Egypt. They obeyed God and they let the boys live. 18 Then the King of Egypt caused the two women to come to him. He asked them: 'Why have you done this? Why have you let the boys live?' 19 The two women answered Pharaoh. They said, 'Israelite women are not like Egyptian women. Israelite women are very strong. Their babies are born very quickly, before we arrive at the house.'

20 Because of this, God was kind to the two women. The people grew in number and they became very strong. 21 Because the two women obeyed God, he gave them families of their own.

22 Then Pharaoh spoke to his people. He said: 'When an Israelite boy is born, you must throw him in the river. But you can let the baby girls live.'

Chapter 2

The birth of Moses

1 At this time, there was an Israelite man who belonged to the big family of Levi. He married a woman who also belonged to that big family. 2 A baby boy was born. His mother saw that he was a very beautiful baby. So she hid him for three months. 3 Then the woman could not continue to hide him. So she took a basket that someone had made from dry river grass. She painted the basket with sticky black paint, to keep the water out of it. The mother put her baby in the basket. Then she put the basket on the edge of the river, among the river grasses.

4 The baby's sister stood not very far away. She wanted to see what would happen to the baby.

5 Now the daughter of Pharaoh came to wash in the river. And her servant girls walked by the edge of the river. Then Pharaoh's daughter saw the basket among the river grasses. So she sent one of her servant girls to fetch it. 6 When Pharaoh's daughter opened the basket, she saw the baby. He was crying and she was sorry for him. She said: 'This is one of the Israelite children.' 7 Then the baby's sister spoke to Pharaoh's daughter. She said, 'Do you want me to fetch one of the Israelite women? She can nurse this baby for you.'

8 Pharaoh's daughter said: 'Yes, do that.' So the girl went and she called the baby's mother. 9 Pharaoh's daughter spoke to the baby's mother. She said: 'Take this baby away and nurse him for me. I will pay you to do this.' So the woman took the baby and she nursed him. 10 When the baby was older, his mother brought him to Pharaoh's daughter. He became her son and she called him Moses. She said: 'I will call him Moses because I pulled him out of the water.'

Moses runs away to Midian

11 Many years later, Moses grew to be a man. At that time, he went out to look at the Israelites. He knew that he was an Israelite too. He saw them as they worked without any rest. Then he saw an Egyptian who was hitting an Israelite. Yes, the Egyptian was hitting someone from Moses' own country! 12 Moses looked in every direction. He saw nobody near. Then Moses killed the Egyptian and he hid his dead body in the sand. 13 Moses went out again the next day and he saw two Israelites. They were fighting together. Moses spoke to the man who was hurting the other man. He said to him: 'Why are you hitting your friend?'

14 The man answered: 'You should not be a ruler and a judge over us. Perhaps you are going to kill me, as you killed the Egyptian.' Then Moses was afraid. He said to himself: 'People know what I have done!' 15 Then someone told Pharaoh about it. Pharaoh tried to kill Moses. But Moses ran away from Pharaoh. He went to the country called Midian and he stayed there. Moses sat down by a well in the country called Midian.

16 Now the priest of Midian had 7 daughters. These 7 girls came to get water out of the well. They filled the long stone dishes with water so that their father's animals could drink. 17 But the shepherds who lived in that place arrived. They made the girls go away. So Moses stood up and he helped the 7 girls. He gave water to their animals.

18 When the girls came to Reuel, their father, he asked them a question. He said: 'Why have you come home so soon today?'

19 They answered: 'An Egyptian saved us from the shepherds. He also took water out of the well and he gave it to the animals.' 20 Reuel said to his daughters, 'Where is the man? You should not have left him there. Ask him to come here so that he can eat bread with us.' 21 Moses was happy to stay with Reuel. Reuel gave his daughter Zipporah to Moses as his wife. 22 After several months, Zipporah gave birth to a baby boy. Moses called the boy Gershom. He called him that because he said: 'I have been a stranger in a foreign country.'

23 After a long time had passed, the king of Egypt died. The Israelites were very sad because they were slaves. They shouted aloud for help from God. 24 God heard them crying because they were slaves. He remembered his promise to Abraham, Isaac and Jacob. 25 So God looked at the Israelites. He knew that they needed his help.

Chapter 3

Moses and the burning bush

1 Moses fed the animals of Jethro the priest of Midian and he kept them safely. Jethro was his wife's father (the same person as Reuel). Moses led the animals to the far side of the desert. He came to Horeb, the mountain of God.

2 There the angel of the Lord showed himself to Moses. The angel looked like a fire that was burning in the middle of a bush. Moses looked at the bush and he saw that it was on fire. The bush was burning but the fire still did not destroy it. 3 Moses said to himself: 'I will go and see this strange thing. I want to see why the bush is not burned.'

4 Then the Lord saw that Moses came to see the bush. And God called to Moses from inside the bush: 'Moses! Moses!' Moses answered: 'Here I am.'

5 God said to Moses: 'Do not come near this place. Remove your shoes from your feet. The place where you stand is holy ground.' 6 Then God said: 'I am the God of your fathers. I am the God of Abraham, the God of Isaac and the God of Jacob.' Then Moses hid his face. He was afraid to look at God.

7 Then the Lord said: 'I have certainly seen the troubles of my people in Egypt. I have heard that they cry because of their slave masters. I know how sad they are. 8 So I have come down to save them from the Egyptians. I will bring them from Egypt to another country. It will be a good country and a wide country. There will be a lot of good food and drink, enough for everyone. It is the place where all these nations live now: the Canaanites, the Hittites, the Amorites, the Perizzites, the Hivites and the Jebusites. 9 And now I have heard Israel's people cry. I have seen how the Egyptians do bad things to them. 10 Now go! I will send you to Pharaoh. You will lead my people, the Israelites, out of Egypt.'

11 But Moses said to God: 'I am not an important person. I cannot go to Pharaoh. I cannot lead the Israelites out of Egypt!'

12 God said to Moses: 'I will be with you. After you have led the people out of Egypt you will worship me on this mountain. That will show people that I have sent you.'

13 Then Moses answered God. He said: 'If I go to the Israelites, they will ask me a question. I shall say: "The God of your fathers has sent me to you." But then they will ask me, "What is God's name?" What then shall I say to them?'

14 God said to Moses: 'I am who I am! Say to the Israelites: "I AM has sent me to you." '

15 God also said to Moses: 'Say this to the Israelites: "This is the God who has sent me to you. He is the Lord, the God of your fathers. He is the God of Abraham. He is the God of Isaac and Jacob." This is my name for all time. People will always remember me by this name.

16 Go and bring together the leaders of Israel. Say to them, "God has shown himself to me. He is the Lord and the God of your fathers. He is the God of Abraham, Isaac and Jacob. And God said to me: 'I have watched you Israelites in Egypt. I have seen what the Egyptians have done to you. 17 I have promised that I will bring you out of your difficult life in Egypt. I will bring you into the country of the Canaanites, the Hittites, the Amorites, the Perizzites, the Hivites and the Jebusites. It is a country with more than enough good food and drink.' "

18 The leaders of the Israelites will listen to you. Then you must go with them to the king of Egypt. Say to him: "The Lord, the God of the Israelites has met with us. Please let us go on a journey of three days, into the desert. We must worship the Lord our God there." 19 I know that the king of Egypt will not want to let you go. He will only let you go if someone more powerful than himself causes him to obey.

20 So I will show him my powerful authority. I will cause very strange and bad things to happen to Egypt. I will do great and powerful things to that country. After that, Pharaoh will let you go.

21 And I will cause the Egyptians to think good things about the Israelites. So when you go, they will give you many gifts. 22 Each Israelite woman must ask for gifts from the Egyptian women. They must ask the Egyptian women who live near them. They must also ask those who live with them in their houses. They must ask for silver things and gold things. They must also ask for expensive clothes. You must dress your sons and your daughters in these clothes. In this way, you will take everything valuable away from the Egyptians.'

Chapter 4

God shows Moses some strange things

1 Then Moses answered: 'But perhaps the leaders of Israel will not believe me. Perhaps they will not listen to my voice. Perhaps they will say: "The Lord did not show himself to you." '

2 Then the Lord said to Moses: 'What is that thing in your hand?' Moses answered: 'It is a stick.'

3 The Lord said: 'Throw it on the ground.' So Moses threw it on the ground. Then the stick became a snake and Moses ran from the snake! 4 But the Lord said to Moses: 'Put out your hand and catch the snake by the tail.' So Moses put out his hand and he caught the snake. Then it became a stick in his hand again. 5God said, 'Do this, and they will believe you. They will believe that the Lord has shown himself to you. It is the Lord, who is the God of their fathers. It is the Lord, who is the God of Abraham, the God of Isaac and the God of Jacob.'

6 Then the Lord said to Moses: 'Put your hand inside your clothes, near to your heart.' So Moses did this. When he took his hand out again, it had become as white as snow. It was like the hand of a man who had the illness called leprosy.

7 Then God said: 'Put your hand back inside your clothes, near to your heart.' So Moses did that. And when he took his hand out, it was well again. It was the same as the other parts of his body.

8 God said, 'They may not believe you. They may not think that the first sign is important. But they may still believe the second sign. 9 But if they will not believe the two signs, you can do something else. If they do not listen to you, then take some water from the River Nile. Pour it on the dry ground. The water that you take from the river will become blood on the ground.'

10 But Moses said to the Lord: 'Oh Master, I cannot speak well. I could not speak well before. And I cannot speak well now, since you have spoken to me. I speak slowly and I speak with difficulty.'

11 Then the Lord said to Moses: 'Who has made human mouths? Who makes a person that cannot speak? Who makes a person that cannot hear? Who makes a person that cannot see? Who makes a person that can see? It is I, the Lord, who does all these things. 12 Now go! I will help you to speak. I will teach you what to say.'

13 But Moses said, 'Oh Master, please send some other person.'

14 Then the Lord became angry with Moses. He said: 'Aaron, the Levite, is your brother. I know that he can speak well. And he is coming to meet you. When Aaron sees you he will be very happy. 15 Then you must speak to him. You must tell him what to say. I will help both of you to speak. And I will teach you what you must do. 16 Aaron will speak to the people for you. You will be like God to him. You will tell Aaron what to say. 17 Take this stick with you. You will use this stick to do the signs.'

Moses returns to Egypt

18 Then Moses went back to Jethro, his wife's father. Moses said to Jethro: 'Please let me return to my family in Egypt. I must see if they are still alive.' So Jethro said to Moses: 'Go in peace.'

19 The Lord had said to Moses while he was still in Midian: 'Go back to Egypt. All the men who tried to kill you are now dead.' 20 So Moses put his wife and his sons on a donkey and they started on the journey back to Egypt. And Moses carried the stick of God in his hand.

21 Then the Lord said to Moses: 'When you return to Egypt you must do the signs. Do all the signs that I gave you the power to do. Do them in front of Pharaoh. But I will make Pharaoh angry and cruel. Because of this, he will not let the people go.

22 Then you must speak to Pharaoh. You must say: "The Lord says, 'Israel is my first son. 23 I have already said to you: "Let my son go so that he can worship me." But if you refuse to let him go, I will kill your first son.' " '

24 On the way to Egypt, there was a house where people can rest on their journey. God met Moses there and God was going to kill him. 25 But Zipporah took a sharp stone and she cut off her son's foreskin with the stone. Then Zipporah threw the foreskin at Moses' feet. She said: 'You are a husband of blood to me.'26 So God did not do anything bad to Moses. Then Zipporah said to Moses: 'You are a husband of blood, because of this circumcision.'

27 The Lord said to Aaron: 'Go into the desert to meet Moses.' So Aaron went. He met Moses at the mountain of God and he kissed him. 28 Then Moses told Aaron all that the Lord had told him to say. He also told Aaron about all the special signs. God had commanded Moses to show these signs to the Israelites and to Pharaoh.

29 Then Moses and Aaron went to Egypt. They brought together all the leaders of the Israelites. 30 Aaron told them all the things that God had said to Moses. Then Moses did the signs in front of the people. 31And the people believed Aaron and Moses. They put their heads down and they worshipped God. They had heard that God had come to his people. God had seen their hard life and he was sorry for them. That is why they worshipped God.

Chapter 5

Moses and Aaron speak to Pharaoh

1 After this, Moses and Aaron went to visit Pharaoh. They said to him: 'Listen to what the Lord says. He is the God of Israel. He says, "Let my people go. Let them prepare a party for me in the desert." '

2 But Pharaoh said: 'I do not know the Lord. I do not know why I should obey his voice. I do not know why I should let the Israelites go. I do not know the Lord. Neither will I let the Israelites go.'

3 Moses and Aaron said: 'The God of the Israelites has met us. Please let us go. We must go on a journey of three days into the desert. There we must give gifts to the Lord our God. If we do not do this, God may attack us with illness. Or he may use soldiers to attack us.'

4 But the king of Egypt said: 'Moses and Aaron, you must not take the people away from their work! Go back to your jobs!' 5 And Pharaoh said: 'Look, there are now many people in the country. But you stop them doing their work.'

6 On that day, Pharaoh gave a command to the masters of the slaves. He also gave the command to the leaders of the work. 7 This was the command: 'Do not give the people any more straw with which to make bricks. They must find their own straw. 8 But they must still make the same number of bricks as before. Do not let the amount become smaller. They are lazy. That is why they ask to go. They say: "Let us go to give gifts to our God." 9 So you must cause them to work harder. They will then be too busy to listen to false words.'

10 So the slaves' masters and the leaders of the work went to the people. They said to them: 'Pharaoh says: "I will not give you straw. 11 You must find your own straw, where you can. But you will still have to make the same number of bricks." ' 12 So the people went everywhere in the land of Egypt, to get straw from the fields. 13 The slaves' masters made the Israelites work fast. They said: 'Finish your work for each day, as when you had straw.' 14 Pharaoh's slave masters hit the leaders who had authority over the people. They said to them: 'Why have you not made as many bricks today, as you did before?'

15 Then the Israelite leaders went to Pharaoh. They asked him: 'Why do you do these things to us, your servants? 16 Our masters do not give us any straw. But they say "Make bricks!" Then they hit us. But it is your people that are doing wrong things.'

17 But Pharaoh said: 'You are lazy! You are only lazy! That is why you say: "Let us go. Let us take gifts to the Lord." 18 Now go and do your work. Nobody will give you any straw. But you must make the same number of bricks.'

19 The Israelite leaders heard Pharaoh say: 'You must make the same number of bricks as you made before.' Then they knew that they were in bad trouble. 20 Then the Israelite leaders met with Moses and Aaron. Moses and Aaron were waiting for them to return from Pharaoh. 21 And the leaders spoke to Moses and Aaron. They said: 'We hope that the Lord will look at you. We hope that the Lord will judge you! You have made us like a bad smell to Pharaoh and to his servants. You have given them a reason to kill us.'

22 Then Moses returned to the Lord. He said: 'Oh Master, why have you done bad things to this people? Why did you send me to them? 23 I came to speak in your name. But since I spoke to Pharaoh, he has done only bad things to the people. And you have done nothing to save your people.'

Chapter 6

God promises to save the Israelites

1 Then the Lord spoke to Moses. He said: 'Now you will see what I will do to Pharaoh. Because of my powerful signs, he will let my people go. Because of my powerful signs, he will command them to leave his country.'

2 And God said to Moses: 'I am the Lord. 3 I showed myself to Abraham, to Isaac and to Jacob, as God Almighty. But I did not let them know me by my name, the Lord. 4 I also made my special promise to them. I promised to give them the country of Canaan. I promised to give them the country where they had lived as foreign people. 5 And I have heard the Israelites when they cry. They cry because the Egyptians cause them to live as slaves. I have remembered my special promise. 6 So you must say this to the Israelites. "I am the Lord. I will remove you from the authority of the Egyptians. You will not be their slaves again. I will bring you back to myself by my powerful authority. I will judge the Egyptians by the great things that I will do. 7 I will make you my own people and I will be your God. Then you will know that I am the Lord. I am your God who saved you from the authority of the Egyptians. 8 And I will bring you to another country. I made a very serious promise to give that other country to Abraham, to Isaac and to Jacob. I will give it to you and it will be your own country. I am the Lord." '

9 Moses reported these words to the Israelites. But they did not listen to him, because their Egyptian masters were so cruel to them. They refused to hope for good things. Their Egyptian masters had broken their spirits and made them very sad.

10 Then the Lord said to Moses: 11 'Go and speak to Pharaoh, king of Egypt. Tell him that he must let the Israelites go out of his country.' 12 But Moses said to the Lord: 'Look! Even the Israelites have not listened to me. So why should Pharaoh listen to me? My lips are unable to speak good words from God.'

13 Then the Lord spoke to Moses and Aaron about the Israelites and about Pharaoh, the king of Egypt. He commanded Moses and Aaron to lead the Israelites out of the country called Egypt.

The Ancestors of Moses and Aaron

14 These were the leaders of the whole families:

The sons of Reuben, Israel's oldest son: Hanoch, Pallu, Hezron and Carmi. These were Reuben's families.

15 The sons of Simeon: Jemuel, Jamin, Ohad, Jachin, Zohar and Shaul. Shaul was the son of a Canaanite woman. These were Simeon's families.

16 These are the names of the sons of Levi from the oldest to the youngest: Gershon, Kohath and Merari. Levi lived for 137 years.

17 The sons of Gershon and their families: Libni and Shimei.

18 The sons of Kohath: Amram, Izhar, Hebron and Uzziel. Kohath lived for 133 years.

19 The sons of Merari: Mahli and Mushi.

These were the families of Levi from the oldest to the youngest.

20 Amram married Jochebed, his father's sister. Aaron and Moses were their sons. Amram lived for 137 years.

21 The sons of Izhar: Korah, Nepheg and Sithri.

22 The sons of Uzziel: Mishael, Elzaphan and Sithri.

23 Aaron married Elisheba. She was the daughter of Amminadab and the sister of Nahshon. Elisheba's children were: Nadab and Abihu, Eleazar and Ithamar.

24 The sons of Korah: Assir, Elkanah and Abiasaph. These are the families of people from Korah.

25 Eleazar, Aaron's son, married one of Putiel's daughters. Phinehas was their son.

These were the leaders of the families of the Levites.

26 This Aaron and Moses are the same men to whom the Lord spoke. He said: 'Lead the Israelites out of the country of Egypt. Lead them out as an army of people.' 27 Yes, it was the same Moses and Aaron who spoke to Pharaoh, king of Egypt. They told him that the Israelites would leave Egypt.

Aaron will speak for Moses

28 When the Lord spoke to Moses in the country of Egypt, 29 he said, 'I am the Lord. Tell Pharaoh, King of Egypt, everything that I tell you.' 30 Then Moses said: 'Look, my lips are unable to speak good words from God. Why should Pharaoh listen to me?'

Chapter 7

1 Then the Lord said to Moses: 'Look, I have made you like God to Pharaoh. And your brother Aaron will be your prophet. 2 You must say everything that I command you. Your brother Aaron must command Pharaoh to let the Israelites go. Pharaoh must let them go out of his country.'

3 'But I will make Pharaoh angry and cruel. He will refuse to listen to you. I will do even more great signs and strange things in the country called Egypt. 4 But Pharaoh will refuse to listen to you. Then I will show my authority to Egypt. And I will remove my army, my people the Israelites, out of the country called Egypt. I will lead them out with powerful authority. 5 Then the Egyptians will know that I am the Lord. They will know this when I judge Egypt. They will know it when I lead the Israelites out of Egypt.'

Moses' stick becomes a snake

6 So Moses and Aaron obeyed all the commands of the Lord. 7 Now Moses was 80 years old when he spoke to Pharaoh. And Aaron was 83 years old.

8 Then the Lord spoke to Moses and Aaron. He said:

9 'Pharaoh will say: "Show me one of your special signs." Then you must say to Aaron: "Take your stick and throw it down in front of Pharaoh. It will become a snake." '

10 So Moses and Aaron went to Pharaoh. They did everything that the Lord had commanded them. Aaron threw down his stick in front of Pharaoh and his servants. And the stick became a snake! 11 Then Pharaoh commanded his clever men to come in. These men, the magicians of Egypt, did the same thing as Aaron. They did it by their bad, powerful authority. 12 Each magician threw down his stick and it became a snake. But Aaron's stick ate their sticks! 13 But still Pharaoh felt angry and cruel. He refused to listen to Moses and Aaron. This was what the Lord had said would happen.

Moses makes water into blood

14 Then the Lord said to Moses: 'There is no change in Pharaoh's thoughts. He refuses to let the people go. 15 Go to Pharaoh in the morning as he goes to the river. Wait for him by the edge of the river. Then take in your hand the stick that became a snake. 16 Then say to him: "The Lord, the God of the Israelites has sent me to you. The Lord says: 'Let my people go. Let them worship me in the desert.' But until now, you have not listened. 17 So this is what the Lord says: 'In this way, you will know that I am the Lord. Moses will hit the water with the stick that is in his hand. And the water will become blood. 18 And the fish in the water will die. And the river will have a very bad smell. Then the Egyptians will not want to drink the water from the river.' " '

19 And the Lord said to Moses: 'Say to Aaron: "Take your stick. Lift up your hand over the waters of Egypt. Lift it up over their rivers and their streams. Lift it up over their ponds and pools of water. They will all become blood. There will be blood in every part of the country called Egypt. There will be blood in all the stone pots. There will be blood also in every bucket that men have made from wood." '

20 Moses and Aaron obeyed the Lord. Aaron lifted up the stick in front of Pharaoh and his servants. He hit the water in the river with the stick. Then all the water in the river became blood. 21 The fish in the river died. The river became bad and the Egyptians could not drink its water. There was blood in every part of the country called Egypt.

22 But the magicians of Egypt did the same thing by their bad powerful authority. So there was no change in Pharaoh's thoughts. He still refused to listen to Moses and Aaron. The Lord had said that this would happen. 23 Pharaoh turned and he went away into his house. He did not think about what had happened. 24 And the Egyptians dug holes near the river to find water to drink. They could not drink the water from the river itself.

25 Seven days went by after the Lord had made the water in the river into blood.

Chapter 8

Moses and Aaron bring frogs out of the water

1 The Lord said to Moses: 'Go to Pharaoh and say to him: "These are the words of the Lord. Let my people go. Let them worship me. 2 But if you do not let them go, I will send thousands of frogs into your country.

3 The river will be full of frogs. The frogs will come into your house. They will jump into your bed. They will come into the houses of your servants. They will come into the houses of your people. They will jump into the hot places where you cook your food. They will jump into the dishes where you mix your flour and water.

4 The frogs will jump up on you. They will jump up on your people and on all your servants." '

5 Then the Lord said to Moses: 'Say to Aaron: "Take your stick in your hand. Then raise your hand. Lift it up over the rivers, the streams and the pools. You will cause frogs to come up over the whole country of Egypt." '

6 So Aaron lifted up his hand over the waters of Egypt. Then the frogs came up over the whole country of Egypt.

7 But the magicians did the same thing by their bad powerful authority. They also made frogs come up on the country of Egypt.

8 Then Pharaoh commanded Moses and Aaron to come to him. He said: 'Ask the Lord to remove the frogs from me and from my people. Then I will let your people go. They can sacrifice to the Lord.' 9 Moses said to Pharaoh: 'You can choose the time when I will speak to God. Then I will ask God to do this for you, for your servants and for your people. I will ask God to remove the frogs from you and from your house. The frogs will remain only in the river.'

10 And Pharaoh said: 'Do it tomorrow.'

Moses answered: 'It will be as you say. Then you will know that there is nobody like the Lord our God. 11 The frogs will leave you and your house. They will leave the houses of your servants and your people. They will remain only in the river.'

12 So Moses and Aaron left Pharaoh. Then Moses prayed to the Lord about the frogs that he had brought on Pharaoh. 13 And the Lord did what Moses asked. The frogs died in the houses, in the yards and in the fields. 14 The people swept the frogs together and there was a very bad smell over the whole country. 15 But when Pharaoh saw that the frogs were dead, he became angry again. He refused to listen to Moses and Aaron. The Lord had said that this would happen.

The gnats arrive

16 Then the Lord said to Moses: 'Say to Aaron, "Lift up your stick and hit the dirt on the ground. It will become gnats in the whole country of Egypt." '

17 Moses and Aaron obeyed God. Aaron lifted up his hand and he hit the dirt with his stick. Then gnats flew on to all the people and on to all the animals. The dirt on the ground became gnats through the whole country of Egypt. 18 Then the magicians tried to make gnats by their bad powerful authority. But they could not do it. And the gnats were on all the people and on all the animals.

19 Then the magicians said to Pharaoh: 'This is the work of God.' But there was no change in Pharaoh's thoughts. He would not listen to the magicians. God had said that this would happen.

The flies arrive

20 Then the Lord said to Moses: 'Get up early in the morning. Meet Pharaoh when he goes out to the water. Then say to him: "The Lord says: 'Let My people go. Let them worship me. 21 If you do not let my people go, I will send thousands of flies on you. I will send them on your servants and on your people. I will send them into your houses. The houses of the Egyptians will be full of flies. The flies will even cover the ground that the houses stand on.

22 But on that day, the country of Goshen will be separate. That is where my people live. There will be no flies there. Then you will know that I, the Lord, am in this country.

23 I will make a difference between my people and your people. This sign will happen tomorrow.' " '

24 And this is what the Lord did. Great numbers of flies came into Pharaoh's house and into his servants' houses. The flies destroyed the whole country of Egypt.

25 Then Pharaoh commanded Moses and Aaron to come to him. He said: 'Go! You can sacrifice to your God here, in the country of Egypt.' 26 But Moses said: 'It would not be right to do that. The Egyptians do not like our sacrifices of animals to the Lord our God. If we sacrifice these animals, the Egyptians will throw stones at us. They will throw them until we are dead. 27 We must go on a journey for three days, into the desert. Then we shall sacrifice to the Lord our God, as he commands us.'

28 So Pharaoh said: 'I will let you go. You can sacrifice to the Lord your God in the desert. But do not go very far away. And pray for me too.'

29 Then Moses said: 'I will leave you now. And I will pray to the Lord. Tomorrow, all the flies will leave the country of Egypt. They will fly away from your servants and from your people. But be careful! Do not do wrong things to us, as you did before. At that time, you did not let the people sacrifice to the Lord.'

30 So Moses left Pharaoh and Moses prayed to the Lord. 31 And the Lord did what Moses asked him. All the flies left Pharaoh and his servants and his people. Not one fly remained! 32 But again, Pharaoh refused to let the people go. There was no change in his thoughts.

Chapter 9

The animals become ill and die

1 Then the Lord said to Moses: 'Go to Pharaoh and say to him: "The Lord, the God of the Israelites says: 'Let my people go. Let them worship me. 2 If you refuse to let them go, you will have trouble. If you still keep them in Egypt, 3 the Lord will send a very bad illness on your animals. All your animals in the fields will become ill. The horses, the donkeys, the camels, the cows, the sheep and the goats will all become very ill.

4 But the Lord will make a difference between the animals of the Israelites and the animals of the Egyptians. None of the animals of the Israelites will die.' " '

5 And God decided when this thing would happen. He said: 'Tomorrow I will do this thing in the country of Egypt.' 6 So on the next day, God did it! All the animals of the Egyptians died. But not one of the animals of the Israelites died. 7 Pharaoh sent men to see what had happened. And they reported that not one of the animals of the Israelites was dead! But there was no change in Pharaoh's mind. He did not let the people go.

The illness of boils

8 Then the Lord said to Moses and Aaron: 'Take in your hands some ashes from the fire. Throw them up in the air as Pharaoh watches. 9 They will become very small bits of dirt over the whole country of Egypt. These will cause boils to appear on the skin. Both people and animals will have these boils on their skin, through the whole country.'

10 So they took ashes from the fire and they stood in front of Pharaoh. Moses threw the ashes up in the air. And boils appeared on both people and animals. 11 Because of the boils, the magicians could not stand in front of Moses. All the Egyptians had boils, even the magicians. 12 But Pharaoh refused to listen to them. The Lord had told Moses that this would happen. The Lord himself made it happen.

Pieces of ice fall on the whole country of Egypt

13 Then the Lord said to Moses: 'Get up early in the morning and go to Pharaoh. Say to him: "This is what the Lord, the God of the Israelites says: 'Let my people go to worship me. 14 Or this time, I will send all my worst troubles against you. I will send them against your servants and against your people. I want you to know that there is nobody like me in the whole earth. That is why I am doing this. 15 Already I could have killed you and your people with one very bad trouble. I could have removed you from the earth. 16 But I have let you live, to show you my power. This is so that people will speak about my powerful name, over the whole world. 17 You still think bad thoughts about my people. You will not let them go.

18 Look! Tomorrow at this time, I will send a very great storm. Heavy pieces of ice will fall. Nobody has ever seen anything like this in Egypt. From Egypt's first day as a country, nobody has seen a storm like this. 19 Now send your servants out. They must bring all your animals from the fields into the buildings. The ice will fall on every human and on every animal that is outside. They will all die.' " '

20 Then those of Pharaoh's servants who were afraid of the Lord's words obeyed God. They quickly brought their slaves and animals inside the buildings. 21 But those who did not listen to the Lord's words left their slaves and animals outside.

22 Then the Lord said to Moses: 'Lift up your hand towards the sky. Then ice will fall over all the country of Egypt. It will fall on every person and on every animal. It will fall on every plant that grows in all the fields in Egypt.'

23 When Moses lifted up his stick towards the sky, the Lord sent a great storm. And the Lord rained large pieces of ice upon the country of Egypt. Also, fire ran along the ground. 24 The ice fell and the fire burned. It was the worst storm that the country of Egypt had ever known. 25 The ice knocked down everything that was in the fields. In the whole country of Egypt it hit both people and animals. It knocked down every plant in the fields and it broke every tree. 26 But in the country of Goshen, there were no pieces of ice. That was where Israel's people lived.

27 Then Pharaoh commanded Moses and Aaron to come to him. And Pharaoh said: 'This time, I have done a wrong thing. The Lord is right. I and my people are wrong. 28 Pray to the Lord because we have had enough storms and ice. I will let you go! You do not need to stay here now.'

29 Then Moses said to Pharaoh: 'When I have left the city, I will lift my hands to the Lord. I will pray to him. Then the storm will stop and there will be no more ice. Then you will know that the whole world belongs to the Lord. 30 But I know you and your servants. You still do not believe in the Lord God.'

31 The large pieces of ice had destroyed the flax and the barley. This was because the barley plants were ready for men to cut them. And the flax plants had buds on them. 32 But the ice had not destroyed the wheat and the spelt. This was because they appeared out of the ground later.

33 Then Moses left Pharaoh and Moses went out of the city. Moses lifted up his hands to the Lord. Then the storms and the ice stopped. The rain also stopped falling on the earth.

34 Pharaoh saw that the rain and the ice and the storms had stopped. But he did a wrong thing again. He and his servants did not do what they had promised to do. There had been no change in his thoughts. 35 Pharaoh still refused to listen to God. He did not let the Israelites go. This is what the Lord had said would happen. Moses had told Pharaoh these words.

Chapter 10

God sends locusts to Egypt

1 Then the Lord said to Moses: 'Go in to Pharaoh. I have caused him not to listen to me. And I have caused his servants also not to listen to me. I have done this so that I can show my signs among them. 2 You can tell your sons and your grandsons how I punished the Egyptians. You can tell them about the signs that I have done among them. In this way, you will know that I am the Lord.'

3 So Moses and Aaron went to Pharaoh. They said to him: 'The Lord, the God of the Israelites says: "You still refuse to obey me. Let my people go. Let them worship me. 4 If you refuse to let them go, I will bring locusts into your country tomorrow. 5 And they will cover the whole country. Nobody will be able to see the ground. They will eat everything that the ice has not destroyed. This will include every tree that is still growing in your fields.

6 They will fill your houses. They will fill your servants' houses. And they will fill the Egyptians' houses. It will be like nothing your father or your grandfather have ever seen. It has never happened before." ' Then Moses turned and left Pharaoh.

7 Pharaoh's servants said to him: 'Stop keeping this man with us, to cause problems. Let the people go, to worship the Lord their God. Surely you know now that they have destroyed Egypt!' 8 So Pharaoh commanded Moses and Aaron to come to him again. He said: 'Go, worship the Lord your God. But which of you will go?'

9 And Moses said: 'We will all go, both young people and old people. We will take our sons and daughters. We will take our animals, because we must have a party for the Lord.'

10 Pharaoh said to them: 'The Lord will certainly be with you, if ever I let you go with your women and children! I can see that you have decided to do something bad. 11 No! Only the men can go and worship the Lord. That is what you have asked for.' And Pharaoh was angry and he sent Moses and Aaron away from him. 12 Then the Lord said to Moses: 'Lift up your hand over the country of Egypt. Then locusts will fly over the country of Egypt. They will eat every plant in the country, all that the ice has not destroyed.'

13 So Moses lifted up his stick over the country of Egypt. And the Lord caused an east wind to blow across the country, for the whole day and the whole night. In the morning, the east wind had brought the locusts. 14 And the locusts flew into every part of the country of Egypt. They landed everywhere, thousands of locusts. There had never been so many locusts in one place before. And it will never happen again. 15 The locusts covered all the ground, until the ground became black with locusts. They ate all the plants in the country. They ate all the fruit of the trees. They ate everything that the ice had not destroyed. Not one green thing remained on tree or plant, in all the country of Egypt.

16 Then Pharaoh quickly commanded Moses and Aaron to come to him. He said: 'I have done bad things against the Lord your God and against you. 17 Please forgive me once more for the bad things that I have done. Please ask the Lord your God to remove this cruel and dangerous trouble from me.'

18 Then Moses left Pharaoh and Moses prayed to the Lord. 19 And the Lord changed the wind to a very strong west wind. This wind lifted the locusts and it carried them into the Red Sea. Not one locust remained in all the country of Egypt. 20 But the Lord caused Pharaoh to change his mind and he would not let the Israelites go.

God makes Egypt completely dark

21 Then the Lord spoke to Moses. He said: 'Lift up your hand towards the sky. Then it will be dark over the whole country of Egypt. It will be so dark that people will be able to feel it.' 22 So Moses lifted up his hand towards the sky and it became completely dark through the whole country of Egypt. It was dark for three days. 23 People could not see each other. Nobody could get up and move about for three days. But all the Israelites had light in the places where they lived.

24 Then Pharaoh commanded Moses to come to him. He said: 'Go, worship the Lord. Even your women and your children can go with you. Only your animals must remain.' 25 But Moses said: 'You must also let us take animals with us. We will sacrifice them and burn them, as gifts to the Lord our God.'

26 'We must take our animals with us. Not one can remain behind. We will use some of them to worship the Lord our God. Until we arrive in the desert, we will not know which animals. But we will use some of them, to worship the Lord our God.'

27 But the Lord caused Pharaoh to refuse. Pharaoh would not listen. He would not let them go. 28 Then Pharaoh said to Moses: 'Go away from me! Never appear in front of me again! On the day that you see my face, you will die!' 29 And Moses said: 'You are right! I will never appear in front of you again.'

Chapter 11

The death of every firstborn son in Egypt

1 The Lord said to Moses: 'I will bring one more bad trouble on Pharaoh and on Egypt. Then Pharaoh will let you go away. He will really cause you to go out of the country completely. 2 Tell the people now what they must do. Every man must ask the Egyptians that live near him for gold and silver. Every woman must do the same thing.' 3 And the Lord made the Egyptians think well of the Israelites. Also, Pharaoh's servants and the Egyptian people thought very well of Moses.

4 So Moses said: 'The Lord says this: "At about midnight, I will walk through the country of Egypt. 5 Then all the firstborn sons in the country of Egypt will die. The firstborn son of Pharaoh, king of Egypt, will die. The firstborn son of the slave, the woman who makes flour, will die. Even the firstborn of the animals will die." '

6 '"Everyone will be crying loudly in the whole country called Egypt. Never before have the people felt so sad or cried so loudly. It will never happen again. 7 But among the Israelites, not even a wild animal will attack any of them. Then you will know that the Lord makes a difference between Egypt and Israel." 8 All these servants of yours will come to me. They will fall down in front of me. They will say to me: "Go! Both you and all the people who follow you." And then, I will leave.' Then Moses was very angry and he left Pharaoh.

9 The Lord had said to Moses: 'Pharaoh will refuse to listen to you. But then I will do even greater signs in the country of Egypt.' 10 Moses and Aaron did all these signs in front of Pharaoh. But the Lord made Pharaoh angry and cruel. So Pharaoh would not let the Israelites go out of his country.

Chapter 12

The Passover

1 The Lord spoke to Moses and Aaron in the country of Egypt. 2 He said: 'This month will be for you the first month of your year. 3 Tell the Israelites that the 10th day of this month is special. Each man must take a young sheep for his family. Take one young sheep for each home. 4 The family may be too small to eat a whole sheep. Then they must eat it with another small family. You must decide this by how much each person can eat. 5 Each young sheep must have nothing wrong with it. It must be a male that is one year old. It can be either a young sheep or a young goat.

6 Keep the young sheep safe until the 14th day of the month. Then all Israel's people must kill the young sheep in the evening. 7 Then they must take some of the blood. They must put it on the wood that is round the door of their houses. They must do this to the houses where they will eat the young sheep. 8 That night, they must cook the meat over the fire and they must eat it. They must eat it with special plants and with bread that has no yeast in it. 9 You must cook the meat, but do not boil it in water. Cook the meat over the fire, with the head, the legs and the inside parts of the animal. 10 You must eat all of the meat before the morning comes. If you cannot eat it before the morning, then you must burn it. 11 This is how you must eat the young sheep: Fix your belt round your coat, put your shoes on your feet. Take your stick in your hand and eat the food quickly.

This meal will be called the Passover of the Lord.

12 I will pass through the country of Egypt on that night. I will kill every firstborn, both men and animals. I will punish all the gods of Egypt. I am the Lord. 13 The blood will be a sign for you, on all the houses where you live. When I see the blood on the house, then I will pass over you. No bad thing will touch you, when I attack the country of Egypt.'

14 'You must remember this day as a special day every year. On this day, you must make a special party for the Lord. You must obey this rule in your families for all time. 15 For 7 days, you must eat bread with no yeast in it. On the first day, you must remove all yeast from your houses. Whoever eats bread with yeast in it, during the 7 days, he does a bad thing. You must remove him from Israel's people. 16 On the first day, you must bring together all the people to a special meeting. And you must do the same thing on the 7th day. On these special days, you must not do any work except to prepare food. This is the only work that you can do.

17 Enjoy the meal of the bread with no yeast in it. It was on this same day that I brought your armies out of Egypt. That is why you must enjoy this day as a special day, for all time. This is a rule that you must always obey. 18 In the first month, you must eat bread without yeast in it. Do this from the evening of the 14th day until the evening of the 21st day. 19 You must not have any yeast in your houses, for 7 days. Whoever eats anything with yeast in it, he does a bad thing. You must remove that person from the rest of the Israelites. You must do this if that person is a foreign person. You must also do it if he was born in that country. 20 Eat nothing that has yeast in it. Whatever country you live in, you must eat bread without yeast in it.'

21 Then Moses commanded the leaders of the Israelites to come to him. He said to them: 'Go and choose young sheep immediately, for your families. Then kill the animals for the Passover party. 22 Take some hyssop. Make it wet with the blood that is in the dish. Then put some of the blood on the wood that is round your door. Nobody must go out of the door of his house until the morning.'

23 'The Lord will pass through the country and he will kill the Egyptians. But when the Lord sees the blood on the wood round the door, he will pass over that house. He will stop the person who kills. The Lord will not let him come into your houses. The Lord will not let him kill you.

24 You must obey these rules always, both you and your sons, for all time. 25 You will come into the country that the Lord promised to give you. Then you must obey these rules.

26 Your children may say to you: "What does this party mean to you?" 27 Then you must say to them: "It is the Lord's Passover party. The Lord passed over the houses of the Israelites when they were in Egypt. He killed the Egyptians but he saved the people in our houses." ' Then the people bent their heads and they worshipped God. 28 And the Israelites did everything that the Lord had commanded Moses and Aaron.

29 At midnight, the Lord killed all the firstborn sons in the country of Egypt. The firstborn son of Pharaoh, the king, died. But also, the firstborn son of any man who was in prison died. Every firstborn son in Egypt died. All the firstborn animals died also. 30 Pharaoh and all his servants got up in the middle of the night. All the Egyptians also got up in the middle of the night. Everyone was crying in Egypt because there was a dead person in every home.

The Israelites leave Egypt

31 Then Pharaoh commanded Moses and Aaron to come to him, during the night. He said: 'Get up! Go away from my people! You and all the Israelites, go! Go. And worship the Lord, as you want to. 32 Take all your animals with you, as you have said. Go away! But ask God to do good things to me too.'

33 The Egyptians really wanted the Israelites to leave. They wanted to send them out of the country immediately. The Egyptians said: 'If we do not send them away immediately, we will all die!' 34 So the Israelites took their bread before they had cooked it. They had not even put the yeast into it. They put the bread in dishes and they covered it with clothes. Then they carried the dishes on their shoulders. 35 The Israelites had obeyed Moses. They had asked the Egyptians for silver and gold. They had also asked them for clothes. 36 The Lord had made the Egyptians think good thoughts about the Israelites. Because of this, the Egyptians let them have all that they asked for. So the Israelites took everything that was valuable from the Egyptians.

37 Then the Israelites travelled from Rameses to Succoth. There were about 600 000 men who walked. There were also many women and children. 38 Many other people travelled with them. And they had a very large number of animals, both sheep and cows. 39 The Israelites cooked the bread that they had brought with them from Egypt. It had no yeast in it, because the Israelites left Egypt quickly. The Egyptians had pushed them out. The Israelites did not have time to make bread with yeast in it. Nor did they have time to prepare any other food.

40 The Israelites had lived in Egypt for 430 years. 41 It was on the last day of the 430 years that all the Lord's people left the country called Egypt. 42 The Lord did not sleep on that night, when he brought the Israelites out of Egypt. Because of this, all the Israelites must not sleep during this special night, every year. They and their families must remember this rule, for all time. They must do this, to thank the Lord.

Rules for the Passover party

43 Then the Lord said to Moses and Aaron: 'These are the rules for the Passover party.

No foreign person can eat the Passover food. 44 If you buy a foreign slave, you must first circumcise him. Then he can eat the food. 45 But if you pay him money for his work, he must not eat the food. A visitor must not eat the food.

46 You must eat the meat in one house. You must not take any of the meat outside the house. You must not break any of the bones in the meat. 47 All the Israelites must enjoy the party together.

48 There may be a foreign person who lives among you. He may want to enjoy the Lord's Passover too. But he must first circumcise himself and all the males in his house. Then he can enjoy the Passover party, like a man who is born in Israel. But no male person without circumcision can enjoy the Passover party. 49 The Israelites and the foreign people who live among you must all obey this rule.'

50 All the Israelites did everything that the Lord had commanded Moses and Aaron. 51 And on the same day, the Lord brought the Israelites out of Egypt, like a large army of people.

Chapter 13

The firstborn males are special

1 The Lord spoke to Moses. 2 He said: 'Keep every firstborn male separate and special for me. Every male who is the first to be born of his mother is mine. He is mine, whether he is man or animal.'

3 Moses said to the people: 'Remember this day, the day when you came out of Egypt. You left the place where you were slaves. The Lord brought you out with powerful authority. Remember! Do not eat anything that has yeast in it on this day. 4 Today you are leaving Egypt. It is the month of Abib. 5 The Lord will bring you to the country of the Canaanites, the Hittites, the Amorites, the Hivites and the Jebusites. God promised your ancestors that he would give that country to you. It is a country where there is plenty to eat and to drink. When the Lord brings you in, you must enjoy the Passover party in this month. 6 For 7 days you must eat bread without yeast in it. Then on the 7th day you must have a party for the Lord. 7 Eat bread without yeast during those 7 days. There must not be anything that has yeast in it among you. Nobody must see any yeast anywhere, in the whole of your country. 8 On that day, you must tell your son the reason for this. Say to him: "I do this because of what the Lord did for me. This is because he brought me out of Egypt." 9 This special time will be like a sign on your hand. It will be like something that you fix between your eyes. It will cause you to remember. Then you will not forget to speak always about the Law of the Lord. It is because the Lord brought you out of Egypt with great power. 10 At the same time, every year, you must obey what I have said.

11 The Lord will bring you into the country of the Canaanites. It is the country that he promised to you and to your ancestors. He will give it to you. 12 You must give to the Lord all the males first. All the male animals that are born first are the Lord's animals. 13 When a donkey is born first, you must kill a young sheep instead of the donkey. If you do not do that, then the donkey must die. You must break its neck. If your son is born first, then you must kill an animal instead of your son.

14 One day, your son may ask you a question: "What does this mean?" Then you must say to him: "The Lord brought us out of Egypt with powerful authority. He brought us from the place where we were slaves. 15 Pharaoh completely refused to let us go. But the Lord killed all the firstborn sons in the country of Egypt. He killed all the firstborn males, both people and animals. That is why I do this. I kill and I give to the Lord all the firstborn male animals. But I do not kill the firstborn sons. Instead, I kill an animal for each firstborn son and I give it to God." 16 So, it will be like a sign on your hand and something between your eyes. It will cause you to remember. You will remember that the Lord brought us out of Egypt with his powerful authority.'

The Israelites cross the Red Sea

17 When Pharaoh let the people go, God did not lead them through the country of the Philistines. This was near, but God did not do that. God said: 'If the people see war, they may change their minds. Then they may return to Egypt.' 18 So God led the people round by the desert road. They went toward the Red Sea. When the Israelites came out of the country of Egypt, they were ready to fight.

19 Moses took the bones of Joseph with him. Joseph had caused the Israelites to promise to do this. He had said: 'God will save you and then you must carry my bones with you from this place.'

20 The Israelites moved on from Succoth. Then they stayed at Etham, on the edge of the desert. And the Lord went in front of them. 21 During the day, God led them in a cloud that went in front of them. During the night, he went in a cloud that had fire in it. This gave them light, so they could travel during the day or the night. 22 The cloud did not leave the people during the day. Nor did the fire in the cloud leave them during the night. It was always in front of them.

Chapter 14

1 Then the Lord spoke to Moses. 2 He said: 'Tell the Israelites that they must stop. Tell them that they must stay near Pihahiroth. This is a place between Migdol and the sea. They must stay by the sea, across from Baal-zephon. 3 Then Pharaoh will think: "The Israelites are confused. They are walking round and round the country. The desert has shut them in." 4 And I will cause Pharaoh to think cruel thoughts. He will go after the Israelites. Then I will show how great I am, by Pharaoh and his whole army. Because of this, the Egyptians will know that I am the Lord.' So the Israelites obeyed God.

5 Someone told the king of Egypt that the Israelites had run away. Then Pharaoh and his servants changed their minds about the Israelites. They said: 'We have done a silly thing. We have let the Israelites go. We have lost our slaves!' 6 So Pharaoh prepared his chariot and he took his army with him. 7 He took 600 of his best chariots with him. He also took all the other chariots of Egypt, with officers to drive them. 8 And the Lord made Pharaoh, king of Egypt think more cruel thoughts. So Pharaoh followed after the brave Israelites, when they marched out.

9 The Egyptians went after the Israelites. They went with all Pharaoh's horses, chariots and soldiers. They came near to the Israelites, who were by the sea. It was near Pihahiroth, across from Baal-zephon.

10 Pharaoh was coming nearer. The Israelites looked up. They saw that the Egyptians had marched after them. Then the Israelites were afraid and they shouted aloud to the Lord. 11 They said to Moses: 'There are many places in Egypt to bury dead people! You did not have to bring us here! Have you brought us here to die in the desert? Why did you bring us out of Egypt? 12 We said to you in Egypt: "Leave us alone. Let us work for the Egyptians." It would have been better for us to do that. Then, anyway, we would not die in the desert!'

13 Then Moses spoke to the people. He said: 'Do not be afraid. Stand quietly. See how the Lord will save you today. The Egyptians that you see today you will never see again. 14 The Lord will fight for you. You will only have to be quiet.'

15 Then the Lord said to Moses: 'Do not shout aloud to me. Command the Israelites to march on. 16 Lift up your stick. Lift up your hand over the sea. Then the water will become two separate parts. Then the Israelites can cross the sea on dry ground. 17 I will make the Egyptians angry and they will follow the Israelites into the sea. And I will show my powerful authority by Pharaoh and by his army and by all his chariots. 18 Then the Egyptians will know that I am the Lord.'

19 The angel of God went in front of the army of the Israelites. Now he moved and he went behind them. The special cloud moved also and it stood behind the army. 20 It stood between the Egyptian army and the Israelite army. During the whole night, the Egyptians were in the dark, because of the cloud. But the Israelites were in the light, because there was fire in the cloud. So the Egyptians stayed away from the Israelites during the whole night.

21 Then Moses lifted up his hand over the sea. During that whole night, the Lord made the sea go back. He did this with a strong wind that made the water into two separate parts. The ground below the sea became like dry land. 22 Then the Israelites walked on the dry ground in the middle of the sea. The water was like a wall on their right side and on their left side.

23 The Egyptians went after them and followed them into the middle of the sea. All Pharaoh's horses and his chariots did this. And so did the men who drove the chariots. 24 In the early morning, the Lord looked down, from the cloud with fire in it. He looked at the Egyptian army and he confused them. 25 Their chariots could not move easily in the sand. It became very difficult for the Egyptians to drive their chariots. So the Egyptians said: 'Let us run away from the Israelites. It is the Lord who fights for them, against Egypt.'

26 Then the Lord spoke to Moses. He said: 'Lift up your hand over the sea. Then the waters will return. They will cover the Egyptians, their chariots and the men who drive them.' 27 So Moses lifted up his hand over the sea. And at dawn, the sea returned to its own place. The Egyptians ran away from the water, as fast as they could. But the Lord killed them. The Egyptians drowned in the middle of the sea. 28 The water returned. It covered the chariots and the men that drove them. The water covered Pharaoh's whole army that had followed the Israelites into the sea. Not one of those men remained alive.

29 But the Israelites walked on dry ground through the sea. The water was like a wall on their right side and on their left side. 30 On that day, the Lord saved the Israelites from the Egyptians. The Israelites saw the dead bodies of the Egyptians, which lay on the shore. 31 Then the Israelites saw what a great thing the Lord had done against the Egyptians. So the Israelites were afraid of the Lord. But they believed that he loved them. They also loved and obeyed Moses, the Lord's servant.

Chapter 15

The song of Moses

1 Then Moses and the Israelites sang this song to the Lord:

I will sing to the Lord, because he is great and powerful.

He threw horses and the men who ride them into the sea.

2 The Lord makes me strong and he gives me a song. He has saved me.

He is my God and I will praise him.

He is my father's God and I will praise him.

3 The Lord is like a great soldier. The Lord is his name.

4 He threw Pharaoh's chariots and armies into the sea.

Pharaoh's best officers drowned in the Red Sea.

5 The deep waters have covered them.

They fell to the floor of the sea, like a stone.

6 Your right hand, Lord, was great and very powerful.

Your right hand, Lord, killed the enemy.

7 With your powerful authority, you killed your enemies.

You were very angry with them. You killed them, like a fire burns dry grass.

8 You blew on the water and it became like a wall.

The deep waters stood up and they did not move.

9 The enemy said: 'I will go after them. I will catch them.

I will take good things from these Israelites and I will give them to my army.

I will be very happy to do this! I will pull out my sharp knife and I will kill them.'

10 But you blew on the waters and the sea covered your enemies.

They went down like heavy metal in the great waters.

11 Oh Lord, there is nobody like you among the gods! There is nobody like you anywhere!

You are so great and so holy. You frighten us with your bright light.

You do great and powerful things.

12 You lifted up your right hand. You caused a hole to open in the ground. Your enemies fell into it.

13 Because your love never changes, you have led your people.

They are the ones that you have saved.

With your strong hand, you will be their guide to your holy home.

14 The people in other countries will hear and they will be very afraid.

You will frighten the people in Philistia with a great pain.

15 The rulers of Edom will feel weak and very afraid.

The leaders of Moab cannot stand. They are so much afraid.

All the people in Canaan will run away.

16 They are very afraid of your powerful authority.

They cannot move. They have become like stones that do not move.

And they will remain like that, until your people pass by them, Lord.

They will not move, until your own people have passed by them.

17 You will bring in your people. You will bring them to live on your own mountain.

Lord, it is the place that you have prepared for your home.

It is the holy place, Lord that you yourself have built.

18 The Lord will rule for all time.

19 Pharaoh's horses and his chariots had gone into the sea, with the men who drove them. Then the Lord had made the waters of the sea come back over them. But the Israelites had walked through the sea on dry ground. 20 Then Miriam, Aaron's sister, who was a female prophet, took a tambourine in her hand. All the other women followed Miriam, with tambourines in their hands. They danced when Miriam sang to them.

21 This is the song that she sang:

'Sing to the Lord!

He is great and powerful.

He threw into the sea the horse and the man who rides it!'

The waters of Marah and Elim

22 Then Moses led the Israelites away from the Red Sea. They travelled into the desert called Shur. They walked into the desert for three days and they could not find any water. 23 Then, when they came to Marah, they could not drink the water there. They tasted the water, but it was bad. That is why they called that place 'Marah'. Marah means 'it tastes bad'. 24 Then the people were not happy and they spoke against Moses. They said: 'What can we drink?'

25 Then Moses prayed to the Lord and the Lord showed Moses a special piece of wood. Moses threw it into the water and then the water became clean and good.

In that place, the Lord made a rule and a law for the Israelites. He checked them there, in that place. 26He said: 'Be careful to listen to the voice of the Lord, your God. Do what he says is right. Obey his commands and all his rules. Then I will not bring on you the illnesses that I gave to the Egyptians. I am the Lord. I make you well again.'

27 Then they came to Elim. There they found 12 wells of water and 70 palm trees. And the Israelites stayed there, by the water.

Chapter 16

God sends bread and meat

1 Then all the Israelites left Elim and they came into the desert called Sin. This is between Elim and Sinai. They arrived in the desert on the 15th day of the second month after they had left the country called Egypt. 2 When they were in the desert, all the Israelites said bad things against Moses and Aaron. 3 The Israelites said to them: 'We wish that the Lord had killed us in Egypt! There, we sat round pots of meat. We ate all the food that we wanted. But now you have brought us into this desert. We shall all die, every one of us, because there is no food to eat.'

4 Then the Lord spoke to Moses. He said: 'I will cause bread to fall down from the sky for you. Each day, the people must go out and pick up enough bread for that day. In this way I will discover what they are like. I will discover whether they will obey my rules. 5 And on the sixth day, they must pick up and prepare twice as much bread.'

6 So Moses and Aaron spoke to the Israelites. They said: 'In the evening, you will know who brought you out of Egypt. It was the Lord! 7 And in the morning, you will see how great and powerful the Lord is. The Lord has heard the bad things that you have said against him. We, Moses and Aaron, are not important. You should not say bad things against us.' 8 And Moses also said: 'The Lord will give you meat to eat in the evening. And in the morning, he will give you all the bread that you want. He will do this because he has heard you. He has heard the bad things that you have said against him. Aaron and I are not important. You have said bad things against the Lord, not against us.'

9 Then Moses spoke to Aaron: 'Say to all the Israelites: "Come near, in front of the Lord. He has heard the bad things that you have said against him." ' 10 While Aaron spoke, the Israelites looked toward the desert. And they saw the glory of the Lord! It appeared in the cloud.

11 Then the Lord spoke to Moses. 12 He said: 'I have heard the bad things that the Israelites have said against me. Tell them this: "In the evening, you will eat meat. And in the morning you will eat all the bread that you want. Then you will know that I am the Lord your God." '

13 That same evening, quails flew down and they covered the whole ground.

And in the morning, there was something like rain on all the ground where the Israelites were living. 14When the ground was dry again, small white pieces of material remained on the ground in the desert. They looked like little pieces of ice. 15 When the Israelites saw these pieces, they said: 'What is it?' They did not understand what it was. But Moses said to them: 'This is the bread that the Lord has given to you. It is for you to eat. 16 This is what the Lord has commanded: "Every man must pick up as much as he needs to eat. Pick up about two litres for each person who lives in your tent." '

17 So the Israelites did this. Some of them picked up a lot of the food. Some of them picked up a little food.18 But when they measured the amount, everyone had the right amount of food. The person who had picked up a lot did not have too much. And the person who had picked up only a little food still had enough food. Each person had picked up what he needed.

19 Then Moses said to them: 'Do not keep any of it until the morning.'

20 But some of them did not listen to Moses. They kept part of the food until the morning. But very small snakes appeared in it. And it began to have a bad smell. Then Moses was angry with those people.

21 Each morning, everyone picked up as much food as he needed. But when the heat of the sun became strong, the food became soft. Then it went away. 22 On the sixth day, the Israelites picked up twice as much food. They picked up four litres for each person. Then the leaders of the people reported this to Moses. 23 Moses said to them: 'This is what the Lord commanded you to do. He said: "Tomorrow is a special day for rest. It is a Sabbath day, for the Lord. Cook the food that you want to cook. Boil the food that you want to boil. And you can keep whatever remains, until the morning." '

24 So they kept the food until the morning, as Moses had said. The food did not have a bad smell and there were no small snakes in it. 25 Moses said: 'Eat it today, because this day is a Sabbath to the Lord. You will not find any food on the ground today. 26 On six days of the week, you must pick it up from the ground. But on the 7th day of the week, there will be none of this food on the ground. That is because the 7th day is the Sabbath day.'

27 But on the 7th day, some of the people went out to pick up food. And they did not find any. 28 Then the Lord spoke to Moses. He said: 'The people always refuse to obey my commands. They always refuse to do what I say! 29 Remember that the Lord has given the Sabbath to you. That is why he gives you enough food for two days. He does this on the sixth day. Then everyone must stay at home on the 7th day. Nobody must go out on the 7th day.' 30 So the people rested on the 7th day.

31 Now the Israelites called the special food 'manna'. It was white, like coriander seed. When they tasted the manna, it was like thin pieces of bread with honey in it.

32 And Moses said: 'This is what the Lord has commanded. He said: "Keep 1 omer of manna (this is equal to 2 litres) for the people in future times. Then they will see the bread that I fed to you in the desert. I gave this to you when I brought you out of the country called Egypt." '

33 So Moses spoke to Aaron. He said: 'Put one omer of manna into a pot. Then put the pot in the tabernacle. We must keep it, so that our people can see it in the future times.'

34 And Aaron did what the Lord had said to Moses. He put the pot in front of the Testimony, to keep it safe.

35 The Israelites ate the manna for 40 years, until they had finished their journey. They ate it until they came to the country called Canaan.

36 (10 omers is equal to 1 ephah.)

Chapter 17

God gives water out of a rock

1 Then all the Israelites travelled away from the desert called Sin. They moved from one place to another, when the Lord commanded them. When they came to Rephidim, there was no water. The people had nothing to drink. 2 Because of this, the people quarrelled with Moses. They said: 'Give us water to drink!' And Moses said to them: 'You should not quarrel with me! You should not try to make the Lord angry!'

3 But the people needed water very much and they said bad things against Moses. They said: 'You should not have brought us out of Egypt! You will kill us and our children and our animals. We will die, because we have no water.'

4 Then Moses shouted aloud to the Lord. 'What shall I do with these people? They will throw stones at me soon. Then they will throw them until I am dead.'

5 The Lord said to Moses: 'Walk in front of the people. Bring some of the leaders of the Israelites with you. Take your stick in your hand, the stick with which you hit the River Nile. Go! 6 I will stand there, in front of you, by the rock at Horeb. Hit the rock, and water will come out of it. Then the people can drink.' So Moses did this, while the leaders of the Israelites watched him. 7 And he called that place Massah and Meribah, because the Israelites quarrelled there. And they tried to make the Lord angry. They said: 'Is the Lord with us, or is he not with us?'

The Israelites beat the Amalekites

8 At Rephidim, the Amalekites came out and they fought against the Israelites. 9 Moses said to Joshua: 'Choose some of our men. Then go out and fight with the Amalekites. Tomorrow I will stand on the top of the hill. And I will hold God's stick in my hand.'

10 So Joshua fought against the Amalekites. He obeyed the words of Moses. Moses, Aaron and Hur went up to the top of the hill. 11 When Moses lifted up his hand, the Israelites were winning in the fight. But when Moses brought his hand down, the Amalekites were winning in the fight. 12 Moses hands became tired. So Aaron and Hur put a stone under Moses and he sat on the stone. Then Aaron and Hur held up Moses' hands. Aaron stood on one side of Moses and Hur stood on the other side. They held his hands up, until sunset. 13 So Joshua and his men beat the Amalekite army in the fight.

14 Then the Lord said to Moses: 'Write these things on a scroll. Then you will remember them. Joshua must hear my words because I will kill all of the Amalekites. Nobody in the whole world will remember them.'

15 Then Moses built a stone table and he called it 'The Lord is my banner'. 16 Moses said: 'I lifted up my hands to the Lord on his seat, where he rules. I prayed to him. Now the Lord has said that he will always fight against the Amalekites.'

Chapter 18

Jethro visits Moses

1 Jethro, the priest of Midian, was the father of Moses' wife. He heard about all the things that God had done for Moses and for the Israelites. He also heard how the Lord had brought Israel out of Egypt.

2 Moses had sent Zipporah, who was his wife, back to her home. Then her father, Jethro, brought her 3and her two sons into his house. One son was called Gershom. Moses said about him, 'I have become a stranger in a foreign country.' 4 The other son was called Eliezer. Moses said about him, 'My father's God gave me help. He saved me from Pharaoh, when Pharaoh wanted to kill me.'

5 Then Jethro came to Moses in the desert. Moses was staying near the mountain of God. Jethro brought with him Moses' sons and Moses' wife. 6 Jethro had sent a message to Moses. He said: 'I am Jethro, your wife's father. I am coming to you with your wife and her two sons.'

7 So Moses went out to meet his wife's father. Moses bent his head and he kissed Jethro. They spoke together and then they went into the tent. 8 Moses told his wife's father about all the things that the Lord had done to Pharaoh. He told him also what the Lord had done to the Egyptians because of the Israelites. He told Jethro about the troubles that had happened to them during the journey. And Moses told him how the Lord had saved his people, the Israelites.

9 Jethro was very happy to listen to Moses. Moses repeated to him how the Lord had saved the Israelites from the authority of the Egyptians. 10 Jethro said: 'Let us thank the Lord, who saved you from the authority of Pharaoh and the Egyptians. He saved all the people also from the authority of the Egyptians.11 Now I know that the Lord is greater than all other gods. The Lord did these things to the people who were cruel towards the Israelites.' 12 Then Jethro, the father of Moses' wife, brought an animal, and other gifts, to God. And Aaron came, with all the leaders of the Israelites. They ate a meal together with Jethro, where God could see them.

13 The next day, Moses sat down to judge the people. They stood round him from morning until evening.14 Jethro saw all that Moses did for the people. Then he said: 'What is this that you do for the people? Why do you sit alone and judge the people? These people stand round you during the whole day.'

15 Moses answered Jethro: 'The people come to me to discover God's commands. 16 When they cannot agree, they come to me. I decide between them and I tell them about God's laws and rules.'

17 The father of Moses' wife replied: 'The thing that you do is not good. 18 Both you and the people who come to you will become too tired. The work is too much for you. You cannot do it alone. 19 Now listen to me! I will give you some good ideas, and God will make you strong. You must be the person who speaks to God, for the Israelites. Bring their quarrels to him. 20 Teach them the rules and laws. Show them how they should live. Explain to them the things that they must do.

21 But you must choose wise men from all the people. They must be men who obey God. They must be good men, who will not do false things. Make these men officers over groups of the people. Some groups will be 1000 people; some groups will be 100 people. Some groups will be 50 people and some will be only 10 people. 22 Let them work as judges for the people, every day. They can decide the small problems, but they must bring the difficult problems to you. That will make your work easier, because they will work with you. 23 If God commands you to do this, please obey him. Then the work will not be too hard for you. You will keep your good health. And all these people will go home and they will be happy.'

24 Then Moses listened to Jethro. And Moses did everything that he suggested.

25 Moses chose good and wise men from all the Israelites. He made them leaders and officers of the people. Some were officers over 1000 people; some were officers over 100 people. Some were officers over 50 people and some were officers over 10 people. 26 They worked as judges for the people at all times. They told Moses about the difficult problems, but they decided the easy problems without his help.

27 Then Moses said goodbye to his wife's father and Jethro returned to his own country.

Chapter 19

The Israelites come to Mount Sinai

1 Three whole months after the Israelites left Egypt, they came to the Desert of Sinai. 2 After they left Rephidim, they arrived in the Desert of Sinai. The Israelites put up their tents in the desert, in front of the mountain.

3 Then Moses went up the mountain to God. The Lord spoke to him from the mountain. He said: 'This is what you must say to Jacob's children and grandchildren and to the Israelites. 4 "You yourselves have seen what I did to Egypt. You know how I carried you. I carried you like a large bird carries her young birds on her wings. And I brought you to myself. 5 Now, obey me completely and love my promises. Then I will make you my special people that I love. I have chosen you only, from all the people in other countries. The whole world is mine, 6 but you will all become my priests. You will become a special family to me, a family that I can love." These are the words that you must speak to the Israelites.'

7 So Moses returned and he brought together all the leaders of the Israelites. He repeated to them all the words that the Lord had commanded him. 8 The people all replied together. They said: 'We will do everything that the Lord has said.' Then Moses repeated their answer to the Lord.

9 The Lord said to Moses: 'I will come to you in a thick cloud. Then the people will hear me speak to you. And they will always believe everything that you say.' Then Moses told the Lord the words that the people had said.

10 And the Lord said to Moses: 'Go to the people. Make them ready to meet with me. Today and tomorrow they must wash their clothes. 11 They must be ready on the third day. On that day, the Lord will come down on Mount Sinai. And all the people will see him. 12 Do not let the people come too near to the mountain. Say to them: "Be careful! Do not go up the mountain or touch the edge of it. Whoever touches the mountain must die. 13 You must throw stones at him until he dies. Or you must shoot at him with arrows. Nobody must touch him. You must not let him live, whether he is a man or an animal. The people must wait until they hear a loud sound of music. Then they can go up to the mountain." '

14 Then Moses came down from the mountain. He commanded the people to make themselves ready for God. And the people washed their clothes. 15 Then Moses said to them: 'Prepare yourselves for the third day. Do not have sex with anyone.'

16 On the morning of the third day, there was a great storm. The people heard loud noises and they saw bright lights. A dark cloud was there over the mountain and the people heard very loud music. They were so afraid that their bodies were shaking.).

17 Then Moses led the people out to meet with God. And they stood at the edge of the mountain.

18 Smoke covered Mount Sinai because the Lord came down on the mountain, like a fire. The smoke rose up from the mountain, like smoke from a great fire. The whole mountain moved about, 19 and the sound of the music became louder and louder. Then Moses spoke and the voice of God answered him.

20 The Lord came down to the top of Mount Sinai. Then he told Moses that he must come to the top of the mountain. So Moses went up the mountain 21 and the Lord spoke to him. He said: 'Go down to the people. Tell them that they must stay away from the mountain. They must not try to see the Lord. If they do, they will die. 22 Even the priests, who come near to the Lord, must make themselves ready for God. If they do not obey this word, the Lord will be very angry with them.'

23 Moses said to the Lord: 'The people cannot come up Mount Sinai. You yourself told us that we must put things round the mountain. You told us that we must make the mountain special. You told us that we must stay away from the edge of the mountain.'

24 The Lord replied: 'Go down. Bring Aaron up with you. But the priests and the people must obey my command. They must not try to come up to the Lord. If they did, the Lord would be very angry with them.'

25 So Moses went down to the people and he repeated these words to them.

Chapter 20

The 10 commandments

1 Then God spoke all these words:

2 'I am the Lord your God. I brought you out of Egypt, out of the country where you were slaves.

3 You must not have any other gods except me.

4 You must not make any false god for yourself. Do not make a false god in the shape of anything in the sky. Do not make one in the shape of anything on the earth or in the water. 5 You must not bend down your head to a false god, nor worship it. I, the Lord your God, will be angry if you do not remember me. I will punish the children for the bad things that their fathers do. I will even punish the grandchildren and their children. I will do this to those who hate me. 6 But I will love thousands of people who love me. These are the people who obey my commandments.

7 You must not use the name of the Lord your God in a wrong way. The Lord will be angry with anyone who uses his name in a wrong way.

8 Remember the Sabbath day and keep it as a special day. 9 You must do all your work for six days. 10 But the seventh day is a Sabbath to the Lord your God. You must not do any work on that day. Your son and your daughter must not work on that day. Your male servant and your female servant must not work on that day. The stranger who lives among you and even your animals must not work on that day. 11 In six days, the Lord made the sky, the earth and the sea. He also made everything that is in them. But on the seventh day, the Lord rested. And he blessed the seventh day and he made it special.

12 Always be very kind to your father and your mother. Then you will live for many years in the country that the Lord will give to you.

13 You must not murder anyone.

14 You must not have sex with another person's husband or wife.

15 You must not take another person's things for yourself.

16 You must not say false things about your neighbour.

17 You must not want to take your neighbour's house, or his wife, or his servants. You must not want to take his cow, or his donkey, or anything that your neighbour has.'

18 The people saw the very bright light and they heard the loud noises. They heard the loud music and they saw the smoke on the mountain. They were so afraid that they could not stop their bodies moving. They would not come near. 19 They said to Moses: 'Speak to us yourself. We will listen to you. But do not let God speak to us. If he does, we will die.'

20 Moses said to the people: 'Do not be afraid. God has only come to test you. He wants you to love him. He wants you to obey him. Then you will not want to do bad things.'

21 So the people stayed away from the mountain. But Moses walked toward the thick, dark cloud, where God was.

22 Then the Lord said to Moses: 'Tell the Israelites this: "You yourselves have heard me speak to you from heaven. 23 Do not make any gods to be equal to me. Do not make for yourselves gods out of silver or out of gold. 24 Make a table out of earth for me. Burn your dead animals upon it and also your other gifts to me. I will cause people in many places to love my name. And in those places, I will come to you and I will make you happy. 25 You can make a table of stone for me also. But do not build it with stones that you have cut. If you use tools on the stones, the table will not be clean for God.

26 Do not climb up to my table on anything, because someone may see parts of your body."

Chapter 21

Israelite slaves

1 These are the laws that you must put in front of the Israelites:

2 If you buy an Israelite slave, he must work for you for six years. But in the seventh year he is a free man. He can leave you. He does not have to pay you any money. 3 If he came to you alone, he is free to leave alone. If he came with a wife, she can leave with him. 4 But if his master gives him a wife, she is her master's slave. And if she has had children, they are also her master's slaves. Only the husband can leave the master.

5 But perhaps the slave may say: "I love my master, my wife and my children. I will not go away like a free man!" 6 Then his master must take him in front of the judges. He must lead him to the door, or to the edge of the door. There the master must push the sharp point of a tool through the slave's ear. Then he will always be his master's slave.

7 Perhaps a man may sell his daughter as a slave. She is not free to leave her master, as the male slaves are, after six years. Her master has chosen her for himself. 8 If he does not like her, he must let someone from her family buy her from him. He cannot sell her to a foreign person. He has not done what he promised to her. 9 If the man chooses the girl to be his son's wife, she must become like his daughter.

10 If the man marries another woman, he must not forget the first woman. He must continue to give her food and clothes. He must be kind to her because she is still his wife. 11 If he does not do these three things, she can leave him. She does not have to pay him any money.

When people attack other people

12 Perhaps a person will hit another person and kill him. This is murder. The person who does it must die.13 But perhaps he did not want to do it, but God let it happen. Then the man must run away to a place that I will show him. 14 But a man may decide to kill another man. Then you must take him away from my table and you must kill him.

15 You must kill anyone who attacks his father or his mother.

16 You must kill anyone who steals another person. He might sell him or keep him.

You must kill the bad man when you catch him.

17 You must kill anyone who curses his father or his mother.

18 Perhaps two men may quarrel. One man hits the other man with a stone or with his fist.

The second man does not die but he has to stay in bed. 19 Then he gets up and walks about outside, with his stick. Then nobody will judge the first man. But he must pay the man whom he hurt. This man cannot work until he is completely well again.

20 Perhaps a man may hit his male or female slave with a stick. If the slave dies because of this, you must punish the man. 21 But if the slave becomes well again after one or two days, do not punish the man. The slave is his own.

22 When two men fight together, perhaps one man may hit a woman. That woman may be with child. Then she gives birth to her child before the right time. If the cruel man has not hurt the child, he must pay money to her husband. He must pay the amount of money that the husband asks. A judge must agree that the amount is fair. 23 But if the man has hurt the child, you must take a life for a life. 24 You must take an eye for an eye or a tooth for a tooth. You must take a hand for a hand or a foot for a foot. 25 You must take a burn for a burn, a wound for a wound, a bruise for a bruise.'

26 'If a man hits the eye of a male or female slave, he may destroy the eye. Then he must let the slave go away free because of his bad eye. 27 Perhaps a man may knock out the tooth of a male or female slave. Then he must let the slave go away free, because of his lost tooth.

28 Perhaps a male cow may attack a person and kill him. Then you must throw stones at the male cow until it dies. You must not eat the meat from that male cow. But do not punish the master of the male cow. 29But perhaps that male cow has attacked people before. Perhaps someone has told his master about this, but the man has not listened. He has not kept the male cow in a safe place and the animal has killed a person. Then you must throw stones at the animal but you must also kill his master. 30 But if the dead person's family demands money, the man can give money instead of his life. 31 This law is true if the male cow attacks a son or a daughter. 32 If it attacks a male or female slave, the animal's master must pay 30silver coins. He must give it to the slave's master and he must kill the animal.

33 If a man finds a hole, he must cover it. If he digs a hole, he must cover it. If he does not do this, a cow or a donkey may fall into it. 34 Then the man who dug the hole must pay for the loss of the animal. He must pay money to the animal's master but he can keep the dead animal for himself.

35 If one man's male cow attacks another man's male cow, it may die. Then they must sell the animal that is alive. Each man can have half of the money and half of the dead animal. 36 But perhaps that male cow has attacked another animal before. Someone has told the animal's master about this, but he has not listened. He has not kept the animal in a safe place. So he must pay the other man for the loss of his animal. But he can keep the dead animal for himself.

Chapter 22

When a man takes something that is not his own

1 Perhaps a bad man may take a cow or a sheep. He may kill it or he may sell it. Then he must pay the animal's master. He must pay five cows for the one cow that he took. And he must pay four sheep for the one sheep that he took.

2 Perhaps someone may catch a bad man, just as he goes into another man's house. He hits the bad man and the bad man dies. This thing is not murder, if it happens at night. But if it happens during the day, it is murder.

3 A man who takes another man's animal must certainly give it back. If he cannot do this, then someone must buy him as a slave. And he must give the money to the man whose animal he took.

4 Perhaps someone will find the animal alive, in the man's field. Then the man must give back two animals. He must do this, whether it was a cow, or a donkey, or a sheep.

5 A man's animals may eat grass in his field or in his garden of grapes. But perhaps he may let them go and eat grass in another man's field.

This is a wrong thing to do. So he must pay back to the other man the best food from his own field.

6 Someone may light a fire in a field and it begins to burn the bushes. Then the fire becomes bigger and hotter. It burns some of the food that is growing in the field. It may even burn the whole field. Then the person who lit the fire must pay money to the farmer. He has destroyed the farmer's food.

7 Perhaps a man may give some silver or other things to his neighbour. He asks his neighbour to keep them safe for him. But a bad man comes and he takes the things from the neighbour's house. If you catch the bad man, then he must pay for these things. He must pay twice the value of the things that he took. 8But if you do not find the bad man, then take the neighbour to the judges. They must agree whether he has taken the other man's things for himself.

9 The judges must judge when there is a quarrel between two people about things.

They may argue about an animal or some clothes or anything that is lost. If one of them says: "This is mine!" they must both come to the judges. The judges will choose which man is wrong. Then that man must pay back twice the value to his neighbour.

10 Perhaps a man may ask his neighbour to keep one of his animals for him. Then someone hurts the animal or it may die. Or perhaps a bad man takes it away while nobody sees him. 11 This problem has an answer. The neighbour can make a special promise, in front of the Lord. He can promise to say what is true. He can say that he did not take the other man's animal for himself. The other man must believe these words. He must not ask his neighbour to pay him any money. 12 But if a bad man did take the animal, then the neighbour must pay for the loss. 13 But perhaps a wild animal killed it. Then the neighbour must show the pieces that are left. Then he will not have to pay for the loss of the animal.

14 Perhaps a man may lend an animal to his neighbour. Then the animal dies while the man is not present. Or someone may hurt the animal. The neighbour must pay for the loss of the animal. 15 But if the man is with his animal, then the neighbour does not have to pay. Perhaps the neighbour gave the man some money, so that he could use his animal. If the animal dies, then that money will pay him back for his loss.

16 Perhaps a man may have sex with a young girl. She has not yet promised to marry anyone. Then that man must marry her. He must pay the bride-price to her father. 17 Her father may completely refuse to give her to the man. But the man must still pay the bride-price for a girl who is not married.'

18 'You must kill any woman who is a magician.

19 You must kill anyone who has sex with an animal.

20 You must kill any person who gives gifts to a false god. People must only bring gifts to the Lord.

21 Always be kind to a foreign person. Do not be cruel to him, because you were strangers in the country called Egypt.

22 Always be fair to a woman whose husband is dead. Be fair also to children whose parents are dead. 23 If you are not fair to them, they will shout aloud to me. I will certainly hear their voices 24 and I will be angry with you. I will kill you in a war. You will leave your wives and children without husbands and fathers.

25 You may lend money to one of my people who needs help. But do not be like the people in other countries. They cause poor people to pay extra money for the help. 26 If you take your neighbour's coat as a pledge, you must return it to him by sunset. 27 He needs his coat, to keep him warm at night. It is the only warm thing that he has. When he shouts aloud to me, I will hear him. I am a kind God and I love men and women.

28 Do not use my name in a bad way and do not curse your ruler.

29 Do not refuse to offer grain or oil from olives to me. 30 You must give your firstborn sons to me.

Do the same thing with your cows and your sheep. Let them stay with their mothers for 7 days. But on the eighth day, you must give them to me.

31 You will be my special people. So do not eat any meat that wild animals have killed. Instead, you must throw it to the dogs. They can eat it.

Chapter 23

God's laws for what is fair and kind

1 Do not make false reports. Do not say false words to give help to a bad man.

2 Do not follow other people, to do wrong things. When you speak in front of a judge, let your words be true. Do not speak false words, to be like everyone else. 3 But do not speak well for a poor man, only because you like him.

4 Perhaps you may find your enemy's cow or donkey as it runs away. You must certainly return it to him. 5Perhaps you may see your enemy's donkey fall down. The basket on its back is too full of heavy things. Do not leave the donkey there. You must certainly give your enemy help with his animal.

6 Always be fair to your poor people when they stand in front of a judge. Do not refuse to be fair to them. 7Refuse to listen to false words against anyone. I will not let anyone go free who has done a wrong thing. So do not kill a person who has not done a wrong thing.

8 Do not accept money as a gift, to do what is wrong. You will not be able to judge properly, because of this gift. Also, it will confuse the words of a good man.

9 Do not be cruel to a foreign person. You yourselves know what it feels like. So do not do it. Remember! You were foreign people in Egypt.

Laws about the Sabbath

10 You must plant seed in your fields for six years and bring in the harvest. 11 But during the seventh year, you must let your fields lie empty. Do not dig them and do not plant them. Then the poor people among you can get food from your fields. And the wild animals can eat any food that remains. Do the same thing with your gardens of fruit.

12 Do your work for six days, but do not work on the seventh day. Then your cow and your donkey can rest. Also, the foreign person and the slave who was born in your home can have some rest. Then they will become strong and happy.

13 Be careful to obey all my words to you. Do not ask any other gods for help. Do not let anyone hear the names of other gods from your lips.

The three parties that happen during each year

14 Three times during each year, I want you to enjoy a party with me.

15 Enjoy the party of bread that has no yeast in it. For 7 days, you must eat bread that you have made without any yeast. I have commanded you to do this. Do it at the right time during the month Abib. It was in that month that you came out of Egypt. Nobody must come to me with nothing in his hands.

16 Enjoy the party of harvest with the first food that you bring from your fields.

Enjoy another party at the end of the year. This will be when you bring in all of your food from the fields.'

17 'Three times during each year, all your men must appear in front of the Lord who is King.

18 If you give to me an animal as a gift, you may offer its blood. But do not offer it together with anything that has yeast in it.

Do not keep the fat from my special gifts until the next morning.

19 When you pick the first food from your fields, put the best food into a basket. Then bring it to the house of the Lord your God.

Do not cook a young goat in its mother's milk.

God's angel will go in front of the Israelites

20 Look! I send an angel in front of you, to keep you safe on the journey. He will bring you to the place that I have prepared for you. 21 Be careful to watch him. Listen to what he says to you. Do not refuse to obey him because he will not forgive you. This is because he is called by my name. 22 Be careful to listen to his words. Do everything that I say to you. Then I will be an enemy to your enemies. I will fight against anyone who fights against you. 23 My angel will go in front of you. He will bring you into the country of the Amorites, the Hittites, the Perizzites, the Canaanites, the Hivites and the Jebusites. I will kill all of them. 24 Do not bend your heads in front of their gods. Do not worship these gods. And do not copy the things that these people do. Destroy the gods and break their special stones into small pieces. 25 Worship me, the Lord your God, and then I will make your bread and water very good. I will remove illness from among you. 26 Your women will all have babies. None of the babies will be born before it is ready. I will give a long life to every person.

27 I will go in front of you and I will make everyone afraid of me. I will confuse the people in every country where you go. I will cause all your enemies to run away from you. 28 I will send in front of you cruel insects that fly. These will cause the Hivites, the Canaanites and the Hittites to run away from you. 29 But I will not remove these people in one year. If I did that, the country would become empty. And then there would be too many wild animals. 30 I will remove them slowly, one group after another group. Then you will become strong and you will fill the country yourselves.

31 I will decide where the edges of your country will be. The country will be from the Red Sea to the Sea of the Philistines. And it will be from the desert to the River Euphrates. I will give to you the people who live in these countries. Then you will send them away from you. 32 Do not make any promises to them, or to their gods. 33 Do not let them live in your country. They will certainly cause you to do wrong things against me. If you worship their gods, you will become their slaves.'

Chapter 24

God repeats his covenant

1 Then God said to Moses: 'Come up to the Lord. Come with Aaron, Nadab, Abihu and 70 of the leaders of Israel. You must worship me, but do not come near. 2 Only Moses can come near to me. And the people must not come with him.'

3 Then Moses told the people all the Lord's words and rules. And the people answered together: 'We will do everything that the Lord has said.' 4 Then Moses wrote down everything that the Lord had said.

The next morning, Moses got up early and he built a stone table. He built it at the lowest part of the mountain. Then he put up 12 large stones, one stone for each big family of Israel. 5 Moses sent young Israelite men to offer gifts of burnt animals and young male cows.

6 Moses took half of the blood of these animals and he put it in pots. He sprinkled the other half of the blood over the stone table. 7 Then he took the scroll of the covenant and he read it to the people. They replied: 'We will do everything that the Lord has said. We will obey him.'

8 Then Moses took the blood in the pots and he sprinkled it on the people. He said: 'This blood will cause you to remember the covenant that the Lord has made with you. He has made the covenant with you, with all these words on the scroll.'

9 Then Moses and Aaron, Nadab, Abihu and the 70 Israelite leaders went up the mountain. 10 They saw the God of Israel. Under his feet was something like a path of valuable blue stone. It shone like the sky itself. 11 God did not attack these Israelite leaders. They saw God. And they ate and drank.

12 The Lord said to Moses: 'Come up to me on the mountain. Stay here and I will give the flat stones to you. I have written on them the Law and the rules. So now you can teach them to the people.'

13 Then Moses went up the mountain of God, with Joshua, his servant. 14 He said to the leaders: 'Wait here for us. We will come back to you. Aaron and Hur are with you. Anyone who cannot agree with his brothers can go to them.'

15 When Moses went up the mountain, the cloud covered it. 16 The Lord's special bright light appeared on Mount Sinai. The cloud covered the mountain for 6 days. Then on the seventh day, the Lord spoke to Moses from inside the cloud. 17 The Lord's special bright light looked like a fire that destroyed everything. When the Israelites looked at it, they saw it like a fire. 18 Then Moses climbed the mountain and he went into the cloud. And he stayed on the mountain for 40 days and 40 nights.

Chapter 25

Gifts for the tabernacle

1 The Lord said to Moses: 2 'Tell the Israelites that they must bring me a gift. Every person who wants to give can do so. You must receive the gifts for me. 3 These are the gifts that you must receive from the people:

    Gold, silver and bronze

4 blue, purple and red materials and special white material goat's hair,

5 red sheep skins and badger skins, wood from acacia trees

6 olive oil for the lights, sweet powder from plants for the special oil, to make a lovely smell

7 many different stones, all valuable, to fix on to the priest's special clothes.'

8 'You must command the Israelites to make a special place for me. Then I will come and live among them. 9 I will show you how to make this tabernacle and everything inside it. But you must make it completely as I tell you.

The Ark

10 The Israelites must make a box of acacia wood. It must be one metre long, three quarters of a metre wide and three quarters of a metre high. 11 Cover it with gold, both inside and outside, and then build up the edges with gold. 12 Make four gold rings and fix them to the feet of the box. Fix two rings on one side and two rings on the other side. 13 Then make two sticks out of acacia wood and cover them with gold. 14 Push the sticks into the rings on the sides of the box. This is how you will carry it. 15 The sticks must remain in the rings of this Ark. You must not remove them. 16 Then put into the Ark the words of the covenant that I have written. I will give these to you.

17 Make a gold lid for the Ark. Make it one metre long and three quarters of a metre wide. 18 And make two angels from gold. Use a hammer to make them the right shape. 19 Make one angel on one end of the lid and the second angel on the other end. The two angels, one at each end, must be part of the lid. 20 The angels' wings must point to the sky and they must make a shadow over the lid. Each angel's face must look toward the other angel and toward the lid. 21 Put the lid on the top of the Ark. Put the words of the covenant that I have written into the Ark. I will give these words to you. 22 I will meet with you there, above the lid, between the two angels. The angels are over the Ark of the Covenant. I will meet with you and I will give to you all my commands for the Israelites.

The table

23 Make a table out of acacia wood. Make it one metre long, half a metre wide and three quarters of a metre high. 24 Cover it with gold, and then build up the edges with gold. 25 Also, fix an extra piece of wood round it, 7 centimetres wide, and build up these edges with gold.

26 Make four gold rings for the table. Fix them to the four corners, where the four legs of the table are. 27 The rings must be very near to the extra piece of wood. They will hold the sticks that you will use to carry the table. 28 Make the sticks out of acacia wood and cover them with gold. Use them to carry the table. 29 Make the plates and the spoons out of gold, also the pots and the dishes. You will use these to pour out the gifts of drink. 30 Put the special loaves of bread on this table. They must be there in front of me always.

The lamp stand

31 Make a lamp stand out of gold. Use a hammer to make it the right shape. Make its cups like open almond flowers and some that are not yet open. You must make every part of the lampstand from one piece of gold. 32 Make six branches on the lampstand, three branches on each side of it. 33 Put three cups like almond flowers on one branch and three on the next branch. Make some of these flowers open and some not yet open. Put three cups on each of the six branches of the lampstand. 34 On the lampst and itself, put four cups like almond flowers, some open and some not yet open. 35 Put one flower, not yet open, under the first pair of branches. Put a second flower, not yet open, under the second pair of branches. Put the third flower, not yet open, under the third pair of branches. There are six branches on the lampstand. 36 You must make the flowers and the branches from the same piece of gold as the lampstand. Use a hammer to make the gold into the right shape.

37 Then make 7 lamps and fix them to the lampstand. Fix them so that they will light the space in front of it. 38 You must make small tools from gold, with which to clean the lamps. You must also make dishes for it. 39 You must make the lampstand and all its tools and dishes from 34 kilos of gold. 40 Be careful how you make all these things. You must copy them completely as you saw them on the mountain.

Chapter 26

The tabernacle

1 Make the tabernacle with 10 curtains of very good material, white, blue, purple and red. Tell a wise worker that he must make pictures of angels in the curtains. 2 All the curtains must be the same size, 12½ metres long and 1¾ metres wide. 3 Join five of the curtains together. Do the same with the other five curtains. 4 On the edge of the last curtain in the set, fix rings of blue material. Do the same thing on the last curtain of the other set. 5 Make 50 rings on one curtain and 50 rings on the last curtain of the other set. Make 50 rings on one curtain opposite to the rings on the other curtain. 6 Then make 50 small pieces of gold to fasten the curtains together. Then the tabernacle will be one piece of work.

7 Make 11 curtains from goat's hair to cover the tabernacle. 8 All the curtains must be the same size. They must be 13½ metres long and 1¾ metres wide. 9 Fix five of the curtains together to make one set. Fix the other six curtains together to make a second set. Hang the sixth curtain over the end curtain of the first set. This will be at the front of the tent. 10 Make 50 rings of material along the edge of the last curtain in the first set. Then make 50 rings along the edge of the last curtain in the second set. 11 Then make 50 small pieces of bronze. Use them to fasten the tent together. Then the tent will be one piece of work. 12 The curtains for the tent will be longer than the curtains for the tabernacle. The extra half of the curtain will hang at the back of the tabernacle. 13 The curtains of the tent will be half a metre longer on both sides. The extra material will cover the sides of the tabernacle. 14 Use red sheep skins to cover the tent. Then use badger skins to cover the sheep skins.

15 Make boards out of acacia wood for the tabernacle. 16 Each board must be 4½ metres long and ¾ of a metre wide. 17 Make two extra pieces on each board, next to each other. Make all the boards of the tabernacle like this. 18 Make 20 boards for the south side of the tabernacle. 1

9 Then make 40 pieces of silver, with a hole in each piece. The boards will stand in the holes. There must be two holes for each board. The extra pieces on each board will fit into the holes.

20 Make 20 boards for the north side of the tabernacle 21 and 40 pieces of silver, two under each board. 22 Make six boards for the west end of the tabernacle. 23 Then make two boards for the corners at the back of the tabernacle. 24 You must fix them together at the lower edge and at the top. Use a ring to fix them together. Make both the corners the same. 25 So there will be 8 boards and 16 pieces of silver, two under each board.

26 You must also cut pieces of acacia wood to fix across the boards of the tabernacle. Cut five pieces for the boards on one side 27 and five pieces for the boards on the other side. Cut five pieces for the boards on the west, at the far end of the tabernacle. 28 The piece of wood in the centre must reach from one end to the other. Fix it at the middle of the boards. 29 Cover the boards with gold and make gold rings. These rings will hold the pieces of wood that you fix across the boards. Then cover the pieces of wood also with gold.

30 Make the tabernacle the same as the plan that I showed to you, on the mountain.

31 Make a curtain out of blue, purple, red and soft white material. A wise man must put into it a picture of angels. 32 Hang it up with gold rings from four sticks of acacia wood. Cover these sticks with gold. Then fix them on four pieces of silver that have holes in the centre. 33 Hang up the curtain and put the Ark of the Covenant behind the curtain. So the Holy Place will be separate from the Most Holy Place. The curtain will hang between them. 34 Put the special lid on the Ark of the Covenant, in the most Holy Place. 35 Put the table outside the curtain on the north side of the tabernacle. Put the lampstand on the opposite side of the tabernacle, on the south side.

36 Make a curtain for the door of the tent. Make it out of blue, purple and red material and out of special white material. Someone who can do wise work with material must make the curtain. 37 Make gold rings for this curtain and make five sticks out of acacia wood. Cover the sticks with gold and make five pieces of bronze to hold them.

Chapter 27

The altar on which to burn animals as gifts

1 Make an altar out of acacia wood. It must be 1¼ metres high and the top must be square, 2¼ metres long and wide. 2 Make four horns, one at each corner. The horns and the altar must be one piece of work. Then cover it all with bronze. 3 Make all the tools for the altar out of bronze. Make pots to remove the ashes. Make spades, dishes and forks for the meat. Make buckets out of metal to carry the fire. 4 Make a square net of bronze with a ring of bronze at each corner. 5 Fix this net under the altar, between the top of the altar and the ground. 6 Make sticks out of acacia wood for the altar, then cover them with bronze. 7 You must put the sticks into the rings when you carry the altar. There will be a stick on two sides of the altar. 8 Make the altar out of boards. You must make it like the thing that the Lord showed you on the mountain.

The yard

9 Make a yard for the tabernacle. The south side must be 46 metres long. It must have curtains of special white material. 10 Make 20 sticks for the curtains and 20 pieces of bronze with holes in them. The sticks will stand in these. Make small pieces of silver and rings of material on the sticks, to fasten the curtains. 11 The north side of the yard must also be 46 metres long. It must also have curtains, sticks, silver pieces and rings of material.

12 The west end of the yard must be 23 metres wide. Make curtains for it and 10 sticks to stand on 10 pieces of bronze. 13 The east end of the yard looks toward the sunrise. It must also be 23 metres wide. 14 Make curtains 7 metres long on one side of the open space where you go in. Make three sticks that stand on three pieces of bronze, for the curtains. 15 Make the same things for the other side.

16 Make a curtain, 9 metres long, for the open space where you go into the yard. Make it out of blue, purple and red material together with special white material. Choose a wise worker to make the curtain. Make four sticks that stand on four pieces of bronze for the curtain. 17 Make small pieces of silver to fix the curtains on all the sticks round the yard. Every stick must stand in a small piece of bronze. 18 The yard must be 46 metres long and 23 metres wide. Make the curtains out of special white material, 2¼ metres long and with pieces of bronze to stand on. 19 Make everything of bronze that you will use in the tabernacle. This includes the small sharp sticks that fix the tent and the yard to the ground.

Olive oil for the lampstand

20 Command the Israelites to bring you clean oil from fresh olives. This oil is to burn in the lamps. They must always give light. 21 Aaron and his sons must keep a light in the lamps from evening until morning. Put these lights in the Tent of Meeting. They are for the Lord to see. Put them outside the curtain that hangs in front of the Testimony. You must make this a rule for the Israelites. It is a rule also for those who are not yet born.

Chapter 28

Special clothes for the priests

1 Fetch Aaron your brother with his sons, from among the Israelites. The names of Aaron's sons are Nadab and Abihu, Eleazar and Ithamar. I want them to be my servants, my priests. 2 Make special clothes for your brother Aaron. These clothes will show that he is important and special to me. 3 I have made certain men very wise so that they can make these clothes. Tell them that they must make Aaron's clothes. The clothes must be ready for the day when I make him my servant, my priest. 4 These are the clothes that the wise men must make:

    a breast piece

    an ephod

    a robe

    a tunic

    a turban

    a long belt.

They must make these special clothes for your brother Aaron and for his sons. Then Aaron and his sons can be my servants,
my priests, 5 The wise men must use beautiful material, gold, blue, purple, red and white.

The ephod

6 Make the ephod out of gold and out of blue, purple and red material. Use also special white material that a wise worker has made. 7 On two of its corners you must fix pieces for Aaron's shoulders. Then you can fasten the ephod. 8 Make the special belt like the ephod. The belt and
the ephod must be one piece of work. You must make them with gold and with blue, purple and red material and with special white material.

9 Take two onyx stones. With a sharp tool, write on them the names of the sons of Israel. 10 Begin with the name of the oldest son and finish with the name of the youngest son. Write six names on one stone and six names on the other. 11 Write these names on the two stones like a wise man draws on valuable metal. Then fix the stones to some thin gold pieces that you have made beautiful. 12 Fasten the stones on the shoulder pieces of the ephod. When the Lord sees the stones, he will remember his promises to the sons of Israel. Aaron will carry the stones on his shoulders and the Lord will see them. 13 Make special pieces of thin gold 14 and two chains of gold. Fix these chains to the thin pieces of gold.

The breast piece

15 A wise worker must make the breast piece. This will give Aaron help when he must decide any matter. Make it like the ephod, out of gold and out of blue, purple and red material. Use special white material too. 16 Bend a piece of cloth to make a square, 22 centimetres long and 22 centimetres wide. 17 Then fix four sets of valuable stones on it. Fix a ruby, a topaz and a beryl in the first set. 18 Fix a turquoise, a sapphire and an emerald in the second set. 19 Fix a jacinth, an agate and an amethyst in the third set. 20 Fix a chrysolite, an onyx and a jasper in the fourth set. Fix each stone in a thin piece of gold that you have made beautiful. 21 There will be 12 stones, one stone for each of Israel's sons. You must write their names on the stones with a sharp tool. Write one name on each stone.

22 Make thin lines out of gold and put them together. This will make a chain. 23 Then make two gold rings for the chains. Fasten them to two corners of the breast piece. 24 Fasten the two gold chains to the rings at the corners of the breast piece. 25 Fasten the other ends of the chains to the shoulder pieces of the ephod, in the front. 26 Make two gold rings and fasten them to the two other corners of the breast piece. Put them inside, next to the ephod. 27 Make two more gold rings. Fix them to the lower edge of the shoulder pieces, on the front of the ephod. Put them just above the ephod's belt. 28 Tie the rings of the breast piece to the rings of the ephod with a line of blue cotton. Fix it to the belt, then the breast piece and the belt will not become separated.

29 When Aaron goes into the Holy Place, he will wear the breast piece over his heart. So he will carry the names of Israel's sons over his heart. And the Lord will always remember the Israelites. 30 Put the Urim and Thummim in the breast piece. Then they will also be over Aaron's heart when he goes into the Lord's home. So Aaron will always carry over his heart the help that he needs. He will always carry this help with him, to decide matters for the Israelites.

Other clothes for the priests

31 Make the robe of the ephod completely out of blue cloth. 32 Make a hole in the centre of the robe, for the priest's head. You must make a collar round this hole, and then it will not
tear. 33 Make pomegranates out of blue, purple and red material. Fix them to the lower edge of the robe, with gold bells between them. 34 Fix a bell, then a pomegranate, a bell, then a pomegranate round the whole lower edge of the robe.

35 Aaron must wear the robe when he works as the Lord's servant. The bells will make a sound when he goes into the Holy Place. And they will make a sound when he comes out. So he will not die.

36 Make a thin plate out of gold and write on it with a sharp tool: HOLY TO THE LORD. 37 Fasten a line of blue cotton to the plate. Then fix the plate to the front of the turban. 38 Aaron will wear the turban, with the plate, on his head for a special reason. When the Israelites bring gifts to God, Aaron himself will carry any bad things in the gifts. Then the Lord will accept the gifts because of the turban on Aaron's head. 39 Make the tunic and the turban out of good white material. A wise worker must make the long belt.

40 Make tunics, long belts and hats for Aaron's sons. These things will make them look important and beautiful. 41 Put these clothes on your brother Aaron and on his sons. Then pour oil on their heads and give them authority. Make them separate from the other Israelites so that they can be the Lord's priests.

42 Make trousers out of white material that will cover the lower parts of the priests' bodies. 43 Aaron and his sons must wear them when they go into the Tent of Meeting. They must also wear them when they go near to the altar in the Holy Place. Then the Lord will not become angry with them, and they will not die. This rule is for Aaron and for all his children and grandchildren. The rule remains the same for all time.

Chapter 29

Priests must be separate from other Israelites

1 When you make the priests separate, do it in this way: Take a young male cow and two male sheep. They must not have anything wrong with them. 2 Make some bread from good flour, with no yeast in it. Use oil to make cakes and biscuits also. 3 Put these things in a basket and bring them, with the three animals. 4 Then bring Aaron and his sons to the door of the Tent of Meeting and wash them there. 5 Then take the special clothes. Dress Aaron in the tunic, the robe, the ephod and the breast piece. Fasten the ephod on him with the special belt. 6 Put the turban on Aaron's head and fix the holy gold plate to the turban. 7 Take the special oil and pour it on his head. 8 Bring his sons and dress them in their tunics. 9 Put the hats on their heads, then tie the long belts on Aaron and on his sons. These men and their sons and grandsons will be priests for all time. This is a special gift to them for always. This is how you must make Aaron and his sons separate:

10 Bring the male cow to the front of the Tent of Meeting. Aaron and his sons must put their hands on the male cow's head. 11 Then kill the animal in front of the Lord, at the door of the Tent of Meeting.

12 Take some of the male cow's blood. Use your finger to put some blood on the horns of the altar. Pour the blood that remains on the ground round the altar. 13 Take all the fat that is round the inside parts of the animal. Take the skin that covers the liver. Take both the kidneys with the fat that is round them. Burn all these things on the altar. 14 But burn the male cow's body outside the camp. You have offered it because of sin.

15 Take one of the male sheep. Aaron and his sons must put their hands on its head. 16 Kill it and take the blood to the altar. Throw some of the blood on to every side of the altar. 17 Cut the male sheep in pieces and wash the inside parts and the legs. Then put them with the head and with the other pieces. 18 Burn the whole male sheep on the altar. It is a gift to the Lord and a good smell. You will offer this gift to the Lord by fire.

19 Take the second male sheep. Aaron and his sons must put their hands on its head. 20 Kill it and put some of the blood on the right ears of Aaron and his sons. Put some blood also on their right hands and on the big toes of their right feet. Then throw some blood on to every side of the altar. 21 Mix together some of the blood on the altar and some of the special oil. Put this on to Aaron and on to his clothes. Put it also on to his sons and on to their clothes. Then Aaron and his sons and their clothes will be holy.

22 Take all the fat from this male sheep. Take the fat tail, the fat round the inside parts and the skin round the liver. Take also the two kidneys with the fat round them. And take the top part of the right leg. (You will use this male sheep when you give authority to Aaron and to his sons.) 23 Take out of the basket a loaf of bread that has no yeast in it. Take also a cake with oil in it and a biscuit. These are all in the basket that is in front of the Lord. 24 Put all these things in the hands of Aaron and his sons. Then lift these things up to the Lord as a gift. 25 Now take them and burn them on the altar, with the animal as a gift. They will make a good smell, a gift to the Lord that you offer by fire.

26 Take the breast of this special male sheep. First lift it up to the Lord as a gift that you offer to him. Then you can eat it.

27 You must make holy the pieces of the sheep that are for Aaron and his sons. These are the breast and the top part of the leg. You have lifted them up first to the Lord. 28 This must always be the regular gift from the Israelites to Aaron and his sons. The Israelites must supply this food for the priests from their gifts to the Lord.

29 Aaron's holy clothes will belong to the males in his family for all time. Those men will become separate and take authority. Then they can wear the clothes. 30 The son who becomes priest after Aaron's death must wear his clothes. When that son comes to the Tent of Meeting, he must wear the clothes for 7 days. He must wear them while he does the Lord's work in the Holy Place.

31 Take the male sheep that is for Aaron and his sons. Cook the meat in a holy place. 32 Aaron and his sons must eat the meat, and the bread from the basket. They must do this at the door of the Tent of Meeting. 33 They must eat these gifts, by which they have paid for their authority and special importance. No other person can eat this meat because it is holy.

34 But if any of this meat remains until the morning, you must burn it. Burn also any bread that remains. You must not eat it because it is holy.

35 Do everything that I have commanded you, for Aaron and his sons. Make them holy and give them authority during 7 days. 36 Kill a male cow each day, as a gift. This animal that you offer dies instead of you, for your sin.'

'Make the altar completely clean. Pay for it with a gift and pour oil on it. This will make it special and holy. 37 Do this to the altar for 7 days, and then it will become very holy. Anything that touches the altar will become holy too.

38 You must offer a regular gift on the altar each day. This gift must be two young sheep that are one year old. 39 Offer one in the morning and the other in the evening.

40 With the first young sheep, offer two litres of good flour. Mix this with one litre of olive oil. Offer also one litre of wine as a gift of drink.

41 Kill the other young sheep in the evening. Offer it with the same gifts of food and drink as in the morning. There will be a good smell from this gift to the Lord, by fire.

42 I give this commandment for all the Israelites who will be born in future years. You must offer this regular gift by fire, to me. Offer it at the door of the Tent of Meeting. I will meet you there and I will speak to you. 43 I will meet the Israelites there also and the place will become holy because of my glory.

44 So I will make the Tent of Meeting holy and separate. I will do the same thing to the altar and to Aaron and to his sons. They will work for me as priests. 45 Then I will live among the Israelites and I will be their God. 46 They will know that I am the Lord their God. I brought them out of Egypt so that I could live among them. I am the Lord their God.'

Chapter 30

The altar for incense

1 'Make an altar out of acacia wood so that you can burn incense on it. 2 The altar must be square. Make it ½ metre long, ½ metre wide and 1 metre high. The altar's horns must be part of it, one piece of wood. 3 Cover every part of the altar with gold. Then fix an extra piece of gold round it. 4 Make two gold rings for the altar, below the extra piece of gold. These rings must be on opposite sides of the altar. They will hold the sticks with which you will carry it. 5 Make the sticks of acacia wood and cover them with gold. 6 There is a curtain in front of the Ark of the Covenant. Put the altar in front of that curtain, in front of the special lid. This lid covers the ark and I will meet you there.

7 Aaron must burn incense with a good smell on the altar every morning. He must do this when he checks the lamps. 8 He must burn incense again when he lights the lamps in the evening. Incense must burn for the Lord every day for all time. 9 Do not offer any different incense on this altar. Do not offer any animals or food plants as gifts on this altar. And do not pour a gift of drink on it. 10 Once every year, Aaron must pay the price for sin on this altar. He must pay this price with the blood of the male cow that he offers. Every year, a priest must do this, for all time. It is most holy to the Lord.'

Money that pays the price for each life

11 Then the Lord said to Moses: 12 'When you count the Israelites, each person must pay the Lord a price for his life. Each person must do this at the time when you count him. Then nothing bad will happen to him at that time. 13 Each person must give a silver coin when you count him. The weight of this coin is six grams and it is a gift to the Lord. 14 You must count every person who is 20 years old or more. And each person must offer his gift to the Lord. 15 Rich people must not give more than six grams of silver. Poor people must not give less when they offer this gift to the Lord. It is the price that each person must pay for his life. 16 Receive this money from the Israelites. Use it for anything that you need for the Tent of Meeting. Then the Lord will always remember that you belong to him. You have paid money for your lives.

17 Then the Lord said to Moses: 18 Make a very large dish for water out of bronze. And make something from bronze for it to stand on. Put it between the Tent of Meeting and the altar and fill it with water.

19 Aaron and his sons must wash their hands and their feet with water from the dish. 20 Every time they go into the Tent of Meeting, they must wash their hands and their feet. Then they will not die. Also, before they offer a gift by fire on the altar, they must wash. 21 Then they will not die when they offer a gift to the Lord. This is a rule for all time, for Aaron and for everyone that is born into his family.'

Special oil to make things holy

22 Then the Lord said to Moses: 23 'Mix together these good spices:

  6 kilos of liquid myrrh

  3 kilos of sweet cinnamon

  3 kilos of sweet cane

| 24 | 6 kilos of cassia |

    4 litres of olive oil.

25 Make these into a holy oil, the special oil that makes things holy. It will be the work of a wise chemist. 26 Then pour a little oil on all of these things:

    the Tent of Meeting

    the Ark of the Covenant

| 27 | the table and all its tools |

    the lampstand and its tools

| 28 | the two altars with their tools |

    and the very large dish for water with its base.

29 You must make all these things separate so that they will be most holy. Then anything that touches them will become holy.

30 Pour some of the holy oil on Aaron's head and on the heads of his sons. Make them separate, and then they can work for me as priests. 31 Say to the Israelites: "This will be my holy oil for all time. 32 Do not pour it on the bodies of men who are not priests. Do not make any of this oil to use for other things. It is holy and you must always think about it as holy. 33 Nobody must make a sweet smell like this oil. Nobody must put this oil on any person except on a priest. Anyone who does not obey this rule must die." '

Sweet incense

34 Then the Lord said to Moses: 'Take sweet spices, (gum resin, onycha, galbanum and frankincense) in equal amounts. 35 Give them to a chemist and let him make them into incense, with a lovely smell. It must have salt in it and it must be clean and holy. 36 Make some of the incense into powder. Put this in front of the Ark of the Covenant, in the Tent of Meeting. I will meet you there. It will be most holy to you. 37 Do not make any incense like this for yourselves. Think about it always as holy to the Lord. 38 Whoever makes any incense like it, with a lovely smell, for himself, he must die.'

Chapter 31

Bezalel and Oholiab

1 Then the Lord said to Moses: 2 'Look! I have chosen Bezalel, the son of Uri, the grandson of Hur, from the big family of Judah. 3 I have filled him with the Spirit of God. I have made him very wise in many different ways. 4 He knows how to draw beautiful pictures of things. Then he makes them out of gold, silver and bronze. 5 He knows how to cut valuable stones. Then he puts them into pieces of gold or silver. He knows how to work with wood. He makes beautiful things and he always does good work.

6 And I have chosen Oholiab, the son of Ahisamach, from the big family of Dan, to help Bezalel. Also, I have made all the workers very wise. They will make everything that I have commanded you. 7 They will make the Tent of Meeting and the Ark of the Covenant with its special lid. They will make all the other things in the tent too. 8 They will make the table and all the things on it. They will make the lamp standout of pure gold and the altar where you will offer incense. 9 They will make the other altar. On that other altar, you will burn the animals that are gifts to me. They will make the very large dish for water and its metal base.

10 These wise men will also make clothes. They will make the special clothes for Aaron the priest and for his sons. His sons will wear these clothes when they work as priests. 11 The wise men will also make the special oil and the incense that has a lovely smell. These are for the Holy Place. They must make them completely as I commanded you.'

The Sabbath

12 Then the Lord said to Moses: 13 'Say to the Israelites: "You must keep my Sabbaths as special days. This will be something special for you and for me. The children that will be born will see it. Then they will know that I am the Lord. It is I who make you holy.

14 Keep the Sabbath special because it is a holy day to you. You must kill anyone who does bad things on the Sabbath. Anyone who works on that day must die. 15 You must work for six days, but the seventh day is a Sabbath for rest. It is a holy day to the Lord. You must kill any person who does any work on the Sabbath day. 16 The Israelites must keep the Sabbath as a special day and they must enjoy it. They must do this for all time. It is a special covenant and it will always be with them." 17 It will be something special between me and the Israelites for all time. This is because the Lord made the sky and the earth in six days. Then, on the seventh day, he did not work but he rested.'

18 The Lord finished his words to Moses on Mount Sinai. Then the Lord gave Moses the two flat stones of the Testimony. God had written on these stones with his own finger.

Chapter 32

The young cow that Aaron made out of gold

1 Moses was on the mountain for a very long time. So the Israelites went to Aaron. They said: 'Get up! Make some gods for us who will lead us. This man, Moses, brought us up out of Egypt. But we do not know where he is now. We do not know what has happened to him.'

2 Then Aaron answered them: 'Take the gold rings from the ears of your wives, your sons and your daughters. Then bring the rings to me.' 3 So all the Israelites removed the rings from their ears and they brought them to Aaron.

4 Aaron took the rings and he made a false god from the gold. He used a tool to make the false god in the shape of a young cow. Then the Israelites said: 'This is your god, Israel. He brought you up out of Egypt!'

5 When Aaron saw this, he built an altar in front of the young cow. He shouted: 'Tomorrow, there will be a party to the Lord.' 6 So, on the next day, the Israelites got up early. They offered gifts of dead animals on the altar and they brought other gifts also. After this they sat down and they ate a meal. They drank and then they played bad games together.

7 Then the Lord said to Moses: 'Go down the mountain. The Israelites that you brought out of Egypt have become bad people. 8 They have turned away from my commandments already. They have made for themselves a false god in the shape of a young cow. They have bent their heads to it. They have brought gifts of dead animals to it. They have said: "These are your gods, Israel, who have brought you out of Egypt." '

9 Then the Lord said to Moses: 'I have seen these people. They are proud and they do not obey me. 10 Now leave me, so that I can be very angry with them. I will kill them and I will make you into a great nation.'

11 But Moses asked the Lord his God to listen to him. Moses said: 'Lord, please do not be so angry with your own family! You brought them out of Egypt with strong and powerful authority. 12 The Egyptians will say: "God led the Israelites out of Egypt so that he could kill them. He wanted to kill them in the mountains. He wanted to destroy them completely." Please stop being angry. Please be sorry for your own people and do not kill them. 13 Remember your servants, Abraham, Isaac and Israel. Remember the promise that you made to them. You said: "I will give you as many children and grandchildren as there are stars in the sky. I have promised to give this whole country to them. And it will be their country for all time." ' 14 Then the Lord was sorry for the people that he had chosen. He did not kill them as he had decided to.

15 Moses turned and he went down the mountain. He carried the two flat stones of the Testimony in his hands. God had written on both sides of the stones. 16 This was God's own work. He himself had written the words on the stones.

17 The Israelites were shouting and Joshua heard the noise. He said to Moses: 'I can hear the sound of war in the camp!' 18 But Moses answered: 'It is not the sound of soldiers who are beating their enemies. It is not the sound of soldiers who run away from their enemies. It is the sound of singers that I can hear.'

19 Then Moses came near to the camp. He saw the young cow and the Israelites who were dancing. He became very angry. He threw the two stones on to the ground. He broke them into pieces where he stood. 20 Then he took the young cow that they had made. He burned it in the fire. He made it into powder and he poured it into the water. Then he commanded the Israelites to drink that water.

21 Moses said to Aaron: 'You should not have caused these people to do such a bad sin. What did they do to you?' 22 Aaron answered: 'Do not be angry, my lord. You know how quickly these people do bad things. 23 They said to me: "Make us some gods that will lead us. This man called Moses brought us out of Egypt. But now we do not know what has happened to him." 24 So I said to them: "If anyone has any gold rings, he must remove them." Then they gave the gold to me. I threw it into the fire and this young cow came out of the fire!'

25 All the Israelites were running about. And Moses saw that they were doing bad things in the camp. Aaron had let them do bad things. They would have felt ashamed if their enemies had seen them. 26 So Moses stood at the edge of the camp. He said: 'Everyone who loves the Lord must come to me.' Then all the Levites went to Moses.

27 Then Moses said to the Levites: 'This is the message from the Lord, the God of Israel. "Every man must take his sword in his hand. You must go from one end of the camp to the other. And each man must kill his brother and his friend and his neighbour." ' 28 The Levites obeyed the command of Moses and about three thousand Israelites died on that day. 29 Then Moses said to the Levites: 'The Lord has made you his special people today. He has blessed you today because you have punished your own sons and brothers.'

30 On the next day, Moses said to the Israelites: 'You have done a very bad thing. But now I will go up to the Lord. Perhaps I can pay the price for your sin.'

31 So Moses returned to the Lord. He said to the Lord: 'These people have done a very bad thing. They have made gods out of gold for themselves! 32 But now, please forgive them! And if you cannot forgive them, then take my name out of your book.'

33 The Lord answered Moses: 'I will take out of my book the name of everyone who has sinned against me. 34 Now go! Lead the Israelites to the place that I have spoken about. My angel will go in front of you. But on the right day I will punish them for their sin.'

35 And the Lord punished the Israelites with a bad illness because of what they had done. They had done bad things with the young cow that Aaron had made.

Chapter 33

1 Then the Lord said to Moses: 'You and the Israelites must all leave this place. You brought them out of Egypt. You must lead them to the country that I promised to Abraham, Isaac and Jacob. I promised to give the country to their children and grandchildren, for all time. 2 I will send an angel in front of you. He will throw out the Canaanites, the Amorites, the Hittites, the Perizzites, the Hivites and the Jebusites. 3 Go to that country where there is enough food and drink for everyone. But I will not go with you because you will not obey my commandments. I might go with you. But then I might kill you as you travel.'

4 The Israelites heard the message and God's words frightened them. They began to cry and nobody put on his beautiful stones. 5 The Lord had said to Moses: 'Speak to the Israelites. Say to them: "You are people who will not obey me. If I go with you, even for a moment, I may kill you. I may kill you as you travel. Now remove your beautiful stones. Then I will decide what I will do with you." ' 6 So the Israelites threw off their beautiful stones near Mount Horeb.

The Tent of Meeting

7 Now Moses put up a special tent outside the camp, in every place where the Israelites stayed. He called it the Tent of Meeting. Anyone could go there and listen to the Lord's words. The Tent of Meeting was outside the camp.

8 When Moses went out to the Tent of Meeting, all the people would stand at the doors of their tents. They would watch Moses until he went into the Tent of Meeting. 9 When Moses went into the tent, the special cloud would come down. The cloud would stay at the door of the tent while the Lord spoke to Moses.

10 Every time that the people saw the special cloud at the door of the Tent of Meeting, they all stood up. Then each person worshipped at the door of his tent. 11 The Lord would speak to Moses as a man speaks to his friend. Then Moses would return to the camp. But Joshua, the son of Nun, stayed in the tent. He was a young man who helped Moses.

Moses wants to see God's glory

12 Moses said to the Lord: 'You have said to me: "Lead these people." But whom will you send with me? You have not told me. You have said: "I know you by your name. You give me pleasure and I love you." 13 If you love me, please tell me your thoughts. I want to understand you. I want you to love me always. Remember that the Israelites are your own family.'

14 The Lord replied: 'I myself will go with you and I will give you rest.'

15 Then Moses said: 'If you do not go with us, do not send us away from here. 16 If you do not go with us, nobody will know about you. Nobody will know that we give you pleasure. We will not be special people. We will be like everyone else in the world.'

17 And the Lord said to Moses: 'I will certainly do this thing that you have asked for. This is because you give me pleasure. Also, I know you by your name.'

18 Then Moses said: 'Please, show me your glory!'

19 And the Lord said: 'I will cause all my goodness to pass in front of you. I will tell you my name that I am the Lord. I will be kind to anyone that I choose. I will show my love to anyone that I choose. 20 But you cannot see my face. Nobody can see my face and live.'

21 Then the Lord said: 'There is a place near me. You can stand there upon a rock. 22 When my glory passes in front of you, I will put you in a hole in the rock. I will cover you with my hand until I have passed in front of you. 23 Then I will remove my hand and you will see my back. But nobody must see my face.'

Chapter 34

Two new flat stones

1 The Lord said to Moses: 'Cut two flat stones like the first stones. Then I will write on them all the words that I wrote on the first stones. You broke the first stones into pieces.

2 'Make yourself ready in the morning and come up Mount Sinai. Show yourself to me there, on the top of the mountain. 3 Nobody must come with you. Nobody must be anywhere on the mountain. Even the animals must not eat grass in front of the mountain.'

4 So Moses cut two flat stones like the first ones. He went up Mount Sinai early in the morning as the Lord had commanded him. And he carried the two flat stones in his hands. 5 Then the Lord came down in the special cloud and he stood by Moses. The Lord spoke with a loud voice and he said: 'The Lord is my name!'

6 Then the Lord passed in front of Moses. He said in a loud voice: 'The Lord! The Lord! The kind God who loves you becomes angry very slowly. He is a God of love who does not change. 7 He loves thousands of people. He forgives the bad things that they do. He forgives many people who do not obey him. He even forgives people who do bad things against him. But he does not forget to punish bad people. He punishes children and grandchildren for the bad things that their fathers did. He continues to punish them, even the children of the grandchildren.'

8 Then Moses bent down his head immediately and he worshipped. 9 He said: 'Lord, if you love me, please go with us! I know that we have often not obeyed you. But please forgive the bad things that we have done. Take us with you as your own family.'

10 Then the Lord said: 'I will make a covenant with you. I will do great and special things in front of all the Israelites. Nobody has done things like these before, in any country in the world. Your neighbours will see these great things that I, the Lord, will do for you. And they will feel afraid of you. 11 Obey what I command you today. Then I will go in front of you. And I will throw out these people: the Amorites, the Canaanites, the Hittites, the Perizzites, the Hivites and the Jebusites.

12 Do not make friends with the people in the country where you are going. If you did, they would teach you to do wrong things. 13 You must break their altars and destroy their special stones. You must cut down the tall sticks that they call holy. 14 Do not worship any other god. The Lord your God will not let you love any god except himself.

15 Be careful! Do not make friends with those people who live in that country. When they do bad things in front of their gods, they will ask you to do it with them. Then they will give you their bad food to eat. 16 Perhaps you may choose some of their daughters for your sons to marry. These daughters will still worship their gods. And they will teach your sons to do the same bad things.

17 Do not make false gods from hot metal.

18 Enjoy the party of bread that has no yeast in it. Eat this bread for 7 days, as I commanded you. Do this on the right date in the month of Abib. This is because you came out of Egypt in that month.

19 Every first child or young animal that is born is my own. You must include every first male that is born of your cows and your sheep. 20 You must pay for every first donkey that is born. You must give a young sheep to me to pay for the donkey. If you do not pay for it, you must break its neck. And you must pay for every first son that is born. Nobody must come to me without a gift in his hand.

21 You must work for six days but on the seventh day you must rest. Even when it is time to plough, you must rest on the seventh day. And when it is time to bring in your harvest, you must still rest on the seventh day.

22 Enjoy the party of weeks when you cut the first of your food plants. Enjoy the party of harvest at the end of the year. 23 Three times in the year, all your men must appear in front of the Lord. He is your king, the God of Israel. 24 He will go in front of you and he will throw out your enemies. He will give you more and more land. And when you leave it, three times in the year, nobody will take it from you.

25 Do not offer to me the blood of an animal with anything that has yeast in it. And do not keep any of the meat from the Passover party until the next morning.

26 When you cut the first of your food plants, bring the best to the Lord's house. Do not cook a young goat in its mother's milk.'

27 Then the Lord said to Moses: 'Write down these words, because I have made a covenant with you and with the Israelites. These words tell you about my covenant.' 28 Moses was there, with the Lord, for 40 days and 40 nights. He did not eat bread or drink water. And he wrote on the flat stones the words of God's covenant. He wrote down the Ten Commandments.

Moses' face shines

29 Moses came down from Mount Sinai with the two stones of the covenant in his hands. But he did not know that his face was shining. His face was shining because he had spoken with the Lord. 30 When Aaron and all the Israelites saw Moses' face, they were afraid to come near him. 31 But Moses shouted to them. So Aaron and the leaders of the people came back to him. Then Moses talked to them. 32 After this, all the Israelites came near to Moses. And he gave them all the commands that the Lord had given to him on Mount Sinai.

33 When Moses had spoken to them, he covered his face with a thin cloth. 34 But when he spoke with the Lord in the Tent of Meeting, he removed the cloth. When he came out, he repeated God's commands to the Israelites. 35 They saw that his face shone. So Moses would put the thin cloth over his face again. The cloth would stay there until he spoke with the Lord again.

Chapter 35

Rules about the Sabbath

1 Moses brought all the Israelites together. Then he said to them: 'These are the Lord's commandments to you. 2 You must work for six days but the seventh day will be your holy day. It will be a day of rest to the Lord. Anyone who works on that day must die. 3 Do not light a fire in any of your homes on the Sabbath day.'

Materials for the tabernacle

4 Moses said to all the Israelites: 'This is what the Lord has commanded: 5 Take a gift for the Lord from the things that you have. Everyone who wants to give can bring a gift of gold, silver and bronze. 6 They can also bring blue, purple and red material, and special white cloth. 7 They can bring goats' hair, red sheepskins, badger skins and acacia wood. 8 They can bring olive oil for the light, many different spices, 9 onyx stones and other valuable stones. And you will put these stones on the ephod and on the breast piece.

10 Every wise person among you must make all the things that the Lord has commanded. 11 Make the tabernacle, with its tent that covers it. Make all the different parts for it, as I have described them to you. 12 Make the Ark, with its sticks, its special lid and the curtain that hangs in front of it.

13 Make the table with its sticks and all its dishes. Make the special bread that you will put on the table. 14 Make the lampstand that will give light, with the lamps and the oil. 15 Make the altar for incense with its sticks, the special oil and the incense that has a sweet smell. Make the curtain for the door of the tabernacle. 16 Make the altar where you will burn animals as gifts to the Lord. Make all the different tools for the altar, as I have described them to you. Make the very large dish for water and its base. 17 Make the curtains for the yard and for the door of the yard. Make the sticks for the curtains and the bases. 18 Make the small, sharp sticks and the strong material that fixes the tents to the ground.

19 Make the special clothes for Aaron and for his sons to wear. They are priests and they will work for the Lord. This is why they must wear special clothes.'

20 Then all the Israelites went away. 21 Many of them really wanted to give a gift to the Lord. So they each brought something to offer for the Tent of Meeting. They also brought materials for the special clothes. 22 Both men and women brought beautiful things of gold that they had worn on their bodies. They all brought their gold things as a special gift of love to the Lord. 23 Everyone who had blue, purple or red material brought it. Also, they brought special white cloth. People who had goats' hair, red sheep skins and badger skins brought them. 24 Those who brought gifts of silver or bronze offered them to the Lord. Everyone who had acacia wood brought it for the Tent of Meeting.

25 Every wise woman worked with her hands. She brought what she had made, blue, purple and red material or special white cloth. 26 Many wise women began to work. They made the goats' hair into cloth. 27 The leaders of the Israelites brought valuable stones to fix on the ephod and on the breast piece. 28 They also brought spices and olive oil. These things were for the light, for the special oil and for the incense with a lovely smell. 29 Many Israelite men and women wanted to offer gifts. They were happy to bring these gifts to the Lord. Moses needed these gifts to make everything for the Lord. That was because the Lord had commanded the Israelites to make all these things.

Bezalel and Oholiab

30 Then Moses said to the Israelites: 'Look! The Lord has chosen Bezalel, who is the son of Uri, and the grandson of Hur. He belongs to the big family of Judah. 31 The Lord has filled him with the Spirit of God and has made him very wise. He knows how to make many different things. 32 He can make beautiful things out of gold, silver and bronze. 33 He can cut and fix valuable stones. He can make things from wood. And everything that he makes is beautiful.

34 Bezalel and Oholiab are both wise men who can teach other people. Oholiab is the son of Ahisamach, from the big family of Dan. And the Lord has made them both wise teachers. 35 The Lord has given them very wise minds that are full of good ideas. They draw plans of beautiful things, and then they make them. They use many different materials to make lovely things. And they are both masters at their work.'

Chapter 36

1 Then Moses said: 'So Bezalel and Oholiab will do the work that the Lord has commanded. And every person that the Lord has made wise will work with them. They will build the Holy Place that the Lord has commanded.'

2 Then Moses brought together Bezalel, Oholiab and every wise person who enjoyed work. These were people that the Lord had prepared. 3 They received from Moses all the gifts that the Israelites had brought. They would use these gifts to build the Holy Place. And the Israelites continued to bring gifts every morning. 4 Then the wise workers who were building the Holy Place left the work. They went to Moses and they said: 5 'The people are bringing more gifts than we need for the Tent of Meeting. This is what the Lord has commanded us to do.'

6 Then Moses gave a command and he sent it round the whole camp. He said: 'No man or woman must offer anything more for the Holy Place.' So Moses did not let the Israelites bring any more gifts. 7 The workers already had more gifts than they needed.

The tabernacle

8 All the wise workers made the tabernacle with ten curtains of soft white material. The same wise people used blue, purple and red cotton to make pictures of angels in the curtains. 9 All the curtains were the same size. They were 12½ metres long and 1¾ metres wide. 10 The workers fixed five of the curtains to make one large curtain. Then they did the same thing with the other five curtains. 11 They made 50 rings of blue material along the edge of the last curtain in each set. 12 These rings were opposite each other. 13 Then they made 50 small pieces of gold to fix each pair of rings. So they fastened the two sets of curtains each to the other and the tabernacle became one thing.

14 The workers made 11 curtains out of goats' hair for a tent to cover the tabernacle.

15 The 11 curtains were all the same size. They were 13½ metres long and 1¾ metres wide. 16 They fastened five of the curtains into one set and six of the curtains into another set. 17 Then they made 50 rings of material along the edge of the last curtain in each set. 18 They made 50 small pieces of bronze to fasten the tent, as one thing. 19 Then they used red sheep skins to cover the tent. And they used badger skins to cover the sheep skins.

20 For the tabernacle, the workers made boards that stood up. They made them out of acacia wood. 21 Each board was 4½ metres long and ¾ of a metre wide. 22 Each board had two extra pieces at one end to join them together. They made all the boards for the tabernacle like this.

23 They made 20 boards for the south side of the tabernacle. 24 And they made 40 pieces of silver with a hole in each one. There were two pieces of silver for each board, one piece under each extra piece of wood. 25 For the north side of the tabernacle they made 20 boards 26 and 40 pieces of silver, two pieces under each board.

27 They made six boards for the west end of the tabernacle. 28 And they made two boards for the corners of the tabernacle, at the far end. 29 At these two corners, they fixed the boards each one to the next, at both ends. They used a ring to fix them. They made both corners the same. 30 So there were 8 boards and 16 pieces of silver, two pieces under each board.

31-32 They also cut pieces of acacia wood to fix across the boards of the tabernacle. They cut five pieces for the boards on one side and five pieces for the boards on the other side. Then they cut five pieces for the boards on the west, at the far end of the tabernacle. 33 They cut a piece of wood for the centre to reach from end to end of the tabernacle. Then they fixed this at the middle of the boards. 34 Then they covered the boards with gold and they made gold rings. These rings held the pieces of wood that they fixed across the boards. They also covered the pieces of wood with gold.

35 The workers made the curtain out of blue, purple, red and soft white material. A wise man put into the curtain a picture of angels. 36 They made four sticks out of acacia wood for the curtain and they covered them with gold. They made gold rings for the sticks and pieces of silver for the sticks to stand in. There was a hole in each piece of silver. 37 They made a curtain for the door of the tent. A person who could do wise work with material made the curtain. This person used blue, purple, red and soft white material. 38 They made five sticks for this curtain and they fixed gold rings to them. They covered the sticks with gold. Then they made five pieces of bronze to hold them.

Chapter 37

The Ark

1 Bezalel made the Ark out of acacia wood. It was one metre long, ¾ of a metre wide and ¾ of a metre high. 2 He covered it with gold, inside and outside, and then he built up the edges with gold. 3 He made four gold rings for it and fastened them to its four feet. He fixed two rings on one side and two rings on the other side. 4 Then he made sticks out of acacia wood and he covered them with gold. 5 He pushed the sticks into the rings on the sides of the Ark, to carry it.

6 He made the special lid for the Ark out of gold. It was one metre long and ¾ of a metre wide. 7 Then he made two angels from gold that he had hit with a hammer. He made these at the two ends of the lid. 8 He made one angel on each end of the lid. The angels were part of the lid so it was one whole piece. 9 The angels' wings pointed to the sky and they made a shadow over the lid. Each angel's face looked toward the other angel, and toward the lid.

The table

10 They made the table out of acacia wood. It was one metre long, ½ metre wide and ¾ of a metre high. 11 They covered it with gold and they built up the edges with gold. 12 They also put an extra edge of gold round it, 7 centimetres wide. 13 Then they made four gold rings for the table. They fastened the rings to the four corners, one by each leg of the table. 14 They put the rings near to the extra edge of gold. These rings would hold the sticks to carry the table. 15 They made the sticks out of acacia wood and they covered them with gold. 16 Then they made gold things to use at the table. They made plates and spoons and dishes. And they made pots and jars to pour out gifts of drink.

The lampstand

17 The workers made the lampstand out of gold. They used a hammer to make it the right shape. They made its cups like open flowers and like flowers that are not yet open. The whole lampstand was one piece. 18 They made six branches on the lampstand, three branches on each side of it. 19 They put three cups like flowers on each of the six branches of the lampstand.

20 On the lampstand itself, they put four cups like almond flowers. Some of the flowers were open but some were not yet open. 21 They put one flower, not yet open, under the first pair of branches.

They put a second flower, not yet open, under the second pair of branches. They put a third flower, not yet open, under the third pair of branches. There were six branches on the lampstand. 22 They made the flowers and the branches from the same piece of gold as the lampstand. And they used a hammer to make the gold into the right shape.

23 They made the seven lamps out of gold. They also made small tools out of gold to clean the lamps. 24They made the lampstand and all its tools from 34 kilos of gold.

The altar for incense

25 They made the altar for incense from acacia wood. It was square, ½ a metre long, ½ a metre wide and one metre high. Its horns were part of it, one whole piece. 26 They covered every part of the altar with gold. Then they made a gold edge round it. 27 They made two gold rings for the altar, below the edge, on opposite sides. They would hold the sticks, to carry the altar. 28 They made the sticks out of acacia wood and they covered them with gold.

29 They also made the special oil that makes things holy and the incense with a lovely smell. This was the work of a wise chemist.

Chapter 38

The altar where you will burn animals as gifts

1 The workers built the altar where Israelites would burn animals as gifts. They made it out of acacia wood. It was 1¼ metres high and the top was square. The top was 2¼ metres long and 2¼ metres wide. 2They made a horn at each corner. The four horns and the altar were all one whole piece. Then they covered the altar with bronze. 3 They made all its tools out of bronze. They made pots to remove the ashes. They made spades, dishes and forks for the meat. They made buckets out of metal, to carry the fire.

4 They made a net out of bronze and they fixed it under the altar. It was between the top and the ground. 5They made rings out of bronze to hold the sticks for the four corners of the net. 6 They made the sticks out of acacia wood and they covered them with bronze. 7 They put the sticks into the rings on each side of the altar, to carry it. The altar was empty because the workers made it with boards.

8 Then they made a very large dish for water from bronze. And they made a special piece of bronze for the pot to stand on. They used the bronze from many small mirrors to make these things. The women who were servants at the Tent of Meeting gave these mirrors.

The yard

9 The next thing that they made was the yard. The south side of the yard was 46 metres long. It had curtains that they had made out of soft white material. 10 For these curtains, there were 20 sticks and 20 pieces of bronze with holes in them. They put the sticks in the holes. There were also small pieces of silver and rings on the sticks. These were to fasten the curtains. 11 The north side of the yard was also 46 metres long. It also had curtains with sticks, and things to fasten them, each one to the other.

12 The west end of the yard was 23 metres wide. It had curtains with 10 sticks that they put into 10 pieces of bronze. On the sticks were silver pieces and rings. 13 The east end of the yard looked toward the sunrise and it was 23 metres wide. 14 The workers made curtains, 7 metres long. They hung these on one side of the open space in front of the yard. They hung the curtains on three sticks that they put on three pieces of bronze. 15 On the other side of the open space they did the same thing. 16 They made all the curtains round the yard out of soft white material.

17 All the sticks stood on pieces of bronze. All the pieces of metal and the rings on the sticks were silver. They covered the tops of the sticks with silver also. So all the sticks in the yard had silver rings.

18 The curtain at the open space of the yard was blue, purple, red and soft white material. A person who could do wise work with cloth made the curtain. It was 9 metres long and 2¼ metres wide.

The curtains of the yard were also 2¼ metres wide. 19 The curtain had four sticks that the workers put on four pieces of bronze. On the sticks were pieces of silver and rings. And they covered the tops of the sticks with silver. 20They made small, sharp pieces of bronze to fix the tabernacle and the yard to the ground.

The workers used these materials

21 The workers used these amounts of materials when they made the tabernacle of witness. Moses commanded Ithamar, son of Aaron the priest, to write down these amounts. And Ithamar caused the Levites to write them down. 22 Bezalel, the son of Uri and grandson of Hur, made everything that the Lord commanded Moses. Bezalel was from the big family of Judah and Oholiab worked with him. 23 Oholiab was the son of Ahisamach, from the big family of Dan. He was a very wise worker who could draw good plans. He also made beautiful pictures on cloth, with blue, purple and red materials. And he worked with soft white material.

24 The workers used 994½ kilos of gold to do all the work of the Holy Place. This gold was offered as a gift by the Israelites.

25 All those Israelites that Moses had counted had given gifts of silver. They had given about 3600 kilos of silver. 26 Each person who was 20 years old or more had given about 6 grams. Moses had counted the people and there were 603 550 men.

27 The workers used much of the silver to make the bases for the Holy Place and for the curtains. They needed 34 kilos of silver to make each base. 28 Then they used the silver that they had not used before. With this, they made the pieces and the rings to fasten the curtains to the sticks. They also used this silver to cover the tops of the sticks.

29 The amount of bronze that the Israelites gave was about 2500 kilos. 30 The workers used it to make the bases for the open space in the Tent of Meeting. They also used the bronze to make the bronze altar, the net and all the tools. 31 They made the bases for the yard that was round the Tent of Meeting and for its open space. They made the small sharp pieces of metal to fix the tabernacle and the yard to the ground. They made all these things out of bronze that the Israelites had given.

Chapter 39

The clothes for the priests

1 The workers made clothes from blue, purple and red material. These clothes were for the priests. They would wear them when they worked in the Holy Place. The workers also made holy clothes for Aaron, as the Lord commanded Moses.

The ephod

2 The workers made the ephod out of gold and out of blue, purple and red material. They also used soft white material. 3 They used a hammer to make gold into very thin pieces. Then they cut the thin pieces into long, thin pieces like hairs. A wise man took these gold hairs and he put them into the special material for the ephod. 4 The workers made pieces for the shoulders of the ephod. They fixed these to two of its corners, to fasten it.

5 They made the beautiful belt for the ephod completely out of the same materials. The belt and the ephod were one whole piece, as the Lord commanded Moses.

0 The workers fixed the onyx stones into thin circles of gold. They used a sharp tool to write on them the names of the sons of Israel. 7 Then they fastened them to the shoulder pieces of the ephod. They would cause all the people to remember the sons of Israel.
The Lord had commanded Moses to do this.

The breast piece

8 A very wise worker made the breast piece. He made it like the ephod, out of the same materials. 9 They bent the cloth to make it a square, 22 centimetres long and 22 centimetres wide.

10 Then they fixed four sets of valuable stones on it. The first set was a ruby, a topaz and a beryl. 11 The second set was a turquoise, a sapphire and an emerald. 12 The third set was a jacinth, an agate and an amethyst. 13 The fourth set was a chrysolite, an onyx and a jasper. They fixed each stone in a thin piece of gold that they had made beautiful. 14 They used 12 stones, one for each of Israel's sons. On each stone, they used a sharp tool to write the name of one son.

15 For the breast piece, they made thin lines of gold and they put them together. They made two chains of gold like this. 16 Then they made two gold rings and two thin pieces of gold that they made beautiful. They fastened the rings to two corners of the breast piece. 17 And they fastened the two gold chains to the rings at the corners of the breast piece. 18 They fastened the other ends of the chains to the beautiful gold pieces. They tied them to the shoulder pieces of the ephod, at the front.

19 They made two more gold rings and they fixed them to the other corners of the breast piece. These were on the inside edge, next to the ephod. 20 Then they made two more gold rings. They fixed these to the edge of the shoulder pieces, on the front of the ephod. They put the rings near to the ephod's belt, a short way above it. 21 They tied the rings of the breast piece to the rings of the ephod with a line of blue cotton. They fastened the breast piece to the belt so that they would not become separate. The workers made all these things as the Lord had commanded Moses.

The other clothes for the priests

22 The workers made the robe of the ephod completely out of blue cloth. A man who made many different materials made this cloth.

23 There was a hole in the centre of the robe, like the hole of a collar. The worker fixed a piece of material round the hole so that it would not tear. 24 They made pomegranates out of blue, purple and red materials and out of soft white material. Then they fixed them to the lower edge of the robe. 25 And they made bells out of gold and they fixed them between the pomegranates. 26 So there was a bell and a pomegranate, another bell and another pomegranate, round the whole lower edge of the robe. The priest must wear this robe when he worked for the Lord. This was the Lord's command to Moses.

27 The workers made tunics out of soft white material for Aaron and his sons. This cloth was the work of a man who made many different materials. 28 They made a turban out of the same material and they made hats and trousers also. 29 A wise worker made the long belt. He put blue, purple and red lines of cloth on soft white material to make the long belt. The Lord told Moses that he must do this.

30 The workers made a thin plate, a holy thing, out of gold. They wrote on it with a sharp tool these words: HOLY TO THE LORD. 31 Then they fastened a line of blue cotton to the plate, to tie it to the turban. The Lord told Moses that he must do this.

Moses checks the tabernacle

32 So the workers finished making everything for the tabernacle, the Tent of Meeting. The Israelites made everything completely as the Lord commanded Moses. 33 Then they brought the tabernacle to Moses. They brought the tent and all the things that were in it. They brought the boards, the sticks, the bases and all the things that fastened it together. 34 They brought the different things that covered the tent and also the curtains. 35 They brought the Ark of the Covenant with its sticks and its special gold lid. 36 They brought the table with all its tools and the special bread. This bread showed that God was with the Israelites.

37 They brought the gold lampstand with its lamps and all its tools and the oil for the light. 38 They brought the gold altar, the special oil, the incense and the curtain for the door of the tent. 39 They brought the bronze altar with all its tools and its sticks. They brought the very large dish for water and its base. 40 They brought all the curtains that they had made for the yard and for its open space. They brought all the tools to fasten the yard to the ground. They brought everything that they had made for the tabernacle, the Tent of Meeting.

41 They also brought the clothes that they had made for the priests. There were the holy clothes that Aaron the priest would wear and the clothes for his sons. They would wear these clothes when they worked as servants of the Lord.

42 The Israelites had done all the work completely as the Lord had commanded Moses. 43 Moses was careful to check all the work. And they had done it completely as the Lord had commanded. Moses saw this and he blessed the Israelites.

Chapter 40

Moses erects the tabernacle

1 Then the Lord said to Moses: 2 'Erect the tabernacle, the Tent of Meeting, on the first day of the first month. 3 Put the Ark of the Covenant in the tabernacle and hide the Ark behind its curtain. 4 Bring in the table and put its own things on it. Then bring in the lampstand and fix its lamps on it. 5 Put the gold altar for incense in front of the Ark of the Covenant. Fix the curtain as a door to the tabernacle.

6 Put the altar, where you will burn animals as gifts, in front of the door. 7 Put the very large dish for water between the Tent of Meeting and the altar and put water in it. 8 Erect the yard round the tent and fix the curtain as a door to the yard.

9 Take the special oil and pour a little of it on the tabernacle and on everything in it. Offer the tabernacle to the Lord with all its things, and then it will be holy. 10 Then pour a little of the special oil on the altar where you will burn animals. Do the same thing to all its tools. Offer it all to the Lord, and then it will be very holy. 11 Pour a little oil on the very large dish for water and on its base and offer them to the Lord.

12 Bring Aaron and his sons to the door of the Tent of Meeting and wash them with water.

13 Then dress Aaron in the holy clothes and pour a little oil on his head. Bring him then to me so that he can work for me as a priest. 14 Bring his sons and dress them in tunics. 15 Pour a little oil on their heads as you did to their father. Then they too can work for me as priests. This special work will be their own for their whole lives. Their sons and grandsons will also be priests. This is a special gift to the family of Aaron for all time.' 16 Moses did everything that the Lord commanded him.

17 So they erected the tabernacle on the first day of the first month. This happened in the second year of the Israelites' journey through the desert. 18 When Moses erected the tabernacle, he put all the different parts in the right places. 19 Then he covered the tabernacle with the tent. He covered the tent also, as the Lord commanded him.

20 Moses took the Testimony and he put it in the Ark. He fastened the sticks to the Ark and he put the special lid over it. 21 Then he brought the Ark into the tabernacle and put the curtain in front of it. So he hid the Ark of the Covenant, as the Lord commanded him.

22 Moses put the table in the Tent of Meeting, on the north side, outside the curtain. 23 He put the bread on the table in front of the Lord, as the Lord commanded him.

24 He put the lampstand in the Tent of Meeting. He put it on the south side, on the opposite side to the table. 25 He erected the lamps in front of the Lord, as the Lord commanded him.

26 Moses put the gold altar in the Tent of Meeting, in front of the curtain. 27 He burned sweet incense on it, as the Lord commanded him. 28 Then he fixed the curtain as a door for the tabernacle.

29 He put the altar, where they would burn animals as gifts, by the door of the tabernacle. He offered on it animals and food as gifts, as the Lord had commanded him.

30 Moses put the very large dish for water between the Tent of Meeting and the altar. He put water in it. 31 Then Moses and Aaron and Aaron's sons used it to wash their hands and their feet. 32 They washed themselves each time that they went into the Tent of Meeting. They also washed themselves before they went to the altar.
The Lord had commanded Moses about this.

33 Then Moses erected the yard round the tabernacle and round the altar. He fixed the curtain to make a door for the yard. And so Moses finished the work.

The glory of the Lord

34 Then the cloud covered the Tent of Meeting. The glory of the Lord filled the tabernacle. 35 Moses could not go into the Tent of Meeting because the cloud covered it. And the glory of the Lord filled the tabernacle.

36 The Israelites followed the cloud during all their journeys. Every time that the cloud rose up from the tabernacle, they would begin their journey again. 37 But if the cloud remained on the tabernacle, the Israelites did not move. They stayed where they were. They stayed there until the day when the cloud rose up. 38 So the cloud of the Lord was over the tabernacle during the day. During the night, there was fire in the cloud. And all the Israelites could see the cloud during all their journeys.

Gifts to God

Leviticus

About Leviticus

> The Lord is showing Israel's people that he is holy. He is showing them how they must live to stay near to him.
>
> The Lord chose Moses to guide Israel's people out of Egypt. Israel's people were slaves in Egypt for 400 years. Aaron was the brother of Moses. He was the first priest that God gave to Israel's people.

Chapter 1

The Lord's rules for the people's gifts to him

1 The Lord spoke to Moses from the Tent of Meeting. He told him the rules that Israel's people must obey. 2 The Lord said, 'Speak to Israel's people. Tell them this. When a person gives an animal to the Lord, it must be a cow or a sheep or a goat. 3 A person may want to give a gift to the Lord. That gift must be a male animal from his group of animals. It must be perfect. He must burn the whole animal as a gift to the Lord. The person must bring it to the door of the Tent of Meeting. If he does, the Lord will accept his gift. 4 The person must put his hand on the animal's head. Then he must kill it. The animal's death will pay for the person's sins. 5 The person must kill the young male cow in front of the Lord. The priests who are the sons of Aaron will take the blood. They will throw it on to the sides of the altar. That is the altar near to the door of the Tent of Meeting. 6 The person must take the skin from the dead animal and then he must cut up the meat. 7 The sons of Aaron the priest will light a fire on the altar. Then they will put wood on it. 8 The priests will put the pieces of meat on the fire. They will put the head and the fat on the fire with the meat. 9 The person must wash the legs and the inside parts with water. Then the priest will burn the whole animal on the altar. The smell of it while it is burning will give the Lord pleasure.

10 A person may want to give a sheep or a goat to the Lord. It must be a male animal. It must be perfect. 11 The person must kill it at the north side of the altar. The priests will throw the blood on to the sides of the altar. 12 The person must cut the animal up. The priests will take the pieces of meat, the head and the fat. They will put them on the fire that is burning on the altar. 13 The person must wash the legs and the inside parts with water. The priest will burn the whole animal on the altar. It is a burnt offering to the Lord. The smell of it while it is burning will give the Lord pleasure.

Moses tells Israel's people what to do with gifts that are birds

14 If a person wants to give a bird to the Lord, it must be a dove or a pigeon. 15 The priest will bring the bird to the altar. He will tear off the head and he will burn it on the altar. The priest will pour the blood on to the side of the altar. 16 Then the priest will remove the part of the bird where the food is stored. He will throw it on the east side of the altar, with the ashes. 17 He will hold the parts that the bird uses to fly. And then he will tear open the body. But he must not tear it completely. He will burn all of it on the fire that is on the altar. The smell of it while it is burning will give the Lord pleasure.

Chapter 2

Moses tells Israel's people what to do with gifts that are grain

1 A person may want to give grain as a gift to the Lord. He must make it into flour. He must put oil and incense on the flour. 2 He must take it to Aaron's sons, the priests. The priest will take some of the flour and oil and all the incense in his hand. He will burn them on the altar as a gift to the Lord. The smell of them while they are burning will give the Lord pleasure. 3 The flour that he did not burn is for the priests. It is very holy. That is because it is part of an offering to the Lord.

4 A person must not use yeast if he bakes his gift of grain. He must make cakes or biscuits with flour and oil. 5 He must not use yeast if he cooks his cake on a flat plate. He must make it with flour and oil. 6 He must break the cake into pieces. He must pour oil on it. It is a gift to the Lord. 7 A person must use flour and oil to cook the cake in a pot. 8 He must give the cake to the priest. The priest will take it to the altar. 9 He will take a piece of it and he will burn it in the fire. It is a gift to the Lord. The smell of it while it is burning will give the Lord pleasure. 10 The part of the cake that he did not burn is for the priests. That is because it is most holy, part of a burnt offering to the Lord.

11 A person must not use yeast when he gives a gift of grain to the Lord. He must not give yeast or honey for the priests to burn as gifts to the Lord. 12 He can give them as the first part of his harvest. He must not burn them on the fire. He cannot use them to give the Lord pleasure. 13 A person must put salt in all his gifts of grain. Salt is a mark of the Lord's promise to Israel's people.

14 A person may want to give the first part of his harvest to the Lord. He must break the grains into pieces and he must cook them in a fire. 15 They are a gift to the Lord, so he must put oil and incense on them. 16 The priest will burn a part of the grain with all the incense. It is a burnt offering to the Lord.

Chapter 3

Moses tells Israel's people what to do with their gifts for the Lord

1 A person might want to give a fellowship gift to the Lord. He must take a perfect animal from his group of animals. The animal can be male or female. 2 The person must put his hand on the animal's head. Then he must kill it at the door of the Tent of Meeting. Aaron's sons the priests will throw the blood on to the sides of the altar. 3 The person must burn some pieces of the animal as a gift to the Lord. It is a fellowship offering. 4 He must bring all the fat from inside the animal. And he must bring the kidneys with their fat and the best piece of the liver. 5 The priests, Aaron's sons, will take the pieces. They must put them on top of the gift on the altar. The smell of them while they are burning will give the Lord pleasure.

6 If a person wants to give a sheep to the Lord as a fellowship gift, it must be perfect. The person can give a male animal or a female animal to the Lord. 7 If it is a young sheep he must offer it to the Lord. 8 He must put his hand on its head. Then he must kill it at the front of the Tent of Meeting. Aaron's sons will throw the blood on to the sides of the altar. 9 The person must cut the tail off the animal. He must give the tail and all the fat from inside the body to the Lord. 10 He must also give the kidneys and the best piece of the liver. 11 The priest will burn them as food on the altar. They are a burnt offering to the Lord.

12 A person may offer a goat to the Lord. 13 The person must put his hand on the goat's head. Then he must kill it at the front of the Tent of Meeting. Then Aaron's sons will throw the blood on to the sides of the altar. 14 The person must take all of the fat round the inside parts. He must give it to the Lord for a burnt offering. 15 He must also give the kidneys with the fat on them and the best piece of the liver. 16 The priest will burn them as food on the altar. The smell of them while they are burning will give the Lord pleasure.

17 Israel's people must not eat any fat or drink any blood. This rule is for them and for their children everywhere. They must obey this rule always.'

Chapter 4

Offerings for sins that people did not really want to do

1 The Lord said to Moses, 2 'Say to Israel's people, "A man may sin, when he did not really want to sin. This is what that person must do.

3 If the man is a priest, his sins will cause the people to sin. He must bring a young bull (male cow) as a gift to the Lord. 4 The priest must bring the young bull to the door of the Tent of Meeting. He must put his hand on the animal's head and then he must kill it.

5 The priest must carry some of the blood into the Tent of Meeting. 6 He must put his finger in the blood. He must shake it in front of the holy curtain seven times in front of the Lord. 7 He must put some of the blood on the corners of the incense altar. The priest must pour the blood that he did not use on to the floor in front of the altar. That altar is near the door inside the Tent of Meeting. 8 He must cut all the fat from inside the dead animal. 9 He must also cut out the kidneys and the best piece of the liver. He must take them from inside the animal. 10 He must burn the fat on the altar. The priest does this when the people give a fellowship offering to the Lord. 11 He must take up the skin and all the meat. He must take the head, the legs and all the inside pieces. He must include the stomach. 12 The priest must take all the pieces to a clean place outside the camp. He must put them on the ashes and he must burn them on a wood fire.

13 All of the people might do bad things when they did not really want to do them. They might not obey some of the Lord's rules. They will have sinned, even if they did not know this. 14 When they do know about it they must bring a young bull (male cow) to the Tent of Meeting. The animal is a sin offering to the Lord. 15 The leaders of the people must put their hands on the young bull's head and then they must kill it.

16 The priest will take some of the blood into the Tent of Meeting. 17 He will put his finger in the blood. He must shake it in front of the holy curtain seven times.

18 He will take some of the blood. Then he will put it on the corners of the altar that is in front of the Lord. He will pour the blood that he did not use on to the floor. He must pour it in front of the burnt offering altar. This altar is in front of the Tent of Meeting. 19 The priest will cut all of the fat from the dead animal. And he will burn all the fat on the altar of burnt offering. 20 He will do with this bull what he did with the bull for the sin offering. This is how the priest will atone (pay) for the sins of the people. The Lord will forgive them when the priest does this. 21 The priest will take the dead animal outside the camp. He will put it on the ashes from the altar fire. He will burn the animal as he did the first bull. This is the sin offering for all the people.

22 A leader might do bad things when he did not really want to do them. He has sinned if he does not obey one of the Lord's rules. 23 People will tell him that he has done wrong things. So then he must give a male goat to the Lord. The animal must be perfect. 24 He must put his hand on the goat's head and then he must kill it. He must do this where they kill animals for the burnt offering. It is an offering for sin. 25 The priest will put his finger in the blood of the dead animal. He will put some of it on the altar's corners. He will pour the blood that he did not use on to the ground. He will pour it in front of the altar. 26 Then the priest will cut all of the fat from the goat. And he will burn it on the altar. He will do this as he did for the fellowship offering. This is how the priest will make atonement for the leader's sin. Then the Lord will I forgive the leader.

27 One of the people might do bad things when he did not really want to do them. He did not obey one of the Lord's rules. That person has sinned. 28 They will tell him that he has done bad things. Then he must give a female goat to the Lord. The animal must be perfect. 29 He must put his hand on the goat's head. Then he must kill it by the altar of burnt offering. 30 The priest will put his finger in the blood of the goat. He will put some of it on the altar's corners. He will pour out the blood that he did not use. He will pour it on to the ground in front of the altar. 31 The priest will cut all the fat from the goat as he did with the fellowship offering. And he will burn it on the altar. This will make atonement for the wrong things that the person has done. The smell of it while it is burning will give the Lord pleasure. Then the Lord will forgive the person.

32 If a person wants to give a young sheep to the Lord, it must be a female. It must be perfect. 33 He must put his hand on the animal's head. He will kill it at the altar of burnt offering. 34 The priest will put his finger in the blood of the sheep. He will take some of it. And he will put it on the corners of the altar. He will pour the blood that he did not use on the ground in front of the altar. 35 The priest will cut all the fat from the sheep as he did with the fellowship offering. He will burn it on the altar. He must burn it on top of the burnt offerings. This is how the priest will make atonement for the person's sin. Then the Lord will forgive the person.

Chapter 5

Sins for which people must give an offering

1 A person may know about something that is wrong. He may not speak about it at a public meeting. That person is sinning.

2 The Lord has said that some animals and insects are not clean. A person may touch a dead animal or an insect like that. If he does, he is doing something wrong. It is a sin even if he did not really want to touch it.

3 A person may touch something that another person has made bad. If he does, he is doing something wrong. He might not know that it is bad. But he is still doing a wrong thing.

4 A person is doing a wrong thing if he says any careless promise. The promise might be good or bad. People will tell him that he has not obeyed God's rules. Then he will know that he has sinned.

5 A person must tell the priest if he has done any of these things. 6 He must give a sheep or a goat for a sin offering. Then the Lord will not be angry with him. The priest will kill the animal as a sacrifice to atone for that sin.

What the people should do if they do not have much money

7 A person may not have money to buy a sheep or a goat. If he does not, he must buy two doves or two pigeons. He must give them to the Lord. One bird will be an offering for wrong things that he has done. The second bird will be for a burnt offering.

8 The priest will bring one of the birds to the altar. It is the offering for sin. He will break the neck of the bird, but he will not pull the head off. 9 He will shake some of the blood on to the side of the altar. He will pour the blood that he did not shake on to the floor. He must pour it in front of the altar. 10 The priest will burn the other bird. The Lord will not be angry with the man when the priest does this.

11 A person may not have money to buy two doves or two pigeons. If he does not, he must give a tenth (1/10th) of an ephah (about two litres or 4 pints) of flour to the Lord. He must not put oil or incense on the flour because it is a sin offering. 12 He must take it to the priest. The priest will burn some of the flour on the altar as a special part of the flour. It is a sin offering. 13 The Lord will forgive the person when the priest does this. The flour that he did not burn is like the grain offering. It belongs to the priests." '

The gift to the Lord when a person does wrong things

14 The Lord said to Moses, 15 'If a person does not obey the Lord's holy rules he is sinning. He must give a male sheep to the Lord. He must do this even if he did not know that he had sinned. It is a gift to the Lord to pay for his sins. It must be a perfect male animal. It must be worth the correct amount of money. 16 He must also give money worth one fifth (1/5th) more. The person must give the sheep and the money to the priest. The priest will sacrifice the sheep to the Lord. It is an atonement for the wrong things that the person has done. The Lord will forgive the person.

17 A person might do wrong things. But he might not know that they were wrong. He is sinning. 18 When he knows about it, he must bring a sheep to the priest. The animal must be a perfect male. The sheep must be worth the right amount of money. The priest will give the sheep to the Lord. It will be an atonement for the wrong things that the person has done. Then the Lord will forgive the person. 19 The sheep is an offering because the person did not obey the Lord.'

Chapter 6

1 The Lord said to Moses, 2 'A person may take something that is not his. Or he may find it and keep it. He may tell his friend that he has not taken it. He might not give him the correct price for something. But then he is not obeying God. 3 A person may speak words that are not true. That is a sin. A person may keep something that belongs to another person. He does not give it back. That is a wrong thing to do. He might find something. And then he might say that it is his. If it is not his, he is not obeying God. 4 He has done something that is wrong. So, he must show that he is sorry. He must give back anything that is not his. He must give back anything that he has found. He must give back anything that he has kept. He must give it to the person to whom it belongs. 5 He must give back everything and one fifth (1/5th) more. He must also, on the same day, give a gift to the Lord. 6 He must bring a sheep to the priest. The sheep must be a perfect male animal. The sheep must be worth the right amount of money. 7 The priest will give the sheep to the Lord. It is an atonement for the wrong things that the person has done. Then the Lord will forgive the person.'

Rules for the priests

8 The Lord said to Moses, 9 'Tell Aaron and his sons my rules. They must burn these gifts for the Lord on the altar. The fire must burn all night. 10 When the morning comes, the priest must dress himself in his linen clothes. The linen must be next to his skin. He must take the ashes from the fire and he must put them at the side of the altar. 11 Then he must dress himself in other clothes. He must carry the ashes outside the camp and he must put them in a special place. 12 The fire that is on the altar must never stop burning. Every morning the priest must put wood on it. He must also put on it the gifts and the fat of the fellowship offerings. 13 The fire must always burn. It must not go out.

14 These are the rules for the gift of grain. Aaron's sons must bring it in front of the altar to give to the Lord. 15 A priest must take some of the flour and oil. He must mix this special part with incense and he must burn all of it on the altar. The smell of them while they are burning will give the Lord pleasure. 16 The priests will make into bread the flour that he did not burn. They must not use yeast to make the bread. They must eat the bread in the holy place, in the yard outside the Tent of Meeting. 17 The bread is for the priests because it is a holy part of a gift for the Lord. It is holy, like the offerings for sin. And it is like the gifts when somebody does anything wrong. 18 Any son, grandson or male of Aaron's family can eat the bread. It is his usual part of the burnt offerings to the Lord. A person who touches the bread will become holy.'

19 The Lord said to Moses, 20 'When Aaron is anointed, Aaron and his sons must give an offering to the Lord. It must be a 10th of an ephah (about two litres or 4 pints) of best flour. They must bring half of it in the morning and half of it in the evening. 21 They must mix it with oil and they must cook it on a flat plate. Then they must break it into pieces and they must offer it to the Lord. The smell of it will give the Lord pleasure. 22 The son whom they will anoint to take Aaron's place must prepare the offering. 23 All of the gifts that the priests give to the Lord must be burnt completely. Nobody should eat them.'

The offering for sin

24 The Lord said to Moses, 25 'Tell Aaron and his sons this rule. When a person does wrong things he must give an animal to the Lord. The animal will be holy. The person must kill the animal at the north side of the altar. That is where they kill the offerings for sin. 26 The priest who offered it will eat his part of the gift in a holy place. That is the yard outside the Tent of Meeting. 27 If anyone or anything touches the meat they will become holy. If the blood touches the clothes of a person, he must wash them in a holy place. 28 If a person cooks the meat in a clay pot, he must break the pot. He must break it when he has cooked the meat. If a person cooks the meat in a metal pot, he must wash the pot. He must wash it well when he has cooked the meat. And he must wash it again with clean water. 29 The meat is holy. Only the priests' sons can eat it. 30 They must take the blood of a sin offering into the Tent of Meeting. It is a sacrifice to atone for sin. Nobody should eat any of that offering. The priest must burn it.

Chapter 7

1 These are the rules for a most holy offering. A person may be sorry for the wrong things that he has done. That person must obey these rules. 2 The priest must kill an animal at the north side of the altar. He must throw the blood on to the sides of the altar. 3 The priest will bring all of the fat from the tail and the inside parts to the altar. 4 He will bring the kidneys and the best piece of the liver. 5 Then he will burn the pieces on the altar. They are a gift to the Lord to make a person clean from sin. 6 Aaron's sons can eat the meat that is not burnt. They must eat it in a holy place because it is most holy.

7 The rules are the same for sacrifices for sin and for a person who is sorry for his sins. The gifts of meat are for the priest who brings them to the altar. 8 The skin of the animal is for the priest. 9 People may give gifts of grain that they cooked over a fire or in a closed flat plate. They should give them all to the priest. 10 Grain that is dry is also a gift. And grain that a man mixes with oil is also a gift. They should give them to Aaron's sons.

The Fellowship Offering

11 These rules are for special gifts (fellowship offerings) to the Lord. 12 If a man wants to thank the Lord, he must give an animal and flat loaves of bread. He must mix the flour for the bread with oil. He must not mix the flour with yeast.

13 He must also give other loaves of bread to the Lord. He must make these with flour, oil and yeast. 14 A man must offer one of each kind of loaf to the Lord. These belong to the priest who throws the blood on the altar. 15 The person must not keep the meat from the animal until the next day. He must eat it on the day that he offers it.

16 The gift to the Lord may be for a promise. The gift may be because the person loves the Lord. That person will not have to eat it all on the same day. He can eat some of it on the next day. 17 On the third day, there may still be some meat that he has not eaten. If there is, he must burn it. 18 If the person eats the meat on the third day, the Lord will not accept the gift. The meat is not good. The person who eats it will not give the Lord pleasure.

19 Some meat may touch something that is not clean. Nobody should eat that meat. People must burn it. Only a clean person can eat the meat that is a gift to the Lord. 20 A person who is not clean might eat the fellowship offering. If he does, they must send him away from Israel's people. 21 A person might touch something that is not clean. That person must not eat the meat. He must not eat it if he has touched an unclean animal or an unclean person. If he does eat it, they must send him away. They must send him away from Israel's people.'

Israel's people must not eat blood or fat

22 The Lord said to Moses, 23 'Tell Israel's people this. They must not eat the fat from sheep, cows or goats. 24 A person can use the fat of a dead animal that he has found. But he must not eat it.

25 They must not eat the fat of an animal that they have burnt as a gift on the Lord's altar. They must send away from the Lord's people anyone who does eat it. 26 You must not eat the blood of an animal or of a bird even if you are living in another country. 27 You must send away from Israel's people any person who eats blood.'

Moses tells the priests which parts of the animal they can eat

28 The Lord said to Moses, 29 'Say to Israel's people, "When a person gives an animal as a fellowship offering, he must bring part of it to the Lord. 30 He must carry the offering in his own hands to the fire. He must bring the fat and the breast and he must lift the breast to the Lord. 31 The priest will burn the fat at the altar. He will lift the meat of the breast to the Lord. Then Aaron's sons can eat it. 32 The top part of the back right leg of the animal is a gift. 33 It is for the priest who offers the blood and the fat. 34 The breast and the top part of the right leg are gifts. They are from the fellowship offering. The Lord wants Aaron and his sons to have them. People must give these parts of the Lord's gift to the priests. 35 The Lord gave this part of the Israelites' offerings to Aaron's sons. He gave it to them on the day when they became priests. 36 The Lord told the Israelites that they must do this. He told them that on the day that Aaron's sons became priests. All their sons and grandsons must always give these offerings to the priests." '

37 These are all the rules that a person must use. They are for when he gives a gift to the Lord. They are the rules for offerings of grain and the fellowship offering. And they are rules for the offerings that people give to take away their sin. The rules tell them how to make Aaron's sons priests. And they tell people who have done bad things what to do. They must show the Lord that they are sorry. 38 Israel's people were in the Sinai desert. The Lord gave the rules to Moses on Sinai's mountain. That was on the day that the Lord spoke to the people. He told them that they should bring their offerings to him there.

Chapter 8

Moses anoints Aaron and his sons

1 The Lord said to Moses, 2 'Fetch Aaron and his sons. Bring their special clothes. Bring the oil. Bring the basket of bread that they made without yeast. And bring the male cow for the offering for sin and the two male sheep. 3 Cause all the people to come to the door of the Tent of Meeting.'

4 Moses and the priests and all the people came to the door of the Tent of Meeting. 5 Moses said to the people, 'The Lord said that I must do this.' 6 Moses washed Aaron and his sons with water. 7 Moses put a shirt on Aaron and he tied a belt round Aaron. He put a robe and an ephod on him. He tied the ephod with its special belt.

8 Moses put the special piece of beautiful work on Aaron's breast. And he put theUrim and Thummim in its pocket. 9 Moses tied a piece of linen as a hat round Aaron's head. On the front of this linen he put a plate of gold with valuable stones on it. The Lord had said that Moses must do this.

10 Moses put some of the special anointing oil on the Tent of Meeting and on everything in it. He did this to make them holy. 11 Moses shook oil on the altar seven times. He put oil on the altar table and on all the tools to use with it. He put oil on the washing dish and on the table on which it stood. 12 Moses anointed Aaron's head with oil to make him holy. 13 He put a robe and a belt and a hat of linen on each of Aaron's sons. The Lord had said that Moses must do this.

14 Moses brought the male cow as a gift to the Lord. Aaron and his sons put their hands on the male cow's head. 15 Moses killed the male cow. He put his finger in the blood. He put the blood on the corners of the altar. That made it holy. Moses poured out the blood that he had not used. He poured it on to the floor in front of the altar. This is how he made the altar ready to make sacrifices to the Lord. 16 He burnt the fat and the kidneys and the best piece of the liver on the altar. 17 Moses burnt the meat with the inside parts and the skin of the male cow outside the camp. The Lord had said that Moses must do this.

18 Moses brought a male sheep to burn as a gift to the Lord. Aaron and his sons put their hands on the sheep's head. 19 Moses killed the sheep. He threw the blood on to the sides of the altar. 20 Moses cut the sheep into small pieces. He burnt the fat and the head and the pieces on the altar. 21 He washed the legs and the inside parts. He burnt them on the altar as an offering to the Lord. The smell of them while they were burning gave the Lord pleasure. The Lord had said that Moses must do this.

22 Moses brought the other male sheep. It was a gift. It showed that the Lord had chosen Aaron's family to become his priests. Aaron and his sons put their hands on the sheep's head. 23 Moses killed the sheep. He put some of its blood on Aaron's right ear. He also put blood on the thumb of Aaron's right hand. And he put some on the big toe of his right foot. 24 Moses did the same to Aaron's sons. Then he threw blood on all the sides of the altar. 25 Moses took the fat tail and the fat and the kidneys from inside the animal. He took the best piece of the liver from inside the animal. He took the top part of the right back leg. 26 Moses took two flat loaves of bread that they had made without yeast and a biscuit from the basket. One of the loaves had oil in it. He put them on top of the fat and the leg. 27 Moses gave them to Aaron and to his sons. They lifted them up as a special gift to the Lord. 28 Moses took the special gift from them and he burnt it on the altar. The smell of it while it was burning gave the Lord pleasure. 29 Moses took the breast, his part of the animal, and he lifted it up to the Lord. The Lord had said that Moses must do this.

30 Moses took some of the oil and some of the blood from the altar. He shook them on Aaron and his sons. He also shook some of the blood and some of the oil on their clothes. He did that to make them holy.

31 Moses said to Aaron and to his sons, 'Cook the meat at the door of the Tent of Meeting. Eat the meat with the bread in the basket by the door of the Tent of Meeting. 32 Burn the meat and bread that you do not eat. 33 You must stay at the door of the Tent of Meeting for 7 (seven) days. This will make you holy. You must stay for 7 days to become holy. 34 The Lord said that you must do this to atone for your sin. 35 Remember that you must stay at the door of the Tent of Meeting. You must stay there for 7 (seven) days and 7 nights. The Lord told me that you must do this. If you do not obey him, you will die.' 36 So Aaron and his sons did everything that the Lord had told Moses.

Chapter 9

The priests begin their work

1 On the 8th (eighth) day, Moses told Aaron and his sons and the leaders of Israel that they must come. 2 He said to Aaron, 'Bring a young male cow for your sin offering. And bring a male sheep for your burnt offering to the Lord. They must be perfect to give to the Lord.' 3 Moses said to Aaron, 'Tell Israel's people that they must bring a male goat for a sin offering. And they must bring a young cow and a young sheep. They are a gift to the Lord. The young cow and the young sheep must be one year old. They must be perfect to burn as an offering to the Lord. 4 Tell Israel's people that they must bring a male cow and a male sheep. They must bring them to sacrifice as a fellowship offering to the Lord. They will sacrifice them. They must mix grain and oil to offer with them. They must do that because the Lord will appear to them today.'

5 The people brought all the animals and the grain to the door of the Tent of Meeting. Moses and all the people came. And they stood at the door of the Tent of Meeting to worship the Lord. 6 Moses said to the people, 'The Lord has told you that you must do this. Do it. And then he will show you how great he is.'

7 Moses said to Aaron, 'Go to the altar. Sacrifice your sin offering and your burnt offering to the Lord. You must do this so the Lord will forgive your sins and those of the people. Then sacrifice the people's gift to the Lord. Their offerings are an atonement for the bad things that they have done. The Lord said that you should do this.'

8 Aaron brought the young male cow to the altar. He killed it. This was his offering to the Lord to atone for his sin. 9 His sons brought the blood to Aaron. He put his finger in the blood and he put it on the corners of the altar. He poured the blood that he did not use on to the floor in front of the altar. 10 Aaron burnt the fat, the kidneys and the best piece of the liver on the altar. This was an offering for his sin. He did it as the Lord had told Moses. 11 He took the meat and the skin from the young male cow outside the camp and he burnt it.

12 Aaron brought the male sheep for the burnt offering to the altar. He killed it. His sons brought the blood to him. He threw the blood on to the sides of the altar. 13 The priests gave the pieces of the animal, including the head, to Aaron. Aaron burnt them on the altar. 14 He washed the inside parts and the legs. He burnt them on the altar on top of the burnt offering.

15 Aaron brought the goat. This was the people's sacrifice to the Lord. Aaron killed it and he burnt it on the altar. It was an offering to atone for the people's sin. He offered this sacrifice in the same way as the first sacrifice for sin.

16 Aaron brought the other young cow. He killed it and he burnt it on the altar. He did it as Moses had told him. 17 He also brought the grain offering. He took some of it and he burnt it on the altar. He burnt it with the Lord's morning sacrifice.

18 Aaron killed the male cow and the male sheep. These were fellowship offerings from the people. The priests brought the blood to him. He threw it on to the sides of the altar. 19 Aaron took the fat tail, the fat and the kidneys and the best piece of the liver. 20 He put them on the animal's breasts. Then he burnt the fat on the altar. 21 Aaron lifted up the meat as an offering to the Lord. Moses had told him that he must do this.

22 When Aaron had finished burning the gifts to the Lord, he lifted up his hands over the people. He had sacrificed the sin offering, the burnt offering and the fellowship offerings. Then he asked the Lord to do good things for the people. And he came down from the altar.

23 Moses and Aaron went into the Tent of Meeting. When they came out, they asked God to do good things for the people. The bright light from the Lord appeared to the people to show how great he is. 24 Then the Lord sent a fire to show that he accepted the gifts. It completely burnt all the fat and the offerings that were on the altar. The people were very happy when they saw this. They shouted and they fell down with their faces to the ground.

Chapter 10

The Lord kills Nadab and Abihu

1 Nadab and Abihu were sons of Aaron. They put hot material in the pots that they used to burn incense. They threw incense over the hot material. They offered the incense to the Lord. This was a wrong thing to do. The Lord had not told them that they should do it. So it was wrong. 2 The Lord was angry and he sent fire to burn them. They died there in front of the Lord's altar. 3 Then Moses said to Aaron, 'This is what the Lord said,

"People may come near to me. But those people must see that I am holy.

All the people must give honour to me." '

Aaron did not reply.

4 Mishael and Elzaphan were sons of Aaron's father's brother, Uzziel. Moses said to them, 'Carry Nadab and Abihu away from the altar. Take your cousins outside the camp.' 5 Nadab and Abihu were still wearing their robes. Mishael and Elzaphan carried Nadab and Abihu outside the camp. Moses had told them that they must do that.

6 Moses said to Aaron and to his sons, 'Comb your hair. Do not tear your clothes. If you do that, you will die. And the Lord will be angry with all of the people. But Israel's people can show that they are sad. They are sad because the Lord has killed Nadab and Abihu with fire. 7 If you go away from the door of the Tent of Meeting you will die. You will die because the Lord's holy oil is on you.' So Aaron and his sons did as Moses had said.

8 The Lord then said to Aaron, 9 'Do not drink wine before you go into the Tent of Meeting. And do not drink anything that contains alcohol. If you do, you will die. This rule is for you and for all your sons and grandsons. 10 You must know what is holy. And you must know what is not holy. You must know what you can use. And you must know what you must not use to worship me. 11 You must teach Israel's people all the rules that I gave to them by Moses.'

12 Moses said to Aaron and to his two other sons Eleazar and Ithamar, 'The grain offering is most holy. Take the part that you did not burn. And make it into bread. Do not use yeast. Take it to the side of the altar and eat it. 13 Eat it in a holy place. The Lord has said that it is your part of the grain offering. It is for you and for your sons. 14 You and your sons and daughters can eat the breast meat that you held up to the Lord. And all your family can eat the top part of the leg. Eat the meat in a place that is clean and ready for the Lord's use. It is your part of the people's fellowship gift to the Lord. 15 Bring the top of the leg and the breast meat. Lift them up to the Lord. The Lord has given them to you and to your children. Lift them up with the fat parts of the burnt offering. He told you that you should do this.'

16 Moses looked for the goat that was to atone for the people's sin. Moses was angry with Eleazar and Ithamar, sons of Aaron. He was angry because they had burnt the goat. 17 Moses said to them, 'This gift was for the Lord. It was a very holy gift. It was to atone for the people's sins. Why did you not take it to the holy place and eat it? 18 You did not bring the blood into the holy place. I told you that you must eat its meat in the Tent of Meeting.' 19 Aaron said to Moses, 'My sons sacrificed their gifts to the Lord today. But very bad things have happened to me today. I would not have given the Lord any pleasure if I had eaten
the sin offering today.' 20 When Moses heard this, he was not angry any longer.

Rules for the people

Chapter 11

The Lord gives rules about food to the people

1 The Lord said to Moses and Aaron, 2 'Some animals walk on the land. Tell Israel's people which of these animals they can eat. 3 Each foot on the animal must have two separate parts. The animal must eat its food and then it must bring the food back into its mouth. And then it must eat the food again. Some animals eat their food twice and they have feet with two parts. You can eat those animals.

4 Some animals have feet that have two separate parts. But they do not eat their food twice. Other animals eat their food twice. But their feet do not have two separate parts. You must not eat those animals. The camel eats its food twice. But its feet are not in two separate parts. The people must not eat the camel. 5 The hyrax eats its food twice. But its feet are not in two separate parts. They must not eat the hyrax. 6 The rabbit eats its food twice. But its feet are not in two separate parts. They must not eat the rabbit. 7 The pig's feet are in two parts. But when the pig eats its food, it does not bring the food back into its mouth. It does not eat it twice. The people must not eat the pig. 8 They must not touch the dead bodies of those animals. They must not eat their meat. They are not clean for you to eat.

9 They can eat some animals that live in the sea or in the river. Those animals must have fins and scales on their bodies. 10 They must not eat any other animals from the sea or the river. They must keep away from them. 11 They must not touch the dead bodies of the animals from the sea or the river. They must not eat the meat from those other
animals. 12 Animals from the sea and the river may
have fins and scales on their bodies. Those are the only ones that you can eat. Those without fins or scales are not clean.

13 They must not eat some birds because they are not clean. They must not eat either the eagle or the vulture. 14 They must not eat the buzzard or the kite. 15 They must not eat the raven. 16 They must not eat any owl, seagull or hawk. 17 They must not eat the cormorant. 18 They must not eat the osprey. 19 They must not eat the heron, the hoopoe or the bat. The people must not eat them nor touch their dead bodies. They are not clean.

20 Some insects fly in the air and walk on the ground. The people must not eat them. 21 Some insects can fly. And they have legs that can jump. They can eat those insects. 22 They can eat any of these. They include the locust, the cricket and the grasshopper. 23 They must not eat any other flying insect that has legs.

24 A person may touch the dead body of an animal that is not clean. If he does, that person is not clean either. They must keep him separate from the other people until the evening. 25 He must wash his clothes immediately.

26 An animal might not have feet that are in two separate parts. It is wrong to touch the dead body of this animal. Some animals do not bring food back into their mouths and eat it again. It is wrong to touch the dead bodies of these animals. 27 Some animals walk on four feet. It is wrong to touch the dead body of an animal that has paws (the kind of feet that animals like cats and dogs have). 28 A person who picks up the dead body of these animals must wash his clothes immediately. They must keep him separate from the people until the evening.

29 Some animals that walk on the ground are not clean. You must not touch a weasel, a rat or a mouse. 30 You must not touch any kind of lizard. 31 A person might touch the dead body of one of those animals. If he does, he will not be clean. So they must keep him separate from the people until evening.

32 A dead animal may fall on to something that someone made from wood, cloth or skin. That thing becomes unclean. A person must put it into water until the evening. Then it will be clean. 33 A dead animal might fall into a pot. Then the pot and the things in it are not clean. The person must break the pot. 34 The food or water from the pot is not clean. A person must not drink it or eat any of that food. Water from the pot may have touched some food. If it did, that food is not clean. You must not eat it. 35 If a dead animal falls on to a cooking pot, then the pot is not clean. You must break the pot. 36 If a dead animal falls into a fresh water stream, the stream stays clean. The pot that a person uses to get fresh water from the stream is clean. 37 If a dead animal falls on to some seeds, they stay clean. 38 A person might pour water on the seeds. A dead animal might fall on the wet seeds. Then those seeds are not clean.

39 An animal that is good for food might die. A man might touch its dead body. If he does, they must keep him separate from the people until the evening. 40 If a person eats meat from the body of the dead animal, he must wash his clothes. He will not be clean until the evening. If a person picks up the body of the dead animal, he must wash his clothes. He will not be clean until the evening.

41 The people must not eat small animals that move across the ground. 42 This means animals that pass across the ground on their stomachs. It also means animals that walk on 4 (four) legs or many legs. 43 The people must not touch them or eat them. 44 The Lord says, "I am the Lord your God. I am holy. Make yourselves holy. Do not touch any small animal that moves across the ground. If you do, you will not be clean or holy. 45 I am the Lord who brought you away from Egypt. I became your God. So be holy because I am holy." '

46 These rules are about animals, birds and all animals that move in water or on the ground. 47 The people must learn to know which animals are clean. They must recognise which animals they can eat. And they must recognise which animals they must not eat.

Chapter 12

What a woman must do when she has a baby

1 The Lord said to Moses, 2 'Say this to Israel's people. When a boy is born, his mother is not clean for 7 (seven) days. When she is bleeding each month, the rule is the same. She is not clean. 3 Eight (8) days after he is born, they must circumcise the boy. 4 The woman must wait for 35 (thirty-five) days after the boy is born. All this time she must not touch anything that is holy. She must not go into the Tent of Meeting. After this time, she will become clean.

5 After a girl is born, her mother will not be clean for two weeks. The rule is the same as for each month, when she is bleeding. She will not be clean then. She must wait 66 (sixty-six) days after a girl is born. Then she will become clean.

6 When the days to wait are finished, the woman must come to the door of the Tent of Meeting. She must bring to the priest a sheep that is one year old for a burnt offering. And she must bring a bird for a sin offering. The bird must be a pigeon or a dove. These are gifts to the Lord. 7 The priest will offer the gifts to the Lord. Then the woman will become clean. These are the rules at the birth of a boy or of a girl.

8 If the woman does not have money to buy a sheep she can give two doves or pigeons (birds) to the Lord. The priest will use one bird for a sin offering and he will burn the other one. That is how he will make atonement for her. Then she will be clean.'

Chapter 13

Rules for illnesses in the skin

1 The Lord said to Moses and Aaron, 2 'A person may have a kind of mark on his skin that might be an illness. He might give the illness to other people. If he has a mark like that, you must bring him to the priest. 3 The priest must look at the mark. If the hair on the mark is white, it might be an illness. If the mark is under the skin and on the skin it might be an illness. The priest must say that the person is not clean. 4 If the mark on the skin is white but not under the skin it might not be an illness. If the hair on the skin is not white, it might not be a bad illness. The priest must keep him separate from the people for 7 (seven) days.

5 On the 7th (seventh) day, the priest must look at the person. The mark may not be any bigger.

If it is not, he must keep the person separate from the people for 7 (seven) more days. 6 On the 7th (seventh) day, the priest must look at the person. The mark may not be so dark and it may not be any bigger. The priest can say that the illness has left that person. The person must wash his clothes. 7 A person might see that the mark on his skin had grown. This might happen after the priest had said that the illness had left him. Then the person must go again to the priest. 8 The priest must look at the person. The mark might be bigger. The priest must say that the person has an illness. It is an illness that he could give to other people.

9 If a person has an illness on his skin, you must bring him to the priest. 10 The priest must look at the person. If the skin has a white mark and white hair on it, the person has an illness. If the mark has no skin on part of it, the person has an illness. But it may not be an illness that he could give to other people. 11 The priest must say that the person is not clean. The priest need not keep him separate from the people. He already has an illness.

12 If the illness is all over the body of the person, the priest must look at the person. 13 If the skin is all white the priest must say that the person is clean. 14 If there is an open hole in the skin, the person is not clean. 15 The priest will see the hole in the skin. He must say that the person has an illness. 16 The hole might close up and the skin might go white. If it does, the person must go to the priest. 17 The priest must look at the skin. It may be white. The priest must say that the illness has left the person. Then he will be clean.

18 A mark on the skin of a person might have water under it. Then it might get better. 19 If there is still a red or white mark on the skin, the person must go to the priest. 20 The priest must look at the person. The red mark might be under the skin and the hair on the skin might be white. The priest must say that the person has an illness. The person is not clean. 21 If the red mark is not under the skin, it might not be an illness. There may not be any white hair on the red mark and the mark may be less red. If that is true, it might not be an illness. The priest must keep the person separate from the people for 7 (seven) days. 22 The red mark may get bigger. The priest must say that the person has an illness. 23 If the red mark is not getting bigger, the illness is getting better. The priest must say that the illness has left the person.

24 A person who has burnt his skin might have a red or white mark. It might be where he burnt himself. 25 The priest must look at him. If the hair on the mark is white, it is an illness. If the mark is under the skin and on the skin, it is an illness. The priest must say that the person is not clean. He might give the illness to other people.

26 There may not be any white hair and the mark may not be under the skin. The illness is leaving the person. Then the priest must keep him separate from the people for 7 (seven) days. 27 On the 7th (seventh) day, the priest must look at the person. If the mark is getting bigger, it is an illness. The priest must say that the person is not clean. 28 If the mark is getting smaller, it is not an illness. The mark is because the person burnt himself. The priest must say that the person is clean.

29 A person may have a mark that hurts on his head. 30 The priest must look at the mark. The mark may be under the skin and on the skin, and it may have thin yellow hair on it. That is a bad illness. He could give that illness to other people. The priest must say that the person is not clean. 31 If the mark is not under the skin, it might not be a bad illness. If there is not any black hair on the mark, it might not be an illness. The priest must keep that person separate from the people for 7 (seven) days. 32 On the 7th (seventh) day, the priest must look at the mark that is hurting. The mark might not be under the skin. There might not be any yellow hair on it. 33 The person must cut the hair off his head. He must not cut the hair for 7 (seven) more days. 34 On the 7th (seventh) day, the priest must look at the mark that is hurting. The mark may be no bigger and not under the skin. The priest can say that the person is clean. The person must wash his clothes. 35 The mark might get bigger after the priest has said that the illness has left the person. 36 The priest must look at the mark. If it is bigger, he need not look for yellow hair. The person is not clean. 37 The mark may be no bigger and black hair may have grown on it. If that is true, the illness has left the person.

38 If a person has white marks on his skin, 39 the priest must look at the marks. If the colour of the marks is not bright, it is not an illness. The person is clean.

40 The hair may fall from the head of a man until he is bald. That man remains clean. 41 If the hair falls from the front of the man's head, it is bald. The man is clean. 42 If the man has a red and white mark on his bald head, it is an illness. 43 The priest must look at the red and white mark on the bald head. 44 The priest must say that the man has an illness. It is an illness that he might give to other people,

45 A person with this illness must tear his clothes. He must not comb his hair. He must cover the lower part of his face. He must shout, "I am not clean." 46 He must be alone all the time that he has an illness. He must live outside the camp.

Rules for clothes that have mildew

47 Clothes might become bad because of mildew. 48 People might have made the clothes from wool, linen cloth or leather. 49 If the mark in the clothes is green or red, the mildew is growing. People must show these clothes to the priest. 50 The priest must look at the mildew. And he must keep the clothes separate from other clothes for 7 (seven) days. 51 On the 7th (seventh) day, the priest must look at the clothes. If the illness is getting bigger, the person must not wear them. 52 The priest must burn the wool, leather or linen clothes. They have an illness that will destroy them.

53 When the priest looks at the clothes, the mildew might not be getting bigger. 54 He must tell the people that they must wash the clothes. The people must keep these clothes separate from their other clothes for 7 (seven) more days. 55 The priest will look at the clothes after the people have washed them. If the mildew still seems the same, the people must not wear the clothes. The people must burn the clothes whether the mark is inside or outside them. 56 The colour of the mark might be less bright, after the people have washed the clothes. If it is, the priest must tear the marked part out of the clothes. 57 If the mildew comes back to the clothes, the people must burn them. 58 If there is no mildew in the washed clothes, the people must wash the clothes again. Then the clothes will be clean.'

59 These are the rules for mildew in linen cloth. They are rules for wool or leather clothes. They tell the priest how to know whether they are clean or not clean.

Chapter 14

Rules for the people after an illness of the skin leaves them

1 The Lord said to Moses, 2 'These rules are for a person who has had an illness on his skin. They are rules about how to make him clean. When the illness leaves the person, you must bring him to the priest.

3 The priest must go outside the camp and he must look at the person. If the illness has gone away, 4 he must speak to the person. He must tell the person that he must bring two birds. They must be birds that are good for food. The birds must be alive. They must also bring wood from the cedar tree, red wool and some hyssop (a plant). 5 The priest will bring a pot with water in it. He will hold one of the birds over the pot and he will kill it. 6 The priest will take the other bird and the wood from the cedar tree. He will take the red wool and the hyssop. He will put all of them into the blood of the dead bird. He will shake the blood over the person who had the illness. He will do this 7 times. The priest will then say that the person is clean. The priest will let the live bird go. It will fly away.

8 The person who had the illness must wash his clothes. He must wash his body with water and he must cut off all his hair. Then he will be clean. He can go into the camp. But he must stay outside the home that he has made from animal skins for seven days. 9 On day seven, he must cut all the hair off his head and his face. He must wash his clothes and his body with water.

10 On the 8th day, the person must bring two young male sheep and one female sheep. The female sheep must be one year old. All the animals must be perfect. He must also bring 3/10th of an ephah of flour (about 6 litres or 12 pints) mixed with oil. And he must bring a log (about 0.3 litres or half a pint) of oil. 11 The priest who is making him clean must be there. He must bring the person to the door of the Tent of Meeting. The person must bring with him his offerings to the Lord.

12 The priest must take one of the male sheep and the oil. He must lift them up to the Lord as a gift. 13 He must kill the sheep at the north side of the altar. That is where they kill the sin offering and the burnt offering. The gift is holy. It is food for the priests. 14 The priest must put some of the blood on the lowest part of the person's right ear. He must put blood on the thumb of the person's right hand. And he must put blood on the big toe of the person's right foot. 15 The priest must pour some of the oil into his own left hand. 16 He must put a finger from his right hand into the oil. He must shake the oil seven times in front of the altar. 17 The priest must put oil on the lowest part of the person's right ear. He must put some of the oil on the thumb of the person's right hand. He must put some of the oil on the big toe of the person's right foot. He will put the oil on top of the offering's blood. 18 The priest must put the oil that he did not use on the person's head. This makes his atonement in front of the Lord.

19 Then the priest must offer the sin offering. That will make atonement for the man who will become clean. Then the priest must kill another sheep. It is a burnt offering. 20 The priest must sacrifice the dead animal. It is a burnt offering. The priest must offer it on the altar. He must burn the flour and the oil with it on the altar. All this will make atonement for the person. This makes the person who had the illness clean.

21 If the person is poor, he must bring one young male sheep. And he must bring 1/10th of an ephah of flour (about 2 litres or 4 pints) mixed with oil. And he must bring a log (about 0.3 litres or half a pint) of oil. The priest must lift them to the Lord. 22 The person must also bring two birds. They must be doves or pigeons. These will be his gift to the Lord. One bird is for a sin offering and the other one is for a burnt offering.

23 On the 8th (eighth) day, the person must bring his gifts to the Lord. He must bring them to the door of the Tent of Meeting. 24 The priest will take the young sheep and the oil and he will lift them up to the Lord. 25 He will kill the sheep. He will put some of its blood on the lowest part of the person's ear. He will put the blood on the thumb of the person's right hand. He will put the blood on the big toe of the person's right foot. 26 The priest will pour some of the oil into his own left hand. 27 He will put a finger from his right hand into the oil. He will shake it seven times in front of the altar. 28 He will put oil from his hand on the lowest part of the person's ear. He will also put oil on the thumb of the person's right hand. He will put oil on the big toe of the person's right foot. 29 The priest will put the oil that he did not use on the person's head. Then the Lord can see that he is clean. 30 The priest will kill the pigeons or doves. 31 One bird is for a sin offering. The priest will burn the other bird with the grain offering. This is how the priest will make atonement in front of the Lord. He will do it for the person who was not clean.

32 These are the rules for a person who had an illness in his skin. They are for an illness that he might give to other people. They are for people who are too poor to buy three sheep.'

Rules for a house that has an illness called mildew

33 The Lord said to Moses and Aaron, 34 'The country called Canaan is my gift to you. I may put an illness called mildew in a house in that country. 35 If a person finds mildew in his house, he must tell the priest. He must say, "I have found something like mildew in my house." 36 The priest will tell the person what he should do. The person must take everything out of the house. If he does, those things will still be clean. Then the priest will go into the house. 37 He will look at the walls of the house. He will look for a green or red mark. If the mark goes into the wall, 38 the priest will leave the house. He will shut it up for 7 (seven) days. 39 On the 7th day, the priest will return to the house. The mildew may be bigger. 40 The priest must say, "You must remove the stones that have mildew." The person must put the stones outside the town. He must put them in a special place. 41 The person must cut the clay from inside the walls of the house. The person must put the clay from the walls outside the town. The person must put it in a place for things that are not clean. 42 The person who lives in the house must get some more stones. He must get some more clay. Then he can mend the wall.

43 A person might find mildew on the wall that he has mended. He must tell the priest. 44 The priest will look at the house. If the mildew is on more of the mended wall, the house is not clean. 45 The person must break the house into pieces. The person who lives in the house must put the stones outside the town. He must put the wood and the clay outside the town. He must put them in the place for things that are not clean.

46 A person may go into the house while it is shut up. If he does, he will not become clean until evening. 47 Any person who sleeps in a house with mildew must wash his clothes. And any person who eats in a house with mildew must wash his clothes.

48 If a person mends his house, the priest must look at it. There may not be any mildew. So, the priest will say that it is clean. 49 The person must take two birds and some wood from the cedar tree. He must take red wool and hyssop (a plant) 50 The priest will bring a pot with water in it. He will hold one of the birds over the pot and he will kill it. 51 The priest will take the other bird and the wood from the cedar tree. He will take the red wool and the hyssop. He will put all of them into the blood of the dead bird. He will shake the blood and water over the house 7 (seven) times. This will make the house clean. 52 The priest will use the birds and the wood from the cedar tree. And he will use the wool and the hyssop to make the house clean. 53 Then the priest will take the bird that is alive outside the town. He will let the bird fly away. And the person can live in the house.'

Moses tells the people what these rules are for

54 These are the rules for an illness in a person's skin. 55 These are the rules for mildew in clothes or in a house. 56 These are the rules for a mark on or under the skin. 57 These rules decide when a person has an illness. And they decide when he is clean. They show when a house has an illness. They are the rules for illnesses in the skin and for mildew.

Chapter 15

What people should do when pus, blood or semen comes out of them

1 The Lord said to Moses and Aaron, 2 'Say to Israel's people, "If pus is coming out of a man's body, he is unclean." 3 The man is unclean if the pus pours. And he is unclean even if it stops pouring.

4 If the man sits on a bed, it becomes unclean. If the man sits on anything, it becomes unclean. 5 A person who touches the bed must wash his clothes and his body. He will be unclean until evening. 6 Any person might sit on anything that he has sat on. That will make him unclean also. He must wash his clothes and his body. He will be unclean until evening.

7 A person who touches the dirty man must wash his clothes. He must also wash his body. He will be unclean until evening.

8 A man who is dirty might make another person wet with water. If the water is from his mouth, the other person must wash his clothes. He must also wash his body. He will be unclean until evening.

9 A dirty man might ride on an animal. The cloth on the back of the animal will become unclean. 10 A person who touches that cloth will be unclean until evening. If a person picks up that cloth, he must wash his clothes. He must also wash his body. He will be unclean until evening.

11 The dirty man might touch another person before the man washes his hands. The person that he touched becomes unclean. The person must wash his clothes and his body. He will be unclean until evening.

12 If the dirty man touches a clay pot, you must break it. Or he may touch a thing that someone has made from wood. If he touches it, you must wash that thing.

13 The pus may stop coming out of a person. When it does, he must count 7 (seven) days. He must wash his clothes and his body with fresh water. Then the man will be clean. 14 On the 8th day, he must take two birds to the door of the Tent of Meeting. They must be doves or pigeons. He must give them to the priest. 15 The priest will sacrifice them. One bird is for a sin offering and the other is for a burnt offering. They are an atonement to the Lord. Then the man will be clean.

16 When semen comes out of a man, he must wash his body. He will be unclean until evening. 17 You must wash any clothes that semen touches. They are unclean until evening. 18 A man might lie with a woman. If semen comes out of him, they are both unclean. They must wash their bodies. They will be unclean until evening.

19 A woman will bleed every month. She is unclean for seven days. A person might touch the woman when she is bleeding. That person will remain unclean until evening.

20 The woman who is bleeding might lie on a bed. The bed will become unclean. If the woman sits on something, it becomes unclean. 21 If another person touches the bed, he must wash his clothes and his body. He will be unclean until evening. 22 Another person might sit on the thing that she sat on. That person must wash his clothes and his body. He will be unclean until evening. 23 A person might touch anything that the woman sat on. If he does, he is unclean until evening.

24 A man might lie down with a woman. If her blood touches him, he is unclean for seven days. Any bed that the man lies on becomes unclean.

25 If a woman is bleeding for more than seven days, she is unclean. She is unclean all the time that she is bleeding. 26 The bed that the woman lies on becomes unclean. Anything that the woman sits on is unclean.

27 If another person touches the chair, he becomes unclean. He must wash his clothes and his body. He will be unclean until evening. If another person touches the bed, he will also become unclean. He must wash his clothes and his body. He will be unclean until evening.

28 When the woman stops bleeding, she must count 7 (seven) days. Then she will be clean. 29 On the 8th day, she must take two birds to the door of the Tent of Meeting. They must be doves or pigeons. She must give them to the priest. He will sacrifice one bird for her sin and he will burn the other. 30 He will kill them as an atonement to the Lord. Then the woman will be clean.

31 The Tent of Meeting is the Lord's house. It is among Israel's people. The priests must keep the people away from anything that makes them unclean. If they are not clean, they will make the Tent of Meeting unclean. So they will die.'

32 These are the rules when pus or semen comes from a man's body. 33 These are the rules for a woman when she bleeds each month. These are the rules for a man who has sex with an unclean woman.

Chapter 16

Rules about the Day of Atonement

1 The Lord spoke to Moses after the two sons of Aaron died. The gift that they gave to the Lord was not holy. So the Lord killed them. 2 The Most Holy Place in the Tent of Meeting is behind the curtain. The Lord said to Moses, 'Your brother Aaron cannot go behind the curtain at any time that he wants to. Tell him that. The Lord appears in a cloud over the lid of the Covenant Box. So Aaron will die if he does not obey the Lord.

3 This is how Aaron must go into the Most Holy Place. He must bring a young bull (a male cow) for a sin offering. He must also bring a male sheep for a burnt offering. 4 He must wash his body before he puts on his special clothes. He must wear his linen robe and linen clothes next to his body. They are holy to the Lord. He must tie a linen belt round his body. He must put the linen hat on his head. These clothes are holy. 5 He must take two male goats for a sin offering. And he must take a male sheep as an offering to burn on the altar. They are a gift to the Lord from Israel's people.

6 Aaron must offer the bull (male cow) as an atonement to the Lord for himself, his family and his servants. 7 He must take the two goats to the door of the Tent of Meeting. They are a gift to the Lord. 8 He must use the Lord's special stones. They will help him to decide what he should do. He must decide which goat is for the Lord. And he must decide which goat he must send away. 9 Aaron must take the goat that is for the Lord. And he must kill it. It is a sin offering. 10 He must not kill the other goat. It is an atonement to the Lord. It will pay for the bad things that the people have done. It is to take away the people's punishment. He must send it away into the desert.'

11 'Aaron must bring the bull (male cow) and he must kill it. It is his atonement for his family's sins. 12 He must take a pot of the hot material that is burning on the altar. He must fill his two hands with incense. He must take the hot material and the incense behind the curtain. 13 He must put the incense on the burning material. The smoke will cover the lid of the Covenant Box. So he will not die. 14 He must take with him blood from the bull. He must use his finger to shake the blood. He must shake it on to the lid of the Covenant Box. He must shake the blood in front of the lid of the Covenant Box. He must shake it seven times with his finger.

15 Aaron must kill the goat for the sin offering. It is a gift to the Lord from the people. He must take the blood behind the curtain. He must shake the blood on the lid of the Covenant Box as he did with the bull's blood. And he must shake the blood in front of the lid of the Covenant Box. 16 This will make atonement for all the sins of Israel's people. This will make the Holy Place clean. Aaron must do the same for the Tent of Meeting. That is because the people have done bad things in the camp. The Tent of meeting is in the middle of the camp. 17 Aaron must give the offerings to the Lord. He must give them for his family and he must give them for his servants. He must give them for all the people. Nobody can go into the Tent of Meeting while Aaron is in the Most Holy Place. He must be alone when he goes in. And he must be alone until he comes out. He must be alone when he gives the offerings to the Lord. Those offerings are for himself, for his family and for all Israel's people.

18 He must go to the altar that is in front of the Lord.

He must make atonement for it. He must take blood from the bull (male cow) and blood from the goat. He must put the blood on the corners of the altar. 19 He must shake blood on the altar seven times to make it clean.

A goat will carry away all the bad things that the people have done

20 Aaron must first atone for the Most Holy Place, the Tent of meeting and the altar. Then he must bring the goat that is alive. 21 He must put his hands on the goat's head. He must speak aloud all the bad things that Israel's people have done. Then all the bad things will be on the goat's head. Aaron must tell a man that he must send the goat away into the desert. 22 The goat will carry all the sins of the people into the desert. The man must send it away into the desert.

23 Aaron must go into the Tent of Meeting. He must take off the holy clothes. The holy clothes must stay in the Tent of Meeting. 24 He must wash his body in a holy place. He must put on his own clothes. He must leave the holy place. Then he must sacrifice the burnt offerings to the Lord. They will make atonement for himself and for the people. 25 And he must also burn the fat from the sin offering on the altar.

26 The person who sent the goat away must wash his clothes and his body. He can return to the camp. 27 Aaron had killed a bull (male cow) and a goat. He took their blood into the Most Holy Place to make atonement. Someone must carry their dead bodies outside the camp. He must burn them. That man must burn the skin, the meat and the inside parts. 28 The man who burnt the animals must wash his clothes and his body. Then he can return to the camp.

29 On the 10th (tenth) day of the 7th (seventh) month, Israel's people must not eat any food. This is a rule that you must obey for all time. The people who are travelling with them must not eat any food. None of them must do any work. 30 This day will make them clean from all their sins. The Lord will see them as clean people. This will be the Day of Atonement. 31 It is a day when you do not eat any food. It is a day for rest. This is a rule from the Lord and you must do this every year. 32 The High Priest is a chosen son of Aaron. And he must make atonement. He will put on the holy clothes. He will bring the people's offerings to the Lord. 33 He will make atonement for the Most Holy Place. He will make atonement for the Tent of Meeting. He will make atonement for the altar. He will make atonement for the priests and for all the people.

34 He will make atonement for all the Israelites' sins once every year. This rule is for now and for all time.'

The people did everything quite as the Lord had told Moses.

Chapter 17

The people must not eat blood

1 The Lord said to Moses, 2 'Tell these rules to Aaron and his sons and all the people. 3 If a person sacrifices a male cow, a sheep or a goat in the fields, that is a sin. Or if a person sacrifices it in the camp, that is a sin. 4 The animal is an offering to the Lord. The person should bring it to the door of the Tent of Meeting. He should offer it to the Lord there. The person who offers a sacrifice anywhere else has sinned. He has sacrificed an animal in the wrong way. He must leave the camp. 5 This rule will stop the people giving sacrifices to the Lord in the fields. They must bring their gifts to the priest. They will be fellowship offerings. The priest will be at the door of the Tent of Meeting. 6 He must shake the blood of the animal on the Lord's altar. That altar is at the door of the Tent of Meeting. The priest must burn the fat. The smell of it while it is burning will give the Lord pleasure. 7 The people give sacrifices in the fields to worship idols that seem like goats. They must never do this again. This rule is for now and for all time.

8 If an Israelite gives a sacrifice or a burnt offering he must offer it at the Tent of Meeting's door. A foreigner may live among you. If he gives a sacrifice he must offer it to the Lord at the Tent of Meeting's door. 9 If they did not offer it to the Lord at the Tent of Meeting's door they are sinning. You must send them away from the camp.

10 An Israelite or a foreigner who lives among you must not eat blood. And they must not drink it. If somebody does, the Lord will turn away from him. He will take that person away from his people.

11 The blood gives its life to an animal. You must put the blood on the altar. The Lord has given the blood to you. It atones for your sins and it gives life to you. 12 For this reason, Israel's people must not eat blood. And the people who are travelling with them must not eat blood.

13 A person may catch an animal or a bird that is clean to eat. If he does, he must pour its blood on the ground. He must cover the blood with some earth. 14 The animal's life is in its blood. That is why no Israelite should eat any animal's blood. You must send any person that eats blood away from your people.

15 An Israelite or a foreign person may find a dead animal. If he eats it, he must wash his clothes and his body. He will be unclean until evening. Then he will become clean. A person might find an animal or a bird that a wild animal has killed. He must wash his clothes and his body. He will be unclean until evening. 16 If that person does not wash clothes and his body, it is his own mistake.'

Chapter 18

Rules for the people about their lives

Rules about sex

1 The Lord said to Moses, 2 'Tell Israel's people that I am the Lord their God. 3 They lived in the country called Egypt. They must not do as the people in Egypt do. I am bringing them to live in Canaan's country. They must not do as the people in Canaan do. 4 They must obey my rules. I am the Lord. 5 If they obey my rules, they will give me pleasure. If they obey my rules, they will remain alive. I am the Lord.

6 A person must not have sex with a person who belongs to his own family. I am the Lord.

7 Do not have sex with your mother. You will cause your father to be ashamed.

8 Do not have sex with a wife of your father. Your father will be ashamed.

9 Do not have sex with your sister. Do not have sex with the sister who has the same mother but a different father from you. Do not have sex with the sister who has the same father but a different mother from you. Do not have sex with your sister even if she lives in the same house as you.

10 Do not have sex with any granddaughter. You will be ashamed.

11 Do not have sex with the daughter of your father and his wife. She is your sister.

12 Do not have sex with your father's sister. She is his sister.

13 Do not have sex with your mother's sister. She is her sister.

14 Do not have sex with the wife who is married to your father's brother. She is your aunt.

15 Do not have sex with your son's wife.

16 Do not have sex with your brother's wife. You will make your brother ashamed.

17 Do not have sex with both a woman and her daughter. Do not have sex with her son's daughter or with her daughter's daughter. They are her family and they are near to her. If you do this you are sinning.

18 Do not take your wife's sister for a 2nd (second) wife. Do not have sex with your wife's sister if your wife is alive.

19 Do not have sex with a woman when she is bleeding. She does this each month.

20 Do not have sex with the wife of another man. You would become unclean.

21 Do not give a child as a sacrifice to the god called Molech. This would destroy the Lord's honour. He is the Lord.

22 Do not have sex with another man. To do this is very wrong.

23 Do not have sex with an animal. To do this is a sin. It would make you unclean. A woman must not have sex with an animal. She would not be obeying the rules of her nature.

24 Do not do these things. They would make you unclean. The people who live in Canaan do these things. It made them unclean. The Lord will send those people out of their country. 25 Canaan is unclean because the people did these things. This is why the Lord pushed the people out of that country. 26 But you and the foreigners with you must not do these wrong things. 27 The people in Canaan did these bad things and the country became unclean. 28 If you do these bad things, I will push you out of Canaan's country. I will send you away, like the people before you.

29 You must send away any person who does any of these bad things. 30 All the people must obey my rules. They must not do the bad things that the people in Canaan did. If they did them, my people would become unclean. I am the Lord your God.'

Chapter 19

1 The Lord said to Moses, 2 'Speak to Israel's people. They must be holy because I am holy. You must tell them that.

3 Each person must respect his mother and his father. All the people must keep the Sabbath as a day for rest. I am the Lord your God.

4 You must not worship idols. You must not use metal to make gods for yourselves. I am the Lord your God.

5 When a person sacrifices a fellowship offering to the Lord, he must obey the rules. If he does, the Lord will accept the gift. 6 The people must eat the meat on the day that the person offers it. Or they must eat it on the next day. The person must burn any meat that he has not eaten after the 2nd (second) day. 7 On the third day, the meat is not clean. 8 If he eats the meat on the third day he makes a holy gift unclean. You must send him away from the camp.

9 When a person cuts the plants in his field, he must not cut to the edge of the field. He must not pick up what he drops. 10 If a person grows fruit to make wine, he must not pick all of the fruit. He must not pick up the fruit that drops. The fruit that drops is for the poor people. And it is for those who are foreign. I am the Lord your God.

11 You must not take something that belongs to another person. You must not say something that is not true. You must obey my rules.

12 You must not use the name of the Lord to say a promise. This will make my name unclean. I am the Lord.

13 You must not rob another person. You must not keep a slave's money until the morning.

14 You must not speak bad words about a person who cannot hear. You must not put something in front of a person who cannot see. The person might fall. I am the Lord.

15 My people must be fair to other people. They must not be more kind to a rich or important man than to a poor one. They must be fair to rich people and to poor people.

16 They must not speak bad words about other people. They must not do anything that would cause a man to die. I am the Lord.

17 You must not think bad thoughts about another person. A person may do something that is wrong. You must tell him that he is doing a wrong thing. If you do, you will not be a part of the wrong thing.

18 You must not hurt another person because he hurt you. And you must not remember for a long time the bad thing that someone did to you. You must love all people as you love yourself. I am the Lord.

19 The people must obey the Lord's rules. They must not let two different kinds of animals have sex together. They must not put two different kinds of seeds in one field. They must not make clothes from two different materials.

20 A slave girl belongs to a man. Another man must not have sex with her. If he does, he is doing a wrong thing. But the girl is not free. He has not bought her. You must punish them. But you must not kill them because the girl was not free. 21 The man must bring a male sheep to the door of the Tent of Meeting. It is an offering to the Lord. 22 The priest will sacrifice the gift to the Lord. The sacrifice will atone for the man's sin. Then the Lord will forgive the man.

23 A person may plant a fruit tree in the country called Canaan. But he must not eat the fruit for (3) three years. 24 In the 4th (fourth) year, the fruit is holy. It is an offering to show that the Lord is great. 25 In the 5th year, the people can eat the fruit. If they do this, the trees will give much fruit to the people. I am the Lord your God.

26 You must not eat any meat that has the blood in it. People must not do magic. They must not use magic to try to discover things that might happen.

27 A man must not cut the hair on the sides of his head. He must not cut the edges of his beard.

28 He must not cut his body to remember the dead people. He must not paint his body. I am the Lord your God.

29 He must not sell his daughter for sex. You would make her ashamed. If he does this, all the people might do the same. The whole country would become full of sin.

30 The Lord has said what the people can do on the day for rest (Sabbath). On the day for rest, the people must do only those things. They must respect the Lord's house.

31 They must not ask people who do magic to help them. That would make Israel's people unclean. I am the Lord your God.

32 The people must stand up when they are with old people. They must respect the old people. They must give honour to their God. I am the Lord your God.

33 A foreign person may live in your country. You must be kind to him or to her. 34 People must love the person from a different country as they love themselves. They must remember the time when they lived in Egypt. Egypt was not their country. I am the Lord your God.

35 They must be fair when they are measuring space or weight or quantity. 36 They must use correct measures and weights. I am the Lord that led them out of Egypt.

37 They must obey all my rules. I am the Lord.'

Chapter 20

What would happen if the people did not obey the rules?

1 The Lord said to Moses, 2 'Talk to Israel's people. Say, "If any Israelite or foreign person gives his children to the god called Molech, he must die." The people must throw stones at him to kill him.

3 I, the Lord, will turn away from that person.

I will make him separate from his people. That person did not respect the Lord. He did not respect the Lord's holy name. 4 Israel's people may not think that his sin was important. So they might not kill him. 5 But the Lord himself will become an enemy of the man and of his family. The Lord will send him away with all the people who worship the god called Molech.

6 A person must not ask someone who does magic for help. They are turning away from the Lord. He will send them away from his people.

7 The people must be holy. I am the Lord your God. 8 They must always obey all the Lord's rules. I am the Lord who makes them holy.

9 If a person says bad things about his mother or his father, you must kill him. He has destroyed their honour. His sin will cause his death.

10 If a man has sex with another man's wife you must kill him and the woman.

11 A man is sinning if he has sex with his father's wife. You must kill the man and the woman. They have destroyed the father's honour. Their sin causes their death.

12 A man is sinning if he has sex with his son's wife. You must kill them both. They have not obeyed the rules of nature. Their sin causes their death.

13 A man is sinning if he has sex with another man. You must kill both of the men. They should be ashamed. Their sin causes their death.

14 A man is sinning if he marries a woman and her mother. You must burn the man and both the women in the fire. Then their sin will not make my people unclean.

15 A man is sinning if he has sex with an animal. You must kill the man and the animal.

16 A woman is sinning if she has sex with an animal. You must kill the woman and the animal. Their sin causes their death.

17 It is a sin if a man marries his sister. She may be the daughter of his father or of his mother. It is a sin if he has sex with her. The people must send them away. He has taken away his sister's honour. He must carry the punishment for his sin.

18 A man must not have sex with a woman when she is bleeding. If he does, it is a sin. They have not obeyed the rules of the Lord. The people must send them away.

19 A man must not have sex with his mother's sister or with his father's sister. They are both doing a wrong thing. They are taking away the family's honour. Their sin causes their punishment.

20 A man is sinning if he has sex with his aunt. He is taking away his father's brother's honour. They will have no children.

21 It makes the people unclean if a man marries his brother's wife. He has taken away his brother's honour. They will not have any children.

22 If the people want to remain in the country called Canaan, they must obey the Lord's rules. 23 The people who are living in Canaan now are doing bad things. I, the Lord, hate them because they did those things. I will send them out of Canaan. 24 I, the Lord, will give their country to Israel's people. I will give it to you and to your children to keep for all time. But you must obey my rules. Everything in the country is good. I am the Lord your God. I want you to be separate from other people.

25 The people must know which animals are clean. And they must know which animals are unclean. They must know which birds are clean. And they must know which birds are unclean.

They must not eat any animal or bird that is unclean. 26 I am holy. So my people must be holy for me. I have made them separate from other people. They belong to me.

27 A man or a woman who uses magic is doing a wrong thing. People must throw stones at that person until they die. Their sin will cause their death.'

Rules for the priests

Chapter 21

1 The Lord said to Moses, 'Say this to the priests. They must not touch a dead body. That would make them unclean. 2 It may be the body of a person from their own family. The priest can touch the dead person if it is his mother or father. He can touch the dead person if it is his son or his daughter or his brother. 3 He can touch the dead person if it is his sister. But he must not touch her if she has a husband. 4 The priest must not touch a dead person who is married to a person of his family. That would make him unclean.

5 A priest must not cut all the hair from his head. He must not cut the sides of his beard. He must not cut his body. 6 A priest must be holy. He must not speak bad words about the Lord. He is the person who sacrifices the people's burnt offerings to the Lord.

7 A priest must not marry a woman who has left her husband. He must not marry a woman if men have paid her to have sex with them. He must not marry a woman whose husband has sent her away. A priest must be holy. 8 A priest is holy because he sacrifices the people's offerings to the Lord. A priest is holy because I, the Lord, am holy.

9 A priest's daughter must not have sex with men who pay her. That would make her unclean. She would take away her father's honour. If she does not obey, you must burn her in a fire.

10 They have poured special oil on the High Priest's head among his brothers. He must wear special clothes. He must comb his hair. He must not tear his clothes. 11 He must not go into a room where there is a dead body. Even if it is the body of his parent, he must not go in. It will make him unclean. 12 He must not leave the house of the Lord. He has the holy oil on his head. He must be separate. I am the Lord.

13 The High Priest must marry a woman who has not had sex before. 14 The woman must not have had a husband who died. She must not have a husband that she has left. Men must not have paid to have sex with her. She must be a woman from Israel's people 15 so their children will be holy. I am the Lord. I make priests holy.'

16 The Lord said to Moses, 17 'Talk to Aaron. Say, "A priest who does not have a perfect body must not sacrifice the burnt offerings to the Lord." This rule is for now and for all time. 18 A priest who cannot see must not sacrifice the food to the Lord. A priest who cannot walk must not sacrifice food to the Lord. A priest with a body that is the wrong shape must not offer food to the Lord. 19 A priest with a hand that is the wrong shape must not offer food to the Lord. A priest with a foot that is the wrong shape must not offer food to the Lord. A priest with a back that is not straight must not offer food to the Lord. Neither must a priest who is very small offer a food gift. A priest who has an eye illness or a skin illness must not offer food to the Lord. Neither must a priest offer food if his testicles (secret parts) are not whole. 21 If a priest's son has something wrong with his body, he must not come near to the altar. He must not give the food offering to the Lord. 22 He can eat God's holy food and God's most holy food. 23 But none of Aaron's family who is not perfect can go near the holy curtain or the altar. He would make the holy place unclean. I am the Lord. I make them holy.'

24 Moses told all these rules to Aaron, to his sons and to all Israel's people.

Chapter 22

1 The Lord said to Moses, 2 'Israel's people give gifts to the Lord. Those gifts are holy. Tell Aaron and his sons that those things are holy. Tell them that they must remember that. They must give honour to my name. I am the Lord.

3 One of your sons may not be clean. That son must not come near the Lord's holy offerings.

But perhaps he may not obey my rule. He might go near to the holy gifts. The priests who are clean must punish him. They must send him away. He must go from the Lord's house. I am the Lord. This rule is for now and for all time. 4 If a son of Aaron has a skin illness, he must not eat the holy gifts. If pus is coming from his body, he is not clean. He must not eat the holy offerings until he is clean. He might touch something that has touched a dead body. Or if he touches an unclean man, he will become unclean. The man may be unclean because semen is coming from his body. 5 Aaron's son might touch an animal that moves on its stomach. Or he might touch a person who is not clean. If he does, Aaron's son will be unclean. 6 The son of Aaron who touches any of these things will be unclean until evening. He must not eat any of the holy gifts until he washes his body. 7 When the sun goes down, he will be clean. He can eat the holy gifts. They are his food. 8 He might find something that is dead. He must not eat it. He must not eat anything that an animal has torn. It will make him unclean. I am the Lord.

9 Aaron's sons must obey the Lord's rules. If they do not obey them, it is a sin. They will die. I am the Lord who makes people holy. 10 Only a person who is from the priest's family can eat the holy gifts. Another person who is living in the priest's house must not eat the holy gifts. If a person is being paid to work for the priest, he must not eat the holy gifts.

11 A slave can eat the holy gifts if he was born in the priest's house. Or he can eat the holy gifts if the priest bought him.

12 A priest's daughter might marry a man who is not a priest. If she has done that, she must not eat the holy food. 13 A priest's daughter's husband might send her away. Or her husband might die. She might not have any children. She may go back to live in her father's house. Then she can eat her father's food.

14 A person might make a mistake and eat a holy gift. He must give back to the priest the same food. He must also give 1/5th (one fifth) more. 15 The priest must not give the holy gifts to people who are not from Aaron's family. The gifts would become unclean. 16 If the people eat them they are sinning. They will have to pay for their sin. I am the Lord and I make them holy.'

Offerings that the Lord will not accept

17 The Lord said to Moses, 18 'Say this to Aaron, to his sons and to all the people. If any person gives a gift to the Lord, 19 he must give a bull (male cow), a sheep or a goat. The gift may be for a promise, or to thank the Lord for something or for a fellowship offering. The animal must be perfect. 20 They must not give any animal that is not perfect. The Lord will not accept that animal. 21 When a person brings an animal to the Lord as a special gift, it must be perfect. If it is, the Lord will accept it. 22 A person must not give to the Lord an animal that cannot see. The animal must not have a skin illness. And pus must not be coming from its body. The person must not burn an animal on the altar that is not perfect. 23 A person may give a male cow or a sheep with a body that is the wrong shape. He can use it as an offering to eat with his friends (fellowship offering). But the Lord will not take this animal as a gift for a promise. That gift must be perfect. You must not put on the altar an animal that is not perfect. 24 A person must not give a gift of an animal that has something wrong with its testicles (male parts). 25 This rule is for Israel's people. You must not take animals that are not perfect from foreigners. You must not offer them to the Lord. The Lord will not accept them because they are not perfect.'

26 The Lord said to Moses, 27 'When a cow or a sheep or a goat is born, it must stay with its mother for 7 (seven) days. From the 8th (eighth) day the people can give it as a burnt offering to the Lord. 28 They must not kill a cow or a sheep and its baby on the same day.

29 When they sacrifice an animal to thank the Lord, they must sacrifice it in the proper way. This will give the Lord pleasure. 30 They must eat it on the day that they kill it. They must not keep any of it until the next day. I am the Lord.

31 The people must obey my rules. 32 I am the Lord. They must give honour to my holy name. My people must believe that I am holy. I am the Lord. I make people holy. 33 I brought you out of Egypt and I became your God. I am the Lord.'

Chapter 23

Rules for the Seasons and for the special days

1 The Lord said to Moses, 2 'Tell Israel's people about the special days when they must worship the Lord. They are holy days. The Israelites must come together and have a feast on these days.

3 There are six days when a person can work. The seventh day is Saturday (Sabbath). A person must not do any work on that day. It is a day when people meet together for worship. You must not work in any place where you live. It is the Sabbath, a day for rest.

Passover and bread without yeast

4 There are other special days. They are holy feasts. On these days you must tell the people how to obey the Lord's rules. 5 One special day is the 14th day of the first month. When the sun goes down, the Passover to the Lord begins. 6 The 15th day of the first month, the feast of Bread without Yeast begins. For 7 (seven) days the people must eat bread that has no yeast in it. 7 On the first day the people must meet together and they must not work. 8 For 7 (seven) days the people must give burnt offerings to the Lord. On the 7th (seventh) day they must stop work and they must worship the Lord.'

Gifts of new grain

9 The Lord said to Moses, 10 'Tell Israel's people this. They will go into the country that I will give to them. And then they must harvest the grain. They must take the first part of the harvest in their arms. They must give this to the priest. 11 The priest will lift it to the Lord. Then the Lord will accept their gift. The priest will do this on the day after the Sabbath day. 12 On the same day the priest will bring a young sheep that is perfect to the Lord. It must be one year old. It is a gift from the people. 13 He will also bring 2/10ths of an ephah (about 4 litres or 8 pints) of the best flour mixed with oil. He will burn the gift as a sacrifice. The smell of it while it is burning will give the Lord pleasure. The people must also give a ¼ hin (about 1 litre or 2 pints) of wine as a gift to the Lord. 14 The people must not eat any of the new grain until they have given their gift to the Lord. They and their children must do this now and always. They must do it in any place that they live.

15 On the day after the Sabbath day the people will sacrifice their gifts to the Lord. After this, they must count 7 (seven) weeks. 16 They must count 50 days until the day after the 7th (seventh) Sabbath. Then they must give another gift of new grain to the Lord. 17 Each family must bring two loaves of bread as a special gift to the Lord. They must make the bread with 2/10ths ephah (about 4 litres or 8 pints) of good flour and yeast. This gift is from the first of their harvest fruits. 18 With the bread, all the people must bring seven perfect sheep. They must be males, each one year old. They must bring a bull (male cow). They must also bring two older male sheep. The priest will burn the grain and the animals as a gift to the Lord. The smell of them while they are burning will give the Lord pleasure. 19 The priest must sacrifice one male goat as a sin offering. The people must give two young sheep. They must be one year old. They are a gift to the Lord. 20 The priest will lift the animals and the bread to the Lord. They are a holy offering to the Lord. They are for the priest. 21 On this day, the people must not do any work. They must not work anywhere that they live. It is a special day to the Lord now and for all time to come.

22 When the people harvest the grain, they must not cut it to the edge of the field. They must not pick up any grain that falls. Some grain must remain in the field. It is for the poor people and for foreign people. I am the Lord your God.'

23 The Lord said to Moses, 24 'Tell Israel's people this. On the first day of the 7th (seventh) month, they must rest. It is a special day. They must worship the Lord together with the sound of trumpets. 25 They must not work. They must burn an offering to the Lord.'

The Day of Atonement

26 The Lord said to Moses, 27 'The 10th (tenth) day of the 7th (seventh) month is the Day of Atonement. On that day, the people must come together. They must not eat any food. They must burn an offering to the Lord. 28 They must not do any work. It is a holy day. On this special day, Aaron (the High Priest) must come near to the Lord. He will make atonement for the sins of the people. 29 You must punish any person who eats any food on that day. Send them away from my people. 30 I will kill any person who works on that day. 31 Nobody must work on that day. This rule is for now and for all time to come. You must obey it in any place where you are living. 32 It is a Sabbath rest for all the people. They must not eat any food. They must rest from the evening of the 9th (ninth) day until the evening of the 10th (tenth) day.'

The Feast of Houses that people have made from branches

33 The Lord said to Moses, 34 'Tell Israel's people that the 15th (fifteenth) day of the 7th (seventh) month is a special day. It is the Day of Houses that people have made from branches. The feast goes on for 7 (seven) days. 35 The first day is a special day. The people must not do any work. 36 For 7 (seven) days each person must give a gift to the Lord. The 8th (eighth) day is holy. The people must come together and they must give a burnt offering to the Lord. This is the last day of the feast. The people must not do any work on that day.

37 These are the rules for the special days of the Lord. You must tell people that they must bring offerings to the Lord on these days. They will bring gifts for burnt offerings each day. They must bring offerings of grain, animals and wine. 38 These are not the usual Sabbath gifts. They are not gifts to give thanks or for promises. But they are extra gifts for special days.

39 When the people have picked the grain, they can enjoy 7 (seven) feast days. The special days will begin on the 15th (fifteenth) day of the 7th (seventh) month. On the first day and on the 8th (eighth) day they can rest.

40 On the first day, they must take fruit and leaves from the trees. Then for 7 (seven) days they must worship the Lord. 41 They must do this for 7 (seven) days of each year. They must obey this rule in the 7th (seventh) month now, and for all the years to come. 42 All Israel's people must live in houses that they have made from branches for 7 (seven) days. 43 The people in the future will know that the Lord brought Israel's people out of Egypt. They will know that he is the Lord. And he caused them to live in houses that they made from branches. I am the Lord, your God.'

44 Moses told the people all that the Lord had told him.

Chapter 24

1 The Lord said to Moses, 2 'Tell Israel's people that they must bring to you the best oil. This will cause the light to burn all the time. 3 Aaron must put more oil in the lamp from evening to morning. The lamp is outside the curtain. That curtain is in the Holy Place. The light must never go out. This rule is for now and for all time to come. 4 The lamps on the gold thing that holds the lamps must burn always.

Rules about the bread that the people give to the Lord

5 The people must bake 12 loaves of bread. They must use the best flour. They must weigh the flour for each loaf. They must use 2/10ths of an ephah (4 litres or 8 pints). 6 They must put the loaves on a table in two rows. There must be six loaves in each row. 7 They must put incense near each row. They must burn the incense as a gift to the Lord instead of the bread. 8 They must put the bread on the table every Sabbath. It is a covenant between Israel's people and the Lord. 9 The bread is for Aaron and for his sons. They must eat it in a holy place. It is their holy part of the burnt offering to the Lord.'

The story of a man who said bad things about the Lord

10 There was a man. His mother was an Israelite and his father was a man from Egypt. The man had a quarrel with an Israelite man. 11 The Israelite woman's son said bad things about the Lord. The people took him to Moses. (The name of the mother was Shelomith. She was the daughter of Dibri from the family of Dan.) 12 They locked the man up. The Lord told them what to do with him.

13 The Lord said to Moses, 14 'Take the man outside the camp. All the people who heard him speak must put a hand on him. All the people must throw stones at him until he is dead. 15 Tell Israel's people, "It is a sin if any man says bad things about the Lord's name. 16 He must die. All the people must throw stones at him until he is dead." You must kill anyone who says bad things about the Lord's name. They may be a foreigner or an Israelite. You must kill them.

17 If any man kills another man you must kill him. 18 A man might kill an animal that belongs to another man. He must give an animal that is alive to the man. You must give a living animal if you take a living animal's life. 19 If a man hurts another man, you must also hurt him. 20 Whatever the man does to another man, the other man can do to him. If he takes an eye, you can take an eye. If he breaks a bone, you can break his bone. If he takes a tooth, you can take his tooth. 21 A man may kill an animal. That man must give back an animal that is alive. But if he kills a man, you must kill him. 22 This rule is for all the people. It is the same rule for Israelites and foreigners. I am the Lord your God.'

23 Moses spoke to Israel's people. A man had said bad things about the Lord. They took him outside the camp. They threw stones at him until he died. Israel's people did as the Lord had told Moses.

Chapter 25

The Sabbath Year

1 Moses was on Sinai's mountain. The Lord spoke to him there. 2 The Lord said, 'Speak to Israel's people. They will go into the country that I will give to them. Then the land must have a Sabbath rest. 3 They can plant seeds in the fields for 6 (six) years. They can cut the leaves of the plants and they can harvest the fruit for six years. 4 In the 7th (seventh) year, the land must have a rest. They must not plant seeds in the fields or cut the leaves. 5 They must not harvest fruit or grain. The land must have a year for rest. 6 All of the people can eat anything that grows by itself in the Sabbath year. That will be food for you and for your servants and for your animals. And other people who live among you can eat it. 7 The wild animals also can eat anything that grows by itself in the Sabbath year.

The Jubilee Year

8 The people must count 7 (seven) lots of Sabbath years (7x7 years). That is 49 years. 9 In the 50th year they must make loud music. They must blow trumpets on the 10th (tenth) day of the 7th (seventh) month. That is the Day of Atonement. They must blow the trumpet through all the country. 10 The year will be special. It is a Jubilee year. It is a time for every one of my people to become free. Everyone can return to his own land and to his family. 11 The 50th year is a Jubilee year. The people must not plant any seed in the fields. They must not harvest anything that grows by itself on the bushes. 12 It is a Jubilee year for the people. And they can eat only food that they take from the fields.

13 In the Jubilee year every person must return to the land of his family.

14 If the people buy and sell land from each other, they must be honest with each other. 15 The person who is selling the land will fix a price. He must count the number of years until the next Jubilee year. 16 When there are many years, the price must be big. When there are few years, the price must be small. What the person is selling are the plants from the fields. 17 Be honest with each other and respect the Lord. I am the Lord your God.

18 The people must obey the Lord's rules. If they do, they will be safe. 19 You will be able to grow food on the land. And the people will have plenty to eat. They will be safe. 20 The people may ask what they shall eat in the seventh year. They will not have planted any seeds. 21 The Lord will cause a lot of food to grow in the 6th (sixth) year. They will have food for three more years. 22 When a person plants seed in the 8th (eighth) year he will still be eating the harvest from the 6th (sixth) year. The next time he will harvest the plants from the fields will be in the 9th (ninth) year.

23 The people must never sell the land for all time. The land belongs to the Lord. He has said that the people can live on it. 24 A person may buy land. But he must remember that he may have to sell it back to the seller.

25 If a man becomes poor, he can sell some of his land. A person from his family must buy the land back for the man. 26 But the man might not have any family. If he stops being poor, he can buy the land back. 27 He must count how many years until the next Jubilee year. He must pay the right amount of money for the land. Then he can live on the land again. 28 If the man is too poor to buy the land back, it will belong to the other person. It will belong to the other person until the next Jubilee year. He must return it to the poor man in the Jubilee year.

29 A man may sell a house in a city with walls. For one year after he sells it, he can buy it back. 30 If the man does not buy back the house, it will belong to the other person and his sons. It will belong to them for all time. They will not have to return it in the Jubilee year. 31 If the house is in a village, a person can buy it back. If he does not buy it back, they will return it to him in the Jubilee year.

32 The Levites (people from the family of Levi) can buy back the houses in their towns. 33 In the Jubilee year, the Levites must get back the houses that they sold. Their towns belong to the Levites. 34 The Levites must not sell the fields that belong to their towns. The Lord gave to them their towns and cities to live in for all time.

People who have a lot of money must lend it to the poor people

35 An Israelite may become poor. He may not be able to feed his family. You must help him. You would help a visitor or a foreigner in the same way. You must help the man so that he can continue to live among you. 36 The man must not pay back more than you gave to him. You must obey the Lord. 37 The person who is feeding the man might give money or food to him. He must not ask for more back than he gave. 38 I am the Lord your God who brought you out of Egypt. I brought you into this country to be your God.

39 If an Israelite becomes poor, he might sell himself to another person. He must not work as a slave for that person. He must be like a paid servant. 40 He must work for that person until the next Jubilee year. 41 In the Jubilee year, you will make him free. He and his children can go back to his own house and family. 42 Israel's people belong to the Lord. I took them out of Egypt. They must not be slaves. 43 You must be kind to all Israelites. Remember to obey your God.

44 Israel's people can buy male and female slaves. Those slaves must come from other countries. 45 And Israelites can buy people from other countries who live among them. They may have children who were born in your country. You can buy them. They will become slaves. 46 You can give the slaves to your children when you die. But you must rule Israel's people in a kind way.

47 A person from another country may become rich. Then he might buy an Israelite who became poor. But the poor man can buy himself back at any time. 48 A person from the family of the poor man can buy him back. 49 A brother or a cousin of the poor man can buy him back. If the poor man becomes rich, he can pay to make himself free. 50 The man and the person who bought him must count the time until the Jubilee year. The man must pay the right amount of money to be free. 51 The Jubilee year may be many years away. If it is, the man must pay a lot of money to be free. 52 There may be a few years until the Jubilee year. If there are, he has to pay only a small amount of money to be free. 53 The person who has bought the man must pay him each year. You must cause the rich man to be kind to the man.

54 Perhaps nobody will pay any money for the man. But the man who bought him must make him free in the Jubilee year. 55 Israel's people belong to me. I brought them out of Egypt. They are my servants. I am the Lord.

Chapter 26

1 You must not make idols from stones and worship them. You must not draw things on stones and bend down in front of them. I am the Lord your God.

2 You must rest on Sabbath days and you must keep them holy. You must respect the Lord's house. I am the Lord.

3 The people must carefully obey the rules. 4 If they do, I will send rain at the proper time. Plants for food will grow in the ground. Fruit will grow on your trees. 5 The people will harvest grain until the grapes are ready to eat. They will harvest the grapes until it is the time to plant seeds. They will have all the food to eat that they need. I will keep them safe in their country.

6 I will stop war in Israel. When the people sleep, they will not be afraid. I will take the wild animals away. Other people will not hurt my people. 7 Israel's enemies will run away from them. They will kill their enemies. 8 Five (5) of you will run after 100 of them. And 100 of you will run after 1000 enemies. You will kill all your enemies.

9 I will do good things for your people and I will give many children to them. Their number will grow. I will do everything that I have promised to do for them. 10 They will have so much food that some will remain after the next harvest. 11 I will live among the people. I will never turn away from them. 12 I will walk among the people. They will belong to me. 13 I am the Lord your God. I brought you out of Egypt. You will not be the slaves of people in Egypt. I saved you so that you need not be ashamed.

People who do not obey the rules will not give any pleasure to the Lord

14 The Lord will be angry if the people do not listen to him. He will be angry if they do not obey his rules.

15 The people may not respect or obey the Lord's rules. So they will not be doing what they promised to him. 16 So the Lord will send illnesses to the people. They will be afraid. The people will have illnesses in their eyes. They will get thin and they will die. They will plant their seed and their enemies will eat the fruit. 17 The Lord will fight against you. Your enemies will win the war. They will become your rulers. Your soldiers will run away even when nobody is running after them.

18 The people may not obey the Lord even after this. If they do not, the Lord will punish them 7 (seven) times more strongly. 19 He will make them ashamed. He will not send any rain and the land will be hard and dry. 20 Even if they do a lot of work, no grain will grow. No fruit will grow on the trees.

21 The people may still not listen to the Lord. If they do not, he will be 7 (seven) times more angry. If they do not obey him, he will cause their lives to be 7 (seven) times more difficult. 22 He will send wild animals to kill their children and their animals. The country will be almost empty.

23 The people may still not listen to the Lord. If they do not, he will be angry. 24 He will become their enemy. If they do not obey him, he will punish them 7 (seven) times more strongly. 25 He will send enemy soldiers to kill the people. They have not done what they promised to do. So he will punish them for that. If they go back to their cities, he will send them illnesses. The enemy will win the war. 26 The people will not have any food. A woman will bake one loaf for ten families. They will weigh it to give one part to each family. When a person eats his piece of bread, he will still be hungry.

27 If the people still turn away from the Lord, he will be even more angry. They will not turn away from their sin. 28 So he will turn away from them. He will punish them 7 (seven) times more again. 29 They will be so hungry that they will eat their own children. 30 The Lord will destroy the places where they worship false gods. He will destroy their very bad incense altars. He will put their dead bodies round their idols. He will hate them. 31 He will destroy the cities. He will destroy the places for wrong worship. Nobody will burn incense to give the Lord pleasure. 32 The Lord will destroy the land. He will cause the enemies who live in your country to hate it. 33 The Lord will push you out. He will send your people away to other countries. He will destroy your cities. He will make your land a desert. 34 The land will have a Sabbath rest while there are no people in it. 35 All the time that it is empty, the land will have rest. It will have the Sabbath rest that it did not have. It did not have it when you lived in it.

36 Some of Israel's people will remain in other countries. They will be frightened. A leaf that is blowing in the wind will cause them to run away. It will be like when an enemy is running after them. They will fall even if no enemy is running after them. 37 They will fall over each other when nobody is running after them. They will not be strong enough to fight their enemies. 38 They will die in the countries where they are living. Those countries will cause their deaths. 39 Those who remain here will die because of their sins. They will die because their fathers and grandfathers did not obey the Lord.

40 Your sons and your grandsons must tell me, the Lord, that they are sorry. They must be sorry because they did not obey my rules. They must be sorry that they turned away from me. 41 They must remember that they made me angry. They caused me to turn away from them. I am the Lord, and I sent them into their enemies' country. They will be sorry until I have punished them enough. 42 Then I will remember my covenant with Abraham, Isaac and Jacob. I will remember that I gave their land to them. 43 Before this, the country will be empty and it will have a rest. My people will pay for the bad things that they did. 44 But I, the Lord, will not kill all of them. The people will be living in their enemies' country. Then I will remember them. I will not leave them alone. I will remember my covenant with their fathers. I am the Lord, their God. 45 The Lord will remember his covenant with the people that he brought out of Egypt. The people in every country saw him do this. He is the Lord.'

46 These are the rules that the Lord gave to Moses on the mountain called Sinai. They are his covenant with Israel's people

Chapter 27

Rules about gifts to the Lord

1 The Lord said to Moses, 2 'Speak to Israel's people. Tell them this. A person might give another person to the Lord for a special promise.

3 They can make that person free.

But they must give the right amount of money to the Lord. For a man between 20 years and 60 years old, they must give 50 pieces of silver. 4 For a woman, they must give 30 pieces of silver. 5 For a male between five years and 20 years old, they must give to the Lord 20 pieces of silver. For a female, they must give 10 pieces of silver. 6 For a boy between one month and five years old, they must give five pieces of silver. For a girl of the same age, the Lord must have three pieces of silver. 7 If a man is older than 60 years, they must give 15 pieces of silver. For a woman, they must give 10 pieces of silver. 8 A person might say this special promise to the Lord. But he might be too poor to pay the money. He must bring the person to the priest. The priest will tell the person how much money to pay. The priest will know how much money the man can give.

9 If the promise is to give an animal to the Lord, the animal becomes holy. 10 The person must not change a good animal for a bad animal. He must not change a bad animal for a good animal. If the person does change one animal for another, both the animals become holy.

11 The animal might be an animal that you must not eat. If it is, the person must bring it to the priest. 12 The priest will decide if the animal is good or bad. 13 The person might want to buy the animal back. He must pay the price of the animal and 1/5 (one fifth) more.

14 A person might give his house to the Lord. The priest will decide if the house is good or bad. The priest will decide the price of the house. 15 The person might want to buy the house back. He must pay the price of the house and 1/5th (one fifth) more. Then it will again belong to him.

16 A person might give part of his land to the Lord. The person will decide the price by how much seed the land needs. The price will be 50 pieces of silver for a homer (220 litres or 6 bushels) of seed. 17 If a person gives his land in a Jubilee year, the price is the same. 18 A person might give his land after the Jubilee year. The priest will count the number of years before the next Jubilee. The price will be less. 19 A person might want to buy the land back. He must pay the price of the land and 1/5th (one fifth) more. 20 He may not buy it back before the year of Jubilee. Then the field becomes holy. But the man may have sold the land to another person. If he has, he cannot get it back. 21 In the Jubilee year the land will become holy. Then it will belong to the priests.

22 A person might buy some land from another family. He might give that land to the Lord. 23 The priest will count how many years there are until the Jubilee year. The person must pay the money on that day. The money is holy to the Lord. 24 In the Jubilee year, the land returns to the family from whom he bought it. 25 The priest must decide the price of the land. He must use the correct measures.

26 The first baby that an animal has is holy. It belongs to the Lord. A person cannot give it as a special gift to the Lord. 27 The animal might be an unclean animal (an animal that they must not eat). The person can pay the price of the animal and 1/5 (one fifth) more to get it back. If the person does not buy it back, the priest will sell it.

28 A man might give to the Lord something that the man has. Everything that a man gives like that is holy. It might be a person, an animal or land. The priest must not sell it. A man cannot take it back. Everything that someone gives to the Lord is most holy.

29 The Lord might decide that a person must die. If he does, nobody can buy him back. The person must die.

30 One tenth (1/10th) of everything that comes from the land is holy. It may be grain or fruit. It belongs to the Lord. 31 If a person buys back any of his gift to the Lord, he must pay the price and 1/5th (one fifth) more. 32 Out of every ten animals, one animal is holy. It belongs to the Lord. 33 A person must not change a good animal for a bad animal. A person must not change a bad animal for a good animal. If he does that, both animals are holy. They belong to the Lord. A person cannot buy them back.'

34 These are the rules that the Lord gave to Moses on the mountain called Sinai. They are the rules for Israel's people.

God gives rules to Israel's people

Numbers

About this book

This is the story of Israel's people. They were travelling from Egypt to the country called Canaan. They were in the desert for 40 years.

Moses was the man that the LORD chose to guide the Israelites out of Egypt. Aaron was the brother of Moses. He was the first priest that the Israelites had.

Chapter 1

1 The Israelites were in the Desert of Sinai. It was the first day of the second month of the second year after they left Egypt. Moses was in the Tent of Meeting. The LORD said to Moses,

2 'Put the people into clans and families and count them. Make a list. Write the name of each man on the list. 3 You and Aaron must record the names of all the men in each group. But only record the names of men who are 20 years old or older. Those men can fight in the army. 4 The most important man from each tribe must help you.

5 These are the men who must help you:

Elizur, who is the son of Shedeur. He is from the tribe of Reuben.

6 Shelumiel, who is the son of Zurishaddai. He is from the tribe of Simeon.

7 Nahshon, who is the son of Amminadab. He is from the tribe of Judah.

8 Nethanel, who is the son of Zuar. He is from the tribe of Issachar.

9 Eliab, who is the son of Helon. He is from the tribe of Zebulun.

10 Elishama, who is the son of Ammihud. He is from the tribe of Ephraim.

Gamaliel, who is the son of Pedahzur. He is from the tribe of Manasseh.

(Ephraim and Manasseh were Joseph's sons.)

11 Abidan, who is the son of Gideoni. He is from the tribe of Benjamin.

12 Ahiezer, who is the son of Ammishaddai. He is from the tribe of Dan.

13 Pagiel, who is the son of Ochran. He is from the tribe of Asher.

14 Eliasaph, who is the son of Deuel. He is from the tribe of Gad.

15 Ahira, who is the son of Enan. He is from the tribe of Naphtali.'

16 The LORD said that Moses must choose those men from among the people. They were leaders of their clans. They were Israel's leaders. 17 Those men helped Moses and Aaron. 18 On the first day of the second month, they said that all the people must come together. The people were in clans and in families. They made a list of all the men who were 20 years old or older. 19 They obeyed the things that the LORD had said to Moses. So he recorded the names in the Desert of Sinai.

20 The men in the tribe of Reuben came first. Reuben was the first son of Israel (Jacob). They recorded the names of all the men in each clan and family. All the men who were 20 years old or older were on the list. Those men could fight in the army. 21 There were 46 500 men from the tribe of Reuben.

22 Next was the tribe of Simeon. They recorded the names of all the men in each clan and family.

All the men who were 20 years old or older were on the list. Those men could fight in the army. 23 There were 59 300 men from the tribe of Simeon. 24 Next was the tribe of Gad. They recorded the names of all the men in each clan and family. All the men who were 20 years old or older were on the list. Those men could fight in the army. 25 There were 45 650 men from the tribe of Gad. 26 Next was the tribe of Judah. They recorded the names of all the men in each clan and family. All the men who were 20 years old or older were on the list. Those men could fight in the army. 27 There were 74 600 men from the tribe of Judah. 28 Next was the tribe of Issachar. They recorded the names of all the men in each clan and family. All the men who were 20 years old or older were on the list. Those men could fight in the army.

29 There were 54 400 men from the tribe of Issachar. 30 Next was the tribe of Zebulun. They recorded the names of all the men in each clan and family. All the men who were 20 years old or older were on the list. Those men could fight in the army.

31 There were 57 400 men from the tribe of Zebulun. 32 Ephraim was a son of Joseph. They recorded the names of all the men in each clan and family. All the men who were 20 years old or older were on the list. Those men could fight in the army. 33 There were 40 500 men from the tribe of Ephraim. 34 Manasseh was a son of Joseph. They recorded the names of all the men in each clan and family. All the men who were 20 years old or older were on the list. Those men could fight in the army. 35 There were 32 200 men from the tribe of Manasseh. 36 Next was the tribe of Benjamin. They recorded the names of all the men in each clan and family. All the men who were 20 years old or older were on the list. Those men could fight in the army. 37 There were 35 400 men from the tribe of Benjamin. 38 Next was the tribe of Dan. They recorded the names of all the men in each clan and family. All the men who were 20 years old or older were on the list. Those men could fight in the army. 39 There were 62 700 men from the tribe of Dan. 40 Next was the tribe of Asher. They recorded the names of all the men in each clan and family. All the men who were 20 years old or older were on the list. Those men could fight in the army. 41 There were 41 500 men from the tribe of Asher. 42 Next was the tribe of Naphtali. They recorded the names of all the men in each clan and family. All the men who were 20 years old or older were on the list. Those men could fight in the army. 43 There were 53 400 men from the tribe of Naphtali.

44 Moses and Aaron made a list of the men. The 12 leaders of Israel helped them to do it. That was one man from each tribe. 45 They recorded the names of all the men in each family. All the men who were 20 years old or older were on the list. Those men could fight in the army. 46 The number of all the men was 603 550.

47 But Moses and Aaron did not count the Levites among the other men. 48 The LORD had said to Moses, 49 'You must not count the tribe of Levi. You must not put the Levites on the list with the other Israelites. 50 The Levites' work is in the Tent of Meeting. They must carry the Tent everywhere. They must carry everything from the Tent and their work is with all those things. And they must put their tents round it. 51 When the people move to another place, the Levites must pack the Tent. When the people make a new camp, the Levites must put the Tent up again. If any other person comes near to the Tent, he must die. 52 All the other Israelites must camp in groups. Each man must camp with his own group. Each group must put up its own flag. 53 But the Levites must camp on each side of the Tent of Meeting. They must keep it safe. Then the LORD will not be angry with the people.'

54 The Israelites did everything that the LORD had said to Moses.

Chapter 2

1 The LORD said to Moses and Aaron, 2 'The Israelites must camp on each side of the Tent of the LORD. They must not be near to it but they should be looking towards it. They must camp in tribes. Each person must be with his own tribe. Each tribe must have its own flag.

3 The people in Judah's tribe must be on the east side of the Tent. They must have their flag with them and they must camp in groups. The leader of the tribe of Judah is Nahshon, the son of Amminadab. 4 There will be 74 600 soldiers in his army.

5 The tribe of Issachar will camp next to them. The leader of the tribe of Issachar is Nethanel, the son of Zuar. 6 There will be 54 400 soldiers in his army.

7 The tribe of Zebulun will be next. The leader of the tribe of Zebulun is Eliab, the son of Helon. 8 There will be 57 400 soldiers in his army.

9 So there will be 186 400 soldiers in the three groups in Judah's camp. They will march first.

10 The tribe of Reuben must be on the south side of the Tent. They must have their flag with them and they must camp in groups. The leader of the tribe of Reuben is Elizur, the son of Shedeur. 11 There will be 46 500 soldiers in his army.

12 The tribe of Simeon will camp next to them. The leader of the tribe of Simeon is Shelumiel, the son of Zurishaddai. 13 There will be 59 300 soldiers in his army.

14 The tribe of Gad will be next. The leader of the tribe of Gad is Eliasaph, the son of Reuel. 15 There will be 45 650 soldiers in his army.

16 So there will be 151 450 soldiers in the three groups in Reuben's camp. They will march second.

17 The Levites must march next. The Levites must carry the Tent of Meeting. They must march between the first two groups of tribes and the last two groups of tribes. Each man must be in his own place. They must march with their flag

18 The tribe of Ephraim must be on the west side of the Tent. They must have their flag with them and they must camp in groups. The leader of the tribe of Ephraim is Elishama, the son of Ammihud. 19 There will be 40 500 soldiers in his army.

20 The tribe of Manasseh will camp next to them. The leader of the tribe of Manasseh is Gamaliel, the son of Pedahzur. 21 There will be 32 200 soldiers in his army.

22 The tribe of Benjamin will be next. The leader of the tribe of Benjamin is Abidan, the son of Gideoni. 23 There will be 35 400 soldiers in his army.

24 So there will be 108 100 soldiers in the three groups in Ephraim's camp. They will march third.

25 The tribe of Dan must be on the north side of the Tent. They must have their flag with them and they must camp in groups. The leader of the tribe of Dan is Ahiezer, the son of Ammishaddai. 26 There will be 62 700 soldiers in his army.

27 The tribe of Asher will camp next to them. The leader of the tribe of Asher is Pagiel, the son of Ochran. 28 There will be 41 500 soldiers in his army.

29 The tribe of Naphtali will be next. The leader of the tribe of Naphtali is Ahira, the son of Enan. 30 There will be 53 400 soldiers in his army.

31 So there will be 157 600 soldiers in the three groups in Dan's camp. They will march last with their flag.'

32 Moses and his helpers had counted all the Israelite men who were able to fight. They had counted them in groups. There were 603 550 soldiers. 33 They did not count the Levites. The LORD had told Moses that they must not count them among the other Israelites.

34 The Israelites did everything that the LORD had said to Moses. They camped in the way that the LORD wanted. Each tribe camped under its own flag. When they started to travel, each man walked with his own clan and his own family.

Chapter 3

About the Levites

1 This is the list of the family of Aaron and Moses, when the LORD spoke to Moses. The LORD spoke to Moses on the mountain called Sinai

2 The names of the sons of Aaron were Nadab, Abihu, Eleazar and Ithamar. Nadab was the oldest son. 3 These are the names of the sons of Aaron. Aaron anointed them. And he gave authority to them to work as priests.

4 But Nadab and Abihu fell down and died in front of the LORD. That happened when they offered unholy fire to the LORD in the Sinai desert. They had no children. So only Eleazar and Ithamar worked as priests while their father Aaron was alive.

The Levites must work for the priests

5 Then the LORD said to Moses, 6 'Bring the tribe of Levi to Aaron the priest. They must help him. 7 They must work for him and for all the Israelites. They must work in front of the Tent of Meeting. They must work at God's Tent.

8 They must work on behalf of the Israelites. They must do all the necessary work with the things that are in the Tent of Meeting. Their work is at God's Tent. 9 Give the Levites to Aaron and to his descendants. So they will be the Israelites who help him. And they do not have to do anything else. 10 But you must make a list of Aaron and his descendants. They will be the priests. If any other person comes near, he must die.' 11 The LORD also said to Moses, 12 'I will not take the first son of every woman of Israel. I will take all the Levites instead. 13 I killed all the first-born children of the Egyptians. Then the first-born of every person and animal of Israel became mine. Now, I will not have the first-born child. I will have all the Levites instead. They are mine. I am the LORD!'

Moses and Aaron count the Levites

14 The LORD said to Moses in the Desert of Sinai, 15 'Put the Levites into clans and families and count them. Make a list of every male who is a month old or older.' 16 Moses obeyed the LORD. So Moses recorded them as the LORD said. 17 The names of the sons of Levi were Gershon, Kohath and Merari. 18 Gershon had two sons. Their names were Libni and Shimei. 19 Kohath's sons were called Amram, Izhar, Hebron and Uzziel. 20 Merari's sons were called Mahli and Mushi. Those were the sons and grandsons of Levi. They had become the leaders of the clans of Levi's tribe.

21 There were two families in Gershon's clan. They were the families of Libni and Shimei. 22 They had 7500 males who were one month or older in their list. 23 Gershon's clans had to camp on the west side of God's Tent. 24 The leader of the clan of Gershon was Eliasaph the son of Lael. 25 The descendants of Gershon had to work with the cloth of the walls and the doors of God's Tent. 26 There was a yard outside God's Tent. This yard was round God's Tent and round the altar. There were curtains that hung round this yard. Those men had to work with these curtains. Also, they had to work with the ropes and the curtain for the place where people went into the yard. And they also did all the work with those things.

27 The descendants of Amram, Izhar, Hebron and Uzziel belonged to the Kohath's clan. 28 There were 8600 males who were one month old or older in this clan. They were one month old or older when Moses counted them. They had to work in God's Holy Tent. 29 Kohath's descendants had to camp on the south side of God's Tent. 30 The leader of Kohath's descendants was Elizaphan the son of Uzziel. 31 They had to work with the Covenant Box, the table and the lamp stands. They had to work with the altar and the tools that the priests used in God's Holy Tent. Also they had to work with the curtain in front of the Most Holy Place in God's Tent. And they also did all the work with those things. 32 Eleazar the son of Aaron the priest was the most important leader of the Levites. He ruled over those people who did all the work in God's Holy Tent.

33 The descendants of Mahli and Mushi belonged to Merari's clan. 34 There were 6200 males in that list. They were one month old or older when Moses counted them. 35 The leader of Merari's clan was Zuriel, the son of Abihail. They had to camp on the north side of God's Tent. 36 They had to work with all the boards of God's Tent and with all the things that held it up. 37 They also had to work with all the things that held up the cloth for the yard round God's Tent.

38 Moses, Aaron and the sons of Aaron had to camp in front of God's Tent. They had to camp on the east side. They were the only people who could go into God's Holy Tent. Any other person who went near it must die. 39 So Moses and Aaron obeyed the LORD. They counted the Levites by their clans. There were 22 000 males who were one month old or older.

The Levites take the place of the first-born sons of the Israelites

40 The LORD said to Moses, 'Record all the first-born males of the Israelites. Record every male who is one month old or older. And count their names. 41 The Israelites' first-born sons are mine. But I will accept all the males among the Levites instead. Also, the Israelites' first-born animals are mine. But I will accept the animals of the Levites instead.'

42 So Moses counted all the first-born males among the Israelites as the LORD had said. 43 He counted 22 273 first-born males who were one month old or older. He made a list of their names.

44 Then the LORD said to Moses, 45 'Do not use the first-born males among the people. Accept the Levites instead.

Do not use the first-born animals of the people. Accept the animals of the Levites instead. The Levites will be mine. I am the LORD. 46 There are 273 more first-born males of the people than there are Levites. The people must buy them back from the LORD. 47 You must accept 5 shekels for each extra first-born male. The shekel must have the same weight as the shekel that the Levites use in God's Holy Tent. There are 20 gerahs in one shekel. 48 Give the money that buys back the extra males to Aaron and his sons.' 49 So Moses took the money to buy back the extra 273 first-born sons. That was because the number of first-born sons was more than the number of Levites. 50 He took 1365 shekels from them. The shekels had the same weight as the shekel that the Levites used in God's Holy Tent. 51 Moses gave the money to Aaron and his sons. The LORD had told him that he must do that. So he did it.

Chapter 4

1 The LORD said to Moses and Aaron, 2 'Write a list of the people in Kohath's clan in their families. That list must be separate from the list of the other Levites. 3 Record the men who can work in the Tent of Meeting. Record them if they are between 30 and 50 years old.

4 These men must work with everything that is most holy in the Tent of Meeting. 5 When the people are ready to move, Aaron and his sons must go into the Tent of Meeting. They must take down the curtain that is in front of the Covenant Box. They must cover the Covenant Box with the curtain. 6 Then they must cover the curtain with good leather. On the top of that, they must put a blue cloth. Then, they must put in its pieces of wood so that they can carry the Covenant Box.

7 They must put a blue cloth over the table for the special bread. The bread must remain on the table. The cloth must cover the plates, bowls and dishes on the table. It must also cover the jars for the wine that they offer to the LORD. 8 Then they must cover all that with a red cloth. On the top of the red cloth, they must put good leather. Then they must put in its pieces of wood so that they can carry the table.

9 They must cover the lamp stand and its tools with a blue cloth. They must also cover the jars for the oil with the blue cloth. 10 Then they must cover all this with good leather. They must carry it on a board.

11 They must cover the gold altar with a blue cloth. They must cover the blue cloth with good leather. Then they must put in its pieces of wood so that they can carry the altar. 12 They must cover all the tools from God's Holy Tent with a blue cloth. They must cover the blue cloth with good leather. They must carry all this on a board.

13 They must remove the ashes from the bronze altar. They must cover the bronze altar with a purple cloth. 14 They must put all the tools on the bronze altar. That includes the pans for the fire, the forks for the meat, the spades and the bowls. They must cover all that with good leather. Then they must put in its pieces of wood so that they can carry the altar.

15 When the camp is ready to move, the men from Kohath's clan must be ready to carry all those things. But they must wait until Aaron and his sons have covered God's Holy Tent and all its holy things. The men from Kohath's clan must not touch the holy things. They will die if they touch the holy things. These are the duties of Kohath's clan. They must carry the things from the Tent of Meeting when the Israelites travel.

16 Eleazar, who is the son of Aaron the priest, must keep the oil for the light. He must keep the incense and the offering of flour. He must keep the special oil. The special oil marks everything that the LORD chooses. Eleazar must work with the whole Tent of Meeting. He must work with God's Holy Tent and with everything in it.'

17 Then the LORD said to Moses and Aaron, 18 'You must not cause the end of Kohath's clan from among the Levites.

19 Do not let the men in that clans die. That will happen if they come near to the most holy things. You must do this: Aaron and his sons must go into the Tent of the LORD. They will tell each man the work that he must do. And they must tell each man the things that he must carry. 20 But the men from Kohath's clan must not look at anything that is holy, even for a moment. If they do look at those things, they will die.'

21 Then the LORD said to Moses, 22 'Also write a list of the people in Gershon's clan in their families. 23 Record the men who can work in the Tent of Meeting. Record them if they are between 30 and 50 years old.

24 The work of the men in Gershon's clan is to carry everything. 25 The men from that clan must carry the curtains of God's Tent. And they must carry the Tent of Meeting with the thing that covers it. And they must carry the good leather that covers all that. And they must carry the curtain for the place where people go into the Tent of Meeting. 26 They must carry the curtains of the yard that is round God's Tent. Also, they must carry the curtain and ropes for the place where people go into the yard. That is the yard that is round God's Tent and the altar. The men from Gershon's clan must carry all the tools that belong with those curtains. They must do everything that all those things need. 27 The men in Gershon's clan must do everything that Aaron and his sons ask them to do. Aaron and his sons must tell them the things that they should carry. And they must tell them everything that they should do. 28 That is the work for the Tent of Meeting that the descendants of Gershon must do. Ithamar, the son of Aaron the priest will tell them the things that they must do.'

29 Then the LORD said to Moses, 'Write a list of the people in Merari's clan in their families. 30 Record the men who can work in the Tent of Meeting. Record them if they are between 30 and 50 years old. 31 This is the work of the men in Merari's clan. They must carry the frames of the Tent of Meeting and its bars. And they must carry its pillars and its bases. 32 And they must carry the pillars, bases, nails of wood and ropes of the yard that is round God's Tent. And the men in Merari's clan must keep all the tools that belong with those things safe. Each man in Merari's clan must keep particular things safe. Tell each man which things he must carry. 33 That is the work of the descendants of Merari in the Tent of Meeting. Ithamar, the son of Aaron the priest, will tell them the things that they must do.'

34 So Moses, Aaron and the people's leaders recorded the names of Kohath's descendants in their clans and in their families. 35 They recorded the men who could work in the Tent of Meeting. They recorded them if they were between 30 and 50 years old. 36 They recorded them in clans. There were 2750 men. 37 Moses and Aaron recorded the descendants of Kohath who worked at the Tent of Meeting. The LORD had told Moses that they must do that.

38 Moses and Aaron also recorded the names of Gershon's descendants in their clans and in their families. 39 They recorded the men who could work in the Tent of Meeting. They recorded them if they were between 30 and 50 years old. 40 They recorded them in clans and families. There were 2630 men. 41 Moses and Aaron recorded the descendants of Gershon who worked at the Tent of Meeting. The LORD had told Moses that they must do that.

42 Moses and Aaron also recorded the names of Merari's descendants in their clans and in their families. 43 They counted all the men who worked in the Tent of Meeting. They counted them if they were between 30 and 50 years old. 44 They recorded them in clans. There were 3200 men. 45 Moses and Aaron recorded the descendants of Merari who worked at the Tent of Meeting. The LORD had told Moses that they must do that.

46 Moses, Aaron and the people's leaders recorded the names of the Levites in their clans and in their families. 47 They counted all the men who worked in the Tent of Meeting. And they counted all the men who carried any of its things. They counted them if they were between 30 and 50 years old. 48 There were 8580 Levites in the list. 49 They told each man the things that he must do. Or they told him what he must carry. Moses recorded all their names. The LORD had told him that he must do that.

Chapter 5

1 The LORD said to Moses, 2 'Speak to the Israelites. They must send any person with an illness of the skin away from the camp. Somebody may have an illness that makes water. Any person like that is not clean. Any person who has touched a dead person is not clean. Send those people out of the camp too. 3 Do those things with both males and females. Send them out of the camp. They must not make the camp, where the LORD lives among the people, not clean.' 4 The Israelites did what the LORD had said to Moses. They sent those people outside the camp.

Gifts to the LORD and to the people when someone sins

5 The LORD said to Moses, 6 'Tell these rules to the Israelites: A person might do a wrong thing against another person. If they do, then they have sinned against me. 7 That person must agree that they have sinned. They must pay the right amount to the other person. Also, they must pay an extra 20% of that amount.

8 But the other person may have died. The other person may not have a relative who can accept the money. If that happens, the money must go to the LORD. The person who did a wrong thing must give the money and a male sheep to the priest. The sheep is a special gift to the LORD to make everything right. Then I will forgive that person. 9 All the special gifts from the Israelites to the LORD are for the priest. 10 The priest will keep all the special gifts.'

How to find out if a wife is doing something wrong

11 The LORD said to Moses, 12 'Speak to the Israelites. Tell them to follow these rules. A woman may do wrong things against her husband. 13 She might have had sex with another man. The husband might not be sure about this. His wife might have kept it secret. Nobody came in while it was happening. So there is nobody to say that it happened. 14 But the man may think that it happened. He will be angry. But she may not have made herself unholy in that way. 15 The man must take his wife to the priest. He must bring 0.1ephahs of flour from barley with him. This is an offering of flour to discover if his wife really did do those things. So he must not put oil or incense on the offering of flour. That is an offering of flour because the man does not trust his wife.

16 Then the priest will bring the woman to stand in front of the LORD. 17 He must pour some holy water into a bowl that someone has made out of clay. He must take some dust from the floor of God's Tent. And he must put the dust into the water. 18 Then the priest must make the woman's hair free. He must put into her hands the offering of flour. That is the offering of flour because the man does not trust his wife. The priest must hold the bowl that contains the bitter water. The bitter water brings a curse. 19 Then the woman must agree to the special promise that the priest speaks. The priest should tell her that she must agree. He must say, "This water brings a curse. If no other man has had sex with you, it will not hurt you. 20 But if another man has had sex with you, 21 the bitter water will cause your female parts to decrease. Your stomach will become very big. 22 That will happen when you drink the bitter water." The woman must say, "That should happen. I agree!"

23 Then the priest must write everything on special paper. Then he must wash off the words into the bitter water. 24 He must tell the woman that she must drink the bitter water. This water that brings a curse will go into her body. It may cause her to be very ill. 25 But first, the priest must take the offering of flour from her hands. That is the offering of flour because the man does not trust his wife. The priest must lift it up in front of the LORD. Then he must bring it to the altar. 26 He must burn a small part of it as a sacrifice. After that, the woman must drink the bitter water. 27 If the woman has had sex with another man, the water will cause her to have very bad pain. Her female parts will decrease. Her stomach will become very big. And people will curse her. 28 But, if she did not do those wrong things, the water will not hurt her. She will be able to have babies.

29-30 Perhaps a man is angry because his wife has had sex with another man. Or a man may think that his wife has had sex with another man. You must do this. This is the rule. The man must bring her in front of the LORD. The priest must obey all these rules. 31 If the woman did not do those wrong things, you must not punish her husband. But if the woman did do those wrong things, you must punish her.'

Chapter 6

People who make special promises to the LORD

1 The LORD said to Moses, 2 'Tell the Israelites this: "A man or a woman may want to make a special promise to the LORD. That will make him or her separate from other people. He or she will become a Nazirite. 3 They must not drink wine. They must not drink any beer or vinegar. They must not drink the juice of grapes or eat grapes or raisins. 4 They must not eat the seeds of grapes for all the time that they are Nazirites. They must not even eat what covers the fruit outside.

5 A person must not cut his hair during the time that he is a Nazirite. He must be different all the time that he is separate from the people. He must let the hair on his head grow long. 6 He must not go near a dead body while he is separate from the people. 7 His hair shows that he is separate for God. So, he must not go near a dead body. He must not go near it even if the dead person is his father mother, brother or sister. 8 During the time that the person is a Nazirite, he is holy to the LORD.

9 He may be with a person when that person dies. Then his head is not still clean. The Nazirite must remove all the hair from his head 7 days after the person dies. Then he will be clean. 10 On day 8, he must bring two doves or two young pigeons to the door of the Tent of Meeting. He must give them to the priest.

11 The priest must sacrifice one bird as a sin-offering and the other bird as a burnt-offering. The priest must do that because the Nazirite sinned. He went too near to a dead body. That will make the Nazirite's head clean again on that same day. 12 He must begin his time as a Nazirite again, with a new promise to the LORD. He cannot include the days before he became unclean. He must bring a male sheep that is one year old. That is a guilt-offering.

13 He is a Nazirite for a certain time. When that time finishes, the people must bring him to the door of the Tent of Meeting. 14 He must offer to the LORD three animals that have nothing wrong with them. He must offer a young male sheep that is one year old. That is a burnt-offering. He must offer a young female sheep that is one year old. That is a sin-offering. He must offer a male sheep. That is a friendship-offering. 15 And he must bring a basket of bread that people have made without yeast. He must bring cakes that people have made with the best flour and oil. Also, he must bring thin biscuits with oil on them. But someone must have made them without yeast too. He must bring the proper offerings of flour and of wine with them.

16 The priest must offer those things to the LORD. And he must sacrifice the sin-offering and the burnt-offering. 17 Then the priest must sacrifice the male sheep as a friendship-offering to the LORD. He must offer the basket of bread. He must give the offerings of flour and of wine with it.

18 Then the Nazirite must stand at the place where people go into the Tent of Meeting. He must remove all the hair from his head. He must put his hair into the same fire where the priest has cooked the friendship-offering.

19 When the male sheep is ready to eat, the priest must take its shoulder. Also, he must take one loaf and one thin biscuit from the basket. The loaf and the biscuit must not have yeast in them. The priest must put these things into the hands of the Nazirite who has removed the hair from his head. 20 The Nazirite must give those things back to the priest. The priest must lift them up to the LORD as a special gift. They are a special gift for the priest. Also, the priest can eat the front part of the sheep and its back leg. After that, the Nazirite can drink wine."

21 Those are the rules about Nazirites. Also, the Nazirite may give anything else that he can give. And he must bring any other gift that he promised to me.'

The priests ask the LORD to help the people

22 The LORD said to Moses, 23 'Tell Aaron and his sons this. They must use these words when they ask the LORD to help the Israelites.

24 They must say, "I pray that the LORD will bless you. I pray that the LORD will keep you safe.

25 I pray that the LORD will smile at you. And I pray that he will be very kind to you.

26 I pray that the LORD will look at you. And I pray that he will give peace to you."

27 Aaron and his sons must say my name. They must ask me to help the Israelites. If they do that, I will bless the Israelites.'

Chapter 7

1 When Moses had raised God's Tent, he marked it for the LORD with oil. He gave the Tent and everything in it to the LORD. He marked the altar and all the tools with oil. He gave the altar and all the tools to the LORD. 2 Then the 12 leaders of Israel's tribes came to God's Tent. They brought gifts. These men were the leaders of the people that they counted. 3 They brought their gifts to the LORD. They brought 6 carts, one cart for every two leaders. They brought 12 oxen. That was one ox for each leader. They brought it all to God's Tent.

4 The LORD said to Moses,

5 'Accept these gifts from the leaders. Give them to the Levites. All the Levites can use them for their work at the Tent of Meeting.'

6 So Moses took the carts and the oxen and he gave them to the Levites. 7 He gave 2 carts and 4 oxen to the descendants of Gershon. 8 He gave 4 carts and 8 oxen to the descendants of Merari for their work. Ithamar was the son of Aaron. He had to tell the descendants of Merari the work that they should do. 9But the descendants of Kohath had to carry everything that was special on their shoulders. So Moses did not give any carts or oxen to the descendants of Kohath.

10 When Moses marked the altar with oil, the leaders brought gifts. They put their gifts in front of the altar. 11 The LORD said to Moses: 'One leader must bring a gift to the altar every day. That is how they will give the altar to the LORD.'

12 On the first day, Nahshon, the son of Amminadab from the tribe of Judah brought his gift. 13 He brought a plate and a bowl that someone had made from silver. The plate weighed 130 shekels. The bowl weighed 70 shekels. They had weighed the silver by the shekel of God's Holy Tent. Both of those were full of best flour that he had mixed with oil. They were for an offering of flour. 14 He brought one small dish that someone had made from gold. It weighed 10 shekels and it was full of incense. 15 He brought one young bull, a male sheep and another male sheep that was less than one year old. Those animals were for a burnt-offering. 16 He brought one male goat for a sin-offering. 17 He also brought 2 oxen, 5 male sheep, 5 male goats, and another 5 male sheep that were less than one year old. Those animals were for the friendship-offerings. That was the gift of Nahshon, the son of Amminadab.

18 On day two, Nethanel, the son of Zuar, from the tribe of Issachar brought his gift. 19 He brought a plate and a bowl that someone had made from silver. The plate weighed 130 shekels. The bowl weighed 70shekels. They had weighed the silver by the shekel of God's Holy Tent. Both of those were full of best flour that he had mixed with oil. They were for an offering of flour. 20 He brought one small dish that someone had made from gold. It weighed 10 shekels and it was full of incense. 21 He brought one young bull, a male sheep and another male sheep that was less than one year old. Those animals were for a burnt-offering. 22He brought one male goat for a sin-offering. 23 He also brought 2 oxen, 5 male sheep, 5 male goats, and another 5 male sheep that were less than one year old. Those animals were for the friendship-offerings. That was the gift of Nethanel, the son of Zuar.

24 On day three, Eliab, the son of Helon, from the tribe of Zebulun brought his gift. 25 He brought a plate and a bowl that someone had made from silver. The plate weighed 130 shekels. The bowl weighed 70shekels. They had weighed the silver by the shekel of God's Holy Tent. Both of those were full of best flour that he had mixed with oil. They were for an offering of flour. 26 He brought one small dish that someone had made from gold. It weighed 10 shekels and it was full of incense. 27 He brought one young bull, a male sheep and another male sheep that was less than one year old. Those animals were for a burnt-offering. 28He brought one male goat for a sin-offering. 29 He also brought 2 oxen, 5 male sheep, 5 male goats, and another 5 male sheep that were less than one year old. Those animals were for the friendship-offerings. That was the gift of Eliab, the son of Helon.

30 On day 4, Elizur, the son of Shedeur, from the tribe of Reuben brought his gift. 31 He brought a plate and a bowl that someone had made from silver. The plate weighed 130 shekels. The bowl weighed 70shekels. They had weighed the silver by the shekel of God's Holy Tent. Both of those were full of best flour that he had mixed with oil. They were for an offering of flour. 32 He brought one small dish that someone had made from gold. It weighed 10 shekels and it was full of incense. 33 He brought one young bull, a male sheep and another male sheep that was less than one year old. Those animals were for a burnt-offering. 34He brought one male goat for a sin-offering. 35 He also brought 2 oxen, 5 male sheep, 5 male goats, and another 5 male sheep that were less than one year old. Those animals were for the friendship-offerings. That was the gift of Elizur, the son of Shedeur.

36 On day 5, Shelumiel, the son of Zurishaddai, from the tribe of Simeon brought his gift. 37 He brought a plate and a bowl that someone had made from silver. The plate weighed 130 shekels. The bowl weighed 70 shekels. They had weighed the silver by the shekel of God's Holy Tent. Both of those were full of best flour that he had mixed with oil. They were for an offering of flour.

38 He brought one small dish that someone had made from gold. It weighed 10 shekels and it was full of incense.

39 He brought one young bull, a male sheep and another male sheep that was less than one year old. Those animals were for a burnt-offering.

40 He brought one male goat for a sin-offering. 41 He also brought 2 oxen, 5 male sheep, 5 male goats, and another 5 male sheep that were less than one year old. Those animals were for the friendship-offerings. That was the gift of Shelumiel, the son of Zurishaddai.

42 On day 6, Eliasaph, the son of Deuel, from the tribe of Gad brought his gift. 43 He brought a plate and a bowl that someone had made from silver. The plate weighed 130 shekels. The bowl weighed 70 shekels. They had weighed the silver by the shekel of God's Holy Tent. Both of those were full of best flour that he had mixed with oil. They were for an offering of flour. 44 He brought one small dish that someone had made from gold. It weighed 10 shekels and it was full of incense. 45 He brought one young bull, a male sheep and another male sheep that was less than one year old. Those animals were for a burnt-offering. 46 He brought one male goat for a sin-offering. 47 He also brought 2 oxen, 5 male sheep, 5 male goats, and another 5 male sheep that were less than one year old. Those animals were for the friendship-offerings. That was the gift of Eliasaph, the son of Deuel.

48 On day 7, Elishama, the son of Ammihud, from the tribe of Ephraim brought his gift. 49 He brought a plate and a bowl that someone had made from silver. The plate weighed 130 shekels. The bowl weighed 70 shekels. They had weighed the silver by the shekel of God's Holy Tent. Both of those were full of best flour that he had mixed with oil. They were for an offering of flour. 50 He brought one small dish that someone had made from gold. It weighed 10 shekels and it was full of incense. 51 He brought one young bull, a male sheep and another male sheep that was less than one year old. Those animals were for a burnt-offering. 52 He brought one male goat for a sin-offering. 53 He also brought 2 oxen, 5 male sheep, 5 male goats, and another 5 male sheep that were less than one year old. Those animals were for the friendship-offerings. That was the gift of Elishama, the son of Ammihud.

54 On day 8, Gamaliel, the son of Pedahzur, from the tribe of Manasseh brought his gift. 55 He brought a plate and a bowl that someone had made from silver. The plate weighed 130 shekels. The bowl weighed 70 shekels. They had weighed the silver by the shekel of God's Holy Tent. Both of those were full of best flour that he had mixed with oil. They were for an offering of flour. 56 He brought one small dish that someone had made from gold. It weighed 10 shekels and it was full of incense. 57 He brought one young bull, a male sheep and another male sheep that was less than one year old. Those animals were for a burnt-offering. 58 He brought one male goat for a sin-offering. 59 He also brought 2 oxen, 5 male sheep, 5 male goats, and another 5 male sheep that were less than one year old. Those animals were for the friendship-offerings. That was the gift of Gamaliel, the son of Pedahzur.

60 On day 9, Abidan, the son of Gideoni, from the tribe of Benjamin brought his gift. 61 He brought a plate and a bowl that someone had made from silver. The plate weighed 130 shekels. The bowl weighed 70shekels. They had weighed the silver by the shekel of God's Holy Tent. Both of those were full of best flour that he had mixed with oil. They were for an offering of flour. 62 He brought one small dish that someone had made from gold. It weighed 10 shekels and it was full of incense. 63 He brought one young bull, a male sheep and another male sheep that was less than one year old. Those animals were for a burnt-offering. 64He brought one male goat for a sin-offering. 65 He also brought 2 oxen, 5 male sheep, 5 male goats, and another 5 male sheep that were less than one year old. Those animals were for the friendship-offerings. That was the gift of Abidan, the son of Gideoni.

66 On day 10, Ahiezer, the son of Ammishaddai, from the tribe of Dan brought his gift. 67 He brought a plate and a bowl that someone had made from silver. The plate weighed 130 shekels. The bowl weighed 70 shekels. They had weighed the silver by the shekel of God's Holy Tent. Both of those were full of best flour that he had mixed with oil. They were for an offering of flour. 68 He brought one small dish that someone had made from gold. It weighed 10 shekels and it was full of incense. 69 He brought one young bull, a male sheep and another male sheep that was less than one year old. Those animals were for a burnt-offering. 70 He brought one male goat for a sin-offering. 71 He also brought 2 oxen, 5 male sheep, 5 male goats, and another 5 male sheep that were less than one year old. Those animals were for the friendship-offerings. That was the gift of Ahiezer, the son of Ammishaddai.

72 On day 11, Pagiel, the son of Ochran, from the tribe of Asher brought his gift. 73 He brought a plate and a bowl that someone had made from silver. The plate weighed 130 shekels. The bowl weighed 70 shekels. They had weighed the silver by the shekel of God's Holy Tent. Both of those were full of best flour that he had mixed with oil. They were for an offering of flour.

74 He brought one small dish that someone had made from gold. It weighed 10 shekels and it was full of incense. 75 He brought one young bull, a male sheep and another male sheep that was less than one year old. Those animals were for a burnt-offering. 76He brought one male goat for a sin-offering. 77 He also brought 2 oxen, 5 male sheep, 5 male goats, and another 5 male sheep that were less than one year old. Those animals were for the friendship-offerings. That was the gift of Pagiel, the son of Ochran.

78 On day 12, Ahira, the son of Enan, from the tribe of Naphtali brought his gift. 79 He brought a plate and a bowl that someone had made from silver. The plate weighed 130 shekels. The bowl weighed 70 shekels. They had weighed the silver by the shekel of God's Holy Tent. Both of those were full of best flour that he had mixed with oil. They were for an offering of flour. 80 He brought one small dish that someone had made from gold. It weighed 10 shekels and it was full of incense. 81 He brought one young bull, a male sheep and another male sheep that was less than one year old. Those animals were for a burnt-offering. 82He brought one male goat for a sin-offering. 83 He also brought 2 oxen, 5 male sheep, 5 male goats, and another 5 male sheep that were less than one year old. Those animals were for the friendship-offerings. That was the gift of Ahira, the son of Enan.

84 The leaders of Israel brought these gifts to the altar when Moses marked it with oil. They brought all the gifts in the list below. They brought 12 plates and 12 bowls that people had made from silver. 85 Each plate weighed 130 shekels and each bowl weighed 70 shekels. All the silver weighed 2400 shekels. That was the shekel of God's Holy Tent. 86 They brought 12 small dishes that people had made from gold. Each small dish weighed 10 shekels. They were each full of incense. All the gold weighed 120 shekels. 87 All the animals for the burnt-offering were 12 young bulls, 12 male sheep and 12 male lambs that were one year old. They also brought the proper offerings of flour with those animals. And they brought 12 male goats for a sin-offering. 88 There were also another 24 oxen, 60 male sheep, 60 male goats and 60 male lambs. The male lambs were one year old. Those animals were for the friendship-offering. That was the offering when they gave the altar to the LORD. That was after Moses had marked it with oil.

89 When Moses went into the Tent of Meeting, to speak with the LORD, the LORD did speak to him. And Moses heard the LORD. The sound came from above the lid which was on the top of the Covenant Box. On the lid, there were two models of angels. The sound came from between those models. That was how the LORD spoke to Moses.

Chapter 8

1 Then the LORD said to Moses, 2 'Speak to Aaron and say to him, "When you put the lamps on the lampstand, the 7 lamps must give light in front of the lamp stand." '

3 So Aaron did that. He put its lamps at the front of the lamp stand, as the LORD had said to Moses. 4 A good worker had made the lamp stand from one piece of gold that he had made flat with a hammer. From its base to the flowers at the top, he had made it in that way. It was completely like the lamp stand that the LORD had shown to Moses.

About the Levites

5 Again the LORD spoke to Moses and he said, 6 'Take the Levites from among the Israelites and make them clean. 7 You will make them clean like this: Put the water that makes people clean on them. They must remove all the hair from their whole body, and they must wash their clothes. Then they will be clean.8 Then they must take a bull with the proper offering of flour and oil. And you must take another bull for a sin-offering. 9 Then you must bring the Levites in front of the Tent of Meeting. You must also bring all the Israelites there. 10 You must bring the Levites in front of the LORD. Then the Israelites must put their hands on the Levites' heads. 11 Aaron must give the Levites to the LORD as a special offering from the Israelites. Then they will be ready to do the LORD's work.

12 Then the Levites must put their hands on the heads of the bulls. Then offer one bull for a sin-offering and the other one for a burnt-offering to the LORD. That will make peace with the LORD for the Levites' sin. 13 And you must cause the Levites to stand in front of Aaron and his sons. So they will be a special gift to the LORD. 14 That is how you will make the Levites separate from the other Israelites. And then the Levites will be mine.

15 Then after that the Levites can go in to work in the Tent of Meeting. But you must make them clean and you must bring them to me as a special gift. 16 That is because all the Levites among the Israelites are mine. All the Israelites' first-born sons are mine. But I have taken the Levites for myself instead. 17 Every first-born son among the Israelites is mine. And all the first-born male animals are mine too. On the day that I killed all the first-born sons in Egypt I made them special for myself. 18 But now I have not taken all the first-born sons among the Israelites. I have taken the Levites instead. 19 And I have given the Levites as a gift to Aaron and to his sons from among the Israelites. They will work at the Tent of Meeting on behalf of the Israelites. And they will make peace with me on behalf of the Israelites. So, there will not be a bad illness among the Israelites because they have come near to God's Holy Tent.'

20 So Moses and Aaron and all the Israelites did those things to the Levites. The Israelites did everything that the LORD had said to Moses about the Levites. 21 The Levites, too, made themselves clean and they washed their clothes. And Aaron brought them in front of LORD as a special gift. Aaron also burnt sacrifices to make them clean. 22 After that, the Levites went in to do their work in the Tent of Meeting. They helped Aaron and his sons. The Israelites did everything with the Levites that the LORD had said to Moses about them.

23 Then the LORD spoke to Moses again and he said, 24 'These are the rules about the Levites: The men who are 25 years old or older must go in to work in the Tent of Meeting. 25 But they must stop that work when they are 50 years old. And they must not do that work after that. 26 But they can help the other Levites in the Tent of meeting. They can help them to do their jobs. But they themselves must not have any jobs. Those are the rules about the Levites and about their jobs.'

Chapter 9

1 The LORD spoke to Moses in the desert called Sinai. The Israelites had left the country called Egypt. It was the second year after the Israelites had left Egypt. It was the first month during that year. The LORD said, 2 'The Israelites must eat the Passover at the proper time. They must eat it as the rules about it say. 3The proper time is during the evening of the 14th day of this month. It is when it starts to become dark. That is when you must eat it. You must obey all its rules and its laws.'

4 So Moses told the Israelites that they should eat the Passover. 5 So they ate the Passover in the first month, on the 14th day when it started to become dark. That was in the desert called Sinai. The Israelites did everything that the LORD had said to Moses about it.

6 But there were some people who were not clean. That was because they had touched a dead body. So they could not eat the Passover on that day. So they came to Moses and Aaron on that day. 7 And those people said to Moses, 'We are not clean because of the dead body that we touched. But we would like to bring our gift to LORD at the proper time with the other Israelites.'

8 So Moses said to them, 'Wait. Then I will ask the LORD about this.'

9 Then the LORD said to Moses, 10 'Say to the Israelites, "Anyone among you or your descendants may become not clean because of a dead body. Or they may be away because they are travelling. They can still celebrate the Passover to the LORD. 11 They must celebrate it during the evening of the 14th day of the second month. They must eat it when it starts to become dark. They must eat it with bread and with bitter herbs. The bread must not have yeast in it. 12 They must not keep any of the food until the next morning. And they must not break any of the bones of the lamb. And they must obey all the rules about the Passover. 13 But perhaps a clean person who is at home does not celebrate the Passover. You must make that person separate from his people. That is because he did not give the proper sacrifices to LORD at the proper time. So that person must have the punishment for that sin.

14 People from foreign countries can celebrate the LORD's Passover too if they are living among you. But they must obey all the rules about the Passover. The rules are the same for a foreign person and for an Israelite." '

The cloud above the Tent of Meeting

15 On the day that Moses raised the Tent of Meeting, a cloud covered it. And in the evening it seemed like fire over God's Tent, until morning.

16 It was like that all the time. The cloud covered it during the day. But at night, the cloud seemed to have fire in it. 17 When the cloud went up from the tent, the Israelites started to travel. And when the cloud came down, the Israelites camped in that place. 18 The LORD decided when the Israelites should start to travel. And the LORD decided where they should camp. During all the time that the cloud was over God's Tent, they stayed in their camp. 19 Even when the cloud stayed over God's Tent for many days, the Israelites obeyed the LORD. 20 Sometimes the cloud stayed over God's Tent for a few days. Then they obeyed the LORD. They remained in their camp. Then the LORD showed that they should travel. So they started to travel. 21 Sometimes the cloud stayed there from evening until morning. But, when the cloud went up in the morning, they started to travel. But sometimes it stayed for one day and one night. Then when the cloud went up, they started to travel again.22 Sometimes the cloud continued to be over God's Tent for two days or for a month or for a year. It stayed above it. Then, the Israelites stayed in their camp. They did not start to travel. But when it went up, they did start to travel. 23 The LORD decided when they should camp. And the LORD decided when they should start to travel. So they obeyed the LORD about everything that the LORD said to Moses.

Chapter 10

The silver trumpets

1 The LORD said to Moses, 2 'Make two trumpets from one piece of silver. Use a hammer to make them in the right shape. Make a noise with them to tell the people that they must come together. Also, use the trumpets to tell the people that they must move the camp. 3 When the people hear the sound from both trumpets, all the people must meet you. They must meet you at the door of the Tent of Meeting. 4 But you may want only the leaders of Israel's tribes to meet you. If you want that, a priest should make the sound from only one trumpet. 5 But when the sound is one short sound, the tribes at the east of the camp must start to travel. 6 When they hear the next short sound, the tribes on the south of the camp must start to travel. Short sounds on the trumpet will tell the people that they must start to travel. 7 But when you want everyone to meet together, make a different sound with the trumpet.

8 The priests, the sons of Aaron must use the trumpets to make a noise. This is a rule for you and for all your descendants. 9 Use the trumpets to tell everyone when an enemy is attacking you in your own country. Make a sound on the trumpets to tell the people that they must fight the enemy. Then the LORD your God will hear and he will save you from your enemies. 10 You must make sounds with the trumpets on your happy days, too. And you must make sounds with the trumpets at your regular festivals and on the first days of your months. And you must make sounds with the trumpets over your burnt-offerings, and over your friendship-offerings. The LORD your God will hear and he will remember you. I am the LORD your God.'

The Israelites leave the Desert called Sinai

11 In the second year, in the second month, on the 20th day of the month, the cloud went up. It went up from over God's Tent of Meeting. 12 Then the Israelites started to travel on their journey away from the desert called Sinai. Then the cloud stopped in the desert called Paran. 13 So they started to travel from Sinai at that time. That was because the LORD used Moses to speak to them. And he told them that they should move.

14 The flag of the camp of the descendants of Judah, with all their armies, started to travel first. And Nahshon the son of Amminadab was over all their armies. 15 Over the army of the tribe of Issachar was Nethanel the son of Zuar. 16 And over the army of the tribe of Zebulun was Eliab the son of Helon. 17 Then the Levites packed God's Tent. And the descendants of Gershon and the descendants of Merari, who were carrying God's Tent, started to travel.

18 Next the flag of the camp of Reuben, and all their armies started to travel. And Elizur the son of Shedeur was over all their armies. 19 And Shelumiel the son of Zurishaddai was over the army of the tribe of Simeon. 20 And Eliasaph the son of Deuel was over the army of the tribe of Gad. 21 Then the descendants of Kohath started to travel. They were carrying the holy things. And the Levites put God's Tent up before they arrived.

22 Next the flag of the camp of the tribe of Ephraim, and all their armies, started to travel. Elishama the son of Ammihud was over all their armies. 23 And Gamaliel the son of Pedahzur was over the army of the tribe of Manasseh. 24 And Abidan the son of Gideoni was over the army of the tribe of Benjamin.

25 Then the flag of the camp of the tribe of Dan and all their armies started to travel last. They could keep the Israelites safe if an enemy attacked them from behind them. Ahiezer the son of Ammishaddai was over all their armies. 26 And Pagiel the son of Ochran was over the army of the tribe of Asher. 27 And Ahira the son of Enan was over the army of the tribe of Naphtali. 28 The Israelites marched out like that every time that they started to travel.

29 Moses spoke to Hobab. Hobab was the brother of Moses' wife. Hobab's father was Reuel who came from Midian. Moses said, 'We are leaving here now. We are going to another place. And the LORD has said, "I will give that place to you." The LORD has promised good things about Israel's people. So come with us and we will do good things for you.'

30 But Hobab said to him, 'I will not come, but I will go to my own country and to my relatives.'

31 Then Moses said, 'But you know where we should camp in the desert. So please do not leave us. You can be like our eyes as we travel. 32 And if you go with us, we will do good things for you. We will do for you all the good things that the LORD does for us.'

33 So the Israelites left the LORD's mountain. They travelled for three days. The Levites carried the Lord's Covenant Box in front of them. That was so that the LORD could show them where to camp. The Covenant Box arrived at the place three days before the other Israelites arrived there. 34 And the LORD's cloud was over them during the day, when they started to travel from the camp.

35 Each time that the Covenant Box started to travel Moses said, 'Rise LORD! Cause your enemies to go in every direction! Cause those who hate you to run away!' 36 And when it stopped moving, he said, 'Return LORD, to the 10 000 thousands of Israel's people.'

Chapter 11

Moses chooses 70 men to be leaders of the Israelites

1 But the people started to say bad words about their problems. The LORD heard them and he became very angry. He sent fire. The LORD's fire burned among them and it destroyed some edges of the camp. 2 So the people asked Moses to help them. And Moses prayed to the LORD, and the fire stopped. 3 So that place was called Taberah, because the LORD's fire burned among them there.

4 Some foreign people were travelling with the Israelites. Those people wanted very much to eat the wrong things. And the Israelites cried again too. And they said, 'We want meat to eat! 5 We remember the fish that we ate in Egypt. It did not cost us anything. And we remember the vegetables called cucumbers, leeks, onions and garlic. And we remember the fruit called melons. 6 But now we do not want to eat anything. There is not even anything to look at except this manna.' 7 The manna was like the seeds called coriander. The colours of the seeds were yellow and white, like the oil called bdellium. 8 The people walked about and they picked it up. They used two stones to make it into flour. Or they hit it with a tool. They boiled it in pots and they made cakes with it. They tasted it. And it was like the cakes that people bake with oil. 9 At night, the air became wet and water fell on the ground in the camp. And the manna fell with it.

10 People from each family were crying at the doors of their tents. And Moses heard them. The LORD became very angry with the people. And so Moses was not happy. 11 So Moses said to the LORD, 'I am your servant. But you have given this problem to me! It seems that I have done something to make you angry. You have given to me the hard job of leader of all these people. 12 They are not my children! But you have said to me, "Be like a baby's mother to them. And carry them to the country that I have promised to their ancestors." 13 They are crying in front of me and they are saying, "Give us meat that we may eat!" But I cannot get meat to give to all these people! 14 I cannot be the leader of all these people without help. This job is too difficult for me. 15 So if you want to do this to me, please kill me now. I do not want to know that I have wasted my life.' 16 So the LORD said to Moses, 'Choose 70 leaders of the Israelites and bring them to the Tent of Meeting. They must stand there with you. 17 Then I will come down and I will speak with you there. And I will take some of the power that I gave to you. I will give it to them. And they will help you to lead the people. So you will not be the only man who is doing that job.

18 And say to the people, "The LORD heard you when you were crying. You said, 'We want someone to give us meat to eat! It was better when we were in Egypt.'

So the LORD will give you meat and you will eat it. So, make yourselves clean for tomorrow, and you will eat meat. 19 You will not eat it for one day, or two days, or 5 days, or 10 days, or 20 days. 20 You will eat it for a whole month, until it comes out of your noses. It will start to seem disgusting to you. That is because you have turned away from the LORD. He is among you and you have wept in front of him. And you have said, 'We do not know why we left Egypt. It was better there.' "
' 21 But Moses said, 'There are at least 600 000 men here. But you have said, "I will give to them meat to eat for a whole month." 22 We would not have enough meat for them if we killed all our sheep and cows. If we caught every fish in the sea, we might not have enough!'

23 Then the LORD said to Moses, 'Perhaps you think that the LORD cannot do some things! I have promised something. Soon, you will see whether it happens!' 24 So Moses went out and he told the people the words of the LORD. Also he chose 70 leaders of the Israelites and he put them round the tent. 25 Then the LORD came down in the cloud. And he spoke to Moses. And he took some of the power that he had given to Moses. And he gave it to the 70 leaders. And God's Spirit stayed on them for a little time. Then they prophesied. But they did not do it again after that.

26 But two men had stayed in the camp. Their names were Eldad and Medad. They were among those that Moses had chosen. But they had not gone out to the tent.

And God's Spirit stayed on them for a little time. Then they prophesied in the camp. 27 So a young man ran to Moses and he said, 'Eldad and Medad are prophesying in the camp.'

28 Then Joshua the son of Nun said to Moses, 'Moses, my master, stop them.' Since Joshua was a boy, he had been Moses' servant.

29 But Moses said to him, 'Perhaps you think that this might make me sad. And that is why you are not happy. But I wish that the LORD would give his Spirit to all his people. I wish that they were all prophets!' 30 Then Moses and the leaders returned to the camp.

The LORD sends birds called quails to the Israelites

31 Then the LORD sent a wind. It blew in birds called quails from the sea. They were everywhere round the camp. They fell to the ground round the camp. There were birds everywhere as far as a person could walk in one day in any direction. There was about a metre (3 feet) of them over the ground. 32 The people were picking up the birds all day and all night and all the next day. Each person got more than 220 litres (465 pints) of birds. And they put their dead bodies on the ground everywhere round the camp. 33 But the LORD became very angry with the people. The meat was still between their teeth, but they had not really even started to eat it. The LORD sent a very bad illness everywhere among the people. 34 They buried there the greedy people who had wanted meat. So the people called that place Kibroth-Hattaavah.

35 From Kibroth-Hattaavah the people started to travel to Hazeroth, and they stayed at Hazeroth.

Chapter 12

Miriam and Aaron speak badly about Moses

1 Moses had married a woman who was a descendant of Cush. And Miriam and Aaron spoke against Moses because had married that woman. 2 They said, 'We do not believe that LORD has really spoken only by Moses. We believe that he has spoken by us too.' And the LORD heard it.

3 But Moses was a very humble man. He was the most humble person on earth.

4 And immediately the LORD said to Moses and Aaron and Miriam, 'You three people come out to the Tent of Meeting.' So those three people came out. 5 Then the LORD came down in a tall cloud and he stood at the door of the tent. And he said that Aaron and Miriam should come nearer. They both came nearer.

6 Then he said, 'Listen to my words! If there is a prophet among you, I, the LORD, will help him to know me by a vision. Or I will speak to him in a dream.

7 But It is different when I speak to Moses. He is faithful among all my people. 8 With him I speak mouth to mouth. I speak clearly to him. I do not say things to him that are hard to understand. And he sees the shape of the LORD. So you should have been afraid to speak against my servant Moses!' 9 So the LORD was very angry with Aaron and Miriam and he left them. 10 But when the cloud had gone away from over the tent, Miriam's skin became white. It was as white as snow. She now had the bad illness called leprosy in her skin. Aaron turned toward Miriam. And he saw that she had leprosy. 11 Then Aaron said to Moses, 'Oh, my master, please do not punish us because we have done this very silly thing. We have sinned. 12 But do not let Miriam be like a baby that is born dead. Sometimes only half of a baby's body seems to be there when he comes out of his mother's body. Do not let her be like that!' 13 So Moses shouted to the LORD, 'Oh God! Please make her well again!'14 But the LORD said to Moses, 'If her father had only spat on her face, she would have to be ashamed for 7 days. So you must keep her outside the camp for 7 days. Then after that you can let her come back inside the camp.' 15 So Moses kept Miriam outside the camp for 7 days. And the people did not start to travel again until they had brought Miriam into the camp again.

16 But after that, the people started to travel from Hazeroth. And they camped in the desert called Paran.

Chapter 13

Moses sends men to explore the country that God had promised

1 Then the LORD said to Moses, 2 'I will give the country called Canaan to the Israelites. Send men to explore that country. Choose one man from each tribe. Each man must be a leader among them.'

3 So Moses obeyed the LORD. He sent the men from the desert called Paran into Canaan. Each man was a leader among the Israelites. 4 This is a list of their names: There was Shammua, Zaccur's son, from Reuben's tribe. 5 From the tribe of Simeon, there was Shaphat the son of Hori. 6 From the tribe of Judah, there was Caleb the son of Jephunneh. 7 From the tribe of Issachar, there was Igal the son of Joseph. 8From the tribe of Ephraim, there was Hoshea the son of Nun. 9 From the tribe of Benjamin, there was Palti the son of Raphu. 10 From the tribe of Zebulun, there was Gaddiel the son of Sodi. 11 From the tribe of Joseph that is from the tribe of Manasseh there was Gaddi the son of Susi. 12 From the tribe of Dan, there was Ammiel the son of Gemalli. 13 From the tribe of Asher, there was Sethur the son of Michael. 14From the tribe of Naphtali, there was Nahbi the son of Vophsi. 15 And from the tribe of Gad, there was Geuel the son of Machi. 16 Those are the names of the men that Moses sent to explore the land. But Moses changed the name of Hoshea the son of Nun to Joshua.

17 Moses sent them to explore the country called Canaan. And he said to them, 'Go north from here. Go through the south of Canaan. Then continue to go north, into the part of the country where there are hills.18 And have a look at the country. See whether the people there are strong or weak. And see whether few people or many people live there. 19 See where their land is good or bad. And see whether their towns have no walls or strong walls. 20 And see whether good food or not much food grows on their land. See whether there are trees in their country or not. Then try to get some fruit from the country.' (It was the time for the first grapes to be ready to eat.) 21 So they went. And they explored the land from the desert called Zin to Rehob, near Lebo-Hamath. 22 When they had gone up into the south of the country, they came to Hebron. That was where Ahiman, Sheshai and Talmai, the descendants of Anak were living. Hebron was 7 years older than Zoan in Egypt. 23 Then the men came to the Valley called Eshcol. There, they cut a branch from a plant. The branch had only one set of grapes on it. But the branch was so large that two men carried it between them on a piece of wood. They also brought some fruits called pomegranates and figs. 24 That valley was called Eshcol. That was because of the set of grapes that the Israelites cut down there. 25 The men returned after they had explored the country for 40 days.

The men bring news to Moses

26 They came to Moses and Aaron and to all the Israelites in the desert called Paran, at Kadesh. They told them about the country and they showed its fruit to them. 27 They said to Moses, 'We went into the country that you sent us to. And there certainly is a lot of milk and honey there, and this is its fruit. 28 But the people who live in the country are strong. Their towns are very big and strong walls keep them safe. Also, we saw the descendants of Anak there. 29 The descendants of Amalek are living in the south of the country. And the people called Hittites, Jebusites and Amorites live in the hills. And the Canaanites live by the sea and by the River Jordan.'

30 Then Caleb made the Israelites quiet in front of Moses. Caleb said, 'We should go into the country. And we should get power over it. We will certainly be able to do it!'

31 But the men who had gone into the country with him said, 'These people are stronger than we are. So we cannot go into the country and beat them.' 32 So they gave to the Israelites a bad report of the country that they had explored. And they said, 'We went through that whole country and we explored it. It seems to eat the people who live there! And all the people that we saw in it were very big. 33 We also saw the people called Nephilim there.' (The descendants of Anak are also Nephilim.) 'And we felt like very small insects when we looked at them. And we seemed like very small insects to them too.'

Chapter 14

The people speak bad words

1 Then all the people started to cry very loudly. And the people cried all night. 2 And all the Israelites spoke bad words against Moses and Aaron. And all the people said to them, 'We wish that we had died in the country called Egypt, or even in this desert! 3 We do not know why the LORD is bringing us into this country. Its people will kill us all with swords. They will take our wives and our little children for themselves. We think that it would be better to return to Egypt.' 4 So they said to each other, 'We should choose a new leader and we should return to Egypt.'

5 Then Moses and Aaron threw themselves on the ground in front of all the Israelites. Their faces were touching the ground. 6 But Joshua the son of Nun and Caleb the son of Jephunneh were among those who had explored the country. And they tore their clothes. 7 And they said to all the Israelites, 'The country that we travelled through to explore is a very, very good country. 8 If the LORD is happy with us, he will bring us into this country. And he will give it to us. And there is a lot of milk and honey everywhere in that country. 9 But do not refuse to obey the LORD. And do not be afraid of the people in that country. We will beat them easily. The LORD is with us and he has made them not safe. Do not be afraid of them.' 10 But all the people wanted to throw stones at Joshua and Caleb until they had killed them. Then the glory of the LORD appeared in the Tent of Meeting to all the Israelites. 11 And the LORD said to Moses, 'These people turn away from me all the time. I did great miracles and they saw them. But still they will not trust me. 12I will send an illness that will kill all those people. And they will not get any of the good things that I wanted to give to them. And I will make you, Moses, the ancestor of a nation greater and more powerful than they are.' 13 But Moses said to the LORD, 'But you brought these people out of Egypt because you are a powerful God. If you do that, someone will tell the people in Egypt about it. 14 And they will tell the people who live in this country about it. Those people already know that you, LORD, are with your people. They know that you talk to your people. They know that your cloud is over the people. And they know that you lead them as a tall cloud during the day and as fire during the night. 15 And there are people in other nations who know a lot about you. So if you kill all your people together now the people in those nations will say, 16 "The LORD could not bring those people into the country that he had seriously promised to them. So he killed all those people in the desert."

17 But now, I am praying. And I am asking you to show how powerful you are. Please do as you promised to do. You said, 18 "I, the LORD, do not get angry easily. My people can trust me to love them very much always. I forgive people if they sin. And I forgive them if they do not obey me. But I do punish people for the wrong things that they do. And I do say that people's children, their grandchildren and their grandchildren's children are guilty because of their sin." 19 I pray that you will forgive the very bad sin of these people. Forgive them because you have promised to love them very much always. You have forgiven these people like that since they left Egypt and until now.' 20 So the LORD said, 'I have forgiven them as you asked me to do. 21 But I live and all the earth will be full of the LORD's glory. 22 And these men have seen my glory and the miracles that I did in Egypt and in the desert. But they have tested me 10 times now. And they have not obeyed me. 23 So certainly, none of them will see the country that I seriously promised to their ancestors. Those men thought that I am not important. So none of those men will see the country. 24 But my servant Caleb has thought differently. And he has obeyed me completely. So, I will bring him into the country that he explored. And it will be his descendants' country. 25 The Amalekites and the Canaanites live in the valleys now. So turn tomorrow and start to travel to the desert past the Red Sea.'

26 And the LORD said to Moses and Aaron, 27 'These bad people have said bad things about me too many times! I have heard the bad things that the Israelites are saying about me. 28 Say to them, "I live," says the LORD. "And I will do to you as you have said. I heard your words. And I will certainly do as you have asked.

29 Your dead bodies will fall to the ground in this desert. All the men that Moses counted will die. All the men who were 20 years old or older will die. All those men said bad words about me and they will die in this desert. 30 None of those men will go into the country that I promised to put you in. The only men who will go in are Caleb the son of Jephunneh and Joshua the son of Nun. 31 You said that the people in Canaan would take your children for themselves. But I will bring those children into the country. And the country that you did not want will be their home. 32 But you will be different. Your dead bodies will fall to the ground in this desert. 33 And your sons will be shepherds for 40 years in the desert. And they will have trouble because you did not trust me. They will have trouble until all your dead bodies are lying in the desert. 34 You explored the country for 40 days. So you will have trouble because of your sins for 40 years. And you will know that I am angry with you. 35 I, the LORD, have spoken. I will certainly do all those things to these very bad people. That is because they have all come together against me. In this desert they will die. So that will be the end of them." '

36 But the men that Moses sent to explore the country had returned. And they had given a bad report to the people about the country. So they caused all the people to say bad things against Moses. 37 So the LORD sent a bad illness. And it killed those men who gave a bad report about the country to the people. 38 But only two men who had gone to explore the country did not die. They were Joshua the son of Nun and Caleb the son of Jephunneh.

39 And when Moses spoke these words to all the Israelites, the people were very sad. 40 But the next morning, they got up early. And they went up to the top of the hills in the country. And they said, 'Here we are. We certainly did sin. But we will go to the place that the LORD has promised to us.'

41 But Moses said, 'I do not know why you are not obeying the LORD. Your ideas will not happen. 42 Do not go into that country. The LORD is not with you. So your enemies will beat you. 43 The Amalekites and the Canaanites will be there in front of you. That is because you have refused to obey the LORD. So the LORD will not be with you. And so they will kill you with their swords.'

44 But the people did not listen to Moses. They went up to the top of the hills in the country. But Moses and the LORD's Covenant Box stayed in the camp. 45 Then the Amalekites and the Canaanites who lived in those hills came down. And they attacked the Israelites. So the people had to run away to Hormah.

Chapter 15

1 The LORD said to Moses, 2 'Say to the Israelites, "You will go into the country that I am giving to you. And you will live there. 3 When you are living there, you can sacrifice bulls, male sheep or goats to the LORD. You will burn them on the altar. That is called a burnt-offering. You can give other sacrifices to the LORD because you have promised to do it. Or you can give sacrifices because you want to do it. Also you can give sacrifices during your regular holidays. The smell of these sacrifices as they burn will make the LORD happy. 4 The person who gives the gift to the LORD must also give a gift of flour. He must mix the flour with oil. It should be 1 kilo (2.2 pounds) of your best flour Mix this flour with 1 litre (2 pints) of olive oil. 5 You must also give a litre (2 pints) of wine for each lamb. You must give that as a drink-offering with each burnt-offering or sacrifice.

6 If the animal is a male sheep, you must also offer 2 kilos (4.4 pounds) of flour. Mix this flour with 1.5 litres (2.6 pints) of olive oil. 7 Also you must pour 1.5 litres (2.6 pints) of wine on the altar as a drink-offering. The smell of the smoke from this sacrifice will make the LORD happy.

8 A person can give a bull as a burnt-offering. Or it can be a special sacrifice. Or he can give it because he promised to give it. Or it may be for a friendship-offering to the LORD. 9 Also you must offer 3 kilos (6.6 pounds) of flour. Mix this flour with 2 litres (4 pints) of olive oil. Do that if the bull is a burnt-offering, or a friendship-offering. Do the same if you offer this sacrifice because of a promise. 10 Also, you must pour 2 litres (4 pints) of wine on the altar as a drink-offering. The smell of this smoke will make the LORD happy.

11 You must do the same thing for each bull, or for each male sheep. And you must do the same thing for each male lamb, or for each young goat. 12 You must do that for every animal that you offer as a gift to the LORD. 13 All the Israelites must do that when they burn a gift to the LORD. The smell of them as they burn will make the LORD happy.

14 A stranger who is living in your country may want to give a gift by fire to the LORD. He must do the same as you do now, and for all future time. 15 These rules will be the same for the Israelites and for all foreign people who live with them. These rules are for now and for all future time. Both you and the foreign person must obey the LORD's rules. 16 There is only one law for you and for the foreign person who is living among you. And there is only one set of rules." '

17 The LORD said to Moses, 18 'Tell the Israelites this. I am bringing them into the country called Canaan. After they have gone into it, they must obey my rules. 19 When they eat the food from that country, they must give a special offering to the LORD. 20 From the first of your dough you must give a cake as a special offering. You must do it as you give your special gift from your threshing-floor. 21 From the first of their dough, all your descendants must give to the LORD a special offering.

22 The people might not obey a rule that the LORD told Moses about. But they might not know that they are not obeying a rule. 23 It might be any rule that the LORD gave to you by Moses. 24 Perhaps all the people did not know that they were not obeying my rules. But they did not obey them all. When that happens, they must sacrifice a bull as a burnt-offering. The smell of the smoke from this sacrifice will make the LORD happy. Also, they must give an offering of flour, a drink-offering and a male goat as a sin-offering. 25 Then the priest will make things right with God for all the Israelites and God will forgive them. That is because it was a mistake. And they have brought their offering, an offering by fire to the LORD. And they have brought their sin-offering to the LORD, for their mistake. 26 The LORD will forgive all the Israelites and the foreign people who live among you. That is because you did not want to sin. It was a mistake. And also you offered the proper sacrifices to me.

27 Also a person may not know that something is a sin. If he does that thing, he must sacrifice a female goat. The goat must be one year old. It will be a sin-offering. 28 The priest will bring the gift to the LORD. That is to make things right. Then the LORD will forgive that person who sinned. The person did not know that he was sinning. 29 The same rule is for the Israelites and for all the foreign people who live among them. That is when it was a mistake. 30 But a person might do something that he knows to be wrong. He does it because he wants to do it. That person is as bad as someone who says bad words against the LORD. It does not matter whether he is an Israelite or a foreign person. You must make that person separate from all the people. 31 That person thought that the LORD's words were not important. And he has not obeyed God's rules. So you must make that person completely separate from the people. He is a guilty person.'

A man does not obey the rules for the day of rest

32 When the Israelites were in the desert, a man was picking up sticks on the day of rest. 33 Some people found him while he was picking up the sticks. The people who found him took him to Moses and Aaron and to all the people. 34 They were not sure what to do with the man. So they put him in a tent. Men stood at the door of the tent so that he could not leave it. 35 The LORD said to Moses, 'This man must die. All the people must take him outside the camp and they must kill him. They must throw stones at him until he is dead.' 36 So the people took the man outside the camp. They threw stones at him until he died. That was what the LORD had said to Moses.

37 The LORD said to Moses, 38 'Tell the Israelites that they must put tassels on the corners of their clothes. They must put the tassels on soft blue rope. They must do this now and for all future time. 39 You will be able to look at the tassels and then you will remember all the LORD's rules. Then you can do them. Then you will not only do what you want to do. And you will not still want everything that you see. 40 When you see the tassels you will remember to obey all my rules. You will be holy for your God. 41 I am the LORD your God. And I brought you out from the country called Egypt to be your God. I am the LORD your God.'

Chapter 16

1 Then Korah the son of Izhar, the son of Kohath, the son of Levi decided to speak against Moses. And Dathan and Abiram, the sons of Eliab, and On the son of Peleth, descendants of Reuben, were with him. 2 So they stood up in front of Moses, together with 250 leaders of the Israelites. Those leaders were famous men that the people had chosen. 3 They all came to Moses and Aaron and they said, 'All the Israelites are special, and the LORD is with them. So, you should not say that you are better than the people.'

4 When Moses heard that, he threw himself on to the ground. He prayed to the LORD.

5 Moses said to Korah and to all the other men, 'Tomorrow the LORD will show us who is special. He will show us which person is near to him. He will make the person that he chooses come near to him. 6 Do this: Get some pots for yourselves, Korah and all your friends. 7 And put fire and incense in them, in front of the LORD tomorrow. Then the LORD will choose the man who is holy. You make yourselves too important, you descendants of Levi!'

8 Then Moses said to Korah, 'Listen, you descendants of Levi. 9 The God of Israel has made you separate from all the other Israelites. And he has brought you near to himself, to work in the LORD's Tent. And he has chosen you to stand in front of all the people and to be their servants. But it seems that that is not enough for you. 10 He has brought you near to himself, Korah, and all the other descendants of Levi. But it seems that you want to be priests as well. 11 You are not speaking bad words about Aaron. You are speaking bad words about the LORD.'

12 Then Moses said to Dathan and Abiram the sons of Eliab, 'Come here.' They said, 'No, we will not. 13 You have brought us up out of a country where there is a lot of milk and honey everywhere. You have brought us here, where we will die in the desert. But it seems that that is not enough for you. It seems that you want to be our master as well! 14 You have certainly not brought us into a country where there is a lot of milk and honey everywhere. And you have not given to us fields and vineyards for us and for our descendants. Perhaps you do not want these men to understand what you are really doing. We will not come up!'

15 Moses was angry. He said to the LORD, 'Do not take any gifts from these men. I did not take anything from them. I did not do anything wrong to them.' 16 Moses said to Korah, 'Tomorrow, you and your men must come to the Tent of Meeting. Aaron will be there. 17 Each of you must take a pot and you must put incense in it. You must put the pots on the altar.' 18 So, each man took a pot. He put incense and fire in it. They stood with Moses and Aaron at the door of the Tent of Meeting. 19 So Korah brought all the people against Moses and Aaron at the door of the Tent of Meeting. And the glory of the LORD appeared to all the people. 20 The LORD said to Moses and Aaron, 21 'Stand away from these men so that I can kill them.'

22 But Moses and Aaron threw themselves on the ground. Their faces were touching the ground. And they said, 'You, our God, are the God of the spirits of all people. When one man sins, will you be angry with all the people?'

23 The LORD said to Moses, 24 'Tell the people that they should stand away from the tents of Korah, Dathan and Abiram.'

25 Moses got up from the ground. He went to Dathan and Abiram. The leaders of the Israelites went with him. 26 And Moses said to all the people, 'Move away from the tents of these very bad men. And do not be touching anything that is theirs. If you do not move away, you might die. You might die when they die because of their sin.' 27 So the people moved away from the tents of Korah, Dathan and Abiram. Dathan and Abiram were standing with their wives and their children at the door of their tents.

28 Then Moses said to the people, 'You will know that the LORD chose me to lead you. This is how you will know. 29 If these men die in a usual way, then the LORD did not choose me. 30 But if the LORD causes a completely new thing to happen, you will know something. See whether the ground opens. See whether these men fall alive into Sheol with all their things. If that happens, you will understand something. These men thought that the LORD was not important. That is what you will understand.'

31 When Moses finished speaking, the ground opened. 32 The ground opened. The men, their families and everything that was theirs fell down into the hole. The earth covered Korah and all his men and everything that was theirs, too. 33 They went alive into Sheol. The ground closed over them and they died. 34 As it happened to them, they were shouting loudly. All the Israelites who were round them heard that. So they ran away and they were saying, 'We might fall into the earth too!'

35 Also fire came out from the LORD. And it killed the 250 men who were offering the incense to God.

36 The LORD said to Moses, 37 'Tell Eleazar, the son of Aaron the priest that he must take the pots out of the burning fire. That is because those pots are holy. Then you must throw all the burning materials over all the ground round that place.

38 And these men died because they sinned. But the pots that they were holding are holy. That is because they were offering the incense to the LORD. So workers must use hammers to make the pots into thin pieces of metal. Then cover the altar with those thin pieces of metal. Then they will be like a sign for the Israelites.' 39 So Eleazar lifted the pots up. He hit them until they were flat. He put the flat metal on the altar. 40 Then the people would know that only people of the family of Aaron could burn incense on the altar.

Aaron saves the Israelites

41 But on the next day, all the Israelites together said bad things about Moses and Aaron. And they said, 'You are the men who have caused the death of the LORD's people.' 42 When they turned towards the Tent of Meeting, a cloud was covering it. There was a bright light. 43 Moses and Aaron went to the front of the Tent of Meeting. 44 The LORD said to Moses, 45 'Get away from the people so that I can kill them.' Moses and Aaron fell to the ground. 46 And Moses said to Aaron, 'God is so angry with the people that he is punishing them. People have started to die from a very bad illness! So take your pot and put into it fire from the altar. And put incense on the fire. Then bring it quickly to all the people and make things right with God for them.' 47 The bad things and illnesses started to happen. But Aaron did what Moses said. 48 He stood between the people who were living and the dead people. The bad things and illnesses stopped. 49 But 14 700 people died because of those things. 50 Aaron went back to Moses at the door of the Tent of Meeting.

Chapter 17

1 The LORD said to Moses, 2 'Tell the Israelites that they must give to you 12 sticks, one for each tribe. Write the name of the leader of one tribe on each stick. 3 On the stick from the tribe of Levi write the name of Aaron. 4 Take the sticks to the Tent of Meeting and put them in front of the Covenant Box. 5 Then leaves will start to grow on the stick of the man that I choose. In that way I will stop the bad words that the Israelites are always saying against you.'

6 Moses spoke to the Israelites. The leaders gave him 12 sticks. 7 Moses put the sticks in front of the Covenant Box that was in the Tent of Meeting.

8 The next day, Moses went to the Tent of Meeting. He saw that the stick of the tribe of Levi was growing. It had the name of Aaron on it. It was growing flowers and almonds. 9 Moses brought all the sticks out of the Tent of Meeting. Each leader took his own stick.

10 But the LORD said to Moses, 'Put Aaron's stick in front of the Covenant Box again. The people will see it there like a sign. And then they will remember that they must not refuse to obey me. That will stop their bad words against me so that they will not have to die.' 11 Moses did as the LORD said to him.

12 The Israelites said to Moses, 'We will die. 13 Any person who comes near the Tent of Meeting will die. We will all die!'

Chapter 18

The work of the priests and the Levites

1 So the LORD said to Aaron, 'You and your sons and your clan will be guilty for any wrong thing that happens in God's Holy Tent. And you and your sons will be guilty for any wrong thing that a priest does. 2 Bring the people of your tribe to the Tent of Meeting. 3 They must do the work in the Tent of Meeting. You must tell them what they should do. They must not go near anything in God's Holy Tent or the altar. If they do, you will die. They will also die. 4 The Levites must work in the Tent of Meeting. No other people must come near the Tent of Meeting when you are working in there.

5 You must work in God's Holy Tent and at the altar. If you do that, I will not be angry with the Israelites again. 6 I chose the other Levites as a gift to you to work in the Tent of Meeting with you. 7 But only you and your sons will be priests. You will work at the altar. I am choosing you as my priests. Any other person who comes near the Holy Place must die.'

Gifts for priests and for Levites

8 The LORD said to Aaron, 'I am giving to you and to your family parts of the gifts that the people give to me. I am giving to you the parts that the people do not burn. They are for you and for your family, now and for always.

9 You must have a part of all the gifts. 10 All the men in your family must eat the gifts. The gifts are holy.

11 Also, you will receive part of the special gifts that the Israelites lift up in front of me. I have given them to you and to your sons and daughters for all time. Every person who lives in your houses can eat it. But they must be clean at the time.

12 I will give to you the best oil, the best wine and the best grain. 13 I am giving to you the best parts of the oil, wine and grain gifts. Any person of your family who is clean can eat them.

14 Everything in Israel that should go to the LORD is yours. 15 Every first-born animal and male child that the people give to me I will give to you. But you must buy them from me. 16 When they are one month old you must buy them from me for 5 shekels of silver each. The shekel must have the same weight as the shekel that the Levites use in God's Holy Tent. There are 20 gerahs in one shekel.

17 You must not buy the first-born of an ox or a sheep or a goat. Those animals are holy. Splash the blood from those animals on the altar and burn the fat from them. The smell will make the LORD happy. 18 And the meat of those animals is yours. It is like the breast and the right back leg of the special gifts that you lift up to me.

19 I have given all the gifts that the Israelites offer to the LORD to you, your sons and your daughters. That is a rule for all time. That is the LORD's special promise to you and to your descendants for all time.'

20 Then the LORD said to Aaron, 'You will have no land in the Israelites' country. And your descendants will not receive any land when you die. Nothing among the Israelites will be yours. Among the Israelites, Levites do not have those things. They have me instead.

21 The Israelites give to me 10% of everything. I will give it to the Levites because they do my work in the Tent of Meeting. 22 And the other Israelites must not come near the Tent of Meeting again. If they do come near it, they will be guilty. And then they will die. 23 Only the Levites must do the work in the Tentof Meeting. And if they do anything wrong there, they will be guilty. That will be a rule for you and for all your descendants. And their children will not receive any land when they die. 24 That is because I have given the tithe of the Israelites to the Levites. The Israelites bring it as an offering to the LORD but I have given it to the Levites. I have said about them, "They will not receive any land among the Israelites as their own land." But I have given the tithes to them instead.'

25 The LORD said to Moses, 26 'Also you must say to the Levites, "You will receive from the Israelites the tithe that I have given to you from them. I have not given any land to you. I have given the tithes to you instead. Then you must give some from it to the LORD. It will be a tithe of the tithe. 27 This gift will be the same as when a farmer is giving grain or wine to me. It will be special. 28 So you will give something to the LORD from your tithes, which you receive from the Israelites. And from it you will give the LORD's gift to Aaron the priest. 29 From all the gifts from the people to you, you must make separate every offering that the LORD should have. The best part of each gift is the part that you must make separate for the LORD."

30 And you must say to them, "After you have made separate from it the best part of it, the other part will be for the Levites. They do not get food because they thresh food plants. And they do not make wine from grapes. They receive that gift instead. 31 They can eat the other part of the gift because they do the work in the Tent of Meeting. 32 And you will not be guilty because you take it. That is because you have given the best part of it to God. But you must do the right things with the holy gifts of the Israelites. If you do the right things you will not die for that reason." '

Chapter 19

1 The LORD said to Moses and Aaron, 2 'This is one rule in the LORD's law that I am telling to you: Tell the Israelites that they must bring to you a young red cow. It must not have anything wrong with it. And nobody must have put a yoke on it. 3 They must take it outside the camp. They must kill it and they must give it to Eleazar the priest.

4 Eleazar must take some of the blood from the cow. He must splash it 7 times in front of the Tent of Meeting.

5 Then the people must burn the whole cow while Eleazar is watching. They must burn its body with the skin, meat, blood and everything inside its body. 6 He must take some wood, some plants and some red wool. He must throw them on the fire. 7 Then priest must wash his clothes and he must bathe his body with water. After that, he can come into the camp but he will not be clean until the evening. 8 And the man who burns it must wash his clothes in water. And he must bathe his body in water. And he will not be clean until the evening.

9 Then a man who is clean must pick up all the ashes of the cow. And he must put them outside the camping a clean place. And all the Israelites must keep them. You must mix them with water to make special water. It will be water for someone who is not clean to make them holy again. It is water to remove sin. 10The man who picks up the ashes must wash himself and his clothes. He will not be clean until evening. This rule is for the Israelites and for all the people who are living with them.

11 Any person who touches a dead body will not be clean for 7 days. 12 He must wash himself on day 3 and day on 7. Then he will be clean. If he does not wash himself on day 3 and on day 7, he will not be clean. 13A person might touch the body of a person who has died. If he does not make himself clean, he has made God's Tent of Meeting not clean. You must make that person separate from the Israelites. Because the special water did not fall on him, he will not be clean. He will still be like a dirty person.

14 This is the rule when a person dies in a tent. Any person who is in the tent will not be clean for 7 days. 15Any pot in the tent that does not have a lid will not be clean.

16 Also, someone might have killed a person with a sword out in the country. Or a person may have died because he was old or ill. Anyone who touches that dead body in the country or a human bone will not be clean for 7 days. Or someone may touch a place where people have buried a dead body. That person will not be clean for 7 days.

17 Then for the person who is not clean, you must take some of the ashes of the young red cow. That is the cow to make people clean. You must put these ashes into a pot and you must mix them with water from a river. 18 Then a person who is clean must take hyssop. He must put it into the water. Then he must use it to throw the water on the tent and on everything that is in it. And he must throw the water on all the people who have been there. And he must throw it on the person who touched the bone or the dead body. Or he must throw it on the person who touched the grave. 19 And the clean person must throw the water on the person who is not clean on the 3rd day too. And he must do it on day 7 too. On day 7 he will make the person clean. And then the person who had not been clean must wash his clothes. And he must bathe himself in water. In the evening, that person will become clean. 20 The person who is not clean might not wash himself and his clothes. If he does not do it, you must make that person separate from the people. That is because he has made the LORD's Holy Tent like something not clean. Because the priest did not splash holy water on him he will not be clean. 21 This rule is for now and for always. The man who splashes the holy water must wash his clothes. Any person who touches the holy water will not be clean until evening. 22 A person who is not clean must not touch anything. Anything that he touches will not be clean until evening.'

Chapter 20

Water from the rock

1 In the first month, the Israelites came to the Desert of Zin. They camped at Kadesh. Miriam died there and the people buried her.

2 The people did not have any water. They came to Moses and Aaron. 3 They said to Moses, 'When the LORD killed our brothers in front of the Tent of Meeting, he should have killed us. 4 We are the LORD's people. You should not have brought us into this desert. Now both we and our animals will die here! 5 You should not have brought us from Egypt to this very bad place. It is not a place where we can get grain or figs or vines or pomegranates. And there is no water to drink.'

6 Moses and Aaron went from the people to the front of the Tent of Meeting. They threw themselves on to the ground. Their faces were on the ground. The special light from the LORD came to them. 7 The LORD said to Moses, 8 'Get the stick. Get your brother Aaron and get the Israelites. Speak to the rock that is in front of you. Water will come from it. It is for the people and for the animals. They can drink it.'

9 So Moses took the stick from in front of the LORD, as the LORD had said to him. 10 Then Moses and Aaron brought all the people to meet in front of the rock. And Moses said to them, 'Listen now, you people who refuse to obey God. It seems that we must bring water out of this rock for you!' 11 Moses lifted up his arm. He hit the rock twice with his stick. Water poured from the rock. The people and the animals drank the water. 12 The LORD said to Moses and Aaron, 'You did not believe in me enough to show the people that I am holy. So you will not lead them into the country that I am giving to them.' 13 That place was called 'The Waters of Meribah', because the Israelites quarrelled with the LORD there. But he showed to them there that he is holy.

14 From Kadesh, Moses sent men to the king of Edom with this message: 'We are Israelites and our ancestor was your ancestor's brother. We should be friendly to each other. We are saying to you, "You know all the bad things that have happened to us. 15 Our ancestors went to Egypt. We lived there for many years. The people in Egypt were bad to us. 16 But when we asked the LORD to help us, he heard us. And he sent an angel and he brought us out from Egypt. Now we are at Kadesh, which is a town at the edge of your land. 17 Please let us travel through your land. We will not go through any fields or through any vineyards. We will not even drink water from your wells. We will go along the king's important road. We will not leave that road on either side until we have gone through all your land." ' 18 The king of Edom said, 'You must not travel through my country. If you do, we will attack you.' 19 The Israelites said, 'We will stay on the road. If our animals drink your water, we will pay for it. We only want to pass through your country.' 20 The king of Edom said, 'No you must not travel through our country.' Then the people in Edom came out to attack the Israelites. 21 The Israelites turned away from Edom.

Aaron dies

22 All the Israelites went from Kadesh to the mountain called Hor. 23 When they were at the edge of Edom, the LORD spoke to Moses and Aaron. 24 He said, 'Aaron will not go in to the country that I am giving to the Israelites. Because you did not obey me, he will die. 25 Aaron and his son Eleazar must climb up the mountain called Hor. 26 Moses must take the priest's clothes from Aaron and he must put them on Eleazar. Aaron will die there.' 27 Moses, Aaron and Eleazar climbed up the mountain called Hor. The Israelites watched. 28 Moses took the priest's clothes from Aaron. He put them on Eleazar. Then Aaron died. Moses and Eleazar walked down the mountain. 29 The Israelites were sad for 30 days because Aaron died.

Chapter 21

1 The king of Canaan was Arad. He lived in the south of the country. People told him that the Israelites were coming. He attacked the Israelites. And he caught some Israelites. 2 The Israelites said to the LORD, 'If you give to us power over the people in Canaan, we will destroy their cities.' 3 The LORD heard the Israelites. They attacked and they got power over the people in Canaan. They destroyed all their cities. The name of the place was Hormah.

The bronze snake

4 The Israelites travelled round the edge of Edom to the Red Sea. The people were angry. 5 They said to the LORD and to Moses, 'You should not have brought us from Egypt to die in the desert. There is no bread. There is no water. We do not like the food that the LORD gives to us.' 6 Then the LORD put snakes among the people. They bit the people and many of the people died. 7 So the people came to Moses and they said, 'We have sinned, because we have spoken against the LORD and against you. Please speak to LORD on our behalf and ask him to remove the snakes from us.' So Moses prayed for the people.

8 The LORD said to Moses, 'Make a snake out of bronze. Put the snake on a stick. If a snake bites a person, the person must look at the bronze snake. Then he will not die.' 9 Moses did what the LORD said. Then when the snake bit anyone, he looked at the bronze snake. Then he did not die.

The Israelites travel to Moab

10 The Israelites camped at Oboth. 11 And they travelled from Oboth, and they camped at Iye-Abarim, in the desert. That place is on the east border of the country called Moab. 12 Then they camped in the Valley called Zered.

13 Then they camped on the north side of the River Arnon. The River Arnon is the border between the Moabites and the Amorites. 14 So someone wrote in the Book of the LORD's Wars about Waheb in Suphah. And he wrote about the valleys of the River Arnon. 15 He wrote, 'The sides of the valleys lead the way to the town called Ar on the edge of Moab.' 16 And from there they continued to travel until they arrived at Beer. That is the well where the LORD said to Moses, 'Bring the people together. Then I will give water to them.' 17 The Israelites sang this song:

'Sing to this well.

Ask it to give water to us.

18 This was the well that our rulers dug.

This was the well that our leaders made.

They dug it with the poles and sticks that showed their authority.'

After that the Israelites went from the desert to Mattanah. 19 They went from Mattanah to Nahaliel. They went from Nahaliel to Bamoth. 20 They went from Bamoth to the valley of Moab. They camped below the top of the mountain called Pisgah.

21 The Israelites said to Sihon, the king of the Amorites, 22 'Please let us go through your country. We will travel on the road. We will not touch your food or drink your water. We will pass through your country.' 23 Sihon would not let the Israelites travel through his country. Sihon and his army marched to Jahaz and they attacked the Israelites. 24 The Israelites fought against the army of Sihon. They got power over the land from the River Arnon to the River Jabbok. 25 They got power over all the cities of the Amorites. They got power over Heshbon and over all the places round it. 26 Heshbon was the city of Sihon, the king of the Amorites. This king had fought against the king of Moab. He won the land as far as the River Arnon from the king of Moab. 27 So the people who say clever things say, 'Come to Heshbon and build it up again. Build the city of Sihon again. 28 An army that was like a fire went out from Heshbon. It was like a flame that went out from Sihon's city. It destroyed Ar in Moab. And it destroyed everything on the high hills near the River Arnon. 29 It is sad for you, people of Moab. Sihon has killed the people of Chemosh. Your god has let the king of the Amorites put the people in a prison. 30 Now, we have killed them. We have destroyed Heshbon as far as Dibon. We have killed them from Nophah to Medeba.' 31 So, the Israelites stayed in the country of the Amorites. 32 Moses sent men to find the best way to attack Jazer. The Israelites attacked Jazer. They caused the Amorites to leave the country. 33 Next, they travelled towards Bashan. Og, the king of Bashan marched out to meet them. He wanted to attack them. They met at Edrei.

34 The LORD said to Moses, 'Do not be afraid of Og. I will give him, his army and his land to you. Attack him in the same way that you attacked Sihon, the king of the Amorites.'

35 So they killed him and his sons and all his people. So all those people were dead and their land became the Israelites' land.

Chapter 22

1 The Israelites travelled to Moab. They lived in tents at the side of the River Jordan. On the other side of the river was the city called Jericho. 2 Balak was the son of Zippor. He saw what the Israelites did to the Amorites. 3 So the people in Moab were afraid because there were very many Israelites. And all the people in Moab became very afraid of the Israelites. 4 So the Moabites said to the leaders of the Midianites, 'This very large group of people will destroy everything round us. They will be like a bull that eats all the grass in a field!' Balak the son of Zippor was king of Moab at that time. 5 He sent men to get Balaam who was the son of Beor. Balaam was near the river at Pethor. Pethor was his home. Balak told them that they should say to Balaam, 'Many people have come from Egypt. And they cover the ground, everywhere. They want to take our land. 6 They are more powerful than I am. Put a curse on them. Then maybe I will be more powerful than I already am. Then I can send them away from our land. When you bless people, it is good for them. When you curse people, they fail. I know that.'

7 The leaders of Moab and Midian went to find Balaam. They took the money for the curse with them. They found him. And they told him what Balak had said.

8 Balaam said to them, 'Stay here tonight. I will talk to the LORD. Tomorrow I will tell you what he says.' The leaders of Moab and Midian stayed with Balaam. 9 Then God came to Balaam and he said, 'Who are these men who are with you?'

10 And Balaam said to God, 'Balak the son of Zippor, king of Moab, has sent a message to me. 11 He said, "Many people have come from Egypt. And they cover the ground, everywhere. So come and curse them for me. Then perhaps I will be able to fight them. And perhaps I will be able to send them away." '

12 The LORD said to Balaam, 'Do not curse these people. They are special people. I have blessed them.' 13 The next day, Balaam said to the men from Moab, 'Go back to Moab. The LORD told me that I should not go with you.' 14 The men went back to Moab. They told Balak that Balaam would not come with them.

15 Then Balak sent more leaders to Balaam. These leaders were even more important than the first group of leaders. 16 They said to him, 'Balak says, "Do not let anything stop you coming to me. 17 I will certainly make you rich and famous. And I will do for you anything that you want. So please come and curse these people for me." ' 18 Balaam said to them, 'No, not even if Balak gives me his house, all his gold and all his silver. I will only do what the LORD says.' 19 Balaam said, 'Stay here tonight as the other men did. I will talk to the LORD.' 20 That night, the LORD spoke to Balaam. He said to him, 'Go with these men. But only do what I say.'

Balaam and his donkey

21 In the morning, Balaam put a blanket on his donkey. He went with the men to Moab. 22 The LORD was angry because Balaam went with the men. He put an angel on the road to stop Balaam. Balaam was riding on his donkey and two servants were with him. 23 The angel was holding a sword. The donkey saw the angel. So it tried to leave the road and it tried to go into a field. Balaam hit the donkey to make it go back to the road.

24 Then the angel stood on a narrow road. There were walls on each side of the road. 25 When the donkey saw the angel, it pushed towards the wall. Balaam had his foot fixed between the donkey and the wall. Balaam hit the donkey again.

26 The angel moved and he stood in another narrow place. There was no space to turn round. 27 When the donkey saw the angel it lay down on the road. Balaam was angry. He hit the donkey with his stick. 28 The LORD made the donkey speak. It said, 'What have I done? Why have you hit me 3 times?'

29 Balaam said to the donkey, 'You have made me look silly. If I had a sword, I would kill you.' 30 The donkey said to Balaam, 'I am your own donkey. Do I usually do things like this to you?' Balaam said, 'No.' 31 Then the LORD let Balaam see the angel who was standing in the road. Balaam lay down with his face on the road.

32 The angel said to him, 'You have hit your donkey 3 times! I have come here to stop you. What you are doing is against me. 33 If the donkey had not turned from me 3 times, I would have killed you. I would not have killed the donkey.'

34 Then Balaam said to the angel of the LORD, 'I have sinned. But I did not know that you were standing in the road to stop me. So, if this is making you angry, I will return to my home.' 35 But the angel of the LORD said to Balaam, 'Go with the men. But you must say only the words that I will tell you.' So Balaam went with Balak's important men.

36 People told Balak that Balaam was coming. Balak went out to meet him at the town in Moab on the river Arnon that is on the border. 37 Balak said to Balaam, 'I will not give anything to you because you did not come to me quickly.'

38 So Balaam said to Balak, 'I have come to you now! But I cannot choose to say the things that I want to say. I can only say the words that God puts into my mouth.'

39 Balaam went with Balak to Kiriath-Huzoth.

40 And Balak sacrificed bulls and sheep. And he sent some to Balaam and to the important men who were with him.

41 The next day Balak and Balaam went to Bamoth-Baal. Balaam saw some of the Israelites.

Chapter 23

1 Balaam said, 'Build 7 altars here. Kill 7 bulls and 7 male sheep.' 2 Balak did this. Balaam and Balak gave a gift of a bull and a male sheep on each altar.

3 Then Balaam said to Balak, 'Stand next to your burnt-offering, and I will go. Perhaps the LORD will come to meet me. And whatever he shows to me I will tell to you.' So Balaam went to the top of a hill where there were no trees.

4 Balaam said to the LORD, 'I made 7 altars. I killed 7 bulls and 7 male sheep. I offered a bull and a male sheep on each altar.'

5 The LORD told Balaam what he should say to Balak.

6 So Balaam returned to Balak, and Balak was still standing by his burnt-offering. And all the leaders of Moab's people were with him.

7 So Balaam started to speak a prophecy. And he said, 'Balak, the king of Moab has brought me from Aram. He brought me from the mountains in the East. He said "Come and curse Jacob's descendants for me. And say bad things about the Israelites!"

8 But I cannot curse these people because the LORD does not curse them. I cannot speak bad words to these people because the LORD does not speak bad words to them.

9 I look at them when I am on the hills. I see people. They are separate from us. They know that the LORD blesses them.

10 Nobody can count Jacob's descendants. They are like the bits of dust on the ground! It would be too difficult to count even a quarter of the Israelites! I would like to die like those good people. And I want the end of my life to be like the end of theirs!'

11 Balak said to Balaam, 'You have not done what I wanted you to do! I brought you to curse these people and you have blessed them.'

12 But Balaam answered, 'I have to be careful. I have to speak only the words that the LORD puts into my mouth!'

Balaam speaks again

13 Then Balak said to him, 'Please come with me to another place where you can see only a small part of the Israelites. You will not be able to see all the Israelites from there. Then curse them for me from there.'

14 They went to the field of Zophim on the top of the mountain called Pisgah. He built 7 altars. He killed 7 bulls and 7 male sheep. And he offered a bull and a male sheep on each altar.

15 Balaam said to Balak, 'Stay here with your gift while I talk with the LORD.'

16 The LORD told Balaam what he should say to Balak.

17 So Balaam went back to Balak. Balak and the men were standing by his gift. Balak said, 'What did the LORD say?'

18 Balaam spoke his message, 'Balak, son of Zippor listen to me.

19 The LORD is not a man. He does not speak words that are not true. If he promises something, it happens. 20 He told me that I must bless the Israelites. He has blessed them, so I must do it too.

21 The LORD is with the Israelites. He blesses them. Bad things will not happen to them in the future. 22 The LORD brought them out of Egypt. He fights for them. 23 Nobody can curse the Israelites. Other people will say about them, "See what the LORD has done." 24 The Israelites are like a lion. It eats the animals that it has killed. It does not rest until it can eat them. It also drinks their blood.'

25 Balak said to Balaam, 'Do not curse the Israelites and do not bless them.' 26 Balaam said, 'I told you, "I must do what the LORD says." '

Balaam speaks again

27 Balak said to Balaam, 'Let me take you to a different place. Perhaps the LORD will let you curse the Israelites from this place.' 28 Balak took Balaam to the top of the mountain called Peor. From there they could look over the desert. 29 Balaam said, 'Build 7 altars here. Kill 7 bulls and 7 male sheep.' 30 Balak did as Balaam asked him to. He offered a bull and a male sheep on each altar.

Chapter 24

1 Now Balaam knew that the LORD wanted him to bless the Israelites. So he stopped looking for ways to change this. He looked over the desert. 2 Balaam looked up. And he saw Israel's people. They were camping tribe by tribe. And the Spirit of God came upon him. 3 And so he said, 'This is the message of Balaam the son of Beor. It is the words of a man. This man understands what the LORD says. 4 This man can hear the LORD. This man sees a picture as in a dream from the LORD.

5 The tents of the Israelites are beautiful.

6 They are like gardens on the side of a river. They are like plants that the LORD puts in the ground. They are like trees at the side of the water.

7 They will always have plenty of water to plant their seeds. Their king will be more powerful than Agag. The LORD will bless their land.

8 God brought them out of Egypt. God fights for them like a wild bull with its dangerous horns. He will destroy the nations who are their enemies. And he will break their enemies' bones into pieces. And he will make holes in their bodies with his arrows.

9 The Israelites are like a lion. When they are sleeping, no other person is brave enough to wake them. The LORD blesses those who bless them. And the LORD curses those who curse them.'

10 Balak was angry with Balaam. He raised his fist to Balaam. He said, 'I asked you to come here and to curse the Israelites. You have blessed them three times. 11 Go home. I said that I would give you money. The LORD has not let you get my money.'

12 Balaam said to Balak, 'I said this to the men that you sent to get me. 13 "I can only say the LORD's words. I cannot do good things or bad things because I want to do them. I will only say what the LORD is saying. Even if Balak gives to me his house full of silver and gold, I cannot do anything different." 14 And so now I will return to my people. But first I will tell you what these people will do to your people in future days'

Balaam speaks again

15 Balaam spoke and he said, 'This is the message of Balaam the son of Beor. It is the words of a man. This man understands what the LORD says. 16 This is the prophecy of a man who hears the words of God. This man knows some things that the Most High God knows. This man sees a vision from the most powerful God. I fall to the ground in front of him but my eyes are still open.

17 I see that at a future time a king will come from the Israelites. He will be like a bright star. He will attack the leaders of Moab. He will attack the people who were born from Sheth (Seth).

18 He will attack his enemies in Edom and Seir. The Israelites will grow strong.

19 A descendant of Jacob will have power. And he will kill all the people who are still alive in the city.' 20 Then, in the dream picture, Balaam saw Amalek. He said, 'Amalek was the most powerful of all the countries. The LORD will destroy it now and for always.' 21 Then he saw the Kenites. He said, 'The place where you live is safe. It is as safe as the home of a bird on the side of a rock. 22 But Assyria's people will take you away as prisoners.'

23 Then Balaam said, 'Almost nobody can live when the LORD does these things! 24 Ships will come from the north. They will bring people from Cyprus who will destroy Assyria and Eber. Then the LORD will destroy them.' 25 Balaam returned to his home. And Balak went away too.

Chapter 25

1 The Israelites were staying in Shittim. The men began to have sex with the women from Moab. 2 The women from Moab took Israel's men to watch them as they gave gifts to the god of Moab. Israel's men ate those women's food. And they prayed to the god of Moab. 3 So the LORD was angry with them. 4 The LORD said to Moses, 'Kill all the leaders of these people. Do this during the day, not at night. Then I will not be angry.'

5 Moses told the leaders of the Israelites that they must kill the men. They must kill the men who prayed to the god of Peor.

6 A man brought a Midianite woman to his family. Moses and all the people could see them. Moses and all the people were at the door of the Tent of Meeting. They were weeping. 7 Then Phinehas the son of Eleazar, the son of Aaron the priest, saw it. So he stood up among all the people and he took a spear in his hand.

8 He went into the man's tent. And he pushed the spear through the body of the man and the Midianite woman. Then, the bad things and illnesses that were hurting the Israelites stopped. 9 But 24 000 people had already died as a result of the illness.

10 The LORD said to Moses, 11 'I am not still angry with the Israelites now. That is because of what Phinehas, the son of Eleazar, the son of Aaron the priest, did. He thought as I thought about this matter. He did not want the people to worship any god except me. That is why I did not kill all the Israelites. 12 So you must say, "I have promised my peace to him. 13 And that promise will be for him and for his descendants after him. They will always be priests. That is because he did not want the people to worship any god except me. And he made things right again after what the Israelites had done." ' 14 The name of the man that Phinehas killed with the Midianite woman was Zimri. He was the son of Salu. Salu was the leader of a family from the tribe of Simeon. 15 The name of the Midianite woman was Cozbi. She was the daughter of Zur. Zur was a leader of a Midianite family.

16 The LORD said to Moses, 17 'The Midianites are your enemies. You must kill them. 18 That is because they have been against you. They deceived you in the matter of Peor, and in the matter of Cozbi. Cozbi was the daughter of a leader of the Midianites. Phinehas killed her on the day when there was the very bad illness among the people. That illness was the result of what happened at Peor.'

Chapter 26

Moses counts the people again

1 When the bad things and illnesses stopped, the LORD said to Moses and Eleazar the son of Aaron, 2 'Count all the Israelites. Count in their clans all the men who are more than 20 years old. Count only those men who can join the army.' 3 So Moses and Eleazar the priest spoke to the Israelites. They were on the flat ground in Moab at the River Jordan. Jericho was on the other side of the river. They said, 4 'Count all the men who are 20 years old or more. The LORD has told Moses that we must do that.' So these are the names of the Israelites who came out of Egypt:

5 There was the tribe of Reuben, Israel's first-born son. Among Reuben's descendants were the descendants of Hanoch and of Pallu. 6 And there were the descendants of Hezron and of Carmi. 7 Those are the clans of the descendants of Reuben. There were 43 730 men in the tribe of Reuben.

8 The son of Pallu was Eliab. 9 The sons of Eliab were Nemuel, Dathan and Abiram.

Dathan and Abiram were the men who did not obey Moses and Aaron.

Korah was their leader. 10 The ground opened. Korah, Dathan, Abiram and their families fell into the hole and they died. And fire killed 250 other men. So they became a warning to the other Israelites. 11 But Korah's sons did not die then.

12 There was the tribe of Simeon. Among Simeon's descendants were the descendants of Nemuel and of Jamin and of Jachin. 13 And there were the descendants of Zerah and of Shaul. 14 Those are the clans of the descendants of Simeon. There were 22 200 men in the tribe of Simeon.

15 There was the tribe of Gad. Among Gad's descendants were the descendants of Zephon and of Haggi and of Shuni. 16 And there were the descendants of Ozni and of Eri. 17 And there were the descendants of Arod and of Areli. 18 Those are the clans of the descendants of Gad. There were 40 500 men in the tribe of Gad.

19 The sons of Judah were Er and Onan. But Er and Onan died in Canaan. 20 These are the clans in the tribe of Judah. Among Judah's descendants were the descendants of Shelah and of Perez and of Zerah. 21And there were the descendants of Hezron and of Hamul. 22 Those are the clans of the descendants of Judah. There were 76 500 men in the tribe of Judah.

23 There was the tribe of Issachar. Among Issachar's descendants were the descendants of Tola and of Puvah. 24 And there were the descendants of Jashub and of Shimron. 25 Those are the clans of the descendants of Issachar. There were 64 300 men in the tribe of Issachar.

26 There was the tribe of Zebulun. Among Zebulun's descendants were the descendants of Sered and of Elon and of Jahleel. 27 Those are the clans of the descendants of Zebulun. There were 60 500 men in the tribe of Zebulun.

28 The descendants of Joseph became two tribes. Those tribes were called Manasseh and Ephraim.

29 So there was the tribe of Manasseh. Among Manasseh's descendants were the descendants of Machir and of Gilead. 30 Among Gilead's descendants were the descendants of Iezer and of Helek. 31 There were also the descendants of Asriel and of Shechem. 32 And there were the descendants of Shemida and of Hepher. 33 Zelophehad the son of Hepher had no sons, but only daughters. And the names of Zelophehad's daughters were Mahlah, Noah, Hoglah, Milcah and Tirzah. 34 Those are the clans of the descendants of Manasseh. There were 52 700 men in the tribe of Manasseh.

35 There was the tribe of Ephraim. Among Ephraim's descendants were the descendants of Shuthelah and of Becher and of Tahan. 36 And there were the descendants of Eran. 37 Those are the clans of the descendants of Ephraim. There were 32 500 men in the tribe of Ephraim. Those last two tribes came from the sons of Joseph.

38 There was the tribe of Benjamin. Among Benjamin's descendants were the descendants of Bela and of Ashbel and of Ahiram. 39 And there were the descendants of Shupham and of Hupham. 40 Among the descendants of Bela there were the descendants of Ard and of Naaman. 41 Those are the clans of the descendants of Benjamin. There were 45 600 men in the tribe of Benjamin.

42 There was the tribe of Dan. Among Dan's descendants were the descendants of Shuham. Those are the clans of the descendants of Dan. 43 There were 64 400 men among the descendants of Shuham.

44 There was the tribe of Asher. Among Asher's descendants were the descendants of Imnah and of Ishvi and of Beriah. 45 And among the descendants of Beriah there were the descendants of Heber and of Malchiel. 46 There was also a daughter of Asher who was called Serah. 47 Those are the clans of the descendants of Asher. There were 53 400 men in the tribe of Asher.

48 There was the tribe of Naphtali. Among Naphtali's descendants were the descendants of Jahzeel and of Guni. 49 And there were the descendants of Jezer and of Shillem. 50 Those are the clans of the descendants of Naphtali. There were 45 400 men in the tribe of Naphtali.

51 There were 601 730 men on the list of the Israelites. 52 The LORD said to Moses, 53 'I will give the land to the tribes. 54 The big tribes will have a big piece of land. The small tribes will have a small piece of land. 55 You must use lots to give land to each tribe. 56 The larger tribes must have more land than the smaller tribes.'

57 The list of the Levites included the clans of Gershon, Kohath and Merari. 58 And it included the clans of Libni, Hebron, Mahli, Mushi and Korah. Kohath was the father of Amram. 59 The name of Amram's wife was Jochebed. Amram and Jochebed were the parents of Moses, Aaron and Miriam. 60 Aaron was the father of Nadab, Abihu, Eleazar and Ithamar. 61 Nadab and Abihu died. They gave wrong gifts to the LORD.

62 There were 23 000 male Levites who were more than one month old. But Moses did not give any land to them among the Israelites. So he did not put them on the list of the Israelites.

63 Those are the men that Moses and Eleazar the priest counted. They counted them on the flat ground in Moab by the Jordan. The place was near Jericho but it was on the other side of the River Jordan. 64 Moses did not count any of these men when he counted the people the first time. This happened in the Desert called Sinai. 65 That was because the LORD had said about them, 'They will certainly die in the desert.' Not one man among them was still alive, except Caleb the son of Jephunneh and Joshua the son of Nun.

Chapter 27

Zelophehad's daughters

1 Then the daughters of Zelophehad the son of Hepher came near to Moses. Hepher was the son of Gilead, the son of Machir, the son of Manasseh, the son of Joseph. So Zelophehad was in the tribe of Manasseh. And his daughters were called Mahlah, Noah, Hoglah, Milcah and Tirzah. 2 They went to the front of the Tent of Meeting. They stood in front of Moses, Eleazar and all the leaders of the people and they said, 3 'Our father died in the desert. But he was not in the group of men who came together against the LORD with Korah. But he died for his own sin, and he did not have any sons. 4 Please give us some of our tribe's land. Then the people will not forget our father.'

5 Moses spoke to the LORD about this. 6 The LORD said to Moses, 7 'What the daughters of Zelophehad said is right. You must give to them some of the tribe of Manasseh's land. Give to them everything that was their father's.

8 Tell the people this. "Sometimes a man only has daughters. He may die. Then, everything that was his must be theirs. 9 And if he does not have any sons or daughters, you must give his land to his brothers. 10 But if he does not have any brothers, you must give his land to his father's brothers. 11 Sometimes the man with no children may have no brothers of his father. If that happens, you must give his land to another person in his family. This is a rule for all the people." '

Joshua is the new leader

12 The LORD said to Moses, 'Go up the Abiram Mountains. Look at the country that I am giving to the Israelites. 13 You will see it. And then you will die as your brother Aaron died. 14 That is because of what happened in the desert at Zin. It was when the people were quarrelling with me there. You did not obey what I said to you. And all the people saw it. So you did not show to the people that I am holy. That was at the water.' (These are the waters of Meribah at Kadesh in the desert called Zin.)

15 Moses said to the LORD, 16 'You are the LORD, the God of the spirits of all people. Please choose another man to be over all the people. 17 Then he can go out and he can come in front of them. He can lead them out and he can bring them in. Then all the LORD's people will not be like sheep without a shepherd.'

18 So the LORD said to Moses, 'Take Joshua the son of Nun. My Spirit is in him. Lay your hand on him.

19 He must stand in front of Eleazar the priest and in front of all the Israelites. Tell Joshua and all the people this. He will be the leader when you die. 20 Tell the people that they must obey him. 21 Eleazar the priest will use everything that is holy. He will know what I am saying. He will tell Joshua. Then the Israelites must obey Joshua.'

22 Moses did as the LORD told him. He took Joshua and he brought him to stand in front of Eleazar the priest. 23 He put his hands on Joshua. So Joshua became the new leader. The LORD had told Moses that he should do that.

Chapter 28

Gifts for the LORD

1 The LORD said to Moses, 2 'Tell the Israelites that they must give their gifts to the LORD at the proper time. The smell of the gifts when they burn will make the LORD happy. 3 And you must say to them, "This is the offering by fire that you must offer to the LORD: It must be two male lambs that are one year old. They must not have anything wrong with them. That is the burnt-offering every day. 4 You must give one lamb in the morning and one lamb in the evening. 5 You must give to the LORD a gift of grain or flour that you have mixed with oil. 6 It is a regular burnt-offering that God told you about. He told you about it on the mountain called Sinai. It is an offering by fire to the LORD. And the smell as it burns makes the LORD happy. 7 Then the drink-offering with it will be one litre (2 pints) of wine for each lamb. In God's Holy Tent you must pour out a drink-offering of the best wine to the LORD. 8 And you must offer the other lamb when it begins to get dark. Offer it with an offering of flour and a drink-offering like the offerings in the morning. You must give it as an offering by fire. The smell of the smoke from these sacrifices will make the LORD happy.

9 Then on the Sabbath day, you must offer two male lambs that are one year old. They must not have anything wrong with them. And you must offer 2 kilos (4.4 pounds) of best flour. Mix that with oil as an offering of flour. And you must give the proper drink-offering with it. 10 This is the burnt-offering for every Sabbath. But you must also give the regular burnt-offering with its proper drink-offering.

11 Also on the first day of every month you must give a burnt-offering to the LORD. It must be two bulls, one male sheep and 7 male lambs. The lambs must be one year old and they must not have anything wrong with them. 12 With each bull and with the male sheep, you must give an offering of flour. Mix together 3 kilos (6.6 pounds) of the best flour with olive oil. Offer it to me with each bull. Mix together 2 kilos (4.4 pounds) of the best flour with olive oil. Offer it to me with the male sheep. 13 And with each lamb you must give an offering of flour. Mix together 1 kilo (2.2 pounds) of the best flour with olive oil. Offer it to me with each male lamb as a burnt-offering to the LORD. The smell of the smoke from these sacrifices will make the LORD happy. 14 And there must be drink-offerings with these sacrifices. The offering must be 2 litres (4 pints) of wine for a bull. It must be 1.5 litres (3 pints) for the male sheep and 1 litre (2 pints) for a lamb. That is the burnt-offering of each month for every month of the year. 15 Also, you must offer one male goat as a sin-offering. You must offer it with the proper drink-offering. But you must still offer the regular burnt-offering.

Remember the Passover

16 On the 14th day of the first month you must remember the Passover. 17 Day 15 is the start of a week when you must eat the flat bread. You must not put anything in the bread to make it rise. You must do that for 7 days. 18 The first day will be a holy day and all the people must meet together. You must not work at your jobs on that day. 19 And you must give an offering by fire, a burnt-offering to the LORD. The offering must be 2 bulls, one male sheep and 7 male lambs that are one year old. But these animals must not have anything wrong with them. 20 Offer the proper grain-offering with each animal. Mix together 3 kilos (6.6 pounds) of the best flour and olive oil. Offer it to me with each bull. Offer 2 kilos (4.4 pounds) of flour with oil with the male sheep. 21 With the 7 lambs, you must give a gift of grain that you have mixed with oil. 22 You must also give one male goat as a sin-offering. That is to make things right with God for you. 23 But you must still give the burnt-offering in the morning that is the regular burnt-offering. 24 You must offer those gifts every day for 7 days. They are the food of an offering by fire. The smell of them as they burn will make the LORD happy. But you must still give the regular burnt-offering with the proper drink-offering. 25 And the 7th day must be a holy day and all the people must meet together. You must not work at your jobs on that day.

26 The day when you offer to the LORD the first part of the harvest must also be a holy day. That is also the day when you give to the LORD an offering of new grain. That is the Feast of Weeks. All the people must meet together. You must not work at your jobs on that day.

27 And you must give a burnt-offering to the LORD. The offering must be 2 bulls, one male sheep and 7 male lambs that are one year old. The smell of the smoke from these sacrifices will make the LORD happy.

28 With the bull and the male sheep you must give a gift of grain that you have mixed with oil. 29 With the 7 lambs you must give a gift of grain that you have mixed with oil. 30 You must also give one male goat. The goat is because of their sins. 31 You must still give the regular burnt-offering with the proper offering of flour. You must give them with the proper drink-offerings. The animals must not have anything wrong with them.

Chapter 29

1 On the first day of the seventh month, all the people must come together for a holy meeting. You must not work at your jobs. It is a day for you to make music with your trumpets. 2 And you must offer a burnt-offering to the LORD. You must give one young bull and one male sheep. Also offer 7 male sheep that are one year old. The animals must not have anything wrong with them. The smell of the smoke from these sacrifices will make the LORD happy. 3 Offer to me the proper offering of flour with each animal. Mix together 3 kilos (6.6 pounds) of the best flour with olive oil. Offer it to me with the young bull. Offer 2 kilos (4.4 pounds) of flour with oil with the male sheep. 4 Offer 1 kilo (2.2 pounds) of flour with each young male sheep. 5 Also offer one male goat as a sin-offering, so that I will forgive the people's sins. 6 Offer these sacrifices with the burnt-offerings, offerings of flour and drink-offerings that you give each month. Offer these sacrifices with the burnt-offerings, offerings of flour and drink-offerings that you give each day. The smell of the smoke from these sacrifices will make the LORD happy.

7 On the 10th day of the 7th month, you must come together for a holy meeting. During that day, you must make yourselves humble. And you must not do any work. 8 You must offer a burnt-offering to the LORD. The smell of the smoke will make the LORD happy. Offer one young bull, one male sheep and 7 male lambs that are one year old. The animals must not have anything wrong with them. 9 Offer to me the proper offering of flour with each animal. Mix together 3 kilos (6.6 pounds) of the best flour with olive oil. Offer it to me with the young bull. Offer 2 kilos (4.4 pounds) of flour with oil with the male sheep. 10 Offer 1 kilo (2.2 pounds) of flour with oil with each lamb. 11 Also offer one male goat as a sin-offering. Give these gifts with the burnt-offering, the flour and the drink-offering that you give each day and each month.

12 On the 15th day of the 7th month, you must come together for a holy meeting. You must not work at your jobs. You must have a feast to the LORD for 7 days. 13 Give an offering by fire as a smell to make the LORD happy. Give a burnt-offering of 13 young bulls, two male sheep and 14 male lambs that are a year old. The animals must not have anything wrong with them. 14 With each of the 13 bulls give an offering of flour. Mix together 3 kilos (6.6 pounds) of the best flour with olive oil. Offer it to me with each bull. Offer 2 kilos (4.4 pounds) of flour with each male sheep. 15 Offer 1 kilo (2.2 pounds) of flour that you have mixed with oil with each male lamb. 16 Include one male goat as a sin-offering. Sacrifice it with the regular burnt-offering with the proper offering of flour and the drink-offering.

17 On the second day give 12 young bulls, two male sheep and 14 male lambs that are a year old. The animals must not have anything wrong with them. 18 With the bulls, male sheep and lambs, give the right offerings of flour and drink-offerings for each animal. 19 Include one male goat as a sin-offering. Sacrifice it with the regular burnt-offering with the proper offering of flour and their drink-offerings.

20 On the third day give 11 bulls, two male sheep and 14 male lambs that are a year old. The animals must not have anything wrong with them. 21 With the bulls, male sheep and lambs, give the right offerings of flour and drink-offerings for each animal. 22 Include one male goat as a sin-offering. Sacrifice it with the regular burnt-offering with the proper offering of flour and the drink-offering.

23 On the 4th day give 10 bulls, two male sheep and 14 male lambs that are a year old. The animals must not have anything wrong with them. 24 With the bulls, male sheep and lambs, give the right offerings of flour and drink-offerings for each animal. 25 Include one male goat as a sin-offering. Sacrifice it with the regular burnt-offering with the proper offering of flour and the drink-offering.

26 On the 5th day give 9 bulls, two male sheep and 14 male lambs that are a year old. The animals must not have anything wrong with them. 27 With the bulls, male sheep and lambs, give the right offerings of flour and drink-offerings for each animal. 28 Include one male goat as a sin-offering. Sacrifice it with the regular burnt-offering with the proper offering of flour and the drink-offering.

29 On the 6th day give 8 bulls, two male sheep and 14 male lambs that are a year old.

The animals must not have anything wrong with them. 30 With the bulls, male sheep and lambs, give the right offerings of flour and drink-offerings for each animal. 31 Include one male goat as a sin-offering. Sacrifice it with the regular burnt-offering with the proper offering of flour and the drink-offering.

32 On the 7th day give 7 bulls, two male sheep and 14 male lambs that are a year old. The animals must not have anything wrong with them. 33 With the bulls, male sheep and lambs, give the right offerings of flour and drink-offerings for each animal. 34 Include one male goat as a sin-offering. Sacrifice it with the regular burnt-offering with the proper offering of flour and the drink-offering.

35 On the 8th day, all the people must come together for a holy meeting. You must not work at your jobs. 36Give an offering by fire as a smell to make the LORD happy. Give a burnt-offering of one bull, one male sheep and 7 male lambs that are a year old. The animals must not have anything wrong with them. 37 With the bull, the male sheep and the lambs, give the right offerings of flour and drink-offerings for each animal. 38 Include one male goat as a sin-offering. Sacrifice it with the regular burnt-offering with the proper offering of flour and the drink-offering.

39 You must offer those gifts to the LORD at the times of the feasts. You must do that even if you have given your usual burnt-offerings, offerings of flour, drink-offerings or friendship-offerings. And you must do it even if you have given other offerings. You might have given those other offerings because you wanted to give them. Or you might have given them because you had promised to give them." '

40 Moses told the Israelites everything that the LORD had said him.

Chapter 30

1 Moses said to the leaders of the tribes: 2 'The LORD says this. A man must do everything that he promised to the LORD.

3 A young woman who lives in the house of her father might make a promise to the LORD. She must do everything that she has said. 4 She must do this if her father does not say anything. 5 But her father may say that she must not do it. Then she does not have to do it. The LORD will understand why she does not do it.

6 But the young woman might marry after she promised something to the LORD. Or she might have promised something when she had not thought carefully about it. 7 If her husband does not say anything about it, she must keep her promise. 8 But her husband may say that he does not agree about the promise. He must say that on the day when he first knows about it. It might be a serious promise. Or it might be a promise that the woman had not thought carefully about. The woman does not have to do the thing now because of what her husband has said. And the LORD will forgive her.

9 If the husband of a woman has died, she must keep her promise. If the woman and her husband do not live together, they are not still married. If she makes a promise, she must do it.

10 A woman who is living with her husband might make a promise. 11 If her husband does not say anything about it, she must do it. 12 Her husband may say that she must not do it. She must obey him. The LORD will let her do that. 13 The husband can let her do what she promised to do. He can also say that she must not do it. 14 If the husband does not say anything about the promise, the woman must do it. 15 The husband may wait for a long time after he hears about the promise. Then, he may say that she must not do it. If that happens, the LORD will be angry with the man. He will not be angry with the woman.'

16 The LORD gave to Moses those rules about a man and his wife. They are also about a father and a young daughter.

Chapter 31

War against the Midianites

1 The LORD said to Moses, 2 'Go to war against the Midianites. After you have done that, you will die.'

3 Moses said to the people, 'Give swords to some of the men. Go to war against the Midianites. This is what the LORD wants you to do.

4 Send 1000 men from each tribe to war.' 5 And 12 000 men were ready for war. There were 1000 men from each tribe. 6 Moses sent those men to the war. There were 1000 men from each tribe. Phinehas the son of Eleazar the priest went with them. Phinehas took with him the things from God's Holy Tent. Also, he took in his hand the trumpets to make warning sounds.

7 They fought against the Midianites. And they killed every man among them. 8 And they killed the kings of Midian with the other men that they killed. Evi, Rekem, Zur, Hur and Reba were the 5 kings of Midian. They also killed Balaam the son of Beor with a sword. 9 Israel's men took the women and children of Midian. They took their animals and everything that was valuable. 10 They burned their towns and camps.11 They took the people, the animals and everything that was valuable. 12 And they brought the prisoners and the things that they took to Moses, and to Eleazar the priest. And they brought it to all the Israelites, to their camp. That was at the flat ground in Moab by the River Jordan. The place was near Jericho but it was on the other side of the River Jordan.

13 Moses, Eleazar and the leaders of the tribes went to meet them outside the camp. 14 Moses was angry with the leaders of the army.

15 He said to them, "Have you let all the women live? 16 These women here caused the Israelites not to obey the LORD by what they did at Peor. Balaam told them how they could do it. So there was a bad illness among all the LORD's people. 17 So kill all the boys. And kill every woman who had had sex with a man. 18 But you can keep for yourselves all the girls who have not had sex with a man.'

19 Moses said, 'Any soldier who has killed any person must stay outside the camp for 7 days. Any soldier who has touched a dead body must stay outside the camp for 7 days. On day 3 and on day 7, you must make yourselves clean. You must also make the people of Midian that you took clean. 20 You must make anything that someone has made out of leather, wool or wood clean.' 21 Eleazar the priest said to the soldiers, 'This is what the LORD told Moses. 22 You must put all the gold and silver in the fire. 23 You must put all the metals that will not burn in the fire. This will make them clean. You must also wash them. You must clean, with water, everything that will burn. 24 On day 7, you must wash your clothes. Then you will be clean. Then you can come into the camp.'

25 The LORD said to Moses, 26 'You and Eleazar and the leaders of the tribes must count all the people and animals that you took. 27 Give anything that is valuable to the soldiers and all the people. Be sure that every person gets some of them. 28 From that which would go to the soldiers, keep one out of every 500Midianite soldiers for the LORD. Do the same with the animals. 29 Give what is for the LORD to Eleazar the priest. 30 From what is for the people give one out of every 50 Midianite soldiers to the Levites. Do the same with the animals.' 31 Moses and Eleazar did as the LORD said.

32 The soldiers took 675 000 sheep, 33 72 000 cows, 34 61 000 donkeys 35 and 32 000 women who had not had sex with a man.

36 The gift for the soldiers included 337 500 sheep. 37 So there were 675 sheep for the LORD. 38 The gift for the soldiers also included 36 000 cows. So there were 72 cows for the LORD. 39 The gift for the soldiers also included 30 500 donkeys. So there were 61 donkeys for the LORD. 40 The gift for the soldiers also included 16 000 people. So there were 32 people for the LORD.

41 Moses gave the gift that was for the LORD to Eleazar, the priest. The LORD had told Moses that he must do that.

42 Moses made the gift that was for the people separate from the gift that was for the soldiers. 43 The gift for the people included 337 500 sheep.

44 It also included 36 000 cows. 45 It also included 30 500donkeys. 46 And it included 16 000 people. 47 From the gift that was for the Israelites, Moses took one out of every 50. And he gave them to the Levites.

48 The leaders of the army went to Moses. 49 They said to him: 'We have counted the soldiers. They are all present. 50 We have brought a gift to the LORD. We have brought gold rings and other gold that people wear. They are gifts for when we sinned.'

51 Moses and Eleazar took all the gold.

52 And they weighed all the gold of the offering that they lifted up to the LORD. That was the offering from the captains over 1000 men and the captains over 100 men. The weight was 16 750 shekels. 53 The soldiers took anything that was gold from the enemy. They took it when they were at war. 54 Moses and Eleazar took all the gold into the Tent of Meeting. It was a gift. It was to remember the time when the LORD told the people to go to war against the Midianites.

Chapter 32

1 The people in the tribes of Reuben and Gad had very many animals. They saw that the land in Jazer and Gilead was good for their animals. 2 They came to Moses, Eleazar and the leaders of the tribes. 3 They said, 'The land at Ataroth, Dibon, Jazer, Nimrah, Heshbon, Elealeh, Sebam, Nebo and Beon 4 is good for animals. We have very many animals. 5 Please let us take this land for our animals. Please do not take us across the River Jordan.'

6 Moses said to the men: 'The Israelites are going to war. It seems that you want to watch them. But you want to stay here! 7 You should not tell the people in your tribes that they should not cross over the River Jordan. The LORD is giving this country to them. 8 Your fathers did the same thing when I sent them from Kadesh-Barnea to look at the country. 9 They went to the valley of Eshcol and they saw the country. But they told the Israelites that it was not a good idea to go into the country. So the Israelites did not go into the country that the LORD had given to them. 10 The LORD was angry with them. 11 He said, "They do not obey me. None of the men who came from Egypt will go into this country. If they are more than 20 years old, they will not go into this country. It is the country that I am giving to them. I promised the country to Abraham, Isaac and Jacob. 12 Jephunneh's son Caleb and Joshua the son of Nun are the only men who will go into the country. It is the country that I am giving to the Israelites. Caleb and Joshua have obeyed me. So they will go in." 13 The LORD was angry with all the Israelites because of those men who would not go in. He caused them to walk about in the desert for 40 years. Then all the men who did not obey him were dead.

14 You are doing the same sins that your fathers did. You are making the LORD even more angry with the Israelites. 15 If you do not obey him, he will not let the people leave the desert. If they die, it will be because of you.'

16 The men said to Moses, 'Let us build houses from stone for our animals, our women and our children. 17Then we will be ready to go to war with the Israelites. When we are at war, our women and children will be safe. 18 We will not return to our homes until all the Israelites receive the land. It is the land that the LORD is giving to them. 19 We will not receive any of the land on the other side of the River Jordan. Our land is here.'

20 Moses said to the men, 'You must really do as you have said. You must go to war. 21 You must cross over the River Jordan with the people to get power over the country. 22 If you really do that, you can return to this land. And the LORD will not be angry. The LORD will give this land to you.

23 But if you do not do it, you will have sinned against the LORD. And be sure that your sin will cause your punishment. 24 Build towns for your families and build pens for your animals. But then do the things that you have promised to do.'

25 The men in the tribes of Gad and Reuben said to Moses, 'We will do what we promised to do. 26 Our women and children will stay here in Gilead. Our animals will stay here in Gilead. 27 But we are your servants. And we will cross over. Everyone among us who has weapons for war will cross over. And we will fight in the LORD's fight, as you have said, my master.'

28 Moses told Eleazar the priest what the men in Reuben's tribe and in Gad's tribe were doing. He also told Joshua the son of Nun and the leaders of the tribes. 29 He said to them, 'The men in Reuben's tribe and in Gad's tribe must cross over the River Jordan to fight with you. If they do, you must give the land called Gilead to them. 30 If they do not do that, they must build their houses in Canaan.'

31 The men in the tribes of Reuben and Gad said, 'We will do what we promised to do. 32 We will go into Canaan to fight, but we will live in Gilead.'

33 So Moses gave to them all the kingdom of Sihon, king of the Amorites and Og, the king of Bashan.

He gave to them the land with its towns and all the land round the towns near those towns. He gave it to the descendants of Gad and of Reuben and half of the tribe of Joseph's son Manasseh.

34 The men in the tribe of Gad built up again Dibon, Ataroth and Aroer. 35 They also built up again Atroth-Shophan, Jazer, Jogbehah, 36 Beth-Nimrah and Beth-Haran. They built houses for their families and their animals. 37 The men in the tribe of Reuben built Heshbon, Elealeh and Kiriathaim up again. 38 They built Nebo and Baal-Meon and Sibmah. They gave new names to the cities that they built up.

39 The descendants of Machir son of Manasseh attacked Gilead. They sent away the people who lived there. 40 So Moses gave Gilead to the descendants of Machir who was the son of Manasseh. And they lived there. 41 Jair, who was a descendant of Manasseh attacked some villages. He got power over them and he called them Havvoth-Jair. 42 Nobah attacked Kenath and the villages round it. He called it Nobah, like himself.

Chapter 33

1 This is the journey of the Israelites. Moses and Aaron led them out of Egypt. They travelled in their tribes. 2 The LORD told Moses that he should write about the journey. This is the journey:

3 They left Rameses in the first month. They started to travel from Rameses on the 15th day of the first month. That was the day after the Passover. The Israelites marched out bravely. And all Egypt's people watched them as they went. 4 As they left, Egypt's people were burying all their oldest sons. The LORD had killed their oldest sons. The LORD had also shown that he is more powerful than their gods.

5 They travelled to Succoth and they camped there.

6 They travelled to Etham. And they camped on the edge of the desert.

7 They travelled from Etham to Pi-Hahiroth, which is east of Baal-Zephon. They camped near Migdol.

8 They travelled from Pi-Hahiroth. They went through the sea into the desert. They travelled for three days and then they camped at Marah in the desert.

9 They travelled from Marah to Elim. At Elim, there were 12 streams and 70 trees. The trees were called palm trees. They camped there.

10 They travelled from Elim and they camped by the side of the Red Sea.

11 They travelled from the Red Sea. And they camped in the Desert called Sin.

12 They travelled from the Desert called Sin. And they camped at Dophkah.

13 They travelled from Dophkah and they camped at Alush.

14 They travelled from Alush and they camped at Rephidim. There was no water here for the people to drink.

15 They travelled from Rephidim. And they camped in the Desert called Sinai.

16 They travelled from the Desert called Sinai. And they camped at Kibroth-Hattaavah.

17 They travelled from Kibroth-Hattaavah and they camped at Hazeroth.

18 They travelled from Hazeroth and they camped at Rithmah.

19 They travelled from Rithmah and they camped at Rimmon-Perez.

20 They travelled from Rimmon-Perez and they camped at Libnah.

21 They travelled from Libnah and they camped at Rissah.

22 They travelled from Rissah and they camped at Kehelathah.

23 They travelled from Kehelathah. And they camped at the mountain called Shepher.

24 They travelled from the mountain called Shepher. And they camped at Haradah.

25 They travelled from Haradah and they camped at Makheloth.

26 They travelled from Makheloth and they camped at Tahath.

27 They travelled from Tahath and they camped at Terah.

28 They travelled from Terah and they camped at Mithkah.

29 They travelled from Mithkah and they camped at Hashmonah.

30 They travelled from Hashmonah and they camped at Moseroth.

31 They travelled from Moseroth and they camped at Bene-Jaakan.

32 They travelled from Bene-Jaakan and they camped at Hor-Haggidgad.

33 They travelled from Hor-Haggidgad and they camped at Jotbathah.

34 They travelled from Jotbathah and they camped at Abronah.

35 They travelled from Abronah and they camped at Ezion-Geber.

36 They travelled from Ezion-Geber and they camped at Kadesh in the Desert of Zin.

37 They travelled from Kadesh. And they camped at the mountain called Hor. It is on the edge of Edom.

38 The LORD told Aaron that he must go up a mountain. The mountain was called Hor. So Aaron went up it. He died there. That was on the first day of the fifth month. It was in the 40th year after the Israelites travelled from Egypt.

39 Aaron was 123 years old when he died.

40 The king of Arad lived in the south, in the country called Canaan. People told him that the Israelites were coming.

41 They travelled from the mountain called Hor. And they camped at Zalmonah.

42 They travelled from Zalmonah and they camped at Punon.

43 They travelled from Punon and they camped at Oboth.

44 They travelled from Oboth and they camped at Iye-Abarim on the edge of Moab.

45 They travelled from Iye-Abarim and they camped at Dibon-Gad.

46 They travelled from Dibon-Gad and they camped at Almon-Diblathaim.

47 They travelled from Almon-Diblathaim and they camped in the mountains of Abarim, near Nebo.

48 They travelled from the mountains of Abarim and they camped in Moab by the side of the River Jordan. They were on the other side of the river from Jericho.

49 They camped by the side of the River Jordan from Beth-Jeshimoth to Abel-Shittim on the flat ground in Moab.

50 Then the LORD spoke to Moses on the flat ground in Moab by the River Jordan. The place was near Jericho but it was on the other side of the River Jordan. He said, 51 'Say to the Israelites, "You will cross over the River Jordan to Canaan. 52 Then you must send out all the people who live in that country in front of you. You must not let any of those people stay in the country. And you must destroy all their stones in the shape of people. And you must destroy all the idols that they have made from metal. And you must destroy all their high places for worship. 53 And you must get power over the country and you must live in it. Do that because I have given the country to you. I have given it to you so that you can live it. 54And you must use lots to give the land to your clans. You must give more land to the larger clans and you must give less land to the smaller clans. Whatever land somebody gets as a result of the lots that will be his land. Each of your ancestors' tribes will get its own land.

55 If any Canaanites remain in the country, they will be a problem to the Israelites. 56 And I will do to you what I wanted to do to them." '

Chapter 34

1 The LORD said to Moses, 2 'Tell the Israelites this: When you go into Canaan, your land will have edges to it.

3 The south edge will include a part of the Desert of Zin. In the east, it will begin at the south end of the Dead Sea. 4 It will go south of the place called Scorpion Pass, on to Zin. And then it will go south of Kadesh-Barnea. It will go to Hazar-Addar and over to Azmon. 5 It will turn and it will join the Wadi of Egypt. It will finish at the sea.

6 The west edge is the coast of the Mediterranean Sea.

7 The north edge is a line from the Mediterranean Sea to the mountain called Hor. 8 From the mountain called Hor it will go to Lebo-Hamath. Then it will go to Zedad. 9 It will go to Ziphron and it will finish at Hazar-Enan.

10 The east edge is a line from Hazar-Enan to Shepham. 11 The line will go down from Shepham to Riblah on the east side of Ain. It will go along the east of the lake called Chinnereth. 12 Then it will go along the River Jordan and it will finish at the Dead Sea.'

13 Moses said to the Israelites, 'Cut this country into parts in the way that the LORD told you. The LORD said that you must give it to 9 and a half tribes. 14 That is because the tribes of Reuben and Gad and half of Manasseh's tribe have their land already. 15 Their land is on the east side of the River Jordan. It is opposite Jericho.'

16 The LORD said to Moses, 17 'Joshua, the son of Nun and Eleazar the priest must cut the country into parts. They must give the parts to the people. 18 One leader from each tribe must help them. 19 These are the names of the men who will help them: Caleb the son of Jephunneh will be the leader from the tribe of Judah. 20 And the leader from the tribe of Simeon will be Shemuel the son of Ammihud. 21 And the leader from the tribe of Benjamin will be Elidad the son of Chislon. 22 And the leader from the tribe of Dan will be Bukki the son of Jogli. 23 These will be the leaders from the descendants of Joseph: Hanniel the son of Ephod will be the leader from the tribe of Manasseh. 24 And Kemuel the son of Shiphtan will be the leader from the tribe of Ephraim. 25 And the leader from the tribe of Zebulun will be Elizaphan the son of Parnach. 26 And the leader from the tribe of Issachar will be Paltiel the son of Azzan. 27 And the leader from the tribe of Asher will be Ahihud the son of Shelomi. 28 And the leader from the tribe of Naphtali will be Pedahel the son of Ammihud.'

29 Those were the men that the LORD chose to help Joshua and Eleazar.

Chapter 35

1 The LORD spoke to Moses in Moab. Moab was by the River Jordan. Jericho was across the river. 2 He said, 'Tell the people this. They must give the Levites towns to live in. They must also give them land round the towns. 3 The Levites must have towns to live in and land for their animals.

4 And you must give the fields of grass round the towns to the Levites. That must include every field that is less than 500 metres (1500 feet) from the town's walls. 5 You must also measure outside the town on the east side 1000 metres (3000 feet), and on the south side. And you must measure 1000 metres on the west side and on the north side. So the town will be in the centre. Those fields of grass will become theirs for their towns.

6 Six (6) of the towns must be places in which a person can hide. He can hide there if he kills another person. They must also have another 42 towns. 7 The Levites must have 48 towns and land for their animals. 8 When the tribes give the towns to the Levites they must take many towns from the big tribes. They must take few towns from the small tribes.' 9 The LORD said to Moses, 10 'Tell the Israelites this. When they cross the River Jordan, they will go into Canaan. 11 They must choose some towns in which a person can hide. He can hide there if he kills another person. 12 And those cities will be places where someone can be safe from the blood-avenger. So the man killer will not die before all the people in the town have judged him. 13 They must choose 6 towns. 14 Three towns must be in Canaan and three towns must be on the other side of the River Jordan. 15 Those towns are places to hide in for the Israelites and for all the people who live with them.

16 A man might hit a person with a thing that someone made out of iron. If the person dies, the man is a murderer. He must die. 17 A man might hit a person with a stone. If the person dies, the man is a murderer. He must die. 18 A man might hit a person with a thing that someone made out of wood. If the person dies, the man is a murderer. He must die. 19 The blood-avenger himself must kill the murderer. He must kill him when he meets him. 20 A man might push another person and kill him. The man must die. A man might throw something at another person and kill him. The man must die. 21 Or a man might hit a person with his hand because he hates him. If the person dies as a result you must kill the man. You must kill the man who hit the other person. He is a murderer. The blood-avenger must kill the murderer when he meets him.

22 If a man pushes another person, it might be a mistake. Or if he throws something at another person, it might be a mistake. 23 Or a man might be holding a stone that could cause death. He might drop it on a person that he did not see. The person might die as a result but the man did not hate the person. The man did not want to hurt the person. 24 If that happens all the people in the town must judge. They must say whether the man killer or the blood-avenger is right. They must use these rules to judge. 25 And all the people will save the man killer from the blood-avenger. And all the people must send him back to the safe city that he ran to. And he will live there until the death of the most important priest that someone put the holy oil on.

26 But the man killer might at some time go outside the border of the safe city that he ran to. 27 If he does that, the blood-avenger might find him outside the border of his safe city. If the blood-avenger kills the man killer in that place, the blood-avenger will not be guilty of murder. 28 That is because he should have stayed in his safe city until the death of the most important priest. But after the death of the most important priest, the man killer can return to his own home.

29 These are the rules from the LORD for now and for all future time.

30 Other people might see a man kill another person. The man must die. But perhaps only one person saw the man kill another person. Then the man must not die.

31 A person must not give money to keep a murderer alive.

32 A person must not give money to a man who killed another person. He must not help the man leave a city that is safe before the death of the most important priest.

33 Do not make the country bad. If you kill people, you make the country bad. The country is bad because men kill other people.

You can make the country good. You must kill the man who kills another person. 34You must not make the country where you live bad. It is the country where I also live. That is because I, the LORD, live among the Israelites.'

Chapter 36

Rules about women who have land

1 Gilead was the son of Machir, the son of Manasseh. And Manasseh was Joseph's son. The leaders of the families in Gilead's clan went to Moses and to the other leaders of the Israelites' clans. 2 And they said, 'The LORD told you, my master, that we should use lots to give the land to the Israelites. Then each man's land would become his sons' land when he died. And the LORD told you, my master, that you should give Zelophehad's land to his daughters. Zelophehad was in our clan. 3 But if the girls marry, the land will become their husbands' land. If they marry men from other tribes, the tribe of Manasseh will lose the land. 4 They are girls. So their land will become part of the land that their husbands already have.'

5 The LORD told Moses what he should say to these men. Moses said, 'What you are saying is right. 6 This is what the LORD has said about the daughters of Zelophehad: "Let them marry men that they want to marry. But they must marry men from the clans of their father's tribe. 7 So none of the Israelites' land that is one tribe's land will become the land of another tribe. So the people in each tribe will keep the land that their ancestors had. 8 And that must happen to every daughter who gets some land of any tribe of the Israelites. She will be the wife of someone in a clan of her father's tribe. So every Israelite will keep the land that was his ancestors' land. 9 So none of the Israelites' land that is one tribe's land will become the land of another tribe. So the people in each tribe will keep the land that their ancestors had.'

10 The daughters of Zelophehad did as Moses said. 11 Mahlah, Tirzah, Hoglah, Milcah and Noah, the daughters of Zelophehad married sons of their father's brothers. 12 They married men from the clans of the descendants of Joseph's son Manasseh. And their land remained with the tribe of their father's clan.

13 Those are the rules that the LORD gave to the Israelites. The LORD used Moses to give those rules to them when they were camping in Moab. They were camping on the flat ground in Moab by the River Jordan near Jericho.

It is Time to Remember

Deuteronomy

About this book

The writer of this book is a man called Moses. God chose him to lead the Israelites out of the country called Egypt. We can read about how God chose Moses in the book of Exodus chapters 2, 3 and 4. Moses knew God and he loved God's Law. God talked to him like a friend. In Deuteronomy, Moses explains God's Law many times to the Israelites. He also tells them how much God loves them. Moses wants the Israelites to obey God. If they obey him, they will be happy. But if they do not obey God, many bad things will happen to them.

The Israelites have now arrived at the Jordan River. On the other side of the river is the country called Canaan. God has promised to give this country to the Israelites. But these men and women are the children of those who left Egypt. They were born during the journey of 40 years from Egypt to Canaan. So Moses teaches them what God is like. He tells them again about the love of God. Deuteronomy is a book about remembering.

Plan of the book

Chapters 1-4 Remembering the journey

Chapters 5-26 Moses repeats the Law of God, to love and obey him

Chapter 1

1 These are the words that Moses spoke to the Israelites. They were in the desert on the east side of the Jordan River. This is the Jordan valley from where you can see Suph. It is between the towns called Paran, Tophel, Laban, Hazeroth and Dizahab. 2 (It is a journey of 11 days from Horeb to Kadesh-Barnea, past Mount Seir.) 3 Moses spoke on the first day of the 11th month, in the 40th year. He repeated to the Israelites all the words that the LORD had spoken about them.

4 This happened after Moses had beaten Sihon, king of the Amorites. Sihon ruled in the town called Heshbon. Moses had also beaten Og, the king of Bashan, at the town called Edrei. Og ruled in the town called Ashtaroth. 5 Moses began to speak on the east side of the Jordan River, in the country called Moab. He explained the Law of God. He said, 6 'The LORD our God said to us at Mount Horeb, "You have stayed for a long time at this mountain. 7 Pack up your tents and begin to travel. Go to the hills of the Amorites and to all the countries near to them. Go to the Jordan valley and to the hills and into the valleys. Go towards the south and to the Mediterranean coast. Go to the country called Canaan, to Lebanon and as far as the great river Euphrates. 8 Look! I have given you all this country. Go in and take it. The LORD promised to give this country to your fathers. He promised to give it to Abraham, Isaac, Jacob and their children."

Moses chose leaders.

9 At that time I, Moses, said these words to you. "I alone cannot lead you and help you with all your troubles. 10 The LORD your God has made you as many people as the stars in the sky. 11 I pray that the LORD, the God of your fathers, will make you a thousand times as many people. And I know that he will cause many good things to happen to you. He has promised to do that. 12 But I alone cannot help you with all your troubles and quarrels. 13 You must choose some wise men who understand you, from each of your tribes. Then I will give them authority over you."

14 You answered me, "That is a good idea!"

15 So I chose the leaders of your tribes who were wise and good men. I gave them authority over you and made them leaders. They were leaders of 1000's, leaders of 100's, leaders of 50's and leaders of 10's. I also chose officers for each tribe. 16 And I said to your leaders at that time, "Listen to the quarrels between Israelites. Decide what is right. Do that when the quarrel is between two Israelites. Do the same thing when the quarrel is between an Israelite and a person from a foreign country. 17 Do not make a difference between important people and poor people. Listen to both of them in a careful way. Do not be afraid of anyone. God always decides what is right. If you cannot answer a question, bring it to me. I will listen to you. Then I will decide what is right." 18 So, at that time, I told you everything that you must do.

Moses sent out men to explore.

19 Then the LORD our God told us to start our journey from Mount Horeb. So we went towards the hills of the Amorites. We walked through all that large and frightening desert that you have seen. And so we reached Kadesh-Barnea. 20 Then I said to you, "You have reached the hills of the Amorites. The LORD our God is giving this to us. 21 Look! The LORD your God has given you this country. Go in and make it your country. The LORD God of your fathers has told you to do this. Do not be afraid. Do not run away."

22 Then all of you came to me. You said, "Let us send some men in front of us. They can explore the country. Then they can bring back a report to us. They can tell us the best road to travel. They can tell us about the towns that we will come to."

23 I thought that this was a good idea. I chose 12 men, one from each of your tribes. 24 They left and went up into the hills. They came to the valley of Eshcol and they explored it. 25 They took some of the fruit that they found. They brought it back to us. And they reported, "The LORD our God is giving us a good country."

The people refuse to obey the LORD.

26 But you did not want to go into the country. You refused to obey the LORD your God. 27 You spoke bad words in your tents. You said, "The LORD hates us. He led us out of Egypt to give us to the Amorites. He wanted to kill us. 28 We do not know where to go. Our friends have made us afraid. They say, 'These people are taller and stronger than we are. The cities are large. They have walls that reach up to the sky. We even saw some descendants of Anak there.' "

29 Then I said to you, "Do not be so frightened. Do not be afraid of these people. 30 The LORD your God is going in front of you. He will fight for you, as he fought for you in Egypt. You watched him do it. 31 And he was with you in the desert. He carried you as a father carries his son. You saw how he carried you all the way. He carried you until you reached this place."

32 But you did not believe in the LORD your God. 33 But he went in front of you, on your journey. He was there in a fire by night and in a cloud by day. He found places for you to put your tents. He showed you the way that you should go.

34 When the LORD heard what you said, he was angry. He made a serious promise. 35 "None of you bad men will see the good country. I promised to give this country to your fathers. 36 Only Caleb, the son of Jephunneh will see it. I will give to him and to his family the land that he walks on. This is because he obeyed the LORD completely."

37 The LORD became angry with me also, because of you. He said to me, "And you will not go into this country."

38 "But your servant Joshua, the son of Nun, will go into the country. You must make him strong by good words. He will lead Israel's people into the country. It will become their country. 39 Your children, too, will go into the country. These children do not yet know the difference between good and bad. You said that they would become slaves. I say that they will go into the country. I will give it to them and it will become their country. 40 But as for you, turn round. Begin your journey towards the desert. Travel along the road to the Red Sea."

41 Then you answered, "We have done wrong things against the LORD. We will go and fight. We will obey the LORD our God." So every one of you picked up his arms. You thought that you could go easily into the hills.

42 But the LORD said, "Do not go up the hill to fight. I will not be with you. Your enemies will beat you."

43 So I repeated the LORD's words to you, but you would not listen. You did not obey the LORD's words. You were proud and so you marched up into the hills. 44 The Amorite people lived in those hills and they came out against you. They ran after you like a large group of bees. They attacked you and you ran down from Seir, all the way to Hormah.

45 You came back and you wept. But the LORD did not change what he was saying. He would not listen to you. 46 And so you stayed in Kadesh for many days. You remained there for a long time.

Chapter 2

40 years in the desert

1 Then we turned back. We began to walk towards the desert. We went along the road to the Red Sea, as the LORD had said. For many days, we walked round the hills in Seir.

2 Then the LORD said to me, 3 "You have walked round this hill for a long time. Now turn to the north. 4These are my words to the Israelites, 'You will soon go through the country that belongs to the descendants of Esau. They have the same ancestors that you have. And they live in Seir. They will be afraid of you, so be very careful.'

5 'Do not make them angry so that they fight against you. I will not give any of their country to you, not even enough to put your foot on. I have given the hills in Seir to Esau. 6 You must pay money to his descendants for the food and water that you eat and drink.

7 The LORD your God has helped you in everything that you have done. He has travelled with you through this very large desert. The LORD your God has remained with you for 40 years. He has given you everything that you needed.' "

8 So we went on. We passed the descendants of Esau, who live in Seir. They have the same ancestors that we have. We left the road through Arabah. This road is from Elath and Ezion-Geber. We travelled through the desert along the road to Moab.

9 Then the LORD said to me, "Do not make the men in Moab angry. Do not make them fight against you. I will not give you any part of their country. I have given Ar city to the descendants of Lot."

10 Some people called the Emites once lived there. There were many of them and they were as strong and tall as the descendants of Anak. 11 Many people called the Emites and the Anakites, 'Rephaites'. But the people from Moab called them Emites. 12 Before this time, the people called the Horites lived in Seir, but the descendants of Esau sent them away. They killed the Horites and they lived in their country. The Israelites did the same thing to their enemies, when the LORD gave the country to them.

13 And the LORD said, "Get up now and cross the Zered Valley." So we crossed the valley.

14 38 years had passed since we left Kadesh-Barnea. All the fighting men of that generation had died. The LORD had said that this would happen.

15 The LORD himself was against them until they had all died.

16 When the last one of these fighting men had died, the LORD spoke to me. 17 This is what he said: 18"Today you will pass by the country called Moab at Ar. 19 You will meet the people from Ammon. Do not make them angry so that they fight against you. I will not give you any of their country. I have given it to the descendants of Lot."

20 (This country also belonged to the Rephaites, who had lived there. But the descendants of Ammon called them Zamzummites. 21 There were many Zamzummites and they were as tall and strong as the descendants of Anak. The LORD killed them when the descendants of Ammon sent them away. Then the descendants of Ammon lived in their country. 22 The LORD had done the same thing for the descendants of Esau. They lived in Seir. The LORD killed the Horites when the descendants of Esau sent them away. The descendants of Esau still live in their country today. 23 Also, people from the island called Crete came. And they killed the Avvites. The Avvites had lived in villages as far as Gaza. But the people from Crete killed them and they lived in their country.)

24 And God said, "Now go! Cross the River Arnon. Look, I have given the country of Sihon the Amorite to you. He is the king of Heshbon and you must fight against him. You must begin to take his country. 25Today I will begin to make all the people in the world afraid of you. They will hear reports about you and they will be very frightened. You will cause them trouble."

The Israelites beat Sihon, king of Heshbon.

26 We were in the desert called Kedemoth when I sent a message to Sihon, king of Heshbon. We did not want to fight him. This is what I said to him: 27 "Please let us travel through your country. We will walk along your widest road. We will not turn to the right or to the left.

28 Please sell us food to eat and water to drink. We will pay you with silver coins. Please let us walk through your country. 29 The descendants of Esau, who live in Seir, let us do this. So did the descendants of Moab who live in Ar. Then we will cross the River Jordan. We will go into the country that the LORD our God is giving to us." 30 But Sihon, king of Heshbon, refused to let us travel through his country. He was angry with us and he would not listen. The LORD your God caused that to happen. He wanted to give the country of Sihon to you. And he has now done that.

31 The LORD said to me, "Look! I have begun to give Sihon and his country to you. Now you must begin to fight him and to take his country."

32 Then Sihon and all his army came out to fight against us at Jahaz. 33 The LORD our God gave him to us and we beat him in the fight. We killed Sihon and his sons and his whole army. 34 At that time we took all his towns and destroyed them completely. We killed men, women and children. We left no one alive. 35But we kept the animals and the good things from every town for ourselves. 36 The LORD our God gave us every town. He gave us all the towns from Aroer, on the edge of the Arnon Valley, all the way to Gilead. He gave us the town in the middle of the Arnon Valley. No town was too strong for us. 37 But you obeyed the word of the LORD our God. You did not go near the country called Ammon. You did not go near the land by the River Jabbok. Neither did you go near the land round any of the towns in the hills.

Chapter 3

The Israelites beat Og, king of Bashan.

1 Then we turned and went up, along the road towards Bashan. Og, king of Bashan, marched out to fight against us. He brought his whole army with him to Edrei. 2 But the LORD said to me, "Do not be afraid of him. I have given him to you with his whole army and his country. You must do to Og as you did to Sihon. Sihon was king of the Amorites and he lived in Heshbon."

3 So the LORD our God also gave Og, king of Bashan, and all his army to us. We killed them and we left no one alive. 4 At that time, we marched into all of his cities. He had 60 cities and we marched into all of them. This was all the land called Argob in Bashan, where King Og ruled. 5 Every city had high walls and gates, which the people locked. There were also very many villages without walls. 6 We destroyed them completely, as we had done to the cities of Sihon, king of Heshbon. We destroyed every city and killed all the men, women and children. 7 But we kept all the animals and the good things from the cities for ourselves.

8 So, at that time, we marched into the countries of these two kings of the Amorites. This country was east of the River Jordan, from the River Arnon to Mount Hermon. 9 (The people from Sidon call MountHermon, Sirion. The Amorites call it Senir.) 10 We marched into all of the towns in the high, flat land and the whole of Gilead. We marched into all of Bashan, as far as Salecah and Edrei. These are towns in the country of Og, in Bashan. 11 (Only Og, king of Bashan, from the descendants of the Rephaites was still alive. He had an iron bed. It was more than 4 metres long and 2 metres wide. This bed is still in Rabbah, a town that belongs to the people from Ammon.)

Moses divides the country.

12 When we marched into the country, I gave certain parts to the tribes of Reuben and Gad. I gave them the land north of Aroer by the River Arnon. This included one half of the hills and the towns in Gilead. 13The other half of Gilead I gave to one half of the tribe of Manasseh. I also gave to them Bashan, the country that Og had ruled. (All the country of Argob in Bashan had been called the country of the Rephaites.) 14 A man called Jair, of the tribe of Manasseh, marched into all the land round Argob. He reached the edges of Geshur and Maacah. Then he gave his own name to that land. To this day, Bashan is called Havvoth-Jair. 15 And I gave Gilead to Machir, from the tribe of Manasseh. 16 But to the tribes of Reuben and Gad, I gave land from Gilead to the middle of the River Arnon. Their land is as far as the River Jabbok, where the country of the people from Ammon begins. 17 The edge of their land on the west was the River Jordan. This is from Arabah and Chinnereth to the Salt Sea, below Mount Pisgah.

18 At that time I said to you, "The LORD your God has given this land to you, for you to live in it. But all your fighting men, with their arms, must cross the River Jordan. You must go over before the other descendants of Israel. 19 But your wives, your children and your animals can stay in your towns. (I know that you have many animals.)

20 You must travel with the other Israelites until the LORD gives them rest. He has already given rest to you. The other Israelites must march into the country which the LORD your God is giving to them. This is the country across the Jordan. Then you can return to the land that I have given to you."

God tells Moses that he cannot cross the River Jordan.

21 At that time, I commanded Joshua, "You have seen with your own eyes everything that the LORD your God has done to these two kings. The LORD will do the same thing to the countries of all the kings where you are going. 22 Do not be afraid of them. The LORD your God himself will fight for you."

23 At that time, I asked the LORD, again and again: 24 "LORD my God! I am your servant. You are showing me how great and how strong you are. There is no other god in heaven or on earth as great as you are. No other god can do the great things that you do. 25 Please let me go over the River Jordan! Please let me see the good country, the hills, the mountains and Lebanon!"

26 But the LORD was angry with me, because of you. He would not listen to me. He said, "That is enough! Do not speak to me any more about this thing. 27 Go up to the top of Mount Pisgah. Look west and north and south and east. Look at the country with your own eyes, because you will not cross this River Jordan. 28 Now you must tell Joshua what to do. Give him help. Teach him to be brave. He will lead Israel's people over the river. He will be the leader in the fight against their enemies. Together they will march into the country that you are going to look at." 29 So we stayed in the valley near Beth-Peor.

Chapter 4

Moses tells the Israelites to remember God's Rules.

1 Listen, Israel's people, to the rules and decrees that I am going to teach you. If you obey them, you will live. You will march into the country and then it will belong to you. This is the country that the LORD, the God of your fathers, is giving to you. 2 Do not put anything new into these rules and do not remove anything from them. But obey the rules of the LORD your God that I am giving to you.

3 You saw with your own eyes what the LORD did at Baal-Peor. The LORD your God killed every one of you who obeyed Baal there.

4 But every one of you who obeyed the rules of the LORD your God is still alive today.

5 Look! I have taught you the decrees and rules as the LORD my God told me to. Now you must obey them when you go into your country.

6 Obey them carefully. They will show people in other countries that you understand right and good ways. These people will hear about all your rules. Then they will say, "These great people really do understand right and good ways." 7 But the LORD our God is always near to us when we pray to him. It is not like that for the people in other countries. 8 And people from other countries do not have the good rules that you have in this Law. This is the Law that I am putting in front of you today.

9 But be careful. Always think about what you do. Do not forget the things that your eyes have seen. Remember these things for as long as you live. Tell your children and your grandchildren about the things that God has done. 10 Remember when you stood in front of the LORD your God at Mount Horeb. He said to me, "Bring all the people to me to hear what I say. Then they will learn to think and speak well about me. They will do this as long as they live in their country. And they will teach my words to their children."11 You came and stood at the edge of the mountain. You saw that it was on fire. The sky was full of black clouds and there was no light. 12 Then from the fire, the LORD spoke to you. You heard him speak but you did not see any shape. There was only a voice. 13 He explained to you his 10 special rules and he wrote them on two flat pieces of stone. He commanded you to obey them. 14 At that time, the LORD told me to teach you all his rules. When you cross the River Jordan, you must obey his rules in your new country.

God says that the Israelites must not have false gods

15 You did not see any shape at all when the LORD spoke to you from the fire. So you must be very careful about everything that you do. 16 Do not change to do very bad things. Do not make a false god for yourselves, because that is wrong. Do not copy the shape of a man or a woman, 17 or the shape of any animal or bird.

18 Do not copy the shape of anything that moves along the ground. Do not copy the shape of any fish that swims in the water. 19 When you look up at the sky, you see the sun, the moon and the stars. They are all shining in the sky. But do not worship them. They are things that the LORD your God has given to everyone on the earth. 20 But you are different. The LORD took you out of Egypt, which was like a place of fire. He took you out, to be his own people. Now you belong to him because he has chosen you.

21 The LORD was angry with me, because of you. He told me again and again that I would not cross the River Jordan. I cannot go into the good country that the LORD your God is giving to you. 22 I will die in this country. I will not cross the River Jordan. But you will soon cross over and God will give to you that good country. 23 Be careful! Do not forget the covenant that the LORD your God made with you. Do not make for yourselves a false god in any shape. The LORD says that you must never do that. 24 That is because the love of the LORD your God is like a burning fire. He cannot let you go away from him. He cannot let you love another god.

25 Even when you have lived in the country for many years, be careful. Do not start to do wrong things. When you have children and grandchildren, do not make a false god in any shape. This would make the LORD your God angry. 26 I want everyone on earth and in heaven to hear what I am saying against you today. If you do not obey me, you will soon die. You will not live long in your country across the River Jordan. The LORD will let people from other countries kill you. 27 He will send you away to live in other countries. Only a few of you will stay alive in the countries where the LORD sends you. 28 There you will obey gods that men have made out of wood and stone. These gods cannot see or hear. They cannot use their mouths or their noses. 29 But even then, if you look for the LORD your God, you will find him. You must really want to find him. If you do, you will certainly find him. 30 When trouble happens to you in future days, you will return to him. When all these bad things have happened to you, you will obey him again.

31 This is because the LORD your God is kind and good. He will not leave you or kill you. He will not forget the promise that he made to your ancestors This is a serious promise and God will not forget it.

The LORD is God.

32 Ask me now about the things that happened many years ago. Ask about the days before you were alive. Ask how God made men and women on the earth. Ask people from every country in the world. Nothing as great as this has ever happened. People have never heard of anything like this. 33 Only you, the Israelites, have heard the voice of God and have not died. You have heard him speaking to you from the fire. And you have still lived! 34 No other god has tried to take one special nation for himself out of another country. The LORD your God did this for you in Egypt. You saw how he used his powerful authority there. He brought bad troubles and war. He did great and frightening things in Egypt.

35 The LORD has shown you all these things. They show you that he is the only God. There is no other God. 36 God let you hear his voice. He spoke to you so that he could teach you. Here on earth he let you see his great fire. He spoke to you from that fire. 37 He brought you out of Egypt because he loved your ancestors. He chose you, their descendants, and he brought you out of Egypt. He did this by himself. He is great and powerful. 38 He sent away the people of other countries who are greater and stronger than you. He sent them away in front of you. He did this to give you their country. This country now belongs to you.

39 Remember today and never forget that the LORD is God. He is God in the sky above you and on the earth below it. There is no other God. 40 Obey his decrees and his rules that I am giving you today. If you do that, everything will be well for you and for your children after you. You will continue to live in your country. The LORD your God is giving it to you for all time.'

Safe cities

41 Then Moses chose three special cities to the east of the River Jordan.

42 These were safe places for any person who killed another person. But only if he did not want to kill him. If the killer was not the enemy of the man, the killer could run into one of the cities. There he would be safe from death. 43 Moses chose Bezer, in the flat desert, for the tribe of Reuben. He chose Ramoth, in Gilead, for the tribe of Gad. And he chose Golan, in Bashan, for the tribe of Manasseh.

Moses teaches the Law to the Israelites.

44 This is the Law that Moses explained to the Israelites. 45 These are the rules, the decrees and the commands. Moses explained them to the Israelites when they left Egypt.

46 At that time they were in the valley, near to Beth-Peor. That is east of the River Jordan. This was the country of Sihon, king of the Amorites. He ruled in Heshbon. Moses and the Israelites beat him when they came out of Egypt. 47 They marched into his country, which then became their own country. They also marched into the country of Og, king of Bashan. These two kings of the Amorites lived east of the River Jordan. 48 This country was from Aroer, on the edge of the River Arnon, to Mount Sion (that is Mount Hermon). 49 This country included all the land east of the River Jordan. To the south, it was to the Dead Sea and to Mount Pisgah.

Chapters 5 6 and 7 - Moses teaches and explains again the 10 special rules that God gave him.

Chapter 5

God's 10 special rules

1 Moses called all the Israelites together and said, 'Listen, Israelites, to the rules that I explain to you today. You can hear what I am saying. Learn the rules and obey them. 2 The LORD our God made a special promise to us at Horeb. 3 He did not make this promise to our fathers. He made it to us, to all of us who are alive here today. 4 The LORD turned his face toward your faces and he spoke to you. He spoke out of the fire on the mountain. 5 (At that time, I stood between the LORD and you. I repeated the LORD's words to you. You were afraid of the fire, so you did not go up the mountain.) And God said:

6 "I am the LORD your God. I brought you out of Egypt, the country where you were slaves.

7 You will have no other gods except Me.

8 You will not make a false god for yourself. Do not make the shape of anything that is in the sky above nor on the earth beneath. Do not make the shape of anything that lives in the water. 9 You must not bend down to them or obey them. I, the LORD your God, love you with a powerful love. I cannot let you love any other god. I punish children because of the bad things that their fathers have done. I do this to the grandchildren and to their children of everyone who hates me. 10 But I show my love to thousands (1000s) of families who love me. These families will obey me.

11 You must not use the name of the LORD your God in a wrong way. The LORD will not excuse anyone who does this.

12 Always make the Sabbath day a special day, as the LORD your God has told you. 13 Work hard for 6 days and do all the necessary work. 14 But the 7th day is a day for rest which the LORD your God has given to you. On that day, you must not do any work. Neither will your children work, nor your servants, nor your animals, nor people from other countries who live with you. Your servants must rest in the same way as you rest. 15 You must remember that you were slaves in Egypt. But I, the LORD your God, brought you out by my powerful authority. So the LORD your God has told you to make the Sabbath day a special day.

16 Always be very kind to your father and mother, as the LORD your God has told you. If you do that, you will have a long life. Also, your life will be good and happy in the country that God is giving to you.

17 You must not kill anyone because you are angry with him. That is murder.

18 You must not have sex with the wife or husband of another person.

19 You must not take another person's things.

20 You must not say things that are not true about anyone.

21 You must not want another man's wife. You must not want the house or the field of another person. You must not want his slaves or his animals or anything that is his."

22 These are the rules that the LORD spoke in a loud voice to you. You were all there. He spoke from the mountain, from the middle of a great fire. There was a cloud, but there was no light. He spoke only these words. Then he wrote them on two flat stones and he gave them to me.

23 There was no light when you heard the voice of God. The mountain burned with fire. Then your leaders and your older men came to me. 24 And they said, "The LORD our God has shown us how powerful and how special he is. We have seen how great he is and we have heard his voice from the fire. This is what we have seen today: A man can live, even if God speaks to him. 25 But now, we do not want to die. This great fire will kill us. We will die if we continue to hear the voice of our God. 26 No other person has ever heard the voice of God and lived. We heard him speak out of the fire. And we are still alive! 27 Please go near to the LORD our God. Listen to all that he says. Then tell us what he tells you. We will listen and obey."

28 The LORD heard what you said to me. He answered, "I have heard what these Israelites said to you. All that they said was good. 29 I really want them to obey me and to love my rules always! If they do that, everything will always be well for them and for their children. 30 Now tell them to return to their tents. 31But I want you to stay here with me. I will give you all the rules and decrees that you must teach to the people. I will give this country to them so that they can keep it. But they must obey all these rules when they are living in that country."

32 So you must be careful to obey the LORD your God. You must not refuse any of his rules.

33 You must live as the LORD your God says. If you do that, you will live for many years in your own country. You will enjoy all your good work.

Chapter 6

Love the LORD your God!

1 These are all the rules. The LORD your God told me to teach them to you. You must obey them when you live in your own country across the River Jordan. 2 You and your children and your grandchildren must be afraid to make the LORD your God angry. You must obey all his rules as long as you live. If you do that, you will enjoy a long life. 3 Listen, Israelites! Be careful to obey God's rules. If you do that, everything will be well for you. Your groups of families will become very large, in a country full of good food and drink. The LORD, the God of your fathers, promised that this will happen.

4 Listen, Israelites! The LORD our God is one LORD. 5 Love the LORD your God with all of your mind and your thoughts. Make him the most important person in your lives. Think about him every day. 6Remember with love all these rules that I give to you today. 7 Teach them and explain them every day to your children. Talk about them when you sit at home. Talk about them when you walk along the road. Repeat them when you lie down. Repeat them when you get up. 8 Tie them like signs on your hands and round your heads. 9 Write them over the doors of your houses and on your gates.

10 The LORD your God is bringing you into the country that he promised to your fathers, Abraham, Isaac and Jacob. This country has large, busy cities that you did not build. 11 There are houses there full of good things that you did not put into them. There are wells of water that you did not dig. There are fields of grapes and olives that you did not plant. You can eat as much as you want. 12 But be careful that you do not forget the LORD. He brought you out of Egypt where you were slaves.

13 You must be afraid to make the LORD your God angry. And you must obey him only. Make all your promises by his authority. 14 Do not obey the other gods of the people who live round you. 15 The LORD your God lives among you. It is very important to him that you love only him. You must not love other gods. If you do love them, you will make him very angry with you. And then he will kill you. That will happen if you obey other gods. 16 Do not make the LORD your God angry with you as you did at Massah.17 Be careful! Obey the rules of the LORD your God. Obey all that he says to you. 18 Do what is right and good. And give pleasure to the LORD. If you do that, all will be well with you. And you will be able to go into the good country. The LORD promised this country to your ancestors. 19 He will help you to beat all your enemies, as he has said.

20 Some day your son may say to you, "The LORD our God has given you all these rules and decrees. But what do they mean?" 21 Then you must tell him this: "We were slaves of Pharaoh in Egypt. But the LORD is very powerful and he brought us out of Egypt.

22 We watched him do great and powerful things to Egypt. And he did them to Pharaoh and to the people who lived in his house.

23 But the LORD brought us out of Egypt. He led us into this country and he gave it to us. He did this because he made a serious promise to our ancestors. 24 The LORD told us that we should obey all these rules. If you do that, we will always do well. And we will continue to live. This is happening to us today. 25 We must be careful to obey all the rules of the LORD our God. When we do this, we become good people. Everything that we do will be right."

Chapter 7

What they should do when God brings them into the country

1 The LORD your God is bringing you into the country that will be your country. He will send away many people from other countries, in front of you. There are seven nations that are larger and stronger than you are. They are
the Hittites, Girgashites, Amorites, Canaanites, Perizzites, Hivites and Jebusites. 2 When the LORD your God has given them to you, you will beat them. Then you must kill them completely. Make no promises to them and do not be kind to them. 3 You must not marry any of these people. Do not let your daughters marry their sons. Do not take their daughters to marry your sons. 4 This is because they will turn your sons away from God's rules. Then your sons will begin to obey other gods. The LORD will be very angry with you and he will quickly kill you. 5 This is what you must do to the people of these countries. Break the stone tables where they offer animals to their gods. Cut down the very tall sticks there that they have used to worship their gods. Burn their false gods in a fire. 6 Do this because you are special people. You belong to the LORD your God. He has chosen you out of everyone who lives on the earth. You are his own people and he loves you very much.

7 The LORD loved you and chose you. This was not because you were the largest nation on the earth. No, you were only a few people, the smallest nation on the earth. 8 But it was because the LORD loved you. And he wanted his promise to your ancestors to become true. So he saved you by his powerful authority and he brought you out of Egypt. Then he made you free from the power of Pharaoh, when you were Pharaoh's slaves. 9 Remember that the LORD your God is the only God. You can always believe in him. He has made a promise to all those who love him.

If they obey him, he will love them and all their children for thousands (1000s) of years. 10 But,

he will kill those who hate him;

he will not be slow to punish them.

11 So be careful! Obey all the rules that I am teaching you today.

12 Listen to these rules and obey them. If you do that, the LORD your God will continue to love you. He promised your ancestors that he would do this. 13 He will love you and he will stay with you always. He will give you many children and he will be with your babies. He will make good food grow in your fields. He will give you plenty of food and drink. He will be with all your animals and give you many cows and sheep. He will do this in the country that he is giving to you. He made this promise to your ancestors.

14 God will make you greater than anyone else on the earth. You will all have children and none of your animals will be without young animals. 15 The LORD will give you good health. He will not send to you any of the bad illnesses from Egypt that you knew about. He will send these illnesses to people who hate you. 16 You must kill the people in every nation that the LORD your God gives to you. Do not be kind to them and do not obey their gods. They will only make you rebel against your God.

17 Perhaps you will say to each other, "The people in these nations are stronger than we are. We cannot send them away." 18 But do not be afraid of them. You must remember what the LORD your God did to Pharaoh and to all the people from Egypt. 19 You saw it all with your own eyes. You saw the great troubles, the strange and powerful things that happened there. And you saw the LORD your God bring you out with great authority. He will do this again to all the people that make you afraid. 20 Also, the LORD your God will send cruel insects among these people. Even those people who hide from you will die.

21 Do not let anyone frighten you. The LORD your God is among you. He is a great and powerful God.

22 The LORD your God will send away the people from those nations, one at a time. He will not let you kill them immediately.

If he did that, wild animals would soon fill the country round you. 23 But the LORD your God will give all the people in these nations to you. He will confuse them completely and he will kill them. 24 He will give their kings to you and no one will remember them any more. No one will be able to beat you. You will kill them all. 25 You must burn their false gods in a fire. You must not want to keep the silver and gold on the gods. The LORD your God hates it. So do not take it for yourselves because it will cause trouble for you. 26 Do not bring anything that God hates into your house. If you do, he will put a mark on you, to destroy both you and the bad thing. God has said that he will destroy it. So you must hate it also.

Chapter 8

Moses talks about the careful love of God during 40 years.

1 Be careful! Obey every rule that I am giving to you today. If you do that, you will live. And you will have many children. You will be able to go into the country. It will become your country. This is the country that the LORD your God promised to your ancestors. 2 Remember how the LORD your God led you all the way in the desert. He led you for 40 years and he sent many troubles to you. He did that for three reasons. He wanted to make you humble. He wanted to know whether you would obey him. And he wanted to know whether you would believe all his words. 3 He caused you to be hungry and then he fed you with special food called manna. Neither you nor your fathers had eaten this food before. By this, he taught you that a man does not live only on bread. A man also needs every word that God speaks to him. These words will teach him how to live a good life.

4 Your clothes did not become too old to wear. Your feet did not become too painful to walk on during all those 40 years. 5 So you can certainly know that the LORD your God is teaching you. And he is punishing you when you do the wrong things. He is doing that in the same way that a man teaches his son to do the right things.

6 Obey the rules of the LORD your God. Always do the things that will give him pleasure. Think about him all the time. 7 Do this because the LORD your God is bringing you into a good country. It is a country with many streams and pools of water. There is water that runs in the valleys and in the hills. 8 It is a country full of good food that grows in the fields. A lot of fruit is hanging on the trees. 9 It is a country where there is enough bread for everyone. You will have everything that you need. It is a country where the stones are full of iron. You can dig other metals out of the hills.

10 You can eat all the food that you want. Then remember to thank the LORD your God. He has given you this good country. 11 Be careful that you do not forget the LORD your God. Always remember to obey all his rules and decrees. I am giving them to you today. 12 In a future time, you will have all the food that you can eat. You will build beautiful houses to live in. 13 You will have many cows and sheep and a lot of gold and silver. You will have more and more things that are yours. 14 Then be careful! You may begin to think too well about yourselves. Then you will forget the LORD your God. He brought you out of Egypt, where you were slaves.

15 He led you through the large and frightening desert. There was no water to drink. The desert was full of dangerous snakes and insects. He made water rise out of a hard rock for you. 16 He gave manna to you to eat in the desert. That was something that your fathers never saw. He sent difficulties to you. He did that for two reasons. He wanted to make you humble. And he wanted to know whether you would obey him. He did those things because he wants to do good things for you in the end. 17 Perhaps you will say to yourself, "I have got all these good things by myself because I am strong!" 18 But you must always remember the LORD your God. It is he who is helping you to get many good things. He wants to do the good things that he promised to your ancestors. And that is what is happening today. 19 Do not ever forget the LORD your God. Do not look at other gods. Do not give things to them and do not worship them. If you do that, God will certainly kill you. That is what I am telling you today. 20 As the LORD killed the people in other nations, because of you, so he will kill you. This will happen if you do not obey the LORD your God.'

Chapter 9

Moses remembers the bad things about Israel's people.

1 Moses said, 'Listen, Israelites! You will soon cross the River Jordan. You will march into your country. You will send away people in many nations who are stronger than you are. They are more powerful and they have large cities with very high walls. 2 The people there are strong and tall. They are called Anakites! You know about them. You have heard people say, "No one can beat the Anakites." 3 But you can be sure today that the LORD your God goes across in front of you. He is like a burning fire. He will destroy your enemies. He will make them do what he says. And you will send them away and remove them quickly. The LORD has promised that this will happen.

4 After the LORD your God has driven them away in front of you, be careful! Do not say to yourself, "The LORD has brought me into this country because I am doing right things." No, it is because these people are doing wrong things. That is why the LORD will send them away from you. 5 It is not because you are doing right things. It is not because you always obey God. This is not the reason that God will give their country to you. The LORD your God will send them away from you because they are doing wrong things. So he will do what he promised to your ancestors, Abraham, Isaac and Jacob. 6 You must understand this. The LORD your God is not giving you this good country because you are doing right things. No, you really think too well about yourselves. You do not like to obey God. You want to do things that give you pleasure.

The young cow that the people made from gold

7 You must never forget how you made the LORD your God angry in the desert. You have failed to obey the LORD. From the day when you left Egypt, until today, you have not obeyed him. 8 When you were at Mount Horeb you made the LORD angry. He was angry enough to kill you. 9 I climbed the mountain to receive the two flat stones from the LORD. On these stones the LORD had written the promise that he had made with you. I stayed with him for 40 days and nights. During those days, I did not eat or drink anything. 10 Then the LORD gave the two flat stones to me. He had written all his rules on the stones with his own finger. The LORD told you these rules, when he spoke from the fire. This was on the day when you all came together to the mountain.

11 After the 40 days and nights, the LORD gave to me the stones with the promise. 12 Then the LORD said to me, "Go down the mountain immediately! The people that you led out of Egypt have become very bad. They have already refused to obey my rules and they have made a false god for themselves."

13 And the LORD said to me, "I know that these people do not like to obey me. They want to do things that give them pleasure. 14 Do not try to stop me. I will kill them and no one on the earth will remember them. Then I will make you into a nation that is stronger and larger than they are."

15 So I turned and went down the mountain. It was burning with fire and the two stones with the promise were in my hands. 16 I looked at you. I saw that you had sinned. You had made a false god for yourselves in the shape of a young cow. You had already refused to obey the LORD. 17 So I threw the two flat stones on the ground. They broke in pieces in front of you.

18 Then again I fell down on my face, in front of the LORD, for 40 days and nights. I did not eat or drink anything. You had sinned. You had refused to obey the LORD. You had made him very angry.

19 I was afraid because the LORD was so angry. He was angry enough with you to kill you. But again the LORD listened to me. 20 The LORD was also angry enough with my brother Aaron, to kill him. But at that time, I prayed for Aaron also.

21 Then I took that sinful thing that you had made. I took that young cow made from gold. I burned it in the fire and I broke it in pieces. Then I broke it into powder and threw the powder into a stream from the mountain.

22 You also made the LORD angry at Taberah, at Massah and at Kibroth-Hattaavah.

23 Then, when the LORD sent you out from Kadesh-Barnea, he said, "March into the country that I have given you." But you refused to obey the words of the LORD your God. You did not believe in him or obey him. 24 You have refused to obey the LORD ever since I have known you.

25 So I lay on my face in front of the LORD for those 40 days and nights. He had said that he would kill you. 26 So I prayed to the LORD. I said, "LORD our King, do not kill your people! They are really your people, because you saved them by your powerful authority. You are so strong that you brought them out of Egypt. 27 Remember your servants, Abraham, Isaac and Jacob. Please forgive your people who have not obeyed you. 28 For if you do not forgive them, the people in Egypt will say, 'The LORD was not strong enough to take them into their country. He had promised to do this. But he took them into the desert to kill them. He did this because he hated them!' 29 But they are your people and they belong to you. You are so strong and powerful that you brought them out."

Chapter 10

The new stones

1 At that time, the LORD said to me, "Cut out two new flat stones. Also, make a box from wood and then come up to me, on the mountain. 2 I will write on these stones the words that I wrote on the first stones. You broke the first stones, but you must put the new stones into the box."

3 So I made an ark from special wood and I cut two new flat stones. Then I went up the mountain. I was carrying the stones. 4 The LORD wrote on the stones the words that he had written before. He wrote the same 10 special rules that he gave you before. He did this on the mountain, when he spoke from the fire. This happened on the day when you came together to the mountain. And the LORD gave the stones to me. 5 Then I came down from the mountain. I put the stones into the special box, the ark that I had made. The LORD told me to do that. And they are still there now.'

6 (The Israelites travelled to Moserah from the wells that belonged to the descendants of Jaakan. Aaron died there and they buried him. Then Eleazar, his son, became priest instead. 7 Then they travelled on to Gudgodah and Jotbathah, a country where there are many streams of water. 8 At that time, the LORD chose the tribe of Levi to carry the ark. He chose them to be his special servants. They had to tell the Israelites that God was always near to them. They still do this today. 9 That is why the Levites do not have any land. The LORD told them that they would always be nearer to him than the other Israelites. He would give them work to do for him. And he would give them everything that they needed. So they would not need any land.)

10 'I stayed on the mountain for 40 days and nights, as I did the first time. The LORD listened to me again. He did not want to kill you. 11 And the LORD said to me, "Go, and lead the people on their journey. Then they can go into the country and make it their country. They can do this because I made a promise to their fathers that I would give it to them."

Obey the LORD always.

12 And now, Israelites, this is what the LORD your God asks you to do. You should always be afraid to make him angry. You should live to give pleasure to him. Be happy, as you love him! Be happy, as you work for him! 13 And you should obey his rules and decrees that I am giving to you today. If you do that, you will do well.

14 The whole of the sky, far beyond what you can see, belongs to the LORD your God. The earth and everything that is in it, also belongs to him. 15 But the LORD loved your ancestors so much that he chose you. You are their children. He chose you from the people of all other countries and you belong to him today.

16 So you must obey the LORD and no other gods. Do not still refuse to obey him. 17 For the LORD your God is greater than all other gods. He is stronger than every other authority. He is very great and very powerful. He is fair to everyone. And everything that he does is completely right. 18 He is very kind to women whose husbands have died. He is very kind to children who have no fathers. They need his help and he loves them. He loves people who are living in a foreign country. He gives them the things that they need. 19 You too must love strangers, because once, you were strangers in Egypt. 20 Always be ready to obey the LORD your God as his servants. Stay near to him and make your promises by his authority. 21Tell God how great and important he is. He is your God. He did great and powerful things for you, which you saw with your own eyes. 22 Only 70 of your ancestors went down to Egypt. Now the LORD your God has made you as many as the stars in the sky!

Chapter 11

Love and obey the LORD.

1 Love the LORD your God always. Obey all his rules and decrees and everything that he commands you. 2Remember this today! Your children have not seen all the great things that God has done. He can punish people so that they learn not to do the wrong things. You saw that he can do that. You saw his great and powerful authority. You saw how special and important he is. No one can ever beat him. 3 You saw the things that God did to Pharaoh, king of Egypt, and to all his people. They were not usual things, but powerful things.

4 You saw it when God removed the whole army of Egypt, with all their horses. They were marching quickly to catch you.

But God caused them to drown in the Red Sea. 5 Your children did not see all the things that the LORD did for you in the desert. But he brought you to this place. 6 Your children did not see what he did to Dathan and Abiram. These men were sons of Eliab, from the tribe of Reuben. God caused the earth to open up, in front of everyone. These men fell into the hole with all their families, their tents and their animals. 7 It was you, not your children. It was you who saw God do all these great things.

The country called Canaan is not like Egypt.

8 Now you must obey all the rules that I give to you today. If you do that, you will be strong and brave. You will cross the River Jordan and you will march into the country. Then it will become your country.9 You will live for a long time in this country. The LORD promised your ancestors that he would give it to you. It is a country where there is enough very good food and drink for everyone. 10 This country is not like Egypt, where you lived before. There, when you planted seeds, you had to give them water to make them grow. 11 But the country into which you will go has mountains and valleys. These receive rain that God gives. 12 The LORD your God is always kind to this country. He watches it every day of the year.

13 So you must obey the rules that I am giving to you today. I tell you to love the LORD your God. Work for him and obey him. And you must really want to do that! 14 If you do that, he will send rain on your country at the right time, in autumn and in spring. Then you can take home the food and the fruit that will grow in your fields.

15 God will make grass grow in your fields for your cows. And you will have all the food that you want.

Remember all God's words.

16 But be careful! Do not let anything cause you to forget the LORD. If something does that, you will begin to think about other gods. Then you will obey them.

17 If you do that, the LORD will be very angry with you. He will not send the rain and nothing will grow from the ground. Then you will soon die in the good country that the LORD is giving to you.

18 Keep my words always in your minds. Write them on pieces of cotton and then tie them on to your hands. Tie them round your heads also. Then they will be like signs for you and you will remember them.19 Teach my words to your children. Talk about them when you sit in your house. Talk about them when you walk along the road. Talk about them when you go to your bed. Talk about them when you get up.

20Write them above the doors of your house and on your gates. 21 If you do that, you and your descendants will live in the country for a long time. You will continue to live there while there is a sky above the earth.

22 Be careful! Every day, you must obey the rules that I am giving to you. These are the rules:

Love the LORD your God.

Do everything that he commands you.

Stay close to him.

23 If you do that, the LORD will fight on your behalf. He will send away the people in all these nations as you go into this country. You will send away people from nations that are larger and stronger than you. 24Every place on which you walk will be yours. All the country from the desert to Lebanon will be yours. And all the country from the River Euphrates to the Mediterranean Sea will be yours. 25 God will not let anyone stop you. The LORD your God has made a promise to you: He will cause everyone to be afraid of you, everywhere that you go.

26 Today I am telling you to choose. God can cause either good things or bad things to happen to you. 27Good things will happen if you obey these rules from the LORD your God.

28 And bad things will happen if you do not obey these rules. Then you will go away from God.

You will obey gods that you do not know. 29The LORD will bring you into the country that will be yours. Then you must pronounce these things with a loud, serious voice. Pronounce the good things from Mount Gerizim and the bad things from MountEbal. 30 You know that these mountains are west of the River Jordan. They are in the country of the Canaanites who live in the Jordan valley. They are not far from the great trees at Moreh, near to Gilgal. 31Soon you will cross the River Jordan. Soon you will take for yourself the country that the LORD is giving to you. When this happens, you will begin to live there. 32 Then be careful and remember! You must obey all the rules and decrees that I am giving to you today.

Chapter 12

God will choose one special place for worship.

1 These are the rules and decrees that you must obey. Be careful! You must obey them in the country that the LORD has given to you. You must obey them all the time that you live there. 2 You must destroy completely all the places where the people in other nations pray to their gods. You will find these places on high mountains. You will find them on hills and under large trees. 3 You must break the tables and the things that they have made from stones for their gods. You must burn their special tall sticks and you must cut down their false gods. And you must remove the names of those gods from these places.

4 Do not pray to the LORD your God as these people pray to their gods. 5 But you must look for the special place that the LORD your God will choose. He will stay there and that place will be his place. You must go to that place 6 to bring your burnt-offerings and other gifts to God. There you must bring one thing from every 10 things that God gives to you. And you must bring the gifts that you lift up to the LORD. So you will bring the things that you have promised and also any extra gifts. Bring the first cows and sheep that are born, too. 7 You and your families will eat and be happy there. You will be with the LORD your God. You will enjoy all your work because the LORD your God will stay near to you.

8 When that time happens, you must live in a different way. Today, everyone is doing the things that he likes. 9 You have not yet reached the country where you can rest. This is the country that the LORD is giving you. 10 But you will cross the River Jordan and begin to live in that country. He will give you rest from all your enemies round you. You will be safe. 11 Then the LORD your God will choose one special place. You must pray to him there. Bring to him everything that I have told you. You must bring your animals to kill and burn as gifts to God. Bring your other gifts to God. You must bring one thing from every 10 things that God gives to you. And you must bring the gifts that you lift up to the LORD. And bring the valuable things that you have promised to the LORD. Bring everything to the place that God will choose.

12 And there you will all be happy, with the LORD your God, you, your children and your servants. Also the Levites from your towns will have no land, but they will still be happy. 13 Be careful! Do not offer your burnt-offerings in any place that you choose. 14 You must only offer your burnt-offerings in the place that the LORD will choose. This will be in the land that belongs to one of your tribes. When you are there, you must obey all my words.

15 But you can kill and eat your animals in any of your towns. You can eat as much meat as you want. The LORD gives it to you. People who are obeying God can eat it. But people who have not yet made themselves ready for God can eat it also. 16 But you must not eat the blood. You must pour it on the ground like water. 17 Do not eat any of your gifts to the LORD in the places where you live. Do not eat there the gifts of one thing out of every 10 things of your food and drink. Do not eat there the first cows or sheep that are born. Do not eat there the valuable things that you have promised to the LORD or your extra gifts to him. And do not eat there the gifts that you lift up to the LORD. 18 Instead, you must eat these things in front of the LORD your God. This will be in the place that he chooses. You and all your family, your servants and the Levites will be very happy. This is because the LORD is very near to you. You will be very happy about everything that you do. 19 Be careful never to forget the Levites, all the time that you live in your country.

20 The LORD your God has promised to give you more and more land. When he does this, you may be very hungry. Perhaps you will say, "I would like some meat." If you think that, you can eat meat. You can eat as much meat as you want. 21 The place that God has chosen may be too far away from you. If it is, you can kill an animal. And you can eat meat at home. The LORD has given your animals to you. I have told you how to kill them. 22 You can eat them in the same way as you eat wild animals. People who are obeying God can eat them. But people who have not yet made themselves ready for God can also eat them. 23 But be careful not to eat the blood. The life of the animal is in the blood. You must not eat the life together with the meat. 24 You must not eat the blood. You must pour it on the ground like water. 25 Do not eat it! If you obey this rule, everything will be well for you and your family. You will do what is right and give pleasure to the LORD.

26 Take all the special gifts that you have chosen. Take also the gifts that you have promised. Bring them to the place that the LORD will choose. 27 Take your burnt-offerings. Put them on the special table of the LORD your God, both the meat and the blood. You must pour the blood next to the special table, but you can eat the meat. 28 Be careful to obey all these rules that I am giving to you. If you do that, you and your children will always do well. This is good and right, and you will give God pleasure.

29 When you march into the country, the LORD your God will remove the people from in front of you. You must kill them and live in their place. 30 But when you have killed them, be careful! Do not let their false gods become important to you. Do not say, "How did these people pray to their gods? How did they obey them? We will do the same as they did." 31 You must not do as they do. When they pray, they do many bad things. The LORD your God hates these bad things. They even burn their children in the fire, as gifts to their gods.

32 Be careful to do everything that I command you. Do not put anything else with it. Do not take away anything from it.

Chapter 13

Be careful! Watch for false gods and false prophets!

1 There may appear among you a person who dreams about future events. He may promise that something special will happen. 2 This is because he wants you to stop thinking about the LORD your God. He wants you to obey other gods. You do not know these gods. The thing that the person spoke about may happen. 3 But you must not listen to him. The LORD your God is using this person to check your thoughts. He wants to know whether you really love him. He wants to know how much you love him. 4 You must follow the LORD your God. You must pray to him and to no one else. Obey his rules and do what he commands you. Work for him and give him pleasure. 5 The man who dreams false dreams about future events must die. He has taught you to say "No!" to the LORD your God. The LORD brought you out of Egypt and saved you from the country of slaves. This bad man has tried to make you do wrong things, not right things. But you must live as God has taught you. You must not let this bad thing remain among you.

6 If anyone says secretly to you, "Let us pray to some other gods", DO NOT LISTEN! This may be your own brother or one of your children. It may be your wife whom you love. It may be a friend who is near to you.

7 (The people round you may pray to these other gods. They may be near to you or far from you. They are gods that neither you nor your fathers have known.) 8 Do not do what your family suggests. Do not listen to your friend when he talks about other gods. Do not be sorry for him or try to save him. 9 You must kill him! You must be the first person to throw stones at him. Then all the people must do the same thing. 10 You must throw stones at him until he dies. He tried to stop you from thinking about the LORD your God. It was the LORD who brought you out of Egypt. Egypt was the country where you were slaves. 11 Then all Israel's people will hear about this. They will be afraid and no one will do such a bad thing again.

12 You will live in the towns that the LORD your God gives you. Then you may hear bad news. 13 Very bad men from among you may have led the people in one town in a false way. They may have said, "Let us go and pray to other gods!" (These are gods that you do not know.)

14 Then you must be very careful to check this news. You must discover if it is true or false. You must know whether people really have done this bad thing among you. 15 If the news is true, you must kill everyone in that town. Kill all the people and the animals. 16 You must bring together all the things that the people of the town have. Put the things in the square place in the middle of the town. Then burn the town and everything in it as a burnt-offering to the LORD your God. Nobody must ever build that town again. 17 You must not keep any of the things for yourselves. Burn them all, as I am telling you. If you do that, the LORD will stop being angry. He will be good and kind to you. He will give you many children, as he promised to your ancestors. 18 This will happen if you obey the LORD your God. You must obey all his rules that I am giving to you today. And you must do right things, that give him pleasure.

Chapter 14

Moses tells the Israelites which food to eat.

1 You belong to the LORD your God. You are like his own family. You weep for people who have died. But you must not cut yourselves. And you must not cut the hair from the front of your head.

2 You are special people because you are the family of the LORD your God.

The LORD has chosen you from all the other people on the earth. You are his special people and he loves you.

3 Do not eat anything that God hates. 4 These are the animals that you can eat: the cow, the sheep, the goat, 5 the deer, the wild goat, the mountain goat, the antelope and the wild sheep. 6 You can eat any animal with feet that grow in two halves. These animals must also bring their food back into their mouths and eat it again.

7 But you must not eat these animals: the camel, the rabbit and the rock badger. They bring back their food but they do not have feet in two halves. For this reason they are not good food for you. 8 The pig is not good food either. It has feet in two halves but it does not bring back its food. You must not eat any of these animals. You must not even touch their dead bodies.

9 You can eat any fish that has fins and pieces of hard skin on its body. 10 But there are things in the water that do not have fins and pieces of hard skin on their bodies. These are not good food for you. Do not eat them.

11 You can eat any clean bird. 12-18 But these birds you must not eat: eagles, vultures, crows, owls, hawks, falcons, buzzards, ostriches, sea-gulls, storks, herons, pelicans, cormorants, hoopoes and bats.

19 Some insects crawl and fly too. Insects like that are not good food for you. You must not eat them. 20 But you can eat any clean thing that has wings.

21 You must not eat anything that you find dead already. You can give it to a foreign person in any of your towns. He can eat it. Or you can sell it to him. But you are special people. You are special to the LORD your God.

You must not cook a young goat in the milk from its mother.

Regular gifts to the LORD

22 You must put away in a special place, a 10th part of all the food that grows in your fields. You must be careful to do this every year. 23 Then take it to that special place that the LORD your God will choose for himself. Eat this 10th part of the food that you grow in your fields, there. Also, you can eat your young animals that are born first. Eat them in front of the LORD your God. Learn to thank him always for everything. 24 But that special place may be too far from your home. Your regular gifts of food may be too heavy to carry, if you have grown a lot of food. (And the special place may be too far away.) 25 If that is true, you can sell your regular gifts for money. Take the money with you to the place that the LORD your God will choose. 26 Then you can use the money to buy whatever you choose: cows, sheep, wine or beer. You can buy anything that you like. And you and your family should eat there in front of the LORD your God and be happy together. 27 Always remember the Levites who live in your towns. Remember them because they have no land.

28 Every third year, store in your towns, a 10th part of the food that you have grown in your fields. 29 This food is for the Levites, who have no land. It is also for the foreign people and the children who have no fathers. It is also for the women whose husbands have died. They can eat until they have had enough. If you do that, the LORD your God will be with you in all your work.

Chapter 15

The year to forget about debts

1 At the end of every 7 years you must forget about every debt.

2 This is how you must do it. Every person who has lent money must forget about this amount of money. He must not demand his money from any Israelite, because another Israelite is like his brother. The LORD himself says that you must forget about all these debts. 3 You can demand your money from a foreign person. But you must forget about every amount of money that you have lent to another Israelite.4

If you obey the LORD your God, he will give you plenty of everything in your country. Not one Israelite should be poor

5 if you obey him completely. So, be careful to obey all the rules that I give to you today. 6 For the LORD your God will make you great, as he has promised. You will lend money to the people in many countries, but they will not lend money to you. You will rule many people, but no one will rule you.

7 Perhaps you will meet a poor man among the Israelites, in one of your towns. If you do meet a man like that, do not refuse to help him. Do not refuse to lend him money. 8 Instead, you must be kind to him and lend him whatever he needs.

9 Be careful not to think this bad thought: "The 7th year will happen soon. That is the year when I must forget about debts!" You must not be cruel to that poor Israelite and give him nothing. He might speak against you to the LORD. If he does, the LORD will be angry with you. He will be angry with you because you have sinned against him. 10 Be very happy to give to that Israelite what he needs. If you do that, the LORD your God will cause everything to be well for you. 11 There will always be poor people in the country. Give to other Israelites and to all poor people, whatever they need. This is my command to you.

Slaves must become free people.

12 Someone may sell you another Israelite, who is a man or a woman. Let him work for you for 6 years. Then in the 7th year, let him go out free. 13 And when you let him go, you must not send him away with nothing in his hands. 14 Give him gifts of sheep, food and drink. Give good things to him as the LORD has given good things to you. 15 Remember that you too were slaves in Egypt. But the LORD your God bought you. This is why I am giving you this rule today.

16 But perhaps your servant will say to you, "I do not want to leave you!" He may say this because he loves you and your family. He is happy with you. 17 If he says that, you must take a metal stick with a sharp point. Push it through his ear, into the door. This will make him your servant for his whole life. Do the same thing for your female servant.

18 You must not be sorry to make your servant free. Remember, that he has worked well for you for 6 years. He has been worth twice as much as a servant whom you pay. And the LORD your God will help you in everything that you do.

The first animals that are born

19 You must keep separate every male animal that is the first to be born from any animal among your animals. They are for the LORD your God. Do not make these animals do any work. Do not cut off the hair from the sheep that are the first to be born. 20 Each year, you and your family must eat these special animals in front of the LORD your God. You must do this in the special place that he will choose. 21 But you must not give to the LORD any animal that has something wrong with it. It must not have weak legs or bad eyes. 22 You can eat these animals at home. People that are obeying God can eat them. But people that are not yet ready for God can eat them also. You can eat them as you would eat deer. 23 But you must not eat the blood. You must pour it on the ground like water.

Chapter 16

Three special parties: Passover, Weeks and Tents

The Passover

1 The month Abib is a special month for you. In this month, you must remember the Passover. Remember that the LORD your God brought you out of Egypt at night in that month. 2 You must go to the special place that the LORD will choose for himself. There you must kill one of your sheep or cows for the Passover party. 3 At this party, do not eat bread that you make with yeast. For 7 days, you must eat bread that you make without yeast, the bread of trouble. This is to make you remember that special night. You ate bread like that when you left Egypt in a hurry that night. You must do it again each year. So you will never forget the night that you left Egypt. 4 No one must keep any yeast in his house for 7 days. You must eat all the meat of your animal on the night that you kill it. You must not leave any of it until the next morning.

5 You must not kill the animal for the Passover in any town that the LORD your God gives you.

6 You must go to the place that he will choose for himself. You must kill the animal for the Passover party there, at sunset. That was the time of day when you left Egypt. 7 Cook the meat and eat it in the special place. The LORD your God will choose the place. Then return to your tents on the next morning. 8 For the next 6 days, you must eat bread that you make without yeast. Then on the 7th day you must all come together to thank the LORD your God. Tell him how great and good he is. You must not do any work on that day.

The party of Weeks

9 Count 7 weeks from the first day that you bring in the food from your fields. 10 Then enjoy the party of Weeks with the LORD your God. Be happy to bring him extra gifts. Do this because he has been so good to you. 11 You and your family will be happy in front of the LORD your God, in his special place. Be happy together with your servants and with the Levites. Worship God happily with the foreign people and with the women whose husbands have died. And worship God happily with the children whose parents have died. All these people live among you. 12 Remember! You were slaves in Egypt, so obey these rules carefully.

The party of Tents

13 When you have brought in the food from your fields, enjoy the party of Tents for seven days. 14 Be happy at your party with your family, your servants and the Levites. Worship God happily with the foreign people and with the women whose husbands have died. And worship God happily with the children whose parents have died. All these people live in your towns. 15 Enjoy this party with the LORD your God for 7 days in the place that he has chosen. Do this because he will cause a lot of food to grow in your fields. He will help you in everything that you do. And you will be completely happy.

16 All your men must come to the LORD your God three times in every year. They must come to the place that he has chosen. They must come at the Passover party, the party of Weeks and the party of Tents. Each man must bring with him a gift to the LORD. 17 This gift can be large or small, as the LORD has given you much or little.

18 You must choose judges and officers from each tribes, in every town that the LORD gives you. They must judge the people in a way that is fair. 19 You must do what is right for every person. You must not accept a gift. A gift makes it difficult for a wise man to know what is right. And a gift can make right words seem wrong. 20 Always be good and fair when you judge. If you do that, you will live. And you will really enjoy your country. This is the country that the LORD your God is giving to you.

Do not obey other gods.

21 Do not put any special tall sticks that you make from wood next to the LORD your God's altar. 22 And do not put up a false god, because the LORD your God hates these things.

Chapter 17

A list of other rules and rules for a king

1 You must bring good gifts to the LORD your God. Do not bring any sheep or cow whose body is not completely right. The LORD hates this.

2 Perhaps a person living in one of your towns may do something bad against the LORD your God. He has not done what he promised to do. 3 He has not obeyed my words, because he has followed other gods. He has obeyed these gods, or he has prayed to the sun, moon or stars. 4 If you hear about this, you must check the report. If this bad thing has happened in Israel, 5 you must take the bad man or woman to the gate of the town. Then you must throw stones at that person until he or she dies. 6 But two or three people must agree that he has done the bad thing. You must never kill anyone because of the words of only one person. 7 These people must throw the first stones at the bad person. Then everyone else must throw stones. You must completely remove this very bad thing from among you.

8 It may be difficult for the judges in your towns to decide between good things and bad things. This may happen when one person has attacked another person. It may happen when people cannot agree about a house or some fields. You must bring those people to the place that the LORD your God will choose.

9 You must go to the priests from the tribe of Levi and to the judge that you have chosen. Ask them to decide for you. 10 Then you must obey them, in the place that the LORD will choose. Be careful to obey all their words. 11 You must do the things that they teach you. You must agree to what they decide. Obey their words completely. 12 You must kill any man who will not obey the judge or the priest. The judge and the priest stand near the LORD your God and do what he says. So you will completely remove bad things from Israel. 13 Then all the people will hear about it and they will be afraid. They will not refuse to listen to the judge or priest again.

The king

14 You are going into the country that the LORD your God has given you. All the countries round you will have kings. Then you will decide that you need a king. 15 Be careful! You must accept the king that the LORD your God chooses. The king must be a man from Israel. Do not choose anyone who is not an Israelite. 16 The king must not get a lot of horses for himself. And he must not send his people back to Egypt to get more horses. The LORD has said to you, "Do not return there!" 17 The king must not marry many wives. They will stop him from thinking about the LORD. He must not store a lot of silver and gold for himself.

The Law of God

18 When he becomes king, he must copy the Law of God on a scroll. This scroll will be a copy of the one that belongs to the priests. They belong to the tribe of Levi. 19 He must keep this scroll near him always and he must read it every day. If you do that, he will learn to love the LORD his God. And he will learn to obey him. He must be careful to read all the words of this Law. He must obey the words and these decrees also. 20 He must not think that he is better than other Israelites. He must not stop thinking about the Law. If he does that, he, his sons and his grandsons will be kings in Israel for many years.

Chapter 18

Gifts for priests and Levites

1 The priests, who are Levites, and the whole tribe of Levi will have no land. They will take their food from the gifts of animals that you give to the LORD. This part of your gift will be theirs, because the LORD has promised it to them. 2 They will have no land. This makes them different from other Israelites, who will all have land. But the LORD himself has promised to supply everything for them.

3 When you bring to God a cow or a sheep as a gift, remember the priests! You must give the shoulder, the face and the stomach to them. 4 You must give to them the first food and drink that you bring from your fields. Give to them also the first hair that you cut from your sheep. 5 The LORD your God has chosen the Levites. He wants them to stand as his servants, ready to obey his words always.

6 Any Levite can come to the place that the LORD will choose. He can leave the town where he lives. 7 If he really wants to, he can work as a servant to the LORD his God. He can join other Levites who work in the special place for the LORD. 8 He may have received money when he sold some of his valuable things. But he must still receive the same amount of food and other good things as the other Levites.

God hates these bad practices!

9 When you go into the country that the LORD your God is giving you, be careful! You must not do the very bad practices of the people who live there. 10 You must not burn your child in a fire, as a gift to a false god. You must not become a servant of Satan and obey him. His servants do very bad things. 11 They are cruel and they often frighten people. They also try to speak to dead people. 12 God hates anyone who does these things. It is because of these very bad practices that the LORD will kill the people in the other nations. 13 You must live in a right way, and always obey the LORD your God.

The prophet. Moses speaks about when Jesus Christ will come.

14 The people who live in your country listen to the servants of Satan. But the LORD your God has commanded you not to do this.

15 He will send you a prophet from among your own people, like me. You must listen to him. 16 Do this because you spoke to the LORD your God. You spoke to him when you came together at Mount Horeb. You said, "Please do not let us hear your voice again. Do not let us see this great fire again. If we do, we will die!"

17 Then the LORD said to me, "The people have said a good thing. 18 I will give them a prophet who will be like you. This special man will be an Israelite. I will tell him what to say. Then he will tell the people everything that I command him. 19 I myself will judge anyone who does not listen to my words. That is because the prophet will speak for me. 20 Perhaps a prophet may give you a false message. He may tell you that it comes from me. Then you must kill him. Or a prophet may say that he has a message from another god. You must kill him."

21 You may say to yourselves, "How can we know when a message has not come from the LORD?" 22 The thing that he speaks about may not happen. If it does not happen, that message was not a true message. The LORD has not spoken. That prophet has given a false message to you. Do not be afraid of him!

Chapter 19

The cities where men are safe

1 The LORD your God will kill the people whose country he is giving to you. You will march into their towns and their houses and you will live in them. 2 Then you must choose three cities. Each city must be in a central place in your country. 3 Make the country into three separate parts and build roads to each city. So then anyone who kills a person can run there. And then that person can be safe.

4 This is the rule for anyone who has killed another person. If it was a mistake, he can run to the city. He will be safe there because the man was not an enemy. 5 For example, two men may go to the forest to cut wood. As one man cuts wood, the metal part of his axe flies off. It hits the other man and kills him. The first man can run to the nearest special city. He will be safe there. 6 If there was only one city, a policeman might catch the killer on his way. The policeman might be so angry that he kills the man. But the man had made a mistake. He killed his friend, who was not an enemy. 7 So I command you to choose three cities for yourselves.

8 The LORD your God promised your ancestors to give you more land. 9 You must love him and you must obey his rules. If you do that, he will give the whole country to you. That is what he has promised. If he does that, you must choose three more cities. 10 You must do this. So then people who are not bad will not die in your country. You must not kill people for murder, when they have made a mistake. Do not do this in the country that the LORD your God is giving you.

11 But perhaps one man may hate another man. He may hide himself and wait for that man. He may kill him and then he may run to one of the cities. 12 If he does that, the leaders of his own town must fetch him back. They must bring him to the policeman and he must die. 13 Do not be sorry for him. You must remove completely from Israel the bad practice of murder. So then people who are not bad will not die in your country. If you do that, everything will be well for you.

God's rule about marks on the ground

14 There may be a stone at the edge of your neighbour's land. Someone put this stone there as a mark before you arrived in the country. You must not move it!

God's rule about reports

15 The report of one man is not enough to check a wrong thing or a sin. Two or three people, who saw the thing happen, must agree about it. They must all have seen the person when he did the wrong thing or the sin.

16 Perhaps a cruel person may say that a man has done something wrong. 17 Then both the men must stand in front of the LORD. They must stand in front of the priests and the judges who are ruling at that time. 18 Then the judges must be careful to discover what is true. The cruel person may be saying things that are not true against another Israelite.

19 If that is true, you must do this: You must do to him the things that he wanted to do to the other Israelite. You must remove bad things like this from among yourselves. 20 So then all the people will be afraid when they hear about this. And this very wrong thing will never happen again among you. 21 Do not be sorry for people who do what is wrong. You must demand:

a life for a life

an eye for an eye

a tooth for a tooth

a hand for a hand

a foot for a foot.

Chapter 20

Special rules for war

1 Do not be afraid when you go out to fight against your enemies. You may meet larger armies with more horses and chariots than you have. Do not be afraid! The LORD your God, who brought you out of Egypt, will be with you. 2 Just before you begin to fight, the priest must come to the front of the army. 3 He must say, "Israelites, listen to me! Today you are going to fight your enemies. Do not be troubled or afraid. Be brave! Do not run away from your enemies because you are frightened. 4 The LORD your God is going with you. He will fight for you and you will win."

5 Then the officers will say to the soldiers, "Has anyone built a new house but has not yet made it ready for God? He must go home. If he does not, he may die in the fight. And someone else may make his house ready. 6 Has anyone planted a field with grapes but has not yet enjoyed the fruit? He must go home. If he does not, he may die in the fight. And someone else will enjoy the fruit.

7 Has anyone promised to marry a woman? If he has not married her yet, he must go home. He may die in the fight and then another man will marry her."

8 Then the officers must also say, "Is anyone afraid? Does anyone not feel brave? He must go home. If he does not, he will make other men afraid too." 9 When the officers have finished speaking to the army, they must choose leaders for it.

10 Before you attack a city, you must do this: Offer peace to the people who live there. Tell them what you want them to do. 11 Perhaps they will open the gates and let you come in. If they do that, you must cause all the people to work hard for you, like slaves. 12 But they may refuse to listen to you. They may even begin to fight you. If they do that, you must fight against that city. 13 When the LORD your God gives it to you, you must kill all the men there. 14 But you can take for yourselves the women, the children, the animals and everything else in the city. You can use all these things that God gives you from your enemies. 15 You must do this to all the cities that are far from you.

16 You will take cities in the country that God is giving you. Then you must kill everything that is alive, people and animals. 17 You must kill completely all the Hittites, Amorites, Canaanites, Perizzites, Hivites and Jebusites. The LORD your God has told you to do this.

18 If you do that, they cannot teach you their bad practices. They cannot teach you to pray as they pray to their gods. If you did that, you would be sinning against the LORD your God.

19 Perhaps you are preparing to take a city. You must not cut down its fruit-trees, but you can eat the fruit. These trees are not your enemies; so do not cut them down. 20 But you can cut down the other trees to use. You can make things from them that will help you to attack the city. You can do this until the city's people open its gates to you.

Chapter 21

Rules about murder, marriage and sons who refuse to obey

1 You may find the dead body of a man that is lying in a field. Someone has killed him, in the country that the LORD your God is giving to you.

2 You may not know who has killed him. If you do not know, you must do this: Your leaders and judges must measure how far the dead man is from the nearest towns. 3 Then the leaders from the nearest town must take a young cow that has never pulled a plough. 4 They must lead her down to a valley that no one has ploughed or planted. There must be a stream full of water. There they must break her neck.

5 The priests from the tribe of Levi must go there too. The LORD your God has chosen them to do his work. They must also decide what is right and wrong among you. 6 All the leaders of that town must wash their hands over the cow whose neck they have broken.

7 And they will say, "We did not kill the man. We did not see anyone kill him. 8 Please accept this animal as a gift, LORD, from your people Israel that you saved from Egypt. This man has not done anything wrong. But do not think that we have killed him." You could not kill the person who did the murder. So you have killed the young cow instead. And so God will not remember this bad thing against you. 9 You will show that you have made yourselves right with God. You have not done this bad thing. And God has seen that you have done the right thing.

When you marry a woman whom you have taken in war

10 When you go to war against your enemies, the LORD your God will deliver them to you. You will take some of them to keep for yourselves. 11 You may see among them a beautiful woman that you like. If you do see one, you can make her your wife. 12 You must bring her into your home. Then she must cut off her hair and cut the hard material at the end of her fingers. 13 And she must change her clothes. Let her live in your house and weep for her parents for a whole month. Then you can become her husband and she can become your wife. 14 You may not like her. You must let her go where she wants. You must not sell her or make her into a slave. You must not do that because she has had sex with you, as your wife.

The rule about the son who is born first

15 A man may have two wives but he may love only one of them. Each wife may give birth to a son. The first son may be the son of the wife that he does not love.

16 But the man must make this promise: After his own death, the first son will have twice as many of his good things as the second son. This is because that son was born first. The man must not promise twice as much to the son of the wife that he loves. Her son was not born first. 17 The man must remember the son of the wife that he does not love. This son was born first and he must have twice as many of his father's good things. He has a special place in the family because he was born first.

The son who refuses to obey his parents

18 Perhaps a man has a bad son who will not obey his parents. They try to teach him right things. But he refuses to listen to them. 19 If that is true, his parents must take him to the leaders of his town. 20 They must say to the leaders, "This is our son. He wants to do bad things and he will not obey us. He is a drunk and he wastes our money." 21 Then all the men in his town must throw stones at him until he is dead. You must remove these bad things from among you. Then all Israel's people will hear about it and they will be afraid.

22 You may have killed a man who has sinned. If you have hung his dead body on a tree, 23 you must not leave it there during the night. Be careful to bury it on the same day. This is because God is very angry with anyone who is hanging on a tree. You must not let bad things destroy your own good country. This is the country that God is giving to you.

Chapter 22

Rules for life

1 You may see the cow or sheep of another Israelite when that animal is running away. If you do see that, you must catch the animal. Do not look away from it. Take it back to him. 2 Perhaps the man does not live near you. Perhaps you do not know him. If you do not know him, take the animal to your home. And then keep it safe. When the man comes to look for it, give it to him. 3 You must do the same thing if you find a donkey or some clothes or anything else. Do not think that you do not have to help.

4 Perhaps you see another Israelite's animal. It has fallen on the road. Do not think that you do not have to help. You must help the other Israelite to lift it up.

5 A woman must not wear the clothes of a man. A man must not wear the clothes of a woman. For the LORD your God hates people who do this.

6 You may find the home of a bird in a tree or on the ground. You must not take away the bird, whether she is sitting on eggs or on young birds. 7 You can take the young birds. But you must let the mother go free. If you do that, everything will be well with you. And you will have a long life.

8 When you build a new house, you must make a wall round the edge of the roof. Even if you have done that, someone may fall from the roof. But even if that person dies, you will not have done anything wrong.

9 You must not plant two different kinds of seed in your field. If you do that, nothing will grow well in that field. The fruit will not be good.

10 You must not tie a cow and a donkey together to plough your land.

11 You must not mix different materials together to make clothes.

12 You must sow tassels on the four corners of your coat.

Rules for marriage

13 A man may marry a girl. Then he may decide that he does not like her. 14 So he says wrong things about her and gives her a bad name. He even says, "I married this girl. Then I discovered that she had already had sex. She had sex before I married her." 15 Then the parents of the girl must bring the blanket. It shows that she had not had sex before. They must bring it to the leaders of the town.

16 And the father of the girl will say to the leaders, "I gave my daughter to this man to be his wife. But now he does not like her.

17 He says wrong things about her. He says, 'Your daughter had sex before I married her.' But here is the blanket. This shows that she had never had sex before." Then her parents must hold up the blanket in front of the leaders of the town. 18 Then the leaders must take the man and punish him. 19 They must make him pay 100 shekels of silver to the girl's father. This man has given a bad name to a young girl in Israel when she has done nothing wrong. She must continue to be his wife. He must continue to be her husband as long as he lives.

20 But perhaps the husband has spoken true words. Perhaps his wife cannot show that she had not had sex before. 21 If she cannot do that, the leaders must bring her to her father's house. There, the men of the town must throw stones at her until she dies. She has done a very bad thing in Israel. She has had sex before she was married. She did this while she lived in her father's house. You must remove this kind of bad thing from among you.

22 You may find a man who is having sex with another man's wife. If you find them, you must kill both the man and the woman. You must remove this bad thing from Israel.

23 Perhaps a man may meet a girl in a town. She has already promised to marry another man, but they have sex together. 24 You must take both of them to the gate of that town. There you must throw stones at both of them until they die. The girl must die because she did not scream for help in the town. The man must die because he had sex with the future wife of another man.

25 But perhaps a man may meet a girl in a country place. He has sex with her because he is too strong for her. But she has already promised to marry another man. Only the man who has done that must die. 26 Do not hurt the girl. She has not done a sin that should cause you to kill her. This thing is like a man who kills another person. 27 This man made the girl have sex with him in a country place. She screamed for help, but there was no one to save her.

28 Perhaps a man may make a girl have sex with him. The girl has not had sex with anyone before and someone discovers them.

She has not yet promised to marry anyone. 29 If that has happened, the man must pay 50 shekels of silver to the father of the girl. He must also marry the girl because he has had sex with her. He must be her husband as long as he lives.

30 A man must not marry his father's wife or have sex with her. This is a bad thing to do against his father.

Chapter 23
These people cannot join with the LORD's people.

1 Perhaps someone has destroyed the sex parts of a man. That man cannot join with the people of the LORD when they come together.

2 No one can join with the people of the LORD unless his parents are married. None of his children or grandchildren can join with the people of the LORD when they come together. Even the 10th generation of his descendants cannot do this.

3 These people cannot join with the people of the LORD when they come together: People from Moab, people from Ammon or their descendants. Even their 10th generation cannot do this. 4 They refused to give bread and water to you when you left Egypt. And they paid Balaam the son of Beor to say very bad things about you. He came from Pethor in Mesopotamia. 5 But the LORD your God did not listen to Balaam. He changed the bad things into good things for you, because he loves you. 6 Do not agree to stop fighting with these people. Do not be friendly with them as long as you live.

7 Do not hate anyone from Edom, because he has the same ancestor as you. Do not hate anyone from Egypt, because you once lived in his country as a stranger. 8 The third generation of their children can join with the people of the LORD when they come together.

Keep the tents prepared for God.

9 Keep away from everything that God would not like. Do this even when you are fighting your enemies.

10 While a man is asleep, something may come out of his sex part. If that happens, he must go away beyond the tents. And he must stay there. 11 In the evening, he must wash himself. Then at sunset he can return to the tents.

12 You must choose a special place beyond the tents. Leave the dirt that comes from inside your body in that place. 13 Always carry with you a small spade. Dig a hole and bury in it the dirt from inside your body. 14 For the LORD your God moves among you in your tents. He keeps you safe and delivers up your enemies to you. So the place where you put your tents must be always ready for God. The LORD will not see anything that is not lovely among you. So he will not turn away from you, because of it.

15 A slave may come to you to be safe. If that happens, keep him with you. Do not give him back to his master. 16 He can live among you in any place that he likes. Let him choose his own town. Do not be cruel to him.

17 No Israelite man or woman must sell his or her body for sex, in the house of a false god. 18 Some people will pay money to a man or a woman for sex. You must not bring this money into the house of the LORD. You must not use this money to buy a gift for the LORD. Even if you have promised a gift to the LORD, you cannot use this money. The LORD hates people who sell their bodies for sex.

19 You can lend money or food or anything else to another Israelite. But do not ask him to give you back more than you lent to him. 20 You can ask anyone from a foreign country to do that. But you must not do this to another Israelite. If you do not do that, the LORD your God will cause all your work to do well, in your country.

21 If you promise a gift to the LORD your God, be careful to bring the gift soon. If you do not bring it, that is a sin. And the LORD will certainly demand it. 22 But if you do not promise to do anything, that will not be a sin. 23 Whatever you say, you must be careful to do. You chose to say the words to the LORD your God. That includes something that you have promised to give to the LORD your God.

24 If you go into your neighbour's field of fruit, you can eat his fruit. You can eat all the fruit that you want. But you must not put any into your basket. 25 If you go into your neighbour's field of corn, you can pick the corn with your hands. But you must not cut his growing corn with a knife.

Chapter 24

1 Perhaps a man will marry a woman and then discover something bad in her. He does not like her, so he writes a letter. This letter finishes the marriage. He gives it to his wife and he sends her out of his house. 2 Perhaps, after she has left his house, she marries another man.

3 Perhaps her second husband also discovers that he does not like her. So he also gives her a letter that finishes the marriage. He sends her away, or perhaps he dies. 4 But her first husband must not marry her again. That is because she has been the wife of another man. To marry her again would be a sin. The LORD hates to see a thing like this. You must not do wrong and bad things in the country that the LORD your God is giving to you.

5 When a man has just married, do not send him to fight in a war. Do not give him any special duties. He should stay at home for one year and make his new wife happy.

6 When you lend money to a man, do not take away his large stones. Do not even take the top one. This is because he needs these stones to make flour from his corn. This is his work.

7 Perhaps you will catch a man who is carrying away another Israelite. He uses him for a slave or even sells him. The man who does this must die. You must remove these wrong things from among you.

8 Perhaps you have the illness that is called leprosy. Be very careful! Do everything that the priests say to you. The priests are Levites. You must obey everything that I have commanded them. 9 Remember what the LORD your God did to Miriam during your journey. This was after you left Egypt.

10 Your neighbour may ask you to lend him something. And he offers you something that is his, as a pledge. Do not go into his house to get it. 11 You must wait outside. Let him bring the pledge out to you. 12 If the man is poor, you must not keep his pledge until the next day. 13 You must give him his coat again before sunset. He can wear it and he can keep himself warm at night. He will ask God to do good things for you. And you will give pleasure to the LORD your God. It is right to do this.

14 Always be kind to a poor servant who needs many things. Do this whether he is an Israelite or a foreign person in one of your towns. 15 You must pay him his money every day before sunset because he is poor. He needs to have the money. If you do not pay him, he may ask the LORD for help against you. You will have sinned.

16 You must not kill fathers for the sins that their children do. You must not kill children for the sins that their fathers do. Each person must die for his own sins. 17 Remember to be completely fair to the foreign person and those who are without fathers. Do not take the coat of any woman whose husband has died, as a pledge. 18 Remember that you were slaves in Egypt and the LORD your God made you free. That is why I tell you to do this.

19 When you bring in the food from your field, perhaps you will leave some of the corn in the field. Do not go back for it. Leave it there for the foreign person, the woman whose husband has died and for her children. If you do that, the LORD your God will cause all your work to be good. 20 When you knock down the olives from your trees, knock them down only once. Leave those that remain for foreign people, women whose husbands have died and their children. 21 When you pick your grapes, pick them only once. Leave those that remain for foreign people, women whose husbands have died and their children. 22 Remember! You were slaves in Egypt. That is why I tell you to do this.

Chapter 25

1 When two men cannot agree, they must both go to the judges. Then the judges will decide who is right and who is wrong.

2 The judge may need to punish the bad man. If he does need to punish him, the judge will cause him to lie down. Then someone will hit him several times. He will hit him many times if he has done a very bad thing. He will hit him only a few times if the thing was not too bad. 3 But he must not hit him more than 40 times. So then you will not all feel that another Israelite has become less important.

4 Do not tie up the mouth of a cow while she walks on your corn to prepare it for you.

5 Perhaps two brothers are living together. One of the brothers may die and leave no son. If that happens, his wife must not marry outside the family. The second brother must take the wife and he must marry her. He is doing what is right for his dead brother. 6 The first son that is born to them will be called the same name as the dead brother. So everyone in Israel will remember that name.

7 But a man may not want to marry his dead brother's wife. If he does not want to do it, she should go to the leaders at the gate of the town. She should say, "My dead husband's brother refuses to do his duty for me. He does not want people to remember my dead husband. He does not want to give my husband's name to our son." 8 Then the leaders of the town must call the man to them and they must talk to him. Perhaps he will continue to say, "I do not want to marry her!"

9 If that happens, his brother's wife must go to him, in front of the leaders. She must pull off one of his shoes and spit in his face. And she must say, "We do this to a man who will not help to keep the family name of his dead brother." 10 Then everyone will call the family of the living brother, "the family of the man who lost his shoe".

11 Perhaps two men are fighting each other. The wife of one of them comes to save him. She takes hold of the sex parts of his enemy. 12 If that happens, you must cut off her hand. Do not be sorry for her.

13 Do not have in your bag two different things with which to measure weight, one heavy and one light. 14 Do not have in your house two different jars with which to measure, one large and one small.

15 You must have true and honest things with which to measure and to weigh. If you do that you will live for a long time in your country. It is the country that the LORD your God is giving to you. 16 The LORD your God hates anyone who is not always honest.

17 Remember what the descendants of Amalek did to you when you came out of Egypt. 18 They met you when you were tired and weak. They killed all the people who could not walk fast. They were not afraid of God. 19 The LORD your God will give you rest from all your enemies in the country. This is the country that he is giving you. On that day you must kill all the descendants of Amalek. Then nobody will remember them. Do not forget to do this!

Chapter 26

The first food from your fields and the regular gifts to God

1 You are going into the country that the LORD your God is giving to you. Now when you have arrived, do this. 2 Take a basket. Put into it some of the first food that you have grown in your fields. This is the country that the LORD your God is giving to you. Then go to the special place that he will choose for himself. 3 Say to the man who is a priest at that time, "Today, I say to the LORD your God that I have come into the country. This is the country that the LORD promised to us. He made this promise to our ancestors." 4 Then the priest will take the basket from you. He will put it down in front of the altar of the LORD your God. 5 Then you must say, in front of the LORD, "My father was a man from Aramea who moved from place to place. He went to Egypt with a few people and lived there. But he became a great nation of many powerful people. 6 But the people in Egypt were cruel to us. They made us work very hard. 7 Then we prayed to the LORD, the God of our fathers. He heard our voices. He saw that we were sad. He saw that the people in Egypt were cruel to us. 8 So the LORD brought us out of Egypt by his strong hands and powerful arms. He made them afraid, because of the great and powerful things that he did. 9 He brought us to this place. He gave to us this country that is full of good food and drink. 10 and now, I bring the first food that has grown in my fields. You, LORD, have given it to me." Then you must put the basket down in front of the LORD your God. You must thank him there. Tell him how great he is. 11 And so you and the Levites and the foreign people among you will be very happy. You will enjoy all the good things that the LORD has given to you and to your family.

12 Every third year you must give a 10th part of the food that grows in your fields. Give it to the Levites, the strangers, the women whose husbands have died and their children. Then they can eat all the food that they need, in every town. 13 Then you can say to the LORD, "None of the 10th part that is special, remains in my house. I have given it to the Levites, the strangers, the women whose husbands have died and their children. I have obeyed your rules. I have not refused to obey your words. I have not forgotten any of them. 14 I did not eat any of the 10th part of the food while I was sad and crying. I did not move any of it while I was not ready for God. I have not put any of it as a gift, in front of a dead person. I have obeyed the LORD my God. I have done everything that you commanded me. 15 Look down from your home, the special place where you live. Come near to your people, Israel's people and give us your help. Do good things also to the country that you have given to us. It is a country full of good food and drink. You promised our ancestors that you would give it to us."

Obey the LORD's rules.

16 Today, the LORD your God commands you to obey these decrees and rules. Be careful to obey them. Be happy to do this because you love the LORD. 17 Today, you have said that the LORD is your God. You have said that you will give him pleasure. You have said that you will obey his rules. You will do everything that he commands. 18 Today the LORD has accepted you as his own people. He has chosen you and you are special to him. He promised that you would be special. And you must obey all his rules. 19 He says that he will make you greater and more famous than every other nation in the world. You will be a special nation that belongs to the LORD your God. He has promised you this.' Moses said all those things.

Chapter 27

The altar on Mount Ebal

1 Moses and the leaders of Israel said to the people, 'Obey all these rules that I give to you today. 2 You will cross the River Jordan and go into the country that the LORD your God is giving to you. On that day, you must put some large stones on the ground and you must cover them with white paint. 3 Then write on them all the words of this Law. Do this when you have crossed over the river into the country.

This is the country that the LORD your God has promised to you.

He is the LORD, the God of your fathers. The country is full of good food and drink. 4 And when you have crossed the river, you must put these stones on Mount Ebal. Do as I command you today. Cover them with white paint. 5 You must build there an altar for the LORD your God. Do not use iron tools to cut the stones. 6 Build this table for the LORD your God with stones from the field. There you must give to him your burnt-offerings on that table. 7 You can also offer friendship-offerings there. Eat them and be happy in front of the LORD your God. 8 And you must write all these rules on the stones that you have put there. You must write the rules very clearly.'

Pronounce the bad things that will happen, from Mount Ebal.

9 Then Moses and the priests (who are Levites) said to all the Israelites, 'Be quiet, Israelites. Listen! The LORD your God has chosen you and made you his own people. 10 Obey the LORD your God. Do whatever he commands you. I am giving you his words today.'

11 On the same day, Moses said to the people:

12 'After you have crossed the Jordan, these tribes must stand on Mount Gerizim. They will promise good things to the people: Simeon, Levi, Judah, Issachar, Joseph and Benjamin. 13 And these tribes must stand on Mount Ebal to pronounce bad things that will happen: Reuben, Gad, Asher, Zebulun, Dan and Naphtali.

14 The Levites will say with a loud voice, to all Israel's people:

15 "God will cause bad things for the man who makes any false god. The LORD hates such a thing, even if the man prays to it as a secret." Then everyone must say, "Yes! I agree."

16 "God will cause bad things for the man who does bad things to his parents." Then everyone must say, "Yes! I agree."

17 "God will cause bad things for the man who moves the stone at the edge of his neighbour's land." Then everyone must say, "Yes! I agree."

18 "A man may lead a person who cannot see, along a wrong path. This path does not go to the place that he wants. God will cause bad things for the cruel man who does this." Then everyone must say, "Yes! I agree."

19 "A man may refuse to do right things for the stranger, the woman whose husband has died, or her children. God will cause bad things for this man." Then everyone must say, "Yes! I agree."

20 "God will cause bad things for the man who has sex with his father's wife. It is very wrong for him to make his father's bed dirty." Then everyone must say, "Yes! I agree."

21 "God will cause bad things for the man who has sex with any animal." Then everyone must say, "Yes! I agree."

22 "God will cause bad things for the man who has sex with his sister. She may be the daughter of his father or of his mother." Then everyone must say, "Yes! I agree."

23 "God will cause bad things for the man who has sex with his wife's mother." Then everyone must say, "Yes! I agree."

24 "Perhaps a man may kill his neighbour. He does this when no one is watching. God will cause bad things for this man." Then everyone must say, "Yes! I agree."

25 "Perhaps a man may accept money to kill another person. This other person has done nothing wrong. God will cause bad things for the man who accepts the money." Then everyone must say, "Yes! I agree."

26 "God will cause bad things for the man who does not obey all God's words and rules." Then everyone must say, "Yes! I agree."

Chapter 28

Good things for people who obey God

1 Today, I am telling you this! You must obey the LORD your God. Be careful to obey all his rules. If you do that, he will make you very important. He will make you more important than any other nation of people in the world.

2 If you obey the LORD your God, all these good things will happen to you. And they will remain with you.

3 The LORD will give you many good things. He will be with you, both in the city and in the fields.

4 The LORD will give you many children, many cows and many sheep. He will make much food grow in your fields.

5 The LORD will give you many baskets of food from your fields. He will be with you as you make your bread. He will make you happy in your work.

6 The LORD will give you good things when you come into your homes. And he will give you good things when you leave them.

7 The LORD will beat your enemies when they attack you. They will come along one path to attack you, but they will run away in all directions.

8 The LORD will make all your work do well. He will fill your buildings with food. The LORD your God will give you many good things in the country that he is giving to you.

9 The LORD will make you his special people for all times, as he has promised. But you must obey his rules and give him pleasure. 10 So everyone in the world will see that the LORD has called you by his own name. And they will be afraid of you. 11 The LORD will give you many children, many animals and much good food. He will do this in the country that he promised to your ancestors.

12 The LORD will send a lot of rain on your country, at the right season. He stores the rain in the clouds. And, at the right season, he will cause it to fall on your land. So then all the food that you plant in your fields will grow well. You will lend to the people in many countries. But you will not need anyone to lend to you. 13 The LORD will make you the leader among the people in many countries. You must not do as they do. Be careful! Always obey the rules of the LORD your God which I give to you today. If you do that, you will always be leaders of the people in other countries. And you will never be their slaves. 14 Do not refuse any of the rules that I give you today. Do not do wrong things. It is wrong to want other gods. You must not have other gods or pray to them.

Bad things for those who do not obey

15 But if you do not obey the LORD your God, all these bad things will happen to you. Be careful! Obey all his rules and decrees that I give to you today. If you do not obey, this is what will happen to you:

16 Bad things will happen to you, whether you are in the city or in the fields.

17 Bad things will happen to the food that is growing in your fields. Even the bread that you make will not be good.

18 Bad things will happen to your children, the food that grows in your fields, your young cows and your sheep.

19 Bad things will happen to you when you come into your homes. And bad things will happen to you when you leave them.

20 If you do not obey the words of the LORD, he will cause bad things, troubles and difficulties for you. These will destroy you because you have done something very wrong.

You have completely refused to remember the LORD and you have forgotten him. 21 The LORD will send bad illnesses to you until he has destroyed you in your country. 22 The LORD will cause you to have cruel illness. You will be very hot and have a lot of pain. He will send great heat and no rain. He will send bad things upon the food that is growing in your fields. These will destroy the food. So at last, you will die. 23 The sky above your head will be like hard metal. The ground under your feet will be like iron. 24 There will be no rain on your country. There will only be dry sand that is flying about in the air. It will come down from the sky until it has destroyed you.

25 The LORD will let your enemies beat you. You will attack them from one direction, but you will run from them in many directions. You will become like a very bad sign to all the people in every country. 26 Your dead bodies will be food for all the birds and the animals. No one will send them away. 27 The LORD will cause you to have hot, painful places on your bodies as he did to the people in Egypt. He will cause you to have many illnesses on your skin. You cannot become well from these illnesses. 28 The LORD will make you so that you cannot see. He will destroy your minds and he will make you confused. 29 You will fall as you walk at midday. You will be like someone who cannot see. You will not do well in anything. Every day, people will rob you and be cruel to you. No one will save you.

30 A woman may promise to marry you. But another man will take her and have sex with her. You will build a house, but you will not live in it. You will plant a garden, but you will never eat the fruit from it. 31 Someone will kill your cow in front of you, but you will not eat any of the meat. Someone will take away your donkey and will not send it back. Your enemies will take your sheep and no one will save them. 32 The people from another country will take your children for slaves. You will look for them every day, but you cannot bring them back to you. 33 Strangers will eat the food from your fields. People will be cruel to you all the days of your life. 34 The things that you see will destroy your minds. 35 The LORD will cause you to have painful hot places on your knees and on your legs. No one will be able to make them well again. They will soon cover the whole of your body.

36 The LORD will send you and your king away to a foreign country. Neither you nor your ancestors ever lived there. There you will pray to gods made from stone and wood. 37 The LORD will send you away to many countries. You will be like a very bad sign to all the people there. And they will not be sorry about your troubles and difficulties.

38 You will plant many seeds in your fields, but you will not bring in much food. Hungry insects will eat it.

39 You will plant gardens for grapes and be careful of them. But you will not drink the wine or bring in the grapes. Animals that are like small snakes will eat them. 40 Olive trees will grow everywhere in your country, but you will have no oil from them. The fruit will drop off the trees.

41 You will have sons and daughters, but you will lose them. Enemies will take them away from you and keep them. 42 Insects will eat all your trees and the food from your fields.

43 Foreign people who live in your country will become stronger and stronger. But you will become weaker and weaker. 44 They will lend money to you, but you will not lend money to them. And, in the end, they will rule over you.

45 All these bad things will happen to you. They will be like an enemy that runs after you and catches you. They will destroy you because you did not obey the LORD your God. You did not obey the rules and decrees that he gave to you. 46 The bad things that happen to you will be a sign to you and your children for always. They will show that God is very angry with you. 47 The LORD made all your work do well. But you were not happy or ready to work for him. 48 So now you must work for the enemies that the LORD will send against you. You will do this while you are without enough food and water, poor and without clothes. He will put cruel masters over you until he has destroyed you.

49 The LORD will bring against you people from a country that is far away. They will drop down on you like a large bird and you will not understand their language. 50 They will have cruel faces. They will neither do good things for your old people, nor be kind to your children.

51 They will eat your young animals and the food from your fields, until they have destroyed you. They will not leave any food, wine or oil for you.

They will take all your young cows and your sheep until nothing remains. 52 They will attack all the cities in your country. You will build high walls to keep yourselves safe. But they will fall.

53 When your enemies attack your cities, you will have no food. You will become very, very hungry. Then you will eat the children that the LORD your God has given to you. 54 Even the best and kindest man among you will do this. He will be so hungry that he will not be sorry for any of his family. He will not even be sorry for his own brother. He will not be sorry for his wife that he loves. And he will not be sorry for his children. 55 He will not give to one of them any of the meat that he is eating. This meat is the body of his child. He will not give any to his brother, or to his wife, or to his children that remain alive. He will have nothing to eat except his children, because your enemies will take away your food. 56 Even the best and kindest woman, who never has to walk anywhere, will do the same thing. 57 She will become so hungry that she will eat her new baby. She will even eat the thing that came out of her body after the baby. She will do this as a secret thing. She will not give any of these things to her husband or to her other children. These things will happen to you when your enemies attack your cities.

58 Be careful! Obey all these rules that I have written in this scroll. Always remember with love, the great and powerful name of the LORD your God. 59 If you do not, the LORD will cause you and your descendants to have very bad illnesses. He will make bad and cruel things happen to you. These things will stay with you always. 60 He will cause you to have all the illnesses that made you afraid in Egypt. These illnesses will remain with you. You will not become well again.

61 The LORD will also cause you to have many illnesses and bad troubles that you do not understand. They are not written in this scroll of the Law but they will destroy you.

62 You were once as many as the stars in the sky. But you will become only a few people because you did not obey the LORD your God. 63 Once, the LORD was happy to give you good things and many children. But then he will be happy to destroy you. He will remove you from the country that will soon become your country.

64 Then the LORD will send you away into many other countries. He will send you from one end of the world to the other. There you will pray to other gods. You will pray to gods made from wood and gods made from stone. Neither you nor your fathers have prayed to these gods before.

65 You will not be happy there. You will not find any place to rest. The LORD will cause you to have a troubled mind and nothing to hope for. You will be very sad.

66 You will be afraid all the time, both in the day and at night. You will always be afraid of death. 67 Every morning you will say, "I want it to be evening very soon!" And every evening you will say, "I want it to be morning very soon!" You will be so afraid of everything that you see. 68 I told you that you would never return to Egypt. But the LORD will send you back to Egypt in ships. In Egypt, you will try to sell yourselves to your enemies, as slaves. But no one will buy you.'

Chapter 29

God repeats his promise.

1 The LORD told Moses to make this promise to the Israelites in the country called Moab. He must join it with the promise that the LORD made to them at Mount Horeb. 2 Moses caused all the people to come together. Then he said to them:

'You have seen what the LORD did to the king of Egypt, to his officers and to his country. 3 You saw with your own eyes all the great and powerful things that he did. 4 But until now the LORD has not let you understand. Your eyes do not really see and your ears do not really hear. 5 The LORD says, "I led you through this desert for 40 years. Your clothes and shoes are still fresh and good. 6 You did not eat bread or drink any alcohol. I am the LORD your God. I wanted you to know that I am your God."

7 When we arrived here, Sihon, king of Heshbon, and Og, king of Bashan, fought against us. But we beat them. 8 We marched into their country and we gave it to the tribes of Reuben and Gad. We also gave some of it to part of the tribe of Manasseh.

9 Be careful to obey the words of this promise. If you do that, everything will be good for you. Everything that you do will be good.

10 You are all standing today in front of the LORD your God. Your leaders, your important men, your officers and your older men are all here. 11 Your children, your wives and the foreign people are all here. The foreign people live with you. They cut wood and carry water for you. 12 You are standing here to agree to a promise with the LORD your God. The LORD is making this promise to you today. He is making it special by using serious and powerful words. 13 He tells you again today that you are his own people. He has promised to be your God. He made the same promise to your ancestors, Abraham, Isaac and Jacob. 14 I am making this promise, using serious and powerful words. It is not only for you. 15 You are standing here with us today, in front of the LORD our God. But I make the promise also to those people who are not here today.

16 You know how we lived in Egypt. You remember how we travelled through other countries on the way here. 17 You saw their gods, which the LORD hates. They made them from wood, stone, silver and gold. 18 Be very careful that no one forgets the LORD our God. Do not let any man, woman or family or tribe pray to the false gods of these countries. This would become like a root of poison among you.

19 Everyone who hears these serious words must obey them. He must not say to himself, "I will be safe, whatever happens. I will do whatever I want!" If you say that, very bad things will destroy you and your fields. This will happen to both good and bad people. 20 The LORD will never forgive such a person. He will be angry and as powerful as a burning fire. The LORD will send on him all the bad things that I have written in this scroll. The LORD will destroy him completely. 21 The LORD will make him a very bad sign to all the Israelites. This scroll of the Law tells about many troubles and bad things. The LORD will cause these things to happen to that man.

22 In future days, your children and your grandchildren will see your troubles. Foreign people also will see your many illnesses and troubles. And they will know that the LORD has done this. 23 The whole country will become a desert of salt and bad dirt. No one will plant seed, because nothing will grow there. Your country will be the same as the cities called Sodom and Gomorrah, Admah and Zeboiim. The LORD destroyed these cities when he was very, very angry. 24 All the people in the country will ask, "Why has the LORD destroyed this country? Why is he so very angry?"

25 And the answer will be: "Because these people stopped obeying their promise to the LORD, the God of their fathers. He made a promise to them when he brought them out of Egypt. 26 They went away and prayed to other gods. They obeyed these strange gods that he had not given to them.

27 So the LORD was angry with the people in this country. The scroll of the Law tells about many troubles and bad things. The LORD caused these things to happen to his people and to their country. 28 The LORD was so angry that he removed them from their country. He would not let them remain there. He made them to go into a foreign country and they are there today."

29 Some secret things belong only to the LORD our God. He does not tell us about those things. But he has told us about many other things. These things belong to us and to our children for all time, so that we will obey all his rules.'

Chapter 30

Good things will happen again when Israel's people come back to the LORD.

1 'I have told you to choose between good things and bad things. When they happen to you, you will remember my words. When God has caused you to go out of your country, you will remember my words. When you have to live among people in other countries, you will remember my words. 2 Then you and your children will come back to the LORD. You will love and obey him completely, in your work and in your thoughts. You must obey all his commands that I am giving to you today.

3 If you do that, the LORD your God will cause good things to happen to you again. He will be sorry for you. He will bring you back from the countries where he sent you away.

4 Perhaps he may have sent you to countries that are very far away. Even from there, he will cause you to come together and he will bring you back. 5 He will bring you to your fathers' country and it will be yours. He will do greater things for you than he did for your fathers. He will make you more in number than your fathers. 6 The LORD your God will make you and your children like different people. Then you will love him completely and you will live. 7 Then the LORD your God will make all these bad things happen to your enemies. They hate you and do cruel things to you. 8 You will obey the LORD again and you will obey all his rules. These are the rules that I give to you today. 9 If you do that, the LORD your God will cause all your work to do very well. He will give you many children, many animals and enough food in your fields for everyone. The LORD will make good things happen to you. You will give him much pleasure, in the same way as your fathers gave him pleasure. 10 This will happen if you obey all the rules and decrees of the LORD your God. I have written them in this scroll. You must obey the LORD your God completely, in your work and in your thoughts.

God offers life or death.

11 The thing that I am commanding you today is not too difficult for you. 12 It is not in God's home. So you do not have to ask, "Who will go up to God's home and bring it down to us? Then we can understand his words and obey them." 13 Nor is it across the sea. So you do not have to ask, "Who will cross the sea to fetch it? Then we can understand his words and obey them." 14 No! God's word is very near to you. It is in your mouth and in your mind, so that you can obey it.

15 Look! I offer you today, life and good things, or death and very bad things. You must choose which you will have. 16 I say this because I am commanding you today to love the LORD your God. Live in a way that will give him pleasure. If you obey all his rules, you will live. And you will have many children. Then the LORD your God will make good things happen to you, in your country. This is the country that you are going into.

17 But you may think about other things and refuse to listen. If you do that, people will lead you to other gods. You will obey them and pray to them. 18 If you do that, God will certainly destroy you. I am saying that to you today. You will not live for many years in your country that is across the River Jordan.

19 Today, I want the sky and the earth to hear my words. I am shouting them aloud. For I have offered you, life or death, good things or bad things. Choose life! If you do that, you and your children will live. 20 Then you will love the LORD your God. You will listen to his voice and you will stay very near to him. You will do this because the LORD is the most important person in your life. He will let you live for many years. You will live in the country that he promised to your fathers, to Abraham, Isaac and Jacob.'

Chapter 31

Joshua will become the new leader.

1 Then Moses went out and he spoke to all the Israelites. He said: 2 'I am now 120 years old and I cannot continue to lead you. The LORD has told me that I will not cross the River Jordan.

3 The LORD your God himself will cross the river in front of you. He will kill the people in these countries in front of you and you will march into their countries. Joshua also will cross the river before you, as the LORD has said. 4 The LORD will do to these people what he did to Sihon and to Og. They were kings of the Amorites, but the LORD killed them. And he destroyed their country. 5 The LORD will deliver them to you. Then you must do to them everything that I have told you. 6 Be strong and be brave! Do not be afraid of them, because the LORD your God goes with you. He will never leave you nor forget you.'

7 Then Moses fetched Joshua. He spoke to him in front of all the people and he said, 'You must go with these people into their country. So be strong and be brave. The LORD promised their ancestors that he would give the country to them. You must give to each tribe its own part of the country. It will belong to them always. 8 The LORD himself goes in front of you and he will be with you. He will never leave you nor forget you. Do not be afraid that you will fail.'

The leaders of Israel must read the rules to the people.

9 So Moses wrote these rules in a scroll. He gave it to the leaders of Israel and to the priests, the sons of Levi.

The Levites carried the Ark of the LORD's promise. 10 Then Moses said to them, 'You must read this scroll to all Israel's people. Read it every 7 years at the party of tents, in the year when you forget about your debts. 11 Everybody will come together to stand in front of the LORD your God. He will choose the place for them. 12 Bring all the men, women and children together. And remember also to bring the foreign people who live in your towns. Then they can listen. They can learn to obey the LORD your God. Then they will be careful to obey all these rules. 13 Their children do not know these rules, so they must hear them. If you do that, they will learn to obey the LORD your God. They must do this for as long as they live in your country, across the Jordan.'

God tells Moses what will happen to the Israelites.

14 The LORD said to Moses, 'You will soon die. Fetch Joshua and bring him to the tent where I meet with you. I will give my authority to him there.' So Moses and Joshua went to the tent where God met with them.

15 Then the LORD came down in a large cloud. The cloud stopped at the door of the tent where God met with them. 16 And the LORD said to Moses, 'You will soon die. After you die, the people will soon stop obeying me. They will pray to the foreign gods of the country to which they are going. They will forget me. They will not keep the promise that we made together. 17 On that day, I will become angry with them. I will go away from them. I will not stay with them, but I will destroy them. Many troubles and difficulties will happen to them. Then they will say, "These troubles and difficulties have happened to us because our God is not with us." 18 And I will certainly refuse to help them on that day. This is because they have done a very bad thing. They have obeyed other gods and prayed to them.

19 Now write this song and teach the Israelites to sing it. So they will remember how often they did bad things against me. 20 I will take them into this country, which is full of good food and drink. I promised their ancestors that I would do this. There they will have all the food that they want. They will have good health and live a comfortable life. But then they will forget me and worship other gods. They will refuse to obey me. They will not keep the promise that we made together. 21 Many troubles and difficulties will happen to them. Then this song will cause them to remember. They will remember the bad things that they have done. Their children will not forget it. Even now, I know what they are thinking. I know it, even before I take them into their country. This is the country that I promised to them, with serious words.' 22 So Moses wrote this song on that day. Then he taught it to the Israelites.

23 Then the LORD said to Joshua, the son of Nun, 'Be strong and be brave! You will lead the Israelites into the country that I have promised to them. And I myself will stay with you. I will not leave you.'

24 So Moses finished writing the whole Law in a scroll. 25 Then he said to the Levites, who carried the Ark of the LORD's covenant: 26 'Take this scroll of the Law. Put it next to the Ark of the LORD your God's promise. There it will remain, so that you will remember. You will remember the bad things that you have done.

27 I know that you like bad things very much.

You do not want to obey God's rules. You enjoy doing wrong things. You have been like this, against the LORD, during my life. You will do even worse things after I die! 28 Bring to me all the leaders of your tribes and all your officers. I want to speak to them. And I want the sky and the earth to hear my words. I am shouting them aloud. 29 I know that you will become completely bad after my death. You will refuse the good commands that I have given to you. In future days, you will have great troubles. This is because you will do bad things against the LORD. You will make him angry because of the bad things that you have made with your hands.'

30 Then Moses spoke the words of this song, from the beginning to the end. And all Israel's people listened to him.

Chapter 32

Moses' song

1 'Sky and earth, hear my words! Listen to me!

2 When I teach people, it will be like the rain when it falls.

My words will do good things to them, like water does to the fields.

They will be like rain on young plants and on new grass.

3 I will pronounce the name of the LORD.

Oh, tell everyone how great and important our God is!

4 He is The Rock that is strong. It does not move away.

His work is completely good. All the things that he does are fair.

He is a God who keeps his promises. He never does anything that is wrong.

He does what is fair and good.

5 But you have done wrong things. You cannot continue to be his people.

You are neither fair nor good. You enjoy doing bad things.

6 This is not the right way to live. The LORD has been very good to you. Do not do these things that make him angry and sad.

You are fools and not people who understand.

He is your Father and he made you. He himself made you from his own plan.

7 Remember the days that are past.

Think of all the people who have died. Ask your father and he will tell you.

Ask the old men. They will explain what happened.

8 The powerful God, who is very important, gave their own place to the people in each country. He decided where the edges of each country should be. And when he was doing that, he was thinking about the number of the descendants of Israel.

9 But the LORD's people are his own people.

He chose the descendants of Jacob to be his special people.

10 The LORD found them in an empty desert where the wind was blowing.

He was careful about them and he loved them.

He did not let anyone hurt them, because they were so valuable to him.

11 He was like a large bird. A bird teaches its young birds to fly.

The large bird flies below them and catches them.

It carries them on its back. They do not fall.

The LORD also was very careful about the Israelites and they were safe.

12 The LORD alone led his people. No foreign god gave the Israelites any help.

13 The LORD made them ride over the high places in the country.

He fed them with fruit that grows in the fields. He gave to them honey out of the rock.

He gave to them oil from a place that was full of stones.

14 Their cows and their sheep gave plenty of milk.

The people ate the best meat that they found in Bashan.

They ate the very best bread and they drank fresh wine.

15 Then the Israelites became lazy. They refused to obey.

They were full of food. But they did not want to obey the God who made them.

They refused to obey God, their Rock.

But he is the God who saved them.

16 They made the LORD angry with their foreign gods.

They made their own gods, which he hated.

17 They obeyed very bad gods and prayed to them.

These are not God. These are new gods, which they had not known.

Even your father was not afraid of them.

18 You refused to obey God, your Rock and your Father.

You forgot the God who caused you to be born.

19 When the LORD saw this, he was angry.

He looked away from his sons and daughters and he said,

20 "I will not continue to be with them. Then I will see what happens to them in the end.

They are children who do not obey me. They refuse to give me pleasure.

21 They made me angry with their false gods. These gods have no value.

So I will make them angry because of those who are not a nation.

I will make them angry, by a nation that does not understand.

22 My anger will be so great that it will seem like a hot fire.

You will meet with it everywhere that you go. You will meet with it in everything that you do.

Even on the day when you die, you will meet with it.

Even the great things that I have made will know the heat of my anger.

23 I will cause them to have many kinds of trouble. I will attack them.

24 They will become very thin because they have no food. They will have many cruel illnesses.

Wild animals will attack them. Snakes will bite them and they will die.

25 War will cause people to die in the streets. War will kill their children.

Even in their homes, they will be afraid.

Young men and young women will die. Babies and old men will also die.

26 I would have caused them to go out of their country completely. So nobody would remember them.

27 But that would give their enemies pleasure. They would not understand.

They would say, 'We have destroyed these people! The LORD has not done it!' "

28 Israel's people do not understand anything. They are all fools.

29 If they were wise, they would understand.

They would know what will happen to them in the end.

30 One man runs after 1000 men!

Two men make 10 000 men run away!

This could only happen if God, their strong Rock, had made them slaves.

This could only happen if the LORD refused to help them.

31 Our enemies know that their own gods are weak.

They are not like the God of Israel.

32 Our enemies are bad and cruel, like the people of Sodom and Gomorrah.

They are like grapes full of poison. They are angry all the time.

33 They make their wine from the poison of snakes.

34 I, the LORD, remember what their enemies have done.

35 I have authority over them. And I will make bad things happen to them because of what they have done. I will punish them.

The time will come when they will fall in front of their enemies.

It will soon be the day for their trouble. My plans will happen quickly.

36 The LORD will judge his people. He will be very kind to his servants.

He will save them when he sees them, weak and without help.

37 Then the LORD will say to them, "Think about the strong gods that you believed in.

38 You fed them with the best part of your gifts of food. You gave them good wine to drink. Let them help you now! Let them save you from your troubles!

39 Remember this: I, and I alone, am God. Other gods are false.

I kill and I give life. I have hurt you, but I can make you well again.

Nobody can stop what I am doing.

40 I am the God who lives for all time.

I raise my hand to heaven, which is my home. And I promise

41 to make my big knife sharp. I will use it to punish my enemies.

I will judge them. And I will make bad things happen to them again.

I will do this to everybody who hates me.

42 Their blood will drop from my arrows. My big knife will kill everyone who is against me.

This will be the blood of the dead people and of the slaves and of the enemy's leaders."

43 All you people in every country, be happy with God's people!

He will punish those who kill his servants. He will punish all his enemies.

But he will pay the price himself for all the bad things that his people have done.'

44 Moses came with Joshua, the son of Nun, and he spoke all the words of this song. And all the Israelites listened to them. 45 When Moses had finished speaking these words, 46 he said to all the people, 'Remember every word that I have said to you today. You must repeat them to your children. Tell them that they must obey all the words of this Law. 47 These words are not silly words. They are the most important things in your life. If you obey them, you will live for many years in the country across the Jordan. It will be your own country.'

Moses will die on Mount Nebo.

48 On the same day, the LORD said to Moses: 49 'Go to the Abarim mountains in the country called Moab and climb Mount Nebo. It is across from the city of Jericho. Look down at the country called Canaan. I am giving this country to Israel's people. It will be their country. 50 You will die on that mountain and join your ancestors. You will die like Aaron your brother. He died on Mount Hor and joined his ancestors. 51 This is because both of you failed to obey me in front of the Israelites. This happened at the waters of Meribah Kadesh, in the desert of Zin. You did not make my special word important among the Israelites. 52 So you will only see the country from far away. You cannot go into the country that I am giving to the Israelites.'

Chapter 33

The last words of Moses to the tribes of Israel

1 Before his death, Moses, the man who knew God so well, spoke these good words to all the Israelites. 2And he said:

'The LORD came from Mount Sinai. He shone like the sun over Edom.

He shone on his people from Mount Paran.

Thousands (1000s) of angels came with him, from the south, from the mountains.

In his right hand, there was a burning Law for them.

3 LORD, you love your people. You are careful about all those holy people who belong to you.

We pray to you. We worship you and we obey your words.

4 We obey your rules, which Moses gave to us.

They are the special gift that you gave to all the descendants of Jacob.

5 You became our king when the leaders of the people and all the tribes came together.

6 Cause the tribe of Reuben live for all time. And do not cause them to be only a few men.'

7 And Moses said about the tribe of Judah:

'LORD, listen to Judah when they ask for help. Bring them back to their own people.

They fight for themselves.

LORD, help them against their enemies.'

8 About the tribe of Levi he said:

'Your Urim and Thummim belong to your true servants, the Levites.

You checked them at Massah and you argued with them at the waters of Meribah.

9 Levi loved and obeyed you more than his parents, more than his brothers or his children.

He studied your words and your promise was very special to him.

10 The Levites teach your rules to Israel's people and your decrees to the sons of Jacob.

They offer powder that has a sweet smell to you, on your altar. And they put burnt-offerings on your altar.

11 LORD, make good things happen to them in everything that they do.

Make all their work give you pleasure.

Destroy all their enemies completely.'

12 About the tribe of Benjamin he said:

'The LORD loves this tribe. They will rest and be safe, near to him.

The LORD keeps them safe every day. He lives among them.'

13 About the tribe of Joseph he said:

'LORD, send good things to their country.

Send rain from the sky above,

and water from under the earth.

14 Make good fruit grow in their fields,

the best fruit of each season.

15 Send them good gifts from the mountains and the hills that are so old.

Make the hills full of good fruit.

16 Fill their country with everything that is good.

Make them very happy with the love of the LORD,

the God who lived in the burning bush.

Send all these good things to the tribe of Joseph,

the man who was special among his brothers.

17 Joseph is as strong as a bull. He has horns like a wild bull.

All the strong men from Ephraim and Manasseh are his horns!

With them, he attacks the people of other countries.

He pushes them to the edges of the world.'

18 About the tribe of Zebulun he said:

'Be happy, Zebulun, as you go out of your home.

Be happy, Issachar, in your home.

19 They ask foreign people to come to their mountain.

Then these people will offer the right gifts there.

They eat good things from the sea. They find special things in the sand.'

20 About the tribe of Gad he said:

'Happy is the man who makes Gad's land wider!

Gad lives there like a lion. He fights anyone who comes into his country.

21 He took the best part of the country for himself.

Moses gave to Gad's tribe the part that belongs to a leader.

When Israel's people came together, the tribe of Gad did good things.

They did what the LORD wanted. They judged in Israel in the way that he commanded.'

22 About the tribe of Dan he said:

'The tribe of Dan are like young lions. They jump out from Bashan and surprise their enemies.'

23 About the tribe of Naphtali he said:

'The LORD has been very kind to the tribe of Naphtali.

They are full of the good things that the LORD has given to them.

They will have all the land, as far as to the south of Lake Galilee.'

24 About the tribe of Asher he said:

'The LORD has given more good things to the tribe of Asher than to all the tribes.

Their brothers will say that they are very important.

They will be rich enough to bathe their feet in oil.

25 They will make the gates of their towns from iron and yellow metal.

They will always be strong.

26 Israelites, there is no god like your God.

He rides across the sky to help you.

He travels to you on the clouds, with great authority.

27 He is the God who has always been alive. He is the safe place where you can hide.

And his strong arms are always under you, to hold you.

He will send away your enemies in front of you.

He says to you, "Destroy them!"

28 So Israel's people will live alone safely. Their fountain of water is safe in a country that has corn and fresh wine. There, dew drops from the sky.

29 Israelites, how happy you are! There is no other nation like you.

The LORD himself has saved you from Egypt and from all your enemies.

He is like a strong wall in front of you. He is like a big, sharp knife against your enemies.

He helps you.

Your enemies will be very afraid of you. And you will destroy the special places where they pray to their gods.'

Chapter 34

The death of Moses

1 Then Moses climbed Mount Nebo. He went from the valley of Moab to the top of Mount Pisgah, across from the River Jordan. There, the LORD showed him the whole country, from Gilead to Dan.

2 He saw all the places that would belong to Naphtali, Ephraim, Manasseh and Judah. He saw all the land, as far as the Mediterranean Sea. 3 He saw the south part of Judah. He saw the valley from Zoar to Jericho. Jericho is the city of tall trees. 4 Then the LORD said to Moses, 'This is the country that I promised to Abraham, Isaac and Jacob. I told them that I would give it to their descendants. I have let you see it. But you will not cross over into it.'

5 And Moses, the servant of the LORD, died there in Moab. This happened as the LORD had said. 6 And the LORD buried him in a valley in Moab. This is near the town called Beth-Peor. But even today, no one knows the place where God buried him. 7 Moses was 120 years old when he died. But he could still see well and his body was still strong. 8 Then the Israelites wept for Moses for 30 days, in the valley of Moab. They wept until the time for them to weep and be sad was finished.

9 Then God filled Joshua, the son of Nun, with his own wise Spirit. Moses had already given his place as leader, to Joshua. So the Israelites listened to Joshua and they obeyed the LORD.

10 There has never been another prophet in Israel like Moses. The LORD spoke to him, face to face. 11 The LORD sent him to do strange and powerful things with great authority. He did these things in Egypt, to Pharaoh, to all his officers and to his whole country. 12 No other man has shown such powerful authority or done such great things. And Moses did these things in front of all the Israelites.

Going in to the land that God promised

Joshua

Introduction

The people of Israel (the Israelites, the sons of Jacob) had lived and walked for 40 years in desert places. All the grown men that God had brought out of Egypt had died. Moses had died, too. Now God had chosen Joshua to be their leader. He was one of the two men who had spoken the true words. He said that the land of Canaan was good. The other 10 men had been afraid of the big, strong men there (Numbers 14). God had promised to give the people the land of Canaan. They had not believed that God could give it to them. So, God made them stay in the desert. They stayed there until they died. But their children did not die. The name 'Joshua' means 'God saves'. The name 'Jesus' means the same in the Greek language.

The book of Joshua is like the books of Judges, Samuel and Kings. All these books tell how God saved and led his people. They tell the story of how God kept his promises to Israel.

Chapter 1

The Lord tells Joshua what to do

1 Moses, the man who had served the Lord, had died. Then the Lord spoke to Joshua, son of Nun, who had helped Moses. 2 'Moses, my servant, is dead. Now you and all these people must get ready to cross the river Jordan. You, the people of Israel, will go into the land that I am going to give you', he said. 3 'I have given you every part of the ground that you walk upon. I promised Moses that I would do this. 4 You will have all the land from the desert in the south to the mountains of Lebanon in the north. It will be from the river Euphrates to the Great Sea on the west. You will have all the land of the Hittite people. 5 No one can stop you from taking this land as long as you live. As I was with Moses, I will always be with you. I will never leave you alone.

6 Be strong and do not be afraid. You will lead these people to take the land. That is the land that I promised to give to their fathers. 7 Be strong and do not be afraid. Be careful to do all the things that Moses told you. Remember to do everything that he told you. Then everything will go well with you. You will win, everywhere you go.

8 You must keep on speaking about the words of God's law. Think about what it says, all the time. Then you will be careful to obey it.

Then you will help yourselves to do well, and to win. 9 Remember that I have told you to do this. So be strong and do not be afraid. Do not be weak but be brave. I, the Lord your God, will be with you, everywhere that you go.'

Joshua speaks to the Israelites

10 So Joshua spoke to the leaders of the people. 11 'Go through all the places where the people live', he said. 'Tell them to get food ready for a journey. In 3 days or less, you will cross the river Jordan to begin to take the land for yourselves. This is the land that the Lord, your God, is giving to you', Joshua said.

12 Moses had given land east of the Jordan to the tribes of Reuben, Gad and half the tribe of Manasseh. Then Joshua spoke to these tribes. 13 'Remember what Moses told you', he said. 'The Lord your God is giving you a rest. He has given you this land.' 14 Your wives, children and animals can stay in this land that Moses gave you, east of the Jordan. But your fighting men must cross the river, with their arms. They must go in front of their brother Israelites. You must help them 15 until the Lord gives them rest as he has given you. When all the other tribes are safe in the land, you may return to the land east of the Jordan. Moses gave this to you.'

16 'We will do whatever you tell us. And we will go everywhere that you send us', they answered Joshua. 17 'As we always obeyed Moses, so we will obey you. The Lord your God was with Moses. We only ask that the Lord will be with you too. 18 Someone might not agree with your word. He might not obey it. We will make sure that he dies. But be very strong and be brave. Do not be afraid.'

Chapter 2

Rahab helps two men of Israel

1 Then Joshua sent out two men from Shittim. He sent them in secret to see what the land was like. 'Go', he said, 'Look at all the country, and look well at the city of Jericho'. When they came to the city, they went into the house of Rahab. They stayed there. She was a woman who had men to stay with her.

2 People spoke to the king of Jericho, 'Look! Some of the people of Israel have come here tonight to see what our land is like', they said. 3 So the king of Jericho sent a message to Rahab. 'Bring out the men who are staying in your house. They have come to see what all our land is like!' he said.

4 But the woman had hidden the two men. 'Yes, some men did come to me. I did not know where they had come from', she said. 5 'When it was getting near the time to close the gate of the city, they left. I do not know where they went. If you go after them quickly, you may catch them.' 6 (But she had taken them up to the roof. She had hidden them under some plants that she was drying there.) 7 So the king's men went out to try to find the two Israelites. They went towards the place where people could cross the river Jordan. As soon as they had gone out, people shut the gate.

8 Rahab went up to the roof. She spoke to the men as they prepared to sleep. 9 'I know that the Lord God has given this land to you', she said to them. 'I know that we are all very frightened of you. Everyone living in this part of the world is very afraid. 10 We heard how you came out of Egypt. And the Lord dried up the Red Sea for you. And we heard what you did to Sihon and Og, the two kings of the Amorites. They lived east of the Jordan, and you destroyed them completely. 11 When we heard all this, we felt very weak. We were very frightened. This is because the Lord, your God, is God. He rules the heaven (the place where God lives) above and the earth beneath. 12 Now, please make me a promise. I have been kind to you. So, say that you will be kind to my family. As you believe in God, make your promise true. Give me something to show that you will keep your promise. 13 Show me that you will save the lives of my family. Save my mother, father, brothers and sisters, and all who belong to them. Please do not let anyone kill us.'

14 'We will give you your life if you save ours. Do not tell the king about us. When the Lord gives us this land we will keep our promise. We will be kind to you', the men said to her.

15 So Rahab put a rope out of the window. (The house that she lived in was part of the city wall.) The men climbed down the rope.

16 'Go to the hills', she told them. 'The men who are looking for you will not find you there. Hide there for 3 days until they return here. Then you can go back to your people.'

17 'We will keep the promise that we have given to you', the men said to her. 18 'This is what you must do. Tie this red rope in the window that we came through. Do this when we come to take your city. Get your father, mother, brothers and sisters and all your family into your house. 19 If anyone goes out into the street, he may die. That will be his own bad mistake. And you will know that we kept our promise. But if anyone in the house with you dies, then we should be punished. 20 It would be different if you told anyone about this. Then we would not have to keep the promise that we have given you.' 21 Rahab agreed with the men, and sent them away. When they had gone, she tied the red rope in her window.

22 The two Israelites went into the hills and hid there. The king's men looked everywhere for them for 3 days. They did not find them, so they returned to Jericho. 23 Then the two men came down from the hills and crossed the river Jordan. They went to Joshua. They told him everything that had happened. 24 'We are sure that the Lord has given us the whole country. All the people there are very frightened of us', they said.

Chapter 3

The people cross the Jordan

1 Early in the morning, Joshua and all the Israelites left the city of Shittim. They put their tents by the river Jordan. They waited to cross the river. 2 Three days later, their leaders went to every tent. 3 'You will see the priests carrying the ark of God's promise', they said to the people. 'Then you must carry your tents and follow them. 4 They will show you the way to go because you have never been here before. But stay about 1000 metres behind the ark. Do not go near it.

5 Joshua told the people to make themselves holy and ready for the Lord. 'Tomorrow the Lord will do great things that will surprise you completely', he said.

6 'Take up the ark, and go in front of the people', Joshua said to the priests. So, they picked it up, and went on in front of the people.

7 And the Lord spoke to Joshua. 'Today I will begin to make you look important in front of all the people of Israel', he said. 'I was with Moses. And they will know that I am with you too. 8 The priests that are carrying the ark will reach the edge of the river Jordan. Tell them, "Go and stand in the river" '.

9 Joshua said to the Israelites, 'Come here and listen to the words of the Lord your God. 10 Your God is alive. He is going to show you that he is with you. He will show you how powerful he is. He will certainly push the Canaanites, Hittites, Hivites, Perizzites, Girgashites, Amorites and Jebusites from this land. 11 See the ark of the Lord of all the earth go into the Jordan in front of you. 12 Now choose 12 men, one from each tribe of Israel. 13 The priests are carrying the ark of promise of the Lord of all the earth. As soon as their feet go into the water of the river, the Lord will stop its water from coming towards them. Instead, the water will rise up like a wall.'

14 So the priests carrying the ark went in front of the people towards the river. 15 There was a lot of water coming down the river at that time of the year. But as soon as the priests carrying the ark went into the river, 16 the water stopped coming. It stopped a long way up the river, at a town called Adam near Zarethan. The water going down to the Salt Sea stopped completely. So, the people crossed the river near Jericho. 17 While the people walked across on dry ground, the priests carrying the ark stood still in the middle of the Jordan. They stood there until all the people had crossed.

Chapter 4

1 When all the people of Israel had crossed the Jordan, the Lord spoke to Joshua. 2 'Choose 12 men from the people, one from each tribe', he said. 3 'Tell them to take up 12 stones from the middle of the Jordan. Take them from where the priests are standing. Carry the stones over with you. Put them down where you stay tonight.'

4 So Joshua called the 12 men that he had chosen, one from each Israelite tribe. 5 He said to them, 'Go in front of the ark of the Lord into the middle of the Jordan.

Each of you must pick up a stone and put it on his shoulder. There will be one stone for each of the tribes of Israel. 6 This will be like a special mark for you. In years to come, your children will ask you, "What do these stones mean?" 7 Then you will tell them that the waters of the river Jordan stopped moving. That was while the ark of God's promise went across the river. These stones will help the people of Israel to remember this for ever.'

8 So the 12 men obeyed Joshua. They took 12 stones from the middle of the Jordan as the Lord had told Joshua. There was one stone for each tribe of Israel. They carried the stones to the place where the people had put their tents. And they put the stones down. 9 Joshua also put 12 stones from the Jordan in the middle of the Jordan, in the place where the priests with the ark had stood. (The stones were still there when people wrote this.) 10 The priests stood in the middle of the Jordan. Then people did everything as the Lord had told Joshua. The Lord had spoken to Joshua as he had spoken to Moses.

The people crossed the river quickly. 11 As soon as everybody was on the other side, the priests took the ark to the other side, too. The people saw them. 12 The tribes of Reuben, Gad and half the tribe of Manasseh led the people, ready to fight, as Moses had told them. 13 About 40 000 men, ready to fight, crossed to the flat land near Jericho.

14 This is what the Lord did that day. It made all the people think that Joshua was a great man. They gave him honour all his life, as they had honoured Moses.

15 Then the Lord spoke again to Joshua. 16 'Tell the priests carrying the ark to come up out of the Jordan.'

17 So Joshua said to the priests, 'Come up out of the Jordan.' 18 And the priests came up out of the river. They were carrying the ark of the Lord. As soon as their feet touched the dry ground, the waters of the Jordan began to return. There was much water and it moved fast.

19 The people went from the Jordan and put their tents at Gilgal on the 10th day of the first month. Gilgal was a city on the east side of Jericho. 20 At Gilgal, Joshua put the 12 stones that they had taken out of the Jordan. 21 He said to the people of Israel, 'Your children will ask, in later years, "What do these stones mean?" 22 Then you must tell them, "Israel went across the river Jordan on dry ground." 23 The Lord your God made the river dry up as he made the Red Sea dry up. He dried the Sea. Then the people could cross it when they left Egypt. 24 He did this so that all the peoples of the world would see how powerful he was. He did it so that you would always fear the Lord, your God.'

Chapter 5

Circumcision at Gilgal

1 All the Amorite kings west of the Jordan, and all the Canaanite kings heard how the Lord had dried up the Jordan. And how the Lord had kept it dry until all the Israelites had crossed to the other side. Then the kings became very afraid, and felt too weak to fight with the Israelites.

2 The Lord spoke to Joshua at that time. 'Make knives of stone and circumcise the men', he said. 3 So Joshua made the knives and circumcised them at Gibeath Haaraloth.

4 All the men who came out of Egypt had died. So Joshua did this. All the men old enough to fight had died in the desert on the way to Canaan. 5 All the people who came out of Egypt had been circumcised. But all the people born in the desert coming from Egypt had not been circumcised. 6 The Israelites had walked about in the desert for 40 years. But all the men who were old enough to fight when they left Egypt had died. This happened because they had not obeyed the Lord. The Lord had made a promise. He had promised to give them the land. But he said that they would certainly not see it. The land would feed their sheep and give other good food, too. 7 Joshua circumcised the sons of the men who had died.

8 All of them were circumcised. Then they stayed there until they were better again. 9 The Lord said to Joshua, 'You are no longer slaves to the people of Egypt. Today I have saved you from being ashamed of this.'

So, the place was called Gilgal and it still has that name. (Gilgal means 'taken away'.)

10 The Israelite people kept the 'feast of Passover' on the evening of the 14th month. They did this while they were at Gilgal, near the city of Jericho. 11 The next day they ate food grown in Canaan for the first time. They ate dry seed and flat bread. 12 The 'manna' stopped falling at the same time, so they did not have it any more. After that time they only ate food that was grown in Canaan.

13 While Joshua was near Jericho, a man appeared, standing in front of him. The man had a sword (a sharp metal stick to fight with) in his hand. Joshua went up to him, 'Are you one of our soldiers, or an enemy?' he asked.

14 'I am neither', he answered. 'I am here as the captain of the Lord's army.'

Joshua fell on the ground to worship and said, 'I am your servant. Lord, what can I do for you?'

15 The captain of the Lord's army said, 'Take your shoes off. You are standing on holy ground.' And Joshua did take off his shoes.

Chapter 6

The fall of Jericho city

1 The people of Jericho kept their gates shut. They watched to see that the Israelites did not get in. No one could go in or out of the city. 2 'I am going to give you Jericho', the Lord said to Joshua. 'I will give you its king and all its brave soldiers. 3 You and all your soldiers must march round the city once each day, for 6 days. 4 Seven (7) priests will walk in front of the ark. They will carry trumpets as they walk. On the 7th day, you and your soldiers must march round the city 7 times. At the same time the priests will blow their trumpets. 5 Then they will make one long loud noise. As soon as you hear this, all the men must give a loud shout. The city walls will fall down. Then the whole army will go straight into the city.' 6 Joshua called the priests. 'Take the ark of God's promise, and make 7 other priests walk in front of it, carrying trumpets', he said to them. 7 He told the people to start marching round the city, with a group of fighting men going in front of the ark.

8 Joshua finished speaking to the people. Then the 7 priests carrying the 7 trumpets went blowing their trumpets. And the priests carrying the ark followed them. 9 Some strong fighting men went in front of the priests with the trumpets, and another group of soldiers followed the ark. The trumpets were blowing all this time. 10 But Joshua had said to the people, 'Do not shout or make a noise. Do not say a word until I tell you to shout. I will tell you to shout one day, then shout!' 11 Joshua made them carry the ark round the city once. Then they returned to their tents, and slept there that night.

12 Joshua got up early the next morning, and the priests took up the ark of the Lord. 13 The 7 priests carrying the trumpets marched in front of the ark, blowing the trumpets. The groups of soldiers went in front of the priests blowing the trumpets, and behind the ark. The priests blew the trumpets all the time. 14 This is how they marched round the city on the second day. They did this once and returned to their tents. They did this for 6 days.

15 On the 7th day they got up at dawn and marched round the city in the same way, but for 7 times. 16 The 7th time, the priests made a long, loud noise on the trumpets. Joshua told the people, 'Shout! Because the Lord has given you the city. 17 The city and all that is in it belongs to the Lord. All the people must die. Only Rahab and the people with her in her house will live. This is because she hid our two men. 18 Keep away from the things that belong to God. If you take any of them, you will die. You would make trouble for the people of Israel, and could cause the Lord to destroy them, too. 19 All the things made of silver, gold and iron and mixed metals are holy to the Lord. They must be stored with his valuable things.'

20 When the trumpets made their loud sound, all the people gave a great shout. When they did this, the walls fell down. Every man went up into the city. And they took the city. 21 They gave the city to the Lord. So they destroyed every living thing in it. They killed men and women, young and old people, cows, sheep and other animals.

22 Joshua spoke to the two men that Rahab had hidden. 'Go into her house. Bring her out with all who are with her', he said. 'This is what you promised to her.'

23 So the young men who had been to look at the city went and brought out Rahab and her whole family. They brought out her father and mother and brothers and all who belonged to her. They gave them a place outside the Israelite tents.

24 Then they burned the whole city and everything in it. They put the gold, silver, iron and metal things into the Lord's store of valuable things. 25 But Joshua saved Rahab and her family and all who belonged to her. Joshua had sent to find out about the city. And Rahab had hidden those men. She still lives among the Israelites.

26 At that time, Joshua made this serious promise.
'The Lord will punish the man who builds this city again', he said. 'When he starts to build, his oldest son will die. His youngest son will die when he puts up its gates.'

27 So the Lord was with Joshua, and people all over the land heard all about him..

Chapter 7

The sin of Achan

1 The people of Israel did not do as God had told them through Joshua. Achan, son of Carmi, son of Zimri, son of Zerah of the tribe of Judah, did not obey God. He took some of the things that belonged to God. So God was very angry with the people of Israel.

2 Now Joshua had sent men from Jericho to Ai. This is a city near to Beth Aven, and east of Bethel. He said to them, 'Go up and look at the land near there, in secret.' So, the men went to see what they could find out.

3 The men came and spoke to Joshua. 'There are not many men there. Do not make all the people tired. 2000 or 3000 men should be enough to take the city.' 4 So about 3000 men went up to Ai. But the men of Ai made them run away. 5 And the men of Ai killed about 36 of the Israelites. They ran after the Israelites from the gate of the city to the place where they cut stone for building. They killed them as they ran over the hill. When the people of Israel heard this, they were very frightened. They felt very weak.

6 Joshua tore his clothes to show that he was very sad. He fell with his face to the ground in front of the ark of the Lord. He stayed there until it began to get dark. The people's leaders did the same, and put dirt on their heads. 7 'Lord, ruler of all, why did you ever bring this group of people over the Jordan?' said Joshua. 'Did you want the Amorites to destroy us? We might have been happy if we had stayed on the other side of the Jordan! 8 Lord, what can I say now that the enemies of Israel have won the fight? 9 The Canaanites and other tribes who live here will hear about this. They will come round us and kill us all. No one will give honour to your name.' 10 The Lord said to Joshua, 'Stand up! Why are you lying on the ground? 11 Israel has sinned. They have not kept their promise. They did not do what I told them. I said that they must destroy everything that was not gold or silver or metal. They have taken some of these things. They took them. Then they said that they had not taken anything. They have hidden them with their own things. 12 That is why
the Israelites cannot stand against their enemies. They run away from their enemies now. The Israelites have sinned and their enemies can destroy them. You must destroy everything that I told you to destroy. If you do not, then I will not be with you any more.'

13 'Get up. Tell the people to make themselves clean. Get ready for tomorrow when you will meet with me. I, the Lord God of Israel say this, "Israel, you have kept some of the things that I told you to destroy. You will not win the fight against your enemies until you have destroyed these things!" 14 So tell them that in the morning they will come before me, one tribe at a time. I will choose one tribe to come in front. The groups of that tribe will come before me, family by family. I will choose a family. Then the men of that family will come before me, one by one. 15 I will choose the man who has taken the things. Then you will burn him with the things that he has taken. You are to burn him and all that he has and all his family. He has caused great trouble to Israel. He made them ashamed, because he did not obey me.'

16 Early the next morning, Joshua made the tribes come in front of him, tribe by tribe. The Lord chose the tribe of Judah. 17 Groups of the tribe of Judah came in front of him, and the Lord chose the group of Zerah. Families of the Zerahites came in front of him, and the Lord chose the family of Zimri.

18 Joshua made each man of the family of Zimri come in front of him, and the Lord chose Achan, son of Carmi, son of Zimri, son of Zerah, of the tribe of Judah.

19 Then Joshua spoke to Achan. 'My son', he said, 'give honour to the Lord, the God of Israel. Tell me what you have done. Do not hide it from me.' 20 Achan replied, 'It is true! I have sinned against the Lord, the God of Israel. This is what I have done. 21 I found a beautiful coat from Babylon and about two kilos of silver and a gold bar that weighed half a kilo. I wanted them so much that I took them. They are in the ground under my tent, with the silver under the other things.' 22 So Joshua sent people with a message. They ran to the tent. They found the things that Achan had hidden. The silver was under them. 23 They took the things from the tent and brought them to Joshua and the other Israelites. They put them all before the Lord.

24 Then Joshua and all the people took Achan, the son of Zerah, and the coat, the gold and the silver to the valley of Achor ('Achor' means trouble). With him, they took his sons, daughters, cows, sheep and other animals and all that he had. 25 Joshua said, 'Why did you cause us so much trouble? The Lord will give you trouble today!' Then all Israel threw big stones at him until he died. They killed his family and his animals with him. They also burnt his family and all that he had. 26 They put many big stones over him that are still there. That is why the place is still called 'Trouble Valley'. Then the Lord was not angry any more.

Chapter 8

They destroyed Ai

1 Then the Lord spoke again. 'Do not be afraid. Do not think that you are weak', he said to Joshua. 'Take the whole army with you and go to attack Ai. I will give the king and all his people and the city and its land to you. 2 You must destroy the city and its king as you did Jericho and its king. But this time you may take their good things and all their animals for yourselves. Hide some of your men behind the city.' 3 So Joshua and the whole army moved out to attack Ai. He chose 30 000 of the best fighting men and sent them off by night. 4 'Listen with great care', he said. 'You are to go and hide behind the city. Stay near to it. Be sure to stay awake! 5 I will march towards the city with all the other soldiers. The men will come out of the city to fight us, as they did before. Then we will run away. 6 They will run after us, until we have gone from the city. They will say, "They are running away from us, as they did before". So, when we run from them, 7 you must get out from your hiding place. You will take the city. The Lord your God will give it to you. 8 When you have taken the city, start to burn it. Do what the Lord has told you. See that you obey my words.'

9 Then Joshua sent the men off. They went to wait and hide to the west of Ai, between Bethel and Ai. But Joshua stayed with the people that night.

10 Early the next morning, Joshua took all the men together to march towards Ai. He and the leaders of Israel went in front. 11 The whole army marched up to the city and stopped in front of it. They put their tents north of Ai. They left a valley between them and the city. 12 Joshua had hidden about 5000 men to the west of the city, between Bethel and Ai. 13 All the soldiers took their places, ready to fight. Some were north of the city, by their tents. And other soldiers were hiding to the west of the city. That night Joshua went into the valley.

14 When the king of Ai saw Joshua's men, the king and his men hurried out of the city. It was early in the morning. They wanted to meet Israel at the same place as before.

And they wanted to fight Israel there.

But the king of Ai did not know that there were Israelite soldiers hidden behind the city. 15 Joshua and his army let the men of Ai push them back, and they ran towards the desert. 16 The king told all the men of Ai to run after them. So they ran after Israel and away from their city. 17 Not one man remained in Ai or Bethel. They all ran after the Israelite soldiers.

18 Then the Lord spoke to Joshua. The Lord said, 'Hold out the throwing stick (a long sharp stick called a 'javelin') that is in your hand. Point it towards Ai. I will give the city to you.' So Joshua held out his throwing stick towards Ai. 19 As soon as he did this, the men hiding behind the city came out at once. They quickly ran into the city. They took it and immediately made it burn.

20 The men of Ai looked back and saw smoke rise over the city. But they could not run away. The Israelites who had been running away had turned to fight them. 21 Joshua and his army had seen that they had taken the city. The men that he had hidden had taken it. Joshua's army saw the smoke from the burning city. So they turned round and began to fight the men of Ai. 22 The Israelites in the city then came down to join the fight. The men of Israel were all round the men of Ai. They killed all the men of Ai. Nobody could run away. 23 The only person that they did not kill was the king of Ai. They took him to Joshua.

24 The Israelites killed all the men in the desert and fields where they had run from the fight. Then they went back to Ai and killed everyone there. 25 All the men and women of Ai died on that day. 12 000 people died then. 26 Joshua had kept pointing his throwing stick at Ai until his army had killed every person who lived there. 27 But the Israelites took the good things and the animals for themselves, as the Lord had told Joshua. 28 Joshua burnt the city and broke it down. It is still like that today. 29 He hanged the king of Ai on a tree and left his body there until evening. At sunset, Joshua told them to cut the body down and throw it in front of the city gate. They covered it with many stones. These stones are still there today.

Joshua reads the Lord's law to the people

30 Then Joshua built an altar on Mount Ebal, to the Lord, the God of Israel ('Mount' is another name for mountain). 31 He made it as Moses had told the Israelites. Moses, the Lord's servant, had written this in a book. This book, the Law of Moses, told him how it should be made. 'The altar must be made of stones that had not been cut with iron tools.' They burnt animals on it to worship the Lord. And they burnt other animals, as 'fellowship offerings' to the Lord. 32 The Israelites watched Joshua as he made a copy of the Law of Moses on the stones. This was the Law that Moses had written. 33 All the Israelites stood on the two sides of the ark, with their faces towards the priests who carried it. The leaders, officers, and judges were there, and the foreign people were with them, too. Half the people stood with their backs to Mount Gerizim. The other half stood with their backs to Mount Ebal. This is how the Lord's servant, Moses had told them to stand (Deuteronomy 11:29). 'Stand like this when I am asking the Lord to give you his blessing', he had said. 34 Then Joshua read the whole Law aloud to them. He read the blessings and the curses, as they are written in the book of the Law. Moses had told him how to bless the people of Israel. 35Joshua read every word to the people of Israel. Moses had told him what to read. Joshua read it to the whole people, including the women, children and the foreign people who lived with them.

Chapter 9

The people of Gibeon tell a lie to Joshua and save their lives

1 When all the kings who lived west of the Jordan heard about these things, they joined together. They were the kings in the hills to the west, and all the places near the Great Sea, as far as Lebanon. (They were the kings of the Hittites, Amorites, Canaanites, Perizzites, Hivites and Jebusites.) 2 They joined together to fight Joshua and Israel.

3 The people of Gibeon heard about what Joshua had done to Jericho and Ai. 4 So they had a clever idea. Some of their men put old bags of food and broken and mended skins of wine (a drink) on their donkeys (animals like small horses for carrying things). 5 They had old mended shoes on their feet, and they wore old clothes. The bread that they took for food was dry. It was going bad. 6 Then they went to Joshua in the camp at Gilgal. They spoke to him and to the men of Israel. 'We have come from a land a long way away', they said. 'Please let us make a promise not to fight each other.'

7 But the men of Israel answered the Hivites, 'Perhaps you live close to us. How then can we make a promise not to destroy you?'

8 'We want to serve you', they said to Joshua.

'Who are you? Where do you come from?' Joshua asked.

9 They answered, 'Your servants have come from a country a very long way away. We heard about your great God. We have heard all about the things that he did in Egypt. 10 And we heard what he did to the two kings of the Amorites. Those kings ruled cities east of the Jordan. They were Sihon, king of Heshbon, and Og, king of Bashan. They ruled in Ashtaroth.

11 Our leaders and the people of our land told us to come to see you. Our leaders said, "Take food and wine (a drink) for your journey. Go to meet them, and speak to them. Say to them, 'We want to serve you, will you promise not to destroy us?' " 12 This bread of ours was warm when we put it in our bags. That was on the day that we left home to come to you. But see how bad and dry it has become. 13 And these skins of wine (a drink) were new, but see how old and mended they are. And our clothes are now old, and our shoes are very thin and mended. They have become old as we made our long journey.'

14 The men of Israel looked at the food and other things, but they did not ask the Lord for help. 15 Then Joshua agreed that they would not kill the people of Gibeon. The leaders of Israel also said that they would keep Joshua's promise.

16 So Joshua and the Israelites made a promise to the Gibeonites. Three days later, the Israelites learnt that the Gibeonites lived near to them. 17 The Israelites left their camp to go to the cities of Gibeon. Three days later, they came to their cities: Gibeon, Kephirah, Beeroth and Kiriath Jearim. 18 The Israelites did not attack them, because of the promise that their leaders had made. They had said to the Lord God of Israel that they would not kill the Gibeonites.

All the people of Israel were angry with their leaders. 19 The leaders said to them, 'We have promised the Lord, the God of Israel, and now we cannot hurt them. 20 But this is what we will do. We will let them live, so that God will not punish us for breaking our promise. 21 Let them live, but make them cut wood and carry water for us', they said. This is how the leaders kept their promise to the Gibeonites.

22 Joshua told the Gibeonites to come to him. 'Why did you tell me those lies? You said that you lived a long way from us. But you really live near to us', he said. 23 'Now you will be punished. You will always be our servants. You will cut wood and carry water for the people of our God.'

24 They answered Joshua, 'The Lord your God had told Moses to give you the whole land. We had heard that clearly. He told you that you must kill all the people who lived there in front of you. So, we were afraid that you would kill us. That is why we did as we did. 25 You must decide what to do with us. Do what you think is right and good.'

26 So Joshua did not let the Israelites kill the Gibeonites, and the Israelites let them live. 27 They made the Gibeonites cut wood and fetch water for them. And they would do this for the altar of the Lord, at the place that the Lord would tell them. They are still doing this.

Chapter 10

The sun stands still

1 The king of Jerusalem, Adoni-Zedek, heard what Joshua had done to Ai and to Jericho and to their kings. He heard that Joshua had destroyed them. He also heard that Israel had promised not to kill the people of Gibeon. They lived near to Joshua. 2 The king and his people were very afraid, because Gibeon was an important city. It was like a king's city and bigger than Ai. All its men fought well. 3 So Adoni-Zedek, king of Jerusalem, asked some other kings to come with him to attack Gibeon. They were Hoham, king of Hebron, Piram, king of Jarmuth, Japhia, king of Lachish and Debir, king of Eglon. 4 Adoni-Zedek said to them, 'Gibeon has promised not to fight Joshua and the Israelites. Please help me to attack Gibeon.'

5 Then the 5 kings of the Amorites joined together. They were the kings of Jerusalem, Hebron, Jarmuth, Lachish and Eglon. They took their soldiers near to Gibeon, and attacked it.

6 Then the Gibeonites sent a message to Joshua in the camp at Gilgal. 'Do not leave us alone. Come quickly and save us. All the Amorite kings from the hills have joined to attack us. We need your help', they said.

7 So Joshua marched his whole army up from Gilgal. He included all his best fighting men.

8 The Lord said to Joshua, 'Do not be afraid of them. I will see that you win the fight. I will not let one of them stand against you.'

9 They marched all night from Gilgal, and Joshua surprised his enemies. 10 The Lord made the enemies confused when they saw Israel. Israel won a great fight at Gibeon. Israel ran after their enemies on the road to Beth Horon. Israel went on killing them all the way to Azekah and Makkedah. 11 The Lord sent stones of hard water on them from the sky as they ran from Beth Horon to Azekah. The Lord killed more men with these stones than the Israelites killed in the fight.

12 Joshua stood in front of Israel and spoke to the Lord on that day. It was the day that he gave them power over the Amorites. Joshua spoke to the Lord and said, 'Sun stand still over Gibeon. Moon stand over the valley of Aijalon.'

13 So the sun stood still and the moon stopped until Israel had punished its enemies. People wrote about this in the book of Jashar.

The sun stopped in the middle of the sky, and did not go down for about a whole day. 14 The Lord has never listened to a man like this before or since that day. The Lord must have been fighting for Israel!

15 Then Joshua and all Israel went back to the camp at Gilgal.

The Israelites kill the 5 Amorite kings

16 Now the 5 kings had run away. They had hidden in a hole in the hill at Makkedah. 17 Joshua heard that they were hiding there. 18 He said to his men, 'Cover the front of the hole with big stones. And put some men there to keep them safe. 19 But do not stop. Go on running after your enemies. Attack them from behind, and do not let them reach their cities. Remember that the Lord, your God has promised to give you power over them.'

20 So Joshua and the Israelites destroyed all of them. Nearly every one died. But the few who were alive reached their strong cities. 21 The whole army returned to Joshua in the camp at Makkedah. All the people in the land were too afraid to say anything bad about the Israelites.

22 Then Joshua said, 'Take away the stones from the hole in the hill. Bring the 5 kings out to me.' 23 So they brought out the kings. They were the kings of Jerusalem, Hebron, Jarmuth, Lachish and Eglon. 24 They brought the kings to Joshua, and he told the men of Israel to come to him. 'Put your feet on the necks of the kings', he said to the officers who had come with him. They did as he told them.

25 Joshua said to them, 'Do not be afraid. Be very strong and brave. This is what the Lord will do to all the enemies that you are going to fight.' 26 Then he hit and killed the kings. The Israelites hung the dead kings on 5 trees until the evening.

27 At sunset, Joshua told his men to take the kings down from the trees. 'Throw them into the hole in the hill where they were hiding', he said. They put big stones over the front of the hole, and they are still there.

28 That day Joshua attacked Makkedah and took it, with its king. He destroyed everyone in it. He did not leave anyone alive. He did to the king of Makkedah what he had done to the king of Jericho.

Joshua attacks cities in the south

29 After this, Joshua and his army went on from Makkedah to Libnah, and attacked it. 30 The Lord gave them power over that city and its king. Joshua destroyed the city and everyone in it. He did not leave anyone alive. They did to the king as they had done to the king of Jericho.

31 After this, Joshua and all the Israelites went on from Libnah to Lachish. They attacked it from all sides. 32 The Lord gave them power over Lachish. And Joshua took the city on the 2nd day. They left no one alive, as they had done at Libnah. They killed everyone in the city. 33 King Horam of Gezer came to help Lachish. But Joshua fought and destroyed him and his army. He killed them all.

34 Then Joshua and his army went from Lachish to Eglon. They went round it and attacked it. 35 They took it on the same day. They killed everyone in that city, as they had at Lachish.

36 After this, Joshua and his army went from Eglon to Hebron in the hills. They attacked 37 and took it. They killed the king and all the people there, and the people in the towns near to it. Joshua destroyed the whole city, as he had done to Eglon. He did not leave anyone alive.

38 Then Joshua and his army went back to Debir and attacked it. 39 He attacked it and took it with all the towns near to it. They killed everyone there. Joshua did to Debir and its king what he had done to Hebron and to Libnah and its king.

40 So Joshua took the whole land. He took the hill country, the hills of the east and the west and the dry country in the south. He took them with their kings. He killed all the people who lived there. He did not leave anyone alive. The Lord God of Israel had told him to do this. 41 Joshua had fought from Kadesh Barnea in the south to Gaza near the sea. This included all of Goshen as far as Gibeon in the north. 42 Joshua won this long list of fights with all these kings and their cities. He won them because the Lord, the God of Israel, was fighting for Israel. 43 After this, Joshua and his army went back to the camp at Gilgal.

Chapter 11

Joshua fights with Jabin and other kings

1 Jabin, king of Hazor, heard what had happened. So, he sent messengers (people with a message) to Jobab, king of Madon, and to the kings of Shimron and of Acshaph. 2 And he sent to the kings of the mountains in the north, in the Arabah, south of Kinnereth. And he sent messengers to the little hills in the west, and Naphoth Dor on the west. 3 Messengers went to the Canaanites in the east and in the west. They went to the Amorites, Hittites, Perizzites and Jebusites in the hills. And he sent them to the Hivites who lived by Hermon near Mizpah. 4 All these kings came with their soldiers and many horses and chariots. It was a great big army. The soldiers were as many as there are bits of sand by the sea. 5 The kings all joined together and made a camp by the Waters of Merom. They wanted to fight against Israel.

6 'Do not be afraid of them', the Lord said to Joshua. 'I will give you all of them. You will kill them all by this time tomorrow. You must cut the backs of the horses' legs, and burn the chariots.'

7 So Joshua and all his army went to fight them at the Waters of Merom. They quickly attacked them 8 and the Lord helped the Israelites to win the fight. Israel ran after them as far as Sidon, Misrephoth Maim and the valley of Mizpah. They went east until they had killed all their enemies. 9 Joshua did to them as the Lord had said. He cut the backs of the legs of the horses and burnt their chariots.

10 Then Joshua went back and took Hazor. He killed its king. (Hazor had been most important kingdom over all the kingdoms who were against Israel.) 11 The Israelites killed everyone who lived there. They killed everything in the city that was alive. They burned the city and destroyed it.

12 Joshua took all these cities and killed all their kings. He destroyed them all, as God's servant Moses had told him to do. 13 But Israel did not burn all the cities built on small hills, except Hazor. Joshua did burn this one. 14 The Israelites took all the animals and good things from the cities, but killed all the people. They did not let one of them live, but destroyed them all. 15 The Lord told Moses what to do. Then Moses told Joshua what the Lord had said. Joshua did what Moses told him to do. Joshua did not forget anything. He did everything that the Lord had told Moses.

16 So Joshua took all these places. He took the hills, the dry country in the south, all of Goshen and the little hills in the west. He took the Arabah and the mountains and hills of Israel. 17 These were from Mount Halak near Seir to Baal Gad in the valley of Lebanon, below Mount Hermon. He took all their kings and killed them all. 18 Joshua was fighting these kings for a very long time. 19 He only left alive the Hivites living in Gibeon, because he had made them a promise. 20 The Lord had made all the peoples want to fight Israel. This was so that the Lord could destroy them all. He did not let them live. This was what the Lord had told Moses. 21 Joshua went at that time to fight the Anakites from the hills. They came from Hebron, Debir and Anab and all the hills of Judah and Israel. Joshua destroyed them all, and all their towns. 22 He killed all the Anakites in Israel, except for a few in Gaza, Gath and Ashdod. 23 So Joshua took the whole country, as the Lord had told Moses. The Lord gave the country to Israel to live in. Joshua gave each tribe its own part.

Then the people did not have to fight any more.

Chapter 12

List of kings that Israel had already destroyed

1 Israel killed these kings. They destroyed them and took their land. It was east of the Jordan, from the Arnon valley to Mount Hermon. All of it was on the east side of the Arabah.

2 Sihon, king of the Amorites, was king of Heshbon. He ruled from Aroer by the middle of the Arnon valley to the Jabbok River. This is near the land of the Ammonites. It included half of Gilead. 3 Sihon ruled the east of the Arabah from the sea of Kinnereth to the sea of the Arabah (the Salt Sea). And he ruled as far as Beth Jeshimoth and to where Mount Pisgah begins.

4 Og, king of Bashan, was one of the last Rephaites. He ruled in Ashtaroth and Edrei. 5 And he ruled Mount Hermon, Salecah and all of Bashan as far as Geshur and Maacah. He ruled the half of Gilead to the edge of Sihon's kingdom of Heshbon.

6 Moses, the servant of the Lord, and the Israelites won the fight with these kings. He gave their land to the tribes of Reuben, Gad and half the tribe of Manasseh to live in.

7 Joshua and the Israelites killed these kings on the west side of the Jordan. They ruled from Baal Gad in the Lebanon valley to Mount Halak, which is near Seir. (Joshua gave each tribe a special part of the land.)8 This was in the hills and in the little hills in the west. And they ruled the Arabah, the sides of the mountains, and the desert and the Negev. They ruled all the land that had belonged to the Hittites, Amorites, Canaanites, Perizzites, Hivites and Jebusites. 9 They took the land of the kings of Jericho, Ai (near Bethel), 10 Jerusalem, Hebron, 11 Jarmuth and Lachish. 12 And they took the land of the kings of Eglon, Gezer, 13 Debir, Geder, 14 Hormah, Arad, 15 Libnah, Adullam, 16 Makkedah and Bethel. 17 And they took the land of the kings of Tappuah, Hepher, 18 Aphek, Lasharon, 19 Madon, Hazor, 20 Shimron Meron and Acshaph. 21 They also took Taanach, Megiddo, 22 Kedesh, Jokneam in Carmel, 23 Dor (in Naphoth Dor), Goyim in Gilgal, 24 and Tirzah. They took all the land of these 31 kings.

Chapter 13

The land that Israel had not yet taken

1 Joshua was very old and had lived for many years. The Lord said to him, 'You are old. There is still a lot of land that you have not taken. This is the land left for you to take. 2 There is all the land of the Philistines and Geshurites 3 and of the Avvim on the south. (The land from the Shihor river east of Egypt to the edge of Ekron's land on the north was part of Canaan. The Philistines lived in Gaza, Ashdod, Ashkelon, Gath and Ekron.) 4 You must take all the land of the Canaanites and Mearah, (which belonged to the people of Sidon). This is the land as far as Aphek, by the edge of the land of the Amorites. 5 You have to take the land of the Gebalites and all of Lebanon to the east. That is from Baal Gad below Mount Hermon to Lebo Hamath.'

6 The Lord said to Joshua, 'I, myself will push out the people of Sidon in front of the Israelites. They will leave the mountains of Lebanon as far as Misrephoth Maim. You must give this land to Israel, as I have told you. 7 Each of the 9 tribes, and the half tribe of Manasseh is to have its own part.'

How Joshua gave each tribe its own land

8 Moses had already given land to the Reubenites, Gadites and the other half of Manasseh. It was east of the Jordan, as Moses, the servant of God, had said.

9 It was from Aroer, on the edge of the Arnon valley and the town in the middle of the valley. It included all the flat land of Medeba to Dibon. 10 And it included all the towns of Sihon, king of the Amorites, who ruled in Heshbon. It went to the edge of the land of the Amorites. 11 It included the land of Gilead, and of the people of Geshur and Maacah. And it included all of Mount Hermon and Bashan as far as Salecah. 12(That was the kingdom of Og in Bashan.) Og had ruled Ashtaroth and Edrei. He was one of the last of the Rephaim (a group of very large people called giants). Moses had won a fight with them and had taken their land. 13 But the Israelites did not send away the people of Geshur and Maacah, so they still live there among the Israelites.

14 Moses had given no land to the tribe of Levi. This was because God had made them a promise. He had said that the other tribes must give them the burnt offerings made to the Lord God of Israel. This was the part for the Levites.

15 This is the part of the land that Moses gave to the families of the Reubenites.

16 He gave them the land from Aroer by the edge of the Arnon valley and the town in the middle of the valley. 17 And he gave them all of the flat land past Medeba in Heshbon. It included Dibon, Bamoth Baal, Beth Baal Meon, 18 Jahaz and Kedemoth. And it included Mephaath, 19 Kiriathaim, Sibmah and Zereth Shahar. Zereth was on a hill in the middle of the valley. 20 Moses gave Beth Peor, and the sides of Mount Pisgah and Beth Jeshimoth town to the tribe of Reuben. 21 And he gave them all the towns on the flat land. He gave them all the land of Sihon, king of the Amorites. Sihon had ruled from Hebron. But Moses had won the fight with him, and the Midianite kings, Evi, Rekem, Zur, Hur and Reba. These kings had lived in that place, and ruled with Sihon. 22 The Israelites had killed Balaam, son of Beor, when they had killed soldiers in the fight. He had wanted to help Balak to fight against Israel (Numbers 22). 23 The end of the land of the Reubenites was by the river Jordan. Moses gave these towns and their villages to the tribe of Reuben to live in, family by family.

24 This is the land that Moses gave to the tribe of Gad, family by family.

25 He gave them the land of Jazer, the towns of Gilead and half the land of the Ammonites. 26 This was from Heshbon to Ramah Mizpah and Betonim, and from Mahanaim to the land of Debir. 27 Moses gave Gad the towns in the valley: Beth Haram, Beth Nimrah, Succoth and Zaphon. He gave them the rest of the land of Sihon, king of Heshbon. (This was on the east of the Jordan, to the end of the sea of Kinnereth.) 28Moses gave these towns and villages to the tribe of Gad to live in, family by family.

29 This is the land that Moses gave to half the tribe of Manasseh. That is, half the families of the sons of Manasseh, family by family.

30 He gave them the land from Mahanaim, the land of Bashan, all the land ruled by Og, king of Bashan. It included all the 60 towns of Jair in Bashan. 31 And it included half of Gilead, Ashtaroth and Edrei. (These were the cities that belonged to Og in Bashan.) This was for half the sons of Makir, son of Manasseh, family by family.

32 Moses gave land to these tribes while he was in the flat land of Moab, east of Jericho. He was across the Jordan then. 33 Moses gave no land to the tribe of Levi. The Lord, the God of Israel, was their part. This is what he had promised to do for them.

Chapter 14

1 Eleazar the priest, Joshua son of Nun, and the leaders of the families of Israel chose different parts of the land for each tribe. This is how they did it. 2 The leaders used lots to decide which parts of the land God had chosen for each of the 9 and a half tribes left. This is what the Lord had told Moses to do. 3 Moses had already given the two and a half tribes land east of the river Jordan. But he had not given any land to the Levites. 4 (The tribe of Joseph was now two tribes, Manasseh and Ephraim.) The leaders gave the Levites towns to live in, with enough land near them to feed their animals. 5 The leaders of the Israelites gave a part of the land to each tribe, as the Lord had told Moses.

Joshua gives Hebron to Caleb

6 Some of the men of Judah came to Joshua at Gilgal. Caleb, son of Jephunneh, spoke to Joshua. He said, 'You know what God said to Moses the man of God, about you and me, at Kadesh Barnea. 7 I was 40 years old when he sent me from there to explore the land. And I brought him a report that was true, and I was sure that we could take the land. 8 The other men who went with us made the people afraid (Numbers 13:26-33). But I did only what the Lord wanted us to do. 9 So Moses made me a promise on that day. Moses said, "The land that your feet have walked on will always belong to you and to your children. This is because you have done everything as the Lord told you" ' (Deuteronomy 1:34-36).

10 Caleb said to Joshua, 'The Lord has kept me alive for the 45 years since Moses said this. Israel was walking about the desert for all this time. Now I am 85 years old.

11 I am still as strong as I was on the day that Moses sent me out. I can fight as well now as I could then. 12 Now then, give to me this hill country that the Lord promised to me. You heard that the Anakites were there then. And you heard that their cities were large and strong. But the Lord will help me to push them out. The Lord said that he would.'

13 Then Joshua asked the Lord to bless Caleb, son of Jephunneh. And he gave Hebron to him as his part of the land. 14 So Hebron has belonged to Caleb, son of Jephunneh, the Kenizzite since that day. He had done everything as the Lord had told him to do. So Joshua gave him the land. 15 (Hebron had been called 'Kiriath Arba' after Arba, the most important man among the Anakites.)

The fighting in the land ended after this.

Chapter 15

The tribe of Judah gets its land

1 Joshua gave the land from the edge of Edom to the Desert of Zin to the families of the tribe of Judah, family by family. The desert was at the south of the land.

2 The south edge of Judah's land was from the south end of the Salt Sea, 3 across the south side of the Scorpion valley, to Zin. He also gave them land south of Kadesh Barnea, as far as Hebron. The edge of their land continued past Addar, round to Karka 4 and to Azmon. The dry valley of Egypt leading to the sea was the south edge of Judah.

5 The Salt Sea was the edge of Judah to the east as far as the mouth of the river Jordan.

The north edge of Judah was from the mouth of the Jordan 6 to Beth Hoglah. Then it went north of Beth Arabah to the stone of Bohan. (Bohan was the son of Reuben.) 7 The edge of Judah's land went from the valley of Achor to Debir. Then it went north to Gilgal. Gilgal is opposite the path of Adummim on the south side of the valley. The edge of Judah then reached to the water springs of En Shemesh to En Rogel. 8 From there it went through the valley of Hinnom to the south side of a hill by the Jebusite city of Jerusalem. The edge of Judah continued to the top of the hill on the west side of the Hinnom valley. This was at the north end of the valley of Rephaim. 9 From there it went to the springs of Nephtoah and on to the cities near Mount Ephron. It went towards Baalah (or Kiriath Jearim). 10 From there it went round Baalah towards the hills of Edom. It went of Mount Jearim (or Kesalon) down to Beth Shemesh, and on past Timnah. 11 The edge of Judah went out to the hills north of Ekron, then towards Shikkeron. It went past Mount Baalah to Jabneel. The land of Judah ended at the sea. 12 The sea was the west edge of Judah's land.

The families of the tribe of Judah lived inside this land.

Caleb takes the cities of Hebron and Debir (Judges 1:11-15)

13 The Lord had told Joshua to give Caleb, son of Jephunneh, part of Judah's land. (He belonged to the tribe of Judah.) Joshua gave him Hebron, the city of Arba. Arba was the father of Anak. 14 Caleb pushed out the 3 sons of Anak from Hebron. Their names were Sheshai, Ahiman and Talmai. 15 From there he marched to fight the people of Debir (also called Kiriath Sepher). 16 Caleb said, 'If a man attacks and takes Kiriath Sepher, he can marry my daughter, Acsah.' 17 Othniel was the son of Caleb's brother, Kenaz. He took Kiriath Sepher, so Caleb gave him his daughter to marry.

18 Acsah spoke to Othniel one day. She wanted him to ask her father for a field. She got off her donkey (an animal like a small horse). 'What can I do for you?' Caleb asked her.

19 'Be very kind to me', she said. 'You have given me land in the dry country in the south, so please will you give me some springs of water, too?' So Caleb gave her the higher and lower springs.

20 This is the land that Joshua gave to the families of the tribe of Judah, to live in.

21 The towns in the south of Judah were near the edge of Edom. They were:

Kabzeel, Eder, Jagur, 22 Kinah, Dimonah, Adadah, 23 Kedesh, Hazor, Ithnan, 24 Ziph, Telem, and Bealoth. 25 Also Hazor Hadattah, Kerioth Hezron (that is, Hazor), 26 Amam, Shema, Moladah, 27 Hazar Gaddah, Heshmon, Beth Pelet. 28 Also Hazar Shual, Beersheba, Biziothiah, 29 Baalah, Iim, Ezem, 30 Eltolad, Kesil, Hormah, 31 Ziklag, Madmannah, Sansannah, 32 Lebaoth, Shilhim, Ain and Rimmon. He gave them 29 towns with their villages.

33 He gave them towns in the small hills of the west:

Eshtaol, Zorah, Ashnah, 34 Zanoah, En Gannim, Tappuah, Enam, 35 Jarmuth, Adullam, Socoh and Azekah. 36 Also he gave them Shaaraim, Adithaim and Gederah, (or Gederothaim). There were 14 towns and villages.

37 He gave them Zenan, Hadashah, Migdal Gad, 38 Dilean, Mizpah, Joktheel, 39 Lachish, Bozkath, Eglon, 40 Cabbon, Lahmas, and Kitlish. 41 Also he gave them Gederoth, Beth Dagon, Naamah and Makkedah. There were 16 towns and their villages.

42 And he gave them Libnah, Ether, Ashan, 43 Iphtah, Ashnah, Nezib, 44 Keilah, Aczib and Mareshah. There were 9 towns with their villages.

45 He also gave to the tribe of Judah, Ekron with the houses and villages that belonged to it. 46 And he gave them all those towns west of Ekron, near to Ashdod with their villages. 47 And he gave them Ashdod and Gaza with their houses and villages. They had the land as far as the valley of Egypt, and to the Great Sea.

48 Joshua gave them land in the hill country:

Shamir, Jattir, Socoh, 49 Dannah, Kiriath Sannah (that is, Debir), 50 and Anab, Eshtemoh, Anim, 51 Goshen, Holon and Giloh. There were 11 towns and their villages.

52 He also gave them Arab, Dumah, Eshan, 53 Janim, Beth Tappuah, Aphekah, 54 Humtah, Kiriath Arba (that is, Hebron) and Zior. There were 9 towns and their villages.

55 Also Maon, Carmel, Ziph, Juttah, 56 Jezreel, Jokdeam, Zanoah, 57 Kain, Gibeah and Timnah. There were 10 towns and their villages.

58 And he gave them Halhul, Beth Zur, Gedor, 59 Maarath, Beth Anoth and Eltekon. There were 6 towns and their villages.

60 And Kiriath Baal, (that is, Kiriath Jearim) and Rabbah. There were two towns and their villages.

61 Joshua gave Judah towns in the desert:

Beth Arabah, Middin, Secacah, 62 Nibshan, the city of salt, and En Gedi. There were 6 towns and their villages.

63 Judah could not push the Jebusites out of Jerusalem. So, Jebusites still live there with the people of Judah.

Chapter 16

Joshua gives Ephraim and Manasseh their land

1 Joshua gave some land east of Jericho to the tribes of Joseph. Their land started at the Jordan and went through the desert into the hills of Bethel. 2 The edge of their land went from Bethel (that is, Luz), to the land of the Arkites in Ataroth. 3 Their land continued to the west, to the land of the Japhletites by lower Beth Horon. It ended near the sea, by Gezer.

4 Joshua gave this land to Manasseh and Ephraim, the sons of Joseph. It was for them and their families.

5 Joshua gave this land to the families of Ephraim:

The edge of their land was from Ataroth Addar in the east to Beth Horon. 6 Then it continued to the west. Michmethath was north of their land. East of Michmethath, the edge of their land went past Taanath Shiloh on the east to Janoah. 7 From there it went to Ataroth and Naarah and through Jericho to the river Jordan. 8 From Tappuah, the edge of their land continued to the west to the little river Kanah. From there, it continued to the sea. Joshua gave all this land to the families of the tribe of Ephraim. 9 He also gave them some towns and villages that were in the land of Manasseh. 10 But the tribe of Ephraim did not push out the Canaanite people who lived in Gezer. Canaanite people still live there, but they have to work as slaves to the Ephraimites.

Chapter 17

West Manasseh

1 Joshua gave part of the land west of the river Jordan to some families of the tribe of Manasseh. Manasseh was Joseph's oldest son. Manasseh's oldest son was Makir, father of Gilead. He had fought very bravely, so Joshua gave him Gilead and Bashan, east of the Jordan. 2 He gave land west of the Jordan to all the other families of Manasseh. These were: Abiezer, Helek, Asriel, Shechem, Hepher and Shemida. They were all sons of Manasseh, and heads of their families. 3 Zelophehad, son of Hepher, son of Gilead, son of Makir, son of Manasseh, had no sons. He had only daughters. Their names were Mahlah, Noah, Hoglah, Milcah and Tirzah. 4 They went to see Eleazar, the priest and Joshua, son of Nun and the leaders. They said, 'The Lord told Moses to give us part of the land. We must have land like the sons of other families.' So, Eleazar and Joshua gave them land, like the other families. 5 That is why they gave Manasseh 10 parts of the land as well as Gilead and Bashan on the east side of the Jordan. 6 They gave some daughters of Manasseh land as well as his sons. They gave the land of Gilead to the rest of the families of Manasseh.

7 The edge of the land of Manasseh was from Asher to Michmethath east of Shechem. It went south to include En Tappuah. 8 Manasseh had the land near Tappuah, but the town of Tappuah belonged to the sons of Ephraim. 9 The edge of Manasseh's land went down to the little river of Kanah. The cities south of the river that belonged to Ephraim were in Manasseh's land. The edge of Manasseh's land was along the north side of the river to the sea. 10 Ephraim was south of the river, and Manasseh to the north. The sea was to the west of them both. Asher was north and west of them, and Issachar to the north and east. 11Beth Shan and Ibleam and the towns near them that belonged to Manasseh were in the lands of Issachar and Asher. Dor (by the sea), Endor, Taanach, Megiddo and the towns near them also belonged to Manasseh. 12 But the people of Manasseh could not push out the people who lived in those cities. So the Canaanite people went on living there. 13 Some of them continued to live there, even when the people of Israel became strong. But the Israelites made the Canaanites work for them.

Joseph's sons ask for more land

14 Joseph's sons asked Joshua, 'Why have you given us only one part of the land to live in? The Lord has been good to us, and there are very many of us.'

15 Joshua said to them, 'If there are so many of you, and the hills of Ephraim are too small for you, take more land. Cut down trees in the land of the Perizzites and the Rephaim.'

16 They replied, 'The hills are not big enough for us. But the Canaanites in Beth Shan and its towns and in the valley of Jezreel have iron chariots.'

17 Joshua said to the tribes of Ephraim and Manasseh, 'There certainly are a lot of you. And you are very strong. I will give you more than one part. 18 You will have the hills. They are full of trees, but you will cut them down. You will take the land from one end to the other. I know that the Canaanites are a strong people. They have iron chariots, but you will push the Canaanites out.'

Chapter 18

Joshua gives land to the other tribes

1 All the people of Israel met together at Shiloh. There they put up the tent where they met with God. They now ruled all the land. 2 But Joshua still had not given 7 tribes a part of the land for themselves.

3 Joshua asked them, 'The Lord, the God of your fathers, has given you the land. How long will you wait before you take it?' 4 Choose 3 men from each tribe. I will send them to look at all the land, and to see what it is like. They must say what they find in each part. Then they must come back to me. 5 You must make it into 7 parts. Judah is to stay in its land to the south, and Joseph's people are to remain in their land in the north. 6 You must write down what each of the 7 parts look like. Then I will ask God to help me to choose which part I will give to each tribe. I will use lots to decide. 7 The Levites will not have any of the 7 parts of the land. This is because their part is to serve the Lord God. And Gad, Reuben and half the tribe of Manasseh already have land on the east side of the river Jordan. Moses, the servant of the Lord, gave it to them.'

8 The chosen men started to go to describe the land. 'Go and look at the land. Write down what you find', Joshua told them. 'Then come back to me in Shiloh. I will use the lots in front of the Lord here.' 9 So the men left and went all through the land. They wrote about each town in a book. They wrote about each of the 7 parts of the land. Then they went back to Joshua in the tents at Shiloh. 10 At Shiloh, Joshua stood in front of the Lord. He used the lots to decide which part of the land each tribe should have.

Benjamin's part of the land

11 The lot showed that the first part of the land was for Benjamin, family by family. It was between the land that Joshua gave to the tribes of Judah and Joseph.

12 The north side of their land began at the river Jordan, and went up the hills to the north of Jericho. From there it went west into the hills, to the desert of Beth Aven. 13 The edge of their land went on to the south of Luz (that is Bethel) to Ataroth Addar. That is on the hill south of Lower Beth Horon.

14 From this hill, the edge of their land went south along the west side to Kiriath Baal (that is Kiriath Jearim). This town belonged to the people of Judah. This was the west edge of Benjamin's land.

15 The south edge went from the edge of Kiriath Jearim to the waters of Nephtoah. 16 Then it went to the foot of the hill across the Valley of Ben Hinnom. This was north of the Valley of Rephaim. It continued down the Hinnom valley south of the Jebusite city to En Rogel. 17 Then it went north to En Shemesh. It went on to Geliloth, opposite the valley of Adummim. Then it went to the stone of Bohan, son of Reuben.18 It continued to the north of Beth Arabah down into the Arabah. 19 Then it went north of Ben Hoglah to the north end of the Salt Sea. This was at the south end of the river Jordan. This was the south edge of Benjamin's land.

20 The Jordan was the west edge of their land.

These are the edges of the land that Joshua gave to the families of the tribe of Benjamin.

21 These are the cities that Joshua gave to the tribe of Benjamin:

Jericho, Beth Hoglah, Emek Keziz, 22 Beth Arabah, Zemaraim, Bethel, 23 Avvim, Parah, Ophrah, 24 Kephar, Ammoni, Ophni and Geba. There were 12 towns and their villages.

25 Gibeon, Ramah, Beeroth, 26 Mizpah, Kephirah, Mozah, 27 Rekem, Irpeel, Taralah, 28 Zelah, Haeleph, the Jebusite city (that is, Jerusalem), Gibeah and Kiriath. These were 14 towns and their villages.

Joshua gave these cities to the families of Benjamin's tribe, to live in.

Chapter 19

Joshua gives land to Simeon

1 The second lot showed that the next part of the land was for the tribe of Simeon. Joshua gave their families some of the land that he had given to Judah. 2 It included:

Beersheba (or Sheba), Moladah, 3 Hazar Shual, Balah, Ezem, 4 Eltolad, Bethul and Hormah. 5 And Joshua gave them Ziklag, Beth Marcaboth, Hazar Susah, 6 Beth Lebaoth and Sharuhen. These were 13 towns and their villages. 7 He gave them 4 more towns and their villages. These were Ain, Rimmon, Ether and Ashan. 8 This included all the villages near them as far as Baalath Beer (Ramah in the Negev).

This is the land that Joshua gave to the families of the tribe of Simeon. 9 He took Simeon's land from Judah's land. Judah did not need all the land that Joshua had given to them. So the tribe of Simeon lived inside the land that Joshua had given to Judah.

Joshua gives land to Zebulun

10 The lot showed that the next part of the land was for Zebulun. The edge of it went as far as Sarid. 11 Then it went west to Maralah, touched Dabbesheth, and went to the valley near Jokneam. 12 From Sarid, the edge of their land went east to the land of Kisloth Tabor. Then it went to Daberath and up to Japhia. 13 It continued east to Gath Hepher and Eth Kazin. It went on to Rimmon, and turned to go to Neah. 14 The edge went north to Hannathon and stopped at the valley of Iphtah El. 15 Twelve (12) towns and their villages were in this part of the land. They were Kattah, Nahalal, Shimron, Idalah and Bethlehem.

16 Joshua gave these towns and their villages to families of the tribe of Zebulun.

Joshua gives land to Issachar

17 The lot showed Joshua that the next part of the land was for Issachar's families. 18 Their land included Jezreel, Kesulloth, Shunem, 19 Hapharaim, Shion, Anaharath, 20 Rabbith, Kishion and Ebez. 21 And it included Remeth, En Gannim, En Haddah and Beth Pazzez. 22 The edge of their land touched Tabor, Shahazumah and Beth Shemesh and ended at the river Jordan. Joshua gave them 16 towns and their villages.

23 Joshua gave these towns and their villages to the families of the tribe of Issachar.

Joshua gives land to Asher

24 The next lot showed Joshua the land that he must give to Asher's families. 25 This is the land that he gave them:

Helkath, Hali, Beten, Acshaph, 26 Allammelech, Amad and Mishal. The edge of the land on the west touched Carmel and Shihor Libnath. 27 Then it went east towards Beth Dagon, to touch Zebulun and the valley of Iphtah El. Then the edge of their land went north to Beth Emek and Neiel. It passed the left side of Cabul. 28 It went to Abdon, Rehob, Hammon and Kanah, as far as Sidon. 29 Then the edge went back towards Ramah to the strong city of Tyre. Then it turned to Hosah and ended at the sea near Aczib, 30 Ummah, Aphek and Rehob. Joshua gave them 22 towns and their villages.

31 These towns and villages Joshua gave to the families of Asher's tribe.

Joshua gives land to Naphtali

32 Joshua gave the land chosen by the 6th lot to Naphtali's families:

33 The edge of their land went from Heleph and the big tree in Zaanannim past Adami Nekeb and Jabneel to Lakkum. It ended at the river Jordan. 34 Another edge went west through Aznoth Tabor to Hukkok. It touched Zebulun on its south side, Asher on its west and the Jordan on its east side. 35 The land contained the strong cities Ziddim, Zer, Hammath, Rakkath and Kinnereth. 36 And Joshua gave them Adamah, Ramah, Hazor, 37 Kedesh, Edrei, En Hazor, 38 Iron, Migdal El, Horem, Beth Anath and Beth Shemesh. He gave them 19 towns and their villages.

39 Joshua gave these towns and villages to the families of Naphtali.

Joshua gives land to the tribe of Dan

40 The next lot showed Joshua the land to give to Dan's families. 41 This is the land that he gave them:

It included Zorah, Eshtaol, Ir Shemesh, 42 Shaalabbin, Aijalon, Ithlah, 43 Elon, Timnah and Ekron. 44 And he gave them Eltekeh, Gibbethon, Baalath, 45 Jehud, Bene Berak, Gath Rimmon, 46 Me Jarkon and Rakkon, with land in front of Joppa.

47 (But the people of Dan could not take their land, so they went to attack Leshem. They took it and killed its people and lived there themselves. They called the city Dan, after their father.)

48 Joshua gave these towns and their villages to the families of Dan's tribe.

The Israelites give land to Joshua

49 When Joshua had given all the tribes their land, the Israelites gave Joshua son of Nun his own land. 50 This is what the Lord had told them to do. He asked for the town Timnah Serah in the hills of Ephraim. And they gave it to him. He built up the town and went to live there.

51 This is the list of all the lands that they gave to each tribe. The lots showed Eleazar the priest, Joshua son of Nun and the leaders which land was for each tribe. They did this by the tent of meeting, in front of the Lord. So they finished giving each tribe a part of the land.

Chapter 20

Safe cities

1 Then the Lord spoke to Joshua. 2 He said, 'Tell the people of Israel to choose special cities. I told you this through Moses. 3 Anyone can be safe in these cities if he has killed someone. But he will only be safe if he had not meant to kill that person. The person who killed a man or woman can run to that city. The person will be safe. They will not let the brother of the dead person kill him there (Numbers 35:6-34).

4 The man who killed someone must go to the city. When he arrives, he must stand in the gate of the city. There he must tell the leaders what he has done. Then they must let him go in. And they must give him a place to live and stay there. 5 The brother of the dead person may follow the man who killed his brother or sister. The leaders must not let the brother hurt that man. This is because he did not mean to kill the dead man. He did not want to hurt him. 6 The man who killed must stay in that city. He may have told them what is true. The judges there will decide. Then he must wait until the High Priest of that time dies. After that, he is free to return to the town that he came from.'

7 So they chose these towns: Kedesh in Galilee, in the hills of Naphtali, Shechem in the hills of Ephraim, Kiriath Arba (that is, Hebron) in the hills of Judah.

8 They chose other cities east of the river Jordan and to the east of the flat land near Jericho: Bezer in the flat desert land of Reuben, Ramoth in Gilead in the tribe of Gad, Golan in Bashan in the tribe of Manasseh.

9 Any Israelite or foreign person living in Israel could run to these cities. They may have killed someone, but had not meant to kill them. They could run to these cities. Then the brother of the dead person could not kill them. The judges had to decide whether they had meant to kill or not. Nobody could kill them before this.

Chapter 21

Towns for the Levites

1 The fathers of the Levite families came to speak to Joshua. They came with the leaders of all the other tribes. 2 They met at Shiloh in Canaan. 'The Lord told Moses that you must give us towns to live in', they said. 'And we must have land to feed our animals.' 3 So the Israelites did as the Lord had told them. They gave them towns with land from the land that belonged to their tribes.

4 They gave towns first to the Kohathite family. They gave them 13 towns from the tribes of Judah, Simeon and Benjamin. They gave these to Levites from the family of Aaron, the priest. 5 They gave to the other Kohathites, towns from the tribes of Ephraim, Dan and half of Manasseh.

6 Then they gave 13 towns to the family of Gershon. The tribes of Issachar, Asher, Naphtali and the half of Manasseh in Bashan gave them these towns.

7 They gave 12 towns to the families of Merari. The tribes of Reuben, Gad and Zebulun gave them these.

8 So the people of Israel gave these towns and the land and fields near to them to the families of Levi's tribe. They did as the Lord had told Moses.

9 These are the names of the towns that the tribes of Simeon and Judah gave. 10 They gave them to the Kohathites, of Aaron's family, because God chose them first.

11 They gave them Kiriath Arba (or Hebron), with land near to it, in the hills of Judah. (Arba was the father of Anak.) 12 But the fields and villages near Hebron belonged to Caleb, son of Jephunneh. 13 So they gave the city of Hebron (a safe city) to the sons of Aaron. They also gave them Libnah, 14 Jattir, Eshtemoa,15 Holon, Debir, 16 Ain, Juttah and Beth Shemesh with their land and fields. These two tribes gave them 9 towns. 17 They gave them Gibeon, Geba, 18 Anathoth and Almon with their fields. These 4 towns were from the tribe of Benjamin.

19 They gave the priests, sons of Aaron, all these 13 towns.

20 They gave to the Levites of Kohath's family, towns from the tribe of Ephraim.

21 They gave them Shechem, a safe city, in the hills of Ephraim, and Gezer, 22 Kibzaim and Beth Horon with their fields. They gave them 4 towns. 23 The tribe of Dan gave them Elthekeh, Gibbethon, 24 Aijalon, and Gath Rimmon. They gave them these 4 towns with their fields. 25 The half tribe of west Manasseh gave them Taanach and Gath Rimmon with their fields. They gave them two towns.

26 They gave the families of Kohath all these 10 cities.

27 They gave the Levites of Gershon's family the towns of Golan in Bashan, a safe city, and Be Eshtarah, two cities with their fields. The half tribe of east Manasseh gave these. 28 They gave them 4 cities from the tribe of Issachar. These were Kishion, Daberath, 29 Jarmuth and En Gannim, with their fields. 30The tribe of Asher gave them 4 towns. These were Mishal, Abdon, 31 Helkath and Rehob, with their fields.32 The tribe of Naphtali gave them Kedesh in Galilee, a safe city, Hammoth Dor and Kartan with their fields. They gave these 3 cities.

33 They gave the families of Gershon all these 13 cities.

34 The other Levites that did not have any towns were the Merarite family. The tribe of Zebulun gave to them the towns of Jokneam, Kartah, 35 Dimnah and Nahalal. They gave to them 4 towns with their fields.

36 The tribe of Reuben gave them four towns. These were Bezer, Jahaz, 37 Kedemoth and Mephaath, with their fields. 38 The tribe of Gad gave them four towns. These were Ramoth in Gilead, a safe city, Mahanaim, 39 Heshbon and Jazer, with their fields.

40 So they gave to these Levites, the family of Merari, 12 towns.

41 The Levites had 48 towns in the land of Israel. 42 Each of these towns had its own fields round it.

43 So the Lord gave all the land to the people of Israel. He had promised it to their fathers. They took it and lived there.

44 The Lord gave them rest, as he had promised. None of the people round Israel attacked them. Not one of their enemies could win a fight with them. The Lord helped them to win all their fights.45 He kept all his good promises to the people of Israel. He did not forget one of his promises.

Chapter 22

The tribes that were living east of the Jordan go home

1 Then Joshua called together the tribes of Reuben, Gad and the half tribe of Manasseh. 2 Joshua said, 'You have done all that Moses, the servant of the Lord, told you to do' (Numbers 32:20-22). He said, 'And you have obeyed me. You have done everything that I told you to do. 3 You have helped your brothers, for a long time. You have stayed even to this day. And you have done the work that the Lord gave you to do. 4Now your brothers have finished fighting for their land, as the Lord promised them. So you can go to your homes on the other side of the river Jordan. Moses, the Lord's servant gave them to you. 5 But you must be very careful to keep the rules and the law that he gave you. This law says that you must love the Lord your God. And you must keep the rules that he gave to you. You must do everything that he tells you. And you must believe him. You must serve him with everything that you have.'

6 Joshua then blessed them and sent them away to their homes. Moses had given land in Bashan to half the tribe of Manasseh. 7 (But Joshua had given land on the west side of the Jordan to the other half of the tribe, with their brothers.) When Joshua sent them home, he blessed them. 8 'Go back to your homes with the good things that you took from your enemies', he said. 'Take many animals, gold and other metals and rich clothes. You and your brothers must each have a part of these things.'

9 So the tribes of Reuben, Gad and half the tribe of Manasseh left their brothers there in Shiloh in Canaan. They returned to Gilead, their own land. Moses had given them this land, as the Lord had told him.

10 The two and a half tribes came to Geliloth, near the Jordan, in Canaan. They built a big altar there, by the river Jordan. 11 When the other Israelites heard that they had built an altar at the edge of Canaan, at Geliloth, they were angry. It was on the side of the Jordan that the Israelites had. 12 They all came together at Shiloh to fight the two and a half tribes.

13 So the Israelites sent Phinehas, son of Eleazar the priest, to the land of Gilead. He went to see Reuben, Gad and the half tribe of Manasseh. 14 They sent 10 of the leaders with him. They chose one man from each of the tribes of Israel. Each man was the leader of his own family group.

15 They spoke to the tribes of Reuben, Gad and the half tribe of Manasseh in Gilead. 16 They said, 'You have not obeyed the Lord God of Israel. All the people of Israel are saying this. Why have you built an altar? The Lord said that you must not do this (Deuteronomy 13:13-14). You are turning away from him.17 The sin at Peor was bad (Numbers 23:27-29). We still feel bad about it and God made us all sick to punish us. 18 Now you seem to be doing another thing that is wrong.'

The leaders said, 'You might do something that is wrong today. The Lord will be angry with all the people of Israel tomorrow. 19 If your land here is not clean, come back to the Lord's land. And we will give you some of it. The Lord's tent is there. Do not turn against the Lord or against us. Do not build an altar for yourselves that is not for the Lord our God. 20 When Achan, son of Zerah, took things that belonged to God, he became angry with all the people of Israel. Achan was not the only one that died' (Joshua 7:1).

21 Reuben, Gad and the half tribe of Manasseh answered the leaders of Israel. 22 They said, 'God, the Lord, is the great one. God the Lord! He knows! So let all Israel know! Punish us today if we have done anything against the Lord. We have not done anything that he told us not to do. 23 We did not build our own altar to burn animals or food, or to give gifts to God. If we did anything wrong, may the Lord punish us himself.'

24 They also said, 'No! We had a very different idea. We were afraid that in later times, your children might speak to ours. They might say, "You have nothing to do with the Lord, the God of Israel. 25 The Lord put the Jordan between us and your tribes, Reuben and Gad. You do not belong to the Lord!" So your children might stop our children from worshipping the Lord.

26 That is why we said, "Let us build an altar". It will not be an altar where we burn food. And it will not be an altar where we give things to God. 27 But it will help us and you, and our children and your children, to remember to worship the Lord at his tent. We will burn animals and seeds and give him gifts there. Then, in later years, your children will not tell our children that they do not belong to the Lord.

28 We said, "If they say this to us, we will answer them. We will say 'Look at this altar. It is a copy of the Lord's altar. It is not for burning food or giving gifts to the Lord. Our fathers built it so that we should remember that we are all part of Israel' ".

29 We never wanted to turn away from the Lord. We wanted to do the things that please him. We would never burn anything at an altar that was not the altar of the Lord our God. His altar stands in front of his tent.'

30 Phinehas the priest and the leaders (the men from each tribe of Israel) heard this. They were pleased with what Reuben, Gad and Manasseh had told them. 31 They said to them, 'You have not done anything that would not please the Lord. So today we know that the Lord is with us. Now he will not be angry with us.'

32 Then Phinehas son of Eleazar, the priest and the leaders went back to Canaan. They told the Israelites what had happened when they had met the men of Reuben and Gad. 33 They were happy to hear about it, and gave thanks to God. They did not talk about fighting them any more. They would not destroy the land where the two and a half tribes lived.

34 Reuben and Gad gave the altar a name. They called it 'Remember, all of us that the Lord is God'.

Chapter 23

Joshua says 'Goodbye' to the leaders

1 After many years had passed, Joshua was very old. The Lord had given the people of Israel a time with no fighting. Their enemies who lived near them all did not attack them any more. 2 Joshua called all the people to him with their leaders, judges and officers. He said to them, 'I am old, many years old. 3 You, yourselves, have seen what the Lord has done to these peoples, to help you. It was the Lord who fought them for you. 4 Remember how I have given each of your tribes a special part of the land. Some other people still live there. I fought for this land and took it from the peoples near you. The land is between the river Jordan and the Great Sea in the west. 5 The Lord himself will push the people out of the land. He will push them out in front of you, and you will live in their land. He promised that he would do this.

6 Be very strong. Do everything that Moses told you to do in his Book of the Law. Obey his rules. Do not turn away from them even a little bit. 7 Do not become friends of the peoples who are near you. Do not call out to their gods. Do not use their names to show that you mean what you say. You must not serve them or worship them. 8 But you must always obey the Lord your God, as you have until now.

9 The Lord has pushed out big and strong peoples in front of you. No one has been strong enough to stand against you. 10 One of you has sent away 1000 men. This is because the Lord your God fought for you, as he promised. 11 You must be very careful to love the Lord your God.'

12 Joshua said to all the people, 'But you may turn away to join with other peoples, those that are left among you. Perhaps you will marry some of them, or mix with them. 13 Then you may be sure that the Lord your God will no more push them out in front of you. Instead, they will catch you and hurt you. They will be like hard sticks on your backs and sharp stones in your eyes. Then you will lose this good land that the Lord your God has given to you.

14 Now I am going to die, as all men do. The Lord has kept every one of the promises that he gave to you. You know that deep in yourselves. He has not failed to keep one of them. 15 The Lord has kept every good promise. And he will also keep the promise to trouble you and to destroy you. He will send you away from this good land that he has given you. 16 He will do this if you do not keep the rules that he gave you. If you do not obey him, he will be very angry with you. If you go to serve other gods and worship them, you will soon die out from this good land.

Chapter 24

Joshua and the people repeat their promises to God

1 Joshua called all the tribes together at Shechem. He made all the men with authority to stand in front of God. They were the leaders, officers and judges.

2 Joshua spoke to the people. He said, 'This is what the Lord, the God of Israel says, "A long time ago, your fathers lived across the river Euphrates, and worshipped other gods. Your fathers included Terah and his sons, Abraham and Nahor. 3 But I took Abraham from that land and brought him all through Canaan. I gave him many sons and daughters. I gave him Isaac, 4 and I gave to Isaac two sons, Jacob and Esau. I gave the hill country of Seir (Edom) to Esau, but Jacob and his sons went down to Egypt.

5 I sent Moses and Aaron to the Israelites in Egypt and did many things to the people of Egypt to make them let you go. 6 When I brought your fathers out of Egypt, you reached the Red Sea. The Egyptians went after them with men on horses and in chariots as far as the Sea. 7 But your fathers cried to the Lord for help. He made it dark between them and the Egyptians, and made the river water cover your enemies. You saw what I did to the Egyptians with your own eyes. Then you lived in the desert for a long time.

8 I brought you to the land of the Amorites, east of the river Jordan. They fought you, but I helped you to win the fight. I destroyed them in front of you, and you took their land. 9 Balak, son of Zippor, king of Moab, got ready to fight you. When he did this, he asked Balaam, son of Beor, to ask me to hurt you. 10 But I would not listen to Balaam. So Balaam blessed you and went on blessing you. And I saved you from the king of Moab.

11 Then you went across the Jordan and came to Jericho. You fought with the people of Jericho and with the Amorites, Perizzites, Canaanites, Hittites, Girgashites, Hivites and Jebusites. I helped you to win all those fights. 12 I made them very afraid of you so they ran away from you. And so did the two kings of the Amorites. You did not do this on your own. 13 So I gave you a land that you had not worked for. I gave you houses that you did not build. You live in the houses. You eat fruit from plants and trees that you did not plant." '

14 Joshua said, 'Now you must give honour to the Lord, and serve him. You must always do only what he says. Throw away the gods that your fathers worshipped across the Euphrates and in Egypt. Worship the Lord. 15 But if you do not want to serve the Lord, you may choose other gods. You may serve the gods that your fathers served across the river. Or serve the gods of the Amorites, in whose land you are now living. But I and my family, we will serve the Lord.'

16 The people answered Joshua, 'We would never leave the Lord to serve other gods! 17 We and our fathers were slaves in Egypt. But the Lord our God brought us out from there. We saw the great things that he did there. He kept us safe all the time on our journey. He saved us from other peoples. 18 He went in front of us. He pushed out the Amorites and the other people who lived in the land. So we, too, will serve the Lord, because he is our God.'

19 Joshua answered them, 'But you cannot serve the Lord. He is a holy God. He will not forget if you turn away from him. He will not forgive your sins. 20 If you leave him and serve other gods, he will turn round and punish you. He will destroy you, after he has been good to you.'

21 'No!' the people said. 'We will serve the Lord.'

22 Joshua said, 'You yourselves have chosen to serve the Lord. See that you keep your promise.'

They replied, 'Yes, we will watch ourselves with great care.'

23 'Now then', Joshua said, 'throw away the false gods, the gods of other peoples that you still keep. And give yourselves completely to the Lord, the God of Israel.'

24 The people said to Joshua, 'We will serve the Lord our God and obey him.'

25 Joshua and the people made these important promises on that day. There at Shechem, he made a list of their rules and laws. 26 And Joshua wrote these things in the Book of the Law of God. Then he took a big stone and stood it there under the oak tree (a big strong tree) that was by the Lord's holy place.

27 'See this stone!' he said to all the people. 'It will help you to remember the promise that you have made. It will make you feel bad if you do not obey your God.'

Joshua dies

28 Then Joshua sent the people away, each to his own part of the land.

29 After this, Joshua died, at the age of 110. 30 The Israelites buried him in his own land, at Timnah Serah in the hills of Ephraim, north of Mount Gaash.

31 The people of Israel served the Lord while Joshua was alive. Other leaders had seen all that the Lord had done for Israel. The people of Israel continued to serve the Lord as long as these leaders were alive.

32 The people of Israel had brought the body of Joseph up from Egypt (Genesis 50:22-26). They buried it at Shechem. This was the land that Jacob had bought from the sons of Hamor, the father of Shechem. Jacob paid them 100 pieces of silver. The land belonged to Joseph's children.

33 Eleazar, son of Aaron, died and people buried him at Gibeah. This was the town in the hills of Ephraim that belonged to his son Phinehas.

God helps people to return to him

Judges

Introduction

This is the story of Israel after Joshua died. Someone wrote it when the Israelites lived among the Canaanites. They had not killed all the Canaanites as God had told them to do. Many Canaanites still lived in cities in the good low land. Most of the Israelites lived in the hills. Because some Israelites had Canaanite wives, they did not obey God. Some obeyed the gods of the Canaanites. God punished his people when they served other gods. When they were sorry, they asked for his help. Then God sent a judge to save them and help them to serve him. The Israelites obeyed God for a short time. Then they stopped obeying God again. God punished them again. They told God that they were sorry. So he sent another judge to save them. This happened again and again. Judges usually decide whether someone has kept the law. In this book a judge is much more than that. These judges are people that God chooses. They lead his people, the Israelites, into fighting and in worship. But God sent his Holy Spirit to make his judges strong. Then they could do the work that he wanted them to do. Judges did not rule the whole of Israel. They ruled in their own tribes. After the death of Joshua, different judges ruled until Saul was made king. This was between the years 1300 to 1000 B.C. (1300 to 1000 years before the Lord Jesus Christ was born).

The word 'Canaanites' includes all the peoples who lived in the land of Canaan. This was the land that God had chosen for the people of Israel. Jebusites, Amorites, Hittites, Hivites and many other tribes were all Canaanites.

Genesis 32:22-32 tell us about the tribes of Israel.

The Israelites had 12 tribes. Each tribe was from one of Jacob's sons. God gave Jacob a new name.

He called him Israel. The names of the sons of Jacob and his first wife, Leah were Reuben, Simeon, Levi, Judah, Issachar, and Zebulun. Jacob and his second wife Rachel had two sons, Joseph and Benjamin. Jacob also had sons with his servants. Their names were Dan, Naphtali, Gad and Asher. Each of Joseph's two sons, Ephraim and Manasseh became a separate tribe, so no one tribe has the name Joseph. Each tribe, except Levi, lived in its own part of Canaan. The tribe of Levi lived on land that was given to them by their brothers. They had a special job. They were servants of God and their brothers. They kept God's house safe and beautiful. They sang and prayed to him. They offered him gifts from the tribes. This was to show that all the tribes belonged to God.

Chapter 1

1 After Joshua had died, the Israelites asked God for a new leader. They were fighting the Canaanites. They wanted to know who should fight the enemy. 2 God told them to send the people of Judah first. 3 The men of Judah asked their cousins, the men of Simeon, to help them. They agreed to go together. They would fight for lands for the tribes of Judah and of Simeon. 4 At Bezek, the Lord helped them to kill 10 000 Canaanites and Perrizites. 5 They found Adoni-Bezek there (the king of Bezek). 6 He ran away. They followed him and cut off his thumbs and big toes.

7 Adoni-Bezek said, 'God punished me because I did this to 70 other kings'. The Israelites took him back to Jerusalem. Adoni-Bezek died there. 8 The men of Judah attacked Jerusalem. They took and burnt the city and killed the people.

9 After this the men of Judah fought the Canaanites in the hills and in the Negev.

10 They attacked the people of Hebron that used to be called Kiriath Arba, and beat Sheshai, Ahiman and Talmai.

11 Then they fought the people who lived in Debir. It was called Kiriath Sepher at that time. 12 Caleb asked his big family to attack Kiriath Sepher. He promised to give his daughter to the one who took the city. His daughter was called Achsah. 13 Othniel, the son of Caleb's brother Kenaz, beat Kiriath Sepher. So Caleb gave Achsah to him as a wife. 14 Othniel told Achsah to ask her father for a field. She got off her donkey. Caleb saw her, and asked what she wanted.

15 She replied, 'Father, please give me water for the land that you gave me'. So Caleb gave her more land. This contained two pools of water.

16 The Kenites were the brothers of Moses' wife. They left Jericho to live with the men of Judah in the desert called Negev, near Arad. 17 Then the men of Judah went with the people of Simeon to attack Zephath. They destroyed the city. They called it Hormah (this means destroyed).

18 The men of Judah also won Gaza, Ashkelon and Ekron in the fight. They won the cities and all their land. 19 The Lord helped the men of Judah. They won all the hill country. They could not take the flat country. The people there had iron chariots to help them. 20 Caleb received Hebron as Moses had promised. He sent away the 3 sons of Anak. 21 The people of Benjamin could not send away the Jebusites. The Jebusites lived in Jerusalem. (Jerusalem had been called Jebus.) The Jebusites and Benjamites now live there together.

22 God helped the people of Joseph (tribes of Ephraim and Manasseh) to attack Bethel. (Bethel was called Luz at first.) 23 Some Israelite men went to look at the city. They wanted to discover its secrets. 24 They found a man who was leaving the city. They told him that he would be safe. But they said, 'You must tell us how to get into the city'. 25 So he showed them. The two tribes killed all the people there, but saved that man's family. 26 Then the man went to the land of the Hittites. He built a city there, and called it Luz. It is still there. 27 But the men of Mannaseh could not send away the peoples of 5 cities. These were Beth Shan, Taanach, Dor, Ibleam and Megiddo. The Canaanites who lived there fought bravely. They wanted to continue to live there. 28 When Israel became strong, they made the Canaanites their servants. They never sent all the people out of the land. 29 The people of Ephraim did not send the Canaanites out of Gezer. These Canaanites continued to live between the people of Ephraim. 30 Nor did Zebulun send the Canaanites from Kitron or Nahalol. But they did make them become their servants.

31 Nor did Asher send away the people of Acco, Sidon, Ahlab, Aczib, Helbah, Aphek or Rehob. 32 Because of this, the people of Asher lived in the land with the Canaanites.

33 The people of Naphthali did not send away the Canaanites who lived in Beth Shemesh or Beth Anath. They too lived with the Canaanites in the land. The Canaanites of Beth Shemesh and Beth Anath became their servants. 34 The Amorites did not let the people of Dan take the cities and valleys for themselves. The people of Dan stayed in the hill country.

35 The Amorites also owned Mount Heres, Aijalon and Shaalbim. But when the people of Joseph became strong, they made the Amorites their servants. 36 The land of the Amorites was between the Scorpion Pass and Sela, and other places.

Chapter 2

1 The Lord God sent an angel from Gilgal to Bokim. The angel said, 'I have brought you from Egypt. You are in the land that I promised to give you. I said that I would always do what I promised in my Covenant.

2 You must not have a covenant with the Canaanites. You must destroy the places where the Canaanites serve these false gods. You have not done as I told you. But you have done what I told you not to do! 3 This is what I will do. I will not send the Canaanites out of the land. They will be your enemies. Their false gods will pull you away from me. They will cause you much pain'.

4 When the angel had said this, the Israelites began to cry aloud. 5 They called the place Bokim (people who cry). They offered gifts there to the Lord.

6 Joshua sent the people to go to their land. Each tribe went to take the part of the land chosen for them. 7 The Israelites obeyed the Lord God for a time. Joshua and the old men had seen how the Lord had done great things for Israel. Whilst some of them were alive, the people obeyed the Lord. 8 Joshua the son of Nun (the servant of the Lord) died at 110 years old. 9 They buried him in the land that was his family's land, at Timnath Heres. This is in the hills near Mount Gaash. It is in Ephraim's part of the land.

10 When all the older men had died, younger men became leaders. They forgot the Lord and all that he had done for Israel. They did not obey him. 11 Then Israel did many bad things. They served the Baals, (gods of some Canaanites). 12 They did not obey the Lord God of their fathers. Yet, he had brought them out of Egypt. They obeyed the many false gods of the people who lived near them. They made the Lord angry, 13 because they served the Baals and Ashtoreths (false male and female gods) and did not obey the Lord. 14 So God punished Israel. He sent enemies to take their animals and food. He let their enemies make the Israelites their servants. 15 Israel went to fight their enemies. But God helped the enemies to win. He had said that he would do this. Israel was very, very sad.

16 Then God made some of the people judges. These judges helped to save Israel from their enemies. 17 But the people would not listen to the judges. They went on following other gods. They were not like their fathers. They soon forgot the Lord. They would not obey him. 18 When the Lord gave them a judge, the Lord helped the judge to save them from their enemies. They obeyed the Lord while the judge was alive. The Lord listened to their cries when other people made their lives difficult.

19 But when the judge died, the people stopped serving the Lord. They became worse than their fathers. They served many false gods. They refused to stop doing all these bad things.

20 Because of this, the Lord God became very angry with Israel. He said to them, 'You have not done what your fathers promised. You have not listened to me. Because of this, I will not help you. 21 I will not send the Canaanites out of the land. They stayed in the land when Joshua died. 22 I will use them to see if you will try to obey me. Your fathers obeyed me'. 23 Some of the Canaanites lived in the land. God did not send them all away. Also, he did not give their lands to Israel soon after Joshua had died.

Chapter 3

1 The Lord let some tribes stay in the land. These tribes were enemies of Israel. They would test the Israelites who had not fought before.

2 He did this to teach the Israelites how to fight their enemies, because they had not fought many battles. 3 These tribes were the Philistines, who had 5 kings, the Canaanites and the Sidonians (who lived in Sidon). There were also Hivites (who lived in the mountains of Lebanon from Mount Baal Hermon to Lebo Hamath). 4 They were to test the Israelites. God wanted to see if the Israelites would obey his rules. Earlier, he had told Moses to write down these rules for the people of Israel. 5 The Israelites lived among other peoples in the land. The Canaanites, Hittites, Amorites, Perizzites, Hivites and Jebusites all lived in the land of Canaan. 6 Some Israelites let their sons marry women from these tribes. Some of their own daughters married men of these peoples. Then they served their false gods.

7 The Israelites forgot the Lord and did many bad things. They served the Baals and Asherahs. 8 God was very angry with them. He let King Cushan-Rishathaim of Aram Naharaim fight against them. This king won the fight and the Israelites became his servants for 8 years. 9 When they cried to the Lord for help, he sent them a leader. This was Othniel, son of Kenaz. He came to save them. Kenaz was Caleb's younger brother. 10 God's Holy Spirit took hold of Othniel. Then he became the judge. He led Israel when they fought other tribes. God helped him to win the fight with Cushan-Rishathaim, King of Aram. 11 So the land of Israel was quiet for 40 years. Then Othniel died.

12 Once again the Israelites did many bad things against the Lord. Because of this, God made Eglon strong. He was the King of Moab. He came and fought with Israel and he won the fight. 13 The Ammonites and Amalekites joined Eglon, and they took the 'City of Palms' (Jericho). 14 Israel served Eglon for 18 years.

15 Again the Israelites cried to the Lord, and he sent a man called Ehud to save them. Ehud's stronger hand was his left hand. He was a son of Gera, of the tribe of Benjamin. He took taxes from Israel to Eglon, King of Moab.

16 He hid a knife that was sharp on both sides, under his clothes. It was about as long as his arm. He carried the knife against the top of his right leg. 17 First, he gave the money to king Eglon, who was a very fat man. 18 Ehud sent back the men who had carried the money. 19 At Gilgal, Ehud turned back to see the king. He said, 'I have a secret message for you, O King!' The king sent away all his servants. 20 Then Ehud went near to the king, who was sitting in his big room. There was nobody with him. Ehud said, 'I have a message from God for you'. The king started to get up. 21 Then Ehud took the knife in his left hand and pushed it into the king's stomach. The whole knife went in. 22 The king's fat covered the handle. The point came out behind the king. Ehud did not pull out the knife, and the fat covered it. 23 Ehud left the room and locked the doors. 24 The servants came and found the doors locked. They thought that the king was at his toilet. 25 They waited for a long time. But the king did not open the doors. So they opened them with a key. They saw that their king was dead on the floor. 26 While they were waiting, Ehud went past the stones that people worshipped, and ran to Seirah. 27 When he arrived, he made a loud noise with a trumpet. He led the Israelites down from the hills of Ephraim. 28 He told them to follow him. He said that the Lord God would save them from the people of Moab. Israel followed him to the river Jordan. They stopped anyone from crossing the river. 29 They killed 10 000 strong Moabites. They killed every one of them. 30 The rest of the Moabites became Israel's servants. And the land was quiet for 80 years. 31 After this, Shamgar, son of Anath, ruled Israel. He killed 600 Philistines with an ox-goad (sharp piece of wood, used to move animals). He too saved Israel.

Chapter 4

1 The Israelites went back to their bad ways again after Ehud died. 2 So God punished them. King Jabin, a Canaanite from Hazor, made them his servants. The captain of his army was called Sisera. He lived in Harosheth Haggoyim. 3 He had 900 chariots of iron. He made the lives of the Israelites very painful for 20 years. They cried to the Lord for help.

4 Deborah, the wife of Lappidoth, was then leading Israel. She was a lady prophet. 5 She sat under a palm tree between Ramah and Bethel. This was in the hill country of Ephraim. Here she judged the people. When the Israelites argued with each other, they came to her. Deborah decided who was right. 6 Deborah told Barak, son of Abinoam to come to her. He came from Kedesh in Naphtali. She gave him a message from the Lord God. The Lord told Barak,

'Go to Mount Tabor. Take with you 10 000 men of the tribes of Naphtali and Benjamin.

7 I will make Sisera (captain of Jabin's army) go to the Kishon river. He will bring the army and their chariots with him. You will beat them all'. 8 Barak said to Deborah, 'I will go if you will come with me. I will not go unless you come with me'. 9 Deborah said, 'Yes, I will go with you. But God will give power to kill Sisera to a woman. This is because you have been slow to obey him. You will not look very big'. So Deborah went with Barak to Kadesh. 10 Barak told the men from Zebulun and Naphtali to come to him. He led 10 000 men. And Deborah went with him.

11 Heber, the Kenite, did not live with the other Kenites. They were cousins of Moses' family. Heber lived in a tent by a big tree in Zaanannim in Kedesh.

12 They told Sisera that Barak (the son of Abinoam) had gone up to Mount Tabor. 13 Sisera and all his soldiers were at Harosheth Haggoyim. They went with 900 iron chariots to the Kishon river. 14 Then Deborah told Barak, 'Go! This day God has given you power over Sisera. God has gone before you!' So Barak went down from Mount Tabor with his soldiers. 15 When they came near to Sisera, the Lord fought for Israel. Israel beat Sisera and all his army. Sisera left his chariot and ran away. All his soldiers ran away. 16 Barak and his men ran after Sisera, his soldiers and his chariots. They followed them to Harosheth Haggoyim. They killed all Sisera's soldiers. They did not leave one.

17 Sisera ran to Jael's tent. She was the wife of Heber, the Kenite. King Jabin and Heber's family were friends. 18 Jael came out. She asked Sisera to come into the tent. She said, 'Do not be afraid'. So he went in, and she covered him up. 19 Sisera asked her for some water. She gave him a drink of milk, and covered him again. 20 Sisera said, 'Stand in front of the door. If someone asks if anyone is here, say, "No" '. 21 But Jael took a sharp stick and a hammer. She hit the stick right through Sisera's head while he was asleep. It went into the ground and he died. 22 Barak came running after Sisera. Jael went out to meet him. She said, 'Come and I will show you the man you are looking for'. He went with her and there was Sisera - dead. The stick was through his head. 23 On that day God made Jabin (the Canaanite king) weak. 24The Israelites became stronger and stronger. Then they ruled Jabin's people..

Chapter 5

The Song of Deborah

1 On that day Deborah and Barak, son of Abinoam, sang this song. 2 "When the leaders of Israel rule. When the people are happy to obey. Tell them that God is good.

3 Hear this, you kings! Listen you rulers! I will sing to the Lord. I will sing. I will sing a song to the Lord God of Israel.

4 Lord, you went out from Seir, you marched from the land of Edom. Then the earth shook. You sent rain from the sky. The clouds rained water. 5 The mountains (even Sinai) shook in front of the Lord, the God of Israel.

6 The roads were empty in the days of Shamgar, son of Anath. There was no one on them in the days of Jael. People walked on secret paths. 7 Nobody lived in the little towns. No one lived there until I came. I, Deborah, became a mother to Israel.

8 When they chose new gods, there was fighting near the city. No one in Israel was ready to fight, not one of the 40 000 in Israel. 9 I will make strong the leaders of Israel. With the people of Israel who want to fight. Tell all of them that God is good.

10 Listen, you rich people as you ride on white horses. Listen while you sit on your animals. And listen you that walk along the road. 11 Hear the singing voices, where you stop for water. They speak about all the Lord has done. They tell of the good things that his soldiers did. Then the people of the Lord went down to the city gates. 12 Wake up, wake up, Deborah! Wake up, wake up and sing. Get up Barak! Lock up your enemies, son of Abinoam.

13 The men who remained went back to their leaders. The people of the Lord came to me with their lords.14 Some came from Ephraim, where Amalek lived. Benjamin followed you. Makir (Manasseh) came too. The leaders of Zebulun came.

15 The leaders of Issachar were with Deborah. Yes, Issachar joined Barak. They ran after him into the valley. Many in Reuben were afraid and did nothing. 16 The men of Reuben stayed with the sheep. Many in Reuben were troubled. 17 Gilead stayed in his land. Dan stayed by the sea. Asher remained near the sea. They hid near its edge. 18 But the people of Zebulun were not afraid to fight. And Naphtali came from the mountains.

19 Kings came and fought. The kings of Canaan fought. They fought at Tannach near the water at Megiddo. But they took no gold or rich gifts. 20 The stars from the sky fought. They fought against Sisera. 21 The very old river Kishon carried away Sisera's soldiers. River Kishon, be strong and do not stop fighting. 22 The horses' feet made a loud noise. They ran fast, their strong legs ran and ran.

23 The Lord's angel said, 'Punish Meroz. Punish its people, because they did not come to fight for the Lord. They did not help the Lord fight his strong enemy'.

24 Jael is blessed. The wife of Heber the Kenite will be the happiest woman who lives in a tent. 25 He asked for water, and she gave him milk. She brought him milk in a lovely dish. 26 Her hand found the pointed stick. Her right hand took the hammer. She hit Sisera, she hit his head. Her stick went through his head.27 He fell at her feet. He stayed there and died.

28 Sisera's mother looked out of the window. She cried out as she looked. 'His chariot is so slow to come. There is no noise'. 29 Her clever ladies replied, and she herself thought, 30 'They are finding riches to bring home and women to please the men. They are finding rich clothes for Sisera. They will find clothes of many colours and win all these riches for him'. 31 May all your enemies die like Sisera, O Lord! But may those who love you be like the sun, which shines in the day".

There was no more fighting for 40 years.

Chapter 6

Gideon

1 The Israelites did things which made the Lord angry again. So he sent the Midianites to fight them. The Midianites won the fight. They ruled Israel for 7 years. 2 They were very cruel to the Israelites. The Israelites made holes in the hills to hide themselves. 3 They planted seeds to grow food. But then the Midianites and Amalekites and the other tribes came and put their tents there. 4 They took all their food, and animals too. They left nothing for Israel. They took sheep, cows and animals to carry heavy things. 5Many enemies came with all their animals. They came like a cloud of insects. They were too many to count. They took everything from the land. 6 The Israelites became so poor that they cried to the Lord for help. 7 The Lord sent a prophet to Israel when they called to him. 8 The prophet said, 'This is what the Lord says. "I brought you out of the land of Egypt. 9 I saved you from being slaves to the Egyptians. I also saved you from all your enemies here. I sent them away and gave you their land. 10 I said to you, 'I am the Lord your God. You must not worship the gods of the Amorites who live in your land'. But you have not listened to me" '.

11 Joash, the Abiezrite, had a farm in Ophrah. The angel from the Lord came and sat there, under a tree. Gideon was taking the seeds out of their hard skins. He was the son of Joash and was hiding from the Midianites. 12 The angel of the Lord said to Gideon, 'The Lord is with you, powerful soldier'. 13 Gideon replied, 'But sir, if the Lord is with us why has all this happened? The Lord helped our fathers to win fights with their enemies. They told us how he brought them out of Egypt. But now he has left us alone. He has let Midianites make us their slaves'. 14 The angel of the Lord turned and said to Gideon, 'Go with the power you have. Save Israel from Midian. I am sending you'.

15 'But sir', Gideon asked, 'How can I save Israel? My family is the smallest in the tribe of Manasseh. And I am the smallest in my family'.

16 The Lord answered, 'I will be with you. Together we will win the fight with Midian'.

17 Gideon replied, 'If I am special to you, please make me sure that you really are the Lord. 18 Please stay here and I will bring you an offering'. The Lord answered, 'I will wait for you'.

19 Gideon cooked a young goat and made many flat cakes of bread. He used an ephah (34-45 pounds weight) of flour. He put the meat in a basket and the soup in a pot. He gave them to the angel under the tree.

20 The Lord's angel said, 'Put the meat and the bread on this rock. Pour the soup over them'. And Gideon did so. 21 The angel touched the meat and bread with the end of his stick. Fire came from the rock and burnt up the bread and meat. Then Gideon could not see the angel. 22 Gideon knew then that he had been an angel from the Lord. He cried out, 'Great Lord, I have seen your angel, face to face'.

23 But the Lord said to him, 'Do not be afraid. You are not going to die'.

24 So Gideon built an altar there. He called it 'The Lord is Peace'. The altar is still there, in Ophrah of the Abiezrites.

25 That same night, the Lord spoke again to Gideon. He said, 'Take your father's second bull, the one which is 7 years old. Break into pieces your father's altar to Baal. Cut into pieces the tree where people give gifts to Asherah. 26 Build a proper altar to the Lord your God in their place. There, on top of the hill, use the broken wood to offer the second bull to me. Offer it to me by burning it with fire'.

27 So Gideon took 10 of his servants, and did as the Lord had said. He was afraid of the men of his family, and of the men of the town. So he worked at night, not in the day.

28 The next day, the men of the town saw that Baal's altar and Asherah's tree were broken. They saw the new altar. They saw that someone had burned the second bull on it.

29 They asked each other, 'Who has done this?' Then they found that Gideon, son of Joash, had done it.

30 The men of the town told Joash to bring Gideon out to them. They said that Gideon must die because he had destroyed Baal's altar. He had destroyed the place where they offered gifts to Asherah.

31 Joash replied to the angry men. He said, 'Are you trying to save Baal? You do not need to save him. If you fight for him, you will die today. If Baal really is a god, he can fight for himself. He will punish anyone who breaks down his altar'. 32 Then they called Gideon 'Jerub-Baal' (Baal must fight for himself). This was because Gideon had broken down Baal's altar.

33 The Midianites, Amalekites and other tribes who lived east of Jordan joined together. They crossed the river Jordan and put their tents in the Valley of Jezreel. 34 The Spirit of the Lord took hold of Gideon. He blew a trumpet. He called the men of his city to follow him. 35 He sent men to the tribe of Manasseh to tell them to fight. He told Asher, Zebulun and Naphtali to fight too. They all met together.

36 Gideon said to God, 'I want to save Israel. You promised to use me. 37 Look, I will put the hair of a sheep out on a dry, stone floor. Please make it wet by the morning, but let the ground stay dry. Then I will know that you will use me'. 38 That is what happened. The next morning the hair contained enough water to fill a large cup.

39 Then Gideon said to God. 'Please do not be angry. Let me ask one more thing. This time could you please make the ground wet, but keep the hair dry'. 40 That night the Lord did so. The ground was wet, but the sheep's hair stayed dry.

Chapter 7

1 Gideon and his men were in tents near Harod, where water came up out of the ground. It was early in the morning. The Midianite army was in tents, north of the Israelite army. They were in the valley near the hill of Moreh. 2 The Lord told Gideon, 'You have too many men. I do not want Israel to say that they won the fight. They must not think that they are strong. I cannot use all your army. 3 Tell the men that they may go back if they are afraid. They may leave Mount Gilead.' So 22 000 men left. But 10 000 remained.

4 The Lord said to Gideon, 'There are still too many men. Take them to the water to drink.

I will choose them for you. If I say that one should go with you, then take him. If I say that one should not go with you, then do not take him'. 5 So Gideon took the men to the water. The Lord said, 'Put the men who stand and drink from their hands here. And put the men who go on their knees to drink there'. 6 300 men stood and drank from their hands. The other soldiers all went on their knees. 7 The Lord said to Gideon, 'I will use the 300 men to save you. I will use them to give you power over the Midianites. Let all the other men return to their tents'. 8 Gideon took the food and trumpets from these men. Then he sent them to their tents. He gave the trumpets and food to the 300 men.

The tents of Midian were in the valley below Gideon. 9 That night the Lord said to Gideon, 'Get up. Go down to the tents of the Midianites. I am going to give them to you. You will win the fight. 10 Perhaps you are afraid to fight. Then go down to their camp (tents). Take Purah your servant with you. 11 Listen to what the Midianites are saying. You will hear something to make you strong to fight'. So Gideon and Purah went near to the edge of the camp. 12 The valley was full of Midianites and the other tribes. There were too many men to count. They had as many camels as there are bits of sand by the sea.

13 When Gideon arrived, he heard a man tell his friend about a dream. The man said, 'I saw a loaf of bread rolling into the Midianite army. It hit a tent hard. The tent fell down'.

14 The friend replied, 'This must be the work of Gideon, the son of Joash. The Lord has given him power to rule us. He will make us all his slaves'.

15 When Gideon heard this, he thanked God. He returned to the Israelite tents. He shouted, 'Get up! The Lord will fight Midian for us'. 16 He put the 300 men into 3 groups. He gave each man a trumpet and an empty pot. Into the pot, each man put a burning branch.

17 'Watch me', he said. 'Follow me. When we get near to their tents, do as I do. You will be all round their tents. 18 I and my men will blow our trumpets. Then you must blow yours. Shout, "For the Lord and for Gideon" '.

19 They reached the Midianite tents in the middle of the night. A new group of Midianite soldiers had just started to watch for the Israelites. Gideon's men blew their trumpets and broke their pots. 20 All three groups of Israelites blew their trumpets and broke their pots. They took their burning branches and trumpets. Then they shouted, 'Fight for the Lord and for Gideon'. Each man stood still. They were all round the camp. 21 Then all the Midianites ran about, screaming.

22 When Gideon's men blew the 300 trumpets, it confused the Midianites. The Lord made them turn and fight each other. Their army ran to Beth Shittar. This was towards Zererah. They ran as far as Abel Meholah, near Tabbath. 23 Gideon called Israelite men from Naphtali, Asher and all Manasseh to run after the Midianites. 24 He sent men into the hills of Ephraim. He told them not to let the Midianites cross the River Jordan. He said, 'Hold it as far as Beth Barah'. So all the men of Ephraim kept their enemies away from the waters of the River Jordan as far as Beth Barah. 25 They caught 2 of the Midianite leaders, Oreb and Zeeb, They killed Oreb at the rock of Oreb. They killed Zeeb at the winepress of Zeeb. (A winepress is a very big basket to make wine from grapes.) They ran after the Midianites and took the heads of Oreb and Zeeb to Gideon. Gideon was by the river Jordan.

Chapter 8

1 The Ephraimites asked Gideon, 'Why did you not ask us to come with you to fight Midian?' They thought that he did not want their help. They were very angry with Gideon. 2 Gideon said that they had done much more than he had. His part was only small. 3 God had given them Oreb and Zeeb. Ephraim's part was much bigger than Gideon's. When Gideon said this, the Ephraimites stopped being angry.

4 Gideon and his 300 men were very tired. But they crossed the Jordan and ran after the Midianites. 5 He asked the men of Succoth for bread to feed his soldiers. He said that they were tired. But they wanted to catch Zebah and Zalmunna. These were the two Kings of Midian. 6 The leaders of Succoth said, 'You have not yet caught Zebah and Zalmunna. We will not give you bread'. 7 Gideon replied, 'I will return when I have taken Zebah and Zalmunna. Then I will punish you with sharp branches. They will tear your skin'.

8 Gideon went on to Peniel. He asked their people for bread. But they gave the same answer as the men of Succoth. 9 Gideon said to the men of Peniel, 'When I have won the fight with my enemies, I will return. Then I will destroy your strongest building'.

10 Zebah and Zalmunna had 15 000 men with them in Karkor. They were the only men left of their great army from the east. 120 000 of their soldiers had died. 11 Gideon followed a quiet, country path to Karkor. He went east of Nobah and Jogbehah. He made a surprise attack on the army there. 12 Zebah and Zalmunna ran away. Gideon ran after the two kings and caught them. The whole Midianite army ran away.

13 Then Gideon, son of Joash returned towards Israel. He went through the Pass of Heres.

14 He caught a young man from Succoth. He made the young man write the names of 77 leaders. 15 Gideon showed Zebah and Zalmunna to the men of Succoth. He said, 'You refused to give us bread because we had not already caught Zebah and Zalmunna'. 16 He took the leaders of Succoth and beat them with sharp branches. He taught them to do as he told them. 17 He also destroyed the building at Peniel, and killed the men of the town.

18 Gideon asked Zebah and Zalmunna what kind of men they had killed at Tabor. The kings answered, 'Men like you, men who stood like kings'. 19 Gideon replied, 'These were my brothers. They were my mother's sons. As sure as the Lord lives, if you had let my brothers live, then I would have let you live'. 20He turned to his oldest son, Jether. 'Kill them', he said. But Jether stood still. He was afraid because he was only a boy. 21 Zebah and Zalmunna said to Gideon, 'Kill us yourself. You are strong'. So Gideon went to them and killed them. He took the valuable ornaments from their camels' necks.

22 The Israelites asked Gideon to be their king. They said, 'Rule over us, you and your sons. You have saved us from the rule of Midian'. 23 But Gideon said to them, 'I will not rule over you. Nor will my son rule over you. The Lord will rule over you'. 24 He said, 'I will ask for one thing. Will each of you give me one ear-ring from the riches you have taken?' (The Ishmaelites wore gold ear-rings.) 25 They answered, 'We are happy to give them to you'. So they put a coat on the ground. Every man threw a ring on to it. 26The weight of all the rings was 1700 shekels (about 40 pounds or 19 kilos in weight). They also had many other valuable things. They had ornaments and rich clothes from the Kings of Midian. And they took the rich ornaments from the necks of the camels. 27 Gideon made the gold into a beautiful ephod. He put this in Ophrah, his own town. All the Israelites came and worshipped the ephod. They made it into a false god. It pulled Gideon and his family away from the true God.

28 Midian could not fight Israel again. While Gideon was alive, Israel kept Midian down. The land had peace for 40 years. 29 Gideon, son of Joash, went back home to live. 30 He had many wives and 70 sons. 31Gideon visited a woman who lived in Shechem. They had a son called Abimelech.

32 Gideon, son of Joash, lived for a long time. Then he died and they put his body into the ground with that of his father, Joash. This was in Ophrah of the Abiezrites.

33 As soon as Gideon had died, the Israelites started to worship the Baals again, They made Baal-Berith their god. 34 They forgot the Lord their God. They did not remember that he had saved them from their enemies. These enemies had been all round them. 35 Nor were Israel kind to the family of Gideon. They did not remember all the good things that he had done for them.

Chapter 9

1 Abimelech, the son of Gideon in Shechem, spoke to his mother's brothers and all her family.

2 He told them to ask the men of Shechem who they wanted as a ruler. He asked if they wanted Gideon's 70 sons or just one man to rule them. He said, 'Remember that I belong to your family'.

3 Abimelech's brothers told all this to the men of Shechem. They decided that they wanted Abimelech as their ruler. They said, 'He is our brother'. 4 They gave him 70 shekels (about 1.75 pounds or 0.8 kilos in weight) of silver from the house of Baal-Berith. Abimelech used this money to pay bad men. Then they became his soldiers.

5 He went to his father's house in Ophrah. There he killed Gideon's 70 sons on one rock. They were his brothers. But Jotham, the youngest son hid himself. He did not die.

6 The men of Shechem and Beth Millo met together. They met at the tree by the tall rock in Shechem. There they made Abimelech king.

7 When he heard this, Jotham climbed up Mount Gerizim. He shouted to the men of Shechem, 'Listen to me, so that God may listen to you. 8 One day, the trees decided to make a king for themselves. They said to the olive tree, "Be our king". 9 But the olive tree answered, "My oil pleases men and the gods. I will not stop making oil to be your king". 10 Next, the trees said to the fig tree, "Come and be our king". 11 The fig tree replied, "I will not stop making my sweet fruit to rule over you". 12 Then the trees said to the vine, "Come and be our king". 13 But the vine answered, "Wine from my fruit makes men and gods happy. I will not stop making fruit to rule over you". 14 At last, the trees said to the thorn bush, "Come and be our king".15 The thorn bush said to the trees, "If you really want me to be your king, come and hide under my branches. If not, fire will come from the thorn bush and burn up all the big cedar trees!"

16 You have made Abimelech king. You have not been good to Gideon's family. You have hurt them. 17 But Gideon fought for you. He did not think about his own life. He saved you from being slaves to the Midianites. 18 Today you threw out my father's family. You have killed his 70 sons. You have made Abimelech king because he is your brother. He is the son of my father's slave-girl. 19 If you have been good to Gideon, I hope that Abimelech will make you happy! I hope that you will make him happy, too! 20 If you have not, I hope that Abimelech will destroy you. And I hope that you men of Shechem and Beth Millo will burn Abimelech!'

21 Jotham ran away to Beer because he was frightened of his brother, Abimelech.

22 Abimelech ruled Israel for 3 years. 23 Then God caused the people of Shechem to argue with Abimelech.24 God was punishing Abimelech for killing Gideon's 70 sons. God was punishing Abimelech and the people of Shechem for their murder.

25 The people of Shechem did not obey Abimelech. They put men on the top of the hills near Shechem. They took money and valuable things from everyone who went past. Abimelech heard about this.

26 Gaal son of Ebed went to live in Shechem with his brothers. The people of Shechem began to want Gaal as their leader. 27 They picked the fruit of the vine and made wine. Then they had a party. This was in the house (temple) where they worshipped their god. As they ate and drank, they said bad things about Abimelech. They wanted Gaal to give Abimelech a lot of trouble. 28 Gaal, son of Ebed, said, 'We should not let Abimelech lead us. He is Gideon's son and Zebul is his officer. We should let men of Hamor (Shechem's father) lead us. 29 If I led this people I would not let Abimelech be king. I would say to him, "Call out your whole army!" '

30 They told Zebul what Gaal, son of Ebed, had said. Zebul ruled the city, and he was very angry.

31 Zebul sent men to Abimelech by hidden paths. They told him, 'Gaal and his brothers are making the men of Shechem want to fight us. They are causing trouble. 32 Come in the night with your men. Hide in the fields until sunrise. 33 Then, in the morning, attack the city. When Gaal and his men come out, fight your best'.

34 So Abimelech and all his army came at night. They hid near Shechem in four groups.

35 Gaal was standing outside the city gates. Abimelech and his men came out from where they were hiding.36 Gaal saw them. He said to Zebul, 'Look, there are men coming from the tops of the mountains'. Zebul replied, 'You are wrong. You are looking at shadows'. 37 Gaal said again, 'Look, there are two groups of people. Some are coming from the centre of the land. Other men are coming from the prophet's tree'. 38Then Zebul spoke to Gaal, 'Where are your big words now? You said that Abimelech should not rule us. These are the men that you said were no use. Now go out and fight them!'

39 Gaal led the people of Shechem out to fight Abimelech.

40 Abimelech ran after him. Many men were hurt. They fell all along the way to the city gate. 41 Abimelech stayed in Arumah. Zebul made Gaal and his brothers leave Shechem.

42 The next day, the people of Shechem went out into the fields. Men told Abimelech about this. 43 He took his men and put them into three groups. When the people came out of the city, he attacked them. 44 Abimelech and his soldiers ran to stand at the city gate. The other two groups ran and killed the people in the fields.

45 Abimelech fought hard all day. He won the fight and killed the people. Then he destroyed the city. He put salt all over it.

46 The people in the strong building of Shechem heard the news. The strong place was in the house (temple) of El-Berith. 47 Men told Abimlelech about the people in the strong building.

48 He took his men up to Mount Zalmon. He cut branches off a tree with an axe. He put the branches on his shoulders. He shouted to his men, 'Be quick! Do as you have seen me do!' 49 So all the men cut branches and followed Abimelech. They put the branches round the strong building. Then they put fire to them. There were about 1000 men and women of Shechem in the building. They all died.

50 Abimelech went to Thebez next. He and his men attacked it. They won the fight for the city. 51 All the people of the city hid in a strong building. The building was inside the city. They locked the door. They went on to the roof. 52 Abimelech and his men attacked the strong building. He went near to the door, to burn it. 53 A woman dropped a very heavy stone on his head and broke his bones. 54 Abimelech said to his army servant, 'Be quick. Kill me. I do not want people to say that a woman killed me!' So his servant killed him with a sharp knife. 55 When the Israelites saw that Abimelech was dead, they went home.

56 This was how God punished Abimelech for murdering his 70 brothers. He had made his father's name look bad. 57 God was also punishing the people of Shechem for all the bad things that they had done. Jotham, son of Gideon had said that these things should happen.

Chapter 10

1 After the time of Abimelech, another man came to save Israel. He was Tola, son of Puah, son of Dodo of the tribe of Issachar. He lived in Shamir, in the hills of Ephraim.

2 He led Israel for 23 years. Then he died and they buried him in Shamir.

3 After Tola, Jair of Gilead became leader of Israel. He ruled Israel for 22 years. 4 He had 30 sons, who rode on 30 donkeys. The sons ruled 30 towns in Gilead. These towns are still called Havvoth Jair (Jair's villages). 5 When Jair died, they buried him in Kamon.

6 Again the Israelites did many bad things. The Lord saw this. Israel served the false gods Baal and Ashtoreth. And they served the gods of Aram, Sidon and Moab. They also served the gods of the Ammonites and the Philistines. They did not serve the Lord any more.

7 He became angry with them, because they had turned away from him. 8 The Lord let the Philistines and the Ammonites attack the people of Israel. He let them win the fight. They destroyed the Israelite armies in that year. The people of Israel served their enemies for 18 years. The enemies ruled the land on the east side of the river Jordan in Gilead. This was the land of the Amorites. 9 The Ammonites also crossed the river Jordan. They fought against Judah, Benjamin and the house of Ephraim. Israel was in bad trouble. 10 Then the Israelites called out to the Lord. They said, 'We have left you and have served other gods. This was wrong'.

11 The Lord replied, 'I have saved you many times when you called to me for help. I saved you from the Egyptians, the Amorites, the Ammonites and the Philistines. 12 I saved you from the Sidonians, the Amalekites and the Maonites (Midianites). They ruled you. You called to me for help and I saved you. 13 But you have left me to serve other gods. I will not save you again. 14 Call to the gods you have chosen. Let them save you from your trouble!'

15 The Israelites said to the Lord, 'We have done very bad things. Do as you will with us, but please save us now'. 16 Then they destroyed all the foreign gods of wood and stone. They began to serve the Lord again. The Lord saw how sorry they were. He did not want them to be hurt any more.

17 The Ammonite army came to Gilead. They were there in their tents. The Israelite men came to Mizpah and put their tents there. 18 The leaders of the people of Gilead made a promise. They said, 'The man who will lead the fight against the Ammonites will become our ruler. He will be the leader of all those living in Gilead'.

Chapter 11

1 Jephthah of Gilead was a brave soldier. His father was Gilead, but his mother was not Gilead's wife. 2 The sons of Gilead's wife became men and sent Jephthah away. They said, 'You will not get any of Gilead's things, because you are the son of another woman'. 3 So Jephthah ran away from his brothers. He went to live in the land of Tob. Other men joined him there. They were a small group of fighting men. Jephthah was their leader.

4 The Ammonite soldiers came to fight Israel some time later. 5 Then the leaders of Gilead went to get Jephthah from the land of Tob. 6 'Come and lead our army', they said. 'Then we can fight the Ammonites'.

7 Jephthah answered, 'You made me leave my father's house. You did not like me. Why do you come to me now that you are in trouble?'

8 The men of Gilead replied, 'But we are asking you to come back to us. Please fight the Ammonites with us. Then we will make you leader over all who live in Gilead'.

9 Jephthah said, 'What if you take me back to fight for you, against the Ammonites. The Lord may help me to win the fight. Then will you really make me your leader?'

10 The leaders of Gilead said, 'God is looking at us. We promise to do as we have said'. 11 So Jephthah went back with them to Gilead. The people made him their ruler and leader. He repeated all that he had said, at Mizpah, in front of the Lord.

12 Jephthah sent men to the Ammonite king. He asked, 'Why have you come to fight our people? What have we done to hurt you?'

13 The King of the Ammonites answered Jephthah's people, 'Israel came up out of Egypt. They took all my land from the Arnon to the Jabbok. They took all the land up to the Jordan. Now give it back to us, without fighting'.

14 Jephthah sent the men back to the King of the Ammonites. 15 They said, 'This is what Jephthah says, "Israel did not take the land of Moab, or the land of the Ammonites. 16 When Israel came up out of Egypt, they went through the desert to the Red Sea and to Kadesh. They went through land where no people live. 17 Then Israel sent men to the King of Edom. They asked him to let Israel go through his kingdom. But the King of Edom would not listen. Israel also sent men to the King of Moab, and he refused. So Israel stayed at Kadesh.

18 Next Israel went round the kingdoms of Edom and Moab. They walked to the east of Moab through desert lands (where no people live). They put their tents on the other side of the Arnon. This was outside the land of Moab.

19 Sihon, King of the Amorites, ruled in Heshbon. Israel sent men to him. They said, 'Let us go through your country to our own place'. 20 But Sihon was afraid. He sent men to get his army. They met together at Jahaz. Then he fought with Israel.

21 The Lord, the God of Israel helped the Israelites to win the fight. Israel beat Sihon and his men. 22 They won all the land of the Amorites who lived in that country. This land was between the Arnon and the Jabbok, and to the Jordan from the desert.

23 The Lord, the God of Israel has made the Amorites run away from the people of Israel. He did not give the land to you.

24 You should take what your god, Chemosh gives to you. We will keep what the Lord, our God, has given to us. 25 You are not better than Balak son of Zippor, King of Moab. He has never argued or fought with Israel. 26 Israel has ruled Heshbon and Aroer and the villages round them for 300 years. Israel has lived in all the towns along the Arnon too. You did not take them back in all that time. 27 I have not done anything wrong to you. You will be doing a wrong thing if you fight me. Let the Lord, the judge, decide whether the Israelites or the Ammonites are doing what is right" '.

28 The king of Ammon refused to listen to the message sent to him by Jephthah.

29 Then the Spirit of the Lord took hold of Jephthah. He crossed the lands of Gilead and of Manasseh. He went through Mizpah in Gilead, and moved towards the Ammonites. 30 Jephthah made a promise to the Lord. He said, 'If you let us win the battle with the Ammonites, I will give you a gift. 31 Whatever comes first out through the door of my house when I return, I will kill and give to you. I will burn it as an offering to you, after we have won the fight'.

32 Then Jephthah went over to fight the Ammonites. The Lord gave him the power to win the battle. 33 He destroyed 20 towns from Aroer to Minnith, as far as Abel Karamim. This is how Israel came to rule Ammon.

34 Jephthah returned to his home in Mizpah. His only daughter came out to meet him, dancing to music. He had no other son or daughter. 35 He cried out when he saw her, and tore his clothes. He said, 'My daughter, you have made me very very sad. I have made a promise to the Lord and I must keep it'.

36 'Father', she said, 'You have made your promise to the Lord. You must do to me what you have promised. The Lord has given you the power to punish your enemies, the Ammonites. 37 But give me this one thing. Give me two months to walk in the hills and to cry with my friends. I am sad that I will never marry'.

38 'You may go', he said. And he let her go away for two months. She and the girls went to the hills. They cried because she would never marry. 39 She returned after two months, and Jephthah kept his promise. The girl had never had sex with a man. This is why 40 the young women of Israel go out for 4 days every year. They are remembering the daughter of Jephthah, the Gileadite.

Chapter 12

1 The men of Ephraim joined together. They crossed over to Zaphon. They said to Jephthah, 'Why did you go to fight the Ammonites without us? You should have asked us to go with you. We are going to burn down your house'.

2 Jephthah answered, 'When my people and I were fighting against the Ammonites, I asked for your help. But you did not come to save us. 3 When I saw this, I crossed over to fight the Ammonites without you. I was afraid that I would die. But the Lord helped me to win. Why have you now come to fight me?'

4 Jephthah asked the men of Gilead to come to him. They fought against Ephraim. The Gileadites won the fight. They were angry because the men of Ephraim had said, 'You are bad men. We sent you away from Ephraim and Manasseh'. 5 The Gileadites guarded the places where the men of Ephraim would cross the river Jordan. They asked a man who returned from the fight, 'Are you an Ephraimite, (man of Ephraim)?' 6 If he replied, 'No', they said, 'Then, say "Shibboleth" '. He might say, "Sibboleth", because Ephraimites could not say, "Shibboleth". Then they would kill him, by the river. 42 000 Ephraimites were killed at that time.

7 Jephthah led Israel for 6 years. Then he died and they buried him in a town in Gilead.

8 After him, Ibzan of Bethlehem led Israel. 9 He had 30 sons and 30 daughters. He let his daughters marry men of other big families. He brought 30 young women from other families to be wives for his sons. He led Israel for 7 years.

10 Then Ibzan died and they buried him in Bethlehem.

11 After him, Elon from Zebulun led Israel for 10 years. 12 Then Elon died, and they buried him in Aijalon. This was in the land of Zebulun.

13 After him, Abdon, son of Hillel, led Israel. He came from Pirathon. 14 He had 40 sons and 30 grandsons. They rode on 70 donkeys. He led Israel for 8 years. 15 Then Abdon, son of Hillel, died. They buried him at Pirathon in Ephraim. This is the hill country of the Amalekites.

Chapter 13

1 Again the Israelites did many wrong things. The Lord was angry. So he let the Philistines fight them, and win. The Philistines ruled Israel for 40 years.

2 Manoah, of the tribe of Dan, lived in Zorah. His wife could not have children. 3 The Lord sent an angel to her. He said, 'You have no children. You thought that you could not have children. But you will have a son. 4 You must drink no wine or other strong drink. You must eat nothing that is not clean. 5 You must not cut the boy's hair. He is to be a Nazirite. He will belong to God from the time that he is born. He will begin to save Israel from the Philistines'.

6 The woman went and told her husband. She said, 'A man of God came to me. He looked like someone sent by God. He was very powerful. I did not ask where he came from. He did not tell me his name. 7 He said to me, "You will give birth to a son. You must not drink any wine or strong drink. You must not eat any food that is not clean. The boy is to be a Nazirite from the day he is born until he dies!" '

8 Manoah asked the Lord God, 'Please, Lord send your angel again. Let him tell us how to teach the boy that is to be born'.

9 God heard Manoah. The angel came again to the woman. She was working in the field. Her husband was not with her. 10 She ran to tell her husband, 'He is here! The man that I saw the other day has come!' 11 Manoah got up and followed his wife. When he came to the man, he said, 'Are you the person who talked to my wife?' 'I am', he said.

12 So Manoah asked, 'When your words come true, how is the boy to live? What rules must he obey?'

13 The angel answered, 'Your wife must do everything that I told her. 14 She must not eat anything from the vine. She must not drink wine or other strong drink. She must obey all the rules that I have taught her'.

15 Manoah said to him, 'Please stay here. We would like to make a meal for you. We will kill and cook a young goat'.

16 The Lord's angel replied, 'I will not eat any of your food, even if you keep me here. If you make a gift, give it to the Lord'. (Manoah did not know that he was an angel from God.)

17 Then Manoah asked the angel, 'What is your name? I want to thank you for being so kind. I will do this when your word comes true'.

18 He replied, 'Why do your ask my name? You could not understand it'. 19 Then Manoah took a young goat and some grain. He burnt them on a rock as a gift to the Lord God. The Lord surprised them. 20 As the fire burnt up, the angel rose up over the light of the fire. When Manoah and his wife saw this, they fell to the ground. 21 They did not see the angel again. Then Manoah understood that it was the angel of the Lord.

22 'We are sure to die!' Manoah said to his wife. 'We have seen God'.

23 But his wife answered, 'The Lord accepted our gift of meat and bread. He would not have shown us these things if he had wanted to kill us. He would not have said anything'.

24 The woman had a baby. She called him Samson. He became a man, and the Lord was good to him. 25 The Lord's Holy Spirit began to work in him. Samson lived in Mahaneh Dan. This is between Zorah and Eshtaol.

Chapter 14

1 In Timnah, Samson saw a young Philistine woman. 2 When he got home, he spoke to his father and mother, 'I have seen a Philistine woman in Timnah. Please get her for me as my wife'.

3 His parents replied, 'Why go to the Philistines for a wife? There are many nice girls in our own family and in Israel. Why go to the Philistines for a wife? They do not obey the Lord'.

But Samson said to his father, 'Get her for me. She is the right girl for me'. 4 His parents did not know that this was what the Lord wanted. God wanted a reason to attack the Philistines. They were ruling Israel at that time. 5 Samson went down to Timnah, with his mother and father. Near the fields of Timnah, an angry young lion ran towards them. 6 The Lord's Spirit gave Samson great power. He tore the lion into pieces with his hands. The lion seemed as weak as a young goat. But he did not tell his father or his mother what he had done. 7 Then he went to talk with the young woman. He liked her very much.

8 Later, Samson returned to marry the girl. He turned off the path to look at the lion's body. There was a big group of bees and some honey inside it. 9 He took the honey out with his hands and ate it as he walked. When he returned to his parents he gave some to them. They ate the honey. But he did not tell them where it came from.

10 Samson's father went to see the young woman. Samson prepared a party meal there. All the men did this when they married. 11 30 young men came to him when he was ready.

12 Samson said to them, 'Let me ask you a difficult question. Give me an answer in the 7 days of my party. Then I will give you 30 valuable coats and 30 sets of clothes. 13 If you cannot tell me the answer, you will give me 30 good coats and 30 sets of clothes'. The young men said, 'Let us hear your question. Do tell us'.

14 Samson replied, 'Out of the eater, something to eat. Out of the strong, something sweet'. They could not find the answer in 3 days.

15 On the fourth day they spoke to Samson's wife. 'Get your husband to tell you the answer for us. If you do not, we will burn you and all in your father's house. You will die. Did you want to take our money when you asked us to your marriage?'

16 Then Samson's wife started to cry. She threw herself at Samson. She shouted, 'You hate me. You do not really love me. You have asked my people a difficult question. But you have not told me the answer'.

'I have not told even my father or mother', he replied. 'So why should I tell you?'

17 His wife cried all the 7 days of the party. So Samson told her the answer on the seventh day. She had made him very tired. Then she told her people the answer to his question.

18 Then the people of the town went to Samson. It was before sunset of the seventh day. They said, 'What is sweeter than honey? What is stronger that a lion?'

Samson said, 'You would not have found the answer on your own. You made my wife ask me'.

19 The Lord's Spirit took hold of Samson. It sent him to Ashkelon. The Spirit gave him great power. He killed 30 Philistines there, and took all their things. He gave their clothes to the men who had answered his question. He was so angry that he seemed to burn inside. He returned to his father's house. 20 And his wife's father gave her to the friend who had stood by him at his marriage.

Chapter 15

1 Later, Samson went to visit his wife. The grain was ready to eat. No one had brought it in from the fields. Samson took a young goat with him. He said, 'I am going into my wife's room'. But the girl's father stopped him.

2 He said, 'I was so sure that you hated her. I have given her to your friend. Her young sister is more beautiful. Take her instead'.

3 Samson said, 'This time you have given me a powerful reason to hurt the Philistines. I will punish them for their bad work'. 4 So he went out and caught 300 foxes. He tied the foxes in pairs by their tails. He tied a dry branch to each pair of tails. 5 He lit the branches. He made the foxes run through the fields of the Philistines. The grain was standing there. Some was ready to take away. He burnt all the grain, the vines and the olive trees.

6 The Philistines asked, 'Who did this?' People told them that it was Samson, who had married the Timnite's daughter. They said, 'He did it because he gave Samson's wife to his friend'.

So the Philistines went and burned the man and his daughter to death. 7 Samson said to them, 'Because you have done this, I will punish you. I will not stop until your punishment is finished'. 8 He fought them with great power. He killed many Philistines. Then he went to live in a hole in the rock of Etam.

9 The Philistines went and put their tents in Judah near Lehi. 10 The men of Judah asked, 'Why have you come to fight us?' 'We have come to take Samson away', they replied. 'We want him because he has hurt us'.

11 3000 men of Judah went to the place where Samson was. They said, 'You must know that the Philistines are our rulers. You are causing us trouble'.

He answered, 'I only did to them as they did to me'.

12 They said to him, 'We have come to tie you up. We must give you to the Philistines'.

Samson said, 'Promise that you will not kill me'.

13 'We agree', they said, 'We will only tie you up and give you to them. We will not kill you'. So they tied him up with two new ropes and led him away.

14 When they came near to Lehi, all the Philistines shouted. They came towards Samson. Then the Spirit of the Lord gave great power to him. The ropes on his arms seemed as weak as grass. The material tied round his hands fell off. 15 He found a new bone from a donkey's face. He took it and killed 1000 men.

16 Then Samson said, 'I have made donkeys of them with a donkey's bone. With a bone I have killed 1000 men'.

17 After this he threw away the bone. The place was called 'Ramah Lehi' (the hill of a donkey's face bone).

18 Samson was very thirsty. He cried out to the Lord, 'You have helped me to win a big fight. Do I have to die of thirst? Your enemies would come and take me'.

19 The Lord made a hole in the ground near Lehi. Water came out of it. Samson drank from it and he became strong again. The name of this water was En Hakkore (water of the one who shouted); it is still in Lehi.

20 Samson led Israel for 20 years in the days of the Philistines.

Chapter 16

1 One day, Samson went to Gaza. He went to have sex with a woman there. 2 The people of Gaza heard that Samson was there. The men waited for him all night at the gate of the city. They said, 'We will stay here. We will kill him at dawn'.

3 But Samson only stayed with the woman until the middle of the night. Then he got up. He took the doors from the gate of the city. He tore them from the walls, with the wood at their edges. He carried them to the top of the hill towards Hebron.

4 Some time later Samson began to love a woman called Delilah. She lived in the valley of Sorek. 5 The rulers of the Philistines went to her. They said, 'See if you can discover what makes Samson so strong. See if you can find a way to get power over him. We want to tie him up and to make him do what we want. We will each give you 1100 shekels of silver (about 28 pounds or 13 kilos)'.

6 Delilah said to Samson, 'Tell me the secret. What makes you so strong? How can you be tied up and kept quiet?'

7 Samson replied, 'You must tie me with 7 new leather ropes. They must not be dried. I will become weak, like other men'.

8 The rulers of the Philistines gave Delilah the 7 new leather ropes. She tied Samson with them. 9 She hid Philistine men in the room. Then she shouted, 'Samson the Philistines are here'. But he broke the 7 ropes as easy as fire breaks a thin line. So they did not discover why he was so strong.

10 Delilah said to Samson, 'You have made me look like a fool. Your words were not true. Come on, tell me how someone can really tie you'.

11 He said, 'If someone ties me with new ropes that have never been used, I will become weak. I will be as other men'.

12 So Delilah took new ropes and tied him with them. Men were hiding in the room. Then she shouted, 'Samson the Philistines are here'. But he broke the ropes as if they had been very thin.

13 Delilah then said to Samson, 'Your words were not true. You have made me look silly. Tell me how someone can really tie you'. He replied, 'If you work the 7 tails of my hair into the cloth you are making I will become weak. You must tie it well and I will be like other men'. Delilah did this while he was asleep. She took the 7 tails of his hair and tied them in with the cloth she was making. 14 She fixed them with a piece of wood. Again she shouted to him, 'Samson, the Philistines are here'. He woke up. She had fixed the cloth to a heavy table. Samson tore the cloth and the piece of wood away from it.

15 Delilah said to him, 'You cannot really love me, when you will not tell me your secret. This is the third time that you have made me look like a fool. You have not told me why you are so strong'. 16 She kept on saying the same thing again and again. Her questions made Samson very tired.

17 So Samson told her everything. 'I have never cut my hair', he said. 'When I was born, God chose me to be a Nazirite. If someone cuts my hair off, I will not be strong any more. I will be as weak as any other man'.

18 Delilah saw that he had told her everything. So she sent a message to the rulers of the Philistines. 'Come back once more. Samson has told me everything'. The rulers of the Philistines came back. They brought silver with them. 19 Delilah made Samson sleep with his head on her knees. She asked a man to cut off the 7 tails of his hair. This was to make him weak. He was not strong any more.

20 Then she shouted, 'Samson, the Philistines are here!' He woke up. He thought that he could become free. But he did not know that God's power had left him.

21 The Philistines took Samson. They pulled out his eyes. They tied him with metal ropes. They made him work in prison. He had to
make grain into flour. 22 But the hair on his head began to grow again.

23 The rulers of the Philistines met together to worship their god, Dagon. They said, 'Our God has put Samson, our enemy, into our power'.

24 When the people saw Samson, they praised their god. They said, 'Our god has given our enemy to us. This enemy destroyed our land. He killed many of us'.

25 The people were all very happy. They shouted, 'Bring out Samson. He can dance for us'. So they brought Samson out of the prison. He had to do as they asked.

They took Samson among the pillars of the temple.

26 A servant held Samson's hand. Samson said, 'Put me against the pillars which hold up the roof. I want to put my weight on them'. 27 The temple was full of men and women. All the leaders of the Philistines were there. About 3000 people were on the roof watching Samson dance. 28 Then Samson prayed to the Lord. 'Remember me, God, powerful Lord and ruler. Please make me strong again, for one more time. I want to punish the Philistines for pulling out my eyes'. 29 Then Samson put his hands on the two pillars in the centre of the building. He got ready to push. He pushed one with his right hand, the other with his left hand. 30 Samson said, 'Let me die with the Philistines'. Then he pushed with the power of his whole body. The building fell down on all the rulers and people in it. So, Samson killed more people when he died than while he lived.

31 Then his brothers and his father's whole family came to get him. They took him back and buried him with his father Manoah's body. This was in the ground between Eshtael and Zorah. Samson had ruled Israel for 20 years.

Chapter 17

1 A man called Micah came from the hill country of Ephraim. 2 He told his mother that he had taken 1100 shekels of silver (about 28 pounds or 13 kilos) from her. She had asked the gods to punish the person who had done this. His mother then asked the Lord to make her son happy.

3 Micah returned the 1100 shekels of silver to his mother. She said, 'You must make this silver into an image and an idol. I am giving it back to you'.

4 Micah's mother took 200 shekels of the silver. She gave them to a man who made things with silver. He made an image and an idol. They were in Micah's house.

5 Now Micah had a special place to worship his gods. He made an ephod and more idols for it. He chose one of his sons to be a priest. 6 There was no king in Israel in those days. Every man did what he thought was right.

7 A young Levite was living in Bethlehem of Judah. 8 He left that town. He was looking for another place to stay. As he travelled, he came to Micah's house in the hills of Ephraim.

9 Micah asked him, 'Where are you from?' 'I am a Levite from Bethlehem in Judah', he said. 'And I am looking for a place to stay'.

10 Micah said, 'Live with me and be my father and my priest. I will give you 10 shekels (110 grams or 4 ounces) of silver a year. And I will give you your food and clothes'. 11 So the Levite agreed to live with Micah. He became like a son to Micah. 12 Micah made the young man a priest at his place of worship. The young man became his priest and lived in his house. 13 Then Micah said, 'Now I know that the Lord will be good to me, because I have made this Levite my priest'.

Chapter 18

1 In those days Israel had no king. The tribe of Dan (the Danites) were looking for a place to live. They wanted their own land to live in. They had not taken the land that Joshua promised to their tribe (Joshua 19:40-48). 2 The Danites sent 5 soldiers from Zorah to Eshtaol to explore the land. These men came from all the families of Dan. They told them, 'Go and explore the land'.

The men went into the hill country of Ephraim. They came to Micah's house and stayed there for a night. 3 As they came near to Micah's house, they recognised the voice of the young Levite. They went in and asked him, 'Who brought you here? What are you doing in this place? Why are you here?'

4 He told them what Micah had done for him. He said, 'He pays me to be his priest'.

5 They said to him, 'Please ask God if our journey will have a good result'.

6 The priest answered, 'Go in peace. The Lord will be with you on your journey'.

7 So the 5 men left and went to Laish. They saw that it was a safe, quiet place. The people of Laish thought that they would never have to fight. The people of Sidon (the Sidonians) thought the same. Their land was good, so they were rich. They lived a long way from the Sidonians. They had no other friends.

8 The men returned to Zorah and Eshtaol. Their brothers asked them, 'What did you find?'

9 They answered, 'Let us go and attack them. The land is very good. You must do something. Do not be afraid to go there. We can win it. 10 The people there think that they are safe. You will find a large land. It has everything. God has given it to you'.

11 600 Danite men prepared for the fight. They took their arms. They left Zorah and Eshtaol. 12 On their way they put up their tents near Kiriath Jearim in Judah. This is why the place to the west of Kiriath Jearim is still called Mahaneh Dan. (Dan's camp.) 13 From there they went to the hill country of Ephraim. They came to Micah's house. 14 The 5 men who had explored the land said to their brothers, 'Do you know that one of these houses has an ephod, an image and an idol? Now you know what to do'. 15 So they went to meet the young Levite in Micah's house. 16 The 600 Danites stood at the gate. They were ready for battle. 17 The 5 men who had explored the land went in. They took all the silver idols and other things. The priest and the Danite soldiers stood outside the gate.

18 So the 5 men went into Micah's house and took his ephod and idols and other gods. Then the priest (the Levite) asked them, 'What are you doing?'

19 They answered him, 'Be quiet! Do not say a word. Come with us, and be our father and our priest. It will be better for you to serve a whole tribe of Israel. It will be better than now, when you are serving only one man's family'. 20 Then the priest was happy. He took the ephod, the other gods and idols, and went with the Danites. 21 The people put their little children and animals in front of them. They took all their own things. Then they left.

22 The men who lived near Micah came together. They ran after the Danites and met them as they travelled. 23 They shouted after the Danites. The Danites turned and spoke to Micah, 'What is the matter? Why are you coming to fight with us?'

24 Micah replied, 'You have taken the gods that I made. You have taken my priest. I have nothing left. How can you ask me what is wrong?'

25 The Danites answered, 'Do not argue with us. Some of us are very quick to get angry. We might attack you and your family and kill you all'. 26 The Danites went on their journey, and Micah went home. He saw that they were too strong for him.

27 They took what Micah had made. They took his priest. Then they went on to Laish. They attacked the people there and destroyed their city by fire. The people of Laish had thought that they were safe. 28 No one came to save them. They lived a long way from Sidon. They had no other friends. The city was in a valley near Beth Rehob.

The Danites built the city again and lived there. 29 They called it Dan, after their father Dan. He had been one of Israel's (Jacob's) 12 sons. The city had been called Laish.

30 The Danites put the idols there. Jonathan, son of Gershom, son of Moses, became their priest. He and his sons served there as priests for Dan. They served until other people started to rule the land of Israel. 31 They continued to use the idols which Micah had made at the time when the House of God was in Shiloh.

Chapter 19

1 There was no king in Israel in those days. A Levite lived in the hills of Ephraim. He took a woman from Bethlehem in Judah to live with him.

2 But she left him and she returned to her father's house in Bethlehem. She stayed there for 4 months. 3 Then her husband went to visit her. He asked her to return to him. He took his servant and two donkeys with him. She took him into her father's house.

Her father was happy to see him. 4 The girl's father asked him to stay there. So he stayed for 3 days. He ate and drank there and slept there also.

5 On the fourth day they got up early and were ready to leave. The girl's father said, 'Have something to eat, and then you may go'. 6 So the two men sat down. They ate and drank together. Then the girl's father asked him to stay that night. He wanted him to enjoy himself. 7 The man got up to go. But the girl's father made him stay. 8 On the morning of the fifth day the girl's father said, 'Have something to eat and drink. Wait until this afternoon and you can go'. So the two of them ate together.

9 The man and woman were ready to go, with the servant. Then her father said, 'It is nearly evening. Sleep here tonight. The day is nearly over. Stay and enjoy yourself. You can leave early tomorrow and go home'. 10 But the man did not want to stay for another night. So he left with his two donkeys and his woman. They went towards Jebus (Jerusalem).

11 When they came near to Jebus, the day was nearly over. The servant said, 'Let us stay in this city of the Jebusites. Let us stop here for the night'.

12 His master replied, 'No, we will not go into a foreign city. These people are not Israelites. We will go on to Gibeah'. 13 He said, 'Let us try to reach Gibeah or Ramah. Then we can stay in one of those cities for the night'. 14 It was sunset when they came near to Gibeah in Benjamin. 15 They stayed there for the night. They sat in the centre of the city. But no one took them in for the night.

16 That evening, an old man from the hill country of Ephraim (but who was living in Gibeah) returned from his work. 17 When he saw the traveller in the square, he asked, 'Where are you going? Where did you come from?'

18 The Levite answered, 'We are going from Bethlehem in Judah to the far hills of Ephraim. I live there. I have been to Bethlehem and now I am going to the house of the Lord. No one has taken me into his house. 19 We have food and material for our animal's beds. We have bread and wine for ourselves. We (this woman, my servant and I) do not need anything'.

20 The old man said, 'Please come into my house. I can give you whatever you need. But do not stay in the open city'. 21 So he took him into his house, and fed the donkeys. When they had washed their feet, they had something to eat and drink.

22 They were enjoying themselves. Then some bad men came from the city and stood all round the house. They hit the door hard and shouted to the old man. They said, 'Bring out the man who came to your house. We want to have sex with him'.

23 The old man went outside to them. He said, 'Friends, do not be so very, very bad. This man is in my house. You would be doing a very bad thing.

24 Here is my daughter, who has never had sex with a man, and this man's woman. I will bring them to you and you can use them as you want. But do not do such a bad thing to this man'.

25 But the men would not listen to him. So the traveller took his woman, and sent her out to them. They made her have sex with them and hurt her all night long. At dawn, they let her go. 26 She went back to the house where the man was staying. She fell at the door. She lay there until it was light.

27 Her master got up and opened the door in the morning. He was ready to continue his journey. He saw the woman lying there. Her hands were reaching towards the door.

28 He said to her, 'Get up. Let us go!' But she did not answer. Then he put her on his donkey and started off for home.

29 When he reached home, he cut the woman's body into 12 parts.

He sent these to all the tribes of Israel. 30 Everyone who saw it said, 'Nothing as bad as this has ever happened before.

Never since the Israelites came out of Egypt. Think about it. Think with care. Tell us what we must do!'

Chapter 20

1 Then all the Israelites from the north to the south of Israel came together. They met at Mizpah, to find out what God wanted. 2 The leaders of all the tribes of Israel stood with the people of God. There were 400 000 men ready to fight. 3 (The Benjamites had heard that the Israelites had gone to Mizpah.) Then the Israelites said, 'Tell us how this bad thing happened'.

4 So the Levite, the husband of the dead woman, spoke to them. He said, 'My woman and I came to Gibeah of Benjamin, to stay the night. 5 The men of Gibeah came and stood round the house. They wanted to kill me. They made my woman have sex with them, and she died. 6 I took her body and cut it into pieces. I sent one piece to each part of Israel. I did this because of the bad thing that they had done. 7 Now, people of Israel, tell us what you think'.

8 All the people of Israel stood together. They said, 'None of us will go home. No, not one of us will return to his house. 9 But this is what we will do to Gibeah. We will use "the lot" to decide how we should go. 10 We will take 10 men of each 100 from each of the tribes of Israel. We will take 100 from each 1000, and 1000 from each 10 000. They will get everything that the army needs. Then, when the army reaches Gibeah, they will punish the men there. The men of Gibeah have done a great wrong. This is the right thing to do to them'. 11 So all the men of Israel met and stood together outside the city.

12 The tribes of Israel sent men to all the places in Benjamin. They said, 'This murder was done by some of your tribe. 13 Send out to us the bad men of Gibeah. Then we can kill them. This will make our people clean from the wrong that the men of Gibeah have done'.

But the Benjamites would not listen to the other Israelites. 14 They came from their towns and met at Gibeah to fight them. 15 They had 26 000 fighting men from their towns. And they had 700 chosen men from Gibeah. 16 Among all these soldiers were 700 men who used their left hands. They could use a leather rope to throw a stone. They could use it to hit a chosen place. They hit it every time.

17 Israel, without Benjamin, had an army of 400 000 fighting men.

18 The Israelites went to Bethel. They asked God which tribe should lead the soldiers against Benjamin. The Lord replied, 'Judah must go first'..

19 The next morning, the Israelites got up and put their tents near to Gibeah. 20 The Israelites prepared to fight the Benjamites at Gibeah. 21 The Benjamites came out of Gibeah. They killed 22 000 Israelites that day, in the fight. 22 The men of Israel decided to stand where they had stood the day before. 23 They went and cried to the Lord until the evening. They asked him, 'Must we go out again to fight the Benjamites, our brothers?'

The Lord answered, 'Go and fight them'.

24 The Israelites went near to Benjamin on the second day. 25 This time, when the Benjamites came out to fight, they killed another 18 000 Israelites.

26 Then all the Israelites went up to Bethel. They sat there, crying to the Lord. They ate no food that day. They offered gifts to the Lord, peace offerings and burnt offerings.

27 They wanted to ask the Lord what to do. (The Ark of the Covenant was there then. Phinehas, son of Eleazar, son of Aaron was the priest who served there.) 28 They asked, 'Should we go up again to fight Benjamin, our brother, or not?' The Lord said, 'Go, for tomorrow you will win the fight'.

29 Then Israel had a good idea. 30 On the third day they went out to fight Benjamin as before.

31 The Benjamites came out of Gibeah to meet them. But the Israelites led them away from the city. The Benjamites began to kill the Israelites again.

They killed about 30 men in the fields and on the roads. These were the roads to Bethel and to Gibeah.

32 The Benjamites were saying, 'We are winning the fight again'. But the Israelites were saying, 'We will run away so that the Benjamites will follow us away from the city'.

33 The men of Israel all moved to Baal Tamar. Men hid to the west of Gibeah and attacked Benjamin. 34 Then 10 000 of Israel's best soldiers attacked the front of Gibeah. The fighting was very strong. Benjamin did not know that the end of the fight was so near. 35 The Lord helped Israel to win the fight with Benjamin. That day Israel killed 25 000 Benjamite fighting men. 36 Then Benjamin saw that Israel had won.

Now the men of Israel had run away from Benjamin. They were waiting for their men to take Gibeah. 37 The men who were hiding ran into Gibeah and went through the whole city. They killed all the people. 38 The leaders had told them to make a big cloud of smoke in the city. 39 Then the other Israelites would turn back to the city.

The Benjamites had begun to kill the Israelites, about 30 (thirty) of them. They said, 'We are winning, as we did in the first fight'. 40 Then they turned and saw the smoke rising from their city to the sky. 41 The men of Israel turned towards them. Then the men of Benjamin were very afraid. They knew that they would soon die. 42 So they ran towards the desert. But they could not get away from the fighting. The men of Israel came from their town and killed them. 43 They were all round the Benjamites and they caught them east of Gibeah. 44 18 000 strong Benjamite fighting men died there. 45 Other men ran through the desert to the rock of Rimmon. The Israelites killed 5000 men along the roads. They continued to run after the Benjamites as far as Gidom. And they killed 2000 more.

46 On that day, 25 000 Benjamite soldiers died. They were all strong fighting men. 47 But 600 men turned and ran to the rock of Rimmon. They stayed there for 4 months. 48 The Israelites went back to Benjamin. They killed the people and animals in all the towns. They burnt all the towns that they could find.

Chapter 21

1 The men of Israel made a promise to the Lord at Mizpah. They agreed that they would not give their daughters to a Benjamite to marry.

2 The people went to Bethel. They sat there until evening, weeping. They cried to the Lord God, and called out to him. 3 'Why has this happened to Israel? Why have we lost one tribe of Israel?'

4 Early next day, the people built an altar. They offered gifts to the Lord there. They burnt some of the gifts, as God had told them.

5 Then the Israelites asked, 'Which people from the tribes did not join us at Mizpah?' For they had decided that everyone should meet there. They would kill anyone who did not meet them.

6 Now the Israelites were very sad. They said, 'Israel has lost one of its tribes. The Benjamites were our brothers. 7 How can we get wives for those who are left? We have promised the Lord that we would not let them marry our daughters'. 8 Then they asked, 'Which Israelites did not come with us to Mizpah?' They found that no one from Jabesh Gilead had come with them. 9 When they counted the people, there were no men from Jabesh Gilead among them.

10 So the Israelite army sent 12 000 fighting men to Jabesh Gilead. They told them to kill everyone there, including the women and children. 11 'This is what you are to do', they said. 'Kill every male, and every married woman'. 12 They found 400 young women in Jabesh Gilead. These girls had not had sex with anyone. The Israelites took them to their camp at Shiloh in Canaan.

13 Then all the Israelites sent a message of peace to the Benjamites. They were still at the rock of Rimmon. 14 So the Benjamites returned at that time. The Israelites gave them the women of Jabesh Gilead who had not been killed. But there were not enough women for all the Benjamites.

15 The people were very sad for Benjamin. This was because the Lord had taken one of the tribes of Israel. 16 The elders of Israel asked, 'How can we get wives for all the other men of Benjamin? All their women are dead. 17 The men of Benjamin that are alive must have children. If they do not, their tribe will die out. 18 We cannot give them our daughters as wives. We promised that we would not do this. We said, "God will punish anyone who gives a girl as wife to a Benjamite. 19 But there will soon be a big party at Shiloh. They worship God there every year in this way. The party is north of Bethel and south of Lebonah. And it is also east of the road from Bethel to Shechem" '.

20 The Israelites told the Benjamites to hide in the fields, 21 and watch. They said, 'When the girls of Shiloh come out to dance, run out and catch one each. Take them to the land of Benjamin. 22 When their fathers or brothers get angry, they will come to us. Then we will say, "Please help the Benjamites. We did not get wives for them in the war. You will not be punished, because you did not give your daughters to them" '.

23 So that is what the Benjamites did. Each man caught a girl as she was dancing. Then he carried her off to be his wife. Then they went back to their own land and built their towns again. Then they lived there.

24 Then the Israelites left that place. They went home to their tribes and families in their own lands.

25 In those days, Israel had no king. Everyone did what he thought was right.

A Stranger Finds Love in Bethlehem

Ruth

About this book

This book is about a woman called Ruth. She was an ancestor of King David and of Jesus. We do not know who wrote the book. Ruth was a good woman who was kind to her husband's mother, Naomi. Naomi's and Ruth's husbands died. They were very poor and Naomi was very sad. But they obeyed God. A man called Boaz helped them. He married Ruth. God was good to Ruth and Boaz. They had children and Naomi became happy again.

Chapter 1

1-2 There was a time when judges ruled Israel. There was not enough food for the people to eat. A man, called Elimelech, lived in Bethlehem in Judah. Elimelech had a wife and two sons. Elimelech's wife was called Naomi and his sons were called Mahlon and Kilion. They were Ephrathites. Because there was not enough food, Elimelech and his family left Bethlehem. They went to live in Moab.

3 Elimelech died while they were living in Moab. Naomi and her two sons remained there and 4 Naomi's sons married women from Moab. Mahlon married a woman called Ruth. And Kilion married a woman called Orpah. 5 Both Mahlon and Kilion died after they had all lived in Moab for about ten years. Naomi was completely alone, without her husband or her sons.

6 Naomi received news from Judah that God had helped his people. There was now enough food in Judah again. Naomi decided to return to Judah. 7 She and her sons' wives left their home in Moab. They began to travel together along the road towards Judah.

8 On the way to Judah, Naomi spoke to Ruth and Orpah. She said, 'Return to your mothers' homes and stay there. Your husbands are dead now. But you were kind to them when they were alive. And you have been kind to me. I pray that God will be as kind to you. I also pray that God will give each of you another husband and a new home.' 9 Naomi kissed them and Ruth and Orpah began to cry.

10 They said to Naomi, 'No! We will go with you to your people.'

11 But Naomi said, 'Return to your own country, my daughters. You should not want to come with me. I will not have other sons. You cannot marry them.

12 Return to your own country, my daughters.

I am too old to have another husband. Think about this. I might even marry another husband tonight. Then I might give birth to sons. Those sons would grow up and they would become men. Then you could marry them. 13 But I am sure that you do not want to wait for so many years, my daughters. This is painful for you. It is more painful for me. God has caused bad things to happen to me.'

14 Ruth and Orpah wept again. Orpah kissed Naomi and she said goodbye. But Ruth would not leave Naomi. She held on to Naomi.

15 Naomi said to Ruth, 'Orpah has returned to her family. She has returned to the gods of Moab. Go with her.'

16 Ruth said to Naomi, 'Do not say that I must leave you. I want to go with you. I want to live with you. You belong to Israel's people. I will belong to them also. Your God will be my God. 17 I want to die in the place where you die. I want someone to bury me there. Even when I die, I want to be with you. I must not leave you before I die. If I do, God should be very angry with me.' 18 Naomi understood that Ruth would not return to her own country. Then Naomi stopped saying that Ruth should leave her.

19 Naomi and Ruth travelled together to Bethlehem. The people in Bethlehem were very surprised when they saw them. The women from the town said, 'Is this really Naomi?'

20 Naomi said to them, 'Do not call me Naomi. Call me Mara. God has made my life very sad. 21 I left here with my husband and my two sons. God has brought me back here without them. You should not call me Naomi. God has caused trouble to happen to me.'

22 So Naomi returned from Moab with Ruth. Ruth was from Moab, and she was the wife of Naomi's son Mahlon. Naomi and Ruth arrived in Bethlehem when the people were cutting down barley in the fields.

Chapter 2

Ruth meets Boaz

1 Boaz was an important man. He was in the family of Elimelech, Naomi's husband.

2 Ruth, the woman from Moab, said to Naomi, 'Let me go to the fields. I will walk behind anyone who lets me. Then I will pick up the barley that he lets fall.' Naomi said, 'Go my daughter.' 3 So she went to the fields. And she began to pick up the barley that the men let fall. It happened that she worked in one of Boaz's fields. Boaz was from Elimelech's family.

4 Just then, Boaz arrived from Bethlehem and he spoke to the workers. 'I ask God to be with you', he said. 'We pray that God will do good things for you', they said.

5 Boaz asked the leader of his workers, 'Whose young woman is that?'

6 The leader said, 'She is that young woman from Moab, who returned from Moab with Naomi. 7 She asked, "Please let me walk behind the workers. Then I can pick up the barley that they let fall." She has worked in the field from morning until now. She only had a short rest in the hut.'

8 Boaz said to Ruth, 'Young woman, listen to me. Do not go and pick up barley in another field. Do not go away from here. Stay here with my servant girls. 9 Watch where the men work. And walk behind the girls. I have said that the workers should not touch you. The workers have filled the jars with water. When you need water, go to those jars. And drink from the jars.'

10 Ruth went down on her knees in front of Boaz. She said, 'Why did you choose to be kind to me? I am a foreign woman.'

11 Boaz said, 'People have told me all about you. When your husband died, you did many things for Naomi. You left your father and your mother and your country. You came to live with people who were strangers to you. 12 You have done many good things. I pray that God will do good things for you. You have come to Israel to be safe. I pray that the God of Israel will give you many good things.'

13 Ruth said, 'Master, you have caused me to feel good by your kind words. I am not as important as one of your servant girls. But you have been kind to me. I hope that you will continue to be kind to me.'

14 When it was time to eat, Boaz said to Ruth, 'Come here. Take some bread and make it wet with the wine vinegar.'

When she sat down with the workers, Boaz gave her some food. It was barley seeds that someone had cooked. She ate all that she wanted. And there was more than she could eat. 15 After this, she returned to work in the field. Boaz said to his workers, 'If she picks up barley near you, do not hurt her. 16 It would be good to help her. You can let some barley drop for her to pick up. And do not be angry with her.'

17 Ruth worked in the field until evening. Then she hit her barley with a stick until the seeds came out. She had about 22 litres of seeds.

18 She carried the seeds to the town. Naomi saw how much Ruth had picked. Ruth also gave to Naomi the barley seeds that Ruth could not eat.

19 Naomi asked her, 'Where did you work today? I want God to do good things for the man who was kind to you.' Then Ruth told Naomi about the man that she had worked with. 'The man that I worked with today is called Boaz', she said.

20 'I pray that God will do good things for him', said Naomi to Ruth. 'God has not stopped being kind to people who are alive. He is kind to those who are dead too. That man is in my husband's family. He is one of our kinsmen-redeemers.'

21 Then Ruth, the woman from Moab, said, 'He even said to me, "Stay with my workers until they have finished the work." '

22 Naomi said to Ruth, 'It will be good for you, my daughter, to go with his girls. The workers in another field might hurt you.'

23 So Ruth worked next to Boaz's servant girls until they finished the work. She lived with Naomi.

Chapter 3

Ruth finds a husband

1 One day, Naomi said to Ruth, 'My daughter, I must find a home for you. There you will have everything that you need. 2 You have worked with Boaz's servant girls. Boaz is in our family. Tonight he will winnow barley on the threshing floor.'

3 'Wash yourself', said Naomi. 'Put oil that has a beautiful smell on yourself. Put on your best clothes. Then go down to the threshing floor. Do not let him know that you are there. Wait until he has finished his food and drink. 4 After that, he will lie down. Then you will see where he is lying. Go and lift the cloth from his feet. Lie down. Then he will say what you should do.'

5 'I will do whatever you say', said Ruth. 6 So she went down to the threshing floor. And she did everything that Naomi had asked her to do.

7 Boaz was happy when he had finished his food and drink. He had put the barley seeds together in one place. Boaz lay down next to the seeds. Ruth was very quiet and she went to him. She lifted the cloth that covered his feet. Then she lay down. 8 In the middle of the night, something caused Boaz to feel afraid. He moved. Then he saw a woman who was lying at his feet.

9 'Who are you?' he asked. 'I am your servant Ruth', she said. 'Put the corner of the cloth that covers your feet over me. You are a kinsman-redeemer.'

10 'Young woman, I pray that God will do good things for you', he replied. 'You were kind to Naomi earlier. Now you have been more kind to me. You have seen young men who are rich.

And you have seen young men who are poor. You have not tried to marry any of these. 11 And now, young woman, do not be afraid. All the people in this town know that you are a good woman. So I will do everything for you that you ask. 12 It is true that I am in your family. But there is another kinsman-redeemer who is nearer to you. 13 Stay here for the night. In the morning, if he wants to help you, let him do it. If he will not do it, I will do it. As God is alive, I will do it. Lie here until the morning.'

14 So she lay at his feet until morning. But she got up before anyone could see her. Boaz said to her, 'Nobody must know that a woman came to the threshing floor.'

15 He also said, 'Bring me your small coat that you are wearing.' She brought the coat to him and Boaz poured barley on to it. Then he put the coat on her. After that, he returned to the town.

16 When Ruth returned, Naomi asked, 'Ruth, what happened in the night?' Then Ruth told her everything that Boaz had done for her. 17 Then she said, 'He also gave me all this barley and he said, "Do not return to Naomi with empty hands." '

18 Naomi said, 'Ruth, you must wait. Soon you will know what will happen. The man will be sure that he finishes everything today.'

Chapter 4

Boaz marries Ruth

1 In the morning, Boaz went up to the gate of the town and he sat down. The kinsman-redeemer that Boaz knew came to the gate. Boaz said to him, 'Come here, my friend, and sit down.' So, the man went to Boaz and the man sat down.

2 Boaz chose ten important men from the town and he said, 'Sit here.' So they sat down. 3 Then he said to the kinsman-redeemer, 'Naomi has returned from Moab. She wants to sell our brother Elimelech's piece of land. 4 I thought that I should tell you about this. Now I ask you, in front of these important people, will you buy this land? If you want to buy it, then you should buy it. If you do not want to buy it, then you must tell me. Then I will know what you want to do. It is right for you to buy it. If you do not buy the land, then I can buy it.' The kinsman-redeemer said, 'I will buy it.'

5 Then Boaz said, 'On the day that you buy the land from Naomi and Ruth, you must marry Ruth. Then the name of Elimelech will stay with the land.'

6 When Boaz said that, the kinsman-redeemer replied. 'I cannot buy the land', he said. 'My family might lose my own land when I die. You buy the land yourself. I cannot buy it.'

7 At this time, in Israel, when a man sold land he removed his shoe. Then he gave it to the man who had bought the land. So then, everyone could see that the first man had sold the land. They had agreed this in the law.

8 So the kinsman-redeemer said to Boaz, 'You buy the land.' And he removed his shoe.

9 Boaz said to all the important people, 'You have all seen today that I have bought the land from Naomi. I have bought all the land of Elimelech, Kilion and Mahlon. 10 I will also marry Ruth, from Moab, who was the wife of Mahlon. His name and his land will stay together. Now his name will remain in his family. And this town will not lose his name. Today you have seen all this happen.'

11 Then the important men and all the other people at the gate said, 'We have seen all that has happened. We want God to be good to the woman who is coming into your home. We pray that he will make her like Rachel and Leah.

They made the family of Israel large. We pray that you will become an important man in Ephrathah. And we pray that you will become famous in Bethlehem.

12 God gave children to Perez. Perez was the son of Tamar and Judah. We pray that God will give children to you by this young woman like that.'

The family of David

13 Boaz married Ruth. God did good things for her and she had a son. 14 The women said to Naomi, 'Thank God! Today, he did not let you have no kinsman-redeemer. We pray that Ruth's son will become famous everywhere in Israel! 15 He will cause you to feel young again. He will be good to you when you are old. Ruth loves you. And she is better for you than seven sons would be. And now she has had this boy.'

16 Naomi took the child. She held him in her arms. She was good to him as she would be to her own son. 17The women who lived there said, 'Naomi has a son.' They called him Obed. He was the father of Jesse, who was the father of David.

18 So this is the family of Perez.

Perez was the father of Hezron.

19 Hezron was the father of Ram.

Ram was the father of Amminadab.

20 Amminadab was the father of Nahshon.

Nahshon was the father of Salmon.

21 Salmon was the father of Boaz.

Boaz was the father of Obed.

22 Obed was the father of Jesse.

Jesse was the father of David.

The King who did not Obey God

1 Samuel

About 1 Samuel and 2 Samuel

The books of 1 and 2 Samuel were once one book. Then men made this book into two separate parts. The name of the book is from the first important person in this book. He was Samuel the prophet. But Samuel died before the end of the book.

Someone wrote the book after King Solomon had died. He died 930 years before Christ was born. After Solomon died, God made the country called Israel into two countries, Israel and Judah. The country called Judah included the tribes of Judah and Benjamin. (See 1 Kings 12:1-24.)

The Israelites called their leaders 'judges'. They were leaders of the Israelites for about 350 years after Joshua's death. Samuel was the last of the judges. He was also a prophet. Samuel anointed Saul to be the first king of Israel. But Saul did not obey God. So God chose another king, David, who would obey him. 1 Samuel tells us about Saul's death at the end of the book. 2 Samuel records the life of David as king.

Chapter 1

Elkanah and his family go to Shiloh

1 There was a man whose name was Elkanah. He lived in the town called Ramathaim-zophim (Ramah). This town was in the hills. It was in a place that God had given to Ephraim's tribe. Elkanah was the son of Jeroham. Jeroham was the son of Elihu. Elihu was the son of Tohu. Tohu was the son of Zuph. Zuph was in the tribe of Ephraim. 2 Elkanah had two wives. One wife was called Hannah and the other wife was called Peninnah. Peninnah had children but Hannah did not have any children.

3 Every year, Elkanah left Ramathaim and he went up to the town called Shiloh. He went there to worship. There he gave sacrifices to God, the most powerful Lord. Hophni and Phinehas were priests to the Lord at Shiloh. Eli was their father. 4 Elkanah gave his sacrifices to God. Then he gave a part of the meat to Peninnah and to her sons and daughters. 5 Elkanah loved Hannah. But she had no children because the Lord had not let her have children. So Elkanah always gave twice as much meat to Hannah.

6 Peninnah was not kind to Hannah. She said things that would cause Hannah to feel sad. She did this because God had not given any children to Hannah. Then Hannah became sad. 7 This happened every year when they went to the Lord's house in Shiloh. Peninnah would say bad things to Hannah to cause her to cry. Then Hannah would not eat anything. 8 Hannah's husband, Elkanah said to her, 'I do not know why you are crying. I do not know why you are not eating. You should not be sad. I am better than 10 sons.'

Hannah and Eli

9 One day they were at Shiloh. They had finished eating and drinking. Hannah stood up. Eli the priest was sitting by the door of the Lord's temple. 10 Hannah was very, very sad. She cried very much and she prayed to the Lord. 11 And she said a promise to God. She prayed, 'You are the most powerful Lord. See how sad I am. I am your servant. Remember me and do not forget me. Please give a son to me. If you do that, I will give him back to you for all of his life. Nobody will ever cut his hair.'

12 Hannah continued to pray to the Lord. Eli watched her mouth while it moved. 13 Hannah was praying inside herself. Her lips moved but Eli could not hear her voice. So he thought that she had drunk too much alcohol. 14 He said to her, 'Stop drinking so much. Put away your wine.' 15 Hannah said to Eli, 'No, sir, I have not drunk wine or strong drink. I have trouble deep inside myself. I told the Lord all about my problems. 16 Please do not think that I am a bad woman. I am praying here because I am sad. And I feel bad inside.'

17 Eli answered Hannah and he said, 'Go and let your mind rest. I ask the God of Israel to give to you the thing that you asked him for.' 18 Hannah said, 'I will try always to do the things that will cause you pleasure.' Then Hannah went away and she ate something. Her face was not sad now.

19 Elkanah and his family got up early the next morning. They worshipped the Lord. Then they went to their home at Ramah. Elkanah had sex with his wife Hannah. And God remembered what she had asked him for. 20 Hannah discovered that she would soon have a baby. She had a son and she called him Samuel. She said, 'His name is Samuel because I asked the Lord for him.'

Hannah gives Samuel to God

21 Every year Elkanah went to Shiloh to give sacrifices. And he did what he had promised to the Lord. His family went too. 22 But Hannah did not go. She said to her husband, 'I will not go until the boy is older. When he can eat proper food, I will take him to the house of the Lord at Shiloh. I will give him to the Lord and he will live there for all his life.' 23 Elkanah said to Hannah, 'You must do what seems right to you. Stay here until the boy begins to eat proper food. The Lord will help you do this.' So, Hannah stayed at her home with her son until he drank no more milk from her.

24 When Samuel was eating proper food, Hannah took him to Shiloh. She took him to the Lord's house there. She took a male cow that was three years old. She also took a big bag of flour and a leather bag full of wine. Samuel was still young. 25 They killed the male cow for the sacrifice. Then Hannah took Samuel to Eli.

26 Hannah spoke to Eli. 'Please believe me sir. I am the woman that was standing here. You saw me here. I was praying to the Lord. 27 I prayed for this boy and the Lord answered me. The Lord gave to me what I asked him for. 28 Now I give this child back to the Lord. He will work for the Lord all of his life.' And Samuel worshipped the Lord there.

Chapter 2

1 Hannah prayed and she said,

> 'I am very happy when I think about the Lord.
>
> The Lord has made me very strong.
>
> I can say that I am stronger than my enemies.
>
> I am happy because you, Lord, have saved me.

2 Nobody else is holy like the Lord.

> There is no other God except you.
>
> You are the only powerful God.

3 You people must not say that you are very great.

> Stop saying that you are important.
>
> The Lord is a God who knows everything.
>
> And he knows whether people are doing good things or bad things.

4 The bows of strong soldiers break.

> But people who fall will become strong.

5 Now the people who had plenty of food have to work for it.

> But the people who were hungry are not hungry any longer.
>
> The woman who could not have any children now has 7 children.
>
> But the woman who had many children has become weak.

6 The Lord kills people. And he makes people alive.

> He causes people to die. And he raises people up.

7 The Lord makes some people poor and he makes other people rich.

> He makes some people not important and he makes other people great.

8 The Lord raises up the poor people from the ground.

> He lifts up the people who need help.
>
> He lets poor people be friends with king's sons.
>
> And he puts poor people in places of honour.

> The deep places of the earth are the Lord's.
>
> He built the world on them.

9 He saves the people who obey him.

> But he keeps bad people quiet in dark places.
>
> Men will not win wars only because they are strong.

10 The Lord will beat his enemies completely.

> His voice against them is like the noise of a storm from the sky.
>
> The Lord will be the judge of all the earth.
>
> He will give power to his king.
>
> He will anoint a king and he will make him strong.'

11 Then Elkanah went to his home at Ramah. But Samuel stayed in Shiloh. He lived with Eli the priest and he became God's servant.

Eli's bad sons

12 But the sons of Eli were very bad men. They did not give honour to the Lord.

13 People brought sacrifices to Shiloh. And this is what these priests did. People boiled their meat in a pot. A priest's servant went to the pot. 14 He pushed a fork into the pot. And the priest kept whatever came out on the fork. They did that to all the Israelites when they came to Shiloh. 15 Often, the servant of the priest came to the people before they had burned the fat meat from the sacrifice. The servant said, 'Give to the priest some meat to bake. He will not accept meat that you have boiled. He will only accept meat that is fresh.' 16 Sometimes, the person said, 'You must burn the fat meat first. Then you can take what you want.' The servant would reply, 'No. Give the meat to me now. If you do not give it to me, I will take it from you.'

17 The Lord saw what the young men did. They thought that the people's sacrifices to the Lord were not important. The Lord saw that their sin was very bad.

Samuel at Shiloh

18 But Samuel was the Lord's servant. He was a young boy. He wore an ephod (a linen coat). 19 Every year, Samuel's mother made a little coat for him. She took it to him when she went to Shiloh. She and her husband went there every year to give their sacrifice to God. 20 Then Eli blessed Elkanah and his wife. He said, 'Hannah prayed for a son and then she gave him back to the Lord. I pray that the Lord will give children to you and Hannah to take the place of Samuel.' Then they returned to their own home. 21 The Lord was good to Hannah. She had three more sons and two daughters. The boy Samuel grew up in the house of the Lord.

22 Eli was very old now. People told him about everything that his sons did in all Israel. Eli's sons had sex with some women servants. Those women worked at the door of the Lord's house. 23 Eli said to his sons, 'I do not know why you do these evil things. People have told me what you do. 24 No, my sons, the Lord's people all give a bad report to me about you. 25 If you do something bad to another person, God can help you. But if you do something against the Lord, nobody can ask him to help you.' Eli's sons did not listen to him because the Lord had decided to kill them.

26 The boy Samuel continued to grow bigger. And he continued to give pleasure to the Lord and to the people.

The prophecy against Eli's family

27 A man of God came and he spoke to Eli. This is what he said:

'The Lord says, "A long time ago your ancestors lived in Egypt. They were slaves to the king of Egypt. I showed myself to your ancestor Aaron. 28I chose him and his family from all of the tribes in Israel. I chose them to be priests. They go up to my altar to burn incense. They can wear the special ephod. I also let them eat part of the sacrifices and burnt offerings that the Israelites give. 29 I said that my people must give these sacrifices and offerings to me in my house. You should not want them for yourself. Eli, you give more honour to your sons than you give to me. You eat all the best parts of the offerings that the Israelites give to me. So you and your sons have become fat."

30 Because of what you have done, the Lord God of Israel says this to you: "I promised your family and your ancestors that they would be my priests for all time." But the Lord says, "That will not happen now. If people give honour to me, I will give honour to them. But some people may think that I am worth nothing. I will give no honour to those people. 31 It will be the time soon when you will die. Also, I will let men kill the young men in your family. Nobody in your family will ever become old.

32 I will cause trouble for the Lord's house. I will do good things for (on behalf of) the Israelites, but there will never be an old man in your family. 33 But I will not completely stop your family working for me at my altar. Some of them will continue to be my servants. But you will cry and you will be sad. All of your family will die when they are young. 34 Hophni and Phinehas, your two sons, will die on the same day. That will show everyone that I have spoken only true words.

35 I will choose a priest. And he will always do the things that give pleasure to me. He will do everything that I want him to do. I will cause his family to continue. They will always be the servants of the man that I anoint. 36 Everyone in your family who continues to live will bend his body down to this priest. They will have to ask him for food and money. 'Please let me help the priests so that I can have a loaf of bread to eat', they will say".'

Chapter 3

The Lord chooses Samuel

1 The boy Samuel became the Lord's servant. Eli the priest taught him. In those days, the Lord did not often speak to people. And he did not give many dreams to them.

2 Eli now had bad eyes and he could not see well. One night, he was lying down to sleep in his usual place.3 The lamp of God was still burning. Samuel was lying down to sleep in the house of the Lord. He was near the covenant box. 4 Then the Lord said Samuel's name. Samuel said, 'Here I am.' 5 He ran to Eli and he said, 'You said my name. Here I am.' But Eli said, 'I did not say your name. Lie down again.' So Samuel lay down again. 6 Again the Lord said, 'Samuel'. Samuel went to Eli and said, 'You said my name. Here I am.' Eli answered, 'My son, I did not say your name. Lie down again.'

7 Samuel did not know the Lord yet. He had not yet heard the Lord's voice. 8 Then the Lord said Samuel's name for the third time. Samuel got up. He went to Eli and he said, 'You said my name. Here I am.' Then Eli knew that the Lord was saying the boy's name. 9 So Eli said to Samuel, 'Lie down again. If he says your name again, you must say, "Speak, Lord. I am your servant and I am listening".' So Samuel went and lay down in his place.

10 The Lord came and he stood there. He said Samuel's name as he had done before. He said, 'Samuel, Samuel'. Samuel said, 'I am your servant and I am listening.'

11 This is what the Lord said to Samuel: 'I will do something among the Israelite people. It will make everyone that people tell about it afraid. 12 I will do everything to Eli and his family that I have said. I will start at the beginning and I will go on to the end. 13 I told Eli that I would punish his family for all time. Eli knew that his sons were doing very bad things. He knew that they would cause me to punish them. But he still let them do those things. 14 So I decided to show them that I was very angry. I said to Eli's family, "I will never forgive you because you have done these things. Even if you give sacrifices and offerings they will never take away your sins".'

15 Samuel lay down until the morning. Then he opened the doors of the house of the Lord. He was afraid to tell Eli about the vision. 16 But Eli called Samuel and he said, 'Samuel, my son.' Samuel answered, 'Here I am.'

17 Eli asked, 'What did the Lord say to you? You must tell me. Do not keep it a secret. If you do keep it a secret, God will punish you. You must tell me everything that he said to you.' 18 So Samuel told Eli everything. He did not hide any of it. Then Eli said, 'He is the Lord. He will do what is right.'

19 The Lord was with Samuel while he grew up. The Lord made sure that all of Samuel's messages from him became true. 20 All the Israelites knew that Samuel was a true prophet from the Lord. All the people from Dan (the north of the country) to Beersheba (the south) knew it. 21 The Lord continued to appear at Shiloh. He showed himself to Samuel and he spoke to him there.

Chapter 4

The Philistines take God's covenant box

1 When Samuel spoke, all the Israelites listened to him.

The Israelites went out to fight against the Philistine people. The Israelite army had their tents near the place called Ebenezer. The Philistine army was in the town called Aphek. 2 The Philistines went out to fight the Israelites. While they fought, the Philistines won the fight with the Israelites. The Philistines killed about 4000 Israelites in the fight. 3 The Israelite soldiers returned to their tents. The leaders of Israel said, 'We do not know why the Lord let the Philistines win today. We will bring the Lord's covenant box here from Shiloh. We will take it with us into the fight. Then it will save us from our enemies.'

4 So the people sent men to Shiloh and they brought back the Lord's covenant box. The great and powerful Lord God sits between the angels on the top of it. Eli's two sons, Hophni and Phinehas, were there with God's covenant box. 5 The men brought the covenant box of the Lord into their army. The Israelites made a great happy noise that caused the ground to move. 6 The Philistines heard them when they were shouting. They asked each other, 'Why is all this noise happening in the Israelite army?'

Then the Philistines found out that the Lord's covenant box had come into the middle of the Israelite army. 7 They were afraid. They said, 'A god has come into their army. We are in trouble. Nothing like this has happened before. 8 This will be very bad for us. Nobody can save us from these powerful gods. They caused great troubles to the people from Egypt and these gods killed them in the desert. 9 Be strong, Philistines. Be strong men. In past days, the Israelites were our servants. Now you must fight like men. If you do not, we will become their servants.'

10 So the Philistines fought strongly and they won again. The Israelites ran towards their own tents. This was a big loss for them. The Philistines killed 30 000 Israelite soldiers. 11 And the Philistines took away God's covenant box. Also, Hophni and Phinehas, Eli's two sons, died.

Eli dies

12 That day a man from the tribe of Benjamin ran from the fight to Shiloh. He had torn his clothes and he had put dirt on his head.

13 Eli was by the side of the road when the man arrived in Shiloh. Eli was sitting on his chair. He was waiting for news. He was not happy because they had taken God's covenant box into the fight. The man from Benjamin came into the town. He told the people what had happened. All the people cried aloud.

14 Eli heard the people crying. He asked, 'What is all this noise about?' The man quickly went to tell Eli. 15Eli was now 98 years old and he could not see. 16 The man from Benjamin said, 'I have come from the fight. Today I ran from it to you.' Eli asked, 'What happened, my son?'

17 The man who brought the news said, 'The Israelites ran away from the Philistines. The Philistines killed many of the Israelite soldiers. Both your two sons, Hophni and Phinehas, are dead. And the Philistines took God's covenant box.'

18 Eli was sitting next to the gate. When the man spoke about God's covenant box, Eli fell off his chair. Eli broke his neck. And he died when he fell. This happened because he was old and heavy. He had been the leader of Israel's people for 40 years.

The glory has left Israel

19 Phinehas had a wife. She would soon have a baby. It was nearly time for the baby to be born. People told her that the Philistines had taken away God's covenant box. They also told her that Phinehas and Eli were dead. When people told her this news, she started to give birth to her baby. But she had a very difficult time. 20 She was dying. Some women helped her to give birth. Just before she died, they said, 'Do not be afraid. You have a son.' But she did not answer them or listen to them.

21 She called the boy Ichabod. She said, 'The glory has left Israel.' She said that because the Philistines had taken God's covenant box. And she was sad because Eli and her husband were dead. 22 She said, 'The glory has left Israel because the Philistines have taken God's covenant box.'

Chapter 5

God's covenant box causes trouble for the Philistines

1 The Philistines took away God's covenant box. And they took it from Ebenezer to the town called Ashdod. 2 They carried it into the temple of their god. The name of their god was Dagon. They put the box next to the idol of Dagon. 3 The next morning, the people in Ashdod got up early and they went to their temple. They saw that Dagon had fallen down in front of the Lord's covenant box. Dagon's face was touching the ground. So, they picked up Dagon and they put him back in his place. 4 They got up early the next morning and they went to the temple of Dagon. Again, they found that Dagon had fallen down in front of the Lord's box. He lay with his face on the ground. His head and his hands had broken off. They were lying on the step of the temple door. Only the other part of his body was not broken. 5 Dagon's priests and other people still go to the temple at Ashdod. But, since this happened, nobody puts a foot on the step of Dagon's temple.

6 The Lord punished the people in Ashdod and the people in the places near to it. They were very afraid. God caused tumours to grow on them. 7 The men in Ashdod saw what was happening. They said, 'God's covenant box must not stay here with us. The God of Israel is punishing us and our god Dagon.' 8 So the Philistine kings met together. The people asked the kings, 'What should we do with the covenant box of the God of Israel?'

The kings answered, 'Take it to Gath.' So the men moved it to the Philistine town called Gath.

9 After they had moved the covenant box to Gath, God punished the people in Gath. He made them all very afraid. He made old and young people ill. And he caused tumours to grow on them. 10 So the people sent God's box to the Philistine town called Ekron.

When the covenant box of God came into Ekron the people in the town shouted. They said, 'They have brought the God of Israel's box to us. It will kill us. It will kill the people who live here.' 11 So they asked the Philistine kings to meet together. The people from Ekron said to them, 'Send away the covenant box of the God of Israel. Send it back to where it should be. If you do not do this, it will kill us. And it will kill all our people.' All the people in the town were very afraid because God was punishing them. 12 Many people died and all the other people had tumours. So, the people in the town shouted out to heaven.

Chapter 6

The Philistines give back God's covenant box to Israel

1 The Philistines had the Lord's covenant box in their country for 7 months. 2 Then they asked their priests and their men who did magic to come to them. The Philistines asked them, 'What can we do with the Lord's covenant box? Tell us how to send it back to its home.'

3 The priests answered, 'Send it back to Israel. But you must not send it back without an offering. You must send an offering to God because he is angry with you. Then you will get well. You will find out why God punished you.'

4 The Philistines asked, 'What offering should we send to God?'

The priests and the men who worked magic replied, 'You should send 5 tumours and 5 mice of gold. You should make

5 of each because you have 5 rulers. Your rulers and your people have all been ill. 5 Make the tumours and mice out of gold. They must be like those that are destroying your country. And give honour to the God of Israel. Maybe then he will stop punishing you and your gods and your country. 6 Do not be like the people from Egypt and Pharaoh their king. They would not change their minds and obey God. So God punished them with great power until they let the Jews leave Egypt.

7 You must make a new cart. Find two cows that have just given birth to little cows. You must use cows that nobody has ever tied to a cart before. Tie them to the cart. Then take their little cows away from them. 8 Put the covenant box of the Lord on the cart. Put the gold tumours and mice in a box. These are your offerings to their God because you made him angry. Put this box next to the covenant box on the cart. Then send the cart away. 9 But continue to watch it. God's covenant box came from Israel. The cart may go to the town called Beth-shemesh in Israel. That would show that the Lord sent this great trouble to us. If the cart does not go there, the Lord has not punished us. We will know that our illness happened for another reason.'

10 So the Philistines did this. They took two cows that had just had little cows. They tied them to a cart. They took away their little cows and they put the little cows in a building. 11 They put the Lord's covenant box on the cart. Then they put their box next to the covenant box. Their box contained the mice and the tumours of gold. 12 The cows went in a straight path towards Beth-shemesh. They kept on the road and they did not turn to the right or to the left. All the way, they made a lot of noise. The Philistine rulers followed them all the way to the edge of Beth-shemesh.

13 The people from Beth-shemesh were in the valley. They were taking in their wheat. They looked and they saw the Lord's covenant box. They were very happy. 14-15 The cows pulled the cart into a field. The field was Joshua's. He lived in Beth-shemesh. The cows stopped next to a large rock. The Levites took the Lord's covenant box off the cart. They put it on the large rock. They also put the box, which contained the gold tumours and mice, on the rock. The people from Beth-shemesh cut up the wood from the cart and they made a fire with it. Then they killed the cows. They burnt them on the fire as an offering to the Lord. That day they sacrificed whole cows as burnt offerings. 16 When the 5 Philistine rulers saw this, they returned to Ekron.

17 The Philistines sent the gold tumours as a gift to the Lord. They sent one from each of their 5 towns. The names of these towns are Ashdod, Gaza, Ashkelon, Gath and Ekron. 18 The Philistines also sent 5 gold mice. They sent one from each of the 5 towns. Each town had walls round it. Each town included the country villages near to it. The large rock that the Israelites put the Lord's covenant box on is still there. It is in Joshua's field in Beth-shemesh.

19 But some of the men from Beth-shemesh looked inside the Lord's covenant box. So God killed 70 of them. Among the 70 men were 50 leaders. The people were very sad because God had punished them so strongly. 20 The men at Beth-shemesh said, 'When God is present, people cannot stand. The Lord is a holy God. We do not know what place we can send the box to.'

21 So they sent people to Kiriath-jearim with a message. They said, 'The Philistines have given the Lord's covenant box back to us. Come and take it from us. Take it to your town.'

Chapter 7

1 So men came from Kiriath-jearim to fetch the Lord's covenant box. They took it to Abinadab's house. His house was on a hill. Eleazar was his son. They consecrated Eleazar so that he could keep the Lord's covenant box safe.

The Lord saves the Israelites from the Philistines

2 The covenant box stayed at Kiriath-jearim for a long time. For 20 years the Israelites were sad. They wanted to give pleasure to the Lord again.

3 Then Samuel said to all the Israelites, 'If you want to obey the Lord, you must do it with all your spirit. You must remove all your foreign gods and idols of Ashtoreth. You must give your lives completely to the Lord. You must worship only the Lord. If you do that, he will save you from the Philistines.' 4 So the Israelites removed all their idols of the gods called Baal and Ashtoreth. They worshipped the Lord only.

5 Then Samuel said, 'Meet together at the town called Mizpah.

I will pray to the Lord for you (on your behalf).' 6 So they all met at Mizpah. They got water from the ground and they poured it out in front of the Lord. They did not eat that day. They prayed to the Lord and they said, 'We have sinned against the Lord.' Samuel ruled the Israelites at Mizpah.

7 People told the Philistines that the Israelites were meeting at Mizpah. So the Philistine rulers went there to attack them. When people told the Israelites about this, they were afraid of the Philistines. 8 The Israelites said to Samuel, 'Pray to the Lord our God and do not stop. Ask him to help us. Ask him to save us from the Philistines.' 9 So Samuel gave a young sheep as a whole burnt offering to the Lord. He prayed to the Lord. Samuel asked him to help the Israelites. The Lord gave a good answer to him. 10 While Samuel was giving the burnt offering to the Lord, the Philistines moved nearer. They were ready to attack Israel. But the Lord caused a very loud noise in the sky against the Philistines. He confused and frightened them. They started to run away. 11 The Israelite men came out from Mizpah. They ran after the Philistines to a place below Beth-car. And they killed them along the way.

12 After that, Samuel took a stone and he put it up between Mizpah and Shen. He called the stone Ebenezer. He said, 'The Lord has helped us all this way.' 13 So the Israelites won the fight with the Philistines. The Philistines did not attack Israel's land again.

The Lord was against the Philistines all the time that Samuel was alive. 14 Earlier, the Philistines had taken towns from the Israelites. But the Israelites won them back. These towns were from Ekron to Gath. Also the Israelite people and the Amorite people did not fight any longer.

15 Samuel continued to be a judge of the Israelites all his life. 16 Every year, he went to the towns called Bethel, Gilgal and Mizpah. He was a judge of the people in those places. 17 But Samuel always returned to his home at Ramah. There also he was a judge of the Israelites. And he built an altar to the Lord at Ramah.

Chapter 8

The Israelites ask for a king

1 When Samuel was old, he made his sons rulers in Israel. 2 His first son was Joel and his second son was Abijah. They were rulers in the town called Beersheba. 3 But Samuel's sons did not do good things as Samuel had done. They tried to get money in ways that were not right. They accepted money from bad people when nobody was looking. Then they would not punish them.

4 So the leaders of Israel met together and they went to Samuel at Ramah. 5 They said to Samuel, 'You are old. Your sons do not do good things as you have done. Give to us a king who will rule over us. The other nations have a king. We want one too.'

6 Samuel was not happy that the leaders asked for a king. So he prayed to the Lord. 7 The Lord said to Samuel, 'Listen to everything that the people say to you. They have not refused to have you as their leader. Instead, they have refused to have me as their king. 8 Today they are doing what they have always done. I brought them out of the country called Egypt. But they left me and they worshipped other gods. Now they are doing the same to you. 9 Listen to the people. But tell them what will happen. Tell them what their kings will do to them.'

10 Samuel spoke to the people who had asked him for a king. He told them everything that the Lord had said. 11 Samuel said, 'The king will rule over you. And this is what he will do. He will take your sons to be his soldiers. They will drive his horses and chariots. And they will run in front of his chariots. 12 The king will make some of your son's leaders of 1000 soldiers each. Other sons will be leaders of groups of 50 soldiers. The king will cause some of your sons to plough his ground. Then they will have to bring to him the food that they have caused to grow. Other sons will have to make weapons for war and weapons for his chariots.

13 The king will take your daughters. They will make him oils that have good smells. They will also cook and bake his food. 14 The king will take your best fields. He will take the places where you find the best grapes and olives. He will give all these to his officers. 15 Then he will take a 10th part of all your seeds and grapes. He will give this to his officers and servants. 16 He will take your male and female servants. He will take your best young men and your donkeys. He will use them for his own work. 17 He will take a 10th of all your sheep. And he will cause you to be his servants too. 18 Then you will shout to the Lord about your king that you have chosen. But the Lord will not answer you then.'

19 But the people would not listen to Samuel. They said, 'No. We want a king to rule us. 20 We want to be like all the other nations with a king to rule us. He will be our leader when we go to war. He will fight for us (on our behalf).'

21 Samuel listened to all that the people said. Then he went and he told the Lord. 22 The Lord said, 'You must do what they want. You must give a king to them.'

Then Samuel told Israel's people, 'Return to your own towns.'

Chapter 9

Saul looks for his father's donkeys

1 Kish was a strong, brave man from the tribe of Benjamin. Kish was the son of Abiel. Abiel was the son of Zeror. Zeror was the son of Becorath. Becorath was the son of Aphiah. Aphiah came from the tribe of Benjamin. 2 Kish had a son whose name was Saul. He was a very handsome young man. No other Israelite was more handsome than Saul. When Saul stood with other people, you could see his head and shoulders above everyone else's head.

3 Kish had some donkeys. But nobody could find them. Kish said to Saul, 'Go and look for the donkeys. Take one of the servants with you when you go to find them.' 4 So Saul and the servant went through the hills in Ephraim's land. Then they went to Shalisha and the places near to it. But they did not find the donkeys there. Then they went to Shaalim's place. The donkeys were not there. The people from the tribe of Benjamin lived all round them. So, Saul and the servant went through all their fields. But they did not find the donkeys.

5 They reached the fields near Zuph. Saul said to his servant, 'We must return to our home now. My father was afraid that he had lost the donkeys. But he will start to think that he has lost us. We must return now.'

6 The servant replied, 'There is a man of God in this town. Everything that he says becomes true. So people give honour to him. We should go there now. Perhaps he will tell us where to find the donkeys.'

7 Saul said to his servant, 'If we go to visit this man we must give a gift to him. But we do not have a gift. We do not even have any food. What can we give to him?'

8 The servant answered, 'I have a small piece of silver. I will give it to the man of God. Then he will tell us which way we should go.' 9 (Sometimes a man from Israel wanted to ask God something. This is what he said to other people: 'Come with me. We will go to the seer.' We now call this man a prophet. But years ago, the Israelites called him a 'seer'.)

10 Saul said to his servant, 'That is good. We should visit this man of God.' So, they went to the town where he was.

11 They went up the hill to the town. Some young women came out of the town to get some water. Saul and his servant said, 'Is the seer here?'

12 They said, 'Yes, he is here. He is in front of you. You must hurry. He came to the town today because the people have a sacrifice. They will sacrifice at the place for worship. 13 When you go into the town, you will find the seer. He is going to the place for worship. The people will not start to eat until he comes. The seer must first ask God to accept the sacrifice. Then the people with him will eat. You will find the seer if you go now.'

Saul meets Samuel

14 Saul and his servant went up to the town. When they went into the town, Samuel came towards them. He was going to the place for worship. 15 God had spoken to Samuel the day before this. God said, 16 'Tomorrow I will send a man to you. He comes from the land of Benjamin. He will arrive at about this time of day. Anoint him as the leader over my people, Israel. He will save my people from the Philistines. I have seen the way that they have hurt my people. I heard the people when they shouted for help.'

17 Samuel saw Saul. God said to Samuel, 'Here is the man that I told you about. He will rule my people.'

18 Samuel was near the gate of the town. Saul went to him and said, 'Please tell me where the seer's house is.'

19 Samuel said, 'I am the seer. You must go in front of me to the place for worship. I want both of you to eat with me today. Tomorrow morning I will answer all your questions. Then you can go to your home. 20 Do not think about the donkeys that you lost three days ago. Someone has found them. I will tell you what all Israel's people want. They want you and all your father's family.'

21 Saul answered, 'I belong to the tribe of Benjamin. It is the smallest tribe in the nation of Israel. And my family group is the least important group in the tribe of Benjamin. Why have you said all this to me?'

22 Then Samuel took Saul and his servant into the place where he would make the sacrifice. He caused them to sit in the most important seats. Samuel had asked about 30 men to come to the meal. 23 Samuel spoke to the cook. He said, 'Please bring me the piece of meat that I gave to you. I said that you must keep it separate.'

24 So the cook took the leg of meat and he put it down in front of Saul. Samuel said to Saul, 'I kept this piece of meat for you. Eat it because this is a special meal. When I first asked the other men, I kept this piece of meat for you.' So, Saul ate with Samuel that day.

25 They left the place for worship and they went into the town. Samuel took Saul on to the roof of his house. They talked together on the roof. 26 They got up at dawn the next day. Saul was on the roof of the house. Samuel shouted up to him. He said, 'Get up and get ready to leave. I will send you on your journey.' Saul got ready to leave. Saul and Samuel went out into the street. 27 They walked to the edge of the town. Samuel said, 'Say to your servant that he must go on in front of us. But you must stay, because I have a message from God for you.'

Chapter 10

Samuel anoints Saul

1 Then Samuel took a jar of oil and he poured the oil over Saul's head. He kissed Saul. He said, 'The Lord has anointed you as the leader of his people. 2 After you leave me today, you will meet two men. They will be near the place where Abraham buried Rachel's dead body. This is on the edge of Benjamin's land at Zelzah. The men will say, 'Someone has found the donkeys that you were looking for. Your father has stopped thinking about his donkeys. Now his mind is full of trouble. He continues to ask, 'What can I do about my son?' "

3 Then you will go on from there until you reach the big tree at Tabor. Three men will meet you there. They are going to the town called Bethel to worship God. One man will carry three young goats. Another man will have three loaves of bread. The third man will have a leather bag full of wine. 4 They will speak to you and they will offer you two loaves of bread. You must accept the bread. 5 Then you must go to the place for worship at the town called Gibeah. A group of Philistine soldiers is there. Near to the town you will meet some prophets. They will be coming down from the place for worship. They will be making music with their harps, tambourines, flutes and lyres. And they will be prophesying. 6 The Spirit of the Lord will give his power to you. And you will prophesy too. You will become a different person inside. 7 All these things will happen. Then do whatever you need to do. God is with you.

8 Go in front of me to the town called Gilgal. I will certainly come down to you there. And I will burn sacrifices and I will give fellowship offerings to God. You must wait for 7 days. Then I will come. And I will tell you what you should do.'

9 Saul left Samuel and went on his journey. When Saul was leaving, God made him a new person inside. And everything happened in the way that Samuel had spoken about. 10 They arrived at Gibeah and a group of prophets met them. The Spirit of God came strongly on Saul. He prophesied with the prophets. 11 There were some people who had known Saul for a long time. They saw him when he was prophesying. They asked each other, 'What has happened to the son of Kish? Has Saul really become a prophet?'

12 A man who lived there asked, 'Who is the leader of these prophets?' So it became a proverb: 'Has Saul really become a prophet?' 13 When Saul stopped prophesying he went up to the place for worship.

14 Saul's father's brother asked Saul and his servant, 'Where have you been?' Saul said, 'We were looking for the donkeys. We could not find them so we went to visit Samuel.'

15 Saul's father's brother said, 'What did Samuel say to you?'

16 Saul said, 'He told us that someone had found the donkeys.' But Saul did not tell his father's brother that Samuel had talked about the kingdom.

Saul becomes the first king of Israel

17 Samuel sent a message to all Israel's people. He said that they must meet with the Lord at Mizpah. 18 He said to them, 'This is a message from the Lord, the God of Israel. The Lord says, "I led you Israelites out from Egypt. I saved you from Egypt's people. And I saved you from other peoples that made you their slaves." 19 The Lord saved you from all your troubles and from people who hurt you. Now you have refused to obey the Lord your God. You said, "No. We want a king to rule us." So, come and stand in front of God. Stand together in your tribes and as families.'

20 Each tribe went towards Samuel. God chose the tribe of Benjamin. 21 Each family group from the tribe of Benjamin went to him. And God chose the family group of Matri. Then God chose Saul, son of Kish, from the family of Matri. They looked for Saul but nobody could find him. 22 So they asked the Lord, 'Has Saul come here yet?' And the Lord said, 'Yes, but he is hiding among the luggage.'

23 So they ran to Saul and they brought him out. When Saul stood with the people, you could see his head and shoulders above everyone else's head. 24 Samuel said to all the people, 'Here is the man that God has chosen. There is nobody like him among all the people.' Then the people shouted, 'We ask God that the king will live for a long time.'

25 Samuel explained to the people all that a king should be. And he explained all that a king should do. He wrote everything in a scroll. He put the scroll in the holy place in front of the Lord. Then Samuel caused the people to go to their own homes. 26 Saul went to his home at Gibeah. A group of brave men went with him. They went with Saul because God caused them to want to do that. 27 There were some other men who caused trouble. They said, 'We do not think that this man can save us.' They did not honour Saul. And they did not bring him any gifts. But Saul did not say anything.

Chapter 11

Saul saves the town called Jabesh

1 Nahash was an Ammonite. He went with his army to beat the men in Jabesh. Jabesh was in the part of the country that was called Gilead. The soldiers were all round Jabesh. The people from Jabesh said, 'Make a covenant with us and we will let you be our ruler.' 2 Nahash said, 'I will make a covenant with you. But I will pull out the right eye of every person in your town. Then Israel's people will be ashamed.' 3 The rulers of Jabesh said to him, 'Wait for 7 days. We will send a message to all the people in Israel. We will ask them to help us. If nobody comes to save us, we will let you be our ruler.'

4 The men took the message to the town called Gibeah. Saul lived in this town. When they told the news to the people, the people started to cry aloud. 5 Saul had been in his field. Now he was returning to his home with the cows. He heard the people crying. He asked, 'What has happened? Why are the people crying?' They told Saul what the men from Jabesh had said. 6 When people told Saul the news, the Spirit of God made him very powerful. Saul became very angry. 7 He killed two of his cows. He cut them into pieces. He gave the pieces to the men from Jabesh. He said that they must take the pieces to all the towns in Israel. The men said, 'Everyone must join Saul and Samuel to fight the Ammonites. They will cut up your cows like this if you do not follow.' The people were afraid of the Lord. So all the men came together as one group. 8 They met together with Saul at the town called Bezek. There were 300 000 men from Israel. And there were 30 000 men from Judah.

9 Saul spoke to the men who had brought the news from Jabesh. He said to them, 'Return to Jabesh and tell the people this message:

"Our people will save you. They will do it tomorrow before midday." ' So, the men went and they gave the message to them. All the people in Jabesh were very happy. 10 The men from Jabesh went and they spoke to Nahash. They said, 'Tomorrow we will come out to you. Then you can do anything that you want with us.'

11 The next day Saul put his soldiers into three groups. At dawn, they attacked the Ammonites' army. The Israelite soldiers killed the Ammonites and won the fight before midday. Some Ammonite soldiers ran away in different directions. Each man ran off by himself.

12 Israel's people said to Samuel, 'Some men said, "We do not think that Saul should rule us." Bring the men who said that to us. Then we will kill them.'

13 Saul said, 'No, you must not kill anyone today because the Lord saved Israel's people today.'

14 Samuel said to the people, 'We will all go to the town called Gilgal. Then we will agree again that Saul is our king.' 15 So everyone went to Gilgal. They went to the place for worship. They all agreed that Saul should be their king. They gave fellowship offerings to the Lord. Saul and all the Israelites had a very good party.

Chapter 12

Samuel speaks to all the Israelites for the last time

1 Samuel said to all the Israelites, 'I have done everything that you asked me to do. I have given a king to you to rule over you. 2 Now you have a king to be your leader. I am old and my hair is grey. My sons are here with you. I have been your leader from the days when I was young until now. 3 Here I am. I have not done any wrong things. If I have, you must tell the Lord and his anointed king. I did not take anyone's cow or donkey. I did not rob anyone. I saw the wrong things that people did. But I never let them give money to me to say that I did not see them. If I have done any of those things, I will make it right.'

4 The Israelites answered, 'You have not robbed any of us. You have not done bad things to any of us. You have not taken any money from anyone.'

5 Samuel said to the Israelites, 'The Lord has heard what you have said today. The Lord's anointed king has also heard that I have not taken anything from anybody.'

They replied, 'He has heard.'

6 Then Samuel said to all the people, 'The Lord chose Moses and Aaron. He brought all your ancestors out from the country called Egypt. 7 You must stand up now. Then I will show you what you are doing. I will tell you again about all the good things that God did. God did these things on behalf of you and your ancestors. 8 He sent Israel's people to Egypt. Then they shouted to the Lord for help. So the Lord sent Moses and Aaron to them. They took your ancestors out of Egypt and they brought them to live here.

9 But your ancestors forgot the Lord their God. Sisera led an army from the town called Hazor. He fought against the Israelites. The Philistines and the king of Moab also fought against the Israelites. The Lord let these enemies win the fight. The Israelites became their slaves. 10 Then the Israelites asked the Lord to help them. They said, "We have sinned. We left the Lord and we worshipped the false gods, the Baals and the Ashtoreths. Save us from our enemies and we will worship you." 11 So the Lord sent Jerubbaal (Gideon), Bedan (Barak), Jephthah and Samuel to you. The Lord saved you from all your enemies. Then you lived safely.

12 But then you saw that Nahash, the king of the Ammonites, was coming to attack you. So you said to me, "No. We want a king to rule us." But the Lord your God was your king. 13 Now here is the king that you chose. He is the man that you asked for. The Lord has made him your king. 14 You should give honour to the Lord. You must do the things that give pleasure to him. You must obey the Lord. You must not do anything against his rules. You and the king who rules you must obey the Lord your God. 15 You might not obey the Lord. You might do things against his rules. If you do, he will fight against you. He will do to you what he did to the Israelites in past times.'

16 Now stand where you are. See the great thing that the Lord will do. 17 The wheat is now ready to bring in. I will pray. The Lord will send storms and rain. Then you will know that you did an evil thing against the Lord. You asked for a king.

18 Samuel prayed to the Lord. That day the Lord sent storms and rain. All the people were afraid of the Lord and of Samuel. 19 All the people said to Samuel, 'We are your servants. Pray to the Lord your God on our behalf. Do not let us die. We have sinned many times in past days. Now we have sinned again. We asked for a king.'

20 Samuel said, 'Do not be afraid. It is true that you have sinned. But do not turn away from the Lord. Obey the Lord with all of your mind and body. 21 Do not worship idols. They cannot help you. They cannot save you. 22 The Lord does not change his mind. He decided to make you his own people. He will not leave you. 23 As for me, I will not stop praying on your behalf. I will sin against the Lord if I stop. I will teach you the good and the right things to do. 24 You must give honour to the Lord. You must do everything that he asks. Remember the great things that he did on your behalf. 25 But if you continue to sin against God, he will remove you and your king.'

Chapter 13

Jonathan attacks the Philistines

1-2 It was now one year since Saul became king. Saul was 30 years old when he became king. He was the king of Israel for 42 years. And when he had ruled over Israel for two more years, he chose 3000 men from Israel. Then 2000 men stayed with him at Michmash. This place was in the mountains of Bethel. But 1000 men stayed with his son Jonathan. They stayed in the town called Gibeah. Gibeah was in the land of Benjamin's tribe. Saul sent all the other men to their tents. 3 Some of the Philistine army were staying at Geba. Jonathan attacked them there. People told the other Philistines about it. Saul said, 'Someone must tell all the Israelites about this.' So Saul sent men out to every place in Israel. They had to make noise with trumpets. Then the Israelites would know that they must come to the fight. 4 They told all the people in Israel the news. They told them that Saul had attacked the Philistines. They told them that the Philistines were now even stronger enemies to the Israelites. So the people came to Saul at Gilgal.

Saul gives the burnt offering to God

5 The Philistines came together to fight the Israelites. The Philistines had 30 000 chariots. And there were 6000 men who rode on horses. And they had many thousands of soldiers. There were so many soldiers that nobody could count them. The Philistines were staying at the town called Michmash which was east of Beth-aven. 6 The Israelites saw the Philistine army. The Israelites knew that they were in a difficult place. Some of them went and hid in the bushes. They also hid among the rocks, in holes in the ground and in wells. 7 Some of the Israelites even crossed to the other side of the river Jordan. They went into the land of Gad and Gilead.

Saul stayed at Gilgal. All the people with him were so afraid that their bodies shook. 8 Samuel had told Saul that he must wait for him. Saul waited for 7 days as Samuel had said. But Samuel did not come to Gilgal. The men with Saul began to leave him. 9 So Saul said, 'Bring the burnt offering and the fellowship offerings to me.' Saul offered the burnt sacrifice to God. 10 Samuel arrived a very short time after he had finished. Saul went to speak to Samuel.

11 Samuel asked, 'What have you done?'

Saul replied, 'The soldiers were leaving me. You said that you would be here at a certain time. But you did not arrive at that time. The Philistines were meeting together at Michmash. 12 I thought that they would come. I thought that they would attack me at Gilgal. But I had not asked God to help me. So I thought that I ought to offer the burnt offering.'

13 Samuel said, 'You have been a fool. You have not obeyed the word of the Lord your God. You should have obeyed the Lord. Then the Lord would have let you and your family rule over the Israelites for all time. 14 But that will not happen now because you did not obey the Lord. Instead, the Lord will find the kind of man that he wants. The Lord will make this man the ruler of his people, the Israelites.'

15 Samuel left Gilgal. He went to the town called Gibeah in the land of Benjamin. Saul counted the men who were with him.

There were about 600 men.

16 Saul, his son Jonathan and the men who were with them were in the town called Geba. Geba is in the land of Benjamin. The Philistines' army was at Michmash. 17 The Philistines sent out three groups of men to attack Saul's men. One group went towards Ophrah in the land of Shual. 18 The second group went towards the town called Beth-horon. The third group went to another place. There they could see across the Valley of Zeboim towards the desert.

19 There were no blacksmiths in the country (Israel). The Philistines had said, 'If the Israelites have blacksmiths they will learn to make swords and spears.' 20 The Israelites used ploughs, hoes, axes and sickles on their farm land. These tools were not sharp when people had used them a lot. So they had to take them to the Philistines' blacksmiths who made them sharp again. 21 The Israelites had to pay 8grams of silver for the Philistines to make each plough or hoe sharp again. They paid 4 grams of silver for each axe, sickle or ox-goad.

22 When the fight started, only Saul and Jonathan each had a sword and spear. The other soldiers did not have any swords or spears.

Jonathan attacks the Philistines

23 A group of Philistine soldiers went to the narrow road in the mountains at Michmash.

Chapter 14

1 A young man carried Jonathan's armour. Jonathan was Saul's son. One day, Jonathan said to the young man, 'We will go across to the Philistine army on the other side.' But Jonathan did not tell his father. 2Saul was staying under a big fruit tree at Migron near Gibeah. There were about 600 men with Saul. 3Ahijah was with Saul. He wore an ephod. Ahijah was the son of Ahitub. Ahitub was Ichabod's brother. Ichabod was the son of Phinehas and the grandson of Eli. Eli was the priest of the Lord in Shiloh. Nobody knew that Jonathan had left.

4 Jonathan had to go along a narrow valley. It was in the mountains at Michmash. There was a high wall of rock on both sides of the road. The name of the wall on one side was 'Bozez'. The name of the other wall was 'Seneh'. 5 One rock wall was on the north side of the road, near Michmash. The other was on the south side, near Geba.

6 Jonathan spoke to the young man who carried his armour. 'Now we will go to the place where those Philistines are. Nobody has circumcised them. Perhaps the Lord will help us. The Lord can help us to win the fight. He can do that whether there are many of us or only a few of us.'

7 The young man said, 'You do anything that you want to do. I will go with you all the way.'

8 Jonathan said, 'We will go across and we will let the Philistines see us. 9 They may ask us to wait for them because they will come across to us. If they say that, we will stay here. 10 But they may ask us to go to them. That will mean that God will help us to win the fight. So we will go to them.'

11 Jonathan and his young man stood where the Philistines could see them. The Philistines said, 'Look at the Hebrews (Israelites). They are coming out of the holes where they were hiding.' 12 The Philistines shouted to Jonathan and his young man, 'Come up here to us. We want to teach you something.'

Jonathan said, 'Follow me. The Lord will help Israel to win the fight.'

13 Jonathan climbed up the rock wall. He was using his hands and his feet to climb up. His young man climbed up behind him. Jonathan attacked and killed some Philistines. The young man followed behind Jonathan and killed more Philistines. 14 Jonathan and his young man killed about 20 men in that small space. This was the first time that they attacked the enemy.

15 All the Philistine soldiers became afraid and confused. This happened to the soldiers in Michmash and to those round the town. And it happened to those other soldiers who had gone out to attack. The ground shook. God had made them all very afraid.

16 Saul was at Gibeah in the land of Benjamin. Some of Saul's soldiers were watching the Philistines. They saw that the Philistines were running away in different directions. 17 Saul said to his army, 'Count our soldiers. Find out who is not here.' They counted the soldiers. Jonathan and the young man who carried his armour were not there.

18 Saul said to Ahijah the priest, 'Bring God's covenant box here.' At that time, it was with the Israelites. 19Saul was talking to the priest. At the same time, the Philistine army made more noise and they were very confused. Saul said to the priest, 'Take your hand away.'

20 Then Saul and all his men went to fight the Philistines. They found that the Philistines were completely confused. They were so confused that they were fighting each other. 21 Before this time, some of the Israelites had joined with the Philistines. Those Israelites who had stayed with the Philistines. Now they went back to the Israelites' army with Saul and Jonathan. 22 Many Israelites had hidden in the mountains in the land of Ephraim. Now somebody told them that the Philistine soldiers were running away. So these Israelites joined the fight and they ran after the Philistines. 23 They fought all the way to Beth-aven and beyond it. That day the Lord saved Israel's people.

Jonathan eats honey

24 But the men among Israel's people were not happy that day. Saul had told them all that they must promise something to him. He had said, 'Nobody should to eat any food before this evening. You must not eat any food before I have won the fight with my enemies. If anyone eats, I will punish him.' So none of Saul's army ate any food. 25 The Israelite army went into a forest. There was honey on the ground. 26 The men saw all the honey in the forest. But none of them ate the honey because they were afraid of their promise to Saul. 27 But Jonathan had not heard what his father had said. He put the end of his stick into the honey. He ate the honey. Then he felt better. 28 One of the soldiers told Jonathan, 'Your father said a promise to all the soldiers. He will punish any man who eats anything today. That is why all the men are weak.'

29 Jonathan said, 'My father has made trouble for the people. I feel so much better because I ate some of the honey. 30 The men took food from their enemies today. It would have been much better if they had eaten some of it. If they had done that, they would have killed many more Philistines.'

31 That day, the Israelites won the fight with the Philistines. They fought them all the way from Michmash to Aijalon. After this, the Israelites were very weak. 32 They took sheep, cows and young cows from the Philistines. The Israelites were so hungry that they killed the animals on the ground. Then they ate the animals with the blood still in them. 33 Someone said to Saul, 'Look at the people. They are sinning against the Lord. They are eating the meat with blood still in it.' Saul said, 'You have sinned. Bring a large stone here.' 34 Then Saul said, 'Go to the people. Tell them that each man must bring his cow or his sheep here. They must kill and eat the animals here. Do not sin against the Lord. Do not eat meat with the blood still in it.' So, every man took his animal and he killed it there. 35 Then Saul built an altar to the Lord. It was the first altar that Saul had built to the Lord.

36 Saul said, 'We will go and we will attack the Philistines tonight until dawn. We will take everything that they have. And we will kill all of them.'

The men answered, 'You decide what seems the best thing to do. Then do that.'

But the priest said, 'We should ask God first.'

37 Saul asked God, 'Should I attack the Philistines? Will you help Israel to win the fight?' But God did not answer Saul that day.

38 So Saul said to all the leaders of the people, 'Come here. We must find out who has sinned today. 39 The Lord lives and he has saved Israel. And even if my son Jonathan has sinned, he must die.' But nobody among the people spoke.

40 Saul said to all the Israelites, 'You stand on this side. My son Jonathan and I will stand on the other side.'

The people answered, 'You decide what seems the best thing to do. Then do that.'

41 Then Saul prayed to the Lord, the God of Israel. He said, 'Give the right answer to me.' God chose Jonathan and Saul. He did not choose the people. 42 Saul said, 'Who has sinned, Jonathan or me?' God chose Jonathan.

43 Saul said to Jonathan, 'Tell me what you have done.'

Jonathan told him, 'I only ate a little honey from the end of my stick. Must I die now?'

44 Saul said, 'Jonathan, I ask God to punish me very much if you do not die.'

45 But the people said to Saul, 'Jonathan won a great fight for (on behalf of) Israel. He will not have to die. We promise by the living God that he will not lose even one hair on his head. God helped Jonathan today in this fight.' So, the people saved Jonathan and he did not have to die.

46 Then Saul stopped fighting the Philistines. The Philistines returned to their own country.

Saul fights Israel's enemies

47 When Saul became king of Israel, he fought against all Israel's enemies all round them. He fought people from the countries called Moab, Ammon and Edom. He fought the kings from the country called Zobah. He also fought the Philistines. Anywhere that Saul went, he won his fights against Israel's enemies. 48 He fought the Amalekites bravely and he won. Saul saved the Israelites from all the people who had robbed them.

49 Saul's sons were Jonathan, Ishvi and Malchishua. Merab was Saul's older daughter. Michal was his younger daughter. 50 The name of Saul's wife was Ahinoam. She was the daughter of Ahimaaz. Abner was the leader of Saul's army. Abner was the son of Ner. Ner was a brother of Saul's father. 51 Saul's father was Kish. Abner's father was Ner and Ner's father was Abiel.

52 Saul fought strongly against the Philistines during all of his life. If Saul found a strong man or a brave man, he caused the man to join his army.

Chapter 15

Saul does not obey the Lord completely

1 Samuel said to Saul, 'The Lord sent me to anoint you as king over his people, the Israelites. So now listen to this message from the Lord. 2 This is what God, the most powerful Lord, says. "Israel's people came out of the country called Egypt and they went to the country called Canaan. But the Amalekites did not want to let them go into Canaan. So I will punish the Amalekites.

3 Go and attack the Amalekites. Completely destroy everything that they have. Do not save anything. Kill the men and women, children and babies. Kill their cows and sheep. Kill their camels and donkeys".'

4 So Saul called his army together. They met at Telaim and he counted his men. There were 200 000 soldiers and 10 000 men from the tribe of Judah. 5 Saul and his army went to a town in the country of Amalek. They waited in a valley to catch their enemy. 6 Saul said to the people from the Kenite tribe, 'Go away. Leave the Amalekites. I will kill the Amalekites. But I do not want to kill you. You were kind to the Israelites when they came out from the country called Egypt.' So the Kenites left the Amalekites.

7 Then Saul attacked the Amalekites. He fought them all the way from Havilah to Shur, which is east of Egypt. And he beat them. 8 Saul brought back their king, Agag, alive. Saul's soldiers killed all the people with their swords. 9 But Saul and the people let Agag live. They did not kill the best old and young sheep or the fat cows. They let all the good animals live. They did not want to kill all the animals. But they killed all the animals that were weak or worth nothing.

10 Then the Lord said to Samuel, 11 'I am sorry that I made Saul king. He has stopped doing the things that cause me pleasure. He has not obeyed my words.' Samuel was very sad. He prayed aloud to the Lord all that night.

12 Samuel got up early the next morning. He went to meet Saul. Someone told Samuel, 'Saul went to the town called Carmel. He put up a tall stone to give honour to himself. Then he went to the town called Gilgal.'

13 Samuel went to find Saul. Saul said to Samuel, 'I ask the Lord to be good to you. I have obeyed the Lord's words.'

14 But Samuel said, 'Why can I hear the noises of sheep and cows?'

15 Saul answered, 'The people took them from the Amalekites. They saved the best sheep and cows. They will sacrifice them to the Lord your God. We killed all the other animals.'

16 Samuel said to Saul, 'Stop talking. I will tell you what the Lord said to me last night.'

Saul said, 'Tell me.'

17 Samuel said, 'In past days you thought that you were not an important person. Now you are the leader of all of the Israelite tribes. God anointed you as king of Israel. 18 The Lord gave to you special work to do. He said to you, "Go and kill all the Amalekites. They are evil people. Fight against them until they are all dead." 19 Why did you not obey the Lord? Why did you keep the best things? Why did you do what God did not want?'

20 Saul said, 'I did obey the Lord. I did what the Lord said. I did what he asked me to do. I killed all the Amalekites. I brought back Agag their king. 21 But the people did not kill the best sheep and cows. They brought them to sacrifice to the Lord your God at Gilgal.'

22 But Samuel replied,

'Is the Lord most happy when people give offerings and sacrifices to him? Or is he most happy when people obey him?

The Lord is most happy when people obey him. That is better than when they sacrifice the best sheep to him.

23 You sin if you refuse to obey the Lord. This sin is as bad as to do evil magic.

You think that you know better than God. That is a sin which is like the worship of idols.

You refused to obey what the Lord said. Now the Lord has refused you as king.'

24 Then Saul said to Samuel, 'I have sinned. I did not obey the Lord or your words. I was afraid of the people. I did what they wanted. 25 Now I am asking you to forgive my sin. Return with me so that I can worship the Lord.'

26 But Samuel said to Saul, 'I will not return with you. You refused to do what the Lord said. Now the Lord refuses you as king of Israel.'

27 Samuel turned away from Saul and left. But Saul pulled the edge of Samuel's coat and it tore. 28 Samuel said to him, 'The Lord has torn the kingdom of Israel from you today. He has given it to someone near to you who is better than you. 29 The Lord is the glory of Israel. He does not say things that are not true. He does not change his mind. He is not like a man who decides to change.'

30 Saul replied, 'I have sinned. But please give honour to me in front of the leaders and people in Israel. Return with me so that I can worship the Lord your God.' 31 So Samuel returned with Saul. And Saul worshipped the Lord.

32 Then Samuel said, 'Bring Agag, king of the Amalekites, to me.'

Agag came to Samuel. Agag was happy because he thought, 'I am sure that now I will not feel the strong pain of death.'

33 But Samuel said, 'You have killed many people. Now some mothers do not have any children that are still alive. Now your mother will have no children.' And Samuel cut Agag into pieces in front of the Lord at Gilgal.

34 Then Samuel left Gilgal and he went to his home in Ramah. But Saul went to his home in Gibeah. 35Until Samuel died, he never saw Saul again. But Samuel was very sad about Saul. And the Lord was very sorry that he had made Saul king of Israel.

Chapter 16

Samuel anoints David

1 The Lord said to Samuel, 'You should not continue to be sad about Saul. I do not still want him to be the king of Israel. Fill your horn with oil and go. I am sending you to a man whose name is Jesse. He lives in the town called Bethlehem. I have chosen one of his sons to be king.'

2 But Samuel said, 'If I go, people will tell Saul about it. Then he will kill me.'

The Lord said, 'Take a young cow with you. Tell the people that you have come to give a sacrifice to the Lord. 3 Say to Jesse, "Come to the sacrifice." I will show you what to do. I will show you the person that you must anoint.'

4 Samuel obeyed the Lord. He arrived at Bethlehem. The leaders of that town went to meet Samuel. The leaders shook because they were afraid of Samuel. They asked him, 'Have you come as a friend and not to bring trouble?'

5 Samuel replied, 'Yes. I have come to offer a sacrifice to the Lord. Make yourselves clean. Then come to the sacrifice with me.' Samuel made Jesse and his sons clean. Then Samuel asked them to come to the sacrifice.

6 When they arrived, Samuel saw Jesse's son Eliab. Samuel thought, 'I am sure that the Lord has chosen this man.'

7 But the Lord said to Samuel, 'Do not look at how handsome or how tall Eliab is. I have not chosen him. The Lord does not look at people in the way that other people do. People look at the face and body of a person. But the Lord looks inside them.'

8 Then Jesse called his son Abinadab. Jesse caused him to walk past Samuel. But Samuel said, 'The Lord has not chosen this man.' 9 Jesse caused his son Shammah to walk past Samuel. But Samuel said, 'The Lord has not chosen this man.' 10 Jesse caused 7 of his sons to walk past Samuel. But Samuel said, 'The Lord has not chosen any of these men.' 11 Samuel asked Jesse, 'Do you have any more sons?'

Jesse answered, 'I have one more son. He is the youngest. He is caring for the sheep.'

Samuel said, 'Ask him to come here. We will not sit down to eat until he arrives.'

12 So Jesse asked them to fetch him and Jesse took him to Samuel. This young man was handsome and strong and he had beautiful eyes.

The Lord said to Samuel, 'I have chosen this man. Go and anoint him.'

13 The name of the young man was David. Samuel took the horn that was full of oil. He poured the oil over David to anoint him. Samuel did this in front of David's brothers. After that, the Spirit of the Lord came on David in a powerful way. Then Samuel returned to Ramah.

14 But the Spirit of the Lord had left Saul. The Lord sent an evil spirit to Saul. It made him afraid and it caused him to have troubles. 15 Saul's servants said to him, 'We know that God sent an evil spirit to give troubles to you. 16 If you will let us, we will go. We will look for a man who can make music on a harp. When the evil spirit comes from God, this man can make music. Then you will feel better.'

17 So Saul said to his servants, 'Find someone who can make good music with a harp. Bring him to me.'

18 One of the servants said, 'Jesse lives in Bethlehem. He has a son who makes good music. This son is a strong, brave soldier. He thinks carefully before he speaks. He is handsome. The Lord is with him.'

19 So Saul sent men to Jesse with a message. He said, 'Ask your son David to come to me. That is the son who is with the sheep.' 20 So Jesse took some loaves of bread, a leather bag that was full of wine, and a young goat. He put them on the back of a donkey. He sent them to Saul with his son David.

21 David came to Saul. He became Saul's servant. Saul loved David. David became one of the men who carried Saul's armour. 22 Saul sent a message to Jesse. He said, 'David gives very much pleasure to me. Let him stay to become my servant.'

23 So, when the evil spirit came from God to Saul, David made music on his harp. Then the evil spirit would leave Saul. And Saul would feel better. And he would be well again.

Chapter 17

David and Goliath

1 The Philistine army came together ready for a fight. They met at Socoh in the land of Judah. They stayed at Ephes-dammim between the towns called Socoh and Azekah. 2 Saul and the Israelites came near together in the Valley of Elah. They put their tents there and they got ready to fight the Philistines. 3 The Philistines were on one side of the hill. The Israelites were on the other side of the hill. The valley was between them.

4 The Philistines had a soldier who had won more fights than anyone else. He came from the town called Gath. His name was Goliath. He was about 3 metres (more than 9 feet) tall. 5 He wore a bronze helmet on his head. His armour included a coat of the same metal. It weighed about 57 kilos (about 125 pounds). 6He had pieces of metal round the front of each leg. He had a bronze javelin that hung on his back. 7 The handle of his spear was very thick. He had an iron point on his spear. It weighed about 7 kilos (about 15 pounds). A man carried Goliath's shield and this man walked in front of him.

8 Goliath stood and he shouted to the Israelite soldiers. He said, 'I do not know why you have got ready for a fight. I am a Philistine. You are Saul's servants. You must choose one of your soldiers. Send him down to fight me. 9 If he can kill me, the Philistines will become your slaves. I will fight this man. If I kill him, the Israelites will become our slaves.' 10 Then Goliath said again, 'I am not afraid to stand against the army of Israel. Send one of your men and we will fight together.' 11 Saul and the Israelites heard what Goliath said. This frightened them very much.

12 David was the son of Jesse. Jesse was from the family of Ephratah. He came from the town called Bethlehem which was in the land of Judah. Jesse had 8 sons. When Saul was king, Jesse was an old man. 13 Jesse's three oldest sons had gone to the war with Saul. Eliab was Jesse's oldest son. Abinadab was Jesse's second son. Shammah was Jesse's third son. 14 David was Jesse's youngest son. Jesse's three oldest sons were with Saul. 15 Sometimes David was with Saul. But sometimes he had to return to Bethlehem. He returned to care for his father's sheep.

16 Goliath shouted to the Israelites every morning and every evening for 40 days.

17 One day, Jesse said to his son David, 'Here are 10 kilos (22 pounds) of wheat that I have cooked, and 10 loaves of bread. Take these quickly to your brothers in the army. 18 Take these 10 cheeses to the officer who is the leader of their group. Find out whether your brothers are well. Bring me back news about them. 19 Your brothers are with Saul and the Israelite army. They are in the Valley of Elah. They are fighting against the Philistines.'

20 So David got up early the next morning. He left the sheep with another shepherd. He took the food. He did what Jesse had asked him to do. David reached the Israelite tents. The army was just going out to the place from which to fight. They shouted while they went. They were shouting because they wanted to fight. 21 The Israelite army and the Philistine army stood in their places ready for the fight. They stood and looked towards each other across the valley. 22 David left all his things with the officer who kept the army's food. David ran to the Israelite army. He went to see his brothers. 23 While David was talking to his brothers, Goliath, the great Philistine soldier, came towards them. Goliath shouted things against the Israelites as usual. David heard what he said. 24 When the Israelites saw Goliath, they were very afraid. They ran away.

25 The Israelites said, 'Look at this man. He shouts bad things at us all the time. King Saul will give a lot of money to the man who kills Goliath. The king will also let this man marry his daughter. The family of that man's father will not have to pay taxes to the king of Israel.'

26 David said to the men who were standing near him, 'If a man kills Goliath, Israel will not be ashamed any longer. What gift will he get? Goliath is only a Philistine. Nobody has circumcised him. He does not give honour to our God. He should not say these things against the army of the living God.'

27 The men told David what they had said. They said, 'This will be done to pay the man who kills Goliath.'

28 Eliab, David's oldest brother, heard David speaking with the men. Eliab was angry with David and Eliab asked him, 'Why have you come here? You have a few sheep in the desert. Who is caring for them? You think that you are great. I know that. But you are evil. I think that you only came here to watch the fight.'

29 David said, 'I do not know what I have done wrong. I only asked a question.' 30 So David went and he asked other people the same question. All the men gave the same answer. 31 Some of the men had heard what David said. They went and they told Saul. Saul asked David to come to see him.

32 David said to Saul, 'I am your servant. Do not think that Goliath will bring trouble to Israel. I will go and I will fight him.'

33 Saul replied, 'You cannot go and fight Goliath. You are only a young man. Goliath has been a strong soldier all of his life.'

34 But David said, 'I have cared for my father's sheep. Sometimes a lion or a bear came and took a young sheep. 35 I ran after the lion or the bear and I attacked it.

I saved the young sheep from its mouth. When the lion or the bear started to attack me, I held its hair. Then I hit it and I killed it. 36 I, your servant, have killed lions and bears. And I will do the same to this Philistine that nobody has circumcised. He has said bad things about the army of the living God. 37 The Lord has saved me from lions and bears. He will save me from this Philistine.'

Saul said to David, 'Go. And I ask the Lord that he will be with you.' 38 Saul put his own clothes on David. He put his bronze helmet on David's head. Then he dressed David with his armour. 39 David put on the sword and the armour. He tried to walk but he had not worn armour before.

David said to Saul, 'I cannot wear all this armour. I have never used it.' So David took it all off.

40 David picked up his shepherd's stick. He went to the stream.

He took 5 round stones from the stream and he put them in his bag. He had his sling in his hand. Then he went to meet the Philistine.

41 Goliath walked towards David. A man walked in front of Goliath and the man was carrying Goliath's shield. Goliath looked at David. 42 He saw that David was a handsome young man with brown skin. That made Goliath very angry. 43 He said to David, 'I do not know why you have come with a stick. Perhaps you think that I am a dog.' Then he asked his gods to cause bad things to happen to David. 44 Then Goliath said, 'Come here. I will feed the birds and the wild animals with your dead body.'

45 David said, 'You have come to fight me with a sword, a spear and a javelin. But I come to fight you in the name of the Lord who is most powerful. You have said bad things about the God of Israel's army. 46 Today the Lord will make me powerful against you. I will hit you and I will cut off your head. Today I will feed the birds and the wild animals with the dead bodies of the Philistine army. Then all the people in the whole world will know that there is a God in Israel. 47 The Lord does not need swords and spears to save his people. Everyone here will soon know that the Lord will win the fight. He will make us powerful against you.'

48 Goliath started to move nearer to David to attack him. David ran quickly to meet him. 49 David took a stone from his bag. He put the stone into the sling and he threw it. The stone hit Goliath on his face above his eyes. It went into his head. Goliath fell with his face on the ground.

50 So David used a sling and a stone to win the fight with the Philistines. David did not have a sword but he killed Goliath. 51 David ran and stood next to him. He took Goliath's sword out of its bag. Then he killed Goliath and he cut off his head with the sword. The Philistines saw that their best fighter was dead. So they ran away. 52 The men from Israel and Judah shouted. They ran after the Philistines all the way to the gate of the town called Gath. And they ran after them to the gates of the town called Ekron. They killed the Philistines. They left their dead bodies on the road to Shaaraim, as far as Gath and Ekron. 53 The Israelites returned when they had finished running after the Philistines. Then the Israelites went and they robbed the Philistines' tents. 54 David took Goliath's head into Jerusalem. But he put Goliath's armour into his own tent.

55 Saul had watched David when he went out to fight Goliath. Abner was the most important officer in Saul's army. Saul said to Abner, 'Abner, whose son is that young man?'

Abner replied, 'My great king, I do not know.'

56 The king said, 'Find out whose son he is.'

57 David returned after he had killed Goliath. Abner brought David to Saul. David was still holding Goliath's head.

58 Saul asked him, 'Young man, who is your father?'

David answered, 'I am the son of your servant Jesse who comes from Bethlehem.'

159

Chapter 18

1 David finished talking with Saul. Then Jonathan, Saul's son, became a very good friend of David. Jonathan loved David as much as Jonathan loved himself. 2 Saul kept David with him from that day. He did not let David go to his home in his father's house. 3 Jonathan loved David so much that he made a special covenant with him. 4 Jonathan was wearing a coat. He took the coat off and he gave it to David. He also gave his armour to David. And he gave his sword, his bow and his belt to him. 5 David did whatever Saul asked him to do. And he always did it well. So Saul made David an important officer in his army. That gave pleasure to all of Saul's officers and people.

6 After David had killed Goliath, he and the soldiers returned to their homes. Women came out from all the towns in Israel to meet King Saul. The women sang happy songs and they danced. They made music with tambourines and lyres too. 7 They sang this while they danced:

'Saul has killed thousands of his enemies.

And David has killed tens of thousands of his enemies.'

8 Saul did not like this song. He became very angry. He thought, 'The women say that David has killed tens of thousands of men. But they say that I have only killed thousands of men. Perhaps they will want David as their king.' 9 Saul had bad thoughts about David after that. He watched David carefully.

10 The next day an evil spirit from the Lord started to use Saul. He was prophesying in his house. And David was making music on his harp as he usually did. But Saul had a spear in his hand. 11 Saul threw the spear. He tried to hit David and to fix him to the wall. But twice he did not hit David.

12 The Lord was with David. But the Lord had left Saul. So Saul was afraid of David. 13 So Saul sent David away from him. He made David the leader of 1000 soldiers. David was their leader in their fights. 14 David won all his fights because the Lord was with him. 15 Saul saw that David was a great soldier. Saul became more afraid of him. 16 All the people in Israel and Judah loved David because he was a good leader.

David marries Saul's daughter

17 Saul said to David, 'Here is my oldest daughter Merab. I will let you marry her. But you must be a brave soldier and you must fight for the Lord.' Saul thought to himself, 'I will not have to kill David. The Philistines will do that.'

18 But David said to Saul, 'I, my family and my father's tribe are not very important in Israel. I cannot marry the king's daughter.' 19 When it was the time for Merab to marry David, Saul gave her to Adriel from Meholah, instead, as his wife.

20 Saul's daughter Michal loved David. When somebody told Saul about this, he was very happy. 21 He thought, 'I will let David marry her. She will cause danger for him. I will cause him to fight the Philistines. Then the Philistines will win the fight and they will kill him.' So Saul said to David, 'Now you can try to win my other daughter as a wife.'

22 Saul asked his servants to talk to David in a secret place. He asked them to say, 'You have given pleasure to the king. His servants like you. You should now marry his daughter.'

23 Saul's servants said this to David. But David said, 'It is a great honour to marry the king's daughter. But I am poor. I am not an important person.'

24 Saul's servants told Saul what David had said. 25 Saul said, 'Tell David this. The king does not want him to pay money for his wife. He can pay for her with the foreskins of 100 dead Philistines. That will punish Saul's enemies.' Saul decided to cause David to do all this. He thought that the Philistines would kill David.

26 Saul's servants told David these things. It made David happy to think that he could marry the king's daughter.

They decided when they would marry each other. 27 Before this time, David and his men went and they killed 200 Philistines. He brought all their foreskins to Saul. Now David could marry the king's daughter. So, Saul had to let him marry his daughter Michal.

28 Saul understood that the Lord was with David. He knew that his daughter Michal loved David. 29 Saul became more afraid of him. Saul was David's enemy until Saul died.

30 The Philistine army leaders continued to go and to fight the Israelites. Every time that they fought, David won more fights than any of Saul's other officers. So David became famous.

Chapter 19

Saul tries to kill David

1 Saul spoke to his son Jonathan and to all his servants.

'You must kill David', he said. But Jonathan liked David very much. 2 So he told David, 'My father Saul is trying to kill you. Be careful tomorrow morning. Hide in a secret place and stay there. 3 I will go out. And I will stand with my father in the field where you are hiding. I will talk to him about you. Then I will tell you what I find out.'

4 Jonathan spoke to his father Saul. Jonathan said good things about David. Jonathan said, 'The king should not do anything that is wrong. He should not punish his servant David. David has not done anything that is wrong. And he has been a great help to you. 5 David was not afraid to die when he killed Goliath the Philistine. The Lord helped him to win an important fight on behalf of all Israel. You saw it and you were happy. I do not know why you want to punish him. He has not done anything that was wrong. You have no reason to kill him.'

6 Saul listened to Jonathan. Then Saul said a promise in the Lord's name. Saul said that he would not kill David. 7 So Jonathan called to David. He told David everything that they had said. Jonathan took David to Saul. So David remained with Saul as before.

8 The war with the Philistines started again. David went out and he fought the Philistines. He beat them. He killed so many of them that the other soldiers ran away.

9 But an evil spirit from the Lord came. It caused Saul to think bad thoughts and to do evil things. Saul was sitting in his house. He had a spear in his hand. David was playing his harp. 10 Saul tried to push his spear through David and into the wall behind him. David moved out of the way and Saul's spear went into the wall. David ran away that night.

11 Saul sent some of his servants to watch David's house. Saul said that they must kill David in the morning. But Michal, David's wife, told him about Saul's idea. She said, 'You must go away tonight. If you do not go away, someone will kill you tomorrow.' 12 So Michal helped David to get down through a window. He ran away and they did not catch him. 13 Then Michal took an idol from their house and she put it in the bed. She put hair from a goat on the idol's head. Then she covered it.

14 Saul sent some men to bring David to him. Michal told them that David was ill. 15 Saul told the men that they must return to David. And Saul said, 'Bring David to me on his bed so that I can kill him.' 16 The men returned to David's house. They found the idol on the bed and the goat's hair was on its head.

17 Saul said to Michal, 'You should have told me what was true. You let my enemy go away. He has run away.' Michal replied, 'David asked me to help him. He said, "I will kill you if you do not help me." '

18 David ran away and he was safe. He went to visit Samuel at Ramah. David told Samuel everything that Saul had done to him. Then David and Samuel went to Naioth and they stayed there.

19 Somebody told Saul that David was in Naioth in Ramah. 20 So Saul sent men to bring David to him. When the men arrived, they saw a group of prophets. Samuel was their leader. They were all prophesying. Then the Spirit of God came and he started to use Saul's men. They started to prophesy too.

21 When people told Saul about this, he sent more men. But they prophesied too. So Saul sent a third group of men. These men also prophesied. 22 Then Saul himself went to Ramah. He went as far as the large well at Secu. He asked the people, 'Where are Samuel and David?' The people replied, 'They are at Naioth in Ramah.'

23 Saul went to Naioth in Ramah. The Spirit of God came and he caused even Saul to prophesy. Saul continued to prophesy until he came to Naioth. 24 Then he took off his clothes and he prophesied in front of Samuel. He lay down and he wore no clothes all that day and all that night. So people still say, 'Has Saul really become a prophet?'

Chapter 20

Jonathan helps David

1 Then David ran away from Naioth at Ramah. He went to Jonathan and asked him, 'What bad things have I done? What have I done to hurt your father? Why is he trying to kill me?'

2 Jonathan replied, 'No. You will not die. My father tells me everything that he does, even the little things. So it is not true! He would not hide this from me.'

3 But David answered, 'Your father knows that you like me. He decided not to tell you. He knew that you would not be very happy. I promise that my words are true. I think that I will soon be dead.'

4 Jonathan said to David, 'I will do anything that you want me to do.'

5 David said to Jonathan, 'Tomorrow we have a special meal because of the new moon. I ought to go and eat this meal with the king. Instead, I will go and hide in the fields. I will stay there until the third evening.6 Your father might see that I am not at the meal. If he does, you say, "David asked me to let him go to his home in Bethlehem. His father and brothers offer a sacrifice at this time every year." 7 Your father may say, "That is good." If he says that, I am safe. And I will know that I am safe. But he may become very angry. If he does become angry, he has decided to hurt me. And you will know that he wants to do that. 8Jonathan, please be a good friend and be kind to me, your servant. The Lord knows about the covenant that you made with me. If I have sinned, you can kill me yourself. Do not let your father kill me.'

9 Jonathan said, 'No, that will not happen. I will find out if my father wants to kill you. If he does, I will tell you.'

10 David said, 'If your father gets angry tomorrow, how will you tell me?'

11 Jonathan said, 'We should go out into the fields.' So they went there together.

12 Then Jonathan said to David, 'I say this promise to you and to the Lord, the God of Israel. Tomorrow or the next day I will find out how my father is feeling. If he is feeling friendly to you, I will send someone to tell you. 13 But my father may want to hurt you. I promise the Lord that I will let you know about it. Then I will send you away so that you can be safe. I pray that the Lord will be with you. I want him to be with you as he has been with my father. 14 The Lord is kind to me. Please be kind to me too while I am alive. Do not let me die. 15 The Lord will remove every one of your enemies from the earth. But please continue to be kind to all my family.'

16 So Jonathan made a covenant with David's family. He said, 'I am asking the Lord to punish David's enemies for what they have done.' 17 Again, Jonathan asked David to say that he loved him. Jonathan loved David as much as Jonathan loved himself.

18 Then Jonathan said to David, 'Tomorrow we will have the special meal because of the new moon. Nobody will be sitting in your chair. People will see that you are not there. 19 Return to the place where you hid at the beginning of this trouble. Go there on the day after tomorrow. Wait by the rock called Ezel.20 I will shoot three arrows by the side of it. I will say that I am shooting at a certain mark. 21 Then I will send a boy to find the arrows. If you are not in danger I will say to him, "The arrows are near to you. Bring them here." That will mean that you are safe. You can come out from the place where you are hiding.

22 But I may say to the boy, "Look, the arrows are beyond you." That will mean that you must go. The Lord has sent you away. 23 Always remember the covenant that we made. The Lord will make sure that we keep this promise.'

24 So David hid in the field. Then it was time for the special meal because of the new moon. The king sat down to eat the meal. 25 He sat by the wall in his usual place. Jonathan sat with his face towards him. Abner sat next to Saul. David's seat was empty. 26 Saul did not say anything about it that day. Saul thought, 'Perhaps something has happened to David that has made him not clean. I am sure that he is not clean.' 27 The next day was the second day of the month. David's seat was still empty at the meal. So Saul said to his son Jonathan, 'Why has the son of Jesse not come to the meal? He did not come yesterday or today.'

28 Jonathan answered, 'David asked me to let him go to Bethlehem. 29 He said, "Let me go. My family is having a sacrifice in the town. My brother told me that I must be there. If you are my friend let me go to visit my brothers." That is why David has not come to eat with the king.'

30 Saul became very angry with Jonathan. Saul said, 'You have done a very bad thing and you do not obey me. I know that you are David's friend. You have made your mother ashamed. You should be ashamed yourself. 31 You will never be king while David is alive. You will never rule the people. Go and bring David to me now. He must die.'

32 Jonathan said, 'Why must David die? What has he done that is wrong?' 33 But Saul threw a spear at Jonathan and tried to kill him. So, Jonathan knew that his father had decided to kill David. 34 Jonathan was very angry. He got up from the table. He did not eat anything on that second day of the month. He was very sad because Saul had not given honour to David.

35 In the morning, Jonathan went out to the field to meet David. Jonathan took a young boy with him. 36He said to the boy, 'Run. And find the arrows that I shoot.' While the boy was running, Jonathan shot an arrow beyond him. 37 The boy reached the place where the arrow landed. Jonathan shouted to him, 'The arrow is beyond you.' 38 Then he shouted, 'Hurry up. Go quickly. Do not stop.' The boy picked up the arrow and he brought it back to Jonathan. 39 (The boy did not know what this meant. Only Jonathan and David knew.) 40 Then Jonathan gave his bow and arrows back to the boy and Jonathan said, 'Go and take them back to town.'

41 So the boy left. David came out from the south side of the rock. He went down on his knees in front of Jonathan. He put his face down on the ground three times. Then David and Jonathan kissed each other and they cried together. But David cried more than Jonathan did.

42 Jonathan said to David, 'Go and God will keep you safe. We promised the Lord that we would always be friends. The Lord will make sure that my family and your family will always keep this promise.' Then David left. And Jonathan returned to the town.

Chapter 21

David goes to the town called Nob

1 David went and he visited Ahimelech the priest. He lived in the town called Nob. Ahimelech shook when he went to meet David. Ahimelech asked David, 'Why are you alone? Why is nobody with you?'

2 David answered, 'The king has asked me to do something special. He said to me, "Do not say to anyone where I have sent you. Do not say what you have to do." And I have sent my men to meet me at a certain place. 3 Do you have anything to eat here? Give to me 5 loaves of bread or anything else that you have.'

4 The priest answered David, 'I do not have any bread that anyone can eat. I only have some special holy bread. You can have it only if your men have not had sex with women.'

5 David replied, 'We have not been near women since we started our journey. The young men always keep themselves clean when we have any kind of journey. So they will certainly be clean today.' 6 So the priest gave the special holy bread to David because he did not have any other bread. Every day the priest went to the holy place where God appeared. The priest took away the old bread and he put hot, fresh bread in its place.

161

7 One of Saul's servants was there that day. He had to remain for a longer time than usual near the place where the Lord appeared. His name was Doeg. He came from the country called Edom. He was Saul's most important shepherd.

8 David asked Ahimelech, 'Do you have a sword or a spear that I could have? The king's business was so important that I left without a sword or anything to fight with.'

9 Ahimelech answered, 'The sword of Goliath the Philistine is here. You killed him in the valley of Elah. We covered the sword in a cloth and we put it behind the ephod. If you want it, you can take it. We do not have any other sword except that one.'

David said, 'Give it to me. There is no sword as good as that one.'

David goes to the town called Gath

10 Saul did not catch David that day. David went to Achish who was the king of the town called Gath. 11 But the servants of King Achish said to him, 'This man is David, the king of the Israelites. The people sing about him when they dance. They sing, "Saul has killed thousands of people, but David has killed tens of thousands of people".'

12 David became very serious. He thought about what the servants said. Then he became very afraid of Achish, king of Gath. 13 When David was near the king or his servants, David did strange things. He was like a man with a sick mind. He made marks on the doors of the gate. He did not keep water in his mouth but he let it go all down his beard.

14 Achish said to his servants, 'Look at that man. He is like a crazy man. Why did you bring him to me? 15 I have enough crazy men already. I do not need to see another one. And I do not want this man to come into my house.'

Chapter 22

David at Adullam and Mizpah

1 David left Gath and he went to a big hole in the rock near Adullam. His brothers and his father's family discovered where he had gone. So they all went to visit him. 2 Everybody who had troubles went to David. Everybody who had debts also went to him. And everyone who was not happy went to him. About 400 men went to David and he became their leader.

3 David then went to the town called Mizpah. It was in the country called Moab. David said to the king of Moab, 'Please let my father and my mother stay with you for a short time. I need to learn how God will help.' 4 So David left his parents with the king of Moab. They stayed with the king all the time that David hid in the safe place.

5 Gad the prophet said to David, 'Do not stay in the safe place. Go to the land of Judah.' So, David left the safe place and he went to the forest at Hereth.

Saul kills Ahimelech's family at Nob

6 Then people told Saul that someone had found David and his men. Saul was on the hill near Gibeah. He was sitting under a large tree. He was holding a spear. All his officers stood round him. 7 Saul said to them, 'Men from the tribe of Benjamin, listen to me. And understand what I say. The son of Jesse will not give fields and vineyards to you. He will not make you officers of men in his army. 8 So I do not know why you have decided to go against me. Nobody tells me when my son says a special promise with the son of Jesse. Nobody thinks about what could happen to me. Nobody tells me that my son is now against me. He has agreed that one of my servants should kill me.'

9 But Doeg, from the country called Edom, was standing with Saul's officers. Doeg said, 'I saw the son of Jesse. He came to the town called Nob and he visited Ahimelech. Ahimelech is the son of Ahitub. 10 Ahimelech asked the Lord what David should do. Then he gave some food and the sword of Goliath the Philistine to David.'

11 Then King Saul asked them to bring to him the priest Ahimelech, son of Ahitub. And with him, they brought all his brothers and their families.

They were priests. And they lived in the town called Nob. They all came to the king. 12 Saul said, 'Listen to me, son of Ahitub.'

Ahimelech answered, 'Yes, master.'

13 Saul said to him, 'You and the son of Jesse seem to be trying to kill me! You gave bread and a sword to him. You prayed to God on his behalf. He does not obey me. Now he is even waiting to attack me.'

14 Ahimelech answered, 'David is the most loyal servant that you have. He is your daughter's husband. He is the captain of the men who keep you safe. Everyone in your family gives honour to him.

15 I have prayed to God on David's behalf many times in past times. This was not the first time. King Saul, do not say that my family or I have done anything wrong. We do not know anything about what is happening.'

16 King Saul said, 'Ahimelech, you and all your brothers and their families must die.'

17 Then the king said to the officers who were round him, 'Go and kill the priests of the Lord. They are helping David. They knew that he was running away from me. But they did not tell me.'

But the king's officers refused to attack the priests of the Lord.

18 So the king said to Doeg, 'Go and kill the priests.' So, Doeg from Edom went and he killed the priests. He killed 85 priests who wore the linen ephod. 19 He also killed all the people in the town called Nob, which was the town of the priests. He killed the men and women, children and babies. He also killed the cows, donkeys and sheep.

20 But the king did not catch Abiathar. He was a son of Ahimelech (who was the son of Ahitub). Abiathar ran away and he met David. 21 Abiathar told David that Saul had killed the priests of the Lord. 22 David said to him, 'When I went to the town called Nob, Doeg was there too. I knew that he would tell Saul about me. I have caused the death of everybody who lives in your father's house. 23 Stay here with me. Do not be afraid. Saul wants to kill you and he wants to kill me too. You will be safe with me.'

Chapter 23

David saves the town called Keilah

1 The Philistines were attacking the town called Keilah. And they were taking away the grain when the Israelites had just brought it in. Someone told David about this. 2 So David asked the Lord, 'Should I go and attack these Philistines?'

The Lord answered him, 'Go and attack the Philistines. Save Keilah.'

3 But David's men said to him, 'We are afraid here in Judah. We will be more afraid if we attack the Philistine army at Keilah.'

4 So David asked the Lord again. The Lord answered, 'Go to Keilah. I will help you to win the fight with the Philistines.' 5 So David and his men went to Keilah. They fought the Philistines and they killed many of them. Also, they took all their animals. So David saved the people who lived in Keilah. 6 (When Abiathar the son of Ahimelech ran away, he came to David at Keilah. And he brought the ephod with him.)

Saul runs after David

7 Someone told Saul that David was now at Keilah. Saul said, 'God has given David to me. David has gone into a town that has a strong gate. He cannot leave.' 8 So Saul caused all his soldiers to join him. They prepared to go to Keilah and to attack David and his men.

9 Somebody told David that Saul was preparing to attack him. David said to Abiathar, 'Bring the ephod here.' 10 David prayed, 'Lord, you are the God of Israel. I am your servant. Somebody has told me that Saul is preparing to come to Keilah. He wants to destroy this town because I am here.

11 Will the people in Keilah give me to Saul? Will Saul really come here? Lord, God of Israel, I am your servant so please tell me.'

The Lord answered, 'Saul will come.'

12 David asked the Lord again, 'Will the people in Keilah give me and my men to Saul?'

And the Lord said, 'They will.'

13 So David and his 600 men left Keilah. They had to move from one place to another all the time. People told Saul that David had left Keilah. So Saul did not go there.

14 David stayed in the safe places in the desert. He also stayed in the hills in the desert places at Ziph. Saul looked for David every day. But God did not let Saul get David.

15 David was at Horesh in the empty places near Ziph. And somebody told him that Saul was coming to kill him. 16 Jonathan, Saul's son, went to visit David at Horesh. He told David that God would help him to be strong. 17 Jonathan said to David, 'Do not be afraid. My father will not hurt you. My father knows that you will be the next king of Israel. I will be your most important officer.' 18 Jonathan and David said a promise together with the Lord. Then Jonathan went to his home. David stayed at Horesh.

19 Some people from Ziph went to visit Saul at Gibeah. They said to Saul, 'David is hiding among us. He is on the hill at Hachilah. He is there in the safe place at Horesh. It is south of Jeshimon. 20 Now, King Saul, you can come to our land at any time. We must help you to catch David.'

21 Saul replied, 'I ask the Lord that he will be good to you. I ask him because you are helping me. 22 Return to your homes and make sure about David. Find out where he usually stays. Find the people who have seen him there. People have told me that David is very clever. 23 Find all the places where he hides. Then return. Tell me everything that you have discovered. Then I will come with you. I will find David if he is still near here. I will look all through the land of Judah for him.'

24 So the people returned to Ziph before Saul. David and his men were in the desert of Maon. This was south of Jeshimon. 25 Saul and his men started to look for David. Somebody told David about this. He and his men stayed in the desert called Maon and they went to a big rock. Somebody told Saul about this. He and his men went to the desert called Maon to follow David.

26 Saul and his men were going along one side of the mountain. David and his men were on the other side of the mountain. They were trying to hide from Saul. Saul and his army were getting nearer to David and his men. They were all round David and his men. They wanted to catch them. 27 But a man came and he gave his message to Saul, 'Come quickly. The Philistines are attacking our land.' 28 So Saul stopped running after David. Instead, Saul went to fight the Philistines. So people call that place 'The rock where they got away safely'.

29 David left that place and he lived in the safe places at Engedi.

Chapter 24

David refuses to kill Saul

1 When Saul had finished fighting the Philistines, he returned to his home. Someone told him that David was in the desert at Engedi. 2 So Saul chose 3000 of the best soldiers in Israel. They went to look for David and his men near Wild Goat Rocks.

3 Saul came to the places where they kept the sheep, near to the road. There was a big hole in the hill near to this place. Saul went into it to use it as a toilet. David and his men were sitting at the back of this hole and they were hiding. 4 The men said to David, 'This is the day that the Lord spoke about. The Lord said to you, "I will give your enemy to you. Then you can do to him what seems to you the right thing to do".' David walked up behind Saul. David was so quiet that Saul did not hear him. David cut off a small piece of cloth from Saul's coat.

5 After that, David felt sorry that he had cut a piece of cloth from Saul's coat. 6 David said to his men, 'I am praying that the Lord will not let me do anything wrong to my master, Saul. The Lord anointed him as king. I must never do anything against Saul, because the Lord has anointed him as king.' 7 David spoke like this so that his men would not attack Saul. David did not let them do it. Saul left the hole in the hill and he continued to go on his journey.

8 Then David went out of the hole and he shouted to Saul, 'My master and my king!' Saul looked behind him. David went down on his knees. He bent down so that his face touched the ground. 9 David said to Saul, 'You should not listen to the people who say, "David wants to hurt you." 10 Today the Lord made me able to hurt you in that place. Some of my men wanted me to kill you. But I let you go. I said, "I will not hurt my master because the Lord has anointed him as king."

11 Look, my father. I have a small piece of your coat. I cut this off the corner of your coat but I did not kill you. Please know that I have not sinned against you. I will not hurt you.

I have not done anything wrong to you.

But you are running after me so that you can kill me. 12 The Lord will be the judge. He will know which one of us has done wrong things. And I ask that the Lord will punish you. I want him to punish you because you have done wrong things to me. But I will not do anything to hurt you. 13 You know that people often say, "Evil people do evil things." But I will not touch you. 14 I do not know whom you have come to fight. I do not know whom you are running after. Perhaps you think that I am like a dead dog or a little insect! 15 The Lord will be the judge. He will know which one of us has done the right things. The Lord will see what I did. I know that I have done only good things. And I pray that he will show that. And I pray that he will save me from you.'

16 When David stopped speaking, Saul asked, 'Is that really you, David my son?' Then Saul started to cry aloud. 17 Saul said, 'You are a better man than I am. You have been good to me. But I have done bad things to you. 18 You have told me all the good things that you did to me. The Lord made you able to hurt me, but you did not kill me. 19 If a person finds his enemy, he does not let him go away. He does not let him be safe. I ask that the Lord will give a lot of good gifts to you. I ask that because you were good to me today. 20 Now I know that you will be the king of Israel. You will rule all the people in Israel. 21 Please promise the Lord that you will not kill all my children and their families. Make sure that people do not forget my family's name.'

22 So David promised that to Saul. Saul went to his home. But David and his men returned to the safe place.

Chapter 25

Samuel the prophet dies

1 Then Samuel died. All the Israelites met together and they were very sad. Then they buried Samuel in his family town, which was called Ramah. David went down to the desert of Paran.

Nabal says bad things about David

2-3 A very rich man lived at Paran. His name was Nabal. He came from the family of Caleb. His wife's name was Abigail. Nabal had some land near Carmel. He had 3000 sheep and 1000 goats. He was cutting the hair from his sheep at Carmel. Abigail was a beautiful and clever woman. But Nabal was a cruel man who did not give anything to anybody.

4 David was in the desert. Somebody told him that Nabal was cutting the hair from his sheep. 5 So David sent 10 young men to the town called Carmel. He said that they must find Nabal. Then they must tell him that David said 'hello'. 6 David asked the young men to say, 'David hopes that you are well. He wants you to have no trouble. He wants your family to have no trouble. He wants everything that you have to be safe. 7 People told David that you were cutting the hair from your sheep. Your shepherds have been with us. We did not hurt them. We did not take anything from them when they were at Carmel. 8 Your servants will tell you that, if you ask them. We have come on the day when you have a special meal. So, please be kind to David's young men. And please give whatever you can to the young men and to your son David.'

9 David's men arrived at Carmel and they gave the message to Nabal. They waited for Nabal to reply. 10Nabal answered David's young men, 'I do not know who David is. Nobody has told me about this son of Jesse. Many slaves run away from their masters these days. 11 I have bread and water. And I have killed some animals. But this is all for the men who are cutting the hair from my sheep. I will not give anything to men that I do not know.'

12 David's men returned to David. They told him everything that Nabal had said. 13 David said to his men, 'Put your swords into your belts.' So, they put them in their belts. David put his sword into his belt too. About 400 men went with David. About 200 men stayed with their food and weapons.

14 One of Nabal's servants spoke to Abigail (Nabal's wife). He said, 'David sent some of his men from the desert to speak to our master. But our master was not very polite to them. 15 These men were very good to us. They did not hurt us. They did not take anything from us while we were out in the fields with them. 16They kept us safe while we stayed with the sheep. They kept us safe during the day and at night. 17 Please think about this. And decide what to do. Very great trouble will happen to our master and to all his family and servants. Our master is such a bad man that he will not listen to anyone.'

18 Abigail quickly got some food. She got 200 loaves of bread, 2 animal skins of wine, 5 sheep that she had cooked. She also got 15 kilos (about 7 pounds) of grain that she had cooked. She also got 100 cakes of grapes that she had made into dry fruit and 200 cakes of figs. She put all this on some donkeys. 19 She said to her servants, 'You go first and I will follow you.' But she did not tell her husband Nabal.

20 Abigail rode her donkey along the valley in the mountain. She saw David and his men while they were coming down the valley towards her. So she met them. 21 David had just said, 'I do not know why I kept Nabal's people and animals safe in the desert. We did not take anything from him. We were good to him, but he has not been good to us. 22 I will certainly go and kill all the men in Nabal's family by tomorrow morning.'

23 When Abigail saw David she quickly got off her donkey. She went on her knees in front of David and her face touched the ground. 24 She was near his feet. She said to David, 'My master, be angry only with me. I am your servant. Please listen to what I say. 25 Please do not think about that bad man Nabal. His name means fool and he is a fool. I, your servant, did not see the young men that you sent. 26 Now the Lord has not let you punish your enemies. And he has not let you kill them. You have enemies and many people want to hurt you. But they will receive their punishment in the same way that Nabal will. I know that this will certainly happen. 27 My master, please accept this gift that I have brought for you and for your men. 28I am your servant. I have done wrong things. Please forgive me. I know that the Lord will always choose someone from your family to be the king. The Lord will do that because you always fight on his behalf. And you do not do anything in your life that is wrong. 29 Someone may run after you and try to kill you. But the Lord your God will always save you. The Lord will throw your enemies away like someone throws away a stone. 30 One day the Lord will do all the good things that he has promised to you. He will make you the ruler of the Israelites. 31 When that happens, you will not feel sorry about anything. You have not killed good people. And you have not tried to punish people yourself. When the Lord has helped you to win all your fights, please remember me.'

32 David said to Abigail, 'I praise the Lord God of Israel. He sent you to meet me today. 33 I pray that the Lord will be good to you. I want him to be good to you because of what you did. You showed me the right thing to do. You have not let me punish or kill people today. 34 The Lord has not let me hurt you. You came quickly to meet me. If you had not come, I certainly would have killed all of Nabal's men by the morning.'

35 David accepted Abigail's gift. He said to her, 'Go to your home and do not be afraid. I have listened to what you have said. And I will do what you have asked for.'

Nabal dies

36 Abigail returned to Nabal. He had prepared a big meal. It was so good that a king could eat it. He had drunk too much wine. He was very happy but his mind was confused. So Abigail did not tell him anything until the next morning. 37 The next morning Nabal was well again. So Abigail told him all that had she had done. Nabal's heart failed and he became like a stone. 38 About 10 days after that, the Lord caused Nabal to die.

39 Somebody told David that Nabal had died. David said, 'I praise the Lord. Nabal said wrong things about me but the Lord saved me. The Lord did not let me do the wrong thing. And now he has punished Nabal.'

Then David sent a message to Abigail. He asked her to marry him. 40 David's servants went to Carmel and they said to Abigail, 'David has sent us to you. We must take you to David so that he can marry you.'

41 Abigail went on her knees and her face touched the ground. She said, 'I am his servant. I will wash the feet of David's servants.' 42 Abigail quickly got on to a donkey and she went with David's men. She took 5 young girls with her. They were her servants. Abigail became David's wife.

43 David had married Ahinoam from the town called Jezreel. So these two women became his wives. 44Saul's daughter Michal had been David's wife. But Saul had given her to Palti as his wife. Palti was the son of Laish who came from the town called Gallim.

Chapter 26

David again refuses to kill Saul

1 Some men from Ziph went to visit Saul at Gibeah. They said, 'David is hiding on the hill called Hachilah which is across the valley from Jeshimon.'

2 So Saul went to the desert of Ziph to look for David. Saul chose 3000 Israelite men to go with him. 3 Saul and his men came to the hill called Hachilah They put their tents next to the road. This was the side away from Jeshimon. But David stayed in the desert. Then somebody told David that Saul had followed him there. 4 So David sent some men to see if that was true. They discovered that Saul was at Hachilah.

5 David went to the place where Saul was staying. Saul was asleep in the middle of the tents. The army was round him. Abner, who was the son of Ner, was the leader of Saul's army. He was asleep too.

6 David spoke to Ahimelech and Abishai. Ahimelech came from the Hittite tribe. Abishai was Joab's brother and Zeruiah was their mother. David said, 'Will one of you come down among Saul's army with me?'

Abishai said, 'I will come with you.'

7 So David and Abishai went among Saul's tents that night. Saul was asleep in the middle of the army. He had put his spear into the ground near his head. Abner and the army were asleep round Saul. 8 Abishai said to David, 'Tonight God has given your enemy to you. I will push the spear through Saul and into the ground under him. I will only have to do it once to kill him. I will not need to do it twice.'

9 But David said to Abishai, 'Do not kill Saul. The Lord anointed Saul as king. If anyone attacks Saul, that will be a sin. 10 I know that the Lord himself will kill Saul. Saul will die either when his time has come or in a fight. 11 The Lord anointed Saul. So I pray that the Lord will not let me hurt him. Take the spear and the pot of water that is near Saul's head. Then we will leave.'

12 So David took the spear and the pot of water that were near Saul's head. Then they left. Nobody saw them. Nobody knew what had happened. Nobody woke up. The men continued to sleep because the Lord caused it to happen.

13 David and Abishai went across the valley to the other side of the hill. David went to the top of the hill. He was a long way away from Saul's soldiers. 14 David shouted to Saul's army. He shouted to Abner, who was the son of Ner, 'Abner, can you hear me?'

Abner replied, 'Who is shouting to the king? Who are you?'

15 David replied to Abner, 'Are you really a great man in Israel? You should have kept your master, the king, safe. Someone came among your tents to kill your master the king. 16 You have failed to keep him safe. I know that you and your men ought to die. The Lord anointed Saul as king. You have not kept him safe from his enemy. The king's spear and water pot were near his head. Where are they now?'

17 Saul recognised David's voice. Saul said, 'Is that you David, my son?'

David answered, 'Yes my master and my king. I am David.' 18 David also said, 'Why are you running after me, my master? What have I done? Have I done something that is wrong? 19 My master and my king, please listen to me. Has the Lord made you angry with me? If that is true, we can give an offering to him. And that will give pleasure to him. Or have men made you angry with me? If they have, I want the Lord to do bad things to them. They have caused me to leave the land that the Lord God gave to me. They want me to go and to worship other gods. 20 Do not let me die a long way away from the Lord's covenant box. The king of Israel is looking for someone who is like a little insect! You are like someone who is looking for one small bird in the mountains!'

21 Then Saul said, 'I have sinned. Return, David, my son. You did not kill me today. I will never hurt you again. I have been like a fool. I have done something that was wrong.'

22 David said, 'Here is your spear. Send one of your young men here to take it from me.

23 The Lord wants every person to do what is right and true. Then he gives gifts to them. The Lord gave you to me today. But I would not hurt the king that the Lord anointed. 24 I did not want to kill you today. I pray that the Lord will want to keep me alive. And so he will save me from all trouble.'

25 Then Saul said to David, 'I pray that the Lord will bless you, my son. You will do great things and you will do many good things.'

So David continued to go on his journey and Saul returned to his home.

Chapter 27

David lives with the Philistines

1 Then David thought, 'I am sure that Saul will kill me one day. But I have a good idea. I will go to the country of the Philistines and I will be safe from Saul. He will stop looking for me in Israel. Then I will be free from Saul.'

2 So David and his 600 men left Israel. They went to Achish, who was the son of Maoch. Achish was the king of the town called Gath. 3 David, his men, and their families lived in Gath with Achish. David had his two wives with him. One wife was Ahinoam. She came from the town called Jezreel. His other wife was Abigail, whose husband Nabal was dead. She came from the town called Carmel. 4 People told Saul that David had run away to Gath. So Saul stopped looking for him.

5 Then David said to Achish, 'Are you happy with me? If you are, I do not need to live in the king's town with you. Please let me have a town somewhere else in this country where I can live.'

6 That day, King Achish gave the town called Ziklag to David. Since then Ziklag has been part of the king of Judah's land. 7 David lived in the country of the Philistines for one year and 4 months.

8 During that time David and his men attacked the tribes of the people called Geshurites, Girzites and Amalekites. These people had lived in that place for a very long time. Their land went down as far as the land near Shur and the country called Egypt. 9 When David attacked them, he killed all the men and women. But he took all their sheep,
cows, donkeys, camels and their clothes. Then he returned to Achish.

10 Achish asked David, 'Which place did you go and attack today?' Sometimes David would tell him that he had gone to the south part of Judah. Other times David told him that he went to the land of the tribe of Jerahmeel or the Kenite tribe. 11 David killed everyone in the places that he attacked. He never took anyone back to the town called Gath. So nobody could tell Achish what David had really done. 12 Achish believed what David had said. Achish thought, 'The Israelites will hate David very much now. So David will have to be my servant for all time.'

Chapter 28

1 After that, the Philistine army met together to fight the Israelites. Achish said to David, 'You must know that you and your men will join my army.'

2 David said, 'Yes, I am your servant. You will see what I can do.'

Achish replied, 'Good. Until you die, you will stay near to me to keep me safe.'

Saul visits a woman who tried to speak with dead people

3 Samuel was dead by this time. All the Israelites had been very sad and they had cried. They buried Samuel in his own town, which was called Ramah. There had been people who tried to speak with dead people in Israel. But Saul had sent them away.

4 The Philistine army came together and they put their tents near the town called Shunem. Saul took the Israelite army and they put their tents by the mountain of Gilboa. 5 Saul saw the Philistine army. He was not happy and he became very afraid. 6 Saul asked the Lord what he should do. But the Lord did not answer him in a dream, or by the Urim or by a prophet. 7 So Saul said to his servants, 'Go. Find a woman who can talk with dead people. I will go to her. I will ask her what will happen.'

His servants said, 'There is a woman at the town called Endor who can do that.'

8 Saul changed his clothes. So nobody recognised that he was the king. At night, Saul and two of his men went to see the woman. Saul said, 'Bring up a certain dead man. Talk to him on my behalf.'

9 But the woman said, 'You know what King Saul has done. He has removed all the people who try to talk to dead people from Israel. Are you trying to catch me so that you can kill me?'

10 Then Saul said a serious promise to the woman. He said, 'Nobody will punish you because you have done this. I promise the Lord that nobody will punish you.'

11 The woman said, 'Whom should I bring here?'

Saul replied, 'Bring Samuel.'

12 The woman screamed when she saw Samuel. She said to Saul, 'You did not say what was true. You are King Saul.'

13 King Saul said to her, 'Do not be afraid. Tell me what you can see.'

She said, 'I can see a spirit that is coming up from the ground.'

14 Saul asked, 'What kind of person?'

She said, 'An old man is coming up from the ground. He is wearing a special coat.'

Saul knew that this was Samuel. Saul went on his knees and his face touched the ground.

15 Samuel said, 'Why have you caused me to come to you? Why have you brought me back?'

Saul said, 'I have a lot of trouble. The Philistines are fighting against me. God has left me. He will not answer me by the prophets or in dreams. So I have brought you here. Tell me what I should do.'

16 Samuel said, 'The Lord has left you and he has become your enemy. So I do not know why you brought me up. 17 I told you what the Lord would do. And he has done it. The Lord has taken the kingdom away from you. He has given it to David instead. 18 The Lord has done this to you because you did not obey him. You did not show the Amalekites how God was very angry with them.

19 The Lord will let the Philistines win this fight. Tomorrow you and your sons will be with me. The Lord will also let the Philistines beat the whole Israelite army.'

20 Saul immediately fell on his face to the ground. He was afraid because of what Samuel had said. Saul was also very weak because he had eaten nothing all that day and night.

21 Then the woman came to Saul. She saw that he was very afraid. She said, 'I, your servant, have obeyed you. I did what you asked me to do. And I might have died because I did it. 22 Please listen to me now. I want to give you some food to eat. Then you will be stronger. And you will be able to travel.'

23 Saul refused and he said, 'I will not eat.'

But the woman and Saul's servants repeated that he must eat. So Saul did what they said. He got up from the ground and he sat down on a bed.

24 The woman had a fat young cow. She went quickly and she killed it. Then she took some flour and she made some flat bread.

25 She gave the food to Saul and to his men and they ate it. They left her house while it was still night.

Chapter 29

The Philistine leaders will not have David in their army

1 The Philistine army met at the town called Aphek. The Israelites stayed by the water at Jezreel. 2 The Philistine kings marched out with their soldiers. The soldiers were in groups of 100 men and 1000 men. David and his men were with King Achish at the back of the army. 3 The Philistine leaders said, 'Why are these Jews here?'

Achish said, 'This is David. He was King Saul's servant. But he came to me more than a year ago. I have not found anything that was wrong with David since then.'

4 But the Philistine leaders were angry with Achish. They said to him, 'Send David back to the town that you gave to him. He cannot go into the fight with us. He might become our enemy and he might start to fight us. He might want to be a friend of his king again. And it would make Saul very happy if David started to kill us. 5 The Israelites danced and sang about David. They sang,

"Saul has killed thousands of his enemies.

And David has killed tens of thousands of his enemies".'

6 So Achish asked to meet David. He said, 'I know that the Lord lives. And I know as certainly that you are my good friend. I would be happy to let you fight with me. Since the day that you came to me, I have never found anything wrong with you. But the other leaders do not want you to fight on my behalf. 7 So return to your home and be happy. Do not make the other Philistine leaders angry.'

8 David said, 'What have I done that is wrong? Have you found anything wrong in me since I joined you? You are my master, the king. I want to go and to fight your enemies.'

9 Achish said, 'I know that you are as good as an angel from God. But the Philistine leaders said that you must not go to the fight with us. 10 You and your master's servants must leave early tomorrow morning. You must get up early in the morning. Then, when it is light, you must go.'

11 So David and his men got up early in the morning. They returned to Ziklag. And the Philistine army went to Jezreel.

Chapter 30

David fights the Amalekites

1 David and his men arrived at Ziklag three days after they left Achish. The Amalekites had attacked part of the south of Judah's land. They had also attacked Ziklag. They had beaten the men there and they had burnt Ziklag. 2 They took women and everyone whether they were important or not important. They took them away but they did not kill anyone.

3 David and his men arrived at Ziklag. They saw that the Amalekites had burnt the city. They had taken away their sons and their daughters. 4 David and his men cried aloud. They continued to cry until they were too weak to cry any more. 5 David had two wives. One wife was Ahinoam from Jezreel. The other wife was Abigail. She had been the wife of Nabal from Carmel. The Amalekites had taken both of David's wives. 6 David was very, very sad because his men wanted to throw stones at him. They wanted to kill him. His men were very angry because they had lost their sons and their daughters. But David believed that the Lord his God would help them. And so he became stronger.

7 Then David spoke to Abiathar the priest, who was the son of Ahimelech. David said, 'Bring the ephod to me.' So Abiathar brought the ephod to David. 8 David asked the Lord, 'Should I go after the men who attacked our town? Will I catch them?'

The Lord answered, 'Run after them and you will certainly catch them. You will save your families from them.'

9-10 So David and his 600 men went out. They arrived at the Besor valley. Some of the men were too tired to go on across the valley. So 200 men remained by the river. David and 400 men continued to run after the Amalekites.

11 David's men found a man from Egypt in a field. They took him to David. They gave to the man some water to drink and food to eat. 12 They gave to him some figs and some grapes that someone had made into dry fruit. He had not eaten any food or drunk any water for three days. So, he felt stronger after he had eaten this food.

13 David asked the man, 'Who is your master? Where do you come from?'

He answered, 'I come from the country called Egypt. I am a slave of an Amalekite man. My master left me here three days ago because I was ill. 14 We attacked the south part of the land of the people called Cherethites. And we attacked the land of Judah and part of Caleb's land. We burned Ziklag too.'

15 David said, 'Can you take me to where these men are now?'

The man from Egypt answered, 'I will do it if you say a promise to me. Do it while God watches us. Promise that you will not kill me. And promise that you will not send me back to my master.'

16 So he took David to the Amalekites. The men were sitting all over the ground. They were eating and drinking. And they were having a party. They were happy because they had taken so many things from the Philistines and from the people in Judah. 17 That evening, David fought the Amalekites. The fight continued until the next evening. They killed all of the Amalekites except for 400 young men. Those 400 men rode away on their camels. 18 David got back everything that the Amalekites had taken. And he saved his two wives. 19 The people had lost nothing. David brought everyone back, the young people and the old people, the sons and the daughters. He also brought back the valuable things and everything that the Amalekites had taken. 20 David took all the sheep and cows and animals. His men caused all these animals to go on in front of them. They said, 'These animals are for David.'

21 David returned to the 200 men who had stayed by the Besor valley. These men had been too tired to go with David. David met the men at the river valley and he said 'hello' to them. 22 But some of the men with David were bad men. They wanted to cause trouble. They said, 'These men did not come with us. We will not give to them any of the things that we have brought back. Each man can have only his wife and his children. Then he must go.'

23 David replied, 'No, my brothers. You cannot do that. The Lord has given all this to us. The Lord kept us safe. He helped us to win the fight. 24 Nobody will agree with what you say. Each person will receive an equal part. Some men stayed with the tents. Some men were in the fight. But each person will receive the same amount.'

25 David made this rule into a law. The Israelites have obeyed this law ever since that day.

26 David arrived at Ziklag with all the things that they had taken from the Amalekites. He sent some of the good things to his friends who were the leaders of Judah. David sent this message, 'Here is a gift for you. We took these from the Lord's enemies.'

27-31 David sent some gifts to the leaders in all these places:

- Bethel
- Ramoth in south Judah
- Jattir
- Aroer
- Siphmoth
- Eshtemoa
- Racal
- the towns of the tribe of Jerahmeel
- the towns of the Kenites
- Hormah
- Chorashan
- Athach
- Hebron.

David and his men had lived in many places. So, David sent some gifts to the people who lived in all those places.

Chapter 31

Saul and his sons die

1 The Philistines fought against the Israelites. Many Israelites died on the mountain of Gilboa. The Israelites ran away and the Philistines killed many of them. 2 The Philistines ran after Saul and his sons. They killed his sons Jonathan, Abinadab and Malchishua. 3 The Philistines fought very strongly against Saul. Their men with bows shot their arrows at Saul and they nearly killed him. 4 Saul spoke to the officer who carried his armour. Saul said, 'Kill me with your sword. I do not want those men that nobody has circumcised to make me ashamed. And I do not want them to kill me.' The officer was afraid. He would not do it. So, Saul took his own sword and he fell on the sharp end. 5 The officer saw that Saul was dead. So, the officer fell on the sharp end of his sword and he died with Saul. 6 So Saul, three of his sons and the officer who carried his armour all died together that day.

7 Israelites lived in the Jezreel valley and across the river Jordan. They saw that the Israelite army had run away. Then people told them that Saul and his sons were dead. So these Israelites left their towns and they ran away. Then the Philistines came and they lived there.

8 The next day, the Philistines came to take all the valuable things from the dead soldiers. They found the dead bodies of Saul and his three sons on the mountain of Gilboa. 9 They cut off Saul's head and they took off his armour. Then they sent men through all the country of the Philistines with the news. These men took the message into the temples of their idols and to the Philistine people. 10 They put Saul's armour in the temple of the female god called Ashtoreth. Then they hung Saul's dead body on the wall of Beth-shan.

11 Some Israelites were in the town called Jabesh Gilead. People told them what the Philistines had done to Saul. 12 So the brave men from Jabesh Gilead marched all night until they arrived at Beth-shan. They took the dead bodies of Saul and his sons off the wall of the town. Then they brought the dead bodies to Jabesh Gilead and they burned them. 13 Then they took the bones and they buried them under a large tree at Jabesh Gilead. The men did not eat any food for 7 days after that.

David is King of Israel

2 Samuel

About 1 Samuel and 2 Samuel

The books of 1 and 2 Samuel were once one book. Then men made this book into two separate parts. The name of the book is from the first important person in this book. He was Samuel the prophet. But Samuel died before the end of the book.

Someone wrote the book after King Solomon had died. He was the king of the country called Israel. He died 930 years before Christ was born. After Solomon died, God made Israel into two countries, Israel and Judah. The country called Judah included the tribes of Judah and Benjamin. (See 1 Kings 12:1-24.)

In the beginning, the Israelites called their leaders 'judges'. They were leaders of the Israelites for about 350 years after Joshua's death. Samuel was the last of the judges. He was also a prophet.
Samuel anointed Saul to be the first king of the country called Israel. But Saul did not obey God. So God chose another king, David, who would obey him. 1 Samuel tells us about Saul's death at the end of the book. 2 Samuel records the life of David as king.

About 2 Samuel

The last chapter of 1 Samuel tells us about the deaths of King Saul and his son, Jonathan. The second book tells us about David as the leader of the Israelites. He obeyed God for almost all his life, and he gave pleasure to God.

David won many fights with Israel's enemies. And he won the country from them for Israel to live in. But he sometimes had problems with his own family.

Chapter 1

A man tells David that Saul is dead

1 David won the fight with the Amalekites and he returned to Ziklag. That was after Saul was dead. David stayed in Ziklag for two days. 2 The next day, a man came from Saul's camp to see David. He had dirt on his head and he had torn his clothes. He fell on the ground when he came to David. That was because he wanted to honour him.

3 'Where have you come from?' David asked him.

'I have run from the Israelite camp', he answered.

4 'Tell me what happened', David said.

The man replied, 'The men ran away and the enemy killed many of them. And Saul and his son Jonathan are dead.'

5 Then David asked the young man who had said this, 'How do you know that Saul and his son Jonathan are dead?'

6 The young man said, 'I was on the mountain called Gilboa. And I saw Saul. He was only standing up with the help of his spear. The enemy army with its horses and chariots were getting very near him. 7 He turned round and he saw me. He shouted to me. I said "What can I do for you?"

8 "Who are you?" he asked me.

"I am an Amalekite", I replied.

9 "Stand over me and kill me", he said. "I am nearly dead but I am still alive."

10 He would die if he fell down. I knew that. So I stood over him and I killed him. And I took the crown from his head and the ring from his arm. And I have brought them here to you, my lord.'

11 Then David and all the men that were with him took their clothes. And they tore them. 12 They cried and they wept until the evening. And they did not eat any food. They were very sad about Saul and Jonathan and the LORD's people and the Israelites. They were sad because so many people had died in the fight.

13 'Where are you from?' David asked the young man who had brought him the report.

'I am the son of a foreign man, an Amalekite', he answered.

14 David said to him, 'You should have been afraid to kill the man that the LORD had anointed!'

15 Then David spoke to one of his own young men. 'Go and punish him', he said. So the man hit him and he died. 16 David had said to the Amalekite, 'This is because you have done a wrong thing. Your blood must pay because you killed the LORD's anointed king. You killed the man that the LORD had anointed. You said yourself that you had done it.'

David's sad song for the deaths of Saul and Jonathan

17 David sang this sad song for Saul and his son Jonathan. 18 He said that the people in Judah should teach this war song to all Judah's men. (It is written in the Book of Jashar.)

> 19 'They have killed the best men from Israel on the mountains.
>
> They have caused great strong men to fall down.
>
> 20 Do not tell the people in Gath about it.
>
> Do not say anything in the streets of Ashkelon.
>
> If you do, the daughters of the Philistines might be happy.

The daughters of men that their parents have not circumcised might feel happy.

> 21 You mountains of Gilboa, I hope that no rain or dew will fall on you now.
>
> I pray, "Do not let those mountains have any fields where grain for offerings to God can grow."
>
> That is because the strong man's shield became disgusting on you.
>
> And Saul was not alive to clean his shield with oil.

22 Jonathan was not afraid of the blood of dead men or of the fat of strong men.

> His bow did not turn away.
>
> And Saul's sword did not return before he had used it.
>
> 23 We loved Saul and Jonathan when they were alive.
>
> They were beautiful.
>
> And they were together when they died.
>
> They moved faster than large birds;
>
> they were stronger than lions.
>
> 24 You daughters of Israel, weep for Saul.
>
> He gave you beautiful red clothes.
>
> He hung pretty stones and gold rings over your clothes.
>
> 25 The strong men have very sadly fallen in the fight!
>
> Jonathan's dead body is lying on your mountain.

26 I am really very sorry that you are no longer here. I am very, very sad, Jonathan, my brother.

> I loved you very much.
>
> Your love was great,
>
> better than the love of women.
>
> 27 The great strong men have very sadly fallen!
>
> Our enemies have destroyed all our weapons.'

Chapter 2

The people anoint David as king over Israel

1 After some time, David asked the LORD, 'Should I go up to any town in Judah?'

The LORD said to him, 'Go up.'

David asked, 'Where should I go?'

'To Hebron', the LORD replied.

2 So David went up there with his two wives. They were Ahinoam of Jezreel and Abigail, Nabal's widow from Carmel. 3 David also brought with him the men who were with him. Each man took his family. They all stayed in Hebron and in its towns. 4 Then the men in the tribe called Judah came to Hebron. And they anointed David as king over Judah. People told David that the men from Jabesh Gilead had buried Saul's dead body.

David says that the men from Jabesh Gilead are good men

5 So David sent men to them with a message.

The message was, 'You were kind to Saul your master; you buried his dead body. So I pray that the LORD will bless you. 6 I pray that the LORD will be kind to you. I pray that he will help you. I too will be kind to you because you have done that. 7 Now be strong and brave because Saul, your master, is dead. And the people of Judah have chosen me as king over them.'

David and his men fight with Saul's descendants

8 Abner, son of Ner, was the ruler of Saul's army. He took Ishbosheth, Saul's son, to Mahanaim. 9 He caused him to rule over Gilead, Asher and Jezreel. He also caused him to rule over Ephraim, Benjamin and all Israel.

10 Ishbosheth, Saul's son, was 40 years old when he became king over Israel. And he ruled Israel for two years. But Judah's people let David rule over them. 11 David remained in Hebron as king of Judah for 7 years and 6 months.

12 Then Abner, son of Ner, left Mahanaim and he brought the servants of Saul's son, Ishbosheth to Gibeon. 13 Joab, Zeruiah's son, went with David's men to meet them at the pool of Gibeon. One group sat on one side of the pool while the other group sat on the other side.

14 Then Abner spoke to Joab. 'I think that some of the young men should stand up. And they should fight in front of us', he said.

'Yes, they can do that', said Joab.

15 So they stood up. They counted 12 men for Benjamin and Ishbosheth, Saul's son, and 12 men for David. 16 Then each man took hold of his enemy's head and pushed his sharp knife into his side. So they fell down together. So people called that place, which is in Gibeon, Helkath Hazzurim.

17 They fought very strongly on that day. And David's men won the fight with Abner's men from Israel.

Abner kills Asahel

18 The three sons of Zeruiah were there. They were Joab, Abishai and Asahel. Asahel could run as fast as the fastest wild animal. 19 He ran after Abner and he did not turn away from him. He did not turn to the right or to the left. 20 Abner looked behind him and he asked, 'Is that you, Asahel?'

'It is', he answered.

21 Then Abner said to him, 'Turn away to the right or to the left and follow a young man. If you do that, you can take his arms.' But Asahel would not stop running after Abner.

22 Abner spoke again. 'Stop running after me. I do not want to knock you down to the ground and kill you. I would never be able to look at your brother Joab again!'

23 But Asahel refused to stop following Abner. So Abner pushed the end of his spear into Asahel's stomach and the spear came out of his back. He fell and he died there in that place. When each man came to that place, he stopped.

The end of the fight

24 But Joab and Abishai continued to run after Abner. They came to the hill of Ammah near Giah when it was almost the end of the day. That was near to the desert of Gibeon. 25 Then Benjamin's men came to be with Abner and they all became one group. And they stood together at the top of a hill.

26 Abner shouted to Joab, 'We might continue to kill like this for all time! The end of this will only make us all very sad. Surely you should tell your men that they must stop killing their brothers now.'

27 'God lives!' Joab replied. 'If you had not spoken, our men would have stopped following yours in the morning.'

28 So Joab caused the trumpet to make a loud noise. Then all his men stopped where they were. They did not run after Israel or fight after that.

29 Abner and his men marched all that night through the Arabah and they crossed the River Jordan. They continued to march through the valley to Mahanaim.

30 Then Joab returned and he brought all his men together. And Asahel and 19 other servants of David were not there because they were dead. 31 But David's men had killed 360 men from Benjamin who were with Abner. 32 They took Asahel's dead body and they buried it next to his father's dead body at Bethlehem. Then Joab and his men marched all night and they arrived at Hebron at sunrise.

Chapter 3

David's sons

1 David's people and Saul's people continued to fight each other and there was war for a long time. David became stronger and stronger but Saul's people became weaker and weaker.

2 While David was in Hebron he had several sons.

First was Amnon, son of Ahinoam from Jezreel.

3 The second son was Chileab, son of Abigail, Nabal's widow from Carmel.

The third son was Absalom, son of Maacah. Maacah was the daughter of Talmai, King of Geshur.

4 The fourth son was Adonijah, son of Haggith.

The fifth son was Shephatiah, son of Abital.

5 The sixth son was Ithream, son of David's wife, Eglah.

David had these sons in Hebron.

Abner wants to work for David now and not for Saul's son

6 Abner was trying to make himself more important to Saul's people. He did that while Saul's people were fighting against David's people. 7 Saul had had among his women one woman called Rizpah, daughter of Aiah. Ishbosheth asked Abner, 'Why did you sleep with my father's woman?'

8 Abner was very angry because of what Ishbosheth had said. 'You cannot think that I would leave you to become David's servant! I have always been a servant to Saul and to his family and his friends to this day. I have helped you in your fight against David. But now you think that I have turned against you because of this woman. 9 Now I will help David to get what God specially promised to him. If I do not do it, God should punish me very much. And I would want God to do it. 10 The LORD gave his sure promise that he would cause David to be king over Israel and Judah from Dan to Beersheba. David would be king and not Saul.' 11 And Ishbosheth was so afraid of Abner that he did not speak another word to him.

12 Then Abner sent men to David with this message: 'Who should rule this country? If you and I can agree a covenant, I will help you to win all Israel to your side.'

David tells Abner that he must bring Michal to him

13 'Good!' said David. 'I will agree a covenant with you. But do one thing for me.

You must bring Michal, Saul's daughter with you. If you do not do that, I will not see you.' 14 Then David sent men to Ishbosheth, son of Saul with this message: 'Give me my wife, Michal. I paid 100 Philistine foreskins to have her as my wife.'

15 So Ishbosheth sent men to take her from her husband, Paltiel son of Laish. 16 But her husband came with her. He wept while he followed her all the way to Bahurim. Then Abner said to him, 'Return to your home!' So he returned.

Abner speaks with Israel's leaders

17 Abner and the leaders of Israel talked together. He said, 'You wanted David to be your king before now. 18 So now do it! Remember that the LORD said about David, "I will use David to save my people, Israel from the Philistines and from all their enemies." '

Abner and David agree

19 Abner also went himself to speak to the men from Benjamin. Then he went to Hebron. He went to tell David what Israel's people and the tribe of Benjamin had agreed to do. 20 Abner came to David in Hebron and 20 men came with him. And David prepared a feast for Abner and the 20 men with him. 21 Then Abner spoke to David. 'Let me go now to bring all the people in Israel together for my lord the king', he said. 'Then they can make a promise that you will be their ruler. And you can have all that you wanted.' So David sent Abner away in peace. He did not let his men hurt Abner.

Joab murders Abner

22 David's men and Joab were attacking some of the enemy's soldiers. Then they returned. They brought with them a lot of things that they had taken from the enemy. But Abner had left Hebron because David had sent him away in peace. 23 When Joab and all his soldiers arrived, they told him, 'Abner, the son of Ner has come to the king. And he has sent him away in peace.' 24 Joab went to the king. He said, 'I do not understand what you have done. Abner came to you. You should not have let him go. Now he is gone. 25 You know what this son of Ner is like. He came to find out everything possible about what you were doing. He wanted you to think that he was your friend.'

26 Then Joab left David and Joab sent men to run after Abner with a message. They brought him from the well at Sirah. But David did not know that. 27 Abner returned to Hebron. Then Joab took him away from the other people. He brought him inside the gate to speak with him alone. There Joab pushed his knife into Abner's stomach. He did it to punish Abner because he killed Joab's brother, Asahel. So Abner died.

David shows that he did not want Abner to die

28 After that, people told David about it. He said, 'The LORD sees that I and my kingdom did not help at all with this murder. Joab poured out the blood of Abner, son of Ner. 29 I hope that this will cause Joab and all his father's family to have trouble! There should always be someone in his family with a bleeding place on his body or leprosy or a bad leg. Or there should be someone who has no food. Or there should be someone who dies by a sword.'

30 Joab and his brother Abishai killed Abner because he had killed their brother Asahel. He killed Asahel in the fight at Gibeon.

31 David spoke to Joab and to all the people with him. 'Tear your clothes and put on rough clothes. Then walk in front of Abner's dead body to show how sad you are', he said. King David himself walked behind Abner's dead body. 32 They buried Abner in Hebron. And the king wept loudly when they put Abner's dead body under the ground. And all the people wept.

33 The king sang a sad song for Abner.

'Abner should not have died like a fool.

34 Nobody had tied your hands or your feet.

You have fallen like someone that wicked men have caused to fall', he sang.

And all the people wept again for him.

35 Then all the people came and they asked David to eat some food before the end of the day. But David said, 'God should punish me if I eat bread or any food before sunset. And I would want him to do it.'

36 All the people heard this, and it gave them pleasure. Like everything that the king did, it gave pleasure to all the people. 37 So, on that day all the people in Israel knew that David had not caused the death of Abner. (Abner was the son of Ner.)

38 The king said to his servants, 'You must understand that a great leader has died today in Israel. 39 I am the king that God has anointed. But I am weak today. These sons of Zeruiah are too strong for me. These wicked men have done evil things. And I pray that the LORD will punish them.'

Chapter 4

Two men kill Ishbosheth

1 People told Saul's son that Abner had died in Hebron. Then he became very afraid. And all the people in Israel were afraid.

2 Saul's son had two men, Baanah and Rechab, who were leaders of small groups of soldiers. Their father was Rimmon from Beeroth, of Benjamin's tribe. At that time, people thought about Beeroth as a part of Benjamin's land. 3 The people from Beeroth ran away to Gittaim. So Beeroth's people still live there but they are like foreign people.

4 Saul's son, Jonathan had a son with two bad feet. When he was 5 years old, the news from Jezreel about Saul and Jonathan reached them. His nurse lifted the boy into her arms and she ran away. But as she ran, he fell. And his feet became hurt. His name was Mephibosheth.

5 The sons of Rimmon from Beeroth, called Rechab and Baanah, left to go to Ishbosheth's house. They arrived in the hot time of the day. And Ishbosheth was resting on his bed at midday. 6 They went inside the house and they were carrying some wheat. But they pushed knives into his stomach. Then Rechab and his brother ran away. Nobody caught them.

7 Ishbosheth was lying on his bed in his bedroom when they went into his house. When they had killed him they cut off his head. They took it with them and they went through the Arabah. They travelled all night. 8 They brought Ishbosheth's head to David in Hebron. They said to the king, 'Here is the head of Ishbosheth, the son of Saul, who was always attacking you. Saul tried to kill you. Today the LORD paid him and his family for the bad things that they did to our lord, the king.'

9 David spoke to Rechab and his brother Baanah, Rimmon's sons from Beeroth, 'The LORD has saved me from all my troubles. And he is certainly alive. 10 When a man told me, "Saul is dead", he thought that he was bringing me good news. But I took him and I caused my servants to kill him in Ziklag. That was the gift that I gave him for his news. 11 But you wicked men have killed a man who was not a bad man. And you killed him in his own house and on his own bed. So there is no reason why I should not cause you to die. You must pay for the evil thing that you have done. The earth will be a better place without you!'

12 So David told his young men that they must kill them. So they did kill them. They cut off their hands and their feet. They hung the dead bodies by the pool in Hebron. But they took Ishbosheth's head and they buried it next to Abner's dead body in Hebron.

Chapter 5

David becomes king over all Israel

1 All the tribes of Israel came to David at Hebron. They said, 'We all come from your big family. 2 When Saul was king over us, some time ago, you were the leader of his army in the wars. And the LORD spoke to you. He said, "You will be like the man that keeps my sheep safe. My people Israel are like my sheep and you will become the ruler over them." '

3 David agreed with the leaders of Israel when they came to him at Hebron. They made promises to each other in front of the LORD. Then they anointed David to be king over Israel.

4 David was 30 years old when he became king. And he was king over Israel for 40 years. 5 He ruled over Judah in Hebron for 7 years and 6 months. And in Jerusalem he ruled over all Israel and Judah for 33 years.

David wins Jerusalem from the Jebusites

6 The king and his soldiers marched to Jerusalem. They wanted to win it from the Jebusites who lived there. The Jebusites said to David, 'You will not get in here. Even men who cannot see could keep you out. Even men who cannot walk well could keep you out.' They thought, 'David cannot get in here.' 7 But they were wrong! David did win the strong city, Zion, that he called 'The City of David'.

8 On that day, David said, 'Some enemies cannot see and some enemies cannot walk well. David hates those people. Anyone who wants to win the fight must go up this way: He must go up the way that water goes up to the city. If he does, he can beat those people.' That is why people say, 'Anybody who cannot see must not go into the house. And anybody who cannot walk well must not go into the house.'

David comes to live in Jerusalem

9 Then David came to live in the strong tall building and he called it the City of David. He built more houses round it to the edge of the hill. 10 David became more and more powerful because the LORD, the strong, powerful God, was with him.

11 Then Hiram, King of Tyre, sent men to David with wood from cedar trees. And he sent men who could work with wood and stone. He sent them to build a house for David. 12 So David knew that the LORD had certainly made him safe as king over Israel. And God had made David's kingdom strong and important for his people, Israel.

13 After he had left Hebron, David married more wives. And he took more ladies to live with him. They lived in Jerusalem and they gave David more sons and daughters. 14 These are the names of the children who were born to him in Jerusalem: Shammua, Shobab, Nathan, Solomon, 15 Ibhar, Elishua, Nepheg, Japhia, 16 Elishama, Eliada and Eliphelet.

David wins another fight with the Philistines

17 People told the Philistines that the people had anointed David as king over Israel. So the Philistines took a big army and they went to look for him. People told David about this, and so he went into a very strong place. 18 The Philistine soldiers were everywhere in the Valley of Rephaim. 19 Then David asked the LORD, 'Should I go and attack the Philistines? Will you help me to win the fight?'

The LORD answered him, 'Go, because I will certainly help you to win against the Philistines.'

20 So David went to Baal Perazim, and there he won the fight. He said, 'The LORD has broken my enemy as waters can break down stone walls.' So that place is called, Baal Perazim.

21 The Philistines did not take their idols when they left there. And David and his men carried them away.

22 Again the Philistines came and they filled the Valley of Rephaim. 23 So David asked the LORD again. And he answered him, 'Do not go straight up, but go round behind them. There you must attack them in front of the balsam trees. 24 When you hear a noise in the tops of the trees like marching men, go quickly to attack them. Do that because the LORD has gone in front of you to hit the Philistine army.' 25 So David did as the LORD had said to him. And he hit the Philistines all the way from Gibeon to Gezer.

Chapter 6

David brings the Covenant Box to Jerusalem

1 David chose 30 000 of the best soldiers in Israel. 2 David brought them with him to Baalah in Judah. He wanted to bring God's Covenant Box from there. The Israelites called it by the LORD's name, the name of the great powerful LORD. He is the LORD who sits as King between the two angels. 3 They put the Covenant Box on a new cart and they brought it from Abinadab's house on the hill. Abinadab's sons, Uzzah and Ahio led the new cart. 4 And they took the cart from the house of Abinadab, which is in the hill. And the cart had the Covenant Box on it. Ahio walked in front of the Covenant Box. 5 David and all Israel's people were singing as well as they could. And they were dancing as well as they could. They meant that the LORD is very great. They made music with harps, lyres, drums, rattles and cymbals.

6 They came to the place where Nacon always hit his wheat. He hit it until the seeds fell out. There the male cows nearly fell. So Uzzah held the Covenant Box to stop it falling. 7 The LORD was very angry with Uzzah because he did that. He was not honouring the LORD. So God knocked him down and he died there, next to the Covenant Box.

8 Then David was angry because the LORD had punished Uzzah. So that place is still called Perez Uzzah..

9 On that day, David became afraid of the LORD. He said, 'I do not know how the LORD's Covenant Box can ever come to me!' 10 He did not want to take the LORD's Covenant Box in to be with him in David's City. He took it instead into the house of Obed-Edom, from Gath. 11 The LORD's Covenant Box stayed in his house for three months. And the LORD blessed Obed-Edom and the people in his house and everything that he had.

12 People told King David, 'The LORD has blessed the people in Obed-Edom's house and all that he has, because of the Covenant Box.' So David went. And he was happy to bring up the Covenant Box from Obed-Edom's house to the City of David. 13 The men who were carrying it walked 6 steps. Then David sacrificed a fat young male and a big male cow. And they continued like that. 14 David wore a linen coat like those that the priests wore. And he jumped as well as he could for the LORD. And he danced too. 15 That is how he and all Israel brought the Covenant Box with them. They shouted and they made a noise with trumpets.

16 While they where bringing the Covenant Box into the City of David, Michal, Saul's daughter, looked out of a window. She saw King David. He was jumping and he was dancing in front of the LORD. And she felt ashamed of him.

17 David had put up a tent for the Covenant Box. So they brought it and they put it in its place inside the tent. Then David sacrificed offerings in front of the LORD. They burnt some of these. But they shared some offerings with each other. 18 After he finished this, he blessed the people. He used the name of the great and powerful LORD, when he blessed them. 19 Then he gave a gift to every man and woman in the crowd of the Israelites. They each received a loaf of bread and a cake of dates and a cake of grapes that someone had dried. And all the people went to their homes.

20 When David returned to his home to bless it, Saul's daughter Michal, came out to meet him. She said, 'The king of Israel seemed very great today! He showed too much of himself in front of his servant's slave girls. A silly fool does that! And he thinks that it does not matter.'

21 David said to Michal, 'I was honouring the LORD who chose me to be the ruler of his people, Israel. He chose me and not your father or any of his family. So I danced in front of the LORD. 22 I will make myself even less important than this, and I will make myself seem very small to myself. But I will seem very great to the slave girls that you spoke about.'

23 And Michal, Saul's daughter, had no children all her life.

Chapter 7

God gives promises to David

1 The king was living in his special king's house. And the LORD kept him safe from all his enemies everywhere round his country. 2 Then the king spoke to Nathan the prophet. 'I am living in a house of cedar wood, but God's Covenant Box is still in a tent!' he said.

3 Nathan replied to the king, 'Do what you think is right. The LORD is with you.' 4 But that night the LORD spoke to Nathan.

5 'Go and speak to my servant David. Tell him that the LORD says, "You are not the man to build a house for me to live in. 6 I have never lived in a house from the time that I brought Israel's people out of Egypt. And I am still not living in a house today. While we moved from place to place I lived in a tent. It was called the Tabernacle. 7 I have moved about to many places with the Israelites. I chose rulers to be leaders of Israel's tribes, who are like my sheep. But, while we travelled, I never said to any of the leaders, 'You should have built a house of cedar wood for me.' "

8 Now speak to my servant David. Tell him that the great and powerful LORD says, "I took you from the fields where you were following the sheep in the fields. I took you from there to be the ruler of my people Israel. 9 I have been with you in every place that you went. I took away all your enemies. Now I will make your name great. It will be as great as the names of the greatest men on the earth.

10 And I have chosen a place for my people Israel to live. They can live there and they can be safe. Wicked men will not hurt them again, as when they first came to this country.

11 Wicked men have done that since I chose leaders for my people Israel until now. But I will cause you to have no trouble from your enemies. And the LORD says to you, 'I will give descendants to you. And that will be like a house that I have built for you.' 12 You will die and people will bury you with your ancestors. Then a son of yours will become king. I will make his kingdom strong. 13 He is the man who will build a house for my Name. And his descendants will rule Israel for all time. 14 I will be his father and he will be my son. If he does wrong things, I will punish him. I will punish him as a father punishes his son. 15 I stopped being good and kind to Saul so that you could rule. But I will not stop being good and kind to your son. 16 You will always have descendants. They will be rulers for all time." '

17 Nathan told David everything that God had said to him. And Nathan told David everything that God had shown to him.

David prays and he thanks God for his promises

18 David went into the LORD's tent. He sat down and he prayed.

He said, 'I am not a special person and my family is not important. But you have done very much for me. 19 But you have promised to do more than this for my descendants. Those promises are for future years. I am only a man but you have shown this to me, my King and my powerful LORD.

20 I cannot say anything more. You know me, your servant, my King and my powerful LORD. 21 Because of your promise you have decided to do all these great things to teach me. 22 You are very great, my King and my powerful LORD. Nobody is like you. Only you are God. We have always known that. 23 There is no other nation on earth like your people Israel. It is the only one that you went to buy for yourself. And it is the only one that you have chosen to be your own people. The great things that you did for them and for your land have made your name great. People among all nations honour you. You pushed out nations and their gods in front of your people that you took out of Egypt. 24 You have chosen Israel as your own people for all time. And you, LORD, have become their God.

25 Now, LORD God, do what you have promised to me and to my descendants. I pray that you will do that. 26 And then your name will be great for all time. People will say, "The great and powerful LORD is God over Israel!" And my descendants will be strong for all time because of you.

27 Great King and LORD, God of Israel, you have shown this to your servant. You have said, "Your descendants will be like a house that I have built for you." So I am not afraid to pray to you like this.

28 Great King and LORD, you are God. Your words are true and you have promised these good things to me, your servant. 29 I pray that it will give you pleasure to be good to your servant's family. And so it will be able to continue for all time. Great King and LORD, you have spoken to me. And if you promise to do good things for my descendants, good things will happen to them for all time.'

Chapter 8

David wins more fights

1 Some time after that, David fought and he won a fight with the Philistines. They stopped fighting and he took from them power over their capital city.

2 He also won a fight with the Moabites. He caused equal groups of them to lie down on the ground. His soldiers killed the Moabites in 2 groups out of every 3 groups. But they did not kill the other men. So those Moabites became David's servants and they began to pay taxes to him.

3 Also David fought Hadadezer, Rehob's son, king of Zobah. This was because Hadadezer had tried to have power again over the land next to the Euphrates River. 4 David took from him 1700 riders of horses and 20 000 soldiers who walked. He kept 100 of the chariot horses. And he cut the legs of the other horses so that they could not run.

5 The Syrians from Damascus sent an army to help Hadadezer, the king of Zobah. And David killed 22 000 out of the Syrian men.

6 David put soldiers to live among the Syrian people in Damascus. And the people there became his servants and they brought taxes to him. The LORD caused David to win all his fights in every place that he went to.

7 Hadadezer's officers had shields of gold, so David took the shields to Jerusalem. 8 Tebah and Berothai were Hadadezer's towns and David took a lot of bronze from them.

9 Then people told Toi, the king of Hamath, that David had won the fight with all Hadadezer's army. 10 Hadadezer had fought against Toi. So Toi sent his son, Joram to tell David what a good thing he had done. And he wanted to ask for peace with David. Joram brought David things of gold, silver and bronze.

11 David took these things and he gave them to the LORD. He had done that with all the silver and gold that he had taken from other nations. That included all the nations that David had beaten. 12 He had won fights with Edom, Moab and the Ammonites, and with the Philistines and the Amalekites. He also gave the LORD things that he had taken from Rehob's son Hadadezer, king of Zobah.

13 David went to the Valley of Salt. There, his army beat 18 000 men from Edom. Many people knew about that. 14 He put soldiers' camps in every part of the country of Edom. David ruled everyone who lived in Edom. The LORD kept David safe in every place that he went to.

David's officers

15 David ruled over all Israel. He did everything that was right and good for his people. 16 Zeruiah's son, Joab was over the army. And Ahilud's son, Jehoshaphat recorded the important things that happened. 17 Ahitub's son Zadok and Abiathar's son Ahimelech were priests and Seraiah wrote things for David. 18 Jehoiada's son Benaiah was leader of the two groups of men who kept David safe. And David's sons helped him to rule.

Chapter 9

David helps Jonathan's son Mephibosheth

1 David asked, 'Does anyone know if there is anyone still alive from Saul's family?' I want to be kind to them because Jonathan was my friend.

2 Saul's family had a servant called Ziba. So they asked him to come to see David. The king said to him, 'Are you Ziba?'

'I am your servant', he replied.

3 The king asked him, 'Is there anyone still alive from Saul's family? I want to be kind to them as God is kind.'

Ziba replied, 'There is still a son of Jonathan. He has two bad feet, so he cannot walk well.'

4 'Where is he?' the king asked.

Ziba answered, 'He lives in the house of Ammiel's son Machir in Lo-debar.'

5 So David sent servants to bring him from the house of Ammiel's son Machir in Lo-debar.

6 Then Mephibosheth, Jonathan's son, grandson of Saul, came to David. He lay on the floor. He was honouring David.

David said, 'Mephibosheth!'

'I am your servant', he replied.

7 'Do not be afraid,' David said to him, 'because I want to be kind to you. I want to be kind to you because your father Jonathan was my friend. I will give you back all Saul's land and I want you to eat here with me always.'

8 Mephibosheth bent his head very low. He said, 'I am not as important as a dead dog. So I do not know why you should be so good to me!'

Ziba says that he will work for Mephibosheth

9 Then David sent men to fetch Saul's servant Ziba. He said to him, 'I have given everything that was Saul's or his family's to your master's grandson. 10 You and your sons and your servants must work on the land for him. You must get the food that grows there. And you must bring it to him. Then he will have food to eat. But Mephibosheth, your master's grandson, will always eat at my table.' (Also, Ziba had 15 sons and 20 servants.)

11 Then Ziba said to the king, 'I am your servant. I will do as my lord the king has said.' So Mephibosheth ate food at the king's table. He was like the king's sons.

12 Mephibosheth had a young son called Mica. And Ziba and all his family and servants became servants to Mephibosheth. 13 So Mephibosheth came to live in Jerusalem because he always ate at the king's table. He had two bad feet, so he could not walk well.

Chapter 10

David and the Ammonites

1 Some time after that, the king of the Ammonites died. His son Hanun became the new king. 2 David thought, 'I will be kind to Hanun, because Nahash his father was kind to me.' David was sorry that Nahash had died. So David sent a group of his officers to tell Hanun that he was sorry. So David's men came to the Ammonites' land.

3 The most powerful Ammonites spoke to Hanun, their lord. 'David wants you to think that he is honouring your father. But we do not believe that he has sent his officers to you because of that. This is what we think. He is not sorry because your father has died. They have come to see how strong your city is. Then his army can fight and they can win it from you.' 4 So Hanun took David's officers and he cut off half the hair from their beards. And he cut off the lower half of their clothes and he sent them away.

5 When somebody told David about this, he sent servants to meet the men. They were very ashamed. The king said, 'Stay at Jericho until your beards have grown again. And then return here.'

6 Then the Ammonites knew that they had made David very angry. So they sent money to get 20 000 Syrian soldiers from Beth-rehob and Zobah. And they also had 1000 men with the king of Maacah and 12 000 men from Tob.

7 People told David about this. Then he sent out Joab with all the soldiers in his army. 8 The Ammonite soldiers came out and they stood in a group in front of the city's gates. The Syrians from Zobah and Rehob and the men from Tob and Maacah stayed in the land round the city.

9 Joab saw that there were the enemy's soldiers in front and behind him.

So he took some of the best of Israel's soldiers and he caused them to look towards the Syrians. 10 He asked his brother Abishai to take all the other men to attack the Ammonites. 11 Joab said, 'If the Syrians are too strong for me, you save me. But if the Ammonites are too strong for you, I will come to you. And I will save you. 12 Be strong. We must be brave when we fight for our people and for God's cities. The LORD will do what seems good to him. And I pray that he will do that.'

13 Then Joab and his group went to fight the Syrians and their enemies ran away from them. 14 The Ammonites saw that the Syrians were running away from Joab. So they ran away from Abishai. They ran into the city. So Joab stopped fighting the Ammonites and he returned to Jerusalem.

15 But then the Syrians saw that Israel had won the fight with them. So, they made another army. 16 Hadadezer got more Syrians from across the River Euphrates. Shobach, his most important officer, led this army to Helam.

17 His servants told David what was happening. And he took all Israel's men across the River Jordan to Helam. The Syrian soldiers stood in front of them and they fought David's army.

18 But they ran away from Israel's men. And David killed 700 of the men in chariots and 40 000 soldiers who walked. He also hit the army leader, Shobach and he died there. 19 Israel had beaten all the kings that Hadadezer ruled. And all those kings knew that Israel had beaten them. So, they said that they did not want to fight against Israel after that. They became the servants of the Israelites instead. So the Syrians were afraid to help the Ammonites after that.

Chapter 11

David sees Bathsheba and he sleeps with her

1 Kings fight each other in the spring. So David sent Joab with the whole Israelite army to fight the Ammonites. They beat the Ammonites completely and Israel's army started to live all round Rabbah. But David stayed in Jerusalem.

2 One evening, David got out of bed and he walked on the roof of the king's house. From the roof he saw a woman who was washing herself. She was very beautiful. 3 And David sent a servant to ask who she was. Someone said, 'She is Eliam's daughter, Bathsheba. And she is the wife of Uriah the Hittite.' 4 Then David sent servants to fetch her. She came to him and he slept with her. (She had cleaned herself from her monthly blood loss.) Then she returned to her home. 5 Bathsheba now had David's baby inside her. So she sent a message to tell David about it.

David asks Joab to send Uriah to him

6 David sent a message to Joab. He said, 'Send Uriah the Hittite to me.' And Joab sent him to David. 7 Uriah arrived. Then David asked him how Joab was. And David asked him how the soldiers were. And he asked him about the war. 8 Then David said to Uriah, 'Now go to your house and wash your feet.' So Uriah left the king's house and David sent a gift after him. 9 But Uriah slept at the door of the king's house with his master's servants. He did not go to his house.

10 David's servants told him that Uriah had not gone to his house. So David asked him, 'You have had a long journey. Why did you not go to your house?'

11 Uriah spoke to David. 'Israel and Judah and the Covenant Box are all staying in tents. My master Joab and your soldiers are sleeping in the fields. So I certainly should not go to my house and eat there. I should not drink there and sleep with my wife. I believe strongly that I must not do anything like that.'

12 David said, 'Stay here one more day, and tomorrow I will let you leave.' So Uriah stayed in Jerusalem that day and the next day. 13 David asked him to eat and to drink with him and David caused him to drink too much wine. But in the evening Uriah went and he slept with his master's servants. He did not go to his house.

David writes to Joab

14 In the morning, David wrote a letter to Joab and Uriah carried it to Joab. 15 In it he wrote, 'Put Uriah in front of all the soldiers, where it is most dangerous. Then pull your men away from him so that he is alone. And so the enemy will kill him.'

16 So while Joab's soldiers were round the city, Joab put Uriah in front of all the other soldiers. And that was where the enemy was strongest. 17 When some of the enemy soldiers came out of the city to fight, some of David's men died. And Uriah the Hittite died too.

Joab tells David that Uriah is dead

18 Joab wrote to David to tell him all about the war. 19 He spoke to the man with the message. 'When you have finished giving my report to the king, 20 the king may be angry. He may ask you, "Why did you get so near to the city? Surely you knew that they would shoot arrows from the walls. 21 Remember what a woman did to Jerub-besheth's son, Abimelech, in Thebez. She threw a heavy stone from the city wall and she killed him. You should not have gone so near to the wall." If he does ask you that, say, "Your servant, Uriah the Hittite is dead too." '

22 The man that Joab sent went to David. And he said everything that Joab had sent him to say.

23 The man said to David, 'The men were certainly stronger than us and they came out of the city to fight. But we pushed them into their own city gate. 24 Some of them shot arrows from the wall and some of your men died. Your servant Uriah the Hittite is also dead.'

25 'Say this to Joab', David said to the man that Joab had sent. 'Do not be too sad, any man can die in a fight. He must fight more strongly and win the city. And he must destroy it. That should help Joab to feel better.'

26 People told Uriah's wife that her husband was dead. And she was very sad and she cried about it very much. 27 Then it was time to stop crying so much. Then David sent men to bring her to his king's house. He married her and she had a baby son. But the LORD was very angry with David because he had done these bad things.

Chapter 12

Nathan tells a story to David

1 The LORD sent Nathan the prophet to David. Nathan came to him and said, 'There were two men who lived in the same town. One man was rich, and the other man was poor', he said. 2 'The rich man had very many sheep and cows. 3 But the poor man had only one young, little female sheep. He had bought it and he had fed it. It had grown up with his children. It ate and it drank with him. It even slept with him. It was like a daughter to him.

4 Then the rich man had a visitor. But the rich man did not kill his own sheep or cow to make a meal for the visitor. Instead, he took the poor man's little sheep to feed his visitor.'

5 David became very angry with the rich man. 'As truly as the LORD is the living God, that man should die', he said to Nathan. 6 'He did this cruel thing and he was not sorry for the poor man. So he must certainly pay the poor man for 4 sheep because he did that.'

The LORD will punish David

7 'You are the man!' Nathan said to David. 'This is what the LORD, the God of Israel says, "I anointed you king over Israel. I saved you from Saul. 8 I gave your master's house and his wives to you. I gave the people in Israel and in Judah to you. And I would have given you even more than that, if you wanted more. 9 But you did not obey the word of the LORD. You did an evil thing. You killed Uriah the Hittite in a fight. You killed him with the Amorite's sword and you took his wife to be your own wife. 10 So now your family will always have wars and death. You thought that I was not important. And so you took Uriah's wife to be your own wife. So I will punish you because of that."

11 This is what the LORD says, "I will cause your own family to give you trouble. I will take your wives. And I will give them to someone that you know very well. And he will lie with them in the day. 12 What you did was a secret. But I will cause this to happen in the light of the sun and in front of all Israel." '

13 Then David said to Nathan, 'I have sinned against the LORD.'

Nathan replied, 'The LORD has taken away your sin. You will not die. 14 But because of what you have done, the LORD's enemies do not honour him. So your son that has been born will certainly die.'

David asks God to save his son

15 Nathan went home. Uriah's wife had given a son to David but after this the child became ill. 16 David asked the LORD to make the child well again. He lay on the floor of his house all night and he ate no food. 17 His servants stood round him. And they tried to help him to get up. But he refused and he would not eat anything with them.

David's son dies

18 After 7 days, the child died. David's servants were afraid to tell him. They thought, 'David did not seem to hear us when we spoke to him. That was when the child was alive. So we cannot tell him that the child is dead. He might do something really bad.'

19 But David saw that his servants were speaking to each other in a quiet way. Then he understood that the child was dead. 'Is the child dead?' he asked his servants.

'Yes', they replied. 'He is dead.'

20 Then David got up and he washed himself. He put on clean clothes and special oil that had a good smell. He went into the LORD's house to worship him. Then he returned to his own house and he asked for food. They gave it to him and he ate it.

21 His servants said to him, 'Why are you doing these things? You ate nothing while the child was alive. And you wept. But now that he is dead you get up. And you eat!'

22 David replied, 'While the child was alive I wept. And I did not eat anything. I thought that perhaps the LORD would be merciful to me. I thought that he might forgive me. Then he might let the child live. 23 But I do not need to do this now that the child is dead. I cannot bring him back to me. I will go to him but he cannot come to me.'

24 Then David went to help his wife, Bathsheba to feel better. He slept with her and she had a son. They called him Solomon, and the LORD loved him. 25 The LORD sent Nathan the prophet to tell them that they should call him Jedidiah. That was because the LORD loved him.

David wins Rabbah

26 At this time, Joab was fighting against the Ammonite city called Rabbah. And he had beaten the soldiers in the king's part of the city. 27 So Joab sent men to David with a message. The message was, 'I have fought against Rabbah. And I have got the river that gives water to it. 28 Now bring the army that is with you to stand round the city. And win the city. If you do not, then I will win the city. And so it will have my name.'

29 So David took all his army and he went to Rabbah. They attacked and they won it. 30 He took the crown of gold from its king's head and they put it on David's head. It weighed about 74 pounds (34 kilos). And there were valuable stones in it. And he took a lot of valuable things from the city. 31 And he brought out the people from the city. He caused them to cut wood. And they had to work with sharp iron tools and with iron axes. And he sent them into the place where people made bricks. He did the same things to the people from all the Ammonite cities. Then David and all the soldiers returned to Jerusalem.

Chapter 13

Amnon loves Tamar

1 After some time, David's son, Amnon, began to love Tamar. She was the beautiful sister of David's son, Absalom. 2 Amnon became ill because he wanted his sister Tamar so much. But she had never slept with a man and it seemed difficult for Amnon to do anything to her.

3 But Amnon had a friend called Jonadab. He was the son of David's brother Shimeah. And he seemed to know what to do about anything. 4 He asked Amnon, 'Why do you seem so sad every morning? Tell me about your trouble.'

Amnon said to him, 'I love Tamar, my brother Absalom's sister.'

Jonadab suggests a bad idea to Amnon

5 'Go to bed. Say that you are ill', said Jonadab. Your father will come to see you. Then you can ask him that your sister Tamar might come to give you something to eat. Say, "Please let me see her make food. And then let her feed me with it." '

6 So Amnon went to bed. He said that he was ill. When the king came to see him, Amnon spoke to him. 'Please let my sister Tamar come. I want her to make some special bread while I watch her. Then she can feed me with it.'

7 David sent a servant to Tamar. 'Go to your brother Amnon and make some food for him', he said.

8 So Tamar went to her brother Amnon's house. He was in his bed. She took flour and water and she mixed them well. She made cakes while he watched her. And she baked them.

Amnon has sex with Tamar

9 Then she took some and she gave them to him. But he would not eat them.

'Send everyone out of here', Amnon said. So everyone left him. 10 Then Amnon said to Tamar, 'Bring the food here into my bedroom so that you can give it to me with your own hands.' So Tamar took the cakes that she had made. And she brought them to Amnon in his bedroom. 11 But when she went to him he took hold of her. And he said, 'Come to bed with me, my sister.'

12 'Do not do it, my brother', she said. 'Do not cause me to do a wrong thing like that. We in Israel should not do things like that. It is an evil thing. 13 Think about me. Nobody would honour me. I would be ashamed and I would not be able to hide myself. And nobody would honour you. People would think that you were like the worst men in Israel. Speak to the king. I am sure that he will let you marry me.' 14 But he refused to listen to her and he was stronger than she. So he took her and he had sex with her.

Amnon causes Tamar to be put out of his house

15 Then Amnon hated her. He hated her more than he had loved her. 'Go away!' he shouted.

16 'No!' she said to him. 'To send me away would be a worse thing to do. It would be worse than the bad thing that you have already done to me.'

But he refused to listen to her. 17 He shouted for his special servant. He said to him, 'Take this woman out of here and lock the door behind her.' 18 So the servant put her out and he locked the door behind her. She was wearing a very beautiful dress. All the king's daughters who were not yet married wore these beautiful clothes. 19 Tamar put dirt on her head. And she tore the beautiful dress that she was wearing. She put her face in her hands. And she wept aloud when she went away.

Everyone is very angry with Amnon

20 When her brother Absalom saw her he said, 'I think that my brother Amnon has hurt you! Now be quiet; he is your brother. Do not let it make you angry.' And Tamar lived in her brother Absalom's house. She was sad and lonely.

21 When someone told King David about all this, he was very, very angry. 22 Absalom hated Amnon because he had done that very wrong thing to his sister, Tamar. So he would not even speak to him.

Absalom kills Amnon

23 After two years, Absalom's servants were cutting the wool from his sheep. That was at Baal Hazor, near to Ephraim's land. Absalom asked all the king's sons to meet him there. 24 He spoke to the king. 'Your servant has men with him to cut the sheep's wool. Would it give the king and his officer's pleasure to come too?' he said.

25 'No, my son', the king replied. 'We should not all go. It would cause you too much trouble.' Absalom asked him again. He refused again, but he gave his blessing to him.

26 'If you will not come, will you let my brother Amnon come?' Absalom asked.

The king said, 'I do not know why he should go with you.' 27 But Absalom asked more strongly, so he sent Amnon with the other king's sons.

28 Absalom told his servants what they must do. He said, 'When Amnon has drunk a lot of wine I will say, "Hit him!" Then you will kill him. Do not be afraid. I am causing you to do this. Be strong and brave.' 29 So Absalom's men obeyed him. Then all the king's other sons ran to their mules. They rode away.

30 While they were returning, men said to David, 'Absalom has attacked all the king's sons. Not one son is still alive.' 31 The king stood up and he tore his clothes. Then he fell on the ground and all his servants stood round him. They had torn their clothes, too.

32 But Jonadab, son of David's brother, Shimeah spoke. 'My lord, do not think that they have killed all the king's sons. Only Amnon is dead. Absalom has wanted to do this since Amnon caused his sister Tamar to have sex with him. 33 My lord should not believe the report that all the king's sons are dead. Only Amnon is dead.'

Absalom runs away

34 While this was happening, Absalom had run away.

A man was standing on the wall of Jerusalem. He watched. And he saw that many people were coming down the hill. They came from the west. He went and he told the king, 'I saw men towards Horonaim, on the side of the hill.'

35 Jonadab said to the king, 'See, the king's sons are here. It is as I said.'

36 While he was speaking, the king's servants came in. They were weeping loudly. The king and all his servants were also weeping. They were very, very sad.

37 Absalom ran to Talmai, son of Ammihud, king of Geshur. But King David continued to weep for his son every day.

38 After Absalom had run to Geshur he stayed there for three years. 39 And the king wanted very much to go to see Absalom. He had stopped being very sad about Amnon's death.

Chapter 14

Joab causes a woman to tell a sad story to David

1 Zeruiah's son, Joab knew how much the king wanted to see Absalom. 2 So he sent a servant to Tekoa to bring a wise woman from there. He said to her, 'Dress in special clothes. The king must think that somebody in your family has died. Do not put oil with a sweet smell on yourself. You must be like a woman who has been sad for a long time. 3 Then go to the king. This is what you must say to him.' Then Joab told her the words.

4 So the woman from Tekoa went to the king. She fell on the floor in front of him because she wanted to honour him. Then she said, 'You are the king. Please help me!'

5 The king asked her, 'What is your trouble?'

She said, 'My husband is dead 6 and I had two sons. They were fighting in the fields and there was nobody near to stop them. One son hit the other son. And he killed him. 7 Now the whole family is against me. They want me to give to them the son who killed his brother. They want to punish him because he killed his brother. They want to kill him now. If they do that, I will have no son. And there will be nobody to continue my husband's name.'

8 The king said, 'Go to your house. I will tell them that they must not kill him.'

9 Then the woman from Tekoa spoke. 'My lord, the king, I want God to punish me for this and not the king or his family.'

10 The king replied, 'If anyone says anything bad to you, bring him to me. After that, he will not cause you any more trouble.'

11 Then she said, 'I do not want the man who should punish my son to kill him. That would be a worse thing than the death of my other son. Please pray to the LORD your God that it will not happen.'

'I promise the living God that he will not touch one hair of his head', he said.

12 Then the woman spoke again. 'Can I say one more thing to my lord the king?'

'Speak', he replied.

13 Then the woman said, 'Why have you done such a wrong thing to God's own people? You have not let your own son return to his home. He is still in a foreign city. You are like someone who has done a wrong thing. I can say that because of what you have just said. 14 We are like water that falls on the ground. We cannot put it into the pot that it fell out of. We must all die. But God does not kill us. He thinks of a way to bring a man back from the place where he sent him away.

15 I am saying this to the king because the people have made me afraid. Your servant thought, "I will speak to the king. Perhaps he will do what I ask. 16 Perhaps he will save me from the man who wants to kill my son. So that man will not take our family from the land that God gave to us."

17 Now I say, "I pray that your promise will keep us safe." That is because the king is like an angel of God. He knows what is good. And he knows what is evil. I pray that the LORD your God will be with you!'

The king knows now what Joab has done

18 Then the king spoke to the woman. 'You must answer to me this one question. Say only what is true. Do not hide anything.'

'Ask me anything, sir', she replied.

19 'Has Joab told you what to say?' he asked.

'I cannot hide the answer to your question, my lord the king', the woman said. 'Yes, it was your servant Joab. He told me what to do. And he told me what to say. 20 He did it to change things. My lord is as wise as God's angels. He knows everything that happens in Israel.'

21 The king spoke to Joab. 'I have decided to do what you want. Go and bring back the young man Absalom.'

22 Joab fell with his face to the ground in front of the king because he wanted to honour him. He said, 'I pray that God will bless you sir. You have given me what I asked for. So now I know that I have given you pleasure.'

Joab brings Absalom back to Jerusalem

23 Then Joab went to Geshur and he brought Absalom back to Jerusalem. 24 But the king said, 'He must go to his own house. I do not want him to come to see me.' So Absalom went to his own house. He did not see the king.

Absalom in Jerusalem

25 Everyone in Israel thought that Absalom was the most handsome man in the whole country. In his body, everything from head to toe was completely good to look at. 26 Sometimes he cut his hair because it was too heavy. The hair that he cut off weighed about 4 pounds (2 kilos).

27 Absalom had three sons and one daughter. He called her Tamar and she became a very beautiful woman.

28 For two whole years Absalom lived in Jerusalem. But he never saw the king. 29 Then Absalom sent a servant to Joab with a message. He wanted Joab to come and to see him. But Joab would not come. So he sent another servant but Joab refused to come. 30 Then Absalom spoke to his servants. 'Joab's field is next to mine. And barley is growing in it. Now go and cause it to burn.' So Absalom's servants did as he asked.

31 Then Joab did go to Absalom's house. 'Why did your servants burn my field?' he asked.

The king lets Absalom come to see him

32 Absalom replied, 'I sent my servants to ask you to come. But you did not come to see me. I wanted to send you to the king. I wanted you to ask him why he had brought me from Geshur to Jerusalem. It would have been better for me to stay there! Now I want to go to see the king. So he can say himself if I have done anything wrong. Then he can kill me for any wrong thing that I have done.'

33 So Joab went to the king and he told the king about it. Then the king sent servants to bring Absalom to him. He came in and he bent down in front of the king. He put his face to the ground. And the king kissed Absalom.

Chapter 15

Absalom causes the people to love him

1 Sometime after that, Absalom bought a chariot and horses. He had 50 men who ran in front of him. 2 He got up early in the morning. Then he went to stand at the side of the road by the city's gate. He shouted to anyone who was coming to see the king. Then he asked, 'Where have you come from?' The man would tell Absalom which tribe of Israel he came from. He knew that the man was arguing with another man about a problem. They wanted the king to tell them the right answer to that problem. 3 Then Absalom would say, 'I am sure that you are right and not the other man. But there is nobody of the king's officers to listen to you.' 4 And Absalom would also say, 'If I became a judge in this country, people with problems would be able to come to me. I would be a fair judge for them.'

5 The man would bend down because he wanted to honour Absalom. But he would put out his hands and he would pull the man to himself. Then he would kiss him. 6 Absalom did this to all the people who came to ask the king for a judgement. That was how he caused all the men in Israel to love him.

7 After 4 years, Absalom spoke to the king. 'Please let me go to Hebron. I have promised something to the LORD. 8 I did it while I was living in Geshur in Aram', he said. 'I promised to worship the LORD in Hebron if the LORD brought me to Jerusalem again.'

9 The king said, 'Go in peace.' So he went to Hebron.

Absalom makes himself king

10 Then Absalom sent men with a message secretly to all the tribes of Israel. The men had to say, 'When you hear the noise of trumpets, shout, "Absalom has become king in Hebron." ' 11 But 200 men from Jerusalem had gone with Absalom. He had asked them to go as friends. They did not know what Absalom would do. 12 Absalom burnt his sacrifices. At the same time he sent men to fetch Ahithophel from Giloh. Ahithophel always suggested to David what he should do. More and more men joined Absalom's men against David. So Absalom became stronger and stronger.

David runs away from Jerusalem

13 A servant came and he told David, 'Israel's men have turned away from you to follow Absalom.'

14 Then David spoke to the officers who were with him in Jerusalem. 'Come, we must run away. If we do not do that, Absalom will beat us all. We must leave now. If we do not do that, he will kill everyone in the city.'

15 The king's servants answered, 'We will do anything that our lord the king chooses.'

16 So the king went out with all his servants and family. But he did not take 10 of his lady friends so that they would be able to keep the king's house safe. 17 He went out and all the people were following him. They stopped at the last house that was near Jerusalem. 18 All his men marched past him with the Kerethites and Pelethites. The 600 men who had come with him from Gath also marched past the king.

19 The king spoke to Ittai from Gath. 'Why are you coming with us? Return and stay with King Absalom. You are from another country. 20 You only came here a short time ago. You do not need to run away with us. I do not even know where I am going! Return and take your people with you. I pray that the LORD will be kind to you. And I pray that he will bless you.'

21 But Ittai replied to the king, 'I promise that I will go with you. As surely as the LORD is alive, I will go with you. I will go to any place that you may go during your whole life. I will go, whether it causes me to live or to die.'

22 'March on then', said David. So Ittai marched on with all his men and their families.

23 All the people that they passed wept with a loud voice. The king crossed the Kidron Valley and all the people moved towards the desert.

24 Zadok the priest was there. The Levites were also there, and they were carrying the Covenant Box. They put it down. Then Abiathar burnt sacrifices until all the people had left the city.

Zadok, Abiathar and their sons take the Covenant Box to Jerusalem again

25 Then the king spoke to Zadok 'Take the Covenant Box into the city. If I have given pleasure to the LORD, he will bring me there again. Then I will see it again in the LORD's house. 26 But if not, I am ready. He must do what seems best to him.'

27 Again the king spoke to Zadok the priest. 'Take your son Ahimaaz and Abiathar's son Jonathan to the city with you. 28 I will wait at the place where we crossed the river. I will wait there until you send me news.' 29 So Zadok and Abiathar took the Covenant Box to Jerusalem and they stayed there.

David sends Hushai to Jerusalem

30 But David continued to go up the hill called the Hill of Olives. He was weeping as he went. He had covered his head and he was not wearing anything on his feet. All the people with him also covered their heads. And they wept as they walked. 31 They had told David that Ahithophel was with Absalom. So David prayed, 'LORD, please cause Ahithophel to give them the advice of a fool.'

32 David arrived at the top of the hill where he worshipped God. Hushai from the place called Archi met him there. He had torn his clothes and he had dirt on his head. 33 David said, 'Do not come with me because you might cause me trouble. 34 Return to the city. You can say to Absalom, "You are the king and I will be your servant. I was once your father's servant, but now I will be your servant." Then you can help me. You can give opposite advice to Ahithophel's advice. 35 The priests Zadok and Abiathar will be there with you. Tell them anything that you hear in the king's house. 36 Their two sons, Ahimaaz and Jonathan are with them. Send them to me with anything that you hear.'

37 So, when Absalom had just gone into the city, David's friend Hushai arrived at Jerusalem.

Chapter 16

David and Ziba

1 When David began to walk down the mountain, he met Mephibosheth's servant Ziba. Ziba was waiting for him with two donkeys. They carried 200 loaves of bread, 100 cakes of figs and 100 cakes of grapes that someone had dried. They also brought a skin that was full of wine.

2 The king asked Ziba, 'Why have you brought these?'

Ziba answered, 'The donkeys are for the king's family to ride. The bread and fruit are for the men to eat. And the wine is so that the very tired men in the desert will feel better.'

3 The king asked, 'Where is your master's grandson?'

Ziba answered, 'He is staying in Jerusalem. He thinks that they will give him back his grandfather Saul's kingdom.'

4 Then the king said to Ziba, 'All that Mephibosheth had is now yours.'

'I am your servant', said Ziba. 'I hope that I will always give you pleasure.'

Shimei throws stones at David and he shouts bad names at David

5 Shimei, son of Gera, came out to meet David. David was coming near to the city called Bahurim. Shimei was from the same family as Saul. Soldiers and David's special men were all round David. But Shimei shouted bad words about David as he came. 6 He threw stones at David and at all his officers. 7 He said, 'Get out! Get out! You are a man who has killed many people. So you are a wicked man! 8 You killed a lot of Saul's people. And this is how the LORD is paying you for that. Saul was king but you became king instead. The LORD has given the kingdom to your son, Absalom. God is punishing you for the murders that you did!'

9 Then Zeruiah's son, Abishai, said to the king, 'This man is like a dog. He should not say these bad things to you. There is no reason for us to let him live. Can I go there and cut off his head?'

10 'You and I think about this in a different way, you sons of Zeruiah', said the king. 'He might be saying these bad things because the LORD has said to him, "Say bad things about David." So we cannot ask why he says them.'

11 Then David spoke to Abishai and to all his officers. 'My son, my own son is trying to kill me. So it is not a surprise that this descendant of Benjamin is angry. He hates me. Do not touch him. The LORD has told him that he should say these things. 12 Perhaps the LORD will see how much it makes me sad. Perhaps he will do good things for me because Shimei is saying bad things today.' 13 David and his men continued to walk along the road. Shimei walked along the hill, where he could see them. He shouted. And he threw stones and dirt at them as he walked. 14 The king and all his men were very tired when they reached the River Jordan. So they rested there.

Hushai and Ahithophel have different ideas

15 So now all Israel's men had come to Jerusalem with Absalom. And Ahithophel was with him. 16 Then David's friend, Hushai from the place called Archi, went to Absalom. He said, 'I pray that the king will live for all time! I pray that the king will live for all time!'

17 Absalom asked Hushai, 'Is this how you show your love for your friend? Why did you not go with him?'

18 Hushai replied, 'No, I will follow the man that the LORD has chosen. I will stay by all Israel's men and with the man that these people have chosen. I will be his man. 19 Clearly, I should work for the son. As I worked for your father, so I will work for you.'

20 Absalom said to Ahithophel, 'Have you any ideas? What do you think that we should do?'

21 Ahithophel answered, 'Sleep with your father's lady friends that are here in his house. Then all the people in Israel will know that you have made your father very angry. Then they will want to help you much more.' 22 So they put up a tent for Absalom on the roof. There he went in to his father's ladies and all Israel watched him.

23 In those days, men thought that Ahithophel's words were like the word of God. David and Absalom both believed that.

Chapter 17

Hushai and Ahithophel do not agree

1 Ahithophel spoke to Absalom, 'I would go tonight to attack David. Please let me choose 12 000 men. 2 I will go after him while he is tired and weak. This will make him afraid, then all the people with him will run away. I will kill only the king. 3 Then I will bring all the people back to you. If we kill this man you will cause all the people to come to you.' 4 This seemed a very good idea to Absalom and to all the leaders of Israel.

5 But Absalom said, 'Send Hushai from the place called Archi to me. Let us hear what he has to say.' 6 Absalom spoke to Hushai when he arrived. 'Ahithophel has suggested that we do this. What do you think? If you do not agree, please give us your ideas.'

7 Hushai replied to Absalom, 'This time Ahithophel's idea is not good. 8 You know that your father and his men are all fighters. They fight like a mother bear when you take away her little bears. And your father has fought many times. He will not stay all night with his soldiers. 9 Even now he is hiding in a hole in the hill or another place like that. He might attack your soldiers first. Someone who saw it would tell other people. He would say, "They have killed Absalom's men!" 10 Then even your bravest soldier would become afraid. He might be as brave as a lion. But even he would be very afraid. Everyone in Israel knows that your father is a fighter. And they know that the men with him are brave.'

They choose Hushai's idea

11 Hushai said, 'This is what I suggest. Bring here all the men in Israel who live in all the country from Dan to Beersheba. Their numbers are as great as the pieces of sand by the side of the sea. Then you yourself should lead them into the fight. 12 In this way we can attack him in any place that we find him. He will not even know that we have found him. He and his men will all die. 13 If he goes into a city, we can pull it down into the valley below. Only small pieces will remain on the hill.'

14 Absalom and all Israel's men said, 'Hushai's idea is better than Ahithophel's.' (The LORD had decided to make Ahithophel's idea seem worse than Hushai's idea. He wanted to cause bad trouble for Absalom.)

15 Then Hushai told the priests Zadok and Abiathar what he had said to Absalom and to his officers. And he told them what Ahithophel had suggested. 16 'Now send servants to David immediately', he said. 'They must tell him that he should not stay this side of the river in the desert. He must cross the River Jordan immediately and all the people with him. If he does not cross it tonight Absalom's men will catch them all. And then they will kill them all.'

Servants go to tell David that he should cross the river

17 Jonathan and Ahimaaz were staying at En Rogel. A servant girl went to tell them what had happened. Then they went and they told it to King David. They did not want anybody to see them as they were going into the city. That was important. 18 But a young man saw them and he told Absalom. So they left quickly and they went to a man's house in Bahurim. He had a well in his yard and they climbed down into it.

A woman hides the two servants

19 His wife took a lid and she put it over the top of the well. Then she threw a lot of seeds on it, so nobody knew anything about it.

20 Absalom's men came to the house. They asked the woman, 'Where are Ahimaaz and Jonathan?'

The woman answered, 'They went across the river.' The men looked everywhere but they did not find anyone. So they returned to Jerusalem.

The servants see David

21 After the men had gone, Ahimaaz and Jonathan climbed out of the well. They went to see David. They said to him, 'Go now and cross the river.' And they told him what Ahithophel had suggested. 22 So David and all the people left immediately and they crossed the river. When it was dawn they had all gone across the river.

Ahithophel kills himself

23 Ahithophel got on his donkey and he left Jerusalem. Absalom had not done as he had suggested. Ahithophel had seen that. He finished all his business and then he hung himself from his neck. He died and they buried him with his father's dead body.

24 David went to Mahanaim and Absalom crossed the River Jordan with all Israel's men. 25 Joab had been the leader of all Israel's soldiers. But Absalom had made Amasa the Ishmaelite leader, instead. Amasa's father, Ithra had married Abigail. She was Nahash's daughter and a sister of Zeruiah, Joab's mother. 26 Absalom and his army put their tents in Gilead.

Three friends give help to David's people

27 When David came to Mahanaim, three men helped him. One man was Nahash's son Shobi from Rabbah. The people called Ammonites lived in Rabbah. The other men were Ammiel's son Machir from Lo-Debar and Barzillai from Rogelim in Gilead. 28-29 They brought beds and pots and cups. They also brought wheat, barley, flour and grain that they had cooked. And they brought beans, lentils, honey, milk, sheep and cheese that they had made from cow's milk. These were for David and his people to eat. They said, 'The people have become tired in the desert and they need food and drink.'

Chapter 18

David prepares his army

1 David brought together all the men who were with him. He chose some to lead hundreds and some to lead thousands of them. 2 He sent them out in three groups. Joab led one group. His brother, Abishai, led another group and Ittai from Gath led the third group. The king said to them all, 'I will go with you myself.'

3 But the men replied, 'You must not go out. If we have to run away they may kill half of us. But they will really want only to kill you. You are worth 10 000 of us. You can send help to us from the city.'

4 'I will do whatever you think is best', the king answered. Then he stood by the side of the gate. And his men marched out in their groups of hundreds and of thousands. 5 The king spoke strongly to Joab, Abishai and Ittai. 'Do not hurt the young man Absalom if you love me', he said. And all the soldiers heard him say this to the three officers.

David's men fight Israel's soldiers

6 The army marched out to fight Israel. They fought in the forest of Ephraim. 7 There David's men won the fight with Israel's men. Many men died. There were 20 000 dead men. 8 They fought over all the land in and round the forest. More men died in the forest than in the fight.

Joab's men catch Absalom

9 And Absalom met some of David's men. He was riding on a mule. It went under a big oak tree and Absalom's hair caught in its branches. He hung there by his hair but the mule continued to walk on.

10 A man saw it and he told Joab, 'I have seen Absalom. He is hanging from an oak tree.'

11 Joab said to the man, 'If you saw him, why did you not kill him? I would have given you 10 silver coins and a special belt.'

12 But the man replied, 'I would not hurt the king's son, even for 25 pounds (11 kilos) of silver. We all heard the king speak to you,

Abishai and Ittai. He said, "Do not hurt young Absalom if you love e." 13 If I had killed Absalom, It would have been very dangerous for me. The king knows everything and then he would have killed me. And you would not have saved me.'

Joab kills Absalom

14 Joab said, 'I cannot stand here and talk with you.' And he took three spears. And he pushed them into Absalom's heart as Absalom was still hanging in the oak tree. 15 Ten of Joab's own men came round Absalom. They hit him and they killed him.

16 Then Joab made a sound with his trumpet and his soldiers stopped running after Israel. Joab had stopped them. 17 They took Absalom's dead body and they put it in a big hole in the forest. They put a lot of stones over it. At the same time, all the Israelites ran to their homes.

Absalom's pillar

18 While Absalom was alive he built a tall pillar of stones in the king's valley. He built it so that people might remember him. He thought, 'I have no son to live after me.' He gave his own name to it and people still call it Absalom's pillar.

Ahimaaz and a man from Ethiopia take the news to David

19 Zadok's son Ahimaaz spoke to Joab. 'Let me run to give the king the news that the LORD has saved him from his enemies', he said.

20 'You must not take any good news today', said Joab. 'You can take it another day, but not today. The king's son is dead.'

21 Then Joab spoke to a man from Ethiopia, 'Go to the king. Tell him what you have seen.' The man bent down in front of Joab and then he ran off.

22 Ahimaaz spoke to Joab again, 'I am not afraid of what may happen. Please let me run after the man from Ethiopia.'

But Joab replied, 'Why do you want to do it? The king will not give you a gift for this news.'

23 He said, 'But I do want to go, whatever happens.'

So Joab said, 'Run!' Then Ahimaaz ran across the flat ground. And he went faster than the man from Ethiopia.

24 David was sitting between the two city gates. A man stood over the gate by the wall. He was watching the road. As he looked he saw a man. The man was running towards the city. He was running alone. 25 The man on the roof shouted to the king to say what he had seen.

The king said, 'If he is alone, the news is good.' And the man came closer and closer.

26 Then the man on the roof saw another man who was running. He called down to the man at the gate, 'Look, another man is also running alone!'

The king said, 'He will bring good news, too.'

27 The man said, 'The first man is running like Zadok's son Ahimaaz.'

'He is a good man', the king said. 'He will bring good news.'

Ahimaaz tells the good news

28 Then Ahimaaz shouted to the king, 'It is good news!' And he bent down with his face to the ground and he said, 'Praise the LORD your God! He has helped you to win the fight with those who were against you.'

29 The king asked, 'Is the young man Absalom safe?'

Ahimaaz answered, 'When your officer Joab sent me I saw many people together. They seemed to be confused. But I did not see what had caused it.'

30 The king said, 'Stand at the side and wait here.' So Ahimaaz stepped to the side and he waited.

31 Then the man from Ethiopia arrived. He said, 'My lord the king, hear my good news! Today the LORD has helped you to win the fight with those who were against you.'

The man from Ethiopia tells David that Absalom is dead

32 The king asked the man from Ethiopia, 'Is the young man Absalom safe?'

The man from Ethiopia replied, 'I hope that all your enemies will be like that young man. And I want the same thing to happen to all those who are against you'

33 The king became so sad that he left the room over the gate. And he wept loudly. As he went, he said, 'My son Absalom, my son, my son Absalom! You should not have died. I should have died instead, Absalom, Absalom my son!'

Chapter 19

Joab tells the king that he is not being wise

1 People told Joab that the king was weeping for Absalom. He was very sad because Absalom was dead. 2 So the whole army was sad too. They had won an important fight. But they could not be happy and they could not have a party. They had heard men say, 'The king is sad because his son is dead.' 3 The soldiers were quiet as they came into the city. Men are ashamed when they have run away from a fight. They came in like that. 4 The king covered his face and he cried, 'Absalom, Absalom my son, my son!'

5 Then Joab went into the king's house. He spoke to the king. 'Today you have made your men ashamed. But they have saved your life and the lives of your sons, daughters and lady friends. 6 You seem to love those who hate you. And you seem to hate those who love you! You have shown today that your officers and soldiers are not important to you. You would be happy if Absalom were still alive. You would be happy even if all of us were dead. 7 Now go out and speak to the men. Tell them that they have fought well. If you do not do that, not one man will remain here tonight. It is as sure as the LORD is alive. That would be worse than anything that has happened to you in all your life.'

8 So the king got up and he went to sit in his seat by the city gate. They told the men, 'The king is sitting by the gate.' Then they all came to stand in front of him. By this time, the people had run to their homes.

David returns to Jerusalem

9 Then the people in their different tribes were quarrelling with each other. They were saying, 'The king saved us from our enemies. He fought the Philistines and he won. Nobody else did that. But now he has run from Absalom that we asked to be our king. He has left the country. 10 We anointed Absalom as king over us but now he has died in the fight. Surely someone should have started to say that we should bring the king back.'

11 People told David what the people were saying. So he sent the priests Zadok and Abiathar to the leaders of Judah with a message. He told them to say,

'Surely, you should not be the last to bring the king back to the king's house? He has heard what the people in all Israel are saying. 12 You are my brothers, my family. So I do not know why you are the last to bring back the king. 13 And say to Amasa, "You belong to my family. From this time on Joab will not be the most important officer in my army. You will be that, instead. I want God to punish me very much if I do not do that." Tell him that.'

14 All the men from Judah turned like one man to follow David. They sent servants to the king. And they asked him to return with all his soldiers. 15 Then the king returned and he went to the River Jordan.

The men from Judah had come to Gilgal to meet the king. They wanted to bring him across the river.

David forgives Shimei

16 Gera's son Shimei came quickly down from Bahurim to meet the king. He came with the men from Judah but he was from Benjamin's tribe. 17 He brought 1000 men from his tribe with him. Ziba, Saul's servant also came with his 15 sons and 20 servants. They all hurried to the River Jordan, where the king was. 18 They crossed where the water was not deep. And they brought the king and his people with them. They wanted to do whatever the king wanted.

When Shimei had crossed the River Jordan he fell down in front of the king. 19 He said to him, 'Please will you forgive me. I did wrong things when you, my lord, left Jerusalem. Please, do not remember those things. Please forget them. 20 I am your servant. And I know that I have sinned. But I am the first to come from the tribes in the north of Israel to meet you here.'

21 Then Abishai, Zeruiah's son said, 'We should kill Shimei. He said wicked things against the king that God has anointed. So we should kill him.'

22 David replied, 'I am not like you and your brother Joab. You will not kill anybody today. This day I have become king over Israel.' 23 So the king gave a promise to Shimei. 'You will not die', he said.

David is kind to Mephibosheth

24 Mephibosheth, Saul's grandson, also went down to meet the king. He had not washed his feet or his clothes since David left Jerusalem. And he had not cut his beard. 25 When he came from Jerusalem to meet the king, David spoke to him. 'Why did you not go with me, Mephibosheth?' he asked.

26 He said, 'My lord, as you know, I cannot walk well. So I asked my servant to prepare a donkey for me to ride so that I could go with you. But Ziba my servant did not obey me. 27 And what he has said to you is not true. But you are like an angel of God. You will do what you think is best. 28 My lord might have killed all the descendants of my grandfather Saul. That would have been a fair punishment. But you gave me a place to eat at your table. I ought not to ask the king for anything more.'

29 The king said, 'Do not say any more about these things. I have decided that you and Ziba must each have half of the fields.'

30 Mephibosheth said to the king, 'He can take them all. I am only happy that you are still safe.'

David wants Barzillai to stay with him in Jerusalem

31 Barzillai from Gilead came down from Rogelim to cross the River Jordan with the king. He wanted to send him on to Jerusalem from there. 32 But Barzillai was a very old man, about 80 years old. He had helped David while David was in Mahanaim. He had given to David much that he had needed. He did that because he was a very rich man. 33 David said to him, 'Cross with me. And come and stay with me in Jerusalem. I can give to you all that you might want.'

Barzillai asks David to take his son Chimham instead

34 Barzillai answered the king, 'I will not live many more years. Why should I go to Jerusalem with the king? 35 I am already 80 years old. And I cannot tell what is good or bad. I cannot taste what I eat. And I cannot taste what I drink. And I cannot still hear people when they sing. I would only cause trouble to you. 36 I will come with you for a short way on the other side of the river, but I cannot accept your gift. 37 Let me, your servant, return to die in my own town. Then they can bury me near the place where they buried my father and my mother. Here is my son Chimham. Let him go across with you. Please do for him whatever you choose. And I hope that it will give you pleasure.'

38 The king said, 'Chimham can go across with me. And I will do for him whatever you want. And I will do whatever you want me to do for you.'

39 So all the people went across the River Jordan and the king followed them. The king kissed Barzillai and blessed him. Then Barzillai returned to his home.

40 When the king went across the river to Gilgal, Chimham went with him. All Judah's army and half of Israel's men took him across the river.

The men from Israel are angry with the men from Judah

41 Then all the men from Israel came to ask the king, 'Why did our brothers, the men from Judah, take you and your people away across the River Jordan?'

42 The men from Judah answered, 'We did it because he belongs to our family. Do not be angry. We have not eaten any of his food and he has not given us anything.'

43 The Israelites replied, 'We have 10 parts in the king but you have only one part. So you should not think that we are not important. And we were the first people to say that we should bring the king back.'

But the words that the men from Judah spoke were even more angry than the words of the Israelites.

Chapter 20

Sheba causes trouble for David

1 A man called Sheba was in Gilgal. He was Bichri's son, from Benjamin's tribe. He liked to cause trouble. He made a noise with a trumpet and he shouted, 'We will not follow David the son of Jesse. Men from Israel, we should return to our homes.' 2 So the Israelites left David and they went with Sheba. But the men from Judah stayed with David and they followed him. They were all the people who lived in places from the River Jordan to Jerusalem.

David keeps his ladies safe

3 David returned to the king's house in Jerusalem. Then he took the 10 lady friends. They had stayed there when he left Jerusalem. Now he shut them away safely in a special house. People were watching them carefully. He gave to them all that they needed. But he did not sleep with them. They stayed there. And they lived like widows until they died.

David sends Amasa to fetch all the men from Judah

4 The king spoke to Amasa. 'Bring all the men from Judah to me here during the next three days. And come with them yourself.' 5 Amasa went to fetch them but he was away for more than three days.

6 David said to Abishai, 'Now Bichri's son Sheba will cause us more trouble than Absalom. Take my men and go after him. If you do not catch him they may hide in towns with strong walls. He might get away from us.' 7 So Abishai took Joab's men, the Pelethites and the Kerethites and all the king's soldiers with him. They marched out from Jerusalem to find Bichri's son Sheba. 8 Amasa came to meet them at the big rock in Gibeon. Joab was dressed for the fight and a sword was hanging from his belt. It fell out of its place as Joab went towards Amasa.

Joab kills Amasa

9 Joab said to Amasa, 'How are you my brother?' And he took Amasa by his beard with his right hand to kiss him. 10 But Amasa did not see the sword in Joab's other hand. Then Joab pushed it completely into Amasa's stomach. All his inside parts fell out on the ground and he died immediately. Joab did not have to hit him again.

Then Joab and his brother Abishai went on. They were following after Sheba.

11 A man stood by Amasa's dead body. The man belonged to Joab's soldiers. He shouted, 'Everyone who wants to follow David, follow Joab!' 12 Amasa's dead body was in the road, covered with his blood. Everyone who saw him stopped there. The man had seen that they stopped. So he pulled the dead body into a field and he covered it with a cloth. 13 After he had taken Amasa's dead body from the road, the men went on with Joab. They were going after Sheba the son of Bichri.

They find Sheba and people kill him to save their city

14 Sheba went through all the tribes of Israel to Abel Beth Maacah. All Bichri's family came together and they followed him into the city. 15 Some people told Joab's men that Sheba was there. So they went and they stood all-round the city. They built the ground up high near to its walls. And they dug under the walls to cause them to fall down. 16 A wise woman shouted to them from the wall. 'Listen, listen. Ask Joab to come here so that I can speak to him', she said. 17 He went towards her. 'Are you Joab?' she asked.

'I am', he answered.

'Listen to what I have to say', she said.

'I am listening', he replied.

18 Then she said, 'A long time ago, people said, "Get your answer at the city called Abel." And that is what they did. 19 We are a peaceful city that is faithful to Israel. Why are you trying to destroy it? Do you want to hurt what is the LORD's?'

20 'I would never do that!' Joab answered. 'I would never hurt or destroy your city. 21 That is not what we want. But a man called Sheba, son of Bichri, has come there from the hills of Ephraim. He has said that he will not follow King David. If you will give me this one man, I will leave your city. I will not destroy it.'

The woman said to Joab, 'I will throw his head to you from the wall.'

22 Then the woman went to all the people in the city. She told them why they should kill Sheba. So they cut off the head of Bichri's son Sheba and they threw it to Joab. Then he made a noise with his trumpet and all his men left the city. Each of them went to his home. And Joab returned to the king in Jerusalem.

David's officers

23 Joab was the officer who led all Israel's army. Jehoiada's son led the Pelethites and the Kerethites who kept David safe. 24 Adoniram ruled over the men that had to work for the king. Ahilud's son Jehoshaphat wrote down all that the king did. 25 Sheva was another writer, and Zadok and Abiathar were priests. 26 Ira from the town called Jair was a priest for David.

Chapter 21

David lets the Gibeonites punish Saul's descendants

1 For three years together no food grew in Israel. So David asked the LORD what had caused this trouble. The LORD said, 'It is because of the blood of the Gibeonites. Saul killed many of them.'

2 The king asked the Gibeonites to come to him. (The Gibeonites were not Israel's people. They were Amorites, but the Israelites had promised not to kill them. Saul had tried to kill them all. He thought that this would be good for Israel and Judah.)

3 David asked the Gibeonites, 'What can I do for you? How can I make things right so that you will bless our people's land?'

4 The Gibeonites answered Saul, 'We do not ask for money or gold from Saul's family. And we do not want to kill anyone in Israel.'

'What do you want me to do for you?' David asked them.

5 They answered the king, 'There was a man who destroyed us. He wanted to kill all of us who were living in Israel. 6 Will you give to us 7 of his male descendants? Then we can kill them and we can hang them in front of the LORD in Gibeah. It is the town of Saul, the man that the LORD chose.'

'I will give them to you', the king said.

The Gibeonites kill 7 of Saul's descendants

7 The king did not choose Mephibosheth, the son of Saul's son Jonathan. That was because of David's promise to Saul's son Jonathan. David used the name of the LORD when he made that promise. 8 But the king took the two sons of Aiah's daughter Rizpah, who were called Armoni and Mephibosheth. Saul was their father. And he took the 5 sons of Saul's daughter Merab. They had grown up as sons of Michal, her sister. They were the sons of Adriel, son of Barzillai from Meholath. 9 He gave them to the Gibeonites. They killed them and they hung them on a hill in front of the LORD. All 7 of them died together. That was at the time when the barley was nearly ready to bring from the fields.

Rizpah protects her son's dead bodies

10 Rizpah, Aiah's daughter, put a cloth over a rock for herself. She stayed there from that time until it rained. The rain came down from the sky on the dead bodies. She kept the birds away from them during the day and she kept the wild animals away during the night.

They bury the bones of Saul's family

11 They told David what Rizpah, Saul's lady friend, had done. 12 Then he went to fetch the bones of Saul and his son Jonathan from the people at Jabesh Gilead. (Their men had taken them from the square in Beth Shan. The Philistines had hung them there. That was after they had killed Saul on the mountain called Gilboa.) 13 David took the bones of Saul and Jonathan and also the bones of the 7 men who had been hung.

14 They buried the bones of Saul and Jonathan with those of Kish, Saul's father, in Zela in Benjamin's land. The king had told them what they should do. And they did it all. Then the LORD answered their prayers for their country.

Wars against the Philistines

15 Israel's people were fighting the Philistines again. David went with his men to fight the Philistines. He became very tired. 16 A descendant of Rapha, Ishbi-Benob said that he would kill David. The point of his bronze spear weighed 7½ pounds (3½ kilos) and he had a new sword. 17 But Zeruiah's son Abishai saved David. He hit the Philistine down and he killed the Philistine. So David's men said to him, 'You must never again come out to fight with us. You are like Israel's light and we do not want anyone to put it out.'

18 Sometime after that, Israel fought with the Philistines at Gob. In that fight, Sibbecai from Hushah killed Saph, a descendant of Rapha.

19 In another fight with the Philistines, Elhanan, the son of Jaare-Oregim from Bethlehem, killed Goliath from Gath. Goliath's spear had a thick handle like a strong tree branch.

20 In another fight, a great big man fought for the Philistines. He had 6 fingers on each hand and 6 toes on each foot. He was also a descendant of Rapha. 21 When he shouted bad things about the Israelites, Shimeah's son Jonathan killed him. Shimeah was David's brother.

22 David and his men killed all these 4 descendants of Rapha from Gath.

Chapter 22

David sings praises to God

1 David wrote this song when the LORD had saved him from Saul and from all his enemies.

2 This is what he sang.

'The LORD is my rock and my strong shelter, and he saved me.

3 My God is the rock that I can hide in.

He is my shield that saves me.

He is my strong shelter and my safe place, and he saves me.

You have saved me from men who would have hurt me.

4 I shout to the LORD because I must praise him.

He has saved me from my enemies.

5 Death was like water that was all round me.

Strong waters covered me over.

6 I felt that they were burying me.

7 I was afraid so I cried to the LORD.

I shouted to my God.

From his holy place he heard my voice.

My loud noise reached his ears.

8 The ground moved and it shook.

And the sky shook itself.

They shook because he was angry.

9 Smoke came out of his nose.

Burning fire came out of his mouth.

Materials started to burn as a result.

10 He broke through the sky and he came down.

He stood on dark clouds.

11 He flew on the backs of angels.

He went like the wind.

12 He made the air dark all round him

with the rain clouds of the sky.

13 From his bright body

swords of light shone out.

14 The LORD spoke with a loud noise.

His great voice was everywhere.

15 He shot arrows that caused enemies to run away.

His swords of light beat them completely.

16 The waters of the sea ran from their deep places.

Men could see the deepest places of the earth.

He caused this by the smoke from his mouth

because he was angry.

17 His hand came out from the sky to hold me.

He pulled me from the deep waters.

18 He saved me from my powerful enemy.

He saved me from those who were too strong for me.

19 When troubles were all round me,

he held me up.

20 He brought me into a safe place.

He saved me because he loved me very much.

21 I do what is right. The LORD helps me because of that.

He blesses me because I do not sin.

22 That is because I have obeyed his laws.

It is because I have not turned away from him.

23 I have obeyed all his laws.

I have not turned away from them.

24 I have done only what is right. He knows that.

I have not sinned.

25 I do what is right. So the LORD has blessed me.

I want only what is good. And he sees that.

26 You are faithful to those who are faithful to you, LORD.

You are completely good to those who are good.

27 All good people know how good you are.

But you are against those who are wicked.

28 You save humble people.

But you bring down proud people.

29 You are like a light in my hand.

You turn dark into light.

30 You make me strong to fight my enemies.

With you, my God, I can jump over a wall.

31 All that God does is perfect.

His words are always good and right.

He is like a shield to all who trust him.

32 The LORD is the only God.

He is the rock that holds us up.

33 It is God who makes me strong.

He makes my path safe.

34 He makes my feet like goat's feet

so that I can stand on high hills.

35 He teaches my hands to fight

so that I can bend an iron bow.

36 You keep me safe in the fight.

Your help has made me great.

37 You have saved me from my enemies

and I have never fallen.

38 I ran after my enemies and I beat them.

I did not turn back until they were all gone.

39 I knocked them down and they could not get up.

They fell under my feet.

40 You made me strong for the fight.

You caused those that I fought to bend down in front of me.

41 You caused my enemies to turn and so they ran away from me.

And I killed all those who were against me.

42 They shouted for help but nobody came to save them.

They shouted to the LORD but he did not answer.

43 I hit them until they were like small stones.

I beat them and I walked over them like the ground.

44 You have saved me when my people were attacking me.

You have made me the ruler of many nations.

People that I did not know obey me.

45 Foreign men come and they bend down to me.

They hear me speak and they obey me immediately.

46 They are not brave now.

They are very afraid as they leave their strong cities.

47 The LORD is alive! Praise him who is my strong rock.

Tell people how great he is. He is the strong God who saves me.

48 He helps me to beat my enemies;

he causes me to rule over the nations.

49 He saves me from my enemies.

You made me stronger than those who were against me.

And you save me from those who would hurt me.

50 So I will praise you, LORD among the nations.

I will sing praises to your name.

51 God wins big and important fights for his king.

He is always kind to the king that he has anointed,

to David and to his descendants for all time.'

Chapter 23

David's last words

1 God chose David, Jesse's son for people to anoint as their king. God made him great and he wrote beautiful songs for Israel. These are David's last words.

2 'The Spirit of the LORD speaks by me.

My mouth speaks his words.

3 The God of Israel has spoken.

He who keeps Israel safe said to me,

"A king who rules over men properly is afraid to make God angry.

4 That kind of king is like morning light when the sun rises.

Yes, he is like a morning when there are no clouds in the sky.

He is like light after rain

that causes the grass to seem bright."

5 The LORD will bless my descendants.

That is because he has given a promise to me.

And that promise will be for all time.

He will not change his promise.

And he will do what he has promised to do.

That is all that I want. And he will keep me safe.

6 But he will throw out evil men like weeds.

Some weeds will hurt your hands if you touch them.

And those men are like those weeds.

7 The man who wants to touch them needs an iron tool or a strong stick.

But men will burn them completely.'

David's strong soldiers

8 These are the names of David's best soldiers.

Josheb-Basshebeth the son of Hachmon was the first of the 'Three'. He stood against 800 men with his spear and he killed them all at the same time.

9 Next was Dodai's son Eleazar from Ahoh's family. He belonged to the three strongest men. He was with David at Pas Dammim when they said words to make their Philistine enemies angry before a fight. Israel's men ran away

10 but Eleazar stood there. And he hit the enemy until his hand was tired. And his hand could not easily leave his sword. On that day the LORD won a big and important victory. The soldiers returned but they only came to take things from the dead Philistines.

11 Next was Shammah the son of Agee from Harar. The Philistines had come together in a field of beans and the Israelites had run away from them. 12 But Shammah had stood in the middle of the field. He fought the Philistines and the LORD gave a big and important victory to him.

13 The time to bring in the grain was near. During that time three out of David's 30 best soldiers came to him near Adullam. He was hiding there in a hole in the hill. A group of Philistine soldiers was in the Valley of Rephaim. 14 David was there at that time and the Philistine army was at Bethlehem. 15 David very much wanted a drink of water. He said, 'I want to have a drink of water from the well by Bethlehem's gate. It would be good if someone brought me some.' 16 So the three best soldiers fought through the Philistines and they got some water from Bethlehem's well. Then they carried it to David. But he refused to drink it. He poured it out in front of the LORD. 17 'I cannot drink it', he said. 'Those men fetched it. But it would seem to me that I would be drinking their blood. They might have died while they were trying to fetch it.' So David would not drink it.

These are the great things that the three best soldiers did.

18 Zeruiah's son Abishai, Joab's brother, was the leader of those three soldiers. He fought 300 men with his sword and he killed them all. So people talked about him a lot when they talked about these three soldiers. 19 Men honoured him more than the other two soldiers. So he was the leader of these three soldiers but he did not belong to the other 'Three'.

20 Jehoiada's son, Benaiah came from Kabzeel. He was a brave fighter and he did many great things. He killed two of Moab's best men. And he went into a deep hole to kill a lion when snow was on the ground.

21 He knocked down a big man from Egypt who had a spear in his hand. He knocked him down with a heavy stick. He took the spear from the man's hand and he killed him with the man's own spear. 22 These were the things that Jehoiada's son Benaiah did. 23 They honoured him more than any of the 30. But he did not belong to the 'Three'. David made him the leader of his own special soldiers.

24-39 These men were among the 30:

Joab's brother Asahel.

Elhanan, Dodo's son from Bethlehem.

Shammah and Elika from Harod.

Helez from Pelet.

Ira, Ikkesh's son from Tekoa.

Abiezer from Anathoth.

Mebunnai from Hushah.

Zalmon from Ahoh's family.

Maharai from Netophah.

Heleb, Baanah's son from Netophah.

Ittai, the son of Ribai, who came from Gibeah in the land of Benjamin.

Benaiah who came from Pirathon.

Hiddai from the valleys near Gaash.

Abialbon from Arbath.

Azmaveth from Bahurim.

Eliahba from Shaalbon, a son of Jashen.

Jonathan.

Shammah from Harar.

Ahiam, the son of Sharar, from Harar.

Eliphelet, Ahasbai's son from Maacah.

Eliam, Ahithophel's son from Gilo.

Hezro from Carmel.

Paarai from the people called Arbites.

Igal, Nathan's son from Zobah.

Bani who came from Gad's family.

Zelek who came from Ammon.

Naharai from Beeroth. He carried Joab's sword and shield.

Ira and Gareb from the people called Ithrites.

And Uriah the Hittite.

Together their number was 37.

Chapter 24

David counts his soldiers

1 The LORD became angry with Israel. So he caused David to cause trouble for them. He said to David, 'Go and count the people in Israel and Judah.'

2 So the king said to Joab and the leaders of the army, 'Go from Dan to Beersheba, through all the tribes of Israel. Count all the men who can fight. I want to know how many they are.'

3 But Joab spoke to the king, 'I pray that the LORD your God will make their numbers very much greater. So then there might be 100 men for each man that there is now. And I pray that you will see it. But, my master, it is not good that you want to do this!'

4 But the king caused Joab and his officers to obey him. So they went out to count the people in Israel.

5 They crossed the River Jordan. And they stayed south of the town called Aroer in a valley. Then they went through Gad to Jazer. 6 They went to Gilead and to Kadesh in the land of the Hittites. Then they went on to Dan and west to Sidon. 7 Then they went south to the strong city called Tyre. And they went to all the towns of the Hivites and the Canaanites. Then they came to Beersheba in the south of Judah.

8 After 9 months and 20 days they had been through the whole country and they returned to Jerusalem.

9 Joab gave a report to the king. The numbers of men who were able to use a sword to fight were 800 000 in Israel and in Judah 500 000.

The LORD punishes David for his sin

10 David had counted the men who were able to fight. But now he was sorry that he had done it. He said to the LORD, 'What I have done was a bad sin. Please forgive me. I have been a fool.'

11 The LORD spoke to Gad, David's prophet, the next morning. He spoke before David got up. 12 He said, 'Go and say this to David: "Choose one out of three things for me to do against you." '

13 So Gad went to David and he said, 'Would you choose three years when you have no food. Or would you choose three months when you are running from your enemies? Or should there be three days of strong illness in the country? Now think carefully. I will take your answer to him who sent me.'

14 David said to Gad, 'I am in a lot of trouble. But I do not want men to punish me. I want the LORD to punish us, because he is kind.'

15 So, from that morning, the LORD caused illness to Israel for three days. And 70 000 Israelites died in that time. 16 The LORD's angel was ready to destroy Jerusalem. But the LORD was sorry for the people and he said to the angel, 'Stop killing the people! Put your hand down now.'
The angel was then at the place where Araunah worked with his grain. Araunah was from the people called Jebusites.

17 David saw the angel who was killing the people. So he spoke to the LORD. 'I have sinned. These people have followed me like sheep. They have done nothing that is wrong. Punish me and my family. Do not punish the people', he said.

David builds an altar

18 Gad went to David on that day and Gad said to him, 'Go up. And build an altar to the LORD at the place where Araunah works with his grain.' 19 So David went up to that place as the LORD had said by Gad the prophet. 20 Araunah looked and he saw the king and his men. They were coming towards him. So he went out in front of the king. He bent with his face to the ground.

21 Araunah said, 'My lord, why have you come to your servant?'

'I have come to buy this place where you work with your grain', David answered. 'I want to build an altar to the LORD. Then he will stop this illness.'

22 'Take anything that you want, my lord', said Araunah, 'Here are male cows, and tools and yokes of wood. 23 My lord, I give all this to the king.' And he said, 'I pray that the LORD your God will accept your offering.'

24 But the king replied to Araunah, 'No, I must pay you for it. I will not sacrifice an offering that costs me nothing.'

So David bought the cows and the land for 1¼ pounds (0.6 kilos) of silver. 25 Then he built an altar and he sacrificed burnt offerings and peace offerings there. Then the LORD answered David's prayer and the illness stopped.

From Solomon to Elijah

1 Kings

About this book

> 1 Kings is a book about the people called Israelites. The Books of 1 Kings and 2 Kings tell us what happened after King David's time. The Book of 1 Kings records how Solomon became king after David.
>
> After Solomon died, the country called Israel became two countries. The south was called Judah. Rehoboam was the first king of Judah. The north was still called Israel. Here Jeroboam became king (chapter 12). There were many other kings after these two kings.
>
> When the kings obeyed God, the people had peace. Sometimes the kings did not obey God and they worshipped other gods instead. Then bad things happened. When the people in Israel stopped obeying God, he sent a prophet. His name was Elijah. He did things that someone could only do with the help of God. He told the people that they should worship God again.

Chapter 1

David makes Solomon king

1 King David was old. He was very old. He could not get warm, even when people put blankets over him. 2 So his servants said to him, 'We will look for a young woman who has never had sex for our master the king. She can be with the king and she can be his nurse. And she can lie at your side so that our master the king will be warm.' 3 So they looked through all the country called Israel for a beautiful girl. And they found Abishag. She was from Shunem. And they brought her to the king. 4 The girl was very beautiful. And she was very kind to the king. She did what the king needed. But the king did not have sex with her.

5 Then Adonijah (David's son) demanded this. 'I want to be the king.' His mother's name was Haggith. He got men that were ready to ride on horses. And he had 50 men to run in front of him. 6 His father had always let him do whatever he wanted to do. (So) his father never asked him, 'Why are you doing that?' Also, Adonijah was very handsome. He was (the son of David that was) born next after Absalom. 7 And Adonijah talked (about this) with Joab and Abiathar. Joab was the son of (David's sister) Zeruiah and Abiathar was the priest. They said that they would help Adonijah.

8 But these people did not join Adonijah's group:

- Zadok the priest
- Benaiah the son of Jehoiada
- Nathan the prophet
- Shimei and Rei
- David's own soldiers.

9 Then Adonijah sacrificed sheep, cows and young fat cows. He did it at the Stone (called) Zoheleth. It was near to the well at Rogel. He asked all these people to come to the meeting:

- all his brothers, who were the sons of the king
- all the men in Judah who were the king's officers.

10 But he did not ask these people to come to the meeting:

- Nathan the prophet
- Benaiah
- David's own soldiers
- (Adonijah's) brother Solomon.

11 Bathsheba was the mother of Solomon. Nathan asked her, 'Have you heard this? Adonijah, the son of Haggith, has become king. Our master, David, does not know about it. 12 Now I will tell you how you can save your life and the life of Solomon your son. 13 Go to King David and say to him, "My master the king, did you not promise this to me, your servant? 'Your son Solomon will become king after me. He will sit on my throne.' So why has Adonijah become king?" 14 While you are still talking to the king, I will come in after you. I will say that your words are true.'

15 So Bathsheba went to see the king in his bedroom. The king was very old. And Abishag, the girl from Shunem, was with him. 16 And Bathsheba bent down on her knees in front of the king. 'What do you want?' the king asked her. 17 And she said to him, 'My master, you promised this to me, your servant, and to the LORD your God. "Solomon, your son, will be king after me and he will sit on my throne", you said. 18 But now, Adonijah has become king. And you, my master the king, you do not know about it.

19 He has sacrificed many cows, fat young cows and sheep. He has asked these people to come to the meeting:

- Abiathar the priest
- Joab the leader of the army.

But he did not ask your servant Solomon to come.

20 My master the king, everyone in Israel is waiting for you to say something. They want to know from you who will sit on the throne of my master the king after him. 21 If you do not tell them, this will happen. Soon after they bury you with your ancestors, they will put me and my son Solomon into a prison.'

22 While Bathsheba spoke to the king, Nathan the prophet arrived. 23 And (his servants) told the king, 'Nathan the prophet is here.' So Nathan the prophet went in to the king's (bedroom). And he bent low, with his face to the ground. 24 Nathan said, 'My master the king, have you said that Adonijah will become king after you? Will he sit on your throne?

25 This is what he has done today. He has sacrificed large numbers of cows, fat young cows and sheep. He has asked these people to be with him:

- all the king's sons

- the leaders of the army

- Abiathar the priest.

Even now, they are eating and drinking with him. They are saying, "We pray that King Adonijah will live for a long time!"

26 But he did not ask these people to be with him:

- me, your servant

- Zadok the priest

- Benaiah the son of Jehoiada

- Solomon your servant.

27 Has my master the king done this? Has he not told his servants who will sit on the throne of my master the king after him?'

28 Then King David answered him. He said, 'Send Bathsheba to me!' So Bathsheba came to the king and she stood in front of him.

29 Then the king spoke a very serious promise. He said, 'I am sure that the LORD is alive! He has saved me from every kind of trouble. 30 As surely as that is true, today I will keep my promise to you. I said it to you and to the LORD, the God of Israel. Your son Solomon will be king after me. He will sit on my throne instead of me.' 31 Then Bathsheba bent down low with her face to the ground. She said this, with her knees on the ground in front of the king. 'I pray that my master King David will live always!'

32 And King David said, 'Send to me Zadok the priest, Nathan the prophet and Benaiah the son of Jehoiada.' And they came to the king. 33 And the king said to them, 'Put my son Solomon on my own donkey. Then take him down to Gihon with all your master's servants. 34 There, Zadok the priest and Nathan the prophet can anoint him king over Israel. Make a noise with a trumpet and shout, "We pray that King Solomon will live for a long time!" 35 Then you must come up with him (to Jerusalem). He must come and he must sit on my throne. He must rule instead of me. I have made him ruler over Israel and Judah.' 36 Benaiah, the son of Jehoiada, answered the king, 'I agree! And I pray that the LORD will say that too. He is the God of my master the king. 37 The LORD was with my master the king. We pray that he will be with Solomon also. We pray that he will make the throne of Solomon even greater than the throne of my master King David!'

38 So these people put Solomon on King David's donkey:

- Zadok the priest

- Nathan the prophet

- Benaiah the son of Jehoiada

- the Kerethites and the Pelethites.

Then they took him down to Gihon.

39 Zadok the priest anointed Solomon. He used oil from a special bottle that was in the holy place. Then they made a loud noise with a trumpet. And all the people shouted, 'We pray that King Solomon will live for a long time!' 40 And all the people went up after him. They used their mouths to make music with things called flutes. And they were very happy. The noise caused the ground to move under them!

41 Adonijah and all the people that were with him heard the noise. They were finishing their special meal. When he heard the sound of the trumpet, Joab asked, 'What does all the noise in the city mean?' 42 Even while Joab was speaking, Jonathan, the son of Abiathar the priest, arrived. Adonijah said to him, 'Come in! You are a good man. I think that you are bringing good news.' 43 Jonathan answered him and said, 'No! Our master King David has made Solomon king.

44 These people put Solomon on to the king's donkey:

- Zadok the priest

- Nathan the prophet

- Benaiah the son of Jehoiada

- the Kerethites and the Pelethites.

Then they took him to Gihon.

45 Zadok the priest and Nathan the prophet anointed Solomon king at Gihon. From there they have gone (to Jerusalem). While they went, they made loud, happy noises. The sound of them is in all the city called Gihon. That is the noise that you can hear.

46 Also, Solomon has sat down on the king's throne.

47 And the king's officers have told our master King David that they are very happy about it. They said, "We pray that your God will make Solomon's name more famous than your name. And we pray that his throne will be greater than your throne." Then the king bent his head down on his bed. He said that God was great, 48 with these words. "The LORD is the great God of Israel. He has let my eyes see who will be king after me. He is on my throne today." '

49 When they heard this, all the people with Adonijah were afraid. They all went away. 50 But Adonijah, because he was afraid of Solomon, went to the holy place. He held the points on the corners of the altar there. 51 Then a servant told Solomon, 'Adonijah is afraid of King Solomon. He is holding the points on the corners of the altar. He is saying, "I pray that Solomon will promise this to me today. (I pray that) he will not kill his servant with the sword." ' 52 Solomon answered, 'If he is a good man, not one hair from his head will fall to the ground. But if he is a bad man, he will die.' 53 Then King Solomon sent men, and they brought Adonijah down from the altar in the holy place. And Adonijah came and he bent down in front of King Solomon. And Solomon said to him, 'Go to your home.

Chapter 2

David dies

1 The day when David should die was near. Then this is what he told his son Solomon. 2 (David) said, 'Soon I will die like everyone else on the earth. So, be strong. And show people that you have grown into a man. 3 Do what the LORD your God asks you to do. Live in his ways. Continue to obey his rules and his laws. Do what he has decided. (Do this because) it is right. Do everything that he wants you to do. Moses wrote it all in his law books. If you do that, you will do well everywhere and in everything.

4 And the LORD will keep his promise to me. This is what he promised to me.

"Someone from your family will always rule Israel. But they must (do these things):

- Live properly.

- Believe in me.

- Try as much as they can to obey me about everything."

5 Also, you know what Joab, the son of Zeruiah, did to me. He killed the two leaders of Israel's armies. He killed Abner, the son of Ner and Amasa, the son of Jether. He did it like there was a war. But there was no war! Their blood is on the belt round his body and on the shoes on his feet. 6 So do the right thing as you thought. Do not let him die in peace as an old man. 7 But be kind to the sons of Barzillai, who lived in Gilead. Let them eat at your table. (Do this) because they were kind to me. (They were kind) when I was running away from your brother Absalom. 8 And remember, Shimei, the son of Gera, is with you. He came from Bahurim, in Benjamin. He prayed that really bad things would happen to me. He did that when I went to Mahanaim. But he did come down to meet me at the (River) Jordan. So I promised him, with the Lord's name, that I would not kill him with the sword. 9 But do not think that he has done nothing wrong. You are a wise man. And so you will do what is right. You know what you must do to him. He is an old man. But you must (cause your servants to) kill him!'

10 Then David (died and he) rested with his ancestors. And they buried him in the City of David, (Jerusalem). 11 David had ruled Israel for 40 years. He was (king) 7 years in Hebron, then 33 years in Jerusalem.

Solomon makes himself safe

12 So Solomon sat on the throne of his father David. He became a strong king.

13 Adonijah was the son of Haggith. He went to Bathsheba, who was the mother of Solomon. And she said, 'Do you come in peace?' He answered, '(I do come) in peace.'

14 Then he said, 'I want to say something to you.' 'Say it', she replied. 15 And he said, 'You know that I should be king. All Israel thought that I should be their king. But things changed, and now my brother is the king. The LORD has made him king. 16 Now I have one thing to ask you. Do not refuse me.' 'Tell me', she replied. 17 So he said, 'Ask King Solomon to give me Abishag, the girl from Shunem, as my wife. He will not refuse you.' 18 And Bathsheba said, 'I will speak to the king on your behalf.'

19 So Bathsheba went to King Solomon, to speak on behalf of Adonijah. The king stood up to meet her. He was polite to her. Then he sat down on his throne. And he ordered (his servants to bring) another throne for his mother. So she sat down at his right side. 20 'I have one small thing to ask you', she said. 'Do not refuse me.' And the king answered her, 'Ask me, mother! I will not refuse you!' 21 So she said, 'Let your brother Adonijah marry Abishag, the girl from Shunem.' 22 And King Solomon said to his mother, 'You are asking that Adonijah can marry Abishag. You are almost asking me that my older brother should become king! (That is what) Abiathar the priest and Joab the son of Zeruiah (want)!' 23 Then King Solomon promised this to the LORD. 'I want God to hurt me very much if Adonijah does not die because of this. And that is what I pray!

24 Now, as surely as God is alive, Adonijah will die today. God has done all these things, which he promised to me:

- He has made me safe.

- He has caused me to sit on the throne of my father David.

- My children will be kings after me.'

25 So King Solomon ordered Benaiah, the son of Jehoiada, to kill Adonijah. And so he attacked him and he died.

26 The king said to Abiathar the priest, 'Go back to your fields in Anathoth. Really, you should die. But I will not kill you now. (That is) because you carried the ark of the LORD God in front of my father David. Also, the trouble that happened to my father happened to you.' 27 So Solomon stopped Abiathar from being a priest of the LORD. The things that the LORD said at Shiloh about Eli's family had now happened.

28 Then the news about this came to Joab. Now Joab had talked with Adonijah, but not with Absalom (about how they could make Adonijah king.) So Joab hurried to the holy place of the LORD. He held the points on the corners of the altar there. 29 And they told Solomon that Joab had hurried to the holy place of the LORD. (They said that) he was next to the altar there. Then Solomon said to Benaiah the son of Jehoiada, 'Go there! Knock him down!' 30 So Benaiah went into the holy place of the LORD. He said to Joab, 'The king says, "Come out!"' But (Joab) answered, 'No! I will die here!' So Benaiah sent a report to the king. He said, 'This is what Joab said to me.' 31 Then the king said to Benaiah, 'Do as he says. Knock him down and bury him. So you will remove from me and from my father's family the blood that Joab poured out. It was the blood of people that he should not have killed.

32 The LORD will punish him because of the blood that he poured out. He attacked two men and he killed them with his sword. My father David did not know about this. Both men were better and more honest than Joab was. (These were the two men :)

- Abner, the son of Ner. He was the leader of Israel's army.

- Amasa, the son of Jether. He was the leader of Judah's army.

33 So Joab and his children and their children will always have troubles because they killed those men. But David's children, their children and his throne will always be in peace with (help from) the LORD.' 34 So Benaiah, the son of Jehoiada, went and he knocked down Joab. He killed him and (Joab's family) buried him in his own land in the country. 35 And the king chose Benaiah, the son of Jehoiada, to be the leader of the army instead of (Joab). Also, the king chose Zadok the priest to (be the leader of the priests) instead of Abiathar.

36 Then the king asked for Shimei to come to him. (The king) said (to Shimei), 'Build yourself a house in Jerusalem and live in it. Do not go out from it to anywhere else.

37 On the day that you leave it to cross the Kidron Valley, you will die. You will die because of what you yourself have done.' 38 And Shimei said to the king, 'Your words are good. Your servant (Shimei) will do as my master the king has said.' So Shimei lived in Jerusalem for many days. 39 But after three years, two of Shimei's slaves ran away. They went to Achish, who was the son of Maacah, the king of Gath. Someone told Shimei, 'Your slaves are in Gath.' 40 So Shimei went out and he prepared his donkey (for a journey). He went to Achish in Gath to look for his slaves. He went out (from Jerusalem) and he brought back his slaves from Gath. 41 Someone reported to Solomon that Shimei had travelled from Jerusalem to Gath. Then he had returned (with his slaves). 42 So the king asked for Shimei to come to him. (The king) said (to Shimei), 'You spoke a very serious promise to the LORD (to obey me). I ordered you not to leave (Jerusalem). If you did, you would die. And you said to me at that time, "Your words are good. I will obey you." 43 But you have not kept your promise to the LORD. You did not do what I ordered you to do.' 44 The king also said to Shimei, 'You know in your mind all the bad things that you did to my father David. Now the LORD will punish you because of the wrong things that you did. 45 But good things will happen to King Solomon. The LORD will make David's throne to be safe for always.' 46 Then the king told Benaiah, the son of Jehoiada, the thing to do. So he went out and he knocked Shimei down. And he killed him. So Solomon now ruled the country. Nobody could say that he was not the proper king.

Chapter 3

Solomon prays for wisdom

1 Solomon made a covenant with Pharaoh, who was the king of Egypt. Solomon married Pharaoh's daughter. He brought her to the city of David. Then Solomon finished the things that he was building. (They were these buildings :)

- his palace

· the temple of the LORD

· the wall round Jerusalem.

2 But the people still sacrificed in high places, because they had not yet built a temple for the LORD's Name.

3 (This is how) Solomon showed that he loved the LORD. He obeyed all the rules of his father David except (one). He burned sacrifices and he burned incense in country places. 4 The king went to Gibeon to sacrifice (to the LORD). That was the most important country place. Solomon sacrificed there a thousand times on the altar. 5 At Gibeon, Solomon saw the LORD during the night, in a dream. And God said, 'Ask me for whatever thing that you want me to give to you.'

6 Solomon's answered, 'You were very kind to your servant, my father David. (This was) because he always believed in you. He was a good man and he was honest. You have continued to be very kind to him. You have given to him a son to sit on his throne to this day. 7 Now, my LORD and God, you have made (me,) your servant king, instead of my father. But I am only a little child. I do not know how to do my duties.8 Your servant is here, among the people (in the country) that you have chosen. It is a great country. There are too many people to count, or to find out how many that there are. 9 So give to your servant a mind that understands things. So I will be able to rule your people. I will be able to see who is right. And I will be able to see who is wrong. That is how I will be able to rule your great country.'

10 It made the LORD happy that Solomon had asked for this.

11-12 So God said to him, 'I will give you what you have asked for. I will do it for (these reasons):

· You have asked for a mind that understands how to rule people fairly.

· You have not asked for a long life or to be very rich.

· You have not asked for the death of your enemies.

I will give to you a mind that is wise. And I will give to you a mind that understands things. As a result, there never has been, or never will be, anyone like you.

13 I will give you more than this. I will give to you the things that you did not ask for. (I will make you) rich. (People will know that you are) great. While you are alive, there will be no better king than you.14 Also, I will give to you a long life, if you (do this). Live as I want you to live. Obey my rules and my laws. That is what David your father did.'

15 Then Solomon awoke. (And he knew) that it was a dream. He returned to Jerusalem and he stood in front of the ark of the covenant of the LORD. He sacrificed (animals) and he burned them. He gave a peace gift (to God). Then he gave a very good meal to all his servants.

Solomon uses his wisdom

16 Then two women came and they stood in front of the king. (The women) were prostitutes. 17 And one woman said (to the king), 'Oh! My lord (and king)! I and this woman live in the same house. And I had a baby while she lived in the house (with me). 18 And three days after (my child) was born, she also had a baby. We were alone in the house. Only the two of us were there. There was no stranger there. 19 But this woman lay on her son in the night and he died. 20 So she got up at midnight and she took my son from my side. I, your servant, was asleep (when she did this). She put him by her breast and she put her dead son by my breast. 21 When I got up in the morning to feed my son, he was dead! So I looked carefully at him in the morning (light). Then I saw that he was not my son. He was not the son that was born to me!' 22 Then the other woman said, 'No! It is my son that is alive. Your son is dead!' But the first woman answered, 'No! The dead boy is yours. My son is alive!' And so they argued in front of the king.

23 Then the king said, 'This (woman) says, "My son is alive and your son is dead." But the other (woman) says, "No! Your son is dead and my son is alive." ' 24 So the king said, 'Bring me a sword.' So they brought a sword to the king. 25 And the king said, 'Cut the child that is alive into two pieces. Give half to one (woman) and half to the other (woman).' 26 Then the woman whose son was alive spoke. She really loved her son. So she said to the king, 'My lord, please give the baby that is alive to her. Do not kill him.' But the other (woman) said, 'Neither you nor I will have him. Cut him in half!' 27 Then this was what the king decided. 'Give the baby that is alive to the first woman. She is its mother. Do not kill it.' 28 Everybody in Israel heard what the king had decided. And they were really afraid of the king. They knew that he used the wisdom from God to decide fairly.

Chapter 4

Solomon's government

1 So King Solomon was the king of all Israel.

2 And these were his important officers:

Azariah, (who was) the son of Zadok. Zadok (was an important) priest.

3 Elihoreph and Ahijah. They were the sons of Shisha. They wrote down (what happened).

Jehoshaphat, (who was) the son of Ahilud. (Jehoshaphat) told people (what Solomon wanted).

4 Benaiah, (who was) the son of Jehoiada. (Benaiah was) the leader of the army.

Zadok and Abiathar (were) priests.

5 Azariah, (who was) the son of Nathan. He told the 12 officers (in verse 7) what to do.

Zabud, (who was also) a son of Nathan. (Zabud was) a priest and he was a friend of the king.

6 Ahishar, (who) kept (the king's) houses and fields well.

Adoniram, (who was) the son of Abda. (Adoniram) told the workers (what they should do).

7 Solomon also had 12 (other) officers. They were in (different) places in all Israel. They supplied food for the king and for the people that lived in his houses. Each (officer) had to supply food for one month in (each) year.

8 These are their names.

Ben-hur. (He supplied food from) the hills in Ephraim.

9 Ben-deker. (He supplied food from) Makaz and Shaalbim and Beth Shemesh and Elon Beth Hanan.

10 Ben-hesed. (He supplied food from) Arubboth. Socoh and all the fields round Hepher were his (also).

11 Ben-abinadab. (He supplied food from) the hills near Dor. (Abinadab) had married Solomon's daughter called Taphath.

12 Baana, (who was) the son of Ahilud. (He supplied food from) Taanach and Megiddo and (from) all of Beth-shean. (Beth-shean) is near Zarethan, (which is) below Jezreel. (He also supplied food) from Beth-shean to Abel-meholah and across to Jokmeam.

13 Ben-geber. (He supplied food from) Ramoth Gilead. The villages of Manasseh's son Jair in Gilead were his. Also, the country round Argob in Bashan (was his). It included 60 large cities. The cities had walls and long pieces of metal (to lock) the gates.

14 Ahinadab, (who was) the son of Iddo. (He supplied food from) Mahanaim.

15 Ahimaaz. (He supplied food from) Naphtali. (Ahimaaz) had married Basemath, (who was) Solomon's daughter.

16 Baana, (who was) the son of Hushai. (He supplied food from) Asher and (from) Aloth.

17 Jehoshaphat, (who was) the son of Paruah. (He supplied food from) Issachar.

18 Shimei, (who was) the son of Ela. (He supplied food from) Benjamin.

19 Geber, (who was) the son of Uri. (He supplied food from) Gilead. (Gilead was) the country where Sihon was king. He was king of the people called Amorites. Also, (Gilead was) the country where Og was the King of Bashan. (Geber) was the only officer in (all) this country.

Solomon's kingdom

20 There were very many people in Judah and Israel. There were as many of them as (there are bits of) sand by the sea (shore). They ate (their food) and they drank (their drink). So they were very happy.

21 And Solomon ruled over all the kingdom. (The kingdom) was from the River (Euphrates in Babylon) to the country where the Philistines live. (They live) near the border of Egypt. The people (from these places) brought gifts (to Solomon) and they were his servants all the days of his life.

22 And this is what (his officers) supplied Solomon each day.

    30 cors (6600 litres or 1700 gallons) of flour

    60 cors (13 200 litres or 3400 gallons) of wheat

23   10 cows that ate in the farm buildings

    20 cows that ate in the fields

    100 sheep

    also (animals called) deer, gazelle, roebuck and chickens.

24 (This is) because (Solomon) ruled all (the land) west of the River (Euphrates in Babylon). (He ruled) from Tiphsah to Gaza. (He ruled) all the kingdoms west of the River (Euphrates). There was no war in any of these places. 25 While Solomon ruled, Judah and Israel were safe. Each (person) lived under their vineor fig tree, from Dan to Beersheba. 26 Solomon had 4000 buildings for horses that pulled chariots. And he had 12 000 horses. 27 The 12 officers supplied food for King Solomon and for everybody that ate with him. (The king) got everything that he needed. 28 (Each officer) brought his part (each month). They brought food and dry grass for the horses that pulled chariots and for the other horses.

Solomon's wisdom

29 God gave Solomon wisdom. He could see what things mean. So he understood them well. (He had more wisdom) than there are bits of sand on the sea shore!

30 Solomon had more wisdom than all the men (that lived) in the East. (His wisdom) was greater than all the wisdom in Egypt. 31 He had more wisdom than any other man. This includes the man called Ethan the Ezrahite. And (it includes) Heman, Calcol and Darda. (Calcol and Darda were) the sons of Mahol. (Solomon) was famous in all the countries round (Israel). 32 (Solomon) spoke 3000 proverbs and (he wrote) 5000 songs. 33 And he described (many) plants: (He described large ones) like the cedar trees that grow in Lebanon. And (he described small ones) like the small plant called hyssop. Hyssop grows on walls. And he taught (people) about all kinds of animals, birds, fishes and things that move on their stomachs. 34 (People) came from all countries to listen to the Wisdom of Solomon. Every king on earth who had heard about his wisdom (sent) someone.

Chapter 5

Solomon prepares to build the temple

1 Hiram (was the) king of Tyre. He heard that Solomon had become king after his father (David). So (Hiram) sent his servants to Solomon, because Hiram had always been a friend of David. 2 And Solomon sent (this message) to Hiram. It said, 3 'You know about my father David. He was unable to build a temple for the Name of the LORD his God. This was because people on all sides fought wars against my father David. (They did this) until God caused him to beat his enemies. 4 But now the LORD my God has made it quiet all round (me). There are no enemies and nothing to destroy anything. 5 So, I have decided to build a temple for the Name of the LORD my God. This is what the LORD said to my father David. (The LORD) said, "I will put your son on your throne after you. He will build the temple for my Name." 6 And you know that none of us can make wood from trees like the men from Sidon. So now, tell (your men) that they should cut down cedar trees in Lebanon for me. And my men will (work) with your men. And I will pay you whatever you ask for your men.'

7 Hiram was very happy when he heard Solomon's message. And he said, 'Praise the LORD today, because he gave David a wise son to rule over this great country.' 8 So Hiram sent this message to Solomon. 'I have received (the message) that you sent to me. I will do all that you ask. (I will send you) cedar wood and pine wood. 9 My men will pull them from Lebanon to the sea. And I will tie several trees together. And then I will pull them along the top of the sea to where you want them. There I will make them into separate trees again, and you will take them away. And you will supply food for my palace, as I want.' 10 So Hiram supplied Solomon with all the cedar wood and pine wood that (Solomon) wanted. 11 Then Solomon supplied Hiram with 20 000 cors (4.4 million litres or 1.1 million gallons) of wheat as food for his palace. He also (supplied) 20 cors (4400 litres or 1100 gallons) of olive oil. Solomon sent this every year to Hiram. 12 And the LORD gave wisdom to Solomon, as (the LORD) had promised to him. Also, there was no war between Hiram and Solomon. They agreed that they would not fight.

13 Then King Solomon caused 30 000 men from all Israel to work for him. 14 He sent them to Lebanon in groups of 10 000 men each month. So, they were one month in Lebanon and two months at home. Adoniram was the master of these men. 15 Solomon had 70 000 men that carried things. And he had 80 000 men that cut stones in the hills. 16 He also had 3300 leaders. They told the workers what they should do. 17 The king ordered them to take large pieces of the best stone that they had cut. They had to take these from the hills where they had cut them. These were the stones that they would build the foundation of the temple with. 18 So the men that worked for Solomon and for Hiram prepared the stone and the wood to build the temple.

Chapter 6

Solomon builds the temple

1 So, Solomon began to build the temple of the LORD. It was 480 years after the Jews had come out from Egypt. Solomon had been king for 4 years. It was in the month called Ziv, the second month (of the year). 2 The temple that Solomon the king built for the LORD was 60 cubits long. It was 20 cubits wide and 30 cubits high. 3 The temple had a group of columns. It was at the front of the larger room (in the temple). (This group) was as wide as the temple. That is, it was 20 cubits wide. It was 10 cubits from the front (of the columns) to the temple itself. 4 And (Solomon) made narrow windows near the tops of the temple (walls).

5 Outside the walls of the temple (Solomon) built rooms at the side. These were outside the larger room of the temple and the holy of holies. (The side rooms) had (three) storeys.

6 The lowest storey was 5cubits wide. The middle storey was 6 cubits wide and the third one was 7 cubits wide. Beams (of wood) kept the (storeys) up.

(The beams) rested on stone pillars so they did not go into the temple walls. 7 When they made the temple, there was no sound of hammers, axes or any iron tools. They used only big stones that they had cut already. They cut them into the right shape at the place where they found them. 8 The door to the lowest storey was on the south side of the temple. And stairs went up to the middle storey and to the top storey. 9 So (Solomon) built the temple and he finished it. He made the roof out of beams (of wood) and cedar boards. 10 And he built the rooms all along the sides of the temple. Each room was
5 cubits high. Cedar beams fastened (the rooms) to the temple.

11 And the word of the LORD came to Solomon. (The LORD) said,

12 'You are building this temple (for me). I will do everything for you that I promised to your father David. But you must (do these things):

- You must obey my laws.

- You must obey my rules.

- You must do everything that I order you to do.

13 If you do those things, I will live among the Israelites. And I will not leave my people Israel.'

14 So Solomon built the temple and he finished it. 15 He put boards (that his men made from) cedar wood on the inside walls. The boards went from the floor of the temple to its ceiling. (The men) covered the floor of the temple with pine wood. 16 (Solomon) made a Most Holy Place at the back of the temple. It was inside the temple and it was 20 cubits long. It had cedar boards from floor to ceiling. It made a very special place (inside the temple). 17 The room in front of this (Most Holy) Place was
40 cubits long. 18 (They made) the inside of the temple with cedar (wood). (They made) pictures (in the wood) of plants like flowers. (They made) everything out of cedar (wood). You could not see any
stone. 19 (Solomon) made the (Most Holy) place inside the temple for the ark of the LORD's covenant. 20 This (Most Holy Place was called) the inside sanctuary. It was 20 cubits long, 20 cubits wide and 20 cubits high. (Solomon) put pure gold on everything (in the sanctuary). He also did this with the cedar altar. 21 Solomon covered everything inside
the temple with pure gold. Also, he put a curtain that they made out of gold in front of the sanctuary. (Everything in the sanctuary) he covered with gold. 22 So he covered everything inside (the temple) with gold. He also covered with gold the altar by the inside sanctuary.

23 In the inside sanctuary, (Solomon) made two cherubs from olive wood. Each one was 10 cubits high. 24 One wing of the first cherub was
5 cubits long. Its other wing was also

5 cubits long. So it was 10 cubits from the end of one wing to the end of the other wing. 25 The second cherub was also 10 cubits long. (This was because) the two cherubs were the same in size and
shape. 26 Each cherub was 10 cubits high. 27 (Solomon) put
the cherubs in the inside room of the temple. Their wings were very wide. The wing of one cherub touched one wall (of the temple). The wing of the other (cherub) touched the other wall. And their wings touched each other in the middle of the room. 28 (Solomon) covered the cherubs with gold.

29 (Solomon) made pictures in the wood of cherubs, palm trees and open flowers. He put them on the walls, all round both the rooms in
the temple. 30 He also covered the floors of both the rooms in the temple with gold. 31 He made the doors to the sanctuary out
of olive wood. The wood that held the doors had 5 sides. 32 And on the doors he put pictures in the wood of cherubs, palm trees and open flowers. Then he covered the cherubs and the palm trees with very thin gold. 33 The olive wood that held the doors to the (temple) itself had 4 sides. 34 (Solomon) also made two doors out of pine wood (for
the temple). Each door had two parts that turned separately. 35 He put pictures of cherubs, palm trees and open flowers on (the doors). He covered them with gold. 36 (Solomon) also built a yard, (called
a courtyard, round the temple). (The wall round the courtyard) was three stones high. There were cedar wood boards on top of it.

37 They put down the first stones of the temple of the LORD in the 4th year (that Solomon was king). It was in the month called Ziv. 38 They finished building the temple in the 11th year (that Solomon was king). It was the 8th month, the month called Bul. Everything was as it was in (Solomon's) plans. It had taken him 7 years to build it.

Chapter 7

Solomon builds his palace

1 Solomon was building his palace for 13 years. Then he finished it. 2 He built the House of the Forest of Lebanon. It was 100 cubits long, 50 cubits wide and 30 cubits high. It had 3 lines of cedar pillars. On top of them were (more) cedar beams, which (his men had) cut. 3 They made the roof (also) from cedar wood. (The roof was over the pillars of) cedar wood. Also, it was over the cedar beams that were on top of (the pillars). There were 45 cedar pillars, in 3 lines of 15. 4 Its windows were very high. There were three groups of them. They were on the other side from other (groups of windows). 5 All the doors were a rectangular shape. The wood that held the doors and the windows was rectangular too. There were three (groups) of windows in the front (of the building). 6 He also made a hall of pillars. It was 50 cubits long and 30 cubits wide. The pillars were at the front of the hall, and there was a low wall in front of them. 7 And he built a room to put his throne (special seat for a king) in. He sat on it to decide who was right. And he decided who was wrong. He covered it with cedar wood from floor to ceiling. 8 And he built his house behind (the room for the king's special seat). This was where he lived. (His house) was like (the room for the king's special seat). He also made a house like it for Pharaoh's daughter. She was (Solomon's) wife.

9 His workers made these buildings from very good, large stones. They cut (the stones) to the right size with a special tool. (They cut) the sides that were towards the inside and towards the outside (of the buildings). (They did this) from the front to the important courtyard behind it. Also, (they did it) from the floor to the roof.

10 (Solomon) had put very good, large stones in the ground. They were 8 or 10 cubits long. He built everything on these. 11 Above (the ground) he used very good stones. (His men) cut them to (the right) size. He also used cedar wood beams. 12 There was a wall all-round
the important courtyard. It was 3 stones high, with cedar beams on top. (Solomon's men) cut the stones (to the right size). (This wall) was like the (wall in the) courtyard of the temple of the LORD. There were pillars at the front of it.

More news about the temple

13 King Solomon sent (a message) to Tyre. (The message) brought Hiram (from Tyre). 14 (Hiram) was the son of a widow from the tribe of Naphtali. His father had come from the city called Tyre. His father was a very good worker with metals. (His son, Hiram,) was also a very good worker with metals. He knew how to make very many metal things. So he came to King Solomon. He did everything that (Solomon) asked him to do.

15 He made two metal pillars. Each pillar was 18 cubits high. A line 12 cubits long would make a circle round each of them. The metal itself was about 7 centimetres thick. The two pillars were the same.

16 He also made two metal pieces, which were the shape of big cups. And he put one on the top of each pillar. Each piece was
5 cubits high. 17 (Each piece) had a group of metal chains. He put 7 of them on the top of each pillar. 18 And he made
two chains of pomegranates. They went round each of the metal chains. They made the tops of the pillars very beautiful. He did the same for each pillar. 19 The shapes on the tops of the pillars were like (flowers called) lilies. Each one was 4 cubits high. 20 There were 200 pomegranates all-round the tops of both pillars. They were above the shapes (of flowers) next to the metal chains. 21 He put these pillars in the hall of pillars in the temple. The pillar at the south he called Jakin and the pillar at the north he called Boaz. 22 The tops of the pillars were in the shape of (flowers called) lilies. And so (Solomon) finished the work on the pillars.

23 And (Hiram) made with metal (what they called) a Sea. It was
10 cubits from one side to the other side. It was 5 cubits deep. (Its shape) was a circle 30 cubits round. 24 All round it, below the top, were (shapes like) the fruit of wild plants called gourds. There were 10 for every cubit. (Hiram) made them in one piece with the Sea. 25 He built the Sea on 12 metal male cows. Three pointed north and three pointed west. Three pointed south and three pointed east. Their backs were towards the middle (of the Sea). 26 The sides of the Sea were 3 inches thick. Its top was like the top of a cup. It was like a (flower called the) lily. (The Sea) contained 44 000 litres (12 000 gallons) (of water).

27 (Hiram) also made 10 metal carts (to carry water). Each one was 4 cubits long, 4 cubits wide and 3 cubits deep. 28 This is how he made the water carts. (He made them) with square pieces (of metal, that he) fastened at the corners.

29 There were (pictures of animals called) lions and oxen on the sides and on the corners. (There were) also (pictures of) cherubs. There were shapes like leaves above and below the lions and the oxen. (The shapes were made) with hammers. 30 Each cart had 4 metal wheels with metal axles. Each (cart) also had 4 corners and a bucket that was on 4 pieces of metal. There were metal shapes like leaves, which he made with hammers (next to the buckets). 31 On the top of the cart there was a round hole. It was one cubit deep and a cubit and a half across. Round the hole there were pictures (that Hiram) made with metal. The pieces of metal on the sides (of the carts) were square. They were not round. 32 There were 4 wheels under each cart. (Hiram) fastened the axles of the wheels to the under sides of the carts. Each wheel was a cubit and a half across. 33 The wheels (of the cart) were like the wheels of a chariot. He cast the metal (to make) the axles and all the parts of the wheels. 34 Each cart had 4 handles. There was one on each corner. (Hiram) made them as one piece with each cart. 35 There was a piece of metal round the top of each cart. It was half a cubit deep. (Hiram) fastened the handles and (square) pieces (of metal) to the tops of the carts. 36 And he cut pictures of cherubs, lions and palm trees. He cut them on the handles and the (square) pieces (of metal on the carts). He put them everywhere! There were also (metal pictures of) leaves everywhere! 37 This was how (Hiram) made the 10 carts. They all had the same size and shape. (That is because) they were all cast in the same mould. 38 And (Hiram) also made 10 metal buckets. Each one contained about 230 gallons. Each bucket was 4 cubits across. There was one bucket for each of the 10 carts. 39 (Hiram) put 5 of the carts on the south side of the temple. He put the other 5 on the north side (of the temple). He put the Sea on the south side of the temple. It was at the south east corner.

40 He also made pots, small shovels and small cups.

So Hiram finished all the work in the temple of the LORD. He had promised to King Solomon that he would do these things:

41-45 (He would make these things):

- 2 pillars

- 2 metal pieces, the shape of big cups, on the top of each pillar

2 groups of chains, which made the shapes of cups on the tops of the pillars more beautiful

400 pomegranates for the 2 groups of chains. There were two groups of pomegranates for each chain. They made the shapes of big cups on the tops of each pillar more beautiful.

- 10 carts with their 10 buckets

- the Sea and the 12 male cows under it

- the pots, small shovels and small cups.

The metal that Hiram used for all these things was bronze. He made them for King Solomon, (who wanted them) for the temple of the LORD.

46 The king made them in sand moulds. He did it near the (River) Jordan, between Succoth and Zarethan.

47 Solomon did not weigh any of these things, because there were so many (of them). They did not discover the weight of the bronze.

48-50 Solomon also made everything that was in the LORD's temple. (He made these things):

- The altar (which he made) out of gold.

The table (which he made) out of gold. On it was the (special) bread. That bread showed (that God) was there.

The things that held the lights. He made them from pure gold.

There were 5 on one side and 5 on the other side of the sanctuary.

- The flowers (that he made) from gold.

- The lights and the tools that held things (for the altar).

- The pure gold plates.

- The tools that (they used) for the lights.

- The cups (with water in them).

- The spoons and the baskets (which made smoke).

Also, the places that held the doors of the sanctuary. (This is) the Most Holy Place.

Also, the places that held the doors of the important hall of the temple.

51 Solomon brought (into the temple) all the things that David his father had put to one side for the temple. (Solomon) did this after he had finished all the things that he had made for the temple of the LORD. They were the things that they made out of wood, silver and gold. He put these things in safe places in the LORD's temple.

Chapter 8

Solomon brings the ark into the temple

1 Then Solomon said that all the leaders of Israel must come to him in Jerusalem. The king wanted all the leaders of the tribes and families of Israel to (do this). He wanted them to) bring the ark of the covenant of the LORD (to the temple). (The ark) was in David's part of the city, called Zion. 2 So all the men from Israel came together, to King Solomon. It was the 7th month, called Ethanim. There was a festival (at this time). 3 When all the leaders of Israel had arrived, the priests lifted up the ark.

4 Together with the ark of the LORD, they brought (these other things):

- the tent where people met.

- the holy tools that were in the tent.

The priests and the Levites carried them up (to the temple).

5 While they did this, all Israel's people were with King Solomon. They sacrificed sheep and oxen in front of the ark. (There were) more than they could count. 6 Then the priests brought the ark of the covenant of the LORD to its place. That place was the inside sanctuary of the temple, called the Most Holy Place. They put it under the wings of the cherubs. 7 The wings of the cherubs were over the place where the ark was. The ark and the handles to carry it were in the shadow (of the cherubs). 8 The handles were very long. (The priests) could see their ends from the Holy Place outside the Most Holy Place. They could not see them from outside the Holy Place. And they are still there today. 9 There was nothing in the ark, except two flat stones. Moses had put them there at Horeb. That was where the LORD made a covenant with the Jews. He did that after they came out from Egypt. 10 And when the priests came out from the Holy Place (in the temple), the cloud filled the LORD's temple. 11 And the priests could not do their work, because of the cloud. Then something like a very bright light filled the LORD's temple to show that the LORD was there.

12 Then Solomon said, 'The LORD said that he would live in a dark cloud.

13 I have built a beautiful temple for you. It is a place where you can always live.'

Solomon speaks to his people

14 While everybody in Israel stood there, the king turned round. He prayed that God would be good to them. 15 And he said, 'Praise the LORD, (who is) the God of Israel. With his own hand he has done what he promised with his own mouth to do for my father David. This is what (God) said: 16 "I brought my people Israel out from Egypt. Since then, I have not chosen a city in any tribe of Israel, to build a temple for my Name. But I have chosen David to rule my people Israel." 17 My father really wanted to build a temple for the Name of the LORD, (who is) the God of Israel. 18 But the LORD said to my father, David, "It was good that you really wanted to build a temple for my Name. 19 You will not build the temple. But, instead, your son will build it. He is (from) your own body and blood. He is the person who will build the temple for my Name." 20 The LORD has done what he promised to do. I am (king) after David (who was) my father. Now I sit on the throne of Israel. This is what the LORD promised. Also, I have built the temple for the Name of the LORD, (who is) the God of Israel. 21 I have made a place there for the ark. In it, is the covenant of the LORD. He made it with our ancestors, when he brought them out of Egypt.'

Solomon prays in the temple

22 Then Solomon stood in front of the altar of the LORD. He was in front of all Israel's people.

He lifted up his hands towards the skies.

23 And (Solomon) said,

'LORD, (you are) the God of Israel. There is no God like you, (either) in the skies above (us) or in the earth beneath (the skies). You continue to do what you have promised to do for your servants. (Your servants are the people) to whom you are always very kind. (Your servants) continue to obey your words as well as they can. 24 You have done what you promised to do for your servant, my father David. Your mouth spoke the promise. Then your hands did (the work, as we see)
today. 25 Now, LORD God of Israel, there is (another) promise that you spoke to your servant, my father David. (I pray) that you will do that also. You said to (David), "There will always be a man to sit on my behalf on the throne of Israel. But for this to happen, your sons must always obey me like you did." 26 So now I pray (to you), God of Israel, "Cause what you promised to your servant, my father David, to happen."

27 But surely God will not really live on the earth! Even heaven, the highest heaven of all the heavens, cannot contain you! How much less will this temple that I have built (contain you)! 28 But listen (to me) while I, your servant, pray (to you), my LORD and my God. I am asking you for mercy. Hear me, while I, your servant, am praying to you today. 29 Watch over this temple day and night. This is the place about which you said, "My Name will be there." (So,) you will hear your servant (the king) when he prays towards this place. 30 Hear the words of your servant, and of your people Israel, when they pray towards this place. Hear (us) from the place called heaven, where you live. And when you hear us, then forgive us.

31 Sometimes, a man does something that is wrong to somebody else. The man must come to this temple. He must promise in front of
the altar that his words are true. 32 Then, listen from heaven. And say who is right. If the man really has done something wrong, punish him. But if he has not done anything wrong, be good to him.

33 Perhaps an enemy will win a war against your people, Israel, because (Israel) has not obeyed you. (Your people) may then turn back to you. (They may do these things :)

· (They may) say that your name (is the name of their God).

· (They may) pray to you.

· (They may) ask you (to forgive them) in this temple.

34 If they do that, hear them from heaven! Forgive the sin of your people, Israel. And bring them back to the land that you gave to their ancestors.

35 Sometimes, the skies will become dry and there will be no rain. This will be when your people have not obeyed you. (Then, they may do these things :)

· They may pray towards this place.

· They may say that your name (is the name of their God).

· They may turn from what they have done wrong. (This is) because you have hurt them.

36 If they do that, hear (them) from heaven. Forgive your servants, your people Israel, for what they have done wrong. Teach them the right things to do. Send rain on to the land, which you gave as a gift to your people.

37 Sometimes, (these things will happen) in the country:

· There will not be enough food.

· The (animals and plants and people) will be ill.

· There will be (insects called) locusts and grasshoppers.

· There will be an enemy all round one of their cities.

· Illness (will hurt people) and (enemies will) kill people.

38 Then, perhaps, only one person from among all of your people Israel will pray to you. He may feel that his heart hurts inside him. So, he will lift up his hands towards this temple. 39 (If he does that,) hear (him). Hear him from heaven where you live. Forgive (the people) and do something. Do to each person what should happen to them. Only you can know what everyone is thinking. 40 So, everybody will be afraid of you, (LORD), while they live in the country. (This is the country) that you gave to
our ancestors.

41 Strangers, who do not belong to your people Israel, will come far from other countries. (They will do this) because (they will hear about) your name. 42 People will hear about your great name and about your strong hand and about the arm that you lift up. The stranger will come and he will pray towards this temple. 43 (When this happens, God,) hear him from your home in heaven. Do what he asks you to do. So, all the people in the world will know your name. They will be afraid of you, as your own people Israel are. And they will know this. The temple that I have built is for you.

44 Sometimes, your people will go to fight against their enemies. (They will go) to where you send them. And when they pray to the LORD, they will look towards the city (Jerusalem). You chose (this city). And I built the temple in it for you. 45 When they pray (to you), listen to them (from your home) in heaven. Do what they ask. And give them help.

46 There is nobody that does not sin (against God). When (your people) sin against you, you will become angry with them. You will give them to their enemies. (The enemies) will take them to their own country. Perhaps it will be far; perhaps it will be near. (Your people will be) in the enemy's prisons. 47 Then, they may become sorry that they have sinned. They may change their minds and they may pray to you. They will be in the country of the people who put them into prisons. In that country, they may pray (these words): "We have sinned. We have done what is wrong. We have been very bad." 48 They may turn back to you in the country of their enemies, who put them into prisons. (They may want to obey you) with all their minds and bodies. They may pray to you. And they will look towards the country that you gave to their ancestors. (They will look) towards the city that you have chosen. (And they will look) towards the temple that I have built for your Name. 49 Then hear them from your home in heaven, when they pray to you. Do what they ask you to do. And give help to them. 50 And forgive your people who have sinned against you. Forgive all the wrong things that they have done against you. And cause their enemies to have mercy on them. 51 (Do this) because they are your people. They belong to you. You brought them out of Egypt. And Egypt was like a very hot fire that could make iron like water.

52 I pray that your eyes will always be open (to two things):

193

- to what your servant (Solomon) asks you.

- to what your people, Israel, ask you.

I hope that you will always listen to them. (Do this) when they pray to you.

53 (Do this) because you chose them from all the countries in the world, to be your own people. This is what you promised to your servant Moses. You did it when you, Lord, our LORD, brought our ancestors out of Egypt.'

54 So Solomon finished praying about everything that he wanted to ask the LORD for. He stood up in front of the altar of the LORD. He had been on his knees with his hands lifted up to the skies. 55 But now he stood up (and he asked God) to do good things to all the people in Israel. He said with a loud voice, 56 'Praise the LORD! He has given rest to his people Israel. This is what he promised (to Moses). Every good promise that (the LORD) gave to his servant Moses has really happened. 57 The LORD our God was with our ancestors. I pray that he will be with us like that. I pray that he will never leave us by ourselves. 58 I pray that (the LORD) will cause us to love him again. So we will do what he wants us to do. And we will obey everything that he asked our ancestors to do. 59 All these words of mine I have prayed to the LORD. I pray that these words of mine will be near to the LORD our God day and night. I want him to help me in what I do. And I pray that he will help (me), his servant. Also, his people, Israel, need his help every day. I pray that he will help them. 60 So, all the people on the earth will know that the LORD is God. And they will know that there is no other (God). 61 But you (people) really must want to be servants of the LORD our God. You must do what he orders you to do. And you must obey his words, as you do now.'

Solomon offers the temple to God

62 Then the king, and all Israel's people with him, offered sacrifices to the LORD.

63 These are the sacrifices that Solomon offered to the LORD:

- 22 000 cows

- 120 000 sheep and goats.

(Solomon) offered these because he and the LORD were friendly. So the king, and all Israel's people, gave the temple to the LORD.

64 On that same day, the king gave the courtyard in front of the temple to the LORD. There, (Solomon) offered sacrifices (to the LORD). He burned animals and he offered wheat and fat (material from inside animals). The fat was the fellowship sacrifice. The bronze altar was too small to contain all the animals, the wheat and the fat of the friendly sacrifice. So Solomon burned all these things in the courtyard and not on the bronze altar.

65 So Solomon had a festival at that time. Everybody in Israel was there. So, there was a very big crowd. There were people from everywhere from Hamath to the Valley of Egypt. Hamath was in the north and the Valley of Egypt was in the south (of Israel). The festival continued in front of the LORD our God for 7 days. Then it continued for another 7 days. So it was 14 days long. 66 The day after (the party, Solomon) sent the people away. They all said good things about the king and then they went home. They were very happy and they felt good inside themselves. This was because the LORD had done so many good things for his servant David and for his people Israel.

Chapter 9

The LORD appears again to Solomon

1 Solomon had finished building the temple of the LORD and the king's palace. He had built everything that he had wanted to build. 2 Then the LORD appeared to (Solomon) a second time, as he had appeared to him at Gibeon.

3 The LORD said to (Solomon),

'I have heard what you have prayed to me. And (I have heard) what you have asked me. I have made this temple special, which you have built. I have put my Name on it for all time. My eyes and my heart will always be there.

4 (I will do good things) for you, if you (will do these things):

- You must be my servant, as your father David was (my servant).

- You must do everything that I ask you to do.

5 Then I will make someone from your family king over Israel for all time. This is what I promised to your father David. (I said,) "You will never fail to have a man (from your family) on the throne of Israel." 6 But you and your sons must not turn away from me. You must not become servants of other gods and you must not worship them. You must not refuse to obey the laws and rules that I have given you. 7 If you do, I will remove Israel from (their) country. (It is the country) that I have given to them. Also, I will destroy this temple that I have made special for my Name. Israel will then become something that people say bad things about. They will all laugh at (Israel). 8 This temple now is really beautiful. Then, everyone that sees it will be surprised. (They will think that) it seems very bad to look at. They will laugh about it! They will ask, "Why has the LORD done this to this country and to this temple?" 9 And people will answer, "He has done it because they have not obeyed the LORD their God. He brought their ancestors out of Egypt. But they have chosen other gods. They have become their servants and they worship them. That is why the LORD has caused such bad things to happen to them (and to their temple)." '

Other things that Solomon did

10 Solomon was building the temple of the LORD and the king's palace for 20 years. After this, 11 he gave 20 towns in Galilee to Hiram, the king of Tyre. (He did this) because Hiram had given him all that (Solomon) needed. (He had given him) cedar and pine wood and gold. 12 So Hiram went from Tyre (to Galilee), to see the towns that Solomon had given to him. But Hiram was not happy with them. 13 'These are not very good towns that you have given to me, my dear friend!' he said. (Hiram) called them the Land of Cabul. They are still called that today. 14 Hiram had sent to king (Solomon) 120 talents of gold.

15 Solomon caused slaves to work for him. They built the LORD's temple, (Solomon's) palace, the Milloand the wall round Jerusalem. (They) also (built) (the towns called) Hazor, Megiddo and Gezer. 16 Pharaoh was the king of Egypt. He had attacked Gezer and it had become his. He had burnt it. He had killed the Canaanites that lived there. He gave it as a gift to his daughter, when she married Solomon. 17 So Solomon built Gezer again. He also built (the town called) Lower Beth Horon. 18 (He also built) Baalath and Tadmor. They were in his country, (in places) where there was much sand. 19 And (Solomon) built cities and towns where he could store things. He also kept his chariots and horses in them. He built everything that he wanted (to build), in Jerusalem, Lebanon and everywhere in his kingdom.

20 Some people who were not Jews lived in Israel. They were called Amorites, Hittites, Perizzites, Hivites and Jebusites.

21 The Jews had not been able to kill all of these people. So Solomon made them his slaves, as they still are today. 22 But Solomon did not make any of the Jews into slaves. They became his soldiers, and they became the people in his government. (Some of the soldiers) were army leaders. Other soldiers told the people that drove chariots what to do.

23 And 550 people were leaders of the people that built things (for Solomon). They told the men that did the work what to do.

24 Pharaoh's daughter came up (from where she lived) in the City of David. She came up to the palace that Solomon had built for her. After this, he built walls (that people could walk on) round it.

25 Three times every year Solomon offered sacrifices. He offered sacrifices that he burned and friendly sacrifices. He did this on the altar that he had built for the LORD. He burned incense to the LORD with everybody else. In this way, he did what he had to do in the temple (of the LORD).

26 King Solomon also built ships at Ezion Geber. (This place) is near Elath in Edom. (It is) by the Red Sea. 27 Hiram had sailors who knew about the sea. (Hiram) sent these men to sail with Solomon's sailors. 28 They sailed to Ophir and they brought back 420 talents of gold. They gave it to King Solomon.

Chapter 10

The Queen of Sheba

1 The Queen of Sheba heard that Solomon was very famous. Also, she heard that (he was a servant) of the LORD. So she came to ask (Solomon) difficult questions. 2 She arrived at Jerusalem with many servants. She had animals called camels. They carried spices. (They also carried) a lot of gold and valuable stones. She came to Solomon. She talked to him about everything that was in her mind. 3 Solomon answered all her questions. There was nothing that was too difficult for the king to explain to her. 4 The Queen of Sheba saw how wise Solomon was. She saw the palace that he had built. 5 (She saw) all the food that was on his table. (She saw) all the important men (in his government) when they met together. (She saw) all his servants in their beautiful clothes. (She saw) all the people that tasted wine at his table. (She saw) all the sacrifices that he burned at the temple of the LORD. And it surprised her very much. So she did not know what to say! 6 She said to the king, 'I heard in my country about what you had done. Also, (I heard) about how wise you were. Everything (that I heard) was true! 7 But I did not believe those things until I came here. Then I saw with my own eyes (that it was true)! Really, they told me less than half (of what was true)! You are very much wiser and a lot richer than the report that I heard (about you). 8 I think that your men should be very happy! The people in your government, who are always with you, should be very happy too. They are always hearing how wise you are. 9 (So, we must) praise the LORD (who is) your God! He is so happy with you and he has put you on the throne of Israel. He has made you king because he will always love Israel. You will always decide fairly and you will always obey God's laws.' 10 And she gave to the king 120 talents of gold, a lot of spices and many valuable stones. Nobody ever brought so many spices (to Jerusalem) as the Queen of Sheba gave to King Solomon.

11 Hiram's ships brought gold from Ophir. They also brought from there large amounts of a special kind of wood called almugwood and valuable stones. 12 The king used the almugwood to make things for the temple of the LORD and for the king's palace. He also used it to make harps and lyres for people to make music on. There was more almugwood than anyone has brought here since that time. Nobody has even seen so much of it since that time.

13 So King Solomon gave to the Queen of Sheba everything that she wanted. (He gave her everything) that she asked for. He also gave her valuable gifts. Then she left (Solomon) and she returned to her own country with her servants.

The valuable things that belonged to Solomon

14 The weight of gold that Solomon received each year was 666 talents.

15 This did not include money from (these people):

·   people who bought and sold things to get money

·   all the kings of Arabia

·   the government in (Solomon's) own country.

16 King Solomon made 200 large shields. They made the gold (for the shields) flat with hammers. They used 600 bekas (about 7.5 pounds or 3.5 kilos) of gold in each shield. 17 (Solomon) also made 300 small shields. They also made the gold (for these shields) flat with hammers. They used 3 minas (about 4 pounds or 1.5 kilos) of gold in each (small) shield. (Solomon) put these (shields) in the House of the Forest of Lebanon. 18 Then the king made a large throne. He used ivory to make the inside (of the throne) and he covered it with gold. 19 There were 6 steps up to the throne. The back (of the throne) was round at the top. There were places to put his arms on both sides of the seat. There was a lion on each side of the throne.

20 There were 12 (more) lions on the 6 steps. (There was) one at each end of each step. No other country had made anything like it.

21 They made all King Solomon's (wine) cups with gold. They made everything in the House of the Forest of Lebanon with gold. They had not mixed the gold (with any other metal). They did not make anything with silver. They did not think (that silver) was valuable in Solomon's time. 22 The king had a number of ships that could sail as far as Tarshish. They sailed with Hiram's ships. Every 3 years they returned (to Solomon). They carried gold, silver and ivory. (They also brought) apes and baboons (which were animals like large monkeys).

23 King Solomon was richer than all the other kings in the world. Also, he had more wisdom than (the other kings). 24 All the people in the whole world wanted to talk to Solomon. They wanted to hear the wisdom that God had put into (Solomon's) mind. 25 Every year, everyone who came (to Solomon) brought him a gift. (They brought) silver and gold things, beautiful clothes, arms, spices, horses and mules.

26 Solomon brought together many chariots and horses. He had 1400 chariots and 12 000 horses. He kept (some of) them in special cities for chariots. And (he kept some of them) with him in Jerusalem. 27 The king made silver as common in Jerusalem as stones (were common)! There were as many cedar trees as there were fig trees in the hills (round Jerusalem). 28 Solomon's horses came from Egypt and from Kue. He sent people to Kue to buy the horses for him. 29 They brought a chariot from Egypt for 600 shekels of silver. A horse cost 150 (shekels). Also, they sold (chariots and horses) to all the kings of the people called Hittites and Arameans.

Chapter 11

Solomon's wives and women

1 Solomon loved Pharaoh's daughter (who came from Egypt). But he also loved many other women from foreign countries. (They were called) Moabites, Ammonites, Edomites, Sidonians and Hittites (because of the countries that they came from). 2 The LORD had said this to the Israelites about these countries. 'You must not marry people (from these countries), because they would cause you to love their own gods.' But Solomon did love (these foreign women). 3 He had 700 wives who were important ladies. Also, he had 300 other women who lived with him. His wives caused him to become the servant of (other gods). 4 This happened when Solomon got older. His wives caused him to love other gods. (Solomon) did not completely love the LORD (who was) his God. David, his father, had always loved (the LORD). 5 (Solomon) made Ashtoreth his god. She was the female god of the people in Sidon. He also made Molech his god. He was the really bad god of the people who lived in Ammon. 6 So Solomon did what the Lorded not like. His father David had (completely obeyed the LORD). But Solomon did not completely obey the LORD. 7 There was a hill east of Jerusalem. Solomon built a high place there for Chemosh and Molech. They were really bad gods of the people who lived in Moab and in Ammon. 8 (Solomon) did the same for all his foreign wives. They burned incense and they offered sacrifices to their own gods (in these places).

9 So the LORD became angry with Solomon. (Solomon's) had stopped loving the LORD (who was) the God of Israel. (The LORD) had appeared to Solomon twice. 10 (The LORD) had told Solomon that he should not become the servant of other gods. But Solomon did not obey the LORD. 11 So the LORD said to Solomon, '(I have seen) what you are doing. You have not obeyed my covenant. You have not done what I ordered you to do. So, I will tear the kingdom away from you. I will give it to one of your servants. 12 But I will not do it while you are alive. This is because of (the promise that I said to) David your father. I will tear (the kingdom) from your son. 13 But I will not tear the whole kingdom from him. I will give to him the one tribe (called Judah). This is because I have chosen Jerusalem. (Jerusalem is in Judah.) Also, it is because of what (I promised) to my servant David.'

Solomon's enemies

14 Then the LORD brought Hadad (to Edom). (He was) an enemy of Solomon. (Hadad) was a man in the king's family in Edom. 15 David had fought against Edom a few years before. (Then) Joab was the leader of (David's) army. He had gone (to Edom) to bury the dead people. He killed all the men in Edom. 16 Joab and all (the army from) Israel stayed in (Edom) for 6 months. They killed all the men in Edom. 17 But Hadad was only a boy at this time. He ran away to Egypt, with some people from his father's government. 18 They started from Midian and they went to Paran. They took men from Paran with them and they went to Egypt. They went to Pharaoh, (who was) the king of Egypt. (Pharaoh) gave Hadad a house and land and food. 19 Pharaoh was so happy with Hadad that he gave him a wife. She was the sister of his own wife, Queen Tahpenes.

20 Tahpenes's sister had a son (with Hadad). (They) called (him) Genubath. He lived with Tahpenes in the king's palace. Genubath lived there with Pharaoh's own children. 21 In Egypt, Hadad heard that David had died. Also, Joab, the leader of (David's) army, was dead. Then Hadad said to Pharaoh, 'Let me return to my own country.' 22 Pharaoh asked him, 'Why do you want to return to your own country? What have you not got here that you want?' 'Nothing', Hadad replied, 'but do let me go!'

23 And God brought another enemy against Solomon. (He was) the son of Eliada, called Rezon. (Rezon) had run away from his master, Hadadezer, the king of Zobah. 24 (Rezon) had men with him and he became their leader. They wanted to fight David, after he had destroyed the army of Zobah). (Rezon's) men went to Damascus. They decided to live there. They became leaders (in Damascus). 25 Rezon was Israel's enemy all the time that Solomon was alive. Like Hadad, he caused trouble (for Solomon). So Rezon ruled in Aram and he was an enemy of Israel.

26 Then, Jeroboam, (who was) the son of Nebat, started to fight against the king. He was one of Solomon's officers. (Jeroboam) came from Zeredah in Ephraim. His mother was a widow. Her name was Zeruah. 27 This happened when Jeroboam started to fight against the king. Solomon had built the Millo on top of the wall of the city of David, (who was) his father. 28 Jeroboam was an important man. And Solomon saw that the young man (Jeroboam) did his work very well. So, Solomon made him the leader of all the workers from the tribe of Joseph. 29 At that time, Jeroboam went out from Jerusalem. He met Ahijah who was a prophet from Shiloh. (Ahijah) was wearing a new coat. They were both alone, in the country (fields). 30 Then Ahijah took off the new coat that he was wearing. He tore it into 12 pieces. 31 Then he said to Jeroboam, 'Take 10 pieces for yourself, because the LORD, the God of Israel, is saying (to you), "I will tear the kingdom away from Solomon and I will give you 10 tribes. 32 But for two reasons (Solomon) will have one tribe:

- I promised something to David.

- I have chosen Jerusalem.

33 I will do this because (Solomon) has gone away from me. He has worshipped Ashtoreth, (who is) the female god of the people in Sidon. (He has also worshipped) Chemosh, (who is) the god of the people in Moab. (He has worshipped) Molech, (who is) the god of the people in Ammon. (Solomon) has not lived in my ways. He has not done what I see to be right. He has not obeyed my words or my rules. David, (who was) Solomon's father, (obeyed all my words). 34 But I will not take all the kingdom away from Solomon. I have made him ruler (of Israel) for all of his life. That is because of my promise to David, (who was) my servant. I chose (David) and he obeyed all my words and my rules. 35 I will take the kingdom away from his son and I will give 10 tribes to you. 36 I will give one tribe to his son. So my servant David will always have a light in front of me in Jerusalem. (Jerusalem) is the city where I chose to put my Name. 37 But I will do this to you. I will take you (from Jerusalem). You will rule everything that you want (to rule). You will be the king of Israel. 38 But you must do everything that I order you (to do). You must live in my ways. You must do what I see to be right. You must obey my words and my rules, as my servant David did. If you do that, I will (always) be near to you. I will build for you a family that will continue as long as David's family. I will give Israel to you. 39 David's family will think that they are not important because of this. But it will not always be like this." ' 40 Solomon tried to kill Jeroboam, but Jeroboam ran away to Egypt. He went to Shishak (who was) the king (of Egypt). And he stayed there until Solomon died.

Solomon dies

41 Other things happened while Solomon was king. They are all are in the Book about Solomon. It includes his wisdom and everything that he did.

42 Solomon ruled all Israel from Jerusalem for 40 years. 43 Then he rested with his ancestors. People buried him in the city of his father, David. And his son Rehoboam was king after him.

Chapter 12

Rehoboam, king of Judah

1 Rehoboam went to Shechem, because all the Israelites had gone there to make him king. 2 Now Jeroboam, (who was the son of Nebat), was still in Egypt. He had gone there when he ran away from King Solomon. But Jeroboam returned from Egypt when he heard (about Rehoboam).

3 Then (the Israelites) sent a message to Jeroboam. They wanted him to come to them. And (Jeroboam) and all the Israelites went to Rehoboam. They said to Rehoboam, 4 'Your father caused us to work too much. Now, make it easier for us. If you make our work easier, we will be your servants.' 5 Rehoboam answered them, 'Go away for three days. Then come back to me.' So the people went away.

6 Then King Rehoboam went to some older men. They had helped his father Solomon, when he was alive. 'What answer should I give to these (Israelites)?' he asked. 7 They said to him, 'If you are like a servant to them today, (they will always be your servants). If you speak kindly to them, they will always work for you.' 8 But Rehoboam did not believe what these older men said. He talked about it to some younger men. They had always been with him and they were his servants. 9 He said to them, 'What do you think that I should do? What answer should we give to the people who say (this) to me? "Make our work easier than your father made it." ' 10 (These young men) had always been with Rehoboam. The young men said, 'Say this to the people who said (these things) to you. "Your father caused us to do work that was not easy. Now make our work easier." Say to them, "My little finger is thicker than my father's body. 11 My father gave you work that was not easy. I will make it even less easy. My father hit you with whips, but I will hit you with snakes." '

12 Jeroboam and all the people returned to Rehoboam three days after that. That was because the king had said, 'Return to me in three days.' 13 The king spoke words that were not kind to the people. He did not say what the older men had wanted him to say. 14 He said what the young men had suggested. 'My father gave you work that was not easy. I will make it even less easy. My father hit you with whips, but I will hit you with snakes!' 15 So the king did not do what the (Israelites) wanted him to do. Really, the LORD caused this to happen. He had said what would happen in his words to Jeroboam the son of Nebat. Ahijah who was from Shiloh (told them to Jeroboam).

16 Then all the Israelites saw that the king would not listen to them. So they said to the king,

'We do not want to be a part of David's (country).

We do not want to belong to Jesse's son.

Israelites, go to your homes!

Now, David's son, you can rule your own people!'

So all the Israelites went home.

17 But Rehoboam still ruled the people that lived in the towns in Judah. 18 A man called Adoniram told the workers what they should do. Rehoboam sent him (to do this). But the Israelites threw stones at him and he died. But Rehoboam, (who was with him,) got into his chariot. He was able to get to Jerusalem. 19 So the people that live in Israel have been against the family of David until now. 20 All the Israelites heard that Jeroboam had returned. They all met together and they asked (Jeroboam) to come to them. They made him king over all Israel. Only the tribe of Judah still remained with the house of David.

21 Rehoboam arrived back in Jerusalem. He brought all the people that lived in Judah and Benjamin together. There were 180 000 of them that could fight. (Rehoboam) wanted to start a war against Israel. He wanted to get back (the tribes in the north of) Israel for himself. (He was) Rehoboam, (who was) the son of Solomon.

22 Then this word of God came to Shemaiah. (Shemaiah) was a servant of God. 23 'Say this to Rehoboam (who is) the son of Solomon. (Solomon was) the king of Judah. Say it to everybody in Judah and in Benjamin. Say it also to everybody else. 24 This is what the LORD is saying. "Do not fight against the Israelites, (who are like) your brothers. Go home, everybody. What is happening is what I want to happen." ' So they obeyed the word of the LORD. They went home again because the LORD said it.

Jeroboam, king of Israel

25 Then Jeroboam made Shechem into a strong (city). He lived there, in the hills of Ephraim. Then he went to (the city called) Penuel and he made it stronger.

26 Jeroboam thought inside himself, 'Now, almost certainly, the kingdom will go back to the family of David. 27 The people (from the north) will go to Jerusalem. They will offer sacrifices there in the temple of the LORD. They will become servants (again) of their lord, Rehoboam. He is the king of Judah. They will kill me and they will go back to King Rehoboam.' 28 (Jeroboam) asked (some people) what he should do. Then, the king (Jeroboam) made two young cows out of gold. He said to the people (that he ruled), 'It is too difficult for you to go up to Jerusalem. (These young cows) are your gods, people of Israel. They brought you up out of Egypt.' 29 He put one young cow in Bethel and he put the other (young cow) in Dan. 30 But that became a sin. Some people went as far as Dan to worship the (young cow) that was there! 31 (Jeroboam) also built places on hills where people could worship (gods). He made priests from many tribes. Many of them were not Levites. 32 (Jeroboam) started a special day on the 15th day of the 8th month. That was like the special day that they had in Judah. But he offered sacrifices in Bethel to the young cows that he had made. He also put priests into the places on hills (where people could worship gods). 33 (Jeroboam) chose the 8th month in his own mind. On the 15th day of that month, he offered sacrifices on the altar that he had made at Bethel. So (Jeroboam) started a special day for the Israelites. They went to the altar (at Bethel or Dan) to offer (their sacrifices to their gods).

Chapter 13

A man that is God's servant visits Jeroboam

1 The LORD ordered a man that was God's servant to go from Judah to Bethel. He came (to Bethel) while Jeroboam was standing by the altar. (Jeroboam) was ready to burn something with a nice smell. 2 (God's servant) shouted loudly against the altar. (He did it) by the word of the LORD. (He shouted), 'Altar! Altar! This is what the LORD is saying (to you). "A son called Josiah will be born in the family of David. He will burn the priests on you, (altar). (They are the priests that work) in the high places. They are offering sacrifices here now. (Josiah) will burn human bones on you!" ' 3 The same day, God's servant (said what else would happen). (He said that) it would be like a sign. 'This is the sign that the LORD has given (to you). (You will see) the altar break in its middle. The ashes on it will pour out.' 4 Jeroboam heard what God's servant shouted loudly against the altar at Bethel. Then (Jeroboam) took his hand away from the altar (and he pointed it at God's servant). 'Hold that man', he said. But after he pointed with his hand, he could not move his arm! He could not pull it back. 5 Also, the altar did break in its middle. And ashes did pour out, as God's servant had said. This was the sign that the word of the LORD gave (to Jeroboam). 6 Then the king said to God's servant, 'Pray for me. (Pray) to the LORD (who is) your God. Pray that my hand will become well again.' So God's servant prayed to the LORD. And the king's hand became well again, as it was before. 7 Then the king said to God's servant, 'Come (to my) home with me. Have something to eat. Then I will give you a gift.' 8 But God's servant said to the king, 'You might give to me half of what is yours. But still I would not go with you! I would not eat bread and I would not drink water here. 9 (That is because) I was sent here by the word of the LORD. (He said), "You must not eat bread or drink water (there). You must not return on the same road that you came on." ' 10 So God's servant returned by another road. He did not go on the road by which he came to Bethel.

The old prophet in Bethel

11 Now a certain old prophet lived in Bethel. And his son came (to him). And he told (the old prophet) everything that God's servant had done there that day. (His sons also) told their father what (God's servant) had said to the king. 12 Their father asked (his sons), 'Which way did (God's servant) go?' And his sons told him on which road God's servant from Judah had gone. 13 Then (the old prophet) said to his sons, 'Get my donkey ready (for me to ride).' When they had got ready the donkey, (the old prophet) got on to it.

14 Then he rode after God's servant. He found (God's servant), who was sitting under an oak tree. He asked him, 'Are you the servant of God from Judah?' 'I am', (God's servant) replied.

15 The (old) prophet said to him, 'Come (to my) home with me and eat.' 16 God's servant said, 'I cannot come with you. I must not go back (to Bethel). I cannot eat bread or drink water with you in that country. 17 The word of the LORD told me, "You must not eat bread or drink water there. You must not return by the way in which you came." ' 18 The old prophet answered, 'I, too, am a prophet like you. But an angel said to me, by the word of the LORD, "Bring him back with you to your house. There, he can eat bread and drink water." ' But what the (old prophet) said was not true. 19 So God's servant went with him. And he ate and drank in his house.

20 They were sitting together at the table, when the word of the LORD came to the old prophet. (He was the old prophet) that had brought (God's servant) back. 21 (The old prophet) said to the servant of God who had come from Judah, 'This is what the LORD is saying. You have not obeyed the word of the LORD. You have not done what the LORD your God ordered you to do. 22 You came here. He said to you, 'You must not eat bread or drink water in that place.' But you ate bread and you drank water here. As a result, they will not bury your body in the same place as (they buried) your fathers' body.' 23 God's servant finished his food and his drink. Then the prophet, who had brought him back, made his donkey ready for him. 24 But when he went on his journey, a lion met him on the road. (The lion) killed him and it threw his body down onto the road. Then, both the donkey and the lion stood by the dead body. 25 Some people, who passed it, saw the dead body. It lay on the road. The lion stood by the dead body. They went and reported it in the city. The old prophet lived (in that city).

26 That was the (old) prophet who had brought (God's servant) back from his journey. When he heard about it, he said, 'It is the servant of God who did not obey the word of the LORD. The LORD has given him to the lion. The lion has attacked him and it has killed him. The word of the LORD had told him that there would be danger.' 27 The (old) prophet said to his sons, 'Make my donkey ready for me (to ride).' So they did (what he had asked them to do). 28 Then (the old prophet) went and he found the body. It lay on the road. The donkey and the lion stood by it. The lion had not eaten the body and it had not attacked the donkey. 29 So the (old) prophet put the body of God's servant on to the donkey. And he brought it back to his own city. There, he was sad about it. Then (he decided to) bury it. 30 He buried the body in the place that he had made for his own dead body. They were (all) sad about it, and they said, 'Oh! My dear friend!'31 When they had buried him, (the old prophet) said to his sons, 'When I die, bury me in the same place. Put me where (we buried) the servant of God. Lay my bones by his bones. 32 This is why (you must do it). Certainly the message that (God's servant) brought will become true. (The message that he brought) was by the word of the LORD. It was against the altar in Bethel. It was also against all the altars on the high places in the towns in Samaria.'

33 Even after this, Jeroboam did not stop doing bad things. He made more priests for the high places from all kinds of people. Anybody who wanted to be a priest, (Jeroboam) made into a priest for the high places.34 This was a big sin in the family of Jeroboam. And that is why it did not continue. (God) destroyed it from the whole earth.

Chapter 14

The prophet Ahijah and King Jeroboam

1 Jeroboam's son was called Abijah. At that time, (Abijah) became ill. 2 So Jeroboam said to his wife, 'Cause yourself to seem different so people will not recognise you as the wife of Jeroboam. Then go to Shiloh. Ahijah the prophet is there. He told me that I would rule the people (of Israel). 3 Take 10 loaves of bread with you. Also (take) some cakes and a jar of honey. Then go to (Ahijah). He will tell you what will happen to the boy.' 4 So Jeroboam's wife did what he said (to her). She went to Ahijah's house in Shiloh. Ahijah could not see because he was very old. 5 But the LORD had said to Ahijah, 'Jeroboam's wife will come to you. She will ask you about her son, who is ill. You must give her the answer (that I tell you). She will (soon) arrive. Then, she will say that she is somebody else.'

6 So, when Ahijah heard the sound of her feet on the ground, he said, 'Come in, Jeroboam's wife! You need not cause yourself to seem like somebody else. (The LORD) has given me bad news for you. 7 Go and tell this to Jeroboam. It is what the LORD, the God of Israel, says (to you). I chose you out of (all) the people and I made you the leader of my people, Israel. 8 I tore the kingdom away from the house of David. I gave the kingdom to you, but you have not been like my servant David. (David) obeyed my rules. He always tried to obey me as much as he could. He always did what was right in my mind.

9 But you have done more really bad things than all (the people) that lived before you. You have made other gods for yourself.

You have made idols with metal. You have made me very angry. You have done to me like when someone throws something (away), behind his back. 10 Because of this, I will destroy the house of Jeroboam. I will kill every male from the (house of) Jeroboam, whether they are slaves or free men. I will take away the house of Jeroboam. It will be like when people sweep away dung. Everything will go! 11 Dogs will eat any of Jeroboam's (family) that die in the city (of Jerusalem). The birds (that fly) in the air will eat those that die in the country (places). This is what the LORD has said! 12 But you, (Jeroboam's wife,) go back home. The boy will die when your feet reach the city.

13 All Israel will cry because of him and they will bury him. He is the only person from Jeroboam's family that they will bury. He is the only person in the house of Jeroboam that Israel's God, the LORD, has found anything good in. 14 The LORD will choose for himself a king of Israel. (That king) will destroy the family of Jeroboam. It will start now, yes, even today! 15 Also, the LORD will hit (the country of) Israel. It will move like a thin plant that is growing in a stream. (The LORD) will take Israel away from this good country that he gave to their ancestors. He will move them beyond the River (Euphrates). (That is because) they made the LORD very angry. (They did that) when they made Asherah poles. 16 (And the LORD) will give Israel (to its enemies) because of Jeroboam's sin. Also, it is because Jeroboam caused Israel's people to sin.'

17 Then Jeroboam's wife stood up. She left (the house) and she went to Tirzah. When she walked through the door of (her) house, the boy died. 18 They buried him and all Israel cried about his death. This is what the LORD had said (would happen) by his servant the prophet Ahijah.

19 There is a book with reports about the kings of Israel. They wrote about everything else that King Jeroboam did, (in this book). (It includes) his wars. And (it includes) how he ruled (his people).20 (Jeroboam) was king for 22 years. Then he died (and they buried him) with his ancestors. His son Nadab was king after him.

Rehoboam dies

21 Rehoboam (was) the son of Solomon. He was the king of Judah. He was 41 years old when he became king. He ruled 17 years in Jerusalem. (Jerusalem) was the city that the LORD had chosen out of all the tribes of Israel. The LORD put his Name (in Jerusalem). Rehoboam's mother was called Naamah. She came from the country called Ammon. 22 (The people in) Judah did what the LORD did not like. Their sins made the LORD angrier than the sins of their ancestors had done. 23 They also had made high places for themselves. They had put Asherah poles on every high hill and under every big tree. 24 There were even temples where men could have sex with other men for money in (Judah). The people did all these very bad things. They were the things that the people did before the Israelites came. God had killed all (those people).

25 After Rehoboam had been king for 5 years, Shishak attacked Jerusalem. (Shishak) was the king of Egypt. 26 (Shishak) took away the valuable things from the temple of the LORD. He also (took) the valuable things from the king's palace. He took away everything. That includes the shields that Solomon had made with gold. 27 So Rehoboam made shields with bronze. His soldiers used these instead (of the shields of gold). (The soldiers) stood at the door of the king's palace to keep out enemies. 28 Every time that the king went to the LORD's temple, the soldiers carried the shields. After that, they took them back to the room where they stored them.

29 There is a book with reports about the kings of Judah. People wrote in it everything that King Rehoboam did. 30 There was always a war between Rehoboam and Jeroboam. 31 So Rehoboam died and they buried him with his ancestors in the City of David. (Rehoboam's) mother's name was Naamah. She came from the country called Ammon. Then, (Rehoboam's) son Abijam became king after him.

Chapter 15

Abijam, king of Judah

1 Abijam became king of Judah. This happened after Jeroboam had been king of Israel for nearly 18 years. Jeroboam was the son of Nebat. 2 (Abijam) was king in Jerusalem for three years. His mother's name was Maacah. She was the daughter of Abishalom. 3 Abijam did all the sins that his father had done before him. He was not a good servant of the LORD (who was) his God. David, his father's grandfather, had been a good servant (of God).

4 But the LORD his God gave (Abijam) a light in Jerusalem. (That was) because of what (God) had promised to David.

So God made Jerusalem strong. He also gave (Abijam) a son (to be king) after him. 5 David had always done what the LORD wanted him to do. David had obeyed the LORD's rules all his life. The only time that he did not do that was about Uriah. Uriah came from the people called the Hittites. 6 There was war between Rehoboam and Jeroboam for all (Abijam's) life.

7 There is a book with reports about the kings of Judah. People wrote in it everything that King Abijam did. There was war between Abijam and Jeroboam.

8 So Abijam died and they buried him with his ancestors in the City of David. Then, (Abijam's) son Asa became king after him.

Asa, king of Judah

9 Asa became king of Judah when Jeroboam had been king of Israel for nearly 20 years. 10 And Asa was king in Jerusalem for 41 years. His grandmother's name was Maacah. She was the daughter of Abishalom.11 And Asa did what his father David had done. Asa did what the LORD wanted him to do. 12 He sent away from the temple the men that had sex with other men for money. (He sent them) away from (Judah). And he destroyed all the idols that his father had made. 13 He even told his grandmother Maacah that she could not continue to call herself 'Queen Mother'. (This was) because she had made (one of the) bad Asherah poles. Asa cut the (Asherah) pole down and he burned it in the Kidron Valley. 14 Asa loved the LORD for all his life. But he did not remove the high places. 15 He brought into the temple silver and gold. He also brought things that he and his father had made special (for God).

16 There was a war between Asa and King Baasha of Israel. It continued all the time that they ruled their countries. 17 Baasha, the king of Israel, attacked Judah. He made (the town called) Ramah very strong. As a result, nobody could go in to or leave the country of Asa, king of Judah. 18 So Asa took all the silver and the gold that they stored in his palace and in the LORD's temple. He gave it to his servants and he sent them to Ben-hadad. He was the king of Aram, who ruled in (the capital city called) Damascus. Ben-hadad's father was Tabrimmon and his grandfather was Hezion. 19 (Asa sent) this message (to Ben-hadad). 'We should agree together, as our fathers agreed together. Look! I am sending you a gift of silver and gold. Do not now help Baasha, (who is) the king of Israel. So (maybe) he will leave my (country).'20 And Ben-hadad did agree with King Asa. He sent his army with its leaders against the towns in Israel. He beat Ijon, Dan, Abel-beth-maacah, all Kinnereth and also Naphtali. 21 When Baasha heard this, he did not build again in Ramah. He (brought his army) back to Tirzah. 22 Then King Asa said that everyone in Judah must do this. They must carry away everything that Baasha was using in Ramah. (This included) stones and wood. King Asa used them to make Geba in Benjamin strong and also Mizpah.

23 There is a book with reports about the kings of Judah. In it, people have written everything that happened during Asa's time.

In the book are these things:

- everything that he did

- the (wars) that he fought

- the cities that he built.

24 So Asa died and they buried him with his ancestors in the City of David. Then, (Asa's) son Jehoshaphat became king after him.

Nadab, king of Israel

25 When Asa had been king of Judah for two years, Nadab the son of Jeroboam became king of Israel. (Nadab) was king of Israel for two years. 26 He did what the LORD did not like. He did what his father had done. He did the same sins as his (father had done). And he caused Israel's people to do them also.

27 Baasha (was) the son of Ahijah. He came from the big family of Issachar. He decided to kill (Nadab).

He did kill him at a town in Philistia called Gibbethon. (This was) while Nadab and (his army from) Israel were attacking (Gibbethon). 28 When Asa had been king of Judah for nearly three years, Baasha killed Nadab. Baasha became king (of Israel) after (Nadab). 29 Immediately after (Baasha) became king, he killed all Jeroboam's family.

He did not leave anybody in Jeroboam's (family) alive. He killed them all. The LORD had said that it would happen. He said it by his servant Ahijah who was from Shiloh. 30 (That was) because of Jeroboam's sins. Also, it was because he had caused Israel's people to do the same sins. This had made the LORD God of Israel very angry.

31 There is a book with reports about the kings of Israel. This book tells about when Nadab was king. It tells about what he did. And it tells about everything else that happened then.

32 There was war between Asa and Baasha, king of Israel, all the time that they ruled (their countries).

Baasha, king of Israel

33 When Asa had been king in Judah for nearly three years, Baasha became the king of all Israel. Baasha was the son of Ahijah. It happened in Tirzah. (Baasha) was king for 24 years. 34 (Baasha) did what the LORD did not like. He did all the sins that Jeroboam did. He had caused Israel's people to do them also.

Chapter 16

1 Then (God) spoke to Jehu (who was) the son of Hanani. The LORD's words were against Baasha. 2 'You were not important, but I made you the leader of my people Israel. But then you did all the bad things that Jeroboam did! Also, you caused my people Israel to sin and you made me very angry because of their sins. 3 As a result, I will take away completely Baasha and his family. I will make the family of Baasha like that of Jeroboam the son of Nebat. 4 Dogs will eat (the dead bodies) of Baasha's family if they die in the city. Some of them will die in country places. The birds (that fly) in the air will eat (the dead bodies of) those people.'

5 There is a book with reports about the kings of Israel. This book tells about when Baasha was king. It tells about what he did. And it tells about everything else that happened then.

6 Baasha died as his ancestors (had died). They buried him in Tirzah. Then (Baasha's) son Elah became king after him. 7 The word of the LORD had come by the prophet Jehu. (Jehu) was the son of Hanani. (The word) came to Baasha and to the family of Baasha. It came because of all the bad things that he had done. He had done what the LORD did not like. (Baasha) had made the LORD very angry by the things that he had done. (The family of Baasha) had become like the family of Jeroboam. The word also came because Baasha had destroyed (the family of Jeroboam).

Elah, king of Israel

8 Elah, the son of Baasha, became king of Israel. (This happened) when Asa had been king of Judah for nearly 26 years. Now (Elah) was king in Tirzah for two years. 9 Zimri was the leader of half of (Elah's) chariots. (Zimri) decided to kill (Elah). Elah was in Tirzah, in the home of (a man called) Arza. (Elah) was drinking too much alcohol. (Arza) said what people must do in (Elah's) palace in Tirzah. 10 Zimri came in (to where Elah was). He hit Elah and he killed him. At this time, Asa had been king of Judah for nearly 27 years. So (Zimri) made himself king instead of (Elah). 11 When Zimri became king on the throne (of Israel), he immediately killed everybody in Baasha's family. He killed every male in the family and (he killed) every friend (of Baasha). 12 So Zimri killed everybody in Baasha's family. The word of the LORD had said that this would happen. The prophet Jehu had spoken (what the LORD had said) against Baasha. 13 (The LORD had said this) because of all the sins that Baasha and his son Elah had done. Also, they had caused Israel's people to do them. Their idols, which had no value, had made the LORD, the God of Israel, very angry. 14 There is a book with reports about the kings of Israel. This book tells about when Elah was king. It tells about what he did. And it tells about everything else that happened then.

Zimri, king of Israel

15 Zimri was king (of Israel) in Tirzah for (only) 7 days. Asa had been king of Judah for nearly 27 years (when this happened).

The army (of Israel) was near a town in Philistia called Gibbethon. 16 The army of Israel heard about what Zimri had done.

(Zimri) had decided to kill the king (Elah) and he had done it. Omri was the leader of the army (of Israel). The army made Omri king of Israel on that day, while they were (in Gibbethon). 17 Then Omri left Gibbethon. All (the army of) Israel left with him. (Omri and his army) attacked Tirzah. 18 Zimri saw that (Omri) had taken the city (Tirzah) from him. So he went into the king's palace, where it was (still) safe. He lit a fire which burned down the palace all round him. So (Zimri) died, 19 because of all the sins that he had done. He had done what the LORD did not like. He had copied the ways of Jeroboam. He had done the sins that Jeroboam had done. Also, he had caused Israel's people to do them. 20 There is a book with reports about the kings of Israel. In it are all the other things that Zimri did. It includes the way that he killed (Baasha's family).

Omri, king of Israel

21 There were two groups of people in Israel. Half (of the people) wanted Tibni, (who was) the son of Ginath, to be the king. The other half wanted Omri (to be the king). 22 But the half that wanted Omri (to be the king) was stronger than the other half. (After 4 years), Tibni (who was) the son of Ginath, died. Then Omri became the king (of Israel). 23 Omri became king of Israel when Asa had been king of Judah for nearly 31 years. (Omri) ruled the people for 12 years. He was in Tirzah for 6 of these years. 24 (Omri) bought a hill called Samaria from Shemer. He paid two talents of silver for it. He built a city on the hill and he called the city Samaria. That was because he bought the hill from Shemer. 25 But Omri did what the LORD did not like. He sinned more than all (the kings of Israel) before him. 26 He did all the bad things that Jeroboam the son of Nebat had done. He did all the sins which (Jeroboam) had caused Israel's people to do. This made the LORD, the God of Israel, very angry, because of the idols which were worth nothing. 27 There is a book with reports about the kings of Israel. This book tells about when Omri was king. It tells about what he did. And it tells about everything else that happened then. 28 So Omri died and they buried him with his ancestors in Samaria. His son Ahab became king (of Israel) after him.

Ahab becomes king of Israel

29 Ahab, (who was) the son of Omri, became king of Israel. Asa had been king of Judah for nearly 38 years (when that happened). Ahab was king of Israel in Samaria for 22 years. 30 Omri's son, Ahab, did more things that the LORD did not like than any of those (kings) before him. 31 He did not think that it was a bad thing to do the same sins as Jeroboam the son of Nebat. So he did something that was even worse. He married Jezebel, who was the daughter of Ethbaal. (Ethbaal) was the king of Sidon. (Ahab) became the servant of Baal and he began to worship him. 32 (Ahab) built a temple for Baal in Samaria. He made an altar for Baal in this (temple). 33 Ahab also made an Asherah pole. He did more things to make the LORD, the God of Israel, angry than all the kings of Israel before him. 34 While Ahab was king (of Israel), Hiel built Jericho again. (Hiel lived) in Bethel. His first son, called Abiram, died when he started to build (Jericho). And his youngest son, called Segub, died when he built the gates (of Jericho). This agreed with the word of the LORD by Joshua, the son of Nun.

Chapter 17

Ravens feed Elijah

1 Elijah came from (a place called) Tishbe in Gilead. (So, Elijah was) a Tishbite. (Elijah) said to Ahab, 'I am a servant of the LORD, (who is) the God of Israel. As surely (as God) is alive, no water will appear on the ground during the night in the next few years. And it will not rain. I will say when it will rain. It will not rain until then.' 2 Then, the word of the LORD came to Elijah. 3 (The LORD said), 'Leave here! Go to the east. And hide by the stream called Cherith, east of the (River) Jordan. 4 You will drink (water) from the stream and the ravens will feed you there. I have said to (them) that they must do this.' 5 So (Elijah) obeyed the word of the LORD. He went. And he lived by the stream called Cherith, east of the (River) Jordan. 6 The ravens brought him bread and meat in the morning and bread and meat in the evening. He drank (water) from the stream.

The widow at Zarephath

7 There was no rain in the country (Israel), so the stream became dry after a time.

8 Then the word of the LORD came (again) to (Elijah). 9 'Go immediately to Zarephath (which is) near Sidon. Stay there. I have said to a widow there that she must supply you with food.'

10 So (Elijah) went to Zarephath. When he came to the town gate, he met a widow. She was getting some small sticks. (Elijah) spoke to her and he asked her, 'Please bring me some water in a jar, so that I can drink (it).' 11 While she was getting it, he said (also), 'And bring me, please, a bit of bread.' 12 She replied, 'As surely as your God is alive, I do not have any bread. I have only a small amount of flour in a jar. I have also a small amount of oil (to cook with). I am getting a few small sticks to take home. Then I will make a meal for myself and for my son. We will eat it. Then we will die (because there is no more food).' 13 Elijah said to her, 'Do not be afraid. Go home. And do what you have said. But first, make a small cake of bread for me. Use what you have got (to make it). Then bring it to me. And (after) that, make something for yourself and for your son.14 This is what the LORD, the God of Israel, says. "You will not use all the flour in your jar. You will not use all the oil (that you cook with). Before (you use them all), the LORD will give rain to the country (called Israel)." ' 15 Then (the widow) went away. And she did what Elijah had asked her to do. And after that, there was food every day for Elijah and for the widow and her family. 16 (She did not) use all the flour in the jar and she did not use all the oil. And that is what Elijah had promised. He did it when he spoke the word of the LORD.

17 Sometime after that, the son of the woman who had the house became ill. He became worse and worse until he died. 18 (The woman) said to Elijah, 'Servant of God, why have you done this to me? Did you come to cause me to think about my sins? (Did you come) to kill my son?' 19 'Give your son to me', Elijah replied. He took (her son) from her arms. (Elijah) carried him upstairs, to the room where he was staying. (Elijah) put (the widow's son) on to his bed. 20 Then (Elijah) prayed this to the LORD. 'LORD, (you are) my God! Did you cause this sad thing to happen to this widow? Did you cause the son of the woman that I am staying with to die?' 21 Then (Elijah) lay on the boy three times. (Elijah) prayed (this) to the LORD. 'LORD, (you are) my God! Cause this boy's life to return to him!' 22 The LORD heard Elijah when he prayed (to God). The boy's life returned to him. He was alive again! 23 Elijah picked up the boy and he carried him downstairs. He took (the boy) from his room into the house. He gave (the boy) to his mother and he said, 'Look! Your son is alive!' 24 Then the woman said to Elijah, 'Now I know that God (sent) you. The word of the LORD that you speak is really true.'

Chapter 18

Elijah and Obadiah

1 Three years after that, the word of the LORD came to Elijah. 'Go and meet Ahab. Then, I will send rain on to the land (in Israel).' 2 So Elijah went to meet Ahab. It was a time when there was almost no food for the people in Samaria to eat. 3 Ahab had asked Obadiah to meet him. (Obadiah) was the leader (of the servants) in (Ahab's) palace. Obadiah was really afraid of the LORD (in a good way). 4 Jezebel had killed (many of) the LORD's prophets. While she was doing this, Obadiah had hidden 100 prophets. He had put them in two caves, 50 in each cave. Also he had supplied them with food and water. 5 Ahab had said to Obadiah, 'Go through all the country (called Israel). (Go to) all the valleys and to places where there is (usually) water. Maybe we can find some grass to feed the horses and other animals. If we do, we will not have to kill (all) our animals.' 6 So Ahab and Obadiah went through the country (called Israel). Ahab went in one direction and Obadiah went in another (direction).

7 While Obadiah was walking along, Elijah met him. Obadiah recognised (Elijah) and he bent in front of him. (Obadiah) said, 'Is it really you, my lord Elijah?' 8 'Yes!' Elijah replied. 'Go. And tell your master that Elijah is here.' 9 'Have I done something (that is) wrong?' Obadiah asked. 'Is that why you are sending (me), your servant, to Ahab? (Ahab) will certainly kill me! 10 As surely as the LORD your God lives, my master (Ahab) has sent people to look for you (everywhere). Every country and kingdom has said that you were not there. He caused them all to say it. It really was true that you were not there. 11 But now you want me to go to my master. And you want me to say, "Elijah is here!" 12 I do not know where the (Holy) Spirit of the LORD will carry you next. (Where will you go) when I leave you? I may go to tell Ahab where you are. But if he does not find you, he will kill me. I am your servant. I have worshipped the LORD since I was a young man. 13 Have you not heard what I have done? While Jezebel was killing the prophets of the LORD, I hid 100 of the LORD's prophets in two caves. (I put) 50 (prophets) in each cave. And I supplied them with food and water. 14 And now you want me to go to my master. And you want me to say, "Elijah is here!" He will kill me!' 15 Elijah said, 'I am the LORD's servant. As (certainly) as he is alive and powerful, I will surely show myself to Ahab today.'

Elijah and the prophets of Baal

16 So Obadiah went to meet Ahab. He told Ahab (where Elijah was.) And Ahab went to meet Elijah.17 When Ahab saw Elijah, he said to him, 'Is that (really) you? (You are) the person that is bringing trouble to Israel.'

18 'I have not brought trouble to Israel', Elijah replied. 'You and your father's family have (done that). You threw away the LORD's rules. Instead, you have become servants of the Baals. 19 Now, fetch people from all over Israel. (Say that they must) meet me. They must meet me on the hill called Carmel. Also, bring the 450 prophets of Baal and the 400 prophets of Asherah, who eat with Jezebel at her table.'

20 So Ahab sent the message through all Israel. He brought the (false) prophets to the hill called Carmel.21 Elijah stood up in front of the people and he said, 'You should not have two ideas still about what you should do. If the LORD is God, worship him. If Baal is God, worship him.' But the people said nothing.22 Then Elijah said to them, 'I am the only prophet of the LORD that is still (here). Baal has 450 prophets.23 Fetch two male cows for us. (The prophets of Baal) can choose one for themselves. Then they should cut it into pieces and they should put it on the wood (on the altar). But they must not light the fire. I will prepare the other male cow and I will put it on the wood (on the altar). I will not light the fire. 24 Then, you pray to your god (Baal) and I will pray to the LORD. The god who sends fire for an answer, (that god,) he is God!' Then all the people said, 'What you say is good.'

25 Elijah said to the prophets of Baal, 'Choose one of the male cows. Prepare it first, because there are so many of you. Pray to your god, but do not light the fire.' 26 So (the prophets of Baal) took their male cow and they prepared it (for the altar). Then they prayed to Baal from morning until noon. 'Baal, answer us!' they shouted. But there was no answer; nobody replied. And they all danced badly round the altar that they had made. 27 At noon, Elijah began to laugh at them. 'Shout louder!' he said. 'He is a god! Maybe he is thinking (about something). Or (maybe) he is busy (in the bathroom), or he is away (from home) on a journey. (Or) maybe he is asleep and you must wake him up!' 28 So they (all) shouted louder. And they cut themselves with swords and knives, as they often did. Soon, there was blood everywhere. 29 They continued what they were doing through the afternoon. They did it until the time came for the evening sacrifice. But nothing happened. Nobody answered (them). None (of the false gods) replied.

30 Then Elijah said to all the people, 'Come here, (near) to me.' When they came, (Elijah) mended the altar of the LORD. (Somebody) had broken it into small pieces. 31 Elijah found 12 stones, one for each of the tribes that Jacob's sons started. (Jacob was the man) to whom the word of the LORD came. It said, 'Your name will be Israel.' 32 (Elijah) built an altar in the name of the LORD with these stones. He dug a hole all round it. (The hole) was big enough to contain 15 litres (4 gallons) of seeds. 33 He put wood on (the altar). He cut the male cow into pieces. Then he put the pieces on to the wood. Then he said to the people, 'Fill 4 large jars with water. Pour it on to the male cow and on to the wood.' 34 'Do it again', he said. So they did it again. 'Do it a third time', he said. So they did it for the third time. 35 The water poured down from the altar. It even filled the hole (that was round the altar).

36 The time came for the (evening) sacrifice. Elijah came to the front (of the altar). He prayed (these words). 'LORD, (you are) the God of Abraham, Isaac and Israel. Cause people to know today that you are (still) God in Israel. (Cause them to know) that I am your servant. I have done all these things because you ordered me to do them. 37 Answer me, LORD, answer me! So these people will know that you, LORD, are (still their) God. And they will know that you have changed their minds back to you again.' 38 Then fire came down from the LORD. It burned the sacrifice, the wood, the stones and the ground (round the altar). It even boiled the water in the hole (round the altar) until it had all gone. 39 When all the people saw this, they fell flat on the ground. They shouted, 'The LORD, he is God! The LORD (really) is God!'40 Then Elijah said, 'Catch the prophets of Baal. Do not let any of them run away!' So they caught them (all) and Elijah brought them down to the Kishon Valley. There, he killed them all.

Elijah waits for rain

41 Then Elijah said to Ahab, 'Go (to where your servants are). Eat and drink there. (Do it quickly), because there is the sound of a lot of rain.' 42 So Ahab went to eat and to drink. But Elijah climbed to the top of Carmel. He bent down to the ground. He put his face between his knees. 43 He said to his servant, 'Go and look towards the sea.' So his servant went and looked. 'There is nothing there', he said (to Elijah). Elijah said (to him) 7 times, 'Go back (and look).' 44 The 7th time, the servant reported, 'A cloud is rising up from the sea. It is as small as a man's hand.' So Elijah said (to him), 'Go and say to Ahab, "Make your chariot ready to go. Then, return down (to Jezreel) before the rain stops you." ' 45 As he said this, the sky became black with clouds. The wind started to blow and heavy rain started. So Ahab rode away to Jezreel. 46 Then the LORD made Elijah strong. Elijah tied his shirt into his belt and he ran in front of Ahab all the way to Jezreel.

Chapter 19

Elijah becomes very sad

1 Then Ahab told Jezebel about everything that Elijah had done. (He told her) how (Elijah) had killed all the prophets (of Baal) with a sword. 2 So Jezebel sent a message to Elijah. 'By this time tomorrow, I will make your life like one of (the prophets of Baal). If I do not, the gods can kill me.' 3 Then Elijah was afraid. He ran away (to save) his life. He came to Beersheba in (the country called) Judah. He left his servant there. 4 (Elijah) himself went into the desert. He travelled for about a day (into the desert). He found a kind of tree called a broom tree there. And he sat down under the tree. There, he prayed that he might die. He said, 'LORD, I have had enough (of this life)! Kill me. I am no better (than the prophets who were) before me.' 5 Then he lay down under the tree and he went to sleep. Soon, an angel touched him and said, 'Get up and eat.' 6 And (Elijah) looked and he saw by his head a cake. (Someone) had baked it on a fire. Also, there was a jar of water. So he ate (the cake) and he drank (the water). Then he lay down again (to sleep). 7 The angel of the LORD came back a second time. He touched (Elijah) and he said (to him), 'Get up and eat (this food). You (must go) on a long journey.' 8 So (Elijah) got up. He ate (the food) and he drank (the water). The food made him strong enough to travel for 40 days and 40 nights to Horeb. (Horeb was) the mountain of God.

The LORD appears to Elijah

9 (Elijah) went into a cave (in Horeb) and he stayed there all night. The word of the LORD came to Elijah. 'Elijah, what (are) you (doing) here?' 10 Elijah replied, 'I have always been a very good servant of the LORD, (who is) the powerful God. But the Israelites have thrown away your covenant. They have destroyed your altars. And they have killed your prophets with swords. I am the only prophet (that is) still (alive). Now, they are trying to kill me also.' 11 Then (the LORD) said, 'Go out (from the cave) and stand in front of the LORD, on the mountain. The LORD will pass in front of you.' Then a very strong and powerful wind tore the mountains into pieces. It broke the rocks in front of the LORD. But the LORD was not in the wind. After the wind, there was an earthquake. But the LORD was not in the earthquake. 12 After the earthquake, there was a fire. But the LORD was not in the fire. And after the fire, he heard someone who was speaking very, very quietly. 13 When Elijah heard (that), he put his coat over his face. He went out and he stood at the way into the cave. Then a voice said to him, 'Elijah, what (are) you (doing) here?' 14 (Elijah) said, 'I have always been a very good servant of the LORD, (who is) the powerful God. But the Israelites have thrown away your covenant. They have destroyed your altars. They have killed your prophets with swords. I am the only prophet (that is) still (alive). Now, they are trying to kill me also.'

15 The LORD said to (Elijah), 'Go back again on the way (by which you came). (Go) to the desert (which is) near Damascus. When you arrive, anoint Hazael, to make him king of Aram. 16 Also, anoint Jehu, (who is) the son of Nimshi, to make him king of Israel. Then, anoint Elisha, (who is) the son of Shaphat, to be a prophet after you. (Elisha comes from) Abel Meholah. 17 Jehu will kill anybody that the sword of Hazael does not kill. Then, Elisha will kill anybody that the sword of Jehu does not kill. 18 But there are still 7000 people in Israel that have not worshipped Baal. Their mouths have not kissed him.'

Elisha becomes Elijah's servant

19 Then Elijah went away from (Horeb). He found Elisha, (who was) the son of Shaphat. (Elisha) was ploughing with 12 pairs of oxen. (Elisha) himself was driving the 12th pair (of oxen). Elijah went to (Elisha) and he threw his coat over (Elisha). 20 So Elisha left his oxen and he ran after Elijah. (Elisha) said, 'Let me kiss my father and my mother goodbye. Then I will come with you.' 'Go back,' Elijah replied. 'Think about what I have done to you.' 21 So Elisha left Elijah. He went back (home). Then, he took a pair of oxen and he killed them. He burned the plough to cook the meat (from the oxen). He gave it to the people (that were there). They (all) ate (what he gave to them). Then he went to follow Elijah and to become his servant.

Chapter 20

Ben-hadad attacks Samaria

1 Ben-hadad was the king of Aram. He got all his army together. He had 32 princes, with their horses and chariots. Then he went to Samaria. (He put his army) all round it and then he attacked it.

2 He sent people with messages into the city (Samaria). (They came) to Ahab, (who was) the king of Israel. They said (to Ahab), 'This is what Ben-hadad says. 3 "Your silver and your gold are mine. Your children are mine and the best of your wives (are mine)." ' 4 (This is what) the king of Israel answered (him). 'It is as you say, my lord. (You are) the king (of Syria). I, and everything that I have, are yours.' 5 The people with messages came again. They said, 'This is what Ben-hadad says. "I want your silver, your gold, your wives and your children. 6 At this time tomorrow, I will send my officers to look in your palace. They will also (look in) the houses of your officers. They will take everything that is valuable. They will carry it away (with them)." '

7 Then the king of Israel said that all the leaders in (his) country must come to him. He said to them, 'You must know (this). This man wants to cause trouble! I did not refuse when he asked for my wives and my children, my silver and my gold.' 8 The leaders and the people answered (him), 'Do not listen to him. Do not agree to what he demands.' 9 So (the king of Israel) said to the people who brought messages from Ben-hadad, 'Say this to my lord, (who is) king (of Aram). "Your servant will do all that you demanded the first time. But I will not let you do what you demand now." ' So they left (Ahab) and they took the answer back to Ben-hadad. 10 Then Ben-hadad sent another message to Ahab. (He said,) 'I want the gods (to be cruel) to me, if I am not very cruel! And I pray that it will happen! I will leave very little dirt in Samaria. There will not be enough (dirt) to fill the hands of each of my soldiers.' 11 (This was) the king of Israel's answer. 'Say to him, "If you put on a soldier's clothes, do not boast. When you take them off (you may not have anything to boast about)." ' 12 Ben-hadad received this message when he and his princes were drinking (alcohol) in their tents. So he said to his men, 'Prepare to attack!' So they prepared to attack the city (Samaria).

Ahab beats Ben-hadad

13 Then a prophet came to Ahab, (who was) the king of Israel. He said (to Ahab), 'The LORD is saying (this to you). "Look at this very large army! You will beat them today. Then you will know that I am the LORD." ' 14 'But who will do this?' asked Ahab. The prophet answered (Ahab), 'This is what the LORD says. "The young officers among the army leaders will do it." ' 'Who will start the war?' asked (Ahab). The prophet answered (him), 'You will.' 15 So Ahab said that the young officers must come to him. There were 232 of them among the army leaders. Then he brought all the other Israelite (soldiers) together. There were 7000 of them.

16 They went out at noon (to where the enemy's army was). Ben-hadad and his 32 princes were like drunks in their tents. 17 The young officers, from among the army leaders, went out first. Now Ben-hadad had put men to watch (the enemy). They said (to him), 'Men are coming from Samaria.' 18 (Ben-hadad) said, 'If they want to stop the war, catch them alive. If they want to fight, catch them alive.' 19 The young officers, from among the army leaders, marched out of the city (Samaria). The army (marched) behind them. 20 Each (of the soldiers) killed an enemy. When that happened, the soldiers from Aram ran away. The Israelites followed them. But Ben-hadad, (who was) the king of Aram, rode away on his horse. Some of his riders on horses (went) with him. 21 The king of Israel attacked the horses and chariots (of the enemies), and he beat them. Many of (the enemies) died.

22 After (the fight), the prophet came to the king of Israel. He said (to the king), 'See what you must do to make your (country) strong. (Do this), because next spring the king of Aram will attack you again.' 23 Also, (after the fight), some of the king of Aram's leaders spoke to him. 'The gods of (the Israelites) are gods of the hills. That is why (the Israelites) were too strong for us. But if we fight them on flat ground, we will be stronger than them.' 24 Do this. Remove all the princes from the army. Put other leaders (in the army) instead of them. 25 Also you must get an army the same size as the one that you lost. There must be the same number of horses and chariots. We will fight Israel on the flat ground. If we do that, surely, we will be stronger than them.' (Ben-hadad) agreed with them. And he did what they had suggested.

26 The next spring, Ben-hadad brought together his (army of) soldiers from Aram. They went to Aphek to fight against Israel. 27 (Ahab) brought all the Israelite (army) together and he gave enough food to them (for the war). They marched out to meet (the enemies). The tents of the Israelites were like two small groups of goats. The soldiers from Aram covered all the land (because there were so many).

28 A man who was God's servant came to the king of Israel. He told the king, 'This is what the LORD says.

"The men from Aram think that the LORD is a god of the hills.

(They think that) he is not a god of the valleys. But you will know that I am the LORD (of both). You will know that because I will give this very large army to you." ' 29 For 7 days, (the two armies) stayed in their tents, on different sides (of the flat ground). On the 7th day, the war started. The Israelites killed 100 000 soldiers from Aram on one day. (These soldiers) did not have horses. 30 The other (soldiers) ran to the city of Aphek. There, a wall fell on 27 000 of them. Ben-hadad hurried into the city and he hid in a room inside (one of the houses).

31 Some of his leaders said to Ben-hadad, 'We have heard that the kings of the family of Israel are kind (men). We should go to the king of Israel. We will wear short, hairy trousers and we will put ropes (thick pieces of line) on our heads. Maybe (Ahab) will not kill you.' 32 So they put on short hairy trousers. They (made hats out of) thick lines and they put them on their heads. They went to the king of Israel and they said, 'Your servant Ben-hadad says, "Please let me live." ' The king (Ahab) answered, 'Is he still alive? He is (like) my brother.' 33 So the men hoped (that they would get a friendly answer). They answered him quickly. 'Yes! Ben-hadad (is like) your brother', they said. 'Go and fetch him', the king said. When Ben-hadad came out (from Aphek), Ahab got him up into his chariot. 34 (Ben-hadad) said, 'I will give you the cities that my father took from your father. You can have your own markets in Damascus, as my father had in Samaria.' Ahab answered, 'We will agree to do this and you can go (home) a free (man).' So they agreed together, and Ahab let (Ben-hadad) go home.

A prophet brings a message to King Ahab

35 The word of the LORD (ordered) one of the sons of the prophets to say (this) to another prophet. 'Hit me with your stick.' But the man refused. 36 So the prophet said, 'You have not obeyed the LORD, so a lion will kill you. It will happen soon after you leave me.' And after the man went away, a lion did find him. (The lion) killed him. 37 The prophet found another man. He said, 'Hit me, please.' So the man hit him and hurt him. 38 Then the prophet went and he stood by the road. He was waiting for the king (Ahab). He did not seem like a prophet, because he pulled his hat down over his eyes. 39 The king passed the prophet, who shouted to him, 'Your servant went into the worst part of the war. Someone came to me with a soldier of the enemy's army that he had caught. He said, "Do not let this man run away. If he does, you will die. Or you must pay a talent of silver." 40 But your servant was busy. He did several things. While (he did them), the man ran away.' 'That is your problem', the king of Israel said. 'You have said yourself what will happen.' 41 Then the prophet quickly took the hat from his eyes. And the king of Israel recognised that the man was one of the prophets. 42 The (prophet) said to the king, 'This is what the LORD is saying to you. "I decided that a man should die. But you have let him go free. So, it is your life for his life, and your people for his people." ' 43 So the king went to his palace in Samaria. He was angry and he would not speak (to people).

Chapter 21

Naboth's vineyard

1 Naboth lived in a town called Jezreel. He had a vineyard. After (the war with Ben-hadad), this happened. (Naboth's) vineyard was in Jezreel, near to the palace of Ahab, (who was) the king of Samaria. 2 Ahab said to Naboth, 'Give me your vineyard. I want to grow vegetables in it, because it is near to my palace. I will give you a better vineyard for it. Or, maybe, you would rather have its value in money.' 3 Naboth replied to Ahab, 'The LORD will not let me give (the field) to you. My ancestors gave it to me.' 4 So Ahab went to his home. He was angry and he would not speak (to people). (That was) because of what Naboth from Jezreel had said. (He had said,) 'I will not give to you (the field) that my ancestors gave to me.' (Ahab) lay on his bed. He was angry and he would not eat (any food).

5 (Ahab's) wife, (who was called) Jezebel, came in (to Ahab's room). She asked him, 'Why are you so angry? Why will you not eat anything?' 6 Ahab answered her, '(It is) because I said to Naboth from Jezreel, "Sell your vineyard to me. Or, if you would like it better, I will give you another vineyard instead of it." But he said, "I will not give you my vineyard." ' 7 (Ahab's) wife Jezebel said, 'You are the king of Israel, so you can do anything. Get up (from your bed) and eat (something). Be happy! I will get the vineyard of Naboth from Jezreel for you.' 8 Then Jezebel wrote letters. They seemed to come from Ahab, because she used his special mark. She sent them to the older men and the leaders that lived in Naboth's city with him. 9 This is what she wrote in those letters. 'Tell everybody that there will be a fast. Give Naboth a seat where everybody can see him. 10 But cause two bad men to sit near him. Order them to say that Naboth has said bad things about God and about the king. Then take him out. Throw stones at him until he is dead.'

11 So the older men and the leaders, who lived in Naboth's city, obeyed Jezebel. They did what she ordered them to do in her letters to them.

12 They said that there must be a fast. They put Naboth in a seat where everybody could see him. 13 Then two bad men came and they sat near to him. They said, in front of all the people, that Naboth had said bad things about God and about the king. So (the people) took him outside their city. They threw stones at him until he was dead. 14 Then they sent a message to Jezebel. '(The people) threw stones at Naboth. He is dead.' 15 So Jezebel knew that Naboth was dead. (He was dead because they threw) stones at him. Then she said to Ahab, 'Get up (from your bed) and take for yourself the vineyard of Naboth from Jezreel. He would not sell it to you, but now he is not alive but dead.' 16 When Ahab knew that Naboth was dead, he got up (from his bed). He went to take for himself Naboth's vineyard.

17 When this (had happened), the word of the LORD came to Elijah from Tishbe. 18 (He said), 'Go to meet King Ahab of Israel. He is the ruler of Samaria. He is now in Naboth's vineyard. He is taking it for himself. 19 Say to him, "This is what the LORD says (to you). You have killed a man and you have taken his (vineyard) for yourself." Then say to him, "This is what the LORD says (to you). In the place where the dogs drank Naboth's blood, dogs will drink your blood. Yes, (they will drink) your blood!" ' 20 Ahab said to Elijah, 'You have found me. (You are) my enemy.' (Elijah) answered, 'I have found you because of all the bad things that you have done. You have decided to do everything that the LORD does not like. It is like you have sold yourself. 21 (The LORD says), "I will kill you. I will take away your children and their children. I will kill every man in Israel from Ahab's family. (It does not matter) whether they are slaves or free men. 22 I will make your family like the family of Jeroboam the son of Nebat. (I will make it like the family of) Baasha (who was) the son of Ahijah. (I will do this) because you have made me very angry. Also, you have caused (the people) in Israel to sin (against me)." 23 Also, the LORD says this about Jezebel. "Dogs will eat Jezebel near the wall of (the city of) Jezreel. 24 Dogs will eat people who belong to Ahab ('s family). (They will eat them) if they die in the city (Samaria). And the birds in the air will eat those people that die outside the city." '

25 Ahab had decided to do everything that the LORD did not like. Nobody (before him) was ever worse than he was. His wife Jezebel wanted him to be like that. 26 (Ahab) did the worst things. He worshipped idols like the people called Amorites did. The LORD had killed those people before Israel (came into their country).

27 When Ahab heard these words, he tore his clothes (into pieces). He wore hairy clothes and he fasted. He made his bed from hairy blankets and he became humble. 28 Then the word of the LORD came to Elijah from Tishbe. (The word of the LORD said to him,) 29 'You have seen that Ahab has become humble in front of me. I will not destroy (his family) while he is alive. (This is because he has become humble (in front of me). (I will destroy his family when he is dead.) I will destroy his family when his son is alive.'

Chapter 22

The prophet Micaiah and Ahab

1 There was no war between Aram and Israel for three years. 2 But after three years, Jehoshaphat, the king of Judah, went to see the king of Israel. 3 The king of Israel had said to his leaders, 'You know that Ramoth Gilead belongs to us. But we are not doing anything to take it from the king of Aram.' 4 So (the king of Israel) asked Jehoshaphat, 'Will you go with me to fight against Ramoth Gilead?' Jehoshaphat said to the king of Israel, 'I am like you are. My people are your people and my horses are your horses.'

5 But Jehoshaphat also said to the king of Israel, 'First, we must know what the LORD wants us to do.' 6 So the king of Israel brought together about 400 prophets. He asked them, 'Should I fight a war against Ramoth Gilead, or not?' And they answered, 'Go, because the LORD will give it into the hands of the king.' 7 But Jehoshaphat asked, 'Can we not ask (someone who is really) a prophet of the LORD?' 8 The king of Israel said to Jehoshaphat, 'There is still one man, called Micaiah, (who is) the son of Imlah. We can ask him what the LORD wants us to do. But I do not like him, because he never says anything good about me.' 'The king (of Israel) should not say that', replied Jehoshaphat. 9 So the king of Israel said to one of his officers, 'Bring Micaiah the son of Imlah (to me), quickly.' 10 The king of Israel and Jehoshaphat the king of Judah were wearing their kings' clothes. They sat on thrones by the gate of Samaria. (The gate) was near (the place where farmers) made flour from wheat. All the (400) prophets were speaking in front of them. 11 Zedekiah (was the) son of Kenaanah. He had used iron to make sharp points like a cow has on its head. (Zedekiah) said, 'This is what the LORD is saying. "With these (sharp points) you will attack the soldiers from Aram. You will kill them all." ' 12 All the other prophets said the same. They said, 'Attack Ramoth Gilead. You will beat it. The LORD will give it into the hands of the king.'

13 The man who had fetched Micaiah said to him, 'All the (400) prophets have said that the king would beat (Aram). What you say must agree with their words. Say something that people want to hear.' 14 But Micaiah said, 'I can only tell the king what the LORD orders me (to say). I say that as surely as the LORD is alive.' 15 When he arrived (at Samaria), the king asked him, 'Micaiah, should we attack Ramoth Gilead or not?' He answered, '(If you) attack it, you will beat it. (This is) because the LORD has given it into the king's hands.' 16 The king (Ahab) said to (Micaiah), 'I always have to order you to say only what is true in the name of the LORD!'

17 Then Micaiah said,

> 'I saw all the people of Israel.
>
> They were moving about on the hills like sheep.
>
> They did not have a leader.
>
> The LORD said (to me), "These people have no master.
>
> Let each of them go home and not fight." '

18 The king of Israel said to Jehoshaphat, 'I told you (what he would say)! He will never say anything that is good about me. (He will only say) bad things.' 19 Micaiah also said, 'So now listen to the word of the LORD. I saw the LORD. He was sitting on his throne. All the armies from God's home were standing round him on both sides. 20 And the LORD said, "Who will cause Ahab to attack Ramoth Gilead, where he will die?" One spirit suggested this (man) and another (suggested) that (man). 21 In the end, the spirit came and stood in front of the LORD. (The spirit) said, "I will cause (Ahab) to do it." 22 "How will you do it?" the LORD asked (him). (The spirit) said, "I will go to all the prophets. And I will put words that are not true into their mouths." The LORD said, "Go and do it. You will be able to cause (Ahab to do it)." 23 So, the LORD has now put a spirit into the mouths of all your prophets. (This spirit will cause them to say) words that are not true. The LORD has decided that you will die.'

24 Then Zedekiah, (who was) the son of Kenaanah, went to Micaiah. (Zedekiah) hit (Micaiah's) face. (Zedekiah) asked (Micaiah), 'Which way did the spirit from the LORD go, when he went from me to speak to you?' 25 Micaiah answered (him), 'You will know on the day that you go to hide in a secret room.' 26 Then the king of Israel said (to his servants), 'Take Micaiah and send him back to Amon. (Amon was the ruler) of the city. Send him also to Joash (who is) the king's son. 27 Say (to them), "This is what the king wants you to do. Put this man (Micaiah) in a prison. Give him only bread and water until I return safely." ' 28 Micaiah said, 'If you ever return safely, the LORD has not spoken by me.' Then he said (to all the people), 'Remember my words, all you people!'

An arrow kills King Ahab

29 So (Ahab) the king of Israel and Jehoshaphat the king of Judah went up to Ramoth Gilead. 30 The king of Israel said to Jehoshaphat, 'I will go into the war and I will wear (a soldier's) clothes. (People will not recognise me.) But you wear your king's clothes.' So the king of Israel caused himself to seem like somebody else. Then he went into the war. 31 Now the king of Aram had said to his 32 chariot leaders, 'Do not fight with anybody, whether they are small or great. Only (fight) the king of Israel.' 32 The chariot leaders saw Jehoshaphat. They thought, 'Surely this (is) the king of Israel.' So they turned to attack him. But Jehoshaphat shouted (something) aloud. 33 Then the chariot leaders saw that (Jehoshaphat) was not the king of Israel. So they did not follow him.

34 Then, someone shot (an arrow from) his bow. He did not shoot at anyone, but he hit the king of Israel. The (arrow) went between holes in the king's war clothes. The king said to the man that drove his chariot, 'Turn the chariot round. Take me away from where they are fighting. (An arrow) hurt me badly.' 35 The soldiers fought all day. The king (of Israel) sat in his chariot. He was looking at the soldiers from Aram. The blood from where the arrow had hit him went down to the floor of the chariot. That evening, (Ahab) died. 36 When the sun started to go behind (the hills), people in the army shouted, 'Every man must now go back to his town or to his farm.'

37 So the king (of Israel) died and they brought him to Samaria. They buried him there. 38 They washed the chariot in a pool (of water) in Samaria. It was where the prostitutes bathed. And the dogs drank (Ahab's) blood. The word of the LORD had said that this would happen. 39 There is a book with reports about the kings of Israel. People wrote in it everything that King Ahab did. It includes the palace that he built. And it includes the cities that he made strong. 40 They buried Ahab with his ancestors. His son Ahaziah became the king (of Israel) after him.

King Jehoshaphat of Judah

41 After Ahab had been king of Israel for nearly 4 years, Jehoshaphat the son of Asa became the king of Judah. 42 Jehoshaphat was 35 years old when he became king. He ruled in Jerusalem for 25 years. His mother's name was Azubah. (Azubah) was the daughter of Shilhi. 43 Jehoshaphat was like his father Asa in everything that he did. He did not do anything that was wrong. He did what the LORD wanted him to do. But he did not remove the (altars) on hills. People continued to offer sacrifices (on the hills) and they continued to burn incense there. 44 Also Jehoshaphat did not fight against the king of Israel.

45 There is a book with reports about the kings of Judah. People wrote in it everything that King Jehoshaphat did. It includes the wars that he fought. 46 He also removed the male prostitutes from their special altars. They were there even when his father Asa was the king (of Judah). 47 At this time there was no king in (the country called) Edom. Someone less important (than a king) ruled (in Edom). 48 Also, Jehoshaphat built some ships. He wanted them to bring back gold from Ophir. But they never went. (A storm) destroyed them at Ezion Geber. 49 At that time, Ahaziah the son of Ahab had said to Jehoshaphat, 'Let my men sail with your men.' But Jehoshaphat refused (when he offered to help). 50 So Jehoshaphat died and they buried him with his ancestors in the city of his father David. Jehoram his son ruled (Judah) after him.

King Ahaziah of Israel

51 Ahaziah (was) the son of Ahab. He became the king of Israel in Samaria. This was nearly 17 years after Jehoshaphat became the king of Judah. Ahaziah ruled Israel for two years. 52 He did things that the Lorded not like. He did the things that his father and mother did. And he did the things that Jeroboam the son of Nebat did. (Jeroboam) had caused Israel's people to sin. 53 (Ahaziah) was the servant of Baal and he also worshipped him. He made the LORD, (who was) the God of Israel, very angry. That was what his father had also done.

Why God Sent His People Away

2 Kings

About this book

2 Kings is a book about the people called Israelites. The Books of 1 Kings and 2 Kings tell us what happened after King David's time. The Book of 1 Kings records how Solomon became king after David.

After Solomon died, the country called Israel became two countries. The south was called Judah. The north was still called Israel.

When the kings of Judah and Israel obeyed God, the people had peace. Sometimes the kings did not obey God and they worshipped other gods instead. Then bad things happened. When the people in Israel stopped obeying God, he sent prophets. The most important prophet in 2 Kings is Elisha. He did things that someone could only do with the help of God. He told the people that they should worship God again.

After Elisha died, many of the kings were very bad. In the end, God decided to send his people out of their country. This happened to the people in Israel first. Then it happened to the people in Judah. God did not let his people go back to their country for 70 years.

Chapter 1

King Ahaziah dies

1 After (King) Ahab's death, (the country called) Moab fought against Israel. 2 (King) Ahaziah lived in Samaria. He fell from the window of an upstairs room. So, he became ill. So he sent people with this message: 'Go to Baalzebub, (who is) the god in Ekron. Ask him if I will become well again after this illness.' 3 Then an angel of the LORD spoke to Elijah who was from Tishbe. (The LORD said,) 'Go and meet the men that the king of Samaria has sent with a message. Say to them, "You should not go to speak to Baalzebub, (who is) the god in Ekron. You seem to think that there is no God in Israel." 4 So this is what the LORD says (to you, Ahaziah). "You will not leave the bed that you are lying on. You will surely die." ' Then Elijah went away.

5 So the people with the message returned to the king. He asked them, 'Why have you returned?' 6 They replied, 'A man came to meet us. And he said (this) to us. Go back to the king who sent you. Tell him, "This is what the LORD says. You should not send men to speak to Baalzebub, (who is) the god in Ekron. You seem to think that there is no God in Israel. You will not leave the bed that you are lying on. You will surely die." ' 7 The king asked them, 'What kind of a man was it who came to meet you? (Who) told you this?' 8 They replied, 'He was a man with hairy clothes and he wore a leather belt.' (Then) the king said, 'That was Elijah from Tishbe.'

9 Then (the king) sent 50 men with their captain to Elijah. Elijah was sitting on the top of a hill. The captain went up to Elijah. He said to (Elijah), '(You are a) man of God. The king says (to you), "Come down." ' 10 This was Elijah's answer to the captain of 50 men. 'If I am a man of God, fire will come down from the sky. It will burn you and your 50 men.' Then fire did fall from the sky. It burnt the captain and his men (so that they died).

11 Then the king sent another captain and 50 men to Elijah. The captain said to him, '(You are a) man of God. The king says, "Come down immediately." ' 12 Elijah answered, 'If I am a man of God, fire will come down from the sky. It will burn you and your 50 men.' Then fire from God did fall from the sky. It burnt the captain and his 50 men (so that they died).

13 So the king sent a third captain, with his 50 men. This third captain went up to Elijah. He fell to his knees (in front of Elijah). 'Man of God', he prayed, 'please be kind to me and to these 50 men. We are your servants. Do not cause us to die. 14 Look! Fire fell from the sky. It burnt the first two captains and all their men, (so that they died). But now, be kind to me.' 15 The LORD's angel said to Elijah, 'Go down with him. Do not be afraid of him.' So Elijah got up and he went down with the captain to the king. 16 (Elijah) said to the king, 'This is what the LORD says. You should not send men with a message to speak to Baalzebub, (who is) the god in Ekron. You seem to think that there is no God in Israel. You will never leave the bed that you are lying on. It is because you have done this. You will surely die.'

17 So (Ahaziah) died. This is what the LORD had told Elijah. Ahaziah had no son, so Joram became king after him. This was in the second year in which Jehoram was the king of Judah. (Jehoram was) the son of Jehoshaphat. 18 Many other things happened while Ahaziah was king. Also, he did many things. People wrote them in a book. It is called 'the reports about the kings of Israel'.

Chapter 2

Elijah goes to heaven

1 The LORD was ready to take Elijah up to heaven in a strong wind. This was while Elijah and Elisha were going away from Gilgal. 2 Elijah said to Elisha, 'Stay here because the LORD has sent me to Bethel.' But Elisha replied, 'I will not leave you. This is as true as the fact that the LORD and you are (both) alive.' So they went down to Bethel. 3 A group of prophets were at Bethel. They came out (of Bethel) to Elisha and they asked him, 'Do you know that the LORD will take your master from you today?' 'Yes, I do know', said Elisha. 'But do not talk about it.'

4 Then Elijah said to Elisha, 'Stay here because the LORD has sent me to Jericho.' But Elisha replied, 'I will not leave you. This is as true as the fact that the LORD and you are (both) alive.' So they went to Jericho. 5 A group of prophets were at Jericho. They went out to Elisha and they asked him, 'Do you know that the LORD will take your master from you today?' 'Yes, I do know', said Elisha. 'But do not talk about it.'

6 Then Elijah said to (Elisha), 'Stay here because the LORD has sent me to the (river) Jordan.' But (Elisha) replied, 'I will not leave you. This is as true as the fact that the LORD and you are (both) alive.' So they continued to walk (together). 7 50 men, from the group of prophets, went and they stood near the (river) Jordan. They were not far away from where Elijah and Elisha were standing. (The prophets) could see them. 8 Elijah took off his coat. He rolled it up. He hit the water with it. The water went to the right (side) and to the left (side). They both crossed (the river) on dry ground.

9 After they had crossed (the river), Elijah said to Elisha, 'Tell me (this). What can I do for you before (the LORD) takes me from you?' Elisha replied, 'Let me have twice the amount of your spirit.' 10 'You have asked a difficult thing', said Elijah. 'But (watch) when (God) takes me from you. If you can see me, it will be yours. (If you cannot see me) it will not (be yours).' 11 So they walked along and they talked together. Then, a chariot that seemed to be on fire appeared. Horses (were pulling it). It went between them. Elijah went up to heaven in a strong wind. 12 Elisha saw this. He shouted, 'My father! My father! (These are) the chariots and the men on horses of Israel!' Then Elisha did not see (Elijah) again. He took off his own clothes and he tore them into pieces. 13 He picked up the coat that had dropped from Elijah. He went and he stood on the edge of the (river) Jordan. 14 Then he took the coat that (Elijah) had dropped. He hit the water with it. And he said, 'I want the LORD, the God of Elijah, to do something for me.' When he hit the water, it went to the right (side) and to the left (side). He crossed (the river).

15 The group of prophets from Jericho watched this. They said, 'The spirit of Elijah is now on Elisha.' And they went to meet (Elisha). They bent down in front of him. 16 And they said to him, 'Look! We are your servants. There are 50 strong men with us. Let them go and look for your master. Maybe the Spirit of the LORD has lifted him up. (Maybe) it has put him on a mountain or in a valley.' 'No', Elisha replied. 'Do not send them.' 17 But they asked him many times. So he was too ashamed to say 'no'. So he said, 'Send them.' And they sent 50 men. They looked for (Elijah) for three days, but they did not find him. 18 Elisha was staying in Jericho. When they returned to (Elisha), he said to them, 'I told you that you should not go (to look for Elijah).'

19 The men in the city (Jericho) said to Elisha, 'Look, our master. You can see that this city is in a good place. But its water is bad and the land does not make good plants.' 20 (Elisha) said, 'Bring to me a new dish. Put salt into it.' So they brought it to him. 21 Then (Elisha) went out to the (bad) water. He threw the salt into it. He said, 'This is what the LORD is saying. "I have made this water clean. It will never cause people to die again. The land will never give bad plants again." ' 22 The water has been good to this day. This is what Elisha had said.

23 From there, Elisha went up to Bethel. While he walked along the road, young (men) came out of the town. They laughed at (Elisha). 'Go up, you bald (man)!' they said. 'Go up, you bald (man)!' 24 (Elisha) turned and he looked at them. He prayed that the LORD would do something bad to them. Then, two bears (wild animals) came out from the forest. They hurt 42 of the young (men). 25 Then Elisha went to the mountain (called) Carmel. From there, he returned to Samaria.

Chapter 3

Moab's people fight against Judah, Israel and Edom

1 Jehoram (was) the son of Ahab. (Jehoram) became the king of Israel in Samaria. (This was when) Jehoshaphat had been the king of Judah for 18 years. (Jehoram) was king for 12 years. 2 The LORD saw that he did very bad things. But he was not as (bad) as were his father and his mother. (Jehoram) did throw away the special stone of Baal that his father (Ahab) had made. 3 But he still did the wrong things that Jeroboam had done. (Jeroboam) was the son of Nebat. He had caused (many people in) Israel to do (those wrong things). (Jehoram) continued to do them.

4 Mesha (was) the king of Moab. He was a sheep farmer. He had to supply the king of Israel with 100 000 young sheep. (He) also (had to supply) the soft hair from 100 000 male sheep. 5 But after Ahab died, the king of Moab decided not to do this for the king of Israel. 6 So, at that time, King Jehoram went out from Samaria. He caused all (the men in) Israel to march (with him). 7 He also sent this message to Jehoshaphat, (who was) the king of Judah. 'The king of Moab will not obey me. Will you go with me to fight against (the king of) Moab?' 'I will go with you', (Jehoshaphat) replied. 'I am as you are. My people (are) as your people. My horses (are) as your horses.' 8 'What road should we go on to attack (Moab)?' (Jehoram) asked. 'Through the sandy part of Edom', (Jehoshaphat) replied.

9 So the king of Israel, the king of Judah and the king of Edom went together (to Moab).

After they had marched round (Edom) for 7 days, there was no more water. (There was no water) for the army or for their animals. 10 'What (has happened)?' said the king of Israel. 'Has the LORD brought us three kings together to give us to the (king of) Moab?' 11 But Jehoshaphat asked, 'Is there not a prophet of the LORD here? We could ask him what the LORD is saying.' A leader of the king of Israel's army answered him. 'Elisha, (who is) the son of Shaphat, is here. He (was the man who) poured water on Elijah's hands.' 12Jehoshaphat said, 'He will tell us what God is saying (to us).' So the king of Israel and Jehoshaphat and the king of Edom went down to (Elisha).

13 Elisha said to the king of Israel, 'We have nothing to say to each other. Go to the prophets of your father and to the prophets of your mother.' 'No!' the king of Israel replied. 'The LORD told us three kings that we must come here together. (He is) giving us to Moab.' 14 Elisha said, 'I am the servant of the very powerful LORD, who is really alive! I would not look at you if Jehoshaphat, the king of Judah, was not with you. (But I think that) he is a good man. (If he were not here), I would not look at you. 15 But now, bring a harpist to me.' While the harpist was making music, the LORD started to use Elisha powerfully. 16 Then Elisha said, 'This is what the LORD is saying. Dig many long holes in this valley. 17 (Do it), because the LORD is saying this. You will not see wind or rain. But this valley will become full of water! You, your cows and your other animals will be able to drink. 18 This is a very easy thing for the LORD to do. He will also give (the people in) Moab to you. 19 You will destroy every city that has strong walls. (You will destroy) every important town. You will cut down every good tree. You will fill every hole where they get water. You will put stones on to every good field, so that they will be of no value.' 20 The water was there on the next morning, at the time when (the priests) burnt food as gifts to (the LORD)! (The water) came from the direction of Edom. The land was full of water!

21 All (the people in) Moab had heard that the kings had come to fight against them. So the (leaders of Moab) asked every man who could fight, whether young or old, to come. They put them on the border (of Moab). 22 When the men (from Moab) got up early (the next) morning, the sun was shining on the water. (They were) the other side of the border. The people from Moab saw that the water seemed red. (They thought that) it was like blood. 23 'That is blood', they said. 'Those kings have fought each other and they have killed each other. Come on, (people from) Moab. We will take what we can find!' 24 So the people from Moab came to where Israel's men were. But then, Israel's men stood up and they fought against (the people from Moab). (The people from Moab) ran away. The men from Israel attacked their country and they killed the people from Moab. 25 They destroyed the towns. Each man threw a stone on to every good field, until they covered them (with stones). They filled every hole where (the people from Moab) got water. They cut down every good tree. Only Kir Hareseth kept all its stone (walls). But men with weapons were all round it. They also attacked it. 26 Then the king of Moab saw that he was not beating his enemies in the war. So he took with him 700 men with swords. They tried to get to the king of Edom. But they failed. 27 So he took his oldest son. (This son) would have been king after him. He killed him on the wall of the city (Kir Hareseth) to make his god happy. They were very angry with (the people from) Israel. So (the people from Israel) left Moab and they returned to their own country.

Chapter 4

Some great things that Elisha did with God's help

1 There was a group of prophets. The wife of one of these men spoke aloud to Elisha. (She said,) 'My husband is dead. He was your servant and he loved the LORD. (My husband) should have given money to a certain man. (But he did not), so that man will come to take my two children. They will become his slaves.' 2 Elisha said to her, 'How can I help you? Tell me, what have you got in (your) house?' She said (to Elisha), 'I, your servant, have nothing in the house, only a pot of oil.' 3 Then (Elisha) said, 'Go to the people who live near you. Ask them all to lend you many pots. The pots (must be) empty. 4 Then go into (your house). Shut the door behind you and behind your sons. Pour (the oil that you have) into all those pots. When each (pot) is full, put it by your side.' 5 So she left (Elisha) and she shut the door behind her and behind her sons. They brought (the pots) to her and she poured (the oil into them). 6 When all the pots were full, she said to her son, 'Bring me another pot.' But he said, 'There are no more pots!' Then there was no more oil to pour (into pots). 7 Then she went and she told (all this) to the man of God. He said, 'Go and sell the oil. Use (some of) the money to pay (that man who wants your sons). (Buy) food for you and for your sons with what you do not need to pay (the man).'

8 There was a time when Elisha went to Shunem. A rich woman was there (in Shunem). She asked him to have a meal (with her family) every time that he passed (her house). So, each time that he passed (her house), he stopped there to eat (a meal). 9 Then she said to her husband, 'Listen! I believe that this (Elisha) is a holy man of God. He often passes our (house). 10 We should make a small room on the roof for him. We can put into it a bed, a table, a chair and a light. Then, when he comes (to visit) us, he can stay there.'

11 There was a certain day when Elisha came there. He went up to his room and he lay there. 12 Gehazi was (Elisha's) servant. (Elisha) said to (Gehazi), 'Ask the woman from Shunem (to come here).' So Gehazi asked her (to come) and she stood in front of him. 13 Elisha said to (Gehazi), 'Say to her, "You have done all this work for us. So, what can (we) do for you? Can we speak on your behalf to the king? Or (can we speak) to the leader of the army (on your behalf)?" ' But she replied, 'I live (safely) among my own people.'14 So Elisha said, 'What can we do (to help) her?' Gehazi said, '(I know that) she has no son. But her husband is old.' 15 (Elisha) said, 'Ask her to come here.' And when (Gehazi) had asked her to come, she stood by the door. 16 And (Elisha) said, 'About this time next year, you will have a son in your arms.' 'No, my master', she said, 'do not say what is not true to your servant. (You are) a man of God.' 17 But the woman did become pregnant. At that time next year she had a son. Elisha had said that this would happen.

18 When the child had grown, he went to his father. (His father was in a field) with the workers. 19 'My head (hurts me)! My head (hurts me)!' he said to his father. (His father) said to (his) servant, 'Carry him to his mother.' 20 So (the servant) lifted him up and carried him to his mother. (The boy) sat on his mother's knees until midday. Then he died. 21 Then she went up (stairs) and she put (the boy) on the bed of the man of God. Then she shut the door (of his room) and she went out. 22 She sent a message to her husband. She said, 'Send to me one of the servants and one of the donkeys. Then I will go quickly to the man of God and return (quickly).' 23 (Her husband) asked, 'Why are you going to him today? It is not a New Moon or a Sabbath.' And she said, 'Do not argue.' 24 So she put a seat on the donkey. And she said to her servant, 'Go! Lead (the way)! Do not go slowly for me, unless I say, "You must (go slowly)".' 25 So she went out (on the road) and she came to the man of God. (He was on) a hill (called) Carmel. (Elisha) saw her when she was a long way away. So the man of God said to his servant Gehazi, 'Look! There is the woman from Shunem! 26 Run now to meet her. Ask her, "Are you well? Is your husband well? Is your child well?" ' And she said, 'Well.' 27 But when she reached the man of God at the hill (called Carmel), she held his feet. Gehazi came to push her away. But the man of God said, 'Do not stop her. She is very, very sad. But the LORD has hidden it from me. (The LORD) has not told me about it.' 28 'My master, I did not ask you for a son', she said. 'I said to you, "Do not cause me to hope (for a son)." ' 29 (Elisha) said to Gehazi, 'Tie your clothes up round your body. Take my stick in your hand and run (to the boy). If you meet anyone, do not speak to him. If anybody speaks to you, do not answer (them). Put my stick on the boy's face.' 30 But the mother of the child said, 'The LORD is alive. You are alive. I will not leave you as surely as both of these things are true.' So (Elisha) got up and he went with her. 31 Gehazi went in front of them. He put the stick on the boy's face. But nothing happened and there was no sound (from the boy). So (Gehazi) went back to meet (Elisha). He said to him, 'The boy has not woken.'

32 When Elisha arrived at the house, the boy really was dead. He was lying on (Elisha's) bed. 33 (Elisha) went in (to the room). He shut the door. He and the boy were together. (Elisha) prayed to the LORD. 34Then (Elisha) went on to the bed. He lay on the boy. He put his mouth to (the boy's) mouth. He put his eyes to (the boy's) eyes and he put his hands to (the boy's) hands. When Elisha lay on the boy's dead body, it became warm. 35 (Elisha) went away (from the bed). He walked round the room. Then he went on to the bed and he lay down again on the boy. The boy made a noise in his nose 7 times and then he opened his eyes. 36 Then (Elisha) spoke to Gehazi. He said, 'Ask the woman from Shunem (to come here).' (Gehazi) did (that). When she came, Elisha said, 'Take your son.' 37 She came in (to the room). She fell down by his feet. She put her face near the ground. Then she took her son and she went out (from the room).

38 Elisha went back to Gilgal. And there was a famine round about (Gilgal). While the group of prophets sat with (Elisha), he spoke to his servant. 'Put the large pot (over the fire). Cook some stew for the group of prophets.' 39 One of (the prophets) went out into the fields to get some vegetables. He found a wild plant and he picked some of its fruits. He filled the pockets of his coat with them. When he returned he cut the fruits (into pieces). He put (the pieces) into the pot of stew. But nobody knew (what they were). 40They poured out the stew for the men to eat. But when they started to eat it, they shouted, 'Man of God, there is poison that would kill us in the pot!' And they could not eat (it). 41 Then (Elisha) said, 'Get (some) flour.' And he put it into the pot. He said, 'Give it to the people to eat.' And there was nothing that was dangerous in the pot.

42 A man came from Baal Shalishah. He brought 20 loaves to the man of God. The baker had made the bread with flour. (It was) from the first corn that was ready (for people) to pick. (He also brought) some of the plant with corn still in it. (Elisha) said, 'Give it to the people to eat.' 43 But his servant said, 'How can I give this to 100 men?' Then (Elisha) answered, 'Give it to the people to eat. (Do it), because the LORD says, "They will eat. But after (the meal) there will still be some (bread)." ' 44 So the servant gave (the bread) to them. And they ate it, but they could not eat all of it. The LORD had said that this would happen.

Chapter 5

God makes Naaman well again

1 Naaman was the leader of the king of Aram's army. (Naaman's) master thought that Naaman was a really great man. (That was) because the LORD had used Naaman. (He had used him) so that (the king of) Aram won wars. (Naaman) was a great soldier. But he had an illness called leprosy. 2 But men from Aram had gone to Israel. They had caught a young girl. She became the servant of Naaman's wife. 3 The girl said to her master's wife, 'I would like my master (Naaman) to see the prophet who is in Samaria. (The prophet) would take away his illness.' 4 (Naaman) went to his master (who was the king of Aram). He told him what the girl had said. 5 The king of Aram replied, 'Go (to Israel)! Go (there)! I will send a letter to the king of Israel.' So Naaman went (to Israel). He took with him 10 talents of silver, 6000 shekels of gold, and 10 suits of clothes. 6 Also, he took the letter for the king of Israel. It said, 'I am sending my servant Naaman to you, with this letter. I want you to take away (from him) his leprosy.' 7 When the king of Israel read the letter, he tore his clothes. He said, 'I am not God. I cannot kill people and make them alive again. This man cannot send someone to me, so that I can take away his leprosy. He is trying to have a quarrel with me.'

8 Elisha, the man of God, heard that the king of Israel had torn his clothes. Then, he sent to him this message. 'You did not have to tear your clothes. Cause the man (from Aram) to come to me. Then he will know that there is a prophet in Israel.' 9 So Naaman went (to Elisha) with his horses and with his chariots. They stopped at the door of Elisha's house. 10 Elisha sent a man with a message (to Naaman). 'Go to the (river) Jordan. Wash yourself 7 times in (the river). Then your skin will be clean. You will not have (leprosy, again).' 11 But Naaman was angry. He went away and he said, 'I thought that he would come out (of his house) to me. (And then he would) stand there. (And then) he would pray to the name of the LORD his God. (And then) he would move his hand over the leprosy. (I thought that) he would make me well again (like that). 12 Abana and Pharpar are rivers in Damascus. They are better than any of the rivers in Israel. Surely, I could wash in them and become clean!' And he turned and he went away. He was very, very angry. 13 But Naaman's servants went to him. (One of them) said, 'My father, the prophet might have asked you to do some great thing. You surely would have done it! Now all that he says to you is, "Wash! Then you will be clean." ' 14 So (Naaman) went down to the river Jordan. He washed himself (in it) 7 times. That was what the man of God had asked him to do. And (Naaman's) skin became well again. It became as clean as a young child's (skin).

15 Then Naaman and all his servants went back to the man of God. (Naaman) stood in front of (the man of God) and said, 'Now I know that there is no God in the whole world except the one in Israel. Now accept a gift from your servant (Naaman). 16 But (Elisha) answered (him), 'As surely as the LORD is alive, I will not accept (a gift). I am (the LORD's) servant.' Naaman asked him many times (to accept a gift) but (Elisha) refused. 17 So Naaman said, 'So, you will not (accept a gift). But give to me, your servant, as much earth as two donkeys can carry. Then your servant will never again worship any God but the LORD. 18 But I want the LORD to excuse your servant for one thing. My master, (the king of Aram, often) goes into the house of the god Rimmon. He bends down (in front of Rimmon). (My master) holds my arm, so I have to bend down also. I want the LORD to excuse me when I do this in the house of Rimmon.' 19 And (Elisha) said (to Naaman), 'Go and do not let it be a trouble (to you).' Then (Naaman) went a little way from (Elisha).

20 Gehazi (was) the servant of Elisha, (who was) the man of God. (Gehazi) said to himself, 'My master (made it too) easy for Naaman, the man from Aram. He did not accept (the gifts) that he brought. As surely as the LORD is alive, I will run after him. I will get something from (Naaman).' 21 So Gehazi hurried after Naaman. Naaman saw that (Gehazi) was running after him. So he got down from (his) chariot to meet him. (Naaman asked Gehazi), 'Is everything well?' 22 'Everything is well', he answered. 'My master sent me to say (this to you). Two young men have come to me. (They are) from a group of prophets in the hills of Ephraim. (Please) give to them a talent of silver (each) and two sets of clothes.' 23 And Naaman said, 'Yes, (I will). But take two talents (for each of them).' He caused (Gehazi to accept them). He tied the two talents of silver into two bags, with two sets of clothes. He gave them to two of his servants and they carried them in front of (Gehazi). 24 When (Gehazi) came to a hill (near Elisha's house), he took the things from the servants. He put them in the house. He sent (the servants) away and they left him. 25 (Gehazi) went into (the house) and he stood in front of his master. And Elisha said to Gehazi, 'Where have you been?' (Gehazi) answered, 'Your servant has not been anywhere.' 26 But (Elisha) said to him, 'My spirit was with you. (It was then) when the man came down from his chariot to meet you. This is not the time to take money, clothes, olive trees, vineyards, groups of animals or male and female servants. 27 Naaman's leprosy will always be with you and your children.' Then (Gehazi) went away from (Elisha). He had leprosy. (His skin was) as white as snow.

Chapter 6

More great things that Elisha did with God's help

1 A group of prophets said to Elisha, 'The place where we meet with you is too small for us. 2 We must go to the (river that is called) Jordan. Each (one) of us can get a piece of wood there. Then we can build a place there in which we can live.' And (Elisha) said, 'Go (there).' 3 Then one of them said, 'Please come with your servants.' (Elisha) replied, 'I will (come with you).' 4 And he went with them. They came to the (river) Jordan and they began to cut down trees. 5 While one of them was cutting down a tree, his iron axe fell into the water. 'My master', he said, 'It was not my (axe)!' 6 The man of God asked (him), 'Where did it fall?' He showed (Elisha) the place. Then (Elisha) cut a stick and he threw it there. It caused the iron (axe) to swim (on the water). 7 'Lift it out (of the water)', (Elisha) said. Then the man took it (out of the water) with his hand.

8 Then there was a war between the king of Aram and Israel. (The king of Aram) talked with the officers (of his army). Then he said (to them), 'I will put my army in a certain place.' 9 The man of God sent a message to the king of Israel. (He said), 'Do not pass that certain place. (The army) from Aram is going down there.' 10 So the king of Israel checked the place, about which the man of God had told him. (Elisha) told (the king) more than once that there was danger (there). (The king) was very careful in that place.

11 This made the king of Aram very angry. He asked the officers (of his army) to come to him. He said to them, 'Tell me (this). Which of us is helping the king of Israel?' 12 One of his officers said, 'None of us (is helping him), my master the king. Elisha is a prophet (who lives) in Israel. He tells the king of Israel every word that you speak in your bedroom.' 13 'Go. And find (the place) where he is', said the king (of Aram). 'Then I will send men and I will catch him.' A report came back (to him), '(Elisha) is in Dothan.' 14 So (the king of Aram) sent horses and chariots and a strong group (of soldiers to Dothan). They went by night and they stayed all-round the city.

15 The servant of the man of God got up early the next morning. He went out (and he saw) an army with horses and chariots all round the city. 'Oh, my master, what can we do?' the servant asked (Elisha). 16 'Do not be afraid', the prophet answered (him). 'There are more people with us than there are with them.' 17 Then Elisha prayed and he said, 'LORD. Open the eyes (of my servant) so that he can see (the angels).' And the LORD opened the eyes of the servant. And he looked. And he saw that the hills (round Dothan) were full of horses and chariots. (The chariots seemed to be on fire. (They were) God's servants, and they were) all round Elisha. 18 When (the enemy) came down towards Elisha, he prayed to the LORD. He said, 'Make these people so that they cannot see clearly.' And (the LORD) did what Elisha had asked. The people could not see clearly (to recognise Elisha). 19 And Elisha said to them, 'This is not the road. And this is not the city (that you are looking for). Follow me! And I will lead you to the man that you are looking for.' And he led them to Samaria.

20 After they had gone into the city (Samaria), Elisha prayed again. 'LORD, open the eyes of these men so that they can see clearly.' And the LORD opened their eyes and they saw clearly. And (they saw that) they were inside Samaria! 21 When the king of Israel saw (the enemy army), he asked Elisha, 'My father! Should I kill them? Should I kill them?' 22 (Elisha) answered, 'You must not kill them. You would not kill men that you had caught yourself with your sword or bow. Give them food and water. Then they can eat and drink. After that, they can go back to their master.' 23 So (the king of Israel) gave a big meal to them. When they had finished the food and the water, he sent them away. So they returned to their master, (who was the king of Aram). After this, small groups of soldiers from Aram did not go into Israel.

24 But after that, King Ben-Hadad of Aram sent his whole army to Samaria. They marched there and they stayed all round (the city). 25 Then there was a bad famine in the city. (The army) stayed all-round the city for so long, that a donkey's head cost 80 shekels of silver. And a quarter of a litre of seeds cost 5 shekels. 26 While the king of Israel was walking past on the wall (of the city), a woman shouted to him. 'Help me, my master the king', she said. 27 The king replied, 'Do not shout to me for help. The LORD must help you, because I cannot (help you). There is no flour and no wine.' 28 Then he asked her, 'What is the matter?' She answered, 'This woman (who is with me) spoke to me. (She said), "Give (to us) your son, so that we can eat him today. Tomorrow we will eat my son." 29 So we cooked my son and we ate him. The next day I said to her, "Give your son (to us), so that we can eat him." But she had hidden him.' 30 When the king heard the woman's words, he tore his clothes. He was walking along the wall. And people saw that under his other clothes he was wearing sackcloth (hairy clothes) next to his body. 31 He said, 'I want God to do this to me, and more. (I want him to do this) if the head of Elisha the son of Shaphat stays on his shoulders today!'

32 Elisha was sitting in his house. The important men of the city were with him. The king sent a man with a message. But before he arrived, (Elisha) said to the important men, '(The king) is sending a killer to cut off my head. When the man with the message comes, shut the door. Keep him outside the door. The sound of his master's feet is behind him.' 33 While (Elisha) was still talking to them, the man with the message came down to him. The man said, 'This bad thing is from the LORD. I cannot wait for the LORD any longer.'

Chapter 7

The end of the war that started in chapter 6

1 Elisha said, 'Listen to the word of the LORD. This is what the LORD is saying. "About this time tomorrow, 7 litres of flour will cost a shekel (of silver). 15 litres of barley will cost a shekel at the gate of Samaria." ' 2 The king was holding on to the arm of an officer. (The officer) said to the man of God, 'This will not happen. Even if the LORD opens windows in the skies, (it will not happen).' (Elisha) answered, 'You will see it with your own eyes. But you will not eat any of it (yourself)!'

3 At this time, there were 4 men who had leprosy. They were at the gate (where people) went in to the city (Samaria). They said among themselves, 'We should not stay here. (If we stay here) we will die. 4 There is a famine in the city. If we go there we will die. And if we stay here, we will die. So we will go to the place where the army from Aram is. We will let them catch us. If they are kind to us, we will not die. If they kill us, we will die.' 5 When the evening came they got up. They went to the place where the (army from) Aram was. When they reached the edge of the place, there was nobody there. 6 The Lord had caused the soldiers from Aram to hear the sounds of horses, chariots and a very big army. So they said among themselves, 'The king of Israel has brought the king of the Hittites and the king of Egypt to attack us!' 7 So, in the evening they got up and they ran away. They left their tents, their horses and their donkeys. They left the place where they were without any changes. And they ran away to save their lives. 8 The men who had leprosy came to the edge of this place. They went in to one of the tents. They ate and they drank. They carried away silver and gold and clothes. They went away and they hid them. Then they came back. They went into another tent and they took some things from it. They also hid them.

9 Then they said among themselves, 'What we are doing is not the right thing to do. This is a day of good news and we are not saying anything about it. If we wait until the morning, something bad will happen to us. We must go immediately and we must tell this to the king's servants.' 10 So they went to the people who kept safely the gate of the city. They spoke to them, and they said, 'We went into the place where the army from Aram was. There was not a man there. There was no sound from anybody. There were only horses and donkeys that they had tied (to something). They had left their tents as they were.' 11 The people who kept safely the gate of the city shouted the news (to everyone else). Somebody reported it to the (people in the) king's house. 12 The king got up in the night and he spoke to his officers. 'I will tell you what the army from Aram has done to us. They know that we have no food. So they have left their tents and they have hidden in the fields. They are thinking, "They will surely come out of (the city). Then we will catch them while they are still alive. We will get into (their) city." ' 13 One of the (king's) officers answered him. 'Send some men with 5 of the horses that are still in (our) city. What will happen to them will be the same as what will happen to all Israel's people in the city. They will be like all those among Israel's people who have died already. They may die. So, send them, to find out what has happened.' 14 So they chose two chariots with their horses. The king sent them to look for the army from Aram. He said to the drivers, 'Go! Find out what has happened.' 15 They followed the army from Aram as far as the (river) Jordan. The road was full of things that the army from Aram threw away. While they were running, (the army) had left clothes and weapons (on the road). So (the men with the chariots) returned to the king. They reported to him the news (about what they had found).

16 Then the people left (the city). They took everything from the army of Aram's tents. So, 7 litres of flour did cost a shekel (of silver). Also, 15 litres of barley did cost a shekel. This is what the LORD had said. 17 The king had put his special officer by the gate (of Samaria). He had held the arm of this officer (earlier). The people caused this officer to fall by the gate (as they ran past him). He fell under their feet and he died. The man of God had said that this would happen. He had said it when the king came down to his (Elisha's) house. 18 The man of God had said to the king that it would happen (like this). 'About this time tomorrow, 7 litres of flour will cost a shekel (of silver)', he had said. '15 litres of barley will cost a shekel at the gate of Samaria.' 19 The officer had said to the man of God, 'This will not happen. Even if the LORD opens windows in the skies, (it will not happen).' The man of God had answered, 'You will see it with your own eyes. But you will not eat any of it (yourself)!' 20 And that had really happened to him! The people had walked all over (this officer) by the gate and he had died.

Chapter 8

More great things that Elisha did

1 Elisha had made a woman's son alive again. (Elisha) had said to the woman, 'Go away with your family. Stay for a time in whatever place you can (stay). (Do this) because the LORD says that there will be a famine in (this) country. It will continue for 7 years.' 2 The woman had done what the man of God had said. She and her family went away. They stayed in the country called Philistia for 7 years. 3 She came back from the country called Philistia after the 7 years. She went to the king to ask for her house and for her fields. 4 The king was talking to Gehazi, who was the servant of the man of God. (The king) had said, 'Tell me about all the great things that Elisha has done.' 5 Gehazi was telling the king that (Elisha) had made dead people alive again. While (Gehazi) was doing this, the woman came in to ask for her house and her fields. It was her dead son that (Elisha) had made alive again. Gehazi said, 'My master the king, this is the woman! And this is her son that Elisha made alive again!' 6 The king asked the woman about it and she told him. Then the king asked for an officer to come to him. (The king) said to him, 'Give everything back to her. This must include all the money from her fields, from the day that she left until now.'

Ben-Hadad's death

7 Elisha went to Damascus. Ben-Hadad, (who was) the king of Aram, was ill. Somebody told him, 'The man of God has come here.' 8 The king said to Hazael, 'Take a gift with you. Go and meet the man of God. Ask him to ask the LORD this question. "Will I get well after this illness?" ' 9 Hazael went to meet (Elisha). He took with him, as a gift, all the best things from Damascus. (They needed) 40 camels to carry them! He went in (to Elisha's house) and he stood in front of him. He said, 'Your son, Ben-Hadad, king of Aram, has sent me (to you). He asks, "Will I get well after this illness?" '

10 (Elisha) answered, 'Go (back to him). Say to him, "Surely, you will get well (after your illness)." But the LORD has shown to me that he will surely die.' 11 (Elisha) looked at him with open eyes until Hazael was ashamed. Then the man of God (Elisha) began to weep. 12 And Hazael asked, 'Why is my master weeping?' 'Because I know that you will hurt Israel's people', answered (Elisha). (Then he said,) 'You will burn their strong (cities). You will kill their young men with the sword. You will knock their children ('s heads) on the ground. You will cut their pregnant women open.' 13 Hazael said, 'How could your servant, who has no more power than a dog, do something like that?' 'The LORD has shown me (this). You will become king of Aram', Elisha answered. 14 Then (Hazael) left Elisha and Hazael returned to his master (the king). Ben-Hadad asked him, 'What did Elisha say to you?' Hazael replied, 'He told me (that) you will surely get well.' 15 But the next day, (Hazael) took a thick cloth. He filled it with water. Then he put it over the king's face until he died. So Hazael became king after (Ben-Hadad).

Jehoram becomes the king of Judah

16 In the 5th year that Joram was king of Israel, Jehoshaphat was still king of Judah. (Joram was) the son of Ahab. Then Jehoram, the son of Jehoshaphat, also started to rule as king of Judah. 17 He was 32 years old when he became king. He ruled in Jerusalem for 8 years. 18 He did all the (bad) things that the kings of Israel (had done). He did what the family of Ahab had done. That was because he married a daughter of Ahab. (Jehoram) did very bad things in the sight of the LORD. 19 But the LORD did not want to destroy Judah, because of his promise to his servant David. (The LORD) had promised always to leave (something like) a light (in Judah) because of David, and because of his descendants.

20 While Jehoram was (king), Edom's people decided not to obey (the king of) Judah. (Edom's people decided) to have their own king. 21 So Jehoram crossed to Zair with all his chariots. (Zair is in Edom.) The men from Edom were all round him and (all round) the leaders of his chariots. But one night, (Jehoram's) army started to fight. They beat (the men from Edom) that were all round him and (all round) the leaders of his chariots. But then his army hurried back home! 22 Even today, Edom's people do not obey (the rulers of) Judah. (The people in a city called) Libnah (stopped obeying the king of Judah) at the same time. 23 Other things happened while Jehoram was king and he did other things. People wrote about them in a book. It is called 'the reports about the kings of Judah'. 24 Jehoram died like his ancestors and people buried him in the City of David. (They buried) him with his ancestors. His son Ahaziah became king after him.

Ahaziah becomes the king of Judah

25 Ahaziah was the son of Jehoram, (who had been) the king of Judah. Joram (was the) son of Ahab (who had been king of Judah). Ahaziah began to rule when (Joram) had been king for (nearly) 12 years. 26Ahaziah was 22 years old when he became king. He ruled in Jerusalem for one year. His mother's name was Athaliah. (She was a) granddaughter of Omri, (who had been) the king of Israel. 27 (Ahaziah) did all the bad things that the family of Ahab had done. (Ahaziah) did very bad things in the sight of the LORD. He did what the family of Ahab had done. That was because he had married (a woman from) Ahab's family.

28 Ahaziah went with Joram to fight against Hazael (who was) the king of Aram. (Joram was) the son of Ahab. (The fight was) at Ramoth Gilead. The army from Aram hurt Joram, 29 so King Joram returned to Jezreel. (He went there) to get well after the army from Aram had hurt him at Ramoth. This happened when he fought Hazael, the king of Aram. Then Ahaziah went down to Jezreel to see Joram (who was the) son of Ahab. (Ahaziah was) the son of Jehoram (who had been the) king of Judah. (Ahaziah went) because (Joram) was ill.

Chapter 9

Elisha and Jehu

1 The prophet Elisha asked a man from the group of prophets to come (to him). (Elisha) said to him, 'Fasten your coat into your belt. Take this bottle of oil with you and go to Ramoth Gilead. 2 When you get there, look for Jehu. (He is) the son of Jehoshaphat, (who is) the son of Nimshi. Go to him and take him away from his friends. Take him to an inside room. 3 Pour the oil from the bottle on to his head. Say to him, "This is what the LORD says (to you). 'I make you king of Israel now.' " Then open the door and run away quickly!'

4 So the young man that (Elisha) the prophet had sent, went to Ramoth Gilead. 5 When he arrived (at Ramoth Gilead), he found the army officers. They were sitting together. 'Captain, I have a message for you', he said. 'For which of us?' Jehu asked. '(Only) for you, captain', the (young prophet) replied. 6 Jehu stood up and he went into the house. The (young prophet) poured the oil on to (Jehu's) head. He said, 'This is what the LORD, the God of Israel, says (to you). "I am making you king over the LORD's people in Israel. 7 You must kill the family of your master Ahab. (In this way) you will punish (Ahab) because he killed my servants the prophets. Also, Jezebel (his wife) killed many of the LORD's servants. 8 The whole family of Ahab must die. I will kill every man from the family of Ahab that is in Israel. (I will kill) every male slave. And I will kill every man who is not a slave. 9 I will make the family of Ahab like the family of Jeroboam (who was) the son of Nebat. It will be like the family of Baasha (who was) the son of Ahijah. 10And dogs will eat Jezebel at a place in Jezreel. Nobody will bury her." ' Then (the young prophet) opened the door and he ran away.

11 Jehu went out to the other officers. 'Is everything well?' one of them asked him. 'Why did this crazy (prophet) come to you?' 'You know this man. And you know what he says', Jehu answered. 12 'That is not true!' they said. 'Tell us (what he said).' So Jehu said, 'This is what he told me. "This is what the LORD says. I am making you king over Israel." ' 13 They hurried to get their coats. They put them under (his feet) on the (stone) steps. Then they made a sound with a trumpet. They shouted, 'Jehu is king!'

14 So Jehu (who was the son of Jehoshaphat) became an enemy of Joram. (Jehoshaphat was the) son of Nimshi. Joram had been in Ramoth Gilead. All the army of Israel (was with him). They were waiting to see what Hazael (would do). (Hazael was) the king of Syria. 15 But King Joram then returned to Jezreel. This was to get well after his illness. (The army of) Aram had hurt him in the war with Hazael. (Hazael was) the king of Aram. Jehu said (to his officers), 'If your purpose really is (to make me king), do not let anyone get out from the city (Jezreel). They will tell the news back in (the city called) Jezreel.' 16 Then (Jehu) got into his chariot and he rode to Jezreel. That was because Joram was resting there (in Jezreel). Ahaziah (was) the king of Judah. He had come down (from Jerusalem) to meet Joram.

17 A man was standing on a tall building in Jezreel and he was there to watch. He saw Jehu's soldiers coming (towards Jezreel). He shouted, 'I can see some soldiers (that) are coming (to us).' Joram said, 'Fetch a man and a horse. Send them to meet (the soldiers). Ask them. "Are you friendly to us?" '

18 The man on the horse rode away to meet Jehu. He said (to Jehu), 'The king asks you, "Are you friendly to us?" ' 'It does not matter to you if we are friends', Jehu replied. 'Ride behind me.'

The man on the tall building reported (to Joram), 'The man with the message has reached them, but he is not coming back (to us).' 19So the king (Joram) sent a second man (who was riding) on a horse. He came to (Jehu). Then he said, 'The king (Joram) says, "Are you coming to us as a friend?" ' Jehu replied, 'It does not matter to you if we are friends. Ride behind me.' 20 The man on the tall building reported (to Joram), 'He has reached them, but he is not coming back (to us) either. The man that is driving (the chariot) drives like Jehu. (Jehu is) the son of Nimshi. He drives like someone that is crazy!'

21 Then Joram said, 'Fetch my chariot (to me).' So they brought (his chariot). Then King Joram of Israel and King Ahaziah of Judah rode to meet Jehu. Each (king) was in his own chariot. They met (Jehu) at the piece of ground that had belonged to Naboth. (Naboth had lived) in Jezreel. 22 When Joram saw Jehu he asked, 'Have you come as a friend, Jehu?' 'We cannot be friends', Jehu replied. '(That is because of) the things that your mother Jezebel did. People still worship false gods. There are women who do magic (in your country) still.' 23 Joram turned his chariot and he drove away quickly. He shouted to Ahaziah, 'Ahaziah, they are not our friends!' 24 Then Jehu used his bow. He shot Joram between his shoulders. The arrow went through his heart. He fell down in his chariot. 25 Bidkar was Jehu's chariot officer. (Jehu) said to him, 'Pick him up! Throw him on to the field that belonged to Naboth. (Naboth was) the man from Jezreel. Remember, you and I rode together in chariots behind Ahab. (Ahab) was (Joram's) father. Then, the LORD said this about (Joram). 26 "Yesterday, I saw the blood of Naboth. (I saw) also the blood of his sons, says the LORD. Surely, I will cause you to pay for this on this piece of ground, says the LORD." So now, pick him up and throw him on to that piece of (ground). Do what the LORD has promised.'

27 Ahaziah (was) the king of Judah. He saw what had happened (to Joram). So, he ran away past the house in his garden. Jehu followed him. (Jehu) shouted, 'Kill him too!' They hurt (Ahaziah) in his chariot. He was on the road to Gur near Ibleam. But he ran away (from them) to Megiddo, where he died. 28 His servants took him in a chariot to Jerusalem. They buried him with his ancestors in his grave. It was in the City of David.

29 Ahaziah had become king of Judah when Joram (had been king) nearly 11 years. (Joram) was the son of Ahab.

30 Then Jehu went to Jezreel. Jezebel heard about it. So she painted her eyes and she combed her hair. Then she looked out of a window. 31 While Jehu was coming through the gate (of the city), she asked him, 'Have you come as a friend, Zimri? You are your master's killer.' 32 (Jehu) looked up at the window (and he saw her). Then he shouted, 'Who is with me? Who?' Two or three eunuchs looked down at him. 33'Throw her down', Jehu said. So they threw her down. Some of her blood went all over the wall. Some of it went over the horses when they were kicking her with their feet. 34 Jehu went into (the king's house). He ate and drank (food and drink). 'Do something with (the dead body of) that bad woman', he said. 'Bury her, because she was the daughter of a king.' 35 But when they went out to bury her, they did not find much. (They found only) the bones of her head, her feet and her hands. 36 They went back and they told this to Jehu. He said, 'The LORD said that this would happen. He spoke by his servant, (who was) Elijah from Tishbe. (He said), "Dogs will eat Jezebel's dead body. (They will do it) on a piece of ground at Jezreel. 37 Jezebel's dead body will be like dirt on the ground, on that piece of ground at Jezreel. Nobody will be able to say, 'This is Jezebel'." '

Chapter 10

Jehu kills Ahab's family

1 Ahab had 70 sons. They were in Samaria. So Jehu wrote letters and he sent them to Samaria. (He sent them) to the officers in Jezreel. (He also sent them) to the important older men and to the people who made Ahab's children safe. 2 (This was what the letter said.) 'When this letter reaches you, your master (Ahab's) sons will be with you. You have chariots and horses, a strong city and weapons. 3 Choose the best person to be king from among your master's sons. Make him king instead of his father. Then fight on behalf of your master's family.' 4 But they were so very afraid. They said, 'Two kings could not beat (Jehu). So we (cannot beat him)!'

5 So these people sent a message to Jehu:

- the servant with most authority in the king's house

- the man that ruled the city (Samaria)

- the important older men

the people who made (Ahab's children) safe.

(The message said), 'We are your servants. We will do anything that you say. We will not make anyone (here) king. You do what is best.'

6 So Jehu wrote to them a second letter. It said, 'If you agree with me, maybe you will obey me. (If you do), bring the heads of your master's sons to Jezreel. Be here by this time tomorrow.' At that time, the 70 sons of Ahab were with the leaders of the city. (The leaders) were teaching them. 7 When the letter arrived, these men went to the sons of King (Ahab). They killed all 70 of them and they put their heads in baskets. Then they sent them to Jehu in Jezreel. 8 The man with the message arrived (in Jezreel). He told Jehu, 'They have brought the heads of King (Ahab's) sons.' Then Jehu said, 'Put them in two groups. Leave them at the gate of the city until the morning.' 9 The next morning, Jehu went out. He stood in front of all the people. He said (to them), 'You have not done anything that is wrong (to Ahab). It was I that decided (to kill) my master. It was I that killed him. But we do not know who killed all these people. 10 You can know this: Everything that the LORD has spoken against the family of Ahab will happen. The LORD has done what he promised to do. (He promised it) by his servant Elijah.' 11 So Jehu killed everybody in Jezreel who was in the family of Ahab. (Jehu also killed Ahab's) officers, his friends and his priests. They were all dead.

12 (Jehu) then left (Jezreel), and he went towards Samaria. He came to Beth Eked. Some men who kept sheep safe were there. 13 And Jehu also met some people from Ahaziah's family. (Ahaziah) was the king of Judah. (Jehu) asked them, 'Who are you?' They said, 'We belong to Ahaziah's family. We have come down here to say "welcome!" to the families of the king and his mother.' 14 'Catch them (while they are) alive!' shouted (Jehu). So they caught them (while they were) alive. Then they killed them by the well of Beth Eked. (They killed) 42 men. (Jehu) left none of them alive.

15 When (Jehu) left (Beth Eked), he met Jehonadab. (Jehonadab) was the son of Rechab and he was coming to meet (Jehu). 'Welcome!' said (Jehu). 'Do you agree with me, as I agree with you?' Jehonadab answered, 'I do!' 'So give me your hand', said (Jehu). So he did, and (Jehu) helped him up into his chariot. 16 (Jehu) said, 'Come with me. You will see that I really want to be the LORD's servant.' So (Jehonadab) rode with (Jehu) in his chariot. 17 So (Jehu) came to Samaria. There, he killed everyone in Ahab's family that was still alive. He killed them all. The LORD had told Elijah that this would happen.

18 Then Jehu caused all the people to come together. He said to them, 'Ahab was not a good servant of Baal. But Jehu will be a much better servant (of Baal)! 19 So, ask all the prophets of Baal to come (here). Also, fetch all (Baal's) servants and his priests. Be sure that they are all (here). (Do this), because I want to have a big sacrifice for Baal. Any person who does not come will not continue to be alive.' But Jehu was being very clever. His idea was to kill all Baal's servant. 20 Then Jehu said, 'Say that there will be a special meeting (to worship) Baal.' So (Jehu's servants) told everybody about it. 21 Then (Jehu) sent a notice to everyone in Israel, and all the servants of Baal came (to the meeting). There was nobody that did not come. They all went into the house of Baal, so that it was full from one end to the other. 22 Then (Jehu) said to the keeper of the clothes, 'Bring out all the special clothes, for the servants of Baal (to wear).' So he brought out the special clothes for them. 23 Then Jehu and Jehonadab, who was the son of Rechab, went into the house of Baal. (Jehu) said to the servants of Baal, 'Look all round (you). Be sure that there are no servants of the LORD here with you. (Be sure) that there are only servants of Baal here.' 24 So they went in (to the house of Baal) to make sacrifices. And they burned (animals) to offer (to Baal). But Jehu had put 80 (of his) men outside the house (of Baal). He had said to them, 'Do not let any of these men run away. If one of you does, it will be your life for his life.' 25 When (Baal's servants) had finished the sacrifice, Jehu said to his soldiers and (to their) officers, 'Go in (to the house of Baal) and kill (his servants). Do not let one of them run away.' So they cut them (into pieces) with their swords. The soldiers and their officers threw (their dead bodies) out (of the house of Baal). Then they went into the inside part of the house of Baal. 26 They brought out the special stones from the house of Baal and they destroyed them. 27 They destroyed the special stone of Baal and they tore down the house of Baal. People have used it as a toilet to this day!

28 So Jehu destroyed Baal in Israel. 29 But Jehu continued (to let people do) the sins of Jeroboam. (Jeroboam was) the son of Nebat. (Jeroboam) had caused Israel to worship young cows. (They had made the young cows) with gold. They were at Bethel and Dan.

30 The LORD said to Jehu, 'You have done well. You have done what is right in my sight. You have done everything to Ahab's family that I wanted (someone to do).

So, your descendants will be kings of Israel for 4 generations.' 31 But Jehu did not try as much as he could to obey the rules of the God of Israel. He did not turn away from the sins of Jeroboam, which he had caused Israel to do.

32 In those days, the LORD began to make Israel smaller. Hazael was stronger than Israel's people in all their country 33 east of (the river) Jordan. (That was) the place called Gilead, where the tribes of Gad, Reuben and Manasseh were. Gilead started in Aroer and it went through the Arnon Valley to Bashan. 34Other things happened while Jehu was king. Everything that he did is in a book. It is called 'the reports about the kings of Israel'. 35 Jehu died like his ancestors and people buried him in Samaria. His son Jehoahaz became king after him. 36 Jehu ruled over Israel in Samaria for 28 years.

Chapter 11

Queen Athaliah and King Joash

1 Athaliah was the mother of Ahaziah. She heard the news that her son was dead. Then, she started to kill all the king's family. 2 Jehosheba was the daughter of King Jehoram. She was the sister of Ahaziah. She took Joash away from the sons of the king, because (Athaliah) was ready to kill them. Joash was the son of Ahaziah. (Jehosheba) put Joash and the woman who fed him from her breast in a bedroom. Athaliah did not kill (Joash) because (Jehosheba) had hidden him. 3 Athaliah ruled the country (Judah) for 6 years. All this time (Jehosheba) hid (Joash) in the house of the LORD (in Jerusalem).

4 In the 7th year (that Athaliah ruled Judah), Jehoiada asked (these people) to come to him:

- the leaders of groups of 100 Carites

- the soldiers that made the palace safe.

They came to him in the house of the LORD. They agreed together with Jehoiada. He asked them to say a special promise, in the house of the LORD. Then he showed to them the king's son (Joash).

5 (Jehoiada) said to them, 'This is what you must do. A third (of your soldiers) that come to work on the Sabbath (must do this). They must make (the door to) the palace safe. 6 (Another) third (of your soldiers must stand) at the Sur Gate. (The other) third must be at the gate of the (LORD's) house. They must be behind the soldiers that usually make the (LORD's) house safe. 7 But two groups of your soldiers do not usually work on the Sabbath. Those soldiers must all make the LORD's house safe for the king. 8 You must stand all-round the king. Each (soldier) must have his weapons in his hand (ready to use). Anybody that comes near to you, you must kill. You must stay near to the king everywhere that he goes.'

9 The leaders of the groups of 100 (soldiers) did what Jehoiada the priest asked them to do. Each (leader) brought his men to Jehoiada the priest. (They brought) those (men) that worked on the Sabbath. They also brought those that did not (usually work on the Sabbath). 10 Then (Jehoiada) gave to the leaders the spears and the shields that had been King David's. They were in the house of the LORD. 11 Each soldier had his weapons in his hand. They stood round the king. They were near to the altar and to the house of (the LORD). They stood from the south side to the north side of the house. 12 Jehoiada brought (Joash,) the king's son (and Jehoiada put him in front of all the people). He put the crown on to his (head) and he gave to him a copy of the covenant. He said that (Joash) was king. They poured oil on to him. They hit their hands together. Then they shouted, 'We want the king to be alive for a long time!'

13 But Athaliah heard the noise that the soldiers and the people made. So she went to the people that were at the house of the LORD. 14 She looked and she saw the king. He was standing in the usual place (where they made someone into a king). The leaders (of the army) and the men with trumpets were by the king. All the people in the country (Judah) were very happy. (Many of them) blew into trumpets. Then Athaliah tore her clothes. She shouted, 'Treason! Treason!' 15 Jehoiada, the priest, said to each leader of 100 soldiers what they must do. 'Bring her out (of the house of the LORD). Keep her between groups of soldiers. (Kill) anyone with a sword that follows her.' That was because the priest had said, 'You must not kill her in the house of the LORD.' 16 So they took her to the place where horses went into the king's palace. There they killed her.

209

17 Then Jehoiada made a covenant. It was between the LORD, the king and the people. (They agreed) to be the LORD's people. He also made a covenant between the king and the people. 18 All the people in the country (Judah) went to the house of Baal. They tore it into pieces. They destroyed the altars and the false gods. Mattan was the priest of Baal. They killed him in front of the altars. Then (Jehoiada) the priest put soldiers to make the house of the LORD safe.

19 (Jehoiada) took with him (these people):

- the leaders of 100 soldiers

- the Carites and the soldiers

- all the people of the country (Judah).

They all brought the king down from the house of the LORD into the palace. They went in (to the palace) through the gate where the soldiers (stayed). Then the king sat on the king's special seat.

20 All the people in the country (Judah) were very happy. And the city (Jerusalem) was quiet. That was because they had killed Athaliah with the sword at the palace.

21 And Joash was 7 years old when he began to rule (Judah)..

Chapter 12

Joash makes repairs to God's house

1 Joash became king (of Judah) in the 7th year that Jehu (was king of Israel). Joash ruled in Jerusalem for 40 years. His mother's name was Zibiah. (She came from) Beersheba. 2 In all the years that Jehoiada the priest taught him, Joash did right things in the sight of the LORD. 3 But he did not remove the high places. The people continued to burn animals and to burn incense (in the high places).

4 Joash said to all the priests, '(There is) money that people offer to God for the house of the LORD. Bring all this money together:

- what each man pays (to the government);

- what each man offers (to the LORD);

- what each man gives (to God's house).

5 Each priest must give something from his own money. They must use the money to make repairs to the house (of the LORD), where people have broken it.' 6 Joash had been king for 23 years. (In that time), the priests had not made any repairs to the house (of the LORD)! 7 So King Joash asked Jehoiada and the other priests to come (to him). He said to them, 'There are no repairs to the parts of the house (of the LORD) where somebody has broken it. (But there should be.) Do not take any more money from the people that give it to you. Give it to (the people that make) repairs to the house (of the LORD).' 8 The priests agreed that they would not take any money from the people. Also, they agreed that they would not make repairs to the house (of the LORD) themselves.

9 Jehoiada the priest got a large box. He made a hole in the top of it. He put it outside the door of the house of the LORD. It was by the altar, on the right side (of the door). (Some) priests made the door (of the house of the LORD) safe. They put into the box all the money that people brought to the house of the LORD. 10 Every time that there was a large amount of money in the box, they counted the money. The leader of the priests and the king's servant who wrote things down (did that). (Then), they took (the money from the box) in the house (of the LORD). And they put it into bags.

11 Then they gave the money that they had counted to some men. They had made these (men) the leaders of the workers in the house of the LORD.

(The leaders) used the money to pay the men that cut the wood.

And (they used it to pay) the builders in the house of the LORD. 12 (They also paid) the men that used stones. And they paid the men that cut stones. They bought wood. And they bought stones that people had cut. They bought them for the repairs to the house of the LORD. And they paid all the other bills for the repairs to the house (of the LORD).

13 But they did not spend any of this money to buy anything that they used in the LORD's house. (This was the money) that people had brought into the house (of the LORD). They did not use it to buy any of these things:

- silver bowls

- tools that they used to cause their lights to burn well

- bowls (that people used) to pour (water or oil on to things)

- trumpets.

14 (They used all the money) to pay the workers. The (workers) used it to mend the house of the LORD. 15 (The priests) gave the money to (the leaders of the workers). But they did not ask (these leaders) to show them the bills. Everybody was very honest. 16 They did not bring other money into the house of the LORD. (People) offered (this money) because they had done wrong things. It was for the priests.

17 Hazael (was) the king of Aram. He went to Gath and (his army) attacked it. (His army) beat (the people in Gath). Then (Hazael) went to attack Jerusalem.

18 Then Joash was (still) the king of Judah. He sent all these special things to Hazael (who was) the king of Aram:

- the gifts that the kings of Judah who were before him had given (to God). (These kings were) Jehoshaphat, Jehoram, and Ahaziah.

- the gifts that (Joash) himself had given (to God)

- all the gold that was in the house of the LORD and in the king's palace

So Hazael left Jerusalem (and he did not attack it).

19 Other things happened while Joash was king. Everything that he did is in a book. It is called 'the reports about the kings of Judah'. 20 (Joash's) officers decided (to kill him). They killed him in the house of Millo, which is on the road down to Silla. 21 The officers that killed him were Jozabad, the son of Shimeath, and Jehozabad, the son of Shomer. (After) he died, people buried him with his ancestors in the City of David. Amaziah, (who was) his son, became king after (Joash).

Chapter 13

Jehoahaz becomes the king of Israel

1 Joash (was) the son of Ahaziah, (who was) the king of Judah. When (Joash) had been king for nearly 23 years, Jehoahaz became king of Israel in Samaria. (Jehoahaz was) the son of Jehu. (Jehoahaz) was king for 17 years. 2 But he did bad things in the sight of the LORD. He did the same sins as Jeroboam did. (Jeroboam was) the son of Nebat. (Jeroboam) had also caused (the people in) Israel to do these sins. And (Jehoahaz) did not stop these things. 3 So the LORD was very, very angry with Israel. For a long time (the LORD) caused Hazael and Ben-Hadad to beat them. (Ben-Hadad was) the son of Hazael, who was the king of Aram. 4 Then Jehoahaz prayed to the LORD again. And the LORD listened to him because of the king of Aram. (The LORD) knew that (the king of Aram) was being very cruel to Israel. 5 The LORD sent someone to help Israel. So they were free from the power of (the king of) Aram. So the people in Israel lived in their own homes, as they had done before (this time). 6 But the people in Israel still did the sins of the family of Jeroboam. They continued to do what Jeroboam had caused Israel to do. So, the Asherah pole still stood in Samaria.

7 The king of Aram had destroyed most of the army of Jehoahaz. But God did not let him kill or destroy these:

- 50 men that rode horses
- 10 chariots
- 10 000 soldiers who had to walk.

(The king of Aram) made everything else into very small bits of dirt.

8 Other things happened while Jehoahaz was king. Everything that he did is in a book. It is called 'the reports about the kings of Israel'. 9 Jehoahaz died like his ancestors, and people buried him in Samaria. Then Jehoash, (who was) his son, became king after him.

Jehoash becomes the king of Israel

10 (Joash) was the king of Judah. When he was 37 years old, Jehoash became king of Israel in Samaria. (Jehoash was) the son of Jehoahaz. (Jehoash) was king for 16 years. 11 But he did bad things in the sight of the LORD. He did the same sins as Jeroboam did. (Jeroboam was) the son of Nebat. (Jeroboam) had also caused (the people in) Israel to do these sins. And (Jehoash) continued to do them. 12 Other things happened while Jehoash was king. Everything that he did is in a book. It is called 'the reports about the kings of Israel'. It includes (the report) of his war against Amaziah, (who was) the king of Judah. 13 Jehoash died like his ancestors and people buried him in Samaria with the kings of Israel. Jeroboam became king (of Israel) after him.

14 Elisha was very ill. It was the illness from which he died. Jehoash, (who was) the king of Israel, went down to see him. (Jehoash) wept by his side. (Jehoash) said, 'My father! My father! The chariots and the men that ride on horses in Israel!' 15 Elisha said to (Jehoash), 'Fetch a bow and (some) arrows.' So he fetched him a bow and (some) arrows. 16 (Elisha) said to the king of Israel, 'Hold the bow in your hands.' When he had done this, Elisha put his hands on the hands of the king. 17 (Elisha) said, 'Open the east window.' And (the king) opened (it). 'Shoot!' said Elisha. And (the king) shot (the arrow). '(It is) the Lord's arrow, that will beat (the enemy). It is the arrow that will destroy Aram!' said Elisha. 'You will completely destroy (the army of) Aram at Aphek.' 18 Then (Elisha) said, 'Take the arrows.' And he took (them). And (Elisha) said to the king of Israel, 'Hit the ground (with them).' (The king) hit the ground three times and then he stopped. 19 The man of God was angry with (Jehoash). He said, 'You should have hit the ground 5 or 6 times. Then you would have beaten (the army of) Aram and you would have destroyed it completely. Now you will beat it only three times.'

Elisha dies

20 So Elisha died and people buried him. But, every spring, men from Moab came into the country (Israel) to rob the people. 21 Once, while they were burying a man, some people saw a group of those men from Moab. So they threw the man's dead body into Elisha's grave. When the dead body touched Elisha's bones, the man became alive again! He stood on his feet.

22 Hazael (was) the king of Aram. He was cruel to (the people in) Israel all the time that Jehoahaz was king. 23 But the LORD was kind to the people (in Israel). He loved them and he helped them. (That was) because of his covenant with Abraham, Isaac and Jacob. He did not want to kill them and he did not want to send them away from himself until now.

24 Then Hazael, (who was) the king of Aram, died. His son, (who was) Ben-Hadad, became king after him. 25 Then Jehoash, (who was) the son of Jehoahaz, got back from Ben-Hadad some towns. They (were towns) that Hazael had taken from Jehoahaz. (Jehoahaz was Jehoash's) father. Jehoash beat (Ben-Hadad) three times and he ruled Israel's towns again.

Chapter 14

Amaziah becomes the king of Judah

1 Jehoash, (who was) the son of Jehoahaz, had been the king of Israel for nearly two years. It was then that Amaziah began to rule Judah. (Amaziah) was the son of Joash.

2 (Amaziah) was 25 years old when he became king. He ruled in Jerusalem for 29 years. His mother's name was Jehoaddin. She (was born in) Jerusalem. 3 (Amaziah) did what was right in the sight of the LORD. But he did not (do everything) as his ancestor David had done. (Amaziah) did everything as his father Joash had done it. 4 But they did not remove the high places. The people continued to burn animals (for Baal). And they continued to burn incense (in those places). 5 (Amaziah) became safe as king (of Judah). Then he killed the officers who had killed his father the king. 6 But he did not kill the sons of these killers. That was because of what (the writer) of the Book of the Law of Moses had written.
The LORD had said that they must not do that. 'Do not kill fathers because their children (have done wrong things). And do not kill children because their fathers (have done wrong things). Each person must die

Chapter 15

Azariah becomes the king of Judah

1 Jeroboam had been king of Israel for nearly 27 years when Azariah began to rule (Judah). (Azariah) was the son of Amaziah, (who was) the king of Judah. 2 (Azariah) was 16 years old when he became king. He ruled in Jerusalem for 52 years. His mother's name was Jecoliah. She (was born in) Jerusalem. 3 Azariah did the right things in the sight of the LORD, as his father Amaziah had done. 4 But he did not remove the high places. The people (in Judah) continued to offer (animals to Baal) and to burn incense there. 5 And the LORD punished the king. The king had the illness called leprosy. He had it until the day that he died. He lived in a separate house. The king's son Jotham had to rule the palace and the people in the country (Judah). 6 Azariah did many other things while he was king. They (wrote) all those things in a book. It is called 'the reports about the kings of Judah'. 7 So Azariah died like his ancestors. And people buried him with them in the City of David. His son Jotham became king after him.

Zechariah becomes the king of Israel

8 When Azariah had been king for nearly 38 years, Zechariah became king of Israel in Samaria. (Zechariah was) the son of Jeroboam and he ruled (Israel) for 6 months. 9 He did bad things in the sight of the LORD, as his ancestors had done. He continued to do the sins of Jeroboam. (Jeroboam was) the son of Nebat and he had caused (the people in) Israel to do these (sins). 10 Shallum (was) the son of Jabesh. He (and his friends) decided to kill Zechariah. (Shallum) attacked (Zechariah) in front of the people. He killed him and he became king instead of him. 11 Other things happened while Zechariah ruled (Israel). They are in a book. It is called 'the reports about the kings of Israel'. 12 So it happened as the LORD had spoken to Jehu. (The LORD had said,) 'You and 4 of your descendants will rule Israel.'

Shallum becomes the king of Israel

13 When Uzziah had been the king of Judah for 39 years, Shallum became the king (of Israel). (Shallum was) the son of Jabesh. (Shallum) ruled in Samaria for one month. 14 Then Menahem went from Tirzah up to Samaria. (Menahem was) the son of Gadi. He attacked Shallum, (who was) the son of Jabesh, in Samaria. He killed him and he became king (of Israel) after him. 15 Other things that happened when Shallum was king are in a book. It is called 'the reports about the kings of Israel'. It includes the way that he killed (Zechariah). 16 When Menahem came from Tirzah, he attacked Tiphsah. (He attacked) everybody that was in the city (Tiphsah) and near it. (He did this) because they would not open their gates. He destroyed Tiphsah and he cut open all the pregnant women.

Menahem becomes the king of Israel

17 When Azariah had been the king of Judah for nearly 39 years, Menahem became the king of Israel. (Menahem was) the son of Gadi, and he ruled in Samaria for 10 years. 18 (Menahem) did what was bad in the sight of the LORD. All the time that he was king, he continued to do the sins of Jeroboam. (Jeroboam was) the son of Nebat. (Jeroboam) had caused (the people in) Israel to do these sins also. 19 Then Pul, (who was) the king of Assyria, attacked the country (Israel). Menahem gave him 1000 talents of silver so that (Pul) would help (Menahem). That would make (Menahem) stronger in his own country. 20 Menahem caused (the people in) Israel to give him this money. He caused every rich man to give 50 shekels of silver to the king of Assyria. So the king of Assyria went (home). He did not stay (for a) longer (time) in the country (Israel). 21 The other things that happened to King Menahem are in a book. People wrote them in a book. It is called 'the reports about the kings of Israel'. Everything that he did (is in that book). 22 So Menahem died like his ancestors. And Pekahiah, (who was) his son, became king after him.

Pekahiah becomes the king of Israel

23 When Azariah had been the king of Judah for nearly 50 years, Pekahiah became the king of Israel in Samaria. (Pekahiah was) the son of Menahem. He ruled (Israel) for two years. 24 Pekahiah did bad things in the sight of the LORD. He continued to do the sins of Jeroboam, (who was) the son of Nebat. (Jeroboam) had caused (the people in) Israel to do these sins also. 25 One of his important officers was Pekah, (who was) the son of Remaliah. (Pekah) decided to kill (Pekahiah). He took 50 men from Gilead with him, and he killed Pekahiah. (He also killed) Argob and Arieh in a strong room in the king's palace. (The king's palace was) in Samaria. So Pekah killed Pekahiah and he became king after him. 26 Somebody wrote the other things that King Pekahiah did in a book. It is called 'the reports about the kings of Israel'. (The book contains) everything that Pekahiah did.

Pekah becomes the king of Israel and Assyria beats Israel

27 When Azariah had been king of Judah for nearly 52 years, Pekah became the king of Israel in Samaria. (Pekah was) the son of Remaliah and he ruled (Israel) for 20 years. 28 Pekah did bad things in the sight of the LORD. He continued to do the sins of Jeroboam, (who was) the son of Nebat. (Jeroboam) had caused (the people in) Israel to do these sins also.

29 While Pekah was the king of Israel, Tiglath Pileser came from Assyria. (He was) the king (of Assyria). He beat (the people in many places in Israel): Ijon, Abel Beth Maacah, Janoah, Kedesh, Hazor, Gilead, Galilee and all of Naphtali. He took (all) the people (that lived in these places) to Assyria. 30 Then Hoshea decided to kill Pekah (who was) the son of Remaliah. (Hoshea was) the son of Elah. (Hoshea) attacked (Pekah) and killed him. So (Hoshea) became king after (Pekah). It was when Jotham had been king of Judah for nearly 20 years. (Jotham was) the son of Uzziah. 31 Somebody wrote the other things that King Pekah did in a book. It is called 'the reports about the kings of Israel'. (The book contains) everything that Pekah did.

Jotham becomes the king of Judah

32 When Pekah had been the king of Israel for nearly 2 years, Jotham began to rule Judah. (Pekah was) the son of Remaliah and (Jotham was) the son of Uzziah. 33 Jotham was 25 years old when he became king. And he ruled in Jerusalem for 16 years. His mother's name was Jerusha. She was the daughter of Zadok. 34 (Jotham) did what was right in the sight of the LORD, as his father Uzziah had done. 35 But he did not remove the high places. The people (in Judah) continued to offer (animals to Baal) and to burn incense on them. Jotham built again the High Gate of the house of the LORD. 36 Somebody wrote the other things that King Jotham did in a book. It is called 'the reports about the kings of Judah'. (The book contains) everything that Jotham did. 37 Then the LORD began to send Rezin and Pekah against (the people in) Judah. (Rezin was) the king of Aram and (Pekah was) the son of Remaliah. 38 And Jotham died like his ancestors and people buried him with his ancestors in the City of his ancestor, David. His son Ahaz became king after him.

Chapter 16

Ahaz becomes the king of Judah

1 When Pekah had been king (of Israel) for nearly 17 years, Ahaz began to rule Judah. (Pekah was) the son of Remaliah and Ahaz was the son of King Jotham (of Judah). 2 Ahaz was 20 years old when he became king. He ruled in Jerusalem for 16 years. He did not do what was right in the sight of the LORD his God. So he was not like his ancestor David. 3 He did the bad things that the kings of Israel did. He even caused his son to walk through fire. He did all the very bad things that people had done earlier (in Canaan). These were (the people that) the LORD had caused to leave (Canaan). He did this before (his people) the Jews (came into Canaan). 4 Ahaz burned animals and other things, and also incense on the high places. (He did it) on the tops of hills and under every wide tree.

5 Rezin (was) the king of Aram. Pekah (was) the king of Israel. (He was) the son of Remaliah. (Rezin and Pekah) marched up to Jerusalem, to fight against it. (Their armies) stayed all-round Ahaz (and his city), but they could not beat him. 6 At that time, Rezin (who was) the king of Aram got Elath back for Aram. He caused the men from Judah to leave (Elath). People from Edom then moved into Elath. They have lived there until now. 7 Then Ahaz sent people with messages to Tiglath Pileser, (who was) the king of Assyria. They said, 'I am your servant.

And I will do anything that you ask me to do.

Come up (to Jerusalem) and save me from the power of the kings of Aram and Israel. They are attacking me.' 8 Also, Ahaz took the silver and gold out of the house of the LORD. He took the valuable things out of his own palace. He sent them (all) as a gift to the king of Assyria. 9 So the king of Assyria did what (Ahaz) had asked. He attacked Damascus and he beat its people. He sent the people that had lived there to Kir. And he killed Rezin.

10 Then King Ahaz went to Damascus to meet King Tiglath Pileser of Assyria. (Ahaz) saw an altar in Damascus. He sent a picture of the altar to Uriah the priest. (He also sent) a plan, so that (people) could make one. 11 So Uriah the priest built an altar. It was the same as the (one in) the plans that King Ahaz had sent from Damascus. (Uriah) finished it before King Ahaz returned. 12 Then the king returned from Damascus. And he saw the altar. He went near it and he climbed up to it. He offered things (to false gods) on it.

13 He offered (these things to his god) on the altar:

- an animal (with its blood)

- something with flour (but no blood) in it

- a drink that he poured (on to the altar)

- the blood (of animals) to bring him peace.

14 A bronze altar stood in front of the LORD (in his house). It was between the new altar and the house of the LORD. (Ahaz) brought it from the front of the house (of the LORD). And he put it on the north side of the new altar.

15 Then King Ahaz said that Uriah the priest must do (these things). 'On the large new altar, offer these (gifts):

- an animal (with its blood) in the morning

- something with flour in it in the evening

- an animal on behalf of the king

- something with flour in it on behalf of the king

- an animal as a gift on behalf of all the people in the country

- something with flour in it on behalf of the people (in the country)

- all the blood from the animals that you kill.

But I will use the bronze altar to ask (God) to guide me.'

16 So Uriah the priest did what King Ahaz asked him to do.

17 King Ahaz also took away pieces from the sides (of the bronze altar). He took the bowls away from the parts that people could move. He took the large bowl for water away from the bronze male cows that it was on. He put it on stone instead. 18 He took away the roof that they had made to cover (the king's path) on the Sabbath. (It was at) the house of the LORD). He removed the door outside the house (of the LORD) that the king used to come in through. The king of Assyria wanted him to do this. 19 Somebody wrote the other things that King Ahaz did, in a book. It is called 'the reports about the kings of Judah'. (The book contains) everything that Ahaz did. 20 So Ahaz died like his ancestors. And people buried him with his ancestors in the City of David. And Hezekiah, (who was) his son, became king after him.

Chapter 17

Hoshea, who was the last king of Israel

1 When Ahaz had been the king of Judah for nearly 12 years, Hoshea became the king of Israel in Samaria. (Hoshea was) the son of Elah and he ruled (Israel) for 9 years. 2 He did things that were very wrong in the sight of the LORD. But he was not like the kings of Israel who were before him. 3 Shalmaneser (was) the king of Assyria. He came up (to Samaria) to attack Hoshea. He had done everything that Shalmaneser had asked him to do. (Every year) he had paid him all the money (that Shalmaneser had asked him for). 4 But Shalmaneser had discovered that now Hoshea was not a good friend (of Shalmaneser). (Hoshea) had sent people with a message to So, (who was) the king of Egypt. (Hoshea) did not pay any more money to the king of Assyria, as he had done every year. So Shalmaneser caught (Hoshea) and put him into a prison. 5The king of Assyria attacked all the country (Israel). (His army) marched against Samaria and it stayed round it for 3 years.

6 When Hoshea had been king (of Israel) for nearly 9 years, the king of Assyria beat the people in Samaria. He sent many of the people from Israel to Assyria. He caused them to live in these places:

- Halah,

- Gozan by the River Habor and

- towns in Media.

7 All this happened because (the people in) Israel had not obeyed the LORD. (The LORD) was their God, who had brought them out of Egypt. (God had) made them free from the power of Pharaoh, (who was) the king of Egypt. (But now) they had worshipped other gods. 8 They had done the things that the people (in Canaan) before them had done. Those people (in Canaan) were the people that the LORD had caused to go to other places. The people in Israel had also done things that the kings of Israel had caused them do. 9The people in Israel did things against the LORD (who was) their God. (Those things) were not right, and they did them secretly. They built high places for themselves in every town. (They built them everywhere) from places where people watched (their sheep) to strong cities. 10 They put up special stones (for their gods) and Asherah poles. (They put them) on every high hill and under every wide tree. 11 At every high place they burned incense. The people that the LORD had sent out (from Canaan) before them had done that. Israel's people did very bad things that made the LORD very angry. 12 They worshipped false gods. The LORD had said, 'You must not do that.' 13 The LORD had sent this message to Israel and to Judah. He sent it by all his prophets and by everyone that he showed things to. 'Do not do more bad things. Obey my words. (Obey) all my rules. Do everything that is in my Law. I told your ancestors that they must obey (my Law). I gave you (my Law) by my servants (who were) the prophets.' 14 But the (people in Israel) would not listen. They were like their ancestors had been. They would not change in their minds. (Their ancestors) did not believe that the LORD (would help them). (The LORD was) their God. 15 They did not obey his Law. They did not agree with the covenant that (God) had made with their ancestors. God had said that bad things would happen to them. But they did not listen. They followed false gods that had no value. So they themselves became of no value. They did what the people that lived next to them did. But the LORD had said, 'Do not do what they do!' But they still did these things. The LORD had said that they should not do them! 16 They threw away all the laws of the LORD, (who was) their God. They made false gods for themselves. The shapes (of those gods) were the same as baby cows. (They also made) an Asherah pole. They fell to their knees to all the stars (in the skies) and they worshipped Baal. 17 They burned their sons and their daughters in fire (for Baal). They used their false gods to tell them what would happen. They used bad spirits (to do strange things). They did very, very bad things in the sight of the LORD. This made him very, very angry. 18 The LORD was so angry with Israel that he sent them away from himself. Only the tribe of Judah remained.

19 Even Judah did not obey the Law of the LORD (who was) their God. They did the same things that Israel had done. 20 So the LORD sent away all the people out of Israel. He hurt them. He gave them to people who would rob them. They had to go away from where he lived.

21 When (God) tore Israel away from David's family, they made Jeroboam into their king. (Jeroboam was) the son of Nebat. Jeroboam caused Israel not to obey the LORD. He caused them to do very bad things. 22The people in Israel continued to do all the sins of Jeroboam. They did not turn away from them 23 until the LORD sent them away from himself. (The LORD) had said by all his servants the prophets that this would happen. So the soldiers from Assyria took the people in Israel away from their own country. They went into exile in Assyria and they are still there.

24 The king of Assyria brought people to live in the towns in Samaria. They came from Babylon, Cuthah, Avva, Hamath and Sepharvaim. They lived (in Samaria) where Israel's people had lived. They lived in its towns and they ruled Samaria. 25 When those people first lived (in Samaria), they did not worship the LORD. So (the LORD) sent lions among them. (The lions) killed some of the people. 26 They reported this to the king of Assyria. (The report said,) 'You sent some people from (your country). You caused them to live in the towns in Samaria. But they do not know what the god of that country wants them to do. He has sent lions among them. The people do not know what to do. So the lions are killing them.' 27 So the king of Assyria said, 'You caught some priests in Samaria. Send one of them back to live there. He can teach the people what the god of that country wants them to do.' 28 So they brought one of the priests that was in exile back to live in Bethel. He taught the people how to worship the LORD.

29 But each group of people, from different countries, made its own gods. They did this in each town where they lived. They did it in the places where the people in Samaria had made altars on the high places. 30The men from Babylon (worshipped the god called) Succoth-Benoth. The men from Cuthah (worshipped the god called) Nergal. The men from Hamath (worshipped the god called) Ashima. 31 The men from Avva (worshipped the gods called) Nibhaz and Tartak. The people from Sepharvaim burned their children in a fire (for their gods). The gods of the people from Sepharvaim (were called) Adrammelech and Anammelech. 32 They (all) worshipped the LORD. But they also made many of their own people priests (of their gods). (They worshipped those gods) at the gods' houses on the high places. 33 They worshipped the LORD, but they also worshipped their own gods. They did what they had always done in their own countries. 34 Even today, they still do those things. They do not (really) worship the LORD, neither do they obey his laws and his rules. (They do not really do) the things that the LORD asked the descendants of Jacob to do. (The LORD) called him (and his descendants) Israel. 35 When the LORD made a covenant with the Jews, he said (to them), 'Do not worship any other gods. Do not get down on your knees to them. Do not be their servants. Do not burn anything for them. 36 But you must worship only the LORD. He brought you out from (the country called) Egypt. He did this very powerfully and he helped you very much. You must fall to your knees to him and you must burn things (on your altar) to him. 37 You must always obey the words that he wrote for you. And (you must) obey him about everything. (You must obey all) his laws and rules. Do not worship other gods. 38 Do not forget the covenant that I made with you. Do not worship other gods. 39 Always worship the LORD (who is) your God. It is he who will save you from the power of all your enemies.' 40 But they would not listen (to him). They continued to do what they had always done.

41 Even while they were worshipping the LORD, they were also the servants of (their) idols. Until today, their children and their grandchildren do what their fathers did.

Chapter 18

Hezekiah becomes the king of Judah

1 When Hoshea had been the king of Israel for nearly three years, Hezekiah began to rule Judah. (Hoshea was) the son of Elah and (Hezekiah was) the son of Ahaz. 2 (Hezekiah) was 25 years old when he became king. And he ruled in Jerusalem for 29 years. His mother's name was Abijah. (She was) the daughter of Zechariah. 3 (Hezekiah) did what was right in the sight of the LORD. He did what his ancestor David had done. 4 He removed the high places. He broke completely the stones (where people worshipped). He cut down the Asherah poles. He broke into pieces the bronze snake that Moses had made. Until then, the people in Israel had burned incense to it. It was called Nehushtan. 5 Hezekiah believed in the LORD (who is) the God of Israel. None of the other kings of Judah was like him, either before him or after him. 6 He really loved the LORD and he always obeyed him. He obeyed the laws that the LORD had given to Moses. 7 And the LORD helped him in everything that he decided to do. So everything that happened was very good! He did not obey the king of Assyria. He did not become his servant. 8 He beat the people in Philistia as far as Gaza and the country that was near it. (He did this) from places where people watched to strong cities.

9 Shalmaneser (was) the king of Assyria. When Hezekiah had been king for nearly 4 years, Shalmaneser marched (his army) to Samaria. (The army) stayed round Samaria (for nearly three years). That was when Hoshea had been the king of Israel for nearly 7 years. (Hoshea was) the son of Elah. 10 After three years, the soldiers from Assyria beat the people in Samaria. So they beat them when Hezekiah had been king (of Judah) for nearly 6 years. Hoshea had been the king of Judah for nearly 9 years.

11 The king of Assyria took all the people out of Israel to Assyria. He caused them to live in these places:

213

- Halah,

- Gozan by the River Habor and

- towns in Media.

12 This happened because they had not obeyed the LORD. (The LORD was) their God. They had not obeyed his covenant. (The covenant contained) all the rules that Moses had told them about. (Moses was) a servant of the LORD. They did not listen to Moses' words and they did not obey them.

13 When Hezekiah had ruled (Judah) for nearly 14 years, Sennacherib attacked all the strong cities in Judah. He made them his cities. (Sennacherib was) the king of Assyria. 14 So King Hezekiah of Judah sent this message to the king of Assyria. (Sennacherib was) at Lachish. 'What I did was wrong. March away from me. Then I will pay everything that you ask me to pay.' The king of Assyria asked King Hezekiah of Judah to send to him 300 talents of silver and 30 talents of gold. 15 So Hezekiah gave (to Sennacherib) all the silver from the house of the LORD. And he gave him all the silver that they found in the king's palace. 16 Hezekiah (was) the king of Judah. He had covered all the doors in the house of the LORD with gold. And he covered the wood on which the doors hung with gold. At this time, he took it all off and he gave it to the king of Assyria.

Sennacherib says that he will attack Jerusalem

17 The king of Assyria sent (three people) from Lachish to King Hezekiah. Hezekiah was at Jerusalem. (They came) with a large army. These were the three people:

- the most important leader of his army

- the leader of his officers

- the leader of his army where they fought.

They came to Jerusalem and they stopped at the aqueduct by the Higher Pool. It was on the road to the field (by the water) where people washed things. (It was called the Washerman's Field.)

18 They asked for the king to come to them. These (three people) went out to meet them:

- Eliakim, (who was) the son of Hilkiah. He decided what would happen in the palace.

- Shebna. He helped the king.

- Joah, (who was) the son of Asaph. He wrote down the things that happened.

19 The leader of (Sennacherib's) army where they fought said this to them:

Chapter 19

The LORD saves Jerusalem

1 When King Hezekiah heard (the report of his servants), he tore his clothes. Then he put on sackcloth (hairy clothes) and he went into the house of the LORD (in Jerusalem). 2 And he sent Eliakim and Shebna and the leaders of the priests to Isaiah (who was) a prophet. (Isaiah) was the son of Amoz. (Eliakim was) the most important servant in the (king's) palace. (Shebna was) the leader of the (king's) government. And (Eliakim, Shebna and the priests) all wore sackcloth (hairy clothes).

3 And they told (Isaiah), 'Hezekiah says, "There are many problems at this time. And (the leader of the army's) words make me ashamed. (The problems) are like a child that is ready to be born. But (its mother) is not strong enough for it to be born.

4 Perhaps the LORD, (who is) your God, will do something about all the words of the leader of the army. His master is the king of Assyria. (The king) sent him to laugh in a bad way at the God who really is alive. Maybe the LORD your God will tell him that his words were wrong. (God) has heard them. So, pray about the people that remain (in Jerusalem)." ' 5 So Hezekiah's servants came to Isaiah. 6Isaiah said to them, 'Tell your master that the LORD says, "Do not be afraid of the words that you have heard. The servants of the king of Assyria are not important. They have said very bad things about me. 7Listen (to me)! I will put a spirit into (the king of Assyria). Then, he will hear a certain report. When (he will hear it), he will return to his own country. And there, I will cause (someone) to kill him with a sword." '

8 Then, the leader of the army heard that the king of Assyria had left Lachish (city). So he left Jerusalem and he found the king (of Assyria). The king was fighting against Libnah (city). 9 But (the king of Assyria) heard (this report) about Tirhakah. (Tirhakah) was the king of Ethiopia. (The report) said, 'He has come out (from Ethiopia) to fight against you.' So again he sent people (to Jerusalem) with a message. They had this message for Hezekiah. 10 'Say this to King Hezekiah of Judah. Say, "You are hoping that your God will help you. But do not let him tell you what is not true. (Your God) says that the king of Assyria will not destroy Jerusalem. 11 But you have heard what the kings of Assyria have done to all (the other) countries. They destroyed them completely. And (your God) will not save you. 12 The gods of (these other) countries did not save them. My fathers destroyed Gozan, Haran and Rezeph. And (they have killed) the people of Eden (that lived) in Tel Assar. 13 The kings of Hamath and Arpad have gone. The king of the city called Sepharvaim has gone. The kings of Hena and Ivvah have gone." '

14 And Hezekiah received the letter from the people that brought the message. And he read it and then he went up to the house of the LORD. He opened the letter in front of the LORD. 15 And Hezekiah prayed to the LORD. He said, 'LORD, (you are) the God of Israel. You sit on a seat between the special angels. Only you are the God of all the countries in the world. You have made the skies and the earth. 16 LORD, turn your ears to me and hear (me). LORD, open your eyes and look (at this letter). Listen to the words of Sennacherib. He sent them to laugh in a bad way at the God who really is alive. 17 It is true, LORD, that the kings of Assyria have made empty places of many countries and their lands. 18 They threw their gods into the fire. They destroyed them because they are not really God. Human hands made them from wood and stone. 19 So now, our LORD and our God, save us from the power of (the king of Assyria)! Then all the people and all the kings in the world will know that only you are the LORD.'

20 Then Isaiah, (who was) the son of Amoz, sent a message to Hezekiah. 'The LORD, (who is) the God of Israel, says, "I heard when you prayed to me about Sennacherib, the king of Assyria." So,

21 this is what the LORD says about him.

"(The) people who live in Zion

do not like you.

They laugh at you.

(The) people who live in Jerusalem

move the head about behind you.

22 Whom have you said bad things about?

They were not true!

Who is it that you have shouted at?

Who is it that you have looked at proudly?

(The answer is) the Holy (God) of Israel!

23 You have used your servants to say bad things about the Lord.

You have said, 'With many of my chariots

I have gone up very high mountains,

the highest (mountains) in Lebanon.

I have cut its tallest cedars down,

and the best of its pine trees.

I went to its highest places and to its best forests.

24 I dug wells and I drank (the) water (from them).

I made all the rivers in Egypt dry with my feet.'

25 Surely, you have heard (this)!

I decided what to do a long time ago!

I decided what to do in past (times)!

Now it has happened.

You have caused strong cities to become mountains of stones.

26 The people in them are not strong.

They are not happy. And they are confused.

They are like plants in a field.

(They are like) the new parts of young green plants.

(They are like) grass on the roof (of a house).

(The hot winds burn them) before they can grow.

27 I know (everything about you).

(I know) when you sit down.

And (I know) when you go out.

And (I know) when you come in.

And (I know) when you shout proudly at me.

28 You have shouted proudly at me

and you have said bad things about me.

So I will put my hook in your nose

and my bit in your mouth.

And I will cause you to return home by the same way that you came."

29 And this will show it to you, (Hezekiah).

"This year, you will eat what grows from its own (seeds).

And in the second year, (you will eat) what grows from (the first year's seeds).

But in the third year you will plant (seeds). And you will pick (what grows from them).

And you will plant again the vineyards and you will enjoy their fruit.

30 And this will happen also to the people that remain in Judah.

(They will be like plants.)

They put roots down below (the ground) and they grow fruit above (it).

(The people will be like that.)

31 (That will happen) because a remnant will come out from Jerusalem.

And the people that remain will come out from Zion Hill.

The great love that the LORD of Everything has (for his people) will cause that to happen!"

32 This is what the LORD says about the king of Assyria.

"He will not come into this city,

and he will not shoot an arrow here.

He will not stand in front of it with a shield.

He will not build mountains of earth against it.

33 He will return (to Assyria) by the way that he came,

and he will not come into this city."

(This is) the promise of the LORD.

34 "So I will make this city safe and I will save it.

(I will do this to keep) my good name.

I promised my servant David (that I would do it). (That is why I will do it.)" '

35 That night, the LORD's angel went and he killed 185 000 men in the army from Assyria. When people got up in the morning, they saw all those dead bodies! 36 So Sennacherib, (who was) the king of Assyria, took his army away. He returned to (Assyria) and he stayed there in Nineveh. 37 (After that time) he was worshipping his god Nisroch in the house (of Nisroch). (Two of) his sons, Adrammelech and Sharezer, killed him with (their) swords. Then, they ran away into the country called Ararat. (So) Esarhaddon, (who was another of) his sons, ruled instead of (Sennacherib).

Chapter 20

Hezekiah's illness and his mistake

1 At that time, Hezekiah was very ill. He nearly died. And Isaiah the prophet, (who was) the son of Amoz, went to (Hezekiah). And (Isaiah) said to (Hezekiah), 'This is what the LORD says. "Make everything ready (for your son), because you will die. You will not get well again." ' 2 Then Hezekiah turned his face to the wall and he prayed to the LORD. 3 And he said, 'Remember, LORD, that I have been your good servant. I have always loved you very much. You have seen that I always did good things.' And Hezekiah wept very much. 4 Then the LORD told Isaiah (again what) to say. This happened before he left the middle (of the king's house). 5 'Go back! Say to Hezekiah, (who is) the leader of my people, "This is what the LORD says. (The LORD) is the God of your ancestor David. I have heard what you prayed. I have seen that you have cried. I will make you well again. On the third day from now you will go to the house of the LORD. 6 I will let you live for 15 more years. I will save you and this city from the power of the king of Assyria. Also, I will keep this city safe, because of my servant David." ' 7 And (Isaiah said), 'Make some medicine with figs in it.' So (the king's servants) did. They put the medicine on the bad place on (Hezekiah's) skin that made him ill. And he was soon well again.

8 Hezekiah had asked, 'How will I know that the LORD will make me well again? (How will I know that) I will go up to the house of the LORD on the third day from now?' 9 Isaiah answered, 'This is a like a sign to you from the LORD. It will show you (that my words are true). (It is a message to you) that (tells you this). The LORD will do what he has promised (to do). Do you want the shadow (on these stairs) to go down 10 stairs? Or do you want it to go back up 10 stairs?' 10 'It is easy to cause the shadow to go down 10 stairs', said Hezekiah. 'So, cause it to go back 10 stairs.' 11 Then the prophet prayed to the LORD. And the LORD caused the shadow to go back 10 stairs. It had already gone down 10 stairs on the stairs that Ahaz had made.

12 When this happened, Merodach-Baladan was the king of Babylon. (He was) the son of Baladan. (Merodach-Baladan) sent Hezekiah letters and a gift. He had heard that (Hezekiah) was ill. 13 Hezekiah met the people with the messages (that the king of Babylon) had sent. (Hezekiah) showed to them everything that he had stored. (He showed them) silver and gold, spices and very good oil. (He showed them) all his weapons and everything else that was valuable. There was nothing in his palace or in his whole country that Hezekiah did not show them. 14 Then Isaiah the prophet went to King Hezekiah and (Isaiah) asked him, 'What did these men say? And from where did they come to you?' Then Hezekiah replied, 'They came to me from the far country called Babylon.' 15 The prophet asked, 'What did they see in your palace?' 'They saw everything (that is) in my palace', Hezekiah replied. 'There is nothing among my valuable things that I did not show to them.'

16 Then Isaiah said to Hezekiah, 'Listen to what the LORD says. 17 "This is what will surely happen. (Soldiers from Babylon) will take everything (that is) in your palace to Babylon. They will take everything that your ancestors have stored here until now. They will not leave anything (here)", says the LORD. 18"And (soldiers from Babylon) will take away some of your own descendants, your sons that will be born to you. And they will become eunuchs in the palace of the king of Babylon." ' 19 And Hezekiah replied, 'You have spoken good words from the LORD.' But what he thought was, 'There will be no war. It will be safe while I am alive.'

20 All the other events while Hezekiah ruled (Judah) are in a book. It is called 'the reports about the kings of Judah'. Everything that he did is in the book. It includes the (story of the) pool and the aqueduct, through which he brought water into the city (Jerusalem). 21 So Hezekiah died like his ancestors. And Manasseh, (who was) his son, became king after him.

Chapter 21

Manasseh becomes the king of Judah

1 Manasseh was 12 years old when he became king. He ruled in Jerusalem for 55 years. His mother's name was Hephzibah. 2 Manasseh did very bad things in the sight of the LORD. He did all the bad things that the people before him (in Canaan) had done. The LORD had sent those people away before Israel's people (had come into the country).

3 He built again the high places that his father Hezekiah had destroyed. He made altars for (the false god) Baal. And he made an Asherah pole, as King Ahab of Israel had done. He fell on to his knees in front of all the stars and he worshipped them. 4 He built altars in the house of the LORD. But the LORD had said (about his house), 'I will put my Name in Jerusalem.'

5 He built altars to all the stars in both courts which were outside the house of the LORD.

6 He burnt his own son in a fire (for one of the false gods). He used bad spirits (to do strange things). He used false gods to try to discover what would happen. He visited bad people to talk to dead people. He visited bad people who used magic. He did very, very bad things in the sight of the LORD. This made (the LORD) very, very angry. 7 He had cut a piece of wood into an Asherah pole. He put it in the house (of the LORD). But the LORD had said to both David and to his son, Solomon, 'I have chosen Jerusalem out of all the tribes of Israel. I will put my Name in this house for all time. 8 I will never cause the feet of the people in Israel go away from this country again. I gave (this country) to their ancestors. But they must do everything that I asked them to do. They must obey all the Law that my servant Moses gave to them.' 9 But the people did not listen (to the LORD). Manasseh caused them not to obey (the Law). Then, the people in Israel did more bad things than the people that the LORD had killed before them.

10 So the LORD said by his servants (who were) prophets, 11 'Manasseh (is) the king of Judah. He has done these really bad sins. He has done more bad things than the people called Amorites. They lived (in Canaan) before him. His false gods have caused (the people in) Judah to do many sins. 12 So the LORD, (who is) the God of Israel, says, "I will cause very, very bad things to happen to Jerusalem and to Judah. Those things will be a bad surprise to everybody who hears about them! 13 I will put a line that measures over Jerusalem. It is the line that I used against Samaria. And it is the plumb line that I used against Ahab's family. I will clean Jerusalem as someone washes a dish. I will clean it and turn it. Its top will be under (the dish)!

14 I will leave the remnant of my people and I will give them to their enemies. All their enemies will rob them. Then they will kill them, 15 because they have done very bad things in my sight. They have made me very, very angry. (They have done that) since their ancestors came out from Egypt until today." '

16 Also, Manasseh poured out so much blood that he filled Jerusalem from one end to the other (with blood). (The blood was from) people who had not done anything wrong. And there were the sins that he had caused (the people in) Judah to do. They did very bad things in the sight of the LORD.

17 All the other events while Manasseh ruled are in a book. It is called 'the reports about the kings of Judah'. It contains everything that he did. And it includes all his sins. 18 So Manasseh died like his ancestors. People buried him in the garden of the palace. It is called the garden of Uzza. And Amon, (who was) his son, became king after him.

Amon becomes the king of Judah

19 Amon was 22 years old when he became king. And he ruled in Jerusalem for two years. His mother's name was Meshullemeth, (who was) the daughter of Haruz. (Haruz) was from Jotbah. 20 Amon did very bad things in the sight of the LORD, as his father Manasseh had done. 21 He did all the (bad) things that his father had done. He worshipped the false gods that his father had worshipped. He went down on his knees to them. 22 He left the LORD, (who was) the God of his ancestors. He did not do the things that the LORD wanted him to do. 23 Amon's officers had some bad ideas against him. Then they killed him in his palace. 24 Then The people (who lived) in the country of Judah killed them. They killed all Amon's killers. They made Josiah, (who was Amon's) son, king instead. 25 The other events while Amon was king are in a book. It is called 'the reports about the kings of Judah'. Everything that he did is in (that book). 26 People buried him in his grave in the garden of Uzza. Josiah, (who was) his son, became king after him.

Chapter 22

Josiah becomes the king of Judah

1 Josiah was 8 years old when he became king. He ruled in Jerusalem for 31 years. His mother's name was Jedidah (who was) the daughter of Adaiah. (Adaiah) came from (a town called) Bozkath. 2 (Josiah) did what was right in the sight of the LORD. He lived like his ancestor David did. He did not fail to obey the LORD in any way.

Hilkiah finds the Law Book

3 When Josiah had been king for nearly 18 years, he sent Shaphan to the house of the LORD. (Shaphan was) the son of Azaliah, (who was) the son of Meshullam. (Josiah) said,

4 'Go up to Hilkiah, (who is) the leader of the priests. Ask him to get ready the money that people have brought into the house of the LORD. The people gave it to the men by the doors (of the house of the LORD). 5 (The priests) must give (the money) to the men who will be leaders for the work in the house (of the LORD). These leaders must pay the men who will mend the house of the LORD. 6 These men will work with wood, and they will build with stones. So they must buy wood. And they must buy stones that people have cut. They must buy them to mend the house (of the LORD). 7 But (the priests) do not need to ask how (the workers) used the money. (The workers) will use the money that (the priests) gave them in the right way.'

8 Hilkiah, (who was) the leader of the priests, said this to Shaphan. (Shaphan) wrote everything (for the king). 'I have found the Law Book in the house of the LORD.' He gave (the book) to Shaphan, who read it. 9 Then Shaphan, who wrote everything (for the king), went to the king, He said to him, 'Your officers have paid all the money that was in the house of the LORD. They have given it to the workers and their leaders in the house (of the LORD).' 10 Then Shaphan, who wrote everything (for the king), said to the king, 'Hilkiah the priest has given me a book.' And Shaphan read from (the book) in front of the king.

11 When the king heard the words from the Law Book, he tore his own clothes. 12 He said that Hilkiah, Ahikam, Acbor, Shaphan and Asaiah must do this. Hilkiah (was) the priest and Ahikam (was) the son of Shaphan. Acbor (was) the son of Micaiah and Shaphan wrote everything (for the king). Asaiah was the king's helper. 13 'Go. And ask the LORD about what is in this book. (Ask) on my behalf, on behalf of the people (in Jerusalem) and on behalf of all (the people in Judah). Ask about this book that (Hilkiah) found. The LORD is very, very angry with us. He is so angry that it is like a fire! (This is because) our ancestors have not obeyed the words in this book. They have not done everything that is in the book. And (it is the same) for us.'

14 So Hilkiah, (who was) the priest, and Ahikam, Acbor, Shaphan and Asaiah went to speak to Huldah. (Huldah) was a prophetess. She was the wife of Shallum (who was) the son of Tikvah. (Tikvah was) the son of Harhas, who kept the king's clothes. Huldah lived in the north part of Jerusalem. 15 She said to them, '(The LORD is) the God of Israel. This is what the LORD says. "Tell this to the man who sent you to me." 16 This is what the LORD is saying. "I will bring much trouble to this place and to its people. It is all in the book that the king of Judah has read. 17 (This is because) they have gone away from me. They have burned incense to other (false) gods. All the false gods that they made with their hands have made me very, very angry. I am so angry with this place that it is like a fire. Nobody will put out (the fire)." 18 The king of Judah sent you to ask for (an answer) from the LORD. Give this answer (to the king). "The LORD, (who is) the God of Israel, says this. (He says it) about the words that you heard (from the Law Book).

19 I heard you (when you prayed to me)," says the LORD. "(I heard you) for these reasons:

- You knew that you needed to do something.

- You made yourself humble in front of the LORD.

You tore your clothes and you wept in front of me.

(You did all that) when you heard (my words). I spoke against this place and its people. I said that bad things would happen to them. (An enemy) will destroy them.

20 So I will bring you to your ancestors. And they will bury you in your grave in peace. You yourself will never see all the bad things that I will cause to happen to this place." ' That was the answer that they took back to the king.

Chapter 23

King Josiah and the covenant

1 So the king (Josiah) asked all the leaders of Judah and Jerusalem to come together.

2 He went up to the house of the LORD. All the people, from the least to the greatest, went with him. These people went:

- the men from Judah

- the people in Jerusalem

- the priests and the prophets.

He read to them, while they listened, all the words in the Book of the Covenant. They had found this (book) in the house of the LORD.

3 The king stood in his place (in the house of the LORD). He promised, in front of the LORD, that he would obey the covenant. He promised these things:

- He would work for the LORD and he would obey him.

He would try as much as he could to obey the LORD's words, his rules and his laws.

So (Josiah) agreed with all the words that were in the Book of the Covenant. Then all the people also promised to obey the covenant.

4 Then the king spoke to Hilkiah and to the other priests. And he spoke to the men who watched at the door (of God's house). He told them what they must do. Hilkiah (was) the leader of the priests. They must take out from the house of the LORD everything that people had made for Baal. And they must take out everything that people had made for Asherah and for all the stars (in the sky). He burned them outside Jerusalem, in a field in the Kidron Valley. Then he took the ashes to Bethel. 5 He sent away the priests of the false gods. The kings of Judah had them to burn incense on the high places. (These were in) the towns of Judah and (the hills) round Jerusalem. (These priests) burned incense to Baal, to the sun and to the moon. They also burned incense to all the stars and to the groups of stars. 6 He took the Asherah pole away from the house of the LORD to the Kidron Valley. (This valley was) outside Jerusalem. He burned the (Asherah pole) there. He made it into a powder and he threw the dirt (from it) over the graves of the people. 7 He also destroyed the houses where the male prostitutes from the house (of the LORD) lived. They were in the house of the LORD. Also, the women made cloth there for Asherah. 8 Josiah brought out all the priests (of false gods) from the towns in Judah. He destroyed the high places, where the priests had burned incense, from Geba to Beersheba. He destroyed the high places at (one of) the gates of the city (Jerusalem). It was called the Gate of Joshua, who was the ruler of the city. It is on the left side of the most important gate (of the city). 9 The priests from the high places did not work at the altar of the LORD in Jerusalem. But they did eat the unleavened bread with the other priests. 10 (Josiah) destroyed Topheth, which was in the Valley of Ben Hinnom. After this, nobody could use it to burn his son or his daughter in the fire to (the false god) Molech. 11 The kings of Judah had made (copies of) horses for the sun (god). (Josiah) removed them from near the door of the house of the LORD. (The horses) were in a court (outside the house). (It was) near the room of an officer called Nathan Melech. Josiah then burned the chariots that they had made for the sun (god). 12 The kings of Judah had built altars on the roof of the house of the LORD. (They were) near the high room of Ahaz. (Josiah) knocked them down. Manasseh had built altars in the two courts of the house of the LORD. (Josiah) took them away from there and he broke them into pieces. He threw the bits into the Kidron Valley.

13 King (Josiah) also destroyed the high places that were on the east (side) of Jerusalem. They were on the south side of the hill called the Hill of Offence. King Solomon had built some of these (high places) for (these false gods):

Ashtoreth. (She was) a very, very bad female god. The people in Sidon (worshipped her).

Chemosh. (He was) a very, bad god. (The people in) Moab (worshipped him).

217

Molech. (He was) the very, very bad god of the people in Ammon.

14 (Josiah) broke the special stones into small pieces. He cut down the Asherah poles. He covered the places where they had been with human bones.

15 (Josiah) even destroyed the altar at Bethel. It was a high place that Jeroboam had made. (He was) the son of Nebat, who had caused the people of Israel to sin. He even destroyed that altar and high place! He burned the high place and he broke (the ash) into powder. He also burned the Asherah pole. 16 Then Josiah looked (at everything that was) round him. When he saw graves in the sides of hills, he sent (someone) to take the bones from them. They burned them on the altar, (so that people would not use it again). He had made it dirty. God had said that this would happen. He had said it by a man of God. 17 Then (the king) asked, 'I can see a (large) stone. What is it?' The men from the city said to him, 'It is the grave of the man of God. He came from Judah. He said things against the altar in Bethel. He said what you would do to it.' 18 'Do not move (his stone)', he said. 'Do not let anyone move his bones.' So they did not move his bones, or the bones of the prophet who had come from Samaria. 19 And Josiah did to all the towns in Samaria what he had done in Bethel. The kings of Israel had built altars (in) the high places, which had made (the LORD) angry. (Josiah) took away all these things. He made them dirty (so that people would not use them again). 20 He killed all the priests (of the false gods) at the high places. (He killed them) on their own altars. He burned human bones on (the altars). Then he went back to Jerusalem.

21 Then the king said what all the people must do. 'Have a special meal (called) the Passover. (Have it) for the LORD, (who is) your God. Obey the rules that are in Book of the Covenant.' 22 There was never a Passover like it, since the days (in the Book of) Judges. There was nothing like it, all the times when there were kings in Judah and Israel. 23 Josiah had been king for nearly 18 years when they had this Passover for the LORD.

24 Josiah did all these things to obey the rules in the Law (Book). This was the book that Hilkiah the priest had found in the house of the LORD.

- (Josiah) sent away the people that tried to speak to dead people.

- (He sent away) the men that did magic.

- (He destroyed) the false gods that were in people's houses.

(He destroyed) all the other really bad things that were in Judah and in Jerusalem.

25 There was never a king like (Josiah). He turned to the LORD like (no other king), either before him or after him. (He obeyed the LORD) with all his mind and with all his soul and with all his strength. He obeyed all the Law of Moses.

26 But the LORD was still very angry with Judah. He was angry because of everything that Manasseh had done to make him angry. He was so angry that it was like a hot fire. 27 So the LORD said, 'I will also send Judah away from where I am. (I will send them) as I sent Israel away. And I will go away from Jerusalem, the city which I chose for my house. I said about (my house), "My Name will always be there." '

28 Other things happened while Josiah ruled (Judah). Everything that he did is in a book. It is called 'the reports about the kings of Judah'.

King Josiah dies

29 While Josiah was king, Pharaoh Neco (was) the king of Egypt. (Pharaoh Neco) went up to the River Euphrates, to help the king of Assyria. King Josiah marched out to meet (Pharaoh Neco). There was a war between them, and Neco killed (Josiah) at Megiddo. 30 Josiah's servants brought his dead body from Megiddo to Jerusalem in a chariot. People buried him in his own grave. And the people in the country (Judah) poured oil on Jehoahaz. They made him king after his father. (Jehoahaz was) the son of Josiah.

Jehoahaz becomes the king of Judah

31 Jehoahaz was 23 years old when he became king. He ruled in Jerusalem for three months. His mother's name was Hamutal, (who was) the daughter of Jeremiah. She came from Libnah.

32 (Jehoahaz) did very bad things in the sight of the LORD, as his ancestors had done. 33 Pharaoh Neco tied him (in a prison) at Riblah, so (Jehoahaz) could not rule in Jerusalem. (Riblah is) in the country called Hamath. (Neco) caused Judah to pay him 100 talents of silver and one talent of gold.

Jehoiakim becomes the king of Judah

34 And then Pharaoh Neco made Eliakim, (who was Josiah's) son, king (of Judah). (He became king) after his father Josiah. (Neco) changed Eliakim's name to Jehoiakim. Then he took Jehoahaz away with him to Egypt. (Jehoahaz) died in Egypt. 35 Jehoiakim paid Pharaoh Neco (all) the silver and gold that he asked for. The people in Judah had to pay money to the government so that he could do this. (They gave) the silver and gold that he asked for.

36 Jehoiakim was 25 years old when he became king. He ruled for 11 years in Jerusalem. His mother's name was Zebidah. (She was) the daughter of Pedaiah. (Pedaiah) came from Rumah. 37 And (Jehoiakim) did bad things in the sight of the LORD, as his ancestors had done.

Chapter 24

Nebuchadnezzar attacks Judah

1 While Jehoiakim was king, Nebuchadnezzar attacked the country (Judah). (Nebuchadnezzar) was the king of Babylon. Jehoiakim had to be his servant for three years. But then, Jehoiakim changed his mind. He decided not to be (Nebuchadnezzar's) servant. 2 The LORD sent armies against (Jehoiakim). They came from Babylon, Aram, Moab and Ammon. (The LORD) sent them to destroy Judah. He had said that he would do that. He had said it by his prophets. (His prophets) were his servants. 3 It is sure that these things should happen to Judah. The LORD had said that they must happen. That is why they happened. (They had to happen) to remove Judah from where the LORD was. That was because of the sins of Manasseh and because of everything that he had done. 4 (Manasseh) had poured out blood from people who had not done anything wrong. He had filled Jerusalem with the blood of those people. The LORD did not want to excuse him. 5 The other things that King Jehoiakim did are in a book. It is called 'the reports about the kings of Judah'. Everything that he did (is in that book). 6 Jehoiakim died like his ancestors. And Jehoiachin, (who was) his son, became king after him. 7 The king of Egypt did not march out (with his army) from his own country again. (That was because) the king of Babylon had taken a lot of his ground. He had taken all the ground from the Valley of Egypt to the River Euphrates.

8 Jehoiachin was 18 years old when he became king. And he ruled in Jerusalem for three months. His mother's name was Nehushta. (She was) the daughter of Elnathan and she came from Jerusalem. 9 (Jehoiachin) did very bad things in the sight of the LORD, as his father had done.

10-11 The leaders of Nebuchadnezzar's (army) marched to Jerusalem. They stayed all-round it. And Nebuchadnezzar, (who was) the king of Babylon, himself came up to the city (Jerusalem). (He came) while his army leaders were there.

12 All these people went out to the king of Babylon (Nebuchadnezzar):

- Jehoiachin, the king of Judah

- his mother (Nehushta)

- (Jehoiachin's) servants, his leaders and his eunuchs.

And the king of Babylon took Jehoiachin away when Nebuchadnezzar had ruled for less than 8 years.

13 Nebuchadnezzar took all the valuable things from the house of the LORD and from the king's palace. He took away all the things that Solomon had made out of gold, for the house of the LORD. The LORD had said that this would happen.

14 Nebuchadnezzar took away all the people from Jerusalem into exile. He took 10 000 people. They were officers, soldiers and people that could make beautiful things. He left only the very poor people in the country.

15 Nebuchadnezzar took Jehoiachin to (a place like) a prison in Babylon.

He also took from Jerusalem the king's mother, his wives, his officers and the important men in the country (Judah). 16 The king of Babylon also took away to Babylon the whole army of 7000 men. They were strong men and ready for war. He also took 1000 people that could make beautiful things. 17 Jehoiachin's father's brother (was called) Mattaniah. (Nebuchadnezzar) made him king instead of Jehoiachin. (Nebuchadnezzar) changed (Mattaniah's) name to Zedekiah.

18 Zedekiah was 21 years old when he became king. And he ruled in Jerusalem for 11 years. His mother's name was Hamutal. (She was) the daughter of Jeremiah and she came from Libnah. 19 (Zedekiah) did bad things in the sight of the LORD, as Jehoiakim had done. 20 All this happened to Jerusalem and to Judah because the LORD was so angry (with them). In the end, (the LORD) sent them away from where he was. Then Zedekiah began to fight against the king of Babylon.

Chapter 25

Nebuchadnezzar destroys Jerusalem

1 Nebuchadnezzar, (who was) the king of Babylon, marched against Jerusalem, with all his army. He did that when Zedekiah had ruled for nearly 9 years, on the 10th day of the 10th month. (The army) stayed outside the city. They built walls all round (the city), which were higher than the walls (of Jerusalem). 2 The army stayed (outside the city), until Zedekiah had been king for nearly 11 years. 3 By the 9th day of the month, the famine was very bad. There was no food for the people to eat. 4 Then the army (from Babylon) broke the city wall. (They did it) on a road near the two walls by the king's garden. The army from Babylon was all round (the city). So the king (of Judah) ran away along (another) road to Arabah. The king (and his servants) went in the night. 5 But the soldiers from Babylon followed the king. They reached him on some flat land near Jericho. All his soldiers became separate from him and they ran away to different places. 6 But (the soldiers from Babylon) caught the king (Zedekiah) and they took him to the king of Babylon at Riblah. There (the king of Babylon) said what would happen to (Zedekiah). 7 They killed all Zedekiah's sons, while (Zedekiah) watched. Then they destroyed Zedekiah's eyes. They tied him with a line of metal pieces that joined together. And they took him to Babylon.

8 When Nebuchadnezzar had been the king of Babylon for nearly 19 years, Nebuzaradan came to Jerusalem. It was on the 7th day of the 5th month. (Nebuzaradan) was an officer (of the king of Babylon). He was the leader of the soldiers that made the king safe. 9 (Nebuzaradan) burned the house of the LORD, the king's palace and all the other houses in Jerusalem. He burned every important building (that was in Jerusalem). 10 All the army from Babylon knocked down the walls round Jerusalem. Their leader was the leader of the soldiers that made king (Nebuchadnezzar) safe. 11 Nebuzaradan was the leader of the soldiers (that made the king of Babylon safe). He sent into exile all the people who remained in the city (Jerusalem). He did the same to all the people (in the country called Judah). He included those who had joined the king of Babylon's army. 12 But (Nebuzaradan) let some of the poorest people stay behind. They had to work in the vineyards and in the fields.

13 The army from Babylon broke the bronze pillars that were in the house of the LORD. They also took everything that they could move. And (they took) the large bronze bowl for water. They carried all the bronze away to Babylon. 14 They also took away the pots, the spades, the tools for the lights and the spoons. And (they took away) everything else that people had used in the work (of the house of the LORD).

15 The leader of the soldiers that made (the king of Babylon) safe also took away things. He took away the things in which they had put fire or water. (He took away) everything that (Solomon had) made out of gold or silver.

16 Solomon had made the two bronze pillars and the large bowl for water. And (he had made) the things that people could move, for the house of the LORD. The bronze in all this was more than they could weigh! 17 Each pillar was 8 metres (8 yards) high. The bronze piece on the top of one pillar was more than a metre (1 yard) high. There were fruits called pomegranates at the top, (that Solomon had) made out of bronze. The other pillar, with its pomegranates, was the same.

18 The leader of the soldiers (that kept Nebuchadnezzar safe) caught some people. These were the people:

· Seraiah, who was the leader of the priests

· Zephaniah, who was the next most important priest

· three people who stood by the door (of the house of the LORD).

19 He also caught some of the people that were still in the city (Jerusalem):

· the leader of the soldiers

· 5 of the men that had told the king (of Judah) what he should do the leader of the men who had caused the men in the country to join the army

· 60 of his helpers whom they found in the city (Jerusalem).

20 Nebuzaradan was the leader of the soldiers that kept Nebuchadnezzar safe. He took all those people and he brought them to the king of Babylon at Riblah. 21 There, at Riblah, in the country of Hamath, the (soldiers of the) king killed them all. So Judah's people went into exile, away from their own country.

22 Nebuchadnezzar (was) the king of Babylon. He made Gedaliah the leader of the people that were still in Jerusalem. (Gedaliah was) the son of Ahikam, (who was) the son of Shaphan.

23 The leaders (of Zedekiah's) army and their men heard that the king of Babylon had made Gedaliah leader (of Jerusalem). So these people came to Gedaliah at Mizpah:

· Ishmael, (who was) the son of Nethaniah

· Johanan, (who was) the son of Kareah

Seraiah, (who was) the son of Tanhumeth, (who came from) Netophah

· Jaazaniah, (who was) the son of a descendant of Maachah

· all their men.

24 Gedaliah promised that all these men would be safe. 'Do not be afraid of the leaders from Babylon', he said. 'Live in the country (Judah), but be servants of the king of Babylon. Then you will not have any problems.' 25 But in the 7th month, Ishmael, (who was) the son of Nethaniah, came with 10 men. They killed Gedaliah, the men from Judah and the men from Babylon who were with him in Mizpah. (Nethaniah was) the son of Elishama, who belonged to the king's (Zedekiah's) family. 26 When that happened, everybody ran away to Egypt. That included the leaders of the army, the poor people and the important people. They were all afraid of the people from Babylon.

27 When King Jehoiachin of Judah had been in exile for nearly 37 years, Evil Merodach became the king of Babylon. On the 27th day of the 12th month, he took Jehoiachin out from the prison.

28 (Evil Merodach) spoke kindly to (Jehoiachin). He gave him a seat that was more important than (the seats) of the other kings with him in Babylon. 29 So Jehoiachin took off the clothes that he had worn in the prison. Until he died, he always ate (his food) at the king's table (in Babylon). 30 Every day, the king (of Babylon) supplied Jehoiachin regularly with everything (that he needed). That happened for as long as (Jehoiachin) was alive.

David, Israel's Second King

1 Chronicles

About this book

1 Chronicles is a book about the Israelites. A lot of the book is about the same time as the Book of 2 Samuel. But there are also many lists of people.

1 Chronicles begins with a list of the families of the Israelites. But after that, it tells us about the time when David ruled over all Israel. But it also tells us a lot about how the people worshipped God. And the last part of the book describes David's ideas for a temple (house of God) in Jerusalem. David gave careful rules to the priests. He wanted everyone in the temple to work properly for God.

The name of the book

In our Bibles, we have 1 Chronicles and 2 Chronicles. They were one book for a long time until there was a translation into Greek. (The name of that translation is the Septuagint.) That was early in the second century BC. They made two books out of the one book because they would fit on two scrolls. The old Hebrew name for the one book was 'The Book of Events'. The name of the two books in the language called Greek was 'Things that are not in the other books'. Several events here are not in the other books. That may be the reason for the Hebrew and Greek names. But now we call them the Books of Chronicles. It means that they are a list of events. The other books that are like the Books of Chronicles are the Books of Samuel and Kings.

When the writer wrote the book

David was the King of Israel between about 1010 BC and 970 BC. But we think that someone wrote the book in about 500 BC.

The writer

We do not know who wrote the Chronicles. But many Jewish people believed that Ezra wrote Chronicles. He wrote the Book of Ezra too. Many Christian students also believe that Ezra wrote the Chronicles. But other students think that Ezra was not the writer of the Chronicles. They think that the writer was not Ezra but someone like Ezra. And he lived during the same time as Ezra did. **The purpose of the book**

The Books of Chronicles are about events. But the books are not only about events. The writer seems to be a Levite. He writes about things like the temple, prayer and the worship of God. He tries to explain what the events in Israel mean. He explains how God was using those events.

The writer gives lists of names. He starts with Adam, the first man. Then he makes a list of those people who came from Noah's family. From them came the nations that the Jews knew about. He then tells about Jacob, who was also called Israel. He was the ancestor of all the Jews. From then on, he gives only lists of all the tribes of Israel. But to him the most important people are those who came from Judah. The kings came from the tribe of Judah. After that, the writer gives lists of people who helped in the worship of God, and soldiers in David's army. He wants to tell people how important those jobs were.

When he wrote the book, the Israelites had just returned to their country after 70 years in exile. So, the writer wants them to know that all Israelites are God's people. He believes that Israel is the Lord's kingdom. David and Solomon were kings over the LORD's kingdom. Those ideas would help the people who had just returned from exile. Israel's kingdom would be safe because God would keep it safe. After some time, God would make it strong again.

These Israelites needed to know that they did belong to Israel's people. So, the writer gives lists of the families of Israel. He records the families of the 12 tribes until the exile. He used several books that are now in the Bible. And he also used many other very old books. We do not have any of those other books now.

One very important thing that we read about in these books is the temple in Jerusalem. The writer tells us how David put the workers in the temple into groups. He made lists of the priests and the Levites who would be leaders of the worship in the temple. God did not let David build the temple. But David prepared the materials so that his son would be able to build it. In another book, 2 Chronicles, we can read how Solomon built the temple.

Chapter 1

Adam to Noah
1 Adam was the father of Seth and Seth was the father of Enosh. Enosh was the father of Kenan. 2 Kenan was the father of Mahalalel and Mahalalel was the father of Jared. Jared was the father of Enoch. 3 Enoch was the father of Methuselah. Methuselah was the father of Lamech and Lamech was the father of Noah.

Noah's descendants

4 The sons of Noah were Shem, Ham and Japheth. 5 Japheth's sons were Gomer, Magog, Madai, Javan, Tubal, Meshech and Tiras. 6 Gomer's sons were Ashkenaz, Diphath and Togarmah. 7 Javan's sons were Elishah, Tarshish, Kittim and Rodanim.

8 Ham's sons were Cush, Mizraim, Put and Canaan. 9 Cush's sons were Seba, Havilah, Sabta, Raamah and Sabteca. Raamah's sons were Sheba and Dedan. 10 Cush was the father of Nimrod. Nimrod grew up to become the first powerful person on the earth. 11-12 Mizraim was the ancestor of the people called Ludim, Anamim, Lehabim, Naphtuhim, Pathrusim, Casluhim and Caphtorim. The Philistines came from the people called Casluhim.

13-16 Canaan's first child was the father of Sidon who was born first and of Heth. And Canaan was also the ancestor of many nations. They included the people called Jebusites, Amorites, Girgashites, Hivites, Arkites, Sinites, Arvadites, Zemarites and Hamathites.

17 Shem's descendants included Elam, Asshur, Arpachshad, Lud, Aram, Uz, Hul, Gether and Meshech. 18 Arpachshad was the father of Shelah and Shelah was the father of Eber.

19 Eber had two sons. The name of one son was Peleg. He had that name because God made the world's nations separate during his life. God sent people away from each other. Peleg's brother's name was Joktan. 20-23 Joktan was the father of Almodad, Sheleph, Hazarmaveth, Jerah, Hadoram, Uzal, Diklah, Ebal, Abimael, Sheba, Ophir, Havilah and Jobab. All those men were Joktan's sons.

Shem to Abraham

24-26 Abram's ancestors included Shem, Arpachshad, Shelah, Eber, Peleg, Reu, Serug, Nahor and Terah.27 God changed Abram's name to Abraham.

Abraham

28 Abraham had sons who were called Isaac and Ishmael.

29-31 These were the sons of Isaac and Ishmael:

Ishmael's first son was Nebaioth. His other sons were Kedar, Adbeel, Mibsam, Mishma, Dumah, Massa, Hadad, Tema, Jetur, Naphish and Kedemah. Those men were Ishmael's sons.

32 Keturah was another woman who also lived with Abraham. He had sex with her too. And her sons were Zimran, Jokshan, Medan, Midian, Ishbak and Shuah. Jokshan's sons were Sheba and Dedan. 33 Midian's sons were Ephah, Epher, Hanoch, Abida and Eldaah. All those men were descendants of Keturah.

34 And Abraham was the father of Isaac. And Isaac's sons were Esau and Israel.

The descendants of Esau and the rulers of Edom

35 Esau's sons were Eliphaz, Reuel, Jeush, Jalam and Korah. 36 Eliphaz's sons were Teman, Omar, Zephi, Gatam, Kenaz, Timna and Amalek. 37 Reuel's sons were Nahath, Zerah, Shammah and Mizzah.

38 Seir's sons were Lotan, Shobal, Zibeon, Anah, Dishon, Ezer and Dishan. 39 Lotan's sons were Hori and Homam. And Lotan's sister was Timna. 40 Shobal's sons were Alian, Manahath, Ebal, Shephi and Onam. Zibeon's sons were Aiah and Anah. 41 Anah's son was Dishon. Dishon's sons were Hamran, Eshban, Ithran and Cheran. 42 Ezer's sons were Bilhan, Zaavan and Jaakan. Dishan's sons were Uz and Aran.

43 These kings ruled in Edom before there were kings in Israel: Bela son of Beor was king of Edom. His city was called Dinhabah. 44 When Bela died, Jobab son of Zerah ruled the people in Edom. He was from Bozrah. 45 When Jobab died, Husham ruled them instead. He was from the country called Teman.

46 When Husham died, Hadad son of Bedad ruled them instead. Hadad won the war against Midian. That happened in the country called Moab. His city was called Avith. 47 When Hadad died, Samlah ruled them instead. He was from Masrekah. 48 When Samlah died, Shaul ruled them instead. He was from Rehoboth. (Rehoboth is by the river.) 49 When Shaul died, Baal-Hanan son of Achbor ruled them instead. 50 When Baal-Hanan died, Hadad ruled them instead. His city was called Pai. Hadad's wife was Mehetabel and she was Matred's daughter. Matred was the daughter of Me-Zahab. 51-54 Hadad died. The leaders of the clans of Edom were Timna, Aliah, Jetheth, Oholibamah, Elah, Pinon, Kenaz, Teman, Mibzar, Magdiel and Iram. Those men were the leaders of Edom.

Chapter 2

The tribes of Israel

The sons of Israel

1-2 The sons of Israel were Reuben, Simeon, Levi, Judah, Issachar, Zebulun, Dan, Joseph, Benjamin, Naphtali, Gad and Asher.

The tribe of Judah

Judah to Chelubai (Caleb)

3 Judah's sons were Er, Onan and Shelah. Their mother was Shua's daughter. She was from Canaan. Judah's first son was Er. Er did wrong things. The LORD said that those things were wrong. So, the LORD killed him. 4 Judah had sex with Tamar, who had been Er's wife. Judah and Tamar had two sons, Perez and Zerah. So, Judah was the father of 5 sons. 5 Perez's sons were Hezron and Hamul. 6 Zerah had 5 sons. They were Zimri, Ethan, Heman, Calcol and Dara. 7 Carmi's son was Achar. Achar caused a lot of trouble for Israel. He did not obey God's rules because he took things for himself. Those things were God's.8 Ethan's son was Azariah. 9 Hezron's sons were Jerahmeel, Ram and Chelubai.

The descendants of Ram

10 Ram was Amminadab's father. And Amminadab was the father of Nahshon. Nahshon was the leader of the tribe called Judah. 11 Nahshon was the father of Salma and Salma was the father of Boaz. 12 Boaz was the father of Obed and Obed was the father of Jesse.

13 Jesse's first son was Eliab and his second son was Abinadab. His third son was Shimea. 14 His 4th son was Nethanel and his 5th son was Raddai. 15 His 6th son was Ozem and his 7th son was David. 16 Their sisters were Zeruiah and Abigail. Zeruiah's three sons were Abishai, Joab and Asahel. 17 Abigail was the mother of Amasa and his father was Jether, a descendant of Ishmael.

The descendants of Caleb

18 Caleb, the son of Hezron, had children by his wife Azubah and by Jerioth. And her sons were Jesher, Shobab and Ardon. 19 When Azubah died, Caleb married Ephrath. And they had a son called Hur. 20 Hur was the father of Uri and Uri was the father of Bezalel.

21 After some time, when Hezron was 60 years old, he married the daughter of Machir. Machir was Gilead's father. Hezron had sex with Machir's daughter. And she had a son called Segub. 22 Segub was the father of Jair. Jair ruled 23 towns in the place called Gilead. 23 But Geshur and Aram won Havvoth-Jair. Also, they won Kenath and the small towns round it. So then they ruled 60 towns. All those people were descendants of Machir, the father of Gilead.

24 Hezron died in Caleb-Ephrathah. Then his wife Abijah had his son, called Ashhur. Ashhur was the father of Tekoa.

The descendants of Jerahmeel

25 Hezron's first son was Jerahmeel and Jerahmeel's sons were Ram, Bunah, Oren, Ozem and Ahijah. Ram was Jerahmeel's first son. 26 Jerahmeel had another wife, called Atarah. She was the mother of Onam. 27 Jerahmeel's first son, Ram, had sons. They were Maaz, Jamin and Eker. 28 Onam's sons were Shammai and Jada and Shammai's sons were Nadab and Abishur. 29 Abishur's wife was called Abihail and their sons were Ahban and Molid. 30 Nadab's sons were Seled and Appaim. But Seled died and he had no sons. 31 Appaim's son was Ishi and Ishi's son was Sheshan. And Sheshan's son was Ahlai. 32 Jada was Shammai's brother. Jada's sons were Jether and Jonathan. And Jether had no sons before he died.33 Jonathan's sons were Peleth and Zaza. Those men were Jerahmeel's descendants. 34 Sheshan did not have any sons but he did have daughters. And he had a servant from Egypt called Jarha. 35 Sheshan gave his daughter to his servant Jarha as his wife. They had a son called Attai. 36 Attai was the father of Nathan and Nathan was the father of Zabad. 37 Zabad was the father of Ephlal and Ephlal was the father of Obed.38 Obed was the father of Jehu and Jehu was the father of Azariah. 39 Azariah was the father of Helez and Helez was the father of Eleasah. 40 Eleasah was the father of Sismai and Sismai was the father of Shallum.41 Shallum was the father of Jekamiah and Jekamiah was the father of Elishama.

More descendants of Caleb

42 Caleb was Jerahmeel's brother. Caleb's first son was Mesha and Mesha was the father of Ziph. And Ziph's son Mareshah was the father of Hebron.

43 Hebron's sons were Korah, Tappuah, Rekem and Shema. 44 Shema was the father of Raham, who was the father of Jorkeam. Rekem was the father of Shammai.

45 Shammai was the father of Maon and Maon was the father of Beth-Zur. 46 Caleb had another woman called Ephah. And she lived with him too. She was the mother of Haran, Moza and Gazez. And Haran was the father of Gazez. 47 Jahdai's sons were Regem, Jotham, Geshan, Pelet, Ephah and Shaaph. 48-49 Maacah was another woman who also lived with Caleb. She was the mother of Sheber, Tirhanah, Shaaph and Sheva. Shaaph was the father of Madmannah. Sheva was the father of Machbenah and Gibea. Caleb's daughter was Achsah.

50-51 Those people were Caleb's descendants. Caleb's son Hur was the first son of his mother Ephrathah. Hur's sons were Shobal, Salma and Hareph. Shobal was the father of Kiriath-Jearim. Salma was the father of Bethlehem and Hareph was the father of Beth-Gader. 52 Shobal, the father of Kiriath-Jearim had other sons. Shobal's descendants were Haroeh and half the people called Manahathites. 53 And Kiriath-Jearim was the ancestor of the people called Ithrites, Puthites, Shumathites and Mishraites. And from them came the people called Zorathites and Eshtaolites. 54 These people were Salma's descendants: Bethlehem, the people called Netophathites, Atroth-Beth-Joab, half the people called Manahathites and the Zorites. 55 Also, he was the ancestor of those people who lived at Jabez. They were writers. Those people were called the Tirathites, Shimeathites and Sucathites. These clans were from the people called Kenites. The ancestor of the Kenites was Hammath. Hammath was the ancestor of the people who came from Rechab.

Chapter 3

The sons of David

1 These sons of David were born in Hebron. The first son was Amnon. His mother was Ahinoam. She was from Jezreel. The second son was Daniel. His mother was Abigail. She was from Carmel. 2 The third son was Absalom. His mother was Maacah. She was the daughter of Talmai, the king of Geshur. The 4th son was Adonijah. His mother was Haggith. 3 The 5th son was Shephatiah. His mother was Abital. The 6th son was Ithream. His mother was David's wife Eglah. 4 Those 6 sons of David were born to him in Hebron. David ruled in Hebron for 7 years and 6 months. And David ruled in Jerusalem for 33 years. 5 Many sons of David were born in Jerusalem. They included Shimea, Shobab, Nathan and Solomon, who were the 4 sons of David and Bath-Sheba. Bath-Sheba was Ammiel's daughter. 6-8 Also born in Jerusalem were 9 other sons. They were Ibhar, Elishama, Eliphelet, Nogah, Nepheg, Japhia, Elishama, Eliada and Eliphelet. 9 Those were all the sons of David's wives and Tamar was their sister. But he also had some sons by other women who lived with him.

The kings of Judah

10 Solomon's son was Rehoboam and Rehoboam's son was Abijah. Abijah's son was Asa and Asa's son was Jehoshaphat. 11 Jehoshaphat's son was Jehoram. Jehoram's son was Ahaziah and Ahaziah's son was Joash. 12 Joash's son was Amaziah. Amaziah's son was Azariah and Azariah's son was Jotham. 13 Jotham's son was Ahaz. Ahaz's son was Hezekiah and Hezekiah's son was Manasseh. 14 Manasseh's son was Amon and Amon's son was Josiah. 15 Josiah had 4 sons. His first son was Johanan. His second son was Jehoiakim. His third son was Zedekiah and his 4th son was Shallum. 16 Jehoiakim's son was Jeconiah and his son was Zedekiah.

The king's descendants after the exile of Judah's people

17-18 Jeconiah's enemies put him in a prison. His sons were Shealtiel, Malchiram, Pedaiah, Shenazzar, Jekamiah, Hoshama and Nedabiah. 19 Pedaiah's sons were Zerubbabel and Shimei. Zerubbabel's sons were Meshullam and Hananiah, and their sister was Shelomith. 20 Zerubbabel also had 5 other sons. They were Hashubah, Ohel, Berechiah, Hasadiah and Jushab-Hesed. 21 The descendants of Hananiah were Pelatiah, Jeshaiah and the sons of Rephaiah. The descendants of Hananiah also included the sons of these men: Arnan, Obadiah and Shecaniah. 22 Shecaniah's son was Shemaiah. And Shemaiah's sons were Hattush, Igal, Bariah, Neariah and Shaphat. So there were 6 men. 23 Neariah had three sons. They were Elioenai, Hizkiah and Azrikam. 24 Elioenai had 7 sons. They were Hodaviah, Eliashib, Pelaiah, Akkub, Johanan, Delaiah and Anani.

Chapter 4

Other descendants of Judah

1 Judah's descendants were Perez, Hezron, Carmi, Hur and Shobal.

2 Reaiah was Shobal's son and Reaiah was the father of Jahath. Jahath was the father of Ahumai and Lahad. Those were the clans of the people called Zorathites. 3 And these are the sons of the leader of Etam: They were Jezreel, Ishma and Idbash. And they had a sister called Hazzelelponi. 4 And Penuel was the father of Gedor, and Ezer was the father of Hushah. Those were the sons of Hur, who was the oldest son of Ephrathah. And Hur was the leader of Bethlehem. 5 Tekoa's father was Ashhur. And Ashhur had two wives called Helah and Naarah. 6 The sons of Ashhur and Naarah were Ahuzzam, Hepher, Temeni and Haahashtari. They were the sons of Naarah. 7-8 Helah's sons were Zereth, Izhar and Ethnan. Koz was the father of Anub, Zobebah and the clans of Aharhel. Aharhel was the son of Harum.

9 There was a man called Jabez. He was a great man and he was better than his brothers. His mother called him Jabez, which means 'pain'. She said, 'I had a lot of pain at his birth.' That is why she chose that name. 10 Jabez prayed to Israel's God. He said, 'Please do very good things for me. Make my borders larger and help me. Save me from danger and do not let anything hurt me.' And God did what Jabez had asked.

11 Chelub, Shuhah's brother, was the father of Mehir and Mehir was the father of Eshton. 12 Eshton was the father of Beth-Rapha, Paseah and Tehinnah. Tehinnah was the father of Irnahash. Those people lived at Recah.

13 The sons of Kenaz were Othniel and Seraiah. Othniel's sons were Hathath and Meonothai. 14 Meonothai was the father of Ophrah and Seraiah was the father of Joab. Joab was the ancestor of the people from Ge-Harashim. That name means,

'The valley where people make things.' The valley had that name because of the jobs of the people there. They made things. 15 Caleb was Jephunneh's son. Caleb's sons were Iru, Elah and Naam. And Elah's son was Kenaz. 16 Jehallelel's sons were Ziph, Ziphah, Tiria and Asarel. 17-18 Ezrah's sons were Jether, Mered, Epher and Jalon. Mered married Bithiah. Her father was the king of Egypt. The children of Mered and Bithiah were Miriam, Shammai and Ishbah. Ishbah was the father of Eshtemoa. Mered also had a wife who was an Israelite. Her sons were Jered, Heber and Jekuthiel. Jered became the father of Gedor. Heber became the father of Soco. And Jekuthiel became the father of Zanoah. 19 Hodiah's wife was Naham's sister. The sons of Hodiah's wife were the fathers of Keilah and Eshtemoa. Keilah's descendants were called Garmites and Eshtemoa's descendants were called Maacathites. 20 Shimon's sons were Amnon, Rinnah, Ben-Hanan and Tilon. Ishi's sons were Zoheth and Ben-Zoheth. 21-22 Shelah was the son of Judah. Shelah's sons were Er, Laadah, Jokim, Joash, Saraph who ruled Moab and Jashubi-Lehem. Er was the father of Lecah and Laadah was the father of Mareshah. Other clans that were descendants of Shelah worked with good cloth at Beth-Ashbea. And other descendants of Shelah lived in Cozeba. (These lists are from old books.) 23 Those people made pots. They lived in Netaim and Gederah. They lived there with the king and they worked for him.

The tribe of Simeon

24 Simeon's sons were Nemuel, Jamin, Jarib, Zerah and Shaul. 25 Shaul's son was Shallum and Shallum's son was Mibsam. Mibsam's son was Mishma. 26 Mishma's son was Hammuel and Hammuel's son was Zaccur. Zaccur's son was Shimei. 27 Shimei had 16 sons and 6 daughters. But his brothers did not have many children. So, their clan did not become as large as Judah's clan did. 28-31 Shimei's descendants lived in cities called Beersheba, Moladah, Hazar-Shual, Bilhah, Ezem, Tolad, Bethuel, Hormah, Ziklag, Beth-Marcaboth, Hazar-Susim, Beth-Biri and Shaaraim. They lived in them until David became king. 32 The 5 villages near those cities were Etam, Ain, Rimmon, Tochen and Ashan. 33 There were also other villages round the same cities all the way to Baal. That is where they lived. And they wrote down the names of their ancestors.

34-38 Each clan had a leader. The leaders were Meshobab, Jamlech, Joshah, Joel, Jehu, Elioenai, Jaakobah, Jeshohaiah, Asaiah, Adiel, Jesimiel, Benaiah and Ziza. Joshah was a son of Amaziah and Jehu was a son of Joshibian. Joshibiah was the son of Seraiah and Seraiah was the son of Asiel. Ziza was the son of Shiphi and Shiphi was the son of Allon. Allon was the son of Jedaiah and Jedaiah was the son of Shimri. Shimri was the son of Shemaiah. And these clans became very large. 39 They travelled to the east side of the valley. They went as far as Gedor. They wanted land so that their sheep would have grass to eat. 40 They found good fields that had plenty of grass. The place was large and there were no troubles in that place. Some people had lived there before these clans came. The people who were living there were descendants of Ham.

41 These clans came to Gedor when Hezekiah was the king of Judah. Then they attacked the people who lived there. Those people were the descendants of the people called Meunites. The men in these clans destroyed their tents and they killed all the people. So now there are none of those people there. Then they lived there instead because there was good grass there for their animals. 42 Then 500 men from Simeon's clan went to the mountain called Seir. Their leaders were Pelatiah, Neariah, Rephaiah and Uzziel. They were Ishi's sons. 43 They killed all the descendants of Amalek who were still there. They lived there instead and they still live there now.

Chapter 5

The tribe of Reuben

1 Reuben was Israel's first son. That is, Reuben was born first. But Reuben had sex with a woman who lived with his father like a wife. So, his father did not let him have the benefits of the first son. Instead, his father gave those benefits to Joseph's sons. Joseph was a son of Israel. So, Reuben does not have the first place in the list of Israel's sons. 2 Judah became stronger than his brothers. And the ruler was from his tribe. But Joseph's sons received the benefits that the oldest son should receive. 3 Reuben was Israel's first son. Reuben's sons were Hanoch, Pallu, Hezron and Carmi.

4 These were the descendants of Joel: Shemaiah was Joel's son. Gog was Shemaiah's son and Shimei was Gog's son.

5 Micah was Shimei's son. Reaiah was Micah's son and Baal was Reaiah's son. 6 Beerah was Baal's son. Beerah was a leader of the tribe of Reuben. Tilgath-Pilneser, king of Assyria took him away.

So Beerah had to live in a foreign country. 7-8 The books of ancestors show Beerah's relatives. The books record these people by their clans. Jeiel was the first, then Zechariah and Bela. Bela was the son of Azaz. Azaz was the son of Shema and Shema was the son of Joel. These people lived in the land between Aroer and Nebo and in the land near Baal-Meon. 9 Their east border was the desert. This is the desert that is next to the Euphrates River. They had too many animals for the place called Gilead. So they had to live in all those other places too.

10 When Saul was king, Bela's people fought a war. The war was against the people called Hagrites. Bela's people beat the Hagrites in that war. Then Bela's people lived in the tents that the Hagrites had used. They lived in all the land that was east of Gilead.

The tribe of Gad

11 The descendants of Gad lived in the place called Bashan. Their border was Salecah. So they lived near Bela's people. 12 Joel was the most important leader and Shapham was the second leader. Janai and Shaphat were leaders in Bashan. 13 Their relatives in their clans were Michael, Meshullam, Sheba, Jorai, Jacan, Zia and Eber. So there were 7 clans. 14 Abihail was their ancestor. Abihail was Huri's son and Huri was Jaroah's son. Jaroah was Gilead's son and Gilead was Michael's son. Michael was Jeshishai's son. Jeshishai was Jahdo's son and Jahdo was the son of Buz. 15 Ahi was Abdiel's son and Abdiel was Guni's son. Ahi was the leader of their clan. 16 The descendants of Gad lived in Gilead and Bashan. And they lived in the small towns near there. They lived in the place called Sharon. Sharon had a lot of fields of grass. And that land was theirs as far as the borders. 17 Gad's descendants wrote down the list of all those names. They wrote it when Jotham was king of Judah. That was when Jeroboam was king of Israel.

18 The tribes of Reuben, Gad and half of the tribe of Manasseh had a large army. They had 44 760 brave soldiers. The soldiers carried shields, swords and bows and they were very good fighters. 19 They started a war against the people called Hagrites. They also fought the people in Jetur, Naphish and Nodab. 20 The soldiers of Manasseh, Reuben and Gad believed God. They prayed to God while they fought. So God helped them. So they won the war against the Hagrites and against all the other people who were helping the Hagrites. 21 And they took all their enemies' animals. They took 50 000 camels, 250 000 sheep and 2000 donkeys. Also they took 100 000 people. 22 Many people died in the fight because it was God's war. Reuben, Gad and half of the tribe of Manasseh lived in the land of the people called Hagrites. They lived there until the exile of Judah's people.

The half tribe of Manasseh in the east

23 There were many people in the half tribe of Manasseh. They lived in the place called Bashan. Their borders were Baal-Hermon, Senir and the mountain called Hermon. 24 These men were the leaders of their clans: Epher, Ishi, Eliel, Azriel, Jeremiah, Hodaviah and Jahdiel. They were brave soldiers and famous men. And they were leaders of their clans.

25 But the clans sinned against God. He was their ancestors' God. But they did not obey him. He had won the war against the people who were living there before them. They had seen that. But they worshipped the gods of those people. 26 So, Israel's God caused Pul, king of Assyria, to attack their country. And he caused Tilgath-Pilneser, king of Assyria, to attack their country. And he took away the people from the tribes of Reuben, Gad and the half tribe of Manasseh. He sent them into exile. Tilgath-Pilneser brought them to Halah, to Habor and to Hara. And he sent them near to the River Gozan. They are still there today.

Chapter 6

The tribe of Levi

1 Levi's sons were Gershon, Kohath and Merari. 2 Kohath's sons were Amram, Izhar, Hebron and Uzziel. 3 Amram's children were Aaron, Moses and Miriam. Aaron's sons were Nadab, Abihu, Eleazar and Ithamar. 4 Eleazar was the father of Phinehas and Phinehas was the father of Abishua. 5 Abishua was the father of Bukki and Bukki was the father of Uzzi. 6 Uzzi was the father of Zerahiah and Zerahiah was the father of Meraioth. 7 Meraioth was the father of Amariah and Amariah was the father of Ahitub. 8 Ahitub was the father of Zadok and Zadok was the father of Ahimaaz. 9 Ahimaaz was the father of Azariah and Azariah was the father of Johanan.

10 Johanan was the father of Azariah. Azariah worked as a priest in the temple that Solomon built in Jerusalem.

11 Azariah was the father of Amariah and Amariah was the father of Ahitub. 12 Ahitub was the father of Zadok and Zadok was the father of Shallum. 13 Shallum was the father of Hilkiah and Hilkiah was the father of Azariah. 14 Azariah was the father of Seraiah and Seraiah was the father of Jehozadak. 15 Jehozadak went into exile. That happened when the LORD sent the people from Judah and from Jerusalem into exile. The LORD used Nebuchadnezzar to do it.

The three clans of Levi

16 Levi's sons were Gershon, Kohath and Merari. 17 The names of Gershon's sons were Libni and Shimei. 18 Kohath's sons were Amram, Izhar, Hebron and Uzziel. 19 Merari's sons were Mahli and Mushi. These are the clans of the Levites. And their ancestors are in this list.

20 Gershon's son was Libni. Libni's son was Jahath and Jahath's son was Zimmah. 21 Zimmah's son was Joah and Joah's son was Iddo. Iddo's son was Zerah and Zerah's son was Jeatherai.

22 Kohath's son was Amminadab. Amminadab's son was Korah and Korah's son was Assir. 23 Assir's son was Elkanah. Elkanah's son was Ebiasaph and Ebiasaph's son was Assir. 24 Assir's son was Tahath and Tahath's son was Uriel. Uriel's son was Uzziah and Uzziah's son was Shaul. 25 Elkanah's sons were Amasai and Ahimoth. 26 Ahimoth's son was Elkanah. Elkanah's son was Zophai and Zophai's son was Nahath. 27 Nahath's son was Eliab. Eliab's son was Jeroham and Jeroham's son was Elkanah. 28 Samuel's first son was Joel and his second son was Abijah.

29 Merari's son was Mahli and Mahli's son was Libni. Libni's son was Shimei and Shimei's son was Uzzah. 30 Uzzah's son was Shimea. Shimea's son was Haggiah and Haggiah's son was Asaiah.

The men who would make music

31 David brought God's Covenant Box into the LORD's house. Then he chose some leaders as the men who would make the music in that house. 32 They worshipped the LORD while they sang at the holy tent. That tent was where the LORD met with the people. They used that tent until Solomon built the LORD's house in Jerusalem. They obeyed the rules for their work.

33 These are the leaders of the music and their sons: From Kohath's clan, there was Heman the singer. Heman was Joel's son and Joel was Samuel's son. 34 Samuel was Elkanah's son and Elkanah was Jeroham's son. Jeroham was Eliel's son and Eliel was Toah's son. 35 Toah was Zuph's son and Zuph was Elkanah's son. Elkanah was Mahath's son and Mahath was Amasai's son. 36 Amasai was Elkanah's son and Elkanah was Joel's son. Joel was Azariah's son and Azariah was Zephaniah's son. 37 Zephaniah was Tahath's son and Tahath was Assir's son. Assir was Ebiasaph's son and Ebiasaph was Korah's son.38 Korah was Izhar's son and Izhar was Kohath's son. Kohath was Levi's son and Levi was Israel's son.

39 Heman worked with Asaph, who belonged to the same tribe as Heman. Asaph stood at Heman's right side. Asaph was Berechiah's son and Berechiah was Shimea's son. 40 Shimea was Michael's son. Michael was Baaseiah's son and Baaseiah was Malchijah's son. 41 Malchijah was Ethni's son. Ethni was Zerah's son and Zerah was Adaiah's son. 42 Adaiah was Ethan's son. Ethan was Zimmah's son and Zimmah was Shimei's son. 43 Shimei was Jahath's son. Jahath was Gershon's son and Gershon was Levi's son.

44 Other relatives of Heman and Asaph worked with them. These men belonged to Merari's clan and they stood on the left side. Ethan the son of Kishi belonged to this group. Kishi was Abdi's son and Abdi was Malluch's son. 45 Malluch was Hashabiah's son. Hashabiah was Amaziah's son and Amaziah was Hilkiah's son. 46 Hilkiah was Amzi's son. Amzi was Bani's son and Bani was Shemer's son. 47 Shemer was Mahli's son and Mahli was Mushi's son. Mushi was Merari's son and Merari was Levi's son.

48 And all the other Levites did everything else that was necessary for the holy tent. The holy tent was the house of God.

Aaron's descendants

49 But Aaron and his descendants gave the gifts to God. They burned the sacrifices on the altar that was for that. And they burned oils with sweet smells on the altar that was for oils with sweet smells. They gave the sacrifices to God so that he would remove the Israelites' sins. They did all the work in the most holy place. They obeyed all the rules that God's servant Moses had told them about. 50 These were Aaron's descendants. Eleazar was Aaron's son. Phinehas was Eleazar's son and Abishua was Phinehas's son.51 Bukki was Abishua's son. Uzzi was Bukki's son and Zerahiah was Uzzi's son. 52 Meraioth was Zerahiah's son. Amariah was Meraioth's son and Ahitub was Amariah's son. 53 Zadok was Ahitub's son and Ahimaaz was Zadok's son.

The cities of the Levites

54 These are the places where the descendants of Levi, Aaron's son, lived. The Kohath clan were first when the leaders used the lot. So they received the first part of the land. (Aaron was from the Kohath clan.)55 They had the city in Judah that is called Hebron. And they had the land round Hebron. 56 But Caleb had the fields round the city. Caleb also had the villages near Hebron. (Caleb was the son of Jephunneh.) 57-58 So the people gave safe cities to the descendants of Aaron. Those cities included Hebron, Libnah with the fields round it, Jattir and Eshtemoa with the fields round it. They also included Hilen with the fields round it and Debir with the fields round it. 59 And they had Ashan with its fields and Beth-Shemesh with its fields. 60 Also, the tribe of Benjamin gave towns and fields to them. Those towns were Geba with its fields, Alemeth with its fields and Anathoth with its fields. So there were 13 towns for all their descendants to live in.

61 And the clans of half of Manasseh gave 10 towns to the other people who belonged to Kohath's clan. They used lots to choose the towns. 62 The tribes of Issachar, Asher, Naphtali and Manasseh chose 13 towns. (That was the part of Manasseh in Bashan.) They gave those towns to the Gershon clan. 63 The tribes of Reuben, Gad and Zebulun chose 12 towns. They used lots to choose the towns. They gave those towns to the Merari clan. 64 So the Israelites gave those towns and their fields to the Levites. 65 The tribes of Judah, Simeon and Benjamin gave certain towns too.

66 And the tribe of Ephraim chose some towns from their land. They gave those towns to some of Kohath's clan. 67-69 And they gave safe cities to Kohath's clan. One city was Shechem with its fields. Shechem is in the hills in Ephraim. The other cities included Gezer with its fields, Jokmeam with its fields and Beth-Horon with its fields. They also included Aijalon with its fields and Gath-Rimmon with its fields.

70 And the half tribe of Manasseh chose Aner with its fields and Bileam with its fields. They gave those towns to the other families that belonged to Kohath's clan.

71 The other half of the tribe of Manasseh chose towns and they gave them to the Gershon clan. They gave Golan in Bashan with its fields. And they gave Ashtaroth with its fields. 72-73 The tribe of Issachar gave towns to the Gershon clan. Those towns were Kedesh with its fields, Daberath with its fields, Ramoth with its fields and Anem with its fields. 74-75 The tribe of Asher gave towns to the Gershon clan. Those towns were Mashal with its fields, Abdon with its fields, Hukok with its fields and Rehob with its fields. 76 The tribe of Naphtali also gave towns to the Gershon clan. The towns were Kedesh in Galilee with its fields, Hammon with its fields and Kiriathaim with its fields. 77 The tribe of Zebulun chose some towns. They gave those towns to the other people who belonged to the Merari clan. The towns were Rimmono with its fields and Tabor with its fields. 78-79 The tribe of Reuben also gave towns to the Merari clan. Those towns included Bezer in the desert with its fields. They also included Jahzah with its fields, Kedemoth with its fields and Mephaath with its fields. The tribe of Reuben lived east of the River Jordan, that is, across from Jericho. 80-81 The tribe of Gad also gave towns to the Merari clan. Those towns included Ramoth in Gilead with its fields and Mahanaim with its fields. They also included Heshbon with its fields and Jazer with its fields.

Chapter 7

The tribe of Issachar

1 Issachar had 4 sons. They were Tola, Puah, Jashub and Shimron. 2 Tola's sons were Uzzi, Rephaiah, Jeriel, Jahmai, Ibsam and Samuel. They were leaders of their clans. Among Tola's descendants there were 22 600 brave soldiers when David was king. 3 Uzzi's son was Izrahiah. Izrahiah's sons were Michael, Obadiah, Joel and Isshiah. All those five men in Uzzi's family were leaders. 4 The books of their clans show that they had many wives and children. So, they had 36 000 men who were ready to fight in the army.5 The books of the clans of Issachar show that they had 87 000 brave soldiers.

The tribe of Benjamin

6 Benjamin had three sons. They were Bela, Becher and Jediael. 7 Bela had 5 sons. They were Ezbon, Uzzi, Uzziel, Jerimoth and Iri. They were leaders of their clans. The books of their ancestors show that they had 22 034 brave soldiers. 8 Becher's sons were Zemirah, Joash, Eliezer, Elioenai, Omri, Jeremoth, Abijah, Anathoth and Alemeth. All those men were sons of Becher. 9 The books of their ancestors include a list of those clan leaders. Also the books show that they had 22 200 brave soldiers. 10 Jediael's son was Bilhan. Bilhan's sons were Jeush, Benjamin, Ehud, Chenaanah, Zethan, Tarshish and Ahishahar. 11 All those sons of Jediael were leaders of their clans. They had 17 200 brave soldiers who were ready to fight in the army.12 Shuppim and Huppim were descendants of Ir. The people called the Hushim were descendants of Aher.

The tribe of Naphtali

13 Naphtali's sons were Jahziel, Guni, Jezer and Shallum. They were Bilhah's grandsons.

The half tribe of Manasseh in the west

14 These are Manasseh's descendants. Manasseh had a woman that he lived with. She was from the country called Syria. She was the mother of Asriel and Machir and Machir was Gilead's father. 15 Machir's wife was from a sister of Huppim and Shuppim. His wife's name was Maacah. Zelophehad was another descendant of Machir. Zelophehad had only daughters. 16 Machir's wife Maacah had a son and she called him Peresh. Peresh's brother was Sheresh and Sheresh's sons were Ulam and Rekem. 17 Ulam's son was Bedan. These were the sons of Gilead. Gilead was the son of Machir and Machir was Manasseh's son.18 Hammolecheth was Gilead's sister. And she had sons called Ishhod, Abiezer and Mahlah. 19 The sons of Shemida were Ahian, Shechem, Likhi and Aniam.

The tribe of Ephraim

20 These are the names of Ephraim's descendants. Ephraim's son was Shuthelah. Shuthelah's son was Bered and Bered's son was Tahath. Tahath's son was Eleadah and Eleadah's son was Tahath. 21 Tahath's son was Zabad and Zabad's son was Shuthelah.

Ezer and Elead were also sons of Ephraim. They went to Gath and they tried to take some cows and sheep from there. So some men who were born in that city killed them. 22 Their father Ephraim cried for them and he was sad for many days. And his family came to help him. 23 Then Ephraim had sex with his wife and they had another son. Ephraim called him Beriah. That name means 'trouble'. Ephraim chose that name because of his family's troubles. 24 Beriah's daughter was Sheerah. She built Lower and Higher Beth-Horon. And she built Uzzen-Sheerah.

25 And Beriah's son was Rephah. And Rephah's son was Resheph. Resheph's son was Telah and Telah's son was Tahan. 26 Tahan's son was Ladan. Ladan's son was Ammihud and Ammihud's son was Elishama.27 Elishama's son was Nun and Joshua was the son of Nun.

28 Ephraim's descendants lived in Bethel and in the villages near it. And they had land there. Also they lived in Naaran in the east. And they lived in Gezer and in the villages near it. Those places were in the west. Also, they lived in Shechem and in the villages near it. And they lived in Ayyah and in the villages near it. 29 Along the borders of Manasseh's descendants' land were other towns. They included Beth-Shean and the villages near it and Taanach and its villages. They also included Megiddo and its villages and Dor and its villages. The descendants of Joseph (son of Israel) lived in those towns and villages.

The tribe of Asher

30 Asher's sons were Imnah, Ishvah, Ishvi and Beriah and their sister was Serah. 31 Beriah's sons were Heber and Malchiel and Malchiel was Birzaith's father. 32 Heber was the father of Japhlet, Shomer, Hotham and their sister Shua.

33 Japhlet's sons were Pasach, Bimhal and Ashvath. They were Japhlet's sons. 34 Shemer's sons were Ahi, Rohgah, Hubbah and Aram.

35 Shemer's brother was Helem and Helem's sons were Zophah, Imna, Shelesh and Amal. 36-37 Zophah's sons were Suah, Harnepher, Shual, Beri, Imrah, Bezer, Hod, Shamma, Shilshah, Ithran and Beera. 38 Jether's sons were Jephunneh, Pispa and Ara.39 Ulla's sons were Arah, Hanniel and Rizia.

40 All those men were descendants of Asher. They were leaders of their clans. They were great and brave soldiers and great leaders. They had 26 000 men ready to fight in the army. There were lists that showed those men's names with their clans.

Chapter 8

The tribe of Benjamin

1 Benjamin was the father of Bela, his first son. Ashbel was his second son and Aharah was his third son.2 Nohah was his 4th son and Rapha was his 5th son. 3-5 Bela's sons were Addar, Gera, Abihud, Abishua, Naaman, Ahoah, Gera, Shephuphan and Huram.

6 Here is a list of the descendants of Ehud. They were the leaders of their clans. But they were still in Geba. They had to leave Geba. They had to go to Manahath. 7 Ehud's descendants were Naaman, Ahijah and Gera. Gera caused them to leave. He was the father of Uzza and Ahihud.

8-11 Shaharaim and his wife Hushim had sons called Abitub and Elpaal. In Moab, Shaharaim sent away his wives Hushim and Baara. After that, Shaharaim and his wife Hodesh had sons who were called Jobab, Zibia, Mesha Malcam, Jeuz, Sachia and Mirmah. They were leaders of their clans.

12-13 Elpaal's sons were Eber, Misham, Shemed, Beriah and Shema. Shemed built the towns called Ono and Lod. He also built villages round them. Beriah and Shema were leaders of the clans who lived in Aijalon. They caused the people in Gath to leave their city. 14-16 Other sons of Elpaal were Ahio, Shashak and Jeremoth. And Zebadiah, Arad, Eder, Michael, Ishpah and Joha were sons of Beriah. 17-18 Elpaal's sons were Zebadiah, Meshullam, Hizki, Heber, Ishmerai, Izliah and Jobab. 19-21 Shimei's sons were Jakim, Zichri, Zabdi, Elienai, Zillethai, Eliel, Adaiah, Beraiah and Shimrath. 22-25 Shashak's sons were Ishpan, Eber, Eliel, Abdon, Zichri, Hanan, Hananiah, Elam, Anthothijah, Iphdeiah and Penuel. 26-27 Jeroham's sons were Shamsherai, Shehariah, Athaliah, Jaareshiah, Elijah and Zichri.

28 The books show that all those men were leaders of their clans. They lived in Jerusalem.

Saul

29 The leader of Gibeon lived in the town called Gibeon. And his wife's name was Maacah. 30-32 His first son was Abdon. His other sons were Zur, Kish, Baal, Nadab, Gedor, Ahio, Zecher and Mikloth. Mikloth was the father of Shimeah. They lived with their relatives in Jerusalem, near other relatives. 33 Ner was the father of Kish and Kish was the father of Saul. And Saul was the father of Jonathan, Malchishua, Abinadab and Esh-Baal. 34 Jonathan's son was Merib-Baal and Merib-Baal was the father of Micah.35 Micah's sons were Pithon, Melech, Tarea and Ahaz. 36 Ahaz was the father of Jehoaddah. Jehoaddah was the father of Alemeth, Azmaveth and Zimri. And Zimri was the father of Moza. 37 Moza was the father of Binea and Binea's son was Raphah. Raphah's son was Eleasah and Eleasah's son was Azel. 38 Azel had 6 sons. Those sons were called Azrikam, Bocheru, Ishmael, Sheariah, Obadiah and Hanan. All those were Azel's sons. 39 Azel's brother was Eshek. Eshek's first son was Ulam. His second son was Jeush and Eliphelet was his third son. 40 Ulam's sons were brave soldiers and they used their bows well. They had many sons and grandsons. There were 150 of them. All those men were descendants of Benjamin.

Chapter 9

The people who lived in Jerusalem

1 All the Israelites were in the lists of ancestors. And those lists are in the Book about Israel's Kings. The people in Judah had to leave it. Their enemies took them away to Babylon. That happened because they did not continue to obey God. 2 The first people who returned after that were Israelites, priests, Levites, and servants in the temple. They lived on their own land, in their own towns.

3-4 And people were living in Jerusalem again. They were from the tribes of Judah, Benjamin, Ephraim and Manasseh.

This is a list of those people. There was Uthai son of Ammihud. Ammihud was Omri's son. Omri was Imri's son and Imri was Bani's son. Bani was a descendant of Perez and Perez was Judah's son.5 From Shelah's clan, there were Asaiah and his sons. Asaiah was the oldest son in his family. 6 From Zerah's clan, there was Jeuel. There were 690 people from Judah's tribe.

7 From the tribe of Benjamin, there was Sallu. Sallu was the son of Meshullam. Meshullam was Hodaviah's son and Hodaviah was Hassenuah's son. 8 There was also Ibneiah son of Jeroham. And there was Elah son of Uzzi. Uzzi was Michri's son. And there was Meshullam son of Shephatiah. Shephatiah was Reuel's son and Reuel was Ibnijah's son. 9 There were 956 people from Benjamin's tribe. There are lists in their books of ancestors. All those men were leaders of their clans.

The priests' clans

10-11 From the priests, there were Jedaiah, Jehoiarib, Jachin and Azariah. Azariah was a son of Hilkiah and Hilkiah was Meshullam's son. Meshullam was Zadok's son and Zadok was Meraioth's son. Meraioth was Ahitub's son and Ahitub was the most important officer in God's house. 12 Also there was Adaiah son of Jeroham. Jeroham was Pashhur's son and Pashhur was Malchijah's son. And there was Maasai son of Adiel. Adiel was Jahzerah's son and Jahzerah was Meshullam's son. Meshullam was Meshillemith's son and Meshillemith was Immer's son. 13 There were 1760 priests. They were leaders of their clans. They were men who could work very well. And they worked in the house of God.

The Levites' clans

14 From the Levites, there was Shemaiah. Shemaiah was the son of Hasshub and Hasshub was Azrikam's son. Azrikam was Hashabiah's son and Hashabiah was from Merari's clan. 15 There were also Bakbakkar, Heresh, Galal and Mattaniah. Mattaniah was a son of Mica. Mica was Zichri's son and Zichri was Asaph's son. 16 Also there was Obadiah, son of Shemaiah. Shemaiah was Galal's son and Galal was Jeduthun's son. And there was Berechiah, son of Asa. Asa was the son of Elkanah. Elkanah lived in the villages of the people called Netophathites.

Some Levites were guards

17 Some men were guards of the temple's gates. Among them, there were Shallum, Akkub, Talmon and Ahiman. Their relatives were with them and Shallum was their leader. 18 All those guards were from Levi's tribe. And they stood next to the King's Gate. That gate is on the east side. 19 Shallum was Kore's son and Kore was Ebiasaph's son. Ebiasaph was Korah's son. Other men from Korah's clan helped Shallum. They were guards at the gates of the tent. That was their work. Their ancestors were also guards at the door of the LORD's tent. 20 Their ancestors included Phinehas. Phinehas was the leader of the guards. He was Eleazar's son. The LORD was with Phinehas. 21 Zechariah, son of Meshelemiah worked outside the LORD's tent. He was the guard. And the LORD met the people there.

22 There were 212 guards for the gates. The books include a list of their names. And the books show their villages. David and the prophet Samuel chose those men to be guards. They were men that they could trust. And that is why they chose them. 23 Those men and their descendants had to work at the gates. They were the guards of the LORD's house. The LORD's house was called the holy tent. 24 The guards were on the 4 sides of the LORD's house. They were on the east, west, south and north sides. 25 Their relatives still lived in their villages. They had to come and help the guards. Each time they came, they worked for seven days. 26 But there were four guards who were more important than the other guards. That was because the leaders trusted them. They kept safe the rooms and the valuable things in God's house. All those men were Levites. 27 They stayed round God's house during the night because they had to keep it safe. And they had to open it each morning.

28 The priests used valuable tools in the temple. And some guards kept those things safe. The priests brought those things in and then the guards counted them. And the guards counted them again when the priests took them out. 29 There were many valuable things in the holy place. Also some guards kept the flour, wine, oil, oils with sweet smells and the spices safe. 30 But some of the priests mixed the spices. 31 Mattithiah was a Levite. He was the first son of Shallum. Shallum was from Korah's clan. Mattithiah was the baker who made the flat bread. 32 Other men who belonged to the Kohath clan prepared the special bread. The priests put this bread on the holy table. They did that each Sabbath day.

Other Levites made music

33 There were clans of Levites who made music in the temple. The leaders of those clans lived in the temple and they had their own rooms there. They had duties during the day. Also, they had duties at night. So they did not do other work in the temple. 34 Those men were the leaders of those Levite clans. Their names were in their clans' books. And they lived in Jerusalem.

Saul

35 The leader of Gibeon lived in the town called Gibeon. He was called Jeiel and his wife's name was Maacah. 36-37 His first son was Abdon. His other sons were Zur, Kish, Baal, Ner, Nadab, Gedor, Ahio, Zechariah and Mikloth. 38 Mikloth was the father of Shimeam. They lived with their relatives in Jerusalem, near other relatives. 39 Ner was the father of Kish and Kish was the father of Saul. And Saul was the father of Jonathan, Malchishua, Abinadab and Esh-Baal. 40 Jonathan's son was Merib-Baal and Merib-Baal was the father of Micah. 41 Micah's sons were Pithon, Melech, Tahrea and Ahaz. 42 Ahaz was the father of Jarah. Jarah was the father of Alemeth, Azmaveth and Zimri. Zimri was the father of Moza. 43 Moza was the father of Binea and Binea's son was Rephaiah. Rephaiah's son was Eleasah and Eleasah's son was Azel. 44 Azel had 6 sons. Those sons were called Azrikam, Bocheru, Ishmael, Sheariah, Obadiah and Hanan. That is the list of Azel's sons.

Chapter 10

Saul fights the Philistines

1 The Philistines fought against Israel. But the Israelites ran from the Philistines. The Philistines killed many Israelites on the mountain called Gilboa. 2 The Philistines fought well against Saul and his sons. They killed Saul's sons Jonathan, Abinadab and Malchishua. 3 The fight was difficult round Saul. The soldiers with bows shot Saul and they hurt him badly.

Saul kills himself and his sons die

4 Then Saul said to the soldier who carried his shield, 'Kill me with your sword. If you do not kill me, these Philistines will be cruel to me. Then they will kill me. They are not like us because nobody has circumcised them.' But the soldier would not do it because he was very afraid. So, Saul got his own sword and he fell on it. 5 The soldier saw that Saul was dead. So, the soldier fell on his own sword and he died too. 6 So, Saul died with his three sons. Saul and his whole family died together.

Philistines come to live in Israel

7 All the Israelites in the valley saw that their army had run away. And they saw that Saul and his sons were dead. So, they left their towns and they ran away. Then the Philistines came to live in those towns.

The Philistines put Saul's head in their temple

8 On the next day, the Philistines came to take clothes and things from the dead soldiers. They found the dead bodies of Saul and his sons on the mountain called Gilboa. 9 The Philistines stripped Saul's dead body. They took his head and his armour. Then they sent men through all their country. They went to tell the news about Saul's death. They told the news in front of their false gods. And then those men told the news to all the people. 10 The Philistines had a temple for their false gods. They put Saul's armour there. And they had another temple for their false god called Dagon. They hung Saul's head there.

The men from Jabesh-Gilead bury the dead bodies of Saul and his sons

11 Someone told all the people in Jabesh-Gilead about what the Philistines had done to Saul. 12 So, all the brave men from Jabesh went. They took the dead bodies of Saul and his sons. They brought the bodies to Jabesh and they buried the bones under the large tree there. Then the people in Jabesh refused food. They did not eat for 7 days.

Why Saul died

13 Saul died because of his sin against the LORD. He did not obey the LORD. Saul wanted to speak to a dead person. He even visited a woman who used bad spirits. He wanted to know what he should do. 14 He should have asked the LORD but he did not ask the LORD. So, the LORD caused his death and the LORD gave the kingdom to Jesse's son, David.

Chapter 11

All the Israelites agree that David must be their king

1 Then all the Israelites came to David in the town called Hebron. They said to him, 'We are like your own family. 2 And you are our leader. Even while Saul was still our king, you were the captain of Israel's army. And the LORD your God said to you, "You will be the ruler of my people, that is, Israel. You will lead them like a man who leads sheep." '

3 So, all the leaders of Israel came to King David. They met him at Hebron. There in Hebron, they promised David that he would be king of Israel. The LORD saw what they did. Then they poured oil on David to show that he was king over all Israel. The LORD had promised by Samuel that this would happen.

David and his men win the fight at Jerusalem

4 David and all the Israelites went to the city called Jerusalem. At that time, the name of Jerusalem was Jebus. And the people who lived there were called the Jebusites. They had lived in the country before the Israelites came. 5 The people who were living in Jebus said to David, 'You cannot come into our city.' But David fought them. He won the very strong building in Zion. And Jerusalem became David's city.

6 David had said to his soldiers, 'The man who attacks the Jebusites first will become the leader and captain of my army.' Joab, the son of Zeruiah, went first. So, he became the captain of the army.

7 Then David made his home in the strong building. That is why the city was called David's city. 8 David built the city round the strong building. He built it from the small hill called the Millo.

He started from there and he built the walls all-round the city. Joab built the other buildings in the city again. 9 The LORD, who is most powerful, was with him. And so David became stronger and stronger.

David's bravest soldiers

10 Here is a list of the leaders of David's greatest soldiers. They helped to make David's kingdom strong. And with all the Israelites, they made him king. He ruled the whole country. And that is what the LORD had promised. 11 This is the list. These men were David's greatest soldiers.

Jashobeam was from Hachmoni's clan. He was the leader of David's officers. He fought 300 men on one day. He used his spear against them and he killed all those men.

12 Then there was Eleazar. He was among the three greatest soldiers. Eleazar was Dodo's son. He was from Ahoah's clan. 13 Eleazar was at Pas-Dammim. He was with David there. Then many Philistines came there to fight them. There was a field there with a lot of barley. The Israelites ran from the Philistines. 14 But David and Eleazar did not run away. They stood in the middle of that field and they fought to keep that field. They killed the Philistines. The LORD saved them. Because he helped them, they won the fight in a great way.

Three brave soldiers fetch water for David from the well at Bethlehem

15 There were 30 captains among David's soldiers. David was living in Adullam's hole in the rock. So three captains went to the rock there. The Philistine army were living there in tents. They were in the Rephaim Valley. 16 David was in his safe place. A lot of the Philistine soldiers were living in Bethlehem.

17 David wanted some water very much. He said, 'Oh, I want water! There is a well in Bethlehem. It is near the gate. I would be very happy if someone would fetch me a drink from that well!'

18 The three famous captains attacked the Philistines and so the three captains passed their tents. Those three captains went into Bethlehem. They found the well that is near the gate. They took water from there and they brought it to David. But David refused to drink that water. He poured it out as a gift to the LORD. 19 He said. 'God knows that I cannot drink this water. This water is like the blood of these men. They might have died when they fetched this water. I would not accept the gift of their blood. And so I will not drink this water.' So, David refused to drink the water. Those three brave men did other things like that too.

David's soldiers do many brave things

20 Abishai was Joab's brother. Abishai was the leader of the soldiers that were called the three brave soldiers. Abishai fought 300 soldiers with his spear and he killed them. He became as famous as those three soldiers were. 21 The other two soldiers honoured him and he became their leader. But he was not as important as the first three great soldiers.

22 Benaiah was the son of Jehoiada. Benaiah was a brave soldier from Kabzeel. He did great things. He killed two great soldiers from Moab. Also, he went down into a hole and he killed a lion. There was snow on that day. 23 Benaiah also killed a man from Egypt who was 2.3 metres (7.5 feet) tall. The man had a very large spear. It was as large as those piece of wood that people use to make cloth. Benaiah only had a heavy stick. But Benaiah took the spear from the man's hand. And Benaiah killed the man with the man's own spear. 24 Those were the things that Benaiah the son of Jehoiada did. He was as famous as the three brave soldiers. 25 He was more famous than the 30 bravest soldiers. But he did not belong to the three brave soldiers. David made him the leader of his own guards.

26-47 These men were also great soldiers:

Asahel. He was the brother of Joab.

Elhanan. He was the son of Dodo from Bethlehem.

Shammoth. He was from the town called Harod.

Helez. He was from the people called Pelonites.

Ira. He was the son of Ikkesh from Tekoa.

Abiezer. He was from the town called Anathoth.

Sibbecai. He was from the place called Hushah.

Ilai. He was a descendant of Ahoah.

Maharai. He was from the town called Netophah.

Heled. He was the son of Baanah. Baanah was also from the town called Netophah.

Ithai. He was the son of Ribai. Ribai was from Gibeah. Gibeah is in Benjamin.

Benaiah. He was from the town called Pirathon.

Hurai. He was from the valleys near Gaash.

Abiel. He was from the place called the Arabah.

Azmaveth. He was from the town called Bahurum.

Eliahba. He was from the town called Shaalbon.

Also there were the sons of Hashem. They belonged to the people called Gizonites.

Jonathan. He was the son of Shagee, who was from among the hills in Judah.

Ahiam. He was the son of Sachar, who was also from among the hills in Judah.

Eliphal. He was the son of Ur.

Hepher. He was from the town called Mecherath.

Ahijah. He was from the people called Pelonites.

Hezro. He was from the town called Carmel.

Naarai. He was the son of Ezbai.

Joel. He was the brother of Nathan.

Mibhar. He was the son of Hagri.

Zelek. He was from the country called Ammon.

Naharai. He was from the city called Beeroth. Naharai carried Joab's sword and shield. (Joab was the son of Zeruiah.)

Ira. He was from the clan called the Ithrites.

Gareb. He was also from the clan called the Ithrites.

Uriah. He was from the people called Hittites.

Zabad. He was the son of Ahlai.

Adina. He was the son of Shiza. Adina belonged to Reuben's tribe. He was the leader of the men from that tribe of Reuben. And he was the leader of 30 brave soldiers.

Hanan. He was the son of Maacah.

Joshaphat. He belonged to the people called Mithnites.

Uzzia. He was from the town called Ashtaroth.

Shama and Jeiel. They were the sons of Hotham. Hotham was from the town called Aroer.

Jediael. He was the son of Shimri.

Joha. He was Jediael's brother. Joha belonged to the people called Tizites.

Eliel. He belonged to the people called Mahavites.

Jeribai and Joshaviah. They were Elnaam's sons.

Ithmah. He was from the country called Moab.

Eliel, Obed and Jaasiel. Jaasiel was from the people called Mezobaites.

Chapter 12

The soldiers who joined David's army at Ziklag

1 David went to the town called Ziklag. He could not move about much because of Saul, the son of Kish. Many men came to David there. They were among the brave soldiers who helped David to fight in war. 2 They came with their bows. They could shoot arrows. And they could use a weapon that throws stones. They could use either their right hand or their left hand to do those things. They were from Benjamin's tribe. (Saul was also from Benjamin's tribe.)

3 Ahiezer was their leader and Joash was his brother. Ahiezer and Joash were sons of Shemaah. (Shemaah was from the town called Gibeah.) There were also Jeziel and Pelet, the sons of Azmaveth. And there were Beracah and Jehu. They were from the town called Anathoth. 4 And there was Ishmaiah. He was from the town called Gibeon. He belonged to the special group of 30 brave soldiers. He was a leader of that group. There were Jeremiah, Jahaziel and Johanan. There was Jozabad, who was from Gederah. 5 There were Eluzai, Jerimoth, Bealiah and Shemariah. There was Shephatiah, who was from Hariph. 6 There were Elkanah, Isshiah, Azarel, Joezer and Jashobeam. They were from Korah's clan. 7 And there were Joelah and Zebadiah. They were the sons of Jeroham. He was from the town called Gedor.

The soldiers who joined David's army while he was living in the desert

8 Many soldiers from Gad's tribe joined David's army in the desert, where David had found a safe place. These men were very brave soldiers in his army and they were ready to fight. They could use shields and spears. They were brave like lions. And they were fast, like the wild animals that run across the mountains. 9 Ezer was the most important officer. The second leader among these soldiers was Obadiah and the third was Eliab. 10 Mishmannah was 4th and Jeremiah was 5th. 11 Attai was 6th and Eliel was 7th. 12 Johanan was 8th and Elzabad was 9th. 13 Jeremiah was 10th and Machbannai was 11th.

14 These descendants of Gad were the leaders of the army. The least important leader among these men had 100 soldiers. And the greatest leader had 1000 soldiers.

15 These were the men who crossed the River Jordan during the first month of the year. The river was a lot wider than it is at other times. And the water was a lot deeper. But they crossed it. And then they fought the people in the valleys and those people had to run away. They ran to the east and to the west.

16 Some other men came to David in his safe place. They were from the tribes called Benjamin and Judah. 17 David went out to meet them. He said to them, 'Perhaps you have come here to be my friends. And you want to help me. If you have come to help me, we can be friends. But perhaps you are here to help the people who want to kill me. Perhaps you want to tell them where I am. But I have not done anything wrong. So I pray that God will be your judge. He is the God of our ancestors. And he will know what you are doing.'

18 Then the Spirit came on Amasai, who was the leader of the 30 bravest soldiers. And he said, 'We are yours, David and we are with you, Jesse's son. Do well! Do well, David! We want you to have peace. And we want everyone who helps you to have peace. Your God will help you.' So, David accepted them. And he caused them to be officers in his army.

Soldiers from Manasseh join David's army at Ziklag

19 Some men from the tribe called Manasseh joined David's army. The Philistines were fighting Saul and David was with the Philistines. But David and his men did not help the Philistines. That was because the leaders of the Philistines decided to send David away. They would not let him fight against Saul. They said, 'David may return to Saul, because Saul is his master. And if David returns to Saul, they might kill us.' 20 So David returned to Ziklag. And these men from Manasseh joined David's army then. These men were Adnah, Jozabad, Jediael, Michael, Jozabad, Elihu and Zillethai. Each man was the leader of 1000 soldiers. Those soldiers belonged to the tribe called Manasseh. 21 All those men were brave soldiers. So they helped David to fight against other armies. And they became officers in David's army. 22 Day after day, more men came to help David. And his army became large. It became a large and powerful army like an army of God.

The soldiers who joined David's army at Hebron

23 These are the numbers of the soldiers who joined David's army. They came to him at Hebron. These soldiers were ready to fight. They came to give Saul's kingdom to David. The LORD had promised that this would happen. 24 There were 6800 men from Judah who carried shields and spears. And they were ready to fight. 25 There were 7100 men from Simeon's descendants. They were brave soldiers and they were ready for war. 26 There were 4600 men from Levi's descendants. 27 Jehoiada was in that group. He was a leader from Aaron's descendants. And there were 3700 men with him. 28 Zadok was also in that group. He was a brave young soldier. And 22 leaders came with him. They were from his clan. 29 There were 3000 men who were from the same tribe as Saul. They were Benjamin's descendants. Lots of them had been in Saul's army and they had obeyed him well. 30 And there were 20 800 men who were descendants of Ephraim. They were brave soldiers and they were famous men in their own clans. 31 And there were 18 000 men who came from the half tribe of Manasseh. Their clans chose those men. And they sent those men to make David king. 32 And there were 200 leaders who were descendants of Issachar. They knew what Israel should do. And they knew the right time to do it. Their relatives were with them and they obeyed those men. 33 There were 50 000 men who came from Zebulun. They were good soldiers in the army. They were ready to fight. And they knew how to use every kind of weapon of war. They would obey David completely. 34 And there were 1000 officers who came from Naphtali. They had 37 000 soldiers with them who carried shields and spears. 35 And there were 28 600 men who came from the tribe of Dan. They were ready for war. 36 And there were 40 000 good soldiers who came from Asher. They were ready to fight. 37 And there were 120 000 soldiers who crossed the River Jordan. They were from the east side of the river. They came from Reuben, Gad and the half tribe of Manasseh. They had every kind of weapon for war.

38 All those men were soldiers. And their leaders had taught them to fight together. So they were ready to go to war. They came to Hebron because they really wanted to make David king over all Israel. All the other Israelites also wanted to make David king. They agreed about that. 39 The men stayed there with David for three days. Their relatives had supplied food for them. So they ate and they drank with him. 40 The Israelites were very happy. So, people also came from as far as Issachar, Zebulun and Naphtali. They brought food on donkeys, camels, mules and oxen. So David and his soldiers had plenty of flour, fig cakes, raisins, wine, oil, cows and sheep.

Chapter 13

David starts to bring the Covenant Box to Jerusalem

1 David talked with all his officers. They were the leaders of his army. Some officers were the leaders of 1000 men. Other officers were the leaders of 100 men. 2 Then David spoke to all the Israelites who were present. 'I want to suggest something. Perhaps you will agree. And perhaps the LORD our God wants us to do this. I think that we should send a message to all the other Israelites. That should include the priests and the Levites who live in their towns and on their land. We should send the message across the whole country. We should ask all those people to come here to meet us. 3 Then we should bring back the Covenant Box of our God. We did not use it to ask God about things while Saul was king.' 4 They all thought that it was the right thing to do. So all the people agreed that they should do that.

5 So, David told all the Israelites that they should come. They came from the River Shihor in Egypt. They came from Lebo-Hamath. And they came from everywhere between those two places. They came to bring God's Covenant Box. It was in the town called Kiriath-Jearim. 6 David and all the Israelites with him went there. They went to Baalah in Judah. (Baalah is also called Kiriath-Jearim.) They went to fetch the LORD God's Covenant Box. The LORD has his throne between the cherubs. They are on the Box, which has his name.

7 The people took God's Covenant Box from Abinadab's house. They put it on a new cart. Uzzah and Ahio were leading the cart. 8 David and all the Israelites were very happy in front of God. They danced. They could not have danced any better. They sang songs. And they used lyres, harps, tambourines, cymbals and trumpets to make music.

9 They reached a certain place. That place was Chidon's threshing-floor. Oxen were pulling the cart. But the oxen had difficulty there, because the yard was not flat. Uzzah thought that the Covenant Box might fall. So he put his hand on it. 10 The LORD was angry with Uzzah because he had touched the Covenant Box. So the LORD hit Uzzah and Uzzah died there in front of God.

11 David was angry because the LORD punished Uzzah. And David called that place Perez-Uzzah. Even today, people still call that place Perez-Uzzah.

12 David was afraid of God that day. He said, 'I do not know how I can bring God's Covenant Box to me.' 13 So, David did not bring the Covenant Box to where he was. He did not bring it into David's city. Instead, he took it to Obed-Edom's house. Obed-Edom lived in the town called Gath. 14 God's Covenant Box stayed there. Obed-Edom's family had it in their house and it stayed there for three months. During that time, the LORD was kind to Obed-Edom's family. And the LORD did good things for everything that Obed-Edom had.

Chapter 14

David becomes famous

1 Huram was the king of Tyre. He sent men to David. Also, he sent some wood from cedar trees. And he sent some workers who could work with stone and with wood. They came to build a house for David. 2 Now David knew that the LORD had made him safe as king over Israel. The LORD had made David's kingdom great. The LORD did that to help his people, that is, Israel.

3 In Jerusalem, David married more wives. And he became the father of more sons and daughters. 4-7 These children were born in Jerusalem: Shammua, Shobab, Nathan, Solomon, Ibhar, Elishua, Elpelet, Nogah, Nepheg, Japhia, Elishama, Beeliada and Eliphelet.

David fights the Philistines

8 People told the Philistines that the Israelites had anointed David as king of all Israel. They all came to attack him. But people told David about it so he went out to fight them. 9 The Philistines had come. And they had attacked the people in the valley called Rephaim. 10 David asked God, 'Should I attack the Philistines? Will you help me to beat them?' The LORD answered him, 'Yes, attack. I will help you to beat them.'

11 So David and his men went to the town called Baal-Perazim. There they won the fight against the Philistines. David said, 'God has used me to stop my enemies. He attacked them, like a river that has too much water.' So, they called that place Baal-Perazim. 12 The Philistines did not take their false gods when they left. David told his men what they should do. And so they burned those things.

13 Again at another time, the Philistines attacked the people in the valley. 14 David prayed to God again. This time God said, 'Do not go by the straight way to attack them. Instead, go round them. Attack them near the trees called balsams. 15 Wait there until you hear a sound. You will hear that sound from the tops of the trees called balsams. It will be like the sound when soldiers march. Then attack because I will march in front of you. I will win the fight against the Philistine's army.' 16 David obeyed God. So he and his men fought the army of the Philistines. And David's men killed Philistines all the way from Gibeon to Gezer.

17 So, David became famous in every country. And the LORD made the people in all the countries afraid of David.

Chapter 15

Levites bring the Covenant Box to Jerusalem

1 David built houses for himself in David's city. And he prepared a place for God's Covenant Box. He put its tent there. 2 Then David said, 'Only Levites can carry God's Covenant Box. That is because the LORD chose them to carry God's Covenant Box. He chose them to work for him for all time.' 3 David told all the Israelites that they should come to Jerusalem. They should bring the LORD's Covenant Box to the place that David had prepared for it. 4 Then David told the descendants of Aaron and the Levites that they must come together. 5 There were 120 people from Kohath's clan. Uriel was their leader. 6 There were 220 people from Merari's clan. Asaiah was their leader. 7 There were 130 people from Gershon's clan. Joel was their leader. 8 There were 200 people from Elizaphan's clan. Shemaiah was their leader. 9 There were 80 people from Hebron's clan. Eliel was their leader. 10 And there were 112 people from Uzziel's clan. Amminadab was their leader.

11 Then David asked the priests Zadok and Abiathar to come to him. Also he asked certain Levites to come. They were Uriel, Asaiah, Joel, Shemaiah, Eliel and Amminadab.

12 David said to them, 'You are the leaders of the Levites' clans. You and the other Levites must make yourselves holy.

Then bring the Covenant Box of the LORD, Israel's God, to the place that I have prepared for it. 13 You did not carry it the first time. And, because of that, the LORD our God was angry with us. We did not ask him how we should move it. So we did not do it in the way that he has said.' 14 Then the priests and the Levites made themselves holy so that they could carry the LORD's Covenant Box. The LORD is Israel's God. 15 The Levites carried God's Covenant Box on their shoulders. And they used the long sticks, as Moses had told the Levites. The LORD had said that this was how to carry it.

Leaders choose some Levites to sing and to make music

16 David told the leaders of the Levites that they must choose some Levites. The men that they chose would sing. And they would make music. They would use lyres, harps and cymbals. And their songs would make people happy.

17 The Levites chose Joel's son Heman. They also chose Asaph and Ethan. Those men were also Levites. Asaph was Berechiah's son. Ethan was from the Merari clan and he was Kushaiah's son. 18 With them, there was a second group of Levites. These were Zechariah, Ben, Jaaziel, Shemiramoth, Jehiel, Unni, Eliab, Benaiah, Maaseiah, Mattithiah, Eliphelehu, Mikneiah, Obed-Edom and Jeiel. All those men were guards at the gates.

19 The singers Heman, Asaph and Ethan had cymbals of bronze that they could use. 20 Zechariah, Aziel, Shemiramoth, Jehiel, Unni, Eliab, Maaseiah and Benaiah had harps. They made the music called Alamoth.

21 Mattithiah, Eliphelehu, Mikneiah, Obed-Edom, Jeiel and Azaziah had lyres. They were leaders for the music called Sheminith. 22 Chenaniah was the leader of the singers. He taught singers how to sing. He did that because he was very good at it. He was the leader of the Levites.

Priests walk in front of the Covenant Box and they make sounds with trumpets

23 Berechiah and Elkanah were guards for the Covenant Box. 24 The priests Shebaniah, Joshaphat, Nethanel, Amasai, Zechariah, Benaiah and Eliezer used trumpets in front of God's Covenant Box. Obed-Edom and Jehiah were also guards for the Covenant Box.

The Levites carry the Covenant Box to Jerusalem

25 So David, the leaders of Israel and the captains over 1000 soldiers went to fetch the Covenant Box. They all went to bring the LORD's Covenant Box from Obed-Edom's house. And they were very happy. 26 And God helped the Levites who were carrying the LORD's Covenant Box. So, they sacrificed 7 male cows and 7 male sheep. 27 David wore clothes of good linen. All the Levites who were carrying the Covenant Box wore clothes of good linen. The singers and Chenaniah, their leader, also wore clothes of good linen. David also wore a special linen shirt. 28 So, all the Israelites brought the Covenant Box of the LORD. They shouted. They used different kinds of trumpets. And they made loud music with cymbals, lyres and harps.

Michal is angry with David

29 The Box of the LORD's special covenant reached David's city. While it was coming into the city, Saul's daughter Michal was watching. She was at a window and she saw King David. He was dancing and he was very happy. She thought that he should not do that. So, in her mind, she thought that he was silly.

Chapter 16

The people worship the LORD

1 The Levites brought God's Covenant Box and they put it in the tent. So it was in the tent that David had prepared for it.

Then they gave sacrifices to God. They gave sacrifices by fire and they gave friendship-offerings. 2 When David had finished the sacrifices by fire and the friendship-offerings, he prayed. He prayed that the LORD would be kind to the people. 3 And he gave food to every Israelite man and woman. He gave a loaf of bread, a piece of meat and a cake of raisins to each person.

David chooses Levites to worship the LORD

4 Then David chose some Levites. Those men would work in front of the LORD's Covenant Box. They would pray and they would thank God. And they would praise the LORD, the God of Israel. 5 Asaph was the leader and Zechariah was the second leader. Then there were Jeiel, Shemiramoth, Jehiel, Mattithiah, Eliab, Benaiah, Obed-Edom and Jeiel. Those men made music with harps and lyres. And Asaph used the cymbals. 6 Regularly, the priests Benaiah and Jahaziel would use trumpets in front of God's Covenant Box.

7 On that day, David first told Asaph and the other Levites that they should thank the LORD with this song.

A song to praise God

> 8 Give thanks to the LORD. Shout to him.
>
> Tell the people among the nations what he has done.
>
> 9 Sing to him. Praise him with songs.
>
> Tell about all the great things that he has done.
>
> 10 Praise his holy name.
>
> All the people who want to know the LORD should be happy.
>
> 11 Look towards the LORD! Because he is strong, ask him to help you.
>
> Always try to find him.
>
> 12 Remember the great things that he has done.
>
> He has done things that we cannot understand.
>
> Remember them too.
>
> He has spoken about things that are right.
>
> Remember what he has said about those things.
>
> 13 You are the descendants of his servant, Israel.
>
> He has chosen Jacob's descendants to be his people.
>
> 14 He is the LORD our God.
>
> He rules the whole earth.
>
> 15 Always remember his covenant.

He said that after more than 30 000 years from now, his people should still remember it.

> 16 He made that covenant with Abraham.
>
> He will do everything that was in his special promise to Isaac.
>
> 17 He gave that special promise for a rule for Jacob's people.
>
> It is a covenant with Israel that will always continue.
>
> 18 He said, 'I will give the country called Canaan to you.
>
> It will be for you and for your descendants.'
>
> 19 At one time, God's people were only a few people.
>
> They were a few people and they were strangers in that country.
>
> 20 They left one country and they went to another country.
>
> They left one kingdom and they went to another nation.
>
> 21 But he did not let anyone hurt them.
>
> He spoke angrily to kings on their behalf.

22 He said, 'Do not even touch my people that I have anointed as mine.

And do not hurt my prophets.'

23 Sing to the LORD. All the people on earth must sing to him.

Say that the LORD saves us, day after day.

24 Speak about his glory. Tell the people in other countries.

Tell everyone about the great things that he has done.

25 The LORD is great. Everyone should praise him very much.

All people should be afraid to make him angry. He is greater than all other gods.

26 All the gods of other countries are false gods.

But the LORD made the skies.

27 His glory shines all-round him. And anyone can see that he is very great.

Those in his temple are happy and powerful.

28 Praise the LORD you nations on earth.

Praise him for his glory and because he is very strong.

29 Always remember that he and his name are both very great.

Come to him with an offering.

Put on holy clothes and then worship him.

30 Be afraid in front of him, everyone who lives on earth.

The world is very safe. Nobody can move it.

31 The stars in the sky should be happy and the earth should be happy.

All the people in the world should say, 'The LORD rules as king!'

32 The sea and all the things in it should make a loud noise.

The fields will be happy and everything in them will be happy too.

33 Then all the trees in the forest will sing.

They will sing to the LORD because they are happy.

They will be happy because he has come to be the judge of all the people on the earth.

34 Thank the LORD because he is good.

Thank him because his kind love will always continue.

35 Say to him, 'Our God, you always save us!

Save us now and bring us to our own country out of all the nations.'

We want to thank you for your holy name.

We want to be happy and we want to praise you.

36 Praise the LORD, the God of Israel

from the beginning to the end of time.

Then all the people said, 'Amen!' and they praised the LORD.

How the people should worship the LORD

37 King David said, 'Asaph and his relatives should always be leaders of the worship there in front of the Lord's Covenant Box. They must do that each day as the rules describe.' 38 He told Obed-Edom and 68 men from his clan that they must help them. Jeduthun's son, Obed-Edom and Hosah were guards at the doors.

39 Zadok the priest and the other priests stayed with the LORD's tent. That was at Gibeon, at the high place there. 40 Their job was to burn sacrifices to the LORD on the altar for sacrifices by fire. They did that every morning and every evening as Moses had written in the LORD's Law. The LORD had given the Law to Israel's people and they had to obey it. 41 Heman and Jeduthun were with them. David had chosen some other men's names and they were there too. They had to give thanks to the LORD for his kind love that would have no end. 42 Heman and Jeduthun also kept the trumpets, cymbals and other things to make music. They made music with them when they were singing to praise God. And Jeduthun's sons stood at the gate.

43 Then all the people left and they all went to their houses. And David went to his house to pray for everyone who lived in his house.

Chapter 17

David wants to build a house for the LORD

1 David's king's house was now his home. Then he spoke to Nathan the prophet. 'Now I am living in a house that men have made from the wood of cedar trees. But the LORD's Covenant Box is in a tent', he said.

2 Nathan replied to David, 'The LORD is with you. So do anything that you want to do about that.'

God speaks to Nathan

3 But God spoke to Nathan that night. He said, 4 'Go and speak to my servant David. This is what I say. "You are not the right man to build a house for me to live in. 5 I have not lived in a house since I brought the Israelites up out of Egypt. I have moved from one place to another and I have lived in different tents. 6 I told the Israelites' leaders that they must be like shepherds to my people. But I did not say in any of those places, 'You should have built a house of cedar for me.' "

7 Now tell David my servant that the most powerful LORD is saying to him, "I took you when you were in the fields with your father's sheep. And I made you the ruler over my people Israel. 8 I have been with you in all the places that you have gone. And I have killed all your enemies before they reached you. Now I will make your name great. It will be as great as the names of earth's greatest men. 9 And I will give to my people Israel a place to stay and to grow. Then they can have their own land and other people will not be able to send them away. Wicked people have attacked them and they have hurt them. But they will not continue to do that. 10 They have done that all the time. They have done it since I chose leaders over my people Israel. But I will cause your enemies to be quiet. I am telling you that the LORD will build a house for you.

11 When it is the right time, you will die. And people will bury you where they buried your ancestors.

Then I will cause a man from among your sons to be king instead. I will make my kingdom strong and safe and I will keep it strong and safe. 12 He will build a house for me. And I will make his kingdom strong and safe for all time. 13 I will be like a father to him and he will be like my son. I will not take my kind love away from him as I took it away from the king before you. 14 He will rule my people and my kingdom for all time.
His kingdom will be safe for all time." '

15 Nathan told David all the words that the LORD had said to him. He told him everything that God had shown to him.

David prays to the LORD

16 Then King David went in and he sat down in front of the LORD. Then he said, 'I am not great or important and my clan is not great or important. But you have already done very many good things for
me, LORD God. 17 But you are my God and you have decided to do many more things for me. You have promised things to me about my
future descendants. You, LORD God, have caused me to seem like a very great man. 18 You know your servant. You have promised to make me very great. And I cannot say any more about that.

19 You have decided to promise these great things to me, LORD. And you are telling me that I will become very great. 20 There is nobody like you, LORD. And you are the only God. Our ancestors have always told us that. 21 Israel is a very special nation. There is no other nation on earth like it. We were slaves in Egypt and you chose to save us for yourself. You did great things and you pushed out our enemies. So the people in all the nations knew that you are very great. And it made them all afraid of you. 22 You chose Israel to be your own people for all time. And
you, LORD have become the God of Israel.

23 Now, LORD please do the things that you have promised to me, your servant, about my descendants. Please do not let anyone change those things. 24 Do that so that your name will always be great. So then people will say, "The great and powerful LORD is Israel's God." And David's descendants will always be your servants.

25 You have told me, your servant, that you will build a house for me. So I was not afraid to pray to you.26 You LORD really are God! You have promised these good things to your servant. 27 Now it has given you pleasure to bless your servant. You have said that I will continue to have descendants for all time. You
have blessed my descendants, LORD and so you certainly will do good things for them for all time.'

Chapter 18

David wins all his fights with his enemies

1 After some time, David had won all his fights with the Philistines. They became quiet and they did not fight him after that. He won Gath and the villages round it from the Philistines.

2 David also fought the Moabites and he beat them. He ruled them and they had to bring gifts to him.

3 David also beat Hadadezer, king of Zobah. He won land as far as Hamath and he ruled the land up to the River Euphrates. 4 David took from Hadadezer 1000 chariots, 7000 men who drove them and 20 000 walking soldiers. David kept 100 horses for his chariots. But he hurt the other horses so that they could not walk well.

5 Men from Damascus in Syria came to help Hadadezer, the king of Zobah. And David killed 22 000 men from Syria. 6 David put some of his soldiers in Damascus in Syria to keep it for him. Then he ruled over the people in Syria and they had to bring gifts to him. The LORD helped David to win his fights everywhere that he went.

7 David took the gold shields that Hadadezer's soldiers carried. And he brought them to Jerusalem.8 David also took a lot of bronze from Tibhath and Cun. Those towns had been Hadadezer's towns. Solomon used that bronze to make the big bowl in the temple. It seemed like a small sea. He also used that bronze to make pillars that held up the temple's roof. And he made the smaller bronze bowls out of that bronze too.

9 People told Tou, king of Hamath, that David had beaten the whole army of Hadadezer, king of Zobah.10 Hadadezer had often fought against Tou.

So Tou sent his son Hadoram to ask King David if he was well. And he wanted Hadoram to tell David that he had done well against Hadadezer. He also sent many kinds of things of gold, silver and bronze to David.

11 King David saved all those things for the LORD. He had done that with all the silver and gold that he had taken from other nations.
Those nations were Edom, Moab, Ammon, Philistia and Amalek.

12 And Zeruiah's son Abishai killed 18 000 men from Edom in the Valley of Salt. 13 He put groups of soldiers in Edom. Then David ruled over all Edom. The LORD caused David to win all the fights that he had in every place.

David's officers

14 David ruled over all Israel. He did only things that were good and fair for all his people. 15 Zeruiah's son Joab was over the army. And Ahilud's son Jehoshaphat recorded the things that happened. 16 Ahitub's son Zadok and Abiathar's son Ahimelech were priests and Shavsha wrote things for the king. 17 Jehoiada's son Benaiah was over
the Cherethites and over the Pelethites. And David's sons were important officers who helped the king.

Chapter 19

David sends men to the new king of the Ammonites

1 After that, Nahash, the king of Ammon, died and his son ruled instead. 2 David said, 'Nahash was kind to me. So I will be kind to his son Hanun.' So David sent some officers to Hanun. He wanted to say that he was sorry about the death of Hanun's father. David's servants came to Ammon to tell Hanun that David was sorry about it. 3 But the leaders of the people in Ammon said to Hanun, 'David has sent these men to you. So perhaps you think that he really wants to honour your father. But really his men have come to look at our country so that he can beat you. He wants to rule our country. That is what we think.'

Hanun makes David's men ashamed

4 So Hanun took David's servants and he cut off all their hair. His men cut off the lower half of their long clothes to the top of their legs. Then they sent them away.

5 Some people came and they told David about the men. So he sent men to meet them because they were very ashamed. The king said, 'Stay in Jericho until your beards have grown again. Then return.'

The people in Ammon fetch help to fight David

6 Then the people in Ammon knew that they had caused David to be very angry. So Hanun and the people in Ammon sent about
1000 talents of silver to Aram-Naharaim, Aram-Maacah and Zobah. That was to buy chariots and their drivers from them. 7 So they bought
32 000 chariots. They also bought the help of the king of Maacah and his army. These men put their tents near Medeba. At the same time the people from Ammon had come together out of their cities. And they were ready to fight.

8 People told David about it so he sent out Joab with all the Israelite army of good soldiers. 9 So the people from Ammon came out. And they stood ready to fight in front of their city's gate. The other kings who had come were outside in the fields.

Joab wins the fight with the two armies

10 Joab saw that there were armies in front of him and behind him too. So he took some of Israel's best soldiers. And he was their leader against the men from Syria. 11 He told his brother Abishai that he must be leader of all the other soldiers against the men from Ammon. 12 Joab said, 'If the army from Syria is too strong for me, you must come to me. And you must help me. But if the army from Ammon is too strong for you, I will help you. 13 We must be strong and brave. We are fighting for our people and for our God's cities. The LORD will do what seems good and right to him.'

14 Then Joab and his soldiers went out to fight the men from Syria. And they ran from him.

15 The men from Ammon saw that the men from Syria had run away. And so they ran from his brother Abishai's men and they went into the city. So Joab returned to Jerusalem.

The men from Syria run away from the Israelites

16 The men from Syria saw that Israel's men had beaten them. So they sent men with a message to fetch more soldiers. More of their men came across the river, from Syria. Shophach, Hadadezer's most important officer, was at the front of those men.

17 Someone told David about it. Then he took all Israel's soldiers and he crossed the River Jordan. They stood in front of the men from Syria, ready to fight. And the men from Syria fought against David. 18 The men from Syria ran away from Israel's men. And David killed 7000 men who drove chariots and 40 000 other soldiers. And he killed Shophach, the leader of their army.

All the kings who had fought him agree to be David's servants

19 The other kings saw that Israel had won the fight against Hadadezer. So they made peace with David. They agreed to be his servants. After that, the people from Syria did not want to help the men from Ammon again.

Chapter 20

Joab wins the fight for Rabbah

1 Joab and the army went out in the spring. It was the time of the year when kings go out to fight. Joab destroyed the land of the Ammonites and he came to Rabbah. He put his soldiers all-round it. But David stayed in Jerusalem. Joab knocked down the buildings in Rabbah and he broke them. 2 David took the crown from the head of Rabbah's king. It was heavy and its weight was about 34 kilos (75 pounds). It was a crown of gold and there was a valuable stone in it. David's men put it on his head. He also took very many good things from the city. 3 He took out the people who were there. And they had to work for him with tools to cut wood and with iron tools and with axes. That is what David did to all the cities in Ammon. Then David and all the people returned to Jerusalem.

The army fights the Philistines

4 Sometime after that, they fought the Philistines at Gezer. Sibbecai from Hushah killed a man called Sippai. Sippai was a descendant of the very large people. So Israel beat the Philistines.

5 In another fight with the Philistines, Jair's son Elhanan killed Lahmi. Lahmi was the brother of Goliath from Gath. And he had a very heavy spear. Its handle was as large as the piece of wood that people use to make cloth.

6 And there was again war at Gath. A very tall man in Gath had 24 fingers and toes. He had 6 fingers on each hand and 6 toes on each foot. He too was a descendant of the very large people. 7 He said that Israel's soldiers were silly. So Jonathan, son of David's brother, Shimea killed him.

8 David and his men killed all those descendants of the very large people in Gath.

Chapter 21

David counts the Israelite men who can fight

1 Then Satan put a bad idea into David's mind. The idea was to count all the men in Israel. 2 So David said to Joab and to all his officers, 'Go and count the people in Israel from Beersheba to Dan. And then come and tell me. Then I will know how many there are.'

3 But Joab replied, 'They are all your servants, my lord and my king. I pray that the LORD will make them 100 times more. But it would be better not to do this. You will cause God to be angry with all Israel.'

4 But Joab had to do what the king had said. So Joab left. And he went through all Israel and then he returned to Jerusalem. 5 He told David the number of men who could fight.

It was 1 100 000 men in all Israel. All those men knew how to use a sword. And 470 000 men who could use a sword came from Judah.

God is angry with David and God punishes Israel

6 But what the king had said seemed disgusting to Joab. So he did not include the men from Levi's and Benjamin's tribes. 7 And God was angry because David had done this thing. So he punished Israel. 8 Then David said to God, 'I have sinned because I have done this thing. Please forgive me. I have done a very silly thing.'

David chooses how God should punish him

9 Gad was David's prophet. The LORD said to him, 10 'Go and say this to David: "You may choose one out of these three things for me to punish you. That is what the LORD says." '

11 So Gad went to David and he said to him, 'This is what the LORD says: "You must choose one out of these things: 12 I might cause three years with very little food for your country. Or I might cause you to run from your enemies' swords for three months while they are killing many people. Or I might cause a very bad illness among your people for three days. The angel of the LORD would kill many people in every part of Israel." Now tell me an answer to take to him who sent me.'

13 David said to Gad, 'I am in great trouble. The LORD is kind and he forgives people. So it is best if he punishes me. I do not want men to punish me.'

The LORD kills many Israelites with a bad illness

14 So the LORD caused a very bad illness in Israel. And 70 000 men died in Israel. 15 God sent an angel to destroy Jerusalem. But then he saw the angel start to kill people. And the LORD was sorry. He said to the angel who was killing them, 'It is enough. Now stop killing them.' The LORD'S angel was standing by the threshing-floor of Ornan the Jebusite at that time.

God stops the angel killing people in Jerusalem

16 David looked up and he saw the LORD's angel. The angel was standing between the earth and heaven. He had a sword in his hand and it was pointing towards Jerusalem. David and the leaders fell down on their faces. They were wearing clothes that were not comfortable.

17 David said to God, 'It was I who caused Joab to count the people. I am the man who has done the bad thing. It was I who sinned. These people are like sheep. They have not done anything that was wrong. LORD God, please punish me and my family. But please take away this illness from your people.'

David buys ground from Ornan and David builds an altar there

18 Then the angel of the LORD spoke to Gad. 'Tell David that he must build an altar to the LORD on the threshing-floor of Ornan the Jebusite', he said. 19 So David obeyed what Gad had spoken on behalf of the LORD.

20 Ornan and his 4 sons were hitting their food plants until the seeds fell out. They turned and they saw the LORD's angel. So his sons hid themselves. 21 Then David came near to Ornan. He looked and he saw David. He left the threshing-floor and he bent his head to the ground in front of David. 22 David said to Ornan, 'Let me buy this ground so that I can build an altar to the LORD here. Then God will stop the illness that is killing people. I will pay the whole price for the land.'

23 Ornan replied, 'Take it. My lord the king may do what he wants to do. Look, I will give the male cows for the sacrifices by fire. And I will give the tools of wood for the fire and the grain for the offering of grain to you. I give everything to you.' 24 But King David said to Ornan, 'No, I must pay the whole price. I must pay for your things. I cannot sacrifice to the LORD an offering by fire that costs me nothing.'

25 So David paid Ornan 7 kilos of gold (about 15 pounds weight) for the place. 26 David built an altar there to the LORD. On it he gave sacrifices by fire and friendship-offerings. He shouted to the LORD and the LORD answered him with fire from heaven. It burnt David's offering that was on the altar for sacrifices by fire.

The LORD stops punishing the people

27 Then the LORD spoke to the angel. And the angel put his sword away into its case. 28 David saw that the LORD had answered him at the threshing-floor of Ornan the Jebusite. So he burnt sacrifices to God there. 29 At that time the LORD's tent was on the high place at Gibeon. That was the tent that Moses had made in the desert. And the altar for sacrifices by fire was also at Gibeon. 30 But David was afraid of the sword of the LORD's angel. So he could not go to the altar there to meet with God

Chapter 22

Before he dies, David prepares everything to build God's temple

1 And then David said, 'We will build the house of the LORD God here. Also, the altar for sacrifices by fire for Israel will be here.' 2 So he told his officers that they must bring together all the foreign men in Israel. From them he chose men to cut the stones so that the people could build the LORD's house. 3 He supplied a lot of iron. That was for things that would hold together its doors and gates and other things. He also gave them more bronze than they could weigh. 4 The people from Tyre and Sidon had brought a lot of cedar wood to David. So David also supplied more pieces of cedar wood than anyone could count.

5 David said, 'The house for the LORD must be great and beautiful. The people in every country must know about it. My son Solomon is young and he has not made anything like this before. I must make things ready for him.' So David prepared a lot of everything for the building before he died.

David tells Solomon why he must build the temple

6 Then David sent someone to fetch Solomon. He told him that he must build a house for the LORD, the God of Israel. 7 He said to Solomon, 'My son, I really wanted to build a house for the name of the LORD my God. 8 But the LORD spoke to me. He said, "You have caused many men to die and you have fought great fights. I know that you have killed many men. So you must not build a house for my name.

9 But you will have a son who will be a quiet man, a man of peace. I will cause all his enemies round this country to give peace to him.

His name will be Solomon. I will cause peace for Israel while he is its king. And there will not be any trouble for the country. 10 He will build a house for my name. He will be my son and I will be his father. I will make it sure that he and his descendants will be kings of Israel for all time."

11 Now, my son, I pray that the LORD will be with you. And I pray that he will help you to finish this building. And so you will build the house of the LORD your God as he said about you. 12 But I pray that the LORD will make you wise. I want him to give wisdom to you when he causes you to rule over Israel. So you will obey the Law of the LORD, your God. 13 Then everything that you do will go well. But you must be careful to obey the laws and the rules that the LORD gave to Moses for Israel. Be strong and brave. Do not be afraid. And do not think that this is too difficult for you to do.'

The things that David has saved to build the temple

14 'I have been very careful to make many things ready for you to build the LORD's house. I have for you 100 000 talents of gold and 1 000 000 talents of silver. And I have more bronze and iron than you can weigh. And I have wood and stone and you must prepare even more. 15 You have many men with you who can cut stone. And you have many men who can work with stone. You have many men who can work with wood. And you have many men who can do any kind of difficult work. 16 And nobody knows how much gold, silver, bronze and iron there is. So now stand up and begin to build. And I pray that the LORD will be with you.'

David tells the leaders that they must help Solomon to build the LORD's house

17 Then David sent messages to all the leaders in Israel. He said that they must help his son Solomon. 18 He said to them, 'The LORD your God is with you and he has let me win fights with all the nations round Israel. Now the LORD and his people rule over all those nations. So he has given you peace everywhere. 19 So you should do only things that will give the LORD your God pleasure. And you should only think things like that. Stand up. Begin to build the LORD God's holy place, the temple, so that you can put the LORD's Covenant Box there. You can also put God's holy things into the house that you will build for the name of the LORD.'

Chapter 23

David gives rules for the Levites to the leaders

1 David was old and his life had nearly finished. Then he caused his son Solomon to rule over Israel.

2 He brought together all Israel's leaders with the priests and the Levites. 3 His men counted all the Levites who were 30 years old or older. Their number was 38 000 men. 4 David said, 'Now 24 000 men from among these Levites must be over the work of the LORD's house. And 6000 will be officers and judges. 5 And 4000 men will keep the gates safe. And 4000 men will praise the LORD with music. They will use the things that I have made to praise him with.'

6 David made the Levites into groups. Each group came from a son of Levi. Those sons were Gershon, Kohath and Merari.

The Gershon clans

7 From the Gershon clan there were Ladan and Shimei.

8 Ladan's three sons were Jehiel the most important, then Zetham and Joel.

9 The three sons of another Shimei were Shelomoth, Haziel and Haran. Those were the leaders of Ladan's clans.

10 And 4 sons of Shimei were Jahath, Zizah, Jeush and Beriah.

11 Jahath was the oldest and Zizah the second. But because Jeush and Beriah did not have many sons the officers counted them as one clan.

The Kohath clans

12 The 4 sons of Kohath were Amram, Izhar, Hebron and Uzziel.

13 Amram's sons were Aaron and Moses. The LORD chose Aaron and his descendants for special work for all time. He chose them to make things holy for him and to burn oils with sweet smells to him. He said that they would work for him. And they would bless the people on his behalf. That would be their work for all time. 14 The tribe of Levi included the sons of Moses, God's servant.

15 The sons of Moses were Gershom and Eliezer.

16 Gershom's oldest son was Shebuel.

17 From Eliezer's family, Rehabiah was the leader. Eliezer had no other sons but Rehabiah had very many sons.

18 From Izhar's sons, Shelomith was the leader.

19 From Hebron's sons, Jeriah was the leader and Amariah was second. Jahaziel was third and Jekameam was fourth.

20 From Uzziel's sons, Micah was the leader and Isshiah was second.

The Merari clans

21 Merari's sons were Mahli and Mushi. Mahli's sons were Eleazar and Kish.

22 Eleazar died without sons but he had daughters. Their cousins, Kish's sons, married them.

23 Mushi's three sons were Mahli, Eder and Jeremoth.

24 Those were the leaders of the Levites' clans with their descendants. The Israelites recorded the names of all the men who were 20 years old or older. Those men were servants in the LORD's house. 25 David had said, 'Now the LORD, the God of Israel, has given rest to his people. And he lives in Jerusalem for all time. 26 So the Levites do not need to carry his tent and the other things to work for him in it.' 27 David had told them that they should count the Levites. But they should only include the Levites who were 20 years old or older. Those were the last words that he said about the Levites.

The work of the Levites

28 The Levites' work was to help Aaron's descendants to be servants in the LORD's house. They kept the yards and the side rooms and the holy things clean. And they helped in God's house in other ways. 29 They kept the special bread that the priests put on the table in the holy place. They kept the good flour for the offering of grain and for the bread that they made without yeast. They mixed the bread for the sacrifices and they baked it. They also helped with the offering that the priests mixed with oil. And they weighed everything and they measured everything. 30 They had to stand every morning to thank and to praise the LORD. And they had to do the same in the evening. 31 They also had to sing when the priests gave sacrifices by fire to the LORD on special days. That included the Sabbaths and the New Moon sacrifices. The correct number of Levites must do everything in the proper way. They must always work in a regular way and at the correct times in front of the LORD. 32 So the Levites had special work. They had to keep the place where people met God and its holy place clean. And they had to help their cousins, Aaron's descendants with their work in the LORD's house.

Chapter 24

The groups of Aaron's sons

1 This is about the groups of Aaron's sons. Aaron's 4 sons were Nadab, Abihu, Eleazar and Ithamar.

2 But Nadab and Abihu died before their father died. And they had no sons. So Eleazar and Ithamar were the priests. 3 Zadok and Ahimelech helped David to put them into groups. Zadok was a descendant of Eleazar and Ahimelech was a descendant of Ithamar. They gave to each group special jobs and regular times to work. 4 They found more leaders among Eleazar's descendants than among Ithamar's descendants. They put 16 leaders of clans from Eleazar's descendants and 8 leaders of clans from Ithamar's descendants over them. 5 They chose in a way that was fair to every group. The descendants of Eleazar and the descendants of Ithamar included officers for the holy place. And both groups included officers to work for God.

6 Nethanel's son Shemaiah the Levite was a writer. He recorded their names in front of the king and the other rulers. So Zadok the priest, Abiathar's son Ahimelech and the leaders of the priests' clans and of the Levites' clans were watching. They chose one group from Eleazar's clan then one group from Ithamar's clan.

7-18 This is the list of the group leaders as they chose them.

1 Jehoiarib

2 Jedaiah

3 Harim

4 Seorim

5 Malchijah

6 Mijamin

7 Hakkoz

8 Abijah

9 Jeshua

10 Shecaniah

11 Eliashib

12 Jakim

13 Huppah

14 Jeshebeab

15 Bilgah

16 Immer

17 Hezir

18 Happizzez

19 Pethahiah

20 Jehezkel

21 Jachin

22 Gamul

23 Delaiah

24 Maaziah

19 Each group followed the group before it to work in the LORD's house. That was the rule that their ancestor, Aaron gave to them. The LORD, the God of Israel had told him how they must do it.

The other Levites

20 These are the other Levites: Shubael was a descendant of Amram and Jehdeiah was a descendant of Shubael.

21 There was Rehabiah's first son Isshiah.

22 From the Izhar clan, there was Shelomoth. And Jahath was a descendant of Shelomoth.

23 There were Hebron's first son Jeriah and his second son Amariah. Then there were his third son Jahaziel and his fourth son Jekameam.

24 There were Uzziel's son Micah and his son Shamir.

25 There were Micah's brother Isshiah and his son Zechariah.

26-27 There were Merari's sons Mahli and Mushi. And the descendants of Merari by his son, Jaaziah were Shoham, Zaccur and Ibri.

28 Mahli's son Eleazar had no sons.

29 There was also Kish's son, Jerahmeel.

30 And there were Mushi's sons, Mahli, Eder and Jerimoth.

That is the list of all the Levites' clans.

31 They, like their brothers, Aaron's descendants, also asked God to choose which jobs each man should do. King David, Zadok and Ahimelech watched them. The leaders of the priests' clans and the leaders of the Levites' clans also did that. They did not give the clans of the oldest brother special places.

Chapter 25

The singers

1 David, with some of his most important army officers, chose some Levites to prophesy with harps, lyres and cymbals. They were from the families of Asaph, Heman and Jeduthun. Here is a list of these men:

2 From Asaph's sons were Zaccur, Joseph, Nethaniah and Asarelah. Asaph was over them. He prophesied when the king wanted him to prophesy.

3 From Jeduthun's sons, there were 6 prophets, who were Gedaliah, Zeri, Jeshaiah, Shimei, Hashabiah and Mattithiah. Their father, the prophet Jeduthun was over them. He used a harp to thank and to praise the LORD.

4 From Heman's sons, there were Bukkiah, Mattaniah, Uzziel, Shebuel and Jerimoth, Hananiah, Hanani and Eliathah. And there were Giddalti and Romamti-Ezer, Joshbekashah, Mallothi, Hothir and Mahazioth. 5 All those men were sons of Heman, the king's prophet. God had promised them to him to honour him. God gave Heman 14 sons and three daughters.

6 Their father was over all those men to make music for the LORD's house. They used cymbals, harps and lyres for worship in God's house. The king tol

7 All those men knew how to make music in a very good way. Other Levites also made music. So, there were 288 Levites who made music for the LORD. 8 They included young men and older men, teachers and students. They chose in a fair way the groups in which they must work.

9 The first group that they chose was a group of the relatives of Asaph's son, Joseph. The second group was 12 men. 10 The third group was 12 men. They were Gedaliah with his brothers and his sons. 10 The third group was 12 men. They were Zaccur with his sons and his brothers. 11 The 4th group was 12 men. They were Izri with his sons and his brothers. 12 The 5th group was 12 men. They were Nethaniah with his sons and his brothers. 13 The 6th group was 12 men. They were Bukkiah with his sons and his brothers. 14 The 7th group was 12 men. They were Jesarelah with his sons and his brothers. 15 The 8th group was 12 men. They were Jeshaiah with his sons and his brothers. 16 The 9th group was 12 men. They were Mattaniah with his sons and his brothers. 17 The 10th group was 12 men. They were Shimei with his sons and his brothers.

18 The 11th group was 12 men. They were Azarel with his sons and his brothers. 19 The 12th group was 12 men. They were Hashabiah with his sons and his brothers. 20 The 13th group was 12 men. They were Shubael with his sons and his brothers. 21 The 14th group was 12 men. They were Mattithiah with his sons and his brothers.22 The 15th group was 12 men. They were Jeremoth with his sons and his brothers. 23 The 16th group was 12 men. They were Hananiah with his sons and his brothers. 24 The 17th group was 12 men. They were Joshbekashah with his sons and his brothers.

25 The 18th group was 12 men. They were Hanani with his sons and his brothers.

26 The 19th group was 12 men. They were Mallothi with his sons and his brothers.27 The 20th group was 12 men. They were Eliathah with his sons and his brothers. 28 The 21st group was 12 men. They were Hothir with his sons and his brothers. 29 The 22nd group was 12 men. They were Giddalti with his sons and his brothers. 30 The 23rd group was 12 men. They were Mahazioth with his sons and his brothers. 31 And the 24th group was 12 men. They were Romamti-Ezer with his sons and his brothers.

Chapter 26

The men who kept the gates of the temple safe

Korah's family

1 These are the groups of guards of the temple's gates. Kore's son Meshelemiah was a descendant of Asaph, who was from the clan of Korah. 2 And Meshelemiah had 7 sons. These were their names: Zechariah was born first and Jediael was his second son. Zebadiah was his third son and Jathniel was his 4th son. 3 Elam was his 5th son. Jehohanan was his 6th son and Eliehoenai was his 7th son.

4 Obed-Edom was another guard. God had blessed him with 8 sons. These were their names: Shemaiah was born first. Jehozabad was his second son and Joah was his third son. Sachar was his 4th son and Nethanel was his 5th son. 5 Ammiel was his 6th son. Issachar was his 7th son and Peullethai was his 8th son.

6-7 Also, his son, Shemaiah had 4 sons. They were called Othni, Rephael, Obed and Elzabad. They were rulers in their clan. They were very brave and their relatives, Elihu and Semachiah were also strong men.

8 All those men were sons of Obed-Edom. They and their sons and their relatives were men who could work well. All those men could work well because they were strong. There were 62 of these men who belonged to Obed-Edom's clan.

9 And Meshelemiah had 18 sons and men from among his relatives who could work well.

Merari's family

10 Also, Merari's son Hosah had 4 sons. Shimri was the most important son. Shimri was not born first but his father made him the most important son among his sons. 11 Hilkiah was second. Tebaliah was third and Zechariah was the 4th son. There were 13 men from Hosah's clan who worked as guards.

12 The leaders of the clans agreed how and when each group should work as guards in the LORD's house.13 They chose their jobs in the same fair way as they had chosen the work for the other Levites. They did that for each gate. They were fair to the large clans but they were also fair to the small ones.

14 They chose Shelemiah for the East gate. They chose his son Zechariah for the North gate and he gave good advice. 15 They chose Obed-Edom to be a guard at the South gate. They chose his sons to be guards at the place where the Levites kept things for their work. 16 Shuppim and Hosah kept the West gate safe and the Shallecheth Gate on the higher road. They chose the times for a group to work each day. 17 Six Levites kept safe the east, four the north and four the south each day. Two worked together each day to be guards at the place where they kept their things. 18 On the west side, there were 4 guards on the road near the yard. And there were two guards on the west side at the yard.

19 That is how they gave their jobs as guards to each group among the clans of Korah and Merari.

The work of other Levite families

20 From the other Levites, Ahijah kept the valuable things safe. That included the valuable things that the priests used in God's house. And it included the valuable things that people had given to God. 21 Ladan was a descendant of Gershon and he was the ancestor of several clans. Jehieli was a leader of one clan. 22 The sons of Jehieli, Zetham and his brother Joel, kept safe the valuable things in the LORD's house.

23 The descendants of Amram, Izhar, Hebron and Uzziel did other work. 24 Gershom's descendant, Shebuel was the most important officer over the valuable things. Gershom was a son of Moses. 25 Gershom's brother, Eliezer was the father of Rehabiah. Jeshaiah was his son and he was the father of Joram. Joram's son, Zichri, was the father of Shelomoth. 26 Shelomoth and his relatives kept safe all the holy things that King David had given to God. The leaders of clans and army officers had also given things to God. Some officers were over groups of 1000 soldiers and some officers were over groups of 100 soldiers. Shelomoth and his relatives kept those holy things safe too. 27 When the Israelites won a fight, they won things from their enemies. Then they took a part of the good things that they had won. Then they gave them to pay for repairs to the LORD's house. 28 That included all the things that Samuel the prophet and Saul the son of Kish had given. And it included the things that Ner's son, Abner had given. And it included the things that Zeruiah's son Joab had given. Shelomoth and his relatives kept those things safe too.

29 Chenaniah and his sons were descendants of Izhar. They did not work in the temple. They were judges and officers over Israel.

30 Hashabiah, Hebron's descendant, had 1700 good workers in his clan. They were over the people to the west of the River Jordan. They made it sure that they worked for the LORD and for the king in a proper way. 31 Jerijah was the most important man among Hebron's descendants. When David had been king for 40 years, people looked in the records of their ancestors and of their descendants. They read there that great soldiers of the Hebron clan were living at Jazer in Gilead. 32 There were 2700 men from Jerijah's clan who were good leaders. King David told them that they must be leaders of Reuben's tribe, Gad's tribe and the half tribe of Manasseh. They were over them for everything that was important to God or to the king.

Chapter 27

The Israelite armies

1 Each month, a group of 24 000 men were the king's servants. They worked for him in everything that was about the army. Among these men were leaders of clans, officers over groups of 1000 or 100 men. Among them, there were also other men who worked for the king. Each group worked for one month each year. This is a list of their names.

2 Zabdiel's son, Jashobeam was the leader of the first group of 24 000 soldiers in the first month. 3 He was a descendant of Perez. He was over all the army officers for the first month.

4 Dodai was from the town called Ahoah. He was the leader of the group of 24 000 men for the second month. Mikloth was his most important helper.

5 Benaiah, the son of the priest Jehoiada, was the leader of the third group for the third month. He was the most important officer and there were 24 000 men in his group. 6 This Benaiah was a great soldier. He was the leader of the special soldiers who were called 'The 30'. His son Ammizabad was the leader of his group.

7 Asahel, Joab's brother, was the leader of the 4th group of 24 000 men for the 4th month. His son Zebadiah was the leader of the group after him.

8 Shamhuth from Izrah's clan was the leader of the 5th group of 24 000 men for the 5th month.

9 Ira was the leader of the 6th group of 24 000 men for the 6th month. He was the son of Ikkesh from Tekoa.

10 Helez was the leader of the 7th group of 24 000 men for the 7th month. He was from the people called Pelonites in Ephraim

11 Sibbecai from Hushah was the leader of the 8th group of 24 000 men for the 8th month. He was from Zerah's clan.

12 Abiezer from Anathoth in Benjamin was the leader of the 9th group of 24 000 men for the 9th month.

13 Maharai from Netophah was the leader of the 10th group of 24 000 men for the 10th month. He was from Zerah's clan.

14 Benaiah from Pirathon in Ephraim was the leader of the 11th group of 24 000 men for the 11th month.

15 Heldai from Netophah was the leader of the 12th group of 24 000 men for the 12th month. He was from Othniel's clan.

Officers over the tribes of Israel

16 And over the tribes of Israel, the ruler of the tribe of Reuben was Eliezer, the son of Zichri. Over Simeon was Maacah's son, Shephatiah.

17 Over Levi was Kemuel's son, Hashabiah. Zadok was over Aaron's clan.

18 Over Judah was David's brother, Elihu. Over Issachar was Michael's son, Omri.

19 Over Zebulun was Obadiah's son, Ishmaiah. Over Naphtali was Azriel's son, Jerimoth.

20 Over Ephraim was Hoshea's son, Azaziah. Over half the tribe of Manasseh was Pedaiah's son, Joel.

21 Over the half tribe of Manasseh in Gilead was Zechariah's son, Iddo. Over Benjamin was Abner's son, Jaasiel.

22 Over Dan was Jeroham's son, Azarel. Those were the officers over the tribes of Israel.

David counts the number of men in Israel

23 The LORD had promised to make Israel a nation with as many people as there are stars in the sky. So David did not count the men who were only 20 years old or less. 24 Zeruiah's son, Joab had begun to count the men but he did not finish. The LORD was angry with Israel because David had started to count them. So nobody wrote the number in the book about King David's life.

Men who kept the king's things safe

25 Adiel's son, Azmaveth was over all the places where the king stored his valuable things. He stored some valuable things outside the city. Uzziah's son, Jonathan was over those things. They were in towns, villages and strong buildings where soldiers watched for enemies.

26 Chelub's son, Ezri was over the men who were digging in the fields.

27 Shimei from Ramah was over the men who worked in the vineyards. Zabdi from Shepham was over the men who stored wine from the vineyards.

28 Baal-Hanan from Geder was over the trees in the lower hills in the west. They were olive and sycamore-fig trees. Joash kept the olive oil.

29 Shitrai from Sharon was over the men who kept the king's animals in Sharon. Adlai's son, Shaphat was over the men who kept his animals in the valleys.

30 Obil, a descendant of Ishmael, kept the camels. Jehdeiah from Meronoth kept the donkeys.

31 Jaziz kept the sheep and goats. He belonged to the people called Hagrites. All those men kept King David's things safe.

32 David's uncle, Jonathan had a good mind. And he helped David to decide what he should do. And he was a writer. Hachmoni's son, Jehiel stayed with the king's sons. 33 Ahithophel helped the king to decide the best things to do. And Hushai, who was born at Archi, was the king's friend.

34 After Ahithophel died, Abiathar and Benaiah's son, Jehoiada helped the king. They helped him to decide what he should do. And Joab was the leader of the king's army.

Chapter 28

David brings all his officers together

1 David asked all the leaders of Israel to come to him at Jerusalem. The leaders of the tribes had to come with the officers over the king's work. That included the officers over the king's things and his animals or his sons' things and their animals. It also included the officers over groups of 1000 or 100 men. All the officers in the king's house and all his brave army officers had to come too.

2 King David stood up and he said, 'Listen to me, my relatives and my people. I wanted very much to build a house for the LORD's Covenant Box to stay. And I wanted it to be a place for our God to put his feet. And I prepared the things that I would need to do it. 3 But God said to me, "You are a fighter and you have killed people. So you must not build a house for my name." '

God has chosen Solomon to be king after David

4 'But the LORD, the God of Israel chose me from all my clan. He chose me to be king over Israel for all time. He chose Judah to rule over the people and he chose my family from the tribe of Judah. And he chose me from my father's sons to be king over all Israel. 5 The LORD has given me many sons and he has chosen Solomon from among them. He has chosen him to sit on the king's seat and to rule over the Lord's kingdom. That kingdom is Israel. 6 He said to me, "Solomon your son will build my house and the buildings round it. That is because I have chosen him to be like my son. And I will be like his father. 7 But he must always do the things that give me pleasure. And he must obey my laws. He must obey me as he is doing now. If he does that, I will make his kingdom strong for all time."

8 Now I am telling you this in front of all the LORD's people, Israel. And God can hear what I am saying. You must be careful to obey all the laws of the LORD your God. You must carefully read about all his rules and you must obey them. Then you will have this good country. And after you die it will be for your descendants to keep for all time.'

Solomon will build God's house

9 'And you, Solomon my son, know your father's God. Be his faithful servant in every way with your whole mind.

The LORD knows what you are thinking. And he understands all your thoughts. If you look for him, you will find him. But if you leave him, he will turn away from you for all time. 10 Think now how the LORD has chosen you. He has chosen you to build a house that will be his temple. Be strong and do this work.'

Solomon learns how to build the temple

11 Then David showed to his son Solomon everything that he had prepared for him to do. He showed him how to build the way into the temple. He showed him how its buildings should be. He showed him how to build the rooms to store valuable things. He described the upstairs rooms and the inside rooms. And he described the room where the Covenant Box with its special lid would be. 12 He gave to him pictures of the house of the LORD. And he gave to him pictures of every room that God's Spirit had shown to him. He included the yards and the rooms where they would keep valuable things safe. And he showed to him the rooms to store all the things that people would give to God.

13 David gave to him lists of all the things that they would need for the work in the LORD's house. And he gave to him the lists of the groups of priests and Levites. And he gave to him the rules about how each group should work in the LORD's house. 14 He said how much gold he should use to make those things. He also said how much silver Solomon should use for all the things for the work in the temple. 15 He said how much gold was for the lampstands and for their lamps. He told him the weight of silver for the silver lampstands and for their lamps. And he told him where they would put each lampstand. 16 He told him the weight of gold for each table on which the priests would put the special bread. And he told him the weight of the silver for the silver tables.

17 He told him the weight of gold to use for the forks, dishes and cups. He told him what the weight of each gold dish should be. And he told him the weight of silver for each silver dish. 18 He told him the weight of best gold for the altar to burn oils with sweet smells. And he showed him how they must make the models of cherubs out of gold. They would be like a chariot to stand over the LORD's Covenant Box. And they would cover it with their wings.

19 David said, 'I have written this as the LORD told me. And he helped me to understand how to do all the work.'

20 David said to Solomon his son, 'Be strong and very brave and do this work. The LORD God, my God is with you. He will not leave you but he will help you. He will stay with you until you have finished all the work. So do not be afraid. And do not think that it will be too difficult for you. Then the LORD's house will be ready for him. 21 Look! The groups of priests and Levites are ready to start work in God's house. The men who are good at any kind of work will be happy to help. And the officers and all the people will do everything that you want them to do.'

Chapter 29

David and the people give gifts for the work on the temple

1 Then King David spoke to all the people who were there. 'God has chosen my son Solomon. But he is young and he has never done anything like this great work. This building must be very beautiful because it is not for man, but for the LORD God. 2 I have given a lot of the valuable things that I had stored for my God's house. They include gold for the gold work. I have given silver for the things that you will make out of silver. I have given bronze for the things that you will make out of bronze. I have given iron for the things that you will make out of iron. I have given wood for the things that you will make out of wood. I have given a large quantity of all kinds of valuable stones. That includes the valuable stones called onyx, antimony, stones of many colours and also a lot of marble. 3 I want very much that we should build this house for my God. So I have also given a lot of my own gold and silver. I am giving that with all the other things that I have prepared for the holy house of my God. 4 I have given 3000 talents of gold from Ophir. And I have given 7000 talents of best silver to put over the walls of the buildings. 5 And good workers can use that gold and silver to make other things out of gold and silver. Now I want to know who else wants to give to the LORD today.'

6 Then the leaders of the clans and the leaders of the tribes of Israel were happy to give gifts. The officers over groups of 1000 men and over groups of 100 men gave their gifts. And the officers who were over the king's work gave their gifts. 7 They gave 5000 talents and 10 000 darics of gold and 10 000 talents of silver. And they gave 18 000 talents of bronze and 100 000 talents of iron. They gave this for the work on God's house. 8 People who had valuable stones gave them to the LORD's house. Jehiel from the Gershon clan stored these in a safe place in the LORD's house. 9 So the people were very happy because it gave their leaders pleasure to give. They were very happy to give to the LORD. David the king was also very happy.

10 David praised the LORD in front of all the people who were present there. He said,

'We praise you LORD.

You are the God of our ancestor, Israel (Jacob).

We praise you now and we should praise you for all time.

11 You, LORD, are greater and more beautiful than anyone else is.

You can do anything and you can beat anyone.

You are the king and everything in heaven and on earth is yours, LORD.

You have a great kingdom and you are over everyone and over everything.

12 All valuable things come from you and only you can make someone great or important.

You are the ruler over all things.

You are able to make people strong and to make them powerful.

You can make them great and you can make everybody strong.

13 Now we thank you, our God, and we praise your great name.

14 But I am not a great person and my people are like nothing. But we are able to give all these things to you. You gave to us everything that we have. We have only given back to you some of your own things. 15 We are like strangers and like foreign people to you, as all our ancestors were. We are only here for a short time. We live for a short time and then we go away like shadows. And nobody lives for a very long time. 16 All these things that we have given have come from you, the LORD, our God. Everything that we have given to build a house for your holy name is yours. And it came from you. 17 You are my God. And you can see what we are really like. I know that. And when we do good things it gives pleasure to you. I am happy that I have given these things to you. That is what I really wanted. And now I have seen that your people here have been happy to give to you. And that has made me happy too. 18 You, LORD, are the God of our ancestors Abraham, Isaac and Israel. I pray that your people will always want to do things like this. I pray that you will help your people always to think like this. And I pray that they will always want to be your servants. 19 I ask that you will cause my son Solomon to obey all your commandments, rules and laws. Please let him build your great house. I have given to him all the things that he will need for that.'

David and the people praise the LORD

20 Then David spoke to all the people who were there together. 'Now praise the LORD, your God', he said. So all the people praised the LORD, the God of their ancestors. They bent down their heads and they worshipped the LORD. And they fell flat in front of the king.

All the people worship the LORD

21 On the next day, they gave sacrifices to the LORD. They burnt 1000 male cows, 1000 male sheep and 1000 young sheep as gifts to the LORD. They also gave the proper offerings of wine with them. And there were many more sacrifices for the Israelites.

The people anoint Solomon as king

22 They were happy on that day. And they ate and they drank there in front of the LORD.

Then, in front of the LORD, they poured oil on the head of David's son Solomon for the second time. That made him their king. And they poured oil on Zadok's head as priest. 23 Solomon's father David had sat on the LORD's throne as king. But now Solomon sat there instead. Everything went well for him and all the people in Israel obeyed him. 24 All King David's officers and all his soldiers promised to obey King Solomon. And even David's other sons promised to obey King Solomon.

25 The LORD caused all the people in Israel to think that Solomon was very great. And they honoured him. The LORD had not made any king of Israel before him so great.

David dies

26 Jesse's son David had ruled over all Israel. 27 He had ruled over Israel for 40 years. He ruled them from Hebron for 7 years and for 33 years he ruled in Jerusalem. 28 He lived for a long time. And he was a good age when he died. God gave many valuable things to him and God made him very great. And his son Solomon ruled instead.

29 The prophets Samuel, Nathan and Gad wrote books about all the things that King David did. They wrote about everything that he did from the beginning to the end. 30 They tell us about the way that he ruled and about his great power. They tell us everything about his life and about what happened in Israel and in all the kingdoms round it.

Israel Becomes Two Countries

2 Chronicles

About this book

> This is the story of Israel from the time of King Solomon. Perhaps the prophet Ezra or another priest or Levite wrote it. This book tells us more about the things that we can read about in the Books of the Kings. It tells the people about the temple worship. God wanted to help the people who had been slaves in another country. They were building the temple in Jerusalem. And he wanted to show them that they were special. They were God's people before they became slaves. They were still his people. So they needed to know what he had done for them. He wanted them to become a strong nation. And he wanted them to worship him again.

Chapter 1

Solomon speaks to his people

1 David's son Solomon made himself strong over his kingdom. The LORD his God was with him. And the LORD made him very great.

2 Solomon spoke to all the people in Israel. He spoke to the officers who were over groups of 1000 men. And he spoke to the officers who were over groups of 100 men. He spoke to the judges and to all the leaders in Israel. And he spoke to the leaders of the families. 3 Then Solomon and all those people went to the town called Gibeon. They went to the place for worship there. The tent where God met with his people was there. Moses, the LORD's servant, had made it in the desert. 4 But David had brought God's Covenant Box from Kiriath-Jearim to Jerusalem. David had made a place for it and he had made a tent for it in Jerusalem. 5 But David put the bronze altar that Bezalel had made in Gibeon in front of the LORD's tent. (Bezalel was the son of Uri, who was the son of Hur.) So Solomon and the people went to meet LORD there. 6 Solomon went up to the bronze altar in front of the LORD. The altar was in front of the holy tent for the people. And he burnt 1000 sacrifices on the altar.

God asks Solomon what he wants

7 That night, God appeared to Solomon and he said to him, 'Ask for anything that you want me to give to you.'

Solomon asks God to make him wise

8 Solomon answered God, 'You have been very kind to my father David. And you have caused me to be king instead.

9 Now, LORD God, do as you promised to my father David. You have caused me to rule over people who seem as many as the dust of the ground. 10 So now please give to me wisdom and knowledge so that I can be the leader of these people. Nobody can rule this big nation without your help, because these people are yours.'

God's answer

11 God said to Solomon, 'You have not asked to become rich or for valuable things. You have not asked for honour or for the death of your enemies. You have not asked for a long life. But you asked for wisdom and knowledge to rule over my people, because I have caused you to rule. And that is what you wanted. 12 So I will give to you wisdom and knowledge. Also, I will make you rich. And I will give to you valuable things. You will have more of those than any king who has lived before you. And you will have more of those than any king who will live after you. And I will cause people to give honour to you. They will give more honour to you than people have given to any king before you or after you.'

13 So, Solomon left the place for worship at Gibeon. He went from the tent where God met with his people. And he returned to Jerusalem. There he ruled over Israel.

Solomon buys horses and chariots

14 Solomon bought many chariots and men to ride horses. He had 1400 chariots and 12 000 men to ride horses. He kept them in special cities for chariots and some with him in Jerusalem. 15 There was a lot of silver and gold in Jerusalem while he was king. People had so much silver and gold that they were like stones in Jerusalem. And they had as much wood from cedar trees as from the common trees that grew in the low hills. 16 Solomon brought horses from Egypt and from Kue. The king's men bought them in Kue at a good price. 17 The chariots came from Egypt. A chariot cost 7 kilos of silver (15 pounds weight) and a horse cost 1.7 kilos of silver (3.25 pounds). Also they sold horses and chariots to all the kings of the people called Hittites and the people from Syria.

Chapter 2

Solomon begins to build the temple

1 Solomon decided to build a house for the LORD's name and a king's house for himself. 2 So Solomon chose 70 000 men to carry all the heavy things that he needed. And he had 80 000 men who cut big stones in the hills. And he chose 3600 men to be over those workers.

Solomon asks Huram for help

3 Solomon wrote a letter to Huram, king of Tyre. It said, 'Send to me the wood of cedar trees as you did for my father David. You sent it for him to build a house to live in. 4 Now I will build a house to honour the LORD my God. It will be a holy place for him. The people and I will burn oils with sweet smells for him. There we will offer special bread to him each day. And we will burn sacrifices to the LORD our God. We will do that every morning, every evening and on Sabbaths and New Moon days and on other holy days. This is a rule for Israel for all time.

5 The house that I will build for our God will be great. It will be great because he is greater than all gods. 6But nobody can really build a house for our God because he is too great. The heavens, even the highest heavens, cannot contain him. I can only build for him a place to offer oils with sweet smells to him.

7 Now send to me a good worker who is able to make pictures on metal. He must be a man who can work with gold, silver, bronze and iron. And he must be able to work with dark red, purple and blue materials. He will work in Judah and in Jerusalem. He will work with the good workers that my father David chose for me.

8 And send to me also the wood of cedar, cypress and algum trees from Lebanon. I know that your servants know how to cut wood from there. And my servants will work with your servants. 9 I will need a lot of wood because I will build a large and beautiful temple. 10 I will pay your servants, the men who cut the wood. I will pay them 4400 kilolitres (1 150 000 gallons) of wheat and 4400 kilolitres of barley. Also, I will give to them 440 kilolitres (115 000 gallons) of wine and 440 kilolitres of olive oil.'

Huram replies to Solomon's letter

11 Huram, king of Tyre replied to Solomon with this letter. 'Because the LORD loves his people, he has chosen you to be their king.' 12 Huram also said, 'Praise the LORD, the God of Israel who made heaven and earth. He has given a wise son to King David. This son is clever and he understands things well. And he will build a house for the LORD and a king's house for himself.

13 I have sent Huram-Abi to you. He is a clever man and he understands things well. 14 His mother came from Dan and his father came from Tyre. He has learnt to work with gold and silver, bronze, iron, stone and wood. He can also work with purple, blue and dark red materials and with linen cloth. He is able to make pictures on metal of any kind that you want. He will work with your good workers and with those of my lord David, your father.

15 So now send to us the wheat, barley, oil and wine that you promised. 16 Then we will cut the wood from Lebanon that you need. We will tie the trees together and we will send them like boats on the sea to Joppa. You can take them from there to Jerusalem.'

Solomon decides which men should build the temple

17 Solomon counted all the men in Israel from foreign countries as his father David had done. There were 153 600 of them.

18 And he chose 70 000 foreign men to carry things and 80 000 men to cut big stones in the hills. He chose 3600 foreign men to be over the other men and to cause them to work well.

Chapter 3

Solomon begins to build

1 Then Solomon began to build the LORD's house in Jerusalem on the mountain called Moriah. That is where the LORD appeared to his father David. David had bought that place and he had prepared it. Before that, it was the place where Ornan made his wheat seeds separate from their hard coat. (Ornan belonged to the people called Jebusites.) 2 Solomon began to build in the 4th year after he began to rule Israel. It was the 2nd day of the 2nd month.

3 Solomon put the strong stones for the floor of God's house in the ground. He made it about 27 metres (90 feet) long and 9 metres (30 feet) wide. (He measured it with the old thing called a cubit.)

4 The large entrance at the front of the temple was about 9 metres (30 feet) long and 54 metres (180 feet) high. It went across the whole front of the temple. He covered it inside with the best gold.

Inside the temple

5 He covered the walls inside the biggest room with pine wood. Then he covered that with good gold. Then his workers drew pictures of palm trees and chains in the gold. 6 He used valuable stones to make the temple beautiful. The gold that he used came from Parvaim. 7 He covered the temple with gold. He covered the beams in the temple's ceiling with gold. And he put gold under the doors. And he covered the walls and doors with gold. He cut pictures of cherubs on the walls.

The Most Holy Place

8 He built the Most Holy Place. It measured 9 metres (30 feet) long and 9 metres wide. It was as long as the temple was wide. He covered the walls inside with about 20 000 kilos (45 000 pounds) of the best gold. 9 The gold for the nails had a weight of about 0.6 kilos (1.25 pounds). Also, he covered the walls of the rooms above with gold.

10 In the Most Holy Place, he made models of two cherubs and he covered them with gold. 11-13 They stood side by side in the Most Holy Place with their faces towards the biggest room. Each cherub had 2 wings about 2.3 metres (7.5 feet) long. They held their wings out at their sides. One wing of a cherub touched a wing of the other cherub. The other wing of each cherub touched a wall of the Most Holy Place. Both pairs of wings measured 9 metres (30 feet) together.

14 He made a blue, purple and dark red linen curtain with pictures of cherubs on it.

The two bronze pillars

15 He made two pillars at the front of the temple. They were about 16 metres (52 feet) long. Each pillar had a top part about 2.3 metres (7.5 feet) long.

16 He made chains and he put them on the top parts of the pillars. And he made 100 models of fruits called pomegranates. And he put them on the chains. 17 Then he put the pillars up on each side of the temple's entrance. He put one pillar on the right side and he put the other pillar on the left side. The pillar on the right side he called Jachin, and the pillar on the left side he called Boaz.

Chapter 4

Solomon makes things for the temple

1 He made a bronze altar. It was about 9 metres (30 feet) long and 9 metres (30 feet) wide and 4.5 metres (15 feet) high. 2 He made a round metal thing like a sea. It was about 4.5 metres (15 feet) across and 2.3 metres (7.5 feet) high. And it was about 13.5 metres (45 feet) round its edge. 3 He made shapes of things like male cows below the edge. He put 5 of these to each 0.5 metres (1.5 feet) and 5 more cows below them. And they were part of the same piece of metal as the metal sea.

4 He put the sea on models of 12 male cows. Three cows looked out towards the north, three towards the west, three towards the south and three towards the east. He put the sea on top of them and their tails were in the centre. 5 The edge of the sea was as wide as a hand. And it was like a cup, the shape of a flower called a lily. It contained about 66 000 litres (17 500 gallons) of water.

6 Then he made 10 bowls to wash in. He put 5 bowls on the right side and 5 bowls on the left side. The priests washed in them all the things that they used for the sacrifices by fire. But the priests washed themselves in the water from the bronze sea.

7 He made 10 lampstands out of gold. And he did it as the rules about them said. He put them in the temple, 5 on the right side and 5 on the left side.

8 He also made 10 tables and he put them in the temple. He put 5 tables on the right side and he put 5 tables on the left side. He also made 100 bowls out of gold.

9 He made the yard for the priests and the big yard outside. He made the doors for the yard and he covered the doors with bronze. 10 He put the sea on the right side in the south-east corner.

11 Huram also made more pots and spades and bowls. So Huram finished the work that he had promised to do for King Solomon for the house of God.

Outside the temple

12 He made the two pillars with their top parts. The top parts were in the shape of bowls. He made the two sets of chains to cover the top parts of the pillars.

13 And he made 400 models of fruits called pomegranates for the two sets of chains. There were two groups of these fruits for each set of chains. They were to cover the two bowls on the top parts of the pillars. One group was below the other group.

14 He made the bowls to wash things in. And he made the things to put the bowls on.

15 He made the very large bowl that was like a sea. And he made the models of 12 male cows under it.

16 He made the pots, spades and forks for meat. Huram, the good worker, made all the things for the house of the LORD. He made them from bronze that he caused to shine. King Solomon had told him that he should do that. 17 The king caused him to make them in the clay at the Jordan valley between Succoth and Zeredah. He made the shapes of these things out of clay. Then he poured the hot metal into the shapes. 18 Solomon made very many things. So nobody knew the weight of the bronze that he used.

Inside the temple

19 And Solomon made all the things that were inside God's house. And he made the altar that he covered with gold. And he made the tables where the priests put the special bread.

20 He made the lampstands and their lamps out of pure gold. The lamps had to burn in front of the Most Holy Place. That was the rule.

21 He made the flowers, the lamps and the tongs out of gold that was the best gold.

22 He made the tools to help the lamps to burn well. He made the bowls, the spoons and the pots to contain burning fire. He made all those things out of the best gold. He made the gate of the temple out of gold. And he made the doors to the Most Holy Place inside the temple out of gold. He made the doors of the biggest room in the temple out of gold too.

Chapter 5

1 So Solomon finished all his work for the house of the LORD. Then Solomon brought into it all the things that his father David had saved for the temple. He brought the silver and the gold and all the other things. And he stored them in rooms of God's house.

Solomon brings the Covenant Box to the temple

2 Then Solomon brought all the leaders of the Israelites and of their tribes and clans to Jerusalem. He wanted to bring up the LORD's Covenant Box from Zion, which is David's city. 3 All the men in Israel came together to the king. It was the time of the feast of the seventh month.

4 When all the leaders in Israel had arrived, the Levites lifted up the Covenant Box. 5 They took the Covenant Box. And they took the Tent where God met with his people. And they took all the holy things that were in the Tent. And the priests and the Levites carried them up to Jerusalem. 6 King Solomon and all the Israelites came together in front of the Covenant Box. They sacrificed more sheep and cows than anyone could count. There were so many that nobody could know the number.

7 Then the priests brought the LORD's Covenant Box to its place. They put it in the inside room of the temple, that is, the Most Holy Place in the temple. They put it beneath the wings of the cherubs. 8 The cherubs' wings covered the place where the Covenant Box was. So the cherubs covered the Covenant Box and the pieces of wood that the Levites had used to carry it. 9 Those pieces of wood were so long that the Levites could see the ends from Holy Place. But nobody could see them from outside it. And they are still there now. 10 In the Covenant Box, Moses had put the two pieces of stone at Horeb. The LORD had given a covenant there to the Israelites when they came out of Egypt. Nothing else was in the Box.

The priests sing to praise the LORD

11 Then all the priests came out of the Holy Place. All the different groups of priests who were there had made themselves holy. 12 The Levites who were singing stood to the east of the altar. They were Asaph, Heman, Jeduthun and their sons and their relatives. They wore clothes of the best linen. And they made music with cymbals, harps and lyres. With them were 120 priests who made sounds with trumpets. 13Those priests and the sound of the trumpets was completely right with the sound of the singers. It was like one sound to praise the LORD and to thank him. The singers sang loudly with those who were making music with trumpets, cymbals and other things. To praise the LORD, they were singing,
'He is good, because his love will continue for all time.'

Then a cloud filled the house, the LORD's house. 14 So the priests could not continue their work because of the cloud. And the shining glory of the LORD filled God's house.

Chapter 6

Solomon prays

1 Then King Solomon prayed. He said, 'The LORD has said that he would live in the dark clouds. 2 But I have built a beautiful house for you. It is a place for you to live for all time.'

Solomon speaks to the people

3 All the Israelites were standing there together. Then the king turned round and he blessed all the Israelites. 4 He said, 'Praise the LORD, the God of Israel. He promised something to my father David. And he has done it. He said, 5 "I brought my people out of the country called Egypt. Since then I have not chosen any city in Israel for you to build a house for my name. And I have not chosen a man to be the leader of my people called Israel. 6 But now I have chosen Jerusalem to become the place where they give honour to my name. And I have chosen David to rule my people called Israel."

7 My father David wanted to build a house for the name of the LORD, the God of Israel. 8 But the LORD said to my father David, "You were good to think that you might build a house for my name. 9 But you will not build the house. But your son who will be born in your own family will build the house for my name."

10 And the LORD has done what he promised to do. I have become king after my father David. And now I sit on the king's seat in Israel, as the LORD promised. And I have built the house for the name of the LORD, the God of Israel.

11 I have put the Covenant Box there. The LORD's covenant that he gave to the Israelites is in it.'

Solomon prays to God

12 Then Solomon stood in front of the altar of the LORD. He held out his hands in front of all the Israelites. 13 He had made a bronze box to stand on. It was about 2.3 metres (7.5 feet) long and 2.3 metres wide. It was about 1.4 metres (4.5 feet) high. He put it in the middle of the yard and he stood on it. And then he went down on his knees in front of all the Israelites. He held out his hands to heaven. 14 He said, 'LORD, God of Israel, there is no God like you in heaven or on earth. Your servants really try to obey you. And you do what you have promised to those people. You love them and you are very kind to them. 15 You have done what you promised to your servant David my father. You spoke with your mouth. And now, today you have done what you said.

16 Now LORD the God of Israel, please do what you promised to your servant David my father. You said, "Your sons must be careful to obey my rules as you have done. If they do that, a man among your descendants will always sit on the king's seat in Israel." 17 LORD the God of Israel, you promised that to your servant David. So now please cause it to happen as you said.

18 But I do not know how it can be possible for God to live on earth with men. Neither the sky, nor the highest heavens can contain you. And this house that I have built is so much smaller than them. 19 So please listen to my prayer. I am your servant. I am asking you to be kind to me, LORD my God. Please listen to what I am saying. And please hear the prayer that I am praying in front of you here. 20 I am asking you to watch this temple always, day and night. You have said that you will put your name here. Listen to the words that your servant is praying towards this place. 21 Your servant and your people Israel will ask for things as they turn towards this place. Please hear them from your home in heaven. And when you hear, please forgive them.

Solomon asks God to forgive people's sins if they are sorry

22 A man may do something wrong to another Israelite. Then people will tell him that he must promise to speak truly. He must speak in front of your altar in this temple. 23 Then, please hear from heaven and be the judge of the two people. Punish the bad man. Do to him as he has done to the other man. But tell everyone that the good man has not done anything wrong. And give to him what good people should have.

24 The Israelites may sin against you. Then you might punish them. You might cause their enemies to win a fight against them. But then they might come to you. And they might give honour to you. They might come to this temple. They might pray in this temple and they might ask you to help them. 25 Then please hear them from heaven and forgive the sin of your people, the Israelites. And cause them to return to the country that you gave to them and to their ancestors.

26 Perhaps you will punish your people for their sin against you. And there will not be any rain. Then they may turn away from their sin and they may pray towards this place. And they may return to give you honour because you are punishing them.

27 When they return, please listen from heaven. And please forgive your servants, the Israelites. Teach them the right way to live. And send rain on your land that you have given to your people to be theirs.

28 Many bad things might happen to your people or to their land. They might have no food, or many people might be very ill. They may have troubles with their plants. Insects may eat their food-plants or enemies may attack their towns. Or there might be very bad illnesses in the country. 29 Then any Israelite might pray towards this house. Or all the people might pray. They might ask you to help. Each person might ask for help about the bad things that are hurting him.

30 Then please hear them from your home in heaven. Please forgive them. You, and only you, know what each person is thinking inside himself. So please do what is right for each person. 31 Then they will be afraid to make you angry. And they will do the things that give pleasure to you. They will obey your rules all the time that they live in their country. It is the country that you gave to our ancestors.

32 A man from a foreign country, not somebody from Israel, may come here. He might have come a long way because of your great name. Someone has told him that you are very strong. He may come and he may pray towards this house. 33 Then please hear him from your home in heaven. And do the thing that he is asking you for. So the people in all the nations on the earth will know your name. They will be afraid to make you angry as the Israelites are afraid to make you angry. And they will know that this house is called by your name. That is why I built it.

34 Your people may go to fight their enemies in a place where you send them. Then they will pray to you. They will pray towards this city that you have chosen. And they will pray towards this house that I have built for your name. 35 Then, from heaven, listen to their prayer. Please hear what they are asking you to do. And help them.

36 There is nobody who does not sin. So they will sin against you. And you will be angry with them. You will let their enemies win the fight. And they will take them away to a country that is near or a long way from here. 37 Then they may change their ideas in that country. And they may be sorry about their sin. They may ask you for help from that country. They may say, "We have sinned and we are very bad. We have done many things that are wrong." 38 Then they will return to you in their minds. They will want to do only the things that give pleasure to you. They will pray from the country where their enemies took them. They will pray towards their country that you have given to their ancestors. And they will pray towards the city that you have chosen. And they will pray towards the house that I have built for your name. 39 Then hear their prayer from your home in heaven. Please listen to what they are asking you for. And help them. And forgive your people who have sinned against you.

40 Now, my God, will you please look at us. And please listen to the words that we are praying in this place.

Solomon asks God to come into his temple

41 Now, LORD God, come up and stay in this, your place. Come with your strong Covenant Box.

LORD God, make your priests holy and good. Let your holy people be happy because you are good.

42 LORD God do not turn away from your anointed king. Remember the great love that you had for your servant David.'

Chapter 7

The glory of the LORD fills the temple

1 When Solomon had finished his prayer, fire came down from heaven. It burnt up the sacrifices by fire and the other sacrifices. And the glory of the LORD filled the temple. 2 And the priests could not go into the LORD's house because the LORD's glory had filled the LORD's house. 3 All the Israelites were watching when the fire came down. And they saw the glory of the LORD over the temple. Then they went down on their knees on the flat stones. And they put their noses to the ground, on the path. They worshipped the LORD and they thanked him. They said, 'He is good, and his kind love will have no end.'

The king and the people give sacrifices to the LORD

4 Then the king and all the people offered sacrifices in front of the LORD.

5 King Solomon offered a sacrifice of 22 000 cows and 120 000 sheep and goats. That is how the king and all the people made God's house right for him to use. 6 The priests and the Levites stood in their places. And the Levites took the things that they used to make music to the LORD. King David had made those things to thank the LORD when he said, 'His kind love has no end.' The priests stood and they were looking towards the Levites. And they made a loud noise with their trumpets. All the Israelites were standing.

7 The bronze altar that Solomon had made could not contain all the offerings of animals and grains and the fat. So Solomon made the middle of the yard that was in front of the LORD's house holy for the LORD. Then he gave sacrifices by fire and he burnt the fat of friendship-offerings there.

8 So Solomon obeyed the rules of the feast for 7 days at that time. And a large crowd of Israelites were with him. They came from everywhere from Lebo-Hamath to the valley near the border of Egypt. 9 On the 8th day, they met together for an important meeting. For 7 days, they had made the altar holy for God. And for 7 days, they had obeyed the rules of the feast. 10 Solomon sent the people to their homes on the 23rd day of the 7th month. The LORD had done many good things for David, for Solomon and for his people, the Israelites. So all the people were very happy when they went to their homes.

The LORD appears to Solomon

11 Solomon finished the house of the LORD and the king's house. He was able to do everything that he had wanted to do for the house of the LORD. And he was able to do everything that he had wanted to do for his own house. 12 Then the LORD appeared to Solomon at night. He said to Solomon, 'I have heard your prayer and I have chosen this place. It will be a place where people can give sacrifices to me.

13 I might cause there to be no rain or I might send insects to eat your food plants. Or I might send bad illnesses to my people. 14 Then my people who are called by my name should be sorry. They should be humble and they should pray. They should try to find me. And they should stop doing the wrong things that they have done. Then I will hear them from heaven and I will forgive their sin. And I will make their country better. 15 Now I will be watching this place and I will be listening to the prayers from here. 16 I have now chosen this temple for me to use and I have made it holy. So my name can be here for all time. I will always be watching it. And it will always be special to me.'

Solomon must obey the LORD

17 'But you must live carefully. You must remember that I am watching you. That is what your father David did. You must obey everything that I have said to you. And you must obey my rules and my laws. 18 If you do that, I will make your descendants kings of Israel for all time. That is what I promised to your father David. I said, "A man among your descendants will always be the ruler of Israel."

19 But that will not happen if you turn away from me. You may stop obeying the rules and the laws that I have given to you. You might go off to become servants of other gods and you might worship them. 20 I have given my country to the Israelites. But if they do those things, I will take them from my country. And I will leave this house that I have made holy for my name to be there. I will make it a thing that the people in other nations think is worth nothing. And the people in all the nations will be talking about that. 21 This temple is now very beautiful. But then all the people who walk past it will be surprised. They will almost feel ill. And they will say, "Why has the LORD done this to this country and to this temple?" 22 Men will answer, "It is because they have left the LORD, the God of their ancestors. He brought them out of the country called Egypt. But they have changed to worship and to be servants of other gods. That is why he has caused them all this trouble." '

Chapter 8

Solomon builds more villages

1 After 20 years, Solomon had built the house of the LORD and his own house. 2 After that, he built in the towns that Huram had given to him. And he sent Israelites to live in them. 3 Then Solomon went to Hamath-Zobah. And he won the fight with the people who lived there. 4 He made Tadmor in the desert and the towns that he had built in Hamath to store things stronger.

5 He built again Higher Beth-Horon and Lower Beth-Horon. He made those cities strong and he put walls with strong gates round them. 6 And he built Baalath and more towns to store things. And he built other towns for his chariots and for his men who rode horses to live in. He built in Jerusalem, Lebanon or in any place that he ruled. He built anything that he wanted to build in all those places.

Solomon causes people who are not Israelites to become his slaves

7 Some people who were not Israelites still lived in the country. They were the people called Hittites, Amorites, Perizzites, Hivites and Jebusites. 8 They were descendants of the people from those nations that the Israelites had not killed. Solomon caused them to work as slaves for him. And they are still slaves today. 9 But Solomon did not cause any Israelites to become slaves for his work. But they were his soldiers, their officers, and the men who drove his chariots. Or they were his soldiers who rode on horses. 10 King Solomon's most important officers were 250 Israelites who ruled over the people.

Solomon gives a house to Pharaoh's daughter

11 Solomon brought Pharaoh's daughter up from David's city into the house that he had built for her. He did that because, he said, 'My wife must not live in the house of David the king of Israel. The Lord's Covenant Box has been there, so that house is holy.'

How the priests and the Levites worked in the Temple

12 Solomon had built an altar in front of the door of the temple. Now he gave sacrifices by fire to the LORD on it. 13 He told the priests and the Levites what they must do every day. Moses had told them what they must do every Sabbath, every New Moon and during three special feasts each year. Those three special feasts were the feast of unleavened bread, the feast-of-weeks and the feast-of-shelters. 14 Solomon gave jobs to groups of priests as his father, David, had described. He caused the Levites to be leaders of the praise. And they had to help the priests as they needed it each day. And he told the guards at each gate when each guard should work. He was doing as David, God's servant, had said. 15 All the priests and all the Levites were careful to do what the king had said about everything. And that included how they kept the valuable things safe. They did not change his words.

16 Solomon's servants did all Solomon's work. They started on the day when they put down the floor of the Lord's house. And they worked until they had finished it. So they finished the house of the LORD.

Solomon's men fetch gold from Ophir

17 Then Solomon went to Ezion-Geber and to Eloth by the edge of the sea. Those towns were in the country called Edom. 18 And Huram sent ships to him with his own men. They had their own officers who knew the sea. Those officers sailed with Solomon's servants to Ophir. And they returned with 17 000 kilos (38 000 pounds) of gold and they gave it to King Solomon.

Chapter 9

The Queen of Sheba visits Solomon

What the Queen of Sheba said to Solomon

5 Then she said to the king, 'People told me about you in my country. And they told me about your wisdom. Everything that they told me was true. 6 But I did not believe it. Now I believe it because I have come here. And I have seen all those things. But people had told me only half of the things that they might have told me. You are much wiser than they said. Everything about you is better than people said. 7 Your men are very happy. And your servants who always stand in front of you are very happy. They can always hear your wise words. 8 I praise the LORD your God. You have given a lot of pleasure to him and so he has put you on his throne. So you are king on behalf of the LORD your God. He loves Israel and he wants to make them strong for all time. That is why he has caused you to be their king. He wants you to rule over them in a fair way. And he wants you to cause them to do right things.'

9 Then she gave to the king 4000 kilos (9000 pounds) of gold, a lot of spices and many valuable stones. There had never been spices in Israel like those that the Queen of Sheba gave to King Solomon.

10 Huram's servants and Solomon's servants brought gold from Ophir. They also brought algum trees and valuable stones. 11 The king used this algum wood to make steps for the LORD's house and for the king's house. And with it he made lyres and harps for the people who made music. Nobody had ever seen things like those in the country called Judah.

12 King Solomon gave to the Queen of Sheba everything that she wanted. And he gave to her everything that she asked for. He gave more things to her than she had brought to him. Then she left with all her servants and she returned to her own country.

Solomon's gold and how he used it

13 Every year 23 000 kilos (50 000 pounds weight) of gold came to Solomon. 14 Men who were buyers and sellers brought more things. And the rulers of the country and all the kings of Arabia brought gold and silver to Solomon.

15 King Solomon's men made 200 large shields out of gold that they hit flat with hammers. They used about of 3.5 kilos of gold (7.5 pounds) to make each shield. 16 Then they made 300 small shields, each with about 1.7 kilos of gold (3.5 pounds). And the king put them in the house of the forest of Lebanon.

17 Then the king made a large king's seat out of ivory and he covered it with pure gold. 18 This seat had 6 steps and on top of them the throne had a gold box for the king's feet. On each side of the throne were places for his arms to rest. Also two models of lions were standing next to his hands. 19 Two lions stood on each step. There was one lion at each side of every step. No other kingdom had anything like it. 20 All King Solomon's cups were gold. Everything that anyone used in the house of the forest of Lebanon was the best gold. People did not think that silver had any value in Solomon's time. 21 The king's ships went to Tarshish with the servants of Huram. And ships from Tarshish came every three years with gold, silver, ivory, monkeys and beautiful birds called peacocks.

Solomon's valuable things

22 King Solomon was more wise and he had more valuable things than any other king on the earth. 23 All the kings on the earth wanted to meet Solomon. They wanted to hear the wisdom that God had put into his mind. 24 Each king brought a gift to him. They brought things of silver, things of gold, clothes and arms to fight with. They also brought spices, horses and mules. And they brought the same amount every year.

25 Solomon had 4000 places for horses and chariots and 12 000 men to ride the horses. And he kept them in the special chariot cities or with him in Jerusalem. 26 He ruled over all the kings from the River Euphrates, past the Philistines' country to the border of Egypt. 27 The king made Jerusalem rich. Silver was like common stones, and cedar wood was like common trees from the low hills. That was because there were so many things like that. 28 And people brought to Solomon horses from Egypt and from all the other countries.

Solomon dies

29 Nathan the prophet wrote about everything else that Solomon did. He wrote all those things from the beginning to the end. Ahijah from Shiloh wrote everything down. And they wrote what Iddo saw in his visions about Jeroboam the son of Nebat. 30 Solomon ruled in Jerusalem for 40 years over all Israel. 31 Then Solomon died and the people buried him in his father David's city. And Rehoboam his son ruled instead.

Chapter 10

The Israelites ask Rehoboam to give them less work

1 Rehoboam went to Shechem, where all the Israelites had gone. They thought that he would become their king there. 2 Jeroboam, son of Nebat was in Egypt when people told him about this. He had run there from King Solomon. But he returned from Egypt when people told him this news. 3 So the Israelites asked Jeroboam to meet with them. All the Israelites went to Rehoboam and they said him, 4 'Your father made our work very difficult, but will you make it easier? If you do that, we will be your servants.' 5 Rehoboam answered, 'Come to me again after three days.' So the people went away.

Rehoboam asks the old men and the young men what they think

6 Then King Rehoboam asked the older men what they thought. Those men had been servants of his father Solomon when he was alive. 'What should I say to these people?' he asked.

7 They replied, 'Be kind to these people. Give to them what they want. And speak good words to them. If you do that, they will always be your servants.'

8 But Rehoboam did not do what the older men had said. He asked the young men who had been children with him. They were standing in front of him. 9 'What answer should I give to these people who have spoken to me?' he said. 'They have said to me, "Your father made our work very difficult, but will you make it easier?" '

10 The young men who had been children with him replied, 'Say this to the people who said, "Your father made our work very difficult, but will you make it easier?" Say, "I am much greater than my father was. 11 My father made your work difficult but I will make your work more difficult. He hurt you a little, but I will hurt you badly." '

Rehoboam refuses to do what the people want

12 Jeroboam and all the people returned to Rehoboam after three days as King Rehoboam had said. He had said, 'Come to me again on the third day after this.' 13 The king did not speak to them in a kind way. King Rehoboam did not do what the older men had said. 14 He did what the young men had said. He said, 'My father caused your work to be difficult but I will make your work more difficult. He hurt you a little, but I will hurt you badly.' 15 So the king did not listen to the people. But this was what God had decided. This was what the LORD had told Jeroboam, Nebat's son, by Ahijah from Shiloh.

Israel and Judah become separate countries

16 All the Israelites saw that the king did not listen to them. Then they answered him, 'We have no part in David, no part in Jesse's son. Israelites, we should return to our tents. David's people can be separate from us.' So all the Israelites went to their homes. 17 But Rehoboam still ruled over the Israelites who lived in the towns of Judah.

18 Hadoram was the officer who caused the people to do very difficult work. King Rehoboam sent him to the Israelites. But the Israelites threw stones at him until he died. Then King Rehoboam got in his chariot and he went away to Jerusalem.

19 So Israel has refused to obey David's descendants to this day.

Chapter 11

1 When Rehoboam returned to Jerusalem, he sent servants to bring all the soldiers in Judah and Benjamin to him. He had 180 000 best soldiers to fight for him against Israel. Rehoboam wanted them to help him to become the king of all the people again.

2 But the LORD said to Shemaiah, the servant of God, 3 'Speak to Rehoboam, son of Solomon, king of Judah, and to all the Israelites in Judah and Benjamin. 4 Tell them that the LORD is saying this: "Do not go up to fight your relatives. Each man must return to his house, because I have caused this to happen." ' So they obeyed the words of the LORD. They turned round and they did not attack Jeroboam.

Rehoboam makes Judah strong

5 Rehoboam lived in Jerusalem. He built cities in Judah to keep it safe. 6 He put more buildings in Bethlehem, Etam, Tekoa, 7 Beth-Zur, Soco, Adullam, 8 Gath, Mareshah and Ziph. 9 And he built in Adoraim, Lachish, Azekah, 10 Zorah, Aijalon and Hebron. He made all those cities in Judah and Benjamin very strong. 11 He made their strong buildings even stronger and he put important officers in them to rule over them. He stored food and olive oil and wine in them. 12 He supplied every city with shields and spears. And he made them very strong. So Judah and Benjamin were his.

13 The priests and Levites from everywhere in Israel joined his group. 14 The Levites even left their lands and their houses to come to him in Judah and Jerusalem. They came because Jeroboam and his sons had not let them be the LORD's priests. 15 Jeroboam chose his own priests for the high places for worship. They were priests for the models of the goats and the young male cows that he had made. 16 But some people from every tribe in Israel followed the Levites to Jerusalem. Those people wanted to be servants of the LORD, the God of Israel. They came to sacrifice to the LORD, the God of their ancestors.

17 They helped to make the kingdom of Judah stronger. They had helped Rehoboam, Solomon's son to be strong for three years. During those three years, they lived in the way that David and Solomon had lived.

Rehoboam's family

18 Rehoboam married Mahalath, daughter of David's son Jerimoth and of Abihail the daughter of Jesse's son Eliab. 19 She gave to him three sons, who were Jeush, Shemariah and Zaham. 20 Then he married Absalom's daughter Maacah and she gave to him Abijah, Attai, Ziza and Shelomith. 21 Rehoboam loved Absalom's daughter Maacah better than he loved any of his other wives or lady friends. He had 18 wives and 60 lady friends. And he was the father of 28 sons and 60 daughters.

22 Rehoboam said that Abijah, son of Maacah was the most important among all his sons. He wanted him to become king. 23 He did a wise thing. He sent his sons to different parts of Judah and Benjamin and to all the strong cities. He gave to them plenty of food to store and he found many wives for them.

Chapter 12

Rehoboam does not do what gives pleasure to the LORD

1 When Rehoboam had become a safe, strong king, he stopped obeying the LORD's Law. And all the Israelites did the same thing. 2 They had not been faithful to the LORD. Because of that, Shishak, the king of Egypt, attacked Jerusalem. That happened 5 years after Rehoboam began to rule Judah. 3 Shishak attacked with 1200 chariots and 60 000 men on horses. Also, there were so many other soldiers that nobody could count them. There were soldiers from Libya and Ethiopia. And there were men called Sukkiim. And they came from Egypt with him. 4 He won the fight for the strong cities in Judah and he came near to Jerusalem.

The LORD uses Shemaiah to speak to Rehoboam

5 The prophet Shemaiah came to the leaders of Judah in Jerusalem. They had come together in Jerusalem because they were afraid of Shishak. Shemaiah told them that the LORD was saying, 'You have gone away from me. So now I have gone away from you and I will let Shishak beat you.'

6 The leaders of Israel and the king made themselves humble and they said, 'The LORD is a fair judge.'

7 The LORD saw that they had made themselves humble. So he said to Shemaiah, 'I will not kill them because they have made themselves humble. I will give some help to them. I was angry but I will not let Shishak destroy Jerusalem now. 8 But they will become his servants. Then they will learn what it is like to be my servants. And they will learn that it is very different to be servants of kings from other countries.'

9 Shishak, king of Egypt attacked Jerusalem. And he took away the valuable things from the LORD's house and the valuable things from the king's house. He took everything. That included the shields of gold that Solomon had made. 10 So King Rehoboam made bronze shields instead. He gave them to the captains of the guards who kept the door of the king's house safe. 11 They carried the shields when they went with the king to the LORD's house. When the king returned, they put the shields in their usual place again. That was in the guards' room.

Rehoboam is sorry that he did wrong things

12 Rehoboam made himself humble. So the LORD was not so angry with him that he killed him. He did not kill him. And some things that happened in Judah were good.

13 King Rehoboam made himself strong in Jerusalem and he ruled there.

He was 41 years old when he began to rule. He ruled for 17 years in Jerusalem, the city where the LORD had chosen to put his name. He chose it out of all the tribes of Israel. Rehoboam's mother was called Naamah and she was an Ammonite. 14 But he did not really want to be the LORD's servant. So he did evil things.

15 Shemaiah the prophet and Iddo, the man that God showed visions to, have written about King Rehoboam in their books. They wrote down everything that he did from the beginning to the end.

They wrote about things that happened to the people in each clan. Rehoboam and Jeroboam fought each other for their whole lives. 16 Rehoboam died and people buried him in David's city with his ancestors. Then Abijah his son ruled as king instead.

Chapter 13

Abijah becomes king

1 Abijah began to rule over Judah when King Jeroboam had been king of Israel for 18 years. 2 Abijah was king in Jerusalem for three years. His mother's name was Micaiah, daughter of Uriel from the town called Gibeah. Abijah and Jeroboam fought a war. 3 Abijah chose his best 400 000 soldiers. And Jeroboam prepared to fight against him with 800 000 strong brave men that he had chosen.

Abijah speaks to Jeroboam and to his army

4 Abijah stood on the hill called Zemaraim in the hills of Ephraim. He said, 'Listen to me, Jeroboam and all you men from Israel. 5 The LORD, Israel's God, has said that David and his descendants would be kings of Israel for all time. And you should know that. It is God's promise and so it must happen. 6 Jeroboam, the son of Nebat, was a servant of David's son Solomon. But this Jeroboam has refused to obey his master. 7 Some evil men with no value joined his group. They made themselves strong against Solomon's son, Rehoboam. Rehoboam was young and he was not brave. So he could not be strong against them.

8 And now you want to be strong against the LORD's kingdom. But David's descendants rule over that kingdom. You are a very large crowd. And you have the young cows of gold that Jeroboam made to be your gods. 9 But you pushed out the LORD's priests, the sons of Aaron. And you sent away the Levites. And you made your own priests as the people in other nations do. You will call anyone a priest who comes with a young male cow and 7 male sheep to sacrifice. But he will become a priest of things that are not gods.

10 But we are different. The LORD is our God and we have not left him. Our priests are the LORD's servants. They are Aaron's sons. And the Levites help them. 11 They burn sacrifices to the LORD and oils with sweet smells every morning and every evening. They put out bread on his special table every day. They put lights on their lampstand of gold every evening. We are obeying the LORD our God. But you have gone away from him. 12 God is with us and he is our leader. His priests will make a loud noise with their trumpets. That will start the fight against you. Men from Israel, you will not win. So do not fight against the LORD, your ancestors' God.'

Jeroboam attacks Abijah and Judah

13 But Jeroboam had sent some soldiers round behind Judah's men. He was in front of them with his army but the other soldiers were now behind Judah's army. 14 Judah's men turned. And they saw Jeroboam's soldiers who were attacking them from the front and from behind them. Then they shouted out to the LORD and the priests started to make a noise with their trumpets.

The LORD helps Abijah to win the fight

15 The men from Judah shouted very loudly. When the men from Judah shouted, the LORD beat Jeroboam and all Israel's men. He helped Abijah and Judah's men to beat them. 16 Israel's men ran away from Judah's men and God caused the men from Judah to win the fight. 17 Abijah and his men completely beat the men from Israel. And 500 000 men from Israel's best soldiers died. 18 On that day, the LORD helped Judah's people to beat the people from Israel. That was because they believed the promises of their ancestors' God. So Israel's men felt silly.

19 Abijah went after Jeroboam. And he won the fight for the towns called Bethel, Jeshanah and Ephron with their villages.

20 After that, Jeroboam was always weak while Abijah was Judah's king. The LORD made Jeroboam ill and so he died.

21 But Abijah became very strong. He married 14 wives and he had 22 sons and 16 daughters.

22 Many other things happened while Abijah was king. The prophet Iddo has written about all those things in his book. He wrote about everything that Abijah had done. And he wrote about everything that he had said.

Chapter 14

Abijah dies

1 Then Abijah died and people buried him in David's city with his ancestors. His son Asa ruled instead. The country had peace for the first 10 years that Asa was king.

Asa obeys God's Law

2 Asa did good things that gave pleasure to the LORD his God. 3 He took away the altars for foreign gods and their high places for worship. And he broke down the tall pillars of stones and he cut down the models of Asherah. 4 Asa said that all the people in Judah must try to obey the LORD, the God of their ancestors. He said that they must obey God's rules and God's Law. 5 He took away the high places for worship. And he removed the altars where people burnt oils with sweet smells. He did that in every city in Judah. And his kingdom had peace while he ruled. 6 He built strong cities in Judah while there was peace for the country. Nobody fought him during that time because the LORD let him rest.

7 Asa said to Judah's people, 'We should make these towns stronger. We will put walls round them with tall buildings and gates and strong pieces of wood across the gates. The country is ours because we have obeyed the LORD our God. We asked him for help and he has given peace everywhere round us.' So they built strong towns and everything was good.

Zerah attacks Asa

8 Asa had an army of 300 000 men from Judah. They carried big shields and spears. And he had 280 000 men from Benjamin's tribe who carried small shields and bows to shoot arrows with. All these were brave men who could fight well.

9 Zerah from Ethiopia marched out to fight them with a big army and 300 chariots. His army contained 1 000 000 men. He reached Mareshah. 10 Asa went out to fight Zerah. And they prepared for the fight in the valley called Zephathah near Mareshah.

Asa asks God for help

11 Then Asa asked the LORD his God to help him. He said, 'There is nobody like you LORD. It is not difficult for you to help the weak against the strong. Help us, LORD our God, because we trust you. We have come to fight this large army because we want people to honour your name. LORD, you are our God. Do not let men win the fight against you.'

The LORD helps Asa to win the fight

12 So the LORD let Asa and the men from Judah knock down the men from Ethiopia. So the soldiers from Ethiopia ran away. 13 Then Asa and his soldiers ran after them until they reached Gerar. So many soldiers from Ethiopia died there that their army could not fight again. The LORD and his army beat them completely and they destroyed their army. And Judah's men carried away very many good things from them. 14 The people in the towns round Gerar had become very afraid of the LORD. So the Israelites destroyed those towns. There were many good things in those towns. So Judah's men took away all those good things. 15 They also attacked the tents of those people there who had animals. And they took very many sheep and camels from there. Then they returned to Jerusalem.

Chapter 15

Azariah speaks to Asa

1 God's Spirit came on Azariah, Oded's son. 2 He went out to meet Asa and he said to him, 'Listen to me Asa and all you men from Judah and Benjamin. The LORD will be with you while you are with him. If you look for him, you will find him. But if you go away from him, he will go away from you. 3 Israel's people have been without the only God that there really is for a long time. They have not had any priests to teach them. And they have not really had God's Law.

4 But when they were in trouble they turned to the LORD, the God of Israel. They looked for him and they found him. 5 At that time it was not safe to go on journeys. The people in all the nations were always fighting. 6 One nation would destroy another nation. The people from one city destroyed another city. God was causing every kind of trouble for all those people. 7 But you be strong and do not be afraid. God will be good to you because your work gives pleasure to him.'

Asa does more things to give pleasure to the LORD

8 When Asa heard those words of Azariah, son of the prophet Oded, he became very brave. He took away all the very bad idols from the country of the tribes called Judah and Benjamin. He also took them from the towns that he had won among the hills in Ephraim. And he did repairs to the LORD's altar that was in front of the first part of the LORD's house.

9 Then he brought all his people together. They were from Judah and Benjamin. And there were some people from the tribes of Ephraim, Manasseh, and Simeon who lived in Judah. Many people like that had come to him from Israel because the LORD, Asa's God was with him.

Asa brings all the people together in Jerusalem

10 These people met together in Jerusalem in the 15th year after Asa had become king. They met in the 3rd month. 11 At that time they sacrificed many animals to the LORD. They killed 700 cows and 7000 sheep that they had taken from their enemies. 12 They promised the LORD, the God of their ancestors, that they would obey all his laws. They really wanted to do that as well as they could. 13 They decided to kill anyone who would not obey the LORD, the God of Israel. They would kill them whether they were important or not important, man or woman. 14 They gave a very serious promise to the LORD. They shouted with loud voices and with the noise of trumpets and horns. 15 All Judah's people were happy because they had given this promise to God. They really wanted to obey the LORD. They really wanted to find him. So he let them find him. Then the LORD gave them peace with all the nations round them.

Asa punishes Maacah because she worshipped idols

16 Asa took away his grandmother Maacah's special honour. He would not let people call her queen. He did that because she had made a very bad idol of the false god Asherah. He cut it down and he broke it into pieces. Then he burned it in the Kidron Valley. 17 Asa did not remove out of Israel the high places for worship to false gods. But Asa loved the LORD as well as he could for his whole life. 18 He took the silver and gold and the other things that he and his father had saved for God. And he put it them into God's house.

19 Judah did not have to fight again until Asa had been king for more than 35 years.

Chapter 16

Baasha, king of Israel, attacks Judah

1 After Asa had been king of Judah for nearly 36 years Baasha, king of Israel, attacked Judah. And he made Ramah a strong town. He did not want to let anyone go in or out of King Asa's country, Judah.

Asa asks Ben-Hadad for help

2 Then Asa took silver and gold from the safe rooms in the LORD's house and in the king's house. And he sent it to Ben-Hadad, king of Syria, who lived in Damascus. He said to him, 3 'We should promise to help each other. My father and your father promised to help each other. I am sending silver and gold to you. Please stop helping Baasha, king of Israel. Then he will go away from me.'

4 Ben-Hadad agreed with King Asa and he sent the captains of his armies to attack Israel's towns. They won the fights at Ijon, Dan, Abel-Maim and all the cities where Naphtali kept their things. 5 When Baasha knew about this, he stopped building Ramah. He stopped his work on it. 6 So King Asa brought all the men from Judah. They carried away the stones and wood that Baasha had used to build with in Ramah. And Asa used them to build in Geba and Mizpah.

Hanani tells Asa that he has done a wrong thing

7 At that time Hanani, the prophet came to Asa, king of Judah. He said, 'You asked the king of Syria for help and not the LORD your God. So the army of Syria's king will get away from you. 8 The armies of Ethiopia and Libya were very large. And they had many chariots and soldiers who rode on horses. But you trusted the LORD then and he helped you to win the fight against them. 9 The LORD can see everything that happens on the earth. He is strong. And he helps those who love him completely. You have done a very silly thing. So now you will always be fighting.'

Asa gets angry

10 Asa was angry with the prophet because of what he had said. He put him in a prison because he was so angry. And at that time Asa caused a lot of trouble to some of the people.

The end of Asa's life

11 Somebody wrote about all the things that King Asa did. They are in the Book about the Kings of Judah and Israel. All the events from the first event to the last event are in that book. 12 When Asa had been king for nearly 39 years, he became ill. His feet became very bad. But Asa did not ask the LORD for help even when he was very ill. He went to the doctors instead. 13 Asa died as his ancestors had done. He had been king for almost 41 years. 14 The people buried him in the place that he had prepared in the city of David. They put him on a table that he had covered with spices and oils with sweet smells. And they lit a large fire to give honour to him.

Chapter 17

Jehoshaphat becomes king of Judah

1 Asa's son Jehoshaphat ruled instead. And he made himself strong against Israel. 2 He put armies in all the cities of Judah that had walls. And he put groups of soldiers in places in Judah. And he put them in the towns of Ephraim that his father Asa had won.

3 Jehoshaphat was like his ancestor David when he was young. He obeyed the LORD's rules as David had done. And Jehoshaphat did not ask the Baals for help. So the LORD was with him. 4 He went for help to the God of his father. He obeyed the LORD's laws. He did not do the wrong things that Israel's people did. 5 The LORD made the kingdom safe with him as its king. And all Judah's people brought gifts to him. So Jehoshaphat became rich and the people gave a lot of honour to him. 6 He really wanted be the LORD's servant. He removed from Judah the high places where people worshipped false gods. And he cut down the models of the false female god called Asherah.

The king sends men to teach the Law in all his towns and cities

7 When he had been king for nearly three years, Jehoshaphat sent his officers to teach in Judah's towns. The names of those officers were Ben-Hail, Obadiah, Zechariah, Nethanel and Micaiah. 8 He sent some Levites with them. The Levites' names were Shemaiah, Nethaniah, Zebadiah, Asahel, Shemiramoth, Jehonathan, Adonijah, Tobijah, and Tob-Adonijah. And he sent the priests Elishama and Jehoram with them. 9 They taught the people in all parts of Judah. They took with them the Book of the LORD's Law. They went to all the towns in Judah and they taught the people.

People in other nations give honour to Jehoshaphat and to the LORD his God

10 The people in all the kingdoms round Judah were afraid of the LORD. So they did not fight against Jehoshaphat. 11 Some Philistines brought gifts to Jehoshaphat. Those gifts included silver as taxes. People from Arabia brought animals to him. They brought 7700 male sheep and 7700 male goats.

Jehoshaphat's army

12 Jehoshaphat became more and more powerful. He built strong buildings. And he built towns in Judah to store his good things. 13 He stored many valuable things in the towns of Judah. And he kept strong, brave soldiers in Jerusalem. 14 These are their names for each clan. From Judah there were officers over groups of 1000 men. Adnah was the officer over 300 000 brave soldiers.

15 Next, there was Jehohanan. He was the officer over 280 000 soldiers.

16 Next, there was Amasiah, Zichri's son. He wanted to be the LORD's servant and there were 200 000 brave soldiers with him.

17 From Benjamin, there was Eliada, a brave soldier, with 200 000 men with bows and shields.

18 Next, there was Jehozabad with 180 000 men with weapons who had prepared themselves to fight.

19 All these soldiers worked for the king. He also had other soldiers that he put in all Judah's strong cities.

Chapter 18

Jehoshaphat becomes a friend of Ahab

1 Jehoshaphat was very rich and people gave a lot of honour to him. And he started to agree with Ahab because his son married Ahab's daughter. 2 After some years, he went to visit Ahab in Samaria. Ahab killed many sheep and cows for him and for the people who were with him. Ahab wanted to attack Ramoth-Gilead. He asked Jehoshaphat to help him. And Jehoshaphat decided to do it. 3 This is what happened. Ahab, Israel's king said to Jehoshaphat Judah's king, 'Will you go with me to attack Ramoth-Gilead?' Jehoshaphat replied, 'I am like you. My people are like your people. We will come with you to the fight.' 4 But Jehoshaphat also said to the king of Israel, 'Please ask the LORD first what he wants us to do.'

5 So the king of Israel brought the prophets. (There were 400 of them.) He asked them, 'Should we go to fight against Ramoth-Gilead, or should I not go?' 'Go', they answered. 'God will help the king to win the fight.'

Jehoshaphat wants to ask the LORD's prophet a question

6 But Jehoshaphat asked, 'Is there another prophet of the LORD here that we can ask?'

7 Ahab replied, 'There is one other man here who will ask the LORD for us. But I do not like him because he only prophesies bad things about me, never anything good. He is Micaiah, son of Imlah.'

'Do not say that!' replied Jehoshaphat.

8 So the king of Israel said to an officer, 'Bring Micaiah son of Imlah to me quickly.'

Ahab's prophets speak

9 The king of Israel and Jehoshaphat, king of Judah were sitting on their special king's seats. And they were wearing their special king's clothes. They were at a threshing-floor. It was near the gate of Samaria and all the prophets were prophesying in front of them. 10 Zedekiah son of Chenaanah had made two iron horns for himself. He said, 'The LORD says, "You will push the people from Syria with these horns until you have killed all those people."'

11 All the other prophets said the same thing. 'Attack Ramoth-Gilead. If you do that, you will win the fight', they said. 'The LORD will help the king to win it', they said.

What Micaiah says

12 The officer who had gone to fetch Micaiah spoke to him. 'All the other prophets are saying good things to the king. Please agree with them and say good things to the king.'

13 But Micaiah said, 'The LORD lives. And I can say to the king only what my God says.'

14 When he arrived, the king asked him, 'Micaiah, should we go to fight at Ramoth-Gilead or should I not go?'

'Attack and win', he said. 'The LORD will help you to beat them.'

15 The king said to him, 'I have to say this to you too many times. You must promise me, in the LORD's name, to say only what is true.'

16 Then Micaiah said, 'I saw all Israel's men and they were running everywhere over the mountains. They were like sheep that had no shepherd. And the LORD said, "These people have no master. Each man should return to his own house and they should not fight." '

17 The king of Israel said to Jehoshaphat, 'I told you that he never prophesies anything good about me. He only says bad things', he said.

18 Then Micaiah said, 'So listen to the word of the LORD. I saw the LORD and he was sitting on his throne. All the angels in the army of heaven were standing either at his right side or at his left side. 19 The LORD said, "Who can cause Ahab, king of Israel to attack Ramoth-Gilead? Then he will die there." One angel said one thing and another angel said something different. 20 Then another spirit came and he stood in front of the LORD. "I will cause him to do it", he said.

"How will you do it?" the LORD asked.

21 "I will go. And I will cause all his prophets to say things that are not true", he said.

"That will cause him to go and fight", said the LORD. "Go and do it."

22 So now the LORD has caused all your prophets here to say things that are not true. The LORD has decided to cause bad trouble for you.'

Zedekiah and Micaiah

23 Then Zedekiah, son of Chenaanah went up and he hit Micaiah on the face. 'Which way did the LORD's Spirit go when he left me to speak to you?' he asked.

24 Micaiah replied, 'You will know that on the day when you go to hide in an inside room.'

25 Then the king of Israel said to his soldiers, 'Take Micaiah to Amon, who rules the city and to Joash my son. 26 Tell them that the king says, "Put this man in a prison. Give to him only bread and water as food until I return alive and well." '

27 Micaiah said, 'If you really return alive and well, the LORD has not spoken by me.' Then he said, 'Remember my words, all you people.'

Ahab and Jehoshaphat go to fight at Ramoth-Gilead

28 So the king of Israel and Jehoshaphat, king of Judah went to fight against the people in Ramoth-Gilead.29 The king of Israel said to Jehoshaphat, 'I will not wear special clothes when I am fighting. But you wear your king's clothes.' So the king of Israel wore soldier's clothes. And they started to fight the enemy.

30 But the king of Syria had said to his chariot officers, 'Do not fight with anyone, important or not important, except the king of Israel.' 31 The chariot officers saw King Jehoshaphat in his special clothes. So they said, 'That is the king of Israel.' And they turned to attack him. Jehoshaphat shouted and the LORD helped him. God caused the officers to turn away from him. 32 The chariot officers saw that it was not the king of Israel. So they stopped running after him.

The enemy hurt Ahab and he dies

33 But a man shot an arrow at the king of Israel.

But the man did not know that it was the king of Israel. He hit the king of Israel between different parts of his armour. The king said to the man who was driving his chariot, 'Turn round. Take me out of the fight because the arrow has hurt me.'

34 They fought all day and the king of Israel stood against the side of his chariot. He looked towards the army of Syria until evening. Then at sunset he died.

Chapter 19

Jehu tells Jehoshaphat that he has made God angry

1 Jehoshaphat king of Judah returned to his house in Jerusalem. He was safe. 2 Jehu the prophet, Hanani's son, went out to meet him. He said to King Jehoshaphat, 'You went to help a bad man. You seem to love people who hate the LORD. The LORD is very angry with you because you have done that. 3 But you have some good things in you. You have destroyed the Asherah idols that people worshipped. And you tried to do the things that give pleasure to God.'

Jehoshaphat chooses men to be judges

4 So Jehoshaphat lived in Jerusalem. But he went out among all the people from Beersheba to the hills of Ephraim. He turned the people to the LORD, the God of their ancestors again. 5 He chose men to become judges in the country's cities. He put them in every strong city in Judah. 6 He said to the judges, 'Be careful how you do your job. Remember that you are not doing it for men but for the LORD. And he will be with you. And he can help you to say what is right. 7 Now be afraid to make the LORD angry. Be careful and do your job well. The LORD our God is fair. Sometimes a judge might decide not to be fair because he likes one man more than another. Or he might not be fair because one person gives things to him. But our God never does those things.'

8 Jehoshaphat also chose men in Jerusalem to be judges. Some judges were priests or Levites. Other judges were leaders of clans in Israel. Their job was to help people to obey the LORD's Law. Sometimes people did not agree with each other. And the judges must say what was right. They lived in Jerusalem.

Rules for judges to obey

9 He said to them, 'You must be afraid to make the LORD angry in the way that you work for him. Obey him faithfully because you really want to do it. 10 Israelites who live in the cities may be arguing. And they will come to you. These problems may be about deaths. They may be about what the Law teaches. They may be about difficulties with God's rules or about some other law. You must speak to everyone that comes to you for these reasons. You must teach them so that they do not sin against the LORD. If they do not sin, God will not be angry with you or with the Israelites. If you tell those things to them, you will not have sinned in that way.

11 Amariah, the most important priest, will be over you about all the things that matter to the LORD. And Zebadiah, the son of Ishmael is the leader of the tribe of Judah. He will be over you about all the things that matter to the king. The Levites will be your officers. Be brave and do these things. The LORD will be with those people who do the right things!'

Chapter 20

Soldiers from Moab and Ammon attack Jehoshaphat

1 After that, men from Moab, men from Ammon and some other people called Meunites came to fight Jehoshaphat.

2 Some men came and they said to Jehoshaphat, 'A large army is coming from this side of Syria. It has come across the Dead Sea to attack you. They are already in Hazazon-Tamar.' (That is another name for En-Gedi.)

Jehoshaphat asks the LORD to help his people

3 Jehoshaphat was afraid. So, he decided to ask the LORD what he should do. And he told all the people in Judah that they should not eat for some time. 4 All Judah's people came together to ask the LORD for his help. They came from every town in Judah to meet with the LORD.

5 Then Jehoshaphat stood up in front of the people from Judah and from Jerusalem. He was standing in front of the new yard of the LORD's house.

6 He said, 'LORD, you were the God of our ancestors. You are the God who is in heaven. You rule over all kings and their nations.

You are strong and powerful and nobody can stand against you. 7 Our God, you pushed out the people who were living in this country. You caused your people, the Israelites to push them out. And you have given this country for all time to the descendants of your friend Abraham. 8 Your people have lived here and they have built a house here to give honour to your name. When they built it, they said, 9 "Perhaps we will have troubles. The trouble might be war, punishment, illness or we might have no food. Then we will come and we will stand in front of you. We will stand in front of this temple because your name is in this temple. Then we will ask you for help when we are in trouble. Then you will hear us and you will save us."

Israel has never hurt Ammon or Edom

10 But now men from Ammon, Moab and the mountain called Seir are here. You would not let the Israelites attack them when the Israelites came out of Egypt. So our people turned away and they did not kill those people. 11 Now see how these people are paying us for that. They are coming to push us out of your country that you gave to us to keep. 12 So, our God, please punish these people. We are not strong. So we cannot fight this very large army that is attacking us. We are too weak to fight them. We do not know what to do. But we hope that you will help us.'

13 All the men from Judah were standing there in front of the LORD. They were standing there with their babies, their wives and their children.

The LORD speaks to Jahaziel

14 Then the Spirit of the LORD came upon Jahaziel. He was the son of Zechariah. Zechariah was the son of Benaiah, the son of Jeiel, Mattaniah's son. He was a descendant of Asaph and he was a Levite. He was standing among the people.

The LORD's reply

15 He said, 'Listen to me all you people who live in Judah and in Jerusalem. And listen to me King Jehoshaphat. The LORD says to you, "This is God's fight, not yours. So do not be afraid. And do not think that this large army will certainly beat you. 16 March down against them tomorrow. They will be climbing up the narrow valley called Ziz. People go to the desert called Jeruel through a valley. You will find the enemy at the end of that valley. 17 You will not have to fight this time. Go to your places. Stand there. And see how the LORD will save you, Judah and Jerusalem. Do not be afraid. And do not think that this army will certainly beat you. Go out to stand in front of them tomorrow. When you do that, the LORD will be with you." '

The people worship the LORD and the Levites praise him

18 Jehoshaphat put his nose to the ground. And all the people from Judah and from Jerusalem fell down in front of
the LORD to worship him. 19 Then some Levites stood up
to praise the LORD the God of Israel with very loud voices. They were from the clans of Kohath and Korah.

The LORD fights for Judah

20 Jehoshaphat and his men got up early the next morning. And they started to go to the Desert of Tekoa. When they were leaving, Jehoshaphat stood up. And he said, 'Listen to me, people from Judah and people who live in Jerusalem! Trust the LORD your God. If you do that, you will be safe. Believe his prophets. If you believe them, you will win the fight.' 21 And Jehoshaphat talked with the people. Then he chose men to sing and to praise the LORD. They had to wear holy clothes. They went in front of the army and they sang, 'The LORD always does what he has promised to do. And his kind love has no end. So give thanks to him.'

22 The soldiers from Ammon, Moab and from the mountain called Seir were coming to attack Judah. God's people started to sing and
to praise the LORD. Then the LORD caused the enemy to have trouble. So Judah's soldiers completely beat the enemy.

23 The men from Ammon and Moab started to attack the men from Seir. They destroyed their army.

When they had done that, they started to fight each other. And they were killing each other. 24 The men from Judah came to the place where they could see the desert. They looked for the very large army. But they saw only dead bodies where the enemies had been. All their dead bodies were on the ground. Nobody was still alive. 25 So Jehoshaphat and his people went to take away everything that was valuable. They found a lot of clothes and other valuable things on the dead bodies. They took the things from the dead bodies. But there were more things than they could carry away. There was so much that it took them three days to carry all the things away. 26 On the fourth day they came together in the Valley of Beracah. There they praised the LORD. That is why it is still called the Valley of Beracah.

Judah's people return to Jerusalem

27 Then Jehoshaphat and all the men from Judah and Jerusalem returned to Jerusalem. Jehoshaphat was walking in front of them. They were very happy because the LORD had made them happy. He had caused them to beat their enemies. 28 They went into Jerusalem
with harps, lyres and trumpets. They went to the Lord's house there.

29 The people in all the kingdoms round Judah became afraid of God when they knew about this. They knew that the LORD had fought against Israel's enemies. 30 Then Jehoshaphat's kingdom had peace. His God stopped all the people who lived round them attacking him.

Jehoshaphat continues to rule Judah

31 So Jehoshaphat was still the king of Judah. He was 35 years old when he started to rule over Judah. And he ruled in Jerusalem for 25 years. His mother's name was Azubah. She was Shilhi's daughter. 32 He lived as his father Asa had done. And he always followed his father's ways. He always did what the LORD wanted him to do. 33 But he did not remove the high places where some people worshipped idols. And the people still did not really want to be the servants of the God of their ancestors.

34 Other things happened while Jehoshaphat was king. Hanani's son Jehu recorded all those things from the first thing to the last thing. He recorded them in the Book about the Kings of Israel.

Jehoshaphat and Ahaziah build ships together

35 After that, Jehoshaphat became a friend of Ahaziah the king of Israel who did very wrong things. 36 They agreed to build ships that would sail to Tarshish. And they built the ships in the town called Ezion-Geber. 37 Dodavahu's son Eliezer from the town called
Mareshah prophesied against Jehoshaphat. He said, 'You have become a friend of Ahaziah. So the LORD will destroy the things that you have made.' The ships broke in the sea. So, they could not sail to Tarshish.

Chapter 21

Jehoshaphat's son, Jehoram becomes king

1 Then Jehoshaphat died as his ancestors had done. And people buried him in David's city, with his ancestors. And Jehoram his son ruled Judah instead. 2 Jehoram had brothers who were also sons of Jehoshaphat. They were Azariah, Jehiel, Zechariah, Azaryahu, Michael and Shephatiah. All these men were sons of Jehoshaphat, king of Israel. 3 Their father had given many gifts of silver, gold and valuable things to them. And he gave to them cities with walls in Judah. But Jehoram was the oldest son. So his father said that he should be the next king.

Jehoram kills his brothers

4 Jehoram made himself a strong king over his father's kingdom. Then he killed all his brothers and some leaders of Israel with the sword. 5 Jehoram was 32 years old when he started to rule. He ruled for 8 years
in Jerusalem.

Jehoram does not give pleasure to the LORD

6 He had married Ahab's daughter. So he did what the kings of Israel had done. He did what Ahab and his descendants did. He did very wrong things that the LORD did not like. 7 But the LORD did not want to destroy David's clan. That was because of what he had promised to David. He had promised that a descendant of David would always rule in Israel.

Edom fights Judah

8 Edom's people decided not to obey Judah's king while Jehoram was king. So they chose their own king to rule over them. 9 So Jehoram went there with his officers and all his chariots. Edom's men went everywhere round him and his chariots. But during the night he got up. He attacked their soldiers and he reached the other side of their army. 10 But since then, Edom's people have refused to obey Judah's king. At the same time, the people in Libnah decided not to obey Jehoram. That was because Jehoram had stopped worshipping the LORD, the God of his ancestors. 11 He also built high places on the hills in Judah. And there he caused the people from Jerusalem to worship false gods. So he caused Judah's people to do wrong things.

A prophet tells Jehoram how the LORD will punish Jehoram

12 Elijah the prophet wrote a letter to Jehoram. This is what it said:

'The LORD, your father David's God says, "You have not done what your father Jehoshaphat and Asa, kings of Judah did. 13 Instead, you have done as the kings of Israel do. You have been like Ahab and his descendants. You have caused Judah's people and the people in Jerusalem to worship false gods. And you have killed your own brothers. They were your father's sons and they were better men than you. 14 So now the LORD will hit your people, your sons, your wives and everything that is yours. He will hit them very badly. 15 You, yourself, will have many illnesses. You will have an illness in your stomach. The illness will get worse each day until in the end your inside parts will come out of your body." '

Enemies attack Judah

16 And the LORD caused the Philistines and the Arabs who lived near Ethiopia to be angry with Jehoram. 17 They attacked Judah and they won a lot of land. They took away all the things in the king's house and his sons and his wives. The only son that did not take was Jehoahaz, the youngest son.

Jehoram dies

18 After all those things, the LORD caused Jehoram to have a bad illness in his stomach. And that illness could not get better. 19 He was very ill for two whole years, and then his inside parts came out because of the illness. He had very bad pain because of this illness and then he died. His people did not make a big fire to give honour to him as they had done for his ancestors.

20 Jehoram was 32 years old when he started to rule. And he ruled in Jerusalem for 8 years. When he died nobody was sad. They buried him in David's city, but not where they had buried the other kings.

Chapter 22

Ahaziah is king of Judah

1 The people who lived in Jerusalem chose Jehoram's youngest son, Ahaziah to be king of Judah instead. Enemies that came in with the Arabs had killed all Jehoram's older sons. So Ahaziah, the son of Jehoram, the king of Judah began to rule over Judah.

2 Ahaziah was 22 years old when he started to rule. And he ruled for one year in Jerusalem. His mother's name was Athaliah, who was a granddaughter of Omri.

Ahaziah does not do what gives pleasure to God

3 Ahaziah's mother taught him to do what was wrong. So he did the things that Ahab and his descendants had done. 4 He did very wrong things that the LORD did not like. They were like the things that Ahab and his descendants had done. Ahab's officers had taught Ahaziah to do those wrong things after his father had died. And those things caused his death. 5 Ahab's officers told him that he should go with Jehoram to fight Hazael, king of Syria at Ramoth-Gilead. Jehoram was the son of Ahab and he was the king of Israel. He did as they said and the soldiers from Syria hurt Jehoram. 6 So he went to Jezreel to get better after what had happened at Ramah. While he was fighting against Hazael, the king of Syria there, Hazael's soldiers had hurt him. Then Jehoram's son Ahaziah, the king of Judah went to Jezreel to see Ahab's son Jehoram because he was ill.

Jehu kills Ahaziah and his people

7 God used this visit to Jehoram to cause Ahaziah's death. When Ahaziah arrived, he went with Jehoram to meet Nimshi's son Jehu. But the LORD had decided to use Jehu to kill all Ahab's family. God's prophet had put oil on Jehu to show him that God would use him. 8 While Jehu was punishing Ahab's family he found the leaders of Judah. He also found some sons of Ahaziah's relatives who had been servants of Ahaziah. And Jehu killed them too. 9 Then he went to find Ahaziah. Jehu's men found him where he was hiding in Samaria. And they caught him. They took him to Jehu. Then they killed him. They buried him because they said, 'He was the grandson of Jehoshaphat. And Jehoshaphat obeyed the LORD as well as he could.' But now there was nobody in Ahaziah's family who could become king.

Athaliah tries to kill all the family of Judah's king

10 Then Athaliah, Ahaziah's mother, knew that her son was dead. So she started to kill everyone in the king's clan in Judah.

Jehoshabeath saves Ahaziah's son, Joash

11 But Jehoshabeath, King Jehoram's daughter, took Ahaziah's son Joash away from the other sons that Athaliah was killing. And she hid him. She was the wife of Jehoiada the priest. She put Joash in a bedroom in the house with his nurse. She hid the child from Athaliah because she was Ahaziah's sister. So Athaliah did not kill him. 12 He stayed secretly with them in the house of God for 6 years. During that time, Athaliah ruled the country.

Chapter 23

Jehoiada causes Joash to become king

1 After nearly 7 years, Jehoiada decided that he must be brave. He told some officers in the army what he wanted to do. And they agreed with him. They were each over 100 soldiers. These men were Jeroham's son Azariah, Jehohanan's son Ishmael, Obed's son Azariah, Adaiah's son Maaseiah and Zichri's son Elishaphat. 2 They went to all the towns in Judah. They brought the Levites from those towns and all the leaders of Israel's clans to Jerusalem. 3 There in God's house all those people promised the king that they would help him.

Jehoiada said to them, 'Here is the king's son. He must rule as the LORD promised about David's descendants. 4 You must do this: You priests and Levites will go in to work in the temple on the Sabbath. There will be three separate groups of you. One group must watch at the doors of the temple. 5 Another group will watch at the king's house. And the last group will be at the gate called Foundation Gate. All the other people will be in the yards round the house of the LORD. 6 Only the priests and the Levites who have to work there can go in to the house of the LORD. They can go in because they are holy. All the other people must stay outside as the LORD has said. 7 The Levites must stand round the new king, each with his sword in his hand. They must kill anyone who comes into the temple. They must stay very near to the king in any place that he goes.'

The people put the crown on Joash's head

8 The Levites and all the men in Judah did everything that Jehoiada the priest had spoken to them about. Each leader took his men who should come into the temple on the Sabbath. And he took his men who should go out of the temple on the Sabbath. Jehoiada the priest did not send anyone to his home. 9 Jehoiada the priest gave spears and large and small shields to the captains over each group of 100 men. Those things had been King David's and they were in the house of God. 10 He told all the men that they must stand with their spears ready. They stood from the north side to the south side of the temple. And they were near the altar and round the king.

11 Jehoiada and his sons brought out the old king's son and they put the crown on his head. They gave to him the laws that kings must obey. Jehoiada and his sons anointed him as king and they shouted, 'We pray that the king will live for a long time.' So he became the king of Judah.

The people kill Athaliah

12 Athaliah heard the noise when the people started to run about. She heard them when they praised the king.

So she went to the people in the house of the LORD. 13 She looked and she saw the new king. He was standing in the king's place by the door of the temple. The officers and the men who made a noise with trumpets were standing next to him. All the country's people were happy and people were making a noise with trumpets. There were singers and they were also making music. They were the leaders of the people while the people praised. Athaliah tore her clothes and she screamed, 'People are fighting against their ruler! They are fighting against their ruler!'

14 Jehoiada the priest sent a message to the captains who were each over 100 men. These captains were over the army. The priest had said to them, 'Do not kill her in the house of the LORD.' So now he said, 'Bring her out between the soldiers. And kill with a sword anyone who tries to help her.' 15 So they took her and they brought her to the Horse Gate, next to the king's house. And they killed her there.

The people destroy the temple of Baal

16 Then Jehoiada, the people and the king promised each other that they would be the LORD's people. 17All the people went to the temple of Baal and they pulled it down. They broke the altars and the idols into pieces. And they killed Mattan, Baal's priest in front of the altars.

Worship in the LORD's temple

18 Then Jehoiada gave authority over the house of the LORD to the priests. They were Levites and David had given to them different jobs at the LORD's house. They gave sacrifices by fire to the LORD as Moses had written in the Law. They were happy and they sang at the same time. David had told them how to do that. 19 Jehoiada also put men at the gates of the LORD's house. So, anyone who was not clean for any reason could not go in.

Joash sits on the king's special seat

20 Jehoiada took the captains who were each over 100 men, the important men and the rulers of the people. And all the country's people went with them. They brought the king down from the LORD's house. They came in through the Higher Gate to the king's house. There they caused the king to sit on the king's special seat. 21 And all the people in the whole country were very happy. The city was quiet because the people had killed Athaliah with the sword.

Chapter 24

Joash is king

1 Joash was 7 years old when he became king. And he ruled in Jerusalem for 40 years. His mother was Zibiah from Beersheba. 2 Joash did the things that gave pleasure to the LORD. And he did that all the time that Jehoiada the priest was alive. 3 Jehoiada chose two wives for him and he had sons and daughters.

Joash wants money for repairs to the temple

4 Sometime after those things, Joash decided to do repairs to the LORD's house. 5 He asked the priests and the Levites to come to him. 'Go into all the towns in Judah. And bring here all the money that Israel's people save each year', he said. 'It is for the repair of your God's house. Do it now.' But the Levites did not hurry to do it.

6 So the king asked Jehoiada, the most important priest, to come to him. 'You have not told the Levites that they must bring in the money from Judah and Jerusalem. It is for the tent of God's promise. You should have caused them to bring it. The LORD's servant Moses and all Israel's people agreed to save this money.'

7 The sons of that wicked woman Athaliah had broken God's house. And they had used the holy things from the LORD's house for the Baals.

People bring money to the temple

8 The king said that the Levites must make a big box. They made a big box and they put it outside, by the gate of the LORD's house.

9 Then he sent men to tell everyone in Judah and Jerusalem that they should bring the money there. God's servant Moses had told the Israelites that they should pay this money. He told them that while they were in the desert. 10 All the officers and all the people were happy to give this money. They brought their part and they threw it into the box. They did that until all the people had given their money. 11 The Levites took the box to the king's officers. They took it when there was a lot of money in it. The king's secretary and an officer of the most important priest came. They took the money out of the box. Then they put the box outside the gate again. They did that regularly, so then they had a lot of money.

The king and Jehoiada pay men to make repairs to the temple

12 The king and Jehoiada gave the money to builders for the repairs to the LORD's house. They used it to pay men who worked there with stone and wood in the LORD's house. And they paid men who worked with iron and bronze for other repairs to the LORD's house.

13 These workers worked well and they soon finished the repairs. They made the house as it should be. And they made it stronger, too. 14 They did not use all the money. So when they had finished the work, they brought some money to the king and to Jehoiada. They decided to make tools to use in the LORD's house. There were things that the priests used for sacrifices by fire and for other work in the house. They also made dishes and cups out of gold and silver. All the time that Jehoiada was alive, they made sacrifices by fire at the LORD's house.

Jehoiada dies

15 But Jehoiada became very old. He had lived for many years. And he died when he was 130 years old. 16They buried him among the kings in David's city. That was because he had done many good things in Israel for God and for God's house.

Joash and the people decide not to obey the LORD's rules

17 After Jehoiada died, the most important leaders in Judah came to the king. They fell down in front of him and then the king listened to them. 18 They stopped worshipping the LORD, the God of their ancestors, in his house. They worshipped Asherahs and idols instead. So God became very angry with the people in Judah and in Jerusalem. That was because they had done those very wrong things. 19 The LORD sent prophets to the people. They told the people that they should begin to worship the LORD again. They told them that they were doing something very bad. But the people would not listen to them.

Zechariah tells the people that God is angry with them

20 Then God's Spirit came upon Zechariah, son of Jehoiada the priest. He stood in front of the people and he said, 'God says, "You are not obeying the LORD's rules. So nothing will go well for you. Because you have gone away from the LORD, he has gone away from you." '

Joash and the people kill Zechariah

21 But the people decided to hurt him. The king told them that they should kill him. So they threw stones at him until he was dead. They did it in the yard of the LORD's house. 22 King Joash did not remember that Zechariah's father Jehoiada had been very kind to him. He killed his son. And when Zechariah was dying he said, 'I pray that the LORD will see this. And I pray that the LORD will punish you because of it.'

An army from Syria attacks Judah and it wins the fight

23 At the end of that year, an army from Syria attacked Joash. They attacked Judah and Jerusalem. They killed all the people's leaders and they sent many valuable things to their king in Damascus. 24 The army from Syria was only a few soldiers. But the LORD helped them to win the fight against Judah's much bigger army. That was because they had stopped worshipping the LORD, the God of their ancestors. So God used those soldiers to punish Joash.

Joash's officers kill him

25 When the army from Syria left, Joash was very ill. His own servants were angry that he had killed the son of Jehoiada the priest. So they decided to kill him and they killed him in his bed. He died and they buried him in David's city. But they did not bury him with the dead bodies of the kings.

Amaziah becomes king

26 The officials who decided to kill Joash were Zabad and Jehozabad. Zabad was the son of Shimeath, a woman from the country called Ammon. And Jehozabad was the son of Shimrith, a woman from the country called Moab. 27 People recorded the things about Joash's sons and the prophecies about him in the Book about the Kings. People also recorded the repairs that he made to the house of God. And his son Amaziah ruled instead.

Chapter 25

Amaziah becomes king

1 Amaziah was 25 years old when he began to rule. He ruled in Jerusalem for 29 years. His mother's name was Jehoaddan and she was from Jerusalem. 2 He did the things that gave pleasure to the LORD. But he did not always really want to do those things.

He kills the men who killed his father

3 He made himself safe and strong as the ruler of the country. Then he killed all his servants who had killed the king, his father. 4 But he did not kill their children. He did as Moses had written in the Law. The LORD had said to Moses, 'You must not kill men because of what their children have done. And you must not kill people because of what their fathers have done. Each person must die because of his own sins only.'

Amaziah's army

5 Then Amaziah brought all the people in Judah together. He chose leaders for their clans. Some were leaders of 1000 men and some were leaders of 100 men from Judah or from Benjamin. He counted 300 000 men who were 20 years old or older. They could fight with spear and shield. 6 And he paid 3500 kilos (7800 pounds) of silver for 100 000 very brave soldiers from Israel to fight for him.

The king sends back the soldiers from Israel

7 But a prophet came to the king and he said, 'You king, do not let these soldiers from Israel go with you because the LORD is not with Israel. He is not with any of those relatives of Ephraim. 8 With them, you may be strong and you may fight well in the war. But God will use the enemy to beat you. God can help you. And he can cause your enemies to beat you.'

9 Amaziah said to God's servant, 'But I have paid 3500 kilos (7800 pounds weight) of silver for the army from Israel. What should I do about that?' God's servant replied, 'The LORD can give you more money than that! He can give you a lot of money!'

10 So Ahaziah spoke to the soldiers who were relatives of Ephraim. He told them that he did not need them. He sent them away to their homes. They were very angry with Judah. They returned to where they had come from with very angry thoughts in their minds.

Amaziah fights men from Seir

11 But Amaziah became brave and he led all his soldiers to the Valley of Salt. There they fought and they killed 10 000 men from Seir. 12 His army also caught 10 000 more men alive. They took them to the top of a tall rock and they threw them from the top of the rock. So, all the men died when they hit the rocks below.

Israelite soldiers attack towns in Judah

13 But the soldiers that Amaziah had sent away were attacking towns in Judah from Samaria to Beth-Horon. He had not let them go to war with his army. They killed 3000 men and they took away many valuable things from those towns.

Amaziah worships idols

14 Amaziah returned to Judah after he had killed all those soldiers from Seir. But he brought the gods that the people in Seir worshipped with him. He put them up as his own gods and he worshipped them. And he burned oils with sweet smells in front of them. 15 So the LORD was very angry with Amaziah and he sent a prophet to him. The prophet said to him, 'You are silly to ask these gods for help! They could not save their own people from you!'

Amaziah will not listen to God's prophet

16 While he was speaking, the king said to him, 'We have not asked you to tell the king what he should do! Stop! If you do not stop, my men will kill you.' So the prophet stopped. But he said, 'I know this: God has decided to kill you because you have done this. And you have not listened to my words.'

Amaziah attacks Israel

17 Then Judah's King Amaziah and his most important officers' spoke together. Then they sent a message to the king of Israel. He was Joash, the son of Jehoahaz, who was the son of Jehu. 'Come and we can fight each other', the message said.

18 But Israel's King Joash replied to Amaziah the king of Judah, 'A small weed in Lebanon sent a message to a great cedar tree in Lebanon. The message said, "Let your daughter marry my son." Then a wild animal that was in Lebanon came. And it walked on the weed and it destroyed it. 19 You say to yourself that you have won the fight with Edom. And now you think that you are great. But stay in your house! You do not want to cause trouble for yourself. If you fight us, we will beat you and Judah.'

God lets Israel win the fight to punish Amaziah

20 But Amaziah refused to listen. God had decided that he would cause Joash's army to win the fight. That was because Amaziah had worshipped Edom's gods. 21 So Joash, Israel's king attacked Amaziah, the king of Judah. They stood at Beth-Shemesh in Judah. And they were looking at each other. 22 Israel's army beat Judah's army completely. So every soldier from Judah ran away to his tent. 23 Joash, the king of Israel caught Amaziah the son of Joash, the son of Jehoahaz, the king of Judah. He caught him at Beth-Shemesh and he took him to Jerusalem. Then Joash broke the wall of Jerusalem, from the Ephraim Gate to the Corner Gate. That part of the wall was about 180 metres (600 feet) long. 24 He took all the gold and the silver from the house of God. And he took all the other things that Obed-Edom was keeping in God's house. Joash also took the valuable things from the king's house and some foreign men that Amaziah had kept there. Then he returned to Samaria.

The end of Amaziah's life

25 Joash's son, King Amaziah of Judah lived for 15 years after Jehoahaz's son Joash, king of Israel died. 26 Men have written down all the other things that Amaziah did from the first thing to the last thing. All those things are in the Book about the Kings of Judah and Israel. 27 After Amaziah had stopped obeying the LORD, men in Jerusalem agreed to kill him. So he ran away to Lachish. But they went after him to Lachish and they killed him there. 28 They brought his dead body to Jerusalem on horses. And they buried him with his ancestors in the city of Judah.

Chapter 26

Uzziah becomes king of Judah

1 Then all the people in Judah took Uzziah and they chose him to be king instead. He was Amaziah's son and he was 16 years old. 2 He built Eloth again after King Amaziah had died. And he made it a part of Judah again.

Uzziah gives pleasure to the LORD

3 Uzziah was 16 years old when he became king. And he ruled in Jerusalem for 52 years. His mother's name was Jecoliah and she was from Jerusalem. 4 He did the things that gave pleasure to the LORD. He was doing as his father, Amaziah had done. 5 He tried to obey God all the time that Zechariah was alive. Zechariah was wise because God showed things to him. All the time that Uzziah tried to obey the LORD, God caused everything to go well for him.

God helps Uzziah to win fights

6 Uzziah went and he attacked the Philistines. He destroyed the walls of Gath, Jabneh and Ashdod. Then he built new towns near Ashdod and in other places among the people called Philistines. 7 God helped him to win fights against the Philistines and against the Arabs who lived in Gur-Baal. And God helped him against the people called Meunites. 8 The people from Ammon paid taxes to Uzziah. He had become very powerful. So all the people everywhere from Judah to Egypt knew that Uzziah was great.

Uzziah makes Jerusalem strong and his men work on the land

9 Uzziah built tall buildings to keep Jerusalem safe. He built them at the Corner Gate, at the Valley Gate and at the corner of the wall. He made them strong and he put men with weapons in them. 10 He also built buildings like that in the desert. He dug big holes there to contain water because he had many animals. They were near the lowest part of the hills and on the flat land. He had men who worked in the fields. And he had men who worked in vineyards on the hills. He loved to use the ground to plant things. So, many men worked for him in places where food plants could grow well.

Uzziah's army

11 Uzziah had an army of soldiers who were ready for war. Jeiel was the king's secretary and Maaseiah was the king's officer. These men counted the soldiers and they put them into groups. And the soldiers fought in those groups. Hananiah, an officer of the king, was over them. 12 The number of leaders of the soldiers' clans was 2600. 13 They ruled an army of 307 500 men who were ready to fight. They were a powerful army to help the king against his enemies. 14 Uzziah gave to all the soldiers enough shields and spears. He gave to them special strong hats and clothes to keep their bodies safe. And he gave bows to them. He even gave stones to them for their things that could shoot stones. 15 Clever men in Jerusalem had new ideas about machines to throw arrows or big stones. Uzziah put them on the tall buildings that he had built on the walls. And he put them at the corners of the walls. God helped him a lot until he became powerful. So the people in places that were a long way away knew a lot about Uzziah.

Uzziah forgets what God has done for him

16 So Uzziah was powerful. But then he began to think that he was more important than anyone. So he began to do wrong things. And he sinned against the LORD his God. He went into the LORD's temple to burn special oils with sweet smells on the altar for special oils. 17 Azariah and 80 other brave priests of the LORD went in after him. 18 They told King Uzziah that he was wrong. They said to him, 'It is not right for you, Uzziah to burn special oils with sweet smells in front of the LORD. God has chosen only Aaron's descendants, the priests, to burn special oils. Go out of this Holy Place because you have sinned. The LORD God will not give honour to you because of this.'

The LORD causes Uzziah to have an illness on his skin

19 Then Uzziah was angry. In his hand, he was holding the thing that priests burn oils with sweet smells in. He was standing by the altar for special oils in the LORD's house. And the priests were there as well. When he was angry with the priests, immediately an illness appeared on the skin at the front of his head. 20 And Azariah the most important priest and all the priests turned toward Uzziah. They looked at him and they saw the illness on the skin at the front of his head. So they quickly took him out of there. And he himself also rushed out of the temple because the LORD had punished him with this illness.

The end of King Uzziah's life

21 King Uzziah had the illness on his skin until the day that he died. Because of the illness he had to live in a house by himself. And he could not go into the LORD's house. Jotham his son was over the king's house and he ruled the people in his country. 22 Amoz's son, the prophet Isaiah, has written about Uzziah. He has recorded all the other things that Uzziah did as king. He has recorded them from the first thing to the last thing. 23 Uzziah died. And his servants buried him in a field that the kings had to bury people in. They did that because they said, 'He had the illness called leprosy.' Then his son Jotham ruled Judah instead.

Chapter 27

Jotham rules Judah

1 Jotham was 25 years old when he began to rule his country. He ruled for 16 years in Jerusalem. His mother's name was Jerushah, the daughter of Zadok. 2 He did the things that his father Uzziah had done. He did things that gave pleasure to the LORD. But he did not do one thing that his father had done. He did not try to go into the LORD's temple to burn oils with sweet smells. But the people still did very wrong things.

Jotham builds many things

3 Jotham built the highest gate of the LORD's house. It was called the Higher Gate. And he did a lot of work on the wall near the hill called Ophel. 4 He built towns in the hills of Judah. And he built strong buildings and tall buildings for soldiers in the forests.

Jotham fights with Ammon's descendants

5 Jotham attacked the king of Ammon's descendants and he beat them. That year, Ammon's descendants gave to him about 3400 kilos (7500 pounds) of silver. They also gave to him 2200 kilolitres (575 000 gallons) of wheat and 2200 kilolitres of barley. Ammon's descendants also gave the same things to him the next year and the year after that. 6 Jotham became powerful because he was careful to obey the LORD his God.

The end of Jotham's life

7 Someone has written about all the wars and about all the other things that Jotham did. All those things are in the Book about the Kings of Israel and Judah. 8 He was 25 years old when he began to rule his country. And he ruled in Jerusalem for 16 years. 9 Then Jotham died and his servants buried him in the city of David. And his son Ahaz ruled the country instead.

Chapter 28

Ahaz rules Judah

1 Ahaz was 20 years old when he began to rule his country. He ruled in Jerusalem for 16 years. But he was not like his ancestor David. He did not do the things that gave pleasure to the LORD.

Ahaz worships idols

2 He did all the things that the kings of Israel did. And he made metal idols of the gods called Baal to worship. 3 He burnt oils with sweet smells in the Ben-Hinnom Valley for them. And he sacrificed his sons in the fire. The people that had lived in the country before the Israelites had done many very bad things. So the LORD had pushed out those people in front of Israel's people. But Ahaz copied those things. 4 He offered sacrifices by fire on high places, on the tops of hills and under every green tree. And he burnt oils with sweet smells in those places.

God punishes Ahaz

5 So, the LORD his God sent the king of Syria against him. He caused the king of Syria to win the fight.

Then the king of Syria took many people from Judah to Damascus and he kept them there. The LORD also let the king of Israel win a fight with Ahaz. And he killed many people. 6 Remaliah's son Pekah from Israel killed 120 000 of Judah's best soldiers in one day. God let that happen because the people in Judah had stopped worshipping the LORD, the God of their ancestors. 7 Zichri, a good fighter from Ephraim, killed Maaseiah the king's son. He also killed Azrikam, the officer over the king's house and Elkanah who was the king's most important officer. 8 The Israelites took away 200 000 wives, sons and daughters from Judah. It did not matter to them that these people were also descendants of Jacob. They also took away to Samaria many good and valuable things.

Oded tells Israel's people that God is angry with them

9 But a prophet of the LORD called Oded lived there. He met Israel's soldiers while they were returning to Samaria. He said to them, 'The LORD, the God of your ancestors was angry with Judah's people. So he let you win the fight against them. But you have angrily killed very many people among them. And the news about that has
reached heaven. 10 And now you want to use people from Judah and Jerusalem as your male and female slaves. But remember that you too have sinned against the LORD your God. 11 Now listen to me.
The LORD is very angry with you. So you should let the people that you have taken away from Judah return to their own country. They have the same ancestors that you have.'

Israel's people obey God's prophet

12 Then some leaders in Ephraim met the soldiers while the soldiers were returning from the war. Those leaders were Johanan's son Azariah, Meshillemoth's son Berechiah, Shallum's son Jehizkiah and Hadlai's son Amasa. 13 'You must not bring these people that you have caught here', they said. 'If you do, it will be a sin against the LORD. The LORD is already angry with Israel because we have sinned. And he may punish us for that. It seems that you want to make it worse.'

14 So the soldiers gave the people and the things that they had taken from Judah to the leaders. All the people were watching them while they did that. 15 Then those 4 leaders gave clothes and shoes to those who had none. They took those things from the things that the soldiers had taken away from Judah. And they gave food, drink and medicines to them. They put on donkeys those people who were too weak to walk. Then they took them to Jericho, the city with many Palms. There they were near where their own people lived. Then those leaders returned to Samaria.

Ahaz asks the king of Assyria for help

16 At that time, King Ahaz asked the king of Assyria for help. 17 The people from Edom had come again. They had attacked Judah and they had taken people away. 18 At the same time, the Philistines had attacked towns in the low hills and in the south of Judah. They won the towns called Beth-Shemesh, Aijalon and Gederoth. They also won Soco, Timnah and Gimzo with the villages near to them. Then they went and they lived in them. 19 The LORD had caused trouble for Judah because of all the wicked things that Ahaz, their king had done. Ahaz let the people in Judah do what was wrong. He sinned badly and he had
stopped worshipping the LORD. 20 Tilgath-Pilneser, the king of Assyria came to Ahaz. But he caused trouble and he did not help Ahaz. 21 Ahaz had taken many valuable things from the LORD's house and from the king's house and from the rulers. He gave them to the king of Assyria but that did not help Ahaz.

Ahaz continues to sin against God

22 In this time of trouble, this same King Ahaz did more and more bad things against the LORD. 23 He gave sacrifices to the gods of the people in Damascus because those people had beaten him. So, he thought, 'The gods of the kings of Syria are helping them. So perhaps they will help me if I give sacrifices to them.' But that caused very bad trouble for him and for all Israel.

24 Ahaz took away all the things that were in God's house. And he cut them into pieces. He shut the doors of the house of the LORD. And he built altars for himself at the corner of every street in Jerusalem. 25 He built high places in every town in Judah to burn oils with sweet smells to other gods. So he made the LORD, the God of his ancestors, very angry.

Ahaz dies

26 Everything about him is in the Book about the Kings of Judah and Israel. And all the things that he did from the first thing to the last thing are in that book. 27 Ahaz died and the people buried him in the city, in Jerusalem. But they did not bury him near the kings of Israel. Then his son Hezekiah ruled the country instead.

Chapter 29

Hezekiah does what gives pleasure to the LORD

1 Hezekiah was 25 years old when he began to rule. And he ruled in Jerusalem for 29 years. His mother's name was Abijah. She was the daughter of Zechariah. 2 He did as his ancestor David had done. He did the things that gave pleasure to the LORD.

Hezekiah tells the Levites that they must make the temple clean

3 He opened the doors of the LORD's house in the first year that he was king, in the first month. And he did repairs to them. 4 He brought the priests and the Levites together in the place at the east side of the temple. 5 He said to them, 'Listen to me you Levites. Make yourselves holy and make the house holy too. It is the house of the LORD, the God of your ancestors. Take out of that holy place anything that is not holy.'

Why God was angry with Judah

6 'Our ancestors have not done the right things. They did very wrong things that the LORD our God did not like. They stopped worshipping him. And they turned away from the LORD's temple. 7 They also shut the doors of the temple and they stopped burning oil in the lamps. They did not burn oils with sweet smells there. And they have not given sacrifices by fire in the holy place to the God of Israel. 8 So the LORD has become angry with Judah and Jerusalem. He made them places where nobody wants to be. You can see this with your own eyes. 9 So our fathers died while they were fighting our enemies. And our sons, our daughters and our wives are in foreign countries because of it. 10 Now I want to give a promise to the LORD the God of Israel. Then he will stop being very angry with us.'

The Levites must make the temple clean

11 'My sons, the LORD has chosen you to stand in front of him. He has chosen you to work for him and to be his servants. And he has chosen you to burn oils with sweet smells to him. So do not waste any time.'

12 Then these Levites began to work.
From Kohath's clan, there were Amasai's son Mahath and Azariah's son Joel.
From Merari's clan, there were Abdi's son Kish and Jehallelel's son Azariah.
From Gershon's clan, there were Zimmah's son Joah and Joah's son Eden.
13 From Elizaphan's clan, there were Shimri and Jeiel.
From Asaph's clan, there were Zechariah and Mattaniah.
14 From Heman's clan, there were Jehiel and Shimei.
And from Jeduthun's clan, there were Shemaiah and Uzziel.

15 They brought all the Levites together and all the Levites made themselves holy. Then they went in to clean the LORD's house and to make it holy. The LORD had told the king that he should do that. 16 The priests went into the inside part of the LORD's house to clean it. They found things in the LORD's temple that were not holy. They carried all those things into the yard of the LORD's house. Then the Levites took them away to the Kidron Valley. 17 They began to make
the temple holy on the first day of the first month. On the 8th day of the month they reached the door of the LORD's house. In 8 more days they had made all the house of the LORD holy. And on the 16th day of the first month they had finished the work.

18 Then they went to King Hezekiah and they said, 'We have made the whole house of the LORD clean and holy. That includes
the altar for sacrifices by fire with all its tools. And it includes the table for the holy bread and all its tools. 19 King Ahaz removed many things from the LORD's house when he stopped worshipping his God. We have prepared all those things and we have made them holy again. They are now in front of the LORD's altar.'

The king and the people give sacrifices to God to make the temple ready for worship

20 King Hezekiah got up early the next morning and he brought the leaders of the city together. Then he and all the leaders went to the LORD's house. 21 They brought with them 7 male cows, 7 male sheep, 7 young sheep and 7 young male goats. These animals were for a sin-offering for the kingdom, for the holy place and for Judah. The king told the priests, Aaron's descendants, that they must sacrifice these on the Lord's altar. 22 So they killed the male cows and the priests took the blood. They threw the blood on the altar. Then they killed the male sheep and the priests threw their blood on the altar. Then they killed the young male sheep and the priests threw their blood on the altar. 23 Then the king and the people who were there put their hands on the male goats. They were a sacrifice for sin. 24 Then the priests killed them. They put their blood on the altar as a sacrifice for sin for all Israel. That was because the king had said, 'You must give the sacrifice by fire and the sacrifice for sin to God for all Israel.'

25 The king caused the Levites to stand in the LORD's house with their cymbals, harps and lyres to make music. They stood as David and David's prophet Gad and the prophet Nathan had told them. The LORD had used his prophets to tell people how they should do it. 26 The Levites were standing ready with David's things to make music and the priests were ready with their trumpets.

27 Then Hezekiah told the priests that they should give the sacrifice by fire on the altar. When they began to give the sacrifice by fire, the singers began to sing to the LORD. The sound of the trumpets also began. And the people with the things of David, the king of Israel, began to make music with them. 28 All the people were worshipping the LORD. At the same time the singers were singing and the priests were making a sound with their trumpets. Everybody did that until the end of the sacrifices by fire.

All the people praise the LORD and they bring offerings to him

29 At the end of the sacrifices by fire, the king and everyone with him bent their bodies to worship. 30 King Hezekiah and his officers told the Levites that they must sing praises to the LORD. 'Use the words of King David and of the prophet Asaph', they said. So the Levites praised God and they bent their bodies to worship God. And they were very happy.

31 Then Hezekiah said, 'Now you have given yourselves to the LORD. Come near and bring sacrifices and offerings to thank the LORD into his house.' So all the people brought their sacrifices and their offerings to thank the LORD. And everyone who wanted to do it also brought sacrifices by fire.

32 For sacrifices by fire, the people brought 70 male cows, 100 male sheep and 200 young sheep. All these animals were for a sacrifice by fire to the LORD. 33 They also put to one side 600 male cows and 3000 sheep and goats for sacrifices. 34 But there were not enough priests to take the skin off all the animals for the sacrifices by fire. So the Levites helped them until they had finished the work. By that time more priests had made themselves holy to work for the LORD. (The Levites had been more careful to make themselves holy than the priests had been.) 35 There were many sacrifices by fire. Also, there was the fat of the friendship-offerings. They also poured the proper offerings of wine with the sacrifices by fire.

That is how they again began to worship in the LORD's house. 36 Hezekiah and all the people were happy because God had helped them to do it so quickly.

Chapter 30

Hezekiah tells the people that they must come to the Passover

1 Hezekiah sent servants with letters to all the people in Israel and in Judah. He also wrote letters to the tribes of Ephraim and Manasseh. He was asking them to come to the house of the LORD in Jerusalem. He was asking them to worship the LORD, the God of Israel with the Passover. 2 The king, his officers and all the people in Jerusalem decided to have the Passover feast in the second month. 3 The proper time was the first month, but not enough priests had made themselves holy. And all the people had not come to Jerusalem. 4 This idea seemed right to the king and to all the people. 5 So they sent men to read a letter to all the people. They sent them through all Israel from Beersheba to Dan. The letter asked them to come to Jerusalem for the Passover feast of the LORD, the God of Israel. God's Law said that the people should come to Jerusalem for this feast. But not many people had done what God's Law said.

6 So the king and his officers sent men with letters to every place in Israel and Judah. The letters said, 'Israelites, start to obey the LORD, the God of Abraham, Isaac and Israel again. Then he will return to you. He has saved a few people from the king of Assyria's army. 7 Do not be like your ancestors and their children who stopped obeying the LORD, the God of their ancestors. He punished them for that in a very bad way, as you can see. 8 Do not refuse to obey him as your ancestors did. Do the things that he wants you to do. Come to the holy place that he has made holy for all time. Become the servants of the LORD your God so that he will stop being very angry with you. 9 If you start to obey the LORD again, your enemies will be kind to your relatives and to your children. They will let them return to this country because the LORD your God is kind. And he wants to be good to you. He will not turn away from you if you start to obey him again.'

10 The men took this letter to every town among the tribes of Ephraim and Manasseh and even to Zebulun. But everywhere the people thought that they were fools. And so they laughed. And they said that the men with the letters were silly. 11 But some people from Asher, Manasseh and Zebulun became humble and they did come to Jerusalem. 12 God was also working in the people in Judah. And so all those people agreed to obey the king and his officers. The LORD had told them in his Book what they should do. And they did it.

13 A very large crowd of people came together in Jerusalem in the second month. They came to have the Feast of Bread Without Yeast. 14 They started to work. And they took away the altars for false gods that were in Jerusalem. And they took away all the altars to burn oils with sweet smells. And they threw them into the Kidron Valley.

15 They killed the young sheep for the Passover on the 14th day of the 2nd month. The priests and the Levites were ashamed. So they made themselves holy to work for the LORD. Then they could bring sacrifices by fire into the LORD's house. 16 They stood in their proper places. God's servant Moses had described these in the Law. The priests threw on the altar the blood that the Levites gave to them. 17Many people in the crowd had not made themselves holy. So they could not kill the Passover sheep. So the Levites had to kill the young sheep for the Passover for them. Then the sheep were holy for the LORD.18 Many people from Ephraim, Manasseh, Issachar and Zebulun had not made themselves holy. So they were not right to eat the Passover. But Hezekiah prayed for them. He said, 'Good LORD, please forgive everyone 19 who really wants to worship the LORD God, the God of his ancestors. They may not be holy as the rules of the holy place say. Please forgive those people.' 20 And the LORD listened to Hezekiah and so he made the people well.

21 The Israelites who were in Jerusalem ate the Feast of Bread Without Yeast for 7 days. They were very happy to do it. The Levites and the priests sang praises to the LORD every day. And they praised the LORD with things that make music.

22 All the Levites really understood how they should work for the LORD. And Hezekiah told them that they were doing well.
They praised the LORD, the God of their ancestors. For 7 days they ate the proper food for the feast and they gave friendship-offerings to God. And they gave thanks to the LORD, the God of their ancestors.

23 Then all the people there agreed to eat the feast for another 7 days. And so they did that happily for 7 more days. 24 Hezekiah, the king of Judah gave to the people 1000 young male cows and 7000 sheep and goats. And the leaders gave to them 1000 young male cows and 10 000 sheep and goats. And many priests had made themselves holy. 25 All Judah's people were happy. And the priests and the Levites and people from everywhere in Israel were happy too. They included the foreign people who had come from Israel. And they included people who lived in Judah. 26 Everyone in Jerusalem was very happy. There had not been anything like this in Jerusalem since the time when David's son Solomon was king of Israel. 27The priests and the Levites stood up and they asked God to be good to the people. And God heard them. Their prayer had reached heaven, the place where he lives.

Chapter 31

After the Passover

1 All the feast finished. Then the Israelites who were there went out to all the towns in Judah. They broke up the tall idols of stones. And they cut down the poles with Asherah on them. They destroyed the places for worship and their altars in all Judah, Benjamin, Ephraim and Manasseh. That continued until they had destroyed all those things. When they had done that, all the Israelites returned to their homes in their own towns.

Hezekiah gives rules to the priests and to the Levites

2 Hezekiah put the priests and the Levites into separate groups. Each group had special work to do. Some priests and Levites had to give sacrifices by fire. Some had to give friendship-offerings to God. Some worked in other ways. Some thanked God and they praised him at the gates of the LORD's temple.

Hezekiah and all the people give gifts to worship God

3 The king gave his own animals for sacrifices by fire. And he gave them for the sacrifices by fire each morning and each evening. He gave them for the sacrifices by fire on Sabbaths and days of the new moon. And he gave them for the sacrifices by fire for the other feasts too. He was obeying the Law of the LORD. 4 He spoke to all the people who lived in Jerusalem. He told them that they must give the proper gifts to the priests and to the Levites. That was so that they would be able to study the Law of the LORD really well. 5 When the people got Hezekiah's message they brought many good things. They brought the first grain that had grown, new wine, oil and honey. And they gave 1 part from every 10 parts of all the things that had grown in their fields. 6 The people from Israel and Judah who lived in Judah's towns also brought gifts. They brought 1 animal from every 10 of all their cows, sheep and goats. And they brought 1 thing from every 10 things that they had made holy to the LORD their God. They put all these things together in one place. 7 They started to put the things together in the 3rd month and they finished in the 7th month. 8 Hezekiah and the leaders saw all the things. And they said good things about the LORD and they blessed his people, Israel.

9 Hezekiah asked the priests and the Levites about all those things. 10 Azariah, the most important priest was from Zadok's clan. He answered, 'The people began to bring their gifts to the LORD's house. Since that time we have had enough food to eat and even more food than that. The LORD has blessed his people and we have all this extra food.'

11 Hezekiah told them that they must make rooms to store the things in the house of the LORD. So they did it. 12 They brought in all the gifts and the holy things. That included 1 thing from every 10 things that the people had. A Levite called Conaniah had to keep all those things safe. His brother, Shimei helped him. 13 Conaniah and his brother, Shimei were over Jehiel, Azaziah, Nahath, Asahel, Jerimoth, Jozabad, Eliel, Ismachiah, Mahath and Benaiah. And those men told other Levites what they must do. King Hezekiah and Azariah, who was the ruler of God's house, gave this special job to Conaniah and Shimei.

How Kore and his helpers gave out the gifts to the Levites and to the priests

14 Imnah the Levite had a son called Kore. And Kore kept the East Gate safe. Kore's other job was to give out what people had given to God. And he had to give out the holy gifts to the priests. 15 He was over Eden, Miniamin, Jeshua, Shemaiah, Amariah and Shecaniah, who lived in the priests' cities. They helped him to give out the gifts to the priests in a fair way. They were fair to the old ones and to the young ones. 16 They gave gifts to all the males with names that were in the lists of Levites. But they must be three years old or older. When they were older, these young men would come into the LORD's house on the right days. They would do the special work for each day that was on those lists. 17 The lists of the priests showed them in their clans. But the list of the Levites only showed those who were 20 years old or older. And it showed the work that each group of Levites had to do. 18 Also, the very young children, wives, sons and daughters received some things from the gifts. That was because they always kept themselves holy for their special work.

19 Some of the priests, Aaron's descendants, lived on the land round the Levites' towns or in other towns. The officers chose men who were fair and honest to take their gifts to them. They gave the proper gifts to every male among the priests. And they gave them to everybody among the Levites who was on the list of Levites.

20 That is what Hezekiah did in all Judah. He did what was good and right. And he obeyed the LORD his God. 21 He tried to obey God in everything that he did for the LORD's house. He tried to obey God's Law and God's rules. In everything that he did for his God he tried to give pleasure to God. So very good things happened to him.

Chapter 32
Sennacherib attacks Judah

1 After Hezekiah had done all these good things, Sennacherib, the king of Assyria came into Judah. His soldiers lived in tents round all the strong cities that had walls. He hoped to win them for himself.

Hezekiah makes Jerusalem strong

2 Hezekiah saw that Sennacherib had come. And he saw that he wanted to fight against Jerusalem's people. 3 So he talked with his officers and with his best soldiers. They decided to stop all the water that came from streams round the city. And the officers and the soldiers helped him to do it. 4 Many people came. And they stopped the big stream that went through the land there. They said, 'We do not want the kings of Assyria to find plenty of water here.' 5 Then Hezekiah's men worked to do repairs to the city's walls where they needed it. All the men worked as well as they could. Hezekiah built tall buildings on the walls. And he built another wall outside the first wall. He made the wall called the Millo round the City of David stronger, too. And he made a lot of weapons and shields too.

Hezekiah prepares to fight

6 Hezekiah chose some men to be captains over the people in the fight. He asked all the captains to come together in front of him. They met in the big place by the city's gate. Then he spoke to make them braver. This is what he said: 7 'Be strong and brave. Do not be afraid of Assyria's king or of his large army. And do not think that they will certainly beat you. There are more soldiers with us than there are with him. 8 He has only human soldiers to help him. But we have the LORD our God to help us and to fight for us.' And the words that Judah's King Hezekiah spoke caused the people to feel brave.

Sennacherib tells Hezekiah that Hezekiah cannot win a fight with him

9 Sennacherib, the king of Assyria and all his army were waiting round Lachish to attack it. Then he sent a message to Judah's King Hezekiah and to all Judah's people with him in Jerusalem. This is what it said:

10 'Sennacherib, king of Assyria says this to you: "You are sitting in Jerusalem and there are soldiers everywhere round you. But I do not know what you are trusting. 11 Hezekiah is saying that the LORD your God will save you from the king of Assyria. But it is not true. You will die because you will have no food or water. And he knows that. 12 Remember that Hezekiah himself removed this god's high places for worship and his altars. He told you people in Judah and Jerusalem that you should worship in front of one altar only. And he said that you should burn oils with sweet smells on that altar only.

13 You know what my ancestors and I have done to all the people in other countries. Their gods were never able to save their country from me. 14 None of the gods of the nations that my ancestors completely destroyed was able to save his people from them. So I do not know how your god can save you from me. 15 So now do not let Hezekiah cause you to believe things that are not true. Do not let him change your thoughts. Do not believe him. No god of any nation or kingdom has been able to save his people from me or from my ancestors. So your god certainly will not save you from me!" '

Sennacherib says that the LORD God has no value

16 Sennacherib's servants also spoke more things against the LORD God and against his servant Hezekiah. 17 He also wrote letters that said bad things about the LORD, the God of Israel. He wrote, 'The gods of other nations could not save their people from me. So the god of Hezekiah will not save his people from me.' 18 Then Sennacherib's servants shouted loudly in the Jewish language to the people who were standing on Jerusalem's walls. They wanted to make them very afraid so that they would be able to win the city. 19 They spoke about Jerusalem's God. They spoke as they had spoken about all the gods of the people in other countries. But those gods were only idols that men had made with their hands.

Hezekiah and Isaiah pray to the LORD

20 King Hezekiah and Amoz's son, Isaiah the prophet, prayed about this. And they shouted towards heaven. 21 Then the LORD God sent an angel. And the angel killed all the strong, brave soldiers in the camp of the king of Assyria. The angel killed the leaders and he killed the officers too. So the king of Assyria was ashamed and he returned to his own country. He went into his own god's house. There some of his own sons attacked him with swords and they killed him.

22 So the LORD saved Hezekiah and Jerusalem's people from Sennacherib, the king of Assyria and from all their other enemies. He kept them safe from the nations everywhere round their country. 23 Many people brought gifts to Jerusalem for the LORD and valuable gifts for Hezekiah, king of Judah. At that time and always after that, the people in all nations thought that Hezekiah was great.

24 Hezekiah became very ill at that time. He nearly died. He prayed to the LORD and the LORD spoke to him. And the LORD showed him that he would get better. 25 But Hezekiah did not thank the LORD for what he had done for him. The king thought that he was too great to do that. So the LORD became angry with him and with the people in Judah and in Jerusalem. 26 But then Hezekiah and the people who lived in Jerusalem made themselves humble. So the LORD did not punish the people while Hezekiah was still alive.

27 Hezekiah was very rich and people gave great honour to him. He had a lot of silver and gold and valuable stones of many colours. He had spices and shields and all kinds of other valuable things. 28 He built places to store grain and new wine and oil. He made buildings for his cows, sheep and goats and all kinds of other animals. 29 He built cities for himself. And he had many sheep and cows because God had given very many things to him.

30 Hezekiah had stopped the water coming from the higher stream that came out of the ground at Gihon. He caused the water to run down inside the west of David's City. And when he tried to do anything, good things happened. 31 But the rulers of Babylon sent some officials to Hezekiah. They came to ask him about the strange thing that had happened in his country. The LORD let Hezekiah decide what to tell them. He wanted to see what Hezekiah would do.

People write about King Hezekiah's life

32 The prophet Isaiah, the son of Amoz, wrote about a vision. And he wrote down all the other things that Hezekiah did. That included the things that gave pleasure to God. Some things are in the book called 'The Vision of Amoz's son, the prophet Isaiah'. Other things are in the 'Book about the Kings of Judah and Israel'. 33 Hezekiah died and people buried him with David's descendants near the top of the hill. All the people in Judah and in Jerusalem gave great honour to him when he died. Then his son Manasseh ruled instead.

Chapter 33

Manasseh becomes king and he does wrong things

1 Manasseh was 12 years old when he started to rule. And he ruled in Jerusalem for 55 years. 2 He did very wrong things that the LORD did not like. The people who lived in the country before the Israelites had done all those things. The LORD had helped the Israelites to push those people out of their country. 3 Manasseh built again the high places for worship that his father Hezekiah had destroyed. He built altars to worship the Baals and the Asherahs. He bent his body to worship all the stars in the sky. 4 The LORD had said about the LORD's house, 'My name will be in Jerusalem for all time.' But Manasseh built altars in the LORD's house. 5 He built altars in the two yards of the house of the LORD to worship all the stars. 6 He sacrificed his sons by fire in the Ben-Hinnom Valley. He did magic and he tried to know about future events in wrong ways. He used people who spoke to spirits. He used people who did magic. He did a lot of very wrong things that the LORD did not like. So the LORD became angry with him.

7 He made an idol out of wood and he put it in God's house. But God had said to David and to his son Solomon, 'I will put my name in this house for all time. I have chosen Jerusalem from the cities of all Israel's tribes. I chose it as the place to put my name for all time. 8 I do not want to take Israel's people away again from this country that I gave to your ancestors. But they must be careful to obey all the rules that are in my Law. And they must be careful to obey all the laws and the rules that I gave to them by Moses.' 9 But Manasseh caused Judah's people and the people in Jerusalem to sin. So they did more evil things than any of the nations that the LORD had destroyed. The LORD had destroyed those nations when he brought the Israelites into their country.

The LORD punishes Manasseh

10 The LORD spoke to Manasseh and to his people. But they would not listen to the LORD. 11 So the LORD brought the officers of the king of Assyria's army to attack them.

They took Manasseh. And they put a piece of metal in his nose and metal chains to tie his feet together. Then they took him to Babylon. 12 When Manasseh had a lot of trouble, he asked the LORD his God to help him. He told the God of his ancestors that he was not a great man.

The LORD lets Manasseh return to Jerusalem as king

13 When he prayed to the LORD, the LORD listened to him. And he listened to what Manasseh was asking for. So he brought Manasseh to Jerusalem again. And he caused him to become king again. Then Manasseh knew that the LORD is God.

14 After that, he built a new wall outside the wall of David's City. He built it to the west of Gihon, in the valley and at the way in to the Fish Gate. The wall went round the hill called Ophel. And he made the wall very high. And Manasseh put officers and soldiers in all the strong cities in Judah.

Judah's people worship the LORD again

15 He took away the gods of other nations and the idol from the LORD's house. He took out all the altars that he had built on the hill of the LORD's house and in Jerusalem. He threw them out of the city. 16 Then he did repairs to the LORD's altar. He sacrificed friendship-offerings and thank-offerings on it. He told Judah that they must be servants of the LORD, the God of Israel. 17 But the people still sacrificed on the high places. But they only burnt sacrifices there to the LORD their God.

The last days of Manasseh's life

18 The other things that Manasseh did are in 'The Book about the Kings of Israel'. The prayer that Manasseh said to his God is in it too. And there were prophets who spoke to him in the name of the LORD, the God of Israel. Their words are in it too. 19 The words that he prayed are in another book. That book is called 'What the Prophets Recorded'. What he asked God for is in it too. The prophets also recorded in it all his sins and how he had not been faithful to God. He had built the high places to worship false gods. He had put up Asherahs and other idols in those places before he made himself humble. The prophets recorded all those places in that book. 20 Manasseh died and his servants buried him in his own house. Then his son Amon ruled instead.

Amon king of Judah

21 Amon was 22 years old when he began to rule. And he ruled in Jerusalem for 2 years. 22 He did all the very wrong things that his father Manasseh had done. The LORD did not like those things. And Amon gave sacrifices to all the idols that his father Manasseh had made. And he worshipped them. 23 But he did not make himself humble in front of the LORD as his father Manasseh made himself humble. Instead, Amon did even more very bad things than his father had done.

Amon dies

24 Amon's servants decided to kill him and they killed him in his own house. 25 Then all the people in that country killed the men who had decided to kill King Amon. And they chose his son Josiah to be king instead.

Chapter 34

Josiah obeys the LORD

1 Josiah was 8 years old when he started to rule. And he ruled in Jerusalem for 31 years. 2 He did the things that gave pleasure to the LORD. He always did things as his ancestor David had done. He did that all the time.

3 When Josiah had been king for nearly 8 years he was still a boy. He began to worship the God of his ancestor David. When he had been king for nearly 12 years he started to destroy the high places for worship.

He did that in Jerusalem and in all Judah.

And he started to take away the Asherahs and idols of wood and metal. 4 He caused the people to pull down the altars to the Baals. He watched them while they did it. Then he cut down the altars to burn oils with sweet smells that were above the altars for Baal. He took away the Asherahs. He broke them and the wood and metal idols into pieces. Then he hit the pieces until they were very small. Then he threw those pieces over the places where they had buried people. The people were those who had sacrificed to those gods. 5 Josiah burned the bones of their priests on the idols' altars. That is how he made Judah and Jerusalem holy again. 6 He went to the towns of Manasseh, Ephraim and Simeon and even into Naphtali. And he did the same in all the old places round them that nobody had used for some time. 7 He pulled down the altars and the Asherahs. He hit their idols until they were very small pieces. He cut down all the altars to burn oils with sweet smells in all Israel. Then he returned to Jerusalem.

Josiah does repairs to the temple

8 When Josiah had been king for nearly 18 years, the country and the temple were clean and holy again. Then he sent men to do repairs to the house of the LORD his God. He chose men to tell them how to do the work. Those men were Azaliah's son Shaphan, Maaseiah the ruler of the city, and Joah, son of Joahaz, who recorded everything.

9 The people had given money to the Levites who kept the doors of the temple safe. The tribes of Manasseh, Ephraim and those who stayed in Israel gave money to those Levites. Also, the people from all Judah and Benjamin and those who lived in Jerusalem gave money to them. They brought this money into the house of God. The three men came to Hilkiah, the most important priest and they gave the money to him. 10 Then they gave this money to the men who were leaders over the work on the LORD's house. Those men gave it to the workers. And they worked to do repairs to the LORD's house and to make it strong. 11 They also gave money to those who worked with wood and with stones. They gave money to the builders to buy stones that were ready to use and wood. The wood was to hold the walls up and for beams. They needed those things because the kings of Judah before Josiah had destroyed the buildings of the temple.

Good men did the work

12 Josiah was able to trust the men and they did good work. The Levites Jahath and Obadiah, Merari's descendants, were over them. Kohath's descendants, Zechariah and Meshullam were also over the men. Those Levites also knew how to make beautiful music. 13 They were also over the men who carried heavy things and over all the other workers. Some Levites worked as writers or officials or they kept the doors safe.

Hilkiah finds the Book of the LORD's Law

14 The Levites brought out the money that people had brought into the house of the LORD. While they were doing that, Hilkiah the priest found the Book of the Law of the LORD. The LORD had used Moses to give this Law to his people. 15 Hilkiah spoke to Shaphan the writer. He said, 'I have found the Book of the Law in the LORD's house.' And Hilkiah gave the book to Shaphan.

16 Then Shaphan brought the book to the king and he told the king about it. He said, 'Your servants are doing everything that you asked them to do. 17 They have taken the money that was in the LORD's house. They have given it to the workers and to the men who are over them.'

Shaphan reads the Book to the king

18 Then Shaphan the writer told the king about it. 'Hilkiah the priest has given a book to me', he said. And Shaphan read from it to the king. 19 When the king had listened to the words of the Law, he tore his clothes.

The king sends Hilkiah and other men to ask the LORD about the Book

20 Then Josiah spoke to Hilkiah, Shaphan's son Ahikam, Micah's son Abdon, Shaphan the writer and Asaiah the king's servant. He told them what they must do. This is what he said to them:

21 'Go to ask the LORD for me and for the people who are still in Israel or in Judah', he said. 'Ask about the words in the book that Hilkiah has found. The LORD will be very angry with us because our ancestors have not obeyed the words of the LORD. They have not done everything that is in this book.'

Hilkiah and the other men visit a lady prophet

22 Hilkiah and those other men that the king had sent went to Huldah. Huldah was a lady and she was a prophet. She was the wife of Tokhath's son Shallum. Tokhath was the son of Hasrah, who kept the king's clothes. Huldah was living in the new part of Jerusalem. And they spoke to her about this.

The LORD will do bad things to the people in Judah

23 She told them what the LORD the God of Israel said to her. This was the message: 'Say this to the man who sent you to me: 24 "The LORD says, 'I will cause very bad things to happen to this place and to all the people who live here. They will be all the bad things that are in the Book. They read that book to the king of Judah. 25 I will do that because they have gone away from me. They have made other gods with their hands and they have burned oils with sweet smells to them. They made me angry by all the things that they made with their hands. So I will punish this place and nobody will be able to make it impossible.' " 26Speak to the king of Judah who sent you to ask the LORD about this. Say, "The LORD the God of Israel says this about the words that you heard: 27 'You were sorry when you heard your God's words about this place and about its people. You made yourself humble in front of your God. You made yourself humble in front of me. You tore your clothes and you wept in front of me. So I have heard you', says the LORD. 28 'So I will let you die in peace and people will bury you with your ancestors. You will not see all the bad things that I will cause for this place and for the people here.' " ' So they took Huldah's answer to the king.

Josiah and the people promise to obey the Law

29 Then the king asked all the leaders in Judah and in Jerusalem to come to him. And they came. 30 Then the king went to the LORD's house. And all the men from Judah, the people from Jerusalem and the priests and the Levites went with him. All the people went, from the most important person to the least important person. He read to all the people the words of the Book that Hilkiah had found in the LORD's house. That book contained the covenant that the LORD made with the Israelites. 31 The king stood there in his special place. And he promised the LORD that he would obey the LORD in every way. He promised that he would obey the LORD's words, rules and laws. He promised to obey them with his whole mind. And he promised that he would really want to obey them. He promised to obey all the words of the covenant that was in the book.

32 Then he caused all the people from Benjamin and all the other people in Jerusalem to promise that too. And so the people who lived in Jerusalem agreed to obey the covenant of God, the God of their ancestors.

All Israel's people worship the LORD

33 Josiah took away all the idols from all the land of the Israelites. He caused all the people in Israel to be servants of the LORD their God. All the time that he was alive, they worshipped the LORD, the God of their ancestors. And they did not stop.

Chapter 35

Josiah has the Passover

1 And Josiah had a Passover feast in Jerusalem for the LORD. They killed the sacrifice for Passover on the 14th day of the first month of the year. 2 He caused the priests to do their special jobs. Then he made them happy to be servants in the LORD's house. 3 He spoke to the Levites who were teaching all the Israelites. These Levites had made themselves holy to work for the LORD. He said, 'Put the holy Covenant Box in the house that Solomon the son of David the king of Israel built. Do not carry it about on your shoulders. Now you must be the servants of the LORD your God and of his people the Israelites. 4Make yourselves ready to do the work that King David and King Solomon chose for each group in each clan. David the king of Israel and his son Solomon wrote about the way that you must do it.'

What the priests and Levites must do

5 'Stand in the holy place. There should be a group of Levites for each clan of the people or of the Levites. 6Kill the young sheep for the Passover. Make yourselves holy. And prepare the young sheep for those who are not Levites. Do it as the LORD said to us by Moses.'

Many people give offerings

7 Josiah gave to the Israelites 30 000 young sheep and young goats to kill for the Passover sacrifices. That was enough animals for all the people who were there. And he gave to them 3000 male cows. All those animals were from the king's own animals.

8 Also, his leaders gave animals freely to the people, to the priests and to the Levites. Hilkiah, Zechariah, and Jehiel were rulers in God's house. They gave to the priests 2600 young sheep and young goats and 300 male cows for Passover sacrifices. 9 Conaniah, Shemaiah, Nethanel, Hashabiah, Jeiel and Jozabad gave animals to the Levites as sacrifices for the Passover. The animals that they gave were 5000 young sheep and young goats and 500 male cows. Shemaiah and Nethanel were Conaniah's brothers. Hashabiah, Jeiel and Jozabad were leaders of the Levites.

The worship begins

10 Everything was ready for the Passover to begin. The priests and the Levites stood in their places, as the king had said. 11 The Levites killed the young sheep for the Passover and they gave the blood to the priests. The priests threw the blood on the altar. At the same time, the Levites were taking the skins from the animals. 12 They put the animals for sacrifices by fire to one side for the people. Then they gave some animals to those who belonged to each clan among the Israelites. They would sacrifice them to the LORD as Moses had written in his book. And they did the same thing with the male cows. 13 They cooked the animals for Passover over fire as is in the rules. And they boiled the holy sacrifices in three kinds of large and small pots. Then they quickly carried the meat to all the people. 14 After that, the Levites prepared the animals for themselves and for the priests. The priests, the descendants of Aaron, were giving the sacrifices by fire and the fat to God. They were doing that until it became dark. So, the Levites prepared the animals for themselves and for the priests, Aaron's descendants.

15 The singers stood where they should stand. They were descendants of Asaph. They were in their places as David, Asaph, Heman and the king's prophet, Jeduthun had said. The men who kept each gate safe did not need to leave their gates. The other Levites prepared everything for them.

The feasts happen in a proper way

16 So, they prepared everything that day to worship the LORD. They had the Passover feast and they gave the sacrifices by fire on the LORD's altar. They did everything that King Josiah had said. 17 Some people from the country called Israel were also there. They had the Passover at that time. And they had the Feast of bread without yeast. That feast continued for 7 days. 18 There had not been a Passover like that in Israel since time when the prophet Samuel was still alive. No king of Israel had a Passover like the Passover that King Josiah had. With him were the priests, the Levites and the people who lived in Jerusalem. All the people from Judah and Israel who were there had the Passover too. 19 They had this Passover in the 18th year that Josiah ruled Judah.

Josiah dies while he is fighting the king of Egypt

20 After Josiah had done all that for the temple, Neco, the king of Egypt came into the country. He came to the city called Carchemish. Carchemish is by the river Euphrates. He came to fight against the people who lived there. And Josiah went to fight against him. 21 But Neco sent men to Josiah. They said to him, 'King of Judah, you and I should not fight. I did not come to fight you. I came to fight my enemies. God told me that I must hurry. God is with me, so do not fight against me. If you do not fight against me, God will not kill you.'

22 But Josiah would not stop his attack. He did not want Neco's soldiers to know that he was Josiah. So he wore different clothes to fight against Neco. God had used Neco to speak to Josiah. But Josiah would not listen to his words. He went to fight Neco on the flat land at Megiddo.

23 Neco's men shot King Josiah with arrows. The king said to his servants, 'Take me away. The arrows have hurt me very badly.' 24 So, they took him out of that chariot and they put him in his other chariot. Then they brought him to Jerusalem and he died there. They buried him near his ancestors. All the people in Judah and in Jerusalem were very sad because Josiah was dead.

25 Jeremiah wrote sad songs about Josiah's death. Even today, all the male and female singers remember Josiah with these songs. These songs became like a law in Israel. They are in a book with other sad songs.

26-27 Everything else that Josiah did is in the Book about the Kings of Israel and Judah. Everything is there from the first thing to the last thing. That includes all the good things that he did. He tried to obey everything that is in the Law of the LORD.

Chapter 36

Judah's people choose Jehoahaz to become king

1 Then the people in Judah chose Josiah's son, Jehoahaz to become king in Jerusalem instead.

Pharaoh Neco chooses Eliakim to be king

2 Jehoahaz was 23 years old when he started to rule. And he ruled in Jerusalem for three months. 3 Then the king of Egypt said that Jehoahaz must not be king in Jerusalem. And he caused Judah's people to pay a lot of money to him. It was about 3400 kilos (7500 pounds) of silver and about 34 kilos (75 pounds) of gold. 4 The king of Egypt chose Jehoahaz's brother Eliakim to be king over Judah and Jerusalem. And he changed Eliakim's name to Jehoiakim. But Neco took his brother Jehoahaz to Egypt.

5 Jehoiakim was 25 years old when he started to rule. And he ruled in Jerusalem for 11 years. He did very wrong things that the LORD his God did not like. 6 Nebuchadnezzar, the king of Babylon came and he attacked him. He tied his hands and his feet together with metal chains to take him away to Babylon. 7Also, Nebuchadnezzar took some things from the LORD's house. He took them to Babylon and he put them in his temple in Babylon.

8 The other things that Jehoiakim did are in the Book about the Kings of Israel and Judah. That includes all the very wrong things that he did. It includes all the things that God did not like about him. And his son Jehoiachin ruled instead.

Jehoiachin becomes king of Judah

9 Jehoiachin was 8 years old when he started to rule. And he ruled in Jerusalem for three months and 10 days. He did very wrong things that the LORD did not like. 10 In the spring, King Nebuchadnezzar sent his soldiers to fetch Jehoiachin and they brought him to Babylon. Also, he brought the valuable things from the LORD's house to Babylon. And Nebuchadnezzar chose Jehoiachin's father's brother, Zedekiah to be king over Judah and Jerusalem.

Zedekiah king of Judah

11 Zedekiah was 21 years old when he started to rule. And he ruled in Jerusalem for 11 years. 12 He did very wrong things that the LORD his God did not like. Jeremiah the prophet spoke the LORD's words to him. But he did not make himself humble when he listened to them. 13 King Nebuchadnezzar had caused Zedekiah to promise in God's name that he would obey Nebuchadnezzar. But he decided not to obey Nebuchadnezzar. And he became proud and he would not change his mind. And so he would not turn to the LORD, the God of Israel. 14 Also, all the leaders of the priests and the people were not obeying the LORD. They were always worshipping all the very bad idols that the people in other nations worshipped. The LORD had made the temple in Jerusalem holy. But they made it like something dirty by the things that they did.

Judah's people make the LORD very angry

15 The LORD, the God of their ancestors, sent men to them with messages from him. He was very careful to tell them that they must not do those things. He knew that he would have to punish them. But he did not want to punish them because he was sorry for his people and for his house. 16 But they said that the men with God's messages were silly. And they thought that God's words were not important. They said that his prophets were saying silly things. Then the LORD became very angry with his people until nothing could help them.

Enemies win the fight for Jerusalem

17 So, the LORD brought the king of Babylon to attack them. The king killed their young men with swords in their holy temple. He did not feel sorry for the young men or for the young women. He did not feel sorry for the old men or for the very old people. God let him take all those people away. 18 And he took all the things that were still in God's house. He took all the big things and he took all the small things too. He took the valuable things from the house of the LORD. And he took the valuable things of the king and of his officers. He took all those things to Babylon. 19 Nebuchadnezzar's men burned the house of God and they broke down the wall round Jerusalem. They burned all the king's houses in Jerusalem and they destroyed all the valuable things in Jerusalem.

20 Nebuchadnezzar took all the people that he had not killed to Babylon. They became slaves for him and for his sons. They were slaves until the king of Persia began to rule everywhere. 21 So, what the LORD had told Israel's people by the mouth of his prophet Jeremiah happened. The country was empty until it had had its Sabbath rest. It was empty and it had rest for 70 whole years.

22 But Cyrus, king of Persia, began to rule Babylon. And during his first year as king, the LORD did what he had promised by the mouth of Jeremiah. The LORD caused Cyrus, king of Persia to decide something. He wrote it down. And he sent servants to read it in every place that he ruled over. And this is what it said:

23 'Cyrus, king of Persia says, "The LORD is the God of heaven. And he has caused me to rule over all the kingdoms on the earth. He has told me that I must build a temple for him at Jerusalem in Judah. I will let anyone among you who belongs to his people go to Jerusalem. I pray that the LORD their God will be with those people." '

God's People Build God's Temple Again

Ezra

> **About this book**
>
> Ezra and Nehemiah are books in the older part of the Bible. They are the last two books in the story of the Jews. Their people had lived as prisoners in Babylon city during 70 years. The books tell us how the people of Israel (Jews or Israelites) returned to Jerusalem from Babylon. Nebuchadnezzar had taken them to Babylon as prisoners. But Persia won a fight with Babylon. Then the king of Persia decided to send Nebuchadnezzar's prisoners back to their own countries. Cyrus, the king, asked the Jews to build God's temple in Jerusalem.
>
> Ezra was a priest who knew God's book. And he knew the rules that it contained. He taught the people how to give pleasure to God. Then God would give a good life to them in their own country.

Chapter 1

Cyrus helps the Jews to return to Jerusalem from Babylon

1 Cyrus, king of Persia had just begun to rule Babylon. He decided to make a new law. Men wrote it down. And he sent out men with the news. He sent them to all the people that he ruled. God had caused him to do this. God had said to Jeremiah years before that he would send the Israelites home (Jeremiah 29:10).

2 This is what Cyrus, the king of Persia said:

'The Lord, the God of heaven, has given me power over all the kingdoms on the earth. He has said that I must build a temple for him at Jerusalem. That is the biggest city in Judah. 3 Any of Israel's people who live in my land can return to Jerusalem. They must build a temple there for the Lord, the God of Israel. He is the God of Jerusalem. I hope that he will be with those people. 4 Many Israelites are living here now. The people who live near to them must give silver and gold to them. And they must give animals and other things to the Israelites for offerings to their God. They will take these gifts to him in Jerusalem's temple.'

5 Then the leaders of Judah and Benjamin's families and the priests and the Levites prepared to go to Jerusalem. God had said that they must build the Lord's house there. And he had caused them to want to do this. 6 All the people who lived near them gave them animals, gold, silver and other things for offerings. They also gave them many valuable gifts. 7 Then King Cyrus remembered the things that Nebuchadnezzar had taken away from the temple in Jerusalem (Daniel 1:1-2). Nebuchadnezzar had put them in his god's house. 8 Mithredath kept Cyrus's valuable things safe. So Cyrus asked him to fetch the things that belonged to Jerusalem's temple. Then Mithredath gave them to Sheshbazzar, an important leader from Judah.

9 They counted the things and they made a list.

    30 gold plates

    1000 silver plates

    29 silver pots

10   30 gold deep dishes

    410 silver deep dishes, all the same as each other

    1000 other things.

11 All the things made from gold and silver were 5400 things. Sheshbazzar took them all with him when he came back with the Israelites to Jerusalem.

Chapter 2

The list of the people who returned

1 These are the people who returned to Jerusalem and Judah. Nebuchadnezzar, king of Babylon had brought them to live as slaves in Babylon. Each person returned to his own town. 2 They went together with Zerubbabel, Jeshua, Nehemiah, Seraiah, Reelaiah, Mordecai, Bilshan, Mispar, Bigvai, Rehum and Baanah. This is the list of the men among Israel's people:

3   2172 descendants of Parosh.

4   372 of Shephatiah.

5   775 of Arah.

6   2812 of Pahath Moab (descendant of Jeshua and Joab).

7   1254 of Elam.

8   945 of Zattu.

9   760 of Zaccai.

10   642 of Bani.

11 623 of Bebai.

12 1222 of Azgad.

13 666 of Adonikam.

14 2056 of Bigvai.

15 454 of Adin.

16 98 of Ater (descendant of Hezekiah).

17 323 of Bezai.

18 112 of Jorah.

19 223 of Hashum.

20 95 of Gibbar.

21 123 men from Bethlehem.

22 56 of Netophah.

23 128 of Anathoth.

24 42 of Azmaveth.

25 743 of Kiriath Jearim, Kephirah and Beeroth.

26 621 of Ramah and Geba.

27 122 of Michmash.

28 223 of Bethel and Ai.

29 52 of Nebo.

30 156 of Magbish.

31 1254 of the other Elam.

32 320 of Harim.

33 725 of Lod, Hadid and Ono.

34 345 of Jericho.

35 3630 of Senaah.

36 The priests,

973 descendants of Jedaiah (by Jeshua's family).

37 1052 of Immer.

38 1247 of Pashhur.

39 1017 of Harim.

40 The Levites,

74 descendants of Jeshua and Kadmiel (by Hodaviah's family).

41 The singers,

128 descendants of Asaph.

42 The men who watch the temple gates,

139 descendants of Shallum, Ater, Talmon, Akkub, Hatita and Shobai.

43 The temple servants,

the descendants of Ziha, Hasupha, Tabbaoth,

44 Keros, Siaha, Padon,

45 Lebanah, Hagabah, Akkub,

46 Hagab, Shalmai, Hanan,

47 Giddel, Gahar, Reaiah,

48 Rezin, Nekoda, Gazzam,

49 Uzza, Paseah, Besai,

50 Asnah, Meunim, Nephussim,

51 Bakbuk, Hakupha, Harhur,

52 Bazluth, Mehida, Harsha,

53 Barkos, Sisera, Temah,

54 Neziah and Hatipha.

55 The descendants of Solomon's servants,

the descendants of Sotai, Hassophereth, Peruda,

56 Jaalah, Darkon, Giddel,

57 Shephatiah, Hattil, Pokereth-Hazzebaim and Ami.

58 392 temple servants and the descendants of Solomon's servants.

59 Some families came from other towns. The towns were Tel Melah, Tel Harsha, Cherub, Addon and Immer. But these families could not show that they were really Israelites. They may not have been descendants of Israel (Jacob).

60 They included 652 descendants of Delaiah, Tobiah and Nekoda.

61 And they included families of the priests. These were descendants of Hobaiah, Hakkoz and Barzillai.

This Barzillai had married one of Barzillai's daughters and he took Barzillai's name. These daughters had lived in Gilead.

62 All these looked to see if their names were written as priests. But they did not find anything. So the leaders did not let them work as priests. 63 They were not clean enough to eat the priests' special food. They must wait until the most important priest could decide. He could use the Urim and Thummim to decide the right thing to do.

64 All together, 42 360 people returned to Jerusalem. 65 And they took with them 7337 men and women servants and 200 men and women singers.

66 They had 736 horses, 245 mules (animals), 67 435 camels (animals) and 6720 donkeys (animals).

68 The most important men in some families came to the Lord's house in Jerusalem. Some of them gave gifts to build it where it had been before. 69 They gave money to build the temple. Rich men gave more and poor men gave less. Together they gave about 500 kilos (half a ton) of gold and nearly 3000 kilos (3 tons) of silver. And they gave 100 special sets of clothes for the priests.

70 The priests, Levites, and some people went to live in or near Jerusalem. The singers, temple servants and workers lived in towns near them. The other Israelites went to live where their ancestors had lived.

Chapter 3

Worship in the Temple begins again

1 When all the people were living in their towns, they met together in Jerusalem. It was the 7th month. 2The priests began to build the altar of the God of Israel. They were priests that included Jeshua, Jozadak's son and Zerubbabel, Shealtiel's son. They were building it to burn sacrifices. This is what Moses, the man of God, wrote in his law. 3 They were afraid of the other people who lived round them. But they built the altar on a flat foundation of stones. On it they burnt sacrifices to the Lord. They did this in the morning and in the evening. 4 Then they had the feast called the 'Feast of Tabernacles' to thank God. He had kept them safe when they left Egypt. And he kept them safe while they crossed the dry land. Nobody lived in that dry land. They lived in huts made out of leaves. And they made sacrifices. Moses had told them how to do this in the law. 5 They burnt sacrifices every day and at the New Moon and at all the times written in the law. Some people brought gifts to offer and to thank the Lord. They wanted to thank him for all the good things that he had done for them. 6 They began to offer burnt sacrifices on the first day of the 7th month. That was before they had started to build the temple.

God's people build the temple again

7 The leaders gave money to men who could work with stone and wood. They sent food and drink and oil to the people in Tyre and Sidon. This was to pay for beams of wood from a tree called cedar. They would bring the wood on the sea. It would come from Lebanon's country to Joppa. Cyrus, king of Persia, had asked Lebanon's people to do this.

8 The Israelites began the work two years after they returned from Babylon, in the 2nd month. Zerubbabel, Shealtiel's son, and Jeshua, Jozadak's son began the work. After this, all the priests and the Levites who worked with them in Jerusalem joined them. Levites who were 20 years old, or older, told the people how to build the Lord's house. 9 These are their names:

Jeshua and his sons and brothers.

Kadmiel and his sons. (They were descendants of Hodaviah.)

Henadad's sons and their sons and brothers.

All of them were Levites.

10 The men who were building the temple finished the foundations. Then the priests put on their special clothes and they made a noise with their trumpets.

The Levites (sons of Asaph) took cymbals and they stood to praise the Lord. Israel's king, David had told them how to do this many years before. 11 They thanked and praised the Lord. They sang, 'He is good. His love for Israel will be for all time.'

And all the people shouted. 'Praise the Lord', they said, 'because we have finished building the first part of the Lord's house!'

12 But many of the older priests and Levites and leaders wept. They were sad because they had seen the earlier temple. And they remembered it. Many other people shouted because they were happy. 13 The shouts and the noise of people who were weeping were very loud. So nobody knew if they were laughing or crying. People far away could hear the noise.

Chapter 4

Enemies do not want the work to continue

1 The enemies of Judah and Benjamin heard that the Jews had begun to build. They were building the temple for the Lord, the God of Israel. 2 Then the enemies went to speak to Zerubbabel and to the family leaders. 'Let us help you to build', they said. 'We want to worship your God. We have lived in this country since Esarhaddon, king of Assyria, brought us here. All this time we have made sacrifices to your God.'

3 But Zerubbabel, Jeshua and Israel's family heads said, 'No. You cannot help us to build the temple to our God. We alone must build it. That is what Cyrus, king of Persia, asked us to do.'

4 Then the people round them tried to make the Israelites afraid. They did not want Judah's people to continue building. 5 They paid men to work against them and to say bad things about the building. They did this all the time that Cyrus was king of Persia. They went on until Darius became king.

6 They wrote to Xerxes when he became king. They said that the people of Judah and Jerusalem were doing a wrong thing.

7 Later, Bishlam, Mithredath, Tabeel and their friends wrote a letter to Artaxerxes, king of Persia. They wrote in the Aramaic language. 8 Rehum, the most important officer and Shimshai wrote this letter against Jerusalem to Artaxerxes. This is what it said.

9 Rehum, your officer and Shimshai, his helper and many other men are writing to you. They are judges and officers with authority over Tripolis, Persia, Erech and Babylon. We are sending this letter also to those who have authority over the people in Susa. (Those people are called Elamites.) 10 We include other people who live in or near the cities in Samaria. The great King Ashurbanipal had sent those people there. Some came from the other side of the River Euphrates.

11 This is the letter that they sent to Artaxerxes:

To King Artaxerxes, from your servants in the land across the Euphrates.

12 The king should know what the Jews here are doing. You sent them here. They are building Jerusalem's city again. It was a bad city whose people did not obey its rulers. They are building the walls and they are beginning to start other buildings.

13 And you should know this. If they build this city and its walls, they will not pay any more money to you. They will take away some of your people's money. 14 We are your servants. We do not want you to lose honour. So we have sent this letter to you. 15 If you look in letters to kings before you, you will find much about this city. Jerusalem's people always did what they chose. And the letters will show you that. For many years Jerusalem's people did not obey those with authority. They did not listen to the kings or their officers. That is why the soldiers from Babylon destroyed the city. 16 We are telling the king that nobody should let these people build up this city and its walls. If they do, you will have no authority on this side of the Euphrates.

17 This is the king's reply:

'To Rehum my officer, Shimshai his helper and all their friends in Samaria and across the River Euphrates.

I thank you for your news.

18 They have translated the letter that you sent into my language. Then they read it to me. 19 I caused them to look in the old letters and they told us about Jerusalem's people. They have always caused trouble to their rulers. They never obeyed their rulers. 20 In past days the kings of Jerusalem were powerful. They ruled all the land on their side of the Euphrates. The people there gave money and other things to them because their kings had authority. 21 Now you must cause them to stop their work. They must not build the city again until I let them. 22 You must be careful to do this. We cannot let them make my authority smaller.'

23 Rehum, Shimshai and their friends took the king's letter to the Jews in Jerusalem. They went as fast as they could. They caused the Jews to stop their work. They would do bad things to them if they did not stop.

24 So the people did no work on God's house in Jerusalem. The work stopped until Darius, Persia's king, had ruled over them for more than one year.

Chapter 5

Tattenai writes to Darius

1 Haggai and Zechariah, Iddo's descendant, gave us messages from God. They obeyed the God of Israel. They were prophets. They told God's message to the Jews in Jerusalem and Judea. 2 Then Zerubbabel, Shealtiel's son, and Jeshua, Jozadak's son, started again to build the temple in Jerusalem. And the prophets worked with them, to help them.

3 At that time Tattenai was the king's ruler of all the land across the River Euphrates. He and Shethar-Bozenai and their friends went to ask them what they were doing. They said, 'Who gave you the authority to start building this temple again?' 4 And they asked, 'What are the names of the men who are building this place?' 5 But God was watching over the Jews' leaders, and nobody stopped them building then. They waited until they could send a letter to King Darius. They waited for him to reply.

6 The ruler Tattenai, Shethar-Bozenai and their friends wrote to King Darius. 7 This is what they said:

We hope that you, King Darius, are well and happy.

8 We went to Judah to visit the temple of the great God. The king should know that the people are building it. They are using big stones and beams of wood to build the walls. They are working hard and the temple is growing fast. Their leaders showed them how to build it.

9 We spoke to them and we asked, 'Who gave authority to you to do this and to build up this temple again?' 10 We also asked them their names. Then we could give the names of their leaders to you.

11 This is the answer that they gave to us:

'We are servants of the God of heaven and earth. A great king of Israel built this temple and finished it many years ago. We are building it again. 12 But our ancestors made the God of heaven angry. So he let Nebuchadnezzar, Babylon's king, fight with them. And Nebuchadnezzar destroyed this temple. Then he took many of our people to Babylon.

13 But Cyrus, king of Babylon said that we must build the house of our God again. He said this in the first year that he was king. 14 And he even gave us the gold and silver things from the Jerusalem temple. Nebuchadnezzar had taken them out of Jerusalem's temple and he put them in the temple in Babylon.

Then King Cyrus gave the valuable things to Sheshbazzar. He had given authority to this man over Jerusalem and the places round it. 15 He said to Sheshbazzar, "Take these things and put them in the temple in Jerusalem. And build again the house of God where it used to be." 16 So this Sheshbazzar came and he built the foundations of God's house in Jerusalem. Since then we have continued to build it, but we have not finished it yet.'

17 If the king should choose, he may look in the letters in his store. It is there in Babylon. King Cyrus did say that we must build up God's temple in Jerusalem. And you will see that in the letters. After this, the king will decide what is right. That is what we hope. We must know whether the king will let us finish this work.

Chapter 6

Darius asks the Jews to go on building the temple

1 King Darius asked his servants to look in his Babylon store. That was where he kept all his valuable things. 2 They found a scroll in a strong building in Ecbatana. This was in Media, a part of Babylon. The words on the scroll were about the temple of God in Jerusalem. This is a copy of those words.

'Remember-

3 King Cyrus told the Jews how to build their temple in Jerusalem. It was the first year that he ruled in Babylon. He said:

"They must build their temple as a place to sacrifice to their God. They must make it 30 metres (90 feet) wide and 30 metres high. They must build it on a foundation. 4 On this they must build a wall from big stones, 3 stones high. On this they must build a wall made out of wood. Money from my store will pay for it. 5 And we will give their silver and gold things back to them. Nebuchadnezzar had taken them from the old temple in Jerusalem. And he brought them to Babylon. They must return them to their places. They must put them in the new temple in Jerusalem. They must put them in their God's house."

6 So you, Tattenai, ruler of the land across the Euphrates, and Shethar-Bozenai and your officers must stay away from them. 7 You must not stop them from building God's temple. The leaders and those Jews with authority must continue to build this house of God. They must build it in its proper place.

8 Now I will tell you what you must do for these leaders. You must pay for everything that they need with the king's money. This money is from the people who live across the Euphrates. Then the work will not stop. 9 Be sure to give each day to the priests the things that they need for sacrifices to the God of heaven. Give them young male cows and young and old male sheep. Give them grain, salt, wine and oil when the priests ask for them. 10 Then their sacrifices will give pleasure to the God of heaven. They can then pray for good things for the king and his sons.

11 Nobody can change any of these rules that I have given to you. If anyone does not obey, men must pull a beam out of his house. They must lift him and push the beam through his body. They must destroy his house because he has not obeyed me. 12 God, has caused his name to live in his temple. He will cause enemies to kill any king or people who change my words. He will be very much against any king or people who try to destroy this temple in Jerusalem. I, Darius, have made this law. You must be sure to obey it.'

They finish the temple

13 Tattenai, ruler of the land across the Euphrates, Shethar-Bozenai and their friends heard this law. Then they were all very careful to obey King Darius. 14 So the leaders of the Jews continued to build the temple. They listened to what Haggai the prophet and Zechariah, Iddo's descendant were teaching them. They finished building the temple. They built it as the God of Israel had told them. They obeyed the rules of Cyrus, Darius and Artaxerxes, the kings of Persia. 15 They finished building it on the 3rd day of the month Adar. King Darius had then been king for 6 years.

16 Then the Israelites had a feast. That included the priests, Levites and the other people. Everyone who had come from Babylon dedicated the temple to God. They were very happy. 17 At this time they offered 100 male cows, 200 male sheep and 400 young male sheep to the Lord. Then they sacrificed 12 male goats because of the sin of all Israel. Each of the 12 large families of Israel gave a goat. 18 They caused the groups of priests and Levites to do their work in the proper way. They did it for God in Jerusalem. Moses had written in his book how to do this.

The Passover

19 On the 14th day of the first month, the people had another party. This was the Passover feast. 20 The priests and Levites made themselves clean for their special work. The Levites killed the Passover lambs (young sheep) for the people, the priests and for themselves. 21 So all the people who had returned from Babylon ate the feast. Other Israelites there had stopped doing the bad things that nations round them did. They made themselves clean. That was because they wanted to worship the Lord, the God of Israel. So they ate the feast. 22 And they all remembered the Feast of Unleavened Bread. This feast was 7 days long. The Lord had made them very happy because the king of Assyria had changed his ideas. Now he was helping them to build their God's house.

Chapter 7

Ezra comes to Jerusalem

1 After these things, Ezra came up from Babylon while Artaxerxes was king of Persia. This is the list of Ezra's ancestors. He was the son of Seraiah, the son of Azariah, the son of Hilkiah. 2 Hilkiah was the son of Shallum, the son of Zadok, the son of Ahitub. 3 Ahitub was the son of Amariah, the son of Azariah, the son of Meraioth. 4 Meraioth was the son of Zerahiah, the son of Uzzi, the son of Bukki. 5 Bukki was the son of Abishua, the son of Phinehas, the son of Eleazar. And Eleazar was a son of Aaron, the most important priest. 6 This Ezra came up from Babylon. He was a teacher who knew the Law of Moses. The Lord, the God of Israel had given that law to Moses. The king had given to Ezra everything that he asked for. That happened because the Lord God had caused the king to do this. 7 Some other Israelites also came up to Jerusalem. They came in the 7th year that Artaxerxes was king. They included priests, Levites, singers, temple servants and men who watched the gates.

8 Ezra came to Jerusalem in the 5th month of Artaxerxes' 7th year. 9 He left Babylon on the first day of the first month. And he came to Jerusalem on the first day of the 5th month. God had made his journey easy. 10 He did this because Ezra had studied God's law carefully. Ezra always obeyed its rules and he taught them to the Israelites.

Artaxerxes' letter to Ezra

11 This is a copy of the letter that Artaxerxes had given to Ezra, the priest and teacher. Ezra knew well all the Lord's rules and laws for Israel.

12 From Artaxerxes, king of kings, to Ezra the priest, a teacher of the God of heaven's law. I hope that you are well.

13 Many Israelites live in my kingdom. Some may want to go with you to Jerusalem. I have decided that they can go. That rule includes priests and Levites with any who want to go. 14 The king and his 7 important officers are sending you there. You must ask whether the people in Judah and Jerusalem are obeying their God's law. You have this law in your hands. 15 And I and my officers have given gold and silver as a free gift to you. You must take them with you. They are for the God of Israel, whose house is in Jerusalem. 16 And take the gold and silver that other people in Babylon give to you. And take too, the gifts that the people and priests have given for their God's temple in Jerusalem. 17 You must buy male cows and old and young male sheep with this money. Also buy drink and grain to offer to your God. Sacrifice them on the altar of Jerusalem's temple.

18 You and all the other Jews can then use the rest of the silver and gold as you want to. You can do anything that your God wants you to do. 19 You must take all the things that you use for worship with you. Give them to Jerusalem's God. 20 Perhaps you may need other things for worship in your God's temple. You can take these from my rich stores.

21 This is what I, King Artaxerxes, will do. I will speak to the rulers of the countries across the River Euphrates. They must help you. Their men keep my money. They must give Ezra anything that he asks for. He is a priest who teaches the law of the God of heaven. They must do that very carefully. 22 You should not give more than this to him:

3400 kilos (3.3 tons) of silver

22 000 litres (5800 US gallons) of grain

2200 litres (580 US gallons) of wine

2200 litres of oil

all the salt that he wants.

23 Be careful to give to Ezra everything that the God of heaven wants for his temple. I do not want the God of heaven to be angry with me or with my sons. 24 You must not take money for any purpose from men who work in this house of God. You have no authority to do this. These men include priests, Levites, singers, servants and those who watch the gate.

25 Your God has helped you to understand things, Ezra. He will show to you which men to choose. They will judge the people. You must choose men to judge small problems in the land across the Euphrates. And other men must judge the bigger problems. All the people must obey the laws of your God. If the people do not know these laws, you must teach them. 26 You must punish the people who do not obey the laws of your God and the king's laws. You may send them away or you may kill them. You may send them out of the country or put them in a prison. Or you may take away some of their things. 27 This is how the king wants to give honour to the Lord's house in Jerusalem. The Lord, the God of our people, has caused him to think like this. We praise God's name! 28 And God has been kind to me in front of the king and his powerful friends and officers. The Lord held me so strongly that I became brave. I could ask the leaders of Israel to go up with me.

Chapter 8

The family leaders who went back with Ezra to Jerusalem

1 These are the leaders and other men in their families who came with me from Babylon. We came during the time that Artaxerxes was king.

2 Gershom, Phinehas's descendant.

Daniel, Ithamar's descendant.

3 Hattush, Shecaniah's son, David's descendant.

Zechariah, Parosh's descendant and 150 men.

4 Elihoenai, Zerahiah's son, and 200 men, Pahath-Moab's descendants.

5 Shecaniah, Jahaziel's son, with 300 men, Zattu's descendants.

6 Ebed, Jonathan's son with 50 men, Adin's descendants.

7 Jeshaiah, Athaliah's son, with 70 men, Elam's descendants.

8 Zebadiah, Michael's son, with 80 men, Shephatiah's descendants.

9 Obadiah, Jehiel's son, with 218 men, Joab's descendants.

10 Shelomith, Josiphiah's son with 160 men, Bani's descendants.

11 Zechariah, Bebai's son, with 28 men, Bebai's descendants.

12 Johanan, Hakkatan's son, with 110 men, Azgad's descendants.

13 Eliphelet, Jeuel and Shemaiah, Adonikam's descendants with 60 men who came later.

14 Uthai and Zaccur with 70 men, Bigvai's descendants.

The return to Jerusalem

15 I caused all the people to come together at the river that goes to Ahava. We stayed there during 3 days. I looked at the people and priests, but I did not see any Levites. 16 So I asked them to send Eliezer, Ariel, Shemaiah and Elnathan. And I asked for Jarib, Elnathan, Nathan, Zechariah and Meshullam. They were all leaders. I also asked for Joiarib and Elnathan. They were men who had learnt much. 17 And I sent them all to Iddo, the leader in Casiphia. Iddo and his family were servants in the temple. But they were living there in Casiphia. I told them what to say to Iddo. They must ask him to bring people to work in the house of our God. 18 This was what God wanted. So they brought Sherebiah to us. He was a man who could do the work well. He was from Mahli's family. Levi was a son of Israel, and Mahli was Levi's son. Sherebiah came with his sons and brothers. Together they were 18 men. 19 Hashabiah came and Jeshaiah, a descendant of Merari came too, with his brothers and the brothers' sons. They were 20 men together. 20They also brought 220 temple servants. These were people that David had said should help the Levites. We had made a list of their names.

21 We were all by the River Ahava. I said that the people should not eat any food. This was to show God that we needed his help. Then we asked him to keep us safe on the journey with our children and all our things. 22 I was ashamed to ask the king for soldiers who walked. And I was ashamed to ask the king for soldiers who rode on horses. They could have kept us safe from our enemies. But we had spoken to the king. We had said, 'Our God is good. He keeps safe those who obey him. But he is very angry with those who turn away from him. And he works against them.' 23 So we ate no food and we prayed to our God about this. And he listened to us.

24 I chose 12 of the most important priests. I put them with Sherebiah, Hashabiah and 10 of their brothers.25 I weighed in front of them many valuable things. These things included the silver and gold offerings and other things that people had given to us. The king, his friends and officers and all the Israelites had given us these. They gave them for the house of our God. 26 I weighed about 20 000 kilos (20 tons) of silver and about 3500 kilos (3.5 tons) of things made from silver. And I weighed 3500 kilos of gold and 2720 deep dishes of gold that weighed about 8.5 kilos (19 pounds). I also gave to them 2 beautiful things that someone had made from metal. But those things were as valuable as gold.

28 Then I spoke to them. I said, 'You people and these things all belong to the Lord. The silver and gold are offerings to the Lord, the God of your fathers. 29 You must be careful to keep them safe until you reach Jerusalem. There in the rooms in the Lord's house you must weigh them. You must do this in front of the leaders of the priests, Levites and other Israelite families.' 30 Then they gave the silver, gold and valuable things to the priests and Levites. They would take them to the temple in Jerusalem.

31 We left the River Ahava on the 12th day of the first month. We left to go to Jerusalem. Our God kept us safe on the journey. No enemies robbed us or hurt us. 32 So we arrived in Jerusalem. And we rested there during 3 days.

33 We went into God's house on the 4th day. Then we weighed out the silver, gold and holy things there. We gave them to Meremoth, Uriah the priest's son. Phinehas's son, Eleazar was with him. The LevitesJozabad, Jeshua's son and Noadiah, Binnui's son, were also there. 34 They weighed and counted everything. They wrote it all in a list.

35 All the people who had returned from Babylon offered sacrifices to the God of Israel. They burnt 12 male cows for all Israel, 96 male sheep and 77 lambs (young male sheep). Then they sacrificed 12 male goats for a sin offering. They burnt all these animals as an offering to the Lord. 36 They also gave the king's letters to his officers. And they gave them to those who ruled the land across the Euphrates. Then those in authority helped the people and they gave things to the house of God.

Chapter 9

Ezra prays about Israelites who have married foreign women

1 When we had done all these things, the leaders came to see me. They said, 'The Israelites have done many wrong things that the people in other countries do. They are like the people called Canaanites, Hittites, Perizzites, Jebusites, Ammonites, Moabites, Egyptians and Amorites. Even some priests and Levites have done these things. They have not kept themselves separate. 2 They and their sons have married some of the foreign men's daughters. They have mixed their blood with that of other peoples. The leaders of our holy nation were the first to do this. They have not been faithful to the Lord.'

3 I tore my shirt and coat when I heard this. I pulled out hair from my head and my beard. I sat down and I was angry and ashamed. 4 Then everyone who was afraid because of the words of the God of Israel came round me. They were afraid because the Israelites from Babylon had not been faithful to their God. And I sat there, very angry, until the time of the evening sacrifice.

5 Then I stood up with my torn shirt and coat. I went on my knees at the evening sacrifice. I was still angry. I held out my hands and I prayed to the Lord, my God. 6 I said,

'My God, I am too ashamed to look up at you. Our sins are very great. They could not be greater. 7 We have done wrong things from the first days of our ancestors. You have punished us, our kings and our priests, because of our sins. Foreign kings have killed our people. And they have taken our things and they have made us prisoners. And they have caused us to be poor people. So today we are poor and we have no honour.

8 But now the Lord our God has begun to be good to us again. A few of us are here. We are safe in his holy place. He has made us happier and he has made our lives easier. 9 We are still slaves, but our God has not left us alone. He has caused the kings of Persia to be kind to us. They have let us live and they have let us build up the house of our God. We have mended it. And now he keeps us safe in Judah and Jerusalem.

10 We can say nothing to you, our God because we have not obeyed your rules. 11 You gave them to us by your servants, the prophets. You said, "You are going into a country that is not clean. The people there have done very bad things and they have made it not clean. It is full of bad things from one end to the other. 12 You must not let your daughters marry their sons. And you must not let your sons marry their daughters. Do not ever make a strong promise to be their friends. Then you will be strong and you will have good food to eat. Your children will live in the same country after you. It will always belong to your families."

13 You have punished us because we did these wrong things. But your punishment, our God, was not as great as our sins. You have brought some of us back to Judah. 14 We do not want to marry people who do those very bad things. We must obey you, or you will be angry with us. You might kill all of us, and none of us would still be here. 15 You do only what is good, Lord God of Israel. Only a few of us are still here.

We come to you. We are sorry and ashamed of the wrong things that we have done. Not one person among us is clean enough to stand in front of you.'

Chapter 10

The people tell God that they are sorry

1 A big crowd of Israelite men, women and children came round Ezra. He was praying and crying. And he was saying 'Sorry' to God. He threw himself down in front of the house of God. And the people were crying very much. 2 Then Shecaniah spoke to him. He was Jehiel's son, a descendant of Elam. Shecaniah said, 'We have not been faithful to our God. We have married foreign women from the countries round us. But we want to make things right with God. 3 We will make a promise to him. We will send away these women and their children. This is what you, Ezra, are telling us to do. And the people who want to obey God's law want it, too. We must obey the law. 4 Get up! Now you must help us to do what is right. We will help you, so you must not be afraid.'

5 So Ezra got up. He caused the leaders of the priests, Levites and all Israel to promise to do as they had said. And they made their strong promise to God. 6 And Ezra went from the front of God's house to Jehohanan's room. Jehohanan was Eliashib's son. Ezra was still very sad because the people had not been faithful to the Lord. So he did not eat any food while he was there. And he did not drink any water while he was there.

7 They wrote a message and they sent it to all the people in Judah and Jerusalem. It said that they must all come to Jerusalem. 8 If they did not arrive in 3 days, they would lose everything. The leaders and officers had decided to say this. And they would push out anyone who did not obey the message. They would send them out of Israel.

9 All the men from Judah and Benjamin reached Jerusalem in 3 days. All the people sat in front of God's house on the 20th day of the 9th month. They were very sad because they had made God angry. And the rain was bad.

10 Then Ezra the priest stood up. He said, 'You have not been faithful to your God. You have married foreign wives. You have done this and so many other sins. 11 Now you must tell the Lord that you are sorry. He is the God of your fathers and grandfathers. You must do the things that he wants. You must make yourselves separate from the people who live in the countries round you. You must make yourselves separate from your foreign wives.'

12 All the people spoke with a loud voice. 'You are right', they said. 'We must do as you say. 13 But we are many people and we cannot stand in the rain. And we shall need more than two days to do this thing. Many of us have sinned like that. 14 Our officers should do this for us. In every town they must make a special time for men to visit the leaders and the judges. Then everyone who has a foreign wife can go to them. God was very angry, but then he will not be angry any longer.' 15 Only 4 men did not agree with this. They were Jonathan, Asahel's son, Jahzeiah, Tikvah's son, with Meshullam and Shabbethai the Levite.

16 So the Jews from Babylon did as the people had said. Ezra the priest chose family leaders for each big family. He wrote down their names. They sat down to decide which men had to send away their wives. They started on the first day of the 10th month. 17 And they finished on the first day of the first month.

A list of the men with foreign wives

18 They found that these people had married foreign women:

From the descendants of the priests,

Jeshua, Jozadak's son and his brothers:

Maaseiah,

Eliezer,

Jarib,

Gedaliah.

19 (They all promised to send away their wives. Each of them gave a male sheep as a sacrifice for their sin.)

20 The descendants of Immer:

Hanani,

Zebadiah.

21 The descendants of Harim:

Maaseiah,

Elijah,

Shemaiah,

Jehiel,

Uzziah.

22 The descendants of Pashhur:

Elioenai,

Maaseiah,

Ishmael,

Nethanel,

Jozabad,

Elasah.

23 The descendants of the Levites:

Jozabad,

Shimei,

Kelaiah (that is Kelita),

Pethahiah,

Judah,

Eliezer.

24 From the singers, Eliashib.

From the men who kept the gate, Shallum, Telem and Uri.

25 And among the other Israelites, the descendants of Parosh:

Ramiah,

Izziah,

Malchijah,

Mijamin,

Eleazar,

Malkijah,

Benaiah.

26 The descendants of Elam:

Mattaniah,

Zechariah,

Jehiel,

Abdi,

Jeremoth,

Elijah.

27 The descendants of Zattu:

Elioenai,

Eliashib,

Mattaniah,

Jeremoth,

Zabad,

Aziza.

28 The descendants of Bebai:

Jehohanan,

Hananiah,

Zabbai,

Athlai.

29 The descendants of Bani:

Meshullam,

Malluch,

Adaiah,

Jashub,

Sheal,

Jeremoth.

30 The descendants of Pahath-Moab:

Adna,

Chelal,

Benaiah,

Maaseiah,

Mattaniah,

Bezalel,

Binnui,

Manasseh.

31 The descendants of Harim:

Eliezer,

Ishijah,

Malkijah,

Shemaiah,

Shimeon,

32 Benjamin,

Malluch,

Shemariah.

33 The descendants of Hashum:

Mattenai,

Mattattah,

Zabad,

Eliphelet,

Jeremai,

Manasseh,

Shimei.

34 The descendants of Bani:

Maadai,

Amram,

Uel,

35 Benaiah,

Bedeiah,

Keluhi,

36 Vaniah,

Meremoth,

Eliashib,

37 Mattaniah,

Mattenai,

Jaasu,

38 Bani,

Binnui,

Shimei,

39 Shelemiah,

Nathan,

Adaiah,

40 Macnadebai,

Shashai,

Sharai,

41 Azarel,

Shelemiah,

Shemariah,

42 Shallum,

Amariah,

Joseph.

43 The descendants of Nebo:

Jeiel,

Mattithiah,

Zabad,

Zebina,

Jaddai,

Joel,

Benaiah.

44 All these men had married foreign women, and some had children by these wives.

God's People Build Jerusalem's City Wall Again

Nehemiah

About this book

The Book of Nehemiah is part of the Old Testament. Nebuchadnezzar, the king of Babylon had destroyed the temple in Jerusalem. Later, Artaxerxes became king of Babylon. The Jews are God's people.

They had to live in Babylon. Nebuchadnezzar had sent the Jews to live there. Later the Jews returned to Jerusalem. This is a careful report of what happened. They found that soldiers had destroyed the city wall. This was very important. In Deuteronomy 7:3-4, God tells the Jews that they must not marry people who were not Jews. This is because people from other countries worshipped other gods. Nehemiah reports what the Jews' enemies did. The Jews were building the city wall again. Then Jerusalem would become a powerful city. So their enemies tried to stop them. The Jews knew that God would keep them safe. He did this while they built the city wall again.

Chapter 1

1 These are the words of Nehemiah, son of Hacaliah. It was the month Kislev. This was when King Artaxerxes had ruled for 20 years. I was in the king's house in the city called Susa. 2 Hanani, my brother and some men arrived. They came from Judah. I asked them for news of the Jews who had earlier returned from Babylon. I asked them about Jerusalem city. 3 They told me, 'The Jews who returned to Judah are in much trouble. And they are ashamed. Their enemies have broken down the city walls and have burnt the gates.'

4 After they told me this, I sat down. And I cried. During many days, I was very sad. I did not eat or drink. I prayed to God.

5 I prayed, 'Oh Lord, God of heaven, you are great and powerful. You are so great that I cannot come near to you. You always keep your promises to the people that you have chosen. You do this because you love them. But they must love and obey you. 6 Listen to my words. I am your servant. I am praying to you. I pray in the day and in the night. I am praying on behalf of the people of Israel. They are your servants. We have all done wrong things. I and my family have not obeyed you. The people of Israel have not obeyed your laws. 7 We have all gone against you. We have not obeyed the laws that you gave to your servant Moses.

8 Remember what you told Moses. You told him, "If you do not obey my laws and love me, I will make you live in foreign lands. I will cause you to become separate. You will not be together. 9 But my people must return to me and obey my laws. Then I will let them live in the place that I have chosen. Even if they live far away, I will find them. They can live in the place that I have chosen for my name." That is what you told Moses.'

10 'Your people are your servants. You saved them from their enemies with your great power. They cost you much. 11 Please listen to my prayer. I am your servant. The people of Israel are your servants. We worship your name. Let the king be happy with me. Let Artaxerxes give me what I ask.'

I was the king's cupbearer.

Chapter 2

1 It was the month of Nisan. King Artaxerxes had ruled Babylon for 20 years. I brought the king's wine. I gave the wine to the king. I was sad. I had not been sad in front of the king before. 2 The king asked me, 'Why are you sad? You are not ill. This must mean that you are not happy.' I was afraid.

3 I replied, 'Let the king live always! I am sad because they have destroyed my ancestors' city. Our enemies have burned the city's gates.' 4 The king asked me, 'What do you want?' So I prayed to God. 5 Then I replied to the king, 'If it gives the king pleasure, might he send me there? Then if he is happy with his servant Nehemiah, I can build the city again. They buried my ancestors there.' 6 The king sat with the queen next to him. The king asked me, 'How long will you be away? When will you return?' The king was happy to let me go to Judah. I told him when I would leave. 7 I said to the king, 'If the king likes the idea, give me some letters. The letters are for your government officers of Trans-Euphrates. The officers will keep me safe on the journey to Judah. 8 Let me have a letter to give to Asaph. He has authority for the king's forest. He will give me wood from the trees to make beams. The beams are for the gates of the city, near the temple. They are also for the city wall and for the house that I will live in.' God was with me. So the king gave me what I asked for.

9 I went to Trans-Euphrates. I gave the government officers the letter. The king sent soldiers with me. Some rode horses and some walked. 10 Sanballat and Tobiah were not happy because I came to help the Jews. Sanballat was from Horon and Tobiah was an Ammonite officer.

11 I went to Jerusalem. I was in Jerusalem for three days. After three days 12 I went out at night. A few men came with me. I did not tell anyone the idea that God had put in my mind. I rode on a horse. We did not take any other horses. 13 I went through the Valley Gate to the Jackal Well and the Dung Gate. I looked at Jerusalem's wall. It was broken. Enemies had broken the wall and they had burnt the gates.

14 I went to the Fountain Gate and the King's Pool. The horse that I was riding could not get through. 15 So I went to the valley to look at the wall. It was dark. I returned past the Valley Gate. 16 The officers did not know what I had done. I had not said anything to the officers or priests. I did not tell the Jews that I wanted them to build the city wall again.

17 I spoke to the priests, Jews and officers. I said, 'We have much trouble. Enemies have broken down the city wall. Fire has burned the gates. We must build the city again. Then Jerusalem will no longer be ashamed.' 18 I told the people how God had helped me. God had put the idea in the king's mind to let me come to Jerusalem. I told them what the king had said to me. The people said, 'We will start to build!' And they began the good work. 19 But Sanballat, Tobiah and Geshem tried to make us seem like fools. They said, 'What are you doing? Are you going against the king?'

20 I replied, 'God will make us strong to finish this work. We are God's servants. We will start to build. But you have no place in Jerusalem.'

Chapter 3

1 Eliashib, the priest, and other priests built the Sheep Gate. They dedicated (gave) it to God and they put on the doors of the gate. Eliashib and the other priests built the wall as far as the Tower of the Hundred. They dedicated this part of the wall. Then they built the wall as far as the Tower of Hananel.

2 The men from Jericho built the next part of the city wall. Zaccur, the son of Imri, built the next part of the wall.

3 The sons of Hassenaah built the Fish Gate. They put up the beams and they put on the doors of the gate. They made the doors so that they could lock the gate. 4 Meremoth son of Uriah, the son of Hakkoz, mended the next part of the wall. Meshullam son of Berekiah, the son of Meshezabel, repaired the wall next to Meremoth. Zadok, son of Baana, repaired the next part of the wall. 5 The men from Tekoa repaired the next part. But their important men did not work hard.

6 Joiada son of Paseah, and Meshullam son of Besodeiah, repaired the Old Gate. They put up the beams of the gate and they put on the doors. They made the doors of the gate so that they could lock them. 7 Men from Gibeon and Mizpah called Melatiah and Jadon repaired the wall next to the Old Gate. Melatiah is from Gibeon. Jadon came from Meronoth that is under the authority of Trans-Euphrates. 8 Uzziel, son of Harhaiah, repaired the next part of the wall. Uzziel is a man who works with gold. Hananiah repaired the wall next to Uzziel. Hananiah makes perfume. Hananiah and Uzziel repaired the wall as far as the Broad Wall. 9 Rephaiah, son of Hur, repaired the next part of the wall. Rephaiah rules over part of Jerusalem.

10 Next to Rephaiah, Jedaiah, son of Harumaph, repaired the wall on the other side of Jedaiah's house. Hattush, son of Hashabneiah, repaired the wall next to Jedaiah. 11 Malkijah son of Harim, and Hasshub son of Pahath-Moab, repaired a part of the wall. They also repaired the Tower of the Ovens. 12 Shallum, son of Hallohesh, repaired the next part of the wall. Shallum's daughters helped him. Shallum ruled over part of Jerusalem.

13 Hanun and the people who lived in Zanoah repaired the Valley Gate. They built it and they put doors on the gate. They made the doors so that they could be locked. The people from Zanoah also repaired 450 metres of the city wall. They repaired the wall as far as the Dung Gate.

14 Malkijah, son of Recab, repaired the Dung Gate. Malkijah put the doors on the gate. He made the doors. Malkijah rules Beth Hakkerem.

15 Shallun, son of Col-Hozeh, repaired the Fountain Gate. Shallun is the ruler of Mizpah and the places round it. Shallun made a roof for the Fountain Gate. He put on the door. He made the doors so that they could lock the gate. Shallun also repaired the wall of the Pool of Siloam near the King's Garden. Shallun repaired the wall as far as the steps from the City of David. 16 Nehemiah, son of Azbuk, repaired another part of the wall. He repaired as far as the pool that people had made and the House of the Brave Men. Nehemiah is a ruler of Beth Zur. 17 Next to Nehemiah, Levites repaired the wall. Rehum son of Bani had authority over the Levites. Next to the Levites, Hashabiah repaired the wall. He ruled over part of Keilah.18 Binnui son of Henadad repaired the wall. Binnui also rules over part of Keilah. Men from Keilah helped him. 19 Ezer son of Jeshua repaired part of the wall. It was in front of the place where the soldiers kept their arms. Ezer rules over Mizpah. 20 Next, Baruch son of Zabbai repaired part of the wall. It was from the corner to the door of Eliashib's house. Baruch worked very well. Eliashib is the leader of the priests. 21 Meremoth son of Uriah, the son of Hakkoz, repaired the next part. It was from the door to the end of Eliashib's house. 22 Next to Meremoth, priests from near Jerusalem repaired the wall. 23 Benjamin and Hasshub repaired the wall in front of their house. Next, Azariah son of Maaseiah, the son of Ananiah, repaired the wall by his house. 24 Binnui son of Henadad, repaired from Azariah's house to the corner. He also repaired the corner of the wall. 25 Palal son of Uzai, worked in front of the tower of the Upper Palace near the guards' yard. Pedaiah son of Parosh 26 and the temple servants repaired the wall towards the east. And they repaired the tower as far as the Water Gate. The temple servants live on the hill of Ophel. 27 The men from Tekoa repaired from the tower to the wall of Ophel.

28 The priests repaired the wall above the Horse Gate. Each priest repaired the wall in front of his house.29 Zadok, son of Immer, repaired the city wall in front of his house. Next to him, Shemaiah son of Shecaniah repaired the wall. Shemaiah is the guard at the East Gate.

30 Next to Shemaiah, Hananiah, son of Shelemiah, repaired the wall. Hanun, the 6th son of Zalaph, also repaired the wall. Next, Meshullam son of Berekiah, repaired the wall in front of the place where he lived.31 Malkijah works with gold. He repaired the wall as far as the temple servants' house. And he repaired as far as the merchants' houses in front of the Meeting Gate. He repaired as far as the room above the corner.

32 Between there and the Sheep Gate the merchants and men who worked with gold repaired the wall.

Chapter 4

1 Sanballat knew that the Jews were building the wall. He was very angry. He wanted people to think that the Jews were fools. 2 Sanballat's officers and Samaria's army were with him. He said, 'Those Jews have great ideas! They are weak. They are trying to repair the wall! They want to give sacrifices to their God. They will take a long time because fire has burned the stones. They cannot use them to build the wall.' 3Tobiah the Ammonite was with him. Tobiah said, 'The wall that the Jews have built is very weak. If a small animal climbs on it, their wall will fall.' 4 I prayed, 'Hear us, our God. Our enemies are against us. Make them seem like fools. Let their enemies take them as slaves. And let their enemies take their land. 5Do not forget their sins. They are saying bad things about you. And the Jews who are building the city wall are hearing their words.'

6 The Jews worked well because they really wanted to build the wall. So they continued to build the city wall. It soon became half as high as the old wall.

7 But Sanballat and Tobiah were very angry. They had heard that the Jews had nearly mended the walls. The holes in them were now small. The people who came from Arabia, the Ammonites and the men from Ashdod were also very angry. 8 They met together. They decided how to fight against the Jews. They wanted to cause trouble for them. 9 But we, the Jews, prayed to God. We made guards watch over the land outside the wall. They watched day and night.

10 While this was happening, the people in Judah said, 'The workers are becoming weak. There are too many small pieces of stone. We cannot build the city. The stones are in the places where we want to build.'11 Our enemies said, 'Before the Jews see us, we will go among them. Then we will kill them. While they are building the wall, we will stop them.' 12 The Jews who lived near them said, 'Anywhere that you go, our enemies will attack us.' They said this to us many times.

13 So I (Nehemiah) put some men behind the lowest part of the wall. They had swords, spears and bows. They stayed near the families who repaired the wall.

14 I looked at everything. I said to the officers and the people, 'Do not be afraid of our enemies. Remember that God is great and powerful. Fight on behalf of your brothers. Fight on behalf of your sons and daughters. Fight on behalf of your wives. Fight on behalf of your homes.'

15 We knew what our enemies had decided to do. They discovered this. Then they knew that God had stopped them. So each of us went back to our work on the wall.

16 After that day, half of my men carried spears, bows and swords. The officers stood behind the people while they built the wall. 17 Those who carried building materials kept one hand on their sword. Everyone who was making repairs to the wall carried a sword. They did their work with one hand and they carried their sword with the other hand. 18 Every man who built the wall carried his sword. And the man with the trumpet stayed near me.

19 I said to all the people, 'Because the wall is long, we are not near each other. 20 When you hear the sound of the trumpet, come to me. Our God will fight on our behalf.'

21 We continued to work on the wall. Half of the men carried spears. They looked for our enemies. We worked from morning until it was dark. 22 I spoke to the Jews and to those who helped them, 'Everyone must stay in Jerusalem at night. You can look for our enemies at night and work in the day.' (I said this to the Jews who did not live in Jerusalem.) 23 Neither I nor my brothers took our clothes off. Nor did my men or the guards take off their clothes. Everyone carried his sword. We were ready always to fight our enemies. Even when we went to get water, we carried our swords.

Chapter 5

1 Some men and their wives were not happy with some other Jews. 2 They said, 'We have many sons and daughters. But we have no food.' 3 Other people said, 'We have no money for food. We have to sell our fields, vineyards and homes for food to stay alive.'

4 Other people said, 'We have no money to pay our debts to the king. 5 We have had to sell our sons and daughters as slaves. Other people buy them because we have no money. Our sons and daughters are Jews like them. But some of our daughters are already slaves. They make us pay for the money that they lent to us. We should not have to do this because we are all Jews. We have no power because we have sold our land to other people.'

6 When I knew about this, I was very angry. 7 I thought about what these Jews had said. Then I said to the rich Jews and their officers, 'You are using other Jews to get more money.' I asked many Jews to meet together. 8 I said, 'We have bought back those Jews who were slaves. They were slaves to people who were not Jews. Now you are making poor Jews become slaves. They are like your brothers. We will have to buy them back again.' The rich Jews did not say anything. They had nothing to say. 9 I said, 'You are doing a very wrong thing. You should be afraid that our enemies will have no respect for our God.'

10 'My brothers and I, together with other men, are lending the people money and food. But we are not getting extra money from them. 11 Please give the fields, vineyards, olive groves and houses back to the poor Jews now. And do not ask them to give back more money than you lend. You have asked for 1/100th part more than you lent! Give that money back to them, too.'

12 The rich Jews said, 'We will give everything back to them. We will not ask them to give back more money than we lent to them. We will do as you say.' I asked the priests to come and join us. I made the rich Jews make a promise. They promised to do as I said. 13 I moved my clothes while I was still wearing them. While I did this, I said, 'Like this, God should move every man out of his house if he does not obey this promise. God should move him away from everything that is his. People should take him away and destroy all his things.' Everyone said, 'Amen'. Everyone worshipped God. All the people obeyed this promise.

14 During all the time that I had authority in Judah, I did not eat the food of those in authority. I did this from the 20th to the 32nd year of King Artaxerxes. For 12 years I did not eat this food. Nor did my brothers.

15 Those in authority before I came took 40 pieces of silver, food and wine from the people. Those who helped them thought of them as more important than other people. I did not do this, because I worship God. 16 I worked together with my men when we built the wall. I did not take any land. 17 150 Jews and officers ate at my table. Also, men from lands near Jerusalem ate with me. 18 Every day, my servants cooked one ox, 6 sheep and some birds for us to eat. Every 10 days I bought much wine. I did not ask for all the things that usually they gave to people in authority. The Jews were poor. They could not give me the food that people in authority could ask for. 19 'Please God, remember me. And do good things to me because of what I have done on behalf of the Jews.'

Chapter 6

1 We had finished building the wall. There were no holes in it, but the doors were not in the gates. Sanballat, Tobiah, Geshem and all our enemies knew that we had finished building the wall. (Geshem came from Arabia.) 2 Sanballat and Geshem sent this message to me, 'Let us meet together in a village on the Ono flat land.' I knew that they wanted to hurt me. 3 I sent a man with my reply, 'I am too busy to meet you. I will not stop this important work to meet you.' 4 They sent me the same message 4 times. My reply to each was the same. 5 Then Sanballat sent his officer to me. He carried a letter that was open. Any person could read this letter. 6 This is what the letter said, 'They are telling the people that you (Nehemiah) and the Jews will cause trouble for the king. Geshem also says that this is true. This is why you are building the city wall. They say that you want to be King of Jerusalem. 7 You have told prophets that they must say, "There is a king in Judah." This report will go to King Artaxerxes. So we must meet together.'

8 I sent this reply, 'What you say is not true. You are saying things that are your own ideas.'

9 Our enemies wanted to frighten us. They thought, 'The Jews will be so afraid that their hands will be weak. They will not finish building the wall.' I prayed to God, 'Make my hands strong.'

10 One day I went to Shemaiah's house. He is the son of Delaiah, son of Mehetabel. He would not go out of his house. He said to me, 'Meet me in the temple of God. We will close the temple doors. Our enemies are coming to kill you. At night, they will come to kill you.'

11 But I said, 'I will not run away. I will not go into the temple to save my life.' 12 Then I knew that my enemies had sent Shemaiah. Tobiah and Sanballat had paid him to say this to me. 13 They wanted to frighten me so that I would hide in the temple. My enemies knew that this would be a sin. If I sinned, they would tell the people about it. Then people would not have respect for me after that. 14 'Please God, remember Tobiah and Sanballat. Remember what they have done. Remember Noadiah the prophetess and the other prophets who want to frighten me.'

15 We finished the wall on the 25th of Elul. It had taken 52 days to build the city wall again. 16 When our enemies knew this, they were afraid. All the people who lived near Jerusalem were afraid. They knew that God had helped the Jews to build the city wall again.

17 The rich men of Judah were sending many letters to Tobiah. Tobiah also sent many replies. 18 Many people in Judah had promised to obey Tobiah. That was because his son Jehohanan had married the daughter of Meshullam. He had helped to repair the city wall. And his wife was Shecaniah's daughter. Shecaniah was Arah's son. 19 The men of Judah told me often about the good things that Tobiah had done. Then they told Tobiah everything that I said. And Tobiah sent letters to people to cause trouble for me.

Chapter 7

1 When we had built the wall I put the doors in their place. We chose men to watch at the gates (these men are called gatekeepers), singers and Levites. 2 I gave my brother Hanani authority over Jerusalem. I also gave authority over the strongest building to Hananiah. He was a good man. He gave God more respect than many men. 3 I said to them, 'Do not open the city gates until the sun is high in the sky. Lock the gates while the gatekeepers are still there. Choose people who live in Jerusalem to watch for enemies. Some people must stand by the gates; other people must stand by their houses.'

4 Jerusalem city was large, but not many people lived in it. We had not yet built the houses completely.

5 God put an idea in my mind. All the people who returned to Jerusalem must write down their family names.

I found the family records of the first people to return to Jerusalem.

6 These families returned to Jerusalem and Judah after King Nebuchadnezzar took the Jews away in the exile. 7 They came with Zerubbabel, Jeshua, Nehemiah, Azariah, Raamiah, Nahamani, Mordecai, Bilshan, Mispereth, Bigvai, Nehum and Baanah. This is a list of the men of Israel:

8 from the descendants of Parosh, 2172;

9 of Shephatiah, 372;

10 of Arah, 652;

11 of Pahath-Moab (by Jeshua and Joab), 2818;

12 of Elam, 1254;

13 of Zattu, 845;

14 of Zaccai, 760;

15 of Binnui, 648;

16 of Bebai, 628;

17 of Azgad, 2322;

18 of Adonikam, 667;

19 of Bigvai, 2067;

20 of Adin, 655;

21 of Ater (by Hezekiah), 98;

22 of Hashum, 328;

23 of Bezai, 324;

24 of Hariph, 112;

25 of Gibeon, 95;

26 the men of Bethlehem and Netophah, 188;

27 of Anathoth, 128;

28 of Beth Azmaveth, 42;

29 of Kiriath Jearim, Kephirah and Beeroth, 743;

30 of Ramah and Geba, 621;

31 of Michmash, 122;

32 of Bethel and Ai, 123;

33 of the different Nebo, 52;

34 of the different Elam, 1254;

35 of Harim, 320;

36 of Jericho, 345;

37 of Lod, Hadid and Ono, 721;

38 of Senaah, 3930;

39 the priests who were descendants of Jedaiah (by Jeshua), 973;

40 of Immer, 1052;

41 of Pashhur, 1247;

42 of Harim, 1017.

43 the Levites who were descendants of Jeshua (by Kadmiel, by Hodaviah), 74.

44 the singers who were descendants of Asaph, 148.

45 the gatekeepers of the descendants of Shallum, Ater, Talmon, Akkub, Hatita and Shobai, 138.

46 the temple servants who were descendants of Ziha, Hasupha, Tabbaoth,

47 Keros, Sia, Padon,

48 Lebana, Hagaba, Shalmai,

49 Hanan, Giddel, Gahar,

50 Reaiah, Rezin, Nekoda,

51 Gazzam, Uzza, Paseah,

52 Besai, Meunim, Nephussim,

53 Bakbuk, Hakupha, Harhur,

54 Bazluth, Mehida, Harsha,

55 Barkos, Sisera, Temah,

56 Neziah and Hatipha.

57 the descendants of the servants of Solomon who were descendants of Sotai, Sophereth, Perida,

58 Jaala, Darkon, Giddel,

59 Shephatiah, Hattil, Pokereth-Hazzebaim and Amon.

60 The temple servants and descendants of the servants of Solomon were 392 men.

61 There were some people who came from the towns of Tel Melah, Tel Harsha, Kerub, Addon and Immer. But they did not have family records. They could not be sure that they were Jewish:

62 the descendants of Delaiah, Tobiah and Nekoda, 642.

63 Among the priests there were the descendants of Hobaiah, Hakkoz and Barzillai. (Barzillai was a man who married a daughter of Barzillai. He came from Gilead and he took that name.) 64 These people could not find family records. Because of this, they could not be priests. They were not clean. 65 The officer in Judah said that they could not eat the priests' special food. They had to wait for a priest to use the Urim and Thummim.

66 The number of all the people was 42 360. 67 There were also 7337 men servants and women servants and 245 men and women singers. 68 There were 736 horses and 245 mules, 69 435 camels and 6720 donkeys.

70 Some of the family leaders gave money to help build the wall. The man with authority in that place gave 8.5 kilos of gold, 50 bowls and 530 sets of special clothes for the priests. 71 Some family leaders gave 170 kilos of gold and 1.3 metric tons of silver. 72 The rest of the people gave 170 kilos of gold and 1.3 metric tons of silver. They also gave 67 sets of special clothes for the priests.

73 The priests, the Levites, the gatekeepers, the singers and the temple servants now lived in their towns. Other people and the rest of the Jewish people also lived in their own towns. All the people were living in their own towns when the 7th month came.

Chapter 8

Ezra reads the Law to the people

1 All the Jews met together in the wide place by the Water Gate. The people asked Ezra to bring the Book of the Law of Moses. The laws that God gave to Israel are in the Book of the Law. 2 On the first day of the 7th month, Ezra brought the Book of the Law to the people. All the men and women who were able to understand were there. 3 Ezra read aloud while he stood there. He read to all those people from morning to noon. Everyone watched him while he read. He read to them while he stood by the Water Gate. Everyone there listened carefully to Ezra while he read the Book of the Law. 4 Ezra stood up above the people on a high floor made out of wood. They made this so that they could see and hear him. Mattithiah, Shema, Anaiah, Uriah, Hilkiah and Maaseiah stood at his right side. Pedaiah, Mishael, Malkijah, Hashum, Hashbaddanah, Zechariah and Meshullam stood at his left side. 5 Ezra opened the book. All the people could see Ezra because he was high above them. When he opened the book, the crowd stood up. 6 Ezra praised God. All the people lifted their hands and they praised God. The people shouted, 'Amen! Amen!' They went on their knees and they worshipped God. 7 The Levites taught the people the law. The names of the Levites were: Jeshua, Bani, Sherebiah, Jamin, Akkub, Shabbethai, Hodiah, Maaseiah, Kelita, Azariah, Jozabad, Hanan and Pelaiah. 8 The Levites taught the Law to the people who stood there. They helped the people to understand what Ezra read to them.

9 Then Ezra, Nehemiah and the Levites said to the people, 'Do not be sad today. Do not cry. Today is holy to God.' They said this because the people were crying. The words of the Law had made them sad. 10 Nehemiah told the people to eat special food and to drink sweet drinks. Nehemiah also told the people to give food and drink to those who had none. He told the people that they should not be sad. They should not be sad because they were giving pleasure to God. This would make them strong. 11 The Levites said, 'Do not be sad. Today is a holy day.' 12 The people went away. They ate and they were very happy. They understood that that day was separate (holy) for God.

13 On the 2nd day of the 7th month, the family leaders met together. They met with the priests, Levites and with Ezra. They wanted to know God's laws. 14 They had heard the Book of the Law. And it said that Jews must live in huts made from tree branches. They must do this in the feast of the 7th month.

15 In the Book of the Law, it says that they must tell everyone in the country to go into the hills. They should bring back branches from olive trees, myrtle trees and from palm trees. They must use these to build their huts.

16 The people went to the hills and they picked branches. They made huts on their roofs and near their houses. They made them outside the temple and by the Water Gate. They made them by the Gate of Ephraim. 17 Everyone who had returned from exile built a hut. The Jews had not remembered a feast with such pleasure since the time of Joshua son of Nun. 18 Every day of the feast, Ezra read aloud from the Book of the Law. The feast went on for 7 days. On the 8th day, the Jews met together, as the law said.

Chapter 9

The people tell God that they are sorry about the bad things that they have done

1 On the 24th day of the same month, the Jews met together. They did not eat or drink. They wore sackcloth and they put dust on their heads.

2 The people from Jewish families had kept themselves separate from foreign people. The Jewish people stood up because they were sorry for their sins. They said that they and their ancestors had done many bad things. 3 The Jews read from the Book of the Law during a quarter of the day. During a quarter of the day they told God their sins and they worshipped him. 4 The Levites stood above the other people on steps made from wood. They cried aloud to God. The Levites were Jeshua, Bani, Kadmiel, Shebaniah, Bunni, Sherebiah, Bani and Kenani. 5 The Levites Jeshua, Kadmiel, Bani, Hashabneiah, Sherebiah, Hodiah, Shebaniah and Pethahiah said, 'Stand up and praise your God. He lives from the beginning for always and always.' They said, 'Your name is great and beautiful. It is above all praising and good words. 6 Only you are the Lord. You made the sky. You made even the highest sky and everything in it and the stars. You made the earth and everything on it. You made the sea and everything in it. You gave life to everything. All things in heaven worship you. 7 You are the Lord God who chose Abram. You brought him out of Ur, the country where the people called Chaldeans live. You called him Abraham. 8 Abraham was faithful. He believed you and he obeyed you. You made a promise to him. You promised to give to his descendants the country where the people called Canaanites, Hittites, Amorites, Perizzites, Jebusites and Girgashites lived. You have always kept your promises because you are good. You do only good things.

9 You saw that our ancestors were not happy in Egypt. You heard them cry aloud to you at the Red Sea. 10 You made great things happen against Pharaoh (the king of Egypt) and all his people and soldiers. You knew their thoughts. They thought that your people had no value. And they did bad things to your people. You showed everyone that you are a powerful God. And people believe this still. 11 You made a path in the sea between two walls. The Jews walked through on a dry path. When Pharaoh and his soldiers followed, you threw the sea over them. You closed the path through the sea. And so Pharaoh's soldiers drowned. 12 During the day, you led the Jews with a tall cloud. At night, you led them with a cloud of fire to give them light. You showed them the way to go.

13 You came to the mountain called Sinai. You spoke to Moses there. You gave him your laws and rules. Your laws are good and true. All that you told them was right. 14 You told the Jews about the Sabbath. And by your servant Moses you gave them your laws. 15 You gave the Jews bread from heaven when they were hungry. You gave them water from a rock to drink. You told them to go and take the land. You had promised to give it to them.

16 But our ancestors did not obey you. They thought that their way was better. 17 They did not listen to you. They forgot all the good things that you had done on their behalf. They chose a leader to take them back to Egypt. They chose to return to where they had been slaves. But you forgave them. You are God who loves his people very much. You do not become angry quickly. So you did not leave your people. 18 The Jewish people made a gold calf to worship. They said that this was a god. They said that the gold calf had brought them out of Egypt. But even then you did not leave your people. 19 You did not leave them in the desert, because you loved your people. In the day, the beam of cloud did not stop showing them the way. The beam of fire did not stop showing them the way at night.'

20 'You gave them your good Spirit to tell them what to do. You continued to give them bread from heaven. You gave them water from a rock to drink. 21 During 40 years you gave them everything that they needed. Their clothes did not become thin. Their feet did not get big and hurt. 22 You gave the Jews countries that other kings had ruled. You gave them the country Heshbon, of King Sihon and the country Bashan, of King Og. 23 The Jewish people had many sons. You brought their sons into the country. You had told their fathers to take it and to live there.

24 The sons of the Jewish people took the land. You gave them power over the Canaanites who lived there.

You gave the Canaanites' kings and people to the Jewish people's sons. They did with the Canaanites as they wanted to do. 25 They took their cities and land. The houses that they took were full of good things. Your people did not have to dig wells. The country was full of fruit and olive trees. They had plenty of food to eat. Everyone said how good God was.

26 But the Jews did not obey you. They stopped obeying your laws. They killed the prophets that you sent. Those prophets had told them that they should return to your ways. Your people had said very bad things about you. 27 So you gave the Jews to their enemies. Their enemies ruled over them. Then the Jews cried aloud to you. From heaven you heard them cry. You loved them very much. So you sent people to save them from their enemies.

28 But when they were safe from their enemies, they did bad things again. So you gave them back to their enemies. Their enemies ruled over them. Your people cried aloud to you again, and again you heard them. You saved them many, many times because you loved them. 29 You told them that they must obey your laws. But they would not listen to you. They thought that their ways were better than yours. They sinned against you. They would not obey your laws. But those laws help people to live. 30 You helped the Jews during many years. You sent your Spirit to them by your prophets. They told them that they should remember your laws. And they told them that they should return to you. But they would not listen to you. So you gave them to enemies from the countries round Israel. 31 You are a God who loves your people. And you are kind to them. So you did not let your people die nor did you leave them alone.

32 Oh God, you are great and powerful and you keep your promises. You continue to love us. Remember how many troubles we have had. They are not small troubles. Our kings, priests, prophets and our ancestors have all had great troubles. We have had trouble since the time of the kings of Assyria. 33 But in all our troubles, you have always been fair to us. When we did wrong things, you were always fair to us. 34 Our kings, leaders, priests and our fathers did not obey your laws. They did not listen to your rules. They would not do as your prophets told them to do. 35 You gave them good land and food. They enjoyed these, but they would not obey you. They did not stop doing things that were wrong. 36 So now we are slaves. We are slaves in the country that you gave to our ancestors. You wanted them to enjoy its food and good things. 37 But we have sinned. So their kings take the food that grows in our fields. You put these kings to rule over us. They use us and our animals as they like. We have many troubles.

38 Because of this we are all making a promise. We are writing our promise. Our leaders, Levites and priests are putting their mark of authority on it.'

Chapter 10

1 These people put their mark of authority on the promise that they had written:

Nehemiah son of Hacaliah (King Artaxerxes gave him authority in Judah) and Zedekiah, 2 Seraiah, Azariah, Jeremiah, 3 Pashhur, Amariah, Malkijah, 4 Hattush, Shebaniah, Malluch, 5 Harim, Meremoth, Obadiah, 6 Daniel, Ginnethon, Baruch, 7 Meshullam, Abijah, Mijamin, 8 Maaziah, Bilgai and Shemaiah. These were the priests.

9 The Levites: Jeshua son of Azaniah, Binnui of the sons of Henadad, Kadmiel, 10 and their friends: Shebaniah, Hodiah, Kelita, Pelaiah, Hanan, 11 Mica, Rehob, Hashabiah, 12 Zaccur, Sherebiah, Shebaniah, 13 Hodiah, Bani and Beninu.

14 The leaders of the people: Parosh, Pahath-Moab, Elam, Zattu, Bani, 15 Bunni, Azgad, Bebai, 16 Adonijah, Bigvai, Adin, 17 Ater, Hezekiah, Azzur, 18 Hodiah, Hashum, Bezai, 19 Hariph, Anathoth, Nebai, 20 Magpiash, Meshullam, Hezir, 21 Meshezabel, Zadok, Jaddua, 22 Pelatiah, Hanan, Anaiah,

23 Hoshea, Hananiah, Hasshub, 24 Hallohesh, Pilha, Shobek, 25 Rehum, Hashabnah, Maaseiah, 26 Ahiah, Hanan, Anan, 27 Malluch, Harim and Baanah.

28 The other people, the priests, Levites, gatekeepers, singers and temple servants made a promise. The people who had kept themselves separate from foreign people because of God's law also made a promise.

They and their wives, sons and daughters agreed to join their leaders. 29 All these people promised to obey everything that was in the Law. That was the Law that God gave to his servant Moses. They asked God to do bad things to them if they did not obey his Laws and rules. They agreed to obey these rules carefully.

30 They said, 'We promise not to let our daughters marry foreign people. We will not let daughters of foreign people marry our sons. 31 We will not buy or sell anything on the Sabbath or any special day. If foreign merchants come to us on a Sabbath, we will not buy their things. Every 7th year we will not work on the land. Every 7th year we will tell people that they do not need to pay their debts. And we will return their land.

32 We will obey the law to give 1/3rd of a shekel each year to the house of God. 33 We will use this for God's special loaves of bread, for grain offerings and for burnt offerings. We will use this for the offerings on the Sabbath, new moon parties and feasts. And we will use it for the sin offerings to take away Israel's sin. And we will use it for all the work in God's house.'

34 The priests and the Levites threw lots. In that way, they told families when they should bring wood for fires. Each family must bring wood to the house of God at a different time of the year. The wood will burn on God's altar. This is what Moses wrote in the Book of the Law. 35 They said, 'We will also bring the first fruit from our trees and the first of our grain. We will bring these to the priests who work in God's house. 36 We will bring our first son to the house of God. We will bring to God's house the first of our young animals that are born. We will bring them to the priests. We read this in God's Law. 37 We will bring the first dough, fruit, wine and oil and other special offerings to the house of God. The priests will store them in its rooms. We will bring our tithes to the Levites. They will take them from our towns to God's house. They will store them there. 38 A priest from the family of Aaron will go with the Levites to get the tithes. The Levites will bring 1/10th part of the tithes to store in God's house. 39 The people of Israel will bring grain, wine and oil to the temple rooms. They will store them with the things that they use for worship. The priests who are working there, the gatekeepers and the singers stay there. We will keep the house of God ready to worship him.'

Chapter 11

1 The leaders of the Jews lived in Jerusalem. The other people threw lots. In that way, they chose where families would live there. From every group of 10 families they chose one family. Then that family would live in Jerusalem, the holy city. The other families could stay in their own towns. 2 The people said that this was good. The families in Jerusalem gave them pleasure.

3 These are the leaders from other towns that came to live in Jerusalem. Some Jews, priests, Levites, and temple servants lived in Judah's towns. Descendants of Solomon's servants also lived in towns in Judah. Each lived in his own house. 4 Other people from Judah and Benjamin lived in Jerusalem. From the descendants of Judah: Athaiah son of Uzziah, Zechariah's son. Zechariah was the son of Amariah, Shephatiah's son. He was the son of Mahalalel, a descendant of Perez. 5 Also Maaseiah son of Baruch, Col-Hozeh's son. Col-Hozeh was the son of Hazaiah, Adaiah's son. Adaiah was the son of Joiarib, son of Zechariah. He was a descendant of Shelah. 6 The descendants of Perez were 468 brave men. They all lived in Jerusalem.

7 From the descendants of Benjamin: Sallu son of Meshullam, Joed's son. Joed was Pedaiah's son, son of Kolaiah, Maaseiah's son. Maaseiah was the son of Ithiel, Jeshaiah's son. 8 Gabbai and Sallai, the people who followed Sallu, were also with him. There were 928 men. 9 Joel son of Zicri was their officer with authority. Judah son of Hassenuah had authority after him.

10 From the priests: Jedaiah son of Joiarib, and Jakin. 11 Also Seraiah son of Hilkiah, son of Meshullam, Zadok's son. Zadok was Meraioth's son, son of Ahitub. Ahitub had authority in the house of God. 12 Their friends worked with them in God's house. There were 822 men; and Adaiah son of Jeroham, Pelaliah's son. Pelaliah was the son of Amzi. Amzi was the son of Zechariah, son of Pashhur, Malkijah's son. 13 They and those with them were leaders of families. There were 242 men; and Amashsai son of Azarel, Ahzai's son. Ahzai was the son of Meshillemoth, son of Immer. 14 And their friends came with them. They were 128 strong brave men. Their officer with authority was Zabdiel, son of Haggedolim.

15 From the Levites: Shemaiah son of Hasshub, son of Azrikam. Azrikam was the son of Hashabiah, Bunni's son.

16 Also Shabbethai and Jozabad who had authority over the outside work of God's house. 17 Also Mattaniah son of Mica, son of Zabdi, Asaph's son. He led the people when they prayed and thanked God. Also Bakbukiah and Abda son of Shammua. He was the son of Galal, Jeduthun's son. 18 The number of Levites in Jerusalem city was 284.

19 The gatekeepers were: Akkub, Talmon and their friends, who watched at the city gates. The number of men was 172. 20 The other Jews and the priests and Levites were in the towns of Judah. They lived at the homes of their ancestors. 21 The temple servants lived on the hill of Ophel. Ziha and Gishpa had authority over them.

22 Uzzi was the Levites' leader. He was the son of Bani, Hashabiah's son and Hashabiah was the son of Mattaniah, Mica's son. Uzzi was one of Asaph's descendants. He had authority over the singers in God's house. 23 The singers had to obey the king. He told them each day what they should do. 24 Pethahiah son of Meshezabel, a descendant of Zerah, Judah's son, spoke for the king. He told the people everything that the king wanted.

25 Many people lived in villages with fields. Some people of Judah lived in Kiriath Arba, Dibon and Jekabzeel and the land round them. 26 Other people lived in Jeshua, Moladah and Beth Pelet. 27 More people lived in Hazar Shual, and in Beersheba and the villages round it. 28 Some people lived in Ziklag, Meconah and 29 En Rimmon. Other people were in Zorah and Jarmuth. 30 Other people lived in Zanoah and Adullam and their villages. Some people were in Lachish and its fields and in Azekah and its villages. They were living from Beersheba to the Hinnom Valley.

31 The descendants of Benjamin from Geba lived in Michmash, Aija, Bethel and its villages. 32 And they lived in Anathoth, Nob and Ananiah. 33 Also they lived in Hazor, Ramah and Gittaim. 34 And they lived in Hadid, Zeboim and Neballat. 35 Also they lived in Lod and Ono and in the Valley of the clever workers. 36 Some of the Levites from Judah lived in Benjamin's land.

Chapter 12

1 This is a list of the priests and Levites who returned with Zerubbabel son of Shealtiel and with Jeshua:

Seraiah, Jeremiah, Ezra, 2 Amariah, Malluch, Hattush, 3 Shecaniah, Rehum, Meremoth, 4 Iddo, Ginnethon, Abijah, 5 Mijamin, Moadiah, Bilgah, 6 Shemaiah, Joiarib, Jedaiah, 7 Sallu, Amok, Hilkiah and Jedaiah. These were the leaders of the priests and the people who helped them in the time of Jeshua. 8 The Levites were: Jeshua, Binnui, Kadmiel, Sherebiah, Judah and Mattaniah. Mattaniah and the people led the songs that thanked God. And other people helped him. 9 Bakbukiah and Unni and other people stood across from them when they sang. And other people helped them. 10 Jeshua was the father of Joiakim. Joiakim was the father of Eliashib. Eliashib was the father of Joiada, 11 Joiada was the father of Jonathan, and Jonathan was the father of Jaddua.

12 This is a list of the priests' family leaders in the time of Joiakim: Meraiah was leader of the family of Seraiah. Hananiah was leader of the family of Jeremiah.

13 Meshullam was leader of the family of Ezra. Jehohanan was leader of the family of Amariah.

14 Jonathan was leader of the family of Malluch. Joseph was leader of the family of Shecaniah.

15 Adna was leader of the family of Harim. Helkai was leader of the family of Meremoth.

16 Zechariah was leader of the family of Iddo. Meshullam was leader of the family of Ginnethon.

17 Zicri was leader of the family of Abijah. Piltai was leader of the families of Miniamin and Moadiah.

18 Shammua was leader of the family of Bilgah. Jehonathan was leader of the family of Shemaiah.

19 Mattenai was leader of the family of Joiarib. Uzzi was leader of the family of Jedaiah.

20 Kallai was leader of the family of Sallu. Eber was leader of the family of Amok.

21 Hashabiah was leader of the family of Hilkiah. Nethanel was leader of the family of Jedaiah.

22 They recorded the names of the leaders of the Levites' families. That was in the time of Eliashib, Joiada, Johanan and Jaddua. They lived when King Darius ruled Persia. I also recorded the names of the family leaders of the priests. 23 I wrote the names of the family leaders who were descendants of Levi, the Levites, in the special book. It was the book where we recorded names. These were their descendants to the time of Johanan son of Eliashib. 24 The leaders of the Levites were: Hashabiah, Sherebiah, Jeshua son of Kadmiel, and the people who helped them. The people who helped them stood across from them to sing and praise and thank God. The Levites sang first. And then the people who helped them replied. They did this as David, God's man, had told the Jews. 25 Mattaniah, Bakbukiah, Obadiah, Meshullam, Talmon and Akkub were gatekeepers. They watched for enemies from the store-rooms by the gates. 26 They were gatekeepers in the time of Joiakim son of Jeshua, son of Jozadak. This was also in the time of Nehemiah, who had authority over Judah. And it was in the time of Ezra, who was a priest and teacher of the law.

27 The Jews brought the Levites to Jerusalem from their homes. The Levites were happy that they could help to dedicate the wall to God. They made music with cymbals, harps and lyres. They sang songs to thank God.

28 The temple singers came together from places round Jerusalem. They came from the villages round Netophah 29 and from Beth Gilgal, Geba and Azmaveth. The singers had built these villages near to Jerusalem. 30 The priests and Levites purified themselves. Then they purified the people. Then they purified the gates and the city wall.

31 I told the leaders of Judah that they should stand on top of the wall. I told two large groups of singers that they should sing songs. They would thank God. I told the first group that they should walk in the direction of the Dung Gate.

32 Hoshaiah and half of the leaders of Judah followed this group. 33 Azariah, Ezra and Meshullam followed. 34 Judah, Benjamin, Shemaiah and Jeremiah followed them also. 35 Some priests with trumpets followed them also. And Zechariah son of Jonathan, Shemaiah's son followed them. Shemaiah was the son of Mattaniah, Micaiah's son. Micaiah was the son of Zaccur, Asaph's son. 36 Other people helped them: Shemaiah, Azarel, Milalai, Gilalai, Maai, Nethanel, Judah and Hanani. They all had things to make music. They did this as David, God's man, had told the Jews. Ezra the teacher of the law led this group of people. They walked towards the Dung Gate. 37 When they came to the Fountain Gate they all went up the steps of the City of David. While they went up the steps, they passed above the house of David. Then they went to the Water Gate on the east.

38 The second group of singers went the opposite way. I followed them along the top of the wall with half of the people. We went past the Tower of the Ovens. We went to the Broad Wall. 39 We went over the Gate of Ephraim. We went over the Jeshanah Gate. We went over the Fish Gate. We went past the Tower of Hananel. We went past the Tower of the Hundred to the Sheep Gate. We stopped at the Gate of the Guards.

40 The two groups of singers went into God's house. I (Nehemiah) went with them. Half of the officers also went into the house of God. 41 The priests Eliakim, Maaseiah, Miniamin, Micaiah, Elioenai, Zechariah and Hananiah went in also. They had trumpets. 42 Also Maaseiah, Shemaiah, Eleazar, Uzzi, Jehohanan, Malkijah, Elam and Ezer went into the house of God. Jezrahiah told the groups of singers how to sing. 43 The Jews gave big sacrifices to God. Men, women and children were very happy. They sang and shouted. People heard them far away from Jerusalem.

44 The people chose men to look after the rooms where they kept the first fruits and tithes. They had to bring the tithes and the first fruits from the fields near the town. They read this in the law. These were for the Levites and priests. The work of the priests and Levites gave pleasure to the people of Judah.

45 The priests and Levites worked on God's behalf. The singers and gatekeepers also worked on God's behalf. They made themselves clean as David and his son Solomon had written. 46 In the time of David and Asaph, special Levites sang the songs to praise and thank God. 47 In the time of Zerubbabel and Nehemiah, all the Jews gave food for the singers and gatekeepers every day. They put on one side what was for the Levites. And the Levites put on one side what was for the priests, the descendants of Aaron.

Chapter 13

1 On that day, we read the book of Moses to the people. The people listened to what Moses had written in the book. One of the laws said that no descendant of Ammon or Moab should be among the people of God. 2 This was because they had not given the Jews food and water. But they had paid Balaam to ask God to do bad things to the Jews. But God did good things for the Jews instead. 3 When the Jews heard this law, they made all the foreign people leave.

4 Before this happened, I had given to Eliashib the priest authority over the store-rooms. They used these rooms to keep the offerings. These rooms were in the house of God. Eliashib was a friend of Tobiah. 5 He let Tobiah use a large room in the house of God. The purpose of the room was to store the temple's grain offerings and incense. They also kept there tithes of grain, wine and oil. These were for the Levites, singers and gatekeepers and for the priests.

6 But when this happened, I (Nehemiah) was not in Jerusalem. In the 32nd year of Artaxerxes, King of Babylon, I had returned to the king. After some time had passed, I asked the king 7 to let me return to Jerusalem. There I heard about the bad thing that Eliashib had done. He had given Tobiah, who was not a Jew, a large room in the house of God. 8 I was very angry. I threw Tobiah's things out of the room. 9 I told people that they must purify the rooms. Then I put God's things back into the room. I put back the things that they used in God's house and the grain offerings and incense.

10 People told me that the Levites did not have any food. The people had not given them anything. So all the Levites and singers had returned to their fields. They were not doing their work in the Lord's temple. 11 I was angry with the officers. I said, 'I am angry because you have forgotten the house of God.' Then I called them all back. I told them that they should stand in their special places in the temple.

12 All the people in Judah brought tithes of grain and wine and oil. They put them into the store-rooms. 13 I gave Shelemiah the priest, Zadok the writer and Pedaiah a Levite, authority. They watched over the things that they kept in these special rooms. Hanan son of Zaccur, Mattaniah's son, helped them. People knew that these men were good. They gave out the grain, oil and wine. They gave it to the people who worked on God's behalf. 14 'Remember what I have done, my God. Do not forget what I have done on behalf of the house of God and its work. I have been faithful.'

15 In those days, I saw men in Judah working on the Sabbath day. They were making wine and they were putting wine, grapes and other fruit on their donkeys. And they brought them into Jerusalem. I told them that they should not work on the Sabbath day. And I told them that they should not sell things on the Sabbath day.

16 Men from Tyre, who lived in Jerusalem, sold fish and other things on the Sabbath day. The Jews then bought things from them. 17 I was angry with the leaders of Judah. I said, 'You are doing a thing that is wrong. It is the Sabbath day. 18 Your ancestors did the same thing. God brought trouble on Jerusalem city because of this. You are making God angry with the Jews by doing wrong things on the Sabbath day.'

19 I said to the gatekeepers, 'You must close the city's gates in the evening before the Sabbath begins.' I did not let them open until the Sabbath was finished. I told my men that they should stand at the gates. They did not let anyone bring things into Jerusalem until after the end of the Sabbath. 20 Once or twice some people who wanted to sell things stayed outside Jerusalem all night. 21 I said to them, 'You should not stay outside the wall all night. If you do this again, I will hurt you.' After this, they did not come to Jerusalem on the Sabbath. 22 Then I told the Levites that they must purify themselves. I told them that they must stand at the gates. This went on during the whole of the Sabbath day. They kept the day holy on God's behalf. 'Remember this, oh my God. Because of your love, be kind to me.'

23 Also at that time, men from Judah had married foreign women from Ashdod, Ammon and Moab. 24 Half of their children spoke the language of Ashdod or the language of another country. They did not know how to speak the language of Judah. 25 I was angry and I said angry words to them. I hit some of them. I pulled out the hair of some of these men. I made them make a promise in God's name. I said, 'You must not let your daughters marry the sons of foreign people. You must not let your sons marry the daughters of foreign people.

26 Solomon, king of Israel sinned against God because he married foreign women. There was no greater king in any other country. God loved him and made him king over all Israel. But foreign women made even Solomon sin.

27 Now we hear that you are doing this bad thing. You are marrying foreign women. You are not faithful to God.'

28 Joiada was the son of Eliashib, the leader of the priests. One of Joiada's sons married a daughter of Sanballat, who came from Horonaim. I sent him away.

29 'Remember them, my God. They were priests, but they sinned. They did not do what you told them to do. They took away people's respect for the priest's work.' 30 So I purified the priests and Levites. I made them clean from anything foreign. I told them what they should do. I gave to each man a special job. 31 I also made sure that people brought wood for the altar. I made them bring their first fruits. 'Remember me, my God. And please be good to me.'

God saves the Jews

Esther

About the Book of Esther

> The Book of Esther is a book in the Old Testament. The writer wrote it in the Hebrew language. The Book of Esther belongs to the third part of the Hebrew Scriptures (Old Testament). The three parts are called the Law, the Prophets and the Writings.
>
> The books that are in the Writings are Song of Songs, Ruth, Lamentations, Ecclesiastes and Esther. The Jews read from one of these books during each of the important Jewish Feasts. The Jews read Esther aloud during the Feast of Purim.
>
> The writer wrote the book after the king of Babylon had sent the Jews away from their own country. He sent them to Babylon. That happened in the year 600 BC. (BC means the years before Jesus was born.) The book tells us what happened in the time of King Xerxes I, the king of Persia (country near Babylon). He ruled from 485-465 BC.

Chapter 1

1 This happened when King Xerxes ruled over 127 parts of the kingdom of Persia. He ruled from India to Cush. 2 King Xerxes lived in the capital, the city called Susa. 3 When King Xerxes had ruled for more than 2 years, he gave a big feast. The feast was for all the important men who had authority in the kingdom.

4 The feast was for 180 days. King Xerxes wanted to show everyone how rich and powerful he was. 5 When this feast finished, he gave another feast. This happened in the palace gardens. It was for 7 days. This feast was for everyone who lived in the city called Susa. It was for people who were important. And it was for people who were not important. 6 The gardens had blue and white curtains. People had made the curtains out of linen. Other curtains were hanging from columns. The colour of those curtains is called purple. There were beds that people had made out of gold and silver. And the floor had many valuable stones in it.

7 People drank from gold cups. Each cup was different. The king let everyone have his own wine. 8 Each man had as much wine to drink as he wanted. But no man had to drink any wine if he did not want to. That is what the king had said to all his officers.

9 Queen Vashti was the king's wife. She gave a feast for all the women in the palace.

10 On the 7th day, King Xerxes was feeling happy. He told his eunuchs that they must come to him. Their names were Mehuman, Biztha, Harbona, Bigtha, Abagtha, Zethar and Carcas. 11 He told them that they must bring Queen Vashti to him. He said that she must wear her royal crown. King Xerxes wanted to show everyone how beautiful his queen was. 12 The eunuchs told Queen Vashti what the king had said. But she would not go to him. This made King Xerxes very angry.

13 The king had men who knew the law. He always asked them what to do when someone did not obey him. 14 He trusted these men. Their names were Carshena, Shethar, Admatha, Tarshish, Meres, Marsena and Memucan. These men always sat next to the king. They had a lot of authority in the kingdom.

15 The king asked them, 'What must I do with Queen Vashti? The eunuchs told her what I said. But she did not obey me. What is the law about this?'

16 In front of the king and all the important men, Memucan (one of the men) replied, 'The queen has not only done something wrong to you. She has done something wrong to all the important men in your kingdom. 17 When other wives hear about this, they will not obey their own husbands. All the women in the kingdom will say, "King Xerxes said that Queen Vashti should come to him. But she would not come." 18 So now, the wives of the king's officers will not obey their husbands. This will make their husbands angry.

19 If it makes the king happy, we suggest this: The king should make a law. Someone should write this law with the other laws of Media and Persia so that nobody can change it. This law should say that Vashti must not stand in front of you again. Then find a better woman to be queen. 20 When people know the law, all women will obey their husbands. They will obey them if they are rich or poor.'

21 The king and his officers liked this idea. And so they did as Memucan said. 22 Men on horses took the law to all the parts of the kingdom. The king said that people must write the law in many languages. They must write it in the languages of all who lived in the kingdom. The law said that every man must rule over his children and his wife.

Chapter 2

1 Sometime after that happened, King Xerxes was not feeling so angry. He thought about Vashti. And he thought about the law that he had made.

2 Some of the king's servants said, 'We think that the king should ask his servants to look for beautiful young women for him. 3 The king could choose officers from every part of his kingdom to do this. They will take the women to the harem at Susa. Hegai, the king's eunuch, will help them and he will keep them safe. The young women will receive beauty treatments. 4 The young woman who makes the king happy will be queen. She will be queen as Vashti was.' King Xerxes agreed with the servants. And he did everything that the servants said.

5 In the city called Susa there was a Jew called Mordecai. Mordecai was the son of Jair. Jair was the son of Shimei. Shimei was the son of Kish. Kish was in Benjamin's family.

6 Nebuchadnezzar, the king of Babylon, had sent Kish (with other Jews) to live away from Jerusalem. That was when Nebuchadnezzar took King Jeconiah of Judah away from Jerusalem. 7 Mordecai had a young cousin called Hadassah. (She was also called Esther.) She lived in his house. Esther's mother and father were dead. Esther was beautiful. Mordecai called Esther his daughter.

8 Esther was with the young women that the officers brought to the city called Susa. The servants brought them to the palace. Hegai had authority over all the young women. 9 Hegai liked Esther. He gave her beauty treatments and special food. He gave her 7 female servants from the king's palace. And he moved Esther and her servants to the best part of the harem.

10 Mordecai said to Esther, 'Do not tell anyone that you are a Jew.' So Esther did not tell anyone. 11 Mordecai wanted to know what was happening to Esther. So he walked by the harem many times each day.

12 Before a young woman went to be with the king she had to have beauty treatments. These went on for 12 months.

13 Then she went to be with the king. And she could take whatever she wanted with her then.

14 She would go to be with the king in the evening. She would stay with him during that night. In the morning, she went to the harem where the king's other wives lived. Shaashgaz, a eunuch, kept the women there safe. The young woman would only see the king again if he liked her. If he did like her, he would ask for her by name.

15 One evening, it was Esther's time to go to the king. And she asked for the things that Hegai had suggested. Everyone who saw Esther liked her. 16 Esther went to King Xerxes in the 10th month. That is the month Tebeth. King Xerxes had ruled for nearly 7 years.

17 The king loved Esther more than he loved any of the other women. He was nice to her because he liked her. He put the crown on her head and he made her queen. So, Esther became queen, as Vashti had been queen. 18 The king gave a great feast called Esther's Feast. All his officers and other important men came to the feast. He gave everyone in the kingdom a day to rest. And he gave many gifts to people.

Mordecai saves the king

19 The officers brought the young women together again. At this time, Mordecai sat at the King's Gate.

20 Esther had not told the king that she was a Jew. Mordecai had told her that she should not tell him. She had obeyed Mordecai when she lived with him as his daughter. And now she still obeyed him like that.

21 Mordecai was sitting at the King's Gate. At that time, Bigthana and Teresh, who were two of the king's officers, became angry. And they wanted to kill the king. 22 Mordecai heard about this. So he told Queen Esther that the officers wanted to kill the king. Queen Esther told the king. She said that Mordecai had discovered this. 23 The king discovered that this was true. He told men that they must kill these officers. They must hang them from gallows until they were dead. The king watched while his servant wrote these things in the Book of Years.

Chapter 3

Haman becomes angry with Mordecai

1 Sometime after that happened, King Xerxes gave a certain officer a lot of authority. The officer was called Haman. Only King Xerxes had more authority in the kingdom than Haman. Haman's father was in Agag's family. 2 The king said that everyone must bend his body down to Haman to show respect. But Mordecai would not bend his body down to Haman.

3 The officers at the King's Gate said to Mordecai, 'You are not obeying the king's law and you should obey it.' 4 They said this to Mordecai every day. But he would not bend his body down to Haman. So the officers told Haman that Mordecai would not bend his body down to him. Mordecai had told them that he was a Jew. So they wanted to know if Haman would excuse Mordecai.

5 Haman saw that Mordecai would not bend his body down. So, he was very angry. 6 Haman discovered that Mordecai was a Jew. Haman did not want to hurt only Mordecai. He decided to kill all the Jews in the kingdom of Xerxes.

Haman has an idea about how to kill all the Jews

7 His men who knew the law threw a pur. The pur chose the 12th month. This was the month called Adar. They would kill all the Jews on this day. 8 So Haman said to King Xerxes, 'There are some people who are living in your kingdom. And they are different from all the other people who live in your kingdom. They do not obey the king's laws. But they live among all your other people. It is not good for you to let them live in your kingdom. 9 If it makes the king happy, the king should make a law to kill all these people. I will pay 10 000 talents of silver into the king's bank. This is for the men who obey your law.'

10 The king took his signet ring from his finger and he gave it to Haman. Haman was the man who really did not like the Jews.

11 He said to Haman, 'Keep your money. You can do anything that you want with these people.'

12 Haman asked the king's writers to come to him. This was on the 13th day of the 1st month. The writers wrote the law in the language of all the people who lived in the kingdom of Xerxes. Haman used the king's signet ring to show that the law had the king's authority.

13 Men delivered the law to the people in all of the kingdom. The law said that on the 13th day of the 12th month people should kill all the Jews. They should kill old people and young people, women and children. All Jews would die. Haman told the people that they could take all the Jews' things. 14 Haman caused people to make copies of the law. They made copies in every language that people in the kingdom spoke. Everybody should be ready for that day.

15 King Xerxes told his officers that they must send the law quickly to all of the kingdom. Then Haman and the king sat down and they began to feast together. While they feasted, everyone in the city (Susa) was afraid.

Chapter 4

Mordecai asks Queen Esther to help the Jews

1 Mordecai discovered what had happened. Then he tore his clothes and he dressed in sackcloth and ashes. He went into the city. He was crying aloud.

2 He stopped at the King's Gate. Nobody who had dressed in sackcloth and ashes could come into the palace. 3 All through the kingdom of Xerxes, Jews were crying aloud and they were fasting. Many of the Jews lay on sackcloth and ashes.

4 Esther's female servants and eunuchs told her what Mordecai was doing. So Esther had troubles in her mind. She sent clothes for Mordecai to put on. But Mordecai refused to wear them. 5 Hathach was one of the king's eunuchs. Esther asked Hathach to discover what was the matter with Mordecai.

6 Hathach went to Mordecai. Mordecai was near the King's Gate. He was waiting outside. 7 Mordecai told Hathach what happened with Haman. King Xerxes had said that people must kill all the Jews. Mordecai told Hathach about that too. And he told Hathach about the 10 000 talents of silver that Haman had promised to pay into the king's bank.

8 Mordecai gave Hathach a copy of the king's law to give to Esther. He spoke to Hathach. He asked him to tell Esther that she must go to the king. She should ask the king to let her people live.

9 Hathach returned to the harem. And he told Esther what Mordecai had said. 10 Esther sent Hathach to tell Mordecai, 11 'A person can only see the king if the king asks for him or her by name. Everyone knows that. There is only one law for anyone who goes to the king. If the king has not asked to see him, that person must die. Only if the king holds out his gold sceptre will the person live. The king has not asked me to go to him for 30 days.'

12 Then Hathach told Mordecai what Esther had said. 13 Mordecai sent back this answer. 'Do not think that you, in the king's palace, will be safer than all the other Jews. 14 If you do not speak on behalf of the Jews at this time, help will come from another place. But you and your family will die. But perhaps you are queen for a time like this.'

15 Esther sent this answer to Mordecai, 16 'Tell all the Jews in Susa that they should fast on behalf of me. They must not eat or drink for three days. They must not eat or drink in the day or night for this time. My female servants and I will also fast. After three days, I will go to the king even when it is against his law. He has not asked for me. So he may tell his officers that they must kill me. If I die, I die.'

17 Mordecai did as Esther had asked him.

Chapter 5

Esther goes to the king

1 After three days, Esther put on her special clothes and she went to King Xerxes. The king was sitting on his special king's seat. Esther stood in the room that was in front of his special seat. 2 When the king saw Esther, he was happy. He held out his gold sceptre. Esther touched the top of the sceptre.

3 The king asked, 'What do you want, Queen Esther? I will give to you whatever you want. Even if it is half my kingdom, I will give it to you.' 4 Esther replied, 'If it makes the king happy, I would like this: I would like the king and Haman to come to a feast that I have prepared.'

5 The king said to his servants, 'Bring Haman quickly. Then we can do what Esther wants.' The king and Haman went to the meal that Esther had prepared.

6 When they were drinking wine, the king asked Esther, 'What do you want? I will give you whatever you want. Even if it is half my kingdom, I will give it to you.' 7 She replied, 'This is what I want. 8 I hope that the king is happy with me. And perhaps the king wants to give me what I want. And this is what I want: I would like the king and Haman to come again tomorrow. Come to a feast that I will prepare for you. Then I will tell the king what I want.'

Mordecai makes Haman angry again

9 When Haman went from Queen Esther's feast he was happy. Mordecai was sitting at the King's Gate. But when Haman passed him, he did not get up. And he did not bend his body down to Haman. Then Haman became very angry with Mordecai. 10 Haman did not say anything to Mordecai. He went home. Then he asked his friends and Zeresh his wife to come to him.

11 Haman told them how rich he was. He told his friends how many sons he had. And he told them how powerful he was. He told his friends and his wife that he was more powerful than any other man in the palace. 12 Haman told his friends and his wife about the feast that Queen Esther prepared for him. He said, 'I was the only other person that the queen asked to come to the meal. The queen has asked me to another feast tomorrow with the king. 13 But all these things do not make me happy when I see the Jew Mordecai. He is sitting at the King's Gate.'

14 Haman's wife and his friends said to him, 'Ask some men to build a gallows so high that everybody can see it. In the morning, ask the king to cause his men to kill Mordecai on the gallows. Then go to Queen Esther's feast and be happy.'

What they had suggested made Haman happy. So he told his servants that they must build the gallows.

Chapter 6

The king remembers Mordecai

1 That night the king could not sleep. He asked a servant to bring the Book of Years. And he asked the servant to read the book to him.

2 The Book of Years included the report of how two officers wanted to kill the king. And how Mordecai had discovered this and he had told Queen Esther. The servant read this report to the king. 3 The king asked his servant, 'When Mordecai saved me, what did I do for him?' The servant told the king that Mordecai did not receive anything.

4 The king said, 'Who is in the palace?' And Haman had just come into the palace. He wanted to ask the king for his officers to kill Mordecai on the gallows. 5 The servants told the king that Haman was in the palace. The king said that Haman should come to him.

6 Haman came to the king. The king asked him, 'What should I do for a man that I want to make very important?' Haman thought to himself, 'I am sure that I am that man. I am sure that the king wants to make me very important.'

7 So Haman replied to the king. 'You should do this for the man that you want to make very important:

8 Your servants should bring the clothes that the king wears. They should bring the king's horse. It should have a royal crown on its head. So, everyone will know that it is the king's horse. 9 Tell your servants that they must give the clothes and the horse to one of your officers. It should be the officer that you trust most. Ask the officer to put the king's clothes on the man that you want to make very important. Tell the officer that he must help the man on to the king's horse. The officer must then lead the man from the beginning to the end of the city. The officer must shout, "This is the man that the king wants to make very important. See what the king does for a man like that!" '

10 The king said, 'Go quickly! Get the clothes and the horse. Do as you have suggested for Mordecai the Jew. He is sitting at the King's Gate. Be sure to do everything that you suggested.' 11 So Haman dressed Mordecai in the king's clothes. And he led Mordecai on the king's horse from the beginning to the end of the city. Haman shouted, 'This is the man that the king wants to make very important. See what the king does for a man like that!'

12 After this, Mordecai returned to the King's Gate. But Haman hurried home. He covered his face because he was ashamed and angry. He was ashamed and angry about what had happened. 13 He told his wife and friends everything that had happened to him. Then his wife, Zeresh, and his friends who knew the law said, 'You have already lost some of your power to Mordecai. If he is a Jew, you cannot fight against him. You cannot win against him.'

14 While they were speaking, the king's eunuchs arrived. They took Haman in a hurry to Queen Esther's feast.

Chapter 7

Haman goes to Queen Esther's feast

1 King Xerxes and Haman went to the feast that Queen Esther had prepared. 2 While they were drinking wine at this second feast, King Xerxes asked his question again. 'Queen Esther', he asked, 'what do you want? Even if you want half the kingdom, I will give it to you.'

3 Queen Esther replied, 'I hope that you are happy with me. And perhaps you want to give me what I ask. If you do, please let me live. And let my people live. That is what I want. 4 Someone has sold me and my people so that we will die. If he had sold us as male and female slaves, I would not have caused trouble for the king.' 5 Then King Xerxes asked Queen Esther, 'Who is he? Where is the man who would do this?' 6Esther replied, 'The man who wants to kill us is this very bad man Haman!' Then Haman was very afraid.

7 The king was very angry. He left his wine and he went into the palace garden. Haman knew that the king would kill him. So, he stayed with Queen Esther to ask her to save him. 8 Just when the king returned, Haman threw himself down. He threw himself down on the bed that Queen Esther was lying on. He asked her to save him. The king shouted, 'You even attack the queen when she is with me in the palace!' When the king said this, servants covered Haman's face with a piece of cloth.

9 Harbona, one of the king's eunuchs said, 'There is a gallows outside Haman's home. Haman's men built it. He wanted to kill Mordecai on the gallows. Two officers wanted to kill the king. Mordecai is the man who told the king about it.' The king said, 'Hang Haman on the gallows until he is dead.' 10 So a servant hung Haman on the gallows until he was dead. It was the gallows that Haman's servants had built for Mordecai. Then the king did not feel so angry.

Chapter 8

The king makes another law

1 That day, King Xerxes gave Queen Esther all of Haman's things. Mordecai came in front of the king. Esther had told the king that Mordecai was her cousin. 2 The king had taken back his signet ring from Haman. He gave the signet ring to Mordecai. Esther gave Mordecai authority over all the things that the king gave to her.

3 Then Esther went to the king. She cried aloud and she threw herself down at his feet. She asked him to stop Haman's very bad idea to kill all the Jews. 4 The king held out his gold sceptre to Esther. Then she stood up in front of the king.

5 Esther said to the king, 'I hope that I make the king happy. And perhaps the king thinks that this is the right thing to do:

If he does, the king should do this. Tell your people that they must not kill all the Jewson the 13th day of the 12th month. 6 If they do kill them, I will have to see the death of all my people.'

7 King Xerxes replied to Queen Esther and to Mordecai, 'Because Haman wanted to kill the Jews, I have given all of his things to Esther. And my officers have killed Haman on the gallows. 8 Write another law with the king's authority. Write a law to help the Jews. My signet ring shows that the law has the king's authority. There can be no change to a law that has the king's authority.'

9 On the 23rd day of the 3rd month (the month Sivan), Mordecai asked certain men to come to him. They were the men who recorded the law. Mordecai the Jew told them what to write. Men who were riding on horses took the law to all the kingdom. Mordecai asked people to copy the law into every language that people spoke in the kingdom. So everyone would know what the new law said. 10 The law that Mordecai wrote had the king's authority. It had the mark of the king's signet ring. Men who were riding on fast horses took the law all through the kingdom.

11 The king's law said this: Every Jew in every city could fight against any person who attacked them. This included the women and children of any man who attacked them. The Jews could take the things of anyone that they killed. 12 The law said that the Jews could do this for one day. This day was the 13th day of the 12th month. That was the month called Adar.

13 A copy of the law reached all the kingdom. Everybody knew the law. The Jews prepared for that day. They would kill all the people who wanted to kill them on that day. 14 The king told his officers that they must travel quickly on their horses. The king's officers also told everybody about the law in the city (Susa).

15 Then Mordecai went from the king's palace. He was wearing beautiful blue and white clothes. He had a large crown of gold on his head and he was wearing special clothes. The colour of the clothes was purple and somebody had made them out of linen. The people in Susa were very happy.

16 The Jews were very happy and everyone respected them. 17 In all the kingdom, the Jews had feasts and they were very happy. Many people became Jews because of what happened.

Chapter 9

The Jews kill the people who wanted to kill them

1 It was the 13th day of the 12th month, the month called Adar. Everyone who really did not like the Jews had hoped to kill them. But because of the king's new law, the Jews could fight to keep themselves safe. 2The Jews came together in their provinces and cities to fight against the people who wanted to kill them. Nobody could fight against them. Everyone was afraid of them.

3 Also, all the officers in the kingdom helped the Jews because they were afraid of Mordecai. 4 Everyone knew that Mordecai had great authority in the palace. And he became more and more powerful. 5 So the Jews could do what they wanted with their enemies. They could kill them.

6 In the city (Susa), the Jews killed 500 men. 7 They also killed Parshandatha, Dalphon, Aspatha, 8 Poratha, Adalia, Aridatha, 9 Parmashta, Arisai, Aridai and Vaizatha. 10 Those men were the 10 sons of Haman, who wanted to kill the Jews. But the Jews did not take any of the things of the people that they killed.

11 Officers told the king how many people the Jews killed in the city (Susa). 12 Then the king said to Queen Esther, 'In the city (Susa) the Jews have killed 500 men and the 10 sons of Haman. So I think that they have killed very many of their enemies in the whole kingdom! Now, what do you want? I will do anything that you want.'

13 Esther replied, 'If it makes the king happy, please let the Jews in Susa do the same tomorrow. Also, please hang the dead bodies of Haman's sons from the gallows.'

14 The king said that this should happen. He made another law in Susa so that the Jews could fight for themselves again. And the king's officers hung the dead bodies of Haman's 10 sons on the gallows. Everyone could see them.

15 On the 14th day of the month called Adar the Jews killed 300 men in Susa. But they did not take the things of the people that they killed. 16 In the provinces, the Jews killed 75 000 of their enemies. The Jews killed all the people who wanted to kill them. But they did not take the things of the people that they killed.

17 They did that on the 13th day of Adar. Then, on the 14th day, the Jews in the provinces rested. They had feasts and they were very happy. 18 But the Jews in Susa killed their enemies on the 13th day and on the 14th day of Adar. On the 15th day they rested. They had feasts and they were very happy on that day. 19 So Jews who live in the provinces have a holiday and a feast on the 14th day of Adar. And they are very happy and they give gifts to each other on that date.

20 Mordecai recorded what had happened. He sent letters to all the Jews who were living in the kingdom of Xerxes. 21-22 He told them that they should have a feast and a holiday on the 14th and 15th days of Adar. He told the Jews that they must do that every year. That was because on those dates they had killed all their enemies. In the month Adar, those who were sad became happy. Mordecai told the Jews that they must remember those days. He told them that they should give gifts and special food to each other. And he told them that they should give those things to poor people too.

23 So the Jews did everything that Mordecai had said. And they had a feast every year to remember what had happened. 24 They remembered how Haman from Agag's family, the enemy of all the Jews, had wanted to kill them. They remembered that he threw pur. He threw it to choose the day when he would kill them. 25 They remembered how Esther went to the king. And they remembered that the king wrote another law. The Jews remembered that the king did not kill the Jews. And they remembered that the king did kill Haman. And they remembered that the Jews killed Haman's sons. They remembered how the dead bodies of Haman and his sons hung on the gallows.

26 So the Jews called the feast Purim. They did all this because of what was in Mordecai's letter. And it was because of everything that they had seen. And it was because of everything that had happened to them.

27 The Jews made a rule. The rule was for themselves and for Jews who were born after them. And it was for anyone who became a Jew. The rule was that everyone must have a feast on the 14th and 15th days of Adar every year. This is what Mordecai had said to them. 28 Every Jew and every Jew who was born after that time everywhere must remember the Feast of Purim.

29 Then Queen Esther, daughter of Abihail, and Mordecai wrote a second letter. In this letter they gave their authority to the Feast of Purim. 30 And Mordecai sent letters to all the Jews who were living in the 127 provinces of the kingdom of Xerxes. The message told them that all the Jews were safe. 31 But it also told the Jews that they should remember the Feast of Purim. And they should remember the times when they fasted. They had asked God for help at those times.

32 Queen Esther made this law for all the Jews. The men who wrote down the law recorded it. They recorded that the Jews should remember the Feast of Purim.

Chapter 10

1 King Xerxes caused everyone to pay tribute. Those who lived on the land had to pay tribute. And those who lived on the islands in the sea had to pay tribute too.

2 The Book of Years of the kings of Media and Persia records all the great and powerful things that the king did. And the book records how Mordecai became powerful. 3 King Xerxes gave very much authority to Mordecai and so Mordecai became very powerful. Only the king had more authority than Mordecai. Many Jews knew that Mordecai was a great man. And Mordecai always did what was right for the Jews.

When Bad Things happen to Good People

Job

About this book

In this book we read the story of a man called Job. Job was a rich man. But Satan destroyed everything that he owned. Job was also a very good man. So he does not understand why such bad things have happened to him. He has three friends who try to give him answers. But their words do not help Job to feel happier. Another man tries to help. But Job does not think that he has really understood Job's problems either. At the end of the story, God speaks to Job. And Job, in the end, understands that he cannot know everything. Only God knows everything. Only God is completely powerful. But we, like Job, must trust God, even if very bad things happen in our lives.

Chapter 1

1 Many years ago, a man lived in a place called Uz. His name was Job and he was a very good man. He was fair to everybody and he did the right things. He was afraid to make God angry. And he refused to do wrong things. 2 Job had seven sons and three daughters. 3 He had 7000 sheep and 3000 camels. He had 500 pairs of oxen and 500 donkeys. And he had many servants. There was no one richer than Job for many miles.

4 Each year, Job's sons had birthday parties in their homes. They had lots to eat and lots to drink. And they always asked their three sisters to come. 5 After each party, Job would ask his children to visit him. He thought that they might have done wrong things. Or perhaps they had had wrong thoughts about God. So he would get up early the next morning and sacrifice an animal to God for each of them. They might have done wrong things. So he would ask God to forgive them for those things.

6 One day, the LORD's angels came to him in heaven. And Satan came with them. 7 The LORD asked Satan where he had been. Satan replied, 'I have been going all over the earth. I have been watching the things that happen there.'

8 Then the LORD asked Satan, 'You have seen Job, who is my servant. What do you think about him? There is no one on earth that is like him. He is a very good person. He is afraid to make me angry and he obeys me. He refuses to do things that are wrong.'

9 'He may be afraid to make you angry and he may obey you', Satan replied. 'There are good reasons why he does that. 10 You do not let any bad things happen to him. So he knows that he will be safe. You do this for all his family. You make sure that all his things are safe. You have helped his business so that he has become very rich. He has many sheep and lots of cows. 11 But take away the things that he has. Then he will certainly let you know that he is cursing you.'

12 So the LORD told Satan, 'Job has many things. Do what you want with any of them. But do not hurt Job's body.' Then Satan left God.

Satan destroys everything that Job owns

13 Job's sons and daughters were at a party in the home of his oldest son. 14 A servant rushed up to Job. He told him about things that had just happened. This is what the servant told Job. 'We were using your oxen to plough the fields. Near where we worked, your donkeys were eating grass in a field. 15 Some bad men from the south came and they attacked us. They took the oxen and the donkeys. And they killed all your servants except me. Instead, I ran away. And I have come to tell you what has happened.' 16 That servant was still speaking, when a second servant ran up to Job. He said, 'God has sent a fire that has killed your sheep and all your servants except me. And I have come to tell you what has happened.' 17 Before that servant had finished speaking, a third servant ran up to Job. He said, 'Bad men from the north have attacked your camels and they have taken them away. They killed all your servants except me. Instead, I ran away. And I have come to tell you what has happened.'

Satan kills Job's children

18 That servant was still speaking, when a fourth servant ran up to Job. He said, 'Your children were at a party. They were drinking wine at the home of your oldest son. 19 There was a bad storm and the wind destroyed the house. The house fell on all your children and it killed them. But I am still alive. And I have come to tell you what has happened.'

What Job did

20 When Job heard all this he was very sad. He tore his clothes and he cut off all his hair. He did this because he was so sad. Then he bent his body to the ground and he worshipped God. 21 And he said, 'When we are born we have nothing. When we die, we take nothing with us. God has given to us all the things that we have. Sometimes he takes away the things that we have. Only the LORD gives us things. It is only the LORD that takes them away again. But I will still praise the name of the LORD!'

22 Even after all the things that had happened, Job still did not do wrong things. Nor did he say that God had done anything wrong.

Chapter 2

1 The next time that the angels came to the LORD, Satan came with them. 2 The LORD asked Satan where he had been. Satan replied, 'I have been going all over the earth.' 3 Then the LORD asked Satan, 'You have seen Job, who is my servant. What do you think about him? There is no one on earth that is like him. He is a very good person. He is afraid to make me angry. He refuses to do things that are wrong. Job had not done anything wrong. But because of what you said I have been against him. And so he has lost everything for no reason. Even then, he did not change. He is still the same good man.'

4 Satan answered, 'A man will only feel pain if he, himself, is hurting. A man will do anything to save his own life. 5 But if you cause Job to have great pain in his own body, it will be different. And then he will certainly let you know that he is cursing you.' 6 So the LORD agreed that Satan could cause Job pain. He could cause him as much pain as he wanted. But the LORD told Satan not to kill him. 7 So Satan left. And he caused Job to have very painful skin all over his body, from his head to his feet.

8 Then Job sat down among the ashes. He did this to show how sad he was. He sat there and removed bad bits of skin with a piece of a broken pot. 9 His wife said, 'You cannot still believe that God is good. You should curse God and die.' 10 Job replied, 'Do not talk like a fool! We take the good things that God gives us. So we should not be surprised if he sends us trouble as well.' Many bad things had happened to Job but he never said any wrong things about God.

Job's friends come to try to help him

11 Three of Job's friends heard about his troubles and so they decided to visit him. The first friend was called Eliphaz. He lived in a place called Teman. The second friend was called Bildad. He lived in a place called Shuah. The third friend was called Zophar. He lived in a place called Naamah. They came because they wanted to help Job. 12 When they came near enough to see Job, they did not recognise him. He looked so ill. They were so sad that they tore their clothes. Then they put ash on their heads and cried a lot. 13 For a whole week, they sat on the ground near Job. All that time, they knew how bad his pain was. So they did not say anything to him.

Chapter 3

Job speaks to God about the things that have happened

1 In the end, Job cursed the day when he was born.

2 He said,

3 'Forget the day of my birth.

Forget the night when a son was born to my parents.

4 Forget about that day because it was a bad day.

5 I want people to think about that day as a dark day.

I want it to be as dark as night.

6 Make it a date that no one remembers.

Hide it from the thoughts of everyone.

7 Do not let children be born on that date.

Do not let people be happy on that date.

8 Some people know how to cause monsters to attack.

Let those people curse that day.

9 On that date, make dark the stars that shine in the morning.

Do not let the sun shine at dawn.

10 I ask all this because on that day I was born into a world full of trouble.

11 It would have been better if I had died at birth.

My mother should have let me die.

12 Instead, she put me on her knee and I drank from her breast.

13 If I had died at birth, I would now be with all the other dead people.

14 Kings and rulers are there, too.

Those kings had lived in buildings that had been beautiful. And I would be with them.

15 I would be with rulers who once were rich with gold and silver.

16 If I had been born dead, my friends would have buried me.

Then I would not have lived to wake each day.

Then I would not have had a life full of trouble.

17 After death, no one causes any more troubles.

This is true for people who have done wrong things during their lives.

And people who have been very tired during their lives can rest.

18 It is a place where no one is in prison.

It is a place where slaves do not hear the voice of a master.

19 Important people and people who are not important are there.

Slaves are free there. They do not have a master there.

20 My life is so difficult that I always feel sad.

So I want to know why God lets people like me live.

21 They want to die. But they are still alive.

They would rather die than discover gold.

22 When, in the end, they are dying, they are very happy.

23 They want to know why they should go on living.

They do not know what will happen to them.

They feel like people that God has put in a prison.

24 I cannot eat because I am crying so much.

I cannot drink because I weep all the time.

25 The things that frighten me most have happened to me.

26 I cannot rest because of all the troubles that I have.'

Chapter 4.

Job's friend Eliphaz speaks to him

1 Job's friend Eliphaz lived in a place called Teman. He spoke with Job. And this is what he said.

2 'You might not like the things that I want to say.

But I have to say something because this is important.

3 Think about this:

You have taught many people.

And you have helped weak people.

4 By your words, you have saved people from great dangers.

And you have helped weak people to hope.

5 But now you have many troubles.

And you feel sad and weak because of your troubles.

6 But you can still hope that your troubles will stop.

Go on being afraid to make God angry.

And try to live the right way.

7 Think about this:

Many people live the right way. They do not die while they are young.

God does not kill people who only do good things.

8 I will tell you what I have seen.

Bad people have trouble in their lives.

In fact they have troubles that they cause for themselves.

They are like a farmer.

The things that he has planted grow in his field.

9 God is angry with people who are like that.

And he will kill them.

When God is angry it is like a strong wind.

When he is angry bad people die. They die like they would in a bad storm.

10 Think about lions. They are strong animals.

But if God breaks a lion's teeth, it cannot eat.

11 So it is hungry and, in the end, it dies.

And the young lions will run away to find their food.

Bad people may be strong too.

But, if God is angry, they cannot fight him.

12 One night I heard a quiet voice.

Someone spoke to me and told me a secret.

13 I was asleep, but my dreams woke me.

14 I was very afraid.

Even my bones were shaking.

15 Then a spirit passed my face.

My hairs stood up.

16 The spirit did not have a shape that I recognised.

Everything was quiet and then I heard the voice. I heard these words:

17 "God made us all. And he sees the things that we do.

He knows that no one is completely good.

18 He says that even his servants and his angels do wrong things.

19 God made us all from clay.

And we are as weak as insects that fly.

So we cannot hope to have lives with no troubles.

20 All our lives are very short.

Insects are born after dawn and they die before the end of the day.

No one will ever see them again.

Our lives are so short that they seem like that.

21 Our lives are like tents.

There are pegs that keep a tent in the right place.

When you remove the pegs, you can take the tent away.

So a small thing can cause us to die.

And often people learn nothing during their lives." '

Chapter 5

1 Eliphaz continued to speak.

'You may shout, Job, and ask someone to help you. But no one will answer you.

Even if you ask the angels, they will not help you.

2 A fool may be so angry with other people that he dies.

He may want to have the things that they have. He may die because he wants them too much.

3 I myself have seen the way that a fool lives. He seems to be happy.

And his life seems to be comfortable. But soon God sends trouble to him.

4 His children are not safe anymore. People will say that they have done wrong things.

Then no one will say that his children are honest.

5 Hungry people take plants from his fields. They even take them from among the weeds.

And other people use his money to buy their drinks.

6 But difficulties do not grow like plants.

And troubles do not come from the ground.

7 You know that from every fire smoke rises into the air.

So every man that is born has troubles in his life.

8 I suggest that you ask God to help you.

I suggest that you tell him about your problems.

9 He does great things that nobody can understand.

Nobody can count the surprising things that he has done.

10 He gives rain for the earth.

He sends water for the fields.

11 He makes humble people important.

Some people are sad because someone has died. But God makes those people safe.

12 Clever people may try to do wrong things.

But God will not let them do such things.

13 He sees the things that clever people are doing.

And he causes them to stop doing those things.

14 They find that it is dark at midday.

They can see no better in the day than at night.

15 He saves poor people from death.

And he stops bad people from hitting them.

16 God helps poor people. So they can hope that their future lives will be good.

But those who do wrong things must be quiet.

17 If God teaches you the right way to live, you should be happy.

He may decide that you should have difficulties in your life.

Do not be sad if the Almighty decides that.

18 He may cause you to have pain. But he will make you well again.

He may hurt you, but he will give you health again.

19 Often he will save you from trouble.

Many times, he will keep you safe from danger.

20 He will keep you alive if there is a famine.

And he will also keep you alive if there is a war.

21 He will not let people say bad things about you.

And you will not be afraid when people attack you.

22 You will laugh if there is a famine. You will smile if there is danger.

You will not be afraid of wild animals.

23 They will not be wild any more when you are near them.

And there will be no danger in your fields.

24 You will know that your home is safe. You will check all the things you have.

And you will find that they are all there.

25 You will know that you will have a large family. You will have many children and grandchildren.

It will not be any easier to count them than to count the grass in a field.

26 You will live for many years. Plants grow until the right time to pick them.

So you will live until it is the right time for you to die. And you will have good health until you die.

27 We have checked all this. And we have found that it is true.

So listen to what we say. And do what we suggest.'

Chapter 6

Job replies to Eliphaz

1 Then Job replied:

2 'It is not possible to measure my troubles

or to weigh my pains!

3 If it were possible to weigh them, they would be heavier than all the sand on the shore.

That is why I have spoken so quickly. And I did not think before I spoke.

4 The Almighty has shot his arrows at me.

Their poison is in my body. I am very afraid of what God is going to do to me.

5 A wild donkey is quiet when it has grass to eat.

An ox does not make a loud noise when it has food.

6 You cannot enjoy food that has no salt in it.

If you only eat the white part of an egg, it will not be very nice.

7 I refuse to eat food like that.

Whatever I eat makes me ill.

8 God will not give me what I ask for. I want to know why this is.

When I pray he does not answer.

9 I want to die. And I have prayed that God would kill me.

10 I have had much pain. But I know that God is holy.

And I have always done what he has told me to do.

So, because I know that, I am ready to die.

11 I am not strong enough to hope for a better life.

There is no reason why I should be patient.

12 I am not as strong as stone.

God did not make my body from bronze.

13 I am not strong enough to help myself.

And there is nowhere that I can go to get help.

14 When a man has many troubles, his friends should be kind to him.

Friends who are not like that have stopped being afraid to make God angry.

15 But, my friends, you are not here to help me when I need you.

You are like some rivers. Sometimes there is water and sometimes there is no water.

16 In the spring, the sun warms the ice and the snow and there is a lot of water.

17 But in the summer, there may be no rain. And the sun is so hot that there is no water.

18 Travellers get lost when they go to look for water.

They leave the proper paths and they die in the desert.

19 Travellers from Tema look for water. People on business from Sheba look for water.

But they are all disappointed.

20 They are sad, because they had hoped to find water.

But when they arrive, they are disappointed.

21 You are like those streams.

You see what has happened to me. And you are afraid.

22 I have never asked you to send me a gift.

Nor have I asked you to pay money so that I could be free.

23 I have not asked you to save me from my enemy.

Nor have I asked you to help me get free from cruel people.

24 Tell me things that are true. Then I will be quiet.

Tell me if I have done something wrong.

25 The true words that an honest man speaks will make the listener sad.

You may argue with me. But the things that you say mean nothing.

26 You do not believe me when I speak to you. So you should not try to argue with me.

There is nothing more that I can hope for in this life. You know that.

27 But you would sell to be slaves, children who had no parents.

You would even sell your best friend.

28 But now, please look at me.

I only tell you things that are true.

29 Please think again about what you say.

Think again. I want people to know that I am an honest man.

30 The things that I say are true.

I know what is right. And I know what is wrong.

Chapter 7

1 Men always have a lot of work to do on this earth.

They have to work every day like servants.

2 A slave waits for the end of the day so that he can stop his work.

A servant waits until his master pays him.

3 But I have nothing to wait for.

Every night, when I lie down to sleep, I am sad.

4 When I lie down I want the night to end.

But it does not end, and I cannot sleep. At last, dawn comes.

5 There are insects all over my body.

All of my skin is painful.

6 My life is passing very fast. It is passing as fast as the shuttle of a weaver.

But I cannot hope that it will get any better.'

7 'Remember, God, that my life is as short as a breath.

I know that I will never be happy again.

8 You see me now but soon you will not see me.

You will look for me, but I will have gone.

9 A cloud passes across the sky and then it is gone. You never see it again.

That is like a person who dies. He never returns to the earth.

10 He will never come back to his house again.

People who knew him soon forget him.

11 So I will not be quiet. I will speak to tell you how angry I am.

I will speak to say how very sad I feel.

12 Perhaps you have to watch the animals that live in the sea.

But I do not understand why you have to watch me every day.

13 I lie down and try to rest.

Perhaps my pain will be less when I am asleep.

14 But even then you cause me to dream and that frightens me.

I am afraid when I see things in the night.

15 I would rather die than continue a life like this.

16 I hate my life and I do not want to live any more.

My life has no meaning.

So let me die alone.

17 You seem to think that men are very important.

You seem to have a lot of interest in men.

18 You seem to watch them every morning.

And you seem to check what they are doing at each moment of the day.

I would like to know why you are like that.

19 It seems that you never stop watching me.

It seems that I cannot be alone, even for a moment.

20 You seem to think that I have done wrong things.

You watch what men do. I know that. But I do not know what I have done to you.

I do not know why you have chosen to watch me.

You seem to think that I have caused trouble for you.

21 I do not know why you do not excuse me.

I do not know why you do not forgive me for my sins.

Soon I will die and my friends will bury me.

Then you will look for me, but you will not find me.'

Chapter 8

Job's friend Bildad speaks to him

1 Job's friend Bildad lived in a place called Shuah.

He spoke to Job. And this is what he said.

2 'You should not continue to say such things.

Your words are like the wind.

3 Surely you know that God is fair.

The Almighty does not change something that is right. He will not make it wrong.

4 Your children did things that were wrong.

Because of the things that they did, God punished them.

5 But you should pray to God

and you should ask the Almighty to help you.

6 If you are honest, God will listen to you.

You may have lived the right way.

Then he will hear you when you speak to him.

And he will give back to you the things that you have lost.

7 You will be very rich.

God will give you much more than you had before.

8 People who lived before us knew many things.

Try to discover what they learned.

9 Our lives are like shadows that pass in a moment.

They are so short that we learn nothing.

10 But the people who lived before us can teach us.

Listen to what they said. Then you will learn from them.

11 You know that some trees only grow tall in wet ground.

And plants can only live if they have water.

12 They may still be growing and they may not be ready for somebody to cut them.

But if they have no water, they will soon die.

13 People who forget about God are like those plants.

They cannot hope to live. They, too, will die before they are old.

14 They believe in something that is weak.

It is as weak as a spider's web.

15 A man like that trusts his family and his things, but they are not strong.

He holds all his things as well as he can. But in the end, they will leave him.'

16 'Bad people are like weeds when there is plenty of water.

The weeds grow all over the garden.

17 Their roots grow round stones

and they find space between rocks.

18 But in the end, someone will dig the ground and destroy the weeds.

Then no one will remember that they had been there.

19 So the weeds die.

But other plants will grow in the ground where they had been.

20 God will not refuse to help an honest man.

Nor will he hurry to help a bad man.

21 He will make you happy.

And you will have reasons to laugh again. And you will smile again, too.

22 Your enemies will be ashamed of what they have done.

And they will even lose their homes.'

Chapter 9

Job replies to Bildad

1 Then Job replied. And this is what he said.

2 'The things that you have said are true. I know that they are true

But God will not agree that anyone is completely honest.

3 We might decide to quarrel with him about that.

But God can ask 1000 questions which we cannot answer.

4 God is very wise and he is very powerful.

It is impossible to argue with him.

5 He is so powerful that he can move mountains.

    When he is angry he can knock them down.

6 He can make the earth itself move.

    He can even move it from the place where it belongs.

7 He can tell the sun not to shine during the day.

    He can stop the stars shining at night.

8 God made the sky and everything that is above the earth.

He did not need anyone to help him. And he tells the seas what they should do.

9 He made all the stars and he put them in their places in the sky.

    He made the Bear, Orion, and the Pleiades.

They are all there in the shapes that he decided.

10 Nobody can understand all the things that he does.

    And nobody can count the surprising things that he has done.

11 When God passes in front of me, I cannot see him.

    He may go somewhere else. And I cannot see where he has gone.

12 He takes what he wants. And no one can stop him.

    No one can ask him what he is doing.

13 God will always be angry with his enemies.

    They may fight against him but they will not beat him.

14 I cannot cause God to change his thoughts about me.

    There are no words that I can use.

15 I may not have done anything that was wrong. But I cannot explain that to God.

    I can only ask him to be merciful.

16 If I call to him he might answer me.

    But even then he would not listen to the things that I say.

17 He would send a storm to cause me pain.

    He would hurt me for no reason.

18 I would not be able to breathe.

    Instead, he would make me very sad.

19 God is much stronger than I am.

    And no one can ask him to explain what he has done.

20 I may not have done anything that was wrong.

    But my words do not show that this is true.

I may be completely honest.

    But when I speak, no one believes me.

21 I have not done anything that was wrong.

    But my life is not important and I hate myself.

22 The same thing happens to everybody in the end.

    So I say, "God kills both good people and very bad people."

23 Sometimes a good man will become ill while he is young.

    But even if he is very sad, God does not do anything to help him.

24 Bad men may rule the countries in the world.

    And the judges do not see what the bad men are doing.

It must be God who lets those things happen.

    I do not know anyone else that would do that.

25 I am becoming old very quickly.

    But even if I live for many years, I will not be happy.

26 A fast boat passes very quickly. My life is like that. It will soon end.

A bird can catch a small animal in a moment. My life seems to be as short as that.

27 I may try to smile.

    And I may try to forget about all my troubles.

28 Even then, I will be afraid of the pain that God causes.

    God does not agree that I am an honest man. I know that.

29 He has decided that I have done wrong things.

    So I do not see why I should continue to argue with him.

30 I might wash myself with soap

    and I might clean my hands with powder.

31 Even then, God would throw me into a dirty hole.

I would be so dirty that I could not wear my own clothes.

32 God is not a man; so I cannot argue with him.

We cannot argue with each other in court.

33 No one can decide which of us is right.

What I say may be true. But no one can check if it is true.

34 No one can stop God when he hurts me.

If that were possible, then I would not be afraid any more.

35 If that were possible, I would not be afraid to speak.

But it is not possible, so I cannot speak.

Chapter 10

1 I do not enjoy my life now. I do not want to live. I am very, very sad.

So I will speak about the thoughts that are in my mind.

2 This is what I will say to God. "Do not say that I am a bad person.

You may believe that I have done wrong things. Tell me what they are.

3 You seem to enjoy it when you hurt me. You made me. So I do not know why you refuse to help me.

And you seem to help very bad people even when they are doing very bad things.

4 Sometimes you seem not to have eyes like men have eyes.

And you seem not to see things as people see them.

5 Your life is not like the life of a human being.

You life does not have an end like ours does.

6 But you seem to be in a hurry to discover the wrong things that I have done.

I do not know why you have to do that.

7 You know that I have not done wrong things.

But you also know that no one can save me from you.

8 You made me with your hands.

But now it seems that you want to kill me.

9 Remember that you made me from dust.

Now it seems that you want to make me into dust again.

10 People make cheese with only a little milk.

So you made my body with only a little material.

11 You joined my bones together

and you covered them with skin.

12 You gave my life to me and you have always loved me.

You have always watched me to save me from danger.

13 But I know what you decided to do.

I know the thoughts that were in your mind.

14 You were watching me to see if I did wrong things.

And then you would not forgive me.

15 If I do wrong things, then you punish me.

But you never see the good things that I do.

Whatever I do, I am ashamed.

Whatever I do, my life is full of trouble.

16 If I do something well, I am happy.

But then you catch me as a lion catches other animals.

And you use your power against me.

17 You continue to say that I do wrong things.

You become more and more angry with me.

You attack me again and again.

18 I do not know why you let me be born.

I should have died before anyone saw me.

19 It would have been better if I had never been born.

Or perhaps I should have died straight after my birth.

20 It seems that I will die soon.

Turn yourself from me so I can be happy for a moment.

21 I want to be happy before I die. I will soon die.

Then I will go to a place from which I cannot return.

22 I will go to a dark place where there are only shadows.

In that place, it is as dark as midnight in the middle of the day." '

Chapter 11
Job's friend Zophar speaks to him

1 Job's friend Zophar lived in a place called Naamah. He spoke to Job. And this is what he said.

2 'Someone must answer all the questions that you ask.

Even if you talk a lot, God will still not excuse you.

3 We will not be quiet while you continue to speak.

You are saying wrong things about God. Someone should stop you doing that.

4 You say to God, "The things that I believe are true.

I am an honest man and I live the right way."

5 I wish that God would speak to you.

And I wish that he would explain to you his thoughts.

6 Then he might tell you the secret of wisdom.

True wisdom is not easy to understand. But know this:

You have done things that were wrong.

But God has forgotten some of those wrong things.

7 You cannot understand the things that God does.

You do not know how powerful he is.

8 His power can reach beyond the sky.

You cannot do that.

He knows what happens after death.

You do not know that.

9 The earth itself could not contain everything that God knows.

Neither is the sea big enough to contain it.

10 If he puts you in prison you will not be able to stop him.

If he accuses you in a court,

you will not be able to answer him.

11 I am sure about this. God knows the people who do wrong things.

He sees the wrong things that they do.

12 Wild donkeys do not change their nature and become friendly.

And fools do not change their nature and become wise.

13 You should live the right way, Job.

You should raise your hands and pray to God.

14 Stop doing things that are wrong.

Do not let people do wrong things in your home.

15 If you do this, you will not be ashamed any more.

Instead, you will be strong. And you will not be afraid.

16 I am sure that you will forget your trouble.

It will be like water that has gone under a bridge long ago. No one remembers it.

17 Your life will be good. And you will be happy again.

All day, it will seem brighter than noon. Even the dark night will seem like the morning.

18 You will be able to hope, so you will trust God.

Then you will know that it is safe to rest.

19 When you sleep, you will not be afraid.

Many people will ask you to help them.

20 But bad people will not be able to hope for a better life.

God will punish them because of the things that they have done.

It would be better if they died.'

Chapter 12
Job replies to Zophar

1 Then Job replied. And this is what he said.

2 'You seem to think that you know everything.

And you think that, after your death, no one else will be wise.

3 But I have a mind too. And you are no better than I am.

Everyone knows the things that you have told me.

4 All my friends think that I am a fool.

But I pray to God and he answers me.

I have always lived the right way.

But still my friends think that I am a fool.

5 Some people have no troubles.

It is easy for them to think that they are better than people with troubles.

It is easy to push a man who is nearly falling already.

   And those people with no troubles are doing something like that.

6 Men who rob other people are safe in their homes.

   They make God angry. But they think that they are safe.

7 But ask the animals, and they will teach you.

   Or ask the birds in the air. They will tell you things that are true.

8 Speak to the earth, and it will teach you.

   Or let the fish that are in the sea speak to you.

9 Any of them can tell you what the LORD has done.

10 He gives life to all the animals.

   And he decides what the lives of men will be like.

11 We can taste food when we put it into our mouths.

   And we learn the things that we hear with our ears.

12 Old people are often wise.

   And they understand more things if they live for a long time.

13 But God is wise. And he helps us to be wise too.

   He is strong and he makes us strong too.

14 No one can repair something that he has destroyed.

   And if God puts someone in prison he must stay there. No one can help that person.

15 If God stops the rain, the land becomes a desert.

   If he sends too much rain, there are floods.

16 God is strong. He will always beat anyone who fights against him.

   He has power over good people and over bad people.

17 He takes away the wisdom of rulers.

   And he causes leaders to seem like fools.

18 He takes from kings the special clothes that they wear.

   He gives them instead cloths to tie round them.

19 God causes priests to lose their jobs.

   Because of what he decides, important men lose their jobs too.

20 He confuses wise men.

   And he removes wisdom from old men.

21 He causes rulers to be ashamed.

   And he destroys the power of strong men.

22 He shows to us things that nobody knew.

   And he makes the shadows of the night shine like the day.

23 He makes nations great, and then he destroys them.

   He makes nations bigger. Then he sends the people in those nations away.

24 He destroys the understanding of kings.

   And then he sends them to walk about in the desert.

25 They have no light while they walk in the dark.

   And he causes them to walk like men who have drunk a lot of alcohol.

Chapter 13

1 I have seen with my own eyes all the things that you have told me.

   I have heard everything that you have said. And I have understood all of it.

2 I know as much as you do.

   You are no better than I am.

3 But I want to speak to the Almighty. I want to tell him how I feel.

   And I want him to explain the things that he has done to me.

4 But you tell me things that are not true.

   You are like doctors who cannot make sick people better.

5 It would be better if you said nothing.

   That would be a wise thing to do.

6 Listen now to me when I speak to you.

   Listen to the things that I say.

7 You should not speak on behalf of God!

   You are saying things on his behalf; but they are not true.

8 You should be fair when you speak on his behalf.

   But I cannot believe that you are really trying to explain his thoughts to me.

9 God may check what you have been doing.

   Other people may not understand.

But he will see the wrong things that you have done.

10 It may be a secret that you have not been fair.

   Even so, God will still punish you.

11 I am sure that his power will frighten you.

   I am sure that you will be afraid of him.

12 The things that you say are worth no more than ashes.

   You are not strong enough to save yourself.

13 So be quiet and let me speak.

   Then I will not cry about the things that happen to me.

14 If anything happens to me, it will be my mistake.

   But I do want to say what I really think.

15 Even if God kills me, I will still believe him.

   But I will explain to him the reason why he should not kill me.

16 No bad man would be brave enough to speak with God.

   So if I speak to him, it will save me.

17 Listen well when I speak.

   Do not forget the things that I say to you.

18 Now I have prepared the things that I want to say.

I have not done anything that was wrong. So I know that he will excuse me.

19 Nobody can tell me any wrong thing that I have done.

   If you can do that, I will be quiet. And then I will die.

20 God, I do not want to hide myself from you any more.

   So I want to ask you to do two things.

21 Stop causing bad things to happen to me.

   And stop making me afraid of you.

22 Call to me and I will answer you.

   Or let me speak, and then reply to me.

23 Tell me how many wrong things I have done.

   Show me one wrong thing that I have done.

24 I would like to know why you hide yourself from me.

You seem to think that I am your enemy. I would like to know why you think that.

25 I am as weak as a leaf that the wind blows along the road.

   I am only as strong as dry grass.

So I do not understand why you want to frighten me.

26 You write down bad things about me.

I may have done wrong things when I was young. And you remember them.

27 You fasten my feet with metal ties.

   You watch me to see where I am going.

You even put marks on my feet so that you can follow me.

28 So my life is worth nothing.

I am like an old coat that the insects have eaten.

Chapter 14

1 Every man that is born will only live for a few years.

   And his life will be full of trouble.

2 Flowers grow and soon die. Our lives are not long, either.

   We are like shadows that soon pass by.

3 So I would like to know why you always watch a weak person like me.

   You always want me to explain the wrong things that I have done.

   I would like to know why you want me to do that.

4 People who are bad do not know the right way to live.

   No one can change them so that they live like that.

5 You have decided whether we will live for a long time or for a short time.

You know the number of months that we will live. And we cannot change that.

6 So do not watch me anymore.

   I may live like a servant. But please let me enjoy my life.

7 If someone cuts branches off a tree, the tree will not die.

Instead, new branches will grow.

8 Its roots may be old.

   Its branches may have fallen off and the tree may be nearly dead.

9 But if there is even a little water, the tree will not die.

   And its branches will start to grow again.

10 But when people are dying, they become very weak.

   Then they die and they can never live again.

11 When there is no water in the river or the lake,

   they both become dry.

12 People are like that. They die and they never live again.

   They will not wake while the sky is above the earth.

13 I want you to hide me among all the dead people.

   Hide me until you are no longer angry with me.

   Then decide when you will remember me.

14 If a man dies, he will not live again.

   So I will wait until my troubles have stopped.

Then I might hope to have a better life.

15 You will call me and I will answer you.

   Then you will have pleasure, because you made me.

16 Then you will watch what I do. And you will watch where I go.

   But you will not still remember the wrong things that I have done.

17 You will forgive me for those wrong things.

   And you will hide them so that you never see them again.

18 In the end, mountains fall

   and rocks move from their places.

19 In the end, water will break stones.

   When the rain falls, nothing remains on the earth.

And in the end, because of the things that you do,

   no man can hope to have a better life.

20 In the end, you kill him. Then he is gone for always.

   You change his face and you send him away.

21 He does not know if his sons become famous.

   Nor does he know if they have wasted their lives.

22 He thinks only about the pain that he feels.

   He does not think about the pain that other people feel.

And when he is sad, he thinks only about himself.'

Chapter 15

Eliphaz speaks to Job again

1 Then Eliphaz replied to Job. This is what he said.

2 'A wise man would not have such silly ideas.

   Nor would he use words that mean so little.

3 No wise man would talk as you do.

   The things that you say do not mean anything.

4 You do not seem to be afraid of God.

   Nor do you want people to pray to him.

5 The wrong things that you say come from bad thoughts in your mind.

   You try to be clever. And you try to make people believe you.

6 I will not say that you are wrong.

   Your words themselves show that you are wrong.

7 You were not the first human to be born.

   You were not alive when God made the hills.

8 You are not with God so you cannot know his thoughts.

   You are not the only wise person in the world.

9 You do not know any more than we know.

   We have as much wisdom as you do.

10 There are men who agree with us.

   They have grey hair and they are older than your father.

11 God is so good to you. And he is kind when he speaks to you.

   That ought to be enough for you.

12 I would like to know why there are wrong thoughts in your mind.

When we look at you, you seem very angry.

13 I would like to know why you are angry with God like this.

You should not say such bad things when you speak to him.

14 No person can say that he is always honest.

Nor can anyone say that he has never done wrong things.

15 God does not even believe that his angels are honest.

When he looks at them, they seem to him to be bad.

16 So people must seem to God to be very bad.

Something inside them causes them to want to do wrong things.

17 Listen to me and I will explain something to you.

Let me tell you what I have seen.

18 Wise men have taught me many things. They have even told me secret things.

They learned such things from people who lived before them.

19 There were no strangers in the country where those people lived.

So they did not learn any foreign ideas.

20 A man who is cruel will not have a happy life.

Instead, he will have pain during all the years that he lives.

21 He will hear things that frighten him.

He may think that he is safe. But bad people will attack him and they will rob him.

22 He will not go out in the dark, because someone may kill him.

23 So that bad man walks about everywhere to look for food.

He is saying, "Where is it?"

He knows that he will soon die.

24 He is afraid and confused.

He is like a king who is frightened before a war.

25 That happens if a man does not obey God.

A man like that thinks that he is more important than the Almighty.

26 He is the kind of man who tries to argue with God.

He even tries to attack God.

27 He may have had plenty of food to eat.

And he may be very fat.

28 But he will live in a town where no one else lives.

And he will not have a home because people will have destroyed his house.

29 He will have lost all his money.

He may have had many valuable things. He will have lost those too.

30 It will be dark and he will not be able to hide. God will find him.

God's breath will be like a fire. And it will destroy everything that he has.

31 He may think that his money will save him. If he thinks that, he is a fool.

He will not get back anything. His money will have no value.

32 Before he is old, his life will end.

He will not be able to do all the things that he wanted to do.

33 A vine may lose its fruit before it is ready for people to eat. Or an olive-tree may lose its flowers before the olives have grown. He will be like that vine or that olive-tree.

34 If people do not obey God, they will have no children.

Such people may have done wrong things to get homes for themselves.

If they have done that, fire will destroy those homes.

35 Such people have only wrong thoughts in their minds.

Other people have trouble because of the things that they do.

And through all their lives they do things that are bad.'

Chapter 16

Job replies to Eliphaz

1 Then Job replied. And this is what he said.

2 'I have heard all these things before. When you speak to me, you do not help me.

Nor do you make me any happier.

3 I want you to stop speaking words that do not help me.

You have no reason to answer me.

4 If your troubles were like my troubles, I could say the same things to you.

I could speak about the wrong things that you have done.

5 But, instead, I would try to help you.

   I would say things that made you happier.

6 But even if I speak, my pain does not go away.

   And if I stop speaking, my pain is still there.

7 God, you have been very cruel to me.

   You have killed my whole family.

8 You and I are enemies.

   And you do not let me move.

I am so thin that people can see my bones.

People think that you made me like this because of the wrong things in my life.

9 God attacks me because he is angry. I look at his face. I look at his eyes.

   And I can see how angry he is.

10 Crowds of people say things about me that are not kind.

   They are not afraid of me and they even slap my face.

11 It was God who let these bad people take me away.

   He let them do these things to me.

   12 I was enjoying my life.

   Then he held me and everything changed.

He held my neck and he hurt me.

   He has made me his target.

13 Soldiers with bows seem to be all round me.

He tears my body and my blood falls on the ground. Still he does not feel sorry for me.

14 He attacks me again and again.

   He rushes at me like a soldier.

15 My clothes show how sad I am.

   I sit among ashes to show that he has beaten me.

16 I have cried so much that my eyes are red.

   I am so tired that there are shadows under my eyes.

17 But I have never done anything that was cruel or wrong.

   And when I pray, I speak honestly to God.

18 I ask the earth not to hide my blood. I do not want people to forget me.

   I want them always to hear my cry for help.

19 Even now there is someone in heaven, who can speak on my behalf.

   I have a friend in that high place who knows about God's rules.

20 My friends do not help me; so I cry to God.

   My tears fall to the ground.

21 Sometimes another person can help friends when they have a quarrel.

   I want someone to speak to God on my behalf.

22 Soon my life will end.

   And I will never again return to this earth.

Chapter 17

1 I am very weak and I will soon die.

   Then my friends will bury me in the ground.

2 All round me people say that I am a fool.

   I have to stand and watch them.

3 God, you must help me.

   There is nobody else who can help me.

4 Because of what you have done, my friends will not listen to me.

   But I do not want them to think that they were right.

5 They have said very bad things about me.

   They wanted people to think that they were clever.

Now I want you to make their children blind.

   Do this, God, because of what they have said about me.

6 When people see me, they are not polite to me.

   You, God, have caused them to be like this.

7 I have cried so much that I can hardly see.

   I am so thin that I am like a shadow.

8 Honest people know that this is not fair.

They are angry because I seem to be so bad.

9 Honest people always know the right thing to do.

And people who only do good things get stronger.

10 But, my friends, come and try again to help me.

I will not find a wise man among you.

11 I will not live for many more days.

I will not be able to do the things that I wanted to do.

12 My friends say, "It is day", when it is still night.

They say that it is nearly morning. But I know that it is still dark.

13 If I die I will go to a dark place.

There I will lie in the dark.

14 There I might speak to the grave where my body will lie.

And I might say to the grave, "You are my father."

Or I might speak to the worms that I find there.

I might say to them, "Hello, my mother. Hello, my sister."

15 I can hope for nothing that is better than that.

No one can find anything that is better for me.

16 When I die, I will go to my grave with nothing.

I will have lost everything that I had hoped for.'

Chapter 18

Bildad speaks to Job again

1 Then Bildad replied. And this is what he said.

2 'You should not talk so much!

Be wise, and then we can talk.

3 You seem to think that we are as silly as cows.

You should not think that we are as silly as that.

4 You are so angry that you will hurt yourself.

You may be very angry, but you will not be able to change anything.

You may be angry. But that will not make the earth move.

Nor will you be able to make the rocks move from their place.

5 The light of a bad person will go out.

His fire will stop burning.

6 He will not be able to see anything in his tent because it is dark.

And the light that is near him will go out.

7 Once he was strong but now his legs are weak.

The things that he decided to do have confused him.

8 Where he is walking there is danger.

9 He cannot move because his foot is in a trap.

10 Someone has hidden the trap on the ground where he walks.

It is on the path in front of him.

11 A bad person is afraid of everything that is round him.

He thinks that there is trouble everywhere.

12 Years ago, he was rich but now he is hungry.

If he makes a mistake, he will have many troubles.

13 An illness will make his skin painful.

When he is nearly dead, he will not be able to use his arms or his legs.

14 He will die. Then, it will like a man who leaves his tent to go to another place.

It will be like a man who goes to meet a bad king. Then the bad person will be really afraid.

15 People will live in his house. They will not be his family.

They will live there after they have lit a fire to clean the house.

16 He is like a tree whose roots have died.

He is like a tree whose branches have fallen off.

17 Then he will not be famous, either in his own country or in any other country.

No one will remember him now.

18 He will have to leave the world where he has lived.

He will go to a place where it is always dark.

19 He will have no children or grandchildren.

He will have no family to live in his house where he lived.

20 People from the east heard about the things that happened to him.

People who lived in the west heard about them too.

And they were all afraid because of what they heard.

21 I am sure that there is a reason for all these things.

They happened because he is a bad man.

And they happened because he did not know God.'

Chapter 19

Job replies to Bildad

1 Then Job replied. And this is what he said.

2 'You are still trying to hurt me with the things that you say about me.

You should not still be doing that after such a long time.

3 Many times, you have been angry because of the things that I have done.

And you have been quick to say bad things about me.

4 It may be true that I have done wrong things.

But the things that I have done have not hurt you.

5 You seem to think that you are a better person than me.

My troubles do not mean that I am a bad person.

But you seem to think that they do mean that.

6 But you should be able to see that God has caused all my troubles.

He is trying to catch me in a trap.

7 God is not fair. He did not have a good reason to cause my troubles.

I shouted and I asked for help. But no one came to help me.

8 He stopped me so that I could not go past.

He made my path dark so that I could not see the way to go.

9 He has removed all the things that I had.

He has caused people to think that I am a bad person.

10 Everywhere I go, God is there to attack me. My life is nearly finished.

I am like a tree that he has dug out of the ground.

There is nothing more that I can hope for in my life.

11 He is very angry with me.

I am one of the people that he sees as his enemies.

12 He sends his army to attack me. They build roads so that they can reach me.

They are all round me.

13 Now my brothers do not want to meet me.

And my friends think that I am a stranger.

14 My relatives have left me.

And my best friends have forgotten me.

15 Visitors to my house think that I am a stranger.

And my servants think that I come from a foreign country.

16 I ask my servant to come to me. But he does not answer me.

Even when I ask him again, he still does not come to me.

17 My wife does not like the smell of my breath.

My brothers will not come near me.

18 Even little boys think that I am a fool.

When I appear, they turn away from me.

19 My best friends hate me.

People that I have loved do not want to be my friends.

20 My body is nothing more than skin and bones.

I could easily have died.

21 Be kind to me, my friends.

Be kind because God has been cruel to me.

22 God looks for me as a hunter looks for an animal.

I want to know why you do the same thing.

23 I want someone to write down the words that I speak.

I want him to write my words on a scroll.

24 I want him to write them on a stone with an iron tool.

I want people to be able to read them always.

25 I know that my Redeemer lives.

I know that, in the end, he will stand upon the earth.

26 One day I will die and people will bury me in the ground.

But in this, my body, I will see God.

27 I will see him with my own eyes.

I really want that to happen soon.

28 You say that I have caused my own troubles.

And because of that, you cause me to have even more trouble.

29 But you should be afraid of what may happen to you.

God will decide if you have done good things or bad things.

He may decide that you have done bad things.

And then he may punish you.'

Chapter 20

Zophar speaks to Job again

1 Then Zophar replied. And this is what he said.

2 'The things that you said have caused me to be very confused.

I have troubles in my mind but I must answer you.

3 You have said bad things about me.

But now I know how to reply to you.

4 I am sure that you know this fact.

It has been true ever since men lived on the earth.

5 A bad man will only be happy for a short time.

He will only enjoy his life for a few moments.

6 He may think that he is very important.

He may be very powerful and his head may seem to touch the sky.

7 But he will die and he will never return.

His friends will ask where he is.

He will be like things that you put into the toilet.

They, too, go away and never come back.

8 You will not find him again. He will be like a dream that you do not see in the morning.

He will have gone, like something that you saw in your dream.

9 People who knew him will not see him again.

No one will see him in the house where he lived before.

10 He was not a fair man and he took money from poor people.

So his children must pay that money back to them.

11 When he was a young man, he was very strong.

But he will die and his bones will lie in the ground.

12 He enjoys the wrong things that he does.

They are like something sweet in his mouth.

13 He continues to do wrong things.

That is like a man who keeps something in his mouth to taste it again and again.

14 But this will be like food that has become bad in his stomach.

It will be like the poison of a snake inside him.

15 He cannot keep all the money that he has taken from other people.

God will say that he should give it all back to them.

16 He will drink the poison of snakes.

An adder will bite him and it will kill him.

17 He might get as much oil from olives as there is water in the stream.

But he will not enjoy that oil.

He may have as much cream as there is water in the river.

But he will not enjoy that cream either.

Nor will he enjoy rivers of cream and other sweet things.

18 He will have to give back everything that he owned.

He will not enjoy the things that he has worked for.

19 This will happen because he took money from poor people.

And he took houses that someone else had built.

20 He will always want to have more money.

But his riches will not save him.

21 Now there is nothing that he can eat.

So his good health will not continue.

22 He may be very rich,

but he will soon have many troubles.

23 When he has filled his stomach with food, God will be very angry with him.

God will show him how angry he is. And God will punish him.

24 He may run from a soldier who has a sword.

But another soldier, with a bow, will catch him and he will shoot an arrow at him.

25 He pulls the arrow out of his back.

Its point hurts him and he is very afraid.

26 He will not be able to save the things that he had.

God will send a fire to kill him and to destroy everything that he had.

27 God in heaven knows about all the wrong things that a bad man does.

People on earth have also seen him do those wrong things.

28 God will very angry. And he will destroy the bad man's home and all his things.

It will be like a flood that destroys a house.

29 This is what will happen to bad people.

God has decided that this will happen to them.'

Chapter 21

Job replies to Zophar

1 Then Job replied. And this is what he said.

2 'Please listen to the things that I say.

You can only help me if you hear my words.

3 Be patient while I speak to you.

You may not agree with me. Then you may want to say bad things about me.

4 It is God that I want to argue with.

I do not understand why I should be patient.

5 Look at me and be surprised.

Put your hand over your mouth.

6 I think about the things that I am saying.

Then I am afraid and my body becomes weak.

7 I do not understand why bad people live for a long time.

As they get older, they become more powerful. I do not know why this happens.

8 They see their children grow up.

Their grandchildren make them happy.

9 Such people feel safe in their homes.

God does not punish them, so they are not afraid.

10 It is easy for their cows to have calves.

And many calves are born without difficulty.

11 Their children jump like lambs.

And the children love to dance, too.

12 Such people enjoy the music of a tambourine or a harp.

And they are happy when they hear the sound of a flute.

13 All through their lives they have plenty of money.

They do not have any troubles until the day that they die.

14 But they say to God, "Do not come near us!

We do not want to know about your ways."

15 They do not want to obey God. Nor do they want to do what he tells them to do.

And they do not see why they should pray to him.

16 They think that they have made themselves rich. But it is not true.

So I do not listen to the things that they say.

17 Bad people may do wrong things. But bad things do not often happen to them.

Even when God is angry, they do not have troubles.

18 They are not often like dry grass that the wind blows away.

Nor are they like something that a storm can sweep away.

19 You say that God will punish the children of bad people.

He will punish them because of the wrong things that the bad people have done.

But I say that God should punish the bad people, and not their children.

Then they will know that they have done wrong things.

20 They must understand what will happen to them.

They should know that God is angry. And they should know what God will do to them.

21 Bad things may happen to their children after they die. But they will not feel sad about those things.

So God should punish them if they do wrong things.

22 No one can tell God what he should do.

He sees the things that important people do. And he decides if those things are right or wrong.

23 One person has good health all his life.

He has been happy and he has had plenty of money.

24 He has always had enough to eat.

And he has never been ill until the day when he dies.

25 Another person has been sad all his life, until the day when he dies.

He has never had good health and he has never enjoyed lots of money.

26 But they lie together in the ground.

And the worms are all round them.

27 I know your thoughts.

You want me to do things that are wrong.

28 You seem to know what happens to bad men.

You say that people destroy their houses.

29 But you should ask people who travel, "What have you seen?"

You should listen to the things that they say.

30 They would tell you this. God does not always punish a bad man.

The bad man may have done wrong things but often nothing will happen to him.

31 No one asks him why he has done wrong things.

And no one punishes him for the things that he has done.

32 When he dies people bury him.

And then they stand near the place where his body lies.

33 The ground is soft where his body lies.

And many people come to say "goodbye" to the man who has died.

34 You have tried to help me and you have told me many things.

But nothing that you have told me is true!'

Chapter 22

Eliphaz speaks to Job a third time

1 Then Eliphaz replied. And this is what he said.

2 'Nothing that a man can do is worth anything to God.

Even a wise man cannot give pleasure to God.

3 It would not make God happy if you lived a good life.

It would not give him pleasure if you always lived the right way.

4 Think about why God punishes you.

It is not because you are a good person.

5 No! It is because you are a bad person.

And you have done so many wrong things that nobody could count them.

That is why he is punishing you.

6 You lent some money to your brother.

But you wanted to be sure that you would get your money back. So you took his clothes.

7 When you met tired people, you did not give them any water to drink.

And when you met hungry people you did not feed them.

8 You, Job, were a powerful man and you owned land.

But you kept for yourself everything that grew on that land.

9 You were not kind to women whose husbands had died.

And you were cruel to children who had no parents.

10 That is why you have so many troubles.

And that is why you are so afraid.

11 That is why you seem to be walking in the dark.

And that is why you seem to be drowning in deep water.

12 God lives in heaven, which is beyond the stars.

From there, he can see everything that happens on earth.

13 But you say, "God does not know.

He cannot see us from so far away."

14 You think that thick clouds hide him.

So he does not see us as he walks on the circle of the sky.

15 You must stop living the wrong way.

That is what bad people have done for a long time.

16 They died while they were still young.

They thought that they were safe.

But they were not safe.

They were like people who had drowned in a flood.

17 They did not believe God.

And they thought that God would not do anything to them.

18 But God gave them all the good things that they enjoyed.

So I do not understand the thoughts of bad people.

19 But, in the end, God punishes bad people.

Good people see that when it happens. And they are happy because they have seen it.

20 "God has killed our enemies", the good people say.

"Fire has destroyed all the things that they owned."

21 So, Job, do not argue with God but obey him instead.

Then your troubles will end and you will be rich again.

22 Listen to what he tells you to do.

And remember all that he says.

23 You should live the way that God wants you to live.

And you should stop doing wrong things. Then your life will be comfortable again.

24 You may have lots of gold but it will not make you happy.

So you should throw it into the dry valley where, years ago, there was a river.

25 Then you will see that God is more valuable than gold.

And he is more valuable than silver.

26 Then you will find that it is a pleasure to know God.

You will enjoy your life more if you worship him.

27 You will pray to him, and he will hear you.

And you will do the things that you have promised to him.

28 You will be able to do all the things that you want to do.

And God will say that you are living the right way.

29 You will pray for people who have difficulties.

And when you pray, God will make their lives better.

30 God will even forgive people who have done wrong things.

He will do that because you have lived a good life.'

Chapter 23

Job replies to Eliphaz.

1 Then Job replied. And this is what he said.

2 'I am still angry because of the things that God has done.

He was cruel to me even when I asked him to help me.

3 I wish that I knew where to find him.

I would like to go to the place where he lives.

4 I would explain to him that I have not done any wrong things.

I would say many things to him.

5 I would want to know how he would reply to me.

I would try to understand all the things that he would say to me.

6 God is much stronger than I am.

But he would be fair and he would listen to me.

7 People may obey him and may live the right way.

He will listen to such people.

If I have lived like that, he will listen to me.

And he will agree that I have not done wrong things.

8 But if I go to the east, God is not there.

And if I go to the west, I cannot find him there either.

9 When he is at work in the north, I do not see him.

And when he goes to the south, I still cannot find him.

10 But he watches where I go. And he knows the things that I do.

Many bad things have happened in my life.

But he will check the way that I have lived.

Then he will see that I am a good man.

I will be like gold that has been in a fire.

People see that it really is gold.

11 I have always lived in the way that he would have wanted.

I have never done things for my own pleasure.

12 I always do the things that God tells me to do. The things that he says are very important.

They are more important than the food that I eat each day.

13 I may want God to change the things that he has decided to do.

But he will not change them. Whatever he wants to do, he does.

14 He will do to me the things that he has decided to do.

And there are many things that he wants to do to me.

15 When he is near me, I am afraid.

And when I think about all this, I am afraid of him.

16 God has frightened me.

The Almighty has caused me to be afraid.

17 So many bad things have happened to me that it seems to be dark all round me.

Everything may be dark. But I will still want to speak about all these things.

Chapter 24

1 The Almighty will not decide when to open his court.

I do not know why he will not decide.

In the end, he will punish bad people for the wrong things they have done.

But good people will have to wait a long time to see this happen.

2 Bad men move the stones that mark the edge of their fields.

They do this to take fields that belong to other people.

Then they take the sheep that belong to those people.

And they bring them to eat the grass in their own fields.

3 Bad men will take a donkey from a child who has no parent.

They will take a cow from a woman who has no husband.

She may have to pay them some money.

So they keep the cow until she pays that money to them.

4 They push away people who need help.

And poor people have to hide because they are afraid of such bad men.

5 Poor people are like wild donkeys in the desert where they have to look for food.

There is nowhere else that they can go to find food for their children.

6 These poor people have to work in the fields of bad men.

They pick the plants and the fruit that grow there.

7 They have no clothes to wear during the cold night.

They do not have anything with which to cover themselves.

8 The rain that falls in the mountains makes them very wet.

So they hide among the rocks where they try to keep dry.

9 Bad men take children without parents and they make them slaves.

These men also take the children of poor people who cannot pay their debts.

10 Poor people have to go out with no clothes to cover them.

They may be hungry. But they cannot eat the plants that they pick from the fields.

11 They make oil from the olives and wine from the grapes.

But they still do not have anything to drink.

12 In the city, men who are dying shout for help.

But God does not do anything to the people who have hurt them.

13 A bad person does not like the light.

He does not understand it. Nor does he follow where it leads him.

14 At sunset, he gets up and he goes out to murder poor people.

In the night, he goes out to take things that belong to other people.

15 A man may want to have sex with another man's wife.

He waits until it is dark.

Then he thinks that no one will see him.

And he covers his face so that no one will recognise him.

16 In the dark, bad men go out to rob other people.

    But in the day, they stay in their homes and sleep.

17 They all like the night rather than the morning.

    And they are not afraid of things that happen at night.

18 If people throw things into a river, they quickly go away.

    Bad people go from the earth as quickly as that.

Nothing grows in their fields.

    And there are no grapes on their vines.

19 Snow on the ground soon goes away when the sun shines.

    And people who do wrong things soon die.

20 Their mothers soon forget them.

    Worms eat their bodies.

No one remembers people who have done wrong things.

    Like a dead tree, they will never live again.

21 They are cruel to women who have no children.

    And they are not kind to women whose husbands have died.

22 But God is strong. And he can kill people who are rich and powerful.

    They may be important. But they do not know when they will die.

23 They think that they are safe. God may let them think that.

    But he always watches them. And he sees the things that they do.

24 For a short time, bad people may be important, but then they die.

They are not different from anyone else and they soon die, like weeds in the ground.

25 I believe that my words are true. But perhaps someone can say that they are not true.

    Then the words that I speak will be as good as nothing.'

Chapter 25

Bildad speaks to Job a third time

1 Then Bildad replied. And this is what he said.

2 'God is great and he is powerful, too. So we should love him and we should be afraid of him.

    In heaven everyone obeys him.

3 No one can count his armies.

    And his light shines over all the earth.

4 God looks at all the people who live on the earth.

    But he does not see anyone who is really good and completely honest.

5 When God looks at the moon and the stars,

    they do not seem to be very bright.

6 So God must think that people are not very important.

    In his mind they are no more important than insects.'

Chapter 26

Job replies to Bildad

1 Then Job replied. And this is what he said.

2 'I am a weak man. But nothing that you have done has saved me.

    And nothing that you have said has helped me.

3 I am a fool. But you have not been able to make me wise.

    And still you think that you are very clever.

4 I think that someone has helped you to speak these words.

    I think that someone has told you the things that you should say.

5 Dead people go to a place that is under the sea.

    But even there, they are afraid of God.

6 God watches the place where dead people go.

    There is nothing that can hide it from him.

7 He puts the sky in the right place so that it covers everything.

    And he hangs the earth in the skies and he holds it there.

8 He puts water in the clouds.

    The clouds are full of water but they do not break.

9 When the moon is big and round, he hides it.

    He causes clouds to cover it.

10 Look across the sea.

    You can see the end of the sea.

There the sky begins.

God decided where that place should be.

11 If God is angry, even the walls of heaven move.

And because he is angry, they are afraid.

12 He is strong enough to fight against the sea.

And he is wise enough to beat everything that lives in the sea.

13 When he blows, the sky becomes bright.

And he is able to kill the sea serpent.

14 These are only a few of the things that God can do.

No one really knows how powerful God is.'

Chapter 27

1 Job continued to speak. And this is what he said.

2 'God has not been fair to me.

And God, who can do anything, has made my life to be very sad.

3 That is what my life has been like.

But while I am alive, I will promise this to God.

4 I will always say things that are true.

And I will always be honest.

5 I will never agree that you are right.

Until my death, I will never say things that are wrong.

6 I will continue to be honest.

During all of my life, my conscience will never say anything bad about me.

7 My enemies are bad people.

I pray that God will punish them.

8 A bad person cannot hope to have a happy life.

In the end, God will cause him to die.

9 God does not hear him when he asks for God's help.

10 He should always ask God to show him the right way to live.

But because he does not do that, he does not enjoy his life.

11 I will teach you about the power of God.

And I will explain to you the things that God will do to bad people.

12 You have all seen this yourselves.

So you should not still say things that mean nothing.

13 I will tell you what God will do to a bad person.

I will tell you how God will punish him.

14 A bad person may have many children, but they will all die.

Some will die in the war. Other people will die because they do not have enough food to eat.

15 Some will live for a longer time but, in the end, an illness will kill them.

And their wives will not weep when they are dead.

16 A bad man may have more money than he can count.

And he may have more clothes than he could ever wear.

17 But, in the end, a good man will wear those clothes.

And an honest man will spend all that money.

18 The house of a bad man will not be any stronger than the home of an insect.

Nor will it be any better than a worker's hut.

19 A bad man may be very rich.

But soon he will find that all his money has gone.

20 He will become afraid as quickly as a flood comes.

A storm will come in the night and it will kill him.

21 The east wind takes him away, and he is gone.

It removes him from his home.

22 It is so strong that he cannot fight against it.

He can only do one thing. He can try to run away from it.

23 People will see a bad man leave his home.

And God will make them happy when they see that.'

Chapter 28

1 Job continued to speak.

'People know how to dig under the ground to find silver.

And they know how to heat gold to remove all the dirt from it.

2 They understand how to get iron from under the ground.

And they know how to choose the stones that they can get copper from.

3 They look for these metals in places that are deep under the ground.

They take lights with them that help them to see in the dark.

4 They dig a very deep hole that is far from towns or cities.

They work alone. And they hang on strong lines to help them climb down into the hole.

5 We grow our food in the fields.

But deep under the ground there is fire.

6 Sapphires come from the rocks deep under the ground.

And among the stones there, people can find pieces of gold.

7 People go to places where birds have never been.

And they find things that birds have never seen.

8 Wild animals do not walk there.

And lions do not go there.

9 Men break into the hard rock.

And they look beneath the mountains.

10 They dig through the rock.

And they discover stones that are very valuable.

11 They look in the places where rivers start.

And they bring into the light the things that they find there.

12 But people do not know where they can find wisdom.

Nor do they know where they can learn to be wise.

13 People do not understand that it is good to be wise.

And in none of the places where people live can anyone find wisdom.

14 No one will find wisdom in the sea.

Even in the deepest sea, no one will find it.

15 You cannot buy wisdom, even if you are very rich.

You may have lots of gold and silver, but you cannot buy wisdom.

16 Wisdom is worth more than all the gold that comes from Ophir.

It is worth more than onyx or sapphires.

17 Neither a gold cup nor a beautiful glass is as valuable as wisdom.

If you sold all your gold, you still could not buy wisdom.

18 Coral and jasper are not as valuable as wisdom.

The price of it is more than the price of rubies.

19 Topaz from Cush is not as valuable as wisdom.

Nor can anyone buy it, not even with the best gold.

20 So people know how to do many things.

But they do not know where to find wisdom.

21 Many people live on the earth, but none of them has found wisdom.

Even the birds that fly above the earth cannot see it.

22 People who have died may have heard about wisdom.

But they cannot tell us where we can find it.

23 Only God understands how we can be wise.

And only he knows where we can find wisdom.

24 He knows this because he knows everything.

And he sees everything that happens on the earth.

25 He decided the power of the wind.

And he decided the size of the seas.

26 He tells the rain where it should fall.

And he decides where storms should go.

27 When he had done these things, he thought about wisdom.

He knew that it was valuable. And he said that it was good.

28 God spoke to all the people. And he said this:

"If you want to live the right way, you must not do wrong things.

If you want to be wise, you should be afraid not to obey me.

You should do these things because I am God." '

Chapter 29

Job explains the way that he feels

1 Job continued to speak. And this is what he said.

2 'There was a time, many months ago, when I was happy.

At that time, God watched the things that I did.

And because he was with me, bad things did not happen to me.

3 He was my guide and he showed me how to live the right way.

His light seemed to shine on my head.

4 At that time, I was strong and I had good health.

God was my best friend and he kept my home safe.

5 He was always with me.

And my children were still alive.

6 At that time, I got plenty of milk from my cows.

And I got lots of oil from my olive-trees.

7 Sometimes I went to the gate of the city.

There I sat down with the people who ruled the city.

8 Young men moved to let me go by.

Even the old men stood up when I arrived.

9 Princes stopped speaking.

And they covered their mouths with their hands.

10 The nobles were quiet.

They closed their mouths and they did not say anything.

11 People heard the things that I said. They saw the things that I did.

And they were happy because of them.

12 When poor people needed help, I saved them.

And if children had no parents, I helped them.

13 I helped men who were near to death. And they thanked me for my help.

I made widows happy again when they were sad.

14 Everyone knew that I always did right things.

I was always fair and I was always honest.

15 If people could not see, I guided them.

If people could not walk, I fetched things for them.

16 If poor people came to me for help, I was like their father.

I helped strangers when they had no one else to speak for them.

17 I destroyed the power of cruel men.

I saved the people that they had attacked.

18 I thought that I would live to be an old man.

And then I would die in my own house with my family round me.

19 I always had good health.

I was like a tree that had plenty of water.

20 I thought that I would always be strong.

I thought that I would always be a great man.

21 Men waited patiently to hear what I would say.

They knew that I was wise. So they waited quietly to learn from me.

22 After I spoke, they did not speak again.

They were happy to hear the things that I said to them.

23 They waited for me to speak to them.

The things that I said were valuable to them, like rain in the spring.

24 They were surprised when I smiled at them.

And my smile made them happy.

25 I told them what they should do. I lived among them like a king who lives with his army.

And when they were sad, I helped them to be happy again.

Chapter 30

1 Now young men are cruel to me and they say bad things about me.

I would not even let their fathers help me with my sheep.

2 These fathers were strong when they were young. But now they are old.

And they are so weak that they cannot do any work for me.

3 They are thin because they do not have anything to eat.

At night, they run and hide in the desert.

4 In the desert, they eat leaves or roots.

And to keep warm at night, they burn the roots of trees and they light fires with them.

5 People tell them to go away from the towns and cities.

The same people shout at them as they would shout at robbers.

6 They live among the rocks in dry valleys where there had been rivers.

Or they live in holes that they make in the sides of hills.

7 The sounds that they make are like the sounds of wild animals.

And they hide together among the bushes to try to get warm.

8 They are like fools and no one recognises them.

And people do not want them to live near them.

9 Now their sons sing songs about me that are not nice.

They enjoy it when they are cruel to me.

10 They do not like me and they stay away from me.

But if they see me, they spit at me.

11 God has made me weak and he has nearly killed me.

So they can do to me anything that they want.

12 From one side, the crowd attacks me. They push me so that I have to run away.

They are like an army that waits to beat the enemy. And I am their enemy.

13 They do not let me get away from them. When they attack, they really want to kill me.

And they know that no one will come to help me.

14 I cannot stop them when they come near me.

When I fall down, they rush to attack me.

15 Every day that I live, I am afraid. No one thinks that I am an important man now.

And my money has gone as quickly as a cloud passes across the sky.

16 My life will soon end.

Every day I have pains in my body.

17 At night, my bones are painful.

The pains that I feel never go away.

18 Because of the things that God has done to me, my clothes do not fit me.

And my skin does not seem to be the right shape any more.

19 He knocks me down and I fall in the dirt.

I am no better than ashes on the ground.

20 I shout to you, God, but you do not answer me.

When I stand to pray, you do not listen to me.

21 You have become cruel to me.

You are strong. And you can attack me when you choose.

22 You send a strong wind to attack me.

And you destroy me in the storm.

23 I know that you will cause me to die soon.

That happens to everyone who lives on this earth.

24 People do not usually attack someone who has fallen.

They do not refuse to help someone who asks for help.

25 I wept when I saw people with troubles in their lives.

I was sorry to see poor people who needed help.

26 I hoped that I would be happy. But bad things happened to me.

And when I looked for light, everything round me was dark.

27 There is never a day when I feel well.

Every day I have pain and I feel sick.

28 I feel sad. And even when the sun shines it seems to me to be dark.

I stand up in a public place and there I shout to ask for help.

29 My voice is like a jackal's voice.

After dark, I make noises like birds in the night.

30 There are holes in my skin, which has become black.

And I have a fever.

31 Before all these things happened to me, I was happy. And I enjoyed music.

Now I am not happy. So I only sing songs that are sad.

Chapter 31

1 I have promised that I will not look at young women in a wrong way.

2 God is angry with men who have thoughts like that.

He will cause bad things to happen to me if I do that.

3 He is angry with people who do any kind of wrong thing.

And bad things will happen to people who do not live the right way.

4 God sees all the things that I do.

And he watches where I go.

5 I have always said things that are true.

And I have always been an honest man.

6 I ask God to be fair when he thinks about me.

He should know that I have never done any wrong things.

7 God may think that I have not lived the right way.

Or he may think that I have not always obeyed him.

Perhaps, in some other way, I have done something that was wrong.

8 If any of these things is true, someone else can dig my fields.

And they can eat the plants that have grown there.

9 I have not decided to have sex with another man's wife.

I have not waited outside her door until she was alone.

10 If I had done those things, my wife should cook food for someone else.

And she should have sex with other men.

But I have not done those things.

11 If I loved the wife of another man, it would be a very bad thing.

I want God to kill me if I ever do something as bad as that.

12 It would be very dangerous if I loved another woman.

It could destroy my whole life as a fire can destroy everything round it.

13 My servants, both men and women, sometimes had problems.

But if they spoke to me about their problems, I always answered them fairly.

14 God might ask me questions about that.

But if I had not listened to them, I could not have answered him honestly.

15 God made me and he made my servants too.

He made us both and we both grew inside our mothers.

16 I have never refused to help people who are poor.

And I have always helped widows.

17 I have never kept my food for myself.

I have always given some of my food to orphans

18 Since I was a young man, I have been kind to orphans.

And I have always been kind to widows too.

19 I have seen people who were too poor to buy clothes.

I have met people who had no coat to wear.

20 So I took material from my sheep's backs and I made warm clothes for them.

And they thanked me because I was very kind to them.

21 I did not have to be kind to orphans.

But I was never cruel to them.

22 The things that I say are true.

But if they are not true, then someone can break my arm.

23 I could never do wrong things because I was afraid of God.

He hates people who do wrong things. And I was afraid that he would kill me.

24 I know that money will not make me happy.

And if I own lots of gold I will still not be a powerful man.

25 I have worked all my life and got a lot of money.

But that has never been the most important thing to me.

26 Sometimes I look at the sun when it shines in the sky.

And sometimes I watch the moon when it shines at night.

27 But I have never believed the sun or the moon to be gods.

Nor have I ever wanted to worship them.

28 That would have been false.

And God would have been angry if I had done something like that.

29 I do not smile if someone beats my enemy in a war.

It does not make me happy when I see my enemy's troubles.

30 I have never wanted to see the death of my enemy.

That would have been a wrong thing for me to do.

31 There are many men who work in my house as my servants.

They know that I always welcome strangers.

32 Travellers are always welcome in my home.

And no stranger has ever slept in the street outside my house.

33 Some people try to hide the wrong things that they have done.

I have never done that.

34 I do not stay inside my house. I do not refuse to speak.

I am not afraid to hear the things that people say about me.

I am an honest man.

And I will speak about the wrong things that I have done.

35 I really need someone to listen to the things that I say.

All the things that I say are true.

God may believe that I have done wrong things.

If he does, then he should write them down.

36 Then I would wear his list on my shoulder.

Or I would put it on my head like a crown.

37 I would tell God everything that I have done.

I would come to speak to him, as a king would come to visit another king.

38 I have not taken land from anyone else.

I have not taken it from other people who owned it.

39 I have paid for the food that I have eaten.

And I have never been so cruel to farmers that they died.

40 But if I have done any of those things, then I want weeds to grow in my fields.

I do not want barley to grow in my fields.

I want very bad weeds to grow there instead.'

That is the end of all the words that Job spoke.

Chapter 32

Elihu had been listening to everyone and now he speaks to Job

1 Job had said again and again that he was a completely honest man. So his three friends did not argue with him anymore. 2 But another man called Elihu was also there. He was the son of Barachel. (Barachel lived in a place called Buz.) And Elihu became very angry with Job because of the things that Job had said. Job had said that he had never done any wrong things. And he had said that God had caused all his troubles.

3 Elihu was also angry with Job's three friends. They had not been able to answer Job's questions. And they had said that Job had caused all his own problems. 4 The three friends were older than Elihu. So he had not spoken to Job. Instead, he had let them speak first. 5 But, in the end, he saw that the three men did not have anything more to say. And he became very angry. 6 So Elihu spoke. And this is what he said.

'I am young and you are old.

So I was afraid to tell you the things that I know.

7 I thought, "Older men should speak.

They should be able to teach other people how to be wise."

8 But it is the Spirit of Almighty God that comes to men.

And the Spirit helps men to be wise.

9 It is not only older people who are wise.

It is not only older people who know the right way to live.

10 So I say, listen to me.

I too will tell you the things that I know.

11 I waited while you spoke. I listened while you explained your reasons to Job.

And I listened while you tried to find the right words to say to him.

12 I listened carefully to you. But Job did not believe the things that you said.

And none of you was able to answer his questions.

13 Do not say, "We are wise."

Do not say, "God, not man, will explain to Job why Job is wrong.

14 Job was speaking to you and not to me.

But I will not answer his questions in the way that you did.

15 Your friends, Job, are sad and confused. They are quiet now because they cannot help you.

There is nothing more that they can say.

16 They stand there and are not able to answer you.

But surely I need not be quiet because they do not say anything.

17 There are things that I, too, want to say to you.

I, too, will tell you what I know.

18 There are many things that I want to say.

It is now time for me to tell you my thoughts.

19 I can hardly wait to speak to you.

   I am like a bottle of wine that is ready to break.

20 Please help me. Let me speak to you.

   I must open my mouth and reply to you.

21 I will not say good things about someone because he is important.

   Nor will I say good things about anyone if they are not true.

22 I am too honest to do that.

   If I am not honest, then God will remove me.

Chapter 33

1 But now, Job, listen to the things that I will tell you.

   Listen carefully to everything that I say.

2 I will speak to you now.

   I am ready to tell you the thoughts that are in my mind.

3 I am an honest man. So you can believe the words that I speak.

   All the things that I will say are true.

4 The Spirit of God has made me.

   I am alive because of him.

5 Answer me now, Job, if you can.

   Prepare yourself and get ready to speak with me.

6 When God looks at us, we are all like each other.

   God made both of us from dirt.

7 There is no reason why you should be afraid of me.

   I will not do anything that might hurt you.

8 But I have heard you speak, Job.

   And these are the words that you spoke.

9 You said, "I am an honest man.

   I have not done anything that was wrong.

10 But God says that I have done wrong things.

   And he thinks that I am his enemy.

11 I cannot go far because he has tied my feet.

   And he always watches me. So he knows where I go."

12 But I tell you this, Job, you are not right.

   You know that God is greater than any man.

13 So you should not argue with him.

   You should not say that he does not answer any of your questions.

14 God does speak to a man.

   He speaks to him again and again.

But often the man does not listen to him.

   And he does not hear the things that God has said.

15 Sometimes God speaks to a man at night, while he is asleep in bed.

   He speaks by the things that he dreams about.

16 When God speaks in that way, a man listens to him.

   And sometimes he is afraid because of the things that God says to him.

17 God speaks to him to tell him that he must not to do wrong things.

   A man may think that he is important.

But God tells him that he is not very important.

18 God will not let anyone kill him.

   He saves him from death.

19 He may have illnesses that are very painful.

   God can send an illness like that to teach a man the right way to live.

20 Then a man feels sick if he looks at food.

   He cannot eat even the food that he likes most.

21 He was well but now he has become very thin.

   He is so thin that people can see his bones.

22 He is so ill that he will soon die.

   Then he will go to the place where all dead people go.

23 God has thousands of angels who can help a man like that.

   Perhaps an angel will say, "This is a good man."

24 Then God will be kind to that sick person.

And God will say, "I have found someone to pay on behalf of this person. So keep him alive."

25 He will become well again.

And he will be strong, like a young man.

26 He will pray to God and God will answer him.

He will again be God's friend.

And he will enjoy that.

God will know him to be a good man again.

27 Then he will say to people, "I did wrong things.

I did not live the right way but God forgave me.

28 God paid to save me from death.

And now I will live to enjoy the light."

29 God does all these things to people.

He does them twice and sometimes three times.

30 He saves them from death.

Then he lets them again enjoy their lives.

31 Now, Job, listen to the things that I will say.

Be quiet, and I will speak to you.

32 There may be something that you want to say. If there is, then say it.

Then I will be able to say to everyone that you are a good man.

33 But you may not want to say anything. If not, then listen to me.

Be quiet and I will teach you about wisdom.'

Chapter 34

1 Then Elihu continued to speak. And this is what he said.

2 'Hear the words that I speak, you wise men.

Listen to me, you men who have learned many things.

3 You recognise nice food when you eat it.

And you ought to understand the words that you hear.

4 We should decide what is right.

And we should agree together what is true.

5 Job has said, "I am an honest man.

But God does not agree with me.

6 I am right.

But nobody believes me.

I have not done anything wrong.

But I am like a man who has his last illness."

7 There has never been a man like Job.

He laughs at God as easily as a man drinks water.

8 He meets with men who do wrong things.

And his friends are bad people.

9 Job says that people should not try to obey God.

If they do, they will not get anything back.

10 So listen to me, you men who understand everything.

Almighty God will not do anything that is wrong.

11 If a man has been kind to other people, God is kind to him.

But God will do to a bad man the things that he has done to other people.

12 No one thinks that God could ever do anything wrong.

All the things that he does, he does fairly.

13 God is the ruler of the whole world.

And nobody gave that job to him!

14 God gave us our lives.

So he can decide if he wants to take them from us.

15 If he did that, everyone would die together.

And people would become dirt again.

16 If you can understand my words, then hear me.

And listen to me when I speak to you.

17 God could not rule fairly if he were not a good God.

He is powerful and he is always fair. So you cannot say that he has been cruel to you.

18 It is God who removes kings and rulers.

He may do this if they have been bad kings or bad rulers.

19 God made us all. So it does matter to him that someone is a king's son.

And he is no kinder to a rich person than he is to a poor person.

20 Anyone can die in a moment, in the middle of the night.

People die, even if no person has tried to kill them.

21 He watches the way that people live.

They can go anywhere that they want. But he will always be able to see them.

22 There is no place dark enough for people to hide from God.

It does not matter where they are. He can always see them.

23 In the end, people will have to explain to God how they have lived their lives.

But God does not need to tell them when they will have to do that.

24 God does not need to ask what rulers have done. He may decide to remove them.

And he will make other men rulers instead of them.

25 He knows that the bad rulers have done wrong things.

So, in the night, he kills them.

26 He punishes them where everyone can see them.

He does this because they have done wrong things.

27 They have not lived in the way that he wanted them to live.

And they have not done the things that he told them to do.

28 Because of the things that they did, poor people had to ask God for help.

And God heard those poor people and he helped them.

29 But God might have decided not to help those poor people.

And no one could say that he was wrong to decide that.

If he hides himself, no one can see him.

But he rules over men and countries.

30 He does not let bad people rule.

In this way, he saves the people from bad rulers.

31 Someone may say to God, "I have done wrong things.

But I am sorry and I will not do them again.

32 I may not have understood that some things were wrong.

Tell me about such things and I will not do them again either."

33 But Job, you refuse to say that you are sorry.

So there is no reason why God should forgive you.

You must decide what you will do. I cannot decide for you.

So give me a true answer - what have you decided?

34 Wise men agree with the things that I say.

This is what they will say to me.

35 "Job speaks like a fool.

He does not understand the things that he says."

36 Job, it is right that bad things should happen to you.

You have spoken like a bad man would speak.

37 You have done wrong things. And now you are refusing to obey God.

You are playing games with us. And you have now said many bad things against God.'

Chapter 35.

1 Then Elihu spoke to Job again. And this is what he said.

2 'The things that you say cannot be right.

"God knows that I have not done anything wrong." That is what you say.

3 But you ask him why you should live the right way.

You ask this also. "What do I get if I only do good things?"

4 I would like to reply to you.

And I will speak, too, to the friends who are with you.

5 Look up at the sky to see what is there.

Look at the clouds that are so high above you.

6 If you do wrong things, that will not hurt God.

If you do many wrong things, it will not change him.

7 You do not give anything to God if you are always good.

He does not receive from you because you do good things.

8 Only you feel the result of the wrong things that you do.

And only other people get something as a result of the good things that you do.

9 People shout when they have a lot of trouble.

They ask for help when powerful people attack them.

10 God made men. And when they are sad, he causes them to be happy.

But none of them asks where he is.

11 He teaches more things to us than he teaches to animals.

And he makes us wiser than the birds. But people still do not ask him to help them.

12 People may ask him to help them.

But he does not help them because they do so many wrong things.

13 They may pray to God. But they do not believe that he will answer them.

So God does not even listen to them.

14 You say that you do not see him. And you say that you wait for him to answer you.

So there is no reason why he should listen to you either.

15 You say that God does not punish bad people. You do things that are wrong.

But you think that he does not see them.

16 So, Job, you do not understand what you say.

And the words that you speak do not mean anything.'

Chapter 36

1 Elihu continued to speak. And this is what he said.

2 'Please be patient and listen to me.

I want to say something else on behalf of God.

3 I have learned many things during my life.

And I know that God is always fair.

4 Everything that I say to you is true.

You can be sure about that because I am a really wise man.

5 God is powerful and he does not hate anyone.

But when he decides to do something, he does it.

6 He does not let bad people live for a long time.

But he is always fair to people who have problems.

7 He sees people who live the right way.

And he makes them famous so that they rule like kings.

8 Sometimes people have trouble in their lives.

And they cannot discover what has caused their trouble.

9 Then he tells them what they have done.

They have done wrong things and they have not listened to him.

10 He causes them to listen to him.

And he tells them that they must not continue to sin.

11 God wants them to be his servants and to obey him.

If they do that, they will be rich. And they will be happy until they die.

12 But some people do not listen to God and they do not obey him.

Such people do not know the right way to live.

And someone will fight against them and kill them.

13 When people do not obey God, they become angry.

Even when God punishes them, they do not ask him to help them.

14 They die while they are still young.

They have wasted their lives. They have lived among men who have sex with other men.

15 But God helps people who have troubles.

And he causes them to hear his words.

16 God does not want you to have trouble in your life, Job.

He wants to make you safe and to take your problems away.

He wants you to have a comfortable life.

And he wants you to have plenty of nice food.

17 But now God is punishing you because of the wrong things that you have done.

But, in the end, he will be fair to you.

18 You are a rich man, but be careful.

Rich people often do wrong things to get even more money.

19 You may be a rich man, but this will not help you.

Even if you try, you will not be able to get out of trouble.

20 Do not wait until it is night.

   Do not take people away from their homes in the dark.

21 God let you have troubles in your life. He did this to make you think about your life.

   So be careful that you live the right way.

22 You know that God is powerful.

   And he is also the best teacher.

23 Nobody can tell God what he should do.

   And no one can say to him, "You have done things that are wrong."

24 People sing songs to say that God is great.

   You should do that, too.

25 Men everywhere have seen the things that God has done.

   But we can only see them from far away.

26 God is so great that we cannot know him completely.

   We do not know how long he has lived.

27 It is God who takes water from the earth.

   Then he makes it into rain.

28 The rain falls from the clouds.

   And so there is enough water for everyone.

29 Nobody understands how the clouds move through the sky.

   And nobody understands the noise that storms make.

30 In a storm, the clouds are dark. But he causes the light to shine brightly.

   It shines even on things that are deep under the sea.

31 This is the way that God rules the world.

   He sends storms. But he gives to people all the food that they need.

32 He sends the storms where he wants them to go.

   And he tells them what they should hit.

33 Loud noises in the sky show that a storm is coming soon.

   Then even the cows in the fields know that there will soon be a storm.

Chapter 37

1 A storm like that makes me very afraid.

2 Listen well to God's words.

   Listen to the loud noise when he speaks.

3 He sends lightning across the sky.

   It goes in all directions.

4 After the lightning comes the sound of his voice.

   When he speaks, it is like the sound of thunder.

5 When God speaks, great things happen.

   He does things that we can never understand.

6 He tells the snow to drop on the earth.

   And when it rains, he causes lots of rain to drop on the ground.

7 People need to see what God can do. He made them and he rules the weather.

   And when the weather is bad like that, people are not able to work.

8 The wild animals hide among the rocks.

   Or they stay in the places where they sleep at night.

9 The storm comes from the south.

   And the cold winds come from the north.

10 Ice covers the rivers and lakes.

   The cold wind that makes the ice is like God's breath.

11 He fills the clouds with water.

   And he sends the lightning through the clouds.

12 The clouds move across all the earth.

   They go where he sends them.

13 He sends the clouds so that there is water on the earth.

   Sometimes he does this when he has to punish people.

Sometimes he does it to show them that he loves them.

14 Listen to the things that I tell you.

   Stop, Job. Think about all the great things that God does.

15 God makes the clouds move.

But you do not know how he does that.

He makes the lightning shine for a moment in the sky.

But you do not know how he does that either.

16 You cannot explain how the clouds stay up in the sky.

Only God can do all these things, because he knows how to do everything.

17 When the warm wind blows from the south in summer, everything is hot.

And you are too warm in the clothes that you wear.

18 Then the sky becomes like a metal mirror that makes everything even warmer.

God has made it like that. And you cannot help him do it.

19 You think that you are wise. So tell us what we should say to God.

Help us, Job, because we do not know what to say to him.

20 I will not ask if I can speak to God.

If I ask, he might kill me.

21 The winds have blown all the clouds away.

Now no one can look at the sun, which shines brightly in the sky.

22 People can see lovely colours in the sky, towards the north. But they cannot see God.

He is too bright and too beautiful for us to look at.

23 God is so powerful that we cannot come near to him.

But he is always kind and fair to everyone.

24 People may think that they are wise.

But they are afraid of him, because only he is really wise.'

Chapter 38

The LORD speaks to Job

1 While a storm continued, the LORD spoke to Job. And this is what he said.

2 'You have asked many questions about the things that I do, Job.

But you do not really understand the things that you say.

3 Now be brave, and listen to me.

There are many things that I want to tell you.

4 You were not there when I made the world.

If you know so many things, tell me about that.

5 I decided how large the world should be.

I am sure that you know that!

6 You do not know how I made the world.

But it was I who put it in the right place.

7 When I did this, the angels sang. They were so happy.

And even the stars seemed to sing, too.

8 At the beginning of time, I made the sea.

I decided where it should begin. And I decided how far it should go.

9 Above the sea, I made the clouds.

And everything was dark.

10 I decided where the land would be.

And the sea could not come there.

11 I said to the sea, "This is as far as you can come.

This is where you must stop."

12 You, Job, have never said when night should end.

And you could not tell the morning when it should start.

13 Bad things happen at night. And when day comes, they stop.

But you could not tell the light when to cover the earth.

14 When the day comes, people can see things clearly.

And the shape of the earth becomes clear, like someone who is wearing a coat.

15 The light of day is too bright for people who do bad things.

In the day, they stop doing things that are wrong.

16 You have not explored where the water in the sea comes from.

Nor have you gone to the deepest part of the sea.

17 You have not seen the place where dead people go.

Nor do you know the way to that place.

18 You do not understand how big the world is.

Tell me, Job, if you know all these things.

19 You do not know where light comes from.

And you do not know how the dark begins.

20 You do not know where to find them.

You do not know how to get there.

21 But you have lived for many years.

So perhaps you do know all these things.

22 You have not visited the place where I keep all the snow.

And you have not seen the place where I keep the hail.

23 I keep the snow and the hail until trouble comes.

I keep them to use when there are wars.

24 You do not understand where lightning comes from.

Nor do you know how the wind from the east blows over the earth.

25 I decide where the rivers should go.

And I tell the storm which way to go.

26 I send the rain to places where no one lives.

And it falls in the desert.

27 It falls on ground where there has been no rain for a long time.

And it makes the grass grow again.

28 The rain does not have a father.

No one knows where dew comes from.

29 Ice does not have a mother.

No one knows why the ground is cold and hard in the morning.

30 In very cold weather, water becomes hard like stone.

And there is even ice on top of the sea.

31 You cannot tie together the beautiful Pleiades.

And you cannot change the shape of Orion.

32 You cannot put the stars in the right place at different times of the year.

And you cannot tell the Great Bear and Little Bear where they should go in the sky.

33 You do not know how everything in the sky stays in the right place.

And you do not understand, either, how I rule the earth.

34 You cannot speak to the clouds.

You cannot tell them to cover the earth with water.

35 You cannot send the lightning to the place where it must go.

Even if you tried to do that, nothing would happen.

36 Wisdom does not come from you, Job.

And you do not understand everything about the weather, either.

37 You are not clever enough to count the clouds.

Nor can you send water from the sky, like a person who pours it from a pot.

38 Rain can make the soil wet.

But you cannot cause the rain to fall.

39 You do not look for food to feed hungry lions.

The mother of the young lions does that herself.

40 She looks for food while the young lions hide in their holes.

She brings them food while they wait in the bushes.

41 You do not feed the ravens.

When the young ravens are hungry, they ask me for food.

Chapter 39

1 You do not know when young goats are born on the mountains.

You are not there to see the young deer when they are born.

2 You do not know how many months it will be until the birth of the young deer.

Nor do you know when they will be born.

3 The deer bend down and the young deer are born.

Then they have no more pain.

4 The young animals become fit and strong.

When they have grown, they leave their parents. And they will not return to them.

5 The wild donkeys are free to run where they want.

I let them do that.

6 I decided that the desert would be their home.

And I decided that they would live there.

7 They do not go near cities where there is a lot of noise.

They do not listen to people who might want them to work.

8 They live on the hills where they look for food.

They look for nice green grass to eat.

9 A wild ox will not do what you tell it to do.

Nor will it stay in your farm at night.

10 It will not let you fasten it to a plough.

Nor will it plough the fields for you.

11 The wild ox is a very strong animal.

But you cannot be sure that it will help you to do your work.

12 It will not help you to pick the plants in your fields.

Nor will it help you to bring them into your farm.

13 The ostrich makes its wings move a lot.

But the ostrich cannot fly, so its wings are not as good as the wings of a stork.

14 The ostrich puts its eggs on the ground.

And it lets them get warm in the sand.

15 It does not know that a person's foot may break them.

And it does not know that a wild animal may walk on them.

16 It is careless with its eggs. It does not know that they are its eggs.

They were the result of its work. But it will not be sad if someone breaks them.

17 This is because I did not make the ostrich wise.

And I did not make it able to think properly.

18 But when the ostrich begins to run, it can run very fast.

It can run past the fastest horse.

19 You, Job, did not make horses strong.

Nor did you give them all the long hair that they have on their necks.

20 You did not make them able to jump like locusts.

And horses also frighten people because of the loud noises that they make.

21 A horse knows that it is very strong.

It hits its foot on the ground when it is ready to fight.

22 A horse is not afraid of anything.

It is not even afraid when it carries a soldier with his weapons.

23 The soldier's sword shines in the sun.

And the horse feels the sword as it hits against its side.

24 It wants to run as fast as it can.

When it hears the trumpet, it wants to run faster.

25 When it hears the sound of the trumpet it makes a loud noise.

People may be far away. But it can hear them when they fight.

It can hear the officers in the army when they shout to the soldiers.

26 The hawk does not learn from you how to fly.

You do not teach it to fly toward the south in winter.

27 You do not tell the eagle that it must fly high into the sky.

You do not show it where to build its home up in the mountains

28 Its home is among the highest rocks where it stays at night.

It knows that it is safe there.

29 From there it can look for its food, even if it is far away.

It can see small animals that it wants to catch.

30 Its food is the small animals that it kills.

And then the young eagles come and they drink the blood of the dead animals.'

Chapter 40

1 The LORD spoke to Job. And this is what he said.

2 'I am God. Do you still want to argue with me?

You say that I have done wrong things. Now you must explain what you mean.'

3 Then Job answered the LORD. And this is what he said.

4 'I am a silly man and I cannot reply to you properly.

I put my hand over my mouth and I will not say anything.

5 I have said too much already.

There is nothing more that I want to say.'

6 Then the LORD spoke to Job out of the storm. And this is what he said.

7 'Stand up and be brave.

I will speak to you, and you must answer me.

8 You think that I am not fair to you.

And you think that you are always right.

9 But you are not as strong as I am.

And your voice is not as loud as mine is.

10 If you were like me, you could put on lovely clothes.

And you could show everyone how beautiful you are.

11 You could show everyone how angry you can be.

People think that they are very clever. You could show them that they are not so clever.

12 You could do that, Job, if you were like me.

And, when you find them, you could kill bad people, too.

13 You could bury them all in the ground.

You could send them to the place where dead people go.

14 If you can do these things, then even I would praise you.

Then I would agree that you could save yourself.

15 Look at the Great Animal.

I made it and I made you. It eats only grass, like a cow.

16 But how strong its legs are!

And how powerful its stomach is!

17 Its tail is as straight as a tall tree.

Its legs are thick and they are strong.

18 Its bones are as strong as bronze.

Its back legs and its front legs are as strong as iron.

19 I have not made anything bigger or better than the Great Animal.

And only I am stronger than the Great Animal.

20 The wild animals may play in the grass on the side of the hill.

But the Great Animal comes and eats the grass next to them.

21 It lies under the bushes.

It hides among the plants that grow at the edge of the lake.

22 It rests under the trees that grow near the river.

Then it can stay cool because the sun does not shine on it.

23 Even when the river is deep and strong, it is not afraid.

The River Jordan may be all round it, but it still feels safe.

24 No one can catch the Great Animal.

No one can put a ring in its nose and lead it away.

Chapter 41

1 You cannot catch a crocodile in the same way that you catch a fish.

Nor can you tie its mouth to stop it biting you.

2 You cannot fasten a line to its nose.

Nor can you put a hook in its mouth.

3 It will not ask you to stop being cruel to it.

And it will not speak to you politely.

4 It will not agree to work for you.

And you cannot make it your slave for always.

5 It is not a friendly animal, like a bird that you can keep in your home.

And it is not the kind of animal that your children can play with.

6 No one will buy it to sell it.

And no one will cut it up and try to sell it in shops.

7 You cannot put long knives into its skin to catch it.

Nor can you put a sharp stick into its head to kill it.

8 If you touch it, you will never forget it.

It will fight with you and you will never touch it again!

9 You cannot hope to catch it, because it will always be too strong.

As soon as you see it, you will be afraid of it.

10 No one is silly enough to wake it. Everyone knows that it is too strong.

And I made it! So no one will be able to fight against me.

11 There is nothing that I must pay to anyone.

Everything in the world is mine.

12 Let me tell you all about this animal.

It is strong and it has a large body and powerful legs.

13 Its skin is so thick that no one could remove it.

And people are afraid to go near it.

14 Nobody would try to open its mouth.

Anyone who sees its teeth would be very afraid.

15 Its back has very thick skin to keep it safe.

There are no spaces into which you could put a knife.

16 Each piece of skin is very near the next one.

Not even air can pass between them.

17 There is no space between the pieces of skin.

And no one can separate them.

18 It makes a loud noise and its eyes are very bright.

Its eyes are as red as the sky at dawn.

19 Fire comes from its mouth.

And sparks come out of its mouth.

20 Smoke comes from its nose.

It is like smoke that comes from a fire of weeds under a pot.

21 The air that comes from its mouth can light a fire.

And flames come quickly out of its mouth.

22 Its neck is very strong.

It frightens people when they see it.

23 There is no weak place anywhere on its skin.

Its whole body is as strong as iron.

24 Its front is hard like rock.

It is as hard as a stone.

25 Even strong and brave people are afraid when it moves towards them.

They run away because it might hit them with its tail.

26 No one can hurt it, even with a sword.

None of your sharp weapons can hurt it.

27 It can break iron as easily as a thin stick.

It can break bronze as easily as an old piece of wood.

28 Arrows do not frighten it.

Stones cannot hurt it.

29 A heavy stick seems to it like a piece of dry grass.

It laughs when it hears the sound of a lance.

30 Its stomach is sharp, like bits of a pot that someone has broken.

When it moves along, it leaves marks on the ground, like a plough.

31 The water seems to boil when it swims in it.

When it swims down deep, the water is like a pot of oil.

32 When it moves through the water, the water behind it shines.

The water seems to have become white.

33 Nowhere in the world is there anything that is as strong as this animal.

And it is not afraid of anything.

34 It is stronger than even the strongest of animals.

It is like the king of all the wild animals.'

Chapter 42

Job replies to the LORD.

1 Then Job replied to the LORD,

2 'I know that you can do all things. Nobody can beat you.

You are powerful. And you can do anything that you want to do.

3 I do not know much. And you asked me why I talk so much.

I have talked about the surprising things that you do.

But I did not understand them.

4 You told me to listen and to answer your questions.

5 I had heard about you from other people.

Now I have seen you with my own eyes.

6 So I do not like the things that I said.

I sit here in the ashes.

I am doing that to show you that I am sorry.'

The end of the story

7 The LORD said to Eliphaz,

'The things that my servant Job has said about me are true. But the things that you said were not true. So I am angry with you and your two friends. 8 I want you to go to Job and to sacrifice 7 bulls and 7 goats. If you do that, I will be happy. After you have sacrificed the animals, Job will pray for you. Then I willforgive you for your silly words. Job, who is my servant, said the right things about me. But you did not.'

9 So Eliphaz, Bildad, and Zophar obeyed the LORD and they sacrificed the animals. And Job prayed for his three friends. Then the LORD did as he had promised. He forgave them for all the wrong things that they had said.

10 So Job prayed for his three friends. After that, the LORD made him twice as rich as he had been before.11 Then Job had a party for his brothers and sisters and for his friends. They each told Job how sad they had been. They had been very sad because the LORD had caused much pain to Job. They each gave a coin and a gold ring to Job.

12 The LORD made Job richer than he had been before. The LORD gave to him 14 000 sheep, 6000camels, 1000 pairs of oxen, and 1000 donkeys. 13 As well as seven sons, Job had three daughters. 14 Their names were Jemimah, Keziah, and Keren-Happuch. 15 They were the most beautiful women in the whole country. Job said what should happen after his death. His sons and his daughters should have all the things that had belonged to him. 16 Job lived for another 140 years. He lived until he had seen his grandchildren and their grandchildren. 17 When, in the end, he died, he was a very old man.

PSALMS

The Two Ways
Psalm 1

Jesus said, "Go in through the narrow gate. The wide gate and the wide road go to death. Many people go that way. The narrow gate and the narrow road go to life that never finishes. Only a few people find it". (Matthew 7: 13 - 14)

Psalm 1

> **v1** The man is very happy that does not:
> ☐ walk as godless people suggest
> ☐ stand in the way near sinners
> ☐ sit with them that scorn (God)
>
> **v2** He likes what the LORD teaches.
> He repeats it day and night.
>
> **v3** "He will become like a tree planted by rivers of water". *(Jeremiah 17:8)*
> "It will give its fruit in its season. Its leaves will not fall" *(Ezekiel 47:12)*
> "Everything that he does will be very good". *(Joshua 1:8)*
>
> **v4** But the godless are like chaff.
> The wind blows them away.
>
> **v5** So godless people will not stand in the judgment.
> Sinners will not stay with righteous people.
>
> **v6** The LORD knows the way of righteous people.
> The way of the godless leads to death.

God Rules OK!
Psalm 2

Jesus said, "Do not be afraid. You believe in God. Believe in me also". (John 14:1)

Psalm 2

> **v1** Why are nations planning together?
> Why are people having such stupid ideas?
>
> **v2 - v3** Why are their kings saying,
> "We will not obey the LORD"?
> Why are their leaders saying,
> "We will not do what his Messiah says"?
>
> **v4** He that is sitting above the skies will laugh.
> The Lord will say that they are stupid.
>
> **v5** Then he will say angry words to them.
> He will make them very frightened because he is so angry.
>
> **v6** He will say, "I myself put my king in Zion.
> I put him on my holy mountain".
>
> **v7** I will tell you what God has decided to do.
> The LORD said to me, "You are my son.
> Today I have given you the *honour that goes with that name.
>
> **v8** Ask me for anything! I will give you nations.
> The whole world can be yours.
>
> **v9** You will rule them with an iron sceptre.
> You will break them like a clay pot".
>
> **v10** So now, you kings, be careful.
> You world leaders, listen to this:
>
> **v11** Become the servants of the LORD.
> Remember that he is very powerful.
>
> **v12** Kiss his son or God will be angry.
> He may be so angry that you will die.
> Only the people that come to the LORD are really happy.
> He will make them safe.

A Morning Song

Psalm 3

Jesus got out of bed very early in the morning. He went somewhere by himself. There he prayed. (Mark 1: 35)

Psalm 3

(This is) a song of David when he ran away from Absalom his son.

> **v1** LORD, every day I have more enemies.
> Many people fight me.
>
> **v2** Many people say about me,
> "God will not save him". **SELAH**
>
> **v3** But LORD, you are a shield over me.
> You are my glory.
> You have lifted up my head.
>
> **v4** I shouted aloud to the LORD.
> He answered me from his holy mountain. **SELAH**
>
> **v5** I lay down and slept.
> I awoke because the LORD kept me alive.
> He kept me safe.
>
> **v6** I will not be afraid of 10 000 enemies that are all round me.
>
> **v7** LORD, stand up! My God, save me!
> In the past, you hit all my enemies in the face.
> You broke their teeth.
>
> **v8** It was the LORD that saved us.
> Lord, do good things for all your people. **SELAH**

An Evening Song
Psalm 4

Jesus said, "Come to me, all you that work hard. Also, all of you that have a lot of trouble. I will give you rest". (Matthew 11: 28)

Psalm 4

(Tell the music leader) to use stringed instruments.
(This is) a song of David.

v1 Answer me when I shout for help, O God.
You are the God that makes me righteous.
Give me help in my troubles.
Show me that you are kind.
Listen to me when I pray.

v2 Sons of man:
- how long will you say that I am bad?
- how long will you love stupid ideas?
- how long will you want to hear lies? **SELAH**

v3 Sons of man:
- the LORD has chosen me
- the LORD has made me separate for himself
- the LORD will listen when I pray to him

v4 Get angry - but do nothing wrong. Go to bed.
Argue with yourself - but say nothing (aloud). **SELAH**

v5 Offer the right gifts and believe in the LORD.

v6 Many people say, "Who will do anything good for us?"
LORD, shine the light of your face on us.

v7 You have made me feel happy deep down inside me.
I feel better than I do at a harvest party.

v8 I will lie down in *peace. Soon I will sleep.
This is because only you, LORD, keep me safe.

Pray about your Enemies
Psalm 5

Jesus said, "Love your enemies. Pray for them that hurt you". (Matthew 5: 44)

Psalm 5

(Tell the) music leader to use flutes.
(This is) a song of David.

v1 LORD, hear my words.
Listen to what I am saying to you.

v2 My king and my God, listen to my voice.
I am praying to you for help.
I am shouting to you!

v3 LORD, at sunrise you will hear my voice.
I will watch and pray early in the morning.

v4 My God, you do not like what is wrong.
Bad people cannot live with you.

v5 Some people think that they are important.
They cannot stay near to God.
God, you hate everyone that does wrong.

v6 You destroy all that do not speak the truth.
The LORD hates all people that do murder.
He hates people that do not keep their promises.

v7 But I will come into your house
because you are so loving and kind.
I will bend low in your holy temple.

v8 Lead me in your righteous way
because of my enemies.
Make your path straight for me.

v9 Nothing that my enemies say is true.
They want to destroy me.
Their mouth is like an open grave.
They only speak what is not true.

v10 God, tell them that they are not right.
Show them that their ideas are wrong.
Send them away because they are bad.
They argued with you.

v11 Make all the people happy that hide with you.
Make them always sing for joy.
Cover them that love your name. Keep them safe.
Then they will rejoice in you.

v12 LORD, you do such good things to the righteous.
Your love is all round them.

David is very ill
Psalm 6

Jesus said, "I am always with you, to the end of time". (Matthew 28: 20)

Psalm 6

(This is) a song of David.
(Tell the) music leader, "Use a harp and male singers".

v1 LORD, do not become angry with me.
Please do not become angry.

v2 LORD, be kind to me because I am not strong.
LORD, give me health because my bones are afraid.

v3 I myself am very frightened. LORD - for how long?

v4 LORD, come back. Give me back my life.
Make me safe because of your kind love.

v5 Nobody that dies can remember you.
Who can praise you in Sheol?

v6 I am weak with crying.
My bed swims on my tears every night.
The place where I sleep is soaked.

v7 My eyes are so sad that they are growing weak.
They are becoming old because of all my enemies.

v8 Go away from me all you bad people.
The LORD has listened to the noise of my crying.

v9 The LORD heard me when I asked him for a kind answer.
The Lord will listen to what I say.

v10 All those that hate me will be very much ashamed.
They will also be disappointed.
They will be disappointed and soon they will turn away.

David and Cush
Psalm 7

Jesus said, "My judgment is fair". (John 5: 30)

Psalm 7

David showed what he felt.
He sang to the LORD because of what Cush said.
Cush was from Benjamin.

v1 LORD, my God, I am hiding in you.
Keep me safe from all those (people) that are trying to catch me.
Make me safe,

v2 or he will tear me to pieces as a wild animal would.
He will tear me to pieces and nobody will find me.

v3 - v4 LORD, my God, if I did this:
- if my hand did something wrong
- if I did something bad to a friend
- if I robbed my enemy without a reason

v5 then I want him to catch me.
I want him to knock me to the ground.
I want him to kill and bury me. **SELAH**

v6 LORD, get up and how that you are angry.
Fight my angry enemies.
Wake up, my God, and tell us who is right.

v7 I want everybody to stand round you.
Rule over them from above.

v8 LORD, tell us who is right when people argue.
LORD Most High, say that I am righteous and honest.

v9 Stop the godless from fighting. Make the righteous safe.
God of the righteous, look at how we think and feel.

v10 God Most High is a shield over me.
He makes everyone that has a clean heart safe.

v11 God is a righteous judge.
God shows his anger every day.

v12 if he does not change his mind, he will make his sword sharp.
He will bend his bow and make it ready.

v13 He will prepare weapons of death for bad people.
He will make ready arrows of fire.

v14 Look! The bad man is pregnant with evil.
He conceives trouble. He gives birth to false ideas.

v15 He digs a hole. He makes it deep.
Then he himself falls into the hole that he has made!

v16 The trouble that he makes for others falls on his own head.
His own violence comes down on the top of himself!

v17 I will thank the LORD because he is righteous.
I will sing praise to the name of the LORD Most High.

The Sky at Night
Psalm 8

The children in the temple said, "Hosanna to the son of David". This made the leaders of the Jews very angry. They said to Jesus, "Do you hear what they are saying?" Jesus said, "Yes! Did you never read, 'From the mouths of children and babies at the breast you received praise'?" (Matthew 21:15-16) Matthew was a friend of Jesus. Hosanna is now a word of praise. Praise is saying good things about someone. The son of David in this story is Jesus.

Psalm 8

The music leader must use Gittith.
(This is) a song of David.

v1 LORD, you are our most powerful king.
Your name is famous in all the wide world.
Your glory is over the skies.

v2 From the mouths of children and babies at the breast
you show (what it is to be) strong.
This is because you have enemies.
You will beat your enemies and the avenger.

v3 When I look at your skies that your fingers made:
☐ I see the moon
☐ I see the stars
☐ You gave them all a place

v4 Then I ask:
☐ why do you remember men (and women)?
☐ what makes you visit them?

v5 You made their place a little below God.
You made them feel as kings.

v6 - v8 You made them to rule everything that your hands made.
You put everything under their feet:
☐ sheep and cows
☐ wild animals in the fields
☐ birds in the air
☐ fish in the waters
☐ monsters in the deep seas

v9 LORD, you are our most powerful king.
Your name is famous in all the wide world.

God will Always Remember you
Psalms 9 and 10

Jesus said, "I did not come to judge the world. I came to save the world". (John 12:47) (Judge here means say who is wrong.)

Psalm 9

The leader (must use the music) "Death to the son".

(This is) a song of David

v1 All my heart sings 'thank you' to the LORD.
I will tell (people) of all your wonderful work.

v2 I will be very happy with you, (LORD). I will rejoice in you.
I will sing praises to your name, Most High God.

v3 Back my enemies went,
they fell down. They died in front of you,

v4 because you judged that what I did was right .
You sat on your throne. You made a righteous judgment.

v5 Clearly you judged the nations and destroyed the wicked.
People will never remember their names.

v6 You caught the enemy. You killed them.
You knocked down their cities. People will just forget them.

v7 Evermore the LORD will rule.
He has built his throne. On it, he will make his judgments.

v8 He will make righteous judgments for the world.
His government will give justice to the people.

v9 For the LORD is a place where the oppressed can hide.
He will be a fortress in times of trouble.

v10 Everyone that knows your name (LORD) will put their trust in you.
LORD, you will never turn away from anyone that looks for you.

v11 Go to the LORD with praises. His throne is in Zion.
Tell all the nations all that he has done.

v12 (God) will remember the people that somebody murdered.
He will not forget the oppressed people that cry to him.

v13 Have mercy on me, LORD.
See how my enemies make my life very difficult.
Make me safe from the gates of death.

v14 Then I will tell your praises in the gates of Jerusalem.
I will rejoice that I am safe with you.

v15 Into the hole that they dug the nations fell.
They caught their own feet in the net that they hid.

v16 You will recognise the LORD by his justice.
The enemies of God will catch themselves in their own nets.
HIGGAION SELAH

v17 Just as the enemies of God go to Sheol,
so will all the nations that forget him.

v18 Know this: God will not always forget the poor.
The oppressed will not have to hope for evermore.

v19 LORD, stand up! Do not let men become too powerful.
Let the nations find justice before you.

v20 LORD, make them afraid.
Make the nations know that they are only human.   **SELAH**

Psalm 10

v1 LORD, why are you standing so far away?
Why do you hide when there is trouble?

v2 in his pride, the wicked man tries to catch helpless people.
I hope that wicked people catch themselves with their bad plans!

v3 The wicked boasts about what he wants.
He says good things about those that want more than is fair.
He says very bad things about the LORD.

v4 In his pride, the wicked does not look for God.
He will not even think of God.

v5 Everything that the wicked does always works well.
He puts the rules of God far from him.
He laughs at the people that do not like him.

v6 He says to himself, "There will be no trouble for me.
Nothing bad will ever happen to me or to my children".

v7 His mouth makes bad promises.
It is full of words that are not true.
He says that he will do very bad things to people.
There is evil on his tongue.

v8 He hides behind the bushes near the villages.
He watches in secret for people to hurt.
He jumps out and murders people that have done nothing wrong.

v9 He lies like a lion under the cover of a bush.
He waits to catch someone that is helpless.
He does catch him and takes him away in his net.

v10 He beats the helpless man.
The helpless man fails and falls under the stronger man.

v11 He says to himself, "God forgot.
He hid his face. He never saw what happened".

v12 Rise up, O God! Lift up your hand.
Do not forget the helpless people.

v13 Why does the wicked man say such bad things about God?
Why does he think, "God will not do anything about it?"

v14 See it all, God, all the trouble,
all the oppressed people.
Decide what to do about it.
The helpless puts his trust in you.
You give help to the fatherless.

v15 The arm of the wicked and evil man ... break it (LORD)!
Tell him to explain what he has done.
He thought that you would not discover it!

v16 The LORD will always be king.
The nations will not remain in his land for evermore.

v17 You hear, LORD, what oppressed people want.
You listen when they pray. You give them something to hope for.

v18 You care for the fatherless and the oppressed.
People from the earth will not frighten the poor again.

Fly Away like a Bird
Psalm 11

Jesus said, "I am the good shepherd. My sheep hear my voice. I know my sheep. They follow me. Nobody will ever take them away from me". (From John 10:14,27,28.) A shepherd is a sheep farmer. Jesus meant that his friends are his sheep. He cares for them.

Psalm 11

(This is) a song of David for the music leader.

v1 (These are words of David.)
I am hiding in the LORD.
How can you say to me,
(These are the words of David's friends.)
Fly away like a bird to the hills?

v2 Look at the godless!
They are preparing their bows and arrows.
They are getting ready to shoot at good people.
They are hiding in the shadows.

v3 When people destroy the foundations
what can the righteous do?

v4 (These are words of David.)
The LORD is in his holy temple.
The LORD is sitting on his throne in heaven.
He is looking down.
His eyes see what the sons of men are doing.

v5 The LORD is (also) checking what the righteous are doing.
But the LORD really hates the godless.
He also hates the people that love to hurt other people.

v6 Burning coal and sulphur will rain on the godless.
A very hot wind will be their inheritance and cup.

v7 The LORD is righteous.
He loves righteous people.
They will see his face.

Good Words and Bad Words
Psalm 12

Jesus said "What I tell you is true". (John 8:45)

Psalm 12

(This is) a song of David.
(Tell the) music leader to use male singers.

v1 LORD, give help!
There are no more kind people.
Nobody is faithful anywhere.

v2 Everybody tells lies to his neighbour.
Their words sound good, but they are not.

v3 LORD, cut off every tongue that tells lies.
Shut every mouth that boasts.

v4 Do this to everyone that says:
☐ what we say will make us powerful
☐ we will say what we like
☐ who will stop us?

v5 The LORD says, "Now I will do something.
This is because bad people attack the poor.
They make the poor cry.
So, I will make the poor safe.
They will be safe from all that scorn them"

v6 The words of the LORD are beautiful words.
They are like silver.
People refine silver 7 times in a very hot fire.

v7 LORD, you will keep the poor safe.
You will never let bad people hurt them.

v8 The godless are winners
when people say that "Wrong is right".

How Long, Lord?
Psalm 13

Jesus said. "With God anything is possible". (Matthew 19: 26)

Psalm 13

(This is) a song of David for the music leader.

v1 How long, LORD, will you forget me? For all time?
How long will you hide your face from me?

v2 How long must I think such sad thoughts? All day long?
How long will my enemy win?

v3 Look! Answer me LORD.
My God, give light to my eyes, or I will sleep in death.

v4 My enemy will say, "I beat him!"
My enemies will be very happy when I fall.

v5 But I will believe in your love that never fails.
My heart will be very happy because you make me safe.

v6 I will sing to the LORD.
He is so good to me.

The World is Full of Fools
Psalm 14

Jesus said, "The Son of man has come to save people that are lost". (Matthew 18: 11)

Psalm 14

(This is) a song of David for the music leader.

v1 A man without shame says in his heart, "There is no God".
Everybody is bad. They are all evil.
Nobody is doing anything good.

v2 The LORD is looking down from heaven on the sons of man.
He is looking to see if there is anyone that understands.
He is looking to see if anyone is looking for God.

v3 But everybody has turned away (from God).
They have all become evil.
Nobody does anything that is good.

v4 Will they never learn? They do evil.
They eat my people (as easily) as they eat bread.
They never talk to God.

v5 There they were afraid. They were very much afraid.
This was because God was with the righteous.

v6 They tried to stop the plans of the poor people.
But the poor people hid in the LORD.

v7 Oh, who will come from Zion and make Israel safe?
When the LORD makes his people rich and happy again,
then this is what will happen:
Jacob will sing and Israel will dance.

A Place for You
Psalm 15

Jesus said, "Where I am going you cannot come now. But you will come with me later". (John 13: 36)

Psalm 15

v1 LORD, who will stay in your house?
Who will live on your holy hill?

v2 He that is always:
- making no mistakes
- doing what is fair
- speaking in his heart what is true

v3 He says nothing bad.
He does nothing wrong to his neighbours.
He does not call his brother a fool.

v4 He does not like bad people,
but he does like the servants of the LORD.
He keeps his promises even when it costs a lot.

v5 He does not lend money to get more money.
He does not take money to do what is not fair.
Nothing can ever move the man that does all this.

And walk with you to Heaven
Psalm 16

Jesus said, 'If anyone leaves their houses, family or land for me, then I will be good to them. I will be good to them in this life. And their inheritance will be life that never finishes'. (Matthew 19:29) Matthew was a friend of Jesus. He wrote a book about Jesus. We call it the Gospel of Matthew. Gospel means good news. See in 'The Story of Psalm 16' for what inheritance means.

Psalm 16

v1 (This is) the secret of David.
Keep me safe, my God, because I come to you for help.

v2 I said to the LORD, You are my Lord.
All the good things in my life come from you.

v3 I have great pleasure in the saints on earth.
It is they that do such good things.

v4 But people that run after other (gods) will be sorry.
They will be more than sorry.
I will not offer gifts of blood (to other gods) with them.
I will not even say the names of these (other gods).

v5 You, LORD, chose my part and my cup.
You make safe what is mine.

v6 The lines fell to me in a pleasing place.
(Or, You chose a part for me that is very pleasing.)
Yes. My part is really very beautiful.

v7 I will say how great the LORD is. He is my teacher.
In the dark nights, my feelings also teach me.

v8 I kept the LORD always in front of me.
With him at my right hand nobody will move me.

v9 My heart is happy. My mouth is always singing.
My body will be safe when I sleep.

v10 You will not send me to Sheol.
You will not let your holy one see the Pit.

v11 You will show me the path of life.
With you, I will enjoy myself a lot.
At your right hand there is pleasure for ever.

David Prays for Help
Psalm 17

Jesus said, 'Ask me for anything in my name. I will do it for you'. (John 14:14)

Psalm 17

v1 LORD, hear what I am saying to you.
What I am asking is righteous.
Listen to me when I cry.
Answer me when I pray to you.
My lips do not tell lies.

v2 I want justice from you.
I want your eyes to see what is right.

v3 You can look at the secrets of my heart.
You can test me at night.
Though you test me, you will find nothing (wrong).
I promise myself that my mouth will not sin.

v4 People do bad things.
The words of your mouth (have given me help).
(They) gave me help not to do bad things.

v5 I put my feet on your path.
My feet did not trip over.

v6 God, I pray to you, because you will answer me.
Listen to me when I pray to you.

v7 Show that your great love is wonderful.
Your right hand saves the people that ask for your help.
It makes them safe from their enemies.

v8 Make me as safe as the apple of your eye.
Hide me under the shadow of your wings.

v9 Very bad men have attacked me.
Enemies that want to kill me are all round me.

v10 Their hearts have become hard.
They speak very proud words.

v11 They found me. They are all round me.
Their eyes are open wide.
They want to put me on the ground.

v12 They are like a hungry lion.
They are like a great lion that is hunting for its food.

v13 LORD, get up! Stand in front of them. Knock them down.
Save me from wicked men by your sword.

v14 LORD, by your hand (take them) from the earth.
Remove them from the world. Their reward is in this life.
You give plenty of food to the people that you love.
Their sons also have plenty.
They will give much to their children.

v15 And I, because I am righteous, will see your face, (LORD).
It will be enough for me when I awake.
Then I will really see you.

God is Alive and Well!   Psalm 18

Peter got out of the boat. He walked on the sea towards Jesus. But then Peter saw that the sea was very angry. Peter became very frightened. He began to fall into the water. He shouted, 'Save me, Lord'. Immediately, Jesus put out his hand. He held on to Peter. They both climbed into the boat. The storm stopped. (Part of Matthew 14:29-32.)

Psalm 18
(This is) for the music leader.
 (It is) for the servant of the LORD.
 (It is) for David.
 David spoke the words of this song.
 David did this when the LORD saved David from his enemies.
 Also, when the LORD saved David from Saul.

(Part 1: God is a Rock for David)

v1 I will love you, LORD.
    In you, I am strong.

v2 The LORD is my rock and my fortress.
    He gives me help.
    God is my rock.
    I run and hide in his shadow.
    He is my shield.
    He is the one that saves me.
    He is my high tower.

v3 The LORD is someone that I must praise.
    He will save me from my enemies.

(Part 2: David asks for help)

v4 Death was all round me.
    God's enemies were following me.

v5 Sheol was tying me down.
    Death was catching me.

v6 in my trouble, I prayed to the LORD.
    I shouted to my God for help.
    He heard my voice from his temple.
    My words went into his ears.

(Part 3: God answers David)

v7 So, the earth moved and shook.
    The foundations of the mountains shook.
    They moved because God was angry.

v8 Smoke rose from his nose.
    Burning fire came from his mouth.
    Burning coals shot out from him.

v9 God opened the heavens and came down.
    Dark clouds were under his feet.

v10 He sat on a cherub and he flew.
    God flew in the arms of the wind.

v11 God covered himself with darkness.
    He was in the dark waters and clouds in the skies.

v12 It was very bright where God was.
    Out of the clouds came hail and lightning.

v13 The LORD sent thunder from the heavens.
    People heard the voice of the Most High.
    There was hail and there was lightning.

v14 (The LORD) shot his arrows (of lightning).
    He made his enemies very frightened.
    He sent a lot of lightning and he beat his enemies.

v15 People saw how deep the sea was.
    They saw the foundations of the earth.
    This was because God blew on them through his nose.

v16 (The LORD) came down to me. He held me.
    He took me out from deep waters.

v17 He saved me from my powerful enemy.
    He saved me from people that hated me.
    They were too strong for me.

v18 It was a bad day for me when I met them.
    But the LORD gave me help.

v19 He led me out to a wide place.
    He saved me because he found pleasure in me.

(Part 4: Why God gives help to people)

v20 - v21 The LORD did this because:
    ☐ I am righteous
    ☐ my hands are clean
    ☐ I obeyed the rules of the LORD
    ☐ I did no evil
    ☐ I did not turn away from God

v22 Really, all his rules are in front of me.
    I did not turn away from him

v23 I did nothing wrong before him.
    I did no sin.

v24 (The LORD) made me righteous.
    My hands are clean when he looks at me.

v25 To people that are kind, you (God) are kind.
    To people that do nothing wrong, you do nothing wrong.

v26 To people that are clean, you are clean.
    To people that turn away from you, you turn away from them.

v27 You will save humble people.
    You will not save people unless they are humble.

(Part 5: Everything that David owns comes from God)

v28 LORD, you make my light burn brightly.
    My God is my light in the dark.

v29 Really, in you I run up to a troop (of soldiers).
    In my God, I can jump over a wall.

v30 The way of God is perfect.
    The word of the LORD is true.
    He is a shield for everyone that hides in him.

v31 Because who is God? Only the LORD!
    Who is a rock? Only our God!

v32 It is in God that I am strong.
    He makes my way perfect.

v33 He makes my feet like the feet of a goat.
    I do not fall on the hills.

v34 He teaches my hands to fight.
    My arms can bend a metal bow.

v35 (God) you made me into a winner.
    You bent down (to earth). You made me great.

v36 You made me take long steps.
    My ankles did not turn.

v37 I ran after my enemies. I caught them.
    I did not turn back until I had killed them.

v38 I knocked them down. They did not get up again.
    They fell beneath my feet.

v39 You made me strong for fighting.
    You made my enemies bend in front of me.

v40 You gave their necks to me.
    I destroyed my enemies.

v41 They cried for help but nobody saved them.
    They cried to the LORD but he did not answer.

v42 I cut them into small pieces in the wind.
    I put them on the streets as sand.

(Part 6: God made David king)

v43 You saved me from the people that attacked me.
    You made me the leader of the nations.
    I even rule people that I do not know.

v44 When they hear about me they obey me.
Foreign people are afraid of me.

v45 They will not fight me.
They do not hide in their fortresses.

v46 The LORD is alive. Praise my Rock.
Lift high the God that saves me.

v47 He is the God that fights for me.
He makes the nations obey me.

v48 He saves me from my enemies.
You lifted me above those enemies.
You saved me from angry men.

v49 LORD, I will praise you in all the nations.
I will praise your name with songs.

v50 (The LORD) will give his king great power.
He will always show kindness to his Messiah, to David.
He will show kindness to his children.

God's Two Books
Psalm 19

There are many other things that Jesus did. If somebody wrote them down, I think that the whole world would not be big enough for all the books! (John 21:25)

Psalm 19

(This is) a song of David for the music leader.

v1 The heavens are telling us about the glory of God.
The sky is showing the things that his hands have made.

v2 One day pours out the story to another day.
One night tells the next night what it knows.

v3 (But) they do not use words and have no languages.
Nobody hears their voice.

v4 (Yet) what they say goes into all the earth.
Their words go to the ends of the world.
God has made a home for the sun (in the sky).

v5 The sun comes out from his home like a bridegroom.
He is very happy to run fast, like a very strong man.

v6 His sunrise is at one end of the heavens.
He travels in a big circle to the other end.
Nothing can hide from the heat of the sun.

v7 The book of the LORD is wonderful.
It makes people feel alive again.
We can trust what the LORD tells us.
He points out the way when we are not sure of it.

v8 What the LORD tells us to do is always right.
It makes us feel happy deep down inside us.
What the LORD commands us is pure.
It makes our eyes shine with new light.

v9 The fear of the LORD is a clean fear.
It will always remain with us.
Every word that the LORD says is true.
Every one of them is righteous.

v10 They are of more value than gold,
even a lot of pure gold.
They are sweeter than honey,
even the best honey that bees make.

v11 Also, they are a guide to your servant.
Good things come if he obeys them.

v12 Who can know when he has made mistakes?
Forgive me all my secret sins.

v13 Also, stop your servant from wanting to sin.
Do not let sin rule over me.
Then nobody will say that I did wrong.
I will be clean (because you help me).
I will not do anything very bad.

v14 Lord, I want everything that I say to make you happy.
I want all my thoughts to please you.
You are my Rock and you are my Redeemer.)

War
Psalm 20

Jesus said, "We are going to Jerusalem. There they will kill the son of man. But 3 days later he will come to life again". (Matthew 20: 18,19) The son of man was a name that Jesus used for himself.

Psalm 20

(This is) a Psalm of David for the music leader

v1 - v3 We are praying that:
☐ the LORD will answer you when trouble comes
☐ the name of the God of Jacob will make you safe
☐ God will send you help from his holy place
☐ he will make you strong from Zion
☐ God will remember all your gifts
☐ he will like all your burnt offerings   **SELAH**

v4 We want God to give you all that you really want
to make all your plans work well

v5 We will shout for joy when you win the war.
We will lift up our banners in the name of our God.
We want the LORD to answer all that you pray.

v6 Now I know that the LORD will save his king.
God will answer him from his holy heaven.
The right hand of God will save the king.

v7 Some people rely on chariots. Others rely on horses.
But we will trust in the name of the LORD our God.

v8 They will falter and fall.
But we will get up and remain strong.

v9 Lord, save the king!
Answer us when we pray.

Peace
Psalm 21

Psalm 21

(This is) a psalm of David for the music leader

v1 LORD, the king is enjoying your power.
He is very happy.
You gave him help to win.

v2 - v5 You gave to him what he really wanted.
You gave to him everything that he asked for.   **SELAH**
You met him and gave to him such good things:
☐ you put a crown of the best gold on his head
☐ he wanted to stay alive and you let him
☐ his life will go on, it will never finish
☐ he has great glory because you gave him help to win
☐ you gave to him honour and he now remains as king

v6 You will always do good things for him.
He is very happy because you are with him.

v7 The king is relying on the LORD.
Because the Most High is loving and kind, nobody will move the king.

v8 Your hand will find all your enemies.
Your right hand will catch everybody that hates you.

v9 When they see you, you will burn them all.
When you are angry, your fire will destroy them.

v10 You will remove their children from the earth.
They will have no families anywhere.

v11 This is because they planned evil against you.
They had really bad ideas and they did not work.

v12 You will make them turn their backs to you.
This is because you will shoot your arrows at their faces.

v13 LORD, you are really strong. You sit on high.
We will sing and praise your power.

The Suffering Servant
Psalm 22

Jesus said to his 12 friends, "We will go to Jerusalem. Everything that the prophets wrote about me will happen. The Jews will give me to the Romans. They will mock me. They will not be kind. They will spit on me. They will hit me. They will kill me. But the third day I will rise again". (Luke 18:31-33)

(spit means shoot out what is in your mouth.)

Psalm 22

(Part 1 ~ David is Suffering)

The leader (must use) the music of "The Hind of the Morning". (This is) a song of David.

v1 My God!
   My God, why have you left me by myself?
   Why is my help far away?
   I am crying out in agony!

v2 My God!
   I cry out for help all day long.
   You do not answer.
   I cry out all through the night.
   You send me no peace.

v3 But you are the Holy God!
   The praise of Israel is like a throne for you.

v4 Our fathers trusted in you.
   They trusted in you and you made them safe.

v5 They cried out to you and you saved them.
   They trusted in you and you did not disappoint them.

(Part 2 ~ Men Hate David)

v6 But I am a worm. I am not a man.
   People scorn me. Everybody hates me.

v7 Everyone that sees me mocks me.
   They say bad things. They shake their heads.

v8 (They say) If the LORD likes him so much
   perhaps he (the LORD) will save him.
   Perhaps he will rescue him.

v9 But you, LORD, you:
   ☐ brought me from the womb
   ☐ made me trust you at the my mother's breast

v10 I trusted in you, LORD, from the womb.
   From the womb of my mother, you were my God.

v11 Do not stay far from me. Trouble is near.
   There is nobody to give me help.

(Part 3 ~ Trouble is All Round Me)

v12 Many bulls are all round me.
   They are strong bulls of Bashan.
   They make a circle with me in the middle.

v13 They open wide their mouths towards me.
   They are like lions that tear their food.
   They roar while they do it.

v14 They are pouring me out like water.
   All my bones have become separate.
   My heart is becoming soft like butter.
   It is changing to milk inside me.

v15 My mouth is dry, like a bit of broken pot.
   My tongue is sticking to the roof of my mouth.
   You laid me down in the dirt of death.

v16 A lot of bad men have made a circle round me.
   They are everywhere like dogs.
   Sharp points are in my hands and feet.

v17 I can count all my bones.
   They look at me all the time.
   They mock me.

v18 They took my clothes.
   They threw dice for my coat.

v19 But LORD, do not stay far away!
   You can make me strong, so hurry to give to me help!

v20 Save my life from the sword.
   Save everything that I love from the dogs.

v21 Save me from the mouth of the lion.
   You heard me from the horns of wild bulls.

(Part 4 ~ David Praises God)

v22 I will tell your name to my brothers.
   I will praise you in the congregation.

v23 Everyone that is in awe of the LORD ... praise him!
   All the seed of Jacob, honour him!

v24 All the seed of Israel, worship him because:
   God did not hate or forget the man that suffered
   God did not hide his face from him
   God heard him when he prayed

v25 I will praise you in the great congregation.
   I will keep my promises.
   The people that are in awe of you will see it.

(Part 5 ~ The Congregation Thanks God)

v26 The poor will eat. They will have plenty.
   The people that look for the LORD will praise him.
   Your heart will always be alive.

v27 People everywhere will remember.
   They will turn to the LORD.
   Families from every country will worship you.

v28 The LORD rules over every nation
   because he is king.

v29 All the rich people on earth will eat well.
   They will worship God.
   All that die will bend in front of him.
   Nobody can keep himself alive.

v30 Our children will become his servants.
   They will tell their children about the LORD.

v31 They will say that the Lord is righteous.
   They will say this to people that are not yet born:
   GOD HAS DONE IT!

God Loves You
Psalm 23

Jesus said, "I am the good shepherd." (John 10:11)

Psalm 23

(This is) a psalm of David.

v1 The LORD is my shepherd.

   I will not need anything.

v2 He makes me lie down in green fields.

   He leads me to waters where I can rest.

v3 He gives me new life.

   He is my guide to the right road.

   He does this to (do what) his name (promises).

v4 I will not be afraid when I walk through the valley of the shadow of death.

   This is because you (LORD) are with me.

   Your rod and staff make me feel brave.

v5 You prepare a table in front of me when my enemies are present.

   You put oil on my head.

   My cup is so full that it overflows.

v6 I am sure that good and loving and kind things will follow me.

They will follow me all the days of my life.

I will always live in the house of the LORD.

Who is the King of Glory?
Psalm 24

Pilate said to Jesus, "Are you a king?" Jesus answered, "You are right to say that I am a king". (John 18:37)

(Pilate was the Roman leader that killed Jesus.)

Psalm 24

(This is) a psalm of David

v1 The earth belongs to the LORD.
Everything in it is his own.
The world belongs to the LORD.
Everybody in it is his own.

v2 The LORD built it on the seas.
He founded it on the waters.

v3 Who can go up the hill of the LORD?
Who can stand in his holy place?

v4 The person that has clean hands and a pure heart.
The person that does not worship idols.
The person that does not believe in lies.

v5 The LORD will do good things to those people.
God will save them. He will say that they are right.

v6 They are the people that are looking for God.
They want to see the face of (the God) of Jacob. **SELAH**

v7 Lift up your heads you gates (of the city).
Lift up your very old doors.
Then the king of glory will come in.

v8 Who is the king of glory?
The LORD that is strong and mighty.
The LORD that is powerful in war.

v9 Lift up your heads you gates of the city.
Lift up its very old doors.
Then the king of glory will come in.

v10 Who is the king of glory?
The LORD Almighty.
He is the king of glory! **SELAH**

I did it God's Way
Psalm 25

Jesus said, "Nobody who starts ploughing and then looks back, will be fit for where God is king". (Luke 9:62)

Psalm 25

(This is a psalm) of David

v1 LORD, I lift myself up to you.

v2 My God, I will trust in you.
Do not let me be ashamed.
Do not let my enemies triumph over me.

v3 No! Do not let anyone that hopes in you be ashamed.
Let the people that say false things without a reason be ashamed.

v4 LORD, show me your ways.
Teach me your paths.

v5 Lead me in your truth.
Teach me, because you are the God that saves me.
I hope in you all the day long.

v6 LORD, remember your love and your kindness.
They have always been, from long ago.

v7 Do not remember my sins when I was young,
or the wrong things I did (when I was older).
LORD, remember your kindness to me,
because you are good.

v8 The LORD is good and always right,
so he will teach sinners in the way.

v9 He will lead the meek in judgment,
he will teach the meek his way.

v10 All the ways of the LORD are kindness and truth
to the people that keep his covenant.

v11 LORD, because of your name
forgive my sin, though it is great.

v12 Who is the man that is afraid of the LORD?
The LORD will show him the way
that the LORD will choose for him.

v13 He will have a good life.
His children will inherit the earth

v14 (People like this) will be the friends of the LORD,
as long as they worship him.
The LORD will show them his covenant.

v15 My eyes are always looking towards the LORD,
so that he can bring my feet out from the net.

v16 Turn yourself to me and be kind to me,
because I am lonely and hurt.

v17 The troubles in my life just get more and more.
Oh, take away from me the things that make me unhappy.

v18 Look at my trouble and pain
and forgive all my sins.

v19 Look at my enemies,
they keep getting more and more.
They hate me very much.

v20 Protect my life and make me safe.
Do not let me be ashamed,
because I am hiding in you.

v21 Protect my life because I am honest and good
and I hope in you.

v22 God, give to Israel help in all its trouble.

Psalm 26

Psalm 26

(This is a psalm) of David

v1 LORD, say that I always walk with you.
Say that I will never stop trusting in the LORD.

v2 Examine me, LORD, and see what I am.
Look inside me, at my feelings and thoughts.

v3 I will always walk in your good ways,
because I can see that you are loving and kind.

v4 I do not sit with worthless men.
I will not go with people that say that they are good, but they are not.

v5 I hate bad people that meet together.
I will not sit with godless men.

v6 I will wash my hands to show that I have done nothing wrong.
I will stand near your altar, LORD.

v7 I will say with a loud voice that you are great.
I will tell people about all the wonderful things that you have done.

v8 LORD, I love the place where your house is.
It is the home of your glory.

v9 Do not put my soul with sinners,
or my life with murderers.

v10 In their hands are bad plans.
Their right hands are full of bribes.

v11 But I will always walk with you.
Make me free and be kind to me.

v12 My foot stands in a flat place.
In the congregation, I will say that the LORD is wonderful.

The Ups and Down of Life
Psalm 27

Jesus said, "I am the light of the world. People that follow me will not walk in the dark. They will have the light of life". (John 8:12.) John was a friend of Jesus.

Psalm 27

(This is) a psalm of David.

v1 The LORD is my light and he makes me safe.
Who will make me afraid?
The LORD is my hiding place.
So, who will make me afraid?

v2 Bad men came near me.
They wanted to eat my body.
But it was my enemies,
the people that fought me,
that tripped and fell.

v3 If an army uses arms against me,
my heart will not be afraid.
Even if they fight against me,
I will be sure (of God's help).

v4 I have asked the LORD for only one thing.
This is what I want:
I want to live in the LORD's house all the days of my life.
Then I will see that the LORD is beautiful.
I will look for him in his palace.

v5 He will keep me safe in his house in the day of trouble.
He will hide me in the hiding place that is his tent.
He will lift me up on a rock.

v6 He will raise up my head above my enemies all round me.
I will give him gifts in his tent.
I will sing and I will make music to the LORD.

v7 LORD, hear my voice. I am praying.
Be kind to me and answer me.

v8 My heart says, "Look for (God's) face".
I will look for your face, LORD.

v9 Do not hide your face from me.
Do not be angry and turn away from your servant.
You gave me help (in the past).
Do not put me out and forget me (now).
You are my God and you make me safe.

v10 If my father and my mother forget me,
the LORD will care for me.

v11 LORD, teach me your way.
Lead me in a straight path, because of my enemies.

v12 Do not give me to my enemies.
They will do what they like with me.
People are saying things that are not true about me.
Others are saying that they want to hurt me.

v13 (What would happen) if I had not believed
to see the goodness of the LORD in the land of the living?

v14 Wait for the LORD. Be strong.
Make your heart become brave.
Again, wait for the LORD.

God Answers Prayer
Psalm 28

Jesus said, "If my words live in your hearts, you can ask for whatever you like, and it will come true for you". (John 15:7 in J B Phillips translation)

Psalm 28

(This is a psalm) of David

v1 LORD, you are my rock. I am praying to you for help.
Do not turn your ears away from me.
If you hide your answer from me,
I will be as those people that go down into the pit.

v2 Hear my voice when I pray for mercy.
I am asking you for help.
I am lifting up my hands towards your most holy place.

v3 Do not drag me away with godless people,
or with people that have done very bad things.
They say kind words to their friends
but plan to do wrong things.

v4 Give them what is fair for what they did
and for the bad things that they have done.
Pay them for the work of their hands
and bring back justice upon them.

v5 (Do it) because they do not understand
the things that the LORD has done,
or the work of his hands.
He will tear them down,
he will not build them up again.

v6 I say that the LORD does good things,
because he heard my voice when I prayed for mercy.

v7 The LORD makes me strong. He is my shield.
My heart trusts in him and he gives me help.
Now my heart jumps for joy and I will thank him with my songs.

v8 The LORD makes (his people) strong.
He is a safe and strong place for his Messiah.

v9 Save your people and do good things for your inheritance.
Be the shepherd of (your people) and always lift them up.

The Storm
Psalm 29

There was a great storm. The wind blew the sea into the ship. It was filling with water. Jesus was asleep on a seat in the back of the ship. They woke him up and said to him, "Teacher, do you not care that we are in danger?"

Jesus got up and told the wind to stop. He said to the sea, "Peace, be still". And the wind stopped and the sea was quiet. And Jesus said to them, "Why are you afraid? Do you not believe in me?" But they were afraid. They said to each other, "What sort of man is this? Even the wind and the sea obey him". (Mark 4:37-41)

Psalm 29

(This is a psalm) of David.

v1 Sons of God, say that the LORD is glorious.
Say that the LORD is powerful.

v2 Say that the LORD has a glorious name.
Say all this to the LORD that is beautiful and holy.

v3 The voice of the LORD is on the waters.
The glorious God is thundering.
The LORD is on the great waters.

v4 The voice of the LORD is powerful.
The voice of the LORD is beautiful.

v5 The voice of the LORD breaks the cedar trees.
The LORD breaks the cedars of Lebanon.

v6 He makes Lebanon jump like a young cow
and Sirion like a young wild animal.

v7 The voice of the LORD makes fire in the sky.

v8 The voice of the LORD makes the desert move,
the LORD makes the desert of Kadesh move.

v9 The voice of the LORD blows strongly on the trees
and he blows everything from the forest.
But in his temple, everyone says that he is glorious.

v10 The LORD was king at the time of the Flood.
The LORD will always be king.

v11 The LORD will make his people strong.
The LORD will give his people peace.

Bless this House
Psalm 30

Two things that Jesus said:

What good will it be to a man if the whole world is his but he loses himself? (Mark 8:36)

You can do nothing without me. (John 15:5)

Psalm 30

(This) psalm of David (is) a song for blessing the house.

v1 LORD, I will praise you
because you have lifted me up (from Sheol).
You have not let my enemies laugh at me.

v2 LORD, my God, I prayed to you for help,
and you gave me health.

v3 LORD, you brought my soul up from Sheol.
You gave me life,
so that I am not with those that go down into the Pit.

v4 Sing to the LORD all you that believe in him.
Praise his holy name.

v5 His anger is for a moment,
but his grace will be for as long as you live.
You may cry all night,
but in the morning, you will sing for joy.

v6 I said that I was safe for ever
because of what I had done.

v7 But LORD, it was your grace that made me safe
and protected my mountain.
When you hid your face (from me), I became very sad.

v8 I prayed to you LORD
and asked you, Lord, for mercy.

v9 What value is there in destroying me in the Pit?
Will my dead body praise you?
Will it say that you keep your promises?

v10 LORD, listen to me and give me mercy.
LORD, be the person that gives me help.

v11 You have changed my crying into dancing.
You have taken away my sad clothes
and given me wonderful clothes.

v12 So my heart will sing to you, nothing will stop it.
LORD, my God, I will always praise you.

David under Stress
Psalm 31

Jesus said, "Father, into your hands I give my spirit". (Luke 23:46) Your spirit lives on after your body dies. "Into your hands" means "to you").

Psalm 31

(This is) for the music leader.
(It is) a psalm of David

v1 LORD, I am trusting in you.
Do not let me ever become ashamed.
Make me free, because you always do what is right.

v2 Listen to me and send me help very soon.
LORD, be a rock for me to hide behind.
Make my house a fortress and keep me safe.

v3 You really are my rock and my fortress.
Because of your name, lead me and be my guide.

v4 You are my fortress.
Make me free from the trap that they hid for me.

v5 I put my spirit into your hand.
Send me help, LORD God of truth.

v6 I hate people that believe in false gods.
I am trusting in the LORD.

v7 I am very happy because of your kind love.
It makes me want to dance.
You saw my trouble.
You knew that I was under stress.

v8 You did not give me into the hands of my enemies.
You made my feet to stand in a wide place.

v9 LORD, give me mercy because I am in trouble.
My eyes and my stomach and my whole body
are sick because I am sad.

v10 My life must come to an end because I am so sad.
My years will finish while I am crying.
I am so unhappy that I have become weak.
My bones are weak.

v11 All my enemies hate me.
People that live near me do not like me.
Even my friends are afraid of me.
People that see me in the street run away.

v12 Everybody has forgotten me.
I am just like a broken pot.

v13 I heard people say unkind things about me.
There is danger everywhere.
They are making bad plans for me.
They want to kill me.

v14 But I am still trusting in you, LORD.
I am saying that you are my God.

v15 My times are in your hand.
Save me from the hand of my enemies
and from the people that are trying to catch me.

v16 Shine the light of your face on your servant.
Send help to me because of your kind love.

v17 LORD, do not let me become ashamed.
I am shouting out to you for help.
Let the godless become ashamed.
Let them be silent in Sheol.

v18 Let the lips that tell lies become silent.
They say unkind things about good people.
They think that they are better than them and they hate them.

v19 You have prepared many good things
for those that are afraid of you.
You did this in front of everybody.
You did it for those that trust in you.

v20 You will hide them from the bad plans that men make.
They will not hear the bad things that people say.
They will be in a secret place with you.

v21 Bless the LORD.
He showed me his kind love when I was under stress.

v22 I said too soon that you were not watching over me.
But you did hear my voice when I prayed to you for help.

v23 Love the LORD, everyone that has enjoyed his kind love.
He will keep safe those that are always his servants,
but he will pay back those that are proud.

v24 Everyone that hopes in the LORD:
be strong and be brave in your heart.

The Hiding Place
Psalm 32

Jesus said, "The Son of Man has power on earth to forgive sins". (Mark 2:10) ("Son of Man" was a name that Jesus called himself.)

Psalm 32

(This is) a maskil by David

v1 - v2 A man is very happy when (God):
☐ forgives his disobedience
☐ covers his sin
☐ does not put it against him when he does bad things
There is nothing false in his spirit

v3 - v4 When I said nothing my bones became weak and I cried all day long.
In the day and in the night your hand was heavy on me.
I felt dried up as in the heat of summer. **SELAH**

v5 (Then) I told you about my sin
and I did not hide the bad things that I had done.
I said, "I will show my disobedience to the LORD".
You forgave the bad things that I had done in my disobedience. **SELAH**

v6 So let everyone that enjoys your kind love pray to you.
(Let them do it) while they can still find you.
Then the great floods of water will not come near to them.

v7 You are my hiding place.
You will keep me safe from trouble.
Your songs will be all around me now that I am free. **SELAH**

v8 I will tell you the way,
I will teach you where you must go.
My eye will be your guide.

v9 Do not be like the horse, or the mule.
They do not understand.
They need special bits in their mouths to make them obey you.

v10 Bad people will be very sad.
People that trust in the LORD
will find his kind love all round them.

v11 So, all you good people that have clean hearts:
☐ show everyone that the LORD has made you happy
☐ praise him in words and in music

Word, Plans, Eye And Power
Psalm 33

Jesus said, "All power is mine, in heaven and on earth.

I will always be with you". (Part of Matthew 28: 18-20)

Psalm 33

v1 Shout to the LORD, everyone that is righteous.

v2 Praise the LORD with a harp.
Make music for him with a lyre that has 10 strings.

v3 Sing to him a new song.
Make beautiful music with a trumpet.

v4 Do this because the LORD says what is right.
Everything that he does is good.

v5 He loves all that is right and fair.
The world is full of his kind love.

v6 The word of the LORD made the skies.
The breath of his mouth made the stars.

v7 He put the waters of the sea together in a bottle.
He hid the deep seas in a safe place.

v8 Let everyone that lives in the earth be afraid of the LORD.
Let all the people of the world fall down in front of him.

v9 Do this because he spoke and it happened.
At his word, everything became fixed in its place.

v10 Governments make plans, but the LORD checks them.
He does not let people do everything that they want to do.

v11 The plans that the LORD makes will always happen.
His ideas will always be with us.

v12 The people that have the LORD as their God will be very happy.
They are the people that he chose to be his own.

v13 The LORD looks down from heaven.
He sees every man, woman and child.

v14 from where he lives, he can see every person that lives on the earth.

v15 He made every separate person.
He knows everything that they do.

v16 A great army will not save a king.
A soldier does not win because he is strong.

v17 A horse will not always give you help to win, even if it is very strong.

v18 Look, the eye of the LORD is on the people that are afraid of him.
It is on the people that trust in his kind love.

v19 He will save them from death and from famine.

v20 We will trust in the LORD.
He will send us help, and he will be our shield.

v21 We are singing happy songs for the LORD.
We are trusting in his holy name.

v22 LORD, we want you to send to us your kind love.
LORD, we are trusting in you.

The Fear of the Lord
Psalm 34

Jesus said, 'This is what I say to my friends. Do not be afraid of them that kill the body. They can do nothing else. I will tell you of whom you should be afraid. Be afraid of him that kills you and has the power to send you to hell. Yes, I tell you, be afraid of him'. (Luke 12:4-5) (Hell is where bad people go when they die.)

Psalm 34

For David, when he made Abimelech think that he was crazy. Abimelech sent David away and he went.

v1 I will always say good things about the LORD.
Every day my lips will sing psalms to him.

v2 My soul will boast about the LORD.
Humble people will hear it. It will make them happy

v3 Let us all make people see that the LORD is great.
We will make his name famous together.

v4 I prayed to the LORD and he answered me.
He saved me from everything that made me afraid.

v5 (Humble people) looked to (the LORD) and were happy.
Their faces were not ashamed.

v6 This humble man prayed and the LORD heard (him).
The (LORD) took him away from all his troubles.

v7 The angel of the LORD made a camp.
He stayed in it, round the people that feared the LORD.
He took them away (from danger).

v8 Oh, taste and see that the LORD is good.
The man that trusts in him will be very happy.

God Help Me
Psalm 35

Jesus said, Which one of you can prove that I have sinned? (John 8: 46) "Prove" means "show it is true". The answer is in the Letter to the Hebrews: He did not sin, Hebrews 4: 15)

Psalm 35

(This is) for David.

v1 Lord, argue with those people that are arguing with me.
Fight against those people that are fighting against me.

v2 Pick up a small shield and a big one.
Get up and give me help.

v3 Pull out a small spear and a long one.
(Use them) against the people that are running after me.
Say to me. "I will make you safe".

v4 Some people want to kill me.
I hope that they will become ashamed.
I hope that everyone else will think that they are very bad.
Some people are planning to destroy me.
Turn them back and confuse them.

v5 Make them become like chaff in the wind.
Let the angel of the LORD send them away.

v6 Make their way dark and dangerous.
Let the angel of the LORD be unkind to them.

v7 (Do this) because they hid a trap for me.
There was no reason for it.
For no reason they dug a pit for me.

v8 Surprise him and destroy him!
Catch him in the trap that he hid! Let him die in his own pit!

v9 Then I will be pleased because of what the LORD has done.
I will be happy when the LORD has made me safe.

v10 All my bones will shout, "LORD, who is like you?
You take the poor man away from the man that is too strong for him.
You take the people that need help away from those that hurt them".

v11 People say that they saw me do bad things.
They asked me about it, but I knew nothing.

v12 They paid me evil for the good things that I did.
I felt as if (my children) had died.

v13 When they were ill I wore clothes made from sacks.
I hurt myself by not eating food.
My prayer came back to my own breast.

v14 I cried when I walked about. I became bent because I was so sad.
I lived as though my friend or my brother or (even) my mother (was ill).

v15 But when I fell down they laughed.
They all met together. They came together against me.
I did not know the people that were attacking me.
They would not stop hurting me.

v16 They were like godless people and they mocked me more and more.
They showed their teeth (like a wild animal).

v17 LORD, how long will you watch (this)?
Take me away from the people that are destroying me.
Save the thing that I love most from the lions.

v18 I will thank you in the great meeting.
I will praise you when all the people are together.

v19 Do not let my enemies laugh at me.
They hate me, but have no reason for it.
Do not let them wink at me with their eye.

v20 They do not talk about peace.
They say false things to the people in the land that do not want trouble.

v21 They open wide their mouth against me.
They say, "Aha! Aha! Our eyes saw it!"

v22 LORD, you saw it (also).
Lord, do not remain silent. Do not stay far from me.

v23 Wake up! Get up and give me justice!
Argue (for me against them), my Lord and my God.

v24 LORD, you are righteous.
Give me justice, my God. Do not let them laugh at me.

v25 Do not let them think in their heart, "Aha! (this is) what we wanted".
Do not let them say, "We have eaten him up!"

v26 (Do this) to them that laughed at me when I became hurt:
☐ make them ashamed and confused at the same time
☐ make them sorry that they said that they were greater than me
☐ make them feel that they are wearing disgrace like clothes

v27 (Other) people will be very happy (when you say) that I am righteous.
They will shout out in their pleasure.
They will always say, "The LORD is great!
He loves it when his servant has peace!"

v28 My mouth will say that you are righteous.
I will praise you all day long."

Reach for the Sky
Psalm 36

Jesus said, "When it is evening and the sky is red you say, It will be good weather. In the morning when the sky is red and dark you say, It will be very bad weather. You are hypocrites. You can understand the signs in the sky. Can you not understand the signs of the times?" (Matthew 16: 2–3) (Hypocrites say lies.)

Psalm 36

(This is) for the music leader.
(He is) the servant of the LORD.
(It is) for David.

v1 – v4 The godless man does not obey (God).
This tells me that: he is not afraid of God
☐ he does not see (that this matters)

(v2) ☐ he tells himself that (God) will not see the bad things (that he does)
☐ (he thinks that God) will not hate these bad things

(v3) ☐ he says things that are bad and not true
☐ he has stopped being honest
☐ he does not do anything good

(v4) ☐ he makes bad plans on his bed (at night)
☐ he decides not to do things in a good way
☐ he does not turn away from doing wrong things

v5 LORD, your kind love is (as high) as the skies.
Your truth reaches the clouds.

v6 Your goodness is like strong mountains.
Your justice is like a deep sea.
LORD, you make men and animals safe.

v7 God, your kind love has great value.
The children of men are safe under the shadow of your wings.

v8 There is enough in your house to give them all that they need.
You give them all a drink of pleasure from your river,

v9 because you have waters that give life.
In your light we will see light.

v10 Go on giving your kind love to the people that know you.
Give your goodness to the people that have clean hearts.

v11 Do not let people that walk proudly hurt me.
Do not let bad people make me run away.

v12 The people that did bad things lay there, where they fell.
(Somebody) knocked them down and they cannot get up again.

Waiting for God
Psalm 37

Jesus said, "Good things will happen to the meek. One day the earth will be theirs". (Matthew 5: 5) (The meek are people that let someone teach them. Here that someone is God.)

Psalm 37: 1 - 11 ~ How to wait

(This psalm is) for David.

v1 Do not make yourself angry because of what evil people do.
Do not feel that you want to be like them.
They are always doing wrong things.

v2 They are like grass that will soon become dry.
They will die just as green plants do.

v3 Trust in the LORD and do good things.
Live in the land and you will be safe.
You will enjoy what it gives to you.

v4 Be happy with the LORD.
He will give to you what you most want.

v5 Promise that you will give yourself to the LORD.
Trust in him and he will do (all this).

v6 You are righteous. That will shine out like the dawn.
You are a fair person. That will be like the sun at midday.

v7 Remain still in front of the LORD.
Wait for him (to do something).
Do not make yourself angry because other people are doing well,
or because they are making bad plans.

v8 Stop being angry (with God) and do not get heated inside.
Do not make yourself angry, it only brings trouble.

v9 Evil people will become cut off,
but people that wait for the LORD will inherit the land.

v10 Soon the godless man will be gone.
If you look for his place, you will not find him.

v11 The meek will inherit the land.
They will enjoy wonderful peace.

Lord, Remember Me
Psalm 38

The man that robbed people said to Jesus, "Jesus, Lord, remember me when they make you king". Jesus said to him, "What I tell you is true. Today you will be with me in paradise". (Luke 23:42-43) (Paradise is a name for God's home, or heaven.)

Psalm 38

(This is) a psalm of David.
(He wrote it so that you, LORD) will remember him.

v1 LORD, do not tell me about my mistakes
when you are not pleased (with me).
Do not punish me because you are so angry (with me).

v2 For your arrows have gone deep into me
and your hand has come down on me.

v3 My body is very ill because you are so angry
and there is no health in my bones because of my sin.

v4 Also, my sin has gone over my head!
Like a heavy weight, it is too heavy for me (to carry).

v5 My wounds are going bad, they are making a bad smell.
(This is) because I was so stupid.

v6 My sins have bent me down, I am very near to the ground.
Every day I walk about in black (clothes).

v7 Also, there is a terrible pain in my stomach.
There is nothing good in my body.

v8 I am very weak. Everything is pushing down on me.
I am making a noise (like a wild animal) because my heart is so sad.

v9 Lord, you know everything that I want.
Nothing can hide me from you when I cry.

v10 My heart is beating fast and my strength is failing me.
There is no light in my eyes.

v11 My family and my friends stay away from my wounds.
The people that live near me stay far from me.

v12 Also, the people that are trying to kill me set traps for me.
Those people that want bad things (to happen to me)
are planning to destroy me.
They only think about (their) lies all day long.

v13 But I am like a deaf man. I hear nothing.
Also, I am like a dumb man. I do not open my mouth.

v14 So, I have become like someone that hears but does not answer.

v15 O LORD, I have waited for you!
(I believe) that you will answer (me), O Lord my God.

v16 I say this so that my enemies will not laugh at me.
When my foot slips, they stand up against me.

v17 For I am ready to fall and my pain is always with me.

v18 But I will say that I have done bad things.
My sin is always a trouble to me.

v19 Many people hate me for no reason.
A lot of people are saying lies about me.

v20 Some people repay evil for good.
They fight me when I try to do what is good.

v21 Do not leave me, O LORD.
O God, do not go far away from me.

v22 Hurry to give me help, O Lord my Salvation.

No Fixed Address
Psalm 39

Jesus said, "Animals have holes and birds have nests but the Son of Man has nowhere to sleep". (Matthew 8:20) (the Son of Man is Jesus)

Psalm 39

(This is) a psalm of David.
It is for Jeduthun, the leader of the music.

v1 I said, I will be careful what I do so that I do not sin.
I will be careful what...

v2 I say.
I will shut my mouth when the godless are near me.

v3 I will be like a dumb man and not speak.
I will not even talk about good things.
But it hurt me to do this and the pain in my heart grew worse.
It was like a fire inside me when I thought about it.
I just had to say something!

v4 O LORD, tell me about my life,
how long it will be and when it will finish.
Then I will know how weak I am.

v5 Look, you have made my life just as wide as my hand!
The length of my life is as nothing to you.
It is true that the life of everybody is like the wind.   SELAH

v6 People walk about just like shadows.
They are like the wind.
They get a lot of money,
but they do not know who will have it when they die.

v7, v8 Now, what do I hope for, O Lord?
I am hoping for you to save me from all the bad things that I do!
Do not put me where fools will laugh at me.

v9 I will not say anything.
I will not open my mouth, because you have done something!

v10 Do not hit me again.
Your hand is hurting and destroying me.

v11 You speak angrily to people about sin and you punish them.
You make all that is pleasant in them fly away like a moth!
It is true that everyone is like the wind.   SELAH

v12 O LORD, hear my prayer.
Listen to me when I cry. Do not be dumb to my tears.
I am an alien to you. I am a stranger, like all my fathers were.

v13 Look away from me.
Then I will be happy until I live no more and die.

Build on a Rock!

Psalm 40

Jesus said, **Everyone that listens to me and obeys me is like a man with good ideas. He built his house on a rock. Then the rain came with a lot of water and the winds blew and there was a storm round that house. It did not fall down because he built it on a rock. Everyone that listens to me and does not obey me is like a man with bad ideas. He built his house on the sand. And the rain came with a lot of water and the winds blew and there was a storm round that house. It fell down with a great crash. (Matthew 7: 24 – 27);** ("crash" means "fall with a big noise")

Psalm 40

(This is) for the music leader.
(It is) a psalm of David.

v1 I was patient while I waited for the LORD.
He turned to me and he heard me when I prayed for help.

v2 He lifted me out of the pit where (bad people) were destroying me
and from very wet ground.
He put my feet on a rock and made me walk without falling.

v3 He gave me a new song to sing.
It was a hymn of praise to God.
Many people will see what happened and be afraid.
Then they will trust in the LORD.

v4 The man that trusts in the LORD will be very happy.
He does not listen to proud people that turn to false gods.

v5 LORD, my God, you have done many wonderful things.
Nobody can tell you about your plans for us.
If I say that I will talk about them,
there would be too many to speak about!

v6 You did not want a sacrifice and an offering.
You have made a hole in my ears.
You did not ask for a burnt offering and a sin offering.

v7 Then I said, "Here I am.
In this book someone wrote about me".

v8 I am pleased to do what you want me to do, my God,
and your rules are in my heart.

v9 I talk about the good news of (how to become) righteous to everybody.
Look, LORD, I never keep my mouth shut, as you know!

v10 I do not keep the righteous things that you do to myself.
I do not hide (from people) that they can trust in you.
I tell everyone that your kind love will save them.
Also, I (show them) the truth.

v11 You, LORD, will not keep your mercy from me.
Your kind love and your truth will always protect me.

v12 But trouble is all round me.
I cannot see how much there is.
My sins have followed me and caught me.
I cannot see anything.

v13 LORD, please save me!
LORD, hurry to give me help!

v14 There are people that want to kill me.
I hope that they will become ashamed and confused.
There are people that want to destroy me.
I hope that everyone will say that they are bad people.

v15 I want all those people that say to me "Aha! Aha!"
to become very sorry for what they have done.

v16 I want everyone that is looking for you to be happy, very happy.
I want everyone that loves it when you save them to say,
"Praise the LORD".

v17 But I am poor and I need help. Lord, you think about me.
You are my help and you save me.
O God, do not be a long time!

The Unkind Friend
Psalm 41

Jesus said, "The Bible says that this will happen: the man that eats food with me will lift up his heel against me". (John 13:18) (We explain "lift up his heel" in "What Psalm 41 means")

Psalm 41

(This is) for the (music) leader.
(It is) a psalm for David.

v1 Anyone that is kind to the poor will be very happy.
The LORD will help him when life is difficult.

v2 The LORD will make him safe and keep him alive.
He will be happy where he lives.
(The LORD) will not give him to his enemies (for them)
to do what they want to do (with him).

v3 The LORD will be like a nurse to him when he is ill in bed.
Every time that he is ill, you will make him well again.

v4 I said, "LORD, have mercy on me.
Heal me, even though I have broken your rules".

v5 My enemies say bad things about me.
(They say) "When will he die?
When will people forget his name?"

v6 And if one (of them) comes to see me, he tells lies.
He fills his mind with bad things to say about me.
Then he goes out and tells (everyone).

v7 All the people that hate me whisper to each other about me.
They hope that worse things will happen to me.

v8 (They say that) "someone put a death-wish on him,
so he will never get up from his bed".

v9 Even my best friend has lifted up his heel against me.
He was someone that I trusted,
someone that I often ate food with (in my home).

v10 But you, LORD, have mercy on me.
Raise me up so that I can repay them.

v11 I know that you are pleased with me
because my enemy does not shout over me (that he has won).

v12 You will help me because I am honest.
You will always keep me near to you.

v13 Say good things about the LORD.
He always was the God of Israel and he always will be!
Amen and amen!

Remember the Good Times
Psalms 42 and 43

Jesus said, "My *soul is so sad that I am nearly dying", (Mark 14:34) and "My *soul is in trouble". (John 12:27)

Psalm 42:1-5

(This is) for the music leader.
(It is) a *maskil for the *sons of Korah.

v1 My *soul cries out for you, (my) God,
*like a *hart crying out for streams of water.

v2 My *soul is *thirsty for God, the God that is alive.
When can I come and see the face of God?

v3 (All) day and (all) night I cry and do not eat.
All day (my enemies) say to me, "Where is your God?"

v4 My *soul cries inside me when I remember that:
    ☐ I went with a crowd (to *worship you)
    ☐ I went to the house of God
    ☐ there was the sound of singing
    ☐ there was a loud noise of people thanking (you) and dancing.

v5 My *soul, why are you so sad?
Why are you so *restless inside me?
Hope in God because I will *praise him again!
When God is with me, he will do great things (for me).

v6 My *soul is sad inside me.
So I will remember you (my God) from:
    ☐ the land of (the) Jordan (river)
    ☐ (the mountains) of Hermon
    ☐ the hill of Mizar.

v7 The deep (waters) make a noise when your *waterfalls thunder.
All your big *waves and all your little waves roll over me.

v8 In the day time the *LORD sends to me his kind love.
At night his song is with me.
My *prayer is to the God of my life.

v9 I will say to the God (that is) my Rock,
"Why did you forget me? Why must I be so sad?
You let my enemy do what he likes to me!"

v10 My enemies hurt all my bones.
The people that fight me are always saying, "Where is your God?"

v11 My *soul, why are you so sad?
Why are you so *restless inside me?
Hope in God, because I will *praise him again!
When God is with me, he will do great things (for me).

Psalm 43

v1 (My) God, say that I am right.
Tell it to the people that do not love (me).
*Rescue me from the man that tells *lies and does bad things.

v2 (This is) because you are my *refuge, God.
Why are you always so *unkind to me?
Why must I continue to be so sad?
You let my enemy do what he likes to me!

v3 Send out your light and your *truth.
Let them be my guide.
They will bring me to your *holy mountain
and to the house where you live.

v4 Then I will come to the *altar of God,
the God that makes me happy.
I will *praise you with a *harp, God, my God.

v5 My *soul, why are you so sad?
Why are you so *restless inside me?
Hope in God, because I will *praise him again!
When God is with me, he will do great things for me.

God Help Us!
Psalm 44

The friends of Jesus came to him. They woke him and said, "*Lord, save us! We are dying". He said to them, "Why are you afraid? You do not have much faith". (Matthew 8:25-26) ("Faith" here means "*trusting in Jesus".)

Psalm 44

(This is) a *maskil.
(It is) for the music leader of the *sons of Korah.

v1 God, we have heard it for ourselves.
Our fathers told it to us.
(They told us) what you did for them a long time ago.

v2 Your hand pushed out the people (that lived in the land)
and put (our fathers) in.
You broke (our enemies) but gave help to (our fathers).

v3 (Our fathers) did not get the land by their own *swords.
Their own power did not win the fight. It was you and
☐ your right hand
☐ your arm
☐ the light on your face
(that did it) because you were their friend.

v4 You are my king. You are my God.
You are the one (that said that) Jacob must win.

v5 Because of you, we pushed back our enemies.
Because of your name, we beat those that fought us.

v6 I do not believe that my bow gave me help.
I do not think that my *sword won (the fight).

v7 This is because you give us help to beat our enemies.
You make the people that *hate us ashamed.

v8 We *praise God *all day long.
We will always *praise your name. **SELAH**

v9 But now you have turned away from us.
You have made us ashamed.
You do not go out with our armies.

v10 You make us run away from an enemy.
Those people that *hate us take what they like from us!

v11 You make us *like sheep so that people can eat us!
You have thrown us into other countries.

v12 You are selling your people (and the price is) cheap.
You have sold them and not got anything for it!

v13 You have made us into something that our *neighbours laugh at.
Everyone round us laughs at us and *scorns us.

v14 We are as nothing among the *nations!
Everybody is sorry for us.

v15 I am ashamed *all day long.
I do not know where to look.

v16 (This is) because of:
☐ the bad things that people say about me
☐ the people that do bad things to me
☐ (the people that are) my enemies
☐ (the people that are) happy because they hurt me.

v17 All this happened to us, but we did not forget you.
We did not forget our *covenant with you.

v18 Our *hearts did not turn away,
nor did our feet turn from your path.

v19 But you broke us where the wild animals are.
You covered us with great *darkness.

v20 If we had
☐ forgotten the name of our God, or
☐ lifted up our hands to a foreign god

v21 would God not have discovered it?
He knows the secrets of (people's) *hearts.

v22 Yet because of you, people kill us *all day long.
They think that we are *like sheep ready for (people to) kill.

v23 *Lord, awake! Why are you asleep?
Get up! Do not throw us away *for ever!

v24 Why do you hide your face (from us)?
Why do you forget our trouble
and the way that people hurt us?

v25 We have fallen down to the earth.
Our bodies are on the ground.

v26 Wake up and give us help!
Save us, because of your kind love.

A Love Song
Psalm 45

Jesus said, "At midnight somebody shouted, Look, the bridegroom is coming. Go out and meet him". (Matthew 25:6) (This is part of a story that Jesus told about a marriage. The bridegroom is the man getting married.)

Psalm 45

(This is) for the music leader.
(It is) for the *sons of Korah.
(It is) a *maskil and a love song.
(Sing it) to (music that they call) "*lilies".

*(Words that the *psalmist says:)*

v1 These good words make my *heart very happy.
I will say these verses to the king.
My *tongue is *like the pen of someone that writes easily.

*(Words that the *psalmist says to the king:)*

v2 You are the most beautiful man (that there is).
You speak words of *grace.
God has made you special *for ever.

v3 Wear your *sword by your side.
(You are) the *Mighty One.
(You are) great and (you are) the king!

v4 (Because you are) the king,
ride out and beat (all your enemies).
Then (people that are) honest and *meek and *righteous
will always win.
Your right hand will show you
that you can do things that (make people) afraid.

v5 Your sharp *arrows will cut into the *heart of the king's enemies.
*Nations will fall down under your (feet).

v6 Your *throne, God, will go on *for ever and ever.
The *sceptre of your *kingdom will be a *righteous *sceptre.

v7 You have loved things that are *righteous
and you have *hated things that are *wicked.
So God, your God, has put you above the people that are with you.
He did this by putting some *oil on you, which made you happy.

333

- **v8** All your clothes (smell) of *myrrh, aloes and cassia.
  The (beautiful) *ivory in big houses
  (and the music that you hear from them) makes you happy.
- **v9** Among your great women are the daughters of kings.
  Your *queen stands at your right hand.
  (She is wearing) gold from *Ophir.

*(Words that the *psalmist says to the *queen:)*

- **v10** Daughter, listen (to me).
  Hear (what I am saying) and think about it.
  Forget your people and your father's house.
- **v11** You are beautiful and so the king loves you.
  He is your *lord, so *worship him, **(v12)** daughter from Tyre.
- **v12** Rich people will make you happy with gifts.
- **v13** The daughter of the king is beautiful inside.
  They made what she wore out of cotton made from gold.
- **v14** They led her to the king in her beautiful clothes.
  The girls that were her friends followed her.
- **v15** They came in with *joy and were very happy
  as they entered the king's *palace.

*(Words that the king says to the *queen; or the *psalmist says to the king:)*

- **v16** You will have sons instead of fathers.
  You will make them *princes over all the land.
- **v17** I will make sure that people always remember your name.
  So, people will *praise you *for ever and ever.

The City of God
Psalms 46, 47 and 48

Jesus said, "Jerusalem, Jerusalem, you killed the *prophets and put to death the people that (God) sent to you. I often wanted to bring you together, *like a mother bird that brings her young birds together under her *wings. But you would not come". (Matthew 23:37) (A *prophet speaks for God. A *wing is what a bird flies with.)

Psalm 46

(This is) for the (music) leader.
  (It is) for the *sons of Korah.
  (It is) a song for women's voices.

- **v1** God is *like a place where we can go, where he will *protect us.
  He will always give us help when troubles come.
- **v2** So we will not be afraid when the earth moves (under our feet),
  or when the mountains fall into the middle of the seas.
- **v3** (We will not be afraid)
  even when the seas make a loud noise and move a lot.
  (We will not be afraid)
  when the mountains move a lot as well.   ***SELAH**
- **v4** (There is) a river (and) the waters from it make the city of God very happy.
  (The city) is the *holy place where the *Most High lives.
- **v5** God is in the middle of it. It will not fall down.
  God will give it help early in the morning.
- **v6** The *nations made a loud noise. *Kingdoms fell.
  When (God) spoke even the earth *melted!
- **v7** The *LORD of Everything is with us.
  The God of Jacob makes us safe.   ***SELAH**
- **v8** Go and look at the things that the *LORD has done.
  (He has done) surprising things in the earth!
- **v9** He is the one that makes wars finish all over the world.
  He breaks bows; he destroys *spears; and he burns *shields in a fire.
- **v10** Be quiet! Know that I am God.
  I will (make them) lift me high among the *nations.
  I will (make them) lift me high in (all the) world.
- **v11** The *LORD of Everything is with us.
  The God of Jacob makes us safe.   ***SELAH**

Psalm 47

(This is) for the (music) leader.
  (It is) for the *sons of Korah.
  (It is) a psalm.

- **v1** Peoples from every (country), *clap your hands (together).
  Shout aloud to God with the sound of happy singing.
- **v2** Because the *LORD *Most High is wonderful.
  (He is) the Great King of all the earth.
- **v3** He won the fight against peoples (that were our enemies).
  He put their soldiers under our feet.
- **v4** He chose for us the place where we live.
  Jacob, that he loved, is very happy with it.   ***SELAH**
- **v5** God has gone up with a great noise.
  The *LORD (has gone up) with the sound of a *shofar.
- **v6** Sing *praises to God, sing *praises!
  Sing *praises to our king, sing *praises!
- **v7** Because God is the King of the whole earth.
  Sing (to him) a *maskil.
- **v8** God is ruling over the *nations.
  God is sitting on his *holy *throne.
- **v9** People that want to be his servants
  have joined the people that belong to Abraham's God.
  The people that rule the earth belong to God.
  (They lifted God up) very high.

*Praise

The Hebrew word for this is zamar, from which we get our word "psalm". Remember, we pronounce "psalm" as "sarm". We pronounce "zamar" as "sarmar". So, psalm means *praise!

Psalm 48

(This is) a song.
  (It is) a psalm for the (music) leader.

- **v1** The *LORD is great. He really is worth our *praise.
  His *holy mountain is in the city of our God.
- **v2** Mount Zion is in a beautiful place,
  and it makes the whole world very happy.
  It is the city of the Great King.
  (It is also called) the High Place of Zaphon.
- **v3** God was in its *defences and he made them very safe.
- **v4** (This was) when we saw the kings meeting each other.
  They crossed (into our country) together.
- **v5** (Then) they saw (something) that really surprised them.
  It made them very frightened (so that) they hurried away!
- **v6** They were so afraid that they felt pain
  *like a woman having a baby.
- **v7** It was *like the east wind that destroys great ships,
  (*like those from) Tarshish.
- **v8** We have seen in the city of the *LORD of Everything
  that it was just as people told us.
  (They told us that) God would keep the city of our God
  safe *for ever!   ***SELAH**
- **v9** When we are inside your *temple, God, we think of your kind love.
- **v10** Your name reaches to the ends of the world
  so that (people) give you *praise.
  Your right hand is full of the good things that you do.
- **v11** Because of the things that you decide to do:
  ☐ Mount Zion will be very happy
  ☐ the daughters of Judah will *praise you.
- **v12** Walk all round Zion, go to every side of it.
  Count the *towers,
- **v13** think about its strong buildings and make a note of its *defences.
  Then you may describe it to your children.
- **v14** For this God is our God *for ever and ever.
  He will be our guide until we die.

You Cannot Buy *Heaven
Psalm 49

Jesus told them this story. The ground of a certain rich man gave him lot of fruit. This is what the rich man thought. "What shall I do? I have nowhere to put the fruit". Then he said, "This is what I will do. I will pull down my buildings, and make bigger ones. There will I put all my fruits and the things that I grow on my land. I will tell myself, You have a lot of things that will help you for many years. Do not work hard any more, but eat and drink and be very happy!" But God said to him, "You fool. Tonight you will die. Then, to whom will all these things belong?" (Luke 12:16-20)

Psalm 49

(This is) for the (music) leader.
(It is) a psalm for the *sons of Korah.

v1 Hear this, people from every country.
Everybody that is passing through this world, listen!

v2 (Listen) together,
whether you are important or not,
or whether you are rich or poor.

v3 I will speak to you words of wisdom.
I will tell you how my *heart understands things.

v4 There is a question that I have heard.
I will (make music on) the *harp while I start to answer the problem.

v5 Must I be I afraid when bad things happen
and bad people are all round me?

v6 (These bad people) think that their money will help them.
They are always saying how rich they are.

v7 A man cannot pay the price for any man.
He cannot give to God what (his life) costs.

v8, v9 The life (of someone) costs very much.
He can never pay enough:
☐ so that he can stay alive *for ever
☐ so that he will not see the *Pit.

v10, v11 Does he not see that *wise people will die?
Fools and people that are not *wise will also die.
Their graves will be their homes *for ever.
That is where they will always be.
They called their land by their own name,
but other people will get their money.

v12 So, even if a man has riches, he will not live *for ever.
He will die, just *like the animals.

v13 This is the way that people that *trust in themselves will go.
(This is also the way) of the people that copy them,
that say that they are right.   *SELAH

v14 They will go to *Sheol, *like sheep. They will feed death!
Their bodies will waste away in *Sheol.
But good people will rule over them in the morning.
They will not (stay in) their big houses!

v15 For God will buy me back from the hand of *Sheol.
He will hold me (in his own hand).   *SELAH

v16 Do not be afraid when a man becomes rich
and his house gets even better.

v17 He cannot take it with him when he dies.
Nothing will go down (to *Sheol) with him, (not even his) fame!

v18 Though good things happened to him in his life
(and people will say good things to you when you have a lot of money)

v19 he will go to his fathers and people *like that.
He will never see the light again.

v20 So, even if a man has riches, he will not (always) understand.
He will die, just *like the animals.

*Judgment Begins at the House of God
Psalm 50

Jesus said, "You will see the Son of man come in the clouds of *heaven". (Matthew 26:64) (The "Son of man" is a name that Jesus gave to himself.)

Psalm 50

(This is) a psalm of Asaph.

v1 God, the powerful God, the *LORD, is speaking.
He is calling (everything on) the earth,
from where the sun rises (in the east)
to where it goes down (in the west).

v2 God is shining out from Zion, that most beautiful place.

v3 Our God is coming and he will not be quiet.
A fire burns up everything that is in front of him.
And there is a great storm round him.

v4 He is calling the skies above and the earth (below)
to say whether his people are good or bad.

v5 (He says) "Bring my people to me.
(Bring to me) the people that have made a *covenant with me
and have made a *sacrifice to me".

v6 Then the skies (above) showed everyone about (God's) *righteousness
and that God himself is the *judge.   *SELAH

v7 Listen to me, my people, and I will speak (to you).
I have something to say against you, Israel.
I am God, your (own) God.

v8 I will not be angry with your *sacrifices,
nor with you for always burning offerings to me.

v9 I do not need a bull from your farm or goats from your fields.

v10 (This is) because all the animals of the forest are mine,
and (all) the cows and bulls on a thousand hills.

v11 I know every bird in the mountains.
(All) the farm animals are mine.

v12 If I am hungry, I will not tell you.
(This is) because the world is mine
and everything that is in it.

v13 Do I eat the meat of bulls? (No!)
Do I drink the blood of goats? (No!)

v14 Offer to God thanks.
Do what you have promised for the *Most High.

v15 Then pray to me when you are in trouble.
I will make you safe and you will say good things to me.

v16 But to the bad people God says:
☐ why do you repeat my rules?
☐ why do you talk about my *covenant?

v17 For you *hate me telling you what to do.
You put my words behind you.

v18 If you see someone robbing (someone else) then you do it with him!
If people have sex with other people's wives or husbands, you do it too!

v19 Your mouth speaks *evil and your *tongue says things that are false.

v20 You sit and say things against your own brother.
You repeat bad things about your own mother's son!

v21 You did all this and I said nothing.
(So) you thought that I was just *like you.
But I will be angry with you
and tell you to your face what you have done wrong.

v22 Now, everyone that forgets God, think about this,
or I will tear you into pieces.
No one will save you.

v23 Anyone that offers me thanks is giving me *praise.
They that live the right way will see that God will make them safe.

A New Man
Psalm 51

Jesus said, "I say this to you. If anyone looks at a woman and wants to have sex with her, he has already had sex with her in his mind". (Matthew 5:28)

335

Psalm 51

(This is) for the music leader.
(It is) a psalm of David.
(It was) when the *prophet Nathan came to him.
(It was) after (David) had sex with Bathsheba.

- **v1** Give *mercy to me, God, because of your kind love.
  Because you have so much love, forget that I did not obey you.

- **v2** Wash me (from the bad feeling that I have)
  because of the bad thing that I did.
  Make me clean from all my *sin.

- **v3** Because I know that I did not obey you
  and my *sin is always in front of me.

- **v4** I have *sinned against you and only you.
  You saw the *evil that I did.
  And so you are right when you talk to me.
  You are not wrong when you say that I am bad.

- **v5** I am sure that I have done bad things since my birth.
  I have always wanted to *sin since the day that I was born.

- **v6** But you want me to be good
  and you want to teach me how to live in the proper way.

- **v7** Make me clean with hyssop and I shall be really clean.
  Wash me and I will be whiter than snow.

- **v8** I want to hear happy words that give me *joy.
  I want the bones that you broke to *rejoice.

- **v9** Hide your face from my *sins
  and forget all the bad things that I have done.

- **v10** *Create a *pure *heart inside me, O God.
  And put a strong spirit in me.

- **v11** Do not send me away from where you are.
  Do not take your *Holy Spirit from me.

- **v12** Give me back the *joy that I get when I am safe with you.
  And (give me) a spirit that makes me strong to give help (to people).

- **v13** I will teach your ways to those people that fight against you.
  Then *sinners will return to you.

- **v14** Take away from me the bad feeling that I have because I killed someone,
  God, the God that makes me safe.
  (Then) my *tongue will sing of your *righteousness.

- **v15** *Lord, open my lips,
  then my mouth will say how great you are.

- **v16** For animal *sacrifice does not bring you pleasure, or I would make it.
  You would not want a whole burnt offering.

- **v17** The *sacrifices that God wants are a broken spirit
  and a broken *heart that knows that it has *sinned.
  . . .

- **v18** In your pleasure, do good things to Zion.
  Build up the walls of Jerusalem.

- **v19** Then:
  - there will be the right kind of animal *sacrifice
  - whole burnt offerings will bring you pleasure
  - they will offer bulls on your *altar.

*Cruel Words
Psalm 52

Jesus said, "Did you not hear what David did? He was hungry and so were the men that were with him. He went into the house of God. He ate the special bread that was there. He broke the rules when he did this, so did all the men that were with him. The rule was that only the *priests should eat the bread". (Matthew 12:3-4) (The special bread told the people that God had fed them with manna. He did this when they came out from Egypt. Manna was another special bread that God sent from *heaven.)

Psalm 52

(This is) for the music leader.
(It is) a *maskil for David.
(It is about) Doeg, the man from Edom.
He went to Saul and told him,
"David went to the house of (the *priest) Ahimelech".

- **v1** Why do you say how great you are, you strong but *evil man?
  The kind love of God is always (with us).

- **v2** Your *tongue talks about ideas to destroy (people).
  (It is) *like a sharp knife.
  You are always doing (something) to hurt (people).

- **v3, v4** You love:
  - to do *evil things
  - not to do good things
  - to say *lies
  - not to say what is true *SELAH
  - every *cruel word
  - a false *tongue.

- **v5** So, God will destroy you completely. He will catch you.
  He will tear you away from your home.
  He will pull you out from the earth where people live. *SELAH

- **v6** And good people will see it and be afraid.
  But then they will laugh at him.

- **v7** "Look at the man that did not make God his *fortress.
  Instead, he *trusted that all his money would make him safe.
  He became strong by destroying (people)".

- **v8** But I am *like an olive tree that is growing well in the house of God.
  I will always *trust in the kind love of God.

- **v9** I will always *praise you for what you have done.
  I will tell your people what a good name that you have.

Will They Never Learn?
Psalm 53

Jesus said, "Have I been with you for such a long time and still you do not know me?" (John 14:9)

Psalm 53

(This is) for the music leader.
(Use the music called) Mahalath.
(It is) a *maskil for David.

- **v1** A fool thinks that there is no God.
  People (*like that) are bad. They are *evil.
  None of them does anything that is good.

- **v2** God is looking down from *heaven on the people on earth.
  He wants to see if there is:
  - anyone that understands
  - anyone that is looking for God

- **v3** But they have all turned away and have become *evil.
  Nobody does anything good, not one person.

- **v4** Will the *evil doers not learn?
  They eat my people (as easily) as they eat bread.
  They do not speak to God.

- **v5** They were very much afraid when there was nothing to fear!
  God threw away the bones of the people that attacked you, (his people).
  He made (the *evil doers) ashamed because God did not like them.

- **v6** Oh, who will come from Zion and make Israel safe?
  When God makes his people rich and happy again,
  Jacob will sing and Israel will dance.

Snakes in the Grass
Psalm 54

Jesus said, "You children of snakes, you are *evil. How can you say anything that is good?" (Matthew 12:34)

Psalm 54

(This is) for the music leader.
   (He must use) *musical instruments.
   (It is) a *maskil for David.
   (It was) when the men that lived in Ziph went to Saul.
   They told him, "David is hiding with us".

v1 God, give me help because of your name.
     Use your power to make me safe.

v2 God, hear my *prayer and listen to what I am saying.

v3 Because my enemies are fighting against me
     and *cruel people are trying to kill me.
     They do not think about God. *SELAH

v4 But God, listen and give me help!
     *Lord, it is you that keeps me alive!

v5 Send back this *evil to my enemies.
     Because you (love what) is true, destroy them.

v6 I want to *sacrifice to you because I am free to do it.
     I want to *praise your name, *LORD, because it is good.

v7 (Your name) saved me from all my trouble.
     When I looked at my enemies I saw (that I had won the battle).

*Betraying a Friend
Psalm 55

Jesus said to him, "Judas, are you *betraying the Son of man with a kiss?" (Luke 22:48) ("Betray" means "tell someone's enemies everything about them".)

Psalm 55

(This is) for the music leader.
   (He must use) *musical instruments.
   (It is) a *maskil for David.

v1 God, listen to my *prayer.
     Do not turn away when I cry for *mercy.

v2 Hear me and answer me.
     I cannot sleep because of my trouble. I am very *unhappy

v3 because of what my enemies say. They give me a lot of pain.
     And they are so angry that they *hate and make trouble for me.

v4 My *heart is jumping inside me.
     And all the fear of death is on every side of me.

v5 Great fear and *shaking have come to me.
     They are all over me.

v6 So I said, "I would like to fly away as a bird.
     Then I would find *peace.

v7 Yes! I would go far away and live in a wild place.   *SELAH

v8 I would hurry to a safe place,
     safe from angry wind and storm".

v9 *Lord, destroy (the *evil people)! Confuse their words!
     Because I see fighting and angry people in the city.

v10 They walk on its walls in the day and at night.
      There are *evil (things) and trouble inside it.

v11 *Cruel men that destroy people are in the city.
      People that tell *lies never leave her streets.

v12 For it was not an enemy that laughed at me.
      That would not have hurt me.
      It was not someone that fought against me and said bad things (to me).
      I could have hidden from him!

v13 But it was you, a man just *like me!
      We did things together, you were my best friend!

v14 We had good times together!
      We used to go with a crowd (of people) to the house of God!

v15 I want death to take (my enemies) by surprise!
      I want them to go down to *Sheol alive!
      Because *evil has made its home in them.

v16 But I will cry to God for help and the *LORD will make me safe.

v17 I will tell (God) that something is wrong,
      and cry (to him) in the evening, in the morning and at noon.
      He will listen to my voice.

v18 He will make me safe and well
      after the many times that I have fought against people
      (that are my enemies).

v19 God will listen to me and he will *punish them.
      (God) will always be King! *SELAH
      He will never change towards the people that are not afraid of God.

v20 But my best friend attacks his friends.
      He does not do what he promised to do.

v21 What he says is as soft as butter, but there is war in his *heart.
      His words are as *soothing as *oil but really they are *like sharp knives.

v22 Take your problems to the *LORD. He will give you help.
      (The *LORD) will never let his people fall.

v23 And you, God, you will make bad people go to the *pit.
      (The *pit) will destroy them.
      (It will destroy) the people that tell *lies and kill (people).
      They will only live half their lives!
      But I will *trust in you, God.

The Silent *Dove Among Strangers
(or Do Not Be Afraid)
Psalm 56

The *Holy Spirit came down on to Jesus. The shape of his body was *like a *dove. A voice from *heaven said, "You are my Son that I love. You give to me a lot of pleasure". (Luke 3:22) (The *Holy Spirit is another name for God. A dove is a bird. The dove is often a sign of *peace or of the *Holy Spirit.)

Jesus said, "Do not be afraid of people that kill the body. They cannot kill the *soul. But rather, be afraid of him that can destroy both *soul and body in hell". (Matthew 10:28) (The *soul is the part of us that lives after our bodies die. *Hell is a place where bad people go when they die.)

Psalm 56

(This is) for the music leader.
   Use (the music that we call) **The Silent *Dove Among Strangers.**
   (It is) a *miktam for David, when the Philistines caught him at Gath.

v1 God, be *gracious to me, because people are fighting me.
     *All day long they are attacking me.

v2 *All day long my enemies are fighting me.
     Many people are attacking me!

v3 *Most High, when I am afraid I will *trust in you.

v4 By God's help I will *praise his word.
     By God's help I will *trust in him. I will not be afraid.
     What can men (on earth) do to me?

v5 *All day long they make my words mean something else
     (that I did not mean).
     All their thoughts about me are bad thoughts against me.

v6 They meet together and hide themselves.
     They watch where I go and hope to kill me.

v7 Do not let them *get away with this!
     God, destroy these people, because you are angry with them.

v8 You count the times when I (cry because I) am not happy.
     Put all my *tears in your bottle.
     (Make sure that) they are all in your book.

v9 Then my enemies will turn back, on the day when I cry (to you).
     Then I will know that God is *on my side.

v10 By God's help I will *praise (his) word.
      By the help of the *LORD I will *praise (his) word.

v11 By God's help I will *trust in him.
      I will not be afraid of what *human beings can do to me.

v12 I have made special promises to you, God.
   I am ready to give you thanks and *praise.

v13 This is because you have saved my life from death.
   Keep my feet from falling so that I may walk before God and stay alive.

(You may know some of the words with asterisks but this psalm uses them in a way that you may not know.)

Danger!
Psalm 57

Everyone in the *synagogue was very angry when they heard Jesus say these things. They got up and took him out of the city. They took him to the top of the hill that they had built their city on. They were going to throw him down. But Jesus just walked away from them and went on his way. (Luke 4:28-30)

Psalm 57

(This is) for the music leader.
   (He must use the music called) "Do not destroy".
   (This is) a *miktam of David, when he ran away from Saul into the *cave.

v1 Be *gracious to me, O God, be *gracious to me.
   I have looked for a place to hide in that is near to you.
   I will hide under the shadow of your *wings until the danger is past.

v2 I will pray to God, the *Most High God,
   to the God who will finish his plan for me.

v3 He will send (a word) from *heaven and he will save me.
   He will stop the people that are trying to catch me.   *SELAH
   God will send me his kind love and his *truth.

v4 There are *lions all round me!
   I must lie down near man-eating animals!
   They are men and their teeth are *like *spears and *arrows.
   Their *tongues are *like sharp *swords.

v5 God, lift yourself up above the skies.
   Lift your *glory above all the earth.

v6 (My enemies) put a *net for my feet.
   I was very sad because of my trouble.
   They dug a hole in front of me, but they fell into it!   *SELAH

v7 God, I have decided to be yours always!
   I will sing your *praises as well as I can!

v8 Wake up, *harp and *lyre.
   I will wake up the dawn!

v9 *LORD, I will thank you in front of all the people.
   I will sing your *praises everywhere.

v10 Your kind love is great. It is *higher than the clouds.
   Your *truth reaches to the skies.

v11 God, lift yourself up above the skies.
   Lift your *glory above all the earth.

Snakes That Will Not Listen
Psalm 58

Jesus said, "These people are *like children that are sitting in the market place. They say to the other (children) there, 'We made music for you, but you did not dance'". (Matthew 11:16-17)

Jesus said, "Why do you call me *Lord, but do not do the things that I tell you (to do). (Luke 6:46)

Psalm 58

(This is) for the music leader.
   He must use (the music called) Do Not Destroy.
   (It is) a *miktam of David.

v1 Do you rulers really say what is fair?
   Do you say what is right when you *judge people?

v2 No! You do not! You think of *evil in your *heart.
   Your hands weigh out *cruelty to the land.

v3 *Wicked people are bad from their birth.
   From the *womb, they start doing wrong and saying *lies.

v4 Their poison is *like the poison of a snake.
   They close their ears *like a *deaf *cobra.

v5 It does not hear the voice of the *charmer, however well he charms!

v6 God, break their teeth in their mouths!
   *LORD, destroy the teeth of those *lions!

v7, v8 May they:
   □ become weak and *flow away *like water
   □ be *like grass that dies after people walk on it
   □ be *like an *abortion that people forget
   □ be *like a child born dead that does not see the sun.

v9 Before their pots can feel (the heat of burning) wood
   I want God to blow them away, *like the wind would in a bad storm.

v10 *Righteous people will be very happy when (God) *punishes (the *wicked).
   They will wash their feet in the blood of the *wicked!

v11 People will say, "There **is** a reward for the *righteous.
   There **is** a God that *judges what happens on earth".

Hungry *Dogs
Psalm 59

Jesus said, "I will always be with you, even to the end of the world". (Matthew 28:20)

Psalm 59

(This is) for the music leader.
   (Use the music that we call) Do Not Destroy.
   (It is) a *miktam of David,
   when Saul sent (men) to watch his house and to kill him.

v1 My God, save me from my enemies.
   Make me strong against the people that are fighting me.

v2 Take me away from men that are doing *evil
   and make me safe from men that kill other people.

v3 Look! They are waiting to kill me!
   *Cruel men are planning together against me.
   *LORD, (I have done) nothing against them and nothing wrong.

v4 (I have done) nothing wrong but they are getting ready to attack me.
   Get up and see (what they are doing)! Bring me help!

v5 For you are the *LORD, a God with *huge armies.
   Get up and *punish the foreign *nations.
   Do not be *gracious to all these *evil and false people.
   *SELAH

v6 They come back to the city every evening.
   They go from place to place and *growl *like *dogs.

v7 Look at their mouths ... *dribbling!
   *Swords come from their lips because (they think that) nobody will hear.

v8 But you, *LORD, you will laugh at them.
   You will also laugh at foreign people.

v9 I will watch for you, My Strength.
   Because you, God, are My *Fortress.

v10 My God, your kind love will come to meet me.
   God will show me (when he wins the battle against) my enemies.

v11 Do not kill them (yet), or my people will forget (them).
   Use your power to make them go from place to place.
   Our *Shield and our *Lord,
   you are stronger than they are so make them do it!

v12 For the *sin of their mouth and the words of their lips,
   catch them in their *pride.
   And (catch them) for the bad things that they say
   and the *lies that they tell.

v13 Destroy them (now) because you are so angry (with them).
    Destroy them and finish their lives.
    Then people will know to the ends of the earth that God rules Jacob.
    *SELAH

v14 They come back to the city every evening.
    They go from place to place and *growl *like *dogs.

v15 They will go from place to place looking for food,
    and they will *growl when they do not find any.

v16 But I will sing that you are My Strength.
    In the morning, I will shout about your kind love.
    Because you were My *Fortress
    where I found *shelter when I was in trouble.

v17 I will raise psalms to you, My Strength.
    Because you, God, are My *Fortress,
    the God that will always show me your kind love.

God, Give Us Help!
Psalm 60

Jesus said, "How can you go into the house of a strong man and take his things? You must first tie him up and then you can take his things". (Matthew 12:29)

Psalm 60

(This is) for the music leader.
    (He must use) "A *Lily of the *Covenant".
    (Psalm 60) is a *miktam of David.
    It was to teach how:
      ☐ he fought armies in Mesopotamia
      ☐ he fought armies in Syria
      ☐ he sent Joab to Edom,
    where he killed 12 000 people in the Valley of Salt.

v1 (You have said) that you will not be our God any more
    and you have broken down our walls.
    Though you are angry, come back to us!

v2 You made the earth move and you tore it open.
    Mend its broken parts because it is falling to pieces.

v3 You showed hard things to your people.
    You made us drink wine that caused us to fall over.

v4 You lifted up a *banner for the people that fear you.
    They will fight for what is true.   *SELAH

v5 Give us help so that the friends that you love will be safe.
    Use your right hand to answer us!

v6 - v8 God did answer us from his *holy place! (He said):
    ☐ I will be the master
    ☐ I will make a parcel of Shechem
    ☐ I will measure the Valley of Succoth
    ☐ Gilead is mine
    ☐ Manasseh is mine
    ☐ Ephraim will cover my head
    ☐ Judah will *judge for me
    ☐ Moab is my bathroom
    ☐ Edom is where I will throw my shoes
    ☐ Philistia will be something for me to laugh at.

v9 Who will lead me into the strong city?
    Who will take me in to Edom?

v10 (You have said) that you would not be our God any more.
    But God, will you really not go with our armies?

v11 Give to us help against the enemy,
    because help from men is of no value!

v12 With God we will beat everybody
    and walk all over our enemies.

Pictures of God
Psalm 61

Jesus said, "I will always be with you, even to the end of the earth". (Matthew 28:20)

Psalm 61

(This is) for the music leader.
    He must use *stringed instruments.
    (It is) a psalm of David.

v1 Hear me when I ask for help, God.
    Listen to my *prayer.

v2 I will shout to you from the ends of the earth when my *heart is weak.
    Lead me to a rock that is *higher than I am.

v3 For you have always been a *shelter for me,
    a *tower against the enemy.

v4 I want to live in your house *for ever.
    I want to hide under the shadow of you *wings.   *SELAH

    . . .

v5 For you, God, have heard my promises.
    You have given (me) the *inheritance (land)
    of the people that are afraid of your name.

v6 Give the king a long life,
    so that he lives for a very long time.

v7 Let him sit with God *for ever.
    Give him your kind love and *truth to make him safe.

v8 Then I will *praise your name *for ever.
    I will keep my promises every day.

Only God!
Psalm 62

Jesus said, "Do not be afraid. Only believe". (Mark 5:36)

Psalm 62

(This is) for the music leader of Jeduthun's (singers).
    (It is) a psalm of David.

v1 **Only** on God is my *soul *resting.
    From him comes my *safety.

v2 **Only** he is my rock. He will keep me safe!
    He is my *fortress, so nothing will move me much.

v3 How long will you shout at a man?
    You all attack (as if he was):
      ☐ a wall that is breaking
      ☐ a *fence that is falling down.

v4 They **only** want to push him off his high place.
    They love to tell a *lie.
    They say good things with their mouths
    but (think) bad things in their *hearts.   *SELAH

v5 **Only** on God is my *soul *resting,
    because from him comes my hope.

v6 **Only** he is my rock. He will keep me safe!
    He is my *fortress so nothing will move me (at all).

v7 (It is) God that made me safe and (put me somewhere) important.
    God is a strong rock and a *shelter.

v8 Everybody (should) always *trust in him!
    Tell him everything that is in your *heart.
    God is our *shelter!   *SELAH

v9 All men are **only** as a *breath! Everyone is as nothing!
    They all weigh less than nothing!
    Everybody together is *like a *breath (of air).

v10 Do not *trust in things that you:
      ☐ make people give to you (or that you)
      ☐ *steal (from people).
    If you become rich do not think in your *heart
    that (money) will give you help.

v11 God has said one thing (and) I have heard two things.
    God is strong,

v12 and you, *Lord, have kind love.
    I am sure that you will give to everyone what they should get.

A Morning Song
Psalm 63

Jesus said, "Good things will happen to people that are hungry and *thirsty for *righteousness. They will have the *kingdom of *heaven". (Matthew 5:10) (The "*kingdom of heaven" is where God is king. "Righteousness" is when everybody does what is right. Only God is really *righteous, and "righteousness" here may mean "God".)

Psalm 63

(This is) a psalm of David, when he was in the wild country of Judah.

v1 God, you are my God. I will look for you early (in the morning).
My *soul is *thirsty for you. All of me wants you.
(It is *like living in) a dry and *thirsty land where there is no water.

v2 I want to see you in your house,
I want to see your power and your *glory.

v3 Your kind love is better than life,
so my mouth will sing your *praises.

v4 Also I will say how good you are all my life.
I will lift up my hands in your name.

v5 My *soul is full, as if I had eaten a lot at a party.
My mouth is full of happy *praises to you.

v6 I remember you when I am in bed
and I think of you through the night.

v7 Because you have given me help
and I will *praise you in the shadow of your *wings.

v8 My *soul stays very near to you
and your right hand keeps me safe.

v9 I ask that (someone) will destroy the people that want to kill me.
Then they will go down deep into the earth.

v10 The *sword will kill them
and wild animals will eat their dead bodies.

v11 The king will sing psalms (of *praises) to God.
Everybody that promises to serve God will be very happy.
(This is) because the mouths of people who tell *lies will be shut.

Words *Like *Arrows
Psalm 64

Simeon said to Mary, "Look, this child (Jesus) is here so that many in Israel will fall down and then rise up again. And many people will say bad things about him. Yes, and a *sword will cut into your *soul also". (Luke 2:34, 35)

(Our *soul is the part of us that will live on when our body dies. It feels sad or happy when things are bad or good.)

Psalm 64

(This is) for the music leader.
(It is) a psalm of David.

v1, v2 God, hear my voice as I tell you my troubles. (Then):
☐ you will make me safe from the enemy that I am afraid of
☐ you will hide me from the secret ideas of bad people
☐ you will keep me from *noisy crowds of *evil people.

v3 - v6 (These *evil people):
☐ make their *tongues sharp *like *swords
☐ shoot words that hurt *like *arrows

(v4) ☐ shoot from secret places at good people
☐ shoot when people do not think it will happen

(v5) ☐ are not afraid (when they have done it)
☐ will not change their *evil ideas
☐ talk about hiding *traps and say, "Who will see them?"

(v6) ☐ say "Who will find out the *crimes that we have done?"
☐ say "We have made a plan that nobody will discover!"
What men think in their *hearts is very deep.

v7 But God will shoot an *arrow at them when they do not think it will happen.
It will hurt them a lot.

v8 Really, they will destroy themselves with their *tongues!
All the people that see it will *shake their heads.

v9 Everyone will be afraid and talk about what God has done.
They will understand what has happened.

v10 Good people will be very happy with the *LORD.
They will *trust in him.
Everybody with an honest *heart will *praise (God)!

A *Harvest Song
Psalm 65

Jesus took bread and he thanked (God). He broke it and gave it to (his friends). He said, "This is my body that I am giving for you. Do this to remember me". In the same way, he also gave them the (wine) cup after supper. He said, "This cup is the new agreement in my blood. (Men) will pour out my blood for you". (Luke 22:19-20) (Other words for agreement are "covenant" and "testament".)

Psalm 65

(This is) for the music leader.
(It is) a psalm of David, a song.

v1 *Silence is *praise to you, God, in Zion.
And we will keep our promises to you.

v2 You are the One that Hears *Prayer.
To you every man and woman should come.

v3 My *sins are too heavy for me.
You (only) can take away (the bad results of) our *disobedience.

v4 The man that you choose will be very happy.
You will bring him near and he will go into your *courts.
We will have plenty of good things in your house, in your *holy *temple.

v5 You answer us by doing things that are *righteous,
(but) they make us afraid.
You are the God that saves us.
You are the hope of people from the ends of the earth and far away seas.

v6 You are so strong that you made the mountains.
Everything that you do shows how powerful you are.

v7 You stop the seas from being angry, so that the waters make no noise.
You do the same with people.

v8 Those that live far away see the great things that you have done.
It makes them afraid.
Where morning starts and evening finishes (they) shout for *joy (to you).

v9 You care for the land.
You send rain on it and you make the ground grow good plants.
The rivers of God are full of water.
They give people *grain because that is how you prepared (the land).

v10 Pour water on the land where the plough was. This will make it flat.
Let the rain make the ground soft. (Then) it will grow good (plants).

v11 The best part of the year is when you give us good things.
Everywhere you go there is plenty.

v12 The fields in wild places pour out good things.
All over the hills there is plenty.

v13 The fields are full of sheep. The valleys are full of *grain.
(They seem) to shout and sing for *joy!

Home and Away
Psalm 66

Jesus said, "They will come from the east, and from the west, and from the north, and from the south. They will sit down in the *kingdom of God". (Luke 13:29)

Psalm 66

(This is) for the music leader.
(It is) a song (and) a psalm.

v1 Shout aloud to God because you are happy, everyone on earth!

v2 Sing to the *glory of his name!
Make the sound of his *praises beautiful!

v3 Say to God, "The things that you do (sometimes) frighten people.
You are so powerful and strong that your enemies are afraid of you.

v4 The whole world will get on its knees in front of you.
It will sing your *praise; it will *praise your name in song".
*SELAH

v5 Come and see the things that God has done.
The things that he did for people frightened many of them.

v6 He made the sea into dry land.
The people walked across the river (Jordan) on their feet!
So, we must *praise him!

v7 He is so powerful that he will rule *for ever.
His eyes are always watching the *nations.
Nobody should fight against him. *SELAH

v8 Say good things about God, you people.
Let everybody hear the sound of (people) *praising him.

v9 He is a God that keeps us alive.
He does not let our feet *slip.

v10 Really, God, you have *tested us.
You have made us *pure as they make *silver *pure.

v11 You brought us into a prison and made people beat our backs.

v12 But you sent a man to lead us.
We went through fire and water,
but you brought us into a place where there was plenty.

v13 I will bring gifts to burn to you in your house.
I will keep the promises that I made to you.

v14 When I was in trouble my lips made a promise.
I said it out aloud.

v15 The gifts that I will offer to you will be fat animals.
You will smell the *rams when they burn.
I will also offer to you *bulls and goats. *SELAH

v16 Come and listen, all you people that are afraid of God.
I will tell you some of the things that he has done for me.

v17 I cried aloud to him, then I *praised him!

v18 If I was thinking bad things in my *heart,
my *Lord would not have listened.

v19 But God did hear me.
He listened to my voice while I prayed.

v20 I will say good things about God.
He has not been *deaf to my voice.
He has shown me his kind love.

The Whole Wide World for Jesus
Psalm 67

Jesus said, "Look at the fields. They are ready for the *harvest". (John 4:35)

Psalm 67

(This is) for the music leader.
(He is) to use *stringed instruments.
(It is) a psalm (and) a song.

v1 God, be *gracious to us and *bless us.
Make your face to shine on us. *SELAH

v2 Then people will know the things that you do on the earth.
People from every *nation will know that you can save them.

v3 So people everywhere will say how great you are, God.
People everywhere will say how great you are.

v4 The *nations will be so very happy that they will sing aloud for *joy!
Because you make fair decisions about everybody,
then you will be a guide to everyone on the earth. *SELAH

v5 People everywhere will say how great your are, God.
People everywhere will say how great you are.

v6 The ground has given us its *harvest
and God, our God, will continue to *bless us.

v7 God - *bless us!
Then everyone that lives on the earth will be afraid of you.

*Gracious, *bless, shine, way, save, people, *nation/s, *joy, *harvest and *awe are all special words in this psalm. "**What Psalm 67 means**" explains them.

Cloud Rider: A Song for the *Nation
Psalm 68

Jesus said, "You will see the Son of man sitting to the right of God. And he will come on the clouds in the sky". (Matthew 26:64) ("Son of man" is a name that Jesus gave himself.)

Psalm 68

(This is) for the music leader.
(It is) a psalm of David, a song.

v1 God will rise up and his enemies will move away in all directions.
The people that *hate him will quickly ride away from him.

v2 (God), blow them away as you would blow smoke away.
As butter becomes *oil in a fire,
when the *godless see the face of God it will destroy them.

v3 But the *righteous will be happy.
They will *rejoice when they see the face of God.
They will shout because they are so happy!

v4 Sing to God, sing psalms to his name.
*Praise the One that Rides on the Clouds.
His name is the *LORD! Shout for *joy in front of him.

v5 God is the father of those that have no father.
He gives help to women whose husbands have died.
(He does this) from the *holy place where he lives.

v6 God gives a home to lonely people.
He leads people out of prison (and they hear) music.
But people that do not obey (God)
will continue to live in a land where the hot sun burns the ground.

v7 God, you went out in front of your people.
You marched through the *wilderness. *SELAH

v8 The ground moved, the skies dropped (rain) when God came to Sinai.
God is the God of Israel.

v9 God, you gave plenty of rain.
It made your Promised Land fresh again when it was dry.

v10 Your people came to live in it.
God, you gave good things to the poor people that needed them.
You made them strong.

v11 The *Lord gave a message
and a large number of women passed on the good news.

v12 Kings of *huge armies ran away. They *fled!
The women at home decided who should have
what their soldiers brought from the war.

v13 Even if you sleep where the sheep sleep,
the *dove will have *wings of *silver and *feathers of gold!

v14 When *Shaddai made (foreign) kings run away in different directions
it was *like snow on Mount Zalmon.

v15 The mountain called Bashan is a Mountain of God.
The mountain called Bashan has many high hills.

v16 High mountains, why do you look at the mountain that God wants to live in?
Why do you want him to live in you instead?
This (mountain) is where the *LORD (himself) will always stay.

v17 God has millions of *chariots.
The *Lord came with them to his *holy (mountain) Sinai.

v18 You went to the high (mountain).
　　　You took with you the *prisoners that you had caught.
　　　You received gifts from men, the men that had fought against you.
　　　The *LORD God will always live here.

v19 Say good things about the *Lord!
　　　Every day he gives us help with what we have to carry.
　　　He is the God that saves us! *SELAH

v20 Our God is the God who will make us free.
　　　The *LORD our God will save us from death.

v21 But God will break the heads of his enemies.
　　　(He will break) the hairy heads of those people
　　　that will not stop doing wrong things.

v22 The *Lord says, "I will bring (my enemies) back from Bashan.
　　　I will bring them back (even from) deep down in the sea.

v23 Then you can put your feet into their blood
　　　and even your *dogs can drink some!"

v24 God, they will see your people walking together.
　　　They will see my God and my King
　　　leading his *procession into the *temple.

v25 The singers will go in front. The musicians will go behind them.
　　　All round them will be girls beating tambourines.

v26 "Say good things about God among all the people there!
　　　All you people of Israel, (*praise) the *LORD!"

v27 Benjamin, the youngest, will go first.
　　　The leaders of Judah will make a noise (*praising God).
　　　(Then will come) the leaders of Zebulun and Naphtali.

v28 Your God sent the power (that gave you help).
　　　God, be powerful (again) as you did (in past times) for us,

v29 from your *temple in Jerusalem.
　　　Kings will (then) bring gifts to you.

v30 Be angry with:
　　　☐ the animals that live in the reeds
　　　☐ the group of bulls among the calves of the *nations.

When they fall on their knees,
　　　they will bring to you pieces of *silver.
　　　Make the people that find pleasure in war
　　　run away from you in all directions.

v31 The government of Egypt will send people
　　　and the people from Cush will lift up their hands to (*praise) God.

v32 Sing to God, you *kingdoms of the earth!
　　　Sing psalms to the *Lord! *SELAH

v33 (Sing) to the One that Rides on the Clouds
　　　and on the *heavens that have always been there!
　　　He is shouting with a powerful voice.

v34 Tell everyone about the powerful God that is the King of Israel.
　　　His power is in the skies.

v35 God, how great you are in your *temple.
　　　He is the God of Israel.
　　　He gives power to his people and makes them strong.
　　　Say good things about God!

**The Whipping Boy
Psalm 69**

Jesus came to his own country, and his own people did not receive him. (John 1:11)

Psalm 69: Verses 1 - 4

(This is) for the music leader.
　　　Use (the music that they call) "*Lilies".
　　　(It is) for David.

v1 Save me, God! Because the waters have come to *(take) my life.

v2 I am going down into deep *mud and there is nowhere to put my feet.
　　　I have come into deep waters and *floods rush over me.

v3 I have shouted so much for help that I am weak.
　　　My mouth is hot and dry. My eyes hurt from looking for God.

v4 More people *hate me than (I have) hairs on my head.
　　　They have no reason to be my enemies.
　　　Many people try to destroy me with their *lies.
　　　They made me give back something that I did not rob them of.

v5 You, God, know that I am a fool.
　　　I cannot hide my *sin from you.

v6 Master, do not let the people that put their hope in you
　　　be ashamed because of me.
　　　You are the *LORD of the armies (of *heaven).
　　　Do not let the people that follow you
　　　be ashamed because of me.
　　　You are the God of Israel.

v7 Because I love you people say bad things about me.
　　　They make me feel ashamed.

v8 I have become a stranger to my brothers
　　　and my own mother's sons do not know me.

v9 I am angry for your house and it burns me up inside.
　　　People *insult you, but they do it by *insulting me!

v10 When I cry and eat no food people still *insult me.

v11 When I wear clothes made from *sacks people laugh at me.

v12 People that sit by the gate talk about me
　　　and people that are drunks sing songs about me.

v13 But me ... I am praying to you, *LORD,
　　　(at a) time when you will hear me.
　　　God, because you have so much kind love,
　　　answer me and make me really safe.

v14 Take me out of the *mud
　　　and do not let me fall into it any more.
　　　Save me from the people that *hate me
　　　and from the very deep waters.

v15 Do not let:
　　　☐ *floods of waters pour over me
　　　☐ the deep seas drown me
　　　☐ the *pit close its mouth round me.

v16 Answer me, *LORD, because your kind love is (so) good.
　　　Turn to me because you have so much *mercy.

v17 And do not hide your face from your servant.
　　　Because of my trouble, answer me very soon.

v18 Come near to my *soul and make it safe.
　　　Buy it back because of my enemies.

v19 You (God) know that people *insult me
　　　and say that I am a *disgrace and make me ashamed.

v20 *Insults have broken my *heart. I feel *helpless.
　　　I looked for *sympathy, but there was none.
　　　I wanted someone to *comfort me, but did not find anyone.

v21 But they put poison in my food
　　　and they gave me *vinegar to drink.

v22 I want (the food on) their table to be a *trap (for them)
　　　and a *trap for all their good friends!

v23 I want their eyes to be in the dark so that they cannot see.
　　　I want their bodies to bend over always,

v24 (because) you are so angry with them.
　　　Pour out your anger on them!

v25 I want the places where they stay to be empty
　　　and nobody to be in their *tents.

v26 For they *persecute the people that you (God) hurt
　　　and talk about (more) pain for the people that you *punish.

v27 Make a note of all their *sins
　　　and do not let them have your *righteousness.

v28 Take their names out of the book of life.
　　　Take them off the list of *righteous people.

v29 But I have pain (in my body) and trouble (in my mind).
　　　God, *protect me and make me safe.

v30 I will *praise God's name with songs
　　　and I will say how great he is by giving thanks.

v31 This will bring more pleasure to the *LORD
than an *ox or a bull with *horns and *hooves.

v32 Poor people will see it and be happy.
People that are looking for God will have brave *hearts again.

v33 For the *LORD hears what people need
and he does not think bad things about his people in *captivity.

v34 Let the skies and the earth *praise him!
And let the seas and everything that moves through them *praise him!

v35 For God will make Zion safe.
He will build again the cities of Judah.
Then (his servants) will live there and it will be theirs.

v36 As for the children of his servants,
it will stay their *inheritance also.
The people that love God's name will always remain there.

Help to Remember
Psalm 70

Jesus said, "Do this to remember me". (Luke 22:19) (These are words that Jesus said when he ate supper the last time with his friends.)

Psalm 70

(This is) for the (music) leader.
(It is) a psalm of David, to give him help to remember.

v1 God, save me!
*LORD, hurry to give me help.

v2 There are people that want to kill me.
I hope that they will become ashamed and confused.
There are people that want to destroy me.
I hope that everyone will say that they are bad people.

v3 I want all those people that say to me '*Aha! Aha!'
to become very sorry for what they have done.

v4 I want everyone looking for you to be happy, very happy.
I want everyone that loves it when you save them to say, '*Praise God'.

v5 But I am poor and I need help.
God, hurry to give me help.
You are my help, and you save me.
God, do not be long!

A Song for Old Age
Psalm 71

Jesus said, "*Trust me until the day that you die. Then I will give to you a *crown of life". (Revelation 2:10)

Psalm 71

v1 *LORD, I am *trusting in you.
Do not let me ever become ashamed.

v2 Take me away from danger and make me free,
because you do what is right.
Listen to me and make me safe.

v3 You really are a rock,
where I can always go to hide from danger.
Tell people to make me safe,
for you are my rock and my *fortress.

v4 My God, take me from the hands of *godless people.
Take me from the *cruel and *evil people that are holding me.

v5 You are my hope, Master.
*LORD, I have *trusted in you since I was young.

v6 Since I was born, I have *trusted in you.
You have given me help since I came out of my mother's *womb.
I will always tell you how great you are!

v7 I make many people think of danger and become afraid.
But you are a strong and safe place for me.

v8 My mouth is full of saying how great you are.
All day I am saying that you are beautiful!

v9 Do not throw me away when I am old.
Do not forget me when I am not strong.

v10 For my enemies say things against me
and the people that want to kill me are making plans together.

v11 They say, "God has forgotten him.
Run after him and catch him! For nobody will save him".

v12 God, do not stay far from me.
God, give me help very soon.

v13 Make my enemies become completely ashamed.
Cover in *scorn and *disgrace the people that want to hurt me.

v14 But I, I will always have hope.
I will go on saying again and again that you are great.

v15 My mouth will say that you are *righteous,
that you make people safe *all day long.
(I will do this) even if I do not know how much (you have done).

v16 I will come and speak about the great things that you have done, Master and *LORD.
I will talk about how *righteous that you are.
You, only you, (are *righteous).

v17 God, you have taught me since I was young.
And until now I have told about the wonderful things that you have done.

v18 And even when I am old and grey, do not forget me, God.
Do not forget me until I tell the people still to be born:
☐ about your great power and
☐ how strong you are.

v19 You are *righteous, God, with *righteousness as high as the sky!
You have done such great things, God, who is *like you?

v20 Even when you made me see troubles, many bad troubles,
you made me live again.
From deep under the earth you brought me up again.

v21 You will make me great again and make me strong.

v22 I will sing about how great you are, with *harp music.
You do what you promise, God.
I will sing about how great you are, with *guitar music.
You are the *Holy One of Israel.

v23 My lips will shout because I am so happy!
I really want to sing about how great you are.
You have bought me back.

v24 My *tongue will talk about your *righteousness *all day long.
The people that want to hurt me will become ashamed
and covered with *disgrace.

The Good, Great King of *Glory

Psalm 72

Psalm 72: 1 - 7 ~ The Good King

(This psalm is) for or by Solomon.

v1 God, give your *justice to the king
and your *righteousness to the king's son.

v2 He will rule your people with *righteousness
and the poor people with *justice.

v3 With *righteousness will the mountains
and the hills bring *peace to the people.

v4 He will *defend the poor people
and save the children of those that are in need.
He will destroy *cruel people

v5 and they will be afraid of him
as long as there is a sun and a moon.

v6 He will be *like rain that falls on grass that people have just cut.
He will be *like showers that bring water to the earth.

v7 When he is king, a *righteous person will do well.
There will be *peace until there is no moon!

Now I Understand
Psalm 73

Jesus said, "Make sure that your valuable things are in *heaven". (Matthew 6:20) (*Heaven is the home of God.)

Psalm 73

(This is) a psalm of *Asaph.

v1 I am sure that God is good to (the people of) Israel,
    to the people whose hearts are clean.

v2 But (this is what happened) to me.
    My feet nearly *slipped and I almost fell over.

v3 Some people had made themselves important.
    Because I was angry, I wanted the things they had.
    I saw that *godless people had plenty!

v4 And so their bodies are fat (and *healthy).
    Even when they die, they feel no pain.

v5 They do not have trouble *like other people
    or the difficulties that hit everyone else.

v6 So they, (the *godless), wear their *pride *like a *necklace.
    The bad things that they do, they wear them *like clothes.

v7 Their eyes look out from fat faces.
    Their hearts are full of *pride.

v8 They laugh (at people) and say bad things (about them).
    In their *pride they talk about *oppressing people.

v9 The mouths (of the *godless) say that the skies belong to them.
    And their *tongues demand the earth.

v10 So his (God's) people turn to them.
    They drink everything from them (the *godless).

v11 And they (God's people) ask, "How can God know?"
    And (they ask) "Does the *Most High see everything?"

v12 This, then, is what *godless people (say and do).
    They have no trouble and plenty of money!

v13 I was sure that I had made my heart clean
    for no good purpose!
    Also, I had washed my hands
    to show that I had done nothing wrong (for no reason)!

v14 I had trouble all day
    and it started to hurt me every morning!

v15 If I had said, "I will agree (with what the *godless say)";
    then I would have let down all your children.

v16 When I thought about this,
    it was so hard for me (to understand).

v17 Then I went into the house of God.
    That was when I understood what would happen to them (the *godless).

v18 (Then) I was sure that you would put them
    in a place where they would *slip!
    You would throw them down and destroy them.

v19 It will take just a moment to destroy them!
    Great *fear will sweep them away completely.

v20 It will be *like when you wake up from a dream.
    *Lord, when you get up, you will forget that they were there!

v21 When my heart hurt me and my stomach was painful...

v22 ...I was *stupid and I knew nothing.
    I was as an angry animal with you!

v23 But really I was always with you.
    (Now) you hold me by my right hand.

v24 What you say to me will be my guide.
    And then you will take me to *glory.

v25 I know nobody in *heaven except you.
    And, with you, there is nothing (else) on earth that I want.

v26 My heart and my body may fail,
    but God will always make me strong.
    He is all that I will ever need.

v27 I am sure that people far from you will die.
    You will destroy everybody that does not obey you.

v28 But it is good for me to be near to God.
    I have made the master and *LORD my safe place.
    I will tell (people) about the good things that you do.

Psalm 74

Jesus said, "One stone will not stay on another. They will all become broken". (Matthew 25:2)

Psalm 74

(This is) a *maskil for *Asaph

v1 God, will you never think about us again?
    Why are you burning with *anger against the people that belong to you?

v2 Think (again) about:
    ☐ your people that you bought a long time ago
    ☐ the people that you chose and saved
    ☐ the Mountain called Zion where you lived

v3 Go and look at everything that the enemy broke.
    He destroyed your *temple!

v4 Your enemies have made an angry noise inside your meeting place.
    They have put their own *flags there as signs.

v5 They seemed *like wild men!
    They used axes to cut the *temple into pieces!

v6 They used hammers and axes to break the doors
    and other things made from wood.

v7 They burned your *temple to the ground!
    They said that the place where your name lived was *rubbish!

v8 They said in their hearts, "We will completely destroy them".
    So they burned every meeting place of God in the land.

v9 Nobody gives us signs (that are *miracles).
    There are no *prophets with us.
    Nobody knows how long this will continue.

v10 God, how long will the enemy laugh at you?
    Will the enemy always laugh at your name?

v11 Why do you hide your hand (from us), even your right hand?
    Take it out from your pocket! Destroy them!

v12 For you, God, have been my king from the beginning.
    You have done great things in the earth.

v13 It was you that *divided the sea, because you are so strong.
    You broke the heads of the *monsters in the waters.

v14 It was you that broke the heads of *Leviathan.
    You gave him as food for the animals in the *desert.

v15 It was you that made *springs and streams.
    It was you that made quick-moving rivers dry!

v16 You made both day and night.
    It was you that put the moon and the sun in their places.

v17 It was you that said where the (dry) land must be.
    It was you that made both summer and winter.

v18 *LORD, think about this:
    ☐ an enemy has laughed at you
    ☐ and *stupid people have *scorned your name

v19 Do not give the life of your *dove to wild animals.
    Do not always forget the lives of your poor people.

v20 Keep your promise!
    Because the earth is full of dark places where bad men hide.

v21 Do not let *oppressed people become ashamed.
    Let the poor people that need help say how great you are!

v22 Stand up, God! Tell everyone that you are right.
    Remember that fools are laughing at you all the time.

v23 Listen to the noise that your enemies make.
    The sound of people fighting against you goes on all the time!

Earthquakes, Horns and A Cup Of Wine!
Psalm 75

Jesus woke up and he was angry with the wind. He said to the sea, "Shut your mouth and stop making a noise!" And the wind stopped blowing and it was very quiet. (Mark 4:39) (The word that Jesus used was one that people used to make their animals quiet.)

Psalm 75

(This is) for the music leader.
  (He must use music called) "Do Not Destroy".
  (This is) a Psalm of *Asaph (and) a Song.

v1 God, we thank you.
  We really thank you because you are still near to us.
  This is what the *wonderful things that you have done tell us!

v2 (God said,) "At the time that I will choose, I will be a fair *judge.

v3 When the earth *shakes and everything in it (is afraid),
  I will stop its *foundations moving.   ***SELAH**

v4 I say to the people that are *boasting, "Do not *boast".
  (I say) to the *godless, "Do not lift up your *horn.

v5 Do not lift your *horn up high.
  (Do not) push your neck up high when you speak".

v6 For nobody
  ☐ from the east
  ☐ or from the west
  ☐ or from the *desert (in the south)
  ☐ or from the mountains (in the north)

v7 will be *judge. Only God (will be *judge).
  He puts one person down and he lifts up another person.

v8 Because there is a cup in the *LORD's hand.
  It is full of *wine, mixing with *spice.
  (The *LORD) will pour it out from this (cup).
  All the *godless people in the world will drink it.
  They will drink the last bit of it.

v9 But I will always talk about (what God did).
  I will sing *praise to the God of *Jacob.

v10 (Because he says) "I will cut off all the *horns of the *godless.
  But I will lift up the *horns of the *righteous".

Sing A Song Of Zion
or
The *Lion's *Den
Psalm 76

They got up and took Jesus out of the city. They led him to the side of a hill, where men had built their city. They wanted to throw him down. But Jesus just walked away from them, and went on his own way. (Luke 4:29-30)

Psalm 76

(This is) for the music leader.
  (He must use) *stringed instruments.
  (It is) a Psalm of *Asaph (and) a Song.

v1 God is famous in Judah.
  His name is great in Israel.

v2 His house is in Salem and his home is in Zion.

v3 There he broke (the enemy's):
  ☐ bow (shooting) fire
  ☐ *shield
  ☐ and *sword
  ☐ and war (*weapons) ***SELAH**

v4 You (God) are the Shining One!
  (You are) the King from the mountains,
  where you robbed your enemy!

v5 (You) took from the brave (enemy) soldiers all (the *weapons) that they had.
  Now they are sleeping and will never wake up.
  None of the soldiers can use their hands.

v6 When you were angry, God of *Jacob,
  both the horses and the men that rode on them fell down dead.

v7 You ... everyone is afraid of you!
  Who can remain standing in front of you when you are angry?

v8 From the *heavens you said that you would *judge (the people).
  All the earth was afraid of you and became quiet.

v9 (This happened), God, when you came to *judge
  and to save the *oppressed people in the land. ***SELAH**

v10 So the *anger of men will *praise you.
  What remains of their *anger you will wear (as *praise).

v11 Make a promise to the *LORD your God and do (what you promise).
  Let everyone that lives near bring a gift to the God that people are afraid of.

v12 He breaks the *spirit of rulers.
  All the kings of the world are afraid of him.

Questions and Answers
Psalm 77

John sent people to ask Jesus, "Are you the One that will come, or must we look for someone else?" Jesus answered and said to them, "Go and tell John the things that you hear and see. Blind people can see again, people with bad legs can walk again, people that are ill become better, the *deaf hear and the dead come back to life". (Matthew 11: 3 - 5) (The "One that will come" is the Messiah or Christ.)

Psalm 77

(This is) for the music leader.
  (His name is) Jeduthun.
  (It is a) psalm of *Asaph.

v1 I cried aloud to God.
  I cried to God so that he could hear me.

v2 When trouble came, I looked for the *Lord.
  All through the night, I lifted my hands (to him while I prayed).
  But I did not get help.

v3 I remembered God and I cried.
  I thought (about my trouble) and my *spirit became weak
  *SELAH

v4 (God), you do not let me close my eyes.
  I have so much trouble that I do not know what to say.

v5 I think about days that have gone
  and the years that have passed.

v6 At night I remember the songs (that I sang).
  I ask myself questions and my *spirit looks for answers.

v7 ☐ "Will the *Lord always say 'No' to us?"
  ☐ "Will he never again be good to us?"

v8 ☐ "Will he for ever stop giving us his kind love?"
  ☐ "Will he not do what he promised for us and our children?"

v9 ☐ "Has God forgotten to be *gracious to us?"
  ☐ "Is he so angry with us that he will not love us?" ***SELAH**

v10 Then I said, "I will think about the times
  when the *Most High did give us help.

v11 I will remember the things that the *LORD has done.
  Yes, I will remember the *miracles that you did in past times.

v12 I will think about all that you have done.
  I will think about all the great things that you have done"

v13 Your way, God, is *holy.
  What god is as great as our God?

v14 You are the God that does *miracles.
  You show people that you are very powerful.

v15 You saved your people with your strong arm.
  You saved the people of *Jacob and *Joseph. ***SELAH**

v16 The waters saw you, God,
  the waters saw you and rolled over and over.
  The deepest seas moved round a lot.

v17 The clouds poured down water.
  The noise of *thunder was in the skies.
  Your *arrows were everywhere.

v18 The voice of your *thunder was in the storm.
    Your *lightning lit all the world.
    The earth moved about and *shook.

v19 Your road went through the sea.
    Your path was through the great waters,
    but nobody saw where your feet went.

v20 You led your people in a group
    with Moses and Aaron at the front.

Tell Your Children
Psalm 78

Jesus said, "Let the little children come to me. Do not stop them". (Matthew 19:14)

Psalm 78: 1 - 8

(This is one) of *Asaph's Psalms that Teach Us (about God).

v1 My people, hear what I am teaching you.
   Listen to the words that I am saying to you.

v2 I will tell you a story.
   I will talk about things hard to understand from past times.

v3 We have heard them and know them
   because our fathers told them to us.

v4 We will not hide them from their children.
   We will tell future children that they should *praise the *LORD.
   (He is) very strong and he has done great things.

v5 He decided what things *Jacob must do and made the *laws in Israel.
   He told our grandfathers that they must teach them to their children.

v6 Then those children would know them, even the children still to be born.
   When the time came, they too would tell their children.

v7 Then they (the children) would:
   ☐ believe that God would give them help
   ☐ not forget what God had done
   ☐ obey his *laws

v8 So they would not be like their grandfathers who:
   ☐ would not listen to God
   ☐ would not obey him
   ☐ did not make God their leader
   ☐ did not continue to follow him

For the *Glory of Your Name
Psalm 79

For the *kingdom is always yours and the power is always yours and the *glory is always yours (Matthew 6:13). (The end of a special *prayer that Jesus taught us; a *kingdom is where a king rules; here, God is the King.)

Psalm 79

(This is) a psalm of *Asaph.

v1 God, countries that do not love you have attacked us.
   They have taken away your land.
   They have done bad things to your *holy *temple
   so that we cannot *worship you in it.
   They have destroyed Jerusalem.

v2 They have given the dead bodies of your people
   to the birds (that fly) in the air for food.
   They have given the bodies of your servants
   for wild animals to eat.

v3 They have poured out the blood (of your servants)
   *like water all round Jerusalem.
   There was nobody to bury your people.

v4 Our *neighbours just laugh at us.
   The people that live near us *scorn us.

v5 How long will this continue?
   (God), will you always be angry?
   Will your *jealousy burn *like a fire for ever?

v6 Be very angry with the countries that do not love you
   and the *nations that do not pray to you.

v7 Because they have beaten *Jacob
   and destroyed the land where he lived.

v8 Do not be angry with us
   because of the wrong things that our fathers did.
   Have *mercy on us soon.
   We have lost all our hope.

v9 God, give us help! (You are the God) that can save us.
   For the *glory of your name, save us.
   So that your name will always be famous, *forgive our *sins.

v10 Why should the countries that do not love God say,
    "Where is their God?"
    We want to see you become angry with these countries,
    because they poured out the blood of your servants.

v11 Listen to the *prisoners that are crying!
    By the power of your arm, save those that are going to die.

v12 *Lord, make the countries that do not love you
    have seven times as much trouble as we have had!
    Because they said bad things to you.

v13 Then we, your people (who are as) sheep in your field,
    will always thank you.
    So will our children and grandchildren.

Make Us United
Psalm 80

Jesus said, "I pray for the people that will believe in me … that they may be united. Then the world will believe that you sent me". (John 17: 20 - 21)

Psalm 80

(This is) for the music leader.
   (Sing it) to (music that they call) '"*Lilies of the *Covenant".
   (It is) a psalm of *Asaph.

v1 *Shepherd of Israel, listen to us!
   You are the one that leads *Joseph *like a *flock.
   You sit *like a king between the *Cherubim.

v2 Shine on Ephraim, Benjamin and Manasseh.
   Get up and show how strong you are.
   Come and make us safe.

v3 God, make us return (to you).
   Make your face shine (on us) and make us safe.

v4 *LORD God (of) *Sabaoth,
   how long will you be angry when your people pray?

v5 You have fed them tears for food
   and buckets of tears for drink.

v6 You have made the people that live near us fight (us)
   and our enemies laugh among themselves (at us).

v7 God (of) *Sabaoth, make us return (to you).
   Make your face shine (on us) and make us safe.

v8 You brought a *vine from Egypt.
   You moved away the people that lived (in the land) and planted it.

v9 You made (the ground) ready for it,
   so that it grew and filled the land.

v10 Its shade covered the mountains (in the south)
    and its branches covered the big cedar (trees in the north).

v11 Its branches reached the (Mediterranean) Sea (in the west)
    and the River (Euphrates in the east).

v12 Why have you knocked down its walls
    so that anyone that passes can rob its fruit?

v13 Pigs from the woods attack it
    and wild animals destroy it.

v14 Come back to us, God (of) *Sabaoth!
    Look down from *heaven and see (us)!
    Be careful with this *vine...

v15 ...that your right hand planted.
     (The *vine is) the son that you made strong for yourself.

v16 You let (the enemy) cut down your *vine and burn it with fire.
     Destroy them (the enemy) because you are angry!

v17 Let your hand be on the man at your right hand.
     (He is) the son of man that you made strong for yourself.

v18 Then we will never turn away from you.
     Give us life and we will (always) *praise your name.

v19 *LORD God (of) *Sabaoth, make us return (to you).
     Make your face shine (on us) and make us safe.

Start The Music!
Psalm 81

Jesus said, "Can the bridegroom's friends be sad when the bridegroom is with them?" (Matthew 9: 15). (A bridegroom is a man getting married.)

Psalm 81

(This is) for the music leader.
(Use) *Gittith.
(It is a psalm) of *Asaph.

v1   Sing to God because you are so happy!
     (Do this because) God makes us strong!
     Shout aloud to the God of *Jacob.

v2   Start the music! Hit the *tambourine
     and make beautiful sounds on the *harp and the *lyre.

v3   Start the New Moon *Festival with the sound of the *shofar.
     Do it at the Full Moon (*Festival) also.

v4   For this is a rule for Israel,
     something that the God of *Jacob said that we must do.

v5   He told it to *Joseph when he attacked the land of Egypt.
     I heard a language that I did not understand.

v6   (It said) "I took the weight off his shoulders.
     His hands did not have to carry a heavy basket (any more).

v7   When you had trouble, you called (to me) and I made you safe.
     I gave you help from the centre of the storm.
     I *tested you at the Waters of Meribah.   *SELAH

v8   My people, hear me! You are near to danger.
     Israel, I really want you to listen to me!

v9   There should not be another god among you
     and you certainly should not go down on your knees to another god.

v10 I am the *LORD your God.
     I brought you out of the land of Egypt.
     Open your mouth wide and I will fill it".

v11 But my people did not listen to my voice
     and Israel did not obey me.

v12 And so I let them follow their own ideas.
     They did whatever they wanted to do.

v13 I want my people to listen to me!
     I want Israel to walk in my ways!

v14 Then I would quickly beat all their enemies
     and fight against all those that are angry with them.

v15 The people that hate the *LORD will be afraid of him
     and this will happen for a long time.

v16 But he would feed him (Israel) with the best *wheat
     and I would give you (Israel) plenty of *honey from the rock.

God And The Gods
Psalm 82

Jesus said, "I saw *Satan fall from *heaven like a light through the sky". (Luke 10: 18)

Psalm 82

(This is) a psalm of *Asaph.

v1   God is the leader of a meeting of the powerful ones.
     He is telling the gods what he has decided.

v2   (He says) "How long will you not be fair to people?
     (How long) will you say that the *godless are right?"   *SELAH

v3   Be fair and give help to:
     ☐ people that are weak
     ☐ children with dead parents
     ☐ people that are poor
     ☐ anyone that has nothing

v4   Make the poor people safe and give them the help that they need.
     Take them away from the power of the *godless.

v5   They (the *godless) know nothing and they understand nothing.
     They walk about in *darkness.
     The ground beneath them moves about.

v6   I (God) say, "You are gods
     and you are all sons of the *Most High.

v7   But you will die like Adam.
     You will fall like rulers".

v8   God, stand up and rule the earth,
     because all the countries in it belong to you.

Enemies All Round Us!
Psalm 83

Jesus said, "I am sending you like sheep into a group of wolves. So, be as clever as snakes but, like the dove, do not hurt anybody" (Matthew 10: 16). (A wolf is a wild animal that eats sheep; a dove is a bird that does not hurt anyone.)

Psalm 83

(This) psalm (is) a song for *Asaph.

v1   God, do not seem to be asleep!
     Do not remain quiet and do nothing, God!

v2   For look, your enemies are (all) doing something.
     The people that hate you are getting ready (to fight you).

v3   They are making clever *plans against your people.
     They are deciding together what to do with those people that you love.

v4   They are saying, "Come on, we will destroy their country.
     Then nobody will ever remember the name of Israel".

v5   They are deciding together what to do.
     They are agreeing to do something against you.

v6 - v7 The people (doing this are) from:
     ☐ Edom and the Ishmaelites
     ☐ Moab and the Hagrites
     ☐ Gebal, Ammon and Amalek
     ☐ Philistia and Tyre

v8   Even Assyria has joined them.
     They have made the sons of Lot (Moab and Ammon) strong.
     *SELAH

v9   Do to them what you did to Midian
     and to Sisera and Jabin at the River Kishon.

v10 They died at Endor
     and they became *like dirt on the ground.

v11 Make their leaders *like Oreb and Zeeb.
     (Make) all their *princes *like Zebah and Zalmunna.

v12 They said, "Let us take all the country that belongs to God".

v13 God, blow them away *like *chaff in the wind!

v14 As fire burns a forest and *lights the mountains,
     so they are on fire.

v15 Go after them with bad weather
     and frighten them a lot with your storms.

v16 Make their faces ashamed
     so that they will look for your name, *LORD.

v17 Let them always be ashamed and very frightened.
     Let them become so ashamed that then they die!

v18 Then they will know that your name is *LORD.
And (they will know that) you are the *Most High over all the earth.

Journey To Zion
Psalm 84

Jesus said, "Foxes have holes and the birds of the air have nests. But the Son of Man has nowhere to rest his head" (Matthew 8: 20). (Holes and *nests are where foxes and birds sleep. Son of Man is a name for Jesus.)

Psalm 84

This is) for the music leader.
(He must use) *Gittith.
(It is) a psalm for *Korah.

v1 *LORD of (*huge) armies
- people love your *temple very much!

v2 I want very much (to go to) the place where the *LORD lives.
(I want it so much) that it is making me feel weak!
All that I am and all that I feel is crying out to the Living God!

v3 Even the *sparrow has found a home
and the *swallow (has found) a *nest.
There she may keep her babies.
(They are in places) near your *altars,
*LORD of (*huge) armies.
You are my king and my God.

v4 The people that live in your house are very happy.
They can always tell you how great you are. *SELAH

v5 The people that you make strong are very happy.
They want to come to you (in Zion).

v6 As they pass through a dry valley,
it (seems) to become a place with wells of water in it.
The autumn rains cover (the valley) with pools.

v7 The people become stronger as they go,
(until) each one appears before God in Zion.

v8 *LORD God of (*huge) armies,
hear the words that I am praying!
God of *Jacob, listen to me! *SELAH

v9 God, look at our *shield!
And look kindly at the face of your king.

v10 One day in your (*temple) *courts
is better than a thousand (days somewhere else).
I would rather stand at the door of God's house
than sit in the houses of *wicked people.

v11 For the *LORD is a sun and a *shield.
He gives *grace and *glory (to people).
He gives good things to people that do what is right.

v12 *LORD of (*huge) armies
- everybody is very happy that *trusts in you!

Turn Again
(or The Kiss Of *Peace)
Psalm 85

Jesus said, "My *peace I give to you". (John 14: 27)

Psalm 85

(This is) for the music leader.
(It is) a psalm of the sons of *Korah.

v1 *LORD, you were good to your land.
You *turned the fortunes of *Jacob.

v2 You *forgave the *sin of your people
and you *pardoned the things that they did wrong.

v3 You were not angry with them anymore
and you turned away from your *fury.

v4 (But now) turn us (again), God.
(You are the God) that makes us safe.
Stop being so angry with us.

v5 Will you be angry with us forever?
Will you always be *furious with us?

v6 Will you not turn to us (again) and give us new life?
Then your people will be happy and *praise you.

v7 *LORD, show us your kind love!
Give to us the help that makes us safe!

v8 I will listen to what God the *LORD is saying.
He will give *peace to his people, to his *saints.
But they must not turn back to become fools.

v9 Certainly he will make safe those that obey him.
Then his *glory will remain in our land.

v10 Kind love will meet *loyalty.
*Goodness and *peace will kiss each other.

v11 *Loyalty will grow (like a plant) in the ground
and *goodness will look down from the *heavens.

v12 Yes! The *LORD will give what is good
and our land will give much fruit.

v13 *Goodness will go before him
and make a way for his feet.

Bits and Pieces
Psalm 86

They said to Jesus, "Teach us to pray". He said, "Ask and you will receive. Look and you will find. Knock and it will open to you". (From Luke 11: 1 and 9)

Psalm 86

Words that David prayed.

v1 *LORD, turn your ear (to me), answer me!
Because I am weak and need (help).

v2 Save me from death because I am one of your people.
Keep (me) your servant safe. You are my God.
(I am) someone that is *trusting in you.

v3 My *Lord, give me *mercy!
All through the day, I am praying (this) to you.

v4 Make (me) your servant happy!
Because I lift up myself to you, my *Lord.

v5 My *Lord, you are good. Also, you *forgive (people).
You give your kind love to everyone that prays to you.

v6 *Turn your ear to what I am praying, *LORD.
And listen to my voice when I cry for *mercy.

v7 On the day that I have trouble I will pray to you,
because you can answer me.

v8 None among the gods is like you, my *Lord.
And nobody can do what you can do.

v9 All the countries that you have made will come
and *worship before you, my *Lord.
They will say how great your name is.

v10 For you are great. You do great things.
You alone are God.

v11 *LORD, teach me your way. I will walk in your *truth.
Make my heart united when I think of your name.

v12 I will *praise you, my *Lord and my God, with my united heart.
I will always tell people that you are really great!

v13 (I will do this) because there is so much of your kind love to me.
You will save me from going to the lowest part of *Sheol.

v14 God, *proud people are attacking me.
A group of cruel men is trying to kill me.
They do not think about you.

v15 But you, my *Lord, are a God that loves (people) and gives (them) *mercy.
You are slow to become angry and (you are) full of kind love.
You do not leave (your people when they have trouble).

v16 Turn to me and give me *mercy. Make (me) your servant strong
and make the son of your woman servant safe.

v17 Show me something that tells me that you are good.
Let my enemies see it and be ashamed.
Because you, *LORD, have given me help and been kind to me.

The Two Jerusalem's
Psalm 87

Jesus said, "You must be born again". (John 3:7)

Psalm 87

(This is) a song with music, for the sons of *Korah.

v1 He built it on the mountains of *holiness.

v2 The *LORD loves the gates of Zion.
 He loves them more than all the places where *Jacob lives.

v3 (People say) *wonderful things about you, city of God.   *SELAH

v4 I will remember the people that I know, from Rahab and Babylon;
 also from Philistia, Tyre and Ethiopia.
 I will remember that this man was born there.

v5 They will say in Zion, "A man ... this man ... was born there".
 So he ... the *Most High ... will build her up.

v6 The *LORD will write in his book (the name of) everyone that says,
 "This man was born there".   *SELAH

v7 The singers and the *musicians (will say),
 "All my *springs are in you".

Down Among the Dead Men
Psalm 88

Jesus went into a town called Nain. Many of his *disciples and a lot of people went with him. Now when he came near to the gate of the town, he saw a dead man. They were carrying him out. His mother was a *widow and the dead man was her only son. A big crowd of people from the town was with her. And when the Lord (Jesus) saw her, he was very sorry for her. He said to her, "Do not weep". And he came and touched the *coffin. The men carrying it stood *still. And he said, "Young man, I say to you, get up". And the dead man got up and began to speak. And Jesus gave him to his mother. And everybody was afraid. They said that God was really great and that a *prophet had come among them. And (they said) that God had visited his people. (Luke 7:11-16)

Psalm 88

(This) song (is a) psalm for the sons of *Korah.
 The music leader (must use music called) "*mahalath leannoth".
 (It is) a *maskil by Heman the Ezrahite.

v1 *LORD, (you are) the God that makes me safe.
 I always cry to you in the day and at night for help.

v2 I want you to hear the words that I am praying.
 Listen to my *cry for help!

v3 Because I have a lot of trouble
 and my life is coming near to *Sheol.

v4 (People) say that I am among those that are going to the *Pit.
 I am *like a strong man that has become weak (and ill).

v5 I am almost with those that are already dead.
 (I am) *like dead people lying in their *graves.
 You do not remember them anymore
 and you cannot give them help where they are.

v6 You are putting me in the lowest *Pit,
 in a very dark and deep place.

v7 You are very angry with me.
 You are like a heavy sea,
 pouring all over me and knocking me down.

v8 You have taken my best friends away from me.
 You have made me seem very bad to them.
 The place that I am in is *like a prison that I cannot leave.

v9 My eyes are weak because I am so sad.
 *LORD, every day I pray to you.
 I lift my hands up to you (while I pray).

v10 Do you do *miracles for people that are dead?
 Do dead people get up and say that you are great?
 *SELAH

v11 Do people talk about your kind love in the *grave?
 (Do they say) in *Abaddon that you continue to be good to people?

v12 Do they know about your *miracles in dark places.
 (Do they know about) the good things that you do
 in the land where people forget (everything).

v13 But *LORD, I cry to you for help.
 Every morning I pray to you.

v14 *LORD, why are you throwing me away?
 Why do you hide your face from me?

v15 I have been ill and near to death since I was young.
 You have let bad things happen to me
 and I do not know what to do.

v16 Your *fury pours over me.
 You are attacking me and destroying me!

v17 (The things that you do), they are all round me *like a *flood.
 They are on every side of me.

v18 You have taken away from me my friends
 and the people that love me.
 My only friend is *darkness.

Make Your *Kingdom Come Soon!
Psalm 89

Make your *kingdom come soon. Make people obey your rules in the earth as they do in *heaven (Matthew 6: 10). (This is part of a special *prayer that Jesus taught us. A *kingdom is where a king rules; here, God is the King.)

Psalm 89: 1 - 4

(This is) a *maskil of Ethan the Ezrahite.

v1 I will always sing about the kind love of the *LORD.
 I will tell (my) children and (my) grandchildren
 that you will do what you have promised.

v2 Yes! I will say that nothing will ever stop your kind love (for us).
 You will do the things that you promised in *heaven.

v3 (God had said in *heaven)
 "I will make a *covenant with the man that I chose.
 I have made special promises to my servant David.

v4 Someone from your family will always be king.
 And there will always be a place where they (will rule) as king".
 *SELAH

v5 In *heaven, they *praise the *wonderful things that you have done, *LORD.
 Also, the *holy *angels that meet together
 (know that) you will do what you have promised.

v6 For who is there in *heaven that is *like the *LORD?
 Which of the *sons of God is *like the *LORD?

v7 God frightens very much the *holy ones that meet together.
 He makes them more afraid than anyone else does.

v8 Most Powerful *LORD God, who is as strong as you are, *LORD?
 And you do everything that you have promised!

v9 You are the ruler of the boiling sea.
 When the water rises up, you make it quiet again.

v10 You broke Rahab and killed it!
 With your strong arm, you destroyed your enemies.

v11 The skies belong to you and so does the earth.
 You made the world and everything that is in it.

v12 You made (places in) the north and in the south.
 Tabor and Hermon *praise you when they hear your name.

v13 You have a strong arm; your hand is powerful;
 you have lifted up your right hand (to use your power).

v14 You have built your *kingdom doing what is right and fair.
 Your kind love and the fact that you keep your promises go in front of you.

v15 The people are very happy when they know how to *praise you.
 *LORD, they will walk in the light from your face.

v16 They will *praise your name all day
      and talk about your *righteousness.

v17 Your *glory will make them strong
      and by your *grace you will lift up our *horn.

v18 Yes! Our *shield is the *LORD's
      and our king belongs to the *Holy One of Israel.

v19 A long time ago, you spoke to your servants.
      It was like a dream. You said (to them),
      "I have given help to a brave soldier.
      I have chosen a young man from the people.

v20 I have found David my servant.
      I have poured my special oil over him (to make him king).

v21 My hand will make him strong and,
      Yes! My arm will make him powerful.

v22 No enemy will win a war against him
      and no *wicked people will *conquer him.

v23 I will destroy his enemies before him
      and kill those that hate him.

v24 I will do everything that I have promised him.
      Also, (I will give him) my kind love.
      And by my name I will raise his *horn.

v25 I will put his (left) hand over the sea
      and his right hand over the rivers.

v26 He (David) will say to me, "You are my Father,
      my God, and the Rock that makes me safe"

v27 Also, I will make him (as) my first born (son).
      (He will be) the most high of the kings of the earth.

v28 I will always give him my kind love
      and my *covenant with him will have no end.

v29 One of his family will always be king,
      as long as there are skies (above us).

v30 - v31 If his *descendants:
      ☐ do not listen to what I am teaching them
      ☐ and do not obey my *laws
      ☐ say that my *laws are bad
      ☐ and do not do what I tell them (to do)

v32 I will *punish their *sin with a stick
      and the wrong things they do with a *whip.

v33 But I will not take my kind love from him (David)
      and I will not *break any of my promises.

v34 I will not *break my *covenant (with him)
      or change any of my promises.

v35 At one time I made a promise.
      Because I am *holy I will not *lie to David.

v36 His *descendants will always continue
      and his *kingdom will go on as long as the sun (shines).

v37 Like the moon, it will always be there.
      From the sky, it will see everything that happens".   *SELAH

v38 But you have said "no" to your *anointed (king).
      You have turned away (from him)
      because you have become angry with him.

v39 You have *broken the *covenant with your servant.
      You threw his *crown to the ground and made it dirty.

v40 You have broken all the walls (round his city).
      You have destroyed all his strong places.

v41 Everyone that goes near him robs him.
      Everybody that lives near him laughs at him.

v42 You have made all his enemies strong,
      you have made them all happy (because they beat him).

v43 You made the edge of his *sword *blunt
      and you have not given him help in war.

v44 You have taken away his authority as king
      and you threw his *throne on the ground.

v45 He does not look *like a young man any more.
      You have dressed him in *shame.   *SELAH

v46 *LORD, how long (will this continue)?
      Will you always hide yourself?
      Will your great *anger (always) burn like a fire?

v47 Remember that my life is so short!
      Have you *created people for no reason?

v48 What man can live and not die?
      Who can save himself from the power of *Sheol (death)?

v49 *Lord, where is the kind love (that you gave us) in past times?
      Where are the special promises that you made to David?

v50 Remember, *Lord, that people have *scorned your servant.
      Many countries have said bad things to me.

v51 *LORD, your enemies laugh at the king that you have chosen.
      They *scorn him everywhere he goes.

v52 Always *praise the *LORD! *Amen and *amen!

God will always be alive!
Psalm 90

Psalm 90

(These are) words that Moses prayed.
      (He was) a servant of God.

v1   *Lord, you have always been (as) a home for us.

v2   You were God before the mountains were born.
      (You were God) before you were as a mother to the earth and the world.
      You always were and you always will (be God).

v3   You make people go back to (being) powder in the ground (when they die).
      You say, "Go back (to the ground), sons of Adam".

v4   For you see a thousand years as just a day (that) passes.
      (The years are as) a few hours in the night when they are over.

v5   You pour the sleep (of death) on them (the sons of Adam).
      They become as new grass in the morning.

v6   In the morning, it grows well;
      but by the evening, it becomes dry and it dies.

v7   You destroy us because you are angry.
      Because you are so angry, you make us very much afraid.

v8   You see in front of you the wrong (things) that we do.
      Your light (even) shows the secret bad (things) that we do!

v9   All our days hurry past because you are angry with us.
      We finish our years in (just the time it takes for) a cry.

v10 The number of our days is 70 years.
      Or maybe 80 years if we are strong.
      Yet, even in the best years of our lives,
      we have trouble and we are not really happy.
      And they soon go and we hurry away (towards death).

v11 (*LORD), who knows how strong you are when you are very angry?
      (The people that) you frighten when you become so angry (will know).

v12 Teach (us) to count well our days.
      Then we will get a heart that thinks (as God thinks).

v13 *LORD, how long (will it be until) you change your mind?
      Be kind to your servants!

v14 Give us your kind love (every) morning.
      Then we will sing and be happy for as long as we live.

v15 Make us happy for as long as you have hurt us.
      (Make us happy) for as many years as we have had trouble.

v16 Let (us) your servants see the work that you do.
      And show how great you are to (our) children.

v17 Let the *Lord our God show how happy he is with us.
      Let him make the work that our hands do continue.
      Let the work that our hands do continue.

My safe place!
Psalm 91

Jesus said, "Jerusalem, I often wanted to get your children together as a mother bird gets her babies under her wings" (Matthew 23:37). (A bird uses its wings to fly.)

In Psalm 91, many Bible students think that there are three people, or groups of people, that speak. We have shown this in the letters. This makes the psalm easier to study. The three are:

- A crowd of people (called the "chorus") in the usual letters: verses 1, 3 - 8, 9b – 13. (9b means the second part of verse 9).

- One person (called the "psalmist") in *leaning letters*: verses 2 and 9a.

- God himself in **dark letters**: verses 14 - 16.

Psalm 91

v1 Whoever stays in the secret place of the *Most High
 will remain under the shadow of the *Almighty.

v2 *I will say to the *LORD,*
 *"(You are) my safe place and my strong *castle.*
 *(You are) my God and I am *trusting in you".*

v3 He (God) really will save you from the *trap that the *bird-catcher (hid).
 And (God will save you) from illnesses that cause death.

v4 He will cover you with his *feathers.
 You will be safe under his *wings.
 (God) will do what he promised.
 And he will be like big and small *shields over you.

v5, v6 Do not be afraid of:
- *bad spirits at night,
- or the *arrow that flies in the day,
- or illnesses that come when it is dark,
- or something bad that may destroy you at midday.

v7 A thousand (people) may die by your side.
 Ten thousand (people may die) by your right hand.
 But (the danger) will not come near to you.

v8 Your eyes will see it and watch,
 while it destroys bad people.

v9, v10 *For you, *LORD, make me safe.*
 (Because) the Most High is your home,
 bad things will not happen to you.
 And there will be no fighting near where you live.

v11 For (God) will tell his *angels what to do for you.
 They will make you safe everywhere that you go.

v12 Their hands will give you help
 so that you will not (even) hurt your feet on a stone.

v13 You will walk on the *lion and the *cobra.
 The young lion and the *serpent will be under your feet.

v14 (God says) **I will make the person safe that loves me.**
 Danger will not hurt him that knows (and trusts in) my name.

v15 **He will pray to me and I will answer him.**
 When he has trouble, I will be with him.
 I will save him and make him famous.

v16 **I will make him happy with a long life.**
 He will enjoy what I will do for him.

A Song for Saturday
Psalm 92

Jesus said, "Thank you, Father". (Matthew 11:25)

Psalm 92

(This) psalm (is a) song (to sing) on Saturday.

v1 It is good to tell the *LORD that he is great,
 and to make music to your name, Most High (God).

v2 (It is good) to talk about your kind love in the morning.
 And (to talk) every night (about) how you do what you have promised.

v3 (It is good) to make music with *lutes and *harps.
 And (it is good) to sing with the *lyre.

v4 Because, *LORD, the things that you have done make me so happy.
 I want to tell you that you are great
 because of the things that your hands have made!

v5 *LORD, how great are the things that you have done!
 Your thoughts are (often) hard to understand!

v6 (Only) a silly man would not know this
 and (only) a fool would not understand it.

v7 That:
- if bad people grow as grass
- and all the very bad people grow as weeds
 (you) will destroy them and they will never (grow) again.

v8 But you, *LORD, will always be the Most High!

v9 Because your enemies, *LORD, your enemies will certainly die.
 You will chase all the people that do bad things to different places.

v10 You have made me very strong, as strong as a big wild animal.
 (You did this when) you poured fresh oil over me.

v11 Mine eyes have seen (you) beat mine enemies.
 Mine ears have heard you beat the bad people that attack me.

v12 *Righteous people will grow as well as a *palm-tree.
 They will grow as the *cedars in Lebanon.

v13 They are as (trees that someone) planted in the house of the *LORD.
 They grow really well (near) the *temple of our God.

v14 When they are old, they will still give fruit!
 They will always be fresh and green.

v15 They will show (everyone) that the *LORD is good.
 He is my rock. There is nothing bad in him.

The *Lord is King!
Psalm 93
(The first *royal psalm)

The Roman leader said to Jesus, "Are you the King of the *Jews?" And Jesus said to him, "(Yes), it is as you say". (Matthew 27:11)

Psalm 93: 1 - 5

v1 The *LORD is King! He is ruling with authority.
 The *LORD is ruling with great power.
 Also, the world will not change.
 Nobody will move it any more.

v2 You (*LORD) have been king for a very long time.
 You were alive before the world started.

v3 The rivers rose up, *LORD,
 the rivers rose up and made a loud noise.
 The rivers rose up as a great storm.

v4 But the *LORD rules over everyone!
 He is greater than all the noise of the waters,
 stronger than the sea itself.

v5 *LORD, the rules that you make will remain.
 Your house will always be beautiful because you are so good.

God, Show that You Are a Great *Judge!
Psalm 94

Jesus said, "I am a good *judge. I do not do what I want to do. I obey the words of (God) that sent me". (John 5:30)

Psalm 94

v1 *LORD, God, you are a great *judge.
 So, God, show people that you are a great *judge!

v2 *Judge of the earth, do something!
 Give to *proud people what they ought to get.

v3 How long will bad people, *LORD,
    how long will bad people laugh (at good people)?

v4 (The bad people) speak many *proud words.
    All the bad people are always saying that they are great.

v5 (The bad people) are as a heavy weight on your people, *LORD.
    They are cruel to the people that belong to you.

v6 They kill *widows and foreign people that live here.
    They *murder children that have no fathers.

v7 They say, "The *LORD is not looking (at us).
    The God of Jacob will not see (what we are doing)".

v8 Be careful, all you fools among the people!
    Fools ... learn to do the right thing!

v9 Does (God) that made the ear not hear?
    Does he that made the eye not see?

v10 Will he that rules the world not *punish (our bad leaders)?
    He teaches people what they know.

v11 The *LORD knows people's thoughts.
    (Their thoughts) are worth nothing.

v12 The man that the *LORD rules is very happy.
    (The *LORD) teaches him (God's) *laws.

v13 You (*LORD) give him rest from days of trouble,
    until someone digs a *pit for bad men.

v14 For the *LORD will not leave his people;
    he will not forget people that belong to him.

v15 Rulers will do what is fair
    and people with good in their hearts will do the same.

v16 Who fought for me against the bad people?
    Who kept me safe from the people that did wrong things?

v17 Unless the *LORD had given me help,
    I would soon have gone to live in the quiet (place of death).

v18 When I thought that my feet were nearly falling,
    your kind love, *LORD, kept me safe.

v19 When I was not happy in my mind,
    you made me strong and happy again.

v20 Can you (ever) agree with bad rulers?
    (No! Because) their rules make people sad.

v21 They join together against good people.
    They say that people that have done nothing wrong must die.

v22 But the *LORD is my strong place.
    And my God is a rock where I can hide and be safe.

v23 He will *punish the bad (leaders).
    He will destroy them because they are so bad.
    The *LORD our God will destroy them.

Do Not Make The Same Mistake!
Psalm 95
(The second *royal psalm)

Jesus said, "Go and do not break God's rules again". (John 8:11)

Psalm 95

v1 Come, we will sing together to the *LORD!
    We will shout aloud to the *Rock that makes us safe!

v2 Come into (God's) house and thank him!
    Tell him that he is great!
    (Do it) with music and with songs!

v3 (This is) because the *LORD is the great God.
    He is the great king that is more important than every other god.

v4 The deep places of the earth are in his hand.
    The tops of the mountains are his.

v5 The sea is his, because he made it.
    Also, his hands made the dry land.

v6 Come, we will fall down on our knees in front of him.
    We will stay on our knees in front of the *LORD that made us.

v7 (We will do this) because he is our God.
    Also, we are the people that he feeds and keeps safe.
    We are as animals and he is as the farmer (that feeds us)!
    Today, if you hear his voice,

v8 do not refuse to listen (to him).
    You did this at *Meribah
    and you did it one day at *Massah, in the *desert.

v9 There, your fathers *tested me to discover what I could do.
    But they had already seen my work!

v10 For 40 years I was angry with those people.
    And I said, "They are people that refuse to obey me.
    They (say that they) do not know what I want them to do".

v11 I was so angry that I said,
    "They will never come into my rest".

Sing A New Song!
Psalm 96
(The third *royal psalm)

Jesus said, "Tell your Father in *Heaven that he is a great (God)". (Matthew 5:16)

Psalm 96

v1 Sing a new song to the *LORD!
    Sing to the *LORD, all the world!

v2 Sing to the *LORD and say good things about him!
    Every day, say that he has made us safe!

v3 Tell every *nation that he is very great!
    Tell everybody the *wonderful things that he has done!

v4 Because the *LORD is great, and everybody should say that he is great!
    People should be more afraid of him than of all (other) gods.

v5 Because all the gods of every country are false.
    But the *LORD made everything.

v6 (People that) are near him can see that he is a very great king.
    (People that) are in his house can see that he is strong and beautiful.

v7 Say to the *LORD, you families of *nations,
    say to the *LORD that he is *glorious and powerful.

v8 Say that the *LORD has a *glorious name.
    Bring a gift and come near his house.

v9 Fall down in front of the *LORD who is beautiful and *holy.
    Be afraid of him, everyone (that lives) on the earth.

v10 Tell all the *nations that the *LORD is King!
    (He has) fixed the world so that nothing can move it.
    He will be a fair *judge of the people.

v11 Earth and sky, be happy!
    Sea and everything in it, *roar (because you are happy!)

v12 Fields, you be happy as well, and everything in you!
    Then, all the trees in the forests will sing because they are so happy!

v13 (They will sing) to the *LORD when he comes.
    He will come to be a *judge of the earth.
    He will be a good *judge and he will be fair to the people.

*Lord of Far-Away People
Psalm 97
(The fourth *royal psalm)

Jesus said, "I have other sheep. They do not live here. I must fetch them also. And they will hear my voice. And there will be one home for sheep and one shepherd". (John 10:16) (A shepherd is a sheep farmer.)

Psalm 97

v1 The *LORD is king! (Everyone) on earth will be very happy!
    (Even) all the (people) on far-away islands will be very happy!

v2 Clouds and black (skies) are all round (the *LORD).
    He is a good and fair ruler.

- v3 Fire goes in front of him.
  It burns up his enemies on every side.

- v4 His *lightning is a light over the (whole) world.
  The earth sees it and is afraid.

- v5 The mountains *melt as butter in front of the *LORD,
  in front of the master of the whole world.

- v6 The skies tell (us) that he is *righteous
  and people (from every country) will see his *glory.

- v7 All the servants of *images (of gods) will be ashamed.
  Also, all those that say that *idols are great (will be ashamed)!
  Because (even) the gods will fall down in front of (the *LORD).

- v8 *Zion will hear about it and be happy.
  The people of Judah will be very happy!
  (This will be) because of what you decide to do, *LORD.

- v9 Because you, *LORD, are the *Most High (God) over all the earth.
  You are much more important than any other god!

- v10 If you love the *LORD, then *hate what bad people do!
  (The *LORD) makes safe the lives of his people.
  He will make them free from the hands of bad people.

- v11 Light will shine on *righteous people
  and honest people will be very happy.

- v12 Everyone that is *righteous, you be happy with the *LORD!
  And say "thanks" to his *holy name.

God Rules The World!
Psalm 98
(The fifth *royal psalm)

Jesus said, "You will see the Son of man sitting by the right hand of the Powerful One. He will come in clouds in the skies". (Matthew 26:64) (The Son of man is a name that Jesus called himself. The Powerful One is a name for God.)

Psalm 98

(This is) a psalm.

- v1 Sing a new song to the *LORD.
  Because he has done *wonderful things.
  His right hand and his *holy arm
  have made (his people) safe.

- v2 The *LORD has made everybody to know
  that he has made (his people) safe.
  He has shown everybody (in the world)
  that he is a *righteous (God).

- v3 He remembered his kind love to the people of Israel.
  And he did what he had promised.
  Everyone (that lives) far away has seen
  that (God) has made (his people) safe.

- v4 Everybody (that lives) on earth,
  shout to the *LORD because you are so happy!
  Start singing and making music!

- v5 Make music to the *LORD with a *harp!
  Make music with *harp and voice!

- v6 With *trumpets and the sound of the *horn
  make a happy noise to the *LORD (who is) King!

- v7 The sea and everything that is in it
  must make a loud noise.
  The earth and everything that lives in it
  must also (make a loud noise).

- v8 The rivers must *clap their hands
  and the mountains must make a happy sound

- v9 to the *LORD.
  Because he is coming to rule the earth.
  He will be a *righteous king.
  He will be a very fair *judge.

God ... He Is *Holy!
Psalm 99
(The sixth and last *royal psalm)

Jesus prayed (to God), "*Holy Father". (John 17:11)

Psalm 99

- v1 The *LORD is king!
  People on earth will be afraid!
  (The *LORD) is sitting between the *cherubim!
  The earth (itself) will *shake!

- v2 The *LORD is great in *Zion.
  And he is king over all the (other) people (in the world).

- v3 They must (all) *praise your great name.
  (It is a name) that makes people afraid.
  Because **he is *holy.**

- v4 (He is) a strong king and he loves what is right.
  You have made everything fair.
  You have done what is right and fair in *Jacob.

- v5 *Praise the *LORD our God!
  *Kneel *before him. **He is *holy.**

- v6 Moses and Aaron were among his *priests
  and Samuel was among those that prayed to him.
  They prayed to the *LORD and he answered them.

- v7 He spoke to them from the *column of cloud.
  They obeyed his rules and they did what he told them to do.

- v8 *LORD our God, you answered them.
  You were a God that *forgave Israel.
  Even if you *punished them when they did not obey you.

- v9 *Praise the *LORD our God and *kneel before him.
  Because the *LORD our God, **he is *holy!**

Psalm 100

Jesus said, "*Thank-you, Father". (Matthew 11:25)

Psalm 100

(This is) a "*thank-you" psalm.

- v1 Everyone on earth, shout to the *LORD!

- v2 Do something for the *LORD to show that you are happy.
  Come to him with songs of *joy.

- v3 Know that the *LORD really is God.
  He made us and we are his people.
  (We are as his) sheep in his fields.

- v4 Say "*thank-you" when you are walking through his gates.
  Stand in front of his *temple and say good things about him.

- v5 (Do all this) because the *LORD is good.
  He is always loving and kind.
  He will always do what he has promised to us.

The King's Song
Psalm 101

Jesus said, "First look for the place where God is king. Do the good things that he does". (Matthew 6:33)

Psalm 101

(This is) a psalm of David.

- v1 I will sing to you, *LORD.
  I will sing about your kind love and *justice.

- v2 I will be careful.
  Then nobody can say that I have done wrong.
  When will you (*LORD) come to me?
  Where I rule, I will do nothing that is wrong.

- v3 I will not let any *wicked people be with me.
  I really do not like what *wicked people do.
  They will not come near to me.

- v4 People with *wicked ideas will be far from me.
  I will not mix with them.

- v5 I will destroy anyone that says bad things about people *in secret.
  I will send away people that have *proud eyes and hearts.

v6   My eyes will look at people who obey (the *LORD).
     They will be with me (in my work).
     My servants will be people that do nothing wrong.

v7   People that are not honest will not stay with me.
     People that do not say what is true will not remain with me.

v8   Every morning I will destroy people that are *wicked in (my) country.
     Nobody that is *wicked will remain in the city of the *LORD.

A Young Man With Trouble
Psalm 102

Jesus said, "Do not let trouble stay in your mind. *Believe in God and believe in me also". (John 14:1) "Destroy this *temple and in three days I will raise it up again". (John 2:19)

Psalm 102

(This is) the *prayer of a man that is weak and in trouble.
He pours out to the *LORD this sad song.

v1   *LORD, hear my *prayer
     and listen when I cry to you for help.

v2   Do not hide your face from me when I am in trouble.
     Turn your ear to me.
     Answer me soon, now that I am praying to you.

v3   Because my life is *disappearing *like smoke (*disappears).
     Also, my bones are burning as a fire burns.

v4   I am so ill that I am as dried grass.
     I (even) forget to eat my food.

v5   Because of my loud *groans,
     I am just skin and bone.

v6   I am as a (wild) bird in a lonely place.
     I am as a (night) bird in a broken building.

v7   I lie awake and feel *like a (small) bird
     by itself on the roof of a house.

v8   All day my enemies say bad things about me.
     People that are angry with me use my name as a *curse.

v9 - v10   Because you are so angry with me:
     ☐ I eat ashes as my food;
     ☐ I mix my drink with my *tears.
     Because you picked me up and then you threw me away.

v11   My days are as an evening shadow.
     I am dying as grass (soon dies).

v12   But you, *LORD, will always be king.
     You will always be famous,
     everybody that will live (will know about you.)

v13   You will stand up and be kind to *Zion,
     because it is time to show her that you love her.
     The time has come when this should happen.

v14   Because her stones are valuable to your servants.
     (Her) broken stones make them very sad.

v15   The *nations will be afraid of the name of the *LORD.
     And all the kings of the earth will *kneel before your *glory.

v16   Because the *LORD will build *Zion again
     and appear in his *glory.

v17   He will answer the *prayers of people that have nothing
     and he will not laugh at what they ask.

v18   Write this down for people that will be alive in future (times).
     Then people (that God has) not yet *created will *praise the *LORD.

v19   The *LORD looked down from his home in the *heavens,
     from the skies he saw the earth.

v20   He heard the *groans of people in prison.
     The people that were going to die he made free.

v21   So people will shout the *LORD's name in *Zion
     and they will *praise him in Jerusalem.

v22   (This will happen) when peoples and *kingdoms
     meet together to *worship the *LORD.

v23   He has made me ill in the middle (of my life).
     He will make my life short.

v24   So I said, "My God, do not let me die in the middle of my life.
     You will always be alive.

v25   At the beginning (of time) you built the earth so that it was strong.
     Also, your hands *created the *heavens.

v26   They will not always remain, but you (*LORD) will.
     They will *wear out as clothes do.
     *Like clothes, you will change them and throw them away.

v27   But you (*LORD) will always be the same
     and your life will never end.

v28   (We are) your servants and our children will live always live here.
     And their children will be safe where you are.

The Love of God
Psalm 103

Jesus said, "Your Father in heaven knows everything that you need". (Matthew 6:32)

(Heaven is the home of God.)

Psalm 103

(This is a psalm) of David.

v1   I say to myself, "*Praise the *LORD!
     Everything that is in me, *praise his *holy name!'

v2   I say to myself, "*Praise the *LORD!
     And never forget any of the good things that he has given you!'

v3   (I say to myself) He *forgives all your *sins.
     He makes you well again when you are ill.

v4   He *redeems you from the *Pit.
     His kind love and *mercy are special things that he gives to you.

v5   He gives you the good things that you want.
     So, you become strong again as a young *eagle.

v6   The *LORD does *righteous and fair things
     for all *oppressed people.

v7   He showed Moses his plans
     and (he showed) the *Israelites what he was going to do.

v8   The *LORD likes (people) and is very kind.
     He is slow to get angry and has a lot of kind love.

v9   He will not always say that we are wrong.
     He will not always be angry.

v10   We do wrong things.
     He does not *punish us for them as much as he should.

v11   The sky is high above the earth.
     So his kind love is great to those people that love him.

v12   As far as the east is from the west,
     so far has he taken our *sins from us.

v13   As a father is kind to his children,
     so the *LORD is kind to people that are afraid of him.

v14   Because he knows (how he) made us,
     he remembers that we are only *dust.

v15   The life of a man is as short as (the life of) grass!
     He lives as short a time as the (wild) flowers in a field!

v16   The wind blows over it and it dies!
     Nothing remembers it any more.

v17   But the kind love of the *LORD
     will always be with those that are afraid of him.
     And his *righteousness will be with their children's children.

v18   (They will be) with those (people) that do what they have agreed (to do).
     (They will be with those people) that remember to obey his rules.

v19   The *LORD has built his *throne in *heaven.
     He is king over everything.

v20 *Praise the *LORD, you (who are) his *angels.
    You are strong and powerful.
    You do what he tells you (to do) and you obey his word.

v21 *Praise the *LORD, all (you) his armies (in *heaven).
    (You are) his servants that do what he wants you (to do).

v22 Everything that he has made
    and (everything) that he rules over, *praise the *LORD!
    I say to myself, *praise the *LORD!

*Creator God, Keeping Everything Alive!
Psalm 104

Jesus said, "Are not two *sparrows sold for a farthing? But not one of them falls to the ground without your Father (knowing)". (Matthew 10:29) (A sparrow is a small bird. A farthing is a small coin.)

Psalm 104: 1 - 9

v1 - v2 I say to myself, "*Praise the *LORD!"
    *LORD, my God, you are very great!
    (As a person wears clothes), you wear *honour and *majesty and light.
    You have put the skies as a roof (over the earth).

v3 You have built your home above the waters that are over the skies.
    The clouds carry you and you ride on the wind.

v4 The winds carry your messages
    and burning fires are your servants.

v5 (The *LORD) built the earth on its *foundations.
    Nobody will ever move it.

v6 You covered it with the deep (sea) as clothes (cover a person).
    The waters were higher than the mountains.

v7 When you shouted (the waters) ran away.
    At the sound of your *thunder they *fled.

v8 (The waters) moved over the mountains.
    They went down into the valleys.
    They went to the place that you had made for them.

v9 You made a mark that they could not cross.
    Never again will (the waters) cover the earth.

Israel in Egypt
Psalm 105

Jesus lived in Egypt until Herod died. So, what the *Lord said to the *prophet really happened. He said, "I have brought my son out of Egypt". (Matthew 2:15)

Psalm 105: 1 - 6

v1 Say "thank-you!" to the *LORD.
    Tell (everybody) his name.
    Tell people in every country what he has done.

v2 Sing songs to him, make music for him.
    Speak about all the great things that he has done.

v3 Be *proud of his *holy name.
    Everybody that goes to the *LORD (in his house), be very happy!

v4 Visit the *LORD, who is so powerful.
    Always go to him (in his house).

v5 Remember the great things that he has done.
    (Remember) his *miracles and what he said (to Pharaoh).

v6 Abraham your *father was (the *LORD's) servant.
    (The *LORD) chose Jacob and you are (Jacob's) *sons.

The *LORD is Good!
Psalm 106

Jesus said, "Father, *forgive them. Because they do not know what they are doing". (Luke 23:34)

Psalm 106: 1 - 5

v1 *Hallelujah! Say "*thank-you" to the *LORD, because he is good.
    His kind love will always (remain).

v2 (Nobody) can tell about all the great things that the *LORD has done.
    (Nobody) can *praise him enough.

v3 (The people) that obey his rules are very happy.
    They always do what is right.

v4 *LORD, do not forget me when you do something good for your people.
    Give me help (also) when you make them safe.

v5 Then I will:
    ☐ enjoy the good things that you do for your people,
    ☐ be happy together with them,
    ☐ *praise you with the people that belong to you.

God Gave Us Help
Psalm 107

Jesus said, "Many people will come from the east and from the west. They will sit down with Abraham, and Isaac, and Jacob, in the *kingdom of *heaven" (Matthew 8:11). (*Heaven is where God lives; a *kingdom is where someone is king.)

Psalm 107: 1 - 9

v1 Thank the *LORD because he is good.
    His kind love will never stop.

v2 People must say that the *LORD has *redeemed them,
    when he has redeemed them from the power of an enemy.

v3 He brought them from countries to the east, to the west,
    to the north; and from the sea.

v4 They moved from place to place in the wild country.
    They did not find the way to a city to live in.

v5 They were hungry and wanted a drink.
    They thought that they were going to die.

v6 **Then they prayed to the *LORD in their trouble.
    And he saved them from the danger that they were in.**

v7 He led them by an easy road to a city where they might live.

v8 They must thank the *LORD for his kind love.
    And they must thank him for the *wonderful things that he does for people.

v9 His people have enough to drink
    and he fills the hungry people with good things.

v10 Some people sat in *darkness and in the shadow of death.
    They were *prisoners behind iron *bars. And they felt *despair.

v11 This happened because they did not obey the words of God.
    They laughed at the plans of the Most High.

v12 Hard work made them listen to him.
    When they fell down, there was nobody to help them.

v13 **Then they prayed to the *LORD in their trouble.
    And he saved them from the danger that they were in.**

v14 He led them out of the *darkness and the shadow of death.
    He broke the *chains that held them.

v15 **They must thank the *LORD for his kind love.
    And they must thank him
    for the *wonderful things that he does for people.**

v16 (They must thank him) because he broke the metal gates
    and destroyed the iron *bars.

v17 Fools went away from the right road
    and were in pain because of their *sin.

v18 They would not eat any food, so they nearly died.

v19 **Then they prayed to the *LORD in their trouble.
    And he saved them from the danger that they were in.**

v20 He sent his word and he *healed them.
    He saved them from death.

v21 **They must thank the *LORD for his kind love.
    And they must thank him
    for the *wonderful things that he does for people.**

v22 They must give *offerings of *praise.
And they must sing about what he has done.

v23 Some went down to the sea, to work in deep waters.

v24 They saw the *wonderful things that the *LORD did there.

v25 He spoke and a wind started. A storm lifted up the sea.

v26 (The sailors) went up to the sky then down into deep places.
The danger made them afraid.

v27 It was not possible to stand up, so they fell over like drunks.
They did not know what to do!

v28 Then they prayed to the *LORD in their trouble.
And he saved them from the danger that they were in.

v29 He stopped the noise of the storm and made the sea become quiet.

v30 They were happy when it became quiet.
He showed them the way to the port that they wanted to reach.

v31 They must thank the *LORD for his kind love.
And they must thank him
for the *wonderful things that he does for people.

v32 The people must say that he is great when they meet together.
Their leaders must *praise him when they sit together.

v33 - v34 The people who live in some places are very bad.
In those places, God will make:
  □ rivers become *desert places
  □ wells of water become dry ground
  □ good ground become salt *marsh

v35 He can make *desert places become pools of water
and dry ground become wells of water.

v36 He can give a place to hungry people where they can build a city to live in.

v37 They can *sow seeds in the fields and plant *vineyards.
Then they will bring home much food.

v38 He will be kind to them so that they grow in number.
Their animals will not decrease in number.

v39 Then they began to decrease in number
because of *oppression, trouble and *despair.

v40 He just laughed at their leaders.
And he took them into roads that led nowhere.

v41 But he lifts people that are in need out of their trouble.
And he makes their families grow like wild animals.

v42 Good people see it and it makes them happy.
Bad people just shut their mouths!

v43 People that are not *stupid will think about these things.
Then they will understand the kind love of the *LORD.

The End of the *Exile
Psalm 108

Jesus said, "The *truth will make you free" (John 8:32).

Psalm 108

This song is a psalm of David.

v1 God, I have decided always to belong to you!
I will sing your *praises as well as I can.

v2 Wake up, *harp and *lyre.
I will sing before the dawn.

v3 *LORD, I will thank you in front of all the people.
I will sing your *praises everywhere.

v4 Your kind love is great. It is higher than the clouds.
Your *truth reaches to the skies.

v5 God, lift yourself up above the skies.
Lift your *glory above all the earth.

v6 Give us help. Make the friends that you love safe.
Use your right hand to answer us!

v7 - v9 God did answer us from his *holy place!
(He said):
  □ I will be the master.
  □ I will make a parcel of Shechem.
  □ I will measure the Valley of Succoth.
  □ Gilead is mine.
  □ Manasseh is mine.
  □ Ephraim will cover my head.
  □ Judah will *judge for me.
  □ Moab is my bathroom.
  □ Edom is where I will throw my shoes.
  □ Philistia will be something for me to laugh at.

v10 Who will lead me into the strong city?
Who will take me into Edom?

v11 (You have said) that you would not be our God any more.
But God, will you really not go with our armies?

v12 Give to us help against the enemy,
because help from men is of no value!

v13 With God we will beat everybody
and walk all over our enemies!

A Man With Trouble
Psalm 109

Jesus said, "You will be happy when people are not kind to you and do bad things to you. You will be happy because you love me, even when they say many bad things about you that are not true" (Matthew 5:11).

Psalm 109

(This is) a psalm of David for the (music) leader.

v1 (You are) the God that I *praise.
Let me hear you speak!

v2 (Do something) because bad men and *liars say bad things about me.
They say things about me that are not true.

v3 Their words of *hate are all round me.
Also, they attack me without a reason.

v4 I love them and pray for them.
But they *accuse me.

v5 I do good things for them, but they pay me back with bad things.
I love them, but they hate me.

v6 Put an *evil man against (my enemy).
Also, make somebody stand by his right hand (side) to *accuse him.

v7 Make him be *guilty at his *trial.
And make his words show that he has done wrong things.

v8 Make his life a short one
and let somebody else be leader (instead of him).

v9 Make his children have no father
and make his wife a *widow.

v10 Make his children go from place to place, asking for money.
Destroy their home and send them away (from it).

v11 Make the lender of money take everything that he had.
And let strangers get everything that he worked for.

v12 Do not let anybody be kind to him.
Do not let anybody be kind to the children that he has left without a father.

v13 I pray that you will destroy everyone in his family after him.
I want people that live later never to know the names (of his family)!

v14 I want the *LORD to remember the bad things that his *fathers did.
I do not want the *LORD to clean away his mother's *sins.

v15 I want the *LORD always to remember these (bad things)
and people on earth never to remember his family.

- v16 (Do this, Lord)
  because he (my enemy) did not remember to be kind (to people).
  Instead, he was not kind to them.
  He killed people that were poor.
  (He killed) people that needed (many things).
  (He killed) people that had nobody to give them help.

- v17 He loved to say bad things about people;
  (so I want) bad things to happen to him!
  He did not like to say good things about people;
  (so I want) nobody to say good things about him!

- v18 He said bad things (about people) as often as he put on clothes.
  (I want these bad things) to go into his body as the water (that he drinks).
  (I want them) to go into his bones like oil.

- v19 Then (the bad things that he says) will cover him like his clothes.
  They will cover him like the belt that he wears every day.

- v20 This is how (I want) the *LORD to pay the people that *accuse me.
  (They are) the people that say bad things about me.

- v21 But you are my *LORD and master.
  Give me help, because of your name!
  Save me, because you are good and you love me.

- v22 Save me because I am poor and need (many things).
  My *heart inside me is hurting.

- v23 I am dying, as a shadow at evening.
  I am like an insect that (the wind) blows away.

- v24 My knees are weak because I am not eating (food).
  My body is thin and not fat (as it was).

- v25 The people that see me just laugh at me!
  They *shake their heads (at me).

- v26 My *LORD and Master, send me help!
  Because of your kind love, save me!

- v27 Make everybody know, *LORD, that you have done something!

- v28 When they say bad things (about me), you will say good things (about me).
  When they attack me, they will be ashamed.
  Then your servant will be very happy!

- v29 The people that *accuse me will have *shame all round them.
  It will be all round them as their clothes are all round them.
  It will be all round them like a coat.

- v30 My mouth will say that the *LORD is very great!
  I will *praise him in front of a big crowd of people.

- v31 He stands at the right hand (side) of the people that need (help).
  He saves the life of (the man) that people are attacking.
  (That is why I will *praise him.)

Melchizedek
Psalm 110

The *Pharisees met together. Jesus asked them a question. He said, "What do you think about the *Christ? Whose son is he?" They said to him, "(He is the son) of David". Jesus said to them, "Why then did David, in his *spirit, call him *Lord? David said, 'The *LORD said to my *Lord, Sit on the right of me until I put your enemies under your feet'. If David calls him *Lord, how can he be his son?" And nobody could answer Jesus one word. Nobody was brave enough to ask him anything after that (Matthew 22:41-46).

Psalm 110

(This is) a Psalm of David.

- v1 The *LORD spoke to my *Lord.
  "Sit on the right of me until I put your enemies under your feet", he said.

- v2 The *LORD will send your great power out from Zion.
  You will rule over all the enemies that are round about you.

- v3 When you fight your enemies, your people will give you help.
  In the early morning (on the day of *battle),
  your young people will be there, on the hills (round Zion).

- v4 The *LORD has made a special promise. He will not change it.
  "You will always be a *priest, as Melchizedek was", (he said).

- v5 The *Lord is standing on the right of you.
  When he gets angry, he will destroy kings!

- v6 He will be the *judge of all the *nations.
  There will be many dead people.
  He will destroy kings over all the earth.

- v7 He will drink from the stream at the side of the road.
  And so, he will lift up his head.

God Is *Righteous
Psalm 111

Jesus said, "Why do you say that I am good? Nobody is good except God" (Luke 18:19).

(*Righteous means "very, very good". Only God is really *righteous.)

Psalm 111

- v1 *Hallelujah! (or, Say that the *LORD is really great!)
  I will say "thanks" to the *LORD with *all my *heart.
  (I will do it) where his people meet together.

- v2 The things that the *LORD does are really great!
  People that find pleasure in them study them.

- v3 (Everything that) he does makes people understand that he is a king!
  He will always be *righteous.

- v4 The *LORD causes (people) to remember his *miracles.
  He is kind and he loves (people).

- v5 He gave food to the people that are his servants.
  He will always remember his *covenant.

- v6 He has shown his people that he is powerful.
  He gave them the lands that belonged to other countries.

- v7 The things that he does are honest and fair.
  People can *trust him when he tells them his rules.

- v8 He made (his rules) to continue for all time.
  (The *LORD) was true and *righteous when he made (these rules.)

- v9 He made his people free.
  He made a *covenant with them for them (to obey) always.
  His name is *holy.
  And it makes people (see him) as powerful and important.

- v10 People who are afraid of the *LORD are starting to be *wise.
  Everyone that (is *wise) will have really understood (the *LORD).
  People should always say that the *LORD is great!

God's Man Is *Righteous
Psalm 112

Jesus said, "The people that always think about good things will be very happy. They will be happy because they will see God" (Matthew 5:8).

Psalm 112

- v1 *Hallelujah!

  (Aleph) The man that is afraid of the *LORD will be very happy.

  (Beth) It will give him pleasure when he obeys the *LORD's rules.

- v2 (Gimel) His children will become powerful in the land.

  (Daleth) (The *LORD) will do good things for the good people in his family.

- v3 (He) He will be a rich man with valuable things in his house.

  (Vav) He will always have (God's gift) of *righteousness.

- v4 (Zayin) A good man is like a light that shines in dark (places).

  (Heth) He is kind and loving and *righteous.

- v5 (Teth) A good man is kind and lends (to people).

(Yod) He is fair in everything that he does.

v6 (Kaph) So (a good man) will never fail.

(Lamed) (People) will always remember a *righteous man.

v7 (Mem) He is not afraid of bad news.

(Nun) His *heart is *steady and he *trusts in the *LORD.

v8 (Samech) His *heart is safe. And he will not be afraid,

(Ayin) until (God) destroys his enemies.

v9 (Pe) He gives a lot to poor people.

(Tsade) He will always be *righteous.

(Qoph) He will be powerful. And people will say that he is good.

v10 (Resh) The bad man will see it and be angry.

(Shin) He will *gnash his teeth together, then *disappear.

(Tav) The things that the bad man wants will not happen.

The Servants' Song
Psalm 113
The First Egyptian Hallel

And when Jesus and his friends had sung a psalm, they went out to the *Mount of Olives (Mark 14:26). (The *Mount of Olives was a small hill near Jerusalem.)

Psalm 113

v1 *Hallelujah!
Servants of the *LORD, tell (him) that he is very great!
Sing aloud that the name of the *LORD is very great!

v2 *Bless the name of the *LORD.
(Do it) now and (do it) always!

v3 *Praise the name of the *LORD!
(Do it) from where the sun rises (in the east)
to where it goes down (in the west).

v4 The *LORD is king over every *nation.
He shines brighter than anything in the sky.

v5 There is nobody like the *LORD our God.
He sits on a *throne that is very high (above us).

v6 He bends down to look at the sky and the earth.
They are far below him.

v7 He lifts up poor people from the ground.
And he lifts up people that need help from the ashes.

v8 He gives them a seat with *princes,
with the *princes of their country.

v9 He makes the woman that is *barren in her home
into a happy mother of children. *Hallelujah!

Seas, Mountains, Rivers And Hills Obey God!
Psalm 114

Jesus said, "If you have *faith as small as a (very small) seed, (this is what you can do). You will say to this mountain, 'Move to that place over there'. And it will go! Nothing will be impossible for you!" (Matthew 17:20) (Faith is to believe that God will answer when you pray.)

Psalm 114

v1 (This happened) when *Israel left Egypt.
(It happened) when the people of Jacob left the people that spoke a strange language.

v2 (The *LORD led them) to a safe place (called) Judah.
(He took them) to the country of Israel where he (became their) king.

v3 The sea looked and ran from (the *LORD).
The (river) Jordan turned back.

v4 The mountains jumped as *rams jump.
The hills jumped as *lambs jump.

v5 What happened, sea, that made you run away?
(What happened), Jordan, that made you turn back?

v6 (What made) you mountains jump as *rams (jump)?
(What made) you hills jump like *lambs?

v7 Earth, be like a man who is afraid, in front of the *Lord.
(Be afraid) when the God of Jacob is near.

v8 He made the rock into a pool of water
and the hard rock into water coming from the ground.

There Is Only One True God
Psalm 115

Jesus said, "Pray like this: Our Father, you are in *heaven. Your name is special. You are king (over everyone). What you want to happen will happen in the earth. It will happen (in earth) as it happens in *heaven. Give us today the food that we need (each day). *Forgive us the wrong things that we have done. (Do this) because we *forgive the people that have done wrong things to us. Do not lead us into difficulties, but take us away from bad places (and ideas). (Do this) because you are the king! You are powerful! You will always be *glorious! *Amen" (Matthew 6:9-13). (*Heaven is the home of God; *forgive means excuse; glorious means "shining very much"; and amen means "we all agree".)

Psalm 115

v1 Do not give to us, *LORD, do not give to us the *glory.
(Keep) it for yourself! (Do this) because of your kind love (to us).
And (do it) because you always do what you have promised.

v2 Why should people say, 'Where is their God?'

v3 Our God is in *heaven. He does what he wants to do.

v4 (People) make their *idols with *silver and gold.
Human hands make them!

v5 (Each *idol) has a mouth ... but it cannot speak!
It has eyes ... but it cannot see!

v6 It has ears ... but it cannot hear!
It has a nose ... but it cannot smell!

v7 It has hands ... but it feels nothing!
It has feet ... but it cannot walk!
Its mouth cannot make a sound!

v8 The people that make them will become like them.
Also, everyone who believes what they say (will become like them).

v9 (People of) Israel ... *trust in the *LORD.
He is their *help and their *shield.

v10 People of Aaron ... *trust in the *LORD.
He is their help and their *shield.

v11 Everyone that is in awe of the *LORD ... *trust in the *LORD.
He is their help and their *shield.

v12 The *LORD will remember us. He will *bless us.
He will *bless the people of Israel.
He will *bless the people of Aaron.

v13 He will *bless everybody that is in awe of the *LORD.
(He will *bless them) whether they are important or not.

v14 (I pray that) the *LORD will give you more (good things).
(I pray that he will) do this to your children also.

v15 I pray that the *LORD will *bless you.
(The *LORD) made *heaven and earth.

v16 *Heaven is where the *LORD lives.
He gave the earth to the people that live there.

v17 Dead people cannot *praise the *LORD.
Neither can anyone that goes to the *Quiet Place.

v18 But we will *bless the *LORD, now and always.
*Hallelujah!

He Saved Me!
Psalm 116

Jesus said, "If the Son (of God) makes you free, you will be really free!" (John 8:36). (Son of God is a name for Jesus.)

Psalm 116

v1 I love the *LORD, because he listens to me.
   He listens to me when I pray to him.

v2 I will always pray to him, because he hears what I say.

v3 The danger of death was all round me.
   I began to be afraid of *Sheol.
   I was sad because (I had) so much trouble.

v4 Then I prayed to the name of the *LORD.
   (I said) "*LORD, please save me!"

v5 The *LORD is kind and good (to people).
   Our God (shows us that he) loves (us).

v6 The *LORD gives help to those (people) that need it.
   When I was in danger, **he saved me!**

v7 (So I could say) to myself, "Now you are safe,
   because the *LORD has been kind to you".

v8 Yes, (*LORD), you saved me from death!
   (You saved) my eyes from crying and my feet from falling.

v9 Now I can *serve the *LORD in this world where people live
   (and not in *Sheol).

v10 I believed (that God would give me help).
    (I believed this) even when I said, "I have much pain".

v11 When I was very sad, I said, "Everybody says what is not true".

v12 What can I give to the *LORD because he has been so kind to me?

v13 I will offer a cup of *wine to the *LORD.
    And I will thank him because **he saved me!**

v14 I will do everything that I have promised to the *LORD.
    (I will do it) in front of all his people.

v15 It hurts God very much when one of his servants dies.

v16 *LORD, I really am your servant.
    I am your servant just as my mother was.
    You have saved me from death!

v17 I will offer you my special "thanks" when I pray to the name of the *LORD.

v18 I will make special promises to the *LORD.
    (I will do this) in front of all his people.

v19 (I will do this) in the *courts of the house of the *LORD.
    (I will do this) in the centre of Jerusalem.

Hallelujah! (or, Tell the *LORD that he is very great!)

The Story of Psalm 116

The Shortest Psalm
Psalm 117
The Fifth Egyptian Hallel

Jesus said, "I have other sheep. They do not live at this farm. I must fetch them also and they will hear my voice. Then there will be one farm and one sheep-farmer" (John 10:16).

Psalm 117

v1 Every country in the world, *praise the *LORD!
   All the people (in the world), *praise him!

v2 His kind love for us is very strong.
   And he will always do what he has promised.
   *Praise the *LORD

Hosanna! (Save Us Now!)
Psalm 118

Jesus said, "Did you not read (this) in the Bible? The *builders threw away a stone. It is now in an important place at the corner (of the building). The *Lord has done this. And we think that it is *wonderful" (Matthew 21:42).

Psalm 118

v1 Thank the *LORD because he is good.
   His *kind love will always be (with us).

v2 Israel must now say,
   "His kind love will always be with us".

v3 The house of Aaron must now say,
   "His kind love will always be with us".

v4 Everyone that is afraid of the *LORD must now say,
   "His kind love will always be with us".

v5 (My enemy) shut me (in a prison).
   There I cried to the *LORD.
   The *LORD answered me and made me free.

v6 The *LORD is with me. I will not be afraid.
   What (bad thing) can anybody do to me?

v7 The *LORD is with me. He gives me help.
   So, I will see (the *LORD destroy) my enemies.

v8 It is better to *trust in the *LORD
   than to *trust in people.

v9 It is better to *trust in the *LORD
   than to *trust in the leaders (of people).

v10 All the *nations were round me,
    (but) I destroyed them *in the name of the *LORD.

v11 They were all round me, yes, all round me.
    (But) I destroyed them in the name of the *LORD.

v12 They were round me like (a cloud of) *bees.
    They burnt (quickly) like a (dry) bush (burns quickly).
    I destroyed them in the name of the *LORD.

v13 (My enemy) pushed me so that I started to fall.
    But the *LORD gave me help (not to fall).

v14 The *LORD makes me strong and gives me psalms to sing.
    He has saved me.

v15 Listen to the happy shouts of God's people in their *tents.
    (They do this) because they have destroyed (their enemies).
    The *right hand of the *LORD is very strong.

v16 The *LORD has lifted his right hand very high.
    The right hand of the *LORD is very strong.

v17 I will not die. I will live.
    I will tell everyone what the *LORD has done.

v18 The *LORD has *punished me a lot,
    but he has not let me die.

v19 Open the gates of the *temple for me.
    I will go in and thank the *LORD.

v20 This is the gate of the *LORD.
    *Righteous people can go in through it.

v21 Thank you because you answered me.
    You saved me.

v22 The men who were building threw away a stone.
    It is now in an important place at the corner (of the building).

v23 The *LORD has done this.
    And we think that it is *wonderful.

v24 This is the day that the *LORD has made.
    We will be happy in it, we will be very happy.

v25 *LORD, save us now!
    *LORD, make us do very well!

v26 The man that comes in the name of the *LORD will be *blessed.
    We *bless you from the house of the *LORD.

v27 The *LORD is God and he has made his light to shine on us.
    With branches in (our) hands
    we will go with the people who are going to the *feast.
    Go to the *horns of the *altar.

v28 You are my God and I will thank you.
    You are my God and I will say that you are great.

v29 Thank the *LORD because he is good.
    His kind love will always be (with us).

The Word of God
Psalm 119

Jesus said, "If you love me you will obey me" (John 14:15).

The Story of Psalm 119

Solomon was king of Israel nearly 1000 years **B**efore **C**hrist came to the earth (B.C.). Solomon built the house of God that was in Jerusalem. We call it "the *temple". About 600 B.C. a nation called Babylon fought the *Jews. A nation is a country with a government. Babylon was 800 kilometres east of Jerusalem. The Babylonians won the fight and they took many *Jews to Babylon. We call this "the *exile". The Babylonians also destroyed the *temple.

After the *exile many *Jews went back to their own country. About 500 B.C. they built the *temple again. Then they made the Book of Psalms to sing in the new *temple. Some were old psalms by David, Moses and Isaiah. Other psalms were new like Psalm 1. Psalm 119 was probably one of these new psalms. It is a very special psalm. There are 176 verses (or parts) in it. Some people think that 176 different people wrote one verse each. Other people think that Ezra wrote all Psalm 119. Ezra was a *Jewish leader about 450 B.C.

There are 22 letters in the Hebrew alphabet. The *Jews spoke Hebrew, so they wrote Psalm 119 in the Hebrew language. The first letter of the Hebrew alphabet is aleph. Verses 1-8 all begin with aleph. Beth is the second letter. Verses 9-16 all begin with beth. Verses 17-24 all begin with the 3rd letter and so on. So, there are 22 times 8, or 176 verses in the psalm. We think that they did this to make it easier for them to remember the psalm. It was probably a psalm that *Jewish leaders had to remember. We have not made the verses start with the right letter in this translation. We have put the psalm into 22 groups with 8 verses in each group.

There are also 8 special words in the psalm. To the *Jews these 8 words were important. They described what God told them to do. They are also important for Christians, because they tell them the ways that God speaks to them. The most important way is through the Bible. Christians call the Bible "The Word of God". Psalm 119 is the longest chapter in the Bible. You will probably find that you can study it more easily in groups of 8 verses.

Way and path both mean the same thing in the psalm. They mean: what we do in our lives. Our way can be good or bad. If we obey Psalm 119, our way will be good. Jesus said, "I am the way" (John 14:6). If we obey Jesus, our way will be good. In Acts 9:2, "in the way" is another name for "being a Christian".

*heart does not mean the same thing each time it comes:

- "a clean *heart" means that God has forgiven us

- "in my *heart" means "in my mind"

- "all my/their *heart" means "all that I/they can do in the body or mind"

Your *heart in the psalms often means all of you! When God *forgives us, he gives our *sin to Jesus. He takes it away. Our *sin is the bad things that we do.

Follow in verses 4, 14, 15, 56, 63, 87, 100, 133, 168 and 173 means "obey".

Psalm 119

ALEPH

v1 The people that make no mistakes in the way are very happy.
They obey the *teaching of the *LORD.

v2 The people that keep to his *instructions are very happy.
They look for him with all their *heart.

v3 Also, they do nothing that is wrong.
They walk in his ways.

v4 You have made *guidelines for me.
I must follow them all.

v5 I want to make sure
that my ways obey your *laws.

v6 Then I will not be ashamed
when I remember all your *commands.

v7 I will *praise you with a clean *heart
when I learn your *righteous rules.

v8 I will obey your *laws.
Do not ever stop giving me help.

BETH

v9 How can a young man keep his path clean?
He must obey your words.

v10 I have looked for you with all my *heart.
Do not let me forget your *commands.

v11 I have hidden your *sayings in my *heart
so that I do not *sin against you.

v12 *LORD, you are *blessed!
Teach me your *laws.

v13 My lips repeat all the *commands of your mouth.

v14 I am happier following the way by your *instructions
than having a lot of money.

v15 I want to think about your *guidelines
and follow your paths.

v16 I am very happy with your *laws.
I will not forget your word.

GIMEL

v17 Be kind to your servant.
Then I will live and obey your word.

v18 Open my eyes
and I will see *wonderful things in your *teaching.

v19 I am a stranger in the earth.
Do not hide your *commands from me.

v20 I love to obey your rules so much
that I have no interest in other things.

v21 You are angry with the people who think that they are important.
Bad things will happen to them
when they walk away from your *commands.

v22 Some people say bad and *unkind things about me
because I keep to your *instructions.
Take me away from those people.

v23 *Princes sit down and make plans against me.
But your servant thinks only about your *laws.

v24 Yes! Your *instructions make me really happy.
They are like people that tell me what to do.

DALETH

v25 I am lying on the ground.
Give me the life that your word promises to me.

v26 I told you about my ways and you answered me.
Teach me your *laws.

v27 Make me to understand what your *guidelines mean.
Then I will always think about the *wonderful things that you do.

v28 My very great *sadness has made me tired.
Make me strong again as your word promises.

v29 Take the false way from me.
Be kind to me in your *teaching.

v30 I have chosen the right way.
I will not forget your rules.

v31 I will keep to your *instructions, *LORD.
Do not make me ashamed.

v32 I will run in the way of your *commands
because you give help to my *heart.

HE

v33 *LORD, give me help to understand your *laws,
then I will always obey them.

v34 Explain your *teaching to me, then I will always obey it.
I will do it with all my *heart.

- **v35** Make me to walk in the path where your *orders send me.
  Do that because it will give me much pleasure.
- **v36** Turn my *heart to your *instructions
  and not to wanting *riches.
- **v37** Turn my eyes away from looking at things that have no value.
  Give me the life that is in your word.
- **v38** Do for your servant the things that your *sayings promise.
  This will make him be afraid of you.
- **v39** I am afraid of being ashamed.
  Do not let it happen, because your rules are good.
- **v40** I really want your *guidelines.
  Keep me alive as you are *righteous.

VAV

- **v41** *LORD, I want your kind love to come to me
  and I want your *sayings to make me safe.
- **v42** Then I will have something to say to the people that laugh at me.
  They laugh at me because I *trust in your word.
- **v43** Do not take a true word away from my mouth,
  because I put my hope in your rules.
- **v44** I will always obey your *teaching,
  I will never stop.
- **v45** I will be free to walk anywhere
  because I look for your *guidelines.
- **v46** I will talk about your *instructions before kings.
  I will not be ashamed.
- **v47** I love your *commands
  and I am very happy with them.
- **v48** I lift up my hands to your *commands, which I love.
  I am always thinking about your *laws.

ZAYIN

- **v49** Remember your word to your servant.
  You made me put my hope in it.
- **v50** Your *sayings *comfort me when I am sad.
  They comfort me because they give me life.
- **v51** *Proud people laugh at me all the time,
  but I do not turn away from your *teaching.
- **v52** *LORD, I remember the rules that you made long ago.
  They make me feel better.
- **v53** I get very angry
  when *godless people turn away from your *teaching.
- **v54** Your *laws are my songs
  in the house where I live.
- **v55** *LORD, in the night I will remember your name.
  I will keep your *teaching.
- **v56** I do this
  because I follow your *guidelines.

HETH

- **v57** *LORD, you are everything to me.
  I promise to obey your words.
- **v58** I ask you, with all my *heart,
  to *have *mercy on me as you have promised.
- **v59** I have thought about my ways,
  and my feet are going back to follow your *instructions.
- **v60** I will hurry to obey your *commands
  and I will not be slow.
- **v61** People who do not know God are all round me.
  They tie me up but still I do not forget your *teaching.
- **v62** I get up in the middle of the night to *praise you
  because your rules are *righteous.
- **v63** I am a friend of everyone that is afraid of you.
  And I am a friend of those who follow your *guidelines.
- **v64** *LORD, the earth is full of your kind love.
  Teach me your *laws.

TETH

- **v65** You do good things for your servant, *LORD,
  as your word says.
- **v66** Teach me. Then I will choose and know what is right.
  I will do that because I *trust your *commands.
- **v67** Before I was in trouble with you I made mistakes.
  But now I keep to your *sayings.
- **v68** You are good and you do good things.
  Teach me your *laws.
- **v69** *Proud men have told me lots of lies,
  but your *guidelines are of great value to me.
- **v70** #Their *heart is fat and they are *stupid;
  but I love your *teaching.
- **v71** My trouble was good for me.
  It made me learn your *laws.
- **v72** *Teaching from your mouth is better for me
  than a lot of *silver and gold.

#This is the *heart of the *proud men in verse 69. It means that they cannot think clearly.

JODH

- **v73** Your hands *created me. And they made me what I am.
  Help me to understand and learn your *commands.
- **v74** The people that are afraid of you will be happy.
  They will be happy when they see me.
  This is because I am *trusting in your word.
- **v75** *LORD, I know that your rules are *righteous.
  You were right when you sent me trouble.
- **v76** Now your kind love makes me feel better.
  You promised this to your servant in your *sayings.
- **v77** Send your love to me and I will live!
  Your *teaching makes me really happy.
- **v78** *Proud men will be ashamed
  because they say lies about me without any reason.
- **v79** The people that are afraid of you will turn to me again.
  They understand your *instructions.
- **v80** My *heart will make no mistakes about your *laws.
  I will not be ashamed.

KAPH

- **v81** I feel weak while I wait for you to save me.
  My hope is in your word.
- **v82** My eyes are closing while I look for your *sayings.
  I say, "When will you *comfort me?"
- **v83** I am like #a *wineskin in smoke
  but I will not forget your *guidelines.
- **v84** The life of your servant is not very long.
  When will you make the people that *persecute me obey your rules?
- **v85** *Proud people have made *traps for me.
  Your *teaching says that they must not do this.
- **v86** All your *commands are true.
  But people still *persecute me with lies. Give me help!
- **v87** People on earth almost destroyed me,
  but I did not stop following your *guidelines.
- **v88** Your kind love gives me life.
  I will obey your *instructions.

We are not sure what this means.

LAMED

v89 *LORD, your word will always rule in the *heavens.

v90 Your *truth will continue from one century to the next.
You have fixed the earth and it will remain.

v91 #They remain today as your rules say they must.
They are all your servants.

v92 If your *teaching had not made me happy
then my great *sadness would have destroyed me.

v93 I will never forget your *guidelines
because in them you give me life.

v94 I am yours, save me!
Do it because I have looked for your *guidelines.

v95 The *godless wait to destroy me,
but I am studying your *instructions.

v96 I see that all that is good on earth will finish.
But your *commands have no end.

#"they" probably means the earth and the stars in the *heavens (skies).

MEM

v97 I love your *teaching very much.
I think about it all day long.

v98 Your *commands teach me more than my enemies.
Your *commands are always with me.

v99 I understand more than all my teachers
because I think about your *commands.

v100 I understand more than the old people
because I follow your *guidelines.

v101 I do not let my feet walk in any *evil path
because I obey your word.

v102 I do not turn away from your rules,
because you teach me.

v103 Your *sayings are like *honey to me.
They are like something that tastes good.

v104 Your *guidelines give me help to understand things,
so I hate every wrong path.

NUN

v105 Your word is a *lamp to my foot
and a light to my path.

v106 I have really promised to keep your *righteous rules
and I will do it.

v107 People have hurt me very much.
Give me the life that your word promises.

v108 *LORD, I pray that you will be happy with what I say.
And I pray that you will teach me your rules.

v109 I am always in danger,
but I never forget your *teaching.

v110 *Wicked people have made a *trap for me,
but I do not go away from your *guidelines.

v111 Your *instructions will always be with me
and they make my *heart very happy.

v112 I will make my *heart obey your *instructions always, to the end.

SAMEKH

v113 I hate the people that do not believe you.
But I love your *teaching.

v114 You are my secret place where I can hide.
I put my hope in your word.

v115 Go away from me, you bad people!
I will obey my God's *commands.

v116 Give me help and life, as your word promises.
And do not make me ashamed, because I hope in you.

v117 Give me help and I will be safe.
I will always obey your *laws.

v118 You turn away from people that do not follow your *laws.
This is because they speak lies.
And they are not honest.

v119 You destroy all the bad people in the world as *rubbish.
For this reason I love your *instructions.

v120 Am afraid of you and it makes my body *shiver.
I am afraid of your rules.

AYIN

v121 I was *righteous and I obeyed the rules.
Do not give me to my *oppressors.

v122 Make sure that good things happen to your servant.
Do not let *proud people become my *oppressors.

v123 My eyes have stopped seeing that you are saving me.
They do not see your *righteous *sayings.

v124 Do with your servant what your kind love suggests.
Teach me your *laws.

v125 I am your servant. Explain your *instructions to me
so that I understand them.

v126 It is time for the *LORD to do something.
People have not obeyed your *teaching.

v127-128 I hate every wrong path because:
☐ I love your *commands more than gold, *pure gold
☐ I think that all your *guidelines are right

PE

v129 I obey your *instructions
because they are *wonderful.

v130 When I read your words they bring light.
They help people that do not know enough to understand things.

v131 My mouth is wide open as I *breathe.
This is because I am so *eager for your *commands.

v132 Turn to me and have *mercy on me.
Your rules say that you will do this.
You will do this to people that love your name.

v133 Make my feet follow your *sayings.
Do not let *sin rule over me.

v134 Make me free from *oppressors
and I will follow your *guidelines.

v135 Show a kind face to your servant
and teach me your *laws.

v136 Streams of water come from my eyes
because people do not obey your *teaching.

TSADHE

v137 *LORD, you are *righteous
and your rules are good.

v138 The *instructions that you gave are very fair.
And we can *trust in them.

v139 I am so *eager that it makes me feel weak.
But my enemies do not listen to your words.

v140 We have found that your *sayings are true.
Your servant loves them.

v141 I am not important and people do not like me.
But I will not forget your *guidelines.

v142 You are always *righteous and fair.
Your *teachings are true.

v143 An enemy brought me trouble,
but your *commands make me happy.

v144 Your *instructions are always fair.
Make me understand them and find life.

KOPH

v145 I cried with all my *heart. "Answer me, *LORD".
"I will obey your *laws", I cried.

v146 "Save me
and I will keep to your *instructions."

v147 I woke up before dawn and cried to you for help.
I want all that you promised in your word.

v148 I stayed up all night
and thought about your *sayings.

v149 Listen to my voice, because you are loving and kind.
*LORD, keep me alive as your rules promise me.

v150 The people that *persecute me are coming near.
They want to do something very bad to me.
They are far away from your *teaching.

v151 *LORD, you are near to me.
All your *commands are true.

v152 I have known about your *instructions for a long time.
And I have known that you made them to continue always.

RESH

v153 Look at my trouble!
Save me because I do not forget your *teaching.

v154 Fight my fight for me and *redeem me.
Keep me alive as your *sayings promise me.

v155 *Godless people are far away from being safe.
They do not look for your *laws.

v156 *LORD, your love is great,
because your rules keep me alive.

v157 Many enemies *persecute me
but I do not go away from your *instructions.

v158 I see people doing such bad things that I hate them.
But, I do not stop obeying your *sayings.

v159 See how I love your *guidelines, *LORD.
Keep me alive through your kind love.

v160 All your words are true.
All your *righteous rules will continue always.

SHIN

v161 *Princes *persecute me for no good reason.
But it is your word that really makes my *heart afraid.

v162 I am very happy with your *sayings.
I am like someone that finds great riches.

v163 I do not like *lies, I hate them.
Your *teaching is what I love.

v164 I *praise you 7 times every day
because of your *righteous rules.

v165 People that love your *teaching have a lot of *peace.
Nothing will make them fall down.

v166 *LORD, I am waiting for you to save me
while I obey your *commands.

v167 I will keep to your *instructions
because I love them so much.

v168 I follow your *guidelines and *instructions
because you see all that I do.

TAV

v169 I am calling to you for help, *LORD.
I want to understand your word.

v170 Hear what I pray and have *mercy on me.
Save me, as your *sayings promise me.

v171 My lips will pour out *praise
because you are *teaching me your *laws.

v172 My *tongue will sing your *sayings
because all your *commands are *righteous.

v173 I want your hand to come to my help
because I chose to follow your *guidelines.

v174 *LORD, I want you to save me.
Your *teaching makes me very happy.

v175 Give me life so that I can *praise you.
May your rules give me help.

v176 I have become like a lost sheep.
Look for your servant,
because I have not forgotten your *commands.

Psalms For Climbing
Psalms 120-134

Jesus said, "We will go up to Jerusalem" (Luke 18:31).

Psalm 120

(This is) a song for climbing.

v1 I cried to the *LORD in my trouble
and he answered me.

v2 *LORD, save me from lips that tell *lies.
And save me from a false *tongue.

v3 What will he do to you
and what else will happen to you, you false *tongue?

v4 The sharp *arrows of a soldier (will hurt you),
like wood that is burning.

v5 It is bad for me to live in Mesech,
with a home among the *tents of Kedar.

v6 I have lived too long with the people that hate *peace.

v7 I want *peace, but when I say this they want war.

Psalm 121

(This is) a song for climbing.

v1 When I look up to the hills I find no help there.

v2 My help comes from the *LORD.
He made the *heaven and the earth.

v3 He will not let your foot *slide.
The one that *guards you will not sleep.

v4 It is certain that he will not sleep.
The one that *guards Israel will never sleep.

v5 The *LORD is the one that *guards you.
The *LORD is near you to *protect you.

v6 The sun will not hurt you in the day,
nor the moon at night.

v7 The *LORD is the one that *guards you from all danger.
He is the one that *guards your life.

v8 The *LORD *guards you when you go out.
And he when *guards you when you come in.
(He will do this) now and always.

Psalm 122

(This is) a song for climbing by David.

v1 It made me very happy when they said to me,
"We will go into the house of the *LORD".

v2 (Now) our feet are standing inside your gates, Jerusalem!

v3 Jerusalem is a city with buildings that fit near together.

v4 The *tribes go up there, the *tribes of the *LORD.
They go there to thank the *LORD. All Israel will see it.

v5 The *thrones of the house of David are there.
Also, they sit there to *judge the people.

- v6 Pray for the *peace of Jerusalem.
  (Pray that) the people that love (Jerusalem) will be safe.
- v7 "I pray that there will be *peace inside your walls.
  And I pray that it will be safe inside your big houses".
- v8 Because of my brothers and friends I will pray,
  "I want *peace inside you."
- v9 Because of the house of the *LORD our God,
  I will hope for good things for you.

Psalm 123

(This is) a song for climbing.

- v1 I lift up my eyes to you (God).
  You are sitting in *heaven.
- v2 Our eyes look to the *LORD our God:
  ☐ like men who are servants look to the hands of their masters;
  ☐ like a woman who is a servant looks to the hand of her *mistress.
  (*LORD), have *mercy on us.
- v3 Have *mercy on us, *LORD, have *mercy on us.
  We have had more than enough *contempt.
- v4 We have had more than enough *contempt
  from the *proud people that are *oppressing us.

Psalm 124

(This is) a song for climbing by David.

- v1 If the *LORD was not fighting for us – now Israel say it –
- v2 - v5 if the *LORD was not fighting for us when men attacked:
  ☐ they would have eaten us alive because they were so angry,
  ☐ waters would have rushed over us
  and a deep river would be over our heads,
  ☐ the angry waters would have gone over our heads and drowned us.
- v6 We will say good things to the *LORD.
  He did not let them eat us.
- v7 We are free and still alive, like a bird that got out of a *trap.
  The *trap became broken and we are free.
- v8 The name of the person that sent us help is the *LORD.
  He made *heaven and earth.

Psalm 125

(This is) a psalm for climbing.

- v1 People that *trust in the *LORD are like the mountain called Zion.
  Nothing will move it; it will always be there.
- v2 Jerusalem has mountains all round it.
  Also, the *LORD is all round his people, now and always.
- v3 *Wicked (people) will not always rule over the land.
  (That is, the land) that (the *LORD) gave to *righteous people.
  If they did, the *righteous people might start doing bad things themselves.
- v4 Do good things, *LORD, to good people.
  (Good people) are *upright in their *hearts.
- v5 But *LORD, take away those people that start doing bad things themselves.
  Take them away with the *wicked (people).
  Let Israel be *at peace!

Psalm 126

(This is) a psalm for climbing.

- v1 An army was attacking Zion.
  When the *LORD turned them away,
  we were like people that were dreaming!
- v2 Then we laughed a lot.
  And we shouted because we were so happy!
  And (people in) other countries said (to each other),
  "The *LORD has done something *wonderful for them!"
- v3 The *LORD has done something *wonderful for us
  and we are very, very happy.
- v4 The *LORD will give back again what we have lost.
  It will be like water coming into a dry place where there is a lot of sand.
- v5 People that are crying will go out and plant seeds.
  (Later) they will sing as they pick the fruits.
- v6 Someone will go out crying, but with a basket of seeds.
  He will come home laughing, with a lot of food.

Psalm 127

(This is) a psalm for climbing by Solomon.

- v1 If the *LORD does not build the house,
  the workers cannot do anything.
  There are men who watch (for danger).
  But if the *LORD does not *guard the city,
  they will be *useless.
- v2 If you work all day for food,
  from early morning to late at night,
  you will get nothing.
  It is God who gives sleep.
  He gives it to the people that he loves.
- v3 Children are something that God gives.
  The fruit of your body is a gift (from him).
- v4 The sons of a young man
  are like *arrows in the hand of a soldier.
- v5 The man with many of them will be very happy.
  He will not be ashamed when he meets his enemies in the city gates.

Psalm 128

(This is) a song for climbing.

- v1 Everyone that is *in awe of the *LORD will be very happy.
  They will *walk in his ways.
- v2 You will eat the things that your hands have worked for.
  You are very sure that you will. You will be happy!
  Good things will happen to you!
- v3 Your wife in your house
  will be like a *vine that grows much fruit.
  Your sons round your table
  will be like branches of an *olive tree.
- v4 The *LORD does good things to the man that is *in awe of him.
  This is how he does it. Make a note of that.
- v5 The *LORD of Zion will do good things to you.
  Then you will see that Jerusalem is a good place
  for as long as you are alive.
- v6 You will see your grandsons
  and there will be *peace in Israel.

Psalm 129

(This is) a song for climbing.

- v1 My enemies have often hurt me since I was a child.
  Israel can now say this.
- v2 They have often hurt me since I was a child,
  but they have not beaten me.
- v3 They ploughed on my back
  like a farmer ploughing long *furrows.
- v4 The *LORD is *righteous.
  He has cut me free from my enemies.
- v5 Everybody that hates Zion will be ashamed.
  So they will turn away.
- v6 They will become like a green plant on a roof.
  It dies before it starts to grow!
- v7 A gardener cannot fill his hand (with it)
  or a farmer (fill) his pocket.

v8 People that go past will not say,
"We want the *LORD to be kind to you!"
(They will not say)
"We want good things to happen to you in the name of the *LORD!"

Psalm 130

(This is) a song for climbing.

v1 *LORD, I am crying to you because I am in great (trouble).

v2 *Lord, listen to my voice.
Turn your ears to hear what I am saying to you.

v3 *LORD, if you make a note of *sins, who will stand?

v4 But you *forgive (people) so that they are *in awe of you.

v5 I will wait for the *LORD.
I will wait for him and *hope in his word.

v6 I want the *Lord more than people want the morning to come,
more than people want the morning.

v7 Israel, hope in the *LORD,
because with the *LORD there is kind love and a lot of *redeeming.

v8 He will *redeem Israel from all his *sins.

Psalm 131

(This is) a song for climbing by David.

v1 *LORD, my *heart is not *proud, neither are my eyes (*proud).
I do not try to do things that are too important for me.
I do not try to do things that are too hard for me.

v2 Really, I have made myself *calm and I have become quiet.
I am like a young child with its mother.
Yes, I am like a young child with its mother.

v3 Israel, put your hope in the *LORD, now and always.

Psalm 132

(This is) a song for climbing.

v1 *LORD, remember David and all his troubles.

v2 He promised the *LORD.
He made this special promise to the *Mighty One of Jacob.

v3 "I will not go into my house or get into my bed.

v4 I will not shut my eyes or go to sleep
until I find a place for the *LORD.

v5 It will be a place where the *Mighty One of Jacob will live".

v6 We heard that it was at Ephratah.
And we found it in the fields of Jaar.

v7 We will go into the place where he lives.
And we will *worship at his feet.

v8 Get up, *LORD. And go into the place where you can rest.
Go in yourself, with the *ark.
The *ark shows that you are strong.

v9 (I pray that) all your *priests will be *righteous
and all your *saints will shout.
They will shout because they are so happy.

v10 Remember your servant David
and do not turn away the face of your *messiah.

v11 The *LORD promised David what would happen.
He will not turn from it.
"I will put the fruit of your body on your *throne."

v12 Your children should obey my rules.
And they should do what I will teach them.
Then their children will always sit on your *throne".

v13 The *LORD chose Zion.
He wants it for a place to live in.

v14 "This is where I will always rest. This is what I want.
So I will live here", he said.

v15 "I will do a lot of good things for her.
I will give food to the poor people in her.

v16 All her *priests will be safe and her *saints will shout aloud.
They will shout because they are so happy.

v17 There I will make David very strong.
The light of my *messiah will never go out.

v18 His enemies will be ashamed.
But his *crown will shine and be bright!'

Psalm 133

(This is) a song for climbing by David.

v1 See how good it is.
And see what pleasure it brings when brothers stay together.

v2 It is as a sweet *oil poured on the head.
It goes down on to the beard, as it did on to Aaron's beard.
It then poured down over his clothes.

v3 It is like the *dew on the mountain called Hermon.
It (also) pours down on to the mountains of Zion.
The *LORD has said that it is a *good place to be.
There is always life there.

Psalm 134

(This is) a song for climbing.

v1 Come, all you servants of the *LORD that stand in his house at night.
And say good things to the *LORD.

v2 Lift up your hands to where he lives.
And say good things to him.

v3 Say good things to the *LORD in Zion.
He made the *heaven and the earth.

A Song of *Praise to God
Psalm 135

They went out and talked about (Jesus) everywhere (Matthew 9:31).

Psalm 135

v1 *Hallelujah! *Praise the name of the *LORD!
*Praise him, you servants of the *LORD!

v2 You are standing in the house of the *LORD.
You are standing in the *courts of the house of our God.

v3 *Praise the *LORD, because the *LORD is good.
*Praise his name with songs, because it is *pleasant to do this.

v4 (*Praise his name) because the *LORD chose *Jacob for himself.
Israel is his own *treasure.

v5 (*Praise his name) because I know that the *LORD is great.
Our *Lord is greater than all other gods.

v6 The *LORD does whatever he wants to do.
(He does this) in the sky and on the earth.
(And he does it) in the deepest parts of the sea.

v7 (The *LORD) makes clouds rise up all over the earth.
He sends rain with *lightning.
He brings winds from where he stores them.

v8 (God) destroyed the *firstborn in Egypt, both men and animals.

v9 He sent signs to *warn Egypt. He did *miracles in Egypt.
(He did them) to *warn *Pharaoh and his servants.

v10 He destroyed many countries and killed many kings.

v11 (He killed) Sihon the king of the *Amorites.
(He also killed) Og the king of *Bashan and all the kings of *Canaan.

v12 Then he gave their lands to his people Israel.
He gave (their lands) to them as a gift.

v13 *LORD, people will always remember your name.
You will always be famous.

v14 And the *LORD will *defend his people.
Also, he will show his love to his servants.

v15 (Other) countries make their *idols with *silver and gold.
Human hands made (those *idols)!

v16 They have mouths ... but they cannot speak!
(They have) eyes ... but they cannot see!

v17 (They have) ears ... but they cannot hear!
(They have) mouths ... but they cannot *breathe!

v18 The people that made them will become as they are.
Also, everyone that *trusts in them (will become as they are).

v19 House of Israel, *bless the *LORD.
House of Aaron, *bless the *LORD.

v20 House of Levi, *bless the *LORD.
(Everyone) that is afraid of him, *bless the *LORD.

v21 Zion, *bless the *LORD that lives in Jerusalem.
*Hallelujah!

The *Kind Love of the *LORD
Psalm 136
The Great *Hallel

Jesus said, "This is how God loved the world" (John 3:16).

Psalm 136

v1 Thank the *LORD, because he is good!
Thank him because his kind love will always continue.

v2 Thank God, (who is) the greatest of the gods.
Thank him because his kind love will always continue.

v3 Thank the *Lord, (who is) the greatest *lord.
Thank him because his kind love will always continue.

v4 - v9 (Thank the *LORD because):
☐ only he does great *miracles
(and) because his kind love will always continue;
☐ he made the skies with understanding
(and) because his kind love will always continue;
☐ he put the earth on the waters
(and) because his kind love will always continue;
☐ he made the great lights
(and) because his kind love will always continue;
☐ (he made) the sun to rule the day
(and) because his kind love will always continue;
☐ (he made) the moon and stars to rule the night
(and) his kind love will always continue.

v10 - v16 (Thank the *LORD because):
☐ he destroyed the *firstborn in Egypt
(and) because his kind love will always continue;
☐ he brought Israel out from (Egypt)
(and) because his kind love will always continue;
☐ (he did this) with a strong hand and a powerful arm
(and) because his kind love will always continue;
☐ he cut the Red Sea into two parts
(and) because his kind love will always continue
☐ he brought Israel through the middle of it
(and) because his kind love will always continue;
☐ he pushed Pharaoh (the king of Egypt) and his army into the Red Sea
(and) because his kind love will always continue;
☐ he led his people through the *desert
(and) because his kind love will always continue.

v17 - v22 (Thank the *LORD because):
☐ he destroyed great kings
(and) because his kind love will always continue;
☐ he killed very strong kings
(and) because his kind love will always continue;
☐ (he killed) Sihon, king of the Amorites
(and) because his kind love will always continue;
☐ (he killed) Og, the king of Bashan
(and) because his kind love will always continue;
☐ he gave their land as a gift
(and) because his kind love will always continue;
☐ (he gave it) as a gift to his servant Israel
(and) because his kind love will always continue.

v23 - v25 (Thank the *LORD because):
☐ he remembered us when we were very sad
(and) because his kind love will always continue;
☐ he made us free from our enemies
(and) because his kind love will always continue;
☐ he gives food to everything that he has made
(and) because his kind love will always continue.

v26 Thank the God of *heaven!
Because his kind love will always continue.

By The Rivers In Babylon
Psalm 137

Jesus said, "You have heard that people used to say, An eye for an eye and a tooth for a tooth. But I say to you, Do not fight against *evil. If someone hits you on the right side of your face, let him hit you on the other side also" (Matthew 5:38-39). ("*Evil" means something that is very, very bad.)

Psalm 137

v1 There we sat down, by the rivers in Babylon.
We cried when we remembered Zion.

v2 There we hung up our *harps
on the willow trees (special kind of tree).

v3 For there the people that made us *prisoners were very *unkind.
"Sing us a song" they shouted.
"Make us laugh with a song from Zion!"

v4 We just cannot sing the *LORD's song in a foreign land.

v5 Jerusalem, if I forget you my right hand (will drop off!)

v6 My *tongue will stick to the top of my mouth
if I do not remember you, Jerusalem.
I think of you more than the things that I like best.

v7 *LORD, remember the people of Edom.
This is what they said in the Day of Jerusalem.
"Knock it down, knock it down to its *foundations!"

v8 Daughter of Babylon, someone will destroy you!
That person will do to you what you did to us.
He will be very happy then!

v9 He will catch your children and hit them with a rock.
He will be very happy then!

Thanks!
Psalm 138

Jesus said, "Offer (to God) the gift that Moses told you (to offer)" (Matthew 8:4).

Psalm 138

(This is) for David.

v1 I will thank you, *LORD, *with all my *heart.
I will sing your *praises in front of the (false) gods.

v2 I will fall down before (you in) your *holy *temple.
I will give thanks to *your name for your kind love that never fails.
(Also we will give thanks,) because you have lifted your name
and your word above everything else.

v3 When I prayed to you, you answered me.
You made me brave and strong.

v4 All the kings in the world will thank you, *LORD.
They have heard the promises that you have made.
That is why they will thank you.

v5 They will sing about what you have done.
(And) they will sing because of your great *glory.

v6 The *LORD is high (above the earth).
But he can see what people below him (need).
Also he can see what *proud people are doing.
They are far away (from him) but he can still see them.

v7 You keep me alive when there is trouble all round me.
When my enemy is angry you fight against him.
You save me with your right hand.

v8 The *LORD will do for me everything that he has promised.
*LORD, your kind love will always continue.
Finish the work of your hands.

God Knows Everything
Psalm 139

Jesus said, "Your Father (God) knows how many hairs there are on your head!" (Matthew 10:30)

Psalm 139

(This is) for the music leader.
(It is) a psalm of David.

v1 *LORD, when you look at me you know all about me.

v2 You know when I sit down.
And you know when I get up.
You understand what I am thinking about
(even when you are) far away.

v3 You see when I go (somewhere).
And you see when I stay (at home).
You remember everything that I do!

v4 For example, before I say a word,
*LORD, you know all about it.

v5 You are all round me, in front (of me) and behind (me).
You have put your *hand upon me.

v6 What you know (about me) is *wonderful.
I cannot understand it.
It is so high that I cannot climb up to it.

v7 Where can I go from your *Spirit?
How can I run away from you?

v8 If I went up to *heaven, you would be there.
If I went down to *Sheol, you would be there also.

v9 If I went:
☐ to where the sun rises (in the east)
☐ to the other side of the sea (in the west)

v10 your hand would be there.
It would be my guide.
Your right hand would give me help.

v11 If I say:
☐ I am sure that *darkness will hide me
☐ or, the light round me will change into night,

v12 *darkness and light are the same to you!
*Darkness is not dark to you.
The night shines as bright as the day (to you).

v13 But you, you made every part of me.
You made me grow in my mother's *womb.

v14 I *praise you for the *mysterious and *wonderful way that you made me.
I know very well that everything that you made is *wonderful.

v15 (Nothing) hid my body from you when I was growing in a secret place.
This happened deep in the earth.

v16 Your eyes saw my body growing.
Before I had lived one day, you wrote in your book how long I should live for!

v17 You have so many ideas, God.
They are so difficult for me to understand.

v18 If I could count them all,
there would be more than the *grains of sand (by the side of the sea).
I would have to live (as long) as you to count them all!

v19 God, I hope that you will kill the *wicked (people)!
And go away from me you *men of blood (murderers).

v20 They are your enemies.
They say bad things about you that are not true.

v21 Do I *hate them that hate you, *LORD?
Do I really hate them that attack you?

v22 (Yes) I do hate them, I really hate them.
I think of them as my enemies.

v23 Look at me, God. And know (what is in) my *heart.
Look into my mind and know my thoughts.

v24 See if I am doing anything bad that might hurt me.
And lead me in the old ways.

Poison!
Psalm 140

Jesus said, "Children of *vipers, how can you say anything that is good? You are *evil people" (Matthew 12:34).

Psalm 140

(This is) for the music leader. (It is) a psalm of David.

v1 Save me, *LORD, from *evil people.
Do not let the men that attack people hurt me.

v2 They have *evil ideas and are always starting wars.

v3 Their *tongues are as sharp as a snake's *tongue.
The poison of vipers (a kind of snake) is on their lips.   *SELAH

v4 Keep me, *LORD, (away) from *the hands of *evil people.
Do not let people that love to fight hurt me.
They want my feet to *trip over!

v5 *Proud people have hidden a *trap for me.
They have put their *nets (where I cannot see them).
They have put *snares along my path.   *SELAH

v6 *LORD, I say to you, "You are my God".
*LORD, hear my *prayer for *mercy!

v7 *LORD, my *Lord, you are my strong *helper.
You cover my head when there is a fight.

v8 *LORD, do not let *evil people do what they want (to do).
They will become *proud if their plans do well.   *SELAH

v9 Pour trouble on the heads of the people round me!
(I mean the trouble) that their lips caused.

v10 Drop burning *coals on them! Throw (these people) into the fire!
(Put them) in holes full of wet mud (dirt and water) so they cannot get out!

v11 Do not let these *slanderers live in the land (of Israel)!
Make *evil follow these people that love to attack (other people).

v12 I know that the *LORD will be fair to poor people.
He will also fight (to help) people *in need.

v13 I am sure that *righteous people will *praise *your name.
Good people will always live near you.

An Evening *Prayer
Psalm 141

Jesus said, "What will a man have if he buys the whole world but loses his own soul?" (Mark 8:36) (The soul is the part of us that lives when our body dies.)

Psalm 141

(This is) a psalm of David.

v1 *LORD, I am praying to you. Come to me soon.
I am talking to you. Please hear what I am saying.

v2 When I pray to you it will be like *incense.
When I raise my hands (to you)
it will be like an evening *prayer.

v3 *LORD, do not let my mouth (speak *evil words).
Listen to what my lips (are saying).

v4 Stop me wanting to do what is wrong.
Do not let me go with *evil people to do what is wrong.
Do not let me eat in their *feasts.

v5 If a good man hits me, he is being kind (to me).
If he is angry with me, it is like *oil on my head.
I will not say "no" to it.
I am always praying against what bad people do.

v6 They will throw their rulers down
    from the rocks on the sides of the hills.
    Then they will know that my words were true.

v7 (They will say) "as people break the earth (to plant seeds),
    so they will throw our bones down to *Sheol'.

v8 But *LORD, my eyes are looking to you, (my) *Lord.
    I am hoping that you will give me help.
    Do not let (people) kill me.

v9 Keep me (away) from the *snares they have put (to catch) me.
    (Keep me away) from the *traps that *evil (people) have hidden for me.

v10 I pray that their own *nets will catch these *evil (people).
    And I pray that I will be safe as I pass the (*nets).

Nobody *Cares About Me
Psalm 142

Jesus said, "Your Father in *heaven feeds the birds (that fly) in the air. You are much better than they are!" (Matthew 6:26) (*Heaven is the home of God the Father.)

Psalm 142

(This is) a *maskil of David.
    (He wrote it) when he was in the cave (hole in the rock).
    (It is) a *prayer.

v1 I am praying aloud to the *LORD.
    I am asking aloud for help from the *LORD.

v2 I am telling him about everything that I think is wrong.
    I am telling him all my troubles.

v3 Sometimes I do not feel brave.
    Then you (*LORD) know what I should do.
    In the path where I walk (my enemies) have hidden a *trap for me.

v4 Look round me and see.
    No (friend) sees that I am here.
    There is no safe place for me to go to.
    Nobody cares about me.

v5 I am praying to you, *LORD.
    You are my safe place (where I can go).
    You are all that I need in this life.

v6 Listen to me as I cry (to you).
    I have a very great need.
    Make me safe from the people that follow me (to hurt me).
    You make me safe because they are too strong for me.

v7 Take me out of this prison
    so that I can *praise *your name.
    Then *righteous people will come to me
    because you are so kind to me.

God Is My Only Hope
Psalm 143

Jesus said, "Father, if it is possible, I pray that this cup will pass from me. But (it must be) what you want (to happen). It must not be what I want" (Mark 26:39). ("Cup will pass from me" is how Jesus said "I do not want to die". The cup was like a picture of death.)

Psalm 143

(This is) a psalm of David.

v1 *LORD, hear my *prayer.
    Listen to me when I ask you for help.
    Answer me, because you are a loving and fair (God).

v2 Do not *judge (me) your servant,
    because nobody alive (on earth) is *righteous.

v3 An enemy is following me.
    He is trying to kill me.
    He wants to put me in a dark place,
    like (people) who have been dead for a long time.

v4 My *spirit inside me is becoming weak.
    My *heart inside me has no hope.

v5 I remember (what happened) many years ago.
    I think about all that you did.
    Also, I see in my mind all that your hands have done.

v6 I raise my hands to you.
    I want you as badly as dry ground (wants rain).   *SELAH

v7 Answer me soon, *LORD. I am losing hope.
    Do not hide your face from me.
    (If you do) I will be as those (people) that go down into the *Pit.

v8 I want to hear news of your kind love in the morning.
    (This is) because I am *trusting in you.
    Show me what I should do.
    Show me because I have asked you (to show me).

v9 *LORD, make me free from my enemies,
    because I am hiding in you.

v10 Teach me what you want me to do.
    Teach me because you are my God.
    Your *spirit is good.
    It will lead me to ground that is flat.

v11 Save my life, *LORD, because of your (great) name.
    Bring me out of trouble, because you are *righteous.

v12 Because you love me, kill my enemies.
    And destroy the people that fight against me.
    (Do this) because I am your servant.

We *Bless God And God *Blesses Us!
Psalm 144

Jesus said, "(God will) *bless people that are good. They will see God" (Matthew 5:8).

Psalm 144

(This is) a psalm of David.

v1 *LORD, I *bless you! You are my Rock!
    You prepared my hands for war.
    You taught my fingers to fight.

v2 You give me your kind love.
    You are my *fortress.
    You are like a strong place that you can take me to.
    You are a *shield that keeps me safe.
    You make my people obey me.

v3 *LORD, why do you want to know about people?
    Why do you think about them?

v4 People are just like the wind.
    They are just like a shadow that passes.

v5 *LORD, open your *heavens and come down (to earth).
    Touch the mountains so that they give out smoke.

v6 Send *flashes of *lightning to frighten (your enemies).
    Shoot your *arrows and destroy them.

v7 Put your hand down from high (in the *heavens).
    Take me from the dangerous waters.
    Make me safe from the hands of foreign people.

v8 Their mouths speak *lies.
    Even when they make a promise, they are saying a *lie.

v9 I will sing to you a new song, God.
    I will make music to you on a *ten-stringed harp.

v10 You give help to kings to win their wars.
    Save your servant David from death by a *sword.

v11 Make me safe from the hands of foreign people.
    Their mouths speak lies.
    Even when they make a promise, they are saying a *lie.

v12 I pray that, when they are young,
    our sons will be like strong plants.
    (I pray that) our daughters will be beautiful,
    like parts of the wall of a great house.

v13 (I pray that you, *LORD,)
    will fill the places where we store many different foods.
    (I pray that) our sheep will have thousands of young sheep.
    Then there will be tens of thousands of them in our fields.

v14 (I pray that) our cows will have good health.
(I pray that) none of them will be sick or have *abortions.
(I pray that) none of them will cry aloud in our fields.

v15 If this happens, then (God has) *blessed our people.
If the *LORD is their God, then (God) will *bless people.

An Alphabet of *Praise
Psalm 145

Jesus said, "Yours is the *kingdom, the power and the *glory, for always, *Amen" (Matthew 6:13). (This is the end of the *prayer that Jesus taught us to say to God. A *kingdom is the country that a king rules. "Amen" is a Hebrew word that means "we agree".)

Psalm 145

(This is) a psalm of David.

v1 Always I will *praise you, my God and my king,
and I will *bless your name!

v2 "*Bless you" I will say every day
and I will always *praise your name.

v3 Clearly the *LORD is great
and we can never *praise him enough.
We will never know how great he really is!

v4 Down from father to son people will say
what *wonderful things you have done.
They will tell each other how powerful you are.

v5 Everyone is talking about your *glory and your *beauty.
I will keep thinking about the *wonderful things that you do.

v6 Famous are the things that you have done.
People talk about them.
I also will say what great things you do.

v7 Good things are what everybody remembers about you.
They all sing about how kind you are.

v8 How full of *grace and *mercy is the *LORD.
He is slow to become angry and is full of kind love.

v9 It is the *LORD that is kind to everybody.
He shows his *mercy to everything that he has made.

v10 Joining together,
everything that you have made will *praise you, *LORD.
Your *saints will *bless you!

v11 "*Kingdom of *Glory" is where you rule.
People talk about it and about how powerful you are.

v12 Let everybody know the powerful things that you have done;
and the *glory and *beauty of your *kingdom.

v13 Many years, even for always, will your *kingdom remain.
You will always rule over it.

Now the *LORD will do as he has promised.
All that he does shows his *mercy.

v14 Out of trouble the *LORD will bring everybody.
He will give help to everyone that has fallen down.

v15 People and other living things look to you.
You give them food when they need it.

v16 Really, you open your hand.
And you give every living thing what it wants.

v17 So the *LORD is fair in all his ways.
Everything that he does shows us his *mercy.

v18 The *LORD is near to all that pray to him.
He is near to all that are honest when they pray to him.

v19 Very soon he will give what they need to those that love him.
He will hear what they say and save them.

v20 *Wicked people will the *LORD destroy.
But he will save the people that love him.

v21 You will hear me speak the *praises of the *LORD.
All that he has made will *bless his *holy name.

*Trust Only In God
Psalm 146
The First *Hallelujah Psalm

Jesus said, "*Believe also in me" (John 14:1).

Psalm 146

v1 *Hallelujah!
I say to myself, '"*Praise the *LORD!"

v2 I will *praise the *LORD all my life.
I will always sing *praises to my God while I am alive.

v3 Do not *trust in human leaders.
Nobody that is only human can save you.

v4 When they die, they return to the ground.
On that day, their plans come to an end.

v5 The person that receives help from the God of Jacob is very happy.
(That person) hopes (for help) from the *LORD their God.

v6 (The *LORD) made the skies and the earth,
the sea and everything that is in them.
He always does what he has promised (to do).

v7 He gives help to people that are *oppressed.
He gives food to the hungry.
He makes people free that are in a prison.

v8 The *LORD makes *blind people see again.
The *LORD lifts up people that have fallen down
(because they carried heavy things).
The *LORD loves people that are *righteous.

v9 The *LORD *protects strangers living in our land,
the children with no fathers and the *widows.
But he does not *protect *wicked people.

v10 The *LORD will always be (your) king.
Zion, he will be your God for all time.
*Hallelujah!

God's Love and *Power
Psalm 147
The 2nd *Hallelujah Psalm

Jesus said, "If God makes the grass green (so that it looks right), how much more will he put (clothes) on you (so that you feel comfortable too)!" (Matthew 6:30)

Psalm 147

v1 *Hallelujah!
It is good to sing *praises to our God.
And it is *pleasant and right to *praise him.

v2 The *LORD is building Jerusalem again.
He is bringing home the *exiles to Israel.

v3 He makes people well again that have *broken hearts.
And he puts *bandages on their *injuries.

v4 He decided how many stars (to make)
and he even gave them all a name.

v5 Our *Lord is great and very powerful.
He understands everything!

v6 The *LORD gives help to poor people
(but) he throws *wicked people to the ground.

v7 Sing to the *LORD and thank him (for what he has done).
Make music to our God with a *harp.

v8 He puts clouds into the sky.
He sends rain to the earth.
He makes the grass grow on the hills.

v9 He gives food for the animals.
He feeds the young *ravens when they cry.

v10 He has no pleasure because a horse is so strong,
nor in the legs of a man (who is riding the horse).

v11 (Instead) the *LORD becomes pleased by people who are *in awe of him.
They *trust in his kind love.

v12 Jerusalem ... *praise the *LORD!
Zion ... *praise your God!

v13 Praise him because he makes your gates strong.
And he is kind to the people inside your (city).

v14 He makes your *borders safe (from an enemy attacking you).
He fills you with the best food.

v15 He tells the earth what to do.
What he says soon reaches it.

v16 He covers (the earth) with snow like a (white) blanket.
He puts *frost everywhere like ashes (that the wind blows).

v17 He sends *hail like small stones.
Nobody can stand up in his *icy wind.

v18 (Then) he sends his word and the ice changes into water.
He makes the wind blow and the water moves.

v19 He showed his word to Jacob.
(He showed) his rules and *laws to Israel.

v20 He has done this for no other country.
They do not know his *laws.
*Hallelujah!

Everything - *Praise The *LORD!
Psalm 148
The 3rd *Hallelujah Psalm

Jesus *commanded the wind and the sea, "Be quiet, and stay quiet!" (Mark 4:39)

Psalm 148

v1 *Hallelujah!
*Praise the *LORD from the *heavens.
*Praise him in the high places.

v2 *Praise him, all his *angels.
*Praise him all his armies (in *heaven).

v3 *Praise him, sun and moon.
*Praise him, all shining stars.

v4 *Praise him, highest *heavens
and the waters above the sky.

v5 They will all *praise the name of the *LORD,
because he created (made) them by his *command.

v6 He has fixed them in their places for all time.
This rule will never change.

v7 - v10 *Praise the *LORD from the earth:
- sea *monsters and all deep waters,
- fire and *hail,
- snow and clouds,
- wind and storm obeying his *commands,
- mountains and all hills,
- fruit trees and all forests,
- wild animals and farm animals,
- *reptiles and flying birds.

v11 - v13a *Praise the name of the *LORD:
- kings of the earth and every country,
- *princes and all rulers on earth,
- young men and young girls,
- old men and children.

v13b (The *LORD's) name is the only great name.
He is king over *heaven and earth.

v14 He has made his people strong.
So all the people that have accepted his kind love will *praise him.
They are the people of Israel who are near to him.
*Hallelujah!

His People
Psalm 149
The 4th *Hallelujah Psalm

Jesus said (to his 12 *disciples), "When the Son of man will sit as king on his *throne, you will also sit on 12 thrones.

You will decide what to do with the 12 *tribes of Israel" (Matthew 19:28). (A disciple is someone that learns from a teacher; Son of man is a name that Jesus called himself; a throne is a special seat that a king sits on; and a tribe is a very large family.)

Psalm 149

v1 *Hallelujah!
Sing a new song to the *LORD.
*Praise him where *his people meet together.

v2 (People of) Israel, be very happy because (God) made you.
Sons of Zion, be very happy because he is your king.

v3 *Praise his name with dancing.
Make music to him with *harp and *tambourine.

v4 (When they do this) his people will give the *LORD pleasure.
He gives help to those who will take it.
He does this so that they can beat (their enemies).

v5 His people will be very happy because he has made them feel important.
They will sing (all night) on their beds because they are so happy.

v6 The *praises of God will always be in their mouths.
Also, *swords with two edges will be in their hands.

v7 - v9 (They must):
- bring (God's) *vengeance on (foreign) countries;
- *punish people (that do not obey God);
- lock their kings (in prison);
- put their leaders in *chains of iron;
- do whatever (God) decided should happen to them.
This is how (God will make) his people feel important.
*Hallelujah!

Jesus said, "If people *held their *peace, the stones would immediately start shouting" (Luke 19:40). ("Held their *peace" means "they said nothing".)

Psalm 150

v1 *Hallelujah!
Shout, "You are the best" to God the *LORD.
Do it in his *temple. Do it in the skies.

v2 Shout, "You are the best" to him because he is very strong.
Shout, "You are the best" to him because he is very powerful.

v3 Sing, "You are the best" to him with music.
Use *horns and *harps and *guitars.

v4 Sing, "You are the best" to him with music.
Use dancing and *drums, *strings and *pipes.

v5 Sing, "You are the best" to him with music.
Use big and small *cymbals.

v6 Everything that is alive, shout to the *LORD, "You are the best".
*Hallelujah!

The Wise Words of a King

Proverbs

About the Book of Proverbs

The Book of Proverbs is about wisdom. King Solomon wrote a very large part of the book.

What God thinks about us is very important. We should do what he wants us to do. The Book of Proverbs teaches us about that. That is the most important lesson about wisdom.

Chapter 1

Important proverbs

1 These are the proverbs of Solomon, David's son, king of Israel.

2 Here are the proverbs that will make you wise. They will help you to understand good messages even when they are difficult.

3 They can help you to understand life. They can teach you how to live a good honest life. And they can teach you how to be fair to everyone.

4 They can cause a person who knows nothing to become clever. And they teach young people what they should know. And they teach them the right way to live.

5 These proverbs can even make wise people more wise. And to those who love to learn, they can give help to know more.

6 In that way, they can understand the thoughts that wise men have hidden in their proverbs and in their words.

Good words for young people

7 You must be afraid of the Lord, even before you begin to learn anything. People who are fools do not listen to wise words. They refuse to learn them.

8 Listen, my son, to the words of your father. And do not forget what your mother taught you.

9 A circle of leaves round your head and a chain round your neck make you more beautiful. In the same way, what your father and mother teach you will make you a better person.

10 When bad men try to cause you to sin, my son, do not do it.

11 They may say, 'Come with us. We will find someone to kill. We will attack people who have not done anything wrong.

12 They may be alive and well when we find them. But they will be dead when we leave them.

13 We will get lots of valuable things and we will fill our houses with them.

14 Come and join us. Our money will be your money. And your money will be our money.'

15 My son, do not go with people like that. Stay away from them.

16 They cannot wait to do something bad. They are always in a hurry to kill.

17 The bird that you want to catch may be watching you. So do not show the bird how you will catch it.

18 In the same way, these men want to kill other men. But in the end, they will die themselves.

19 This is the end of everyone who will kill people to take things from them. That person will die himself as a result.

Someone wise is shouting

20 Listen! Someone wise is shouting in the streets. She is speaking loudly in the market places.

21 She speaks in the city. She shouts loudly at the gates, and in all places where people meet.

22 'Some silly people enjoy being silly. Some people enjoy laughing at those who want to learn. And fools refuse to listen to wise words. All of those people should stop doing those things.

23 I will let you know my thoughts and how I feel. Listen when I tell you about danger.

24 I shouted to you and I asked you to come. But you refused to come. Nobody listened to what I was saying.

25 You refused to listen to my wise words. I told you that you were wrong. But you did not want to hear.

26 So, when you are in trouble, I will laugh at you. When you are afraid, I will laugh at you.

27 You may be afraid as if you were in a storm. Your troubles may be dangerous like a very strong wind. Pain and problems may happen to you.

28 Then you will shout to me, but I will not answer. You will look for me everywhere, but you will not find me.

29 You have never liked to hear wise words and you have always refused to be afraid of the Lord.

30 You have never wanted to listen to my wise words. I told you that you were wrong. But you thought that my words were not important.

31 So now other people will punish you. And everything that you do will make life very difficult for you.

32 Silly people and fools love only themselves. They will die when they do not listen to wise words.

33 But whoever listens to me will live safely. And so he will be really quiet. And he will not be afraid of bad things that might happen to him.'

Chapter 2

The good results of wise words

1 Learn what I teach you, my son. And never forget what I ask you to do.

2 Listen to my wise words and try to understand them.

3 Yes, do not stop asking for wise words. Do not stop asking until you understand.

4 Look for wisdom as you would look for silver. Look for it as for valuable stones that someone has hidden under the ground.

5 So you will know how to be afraid of the Lord. And you will learn about God.

6 It is the Lord who says wise words. He helps us to understand the things that are too difficult for us. He helps us to know what we need to know.

7 He helps good people to be wise. And he keeps honest people safe.

8 He keeps people safe who are fair to other people. And he watches over those people who obey him.

9 Listen to me. So you will know what is right. You will know what are true and fair words. You will know what you should do.

10 You will become wise. And you will have pleasure in the things that you understand.

11 Your good thoughts and the things that you understand will help you. They will be like someone who is watching over you to keep you safe.

12 So you will not do the wrong thing. They will keep you from people who want to cause trouble.

13 Those people are like people who leave the straight paths. They are like people who walk in dark ways.

14 Those people enjoy doing the wrong things. They enjoy doing bad things for no good reason.

15 Those people will not do the right thing. They always do very bad things.

16 An adulteress may say nice things to you. But she will be trying to cause you to do the wrong thing. But, if you have listened to wise words, your mind will be strong. And so you will be safe from that woman.

17 She leaves her own husband. And she forgets the promises that she said to God at the time of her marriage.

18 If you go to her house, you will travel the road to death. Her paths will lead to where dead people are.

19 Nobody who visits her will ever return. He will never return to the way to life.

20 So you must do as good people do. And you must live a good life.

21 People who are good will live in the country. Perfect people will stay in it.

22 But God will remove the bad people from this country. He will pull sinners out like plants from the ground.

Chapter 3

More good words

1 Do not forget what I teach you, my son. Always remember what I ask you to do.

2 What I teach will give you a long and good life. And it will give you peace.

3 Do not let love go, and always do right things. Keep them like valuable stones round your neck and never forget them.

4 If you do that, you will make God happy. And you will make people happy too.

5 Always trust the Lord completely. Do not think that your own wisdom is enough.

6 Remember the Lord in everything that you do. If you do, he will show you the right way to go.

7 Do not think about yourself as wiser than you really are. Be afraid of the Lord and refuse to do wrong things.

8 If you do, it will be like good medicine. It will be like medicine that makes your body well. And it will be like something that makes your bones strong.

9 Obey the Lord's rules with your money and offer him the best things from your farm.

10 If you do, you will not have enough places to store everything from your farm. And you will have more wine than you can keep.

11 My son, the Lord will sometimes punish you. And he will sometimes tell you that you have done wrong things. Do not be angry when he does. And, when the Lord wants you to change something, obey him.

12 A father may be happy that his son is doing good things. But he will tell him if his son has done something wrong. The Lord will do the same to the people that he loves.

13 Happy is anyone who becomes wise. And happy is anyone who finds out what to do.

14 It is better than silver or the best gold.

15 It is better to be wise than to have very valuable stones. Nothing that you want could have more value.

16 If you are wise, you will have a long life. And you will have money, and people will call you a great person.

17 When you are wise, your life will be really good. And you will always be safe.

18 Wise people are happy. They will take hold of the good things of life.

19 The Lord, who is wise, made all the earth. And by wisdom he put the sky where it is.

20 The Lord who is wise, created the rivers and the clouds to give rain to the earth.

21 My son, remember my wise words and do not lose your wisdom. Always be wise when you are choosing what to do.

22 That will keep your soul alive. And your life will be good.

23 You will walk and you will not fall. Your feet will keep to the path.

24 You will not be afraid when you go to bed. And you will sleep well.

25 Bad things happen to bad men. But you will not have to be afraid about bad things that might surprise you.

26 You will be able to trust the Lord. He will not let you fall into a hole that bad men have dug.

27 Do not refuse to do good things to those that need it. Always do good things to them when you can.

28 Do not ask anyone to wait until tomorrow if you can help them today.

29 The man who lives next to you trusts you. So do not think about doing bad things to him.

30 Do not quarrel with other people for no good reason when they have never done anything wrong to you.

31 You should not want to be like bad people. Do not do anything that they do.

32 The Lord hates people who do bad things. But he shows his purposes to good people.

33 The Lord will cause bad things to happen to the homes of bad people. But he does good things to the homes of good people.

34 The Lord laughs at people who laugh at other people. But he is kind to people who have problems.

35 Wise people will be called great. But silly people will not be called great.

Chapter 4

The importance of wise words

1 Listen to what your father teaches you my sons. If you listen, you will understand.

2 The things that I am teaching you are good. So remember them.

3 When I was a little boy, the one son of my parents,

4 my father taught me. He said,

'Remember what I say. And never forget it. Obey my words. If you do, you will live.

5 Look for words that are wise. Look for wisdom! Do not forget my words and do not turn your ear away from them.

6 If you obey my wise words, they will keep you from trouble. If you love them, they will keep you safe.

7 To learn wise words is the most important thing that you can do. Whatever else you get, get wisdom.

8 If you love wise words, they will make you great. Remember that wise words are important. If you do, it will cause people to speak well about you.

9 Everyone will speak well about you when they hear your wise words.'

10 Listen to me, my son, and accept my words. If you do, the years of your life will be many.

11 I have taught you wise words. And I have taught you the right way to live.

12 When you walk, your steps will be sure. And when you run, you will not fall.

13 Always remember what you have learnt. Do not forget it. The things that you have learnt will give you life. So keep them well.

14 Do not go where bad people go. Do not follow the ways of bad people.

15 Do not do it! Keep away from every bad thing! Refuse it and go on your way.

16 Bad people cannot sleep unless they have done something wrong. They lie awake unless they have caused someone to fall.

17 To do bad things is like food and drink to bad men.

18 But the road that good people travel along is like the sunrise. It gets brighter and brighter until it is really day.

19 But the road of bad people is as dark as night. They fall. But they cannot see what has caused them to fall.

20 Listen to what I say, my son. Listen to my words.

21 Never let my words leave you. Think about them and obey them.

22 They will give life to anyone who understands them. And they will give health to their whole body.

23 Be careful how you think. Your thoughts make you the person that you are.

24 Never say anything that is not true.

25 Look straight in front of you. And watch where you are going.

26 You must decide to do things carefully. So whatever you do will be right.

27 Keep away from bad people and walk on a straight path. Do not go one step off the right way.

Chapter 5

A husband who does right things is the best husband

1 My son, listen to my wisdom. And listen to my words that cause you to know.

2 If you do, you will always choose to do the right thing. And your words will show that you are wise.

3 The lips of the wife of another man will be as sweet as honey. Her kisses will be as soft as oil.

4 But in the end, she gives you something that is like a bitter food. It is like a very sharp sword. And you will be sad and angry.

5 She will take you down to the world of dead persons. The road that she walks is the road to death.

6 She does not think about the way to life but she walks away. She does not understand what is happening.

7 So listen to me, my sons. Never forget what I am saying.

8 Keep away from a woman like that! Do not even go near the door of her house.

9 If you do, other people will not speak well about you. You will die young because a cruel person will kill you.

10 Strangers will take all your money. What you have worked for will go into a stranger's house.

11 Near the end of your life, you will shout out because your body will be so sick and weak.

12 You will say, 'I certainly should have learned. People told me that I was doing the wrong things. But I thought that it was not important.

13 I did not listen to my teachers. I did not want to do what they said.

14 In front of all the people I lost the importance that they once gave to me.'

15 Enjoy sex with your own wife.

16 If you have children by other women, they will not help you.

17 Your children should grow up to help you. They should not grow up to help strangers.

18 So be happy with your wife. You married her when you were young. Enjoy the woman that you married.

19 She is pretty and she is as nice to watch as a young animal. Let her body keep you happy at all times. Always enjoy her love.

20 You should not give your love to another woman, my son. You should not go to another man's wife.

21 The Lord sees everything that you do. He is watching you everywhere that you go.

22 The bad things that a bad person does cover him like a net. And his own sin is like ropes that tie him.

23 He will not let anyone tell him that he is wrong. So he will die. He will be like a fool who goes the wrong way.

Chapter 6

The father tells his son again that he must be careful

1 You may have promised to pay the debts of a friend or of a stranger.

2 You may have let a man use your words and promises for his own purposes.

3 So now, you are in the power of that man. Hurry to him and ask him quietly to make you free from your promise.

4 Do not let yourself sleep or even stop to rest.

5 Like a bird or a wild animal that runs away from the hunter, make yourself free.

6 Lazy people should learn a lesson from the way that ants live.

7 They have no leader or ruler,

8 but they prepare their food during the summer. They get it at the time of harvest to prepare for winter.

9 You lie in bed too long, you lazy man! It seems that you will never get up out of bed!

10 'I will have only a short sleep', he says. 'I will stop work and I will rest for a short time.'

11 But while you sleep you will lose all your things. It is as if someone robs you.

12 Bad people go about and they tell everybody false things.

13 They send messages with their eyes, their feet and their fingers. They want people to believe what is false.

14 They think about how to say what is not true. They decide to do bad things all the time. They cause quarrels everywhere.

15 Because of this, very bad trouble will happen to them. It will happen quickly and they will not be able to make things better.

16 There are 6 things that the Lord does not like. There are 7 things that he hates.

17-19

- a person who thinks that he is great

- a mouth that speaks false things

- hands that kill people that have done nothing wrong

- a mind that decides to do what is wrong

- feet that hurry to do bad things

- a person who gives false reports of what he has seen

- someone who causes trouble among friends.

The father tells his son that he should keep away from adulteresses

20 Obey your father's rules, my son. And never forget what your mother taught you.

21 Do not forget their words. Think about them often.

22 When you walk, they will lead you. When you sleep, they will keep you safe. When you wake up, they will speak to you.

23 Their rules and what they taught you are like a light. They told you when you did wrong things. And that showed you how to live.

24 They can keep you away from bad women. An adulteress will say nice things to you. But she wants to cause you to do wrong things.

25 Do not want these beautiful women. And do not let them cause you to do wrong things.

26 A prostitute makes a man poor. He can only buy a loaf of bread. She will rob you of your life.

27 You cannot carry fire next to your body and not burn your clothes.

28 A man cannot walk over a fire and not burn his feet.

29 It is like that when a man sleeps with another man's wife. Punishment will happen to whoever touches her.

30 Someone may rob to get food when he is hungry. So people do not think that he is bad.

31 But if someone catches him, he must pay back more. He must pay back 7 things for each thing that he took. He must give up everything that he has in his house.

32 But an adulterer does not know anything. He destroys himself.

33 Men will hit him. They will no longer think that he is a good man. They will never forget his shame.

34 The husband will have bad thoughts about the adulterer and he will be angry with him. He will punish the adulterer very much.

35 He will not accept any money. He will refuse any amount of gifts.

Chapter 7

1 Remember what I say, my son. Never forget my rules.

2 If you obey my rules, you will live. Keep my words as you keep your eyes safe.

3 Remember my words. Think about them all the time.

4 Love wise words in the same way as you love your sister.
Love wisdom in the same way as you love your special friend.

5 Wisdom will keep you away from the bad wives of other men. They will keep you away from the adulteress. She says nice words but they could cause you to sin.

The adulteress

6 Once I was looking out of the window of my house.

7 I saw a group of young men who did not know very much. Among them was a boy who was not wise.

8 He was walking along the street near the house of a certain woman, and he passed her house.

9 It was in the evening after it was dark.

10 Then she met him. Her clothes were like those that an adulteress wears. And she knew what she wanted to do.

11 She was a bad woman. She never did what she should do. Her feet never stayed at her home.

12 Sometimes she stood in the streets and sometimes she stood in the market place. She waited at the corners of the streets.

13 She put her arms round the young man and she kissed him. She looked into his eyes.

14 She said, 'I have meat from the sacrifices that I made today. Today I have given what I promised to God.

15 So I came out to meet you. I was looking for you, and I have found you.

16 I have covered my bed with cloths from Egypt.

17 And the colour of it and the smell of it are beautiful.

18 Come, let me lie all night in your arms. We can enjoy ourselves with love all night long.

19 My husband is not here. He has gone away on a long journey.

20 He took plenty of money with him and he will not be back for two weeks.'

21 She tried to cause him to sin with her many words of love. She said very nice things to him. So he did everything that she wanted.

22 Immediately he followed her like an ox that men kill for food. He was like a fool that people tie with chains to punish him.

23 Then they kill that man with sharp sticks. He was like a bird that hurries into a net. He did not know that this could be the end of his life.

24 So, my sons, listen to me. Listen to what I say.

25 Do not love that kind of a woman. Do not go after her.

26 She has caused the death of many men. They are too many to count.

27 If you go to her house, you are on the path to the world of dead persons. It is a quick way to die.

Chapter 8

Remember that wise words are important

1 Listen. You should be able to hear the wise words. Wisdom is like a woman who is causing people to hear her.

2 You will hear these words high on the hills along the way. You will hear these words where the paths meet.

3 Next to the gates that go into the city, you will hear these words. Someone will be shouting them aloud at the doors where you go in.

4 'I shout out to all of you, to everyone on earth.

5 You who do not have wisdom, be wise. You who are fools, learn to understand.

6 Listen to my very good words. All that I tell you is right.

7 What I say is true. I hate words that are not true.

8 Everything that I say is true. None of my words are false. They do not turn people on to the wrong path.

9 Wise words are clear to people who understand. Wise words are easy to understand for people who want to learn.

10 Choose my wise words rather than silver. Choose to learn rather than the best gold.

11 Wisdom is more valuable than valuable stones. Nothing that you want can be equal to it.

12 I, wisdom, am like a woman who lives with careful people. She knows many important things. And she knows when to speak.

13 Those who are afraid of the Lord hate wrong things. Some people think that they are great. They think of themselves as better than they really are. And they say false things. I do not like those people.

14 I tell people how to do the right things. I am wise and I am strong.

15 I help kings to rule, and I help rulers to make fair rules.

16 I help rulers to rule. And I help officers who work for the king. I help all the fair judges in the world to do their work.

17 I love those who love me. Whoever looks for me will find me.

18 I make people rich and great. I help people not to waste their money. And I help them to do the right things.

19 What you get from me is better than gold. It is better even than the best gold. It is better than the best silver.

20 I walk the way that is good. I follow the paths that are fair.

21 I make those people rich who love me. I fill their houses with valuable things.

22 A long time ago, the Lord had me. He had me before he created anything.

23 The Lord chose me in the beginning, before the world began.

24 I appeared before he created the seas. I appeared when there was no water on earth.

25 I appeared before he created the mountains. I appeared before he created the hills.

26 I was with him before he created the earth and its fields or even the ground.

27 I was there when he created the sky. I was there when he made the sky separate from the sea.

28 I was there when he put the clouds in the sky. I was there when he opened the streams of waters in the sea.

29 He said how high the waters of the sea should rise. They must not rise any higher than what he said. I was there when he created the earth.

30 I was next to him and I was a help to him every day. I gave him pleasure always. I was happy to be with him.

31 I was happy in his whole world and all the people gave me pleasure.

32 So, my sons, listen to me. Do as I say. If you do, you will be happy.

33 Listen to your teacher. If you are wise, you will not forget his words.

34 Happy is the man who listens to me. He watches every day at my gates, and he waits at my door.

35 Those who find me find life. The Lord will enjoy them.

36 Those who do not obey me hurt themselves. Everybody who does not like me loves death.'

Chapter 9

The wise woman and the silly woman

1 Wisdom is the name of the woman who has built her house. And she has made it beautiful.

2 She has prepared her meat and she has mixed her wine. Also, she has made her table ready.

3 She has sent her servants to shout out from the highest places in the town,

4 'Come in, you people who are not wise yet. Come in you people who are fools.

5 Come, eat my food. Drink the wine that I have mixed.

6 Leave the ways of fools. If you do, you will continue to live. Do what wise people do.'

7 Some people think that they are great. You may tell them that they should not say bad words. But they will say bad things about you. Do not tell a bad man that he is wrong. If you do, he will attack you.

8 Do not tell these people that they are wrong. If you do, they will hate you. You can tell a wise man that he is wrong. If you do, he will love you.

9 Anything that you say to wise men will cause them to be more wise. Good men will learn whatever you tell them.

10 To be afraid of the Lord is the beginning of wisdom. If you know the Holy God you will be wise.

11 Wisdom will give to you more days and even more years of life.

12 If you are wise, you will receive good things. But you may think that wise words are not important. If you do, bad things will happen to you.

13 Some women are not wise. They make a lot of noise. They do not know anything. They are like a woman who is not ashamed.

14 That kind of woman sits at the door of her house. Or she may have a seat at the highest part of the city.

15 She shouts out to people when they pass by. She shouts to those who want to go straight on their way.

16 'Anyone who is silly should come in here', she says. And she says to any man who has no wisdom,

17 'Water that someone did not get honestly seems better to drink. Food that someone eats secretly seems better to eat.'

18 But he does not know that dead people are there. They are down deep where dead persons go.

Chapter 10

The Proverbs of Solomon

1 These are the proverbs of Solomon.

A wise son makes his father happy. A fool makes his mother a sad woman.

2 If you are not honest, your money will not help you. But you should live in the way that God wants you to live. If you do that, it will save you from death.

3 The Lord will not let honest people be hungry. But he will not let bad people get what they want.

4 If a man is lazy, he will be poor. But if he does good work, he will be rich.

5 The man who cuts the plants in his field in the summer is a wise son. But another man sleeps when it is time to work in the field. That man causes his father to be ashamed.

6 God will do many good things for people who live good lives. The words of bad people hide the fact that they are very angry.

7 It is a pleasure to remember good people. But when bad people die, everyone will forget their name.

8 Wise people listen to wise rules. But a fool who talks too much will destroy himself.

9 Honest people are safe. But everyone will know about people who are not honest.

10 Someone who does not speak true words causes trouble. But a fool who talks too much will destroy himself.

11 The words of a good man are like the water that gives life. But the words of bad people hide the fact that they are very angry.

12 People who hate you cause quarrels. But love covers over all sins.

13 Wise people speak wise words, but punishment happens to silly people.

14 Wise people get all the wisdom that they can. But when fools speak, trouble is near.

15 Money keeps rich people safe. But poor people die because they do not have money.

16 The money that good people receive for their work keeps them alive. But what bad people receive is punishment.

17 People may tell a man that he is wrong. If he listens, he will live. But the man who refuses to listen is making a big mistake.

18 Some people say what is not true. They hide the fact that they hate other people. Anyone who says false things about other people is a fool.

19 The more you talk, the more possible it is for you to sin. If you are wise, you will keep quiet.

20 The words of a good person are like the best silver. The ideas of a bad person have no value.

21 The words of a good person will help many people. But you can kill yourself if you are not wise.

22 Good things from the Lord make you rich. And he does not make you sad at the same time.

23 A fool enjoys doing wrong things. But a wise man enjoys doing things that are right.

24 Bad people will get what they are afraid of. Good men will get what they want.

25 When the storm has finished, bad people are no longer there. But good people are always safe.

26 Do not send a lazy person with a message. He will be like bad wine to your teeth, or like smoke to your eyes.

27 If you are afraid of the Lord, you will live longer. Bad people die before their time.

28 What good people hope for makes them happy. What bad people hope for does not happen.

29 The Lord keeps honest people safe. But he punishes those who do wrong things.

30 Good people will always be safe. But bad people will not stay in the country.

31 Good people speak wise words. But the Lord will take away the tongue that speaks bad words.

32 Good people say kind things. But bad people say things that are not kind.

Chapter 11

1 The Lord hates people who do not measure weights honestly. He is happy when they measure things honestly.

2 Some people think that they are great. But they will really be ashamed. But people who do not think like that speak wise words.

3 Good people are honest. So they will always know what is the right thing to do. Bad people say things that are not true. That will destroy them.

4 Much money will not help you on the day of your death. But if you are a good person you can save your life.

5 An honest man walks a straight path. But the bad things that a bad man does will destroy him.

6 The good things that good men do will keep them safe. But the bad plans of cruel men will cause trouble for them.

7 A bad man dies. And then what he wants dies with him. All that he wanted from his power becomes nothing.

8 Trouble does not destroy a good man, but it happens to the bad man instead.

9 People without God can destroy you by the way that they talk. But wise words keep good people safe.

10 When good men do well, people in the city will be happy. Also, people will be happy when bad men die. The people will shout because they are happy.

11 A city becomes great when good men want it to be happy. But the words of bad men destroy it.

12 A silly man thinks that the people near to him are not important. But a man who is wise will not speak.

13 If a man talks too much, he tells people secrets. You can tell your secret to a man who is wise. He will keep it secret.

14 The people in a country will fall if it has no wise men to lead it. But the words of many wise men make the country safe.

15 If you promise to pay the debt of a stranger, you will be sorry. If you do not promise things like that, you will be safe.

16 People think that a beautiful woman is great. But strong men only get money.

17 A kind man causes good things to happen to himself. A cruel man causes trouble for himself.

18 The money that bad men get because of their work will not do any good thing on their behalf. But the man who does the right things will receive good things.

19 The man who decides to do right things will live. But anyone who does wrong things will die.

20 The Lord hates people who make plans to do bad things. But he loves those people who always do the right thing.

21 Be sure about this: The Lord will punish bad people but he will save the children of good people.

22 A beautiful woman may refuse to know what is good. A woman like that is like a gold ring in a pig's nose.

23 What good people want always causes good things to happen. Bad people may get what they want. But then God will punish them.

24 One man gives away his money and he gets even more. Another man refuses to pay his servants for what they have done. And he becomes poor.

25 If you give away your money, you will receive more. If you help other people, they will help you.

26 A man may want to keep the seeds that people can eat from the plants in his field. People will speak bad words against him if he is waiting to get more money. But they will say good things if he sells those seeds to them.

27 The man who looks for good things will be very happy. But the man who looks for trouble will get trouble.

28 A man may think that his money will save him. But he will fall like the leaves in autumn. But the good man will not fall. His valuable things will be like the green leaves in summer.

29 The man who causes trouble for his family will have nothing in the end. And the fool will always be the servant of the wise man.

30 The man who decides to do good things lives a really good life. The man who wins souls is wise.

31 Men who are good receive many good things. You can be sure that bad men will receive punishment.

Chapter 12

1 Some people like to know things. And they want to know when they are wrong. But fools do not want to know when they are wrong. They hate it when someone tells this to them.

2 Good people give pleasure to the Lord. But he punishes those who make plans to do bad things.

3 A man who is bad will never be safe. But good people will never need to be afraid.

4 A good wife gives pleasure to her husband and she makes him happy. But a bad wife makes her husband ashamed. She causes him to be like a man who has weak bones.

5 The plans of honest people are fair. But bad people only want you to believe the false things that they say.

6 The words of very bad people can cause murder. But the words of good people can save lives.

7 Bad men will die and they will not have any children. But the families of good men will live.

8 People speak well about a wise man, but they do not listen to a fool.

9 A man may let people think that he is important. But this same man may not have enough food to eat. It is bad to be a man like that. People may think that another man is not important. But, if that man has a servant, it is better to be a man like that.

10 Good people are kind to their animals. But very bad people are always cruel.

11 A farmer who does much work has plenty to eat. But a fool wastes time on dreams.

12 Bad people look for bad things to do. But good people do well in everything that they do.

13 The words of bad men get them into trouble. But a good man will get out of trouble.

14 When you say all things well, you will get many good things. And when you do all things well, people will give you many good things.

15 The way of a fool seems right to him. But wise people listen to words that help them.

16 A fool lets people know when he is angry. But it is not easy to make a wise man angry.

17 You can believe a man who usually speaks true words. But you cannot believe a man who speaks lies.

18 Careless words can cut like a sharp knife. But to speak wise words can make people well.

19 A false word continues for only a short time. But true words continue for all time.

20 Those people who are bad decide to do bad things. But those people who help other people to live without trouble will be happy.

21 Nothing bad will happen to good people. But nothing but trouble will happen to bad people.

22 The Lord hates people who speak false words. But it gives him pleasure when people are fair to other people.

23 Wise men keep quiet about what they know. But fools shout out silly words.

24 Much work will give you power. But if you are lazy, you will become a servant.

25 If you are afraid, you will not be happy. But kind words will make you happy.

26 A good man is like a guide to his friend. But bad people are like someone who has gone on to the wrong path.

27 The lazy man does not cook the animals that he caught. But another man works well. His good things are very important to him.

28 Good men are like men who follow the road to life. Along that path, there is no death.

Chapter 13

1 A wise son listens to the words of his father. And he does what his father says. But a silly person refuses to listen to anyone. Someone may tell him that he is doing wrong things. But he thinks that it is not important. He laughs about it.

2 Good people will get good things for what they say. Bad people like to fight.

3 The man who is careful with his words keeps his life safe. But the man who is careless with his words destroys himself.

4 A lazy person may want something, but he will not get it. A person who does a lot of work will receive many good things.

5 Honest people hate to speak false words. But the words of bad people make them ashamed. And nobody likes those people.

6 When good people do right things, it keeps them safe. But when sinners do bad things, it causes them trouble.

7 Some people want other people to think that they are rich. But really, they have nothing. Other people want people to think that they are poor. But really, they have a lot of money.

8 A rich man must use his money to save his life. But a poor man has no reason to think that he might lose his life.

9 Good people seem to shine like a bright light. But bad people are like a light that is going out.

10 A man may think that he is great. But he only causes quarrels. But the man who listens to good words is wise.

11 If you have not received your money in an honest way, you will lose it. The man who works to get his money slowly sees it grow.

12 Someone may not receive what he hopes for. So he is very sad. But he may get what he wants. If he does, he is very happy.

13 Do not refuse to listen to wise words. If you do, trouble will destroy you. If you obey wise words, good things will happen to you.

14 The words of wise men are like the water that gives life. They will help you when you might lose your life.

15 People like anyone who speaks wise words. But the person that you cannot trust will be in trouble in the end.

16 Careful people think before they do anything. Silly people let everybody see how silly they are.

17 A bad man brings a message and he causes trouble to himself. But you can trust other people to take a message. And they cause you to feel better.

18 If a man refuses to learn he will be poor. He seems like a fool. But you may tell another man that he is doing wrong things. And he may listen to you. He may think that your words are important. People will think that he is a great man.

19 How good it is to get what you want! But silly people hate to turn away from what is bad.

20 The man who has wise friends will be wise. The man who has silly friends will be in trouble in the end.

21 Trouble seems to follow sinners, but good people will receive good things.

22 When a good man dies, his grandchildren get his money. But a sinner's money will go to those who are good.

23 A poor man may have a lot of food from his farm. But a bad man near to him may destroy it.

24 If you do not punish your son, you do not love him. If you do love him, you will punish him.

25 The good man has enough food to eat, but bad men are always hungry.

Chapter 14

1 The wise woman builds her home. But the silly woman destroys her home with her own hands.

2 An honest man is afraid of the Lord. But some men are not honest. A man like that thinks that the Lord is not important.

3 Fools think that they are great. So, they talk too much. But the words of wise men keep them from what is bad.

4 When a farmer has no oxen, his building will be clean. But if he has oxen, his building will be full of seeds from his farm.

5 An honest person always speaks true words about what he has seen. But a bad person always speaks false words about what he has seen.

6 Some people laugh about wise words. They would like to become wise but they cannot. But wise people learn easily.

7 Stay away from silly people. They have nothing to teach you.

8 A clever person knows what to do. So he is wise. But a silly person is a fool. He only thinks that he knows what to do.

9 Silly people are not sorry when they sin. They laugh about it. But everyone likes good people.

10 When you are happy, you yourself are happy. When you are sad, you yourself are sad. Nobody else is happy or sad with you.

11 The house of a good person will not fall, but anything can destroy the house of a bad person.

12 There is a way that seems right to a man. But in the end, it leads him to death.

13 A man may be sad even when he is laughing. He may smile but he may still not be happy in the end.

14 A man who was good may now be bad. A man like that receives a lot of bad things. But a good man receives a lot of good things.

15 A fool will believe anything. But a careful man will think before he does anything.

16 A wise man is careful to stay out of trouble. But a silly man is careless and he does things too quickly.

17 An angry man does silly things. And people hate a man whose plans cause trouble.

18 People who do not know anything get into trouble. But careful people become wise.

19 Bad people must bend their knees to good people. And they must ask the good people to be kind to them.

20 Nobody likes poor people, not even those near to them. But rich people have many friends.

21 A man may think that he is better than those near to him. A man like that is a sinner. But God does good things on behalf of a man who is kind to poor people.

22 People who try to do bad things make a mistake. But those who do good things for other people will find love and honest friends.

23 All work causes you to have money. But people who talk too much become poor.

24 To a wise man, money is like what a king wears on his head. But a fool does not have anything like that.

25 Someone may speak true words about what he has seen. If he does, he will keep lives safe. But when a man speaks false words, he causes people to believe false things.

26 When a man is afraid of the Lord, he and his family will be safe.

27 To be afraid of the Lord is like the water that gives life. It keeps a man safe, even from death.

28 When a king rules many people, he is great. But without the people, he is nothing.

29 A patient man can understand many things, but an angry man does not know anything.

30 A mind that does not have trouble causes the body to be well. But when someone thinks bad thoughts about other people, he becomes sick.

31 A man may be cruel to poor people. But really he thinks bad things about God who created them. But whoever is kind to poor people worships God.

32 When bad men do wrong things, they destroy themselves. But good men have hope even in death.

33 Wise people think wise thoughts. But fools show everyone that they know nothing about wise thoughts.

34 A country becomes great when it does right things. But sin makes its people ashamed.

35 A wise servant gives the king pleasure. But the king is angry with the servant who causes shame.

Chapter 15

1 A person stops being angry when people answer him kindly. But a cruel word makes a person angry.

2 When wise people speak, other people want to learn from them. But fools say many silly things.

3 The Lord sees what happens everywhere. He is watching everyone - whether they are good or bad.

4 Kind words cause life for other people. But words that are not honest make you sad.

5 A fool hates his father's rules and punishment. But a wise son listens to him and learns.

6 Good people have many valuable things in their house. But the valuable things of bad people cause them trouble.

7 It is wise people, not fools, who teach wise words.

8 The Lord hates the animals that bad people give to him. But it gives pleasure to the Lord when good people pray.

9 The Lord hates the way of bad people. But he loves the way of good people.

10 If you do wrong things, you will receive punishment. Someone may tell you that you are doing wrong things. If you hate that, you will die.

11 Death and the things that destroy people lie open in front of the Lord. Even more open to him are the secret thoughts of men.

12 Some people laugh about wise words. A man like that does not love someone who says to him, 'You are doing wrong things.' He will not go to wise people.

13 When people are happy, they smile. But when they feel sad inside themselves, their spirit is in trouble. They seem to lose their love of life.

14 Wise people want to learn. But silly people want to know about silly things.

15 All the days of poor people are sad. But happy people enjoy life.

16 You may be poor but you obey the Lord. That is better than if you are rich and in trouble.

17 It is good to eat vegetables with people that you love. That is better than to eat good meat with people who hate you.

18 Angry people cause quarrels, but patient people cause everything to be quiet.

19 If you are lazy, you will find difficulty everywhere. But if you are honest, everything will be easy.

20 A wise son makes his father happy. But a silly man thinks that his mother is silly.

21 Fools are happy when they do silly things. But wise people will do what is right.

22 Good ideas become like nothing without the wise words of many people to help. But if you listen to those wise words, you will win.

23 When you hear the right word at the right time, it makes you happy.

24 A wise man walks a path that causes him to have life, not death.

25 The Lord will destroy the homes of bad men. But he keeps valuable things safe on behalf of women without husbands.

26 The Lord hates bad thoughts, but friendly words give him pleasure.

27 A man may want to get a lot of money in ways that are not honest. A man like that causes trouble for his family. But a man who refuses to speak false words for money will keep himself alive.

28 Good people think before they answer. Bad people answer quickly, but the answer causes trouble.

29 The Lord does not listen to bad people. But when good people pray, he does listen.

30 A face that smiles makes you happy. Good news makes you feel better.

31 You can tell some men that they have done wrong things. Your words could save their life. If they listen to you, they will live among wise men.

32 Some men hate punishment. But a man like that really thinks that his own life is not important. But another man wants to learn and he obeys wise words. That man becomes wise.

33 When a man is afraid of the Lord, it teaches him to be wise. And some people do not think that they are great. But other people will say that they are great.

Chapter 16

1 We may have good ideas. But only God can help you to say the right thing.

2 Whatever you do may be right in your own mind. But the Lord knows why a man wants to do things.

3 If you bring your ideas to the Lord, he will help you to do them well.

4 The Lord has created everything for his purpose. And the purpose of bad people is death.

5 Some people think that they are great. The Lord hates them and he will punish them always.

6 God will cover your sins if you are kind and honest. And if you are afraid of the Lord, you will turn away from bad things.

7 When you give pleasure to the Lord, God will make even your enemies into your friends.

8 It is better to be poor and good than to get rich and not to be fair.

9 You may have your ideas. But it is God who leads you.

10 The king speaks with authority from God. He will be a good judge.

11 The Lord wants people to be honest when they weigh anything. And he wants people to be honest when they measure anything. He wants those people who sell things to be fair.

12 Kings hate to do wrong things. When a king does the right things, he becomes strong.

13 Kings like to hear honest words. They will love those people who speak true words.

14 If the king becomes angry, someone may die. So a wise man will try to make the king happy.

15 When the king smiles, it means life. It is like a cloud that gives rain in the spring.

16 It is better to become wise than to get gold. It is better than to have a lot of silver.

17 A good man keeps away from what is bad. So watch where you are going. It may keep your life safe.

18 A man may think that he is great. He will really destroy himself in the end. A man may think that he is better than everyone else. A man like that will soon fall.

19 A man may think that he is great. So he robs other people. You should not receive any of those things when he gives them out. It is better not to have those things and to live among poor people. It is better to think that you are not important.

20 If you listen to good words, you will do well. A man who trusts the Lord is happy.

21 A wise man understands many things. So people call him a clever man. It is easy to learn when the words are nice.

22 For a wise man, wisdom is like the water that gives life. But fools cause their own punishment because they are silly.

23 Wise people think before they speak. What they say helps other people to learn.

24 Honey is sweet to taste and it is good for your health. Kind words are like that.

25 There is a way that seems right to a man. But, in the end, it causes his death.

26 It is not a bad thing when a worker feels hungry. It causes him to work more.

27 Bad people look for ways to hurt other people, and even their words are like a fire.

28 A bad man causes quarrels. And the careless words of a man can cause friends to be separate.

29 A cruel man causes those near to him to believe false things. And he causes them to do wrong things.

30 A man may close one eye when he looks at you. Or he may move his lips in a strange way. Be careful, because he may be thinking about something bad.

31 Long life is a gift to good people. Grey hair is like the beautiful thing that kings wear on their heads.

32 A patient man does not become angry quickly. He is better than a strong man. A man like that is better than a soldier who beats the enemies in a city.

33 People use lots to choose the right thing. But God causes the result.

Chapter 17

1 You may have to eat a bit of dry bread. But to eat it with a quiet mind is better than to eat plenty in a house full of quarrels.

2 A wise servant will rule over a son that makes his father ashamed. He will receive part of the valuable things of his master when his master dies.

3 Fire will show how good gold and silver are. In the same way, the Lord shows what a man is like.

4 Bad people listen to bad ideas. Those who speak false words listen to false words.

5 You should not say things that are not kind about poor people. If you do, you are not speaking well about God. You should not be happy when trouble has happened to someone. If you are, God will punish you.

6 Grandparents enjoy their grandchildren. In the same way, children think that their parents are great.

7 It does not seem right when a fool speaks very good words. It seems even worse when a ruler does not speak true things.

8 Some people think that a bribe does impossible things. They believe that it can do anything.

9 People may do bad things to you. If you want them to love you, do not remember those bad things. Remember that those bad things can cause a quarrel among very good friends.

10 You can tell a wise man that he has done something wrong. He will learn from that, but a fool learns nothing. He will not learn, even if someone hits him 100 times.

11 A man that always causes trouble wants bad things to happen. So a cruel man will tell him bad news.

12 When someone takes a young animal away from its mother, the mother is very angry. But it is better to meet this mother animal than to meet a fool who is doing silly things.

13 Do not give bad things for what is good. If you do, bad things will always happen to you and to your family.

14 To start a quarrel is like the first small hole in a dam. Stop it before it is too late.

15 People may let a man be free when he has done wrong things. Or they may punish a man who has not done anything wrong. The Lord hates it when people do those things.

16 Money does not do anything good for a fool because he does not want to be wise.

17 A friend loves at all times and a brother is always there to help at the bad times.

18 Only a fool promises to pay the debts of another man.

19 A man who loves a quarrel really loves sin. And a man may think of himself as great because of what he does. Or he may build a better house than he has money for. But he is really causing trouble for himself in the end.

20 A man who thinks wrong things cannot do well. The man who speaks false words gets into trouble.

21 To have a foolish son makes parents sad. The father of a fool is never happy.

22 A happy mind is like good medicine. But when you are sad and lonely you will become ill.

23 Bad judges may take money secretly. Then they are not fair to anybody.

24 A wise man judges things with wisdom. But a fool looks everywhere.

25 To have a foolish son makes his father sad. And it makes his mother very sad.

26 It is not good to punish a man who has done nothing wrong. And it is not good to hit officers because they have been honest.

27 A wise man is careful with the words that he uses. A man who is wise always keeps quiet.

28 Even a fool seems to be wise if he keeps quiet. He should keep his mouth shut. So people will think that he is wise.

Chapter 18

1 People who are not friendly with other people think only about themselves. They will refuse to listen to what everyone else knows to be right.

2 A fool finds no pleasure in wisdom, but he likes to show his own thoughts and ideas.

3 Sin and shame happen together. And shame means that people do not like you.

4 The words that a wise man speaks are like deep waters. They are like a cool stream.

5 You should not refuse to punish bad people. That would not be good. But do not punish people who have not done anything wrong.

6 When a fool speaks, he starts a quarrel. Then, he will receive punishment.

7 When a fool speaks, he causes trouble for himself. He cannot escape from the results of his own lies.

8 Lies about other people have much interest and often we believe them.

9 A lazy person is like someone who destroys things.

10 The name of the Lord is like a strong building. Good people can run there and then they will be safe.

11 Rich people think that their money makes them safe like high, strong walls round a city.

12 Something will happen to destroy a proud man. But people will like a man who is not proud. They will think that he is great.

13 Listen before you answer. If you do not listen, you are a silly fool.

14 When a man is sick, his spirit helps him. But nobody can live if his spirit is not strong.

15 Wise people are always learning. Wise people always want to listen.

16 If you want to meet a great person, take a gift to him. Then it will be easy.

17 Two men may argue with each other. The first man will seem right until the second man speaks.

18 Two powerful men may argue. Then they can use lots to find the right answer.

19 You may make a brother angry. It will be difficult to become friends with him again. It will be more difficult than it would be to beat the people in a strong city. And it is more difficult to stop quarrels than it is to get into a strong building.

20 You have to live with the result of the words that you speak.

21 Words are able to save life and to cause death. So you must accept the result of what you say.

22 If you find a wife, you find a good thing. It shows that the Lord is good to you.

23 A poor man asks for help, but a rich man replies with angry words.

24 A man with many friends may lose them. But there is a friend who keeps nearer than a brother.

Chapter 19

1 It is better to be poor but honest than to be a fool that speaks lies.

2 Not to know the facts is not good. And if you hurry, you will get into trouble.

3 Some people do silly things and so they destroy themselves. Then they get angry with the Lord.

4 Rich people are always finding new friends. But poor people only have a few friends. And poor people cannot even keep those friends.

5 If you tell lies to an officer he will put you in a prison. A man who tells lies will not be a free man.

6 Many people try to be a friend of an important person because of the gifts that he gives to them.

7 The family of a poor man does not want to know him. His friends do not want to know him. Even if he shouts to them, he cannot find them.

8 It is good for a man to learn all that he can. Remember what you learn. If you do, you will get good things.

9 If you tell lies to an officer he will put you in a prison. A man who tells lies will die.

10 Fools should not live in rich houses and slaves should not rule over sons of kings.

11 A man who speaks wise words is patient. It is good to forget a wrong thing.

12 When the king is angry he makes a noise like a lion. But when he is kind, it is like nice rain.

13 A father loses all his money when his son is a fool. A woman who quarrels with her husband makes him tired. Her words are like rain that never stops.

14 When his parents die a man can receive their house and money. But only the Lord can give him a wise wife.

15 A lazy man sleeps during the day. And that kind of man will be hungry.

16 If you obey God's rules, you will live. If you are careless about them, you will die.

17 To be kind to a poor man is the same as to give money to the Lord. He will give it back to you.

18 When your son is young, do not help him to his death. Punish him until he obeys the rules.

19 Do not help an angry man, because he will get into trouble all the time. If you help him, you will have to do it again and again.

20 If you listen to wise words, you also will be wise at the end of your life.

21 A man may have lots of ideas. But the Lord will do what he wants to do.

22 It is a good thing for a man to be kind. And it is better to be poor than to tell lies.

23 If you are afraid of the Lord, you will live a long life. You will be happy and safe from trouble, even while you are asleep.

24 A lazy man puts his hand into his food. But then he is too lazy to put the food into his own mouth.

25 Punish a fool. So people who do not know any better can learn a lesson. But someone who is wise will learn. He will learn what other people teach him.

26 The man who robs his father is a bad son. And the man who sends his mother away from his home will make her ashamed.

27 Son, listen when someone is teaching you. If you do not, you will soon forget their wise words. And you will soon forget what you have already learnt.

28 Nobody can stop a bad witness telling lies. And bad people love to do wrong things.

29 People will punish someone who laughs about wisdom. And they will hit fools.

Chapter 20

1 When you drink too much alcohol you become loud and silly. And you want to fight people. It is not wise to become a drunk.

2 An angry lion frightens you, so also should an angry king. If you make him angry, it will cause you to die.

3 Any fool can quarrel, but a wise man will not quarrel.

4 A lazy farmer who does not plough his fields in winter will have nothing to eat in the summer.

5 The thoughts of a man are like deep waters. But a wise man understands them.

6 Many men say that they love other people. But there are not many men that you can trust.

7 An honest father does what is right. He has happy children.

8 A king looks at a man. Then he will know if that man is bad.

9 Nobody can say, 'I have done nothing wrong.' Nobody can say, 'I have not sinned.'

10 Some people weigh or measure things in a wrong way. The Lord hates people who are like that.

11 What children do is important. It shows what they are like. And you will know if they are honest and good.

12 The ears are to hear with and the eyes are to see with. The Lord made them both.

13 Too much sleep will make you poor. If you keep awake, you will have plenty of food.

14 A man may buy something at a good price. But he says that the price is too much. He goes away. Then he likes to say that he was really clever. He was clever because he bought something so cheap.

15 Wise words are better than gold or many valuable stones.

16 You should not promise to pay the debts of a stranger. That would be silly. If you do, you might lose your own clothes or your things.

17 You may eat something that is not yours. It may seem good when you taste it. But soon it will seem like sand.

18 Ask for help when you do not know what to do. If you do, you will do well. Do not go to war unless you prepare for it. First ask wise people what you should do.

19 Stay away from people who talk too much. They will tell everybody about your secrets.

20 Do not speak bad words to your parents. If you do, you will soon die. Your life will be like a light that goes out in the dark.

21 The more easily you get rich, the less good it will do to you in the end.

22 Do not say, 'You have hurt me so I will hurt you.' The Lord himself will make it right.

23 The Lord hates people who rob customers. It is not good to do that.

24 The Lord decides the way that a man should go. Nobody knows the way that he should go.

25 Be careful before you say a promise to God. You might not be able to do what you promised.

26 A wise king will know who is doing wrong things. He will be angry and he will punish that person very much.

27 The Lord knows the spirit of a man. He knows him completely.

28 A king will continue to live for as long as he rules honestly and fairly. And he will continue to be king while he does the right things.

29 Young men show how strong they are. Grey hair shows that a man is old and wise.

30 Often only pain can cause us to change what we do.

Chapter 21

1 The Lord can change the king's mind. The Lord does what he wants to do. The Lord can change the direction of a stream. In the same way, the Lord can change the thoughts of a king.

2 Everybody thinks that he always does right things. But it is the Lord who knows your thoughts.

3 Do what is right and fair. That gives pleasure to the Lord more than sacrifice.

4 Bad people think that they are better than anyone else. That is a sin.

5 A careful man thinks before he does anything. So he will have plenty. A man may not think before he does anything. That man will become poor.

6 You may get money because you tell lies. If you do, that money will go soon. But it will cause your death.

7 Punishment happens to bad people who do bad things. They refuse to do what is right.

8 Bad people do wrong things. Good people do what is right.

9 It is better to live on the roof of your house than to live with a wife that argues.

10 Bad people want to do bad things all the time. They are not kind to anyone.

11 A fool laughs about wise words. You should punish that man. That will help to teach the man who is not wise. When you teach a wise man, he will understand more.

12 The righteous God knows what happens in the homes of bad people. They will become poor because God will make them poor.

13 Some people refuse to listen when poor people ask for help. So nobody will listen when they ask for help.

14 If someone is angry with you, give him a gift. This secret gift will make him quiet.

15 When anyone does right things, good people are happy. But bad people are often very much afraid.

16 A man may refuse to understand what is right. If he refuses, he will die.

17 The man who loves pleasure will become poor. A man who eats expensive food will never get valuable things. A man who drinks too much alcohol will never get valuable things.

18 Bad people cause to themselves the pain that they try to cause to good people.

19 It is better to live in wild places than to live with a wife who is always quarrelling.

20 Wise people are rich. And there is good food in their house. But when silly people get money, they waste it immediately.

21 If you are kind and honest, you will live a long life! Other people will be fair to you. And they will think that you are great.

22 A wise man attacks the city of strong men. They think that its walls will keep them safe. But the wise man destroys the walls.

23 Be careful what you say. If you are careful, bad things will not happen to you.

24 A proud person thinks that he is better than other people. He thinks only about himself. And he laughs about wise words.

25 Lazy people refuse to work. They will die before they need to die.

26 They think only about what they would like to have. But a good man gives away his money and he does not count the cost.

27 The Lord will hate sacrifices from bad people. Sometimes they do it because of the wrong reasons. So he hates it even more.

28 You cannot believe a man who tells lies. And he will die. But a careful man listens before he speaks. You can believe him. And he speaks for all time.

29 Good people believe in themselves. But bad people hide what they really believe.

30 You cannot know anything if the Lord is against it. And you cannot understand anything if the Lord is against it. And you cannot be cleverer than he is.

31 You can make horses ready for war. But it is the Lord who helps you to beat your enemies.

Chapter 22

1 If you have to choose a good name or lots of money, choose a good name. You should want people to think that you are great. That is better than silver or gold.

2 Rich people and poor people meet together. The Lord created them all.

3 A wise man sees the danger and he hides himself. But a man who does not think will walk immediately into danger and punishment.

4 Do not think that you are important. And be afraid of the Lord. If you do those things, you will get many valuable things. And you will have a long life. And people will say that you are very good.

5 Stay away from the paths of bad people. They are dark and dangerous.

6 Teach children how they should live. They will remember it all their lives.

7 People lend money. They rule over those who receive it. And rich people rule over poor people.

8 A bad man who causes trouble for other people will cause trouble for himself. He will no longer have the power to rule over other people.

9 Give some of your food to poor people. The Lord will bless you because you do.

10 Send away a man who is too proud. Then there will be nothing to argue about. It will be the end of all quarrels and shame.

11 Some men love to do what is right in front of the Lord. They speak well to everyone. They will have the king as a friend.

12 The Lord watches over words that are true. And he does not forget the words of bad men. He does not let them become true.

13 A lazy man stays in his house. He says, 'There is a lion outside. It might kill me in the street.'

14 The mouth of an adulteress is like a deep hole. The Lord is angry with those who fall into it.

15 A child loves to do silly things. You must hit him when he does wrong things. If you do, he will learn to do right things.

16 A man may take money from poor people because he hopes to become rich. Another man may give gifts to rich people because he hopes to become rich. But both those men will become poor.

17 Listen. I will teach you what wise people have said. Study what they have taught.

18 If you remember those things, you will be happy. Try to remember them and to repeat them.

19 I want you to hope in the Lord. So, I will tell you now what they have taught.

20 I have written down 30 proverbs for you. They will make you wise. They will give good ideas to you. And they will teach you what is true.

21 Someone may send you to discover what is true. If he does, you should bring back the right answer.

22 You are stronger than poor people. It is wrong to do cruel things to them. Sometimes, when they bring people to the rulers, those people do not have anybody to speak on their behalf.

23 The Lord will speak on their behalf. A rich person may try to take everything that poor people have. If he does, the Lord will take away the life of that rich person.

24 Do not be a friend to people who are very, very angry.

25 You might become like them and you might always be an angry person.

26 Do not promise to pay the money that someone else should have paid.

27 If you are unable to pay, they will take away even your bed.

28 Do not move the old stones that your fathers and their fathers put there. They show the border of your land.

29 The king will give work to a man who works well. But he has to do better than most men.

Chapter 23

1 When you sit down to eat with a ruler be careful.

2 Even if you enjoy your food, do not eat too much of it.

3 Do not want his special food. He put it there so that you would seem like a fool.

4 Do not try to get rich and so make yourself ill.

5 Your money can go very quickly. It can seem to grow wings and to fly away like a big bird.

6 A man can be too careful about his money. His food seems good when you taste it. But do not eat it or want it.

7 He says, 'Please have some more', but he is thinking, 'Do not have any more.'

8 The food will make you sick and all your nice words will mean nothing.

9 Do not speak wise words to a fool. He will not understand them. And he will think that they are silly.

10 Never move an old stone that shows the border of someone's land. Never take the land from children who have neither father nor mother.

11 The Lord is strong on their behalf. He will speak against you.

12 Listen to your teacher. And learn all that you can.

13 Your children must obey you. If you hit them with a stick, you will not kill them.

14 Hit them with a stick. It will save their lives.

15 Son, if you become wise, I will be very happy.

16 I will be very happy when I hear you speak words of wisdom.

17 Do not want to be the same as very bad people. Obey the Lord during all your life.

18 If you do, you will be happy in future days. And what you hope for will not come to an end.

19 Listen, my son, and remember to live a wise life.

20 Do not be a friend of people who drink too much alcohol. Do not be a friend of people who eat too much.

21 They will become poor. And if you sleep too much, your clothes will soon have holes in them.

22 Listen to your father. You would not be alive without him. Your mother will get old. But do not think that she is not important then.

23 Buy wise words and do not sell them. They are worth the money. They are too valuable for you to sell. Get wisdom. Learn all that you can.

24 The father of a good man will be happy. He can have pleasure in a wise son.

25 Give pleasure to your father and mother. And make your mother happy.

26 Watch me, my son. Be happy to live as I live.

27 Prostitutes cause men to sin. And an adulteress is very dangerous.

28 They take husbands away from their wives. They take men who are not theirs. This happens to more men all the time.

29-30 Show to me someone who drinks too much alcohol. And he likes to taste new drinks. Then I will show to you someone who is sad and sorry for himself. He always causes quarrels. He is always saying that something is wrong. His eyes are red. His body has marks where he has hurt himself.

31 Do not look at wine when it is red. Do not look at it when it shines in the cup. Do not look at it when it goes down easily.

32 In the end, it bites like a snake with all its poison.

33 Your eyes will see strange things. And you will not think or speak easily.

34 You will be like a man on a ship who is asleep in a storm.

35 'They hit me', he says, 'but they did not hurt me. They hit me and I do not remember it. I hope that I will wake up soon. I need another drink.'

Chapter 24

Wise words

1 Do not want for yourself what bad people have. Do not want to be with them.

2 To cause trouble is all that they think about. They say that they will hurt people.

3 A wise man needs good plans to build a house.

4 When he knows what to do, he can fill his rooms with beautiful and valuable things.

5 A wise man is better than a strong man. To know about things makes a man stronger.

6 You must think carefully before you go to war. You can win only if you listen to the words of many wise men.

7 A fool cannot understand wise words. He has nothing to say about important things.

8 People will know the man who makes plans to do bad things.

9 Any idea that a fool thinks about is a sin. People hate a person who causes other people to seem like fools.

10 If you are weak in times of trouble, you are very weak.

11 You may see people who are leading a man to his death. Or you may see people who are going to their own death. Then you should save those people.

12 You may say that you knew nothing about this. But God knows your thoughts. He knows whether they are right or wrong. He always watches you. He will give gifts to you because of what you have done. He will punish you for what you have not done.

13 Son, eat honey. It is good for you. Honey is sweet when you taste it.

14 In the same way, wise words are good for your life. If you find them, you will have hope for future days. What you hope for will not come to an end.

15 Some bad people rob honest people. Do not be like them. Do not destroy the homes of honest people.

16 Trouble might happen 7 times to honest people and they may make mistakes. But in the end, all will be well. But trouble will destroy bad people.

17 Do not be happy when trouble happens to your enemies. Do not feel happy when they make mistakes.

18 The Lord will know if you laugh about the troubles of your enemies. He will not like it. Then he might not punish them.

19 Do not be afraid of bad people. Do not want to be like them.

20 A bad man will not have anything good in future times. He will not have anything to hope for.

21 Be afraid of the Lord and of the king, my son. Obey them. Do not be friends with people who do not obey them.

22 The life of a man can change in a moment. God and the king can cause problems that could destroy those men.

More wise words

23 These are also proverbs of wise people.

Judges must say fairly who is wrong or right. They should not always say that their friends are right. And they should not always say that their enemies are wrong. It is not good if they do those things.

24 A judge must not say to a bad person, 'You are a good person.' If the judge does say that, everyone will shout bad words against him.

25 It will be well with judges who punish bad people. God will do good things on their behalf.

26 A true friend gives an honest answer.

27 Finish the work outside and in your fields. After that, build your house.

28 Do not say wrong things about a person who lives near to you. Do not tell lies about him.

29 Do not say, 'I will do to him what he did to me. I will punish that man because of what he did.'

30 I walked past the field of a lazy person. And I walked past the vineyard of a silly person.

31 There were weeds over all the ground. And the wall of stones round them had fallen down.

32 I looked at this and I thought about it. Then I learned a lesson.

33 Perhaps you say, 'I will sleep for a short time. I will put my hands together and I will rest.'

34 But while you are asleep you will become poor. You will become as poor as when a man had robbed you. You will be as if a soldier had taken away all your things.

Chapter 25

More of the Proverbs of Solomon

1 These are more of the proverbs of Solomon. Hezekiah's men wrote them down when Hezekiah was king of Judah.

2 God hides things because he is great. But great kings discover things.

3 You never know what a king is thinking. His thoughts are beyond us like the sky that is so high above us. His thoughts are beyond us like the earth that is so deep beneath us.

4 Take the dirt out of the silver. Then the man that works with the silver can make a beautiful thing.

5 Keep very bad men away from the king. Then his government will be good.

6 Perhaps you may stand in front of the king. Do not try to cause him to think that you are great. And do not stand where the important people stand.

7 It will be good if the king asks you to sit on a more important seat. That would be better than if he asks you to give your seat to someone more important than you.

8 Do not be too quick to tell a ruler about something that you have seen. Another man may tell the ruler something different. You may be wrong. Then you will not know what you should do.

9 If you and another man argue, try to agree with him. Do not tell his secrets.

10 If you do tell his secrets, everyone will hear them. People will always think that you are a bad person.

11 A wise word is like apples of gold on a silver plate.

12 The words of a wise man are like a gold ring for the ear. They are like gold round the neck. Only someone who wants to learn will hear them.

13 A good man may bring messages from his master. He helps his master who sent him. He is like cold water during the time of harvest. He helps his master to feel better.

14 Some people promise things that they never give. They are like clouds and wind that bring no rain.

15 A careful man who works slowly can change the thoughts of a ruler. And a careful word can change the thoughts of an angry man.

16 Never eat more honey than you need. If you eat too much honey, you will be a sick man.

17 Do not visit the people who live near to you too often. They may get tired of you and you will make them angry.

18 Some men tell lies about those people who live near to them. They are like the heavy sticks or the sharp knives or the arrows that soldiers use.

19 A man who is not honest in times of trouble is like a bad tooth or a bad foot.

20 To sing to a sad man is the same as to put salt into places on his body that hurt. Or it is like someone who takes away his coat on a cold day.

21 If your enemy is hungry, feed him. If he needs a drink, give it to him.

22 You will make him ashamed and the Lord will give gifts to you.

23 The north wind brings rain. And a man who tells lies about people makes them angry.

24 It is better to live on the roof than to live in a house with a quarrelling wife.

25 As cold water is to a tired person, so is good news from a faraway country.

26 Sometimes a good person does what a very bad person wants him to do. It is like when you drink dirty water. It is like when you take water from a dirty well.

27 Too much honey is bad for you. It is wrong, also, when you want people to speak well about you.

28 An angry man is a weak man. He is like a city without walls that an enemy attacks.

Chapter 26

1 It is not right to say good words about a fool. It is like snow in summer. It is like rain at the time of harvest.

2 Sometimes people may say bad words about you. They may hope that bad things will happen to you. But if you have not done anything wrong, those words will have no power over you. They are like birds that never stop flying.

3 You have to hit a fool like you have to hit a horse or a donkey.

4 You are silly if you answer a silly question. You are as silly as the person who asked the question.

5 If someone asks a silly question, give him a silly answer. So he will know that he is not so wise. He is not as wise as he thinks.

6 If you let a fool deliver a message there will be trouble. It will be as bad as to cut off your own feet.

7 A fool cannot use a proverb. It is like the legs of a man who cannot walk.

8 To speak well about a fool is as silly as to fight with a sword that you have broken.

9 When a fool speaks a proverb, he is like a drunk. He is like a man who has drunk too much alcohol. He cannot even pick a sharp hard point of wood from his hand.

10 A soldier who fights everyone is no help to his master. The man who gives work to a fool is like that soldier. Someone who gives work to a stranger is as silly.

11 A sick dog cannot keep in its stomach what it has eaten. But then the dog eats it again. That is like a fool who makes the same mistakes again.

12 Some men think that they are wise. But really, they are not. Silly fools are better than those men.

13 A lazy man does not go out of the house. He says that there is a lion in the street.

14 A lazy person turns over in bed. A door opens and closes. And he is like that door.

15 A lazy man puts his hand into his food. But then he is too tired to put the food into his own mouth.

16 A wise man can give a good answer to any question. But a lazy person thinks that he is wiser than 7wise men.

17 Only a fool speaks in a quarrel among strangers. He is like someone who holds on to the ears of a dog.

18-19 A man may tell lies and then laugh about it. Do not listen to him. He is like a man who shoots everywhere with arrows. He is like a man who throws burning sticks about.

20 Without wood, a fire goes out. When nobody argues about other people, quarrels stop.

21 With wood, a fire continues to burn. In the same way, a man who causes trouble causes a quarrel to continue.

22 To say bad things about other people is like when you eat nice food.

23 Nice words from a bad man are like a cheap pot that shines.

24 A man who hates somebody can speak good words. But he is speaking lies. And nobody knows what he is really thinking.

25 The words of a bad man may seem good. But do not believe him, because there are 7 sins in his mind.

26 He may hide his sin. But everyone will see the bad things that he does.

27 If a man digs a very deep hole, he will fall into it. If a man rolls a stone, it will roll back on him.

28 If you tell lies about someone, you hate them. Bad words destroy the man who listens to them.

Chapter 27

1 Do not say what great things you will do tomorrow. You do not know what will happen between now and then.

2 Let other people say how good you are. Let a stranger do it. Never do it yourself.

3 Stone is heavy and sand is heavy too. But the silly words of a fool are like something that is heavier than both.

4 An angry man is a cruel man who destroys everything. But a man is worse who will do anything to get other people's things.

5 A good friend will tell you when you have done something wrong. He will tell you even in front of other people. That is better than someone who loves you secretly.

6 Do not let the painful words of a friend frighten you. But be careful when an enemy meets you with a kiss.

7 A person who is full of food will refuse honey. But to a hungry person, any bitter thing seems sweet.

8 A man may leave his home. Then he is like a bird that leaves its home.

9 Oil that has the smell of flowers makes you happy. Also, wise words from a friend make you happy.

10 Do not forget your friends and do not forget the friends of your father. If you are in trouble, do not ask someone from your family for help. A friend who lives near to you can help you. He can help you more than your family if they live far away.

11 If you are wise my son, I will be happy. And I will be able to answer anyone that uses bad words against me.

12 A careful man can see danger and he will hide himself. But the fool never stops and he goes into danger.

13 Take a coat from someone who promises to pay the debts of a stranger or of an adulteress.

14 Do not say nice things to your friends early in the morning with loud words. They will think that you are using bad words against them.

15 On some days, the rain continues to fall and it never stops. A wife who always quarrels is like that.

16 You can never keep her quiet. Anyone who can keep her quiet could stop the wind! And he could hold oil in his hand!

17 People learn from each other, as an iron tool makes iron sharp.

18 A careful man will eat the fruit from his own trees. And a master will give gifts to a man that is a good servant.

19 A man can see his face in water. In the same way, a man can understand the thoughts of another man.

20 The place of the dead people is never full. In the same way, the eyes of a man never get tired because they continue to look.

21 Fire cleans gold and heat cleans valuable metals. In the same way, if a man hears good words about himself, he will show his true nature.

22 Even when you hit a fool with a big stick it is not possible to remove all his silly ideas.

23 Always watch over your sheep and your cows.

24 A man can lose his valuable things and a country can lose its king.

25 You cut the yellow grass and new grass appears. Then you cut the green grass on the hills.

26 You make clothes from your sheep. When you sell your goats, you can use the money to buy a field.

27 Your other goats will give enough milk for you, for your family and for your servants.

Chapter 28

1 The bad man runs when nobody is running after him. But a good person is as brave as a lion.

2 When the people in a country sin, they will have many rulers. But a country will be strong when it has a wise leader.

3 A poor man that does bad things to weak people is like a lot of rain. It is like rain that destroys the harvest.

4 Men that do not obey the rules speak well about bad people. But men that obey the rules are against bad people.

5 Bad people do not understand what is fair. But there are people that want to know the Lord more than anything else. They are the people that do fair things.

6 It is better to be poor and honest than to be rich and not honest.

7 A son that obeys the rules is wise. But the man who has bad friends makes his father ashamed of him.

8 Some men get rich when they demand too much money from people. But their valuable things will go to someone that is kind to poor people.

9 Someone may not obey God's rules. God will not listen to the words that he prays. God hates them.

10 If you cause an honest person to do wrong things, bad things will happen to you. But a man who never does wrong things will receive valuable things.

11 Rich people always think that they know everything. But a poor person who understands people knows better.

12 When good people have power, everybody is happy. But when bad people have power, good people hide.

13 The man who hides his sins will never do well. A man should say that he is sorry. And he should stop doing bad things. If he does, God will be kind to that man.

14 Always be afraid of God and obey him. If you do, you will be happy. But trouble will happen to the person who hates authority.

15 Poor people have no help against a very bad ruler. He is as dangerous as an angry lion or as frightening as a bear.

16 A silly ruler will become a cruel master. An honest ruler will rule for a long time.

17 Someone that has done a murder will have to run. And he will have to hide. He will have to hide until the day that he dies. No man should help him.

18 If you are honest, God will save you. But the man who is not honest will be in danger.

19 A farmer that works well will have plenty of food to eat. But the man that loves to dream during the day will always be poor.

20 The lives of honest people will be very happy. But if you are in a hurry to get rich, God will punish you.

21 Judges must say fairly who is wrong or right. They should not always say that their friends are right. And they should not always say that their enemies are wrong. It is not good if they do those things. A judge like that would sin even to get a small piece of bread.

22 Some people think only about themselves and they never give gifts. People like that are in a great hurry to get rich. They do not know how soon they will become poor.

23 A man may tell his friend that the friend has done something wrong. In the end, the friend will like that man. He will like him more than a man who says nice words to him.

24 Some people think that it is not wrong to rob their parents. But a person like that is as bad as a destroyer.

25 Some people think that they are great. They cause many quarrels. But someone who trusts the Lord will enjoy many good things.

26 He that trusts himself is a fool. But people that obey wise words will receive help. And God will keep them safe.

27 If you give to the poor people, you will never need anything for yourself. If you do not help the poor people, many people will say bad words about you.

28 People hide when bad men become rulers. But good men will get their power, and the good men will rule again.

Chapter 29

1 A man should not refuse to listen when someone checks his words. If he refuses to listen again and again, something will destroy him very quickly. And nothing will be able to make it better.

2 If you show to me a good ruler, I will show to you happy people. If you show to me a bad ruler, I will show to you sad people.

3 A man that loves wise words makes his father happy. But if he likes to be with prostitutes he will waste his money.

4 When the king makes fair rules, he will have a strong country. But when he takes money to do wrong things, he will destroy his country.

5 Do not tell your friends that they are really great. If you continue to tell this to them, it will cause you to have a difficult time.

6 A bad man cannot escape from the results of his sins. But an honest person is so happy that he sings.

7 Good people want good rules for poor people. Bad people have no interest in poor people.

8 People that laugh at other people can cause difficult problems in a city. But wise men keep things quiet.

9 If a wise man goes to a judge with a fool, the fool will laugh. Or he will shout. There will be trouble.

10 Men that want to kill people will hate an honest man. They will try to kill him.

11 Silly people show that they are angry. Wise people are patient people. They do not show that they are angry.

12 When a ruler listens to lies, all his officers will become bad men.

13 The Lord gave eyes to the poor person and also to the officer that is cruel to him.

14 If the rules of the king are fair to the poor people, he will rule for a long time.

15 Do not let a child do always what he wants to do. If he is wrong, hit him. Or tell him that he must not do it. You should not let a child do whatever he wants to do. If you do, he will make his mother ashamed.

16 When rulers are bad people, more and more people will sin. But good people will live to see those rulers lose their power.

17 Do not let your children do always what they want to do. So they will not make you ashamed of them. They will always make you happy.

18 Only God can be the leader of a country. Without him, people do what they want to do. Happy are those people who obey God's rules.

19 If you use only words you cannot cause servants to obey you. Even if they understand you, they will not obey you.

20 A man may speak before he thinks. Better things will happen to a fool than will happen to that man.

21 You may give to a servant everything that he wants. You may have done this since he was a child. If you do, one day he will be like a son. He will take everything that is yours.

22 An angry man causes quarrels and angry men sin often.

23 People will not always like a man that is proud. They will not think that he is great. But they will like a man that is not proud. They will think that he is great.

24 When a man helps someone to rob other people he becomes his own enemy. The judge asks him what happened. But he does not tell the judge what happened. So God will punish him.

25 If you are afraid of other people you will never feel safe. But if you trust the Lord, he will keep you safe.

26 Everybody wants to speak with the ruler. But only the Lord is fair.

27 The good man does not like the bad man, and the bad man does not like the good man.

Chapter 30

The wise words of Agur

1 These are the wise words of Agur the son of Jakeh. The man spoke to Ithiel and to Ucal.

2 I am sillier than any other man is. And I do not have the wisdom of a man.

3 I have never known words of wisdom and I do not know anything about God.

4 Tell me who has gone to God's home. And tell me who has come back. Tell me who has held the wind in his hands. Tell me who has covered the waters with his coat. Tell me who has created the world. If anybody has done this, tell his name to me. Tell his son's name to me. Tell me, if you know.

5 God does everything that he promises to do. You can trust him and be safe. He is like something that you can hide behind.

6 Do not mix your words with his words. If you do, he will say, 'You are wrong.' And he will show that you tell lies.

More wise words

7 I ask you, God, to do two things for me before I die. Please do not say, 'No'.

8 Keep me from lies. Do not let me be rich or poor. Give me only as much food as I need.

9 I might have more than I need. Then I might say that I do not need you. But if I am poor, I might rob people. Then I would make you ashamed of me.

10 Do not say bad words to a servant about his master. If you do, the servant will punish you.

11 There are people who say very bad words about their fathers. They are not kind to their mothers.

12 Some people think that they are always right. But they do bad things anyway.

13 Some people think that they are very good. Oh, how good they think that they are!

14 Some people seem to have teeth like knives. They rob and destroy the poor people. That is the work that they do.

15-16 A leech has two daughters. 'Give! Give!' they shout.

There are 3 things that are never happy. And there are 4 things that are never full:

- the world of dead people

- a woman without children

- dry ground that needs rain

- a fire that never stops.

17 There is a man who looks at his father. And he says bad things to him. There is a man who laughs at his old mother. Big birds will pick out that man's eyes and they will eat them.

18-19 There are 3 things that are too difficult for me to understand. There are 4 things that I do not know about:

- how a large bird flies in the sky

- how a snake moves on a rock
- how a ship sails over the sea
- the way of a man with a young woman.

20 This is the way of an adulteress.

She eats and she washes her mouth. Then she says, 'I have not done anything wrong.'

21-23 There are 3 wrong things on the earth and there are 4 very bad things:

- a slave who becomes a king
- a fool that has all that he wants to eat
- a woman who has not had a husband then gets one
- a servant woman who takes the place of the woman that she works for.

24-28 There are 4 small animals in the world that are very wise:

- Ants are weak, but they prepare their food in the summer.
- There are small animals that are weak. But they make their homes among the rocks.
- Locusts have no king. But they all fly together in one direction.
- You can catch a lizard with your hand. But you can find them in kings' houses.

29-31 There are 3 things that seem powerful. They seem powerful when they walk. There are 4 things that are good to see. They are good to see walking:

- Lions are the strongest of all animals and they are not afraid of anything.
- the cockerel that wakes the farmer in the morning
- a male goat
- a king with his army round him.

32 You may think about yourself as good when you really are not so good. If you think like that, you are silly. Put your hand over your mouth. Also put your hand over your mouth if you want to do bad things.

33 If you mix milk for a long time you will make butter. If you hit someone's nose, it bleeds. If you make people angry, you will cause a quarrel for yourself.

Chapter 31

Good words for a king

1 These are the serious words that King Lemuel's mother taught to him.

2 You are the son that I prayed for. Let me tell you this.

3 Do not spend all your money on women. They have destroyed kings.

4 Listen, Lemuel. Kings should not drink wine. And rulers should not ask for alcohol.

5 When kings drink alcohol, they forget the rules. And they are not fair to poor people.

6 Alcohol is for people who are dying. And wine is for people who are very sad.

7 They should drink alcohol. Then they will forget that they are poor. And they will no longer remember that they are sad.

8 Speak on behalf of people that cannot speak on behalf of themselves. Watch over poor people. And supply what they need.

9 Speak on behalf of them and rule with wisdom. Watch over poor people. And supply what they need.

The wife who does all things well

10 How difficult it is to find a wife that does all things well! She is worth much more than valuable stones.

11 Her husband knows that she will help him. He will never be poor.

12 As long as she lives, she does only good things for him.

13 She is always busy. She makes cloth and she enjoys her work.

14 A ship brings food from all parts of the world. In the same way, she brings food from faraway places.

15 She gets up while it is still night to prepare food for her family. She tells her servant women what they should do.

16 She thinks about a field and she buys it with her own money. And she plants fruit bushes to make wine.

17 She is strong and she works well.

18 She knows the cost of everything that she makes. And she works late into the night.

19 She makes her own cloth from the beginning to the end.

20 She gives money to poor people. And she helps people that need help.

21 All her family have warm clothes, so snow is not a problem.

22 She makes beautiful cloths to cover all her beds. She wears good clothes of beautiful colours.

23 Everybody in the city knows her husband. He is one of the rulers of the country.

24 She makes clothes and she sells them. Some men buy and sell all things. She makes belts to sell to them.

25 She is strong and future times have no problems for her. People think that she is great.

26 She speaks with wise words. And she teaches kind rules to people.

27 She is always busy. And every day she carefully watches everything that happens in her house.

28 Her children love her. They say that she is good. Her husband says that too.

29 He says, 'Many women are good wives, but you are the best of them all.'

30 A beautiful woman may not be honest. And she may not be beautiful when she is old. But all men speak well about a woman who is afraid of the Lord.

31 Give her the things that she herself has made. Remember her because of all that she has done. Everyone should speak well about her.

The Teacher's Words

Ecclesiastes

About Ecclesiastes

We do not know the name of the person who wrote Ecclesiastes. But we know that he was a son of David. And we know that the writer was a king. So, many students think that King Solomon wrote it. Its writer was certainly a very wise man. He calls himself 'the Teacher'. The Teacher said some strange things. This is the reason. Many people do not know about God. So they try to find reasons for all the things that happen.

But they cannot find reasons. The Teacher tells us what these people think.

Sometimes people do things that have no purpose. He tells us what this is like. It is like somebody who tries to catch the wind. He means that it is very silly. The Teacher tells us how these people think. He does this when he uses the words 'on the earth'. These people find that life on the earth has no purpose.

The Teacher uses the words wise and wisdom many times. In the Word List, you can read what these words mean. Often people who do not know God try to be wise. But if you want to be really wise, you need to know God. The Teacher wants us to know God. And he wants us to believe God. Also, he wants us to obey God. He wants us to enjoy the good things that God has given to us. We will still have questions about our life on the earth. Some of them are questions that nobody can answer. But God will be with us during our lives. At some future time, each of us will die. The Teacher is not sure what will happen then. He says, 'Our spirits will return to God' (Ecclesiastes 12:7). In the New Testament, we learn what else will happen.

Chapter 1

1 These are the Teacher's words. The Teacher was David's son. The Teacher was a king. He lived in a city that was called Jerusalem. There he ruled his country.

2 'Nothing has a purpose', he said.

'None of the things that happen has a purpose.'

3 People work for their whole lives.

But they get nothing for the work that they do here on the earth.

4 People are born and they live on the earth. At the end of their lives, they die.

But the earth continues as it has always continued.

5 The sun still rises in the morning and it goes down in the evening.

And it does the same thing each day.

6 The wind blows to the south and it turns to the north.

It blows round and round, but it always returns.

7 All rivers go to the sea, but they never fill the sea.

In the end, the water returns. It returns to where it came from.

8 Life makes us tired. It makes us so tired that we could not tell anyone about it.

Nothing that we see can ever make us happy.

Nothing that we hear will ever cause true pleasure for us.

9 Future events will be the same as past events were.

What people have done, they will do again.

There is nothing that is new anywhere on the earth.

10 We can say, 'Look! Here is something new.'

But it is not true! It was here already, many years ago.

It was here before we were born.

We soon forget people who have died.

11 We do not remember what they did many years ago.

It will be the same in future years.

People will remember things that they have seen during their lives.

But many events happened before they were born. They will not remember those events.

12 I said these things when I was the king of my country, Israel. I lived in the city called Jerusalem. There I ruled my country. 13 I also studied a lot and I was very wise. I thought about the things that happen here on the earth. And I tried to understand them. But God has made this very difficult for us to do. 14 I have seen all the things that happen on the earth. There is no reason for any of them. It is like somebody who tries to catch the wind.

15 People may do things that are wrong.

This is like something that you have bent.

When you have bent it, you cannot make it straight again.

Neither can you count things that are not there.

16 'I have become a really great man', I told myself. 'There have been other kings who have ruled in Jerusalem. But I am more wise than any of them', I thought. 17 I wanted to learn all that I could learn about wisdom. I also wanted to know how a fool thinks. But this, too, was like somebody who tries to catch the wind.

18 If I learn to be very wise, I will be very sad.

If I learn a lot about many things, that will be very painful for me.

Chapter 2

1 'I will enjoy my life', I thought. 'I will make myself happy. That will be good.' But it was not good. I enjoyed myself, but my life was not worth anything. 2 It was silly to laugh all the time. I could look for things to make me happy. But they would not make my life worth anything. 3 So I decided to drink wine to make myself happy. I wanted to understand how a fool thinks. But I did not want to be a fool myself. We only live for a short time on the earth. And I wanted to know the best way to use that time.

4 I made some great things. I built houses for myself and I planted many vines. 5 I made gardens and parks. I planted many fruit trees in the gardens and parks. 6 I made large pools to give water for the trees.7 I bought male slaves and female slaves. Their sons and their daughters became my slaves too. Many people lived in Jerusalem before I did. And many of them had animals. But I had more cows and sheep than anyone else had. 8 I ruled many countries. And I got silver and gold for myself from their kings. Men and women sang for me. I got many wives to make me happy. These are all things that people enjoy. 9 I was the most famous person who had ever lived in Jerusalem. And I was very wise.

10 If I wanted to have something, I took it.

If I wanted to do something, I did it.

And I enjoyed my work.

I liked what I got from it.

11 Then I thought about the things that I had done.

I thought about all my difficult work.

But, in the end, I still saw that nothing had a purpose.

It was like somebody who tries to catch the wind.

None of the things that I had done had any value.

12 Then I decided to think about how a wise person lives.

I wanted to think also about how a fool lives.

I said to myself, 'The next king will not do any more than I have done.'

13 I know that light is better than the dark.

And I saw that it is better to be wise.

To be a fool is worse.

14 A wise man looks where he is going.

A fool shuts his eyes when he walks.

But at the end of their lives, they both die.

15 Then I thought to myself, 'Like the fool, I will die.

So, if I am wise, there is no value in it.'

I said to myself, 'This too means nothing.'

16 People do not remember wise men or fools.

That is because people will forget everything at some future time.

Even wise men, like fools, must die in the end!

17 So I was not happy with my life. And my work on the earth does not make me happy now. All of my work was worth nothing. It was like somebody who tries to catch the wind. 18 I will die in the end. Then some other person will enjoy the things that I have made. 19 That person may be a wise man or he may be a fool. But he will have all the things that I have worked for on the earth. This, too, is not good. The fact that I was wise means nothing. 20 So I became sad about all my work on the earth. 21 A man may know how to do his job well. He may do his work well and after that, he dies. Then all that he had will become another man's things. And that man will not have worked for it. This too means nothing and it is very sad.22 People have to do a lot of work on this earth. But they get nothing that they can keep. 23 Every day, their work disappoints them and it makes them sad. Even at night, their minds do not rest. All their work means nothing.

24 We should eat and we should drink. And we should enjoy our work. There is nothing better that we can do than those things. I believe that these are gifts from God. 25 Without God's help, nobody can have enough food to eat. And nobody can be happy. 26 If we obey God, he will help us. He will make us wise. He will make us clever. And he will help us to enjoy our life. But if we do not obey God, our lives will be difficult. He will give what is ours to another person. This, too, is not good. It is like somebody who tries to catch the wind.

Chapter 3

1 There is a right time for everything that we do under the sun.

2 There is a time to be born. And there is a time to die.

There is a time to plant seeds. Then the seeds will grow and they will become plants. And there is a time to pick the plants.

3 There is a time to kill. And there is a time to make people well.

There is a time to destroy something. And there is a time to build it again.

4 There is a time to weep. And there is a time to laugh.

There is a time to be sad. And there is a time to dance.

5 There is a time to throw stones away. And there is a time to pick them up.

There is a time to kiss. And there is a time to say goodbye.

6 There is a time to look for something. You look for something that you have lost.

And there is a time to stop looking for it.

There is a time to keep things.

And there is a time to throw them away.

7 There is a time to tear something down. And there is a time to mend it.

There is a time to be quiet. And there is a time to speak.

8 There is a time to love. And there is a time to hate.

There is a time to fight. And there is a time not to fight.

9 People get nothing for all the work that they do. 10 Their work is very difficult. And God has caused it to be like that. 11 But he also causes all things to happen at the right time. He puts questions in our minds. We want to know what happens after our death. We cannot understand all the things that God has done. 12 We should enjoy our lives. There is nothing better that we can do than that. We should also do good things during our lives. 13 We should get pleasure from what we eat. We should enjoy what we drink. And we should be happy when we are doing our work. These are all gifts from God.

14 Everything that God does will be for all time. We cannot do anything more than what God has done. We cannot take anything away from what he has done. God wants us to worship him. That is the reason for all that he does.

15 Future events will be the same as past events were.

God causes the same things to happen again and again.

16 I saw something else about the people who live in this world.

People should say if something is wrong. But they say that it is right.

They should be fair to each other but they are not fair.

17 'God will be the judge of all good people and of all bad people', I told myself.

Everything will happen at the right time.

18 'Perhaps God wants us to know that we are like animals', I thought. 19 Like animals, we live and then we die. We really are the same as animals. So our life means nothing for us or for them. 20 People and animals go to the same place. God made animals and people from the same dry material on the ground. And when they die, they both become dry material on the ground again. 21 We need to know what happens after our death. We think that the spirit of a man goes up. And we think that the spirit of an animal goes down towards the ground. But nobody really knows. 22 So we should enjoy our work. That is the best thing that we can do. That is what God wants us to do. But we do not know what there is after death.

Chapter 4

1 In every place on the earth, I saw cruel people.

Some people were crying because the cruel people were hurting them.

There was nobody to help them.

They were too weak to help themselves.

2 'It is better to be dead. That is better than to be alive', I said to myself.

3 'The most happy people are those who have not been born.

They do not see the bad things that happen on the earth.'

4 We do not like other people to have more than we have. That is why we work for many hours each day. That is why we try to do very many things. This, too, is like somebody who tries to catch the wind.

5 Fools refuse to work.

They die because they have no food.

6 It is better to be happy with a little food.

Some people work for more food than they need. But that is not right.

It is like somebody who tries to catch the wind.

7 Again, on the earth I saw something else that has no purpose.

8 Some people live alone.

They cannot give things to friends or to children,

because they have no friends or children.

They are not happy with the things that they have.

But they continue to work so that they can get more.

They should ask themselves, 'Whom are we working for?'

They should ask themselves why they do not enjoy their life more.

After their death, all that they have will not be theirs any longer. All those things will be another person's things.

Their lives will have meant nothing. This is like sad work.

9 It is good to have a friend.

You can enjoy the work that you and your friend do together.

10 If you fall, a friend can help you.

You may fall when you are alone.

If you do that, you really are in trouble.

11 If two people sleep together, they keep each other warm.

If you sleep alone, you will be cold in the night.

12 A strong person might hurt you.

But if you have a friend, your friend can help you. And you can fight so that the strong person will not hurt you.

Somebody has said, 'A rope can have three parts rather than one part. If it has three parts, it is difficult to break it.'

13 You may be poor and you may be young. But anyway it is a good thing to be wise. A king will not always listen when people speak to him. If you are wise, you are better. You are better than that kind of king. He is a fool.

14 You may have been in a prison and you may be very poor. Your father may not be a king, but you could become a king. 15 I once knew a young person. That young person became a powerful king after another king had died. 16 Many people thought that he was a good king. Nobody could even count the people who thought that. But in future years, nobody will remember him. This, too, is like somebody who tries to catch the wind.

Chapter 5

1 Be careful about anything that you do in the temple. Listen well when you worship God. Some fools go to the temple and they give sacrifices to God. But they do it for the wrong reasons. They do not know that they have done a wrong thing!

2 You should think before you speak.

You should think before you promise something to God.

God is in heaven and he knows you well.

You are here on the earth.

And you do not see as much as God sees.

Do not say to God more than you have to say.

3 If you think about your troubles too much, you will dream about bad things.

If you talk too much, you will say silly things.

4 You should do what you have promised to God. You should do it when you can. You should not wait before you do it. Only a fool would not do what he had promised to God. 5 Do not promise to do something that you might not do. It would be better not to promise anything. 6 Only say things that are true. You should not say to the priest, 'The promise that I said was a mistake.' That would make God angry. God might destroy the things that you have worked for. 7 It is silly to dream all the time. Remember that. It is also silly to talk all the time. But you should obey God because he is a great God.

8 The poor people who live in your country may be hungry. But the government does not help them, and the government is not fair to them. Do not be surprised about that. The government's officers do not decide what to do. Other more important people tell them what they must do. The king is the most important person in the country. 9 When people pay money to the government, the king receives a lot of it.

10 You may love money.

But you will never have enough money.

You may like to have valuable things.

But you will always want to have more of them. This is silly.

11 If you have a lot of money, other people will want some of it.

You will not enjoy the money that you have.

Other people will spend it for you.

12 A man who has worked all day will sleep well at night.

This is true even if he did not eat very much food.

But the rich man cannot sleep well because he has eaten too much.

13 I have seen something else that is not fair on the earth.

People may get a lot of money.

But, if they try to keep it,

it will be bad for them.

14 At a future time, they may discover that they have lost all their money.

Then, after they die, there will be no money for their children.

15 They were born with nothing.

When they die, they will have nothing.

They cannot take anything with them when they leave this earth.

They will have nothing for all their work.

16 That is not fair.

People leave this earth, as they came into it, with nothing.

They live as if they were trying to catch the wind.

But after all their work, they have nothing.

17 During their lives, they are always sad, angry and sick.

18 God has given to us a short life on this earth. I think that we should enjoy our lives. We should eat and drink. And we should do our work well. That is what God wants us to do.

19 If you are rich, you will have many things. You should enjoy those things. You should enjoy your work, too. This is a gift from God to you. 20 God will keep you busy and he will make you happy. You will be too busy to think about your troubles each day.

Chapter 6

1 On this earth, there is something else that is not fair. 2 God may give to you all the things that you want. He may give riches to you. And he may give to you money to spend. He may give to you a house to live in. But he may not let you enjoy those things. Somebody that you do not even know may get them all. That is not fair and it will confuse you a lot. 3 You may live for a long time and you may have many children. But you may not enjoy your life. When you die, people may not bury you properly. A child that is dead at its birth does not have a good life. But your life is worse than that. 4 A child like that will never live to see the sun. 5 It will not even have a name. It will leave this earth and it will go to a dark place. But that child will have more peace than you do. 6 You may live for a very long time, but you may not enjoy your life. We all go to the same place after we die. This is what will happen. Remember that.

7 We work so that we will have food.

But we never have enough food.

8 Our lives have not been more happy because we have been wise.

A fool would be as happy as we have been.

We may try to live in the right way.

But that does not make us happier if we are still poor.

9 It is not good always to want more things.

> We should enjoy the things that we have. That is better.

Somebody who wants more things all the time is silly.

> He is like somebody who tries to catch the wind.

10 God decided a long time ago what we should be like.

We cannot argue with God about that. He is very much stronger than we are.

11 If we talk too much, we will say silly things.

> It is better not to talk a lot.

12 We live for only a few years and our lives mean nothing. Our lives are like shadows that pass over the earth. We do not know the best way to live. We do not know what will happen after our death.

Chapter 7

1 You may be a nice person.

> So it is good if people know that.

There was a day when you were born. But the day when you die will be better.

> 2 You may enjoy a party.

But it is better for you if you go to a funeral.

> There, you will think about the day when you will die.

We will all die in the end. It is good to remember that.

> 3 It is better to be sad than it is to be happy.

We learn more about ourselves when we are sad.

> 4 A wise person thinks about death.

A fool thinks about how to enjoy his life.

> 5 You can listen to a fool who is singing songs.

But it is better to listen to a wise friend.

> He can tell you if you do a wrong thing.

6 Some sharp, hard plants make a lot of noise when they burn. But they do not make much heat.

Fools make a lot of noise when they laugh. But they never do anything good.

7 Wise people become fools if they are not fair to other people.

> It is wrong to receive a bribe.

8 It is good when you start to do some new work.

> But it is better to finish that work.

Do your work well even if you have to do it slowly.

> Some people may be proud. But it is better to do your work well.

9 Do not get angry quickly. That is what fools do.

> Try to forget the bad things that people may have done to you.

10 You may think that your life is difficult.

> You may think that it was easier before now.

It is not wise to think like that.

> So do not think like that.

11 It is as good to be wise as it is to receive a lot of money.

12 Money can keep you safe. And wisdom can keep you safe.

> But if you are wise, you will know the best way to live.

13 Think about the things that God has done.

> If God has bent something, you cannot make it straight.

14 If your life is good, you should be happy.

> But bad things may happen to you.

God causes good things to happen and he also causes bad things to happen. Remember that.

> You do not know what will happen next.

15 I do not know why I am alive.

> But I have seen two things during my life.

I have seen that good people have died. They died when they were young.

> They always did the right thing but they died like everyone else.

I have seen that some bad people live for many years.

> 16 Be careful that you do not kill yourself.

That might happen if you try to be too good or too wise.

> 17 Be careful that you do not die too soon.

That might happen if you are a fool or a bad person.

18 Try to live your life in a way that is in the middle.

You can do that if you try to love God. And you can do it if you try to obey him.

19 A wise man can do greater things than ten leaders in a city can do.

20 But even good men do not always do what is right.

Sometimes they make mistakes.

21 Do not listen to all the things that people say about you.

Even your servant may say bad things about you.

22 Do not forget that you, too, have said bad things.

23 I wanted to be wise.

Many things have happened to me during my life.

And I wanted to discover the reason for them.

24 But I could not discover a good reason.

It was too difficult for me.

25 So I decided to learn many things.

I wanted to become wise.

And I wanted to get answers to all my questions.

I believed that it was silly to be a fool.

I wanted to discover if this was true.

26 I learned that it is dangerous to meet a bad woman.

She is a worse thing than death itself.

She says that she loves you.

But if you listen to her, you will do wrong things.

Do what God wants people to do. If you do that, a woman like that will not catch you.

But that bad woman will catch the man who does not obey God's rules.

27 I used all my wisdom. And I looked for answers to my questions.

28 But I have failed.

I do know that there is one good man in every thousand men.

But I have not found a good woman.

29 I did learn one thing.

God made us to be good people.

But we have become bad people.

Chapter 8

1 A person's wisdom will cause his face to be like a happy man's face.

It will do that, even when things have made him sad.

But only a few people are wise.

And only a few people really understand things.

2 Perhaps you promised to God that you would obey the king. You should do what you promised to do. 3 If you are with the king, do not leave too quickly. The king can do anything that he wants to do. So do not join a group of people who do not want to obey him. 4 Do not argue with the king because he is very powerful. Nobody can tell him that he must not do something.

5 Everyone who obeys the king will be safe.

And a wise man knows what he should do.

And he knows when he should do it

And he knows how to do it.

6 You may have a difficult life.

But there is a right time for things to happen.

There is a right way to do things.

7 Nobody can tell what will happen in future days or years.

8 We do not know the day when we will die.

And we can do nothing to change that day.

We may fight against death, but we cannot win that fight.

Not even a bad person can do that.

9 I saw all these things and I thought about them a lot. I thought about the things that happen on the earth. I saw people who had power. They used that power to hurt people. 10 I saw people bury the dead bodies of bad men. Those bad men had gone in and out of the holy place. The people in their city forgot all the bad things that those men had done. There is no good reason for any of this.

11 When bad people do wrong things, the judges should punish them. This should happen very fast. If it does not happen fast, other people will do wrong things. 12 A man may do many bad things and that bad man may live to a very old age. But I believe that God is fair. If you obey God, you will have a good life. 13 If you do not obey God, you will not have a long life. Your life will be short, like a shadow. 14 Here is something else that is not right. The judges should not punish good people. But sometimes they do that. And the judges do not punish the bad people that they should punish. I have not discovered any good reason for this.

15 So we should enjoy our lives as much as possible. The best thing that we can do is to enjoy everything. We should enjoy what we eat. And we should enjoy what we drink. We should all try to be happy. There are no other good things on this earth. God has given us each day in our life. We will have easier lives if we enjoy ourselves.

16 I have tried to understand the things that happen on this earth. I thought about those things all day and all night. I did not go to sleep. 17 Then I saw all the things that God has done. Nobody can really understand the things that happen on the earth. That is what I discovered. We may be very wise. We may try many times to learn more and more. We may learn many things. But there will still be things that we will not understand.

Chapter 9

1 I thought about all these things. I saw that God is very powerful. He decides what our lives will be like. That is true even if we are wise. It is true even if we live in the right way. We do not know the things that will happen during our lives. So we never know if we will be happy or sad. We may live in the right way and we may obey God. Or we may do wrong things. 2 But what happens to us in the end will be the same. We may give sacrifices to God or we may not do that.

We may be good or we may be bad.

When we have promised something to God, we may do that thing. Or we may not do it.

What happens to us in the end will be the same, anyway.

3 After our death, the same thing will happen to us. There will be no difference in that. That is not fair. So people decide to live like fools. They do not try to be good. And then they die. 4 It is not very good to be a dead lion. It is better to be a dog that is alive. A person that is alive can hope to have a good life.

5 We know that we will all die in the end.

But dead people do not know anything.

And when they are dead, they cannot enjoy their life.

6 Dead people have gone from the earth and people do not remember them.

Nobody that is dead can love another person.

Nobody that is dead can hate another person.

Dead people cannot change the things that happen on the earth.

7 It is good to be happy. It is good to enjoy what you eat. And it is good to enjoy what you drink. God has pleasure in what you do. 8 You should put on your best clothes and you should comb your hair well. 9 Your life will be short and it will be difficult. But you love your wife, so enjoy your life together. That is the way to live on the earth. 10 And do your work well. You will soon leave the earth. Then it will not be possible for you to work. You will not think about future events. You will not know anything.

11 I saw another thing that happens on the earth.

The runner who can run most quickly does not always finish first.

The strongest soldier may not win the war.

People will not always feed you because you are wise.

If you are clever, good things will not always happen to you.

You may not become rich even if you do your work well.

Good things and bad things happen to us all.

12 Bad things can happen to all of us.

A fish does not know when somebody will catch it.

A bird does not know when somebody will catch it.

That is like us. We do not know when something bad will happen.

13 I saw another example of wisdom. 14 There was a city that only a few people lived in. A foreign king attacked that city. His army was ready to knock down the walls round the city. 15 But a poor man, who was very wise, lived in the city. And he knew how to save the city. He saved it, but people soon forgot him. 16 So, it may be good to be strong. But it is better to be wise. That is what I thought about it. But if you are poor, nobody listens to you. It does not matter how wise you are. People will not listen to you, anyway.

17 A wise man will speak quietly.

When he speaks quietly, it is good to listen to him.

The loud words of a king that is a fool do not mean a lot. The quiet words of a wise man mean more.

18 A wise person can do more than a soldier can do.

You may be wise. But one bad person can destroy all the good things that you have done.

Chapter 10

1 A jar of perfume soon has a bad smell if there are even a few dead flies in it.

So one silly thing can destroy the good things that a wise man has done.

2 If you are wise, you can do the right thing. You will know what is right. That is why you can do the right thing.

If you think like a fool, you will do wrong things.

3 We know that fools are silly.

It is easy to recognise a fool.

You have only to watch what he does.

Then you will see that he is a fool.

4 Do not leave your job when your master gets angry.

Be quiet and say nothing to him.

Your master will forget that you have made him angry.

He will still let you work for him.

5 I have seen something on the earth that is very bad.

I saw a ruler who did the wrong thing.

6 Rulers give power to fools. But they do not give it to rich people.

7 Rulers let slaves ride on horses.

    But the masters of those slaves have to walk.

8 If you dig a deep hole, you will fall into it.

    If you knock down a wall, a snake will come out. And it will bite you.

9 You will hurt yourself when you are getting stones from under the ground.

    If you are cutting wood, a piece of it might hurt you.

10 If your axe is not sharp, it will be difficult to use.

If you are wise, you can do the right thing. You will know what is right. That is why you can do the right thing.

11 You may know how to cause a snake to do what you want it to do.

    But that will not help you if the snake bites you first.

12 People like a wise man because of the things that he says.

    But a fool's own words can hurt the fool badly.

13 Fools do not think before they speak.

They say things and then those things cause problems for them. And those things cause problems for other people, too.

14 And fools always talk a lot.

    They talk about things that may happen.

But none of us really knows what future things will be like.

15 When a fool does some work, it soon makes him tired.

    He is so tired that he forgets the way to town.

16 Sometimes a country will have a very young king.

    If he rules like a child, there will be bad problems in that country.

And the leaders of the country might go to parties all the time. And then the problems will be worse.

    17 But a country will become rich if its ruler is wise.

It will become rich if its leaders do not go to parties all the time.

18 A man may be too lazy to do repairs to the roof on his house.

If he does not do the repairs, water will get into the house. And the house will fall down.

19 Eat good food and drink good wine. If you do that, you will be happy.

When you have a lot of money, you can buy anything. You can buy anything that you want.

20 Do not say bad things about the king.

    Do not say bad things about rich people.

Do not even think that you might do that.

    A little bird may hear you. And it might tell people what you said.

Chapter 11

1 Give money to anybody who needs it.

At some future time, you may be poor and other people will then give money to you.

2 You do not know when you will need help.

    So, if seven or eight people need money, give it to them.

3 When clouds are full of water, there will be rain on the earth.

If there is too much wind, a tree will fall. Wherever the tree falls, there it will lie.

4 If you are always thinking about the wind, you will not plant seeds.

If you are always watching the clouds, you will never pick any plants.

5 Before a baby is born, it grows inside its mother.

    Nobody can explain how that happens.

Nobody can explain the things that God does.

    So do not be surprised about that.

Remember that God made the world.

    And he made everything that is in the world.

6 Plant your seeds early in the morning.

    You should plant seeds all day, until the evening.

Some of the seeds may grow.

    Perhaps all the seeds will grow.

7 Light is good.

    So people are happy when they see the sun.

8 You should enjoy the things that you do each day.

    You should do that even if you live to a very old age.

You may live for many years but, in the end, you will die.

And you will be dead for a very long time.

There is nothing that means anything after that.

9 Enjoy your life while you are young.

Do the things that you want to do.

The things that you see will give you pleasure, too.

But God watches the things that you do. You should remember that.

He will want to know why you did those things.

10 Do not think about the good things that you do not have.

And do not do things that cause pain in your body.

You cannot always be young.

We all become old.

Chapter 12

1 While you are young, you should worship God.

In future years, you will say, 'I do not enjoy my life longer.'

2 In the end, you will not see the light that comes from the sun.

And will you not see the moon or the stars.

There will always be black clouds in the sky.

3 Your arms will move from one side to the other side when you do not want them to move.

Your legs will become weak.

You will have only a few teeth.

Your eyes will not see well.

4 Your ears will not hear well.

You will not hear the noise of people at their work.

At night, you will not sleep well.

But you will hear the birds when they sing. Then you will wake up because of that.

5 You will be afraid to climb up a hill.

You will be afraid to walk along a road.

Your hair will become white.

It will be like white flowers on a bush.

You will feel very tired all the time.

And you will not want to have sex any longer.

We will all die in the end.

When we die, people will be sad.

Many of them will be on the streets.

And they will cry because we have died.

6 In the end, the valuable jar will break.

The water pot will break. The rope at the well will break.

You will not get water from the well any longer.

7 So, in the end, we will all die.

People will bury our dead bodies under the ground.

Our spirits will return to God.

8 Nothing on the earth has a purpose.

I have seen all the things that happen on the earth.

None of them has a purpose.

9 I was a wise teacher and I saw many things. I wrote down all the proverbs that I had studied. 10 I saw all the things that happen on the earth. I tried to explain them. My words are all true. 11 A farmer uses a stick when he wants his animals to move. Proverbs are like the stick that the farmer uses. Proverbs come from God. He is like a guide because he shows us the way to live. He uses proverbs to do that.

12 You are my son. So listen to what I say. Do not listen when people teach you other things. There are many books. If you study them all, you will be very tired.

13 With a few words, I can describe everything that you must know. You should worship God. He says to you what you should do. And you should do what he says. That is our duty. 14 We may do good things. Sometimes we do wrong things. We think that nobody sees us. But God sees the things that we do. And he will ask us to explain the answer to this question: 'What have we done with our lives here on the earth?'

A Love Story

Song of Songs

About the Song of Songs People in the book

This is a book about love. It is a story about a man and a woman. The man loves only the woman. The woman loves only the man.

We read about the woman's brothers. We read about the woman's mother. We do not read anything about her father. There is also a group of friends. All or almost all of them are women.

We do not know a lot about the man or about the woman. In parts of the story, the writer calls the man a king. He may be King Solomon. But maybe the writer uses the word 'king' only to show that the woman respects him.

Also, we must ask, 'Did the man and woman really live? Or, is this about any man and woman who love each other?'

The words in the book

Some people believe that this book is a set of songs. Together they make one larger song. The songs are like each other. The songs may be words only with no music. The songs have the same ideas. The writer repeats ideas in different ways. Maybe the songs are about different people. It is difficult to find the beginning and the end of each song.

Other people believe that this is one song, not a set of songs. It tells one story only. It is about the same people. It is not the whole story from beginning to end. It seems that the writer has told only parts of the story. The story is not easy to understand. But love is not easy to understand!

The person who wrote this book was from the East. The way that the writer puts the words together shows this fact to us. Sometimes we have to ask, 'Has an event already happened?' 'Is this happening now?' 'Will this happen at some future time?' We are not always sure.

We do not know, always, who is speaking. Also, we may not know which person they are speaking to. For example, the woman sometimes speaks to the man. Sometimes she speaks to the group of women friends. Sometimes she may only be speaking aloud. This is to show her thoughts to us. Maybe sometimes the woman is only thinking and hoping. It may not be happening outside of her mind. To help you, we have put the names of the people above their words. This is how we understand it.

When you read this book, you may feel certain things. You may think that you are with the man and woman in the story. The writer has caused this to happen. We read about how the man and the woman touch. And we read about how they kiss. We read about how they taste wine and apple. We read about the smell of things. We know that the story is really happening!

Marriage in the book

In some countries, the parents decide about the person that their child will marry. The man and woman may not know each other much until after they are married. In other countries, they meet each other. But their parents have not decided this. The man and woman may have a long time to be best friends. Then they marry.

This book does not say anything about the marriage. It seems that the man and woman do have some time together before the marriage. They enjoy that time. But they do not have sex until after the marriage.

There may be a time when the husband and his wife become parents. The book seems to say that they can have children. But it is not about the birth of children. It is not about families. The book is about the man and woman as best friends.

How the writer describes things in the book

The book describes what God has made. It also describes things that people have made. These ideas cause the reader to think about the man and woman. For example, we read about land where there are farms. This gives the idea that a man and his wife can make a new life. They may have a baby together. The man can see a long way from the hills. This shows that his love can become larger. Valuable stones show that the man and woman are very valuable to each other.

Often a word or a group of words can mean two things. For example, the word vineyard can mean that the woman is in a vineyard. Also, the word vineyard can mean that she is like a vineyard. The word garden can mean that the man and woman are in a garden. But it can also mean that the woman's body is like a garden. The writer uses the word garden to mean the woman's body in chapter 4. This is when the man and woman are enjoying sex.

Chapter 1

The writer

1 Solomon's Song of Songs.

Solomon was a very rich king. He lived more than 900 years before Christ (BC). He had a group of about 1000 songs. This is the most important song. Perhaps he liked this song best.

Solomon may have written the book. Or it may be a book about Solomon, or about another rich man. Many people respected King Solomon. So the writer may have used Solomon's name here. Another person may have written the book. He or she put it with Solomon's other songs.

King Solomon accepted this book. He had a very good mind. He understood many things. This is how it became part of the Bible.

The book is more about the woman than about the man. Also, the book is more about how a woman, rather than a man, thinks. And it is more about how a woman feels. So a woman may have written the book.

Woman

2 I really want him to kiss me with his lips.

Your love makes me happier than wine does.

3 You have put something on your body.

Certainly, it has a lovely smell.

The sound of your name causes me pleasure like that too.

I am not surprised that the young women love you!

4 Take me away with you. Come quickly.

I want the king to take me into his rooms.

Women friends

We are very happy!

You make us happy.

> Your love is better than wine. We will speak and sing about it.

Woman

I agree! They are right to think about you like that. And they are right to love you like that.

5 Daughters of Jerusalem, my skin is dark but lovely.

> It is dark like the tents of Kedar.
>
> It is dark but lovely like the curtains in Solomon's tent.

6 Do not continue to look at me because my skin is dark.

> The sun has made my skin like this.

My mother's sons were angry with me.

They caused me to work in the vineyards. I had to watch over the vineyards.

> So I could not watch over my own vineyard.

Woman

7 I love you.

Tell me where your sheep eat the grass.

> Where do you lead your sheep so that they can rest at midday?

When I am near your friends with their animals,

I do not want to wear a veil over my face!

Man

8 You are the most beautiful woman of all.

If you do not know where to find me,

> follow the marks from the feet of the sheep.

Let your young goats eat grass by the tents of those who watch over the sheep.

Man

9 You are my best friend. I love you more than anyone else.

You seem to me like a female horse that pulls one of Pharaoh's chariots.

10 Your face is beautiful with ear-rings.

> Round your neck are valuable stones, which make it very pretty.

11 We will make ear-rings for you. We will make them out of gold with pieces of silver in.

Woman

12 The king was lying down and he was eating.

> I had put something on my skin that has a lovely smell.
>
> This smell moved into the air.

13 To me, the man that I love is like a little bag of myrrh.

> He is like the little bag of myrrh that lies between my breasts.

14 To me he is like a group of henna flowers.

> He is like flowers that grow in the vineyards at En Gedi.

Man

15 How beautiful you are!

> My best friend, you are very beautiful! Your eyes are like doves.

Woman

16 You are very handsome and you love me.

> You are very lovely!

This green field of fresh, long grass is our bed.

Man

17 The beams of our house are the cedar trees.

The trees, with green leaves all of the time, are above us like a roof.

Chapter 2

Woman

1 I am a wild flower of Sharon.

> I am a lily from the valleys.

Man

2 Among other young women, my best friend that I love is like a lily among thorns.

Woman

3 Among the other young men, the man who loves me is like an apple tree.

> He is like an apple tree among the trees of the forest.

I love to sit in his shade.

> His fruit is sweet.

> It tastes nice.

4 He has taken me to the banquet hall.

> Everyone can see that he loves me.

5 I am weak with love.

> So, give raisins to me to make me strong.

> Give apples to me to keep me awake.

6 His left arm is under my head.

> His right arm draws me near to him.

7 Daughters of Jerusalem,

> please do not cause someone to feel love for another person;

> not until he or she wants to.

I am saying this because I really mean it.

I beg you on behalf of the gazelles and the young female deer in the field.

8 Listen! I hear the man who loves me!

> Look! He is coming!

> He moves quickly across the mountains.

He runs and he jumps. He comes over the hills.

9 The man who loves me is like a gazelle or like a young male deer.

Look! There he is! He is standing behind our wall.

He is looking through the windows.

> He is trying to see through the lattice.

10 The man who loves me spoke. He said to me.

> 'My beautiful best friend, I love you.

> Please get up and come with me.

11 See! The winter is past. The rains have finished.

> 12 Flowers are appearing in country places.

> It is now the season to sing.

Near here, we can hear the lovely sound that the doves are making.

13 The new fruit on the fig trees is growing.

> The smell from the flowers on the vines is moving into the air.

My beautiful best friend, I love you.

> Please get up and come with me.'

Man

14 You are like a dove that is hiding in a rock.

> You are like a dove that is hiding in the mountains.

Show your face to me because it is lovely.

Let me hear your voice because it has a beautiful sound.

15 Catch the foxes for us.

> Catch the little foxes that destroy the vineyards.

> They destroy our vines when the flowers are appearing.

Woman

16 The man who loves me is mine.

> And I am his.

> He eats slowly among the lilies.

17 My best friend that I love,

> turn round until the dawn.

Until the shadows have gone, be like a gazelle.

> Or be like a young male deer on the hills of rock.

Chapter 3

Woman

1 All night I lay in bed.

> I looked for the man that I love.

> I looked for him but he did not appear.

2 I thought, 'I will get up now and I will go into the city.

> I will look everywhere for the man that I really love.

> I will go through all the streets.

> I will look in all the market places.'

So I looked for him.

> But I did not find him.

3 The security guards were working.

> They walked through the streets of the city.
>
> They found me.
>
> I said, 'Have you seen the man that I love very much?'

4 I passed them.

Just then, I found the man that I love!

> I hugged him. I would not let him go.
>
> I held him until I had brought him to my mother's house.

I brought him to my mother's room.

> (There my life started, in my mother's body.)

5 Daughters of Jerusalem,

> please do not cause someone to feel love for another person;
>
> not until he or she wants to.

I am saying this because I really mean it.

I beg you on behalf of the gazelles and the young female deer in the field.

The Writer

6 Who is this who is appearing from the empty land?

> What is this smoke that is rising?
>
> There is a lovely smell of myrrh and incense.

The smell of the trader's spices fills the air.

7 Look! It is King Solomon's sedan chair and 60 soldiers are travelling with it.

> The soldiers are very brave. They are the best in Israel.

8 All of them wear a sword. Each man is ready to use it.

> They have all fought in many wars.
>
> They are ready for the dangers of the night.

9 King Solomon made the sedan chair for himself.

> He made it out of wood from Lebanon.

10 He made the posts out of silver.

> He used gold for the part where the passenger's feet rest.

The Daughters of Jerusalem put a comfortable purple cloth over the seat to cover it.

> They were careful to make it beautiful inside.

11 Daughters of Zion, come out.

Look at King Solomon who is wearing his crown.

> His mother put the crown on him.
>
> She put it on him on his marriage day.
>
> It was the day that he was very happy.

Chapter 4

Man

1 How beautiful you are!

> My best friend that I love, you are certainly very beautiful!
>
> Your eyes behind your veil are like doves.

Your hair is like a group of goats.

> It is like goats that are coming down Mount Gilead.

Man

2 Your teeth are white like a group of sheep.

> They are like sheep after someone has cut off their dirty wool.
>
> They are like sheep that are coming out of the pool of water.
>
> Each tooth is one of a pair. Not one of them is alone.

3 Your lips are bright red.

> They are bright red like a ribbon.
>
> Your mouth is lovely.

The sides of your face are round like the halves of a pomegranate.

> Your veil hides them.

Man

4 Your neck is like the beautiful, important tower that King David built.

> The shields of 1000 soldiers hang from the stones round it.

Man

5 Your breasts are like two young gazelles that were born to their mother on the same day.

> They walk slowly among the lilies and they eat the grass.

6 Until the dawn, I will go to the mountain of myrrh.

> Until the shadows go, I will go to the hill with the lovely smell.

7 You are my best friend and I love you.

> I find that every part of you is beautiful.

> There is no part of you that is not lovely.

8 Come with me from Lebanon.

> You are my new wife.

Come with me from Lebanon.

> Come down from the top of Amana, from the top of Senir.

> Come down from the highest part of Hermon.

> Come away from the lions' homes

> and from the places in the mountains where there are leopards.

Man

9 I love you so much that I never want to leave you.

> You are my sister and my new wife.

After one glance of your eyes, I knew that I wanted you more than anyone else.

I see one of the valuable stones that hang round your neck.

> And then I know that you are the most valuable person to me.

Man

10 Your love to me is certainly very good, my sister, my new wife.

> It gives to me more pleasure than when I drink wine.

You have a smell that is lovelier than any spice!

11 Your lips taste sweet, my new wife.

They taste like honey that falls from the honeycomb.

> Milk and honey are under your tongue.

The smell of your clothes is like the smell of Lebanon.

12 You are like a garden that you have locked up, my sister, and my new wife.

> You are like a spring that someone has covered.

> You are like a fountain that nobody has opened.

> Water cannot rise from it.

13 Your garden is full of pomegranate trees with their sweet fruit.

> There are fruits that many people like.

There are henna and nard.

14 There are nard, saffron, calamus and cinnamon.

There are many different plants that have lovely smells.

> There are myrrh and aloes.

> All the best spices are there.

Man

15 You are like a fountain in a garden.

> You are like a well that is full of water.

> The water now comes quickly down from Lebanon.

Woman

16 Awake, north wind! Come, south wind!

Blow on my garden so that its lovely smell will move all over the place.

I really want the man that I love to come into his garden.

> Let him taste the best fruits.

Chapter 5

Man

1 I have come into my garden, my sister and my new wife.

> I have taken my myrrh with my spice.

> I have eaten my honeycomb and my honey.

> I have drunk my wine and my milk.

The Writer

Eat, friends, and drink. You love each other!

> Drink until you no longer need a drink.

Woman

2 I slept but my heart was awake.

> Listen! The man who loves me is knocking.
>
> 'Open the door for me, my sister', he said.
>
> 'You are my best friend that I love the most.
>
> To me you are like a dove.
>
> Nobody is lovelier than you.
>
> Water from the night air covers my head.
>
> My hair is very wet.'

3 I said, 'I have taken off my day clothes.

> I do not want to put them on again.
>
> I have washed my feet.
>
> I do not want them to get dirty again.'

4 The man who loves me pushed his hand through the hole in the door.

> My heart began to go quicker for him.
>
> I could feel it and I could almost hear it.

5 I stood up to open the door for the man who loves me.

> My hands were wet with myrrh.
>
> Myrrh was dropping from my fingers onto the door handle.

6 I opened the door for the man who loves me. But he had left.

> He was gone.

I felt full of love for him when he spoke.

> I looked for him but I did not find him.
>
> I spoke his name loudly but he did not answer.

7 The security guards were working.

They found me while they were walking through the streets of the city.

> They hit me and they hurt me.
>
> And the marks on my body show this.
>
> Those security guards of the walls took away my shawl.

8 Please find the man who loves me, Daughters of Jerusalem!

> If you find him, please speak to him about me.
>
> Please tell him that I am weak with love.

Friends

9 You are the most beautiful among women.

> How is the man that you love better than other men?
>
> How is he better than other men, that you ask us to say this?

Woman

10 His face and his body shine because of the sun.

> He is the greatest among 10 000 men.

11 His head is valuable like pure gold.

> The hairs on his head are black, but they are not straight.
>
> They are black like the night with no moon.

12 His eyes are like doves by the water streams.

> They are like doves that someone has washed in milk.
>
> They sometimes shine like valuable stones.

13 The sides of his face are like spice plants in the ground that have a lovely smell.

> His lips are like lilies with myrrh that falls from them.

14 His arms are like long round pieces of gold

> and some valuable stones are over them.

His body is like ivory that someone has caused to shine.

> A few valuable, blue stones make it even more beautiful.

15 His legs are straight and strong like round pieces of beautiful stone.

> His feet are of pure gold.

He is tall like Lebanon, quite as handsome as its best cedars.

16 His mouth is very nice in every way.

> Everything about him is lovely.
>
> This is the man who loves me.
>
> This is my friend, Daughters of Jerusalem.

Chapter 6

Friends

1 You are the most beautiful among women.

> Where has the man who loves you gone?

> Which way did he turn so that we can look for him with you?

Woman

2 The man who loves me has gone down to his garden.

> He has gone to where the plants with a lovely smell grow.

> He has gone there to walk in the gardens and to pick lilies.

3 This man loves me and I am his. And he is mine.

> He is walking among the lilies.

Man

4 You are my best friend that I love the most.

> You are as beautiful as Tirzah.

> You are as lovely as Jerusalem.

> Everyone sees you easily.

You are like an army that is holding up its beautiful cloth with bright colours.

5 Turn your eyes away from me.

> They cause a lot of pleasure for me.

> But the pleasure is too strong for me!

Your hair is like a group of goats.

> It is like goats that are coming down from Mount Gilead.

6 Your teeth are white like a group of sheep.

> They are like clean sheep that come out of the pool.

> Each tooth is one of a pair. Not one of them is alone.

7 The sides of your face are round like the halves of a pomegranate.

Your veil hides them.

Man

8 There may be 60 queens.

And a king may have 80 other wives.

He may have many young women who do not yet have children.

> There may be too many for him to count!

9 But there is only one woman that I want.

> Nobody is like her in any way.

> She is lovely like a dove.

> She is mine.

> Nobody else is lovelier.

She is the special daughter of her mother.

The woman who gave birth to her likes her best among all her children.

The young women saw that she was now happier.

The queens and the other wives said 'Well done!'

> They all said,

10 'She appears like the dawn.

> She is lovelier every moment like the sunrise.

> She is as pretty as the moon.

> She is very beautiful to look at!

> She is bright, like the sun.

There she stands, beautiful and important.

It is like the way that God has put each star like a king or a queen in its place.'

Man

11 I went down to the small wood where there are trees with dry, hard fruit.

> I wanted to see what had started to grow in the valley.

> I wanted to see if the vines had flowers now.

> I wanted to see if the pomegranates had flowers.

12 I did not have time to understand everything about it.

> But I knew that I really wanted her.

> This put me among the king's chariots with the king's men.

Friends

13 Come back, come back, Shulammite woman.

> Come back! Come back!

We want to look at you for a long time.

Man

Do not look for a long time at the Shulammite woman.

Do not look at her as you would look at the dance at Mahanaim.

Chapter 7

Man

1 How beautiful are your feet in sandals, my princess!

> How beautifully your legs move!

> They are like valuable stones

> that a craftsman's hands have made into a lovely shape.

Man

2 Your navel is like a round cup that is full of good wine.

> Your stomach is the shape of many plants that a farmer has picked for food.

> Lilies are round the edge.

3 Your breasts are like two young gazelles

> born to their mother on the same day.

4 Your neck is like an ivory tower.

Your eyes are like the pools in Heshbon, by the gate that is called Bath Rabbim.

Your nose is like the tower of Lebanon,

> the building from where people can look towards Damascus.

Man

5 At the top, your head is like the mountain that is called Mount Carmel.

> Like a crown, it makes your whole body even more beautiful.

Your hair hangs down and it shines like long, thin pieces of silk.

> It is like silk that queen's use for their clothes.

It is so beautiful that a king would keep his eyes towards it all the time!

6 You are very, very beautiful.

> I love you.

> Many things about you give a lot of pleasure to me.

7 You are tall like a palm tree.

Your breasts are like groups of fruit that are very near to each other.

8 I said, 'I will climb the palm tree. I will take hold of its fruit.'

> I want your breasts to be like the groups of fruit on the vine.

> I want the smell from your mouth to be like apples.

9 I want your mouth to be like wine.

Woman

> I want the wine to go immediately to the man who loves me.

> I want to pour it slowly over his lips and over his teeth.

10 This man loves me and I am his.

> He wants me very much.

> 11 You love me!

> Come! I want us to go away from the towns.

> I suggest that we stay in the villages for the night.

12 We can go early to the vineyards.

> We can see if the vines have flowers on them now.

> We can see if the flowers have opened.

> We can see if the pomegranates have flowers.

> There I will give my love to you.

13 The mandrakes send out their lovely smell.

> There is every good thing to eat at our door.

> You love me and I have stored new and old things for you.

Chapter 8

Woman

1 I want you to be like a brother who drank at my mother's breasts!

I want us to be like a brother and sister.

So, if I found you outside, I would kiss you.

And nobody would think about me as a bad person.

2 I would lead you to my mother's house.

I would bring you to the mother who has taught me.

I would give to you wine with spices to drink.

I would give to you my pomegranate drink that tastes lovely.

Woman

3 His left arm is under my head and his right arm draws me near to him.

4 Daughters of Jerusalem,

please do not cause someone to feel love for another person;

not until he or she wants to.

I am saying this because I really mean it.

I beg you not to do it.

Friends

5 Someone is coming up from the dry, empty place with the man who loves her!

Her head is against the man's shoulder.

Woman

Under the apple tree, I woke you.

There your life started in your mother's body.

There your mother was in pain during your birth.

6 Draw me near to you like a seal over your heart.

Put me like a seal over your arm.

Keep me there always because love is as strong as death.

A dead person in a hole in the ground never comes out alive again.

A man who loves his wife will never let another man take her away from him.

And I do not want you to love another woman.

Love burns like a red-hot fire.

It burns like the hottest part of a large fire.

7 Lots of water cannot put it out.

Rivers cannot carry it away.

A rich man might give everything that he has to buy someone's love.

But people would tell him that he was very silly!

Woman

8 My brothers had said:

'We have a younger sister.

Her breasts have not yet grown.

What will we do on her behalf when it is the time for her to marry?'

9 My friends said:

'If she is a wall, we will build towers out of silver on her.

If she is a door, we will put boards of cedar wood over her.'

10 I am a wall.

My breasts are like towers.

So, to him, I have become like someone who gives pleasure to him.

11 King Solomon had a vineyard in Baal Hamon.

People could come and they could pay 11 kilos of silver for its fruit.

12 But my own vineyard is mine. It is a gift to you, my king.

The 11 kilos of silver are for you, my Solomon.

I give 2 kilos of silver to those who watch over its fruit.

Man

13 You have been in the garden with your friends for a long time.

Let me hear your voice!

Woman

14 You love me. Come away.

Be like a gazelle or like a young deer on the mountains that are full of spice.

Isaiah Tells Us God's Good News

Isaiah

A note on the book of Isaiah

There are 66 chapters in Isaiah's book. The book is easier to understand if we put it into 5 parts. We have done this below. The word list explains the words prophet and messiah. The words king, servant and messiah do not always mean the same people in Isaiah's book. This often confuses us in Isaiah's book.

The five parts of Isaiah

PART 1 (Chapters 1-5) Isaiah describes the people in the country called Judah and its capital city Jerusalem.

PART 2 (Chapter 6) God makes Isaiah into a prophet.

PART 3 (Chapters 7-37) God's **KING** rules God's people.

PART 4 (Chapters 38-55) God's **SERVANT** saves God's people.

PART 5 (Chapters 56-66) God's **MESSIAH** beats God's enemies.

PART 1: Chapters 1-5 Isaiah describes the people that live in the country called Judah and its capital city Jerusalem

Chapter 1

1 This is what Isaiah, the son of Amoz, saw. He saw things about the country called Judah and the city called Jerusalem. It happened when Uzziah, Jotham, Ahaz and Hezekiah were kings of Judah.

The problems of the country called Judah

2 Hear (the LORD, you) skies! And listen (to him, you) earth, because the LORD, he has spoken! (He has said,) 'I have helped (my) sons to grow. And I have loved them. But even they have fought against me!

3 A cow knows its master. And a horse (knows) where its keeper feeds it. But Israel, they do not know (me). My people, they do not understand (me).'

4 Oh! (You are a) country that does not obey me. (All your) people are (like people who are) carrying a heavy weight. (It is) the wrong things (that you have done). (You are a) family (of people)

that is always doing bad things. (You are) sons that destroy (everything). They have left the LORD. They think that the Holy (God) of Israel is silly. They have become strangers. Their backs are towards (him).

5 So, you continue to fight (against God). (The enemy) will only hurt you again. (Your) whole head is not well and (your) whole heart is ill.

6 From the under part of the feet, even to the head, there is no health in you. (There are) places (where people have) hit (you). (There are) places that hurt. People have cut some places until they bleed. Nobody has cleaned those places. Nobody has tied a cloth round them. Nobody has put medicine on them.

7 Your country is empty. Fire has burned your cities. Foreign people have taken everything from your fields. (They did it) in front of you. Strangers have destroyed (your country).

8 The Daughter of Zion, (Jerusalem,) remains like an empty hut in a vineyard. (She is) like a hut in a field of fruit. (She is) like a city that an enemy is attacking.

9 Unless the LORD of Everything had left some people to continue living, we would have been like Sodom. We would have been like Gomorrah.

The problems of the religion of the country called Judah

10 Hear what the LORD says, (you) rulers of Sodom. Listen to our God. He is saying what you must do, (you) people in Gomorrah.

11 'All your sacrifices do not matter to me.' (This is what) the LORD is saying. 'I have had enough (sacrifices) that you have burned as gifts to me. (I have had enough) male sheep and the best bits of fat animals. (I have had enough) of the blood of male cows, goats and young sheep. They do not give me pleasure.

12 (There are times) when you come to appear in front of me. But nobody asked you to do this. Do not walk heavily round my temple.

13 Do not bring gifts (to me) that mean nothing! I do not like your incense. I do not like your new moons, (your) Sabbaths and (your) special meetings. These meetings are bad.

14 I really do not like your new moon meetings and your holy days. They have become like a heavy weight for me. I am tired because I have to carry them.

15 I will hide my eyes from you, when you lift up your hands (to me). I will not listen (to you), even if you pray (to me) often. Your hands are full of blood.

16 Wash yourselves (and) make yourselves clean! Take away the bad things that you are doing. Then I will not see them. Do not continue to do what is wrong.

17 Learn to do what is right. Make justice your purpose. Do not let masters be very cruel (to people). Do not let people hurt children who have no father. Say good things on behalf of women whose husbands are dead.

18 Come, now', the LORD is saying. 'We should talk about this together. Even if your sins are as bright red, they shall be as white as snow. Even if they are as dark red, they shall be like wool.

19 Agree (with me). And obey (me). If you do (these things), you will eat the best food in the country.

20 But (if you do not do these things), the sword will kill you. (It will kill you) if you do not obey me. (It will kill you) if you continue to fight against me.' This is what God himself has said.

The problems of the people that live in the country called Judah

21 Oh! The City that Loved Me (as a wife) has become like a prostitute! (The city was) full of justice. Good people lived in her, but now there are people who murder (other people there).

22 Your silver has become dirt and you have mixed water with your best wine.

23 Your rulers are fighting against (God). And they are friends of robbers. They all accept things to help people (that they should not help). And (they all) hope for gifts like these. But they do not help children that have no father. (They do not help these children) when people hurt them. The women whose husbands are dead have problems. But (the problems) do not come to the (rulers).

24 So the Lord says this. (He is) the LORD of Everything (and he is) the Powerful (God) of Israel. 'Oh! I will get rest from my enemies. And I will punish those people who fight against me.

25 And I will turn my hand against you and I will wash away all your dirt with soap and brush. So I will remove everything that is not clean.

26 And I will give back to you your judges, as (you had them) a long time ago. And (I will give back to you) the people that say what you must do, as at the beginning. After this, you will be called The Good City, and The City that Loves Me.'

27 (God) will use justice to make Zion free. (He will make things) right for the people that return (to him).

28 But he will destroy people that sin. (And he will destroy) those people that continue to fight (against him). The LORD will kill everybody that goes away from him.

29 Really, they will be ashamed of their special trees (called) oaks. You have found a lot of pleasure in them. The gardens that you have chosen will make you really ashamed.

30 You will be like an oak tree whose leaves are dying. (You will be like) a garden without water.

31 The strong man will become like something that burns easily. His work will be like something that causes things to burn. They will both burn together and nobody will put out the fire.

Chapter 2

1 This is what Isaiah, the son of Amoz, 'saw' about Judah and Jerusalem.

Words that cause us to hope in God

2 This is what will happen in the last days. The mountain, where the house of the LORD is, will always be there (in Jerusalem). It will be the most important mountain. It will be higher than the hills (round it). (People from) every country will come towards it.

3 And people from many countries will come (to it). And they will say, 'Come! We shall go to the mountain of the LORD. We must go to the house of the God of Jacob. Then he will teach us his ways, so that we can walk in his paths.' So, the word (of God) will go out from Zion. The LORD's words will go out from Jerusalem.

4 (God) will be the judge between the nations. He will say (who is right. And he will say) who is wrong. They will use hammers to change their swords into parts of ploughs. And they will use their knives to prune plants. Nations will not attack other nations with swords, neither will they learn how to fight again.

5 House of Jacob, come and we shall walk in the light of the LORD.

The problems of religion in Judah and Israel

6 But you, (LORD), have gone away from your people. They are the house (family) of Jacob. They are full (of magic) from (countries in) the east. They are like the people called Philistines. They have people who use magic to find out what will happen. Also, they join hands with foreign people.

7 Their country is full of silver and gold and they have many valuable things. Their country is full of horses and they have many chariots.

8 Idols that are worth nothing fill their country. They get down on the ground in front of things that their hands have made. (They are things) that their own fingers have made.

9 So, (the LORD) makes people humble and everyone becomes low! (LORD), do not lift them up again!

10 Go into (the holes in) the rocks and hide in the ground. (Hide) because you are afraid. (You are afraid) of (what) the LORD (will do). And (hide from) his great power.

11 (The LORD) will stop the way that proud people look at other people. And (he will make) very proud people humble. On that day, only the LORD will be important.

12 Yes! The LORD of Everything will choose a day. Then, (in that day, the LORD) will make humble everyone that is proud, very proud and important.

13-16 (The LORD will be) against all these things:

·   the high, the really high cedar trees in Lebanon

·   the oak trees in Bashan

·   the very high mountains

·   the highest hills

·   tall buildings

·   strong walls

·   boats from Tarshish

·   beautiful ships.

17 (The LORD) will stop the way that proud people look at other people. And he will make very proud people humble. On that day, only the LORD will be important.

18 And nobody will see any of the idols again.

19 And (people) will run to holes in the sides of the rocks and to holes in the ground. (They will run) because they are afraid of the LORD. (They will run) from his great power. (They will run) when he comes to punish the earth.

20 In that day people will throw away their silver idols and their gold idols. (They will throw them) to (animals) called rats and bats. They made (these idols) so that they could worship them.

21 Then people will run to large holes in the rocks and to holes in (the sides of) mountains. (They will run) because they are afraid of the LORD. And (they are afraid) of his great power, when he comes to punish the earth.

22 Do not ask human people (to help you). They get air through their noses! They are worth (nothing).

Chapter 3

The problems of the people in Judah and Israel

1 I will show you what the Lord, the LORD of Everything (will do). He will remove from Jerusalem and Judah everything that helps them. (He will take away) everything that supplies their food and their water.

2-3 (He will take away these people):

- the strong man and the soldier

- the judge and the prophet

the person who uses magic to find out what will happen and the older (leader)

- the captain of 50 (soldiers) and the very important man

- the person that tells people what to do and the good worker

- the person that uses magic.

4 'And I, (the LORD), will make boys their leaders and children will rule over them.'

5 The people will be cruel to each other. (It will be) man against man. (It will be) man against the person that lives near him. Young people will say bad things to older people. And bad people will say bad things to good people.

6 Then a man will hold his brother strongly in the house of his father. (The man will say), 'You have a coat. So, you can be our leader! Then you can rule over these buildings that (the enemy) destroyed!'

7 On that day, (the brother) will refuse. He will say, 'I cannot help! There is no food and no coat in my house. Do not make me a leader of people.'

8 (This will happen because the leaders of) Jerusalem and Judah have started to fall. Then they have fallen down. Their words and the things that they do are against the LORD. They have said bad things about his great glory.

9 Their faces show what they are really like. It is clear that they have sinned, like the (people in) Sodom. They do not hide it. It is so sad! They have brought great trouble to themselves.

10 Tell the very good people that things will be well for them. They will enjoy the results of the good things that they have done.

11 The very bad person will be very sad. He will have great trouble. (Here is the reason.) What his hands have done (to other people) will happen to him.

12 Children are cruel to my people and women rule over them. My people, your leaders have not ruled you well. They have led you away from the (right) paths.

13 The LORD stands up to tell (his enemies) that they have done wrong things. He stands as a judge of (many) countries.

14 The LORD comes as judge of those people who are in the government. (He comes as judge) of the leaders. (He says that) they burned the vineyard. Also, they kept what they took away from the poor people.

15 The LORD of Everything asks (them these questions):

'Why do you hit my people, so that they break into pieces?' (which means, 'Do not hit my people, so that they break into pieces.')

'Why do you walk on the faces of the poor people?' (which means, 'Do not walk on the faces of the poor people.')

16 The LORD says, 'The Daughters of Zion are very proud. They lift up their necks when they walk. They glance to see (if the men are looking at them). They walk (so that men do look at them). The little bells on their ankles make a sound when they walk.

17 So the LORD will make places that hurt them on their heads. He will make their heads bald.'

18-23 In that day the Lord will take away the valuable stones that they wear on their ankles, heads, necks, ears, arms, fingers and noses. He will take away their beautiful clothes and belts, their perfumes and charms.

24 There will be a bad smell instead of perfume. There will be a rope instead of a belt. They will not have lovely hair. They will be bald instead. Instead of good clothes (they will wear) cheap hairy cloth. They will not be beautiful. Instead, there will be only shame.

25 Swords will kill your men. Your strong men will die in wars.

26 And the gates (of Zion) will be (like) sad (people). And they will (be like people who) cry. Zion will (be like people who) sit on the ground. (And the city will be) empty.

Chapter 4

1 In that day, 7 women will (find and) hold one man. They will say, 'We will eat our own bread and we will wear our own clothes. But, let us call ourselves by your name. Take away our shame.'

More good news

2 In that day, the Branch of the LORD will be something pretty and something that has glory. And the fruit of the land will be as something proud and something beautiful. (They will be) for Israel's people that will become free. 3 Everyone that remains in Zion will be called holy. Also, (everyone) who stays in Jerusalem (will be called holy). All their names will be on a list of people who are living in Jerusalem. 4(This will happen) when the Lord will wash away the dirt from the Daughters of Zion. Also, (then) he will make Jerusalem clean from the marks left by blood. (He will do this) by a spirit that will be a judge and by a spirit of fire. 5 (This is what) the LORD will make over all the mountain called Zion. And (it will be over) all the people that come together there. (He will make) a lot of smoke during the day. And (he will make) a fire, which shines in the night. The glory will be like a coat over everything. 6 It will be a place to hide from the heat in the day. And it will be a place to hide from storms and rain.

Chapter 5

God punishes his people

The song of the vineyard

1 Now I will sing for the person that I love. (I will sing) a song of love about his vineyard.

'The person that I love has a vineyard. It is on a hill where plants grow well.

2 He dug (the ground) and he removed the stones. He planted the best vines in it.

    He built a place where he could watch (the vineyard).

He also made a place to store grapes in it. Then he waited for (the vineyard) to grow (good) grapes.

    But it grew bad grapes.'

3 And now, (listen to me,) you people that live in Jerusalem. And (listen,) all you people that live in Judah. You decide who was wrong, me or my vineyard.

4 There was nothing else that I ought to have done for my vineyard. I had done everything for it! I waited for (good) grapes. (Tell me) why it gave bad grapes!

5 And now I will tell you what I will do to my vineyard. I will take away its wall. Then (animals will come in and) eat (the vines). I will knock down its wall and (the animals) will walk all over (the vineyard).

6 I will make the land so that nobody can use it. Nobody will prune the vines or dig the ground round them. So weeds and thorns will grow there. I will say to the clouds, 'Do not (drop) rain on it.'

7 Now the vineyard of the LORD of Everything is like a picture of Israel. The plants (in it) that he likes are the people in Judah. The LORD looked for justice, but he saw only the opposite. (He wanted) people to be very good. But he only heard people that were crying for help.

The wrong things that the people in Jerusalem and Judah have done

8 The people who build (one) house (next) to (another) house will be very sad. Also, they join (one) field to (another) field. (They do this) until there is no more room. Then you live alone on the land.

9 I have heard the LORD of Everything (promise this. He said this.) 'I am sure that many houses will be empty. There will be large and beautiful houses that nobody lives in.

10 Also, large parts of the vineyard will give only a small amount (of wine). Very large amounts of seed will cause only a few plants to grow.'

11 The people that get up early in the morning will be very sad. (They do this) so that they can get a drink of alcohol. They go to bed late in the evening, so that wine can cause them to become drunks.

12 At their parties there is (music from) lyre and harp, tambourine and flute. (They enjoy) their wine. But they think that God's works have no value. They do not really like what he has made.

13 So my people will go into exile, because they do not understand (God). Their leaders will die because they do not have enough food. And very many people will not have anything to drink.

14 So Sheol will open its mouth very wide to eat more (people). The leaders and the people will go into it. (Death will take in) the crowds that make a lot of noise. Also, (it will take in) the people that have parties (in Jerusalem).

15 So (the LORD) will make people humble. Then (God) will make everybody low! (He will) take away their proud faces.

16 But his justice will make the LORD of Everything great! The Holy God will show that he is holy because he is so very good.

17 Then the sheep will eat grass as (they do in) their own fields. Young sheep will eat in the large houses (that the enemy) destroyed.

18 The people who tie themselves to sin with silly (pieces of) line will be very sad. (They pull) sin as (a horse pulls) a cart with ropes.

19 Those people who say, '(The LORD) must hurry!' will be very sad. (They say) 'He must do his work quickly, so that we can see it. We want to hear the ideas of the Holy (One) of Israel. We want them to happen! Then we will really know (that they are true)!'

20 The people that call wrong things right and right things wrong will be very sad. They say that it is light when it is dark. And (they say) that it is dark when it is light. They say that bitter things are sweet. And (they say) that sweet things are bitter.

21 Some people think that they are clever. Those people will be very sad. They think that they are clever.

22 Some people think that they are great. Those people will be very sad. (They think this) because they drink much wine. Also, some people are strong when they mix strong drink. (Those people will be very sad.)

23 They do not punish guilty people, when (the guilty) people give them money. There is no justice for people that are not guilty.

24 So as (surely as) fire burns dry plants, parts of them will fall into pieces. And as fire burns away dry grass, their flowers will blow away like small pieces of dirt. (This will happen) because they refused to obey the LORD of Everything. He said what they should do. (But they did not do it.) And they thought that the words of the Holy One of Israel were silly.

25 For this reason the LORD became angry with his people. He punished them, as if someone had hit them with his hand. And the mountains moved and (his people's) dead bodies became like dirt in the streets. (The LORD has done) all this but he is still angry with them. And his hand is still ready (to hit them again).

God will send a message to another nation from far away to punish His people

26 (The LORD) will send a message to nations that are far away. And he will (blow on his) whistle to (a nation at) the ends of the earth. And look! Here (its army) comes, very quickly!

27 Nobody is tired; nobody falls down. Nobody rests; nobody sleeps. Nobody has a belt that they have not fastened. And nobody has broken a part of a shoe.

28 Their arrows are sharp and their bows are ready to shoot. Their horses' feet are (as hard) as stones. And the wheels (on their chariots go as fast) as a strong wind.

29 They roar like a lion, they make a noise like a young lion. They roar while they catch an animal to eat. They carry it away and nobody can save it.

30 On that day, (the enemy) will roar over what they catch. Their roar will be like the sea. And if anybody looks to the land they will see darkness. And (they will see) people that are very much afraid. Also, clouds will hide the light (of the sun).

PART 2: Chapter 6 God makes Isaiah into a prophet

Chapter 6

1 (It happened) in the year when King Uzziah died. I saw my Lord. He was sitting on a very high seat. The ends of his very long coat filled the temple. 2 Above the (Lord) were seraphs. They were waiting to do what he wanted them to do. Each one had 6 wings. Two (of the wings) were covering their faces. Two of them were covering their feet. With two of them they were flying.

3 One (seraph) spoke to another. They said, 'Holy, holy, holy is the LORD of Everything! The whole earth is full of his glory.'

4 When each (seraph) spoke, the door-steps of the temple moved. Also, the temple was full of smoke.

5 Then I said, 'I am very sad, because I must not speak! I am a man with lips that are not clean. And I live among people with lips that are not clean. And with my own eyes I have seen the King, the LORD of Everything!'

6 Then one of the seraphs flew towards me. In his hand was a (piece of) coal that was burning. He had taken it from the altar with a special tool.

7 And he touched my mouth (with it). And he said, 'Look! This has touched your lips and it has taken away your guilt. It has covered your sin.'

8 Then I heard the voice of the Lord. He said, 'Whom shall I send and who will go for us?' Then I said, 'I am here. Send me.'

9 And (God said), 'Go! And tell this to the people (in Judah):

· "Always listen, but you will never understand!

· Always look. But you will never see what it means!"

10 Make the heart of these people fat. Close their ears and shut their eyes. If (you do not do this) they will see with their eyes. They will hear with their ears and they will understand with their hearts. (Then they will) turn and they will be well again.'

11 Then I said, 'For how long, Lord, (must I do this)?' And (this is what) he answered:

'(Do it) until (their enemy) destroys the cities. Then nobody will live there.

· (Do it until) nobody lives in the houses.

· (Do it until) they cannot use the land in any way.

· 12 (Do it until) the LORD removes people to far away (places).

And (do it until an enemy has) destroyed many places inside the country (called Israel).

13 And even if one in every 10 (places or people) stay, an enemy will burn them again! (They will do it as they burn) trees called terebinths and oaks. But from what remains of such a tree, an holy people will grow.'

PART 3: Chapters 7-37 God's king rules God's people

Chapter 7

King Ahaz refuses to ask God for a message

1 Ahaz became the king of Judah. He was the son of (King) Jotham. (Jotham was) the son of (King) Uzziah. (When Ahaz was king), Rezin, the king of Syria, and Pekah, the king of Israel, both attacked Jerusalem. But they did not win the fight. (Pekah was the) son of Remaliah. 2 (People that were in the government) told (this to) Ahaz. He was from (the family of David. (They said,) 'Syria and Ephraim have agreed (to attack you).' Ahaz and his people (were afraid). Their hearts moved, as trees in the forest move in the wind.

3 Then the LORD said to Isaiah, 'Go out and meet Ahaz. You and Shear Jashub, your son, will meet him at the end of the water stream. That (stream) pours from the higher pool down to where people wash clothes.' 4 (The LORD said,) 'Say (to Ahaz), "Be careful. And be very quiet. Do not be afraid. Do not be afraid because Rezin and the people from Syria and Pekah, the son of Remaliah, are angry. They are trying to 'start a fire', but their 'fire' will soon finish. 5 (Do not be afraid) because (the king of) Syria and the son of Remaliah have made bad plans against you. They have said, 6 'We must attack Judah. We will frighten the people). We will destroy (their country) and it will become ours. We will make the son of Tabeal king there.' 7 The LORD, who is Lord, says this. 'It will not happen, it will never happen! 8 (It will not happen,) because the capital (city) of Syria is Damascus. Now the king of Damascus is Rezin. And 65 years from now Ephraim will not be (a country)! There will be no people (of Ephraim) there. 9 And the capital (city) of Ephraim is Samaria. And the king of Samaria is the son of Remaliah. And if you do not believe this, you will not be alive (either).' " '

10 And the LORD spoke again (to Isaiah. 'Say this) to Ahaz. (') 11 He said, 'Ask the LORD your God for a message. Ask for it deep (in the earth) or high (in the sky).' 12 But Ahaz said, 'I will never ask (for a message) or ask the LORD to do something.' 13 And he (Isaiah) said, 'Now listen, (Ahaz. You belong to the) family of David! You are making (your) people angry (with you). And you are making God angry with you too.

14 So the Lord himself will give you a message. Look, the virgin will become pregnant. She will have a son and she will call his name Immanu El. 15 (One day) he will know (the difference between) right things and wrong things. Then he will (be old enough) to eat butter and sugar. 16 But even before the child knows (the difference between) right things and wrong things, (Assyria) will destroy (Ephraim and Syria). The two kings that you are afraid of will be (in other countries themselves).

17 The LORD will bring the king of Assyria to you and to your people. (He will come) to the house of your father. It will be a special time. There have been no days like it since Ephraim became separate from Judah.' 18 On that day the LORD will tell the flies at the higher end of the river in Egypt that they must come. And he will tell the bees in the country called Assyria that they must come. 19 And they will all come and they will land on (these places):

· the valleys with high sides

· the holes in the rocks

· all the thorn bushes

· all the places where there is water.

20 On that day the Lord will use the king of Assyria. He will come from beyond the river. He will cut off the hair from your head, your legs and your beard.

21 On that day a man will keep alive a young cow and two goats. 22 They will give a lot of milk, so he will have butter to eat. Everyone that remains in the country will eat butter and sugar. 23 On that day, in every place where there were 1000 vines, there will be weeds and thorns. (1000 vines) are worth 1000 pieces of silver. 24 A man will go there with a bow and arrows. (He will do this) because there will be brambles and thorns on all the land. 25 Nobody will go to the hills because they are afraid of the brambles and thorns. (These are the hills where) people would dig to grow plants. Now cows go there and sheep run about.

Chapter 8

God will use Assyria to destroy Israel and Syria

1 And the LORD said to me, 'Get something big to write on. Then write on it, with a tool that will write (words on stones. Write "This is) about Maher-shalal-hash-baz." 2 And I will ask (two) special people to come to me. They must say what is true. (One will be) Uriah the priest and (the other will be) Zechariah the son of Jeberechiah. They will be my special people. They must say what is true.' 3 Then I went to the prophetess. She became pregnant and she had a son. And the LORD said to me, 'Call his name Maher-shalal-hash-baz. 4 Before the child knows how to say "my father" or "my mother" (this will happen). The king of Assyria will carry away the valuable things from Damascus and from Samaria.'

5 The LORD spoke to me again. (He told me) that I must say,

6 'This people has refused (to accept) the waters of Shiloah, which move quietly. And (they have said that they) are very happy about Rezin and the son of Remaliah.

7 So, see (what will happen). The LORD will bring against them the waters of the River (Euphrates). (The waters will be) strong and powerful. (Really, the waters will be) the king of Assyria and his powerful (armies). (They will come) like a great river that rises. And it goes over its sides.

8 Then it will pour quickly into Judah. It will rise over its sides and it will go over (the land). It will even reach the neck! His wings will open out and cover all your country, Immanu El.

9 Join together (against your enemies), you people, but they will kill you all. Listen carefully, all you far countries.

Get ready for war, but (your enemies) will kill your people. Get ready to fight, but (your enemies) will kill you.

10 Make plans together, but (the plans) will fail! Talk about what you will do. But it will not happen. (Your plans will fail) because Immanu El (God is with us)!'

11 Now the LORD spoke to me. (He said this) while his strong hand was upon me. He said that I must not to do what this people (the people in Judah) were doing. He said,

12 'You must not think, "Everything that this people call a secret plan is a secret plan." Also, do not be afraid of what they are afraid of. And do not let it frighten you.

13 Instead, be afraid of the LORD of Everything! You should think of him as holy. You should be afraid of him,

14 because he, (the LORD,) will be a safe place.

But for both houses of Israel (he will become like) a stone that will make people angry. And (he will become like) a rock that will cause them to fall over. To the people in Jerusalem, (the LORD) will become someone to catch and to hold them.

15 Many people's feet will hit something and they will fall. (The LORD) will hurt them very badly. He will catch and hold them!'

16 Tie up what I have said (in a scroll). Fasten what I have taught to my disciples. 17 And I will wait for the LORD. He is hiding his face from the house of Jacob (Israel's people). But I believe that he (the LORD will do something). 18 Here am I and the children that the LORD has given to me. We are messages, messages from the LORD of Everything to (the people in) Israel. He lives on the mountain (called) Zion.

19 And they will say to you, 'Ask the mediums and wizards. They will tell you what you should do.' (Mediums and wizards) make noises like birds or animals! People should ask their God what to do. People who are alive should not talk to dead people. 20 (Listen again) to what I have said. And (listen) to what I have taught you. (If you listen to) their words, then there will be no dawn! 21 Then they will go through the country and they will not be very happy. They will not have enough to eat. Because they do not have enough to eat, they will become angry. They will look up (to where God lives). Then they will say bad things about their king and about their God. 22 And they will look to the earth. But they will see that it is dark and (that people are) not very happy. In the dark, (people will be) very sad. It will push (people) into something even blacker.

Chapter 9

Good news for God's people

1 But there will be no dark places for the people that were not very happy. In past years, (God) let trouble happen to the people in the places called Zebulun and Naphtali. But in future years, he will send glory to (these places):

- the country by the sea

- the land at the other side of the (River) Jordan

- the part (of Israel) that people in other countries (call) Galilee.

2 The people that walk in the dark will see a great light. The light will shine on those (people) that live on land full of dark shadows.

3 You (LORD) will make the country bigger. And you will make its people much happier. They will be happy with you as when people are happy at harvest time. Soldiers are also happy, because of what they have won in war. And its people will be happy like them.

4 (This is) because, as in the time of Midian, (you will kill our enemies). You will break (these things):

- the yoke (that carries) their heavy weights

- the sticks (that they hit) our backs with

- the rod that hurts us.

5 Then they will burn as material for the fire every boot that soldiers wore in war. And (they will burn) the clothes with blood on them.

6 (They will do this) because a child is born for us. (God has) given us a son. And that son will always have authority (to rule the people). And (people) will call him by these names:

- Wonderful Friend

- Great God

- Father for Always

- Leader who brings Peace

7 His authority will become greater. And the peace that he will bring will never come to an end. He will be king over (the land) that David ruled. He will make it safe. He will make sure that it has justice. And its people will be very good, now and always. The LORD of Everything will cause this to happen, because he loves (his people).

God has punished Israel and he will do it again

8 The Lord sent a message against Jacob and it came to Israel.

9 And all the people (that live in) Ephraim and Samaria know about it. They praise themselves (with these words).

10 '(Our) brick (houses) fell down. But we will build them again with stones that we have cut. They have knocked down (buildings that we made from) sycamore trees. But we will build them again with cedar (trees, which are better).'

11 But the LORD will make the enemies of Rezin stronger against him. Also, he will help those enemies.

12 The people from Syria on the east and the people from Philistia on the west have opened their mouths. And they have eaten Israel. **But (the LORD) is still angry and his hand is still ready (to hit them again).**'

13 But the people did not turn to him who hit them. Neither did they go to the LORD of Everything.

14 So in one day the LORD will cut off from Israel head and tail. (He will also cut off) palm branch and reed.

15 The head means the older men and the important people. The tail means the (false) prophets. They teach what is not true.

16 The leaders of this people lead them away from what is true. They confuse the people that they are leaders of.

17 So the Lord will not feel happy with their young men. And he will not be kind and help (children) without fathers. (He will not help) women whose husbands are dead. This is because nobody obeys God. (Everyone) does wrong things. What everyone says tells us this. They are fools. **But (the LORD) is still angry and his hand is still ready (to hit them again).**

18 The wrong things (that people do) burn like a fire. They eat up briars and thorns. They burn up the bushes in the forest. And they rise up (into the sky) like a lot of smoke.

19 He is very angry, so the LORD of Everything will burn the land. Also, the people will be like material for the fire. No man will be kind to his brother (another Jew).

20 They will take food on their right (side), but they will remain hungry. And they will eat what is on the left (side), but it will not fill them. Everyone will eat the body of the person that lives near him.

21 Ephraim will eat Manasseh and Manasseh will eat Ephraim. And both of them (will fight) against Judah. **But (the LORD) is still angry and his hand is still ready (to hit them again).**

Chapter 10

1 (Some) people make rules that are not fair. (They also make) rules that are cruel to people. Those people will be very sad.

2 (They do these things :)

(Some) people need many things. (Their rulers) do not let them get what is fair.

- They take away what poor people should have.

- They rob women whose husbands are dead of everything.

- And they are cruel to children whose parents are dead.

3 You can do nothing when God punishes you. And (you can do nothing) in a storm that comes from far away. Nobody will help you and there will be nowhere to hide your valuable things.

4 You can only go to be with the people that are in a prison. Or perhaps you will die with those (that the enemy) kills in war. **But (the LORD) is still angry and his hand is still ready (to hit them again).**

Then God will punish Assyria

5 (The people) in Assyria (will be very sad). (I will use them) like a stick, because I am angry. They (will be like someone who hits Israel) with a heavy stick. (They will do that) because I am so very angry.

6 I will send (the people from Assyria) against (Israel, because Israel) does not obey God. I will tell (them that they must attack Israel). I am angry with the people (in Israel). (The people from Assyria) will take what (the people in Israel) have. And they will rob them of their things. Then (the people from Assyria) will walk all over them, as (if Israel's people were) dirt in the streets.

7 But this is not what (Assyria's people) are thinking. Their ideas are different. They want to beat as many countries as they can. (They want) to destroy them.

8 (The king of Assyria) boasts, 'All the leaders of my armies are (like) kings!

9 (The city that is called) Calno is like Carchemish. Hamath is like Arpad and Samaria is like Damascus.

10 My hand took all these places and their idols. They had more idols than Jerusalem and Samaria.

11 So I will do to Jerusalem and her idols what I did to Samaria and her idols.'

12 The Lord will finish all his work against the hill called Zion and Jerusalem. Then (he will say), 'I will punish the king of Assyria. He boasts in his mind and there is pride in his eyes.'

13 (This is what the king of Assyria) says. 'I have done this because I am so strong. Also, I am very clever. (So) I know (what to do). I have removed the boundaries between countries. Also, I have taken their valuable things. Like a wild animal, I have attacked their people.

14 My hand found the valuable things of (many) countries. (I did this) as one finds a (bird's) home. I have got all the earth (as easily) as people take eggs from an empty bird's home. And nobody moved a wing or opened a mouth to make a noise.'

15 (The LORD says,) 'The axe is not more powerful than the person that uses it. A tool is not more important than the person that uses it. (Also, it is silly) to think that a stick can move its user! Or (it is silly to think) that a thick stick can move a man!

16 So the Lord, the LORD of Everything, will send an illness to (Assyria's) fat soldiers. They will become thin! He will light a fire under their pride. It will burn with a bright light.

17 (The LORD, who is) the Light of Israel, will become a fire. The Holy One (of Israel) will become a bright fire. And it will burn and destroy (Assyria's) thorns and briars in one day.

18 (The LORD) will completely destroy (Assyria's) great forests and its good fields. Its people's spirit and body will become as nothing.

19 Only a few forest trees will remain, so that even a child will be able to count them!

But God will help the people that continue to love him

20 When that happens, (this will happen to) the remnant of Israel. (They are) the people of Jacob that are still alive.

- They will not get help from (Assyria), which beat them.

Instead, they will get all their help from the LORD, the Holy One of Israel.

21 A remnant, a remnant of Jacob, will return and get help from the Great God.

22 Israel, only a remnant (of you) will return. (This is) even when there are so many of you. (There are as many of you) as there are bits of sand on the sea shore.

23 This will happen because the Lord, the LORD of Everything, will destroy the whole country. (He will destroy it), as he promised to do.'

24 So, this is what the Lord, the LORD of Everything says. 'My people who live in Zion, do not be afraid of the people from Assyria. They will be like someone who hits you with a stick. They will lift up a big stick against you like the people in Egypt did. 25 But soon I will not be angry with you. Instead, I will be angry (with the people from Assyria) and I will kill them. 26 And the LORD of Everything will use a whip against them. He will do this as when he killed Midian's people at the Rock of Oreb. His stick will be over the sea, and he will lift it up. (He will lift it up) as he did in Egypt. 27 In that day the weight will come off your shoulder. (The LORD) will destroy the yoke on your neck.'

28 (Assyria) will start from Rimmon and he will go to Aiath. He will pass through Migron. He will store his things at Michmash.

29 They will pass (through the hills), and they will stay for a night at Geba. (The people in) Ramah will be afraid and (the people in) Gibeah of Saul will run away.

30 People in Gallim, shout (for help)! Listen, (people in) Laish. Answer them, (people in) Anathoth.

31 (The people in) Madmenah will run away. And those that live in Gebim will rush to a safe place.

32 He will remain at Nob the day (that he arrives there). He will move his fist angrily towards the people who live in Zion and on the hill of Jerusalem.

33 But look! The Lord, the LORD of Everything, will cut off the branches with (his) power which frightens (people). He will cut down the tallest trees. And he will cause those that are very high to lie low.

34 He will cut down the trees in the forest with an axe. Also, (the great trees from) Lebanon will fall down.

Chapter 11

The good king, called the Branch, that God will send

1 The part of the Tree of Jesse that remains will start to grow. Then a Branch will grow from the part of it that is under the ground.

2 The Spirit of the LORD will come on him. (It will be like this:)

a spirit that knows what is right; and (a spirit that) knows what things mean

· a spirit that tells people the (right) thing to do and that has authority

· a spirit that knows everything and that is afraid of the LORD.

3 To obey the LORD will give pleasure (to the Branch). He will not decide about things (only) with what his eyes see. (He will not) decide (only) with what his ears hear.

4 But what he decides about poor people will be with justice. Also, he will decide about people who are not powerful. He will be fair. He will punish bad people and his words will kill them.

5 (He will wear) true justice like a belt round him. (He will) also (wear) as clothes (the fact that he is) always there.

6 Wolves will live with young sheep (and will not eat them)! And leopards will lie down with young goats! Young cows and lions will feed together and young children will lead them!

7 Cows and bears will feed (together) and their young (animals) will lie down together. And lions will eat dry grass like cows.

8 And a small baby will play (safely) near the hole where a dangerous snake (lives). And a young child (will be safe) if he puts his hand on to the home of (another) dangerous snake.

9 They will not hurt nor kill (each other) in all my holy mountain. Then the earth shall be as full of facts about the LORD as water fills the sea.

10 In that day, the part (of the tree) of Jesse will be a like a sign to (all) peoples. Other countries will come to him. And the place where he lives will be wonderful.

11 And on that day, my Lord will do something for the second time. He will save the remnant of his people that are still (alive). He will take them from Assyria, Egypt, Pathros, Elam, Shinar, Hamath and from countries by the sea.

12 (The Lord) will lift up a sign for these countries (to see). He will bring together the people from Israel (that Assyria) took away. He will bring back the exiles of Judah from all over the earth.

13 No longer will Ephraim not like (Judah) and Judah will not attack (Ephraim) any longer. Ephraim will no longer want what Judah has.

Also, Judah will not cause trouble for Ephraim again.

14 But together they will attack the low hills of Philistia to the west. They will beat the people to the east (of the River Jordan). They will fight against Edom and Moab, and the people in Ammon will obey them.

15 The LORD completely destroyed part of the Sea of Egypt. He will lift his hand over the River (Euphrates). Then he will send a hot wind that burns things. It will make (the river) into 7 streams, so that people can cross it with dry feet.

16 And there will be a good road from Assyria for the remnant. (They are the LORD's) people that remain. It will be (as good a road) as when Israel came up from the country called Egypt.

Chapter 12

Isaiah's psalm (or song to God)

1 You will say in that day, 'I praise you, LORD. You were angry with me, but now, you are not angry (with me). Now you are being kind to me.

2 Listen! God has made me safe! I will continue to believe (in him). And I will not be afraid because the LORD, the LORD, has made me strong. He is the person that I am singing about. He has made me safe.

3 You will get water happily from the wells. (This water) will make you safe.'

4 And you will say in that day, 'Praise the LORD! Shout (aloud) his name! Tell everybody what God has done. Cause them to remember that he is very great.

5 Sing psalms to the LORD because he has done wonderful things! Cause everyone in the world to know it!

6 Everyone that lives in Zion, shout! And sing because you are so happy! The Holy One of Israel is great and he is (living) with you.'

Chapter 13

God will destroy Babylon

1 (These are) serious words (about) Babylon that Isaiah the son of Amoz 'saw'.

2 Lift up a sign on an empty hill. Shout aloud to them and lift a hand! Then they will go through the gates of the kings.

3 I myself have sent my holy ones. I have told them what they must do. Also, my brave soldiers (must say) that I am very angry. I have sent them. (They are) my proud (soldiers). Nobody has ever beaten them.

4 (Listen to) the sound of a very big crowd! (They are) people (that are) on the mountains! (Listen to) the sound of these people. They are shouting while they come together from many countries! The LORD of Many (Armies) is preparing an army ready for war.

5 People are coming from a country that is far away. (They are coming) from the ends of the skies. The LORD (is coming) with arms, (because he is) angry. He will destroy the whole country (of Babylon).

6 Weep, because the day of the LORD is near. It will happen when Shaddai destroys (your country).

7 Everybody's hands will become weak because of this. And every human heart will fail,

8 and they will be very much afraid. They will hurt and they will be in much pain. They will be (afraid) like a woman that is having (a baby). They will look at each other and their faces will frighten each other.

9 Look! The day of the LORD will happen (soon!) (It will be) cruel. (The LORD) will be angry. He will be like an angry fire! It will make the country (of Babylon) empty and it will kill (all the) sinners in it.

10 Yes! The stars in the skies, all of them, will give no light. When the sun appears (in the morning), it will still be dark. The moon will not shine.

11 I will cause very bad things to happen to the world. And (I will punish) bad people for their sins. I will not let proud people think that they are better (than anyone else). And I will beat strong people that hurt (weak people).

12 I will make men harder to find than the best gold. And men and women will be more difficult to find than gold from Ophir.

13 So I will cause the skies to move. The earth will move. And (people) will see how angry the LORD of Many (Armies) is.

14 And people will look at each other and they will run away to their own country. They will be like wild animals that run away from the hunter. Or (they will be) like sheep with nobody to lead them.

15 (The foreign army) will (kill) with sharp knives anyone that tries to run away. And they will kill with the sword anyone that they catch.

16 They will break young children into pieces while (the children's parents) watch. They will rob the people's homes and they will have sex with their wives.

17 Look, I will cause the Medes to come (to fight) against (Babylon). (The Medes) do not ask for silver or gold.

18 Their bows will kill the young men. They will not be kind to babies. And they will not seem sorry for the children.

19 And Babylon will be like Sodom and Gomorrah when God destroyed them. (This will happen even if other) countries think, 'Babylon is beautiful.' The people in Chaldea are proud of (Babylon).

20 People will never live there again. And none of its children will ever live there again. No Arab will put his tent there. No farmers will cause their animals to lie down there.

21 Only wild animals will lie down there. Its houses will be full of owls that scream. And ostriches will live there. Wild goats will dance about in it.

22 Hyenas will make a noise in its tall buildings and jackals will live in its beautiful palaces. (The Medes) will soon destroy it. It does not have many more days.

Chapter 14

A few words about Israel

1 The LORD will be sorry for Jacob and he will choose Israel again. Then he will give them rest in their own country. Also, people from a foreign country will join themselves to the people of Jacob. They will really become united with them. 2 And the (foreign) people will take the people (of Israel) and bring them to their own country (Israel). Then the people of Israel will rule the foreign people in the LORD's country. They (the foreign people) will become male and female slaves. So the people that made (Israel) prisoners, will be prisoners themselves! (Israel) will rule over the people that were cruel to them.

More about Babylon

3 On that day, this will happen. The LORD will give you rest from these things:

- all your pain and illnesses
- the cruel way that (your enemies) caused you to work.

4 You will laugh at the king of Babylon. Then you will say (to him), 'Now you cannot be cruel to us, nor can you attack us!

5 The LORD has destroyed the authority of bad people. He has removed the power of the rulers (of Babylon).

6 (The rulers of Babylon) hit many people because they were angry with them. They never stopped hitting them. They were very angry, so they attacked (other) countries. They never stopped fighting them.

7 (But now) there is no war in the whole world and it can rest. Everyone is singing (because they are so happy)!

8 Even the pine trees and the cedar trees in Lebanon are happy. (They say this) to you, (king of Babylon): "Since (the LORD) beat you, nobody has come to cut us down!"

9 When you arrive there, you will get much interest from (the people in) Sheol. People there will (come) to meet you! You will wake up the Rephaim, who were all leaders on the earth. (They will come) to say, "welcome" to you. All who were kings of their countries will stand up from their seats.

10 All of them will speak to you and say this. "Even you have become as weak as we (are)! You have become like us!"

11 Your pride will bring you down to Sheol with the noise of your harps. Under you will be a bed of maggots and (over you) a blanket of worms.'

More words about Babylon

12 'Look at you! You have fallen from the skies!

    You shine. (You are called the) Son of the Dawn!

    You made many countries low, but now you are low yourself!

13 You said in your mind, "I will go up into the heavens.

    I will put my seat above the stars of God.

    I will sit in the mountain in the far north with God's leaders.

14 I will rise above the tops of the clouds. I will be like the Most High."

15 But he has brought you down to Sheol, to the deepest Pit!'

More words about Babylon

16 'Those (people) that see you will really look at you. They will think this about you. "This is the man that caused the earth to move. He caused countries to shake.

17 (This is the man) that made the world like a desert. He destroyed its cities. He did not let his prisoners go (back to their) homes."

18 All the kings of all the countries – yes! all of them – lie down in a good place. Each (king lies) in his own grave.

19 But you, they will throw you out without a grave! You will be like a branch (that people throw) away. Or (you will be like) the clothes of a dead man that a sword has cut. (You will be like) someone that fell on to the stones in a big hole. Or (you will be like) a dead body that people have kicked.

20 They will not bury you with the other (kings of Babylon). Here are the reasons:

·   You have destroyed your country.

·   You have killed your (own) people.

Nobody will ever remember again this son of very bad people!

21 Prepare a place where they will kill his children. (They will kill them) because their parents sinned. Then his children will not rule the world or fill it with cities.'

22 'I will fight against them', says the LORD of Many Armies. The LORD of Many Armies also says, 'I will remove the name of Babylon. (I will remove its) people that remain, their children and their children's children.' 23 The LORD of Many Armies says this also: 'I will make (Babylon) a place where owls live. Also, (it will be a place) where there are pools of water. And I will take it away completely (like a man sweeps things away) with a brush.'

A few words about Assyria

24 The LORD of Many Armies has made a serious promise. 'It will happen as my plan says. I will really do what I have decided to do. 25 I will kill the man from Assyria in my country. Also, I will put him under my feet on my mountains. Then, he will not be cruel to my people. Also, they will not have to carry his heavy weights again.' 26 This is the plan that (he) made for the whole earth. And this is the hand that (he) lifted over all
the nations. 27 This is the plan of the LORD of Many Armies. Nobody can change it. He has lifted up his hand. Nobody can change this.

A few words about Philistia

28 In the year that King Ahaz died, (Isaiah) received this message:

29 'Do not feel happy, you people in Philistia. (God) has broken the stick that hit you. But from that snake a more dangerous snake will come. And from that (snake) will come a snake that can fly!

30 But poor people will feed their (animals) that were born first. And people that need (help) will sleep safely. Then I will cause your people (in Philistia) to die because there is no food. And I will kill the people that remain.

31 Gate (of the city), cry! City (itself), scream! Move away, all you people in Philistia! (Do this) because smoke will come from the north. Everybody in (that) army will march quickly.'

32 'What shall we say to the people that bring messages from the government? Say that the LORD has built Zion. And (say) that his poor people will be safe there.'

Chapter 15

Words about Moab

1 (This is) a serious message (about) Moab.

It is true! In one night (an enemy) destroyed Ar (and) Moab made no noise.

It is true! In one night (an enemy) destroyed Kir in Moab (and Moab made) no noise.

2 (The people in) Dibon have gone up to their temple to weep. (They have gone up to) the high places. Moab is crying about Nebo and Medeba. Every head is bald and (they have) cut off every beard.

3 They are wearing hairy cloth in the streets. On the roofs (of their houses) they are weeping. And in the open places (in their towns they are weeping). Tears cover their faces.

4 Then (the people in) Heshbon and Elealeh cried aloud. (People) as far away as Jahaz heard the sound! The soldiers of Moab cry aloud (because they are afraid). The minds (of Moab's people) are afraid.

5 Inside, I feel like a man who is crying aloud for Moab! Its people have run away as far as Zoar (and) Eglath Shelishijah.

It is true! They weep while they climb up the hill to Luhith.

It is true! On the road to Horonaim they shout aloud, '(An enemy) has destroyed (us)!'

6 It is true! It is not wet; it is dry in (the Valley of) Nimrim.

It is true! The grass is dead. Nothing new is growing. (And) there is nothing (that is) green.

7 So, they are carrying away over the Wadi Arabim whatever they found still (in the fields). And they are carrying away what they have saved.

8 It is true! The sounds (of people that ask for help) reach the edges of Moab. (People) as far as Eglaim heard (Moab's) sad songs. (Moab's) sad songs reached Beer Elim.

9 It is true! Blood fills the waters of Dimon.

It is true! More (bad) things will happen to Dimon. A lion will wait for those that run away from Moab. And (it will wait) for those that remain (in the) country.

Chapter 16

More about Moab

1 Send young sheep from the ruler of the country (to Jerusalem). Send them from Sela across the desert to the mountain of the Daughter of Zion (Jerusalem).

2 The women from Moab (are crossing) the River Arnon. (They are) like birds that are learning to fly. (The mother bird) has pushed them out from their home.

3 Tell us what we should do! Be fair about what you say! Cause your shadow (over us) to seem like it is night in the middle of the day! Hide the refugees! Do not show (to their enemies) the people that have run away!

4 Let the people from Moab who are running away stay with you. Hide them from (the enemy that is) killing them.

It is true! People will not be cruel to those who are weak. People will not destroy things. People that fight will disappear from the country.

5 Someone from David's family will build a kingdom. The man that rules it will be fair and honest. He will be a fair judge. He will decide rightly. And he will quickly cause (his people) to do what is right.

6 We have heard about the pride of Moab. (Moab was) very proud. In its pride, (Moab) thought that it was better (than other people). And Moab said things that were not kind (to them).

7 So Moab weeps. All Moab weeps for itself. Sing a sad song. And cry for the cakes made with very dry grapes from Kir Hareseth!

8 It is true! There are no (fruits) in the fields in Heshbon. And (there is nothing on) the vine of Sibmah. The rulers of (other) countries have destroyed its branches. (The branches) reached to Jazer (in the north-west) and as far as the desert (in the east). Its new branches grew and they crossed over (the Dead) Sea.

9 Because of this, I weep for the vine of Sibmah, as Jazer weeps. I put my tears all over you, Heshbon and Elealeh.

It is true! The noise of war has fallen on your plants and on your fruit.

10 Nobody is really happy in the fields. Nobody sings or shouts (because they are happy) in the vineyards. Nobody jumps on the grapes in the places where they make wine. I have caused the noise to stop.

11 So, I cry deep inside me for Moab. It is like the sad sound of a harp. And I am hurting for Kir Hareseth.

12 And when the people in Moab come to their high place, they will become very tired. When they come to pray at their temple, nothing will happen.

13 Those are the words that the LORD has already spoken about Moab. 14 But now the LORD says, 'In three years, everybody will laugh at Moab. Count these years like (the years that) people pay a worker. Then (God) will make all Moab's many proud people humble. And only a few of them will remain, a very small number.'

Chapter 17

Words about Damascus

1 (This is a) serious message (about) Damascus. Look! (The enemy) broke the city called Damascus into a lot of stones.

2 Nobody lives in the cities of Aroer. They have become (places) where groups (of animals) lie down. Nobody makes them afraid.

3 There are no strong cities in Ephraim and no kings in Damascus. The few people that remain in Aram are as great as the people of Israel! (This is what) the LORD of Many Armies is saying.

4 On that day the LORD removed the things that Jacob was proud of. His fat body became thin!

5 And it was like when a farmer got all the grain. He did it while it was still (in a field). With his arm he cut off the fruit from the plants. Then it was like when someone gleans some of the grain in the Valley of Rephaim.

6 There was not much in (Israel). It was like someone that hit an olive tree. There were only two or three small olives on the highest branch. And (there were only) 4 or 5 fruits on the branches of a fruit tree. (This is what) the LORD, the God of Israel, (is) saying.

7 On a day (like) that, people should obey their Maker. They should turn to the Holy One of Israel.

8 They should not think that the altars (can help them). Their hands have made (these altars). They should not turn to what their fingers have made. These are (images of the female god called) Asherah. And the altars (are where they burn) incense.

9 On that day, (Israel's) strong cities became like empty cities. (They were like) those (other) empty forests and woods. People had left them when Israel (first attacked them). So (the cities) were empty groups of stones, 10 for these reasons. You forgot the God that made you safe. You did not remember the Rock that hid you (from danger). You planted gardens for a false god and you planted vines for a foreign god.

11 So, there were no fruits. On the day that you planted them, you caused them to grow well. They had flowers on the morning that you planted them! But all this finished in a day that was very sad. And (there was) pain that nothing could take away.

12 Oh, (listen)! (The people in) many countries are roaring. They are making a noise like an angry sea! And (listen)! The (people in those) countries are roaring, they are roaring like great amounts of water!

13 The (people in those) countries are roaring; they are roaring like great amounts of water! But when (the LORD) will shout at them, they will run far away. The wind will blow them away like dead bits of plants on the hills. Or it will blow them away like dirt that blows about before a storm.

14 Look! In the evening everyone is very much afraid. And in the morning nobody is there! This is what will happen to anyone that takes things from us. (It will happen to anyone who) robs us.

Chapter 18

Words about Cush

1 Oh! (There is) a country (where the) ships have wings. It is near the rivers of Cush.

2 It is sending messages by people in boats (that they) made from papyrus. They sail on the top of the waters. Go, take a message quickly. (Go to) a country where (the people) are tall. And their skins are not hairy. (It is a country where everyone), both near and far, is afraid of its people. The country is very strong and rivers cut the land into parts.

3 Everybody that lives (in the) world and (on the) earth, (listen to this). You will see a sign on the tops of the mountains. You will hear the sound of a trumpet.

4 This (is what) the LORD said to me. 'I will watch quietly from my place. I will be as quiet as the heat that shines from the sun. (I will be as quiet as) the mist that rises at harvest time.'

5 Then, before the harvest, (the LORD) will cut off the new parts of the plants. He will use a special knife. He will cut off the wide branches and take them away. (He will do this) after the flowers have gone. But (he will do it) before the fruit is ready to pick.

6 (He) will leave them all for the birds that catch small animals in the mountains to eat. (He will leave them) to the wild animals on the land. The birds (will feed) on them all the summer. And the wild animals will (feed) on them all the winter.

7 At that time (people) brought gifts to the LORD of Many Armies. The people are tall and their skins are not hairy. Everyone both near and far is afraid of these people. The country is very strong, and rivers cut the land into parts. (They will come) to a place where the Name of the LORD of Many Armies is. It is a mountain called Zion.

Chapter 19

Words about Egypt

1 (This is a) serious message (about) Egypt.

Look! The LORD will come to Egypt. He will ride on a cloud that will move quickly. The false gods of Egypt will be afraid when he comes. Also, the heart of Egypt will turn into water inside.

2 'I will cause Egypt's men (to fight) against Egypt's men. A man will fight against his brother. A man will fight against the man that lives near him. A city (will fight) against a city and a kingdom will fight against a kingdom.

3 (I will) pour out the spirit of Egypt from inside it. And I will confuse their plans. (So) they will ask (for help from) their false gods. And (they will ask for help from) the spirits of dead people, and from mediums and from wizards.

4 And I will give Egypt into the power of a cruel master. And a powerful king will rule over them.' (This is what) the Lord, the LORD of Many Armies says.

5 And the waters of the sea will become dry. And the river will have no water and so it will become dry.

6 And the canals will have less (water) and they will have a bad smell. And the streams of Egypt will become dry. The reeds and the other plants that grow by the river will die.

7 (And) the plants at the side of the river (Nile) will die. And (the plants near) where the river goes into the sea (will die). Everything (that people) plant by the river will become dry. (The wind will) blow it away and (there will be) nothing there.

8 And the fishers will be very sad. Then, everyone that throws a bent piece of metal and a line into the river will cry. Also, those people that put something on the water to catch fish will have nothing (to eat).

9 The people that work with the flax will not know what to do. The women that comb (the flax) will not be happy. Neither will the men that make it into cloth (be happy).

10 This will destroy the spirit of the workers (in Egypt). Everyone that works for money (will feel) sick inside them.

11 The leaders of Zoan are really fools! The best people in Pharaoh's government say that he must do silly things! You cannot say to Pharaoh, 'I am a son of a man who knows nearly everything. (I am) a son of (someone who was) king a long time ago.'

12 Where, then, (Pharaoh), are your clever men? (Or, Pharaoh, you have no clever men!) Cause them to tell you now what they know. They know what the LORD of Many Armies will do against Egypt.

13 The leaders in Zoan have made themselves into fools. The leaders of Noph have confused each other. The leaders of (these) groups (of people) have caused Egypt to choose wrongly.

14 The LORD has mixed into the people (of Egypt) something that confuses their spirits. In everything that they do they choose wrongly.) They choose wrongly like a drunk that is being sick.

15 There is nothing that anybody in Egypt can do. They may be like a head or like a tail, a branch on a palm tree or a reed. (There is nothing that they can do.)

16 In that day the people in Egypt will be afraid, like women. They will be afraid when the LORD of Many Armies uses his power against them. 17 The (name of the) country called Judah will frighten the people in Egypt very much. When people say (the name Judah), they will be afraid of the LORD of Many Armies. They will be afraid of what he has decided to do against them.

18 In that day 5 cities in the country called Egypt will speak the language of Canaan. (The people in them) will promise to obey the LORD of Many Armies. One of the towns will be called Sun City.

19 In that day there will be an altar to the LORD in the middle of the country called Egypt. Also, (there will be) a tall stone to the LORD at the edge (of Egypt). 20 Those (two things) will be like notices to tell (everyone in) the country called Egypt about the LORD of Many Armies. (The people in Egypt) will pray to the LORD because other people are cruel to them. Then, this is what he will do. He will send someone to make them safe. And he will send a judge who will remove the danger from them. 21 And the LORD will know the people in Egypt. And also, the people in Egypt will know the LORD in that day. And they will worship (the LORD) and they will offer gifts to him. They will make promises to the LORD. And they will do what they have promised to do. 22 And (if) the LORD should send to Egypt a plague, he (really) will hurt them. But then he will make them well again. And then they will return to the LORD. And he will answer their prayers and he will make them well.

23 In that day there will be a road from Egypt to Assyria. (People from) Assyria will go to Egypt and (people from) Egypt will go to Assyria. People from Egypt and Assyria will worship together.

24 In that day Israel will be the third (country) with Egypt and Assyria. Good things will happen in the middle of the country. 25 The LORD of Many Armies will do good things for them. He will say, 'I will do good things for my people Egypt, and Assyria, which I have made. And I will do good things for Israel that I have chosen.'

Chapter 20

Words about Egypt and Cush

1 In the year (711 B.C.) (the man called the) Tartan came to Ashdod. (This was) when Sargon, the king of Assyria, sent him. He fought against Ashdod and he destroyed it. 2 In that time the LORD spoke by Isaiah the son of Amoz. (He) said, 'Go and take the hairy clothes off your body and the shoes from your feet.' And (Isaiah) did this. He walked about without clothes and without shoes.

3 And the LORD said, 'My servant Isaiah walked without clothes and without shoes for three years.

It was a message and a prophecy against Egypt and Cush. 4 This is what the king of Assyria (will do). He will take away (people) from Egypt as prisoners. And (he will take people) from Cush as exiles. Young people and old people will go. They will have no clothes or shoes. (People) will see their bottoms (where the backs of the legs and the body join). This will make the people in Egypt ashamed. 5 They will not be very happy and they will be ashamed. They had hoped that Cush (would help them). And they had said that Egypt (would help them also). 6 The people that live along this coast will say in that day, "Look! This happened to the people that we hoped (would help us). We went to them for help. (We did this) to get away from the king of Assyria. And now, we do not know how to get away (from him)." '

Chapter 21

Words about Babylon

1 (This is) a serious message about the desert near the sea. It comes from the desert. (It comes) from a frightening place. It is like a storm from the Negev desert.

2 I received a difficult message. The robber robs and the destroyer destroys. Elam, go up (to Babylon)! Media, attack (Babylon)! (The LORD says,) 'I will stop (Babylon) crying.'

3 (All) this hurts me. Bad pains attack me. (They are) like the bad pains that a woman feels. (She feels them) when she has a baby. What I hear bends me over. And that is why I cannot listen. What I see frightens me. And that is why I cannot look.

4 It confuses my mind. I am very much afraid. I wanted a quiet evening. But now that quiet evening has become (a time) when I am very much afraid.

5 They prepare a special meal. They put down the carpets. They eat and drink. Officers, make your shields ready!

6 This is what the Lord said to me. 'Go! And cause somebody to stand and to watch (what will happen). (Ask) him to report what he sees.

7 If he reports (one of these) then cause him to watch.

· a rider

· a pair of (men on) horses

· a rider on a donkey

· a rider on a camel.

And he must watch very well.'

8 Then the man that watched shouted. (He said), 'Lord, I am standing every day on a building (from which I can see everything). I am standing at my place every night.

9 And look! Someone is coming! (It is) a rider, (it is) a man with a pair of horses!' (The man) reports and says this. '(An enemy) has destroyed Babylon! (The enemy) has destroyed it! All the images of its people's gods lie in pieces on the ground!'

10 (Judah), they have hurt you. They have hurt you very much. (But) I have told you what I have heard from the LORD of Everything. (He is) the God of Israel.

Words about Edom

11 (This is) a serious message about Dumah. Someone is shouting to me from Seir. (They are asking,) 'Keeper, how much more of the night (is there)? Keeper, how much more of the night (is there)?'

12 The keeper said, 'The morning will come, (but) so will the night. If you want to ask (again, then) come back. Come (and) ask!'

Words about Arabia

13 (This is) a serious message about Arabia. Caravans of people from Dedan, you will find a safe place (behind) the bushes in the wild country.

14 (There) you will give water to (people) who need a drink. People that live in Tema will give bread to the refugees.

15 (Do this) because they are running away from (all this):

- swords

- swords (that are) ready to fight

- bows (that soldiers have) bent

- the dangerous battle.

16 This is what my Lord has said to me. 'In less than a year, all the important people in Kedar will have gone. A servant (that someone has) paid counts a year. Count the year like that. 17 Only a few of the men that use bows (from the) soldiers of the men from Kedar will remain. (This will happen) because the LORD, the God of Israel, has spoken.'

Chapter 22

Words about Jerusalem

Words about the city itself

1 (This is) a serious message about the Valley (in Jerusalem that Isaiah 'saw') in a vision. Something is the matter with you. You have all gone up on to the roofs of your houses!

2 (Your) city is full of noise. And (it is full of people that are) rushing about. The town is having a party! The sword did not kill the people that are dead. They did not die in a war.

3 (The enemy) caught all your leaders that ran away. (The enemy) did not have to use one bow. Some of them ran a long way away, but (the enemy) caught them all!

4 So I said, 'Leave me alone! Let me cry the saddest tears. Do not try to make me happy, because (the enemy will) kill many of my people.

5 (This is) because my Lord, the LORD of Everything, will have a day of noise. (It will be) in the Valley of Vision (in Jerusalem). There will be feet that are running and (it will) confuse people. (The enemy) will destroy walls and people will shout (for help) to the hills.'

6 (People will say), '(People from) Elam carried baskets of arrows. (There were) men with chariots and horses and (soldiers from) Kir lifted up (their) shields.'

7 So your best valleys will be full of chariots and men on horses will attack (your city's) gates.

8 (The LORD) will take away from Judah the place where its people hide themselves. So, in that day, you will look for arms in the House of the Forest (in Jerusalem).

9 You will see that there are many holes in the walls of the City of David. Also, you will get water from the Lower Pool.

10 Then you will count the houses in Jerusalem. And you will knock down the houses to make the walls (of Jerusalem) stronger.

11 You may have built a place inside the walls (of Jerusalem) to put water from the Old Pool. But you have not looked to its Maker. And you did not see the person that made plans for it long ago.

12 And in that day my Lord, the LORD of Everything, will ask for (people) to weep and to cry aloud. He will ask them to cut the hair off their heads. Also, they must wear hairy clothes.

13 But look! (Everybody is) happy, they are very happy. They are killing cows and sheep. They will eat meat and drink. (They are saying,) 'We will eat and drink, because tomorrow we will die.'

14 But this is what the LORD of Everything has told me. '(I will) certainly not excuse this sin until you (all) die.' (This is what) my Lord, the LORD of Everything said.

Words about one of the leaders in Jerusalem called Shebna

15 This (is what) my Lord, the LORD of Everything, said. (He said,) 'Stand up and go to this (man) Shebna. He has authority in (the king's) house.

16 (Say to him,) "You should not be here. (God did not say) that you (could be) here. You have cut (in the rock) here for yourself a tomb. You have cut a tomb in the side of the hill. You have cut for yourself a place in the rock to put your dead body.

17 Look! The LORD will throw you; he will throw you (away, you) strong man! (First) he will hold on to you in his strong hand.

18 (Then) he will make you like a ball; he will make you like a ball. (Then he will) throw you like a ball into a wide country. You will die there. (There) your great chariots will make your master's family ashamed."

19 I will remove you from your job. And he will throw you down from the place where you are an officer.'

Words about another leader, called Eliakim

20 'And this is what will happen in that day. I will tell my servant Eliakim, the son of Hilkiah that he must come.

21 And I will put on him your (Shebna's) special clothes and I will tie your special belt round him. And I will give him your authority. Then he (Eliakim) will become (like) a father to everyone that lives in Jerusalem and to the people of Judah.

22 And I will put the key of the family of David on his shoulder. What he opens, nobody will close. What he closes, nobody will open.

23 And I will fix him in place (like a) strong bent piece of metal. And he will make his father's house famous.

24 But the whole weight of his father's family will hang on him (like that piece of metal). All his children and their children, like cups and bottles that contain things, (will hang on him).' 25 (This is what) the LORD of Everything says: 'In that day the bent piece of metal that (they) fixed strongly, will not hold. (I will) cut it down and it will fall. And the weight on it will fall off because the LORD has spoken (it).'

Chapter 23

Words about Tyre

1 (This is) a serious message about Tyre.

Cry aloud, (you people in) the ships (that go) to Tarshish. (An enemy) has destroyed it. There is no house to come home to. They heard about this in the country called Cyprus.

2 Weep, (you people) that live on the island. (Weep, you) merchants of Sidon, that the sailors made rich.

3 Grain came from the River Nile on the great seas. The fruits from the River Nile brought money (to Phoenicia). So it became a market place for (many) countries.

4 (You people that live in) Sidon, be ashamed. (Be ashamed,) because the sea has spoken. The power of the sea, (Tyre), has said, 'I have not been in labour. (Children) have not been born. I have not had sons nor been a parent to daughters.'

5 When (the people in) Egypt receive the news, they will be in much pain at the report from Tyre.

6 Cross over to Tarshish! Cry aloud, you people that live on the island.

7 (This is) the city where you had many parties. It is old, very old. (Now) their feet have taken its people to live in countries that are far away.

8 People do not know who made these plans against Tyre. (Tyre is the city that) gives crowns (to people). Its merchants are like kings. Its merchants are famous in (all) the world.

9 The LORD of Everything thought that he should do this. (He did not want) people to feel more important than they were. And (he wanted) to cause all the famous people in the world not to feel important. (That is why he did it.)

10 Travel through your country, people in Tarshish, as (easily as the people in Egypt travel along) the River Nile. (Travel) because now, nobody will stop you.

11 The LORD has lifted his hand over the sea. He made kingdoms afraid. He told (his armies) what they must do in Phoenicia. (They had to) destroy all (Phoenicia's) strong buildings.

12 Then he said, 'Do not continue your parties. (The enemy) has destroyed you, you people that live in Sidon. Get up! Cross over to Cyprus. Even there you will not find rest for yourself.'

13 Look at the country called Babylon! Its people are all dead! (The armies) from Assyria made it a place for wild animals (to live in). They (the men from Assyria) built small mountains (of earth that they climbed on) to attack it. They took everything away from its strong buildings and they destroyed (Babylon).

14 Cry aloud, you ships of Tarshish. (Your enemy) has destroyed your strong port.

15 At that time (people will) forget Tyre for 70 years. This is how long one king lives. At the end of 70 years something will happen to Tyre. It is like the song about the prostitute.

16 'Prostitute that (people) have forgotten,

walk about the city with your harp.

Play it well. Sing many songs.

Then (people) will remember you again.'

17 At the end of 70 years the LORD will be kind to Tyre. It will 'become a prostitute' again! (This means that) its merchants will go to all the kingdoms of the world on the earth. 18 And this will happen: All the money that (Tyre) gets and all the profit will go to the LORD. (Tyre) will not hide it or store it. Rather, the profit (will go) to the people that live near the LORD. (They will have) plenty of food and good clothes.

Chapter 24

Things that will happen to bad people

1 Understand (this)! The LORD will make the country empty and he will destroy it. He will destroy the ground. And he will move the people that live in it in all directions.

2 It will be the same for (all these people):

- the people and the priest

- the servant and his master

- the girl that is a servant and her mistress

- the buyer and the seller

- the lender and the borrower

- the person that has lent money and the person that has borrowed money.

3 (Enemies) will completely destroy the land. (They) will take everything from it. The LORD says that (this will happen). (So it will happen.) 4 The land will be dry and it will die. The world will become weak and it will die. The important people in the country will become weak.

5 The people that live in the country have made it dirty. (This happened) for these reasons:

- They have not obeyed (God's) rules.

- They have changed (God's) rules.

- They have decided to forget (God's) covenant that will always be true.

6 That is why a curse is destroying the country. And the people that live in it are hurting. This is because they have done wrong things. (Something) burns the people that live in the country. Only a few of them remain.

7 The wine dries up and the vine dies. The people that want to drink (the wine) are not happy.

8 The happy sound of the tambourine stops. The noise from parties has finished. The harp does not make any happy music.

9 People do not sing while they drink wine. The beer does not taste nice to those that drink it.

10 (Enemies) have destroyed the city (so that) it is without shape. (People) locked every house so that (the enemy) could not get in.

11 People shout for wine in the streets. Everybody that is happy becomes sad. Nobody in the country laughs.

12 (Enemies) have destroyed the city. (They) knocked down the gates (of the city) and they destroyed them.

13 This will happen through all the country and among (other) countries. They will be empty like an olive tree that people hit. Or (they will be empty like a vine) with a few grapes (that people have) not picked.

The song of the few people that remain (verses 14-16a)

14 These (are the people) that use their voices to shout aloud! From (the sea in) the west they say that the LORD is great!

15 So, in (the countries in) the east give praise to the LORD. (Give praise) to the LORD God of Israel. (Give praise) from the islands in the sea.

16 From every part of the country we hear songs that give praise to the Righteous One.

Isaiah's sad song (verses 16b-23)

But I said, 'I have become thin and weak! I have become thin and weak! I am so sad! Bad people are doing bad things. Yes, the bad people are being really very bad!'

17 People in the country, terror, a big hole in the ground and a trap will kill you!

18 The person that runs away from the sound of terror will fall into the big hole. A trap will catch the person that climbs out of the big hole. (It will happen because (someone has) opened the windows of the sky. Also, (they have) moved what is under the land.

19 All this has completely broken the land. It has torn the land into pieces. It has moved the land very much.

20 The earth walks like a man that is a drunk. It moves about like a tent (in the wind). The wrong things that (the people in the country) have done feel heavy upon the country. So it will be like someone who falls down. And it will be like someone who never gets up again.

21 On that day the LORD will punish (anything with) power in the skies above. And (he will punish) the kings on the land below.

22 (The LORD) will bring them together like prisoners in a hole in the ground. He will lock them in a prison and after a long time he will punish them.

23 The white (light of the moon) will disappear. And the heat (of the sun) will become cold. (This is) because the LORD of Everything will be king on the hill called Zion. Then, his leaders in Jerusalem will see that he is very great.

Chapter 25

A song that gives praise to God, because God killed the enemies

1 LORD, you are my God and I will give you praise. I will say that you are very great. And I will give praise to your name, because you have done wonderful things. You said long ago what you would do. And you have done it. (You were) honest and (your promises) were true.

2 And you have broken the city into a hill (of stones). (You have) destroyed the strong city. The strong city that foreign people (live in) has gone. Nobody will build it again.

3 So, a strong country will give you praise. The city in a cruel country will be afraid of you.

4 (This is) because you (LORD) have made (your) poor people safe. (You have) made safe the people that needed (help) in their trouble. (You) hid them from the storm (and you were their) shade from the heat. The attack of the cruel people was like a storm that knocked against a wall.

5 (And the storm was) like heat in a dry sandy place. You, (LORD), stopped the noise of the foreigners. The shade of a cloud makes less the heat (of the sun). In the same way, you took away the songs of the enemies. They thought that they had beaten us. (That is why they sang.)

6 The LORD of Everything will make a feast for all people upon this mountain (in Jerusalem). It will be a feast of the very best meat, a feast with the very best wine. (It will be a feast) of the very best meat that makes people strong. It will be a feast with the best wines.

7 And on this mountain (the LORD) will destroy the shroud that covers all people. It is a shroud that is over every country

8 He will destroy death for always. The LORD, my master, will dry the faces of everyone that has tears (in their eyes). People will not feel ashamed again, over all the earth. This is what the LORD has promised to do.

9 On that day they will say, 'Look! This is our God! We have waited for him to come and to make us safe. This is the LORD! We have waited for him. So we shall be happy, very happy, because he has saved us.'

10 The power of the LORD will stay on this mountain. And he will walk on the people from Moab as people walk on dead grass and animal dirt.

11 And (the people from Moab) will put their hands into it. (They will be) like someone that puts out (his hands) to swim. But they will go down deep in the water, even if they are able (to swim) with their hands.

12 And (the LORD) will knock down their high, strong walls. He will throw them down. He will make them low and he will turn them into small bits of dry dirt on the ground.

Chapter 26

Another song that gives praise to God

1 In that day, (people) will sing this song in the country called Judah.

We have a strong city. (The LORD) made walls inside and outside (the city), to make us safe.

2 Open the gates (of the city), so that the righteous people can come in. (The righteous people) are those people that continue to believe (the LORD).

3 You, (LORD), will make safe the person whose mind is always thinking about you. (You will keep him) safe, because he believes you.

4 Always, always believe the LORD! (Do this) because the LORD, the LORD is a (like a) Rock. He will always be alive.

5 He brings down low the people that live in high places, in a city on tall (hills). He makes it low. He brings it down to the ground. He throws it into the dirt.

6 Feet will walk on it. The feet of the poor people and of the weak people (will walk over it).

7 The path that righteous people walk on is flat. You, (LORD), make clear the way of righteous people.

8 Yes, LORD, we wait for you in the path that your rules (point us to). In our minds, we want (everybody to know) your name. And (we want everybody to know) that you are famous.

9 My mind wants you in the night time and my spirit wants you in the morning. The people in the world will learn what 'righteous' means. (This will happen) when you are ruling in the country.

10 Bad people will not learn, if nobody punishes them. (They will not learn) what 'righteous' means. In a country where people are honest, (bad people) will continue to do bad things. They do not obey the rules of the LORD.

11 LORD, you have lifted up your hand (to hit them), but they do not see it. (But one day) they will see that you really love your people. Then, I pray that they will become ashamed. I pray that fire will burn up your enemies.

12 LORD, you will keep us safe. Really, all that we have done, you have done on our behalf.

13 LORD, our God, other lords than you have ruled over us. But only to your name do we give praise.

14 Now (the other lords) are dead. They are not alive. Their spirits have gone and they will not rise up (again). You punished them and you killed them. You have done it, so that we do not remember them.

15 LORD, you have made the country larger. You really have made the country larger. You have received praise for yourself. You have made all the edges of the country bigger.

16 LORD, they came to you when they had trouble. They prayed quietly to you when you punished them.

17 LORD, we were with you, like a woman who would soon have a baby. Just before she had her baby (we were like her). We could not keep still and we cried with the pain.

18 We were going to have a baby. We could not keep still and we cried with the pain. But we gave birth only to wind! We have not made the earth safe. We have not killed the people in the world.

19 But your dead (people) will live (again). Their bodies will rise up (from the grave). Wake up! Shout because you are so happy, you (people) that live in the ground! (Shout), because your dew is like the dew of the morning. The earth will give birth to the dead (people) in it.

20 My people, go into your rooms and shut the doors behind you. Hide yourselves for a short time, until (the LORD) is not angry.

21 Look, the LORD is coming out of his house. He will punish the people on the earth because they have not obeyed him. The earth will show (him) the blood (that people) poured out on it. It will not hide any longer the (dead) bodies (that people have) killed.

Chapter 27

1 In that day the LORD will punish Leviathan. (The LORD will use) his sword. (His sword is) great, powerful and strong. (Leviathan is) a snake that moves quickly (in the sea). (It is) a snake that puts itself (round things). He will kill that great animal in the sea.

God will guard his people

2 'In that day, sing about a field where vines are growing. It is full of fruit!

3 I, the LORD, will guard it. I will continue to put water on it. I will guard it night and day, so that nobody will destroy it.

4 I am not angry. If there was a thorn or a briar (in my field of vines), I would march against it in a war. I would make fire out of (the thorns and briars).

5 Or (the field) should come to me. I will make it safe. It should not fight with me. It should rest with me.

6 The days will come when Jacob will grow (like a plant) in the ground. Israel will grow and make flowers. They will fill all the world with fruit.'

God has a purpose when he punishes people

7 (The LORD) has hit (those enemies) that hit (his people). He has hit (his people) like that. (The LORD) has killed (those enemies). He has killed (his people) like that.

8 (LORD) you fought (against your people). You sent them into exile. He made them go with a cruel wind. It was like a day when the east wind blows.

9 This, then, is how Jacob will be sorry because of his sins. And this will be the result when (God) has taken away (Jacob's) sin completely. (The LORD) will break all the altar stones to pieces like chalk stones. (He will) not leave the Asherah poles or incense altars standing.

10 Then the strong city will be empty. Everybody that lived there will leave it. It will be like a dry sandy place. Nobody will go there. Young cows will eat the grass and they will lie down there. They will eat everything on the branches (of the trees).

11 When their branches become dry, people will break them off (the trees). The women will come and make fires with them. (This will happen) because these people do not understand things. So, their Maker will not help them. Also, their Creator will not be kind to them.

12 And in that day (this) will happen. The LORD will pick (fruit) from the River (Euphrates) to the stream of Egypt. So (the LORD) will fetch you one by one, (you) sons of Israel.

13 And in that day (this) will happen. (Someone) will make a sound on a great trumpet. And people that are dying in the country called Assyria will come. Also, people in exile in the country called Egypt (will come). They will worship the LORD in the mountain at Jerusalem.

Chapter 28

A sad song about Ephraim

1 (There will be a) very sad (day in) Ephraim! The leaders (of Ephraim) are very proud, (but they) are drunks. (Ephraim is like) a beautiful flower, but it will die. It will not always be beautiful. (Ephraim) is at the top of a valley where there are good plants. But wine causes (its people) to fall over.

2 Look! The Lord has (somebody who is) powerful and strong. He is like a storm of ice (from the skies) and (he is like) a wind that destroys (things). (He is) like a storm of rain with a great amount of water. He will throw (Ephraim) to the ground with (his) hands!

3 (His) feet will walk on the proud leaders. These (leaders) are the drunks of Ephraim.

4 And (Ephraim) will be like a (fruit called a) fig. It is ready to eat when they pick it. When someone sees it, he will pick it. And he will eat it! (This Ephraim is like) a beautiful flower. But it will die, and it will not be beautiful. It is at the top of a valley. Good plants are there.

5 In that day the LORD of Everything will be a wonderful leader. And (he will be) a beautiful ruler for his people that remain (in their country).

6 (The LORD) will help people to decide what is right. He will make the people strong who guard their city.

7 But wine also causes most (people in Jerusalem) to fall down. And beer makes them into drunks. Beer causes priest and prophet to fall over. And wine confuses (their minds). Beer causes them to fall over. And when they see visions they cannot understand them. They become silly when they decide what to do.

8 They are sick over all their tables. And there is nowhere that is not dirty.

9 (They say,) 'He is teaching what he knows (to us)! He is explaining his message (to us)! (He thinks that we are babies!) (And he thinks that) we have just stopped drinking milk! (He thinks that) we have just come from (our mother's) breast!

10 (It sounds like,) "Tsaw latsaw tsaw latsaw; qaw laqaw qaw laqaw; zeir sham, zeir sham." '

11 So, with foreign lips and a strange language (God) spoke to this people.

12 He said to (this people), 'This (is your) place to rest. Let the tired (people) rest.' And (he said), 'This (is your) place to be quiet in.' But they would not listen.

13 So then, the LORD's message will sound to them like, 'Tsaw latsaw tsaw latsaw, qaw laqaw qaw laqaw, zeir sham, zeir sham.' So they will go, but they will fall over. (An enemy) will hurt them, and he will catch them in a trap.

14 So, listen to the LORD's message. (Hear it) you people that laugh in a bad way (at me). And (obey it), you rulers of this people in Jerusalem.

15 What you are really saying (is this). 'We have made a covenant with death and we have agreed with Sheol. When the waters rise, they cannot touch us. (This is) because we believe in lies. And what is not true will keep us safe.'

16 So the Lord, (who is) LORD, says, 'Look! It is I who has put a stone in Zion. (People now know) that this is a good stone. (It is) a valuable stone, because (it makes) the corners (of buildings). (It is) a strong stone to build on. The person that believes (in the LORD) will never be sorry.

17 If you do what is right and fair, I may be able to help you. (But if not), the rain of ice will carry away the lies that you believe. And water will pour into your safe place.

18 (I will) stop your covenant with death. What you agree with Sheol will not continue. When the water rises, it will pour over (you). (It will drown) you.

19 Every time that it comes to you, it will carry you away. Certainly, every morning, any day and any night, it might pour over you. And, if you understand the message, then you will be very much afraid.'

20 (You know what people say.) 'The bed is so short that you cannot lie in it. The blanket is so narrow that you cannot put it round yourself.'

21 But the LORD will do something, like he did at Mount Perazim. He will be very angry, as he was in the Valley of Gibeon. He will do something that is very strange. He will do something that is not usual.

22 So, do not laugh in a bad way (at me). (If you do), your chains will be even heavier. The Lord, the LORD of Everything, told me that (he has) decided to destroy all the land.

23 Listen and hear my voice! Listen (to me). And hear what I am saying!

24 When the farmer ploughs to plant (seeds), he does not plough every day. He does not always break his ground into small pieces.

25 When he has made the ground flat, he plants carraway and cummin. He plants all the different grain seeds in their own places (in his field).

26 His God teaches him and (his God) tells him the right (thing) to do.

27 (Farmers) do not remove carraway (seeds) with a special machine. Nor do they get cummin seeds like this. They hit carraway (seeds) and cummin (seeds) with a stick.

28 (But they do use) a special machine to get (grain) to make bread. But they do not do it for too long. (The farmer) does not drive the wheels of the special machine over (the grain). And his horses do not walk on it.

29 The LORD of Everything causes them to know all this. What he tells them to do is wonderful. And his wisdom is great.

Chapter 29

A sad song about Ariel

1 (There will be a) very sad (day in) Ariel. Ariel (is) the city that David attacked. Continue to have your usual feasts every year.

2 But I will bring trouble to Ariel. And (Ariel) will not be happy. It will be very sad. And (Ariel) will be my Ariel, (my fire place).

3 And I will do (these things): (My army will) attack you. (They will be) in a circle round you. (I will) put an army against you on every side. (I will) build things against you to attack you.

4 Then you will become humble and you will speak from the ground. And, from low in the dirt, what you say will be difficult to hear. And your voice will come from the ground like (the voice of) the spirit of a dead person. And from the dirt, you will speak very quietly.

5 But your enemies will become like many small bits of dirt. And the crowds of cruel (soldiers) will be like dead bits of a plant in the wind. (This is) because, in a moment,

6 the LORD of Everything will visit you! (It will be like) thunder, or when the ground moves. (It will be like) a very loud noise. (It will be like) a very strong wind and a great storm. And (it will be like) a fire that burns up everything.

7 This will happen to all the many countries that attack Ariel. (It will happen to) everyone that fights against it and its strongest building. (It will happen to) all (the soldiers) that are in a circle round it. They will be like a dream that people see in the night!

8 It will be like a hungry man who dreams. (He dreams) that he is eating (something). But, look! He wakes up hungry! Or it will be like a thirsty man. He dreams that he is drinking. But, look! He wakes up and look! He is still weak because he is still thirsty! This will happen to the many (soldiers) from all the countries that fight against the hill called Zion.

9 (This will) hit you (so that you become) like fools. And you will not believe it! You will become blind, so that you cannot see anything! You will become drunks, but not from wine! You will fall over, but not (because you have drunk) beer!

10 (But it is) because the LORD has caused you to go into a deep sleep. He has shut the eyes of your prophets and he has covered the heads of your seers.

11 And all this vision is for you. (It is) the words in a closed book. Give the book to someone that can read. And say (to them), 'Read this, please.' But he will answer, 'I cannot (read it, because) someone shut it.' 12Or, give the book to someone that cannot read. Say, 'Read it, please.' But he will answer, 'I do not know how to read.'

13 The Lord says, 'These people pray to me with their mouths. And their lips say that I am important. But their hearts are far from me. And to worship me they use rules that men have made.'

14 'So look! I will surprise these people again. (I will) surprise (them) again and again! (Some) people are able to use what they know rightly. But they will not be able to. The people with good minds will not be able to use them.'

15 (There will be a) very sad (day) for those people who (do these things):

- They really try to hide from the LORD what they tell (to the king).

- They work in dark places (where nobody can see them).

- And they say, 'Nobody knows us.'

- (And they say,) 'Nobody sees us.'

16 You turn things the wrong way up! You confuse the person who makes pots with the clay! The thing that somebody made cannot say to its maker, 'You did not make me!' The pot cannot say to the person who makes pots, 'You do not know anything!'

17 In a very short time, (the country called) Lebanon will become a garden of fruit trees. And Carmel will be like a forest.

18 At that time, people who were not able to hear will hear someone read words from a book. And people who were not able to see will see. And they will not remain in shadows and in the dark.

19 And the LORD will make humble people happy again. And the poor people will sing songs to the Holy (God) of Israel, because they are so happy.

20 (This is) because cruel people will go. People that laugh in a bad way (at God) will not appear anywhere. And (the LORD) will kill everybody that is preparing to do bad things.

21 These (bad) people (do these things):

- They say that a man has done something wrong with (only) a word.

- They set a trap for the judge at the city gate.

- And they do not let a man who has done nothing wrong get a fair result.

22 So this is what the LORD says to the house of Jacob. (He is the LORD) who saved Abraham. 'Jacob will not be ashamed again. And his face will never lose colour (because he is afraid).

23 They will see their children, which my hands made, among them. Then they will keep my name holy. They will praise the Holy (God) of Jacob and they will show great love for the God of Israel.

24 Also, people whose minds are confused will understand (things). (Some) people always say that something is wrong. Then, they will be happy to learn (things).'

Chapter 30

A sad song for those who want to join with Egypt

1 '(It is) a very sad (day) for children who do not obey (their father)', says the LORD. 'They have decided what to do, but they did not ask me (about it). They have decided to agree (with Egypt), but without my Spirit's (help). They have done more and more sins as a result.

2 They hurry to go down to Egypt. But they do not ask me what to do. They ask for Pharaoh's help to make them safe. And they look for the shadow of Egypt to cover them.

3 But Pharaoh's help will make you ashamed. And you will not receive help in Egypt's shadow.

4 Their leaders have arrived in Zoan and their people with authority have gone to Hanes.

5 Everyone will be ashamed because the people (in Egypt) will not be able to help them. They will not bring any help to you. (They will) not really (bring to you) any help. (They will) only (make you) very much more ashamed.'

6 (These are) sad (words) about the animals (that go through) the Negev. It is a place where there is trouble and danger. (These wild animals live) there:

- lionesses and lions that roar

- snakes and dangerous snakes that fly.

(Here the leaders of Judah) carry their valuable things on the backs of horses. And they carry their very valuable things on the backs of other animals. They do this on behalf of people that cannot help them!

7 Egypt has no value. They will not send any help. So, I call (Egypt) 'Rahab' or 'She shouts while she does not move'.

8 Now go! Write it down on a piece of stone for them. Also, write it in a book. Then, in future days, it will always be there to read.

9 These (people) are people that do not obey (the LORD). They are his children and they disappoint (him). They are children that do not want to listen to the LORD's words.

10 They say to the seers, 'Do not see anything!' And (they say) to the prophets, 'Do not tell us what is the right (thing to do). Tell us nice things. Say what is not true!

11 Leave this path. Get off this road. Do not hold the Holy (God) of Israel in front of us.'

12 So, this is what the Holy (God) of Israel says. You have not listened when my word told you about the danger. And you thought that it was right to be cruel to people. And you have believed in lies.

13 So this will happen. This sin will be for you like a high wall that is not safe. It will bend over, and in a moment, it will fall down.

14 He (the LORD) will break it into pieces as (easily as someone breaks) a piece of pot. He will destroy it, and he will not feel kind about it. There will not be a (big) piece (of pot) among the bits. It cannot lift a stick that is burning from a fire. It cannot bring water from a pool.

15 Now this is what the Lord said, the LORD (who is) the Holy (God) of Israel: 'You will be safe if you return (from Egypt) and rest. Be quiet and believe (in God). Then you will be strong. But you would not (listen).'

16 But you said, 'No! We will run away on horses.' So you will run away. (You said) 'We will ride away very quickly.' So the people that run after you will move quickly.

17 A thousand (1000) (of you will run away) from only one enemy. You will (all) run away from 5 of them! They will leave you like a sign on the top of the mountain, or like a flag on a hill.

God is kind and fair

18 So the LORD will wait (before) he is kind to you. So, also, (one day) he will start to show you his great love (for you). (It is) because the LORD is a fair God. He will make everyone that waits for him very happy.

19 Yes! You people of Zion that live in Jerusalem, you will not weep again. (The LORD) will be very kind to you when you shout for help. When he hears you, he will answer you. 20 (In the past) the Lord has given you trouble as your bread and he has given you pain as your water. But then your Teacher will not hide himself from you. You will see him with your own eyes. 21 And your ears will hear a word near you, but behind you. When you turn to the right or to the left it will say, 'This is the way. Walk in it.' 22 And you will not use your idols. You cut them from wood with a knife. Then you covered them with silver. You will not use your idols that you made from metal. You covered them with gold. You will throw them away like dirty things. You will say to them, 'Go!'

23 He (the LORD) will send rain for your seeds that you plant in the ground. And plenty of good food will come from the ground. In that day your cows will eat (grass) in wide fields.

24 And the cows and the horses that work (on) the ground will eat the best food for animals. (Farmers) will use a big farm fork and a spade to give it to them. 25 And on every tall mountain and on every high hill, water will pour down in streams. (This will happen) on the day when high buildings fall. And many people will die. 26 Also, the moon will shine as bright as the sun. And the light of the sun will be 7 times brighter. It will be like the light of 7 days (at the same time)! This will happen when the LORD puts soft cloths on his people. He will put the cloths where (the LORD) hit them hard. And he will make them better where he hurt them.

27 Look! The LORD himself is coming from far away. There is fire in his nose and smoke like thick clouds (are all round him). His lips show that he is angry. His tongue eats things like a fire (burns them).

28 From his mouth (comes something) that is like a lot of water. It will reach up to (someone's) neck. He moves (many) countries to make them separate and to destroy them. And he (will be like a man who) puts a bit in (horses') mouths, to lead them away.

29 And you, (my people,) will sing! It will be like the night when there is a big party for everyone in your church. You will feel very happy inside you! It will be like when people go up to the LORD's (temple). There will be music. (Another name for the LORD) is the Rock of Israel.

30 Then the LORD will cause people to hear his voice. (It will be) like the voice of a great king! He will cause (people) to see his arm when it comes down (to hit them). He will cause people to know that he is very, very angry. (He will be) like a fire that burns everything. (He will be) like a cloud that drops (much rain). (He will be) like a storm that makes a lot of noise. (He will drop like) bits of ice.

31 The voice of the LORD will completely destroy Assyria. He will knock them down with his stick to show to everybody that he is a king.

32 He will hit them with his stick. He will use his stick to punish them. It will sound like the music of harps and tambourines while the LORD fights them in a war. (He will use) his arms to hit them.

33 (The LORD) has already made (the fire called) Topheth ready. He prepared it for the king (of Assyria). The hole in the ground for the fire is deep and wide. There is plenty of wood for the fire. The air from the LORD's mouth will light the fire. (The air) is like a stream of sulphur that is on fire.

Chapter 31

God's help is better than help from Egypt

1 (It will be) a sad (day) for those people that go down to Egypt. They want help and horses (from Egypt). They think that chariots will help them. (This is) because there are very many (chariots in Egypt). And (they hope for help from) men that ride on horses. (This is because these (men) are very strong. And they do not ask the Holy (God) of Israel for help. And they do not ask LORD to tell them what to do.

2 But (the LORD) knows the best thing to do. Also, he can kill people. He does not change what he says. And he will do something against the people that do bad things. (And he will do something against) those people that help people to do bad things.

3 The men in Egypt are (only) men. They are not God. Their horses are animals, not spirits. When the LORD puts out his hand, the helper will fall down. And the person that he helps will fall down too. They will all come to an end together.

4 This is what the LORD said to me. 'The LORD of Everything will come down to fight on the mountain of Zion and on its hill. He will make a noise like a lion or a young lion. It makes noises over what it has caught. He will not be afraid of the group of sheep farmers when they come out against (the lion).'

5 The LORD of Everything will make Jerusalem safe. He will fly round it like a bird. He will make it safe, and he will make it free. He will pass over it and he will save it.

6 People of Israel, turn (back) to him. You have caused him to feel very sick and ill. 7 (Turn back to him) because in that day everyone must throw away their gold and silver idols. Your hands made them for you, which was wrong.

8 A sword will kill the man from Assyria. A man will not do it. And a sword, that is not held by a man, will kill him. And (he) will run from the sword. And it will cause his young men always to do difficult work.

9 'The (king of Assyria), (who is like) their rock, will run away. (He will run away) because he is so afraid. And his (army) leaders will run away because they are all afraid of the war flag.' This is what the LORD says. His fire is in Zion and his Ariel is in Jerusalem.

Chapter 32

God promises that his people will have a good king

1 A king will be a good judge. And leaders will be fair judges. Think about those things.

2 Then each (ruler) will be like a place to hide from the wind. And he will be like someone who covers us from the storm. (He will be) like streams of water in a dry place. And he will be like the shadow of a big rock in very dry land.

3-4 Now think (about these things):

- The eyes of people that see will never shut.

- And the ears of people that hear will really listen.

- And people who are too quick to speak will wait to understand.

- And the tongues of people that speak with difficulty (now) will speak clearly (then).

5 Then they will not again call a fool clever. They will not say that a cheat is honest.

6 What a fool says is silly and his mind thinks about bad (things):

- He does things that do not obey God's rules.

- He says wrong things about the LORD.

- He does not give food to hungry people.

- And he does not give thirsty people a drink.

7 The things that a cheat does are bad. They cause people to believe what is not true. Also, his ideas are bad. (He decides) to hurt poor people. What he says about them is not true. And he gives false reasons, even when (the poor) people speak the truth. (They are people) who need (help).

8 But a good person wants (to do) good things. Also, he does the good things that he promised to do.

An enemy (Assyria) will attack you before your good king comes

9 You women that have no problems, get ready. Listen to my voice. You ladies that feel so safe, hear my words (to you).

10 In less than a year, you (women) that feel so safe will worry. (You will worry because the grape harvest will fail. The harvest of fruit will not happen.

11 Shake, you women that have no problems. Be afraid, (you ladies) that feel so safe. Take off (your clothes) so that you are wearing nothing. Then put a cloth about the tops of your legs.

12 Hit your breasts for these (reasons). (There are no) good fields. The vine has no fruit.

13 The ground where our people work gives (only) thorns (and) briars. Also, (this is) because (there are no) happy homes in the happy city.

14 It is a fact that (the king) will go from his beautiful house. The city where many people live will be empty. The hill (in Jerusalem) and the tall building, where people watch (for enemies), will always be homes for animals. (They will be) a happy place for wild horses (to live in), and fields where groups (of animals feed).

15 (This will happen) until (God) pours his Spirit on us from above (the earth). Then, the wild places will become gardens and the gardens will become forests.

16 Then (people) will decide fairly in the wild places. And (they will say) good things in the fields that contain plenty of fruit.

17 And when people do good things, there will be no war. When people do good things there will be a quiet and safe life. It will continue for a long time.

18 My people will live in a place where there is no war. Their homes will be safe and they will sleep without pain.

19-20 Ice may knock down the trees in the forest. But, even then, people who plant seeds by the stream will be happy. (Even if a storm) completely destroys the city, they will let their cows and horses go to the fields freely.

Chapter 33

Another sad song

1 It will be very sad for you, the country that destroys (other countries). But no (other country) has destroyed you, yet. (It will be sad for) you, the country that is not honest (with other countries). But no (other country) has not been honest with you yet. When you stop destroying (other countries, one of them) will destroy you. When you stop not being honest (with other countries,) they will not be honest with you.

2 LORD, be kind to us. We look to you for help. Make us strong every day. Save us when trouble happens.

3 At the sound of a voice, people run away. When you go to war, (the people in other) countries run away.

4 People get things together (after a war), as a locust gets (food). As locusts rush (to their food), so people rush (to those things).

5 The LORD is more important (than anyone else). He lives high above (the earth). He will fill Zion with fair answers to questions. And (everybody will do) what is right.

6 He will make your lives safe and you will keep your money. Here are the valuable things that he gives (to you):

- You will have the right answers for questions.

- You will know everything (that you need to know).

- You will be (properly) afraid of the LORD.

7 Look! The brave men (from Jerusalem) weep in the streets. Officers went (to Assyria). They asked for the war to stop. Now they cry very sad tears.

8 The important roads are empty and nobody travels on the smaller roads. (The enemy) stopped the covenant. He does not like the cities and he does not love anyone.

9 The land itself is very sad and it is becoming dry. Lebanon is ashamed and it is dying. Sharon is like a sandy place and the leaves in Bashan and Carmel are dying.

10 The LORD says, 'Now will I stand up. Now I will lift myself up. Now I will raise myself up.

11 You make dry grass and you call it straw. Your own breath will destroy you as fire (burns up that dry grass).

12 (It) will burn the bones of people to make lime. They will burn as easily as thorn bushes, (when people) cut them down.

13 You people (that are) far away, listen. Listen to what I have done! And you people (that are) near, understand. Understand that I am very powerful.'

14 The sinners (that live) in Zion are afraid. (Some) people are not clean (as God sees them). (They are also) afraid. (They ask this.) 'Which of us can live with a fire that burns everything? Which of us can live with a fire that will never stop burning?'

15 (The answer is) the person that (is like this):

- He is very good and he speaks what is right.

- He gets nothing when he is cruel to people.

- His hands will not accept money to do wrong things.

- He closes his ears against ideas to kill (people).

- And he shuts his eyes, so that he does not think about bad (things).

16 (That person) will be the person that lives on high places. That person's safe place will be in the rocks. People like that will always have food and their drink will not stop.

17 Your eyes will see that the king is beautiful. (Your eyes) will see a country that reaches too far away.

18 Your mind will think about when were afraid. (You will say,) 'The (enemy) officer who counted (things) has gone! (The man who) weighed (everything) has gone! (The man who) counted high buildings has gone!'

19 You will never see those cruel people again. They speak words that are difficult to understand. Their language is strange. It is difficult to understand it.

20 Look at Zion. It is the city where we have our parties. Your eyes will see Jerusalem. It is a place where there is no war. It is (like) a tent that people will never remove. They will never pull up its pegs. They will never break any of its ropes.

21 It is there (in Jerusalem) that the LORD will be our powerful (God). It will be (like) a place with wide rivers and streams. No boat that men push along will go on them. No great ship will sail on them.

22 The LORD is our judge. The LORD gives us our rules. The LORD is our king. It is (the LORD) that will make us safe.

23 The ropes on your ship hang down. The wood that they hang from is not safe. They have not put the sail up.

Then people will have the many things (that they took from their enemies). And even people who cannot walk well will carry away something!

24 Nobody that lives in Zion will say, 'I am ill.' And (God will not) punish people that live there again.

Chapter 34

God punishes the people in Edom

1 Come near (to me), you (people in all) countries, and listen (to me).

    (All) you people, think about what I am saying to you.

    Hear (me, all) the earth, and everything that is in it.

    (Listen, all the) world, and all that comes from it.

2 Yes! The LORD is (right to be) angry against every country.

    And (he is right to be) very angry against all their armies.

    (The LORD) will destroy them.

    He will send them to their deaths.

3 Nobody will bury the dead bodies.

    The dead bodies will fill the air with a very bad smell.

    Their blood will go down into the mountains.

4 And every army in the skies will be like water.

    And the skies will close up like a book.

    And all their armies will fall

    like leaves that fall from a vine.

    (They will fall) like the fruit called figs from a fig tree.

5 When my sword has done its work in the skies,

    it will come down on Edom.

    (It will fall) on the people that I have decided to kill.

6 The LORD (is right) to use a sword!

    (He will) put it into blood. (He will) cover it with meat.

    It is the blood of young sheep and goats.

    It is the meat from inside male sheep.

    Yes! The LORD (is right) to make a sacrifice in Bozrah.

    He will kill many people in the country called Edom.

7 And wild cows will fall with them.

    Young male cows (will die) with old cows.

    Blood will go into their land.

    Meat will go into their earth.

8 Look! The LORD (is right) to have a day when he will punish (people).

    It will be a year when (the LORD) helps Zion.

    (It will be a year) when he punishes (Zion's enemies).

9 The streams in sandy places (in Edom) will turn into pitch.

    Its ground will turn into sulphur that is burning.

    Its land will become pitch that is on fire.

10 Nobody will put out (the fire) in the day or in the night.

    Smoke from (the fire) will rise up for a long time.

    (The land) will be empty from one century to the next century.

    Nobody will ever pass through it again.

11 But (these owls) will be in it:

    the sandy owl, the owl that screams and the great owl.

    And the large black bird called a raven will build its home there.

    And (the LORD) will hold over it a line that measures.

    (It will make it) without shape.

    (He will hold over it) a special line (that will make it) empty.

12 (Edom's) leaders will have nothing there that they can call a kingdom.

    And all its officers will vanish.

13 And thorn bushes will cover its beautiful houses.

Weeds and briars (will cover) its castles.

The country will be a home for jackals. And ostriches will live in it.

14 Wild animals and hyenas will come together.

And wild goats will make a noise to each other.

Also, the bad female spirit called Lilith will rest there.

And she will find for herself a place in which to stay.

15 The owl will build a home there.

And she will keep her eggs there until they become baby birds.

And she will keep them safe under the shadow (of her wings).

Vultures will meet there too. Each has her mate.

16 Look in the LORD's book and read this!

'Not one of them will not be there.

Not one of them will be without her mate.

(This is) because (the LORD's) mouth said that it must happen.

And his breath will bring them together.

17 He (the LORD) will give their places (to them).

And his hand will give (these things) to them with the line that measures.

They will have (that country) always.

They will live in it from one century to the next century.'

Chapter 35

God gives gifts to his people

1 The sandy place and the dry land will be happy.

The wild places will feel happy and (flowers) will grow there.

2 Flowers will appear quickly on the (plant that is called) crocus

(The land) will be very happy.

It will be so happy that it will shout (aloud)!

It will be as beautiful as Lebanon.

(It will) seem like places in Carmel and Sharon.

(These places) will see that the LORD is very great.

(They will see) that our God is very, very good.

3 Make (your) weak hands strong.

Make the knees that will not hold (you) up strong.

4 Say to the people who are very much afraid,

'Be strong! Do not be afraid! Your God will come.

He will come to punish (his enemies). He will punish them fairly.

He will come and he will save you.'

5 Then (the LORD will) open the eyes of people that are not able to see.

And he will clear the ears of people that are not able to hear.

6 Then people that cannot walk will jump like deer.

And people that cannot speak will shout.

(This is) because they are so happy.

Yes! (God) will pour water into the wild, dry places.

And (he will) pour streams (of water) into the sandy places.

7 Then the hot sand will become a pool (of water).

And water will come up from the ground that is very dry.

In the places where jackals had lived,

reeds and plants like that will grow instead of grass.

8 And there will be a high road there, a way.

Its name will be 'The Holy Way'.

People that are not clean will not go on it.

It will be for those (people) that walk in the Way.

Fools who are very bad people will not walk on it.

9 No lions will be there.

No dangerous wild animals will walk on it.

Nobody will find those (animals) there.

Only people (that the LORD has) bought back (from death) will walk there.

10 And the people that the LORD has bought back (from death) will return.

And they will sing while they go into Zion.

And they will never stop enjoying themselves. It will show on their faces.

Everywhere that they go they will be very, very happy.

Chapter 36

Assyria's army arrives in Judah

1 King Hezekiah had ruled (Judah) for nearly 14 years. Then, King Sennacherib of Assyria attacked all the cities in Judah that had high, strong walls. He beat them and they became his.

2 And the king of Assyria sent the leader of his soldiers from Lachish. (He came) to King Hezekiah in Jerusalem. This leader had a large army with him. He stopped at the water stream (that went) from the higher pool. It was on the road, near the place where people wash clothes.

3 And these people came out to (meet) him:

Eliakim, the son of Hilkiah. (He was) the most important (servant) in the (king's) beautiful house.

- Shebna, the leader of the government.

- Joah, the son of Asaph. He was (the king's) writer.

4-5 And the (soldiers') leader said to these men, 'Now (please) say (this) to Hezekiah. This is what the Great King, the king of Assyria, says (to you):

- "You should not believe (that God will help you)!

- Words alone cannot tell you what to do!

- And they cannot give you the power (that you need) for war!

- I do not know anyone who will help you to fight against me!

6 Look, (I know that) you are hoping for help from Egypt. (Egypt is like) a stick that people use. It helps them to walk. But it will break! If you push on it, it will go into your hand, like a sharp piece of reed. That is what will happen to anybody that hopes for help from Pharaoh, the king of Egypt. 7 But you might say to me, 'We are hoping that the LORD our God will help us.' (Then I will answer this.) He is the (God) whose high places and altars Hezekiah removed! (Hezekiah) said to Judah and to Jerusalem, 'You must worship (God) only at this (one) altar.' " 8 And now', (said Rav Shakeh, the leader,) 'agree today with my master, (who is) the king of Assyria. And I will give you 2000 horses, if you can put (2000) riders on them! 9 You cannot refuse (what I offer. I am) the least important of my master's officers. But you are (still) hoping that Egypt will send chariots and riders on horses. 10 And (there is) something else. Surely I would not attack and destroy this country without help from the LORD! The LORD told me, "March against this country and destroy it." '

11 Then Eliakim, Shebna and Joah spoke to Rav Shakeh. (They said,) 'Please, speak to your servants in (our) Aramaic language, because we do understand it. Do not speak to us in Hebrew, or the people on the (city) wall may hear (you).' 12 But Rav Shakeh said, 'My master did not send me to say these things only to you and to your master. Also, he sent me to say them to the people that are sitting on the (city) wall. Like you, they will have to eat the material that their own body wastes. And they will have to drink the water that their own body wastes.'

13 Then Rav Shakeh stood up. He shouted in a loud voice in Hebrew. 'Hear the words of the king. (They are what) the Great King of Assyria (is telling you). 14 This is what the king (of Assyria) says (to you). "Do not let Hezekiah tell you what is not true. Hezekiah cannot save you.

15 And do not let Hezekiah cause you to agree with him. (He wants you) to believe in the LORD. He tells you that the LORD really will make you free (from Assyria). (He says that the LORD) will not give this city to the king of Assyria. 16 Do not hear (and obey) Hezekiah!" This is what the king of Assyria says (to you). "Do not have a war with me. Come out (of your city) to me. Then you will all eat (the grapes) from your own vines and (the figs) from your own fig trees. And you will all drink the water from your own wells. 17 (Do this) until I come (to you). Then I will take you away to a country like your own country. (It is) a country where grain and new wine grow. (It is) a country (where they make) bread. And (it is a country) where vineyards grow. 18 Do not (hear and obey) Hezekiah. He will (be like a man who) leads you the wrong (way). He says that the LORD will save you. No other country's god has saved his people from the power of the king of Assyria. 19 The gods of (the cities called) Hamath and Arpad (could not help them). The gods of (the city called) Sepharvaim (could not help them). None (of these gods) saved Samaria. 20 None of these gods has saved his own country from my power. Can the LORD save Jerusalem from my power?" '

21 But the people were quiet and they did not answer him one word. (They did this) because King (Hezekiah) had said, 'Do not answer him.'

22 Then (these people) came to Hezekiah:

Eliakim, the son of Hilkiah. (He was) the most important (servant) in the (king's) beautiful house.

- Shebna, the leader of the government.

- Joah, the son of Asaph. He was (the king's) writer.

They tore their clothes. And they told the king all the words that Rav Shakeh (had said).

Chapter 37

Hezekiah sends a message to Isaiah

1 When King Hezekiah heard (the report of his servants), he tore his clothes. Then he put on cheap hairy cloth and he went into the temple. (It was the temple) of the LORD (in Jerusalem). 2 And he sent Eliakim and Shebna and the leaders of the priests to Isaiah the prophet. (Isaiah) was the son of Amoz. (Eliakim was) the most important servant in the (king's) house. (Shebna was) the leader of the (king's) government. And (Eliakim, Shebna and the priests) all wore cheap hairy clothes. 3 And they told (Isaiah), 'This is what Hezekiah says. "There are many problems at this time. And (Rav Shakeh's) words make me ashamed. (The problems) are like a child that is ready to be born. But (its mother) is not strong enough for it to be born. 4 Perhaps the LORD, (who is) your God, will do something about the words of Rav Shakeh. Rav Shakeh's master is the king of Assyria. (The king) sent (Rav Shakeh) to laugh in a bad way at the God who is really alive. Maybe the LORD your God will tell (Rav Shakeh) that his words were wrong. (God) has heard them. So, pray for the people that remain (in Jerusalem)." ' 5 So Hezekiah's servants came to Isaiah. 6 Isaiah said to them, 'Tell your master that the LORD says this. "Do not be afraid of the words that you have heard. The servants of the king of Assyria are not important. They have said very bad things about me. 7 Listen (to me)! I will put a spirit into (the king of Assyria). Then, he will hear a certain report. When (he hears it), he will return to his own country. And there, I will cause (someone) to kill him with a sword." '

8 Then, Rav Shakeh heard that the king of Assyria had left Lachish (city). So (Rav Shakeh) left Jerusalem and he found the king (of Assyria). The king was fighting against Libnah (city). 9 Now (the king of Assyria) heard (this report) about Tirhanah. (Tirhakah) was the king of Ethiopia. (The report) said, 'He has come out (from Ethiopia) to fight against you.' And when (the king of Assyria) heard this, he sent people (to Jerusalem) with a message. They had this message for (King) Hezekiah. 10 'Say this to King Hezekiah of Judah. Say, "You are hoping that your God will help you. But do not let him tell you what is not true. (Your God) says that the king of Assyria will not destroy Jerusalem. 11 But you have heard what the kings of Assyria have done to all the (other) countries. They destroyed them completely. And (your God) will not save you. 12 The gods of (these other) countries did not save them. My ancestors destroyed Gozan and Haran, Rezeph and the people of Eden (that lived) in Tel Assar. 13 The kings of Hamath and Arpad have gone. The king of the city called Sepharvaim has gone. And the kings of Hena and Ivvah have gone." '

14 And Hezekiah received the letter from the people that brought the message. And he read it and then he went up to the temple of the LORD. He opened the letter in front of the LORD.

15 And Hezekiah prayed to the LORD. He said, 16 'LORD of Everything, (you are) the God of Israel. You sit on a seat between the very important angels. Only you are the God of all the countries in the world. You have made the skies and the earth. 17 LORD, turn your ears to me and hear (me). LORD, open your eyes and look (at this letter). Listen to all the words of Sennacherib. He sent them to laugh in a bad way at the God who really is alive. 18 It is true, LORD, that the kings of Assyria have made empty places from many countries and their land. 19They threw their gods into the fire. They destroyed them because they were not really gods. Human hands made them from wood and stone. 20 So now, our LORD and our God, save us from the power of (the king of Assyria)! Then all the (people in all the) kingdoms in the world will know that only you are the LORD.'

God answers Hezekiah

21 Then Isaiah, (who was) the son of Amoz, sent a message to Hezekiah. 'This is what the LORD, (who is) the God of Israel, says.

"You have prayed to me about Sennacherib, (who is) the king of Assyria." So, 22this is what the LORD says about him.

"(The) Virgin Daughter of Zion (Jerusalem),

she does not like you; she laughs at you.

(The) Daughter of Jerusalem,

she moves her head about after you.

23 Who is it about whom you have said bad things? They were not true!

Who is it that you have shouted at?

Who is it that you have looked at proudly?

(The answer is) the Holy (God) of Israel!

24 You have used your servants to say bad things about the Lord.

You have said, 'With many of my chariots

I have gone up very high mountains,

the highest (mountains) in Lebanon.

I have cut its tallest cedars down

and I have cut down the best of its pine trees.

I went to its highest places and to its best forests.

25 I dug wells and I drank (the) water (from them).

I made all the rivers in Egypt dry with the parts under my feet.'

26 Surely, you have heard (this)!

I decided what to do a long time ago!

I decided what to do in past (years)!

Now it has happened.

You have caused strong cities to become mountains of stones.

27 The people in them are not strong.

They are not happy. And they are confused.

They are like plants in a field.

(They are like) the new parts of young green plants.

(They are like) grass on the roof (of a house).

(The hot winds burn them) before they can grow.

28 I know (everything about you).

(I know) when you sit down.

And (I know) when you go out.

And (I know) when you come in.

And (I know) when you shout proudly at me.

29 You have shouted proudly at me

and you have said bad things about me.

So I will put my hook (a bent piece of metal) in your nose.

And I will put my bit in your mouth.

And I will cause you to return home by the same way that you came."

30 And this will be a sign for you, (Hezekiah).

"This year, you will eat what grows from its own (seeds).

And in the second year, (you will eat) what grows from (the first year's seeds).

But in the third year you will plant (seeds) and you will pick (plants for food).

And you will plant again the vineyards and you will enjoy their fruit.

31 And this will happen also to the people that remain in Judah.

(Like plants), they will put roots down below (the ground) and they will grow fruit above (it).

32 (This will happen) because a remnant will come out from Jerusalem.

And the people that remain will come out from the hill (called) Zion.

The great love that the LORD of Everything has (for his people) will cause this to happen!"

33 This is what the LORD says about the king of Assyria.

"He will not come into this city,

and he will not shoot an arrow here.

He will not stand in front of it with a shield.

He will not build mountains of earth against it.

34 He will return (to Assyria) by the way that he came,

and he will not come into this city."

(This is) the promise of the LORD.

35 "So I will make this city safe and I will save it.

(I will do this to keep) my good name.

I promised my servant David (that I would do it). (That is why I will do it.)" '

God destroys Assyria's army

36 Then an angel of the LORD went and he killed 185 000 men in the (army) from Assyria. When people got up in the morning, they saw all these dead bodies! 37 So Sennacherib, (who was) the king of Assyria, took his army away. He returned to (Assyria) and he stayed there in Nineveh. 38 He was worshipping his god Nisroch in the house (of Nisroch). (Two of) his sons, Adrammelech and Sharezer, killed him with (their) swords. Then, they ran away into the country called Ararat. (So) Esarhaddon, (who was another of) his sons, ruled instead of (Sennacherib).

PART 4: Chapters 38-55 God's Servant saves God's people

Hezekiah's mistake and God's promises (chapters 38-40)

Chapter 38

Hezekiah becomes ill

1 At that time, Hezekiah was very ill. He nearly died. And Isaiah the prophet, (who was) the son of Amoz, went to (Hezekiah). And (Isaiah) said to (Hezekiah), 'This is what the LORD says. "Make everything ready for your son, because you will die. You will not get better." ' 2 Then Hezekiah turned his face to the wall and he prayed to the LORD. 3 And he said, 'Please remember, LORD, that I have been your good servant. (I have) always obeyed to you. I have worked for you with all my power. You have seen that I did good things.' And Hezekiah wept sad tears. 4 Then the LORD told Isaiah (again what) to say. 5 'Go and say this to Hezekiah. "This is what the LORD says. (The LORD) is the God of your ancestor David. I have heard what you prayed. I have seen your tears. So, I will let you be alive for 15 more years. 6 I will save you from the power of the king of Assyria. Also, I will keep this city safe, this city (Jerusalem)." ' 7 And (Isaiah said), 'This is a message to you from the LORD. (It is a message) that the LORD will do what he has promised (to do). 8 You can see the shadow of the sun when it falls on the stairs. (They are the stairs) that (King) Ahaz built. I will cause the shadow to go back ten steps (on these stairs).' And the shadow did go back ten steps!

9 (This is) a poem that Hezekiah the king of Judah wrote. He wrote it after he got better from his illness.

10 I said, 'I hope that I will not really go through the gates of Sheol during the best days of my life.

> I hope that (death) will not take from me my other years.'

> 11 I said, 'I will not see the LORD (again).

> (I will not) live on this earth and (see) the LORD.

I will never see these people (again).

I will never be with the people that are living in this world.

12 (The LORD) has knocked down my house and he has taken it from me.

(He did it) as (easily as someone packs away) the tent of a sheep farmer.

(He has) caused my life to come to an end.

It is like when someone finishes making a carpet. He rolls it up.

It is like when someone has made some cloth.

He cuts it away from the machine that he uses to make the cloth.

(In a) day and (in a) night God brought me to my end.

13 I waited quietly until the dawn.

Then, like a lion (does), (God) broke all my bones.

(In a) day and (in a) night God brought me to my end.

14 I cried like a small bird, (perhaps) a thrush.

I made a sad noise like a dove makes.

My eyes became weak (while I looked) to the skies.

Lord, save me from my trouble!

15 I do not know what I can say. (The LORD) has spoken to me

and (the LORD) has done (all this to me).

I will live quietly, because I felt so sad (inside me).

16 Lord, by these things, (people) have life.

By all these things, my spirit has life.

You gave me back my health and you have let me live.

17 Really, it was good for me to have such trouble.

Your love did not let the Pit kill me,

because you threw all my sins behind your back.

18 (People that are in) Sheol cannot thank you.

Dead (people) cannot sing and praise you.

People that go down to the Pit cannot enjoy your love.

19 People that are alive and not dead can thank you.

I am doing it today.

A father tells his children about your love.

20 The LORD will save me (from death).

Then we will sing in the temple of the LORD every day of our lives.

(We will sing with the music of) stringed instruments.'

21 Now Isaiah said (this earlier). 'Make a hot cake of figs and put it on the bad place on (Hezekiah's) skin. Then he will get better.'

22 And Hezekiah had asked, 'What will show me that I will be able to go up to the temple of the LORD?'

Chapter 39

Hezekiah's mistake

1 When this happened, Merodach-Baladan was the king of Babylon. He was the son of Baladan. (Merodach-Baladan) sent Hezekiah letters and a gift. He had heard that (Hezekiah) was ill. But (now he heard) that Hezekiah was better. 2 Hezekiah was happy to meet the officers that (the king of Babylon) had sent. (Hezekiah) showed to them the places where he stored (his valuable things). He showed them what was there. (He showed them) silver and gold, spices and very good oil. (He showed them) all his arms and everything else that was valuable. There was nothing in his beautiful house or in his whole country that Hezekiah did not show them. 3 Then Isaiah the prophet went to King Hezekiah and (Isaiah) said to him, 'What did these men say? And from where did they come to you?' Then Hezekiah said, 'They came to me from the far country called Babylon.' 4 And (Isaiah) asked, 'What did they see in your house?' So Hezekiah said, 'They saw everything (that is) in my house. There is nothing among my valuable things that I did not show to them.' 5 Then Isaiah said to Hezekiah, 'Hear what the LORD of Everything says to you.

6 "This is what will certainly happen. (Soldiers from Babylon) will take everything (that is) in your beautiful house to Babylon. They will take everything that your ancestors have stored here until now. They will leave nothing (here)", says the LORD.

7 "And some of your own sons, your grandsons (and their sons, too), will go to Babylon. (Soldiers from Babylon) will cause them to go there. And they will become eunuchs in the beautiful house of the king of Babylon."
' 8 And Hezekiah said to Isaiah, 'The words that you said from the LORD are good.' But what he really thought was, 'There will be no war. And it will be safe while I am alive.'

Chapter 40

God's promises

1 'Say kind words to my people. Say kind words (to them)', says your God.

2 'Speak to the minds of the people in Jerusalem and tell this to them:

- (Your) life as soldiers in a war has finished.

- (God has) excused (your) sins.

- And the LORD's hand has punished you twice for all (your) sins.'

3 A voice is shouting, 'Prepare a road for the LORD in the sandy places. Make a straight road on higher ground for our God in the Arabah.

4 (God's servants will) raise up (the lower parts of) every valley. And (they will) make every mountain and hill lower. The ground that nobody has dug will become like a garden. And (they will make) the hilly places flat.

5 Then, (people will) see the glory of the LORD. Everybody that lives on the earth will see it together. These are words that the LORD himself has spoken.'

6 A voice is saying, 'Shout (something) aloud!' But I say, 'What shall I shout?' (The voice answered), 'Everybody is like grass and all their glory is like a flower in the field.

7 Grass will die and a flower will fall (to the ground). (This will happen) because the LORD's breath will blow on them. Surely, everybody (is like) grass.

8 Grass will die and a flower will fall (to the ground). But a word that our God (speaks) will be true for all time.

9 You, (the servant that is) bringing good news to Zion, go up on to a high mountain. You, (the servant that is) bringing good news to Jerusalem, shout loudly with your voice. (Shout) aloud, and do not be afraid. Say to the towns in Judah, "Here is your God!"

10 Look! Your master, the LORD, is coming with power. And his arm will rule (the people) for him. Look (again)! (He is bringing) his gifts with him. And he will pay something (to his people).'

11 'He will love his sheep like a shepherd does. He will carry the young sheep in his arms. And he will hold them near to his heart. He will carefully lead (the sheep) that have young (sheep).'

12 (He is the God) who has (done these things):

- (He) measured (all) the waters (in the sea) in (one of) his hand(s).

- (He saw that) the skies were as wide as (one of) his hands.

- (He) put (all) the dirt of the earth into a bucket.

- (He) weighed the mountains on the scales.

- (He weighed) the hills in a balance.

13-14 (There is nobody) who has (done these things).

- (Nobody) understood the mind of the LORD.

- (Nobody,) as his helper, told him what to do.

- (Nobody) told (God) what to do when the LORD asked him.

- (Nobody) taught him the proper way to do things.

- (Nobody) taught him what things to know about.

- (Nobody) showed him the way to understand things.

15 Surely, the countries are like a small quantity (of water) in a bucket. They are like a small bits of dirt on the scales. (The LORD) weighs the islands like small bits of dirt.

16 (A tree from) Lebanon is not enough to make a fire for his altar. Neither are its animals enough to burn on the altars (to make God happy).

17 All the countries in the world are like nothing in front of (the LORD). He thinks about them like they had no value. (They seem) less than nothing.

18   You cannot find anyone else that is like God.

   You cannot say that he is like any false god.

19 An able man makes a false god. An able worker covers it with gold. He also makes something from silver for it.

20 Some people are too poor to give a gift like that. They choose a wood that will not soon fall into pieces. They will look for an able man that will make a false god (from the wood). (But that false god) cannot move.

21 (Think about the things in verses 22-24.)

· You should know (these things).

· You should have heard (these things).

· (Somebody) should have told (them) to you from the beginning

You should have understood (them) since (God) made the earth.

22 (God) sits on a special seat where the earth and the sky meet. And the people (on the earth seem) like small insects (to him). He hangs out the skies like a curtain. And he makes them like a tent (that he can) live in.

23 He is the (God) that makes kings into nothing. He takes away (the power) from world leaders, so that they have none.

24 (Those leaders are like plants.) As soon as (somebody) plants them, (God) will blow on them. And as soon as (somebody) puts them into the ground, they will die. As soon as they put roots down, a strong wind will blow them away like dead plants.

25 The Holy (God) says (these things):

· 'You cannot say that I am like anybody.

· Nobody is as good as (or better than) I am.'

26 Turn your eyes up and look at the skies. (He is the God) who created them. (God) made the very large number (of stars) and he gave each one of them a name. He did not forget to give a name to any of them, because of (his) great power. (God) is very, very strong.

27 You people of Jacob (Jewish people) say, 'The LORD has forgotten what I am doing.' And you people of Israel say, 'My God is not fair to me.' But you should not say those things.

28 You surely know this. You surely have listened to it! The LORD is the God that will always be alive. He is the Creator of (even) the parts of the earth that are very far away. He will never become tired or lose his strength. Nobody will ever understand his mind.

29 He makes tired people strong and he gives more strength to weak people.

30 Even young people get tired and they lose their strength. And young men will fall over (something) and they will fall (to the ground).

31 But people who hope (for help from) the LORD will get back (their) strength. They will fly high on wings like (large birds called) eagles. They will run and they will not become tired. They will walk and they will not fall over.

Chapter 41

God is the Judge of the World

1 'You islands, be quiet when you come to me. And everybody must become strong again. They must move towards the front (of the court) and they must speak. We must meet together so that (I, the LORD) can be your judge.

2 (The LORD) will awake a man in the east (as from sleep). The good (God) will ask the man to follow (the LORD).

· (The LORD) will give (many) countries to him.

(The LORD) will cause kings to go down on their knees in front of him.

(The LORD) will make (people) into dead bodies with that man's sword.

(The LORD) will make) them like dry dead bits of plants. That man's bow will blow them away.

3 He (the LORD's servant) will run after them, but he himself will move on safely. He will go on a path (very quickly). His feet (will almost not touch the ground) while he travels.

4 (I am the God) who will do this. And I will cause it to happen', (says the LORD). '(I am the God) who told you about everything from the beginning. I, the LORD, am the first (person). But I am he (who will be) with people at the end.'

5 The (people on the) islands heard this and they were afraid. It frightened the people at the far places of the earth very much. They came near (to each other). They met together.

6 Each (country) helped the other (country). Each person said to his brother, 'Be strong!'

7 The careful worker let the worker who makes things out of gold hope. The man with a hammer said to the man with the large bit of iron, 'What you have put together is good.' Then he made (the idol) safe with bits of iron so that it could not fall over.

8 'But you, Israel, are my servant. Jacob, I have chosen you. You are the descendants of my friend Abraham.'

9 'I brought you from the ends of the earth. I brought you from its far corners. I have said, "You are my servant. I have chosen you. I have not refused to say that you are mine.

10 So do not be afraid, because I am with you. Do not be sad, because I am your God. I will make you strong and I will help you. Really, I will hold you with my right hand. (It is strong and) it wins wars."

11 Everybody that is angry with you will surely be ashamed. They will lose their good name. Those that fight you will become like nothing. And they will die.

12 Even if you look for your enemies, you will not find them. The people that fight against you will disappear.

13 (This will happen) because I am the LORD. (I am) your God. I will hold on to your right hand. And I will say to you, "Do not be afraid. I will help you."

14 Do not be afraid, you worm Jacob, you (people of) little Israel. I myself will help you.' This is what the LORD says. He is your Redeemer. (He is the) Holy (God) of Israel.

15 'Look! I will cause you to become like a machine that threshes. It will be new and sharp, with many sharp metal points that are like teeth. You will thresh the mountains and you will break the hills. They will become (like) chaff.

16 You will make them into separate (small pieces). Then the wind will pick them up and a strong wind will blow them away. But you will be happy with the LORD. You will (have some of) the glory of the Holy (God) of Israel.

17 Poor people and people who need (water) look for water. But there is none. Their mouths are dry because they need a drink. I, the LORD, will answer them. I, the God of Israel, will not forget them.

18 I will make rivers on hills where nothing grows. And (I will make) wells of water in the valleys. I will make pools of water in the sandy places. And (I will make) wells where the ground is dry.

19 I will put these kinds of trees into the sandy places: cedar, acacia, myrtle and olive. And I will put together into the Arabah these kinds of trees: pine, fir and cypress.

20 Then people will see this. They will know that the hand of the LORD has done it. They will think about it. And they will understand that the Holy (God) of Israel has created it.'

21 The LORD says, 'Tell me the reasons (for your thoughts).' Jacob's king says, 'Say what you believe.

22 Bring (your idols) into (court). Cause them to tell us what will happen (in future years). Tell us about past things. Then we can think about them. And we will know what happened. Or tell us about events that will happen.

23 Tell us what will happen in future years. Then we will know that (your idols) are gods. Do something good or bad that will make us sad and afraid at the same time.

24 But your (idols) are less than nothing. And the things that you have made are really worth nothing. Anybody that chooses you is really very bad!'

25 'I will awake somebody from the north. And he will come from (the direction of) the sun where it rises. He will tell my name to people (by what he does). He will walk on the rulers (of the people) like they were mortar. And like a person who makes pots, he will make shapes with the clay.

26 Tell me who told (this) to you from the beginning. Then we would know (what would happen). Or (tell me) who told this to you. They told it to you) before it happened. Then we could say, "He was right."

27 Remember, I (God) was the first (person) to tell this to Zion. "Look, they are here!" I gave to Jerusalem somebody that brought good news.

28 I looked, but there is nobody (among the people). There is nobody to teach them what to do. There is nobody to answer (the questions that) I ask them.

29 Look! All (the idols) are false. What they do comes to nothing. Their idols are only like wind and they confuse people.'

Chapter 42

The First Servant Song

The Song: God speaks about his servant

1 'Look at my servant, to whom I will give a lot of help. I chose him and he gives pleasure to my Spirit. I will put my Spirit on him and he will be a fair judge for every country.

2 He will not talk loudly, nor scream. And he will not shout with a loud voice in the streets.

3 He will not break a reed that somebody has bent. And he will not put out a fire that has almost stopped burning. He will always be kind (to his people) and he will be a fair judge.

4 Nothing will cause him to make a mistake. Also, he will always be brave, until there is justice (everywhere) on the earth. The islands will hope for what he has promised (to happen).'

God speaks to his servant

5 God (is) the LORD. This is what he says. (He is the God) who created the skies. He hung them up (like a curtain). He made the shape of the whole earth. (He made) everything that grows in it. He gives (air) to its people so that they can breathe. And he causes everybody to live that walks on (the earth).

6 (He says), 'I (am) the LORD. I have asked you (to work for) Righteousness. I will hold your hand. I will keep you safe. And I will cause you to be a Covenant for the people. (You will be like) a light for the countries that are not Jewish.

7 (You will) cause blind eyes to see. You will make the prisoners free from (their) prison. And you will make free those people who sit in a dark prison, deep in the ground.

8 I am the LORD. That is my name. I will not give my glory to anybody else. (I will) not let people praise idols. (They should praise) me.

9 Everything (that I promised) in past years has happened. Now I will tell you about new things. Before they happen, I will talk about them to you.'

Words from Isaiah

10 Sing a new song to the LORD, you people that go down to the sea. And everything that is in (the sea), (sing a new song). Praise him from the far places of the earth, you islands and everybody that lives in them.

11 (The people in) the sandy places and in the towns near them should use their voices (to praise God). The places (where the people) of Kedar live should be very happy. The people in Sela should sing because they are so happy. They should shout from the tops of their mountains.

12 They should give glory to the LORD and they should praise him in the islands.

13 The LORD will march out like a strong man. He will awake like a soldier who is ready (to fight). He will shout the war song loudly. And then he will beat his enemies.

God speaks again

14 'I have been quiet for a long time. I have held myself back and I have done nothing. I am like a woman that is having a baby. I cry. I try to breathe. And I breathe out with difficulty, all at the same time.

15 I will make the mountains and hills into empty places. And I will make all the plants (that grow) there dry. I will make rivers into islands and I will make all the pools dry.

16 I will lead blind people by ways that they did not know. I will be their guide along paths that are new to them. I will make the dark places in front of them into light places. And I will make the rough places flat. These are the things that I will do. I will not leave (my people by themselves).

17 I will turn back (people) that believe in idols. And (people that) say to idols, "You are our gods" will be ashamed.

18 Listen (to me), you (people) who are not able to hear! You blind (people), look and see!

19 Who is blind? (Only) my servant (Israel is blind). Who is not able to hear? The man with the message that I send. (He is not able to hear.) Of all people, the person that believes me is really blind! Of all people, the servant of the LORD is really blind!

20 You have seen many things, but you have not thought about them. He (Israel) has opened his ears (to listen), but he hears nothing.'

More words from Isaiah

21 It gave pleasure to the LORD to make his great and fair rules. (He did this) because he was righteous.

22 But (an enemy) has robbed this people and he has taken things from them. (The enemy) has caught them all in holes in the ground or he has hidden them in prisons. (The enemy) took this people and nobody has saved them. They themselves are what the robber took. And nobody said, 'Send them back.'

23 Not many among you will listen to this! Not many (of you) will think about it in the future!

24 Who gave Jacob (for the enemy) to rob? Who gave Israel's people to those who robbed them? (The answer is) that it was the LORD. We have sinned against him. They would not walk in his ways. Also, they did not obey his rules.

25 So (the LORD) was very, very angry with them. (He caused) a very, very bad war. (He was so angry that) it was like a fire round them. But they did not understand (what he was doing). (The war) killed their people. But they did not know what it meant.

About the Servant of the LORD

Many Bible students, perhaps hundreds, have written about 'the servant of the LORD'. The words come in other places in the Old Testament, but it comes most importantly in Isaiah chapters 41-55. The word LORD, with 4 capital letters, translates the Hebrew word YHWH. Some people pronounce it JEHOVAH. Nobody is sure what YHWH means. It may mean the same as God's name in Exodus 3:14: 'I AM THAT WHICH I AM' or 'I AM BECAUSE I AM'. It tells us that God is always alive!

There are 4 parts of Isaiah that Bible students call 'Servant Songs'. They are Isaiah 42:1-4; 49:1-6; 50:4-9 and 52:13-53:12. In Acts 8:30-35, we can read part of the story of a man from Ethiopia. Philip heard him read from the 4th Servant Song. Philip asked him if he understood what he was reading. The man did not understand, so Philip explained it to him. The question the man asked was this. 'Is the prophet (Isaiah) speaking about himself, or about somebody else?' Philip's answer was, 'Somebody else, Jesus'. Also, Matthew tells us that Isaiah wrote about Jesus in the first Servant Song, Matthew 12:14-21.

But the servant in Isaiah chapters 41-55 (not only the 4 Servant Songs) is not always Jesus. Also, Jewish Bible students do not have the same answers as Christians. Lastly, the servant in some places in Isaiah chapters 41-55 is one person (or group of persons). But in other places it is somebody else. Here are some of the answers that Bible students have given.

1) Usually, Jewish Bible students say that the servant is nearly always the country called Israel.

Christians agree that in some places, like Isaiah 41:18-20, Israel is called the servant of the LORD. Even in Babylon, after God has punished Israel, Israel continues to be God's servant, as in Isaiah 43:21.

2) In Isaiah 44:28 and 45:1 the servant is King Cyrus of Persia. Isaiah 44:28 calls him the Lord's 'shepherd'. And 45:1 says that the LORD has 'anointed' him. A shepherd is a sheep farmer. He is a like a picture of somebody that is careful for his people. 'Anointed' means 'someone poured oil on him'. Oil in the Bible often means God's Holy Spirit. This gives the anointed person something to do and it gives him the authority and power to do it. The kings that lived after Cyrus are also God's servants, Darius and Artaxerxes.

3) But Jesus is also a shepherd (John 10:11) and God has anointed him with the Holy Spirit (Matthew 3:16).

And Christians believe that Isaiah 53 can only be about Jesus. Also, it is true that Isaiah 42:1 may be about both Israel and the kings of Persia. But it is mostly about Jesus.

So, when we read the words 'the servant of YHWH', they can mean several things:

- the country called Israel
- the prophet Isaiah
- the rulers of Persia
- Jesus Christ.

'Christ' is the Greek word for 'anointed'. Greek is a language. For Christians, the servant of YHWH is JESUS THE ANOINTED! He is doing what Israel, Isaiah and Cyrus did 2700 years ago.

God redeems Israel (chapters 43-45)

Chapter 43

1 But now, this is what the LORD says. He (is the LORD) who created you, Jacob. And he (is the God) who gave shape to you, Israel. (He says this.) 'Do not be afraid, because I have redeemed you. I have called you by (your) name. You are mine.

2 I will be with you, when you go through (dangerous) waters. (And when you go through) rivers they will not carry you away. When you walk through fire it will not burn you. And the fire will not make a fire out of you.

3 I will save you, because I, the LORD, am your God. (I am) the Holy (God) of Israel. I gave Egypt to ransom you and I gave Ethiopia and Seba in your place.

4 I think that you are valuable and very good. Because of this, and because I love you, (I will do this). I will take men for you and I will take people for your life.

5 Do not be afraid, because I am with you. I will bring your child (ren) from the east and I will fetch you from the west.

6 I will say to (people in) the north, "Give them back!" And I will say to (people in) the south, "Do not stop them from coming back." Bring my sons from far (places) and my daughters from the ends of the earth.

7 (Bring) everyone who is called by my name. I created them. I gave them a shape and yes, I made them for my glory.

8 Lead out those (people) with eyes who are blind. (Lead out) those (people) with ears who cannot hear.

9 Bring every country together. And bring together all the people. Perhaps some of them said that this would happen. And (perhaps some of them) told us about what happened a long time ago. (If they did,) they should bring their witnesses. (They could) prove that they were right. Then other people will hear it and they will say, "It is true."

10 You are my witnesses', says the LORD. 'You are my servant whom I have chosen. (I chose you) so that you may know (me). Also, (I wanted you to) believe that I am (God). And (I wanted you) to understand (that I am God). That is why (I chose you). Before me, nobody made a god. And there will not be (a God) after me.

11 I, only I, am the LORD. And, without me, there is nobody to save (you).

12 It was I, and not a foreign god among you, that showed (this to you). And I saved (you) and I told (this to you). You are my witnesses that I am God', says the LORD.

13 'Yes! From a long time ago, I am (God). Nobody can save himself from my power. When I do something, nobody can change it.'

14 This is what the LORD says. (The LORD) is your redeemer (and he is) the Holy (God) of Israel. (He says), 'I will send (an army) to Babylon because of you, (Israel). And I will make all the people from Babylon into prisoners. (They will be) in their ships. They think that they are very good.

15 I am the LORD (who is) your Holy (God). (I am) Israel's Creator and your King.'

16-17 This is what the LORD says. (He is the LORD who did these things:)

- He made a road through the sea.

- (He made) a path through the great waters.

He drew chariots and (their) horses, the army and (its) leaders, out (into the sea).

(He caused them) to lie there so that they would never get up again. He put them out and he blew them out, like a light.

18 (The LORD says,) 'Forget what happened a long time ago. Do not think about that.

19 Look! I will do something that is new! Now it appears quickly. Surely, you can see it. I am making a road in the sandy places. And (I am making) streams in the wild places.

20 The wild animals, jackals and owls, give me praise. (They do this) because I give them water in the sandy places and streams in the wild places. (I want) my people that I have chosen to be able to drink. (That is why I do this.)

21 (They are) the people that I made for myself. (I did it) so that they could praise me aloud.

22 You did not pray to me, Jacob. You have not worked for me, Israel.

23 (It was) not to me that you brought sheep. (You did not) burn them to offer them to me. What you put at one side did not give me praise. I have not caused you to carry heavy grain to offer to me. I have not made you tired because I demanded incense (from you).

24 You did not bring (the plant called) calamus, which had a nice smell, for me. You did not give large amounts of meat from the animals that you burned to me. Instead, you caused me to carry your sins like a heavy weight. And you have made me tired every time that you did not obey me.

25 I, (but yes,) I am he who sweeps away your sins. (I do it) to keep my good name. I will not remember that you have not obeyed me.

26 Remember with me (what happened a long time ago). We should talk about it together. You think that you have not sinned. Tell me why you think that.

27 Your first ancestor did not obey me. And the people that spoke (to me) on behalf of you sinned against me.

28 So I made your holy leaders ashamed. Then I destroyed everything in Jacob (that I did not like). (Also, people) laughed in a bad way at Israel.

Chapter 44

1 But now listen (and obey me), my servant Jacob. (Listen to me) Israel, whom I have chosen.'

2 This is what the LORD says. He (is the LORD) who made you. He gave you a shape when you were still inside your mother. And he will help you. (He says), 'Do not be afraid, Jacob my servant and Jeshurun, whom I chose.

3 (Do not be afraid) for these reasons:

- I will pour water on to land that is very dry.

- I will pour streams (of water) on to dry ground.

- I will pour out my Spirit on to your children.

- I will do good things for your children's children.

4 They will grow up like grass in a field. (They will grow) like tall trees by streams of water.

5 One (of them) will say, "I (belong) to the LORD." And another (person) will call (himself) by the name Jacob. Then another (person) will write on his hand, "(I belong to) the LORD", and he will call (himself) Israel.'

6 This is what the LORD says. (He is) the King and Redeemer of Israel and (he is) the LORD of Everything. (He says,) 'I am the first (God) and I am the last (God). There is no God without me.

7 Is there (any God) like me? (If there is), he should say so. He must say it. And he should tell me (this):

- What has happened since I made my people a long (time) ago?

- What will happen in future years?

Yes! He should say what will happen!

8 Do not move and do not be afraid. I told you this long ago. And I said that it would happen. You are my witnesses. Is there any God without me? No! There is no (other) Rock. I do not know about any (other God).'

9 Everybody that makes an idol (is) of no value. And the things that they have pleasure in will bring no help. Their witnesses cannot see (anything). Also, they will be ashamed, because they know nothing. 10 Everybody who has made the shape of a god has made (only) an idol. It will not help them. 11 Really, everybody like them will be ashamed. People who make (these things) are only human. They should all come and they should stand together (by their idols). They will be very much afraid. Also, they will quickly understand what fools they are.

12 A man that works with iron (takes) a tool. He holds (the iron) in the fire (with the tool). Then he uses a hammer. He gives (the iron) a shape. He has made (an idol) with his strong arms. But (then) he becomes hungry and he is not strong. He drinks no water and he feels weak. 13 A man that works with wood measures (it) with a ruler. Then he draws a shape with a pencil. He uses one tool to give (the wood) its first shape. He uses another tool to make the shape better. Then he causes its shape to seem like a man. (He has made) a beautiful human (shape). It will remain in a house. 14 (A man went) to cut down cedar trees for himself. He had taken cypress and oak (trees). And he had let them grow for himself, among the trees in the forest. He had planted a pine tree and the rain had caused it to grow. 15 It is (wood) for (the) man to burn. So he takes some of it and he makes himself warm. Yes, and now he lights a fire and he bakes bread. And then he makes a god and he worships it. He makes an idol and he goes down on his knees in front of it. 16 Half (of the wood) he burnt in the fire. He made his meal with (that) half. He cooked his meat. And he ate as much as he wanted. He also made himself warm and he said, 'Good! I am warm. I can see the fire.' 17 From the other half he makes a god. (It is) his idol. He goes on his knees in front of it and he worships it. And he prays to it and he says, 'Save me, because you are my god.'

18 These people know nothing. They understand nothing. (This is) because something is covering their eyes. So, they cannot see (anything). Their minds cannot understand (anything). 19 Nobody really thinks about it. Nobody knows about it, or understands it. (Nobody) says, 'I burnt half of it in the fire. I even baked bread with the wood from it. I cooked meat and I ate (it). (Perhaps) I will make something to worship from what is still there. (Perhaps) I will go down on my knees in front of a piece of wood.'

20 It is like he is eating ashes. His mind has made a mistake. And it leads him away (from what is true). He cannot save himself. He does not understand that the thing in his right hand is a false (god).

21 'Jacob, remember these things, because you, Israel, are my servant. I caused you (to be) my servant. Israel, I will not forget you.

22 I have swept away your sins like (the wind sweeps away) a cloud. The wrong things that you have done (have disappeared) like clouds in the morning. Return to me, because I have redeemed you.'

23 Skies above (us), sing because you are so happy. (Sing), because the LORD has done this! Earth beneath (us), shout as loudly (as you can). You mountains, start to sing. (Do the same), you forests and all your trees! (Do this), because the LORD has redeemed Jacob. He has shown his glory in Israel.

24 This is what the LORD says. He is your Redeemer. He gave you a shape (when you were still) inside your mother. 'I am the LORD, who has made everything. I alone hung out the skies (like a curtain). I made the earth by myself.

25 I will destroy the messages of the false prophets. Some people try to say what will happen in future years. I will cause them to seem like fools. Some people think that they are clever. They think that they know everything. But I will change that. (What they know) will mean nothing. My servants say what I will do. My prophets say what will happen. I will do (all those things).

26 I say about Jerusalem, "People will live there (again)." (I say) about the towns in Judah, "(People) will build them." (And I say) about the (places that the enemy) destroyed, "I will build them again."

27 I said to the watery deep (sea), "Be dry! And I made your streams dry."

28 I say about Cyrus, "He is (like) my shepherd (sheep farmer). And he will do everything that gives me pleasure." (Cyrus) will say about Jerusalem, "Build it again!" And (he will say) about the temple, "Lay out the stones to build it on." '

Chapter 45

1 The LORD will say this to Cyrus, whom he has anointed. I will hold his right hand. Then he will beat the countries where he goes. He will take their (war) arms from kings. He will open doors in front of him, so that the gates will not be closed. (He will say,)

2 'I will go in front of you and I will make the mountains flat. I will break down bronze gates and I will cut through iron bars.

3 Also, I will give to you the valuable things (that people hide) in dark places. (I will give to you) the valuable things that they store secretly. Then you will know that I am the LORD. (I am) the God of Israel who will cause you to come. He will call you by (your) name.

4 I will cause you to come. I have called you by (your) name, because of my servant Jacob and because of Israel. I have chosen you (Israel). And I will give you a good name, even if you will not recognise me.

5 I am the LORD and there is no other (LORD). There is no God without me. I will make you strong, even if you will not recognise me.

6 Then, from east to west, people will know this. There is no (God) without me.

7 I made the light and I created the dark. I cause (people) to do well and I create trouble. I (am) the LORD. I do all these things.'

8 I will ask the skies to send down good things. They will come down like rain. And I will prepare the earth to receive my power to save. That power will become great, like a plant that is growing. And good things will grow with it. I, (who am) the Lord, will cause this to happen.

9 Bad (things will happen) to people who quarrel with their Maker. (They are like) bits of pot (that are lying) among other bits of pot on the ground. The clay does not say to the person who makes the pots, 'What are you making?' And the things that you make (do not say), 'He has no hands.'

10 Bad (things will happen) to people who say to their fathers, 'What have you been father to?' Or (bad things will happen to people) that say to their mothers, 'What have you given birth to?'

11 The LORD says this about things that will happen in the future. (The LORD is) the Holy (God) of Israel and he is its Maker. (He says this :)

'You should not ask me questions about my children.

You should not tell me what to do with what my hands have made.

12 It is I who made the earth. Then I created the people on it. (It was) I who, with my own hands, hung up the skies (like a curtain). I put all (the stars) in their places.

13 My good help will make (Cyrus) into a great leader. I will make all his paths straight. He will build again my city (Jerusalem) and he will make my exiles free. He will not get money or gifts because (he will do) this', says the LORD of Everything.

14 This is what the LORD is saying. 'This is what will come to you and what will become yours.

- everything that (the people in) Egypt make

- everything that (the people in) Cush sell

- the tall people from Sabea.

They will walk behind you. Metal lines (will tie them up) when they come to you. They will go down on their knees in front of you. They will pray to you. They will say, "Surely God is with you. And there is no other God." '

15 It is true. You are a God that hides himself! (You are) the God that makes Israel safe!

16 Everybody that makes idols will be ashamed. And nobody will give them praise. Together, they will have no praise.

17 The LORD will make Israel safe. (Israel) will be safe for all time. You will never be ashamed. And you will always have praise. This will always be true.

18 This is because the LORD says it. He (is the LORD that) created the skies. He is God. He made the earth and he gave to it its shape. He built it. He did not create it to be empty. He made it for people to live in. He says, 'I am the LORD. And there is nobody else (that is LORD).

19 I have not spoken secretly. (I have not spoken) from somewhere that is a dark country. I did not say to the people whose ancestor is Jacob, "Look for me, but do not find me." I am the LORD. I speak what is true. I say what is right.

20 Bring (yourselves) together! And come and put yourselves into a group. You (are) people that are running away from (other) countries. Some people that carry idols that they made from wood. Those people do not know anything. (They are people that) pray to (false) gods. (Those gods) cannot make them safe.

21 Speak! Tell us (what will happen)! Also, decide this together. Who said a long time ago that this would happen? Who said it in past years? It was I, the LORD! There is no God without me. I am a righteous God that saves (my people). There is (no other) God but me.

22 Turn to me and I will make you safe. (Do this), everybody on the earth. (Do this) because I am God. I am God and there is no other (God but me).

23 I, myself, have given you a promise. Because I am honest I have said this. I will change nothing that I have said. Everybody will go down on their knees in front of me. People will say their promises in every language in my (name).

24 People will say this about me. "Only with the LORD are things that are righteous and strong." Everybody that was angry with (God) will come to (God). They will be ashamed.

25 With the LORD, everybody that has Israel for an ancestor will be righteous and they will be very, very happy.'

God will send Cyrus to beat Babylon (chapters 46-47)

Chapter 46

1 Bel bends down. Nebo lies low. Animals that can carry heavy things carry these idols. (The animals) carry the idols, which are very heavy. They are very heavy for tired (animals).

2 (The false gods) fall down and they lie together. (The animals) cannot carry the heavy weights. (The false gods) themselves go away (into another country) as slaves.

3 'Listen to me, you people (that live) in Jacob. (Listen to me), everyone that remains from the people in Israel. I have helped you since you began to live inside (your mother). And I have carried you since you were born.

4 (I will do this) even until you are old. (Then) you will have grey hairs. I am he who will supply everything. I (will supply everything) that you need. I have made you and I will carry you. I will supply everything that you need. And I will save you.

5 No (god) is like me! (Bel, or Nebo) are not as good as me. You cannot say that any god is like me. You cannot say that I am the same (as them).

6 Some (people) pour out gold from a bag. And they weigh out silver on the scales. Then they pay someone who can work with gold. He makes it into a god. Then they bend down and they worship it!

7 They lift it on to their shoulders and they carry it. They put it in its place and it stands there. It cannot move from that place. If anyone shouts out to it, it does not answer. It cannot save anybody from his troubles.

8 Remember this and fix it in (your) mind. Do not forget it, you people that fight against me.

9 Remember the things that happened long ago. I am God and there is no other (God). I am God and there is nobody like me.

10 I told (you) at the beginning what will happen at the end. (I told you) from long ago about future things that will happen. I am the Person that says (this). My purpose will not change. And I will do everything that I want (to do).

11 I will send someone from the east like a bird that catches small animals. And (I will get) a man from a country that is far away. He will cause my purposes to happen.

I really will do the things that I have promised to do. I have made a plan and I will really will cause it to happen.

12 Listen to me, you people that will not change your minds. (Listen), you people who are not righteous in any way.

13 Soon, I will come to do what is right. I am not far away. I will not wait any longer to come and save you. I will save (the people in) Zion (Jerusalem). (I will make) Israel beautiful.'

Chapter 47

1 'Get down (on to the ground) and sit in the dirt, Virgin Daughter of Babylon. Sit on the ground without a high seat, Daughter of the people in Chaldea. Nobody will say that you are quiet and pretty again.

2 Use a stone to break (grain) into flour. Uncover your face. Lift up your skirt and make your legs bare. Walk through streams (of water).

3 Everybody will see that you are bare. Nothing will hide your sex parts. I will punish (you) and I will not leave anybody out.'

4 Our Redeemer is the Holy (God) of Israel. His name is the LORD of Everything. (He says this.)

5 'Daughter of the people in Chaldea, sit and make no noise. And go into dark (places). Nobody will call you the queen of kingdoms again.

6 I was angry with my people (Judah). I made what was mine not clean. I gave them into your power, but you were not kind them. You even made the old people into slaves.

7 You said, "I will always continue to be queen. (I will) always (be queen)!" But you did not think about these things. You did not think about what might happen (to you).

8 Now, listen (to me), you (women) that love pleasure. You do not say what is true about your safety. And you say (this) to yourself. "(Here) I am, and there is nobody except me. I will never be a widow and I will never lose (my) children."

9 Both of these things will happen to you in one moment. (They will happen) in only one day. You will lose your children and you will become a widow. It will all happen to you, even if you (try to stop it) with much magic and powerful magic words.

10 You have believed this: The bad things that you have done would help you. And you have said, "Nobody sees me (when I do them)." But you are clever and you know so much. It has caused you to make mistakes. This happened when you said to yourself, "(Here) I am, and there is nobody except me."

11 Then bad things will happen to you. And you will not know what magic words (will remove them). So they will destroy you and you will have no ransom for them. They will destroy you quickly, in a way that you have known nothing about.

12 Continue, then, with your magic! (Continue to say) your many magic words! You have worked a lot with them since you were children. Perhaps you will cause the magic things really to happen. Perhaps you will frighten (your enemies)!

13 All the things that you have learned have made you very tired! The people that (look at) different parts of the skies should stand up. Those people that study the stars should (stand up). They say what will happen each month. Cause them to save you from what will happen to you.

14 Surely, they are like dry grass! Fire will burn them (away). They cannot save themselves from the heat of the fires. This is not the wood that will bake their bread. (It is) not a fire to sit by.

15 This is (all) that they (have done) on your behalf. You worked with them since you were children. They were your friends. (But now) each of them continues to make mistakes. There is nobody to save you.'

Chapter 48

God will send Cyrus to make his people free from Babylon

1 'Listen to this, you people of Jacob. Your name is Israel and you belong to the family of Judah. You (are people) that promise in the name of the LORD. Also, you ask the God of Israel for help. But you do not (do these things) honestly and fairly.

2 They even call themselves (people who live) in the holy city. And they hope that the God of Israel will help them. His name is the LORD of Everything.

3 I said (a) long (time) ago the things (that would) soon (happen). I myself said that they would happen. And I caused (everybody) to know (about them). Then, quickly, I did something and they happened!

4 (This is why) I did it. I knew that it would be difficult to cause you to think differently. It seems that your necks have become (as hard) as iron! The front of your head is like bronze!

5 So I told you these things long ago. Before they happened, I told you about them. Then you could not say, "My idol did them. My wood idol and my metal god decided that they would happen."

6 You heard (these things). Now look at them all. Agree that it is true! From now, I will tell you new things. They will be things that you do not know. (They will be things that I) hid from you.

7 (I) created them now. I did not (create them) a long (time) ago. You did not hear about them before today. So you cannot say, "Yes. I knew about them."

8 You have not heard them and you have not understood them. From (a) long (time) ago your ear has not listened to them. I know well that you do not always obey me. (People) said that you fought against (me) from (your) birth.

9 I will not be angry immediately, because of the name that I have. (So that people will give) me praise, I will not be angry with you. Then (nobody) will kill you.

10 I have made you clean, but not as (people make) silver (clean). I have let you have much trouble. It is like I put you in a fire. This has been to check how good you are.

11 I do this on my own behalf, (yes), on my own behalf! Really, I cannot let people say bad things about me. And (so), I will not give my praise to another (person or god).

12 Listen to me, (you people of) Jacob! (Listen to me, you people of) Israel. I have asked you to follow me. I am (your God). I am the first (God) and (I am) the last (God).

13 My own hand put out the parts that are under the earth. And my right hand hung up the skies. When I speak to them, they all stand (up) together.

14 All of you, come together and listen (to me). Not one (of your idols) said what would happen. The LORD has chosen a friend to help him. (This friend) will do what God wants to happen against Babylon. His arm (will be against) the people in Chaldea.

15 I, (yes,) I have spoken. Also, I have asked him to follow me. I will bring him (to Babylon). And he will do well in what he has to do.

16 Come near to me and listen to this. From the first time that I spoke (about it), it was not a secret. When it happens, I will be there. And now the LORD and Master has sent me with his Spirit', (says God's servant).

17 This is what the LORD says. He is your Redeemer, the Holy (God) of Israel. 'I am the LORD your God. I will teach you what is the best (thing) for you. I will send you in the way that you should go.

18 I told you what you should do. You should have listened to what I said. Then your peace would be like a river. Also, the good things that you do would be like the waves in the sea.

19 Your children, and your children's children, would be as many as there are little bits in some sand. Nobody would ever forget their names. Nobody would kill them in front of me.

20 Leave Babylon! Run from the people in Chaldea! Talk about it with happy shouts. Talk about it and send (the news) to the ends of the earth. Say that the LORD has redeemed Jacob his servant.'

21 They did not need a drink when he led them through sandy places. He caused water to pour from a rock for them. He broke the rock and water rushed out.

22 'There is no peace for bad people', says the LORD.

Chapter 49

The Second Servant Song

1 Listen to me, (you) islands. And hear (this, you) countries that are far away. The LORD chose me when I was inside my mother. From (when I was) inside her body he said my name.

2 And he made my mouth like a sharp sword. He hid me in the shadow of his hand. And he made me into an arrow (that he had caused) to shine. He hid me in his basket of arrows.

3 He said to me, 'You are my servant. (You are) Israel. In you I will show (to everybody) that I am beautiful.'

4 But I said (that) my work had no purpose. I had done all that work for nothing. But the LORD will be my judge and my God (will know) the result of my work.

5 And now the LORD says (this). He (is the LORD) that made me inside my mother to be his servant.

· (He did this) to bring Jacob back to him.

· Also, (he did it) to bring Israel to himself.

And I will have praise in the eyes of the LORD. My God will make me strong. He says,

6 'It is too small a thing for you, as my servant (to do these things):

· Bring back the families of Jacob.

· And bring together the people of Israel that I have kept alive.

I will also make you (like) a light for the (people in other) countries. Then you will bring (the news) that I can save people to the ends of the earth.'

7 This is what the LORD says. (The LORD is) the Redeemer and the Holy (God) of Israel. (He says it) to him, (the servant). The country (Judah) thought that he was not important. And they did not like (him). (He was) the servant of rulers. (God says), 'Kings will see you and they will rise up. Also, leaders will get on their knees (in front of you). (They will do this) because the LORD will always help (you). (He is) the Holy (God) of Israel, who has chosen you.'

8 This is what the LORD says. 'When I am ready to do something for you, I will answer you. And in the day when I am ready to save you, I will help you. Also, I will keep you alive and I will cause you to be a covenant for the people. You will make the country safe, and you will cause (people) to live in the empty places.

9 You will say to the people (that are) in a prison, "Come out." And (you will say) to those people that are in the dark, "Be free!"

They will eat food at the sides of the roads. And there will be food for them on every empty hill.

10 They will not be hungry and they will not need a drink. The heat of the sun in the sandy places will not hurt them. He who loves them will be their guide. And he will lead them to water that comes up (from the ground).

11 I will make all my mountains into roads. And I will build up all my roads on higher ground.

12 Look! People will come from far away. And look! Some people will come from the north and some (will come) from the west. Some will (even) come from round Sinim.'

13 (Everything in) the skies, shout because you are so happy! (Everything on) the earth, be very happy! Sing loudly, you mountains! (Do this) because the LORD is being kind to his people. He will show his love to his people that are hurting.

14 But Zion said, 'The LORD has left me. The Lord has forgotten me.'

15 (The LORD answered), 'Can a mother forget the baby at her breast? Can she have no love for the child that came from inside her body? Yes, these (mothers) may forget, but I will not forget you.

16 Look! I have written (your names) on my (own) hands. Your walls (of Jerusalem) are always in front of me.

17 Your sons will hurry back (to you). People beat you and they destroyed you. But those people will leave you.

18 Use your eyes and look all round you. All your (sons) will come (together). They will return to you. Because I am alive', says the LORD, 'you will surely wear all of them as something beautiful. You will put them on as a woman does at the time of her marriage.

19 (The enemy) broke you and they destroyed you. They made your land empty. But now your (land) will be too small for the people (that will come to) you. The people that destroyed you will be far away.

20 Children were born to you while you were a widow. They will say (this). "This place is too small for us. Give us more room to live in."

21 Then you will say in your mind, "I do not know how these (people) were born to me. I was a widow and I could not have any (children). I was in exile and (God had) thrown me away. So I do not know who brought them up. Look, (he) left me alone. So I do not know where they have (come from)." '

22 The LORD, (who is) the Lord, says, 'Look! I will point with my hand to (many) countries. I will lift up a mark to the people (in many countries). And they will bring your sons in their arms and they will carry your daughters on their shoulders.

23 Then kings will be (like) fathers for you and their queens will be (like) mothers (to your children). They will go down on their knees in front of you. Their faces will look to the ground. And they will taste the dirt by your feet. Then you will know that I am the LORD. I will not disappoint people that hope in me.

24 You cannot take things away from strong soldiers. And you cannot save prisoners from people that are right to keep them.'

25 But this is what the LORD says. 'Yes! (I) can take the prisoner from the strong soldier. And I will take back what the cruel man took away. I will fight with those people that fight with you. And I will make your children safe.

26 I will cause the people that are cruel to you to eat their own bodies. They will become drunks with their own blood, like it was wine. Then everybody will know that I, the LORD, have made you safe. (I am) your Redeemer, the Strong (God) of Jacob.'

Chapter 50

1 The LORD says, 'Your mother (Jerusalem) does not have a divorce notice. (I mean) that I did not send her away with (a notice). I did not sell you to any of the people with whom I had a debt. I sold you because of your sins. I sent your mother away because of wrong things (that she did).

2 Nobody was there when I came. Nobody answered when I spoke to them. My arm was not too short to ransom you. I was strong enough to save you. Look! With only a word I can make the sea dry. I can make rivers into sandy places. The fish in them will die because there is no water. And they will die because they need water.

3 I can make the sky dark and I can cover it with hairy cloth.'

The Third Servant Song

4 (The servant says,) 'The Lord, who is LORD, has given to me a tongue. It has learned (what to say). I know what to say to give hope (for something good) to very tired people. He wakes me every morning. He wakes my ear to listen, like someone that he is teaching.

5 The Lord, who is LORD, has opened my ears. I have obeyed him and I have not turned back.

6 I offered my back to the people that hit me. And (I offered) my face to the people that pulled out my beard. I did not hide my face when (they did these things). They laughed in a bad way at me and they spat at me.

7 The Lord, who is LORD, will help me. So, I will not be ashamed. I have made my face (hard) like a stone. So, I know that I will not be ashamed.

8 He (the LORD) says that I am right. He is near (to me). Some people are saying bad things about me. We should talk to each other! Some people have said that I have done wrong things. We should talk about it together!

9 Look! The Lord, who is LORD, will help me. Some person may say that I have done wrong things. But people like that will all become like very old clothes. The moths will eat them up!'

10 Perhaps someone among you is afraid of the LORD. And perhaps someone obeys the word of his servant. Some people walk in the dark and they have no light. They should believe in the LORD and they should hope for help from their God.

11 But now, go and walk in the light of your fires. Everyone who has lit a fire (must do this). (So must) everybody that has got for themselves something on fire. (You must) go in the light of the fires that you have made. This is what you will receive from me. You will lie down in very great pain.

Copy God's servant (Isaiah 51:1-52:12)

Chapter 51

1 'Listen to me, you people that are trying to be very good (like my servant). And (listen to me,) you people that are coming to the LORD. Think about the rock from which he cut you. And (think about) the rocky place from which he took you.

2 Think about your father Abraham. And think about Sarah who gave you birth. When I spoke to (Abraham), there was only one (of him). Then I blessed him and I made (from) him many (people).'

3 Surely, the LORD will be kind to Zion. And he will make it strong again, when he looks at its buildings. (These are the people whose land the enemy) destroyed. He will make its sandy places like (the garden of) Eden. (He will make) its wild places like the garden of the LORD. (People will) be happy there. They will feel very happy there. (People will) hear songs that thank (God).

4 'Listen to me, my people. And hear me, my country. The law will go out from me. And what I fairly decide will be (like) a light to every country.

5 The good things that I do (will be) near (to you). I will soon make you very safe. And my arm will decide fairly for every country. The islands will look to me and they will hope for my arm (to arrive).'

6 'Lift up your eyes to the skies and look at the earth beneath (them). The skies will disappear like smoke and the earth will become old like a coat. The people that live there will die in the same way. But the safe place that I give will be there always. The very good things that I do will never fail.'

7 'You people know that I am very good. (So) listen to me. You people have my law in your minds. (Listen to me.) Some people say that you are wrong, But do not be afraid of those people. Do not let them make you afraid with their bad words.

8 (Do not be afraid) because a moth will (seem to) eat them up! (It will seem to eat them) like (it eats) clothes. A grub will (seem to) eat them like (a grub eats) clothes. But the very good things that I do will never have an end. The safe place that I (offer to you) will never have an end.'

9 Awake, awake (you) arm of the LORD! Put on strength like (you put on) clothes! Awake, as you did in past days. (Awake) as you did for people many years ago. You cut Rahab into pieces. You pushed (your sword) into that large animal.

10 You made the sea and the deep waters dry. You made a road deep in the sea. The people that you redeemed crossed over.

11 And the people that the LORD has ransomed will return. And they will sing while they go into Zion. And they will be so happy that it will always show on their faces. They will continue to be happy, so very happy. Then, they will no longer feel sad and they will not want to cry.

12 'I, (the LORD, yes,) I am he that (will always) make (everybody) strong.

You (people in Zion, you) do not have to be afraid of men that will always die. They are (only) the sons of (other) men and they are only like grass.

13 But (you all) forget the LORD that made you! He put the skies in their place. And he made what is beneath the earth. (Do not) be afraid every day of your life, because your oppressor is very angry. The oppressor wants to destroy things. But really he can do nothing, even if he is angry.

14 The people that are so afraid will be made free. They will not die in a hole in the ground. They will not be without their bread, 15 because I am the LORD your God. I am (the God) that moves the sea so that its waters make a great noise! His name is the LORD of Everything. 16 I have put my words into your mouth, (my servant). And I have covered you with the shadow of my hand. (It is I) that will put the skies in their place. And I will make what is beneath the earth. And I will say to Zion, "You are my people." '

17 Awake, awake! Get up, (people in) Jerusalem! The LORD has been angry with you and he has punished you. When he punishes you it is like you are drinking something bad from a cup. You have drunk everything from the cup that makes people afraid (in front of God).

18 There was nobody to be her guide, from all the sons that she gave birth to. There was nobody to lead her by the hand, from all the sons that she had taught.

19 These two things have (destroyed) you. I do not know anyone who can make you strong again. (An enemy) broke and they destroyed (your buildings). The sword (killed your people). And (they died because) there was no food. I do not know anyone who can make you happy again.

20 Your sons have fallen down. They lie at the end of every street. (They are) like animals that something has caught. The LORD was angry and the serious words of your God punished them.

21 So, hear this, you people that (God is) hurting. You are (like) drunks, but it is not because you have drunk wine.

22 This is what the Lord who is your LORD says. (He is) your God, that fights for his people. 'Look! I have taken out from your hand the cup that makes you afraid. You will never drink again from that cup, the cup that contains my anger.

23 I will put it into the hands of the people that are cruel and unkind to you. (They are) the people that said, "Lie down flat (on the ground), so that we can walk over you." And you made your backs like the ground. (You made them) like a street that people could walk over.'

Chapter 52

1 Awake, awake, Zion! Put on strength like (you put on) clothes. Put on your beautiful clothes, Jerusalem, the holy city. People who are not God's people will not come into you again.

2 Remove the dirt (from yourselves). Get up and sit on your special high seat, Jerusalem. Make yourself free from the chains round your neck, Daughter of Zion (Jerusalem) (who is now) (like someone) in a prison.

3 (Do this) because the LORD says, 'You sold yourselves for nothing, and I will redeem you without money.' 4 And the Lord who is LORD says, 'Firstly, my people went down to live in Egypt. Then, not long ago, Assyria was cruel to them. 5 And now, this is what I (have got) here', says the LORD. He says, '(An enemy) took my people away for nothing. And the rulers (of my people) are crying. And for all of every day (enemies) continue to say bad things about me. 6 So, my people will know my name. So, in that day, (my people) will know this. I said what would happen. Yes, I (said it)!'

7 The feet of the people that bring good news will be beautiful. (They will be beautiful while they run) on the mountains. The people that bring good news will tell you, 'There is no war and there is no danger.' They will say to Zion, 'Your God rules (as king)!'

8 Listen! The men that watch over (your city) are saying (something). They are (all) shouting together because they are so happy. When the LORD returns to Zion, they will see it with their own eyes.

9 Sing aloud together, (you places in) Jerusalem that the enemy destroyed. (Do this) because the LORD has made his people happy again. He has redeemed Jerusalem.

10 The LORD has made his holy arm bare. (He has done it) in front of the eyes of the people in every country. Now, all parts of the earth can see that our God makes people safe.

11 Leave! Leave! Go out from there. Do not touch anything that is not clean. Go out from inside it! Those (people) that will carry the LORD's special things, be clean!

12 But you will not go out quickly, or hurry away. (This is) because the LORD will go in front of you. And the God of Israel will be like an army behind you.

The Fourth Servant Song (52:13-53:12)

13 Look! Everything that my servant says will be good. (It will be) right. (I will) raise him up and I will lift him up (to an important place). And I will make him very important.

14 (They) hit his body, so that it did not seem like (the body) of a man. (They) changed his shape, so that it was not like the shape of any human person. And when many people looked at him, they felt sick.

15 But he will pour (water or something like water) on many countries! Kings will shut their mouths because of him. (Here are the reasons :)

- They will see things that nobody told them about.

- And they will understand things that they have not heard about.

Chapter 53

1 Who has believed our message? And to whom has the LORD shown his Arm?

2 (The Servant) grew up in front of him like a weak plant. And (he grew) from a root in dry ground. He was not beautiful and he did not seem like a king. We had no interest in him. We looked at him. But there was nothing to cause us to want him.

3 People did not like him. And they caused him to go away. (He was) a man who often felt very sad. And he knew what pain felt like. He was like someone from whom people hid their faces. People did not like him. And we decided that he was worth nothing.

4 Surely, he lifted up our pain (from us)! And he took away the things that cause us to feel sad. But we thought that he had become ill. (We thought that) God had hit him very badly. And (we thought) that he was sick.

5 They put a sword into him, but we had done the wrong things. They hurt him and they broke him because of our sins. (They gave) to him the punishment (that brought) peace to us. His wounds have given us health.

6 We have all gone away, like sheep. Each (of us) has turned to his own way. And the LORD has put all our sins on him.

7 They were very cruel to him, but he was always quiet. And he did not open his mouth. They led him away like a lamb to kill him. A sheep is quiet when they cut off its hairy coat. In the same way, he did not open his mouth.

8 They took him to a court. After this, they decided to take him (to die). And none of his people said that it was wrong. They did not let him stay in the country where people are alive. They hit him very badly because of the sins of my people.

9 They gave him a grave with very bad people. And he was with a rich (man) in his deaths. (They did this), but he had done nothing to hurt people. Also, he had said nothing that was not true.

10 But it was the LORD's idea to hurt him and to break him. (The LORD) caused (people) to hurt (him). The LORD offered his life for sin, but (the servant) will see his seed. He will continue to live (after his death).

11 (Death) will hurt his spirit. But, after that, what he sees will make him happy. My very good servant will make many (people) very good, because they know him. And he will carry their sins (away).

12 So, I will give to him many (peoples). And he will have the strong (people) as his gift. (The facts are these.) He poured out his life until he died. He let people count him in with bad people. Also, he carried the sin of many (people) and he prayed for the very bad people.

Enjoy the results of the Servant's work (chapters 54-55)

Chapter 54

1 'Sing, woman that cannot have a child. (Sing), you who have never had a baby. Sing a song and shout! Then, you will be so happy! (Sing), you, who never had the pain of giving birth (to a baby). (Do this), because the lonely woman will have more sons than the woman with a husband.' This is what the LORD is saying.

2 'Make bigger the space that your tent covers. Make the curtains of your tent wider. Do not make it smaller! Make the sides longer and make the tent pegs stronger.

3 (Do this), because you will become larger, both to the right (side) and to the left (side). Your children (and their children) will cause people to go (from their own countries). (Your children) will live in the empty cities (of the people that go away).

4 Do not be afraid. You will not be ashamed. Nobody will take away your good name. You will not seem to be unimportant. Then, you will forget this: You were ashamed when you were young. You will not remember how bad you felt as a widow.

5 (This is) because your Maker is now your husband. His name is the LORD of Everything. The Holy (God) of Israel is your Redeemer. (People) call (him), "The God of all the earth".

6 (This is) because the LORD has asked you (to come) back. (You were) like a wife (whose husband had) left (her) alone. (He has asked you to come to him, like a wife) who was not happy. (That) wife married when she was young. Then, (her husband) sent her away.' This is what God is saying.

7 'For a short time I left you alone. But (now), because I love you very much, I will bring you back.

8 When I was angry, I hid my face from you, for a moment. But (now), with kind love that will always stay (with you), I will help you.' This is what the LORD, (who is) your Redeemer, is saying.

9 'This is like the waters of Noah for me. Then, I promised that the waters of Noah would never again cover the earth. So, now I have promised not to be angry with you. I will not punish you again.'

10 'Even if the mountains move, my kind love for you will not fail. Even if (someone) removes the hills, no (body) will remove my covenant of peace (with you).' This is what the LORD, who loves you, is saying.

11 '(My city, that the enemy) hurt, storms hit you. No (body) made you strong. Look! I will build you (again) with turquoise stones. (I will build you) on the top of very valuable blue stones called sapphires.'

12 'I will build your castles with valuable red stones called rubies. (I will build) your gates with valuable stones that shine (in the light). (I will build) your walls with very valuable stones.

13 The LORD will teach all your sons. And your sons will have great peace.

14 (The LORD) will build you on (a base of) what is right. You will be far away from cruel (people). Really, you will have nothing to be afraid of. Nobody will ever frighten you again. (People that frighten you) will not come near to you.

15 If anybody attacks you, I will not have sent them. You will beat anyone who attacks you.

16 Look! I, I created the man that works with iron. He causes the coal to burn strongly. He makes arms that are good for their work. But it is I that have created the destroyer. That (destroyer) can destroy everything.

17 No arms that anybody will make will beat you. And you will show that this is true. Everything that people say against you is not true. This is what the servants of the LORD will enjoy. And their righteousness will be from me.' These are the words of the LORD.

Chapter 55

1 'Hoy! Everyone that needs a drink, come to the waters! And the person without money, come (to me). Buy (food) and eat! Come and buy wine and milk!

2 Do not spend money on (that which is) not bread. And do not work for (things which) do not make (you) happy. Listen! Listen to me. And eat (what is) good! Then your spirit will have pleasure in the best (things).

3 Listen and come to me! Hear (me), so that your spirit may live! Then I will make a covenant (of peace) with you (all) that will never end. (It will be) the kind love that I promised to David.

4 Look! I have made (David) someone that every country can listen to. (And I have made him) a leader and a ruler of all the countries.'

5 'Surely, you will ask a country that you do not know to come to you. And a country that does not know you will hurry to you. (This will happen) because the LORD (is) your God. (He is) the Holy (God) of Israel. And he has made you really great!'

6 Come to the LORD while you can find him. Talk to him while he is near (to you).

7 The very bad (man) must stop doing bad things. And the very bad man (must stop having) his (bad) thoughts. He must turn to the LORD, who will be kind to him. And (he must turn) to our God, because (God) will certainly excuse him.

8 '(This is) because my thoughts are not your thoughts. And neither are your ways my ways.' These are the words of the LORD.

9 'As the skies are higher than the earth, so are my ways higher than your ways. Also, my thoughts (are higher) than your thoughts (like that too).'

10 The rain and the snow come down from the skies. And they do not return (to them) until they have put water on to the earth. And they cause (plants) to grow in the earth. Then (the plants) become strong. Then they give seeds for the gardener and they give bread for the eater.

11 It is the same with the word that I speak. It will not return to me empty. It will do what I want it to do. And it will cause to happen the purpose for which I sent it.

12 You will go out and you will be happy. And you will follow (your leader). You will have peace. The mountains and the hills will sing songs in front of you. And all the trees in the field(s) will hit their hands together!

13 Pine trees will grow in the place of thorn bushes, and myrtle bushes will grow in the place of briars. This will make the LORD famous. It will always be something that nobody will destroy.'

PART 5: Chapters 56-66 God's Messiah beats God's enemies
A place where everyone can pray (chapters 56-57)

Chapter 56

1 This is what the LORD is saying (to you). 'Always be fair. And do what is right. (Do this) because I will make you safe. It will happen very soon. Also, soon I will show (everybody) that I am righteous.

2 (God) will bless the man that does this. (He will bless) the man that really does this. (That man) does not do the wrong things on the Sabbath and he does not make it dirty. And he does not let his hand do anything that is really bad.'

3 (A foreigner) may have promised to obey the LORD. That foreigner should not say, 'The LORD will surely not let me join his people.' And no eunuch should say, 'I am only like a dry tree.'

4 The LORD says this to the eunuchs that do the things in this list:

- They do not do wrong things on my Sabbaths.

- They choose to do what makes me happy.

- They really obey my covenant.

5 (He says,) 'Then I will give to them these things inside the walls of my temple:

- something to (cause people) to remember them

- a name that is better than sons and daughters.

I will give them a name that will always stay. Nobody will cut it off.'

6 '(This will happen) to foreigners who (do these things):

- They promise to obey and to be the LORD's servants.

- They love the name of the LORD and they worship him.

- They all do the right things on the Sabbath and they do not make it dirty.

- They hold strongly to my covenant.'

7 'I will bring them to my holy mountain. And I will make them happy in my house for prayer. I will accept what they offer. (I will accept) what they burn as sacrifices on my altar. (This is) because (people will) call my house, "A house for prayer for people from every country".'

8 The LORD (is the God) that brings the exiles of Israel together. The LORD (who is) Lord says, 'I will bring even other (people) to them. (They will be) with those people that I have brought already.'

9 (God says this about bad people.) 'Come here, you wild animals (that live) in fields! (Come,) you wild animals (that live) in the forest! Come and eat everything!'

10 Israel's watchmen cannot see anything. They do not know anything. They are all (like) dogs that cannot make a noise. They cannot make the noise that dogs usually make. They lie about and they dream. They like to sleep.

11 They are (like) dogs that like to eat a lot. And they never have enough. (Also,) they are (like) shepherds who understand nothing. They all turn to their own way. Everybody (tries) to get (what he can for himself).

12 (Each one of them) shouts, 'Come, I must get wine! We must drink as much beer as we can! And tomorrow will be like today. It might be much better!'

Chapter 57

1 When a very good man dies, nobody really thinks about it. (Death) takes away men that (God) loves. But nobody understands why (death) takes them away. It is to save the very good man from trouble that will come soon.

2 (When a good man dies) he goes into (a place where there is) peace. They lie on their beds. He is the man that walks in the right (way).

3 But you, come here! (You are) sons of a woman that does magic. (You are) the children of an adulteress. (You are the children of) a woman that sells her body for sex.

4 Tell me whom you are you laughing at in a bad way. Tell me about whom you are saying bad things. You push your tongue out of your mouth! You are a crowd of people that do not obey (God's) rules. You do not say what is true.

5 You like to have sex among the big trees. Also, (you have sex) under every tree that hangs out (its branches). You kill and burn your children (for false gods). (You do this) in the deep valleys and under the rocks that hang over (the sides of hills).

6 Your place is among the flat (stones) in the deep valley. Yes, they, they are where you should be. Yes, you have poured out drink, to offer it to (your false gods). And you have offered (them) grain. Because of this, I, (God), will not change my mind.

7 You have made your bed on a high and tall hill. You went there to offer things to your (false gods).

8 You have put your notice behind your door, where the door opens. But you left me and you opened your bed. You climbed into it and you opened it wide. You agreed with those people whose beds you loved. You saw a hand (to help you).

9 You went to the king with olive oil and you made more perfumes. You sent your leaders far away and you even went down to Sheol.

10 All your journeys made you very tired. But you would not say, 'We cannot continue to hope.' You became strong again and so you did not stop trying.

11 Perhaps someone is frightening you, so that you do not worship (me). Perhaps you are so afraid of someone that you cannot remember me. And you have not thought about me in your minds. Perhaps you are afraid of me because I have not said anything for a long time.

12 I will show (to everybody) the very good things that you do. (Only you think that they are good!) And they will not be a benefit to you.

13 You will shout for help. Then I will let all (your false gods) save you (if they can)! The wind will carry them all away. (Somebody's) breath will blow them away. But anyone that comes to me for help will have the land. (He or she) will have my holy mountain.

14 He will say, 'Build up (a road)! Build (it) up. Make a road. Remove the things that stop my people from using the road.'

15 The High (God), who is Above (Everything), is speaking. He (is the God that) will always be alive. His name is holy. (He says,) 'I live in a high and holy place. But (I will live) also with anyone who has a lowly and a humble spirit. I will cause the spirit of the humble person to continue to live. I will also cause the heart of the lowly person to stay alive.

16 I will not always say that someone is bad. (I will not always) be angry (with him). (If I did, his) spirit would become weak in front of me. I made (him) alive when I made man.

17 His sin, greed made me angry and I punished him. I was angry and I hid from him. But he continued to do what he wanted to do.

18 I have seen what he is doing. But I will give him health again. Then I will be a guide to him and I will make him strong again.'

19 (God) will cause the people who are sad to speak words of praise. The LORD says, '(I will give) peace. (There will be) peace to the people that are far away. And (there will be peace) to those that are near. And I will give them health.

20 But bad people are like a sea that is always moving. Its waters throw up dirt. And they throw up wet material that is not clean.

21 There is no peace', says my God, 'for bad people.'

Chapter 58

Fast or Feast

1 (God says),'Shout with (your) voice! Do not keep (the sound) quiet! Make a sound with your voice like a trumpet! Tell my people that they have not obeyed me. Also, (tell) the house of Jacob about their sins.'

2 '(Do this) because every day (my people) look for me. And it seems that they really want to know my ways. They are like a country that does what is right. And they seem not to have turned away from what their God wants them to do. They ask me to decide fairly. And they seem to want God to come near to them.'

3 (They say this.) 'We have fasted and you, (God), did not see it. We made ourselves humble and you did not seem to see it.' (God answers), 'Look! On the day when you fast, you make yourselves happy. And you are not kind to the people that work for you.

4 Look! While you fast, you quarrel. Then you fight. And you hit each other with your fists. You cannot fast today so that (I, God) will hear your voice in (heaven).

5 I did not want you to do these things when you fast:

· A man makes himself humble (only) for a day.

· (A man) is humble, like a plant that is dying.

· And (a man) lies on hairy cloth and ashes.

That is what you do when you fast. (Do not think) that the LORD will accept that.

6-7 This is the way that I want you to fast:

· Remove the chains that wrongly tie (people) up.

· And take off the chains (that hold) the yoke.

· Let the people that the enemy has been cruel to go free.

· And break every yoke.

· Give some of your food to hungry people.

And give a safe place to the poor person who goes from place to place.

· When you see bare people, give them clothes.

· And do not turn away from your own family.

8 Then your light will shine like the (light at) dawn. And soon (everyone) will see that you are well again. Then your righteous (God) will go in front of you. And the glory of the LORD at your backs will make you safe.

9-10 Then you will pray and the LORD will answer (you). You will ask for help and immediately he will say, "Here I am."

(You must do these things :)

· Remove the yoke.

Do not point with the finger (at people) and say bad things (about them).

· Use all your power to give help to hungry people.

· Give to oppressed people the things that they need.

Then your light will shine in the dark places and your night will be like midday.

11 (Then) the LORD will always be your guide. He will give to you plenty of everything, in a country where the sun is burning (everything). And he will make your bodies strong. You will become like a garden that has plenty of water. (You will be) like a well whose waters never fail.

12 You will build again the old (places that the enemy) destroyed. And you will build the old houses again. (People) will call you "The Person who Mends Broken Walls" and "The Person who Builds Again Streets with Houses".

13-14 If you (do these things), then you will enjoy yourselves with the LORD:

- Do not do wrong things on the Sabbath.

- Do not do what only what makes you happy you on my holy day.

- Call the Sabbath a lovely day.

- Call the LORD's holy day a good day.

- Think good things about (the Sabbath). (You will do this) when you do not do things in your own way.

- Do not do things to make yourself happy (on the Sabbath). And do not speak words that are not important (on the Sabbath).

(If you do these things,) I will cause you to ride on the high places in the country. Also, you will have a feast with what your ancestor Jacob gave to you.' (Do these things) because the mouth of the LORD has said them.

Chapter 59

1 Look! The hand of the LORD is not too short to save you. Neither is his ear too weak to hear you.

2 But the wrong things that you have done have made you separate from your God. Your sins have hidden (his) face from you, so that he will not listen (to you).

3-4 (This is true) for these reasons:

- Blood makes your hands red. The wrong things that you do are on your fingers.

- Your lips have said things that are not true. Also, your tongue quietly says bad things.

- Nobody asks for a judge to be fair. Nobody says things that are honest.

- People give reasons that mean nothing. People say things that are not true.

- People conceive trouble and they give birth to bad (things).

5 It is like when a snake causes young snakes to come out of the snake's eggs. And they are always making spiders' webs. People that eat the eggs (of spiders) will die. And when they break (a snake's egg) a worse snake will come out.

6 They cannot use (spiders') webs (to make) clothes. They cannot cover themselves with the things that they make from them.

The things that they do are bad. And they use their hands to hurt people.

7 Their feet hurry (them) to do bad things. They rush to pour out the blood of people who have not done anything bad. Their thoughts are bad thoughts. They break and destroy things. They do that everywhere that they go.

8 They do not know the way to peace. Their paths are never honest. Their roads turn away (from what is good). Nobody that walks on them will have peace.

9 So, (God's) rules are far away from us! So, righteousness does not reach us! We look for light, but everything is dark. (We look) for a little bit of light, but we see only dark shadows.

10 Like blind people, we touch the wall (to find our way). We find our way (when we touch things), like men without eyes. At midday, we fall down. (We are) like (people that are in) bad light. We are like dead people among strong people.

11 We all make angry noises, like bears (make). And we make sad noises, like doves make. We look for (people to obey God's) rules, but we do not find any. (We look) for people to help us, but they are far away.

12 (This is) because we have done many (wrong) things. You, (God) think that they are wrong. And our sins speak against us. The things that we have done wrong are always with us. And we know about our sins.

13 We have not obeyed the LORD. And we have not tried to do what he wanted us to do. We have turned away from our God. We have spoken about being cruel to people. And we have spoken about fights against (God). We have thought about things in our minds that were not true. Then we have said those things.

14 So, (it is like) we have sent away (God's) rules. And righteousness (is like a person who) is standing a long way away. Things that are true have fallen down in the streets. We will not let people be honest.

15 (People) cannot find what is true anywhere. Also, good people become (people that bad people) try to kill.

And the LORD looked (at his people). And it did not make him happy that (people did) not obey his rules.

16 He saw that there was nobody to do anything (about it). And he thought that this was bad. So his own arm made his people safe. And (with) his own righteousness he made himself strong.

17 He put on righteousness to cover his body. And (he put on) what makes people safe to cover his head. He put on (these things as) clothes to fight against his enemies. And he wanted so much (to fight his enemies) that these (clothes) were like a coat all round him!

18 He will pay again to people what they should have.

- He will be angry with the people that fight against him.

- (There will be) a fair punishment for his enemies.

- (He will) pay a fair price to the islands.

19 People will be afraid of the name of the LORD in the west. And from where the sun rises (in the east) they will see his glory. (They will say that) it is very good. (This is) because he will rush along like a river. The Spirit of the LORD will push him along.

20 'The Redeemer will come to Zion. (He will come) to the people of Jacob who are sorry because of their sins', says the LORD.

21 'Now I myself have this covenant with them', says the LORD. 'My Spirit is with you and I have put my words into your mouth. They will not go from your mouth. (They will not go) from the mouths of your children, or from the mouths of their children. This will be (true), now and for always', says the LORD.

Chapter 60

The first Song of the Messiah

1 Stand up and shine! (Do this) because your light has come! And the glory of the LORD has risen over you.

2 Look, because a dark cloud covers the earth. It is very dark over the people. But the LORD will rise up above you and (the world will) see his glory over you.

3 Then, people will come to your light from foreign countries. Also, kings will come to the bright light that is beginning to shine over you.

4 Open your eyes and look all round you. Everybody is coming together and they are coming to you. Your sons will come from far away and (you will) carry your daughters in your arms.

5 Then you will look and you will shine! And you will feel like your heart is jumping. And (it will) feel bigger (inside you). (This will happen) because they will bring valuable things from across the seas to you. The valuable (things) from other countries will come to you.

6 Groups of camels will be in your country. Young camels (will come from) Midian and from Ephah. And everybody from Sheba will come. They will carry gold and incense. Also, they will talk about how great that the LORD is.

7 (People) will bring to you all the farm animals from Kedar. They will offer the male sheep from Nebaioth to you. I (God's Messiah,) will accept them when people offer them (to me) on my altar. So, I will make my great temple beautiful.

8 These are the people that fly along (quickly) like clouds. They come like birds to their homes.

9 (They do this) because the islands are looking for me to come. The ships from Tarshish are at the front (of the people that are coming). They bring your sons from far away. And they bring silver and gold. They will come to (the place where) the name of LORD your God (is important). (He is) the Holy (God) of Israel. (They do this) because he has made you beautiful.

10 And the sons of strangers will build your walls again. Also, their kings will be your servants. I hit you when I was angry. But I will be kind to you now that I am not angry (with you).

11 Your gates will always be open. (People) will never close them, during the day or during the night. Then, people can bring in (to you) valuable things from other countries. Their kings will come with them.

12 (Somebody will) destroy the country or the kingdom that will not be your servant. (That country) will really destroy itself completely.

13 The glory of Lebanon will come to you. (Its glory is its) pine trees, fir trees and cypress trees. They will make my temple beautiful. And I will put my glory where my feet touch the earth.

14 The people that were cruel to you will come (to you). They will bend in front of you. And everybody that did not like you will come (to you). (They will) bend on their knees at your feet. And they will call you, 'The City of the LORD. (You are) Zion. (You) belong to the Holy (God) of Israel.'

15 People have kept away from you and they have not liked you. Now, everybody will always think that you are great. Nobody may travel through you, but everybody will (always) be happy because of you.

16 And you will drink the milk of other countries and the breasts of queens will feed you. Then you will know that I, the LORD, have made you safe. And I am your Redeemer. I am the very strong (God) of Jacob.

17 I will bring you gold, (I will not bring you) bronze. And (I will bring you) silver. (I will not bring you) iron. And you will not have wood, (but you will have) bronze. And (I will bring you) iron; (I will not bring you) stones. And I will make peace your ruler and righteousness will rule over you.

18 You will not hear in your country (the noise that) cruel people make. Nobody will break or destroy anything inside the edges of your country. And you will call your walls 'A Safe Place' and (you will call) your gates 'Praise'.

19 The sun will not give you light in the day again, neither will the moon shine brightly on you. But (instead) the LORD will always be your light and your God will be your glory.

20 Your sun will never go down again and your moon will never disappear. (This is) because the LORD will always be your light. Then your sad days will end.

21 Then all your people will be righteous and they will always have the land. They will be like a small plant that I have planted. (They will be) the work that my hands have made. (They will) show that I am beautiful.

22 The least (person) will become a thousand (1000) people and the smallest (person) will become a strong country. I am the LORD. When it happens, I will do it quickly.

The 2nd and 3rd Songs of the Messiah (chapters 61-62)

Chapter 61

The second Song of the Messiah

1 The Spirit of the Lord, (who is) LORD, (is) upon me. (This is) because the LORD has anointed me to tell good news to poor people. He has sent me to make people happy again. (These are the people that trouble) has caused to be very sad. (He has sent me) to tell the people in a prison that they are free. And (he sent me) to tell the people in a prison that they can come out of the dark places.

2 (He has sent me) to say (this. Now is) the year when the LORD will be kind. Also, the day when God will punish people (is near). (He has sent me) to make everybody who is very sad happy again. (They are so sad) that it causes them to weep.

3 (He has sent me) to do (these things). (I will do them) on behalf of all those people in Zion whose spirits are hurting:

· (They will have) flowers on them; (they will not have) ashes (on them).

· (They will have on them olive) oil that will make them happy. Then, they will not weep.

· No longer will their spirits have no hope. Praise will be like a coat for them, instead.

People will say that they are like large trees of righteousness. They will be (like trees) that the LORD has planted. They will show to people that the LORD is beautiful.

4 They will build again what (enemies) broke into pieces long ago. And they will make places new again (that enemies) destroyed long ago. They will mend the cities that (somebody) destroyed. (Someone) destroyed (the cities) when their grandparents were alive!

5 Foreigners will come and they will be shepherds to your animals. People from foreign countries will work in your fields and in your vineyards.

6 And (people) will call you 'priests of the LORD'. Your name will be 'servants of our God'. You will have valuable things from every country. And you will tell everybody about how rich they (have made you).

7 You will not be ashamed, (because you will be) twice as (happy) instead. And (things will not) disappoint (them). They will sing aloud about what (the LORD has) given (to them). So, they will have twice as much (as they had) in their land. And they will always be very happy.

8 (This is) because I, the LORD, love justice. I do not like people that take things for themselves. (I am speaking about the things) that they offer on my altar. And I will give a gift to them, because I will always be kind to them. I will make a covenant with them that will never end.

9 And every country will know their seed. People from every country will know their children. Everybody that sees them will agree to this. They are the seed that the LORD has blessed.

The third Song of the Messiah

10 I have great pleasure in the LORD. My spirit is very happy in my God. He has put the clothes on to me that make me safe. He has dressed me in the clothes of righteousness. (I am) like a man at his marriage, with a special hat like a priest's. And (I am) like a woman at her marriage whose valuable stones make her beautiful.

11 So the Lord, (who is) LORD, will cause righteousness and praise to appear to every country. It will be like the ground that causes the young plant to come up. And (it will be like) a garden that causes seeds to grow.

Chapter 62

1 I will not be quiet, on behalf of Zion. On behalf of Jerusalem, I will not stay quiet. (I will be like this) until her righteousness shines out like the dawn. She will be so safe that it burns like the brightest torch.

2 Then, the people in every country will see your righteousness and every king (will see) your glory. And they will call you by a new name. The mouth of the LORD will give it to you.

3 And you will be like a beautiful crown in the LORD's hand. In the hand of your God (you will be like) what a king wears on his head.

4 They will not call you 'Alone' again. The name of your country will not be 'Empty, Sandy Place'. But they will call you 'Hephzibah' and they will call your country 'Beulah'.

5 As a young man marries a young woman, so your sons will marry you. As a man at his marriage is happy with his new wife, so your God will be happy with you.

6 I have put people on your walls, Jerusalem, to keep them safe. They will not be quiet, during all the day and during all the night. Those (people) that remember the LORD do not rest.

7 And do not let (the LORD) rest, until he has built Jerusalem again. He will make (Jerusalem the place) that all the people in the world praise. (Do not let him rest) until he does that.

8 The LORD has promised (these things). (He will do them) with his right hand and with his strong arm.

· 'I will never give your grain to your enemies for food again.

· And never again will foreigners drink the new wine that you have worked carefully to make.'

9 'But the people who pick it will eat it. Then they will praise the LORD. And those (people) who pick the grapes will drink (the wine). They will do it in the yards that are round about my temple.'

10 Pass through, pass through the gates. Prepare the way for the people. Build up, build up the road on higher ground. Remove the stones. Lift up a sign for the people (from foreign countries).

11 Look! The LORD has said this to the parts of the earth that are far away. 'Say to the Daughter of Zion (Jerusalem), "Look! The (Messiah that will) make you safe is coming! Look! His gifts are with him! He is bringing with him what he will give back (to you)." '

12 Their name will be the Holy People. (They are the people) whom the LORD has redeemed. And people will call you (by these names): '(Whom somebody) Looked For' (and) 'The City that Nobody Keeps Away From'.

The 4th Song of the Messiah and Isaiah's Prayer (chapters 63-64)

Chapter 63

The fourth Song of the Messiah

1 Someone is coming from Edom and from Bozrah. A bright colour makes his clothes (red). It is someone that is wearing beautiful clothes. He marches on his way and he is very strong. (He says), 'I am speaking (to you). I am righteous. I am strong enough to save you.'

2 Why are your clothes red? They are like (the clothes) of somebody that has worked in a winepress.

3 'I have worked in the winepress alone. From (all) the countries, nobody was with me. I walked on them because I was angry. And I put them under my feet because I was angry. Their blood went all over my clothes and I made all my clothes (red).

4 (I did this) because I was thinking about (a certain) day. (On that day) I would punish people. Also, the year when I would redeem people had come.'

5 'I had looked, but there was nobody to help (me). And I was not happy, because nobody helped (me). So my own arm did the work to save them. And I was so angry that it helped me.

6 I walked on (all) the countries, because I was angry. I was so angry that I caused them (to seem) like drunks. Then, I poured their blood on to the ground.'

Isaiah's Prayer

7 I will tell (people) that the LORD is kind. (I will talk about) how people praise the LORD. (This is) because of all that the LORD has done on our behalf. He has done many good things on behalf of the house of Israel. (He did this) because of his great love on their behalf. And (he did this) (because) he was very kind (to them).

8 And he said, 'Surely, they are my people. (They are) sons who will always follow me.' So he became the person that saved them.

9 When they were in trouble, he was in their trouble with them. And the angel, that was there with him, saved them. And in his love and in his mercy he redeemed them. Also, he lifted them up and he carried them. (He did this) as he had done it in past years.

10 But they did not obey him and they made his Holy Spirit angry. So, he turned against them and he became their enemy. He fought against them.

11 Then he remembered past years. (He remembered) Moses and his people. (They said,) '(We need) the Person that brought them up out of the sea, with the leaders of his people. (We need the Person) that put his Holy Spirit on him.

12 His arm shone while he went at Moses' right hand. (We need that Person.) (We need the Person) who caused the waters (of the River Jordan) to become separate. (Because of that,) he caused his name always to be famous.'

13 '(We need the Person) who led them through the deep (places in the sea). As a horse (runs) in flat country, so they did not fall.

14 The (Holy) Spirit of the LORD gave them rest, like cows and sheep that go down to their fields. This is how he was the guide of your people. And you made for yourself a famous name!'

15 Look down from your holy and beautiful house in heaven and see (us). You want (to do what you have promised to us). And you are strong. And you love (us) and you want to be kind to us. But you are not doing anything on our behalf!

16 But you are our father, even if Abraham does not know us. (You are our father) even if Israel does not recognise us. You, LORD, are our father. Your name is our Redeemer, from days long ago.

17 LORD, we do not know why you let us go away from your ways. (You let us make) our hearts so hard, so that we do not love you. (We do not know why you let us do that.) Come back to us, on behalf of your servants. (We are) the families that belong to you!

18 Your holy people will have (their own land) only for a short time. Our enemies will walk all over your holy place.

19 For a long time, we are like people that you have not ruled. (People) did not call us by your name!

Chapter 64

1 Oh, I wanted you to break open the skies and I wanted you to come down! Then the mountains would have moved in front of you.

2 (It would have been) like a fire that burns up bits of wood. And (it would have been) like a fire that boils water. (These things would have happened) when you came down. And you would have caused your enemies to know your name. The countries would have moved away in front of you.

3 (You did things) that made us afraid. (And it would have happened) while you did those things. They were things that we did not think would happen. (It would have happened) while you came down. And the mountains would have moved in front of you.

4 And, for a long time, nobody has heard of, or thought about, a God like you. Nobody has seen (a God like you). He does things on behalf of those (people) that wait for him.

5 You help the people that are happy. (You help them) to do what is right. They (are the people that) remember your ways. But you are angry because, for a long time, we have sinned against your rules. So, we do not know if (anyone) can save us.

6 We have all become like someone who is not clean. And all the good things that we do are like very dirty bits of cloth. We all become dry, like a leaf. And, like a wind, our sins sweep us away.

7 And nobody shouts your name or tries to pray to you. (This is) because you have hidden your face from us. And you have caused us slowly to become weak, because our sins are so strong.

8 But LORD, you are still our father. We are like the clay. And you are like the person that makes the pots. Your hand made all of us.

9 Do not be too angry with us, LORD. And do not always remember our sins. But help us again, because we are your people.

10 Your holy cities will become empty, sandy places. Zion will be an empty, sandy place and Jerusalem will be full of dirt.

11 Our ancestors praised you in our holy and beautiful temple. (But soon,) fire will burn it. (An enemy will) destroy everything that is valuable to us.

12 After all this, LORD, we hope that you will not still do nothing. We hope that you will not continue to be quiet. We hope that you will not continue to punish us.

The New Jerusalem (chapters 65-66)

Chapter 65

1 'I spoke to people who did not ask for me. People who did not look for me found me. I said, "Here I (am), here I (am)!" (I said it) to a country that was not called by my name.

2 All day long I hold my hands out to people who will not listen (to me). They continue to walk (live) in ways that are not good. They still do what their thoughts (want them to do).'

3 'They are people that continue to make me angry. (They do it) in front of me! They offer gifts in (their) gardens (to false gods). They burn them on stones.

4 They sit among the graves and they watch all night in secret places. They eat meat from pigs. And (they eat) dishes of soup (that they made) from unclean meat.

5 They are people that say, "Keep away from me, and do not come near me. I am too holy for you!" These people are like smoke in my nose! (They are like smoke) from a fire that burns all day.

6 Look! The words are (in a book) in front of me. I will not stay quiet, but I will punish them completely. I will pay them back completely, like someone who puts things into their hands.

7 (I will pay back) both your sins and the sins of your ancestors', says the LORD. '(I will do this) because they burned gifts (to false gods) on the mountains. And they said bad things about me on the hills. And, firstly, I will measure to them the right punishment for what they have done.'

8 This is what the LORD says. 'Sometimes people find juice in a group of grapes. Then men say, "Do not destroy it, because there is something good in it." I will do something like this on behalf of my servants. I will not kill them all.

9 I will cause there still to be seed in Jacob's family. There will be people in Judah to live on my mountains. The people that I have chosen will live on them. And my servants will live there.'

10 'And Sharon will become a field for groups (of sheep). Also, groups (of cows) will rest in the Valley of Achor. (They will be places) for my people who are looking for me.

11 (This will happen) to you (people) who go away from the LORD. And (it will happen to you people) that forget my holy mountain. Also, (it will happen to people) who put food on a table for (the false god called) Luck. And (it will happen to people) who fill dishes of wine for Fate.'

12 'Your "luck" will be that a sword (will kill you). And you will all bend down for death. I spoke (to you), but you did not answer. I spoke, but you did not listen. You did bad things in front of me, where I could see them. And you chose (to do things) that did not make me happy.'

13 So the LORD (who is) Master says this. 'Look! My servants will eat (food), but you will be hungry. Look! My servants will (have something to) drink, but you will have nothing to drink. Look! My servants will be very happy, but you will be ashamed.

14 Look! My servants will sing because they feel so happy. But you will cry because there is so much pain in your minds. You will weep because your spirits are so sad.

15 And you will leave your name as a curse to the people that I have chosen. And the LORD (who is) Master will kill (all of) you. But he will give to his servants another name.

16 Whoever asks for a blessing in the country will do it by the God of Truth. Whoever makes a promise in the country will do it by the God of Truth. (This is because God) will forget troubles in past years. Really, (something) will hide them from my eyes.'

17 'Listen, because I will create new heavens and a new earth. And (people) will not remember how things were.

They will not even (be ideas that) come to their minds.

18 But rather, be happy! And always, (yes), always be very happy about what I will create! (Do this), for these reasons:

- The Jerusalem that I will create will be a pleasure (to me).

- The people that live there will make (me) very happy.

19 Then, I will be very happy with Jerusalem and I will have great pleasure in my people. Nobody will hear the sound of (people) crying (in Jerusalem). People will not weep there again.

20 Never again will there be (in Jerusalem) a baby that only lives for a few days. (Nor will there be) an old man that does not live a long life. But a man that dies 100 (years old), people will call a young man. And a man may not live to be 100 (years old). But then people will think that someone has said a curse about him.

21 People (in Jerusalem) will build houses and they will live in them. They will plant vineyards and they will eat the fruit from them.

22 They will not build houses for other people to live in. They will not plant things for other people to eat (the fruit). (This is) because the days of my people will be as many as the days of a tree. The people that I have chosen will enjoy things. (They will enjoy) what their hands have made for a long time.

23 They will not work without result. Neither will they have children that will have bad times. (This is) because they are the seed. (They are the seed) that the LORD will bless. (He will bless) them and their descendants with them.

24 Before they pray (to me), I will answer (them). While they are still speaking, I will hear (them).

25 The wolf and the young sheep will eat together. And the lion will eat dry grass like the cow. But the food of the snake will be dirt. They will neither hurt nor kill (anything) on all my holy mountain', says the LORD.

Chapter 66

1 This is what the LORD is saying. 'Heaven is my high seat. And the earth is the place where I will put my feet. I do not know where you could build a house for me. You could not make a place where I will rest.'

2 'My hand has made all these things. That is how they happened', says the LORD. 'I think that this kind of person is valuable. He will be humble and he will have a lowly spirit. And he will be afraid when he hears my word.

3 Some people kill a male cow for me. Some people kill a man. Some people offer me a young sheep. Some people break a dog's neck. Some people offer grain. Some people offer pig's blood. Some people (burn) incense to remember (me). Some people worship false gods. Some people have chosen their own ways. Their spirits have pleasure in bad things.

4 So I will choose to punish them a lot. And I will send to them the things that will make them very afraid. (This is) because nobody answered when I spoke. And when I spoke, nobody listened. They did bad things (even while) I watched them! And they chose (to do) things that did not make me happy.'

5 Listen to the LORD's message, you people that were afraid of his words. 'Your (bad) brothers did not like you. They do not let you belong (to the people of Judah). They do this because of my name. They said (to you), "Give praise to the LORD. Then we will see that you are happy." But (your brothers) will be ashamed.'

6 'A voice (comes like) a loud noise from the city! A voice (comes) from the temple. The voice (is) the Lord's (voice). He is giving to his enemies all that they should have.'

7 'Before she has labour, she has a baby. Before the pains come to her, a son is born!

8 Nobody has ever heard of such a thing. Nobody has ever seen things like this. A country cannot be born in one day. Nor can a country have birth in a moment. But as soon as Zion has labour, her children are born!

9 When I bring (someone) to the moment of birth, then the baby is born.' This is what the LORD is saying. 'I do not close up the mother's body before the baby is born', says your God.

10 'Be happy with (the people in) Jerusalem and be very happy for Jerusalem. (Do this), everybody that loves Jerusalem. Be very happy with Jerusalem, everybody that cries for Jerusalem.

11 (Jerusalem) will be like a mother to you. And she will give to you all that you need. Her breasts will cause you to feel happier. You will drink a lot (of her milk). And you will be very happy with the glory that pours (like a stream of water) from her.'

12 (This will happen) because the LORD says, 'Look! I will give peace to (Jerusalem) like a river. And (I will cause) the valuable things from every country to pour in like a stream (of water). Jerusalem will be like a mother to you and she will carry you by her side. And you will (be like a baby that) sits on its (mother's) knees.

13 I will cause you to feel happier as a mother causes her child to feel happier. (You felt sad because an enemy destroyed Jerusalem.) I will cause you to feel happier about Jerusalem (now).'

14 And when you see (this), you will feel very happy! And your bones will grow easily, like grass. The LORD will cause his servants to know that his hand (is good). But he will show his enemies that he is very angry.

15 Look! The LORD will come with fire and his chariots will be like a strong wind. He will come down (from heaven) because he is very angry. He will speak against them with words of fire.

16 And so the LORD will be the judge of all people with fire and with his sword. Then the LORD will kill many people.

17 'Some people are servants of their gods. And some people make themselves very clean for their gods. They go into the gardens. They follow the people who eat the meat from pigs and rats and other dirty things. They will all come to their deaths together', says the LORD.

18 'And I will come and I will bring together the people from all countries. And I will bring together the people who speak all languages. (I will do this because) of what they have done and (because of) their thoughts. And they will come and they will see my glory.

19 And I will put a sign among them. And I will send some of those people that run away (from me) to other countries. (They will go to):

- Tarshish (in Spain)

- the people in Libya

- the people in Lydia, who are famous because they shoot arrows (so well)

- Tubal

- Greece

- far away islands that have not heard of my name and have not seen my glory.

These people will tell other countries about my glory.

20 And they will bring all your brothers to my holy mountain in Jerusalem. (They will bring them) from all the countries to offer (them) to the LORD. (They will come) on horses, in chariots and in trucks. (They will come) on mules (animals like small horses) and on camels', says the LORD. 'They will bring them as the Jews bring grain. (This is what) they offer to the LORD in the temple. (The grain is in) the special dishes that they use to worship me. 21 And I will choose some of them to be priests. And I will choose some of them to be servants of God (like my servants) from Levi's family', says the LORD.

22 'The new heavens and the new earth that I will make will always be there', says the LORD. 'Also, your name and (the names of) your seed will stay there.'

23 'Everybody will come and they will bend down on their knees in front of me', says the LORD. '(They will come) from one New Moon to the next (New Moon) and from one Sabbath to another.

24 And they will go out (of the New Jerusalem). And they will look at the dead bodies of the people that did not obey me. Their worm will not die and their fire will not go out. And everybody will see how dirty that they are.'

Jeremiah Speaks God's Words

Jeremiah

About Jeremiah

Jeremiah was a priest. He was born in Anathoth, a town in Israel in about 650 BC. The LORD spoke to him. 'You must be a prophet', he said. He told Jeremiah what he must say to the people in Judah. Jeremiah was afraid, but the LORD promised to make him strong. He went. And he told the people what the LORD had told him to say. He did this for 40 years, but it was very difficult. The LORD told the people that they were very bad. So the people got angry. Jeremiah was very brave and he continued to speak the Lord's words. He was sad for another reason. He wanted people to stop doing bad things. The LORD would not punish them if they were sorry. Jeremiah knew that. But the people did not listen, so God had to punish them. They were not kind to Jeremiah. But he was only telling them what God had told him to say. Jeremiah knew that the LORD wanted people to worship him, and only him. Their ancestors had promised to do that. If they obeyed the LORD, he would give them many good things. But now they were worshipping many false gods. Jeremiah had to tell them that God would punish them for that.

The LORD sent other prophets to Israel at nearly the same time as Jeremiah. God spoke by his prophets. Most of the people did not listen to their words. But they listened to false prophets. They spoke things that the people wanted to hear.

People would not listen to God's message. But Jeremiah still obeyed God. So God showed Jeremiah how God himself would, one day, bring people to know him. He told him about the gift of the Holy Spirit. He sent the LORD Jesus Christ to give this gift. But that was many years after Jeremiah had died.

Chapter 1

1 Jeremiah, son of Hilkiah, spoke to the people of Israel. He was a priest. He lived at Anathoth, a town in the land that God gave to the tribe of Benjamin. 2 God spoke to him when Josiah, son of Amon, had been king of Judah for 13 years. 3 God continued to speak to him all the time that Josiah's son, Jehoiakim, was king. And he went on speaking to Jeremiah for the 11 years and 5 months, that Zedekiah was king. Zedekiah was a son of King Josiah. After this, enemies took the people from Jerusalem away to a far country.

God chooses Jeremiah.

4 God spoke to me. 5 'I knew you even before I made your body inside your mother's body. I chose you before you were born. I decided that you must be a prophet to all the countries in the world', he said.

6 'Great and powerful LORD', I said. 'I do not know how to speak. I am only a child.'

7 The LORD said to me, 'Do not say, "I am only a child." You must go to everyone that I send you to. You must say whatever I tell you to say. 8 You need not be afraid of them, because I am with you. I will save you', he said.

9 Then the LORD touched my mouth with his hand. 'Now I have put my words into your mouth', he said. 10 'Look, I give you authority over countries and kingdoms. You can pull them down or break them up to destroy them. You can build them up and make them safe.'

The LORD shows Jeremiah two pictures.

11 The LORD spoke to me. 'What do you see, Jeremiah?' he said.

'I see the branch of an almond tree', I replied.

12 'Yes that is correct', he said. 'I am watching my words. And I will cause them to happen.'

13 The LORD spoke to me again. 'What do you see?' he said. 'I see a boiling pot. It is in the north and it is pouring this way', I answered. 14 'People from the north will pour out. And they will kill all the people who live in this country', the LORD said. 15 'I will bring all the nations who live in the north', he said. 'Their kings will come and they will sit in the gates of Jerusalem. They will rule there. They will be round its walls. They will be round all the towns of Judah. 16 I will be the judge of my people, because they have turned away from me. They have done very wrong things. They have given gifts to false gods. They have worshipped things that they have made with their own hands. 17 You must get ready! Stand up. And say whatever I tell you. Do not be afraid of them. If you are afraid of them, I will make you afraid in front of them! 18 Today I have made you as strong as a city with great walls. You will be like a tree that someone has made out of iron. You will be like a metal wall to stand against the whole nation. You will stand against the kings of Judah and their officers. You will stand against the priests and the people of the country. 19 They will fight against you. But they will not win, because I am with you. I will save you', says the LORD.

Chapter 2

Israel's people have turned away from the LORD.

1 God spoke to me again. 2 'Speak to the people in Jerusalem', he said.

'I remember how you used to love me. That was when I first made you my people.

You loved me as a young wife loves her husband.

You followed me through a wild place,

where nobody grew any food.

3 Israel belonged to me. It was special.

It was like the first food that grew on my land.

Anyone else who ate that food was doing something bad.

And I caused bad things to happen to them.'

The LORD said this.

4 'Listen to what the LORD says, you sons of Jacob,

and all the families in Israel.'

5 This is the LORD's message.

'Your ancestors were angry with me.

But I did nothing that was wrong. But they went a long way from me.

They went to gods of wood and stone that could not do anything for them.

And then they could not do anything for themselves.

6 They did not ask the LORD for help.

He brought them out of Egypt.

He led them through the place where nothing grows,

an empty place with many valleys.

It was a dry and dark place.

Nobody goes through it and nobody lives in it.

7 I, the LORD, brought you to a good country,

where you could eat very good food.

But you came and you made my country like something dirty.

You made it too bad for me to look at.

8 The priests did not ask "Where is the LORD?"

And the judges did not know me.

Your leaders did not obey me.

The prophets asked Baal what to say to you.

They hoped that gods of wood and stone would help them.

Those gods cannot help anyone.'

9 'So I must be your judge', says the LORD.

'And I will be the judge of your children and their children.

10 Go to the people who live in the east and the west.

Ask them if anyone has ever done this before.

11 Other nations have not changed their gods.

But their gods are not really gods.

But my people have changed him who is greater than any god.

They have changed him for things of wood and stone that cannot help them.

12 You skies, be very surprised.

Shake and be afraid', says the LORD.

13 'My people have sinned twice.

They have left me. I am like a river of living water.

And they have dug holes in the earth for themselves.

These holes cannot hold water. They let water run away.

14 Israel's people are not slaves, born to be servants.

But they have become slaves to their enemies.

15 The enemies attacked them like lions.

They have destroyed their country.

They have burnt their towns and nobody lives in them.

16 The men from Memphis and Tahpanhes have removed all the hair from your heads.

So they have made you ashamed.

17 You have caused this to happen.

It is because you stopped following the LORD, your God.

He was leading you in the way that you should go.

18 The water of the River Shihor in Egypt is not better to drink than yours is.

And the water from the river of Assyria is not better to drink than yours is.

19 The very bad things that you have done will punish you.

And your backslidings will show to you that you have done wrong things.

You have gone away from the LORD your God.

And you are not afraid to make me angry.

Those are very bad things and they will cause you to have very bad pain.

You must think about that and you must understand it.'

That is what the great, powerful LORD says.

20 'You stopped working for me a long time ago.

You cut through anything that tied us together.

You said, "I will not work for you!"

So you sold yourselves to any people that would take you.

You were like a woman that sells sex.

21 But I had planted you like a young vine.

You were strong and you had good strong ancestors.

Tell me how you became weak, dirty and really bad.

22 You may wash yourselves with clean water,

and you may use a lot of soap', says the most powerful LORD.

'But you will always seem dirty to me.

23 You say that you are not dirty.

And you say that you do not run after false gods.

But remember what you did in the valley.

Think carefully what you have done.

You are like a fast female animal.

You run all over the country.

24 You are like a wild female horse

that lifts its nose in the air.

It is looking for a male horse.

Nobody can keep it from what it wants.

Any males who follow it will catch it easily.

You are like that.

25 Do not run for so long that you become tired.

Do not run for so long that your feet hurt.

"I cannot change", you say.

"I love foreign gods. I must obey them!"

26 A man may take things that are not his.

He is ashamed when people catch him.

So the people of Israel are ashamed.

They, their kings, their officers, and their prophets all do what is wrong.

27 They say to a piece of wood, "You are my father."

They call a stone their mother.

They have turned away from me.

They do not show their faces to me.

But then troubles happen to them.

"Come and save us!" they ask me.

28 I tell them to ask the gods that they made for themselves.

Ask them to come and save you.

Ask for their help when you have troubles.

Judah, you have many towns.

And you have as many gods.'

29 'You must not judge me.

You have all turned against me', says the LORD.

30 'I punished your people.

But they would not turn back to me.

You have killed your prophets.

You are like hungry animals.'

God will punish Judah.

31 'Think about my message, you people who are alive today', says the LORD.

'I have not been like a place where nothing grows.

I have not been like a dark place where nobody lives.

But my people say, "We can go where we like.

We do not want to visit you any more."

32 A young woman does not forget her pretty things.

A wife does not forget her valuable gifts.

But my people have forgotten me for many years.

33 You are so clever. You can always find love!

Very bad women, even, can learn from you.

34 Your clothes have blood on them.

That blood gave life to people who never hurt you.

It was the blood of people who never took your things.

35 But still you say, "I have not done anything that is wrong.

God is not angry with me!"

But I will judge you.

You say "I have not sinned."

So I will judge you.

36 You look at nations who live near to you.

You want to change.

You know now that Assyria cannot help you.

And you will soon know that Egypt cannot help you.

37 You will become slaves.

You will leave your country with your hands on your heads.

The LORD has not chosen the people that you have chosen.

They will not help you.'

Chapter 3

1 'A man may divorce his wife.

Then she may leave him and marry another man.

If her first husband returned to her, he would not be clean.

He would make the whole country bad.

But you have lived with many lovers.

And you want to return to me', says the LORD.

2 'Look at the tops of the hills.

You have loved other gods on all of them.

You sat by the side of the road, waiting for lovers.

You waited to catch men.

You have made the country bad.

It is dirty with all the wrong things that you have done.

You have loved other gods when you should have loved me.

3 That is why I have not sent any rain to you.

And that is why the spring rains have not come.

But you seem to be quite happy.

You are not ashamed.

4 But you say to me, "You have been my friend, who has loved me all my life.

5 Surely you cannot be angry with me!

You cannot always be angry."

Those are the things that you say.

But you do as many wrong things as you can.'

Israel is not faithful to God.

6 The LORD spoke to me while Josiah was king. 'Look at what Israel's people have done', he said. 'They have not been faithful to me. They have worshipped false gods under every big tree and on every high hill. They have been like a wife who is not faithful to her husband. 7 I thought that they would come back to me. But they did not return when it was over. Israel's sister, Judah, saw what Israel did. 8 I sent Israel away, like a wife after her husband has divorced her. I sent her away because she had loved so many other gods. But Judah's people, who had not been faithful, were not afraid. Judah's people also went out and they found other lovers. 9 Israel's people were not sorry that they had not been faithful to me. So they worshipped gods that they made from wood and stone. They made the country like a dirty place because they did very many bad things. 10 Judah saw this, but Judah was not faithful. Judah's people did not really return to me. They only made it seem that they had returned to me', says the LORD.

11 And the LORD said to me, 'Israel's people have not been faithful to me. So Israel's backsliding is not as bad as the things that Judah's people have done. 12 Go. Turn to the north, and say,

"You people in Israel who have not been faithful, return to me", says the LORD.

"I will not always be angry with you,

because I am full of mercy", says the LORD.

13 But you must believe that you have done many wrong things.

You must agree with me that you turned against me.

You loved many foreign gods.

You worshipped them under big trees.

You have not obeyed me" ', says the LORD.

14 'Return to me, you people who are backsliding', says the LORD. 'I am your husband. I will bring some of you to Zion. I will choose one from a town and two from a family.

15 Then I will give shepherds to you that I can trust. They will lead you and they will teach you good things.

16 After some time, the number of your people will grow. Then you will think in a new way', says the LORD. 'You will not talk or even think about the ark of the LORD. You will forget all about it, and you will not make another one. 17 Then they will call Jerusalem "The Throne of the LORD". At that time, people from all countries will come to Jerusalem. They will all give honour to the name of the LORD. They will not do the wrong things that they want any more. 18 Then the people from Israel and the people from Judah will join together in Jerusalem. They will come from a country in the north. They will come to this country that I gave to your ancestors. I gave it to you and to your ancestors to keep.

19 I myself said,

"I want very much to make you my sons.

I want to give a good country to you.

It is more beautiful than the country that any other people enjoy."

And I said, "You will call me 'Father'.

And you will not stop obeying me."

20 But you have been like a woman who has left her husband to go to another man.

You, Israel's people, have not been faithful to me', says the LORD.

21 I can hear a noise on the high places.

Israel's people are crying and they are asking for help.

They are crying because they have left the good ways.

They have forgotten the LORD, their God.

22 Return to me, you backsliding children.

I will cause you to stop doing that.'

'Yes, we will come to you

because you are the LORD our God.

23 You hope for help from the other side of the hills and the mountains.

But it will not come.

Only the LORD our God can really save Israel.

24 Since we were young,

we have lost all our good things.

False gods have used them up.

They ate the things that our fathers worked for.

They took their sheep and cows.

They took their sons and daughters.

25 We are ashamed.

We want to lie down and hide ourselves.

From many years ago until now,

we and our ancestors have not obeyed you.'

Chapter 4

1 'If you want to return, then return to me', the LORD says.

'Throw away your gods that I hate.

You must not go away from me again.

2 And if you make a true, good and fair promise to me,

then you can say, "It is sure that the LORD is alive."

He will bless all the nations in the world.

And they will be very happy to give honour and praise to him.'

3 This is what the LORD says to the people in Judah, and in Jerusalem.

'Break up your hard ground.

Do not put seed among weeds.

4 Give all of yourselves to the LORD.

Cut off everything that is not his.

Men in Judah and people in Jerusalem, you must do that.

If you do not do it, I will be angry.

My anger will burn you like a fire.

I will hurt you because of the bad things that you have done.

Nobody will save you.'

An enemy will attack from the north.

5 'Shout to the people in Judah. Tell this to the people in Jerusalem.

"Blow the trumpets in all the country!"

Shout to them and say,

"Come together!

We must all run to the cities with strong walls!"

6 Tell everyone to go to Zion!

Do not wait to run to a safe place

because I will bring trouble from the north.

I will destroy your country.

7 A lion was hiding in the hills.

It has come out to destroy the nations.

It has left its home to destroy your country.

It will break down your towns.

They will be empty.

8 So put on special clothes to show that you are sad.

Cry and be very sad.

Cry because the LORD is still angry with us.

He has not forgotten his anger.'

9 'The king and his officers will not be happy on that day',

says the LORD.

'The priests will be very sad,

and the prophets will be very, very sad.'

10 'Oh, great and powerful LORD', I said. 'You have not spoken what is true to this people and to Jerusalem. You said, "You will have peace." But now our enemies will attack us!'

11 'A hot wind from the empty mountains will blow towards my people', the LORD will tell them at that time. 'But it will not make them clean. It will not blow away the wrong things that they have done.' The LORD will tell them this. 12 'I will send a wind that is too strong for that. Now I will tell you how I will judge them.'

13 Look! He is coming like the clouds.

He is like a strong, fast wind.

He flies faster than a great bird.

We are really in trouble. We will lose everything!

14 Jerusalem, wash away your bad thoughts.

Then the LORD will save you.

You must not hold on to your bad thoughts.

15 A voice is calling out from Dan.

It says that trouble is coming from the hills of Ephraim.

16 'Tell this to all the nations,

shout it to Jerusalem.

"An army is coming from a far country.

It will attack Jerusalem.

17 Their soldiers are round its walls.

This is because Jerusalem's people have not obeyed me" ',

says the LORD.

18 'I have done this to you

because of the wrong things that you have done.

You have caused this trouble.

I am punishing you.

Yes, it is painful.

The pain goes all through you.'

19 I am in such great pain!

All my body hurts. I have to go on moving.

My thoughts are full of pain.

My heart keeps hitting hard inside me.

I feel that I have to shout.

I have heard the noise of the trumpet.

I have heard the enemy when they were shouting.

20 It is bad, but it is getting worse!

Our enemies have destroyed everything in the country.

They have quickly broken down my tents.

They did not wait to destroy my home.

21 I do not know how long the battle will last.

I can still hear the sound of people who are fighting.

22 The LORD says, 'My people are fools.

They do not know me.

They are like children who do not know anything.

They understand nothing.

They know how to do bad things.

But they have no idea how to do good things.'

23 I looked at the earth,

and it had no shape.

I looked at the sky,

and its light was gone.

24 I looked at the mountains,

and they kept moving about.

All the hills were moving.

25 I looked, and I did not see any people.

All the birds had flown away.

26 I looked at the good country, but no plants grew there.

Our enemies had knocked down all its towns.

The LORD was very angry. He caused them to do all this.

27 'I will cause bad things to happen in the whole country',

the LORD says.

'But I will not completely destroy it.

28 So the whole earth will be sad.

The sky will become dark.

This will happen as I have said.

And I will not change my plan.

I have spoken and I will not turn back.'

29 The people in every town will run away

when they hear the sound of soldiers and horses.

Some of them hide in bushes.

Some of them climb up among the rocks.

All the towns are empty.

Nobody lives in them.

30 You are like a woman who wears bright red clothes.

You are like a woman who wears things of gold.

You paint your eyes,

but that does not help you.

The men that you loved do not give honour to you.

They want to kill you.

31 I can hear that people are shouting. It is like the noise of a woman while her baby is being born.

It is like the noise of a woman while her first child is being born.

It is the people in Jerusalem, who are shouting for help.

They shout and they say,

'I am very weak, and I am getting weaker.

I am afraid that they will kill me.'

Chapter 5

1 'Go along the streets of Jerusalem, and come back again.

Look all round you, carefully.

Look in all parts of the city.

Try to find one person who is honest. Try to find a person who wants to know the truth.

If you find one, I will forgive all the people in the city.

2 They may say, "As the LORD lives".

They want people to think that they are honest.

But what they are saying is false.'

3 LORD, you want us to speak words that are true.

But the people that you have hurt do not feel any pain.

You hit them, but they would not change.

They would not do the things that you wanted.

They held on to the bad things that they were doing.

And they refused to turn away from them.

4 'These are poor people, and they are fools', I thought.

'They do not know what the LORD asks them to do.

They have no idea what he wants.

5 So I will go to speak to the leaders.

They will certainly know what the LORD wants.

They will know what they must do to please him.'

But every one of them turned away from him.

They said that they were not his slaves.

6 A big wild animal from the forest will attack them for that.

Another animal will tear them into pieces.

Other animals will wait near their towns to hurt anyone who leaves.

That is because they have turned so far from the LORD.

It is because they have done very many bad things.

7 'I cannot forgive you.

Your children have gone away from me.

They have trusted gods that are not gods.

I gave to them everything that they needed.

But they left me and they went to the houses of false gods.

They are like men who have sex with other men's wives.

8 They are like wild horses.

Wild horses run after any female that they want.

9 I must punish them for that', the LORD says.

'They have hurt me so much.

They are such bad people that I must punish them.'

10 Go through the gardens where their grapes are growing. And destroy their fruits.

But do not completely destroy them.

Pull the branches from the trees

because these people do not belong to the LORD.

11 All the families in Judah and in Israel

have gone far from me', says the LORD.

12 They spoke about the LORD. They said what is not true.

'He will not do anything', they said.

'He will never hurt us.

We will have enough to eat. Soldiers will not kill us.

13 The prophets speak empty words.

They do not know what the LORD says.

So they may say that something bad will happen.

If that is true, let it happen to them.'

14 'So the people have said this',

says the strong and powerful LORD.

'I will make the words in your mouth like a fire.

And the people will burn like wood in that fire.'

15 'People in Israel', the LORD says,

'I will send soldiers to attack you.

They will come from a country far away.

They have lived there for a long time.

You do not know their language.

You cannot understand what they say.

16 They want to kill you and they want to destroy your land.

They are all powerful soldiers.

17 They will eat all the food in your fields

and the food that you have stored.

They will take your sons and daughters.

They will eat your sheep and cows.

They will take the fruit from your trees.

They will fight and break down the strong cities.

You thought that those cities would keep you safe.'

18 'But even at that time', says the LORD, 'I will not destroy you completely. 19 And when the people ask, "Why has the LORD, our God, done this to us?" you will speak to them. Say, "You have left me, and you serve foreign gods in your own country. So now you will serve foreign people in a country that is not your own."

20 Tell this to the families of Jacob. Shout it in the country called Judah.

21 Hear this, you people who are fools with no understanding.

You have eyes, but you do not see.

You have ears, but you do not hear.

22 You should be afraid of me', says the LORD.

'Your knees should knock together when you are near to me.

I made the sand to be an edge to the sea.

It is like a wall that the sea cannot cross.

The water of the sea may attack it, but it cannot win.

It can make a loud noise, but it cannot cross the sand.

23 These people will not obey me.

They have turned and they have gone away from me.

24 They do not say to themselves,

"We must honour and obey the LORD our God.

He gives the autumn and spring rains to us.

Each year he makes sure that we have food."

25 But you have done many wrong things.

So he has not sent rain or food to you.

He has taken away good things because you have sinned.

26 Many bad men belong to my people.

They hide like men who catch birds.

They are like people who try to catch men.

27 Their houses are full of valuable things

that they have taken with false words.

They are rich and powerful.

28 Now they are fat and they seem good.

They will never stop doing bad things.

They do not try to help children who have no fathers.

They do not help poor people to get what is theirs.

29 I certainly must punish them for this',

says the LORD.

'I must show them how angry I am.

The people are very, very bad.'

30 A really bad thing has happened in this country.

31 The prophets tell people things that are not true.

The priests make their own rules.

And my people like what they do.

I will stop all this. Then they will not know what to do.

Chapter 6

Enemies are all round Jerusalem.

1 'You descendants of Benjamin, you must run away to be safe!

Run away from Jerusalem!

Make a noise with the trumpet in Tekoa!

Shout over to Beth-Haccerem!

Big trouble is coming from the north.

2 I will send enemies to destroy Jerusalem and its people.

It is such a lovely city.

3 Men will come with the sheep that they keep.

They will put their tents all round it.

Each man will have a small part of the land.'

4 'Get ready to fight against it!

Let us get up and attack at noon!

But the day is getting dark.

It is already evening.

5 Rise up. Let us attack in the night.

Let us destroy their strong cities!'

6 The strong and powerful LORD spoke.

'Cut down the trees', he said.

'Build high hills up to the walls of the city.

I must punish Jerusalem.

It is full of men who hurt other people.

7 It contains so many people who do bad things.

Bad things pour out from it, like water from a well.

It is full of fights and of men who destroy.

All the time I can see how sick and weak it is.'

8 'Listen to my words', says the LORD, to the people in Jerusalem.

'If you do not listen, I will turn away from you.

I will destroy your country.

Then nobody will be able to live in it.'

9 The strong, powerful LORD spoke again.

'I will let the enemy take everything from Israel.

They will take things like a farmer who is picking his fruit', he said.

10 I want to speak to people. And I want to tell them what may happen.

But nobody will listen to me.

They close their ears so that they cannot hear.

They hate the LORD's message.

It does not give any pleasure to them.

11 But the LORD is full of anger.

He is so angry that he cannot contain it.

His anger will be like water that pours out on the children in the street.

It will pour out on the groups of young men.

It will cover both husbands and wives.

It will pour over the very old people.

12 I will give their houses to other people.

Other people will take their fields and their wives.

This will happen when I decide to punish the people in this country',

says the LORD.

13 'All the people, important and not important, want to get more and more things.

Priests and prophets are all the same.

They all say things that are not true.

14 They tell my people that there is no great trouble.

They say that there is nothing to be afraid of.

"Peace, peace", they say.

But they do not have any peace to give.

15 They are not ashamed of the wrong things that they do.

They seem to think that there is nothing wrong about those things.

They have forgotten how to be sorry.

So they will fall when other people fall.

I will bring them down when I decide to punish them',

says the LORD.

16 The LORD spoke to the people.

'Stand at the place where the roads cross. And look', he said.

'Ask where the old ways lead.

Find the good way, and walk along that way.

Then I will give proper peace to you.

But you said, "We will not walk that way."

17 I gave you men to help you and to lead you. I said,

"Listen for the noise of the trumpet!"

But you said, "We will not listen."

18 So listen to me, all you countries.

Look. And you will see

the things that I will do to them.

19 Hear me, people on the earth.

I am causing great trouble for these people.

They will have trouble because they have done many wrong things.

And they have not listened to my words.

They have not obeyed my law.

20 I do not want nice smells from Sheba.

I do not want oils from countries far away.

The food and drink that you give to me

do not give pleasure to me.'

21 So this is the message from the LORD.

'I will make things very difficult for you people.

Both sons and their fathers will have difficulties.

Friends and people who live near to each other will die.'

22 The LORD spoke again.

'Look, an army is coming from the country in the north.

I am calling up a great people from the ends of the earth.

23 They are carrying bows and spears.

They are never kind and they never forgive.

They ride on their horses and

it is like the noise of the sea.

They are ready to fight,

and they are coming to attack you, Jerusalem.'

24 We have heard about them,

and we are afraid.

Pain is all over our bodies.

It is like the pain of a woman who is having a baby.

25 Do not go out into the fields.

Do not walk along the roads.

Our enemies have long, sharp knives.

We are afraid that they are all round us.

26 My people must become very sorry.

They wear special clothes when someone dies.

They must wear clothes like those.

They cry with loud voices.

They cry like a man whose only son has died.

They do that because the enemy will quickly come to destroy us.

27 'My people are like metals.

And you must test them to see if they are good.

I want you to watch them.

Then you can see what they do.'

28 They never obeyed God.

They tell stories that are not true. And they enjoy it.

Their minds are as hard as iron.

They all do very bad things.

29 A very hot fire makes metals clean.

I send punishment like a fire.

But it does not cause bad men to do what is good.

30 God will throw them out like dirty metal.

The LORD will not receive them.

Chapter 7

To worship false gods is wrong.

1 The LORD spoke to Jeremiah. 2 'Stand at the gate of the LORD's house and speak to the people there. Say, "Hear the LORD's message, all you people in Judah. You come through this gate to worship the LORD." ' 3 The great, powerful God of Israel says, 'Change the things that you do. Do the right things. If you do that, I will let you live in this place. 4 People may say, "We are safe. This is the temple of the LORD, the temple of the LORD!" But do not believe words that are not true. 5 You must really change. You must be fair to each other. 6 You must not be cruel to foreigners, to children without living parents or to widows. You must not kill people. You must not worship other gods. If you do those things, I will destroy you. 7 If you obey me, then I will let you live in this country. This is the country that I gave to your ancestors. I gave it to them to live in for all time. 8 But you believe in words that are not true. They cannot help you.

9 You take things that are not yours. And you kill people. You tell judges things that are not true. You have sex with wives or husbands of other people. You offer gifts to the false god, Baal. You worship other gods. 10 And then you come to this, my house! You stand in front of this house that is mine. You say, "We are safe!" 11 My temple is not a place for people who hurt other people. It is not a place for people who kill other people. And it is not a place for people who speak lies! I have seen what you are doing', says the LORD.

12 'Go to Shiloh. It was the first place that I chose as a house for my name. See what I did to it. I destroyed it because you had done so many bad things. 13 I spoke to you while you were doing those bad things', the LORD said. 'I spoke to you again and again, but you would not listen. I called you, but you did not answer.14 I gave this temple to you and to your ancestors. But I will do to it what I did to the house at Shiloh. You think that the house for my name will save you. 15 But I will push you away from me, as I pushed away the other Israelites, Ephraim's tribe.'

16 'Jeremiah, you must not pray for this people. You must not ask me to help them. If you ask me, I will not listen to you. 17 You can see what they are doing in the towns in Judah. You see what they are doing in the streets in Jerusalem. 18 The children fetch wood and their fathers light a fire. The women prepare and cook cakes of bread. Then they offer them to the "Queen of Heaven". And they offer gifts of drink to other false gods. That makes me very angry. 19 I am angry. But they are the people who will hurt themselves', says the LORD. 'They will be ashamed.'

20 'So I will send out my anger', says the strong, powerful LORD. 'I will send it, like fire, on this place. I will send it on men, animals, trees and fruits. It will burn them up, and nothing will stop it.'

21 'Continue to give your offerings to me. Give burnt-offerings of meat and other things, and eat the meat yourselves! 22 I brought your ancestors out of Egypt. Then I did not only tell them how to give burnt-offerings. 23 I also told them to obey me, and to keep all my laws. Then I would be their God, and they would be my people. I said that they should obey me. They would have good lives if they did that.

24 But they did not listen. They did not think that my words had any value. Instead, they did the bad things that they liked to do. They went away from me, and they did not want to come to me.

25 I sent my servants, the prophets to you again and again. I did that from the day that you left Egypt until today. 26 But they did not listen to me. They did not try to do as I asked them. They went on doing the same bad things. And they did even worse things than their ancestors had done.'

27 'Jeremiah, you will tell them all that I have said. But when you tell them, they will not listen to you. When you call them, they will not answer. 28 So you will have to speak to them. "The people in this country have not obeyed the LORD, their God. They have not turned away from the wrong things that they were doing", you must say. "Nobody now says anything that is true. 29 Cut off your hair. Sing sad songs on the empty hills. The LORD has turned away from the people who are still alive. He has left them because he is so angry." '

The valley of death

30 'The people in Judah have done wrong things. I told them that those things were wrong', says the LORD. 'They have put false gods in my house. I hate that. They have made it like a dirty thing. 31 They have made big fires in Topheth. There, in Ben-Hinnom Valley, they burn their sons and daughters. I did not tell them to do that. I never thought to ask them to do such a thing. 32 So you must be careful. The day will come when it will not be called Topheth or the Valley of Ben-Hinnom. No, it will be called Death Valley. They will put dead persons in the earth there, until it is full up. 33 Birds and animals will eat the dead persons, and nobody will make them afraid. They will not go away. 34 I will make the place quiet. Nobody will sing or be happy there. Nobody in the towns in Judah or in Jerusalem will have marriage parties. Nobody will live in the country any more.'

Chapter 8

1 'Enemies will remove the bones of the kings of Judah and their officers. And they will remove the bones of the priests and prophets and the people from Jerusalem. They will take them out of the earth at that time. 2 The sun will shine on them, and the moon, too. My people worked for and loved the sun and moon. They worshipped them. Nobody will take the bones and put them back in the ground. They will be like dirt. 3 All the people in this bad country will want to die, and not to live', says the great, powerful LORD.

God will punish people who choose to do wrong things.

4 Speak to the people, and tell them,

'When men fall down, they get up again.

When a man goes away, he comes back.

5 I ask why these people have turned away.

The people in Jerusalem always turn away.

They choose to believe things that are not true.

They refuse to return to me.

6 I have listened carefully.

But they do not say what is right.

Nobody is sorry for the bad things that they have done.

They think, "Nobody knows what we have done."

Each person does the things that he wants.

He is like a horse that is running to the fight.

7 Even a big bird in the sky knows when it should go away.

Small birds know when it is time for them to fly away.

But my people do not know

what I want them to do.'

8 'You must not say, "We know what is right.

We know it because we have the law of the LORD."

Your writers have written what is not true!

9 Some people think that they are clever.

Those people will be ashamed. Enemies will catch them like animals in a field.

They have refused to hear the LORD's message.

They are not very clever.

10 So I will give their wives to other men.

Other men will have their fields.

All people, rich and poor, want to have more and more things.

Both priests and prophets

tell people things that are not true.

11 They can see that my people have pain.

But they say that it is not important.

They say, "Peace, peace", when there is no peace.

12 They are not ashamed of the wrong things that they do.

They are not sorry.

Their faces do not get red.

So they will fall when other men fall.

I will bring them down when I punish them',

says the LORD.

13 'I will take away the fruit and seed from their fields',

says the LORD.

'No figs or grapes will grow on their trees.

The leaves of the trees will dry up and die.

I will take away everything that I have given to them.'

14 We say to ourselves,

'We should not be sitting here like this.

We must come together.

Let us run to the cities with strong walls.

We will die there!

The LORD our God has said that we must die.

He has given to us water to drink that has poison in it

because we have not obeyed him.

15 We wanted peace, but it has not happened.

We wanted God to make us well, but he made us afraid.

16 The people can hear the noise of the enemy's horses.

They can hear them, even from Dan.

All the country shakes when they hear their noise.

They have come to destroy the country and everything in it.

They will get power over the city and over all the people who live there.'

17 'I will send snakes to you that have poison in their mouths.

Nobody can cause them to sleep.

They will bite you', says the LORD.

18 LORD, you made me happy when I was sad.

But now I feel weak and afraid.

19 Listen to your people who are crying from a country far away.

They ask if the LORD is still in Jerusalem.

They think that their king has gone away.

'They have made me angry with their false gods.

Their foreign gods do not have any value.'

20 'We have taken in all the food from the fields.

The summer is finished.

And you have not saved us.'

21 I am very sad because my people are so sad.

I feel sad as if they were dead. And I am afraid for them.

22 God has hurt his people so that no doctor can help them.

He will not make them better.

Chapter 9

1 My head should be like a river of water,

and my eyes like a pool of tears.

Then I would cry all day and night

for my people who have died.

2 I would like to have a place to stay in the desert.

Then I could leave my people.

I could go away from them.

They have all gone away from God like men who have left their wives for other women.

Not one person trusts him.

3 Their tongues are like bows.

They shoot words that are not true.

These people win their fights when they say false things.

They sin many times.

They do not give honour to me',

says the LORD.

4 'Watch your friends.

Every brother says words that are not true.

So do not trust in your brothers.

And every friend speaks words that can hurt you.

5 One friend will say words that are not true to another friend.

Nobody speaks true words.

They have taught their tongues to say things that are false.

They have sinned so much that they are tired.

6 False words are all round you.

People say so many things that are not true.

So they refuse to know me',

says the LORD.

7 So this is what the great, strong LORD says:

'I will see how clean they are.

I want to make them more clean.

A man uses a very hot fire to remove other metals from gold.

It will be like that.

I must do that because my people have sinned.

8 Their tongue is like poison.

It does not say things that are true.

A man may speak kind words to his friend,

but he is really trying to hurt him.

9 I must punish men for that',

says the LORD.

'I must be angry

because the people in this country do not give honour to me.

10 There are no people on the mountains.

So I will cry and I will be sad.

No animals live on the hills where they ate the grass.

The hills and mountains are empty.

Nobody can hear the sound of cows and sheep.

No birds fly in the air,

and the animals are gone.

11 I will make Jerusalem a hill of broken stones.

Wild animals will live there.

I will destroy the towns in Judah

so that nobody can live there.'

12 Nobody can understand this. The LORD has not told anyone how it happened. No man can say why the LORD has made the country into a desert. Now nobody can walk across it.

13 'It is because they have not obeyed my law', the LORD said. 'They have not obeyed the law that I gave to them. They have gone away from it and they have chosen to do bad things. 14 They have left me and they have gone to worship the Baals. They are doing as their ancestors taught them.' 15 So the great, strong LORD, the God of Israel says, 'I will cause these people to eat food that is bad. I will put poison in the water that they drink. 16 I will send them to many foreign countries. Neither they nor their ancestors knew these countries. I will send enemies after them to kill and to destroy them.'

17 'Call the women who cry for people in trouble. Call them now!'

the great powerful LORD says.

'Send for those who cry the loudest.

18 Tell them to come quickly to make their sad noise.

Then our eyes will make water.

And it will be like rivers that fall from them.

19 We can hear the sound of people who are crying in Zion.

"People have taken all our good things! We are very ashamed!

We have to leave our country

because our enemies have destroyed all our houses." '

20 Now hear the LORD's message, you women.

Listen to the words of his mouth.

Teach your daughters how to cry about their troubles.

Teach each other sad songs.

21 We are all dying. Dead bodies fill our strong cities.

No children play in the streets.

The open places of the city are empty.

The young men have all gone.

22 'Men's dead bodies will lie on the open fields.

Nobody will take them away', says the LORD.

'They will lie like plants that people have cut for food.

But nobody will pick them up.'

23 'The wise man must not say that he is wise.

And the strong man must not say that he is strong',

says the LORD.

24 'But they can say that they know me. And they can say that they understand me.

Then they would be able to say that they were clever.

They would know that I am the LORD.

They would know that I am kind.

And I do only good things.

I am fair when I judge the earth.

They would know that too.

Those are the things that give pleasure to me', says the LORD.

25 'Very soon', says the LORD, 'I will punish many people. Those people have bodies that their parents have not circumcised. Other people have bodies that their parents have circumcised. But I will punish those people at the same time. 26 I will punish the people in Egypt, Judah, Edom, Ammon and Moab. And I will punish the people who remove the hair from the front of their heads. And I will punish the people who live in the desert. Their parents have not circumcised the people who live in other countries. And all the descendants of Israel live like people that their parents have not circumcised. That is because they have never really wanted to obey me.'

Chapter 10

1 People in Israel, listen to what the LORD says to you.

2 'Do not do the things that people in other countries do', he says.

'You should not be afraid of things that happen in the sky.

You must not be like people in other countries.

3 The things that those people do have no value.

They take a tree from the forest,

and a worker gives shape to it with a knife.

4 They make it pretty with silver and gold.

They fix it to the floor so that it will not fall.

5 We put things like them in the fields.

Our things save the fruit from the birds.

And they cannot speak.

Men carry idols, because they cannot walk.

Do not be afraid of them.

They cannot hurt you

and they cannot help you.'

6 There is nobody like you, LORD.

You are great and your name is powerful.

7 Everyone should honour you,

King of the countries.

That is their duty.

There is nobody like you in all the countries.

No men are as wise as you are.

There is no king like you.

8 All men are fools, and they learn from fools.

Things that people have made out of wood cannot teach them anything.

9 They cover the wood with silver from Spain.

They make it pretty with gold from Uphaz.

Then they take expensive clothes that men have made with their hands.

They put them on this idol that other men have made.

10 But the LORD is really the only God.

He is the God who is alive. He is the King who will always be alive.

When he is angry, the earth moves like a leaf in the wind.

When he is angry, the people in a country cannot stand.

11 Speak to them. Say, 'Your gods did not make the earth or the sky. The LORD will destroy them. He will push them out of the earth and from all places under the sky.'

12 But God made the earth by his power.

Only he could do that.

It was he who put the sky over the earth.

13 When he shouts, there are loud noises in the sky.

He causes clouds to rise from the ends of the earth.

He causes the lightning with the rain.

And he brings the winds from the place where he hides them.

14 Nobody knows God or understands him.

Men who work to make things from metal are ashamed.

Idols that they make have no life in them.

15 They are silly because they do not have any value.

God will destroy them when he judges them.

16 The God of Jacob is not like those idols.

He made everything.

He made Israel to be the people that he chose.

He is the great and powerful LORD.

17 Get all your things together, ready to leave the country.

Your enemies are all round you.

18 This is what the LORD says,

'I will now throw out those people who live in this country.

I will make their lives difficult,

then their enemies will take them as their prisoners.'

19 I am hurt and in great pain.

Nobody can make me well.

I said to myself, 'This is my pain, and I must live with it!'

20 They have destroyed my tent.

They have broken all its ropes.

My sons have gone away, and they are dead.

Now nobody will put up my tent.

21 The shepherds are fools.

They do not ask the LORD to help them,

so their work does not make them rich.

And all their sheep have run away.

22 Listen to the noise!

People are coming from the country in the north.

They will take the people out from the towns in Judah.

Only wild animals will live there.

Jeremiah's prayer

23 I know, LORD, that you give life to each man.

Only you can say where he should walk.

24 Please lead me back to the right path, LORD, but be fair to me.

Do not be angry with me.

If you become angry, you might completely destroy me.

25 Be angry, LORD, with the people in the countries that do not honour you.

Be angry with the nations who do not ask you to lead them.

The people in those countries have completely destroyed your people,

the descendants of Jacob.

They have destroyed the country that you gave to your people.

Chapter 11

The people have not obeyed the rules of the covenant that they had with God.

1 God spoke to Jeremiah, the prophet. 2 'Listen to the rules of this covenant', he said. 'Tell them to the people in Judah and the people who live in Jerusalem. 3 Tell them that the LORD, the God of Israel says. "I will send curses to the man who does not obey the rules of this covenant. 4 I gave the rules to your ancestors when I brought them out of Egypt. Enemies caught your ancestors like wood in a fire, but I took them out. I said, 'Listen to me. And obey me about everything that I say to you. Then you will be my people and I will be your God.' 5 Then I will do what I promised to your ancestors. I promised to give to them a country that would give to them plenty of milk and honey. This is the country that you now live in." '

I answered, 'Amen, LORD.'

6 'Speak out all these words in the towns in Judah and the streets in Jerusalem', the LORD said to me. 'Say, "Listen to these rules of the covenant, and obey them. 7 I have said that all the time since I brought your ancestors out of Egypt. Again and again, until now, I have said, 'You must obey me.' 8 But they did not listen. They did not think that my rules were important. Instead, they did all the bad things that they wanted to do. All their thoughts were evil. So I had to punish them. I sent to them all the curses that I promised. I promised those curses if they did not obey me. I punished them because they did not obey the rules of the covenant."'

9 'The people in Judah and those who live in Jerusalem have agreed together. They have agreed to do wrong things. 10 They are doing the same sins that their ancestors did. Their ancestors refused to listen to my words. They left me and now they work for other gods. I made a covenant with their ancestors. None of the people from Judah or Israel has obeyed the rules of the covenant.' 11 Because of that, the LORD says, 'I will bring great trouble to you. You will not get away from it. Even if you call out to me, I will not listen to you. 12 The people in the towns in Judah and in Jerusalem will shout to the gods that they worship. But those gods will not help them when trouble happens to them. 13 Judah, you have different gods in every town. You have made altars for the god that you should be ashamed of. You have made altars to burn oils that make nice smells for Baal. You have built as many altars as there are streets in Jerusalem.

14 Jeremiah, do not pray for these people and do not ask me to do anything for them. I will not listen to them when they ask me for help.

15 The people that I love are doing evil things in my temple.

They cannot stop me from punishing them.

If you give gifts of meat to me, I will still punish you.

You enjoy doing these wrong things.'

16 The LORD said that you were like an olive tree.

It was beautiful and it gave much fruit.

But now he will burn the tree with a loud noise,

and he will break all its branches.

17 The LORD, who has all power, planted you like a tree. Now he will cause great trouble to Israel and to Judah. That is because you have burnt oils with nice smells to worship the god Baal. You have caused the LORD to be very angry.

The men in Anathoth want to kill Jeremiah.

18 I knew what the people wanted to do. The LORD had showed me what they were doing. 19 I was like a young animal that is waiting for men to kill it. I had no idea what they had been saying.

'Sometimes people have to destroy the tree and its fruit', they said. 'In the same way, he must not go on living. Men will forget all about him.'

20 'But LORD of all power, you judge in a fair way. You can see into the thoughts and minds of men. I believe that I have not done anything wrong. So I ask you to punish them.

21 The men in Anathoth wanted to kill me. "Do not go on telling us what the LORD says", they said. "If you do continue to give his messages to us, we will kill you." ' 22 So the LORD of all power spoke to me. 'I will punish them. Their young men will die as they fight. And their children will not have enough food and so they will die', he said. 23 He said, 'I will destroy all the men in Anathoth when I punish them. There will not be one living man there at that time.'

Chapter 12

Jeremiah tells the LORD about his troubles.

1 You always judge me in a good and fair way LORD,

when I tell you about my problems.

But I must ask you some questions.

Why do bad people have such an easy life?

Why does everything seem to happen in the way that pleases them?

Why do you help the people who do not obey you to be very comfortable?

2 They are like plants that you have planted. And they are growing.

They grow and they make fruit.

They talk about you a lot.

But they do not think about what you want them to do.

3 But you know me, LORD.

You watch me. And you judge the thoughts that I have about you.

Take those bad men away like animals to kill them!

Put them in a special place, ready to die.

4 The country has been dry for a long time.

The grass in every field is brown and dry.

The people who live in this country are bad.

So all the animals and birds have died.

It is even worse than that. People are saying,

'He will not see what happens to us.'

God answers Jeremiah.

5 'You get very tired when you try to run faster than other men.

So you will never run faster than horses.

You fall over on flat fields.

So you will certainly fall near the River Jordan,

when you are among many trees and bushes.

6 Even your brothers and your own family

are against you.

They join in the attacks against you.

Do not believe them,

even when they speak kind words about you.'

7 'I will leave my house and I will go away.

And my people's country will be empty.

I will let their enemies take the people that I love.

8 The people that belong to me

are like a lion.

They are like a lion that is hiding in the trees.

They shout, ready to jump on me.

This is why I hate them.

9 The people that I chose are like a small bird.

Their enemies are like big birds. They will attack them and they will kill them.

Call to the wild animals

to come and to eat them!

10 My people are like a garden where soft plants grow.

But the men who keep the garden are walking all over it.

They are making my garden into a desert.

11 It will become dry and empty

and nothing will grow there.

The whole country will become empty

because nobody cares for it.

12 Enemies will come over the empty country.

They will come to destroy my people.

Nobody will be safe in any part of the country.

13 They will plant good seed, but bad plants will grow.

My people will work very hard, but they will get nothing.

Because I am very angry, they will not have any food.

14 I will remove all the enemies who took this country. They took the country that I gave to my people, Israel. I will take them out of their countries. I will separate the people of Judah from them', says the LORD. 15 'But after I have taken away the people from Judah, I will be kind to them. I will bring them back, each to the country of his ancestors. I will bring them back to their own country. 16 Then they must learn to obey the rules of my people. They must give honour to me. They must not continue to believe in the name of Baal. They must learn to say, "As the LORD lives". Then they will become part of my people. 17 But if the people in any country will not obey these rules, I will destroy it completely', says the LORD.

Chapter 13

A belt that someone has made from cloth

1 'Go. And buy a belt that someone has made from cloth. And put it round your body', the LORD said to me. 'But you must not put it into water.' 2 So I bought a belt, as the LORD had said. I tied it on.

3 The LORD spoke to me again. 4 'Take the belt that you bought. You are now wearing it. Take it to the River Euphrates and hide it in a hole in the rocks.' 5 So I went. And I hid it at the River Euphrates as the LORD had said to me.

6 Many days after that, the LORD said to me, 'Now go to the River Euphrates. Get the belt that I sent you to hide there.' 7 So I went to the River Euphrates, to the place where I had hidden the belt. I dug it up. But it was dirty and I could not use it.

8 Then the LORD spoke to me.

9 'I will destroy everything that has any value in Judah and in Jerusalem. I will make it like this belt. 10 These people are very bad. They refuse to listen to my words. They do what they want. They work for other gods and they worship them', he said. 'They will be like this belt. Nobody will be able to use them for anything. 11 My people are like a belt. I tied all Israel's people and all Judah's people round myself. They should have been my people and they should have brought honour and praise to me. But they have not listened to me.'

12 'You must speak to them. Say, " 'People should fill with wine every skin of a goat that is to keep wine in', says the LORD." They may answer, "We know that."

13 Then say to them, "I will make all the people who live in this country like drunks. All the kings, prophets, priests and people who live in Jerusalem will be like drunks. 14 I will hit them against each other like jars, whether they are old or young", says the LORD. "I will not be sorry for them and I will not be kind to them. I will destroy them, and nothing can stop me." '

The people must not think that they are better than other people.

15 Listen to me.

Listen very carefully.

Do not think that you do not need to listen!

The LORD has spoken.

16 Give honour to the LORD your God,

before he makes it dark.

Then your feet will not find the path,

as the hills become dark.

You want it to get light.

But God will make it very dark.

17 If you do not listen,

I will weep in secret.

You think that you do not need the LORD.

That is why I will cry.

Water will fall from my eyes

like a great river.

This will happen because the LORD will make his people prisoners.

18 Speak to the king and to the queen, his mother.

Say, 'Come down from your thrones.

The gold crowns will fall from your heads.'

19 The cities in the south of Judah will not be open,

and there will be nobody to open them.

Enemies will take all the people in Judah to a foreign country.

They will take them away completely.

20 Look up. See people who are coming from the north.

The people that made you important are gone.

You are like shepherds who have lost their sheep.

21 The LORD will give your authority to other people.

People from the country that was your special friend will rule over you.

You will have pain,

pain like the pain of a woman who is having a baby.

22 You may ask, 'Why is this happening to me?'

It is because of the many wrong things that you have done.

That is why people have torn off your clothes.

And they have hurt you.

23 A black man cannot make himself white,

and an animal cannot change its colour.

In the same way, you cannot do good things

if you have always done evil things.

24 'I will blow you away

as the desert wind blows a leaf.

25 That is what I have decided to do to you', says the LORD.

'I will do it because you have forgotten me.

And you have listened to false gods.

26 I will pull off your clothes.

You will be ashamed.

27 You have had sex with women who are not your wives.

And everyone will see that you have done that.

They will know that men have paid women

to have sex with them.

I have seen the bad things that you do

on the hills and in the fields.

People in Jerusalem, you will never be happy.

You should not always do wrong things.'

Chapter 14

God will stop sending food and water and he will send wars.

1 This is what the LORD told Jeremiah. He said that he would stop sending rain.

2 'Judah's people are very sad. The people in their cities are tired.

They are sitting on the ground and they are crying.

Jerusalem's people are weeping.

3 Rich men send their servants for water.

But they do not find any water

in the big holes where they keep it.

They return with empty water jars.

Their trouble is great and they are sad.

They cover their heads.

4 The ground has long holes in it

because God has sent no rain.

The farmers have great trouble.

They cover their heads.

5 Mother animals let their new babies lie in the fields and they will leave them

because the grass is dead.

6 Wild horses stand on the empty hills and they are breathing very fast.

They cannot see well because they do not have any food.'

7 We know that we have done many bad things.

But please help us, LORD.

People will give honour to you if you will help us.

We have been backsliding people many times.

We have not obeyed your laws.

8 We trust you. Israel's people trust you.

You saved us from our troubles.

But now you are like a foreigner.

You are like a visitor who stays for only one night.

9 You are like a man who is surprised.

He is surprised when enemies make him a prisoner.

Yes, you are like a soldier who cannot save anyone.

You are among us, LORD.

People call us by your name.

Do not leave us alone!

10 'This people love to go away from me.

They let their feet go anywhere that they like.

So they cannot please the LORD.

Now he will remember the bad things that they have done.

And he will punish them for their sins.'

That is what the LORD says.

11 The LORD spoke to me again. 'Do not pray that I will do good things for this people. 12 Even if they stop eating food, I will not listen to them. If they burn meat and seeds to offer to me, I will not accept their gifts. Instead, I will kill them. They will not have any food. Or they will become ill and they will die. I will send men to kill some of them', the LORD said to me.

13 'LORD, ruler of all, the prophets say other things', I said. 'They say that soldiers will not kill the people. They do not believe that they will not have any food. The prophets say that they will not have any troubles. They say that their peace will continue.'

14 'The prophets are saying what is not true', the LORD said to me. 'And they said that I had said it. I did not send them. And I did not give my authority to them. I did not speak to them. Their words are false. They are telling to you prophecies and pictures that their own minds have made. They worship false gods.15 So this is what the LORD says about these prophets. "I did not send them. But they are saying that I have spoken to them." They say, "Enemies will not kill anyone in this country. Nobody will die because they do not have any food." But I say, "Those same prophets will not have any food and they will die. Or soldiers will kill them. 16 And men will throw the people that listened to them into the streets of Jerusalem. They will die because they do not have any food. Or they may die because soldiers will kill them. Nobody will bury the dead people. They and their dead wives, sons and daughters will lie in the street. I will punish them because they did not obey me." '

17 Say this to them.

'Water runs from my eyes

all day and all night and it does not stop.

I am crying because a heavy weapon has broken my own people.

They have a very bad illness.

18 I see dead people

when I go into the country.

Soldiers have killed them.

In the city, I see dead people.

They died because they did not have any food.

Both prophets and priests

have gone to a place that they never knew.'

Jeremiah asks the LORD to save his people.

19 I cannot believe that you have completely turned away from Judah.

I cannot believe that you hate Zion.

You have hurt us so much

that nobody can make us well again.

We trusted you to save us from trouble.

But you have not done anything good for us.

We trusted you to make us well.

But we are only very afraid.

20 LORD, we agree that we have done many bad things.

We remember, too, the bad things that our ancestors did.

We have not obeyed you, and we have hurt you.

21 We are bad. So people may think that you are bad because of that.

We do not want that.

We want people to give honour to you.

Remember that you promised something to us.

Please do what you promised to do.

22 Gods that men made from wood and stone belong to other countries.

They cannot bring rain.

The sky itself does not make rain.

No, you our LORD, our God,

you bring rain.

Only you can do all these things.

So we hope that you will help us.

Chapter 15

1 'Even if Moses and Samuel asked me not to punish my people, I would not listen to them', the LORD said to me. 'Send my people away from me. Let them go! 2 They may ask you, "Where should we go?" Then tell them that the LORD says,

"Those who should die will die.

Other soldiers will kill those who are soldiers.

Those that should not have any food will not have any food.

Those who should be prisoners will become prisoners." '

3 'I will send 4 kinds of punishments to destroy them', the LORD says. 'I will send soldiers to kill them and dogs to carry them away. And I will send birds from the air and wild animals to eat and to destroy them. 4 I will cause all the nations on the earth to hate them. I will do that because of the evil things that Manasseh, Hezekiah's son, did in Jerusalem.'

5 'Nobody will be sorry for you, people in Jerusalem.

Nobody will weep for you.

Nobody will stop to ask how you are.

6 You have turned away from me', says the LORD.

'You are often backsliding people.

So I will attack you and I will destroy you.

I am tired of being sorry for you.

7 I will judge you at the gates of the country.

Many of you will see your sons die.

And I will kill many people

because they have not returned to me.

8 I will kill many husbands.

More men will die than you can count.

I will send an enemy at midday

against mothers and young children.

They will become afraid quickly.

9 A mother who has 7 children will fall.

And she will die.

Her life will finish before she is old.

She will be ashamed and without honour.

I will send soldiers to kill

those people who are not already dead',

says the LORD.

Jeremiah is angry with the LORD.

10 I am sorry, mother, that I was ever born.

Everyone in the country is against me.

I have not lent money and I have not taken it.

But everyone says bad things about me.

11 'I will save you so that I can do good things.

I will cause your enemies to ask you for help.

They will come to you when they have great trouble', the LORD said to me.

12 'A man cannot break iron or other metals.

He cannot break the iron from the north.'

13 'I will give all your valuable things and all your money

to enemies who will attack you.

They will not pay for them

because you have done so many wrong things.

You have done bad things all over the country.

14 Your enemies will make you slaves.

They will take you to a country that you do not know.

I am very angry. And so I am like a fire that will burn you.'

15 You understand my problems, LORD.

Remember me and care for me.

Please punish those who cause so much trouble to me.

You are patient but do not let them kill me. Remember me.

They have made my life difficult because I work for you.

16 Your words were like sweet food to me.

They made me very happy.

I belong to you, LORD, powerful God.

17 I never sat with happy people at a party.

I sat alone, because you had touched me.

You had made me very angry.

18 My pain has no end.

And there is nothing that can help me to feel better.

It seems to me that you are not always there.

You are not always there when I need your help.

19 So the LORD spoke to me.

'If you will turn to me, I will take you back.

Then you can be my servant.

If you will speak good words and not bad words,

you can speak for me.

These people will return to you,

but you must not become like them.

20 I will make you like a wall to this people.

You will be like a wall of strong metal.

They will fight against you,

but they will not win the fight.

They will not win because I am with you.

I will save you', says the LORD.

21 'I will save you from bad men who attack you.

I will save you from people who want to hurt you.'

Chapter 16

The LORD tells Jeremiah about great troubles that he will cause for his people.

1-2 The LORD said to me, 'You must not marry and you must not have sons or daughters here. 3 Sons and daughters who are born in this country will die from bad illnesses. Their mothers and fathers will die, too. 4 Their bodies will lie on the ground. And nobody will be sad and nobody will bury them. Nobody will give any honour to them. Soldiers will kill them. Or they will die because they do not have any food. Birds and wild animals will eat the dead bodies.'

5 'Do not go into a house where they are eating a meal to remember a dead person. You may be sorry that the person is dead. But do not show them that you are sorry. Do that because I have taken my love and my blessings away from them', says the LORD.

6 'Nobody will bury dead persons. Nobody will bury them, whether they are rich or poor. Nobody will be sad. Nobody will show other people how sad they are. They will not cut themselves, or remove the hair from their heads. 7 Nobody will give food to families when someone has died. They will not even give food to them if their mother or father has died. And nobody will give a drink to them to try to make them happy.

8 And do not go into a house where they are having a party. Do not sit down with them to eat and to drink.' 9 And the LORD of power, the God of Israel, said to me, 'That is because I will stop their happy songs and marriage parties in this place. I will do that while you are still alive. And you will see it.

10 You must tell to the people everything that I have said. Then they will ask questions.

"Why has the LORD said all these bad things about us? What wrong things have we done? What sin have we done against the LORD, our God?" 11 Then you must speak to them. "It is because
your ancestors went away from me", says the LORD.
"They worshipped other gods and they became their servants. They turned away from me and they did not obey my law. 12 But you have done worse things than your ancestors. Each of you does what he wants. You know that. You do it even when it is wrong. You do not obey me. 13 So I will throw you out of this country into a country that you and
your ancestors have not known. There you will be servants to other gods, day and night, because I will not help you." '

14 'But a better time will come', says the LORD. 'Men will not talk about the time when I, the living God, took them out of Egypt. 15 I will bring them back to the country that I gave to their ancestors. So, instead they will say, "The LORD brought the people out from the country in the north. He brought them out from all the countries that he had sent them to. Certainly the LORD lives." '

16 'But now I will make them like fish. I will send for many men to fish for them', says the LORD. 'And these men will catch them. Then I will send hunters to run after them like wild animals. The hunters will find them in the mountains and hills and in holes in the rocks. 17 I am watching them all the time. They cannot hide from me. And they cannot hide the wrong things that they do. 18 I will punish them twice as much for their sin and for the bad things that they have done. That is because they have made my country like a place full of dirt. They have filled it with their idols that do not have any life. They have made the country that I gave to you full of their disgusting idols.'

19 LORD, you are the person who makes me strong.

You are like a city with strong walls – a city that I can hide in.

I can hide in you when troubles happen to me.

People will come to you from countries all over the earth.

They will say, 'Our ancestors had only false gods.

They did not have any power and they did not help us.

20 Men make "gods", but they are not really gods.'

21 'So I will teach them.

This time I will teach them

how strong and powerful I am.

Then they will know that the LORD is my name.'

Chapter 17

1 'All the people in Judah are full of sin.

It is deep in every part of their bodies.

It is like something that someone has written with a pen of iron.

And they use their altars to sin against me.

It is like something that someone has written on those altars too.

2 Even their children

use their altars and sticks that they call gods.

They put those tall sticks on high hills

and under big trees.

3 Enemies will come to my mountain that is in your country.

They will take away all the valuable things from there.

They will take away all the things that make you rich.

I will do that because of the sin of the people in all my country.

4 You will lose the country that I gave to your ancestors.

You will lose it because of your own sin.

Your enemies will make you their slaves.

You will live in a country that you do not know.

You have made me very angry,

and you cannot stop me being angry.'

5 The LORD spoke again.

'Some people trust human people.

I will punish everyone who thinks like that.

They think that human people can make them strong.

They do not ask the LORD for help.

6 Those people will be like a bush in a wild place.

They will not become rich when other people become rich.

They will stay in dry salty places where nobody lives.

7 The person who lets the LORD lead him is not like that.

The LORD will bless the man who follows him.

8 He will be like a tree near water

that drinks from the river.

He will not be afraid of the sun's heat.

He will be like a tree that is always green.

The tree gives much fruit and it always has enough water.

9 A man's mind can decide what he will do.

But that can cause trouble for him.

I do not know anybody except me who can understand the things in a man's mind.

It is bad and sick and nobody can make it better.

10 But I, the LORD, can look inside a man.

I can see what he feels. And I can see what he thinks.

I will give good gifts to him if he does good things.

And I will punish him if he does bad things.

11 A man may get rich because he is not fair to other people.

He is like a bird that sits on eggs. But the eggs are not its own.

He will lose his riches before he is old.

At the end of his life, people will see that he is a fool.'

12 Our God's throne was from the beginning.

It is high up in the holy place.

13 LORD, Israel's people are your people. And they trust you.

All who go away from you will be ashamed.

Those who turn away from you will die.

They will die because they have gone away from the LORD.

He is the living water that gives life to them.

Jeremiah tells the LORD about his troubles.

14 LORD, make me well, and I will be well.

Save me and I will be safe.

Save me because I praise you.

15 People keep asking me questions.

'Where are the words of the LORD?

When will they come true?'

16 LORD, I have not stopped giving help to your people who are like your sheep.

You know that I did not want bad things to happen to them.

You know that I have spoken your words.

17 Please do not make me afraid!

When bad things happen, I run to you to hide me.

18 I want you to make the people ashamed who hurt me.

Please make them very afraid.

But help me not to be afraid.

Cause them to have a lot of trouble.

Destroy them again and again.

The LORD tells Jeremiah about his rules for the Sabbath.

19 'Go and stand in the gate of the city', the LORD said to me. 'Stand in the gate that the kings of Judah use to go in and out of the city. And stand at the other city gates, too. 20 Speak to the people. Say, "Listen, you kings of Judah, people of Judah, and everyone who lives in Jerusalem. Hear the message from the LORD. 21 This is what the LORD says. 'Do not carry anything on the Sabbath day. Do not carry anything through the gates of Jerusalem. 22 Do not carry anything out of your houses and do not do any work on the Sabbath day. You must keep the Sabbath day holy as I told your ancestors. 23 But they did not listen to me and they did not obey me. They thought that my words did not have any value. They would not listen when I corrected them. 24 But you must be careful to listen to me and to obey me. Then you will neither carry things through these gates nor work on the Sabbath. You will keep the Sabbath day holy', says the LORD. 25 'Then kings who sit on David's throne will come to the city. They will come through the gates with their officers. Some kings will ride on horses. Some kings will ride in beautiful chariots that horses are pulling. The men of Judah and those who live in Jerusalem will come with them. Then people will always live in this city. 26 People will come from the towns and villages in Judah. They will come from the land that belongs to Benjamin. They will come from the hills and the little hills in the west. They will come from the south. They will bring animals, grain and oils with nice smells. They will offer those things to the LORD in his temple. They will offer them to the LORD to thank him. They will thank him for all the good things that he has done. 27 If you do not obey me, I will punish you. You must not carry things on the Sabbath day. You must not even take them through the gates. If you do not obey me, I will send fire to the gates of Jerusalem. You will not be able to put it out. Your strong city will burn down.' " '

Chapter 18

Jeremiah at the potter's house

1 The LORD spoke to Jeremiah. 2 'Go down to the potter's house, and there I will tell you my message', he said. 3 So I went down to the potter's house. There I saw him when he was working at his wheel. 4 He was working with clay to make a pot with his hands. But, as he worked, it became the wrong shape. So he made it into a pot of another shape, as he chose.

5 Then the LORD spoke to me. 'You know that I can change the Jewish people. I can change them as the potter changes the shape of the clay', he said. 6 'You Jewish people are in my hands. I hold you as the potter holds the clay in his hands. 7 I may say at any time that I will break down a country. I may say that I will destroy it. 8 But the people in that country might hear my words. And they might stop doing the things that made me angry. Then I would change my mind. I would not cause the trouble that I had promised. 9 Or I might say that I will build up a country. I might say that I will make it strong. 10 But the people in that country might do wrong things, and they might not obey my rules. Then I would think again about the good things that I had said. I might not do them.'

11 'So now you must speak to the people who live in Judah and in Jerusalem. Tell them that the LORD says, "Look! I will cause great trouble for you. I have decided to come against you. So each person must stop doing bad things and he must start to do good things. You must live in the way that gives pleasure to me." 12 But they will say to you, "We do not want to do that. We will continue to do what we want to do. We will do every bad thing that we choose to do." '

13 So the LORD said to Jeremiah,

'The people in other countries have never heard about anything like this.

My people, Israel, have done a very wrong thing.

14 The snow stays on the rocky sides of Mount Lebanon.

Cold water never stops falling from its high rocks.

15 But my people have forgotten me.

They burn oils with a nice smell

to give pleasure to gods that do not have any value.

Those gods cause them to become lost.

They go away from the right paths.

They walk alongside paths and poor roads.

16 I will send their enemies to get power over their country.

They will destroy everything in it.

My people will be ashamed.

Men who pass the country will be very surprised.

They will show how sad they are.

17 I will come to my people like the east wind.

I will blow them like sand in front of their enemies.

I will not show my face to them.

I will turn my back to them when that day comes.'

18 The people said, 'Let us attack Jeremiah. We do not need him. The priests will still teach the law, and wise men will still lead us. We will still have the words of the prophets. So we will speak against Jeremiah with our tongues. We will not listen to anything that he says.'

19 Listen to me, LORD.

Hear what people are saying against me.

20 I have tried to teach them well,

but they will do bad things to me.

Remember that I stood in front of you. And I spoke to you.

I asked you not to be angry with them.

21 So now cause them not to have any food.

Let their enemies kill them with sharp knives.

I want their wives to lose their husbands and their children.

Let their enemies kill the men.

And let the young men die while they are fighting.

22 They will shout from their houses

when you bring enemies to surprise them.

They are trying to catch me in a hole

or to tie me like an animal.

23 But you, LORD, know

the bad things that they want to do to me.

Please do not forgive them.

And do not forget the bad things that they have done.

Watch as their enemies win the fight against them.

Punish them while you are angry.

Chapter 19

The LORD sends Jeremiah to a valley.

1 The LORD said to me, 'Go. And buy a pot from a potter that he has made out of clay. Take some of the leaders of the people and some priests with you. 2 Go out into Ben-Hinnom Valley, near to the Piece of Pot gate. There you must speak the words that I will give to you. 3 Say, "Hear the LORD's message, you kings of Judah and people in Jerusalem. The great and powerful LORD says, 'Listen! I will bring very great trouble to this place. It will be very bad. It will hurt the ears of everyone who hears about it. 4 I will do that because you have brought foreign gods to this place. People have burnt animals here to offer to these gods. Neither their ancestors nor the kings of Judah knew those gods. People have killed those who had not done any wrong thing. 5 People burned their own sons in fires on the high hills. They offered them to the false god, Baal. That is something that I never asked you to do. I would never have thought to ask it. 6That is why this valley will have a new name', says the LORD. 'At a future time, it will not be called Topheth or Ben-Hinnom Valley. No, it will be called "Death Valley".

7 Judah and Jerusalem will not grow in the way that they want. In this place, I will cause their enemies to destroy them. They will kill those who live here. I will give their dead bodies to the birds and to the wild animals for food. 8 I will completely destroy this city so that people will be ashamed. Anyone who walks past it will see it. They will see that I have destroyed it. They will think that it did not have any value. That will be because of all its troubles. 9 Enemies who want to kill its people will be all round the city. And its people will not have any food. They will be so hungry that they will eat the dead bodies of their children and of each other.' "

10 Then break the pot that you bought. Break it in front of all those people who are watching you.

11 Say to them, "The great and powerful LORD says, 'I will break this country. I will break this city as someone breaks a pot. Nobody will be able to mend it. Topheth will not be able to hold all the dead bodies. 12 I will make this city like Topheth. That is what I will do to this city. And I will do it to those who live here. 13 I will make the houses in Jerusalem and those of the kings of Judah full of dead bones like Topheth. I will do that to all the places where they burned nice oils. And I will do that to all the places where they poured drinks. That is because they offered them to the stars in the sky and to other gods.' " '

14 Jeremiah returned from Topheth where he had given the LORD's message to the rulers. Then he went and he stood in the outside part of the LORD's temple. He spoke to the people. He said, 15 'The great and powerful LORD is saying to you, "Listen! I will do all the really bad things that I promised to do. I will destroy this city and the villages near to it. I will do it because the people in them did not listen to me. I will do it because they would not obey my words." '

Chapter 20

Jeremiah and Pashhur

1 Pashhur, son of Immer, was the leader of the priests in the LORD's temple. He heard the things that Jeremiah was prophesying. 2 So he caused his men to hit Jeremiah, and to tie him up. They tied him on a seat by the highest gate. That is the gate of Benjamin at the LORD's temple. 3 The next day, Pashhur let Jeremiah go. 'The LORD's name for you is not Pashhur, but Magor-Missabib', Jeremiah said.

4 'The LORD says, "I will make you afraid of yourself and your friends will be afraid of you too. With your own eyes, you will see their enemies kill all your friends. I will give all the people in Judah to the king of Babylon and he will take them away. He will take them to Babylon or he will cause his soldiers to kill them. 5 I will give all the valuable things in the city to the people's enemies. I will give all your valuable things, the things that you have made, to them. They will take all the valuable things of the kings of Judah. They will take them away to Babylon because they have won their fight against you. 6 And they will take you, Pashhur, and everybody who lives in your house, to Babylon. You will die there and all your friends will die there too. You spoke false prophecies to them. They will bury you there." '

Jeremiah cries out to the LORD.

7 LORD, you did not tell me how bad they would be to your prophet.

You caused me to believe something that was not true.

You fought against me.

You are stronger than I am. And you won.

Nobody believes the words that I speak. They think all the time that I am a fool.

8 Every time that I speak, I have to tell them bad things.

I shout out that their enemies are all round them.

And I shout that their enemies will fight. I shout that they will kill them.

These words of yours make them angry with me.

So they say bad things about me all the time.

9 I want to keep quiet. I do not want to talk about you.

I tried to do that. I said that I would not speak on your behalf.

But then your words burned like a fire inside me. They did not give me any rest.

I am too tired to hold them in. I cannot do it.

10 I hear voices that say, 'Everything round you should make you afraid!

Let us tell the officers what he is saying.'

All my friends are waiting for me to make a mistake. They say,

'Perhaps we can cause him to believe something that is not true.

Then we can punish him for the bad things that he has said.'

11 But the LORD is with me like a strong soldier.

So those who are against me will fail. They will not win.

They will fail completely. They will be very ashamed for all time.

People will never forget that nobody should honour them.

12 Great and powerful LORD, you look at all the people.

You know what they think. They think that they are right.

Let me see you punish them. Do that because I am trusting you to help me.

13 Sing to the LORD!

Give praise to the LORD!

He saves the lives of poor people from the things that bad men do.

14 I will put a curse on the day that I was born.

I do not want the day that I was born ever to be happy.

15 I will put a curse on the man who told the news to my father.

He made my father very happy. He said,

'You have a son!'

16 I want the LORD to kill the man who said that.

The LORD was not sorry to destroy our towns.

Destroy that man like that.

I want him to hear people who are crying in the morning.

I want him to hear the shouts of men who fight at noon.

17 The LORD did not kill me before I was born. I am angry about that.

I was not a dead body buried inside my mother.

That body would have kept her big for her whole life.

18 I do not know why I came out from my mother.

I only get troubles and things that make me sad.

People will only say bad things about me when I die.

Chapter 21

King Zedekiah asks the LORD for help.

1 King Zedekiah sent Pashhur, son of Malchijah, and the priest Zephaniah, son of Maaseiah, to Jeremiah. 2 'Nebuchadnezzar, king of Babylon, is attacking us', they said. 'Ask the LORD for us if he will do something great for us. He did many good things for us before now. Perhaps he will cause Nebuchadnezzar to go away.'

The LORD uses Jeremiah to speak to them.

3 'Tell Zedekiah', Jeremiah answered them, 'that the LORD says this: 4 "You have weapons in your hands to fight the king of Babylon and his soldiers. But I will turn your weapons against you. The enemy are everywhere round your city's walls. And I will bring them together inside this city. 5 I will fight against you myself with my own hand. I am very strong and very angry. 6 I will attack all the people who live in this city. I will kill them with a very bad illness, both people and animals. 7 After that", the LORD says, "I will take Zedekiah, king of Judah. With him, I will take any of his officers or people that are still alive. I will take anybody that the soldiers have not killed. And I will take everybody who has not died from illness. I will give them to Nebuchadnezzar, king of Babylon. I will give them to the enemies who want to kill them. He will kill them. He will not be sorry and he will not be kind to them."

8 And tell the people more. Tell them that the LORD says, "I am showing two different paths to you. One path is the way to life and the other path is the way to death. 9 Anyone who stays in the city will die from hunger or illness. Or soldiers will kill them. But anyone can go out and he can give himself to the soldiers from Babylon. If he goes outside the city, he will save his life. 10 I have decided to hurt this city and not to help it", says the LORD. "I will give it to the king of Babylon, and he will destroy it with fire."

11 Then to the king of Judah and to his family, say this: 12 "Descendants of David, the LORD says this:

'You must judge people fairly every day.

Perhaps men have taken things from another man.

Then save that man from those who have taken his things.

If you do not do that, I will be very, very angry.

I will be angry because of the bad thing that you have done.

I will be so angry that my anger will burn like a fire.

Nobody can put out that fire.

13 I am your enemy, people in Jerusalem.

You live over this valley on a rocky hill',

the LORD says.

'You say, "Nobody can attack us.

Nobody can get into our strong city."

14 But I will punish you for all the bad things that you have done',

says the LORD.

'I will light a fire in your trees.

Then that fire will destroy everything that is round you.' " '

Chapter 22

The LORD will judge kings that are evil.

1 'Go down to the house of the king of Judah', the LORD said to me. 'You must say this to them there. 2"Hear the LORD's message, king of Judah, who sits on the throne of David. These words are for you. And they are for your officers and for all the people who come here.

3 The LORD says, 'You must do the things that are right and fair. If someone has taken away a person's things,

you should save that person. Save him from the man who took them. Do not hurt foreign people or children without living parents. Do not hurt widows. Do not kill anyone who has not done anything wrong. 4 If you are careful to obey all these rules, your kings will stay here. The descendants of David will ride in on horses, and on chariots. Their officers and people will come with them. 5 But you will have trouble if you do not obey my rules', the LORD says. 'I, myself, promise that your enemies will break down your house.' " '

6 The LORD says this: He is speaking about the palace of the king of Judah.

'I will make you like a desert.

You may be like Gilead or like the mountains of Lebanon.

But I will make you like towns where nobody lives.

7 I will send enemies against you with their weapons.

They will cut down your strong walls of wood

and they will throw them into the fire.

8 People from many countries will pass by. They will ask, "Why has the LORD done this to such a great city?" 9 Other people will answer, "They have not done what they promised to the LORD, their God. They have worshipped other gods, and they have become their servants. That is why he has done this." '

10 Do not cry because the king is dead. Do not be sad that he is gone.

But cry much for the people that enemies have taken to a foreign country.

Cry because they will never come back.

They will never see their own country again.

11 The LORD says this about Shallum, son of Josiah: 'He became king after his father, but he has gone away. He will never return to this place. 12 He will die in the place that they have taken him to. They have put him in a prison there. He will not see this country again.'

13 'A man might use the bad things that he does to build his palace.

But he will never be happy.

The person who is not fair to his workers will also never be happy.

He causes people in his own country to work for nothing.

He does not give to them the money for their work.

14 He says, "I will build myself a great palace.

I will build rooms on the ground and big rooms over them.

I will make big windows and I will cover the walls with nice smelling wood.

I will make it beautiful with red paint."

15 But red wood does not make you a greater king. Your father had enough food and drink.

And he did what was right and fair. So his life was good.

16 He helped people who were poor. And he helped those who needed his help.

So everything was good for you.

That happens when people know me',

the LORD says.

17 'But you only want to get rich in ways that are not fair.

People do not do anything wrong, but you kill them.

And you cause people to give money to you that is not yours.'

18 So the LORD says this about Jehoiakim, son of Josiah, king of Judah.

'They will not be sad when he dies.

They will not say, "My brother, how sad, my sister."

They will not say, "My poor master, how great he was."

19 They will bury him like a dead animal.

They will pull his dead body to the gate and they will throw it outside Jerusalem.

20 Go up to Lebanon and shout.

Shout loudly in Bashan.

Shout out from Abarim.

Shout because all your friends are gone.

21 I did tell you that it would happen.

But you thought that you were safe.

And you said, "I will not listen!"

You have been like that since you were young.

You have not obeyed me.

22 Your rulers will leave you, as if the wind had blown them away.

Enemies will take your friends to a country far away.

Then you will be ashamed and you will feel sad.

You will be sorry for all the wrong things that you have done.

23 Some of you live in Lebanon in houses of wood that smells nice.

But you will shout with pain when you start to have troubles.

It will be like the pain of a woman who is having a baby.'

24 'This is as sure as the fact that I am alive', says the LORD. 'I will let this happen to you, Coniah, son of Jehoiakim, king of Judah. I will pull you off as I would pull a valuable ring from my right hand. 25 I will give you to those men that you are afraid of. I will give you to those people who want to kill you. I will give Nebuchadnezzar and the people from Babylon power over you. 26 I will throw you and your mother into another country. I will send you both to a country that you do not know. It is a country where neither of you was born. You will both die there. 27 You will never return to the country where you want to be.'

28 This man Coniah must be like a pot that somebody has broken. Nobody seems to want him.

He and his children will go out into a country that they do not know.

29 Country, country, country, listen to the LORD's message!

30 'Write this man's name. Write it as the name of a man without any children.'

The LORD says,

'Nothing good will happen to this man while he lives.

And no good thing will happen to his descendants.

Not one descendant will sit on the throne of David.

None of them will rule in Judah.'

Chapter 23

A son of David will rule one day. He will rule in the right way.

1 'I will cause trouble to the rulers who are destroying my people. They cause them to run away', the LORD says. 2 So he says to them, 'You rulers should care for my people as a shepherd cares for his sheep. I will punish you because you have done this evil thing. You have caused my people to run away to many different places. You have not cared for them', says the LORD. 3 'I myself will fetch all my people who are still alive. I will fetch them from the countries that they ran to. I will bring them back to their own country. There they will have children and they will grow in number. 4 I will give to them rulers who will care for them. My people will not be afraid. Not one person will be missing', says the LORD.

5 'The time is coming', says the LORD,

'when I will give a good son to David's descendants.

He will rule in a right way and with understanding.

He will judge fairly in the country.

6 When he is ruling, Judah will be safe.

And Israel will not be afraid then.

People will give this name to him:

"The LORD makes us right and good".'

7 'People will speak in a new way at a future time', says the LORD. 'They will not say again, "This is as sure as the fact that the LORD is alive. I am sure that he brought Israel's people out of Egypt."

8 But they will say, "This is as sure as the fact that the LORD is alive.

I am sure that he brought Israel's descendants out of the countries in the north. And he brought them out of all the countries that he had sent them to." Then they will live in their own country.'

Prophets who say things that are not true

9 I must speak about the prophets.

My mind is not happy.

My body feels weak and ill.

I am like a man who has drunk too much wine.

The LORD has spoken to me, and his words are holy.

10 The country is full of men who have sex with other men's wives.

Because of that, the country is as dry as dead bones.

And all the plants in the fields are dead.

The prophets are doing things that are wrong.

And they do not use their power in the right way.

11 'And the prophets and the priests do not give honour to me.

Even in my temple I see them. And they are doing things that are very wrong',

says the LORD.

12 'Because of that, I will make it difficult for them to do their work.

I will send them away to a dark place where they will fall.

Many bad things will happen to them when I start to punish them',

says the LORD.

13 'I saw a very bad thing that the prophets in Samaria did.

They were speaking the name of the false god, Baal when they were prophesying.

They did not tell my people things that were right.

So they caused them to do wrong things.

14 Some prophets in Jerusalem

were doing wrong things too.

I saw them having sex with other men's wives.

But they let people think that they were good.

They say that it is good for men to do evil things.

So they let them continue to do things that are wrong.

They seem as bad to me as were the people in Sodom.

The people in Jerusalem are as bad as the people in Gomorrah.'

15 So the great and powerful LORD says this about the prophets:

'I will cause them to eat food that tastes bad.

And I will cause them to drink water that will make them ill.

That is because of the things that the prophets in Jerusalem have done.

They have caused all the people in the country to turn away from God.'

16 The great and powerful LORD says:

'Do not listen to the words that the prophets are prophesying to you.

They cause you to believe things that are not true.

They tell you about pictures that they have made in their own minds.

They do not speak the words that come from the LORD's mouth.

17 They continue to think that I am worth nothing.

And they cause other people to think as they think.

They say that the LORD has said to them,

"You will have peace.

Nothing bad will happen to you."

Some people refuse to change the things that they are doing.

But the prophets say those good things to all those people.

18 But none of them has been with the LORD.

They have not seen him and they have not heard his word.

They have not listened to him.

19 But you will see that the LORD will be very angry.

He will be angry like a storm and a strong wind.

He will knock down people who do wrong things.

20 Nothing will cause the LORD to stop being angry.

He will finish completely everything that he wants to do.

At a future time, you will understand all of this.

21 I did not send these prophets.

But they have still run to tell their message to you.

I did not speak to them,

but they have prophesied.

22 If they had met with me,

they would have spoken my words to the people.

Then my people would have turned away from the things that are wrong.

They would have stopped doing bad things.

23 I can see things that happen a long way away.

I do not see only what is close to me.

24 Nobody can hide in a secret place

so that I cannot see him', says the LORD.

'I am in all the earth and in all the sky', says the LORD.

25 'I have heard the things that these prophets say. They say things that are not true. They give false messages. They say that they are messages from me. They say, "I had a dream." 26 They should stop speaking false words. They make pictures in their own minds. And they say that they are prophecies. 27 They tell their dreams to each other. They think that their dreams will cause my people to forget my name. Then they would be like their ancestors who forgot me. They forgot me when they worshipped the false god, Baal. 28 A prophet may have a dream. That prophet can tell people that it is only a dream. But anyone who has heard my words must be sure to give my message to people. The dream and my message are very different. Their dream is nothing but my message is everything good', says the LORD. 29 'My word is like a fire', says the LORD. 'It is like a hammer that breaks a rock in pieces.'

30 'The prophets take each other's words. Then they say that they came from me. That is why I am against them', says the LORD. 31 'Yes', says the LORD, 'They tell people what they think. But they say, "The LORD says." ' 32 'Yes, I am against those who prophesy false dreams', says the LORD. 'Those dreams that they tell to the people lead the people away from me. Their stories cause people to believe things that are not true. I did not send them and I did not give my authority to them. They do not help my people', the LORD says.

False prophets and their false prophecies

33 'These people or a prophet or a priest may ask you, "What is the LORD saying?" Then you must say to them, "'I will leave you', he says". 34 If a prophet or a priest says, "This is a message from the LORD", I will punish him. I will punish that man and all the people who are in his house. 35 You can ask your friends and families questions. "What is the LORD's answer?" or "What has the LORD said?" you can say. 36 But you must not speak again about the LORD's message. You say that it is a message from the LORD. But you are really speaking your own words. In that way, you change the words of the living God. You change the words of the great powerful LORD, our God. 37 You can ask a prophet, "What is the LORD's answer to you?" or "What did the LORD say?" 38 You might say, "This is the LORD's message." But the LORD says to you, "You said that your words were my message. You did that. But I had told you not to use the words, 'This is the LORD's message.' " 39 Because of that, I will certainly forget you. I will push you away from me and from this city. You will leave the city that I gave to you and to your ancestors. 40 I will make you ashamed. People will always remember that I made you ashamed. They will not forget.'

Chapter 24

The LORD shows another picture to Jeremiah.

1 Nebuchadnezzar, king of Babylon took Jeconiah away to Babylon. Jeconiah was the son of Jehoiakim, king of Judah. He took with him all Jeconiah's officers and all the men who had clever hands. After that, the LORD showed two baskets of figs to me. 2 One basket had very good fruit, like the first fruit on a tree. The other basket had very bad fruit. It was so bad that nobody could eat it.

3 Then the LORD asked me, 'What do you see, Jeremiah?'

'Figs', I answered, 'the good ones are very good. But the bad ones are so bad that nobody can eat them.'

4 Then the LORD spoke to me,

5 'The LORD, the God of Israel, says, "The people that I sent away from Judah are like the good figs. I see them as good. I sent them away from this place to Babylon. 6 I will watch them, and I will cause good things to happen to them. I will bring them back to this country. I will build them like a strong building and I will not destroy them. I will put them where they can grow like a plant. And I will not pull them up. 7 I will cause them to want to know me, the LORD. They will be my people and I will be their God. That will happen because they will completely return to me.

8-9 But Zedekiah, his officers and the people who are still in Jerusalem are like the bad figs. They are like the figs that nobody can eat. They may stay in this country or they may live in Egypt. But I will cause them to have to run from one country to another country. The people in all the kingdoms on the earth will hate them. People will not want them. And they will say that they are silly. And they will say bad things about them and they will curse them. They will do that in every place that I send them to. 10 I will send soldiers and illness to kill them. They will not have enough food to eat. So I will kill all the people still in the country that I gave to their ancestors." '

Chapter 25

Israel's people will be prisoners for 70 years.

1 The LORD spoke to Jeremiah in the 4th year of Jehoiakim. Jehoiakim was the son of Josiah king of Judah. The LORD spoke about the people in Judah. It was the first year when Nebuchadnezzar was the king of Babylon. 2 So Jeremiah the prophet spoke to all the people in Judah and to those who were living in Jerusalem. He said, 3 'For 23 years the LORD has spoken to me. And I have told you the words that he has said. I have done that since the 13th year of Josiah. He was the son of Amon, king of Judah. I have spoken to you again and again, but you have never listened.

4 And you have not listened to the prophets, the LORD's servants, at all. Even when the LORD sent them again and again, you would not listen to their words. 5 "Turn away from all the wrong things that you are doing. You know that they are bad", they said. "If you stop doing evil things, you can stay in the country. It is the country that the LORD gave to you and to your ancestors for all time.

6 Do not work for other gods and do not worship them. You must not do the things that their servants do. Stop making the LORD angry. You are making him angry because you are making false gods with your hands. If you stop making the LORD angry, he will not hurt you." '

7 'But you did not listen to me', the LORD says. 'And you have made me angry because of the things that you have made. So I will cause trouble for you. That is only because you refused to obey me.'

8 The great and powerful LORD says, 'You have not listened to my words. 9 So I will call the nations in the north. And I will call my servant Nebuchadnezzar, the king of Babylon', he says. 'And I will bring them to fight against this country and against the people who live here. They will also fight against all the countries round you. I will destroy all of those countries completely. They will be places that people are afraid of. They will say that people could not keep their countries safe. They will remain like a desert for all time.

10 I will stop any sounds of happy parties. Nobody will get married here. Nobody will make flour here. No lights will shine here.

11 The whole country will be empty and nobody will live here. The people from all these countries will work for 70 years for the king of Babylon. 12 But after the 70 years, I will punish the king of Babylon and his country. I will punish the people in Babylon for the bad things that they did', says the LORD. 'I will make Babylon empty for all time. Nobody will live there. 13 I will cause everything to happen to it that I have spoken about. You can read all those things in this book. They are the prophecies of Jeremiah against the countries. 14 Many countries and great kings will take the people from Babylon themselves as slaves. I will do to them all the bad things that they did to other nations.'

Jeremiah takes a cup from the LORD.

15 The LORD, the God of Israel, said to me, 'Here is a cup that is full of wine. The wine is a picture of my anger. In the countries that I send you to, you must cause the people there to drink this wine. 16 I will send armies against them. Then when they drink the wine of my anger they will become crazy.'

17 So I took the cup from the LORD's hand. As in a picture, I saw all the countries that he had sent me to. Their people were drinking from the cup. 18 The people in Jerusalem and in all the towns in Judah drank from it. And their kings and officers also drank. Then God would break up all their country. He would make it a thing that people would turn away from. People would think that they did not have any value. And they would curse them. That is what they do today. 19 Pharaoh, king of Egypt and all his officers, his slaves and all his people would drink from the cup. 20 And all the foreign people in Egypt would drink from it too. The kings that must drink from the cup include the kings of Uz and all the kings of Philistia. (The kings of Philistia include the kings of the people in Ashkelon, Gaza, and Ekron. And they include the king of all the people who are still at Ashdod.) 21 Edom, Moab and Ammon 22 and all the kings of Tyre and Sidon would drink, too. The kings of the countries across the sea, 23 Dedan, Tema, and Buz would drink from the cup. And everyone in far places would drink from the cup. 24 All the kings of Arabia and the kings of the foreign people who live in the desert would drink. 25 And all the kings of Zimri, Elam and Media would drink. 26 All the kings of the north would drink whether they live near or a long way away. The people in all the kingdoms on the earth will drink, one after another. The last to drink will be the king of Sheshach (Babylon).

27 Then tell them that the great and powerful LORD, the God of Israel, says, "Drink. Become ill with drink and be sick. Fall down and never get up again. I will send men with swords to hurt you." 28 But they may refuse to take the cup and to drink from it. Then you must tell them that they must drink my wine. Say, "The great and powerful LORD says, 29 'See the things that I am beginning to do. I am beginning to destroy the city that has my name. And I will punish all you people. I will bring war against everyone who lives on the earth. And that is the time when I will punish you.' The great and powerful LORD is saying those things."

30 Now prophesy all these words against them. Say to them,

"The LORD will shout from his high place.

He will make a noise like a storm from his holy place.

His great voice will shout against this country.

He will shout like the men who jump on grapes to make wine.

He will shout against all people who live on the earth.

31 The noise will be so great that all the earth will hear it.

That is because the LORD will punish all the countries.

He will judge all the people on the earth.

Soldiers will kill those people who have done any wrong things."

Those are the LORD's words.'

32 The great and powerful LORD says,

'Look! I am destroying one country after another.

A great storm is coming from the ends of the earth.'

33 At that time dead bodies will lie everywhere. They will cover the earth. Nobody will cry because they are dead. Nobody will take them to bury them in the ground. They will lie there like things that people have thrown away.

34 You shepherds of my people will cry aloud.

Roll on the ground, you who lead them.

The time for you to die has come.

You will fall and you will break in pieces, like a pot.

35 The shepherds will not find anywhere to run and to hide.

The leaders will not be able to run away.

36 You will hear the leaders shout out.

They will shout loudly

because the LORD is destroying their country.

37 The LORD will destroy the quiet fields

because he is very angry.

38 He will come out of his home like a lion.

And he will make their country a desert.

It will be empty because of the enemy's army.

It will be empty because the LORD is very angry.

Chapter 26

Men say that they will kill Jeremiah.

1 The LORD spoke to Jeremiah soon after Jehoiakim, son of Josiah, became king. He said, 2 'The LORD says. "Stand in front of my house and speak to all the people there. People from all the towns in Judah come to worship in the LORD's house. Tell them everything that I say. Do not leave out one word. 3Perhaps they will listen. And perhaps they will each turn away from the evil things that they are doing. Then I will change the thing that I had decided to do to them. I will not send very bad trouble to them." 4Say to them, "The LORD says, 'You must obey the law that I have given to you. 5 You must obey me and you must listen to the words of my prophets. If you do not obey me, I will punish you. I have sent my prophets to you again and again. But you have not listened to them. 6 So I will destroy this house. I will make it like Shiloh. And people in other countries will call this city a curse.' " '

7 The priests, the prophets and all the people heard Jeremiah while he was speaking. He spoke the Lord's words in the LORD's house. 8 Jeremiah said everything that the LORD had given to him to say. When he had finished, the priests, prophets and people took him. They said, 'You must die! 9 You should not prophesy that this house will be like Shiloh. You have said, "Enemies will destroy this city. And it will be empty after they have gone." But you must not say that.' And all the people became a crowd round Jeremiah in the LORD's house.

10 The officers of Judah heard those words. So they left the king's house and they went up to the LORD's house. They sat in their places at the way into the New Gate. 11 Then the priests and the prophets spoke to the officers and to all the people. They said, 'You must decide to kill this man. He has prophesied against this city. Your ears heard him say it!'

12 Then Jeremiah said to all the officers and to all the people, 'The LORD sent me to prophesy against this house and against this city. He told me that I must say those things. And you have heard the words that he gave to me. 13 Now you must turn away from the wrong things that you are doing. You must obey the LORD your God. Then the LORD will change his thoughts. He will not do all these bad things that he has told you about. 14 I am in your power. Do with me whatever you think to be good and right. 15 But I am sure that I have not done any wrong things. If you kill me, God will punish you. And he will punish your city and all the people who live in it. The LORD really did send me to speak all these words for you to hear. They are true.'

16 Then the officers and all the people spoke to the priests and to the prophets. They said, 'This man should not die. He has spoken to us on behalf of the LORD.'

17 Some of the leaders of the people came to speak to everyone who was there. They said, 18 'Micah from Moresheth prophesied when Hezekiah was king of Judah. He told all the people in Judah the words that the LORD had said. He said,

"Zion will be like a field.

Jerusalem will become a lot of stones.

The hill that the temple is on will have weeds everywhere."

19 Neither King Hezekiah nor anyone else in Judah caused Micah to die. Hezekiah was afraid to make the LORD angry and he wanted to honour the LORD. And he wanted to give pleasure to him. And then the LORD changed what he had decided to do. He did not send to them what he had promised to send. We will cause a lot of trouble for ourselves!'

20 (Uriah, son of Shemaiah from Kiriath-Jearim, was another prophet. He prophesied on behalf of the LORD against this city and against this country. He prophesied with the LORD's authority against this city and against this country. He said things like the things that Jeremiah said. 21 When King Jehoiakim and all his officers heard those words, the king wanted to kill Uriah. But Uriah was afraid when people told him about that. So he ran away to Egypt. 22 But King Jehoiakim sent Elnathan, son of Achbor, to Egypt. He went with some other men. 23 They brought Uriah back to King Jehoiakim. The king caused his soldiers to kill Uriah. And they threw his dead body down in the place where they buried poor people.)

24 Ahikam, son of Shaphan, also said that Jeremiah spoke the true words of the LORD. So the officers did not let the people kill Jeremiah.

Chapter 27

God tells Jeremiah that people from many countries will become Nebuchadnezzar's servants.

1 The LORD spoke to Jeremiah soon after Zedekiah became king. Zedekiah was the son of Josiah and he had become king of Judah. 2 The LORD said to me, 'Make a yoke from wood and leather, and put it on your neck. 3 Then send for the messengers in Jerusalem. They have come from other countries to see Zedekiah, king of Judah. The kings of Edom, Moab, Ammon, Tyre and Sidon sent them here. 4 Give to them a message for their masters. Say, "The great powerful LORD, the God of Israel, says this: 'Tell this to your masters: 5 I made this earth with my long arm and with my great power. I made the people and the animals on the earth. And I will give it to anyone that I choose. 6 Now I will give all your countries to my servant Nebuchadnezzar, king of Babylon. He will have power over you and even over the wild animals. 7 People from all countries will serve him and his son and his grandson. They will serve him and his sons for as long as I let him and his sons rule. Then people from many countries will join together and they will take away his power.

8 If the people from any country will not serve Nebuchadnezzar, king of Babylon, I will punish those people. I will send soldiers or illness or I will destroy their food.

I will cause Nebuchadnezzar to do that if the people in that country will not be his servants. 9 So do not listen to your prophets, or to your people. They think that they know about future things. But they do not know. Do not listen to those who ask spirits for help. Do not listen to those who try to understand dreams. They might tell you that you will not become servants of the king of Babylon. 10 They would not be telling you what is true. That would make it sure that an enemy would take you a long way from your own country. I would send you away and you would die there. 11 But the people from a country might decide to obey the king of Babylon. They might become his servants. Then I would let those people remain in their own country. They could continue to live there' " ', says the LORD.

12 I gave the same message to the king of Judah. I said, 'Put on the yoke of the king of Babylon. You and your people must become his servants. Then you will live. 13 You and your people do not want to die. Any people who do not serve the king of Babylon will die. The LORD has promised this. He will kill those people with soldiers or with illness. Or they will die because they do not have any food. 14 Do not listen to the words of the prophets who say, "You will not serve the king of Babylon." They are prophesying lies. 15 "I have not sent those prophets", says the LORD. "They are using my name. But they are saying things that are not true. So I will send you away and you will die. You and the prophets who are prophesying to you will die." '

16 Then I spoke to the priests and to all the people. I said, 'The LORD says, "Do not listen to the prophets. They tell you that people will soon bring back from Babylon the things from the LORD's house. But the things that they say are not true. 17 Do not listen to them. If you serve the king of Babylon, you will live. You do not want him to destroy this city! 18 Proper prophets who had heard the LORD's message would ask him for help. They would ask the great powerful God to let the things still in the LORD's house stay there. They would ask him not to let people take them to Babylon. They would ask that the things from the king's house and in Jerusalem would remain there." 19 The LORD says that there are beautiful things of stone and metal still in the city. 20 Nebuchadnezzar let them remain here when he took Jehoiakim, king of Judah, away. He took him then with all the great people in Judah and in Jerusalem. He took them from Jerusalem to Babylon. 21 Yes, the LORD says. He says this about all the things that they had let remain in the LORD's house and in the king's palace: 22 "Nebuchadnezzar's people will take them to Babylon. They will stay there until I come for them. Then I will bring them and I will put them back in this place." '

Chapter 28

The false prophet Hananiah

1 The prophet Hananiah, son of Azzur, spoke to me. He spoke to me in the house of the LORD that same year. It was the 5th month of the 4th year, soon after Zedekiah had become king of Judah. Hananiah came from Gibeon. He spoke to me in front of the priests and all the people. 2 'The great and powerful LORD, the God of Israel says this', he said. 'I will break the yoke of the king of Babylon.

3 Nebuchadnezzar king of Babylon took many things from the LORD's house. He took them to Babylon. In less than two years, I will bring them back to this place. 4 I will also bring back Jeconiah, king of Judah, and many other people. I will bring back all the people that Nebuchadnezzar took to Babylon. I will break his yoke', says the LORD.

5 Jeremiah replied to the prophet Hananiah in front of the priests and in front of all the people. They were all standing in the house of the LORD. 6 'Amen!' he said. 'I want the LORD to do that! I want him to bring back all the things to the LORD's house. I want him to bring back all the people that Nebuchadnezzar took to Babylon. I want him to do as you have prophesied. 7 But hear what I say to you and to all the people here. 8 Many prophets have prophesied for many years before us. They said that war and illness would happen. They said that people would not have any food. Those things would happen in many countries and kingdoms, they said. 9 Other prophets say that peace will happen. That peace may happen. Only then can we know that their words are true. And we will know that the LORD has sent them.'

10 Then the prophet Hananiah took the yoke off the neck of the prophet Jeremiah and he broke it. 11 He said in front of all the people, 'The LORD says, "I will break the yoke of Nebuchadnezzar king of Babylon like that. In less than two years I will break his yoke from the neck of all the countries." ' After that, the prophet Jeremiah went away.

12 A short time after Hananiah had broken the yoke from Jeremiah's neck, the LORD spoke to Jeremiah. 13 'Go. And tell my words to Hananiah', he said. 'Tell him that the LORD says, "You have broken a yoke of wood, but I will give to you a yoke of iron in its place."

14 The great and powerful LORD says this: The God of Israel says, "I will put an iron yoke on the neck of all those countries to make them slaves. They will serve Nebuchadnezzar king of Babylon. I will even give to him power over the wild animals." '

15 Then the prophet Jeremiah said to the prophet Hananiah, 'Listen! The LORD has not sent you, Hananiah. But you have spoken things that are not true to the people in this country. And they believed that they were the LORD's words. 16 So the LORD says, "I will cause you to die this year because you have taught people not to obey the LORD." '

17 In that same year, in the 7th month, Hananiah the prophet died.

Chapter 29

Jeremiah's letter

1 Jeremiah sent a letter from Jerusalem to Babylon. He sent it to the Jewish leaders and to the priests, prophets and people who were still there. Nebuchadnezzar had taken them from Jerusalem to Babylon. 2 (That was after Nebuchadnezzar had taken King Jeconiah and his mother. He had taken them to Babylon with Jeconiah's officers. The leaders of Judah and Jerusalem and all the men who worked with clever hands had gone with them.) 3 Zedekiah was the king of Judah. He sent some men to King Nebuchadnezzar in Babylon. They were Elasah, son of Shaphan, and Gemariah, son of Hilkiah. Jeremiah gave his letter to them. It said this:

4 The great and powerful LORD, the God of Israel, says this to all the people. They were the people that he sent away to Babylon. 5 'Build houses and get comfortable. Plant gardens. And eat what grows in them. 6 You must marry each other and you must have sons and daughters. Find wives for your sons, and let your daughters marry. Then they too can have sons and daughters. I want the numbers of the people of Israel in Babylon to grow more. I do not want them to become fewer. 7 Try to make the city where you are living rich. Pray to the LORD that it will do well. If it does become rich, you will become rich too.' 8 Yes, the great and powerful LORD, the God of Israel says, 'The prophets and the people look for signs. They tell false stories to you. Do not listen to them. Do not listen to the dreams that you ask them to have. 9 They say that they are prophesying with my authority. But the things that they are telling you are not true. I have not sent them', says the LORD.

10 The LORD says, 'I will come to you when you have been in Babylon for 70 years. Then I will do as I kindly promised you. I will bring you back to this place. 11 I want to do many good things for you', the LORD says. 'I want you to become rich and strong, and I do not want to hurt you. I want you to believe that you will have a good future life.

12 Then you will ask for my help. And you will come and you will pray to me. And I will listen to you. 13 You will look for me. And you will find me when you really want to find me.' 14 'You will find me', says the LORD. 'And I will bring you back from the foreign countries where you were slaves. I will bring you back from all the countries and from among the people that I sent you to', he says. 'I will bring you back from the places that I sent you away to.'

15 You may say, 'The LORD has made prophets for us here in Babylon.' 16 But I must tell you what the LORD says about all the people in this city (Jerusalem). He is speaking to the king who sits on David's throne. And he speaks to all his people who are still in this city. They are the people who did not go with you to Babylon. 17 Yes, the great powerful LORD says, 'I will send men with swords to hurt them. They will not have enough to eat and I will make them ill. They will be like bad figs that nobody can eat. 18 I will send men to run after them with swords. They will not have any food and I will make them ill. I will cause the people in all the other countries to hate them. People will say many bad things about them. I will send them too many nations. The people in other countries will all think that they are worth nothing. 19 I will cause that to happen because they have not listened to my words', says the LORD. 'I sent these words to them again and again by my servants the prophets. And you, my people in Babylon, have not listened either', says the LORD.

20 'So you people that I have sent away from Jerusalem to Babylon must listen to me. 21 The great and powerful LORD, the God of Israel, says this: Ahab, son of Kolaiah, and Zedekiah, son of Maaseiah, say that they are prophesying with my authority. But they are telling you things that are not true. So I will give them to Nebuchadnezzar king of Babylon and he will kill them in front of you.

22 Because of them, the people from Judah that I sent to Babylon will use this curse. "We want the God of Israel to make you like Zedekiah and Ahab.

He caused them to burn in the fire." 23 That is because they have done very bad things in Israel. They have had sex with other men's wives. They have used my name to speak words that are not true. I did not tell them to say those words. I know this and I have seen it', says the LORD.

A message to Shemaiah

24 You must say to Shemaiah from Nehelam, 25 'You sent letters on your own behalf to all the people in Jerusalem', says the great and powerful LORD, the God of Israel. 'You wrote to Zephaniah, son of Maaseiah the priest, and to all the other priests. You said to Zephaniah, 26 "The LORD has made you priest instead of Jehoiada to care for the house of the LORD. You should put silly men who say that they are prophets into the stocks. You should put their feet between two pieces of wood and you should put their neck in an iron ring. 27 So I do not know why you have not punished Jeremiah from Anathoth. He is among us. And he says that he is a prophet. 28 He has sent a message to us in Babylon. He says that we will be here for a long time. He tells us that we should build houses. He says that we should make ourselves comfortable. And he says that we should grow food to eat." '

29 But Zephaniah the priest read the letter to Jeremiah the prophet. 30 Then the LORD said to Jeremiah, 31'Send this message to all the Jews in Babylon', he said. 'The LORD says about Shemaiah from Nehelam. "Shemaiah has prophesied to you. But I did not send him. And he has caused you to believe a lie." 32 So the LORD says, "I will certainly punish Shemaiah and his descendants. He will not have any descendants that are still alive among my people. He will not see the good things that I will do for my people", says the LORD, "That is because he has taught my people not to obey me." '

Chapter 30

The LORD promises to bring his people back to Israel.

1 This is the word that the LORD spoke to Jeremiah. 2 'The LORD, the God of Israel, says, "Write all the words that I have spoken in a book. 3 The time is coming", says the LORD, "when I will bring back my people. I will bring Israel's people and Judah's people back from the countries where they are prisoners. I will take them back to the country that I gave to their ancestors", says the LORD.'

4 The LORD spoke these words about Israel and Judah. 5 'The LORD says,

"People will shout because they are afraid. They will not have any peace.

6 Men cannot have children.

But every strong man is holding his body

like a woman who is giving birth to a child.

Every face is as white as death.

7 That will be a day when everyone is afraid.

There will not be any other day like that day.

It will be a time of trouble for Jacob.

But I will save him out of all that trouble."

8 "On that day I will break the yoke from your necks.

The LORD will save his people so that they will not continue to be slaves in Babylon.

I will destroy the things that make them prisoners.

They will not be still slaves to people from other countries.

9 Instead they will serve the LORD their God.

And they will serve David their king.

I will raise him up for them.

10 So do not be afraid, Jacob my servant.

Do not let yourself be afraid, Israel", says the LORD.

"I will certainly bring you from a place that is far away.

I will save your sons from the country where they are prisoners.

Jacob (Israel) will again have peace and he will be safe.

And nobody will make him afraid.

11 I am with you and I will save you", says the LORD.

"I may destroy completely all the countries that I send you to.

But I will not destroy you completely.

I will punish you in a fair way.

I certainly will punish you."

12 The LORD says,

"Your enemies have hurt you so badly that nobody can make you better.

Nobody can make you completely well.

13 There is nobody who will ask people to help you.

There is no medicine that can make you well.

14 All those who were your friends have forgotten you.

They do not feel pain for your troubles.

I have hit you as an enemy would hit you.

I have punished you because you have not obeyed me very many times.

I have punished you because you have done many very bad things.

15 You shout because you people have hurt you.

And nobody can make you well again.

Your sin is great and you have done many wrong things.

So I have done these things to you.

16 People have hurt you and they have killed you. But I will hurt those people and I will kill them.

I will send all your enemies away to be prisoners in other countries.

I will take away the good things

from those people who took away your good things.

17 I will give back your health to you.

I will take away everything that hurts you", says the LORD.

"I will do that because of the words that people say.

They threw you out.

They call you the people from Zion that nobody wants."

18 The LORD says,

"I will repair the places where Jacob (Israel) lives.

I will be kind to his descendants.

You will build the city again over its broken stones.

The palace will stand again in its proper place.

19 You will hear people who are singing with thanks to God.

They will be making a happy noise.

I will make the number of my people larger.

It will not become less.

I will cause the nations to honour my people.

They will not think that my people have no value.

20 My children will be as they were before now.

I will make them into one strong people.

I will punish all the people who try to make them their slaves.

21 A Jew will lead them.

A Jew will become their ruler.

I will bring him near and he will come close to me.

Nobody can come to me if I do not call him", says the LORD.

22 "So you will be my people and I will be your God." '

23 Look! The LORD will rush like a storm when he is angry.

He will be like a powerful wind that blows people away.

It blows away the people who do wrong things.

24 The LORD will not turn away his great anger.

He will completely finish all the work that he decides to do.

Only then will he stop being angry.

You will understand these things at a future time.

Chapter 31

Israel's return to their own country

1 'When that time comes', says the LORD, 'I will be the God of every family in Israel. And they will be my people.'

2 The LORD says,

'I was kind in the desert to the people who did not die.

That was when Israel's people wanted to rest.'

3 Before now, the LORD showed himself to us. He said,

'I have loved you with a love that has no end.

So I am showing my love to you so that you will move towards me.

4 I will build you up again.

You will again make music together,

and you will dance a happy dance.

5 You will again plant vines on the hills in Samaria.

Farmers will plant vines and they will enjoy their fruit.

6 In a future day men who watch

will shout from the hills of Ephraim.

They will say, "Let us go up to Zion,

to the LORD our God." '

7 The LORD says,

'Sing and be happy for Jacob (Israel).

Shout for your great country.

Let the LORD hear you while you praise him.

Say, "LORD, save your people.

LORD, save the few people from Israel who are still alive."

8 Look, I will bring them from the country in the north.

I will bring them from the ends of the earth.

They will bring with them those who cannot see.

And I will bring also those who cannot walk well.

Women who will soon have babies will come.

And those who will very soon give birth will come.

A very big crowd of my people will return here.

9 They will be crying as they come.

They will pray while I am bringing them back.

I will lead them along by streams of water.

They will walk along flat paths so that they will not fall.

I will do that because I am Israel's father.

And Ephraim (Israel) is my oldest son.

10 People in many countries, you must hear the LORD's message.

Shout it by the coasts of countries that are far away.

"He who pushed Israel's people away will fetch them back.

And he will watch them as a shepherd watches his sheep."

11 The LORD will buy back Jacob (Israel).

He will take them away from the people who were stronger than them.

12 They will come and they will shout on the top of Mount Zion.

They will shout because they are very happy.

They will be happy with all the good things that the LORD gives to them.

He will give bread, new wine and oil to them.

The sheep and cows will have young ones.

Israel will grow like a garden that has much water.

Its people will not still be sad.

13 Girls will dance and they will be happy.

The young men and the old men will dance too.

I will make them happy and they will not be sad.

I will do things for them that will help them to feel better.

Their faces will smile and they will not be sad.

14 I will give plenty of good things to the priests.

And I will give to my people plenty of good things. They will have more than they need', says the LORD.

15 The LORD says,

'You will hear a voice in Ramah,

a loud voice that cries sadly.

It is the voice of Rachel (Israel's people). She is crying for her children.

Nobody can stop her crying,

because her children are dead.'

16 The LORD says,

'Stop the loud noise of your voice,

and stop your eyes from crying.

I will be happy about the work that you do', says the LORD.

'Your children will return from the country of your enemies.

17 You are right to believe that your future days will be better',

says the LORD.

'Your children will return to their own country.'

18 I have certainly heard my people when they were crying.

"You have punished me.

I feel like an animal that does not obey", they said.

"And you did punish me.

Bring me back, and I will return.

I will come back because you are the LORD, my God.

19 After I had gone away from you, I became very sorry.

After you helped me to understand, I felt pain inside.

I was ashamed and I felt very small.

I had done wrong things when I was young.

I became ashamed of those things."

20 But Ephraim (Israel) is the son that I love.

He is like a child that gives pleasure to me.

I may often say that he is doing wrong things.

But while I have been speaking against him, I have always remembered him.

So I want very much to see him again.

I love him very much.

And I will certainly be merciful to him', says the LORD.

21 'Put up signs along the roads,

to show people the way.

Return, Israel, the people that I love. Return to your towns.

22 You have been away from me for a long time.

You are like a daughter who loved another man.

The LORD will do a new thing.

A woman will keep a man safe.'

23 The great and powerful LORD, the God of Israel, says, 'I will bring my people back from the country where they are prisoners. Then the people in Judah and in its towns will again say, "We pray that the LORD will be good to the holy mountain. It is the special place where he lives!" 24 People will live together in the towns in Judah. Farmers and shepherds will work in the fields. 25 I will make the tired people feel less tired. I will make the weak ones strong.'

26 Then I woke from my dream. My sleep had been good.

27 'There will be a time', says the LORD, 'when I will be like a gardener to my people. Young men and animals will be like plants that I will plant. I will put young men and animals in the nations called Judah and Israel. 28 Before now, I pulled up the roots of those "plants" to bring them down and to destroy them. Now I will plant them and I will watch over them. I want to cause them to grow', says the LORD. 29 'When that happens, people will not say, "The fathers have eaten sour fruit but the children's mouths will taste bad."

30 Instead, the mouth of anyone who eats sour fruit will taste bad. I will punish everyone for his own sin.'

31 'A time is coming', says the LORD,

'when I will make a new covenant.

I will make it with Israel's people and with Judah's people.

32 It will not be like the covenant that I made with their ancestors.

When I took them to lead them out of Egypt,

I was like a husband to them.

But they did not obey the rules in my covenant', says the LORD.

33 'This is the covenant that I will make with Israel.

I will make it when that time comes', says the LORD.

'I will put my law in their minds,

and they will always remember it.

I will be their God, and they will be my people.

34 A man will not teach his friend then.

And he will not teach his brother how to know the LORD.

That will be because they will all know me.

From the least of them to the greatest of them, they will all know me.'

The LORD says,

'I will forgive all the wrong things that they have done.

I will not continue to remember their sins.'

35 The LORD is the God who causes the sun to shine in the day.

He causes the moon and the stars to shine at night.

He causes the sea to move and to make a loud sound.

He is the great, powerful LORD. That is his name.

And he says,

36 'I will never stop watching over Israel's children.

They will always be a nation

unless I forget those laws (about the sun, moon, stars and sea) completely.'

37 The LORD says,

'I will leave the children of Israel alone only if these things happen.

I will leave if men can measure the sky above.

Men can try to find the rock that I built the earth on.

I will leave if they can find that rock.

Then I will leave the children of Israel alone

because of all the things that they have done', says the LORD.

38 'At a future time', says the LORD,

'you will build this city again. You will build it for me from the tower of Hananel to the corner gate. 39 The wall will go straight from there to Gareb. Then you must turn and cause it to go to Goah. 40 The whole valley will be holy to the LORD. It will include the place where they throw dead bodies. They throw things that they have burnt there. And it will include all the big steps to the east of the Kidron valley. It will end at the corner of the Horse Gate. I will never again destroy the city and I will never again take away its people.'

Chapter 32

Jeremiah buys a field.

1 The LORD spoke to Jeremiah when Zedekiah, king of Judah, had ruled for 10 years. Nebuchadnezzar had ruled for 18 years. 2 The army of the king of Babylon was all round Jerusalem at that time. They would not let anybody take food into the city. Jeremiah was in a prison in the soldiers' yard. That was in the king's house.

3 Zedekiah had put Jeremiah there. He did not like this message that the LORD had given to him by Jeremiah: 'I will give power over this city to the king of Babylon. And he will win the city. 4 Zedekiah, the king, will not be able to run away. They will take him to the king of Babylon and he will see his face. They will speak to each other. 5 Then he will take Zedekiah to Babylon. He will stay there until I come to see him. If you fight against the soldiers from Babylon, you will not win.' The LORD had said that to Zedekiah.

6 Jeremiah said, 'The LORD has spoken to me. 7 He told me that Hanamel, the son of my uncle Shallum, will come to see me. He will ask me to buy his field in Anathoth. I should do that because I am the cousin closest to his family. It is the right thing for me to do.'

8 Then my cousin Hanamel came to the prison in the soldiers' yard where they kept me. He said, "Buy my field at Anathoth. It is in the land of Benjamin. You must do that because it is right for you to buy it. You are the closest cousin. So buy it back and keep it for yourself."

I knew that this was the LORD's message. 9 So I bought the field at Anathoth from my cousin Hanamel. I weighed 17 shekels of silver. 10 I wrote my name on a special piece of paper and I closed it up. The paper showed that the field was mine. I did that in front of other men who put their names on it. Then I gave to Hanamel the silver that I had weighed. 11 I took the paper that I had closed up and a copy of that piece of paper. 12 I gave both pieces of paper to Baruch, the son of Neriah. Neriah was the son of Mahseiah. I did that in front of Hanamel and the other men who had written their names. And I did it in front of all the Jews who were sitting in the soldiers' yard.

13 The men watched me as I spoke to Baruch. I said to him, 14 "The great and powerful LORD of Israel says this: Take these two pieces of paper. Take the piece that is closed and the piece that is open. Put them in a jar of clay to keep them safe. They will be safe there for a long time. 15 The great and powerful LORD, the LORD of Israel, says, 'Men will again buy houses, fields and fields of vines in this country.' "

16 After I had given the important paper to Baruch, the son of Neriah, I prayed to the LORD.

17 I prayed, "LORD, king of all people, you have made the earth and the sky by your great power. Your hands have made them. Nothing is too difficult for you to do. 18 You teach thousands of people to understand that you love them. But you punish children for the sins that their ancestors did in past times. Great and powerful LORD, your name is 'All-powerful LORD'. 19 You are so wise that you do very great things. You see everything that men do. You give good things to those who give pleasure to you. Those who do good things give pleasure to you. And you punish everyone who has done wrong things. 20 You did miracles in Egypt. And you continue to do miracles in Israel and for all people. So your name is great and all people know it. 21 You brought your people out of Egypt with many great miracles. You put out your strong hand and arm to save them. So you caused men to be afraid of you. 22 You gave this country to your people as you had promised to their ancestors. Much good food grows in this country and cows give much milk. 23 Your people came in and they got power over this country. But they did not obey you. They did not obey the law that you had given to them. They did not do the things that you wanted them to do. So you caused them to have this great trouble. You sent it to them.

24 You can see the great hills that enemies have built to attack the city. Because of their sharp knives, they will win the fight. And because we are hungry and ill, they will win the fight. The soldiers from Babylon who are attacking the city will get power over it. You said that it would happen. You can see that all those things have happened. 25 The soldiers from Babylon will get power over the city. But you still told me that I must buy this field. You told me that I must buy it with silver. And men must see certainly that I had bought it." '

26 Then the LORD spoke to Jeremiah. He said, 27 'I am the LORD, the God of all people. Nothing is too difficult for me to do. 28 So I say this: I will give this city to the soldiers from Babylon. I will give it to Nebuchadnezzar, king of Babylon. They will get power over it. 29 The soldiers from Babylon who are attacking it will come in. And they will burn it with fire. They will burn down the houses where people made me angry. There they burned oils that smell nice on their roofs for Baal. They made me angry because they gave gifts to other gods.'

30 'The people in Israel and Judah have done only evil things from the time when they were young. Israel's people have always done the things that made me angry. They did that with the things that they have made with their hands', says the LORD. 31 'This city has made me angry from the time when they built it even until this day. So I must destroy it. 32 The people in Israel and in Judah have made me very angry. I became angry because of all the evil things that they and their kings and their officers have done. And the men in Judah and Jerusalem and

their prophets and priests did many evil things. 33 They turned away from me and they would not look at me. They would not listen to me when I punished them. And they would not turn back to me. Again and again, I taught them the right things to do. 34 People have made the house that is called by my name disgusting. They have a put a "god" that is not God in my house. 35 They have built high places to worship Baal in Ben-Hinnom Valley. There they kill their sons and daughters to offer them to Molech. I never told them to do such a bad thing. I never thought that they would do such a wrong thing. It caused Judah's people to sin.'

God promises his people that they can continue to trust him.

36 'You are hungry and you do not have any food. So you say that swords and illness will cause the king of Babylon to get power over this city. But the LORD, the God of Israel says, 37 "I am very angry with them. So I will send them to countries that are far away. But I will certainly bring my people back to this place. I will let them live here and they will be safe. 38 They will be my people and I will be their God. 39 I will give the same purpose to all the people. I will do that so that their lives and their children's lives can be good. They will always give honour to me. 40 I will make a covenant with them that will last for all time. I will never stop doing good things for them. I will cause them to want to give honour to me so that they will never turn away from me. 41 I will be happy when I do good things for them. I really want to plant them in this country to grow, like trees. Nobody wants to do anything more than I want to do that." '

42 The LORD says, 'I have caused much trouble to this people. In the same way, I will give great riches to them as I promised. 43 Men will buy fields in this country again. You say, "It is an empty country, without people or animals, because the soldiers from Babylon have taken them." 44 But people will buy fields in this country for silver. And people will write on papers to show who owns the land. People will close the pieces of paper and they will keep them in a safe place. Men will watch to see that they do it in a fair way. They will sell fields again in the land of Benjamin and the in the villages round Jerusalem. They will sell land in the towns of Judah. And they will sell it in the hills in the west and in the south. I will give back to them the good things that they lost. Those are the words of the LORD.'

Chapter 33

The promise that God will bring the people back

1 Jeremiah was still in the prison in the yard where the king's soldiers were. God spoke to Jeremiah a second time while he was there. He said, 2 'I am the LORD who made the earth. I gave a shape to it and I put it in its place. The LORD is my name. And I say, 3 "Call to me and I will answer you. I will tell you great, strange things that you do not know."

4 The LORD is the God of Israel. And he says this about the houses in this city and about the houses of the kings of Judah: "The people had broken them down. They used the stones to make the city's walls stronger against the enemy.

5 That was during their battle with the army from Babylon." The LORD says, "The houses will be full of dead bodies.

I will kill the people when I am very angry with them. I will not be kind to this city. That is because of all the bad things that the people have done. 6 But I will make the people in this city well again. I will make my people well. They will enjoy peace. 7 I will bring back Judah's people and Israel's people and I will make them safe and comfortable. I will build them up again. Then they will be as they were before. 8 I will make them clean from all their sin. They refused to obey me. But I will forgive all the wrong things that they did. 9 Then this city will cause the people in all the countries on the earth to praise me. They will hear about all the good things that I am doing for Jerusalem. So they will give honour to me. I will make the city rich and I will give peace to it. They will be afraid when they see that." '

10 The LORD says, 'You say that this place is empty, without men or animals. But people will return to the empty streets in Jerusalem. People will make a happy noise where now there are no men and no animals. 11 You will hear the voices of men and women who are just married. People will bring gifts to the house of the LORD to thank him. You will hear their voices as they say,

"Give thanks to the great, powerful LORD,

because the LORD is good.

His love lasts for all time."

I will make the country as rich as it was before', says the LORD.

12 The great and powerful LORD says, 'This place is empty now, without people or animals. But I will put grass round its towns where sheep can rest with their shepherds. 13 Shepherds will count their sheep again in the towns among the hills. And they will do that in the towns in the west and in the south. And they will count them in the land of Benjamin. They will do it again in the villages round Jerusalem. And they will count them in the towns in Judah', says the LORD.

14 'At a future time', says the LORD, 'I will do the kind things that I have promised to do. I promised those things to the people of both Judah and Israel.

15 David and his descendants are like a tree. In that day, when the time is right, I will cause a good branch to grow from that tree. He will do things that are good and fair in my country. 16 At that time, the people from Judah and Jerusalem will come back and they will be safe. People will call the city, "The LORD makes us right and good." '

17 The LORD says, 'A man from David's descendants will always be a king of Israel. 18 And there will always be a priest from Levi's descendants to offer meat and food to me. They will burn their gifts on the altar to show honour to me.'

19 Jeremiah heard the LORD who was saying to him, 20 'The LORD says, "You can never change my rules about the day and the night. They will always come at their proper times. 21 My promise to David my servant, and to the Levites is like that. They will always be priests who will serve me. And David will always have a descendant to sit on his throne. 22 I will cause David my servant and the Levites to have many descendants. There are many stars in the sky. And there are many pieces of sand by the sea. The number of their descendants will be like the number of those stars and like the number of those pieces." '

23 The LORD spoke to Jeremiah. 24 And he said, 'The people are saying that the LORD has left his people. But they are the people that he chose. They say that he is not still the God of Israel and Judah. They think that Israel and Judah are not still a nation. They do not think that they are important.' 25 But the LORD says, 'Nobody can change my rules about the day and the night. And I have made the laws about earth and sky. 26 I will never turn away from the descendants of Jacob and of David my servant. I will always choose one from among their descendants to rule over the descendants of Abraham, Isaac and Jacob. I will bring them back to the place that is theirs. I will be kind to them.'

Chapter 34

A message to Zedekiah

1 Nebuchadnezzar and his army and all the people from all the countries that he ruled were fighting.

They were attacking Jerusalem and the towns that were near to it. At this time, Jeremiah heard the LORD who was saying to him, 2 'The LORD, the God of Israel says this: Go to Zedekiah, king of Judah, and say to him, "The LORD says this: I will give power over this city to the king of Babylon and he will burn it down. 3 You will not be able to run away because his soldiers will certainly catch you. They will give you to him. You will see the king of Babylon with your own eyes. And you will speak with him and you will see his face. Then you will go to Babylon.

4 But listen to the promise of the LORD, Zedekiah, king of Judah. The LORD says this about you: They will not kill you with a sword, 5 but you will die in peace. People will make a big fire when they die to give honour to you. People were sad when the kings, your ancestors, died. They will cry when you die, too. And they will be sad. They will say, 'Our master has died!' This is my promise", says the LORD.'

6 Then Jeremiah, the prophet, told all this to Zedekiah, the king, in Jerusalem. 7 At this time, the king of Babylon and his army were fighting against Judah. He was fighting against Jerusalem and Lachish and Azekah, the cities that he had not got power over yet. They were the only walled cities in Judah that he had not got power over.

Zedekiah and the slaves

8 King Zedekiah promised the people in Jerusalem that he would let their slaves go. After that, the LORD spoke to Jeremiah. 9 The king had said that no Israelite, neither man nor woman, should be a slave. They must all be free people. 10 All the officers and the people who promised to do that agreed with the king. They would not continue to have male or female slaves. They made them free men and women. 11 But after that, they did not do what they had promised to do. They took the people back and they made them slaves again.

12 Then the LORD said to Jeremiah, 13 'The LORD, the God of Israel, says this: I made a covenant with your ancestors when I brought them out of Egypt. They were slaves when they were there. 14 I said that you must do something. Each 7th year you must let any of your Jewish brothers that you had bought become a free person. After he has worked for you for 6 years, you must let him go. But your ancestors did not listen to me. They did not obey me. 15 A little time ago, you were sorry that you had not obeyed me. I had said that you must do a good thing. And you did it. Each man made his Jewish slaves free men and women. You even made a promise to me in my house, the temple. 16 But now you have turned back to your old ways. You have taken away my honour. You have said to your slaves, "You can go where you want to go." But now you have taken them back. You have caused free men and women again to become your slaves.

17 So the LORD says: You have not obeyed me. You have not let your slaves become free men and women. So now I will make you free, he says. I will make you free to die. Men will kill you with swords. You will not have enough to eat. And you will become ill and you will die. All the people in all the countries on the earth will hate you. 18 I will do this to the men who did not obey me. They will be like an animal that people offer to me. They will be like the young cow that they cut in half. They cut it in half so that they could walk between the pieces.'

19 'I will punish the leaders of Judah and Jerusalem. I will punish the king's officers, the priests and all the people in the country. I will punish all the people who promised that to me. They walked between the pieces of the young cow. 20 I will give to their enemies power over them. The enemies will kill them and I will give their dead bodies to the birds and wild animals for food.'

21 'I will give Zedekiah, king of Judah, and his officers to the enemies who want to kill them. The army of the king of Babylon has left you. But I will give to them power over Zedekiah and his officers. 22 I will tell their army that they must return to this city. They will fight and they will get power over it. And they will burn it down. And I will destroy the towns in Judah so that nobody can live there.'

Chapter 35

Rechab's descendants

1 The LORD spoke to Jeremiah in the time that Jehoiakim, son of Josiah, ruled Judah. He said, 2 'Go to Rechab's descendants and ask them to come to the temple. Take them into a little room at the side of the temple and give to them wine to drink.'

3 So I went to get all Rechab's descendants. They were Jaazaniah, son of Jeremiah, son of Habazziniah, and his relatives and all his sons. 4 I took them into a room in the LORD's house. It was the room of the sons of Hanan. He was the son of Igdaliah, the man of God. It was next to the officer's room, and that was over the door keeper's room. The keeper of the door was Maaseiah, son of Shallum. 5 Then I took some bowls of wine and some cups. I put them in front of the men from Rechab's descendants and I said, 'Drink some wine.'

6 They replied, 'We do not drink wine. Our ancestor Jonadab, son of Rechab, said to us, "You and your descendants must never drink wine. 7 And you must not build houses, or plant seed or vines. You must never have any of those things, but you must always live in tents. Then you will live for a long time while you move through the country." 8-9 We have obeyed all the rules that our ancestor Jonadab, son of Rechab, gave to us. We have never drunk wine. We have never built houses. And we have never planted seeds. And our wives and children have never done any of those things. 10 We have obeyed completely all our ancestor Jonadab's rules. 11 But, when Nebuchadnezzar king of Babylon came into this country, we came to Jerusalem. We said, "We must go to Jerusalem. We must save ourselves from the armies of Babylon and Aram." So we stayed in Jerusalem.'

12 Then the LORD said to Jeremiah, 13 'The great, powerful LORD, the God of Israel, says this: Go and speak to the people in Judah and in Jerusalem. Ask them to learn a lesson from the descendants of Rechab. 14 Jonadab, Rechab's son, said that his descendants must not drink wine. And they have always obeyed him. They have not drunk wine even to this day. They have always obeyed their ancestor's rules. But I have spoken to you again and again and you have not obeyed me. 15 I have sent my servants the prophets to you again and again, but you have not obeyed me. The prophets said, "Each of you must stop doing wrong things. You must change the things that you do. Start doing the things that are right. Do not be servants of other gods. Then you will live in the country that I have given to you and to your ancestors." But you did not think that this was important. You did not listen to me. 16 The descendants of Jonadab, Rechab's son, obeyed the rules that their ancestor gave to them. But these people have not obeyed me.

17 So the great and powerful LORD says, "Listen! I will send all the bad things that I told you about. I am sending them to all those people who live in Judah and in Jerusalem. I spoke to them, but they did not listen. I called to them but they did not answer." '

18 Then Jeremiah spoke to the descendants of Rechab. 'The great and powerful LORD, the God of Israel, says, "You have obeyed the rules of your ancestor Jonadab. You have done everything that he asked you to do." 19 So the great and powerful LORD, the God of Israel, says to you, "Jonadab, son of Rechab, will always have a male descendant to be my servant. This promise is for all time." '

Chapter 36

Jehoiakim burns the words that Jeremiah had written.

1 The LORD spoke to Jeremiah in the 4th year that Jehoiakim was king of Judah. He said, 2 'Write down all the words that I have spoken to you about Israel, Judah and the other countries. I began to speak to you when Josiah was king. Write everything that I have said from that time until now. 3 Perhaps the people of Israel will listen to my words. Perhaps they will hear about all the punishments that I will do. Then they may each turn away from the wrong things that they are doing. Then I will forgive those bad things and their sin.'

4 So Jeremiah asked Baruch, son of Neriah to come. While Jeremiah spoke all the LORD's words, Baruch wrote them down. He wrote them on a long dry piece of a sheep's skin. 5 Then Jeremiah said to Baruch, 'They will not let me go to the LORD's temple. 6 So you must go to the temple on a day when people choose not to eat. Read these words to the people. You wrote the LORD's words as I spoke them to you. Read them to all the people. Do that when they come from the towns in Judah. 7 Perhaps they will ask the LORD for help and they will stop doing wrong things. Perhaps they will stop because of the LORD's words. He has said that he will punish them. He will punish them because he is very angry with them.'

8 Baruch, son of Neriah, did everything that Jeremiah the prophet had said. He read out the words of the LORD in the LORD's temple. 9 The king said that he wanted the people to fast in the temple for one day. That was in the 9th month of the 5th year since he became king. He caused all the people to come from Jerusalem and from the towns in Judah. 10 Baruch stood in the room of Gemariah the secretary. He was the son of Shaphan. The room was in the yard by the temple's New Gate. There Baruch read the LORD's words to all the people. He read to them the words that Jeremiah had caused him to write.

11 Micaiah, son of Gemariah, heard all the words of the LORD that Baruch had read out. 12 Then he went to the secretary's room in the king's house. All the king's officers were sitting there. They included Elishama who was the secretary and Delaiah, son of Shaphan. Elnathan, Achbor's son, Gemariah, Shaphan's son and Zedekiah, Hananiah's son were also there. 13 Micaiah told everything that he had heard to them. He heard it when Baruch read to the people. 14 The officers sent Jehudi to speak to Baruch. (Jehudi's father was Nethaniah, the son of Shelemiah, the son of Cushi.) They said, 'Bring the piece of skin with the words that you read to the people. And come here.' So Baruch, Neriah's son, went to them and he took the skin with him. 15 'Please sit down and read it to us', they said. So Baruch read it to them.

16 They heard the words that Baruch had written. And they became afraid. They looked at each other and they said to Baruch, 'We must tell the king what these words say.' 17 They asked Baruch, 'How did you write these words? Did you write them down as Jeremiah spoke them to you?'

18 'Yes', said Baruch, 'he spoke the words and I wrote them in ink on this skin.'

19 'You and Jeremiah go and hide yourselves', the officers said to Baruch. 'Do not tell anyone where you are.'

20 The officers put the skin into Elishama's room. Elishama was the secretary. Then they went to the king, who was in the yard. They told him all that they had heard. 21 They told the king about the skin on which Baruch had written God's words. So, he sent Jehudi to fetch it. Jehudi brought the skin from the room of Elishama the secretary. Then he read the words to the king and to all the officers who there. 22 The king was in his winter rooms. A fire was burning because it was the 9th month. 23 Jehudi read a small part of the words that Baruch had written on the skin. Then the king took a knife and he cut off that part of the skin. He threw it into the fire. Soon he had burned all the skin in the fire. 24 Neither the king nor the officers who were with him were afraid. And they did not want to show that they were sorry. So they did not tear their clothes. 25 Elnathan, Delaiah and Gemariah asked the king not to burn the skin on which Baruch had written. But he would not listen to them. 26 Instead, the king told his son Jerahmeel that he should take Baruch the secretary and Jeremiah the prophet. Then Jerahmeel should put them in a prison. But the LORD had hidden them.

27 So the king burnt the piece of skin on which Baruch had written Jeremiah's words. After that, the LORD spoke to Jeremiah. 28 'Take another piece of skin', he said. 'Write on it all the words that were on the other skin. That was the skin that Jehoiakim king of Judah burned up.

29 Also say to the king, "You burned the skin. And you asked why I wrote such bad things about Judah. You did not believe that the king of Babylon would come to destroy this country. You did not think that he would take both men and animals away from it." 30 So the LORD says this about Jehoiakim, king of Judah: None of his descendants will become king of Judah. People will throw out his dead body. And the sun will burn it in the day and it will be cold at night. 31 His children and his servants have done bad things. I will punish them. I will do all the bad things that I promised to do. I will do them to your children and to the people in Jerusalem. I will punish them and the people in Judah for all the wrong things that they have done. I will do that because they have not listened to me.'

32 So Jeremiah took another piece of skin and he gave it to the secretary, Baruch, Neriah's son. Then Jeremiah spoke the words that had been on the first skin. King Jehoiakim had burnt the first skin in the fire. And Baruch wrote the words down with many other words that said the same things.

Chapter 37

Jeremiah in the prison

1 Nebuchadnezzar, king of Babylon would not let Coniah, son of Jehoiakim continue to be king of Judah. He chose Josiah's son Zedekiah to be the king of Judah instead. 2 Zedekiah did not listen to the words of the LORD that Jeremiah had told him about. And neither the king's servants nor the people of the country listened to the LORD's words.

3 But King Zedekiah sent a message to Jeremiah the prophet. He sent Jehucal, son of Shelemiah, with the priest Zephaniah, son of Maaseiah, to deliver this message. 'Please pray to the LORD our God for us.'

4 Jeremiah was a free man at this time. They had not yet put him into the prison. He could walk among the people.

5 The army of Pharaoh, king of Egypt, had marched out of Egypt. People told the soldiers from Babylon who were round Jerusalem about that. So they went away.

6 Then the LORD said to Jeremiah the prophet, 7 'Speak to the king of Judah, who sent you to ask for my help', he said. 'Say to him, "Pharaoh's army, which marched out to help you, will turn back. They will return to Egypt, their own country. 8 Then the soldiers from Babylon will return and they will attack this city. They will get power over it and they will burn it completely."

9 The LORD says, "Do not make a mistake. Do not think that the soldiers from Babylon will go away. They will not go away! 10 You might win the fight against the whole army that is attacking you. There might be only sick men in their tents after you had beaten them. But those sick men would still come and they would burn down this city." '

11 The army from Babylon had left Jerusalem because of Pharaoh's army. 12 So Jeremiah started to leave the city to go to the land of Benjamin. He wanted to visit his part of the country that was among his people. 13 When he came to the Benjamin gate of the city, Irijah, Shelemiah's son, stopped him. He was the captain of the soldiers at the gate. And he put Jeremiah into the prison. 'You are going to join the soldiers from Babylon!' he said. 14 'That is not true!' said Jeremiah. 'I am not going to join the soldiers from Babylon.' But Irijah would not listen to him. So he took Jeremiah, his prisoner, to the king's officers. 15 The officers were angry with Jeremiah. They hit him with a stick and they put him in the house of Jonathan the secretary. They had made Jonathan's house into a prison.

16 They put Jeremiah in a small room with a high ceiling. It was deep under the house. He stayed there for a long time. 17 Then King Zedekiah sent for him and he brought him to his house. When they were alone, the king asked him, 'Is there any message from the LORD?'

'Yes', Jeremiah replied, 'they will deliver you to the hands of the king of Babylon.'

18 Then Jeremiah spoke to King Zedekiah. 'I do not know what bad things I have done to you or to your officers. I do not know why you have put me into the prison. 19 Your prophets told you things that were not true. They said that the king of Babylon would not attack you or your country. 20 I want you to help me. Do not send me back to the house of Jonathan the secretary. If you do, I will die there.'

21 Then King Zedekiah told his officers to put Jeremiah into the yard of his house with his soldiers. He told them to give bread from the bakers to him until there was no more bread in the city. So Jeremiah stayed in the yard with the soldiers.

Chapter 38

Men put Jeremiah into a large hole where they had stored water.

1 Some men heard the things that Jeremiah was telling all the people. They were Pashhur's son Shephatiah, Shelemiah's son Jehucal and Malchijah's son Pashhur. 2 Jeremiah had told the people that the LORD had said, 'Any people who stay in this city will die. Soldiers or illness will kill them, or they will not have any food to eat. But those people who join the soldiers from Babylon will not die. They will live. 3 And the LORD says, "I will give this city to the soldiers from Babylon. Their king's army will get power over it." '

4 Then the officers spoke to the king. 'You should kill this man', they said. 'He is making the soldiers who remain in the city afraid. And the people are becoming afraid because of the things that he is saying to them. This man does not want to help these people. He wants to destroy them.'

5 'You can do what you want to do', King Zedekiah said. 'I cannot stop you.'

6 So they took Jeremiah. And they put him in a big hole in the yard where the soldiers were. Malchijah, the king's son had made the hole to store water. They tied a long piece of rope round Jeremiah and they held the end of it. Then they slowly dropped him into the deep hole. There was no water in the hole, but only wet ground. The ground pulled Jeremiah down.

7 Ebed-Melech was an officer in the king's house. He came from the country called Ethiopia. People told him that other people had put Jeremiah into the hole in the yard. 8 He went out of the king's house and he spoke to the king. The king was sitting in the Benjamin gate of the city. 9 'My master, the king', he said. 'these men have done very bad things to Jeremiah the prophet. They have put him in a deep hole. He will die there when there is no food in the city.'

10 Then the king told Ebed-Melech what he should do. 'Take 30 men with you', he said. 'And lift Jeremiah the prophet out of the hole before he dies.'

11 So Ebed-Melech took the men with him. He went to a room under the king's house and he found some old clothes and some pieces of cloth. He tied them to ropes. And he let them drop down into the hole where Jeremiah was. 12 'Put these clothes under your arms', he said. 'Then tie the ropes over them so that they will not hurt you.' Jeremiah did as Ebed-Melech had said. 13 Then they pulled Jeremiah out of the hole. And he stayed in the yard with the soldiers.

Zedekiah asks Jeremiah more questions.

14 Then King Zedekiah sent messengers to bring Jeremiah the prophet to see him. They brought him to the third gate of the LORD's temple. 'I will ask you something', the king said to Jeremiah. 'Do not hide anything from me.'

15 'If I give an answer to you, you may kill me', Jeremiah said to the king. 'I might tell you the things that you should do. But you would not listen to me.'

16 But King Zedekiah made a secret promise to Jeremiah. 'I believe that the LORD lives. So I will not kill you. And I will not give you to the men who are trying to kill you.'

17 Then Jeremiah spoke to Zedekiah. 'The great and powerful LORD, the God of Israel says this: "If you let the officers of the king of Babylon get power over your kingdom, you will not die. And they will not burn down this city. You and your family will live. 18 But you must let those officers get power over your kingdom. If you do not do that, I will cause much trouble for you. I will give this city to the soldiers from Babylon and they will burn it down. And they will make you their prisoner." '

19 'I am afraid of the Jews who have left to join the king of Babylon', King Zedekiah said to Jeremiah. 'Perhaps the soldiers from Babylon will give me to them, and they may hurt me.'

20 'They will not give you to those Jews', Jeremiah replied. 'Do as I tell you. That is how you can obey the LORD. Then your life will be good and you will not lose it. 21 But if you do not give power over your kingdom to the officers from Babylon, these things will happen: The LORD has shown them to me. 22 Your enemies will bring out all the women in the king of Judah's house. They will give them to the officers of the king of Babylon. Those women will say this to you:

"You have believed the words of your friends. But they have said to you things that are not true.

Your feet are stuck in the ground and your friends have left you alone."

23 The officers from Babylon will give all your wives and children to the soldiers from Babylon. You yourself will not get away. The king of Babylon will make you his prisoner and his soldiers will burn down this city.'

24 'Do not tell anyone what we have talked about', Zedekiah said to Jeremiah. 'If you do tell them, you might die. 25 My officers may come. And they may ask you what we talked about. They may want to kill you if you do not tell them. 26 So say, "I was asking the king not to send me back to Jonathan's house where I might die." '

27 All the officers did come to Jeremiah to ask about his meeting with the king. And he said everything that the king had told him to say. Nobody had heard what Jeremiah and the king had really said. So the officers did not ask him again.

28 And Jeremiah stayed in the yard where the soldiers were. He stayed there until the day when the soldiers from Babylon got power over Jerusalem.

Chapter 39

The soldiers from Babylon get power over Jerusalem.

1 This is how the soldiers of the king of Babylon got power over Jerusalem. After King Zedekiah had ruled Judah for eight years, Nebuchadnezzar marched to Jerusalem. His whole army went round the city to attack it. 2 And 10 years, 4 months and 9 days after Zedekiah had become king, soldiers from Babylon attacked Jerusalem. And they broke through the walls of the city. 3 Then the officers of the king of Babylon came into the city. And they sat in the Middle Gate. They were Nergal-Sar-Ezer, Samgar-Nebu, Sar-Sekim, an important officer and Nergal-Sar-Ezer, another important officer. There were also all the other officers of the king of Babylon. 4 Zedekiah, king of Judah, and all his soldiers ran away when they saw them. They left the city at night, through the king's garden. They left through the gate between the two walls. And then they ran towards the flat land called the Arabah.

5 But the soldiers from Babylon ran after them. And they caught them on the flat land near Jericho. They took Zedekiah to Nebuchadnezzar king of Babylon. He was at Riblah in the place called Hamath. 6 In that place, Nebuchadnezzar decided how he would punish Zedekiah. He caused the soldiers to kill all Zedekiah's sons. Zedekiah had to watch while they killed his sons. And Nebuchadnezzar killed all the important men from Judah. 7 Then the soldiers destroyed Zedekiah's eyes. Then they put metal rings round his legs and they tied them together. Then they took him to Babylon.

8 The soldiers from Babylon burned the king's house and the people's houses. They broke down the walls of Jerusalem. 9 Nebuzaradan, the captain of the king's own special soldiers, took away all the people who remained in Jerusalem. He took them as prisoners to Babylon with all the other people. With them, he took those who had joined the soldiers from Babylon. 10 But captain Nebuzaradan let some very poor people, who had nothing, remain in Judah. At that time he gave fields to them. Some of those fields had vines on them.

11 Nebuchadnezzar, king of Babylon, had told Nebuzaradan, captain of his own soldiers, about Jeremiah.12 'Take him and be good to him. Do not hurt him. And do anything that he asks you to do', he had said. 13So Nebuzaradan, an important officer called Nebushazban, Nergal-Sar-Ezer and all the other officers of the king of Babylon obeyed Nebuchadnezzar. 14 They sent for Jeremiah and they took him out of the yard. It was where Zedekiah's soldiers had put him. Then Gedaliah, who was Ahikam's son and Shaphan's grandson, took Jeremiah back to his own home. So Jeremiah stayed with his own people.

15 The LORD had spoken to Jeremiah while he was still a prisoner in the king's house. 16 'Go. And tell Ebed-Melech from Ethiopia, this', the LORD said to him. 'The great and powerful LORD of Israel says this: Now I will to do as I promised. I will destroy this city. I will not make it rich. You will see it when it happens. 17 But I will save you on that day. They will not give you to the people that you are afraid of. 18 I will save you and soldiers will not kill you. You believed that I could keep you safe. So I will keep you safe, says the LORD.'

Chapter 40

The soldiers from Babylon make Jeremiah free.

1 Nebuzaradan, captain of the king's special soldiers, found Jeremiah at Ramah. They had tied him up with all the prisoners from Jerusalem and Judah. Nebuzaradan caused the soldiers to let Jeremiah go free. Then the LORD spoke to Jeremiah. They were taking the prisoners to Babylon. 2 Nebuzaradan said to Jeremiah, 'The LORD your God promised that he would help me to destroy this place. 3 And now, your God has done that. He has done all that he promised. He did that because your people did not obey the LORD. That was their sin. 4 But today I am taking off the ropes that tie you up. You are a free man. You can come with me to Babylon if you want to do that. If you do come, I will help you. But you do not have to come with me. You can go to any part of the country that you like.' 5 But before Jeremiah left, Nebuzaradan said, 'Return to Gedaliah, who is Ahikam's son and Shaphan's grandson, and to the people. The king of Babylon has chosen Gedaliah to rule over the towns in Judah. Live with Gedaliah and all the people there. Or you can go to any other place that you want to go to.'

Then Nebuzaradan gave food and a gift to Jeremiah and he let him go. 6 So Jeremiah went to Gedaliah, Ahikam's son, at Mizpah. He stayed there with him and with the people who remained in Judah.

Some people kill Gedaliah.

7 Some Jewish army officers and soldiers were living in the fields in Judah. Somebody told them that the king of Babylon had chosen Gedaliah, Ahikam's son, as the ruler over the people. These people were the poorest men, women and children in the country. The soldiers from Babylon had not taken them to Babylon. 8 Some army officers and their men came to Gedaliah at Mizpah. They were Nethaniah's son Ishmael, and Johanan and Jonathan, who were Kareah's sons. They came with Seraiah, who was Tanhumeth's son. The sons of Ephai from Netophah came. And the son of Jaazaniah from Maachah and their men also came. 9 Gedaliah, Ahikam's son, saw that they were afraid. So he said, 'Do not be afraid to be servants to the soldiers from Babylon. Stay here and serve the king of Babylon. If you do that, good things will happen. 10 I myself will stay with you. I will speak on your behalf when the men from Babylon come. But you can take in the summer fruits and the food seeds and you can make wine and oil. Then you can store them in jars. And you can live in the towns that you have got power over.'

11 People told this news to the Jews in Moab, Ammon, Edom and all the other countries. People told them that the king of Babylon had let a few people remain in Judah. And they told them that he had chosen Gedaliah, son of Ahikam, son of Shaphan, as their ruler. 12 So all those Jews came back to Judah. They came to Gedaliah at Mizpah. They came from all the countries where they were hiding. And they took very much wine and summer fruit from the fields and they stored them.

13 Kareah's son Johanan and all the officers that were in the fields came to Gedaliah. 14 'You should know that Baalis, king of Ammon, has sent Ishmael, Nethaniah's son, to kill you', they said to him. But Gedaliah, son of Ahikam, did not believe them.

15 Johanan, son of Kareah, went to speak to Gedaliah secretly. 'Let me go and kill Ishmael, son of Nethaniah. And nobody will know about it', he said. 'We should not let him kill you. There are many Jews with you. If he kills you, all those Jews will run away to different places. Then the few people from Israel that remain will die.'

16 But Gedaliah, son of Ahikam, spoke to Johanan, son of Kareah. 'Do not do anything like that', he said. 'The things that you are saying about Ishmael are not true.'

Chapter 41

1 Ishmael, Nethaniah's son, came to Gedaliah, Ahikam's son, at Mizpah in the 7th month. Ishmael was a relative of the king and he had 10 men with him. He had been an officer of the king. They were all eating a meal together. 2 During the meal, Ishmael and his

10 men stood up and they killed Gedaliah, Ahikam's son. Ahikam was the son of Shaphan. They killed Gedaliah with their swords. They killed the man that the king of Babylon had chosen to rule the country. 3 Ishmael also killed the Jews who were with Gedaliah at Mizpah. And he killed the soldiers from Babylon who were there.

4-5 The day after Gedaliah died, 80 Jews came to the temple with grain and with nice oils. They came from Shechem, Shiloh and Samaria to offer them to the LORD. Nobody knew that Ishmael had killed Gedaliah. 6 Ishmael, son of Nethaniah, went out from Mizpah to meet them. He was crying while he went. 'Come to Gedaliah, son of Ahikam', he said, when he met them. 7 They came into the city. Then Nethaniah's son Ishmael and the men who were with him killed them. They threw their dead bodies into a hole in the ground. 8 But 10 men said, 'Do not kill us! We have wheat, barley, oil and honey that we have hidden in a field.' So he let them go and he did not kill them with the other men. 9 He had thrown Gedaliah's body into a hole that King Asa had dug. Asa had dug many holes to save himself from Baasha king of Israel. Ishmael, son of Nethaniah, filled this hole with dead bodies.

10 Ishmael caused all the other people who were in Mizpah to become his prisoners. He took the king's daughters and all the other people who remained there. Nebuzaradan, captain of the king's special soldiers, had said that Gedaliah, Ahikam's son, must rule over those people. Ishmael, Nethaniah's son, made them his prisoners. And he started to take them to the country called Ammon.

11 People told Johanan, Kareah's son, and the army officers with him about the bad things that Ishmael had done. 12 So they took all their men and they went to fight Ishmael, Nethaniah's son. They found him near the big pool in Gibeon.

13 All the people that were with Ishmael saw Johanan and the soldiers with him. They were happy when they saw them. 14 All the people that Ishmael had taken as prisoners at Mizpah left Ishmael. They went to join Johanan, son of Kareah. 15 But Ishmael, son of Nethaniah, ran away from Johanan. He and 8 men went to Ammon.

Johanan takes the people to Egypt.

16 Johanan, Kareah's son, and the officers with him took away the people who had come from Mizpah. They were the people that he had saved from Ishmael, son of Nethaniah. Ishmael had killed Gedaliah, son of Ahikam. These people were the soldiers, women, children and officers that Johanan brought from Gibeon. 17 These people went towards Egypt. They stopped at Geruth-Chimham on the way to Egypt. That is near Bethlehem. 18 They wanted to run away from the soldiers from Babylon. They were afraid because Ishmael, son of Nethaniah, had killed Gedaliah. And the king of Babylon had said that Gedaliah should rule Israel.

Chapter 42

1 Then all the army officers and the people went to speak to Jeremiah the prophet. They included Johanan, son of Kareah, Jezaniah, son of Hoshaiah, and other people. The important people went. And those who were not important also went. 2 'Please listen to us and pray for us', they said. 'Pray to the LORD your God for us who remain here. You can see that we are now only a few. But before now, we were many people. 3 Ask the LORD to tell us where we should go. Ask him what we should do.'

4 'I have heard you', Jeremiah the prophet replied. 'I will certainly pray to the LORD your God as you have asked me. I will tell everything that the LORD says to you. I will not hide anything from you.'

5 'We will do everything that the LORD has sent you to say to us. We want the LORD to punish us if we do not do that', they said to Jeremiah. 6 'We have asked you to pray to the LORD our God and we will obey him. We will obey him whether he tells us good things or bad things. We will obey him because we want good things to happen to us.'

7 Ten days after that, the LORD spoke to Jeremiah. 8 So Jeremiah brought Johanan, son of Kareah, and the soldiers and all the people together. He brought together all the people who were with him. He brought the important people and those who were not important. 9 'You sent me to the LORD, the God of Israel. He says this', he said to them.

10 'If you will stay in this country, I will build you up. I will plant you like a seed and you will grow. I will not pull you up and I will not kill you. I am sad about the way that I hurt you. That is why I will do this. 11 Do not be afraid of the king of Babylon. You are afraid of him now but do not be afraid of him', says the LORD. 'I am with you and I will save you from him. 12 I will be kind to him. So then he will be kind to you and he will give your country back to you.'

13 'But you may not obey the LORD your God. Or you may say, "We will not stay in this country." 14 You may say, "No, we will go to live in Egypt where we will not have to fight. And we will have enough food there." 15 Then listen to me, you few people from Judah who remain here. The great and powerful LORD, the God of Israel, says this. I will cause this to happen if you decide to live in Egypt: If you make it your home, 16 you will die there. The soldiers that you are afraid of will kill you. Or you will not have enough food. 17 But all the people who decide to go to make their home in Egypt will die there. Soldiers will kill some of them. I will cause other people to die because they become ill. And other people will die because they do not have any food. Nobody will save any of them from the trouble that I will send. 18 The great and powerful LORD, the God of Israel, says this: I was very angry with the people who lived in Jerusalem. In the same way, I will be very angry with you when you go to Egypt. People will hate you and they will shout bad things about you. They will say that you have done wrong things. You will never see this place again.

19 You people from Judah that are still here, I am speaking to you. The LORD has said what you must do. He has said, "Do not go to Egypt." 20 You made a bad mistake when you asked me to pray to the LORD for you. You said, "Tell us everything that he says. And then we will do it." 21 I told you today, but you still have not obeyed the LORD your God. You have not done anything that he sent me to tell you to do. 22 I will tell you something. You will die in the place where you want to live. Soldiers may kill you. Or you may die because you are ill. Or you will die because you do not have any food.'

Chapter 43

1 So Jeremiah finished telling the people all the words of the LORD their God. He told them everything that the LORD had sent him to tell them.

2 Then Hoshaiah's son Azariah and Kareah's son Johanan and some other men spoke to Jeremiah. All those men thought that they knew everything. They thought that they were better than other people. 'You are speaking lies!' they said to Jeremiah. 'The LORD our God has not sent you to say that we must not go to Egypt to live there. 3 But you are doing what Baruch, son of Neriah, wants. He is against us. He wants the soldiers from Babylon to kill us or to take us as prisoners to Babylon.'

4 So Johanan, son of Kareah, and all the officers in the army did not obey the LORD's message. They did not stay in Judah. 5 Instead, Johanan and the officers led the people away from Judah. These were the few people who had returned to Judah. They had come from all the countries where their enemies had sent them. 6 They took with them the men, women and children and the king's daughters. Nebuzaradan, the captain of Nebuchadnezzar's special soldiers, had let those people remain with Gedaliah. (Gedaliah was Ahikam's son and Shaphan's grandson.) And Nebuzaradan had let Jeremiah the prophet and Baruch, son of Neriah, remain there with them. 7 So they did not obey the LORD. They went into Egypt and they went as far as Tahpanhes.

8 The LORD spoke to Jeremiah in Tahpanhes. 'The king of Egypt's house is in Tahpanhes. 9 Choose some large stones while the Jews are watching you', he said. 'Take them and put them under the path to the king's house. 10 Then you must speak to the people. Say, "The strong, powerful LORD, the God of Israel, says this: I will send my servant, Nebuchadnezzar, king of Babylon, here. He will put his throne here, over these stones that I have hidden. He will make his king's tent over him. 11 He will come and he will attack Egypt. He will kill those people that I have chosen to die. He will take as prisoners those that I choose to be prisoners. His soldiers will kill those people that I choose to die in that way. 12 He will use fire when he attacks the temples of the gods of Egypt. He will burn them and he will take away their gods. He will do what he wants with Egypt. Nobody will stop him. 13 He will break down the places where the people in Egypt worship in the temple of the sun. And he will burn down the temples of the gods there." '

Chapter 44

God will judge his people.

1 The LORD spoke to Jeremiah. He spoke about the Jews who lived in Egypt. They lived in Migdol, Tahpanhes and Memphis and in other places. He said,

2 'The great and powerful LORD, the God of Israel, says, "You saw the great trouble that I caused to Jerusalem and to all the towns in Judah. Your enemies have broken them down and nobody lives there now. 3 That is because of the evil things that the people did there. They made me angry because they made nice smells to give pleasure to other gods. And they worshipped those gods. Neither they nor their ancestors knew those gods. 4 Again and again I sent my servants the prophets to them. They gave my message to them. 'Do not do this bad thing that I hate!' they said. 5 But the people did not listen to my words and they did not obey me. They did not stop doing wrong things. And they did not stop making nice smells to give pleasure to other gods. 6 So I became very angry. I punished the towns in Judah and the streets in Jerusalem. I destroyed them. And I broke those places down as you can see today.

7 Now the great and powerful LORD, the God of Israel, says, 'You are causing more trouble for yourselves. You are taking all the men, women, children and babies out of Judah. You have not let anybody stay in Israel. 8 You are making me very angry by the things that you have made with your hands. You are making nice smells to give pleasure to the gods of Egypt where you have come to live. Those things will destroy your nation. You will become a nation that all other nations hate. They will think that you do not have any value. 9 You must remember the evil things that your ancestors did. The kings and queens of Judah and you and your wives also did many wrong things. You did evil things in Jerusalem and in all Judah. 10Even now your people have not become sorry. They have not agreed that they have done wrong things. They have not given any honour to me. They have not obeyed the rules that I gave to them and to their ancestors.' "

11 So the great and powerful LORD, the God of Israel, says, "I will certainly give much trouble to you and I will destroy all Judah. 12 I will take away the few Jews who decided to come to Egypt. They will all die there. Soldiers will kill them. Or they will die because they do not have any food to eat. Other people will hate them and they will make them ashamed. They will say how bad the Jews are. They will tell them that they have done wrong things. 13 I will punish those people in Egypt. I will use soldiers with swords. Or I might make them ill. Or I will not give any food to them so then they will die. I will punish them, as I punished the people in Jerusalem. 14 None of the few people from Judah who went to live in Egypt will return. They want very much to return to Judah. But not one Jew will be able to leave Egypt, except for a very small group who will run away." '

15 A large crowd came together from all the places in Egypt where they lived. The men knew that their wives were burning nice smelling oils to other gods. And there were many women with them. They spoke to Jeremiah. 16 'You have said that the LORD has given a message to you. But we will not listen to you', they said. 17 'We will certainly do everything that we want to do. We will make nice smells for the Queen of Heaven and we will offer drinks to her. We will do what our ancestors did. We and our kings and our officers did this in Jerusalem and in all the towns in Judah. We had plenty of food then. We were rich and we did not have any troubles. 18 But since we stopped offering those things to the Queen of Heaven we have not had anything. Some of us have died because they did not have any food. And soldiers have killed other people.'

19 The women spoke. 'Our husbands knew that we were burning oils to make nice smells to the Queen of Heaven. And we made cakes in her shape and we offered wine to her, too', they said.

20 Then Jeremiah spoke to all the men and to all the women who had answered him. 21 'The LORD knew about the things that you and your ancestors, your kings and officers and all the people did. He knew that you burned those oils with nice smells in the towns in Judah. He knew that you burned them in the streets in Jerusalem', he said. 22 'He saw the things that you were doing. So he made your country empty and he did not let anything grow there. The LORD saw the bad things that you were doing. So he made the country a place where nobody wanted to live. He caused it to become empty and now nobody lives there.23 The LORD did that because of the wrong things that you were doing. He would not let you continue to do them. You burned the nice oils. You did not obey his rules. And you did not do any of the things that he wanted you to do. So he has caused these bad things that you see.'

24 'Hear the LORD's word, all you people from Judah who are in Egypt', Jeremiah said. 'I am speaking to the men and to the women. 25 The great and powerful LORD, the God of Israel, says this: You and your wives have certainly done as you promised. You said, "We will do the things that we have said. We will burn nice smelling oils and we will offer drink to the Queen of Heaven." So go. And do what you promised to do!

26 But listen to the words that the LORD has to say to all you Jews in Egypt:

"I am promising something to you. I will do this as certainly as I am alive", says the LORD. "Nobody from Judah who lives in Egypt will again be able to say, 'As certainly as the LORD, the ruler, lives.' 27 I will not help the Jews in Egypt. I will kill all those Jews. They will die because they do not have any food. Or soldiers will kill them. 28 Only a few of those people that they do not kill will leave Egypt to return to Judah. Then all the Jews who came to live in Egypt will know this. They will know that my word and not theirs is true."

29 "I will punish you in this place", says the LORD. "I will tell you something that will happen soon. Then you will know that my promise to destroy you is a true promise." 30 The LORD says, "I will deliver Hophra king of Egypt to his enemies. They want to kill him. I will do that in the same way that I delivered Zedekiah king of Judah to Nebuchadnezzar king of Babylon. Nebuchadnezzar wanted to kill Zedekiah." '

Chapter 45

God's message to Baruch

1 Baruch wrote down on a scroll the words that I gave to him. That was in the 4th year that Jehoiakim, Josiah's son, was king of Judah. Then I told him 2 these words that the LORD the God of Israel had said to me: 'Baruch, 3 you said, "I am not a happy man! I have pain and now the LORD has made me sad too. I am so sad that it has made me feel very tired. And there is no rest for me." '

4 Then the LORD asked me to say this to Baruch. 'But I, the LORD, am pushing down the things that I have built. And I am pulling up the things that I have planted. I will do that to all the country. 5 You may want to be very important. Do not want that. I will punish all men and women. But in any place that you go to, I will let you keep your life safe.'

Chapter 46

God tells Jeremiah about the things that he will do to Egypt.

1 The LORD told Jeremiah the prophet about the things that he will do to the people in many countries.

2 This is the message against the army of King Neco of Egypt. Nebuchadnezzar, Babylon's king, fought with them at Carchemish on the River Euphrates.

Nebuchadnezzar won that fight in the 4th year after Josiah's son Jehoiakim became king of Judah.

3 'Get ready to march to the fight!

Prepare your shields, whether you are important or not.

4 Make the horses ready to obey you.

Stand ready with hard hats on your heads.

Make sharp the knives that you throw.

Put on strong clothes of leather and metal.

5 I see that the army are afraid.

They are running away.

Their soldiers have not won the fight.

They are running away fast.

They do not look behind them.

Everything round them makes them afraid',

says the LORD.

6 But they cannot run as fast as they need to run.

The strong men cannot run away.

They are falling by the River Euphrates.

In the north, they fall down.

7 A country is rising up.

It rises like the great waters of the River Nile.

8 Egypt is rising like the River Nile,

like rivers of fast waters.

Egypt says, 'I will rise up and I will cover the earth.

I will destroy cities and I will kill their people.'

9 The horses run fast.

Men in their chariots cause them to go faster.

The soldiers continue to march.

Men from Ethiopia and Put are carrying their shields.

Men from the people called Lydians are bringing their bows.

10 But that day is a day when the LORD, the great powerful LORD will punish his enemies.

He is angry with his enemies and he will punish them.

His soldiers will kill with their swords.

They will kill many people.

They will be like a hungry man. He eats until he is not still hungry.

The LORD, the great and powerful LORD, will offer up the dead people.

He will offer them in a place in the north by the River Euphrates.

11 Go to Gilead to get medicine to make you well.

Go, you young women in Egypt.

But many medicines will not make you better.

Nothing will make you well.

12 All countries will see that you are ashamed.

All the people on earth will hear you when you cry.

Two soldiers will knock against each other.

They will fall down together.

13 This is the message that the LORD spoke to Jeremiah the prophet about Nebuchadnezzar. He, the king of Babylon, would come to attack Egypt.

14 'Tell this to the people in Egypt and shout it in Migdol.

And tell it to the people in Memphis and in Tahpanhes.

"Get ready to fight because they are killing all the people round you."

15 Enemies will knock down your soldiers.

They cannot stand because the LORD will push them down.

16 They will go on falling.

They will fall over each other.

They will say, "Get up. Let us return to our own people and to our own country.

We want to run from these fights and from our enemies."

17 When they get back they will shout,

"The king of Egypt is weak. He is like a loud noise.

He is too late to win the fight." '

18 The King, the great and powerful LORD says,

'I am giving a promise to you. Someone will come who will be great.

He will be as great among men as Tabor and Carmel are great among the mountains.

19 You people who live in Egypt, pack your things ready to go to a far country.

They will destroy Memphis. Its buildings will lie in pieces and nobody will live there.

20 Egypt is like a good cow that a fly from the north is coming to hurt.

21 Egypt has bought soldiers. But they are like animals that men are ready to kill.

They will run away together. They will not stand and fight.

Now the day is coming when the LORD will kill those soldiers.

22 Egypt's people will run from the enemy when many men come near to attack it.

They will attack it with axes.

They will be like men who cut down trees,

23 to destroy thick forests', says the LORD.

'There are too many enemies to count.

They are like many insects that seem like a great cloud.

24 They will make the people in Egypt ashamed.

The people from the north will make them their prisoners.'

25 'Now I will punish Amon, god of Thebes. And I will punish Pharaoh, the king of Egypt. And I will punish their other gods and kings, and the people that they rule. 26 I will give them to those who want to kill them. Nebuchadnezzar king of Babylon and his officers will take them', says the great and powerful LORD. 'But in later years, people will again live in Egypt as they did before', he says.

27 'Do not be afraid, my servant Jacob. Do not be afraid of trouble, Israel.

I will certainly bring you from a far country.

I will save your children from the places where they went as prisoners.

Jacob (Israel) will again have peace and he will be safe.

Then nobody will make him afraid.

28 Do not be afraid, Jacob my servant,

because I am with you', says the LORD.

'I may completely destroy all the countries where I send you.

But I will never completely destroy you.

I will be fair when I punish you. But I certainly will punish you.'

Chapter 47

The LORD tells Jeremiah about the things that he will do to the Philistines.

1 The LORD told this to Jeremiah the prophet before Pharaoh, king of Egypt, attacked Gaza. He spoke about the Philistines.

2 The great and powerful LORD, the God of Israel says,

'See how the armies in the north are rising like water.

I will make them as strong as a great fast river.

They will cover the country and everything in it.

They will cover the towns and the people who live in them.

The people will shout. All the people who live in the country will cry.

3 They will cry when they hear the sound of horses

and the noise of their enemies' war chariots.

They will hear them when they are coming.

Fathers will not turn to help their children.

Their hands will not move.

4 This is the day when God will kill all the Philistines.

He will not let anybody live to help Tyre and Sidon.

The LORD will soon remove the Philistines.

He will remove those who remain by the sea. He will remove them from the country called Caphtor.

5 The people in Gaza will be very sad.

No voice will speak in Ashkelon.

Stop cutting yourselves, you who live near the sea!'

6 'You shout to the LORD, "Your sword is attacking.

We want it to stop!

Put it back in its bag and make it still."

7 But it cannot rest because the LORD has caused his sword to do this.

He has caused it to attack Ashkelon and the country by the sea.'

Chapter 48

A message about Moab

1 The great and powerful LORD, the God of Israel says,

'I will cause the people in Nebo city to cry, because I will destroy it.

The people in Kiriathaim city will be ashamed and its enemies will get power over it.

They will break its strong buildings, and its people will be ashamed.

2 Nobody will again say good things about Moab.

In Heshbon, men will think about how they can destroy Moab.

They will say, "Let us completely destroy that nation."

And the town called Madmen will become completely quiet.

3 You will hear sad voices from Horonaim.

Its people will be afraid. And they will cry while enemies destroy it.

4 The LORD will break the country called Moab.

The children who live there will cry.

5 They will go to Luhith. And they will cry while they walk.

They will go towards Horonaim. And they will cry while enemies destroy their cities.

6 Go! Run away to save your lives!

Live like bushes in the empty country where no people live.

7 You thought that your rich things would save you.

But your enemies will take you away too.

The people and the god Chemosh will go to a foreign country

together with their priests and their officers.

8 The enemy's armies will attack every town.

They will not save one town.

They will destroy the valley and the flat country.

The LORD has spoken.

9 They will put salt on Moab's country so that nothing will grow there.

Nobody will live in their towns. They will be empty.

10 The LORD will punish any man who will not do God's work!

He will punish anyone who does not kill with his sword!

11 Moab's people have had peace since they became a nation.

They have been like wine that rests in a cupboard.

Nobody has ever taken them away to a foreign country.

So it is the same as it always was.'

12 'But the time will come', says the LORD,

'when I will send men to it.

They will pour out Moab's people like wine. They will empty Moab like wine jars.

They will break the jars completely.

13 Then the people from Moab will be ashamed of Chemosh.

They will be like the people in Israel who worshipped the god at Bethel.

Those people became ashamed when they did that.

14 You should not say, "We are soldiers who are strong in a fight."

15 I will destroy Moab. Enemies will get power over its towns.

They will kill the best of its young men.'

The King, the great and powerful LORD says,

16 'Moab will fall very soon.

Enemies will destroy it quickly.

17 The people who live round it must be sorry for it.

They all knew how great it had been.

They will say, "Moab's great kingdom is broken.

Their king is not still ruling there!"

18 You people who live round Dibon, sit on the ground.

Come from your beautiful houses and sit in the dirt.

The enemy who is destroying Moab will come to attack you.

He will break down your cities that have walls round them.

19 Stand by the road, you people who live in Aroer. And watch.

You will see men and women who are running away.

Ask them, "Why are you running away from the city?"

20 Moab is ashamed because enemies have broken it.

Shout!

Tell the people by the River Arnon that enemies have destroyed Moab.

21 The LORD has judged the cities on the flat country.

He has judged Holon, Jahzah and Mephaath,

22 and Dibon, Nebo and Beth-Diblathaim.

23 Tell Kiriathaim, Beth-Gamul and Beth-Meon,

24 Kerioth and Bozrah that he has judged them.

Tell the people in all the towns in Moab, near or far away.

25 Moab does not have any power now.

Their enemies have destroyed the things that made them strong',

says the LORD.

26 'Moab has not obeyed the LORD. So make it like a woman who is drunk.

She will be sick and she will sit in her own dirt.

People will point at Moab. They will not give any honour to their people.

27 You said things that were not kind about Israel.

You said that they did not have any value.

You did not find Israel's people when they were with many robbers.

So you do not have any good reason to speak like that about them.

28 You people in Moab,

leave your towns and go to live among the rocks.

Live like a bird that builds its house by a hole in the hill.

29 We have heard about the people in Moab.

They think that they are better than anyone else.

They think that other people are like dirt.

They think that nobody is good enough to speak to them.

30 I know about Moab's thoughts.

They think that Israel does not have any value.

But their thoughts do not have any value', says the LORD.

'The loud words that they say will not help them.

31 So I am sad for Moab. I am crying for all their people.

I am sorry for the men in Kir-Heres.

32 I am weeping for your vines of Sibmah.

They reach as far as the sea.

Their branches reach to the sea called Jazer.

The enemy is destroying their fruit and their grapes.

33 The fruit farms and the fields of Moab are empty.

They make people sad.

They are not happy

because I have stopped them making wine.

They are not singing now and they are not happy now.

34 They are crying with a loud voice.

The noise rises from Heshbon to Elealeh and Jahaz.

It reaches from Zoar to Horonaim and Eglath-Shelishiyah.

Even the River Nimrim has become dry.

35 'The people in Moab worship other gods.

They offer food to them on the high places.

They burn nice smelling oils to their gods.

I will cause them to stop that', says the LORD.

36 'So I am very, very sad for the people in Moab.

I will sing a sad song.

It is a song for the men in Kir-Heres

because they have lost their valuable things.

37 All the men have cut off the hair from their heads and faces.

They have cut their hands.

And they are wearing hard material.

38 On all the roofs and in the streets,

the people are sad and they are crying.

They are sad because I have broken Moab.

I have broken it like a jar that I do not want',

says the LORD.

39 'I have really broken Moab. So its people cry with loud voices.

They are ashamed and they turn away.

People look at Moab's troubles. They do not give any honour to its people.

All who live near there are afraid to look at Moab.'

40 The LORD says,

'Look! A big bird is flying down.

Its wings are open while it flies over Moab.'

41 'An enemy will win the fight for Kerioth

and he will get power over its strong buildings.

Then Moab's soldiers will be afraid.

They will be afraid like a woman who is having a baby.

42 The LORD will destroy the nation of Moab

because they have not obeyed him.

43 He will catch their people and he will punish them.

And they will be very afraid', says the LORD.

44 'People who run from dangerous things will fall into holes.

They will fall into holes that their enemies have dug.

And the enemy will catch those who climb out of the holes.

That will happen because now I will punish Moab', says the LORD.

45 'Those people who tried to run away will stand near to Heshbon.

Nobody will help them.

I have been like a fire that is coming from Heshbon.

It is like a fire from the centre of Sihon.

It burns the faces of Moab's people.

And it burns the heads of the drunks who make a lot of noise.

46 Cry, you people in Moab!

I have destroyed the people of Chemosh.

The enemy has taken your sons to a far country.

They have taken your daughters to become slaves.

47 But one day I will cause Moab to become a nation again.'

That is what the LORD says.

That is what the LORD says as the judge of Moab.

Chapter 49

A message about Ammon

1 The LORD says,

'You have let Molech rule the people from Gad.

Your sons have not sent him away.

His people live in the country that I gave to Gad.'

2 'But at a future time, I will call my people to fight', says the LORD.

'They will fight against Rabbah, that city in Ammon.

They will pull it down to become a lot of stones.

And they will burn the villages round it with fire.

Then Israel's people will push out the people who pushed them out', says the LORD.

3 'Cry, you people in Heshbon, because they have destroyed Ai.

Cry aloud, you people who live in Rabbah.

You wear hard material when a friend has died.

Put on those clothes now and be very sad.

You do not know what to do. So you will run about.

Enemies will take the people from Moab to a far country.

They will take them with their priests and their officers.

4 You say to everyone that your valleys are full of fruit.

You are like a daughter that does not obey me.

You think that your valuable things will save you from your enemies.

5 But I will make you afraid of all the people who live round you',

says the great and powerful LORD.

'Enemies will push everyone away from his home.

Nobody will save those people who are running away.

6 But, after this, I will bring back Ammon's people', says the LORD.

A message about Edom

7 The great and powerful LORD says this about Edom:

'The men from Teman do not have any more clever thoughts.

Their great ideas have left them.

8 You people in Dedan, turn and run away. Hide in deep holes.

I will punish Esau's descendants and I will cause a lot of trouble for them.

9 I will not be like men who pick fruits. They let a few fruits remain behind.

And I will not be like a robber who takes only a few things.

10 No, I will take everything and Esau's country will be empty.

I will show enemies where Esau's descendants hide. And they will find Esau's descendants.

They will kill all their children, family and friends.

And they will die.

11 Leave those who do not have living fathers. Then I will save them.

And widows will be safe with me.'

12 The LORD says, 'Not all the people that I have punished were bad. So I must certainly punish you people who are bad. 13 I will do that as certainly as the fact that I am LORD. Enemies will destroy Bozrah. People will see that enemies have broken it down. And they will be afraid. They will point to it. And they will say how bad it was. All its villages will be heaps of stones for all time.'

14 I have heard a message from the LORD. He has sent his messenger to the nations. He says, 'Get ready to attack Edom. Prepare to fight!'

15 'The LORD will make you (Edom) weak and nobody will honour you.

16 You made people afraid. So you thought that you were great and strong.

But your thoughts were wrong.

You may hide in small holes in the rock or high up on the hill.

Even if you live as high as the homes of great birds, I will bring you down.'

Those are the words of the LORD.

17 'Edom will change so much that people will not want to look at it.

Those who walk past will say bad things about it.

They will turn away from it because its enemies have destroyed it completely.

18 Nobody will live there, not one man.

It will be like Sodom and Gomorrah

when men destroyed them and the towns near them',

says the LORD.

19 'I will be like a lion that comes into green fields.

I will come like a lion out of the trees by the River Jordan.

I will push Edom's people quickly out of their country.

The leader that I choose will rule the people.

Nobody is like me. Nobody can say that they are as great as me.'

20 So listen to the things that the LORD will do to Edom.

Listen to the things that he will do to the people in Teman.

Your people will be like sheep. He will take away their young sheep.

He will completely destroy their country

because they do not obey him.

21 The whole earth will move with the noise when they fall.

They will cry by seas that are far away.

People will hear them when they cry.

22 God will make the men who fight in Bozrah afraid.

They will feel like an animal that sees a big bird. The bird is flying to catch it.

They will be afraid like a woman who will soon have a child.

A message about Damascus

23 The LORD says about Damascus,

'People have brought bad news to the people who live in Hamath and in Arpad.

They are afraid. Their minds are full of trouble.

Their thoughts move like the waters of the sea.

24 Damascus has become weak.

Its people want to run away.

They are so afraid that they feel pain.

Their pain is like the pain of a woman who is having a baby.

25 They have not left their famous city,

a city that gives pleasure to me.

26 The young men in it will die in its streets.

Then enemies will kill all its soldiers', says the great and powerful LORD.

27 'I will burn the walls of Damascus.

Fire will burn up the strong places of Ben-Hadad.'

A message about Kedar and Hazor

28 Nebuchadnezzar king of Babylon had attacked Kedar and the kingdoms of Hazor. The LORD said about them,

'Get up and attack Kedar.

And take all their valuable things from the people in the East.

29 Enemies will take their tents and their animals.

They will take their homes and all their things and their camels.

Men will shout at them, "Everything round you makes you afraid.

30 Run away as fast as you can!

You people in Hazor, hide in deep holes in the ground" ', says the LORD.

'Nebuchadnezzar king of Babylon has decided to attack you.

He wants to get power over your country.

31 They think that they are safe. But he will attack them', says the LORD.

'The nation is comfortable. It does not have any gates. Its people live alone.

32 His soldiers will take their camels.

And they will lead away their animals.

I will send people who live far away to places all over the earth.

33 Only wild animals will live in Hazor.

It will always be a place where no people live.'

A message about Elam

34 The LORD spoke to Jeremiah the prophet soon after Zedekiah became king of Judah. He spoke about Elam. 35 The great and powerful LORD said,

'I will destroy the weapons of Elam that make them strong.

36 I will bring against them the winds from every direction.

The wind will push them to the far places of the earth.

Some people from Elam will run to every nation.

37 Their enemies want to kill them.

They will run away from those who attack them.

I am very angry with them and I will cause much trouble to them',

says the LORD.

'I will send enemies to run after them with swords

until they are all dead.

38 I will become the ruler of Elam.

And I will kill their king and his officers', says the LORD.

39 'But at a time that is still future,

I will make Elam a nation again', says the LORD.

Chapter 50

A message about Babylon

1 The LORD spoke about the people in Babylon and about their country. He spoke by the prophet Jeremiah. He said,

2 'Tell this to the nations. Shout it out to the countries.

Write it on a large piece of material and lift it up.

Do not hide anything but say,

"Enemies will get power over Babylon.

Bel will be ashamed and Marduk will be afraid.

All the gods that they have made with their hands will be ashamed." '

3 'A nation from the north will attack Babylon and they will destroy that country.

Nobody will live in it. Men and animals will run away.'

4 'When that happens', the LORD says,

'The people from Judah and from Israel will be sorry.

They will cry while they go to find the LORD their God.

5 They will ask for the way to Zion. And they will go towards it.

They will return and they will promise to be the LORD's servants.

They will make a covenant that will be for all time.

Nobody will forget that covenant.

6 My people have been like sheep that are lost.

Those who should have led them to me have led them away.

They have been walking on the mountains and hills.

They have walked about and they have forgotten their place to rest.

7 Anyone who found them killed them.

Their enemies said, "They have caused this trouble to themselves.

They did many wrong things.

They did not obey the LORD who was really their leader.

He was the leader that their ancestors followed. They trusted him."

8-9 I will wake up the people in many nations. I will bring many great nations together from the country in the north. They will get ready to fight against Babylon.

They will come against Babylon from the north. And they will take its people away to be prisoners.

Their arrows will kill many people.

So run away from Babylon. Leave the country called Babylon.

Be the first people to leave Babylon.

10 Enemies will take all the things that they want from Babylon.

Every enemy will have enough things', says the LORD.

11 'Listen, you people who take away my things.

You are so happy that you dance like young cows.

You shout aloud like a horse that wants sex.

12 Your country will be like a mother who is very ashamed.

Her child does not bring honour to the woman who gave life to him.

Your people will be less important than other nations.

Your country will be a desert, dry and empty.

13 Nobody will live there because the LORD is angry with you.

Your country will be completely empty.

All who pass Babylon will be very afraid.

And they will say all kinds of bad things about it when they see its troubles.

14 All you men who can shoot arrows with a bow,

stand round Babylon.

Shoot at it! Use all your arrows.

Shoot because its people have done bad things against the LORD.

15 Shoot at them from all sides.

Its people will let you get power over it. Its strong buildings will fall.

You will pull down its walls.

That is how the LORD will punish them. You will punish them.

You must do to them what they have done to other people.

16 Do not let anyone remain in Babylon to work on the land.

And do not let anyone remain to get food from the fields at the proper time.

All the foreign workers will return to their own nation because they are afraid of the attacking enemies.

All those workers will run away to their own country.

17 Israel is like a group of sheep that have all run to different places.

They ran away because lions ran after them.

The first to eat them was the king of Assyria.

The man who finished the meal was Nebuchadnezzar, king of Babylon.'

18 So the great and powerful LORD, the God of Israel says,

'I will punish the king of Babylon and his country

as I punished the king of Assyria.

19 But I will bring Israel back to their own country.

And their cows will feed on Carmel and in Bashan.

They will eat and they will be full on the hills of Ephraim and Gilead.

20 At that time', says the LORD,

'I will forgive the people in Israel and Judah that remain.

Nobody will find any sin in Israel.

There will not be any sin in Judah or in Israel.'

21 'Attack the place called Merathaim. And attack the people who live in Pekod.

Run after them and kill all those people', says the LORD.

'Do everything that I have asked you to do.

22 There is a noise of fights in the country.

It is like the noise when enemies are destroying everything.

23 Babylon was like a hammer to the whole earth.

But now enemies have broken it into small pieces.

It is now alone among the nations.

24 I meant to catch you, Babylon, but you did not know.

And now I have caught you!

Your enemies found you and they got power over you. They got power over you because you did not obey the LORD.

25 The LORD is angry.

He has taken out the weapons from where he had stored them.

The great and powerful LORD has work to do in the country called Babylon.

26 He will send people against Babylon from far places.

They will break open the places where people had put their food.

503

They will break its buildings into pieces.

They will destroy it completely. Nothing will still be there.

27 They will kill all its young male cows.

They will be sorry. They will all die. It is time for me to punish them.'

28 'People have run away from Babylon to Zion.

They will tell how the LORD has punished Babylon.

The LORD has punished Babylon because Babylon destroyed the LORD's temple.

29 Bring the men with bows and arrows against Babylon.

They will stay all round it so that nobody will be able to run away.

You must punish it for all the bad things that its people have done.

Do to them as they did to you.

Do that because they proudly refused to obey the LORD, the holy God of Israel.

30 So, on that day, their young men will die in their streets.

Then none of their soldiers will be able to fight', says the LORD.

31 'You think that you are very important.

But you will see that I am against you', says the great and powerful LORD.

'That is because the day for your punishment has come.

32 Your proud people will trip and they will fall.

And nobody will help them to get up.

I will make a fire in your towns to burn up all who are near to it.'

33 The great and powerful LORD says,

'You have been cruel to the people from Israel and Judah.

You have taken them as prisoners,

and you will not let them go.

34 But the powerful LORD is great and strong.

He will come to redeem them.

He will fight hard to save them.

Then their country will have rest.

But Babylon's people will not have any rest.'

35 'I am sending an army against Babylon', says the LORD.

'I am against those who live in Babylon.

And I am against its officers and its clever men.

36 I am against its false prophets.

I will cause them to become fools.

My sword will make its soldiers afraid.

37 My army will attack its horses and its chariots

and foreign men who fight for it.

They will be as weak as women.

I will cause them to give their valuable things to you.

You will take them away.

38 I will not send any rain and so its wet places will become dry places.

Their country is full of idols.

Their false gods will be afraid.

39 Wild animals, including wild dogs, will live there.

Birds that fly at night will live there, too.

Men will never live there again.

Nobody's sons or grandsons will live there.

40 God destroyed Sodom and Gomorrah

and the towns near to them', says the LORD.

'Babylon will be like those towns,

so nobody will live there, not one man.

41 Look. You will see an army that is coming from the north.

A great nation and kings from all over the earth

are coming towards Babylon.

42 They have bows and knives that they throw.

They are cruel and they are not kind.

They make a noise like the moving sea while they ride on their horses.

They are an army that is ready to attack you, people in Babylon.

43 The king of Babylon has heard about them.

He is weak because he is afraid.

He feels pain like the pain of a woman who is having a baby.

44 I will be like a lion

that is coming out of the woods by the River Jordan.

I will come into your rich fields.

I will soon cause the people in Babylon to run from their country.

I will choose a man to do that, and nobody can stand against me.

Nobody can stop me.'

45 So now listen to the things that the LORD will do to Babylon.

Hear about the things that he will do to their country.

He will pull the young children away from their mothers.

And he will completely destroy their good country

because of the bad things that they have done.

46 All the people in the world will hear how your people got power over Babylon.

Then people will be afraid.

All the nations will hear when its people shout with pain.

Chapter 51

1 The LORD says,

'I will wake up those people who want to destroy Babylon and the people in Leb-Kamai.

2 I will send foreign armies to Babylon.

They will break it and they will destroy its country.

They will be all round it at that time.

3 Its men will not have time to shoot

or to pick up their weapons.

You will kill all its young men.

You will completely destroy its army.

4 Babylon's soldiers will lie dead in the streets.

5 The great, powerful LORD is with Israel and Judah.

They have done many wrong things.

And they have not obeyed him.

But he has not left them.

6 Run away from Babylon!

Run to save your lives!

My armies are coming to punish Babylon.

Do not let them hurt you.

The time has come to punish Babylon.

The LORD will punish them for the bad things that they have done.

7 Babylon was like a great cup of wine.

The LORD saw that the wine made the whole earth drunk.

The nations drank the wine and they became angry.

8 Babylon will fall quickly. Cry about it!

If you get medicine, perhaps you may make it well.

9 We would have made Babylon well if we could.

But nobody can make it well.

We will leave it and each person will go to his own country.

Its punishment is very great.

It is as great as how far the sky is from the earth.

10 The LORD has saved us.

We must tell the people in Zion

about the things that our God has done.

11 Get your arrows ready and prepare your weapons.

The LORD has caused the kings of Media to prepare for war.

He wants them to destroy Babylon.

The LORD will punish its people because they destroyed his temple.

12 Get ready to attack the walls of Babylon.

Watch. And be ready to catch those who try to run away.

The LORD will do as he has promised against Babylon's people.

13 It is the time for the end of their lives.

I speak to those rich people who live by the rivers of Babylon.

14 The LORD has given a serious promise that he will not change. He used his own name to promise this:

I will fill Babylon with men. They will come like a very big number of insects. And they will shout happily because they have beaten you.

15 The LORD used his power to make the earth.

He was so wise that he made it and the sky over it.

16 When he shouts, the waters in the sky make a loud noise.

He causes the clouds to rise from the ends of the earth.

He sends arrows of light with the rain.

And he causes the wind to blow.

17 No man is really clever. Nobody knows anything.

Men who work with gold should be ashamed.

They make idols, but those are not gods. They are not alive.

18 Idols do not have any value. We do not give any honour to them.

The LORD will judge them and he will destroy them.

19 The God of Jacob is the God who made all things.

So he is not like the idols.

He chose Israel's people to be his own people.

His is called the great and powerful LORD.

20 You people are my weapons for war.

I use you to fight for me.

You will break the nations for me.

I will use you to destroy kingdoms.

21 With you I will break horses and those who ride on them.

With you I will break chariots and the men in them.

22 With you I will break men and women.

With you, I will break old men and young men.

With you, I will break young men and girls.

23 With you I will break sheep and the men with them.

With you, I will break farmers and their animals.

With you, I will break those in authority and their officers.

24 I will punish Babylon and all the people in it.

I will punish them for all the evil things that they did to Jerusalem.

You will see it with your own eyes', says the LORD.

25 'Babylon, you are like a mountain that destroys the whole earth',

says the LORD.

'I will put out my hands towards you and I will push you down.

I will burn you up.

26 Nobody will ever use any of your stones for a new building.

You will be like a desert for all time', the LORD says.

27 'Show to the people in the country that you are ready to fight.

You must make a noise with the trumpet so that all the nations can hear.

Cause the nations to prepare for war against Babylon.

Ask the armies of the kingdoms called Ararat, Minni and Ashkenaz to attack it.

They must choose their captain to lead them. They will have many horses.

Their horses will be like so many insects that they seem like a cloud.

28 Send messengers to the kings of Media

and to their officers and leaders.

Ask them to prepare for war against Babylon.

Cause them to bring armies from the places that they rule.

29 The LORD has decided to punish Babylon. He will not change.

The country is shaking because it is afraid.

The LORD will destroy Babylon and he will make it a desert.

Nobody will live there.

30 The strong men from Babylon have stopped fighting.

They are staying in their strong buildings.

They are very tired and they have become like women.

Soldiers are burning the city.

They have broken down its gates and they have burnt its houses.

31 One messenger follows another to the king of Babylon.

They all tell him that his enemies have got power over his city.

32 And they have got power over the places where men cross the rivers.

Enemies have made the country like a fire and the soldiers of Babylon are afraid.'

33 The great and powerful LORD, the God of Israel says this:

'Babylon is like the place where men walk on the grain to make the seeds separate from everything else.

It is time for men to walk over the city.

It will soon be time for men to take away the city's valuable things.'

34 'Nebuchadnezzar king of Babylon has destroyed us.

He has confused us. He has made us like an empty jar.

Like a snake, he has eaten us and he has filled himself with our good things.

Then he threw us away.'

35 That is what Zion's people will say. They will also say, 'We are asking the LORD to punish Nebuchadnezzar.

'We are asking him to do to Nebuchadnezzar all the bad things that he did to our people.'

'We ask him to punish Babylon's people because they killed our people', say Jerusalem's people.

36 So the LORD says,

'Watch. And see that I will fight for you. I will punish them.

I will cause its sea and its rivers to become dry.

37 I will make Babylon a hill of stones.

Wild animals will live there.

Men will hate the place and nobody will live there.

38 Its people may make a loud noise

like angry lions or like their young ones.

39 But even when they are shouting, I will prepare a feast for them.

I will cause them to get drunk. And so they will laugh.

They will sleep and they will never wake again', says the LORD.

40 'I will bring them down. They will be like sheep that people will soon kill.

They will be like sheep and goats and their young animals.

41 Enemies will get power over Sheshach (Babylon), the city that was the greatest city on the earth.

None of the nations will want to look at Babylon.

42 The sea will rise over it. Its water will cover it.

43 Its towns will be empty. Its land will be a dry desert.

Nobody will live there. Nobody will walk on its land.

44 I will punish Bel.

I will cause him to give back everything that he has taken.

Nations will never run to him again.

And the walls of Babylon will fall.

45 Come out of it, my people! Run away and save your lives!

Run away because the LORD is very angry with it.

46 You must not be afraid

when people say things to make you afraid.

They will tell stories this year and they will tell more stories next year.

They will tell stories about men who hurt each other badly.

They will say that rulers will fight each other.

47 Certainly the time will come

when I will punish the idols of Babylon.

Men will be ashamed of its whole country.

And its dead people will lie in its streets.

48 Then the earth and the sky and all the people in them will shout.

They will be so happy that they will shout. And they will dance.

They will be happy because people will come to destroy Babylon.

They will come from the north to attack it', says the LORD.

49 'Enemies must destroy Babylon because its people have killed many people in Israel.

People killed the people in Babylon as they caused many to die in all the earth.

50 You Jews who have not died must run away.

Do not wait for anything, but go quickly.

Remember the LORD. Think about Jerusalem, you who are far away.'

51 We are ashamed. They have taken away our honour.

We cannot look at people's faces.

We are ashamed because foreigners have gone into the holy places of the LORD's house.

52 'But the time will come', says the LORD,

'when I will punish Babylon's idols.

And I will hurt many people all over that country.

They will cry with pain.

53 Babylon's people may build their city very high.

They may make its walls very strong.

But I will send men to destroy it', says the LORD.

54 'The sound of people who are shouting will come from Babylon.

It will be the noise of the country of Babylon as men destroy it.

55 The LORD will destroy Babylon. It will not continue to make any noise.

Enemies will come against it like a hill of waters.

Their voices will sound like the sea when it is moving like an angry person.

56 They will come against Babylon to destroy it.

They will take its soldiers and they will break their bows.

The LORD will be paying back those who have hurt his people.

He will give full punishment to them.

57 I will make its officers and its wise men drunk.

I will do that also to its rulers and to its soldiers.

They will sleep and they will never wake up', says the King.

He is the great and powerful LORD.

58 The great and powerful LORD says,

'They will knock down the thick walls of Babylon.

They will burn its high gates.

The nations run about and are tired. But they cannot do anything.

All the things that the nations do only make the fire worse.'

59 This is the message that Jeremiah gave to the officer Seraiah. He was the son of Neriah, the son of Mahseiah. Seraiah gave it when he went to Babylon with Zedekiah, Judah's king. It was in the 4th year of his rule. 60 Jeremiah had written his message on a piece of clean dry skin. He had written down all the punishment that the LORD would cause to happen to Babylon. 61 Jeremiah spoke to Seraiah. He said, 'When you reach Babylon, certainly read all these words aloud. 62 Then say, "LORD you have said that you will destroy this place. Then no man or animal will live in it. It will be empty for all time." 63 When you have finished reading all the words, tie a big stone to the skin. And throw the stone and the skin into the River Euphrates. 64 Then say, "Babylon will go down like that stone and it will never rise again. I will cause all these bad things. Its people will be too tired and too weak to do anything about it." '

That is the end of Jeremiah's words.

Chapter 52

Nebuchadnezzar gets power over Jerusalem.

1 Zedekiah was 21 years old when he became king. He ruled in Jerusalem for 11 years. His mother's name was Hamutal, daughter of Jeremiah. She came from Libnah.

2 Zedekiah did not obey the LORD. He did all the bad things that Jehoiakim had done. 3 The LORD was angry, so he caused these things to happen to Jerusalem and Judah. They became so bad that the LORD sent his people away. He did not want them to be near to him. The king of Babylon had told Zedekiah what he must do. But Zedekiah did not do it. 4 So Nebuchadnezzar, king of Babylon, and all his army marched against Jerusalem. That was when Zedekiah had been king for almost 9 years, on the 10th day of the 10th month. The army stayed outside the city. They built hills round it so that they could attack it from those hills. 5 The army stayed there until the 11th year of King Zedekiah.

6 By the 9th day of the 4th month there was no food in the city. The people had nothing to eat. 7 The soldiers from Babylon broke down part of the city's wall. The whole army of Judah ran away at night. They went out between the two walls near the king's garden. The soldiers from Babylon were still round the city. The Jews ran towards the flat land called the Arabah. 8 But the soldiers from Babylon ran after King Zedekiah. They caught him near Jericho. All his soldiers ran different ways 9 and the enemy caught Zedekiah.

They took him to the king of Babylon. Nebuchadnezzar the king was at Riblah in the country called Hamath. There Nebuchadnezzar decided what to do to him. 10 At Riblah, he killed all Zedekiah's sons in front of their father's eyes. He also killed all the officers of Judah. 11 Then he took out Zedekiah's eyes and he tied him with metal ropes. He took him to Babylon. And he kept him in a prison until he died.

12 Nebuzaradan, the leader of the king's special soldiers, came to Jerusalem. It was the 19th year of Nebuchadnezzar's rule. He came on the 10th day of the 5th month. 13 He burned the LORD's temple and the king's house and all the houses in Jerusalem. He burned down every important building. 14 He told the whole army to break down the walls round Jerusalem. 15 Nebuzaradan took away some of the very poor people and those who remained in the city. And he also took those who had clever hands. 16 But he let the poorest people stay to work with the vines and in the fields.

17 The soldiers from Babylon broke up all the big things of bronze that were in the temple. And they took the bronze to Babylon. 18 And they took away all the small bronze tools that the priests used in the temple. 19 The leader of the king's soldiers took all the bowls. And he took all the things that people had made from gold or from silver.

20 They had a lot of bronze from the things that King Solomon had made for the temple. There was so much that they could not weigh it. 21 The metal parts of the doors were more than 6 metres high and 4 metres round. Each was as thick as 4 fingers and they were empty inside. 22 Over each of these two parts there were two very beautiful metal tops nearly two metres high. 23 They had 96 bronze fruits round their sides and 100 bronze fruits above those.

24 Nebuchadnezzar's captain took Seraiah the leader of the priests and his most important helper as his prisoners. And he took the three men who were keepers of the doors of the temple. 25 He also took the most important officer of the soldiers who remained in the city. Seven men had helped Judah's king to decide what he should do. Nebuchadnezzar's captain took them also. He took away the most important man who chose men to become soldiers and 60 of his helpers.

26 Nebuzaradan, Nebuchadnezzar's most important officer, took all those men to the king of Babylon at Riblah. 27 There, at Riblah in the country called Hamath, the king's soldiers killed all those men.

So he took the people from Judah to live as prisoners in a country far away. 28 This is the number of the people that Nebuchadnezzar took away:

He took 3023 Jews in his 7th year.

29 He took 832 people from Jerusalem in his 18th year.

30 And he took 745 Jews in his 23rd year.

So Nebuzaradan, Nebuchadnezzar's captain, took 4600 people away.

31 Jehoiachin had been in prison for 37 years when Evil-Merodach became king of Babylon. Evil-Merodach let Jehoiachin king of Judah go free. He let him go out from the prison on the 25th day of the 12th month. 32 He spoke kind words to him. He gave to him a more important place than the other kings who were with him in Babylon. 33 So Jehoiachin took off the clothes that he had worn in the prison. And he ate his food at the king's table until the day that he died. 34 The king of Babylon gave something to Jehoiachin every day until he died.

A Very Sad Man Prays to God

Lamentations

About this book

We call this book Lamentations because it is a sad book. It has five parts. All five parts are about the city called Jerusalem.

God wanted people to look after Jerusalem and the special house there. God wanted people to worship only him in that house. But the people who lived in Jerusalem did not obey God. In the end, he was angry with those people. He let armies come from another country. Those armies came to destroy Jerusalem and to take the people away. The writer lived in Jerusalem. We think that he was a man called Jeremiah. We can read a translation of Lamentations in a very old book called the Septuagint. It says that Jeremiah wrote Lamentations. He certainly wrote another book in the Bible, which is called Jeremiah. Jeremiah was a man who loved God and his own people. He was very sad when they destroyed his city, Jerusalem. Jeremiah wrote the book about 586 years before Jesus was born.

In the first two parts of the book, Jeremiah writes sometimes as if he himself is speaking. Other times he writes as if Jerusalem city and its people are speaking. The city speaks as if a woman is speaking. In the next two parts, only Jeremiah speaks. In the last part, he writes as if the city's people are praying to God.

The first part is about the lonely city. The second part says that God was like an angry enemy. In the next part, Jeremiah remembers how good God is. If people really love God, they can hope for better things always. After that, Jeremiah talks about the cruel enemies. He remembers what those enemies did to the people in the city. In the last part, the city's people know that they have done many wrong things. So they ask God to forget those bad things.

Lamentations shows us that God gets angry about sin. He is happy when we change. This book also shows us what God wants. He wants us to love him. He wants us to obey him. If we do that, he helps us. He will help us to be good and to do good things.

Chapter 1

Jeremiah is speaking

1 The city that was full of people is lonely now.

The city is like the wife of a dead husband.

Once she was great.

She was like a queen among the other places in the country.

Now she is a slave.

2 She weeps in the night

and there are tears on her face.

Not one of her lovers will help her to feel better.

All her friends have left her.

They have gone against her and they are now her enemies.

3 The enemies have taken Judah's people away as slaves.

The slaves have only trouble and difficult work.

They now live among strangers.

They have no rest, and they live far away from home.

They cannot go away from those who do cruel things to them.

4 Zion's streets are sad places now.

Nobody comes to worship God there any longer.

There is nothing to hear at the city gates.

The priests are sad.

Strangers are cruel to the young women.

The people in Zion are very sad.

5 The people's enemies rule them now.

Those who hate them have plenty.

The Lord has caused trouble for the people

because they did so many wrong things.

The enemies took the children away to work as slaves.

6 Zion is not beautiful any longer.

Her leaders are like animals without food.

They are too weak to run from their enemies.

7 Jerusalem's people are in trouble and they are away from their homes now.

So, they remember the good things

that they had a long time ago.

When their enemies came, nobody was there with them.

Nobody helped them.

Their enemies laughed when they destroyed Jerusalem.

8 Jerusalem's people have sinned very much.

That is why this city is not clean any longer.

People thought that this city was the best.

Now they think that it is not important.

They see it as it is.

Jerusalem's people make sad noises and they want to hide themselves away.

9 Jerusalem seemed dirty because the people were so bad.

They never thought that the end would be like this.

But their enemies destroyed the city.

They do not have anyone who can help them to feel better.

God did not listen any longer when they asked for his help.

'Lord, see our troubles.

See how happy our enemies are', the people pray.

10 The enemies have taken away all Jerusalem's valuable things.

Foreign people have walked into God's holy house.

But God had said that people like that must not go in there.

They are not his people.

11 Jerusalem's people are making sad noises.

They are sad as they look for food.

They sell things that they love.

They use them to buy food.

That way, they can keep themselves alive.

The city's people are speaking like one person

'Lord, see what is happening.

Think about me,

because nobody else does', the people pray.

12 'Come and really look at me!

All you people who pass me do not show any interest in me.

But you have never seen anything as sad as I am.

The Lord was very angry with me.

So it was the Lord who did this to me.'

The city's people are speaking

13 'It is like God has sent fire down into our bones to hurt us.

He wants us to turn towards him again.

So he has caused things to be very difficult for us.

All day he causes us to feel lonely and weak.

14 He has caused our sins to seem like something very heavy that lies on our necks.

It makes us weak.

He has let the enemy be very strong.

He let them win against us.

So we cannot beat them.

15 The Lord has let the enemy beat all our strong men.

He brought a big army to fight our young men.

And the enemy won that fight.

People walk on grapes to break them.

Like that, the Lord let the enemy hurt our young women here in Judah.'

16 'We weep because of these things.

Tears run down our faces because God is not with us.

Nobody will help us.

We are the children of this city

and we have nothing now.

The enemy has won.'

Jeremiah is speaking again

17 Zion's people ask for help,

but nobody is their friend.

They are Jacob's children.

But the Lord has said that he will cause their enemies

to come from every country near them.

Those other people think about Jerusalem as they would think about something dirty.

The city's people are speaking again

18 'The Lord is right to punish us.

We have not obeyed him.

Listen, all people everywhere, and look at us.

We are in very bad trouble.

The enemy has taken away our young women

and our young men to be slaves.'

19 'We shouted to our friends.

They had said that they would help us.

But they did not help us.

Our priests and our leaders died in the city.

They were looking for food to keep them alive.

20 Look, Lord, we are in a lot of trouble.

We are very sad.

We are weak deep inside ourselves

because we have done so many bad things.

They are killing our people in the streets.

People are dying in the houses.'

21 'Everybody knows that we are very sad.

Nobody wants to help us.

All our enemies know about our trouble.

They are happy, God, that you caused that trouble.

Please cause trouble for those enemies too, as you promised.

22 You know that they have done many bad things.

Punish them as you have punished us.

You punished us because we did many bad things.

Now we are ashamed and we are very sad.'

Chapter 2

Jeremiah is speaking

1 The Lord was very angry.

He wanted Zion's people to be ashamed.

Zion was the most beautiful city in Israel.

But he has put it down to the ground from its high place.

Zion was like a place where he had rested his feet.

Now that he is angry, he has forgotten about that.

2 The Lord has destroyed all the houses where Jacob's people lived.

He decided that he must punish them.

Because he is angry,

he has destroyed all Judah's strong towns.

Yes, he has destroyed all the buildings.

And he has killed the rulers and all the people.

3 Yes, because he is very angry,

he has destroyed Israel's whole army.

He did not help them when they were fighting the enemy.

He was like a big hot fire

that burned Jacob's people from all sides.

4 He has bent his bow like an enemy ready to kill people.

And, like an enemy,

he has killed all those who once gave him pleasure.

He has shown how angry he was.

He has sent a fire and he burned all Zion's houses.

5 The Lord has become like an enemy.

He has destroyed Israel

and all the beautiful houses there.

He has destroyed all the strong towns that had walls.

He has caused Judah's people to weep.

They are very sad.

6 He has knocked down his own holy house

as easily as someone can knock down a hut in a garden.

He has destroyed this place where people once met him.

He has caused Zion's people to forget

the special events and the Sabbaths in his holy house.

He was very angry.

So he thought that our king and our priests were not important.

He refused to help them.

7 His holy house and his altar there

no longer give pleasure to the Lord.

He has given Zion's most beautiful houses to the enemy.

They shout in the holy house of the Lord

as people shout on a special holy day.

8 The Lord decided to destroy the strong walls of Zion.

He carefully broke away each stone.

It causes us to weep when we look at those walls.

He destroyed them all.

He destroyed the inside walls and he destroyed the strong outside walls.

9 Zion's gates fell down on the ground.

He destroyed them and he has broken them in pieces.

The enemies have taken away our king

and his sons to a foreign country.

The people have nearly forgotten God's rules.

And God does not send messages to us any longer.

His prophets have nothing to say to us.

10 Zion's leaders sit on the ground and they are saying nothing.

They have dressed themselves in sackcloth

and they throw dirt on their own heads.

They are showing everyone that they are very sad.

And the young women of Jerusalem can only look down to the ground,

because they are very sad too.

11 I have cried so much that my eyes are red now.

Even the parts inside my body hurt,

because my people are dying.

I feel ill because I am so sad.

The children and babies fall in the city's streets

because they are so weak.

12 'Where has all the food and drink gone?'

the hungry children ask their mothers.

Then they fall down in pain on the streets of the city.

They die in their mothers' arms.

13 I want to help you people of Jerusalem.

But there is nothing that I can say to you.

I do not know about anything like what has happened to you.

God has destroyed Zion completely!

I do not know anyone who can make you people better.

14 Your prophets have promised you many good things.

Those good things will not happen.

They should have told you that you should not do wrong things.

If they had told you that, none of these troubles would have happened.

The prophets do not tell you true messages from God

and their dreams are false.

15 Everyone who goes by laughs.

They are happy because you are sad.

They see how the enemy has destroyed everything in Jerusalem.

"Surely this cannot be the city that men called 'most beautiful' ", they say.

"People have said that this city is the best city on earth."

16 All your enemies make noises through their teeth

because they are very happy.

'We have won!' they say.

'We have waited for this day.

Now we have beaten you!

Now we have seen it!'

17 The Lord has done what he decided to do.

Yes, he has done what he told you about a long time ago.

He has destroyed your city and he has not felt sorry about it.

He has caused your enemies to be happy.

He has made them strong

so that they could win against you.

18 Day and night, cause your tears to run like a river round the walls of Zion.

Cry to the Lord all the time, you people.

Do not rest.

Do not let your eyes stop crying.

19 Stand up and pray for God's help.

Talk to God all night.

Pour out your words and thoughts to God

as you pour out water from a jar.

Lift up your hands to him when you ask him.

And ask him to save the lives of your children.

They fall down to die at the end of every street

because they are so hungry.

Jerusalem's people speak

20 'Look at us, Lord', you should say.

'You have done all this to your people.

Women eat their own children now!

But they are the children that they looked after.

People have killed your own priests and prophets

in your holy house!

21 Young people and old people lie dead in the streets.

The enemy has killed the young men and women with long knives.

But it was really you who killed them.

You were very angry with us.

So you killed them and you did not feel sorry.

22 You asked our enemies to come round us

as people come to a special party.

They killed our people because you were angry.

Nobody could hide or run away.

They all died.

We saw the enemy kill our own children.'

Chapter 3

1 I am the man who has seen trouble.

God punished me because he was angry with me.

2 He has led me into the dark.

There is no light, so I cannot see the right way.

3 He is completely against me;

so again and again, he causes me trouble all day long.

4 God has caused my skin and my whole body to become old.

He has broken my bones.

5 He has fought against me from every side.

He caused much trouble for me,

so that I am very sad.

6 He has brought me to this dark place.

So I am like a person who has been dead for a long time.

7 I am like a person inside high walls that God has built.

And I cannot go out.

My troubles are very bad.

They are like heavy metal and they hold me down.

8 I shout and I pray for help,

But God does not listen.

9 I am like a person on a path with lots of curves,

because he put big rocks in my way.

10 God is like a strong wild animal.

He hides and he waits for me by the path.

11 He is like an animal that pulls a person away from the path.

Then it tears the person in pieces.

He has made me very lonely.

12 God is like a soldier with a bow.

He bent the bow and he shot at me.

13 It was as if he shot me in the heart.

14 All the people see me and laugh.

They even sing silly songs about me all day long.

15 God has caused my life to become a thing of pain.

It is as if he filled a cup with a very bitter drink for me.

16 It is as if he caused me to eat small stones.

And the stones broke my teeth.

Then he put me on the ground,

and he covered me with ashes.

17 He has taken peace away from my mind.

I have forgotten what good days are like.

There were good days when I had plenty.

And there were good days when I was happy.

But I have forgotten what that was like.

18 'Everything good has finished for me!

The things that I hoped for from the Lord have not come!' I tell myself.

19 Remember (Lord) all my troubles because I am sad.

Remember that I am very lonely.

And my mouth tastes bad as I think about it.

20 I think about all those things,

and I feel small and alone.

21 But then I choose to remember God,

and then I hope again:

22 God is good and he never stops being kind to us.

That is why we are alive at all.

23 Each new day we can remember

that God's promises will certainly happen.

24 'He is my Lord', I say to myself.

'He is the reason why I can hope again.'

25 The Lord does good things for people who wait for him.

He is kind to everyone who looks for him.

26 It is good when people go on hoping.

It is good when they quietly wait for God,

because he will save them.

27 It is also good for people to obey God when they are young.

They should work well for him.

28 Also, they should sit alone quietly,

when God causes them to be in trouble.

29 They should lie down on the ground in front of God.

Then they can hope again.

30 Cruel people will want to hurt them.

And those people will want to say cruel things to them.

They should let them do it and they should not fight them.

31 The Lord does not turn away from people for always.

32 God does cause people to feel sad sometimes,

but he is sorry for us.

He is also very kind to us,

because he loves us very much.

33 He does not enjoy seeing people who are in pain.

He does not enjoy causing trouble for them.

34 Bad people may be cruel to those who are in a prison.

But God does not like to see that.

35 Bad people may take other people's things.

But God does not like to see that.

And God is the greatest of all.

36 People with authority may not be fair to other people.

But the Lord is not happy when he sees that.

37 The Lord causes things to happen.

Nobody can cause things to happen without him.

38 God is the greatest of all and he causes things to happen.

He causes good things and bad things when he speaks.

39 He only punishes us when we do wrong things.

We are still alive, so we should not be angry with God.

40 Instead, we should think a lot about what we do.

And we should turn back to the Lord again.

41 God is in his home and we should pray to him.

We should offer ourselves completely to him.

42 'We have done wrong things,

and we have gone against you.

And you have not forgiven us', we say to God.

43 'You have hidden yourself from us because you are angry.

You have followed us so that you could kill us.

You were not sorry about it.

44 You have hidden from us in a cloud.

So you do not listen to us when we talk to you.

45 You let people from other countries think bad things about us.

They think that we have no value.

We are like things that nobody can use any longer.

46 All our enemies say bad things to us.

47 And we are very afraid of the people who have beaten us.

They have caught us like animals.

They have killed us.

And they have destroyed all the things that we had.'

48 I weep, and my eyes are red with all my tears.

It is because the enemy has killed my people.

49 Tears come like a river from my eyes.

And they will not stop,

50 until the Lord looks down on us from his home in heaven.

He will see us and he will help us.

51 I see our city.

I see what has happened to all the people here.

And so I am very sad.

52 My enemies had no reason to follow me.

But they caught me as they would catch a bird.

53 They put me alive into the well,

and they threw stones down on me.

54 The water covered my head.

Then I said, 'I shall die.'

55 I shouted your name, Lord,

when I was in the well.

56 'Please listen to me, Lord', I shouted.

'Help me! Save me!' I shouted,

and you heard me.

57 You came near to me when I prayed to you.

'Do not be afraid', you said.

58 Lord, you have given me help.

You have paid the price to keep me alive.

59 You saw the bad things that they did to me.

So please agree with me that they were not fair!

60 You know all the bad things that they did to me.

And you know about all the bad things that they want to do to me.

61 You have heard their cruel words against me, Lord.

Yes, you know about all the bad things that they want to do to me.

62 These people have been cruel to me.

They attack me with cruel words every hour of the day.

63 Look at them as they sing cruel things about me.

They sing when they are sitting.

And they sing when they are standing.

64 Punish them for what they have done, Lord.

65 Cause them to think that they cannot hope for anything good.

Cause bad things to happen to them.

66 Run after them angrily.

Kill them all because you are angry with them.

Let nobody on earth remember them any longer.

Chapter 4

1 Look! The gold has stopped shining!

Look how the best gold has changed!

The valuable stones from the Holy Place lie at the end of every street!

2 Jerusalem's men were valuable, like the best gold.

Now they lie in the streets, because God has broken them.

They are like common pots that a potter makes.

3 Even the wild animals offer the breast to their young animals.

But Jerusalem's young women have become cruel.

They are like ostriches that put their young ostriches in wild places.

4 The mouths of the babies in Jerusalem are completely dry, because they are so thirsty.

And the young children ask for food, but nobody gives them anything to eat.

5 There are people here who had been very rich.

They ate the best foods, but now they are hungry.

Now they lie in the streets with nothing to eat.

They wore the best clothes, but now they sit in the ashes.

6 God has punished my people.

He punished us more than he punished Sodom's people.

God destroyed that city in a moment,

and no human person helped him.

7 The leaders of Jerusalem were more clean than the cleanest cold water.

They seemed to be more white than milk.

Their bodies had very good health,

and they seemed to shine like valuable stones.

8 Now their faces are black like wood that somebody has burnt.

People see them in the streets, but do not recognise them.

Their skin hangs on their bones.

Their skin is as dry as wood for a fire.

9 Our enemies have killed many people with long knives.

It is better for those dead people

than for the people who have no food.

They are very hungry.

And they die slowly because they have nothing to eat.

10 Women who once were very kind

have boiled their own children.

Their children became their food,

when the enemies were destroying the city.

11 The Lord was very angry.

So he sent fire to burn Zion.

It destroyed the whole city, even the strongest houses.

12 The kings in the other cities on earth could not believe it.

None of the people on earth could believe it.

They thought that no enemy could go through Jerusalem's gates.

13 God punished Jerusalem and its people because their leaders sinned.

God did not like the things that their prophets and priests did.

They had caused good people to die.

14 Those leaders walked in the streets like men who cannot see.

There was blood on their clothes and everybody was afraid to touch them.

15 'Go away!' people shouted at them.

'Do not touch us!

You are too dirty to be among God's people!'

So they went away to other countries, but the people there did not want them.

'They cannot stay here with us!' those people said.

16 The Lord himself has sent them away because he is angry with them.

He will not be kind to them any longer.

Nobody likes bad priests and nobody likes bad leaders.

17 Our eyes became red as we watched.

We were looking for help, but it did not come.

The people from other countries could not save us.

18 Enemies ran after us, so that we could not go into the streets any longer.

We knew that we would die soon.

We could not live like this any longer.

19 The enemy was quicker than big birds that fly in the air.

They followed us so that they could catch us out on the mountains.

They hid and they waited for us in the wild places.

20 God had chosen a man to be our king.

We thought that he would save us.

'Under his shadow we will live among the other countries', we had always said.

But the enemy caught him.

21 You, Edom's people, live in the country called Uz. And you are happy now.

But at a future time, God will hurt you also.

The enemy will take away everything that you have.

So you will become like drunks.

22 God has finished punishing Zion's people.

He will let them return to their homes soon.

But you, Edom's people, God will certainly punish you.

He will discover everything that you have done wrong.

Chapter 5

1 Lord, please remember the trouble that has happened to us.

Look at us, because we are ashamed.

2 Strangers have taken the land that our fathers gave to us.

Foreign people live in our homes.

3 We are children whose fathers are dead.

Our mothers no longer have husbands.

4 We must pay money for the water that we drink.

We must buy wood for our fires.

5 Our enemies cause us to work like animals.

But the work is too difficult

and they will not let us rest.

6 We gave ourselves to the Egyptians and to the Assyrians,

so that we could get food to eat.

7 Our fathers sinned, but they are dead.

Now we have the troubles that you caused because of them.

You punished us because of their sin.

8 Slaves now rule us.

And there is nobody to save us from their power.

9 We meet danger when we work in the fields.

Enemies are everywhere and they want to kill us.

10 Our skin feels as if we are burning.

We are so hungry that we are ill.

11 Enemies do what they want with the women in Zion.

They are cruel to the young women in Judah's cities.

12 They hang our leaders by their hands.

And they are cruel to our old men also.

13 They took the young men to work as slaves.

Those young men make flour for them.

And our boys carry wood.

They fall down under big bags of wood.

14 Our enemies no longer let our old men decide things.

The old men cannot say what is right or fair for us.

And the young men have stopped their music.

15 We are not happy any longer.

Instead, we are very sad,

so we do not dance any longer.

16 And we have no king in Jerusalem any longer.

We have sinned and so very bad things have happened to us.

17 So our bodies feel ill and we feel ill deep inside us.

Our eyes are very tired and we cannot hope for good things any longer.

18 We are so sad because they destroyed Zion's walls and buildings.

Wild animals walk on them now.

19 But you, Lord, are always king.

You will always rule us.

20 Tell us why you have forgotten us.

Tell us why you have left us for so long.

21 Help us to come back to you, Lord.

We really want to make a new start with you.

We were great before our enemies beat us.

We pray that you will make us as great as that again.

22 That could happen unless you have turned away from us completely.

That could happen unless you will continue to be very angry with us.

Prophet in Babylon with a message for Jerusalem

Ezekiel

About Ezekiel

Ezekiel was from the tribe of Levi. He knew all about the work that the priests in Israel did. But he could not do a priest's work in God's house (the temple) in Jerusalem. He was living in Babylon. Nebuchadnezzar had taken many important people from Jerusalem. He had taken them to his city, Babylon. God had let him do this because Israel's people had worshipped other gods.

God chose to speak to Ezekiel and God made him a prophet. Bible students think that God began to give him messages in the year 593 BC. Ezekiel became God's messenger to Israel's people. He spoke to all the Jews who lived in Babylon.

Some Jews remained in Jerusalem. They thought that they were important. They thought that they were better than the Jews in Babylon. (Nebuchadnezzar had taken some of them there.) God said that Ezekiel must speak to the people in Babylon. He said that he would punish the people in Jerusalem. That was because they had not obeyed his rules.
The prophet Jeremiah had already said this to the people in Jerusalem. But they would not listen to Jeremiah.

The Bible says that the Lord God rules all the earth. Ezekiel believed this. He believed that God was holy. And he gave great honour to God. The Israelites in Babylon listened to Ezekiel. They believed that he was God's prophet. Sometimes God spoke to Ezekiel in dreams. Or he said that he must do strange things. Ezekiel had to explain the dreams to Israel's people.

Chapter 1

God gives Ezekiel a dream

1 God spoke to me on the fifth (5th) day of the fourth (4th) month.

I was among the Jews by the side of the river Kebar. Nebuchadnezzar had taken them there from Israel. God opened heaven (God's home) and I saw pictures of him in the sky.

2 Nebuchadnezzar had kept King Jehoiachin in Babylon for five (5) years. On the fifth (5th) day of the month, 3 God spoke to Ezekiel the priest. He was the son of Buzi. He was standing by the River Kebar in the country called Babylon. This was the place where the Lord God spoke to Ezekiel. He told him what he wanted him to do.

4 I, Ezekiel, looked. And I saw great clouds that were coming from the north. They came with a strong wind and bright lights. Light shone all-round the clouds. It was like a fire that had burning metal in the centre. 5 I could see something like four (4) living things in the fire. Each of them had the shape of a man. 6 But each of them had four (4) faces and four (4) wings. 7 Their legs were straight and their feet were like the feet of a young cow. They shone like bright metal. 8 They had hands under their wings on the four (4) sides. They were like the hands of a man. Each of these four living things had faces and wings. 9 And their wings touched each other. Each living thing went straight towards the front. They did not turn from their straight path.

10 I saw their faces. The face at the front was the face of a man. On the right side each had an ox's face. And on the left side each had a lion's face. Each also had the face of a great bird. 11 That is how I saw their faces. Each of them held two wings up from their sides. The wings of each living thing touched the wings next to them. 12 Each living thing covered its body with two wings. Each living thing moved straight towards the front. They did not turn when they moved. So they went where the spirit wanted. 13 They looked like hot fires or burning sticks of wood. Fire moved between the living things. It shone brightly, and it sent out light like sharp knives. 14 The living things moved very quickly. They went one way and then they went another way.

15 I continued to look at them. And I saw four (4) wheels on the ground. Each was by the side of a living thing. 16 The wheels were all the same. They shone like bright glass. Each was like a wheel across another wheel. 17 They moved any way that the living things moved. 18 The wheels had high edges. Eyes covered their edges. 19 When the living things moved, the wheels moved with them. If they rose from the earth, the wheels rose with them. 20 They went where the spirit wanted, and the wheels went with them. The wheels also had the spirit of the living things. 21 The wheels moved when the living things moved. The wheels stood in the same place when the things stopped. When the living things rose from the ground the wheels also rose. The same spirit moved the living things and the wheels.

22 A roof that looked like shining ice was over the heads of the living things. 23 The living things stood under the roof. Each stood with their wings held towards the things next to them. They covered their bodies with their other two wings. 24 I heard a noise like a fast river or like a great army when they flew. It was like the voice of the great, powerful God. They put their wings down when they stood still. 25 A voice spoke while they stood still with their wings down. It came from above their heads.

26 Over the roof like ice I saw a kind of throne. Someone had made it out of blue stone. And high above the throne I saw something like a man. 27 He shone like bright metal in the centre of a fire. The light of many colours was all round him. 28 It was like the ring of light over the earth on a wet day. This light showed that the Lord was there, in his glory. When I saw it, I fell down on my face. Then a voice spoke to me.

Chapter 2

God chooses Ezekiel to be his messenger

1 'Son of man, you must stand up on your feet', the Lord said to me. 'Then I will speak to you.' 2 His Spirit came into me while he spoke. He made me stand up and I heard him speak to me.

3 'Son of man', he said. 'I am sending you to Israel's people. They are people who have not obeyed me. Their nation has turned away from me. They and their fathers have never obeyed my rules. 4 I am sending you to a people who do not listen to me. They think that their ideas are better than mine. This is what you must say to them. "This is what the great, powerful Lord says."

5 They may listen or they may not listen. But they will know that you are a prophet. They are not an obedient people. But they will know that I have sent a prophet to them. 6 You, son of man, must not be afraid of them or their words. You may feel like you have sharp branches all round you. You may think that they can bite you like animals. But they cannot hurt you. Do not be afraid of what they say. They are all against me. 7 You must speak my words to them, whether they will listen or not. They are a people that do not obey me. 8 But you, son of man, must listen to what I say to you. Do not turn against me, like those bad people. Open your mouth. And eat what I give you.'

9 Then I looked and I saw a hand. It held a very long piece of skin. Someone had written words on the skin. The hand offered it to me. 10 When the hand opened the skin, I saw words on both sides of the skin. I read them. They were not happy words, but were very sad.

Chapter 3

1 'Son of man, eat what is in front of you', he said to me. 'Eat this skin with words on it. Then go and speak to the Israelites.' 2 Then I opened my mouth and he gave me the skin to eat.

3 'Son of man, eat this and fill your stomach with it', he said. So I ate it, and it was very sweet in my mouth.

4 Then he said to me, 'Now go, son of man. Speak my words to Israel's people. 5 I am sending you to them. I do not send you to a people whose words you cannot understand. 6 And I do not send you to people who speak a foreign language. I could have sent you to those people. And I am sure that they would have listened to you. 7 But Israel's people will not listen to you. That is because they will not listen to me. They have all decided not to obey me, and they will not change. 8 But I will make you as strong as they are. You will not stop obeying me. 9 You will be strong and you will not change. They may refuse to do as I say. But you must not be afraid of them, even when they do.'

10 And he said to me, 'Son of man, listen carefully to all that I say. Remember the words that I speak to you. 11 Now you must go to Babylon. Speak to Israel's people who are there. Say this, "This is what the great powerful Lord says." They may listen or they may refuse to listen.'

12 Then the Lord's Spirit lifted me up. I heard a loud noise and a voice spoke. 'Praise the glory of the Lord in his home above', it said. 13 I heard the sound of the living things' wings. Their wings were hitting each other. And the wheels made a noise like the sound of the earth when it moves about. 14 Then the Spirit lifted me up and he took me away. He carried me with great power. I felt angry and hurt in my mind. 15 I came to Tel Abib near the river Kedar. The people who had come from Israel lived there. I stayed there with them for seven (7) days. I was very tired and confused.

The Lord tells Ezekiel that he will become a watchman

16 When the seven (7) days were finished, the Lord spoke to me. 17 'Son of man, I have made you a watchman for Israel's people. So listen to what I say. They may not obey me. Then tell them what will happen. 18 I may say to a bad man, "I am going to make you die." You must tell him this. Or you must say that he must stop doing wrong things. Then he will save his life. If you do not tell him this, he will die. He will die because of the bad things that he has done. But I will punish you, because you did not give him my message. 19 You must tell him what I have promised. But he may not listen. Then he will die because he has not obeyed me. But you will have saved yourself.

20 A very good man may start to do bad things and I can make his life difficult. But he will die if you do not tell him about his sin. He will die because of his sins. I will not remember the good things that he did. But you did not tell him what I would do. Then I will punish you. 21 If you give him my message, he may stop sinning. Then he will stay alive. He will not die, because he stopped doing wrong things. And you will not die.'

22 The Lord was very near to me. 'Go into the flat land and I will speak to you there', he said. 23 So I got up and I went out to the flat land. And I saw the glory of the Lord there. It was like the glory that I had seen by the River Kebar. I fell down with my face to the ground.

24 Then the Lord's Spirit lifted me up and he made me stand up. 'Go into your house and shut the door', he said. 25 'I will stop you from moving. You will be like a man that men will have tied up. You will not be able to go out among the people. 26 I will stop your tongue from moving so that you cannot speak. You will not be able to tell my people that they have not obeyed me. But they have done wrong things. 27 I will speak to you again. Then you will be able to give them my message. "This is what the great and powerful Lord says", you will say. Some of my people will listen to my words, but some people will refuse to listen. They are people who will not obey me.'

Chapter 4

A picture with a message about Jerusalem

1 'Now, son of man, make a square flat plate out of soft earth. Draw a picture on this plate. Draw a picture of the city, Jerusalem. 2 Then build hills round it for soldiers to attack the city. Put your tents round the city. Prepare very heavy long sticks to hit its gates. 3 Then you must turn your face towards it. Take an iron plate and put it between your face and the city. This will be a wall between you and the city.

The army is round the city. But you will attack it. This is to show Israel's people what I will do.

4 Then lie on your left side. I will put on you the sin of the Israelites. You will stay there for 390 days and you will suffer because of their sin. 5 This means that I will punish Israel for 390 years. 6 After you have finished this, lie down on your right side. You will stay there for 40 days. You will suffer for the sin of Judah's people. This is to show that I will punish them for 40 years. 7 Turn your face towards the picture of the soldiers who are attacking Jerusalem. Point to it and prophesy against the city. 8 I will tie you up so that you cannot turn from one side to another. You will stay on one side until the day when the soldiers round the city go away.

9 You must take different kinds of food grains. Then put them in a jar. Use them to make bread for yourself. You must eat this for 390 days. Those are the 390 days that you are on your left side. 10 Weigh out 20 shekels (about 8 ounces or 220 grams) of food for each day. This is all the food that I will let you eat in one day. 11 You can have a sixth (1/6th) of a hin (two cups) of water a day to drink. 12 Bake the food like a cake. Bake it in front of the people on a fire that you have made with human dirt.' 13 The Lord said, 'I will send Israel's people to live in foreign lands. This is to show them that they will eat bad food there. That food will not be clean.'

14 'No, great and powerful Lord', I replied. 'I have never eaten anything that would make me not clean. Even when I was a child, I obeyed your rules. An animal might have died when nobody had killed it. I did not eat that meat. Nor did I eat meat that wild animals had killed. I have never eaten any food that was not clean.'

15 So God spoke to me. 'It is good', he said. 'You can use dirt from cows instead. You can cook your bread on that.'

16 Then God said, 'I am going to take away the bread from the people in Jerusalem. They will have to measure the food that they eat.'

And they will measure the water that they drink. I will give them great trouble. 17 They will have no more bread or water. They will be very sad and their bodies will become thin. This is because they have done so many bad things.'

Chapter 5

Ezekiel cuts his hair

1 'Now, son of man, take a sharp sword. Use it to cut all the hair from your head and face. Then take the hair and weigh it. Make it into three (3) equal parts.

2 Keep this hair until the end of the days that you lie still. Then you will not watch the soldiers round your picture of Jerusalem any longer. Take one part of the hair and burn it inside the city. Take another part and hit it all round the city with a sword. And take the third (3rd) part and throw the hairs to the wind. I will run after them with a sword. 3 But take a few hairs and keep them in your clothes. 4 Then take out some of these hairs and burn them in the fire. This fire will grow and go out to all Israel.'

5 The Lord, the King who rules Israel, says this. 'I have put Jerusalem in the centre of all the nations. There are countries all round it. 6 But the people who live there have not obeyed my rules. They have been very wicked.' 7 So this is what the Lord, your King says: 'They have done more bad things than any of the nations round them have done. They have refused to obey my rules. I said that they must not do certain things. But they have done them. They have done even worse things than the nations round them have done.'

8 So this is what the Lord, your King, says: 'I am against you, people in Jerusalem. I will punish you in front of all the nations. 9 I will punish you as I have never punished anyone before. And I will never do it again. I will punish you because you worship so many wrong things. You worship idols. But they are not gods. 10 You will have among you fathers who will eat their children. And children will eat their fathers. I will punish you. I will send far away those few people who do not die. They will go to all parts of the earth.

11 You can be sure that I am alive. I will surely not help you again. You have put your bad things (idols) in my house, and you have done wrong things there. Because you have made my house not clean, I will not be sorry for you. I will not save you. 12 A third (1/3rd) of the people will die. They will die inside your city because they are ill. Or they will die there because they have no food. Soldiers will kill a third (1/3rd) of the people outside your walls. And I will send a third (1/3rd) away. Their enemies will run after them with a sword.

13 When I have done this I will not be angry any longer. I will not punish them anymore, because it is enough. They will know that I, the Lord, have spoken to them. And I hate the wrong things that they have done.

14 I will break down your walls and your buildings. People from other nations who walk past you will be afraid. 15 They will look at you. They will see what I did to you. I did it because I was angry. They will think that you have no value. They will know what I told you. You should not do bad things. And they will say that I punished you because you did not obey me. And they will be afraid.' I, the Lord, say this. 16 'I will take away your food in order to kill you. You will have pain because you will be very hungry. I will make it more and more difficult for those in the city to get food. 17 You will have nothing to eat and wild animals will attack you. They will kill your children. I will send illness, armies and swords to kill you.' I, the Lord, have spoken.

Chapter 6

1 The Lord spoke to me again. 2 'Son of man, you must turn to speak against the mountains of Israel. Give my prophecy to them. 3 "You mountains of Israel", you must say. "This is what the Lord, your ruler, says to you. I am speaking to the mountains, the hills and valleys. 'I am going to attack you. I will destroy your high places where men worship other gods. 4 I will break down your altars where they burn food to idols. I will destroy the altars where they offer their sweet smelling oils to false gods. And I will kill the people in front of those idols. 5 Their dead bodies will lie in front of their false gods. And soldiers will throw their bones round the idol's altars. 6 In every place that they live, they will destroy their towns.

They will break the altars on the high places. And they will pull down the altars where you burnt the sweet oils.

They will destroy your idols. 7 You will see your dead people. And then you will know that I am the Lord.

8 But some of you will not die. These people will run to other countries and nations. 9 When they are there, far away, they will remember me. They will remember how they made me very sad. They turned away from me and they did wrong things. They worshipped idols and they did not obey me. Then they will be angry with themselves. They will be ashamed of the evil things that they did. 10 And they will know that I am the Lord. They will know that I kept my promise to punish them.' "

11 This is what the Lord, your King, says. "Make a loud noise. Hit your hands together. Hit the ground with your feet. Shout 'Help!' Do this because of all the bad, evil things that Israel's people have done. I will send soldiers and illness to kill them. Or they will die because they do not have anything to eat. 12 People who are far away will become ill. And they will die. Soldiers will kill those who are near to the city. The people in the city will die because they do not have any food. That is how I will punish them. I am very angry.

13 They will see their dead bodies. Then they will know that I am the Lord. The bodies will be lying in front of their idols and their altars to false gods. They will see dead bodies on every high hill and mountain and round their altars. They will see them in every place. Their bodies will lie under big trees. That is where they offered sweet oils to their idols. 14 I will make the land from Diblah to the desert empty. I will change the land where they live into a desert. Then they will know that I am the Lord." '

Chapter 7

The day has come for the Lord to punish Israel

1 The Lord spoke to me. 2 'Son of man, the Lord, your King, is speaking to the land in Israel. He says, "This is the end. Now I am going to finish with all the land. 3 Now I will show you how angry I am. I will punish you because of all the wrong things that you have done. The punishment will be as great as the wrong things that you have done. 4 I will not be sorry for you or save you. I will punish you. I will punish you because of all the wrong things that you have done. Then you will know that I am the Lord."

5 This is what the Lord says. "Great trouble! I am going to send you greater trouble than anyone has ever seen. 6 No time is left. It is finished. 7 I will destroy the lives of the people who live in this country. They will not have parties where they worshipped idols. They will have no more parties in the high places. People will be confused, not happy. 8 I will soon cause you to know how angry I am. I am going to be your judge for all that you have done. And I will punish you because of all the wrong things that you have done.9 I will not make your punishment less. I will give you great punishment for all the sins that you have done. Then you will know that I, the Lord, am punishing you.

10 It is time now. The people have done enough wrong things. The time to punish them has come. 11 I have become very angry. I will punish the wicked people. I will punish all of them. None of their dear things will remain, not anything that has any value. 12 The day when I punish my people has come. The person who buys will not be happy. Nor will the person who sells. I am angry with every one of them. 13 Any man who sells his land will not get it back. I will keep my promise. Nobody who has done wrong things will stay alive. 14 They may prepare for war, but nobody will go out to fight. The whole nation has made me very angry.

15 The enemy is outside the city. Inside the city, people are ill and they have no food. Soldiers will kill the people in the country. The people in the city will die from illness, or because they do not have any food. 16Some people will stay alive. They will leave the city and they will run to the mountains. They will be like birds that are flying from the hunters. They will all cry because of their sins. 17 Their hands will be weak and their knees will knock together. 18 They will want to show that they are sorry. So they will wear clothes that are not comfortable. They will be very afraid. They will be ashamed and they will cut all the hair from their heads. 19 They will throw their silver and gold away like dirt. They will know that neither silver nor gold can save them from God's anger. Neither will buy them food or anything that they want. These valuable metals have made them sin. 20 They were happy because they had beautiful things. But they used them to make idols. That is why the Lord has made them hate their silver and gold. 21 He will give their silver and gold to foreigners and to robbers. People will think that their idols have become not clean. 22 I will turn away from my people. Bad men will go into my special house (temple) and they will make it not clean. Nobody will worship me there.

23 Nothing is safe. The country is full of men who kill. People are fighting in the city. 24 I will bring the most evil people here and they will live in your homes. Your strongest men will feel weak when they see the temple. Evil men will have made it not clean.

25 When people are afraid, they will look for peace. But they will not find it. 26 Many bad things will come, one after another. Men will bring bad news all the time. They will ask the prophet to tell them what will happen. The priests will not have anything to teach the people. And the leaders will have not have anything to say. 27 The king will be very sad and his son will not be able to hope for anything. The people will be very afraid. And their bodies will move about like leaves in the wind. I will punish them because of the wrong things that they have done. I will be their judge in the same way that they were judges for other people. Then they will know that I am the Lord." '

Chapter 8

God shows Ezekiel the bad things that men are doing in his temple

1 I was sitting in my house. The leaders of Judah sat in front of me. It was the sixth (6th) year and the fifth (5th) day of the sixth (6th) month. While I sat there, the Lord showed me a picture in my mind.

2 I saw something that looked like a man. The top half of his body looked as bright as burning metal. The half of his body that was below looked like fire. 3 He put out something like a hand. Then he held me by my hair. The Lord's Spirit lifted me up in a dream, high in the sky. And, in my dream, God took me to Jerusalem. He took me to the north gate of the temples inside yard. Enemies had put an idol there that had made God angry. 4 And in front of me I saw the bright light of the Lord. It was like the light that I had seen by the River Kebar.

5 Then the Lord spoke to me. 'Son of man', he said, 'Look towards the north.'

When I looked, I saw the idol. It made God angry. It stood near the altar by the north door.

6 'Son of man, you see what they are doing', he said to me. 'Israel's people are doing very bad things here. They are keeping me a long way away from my holy temple. But I will show you worse things than these.'

7 Then he took me to the gate of the inside yard. There he showed me a hole in the wall. 8 'Son of man, make a hole in the wall here', he said. So I dug into the wall and I found a door. 9 'Go in. And see the very bad things that they are doing there', he said. 10 So I went in and I saw pictures on the walls. They were pictures of snakes and other animals. They were all animals that God did not let us touch or eat. And there were other pictures there. Israel's people were worshipping them. 11 Seventy (70) leaders were there. Jaazaniah, son of Shaphan, was among them. Each man held a pot with burning sweet-smelling oil in it.

12 'Son of man', said the Lord. 'Look at what these leaders are doing! Each man is burning oil to offer worship to his own idol. It is their secret. They say, "The Lord does not see us. He has gone away from us." '

13 'You will see even worse things than that', the Lord said to me. 14 Then he took me to the north gate of the temple. Women there were crying because the god Tammuz was dead.

15 'You saw that', he said. 'But I will show you more things that are even worse.' 16 He took me to the inside yard, between the altar and the gate. About twenty-five (25) men were standing there. Their backs were turned away from the Lord. And their faces were looking to the east. Then they bent their heads down to worship the sun when it rose.

17 'Son of man, you saw that', the Lord said to me. 'This is not a small thing. The people in Judah are doing the wrong things that you have seen here. And they are fighting and killing in all the country. They are making me angry all the time. They are worshipping other gods in my holy temple. They are taking away the honour of my name. 18 So I will show them how angry I am. I will not be kind to them or save them. They may shout to me, but I will not listen to them.'

Chapter 9

God kills the people who worship idols

1 I heard God's Spirit speak in a loud voice. 'Bring here the men who keep the city safe. Tell them that they must bring their arms with them.' 2 And I saw (6) six men. They came out of the higher gate. People can look towards the north from that gate. Each man carried his powerful arms. A man who was wearing white clothes came with them. He was carrying tools with which to write. They came in and they stood next to the altar of yellow metal.

3 The bright light that was the glory of Israel's God moved away from the living things. It went to the door of the temple that was outside. Then the Lord called out to the man with the writing tools. 4 'Go through all the city (Jerusalem)', he said. 'Some people are very sad. They are sad because of the evil things that men are doing there. Put a mark on those people who are so sad. Put it on their faces.'

5 While I listened, the Lord spoke to the other men. 'Follow that man through the city. And kill anyone who does not have the mark. 6 Kill the old men, young men and women. Kill the women and the children. Do not be kind or save any of them. But do not touch anyone that has the mark on their face.' So they started to kill. The leaders were in front of the temple. They began with them.

7 'Fill the yard of the temple with dead bodies. Then the people cannot use the temple for worship', he said. 'Go now!' So they went out and they started to kill people all over the city. 8 They left me alone while they were doing this. I fell down on my face. 'Great and powerful Lord', I cried. 'Jerusalem has made you very angry. Will you kill all Israel's people who remain?'

9 This was his answer. 'Both Israel and Judah are very, very bad. They have hurt and killed each other. And they have not been fair to each other. They say, "The Lord has forgotten his country. The Lord does not see us." 10 So I will not be sorry for them. I will punish them because of what they have done.'

11 Then the man with the writing tools came back 'I have done what you asked me to do', he said.

Chapter 10

God's glory leaves the temple

1 I looked and I saw something like a throne of blue stone. It was high over the heads of the living things. 2The Lord spoke to the man with white clothes. 'Go between the wheels under the living things', he said. 'See the stones that are burning among the living things. Fill your hands with them. Then throw them all over the city.' The man went in. And I watched him while he went in.

3 The living things stood at the south side of the temple. A cloud filled the inside yard. 4 Then the Lord's glory rose up. It went from above the living things. Then it moved to the outside door of the temple. The cloud filled the temple. And the Lord's glory shone through the whole inside yard. 5 I could hear the noise of the living things' wings as far as the outside yard. The noise was like the voice of the great and powerful God when he speaks.

6 The man in white clothes went and he stood next to a wheel. He did this when the Lord said 'Take fire from among the wheels. Take it from under the living things.' 7 Then one of the living things put his hand into the fire. He took some fire. He put it into the man's hands. Then the man in white clothes went out. 8(The living things had hands under their wings. They were like the hands of a man.)

9 I looked and I saw four (4) wheels next to the living things. There was one wheel next to each living thing. And the wheels shone like broken ice. 10 All the four (4) wheels looked the same. Each had a wheel inside a wheel. 11 When the living things moved, they could go in any direction. They all moved together to go where they wanted. They did not have to turn round to change their direction. 12 All their bodies were covered with eyes. This included their backs, hands and wings. And eyes covered the wheels. 13 A voice gave the wheels the name, 'fast moving wheels'. (See Ezekiel 1:15-21.)

14 Each of the living things had four (4) faces. One face was the face of a male cow. And the second (2nd) was the face of a man. The third (3rd) face was a lion's face. And the fourth (4th) face was the face of an eagle (a great bird).

15 I had seen the same living things by the River Kebar. 16 When they rose in the air, the wheels rose too. They put out their wings to fly. And then the wheels stayed by them. 17 When the living things stood still, the wheels also stood still. And when the living things rose in the air, the wheels rose also. This was because the same spirit ruled them all.

18 Then the glory of the Lord left the outside door of the temple. It moved to a place above the living things.

19 They put out their wings. So they flew up from the earth. And the wheels went with them. They stopped by the east gate of the Lord's house. And the glory of the Lord was above them.

20 They were the same living things that I had seen before. They were under the Lord's glory. And I knew that they were called cherubs. 21 Each of them had four (4) faces and four (4) wings. And they had something that looked like a hand under each wing. 22 Their faces were the same as those that I had seen by the river Kebar. Each of them moved along a straight path.

Chapter 11

1 Then the Spirit lifted me and he took me to the Lord's house. We stood by the east gate. I saw Jaazaniah, Azzur's son and Pelatiah, Benaiah's son among them. They were leaders of the people. 2 The Lord spoke to me. 'These are the men who want to do evil things in this city', he said. 'They are saying wrong things to the people. 3 They are saying, "It will soon be time to build houses. This city is like a pot to cook meat. And we are that good meat." 4 Son of man, you must prophesy against them.'

5 Then the Lord's Spirit told me what I should say. 'I know what you are saying, Israel's people. And I know what you want to do. 6 You have killed so many people that the streets are full of dead bodies.

7 So this is what the great and powerful Lord says: "The bodies that you threw into the street are the meat. And the city is the pot in which to cook them. But I will push you out of the city. 8 You are afraid of swords. So I will send men with swords to attack you", says the Lord. 9 "I will make you run from the city. I will send foreign men
to punish you. 10 Their swords will kill you in your own country. This is how I have decided to punish you. Then you will know that I am the Lord. 11 This city will not be like a pot that holds the meat inside it. And you will not be the meat in the pot. I will punish you near the edges of Israel. 12Then you will know that I am the Lord. This is because you have not obeyed my rules. Instead you have done the same things as the nation's round you." '

13 While I was speaking the words from the Lord, Pelatiah, Benaiah's son, died. Then I fell with my face down. And I shouted to the Lord. 'Great and powerful Lord, will you kill all Israel's people who remain?'

14 The Lord spoke to me. 15 'Son of man, this is what the people in Jerusalem say. They say that your family and all Israel's people are far away from me. They say that I gave them this country to keep.'

The Lord promises that some of the people will return to their country

16 'So say this to them. "This is what the Lord, your King, says. 'I did send them to many different lands far away. But for that short time I have kept them safe in those countries.' "

17 Then say, "This is what the Lord, your King, says. 'I will fetch you and bring you home. I will bring you back from the countries where I sent you. I will give the land of Israel back to you.' "

18 The people will return and burn their idols and their evil things. 19 They will want to worship only me. I will put a new spirit into them. I will take away the bad spirit that is in them. I will make them understand how I want them to live. 20 Then they will know my rules. They will be careful to obey them. They will be my people and I will be their God. 21 But I will punish those who continue to worship idols. I will punish them because of the evil things that they do', says the Lord, your God.

22 Then the living things put out their wings to fly. The wheels were by their sides. And the glory of Israel's God was above them. 23 The glory of the Lord rose up from the city. It stopped to the east of it. The glory was above the mountain. 24 In my dream, the Spirit took me back to Babylon. I went to the Israelites who were there. That was the end of the dream. 25 I told the people everything that the Lord's dream had showed me.

Chapter 12

1 The Lord spoke to me again. 2 'Son of man, you live among a people who refuse to obey me. They have eyes to see, but they do not see. They have ears to hear, but they do not hear. Then they refuse to obey me.

3 So you must prepare your things for a journey. Enemies will take you as a prisoner to a country far away.

Go to another place while it is day. Then the people can watch you go. They do not obey me but perhaps they will understand. 4 Bring out the things that you have prepared. Bring them out during the day while the people are watching you. Then go out in the evening while they watch you. Go like someone who is leaving the country. 5 While they watch, dig a hole in the wall. Go through it and take your things with you. 6 Put your things on your shoulder while they watch you. Carry them out while the light starts to go away. Cover your face so that you cannot see the land. This is how I have made you a picture for Israel's people.'

7 So I did what the Lord had said. I brought out the things that I had prepared. I would take them with me out of the country. I did this during the day. Then evening came. I dug a hole in the wall with my hands. I took my things out when it became dark. I carried them on my shoulders while the people watched me.

8 In the morning, the Lord spoke to me again. 9 'Son of man, you know about those people who refuse to obey me. They did not even ask you what you were doing', he said to me.

10 'You must speak to them. Say, "This what the Lord, your King says. 'This is a picture of the king in Jerusalem and all the people there.' " 11 You must say to them, "I am a picture of what the Lord will cause to happen. The people will do what I have done. Enemies will take them far away to another country as prisoners." 12 Their king will leave when it starts to become dark. He will carry his things on his shoulders. They will dig a hole in the wall for him to go through. He will cover his face so that he cannot see the land.13 I will catch him and take him to Babylon. That is the country where the people called Chaldeans live. But he will not see the land, and he will die there. 14 I will make all his officers and soldiers run away. I will make their enemies run after them with swords. Their enemies will be ready to kill them.

15 I will send the people away from their city. Then they will know that I am the Lord. They will know this when I send them too many different countries. 16 But I will save a few of them. I will not make them all die. In those far countries they will be sad. Then they will be sorry because of the many bad things that they have done. And they will know that I am the Lord.'

17 The Lord spoke to me again. 18 'Son of man, let your body shake while you eat your food. Be afraid and shake your body. You will shake while you drink your water. 19 Speak to the people in this country. Say, "This is what the Lord, the King, says. He is speaking about those who live in Jerusalem and in Israel. They will be afraid while they eat their food. They will be very afraid. They will shake while they drink their water. This is because nothing will remain in their country. All who live there are angry. Then they hurt each other. 20 Enemies will knock down the towns where people live. The country will be empty. Then you will know that I am the Lord." '

21 The Lord spoke to me again. 22 'Son of man, there is a thing that people say in Israel. They say, "People see pictures in the mind. But what they see never happens. Time passes and people forget about it." 23 But you must say to them. "This is what the Lord, your King, says. 'I will stop you from saying these words. I say that soon every one of your dreams will become true. I will do it. 24 Nobody in Israel will again dream things that are false. Nobody will say that bad things will not happen. 25 But I, the Lord, will say what I want to say. I will make it happen immediately. I say this to you people who do not obey me. I will do this while you are alive. I will do all the things that I have said', says the Lord, your King." '

26 The Lord spoke to me. 27 'Son of man, Israel's people are saying wrong things. "Your message will not become true for many years. That day will not be soon." That is what they say. 28 So you must speak to them. "This is what your Lord, the King says, 'I will not wait any longer to do what I have said. I will do everything that I told you' ", says the Lord.'

Chapter 13

The Lord is against false prophets

1 The Lord spoke to me. 2 'Son of man, prophesy against the prophets who are now speaking to Israel's people. Their prophecies are their own ideas. Say to them, "Listen to what the Lord says. 3 This is what he says. 'You will not be happy, you fools. You have not seen anything. You are speaking your own words.

4Israel's prophets are like wild dogs that live in broken houses.

5 They have not built up the broken walls for Israel's people.

So they will not be strong when I send enemies to attack them. 6 These prophets describe false dreams and their words are not true. They say, "The Lord says". But I have not sent them. The things that they tell the people will not happen. But they think that they will happen. 7 Their dreams are false. And they have said things that are not true. You know that they said, "The Lord says". But I have not spoken to them.' "

8 So this is what the Lord, your King, says to them. "I am against you because of your words and dreams that are not true", says the Lord. 9 "I will punish the prophets who see false dreams. I will punish those who say false things. They will not become leaders of my people. People will not remember them. They will not go into the country called Israel. Then you will know that I am the Lord, your King."

10 They are leading my people away from me. They say that there will be peace. But there is no peace. They are like men who build a thin wall. And they paint it white. 11 You must speak to the men who painted the wall. Say that it will fall. I will send much rain and hail (rain like stones) and strong winds. 12The wall will fall. And people will ask why the paint did not hold it up.

13 This, then, is what the Lord, your King, says. "I am very angry. So I will send strong winds and hail (rain like stones). Hard rain will fall and it will destroy much. 14 I will break down the wall that you painted. The wall will fall flat. Then you will see the ground on which it was. When the wall falls it will kill you. And you will know that I am the Lord. 15 By this, I will show you that I am very angry. I will destroy the wall and those who painted it white. I will say to you, 'The wall is gone. And so are those who painted it.' 16 I am speaking about the prophets of Israel. They promised that Jerusalem would have peace. But I will send no peace to Jerusalem", says the Lord, your King.'

17 'Now, son of man, you must turn against the women prophets. They say to your people things that are not true. They tell them things that are their own ideas. You must prophesy against them. 18 Say, "This is what the Lord, your King, says. 'I will punish those who tie special things on their arms. They think that these can make good things happen for them. They wear special cloths over their heads to give them power over people. They want to have power over other people so that they can save themselves. 19 You have taken away my honour so that you can get a little bread. You have said things that are not true. This is how you have caused people to die. But they should not have died. And you have caused people to stay alive who should not stay alive. You say what is not true to my people. And they believe you.' "

20 Now this is what the Lord, your King, says. "You catch people as you catch birds with your special cloths and things. But I will tear the special things from you. I will make everyone free from your power. 21 I will tear the cloths from your heads. And you will have no power over people. Then you will know that I am the Lord. 22 The false things that you said made the good people sad. But I did nothing to make them sad. And you did not try to make the bad people stop doing wrong things. You did not try to save their lives. 23So you women will not see false dreams or have power over people. I will save my people from the things that you do. And then you will know that I am the Lord." '

Chapter 14

1 Some of the leaders of Israel came. They sat down in front of me. 2 Then the Lord spoke to me. 3 'Son of man', he said, 'These men worship idols. They will not listen to me. I do not want them to ask me for anything. 4 You must speak to them. Say, "This is what the Lord, the King, says. 'A man who worships idols may come to ask me something. And I will answer him. I will show him that his idols have no value. 5I will do this so that Israel's people will turn back to me. Those who worship idols will again worship me.' "

6 So you must speak to Israel's people. Say, "This is what the Lord, your King says. 'Be sorry about the bad things that you have done! You must not worship idols. Stop doing all the wrong things that you were doing."

7 An Israelite or a foreigner who lives in Israel may not want to be my servant. He may turn from me and worship idols. Then he may go to ask a prophet for help. I myself, the Lord, will answer him. 8 I will be against that man. I will make bad things happen to him. People will see what I have done. I will make him an example to them and they will push him away. He will no longer belong to my people. Then you will know that I am the Lord.

9 I can make a prophet give a false answer. He will give a false prophecy. But I have made him say it. 10 I will punish both the prophet and the person who asked him for a prophecy. 11 Then Israel's people will stay close to me. They will no longer be like a bad smell to me because they do so many bad things. They will be my people and I will be their God' ", says the Lord.'

12 The Lord spoke to me. 13 'Son of man, a country's people may not obey me. Then this is what I will do.

I will not give its people any food if they turn away from me. The men and animals that live there will die because they do not have anything to eat. 14 I would only save men like Noah, Daniel and Job, if they lived there. They would save themselves because they did good things', says the Lord, your King.

15 'Or I might send wild animals to kill the people in that country. Nobody would be able to travel through it because of the animals. 16 I am surely alive', the Lord, your King says. 'And I say what is true. Even if these three (3) men lived in that country, they could not save their own children. I would save only those three men.

17 Or I might bring men with swords to fight against that country. I would let them kill the men and their animals. 18 I am surely alive', says the Lord, your King. 'And my promise is true. Even if these three (3) men lived there, they could not save their own children. I would save only those three men.

19 Or I might be angry and send illness into that country. It would kill the men and animals that lived there. 20 I am surely alive', says the Lord, your King. 'And what I say is true. Even if Noah, Daniel and Job lived there, they could not save their sons or daughters. They would save only themselves because they had done good things.'

21 This is what the Lord, your King says. 'Jerusalem's people will have a very bad time when they do not have any food to eat. And I will send soldiers and wild animals and illness to punish them. 22 But they will not all die. Some sons and daughters will remain alive. They will come to you. You will see that they stay alive. And then you will be happy. You will be happy that I sent all these things to punish Jerusalem's people. 23 Then you will know that I had a good reason to do these things', says the Lord, your King.

Chapter 15

Jerusalem is like a tree that has no value

1 Again the Lord spoke to me. 2 'Son of man', he said. 'The wood of the vine is no better than any other wood that grows. 3 Nobody takes its wood to make into a thing that they can use. They cannot even make from it a little thing on which to hang clothes! 4 They can burn it in the fire. Then only the black, burnt centre remains. But they still cannot use it. 5 They could not use it while it was green. So they surely cannot use it after they have burnt it black.

6 So this is what the Lord, your King, says to you. "I have burnt the wood of the vine. In the same way, I will burn the people who live in Jerusalem. 7 I will not save them. If the fire has not burnt them yet, it will still burn them. I will do this. Then you will know that I am the Lord. 8 I will cause the land to be empty. I will do this because they have not continued to worship me" ', says the Lord, your King.

Chapter 16

1 The Lord spoke to me. 2 'Son of man, make Jerusalem's people see what bad things they have done. 3 Say to them, "This is what the Lord, your King says to Jerusalem's people, 'Your mother gave you birth in the country called Canaan. Your father was an Ammonite and your mother a Hittite. 4 They did not wash you on the day that you were born. They did not cut you from your mother's body. They did not make you clean or tie you in cloths. 5 Nobody was sorry or wanted to do these things for you.

No, they threw you out on the day that you were born. They threw you into a field. They thought that you had no value.

6 Then I came. I was walking by and I saw you. You were lying there. You were kicking and blood covered you. Then I said to you, "Stay alive." 7 I made you grow like the plants in a field. You became beautiful, like a valuable shining stone. Your breasts and your hair grew. You had no value before, but I had made you beautiful.

8 I walked by again. Then I saw that you were old enough for me to love you. I covered you with my coat. I gave you clothes. I made a promise to you that was true. We agreed that you would belong to me', said the Lord, your King.

9 'I washed you with water. I washed away the blood and I put oil on your body. 10 I put a beautiful dress on you and leather shoes on your feet. The clothes that I gave you were very good. They were the best and most expensive that I could find. 11 I made rings out of pretty stones. Then I put them round your neck and your arms.

12 I put valuable rings in your nose and ears. And I put a beautiful ring round your head. I dressed you like a queen. 13 I made you beautiful with gold and silver. I gave you pretty, expensive clothes and I fed you with the best food. You became very beautiful and then you became a queen. 14 The people in all countries heard how beautiful you were. I was the person who had made you so beautiful. I had given you all your good things', says the Lord, your King.

15 'But you used your beauty to do wrong things. You wanted to do what you liked. You thought like this because you were so beautiful. You had sex with those who were not your husband. You had sex with any traveller who came past. He tasted your beautiful body. 16 You took some of your good clothes. You used them to make beautiful the places where they worship idols. 17 You took the things of gold and silver that I had given to you. You made male idols for yourself. You had sex with them. 18 You put your beautiful clothes on them and you gave them my oil and wine. 19 You offered to idols the food that I gave to you. You worshipped them with sweet smells. You made all this happen', says the Lord, your King.

20 'And you took the sons and daughters that I had given to you. 21 You offered them to those idols for food. You did what was wrong. You worshipped other Gods. But you did a much worse thing. You killed my children and you offered them to idols. 22 When I found you, then you had no clothes. And blood covered you. You did not remember this when you had sex with idols.

23 Be very sad. I will bring great trouble to you!' says the Lord, your King. 'You have done even more evil things. 24 In the centre of every town, you have built hills. On each hill you have built a place to worship other gods. 25 You have put these places at the end of every street. There you offered yourself to anyone who went past. You have made yourself of no value. 26 You had sex with the Egyptians, who wanted you. All this made me very angry. 27 So I took away some of your land. I gave your enemies, the people who live in Philistia, power over you. They were ashamed because you were not faithful to me. 28 You gave your body to the people who live in Assyria, too. You could not get enough sex! 29 You had sex with the people from Babylon, who sell things. But even then you had not had enough sex.' " ' 30 'Your mind is so weak', says the Lord, your King. 'You do these things like a woman who is not ashamed. She asks a man for money to have sex with her. 31 But you are not like one of those women. You built places to worship idols in every street. But you did not let men pay you when they had sex with you.

32 You are like a wife that is not faithful wife to me. You want to have sex with strangers more than with your own husband! 33 Men pay bad women who let them have sex with them. But you give gifts to the men who have sex with you. You pay them to come and have sex with you. 34 So you are very different from those other women. You pay your men, and they do not pay you.'

35 So listen to what the Lord is saying to you. 'You are not a faithful wife. 36 You gave your good things to those who were not your husband. And you showed them your body without any clothes. You offered them your children's blood. 37 So I will bring all those with whom you had sex round you. I will bring those that you liked. And I will bring those that you did not like. Then I will remove your clothes in front of them all. They will see you without clothes. 38 They punish wives who are not faithful. You are like those who kill people. So I will punish you. I will show you that I am very angry. I am like a good husband who is angry with a wife. He is angry because she is not faithful. 39 I will make those men who loved you punish you. They will destroy the high places where you worshipped idols. They will take away your beautiful clothes and your things of gold and silver. They will leave you with no clothes. 40 They will bring a crowd of men with swords to cut you up. They will throw stones at you. 41 They will burn down your houses. Women will watch while they punish you. I will stop you from having sex with other men. You will not pay them to have sex with you. 42 After this, I will no longer be angry with you. I will be quiet, and not angry.

43 I will surely punish you because of what you have done', says the Lord, your King. 'You forgot what I did for you. I was kind to you when you were young. You did many things to make me very angry. And you were not ashamed of the bad things that you did.

44 You say that a daughter will be like her mother. 45 Yes, you are a true daughter of your mother! She thought that her husband and her children were not valuable. And you are like your sisters. They thought that their husbands and their children had no value. Your mother was a Hittite and your father was an Amorite.

46 Your older sister was Samaria. She and her daughters lived north of you. Your younger sister was Sodom. She and her daughters lived south of you. 47 You did all the bad things that they did. But you did even worse things, too. 48 Your sister Sodom and her daughters never did such bad things as you and your daughters have done', says the Lord, your King.

49 'This is the sin that your sister Sodom did. She and her daughters (people) thought that they were better than other people. They ate too much and they did not try to help poor people. 50 They thought that they could do what they liked. And I saw them do all kinds of bad things. So I took them away, as you have seen. 51 Samaria's people did only half as many bad things as you have done. You have done much worse things than your sisters. The things that you have done make your bad sisters seem good! 52 Now I must punish you. You have done such bad things that you should be ashamed. After I have looked at you, your sisters seem to be good.

53 But I will give things back to Sodom and her daughters (people). I will give to Samaria and her daughters the things that I took from them. And I will give you back the things that I took away from you. 54 You will be sorry that you did such bad things. And your sisters will be happy that I punished you. 55 I will make your sisters, Sodom and Samaria with their daughters, the same as they were before. And you and your daughters will become what they were before. 56 Before I punished you, you would not speak about your sister Sodom. You thought that you were much better than she was. 57 But then I showed everyone how bad you were. Now the people in Edom and the people near to that country think that you have no value. The people in Philistia and all the people round you think that you have no value. 58 This is because you were not a faithful wife to me. And you did so many wrong things', says the Lord.

59 'You have not kept your promise to me. You did not think that it was important', says the Lord, your King. 'Because of this, I must punish you. 60 But I will remember my promise. I agreed it with you when you were young. And I will make a promise with you that will always remain. 61 Then you will remember the bad things that you did. You will be ashamed when you meet your sisters. I will make them like daughters to you. That was not part of my promise but I will do it. 62 I will keep this promise. And then you will know that I am the Lord. 63 When I pay the price of your sin, you will remember. And you will be ashamed. You will remain quiet because you will be so ashamed', says the Lord, your King.

Chapter 17

God's picture of two big birds and a vine

1 The Lord spoke to me. 2 'Son of man', he said. 'I want you to tell a story. This story is a picture of Israel's people. 3 Say this to Israel's people. "A big bird had great powerful wings. Feathers of beautiful colours covered his wings. He came to Lebanon. 4 There he broke the top from a big tree. He took this top branch to a city. In that city, men buy and sell many things. There he planted his branch.

5 The bird took seed from your land. And he planted it in good ground. He planted it near to much water where trees grow. 6 The branch grew along the ground and it became a vine. The branches turned up towards the bird. And the roots went down into the ground. The vine grew and it covered itself with branches and leaves.

7 Another big bird came, with great wings and many feathers. Then the vine made its branches and roots grow towards this bird. The vine thought that the new bird would give it even more water. 8 But the vine was in a lovely garden where there was good ground and much water. It could grow leaves and fruit (grapes) there, and become big and strong."

9 Ask the people a question', said the Lord. 'Do they think that the vine will stay alive? No, enemies will pull it up and take its fruit. They will let it die. All its new branches will die. It would not be difficult for a strong man or a few people to pull it up. 10 It would die even if they put it into good new ground. The east wind would kill it where it grew.'

11 The Lord spoke to me again. 12 'This people do not obey me. Perhaps they do not know what these things mean', he said. 'Speak to them. Say, "The king of Babylon came to Jerusalem. He took away the king and his officers. He took them back with him to Babylon. 13 Then he agreed to let one of the king's family rule Jerusalem as its king.

This king made a promise to the king of Babylon. He said that he would obey Babylon's king. 14 The king of Babylon wanted to make Israel weak. So he took Jerusalem's important men away to Babylon. He did not want them make Israel strong enough to fight him. 15 But the king of Jerusalem did not keep his promise. He sent messengers to the king of Egypt. He asked him to send an army with horses to save Jerusalem. I tell you that he did a bad thing. He has done the thing that he had promised not to do. The king of Babylon will punish him.

16 I am surely alive", says the Lord, your King. "The king of Israel will die in Babylon. The king of Babylon gave him authority to rule Israel. Israel's king will die in his country. This is because he did not remember his promise to the king of Babylon. He thought that the promise was not important. 17 Pharaoh (the king of Egypt) will not be able to help him with his big army and many soldiers. An enemy will build hills round the city. Then they will attack it. And soldiers will attack Jerusalem and they will kill many people. 18 Your king did not remember his promise. He did not keep it.

Because he did all these things, I will punish him." ' 19 So this is what the Lord, your God, says. 'He did not obey me. So I will do all the bad things that I promised. He promised to do good things. But he did not do them. He thought that his promise to me had no value. 20 I will catch him like a hunter that catches an animal. I will take him to Babylon and I will punish him there. I will punish him because he was not faithful to me. 21 His soldiers will run away and enemies will kill them. A few of them will run to countries that are far away. Then you will know that my words are true.'

22 The Lord, your King, says this: 'I myself will take a small branch from the top of a great tree. I will take it and I will plant it on a high mountain. 23 I will plant it on a high mountain in Israel. It will grow more branches and make fruit. It will become a great tree. Many kinds of birds will live in the tree. They will make their homes in it. Its branches will keep them safe from the sun. 24 Then all the trees in the field will know that I am the Lord. I break down big trees and I make small trees grow. I make the green tree dry and I make the dry tree grow well.

This is what I, the Lord, have said. And I will do it.'

Chapter 18

1 The Lord spoke to me. 2 'Your people say this about the country called Israel. "Fathers have eaten fruit that makes their mouths dry. But their children have the dry mouths." 3 Now I am sure that you will no longer say this. 4 Everything that is alive is mine, says the Lord. Both the father and the son are mine. I will punish any person who does wrong things. 5 Think about a good man. He does only what is good.

6 He does not eat with people who worship idols. He does not himself worship idols. He does not have sex with another man's wife. He does not have sex at the time that the woman is not clean.

7 He does not hurt other people. He may take something from a man and lend him money. He will keep the thing until the man has paid him back. But he will always give the man's thing back.

He does not take things from other people. But he gives food to hungry people.

And he gives clothes to people who have no clothes.

8 He does not lend money and then ask the man to give back a lot more money.

He will not do anything that is wrong.

Sometimes men do not agree. He decides what is right.

9 He obeys all my rules.

Surely he is a good man. And I will let him stay alive', says the Lord, your King 10 'Now think about that man's son. He might be angry. And he might hurt or kill people.

He might do other bad things. 11 (But the father has not done any of these things.)

The son might eat with people who worship idols.

He might have sex with another man's wife.

12 He might hurt people who are poor or sick.

He might take things that are not his.

He might not give back things that he took from other men.

He might worship idols and do other bad things.

13 He might lend money and take back much more money.

I will not let any man that does these things stay alive. I will kill him because he has not obeyed me. I am a fair judge.

14 But this bad man might have a son. The son would see all the wrong things that his father had done. But he would not do them himself.

15 He would not eat with people who worship idols.

He would not worship idols.

He would not have sex with another man's wife.

16 He would not hurt anyone.

He would not take anything when he lent money to someone.

He would not take things that belonged to other people. But he would give food to hungry people.

He would give clothes to people who had none.

17 He would not do any wrong thing. He would not take back too much money from people to whom he had lent it.

He would obey my rules. And he would do the things that give me pleasure.

This son will not die because his father did bad things. He will stay alive. 18 But his father did things that were wrong. So he will die. He took too much money from people to whom he had lent it. He took things from his brother.

19 You do not understand why I do not punish the son with his father. The son has done what is good and right. And so he will stay alive. He obeyed all my rules, so he will stay alive. 20 But I will punish people who do wrong things. They will die. I will not punish the son because of the bad things that his father did. And I will not punish the father because of the bad things that his son did. Men who do good things give me pleasure. But I will punish those men who do bad things.

21 A bad man might not do the wrong things that he did any longer. And he might start to do good things. He would begin to obey me. Then he would stay alive. I would not kill him. 22 I would not remember any of the bad things that he did. 23 I do not want to kill anyone. That does not give me pleasure', says the Lord, your King. 'When bad men start to do good things, it gives me pleasure. Then they stay alive.

24 A good man might not do things that are good and true any longer. He might start to do the same wrong things as bad men. Then I will not remember any of the good things that he did. I will punish him because of the wrong things that he has done. He will die because he has not been faithful to me.

25 You say that I am not fair. But listen to me, Israel's people. The things that you do are not fair. 26 A good man might stop doing good things. If then he does bad things he will die. He will die because he has done wrong things. 27 A bad man might not do bad things any longer. Then if he does good things he will stay alive. 28 He has seen that he had done wrong things. And so he has started to do good things. I will not kill him and he will stay alive. 29 But you, Israel's people, say that I am not fair. You must see that you are not fair to me. The things that you do are wrong.

30 So I will be a judge for each of you. I will punish those people who do bad things. And I will save the people who do good things', says the Lord, your King. 'You must be sad if you have done bad things. You must be sorry and you must start to do good things. Stop doing bad things and I will not punish you. 31 You must live in a different way. You need new thoughts. You must want to do good things. I am sure that you, Israel's people, do not want to die. 32 I do not want anyone to die. That gives me no pleasure', says the Lord, your King. 'Be sad. Turn back to me and stop doing wrong things. Then you will stay alive.'

Chapter 19

1 'Say this to the leaders of Israel. It is a sad song and it is about them.

2 "Your mother was a strong female among the great wild animals.

She lay among her young animals. She kept them safe among the males.

3 One of her young animals became a great strong male.

He caught animals for food and he tore them into pieces.

He also ate men.

4 Men in other countries heard what he did.

So they dug a hole and they caught him in it.

They pulled him out and they took him to Egypt.

5 The mother saw that her strong son was taken away.

So she took another of her sons and she made him big and strong.

6 Now he was big. And he learned to kill and tear his food.

And he killed and ate men.

7 He attacked their towns and he broke down their strong buildings.

All the people in the country were afraid. The noise that he made frightened them.

8 Men from countries round them came to attack him.

They dug a hole and they made him run into it.

They caught him and they put him in a box.

9 They took him to the king of Babylon.

There they put him in prison.

The people on the hills of Israel could not hear his voice any longer.

10 Your mother was like a vine that was growing in a field of vines.

Her vine grew near the water and its branches had much fruit.

11 The branches were strong enough to use as a stick to show a king's power.

The vine grew high above other trees.

It was very tall and it had many branches.

12 But I was angry with it. So I threw it to the ground.

The east wind dried it up and its leaves died.

They took its fruit.

Its strong branches dried and they burnt them in a fire.

13 Now the vine is growing in a dry and empty land (a desert).

14 Fire from one of its big branches burnt up its fruit.

Now it has no big branches that men can make into a special stick.

That stick is for the king.

This is a sad story for people to sing." '

Chapter 20

1 In the tenth (10th) day of the fifth (5th) month some of Israel's leaders came to me. That was in the seventh (7th) year in Babylon. They sat in front of me. They wanted me to ask the Lord for his help.

2 Then the Lord spoke to me. 3 'Son of man, say this to the leaders of Israel. "This is what the Lord, your King, says. 'I see that you have come to ask for my help. Be sure that I am alive. But I will not let you ask me anything' ", he says.

4 You must be a judge for them, son of man. Make them remember all the wrong things that their fathers did. 5 Say to them, "On the day that I chose Israel's people, I the Lord, your King said: 'I made a promise to all Jacob's sons and their sons. I showed myself to them in Egypt. I promised to be their God. 6 I said that I would take them out of Egypt.

And I promised to take them to a country that I had chosen for them. It was a most beautiful country and it would give them milk and sweet food. 7 I said to them: "You must each destroy the idols that you worshipped in Egypt. You are not clean. I am the Lord, your God."

8 But your fathers would not obey me. They would not listen to me, and they did not destroy their idols. They continued to worship the idols of Egypt. So I was very angry. I said that I would punish them there in Egypt. 9 But the people who lived near to Egypt knew about me. They had seen that I had taken the Israelites out of Egypt. I did not want them to say bad things about me. 10 So I took the people out of Egypt. Then I led them into the desert. 11 I gave them my rules. I told them how I wanted them to live. The man that obeys my rules will live a good life. 12 And I gave them the Sabbath, the seventh (7th) day of the week. This special day showed them that I had chosen them to be my holy people. It helped them to remember our promises to each other.

13 But when Israel's people were in the desert, they did not obey me. They did not obey my rules. I told them what they should do. But they did not do those things. (But the man that does these things will stay alive.) And they did not obey my rules about the Sabbath. I was very angry. So I said that I would destroy them there in the desert. 14 I wanted the nations who had seen me take them from Egypt to give me honour. I did not want them to think that I could not save my people.

15 But I spoke to my people in the desert. I had chosen a beautiful country that gave milk and sweet food for them. But I said that I would not bring my people into their country. 16 I would not do this because they had not obeyed my rules. And they had done so many wrong things. They wanted to worship their idols and not to worship me. 17 But I was kind to them. I did not kill them in the desert. 18 I spoke to their children in the desert. "Do not do the wrong things that your fathers do", I said. "Do not obey their rules or worship their idols. 19 I am the Lord your God, so obey my rules. Be careful to do the things that give me pleasure. 20 Make the Sabbath a holyday. Then I will know that you remember my promises. You will know that I am the Lord your God."

21 But the children did not obey my rules. They did not do the things that give me pleasure. (But people who obey my rules will stay alive.) And they did not make the Sabbath day a holy day. So I showed them there in the desert that I was angry. 22 But I did not kill them. All the nations round Israel had seen me take my people out of Egypt. I wanted the nations to give me honour. I did not want them to say bad things about me. 23 There in the desert I made a strong promise to my people. I said that I would send them too many different countries. 24 This was because they had not obeyed my rules. Nor had they made the Sabbath a holy day. And they had chosen to worship their father's idols. 25 So I let them obey their own rules. They were bad rules and they could not give life. 26 I let them kill their first-born children to offer to idols. This would make them so sad that they would be sorry. Then they would know that I am the Lord.' "

27 Son of man, you must speak to Israel's people and say, "This is what the Lord, your King says, 'This is how your fathers took away my honour. They stopped obeying me. 28 They came to the country that I had promised to give them. They looked at the mountains and high hills When I took them there they offered gifts to idols on those high hills. They offered them gifts under the tall trees. This made me angry. And they made sweet smells and they gave food and drink to those idols. 29 They did this on the high places that they all turn to.' "

30 Say this to Israel's people. "This is what the Lord, your King says: 'The things that you are doing are not right. They are quite as bad as the wrong things that your fathers did. You still want to worship things that they made out of wood and stone (idols). 31 You offer your sons to them in the fire as gifts. This shows how bad you are. You must see that. But you still do it even to this day. I cannot let you ask me for help. I am surely alive and I will not let you do this.

32 You say: "We want to be like people in other countries. They worship things that they have made out of wood and stone (idols)." But I will not let this happen. 33 I am alive', says the powerful Lord. 'I will rule over you. I will rule you with my strong power. And I will punish you when you make me angry. 34 I will bring you back from the nations where I sent you. I will do this with my strong power. I am still angry with you. 35 I will take you away to a desert where I will punish you. 36 As I punished your fathers in the desert of Egypt, so I will punish you', says the Lord, your King. 37 'I will look at each of you and I will remember my covenant with you. 38 I will remove those who will not obey my rules. I will bring them out of the country where they are living. But I will not bring them into the country called Israel. Then you will know that I am the Lord.

39 Israel's people, this is what the Lord, your King says: "Go, every one of you, to be servants to your idols! But after you have gone to do it you will listen to me. I am sure about that. And you will no longer give gifts to idols. You will no longer give them honour. You should give me that honour. 40 The high mountain of Israel is my holy mountain, says the Lord, your King. There in the country called Israel you will all be my servants. This will give me pleasure. There you will bring me your good gifts. I want you to offer me your holy gifts there. And you will burn them on my altar. 41 You will be like a sweet smell to me when I bring you home. I will bring you back from all the nations. I will bring you back from all the countries to which I sent you. I will show you that I am holy. And those nations will also see that I am holy. 42 Then you will know that I am the Lord. You will know this when I bring you into the country. I promised to give your fathers that country. 43 Then you will remember all the wrong things that you did. You will be sorry. You will be ashamed of the evil things that you have done. 44 Then I will be good to you. And you will know that I am the Lord. I will forget the bad things that you did and your wrong thoughts. This will bring honour to me, you Israel's people" ', says the Lord, your King." '

45 The Lord spoke to me again. 46 'Son of man', he said. 'Turn and look towards the south. Speak my words to the people there. Prophesy against the forests in the south. 47 Say this to those forests: "Listen to what the Lord says. I am going to make you burn with fire. The fire will destroy all the young trees and the dry trees. You will not be able to stop the fire. It will burn the faces of people. It will burn those in the south and in the north. 48 Everyone will see that I, the Lord, started the fire. Nobody will put it out." '

49 Then I told the Lord what the people thought. They said that I was only telling them stories.

Chapter 21

The Lord uses the people from Babylon to punish Israel

1 The Lord spoke to me. 2 'Son of man', he said. 'You must look towards Jerusalem. Then tell them what I say. They are doing things in my holy place that are wrong. Speak to the people in Israel. 3 Say to them, "This is what the Lord says. 'I will fight against you. I will take out my sword and I will use it to kill everyone. I will kill the good people and the bad ones. 4 Because of this, I will attack all the people from the north to the south. 5 Then all the people will know that I am attacking them with my sword. And I will not put my sword back in its place.' "

6 So cry with a loud voice, son of man. Let them see how sad and sorry you are. 7 They will ask you why you are so sad. Then you will say, "Because of the bad news that is coming to you. Every one of you will be afraid and will become weak. Your hands will hang down and your knees will bend. You will be very afraid. You can be sure that I am coming to punish you", says the Lord, your King.'

8 The Lord spoke to me again. 9 'Son of man, prophesy to them. Say, "This is what the Lord says:

I have a sword. It is sharp and it shines.

10 It is ready to kill. It shines like the light that shoots from the sky!"

This sword will destroy all arms made from wood. So we cannot be happy.

11 I have made it ready to hold in the hand.

It is sharp and it shines. My sword is ready for the hand of the person who kills.

12 Cry with a loud voice, son of man,

because the sword is coming against my people.

It is coming against the princes of Israel.

I will throw the princes and the people to the sword.

So you must show them that you are very sad.

13 I will surely be a judge for my people.

And if they do not obey me, these things will happen', says the Lord, your King.

14 'So prophesy, son of man.

Hit your hands together.

The sword will hit them more than once.

I made the sword to kill. It will kill many times.

The swords come from all round the city.

15 The people are very afraid. Swords will kill many of them.

Swords wait at every gate. They move fast to kill.

16 Sword, hit out to your right side. Then hit to the left. Turn every way to kill.

17 I, too, will hit my hands together. Then I will not be angry any longer.

I, the Lord have spoken.'

18 The Lord spoke to me. 19 'Son of man, draw two roads for the king of Babylon to follow. They must both start from the same country. Put a sign where the two roads go away from each other. 20 Mark one road for the sword to go to Rabbah of the Ammonites. The other road goes towards Judah and the strong city, Jerusalem. 21 The king of Babylon will stop when he comes to the sign. He will try to find which way to go. He will ask his idols. He will ask his priests to throw down sticks. Then they will look at the insides of animals. But this sword will destroy all arms that people have made from wood. 22 The priests will say that he should go to Jerusalem. There he will build hills round the city, to attack it. He will make his men shout while they attack it. They will hit the gates with very heavy long sticks. They will climb up its walls. 23 The people in Jerusalem may think that the king of Babylon is their friend. He should be their friend because of the promises that they made to each other. They think that he will not attack them. But he will attack because the people in Jerusalem have done many wrong things. That is what I say. He will make them his prisoners.

24 This then is what the Lord, your King says: "People see that you have not obeyed me. You do evil things all the time and in all the places where you go. You are not ashamed of your sin. So your enemies will make you their prisoners.

25 King of Israel, you are evil. I told you what you should do. But you have not done those things. The day has come when I will punish you." 26 This is what the Lord, your King says: "Take off the special hat that you wear. Remove your crown. I will change things. Some people think that other people have no value. But those same people will become important. Other people thought that they themselves were important. Then they will learn that they are not important. 27 I will break down your city. This will not happen until my chosen man comes. I will give the city to him. It belongs to him."

28 You, son of man, must prophesy about the people in Ammon. They have said bad things about you. This is what the Lord, your King says:

"A sword, a sword, it is ready to kill.

It shines like the light that moves quickly from the sky.

29 Your prophets have said nothing that is true.

They have told you about pictures that I have not given them.

They say that things will happen. But I did not tell them that they should say those things.

The sword will cut through the necks of people who are evil.

The time has come when I will punish them.

30 Put your sword back in its place.

I will be your judge in the place where I made you.

In the country that I gave to your fathers, I will punish you.

31 You will see that I am angry with you.

I will give you to men who are not kind.

They are men who like to kill.

32 You will be like wood in the fire.

They will pour your blood on the land.

Nobody will remember you.

I, the Lord, have spoken." '

Chapter 22

The Lord is a judge for Jerusalem (and all its people)

1 The Lord spoke to me. 2 'Son of man, you must tell the people in this city that I am going to be their judge. They have killed many people. Make them see how many wrong things they have done. 3 Say to them, "This is what the Lord, your King says: 'You are a city that destroys itself. 4 I will punish you because you poured blood over your streets. You have made idols for yourselves and you are no longer pure. I will cause your days to end. I have finished your years as a city. Nations will not give you any honour. Men from all countries will laugh because I have punished you. 5 Those who live near and those far away will laugh. You are a city full of evil things. And all the people in you are always fighting.

6 In you, each leader of Israel used his power to kill men. 7 In you they have not given any honour to father or mother. In you they have not been kind to foreigners, widows or children with no parents. 8 You gave no honour to my holy things. You have not made my Sabbaths holy. 9-10 In you, are men who say wrong things. They say what is not true. They say it in order to kill other people. In you, there are men who have sex with other men's wives. They do the bad things that they did in Egypt. The people there give food to idols. And then those people eat it. In you, there are men who do the same thing. And they do other bad things. Some men have sex with women who are not pure. 11 There are men who have sex with other men's wives. There are those who have sex with their daughters or their son's wives. Some have sex with their sisters, the daughters of their own fathers. 12 In you, men pay money for one man to kill another. They lend money to people. But they make those men give them a lot more money back. In you, men make people give them money in ways that are not fair. And you have forgotten me', says the Lord.

13 'I am very angry because you have killed people. You have not been fair. You have taken more money than was right. 14 I will punish you and that will make you feel weak. I am the Lord. I have said what I will do. And I will do it. 15 I will send you too many different countries. I will make you pure again. 16 All nations will think that you have no value. Then you will know that I am the Lord.' " '

17 The Lord spoke to me. 18 'Son of man, Israel's people are like dirt to me. Men burn metals in a fire so that they can take out the silver. My people are like the metal that remains in the pot. 19 So this is what the Lord, your King says: "I will bring you all into Jerusalem because you are like dirt. 20 Men bring metals into a hot fire to make them soft. I will do the same thing to you. I will bring you into the city and I will make you soft. I will do this because I am so angry. 21 I will bring you into Jerusalem. And I will burn you with my anger. 22 They make silver soft in a hot fire. In the same way I will make you soft with my hot anger. Then you will know that I am the Lord. And you will know that I have burnt you with my hot anger." '

23 The Lord spoke to me again. 24 'Son of man, speak to the land. Say, "I am angry and I will not send you any rain." 25 Your leaders agree to hurt people. They take valuable things from the people and they kill many women's husbands. They are like wild animals that tear up their meat. 26 The priests do not obey my rules. They do not use my holy things as they should. They think that holy things are not special. They teach men that pure things and things that are not pure are the same. They do not teach men to keep my Sabbath holy. Because of this, men do not give me any honour.

27 Their officers are like wild animals that tear their meat. They do not judge in a fair way. And they kill people to get their money.

28 Their prophets say that they are not doing any wrong thing. But those prophets see false dreams and they tell false stories. They say, "This is what the Lord, your King says." But I have not spoken to them. 29 The people in this country make people afraid and take their money. They are not kind to poor people or to those people who are weak. They hurt foreigners and they do not judge them in a fair way.

30 I tried to find a man who would help me to save the land. Then I would not have to destroy it. But I could not find a man to help me. 31 So I will burn the people up with my great anger. I will punish them because of the wrong things that they have done', says the Lord, your King.

Chapter 23

A story about two bad sisters

1 The Lord spoke to me. 2 'Son of man, a woman had two daughters. They were sisters. 3 Men in Egypt paid to have sex with them. They sold themselves to men from the time that they were young. Men touched their young breasts and made love to them. 4 The older sister was called Oholah. The younger one was Oholibah. They belonged to me, and they gave birth to sons and daughters. Oholah is Samaria and Oholibah is Jerusalem.

5 Oholah sold herself to other men while she was still mine. She wanted to have sex with the people who live in Assyria, her lovers. 6 Their soldiers wore red and blue clothes. They were officers and rulers and they were all very beautiful. They rode on horses. 7 Oholah had sex with all the important people who live in Assyria. And she worshipped their idols. 8 She continued to sell her body as she had done in Egypt. She had sex with men. She was quite as bad as when she was young.

9 I gave her to her lovers, the people who live in Assyria. That was because she had not been faithful to me. 10 They took off all her clothes and they took all her sons and daughters. Then they killed her. Her story made women afraid because I punished her.

11 Oholibah, her sister saw this, but did even worse things than her sister. 12 She, too, wanted to have sex with the people who live in Assyria. She wanted the beautiful young officers and the rulers on horses to love her. 13 I saw that she, like her sister, was not faithful to me. She became not clean.

14 But she did more bad things than her sister. She saw pictures on the walls. They were pictures of men from Babylon They wore red clothes. 15 They had belts round their bodies and cloths round their heads. They looked like officers who drove chariots. 16 As soon as she saw the officers, she wanted them. She sent messengers to them in Babylon. 17 Then they came to her from Babylon. And they had sex with her. They made her not clean. After they had done this to her, she did not want them any longer. She turned away from them. 18 I turned away from her when she had sex with other men. She was quite like her sister. 19But she wanted more and more men to love her. She had had sex with when she was young. She remembered about that. At that time she had sex with men in Egypt. 20 They had loved her more like animals than men.21 She very much wanted to have sex like that again.

22 So this is what the Lord, your King says to you, Oholibah: "The men that you had sex with will turn against you. I will make them do this. You turned away from them. But I will bring them all round you. 23Men from Babylon and Chaldea will come. And men from Pekod, Shoa and Koa will come. All the people who live in Assyria will come with them. They will be beautiful young men, officers, rulers and important men. They will all ride on horses. 24 They will fight you with arms and chariots and with many soldiers. They will come to attack you from every side. They will have shields (flat metal or leather plates to save them from sharp knives and stones) and they will wear strong hats on their heads. I will let them punish you as they think best. 25 I am very angry with you. And they are angry with you. They will cut off your noses and ears. They will kill any men that remain. They will take away your sons and daughters. And they will burn the rest of your people with fire. 26 They will take away your clothes and all your valuable things.27 You will no longer do the wrong things that you began to do in Egypt. I will stop you. You will never want to think about them or remember Egypt any longer."

28 So this is what the Lord, your King says: "I will give people power over you. I will give that power to people that you hate. You turned away from them because they did bad things to you. 29 They will show you how much they hate you.

They will take away everything for which you have worked. You will have no clothes or food. You will be ashamed of the things that you did. Everyone will know what you did. 30 I am punishing you because you did those things. I am punishing you because you wanted to be like other nations. And because you worshipped their idols. 31 You have done the same bad things that your sister did. So I will punish you as I punished her."

32 This is what the Lord, your King says:

"I will give you the same punishment that I gave to your sister.

It will be a strong punishment.

It will make people laugh. And they will think that you have no value.

33 You will all be sad and you will get drunk.

They will break down your cities and your country will be empty.

It will be like your sister Samaria.

34 Your punishment will be complete and you will be very sad.

That is what I have said", says the Lord, your King.

35 "So this is what I say to you", says the Lord, your King. "You have forgotten me and men have paid to have sex with you. You were not ashamed. You thought that I could not see. But now I will punish you because of the bad things that you have done." '

36 The Lord spoke to me. 'Son of man, you must judge Oholah and Oholibah. Make them see that they have done wrong things. 37 They have not been faithful to me and they have caused men to die. They worshipped idols and they even offered their children to the idols as food. 38 At the same time, they did not keep holy the place where they should have worshipped me. They did not keep the Sabbaths as my special days. 39 The same day that they gave their children to idols they made my house not clean. That is what they did to my house.

40 The sisters sent messages to men in a far country. When the men came to visit them they made themselves beautiful with paint and pretty stones. 41 They sat on a soft seat and they put a table in front of it. On the table they put oils with sweet smells. But those oils belonged to me.

42 Men from the desert (Sabeans) came with a crowd who were making a noise. Some of them put pretty things on the women's arms and crowns (special hats that rulers wear) on their heads. 43 I said: "Let them have sex with the woman. She has had so much sex that she is tired. That is now the only way that anyone can use her." 44 So the men used her for sex. They paid Oholah and Oholibah to have sex with them. 45 But men who do good things will punish them. They will punish them because they were not faithful to me. And because they caused men to die.

46 This is what the Lord, your King says: "You good men must take a crowd to attack them. You will make them afraid and you will take their things. 47 The crowd will throw stones at them and cut them with swords. They will kill their sons and daughters and they will burn down their houses.

48 So I will stop people from using their bodies in a wrong way. I will make women want to do what is good and right. 49 I will punish you because of the bad things that you have done. And I will punish you because you have worshipped idols. Then you will know that I am the Lord, your King." '

Chapter 24

The pot to cook meat

1 The Lord spoke to me on the tenth (10th) day. That was in the tenth (10th) month of the ninth (9th) year.

2 'Remember this day, son of man. On this day, the king of Babylon is starting to attack Jerusalem. 3 Tell a story to this people who do not obey me. Say, "This is what the Lord says:

'Put the pot on the fire. Fill it with water.

4 Put into it the best pieces of meat, the leg and the shoulder.

Fill it with all the best bones. 5 Take them from sheep that are the best to eat.

Put wood under the pot and boil it to cook the meat and the bones.'

6 This is what the Lord, your King says.

'I will make sorry the city where they killed men.

This city is like a pot that nobody has cleaned. They have taken out every piece of meat. They have not left one piece. 7 Men can see the blood that poured out on the streets. No dirt covers it. 8 I am very angry. So I let all men see the blood that you poured out.'

9 So this is what the Lord, your King says.

'I will make the city that poured out this blood very sad.

And I will put wood on the fire.

10 So make the fire burn and cook the meat well.

Put in more things that will make it taste good. Let the bones burn.

11 Put the empty pot on the fire so that it becomes red and hot.

The fire should burn away all its dirt.

12 But the dirt will not burn away. Even fire cannot do this.

13 The bad things that you do are like your dirt. I tried to make you clean, but you would not let me. You will not become clean until I am no longer angry with you.

14 I, the Lord have spoken. Now I am beginning to do the things that I promised.

I will not stop. I will not be kind or make the punishment less. I will judge you because of the many bad things that you have done', says the Lord, your King." '

Ezekiel's wife dies

15 The Lord spoke to me. 16 'Son of man I will take away the one person who gives you great pleasure. I will do it quickly. But you must not look sad or cry. 17 You must not make a lot of noise. You must not show people how sad you are. Keep your head covered and your feet. Do not cover part of your face. People eat special food when someone dies. But you must not do this.'

18 That morning I spoke to the people. In the evening my wife died. The next morning I did what the Lord had said.

19 Then the people asked me what this meant for them. 20 So I said to them, 'The Lord spoke to me. He said, 21 "Say this to Israel's people: 'This is what the Lord, your King says:

"I will make my holy place not clean. You think that it is a beautiful place. And you love it. I will take away the things that you love. And they will kill your sons and daughters that you left in Jerusalem. 22 Then you will do the same things that I have done. You will not cover part of your face. You will not eat special food. People eat special food when someone dies. But you will not do that. 23 You will not cry or look sad. You will wear your hats and shoes. You will be sorry. You will become thin because of the bad things that you have done.

24 I have made Ezekiel show you what I will do to you. Then you will know that I am the Lord." ' 25 On that day, son of man, I will destroy all the things that they love. I will destroy their beautiful buildings and I will take away their sons and daughters. 26 A man will run away from Jerusalem. He will bring you the bad news on the day that I cause these things to happen. 27 At that time you will become able to speak. You will talk with him. You will no longer be quiet. This will show the people that I am the Lord." '

Chapter 25

The Lord speaks against Ammon

1 The Lord spoke to me. 2 'Son of man', he said. 'Turn your face towards the people in Ammon. You must prophesy against them. 3 Say to them, "Listen to the message from the Lord, the King. This is what he says: 'You were happy when enemies made my holy place not clean. And you were not sorry when I destroyed the land in Israel. Nor were you sad when I took the people in Judah away to a foreign country. 4 So I will give you to the people in the East as a gift. Their armies will come and they will put tents all round you. They will eat your fruit and they will drink your milk. 5 I will make Rabbah a place where camels (animals that carry men and their things over deserts) feed. I will make Ammon a place where sheep rest. Then you will know that I am the Lord.' 6 So this is what the Lord, the King says: 'You hit your hands together and you jumped about. You were happy when I punished Israel. 7 Because of this I will attack you. Nations will come and I will give them all your good things. You will not be a nation any longer. I will destroy you and you will not have your own country. And you will know that I am the Lord.'

The Lord speaks against Moab

8 The Lord, the King says this to the people in Moab and Seir. 'You said that the people in Judah have become like all the other nations. 9 Because of this, I will make the towns at the edge of Moab weak. These are Beth Jeshimoth, Baal Meon and Kiriathaim. They are the best towns in the country. 10 I will give Moab with the Ammonites as a gift to the people in the East. Nobody will remember that Ammon was a nation. 11 and I will punish Moab. Then they will know that I am the Lord.' " '

The Lord speaks against Edom

12 "This is what the Lord, the King says: 'Edom was angry with the people in Judah. So they attacked them. They caused me to become very angry.' 13 'Because they did this', the Lord says, 'I will attack Edom. Enemies will kill its men and its animals. I will make Edom into a desert. Israel will take their words. And they will kill the people from Teman to Dedan. 14 I will use Israel's people to punish Edom. They will make Edom know that I am very angry with them. They will know that I am punishing them', says the Lord, the King."

The Lord speaks against the Philistines

15 "This is what the Lord, the King says. 'The Philistines hated Judah. They sent armies to kill and to hurt them. They tried to destroy Judah.' 16 So this is what the Lord, the King says. 'I will punish the Philistines. I will kill their people who remain by the edge of the sea. 17 I am very angry with them and I will punish them strongly. I will do this. Then they will know that I am the Lord.' " '

Chapter 26

The Lord speaks against Tyre

1 The Lord spoke to me on the first day of the month. It was the eleventh (11th) year.

2 'Tyre's people have said: "Good! Now we have broken down the walls of Jerusalem. Its doors are open to us. Tyre will become a rich city because we have destroyed Jerusalem."

3 So this is what the Lord, the King says: "I am against you, Tyre, I will bring many nations to attack you. They will be as strong as the waves of the sea.

4 They will destroy the walls of Tyre and they will pull down its strong buildings. I will pull away all the stones that they used to build it. 5 There, men will dry the things that they use to catch fish. They will dry them on the rock where Tyre was before. That is what I say", says the Lord, the King.

6 "Armies with swords will destroy all the towns near the city. Then they will know that I am the Lord." '

7 Now this is what the Lord, your King says: 'I will bring Nebuchadnezzar king of Babylon against Tyre. He will come from the north. He is a great king with men on horses, chariots (war cars) and a great army. 8 He will attack and destroy all your towns and villages on the land near the sea. He will build hills to attack your walls. 9 He will hit your walls with very heavy long sticks. And he will destroy your high buildings. 10 He will have many horses. Their feet will cause dirt to cover you. He will break through your walls and he will bring in his horses and chariots (war cars). The noise that they make will cause your walls to shake. 11 While his horses go along your streets, his soldiers will kill people. They will kill them with their swords. They will break down all your tall buildings. 12 They will take away all your food and the things that you sell. They will break down your beautiful buildings. And you will throw into the sea all the wood and stone that made them. 13 Nobody will sing your songs any longer. Nobody will hear your music any longer. 14 I will cause you to become just a rock in the sea. Men will dry there the things that they use to catch fish. They will never build you again. That is what I say', says the Lord, the King.

15 This is what the Lord, the King says to Tyre. 'All the people who live by the sea will hear. They will hear that I have made you fall. Then they will be very afraid. They will hear the cries of people who are hurting. 16 Then the princes of those towns will take off their beautiful clothes. They will sit in the dirt and they will be sad and afraid. Their bodies will shake because they are so afraid. 17 Then they will make a sad song about you:

"Great city of men of the sea, I have completely destroyed you.

You and your people were the strong men of the sea.

You made everyone else afraid of you.

18 Now people on the land are afraid on the day that you fall.

The islands in the sea are afraid because I have made you fall." '

19 This is what the Lord, your King says. 'I will make you like an empty city. And the sea will cover you with its great waters. 20 Then I will make you fall into the earth. You will go to be with men who have died. You will not return. Nobody will ever live in you again. 21 I will completely destroy you. People will look for you but they will never find you", says the Lord, your King.'

Chapter 27

A sad song about Tyre

1 The Lord spoke to me. 2 'Son of man, you must sing this sad song for Tyre. Tyre is like a gate to the sea. From there, men go to sell things to many peoples. 3 Say to Tyre's people, "This is what the Lord, the King says:

'You say that the beauty of Tyre is complete.

4 You ruled the great seas. Men made you a beautiful city like a boat on the sea.

5 They used wood from the pine trees of Senir.

They took the trunk of a cedar of Lebanon. From it they made a tall round stick to stand in the centre of the boat.

6 They made flat sticks (oars) from oaks of Bashan. They used them to push you through the water.

They made your deck with ivory and wood from the coasts of Cyprus.

7 They made your sail out of the best white cloth from Egypt. They made it pretty with many colours.

The beautiful sail told people who you were.

Over your deck they put tents of blue and purple cloth.

It came from Elishah's country by the sea.

8 Men from Sidon and Arvad pushed you through the water.

Your men from Tyre told them how to do this. And they told them where to go.

9 Men from Gebal went with you. They had made boats for many years.

Sailors from many ships bought and sold things in your shops.

10 You had men from Persia, Lydia and Put (Libya) in your army.

They hung their arms in the houses where your soldiers lived.

They fought and won your fights for you.

They brought you honour.

11 Men from Arvad and Helech stood on your walls.

And men from Gammad kept your tall buildings safe.

They hung their arms on your walls. They made you beautiful.

12 You had many different things to sell. So men from Tarshish came to buy from you. They brought silver and other metals to pay for those things.

13 Men from Greece, Tubal and Meshech came. They paid you with slaves and metals.

14 Men from Beth Togarmah came. They sold you horses to use for war or for work.

15 Men from Rhodes and other countries by the sea came to you. They paid you with ivory and hard black wood.

16 People from Aram came because you had so many things to sell. They brought you coloured stones of great value. And they brought the best cloth with pretty colours on it.

17 People from Judah and Israel came to buy things from you. They paid you with food grains from Minnith and sweet cakes.

18 Men from Damascus came to buy your things. They came because you had many different things to sell. They sold you wine from Helbon and white wool.

19 Men from Dan and Greeks from Uzal came and they bought your things. They paid you with iron and plants to make food taste good (spices).

20 People from Dedan sold you blankets for your horses.

21 Men from Arabia and the leaders of Kedar all came to buy your things. They bought and sold young sheep, male sheep and goats.

22 Men from Sheba and Raamah came to buy and to sell many valuable things. These were pretty stones, gold and things to make food taste good (spices).

23 Men from many towns came to you to buy and sell things. They came from Haran, Canneh and Eden. Other men came from Sheba, Asshur and Kilmad. 24 They came to the centre of your town. There they bought and sold beautiful clothes, good blue cotton cloth and strong carpets.

25 You were like a ship from Tarshish.

You carried the things that you wanted to buy and sell.

You sailed on the sea. You were full of heavy things.

26 Men took sticks that they had made from wood (oars). With them they pushed your boats. The boats went over the deep sea.

But the east wind there will break you into small pieces.

27 All your valuable things and all the people in the boat

will fall into the deep sea.

The men who buy and sell will fall.

The soldiers and the sailors in the ship will all fall.

They will fall into the sea when the boat breaks.

28 The land by the sea will shake.

It will move when people hear your sailors cry out.

29 The men who push the boat will jump out of the ship. They push the boat with sticks that they made from wood (oars).

Sailors and people by the sea 30 will stand there and cry. They will make a loud noise.

They will put dirt on their heads and on their clothes.

31 They will cut the hair from their heads and they will wear old clothes.

They will do this because God is punishing you.

They will be very sorry and they will cry about you.

32 They will sing a sad song about you while they walk up and down.

"Nobody ever destroyed a city as God has destroyed Tyre.

Tyre was a city with sea all round it."

33 You gave good things to many nations.

You had valuable things and you sold them to kings.

You made all the kings in the world become rich men.

34 Now the sea has broken you up.

You are under its waters.

All your things and your people are under the sea.

35 The people who live by the sea are afraid.

They are afraid because they have seen you fall.

Their kings shake because they are afraid.

Their faces have become long and sad.

36 Men from other nations who buy and sell are afraid.

They are afraid that they too will fall.

God has destroyed your city. You will never return.' " '

Chapter 28

God's prophecy against the king of Tyre

1 The Lord spoke to me. 2 'Son of man, say this to the ruler of Tyre. "This is what the Lord, your King says:

'You thought that you were very great.

You said to yourself, "I am a god.

I am sitting on a throne. I am like a god with seas all round me."

But you are a man and not a god.

You think that you are as wise as a god.

3 But you are not as wise as Daniel.

You do not know all secrets.

4 You have been clever enough to get many valuable things.

You have stored much gold and silver in a safe place.

5 You buy and sell in a clever way, so you have many valuable things.

You think that you are great. You think that because you are so rich.

So this is what the Lord, your King, says:

6 "You think that you are as wise as a god.

7 So I am bringing foreign soldiers to fight you.

They will be less kind than people from any nation.

Their swords will destroy your beautiful city.

It will no longer be beautiful.

8 They will kill you and they will send your bodies into the sea.

9 Your enemies will come to kill you.

Then you will no longer say that you are a god.

10 They will kill you in the same way as they kill other people. They will kill you like people who do not belong to God.

That is what I say", says the Lord, your King.' " '

11 The Lord spoke to me,

12 'Son of man, you must make a sad song about the king of Tyre. Speak to him. Say, "This is what the Lord, the King, says:

'I did not see anything bad in you.

You were completely beautiful. You were wise in every way.

13 You lived in the garden of God (Eden).

I had covered your body with beautiful stones of every kind.

They were of different colours, red, blue, green, yellow and other colours too.

Gold held the stones together.

I made them for you on the day that I made you.

14 I chose you to keep my garden safe.

I gave you that work to do for me.

You lived on my holy mountain.

You walked among the burning fires.

15 You were not bad in any way.

You were completely pure on the day that I made you.

But later, I saw that you had become bad.

16 You bought and sold things. You fought for the things that you wanted.

That was your sin.

So I sent you out of my mountain to make you ashamed.

You no longer walked among the fires.

17 But you still thought that you were very great.

You liked to think that you were very beautiful.

You used your wisdom to do things that were wrong.

Because of this, I threw you down to the earth.

Their kings saw how you had fallen.

18 You bought and sold things. But you did it in a way that was not fair.

That is how your temples became no longer pure.

So I made a fire come out of you to burn you up.

Everyone saw you become ashes on the ground.

19 The nations who knew you are very afraid. They were not happy at all.

They saw that your life had such a bad end. So they were not happy.

You will not be alive again.' " '

A prophecy against Sidon

20 The Lord spoke to me. 21 'Son of man, you must turn against Sidon. Prophesy against its people and say, 22 "This is what the Lord, your King says:

'I am against you, Sidon.

But the people in you will give me honour.

I will punish their city.

Then they will know that I am the Lord.

Then they will know that I am holy.

23 I will cause them to become ill.

I will make blood run through its streets.

They will kill the men in the city.

Enemies will attack Sidon from every side.

Then its people will know that I am the Lord.

24 I will kill the people in the countries round Israel.

They will no longer be like sharp points on plants that cause Israel's people pain.

Then they will know that I am the Lord, their King.'

25 This is what the Lord, the King, says: 'I will bring back Israel's people from the countries where I sent them. Then all the nations will see that I am holy. My people will live in their own country. I gave that country to my servant, their father Jacob. 26 I will make them safe while they live there. They will build houses and they will plant vines in their fields. I will punish all those nations round them. I will punish them because they said bad things about my people. Then my people will be safe. And they will know that I am the Lord their God.' " '

Chapter 29

A prophecy against Egypt

1 The Lord spoke to me. It was the twelfth (12th) day of the tenth (10th) month of the tenth (10th) year.

2 'Son of man', he said. 'Turn against Pharaoh, the king of Egypt. You must prophesy against him and against all Egypt. 3 Speak to him and say, "The Lord says this:

'I am against you, Pharaoh, king of Egypt.

You are like the great wild animal that lies in your streams.

You say, "The River Nile is mine; I made it for myself."

4 But I will catch you like a fish.

I will catch your mouth with a piece of bent metal.

I will pull you out of your streams.

Little fish will hang on the points of your skin.

5 I will leave you and your little fish in the desert.

You will lie on the ground.

And nobody will pick you up.

I will give you as food to the wild animals and birds.

6 Then all the people in Egypt will know that I am the Lord.

Israel's people thought that you would help them. 7 But your help was like a thin stick. It broke. And it tore their shoulders when they held it. And it hurt their backs when they put weight on it.'

8 So this is what the Lord God of Israel says, 'I will bring men with swords to kill your men and their animals. 9 I will make Egypt become a desert where nobody lives. Then they will know that I am the Lord.

I am against you because you said, "The River Nile is mine. I made it." 10 I am against you and your streams. I will destroy the country called Egypt. I will destroy it from Migdol to Aswan, as far as Cush. I will make it a desert where nobody lives. 11 No men or animals will walk there and nobody will live there for forty (40) years. 12 It will become a desert among desert lands. Its broken cities will be empty for forty (40) years. I will push the Egyptians out to other lands. They will go to many other countries.'

13 But this is what the Lord, the King says, 'I will bring back the Egyptians from the lands where I sent them. I will do this after the forty (40) years. 14 I will bring them back from their prisons. I will bring them to Pathros, the country of their fathers. There they will not be important. 15 Their king will be the least important of all kings. People will never again think that Egypt is important. I will make it so weak that it can never rule over other nations. 16 Egypt's people will no longer be able to help Israel. But they will make Israel's people remember their sin. Their sin was to ask Egypt for help.' Then they will know that I am the Lord, their King." '

17 The Lord spoke to me in the twenty-seventh (27th) year. It was the first day of the first month. 18 'Son of man', he said. 'Nebuchadnezzar, king of Babylon fought to win the city called Tyre. His soldiers carried such great weights that their skin broke. And it bled. But they did not find there any things of value to pay for their work.' 19 So this is what the Lord, the King, says: 'I will give Egypt to the king of Babylon. He will take away all its valuable things. He will go through the country to find things to give to his soldiers. 20 I will do this to pay him. He and his army did what I wanted. So I will pay him', says the Lord, your King.

21 'When that happens, I will make Israel's people strong. Then I will open your mouth to speak to them. Then they will know that I am the Lord.'

Chapter 30

The Lord will punish Egypt

1 The Lord spoke again. 2 'Son of man', he said. 'Prophesy to the people. Tell them what I, the Lord, your King, say. You must shout these words,

"A day is coming that will frighten you all!"

3 That day will be very soon. It is the day when the Lord will do this.

He will bring clouds and trouble to the nations.

4 Enemies will come to fight with Egypt.

The people in Cush will be sad.

Many men in Egypt will die

and enemies will carry away their valuable things.

They will break its cities into pieces.

5 Soldiers who fight for Egypt will die, too. They came from Cush, Lydia, Libya, Put and the Arab nations. Some men even came from my own people.

6 The Lord says, "Enemies will kill all the people who fight for Egypt. All the people will die. They will die from the north to the south. They will die from Migdol to Aswan. Enemies will destroy all the army of Egypt." I, the Lord your God, say this. 7 "Egypt will have more desert than any other country. Enemies will break all its cities into pieces. 8 I will cause them to burn Egypt and those who fight for Egypt. Then they will know that I am the Lord.

9 On the day that I destroy Egypt, I will send messengers to Cush. I will send them on ships. The people there think that they are safe. The news from Egypt will make them very afraid. That day is coming soon!

10 I will use King Nebuchadnezzar of Babylon to kill all the people in Egypt. He and his army will take away all Egypt's good things. 11 They will come to destroy the country. They will attack Egypt's people with swords. They will fill the country with dead bodies. 12 I will cause the river Nile to become dry. Evil men will rule Egypt. Foreign men will destroy the whole country." This is what I, the Lord, say.

13 The Lord, your King says, "I will destroy the idols and false gods in Memphis. Egypt will no longer have its own ruler. Everyone will be very afraid.

14 I will make Pathros a desert and I will burn Zoan with fire.

I will punish the great city called Thebes.

15 Pelusium is the strongest city in Egypt.

I will show it that I am very angry.

Enemies will take away all the valuable things from Thebes.

16 I will make fire burn the country of Egypt.

The pain of Pelusium will be very great.

Enemies will come like a storm and they will take Thebes.

The people in Memphis will always have trouble.

17 Soldiers will kill the young men in Heliopolis and Bubastis.

They will make all the other people their prisoners.

18 I will take away Egypt's power.

Then the people in Tahpanhes will feel that they are in a dark place.

A cloud will cover Egypt.

Enemies will take away the people from the villages.

19 This is how I will punish Egypt.

Then they will know that I am the Lord." '

20 The Lord spoke to me on the seventh (7th) day. It was the first month of the eleventh (11th) year. 21 'Son of man', he said. 'I have broken the arm of Pharaoh king of Egypt. He will never again have great power. He will always be weak. 22 So this is what the Lord, your King says, "Pharaoh king of Egypt is my enemy. But I will make him like a man with two broken arms. He will drop his sword. He will not be able to fight again. 23 I will send his people away to many other countries. 24 I will make the king of Babylon strong. I will give him power over Pharaoh. The king of Egypt will cry out like a man who is dying. 25 I will make the king of Babylon strong. But the king of Egypt will have no power. Then they will know that I am the Lord. They will see that I gave Babylon the power to win the fight. 26 I will send the people in Egypt to many different countries. They will live among the nations. Then they will know that I am the Lord." '

Chapter 31

1 The Lord spoke to me on the first day of the third (3rd) month. That was in the eleventh (11th) year. 2 'Son of man', he said, 'Speak to Pharaoh king of Egypt and his soldiers:

"Nobody is as great or powerful as you are.

3 Think about Assyria. It was like a great cedar tree before.

It had beautiful branches that covered other trees.

It was very tall and it had many leaves.

4 Waters fed the tree and streams made it grow tall.

The streams went round it. And they sent some water to all the other trees.

5 So it became taller than any of the trees in the field.

Many long branches grew from it.

They grew because it had so much water.

6 All kinds of birds lived in its branches.

Under its branches, the wild animals gave birth to their young animals.

It kept safe all the great nations.

7 It was as beautiful as a king in his best clothes.

It drank the deep waters.

8 It was more beautiful than the cedars in God's garden.

The pine trees were not as tall.

Other trees had fewer branches.

No other tree in God's garden was nearly as beautiful.

9 I made the tree beautiful and I gave it its branches.

All the trees in Eden (God's garden) wanted to be as beautiful as the cedar.

10 So this is what the Lord, your King says:

'Assyria was like that tree. It knew that it was very tall. And it thought that it was more important than any other tree. These thoughts were bad thoughts. 11 So I made the ruler of the nations punish it. I have destroyed it because it was so bad. 12 Cruel foreigners cut it down and they went away. They broke all its branches. Its branches fell on the mountains and in the valleys. The nations that it had kept safe all went away from it. 13 The birds sat on the tree that had fallen. And the wild animals walked over its branches. 14I will never again let a tree become so tall. No tree that grows by the waters will grow as big. It grew taller than other trees. Its top was in the clouds. So it thought that it was more important than the other trees. All the trees will die, like men. They will die even when they have much water. They will never grow so high again. They will die like men. And other men will bury them in the ground.'

15 This is what the Lord, your King says: 'They buried the tree. Then I made the deep streams cover it. But I will stop the rivers from sending streams of water to the earth. I will make the mountains of Lebanon dark. All the trees in the forest will become dry and they will die. 16 The nations will shake when they hear the tree fall. They will bury the tree with all those in the earth below. After I have done this, the other trees in the earth will become happy. They were the trees from God's garden (Eden) and from Lebanon. 17 Some trees are already in the earth. Men will bury the cedar tree with those trees. I will send the people who lived under the tree to live in other nations.

18 The king of Egypt and all his people are also like a tree. You are great and powerful. But I will cut you down like the trees of Eden (God's garden). Men will bury you with your dead soldiers. You will lie with those that men have killed with swords.

This is what I will do to Pharaoh and all his armies' ", says the Lord, your King.'

Chapter 32

The king of Egypt is like a great animal that swims in rivers

1 The Lord spoke to me in the twelfth (12th) year. It was the first day of the twelfth (12th) month. 2 'Son of man', he said. 'Make this sad song about Pharaoh, king of Egypt. And say to him,

"You are the strongest among the nations.

You are like the greatest of animals in the seas.

You move about in the rivers

and you hit the water with your feet.

You mix dirt with the clean water." '

3 This is what the Lord, the King says:

'I will send a great crowd of people

and they will catch you in their net.

4 I will pull you out of the water

and I will throw you on dry ground.

I will let the birds land on you in the field.

I will give your meat to the wild animals. I will fill their stomachs.

5 I will cause parts of your body to lie on all the mountains

and they will fill the valleys.

6 I will cover the ground with your blood. It will run up to the mountains.

And your meat will fill the deep valleys.

7 I will hide the stars and I will make the sky dark.

I will do this when I make you nothing.

I will cover the sun with a cloud

and you will not see the moon.

8 I will make the lights in the sky become dark.

Your whole country will become dark.

I will make it dark', says the Lord.

9 'I will destroy your nation.

Then many nations that you do not know will become afraid.

10 They will think that I will give them trouble.

And their kings will be afraid because I destroyed you.

They will see me shake my sword in front of them.

They will think that I will kill them.

So each of them will be afraid and they will shake.'

11 So, this is what the Lord, your King says.

'The king of Babylon will attack you.

12 His great army will fight against you.

I will give his strong men power to kill your soldiers.

His people are the most cruel of all nations.

They will change Egypt into a poor weak nation.

They will destroy all its armies.

13 Egypt's people have many cows near its great rivers,

but I will destroy them.

No men's feet will mix dirt with the water any longer.

No animal's feet will remain to make the water dirty.

14 Then I will make the waters quiet.

They will move like oil', says the Lord, your King.

15 'I will destroy Egypt.

I will take away all that you have.

I will kill all the people who live there.

Then they will know that I am the Lord.

16 They will sing this sad song for Egypt. Women in all nations will sing it. They will sing it for the land of Egypt and its many people.' This is what the Lord, your King says.

17 In the fifteenth (15th) month of the twelfth (12th) year, the Lord spoke to me.

18 'Son of man', he said. 'Be sad and make a loud noise for the many people in Egypt. Send them down to the place of dead people. Send them there with the dead bodies of all the strong nations' men. 19 Tell them that they are no better than any other people. They will all go to that place. They will be with those who are not circumcised. 20 The people in Egypt will die with the other soldiers who die. A sword is ready to kill them all. 21 Great leaders lie in the home of dead people. They will speak about Egypt and its friends. They will say: "Many men died in the fight. They have come down to lie with all of them. They are with those who are not circumcised."

22 Assyria is there with its whole army. All its men who died in the fight lie there. They lie round it in the home of dead people. 23 Their dead bodies are in the deepest parts of that place. Its dead soldiers are all round it. Many armies made people afraid. All their men are now in the country of dead people. Their enemies have killed them.

24 Elam is there with all its dead soldiers round it. Its enemy's swords have killed them all. All the men who made people afraid are down there. They are there with those who are not circumcised. They are ashamed. They are in the place of dead people. 25 Elam lies on a bed with all its soldiers round it. Not one of them is circumcised. Swords have killed them all. They will be ashamed because they made people afraid. They did that when they were alive. So I will make their bodies lie among the men who died.

26 Meshech and Tubal are there in the home of dead people. The dead bodies of their soldiers are round them. They are all in the home of dead people. Not one of them is circumcised. They made people afraid when they were alive. So men killed them with swords. 27 Now they lie with other dead soldiers who were not circumcised. They are in the home of dead people with their arms and their swords under their heads. Their armies made all people very afraid when they marched through the country. But I have punished them because of their sins.

28 I will kill you too, Pharaoh. And your dead body will lie with those men. You will lie with men who are not circumcised. You will lie with men whose enemies killed them with swords.

29 Edom is there. Its kings and leaders are there. Soldiers killed many of their men with swords. The kings and leaders are with those men. They had great power. But now they lie in the home of dead people. They lie with men who are not circumcised.

30 The kings of the north and from Sidon are there. They had great power but they are ashamed. They made men very afraid. But now they lie in the home of dead people.

They are with those that men killed with swords. They are with those dead men who are not circumcised.

31 Pharaoh felt sad because men had killed all his soldiers. When he and his army see those other dead men, they will feel better', says the Lord, your King. 32 'Pharaoh and his armies will lie among men who are not circumcised. They made men very afraid.

But their dead bodies will lie with other men's bodies. They will lie with men that enemies 'swords had killed.'

Chapter 33

The Lord tells Ezekiel that he must watch over his people

1 The Lord spoke to me. 2 'Son of man', he said. 'Speak to the people in your nation. Tell them that they may choose a man to watch over my people. I may send men with swords to attack you. Then you must do this. 3 The man must blow a trumpet to tell them if he sees an enemy. The enemy may come to attack them with swords. 4 The people will hear the trumpet and they will prepare to fight. If they do not prepare, then they may die. They will die because they did not listen. 5 A man may hear the trumpet but he may not prepare to fight. Then the enemy may kill him with a sword. He will die because he did not obey the noise of the trumpet. He would not have died if he had listened to the trumpet's noise. He did not save himself. 6 But the man who is watching may see the enemy. He may see them when they come with swords. But then he may not blow his trumpet. The men in the city will not hear anything. Then soldiers will come and kill them. The people may have done bad things. They will die because they did not obey me. But they did not know that the enemy was coming to attack them. They could not prepare to fight the enemy. Then I will punish the man who saw the soldiers. I will punish him because he did not blow the trumpet. He did not tell the people that an enemy was attacking them.

7 Son of man, I have made you like the man with the trumpet. You must watch Israel's people. You must tell them when they do wrong things. 8 I may say to a bad man, "You are doing something that is wrong. You will die." Then you must tell him that I am angry. Tell him that I will kill him. If you do not tell him this, he will surely die because of his sin. But I will punish you because you have caused his death. 9 That man is doing something that is wrong. You must tell him that. He may not listen to your words. He may not stop doing those things. Then he will die because of his sins. But you will not have caused his death. I will not punish you.

10 Son of man, speak to Israel's people. "You say: 'We have done many wrong things and we are dying. We want to stay alive!' " 11 Tell them, "It does not give me pleasure to kill men that do bad things. I want them to stop doing those wrong things and to stay alive. Stop doing things that are wrong, Israel's people. I do not want you to die!"

12 So you must speak to the people in your country, son of man. Say, "If a good man starts to do bad things, I will punish him. The good things that he did will not save him. They will not save him if he does not obey me. But I will not punish a bad man who stops doing wrong things.

A good man may stop doing good things. He may start to do bad things. Then he will die. The good things that he had done will not save him." 13 He may think about the good things that he has done. He may think that they will save him. But I will not remember those good things if he then does bad things. I will cause him to die because of the wrong things that he has done.

14 I may say to a bad man: "You must die." But then he may stop doing wrong things and do good things. 15 He might give back to a man something that he had taken (something that would make sure that the man would return his money). Or he might return things that were not his. He might start to obey me. If he then does only good things he will stay alive. 16 I will not remember any of the wrong things that he has done.

He has done what is good and right. So he will surely stay alive.

17 Israel's people are saying: "The Lord's rules are not fair!" But you people are those who are not fair. 18 A good man may stop doing good things. If he then starts to do bad things he will die. 19 And a bad man may stop doing bad things. Then he might start to do things that are good and right. Because he has done these good things, he will stay alive. 20 But Israel's people say: "The Lord is not fair!" But I will judge each man because of the things that he has done.'

The Lord tells Ezekiel why enemies have taken Jerusalem

21 A man ran away from Jerusalem. He came to me when we had been in Babylon for twelve (12) years. He came on the fifth (5th) day of the tenth (10th) month. He said, 'Enemies have taken the city.' 22 The Lord had touched me in the night. That was the night before the man came to me. He had opened my mouth so that I was able to speak again.

23 Then the Lord spoke to me. 24 'Son of man', he said, 'People live in the broken cities of Israel. This is what they are saying. They say, "Abraham was only one man, but God gave him the country called Israel. But we are many men. Now God has given the country called Israel to us." 25 So speak to them. Say, "This is what the Lord, your King says. 'You eat meat with the blood still in it. You worship your idols and you kill people. The country is too good for you. 26 You fight to get the things that you want. You do bad things. You have sex with each other's wives. I cannot give the country to you.' "

27 Say this to them. "This is what the Lord, your King says: 'I will make a promise. Enemies will kill the people in the destroyed city with swords. Wild animals will kill and eat people in the country. Some of these people will hide in strong buildings. Or they might hide in holes in the sides of mountains. They will become ill and die. 28 I will make the country empty, like a desert. Israel will no longer be strong or powerful. I will make its mountains wild and empty. No people will walk across them. 29 Then they will know that I am the Lord. I have made the country a desert because they have done such evil things.' "

30 Son of man, your people are talking about you in the streets. They are saying, "Come and hear the message that has come from the Lord." 31 My people will come and sit in front of you. They often do that. They will listen to your words. But they will not obey them. They say that they love me. But they really want to become rich people. They take things from other people. They are not fair. 32 They do not believe your words. You are like a man who sings beautiful love songs. They listen to your words but they do not obey them.

33 All these things will happen. Then they will know that a prophet has spoken to them.'

Chapter 34

Sheep and the shepherds who keep them safe

1 The Lord spoke to me. 2 'Son of man', he said. 'You must prophesy against the shepherds of Israel. Say to them, "This is what the Lord, your King says, 'I am angry with the shepherds of Israel. They only think about themselves. But shepherds should keep the sheep safe and well. 3 You eat their milk and you make warm clothes from their wool. You kill the best animals to eat. But you have not kept my sheep well and safe. 4 You have not helped the weak sheep to grow strong. You have not made the sick ones well. Nor have you tied up those who were hurting. You have not found the lost sheep and brought them back. You have not ruled them in a kind way. You have been cruel to them. 5 So my sheep went away to many places because they did not have a shepherd. Then the wild animals ate them. 6 My sheep went over the mountains and the high hills. They were all over the land. Nobody went to find them.' " '

7 So I say this to you, my shepherds, says the Lord: 8 'My sheep do not have any shepherds. You shepherds have not kept my sheep safe and wild animals have eaten the sheep. You did not look for those that were lost. You only wanted good things for yourselves. 9 So listen to what I say, you shepherds. 10 The Lord, your King says this, "You can be sure that I am against the shepherds. They should have kept my sheep safe. Because they did not do this they will no longer be shepherds. They will no longer keep my sheep. Then they will not have any food to eat. I will take away my sheep so that no shepherds can eat them." '

11 So this is what the Lord, your King says, 'I myself will look for my sheep and I will keep them safe.

12 I will be like a shepherd who looks everywhere to find his lost sheep. I will be with them and I will keep them safe. I will bring them back from places that are far away. They went away on a dark day when I let bad things happen. 13 I will bring them back from other countries to their own land. They will eat grass on the mountains of Israel. They will eat it in its valleys and villages. 14 I will keep them on good land. And they will eat grass on Israel's high places. They will lie down in the good land. They will eat good food on Israel's mountains. 15 I will keep them safe myself. I will make them lie down and rest', says the Lord, your King. 16 'I will find the lost sheep and I will bring them back. I will tie up the ones that are hurting. I will help the weak ones to become strong. But I will kill the fat sheep in a way that is fair.

17 This is what the Lord, your King says to his sheep, "I will decide how to judge between my sheep. I will decide how to judge between male sheep and goats. 18 You have much good food, so you must not destroy other grass. You have clean water to drink. So you must not make dirty that which remains. 19 I do not want my sheep to eat grass that you have made too dirty to eat. I do not want them to drink water that you have made dirty with your feet." '

20 So this is what the Lord, your King says to them, 'I myself will judge between the fat sheep and the thin sheep. 21 You attack them with the sharp points (horns) on your heads. You push them away with your shoulders. Because you do this, 22 I will save my sheep. No longer will anyone take them away. I will judge between one sheep and another sheep. 23 I will make my servant David one shepherd over them all. He will keep them safe. He will be their shepherd. 24 I, the Lord will be their God and David will rule them. He will be their king. I the Lord have spoken.

25 I will make a promise to them. I will give them peace. I will take away the wild animals. Then they can live in the desert. Then they can sleep in the forests. They will be safe there. 26 I will bless them (give them many good things). I will bless all the places round my hill. I will send them rain at the right seasons. The rain will be a picture of how kind I will be to them. 27 The trees will give them their fruit. Seeds that they plant in the ground will give plenty of food to eat. The people will be safe in their country. I will make them free from the men who made them their servants. They will no longer be slaves. Then they will know that I am the Lord. 28 Other nations will no longer take their things. And no longer will wild animals eat them. They will be safe and nobody will make them afraid. 29 I will give them a country that gives much good food. So then they will always have enough to eat. They will never be hungry. Other nations will not say bad things about them any longer. 30 Then they will know that I, the Lord their God, am with them. They will know that they are my people', says the Lord, the King. 31 'And you are like my sheep, the sheep of my grass-lands. You are men and I am your God', says God, the Lord.

Chapter 35

A prophecy against Edom

1 The Lord spoke to me. 2 'Son of man, look towards Mount Seir. Then you must prophesy against it. 3 Say, "This is what the Lord, your King says: 'I am against you, Mount Seir. I will attack you and I will make you a desert. 4 I will destroy your towns and nobody will live there. Then you will know that I am the Lord.

5 You continued to hate Israel's people for many years. Before, I punished them and they had no friends. But you let people attack them with swords. 6 So I make this promise to you. I will surely do this. Your blood will fall to the ground. You will run away from your enemies but you will still die. You were not afraid to kill people, so I will not be afraid to kill you. 7 I will make Mount Seir a desert where nobody lives. No longer will anyone visit it. 8 Dead bodies will cover your mountains. Men that enemies' swords have killed will lie on your hills. And their bodies will lie in your valleys. 9 I will make you into a desert for all time. Nobody will live in your towns. Then you will know that I am the Lord.

10 You say, "We will take these two nations (Israel and Judah) and then they will become ours. We will take them, even if the Lord is there." 11 So I will surely punish you', says the Lord, the King. 'You hurt them because you were angry. You hated them. I will hurt you in the same way that you hurt them. My people will know me when I judge you.

12 Then you will know this. I, the Lord have heard all the bad things that you have said. You spoke about the mountains of Israel "Men have made them into a desert. We can take them for ourselves."

13 You said bad things about me. You said that I had only a little power. And you said that I could not help my people.

And I heard you say it.' 14 So this is what the Lord, the King says: 'I will make you a desert. All the nations will see this and they will be very happy. 15 You were happy when you saw me punish Israel. You were happy when Israel became a desert. Because you were happy, I will make your country a desert. Mount Seir and all the country of Edom will become an empty desert. Then they will know that I am the Lord.' " '

Chapter 36

A prophecy to the mountains of Israel

1 'Son of man, prophesy to the mountains of Israel. Say to them, "Listen to the word of the Lord, you mountains of Israel. 2 'This is what an enemy has said to you: "Your old mountains now belong to us." 3 So prophesy to them. Say, "This is what the Lord, the King says: 'Enemies attacked you from every side. Many nations took parts of you to keep for themselves. People said many bad things about you.' " ' 4 I am speaking to you, mountains of Israel, because they did this. This is what I say to the mountains and hills and to the valleys. This is what I say to the empty, broken towns. Enemies took away all their good things and they laughed at their people. 5 'I am very angry', says the Lord, the King. 'I have judged against Edom and the other nations. This is because they took my land. They wanted it for their cows and sheep. And they hated my people. They hurt them. They were happy to hurt them.' 6 So prophesy about the country of Israel to the mountains, hills and valleys. Say, 'This is what the Lord, the King says, "I am angry because other nations have laughed at you. They thought that you had no value." 7 So this is what I say: "I promise that people will laugh at the nations round you. That is my true word.

8 But you mountains of Israel will give much food for Israel's people. I promise that my people will soon come home. 9 I love you and I want to give you good things. Men will dig your ground and they will plant seeds in it. 10 The number of people who live there will grow. They will live in the towns and they will repair the broken buildings. 11 I will make more men and animals live on you, and they will have many children. People will live on you as they did many years ago. I will give them many good things. They had food before I sent them away. But they will have more. Then you will know that I am the Lord. 12 I will cause my people, Israel's people, to walk upon you. You will be their land, and you will belong to them and to their children. You will never again lose them."

13 This is what the Lord, your King says. "People say that you destroy men. They say that you kill the nation's children. So I am making a promise to you. 14 You will no longer destroy or kill the nation's people', says the Lord, your King. 15 People from other nations will no longer laugh at you. You will no longer feel sad or cause your nation to fall', says the Lord, your King." '

16 The Lord spoke to me again. 17 'Son of man, Israel's people made their own country not clean when they lived there. They did many wrong things. I saw that they were an evil people. 18 So I became angry and I punished them. I punished them because they had killed people there. And they had made the country not clean with idols. 19 I sent them to many different nations. They went to many countries. I judged them because of the bad things that they had done. 20 But they still did the things that took away my honour. Men said bad things about my name. "These are the Lord's people, but they had to leave their country", they said. 21 I wanted them to give honour to my holy name. But Israel's people who lived in other nations had given me no honour. 22 So you must speak to Israel's people. Say, "This is what the Lord, the King says, 'I will not do this for you, Israel's people. But I will do it so that men will give honour to my holy name. You took away my honour from the nations where you live. 23 I will show them that my name is great and holy. You made them think that it was not clean. Then the nations will know that I am the Lord', says the Lord, your King. 'I will do this for you. Then they will see that I am holy.

24 So I will take you out from the nations. I will bring you back to your own country. You will return from all the places where I sent you. 25 You will become pure. You will be like a man whom I have washed with clean water. You will no longer be not clean, but you will be clean. You will turn away from your idols. 26 I will make you new inside. I will give you a new spirit. You will no longer turn away from me. I will make you want to do the things that give me pleasure. 27 And I will put my Spirit in you, and you will want to obey my rules. You will want to obey me. 28 You will live in the country that I gave to your fathers. You will be my people and I will be your God. 29 I save you from the bad things that made you not clean. I will make seeds grow to give plenty of food. You will always have enough to eat. 30 I will make the trees give much fruit. And plants will grow well in the fields. Then you will not feel ashamed because you have no food. Other nations will no longer think that you have no value. 31 Then you will remember the evil things that you did. And you will be sorry and ashamed that you did those wrong things. 32 I want you to know that I am not doing this for your honour, says the Lord, your King. 'You must feel very sorry and ashamed because of the bad things that you did, Israel's people!'

33 This is what the Lord, the King says: 'I will make you clean from the evil things that you did. On that same day, I will send you back to your towns. You will build them up again. 34 You will again make food grow on the empty land. No longer will people who pass it think that it is a desert. 35 They will say, "This land was like a desert, but now it is like the Garden of Eden (Genesis 2: 8-9). People now live in the cities that were broken and empty. But now they have built them with strong walls." 36 Then the nations who still live round you will see this. They will know that I have built up the broken cities. They will know that I have planted them again. I will plant what enemies destroyed. I, the Lord, have spoken and I will do it.'

37-38 This is what the Lord, the King says: 'Israel's people ask for my help. I will listen to them again. Men bring many sheep to Jerusalem to offer to the Lord. They bring them on a feast day. I will make them as many as those sheep. So I will fill the broken cities with people. Then they will know that I am the Lord.' " '

Chapter 37

The valley of dry bones

1 The Lord showed me a picture in my mind. His Spirit took me and put me in the middle of a dry valley. It was full of bones. 2 He made me walk up and down among them. There, on the ground in the valley, I saw many very dry bones. 3 'Son of man', he asked me. 'Can these dry bones become alive?' 'Lord my King', I said. 'Only you know the answer.'

4 'Prophesy to these bones', he said. 'Say to them, "Dry bones, listen to the Lord's word." 5 This is what the Lord, the King says to these dry bones. "I will make you become alive. 6 I will make your bones join together and I will put meat on your bones. I will cover you with skin. I will blow air into your bodies. You will become alive. Then you will know that I am the Lord." '

7 So I prophesied as he had said. While I did this, I heard noises. The bones hit each other when they came together. 8 Then I looked. And I saw meat and skin cover the bones. But the bodies were not alive. They did not move or take in air.

9 Then the Lord spoke to me. 'Prophesy to the air', he said. 'Say that the four (4) winds must come. And they must blow air into these dead bodies. Then they can become alive.' 10 So I prophesied and air blew into them. They became alive and they stood on their feet. They were a great army. 11 Then the Lord said, 'Son of man, these bones are all Israel's people. They say, "Our bones are dry and we cannot hope for anything. We are lost." 12 So prophesy and say to them, "This is what the Lord, the King says: 'My people, I am going to open the places where men bury your bodies. I will take you out of them and I will bring you back to the country called Israel. 13 I will open the places where they buried you. I will bring you out. Then you, my people, will know that I am the Lord. 14 I will put my Spirit in you and you will become alive. And you will stay in your own country. Then you will know that I, the Lord have spoken. You will know that I have done this', says the Lord." '

15 The Lord spoke to me. 16 'Son of man', he said. 'Take a wooden stick and write on it. Write, "This stick belongs to Judah and all the people with him." Then take another stick and write on it, "Ephraim's stick belongs to Joseph and all Israel's people that are with him." 17 Make the two sticks join together to become one stick in your hand. 18 Your people, Israel's people, will ask you why you did this. They will ask, "Please tell us what this means." 19 Say to them, "This is what the Lord, the King says: 'Joseph's stick is the land of Ephraim and all the Israelite tribes who are with him. I will cause it to join Judah's stick and I will make them one stick in my hand.' " 20 Hold the sticks with words on them in front of their eyes. 21 Say to them "This is what the Lord, the King says: 'I will take Israel's people out from the nations where they have gone. I will fetch them back from all the places round them. I will bring them into their own country. 22 I will make them become one nation. They will be in the country. They will live on Israel's mountains. They will have one king over them all. They will never become two nations or two kingdoms again. 23 They will no longer worship idols and make themselves not clean. They will no longer do those things that make me angry. I will save them from all the wrong things that they did. I will make them clean. They will be my people and I will be their God.

24 My servant David will be their king and he will be their shepherd. They will all have one ruler. And they will obey all my rules. 25 They will live in the country that I gave to my servant Jacob and his sons. It is the country where your fathers lived. My people and their children and grandchildren will live there. They will live there until the end of time.

And David my servant will always be their king.

26 I will make a promise with them to give them peace. It is a promise that will never change. They will remain there and I will keep them safe. Their numbers will grow greater. 27 I will put my temple there and it will always remain there. I will live among them. I will be their God and they will be my people. 28 I have put my temple among them. It will remain until the end of time. Then the nations will know that I, the Lord make Israel holy.' " '

Chapter 38

1 The Lord spoke to me. 2 'Gog rules the country of Magog. Son of man, turn your face against him', he said. 'Gog is the most important prince of Meshech and Tubal. Prophesy against him 3 and say, "This is what the Lord, the King says. 'I am against you, Gog, important prince of Meshech and Tubal. 4 And I will turn you round. I will catch your mouth with a sharp piece of metal like a fish. I will catch you and your great army with its men on horses. I will take you and all your soldiers. They have small shields. They hold their swords high. 5 Persia, Cush (Sudan) and Put (Libya) will be there with their metal hats and their shields. 6 Gomer will be there with its armies. And Beth Togarmah and its armies from the north will be with them. I will catch all these many nations with you.

7 Prepare to fight. Make all the armies round you ready. You must tell them what they should do. 8 After many days you will fight. In a future year, you will attack a country. That country's people will not have fought for a long time. The people there came back to Israel's mountains from many nations. I had brought them out from the nations and they were safe there. 9 You, your armies and all the nations with you will go to attack them. You will be like a storm cloud that is moving over the country.'

10 This is what the Lord, the King says, 'On that day you will have bad thoughts. You will decide to do an evil thing. 11 You will say: "We will attack a country whose villages have no walls. The people have peace. So they do not think that anyone will attack them. They have no walls or gates to keep them safe. 12 I will turn against the people who have returned to build up their broken cities. I will take their good things and their many animals. Now they are in the middle of the land." 13 The men in Sheba and Dedan will ask you questions. So will those from Tarshish and its villages. Their people buy and sell things. They will say, "Have you come to take away their good things? Have you and your armies come to carry away their silver and gold? Will you take their animals and other things?" ' "

14 So, son of man, you must prophesy to Gog. Say, "This is what the Lord, the King says: 'Now you see my people Israel. They are living in peace. 15 So you will come from your country far in the north. You will come with your great armies. All the soldiers will ride on horses. You will be very many men. 16 Your armies will be like a cloud that covers the land. I will make you, Gog, attack my country on a future day. I will use you to show the nations that I am holy. Then they will know me.'

17 This is what the Lord, the King says: 'I spoke to you in days long ago. I spoke by my servants, the prophets of Israel. For many years they have said that I would bring you against my people. 18 When that day comes, I will become very angry. Gog will attack Israel', says the Lord, the King. 19 'Then I will make the whole country of Israel shake because I am so angry. 20 The fish in the sea, and the birds in the air will be very afraid. And all the animals on the land will be afraid. Everything that moves and all the people on the earth will be afraid. They will all shake when they see that I am so angry. I will make the mountains fall and break into pieces. All the walls will fall down. 21 I will call the men on the mountains to show their swords', the Lord, the King says. 'Every man of yours will fight his brothers. 22 I will judge Gog. I will make his men ill and they will die. I will send rain and fire and stones from the sky on him and his armies. 23 I will show the nations how great and holy I am. Then they will all know that I am the Lord.' " '

Chapter 39

1 'Son of man, you must prophesy against the nations. Say to them, "This is what the Lord, the King says: 'I am against you, Gog, prince of Meshech and Tubal. 2 I will turn you round and I will pull you along. I will bring you from the far north to attack the mountains of Israel. 3 Then I will knock your arms out of your hands. 4 You will fall on Israel's mountains. You and your soldiers and the nations with you will all fall there. Birds of many kinds and wild animals will feed on your dead bodies. 5 I have decided that you will fall in the fields.' That is what the Lord, the King says. 6 'I will send fire to burn Magog and the people who live in safe towns by the sea. Then they will know that I am the Lord.

7 My people, Israel will know that my name is holy. No longer will I let them say bad things about me. And the nations round you will know that I, the Lord am holy. 8 I promise that I will cause this to happen. You can be sure that this day will come', says the Lord, the King. 'I told you that this day would come.

9 Then those who live in Israel's towns will go out. They will pick up the arms and they will burn them. They will burn the small and large shields, the heavy sticks, the throwing sticks and the sharp pointed sticks (swords). They will use them to make their fires. They will have enough wood for seven (7) years of fires. 10 They will not have to go into the fields or forests to find wood. They will take away the things from those who took their things', says the Lord, the King.

11 'They will bury Gog in the valley east of the sea. They will bury Gog and all his armies there. So men will not be able to walk through this valley. They will call it the valley of Hamon Gog (Gog's army).

12 Israel's people will need seven (7) months to bury all the dead bodies. Then the land will be clean. 13 All the people in the country will bury the dead bodies. They will always remember that day, the day that I won the fight. They will give me glory', says the Lord, the King.

14 'They will choose some men to clean the land. They will travel through all the country. Other men will bury the dead bodies that remain on the ground. They will begin to do this at the end of the seven (7) months. 15 The men who walk through the country will find dead men's bones. They will put a sign by each one. Then the men who bury the bodies will bury them in the valley of Hamon Gog. 16 (A town called Hamonah is also there.) That is how they will make the land clean.' "

17 Son of man, this is what the Lord, the King says: "Shout to all kinds of birds and wild animals, 'Come here from all the country to eat the meal that I have prepared for you. It is a great sacrifice on Israel's mountains. There you will eat meat and you will drink blood. 18 You will eat the meat of great men and you will drink the blood of kings. You will eat them like the fat sheep, cows and animals from Bashan that you eat. 19 At this sacrifice, you will eat so much fat that you cannot eat any more. You will drink so much blood that you become drunk. 20 I will give you horses and their riders to eat. I will give you great men and many kinds of soldiers to eat', says the Lord, the King.

21 'I will show my glory to all the nations. They will see that I can punish people. And they will know that I decide how and when to punish them. 22 From that time and for all the time after that, Israel's people will know that I am the Lord their God. 23 And the nations will know that I sent Israel's people away from their country. They will know that I punished my people because of their sin. They had not been faithful to me so I turned away from them. I let their enemies take them and kill them with swords. 24 I punished them because they had not kept themselves clean from sin. I hid myself from them because they had done so many evil things.' " '

25 So this is what the Lord, your King says. 'Now I will bring back Jacob (Israel) from the countries where his people are prisoners. I will be kind to all Israel's people. And I will make them see that I am holy. 26 They will forget that they were ashamed. They will forget that they failed to keep their promises to me. That was when they lived in a safe country. In that country, nobody made them afraid. 27 I will bring them back from the lands where their enemies took them. The nations will see what I have done. So all the nations will know that I am holy. 28 Then Israel will know that I am the Lord their God. I sent my people away to far countries. But I will bring them all back to their own country. I will not leave any behind. 29 No longer will I turn away from them. I will pour my Spirit over Israel's people', says the Lord, the King.

Chapter 40

A picture of the Temple

1 The Lord touched me on the tenth (10th) day of the year. It was our twenty-fifth (25th) year in a foreign country. He took me to our city (Jerusalem). Enemies had taken the city fourteen (14) years earlier. 2 He showed me a picture of the country of Israel. I was standing on a very high mountain. Some buildings that looked like a city were there on its south side. 3 The Lord took me there. And I saw a man that looked like bronze. He was standing in the gate. The man had a thin rope and a stick in his hand to measure the ground and walls. 4 The man spoke to me. 'Son of man', he said, 'Look and listen carefully to me. Remember everything that I show to you. That is why God has brought you here. Tell Israel's people everything that you see.'

The east gate to the yard

5 I saw a wall all the way round the place where the temple was. The stick in the man's hand was three (3) metres long. He measured the wall with this stick. It was three (3) metres wide and three (3) metres high.

6 Then he went to the gate on the east side. He climbed its steps and he measured the size of the entrance. It was three (3) metres deep. 7 Beyond this was a passage with three (3) rooms on each side. They were rooms for the guards. Each of these rooms was three (3) metres long and 3 (three) metres wide. The walls between the rooms were two and a half metres thick. Beyond them was a passage that was three (3) metres long. This went to a room towards the temple. 8-9 This room was four (4) metres wide. It was the nearest part of the gate to the temple. Its walls were one metre wide at the far end. 10 The rooms on each side of the passage were all the same size. So were all the walls between them.

11 Then the man measured across the passage through the gate. It was six and a half (6½) metres wide. The space between the two open gates was five (5) metres. 12 A wall half a metre high and half a metre wide was in front of each of the rooms. (The rooms were three (3) metres square.) 13 He measured the space between the back wall of one room and the back wall of the room opposite. It was twelve and a half (12½) metres long. 14 The room at the other end opened into a yard. That room measured ten (10) metres wide. 15 The gate measured twenty-five (25) metres from the outside wall to the other room's end. 16 All the rooms had windows in their outside walls. And they had windows on the walls between the rooms. Men had cut shapes of palm trees inside the passage walls.

The yard outside the temple

17 The man took me through the gate into the yard. They had built thirty (30) rooms against the outside wall. Flat stones covered the space in front of them. 18 This space went all round the yard. The outside yard was lower down than the inside yard.

19 There was a gate to the inside yard. The man measured fifty (50) metres between the two gates.

The north gate

20 Then the man measured the gate on the north side of the outside yard. 21 He measured the entrance room. Then he measured the three rooms on each side of the passage and the walls between them. They measured the same as those in the east gate. The whole gate was twenty-five (25) metres long and it was twelve and a half (12½) metres wide. 22 The entrance room, the windows and the palm trees were the same as those in the east gate. Seven (7) steps went up to the gate. And there was a room at the end by the yard. 23 From this gate across the yard was the gate to the inside yard. It was the same as on the east side. The man measured fifty (50) metres between the two gates.

The south gate

24 Next, the man took me to the south side, and we saw another gate there. The man measured its walls and the entrance room and they measured the same as the other walls. 25 The rooms in this gate had windows that were the same as those in the other gates. The whole gate was twenty-five (25) metres long and twelve and a half (12½) metres wide. 26 Seven (7) steps went up to it. The way in was also at the end by the yard. They had cut the shapes of palm trees on the inside walls of the passage. 27 Here too, was a gate into the inside yard. The man measured fifty (50) metres between the two gates.

The south gate of the inside yard

28 The man took me through the south gate into the inside yard. He measured the gate. It was the same size as the gates in the outside wall. 29-30 The guards' rooms, entrance and inside walls were the same as those of the other gates. And its rooms had windows. It was twenty-five (25) metres long and twelve and a half (12½) metres wide. 31 Its entrance room opened towards the outside yard. Men had cut shapes of palm trees. They were along the walls inside the passage.

The east gate of the inside yard

32 The man took me through the east gate into the inside yard. He measured the gate. He found that it was the same size as the other gates. 33 The guards' rooms, entrance and inside walls all measured the same as those in the other gates.

They had made windows all round and in the entrance room. The whole gate was twenty-five (25) metres long and twelve and a half (12½) metres wide. 34 The entrance room's door opened towards the outside yard. They had cut shapes of palm trees along the walls. They were inside the passage. Eight (8) steps went up to this gate.

The north gate of the inside yard

35 The man took me to the north gate. He measured it. He found that it was the same size as the other gates. 36 Like them, it had rooms for the guards and pictures on the inside walls. It had an entrance room with windows all round. It was twenty-five (25) metres long and twelve and a half (12½) metres wide. 37 The entrance room's door opened towards the outside yard. Men had cut palm tree shapes on the walls of the passage. Eight (8) steps went up to this gate.

Buildings near the north gate

38 They had put a small building in the outside yard. It was next to the north side of the inside gate. Its door opened from the entrance room by the yard. There the priests washed the dead bodies of animals that they burnt whole as sacrifices. 39 In the entrance room they had put four (4) tables, two on each side of the room. They killed the animals for sacrifice on these tables. They burnt some of these animals whole. But they burnt other animals for sin offerings. They killed other animals as sacrifices when people had done wrong things.

40 They had put four (4) more tables outside the room by the north gate's entrance. They put two on each side of the north gate. 41 I counted eight (8) tables on which they killed animals for sacrifices. Four (4) tables were in the room and four (4) were in the yard. 42 Someone had made the tables in the room out of stone. They put the animals on them. There they would kill the animals that they burnt whole. These tables were fifty (50) centimetres high and their tops were seventy-five (75) centimetres square. They kept all the things that they used to kill the animals on these tables. 43 They had raised the edges all round each table by seven and a half (7½) centimetres. They put all the meat that they would sacrifice on these tables.

44 Then the man brought me into the inside yard. Two rooms had doors to the inside yard. One was by the north gate and its door opened towards the south. The other room was by the south gate and its door opened towards the north. 45 The man told me that one room was for the priests. That room's door opened to the south. 46 The other room's door opened to the north. The priests who worked for God at the altar used that room. All the priests belong to Zadok's family. They are the only people that the Lord lets near to work for him in his temple. All Zadok's family come from Levi's tribe.

The inside yard and the temple building

47 The man measured the inside yard. It was square, fifty (50) metres long and fifty (50) metres wide. The temple was on the west side of the yard. An altar was there in front of the temple. 48 Then he took me into the entrance room of the temple. He measured the entrance. It was two and a half metres long and seven (7) metres wide. The walls were one and a half metres thick on each side. 49 Steps went up to the entrance room. This room was ten (10) metres wide and six (6) metres long. Two pillars were there, one on each side of the entrance.

Chapter 41

1 Then the man took me into the room in the centre, the Holy Place. He measured the entrance to it. It was three (3) metres deep 2 and five (5) metres wide. The walls on either side were two and a half (2½) metres thick. The room itself measured twenty (20) metres long and ten (10) metres wide.

3 Then he measured the passage that went to the inside room. He went in. It was one metre long and three (3) metres wide. The walls on either side were three and a half (3½) metres thick. 4 The room measured ten (10) metres square. It was behind the Holy Place. 'This is the Most Holy Place', he said to me.

5 Then the man measured the wall of the temple. It was three (3) metres thick. They had built rooms two metres wide all-round the temple. They were against the wall. 6 Three (3) rooms were on top of each other. They were all round the temple. I counted thirty (30) rooms at the top, thirty (30) rooms below them and thirty (30) rooms below them.

The wall of the temple in each group of 30 rooms was thinner than the wall below. So the floor of the room at the top could rest on the wall's edge. They did not have to fix it to the temple wall. 7 The walls at the top of the temple were thinner than the walls below them. So the rooms at the top were wider than the rooms below them.

Against the temple walls, they had built two wide sets of stairs. People could walk up these stairs to the rooms above. 8-11 The outside wall of these rooms was two and a half (2½) metres thick. One door opened into the north side rooms of the temple. And one door opened into the south side of the temple. I saw a path two and a half (2½) metres wide all-round the temple. It was three (3) metres above the yard. It was as high as the lowest rooms against the temple wall. The yard was between this path and the buildings for the priests. It was ten (10) metres wide and it went along the sides of the temple. 12 A building was at the west side of the temple. It was at the far end of the yard. It measured forty-five (45) metres long and thirty-five (35) metres wide. Its walls were two and a half (2½) metres thick.

13 Then the man measured the outside of the temple. It was fifty (50) metres long. He measured from the back of the temple to the building's west side. It measured fifty (50) metres. 14 He measured the space across the front of the temple. Then he measured the yard on each side. Each of these measured fifty (50) metres. 15 The building at the west, with its passages also measured fifty (50) metres. 16 They had covered the inside walls of the entrance room of the temple, the Holy Place and the Most Holy Place with wood. The wood covered the walls from the floor to the windows. They could also cover the windows. 17-18 Men had cut shapes above the doors and all over the walls. They were shapes of palm trees and animals with wings. They covered all the inside walls of the temple. First they cut a palm tree then an animal, then another palm tree, and so on, all round the room. Each animal had two faces. 19 On one side, a human face looked at the palm tree. A lion's face looked at the tree on the other side. The walls were like this all round the room. 20 These pictures went from the floor to above the doors. 21 The bases of the pillars that were holding the doors were square. And the front of the Holy Place seemed the same.

The altar

22 There was an altar in front of the Holy Place's entrance. They had made it out of wood. It was one and a half metres high and one metre wide. Its corners, sides and part below the top were all wooden. 'This is the table that is in front of the Lord', the man said to me.

The doors

23 A door opened into the passage to the Holy Place. Another door went to the Most Holy Place. 24 Both of these doors opened down the middle. 25 Men had made pictures on the doors. They were pictures of palm trees and animals with wings. They were like the shapes that they had cut on the walls. Men had put a cover over the door to the entrance room. 26 This room had thin windows in its sides. Men had cut shapes of palm trees on its walls. They had also made covers over the side rooms.

Chapter 42

Two buildings near the temple

1 Then the man took me into the outside yard. We went to a building near the temple. It was on the north side of the temple. It was not far from the other building (that was on the west side of the temple). 2 This building was fifty (50) metres long and twenty-five (25) metres wide. There was a ten (10) metre space between it and the temple. The building's other side was by the yard that they had covered with flat stones. 3 It had three (3) sets of rooms. They were on top of each other. Each was a little way behind the one below it. 4 A path went along inside its north side. It was fifty (50) metres long and five (5) metres wide. The entrances to the building were on the same side. 5 The rooms at the top were not as wide as the rooms below them. And they were not as wide as the rooms below them. 6 Each of the two groups of rooms at the top was on a wide wall. They were not on pillars like the other buildings in the yard. 7 The wall in front of the lowest rooms had no doors for twenty-five (25) metres. Rooms filled the other 25 metres. 8 At the top, there were rooms from one end to the other. 9 They had made an entrance to the rooms below from the outside yard. It was at the east end of the building. The wall of the yard started there.

10 A building like this one was at the south side of the temple. It was not far from the other building (that was at the west end of the temple). 11 A path went along its side. The sizes and entrance were the same as those of the other building.

12 They had made a door at its east end. The door went to the set of rooms that was below the other sets of rooms. The door was on the building's south side, where the wall began.

13 The man spoke to me. 'The north and south rooms towards the yard are for the priests. They are holy. In them, the priests who work there will eat the most holy sacrifices. They will keep the most holy things there. For example, they put there the grain and other offerings that people gave. Those people were sorry about the wrong things that they had done.

14 The priests may want to go into the outside yard. Then they must take off the special holy clothes that they wear to work for the Lord. They must leave them in these rooms and they must put on other clothes. Then they can go out to meet the people.'

15 Then he had finished measuring everything inside the place where the temple was. He took me out through the east gate and he measured the space all round. 16 He measured the wall of the east side with his stick. It was two hundred and fifty (250) metres. 17-19 Then he measured the north side and the south side and the west side. Each one measured the same as the east side, two hundred and fifty (250) metres. 20 So the walls made a square round the holy place. They separated the holy place from the common place.

Chapter 43

The Lord returns to the Temple

1 Then the man brought me to the east gate. 2 And I saw the shining glory of the God of Israel. It came from the east. His voice was loud like the noise of the great sea. The earth shone with the bright light of his glory. 3 I had seen a dream picture like this by the River Kebar. That was when God had come to destroy the city. I fell down on my face. 4 The shining light went through the east gate into the temple. 5 Then the Lord's Spirit lifted me up. He took me into the temples inside yard. And I saw that the glory of the Lord filled the temple.

6 The man stood there by my side. I heard the Lord's voice come from inside the temple. 7 'Son of man', he said. 'Here is my throne. I will live here among Israel's people. I will rule over them for all time. They will never again do things that take away my honour. Neither they nor their kings will worship other gods or put their kings' dead bodies in this place. 8 They built the entrances and doors of their houses here. They were next to my temple's doors. Only a wall separated us. They did many evil things and they took away the honour of my holy name. 9 Now they must stop doing those evil things. They must take away their kings' dead bodies. If they do this, I will live among them for all time.

10 Son of man, tell Israel's people about the temple. It should make them ashamed of the evil things that they have done. Let them think about it. 11 Then they will become ashamed of what they have done. You must tell them all about the way to build the temple. Describe its entrances, its shape, its rules and how they must do everything. You must write all this down. Then they can copy the whole thing and they can correctly obey its rules.

12 All the top of the mountain round the temple will be most holy. That is the important rule about the temple.'

The altar

13 The man measured the altar with the same measuring stick. They had dug a hole that was half a metre deep and half a metre wide round the altar. Round its outside edge they had built a wall twenty-five (25) centimetres high. 14 The lowest part of the altar was one metre high. The next part was fifty (50) centimetres inside the part below all round. It was two metres high. The edge above that was again fifty (50) centimetres inside the middle part. 15 This top part was two metres high. They burnt the sacrifices on this top part. Its corners had points that were higher than the flat top. 16 The top of the altar was square and each side was six (6) metres long. 17 The middle part was also square, with sides seven (7) metres long. It had a wall twenty-five (25) centimetres high round its edge. (They had left a space fifty (50) centimetres wide between the top two parts of the altar.) They had built steps up to the altar on the east side.

They must make the altar holy

18 'Son of man', the Lord, the King said to me. 'Listen to me. They must make the altar holy for my worship.

To do this they will burn sacrifices on it. And they will shake over it the animal's blood that you sacrificed. 19 The sons of Zadok are the only priests who can come into my house to work for me. I, the Lord, your King say this very strongly. You will give them a young male cow to offer as a sacrifice for sin. 20 You will take some of its blood and put it on the points on the altar. Those are on the corners of its top part. And you will put its blood on the corners of its middle part. And you must put blood all-round its edges. This is how you will make the altar clean and holy, separate for my worship. 21 You must choose the male cow to become the sacrifice for sin. Take it to the special place. Burn it outside the holy place. 22 The next day, choose the best male goat that you can find. Offer it as a sacrifice for sin. Use its blood to make the altar clean and holy, as you did with the cow's blood. 23 After that, take the best young male cow and young male sheep 24 and bring them to me. The priests will shake salt on them. They will burn them as a gift to me. 25 Each day for a week you must offer sacrifices to me. They are for your sins. Sacrifice a goat, a male cow and a male sheep each day. They must all be your best animals that have nothing wrong with them. 26 The priests must make the altar clean and holy for each of seven (7) days. Then it will be ready to use. 27 The priests can begin to make burnt offerings when the seven (7) days are finished. They will offer the burnt offerings and the people's fellowship offerings on the altar. You will all give me great pleasure when you do this. I, the Lord, your King, say this.'

Chapter 44

Rules about how to use the temple

1 Then the man brought me back to the outside gate of the holy place. That gate opened to the east. But it they had shut it. 2 'This gate must stay shut', the Lord said to me. 'Nobody can go through it. It must remain closed because the Lord, the God of Israel, has gone through it. 3 Only the king himself can sit inside the gate to eat a holy meal in front of the Lord. He must go in and out through the inside entrance room.'

4 Then the man took me through the north gate. We went to the front of the temple. I saw that the Lord's glory filled his temple. And I fell flat on my face.

5 'Son of man, look and listen carefully', the Lord said to me. 'You must listen very carefully to everything that I tell you. These are the rules for the Lord's temple. Understand which people can go into the temple. And learn which people can go out of the temple. 6 Speak to those Israelites who do not obey me. Say, "This is what the Lord, the King says. 'You have done enough evil things. 7 You even brought foreigners into my holy place. But they were not circumcised and they did not obey my important rules. You made my temple not clean. It was no longer holy. And you offered me food, fat and blood there. You did not keep your promise to me, your covenant promise. 8 You did not do the work yourselves. But you made people that I had not chosen work in my holy place.' 9 This is what the Lord, your King says. 'No foreigner who is not circumcised can go into my holy place. He must not go in because he does not obey my rules. Even if that foreigner lives among my people, he must not go in.

10 Some men from Levi's tribe turned away from me to worship idols. I will punish them because of their sin. 11 They can work for me in the holy place. They can open and close the doors. They can make offerings and sacrifices. And they can stand and work for the people. 12 But I have decided that I must punish them. That is because they helped the people to worship idols. And so they caused them to sin. I promise that I will do this. 13 They must not come near to me to work for me as priests. They must not come near to my holy things or my most holy offerings. They must become ashamed of the evil things that they have done. 14 But I will let them do the work of the temple that is not special priest's work. 15 Only the priests, sons of Zadok, Levi's son, can offer sacrifices to me. Only they worked for me and obeyed me. They remained faithful to me when other Israelites worshipped false gods. They can offer sacrifices of fat and blood to me', says the Lord, the King. 16 'Only they can come into the holy place. They are the only men who can come near to my table to work for me.

17 When they come into the inside yard, they must wear linen clothes. They must not wear anything woollen while they are working. They must not wear them inside the yard or inside the temple. 18 They must wear linen cloths round their heads and linen clothes next to their skin. They must not wear anything that makes them hot and sticky. 19 They must take off their special clothes when they leave the holy place. They must leave them in the holy place when they go out to meet the people. Then their special clothes will not make the people holy.

20 They must keep the hair on their heads short. They must not cut it all off, or let it grow long. 21 A priest must not drink wine when he goes into the inside yard.

22 He must not marry a woman whose husband has died. And he must not marry a woman whose husband has sent her away. Priests can only marry women who have never had sex. Or they can marry the wives of priests who are now dead. 23 They must teach my people that holy things are different from common things.

24 If people do not agree with each other, the priests must be their judges. They must decide who is right. They must use my rules to decide. They must obey the rules about my special feasts and they must keep my Sabbaths holy.

25 A priest must not go near to a dead person. It would stop him from being holy. But he can go near to a dead person who is his father or mother. He can also make himself not clean (not pure) for a son, daughter or a sister who is not married. 26 After this, he must make himself clean. Then he must wait seven (7) days. 27 And he can go back into the inside yard of the holy place to work for me there. Then he must offer a sin offering for himself', says the Lord, the King.

28 'The priests must not own any land in Israel to keep for their children and grandchildren. I will be like the land that belongs to them. 29 They will eat the offerings of grain and the offerings because of sin. They can also eat some other offerings that people bring. All the Lord's special things will belong to them. 30 The best of your first fruits and all your special gifts will belong to the priests. You must also give them the first flour that you make from your grain. Then I will bless those who live in your house. 31 The priests must not eat anything, bird or animal, that men find dead.' " '

Chapter 45

The Lord separates the land into different parts

1 'You must separate the land into different parts for each tribe. When you do this, you must give one part to the Lord. Make it twelve and a half (12½) kilometres long and ten (10) kilometres wide. All of this land will be holy. 2 You will keep a piece of this land, two hundred and fifty (250) metres long and two hundred and fifty (250) metres wide for the temple. You must keep an empty space twenty-five (25) metres wide all-round the temple. 3 Half of this space that measures twelve and a half (12½) kilometres by five (5) kilometres will contain the temple. This will be the most holy part of the land. 4 The priests will have this holy part of the country to work for the Lord in his temple. They will build their houses there as well as the temple. 5 Some Levites work in the temple. They will own the other half of the land. There they will build their towns to live in.

6 You must give a piece of land to the city. It is the part next to the holy part. This part will measure twelve and a half (12½) kilometres long, and two and a half (2½) kilometres wide. Any of Israel's people can live there.

7 You must keep some land for the king. His land will include that from the west of the holy land to the sea. From the east, his land will include all the land to the country's east edge. So his land will be as long as a tribe's part of the land. 8 This is the part of the land that will belong to the king who rules Israel. Then he will no longer try to make the people do what he wants. And they can all live in their own parts of the country. I will give parts to each of them.

9 "Stop arguing and fighting, you leaders of Israel. You have done enough bad things!" says the Lord, your King. "Do the things that are right and good. Stop taking away the things that belong to my people." That is what the Lord, the King says. 10 "You must use correct measures for size and weight. 11 The ephah for dry things must be the same as the bath for wet things. Ten ephahs will be equal to one homer. Ten baths will be equal to one homer. 12 Twenty (20) gerahs will be equal to one shekel. Sixty (60) shekels will be equal to one mina (about 24 ounces or 660 grams).

Offerings and holy days

13 You must take 1/6th of a homer of grain to offer as a special gift. 14 The correct oil gift is 1/10th of a bath from each cor (a cor is equal to 10 baths or one homer). 15 You must take one sheep from every two hundred (200) sheep that live in the green land in Israel. You will use these gifts to offer to me. They are grain offerings, animals to burn and fellowship offerings. These are sacrifices so that I can forgive your sin." I, the Lord, your King, say that you must do this.

16 "All Israel's people must bring these offerings to the king in Israel." This is what the Lord, the King says:

17 "The king must give the animals for the burnt sacrifices. He must give the grain and wine to offer at the people's feasts. He must give them for the New Moon feasts and the Sabbaths. He must give them the sin offerings, grain offerings, burnt offerings and fellowship offerings. These are to pay for the sin of Israel's people.

18 On the first day of the first month you must take a male cow to make the holy place clean. The animal must not have anything wrong with it. 19 The priest will take some of the blood of this sin offering. He will put some blood on the posts of the temple doors. And he must put blood on the corners of the altar. And he will put some on the gate posts of the inside temple yard. 20 You must also do this on the seventh (7th) day of the month. A person might sin by mistake and this will make the temple clean from their sin.

21 On the fourteenth (14th) day of the first month you must have a feast. You will have a feast for seven (7) days. It is the Passover feast. And for that time you must not eat any bread that you have made with yeast.

22 On that day the king must give a male cow as a sin offering. It is an offering for himself and for all the people. 23 Every day of the feast he must give seven (7) male cows and seven (7) male sheep for burnt offerings to the Lord. He must also give a male goat each day for a sin offering. None of the animals can have anything wrong with it. 24 The king must give an ephah of grain with each cow and an ephah with each sheep. He must give a hin of oil with each ephah.

25 You will have a feast for seven (7) days. It will begin on the fifteenth (15th) day of the seventh (7th) month. The king must give the same offerings for these seven (7) days." '

Chapter 46

1 'You must keep shut the door of the inside yard that opens to the east. You must do this for the six (6) days that you work. You must only open it on the seventh (7th) day and on the New Moon day. 2 The king must go through the entrance room by the gate. It is his way in from the outside yard. He must stand by the gate's posts. The priests must burn his sacrifice and offer his fellowship gifts. He can worship there and then go out. But they must not shut the gate until the evening. 3 The people must also worship the Lord in front of the gate each Sabbath and New Moon feast. 4 Every Sabbath day, the king must bring a male sheep and six (6) young male sheep. The priests will burn them as a sacrifice to the Lord. None of them should have anything wrong with them. 5 The king must bring an ephah of grain to sacrifice with the male sheep. He can give as much grain as he likes with the young sheep. And he must give a hin of oil with each ephah. 6 On the day of the New Moon he must offer a young male cow, a male sheep and six (6) young sheep. None of them can have anything wrong with it. 7 He must give an ephah of grain with the cow and an ephah with the sheep. He can give as much as he chooses with the young sheep. And he must give a hin of oil with
each ephah of grain. 8 When the king goes in, he must go through the gate's entrance room. And he must go out by the same way.

9 The people will come to worship the Lord at the feast times that I give to them.

Then if they come in by the north gate they must go out by the south gate. And if they come in by the south gate they must go out by the north gate. Nobody can go out of the gate through which they came in. He must go out by the opposite gate. 10 The king must go with them. He must go in when they go in. He must go out when they go out.

11 They must offer an ephah of grain with a male cow. And they must give an ephah with a sheep. They can give as much as they choose with a young sheep. They must give a hin of oil with each ephah.

This is what they must do on feast days. They must do it on each of the days that I have given to them for worship. 12 They must open the east gate for the king. He may want to make a special offering to the Lord. He can go in. He can make his burnt offering or fellowship offering as he does on the Sabbath day. Then he must go out and they will shut the gate after him.

13 Every day, you must give a sheep one year old to burn as an offering to the Lord. It must have nothing that is wrong with it. You must sacrifice this sheep every morning, day after day. 14 And you must give a sixth (1/6th) of an ephah of grain with it.

And you must put with it a third (1/3rd) of a hin of oil. That is to keep the flour together. You must continue to offer the grain to the Lord until the end of time. 15 Every morning, you must offer the young sheep, the grain and the oil for a burnt sacrifice.

16 The king can make a gift to one of his sons. He can make it from the land that I gave him.' This is what the Lord, your King says, 'That land will belong to the son and to his children and grandchildren. It will become their land for all time. 17 But the king may give land to one of his servants. The servant can keep the land until the year of jubilee. (See Leviticus 25:10.) Then they must give the land back to the king. The land belongs only to the king and his sons for all time. 18 The king must not take any land that belongs to the people. He can give only land that I have given to him to his sons. Nobody among the people must be without his land.'

19 The man took me through the entrance by the gate. We came into the priest's holy rooms. These opened to the north. He showed me a place at the west end. 20 'This is the place where the priests will cook the offerings to pay for sin and other wrong things', he said. 'They will bake the grain offerings here, too. In this way, they will not have to go into the outside yard. If they did that, they would make the people holy.'

21-22 Then he took me to the outside yard. He showed me the four (4) corners. In each corner I saw another yard twenty (20) metres long and fifteen (15) metres wide. 23 These smaller yards had walls round them. Under the walls they had made places for fire. 24 'The temple priests will work in these kitchens. Here they will cook the people's sacrifices', he said to me.

Chapter 47

The river from the temple

1 The man brought me back to the entrance of the temple. There I saw water. It was coming out from under the entrance and it was running to the east. (The temple looked towards the east.) It came from under the south side of the temple. Then it ran past the south side of the altar. 2 The man took me out of the temple by the north gate. We went to the gate that opens to the east. Another small stream of water came out. That was at the south side of the gate. 3 The man measured five hundred (500) metres down the stream. He told me that I must walk through it. The water came up to my ankles. 4 Then he measured another five hundred (500) metres along the stream and the water came up to my knees. He measured down another five hundred (500) metres. The water came to the middle of my body. 5 When he measured another five hundred (500) metres the river was so deep that nobody could walk through it. 6 'Son of man', he said, 'remember this.'

Then he took me back to the river's edge. 7 There I saw very many trees. They were on each side of the river. 8 'This water goes through the land to the east. It runs into the River Jordan's valley and out into the Dead Sea. When it goes into the sea, the water there will lose its salt. 9 Many kinds of animals and plants will live where the river goes. Many fish will live where the river goes. They will live there because there is no salt in the water. 10 Men by the sea will catch fish. They will find fish from the River Engedi to the streams of Eneglaim. They will dry their fishing nets by the side of the sea. Many kinds of fish, like the fish of the Great Sea, will live there. 11 But the wet lands near the Dead Sea will still contain salt. You can use their water to get salt for yourselves. 12 All kinds of fruit trees will live there. They will live on each side of the river. They will remain green and give fruit every month. That is because they live by special water. That is the water that comes from the holy place. You will eat their fruit. And you can use their leaves to make sick people well.'

The edges of Israel's land

13 This is what the Lord, your King says. 'This is the land that I am giving to you to keep. Each of your twelve (12) tribes must have a part. You must give Joseph's sons two parts. 14 Each tribe must have a part of the same size. I made a promise to your fathers that I would give them this country to live in. I gave it to them and their children to keep for all time.

15 These are the edges of your country. The north side goes from the Great Sea to the city called Hethlon. Then it passes Lebo Hamath and goes to the city called Zedad. 16 From there, it continues through Berothah and Sibraim. They are on the edges of Hamath's and Damascus's lands. Then it goes to the city called Hazarhatticon. It goes by the edge of Hauran's land. 17 That is the north edge of your country. It goes from the Great Sea to the city called Hazarenan. That is the north edge of Damascus's land. The land of Hamath is north of it.

18 On the east side, your land goes along the River Jordan. It starts between Hauran and Damascus. It goes between Gilead and Israel as far as Tamar on the Dead Sea.

19 On the south side, it goes from Tamar to the waters of Kadesh Meribah. Then it goes north-west along the edge of Egypt to the Great Sea.

20 The Great Sea is the west edge of your country. It goes north as far as the west of Lebo Hamath. That is the west side of your country.

21 You must give each tribe a part of the land. 22 You will keep it for yourselves and the foreigners and their children who live among you. You must think of them as Israel's people. You must give them land to live on. 23 They can have land in any tribe's land where they decide to live', says the Lord, your King.

Chapter 48

Each tribe gets its part of the land

1-7 'The north edge of your country starts at the Great Sea. It goes from Hethlon through Lebo Hamath. From there, it goes to the city called Hazarenan. It ends where the lands of Damascus and Hamath meet. You must give each tribe a part of the land. Each part must go from the east edge to the Great Sea. From north to south, the tribes will be,

Dan

Asher

Naphtali

Manasseh

Ephraim

Reuben

Judah.

Each tribe will be next to the one to its north side.

8 The next part of the land will be different. It will be as wide as the parts of the land that I am giving to the tribes. It will measure twelve and a half (17½) kilometres from north to south. You must put the temple in the middle of it.

9 A special part twelve and a half (12½) kilometres by ten (10) kilometres will be holy to the Lord. 10 Here the priests will have their part. It will measure twelve and a half (12½) kilometres from east to west. And it will measure five (5) kilometres from north to south. You must build the Lord's temple in the middle of this part. 11 The priests who are the sons of Zadok will have this part. They were my faithful servants. They obeyed me when the other Levites and Israel's people did not obey me. 12 So the priests will have a special part, next to the Levite's part. And the priest's part is the most holy part. 13 The Levites will also have a special part, south of the priest's part. And it will measure the same. It will measure twelve and a half (12½) kilometres from east to west. And it will be five (5) kilometres from north to south. 14 The Lord's part of the land is the best of the land. You must not give or sell his land to anyone else. It is holy and it belongs to the Lord.

15 The people can use the rest of this special part. It measures twelve and a half (12½) kilometres by two and a half (2½) kilometres and it is not holy. You must build the city in the middle of it. 16 You will make it square. It must be 2250 metres long on each side. 17 You must leave an open space one hundred and twenty-five (125) metres wide on each side of the city. 18 When you have built the city south of the holy place, the land on each side will be left. People who live in the city can use it to grow food and to feed their animals. 19 The farmers can be from any of Israel's tribes.

20 This middle of the Lord's part will be a square. It measures twelve and a half (12½) kilometres on each side. The city will be in this middle part. 21 The parts on either side of the square will be the king's land. They will go east to the edge of the country. They will go west to the Great Sea. And the holy part and the most holy place will be in the middle. 22 So the land that belongs to the Levites and the priests is in the king's land. It is in the middle of it. Judah's land is north of these lands. And Benjamin's land is south of it.

23-27 The other tribes will each have a part of the land south of this special part. From north to south they will be

Benjamin

Simeon

Issachar

Zebulun

Gad.

Each tribe's part will be south of the next tribe's land.

28 The south edge of Gad's land goes south. It goes from Tamar to the waters of Meribah Kadesh. Then it goes along the edge of Egypt. It goes to the Great Sea.

29 This is how you must give the land to the tribes. You must give a part to each tribe', says the Lord, your King.

The city gates

30 'Each side of the city is 2250 metres long. 31 You will give the gates the names of Israel's tribes. You will give the three gates in the north wall the names of Reuben, Judah and Levi. 32 You will give the three gates in the east wall the names of Joseph, Benjamin and Dan. 33 You will give the three gates in the south wall the names of Simeon, Issachar and Zebulun. 34 You will give the three gates in the west wall the names of Gad, Asher and Naphtali. 35 The walls all-round the city will measure 9000 metres. And then you will give the city the name, "The Lord is there."'

God's man Daniel

Daniel

About this book

The events in the book of Daniel happened about 600 years before Jesus was born.

There is only one God. He made everything. But God's special people, the Jews, did not obey God. So he punished them. He let Nebuchadnezzar, the king of Babylon, and his army beat them. Nebuchadnezzar brought almost all the Jews who were in Judah to live in Babylon.

The first part of the book tells us about events that happened during the lives of Daniel and his friends. Many times the people in Babylon tried to cause them to forget God. They wanted them to worship images. The people in Babylon even tried to kill Daniel and his friends because they would not worship the images. But Daniel and his friends knew that images are not really gods. So they continued to worship the only God. Daniel became a very important man in the government of Babylon.

The second part of the book tells about Daniel's dreams. They were strange dreams. Sometimes Daniel was awake when he had his dreams. They were special dreams that God sent to Daniel. God sent them to tell Daniel what would happen in future years. Some things that Daniel saw in his dreams have now happened. Other things that God told Daniel in his dreams have not happened yet. But God rules over events. God will do what he has promised.

God used Nebuchadnezzar, to punish the Jews, but Nebuchadnezzar did not know that. The book teaches us that God rules over events. He can use people who do not know him to teach us.

Chapter 1

God makes his servant Daniel ready for his work

Israel's enemies take Daniel and his friends to Babylon

1 Nebuchadnezzar was the king of Babylon. He came to Jerusalem with his army. Then he caused his soldiers to live round the city. This happened when Jehoiakim had been king of Judah for longer than two years. 2 God caused Nebuchadnezzar to take Jehoiakim, king of Judah. God helped Nebuchadnezzar to take some holy things from God's house there also. Nebuchadnezzar took those things back to Babylon. He put them among the valuable things in the house of his own god.

3 Nebuchadnezzar said to Ashpenaz, his most important officer, 'Bring some of the Jews from Israel to me. Choose young men from the king of Israel's family. And choose young men from the other important families in Israel.' 4-5 Nebuchadnezzar wanted young men who were strong and handsome. The young men must be clever. And they must be able to learn and to understand quickly. These young men would be able to become King Nebuchadnezzar's servants. They must learn the language of Babylon and they must learn from the country's books. King Nebuchadnezzar also sent to them each day some of the same food and wine as he had. After three years, they would then be ready to work for him.

6 Daniel, Hananiah, Mishael and Azariah, who were from Judah, were among these young men. 7 The important officer gave new names to them. He gave the name Belteshazzar to Daniel and he called Hananiah, Shadrach. He gave the name Meshach to Mishael and he called Azariah, Abednego.

Daniel refuses to eat the king's food

8 But Daniel thought that God did not want him to eat the king's food and wine. He wanted God to be happy with him. So, he decided that he would not have the food. So, he asked the important officer that he might not have to eat the king's food. 9 God had caused that officer to like Daniel. And the officer understood what Daniel was thinking. 10 But he spoke to Daniel. 'I am afraid of the king, who is giving your food and drink to you', he said. 'He might see that you are not as strong as the other young men. And then he will kill me.'

11 The officer had chosen a man to help Daniel, Hananiah, Mishael and Azariah. So Daniel spoke to this man. 12 'We are your servants. Please watch us for 10 days. Give to us only vegetables to eat and water to drink. 13 Then see whether we have good health. Look at us with the young men who eat the king's food. Then decide what to do with us, your servants.' 14 So the man agreed and he watched them for 10 days. 15And after 10 days, their faces and bodies seemed more handsome than the young men who ate the king's food. 16 So the man took away the king's food and wine and he gave only vegetables and water to them.

God makes Daniel and his friends wise

17 God gave clever minds to these 4 young men. While they studied, he helped them to learn from books. And he helped them to understand the books. And Daniel could understand all kinds of dreams too.

18 The king had said that they must wait for a certain time. That time finished. Then the important officer brought the young men to Nebuchadnezzar. 19 The king talked with them. He discovered that there was nobody else like Daniel, Hananiah, Mishael and Azariah. So they became the king's servants.

20 The king continued to ask them to help him. They helped him to understand everything and to do good things. The king's other wise men used every kind of magic to suggest what he might do. These other men came from every country that Nebuchadnezzar ruled. But the answers that Daniel and his friends gave seemed 10 times (10 ×) better than the other men's words.

21 And Daniel lived there until the year when Cyrus became king.

Chapter 2

Nebuchadnezzar's dream

The king asks his wise men to explain his dream

1 When Nebuchadnezzar had been king for almost two years, he had dreams. His mind was not comfortable and he could not sleep.

2 He told his servants that they must bring the magicians, enchanters, sorcerers and wise men to him. He wanted them to tell him what he had dreamed. So they came in and they stood in front of the king. 3 Then the king said to them, 'I have had a dream that takes away my sleep. And so I want to know what it means.'

4 Then the wise men answered the king in the Aramaic language. 'We want the king to live for all time', they said. 'We are your servants. Tell us the dream. And then we will tell you what it means.'

5 The king replied to the wise men. 'I have decided what to do', he said. 'You tell me what my dream was. And you must tell me what it means. If not, I will cause people to cut you into pieces. And they will make your houses into hills of stones. 6 You must tell me the dream and what it means. If you do, I will give gifts to you. I will give many gifts and great honour to you. So, tell me my dream. And tell me what it means.'

7 They answered him again. 'We are your servants, so please tell us your dream. Then we will tell you what it means.'

8 And the king answered them. 'I certainly know that you are trying to get more time. You know what I have decided. 9 If you do not tell me the dream, you will all receive the same punishment. You are continuing to tell me lies and bad things. And you have agreed to do that. You hope that I will change my mind. So now, tell me the dream. Then you can tell me what it means. And I will be able to believe what you say.'

10 The wise men answered the king, 'There is not a man on earth who can do that! No king has ever asked anyone to do anything like this. No magician, or man with the power to understand has ever done this. Even the greatest and most powerful king of all has never asked this. 11 You are asking a very difficult thing. Nobody can do it, except the gods. And they do not live among men.'

12 This made the king very, very angry. So he said to his soldiers, 'Kill all the wise men in Babylon.' 13 He sent them a message to kill all his wise men. So some men went to look for Daniel and his friends. They wanted to kill them too.

14 Arioch, the captain of the king's soldiers, went to kill the wise men in Babylon. But Daniel spoke to him carefully. 15 He said to Arioch, the king's captain, 'Why is the king's message so cruel?' Then Arioch explained everything to Daniel. 16 So Daniel went to see the king. He asked the king for more time. Then he would be able to tell the king what the dream meant.

God shows the dream to Daniel

17 Then Daniel went to his home and he explained the problem to his friends, Hananiah, Mishael and Azariah. 18 He told them that they should pray to God in heaven. They should pray about this problem. He told them that they should ask God to keep them safe. Then they would not die with all the other wise men in Babylon. 19 During the night, Daniel had a dream. God showed him in the dream what it meant. Then Daniel gave honour to the God of heaven. 20 He said,

'Give honour to the name of God always

because he is great.

And he knows everything.

21 He changes times and seasons.

He chooses kings to rule. And he stops them ruling.

He causes some people to become wise.

And he helps people to understand the things that they learn.

22 He explains difficult problems and secret things.

He knows about all things, even when they are in dark places.

But he lives in the light.

23 I thank you. And I give honour to you, because you were my ancestors' God too.

And you have made me wise and you have made me strong.

You have shown me your answer to what we asked.

You have explained the king's problem to us.'

24 So Daniel went to Arioch. He was the officer to whom the king had said, 'You must kill the wise men in Babylon.' Daniel said to Arioch, 'Do not kill the king's wise men in Babylon. Take me to the king. Then I will tell the king what his dream means.'

25 Then Arioch quickly took Daniel to the king. He said, 'I have found a man. He can tell the king what his dream means. He is one of the people that you brought from Judah.'

26 The king spoke to Daniel (whose other name was Belteshazzar). He said, 'Can you tell me my dream? And can you tell me what it means?'

27 Daniel answered the king.
'No wise men, enchanters, magicians or diviners can explain this dream to the king', he said. 28 'But there is a God in heaven. And he explains hidden things. He is showing King Nebuchadnezzar what will happen in future years. This is the dream and the thoughts in your head while you lay on your bed.

29 While you lay on your bed, you dreamed about future years. God showed you what will happen in future years. He explains hidden things. 30 I am not more clever than anyone else. But God explained the dream to me. He wants you to know what it means. And he wants you to understand the thoughts in your mind.

The dream

31 You looked, and you saw a large image with a man's shape. This big image was in front of you. It was very bright and it frightened people. 32 Someone had made its head from clean gold. The top of its body and its arms were silver. Its lower body was bronze. 33 The image's legs were iron and the feet had parts of iron and parts of clay. 34 While you looked, someone cut out a stone. But no human hand did this. The stone hit the image on its iron and clay feet and the stone broke them into pieces. 35 Then the iron, clay, bronze, silver and gold all fell into pieces. They became like powder. The wind blew them away until nobody could see them. But the stone that had hit the image became a large mountain. And it filled the whole earth.

Daniel explains the dream to the king

36 This was the dream. Now we will tell the king what it means. 37 You are a great king who rules other kings. The God of heaven has made you king and he has given power and honour to you. He has made you strong. 38 He has given all the people, the animals on the earth and the birds in the air to you. He has made you king of them all, in every place that they live. You are like the head of gold in your dream.

39 After you, there will be another kingdom that is not as great as yours. Then a third (3rd) kingdom will rule the whole earth. It will be like bronze. 40 And there will be a fourth (4th) kingdom that is as strong as iron. Iron breaks everything and it destroys everything. So, like iron, that kingdom will destroy the other kingdoms. 41 You saw that someone had made the feet and toes from parts of clay and parts of iron. This means that it will not be a united kingdom. But some will be strong, like iron, because you saw iron with the clay. 42 Parts of the toes were iron and parts of them were clay. So that kingdom will be strong in some parts and weak in other parts. 43 You saw iron and clay mixed together. So, the people will mix with each other but they will not stay together. This is like iron that cannot mix with clay.

44 In the days when those kings rule, the God of heaven will begin a kingdom. And that kingdom will never end. No other people will have power over it. It will break up all these other kingdoms and it will destroy them. And it will continue for always. 45 You saw the stone that no human hand cut out. The stone broke up the iron, the bronze, the clay, the silver and the gold. The great God has shown to the king what will happen in future years. That was the dream. And that is what it means. And you can be sure about that.'

The king gives important jobs to Daniel and to his friends

46 Then King Nebuchadnezzar lay flat on the ground in front of Daniel. This showed that he gave honour to Daniel. He said that his servants must give to Daniel gifts and things to make nice smells. 47 The king said to Daniel, 'It is true that your God is greater than all other gods. He rules over kings and he explains hidden things. I know this because you were able to explain this dream to me.'

48 Then the king made Daniel an important man and the king gave many great gifts to him. He made Daniel ruler over the whole of Babylon. He made Daniel the leader of all the wise men.

49 Then Daniel asked the king to give important work to Shadrach, Meshach and Abednego. So the king told them that they must rule things in Babylon. But Daniel remained with the king.

Chapter 3

Nebuchadnezzar's image of gold

The king says that everyone must worship the image

1 King Nebuchadnezzar caused his workers to make a golden image. It was 30 metres (90 feet) high and 3 metres (9 feet) wide. He built it on the flat land called Dura, in a part of Babylon. 2 Then King Nebuchadnezzar told the king's family, the rulers and the captains that they must all come together. He also told all the other officers the same thing. And he told the men who knew the law. And he told the men who kept the money. He told them that they must come together. They must meet in front of the image that his men had made. 3 So the king's family, the captains and the other people came to the meeting in front of the image. Those who kept the money and all the officers and other important people came too. They all stood in front of the image that King Nebuchadnezzar had built.

4 Then an officer shouted aloud. 'You, people in every country who speak every language, listen. This is what the king says to you. 5 Listen for the sound of all kinds of music. When you hear it, you must go down on your knees. You must worship the golden image that King Nebuchadnezzar has built. 6 "I will punish anyone who does not do this", the king said. "My servants will throw them immediately into a very hot fire." ' 7 So, when the people heard the different kinds of music, they obeyed. All the people went on their knees. They were worshipping King Nebuchadnezzar's golden image.

Daniel's friends refuse to worship the image

8 Then some astrologers came to the king and they told the king about the Jews.

9 They said to the king, 'We want the king to live for all time. 10 You, the king, made a rule. You said that everyone must listen for the sound from all kinds of music. Then they must go down on their knees and worship the golden image. 11 You said that everyone must obey you. You would throw them into a very hot fire if they did not obey you. 12 There are some Jews who do not obey you. You put them to rule everything that happens in Babylon. They are Shadrach, Meshach and Abednego and they do not give honour to your gods. They do not worship your golden image.'

13 Then Nebuchadnezzar was very, very angry. So he told his servants that they must bring Shadrach, Meshach and Abednego to him. And they brought these men to the king. 14 Then Nebuchadnezzar spoke to them. He said, 'Is it true, Shadrach, Meshach and Abednego, that you do not give honour to my gods? And you do not worship the golden image that I have made? 15 You will hear again the sound of all kinds of music. You must be ready, when you hear the music. You must go down on your knees. Then you will show honour to the image that I have made. If you do not worship my image, my servants will throw you immediately into a very hot fire. And no god can save you from my power.'

16 Shadrach, Meshach and Abednego answered the king. 'King Nebuchadnezzar, we know that we did the right thing', they said. 17 'You may throw us into the very hot fire. But the God that we worship can save us. He will save us from your power if he wants to. 18 But if he does not save us, it does not make any difference. We want you to know that we will not worship your gods. And we will not give honour to the image that you have made.'

The king's servants throw Daniel's three friends into a very hot fire

19 Then Nebuchadnezzar was very angry with Shadrach, Meshach and Abednego. His face became red. He said to his servants, 'Make the hot fire 7 times (7 ×) hotter than usual.' 20 He told the strongest men in his army that they must tie Shadrach, Meshach and Abednego. And then he said to them, 'Throw Shadrach, Meshach and Abednego into the very hot fire.' 21 Shadrach, Meshach and Abednego were still wearing their clothes. They were wearing their coats, hats and other clothes when the men threw them into the fire. 22 The king's word was very powerful and the fire was very hot. So the fire killed the men who threw Shadrach, Meshach and Abednego into it. 23 But Shadrach, Meshach and Abednego, still tied up, fell into the very hot fire.

The king sees that God has kept Daniel's friends safe

24 What King Nebuchadnezzar saw next surprised him very much. So he jumped up and he asked his officers, 'Did we not tie up 3 men and throw them into the fire?' 'You are right, our king', they answered. 25 The king said, 'But I see 4 men walking about in the fire! They are free and the fire has not hurt them. The fourth (4th) man seems like a son of the gods.'

26 King Nebuchadnezzar went to the door where the very hot fire was. He shouted aloud to the men inside, 'Shadrach, Meshach and Abednego, who give honour to the true God, you come out here.' So Shadrach, Meshach and Abednego came out of the fire. 27 The king's family, rulers, captains and his officers came close to look at them. They saw that the fire had not hurt Shadrach, Meshach or Abednego. The fire had not touched their hair or their clothes. There was not even the smell from the smoke.

Nebuchadnezzar's new rules

28 Nebuchadnezzar spoke. 'Give honour to the God of Shadrach, Meshach and Abednego', he said. 'He sent his angel to save his servants. I am the king. But they believed that their God would save them. So they did not obey me. They might have died. But they would give honour only to their own God and not to any other god. 29 No other god can save like this. So I make a rule for the people in every country who speak every language. They must not say anything against the God of Shadrach, Meshach and Abednego. My servants will cut into pieces anyone who does not obey. I will also destroy those people's houses.'

30 Then the king gave more important jobs in Babylon to Shadrach, Meshach and Abednego.

Chapter 4

The big tree

Nebuchadnezzar writes a letter

1 I, King Nebuchadnezzar, am sending this message to everyone in the world. I am writing to the people in every country who speak every language. I pray that you all have good and happy lives.

2 It makes me happy to tell you what the great God has done.

God has given many good gifts to me. He has done great and special things.

3 The things that he does are very great.

God's kingdom will never end. He rules for all time.

The king's wise men fail again

4 I, Nebuchadnezzar, was at home in my king's house. I was comfortable and I was happy. 5 Then I had a dream that made me afraid. I lay on my bed and the thoughts in my head made me afraid.

6 So I asked all the wise men in Babylon to come to me. I wanted them to tell me what the dream meant.

7 When the magicians, enchanters, astrologers and diviners came, I told them the dream. But none of them could tell me what the dream meant. 8 Last of all, Daniel came to me. I call him Belteshazzar like my god's name. The spirit of the holy gods is in this man, Daniel. So I told him the dream.

9 'Belteshazzar', I said, 'you are the leader of my wise men. I know that the spirit of the holy gods is in you. I know also that no problem is too difficult for you. So, here is the dream that I saw. Tell me what it means.'

The king tells Daniel about his dream

10 'This is what I saw in my mind. I saw it while I was asleep. I saw a tree in the middle of the earth and it was very tall. 11 The tree grew taller and stronger. Its top touched the sky, so everyone in the world could see it. 12 It had beautiful leaves and lots of fruit. There was enough food on it for everyone. It was a home for the animals. And birds lived in it. Every living thing ate its food.'

13 'While I was still sleeping, I saw an angel. He was holy and he came from heaven. 14 He shouted aloud. "Cause the animals that are under the tree go away", he shouted. "Cause the birds that are in its branches to fly away. Cut down the tree. Cut off its branches. Tear off its leaves. Let its fruit fall on the ground. 15 But leave the part of the tree that is in the ground. Tie it up with iron and bronze. Then leave it in the grass.

Make him wet with dew from the sky. Cause him to live in the fields with the animals. 16 Take his own mind away from him. And give the mind of an animal to him for 7 years.

17 The angels who watch human people have said this. And this is what they have chosen. So now everyone will know that God rules in the kingdoms of men. He can give kingdoms to anyone that he wants to. And he can cause men who are not important to become kings."

18 This was my dream', I said to Belteshazzar. 'Now, you tell me what it means. None of the wise men in any of my countries can tell me what it means. But you can tell me, because the spirit of the holy gods is in you.'

Daniel explains this dream to the king

19 Daniel, whose other name was Belteshazzar, was not happy for a time. His thoughts caused him trouble. The king said, 'Belteshazzar, do not let the dream or what it means cause you trouble.' Then Belteshazzar answered the king. 'Sir, I wish that the dream was about your enemies and not about you. 20 You saw a tree that grew. And it grew taller and stronger until its top touched the sky. Everyone in the world could see it. 21 It had beautiful leaves and lots of fruit. There was enough food on it for everyone. It was a home for the animals. And the birds built their houses in it. 22 You, the king, are like that tree. You have become stronger and more powerful. You have become very great. They have heard about you in heaven. You have power over the whole land.

23 Then you saw an angel. He was holy and he came from heaven. "Cut down the tree and destroy it", he said. "But leave the part of the tree that is in the ground. Tie it up with iron and bronze. Then leave it in the grass.

Make him wet with dew from the sky. Cause him to live in the fields with the animals for 7 years."

24 This is what the dream means. The true God has decided what he will do to my lord, the king. 25 People will push you out, so that you will have to live with the animals. And you will eat grass as cows do. Dew from the sky will make you wet. And you will live in this way for 7 years. Then you will know that God rules in the kingdoms of men. He can give kingdoms to anyone that he wants to. 26 The angel said, "Leave the part of the tree that is in the ground." This means that you will be king again later. But before that, you will have to agree that God rules the world. 27 So my king, please do as I suggest. Stop doing bad things. Start doing what is right. Do not do bad things. But be kind to the people who are not happy. Then, perhaps, you will continue to be happy.'

Nebuchadnezzar's pride

28 All this happened to King Nebuchadnezzar. 29 One year later, he was walking on the flat roof of the king's house in Babylon. 30 Then the king spoke aloud and he said, 'Look how great Babylon is. My power has built this city to be the king's home. It shows that I am great and powerful.'

The bad things that were in the dream happen to Nebuchadnezzar

31 While he was still speaking about his power, he heard a voice from heaven. 'I am speaking to you, King Nebuchadnezzar', the voice said. 'I have taken the king's power away from you. 32 People will push you away. You will live with the animals. And you will eat grass as cows do. I will cause you to live like this for 7 years. Then you will know that God rules the kingdoms of men. And he can give kingdoms to anyone that he wants to give them to.'

33 Then it all happened to Nebuchadnezzar as he had dreamed. People sent him away. And he ate grass as cows do. Dew from the sky made his body wet. His hair grew long. It seemed like what a large bird has over its body. And his feet seemed like bird's feet.

God makes Nebuchadnezzar better

34 At the end of that time, I, Nebuchadnezzar, looked up towards heaven and I prayed. I got my proper mind back and I thanked the true God. I gave honour to him who never dies.

His kingdom will never end

because he rules always and for all time.

35 All the people on the earth are worth nothing.

He does what he wants with the angels in heaven.

And he does what he wants with the people on the earth.

Nobody can stop him.

Nobody can say to him, 'You should not be doing that.'

36 When I got my proper mind back, I also got my power back. People gave honour to me. My officers and important men came back to me. So I became the king again. And I became greater than I was before. 37 Now I, Nebuchadnezzar, give honour to the King of heaven and I thank him. He does what is right all the time. He is always fair. And some people may think that they are great. He can teach them that they are not great.

Chapter 5

Chapter 5 A message on the wall

Belshazzar's big party

1 King Belshazzar had a big party. He asked 1000 important people to come, and he drank wine with them. 2 When Belshazzar drank wine, he spoke to his servants. He said that they must bring to him the gold and silver cups from God's house.

Nebuchadnezzar, his father, had taken these cups from God's house in Jerusalem. Belshazzar wanted his friends, his wives and his other women to drink their wine from these cups. 3 So his servants brought the gold cups that had come from God's house in Jerusalem. Then the king, his wives, his other women and all the important people drank wine out of those cups. 4 And when they drank the wine, they also gave honour to their gods. Their gods were images that people had made out of gold, silver, bronze, iron and stone.

A hand writes on the wall

5 Immediately, the fingers of a man's hand appeared and the fingers wrote on the wall of the king's house. They wrote near the light that stood in the room. So the king saw the hand while it wrote. 6 The king's face became white and he was afraid. His knees started to knock together and his legs became weak.

The king's wise men cannot help him

7 The king shouted for his wise men:
the enchanters, astrologers and diviners. When they came, the king spoke to them. He said, 'Who can read these words? Who can tell me what they mean? I will put purple clothes on that person and he will have a gold ring round his neck. And I will make him the third (3rd) ruler in the kingdom.' 8 Then all the king's wise men came in, but they could not read the words. They could not tell the king what the words meant. 9 So King Belshazzar became very afraid and his face became very white. His officers did not know what to do.

The queen tells Belshazzar about Daniel

10 The queen heard the words of the king and his officers. So she came into the room where they were having the party. Then she spoke to the king. 'I want the king to live for all time', she said. 'Do not be afraid. Do not let your face be so white. 11 There is a man in your kingdom who has the spirit of the holy gods in him. He showed your father in his time, that he was very, very wise. He was wise like the gods. Your father, Nebuchadnezzar, made him the leader of all
the magicians, astrologers, enchanters and diviners. 12 His mind was clever and he knew many things. He could tell what dreams mean. He could explain hidden things and answer problems. His name was Daniel, but the king called him Belteshazzar. Send a man to fetch Daniel. He will tell you what the words mean.'

Belshazzar asks Daniel to explain the message

13 Then people brought Daniel to the king. The king said to Daniel, 'Are you Daniel? Are you one of the men that my father the king brought from Judah? 14 I have heard that the spirit of the gods is in you. You are wise and you understand many things. 15 I told my servants that they must bring the wise men and enchanters. I wanted the wise men to read these words. I asked them to tell me what the words mean. But they could not explain them to me. 16 I have heard that you can understand dreams. And I have heard that you can answer problems. So, can you read these words? And can you tell me what they mean? If you can do that, then I will put purple clothes on you. You will have a gold ring round your neck. And you will be the third (3rd) ruler in the kingdom.'

Daniel tells the king that he has been bad and silly

17 Then Daniel answered the king. 'You can keep your gifts for yourself. You can give them to someone else. But I will read the words for the king. And I will tell him what they mean. 18 The God who is great and true made your father Nebuchadnezzar king. God made him great and God gave honour to him. 19 Because God made him so great, the people in every country were afraid of him. The people who spoke every language were afraid of him. He killed anyone that he wanted to kill. And if he wanted someone to live, he let him live. He made people important if he wanted to. And if he wanted to make someone less important, he made that person less important. 20 He thought that he was the most important person. He thought that he could do anything. Then God took away his kingdom and his honour. 21 People pushed him out because he had an animal's mind. So he lived with the wild horses. People fed him with grass that cows eat. Dew from the sky made his body wet until he changed his mind. But then he agreed that the great and true God rules the kingdoms of men. God gives authority over them to anyone that he wants to give it to.

22 You, Belshazzar, are Nebuchadnezzar's son and you knew all this. But you did not keep pride out of your mind.

23 You think that you are more important than the Lord of heaven. You demanded the cups from his house. And you, your wives, your other women and your important friends drank wine from them. Then you gave honour to gods that people had made from silver, gold, bronze, iron, wood and stone. These gods cannot see or hear. And they cannot understand. But you gave honour to them and you did not give honour to the true God. He gave your life to you. He has power over everything that you do. 24 That is why he sent the hand that wrote these words. 25 And these are the words:

Mene, Mene, Tekel and Peres.

Daniel explains the words on the wall

26 This is what the words mean:

Mene means that God has counted the days of your kingdom. Now these days are finished and he has finished your kingdom.

27 Tekel means that God has measured you. He has measured you to see if you are right (as you should be). But you were too small when he measured you.

28 Peres means that God has cut your kingdom into two parts. He has given it to the people from Media and from Persia.'

The things that were in the message happen

29 Then Belshazzar caused his servants to put purple clothes on Daniel. They put a gold ring round his neck. Then the king told all the people that Daniel was the third (3rd) ruler in the kingdom. 30 That same night someone killed Belshazzar, king of Babylon. 31 And Darius from Media became king. He was 62 years old.

Chapter 6

Chapter 6 Daniel and the lions

Some men are not happy because Daniel is very important

1 Darius decided to make 120 men rulers. Together, they would rule the whole kingdom. 2 He also made 3 other men officers. He made them more important than the rulers. The 3 men would watch over the work of the rulers. Then the king would know that they were working well. Daniel was one of these 3 officers. 3 But Daniel did his work much better than the other officers and rulers. He was very good at his job. So the king wanted to make him ruler over the whole kingdom. 4 The other officers and rulers watched how Daniel worked for the king. They tried to show that he was doing something wrong. But they could not find that he did any wrong thing. That was because Daniel was a good and honest servant. He always did everything that the king wanted him to do. 5 Then these men said to each other, 'We cannot find anything that Daniel does wrong. We can beat him only with something from the laws of his God.'

The men decide that they will make the king angry with Daniel

6 So these officers and rulers went together to the king. 'King Darius, we want you to live for all time', they said. 7 'All the officers and rulers in the kingdom including the king's sons, rulers and captains have agreed. The king should make a law. For 30 days, the people must pray only to you, the king. If they pray to any other man or god, then your servants must take them to the prison. The servants must throw them into the deep hole where your lions live. 8 Now, you, the king, should make the law and sign it. Then it will be a law for the Medes and the Persians, and nobody can change it.' 9 So King Darius wrote the law and he signed it.

Daniel refuses to obey the king's new rule

10 Daniel heard that the king had signed the law. Then he went home. He went upstairs to his room where the windows opened in the direction of Jerusalem. He went on his knees and he prayed to God. He also thanked God. He did this three times every day. This is what he had always done. 11 Then the officers and rulers met together to see what Daniel would do. They saw that Daniel was praying to God. And he was asking God for help.

12 So they went to the king. They spoke to him about the law that he had made. 'Do you remember that you signed a law?' they said to the king. 'For 30 days, nobody must pray to any god or man, except to you, the king. If they do pray to someone else, your servants must throw them into the deep hole where your lions live.' The king answered them. 'It is true. It is a law for the Medes and the Persians and nobody can change it.' 13 Then the officers and rulers said to the king, 'That Daniel, whom Nebuchadnezzar brought from Judah, does not obey you. He does not obey the law that you signed. He still prays three times every day to his God.' 14 When the king heard this, he was very sad. He tried to think of a way to save Daniel. Until evening, the king tried every way to save Daniel. 15 Then the officers and rulers came back to the king. 'Remember that it is a law for the Medes and the Persians. Nobody can change a law that the king has made', they said to him.

Daniel in the lions' hole

16 Then the king sent his servants to take Daniel to the prison. So they threw him into the deep hole where the lions lived. And the king spoke to Daniel. 'You obey your God's rules and you are his good servant. He will save you', he said. 17 Then they brought a stone. And they put it over the top of the lions' hole. The king put a mark on the stone with his ring of authority. He also marked it with the rings of his important men. This meant that nobody could move that stone. Nobody could change it. 18 Then the king returned to his own house. He ate no food. And nobody brought to him anything that he could enjoy. And he was unable to sleep.

God has shut the lions' mouths

19 The king got up very early in the morning. He hurried to the deep hole where the lions were. 20 When he got near to it, he shouted aloud. His voice showed that he was very afraid. 'Daniel, you are a good servant of the living God. Was your God able to save you from the lions?' he said. 21 Then Daniel said to the king, 'I want you, the king, to live for all time. 22 My God sent his angel, who shut the lions' mouths. So the lions have not hurt me. God knows that I have done no wrong thing. I have not done anything to hurt you, the king, either.' 23 The king was very happy when he heard Daniel's voice. He told his servants that they must lift Daniel out of the lions' hole. So they pulled him out and they looked at him. They saw that the lions had not hurt him. Daniel had believed that his God could save him. That is why the lions had not hurt him.

King Darius punishes the bad men and he writes a letter about God

24 Then the king spoke to his servants. So the servants brought the men who had said bad things about Daniel. They threw those men and their wives and children into the deep hole where the lions were. Before they reached the floor of the hole, the lions attacked them. The lions broke all their bones when they killed them.

25 After this, King Darius wrote to all the people. He wrote to every country in the world. He wrote in every language. 'I pray that you all will have good and happy lives.

26 I have made a law. In every part of my kingdom, the people must give honour to Daniel's God. And they must be afraid of him.

He is the living God

and he will live always.

Nobody will ever destroy his kingdom.

It will never end.

27 He saves people. He keeps them safe.

He does great things in heaven and on earth.

He has saved Daniel from the lions' power.'

28 So Daniel was a powerful ruler while Darius was king. And he continued to be a powerful officer, when Cyrus from Persia (Iran) became king.

Chapter 7

Daniel's dream

Four animals and a little horn

1 It was the first year that King Belshazzar ruled Babylon. Daniel had a dream. He saw pictures in his head while he lay on his bed. And he wrote down what he saw in the dream.

2 Daniel wrote, 'I had a dream at night. I saw the 4 winds of heaven causing the great sea to move up and down. 3 Then 4 large animals came out of the sea. They were all different. 4 The first one seemed like a lion, but it had wings like a great bird. As I watched, someone pulled its wings off. They lifted it up and it stood on two feet like a man. They gave a man's mind to it. 5 Then I saw a second animal. It seemed like a bear. It raised itself up on one side and it had three bones between its teeth. Someone said to it, "Stand up and attack! Eat lots of meat." 6 Then I saw another animal. It seemed like a leopard, but it had 4 wings like a bird's wings on its back. Also, this animal had 4 heads, and it had authority to rule. 7 Then I saw a fourth (4th) animal in my dream. It frightened me more than the other animals. It was very strong and it had large iron teeth. It broke things and people into pieces and it ate them. It destroyed everything else with its feet. It was different from the other animals because it had 10 horns. 8 While I was looking at the horns, I saw another little horn. It came up among the other 10 horns. It pushed out three of those other horns to make room for itself. This little horn had eyes like a man's eyes. And it had a mouth that spoke strong words. That animal thought that it was the most important of all things.'

The time when God will judge people

9-10 Daniel continued to write about his dream.

'I saw that the great authority of those animals ended.

Then God, who is always God, sat down to be their judge.

His clothes were as white as snow.

His hair was white like clean wool (soft hair of a sheep).

He caused thousands of people to become his servants.

Many thousands of people stood in front of him.

The books were open, and God began to judge the people.

God's seat had wheels and it burned like a fire.

A river of fire came out in front of him.

11 The horn was saying how important he was. So I was watching. While I watched, someone killed the fourth (4th) animal. They destroyed its body and they burned it with fire. 12 The other animals lost their power too, but they continued to live for a certain time.'

13 'In my dream at night', Daniel wrote, 'I continued to watch.

Then I saw someone who seemed like a man. He seemed like a son of man. He came with the clouds of heaven.

He came near to God, who is always God.

God's servants brought him close to God.

14 Then God gave authority, honour and a king's power to him.

So the people in every country who spoke every language worshipped him.

His kingdom will continue always.

And nobody will ever cause it to become nothing.

Nobody can destroy it.

An angel explains some things to Daniel

15 I, Daniel, had much trouble in my mind. The thoughts in my head frightened me. 16 So I spoke to someone who was standing near me in my dream. And I asked him what all this meant. Then he explained it to me. 17 "The 4 great animals are 4 kings. They will rule with power on the earth. 18 But the true God will give the kingdom to his own people. Then they will have the kingdom always."

The angel tells Daniel many more things about the fourth animal and about the time when God will judge people

19 Then I wanted to know about the fourth (4th) animal', Daniel wrote. 'It was different from the other animals. It made me very afraid because it was so bad and so strong. It had large iron teeth and bronze fingers. It broke things and people into pieces and it ate them. And it destroyed everything else with its feet. 20 I wanted to know about the 10 horns on its head. I also wanted to know about the little horn that came up among them. It pushed out three of the other horns to make room for itself. This horn had eyes, and a mouth. This mouth said that it was most important. And this little horn seemed greater than the other horns. 21 I continued to watch. And this horn fought against God's holy people. It nearly won the fight. 22 But I continued to look. And God, who is always God, came. He was the judge. He said that the horn must not kill God's holy people. Then the time came when he gave the kingdom to his holy people.

23 Then the person who was near me explained it to me. "The fourth (4th) animal means that there will be a fourth (4th) kingdom on the earth. It will be different from the other kingdoms. It will be as if its king eats up the whole earth. He will walk on the earth and he will break it into pieces. 24 The 10 horns mean 10 kings who will come from that kingdom. They will rule and after them, another king will come. He will be different from the other kings. He will fight and he will kill three of the other kings. 25 He will speak against God. And he will stand against God's holy people. He will try to change the times and God's Law. He will have power over God's people for three and a half years. 26 Then God will judge him. He will take away this king's power and he will destroy it. 27 Then God will give the kingdom to his own people. It will be a great kingdom and they will have great power. And they will rule all the kingdoms of the world on behalf of God. God's kingdom will never end. And all rulers will obey him and they will be his servants."

28 This is the end of my dream', wrote Daniel. 'And I, Daniel, had much trouble because my thoughts made me afraid. My face became white, but I did not tell anyone about these things.'

Chapter 8

The male sheep, the male goat and the little horn

The male sheep and the male goat

1 In the third (3rd) year that King Belshazzar ruled Babylon, I, Daniel, had another dream. 2 In my dream, I saw myself in the king's strong house in the city called Susa. Susa is in the part of the country called Elam. I was standing by the stream called Ulai. 3 I looked up and I saw a male sheep by the stream. He had two long horns. But the longer horn grew up after the other horn. 4 I watched the male sheep while he was running to the west, and to the north, and to the south. He was more powerful than all other animals. Nobody could save any of them from him. He did whatever he wanted to do. And he became great.

5 While I was thinking about this, immediately a male goat came from the west. He went across the whole earth so quickly that his feet did not even touch the ground. The goat had a very big horn between his eyes.

6 He came towards the sheep that I had seen. The sheep had two horns and he was standing by the stream. But the goat was very angry and he ran at the sheep. 7 I saw him attack the sheep because he was so angry with the sheep. He hit the sheep and he broke the sheep's two horns. The sheep had no power against the goat, so the goat knocked the sheep down. And the goat walked over him and killed him. And nobody could save the sheep from the goat.

The little horn

8 The male goat became very great. But when he was greatest, his big horn broke. Instead, 4 other large horns grew up in its place. Each one pointed in a different direction. 9 Out of one of these horns another little horn grew. It became powerful towards the south, and towards the east and towards the Beautiful Country. 10 It became so great that it attacked the stars in the sky. They are the army of heaven. It threw some of the stars to the ground and it walked over them. 11 It thought that it was as great as God, the leader of heaven's army. It took away the gifts that the people offered to God each day. And it destroyed the honour of God's house. 12 Because of the bad things that the people had done, the horn received power over God's people. So God's people did not give gifts to God each day. They gave them to the horn. The horn did not let people worship God any longer. It was able to do all that it wanted to do.

13 Then I heard two angels talking. One angel asked, 'How long will the things in the dream go on? How long will the horn stop people giving the gifts to God each day? How long will God let the horn rule his house? How long will he let the horn walk on his people? How long before they can worship God again?' 14 The other angel answered, 'It will go on for 2300 evenings and mornings. Then they will make God's house holy again.'

An angel called Gabriel explains the dream

15 When I, Daniel, had seen the dream, I tried to understand it. Then someone who seemed like a man appeared in front of me. 16 I heard a man's voice. It was coming from the stream Ulai. 'Gabriel, tell this man what the dream means', the voice said. 17 So Gabriel came near to me. I was very afraid, so I fell down in front of him. But he spoke to me. 'You are only a man, but you must understand the dream. It is about the end of time.' 18 While he was speaking to me I was really asleep. So he touched me and he caused me to stand up. 19 Then he spoke to me again. 'I will tell you what will happen at the end of time. It will happen because God is angry. The end will be at the time that God has decided.'

20 The angel continued to speak. 'You saw a male sheep with two horns. These horns mean the kingdoms of Media and Persia. 21 The male goat means the kingdom of Greece. The big horn between his eyes means the first king. 22 Four horns grew to take the place of the broken big horn. They will make the Greek people into 4 kingdoms. But they will not be as powerful as the first Greek kingdom.'

23 The angel continued to speak. He said, 'Near the end of the time when they rule, people will do many bad things. God will have to punish them. A very cruel king will appear. He will say things that are not true. And he will be very clever.

24 He will become very powerful, but this will not be his own power. He will destroy many things. And he will be clever. So he will be able to do anything that he wants to do. He will kill strong leaders and he will even kill God's people. 25 He will kill people for no good reason. People will think that they are safe. But then he will kill them. He will think that he is very important. He will fight against the greatest of all kings. Then he will fail, but no human hand will do this to him.'

26 The angel continued to speak. He said, 'This is the dream about the evenings and the mornings. And I have told you what it means. It is true, but keep the dream as a secret now. It will be a long time before all this happens.' 27 After this dream, I, Daniel, was weak. I was sick for many days. Then I got up and I returned to my work for the king. The dream caused great trouble in my mind and I could not understand it.

Chapter 9

Daniel's prayer and the 490 years

Daniel reads something in the Book of Jeremiah

1 This is what happened in the first year that Darius ruled the country. He was the son of Xerxes and he came from the country called Media. He became king of Babylon.

2 Before he had been king for one year, I, Daniel, was studying the words in God's book. I read what the Lord had told Jeremiah the prophet. He told him that Jerusalem would continue to be broken and empty for 70 years. Nobody would live there.

Daniel prays about the words that he has read

3 So I started to pray very much to the Lord God, and I stopped eating food. I put on old clothes and I threw ashes over myself. I wanted to show how sad I felt.

4 I prayed to the Lord my God. And I said to him that we had done wrong things. 'Lord, you are the great God and we give honour to you', I prayed. 'You keep your promises to those who obey your Laws. You always love those who love you.'

5 'We have been very bad', I prayed. 'We have done wrong and evil things. We have not obeyed your rules. 6 We did not listen to the prophets who are your servants. They told your message to our kings, to our rulers, to our fathers and to all the people. 7 Lord, you always do what is right. We are people from Judah, from Jerusalem and from all Israel. We have done bad things and we are ashamed. We have not been faithful to you. So some of us are near here, but you have sent some of us to countries far away. 8 Lord, we are ashamed because we have not obeyed you. Our kings, their sons and our fathers are ashamed. 9 Lord our God, we have not been faithful to you, but you forgive us. 10 We have not obeyed you, the Lord our God. You sent your servants, the prophets with your message. They gave your rules to us. But we have not obeyed those Laws. 11 None of the people from Israel have obeyed your Laws. We have turned away from you. We have refused to obey you. We read the book that your servant Moses wrote. We read about your punishments, but we did not do anything about it. So now, you have punished us because we did not obey you. 12 You did what you promised to do to our rulers and to us. So you punished us. You punished Jerusalem more than anywhere else under heaven. 13 You have punished us as Moses wrote in his book. And still we have not tried to make you happy, the Lord our God. We do wrong things still and we do not obey your Laws. 14 So you remembered the punishments that you had told us about. Everything that you, the Lord God, do is right. And we did not obey you.'

15 'Lord our God', I said, 'you brought your people out of the country called Egypt by your power. You caused many people to know your name. Many people know about you still. But we did more wrong things and we have been very bad.

16 Lord, you have always done what is right. Please stop being angry with the people from Jerusalem. It is your special city. All the people that live round us laugh about Jerusalem in a bad way. And they laugh about your people. That is happening because our fathers were so bad. And we have been evil also.

17 So now, our God, I am praying to you. Please listen to me because I am your servant. Listen to me while I pray! So then people will know that you are God. Lord, be kind to your empty house. 18 Listen to us, Lord. Look at the city that belongs to you. Nobody lives there now. We do not pray for things because we are good. We pray to you because you are kind. 19 Lord, listen. Lord, forgive us. Lord, listen because the city and your people are yours. Do something quickly. Then people will know that you are God.'

God sends the angel called Gabriel to Daniel

20 I continued to pray. I was saying that all the people of Israel had done wrong things. I was praying to the Lord my God about his holy place.

21 And while I was praying, Gabriel came to me. He was the same man that I had seen in the first dream. He flew quickly to me. It was about the time of the evening sacrifice. 22 He came and he spoke to me. 'Daniel, I have come so that you can understand', he said. 23 'As soon as you started to pray, God sent the answer. I have come to tell you the answer because God really loves you. Now listen to me. I will explain what you have seen.'

24 'God has chosen 490 years (in other words, 70 × 7 years)', Gabriel said. 'This is about your people and the holy city. Then God will stop people doing bad things. He will pay for the wrong things that people have done. He will make everything completely good for always. All that the prophets wrote about will happen. And he will anoint the most holy one.

The 490 years

25 I want you to know and understand.

Someone will tell men that they must build Jerusalem again. After 49 years (in other words, 7 × 7), people will build Jerusalem city again. They will build streets and a wall. But God's people will have much trouble during this time. Then there will be 434 years (in other words, 62 × 7) more. Then, the special ruler that God has chosen will come. 26 After the 434 years, people will kill the special ruler that God has sent. He will have nothing. Then a foreign ruler will come with his army and he will destroy the city and the holy place. The end will be like a fast river. War will continue until the end of that time. God has said that people would destroy things. 27 The ruler will agree with many people for 7 years. In the middle of the 7 years he will stop all the sacrifices. He will put a thing that is not holy in the holy place. And it will stay there until God decides to kill this ruler. Then his end will happen.'

Chapter 10

God sends another angel to Daniel

When Daniel had his next dream

1 In the third (3rd) year that King Cyrus ruled Persia, God gave a message to Daniel. (Daniel's other name was Belteshazzar.) The message was true, and it was about a great war. Daniel had a dream. This showed him what the message meant. 2 He wrote down this message:

At that time I, Daniel, was sad for three weeks. 3 I did not eat any good food. I had no meat or wine. I did not put anything good on my skin or my hair until the three weeks finished.

The angel appears to Daniel

4 On the 24th day of the first month, I was standing by the great river Tigris. 5 I looked and I saw a man. He was wearing good white clothes. He wore a gold belt. 6 His body was bright like a beautiful stone. His face was like a bright light. His eyes seemed like tongues made from fire. His arms and legs seemed like shining bronze. When he spoke, his voice was like the noise of many people's voices.

Daniel and his friends become afraid and weak

7 Only I, Daniel, saw this picture. The people who were with me did not see anything. But they were very afraid, so they ran away. And they hid themselves.

8 Then I was alone while I looked at this great person. My face became very white and I became weak. 9 When I heard his voice, I fell down. I lay with my face on the ground and I started to sleep.

The angel explains why God has sent him

10 Then a hand touched me and it helped me to get up. I was on my hands and knees. But my body moved because I was afraid. 11 He spoke to me. 'Daniel, God loves you very much', he said. 'Listen carefully to what I say to you. Stand up, because God has sent me to you.' When he said this, I stood up. But I was afraid still. 12 Then he said, 'Daniel, do not be afraid. You wanted to understand God. You became ready to do what he had decided. As soon as you did this, God heard your words. So I have come to bring the answer to your prayers. 13 The ruler of the kingdom of Persia stood in my way for 21 days. But then Michael, who is one of God's most important servants, came to help me. Until then, I had to stay there with the kings of Persia. 14 Now I am here to explain this dream about future years. The dream tells what will happen to your people then.'

The angel makes Daniel stronger

15 While he was saying these words to me, I looked down at the ground. I could not speak. 16 Then someone who seemed like a man touched my lips. I opened my mouth and I was able to speak again. So I spoke to the person who stood in front of me. 'My lord, the dream has given great pain to me and now I am weak. 17 My lord, I am your servant. I am not important enough to talk with you. I am very weak. I can hardly pull air into my body.'

18 He who seemed like a man touched me again. He made me strong. 19 'Do not be afraid, man', he said to me, 'because God loves you very much. I want your mind to rest. I want you to be strong, very strong.' When he said this, I felt stronger. So I spoke again. 'My lord, speak to me, because you have made me strong again', I said.

The angel's fights

20 Then he spoke to me again. 'I will tell you why I have come to you. Soon I will return to fight against the ruler of Persia. When I have won that fight, the king from Greece will come. 21 But now I will explain to you what the words in the True Book mean. (Only Michael, your people's ruler, will help me against God's enemies.)'

Chapter 11

North, South and the very bad man

Darius and the kings of Persia and of Greece

1 'Since the first year that Darius from Media ruled, I helped him. And I saved him from his enemies.'

2 'Now I will explain to you the things that will happen', the messenger said. 'There will be three more kings in Persia and then a fourth (4th) king will come. He will be richer than all the other kings. He will become powerful because he is so rich. Then he will cause everybody to become angry with the kingdom called Greece.'

3 'Then a very strong king will come', he told me. 'He will rule with great power. And he will do whatever he wants to do. 4 After he comes, his kingdom will break into 4 parts. Those parts will be in the north, south, east and west. His children and grandchildren will not rule his kingdom. Other people will rule his kingdom, but they will not be as powerful.'

Wars in the countries near Israel

5 'Then the king in the south will become strong, but one of his officers will become even stronger. He will rule his own kingdom and he will be very powerful.

6 After some years, the king in the south and the king in the north will agree not to fight each other. The daughter of the king in the south will marry the king in the north. This should cause the two kingdoms to become friends. But the plan will fail and they will lose their power. Someone will kill her and her husband and her father and her servants.

7 Later, someone from her family will become king in the south. He will attack the army of the king in the north and he will go into the strong city. He will fight against the army and he will win the fight. 8 He will take away their gods that they have made out of wood or stone. And he will take away their valuable gold and silver dishes. He will take these things back to the country called Egypt. Then for several years, he will not attack the king in the north again.

9 After that, the king in the north will attack the country where the king in the south lives. But they will cause him to return to his own country. 10 Then his sons will prepare for war. They will bring together a large army, which will go to the south like a powerful river. The army will attack the strong city of the king in the south. 11 Then the king in the south will be angry. He will bring out his army to fight the king from the north. The king from the north might have a large army, but the king in the south will win the fight. 12 The king in the south will destroy this large army. So then he will think that he is great. He will kill many thousands of people, but his power will not continue.

13 The king from the north will again bring together a large army. It will be even bigger than the first army. After a few years, he will come back with his larger army. And this army will have all the arms that it needs to attack other countries. 14 At that time, many people will stand against the king in the south. And the angry men from your own people will also rise up. They will fight against him. This is what the dream tells us. But they will fail. 15 Then the king from the north will come. He will build up earth round a strong city. He will take the city because the army in the south will not be able to stand against him. Even their best soldiers will not be strong enough to win the fight. 16 The king from the north will do whatever he wants to do. Nobody will be able to stand against him. He will stay in the Beautiful Country and he will have the power to destroy it.

17 Then the king from the north will decide to go south with all his power. He will agree not to fight with the king in the south. He will give a daughter to marry the king in the south. He will want very much to stop that king ruling. But his plan will fail. She will not help him.

18 After this, he will turn and attack the countries by the sea. He will take many of those countries, but one officer will stop him. He will even cause the king from the north to stop fighting.

Then he will not be able to take power over other countries. 19 So the king from the north will return. He will return to the strong cities in his own country. But he will lose another fight. And he will fall so that nobody will see him again.

20 Then the next king in the north will try to make himself even more rich. He will send out someone to take money from his people, but soon God will cause him to die. This will not happen in an attack or a fight.

The life of the very bad man

21 The person who comes after him will be a very bad man. He will not become a king but he will come to take power. The people will think that they are safe. That is when he will come. He will tell lies and he will do wrong things to become king. 22 He will fight a great army and he will destroy it. He will even kill the ruler of the promise. 23 He will try to agree with people from other countries. But he will tell them things that are not true. Only a few people will help him but he will become powerful. 24 He will attack the richest places. They will think that they are safe. That is when he will attack them. He will do things that his father and grandfathers did not do. He will take valuable things in war and he will give some to his servants. And he will try to discover how he might attack strong cities. But this will only happen for a short time.

25 He will feel strong and brave against the king in the south because he has a large army. And the king in the south will fight back with a large and powerful army. But the king in the south will not win, because people will make a way to stop him. 26 Even those who eat the king's food will try to kill him. They will push his army away and many soldiers will die. 27 These two kings will want to do many bad things. They will sit together at the same table. But they will tell each other things that are not true. God has decided the time of the end already. So he will not let them do those bad things.

28 The king from the north will return to his own country. He will be very rich. He will hate those who worship the true God. He will do whatever he wants to do against them. Then he will continue his journey back to his own country.

29 At the time that God has decided, the king will go to the south again. This time the result will be different. 30 People from the west will come in ships and they will stand against him. He will be afraid and he will turn back. He will be angry with people who worship the true God. He will give benefits to those people who have not kept their promises to God. 31 He will send some of his soldiers into God's strong and holy place to make it dirty. Then it will not be holy any longer. Nor will they let people sacrifice gifts to God. They will put something that God hates in there. 32 The king will say that some people are good. Those are the people who do not obey God. But those who know their God will be strong. And they will work. 33 The wise leaders will teach the people, but the people will attack them for some time. People will kill some with sharp knives or they will burn them. They will rob them and they will put some of them in a prison. 34 When God's people are dying, they will receive a little help. Many people who do not really know God will join them. 35 Some of the wise people will fall. Then God can make them clean (holy). And they will become the people that God wants them to be at the end. God has decided when the end will come.

36 And this king will do whatever he wants to do. He will say that he is greater than any god. He will even say very bad things against the God of gods. This will happen until God is not angry with his people any longer. God must do what he has decided to do. 37 This king will not have any interest in the gods that his father and grandfathers worshipped. He will not have any interest in the god that women love. He will think that he is greater than any of the gods. 38 Instead, he will give honour to the god that saves strong cities. His father and grandfathers did not give honour to that god. But he will give gold, silver, pretty stones and gifts to that god. 39 He will give honour to this foreign god who will help him to fight strong cities. Then he will give gifts to those people who give honour to his god. He will let them rule many people. And he will sell parts of the land to them.

The end of the very bad man's life

40 In the end, the king from the south will attack him. The king in the north will fight back like a storm. He will have soldiers on horses and many ships. He will attack many countries and he will go through them like a great powerful river.

41 He will also attack the Beautiful Country and he will kill many thousands of the people there. But he will not take the people in the countries called Edom and Moab or the leaders from Ammon. 42 He will have power over many countries, including the country called Egypt. 43 He will take all the gold, silver and other valuable things in Egypt. He will also rule the countries called Libya and Cush. 44 But he will hear news from the north and the east that will cause trouble in his mind. So he will be very angry. And then he will go to destroy things and to kill many people. 45 He will stay with his soldiers between the sea and the holy mountain. But he will die there and nobody will help him.'

Chapter 12

The time of the end of the world

Trouble and the time when dead people come back to life

1 'At that time Michael will come', the same man said. 'He is the great angel who is good to your people. There will be a time of very great trouble. It will be the worst time since God made man. Then God will save those among your people whose names are in his book. 2 Many of those who have died will come back to life again. God will give life that will never end to some of them. But some will be ashamed and have no honour for all time. 3 And those who are wise will shine like the bright sky. Those who help many people to obey God will shine like the stars always.

Daniel must close the book and he must keep it secret

4 Now you, Daniel, do not change this message. Close the book and keep it secret until the end. Many will try to learn more about this.'

An angel says that the surprising things will finish after three and a half years

5 Then I, Daniel, looked up and I saw two other people. One of them was on this side of the river with me. The other one was on the other side of the river. 6 One of them spoke to the man who was wearing white clothes. He was beyond them over the water. He asked him, 'How long will it be before these surprising things end?'

7 The man who was wearing white clothes lifted up both his hands towards the sky. I heard him make a promise by God, who lives always. 'It will end after three and a half years. Then the enemies who fight against the power of the holy people will stop. And that will be the end of all these events.'

The angel tells some more things to Daniel and he tells Daniel about God's promise to him

8 I heard his words, but I did not understand. So I said, 'My lord, how will it all end?' 9 'You go now, Daniel,' he said. 'This message will remain secret until the end comes. 10 God will make many people holy and good. But evil people will continue to do things that are wrong. Those bad people will not understand what God wants. But wise people will understand. 11 From the time that there is no sacrifice each day there will be 1290 days. That is from the time that they put the thing that God hates in his house. 12 The people who wait in a patient way for 1335 days will be happy. 13 You yourself must be patient and you must continue until the end. You will die. But then you will live again. And then you will receive the good things that God has promised at the end of time.'

Return to God

Hosea

About this book

Hosea wrote his book in the middle of the 8th century B.C. (Before Christ). He usually gave his messages to Israel's people. Israel was the name of the country in the north. But some messages were for Judah's people, the country in the south. The book has many good things and many bad things to say to the people in Israel. If we want to understand this book, we need to understand the covenant at Sinai. Sinai was the place where God gave his rules to Moses.

The good things and bad things in Hosea are part of this covenant. Hosea's job was to tell his people that there was danger.

God would make sure that people in Israel obeyed the covenant. Israel's people will have to live in the right way. It is the same message that many of the prophets gave before the exile. Hosea says that there will be death and illness in Israel. He also says that soldiers from another country will destroy their country. They will take the people in Israel away. These things will have to happen. After that, God will be able to do good things for Israel again. We must understand what these promises mean. There is no hope that God will not be angry. Israel's people have not obeyed the covenant and so bad things will happen soon.

There were only a few people in Israel who worshipped God in the right way at this time. There were more people in Judah who obeyed God's rules. Israel was a strong and rich country and they could often beat other countries in war. Because of this, people from Israel met people from other countries. So they knew about other people's gods. People forgot the rules that God gave to them at Sinai. It was a time when things were not easy in Israel. Very bad leaders killed their kings. Also, Assyria and Israel were fighting each other in 734 B.C. After that, Israel became a much smaller country. This was the beginning of the end for Israel. Then, in 722 B.C., Assyria destroyed Israel.

None of Hosea's messages have dates. We know that Hosea wrote his messages. We do not know if Hosea spoke his messages also. Hosea 5:1 may mean that he did.

We know very little about Hosea and his family. Hosea tells us only a few things about himself. We do not know for sure if Gomer really was a prostitute. There are other difficult questions with these chapters.

To know God as a person is important to Hosea. He wanted the people's sacrifices to really mean something to God. He wanted people to obey God. If they did that, they could know God in a true way.

Chapter 1

1 This is the message that the Lord gave to Hosea, the son of Beeri. He gave this message during the time that Uzziah, Jotham, Ahaz and Hezekiah were kings of Judah.

This was during the time when Jeroboam, son of Joash, was the king of Israel.

Hosea's wife and their children

2 The Lord began to speak to Israel's people by Hosea. The Lord said to Hosea, 'Go, and marry a prostitute. I want you to have children by her. The children will be like her. In the same way, my people have left me and they have loved other gods.' 3 So Hosea married a woman called Gomer, the daughter of Diblaim. After this, a child began to grow in her and she gave birth to their first child, a son. 4 The Lord said to Hosea, 'Call him Jezreel. This is because I will soon punish the family of Jehu. I will hurt them because of the murders by Jehu at Jezreel. Then I will cause the end of the country called Israel. 5 And, in the Valley of Jezreel, I will at that time completely destroy the armies of Israel.'

6 Gomer had a second child. This time it was a daughter. The Lord said to Hosea, 'Call her Lo-Ruhamah. This is because I will not continue to show great love to the people in Israel. I will not forget their sins. 7 But I will show love to the people in Judah. I, the Lord, will save them. I will not do it by war. I will not use weapons. I will not use horses or people who ride horses.'

8 After Gomer gave her own milk to Lo-Ruhamah, another child began to grow in Gomer. A son was born to her. 9 Then the Lord said to Hosea, 'Call him Lo-Ammi. This is because the people in Israel are not my people. And I am not their God.'

10 At a future time, the number of Israel's people will be like the sand by the sea. You cannot measure the sand or count it. Now God says to them, 'You are not my people.' But there will be a future day when he will say to them, 'You are the children of the living God!' 11 The people from Judah and the people from Israel will come together again. They will choose for themselves a single leader. And they will go out of a foreign country. The day of Jezreel will be an important day.

Chapter 2

1 Then you will tell your brothers, 'You are my people.' And you will tell your sisters, 'He has shown great love to you.'

The Lord speaks to the people in Israel

2 My children, argue with your mother. Tell her that she is wrong. Tell that to her because she is not my wife. And I am not her husband. Tell her that she must stop living like a prostitute. She must take away the men that she loved from between her breasts. 3 If she does not do that, I will take away all her clothes. It will be like the day when she was born. I will leave her to die. She will die because she will have no water. I will let her stay in a dry desert. 4-5 I will not show great love to her children. They are the children of a prostitute. This prostitute does not think about what she does. She herself said, 'I will go to the men that I love. They give me food and water, clothes and cloth, oil from trees and wine.'

6 So I (the Lord) will put something in the way of your (Israel's people's) road. I will use plants that hurt. I will build a wall so that she cannot find her way. 7 She will run after the men that she loves. But she will not catch them. She will look for them, but she will not catch them. Then she will say, 'I will return to my first husband (God). Life was better for me when I was with him. Life was better then than it is now.'

8 'She (Israel) did not believe that I (the Lord) had given grain, wine and oil from trees to her. She thought that another God had given them to her. It was I who gave her plenty of silver and gold. She used this silver and gold when she wanted to worship Baal. 9 So I will take back my grain at the time when it is ready. I will take back my new wine when it is ready. I will take back my clothes and cloth. They were what should have covered the body. 10 Now I will take away her clothes. So all the men who loved her will see her. They will see her as she is. Nobody will be able to take her from my power. 11 I (God) will stop the special times when she enjoys herself. I will stop her religious holidays and the meals that she has at a new moon. 12 I will destroy her grapes and her fruit trees. She said that men loved her. These men paid her with those things. But I will change her gardens. They will become like a wild forest. Wild animals will come and they will eat from those plants. 13 I will punish her for the times that she burnt special plants to the god, Baal. I will punish her because she wore special stones. Then she could run after the men who loved her. But she forgot me.' The Lord has said this.

The Lord's love for his people

14 So I (the Lord) will say words of love to her. I will lead her into the desert and I will speak kind words to her. 15 There, I will give back to her the grapes that she had. I will give her Trouble Valley. This will be a way for her to hope in me. Then she will answer me like the time that she came out of Egypt. 16 Then, at a future time, she will call me her husband. She will not call me her god, Baal again. 17 I will never let her speak the name of the god, Baal again. Then people will not use Baal's names again. 18 At that time, I will promise to do things for Israel's people. I will cause the animals in the fields and the birds in the sky to be their friends. I will cause the animals that move along the ground to be their friends too. I also will break the things that Israel's people used in war. I will remove the things that men use to fight in wars. None of these things will remain in the land. My people will live in a time when people do not attack them. They will be safe.

19 I (the Lord) will make you my wife for always.

   I will be good and fair. I will always love you and I will always show mercy to you.

   I will make you mine for always.

20 I will make you a wife that follows me.

   Then you will know the Lord in a true way.

21 At that time, I will answer the sky.

   I will speak to the sky and then rain will fall on the earth.

22 The ground will give back grain, wine and oil from trees.

   They will have an answer for Jezreel.

23 I will plant many seeds on Israel's land.

   To Lo-Ruhamah, I will show great love.

   To Lo-Ammi, I will say, 'You are my people.'

   And they will say to me,

   'You are my God.'

Chapter 3

Hosea returns to his wife

1 Then the Lord said to me again, 'Show love to a woman again. Another man loves her but you must love her. She goes after other men but you must continue to love her. You must love her in the same way that the Lord loves Israel's people. But they continue to worship other gods. And they like to offer fruit to these gods.' 2 So I bought the woman with 15 pieces of silver and 1.5 homers (about 330 litres or 9 bushels) of grain. 3 Then I told her, 'You must stay at home with me for a long time. You must not be like a prostitute. You must not be too friendly with another man. So then I will live with you.'

4 In the same way, Israel's people will continue to live for a long time without a king or a leader. They will not have sacrifices, or stones to help them to remember God. They will not have any ephods and they will not have any gods in their homes. 5 At a future time, Israel's people will return. Then they will look for the Lord their God and they will look for David, their king. They will come to the Lord and they will receive his gifts.

Chapter 4

The Lord is angry with the people in Israel

1 People in Israel, listen to the Lord's message! The Lord will argue against the people that live in this country. 'People in this country do not really know God. The people are never kind to other people. And they do not do what they have promised to do. 2 They hope that bad things will happen to people. They tell people things that are not true. They kill people and they rob people. They do the sin of adultery. They kill more and more people. 3 So the people cry. And everything that lives is slowly dying. All the animals and birds, and even the fish, are dying. 4 Nobody among you should argue. And nobody among you should say that another person is wrong. You people are like people who argue with a priest. 5 You fall over during the day and during the night. And the prophets fall with you. And I will destroy your mother (Israel). 6You are destroying my people because they do not know me. You have refused to learn. So I will refuse to let you be a priest for me. You have forgotten your God's rules, so I will forget your children.'

7 'The more priests that there are of you, the more you sin against me. So I will change the way that you are great into something else. You will not like what will happen to you. 8 The priests eat when the people sin. So the priests are happy when the people sin. 9 The priests are not different from the people. I will tell them both what they should do. They will have to change the things that they do. I will punish them for the wrong things that they did. 10 You people will eat your part of the sacrifices, but you will still be hungry. You will live like prostitutes, but you will not have babies. This is because you have turned away from me to follow other gods.'

11 'My people cannot understand anything because they drink too much old wine and new wine. And they have wrong sex. 12 My people are asking a piece of wood for help. They want those sticks to tell them what they want to know! They think that those sticks can do that. That is because they have followed those false gods like prostitutes. So my people have stopped worshipping their God. 13 They give sacrifices on the tops of the mountains. They burn incense on the hills. They do this under many different kinds of trees. The shade under those trees is very nice. So your daughters become like prostitutes. Also your son's wives do the sin of adultery. 14 Your daughters are prostitutes. Your son's wives do the sin of adultery. But I will not punish them. I will not do it because the men, too, go to be with prostitutes. And they offer sacrifices with prostitutes. So these silly people will cause their own death.'

The sins that will cause God to punish the people in Israel

15 'Israel's people, you live like a prostitute. But do not let Judah's people also do wrong things. Do not worship at Gilgal or at Beth Aven. Do not say promises there in the name of the Lord. Do not say, "As the Lord lives". 16 Israel's people are like a young cow. This young cow does not let you lead it. It is not possible to feed my people. A farmer takes young sheep to a field where there is much grass. I want to be kind to my people as the farmer is kind to those young sheep. 17 The people in Israel have become friends with idols. Let them go their own way. 18 After they have drunk wine, they are happy to be with prostitutes. They do not think about what people will say about them. 19 A wind will take them away. Now they cannot think any longer. Their sacrifices will cause people to think bad things about them.'

Chapter 5

1 'Listen to this, you priests! Be careful how you listen, people in Israel! Listen, you that belong to the family of kings! I (God) have decided what to do with you. You have tried to catch people at Mizpah. You were like a net on the ground at Tabor. 2 The people who will not obey me have killed very many people. So I will tell them all that they should not have done it. And I will punish them. 3 I know what the people from Ephraim are like. They cannot hide from me. They live like a prostitute and they have become very bad. 4 Israel's people have done bad things. This makes it impossible for them to return to their God. They are like prostitutes. They do not know the Lord. 5 Israel's people think that they are too good. This is something that has made me angry with them. Their sins cause them to fall. But Judah's people will fall with them. 6 They take their sheep and cows to offer as sacrifices to the Lord. But it does not help them. They cannot find the Lord because he has left them. 7 They have not obeyed the Lord. Their children are not his. They have times when they enjoy themselves at the beginning of every month. But at the beginning of the month I will destroy their fields and they themselves will die.'

Judah and Israel will fight each other in a war

8 'Make a noise with the horn in Gibeah!

   Make a noise with the trumpet in Ramah!

   Shout about war at Beth Aven!

   Go into war, men in Benjamin's family!

9 The day will happen. Then I will tell them that they are wrong.

   None of Ephraim's people will still be alive.

   People in Israel, you can be sure that this will happen.

10 The leaders of Judah are like people who rob. They have robbed land. So I (God) will punish them very much because I am so angry with them.

11 Israel's people are in trouble because people attack them. Other countries have come as judges. This is because Israel's people wanted help from idols.

12 I (God) will destroy Israel,

   as an insect destroys a piece of cloth.

   I will destroy Judah,

   as water destroys a piece of wood.

13 Ephraim's people saw that they were like a sick man.

   Judah's people saw that they were like a man with wounds.

   So they went to Assyria for help.

   They told their problems to King Jareb,

   but that king cannot bring you health.

   He cannot stop you hurting.

14 I will attack Ephraim's people like a lion.

   I will attack Judah's people like a young lion.

   I, the Lord, will break them into pieces.

   I will carry them away.

   And no person will be able to save them.

15 At a future time, the people will see that they have done something wrong.

   I will return to my place until then.

   Then they will come to look for me.

   They will try to find me when their troubles are very bad.'

Chapter 6

The people do not obey God

1 'Come. We should return to the Lord.

   He attacked us, but he will bring us health.

   He has caused us pain.

   But he will help us.

   People cover, with pieces of cloth, the parts that hurt other people.

   And he will be like someone who does that for us.

2 After two days, he will cause us to live again.

   He will raise us up on the third day.

   Then we can live near him.

3 We should try to know the Lord. We can be sure that he will come.

   It will be like the sun when it rises at the beginning of the day.

   He will come to us like the rain.

   It will be like spring rain. It will bring water to the ground.'

4 'Israel's people, I do not know what I should do with you.

   Judah's people, I do not know what I should do with you.

   You soon stop loving me. You are like the morning cloud.

   Your love is like the low cloud that goes away early in the morning.

5 That is why I have sent my prophets to you.

   I wanted to cut you in pieces.

   I wanted to kill you with words.

   I will judge you. Then things will become clear.

6 I will judge you because I want you to love in the right way.

   I do not want your sacrifices of animals.

   I want my people to know me.

   I do not want them to bring sacrifices.

7 But like Adam, the people did not obey the covenant.

   They did not do in their country what they had promised to me.

8 Gilead is a city of men who do very bad things.

People have killed each other.

9 There are people who rob. They hide and they wait to attack someone.

In the same way, priests wait on the road to Shechem.

They attack people who pass by.

They have done very bad things.

10 Yes, I have seen many bad things in Israel.

Ephraim's people are like a prostitute.

This prostitute is very bad.

11 People in Judah, I have made a special time for you.

I will bring in the crops. At that time, I will tell you what you should do.

But I wanted very much to cause the good times again for my people!' God says.

Chapter 7

1 'When I wanted to give health to my people, they did very many wrong things!

Samaria is full of people who do not say true things.

It is full of people who rob from houses.

They also rob people in the streets.

2 They do not know that I (God) will remember their sins.

The sins that they did are everywhere to see.

I can see these sins in a clear way.

3 The very bad things that they do make their king happy.

The very bad things that they do make their leaders happy too.

4 They are all bad and they do not obey me.

A baker takes flour to make bread.

He starts to cook the bread.

The bread rises. But the baker does not make the fire hotter.

Israel's people are like a baker who is always making his fire hotter.

5 On holidays for the king, the leaders drink too much wine.

The wine causes them to do things in a silly way.

The king has become a friend of bad people. Those people think that good things are silly.

6 The people decide to do secret things.

They are very angry. So they feel that their hearts are like an oven.

It is like the time when they were cooking bread.

During the night, they became angrier.

And in the morning, there was a fire.

7 They were so angry that they killed their leaders.

They killed their kings.

All of their kings fell.

Nobody prays to me for help.'

Israel's people do not know that other people will kill them

8 'Israel's people mix themselves with people from other countries.

Israel is like a cake that someone did not cook on both sides.

9 People in Israel mix themselves with foreign people.

Israel's people do not know that this makes my people weaker.

Israel is like an old man with grey hair.

He does not know how old and weak he is now.

10 Israel's people think that they are very important.

This is something that makes me angry with them.

The people had many troubles.

But even then they did not return to the Lord their God.

The people did not look to him for help.

11 Ephraim is like a silly dove (a bird),

a dove that does not understand anything.

The people looked to Egypt for help.

The people went to Assyria for help.

12 When they do that, I will throw my net over them.

I will catch them like birds as they go by.

I will tell them about the bad things that they have done.

And I will punish them.

13 It will be very bad for them.

They have left me. They refused to obey me.

So they will die.

I wanted to redeem them.

But they do not say true things about me.

14 They do not pray to me from deep inside themselves.

But they cry on their beds.

When they pray for grain and wine, they cut themselves.

They have left me.

15 I taught them and I made them strong.

But they have decided to do very bad things against me.

16 They have returned to false gods.

They are like a weapon that does not work.

Their leaders think that they are very important.

They will die quickly.

Then the people in Egypt will think that they are silly.'

Chapter 8

God does not like Israel's people because they pray to idols

1 'People must know about what will happen! Make sure that they do know.

The enemy will come down like an eagle.

They will come on to the Lord's people

because the Lord's people have not obeyed my covenant.

They have not obeyed the things that I taught them.

2 Israel's people shout out to me. They say, "We in Israel know you."

3 But they refused what is good.

So the enemy will run after them.

4 My people chose kings, but they did not ask me for help.

My people chose leaders. But they did not choose men that I knew.

The people used their silver and gold to make idols for themselves.

I will cause their enemies to kill them because of this.

5 I do not like the gold bull that the people in Samaria worship.

I am very angry with the people in Israel.

It will be a long time before they are without sin.

6 A worker from Israel made that idol.

It is not God.

I will break Samaria's bull into pieces.

7 Israel's people did a silly thing.

It was like a man who is trying to plant the wind.

But they will only get troubles.

They will get back something that is like a very strong wind.

The plants in the field will grow, but they will not give any food.

If the plants did grow, then foreign people would eat them.

8 Israel has become like the other countries.

It is like a pot that someone has broken.

Nobody can use it.

9 Israel's rulers have gone to Assyria for help.

They are like a wild animal that walks without any direction.

The people in Ephraim have sold themselves to other countries.

They wanted to love those countries.

10 They will try to get friends among those countries. But I will bring Israel's people together.

They will feel some pain.

This pain will come from a foreign king.

11 Israel's people built more and more altars.

They built them so that God would not see their sin.

But they have used those places to sin even more!

12 I gave all my rules to Israel's people.

But they look at those rules as if they were strange.

13 Israel's people love sacrifices.

   They offer meat in those sacrifices and then they eat it.

   The Lord does not accept these sacrifices.

   He remembers their sins.

   And he will punish them for their sins.

   They will have to return to Egypt.

14 Israel's people built houses for kings.

   But I made Israel and they forgot me!

   Judah's people have made their towns strong.

   But I will send fire on the cities in Judah.

   And the fire will destroy those strong towns!'

Chapter 9

God will tell the people in Israel what they must do

1   People in Israel, do not be happy at special times as the people in foreign countries do!

   You were like a prostitute and you left your God.

   You are like a prostitute because men pay her to have sex.

   She loves the money that they give to her.

   And you loved all the grain that people gave to you.

   So you have worshipped false gods on the floors where people work with grain.

2   But soon you will not have enough grain or wine.

   There will be no more wine.

3   You will not stay in the Lord's country.

   You will have to return to Egypt.

   In Assyria, you will have to eat food that you should not eat.

4   Israel's people will not be able to offer wine to the Lord.

   Their sacrifices will not make God happy.

   People eat special bread when other people die. Their sacrifices will be like that bread.

   Whoever eats that bread will not be holy.

   This food will be only for themselves.

   It will not come into the temple of the Lord.

5   Israel's people will not be able to enjoy special days.

   Those are the special days when people remember God.

6   Perhaps Assyria will not destroy your country.

   But Egypt will take the people in war.

   People in Memphis will bury them. Weeds will grow over their silver.

   Weeds will grow over the places where they live.

7   The time is now. Now I will tell you what you must do.

   Now is the time when I will have to hurt you.

   I will have to hurt you because of what you have done.

   And Israel's people will know it!

   You do very many sins. You are very angry with me.

   So you think that I am a silly person.

   You think that I have God's Spirit. But I am crazy, you think.

8   God has sent me as a prophet to make sure that Israel's people know things.

   But people try to say bad things about me in the places where I go.

   And people do not like a prophet in the house of God.

9   They have done some very bad sins.

   They were like the sins that Israel's people did at Gibeah.

   The Lord will remember their very bad sins.

   He will punish them for their sins.

The people in Israel will cause God to punish them by their worship of idols

10 'I found Israel.

   It was like when someone finds grapes in the desert.

   I saw your ancestors.

   It was like when someone finds fruit on a fig tree before the usual time.

   But then they came to the god, Baal-Peor.

   They began to worship that very bad idol.

They became like the idol that they loved very much.

11 Israel is great. But this special time will finish.

It will be like a bird.

There will be no more times when babies grow inside women.

There will be no more times when women give birth to babies.

There will be no more children.

12 But even if Israel's people have children,

the children will die.

I will cause that to happen.

There will be none still alive.

I will leave them. They will have nothing but trouble.

13 Lord, I can see that Ephraim's people are going to a difficult place.

They are going to someone who will kill them.

14 Lord, give to these people the things that you want to give to them.

Make it impossible for their women to have babies!

Make it impossible for their breasts to give milk to their babies!

15 They started to do all their very bad things at Gilgal.

It was there that I began not to like them in any way.

I will tell them that they must leave my country.

I will not love them any longer.

Their leaders have not obeyed me.

16 Ephraim's people are in bad trouble.

They are like a plant that has no water.

This plant will have no fruit.

They will have no children.

Even if they have children, I (God) will kill the children.

They think that these children are very important.

17 My God will refuse to accept them.

That is because they have not obeyed him.

They will have to travel from place to place in different countries.'

Chapter 10

Because the people were rich, that caused them to worship idols

1 'Israel is like a vine that has plenty of fruit.

But Israel became more and more rich,

and so the people built more altars.

Their land became better and better.

So they could build special stones that they could worship.

2 Their minds are not honest.

But now they must understand that they have done wrong things.

The Lord will destroy their altars.

He will destroy their special stones.

3 Soon these people will say, "We have no king.

We do not worship the Lord in a true way.

But if we had a king, he could not do anything for us."

4 They promise to do many things. But what they say is not true.

They agree about things with other countries.

People do not agree with each other in courts.

These things are like weeds that have poison.

Weeds that are growing in a field will soon grow into plants.

5 The people who live in Samaria will be afraid.

They will cry because their idol at Beth Aven has gone.

Their very bad priests will cry too.

They were very happy with their beautiful idol.

But now someone will carry the idol away.

6 Assyria's people will carry the idol away.

It will be a gift for the king of Assyria.

Ephraim's people will feel very sad.

They will be very sorry that they worshipped their idol.

7 God will destroy Samaria and he will kill Samaria's king.

He (the king) will be like a piece of wood that water carries away.

8   God will destroy these high places at Aven.

   These are places where Israel's people have sinned.

   Weeds will grow on their altars.

   Then the people will say to the mountains, "Hide us!"

   They will say to the hills, "Fall on us!" ', God says.

God will punish the people in Israel because of their sin

9   'Israel's people, you have sinned since the time of Gibeah.

   You have continued to sin since then.

   But those very bad people at Gibeah had a war.

10 I (God) will punish these very bad people.

   Countries will join together to attack them.

   They will put the people from Israel in prisons because of their very bad sins.

11 Ephraim's people are like a young cow that someone has taught.

   They are like a cow that loves to walk on grain.

   But I decided to be like someone who puts a yoke on the cow's beautiful neck.

   I wanted to show Ephraim's people the right way

   so they could work hard.

   I wanted Judah's people to be like a farmer who breaks up the ground.

   Jacob's people, too, must be like that.

12 If a farmer plants good plants, those plants will grow.

   A farmer may have some ground that he has not used for more than a year.

   He should dig that ground to make it not so hard.

   You should be like that farmer.

   You should start to do the right things and the good things.

   Then the Lord will show his love to you.

   Do these things because it is time for you to look for the Lord.

   When he comes, he will cause good to things come down on you like rain!

13 But you are like someone who planted very bad things.

   Bad plants grow.

   And you are in trouble.

   You have said things that are not true. So you have had the results of this.

   But you believed that you could help yourselves.

   And you believed that your soldiers would help you.

   That is why bad things have happened to you.

14 Your people will hear the noise of war.

   Your enemies will destroy your strong places.

   It will be like the time that King Shalman destroyed Betharbel city in war.

   At that time, people killed mothers with their children.

15 The same thing will happen to you at Bethel.

   That is because you did so many very bad things.

   When that day begins, the king of Israel will die.'

Chapter 11

The people in Israel have forgotten the Lord

1   'Israel is like a man. I, (the Lord), loved him when he was a child.

   I brought him out of Egypt as my son.

2   But the more I spoke to him,

   the more he turned away from me.

   My people gave sacrifices to the god, Baal.

   They burned incense and they offered this to idols.

3   But it was I who taught this child to walk!

   I took my people up in my arms!

   I gave them health.

   But they did not know this.

4   I led them with love and with kind words.

   I was like a person who let them be free.

   I bent down to feed them.

5   Israel's people refuse to return to me.

    So they must return to Egypt.

    Assyria will rule over them.

6   Their cities will have war.

    People will break down the city gates.

    Their strong places will not help them.

7   My people are trying very much not to obey me.

    They will shout to God above.

    But I will not listen to them.'

The Lord does not want to destroy Israel

8   'Ephraim, I do not want to forget about you.

    I do not want to give you to someone else.

    I do not want to make you like Admah.

    I do not want to make you like Zeboiim.

    My love for you will not let me do it!

    My love for you is too strong.

9   I will not punish you any longer.

    This is even when I am angry.

    I will not destroy Israel again.

    This is because I am God and not a man.

    I am the Holy God and I am with you.

    I will not show you that I am angry.

10 I will make a loud sound like a lion.

    I will make a loud sound and my children will come.

    They will follow me.

    My children will come from the west.

    They will be afraid when they come.

11 They will be like birds from Egypt.

    They will be like birds from Assyria.

    They will be afraid.

    I will bring them back to their homes again.

    I, the Lord, have spoken.'

The Lord is against the people in Israel

12 Israel's people say things that are not true.

    Those things are all round me.

    Israel's people have not told me true things.

    But Judah's people have not obeyed God.

    I, the Holy God, always do what I have promised to do.

    But Judah's people do not obey me.

Chapter 12

1   There is much that the people in Israel do from morning to night.

    But it has no value and it destroys things.

    The people also do not say true things.

    Israel's rulers and Assyria's rulers come together to agree about things.

    They carry their olive oil to Egypt.

2   The Lord says,

    'I want to take Judah's people to a court.

    I will punish Jacob's family for the way that they have lived.

    I will punish them for the things that they have done.

3   Their ancestor Jacob held on to his brother's foot.

    He did that when they were both inside their mother's body.

    When Jacob was a man, he fought with God.

4   Jacob fought against the angel and Jacob won.

    He cried and he asked for blessings.

    He met God at Bethel. God spoke with him there.

5   This was the Lord God Almighty.

    The Lord is his name.

6   So you must return to your God.

You must love each other. You must be fair in your rules.

You must be patient. And you must wait for your God to do what he wants.

7   There are people in business who are not fair.

They are not fair when they measure food and other things.

8   Ephraim's people say, "We are rich! We are now very rich!

Because we are rich, people will not find any sin in us."

9   But I am the Lord your God.

I brought you out of Egypt.

I will make sure that you live in tents again.

It will be like the time when you had religious holidays.

10   I spoke to the prophets. I gave them many visions.

I told parables so that they could teach my lessons to the people', God is saying.

11   The people in Gilead are very bad.

They are not worth anything.

There are many very bad idols in Gilead.

These idols are not worth anything.

They gave animals as sacrifices at Gilgal.

Their altars will become like stones in a field.

12   Our ancestor Jacob ran away to the country called Aram.

He worked there so that he could get a wife.

He kept sheep safe so that he could pay for her.

13   The Lord used a prophet to bring Israel's people out of Egypt.

He used a prophet to keep them safe.

14   Ephraim's people have made the Lord very angry.

They have killed many people.

So I will punish them.

This is because of the wrong things that they have done.

They will know that the Lord will think very badly about them.

Chapter 13

The Lord is angry with the people in Israel

1   In past times, when Ephraim spoke, other people in Israel were afraid.

People thought that Israel was important.

But the people sinned by their worship of the god, Baal.

And because of that, they died.

2   Now the people in Israel sin more and more.

They make idols for themselves from their metals.

They are clever in the way that they make these idols.

And then they say, 'Offer sacrifices to them!'

It is silly to kiss idols!

They are idols in the shape of animals!

3   That is why those people will soon go away.

They will be like the cloud in the morning.

They will be like the low cloud that goes away early in the morning.

Israel's people will be like seed that a wind blows from the floor.

They will be like smoke that goes out of a window.

4   The Lord says,

'I am the Lord your God who led you out of Egypt.

You do not know any other God except me.

I only am the person who can redeem you.

5   I did not forget you in the desert.

That was when you were in a hot dry country.

6   I gave food to Israel's people.

They ate that food. They became full and they really liked the food.

They began to think that they were important.

And they forgot me.

7   That is why I will be like a lion to them.

I will be like a lion that is waiting by the road.

8   I will attack them like an animal that has lost her children.

I will break Israel's people into pieces.

I will eat them like an animal.

I will break them in pieces like an animal.

9   I will destroy you, Israel.

There will be nobody to help you.

10 Nobody can find your king. He cannot help you.

Nobody can find your leaders.

In past times, you asked for a king and leaders.

11 I was angry, so I gave you a king.

And when I became very angry, I took him away.

12 I have written about Ephraim's people's guilt and sin.

I will keep the words that I wrote in a safe place.

13 Ephraim's people will be in pain like a woman who is having a baby.

They are very silly!

They are like a child inside a woman.

It is time for the child to come out.

But the child does not come out at the right time.

14 I will redeem these people. People will not have to bury them.

I will redeem them from death.

Death, your illnesses have gone.

Death, you cannot kill any longer.

I will not be sorry for this people any longer.

15 Israel was like a plant that grew well among other plants.

But a strong east wind will come.

It will blow in from the desert.

Then Israel's wells will become dry.

The water that comes from the ground will stop.

The wind will take everything away that has value.

16 Samaria will become like an empty country.

They are guilty because they did not obey their God.

Their people will die in war.

Their enemies will throw Samaria's children to the ground.

Their enemies will break women into pieces.

These are women who have babies inside them.'

Chapter 14

New life for Israel's people

1   Return to the Lord your God, Israel's people.

Your sin has destroyed you.

2   Think about the things that you will say.

And return to the Lord.

Say to him, 'Forgive all our sins.

Accept the good things that we are doing.

We will praise you with our lips.

3   Assyria cannot save us.

Our war horses cannot keep us away from trouble.

We will never again say to idols that they are our God.

Our hands had made those idols.

But you are someone who shows great love.

You show great love to children who have no parents.'

4   The Lord says, 'They left me. But I will forgive them for that.

I will love them very much.

I am not angry with them now.

5   I will be like the rain in the morning to Israel's people.

They will become like flowers.

They will be like the tall trees in Lebanon.

These trees will be very strong in the ground.

6   They will become alive with new branches.

They will be beautiful like olive trees.

They will have a smell like the tall trees in Lebanon.

7 Israel's people will live again in a shade.

    They will grow well like grain.

    They will grow well like a vine.

    They will be famous like the wine from Lebanon.

8 Ephraim's people, I do not want to see any more idols.

    I will answer the people's prayers. I will show an interest in them.

    I (God) am like a tree that is always green.

    Your fruit comes from me.'

9 A wise person understands these things.

    A wise person learns about these things.

    The things that the Lord does are correct.

    Good people will live because of these things.

But sinners will be like someone who falls down because of these things.

God promises to send his Spirit

Joel

About this book

Joel may have lived in the country called Judah. He was a prophet. And he told Israel's people, and their enemies, that God would punish them. They thought that on the 'Day of the Lord' he would bless them. But on that day he would punish them. But after God had punished his people, he would again show his love to them. He would send them his Holy Spirit.

The 'Day of the Lord' was an idea that several prophets had given to Israel. Most people thought that the Lord Jehovah would then make Israel rule all the other countries in the world.

Chapter 1

Locusts eat all the plants in Israel

1 This is the word of the Lord that came to Joel, son of Pethuel.

2 You older men, hear this! Listen, all people who live in this country.

Nothing like this has happened while you have been alive.

Nothing like this happened while your fathers were alive.

3 Tell this to your children.

And they must tell it to their children.

And their children must tell it to their own children.

4 The great locusts have eaten what the big group of locusts left.

The young locusts have eaten what the great locusts left.

Other locusts have eaten what the young locusts left.

5 Wake up, you who have drunk too much wine!

Cry, all people who drink wine!

Cry because you will have no new wine.

Someone has taken it away from you.

6 A group has come to fill my country.

It is powerful, and great in numbers.

It has the teeth of a strong animal.

And the teeth are long and dangerous.

7 It has broken my vines

and destroyed my fig trees.

It has eaten the hard skins and it threw them away.

It has left their branches white.

8 Cry like a girl that no man ever loved.

She is crying because her promised husband is dead.

9 There will be no more gifts of food or drink.

They will not reach the house of the Lord.

The priests, the servants of the Lord,

are very, very sad.

10 Nobody can use the fields.

They are all dry.

The new wine has all gone.

The oil has all gone.

11 You farmers, you cry.

You who grow vines, cry.

Be sad for the seeds that are food.

Be sad because the fields are dry. And the plants have died.

12 The vine has become dry

and the fig tree is dead.

The apple trees and other fruit trees -

all the trees have no more fruit.

Men have no more joy.

It has all gone.

Joel tells people that they must repent

13 You priests, wear clothes that are not comfortable.

That will show that you are sad.

You cry, you who serve the Lord in his temple.

Come, you who serve in front of my God.

Sleep in the clothes that are not comfortable.

Cry for the gifts of food and drink.

Cry because they do not come to the house of your God any longer.

14 Tell everyone that they must not eat any food.

Tell the people that they must all come to hear the Lord.

Speak to the older leaders,

and all the people who live in this country.

Tell them that they must all come.

They must come to the house of the Lord your God

and they must shout out to the Lord.

15 Be afraid because of that day.

Be afraid because the day of the Lord is near.

It will be as if the great God would destroy everything.

16 No food has come.

We saw this with our own eyes.

The house of our God cannot make us happy.

17 The seeds under the earth are dry.

The places where they were stored have fallen down.

Someone has broken them up

because the seed does not grow.

18 The cows make a sad noise.

They all move about

because they cannot find any grass.

Even groups of sheep are hungry.

19 I speak to you, my Lord.

Fire has destroyed the grass,

and it has burned up all the trees.

20 Even the wild animals are thirsty and they want your help.

The rivers have no water in them.

Fire has destroyed the grass in the fields.

Chapter 2

The army of locusts

1 Blow the trumpet in Zion.

Tell the people on the Lord's hill that they must watch for trouble.

All the people who live in this country will be afraid.

They will be afraid because the day of the Lord is coming.

It is very near.

2 That day will be sad and dark.

It will be cloudy and black.

A great big army is coming.

It comes across the sky like light in the morning.

A great army like this has never come before.

And it will never come again in future years.

3 Fire goes in front of the army.

It burns everything behind them.

The land in front of them is like the Garden of Eden.

Behind them it is like a desert.

They leave nothing behind them.

4 They look like horses.

And they run fast to the war.

5 Their noise is like the noise of many feet.

They jump over the mountains

as fast as fire burns dry grass.

They are like a great army ready for a fight.

6 Nations that see them are very afraid.

Every face changes colour.

7 They run together like an army into a fight.

They climb walls like soldiers.

They march on in a straight line.

They do not turn away.

8 They do not push each other away.

Each one of them goes straight on.

You can put weapons in their path

but they go straight on.

9 They run towards the city.

They run along the wall.

They climb into houses.

They go through the windows like thieves.

10 The earth in front of them moves.

The sky itself moves.

The sun and moon are dark

and the stars do not give any light.

11 The Lord shouts aloud

as he leads his army.

We cannot count his soldiers.

Those who obey him are very strong.

The day of the Lord is powerful.

It makes us afraid.

Not many of us will be alive after it has gone.

Show the Lord that you are sorry

12 'Even now', the Lord says,

'return to me and put me first.

Eat no food. Cry and be very sad.

13 Stop pulling your clothes to pieces. That does not help.

Show me instead that you are really sorry.'

Return to the Lord, your God.

He is kind and full of grace.

He is slow to get angry, and he is full of love.

He is sad that he had to cause troubles for you.

14 Perhaps he will change his mind and he will be sorry.

He may send you blessings of food and drink.

Then you can offer gifts to the Lord your God.

15 Blow the trumpet in Zion.

Tell the people that they must not eat any food.

Tell the people that they must all come to worship him.

16 Tell the people that they must all come.

Make them all ready to serve the Lord.

Bring the old people together.

Bring the children - even the smallest ones.

Every new husband must leave his room.

Every wife must leave her secret room.

17 There are priests who go in front of the Lord.

They must cry as they go from the temple door to the altar.

They must say to the Lord, 'Do not hurt your people.

Do not let the people in other countries laugh at your own people.

They will point at them. And they will say that they have no value.

They will say that we have no God.'

The Lord's answer

18 Then the Lord will be careful for his land.

He will be kind to his people.

19 He will answer them and he will say,

'I am giving you new wine and food and oil.

You will have enough to fill you up.

I will never again let people in other countries laugh about you.

20 I will send the army from the north far from you.

I will push it into empty land where nothing grows.

I will make the front of it go into the sea on the east.

And I will make the back of it go into the sea on the west.

I will make its smell rise up high

because it has done great things.'

21 Be not afraid, land in Israel.

Be very happy.

Be sure that the Lord has done great things.

22 Do not be afraid, wild animals.

The fields are becoming green.

Fruit is growing on the trees.

The fig tree and the vine are giving much fruit.

23 Be happy, people in Zion!

Rejoice in the Lord your God.

He has given you just enough autumn rain.

He has given you the winter rain,

and the summer rain, as before.

24 He will fill your stores with seeds to make bread.

And he will fill your jars with new wine and oil.

25 'I will give you back the years that the locusts have eaten.

I will give you all that the great locust and the young locust,

and other locusts and their groups have eaten.

All that my great army has eaten I will give you.

26 You will have plenty to eat. You will be full.

You will praise the name of the Lord your God.

He has done great things for you.

My people will never again be ashamed.

27 Then you will know that I am in Israel.

You will know that I am your God.

And you will know that there is no other God.

My people will never again be ashamed.'

The day of the Lord

28 After that, I will pour out my Holy Spirit on all people.

Your sons and daughters will be prophets.

Your old men will dream and

your young men will see pictures in their minds. (The Lord will send these to them.)

29 I will pour out my Spirit on all my servants,

on men and on women in those days.

30 I will do strange things in the sky and on the earth.

I will send blood and fire and clouds of smoke.

31 The sun will become dark and the moon will become red.

Then the great and frightening day of the Lord will come.

32 Everyone who asks the Lord for help

will be safe.

They will be safe if they believe in his name.

The Lord will save the people on Mount Zion and in Jerusalem.

He has promised this to those people whom he has asked to come to him.

Chapter 3

The Lord judges the nations

1 'Judah and Jerusalem were once great.

One day, at that time, I will make them great again.

2 Then I will bring all the nations together.

I will bring them down to the valley of Jehoshaphat (a place of judgement).

There I will judge against them

because of what they did to my children, my people Israel.

Those nations pushed my people out into other countries.

They broke up my land and each took pieces.

3 They played games to win my people.

They gave boys to buy women to have sex with them.

They sold girls so that they could get wine to drink.

4 You people in Tyre, Sidon, and of all the land of the people called Philistines, listen. You cannot say that I have done anything wrong. You want to punish me. If you do this, I will soon do the same to you. 5 You took my silver and my gold, and you put all my riches in your temples. 6 You sold the people from Judah and Jerusalem to the Greek people. You wanted to send them a long way from their own country. 7 Now I am going to bring them back from the places to which you sold them. I will do to you what you have done to them. 8 I will sell your sons and daughters to the people in Judah. And they will sell them to the people called Sabeans, who live far away. I, the Lord, have spoken.'

9 Tell this news to the people in all the countries.

Get ready for war!

Shout to the soldiers.

Make all the men who fight get ready to attack.

10 Make your digging tools into sharp knives.

Make the tools that you use on the farm into pointed fighting sticks.

The weak man must say, 'I am strong!'

11 Come quickly, you people who live round Israel.

And get together in the valley.

Lord, send down your army to attack them.

12 Wake up the people in all the countries!

Bring them into the Valley of Jehoshaphat (place of judgement).

I will sit there to judge the people from every place.

13 Now is the time to cut down the fruits.

They are ready for you to bring them in.

Walk all over the grapes.

The winepress is full of them.

They come over the top.

The people in all countries have done so many bad things.

14 Many, many nations are in the Valley of Judgement.

It is there that the day of the Lord will soon come.

15 The sun and moon will grow dark,

and the stars will not shine.

God will bless his people

16 The Lord will shout from Zion.

He will make a great noise from Jerusalem.

The earth and the sky will move about.

But the Lord will keep his people safe.

17 Then you will know that I am your God.

You will know that I live in Zion, my holy hill.

Jerusalem will be holy.

Strangers will never take it again.

18 In that day new wine will run from the mountains.

And milk will run from the hills.

All the valleys of Judah will have rivers of water.

Water will come from the house of the Lord

and it will water the Valley of Acacias (special trees).

19 But Egypt will be an empty desert.

I will destroy Edom (a country near Israel)

because their people hurt the people in Judah.

The people in Judah had not done anything wrong,

but the people from Edom made them give up their blood.

20 My people will always live in Jerusalem and Judah.

21 I will forgive all the wrong things that they have done.

The Lord lives in Zion!

Bad Things Will Happen Soon

Amos

About this Book

Amos lived in the town called Tekoa. It was near Jerusalem, on the south side. He had sheep. And he watched them to keep them safe. And he gave to them what they needed. He also sold them.

The country where the Israelites lived had 2 parts, a north part and a south part. The south part was called Judah and the big city there was Jerusalem. The king there was called Uzziah. The north part was called Israel and the big city there was Samaria. The king there was called Jeroboam. He was Israel's second king that was called Jeroboam. There had been another King Jeroboam there earlier.

God's temple was in Jerusalem, which was in the south part. The Israelites met there to pray to God. And they gave gifts to God there. But the kings of the north part did not like it when their people went to the south. They were afraid that the people would stay there. So a long time ago the first king called Jeroboam had made a holy place in the north. It was in Bethel town. He made a young cow from gold and he put it in that place. People came there and they said 'thank you' to that young cow. And they brought presents to it. But God was not happy about that. He had told the people not to do those things. But they were not listening to him. So, God chose Amos to speak a message to those people. Amos spoke to the Israelites that lived in the north.

In this book, we read God's message that Amos spoke. Amos also explains the dreams that God showed to him. Two years after Amos spoke the message, there was an earthquake.

Amos 1:1–2:5

First, Amos spoke about the people that lived near Israel. They lived in the countries round Israel. He told those people, 'You have done wrong things. God will send trouble to you.' When the Israelites in the north heard that, they agreed. They said, 'Yes, God should send trouble to them.'

Amos 2:6–6:14

But then Amos spoke to those Israelites that lived in the north. He told them, 'You also have done wrong things. The rich people have not been fair to poor people. They have taken money and land away from the poor people. Rich people have sold poor people to other rich people. So then those poor people have to work for those other people.'

God is good and kind. But sometimes his people do not listen to him any longer and they do not obey him. Then he will send trouble to them. That will help them stop the wrong things that they are doing. God loves his people. He gives to them what they need. He does what is best for them. Sometimes he must shout loudly at them. It is like when a wild animal makes a loud noise. God must shout, 'No, no, no! Do not do wrong things. I am not happy when you do wrong things.' When God sends trouble to people, he wants them to listen to him again. He wants them to obey him again. He wants them to choose good things instead of wrong things.

Amos 7:1–9:10

Amos told the people, 'God will send trouble.' He told them about the dreams that God showed to him.

Amos 9:11-15

God made a promise to the people that lived in Israel. He said, 'After the bad things have come, I will save Israel's people. I will again send good things to those that have not died.'

Chapter 1

1 Amos was among men who were near the town called Tekoa. They watched sheep to keep them safe. And they gave the sheep what they needed. God spoke to him. And God showed to Amos the trouble that was coming to Israel. God showed it to him two years before the earthquake came. When God showed the trouble to Amos, Uzziah was the king of Judah. And Joash's son, Jeroboam was the king of Israel.

2 Amos said, 'The LORD speaks loudly from Zion and from Jerusalem. He is like a wild animal (lion) that makes a loud noise. He says, "The fields are green now. So the sheep can eat lots of grass. But those fields will become dry and so the grass will die. In the whole country, the grass will become dry and it will die. That will happen even on top of the mountain called Carmel." '

These are the messages to the people near Israel

This is the message to the people in Aram (Syria). The very big city of Aram was Damascus.

3 The LORD says, 'The people in Damascus have done wrong things. Many times, they have done wrong things.

The people in Damascus were cruel. They had sharp tools that they had made from iron. And they used those tools to beat the people in Gilead. So I will send trouble to the people in Damascus. 4 I will start a fire. The fire will destroy King Hazael's big house. And it will destroy the strong buildings that belong to his son Ben-Hadad. 5 I will also break the strong gates of Damascus city. I will remove all the people who live in the Aven valley. And I will remove the king of Beth-Eden. The people's enemies will take all the people in Syria far away to the place called Kir.' That is what the LORD says.

This is the message to the people called the Philistines. Their biggest city was Gaza.

6 The LORD says, 'The people in Gaza have done wrong things. Many times, they have done wrong things. The people from Gaza took my people away. They sold my people to those that lived in Edom. 7 So I will start a fire. And the fire will destroy the walls of Gaza. It will also destroy the strong buildings in Gaza.

8 I will remove the king of Ashdod city. And I will remove the king of Ashkelon city. I will send trouble to the people that live in Ekron city. I will send trouble to every Philistine, until they are all dead.' That is what the great LORD says.

This is the message to the people on the island called Tyre

9 The LORD says, 'The people in Tyre have done wrong things. Many times, they have done wrong things. So I will send trouble to the people in Tyre. Before, they had agreed with the people in Israel. They had promised to those people, "We will be like brothers." But the people from Tyre did not do what they had promised. They took my people away. They sold my people to the people in Edom and my people became slaves. 10 So I will start a fire on the walls of Tyre city. And the fire will burn all the strong buildings. It will destroy them completely.'

This is the message to the people in Edom

11 The LORD says, 'The people in Edom have done wrong things. Many times, they have done wrong things. So I will send trouble to them. They took long knives in their hands and they ran after their cousins, the Israelites. They were not kind, but they were very angry. And they continued to be angry all the time. They did not stop it. 12 So I will start a fire. And the fire will destroy the big city called Teman. The fire will also burn the strong buildings in the big city called Bozrah.'

This is the message to the people in Ammon

13 The LORD says, 'The people in Ammon have done wrong things. Many times, they have done wrong things. So I will send trouble to them. People from Ammon fought in the place called Gilead. (Gilead was next to their country.) Ammon's people fought there to get more land for themselves. While they were killing people there, they also cut women open. Those women had babies inside them. 14 So I will send fire. And the fire will destroy the walls of the big city called Rabbah. It will destroy the strong buildings too. People will fight and they will shout. They will shout loudly, like the noise that a strong wind makes in a storm. 15 The enemies will take away their king and their leaders. They will take them to another country. The king and the leaders will not be free to return.' That is what the LORD says.

Chapter 2

This is the message to the people in Moab

1 The LORD says, 'The people in Moab have done wrong things. Many times, they have done wrong things. So I will send trouble to them. They dug up the bones of a king of Edom. They also burned those bones until they became ashes. That was not good. 2 So I will send fire to the country called Moab. The fire will destroy the strong buildings in Kerioth town. The people will hear their enemies shout. And they will hear the sounds that their enemies' trumpets make. And the people will die. 3 I will let the enemies kill the ruler of Moab. And I will let them kill all its leaders too.' That is what the LORD says.

This is the message to the people in Judah

4 The LORD says, 'The people in Judah have done wrong things. Many times, they have done wrong things. So I will send trouble to them. I, the LORD, told to those people the things that they must do. And I wrote those things for them. But they have not done those things. Those people have not listened to what I said to them. They have listened to someone else, who was not saying true things. And so Judah's people did wrong things. They lived like their family that lived a long time ago. They lived in the same bad way. 5So I will send fire to Judah. The fire will completely burn the strong buildings that are in the big city called Jerusalem.'

This is the message to the people in Israel

6 The LORD says, 'The people in Israel have done wrong things. Many times, they have done wrong things. So I will send trouble to them. They sold people that did not do wrong things. They sold them for silver. And they sold poor people for only the price of shoes. 7 They are not kind to poor people and they do not help them. A father and his son have sex with the same woman. I told them not to do that, but they do not listen to me. 8 Those men take clothes from poor people, because those poor people have a debt to them. Then they sleep on those poor people's clothes. And they do that in the special places where they pray. The rich people in Israel do this wrong thing also. Poor people give some money to rich people to pay for their debts. The rich people take the money and then they go to buy alcohol. Then they drink the alcohol at the special places where people pray.'

9 'Remember the Amorites. They were big and strong. They were like the tallest and strongest trees. But I removed all of them. 10 I brought you out of the country called Egypt. After that, I guided you for 40 years. I led you through a large dry place where nobody lived.

Then I gave to you the country where the people
called Amorites lived. 11 I chose some men among you to be prophets. I chose some young men among you to be Nazirites. You Israelites know that it is true', says the LORD God. 12 'But you told this to the people that should not drink alcohol (the Nazirites). You told them, "Be like everyone else. Drink alcohol." And you said to the people that speak my message (the prophets), "Do not speak it." '

13 'I will hurt you. A wagon that is full of food pushes down on the ground. I will do to you like the wagon does to the ground. 14 You might try to run away. But nobody will get free. The fastest runner will not get free. The strong people will not be strong enough to stop me. The soldiers will not be able to save themselves. 15 Men that shoot arrows will not live. Fast runners will not get free. All soldiers on horses will die. 16 At that time, strong and brave soldiers will run away without clothes on.' That is what the LORD God says.

Chapter 3

The LORD has decided what he will do

1 You Israelites, listen to this message that the LORD has spoken against you. This message is to all you people that he saved from Egypt. 2 He says, 'There are many groups of people on Earth. But I chose you for myself. You have done wrong things, so I have not been very happy with you. Now I will send trouble to you because of that.'

The prophet's work

3 If two people travel together, they have first agreed to travel. 4 If a lion (a wild animal) makes a loud noise in the forest, it is happy. It is happy because it has attacked an animal to eat. (If it has not caught anything, it is quiet. It looks quietly for something to eat.) If a young lion (a wild animal) makes a happy noise in his home, he has caught an animal. He has caught it to eat. (If he has not caught anything, he will be quiet.)

5 If there is no food in a trap, a bird will not fly into it. If there is no bird inside, the door of the trap will not shut. 6 If the people in a city hear a trumpet's sound, they are very afraid. And they may see soldiers go away to fight. Then, too, they are very afraid. Trouble may come to a city. Then we can know that the LORD has sent it.

7 Before the great LORD decides to send trouble, he first tells someone. He tells those that speak his message to all the people. They speak because God wants them to do it. This is true.

8 We are afraid now, because the lion has made a loud noise. The great LORD has spoken, so we must tell his message.

9 Go to Ashdod city and go to Egypt. Tell this to the people who live in beautiful buildings. 'Come to the mountains in Samaria. Look at the people there. They are hurting each other and they are afraid of each other.' 10 The LORD says, 'People take things from other people. They keep those things for themselves in their strong buildings. They become rich from those things. That is wrong.'

11 So the great LORD says, 'Enemies will come all round your country and they will destroy your strong buildings. They will take all your good things from you.'

12 The LORD says, 'A wild animal might attack a young sheep. The worker that watches the sheep might try to save them. He might save two legs and a small part of the ear. But he does not save the whole sheep. In the same way, the LORD will not save all the Israelites that live in Samaria and Damascus. The ones in Samaria lie on beautiful beds. And the ones in Damascus sit on comfortable chairs. But God will only save a few of those people.' 13 The LORD, the powerful God, said to me, 'Hear all this. And tell the Israelites that they have done wrong things.' 14 'I will punish them. And I will destroy the altars at Bethel at the same time. You will not be able to hold their tall corners. Their corners will break off and the corners will fall to the ground. 15 I will destroy all the big houses. Rich people live in special houses when it is cold. And they live in special houses when it is hot. I will destroy all those houses. There are houses with beautiful things that people have made from elephants' tusks. I will destroy those houses too', says the LORD.

Chapter 4

The LORD speaks against the people in Samaria

1 Listen to this message, you women who live on the hill in Samaria. You are like fat cows that do not work hard for food. You are like the cows in the place called Bashan. They eat on very good land by the Jordan river. You do not give to weak people what they need. You are not fair to poor people. Then you sit down and you say to your husbands, 'Bring us alcohol to drink.' 2 The great LORD has made this promise and he speaks only true words. He says, 'The time will come, when your enemies will take you away with meat hooks and fish hooks. 3 There are places in your city's walls where people have broken the walls. Your enemies will pull you through those places and they will throw you out. They will take you to that bad place called Harmon. None of you will stay here.'

The people in Israel have not learned to listen to God

4 The LORD also says, 'You like to go to Bethel. You say that it is your holy place. And when you go there, you do wrong things. So go there and sin. Do that if you want. You like to go to that other place, Gilgal. You say that it is a holy place. You do lots of wrong things there. So go there and sin. Do that if you want. You take your meat to burn it there every morning as a gift. But that does not make me happy. Every three days, you bring food that you have picked from your fields. But that also does not make me happy. 5 'You bring bread to say "thank you". You even bring lots of it and you tell everyone, "Look at how much I have brought." You really like to do that. So continue to do it but it does not make me happy', says the great LORD.

6 'Earlier I made you hungry in all your cities. There was no food anywhere. But you did not start to pray to me again', says the LORD. 7 'Three months before your food was ready to pick, I did not send rain. So all the food became too dry. Sometimes I sent rain to one city, but I did not send it to other cities. I sent rain to one person's land, but I did not send it to another person's land. So that other person's land became too dry. 8 People became weak. They went from city to city to look for water. As they went, they could hardly walk. There was not enough water. But still you did not start to pray to me again', says the LORD. 9 'I sent hot winds from the east. They burned the small plants, so those plants died. Worms (small, narrow, soft animals with no legs) made the other plants sick. So the other plants died. Locusts ate your trees that give fruit. But still you did not start to pray to me again', says the LORD.

10 'I caused many people among you to become very sick. It was like what happened many years ago in Egypt. At that time, very many people got sick. Then I sent soldiers to you. And they killed your young men and they took away your horses. The smell from dead bodies was very bad. But you still did not start to pray to me again', says the LORD. 11 'I killed many people among you, as I destroyed the cities called Sodom and Gomorrah. Some of you did not die. You were like a stick that is already burning. And someone saves it from the fire. But still you did not start to pray to me again', says the LORD. 12 'So I will send trouble to you Israelites again. Get ready! You will see it. Then you will know that it is I.'

13 I made the mountains and I made the wind. I tell people what I am thinking. I change dawn into night. I walk on the high places of the Earth. My name is the LORD, the powerful God.'

Chapter 5

Amos is sad

1 'Listen, you people in Israel, to the sad song that I am singing to you. 2 You are like a young woman that died early without children. No more good things will happen to you. You will not be important again. There are no people on your land to help you. They have all left.' 3 This is what the great LORD says. '1000 soldiers will go out from a city to fight, but only 100 soldiers will come back. From another city, 100 soldiers will go out to fight. But only 10 will come back.'

Look for God

4 To the people in Israel, the LORD says, 'Look for me and you will live. 5 Do not go to Bethel, Gilgal, or Beersheba. Do not try to find me there, because I am not there. I will send enemies to destroy those places. And they will take the people away as slaves.

6 Look for the LORD and you will live. If you do not look for him, he will come like fire. Bethel will burn and all the people there will burn. Nobody will be able to put out the fire. 7 You people do not speak true words. You are not fair to other people and you are not honest with them.'

8 The LORD made the groups of stars called Pleiades and Orion. They show you when it will become warmer or colder. The LORD changes the dark (night) into dawn and he changes the day into night again. He takes the water in the sea, and he pours it out on the earth. The LORD is his name.

9 He kills strong people. And he destroys their strong buildings and walls.

10 Some men are not afraid to speak against people. They are not afraid to say that people have done wrong things. You hate those men very much. And some men speak true words. You think that those men are not important. 11 You cause poor people to give you too much food from their fields. And you make them give too much money to you. You do not keep them safe. You have built big houses, but you will not live in them. You have planted many plants that give grapes. But you will not drink alcohol from them.

12 'I, the LORD, know the wrong things that you have done. You have hurt people that have not done wrong things. Sometimes a person gives money to you and he says, "Now do not speak true words." You take that money and you do not speak true words. Also, you do not speak true words for poor people. So other people do wrong things to them for no reason.' 13 This is such a bad time. Some people will think about how bad it is. And so, they will keep quiet. They will keep themselves safe.

14 You say that the LORD, the powerful God, is with you. So stop doing wrong things. Do good things. Then you will live. And the LORD, the powerful God, will really be with you. 15 Stop doing what is wrong. And choose what is good and right. Some of you decide whether a person has done right or wrong things. You people, be fair and speak true words. There are a few people that are still alive in Israel. Maybe the LORD, the powerful God, will be kind to them.

16 But the great LORD, the powerful God, says, 'Many people will be sad. They will cry loudly in all the streets. People on the farms will cry too. People will pay other people to help them cry because of the dead people. 17 And in all the places where fruit grows, people will cry. They will cry because I am sending trouble to you. I, the LORD, have spoken.'

The special Day of the LORD

18 You are hoping for the special Day of the LORD. You hope that he will save you from your enemies on that day. But that day will not be good for you. It will be sad and dark. It will not be happy and sunny. 19 It will be like a man that runs from a lion. But then he meets a bear. Or it will be like a man that goes into his house. He rests against a wall, and then a snake bites him.

20 The special Day of the LORD will be dark. It will have lots of trouble for you. It will not be bright, but it will be dark. It will not be happy, but it will be sad for very many people.

21 The LORD says, 'You come together to eat and to drink. And you come to bring gifts to me. When you do that, I do not like it at all.

22 When you bring fat animals to burn for me, I will not happily accept them. You might give food to me, but I will not take it.

23 I will not listen when you sing songs to me. I will not listen as you play music on harps. 24 A river never stops moving. So, like the river, never stop being fair to people. Never stop doing right things.

25 You people in Israel, listen to me. I led you through the large dry place for 40 years. You did not bring gifts to me to thank me there.

26 You made things for yourselves to pray to. You made the thing called Sakkuth. You say that it is your king. And you made that other thing, which is like a star. You call it Kaiwan. You continue to pray to them and you do not pray to me. 27 So I will send your enemies to take you away past Damascus. I, the LORD, the powerful God have said it.'

Chapter 6

God has promised to send enemies

1 You people in Jerusalem and on the hill in Samaria, you think that you are safe. And you think that everything is good and easy. But it will be bad for you. You leaders think that you are important people. And you think that you live in an important country. People come to you to get help. But bad things will happen to you people in the south and in the north.

2 Go and look at the city called Calneh. And go and look at the big city called Hamath. Those cities are in the north and their people are your enemies. Look at Gath city, where the Philistines live. It is in the south and its people too are your enemies. The people in those places are not stronger than you are. And their lands are not larger than your lands. 3 But you are not thinking that God might send trouble to you soon. Instead, you never stop doing wrong things. And so you cause trouble to come to you sooner. 4 You lie on beautiful, expensive beds and you do not work. You are resting all the time. You eat lots of young sheep and fat young cows. 5 Like King David, you play music on your harps and you make songs. 6 You happily drink lots of alcohol. You put the best smelling oils on your bodies. But you are not sad that Israel is destroying itself.

7 You will be the first people that your enemies will take away from there. You will be slaves for them. You will stop having parties and you will stop resting.

8 The great LORD, the powerful God, has promised this. He has spoken this strong message. 'The Israelites think that they are so good. But I do not like that. I do not like their strong buildings. So I will let their enemies have the Israelites' big city. The enemies can take away everything from it.'

9 At that time, ten people might still be in one house. But they will all die. 10 Then someone from a person's family will come to the house. And he will carry the person's dead body outside to burn it. Then he will ask anyone who is still inside, 'Is there anyone with you?' The person will answer, 'No.' Then the person from the family will say, 'Be quiet now. We must not speak the name of the LORD.' 11 When the LORD speaks to enemies, they destroy big and little houses. They will break those houses into pieces.

12 Horses cannot run on rocks. People do not try to plough the sea. But you have changed what is good to something bad. Some people are fair and honest. But you have made that seem like poison. 13 You are so happy. You think to yourselves, 'We are very strong. We fought against the people in Lo-Debar and Karnaim. And we won.' 14 But the LORD, the powerful God, says to you people in Israel, 'I am sending enemies to your country, from the way into Hamath to the river in Arabah. They will fight against you. And they will cause trouble in all your country.'

Chapter 7

Locusts

1 The great LORD showed locusts to me. He was getting ready to send them to us. They destroyed the food that was growing in the fields. That happened after we had cut down the first plants. We had given the food from those plants to the king. The locusts destroyed the next plants before the plants grew big. The plants were still only small. 2 The locusts ate everything. After that, I asked the LORD, 'Great LORD, please forgive us. We cannot live if those locusts come. We are a small number of people and we are weak.' 3 Then the LORD changed what he had decided. And he said to me, 'That will not happen.'

Fire

4 After that, the great LORD showed a fire to me. He was getting ready to send it to us. It dried the water under the land and it was burning the land. 5 Then I said, 'Great LORD, please do not send fire. We cannot live if that fire comes. We are a small number of people and we are weak.' 6 Then the LORD changed what he had decided. And he said to me, 'That too will not happen.'

The LORD measures the wall

7 Then the great LORD showed this to me. It was like a picture in my mind. The Lord was standing next to a wall. In his hand was a string. Someone had tied a big stone to the end of the string. The Lord was hanging the string down the wall. And he was looking to see whether the wall was straight.

8 And he asked me, 'Amos, what do you see?' I said, 'You are measuring the wall. Maybe it is straight or maybe it is not.' The Lord said, 'It is like this. I am measuring my people. I want to see whether they are good and honest. But they are not good and honest. I will now send trouble to them. I will not change what I have decided.

9 I will send enemies to destroy the holy places (special places where the Israelites pray). And the enemies will use long knives to kill King Jeroboam and his family.'

Amaziah speaks with Amos

10 Then Amaziah, the priest at the holy place called Bethel, sent a message to Jeroboam, the king of Israel. It said, 'Amos is speaking against you among Israel's people. He says that you will die. We will not listen to his words because he is saying bad things. And those things would destroy our country. 11 Amos is saying, "Our enemies will fight against us and they will kill you, Jeroboam. They will take all the people to the enemies' country, so that the people can be slaves for them." '

12 Then Amaziah spoke to me. He said, 'Go, you prophet, get out of here! Go back to the south, to Judah. Work for your food there. Speak your messages from God there. 13 Do not speak words from God here in Bethel again. It is King Jeroboam's temple. He and the people in Israel worship here.'

14 Then I answered Amaziah and I said, 'I am not a prophet or the son of a prophet. People do not pay me to do it. My work is to watch sheep. I keep them safe. And I give to them what they need. I also do to fig trees what they need. (A fig is a soft sweet fruit with lots of seeds.) 15 But the LORD told me to leave my sheep. He told me to speak his message. And he sent me to his people Israel in the north.

16 Now you are telling me, "Do not speak against Israel. Do not say that trouble is coming." 17 The LORD says this to you, Amaziah. "Your wife will sell herself to men so they can have sex with her. Your enemies will kill your sons and daughters. The enemies will give your land to people that are enemies. They will take your people away from this country. They will take them far away to another country. The enemies will take your people to be slaves. And you will die in your enemies' country." '

Chapter 8

Fruit that is ready to eat

1 Then the great LORD showed to me a basket of summer fruit. 2 He asked me, 'Amos, what do you see?' I answered him, 'I see a basket of summer fruit.' Then the LORD said to me, 'The time is ready. I will now send troubles to my people.

3 On that day, people will not sing in the temple. Instead they will cry loudly, because there will be dead bodies everywhere. Be quiet, because I have spoken. I am the great LORD.'

Trouble will come

4 So listen to me, you people that are not fair to poor people. You try to kill them. 5 You say to yourselves, 'We want this special party to finish. We are having a party because the moon is new (it is still very narrow). But we do not want to have a party. We want to sell food again. We want our day for rest to finish. We do not want to rest. We want to continue to sell food.' But you rob other people. You lie. You say, 'This is the right amount of food.' But it is not the right amount. You say, 'This is good food.' But it is not good. It has dirt in it. And it has other bits in it that are not good. And you make the price too high. 6 Sometimes a poor person cannot pay money back to another person, because he does not have enough money. It is a small amount of money. It is the amount of money that a person pays for shoes. But you buy that poor person for that small amount of money. So then he will be a slave for you. And you sell the bad bits of food plants. It is wrong that you do those things. 7 The LORD has strongly promised this: 'I will never forget the wrong things that they have done. 8 The whole country will start to move because they did wrong things. It will shake (move quickly up and down). It will go up and it will go down, like the Nile river. Everyone will be afraid and everyone will cry.'

9 The great LORD says, 'At that time, I will make the sun go down at noon. I will make light become dark. 10 Your parties and happy songs will finish. Instead, you will be very sad and you will cry.

You will cut your hair. And you will wear special clothes. Those clothes will show that you are very sad. It will be as if your only son died. It will all be very sad.

11 I, the great LORD, speak true words. At that time, I will cause you to be very hungry. It will not be because you have no food and water. You will be hungry to hear a message from me, the LORD. 12 You will go all over your country, because you will want to hear a message from me, the LORD. But you will not hear one.

13 At that time, your beautiful young women and young men will feel that they need to drink. So they will become very weak and tired. 14 People did not want me to help them. They made idols (things to worship) in Samaria and Dan and Beersheba. And then they said, "They will help us." These people will fall down and they will never get up again.'

Chapter 9

The LORD is powerful

1 Then Amos said, 'I saw the Lord. He was standing in the temple, by the altar. The Lord said, "Hit the top of the temple very hard. Hit it hard so that the floor under it will move. Cause everything to fall on to the heads of all the people there. Nobody will be able to run away. If anyone is alive after that, your enemies will kill him or her with long knives. 2 They might try to dig very deep into the Earth to save themselves. But my strong hand will take them out of the deep place. They might climb up to the sky. But I will bring them down from there. 3 They might run away to the top of the mountain called Carmel. But I will look for them and I will take them from there. They might try to hide from me deep down in the sea. But I will tell the big sea-snake that it must bite them. 4 Their enemies might take them away to be their slaves in the enemies' country. I will tell people there that they must kill them with long knives. And they will certainly kill them. I will not help them." '

5 When the LORD, the powerful God, touches the earth, it moves. It goes up and down like the Nile river, and many people die. Those people that are alive cry loudly because of the dead people. 6 The LORD makes his place in the sky and he puts the sky over the earth. He takes the water in the sea, and he pours it out on the earth. The LORD is his name.

The LORD will not kill everyone

7 The LORD says to his people, the Israelites, 'I like you. But in the same way, I like the people in Ethiopia. It is true that I led you safely from Egypt. But I also led other people too. I led the Philistines from Crete. And I led the people in Aram (Syria) from Kir.' 8 'I, the great LORD, am carefully watching you Israelites. And I see that you have done wrong things. I will remove you from the Earth. But I will keep a few Israelites alive', says the LORD.

9 'I will tell the enemies that they must separate you. And they will separate the good people from the bad people. A person shakes a sieve (moves it quickly up and down) and the good food falls through the holes. But the bad food stays in the sieve. The enemies will separate you like that. And then they will kill all the bad people. 10 The people that do wrong things say, "God will not send trouble to us." But their enemies will kill those people in war.'

The Israelites will be strong again

11 'The time will come when you will be powerful and important again. It will be like the time when David was your king. Now you are like a house that someone has destroyed. But I will repair you and I will make you good and strong again. 12 You Israelites will fight and you will win a war against the Edomite's. You will also be winners in wars against other countries. And you will have all the land that you had before.' The LORD says it and he will do it.

13 'The time will come', says the LORD, 'when food will grow very quickly and well. People will work hard. They will pick all the food and they will put it into baskets. Before they have finished, they will see more food. It will grow very quickly. Much fruit (grapes) will grow too. People will work hard and they will make a drink from the fruit (grapes). But before they have finished, they will see much more fruit. That fruit (grapes) will be big and it will be ready to pick. The fruit (grapes) grows on mountains. It will give so much wine that the wine will flow (move like water) down the mountains.

14 I will bring my people back to their country.

They will again build their cities, the ones that their enemies destroyed. And they will live there. In some fields, my people will put plants that give grapes.

And they will drink the wine from them. In other fields, my people will put plants that give food. And they will eat what grows there. 15 And I will put you back again on the land that I gave to you. And your enemies will never take you away again from the land that I have given to you.' That is what the LORD, your God, has said.

God's Message about Edom

Obadiah

About this book

> The book called Obadiah is in the Old Testament. The events in the Old Testament happened during a long time. All that time, there were many wars between the Israelites and the people from Edom. Genesis chapter 27 and Numbers 20:14-21 tell us why these wars happened.
>
> God gives to Obadiah a message for the Israelites. He does this just after people from Babylon have destroyed Jerusalem. People from Edom helped those people from Babylon. So God is angry with the people from Edom. And he warns them that he is angry. He warns them in this message that God gives to Obadiah. In the message, God also tells the Israelites that he remembers them. And he remembers what the people from Edom did. God tells the Israelites that he will punish the people from Edom.

Chapter 1

God will punish Edom's people

1 God, who is the LORD, gave a message to Obadiah. The message is about Edom.

This is the message from the LORD to the Israelites.

We have heard what God said.

And someone has taken a message to the countries.

'Stand up and fight against Edom.'

2 God said to Edom,

'I will make you small among other people.

They will think that you are not worth anything.

3 You think that you are better than other people. And so you believe something that is not true.

You live in a place that is difficult to reach.

Your home is high up in a place among rocks.

You say to yourself,

"Nobody can reach us up here."

4 You may like a strong bird that flies high.

And you may make your home in the highest places among the stars.

But I will bring you down from there,' says the LORD.

5 God says,

'Men might come in the night

to take away what is yours.

(Oh, what a very bad thing will happen to you!)

But they would not take everything.

If people came to take fruit from your trees,

they would leave some fruit on the tree.

6 But people will take everything from Esau's people (also called Edom).

They will even take the valuable things that you hide.

7 People who have helped you to fight

will push you out from your country.

They will tell you what is not true. You will believe them.

They will be stronger than you

because you will believe their words.

They will make a trap for you.'

8 The LORD says,

'Some men in Edom know what is right. But, at that time, I will kill them.

Some men in the mountains know what is good. (These are the mountains where Esau's people live.) But I will kill those men.

9 There are men from Teman city that fight. But I will make them afraid.

Esau's people live in the mountains. And everyone there will die.

10 This will happen because you were cruel to your brother Jacob (the people in Israel).

God will make you ashamed because of this and you will die.

11 Men from other countries came into Jerusalem. They took away all the good things from Jerusalem. They played a game for the best things. You were as bad as they were. You did not help the Jews.

12 Your brothers in Judah were in great trouble.

You thought that you were better than they. But you were wrong to think that.

You should not have been happy when the people in Judah were dying.

You should not have been happy when they were in trouble.

13 You should not have walked like soldiers through my people's gates.

You did that at the time when they were in trouble.

You should not have thought that you were better than they.

You thought it at the time when they were in trouble.

You should not have taken what was theirs.

14 You waited at the place where the roads joined each other.

You wanted to kill those that ran away from the enemy.

That is why you waited there.

You should not have done that.

Some Jews were still alive, but they were in trouble.

You should not have taken them to the enemy.

The Day of the LORD and what will happen then

15 The Day of the LORD will come soon for all the world's people.

God will do to you what you did to other people.

God will be angry with you because you did those things to them.

16 You drank on my special hill.

In the same way, people from all countries will drink and they will not stop.

They will drink until God has killed them.

17 But on the mountain called Zion, people will be free.

It will be special to me.

Jacob's family will have the country that is theirs.

I will give it to them.

18 The people in Jacob's and Joseph's family will kill all the people that belong to Esau's family.'

This is what the LORD said.

19 People will come from the Negev. They will come to live in the mountains where Esau's people (the people in Edom) lived.

People will come from the small hills near the mountain. And they will get the Philistines' country.

They will live in the fields in Ephraim and Samaria.

Benjamin's people will get Gilead.

20 Some people lived in Israel,

but they now have to live with the Canaanites.

They will get the country as far as Zarephath.

Some people lived in Jerusalem, but now they have to be in Sepharad.

They will get the towns in the Negev.

21 Men will come to make Jerusalem free

and they will rule over Edom.

And that country will belong to the LORD.

God Loves People From Every Country

Jonah

About the Book of Jonah

This book records what happened to a man called Jonah. Jonah lived in Gath Hepher, a town in Israel. Israel is east of the Mediterranean Sea. It is the home of God's special people, the Jews.

We also read about Jonah in one other part of the Old Testament. This is in 2 Kings 14:25. The king was Jeroboam the Second. He ruled in the 8th century BC. A country near Israel, called Syria, had taken some of Israel's land by war. We read that Jonah spoke God's words to the Jews. He said that the people in Israel would win back this land by war from Syria. And that is what had happened. So people knew Jonah as a prophet. But Jonah's book is not about the words that Jonah spoke. It records something that happened in his life.

We do not know when the writer wrote the book. It may have been about 750 BC. Jonah may have written the book. Or another prophet may have written it. Usually these prophets of God spoke only to the Jews in Israel and Judah.

Chapter 1

1 The LORD spoke to Jonah, Amittai's son. 2 He said 'Go to the large, important city called Nineveh. Tell the people in the city that they do wrong things. I have seen what the cruel people there are doing. Lots of really bad things happen there.'

3 But Jonah ran away from the LORD. He went towards Tarshish. He went down to Joppa. There he found a ship that was ready to sail to that port. After he had paid for the journey, he got into the ship. He sailed to Tarshish to run away from the LORD.

4 Then the LORD sent a strong wind on the sea. There was a powerful storm. The storm almost broke the ship into pieces. 5 All the sailors were afraid. Each of them shouted in a loud voice to his own god. They threw the things that the ship carried into the sea. They made the ship's weight as light as they could. But Jonah had gone below deck. He lay down and he slept. He slept in a way that it would be difficult for anyone to wake him up.

6 The ship's captain went to Jonah. He said, 'You should not be sleeping! Get up and speak in a loud voice to your god! Maybe he will listen to us and we will not die.' 7 Then the sailors said to each other, 'We will throw dice to find out who has caused this trouble.' They threw dice. And they found out that Jonah had caused the storm.

8 So they asked Jonah, 'Who has caused all this trouble for us? What is your job? Where do you come from? What country do you live in? Where were you born?'

9 Jonah explained. He said, 'I am a Jew. I worship the LORD, the God of heaven. He made the sea and the land.' 10 This made the sailors really afraid. They asked Jonah, 'What have you done?' They knew that he was running from the LORD. He had already told them that.

11 The water in the sea was moving up and down. It was so high now that water sometimes came into the ship. So the sailors asked Jonah, 'What should we do to you? The water is coming into the ship. How can we stop that?' 12 Jonah replied, 'Lift me up and throw me into the sea. The sea will not move up and down any longer. It will become flat again. I have done something wrong. So you are in a storm.'

13 But the men did not throw Jonah into the sea. They rowed and they tried to return to the land. But they could not do that. Still the water in the sea moved up and down. It was even higher than before.

14 Then the men spoke in a loud voice to the LORD. They said, 'This man has done nothing wrong. But we will have to kill this man. But LORD, please do not let us die because of this. Do not say that we have done something wrong. LORD, you have sent this storm for your own reasons.'

15 Then the sailors took Jonah and they threw him over the side of the ship. The water in the sea did not continue to move up and down. It became flat. 16 When they saw this, the men were afraid of the LORD. They respected him and they offered a sacrifice to him. And they promised God that they would do certain things. This was a serious promise.

17 But the LORD had made a very large fish or sea animal. The fish caught Jonah in its mouth. God had chosen the fish to take the whole body of Jonah. Jonah went down immediately from the mouth into the fish's stomach. Jonah was inside the fish's stomach for three days and three nights.

Chapter 2

1 From inside the fish, Jonah prayed to the LORD his God.

2 He said,

'I was really afraid.

So I spoke to the LORD about my trouble.

And he answered me.

From the deep hole, I shouted for help.

And you listened when I cried.

3 You threw me into the deep water.

I fell into the middle of the sea.

The water moved all-round me.

It carried me along.

The high water came down over me.

The white water covered my head.

4 I said,

"You have sent me away so that you can no longer see me.

But I will look again towards the place where I can worship you."

5 The water all-round me made me afraid.

The deep water caused me to think that my life was in danger.

Plants in the sea covered very near round my head.

6 I went far down in the water.

I went down to the ground.

I could not go any deeper.

I did not know how I would ever come up again.

But you brought me up from the deep hole.

You are my LORD, my God.

7 While I was dying, I remembered you, LORD.

I prayed. And you heard me in the place where I can worship you.

8 Some people want to keep things that have no value.

They worship them.

So they do not receive God's love that could be for them.

9 But I will give sacrifices to you.

I will sing and I will thank you.

I will do what I have promised to do.

The LORD has saved me.'

10 And the LORD spoke to the fish. The fish caused Jonah to leave its stomach and to come back out of its mouth. Jonah landed on to the dry ground.

Chapter 3

1 God spoke to Jonah for the second time. 2 He said, 'Go to the large, important city called Nineveh. Tell all the people there the message that I will give to you.' 3 Jonah obeyed the LORD and he went to Nineveh.

Nineveh was a very large city. A person would need three days to travel all through it.

4 Jonah started to travel into the city. When he had travelled for a day, he shouted out to the people. He said, '40 more days and God will destroy Nineveh.'

5 The people who lived in Nineveh believed God. They were ashamed about how they had lived. So they told everyone that they must not eat anything for several days. All the people put sackcloth on. The most important people and the least important people did that.

6 When the king of Nineveh heard about this, he got up from his throne. He took off his king's clothes. He covered himself with sackcloth and he sat down on the dirty ground.

7 Then the king spoke to all the people in Nineveh. He said, 'I and the important people who work for me have made a rule.

No man or animal or any group of animals must taste anything. They must not eat or drink. 8 Men and women must cover themselves with sackcloth. They must cover all the animals with sackcloth, too. Everyone must shout in a loud voice to God. They must do this immediately. Everyone must do good things, not bad things. They must not fight other people. They must not be cruel people any longer. 9 Nobody knows what will happen. Even now, God may change his mind. He may not be angry any longer. He may be kind to us and so we may not die.'

10 God saw what the people in Nineveh did. He saw that they did good things now. They no longer did wrong things. So he was kind to them. He did not destroy their city as he had said.

Chapter 4

1 But Jonah did not like that. He was certainly not happy. He became angry. 2 He prayed to the LORD. He said, 'LORD, I spoke to you about this when I was at home. So I went quickly to Tarshish. I knew that you are a kind God. I knew that you understand people. You help them. You are full of love and you do not become angry easily. You are a God who thinks about causing bad things to happen to people. But then you decide not to do it. 3 Now, LORD, kill me. It is better for me to die than to live.'

4 But the LORD replied, 'You have no reason to be angry.'

5 Jonah went outside and he sat down at a place to the east of the city. There he made a small hut for himself. He sat under it so that the sun would not burn him. He waited. He wanted to see what would happen to the city.

6 But God made a plant. The LORD God caused it to grow up over Jonah so that the sun would not burn Jonah's head. He made it so that Jonah would feel good. Jonah was very happy about the plant.

7 But God had also made a worm. At dawn on the next day the worm ate some of the plant. So then the plant died. 8 When the sun rose, God caused the wind to blow from the east. The wind was very hot. The sun made Jonah's head very hot. He became weak and ill. He wanted to die. He said, 'It would be better for me to die than to live.'

9 But God said to Jonah, 'Should you be angry about the plant?'

'I should', he said. 'I feel so angry that I want to die.' 10 But the LORD said, 'You like this plant. It is important to you. But you did not plant it or cause it to grow. It grew up quickly during the night and it died before dawn. 11 But Nineveh has more than 120 000 people. They cannot understand the difference between right ways and wrong ways. Also, they have many cows. That large city is important to me.'

Micah's Message to God's People

Micah

About this book

God told Micah to speak to Israel's people (the Jewish people). Micah was a prophet because he spoke messages from God. He lived a long time before Jesus lived on this earth. He spoke God's messages between about 740 BC (Before Christ's birth) and 686 BC. The prophet Isaiah also spoke messages from God to Israel's people at that same time.

When Micah was alive, the country of Israel was two separate parts. The name of the north part was Israel and the name of the south part was Judah. A king ruled each part. Micah's home was in Moresheth, which was a small town in the part called Judah. It was about 5 hours' walk (about 32 kilometres) south and west from Jerusalem, Judah's capital city.

In this book, Micah tells Israel's people that God is angry with them. God is angry because they have refused to obey him.

So, he will cause enemies to attack them. But Micah also speaks about what God has promised. God has promised to save his people in the end.

In most of this book, Micah speaks God's words to the people. But sometimes he speaks to God on behalf of the people, and sometimes he speaks for himself.

Chapter 1

1 These are the messages that the Lord gave to Micah. Then Micah told them to the people during the times that Jotham, Ahaz and Hezekiah ruled the country called Judah. Micah was born in a small town called Moresheth. God showed Micah about what would happen to the cities called Samaria and Jerusalem.

God will destroy Samaria city

> 2 Listen, all of you people everywhere!
>
> Hear this, everyone who lives on the earth!
>
> The Lord who is ruler of everyone will speak against you.

You have done what is wrong. That is why he will speak against you.

> He will speak from his special house.

3 Look! The Lord is leaving his place and he is coming down to the earth.

> He will come to the high places (where you worship false gods).
>
> He will destroy those places when he comes.
>
> 4 The mountains will melt when he comes,
>
> like wax melts near a fire.
>
> The valleys will break too.
>
> They will move like water when it rushes down a hill.

5 All these bad things will happen because Jacob's people have refused to obey God.

These things will happen because Israel's people have done wrong things.

> You may ask who has caused this.
>
> It is the leaders in your capital cities,
>
> Samaria city and Jerusalem city.

They have kept the high places there for people to offer gifts to false gods.

6 So God says to you:

'I will destroy Samaria so that just a few stones are lying in the fields there.

> Then people will plant vines in that place.
>
> I will throw the stones from the city down into the valley,
>
> when I completely destroy all the buildings.
>
> 7 I will break all the false gods into pieces and I will destroy them.
>
> I will burn all the gifts that the people brought for those false gods.

The people have paid so that they could have sex with bad women in those places.

> Your enemies will come and they will take away this money.
>
> They will give it to their gods in the same way.'

Micah is sad for the people in Israel and Judah

> 8 Because of what God has said, I will cry aloud. And I will weep.
>
> I will walk about without shoes or clothes.
>
> I will scream like a wild dog,
>
> and I will cry like a bird in the night.

9 Because Samaria has such bad wounds that it can never get well.

> And the same will happen also to Judah's people.

The enemies have already reached the gates of my people, that is, Jerusalem itself.

> 10 Do not talk about this in the city called Gath.
>
> Do not even weep there.
>
> But you people at Beth Leaphrah,
>
> roll on the ground to show how sad you are.
>
> 11 You people who live in Shaphir, go on your way.

Your enemies will not let you wear any clothes while they take you away.

> So you will be ashamed.
>
> The people who live in Zaanan will be afraid to leave their city.

The people at Bethezel will cry because nobody comes to help them.

> 12 The people at Maroth are in pain while they wait.
>
> They were waiting and hoping for something good.
>
> But the Lord sent only something bad.
>
> He brought trouble even to the gates of Jerusalem.

13 You people who live in Lachish, get your war-carts and horses ready to go!

> You were the first people in Judah to do what is wrong.

You are exactly like Israel's people, because, like them, you refused to obey God.

> 14 You will need to give gifts to the people in Moresheth Gath,
>
> because they must go away.
>
> The houses in Achzib town will disappoint the kings of Israel.
>
> 15 People in Mareshah, I (God) will bring an army against you,
>
> to fight your town. And it will win.
>
> And Israel's leaders will need to hide at Adullam.
>
> 16 People in Judah, cut off all your hair.
>
> Make yourselves bald like vultures,
>
> because you will be very sad.
>
> Your enemies will take your children away.

They will take your children, whom you love so much, away to another country!

Chapter 2

God says that bad things will happen to the bad people

1 Micah continues:

> People who prepare to do bad things should be afraid.
>
> God will do bad things to them!
>
> While they lie in bed, they think about bad things to do.
>
> Then, when the morning comes, they do those bad things.
>
> They have the authority to do whatever they want to do.
>
> 2 When they want fields, they take them from other people.
>
> When they want houses, they take them.
>
> These cruel people take other people's homes and fields;
>
> then those people's families have nothing.

3 So the Lord says this to them:

> 'I am against you.
>
> You cannot save yourselves.
>
> I will prepare trouble for you.
>
> Then you will stop thinking that you are so very clever and important.
>
> It will be a time of much trouble for you.
>
> 4 At that time, people will say that you are fools.
>
> They will sing this sad song on your behalf:
>
> God has completely destroyed us!
>
> We no longer have any fields, because God has taken them away from us.
>
> He has given them to our enemies, who have turned away from what is right.
>
> 5 So, when the Lord's people measure the land again to give fields to everyone,
>
> you will get none.
>
> You will have nobody to speak on your behalf.'
>
> 6 The bad people say to Micah: 'Do not prophesy like this to us!
>
> Do not say that we will have trouble.
>
> God will not make us ashamed!'

7 Micah replies: It is wrong for you to say that the Lord's Spirit is not angry with Jacob's people.

> God does not do bad things.
>
> My (God's) words do good things.
>
> He is kind to people who do the right things.
>
> 8 'Even in days that have only just passed,
>
> you have become enemies among my people', God says.
>
> 'You rob people of their coats when they pass by.
>
> Even men who thought that they were safe now.
>
> You even rob men who are returning home from war.
>
> 9 You rob the women among my people too.
>
> You take away their happy homes.
>
> So, you take away what I want their children to enjoy.

10 Get up and go away!

> You cannot remain in this place because you have made it bad.

> It is so bad that it will completely destroy you.

11 When a person speaks false messages to you, then you believe them.

They might say that you would have plenty of wine and strong drink.

> That is the message that you would like!'

God promises to bring his people back together

> 12 'You people of Israel, I promise to bring all of you together.

> I will bring back together all Israel's people who remain.

> I will put all of you together like sheep in a field with a wall round it.

> You will be like a field full of sheep.

> There will be a loud noise because there will be so many of you.

> 13 The person who breaks open the way will go in front of you.

> Then you will go out through the gate.

> I am the Lord, your king, and I will lead you out.'

Chapter 3

Micah speaks against the bad leaders of Israel

1 Then I spoke to the leaders:

> Listen to me, I said.

> You are the leaders of Jacob's people,

> you are the rulers of Israel.

> You ought to know what is right or wrong.

> 2 But you hate what is good.

> And you love what is bad.

> You would like to tear the skin off my people,

> and pull the meat from their bones.

> 3 You look at my people and you are like butchers.

> They strip the skin off an animal and they break its bones.

> Then they cut the meat into pieces and they cook it in a pot.

> They are happy when they eat the meat.

> 4 One day you will shout to the Lord for help,

> but he will not answer you.

> Instead, God will turn away from you at that time,

> because you have done those bad things.

5 The Lord has spoken about you prophets who tell false messages. You lead my people the wrong way with false promises. If people give food to you, then you are happy. So, you promise that there will be no war. But, if people do not feed you, then you are angry. You promise that war will come.

6 God says to you: 'It will be like night for you because it will be dark.

> You will not see anything.

> You will no longer be able to see what will happen in future times.

> The sun will go down over you prophets,

> and the day will become dark for you.

7 You saw what would happen in future times. That is what you said.

> But you will be ashamed.

> And you try to tell what will happen in future times.

> But I will confuse you.

> All of you will hide your faces because I will not answer you.'

8 'But the Spirit of the Lord fills me, to make me powerful', I told them.

> He helps me to know what is right and fair.

> He makes me brave so that I can speak to you, Jacob's people.

> I can tell you what you have done wrong.

> You are Israel's people,

> but you have not obeyed God.

> 9 So listen to this, you leaders of Jacob's people.

> You are Israel's rulers.

> But you never do what is right and fair.

> You take what is good.

> And you make it seem bad.

10 You rule Zion city, which is Jerusalem.

>But you are cruel, and you kill honest people.

>11 You are the city's rulers, but you accept money from people.

>Then you decide what is right or wrong.

>You listen to the people who give the money to you.

>Then they tell you what to decide.

>You priests teach only if the people pay you to teach.

>You prophets speak about what will happen in future times.

>But you only speak if you receive money.

>But all of you, the leaders, still say that you believe the Lord.

>'The Lord is with us, so nothing bad will happen to us', you say.

>12 So God says: 'Because of you,

>I will make Zion like a field that people have ploughed.

>I will destroy Jerusalem so that only stones are lying there.

Weeds and bushes will grow all over the hill where they built my house.'

Chapter 4

God's mountain

>1 In the last days,

the mountain where the Lord's house is will be the highest mountain.

>It will be the most important of all the mountains.

>It will be higher than the hills,

>and people from many countries will go to it.

>2 Many people will speak about it.

>'Come! We will go up to the Lord's mountain', they will say.

'We will go to the Lord's house because he is the God of Jacob's people.

>He will teach us what he wants us to do.

>He will show us the right way; so then we will be able to obey him.

>The Lord will speak his rules from Zion.

>He will send out his message from Jerusalem.'

>3 He will decide what is right or wrong between many countries.

He will cause strong countries everywhere to stop fighting each other.

>They fight with swords and spears.

>But then, they will use hammers to make their swords into ploughs.

>They will make their spears into tools to cut plants.

>One country will not fight another country any longer.

>They will never prepare for war again.

>4 Everyone will sit under his own vine and his own fig tree.

>Nobody will make them afraid any longer.

>The Lord, who has all authority, has promised this.

>5 People from other countries may be the servants of other gods.

>But we will be servants of the Lord our God.

>We will obey him always.

God will make Israel and Jerusalem strong again

6 The Lord speaks again:

>'At that time I will bring together the people who cannot walk well.

>I will bring back the people that I sent away.

>I caused trouble for those people,

>but I will bring them back together.

7 I will make a new beginning with those people who cannot walk well.

>Together with some of those people that I sent far away,

>I will make them my own special people.

>They will be strong,

>and I will rule over them from Zion's mountain.

>I will be their king from that time and always.

>8 And as for Jerusalem city,

>it was a strong, safe place for Zion's people.

>It was like a tall building,

>from which a man can watch over his sheep.

Then it will again be a place where a king rules with great authority.'

> 9 You people in Jerusalem,
>
> you are crying aloud like people who have no king.
>
> You cry like people who have nobody to advise them.
>
> You have bad pains like a woman who is giving birth to a baby.
>
> 10 People in Zion, you will have a lot of pain,
>
> like a woman who is giving birth to a baby.
>
> She rolls about and she screams with pain.

Soon you will have to leave your city and you will have to live in the fields.

> You will have to go to Babylon,
>
> but there the Lord will save you.
>
> He will make you free again from the authority of your enemies.

11 But now, at this time, many countries have come together to attack your city.

> They say: 'We will destroy Jerusalem and we will enjoy ourselves.
>
> We want to see Zion's people in trouble.'

12 But they do not know the Lord's thoughts.

> They do not understand how he will punish them.
>
> He will bring them together,
>
> as people bring bundles of wheat together at harvest time.
>
> He will punish them,
>
> as people thresh wheat to get the seeds out.

13 'People in Zion, get up and fight your enemies', God says to you.

> 'Hit them like people thresh the wheat.
>
> I will make you very strong.

Then you will be like dangerous animals with iron horns and metal feet.

> You will beat enemies from many countries,
>
> as men crush things into small pieces.
>
> The people from those countries became rich,
>
> because they did bad things.

> But you will bring their riches to me,
>
> because I am the Lord of all the earth.'

Chapter 5

The ruler that God chooses will be born in Bethlehem

> 1 Soldiers in Jerusalem, come together!
>
> Get ready, because your enemies are attacking you.
>
> They are all round the city, ready to fight.
>
> They will hit Israel's ruler on his face with a stick.

2 But God tells us this:

> 'Bethlehem Ephrathah is only a little town,
>
> among all the many towns in Judah', God says.
>
> 'But I will choose someone who is born there.
>
> He will rule Israel for me.
>
> Long, long ago, I prepared for him to come.'

3 So God will turn away from his people,

> until the time that the woman gives birth to this baby in Bethlehem.
>
> Then this ruler's own people who are still alive will return to Israel.

4 And this ruler will stay strong because the Lord will make him strong.

> He will supply what his people need.
>
> He will be like a man who supplies everything for his sheep.
>
> He will rule with authority from the Lord his God,
>
> and his people will be safe.
>
> So then, all over the world, people will know that he is great.

5 And he will cause the people to rest,

> so that they have no trouble.
>
> Assyria's soldiers will come to attack our country.
>
> They will march through our large, strong buildings.
>
> Then we will choose seven or eight leaders to fight against them.

6 These leaders will use their swords to destroy Assyria.

They will beat the people in the country called Nimrod with swords in their hands.

> Assyria's soldiers will come into our country.
>
> They will march across our borders,
>
> but our ruler will save us from them.

God's people will be strong again

7 And later, Jacob's people who are still alive will be in many countries.

> They will be everywhere,
>
> like water on the ground in the early morning,
>
> or rain on the grass.
>
> The Lord sends the water to help the plants,
>
> but no human person can make it stay.

8 Jacob's people who are still alive will be living among people in many other countries.

> They will become like a dangerous lion among the other animals in the forest.
>
> They will become like a young lion among people's sheep.
>
> The lion attacks other animals.
>
> It knocks them down and it tears them in pieces.
>
> Nobody can save them.

9 You will be strong like that and so you will beat your enemies.

> You will kill all of them.

God wants people to obey him

10 'At that time', the Lord says, 'I will take your horses away from you.

> I will destroy your war-carts.

11 I will destroy the cities in your country.

> I will knock down all your strong buildings.

12 You make bad spirits help you.

> But I will destroy the things that you use to talk to them.
>
> You will have nobody to tell you about future times.

13 You bend down to worship tall stones and idols.

> But I will destroy all of them.
>
> You will stop worshipping things that you have made with your own hands.

14 You worship the false god Asherah,

> but I will pull her poles from the ground.
>
> I will even destroy your cities.

15 Also I will punish all the people in other countries who refuse to obey me.

> I will show them that I am very angry with them.'

Chapter 6

God has a quarrel with Israel's people

1 Now listen to what the Lord says:

> 'Stand up! Explain in front of the mountains what I want to say.
>
> Speak loud so that the hills can hear your voice.

2 Listen, you mountains.

Hear this, you strong places that have always been there deep in the earth.

> God has a quarrel with Israel's people.
>
> Hear the reasons why God is angry with you, his people.'

3 'My people, what bad thing have I done to you?' God asks.

> 'How have I made you tired of me?
>
> Answer me.

4 I brought you out of Egypt.

> You were slaves in that country,
>
> but I made you free people.
>
> I sent Moses to lead you,
>
> and Aaron and Miriam with him.

5 My people, please remember the bad things that King Balak of Moab tried to do.

> And remember what Balaam, Beor's son, answered him.
>
> Remember your journey from Shittim to Gilgal.
>
> Then you will remember that I, the Lord, do good things.'

What God wants from his people

> 6 'I come to meet with the Lord', you say.
>
> 'I must know what to bring when I come.
>
> I bend down to worship him.
>
> I must know what to offer when I bend down.
>
> He is God and he is greater than everything.
>
> Perhaps he would like it if I burn young cows one year old for him.
>
> 7 He might be happy with thousands of male sheep,
>
> or ten thousand rivers of olive oil.
>
> I have not obeyed God.
>
> I might even kill and burn my oldest son, because of that.
>
> I have done wrong things and I must pay God for that.
>
> Perhaps, if I give my own child to him, that will be enough to pay.'

8 But God has told us what is good. This is what the Lord wants from us:

> 'You must be fair to other people', God says.
>
> 'You must want to be kind.
>
> And you must be careful to do what I show you.'

God will punish people that are not honest

> 9 The Lord shouts to the people in Jerusalem city.
>
> So, it is good for us to listen carefully to what he says.

'Listen to me, because I have the authority to punish you', God says.

10 'You bad people still hide valuable things that you have taken from other people.

> I will not forget this.

You bad people use false weights to measure the food that you sell.

> I hate that.
>
> 11 I will not excuse you people who use false weights.
>
> You are not being honest if you weigh things like that.
>
> 12 You rich people in the city are very cruel.
>
> Everyone there says things that are not true.
>
> All of them speak false words.
>
> 13 So, I will make you so sick that you will never get well.
>
> I have begun to destroy you because you have done bad things.
>
> 14 You will eat, but you will still feel hungry.
>
> You will store things and you will try to keep them safe.
>
> But you will fail to save them.
>
> I will cause enemies to destroy all your things in the war.
>
> 15 You will plant seeds,
>
> but you will not bring in the harvest.
>
> You will crush olives,
>
> but you will not use the olive oil for yourselves.
>
> You will crush grapes,
>
> but you will not drink the wine from them.
>
> 16 You have obeyed the rules of King Omri.
>
> You have done what King Ahab and all his people did.
>
> You have copied their bad example.
>
> So, I must destroy you and all your things completely.
>
> Then people from other countries will not be kind or polite to you.
>
> Instead, they will make you ashamed.'

Chapter 7

Israel's people are very bad, but Micah still believes God

> 1 I am very sad!
>
> I am like someone who comes to trees with no fruit on them.
>
> Other people have picked the fruit already.
>
> So, I am like those people who can only pick the last grapes.
>
> Those are the grapes that other people leave behind.
>
> Really, there are no grapes there to eat.
>
> There are none of the first figs that I like so much.
>
> 2 There are no longer any people here who obey God.

There are no good, honest people.

    Everyone is waiting to kill someone else.

    They are all like hunters, who try to catch each other.

3 They know very well how to work together to do bad things.

    Rulers demand gifts and judges ask for money.

    Powerful bad people always get what they want.

    All these people work together to do what is bad.

4 The best of them are dangerous like wild plants with thorns.

    The most honest of them are worse than thorn bushes.

    The bad time that your prophets told you about is coming.

    Soon God will punish you,

    and you will be confused.

5 Do not believe anyone, even somebody that you know well.

    You cannot be sure that your friend will always be honest with you.

    Be careful what you say to your wife.

    Be careful even when you are hugging her.

6 Sons think that their fathers are fools.

    And daughters refuse to obey their mothers.

    Wives quarrel with their husbands' mothers.

    A man's enemies are the people who live in his own house now.

7 But as for me, I will watch for what the Lord will do.

    I will wait for God, who saves me.

    I know that he hears me.

Israel's enemies will be ashamed

    8 My enemy, do not be happy because I am in trouble.

    I have fallen down, but I will get up.

    I am in the dark, but the Lord will be a light to me.

    9 I have not obeyed the Lord,

    so he is angry with me.

    He will continue to punish me,

    until the time when he speaks for me.

    Then he will make things right for me.

    He will bring me out into the light.

    He always does what is really right.

    And I will see that then.

10 'Why does the Lord your God not help you?' my enemies say to me.

    They will see what God does for me.

    Then they will be very ashamed.

    And I will see the bad things that happen to them.

    Soon other people will crush them and beat them.

    Then they will be like wet ground in the streets under people's feet.

Jerusalem city will be great again

11 But the time will come for you to build the walls of your cities again.

    You will make the borders of your country much wider then.

12 At that time many of Assyria's people and Egypt's people will come to you.

People will come to you from the countries between Egypt and the River Euphrates.

    They will come to you from all over the earth,

    from sea to sea and from mountain to mountain.

13 The other parts of the earth will become sad places where nobody lives.

    God will destroy them because of the people who live there.

    Those people have done what is bad.

Micah talks to God

    14 Rule us and lead us, Lord.

    You are like a man who leads his sheep.

    He uses a strong stick to lead them.

    We are your own special people.

    We are like a group of sheep that lives by itself in a forest.

There is good grass all round them.

Let your sheep eat grass in Bashan and Gilead,

as they did a long time ago.

15 Lord, you did great things long ago,

when you brought us out of the country called Egypt.

Do great things like that again.

16 The people in other countries will see what you do.

They will understand that they are not really powerful.

So then they will be ashamed.

They will be like deaf and dumb people (people who cannot speak or hear).

17 They will be like snakes that move along the ground.

They will eat the ground like snakes because they will be very afraid.

They will come out of their safe places,

because they will be afraid of you, the Lord our God.

18 No other god is like you.

You chose us to be your people.

And you decide not to remember what we have done wrong.

Not many of your people remain and we have done bad things.

But you choose to forget those bad things.

You will not always be angry,

because you want very much to be kind.

19 You like to be kind because you love us.

So, again you will remove everything that we have done wrong.

You will crush those bad things.

You will throw all of them into the deep sea.

20 You will continue to be kind to us,

because we are Jacob's and Abraham's people.

That is what you promised to our grandfathers a long time ago.

Nahum's message for Nineveh

Nahum

About the Book of Nahum

Nahum is telling the people in Nineveh (the capital of Assyria) that God will punish them. They are enemies of Israel and Judah. And they have hurt God's people and people from other countries too. Now God is going to punish them for all the wrong things that they have done. Until now, he has been very patient. We can read about that in the book of Jonah. But now he is very angry with the people in Nineveh.

Chapter 1

1 Nahum lives in Elkosh and this is his prophecy about the people in Nineveh.

2 God is angry with the people in Nineveh. The LORD loves his people. But he is very angry with his enemies. He is so angry with them that he must punish them. He will be angry until he has killed his enemies. 3 The LORD will punish those who do wrong things. But he does not get angry quickly. He is a powerful God. The LORD does not get angry quickly. But he gets angry when people do wrong things. Then he punishes those people.

He is very powerful. You can see his power in the whirlwind and in the storm. A man moves small bits of dirt when he walks. The clouds are like that to God. 4 He can cause the sea and the rivers to become dry by one word. The fertile places of Bashan and Carmel become dry and the green forests of Lebanon die too. 5He causes the mountains to shake and he causes the hills to become flat. The earth and all the people in the world are afraid of God.

6 Nobody can fight God when he is very angry. The LORD pours his anger out like fire and he breaks the rocks in his path. 7 The LORD loves those who believe him. When they are in trouble, they can put their hope in God. 8 But the people in Nineveh are his enemies and he will kill them. 9 The LORD will stop their plans against him at once. 10 He will kill them. And then it will be like when thorny bushes have caught people. Or it will be like they have drunk too much alcohol. It will be like when someone burns very dry stubble. 11 The LORD tells the king of Nineveh that he has done bad things against God. And the king has told his people that they should do wrong things.

12 The LORD has said, 'The people in Nineveh are many. And they think that they are safe. But I will kill them. I have punished you, my people, before now but now I will stop punishing you. 13 Now I will make you free from the people from Nineveh. And I will break the things that are holding you like iron.'

14 Nineveh, the LORD has said what will happen to you. He has said, 'You will have no children and your family name will have an end. I will destroy the statues that you made out of wood and metal. You worship those statues in your temples. There I will make graves for you because you are bad.'

15 People in Judah, look at the mountains. You will see the feet of the person who will bring good news. He causes peace. You can have religious parties now. And now you can do what you promised to me. The bad people will not win a war against you because I have killed them.

Chapter 2

1 An enemy is going to attack you, people in Nineveh. Watch the fortress. Prepare your army to defend the city. Watch the road. Get ready.

2 Armies have destroyed the countries called Israel and Jacob. They have destroyed their grape plants. But, the LORD will make Israel and Jacob great again.

3 The soldiers have red shields and bright red clothes. The soldiers move their spears in their hands very fast. The metal on their chariots is very bright. 4 When the soldiers are ready for war they move fast through the streets. Their chariots move like torches with fire and lightning. 5 The king of Nineveh chooses his best soldiers but they fall on the way. They hurry to their city wall to prepare their defences. 6 But their enemies open the river gates. Then the water goes into the city and it destroys the palace. 7 The enemy tells its soldiers that they must take the idol from Nineveh. Her women cry like doves and they hit their breasts.

8 Nineveh is like a pool. Its people run like water that is going away. 'Stop, stop!' they shout, but nobody comes back.

9 Take the silver. Take the gold. The city has so many valuable things.

10 They take the valuable things from the city. They take everything that they can. And they destroy everything else. The people are very sad. Their knees and their bodies shake. Their faces become white because they are afraid. 11 The home of the lions has gone. The place where they fed their young lions has gone. This was the place where the lion and the lioness went. It is here where their young lions were not afraid. 12 The lion killed to give enough food to his young lions and he strangled animals to feed his female lion. He filled his home with the animals that he had killed.

13 The LORD says, 'I am against you. I will burn your chariots and the sword will kill your young lions. I will take away all the animals that you attack. Nobody will hear the voices of your messengers.'

Chapter 3

1 You will have many troubles Nineveh, city of blood, full of lies and stolen valuable things. 2 Listen to the loud noises of the whips, the chariots, the wheels and the feet of the horses. The chariots are moving fast towards Nineveh. 3 See the bright swords and spears in the hands of the horses' riders. There are dead bodies that are lying in the streets. It is like mountains of dead bodies everywhere. There are so many dead bodies that men fall over the bodies. 4 This is because Nineveh has sold herself to the enemies of God. She is like a beautiful prostitute. She uses her body and her bad magic to make all the people in other countries her slaves.

5 This is why I am against you, says the great LORD. I will make you like a woman whose skirt is up over her face. I will show the countries that you are like that woman. You will be like a woman who is not wearing any clothes. 6 I will throw garbage at you. I will do with you like you were nothing. And I will make everyone ashamed of you. 7 When people see you, they will run away. And they will say, 'They have destroyed Nineveh. Nobody will be sad.' There will be nobody to help you.

8 Remember the city called Thebes that was near the River Nile. It had water on all sides and it had the river like a wall. Nineveh is not better than Thebes was. 9 The countries called Cush and Egypt were strong friends. And Put and Libya were strong friends too.

10 But the enemies of Thebes took its people away and they made them slaves. They cut their babies to pieces in every street. They played games with the great men from Thebes and they put them in iron chains. 11 You will be like a man who has drunk too much alcohol. And you will try to hide. You will try to get help from your enemy. 12 All your fortresses are like fig trees. They will fall very easily when the enemies shake them. And your valuable things will be like figs that fall into people's mouths. 13 Look at your soldiers, they are all like women! Your enemies have burned your gates and they have pushed them wide open.

14 Take as much water as you can for the attack. Make your defences strong. Do repairs to your buildings. 15 The fire will burn you. The sword will cut you and it will kill you like grasshoppers. Grow in number like the grasshoppers and locusts.

16 You welcomed sellers into your city until there were more than all the stars in the sky. But they are like locusts. They take everything from the land and then they fly away. 17 Your army and officials are so many that they are like locusts. Locusts stay on the walls on a cold day. But when the sun comes out, they fly away. And then nobody knows where they go.

18 King of Assyria, the people who keep your people safe are asleep. Also, your powerful men are lying down to rest. Your people have run away to the mountains with nobody to get them together.

19 Your wounds will kill you. They are too bad to make better. People have heard about what happened to you. Everyone who has heard about it is very happy. They are so happy that they clap their hands. This is because you have done bad things to all of them.

Do Not Be Afraid

Habakkuk

About this book

Habakkuk lived about 600 years BC. He lived in the country called Judah. Here is a list of the kings of Judah at that time:

640 - 639: Amon

639 - 609: Josiah

609: Jehoahaz

609 - 598: Jehoiakim

598: Jehoiachin

597 - 586: Zedekiah

The country that ruled that part of the world until 612 BC was Assyria. In 612 BC, a country called Babylon beat Assyria. Then the Babylonians ruled that part of the world. Both the Assyrians and the Babylonians loved and worshipped false gods. Habakkuk thought that the king and other leaders of the people in Judah did not rule well. Many leaders did bad things and nothing could stop them. These leaders did very cruel things to the people in Judah. These leaders did not obey the covenant that they had with God. A covenant is when two people or groups agree. Here the two are God and the people in Judah. God said that he would be kind to the people in Judah. They promised to love God and to obey him. But the leaders did not love and obey God. So, God said that he would punish Judah's people.

God chose the Babylonians to punish the leaders of Judah. The trouble was that they punished the people in Judah with the leaders. Starting in about 625 BC, Babylon had become a powerful country. They destroyed many countries and, in 612 BC, they destroyed Assyria. Then they destroyed Egypt in 605 BC. Then, in 586 BC, they destroyed Judah too. There is more about Assyria in our commentary on Nahum, Habakkuk and Zephaniah. That commentary is called 'The Problem of Assyria'.

Habakkuk could not understand why God had chosen the Babylonians. He knew that someone must punish Judah. But he did not know why it should be the Babylonians. The Babylonians were very bad and cruel people. The Babylonians loved and worshipped false gods. In his book, Habakkuk talks to God:

· In chapter 1, he asks God a question. Would God ever answer when Habakkuk prayed to him?

· In chapter 2, he waits for God's answer. God says that he will punish the Babylonians later. The whole world would see what God would do.

· In chapter 3, we read something else. Habakkuk believes that God will punish the Babylonians. And he believes that God will make Judah safe.

The Story of Habakkuk

We know very little about Habakkuk. The name means 'he who holds somebody close to him'. Bible students think that he lived about 600 BC.

This was a very important time for the Jews. After the kings called Saul, David and Solomon, their country became two countries. The north part was called Israel. The south part was called Judah. About 720 BC, the Assyrians destroyed the north part. That was because Israel's people did not obey God's rules. But the south part did not think that this would happen to them. They too did not obey God's rules. And Habakkuk said that it **would** happen to them. He was right. In 586 BC, the Babylonians destroyed Jerusalem. They took the people away to Babylon. We call this 'the exile'.

Habakkuk had two problems:

1) In Judah, many people did not obey God's rules. Habakkuk did not understand why God did not make them obey him (Habakkuk 1:2-4).

2) God told Habakkuk about something that he would do. But Habakkuk did not think that it was possible. He did not understand how God could use wicked people (like the Babylonians) to punish Judah's people. Judah's people were not as wicked as the Babylonians! (See Habakkuk 1:12-17.)

God still has authority today. It may not always seem to us that he has authority. But we must believe that he does have it. Then we say that we are 'living by faith'. Habakkuk 2:4 says, 'righteous people will live by their faith in God'.

That means two things:

· They will continue to believe that God will help them.

· After they die on this earth, they will live with God.

At the end of his book, Habakkuk writes a psalm. A psalm is a song with music. In it, he praises God. He also says this: Whatever happens, he will still praise God. That is the message of Habakkuk: God knows what he is doing. But he does not always do what we might want him to do. **But, whatever happens, praise God!**

Chapter 1

1 These are the important words that Habakkuk the prophet received (from God).

Habakkuk has a problem

2 LORD, how long must I cry to you for help and you will not listen? How long must I shout aloud to you, 'Violence!' and you do not make us safe?

3 Why do you cause me to see things that are not right? Why do you let people do what is wrong? People destroy things and there is violence everywhere. People argue and fight a lot.

4 So the law can do nothing and justice never wins. There is a circle of very, very bad people round the righteous people and judges give the wrong answers.

The LORD answers

5 'Look at other countries and watch. You will become very, very surprised because of the things that I will do during your lifetime. And you will not believe it. You will not believe it even when I tell you about it!

6 I will make the Babylonians strong. They will be cruel and they will do things fast and without thought. They will go across the whole earth. And they will take homes that are not theirs.

7 People will be afraid of them. They will really frighten people. The Babylonians will make their own rules and they will write their own laws.

8 Their horses will run faster than leopards. And they will be more cruel than wolves in the night. Their men on horses will ride fast (and they will frighten people). The riders on horses will come from far away. They will fly as vultures that hurry to eat something.

9 They will all come for violence. Large crowds of them will come like a wind in the places where there is a lot of sand. They will put as many people into prisons as there are bits of sand in those places.

10 They will say things that are not kind about kings. And they will say that the leaders of the people are silly. They will know that city walls will not keep them out. They will build earth as high as the walls and they will get into each city.

11 Then they will rush past like the wind and they will go on to somewhere else. They will think that their own god has made them strong.'

Habakkuk has another problem

12 LORD, you have always been alive. You are my very holy God, so we will not die. LORD, you have given a job to the Babylonians. It is to bring justice to us. You are like our rock, but you have sent them to punish us.

13 But your eyes are too holy to look at very bad men. You cannot look at anything that is wrong. So why do you let these bad men live? Why do you say nothing? These bad people are killing those who are better than them.

14 And you have made people like fishes in the sea. You have made them like animals that move with no rulers.

15 The Babylonians will catch all of them, with the hooks that they use to fish with. They will catch them in their fishing nets and they will put them in their special holding nets. This makes the Babylonians very happy and it gives a lot of pleasure to them.

16 So they give sacrifices to their nets and they burn incense to their special holding nets. They do that because they catch a lot of fish in their nets. And so they have the best food.

17 So will they pour fish out of their net always? Will they destroy countries without mercy?

Chapter 2

Habakkuk waits for an answer

1 I will stand and I will watch. I will stay on the walls (of the city). I will look to see what God will say to me. And I will see what answer I will have for my problem.

The LORD answers

2 Then the LORD replied to me. And he said, 'Write down what I will show to you. Make it very clear on the page where you write it. Then the runner can tell people all about it.

3 What I will show to you must wait for the proper time. But at that time, it will happen. It will happen as I have said. It may not happen for a long time but wait for it. It will certainly happen and it will not be late.

4 Look, the Babylonians are proud. The things that they want are not good. But righteous people will live by their faith in God.

5 And also, wine will destroy Babylon. Yes, they are proud and they never stop taking things from people. They never have enough, as Sheol and death never have enough. They take people from all countries for themselves and they take people from everywhere.

6 The people in all those countries will write a song that is against Babylon. They will say that its people are silly. And they will say other bad things about it. They will say, "Some people rob other people. And they keep what they take. A sad time will come to those people. Some people get a lot of money by the very bad things that they do. A sad time will come to those people. They will not always be able to do those things."

7 The people that you people in Babylon have taken things from will wake up. It will happen when you are not thinking about it! They will get up and they will make you afraid. Then you will be the people that they will rob!

8 You have robbed many countries. So the people who remain will rob you. That is because you have killed people. And you have destroyed their towns and their lands. You have killed everyone who lived there.

9 Some people get things for themselves by ways that are not fair. A sad time will come to those people. You build your homes high up so that nobody can take you to do bad things to you.

10 You decided to kill the people from many countries. Because of that, you will be ashamed. And you will pay with your own life.

11 Even the stones in the walls will cry. The beams that you made from wood will do it as well.

12 A man might build a city because he kills people. A man might make a town great because he has been very bad. A sad time will come to that man.

13 The work that people do will go into the fire. The LORD of everything has decided that it will. People in many countries will make themselves tired for nothing!

14 But the earth will become filled with people who know about the glory of the LORD. This will be as the waters cover the sea.

15 A sad time will come to him who gives strong drink to his neighbours. He pours out wine until they are drunk. Then he looks at them when they have no clothes on!

16 You will be really ashamed. Nobody will think that you are great. Then you will drink and people will see you with no clothes on! The cup in the LORD's right hand will come round to you. You will be ashamed. You will not always be great.

17 The violence that you did to Lebanon will cover you. You will be very frightened because you killed animals. And you have killed people. And you have destroyed their towns and their lands. You have also killed everyone who lived there.

18 An idol cannot do anything. It was a man who made it! It is a copy of a false god. It teaches him things that are not true. That is because he is trusting his own work. He has made idols that cannot speak!

19 It will be very bad for someone who says to a piece of wood, "Wake up!" He says to a stone that cannot speak, "Get up and be my guide!" Look at it! It has gold and silver over it but it is not alive.

20 But the LORD is in his holy temple. Everything in the world should be quiet in front of him.'

Chapter 3

Habakkuk prays

1 These are the words that the prophet Habakkuk prayed. He used music called Shigionoth.

2 LORD, I have heard what people say about you. I see the things that you have done, LORD. Then I am afraid. But do them again now. Cause people to know what you can do in our lifetime. You are angry, but still remember mercy!

3 God came from Teman. The Holy God came from the mountain called Paran.

Selah

His glory covered the skies and his praise filled the earth.

4 He was as bright as the sunrise. Light fell from his hands, where he hid his great power.

5 Plague went in front of him and pestilence followed his feet.

6 (God) stood and he caused the earth to shake. He looked and countries were afraid. Old mountains broke into rocks and very old hills fell down. That always happens everywhere that he goes!

7 I saw the places where Cushan lived. The people there were not happy. The people who live in the houses of Midian were afraid.

8 I do not think that you were angry with the streams and rivers, LORD! You rode through the sea with horses and chariots! But I do not think that you were angry with the sea. You did that to win the fight.

9 You showed people your bow and you asked for many arrows.

Selah

You cut the earth into pieces with rivers.

10 The mountains saw you and they shook. Deep waters moved very fast. The sea made a loud noise and it lifted its waters high.

11 The sun and the moon stopped moving in the skies. The light from your arrows that were flying past and the light from your shining spear stopped them.

12 You marched through the country because you were angry. Because you were so angry, you hit the people in many countries with your stick.

13 You went out to make your people safe. You went out to save the person whom you have anointed. You beat the leader of the wicked country. You took away his clothes from head to foot.

Selah

14 You, LORD, pushed your own spear into his head. You did that when his soldiers came out to fight us. They were laughing when they came out to kill the poor people. The poor people were hiding from them.

15 You marched through the sea with your horses. You shook the waters.

16 I listened and my heart was afraid. My lips shook at the sound. My bones began to fall into pieces. My legs would not stop moving. But I will be patient. And I will wait for the very bad days that will come. They will come to the people who are attacking us.

17 There may be:

- no flowers on the fig tree

- no fruit on the vines

- nothing on the trees that have fruits called olives

- no food in the fields

- no sheep in the hills

- no cows on the farms

18 but I will still sing praises to the LORD! I will be happy with the God that makes me safe.

19 The LORD, who is my master, will make me safe. He makes my feet like the feet of a deer so that I can climb mountains.

The music leader must use things that have strings to make music.

Your God Will Sing

Zephaniah

About the Book of Zephaniah

> Zephaniah was a man who knew God. He was a prophet. He lived when Josiah was king of God's people. These were the people who lived in Judah.
>
> Zephaniah wrote this book between the years 630 and 625 B.C. (B.C. means 'before Christ lived on earth'.) The book is in three parts. In Chapter 1, Zephaniah told the people in Judah that God would punish them. In Chapter 2, Zephaniah was speaking to people in many countries. These were the countries on every side of Judah. He told them that God was angry with them. He also told them that God would punish them. Chapter 3 is another message to the people in Judah.
>
> At that time, the prophet Jeremiah also was giving God's messages to the people in Judah. Both prophets (Zephaniah and Jeremiah) said that God loved his people in Judah. But these prophets taught that God was also angry. The people had done what God does not like. That is why God was angry. God did not want to punish his people. He wanted to be kind to them. But he told them that they must stop doing wrong things. They should love him again. If they continued to love false gods, God would certainly punish them.
>
> King Josiah was a good man. He listened to the prophets. He punished the false prophets. He took away the false gods that they had made out of wood or stone or metal. He also broke down the special tables of stone on which they burned gifts to God (sacrifices). That was because they did it in the wrong place or in the wrong way.
>
> Some people in Judah listened to the prophets. Those people loved God. But many people did not listen. So about 40 years after that, God sent the army of Babylon to destroy Jerusalem. Jerusalem was the city where the Temple (God's holy house) was. Babylon was an important city in another country. This happened in the year 586 B.C. Four more kings had ruled Judah after Josiah.
>
> The people from Babylon began to take Judah's people away from their homes to Babylon. In that way, God punished Judah's people. They had done what God does not like. So he punished them. But God had not finished with his people. He had said that his people would return to Judah at some time. Then the people would really love God and they would obey him. This will happen at the future time when God is king of the whole world. Then there will be a good and happy time.

Chapter 1

1 This is the LORD's message, which he gave to Zephaniah, Cushi's son. Cushi's father was Gedaliah. Gedaliah's father was Amariah, and Amariah's father was Hezekiah. The LORD gave this message to Zephaniah when Josiah was king. Josiah was the son of Amon, who was the king of Judah.

2 'It is the LORD who is speaking now.

I will remove everything from the ground.

3 I will remove men and animals.

I will remove the birds that fly in the air.

I will also remove the fish that live in the sea.

I will remove all the bad people.

Bad people cause trouble for other people.

Yes, I will remove all the people from the ground.

It is the LORD who is speaking.

4 I will destroy Judah.

I will remove all the people who live in Jerusalem.

I will remove all those who believe in the false god Baal.

I will remove Baal's priests.

5 Some people stand on the roof tops to worship the sun, the moon and the stars. I will remove those people.

Some people say that they love me. But they say also that they love Malcam (a false god). So I will remove them, too.'

6 'I will remove those who have turned away from the LORD.

I will also remove those who decide things without the LORD.

7 Be quiet! God, the LORD is here.

It will soon be the day of the LORD.

The LORD has made his sacrifice ready.

He has made the people ready who will give the sacrifice to him.'

8 'When it is time for the LORD's sacrifice, I will punish the rulers and the king's sons.

I will punish the people who wear heathen clothes, too.'

9 'I will also punish the people who rush into other people's houses. They do that because they want to rob those people.

On that same day, I will also punish other robbers. Those people fill their masters' houses with the things that they take.'

10 'On that day', says the LORD, 'you will hear the noise of people who are shouting from one gate of the city. It is the gate called Fish Gate.

And there will be sad sounds from the next gate.

There will be loud noises from the hills.

11 Shout out, you who live in Maktesh! Weep!

The LORD will remove those who do business in your town.

Some people have lots of money there. But all those people will be dead then.'

12 'At that time,

I will look in all Jerusalem's dark corners. I will take lights with me.

I will find the drunks and I will punish them. These people say in their minds,

"The LORD will do neither good things nor bad things to us."

13 So I will take away from them everything that they have.

I will take away their houses also.

They will build houses, but they will never live in them.

They will plant plants to get grapes. But they will never have wine from them.'

14 The time for the great day of the LORD is soon, very soon.

It will happen quickly.

Strong men will weep when they hear the noise of it.

15 The LORD will be very angry at that time.

It will be a time when there will be trouble.

On that day, he will destroy everything bad.

It will be very dark. At that time, there will be thick dark clouds.

16 At that time, people will make a noise with trumpets. They will shout when they go to fight in a war.

In the fight, they will try to destroy the strong walls of cities.

And they will try to destroy the strong high parts of the walls.

17 I will cause trouble for people.

So they will walk like people who cannot see.

This is because they have not obeyed the LORD.

Their blood will fall to the ground.

Yes, they will fall to the ground and they will die. After that, they will be nothing.

18 Their money will not save them

on the day when the LORD is angry.

He watches.

And he is angry when his people love other gods.

So, he will send fire on the earth.

Yes, he will quickly kill all the people who live in Judah.

Chapter 2

1 Come together!

Yes, you people, come together and think.

You do not know how to be ashamed!

2-3 The wind takes away the dry parts of a plant that covered the seed.

It will be like that when I punish you.

Before it is the time for me to punish you, look for me.

Before this time is past, look for me.

Look for me, before I become very, very angry with you.

There will be a day when God will be angry. Look for me, before that day.

Yes, look for the LORD, all you people who want to make him happy.

You have done what the LORD wants.

Continue to do what is good.

But do not think that you are great.

Perhaps you will find a safe place

on the day when God is angry.

4 Then, the people who have lived in Gaza city and Ashkelon city will not be there.

Enemies will also send away the people in Ashdod city at midday. And those enemies will destroy Ekron city.

5 It will be very bad for you people called Cherethites, who live by the sea!

The LORD's message is against you.

I will also kill all you people called Philistines, who live in the country called Canaan!

You will all die. So nobody will live there.

6 By the sea, there will be houses for people who feed sheep.

There will be safe places for their sheep.

7 Those people in Judah who love God will live there, by the sea.

They will have food there.

They will lie down to sleep in Ashkelon city's houses.

The LORD, their God, will be with them.

He will stop their troubles.

8 The LORD of all his armies says, 'I have heard the cruel people in the countries called Moab and Ammon.

They laugh about you and they say cruel things about you, my people.

They have thought that they were greater than you.

They have come against you.'

9 The LORD of all his armies,

the God of Israel, says,

'You can be sure that I live.

In the same way, you can also be sure that my people will take everything.

It will be theirs to keep.

God will destroy Moab as he destroyed Sodom.

He will destroy Ammon as he destroyed Gomorrah.

After this, the ground will have lots of salt on it. Weeds will grow there.

Nobody will build anything there again.

The small number of my people that enemies have not killed will have Ammon's peoples' things and Moab's peoples' things.'

10 That will happen to all proud people.

The proud people said cruel words to God's people.

The cruel people thought that they were greater than the people of the LORD of all his armies.

11 The LORD will make them afraid.

He will destroy all the false gods.

People will worship him instead. Every person, in his own place, will worship God.

They will also worship him in the places where the people now believe in false gods.

12 'I will also punish you people in the country called Ethiopia.

Other people will kill you with a big knife', the LORD says.

13 The LORD will go against the north.

There, he will destroy the country called Assyria.

He will also destroy Nineveh city. That place will become only dry sand.

14 Sheep will lie down there.

All the wild animals of that place will live together there.

Vultures and owls will rest on top of the high, thin parts of the buildings.

They will sing in the windows.

Bits of doors will lie on the ground.

The LORD will tear down all the things in the houses that they have made out of dear wood.

15 All this will happen to that city, the proud city.

That city's people said in their minds,

'Here we are. We are greater than all the other people.'

But then, other people will destroy their city! Only bits of it will still be there.

Then wild animals will come and they will lie down in it. People will see this.

So, any people who pass by the city will make noises with their lips.

And they will hold their fists up. In this way, they will show that they think bad things about the city.

Chapter 3

1 It will be very bad for the city!

It is like something that is dirty.

Its people will not obey me. They like to fight weak people. They also like to do bad things.

2 They do not listen to anyone's voice.

They accept no correction.

They do not trust in the LORD.

They do not come near to their God.

3 The rulers of the city make a very loud noise with their voices like big wild animals.

Its judges are like hungry wolves.

They are like wolves that have even eaten all an animal's bones before morning.

4 Its prophets do not know what to think.

People cannot trust them.

Its priests have done wrong things,

even in God's holy house.

They have also made changes to God's rules.

They have made changes that they want.

5 But the LORD is among all the people in the city.

He will do what is right.

He is always the honest judge.

He never fails.

But the bad people do not know how to be ashamed.

6 'I have destroyed nations', the LORD says.

'There is nobody in their strong towers now.

I have made their streets empty, so no people are there.

I have destroyed their cities.

So, nobody lives in them now.

7 I said, "I hope that the people in the city will obey me.

Accept correction."

The people would have been safe if they had accepted it.

Then I would not have to destroy them.

But it did not happen. I had to punish them.

Still, the people got up early to do bad things.'

8 'So wait for me', says the LORD.

'I will stand up and I will punish the nations.

I have decided to bring together the nations and the people that kings rule over.

Then I will punish them very, very much.

They will see how angry I am.

They will see it because, on that day, I will burn all the earth.

9 Then I will give to people lips that I have made pure.

With those lips, they will call me LORD.

And then, all the people will agree to work together for me.'

10 'Some people live a long way beyond the rivers of Ethiopia.

Yes, my people who pray went away to many other countries.

They will return and they will carry their gifts to me.

11 At that time, you will not have to be ashamed

of the wrong things that you have done against me.

But I will take away those who do not see anything wrong in themselves.

Those people will not call each other

"the people who live on God's holy mountain".

12 But I will let the poor people remain there.

These are the people who have had bad times.

These are the people who will trust me. And they will call me LORD.

13 I will let those people stay there.

They will not do any bad things.

They will only say things that are true.

They will say honest things.

They will eat well and they will sleep well.

Nobody will make them afraid.'

14 Sing, you people in Zion. You are my own people, like my own daughter.

Shout, you people in Israel!

Be very, very happy, my people in Jerusalem!

15 The LORD has not punished you as he would have done.

He has sent your enemy away.

I, the King of Israel, am with you!

The bad times have gone.

They will not happen again!

16 On that special day, this will be my message for Jerusalem.

'Do not be afraid now! Do not be weak now!

17 The LORD, your God, is with you.

He is strong. He will save you.

He will be very happy about you!

He will quietly love you.

He will sing, because he is so happy about you!

18 I will bring together those people among you who want to meet together again.

You want to meet again to pray. And you want to meet again to praise God.

You have had enough cruel words from your enemies.

19 Look! At that time, I will punish

all those people who hurt you.

I will save those who cannot walk well.

I will bring back the people that the enemy has sent away.

I will cause people in every country to know about you. I will cause them to praise you.

20 At that time, I will bring you back to your home.

I will bring you back together.

I will give you a good name among all the people on the earth.

That is what I will do. I will stop your troubles. And you will see it happen.'

That is what the LORD says.

Build God's Special Building Now

Haggai

About this book

> The Jews were people that God chose to be his special people. But the Jews forgot God and they did not obey him. And so God sent them to live as slaves in a country called Babylon. After 60 years, they returned to their own country. Even then, they forgot God. But he sent Haggai to speak to them. This book is about the message that God gave to Haggai for them. And it is about what the people did after that.

Chapter 1

1-2 Darius was a king. He was the king of a country called Persia. He had been king for 1 year and 5 months. On the first day of the next month, the Lord Almighty spoke to Haggai. (Haggai was a prophet of the Lord.) This is what the Lord said. 'Everyone says that this is not the right time to build a temple for me.' The Lord told Haggai that he must speak to the ruler of Judah and to the high priest. The ruler was called Zerubbabel. (His father was called Shealtiel.) The high priest was called Joshua. (His father was called Jehozadak.) 3 So Haggai, the prophet, told Zerubbabel and Joshua what the Lord had said.

4 This was the Lord's message. 'You seem to think that it is right for you to live in expensive houses. But you still have not built my temple. 5 But think about what has happened to you. 6 You plant seeds but not many plants grow. You never have enough food to eat. You drink but you are still thirsty. You put on clothes but your clothes do not keep you warm. And the money that you get for all your work is not enough. It is like when you put your money into pockets with holes in them. 7 Think about what has happened to you!

8 And now, get wood from the hills to build my temple again. I want to look at my temple with pleasure. I want people to worship me there. 9 You thought that many food plants would grow in your fields. But only a few plants grew and that disappointed you. And when you brought your food to your home, I destroyed it. You may ask why I have done this. I did it because your first thought was to build your own houses. But your first thought should have been to build my temple again. And you have not done anything about that. 10 That is why your fields are dry. That is why your plants do not grow. 11 I have stopped the rains so that nothing will grow. Your plants will not grow. Your cows will not have enough grass to eat. Your vines and your olive trees will have only a little fruit. No young animals will be born. And you will not have any children. For all your work, you will get nothing.'

12 Some years before this, the people had returned to live in their own country. Zerubbabel and Joshua had returned with them. (Zerubbabel was Shealtiel's son. Joshua was the high priest and he was Jehozadak's son.) Now everyone heard the message that Haggai brought to them from the Lord. They were afraid because of what Haggai told them. And they all decided to obey the Lord their God and to worship him. 13 Haggai was the Lord's prophet. This was Haggai's message from the Lord: '"I am with you", says the Lord.' 14 So the Lord changed what Zerubbabel and Joshua and the people thought. Soon, all the people wanted to build the temple for the Lord. Zerubbabel and Joshua, too, wanted to build the temple. (Zerubbabel was the ruler of Judah and he was Shealtiel's son. Joshua was the high priest and he was Jehozadak's son.) They all came and they worked at the temple of the Lord Almighty, their God. 15 And so the work began on the 24th day of that same month. Darius had been king for more than 1 year and 5 months.

Chapter 2

1 On the 21st day of the next month, the Lord spoke to Haggai, the prophet. 2 The Lord told Haggai that he must speak to Zerubbabel and to Joshua. (Zerubbabel was Shealtiel's son and he was the ruler of Judah. Joshua was the high priest and he was Jehozadak's son.) The Lord also told Haggai that he must speak to all the people. This was the message that the Lord sent:

3 'Some of the people will remember that my temple was once very beautiful. You think that it is really not beautiful now. 4 But now, be strong and brave, Zerubbabel! And be strong and brave, Joshua, high priest, son of Jehozadak! And be strong and brave, all you people in this country, and work! Work because I am with you', says the Lord Almighty. 5 'A long time ago, my people returned to their own country from Egypt. I promised them then that I would be with them. And I was with them. I will be with you, too. So, do not be afraid. And do not think that the work will be too difficult for you. My Spirit will stay here among you.

6 Soon, people will see that I am a powerful God. Soon, I will cause the skies and the earth to move. I will cause the sea and the land to move. 7 I will cause people in many countries to be afraid. They will come to your country and they will bring with them valuable gifts. And I will make my temple beautiful', says the Lord Almighty. 8 'All the silver and gold in the world is mine', says the Lord Almighty. 9 'I promise that this new temple will be more beautiful than the old temple. People will see my temple. And then they will know that I am a great God. I will also make this city a place where there is peace', says the Lord Almighty.

10 Darius had been king for 1 year and 8 months and 23 days. Then the Lord Almighty spoke to Haggai the
prophet again. 11 The Lord Almighty told Haggai that he must ask the priests a question about God's rules. 12 This was the question. 'A person might be carrying some meat in his clothes. It is meat that he wants to give to God as a sacrifice. His clothes might touch some food. It might be bread. Or it might be food that he has cooked. It might be wine or oil. Or it might be some other food. Would the food that his clothes had touched become holy?' The priests replied, 'No.'

13 Haggai asked the priests another question. 'If you touch a dead person, you become not holy. You know that. If you then touch any of these foods, would they become not holy?' The priests replied, 'Yes, they would.'

14 So Haggai answered, 'That is how I thought about all the people in this country', says the Lord. 'I was angry about all the things that you had done. I did not accept your sacrifices. 15 You have now started to build the Lord's temple again. Try to remember what life was like before that. 16 You wanted 20 pots of grain. But you found that there were only 10 pots. You wanted 50 jars of wine. But you found that there were only 20 jars. 17 I sent bad weather and I destroyed all your work. And the things that you picked from your fields were not good to eat. So you had to waste them. But you still did not return to me. And you did not say that I was your Lord. 18 Today, the 24th day of the 9th month, you have started to build my temple. Now this is what will happen to you: 19 You have not yet picked any seeds or grapes. You have not yet picked
any figs or pomegranates. You have not yet picked any olives. But after today, I will be good to you. So then you will have as much as you need of all these things.'

20 On the same day, the 24th day of the month, the Lord spoke to Haggai again. This is what he said. 21 'Speak to Zerubbabel, who is the ruler of Judah. Tell him that I will because the skies and the earth to move. 22 tell him that I will remove foreign kings. And I will destroy their countries. I will destroy their chariots. And I will kill the soldiers who ride in them. The soldiers who ride on horses will start to kill each other. And they will kill each other's horses. 23 But I am the Lord Almighty and you, Zerubbabel, son of Shealtiel are my servant. I have chosen you. And so, on that day, I will cause you to be like my special ring. I will keep you safe. And you will rule this country for me', says the Lord Almighty.

God's Servant who is called The Branch

Zechariah

About this book

> The enemies of the Jews took them to a country called Babylon. After 70 years, the king of Babylon let the Jews return to Israel to build the temple again. Zechariah was one of those Jews. He lived 520 years before Jesus was born. The Lord told Zechariah what to say to God's people in Israel. We can say that an important part of his message was, 'If you return to me, I will return to you.' The Lord gave Zechariah 8 dreams. These dreams from the Lord showed Israel's people what would happen in future years.
> The Lord would bless them and he would fight against their enemies. The last chapters tell that Jesus will come back to be king of all the earth.

Chapter 1

Return to the Lord

1 Zechariah the prophet heard a message from the Lord. He heard this when Darius had been king for two years. It was the 8th month of the year. Zechariah was the son of Berechiah and Berechiah was the son of Iddo.

2 The Lord told Zechariah to say to the people,

'I, the Lord, was very angry with your fathers and their fathers. 3 Now I, the Lord Almighty, say this to you, "If you return to me, I will return to you." 4 Do not be like your fathers. Many years ago the prophets gave them a message from me. The message was, "Stop doing those things that are wrong." They did not listen to me. And they did not think that my words were important.

5 Your fathers and their prophets have been dead for a long time. 6 I told my servants the prophets that they should say my words. They continued to say my words until my words made your fathers sorry. I had done to your fathers what I promised to do. They knew that. They said that they were very sorry.'

The man on the red horse

7 Shebat is the name of the 11th month. On the 24th day of Shebat, the Lord spoke to Zechariah the prophet. This was when Darius had been king for two years.

8 During the night I, Zechariah, had a dream from the Lord. I saw a man on a red horse. The horse was standing among some trees called myrtle trees, in the valley. And behind him were red, brown and white horses.

9 I asked him, 'My lord, what are these horses?' The angel who talked with me said, 'I will show you what they are.'

10 The man who was standing among the trees answered. 'The Lord has sent these horses to go to all the places on the earth.'

11 And the horses spoke to the angel of the Lord who stood among the trees. They said, 'We have gone all over the earth. All the earth is without trouble.'

12 Then the angel of the Lord said, 'Oh Lord Almighty, how long will you be angry with Jerusalem? How long will you be angry against the cities of Judah? You have already been angry for 70 years.' 13 And the Lord answered the angel with kind words.

14 The angel said to me, 'Tell this to the people. This is what the Lord Almighty says: "I love Jerusalem. Jerusalem is mine. 15 I am very angry with the countries that are safe and without danger. Those countries were too cruel to my people, when I was only a little angry with Jerusalem." 16 So, this is what the Lord says: "I will return to Jerusalem to be kind to the people there. I will build my house again", says the Lord Almighty, "and I will build the city again." '

17 The angel told me that I must say this: 'The Lord Almighty says, "My towns will be rich again. I will again speak kind words to Jerusalem. I will choose Jerusalem again as my own city." '

Four horns and four good workers

18 And I looked up and I saw four horns. 19 And I asked the angel that talked with me, 'What are these horns?' Then the angel said to me, 'These are the strong enemies of my people. They took my people out of Judah, out of Israel and out of Jerusalem.'

20 Then the Lord showed me four workers with hammers. 21 I said, 'What are these men coming to do?' The Lord answered, 'The horns are the enemies that destroyed Judah. They destroyed Judah so that they will all be ashamed. The workers came to frighten and to destroy the enemies because they killed many of my people. The enemies took many of my people out of Judah.'

Chapter 2

The dream about Jerusalem that God gave to Zechariah

1 Then I looked up and I saw a man in front of me. He had a line in his hand. The line was to measure something. 2 Then I said, 'Where are you going?' He said to me, 'I am going to measure Jerusalem. I want to see how broad and how long it is.' 3 The angel that talked with me went away. Another angel came to meet him. 4 The second angel said to the first angel, 'Run to that young man with the line in his hand. Say that Jerusalem will be a city without walls. This is because of the many people and many animals that will live in it.

5 The Lord himself promises that he will be like a wall of fire round Jerusalem. He will shine as a beautiful light inside the city.'

The Lord will be among his people

6 'Come! Come! Run away from the country in the north', says the Lord. 'As the four winds blow in different directions, I sent you to many far countries.

7 Come, my people. Run away from Babylon and return to Jerusalem.' 8 Return because the Lord says, 'Anyone that attacks you is attacking the Lord's people. He is attacking the people that the Lord loves.' So the Lord Almighty sent me, Zechariah, with this message about the countries that have robbed his people. 9 'The Lord himself will fight against your enemies and their own slaves will rob them. Then you will know that the Lord Almighty has sent me, Zechariah, to you.'

10 'Sing and be happy, you people in Jerusalem. This is because I will come. And I will live among you', says the Lord. 11 'On that day, the people from many countries will come to me, the Lord, and they will become my people. I will live among you. You will know that the Lord Almighty has sent me. 12 The Lord will choose Judah for himself again. Jerusalem will be the city that he loves most of all cities. 13 Be quiet, all people, because the Lord has left his home in heaven to come among you.'

Chapter 3

Clean clothes for Joshua the most important priest

1 Then the angel of the Lord appeared to me, Zechariah, and he showed me Joshua, the most important priest. Joshua was standing in front of the angel of the Lord. Satan stood on the right side of Joshua. He was ready to say that Joshua had done bad things. 2 The Lord said to Satan, 'The Lord says that you are wrong. The Lord has chosen Jerusalem. And he says that you are wrong. Joshua is certainly like a burning stick that someone pulls quickly out of the fire.'

3 Joshua was wearing very dirty clothes and he stood in front of the angel. 4 The angel said to the other angels that stood in front of him, 'Remove his very dirty clothes.' Then the first angel said to Joshua, 'See, I have taken away your sin. I will put the clothes on you that a priest should wear.'

5 Then Zechariah said, 'Put a clean hat on his head.' So, they put a clean hat on his head and they dressed him in clean clothes. The angel of the Lord stood near to them.

6 The angel of the Lord spoke to Joshua with these serious words. 7 'These are the words of the Lord Almighty. Listen to them and obey them. "You will rule in my house. You will rule inside the walls of my house. I will give you a place among the angels that are standing here.

8 Listen, Joshua, most important priest of the Lord. Listen you priests that sit with Joshua. You are like a sign. People can look at you. And they can know that good things will happen in future years. See! I will bring to you my servant who is called The Branch. 9 See the stone that I have put in front of Joshua! It is a stone with seven sides and I will cut words in the stone", says the Lord Almighty. "I will remove the sin of this country's people in one day." 10 "On that day", says the Lord Almighty, "each of you will ask your friends to come. You will ask them to come and to sit under your own vines and fig trees." '

Chapter 4

The burning lights and the olive trees

1 The angel that talked with me before woke me. I, Zechariah, was like a man who wakes out of his sleep. 2 The angel said to me, 'What do you see?' I said, 'I see a thing that someone has made out of gold. And it contains oil. The oil burns to make light. It has a dish on top of it. And it has seven things like branches that someone has made out of gold. Each branch has a burning light on top of it. 3 And two olive trees are standing by the burning lights. One tree is on the right of the lights and one tree is on the left of the lights.'

4 I, Zechariah, said to the angel that talked with me. 'What does this light mean, my lord?'

5 He said, 'Do you not know what these are?'

I said, 'No, my lord.'

6 Then the angel said to me, 'The Lord said this to Zerubbabel: "You will need my Spirit. You yourself are too weak. And you do not have enough power." This is what the Lord Almighty says: 7 "Big mountain, you are no problem. You will become flat ground in front of Zerubbabel. Then he will bring out the last and biggest stone of my house. The people will shout, 'God bless it! God bless it!' " '

8 Then the Lord's message came to me, Zechariah. He said, 9 'Zerubbabel has put down the first stone of my house. He will also finish it.' Then you will know that the Lord Almighty has sent me to you.

10 Everyone should know that the day of small things is important.

Men will see Zerubbabel. Then they will sing and they will be happy. They will see him with a line in his hand to measure the walls.

The Lord sees everything in the whole earth. (The 7 lights are the 7 eyes of the Lord.)

11 Then I said to the angel, 'What are these two olive trees on the right and on the left of the light?'

12 A second time I spoke to the angel, 'What are these two branches of the olive trees? They are next to the pipes of gold and oil comes from those pipes.'

13 The angel replied, 'Do you not know what these olive trees mean?'

'No, my lord', I said.

14 So the angel said, 'These are the two men that the Lord of all the earth has chosen to be his servants.'

Chapter 5

Words for everyone to read

1 Again, I looked and I saw a large paper. It was moving through the air. There were many words on the paper.

2 The angel said to me, 'What do you see?' And I answered, 'I see a paper that is flying through the air. It is twice as long as it is wide. And it is as long as 5 men.'

3 Then the angel said to me, 'The words on the paper tell about bad events for the whole earth. This will be in future years. On one side of the paper, it says that a man must not rob anyone. If he does, people will send him away from his own country. On the other side of the paper, it says that a man must not speak false words. If he does, people will send him away from his own country. 4 The Lord Almighty says, "I will cause bad things to happen in the house of the man that robs anyone. I will cause bad things to happen in the house of the man that speaks false words. It is as if the words on the paper will destroy the houses of those bad people." '

The woman in the basket

5 Then the angel that talked to me came near to me. He said, 'Look. And see the thing that has just appeared.'

6 I said, 'What is it?'

He said, 'It is a basket that people measure with.' Then he said, 'It is the sin of all the people in this country.'

7 He lifted the heavy metal lid and there was a woman. She was sitting in the basket!

8 The angel said, 'This is sin.' He pushed her into the basket again and he put the heavy metal lid on top of the basket.

9 Then I looked up and I saw two women. They flew towards me with strong wings. The wind carried them as the wind carries large birds. They lifted the basket between the earth and the sky.

10 Then I said to the angel that talked with me, 'Where will these women take the basket?'

11 The angel said to me, 'They will take the basket to the country called Babylon. They will build a house for it there. When the house is ready, they will put the basket inside the house. They will put it where people can see it.'

Chapter 6

Four chariots

1 Again I looked up and I saw 4 chariots! They came out from between two mountains and the mountains were mountains of shining metal! 2 The first chariot had red horses and the second chariot had black horses. 3 The third chariot had white horses and the fourth chariot had grey horses. All the horses were strong. 4 Then I spoke to the angel that talked to me. 'What are these chariots, my lord?' I said.

5 The angel answered me, 'These are the 4 spirits of heaven. They have come from the Lord of the whole world. 6 The chariot with the black horses goes towards the North Country. The chariot with the white horses goes after them. The chariot with the grey horses goes towards the south country.'

7 When the strong horses came out, they were in a hurry to leave. The angel said, 'Go through all the earth.' So the horses went through all the earth.

8 Then the Lord told me, 'The chariot that goes to the North Country has caused my Spirit to rest in the north country. I am now no longer angry about the north country.'

A crown for Joshua

9 The Lord spoke to me.

10 'Three men have arrived from Babylon', he said. 'Their names are Heldai, Tobijah and Jedaiah. Take the gold that they have brought with them. On the same day, take the gold to the house of Josiah, the son of Zephaniah.

11 Take the gold and other valuable metal and make a crown. Put it on the head of Joshua the most important priest. He is the son of Jehozadak. 12 Say to Joshua, "The Lord Almighty says, 'I have chosen a man. His name is the Branch. He will be a great man and he will build the house of the Lord.

13 It is he who will build the house of the Lord. He will sit on his special high seat and he will rule all the people. He will be a priest on the seat of a king. This one man will be priest and king.' " 14 They will put the crown in the house of the Lord. This is to remember Heldai, Tobijah, Jedaiah and Hen the son of Zephaniah. This is because they brought the gold from Babylon.

15 People will come a long way and they will help to build the house of the Lord. Then you will know that the Lord Almighty has sent me to you. All this will happen if you completely obey the Lord your God.'

Chapter 7

God wants people to be fair and kind

1 The Lord spoke to Zechariah when Darius had been king for four years. It was the 4th day of the 9th month. The name of the month was Chislev. 2 Then the people in Bethel sent Sharezer and Regem-Melech and their men to Jerusalem. They came to ask the Lord to help them. 3 They came to the house of the Lord Almighty to speak to the priests and to the prophets. They asked, 'Should we cry and not eat our food in the 5th month? We have done this for many years.'

4 The Lord Almighty spoke to me, Zechariah. 5 He said, 'Say this to all the people in this country and to the priests. "You lived in Babylon for many years. You ate no food and you were sad in the 5th month and in the 7th month. But you did not do this for me. 6 You ate and you drank. But you ate and you drank for yourselves. 7 These are the words that I, the Lord, spoke by my prophets in past years. At that time, the people in Jerusalem lived without trouble. Many rich people lived in Jerusalem. Also the people to the south and to the west of Jerusalem lived without trouble." '

8 The Lord spoke again to Zechariah. He said, 9 'The Lord Almighty has said, "Be sure that you are fair to all people. Be kind to each other. 10 Be kind to a woman after the death of her husband. Be kind to a child after the death of his father. Be kind to strangers and to poor people. Do not think bad thoughts against your brother."

11 But the people would not listen and they turned away. They put their hands over their ears, because they did not want to hear. 12 They decided that they would not listen to God's rules or to the messages from the prophets. But the Lord Almighty had sent those messages by His Spirit. So I, the Lord Almighty, was very angry.

13 When I spoke to them, they did not listen. So when they prayed to me, I did not listen to them', says the Lord Almighty.

14 'As a storm takes things away, I took my people away to strange countries. The country that they left became an empty country. Nobody lived in it. That is how they made the good country an empty country.'

Chapter 8

The promises of God for Jerusalem

1 The Lord Almighty gave this message to Zechariah. 2 'I have wanted to help Jerusalem because I love its people very much. My love causes me to be very angry with the enemies of Jerusalem', says the Lord Almighty.

3 'Jerusalem is the city that I have chosen. I will return there and I will live there. Then Jerusalem will be called the city that obeys God. And the mountain of the Lord Almighty will be called the mountain that God has chosen.'

4 The Lord Almighty says, 'Old men and old women will sit in the streets of Jerusalem again. Each will have a stick in his hands because he is so old.

5 Many boys and girls will play in the streets of the city again.'

6 'This may seem impossible to the few people that remain', says the Lord Almighty. 'But nothing is impossible to me', says the Lord Almighty.

7 'I will bring my people back from the east country and from the west country', says the Lord Almighty. 8 'I will bring them back to live in Jerusalem. They will be my people and I will be their God. I will do for them what I promised to do.'

9 The Lord Almighty says, 'Be strong, you people who now hear these words from the mouths of the prophets. The prophets spoke the same words when you prepared the ground for the temple of the Lord Almighty. Now be strong and continue to build. 10 Before that time, there was not enough money to pay for work that men or animals did. No man was safe from the enemy because I made all men angry with each other.'

11 'But now it is different. I will not be angry with the few people that have returned', says the Lord Almighty.

12 'The seeds and the plants will grow well. The trees will give fruit. There will be water from the skies. I will bless the few people that will return. 13 In past years, people from other countries have said bad things against you, Judah and Israel. But now I will help you. You will bless many people. Do not be afraid. Be strong.'

14 The Lord Almighty says this: 'When your parents and their parents made me angry, I decided to punish them.' 'I have also punished you', says the Lord Almighty.

15 'Do not be afraid. I have now decided to do good things to Jerusalem and to the people in Judah again. 16 These are the things that you should do. Speak true words to each other. Leaders, be fair to all people. 17 Do not think to do bad things against other people. Do not use my name to promise things and then not do those things. All these things make me very angry.'

18 Again Zechariah the prophet heard this message from the Lord Almighty. 19 'On special days in the year you eat no food. Those days are in the 4th, 5th, 7th and 10th months. But I want you to enjoy those days', says the Lord Almighty. 'I want the people in Judah to be happy. So speak true words and live quiet lives.'

20 'People that live in many countries will come to Jerusalem', says the Lord Almighty. 21 'The people from one city will go the people in another city. They will say, "Come with us to worship the Lord Almighty. Come and ask the Lord to help us." 22 People from many strong countries will worship the Lord Almighty in Jerusalem. And they will ask the Lord to help them.'

23 'Then, 10 men from foreign countries will hold the coat of one Jew', says the Lord Almighty. 'They will say, "People have told us that the Lord is with you. So we want to go with you."'

Chapter 9

God speaks against Israel's enemies

1 The Lord speaks against the country called Hadrach and against Damascus city.

The Lord watches all men and all the groups of people in Israel.

2 The Lord speaks against the country called Hamath. (It is next to the country called Hadrach.) The people in Tyre and Sidon cities are very wise. But the Lord also speaks against them.

3 Tyre's people have built strong walls to keep enemies out.

They have swept up rich metals like dirt.

They have swept up gold like dirt in the streets.

4 The Lord will take away all the things that Tyre's people have.

And he will remove their ships from the sea.

Fire will burn every part of the city.

5 The people in Ashkelon city will see it and they will be afraid.

The people in Gaza city will see it and they will be afraid.

The things that the people in Ekron city hope for will not happen.

The king of Gaza will die

and there will be no people in Ashkelon any longer.

6 Foreign people will live in Ashdod city.

I will show the Philistines that they are not clever. They are not as clever as they believe.

7 I will take the blood from their mouths.

I will take the food from their teeth, because it is bad food.

Those that remain will still be my people.

They will become leaders in Judah.

Ekron will be like a part of Judah, as the Jebusites were.

8 Then I will keep my house safe against my enemies.

No army will ever again beat my people,

because I am watching them.

The King of Zion comes

9 Sing loudly, people in Zion.

Shout, people in Jerusalem.

Look! Your king comes to you.

He will save you because he does everything well.

But he is quiet and he is riding on a donkey.

He will ride on a young animal. Its mother is a donkey.

10 I will take away the chariots from Ephraim

and the horses of war from Jerusalem.

The bows of war will be broken.

He will speak to all the countries and wars will finish.

He will rule from sea to sea. He will rule from the river Euphrates to the ends of the earth.

11 But I made a promise to you. I made that promise true with blood. I will free your people that are in a prison, in deep dark holes without water.

12 All you people who hoped to see your own country again, return to Jerusalem.

I tell you this now: I will give back to you twice as much as you have lost.

13 I will use Judah and Israel to attack my enemies.

I will use you, men from Zion, to attack the men from Greece.

I will make you like the long metal knife of a soldier.

The Lord will appear

14 Then the Lord will appear over them.

His arrow will be like the bright light in the sky that you see during a storm.

The Lord will make a great sound.

He will march in the storms from the south.

15 And the Lord Almighty will watch over them.

They will beat the stones that their enemies throw at them.

When they go to war, they will shout.

They will shout like men

Who have drunk too much wine?

They will be as full of joy as the dish is full.

This is the dish filled with the blood of animals in the house of God. The priest pours it on the altar.

16 On that day, the Lord will save them.

They are his people.

They will shine in his country

Like beautiful stones that shine in a crown.

17 The people will be beautiful and good.

The young people will become strong

When they eat good bread.

The young women will become strong

When they drink new wine.

Chapter 10

The Lord will watch over Judah

1 Ask the Lord for rain in spring.

It is the Lord who makes the clouds and the storms.

He gives the rain to men.

He gives the plants of the field to everyone.

2 People ask idols for help,

But the idols do not speak true words.

Some people explain what a dream means.

But they do not speak true words.

The help that they give is not good.

So the people move from place to place like sheep.

They are not safe. They have no leaders.

3 'I am angry with the leaders.

I will cause them to be sorry.

Judah's people are mine', says the Lord Almighty. 'I will watch over them.

I will make them as strong as horses that are ready for war.

4 From Judah's people will come the man called the Cornerstone.

A strong leader will come from Judah.

A strong soldier will come from Judah.

Every ruler will come from Judah.

5 Together they will be like strong soldiers

who march through the dirty streets of the enemy.

The Lord is with them and they will fight their enemies.

They will pull down the soldiers from their horses.

6 I will make Judah's people strong

and I will make Israel's people free men.

I will bring them back to me,

because I am sorry for them.

I am their God

and I will answer them.

It will be as if I had never turned away from them.

7 Israel's people will become like strong men.

They will be as happy as men that drink wine.

Their children will see their happy fathers

and so the children will be happy.

They will sing to the Lord.

8 I will cause my people to come to me and I will bring them all together.

I will buy them and I will make them free people.

And there will be as many people as there were before.

9 I will send them to foreign countries among foreign people.

But, in these far countries, they will remember me.

They and their children will not die.

They will return to Jerusalem.

10 I will bring my people back from Egypt

and I will bring them here together from Assyria.

I will bring them to Gilead and to Lebanon.

There will not be enough room for them all.

11 And he will come to the difficult sea.

But it will be no trouble to him.

He will stop the waves in the sea.

He will make the river Nile dry.

Proud Assyria will have nothing to be proud about and

the power of Egypt's people will finish.'

12 'I will make my people strong.

They will obey me because they love my name.'

Chapter 11

The sheep and the shepherd

1 Open your gates, Lebanon,

so that the fires can burn down your cedar trees.

2 Cry aloud, cypress tree, because the cedar tree has fallen.

Enemies have cut down the tall and beautiful trees.

Cry aloud, oak trees in Bashan,

because they have cut down the thick forest.

3 Listen to the shepherds. They are crying

because enemies have destroyed their fields.

Listen to the noise of the lions

because the wood along the river Jordan

Is no longer there.

The two shepherds

4 This is what the Lord said to me, Zechariah. 'My people are like sheep. There will be a time when men will buy them. And then they will kill them. But feed them until that time.

5 Those men who buy the sheep will kill them. Nobody will punish them. They will sell them. And they will say, "Thank you Lord, because I am a rich man." Their own shepherds do not give the sheep any help.'

6 The Lord says, 'The people in this country were my people, but they are not my people now. I will not go on being kind to them. I myself will give them to their enemies and to foreign kings. The foreign kings will do very bad things to the country, but I will not come to help.'

7 So I was a good shepherd to the sheep that men would soon kill. I thought specially about the weakest sheep. Then I took two sticks. And I called one stick 'Grace' and I called the other stick 'Together'. I fed the sheep.

8 In one month, I sent away three shepherds. They did not like me and I was not patient with them.

9 I said to the sheep, 'I will not be your shepherd and you will die. The sheep that do not die will eat each other.'

10 I took 'Grace', which was my first stick. I broke it into two pieces. The Lord's promise to his people finished.

11 On the day that the Lord's promise finished, the oppressed sheep watched me. They knew that it was the Lord's message.

12 I said to them, 'You may think that I should have some money for my work. If you do think that, pay me my money. If you do not want to pay me, keep it.' So they paid me 30 silver coins.

13 The Lord said to me, 'Throw the 30 silver coins to the man who makes pots in the house of the Lord.' They thought that I was not worth very much! I took the 30 coins. And I threw them to the man who makes pots. He makes them for the house of the Lord.

14 Then I broke the second stick called 'Together'. I made the country called Judah separate. I made it separate from the country called Israel. 15 Then the Lord said to me, Zechariah, 'Take again the tools of a bad shepherd.

16 I have chosen a man to watch the sheep. He will not help the sheep that are dying. He will not look for the sheep that have gone away. He will not help the sick sheep or feed the strong sheep. He will eat the meat of the fat sheep. He will tear off their feet to get all the meat.

17 Bad things will happen to the bad shepherd who leaves his sheep.

His enemy's knife will cut his arm and his right eye.

His arm will become like a dry stick. And his right eye will no longer be able to see anything.'

Chapter 12

God will beat the enemies of Jerusalem

1 This is the Lord's message about Israel. The Lord made the skies and the whole wide earth. He makes men and women.

2 'I will frighten the enemies that live round Jerusalem. I will frighten them so much that they will run. They will run as fast as they can from Jerusalem and from Judah.

3 There will be a time when all the countries of the earth will be ready to attack Jerusalem. Then I will make Jerusalem like a heavy rock that nobody can move. All those who try to lift it will hurt themselves very badly.

4 On that day', says the Lord, 'I will make every horse very afraid. I will make all the men that ride them crazy. I want to help Judah's people. And so, I will not let the horses of the enemy see any longer.

5 Then the leaders of Judah will say to themselves, "The Lord Almighty, their God, makes the people in Jerusalem strong. And they will help us."

6 On that day, I will make the leaders of Judah like fire in a forest. I will make them like fire among wheat that the farmer has cut. They will kill all the people from round Jerusalem, but the people in Jerusalem will be safe.

7 The Lord will save the homes of the people from Judah first. So David's family and the people who live in Jerusalem will not be greater than the people from Judah.

8 On that day, the Lord will save the people who live in Jerusalem. Even sick people will be as strong as King David was. The family of David will lead the people from Jerusalem like the angel of the Lord. God himself will go before them.

9 On that day, I will destroy all the countries that fight against Israel.

They will weep for the man that they killed

10 I will cause the family of David and the people in Jerusalem to think seriously about me. Then they will know that I am kind to them.

And they will want to pray to me. They will look at me whom they pierced (made holes in). They will weep about him as those that weep after the death of their only son. They will cry aloud as if their only son was dead.

11 On that day, people will weep loudly in Jerusalem. It will be like when they were weeping about Hadadrimmon in the fields of Megiddo.

12 All the people will weep. Each family will weep by itself. The family of King David will weep by itself. And their wives will weep by themselves. The family of Nathan will weep by itself. And their wives will weep by themselves.

13 The family of Levi will weep by itself. And their wives will weep by themselves. The family of Shimei will weep by itself. And their wives will weep by themselves.

14 And all the families that have not died will weep by themselves. And their wives will weep by themselves.'

Chapter 13

The Lord takes away the sin of the people

1 'On that day, something will be like water that comes up from the ground. And it will clean away the sin from the family of David. It will clean away the sin from the people in Jerusalem.

2 On that day, I will remove the names of false gods from the country', says the Lord Almighty. 'Everyone will forget them. I will remove all the false prophets. And I will remove the bad spirit that is not holy.

3 And if anyone appears as a prophet again, his father and his mother will say to him, "You must die. You do not speak true words. The Lord has not spoken to you." Then they will kill him.

4 On that day, every prophet will be ashamed that he was ever a prophet. He will not put on the clothes of a prophet that they make from hair. Then people will not know that he is a prophet.

5 He will say, "I am not a prophet. I am a farmer. From the time that I was a boy, I have worked on the land."

6 If someone asks him, "Who cut your body?" he will answer, "My friends cut me when I was at their house." '

Kill the shepherd and the sheep will run away

7 'Attack my shepherd with a sharp knife.

Attack the man that is next to me',

says the Lord Almighty.

'Kill the shepherd and then the sheep will run away.

Then I will attack the young sheep.

8   In the whole country', says the Lord,

'two thirds of the people will die.

But one third will still be living there.

9   I will bring these people through fire.

As men clean silver in the fire, so I will clean them.

As men test gold in the fire, so I will test them.

They will speak my name and I will answer them.

I will say, "They are my people."

They will say, "The Lord is our God." '

Chapter 14

The lord and ruler comes

1 There will be a day when your enemies will take away everything. They will take away everything that is yours. They will each have some of your things.

2 I will bring soldiers from all countries to fight against Jerusalem. They will go into the city and they will rob the houses. They will have sex with the women. They will lead away half the people to other countries. They will let the other half stay in Jerusalem.

3 Then the Lord will go out. And he will fight against the people from those countries as in past years.

4 On that day, the Lord's feet will stand on the mountain of Olives. This mountain is east of Jerusalem. It will break in two from east to west and it will make a wide valley. Half of the mountain will move north and half of the mountain will move south.

5 In the time of Uzziah, king of Judah, you ran away when the earth moved. You will do this again. Then the Lord will come. And all those who are holy will come with him.

6 On that day, it will not be light in some places and dark in other places.

7 It will be a day like no other day. There will be no night. When it is evening, there will still be light. Only the Lord himself will know that day.

8 On that day, water will come out from Jerusalem. Half of this water will go towards the sea in the east. Half of this water will go towards the sea in the west. This will go on during summer and winter.

9 The Lord will be king over the whole earth. On that day, there will be only one Lord and he will have only one name.

10 All the land, from Geba to Rimmon, south of Jerusalem, will become flat. But Jerusalem will rise and it will be high in its place. The city will be from the Gate of Benjamin to the Corner Gate and to the High Building of Hananel. The place where the servants of the king make his wine will be in it too.

11 Jerusalem will be safe. People will live there. Nobody will destroy Jerusalem ever again.

12 The Lord will make the people sick that fought against Jerusalem. Their bodies will become bad as they stand on their feet. Their eyes will become bad and they will fall out. And their tongues will become bad in their mouths.

13 On that day, the Lord will make men so afraid that each man will attack the man next to him.

14 Judah also will go to Jerusalem and they will fight. They will take every good thing from all the countries. There will be a lot of expensive metals and many rich clothes.

15 The horses and all the other animals will be sick. And they will die as the soldiers died.

16 Some of the soldiers from the countries that attacked Jerusalem will not die. They will go to Jerusalem year after year to worship the King, the Lord Almighty. They will worship him at the Feast of Tabernacles.

17 All the people on the earth will have to go to Jerusalem to worship the King, the Lord Almighty. If any people on the earth do not go, they will have no rain.

18 If the people from Egypt do not go to Jerusalem to worship the Lord, they will have no rain. And the Lord will make them sick. If the people from other countries will not go to Jerusalem, the Lord will make them sick. They will die.

19 This will happen to the people from Egypt. This will happen to the people from all the countries that do not go up to Jerusalem at that time.

20 On that day, men will write the words, 'This is for the Lord' on the bells of the horses. The pots that anyone uses to cook with in the house of the Lord will be special. They will be as special as the dishes in front of the altar.

21 Every pot in Jerusalem and Judah will be for the Lord Almighty. All the people who come to offer animals to the Lord will cook in those pots. On that day, nobody who sells things will come into the house of the Lord Almighty.

Offer Your Best Gifts To God, Who Is Coming Soon

Malachi

About the Book of Malachi

> Malachi is the name of the man who wrote this book. He spoke God's message to the people. Many years ago, a powerful enemy had come. The enemy had sent the people away from their own country. After a long time, they returned home. They built the temple again. The date when this happened was about 516 B.C. Malachi wrote this book in about 460 B.C. God had promised the people that they would have plenty of good things. But they only had a little rain and so their crops did not grow. They did not have enough food to eat. So, the people thought that perhaps God did not love them. They began to be careless. They did not obey the rules that God had given to them. Malachi found out how the people were thinking. And he put this into words. He then told them what God wanted to say to them. He told them how they could come back to God. And he told them how they could love God again. If they did not do that, there would be bad news for them.

Chapter 1

1 This is the message that God told to Malachi. Malachi knew that he must tell the Israelites this message.

2 'I have loved you', says the Lord. 'But you ask, "How have you loved us?" '

'Esau was Jacob's brother', the Lord says. 'I have loved Jacob and all his descendants.

3 But I have not loved Esau and his descendants.

Esau is like my enemy and I have caused trouble for him. Esau's mountains are now empty. Nobody uses the land any longer. There are only jackals there now. They have the things that Esau used there.'

4 Edom may say, 'Our enemies have beaten us. They have knocked our houses down. But we will build them again.' But the Lord Almighty says, 'They may build. But I will knock everything down. People will call Edom the Very Bad Country. They will say that the people in Edom always have trouble from God. He is very angry with them. 5 You will see it with your own eyes. You will say, "Great is the Lord, even beyond Israel's borders." '

6 'A son respects his father. A servant respects his master. If I am like a father, show respect for me as a father. If I am like a master, respect me as a master', says the Lord Almighty. 'You are priests. But you show that you scorn my name. But you ask, "How have we shown that we have scorned your name?"

7 You put food that is not clean on my altar.

But you ask, "How have we made you not clean?" You have said that the Lord's Table is not important.'

8 'You bring for sacrifice animals that cannot see. That is not right. You sacrifice animals that cannot walk. That is a wrong thing to do. You sacrifice animals that have an illness. And that is a wrong thing to do, too. Offer these to your ruler. And see what will happen. He will surely not accept you. He will not be happy with you', says the Lord Almighty.

9 'Ask God to be kind to us. Explain to him that this is really important to you. Tell him often about this. But your offerings are not clean. So they will not change how God thinks. He will not accept you', says the Lord Almighty.

10 'It would be better if one of you shut the temple doors! Then you would not light fires that have no value on my altar. I am not happy with you', says the Lord Almighty. 'I will not accept any gift from your hands. 11 My name will be great in the whole world, in every country. From the East to the West, people will respect my name. So, in every place, people will bring incense to me. They will give clean offerings to me', says the Lord Almighty.

12 'But you are saying that the Lord's Table is not clean. So you are scorning my name. You say that the food on it has little value. 13 And you say, "The duty that we must do is like a heavy weight on us. We do not want to do this." You think that you are too important to do it', says the Lord Almighty.

'I will not accept ill animals from you as sacrifices. I will not accept hurt animals or animals that cannot walk', says the Lord. 14 'Someone may have a good male as one of his animals. He may promise to give it to God. He says to God, "I will give it." But he may then sacrifice an animal that is not clean. So God will curse him. That is because I am a great king', says the Lord Almighty. 'Everyone on earth will know that my name is very serious. They will respect it.'

Chapter 2

1 'And now, priests, I am talking to you. So be careful. 2 If you do not listen', says the Lord Almighty, 'I will curse you. If you do not decide to respect my name, I will curse your blessings. You have not yet decided to respect my name. So I have already cursed your blessings.'

3 'I will tell your descendants that they have done wrong things. This is because you have done wrong things. I will tell them that I am not happy with them. I will tell them that they must not do wrong things again. I will cover your faces with the offal from your festival sacrifices. Someone will carry you away with it.'

.4 'I have told you that you must be careful. This is so that my promises with Levi can continue', says the Lord Almighty.

5 'I promised to Levi a good life and many blessings. He received what I promised him. So, he did what I asked him to do. He worshipped me, and he respected me. He knew that my name is very great. He was afraid of me. So, he was careful when he was with me. 6 He taught what was right. He told people only facts. He often talked to me. And he enjoyed the times when he was with me. He did what was right. And we agreed about how he should live. He caused many people to stop doing wrong things.

7 Priests are men that the Lord Almighty has chosen. They must speak his messages for him. The priests should tell people what they know about God. They should tell people about what God has asked them all to do. If they did that, everyone would remember these important facts. People should ask the priests what they need to know. 8 People who love me want to do certain things. But you have stopped doing those things. What you teach causes many people to make mistakes. What I agreed with Levi does not happen any longer', says the Lord Almighty.

9 'So people have scorned you. They have then shown other people what you have done. Everyone now thinks that you are fools. I have caused this to happen. You have not done what I asked you to do. In your jobs as priests you have not used the same rules for everyone.'

10 We all have one Father. One God made us from nothing. We have agreed to do things for each other. But we do not do them. So we scorn what God agreed with our fathers. We ought not to do this.

11 Judah's people no longer do the things that God teaches. A very bad thing has happened in Israel and in Jerusalem. God certainly does not like it. Judah's people have married women who worship a foreign god. Then they meet with God in a place that he loves. And so they have made that place dirty. 12 I pray that the Lord will send all people like that away from the Israelites and from that place. And I do not want them to come back into this group of people. I pray that the Lord will not let them. Even send away someone like that who is bringing gifts to the Lord Almighty.

13 Also, you cry. You cry so much that the water covers the Lord's altar! The Lord no longer looks at your gifts. He does not accept them with pleasure from your hands. So, you weep and you shout out in pain. 14You ask 'Why?' The Lord was there when you were a young man. He was there when you agreed to marry your wife. He heard what you said. You promised to be with her until the end of your life. He sees that you no longer live together as man and wife. That is why the Lord no longer accepts your gifts.

15 The Lord has made a man and his wife to be as one person. He has made them with a body and a spirit and they are his. Why should a man and his wife be as one person? It is because the Lord wants their children to be good. And he wants them to respect him. So, think carefully about your spirit. Do not forget the promise that you said to your wife. Do not leave her.

16 Sometimes a man and his wife completely leave each other. They decide this with a judge and with other people there. 'I strongly do not like it when a man and his wife decide never to live together again', says the Lord God of Israel. 'If a man leaves his wife like this, the result will be very bad for her. He has done a cruel thing to her. I strongly do not like that', says the son Almighty. 'So watch over your spirit and do not forget your promise.'

17 The Lord is tired from your words. 'Why is he tired? How have we caused that?' you ask. He is tired because of the things that you have said. You say, 'The Lord sees all who do very bad things. He thinks that they are good. He is happy with them.' Or you say, 'The God who is a fair judge is not doing anything here.'

Chapter 3

1 'See, I will send someone with my message. He will prepare the way before me. And so the Lord that you are looking for will return to his temple. He will come quickly.

And you do not know when he will come. It is he that you want so much. The man who brings the message about the promise will come', says the Lord Almighty.

2 'But nobody will be able to stand when the Lord appears. It will be impossible for anyone to remain the same on the day that he comes. That is because he will be like a refiner's fire. He will be like the soap that people use to make cloths white.'

3 'He will sit as a refiner of silver. The refiner works until the silver shines. He will make the priests clean as a refiner works with gold and silver. Then the Lord will have righteous people who will bring proper offerings. 4 The Lord will accept all the gifts of Judah and Jerusalem that people give in a right way. It will be as it was earlier. It will be as it was a long time ago.'

5 The Lord Almighty says, 'So I will come near to you as your judge. And I will decide how to punish those who have done wrong things. I will immediately speak against magicians, adulterers and perjurers. I will speak against those who do not pay their workers.

Some women's husbands have died. I will speak against anyone who does cruel things to these wives and to their children. And some of you are deciding things about foreign people in ways that are not fair.

All these people are doing wrong things. They do not think that I am being serious. They are not afraid of me and they do not respect me.'

6 'I am the Lord and I do not change. So I have not killed you who are descendants of Jacob. 7 I have told you what I want you to do. But you do not listen to me any longer. You have not obeyed me. All Jacob's descendants have done the same. Return to me and I will return to you', says the Lord Almighty. 'But you ask, "How do we return?" 8 A man should not rob God. But you rob me. But you ask, "How do we rob you?" You rob tithes and offerings from me. 9 You, and everyone who is an Israelite, are robbing me. So you are all receiving the results of a curse. 10 Give me all that is mine. Store it so that there will be food in my house. Do this. And find out what I will do', says the Lord Almighty. 'You will receive so much blessing that you will not have enough room for it. It will be like rain that I pour out of the sky. It will be like rain that covers the ground with a lot of water. 11 I will not let insects eat your crops. The grapes will not fall from the vines before they are ready to eat. 12 You will enjoy your land', says the Lord Almighty. 'So all the people on earth will say that God has blessed you.'

13 'You have said cruel words against me', says the Lord. 'But you ask, "What have we said about you?" 14You have said, "We work for God. But nothing good happens because of this. We do what he asks us to do. We are sorry when we do wrong things. And we show him that we are sorry. There are no good results from this.

15 Some people think that they are better than other people. We now think that those people have blessings from God. Surely, those who do wrong things enjoy a good life. Even those who fight against God do not have trouble." '

16 Then those people who respected the Lord talked to each other. The Lord listened and he heard. Someone, who was with God, wrote on a scroll. God watched while this person wrote. He wrote about all the people who worshipped God. These are the people who respected God's name. Now everyone would remember these people.

17 'These people will be mine', says the Lord Almighty. 'One day I will bring together all my own people. They are worth a lot to me and I really want them. A man is merciful to his son who works for him. I will be merciful to my people like that. 18 Then you will again see how the good people are different from the very bad people. Also, some people are God's servants and some people are not God's servants. And you will again see that difference too.'

Chapter 4

1 'This future day is a fact. It will burn like a great fire. It will be like a fire that a man uses to burn stubble. When this happens, no branch or any part of a plant will be there any longer. The people who have done very bad things are like that stubble. No bad person will be there any longer. Some people think that they are better than other people. All the people who are like that will burn in the heat.' That is what the Lord Almighty says.

2 'But for you who respect my name it will be different. The "Sun of Righteousness" will rise to make you well. You will go out and you will jump up and down. You will be like baby cows when someone lets them go out of their stalls. 3 Then you will put your feet down in a heavy way and you will walk on the bad people. They will be like ashes under your feet. All this will happen on the day that I do these things', says the Lord Almighty.

4 'Remember everything that my servant Moses told you. Do not forget the rules that I gave to him at Sinai. They were for all the Israelites and you must still obey them.'

5 'See. I will send you a man called Elijah. He will speak God's message. He will come before that great and frightening day of the Lord.

A man called Matthew wrote this book at some time between the years AD 59 and AD 70. Matthew was a Jew and he was sometimes called Levi. He received taxes for the government before he became a disciple of Jesus. He may have written his book when he was living in Israel. But he may have written it when he was living in Antioch. Antioch is a city in the country called Syria. Matthew wrote the book in the Greek language. He wrote it for Jews who understood Greek. In his book, Matthew wrote many things about the messages that God's prophets had written a long time ago. The Jews who read Matthew's book would know all about these things.

Matthew tells us the Good News about the Kingdom of God. He tells us about the birth of Jesus and how he lived. He tells us how Jesus died. He tells us how he went to live with God again. He also tells us who Jesus is. And he tells us why he came to live in the world. Matthew explained the things that Jesus taught the people. And he tells us about many things that Jesus did.

The Jews were waiting for God to send a special person to them. They called this person the Messiah. God had promised to send him. It means the person whom God sent to save people from punishment. He would also be the king of the Jews. He is the only person who can put us right with God. In the Greek language, the special person was called Christ. Matthew knew that Jesus was that special person. He wanted other people also to know this.

Matthew wrote his book in 8 parts:

1:1 – 2:23 ~ what happened when Jesus was born.

3:1 – 4:11 ~ what happened when Jesus began his work.

4:12 – 14:12 ~ what happened when Jesus was working in Galilee.

14:13 – 17:21 ~ what happened when Jesus went to other places in the north of Israel.

17:22 – 18:35 ~ what happened when Jesus returned to Galilee.

19:1 - 20:34 ~ what happened when Jesus taught the people in Judea and Perea.

21:1 – 27:66 ~ what happened in the city called Jerusalem in the last week of Jesus' life.

28:1 – 28:20 ~ people see Jesus alive again after he died.

(Galilee, Judea and Perea were all different parts of the country called Israel.)

6 He will cause fathers and their children to be friendly again. If not, I will come in a hurry and I will curse the land.'

Matthew tells us the Good News about Jesus

Matthew

This is about the book that Matthew wrote

Chapter 1

The ancestors of Jesus

1 These are the names of people in the family of Jesus Christ. Jesus was in the family of King David. David was in the family of Abraham.

Jesus was a Jew. Abraham was the ancestor of all the Jews. The Jews are also called Israel, and they called their country Israel. We can read about Abraham in the book called Genesis 12-25. We can read about King David in the books called 1 Samuel (chapters 16-31) and 2 Samuel.

2   Abraham was the father of Isaac.

　　　　　　　　　Isaac was the father of Jacob.

　　　　　　　　　Jacob was the father of Judah and his brothers.

3   Judah was the father of Perez and Zerah. Their mother was called Tamar.

　　　　　　　　　Perez was the father of Hezron.

　　　　　　　　　Hezron was the father of Ram.

4   Ram was the father of Amminadab.

　　　　　　　　　Amminadab was the father of Nahshon.

　　　　　　　　　Nahshon was the father of Salmon.

5   Salmon was the father of Boaz (his mother was called Rahab).

Boaz was the father of Obed (his mother was called Ruth).

　　　　　　　　　Obed was the father of Jesse.

6   Jesse was the father of King David.

David was Solomon's father. Solomon's mother was the wife of Uriah.

7   Solomon was the father of Rehoboam.

Rehoboam was the father of Abijah.

Abijah was the father of Asa.

8   Asa was the father of Jehoshaphat.

Jehoshaphat was the father of Jehoram.

Jehoram was the father of Uzziah.

9   Uzziah was the father of Jotham.

Jotham was the father of Ahaz.

Ahaz was the father of Hezekiah.

10 Hezekiah was the father of Manasseh.

Manasseh was the father of Amon.

Amon was the father of Josiah.

Josiah was the father of Jeconiah and his brothers.

11 This was when soldiers from Babylon took the Jews away to Babylon.

12 Here is a list of the people who lived after that time:

Jeconiah was the father of Shealtiel.

Shealtiel was the father of Zerubbabel.

13 Zerubbabel was the father of Abiud.

Abiud was the father of Eliakim.

Eliakim was the father of Azor.

14 Azor was the father of Zadok.

Zadok was the father of Akim.

Akim was the father of Eliud.

15 Eliud was the father of Eleazar.

Eleazar was the father of Matthan.

Matthan was the father of Jacob.

16 Jacob was the father of Joseph.

Joseph married Mary. Mary was the mother of Jesus Christ. Jesus was the special person that God sent to save his people.

17 So then, there were 14 generations from Abraham to David. There were 14 generations from David to the time the Jews went to Babylon. There were 14 generations from then until Jesus was born.

Jesus is born

18 Now this is how Jesus Christ was born. His mother's name was Mary. She had promised to marry a man called Joseph.

Then she discovered that a baby was growing inside her. This happened before she married Joseph. The powerful Holy Spirit had caused this to happen to her. 19 Joseph always wanted to do what was right. He did not want everyone to know about Mary's baby. He did not want her to be ashamed. So he had a plan to stop the marriage secretly.

20 Joseph thought about what to do. Then an angel came from God to see him. While he was dreaming, the angel said, 'Joseph, you who are from the family of King David, do not be afraid to take Mary as your wife. The baby that is growing inside her is from God's Holy Spirit. 21 Mary's baby will be a boy. He will save his people from the wrong things that they have done. Because of this, you must name him Jesus.'

22 Many years before, God had spoken to one of his prophets about this. Now God's words would soon become true. The prophet called Isaiah had said, 23 'There will be a young woman who has never had sex. A baby boy will grow inside her. People will call him Immanuel **[Isaiah 7:4]** . This name means "God is with us".'

24 Then Joseph woke up from his sleep. He did what God's angel had asked him to do. He married Mary. 25 Joseph did not have sex with Mary before the baby boy was born. Joseph said that the baby should be called Jesus.

Chapter 2

Some men come to visit Jesus

1 Jesus was born in the town called Bethlehem in Judea. At that time, King Herod ruled Judea. Soon after Jesus was born, some clever men came from the east to Jerusalem.

2 The men arrived in Jerusalem and they asked people, 'Where is the baby who was born a short time ago as the King of the Jews? We ask because we saw a special star. This star rose in the east. We knew about the baby king when we saw this star. We want to bend our knees in front of him. We *want* to tell him how great and important he is.'

3 Herod heard what the men were saying. And he became anxious. Many people in Jerusalem were also anxious. 4 Then Herod asked all the leaders of the priests and the teachers of the Law to meet with him. He asked them, 'God promised to send a special person. Where will that special person be born?' 5 Then the leaders of the priests and the teachers of the Law replied, 'The special person will be born in Bethlehem in Judea. This is what the prophet wrote about Bethlehem. 6 "God said: People in Bethlehem, your town is one of the most important towns in Judea.

A person born in your town will rule my people Israel. He will guide my people." ' **[Micah 5:2]**

7 Herod listened to all these things. So he asked the visitors to meet with him by himself. Herod asked them some questions. And he discovered the time that the star had appeared. 8 Then Herod sent the men to Bethlehem. 'Go and look everywhere for this child', he said. 'And when you find him, come back here. Then you can tell me where he is. After that, I can also bend my knees in front of him. I can tell him how great and important he is.'

9 After the men had heard the king, they continued their journey. While they were travelling, the same star appeared again. 10 The star moved along in front of them. Then it stopped above the place where the child was staying. The men were very happy when they saw the star. 11 They went into the house and they saw the child. He was with Mary, his mother. They went down on their knees in front of the child. They said to him, 'You are very great and important.' Then they opened their bags. They took out valuable gifts and they gave them to the child. The gifts were gold, incense called frankincense and myrrh. 12 God said to them in a dream, 'Do not go back to see Herod.' So the men returned to their own country by a different road.

Gold is a very valuable metal. People would give gold to a king. Incense makes a sweet smell when it burns. Myrrh was an expensive medicine.

Mary, Joseph and Jesus go to Egypt

13 That night, after the men had gone away, Joseph had a dream. He saw one of God's angels who said to him, 'Herod will be looking for the child, so that his soldiers can kill him. You must get up and take the child and his mother with you. Go immediately to the country called Egypt. You will all be safe there. I will tell you when you can leave. You must remain there until then.'

14 So Joseph got up and he took the child and the child's mother with him. They started on the journey to Egypt that same night. 15 They all remained in Egypt until Herod died. This happened to cause the words of the prophet to become true. God had said by the prophet, 'I have brought my son out of Egypt.' **[Hosea 11:1]**

Herod's soldiers kill the baby boys in Bethlehem

16 Then Herod understood that his visitors from the east would not return to him. He was very angry. He sent his soldiers to Bethlehem. He said to them, 'Kill all the baby boys in Bethlehem. Kill those boys also who live near there. Kill all those who are not more than 2 years old.' The visitors had told Herod that they had first seen the star 2 years ago. So he chose to kill the baby boys of that age. 17 In this way, the words that Jeremiah the prophet spoke became true.

'People heard a noise in the town called Ramah.

They heard someone weeping with a loud voice.

It is Rachel and she is crying for her children.

Her children are dead,

So nobody can help her to feel better.' **[Jeremiah 31:15]**

Joseph, Mary and Jesus return to Israel from Egypt

19 After Herod died, Joseph saw one of God's angels in a dream. 20 'Get up', said the angel. 'The people who wanted to kill the child are dead. Take the child and his mother. You can return with them to Israel.'

21 So Joseph got up. He took the child and the child's mother and they travelled to Israel. 22 But then, Joseph heard that Archelaus, Herod's son, was now king of Judea. So Joseph was afraid to go to Judea. Joseph had another dream. An angel explained to him what to do. 'Go to Galilee instead', he said. 23Joseph made his home in a town called Nazareth. So what the prophets had said became true. 'He will be called a person from Nazareth.'

Chapter 3

John the Baptist prepares a way for Jesus

1 Some years later, a man called John the Baptist went to the desert in Judea. He began to tell people a message from God.

2 John said, 'Stop doing wrong things. Say sorry to God and obey him. You must do this because the Kingdom of heaven is coming soon.'

A kingdom is the place where a king rules. The Kingdom of God is where God rules. Matthew used Kingdom of heaven in his book. Heaven is God's home. The Jews did not speak God's name because he is so much greater than everyone else.

3 John the Baptist is the man that the prophet Isaiah spoke about. Isaiah said,

'You will hear someone shouting in the desert these words:

"The Lord is coming, so prepare a road for him to travel on.

Make the path straight." ' **[Isaiah 40:3]**

Isaiah was telling people about a man called John. John told the people to get ready for King Jesus to come. People mend roads before a king travels along them. Isaiah is using this as a picture. It helped the people to understand how to prepare themselves for Jesus.

4 Now John always wore a coat that he had made out of hair from a camel. He also wore a leather belt. His usual food was large insects and honey from the desert.

Judea was part of Israel. A camel is a large animal that lives in the desert. It can carry heavy things on its back like a horse. The insects that John ate were called locusts. An insect called a bee makes honey. It is sweet like sugar.

5 Many of the people went to listen to John. They lived in Jerusalem and Judea and all the other places near the river Jordan. 6 The people told God about all the wrong things that they had done. Then John baptised the people in the river Jordan.

John baptised people who wanted to stop doing wrong things. These people told God that they were sorry. They were sorry about the wrong things that they had done. God then forgave them.

7 Many Pharisees and Sadducees came to John. They wanted John to baptise them. He said to them, 'You are like dangerous snakes. You are trying to run away from God because he is angry with you. He will soon punish people who do wrong things. 8 Stop doing the things that God does not like. Do things to show God that you are sorry. 9 Do not say to yourselves, "We are in the family of Abraham. So God will not punish us." Listen! God can make children for Abraham out of these stones! 10 You are like trees. God has an axe ready at the lowest part of the trees. He will cut down every tree that does not make good fruit. He will throw these trees into the fire.'

The Pharisees were a group of Jews. They thought that they obeyed all God's rules. They thought that they did not do any wrong things. Sadducees were an important group of Jewish leaders at the time of Jesus.

11 'I baptise you with water. This shows God that you are sorry. You are sorry about the wrong things that you have done. It shows him that you now want to obey his rules. But a person is coming soon.

He is more important than I am. I am not at all good like he is. I am no good even to carry his shoes for him. He will baptise you with the Holy Spirit and he will baptise you with fire. 12 He is like a farmer with a special tool in his hand. A farmer throws the wheat up in the air with this tool. He does this to remove the dry hard part that is outside of the seed. He cannot use this hard part for anything, so he burns it in a fire. Nobody can put out this fire. But he will put the seeds in a building to keep them safe.'

Jesus is the important person who is coming. John is using a story to teach the people about the work that Jesus will do.

John baptises Jesus

13 Then Jesus came from Galilee to the river Jordan. He wanted John to baptise him. 14 But John did not want to baptise Jesus. He said to Jesus, 'I should come to you instead, and then you can baptise me. But you are asking me to baptise you.'

15 Jesus replied, 'This time, do what I ask you. God wants you to baptise me. And we must do everything that is proper.' So John did what Jesus asked him to do.

16 When John baptised him, Jesus came up out of the water. Then God opened the sky and Jesus saw God's Spirit coming down. He came down like a bird, which sat on Jesus. 17 Then Jesus heard a voice in the sky. 'This man is my Son. I love him and he makes me very happy.'

Chapter 4

The devil tries to cause Jesus to do wrong things

1 God's Spirit led Jesus into the desert. Here the devil tried to cause Jesus to do wrong things.

2 Jesus did not eat anything for 40 days and 40 nights. He was very hungry at the end of this time. 3 Then the devil came to Jesus and said to him, 'If you are the Son of God, you can talk to these stones. Tell the stones that they must become bread.'

4 But Jesus answered the devil, 'Moses wrote this in God's book. "People need more than bread to really live. They need to hear every word that God speaks. Then they can really live." ' **[Deuteronomy 8:3]**

5 Then the devil led Jesus to Jerusalem. He took Jesus to stand on the highest point of God's Great House. 6 He said to Jesus, 'If you are God's Son, jump down from here to the ground. Someone wrote in God's book,

"God will ask his angels to take care of you.

They will hold you in their hands while you fall. And so you will be safe.

They will not even let you hurt your feet on a stone".' **[Psalm 91:11-12]**.

7 Jesus answered the devil, 'Moses also wrote in God's book. "You must not do something dangerous to see if God will save you".' **[Deuteronomy 6:16]**

8 Then the devil led Jesus up a very high mountain. He showed Jesus all the countries in the whole world. They were all very great and beautiful. 9 'I will give you everything that you can see', said the devil. 'Go down on your knees in front of me. Say that I am great and important and beautiful. And I will give it all to you.'

10 Jesus then said to him, 'Go away. Moses also wrote this in God's book. "We must only go down on our knees in front of God. We must only tell him, 'You are great and important'. We must obey him first".'**[Deuteronomy 6:13]**

11 Then the devil left Jesus alone. After that, angels came to Jesus and they took care of him.

Jesus starts his work in Galilee

12 Now Jesus heard that Herod's soldiers had put John the Baptist in prison. So Jesus returned to Galilee.

13 He did not stay in Nazareth. He went to live in a town called Capernaum. Capernaum is on the shore of Lake Galilee. It was in the part of Israel called Zebulun and Naphtali.

14 Jesus went to live in Capernaum. And this caused the words of God to become true. God had said this to his prophet who was called Isaiah.

15 'I am speaking to you people who live in Zebulun and Naphtali.

Your part of this country is on the way to Lake Galilee.

It is across the River Jordan in the part of the country called Galilee.

Some people who are not Jews live there.

16 They are like people who are living in the dark.

They live in the shadow which death brings.

God will send a light to shine on them.' **[Isaiah 9:1-2]**

.17 Then Jesus began to teach the people. 'Stop doing wrong things. Say to God that you are sorry', Jesus said. 'Begin to obey God. You must do all this because the Kingdom of Heaven is coming soon.'

Jesus asks some men to be his disciples

18 One day, Jesus was walking along the shore of Lake Galilee. He saw two men. One man was called Simon, and he was also called Peter. The other man's name was Andrew, and he was Simon's brother. Their job was to catch fish. They were throwing their nets into the lake to catch some fish. 19 'Come with me and be my disciples', Jesus said to them. 'And I will teach you how to catch people.'

20 Peter and Andrew immediately stopped working with their nets. They went with Jesus and they became his disciples.

21 Then Jesus continued to walk along the shore of Lake Galilee. Soon he saw two more men. Their job also was to catch fish. They were called James and John.

They were brothers and their father was called Zebedee. John, James and Zebedee were in their boat and they were mending their nets. Jesus said to James and John, 'Come with me and be my disciples.' 22 Then the brothers immediately left the boat and their father behind. They went with Jesus and they became his disciples.

Jesus teaches the people about God and he makes sick people well again

23 Jesus went everywhere in Galilee. He went into the building where the Jews met to pray. Then he taught the people the good news about the Kingdom. People who had many different illnesses and problems came to Jesus. He caused all these people to become well again. 24 So people began to hear about Jesus more and more. People in Syria also heard about Jesus, so they brought all the sick people to see him. They wanted Jesus to cause them to become well again. They had many different illnesses and some had pains. Bad spirits were living inside some of them. Some people had sick minds, and some people could not move. Jesus caused all these people to become well again. 25 Because of this, large crowds followed him. These people came from Galilee and the Decapolis, and from Jerusalem. They also came from the part of Judea that is on the other side of the River Jordan.

Syria was a part of Israel that was on the east side of Galilee. The Decapolis was another part of Israel.

Chapter 5

Jesus teaches those who followed him

1 Jesus saw all the crowds following him. So he went up a hill and he sat down there to teach. Jesus 'disciples went close to listen to him. 2 And he began to teach them.

3   'Some people', he said, 'know that they need God very much. God will cause those people to be happy because they will be part of the Kingdom of Heaven.

4   Some people are sad now. God will help them to feel better. They will be happy.'

5   'Some people know that they are not powerful. They will be happy. God will give them what he has promised them.

6   Some people want to obey God more than they want to do anything else. God will give to them all that they need.

7   Some people are kind and they forgive other people. They will be happy. God will be kind to them and he will forgive them.

8   Some people do not want to do wrong things. They will be happy because they will see God.

9   Some people help other people to be friends and to agree together. They will be happy because God will call them his children.

10   Some people will have pain because they obey God. They will be happy because they are part of the Kingdom of Heaven.

11 You will be happy when people say bad things about you. Sometimes people will hurt you. Sometimes people will say things about you that are not true.

People will do these things to you because you are my disciples. 12 You should be very happy when people do these things to any of you. You should shout because you are so happy. God has kept many good things for you. He will give you these things when you go to heaven. People did all these same things to the prophets who lived a long time ago.'

Jesus' disciples are like salt and light

13 'You are like salt', Jesus said, 'for all people to taste and use. Salt is good. But sometimes it does not taste like salt any longer. That salt cannot become good again. It is not good for people to use for anything. They throw it outside and they walk on it.

14 You are like the light that everybody needs in this world. If people build a city on a hill, then other people can see it easily. 15 Nobody lights a lamp and then puts it under a can. He will put the lamp in a high place. Everybody who is in the house can then see the light from the lamp. 16 You must be sure that you shine like that light. Then everybody will be able to see. People will see all the lovely things that you do. Then they will say good things about God. He is your Father in heaven.'

Jesus talks about the Laws that Moses gave to the Jews

17 Jesus said, 'You should not think that I have come to destroy the Law. Also, I have not come to destroy the messages that the prophets wrote down. No, I have not come to destroy their words. I have come to cause what they taught to become true. 18 Remember my words. The sky and the earth will remain for a long time. While they remain, the Law will also remain. Not even a small change in the Law will happen. When everything in it has happened, then the Law will finish. 19 So then a person may think to himself, "This rule is not very important. I will not obey it." He may also teach other people to think like that. But this teacher will be the least important person in the Kingdom of Heaven. On the other hand, a person who obeys all God's rules will be important. He teaches other people also to obey, so he will be great in God's Kingdom. 20 I am telling you this. You will be able to come into the Kingdom of Heaven if you obey him. But you must obey him better than the teachers of the Law and the Pharisees do.'

Jesus teaches about angry people

21 'You have heard the words to your people long ago. "You must not kill another person. And any person who does kill will stand in front of a judge. This judge will say that he has done something wrong. And he will punish him." 22 But now, I say this to you about it. Anybody who is angry with his brother without a good reason will stand in front of a judge. The judge may say that this angry person has done a wrong thing. Someone might call his brother by a bad name. Then, the most important rulers will judge him. They may say that he must be punished. But whoever says, "You are a fool", to their brother, God will judge him. He may say to him, "You should go into the fire in hell."

23 'Maybe you go to give your gift to God', said Jesus to them. 'You take it to the special table in God's Great House. But then you remember that your brother is angry with you. 24 You must leave your gift there in front of God's special table. And you must first go and find your brother. Say to him that you are sorry. Then you can both become friends with each other again. After that, you can go back and give your gift to God.

25 A person may say that you have done something wrong. So he will take you to stand in front of the judge. You should try to agree with this person. You should decide with him what is right. Do this even while you are going with him to the judge. Do it so that he will not speak against you to the judge. The judge may agree with him that you have done a wrong thing. Then he will give you to his officer who will put you in prison. 26 What I say is true. You will remain in prison until you have paid all the money.'

Jesus teaches people about not doing wrong things

27 'You know what God said to your people long ago. "You must not have sex with a person who is not your husband or wife.

If you do, then you have done a wrong thing." 28 But I tell you this. A man looks at a woman who is not his wife. And he wants to have sex with her. Now this man has also done a wrong thing.29 If your right eye makes you do wrong things, then you should take it out. You should throw it away. You will lose one eye. But it will be much worse if God throws you with your two eyes into hell. 30 If your right hand makes you do wrong things, then you should cut it off. You should throw it away. You will lose one hand. But it is much worse if God sends you with your two hands into hell.'

Jesus talks about when a man sends his wife away

31 'These words are also in God's Law. "Any man who wants to stop being married to his wife must give her a paper. This paper shows that they are now separate." **[Deuteronomy 24:1-4]** 32 But now, I tell you this. A man must only become separate from his wife because of one reason. This reason is that his wife has had sex with another man. If his wife has not done this, then she is still his wife. The paper does not cause the man and his wife to be separate. Now, if his wife marries another man she is doing a wrong thing. And the other man who marries her is also doing a wrong thing.'

Jesus teaches people about promises to God

33 'You know what God also said to your people long ago. "If you make a promise to God and use his name, do what you have said." **[Numbers 30:2]** 34 But I tell you this. Do not use God's name to make a promise. Do not use the words "by heaven" to make a promise. Heaven is the place where God rules. Do not use the words "by the earth" to make a promise. The earth is the place where God rests his feet. 35 Do not use the words "by Jerusalem" to make a promise. Jerusalem is God's city. He is the great King there. 36 Do not use the words "my head" to make a promise. You cannot make the colour of your hair black or white. 37 You should say only "Yes" if you mean, "Yes, I will do it." And you should say only "No" if you mean, "No, I will not do it." If you say more than this, what you say comes from the Devil.'

Jesus teaches them about how to love people

38 'So, this is also in God's Law. "If a man destroys somebody's eye, then somebody should destroy that man's eye. If a man destroys a man's tooth, then somebody should destroy that man's tooth." **[Exodus 21:24]** 39 But I tell you this. If somebody does something bad to you, do not try to do something bad back to him. Somebody may slap you on one side of your face. Then you should let him slap you on the other side of your face also.'

40 'Maybe somebody wants to take you to the judge. He says to the judge, "This man has done a wrong thing against me. So I want him to give me his shirt." Give the man your shirt. Give him also your coat. 41A soldier may say to you, "Carry my luggage for one mile (1500 metres)." Help him. Carry it for two miles (3000 metres). 42 When somebody asks you for something, you should give it to him. If somebody asks you to lend him something, then you should not refuse.

43 You hear people say, "Love the people who are your friends. Do not love those who want to hurt you." 44But I tell you this. You should love the people who want to hurt you. Some people hurt you because you obey God. You should pray to God that he would help them.

45 If you do this, you will be sons and daughters of your Father above. He causes the sun to shine on people who obey him. He also causes the sun to shine on people who do not obey him. God causes the rain to fall on people who obey him. He also causes the rain to fall on people who do not obey him. 46 You might only love people who love you. But then, God will not pay you for doing that. Even men who take the taxes do it!'

47 'When you only speak to your friends', said Jesus, 'then you are not doing anything extra. Even people who do not believe in God do that. 48 So you must be good in every way, as your Father above is good in every way.' **[Leviticus 19:2]**

Chapter 6

Jesus teaches people how to help poor people

1 Jesus still spoke to them. 'You may do good things and help somebody. But be careful that you do not want other people to see you. Let it be a secret. If you do these things to show people, God, your Father in heaven will not pay you back.

2 When you give something to a poor person, do not tell anyone about it. The hypocrites do this in the buildings where people meet to pray. They also do it outside in the busy streets of the town. They do this so that other people will say, "These men are good." What I say is true. They have already received good words from other people. So, God will not give them anything more.'

3 'When you give something to a poor person, keep it a secret. Do not tell even your best friend. Let it be as if your left hand did not know about your right hand's actions. 4 Nobody else will know about what you gave to the person. It will be a secret. God sees things that are secret. And he will give you good things.'

Jesus teaches people how to pray

5 'So, you must not pray like the hypocrites pray. They like to stand and pray in the Jewish meeting places and on the busy corners of the streets. Then many people can see them praying. What I say is true. They have already received good words from people and they will not get anything more.'

6 'I will tell you how to pray. Go to a place in your house where you can be alone. There you can pray to God your Father. He is in that secret place. And he sees what you do. He will give you good things. 7 When you pray, do not say the same words many times. And do not use many words that mean nothing. People who do not believe in God do that. And they think that God will hear them. 8 Do not be like them. God your Father already knows what you need. He knows this even before you ask him.

9 This then is how you should pray,

"God our Father, you live in heaven.

You are powerful and important.

We want more and more people to know that your name has great authority.

10   We want you to rule everyone.

We want everyone to obey you on earth, like everyone in heaven obeys you.

11   Please give us the food that we need each day.

12   Please forgive us for all the wrong things that we have done.

We have forgiven everyone who has done wrong things to us.

> Forgive us in the same way.

13   Do not let anything cause us to do wrong things.

> Keep us safe from the Devil." '

14 Then Jesus said, 'You must forgive other people for the wrong things that they have done to you. Then God, your Father in heaven will also forgive you for the wrong things that you have done to him. 15 But if you do not forgive other people, then your Father will not forgive you.'

Jesus teaches the people about how to stop eating for some time

16 'Be careful when you stop eating for some time. Do not look sad. Then people will not know what you are doing. That is what the hypocrites do. A hypocrite wants people to think about how good he is. He will let his face become dirty. Then other people can see that he has stopped eating. You should remember that God will not give the hypocrites anything else. Other people think that they are good. And that is all that they will get. 17 But when you stop eating for some time, you should wash your face. You should cause your hair to look nice. 18 Then other people will not know that you have stopped eating for some time. But God your Father knows. He sees what you do in that secret place. So he will give you good things.'

Jesus teaches the people about the valuable things that they have in God's place above

19 'Do not have many valuable things here in the world. Here there are insects and water that can destroy them. There are also men who can come into your house. They can rob you of all your valuable things. 20 Instead, you should put all your valuable things in God's place above. The insects and water cannot destroy your valuable things there. Men cannot rob you of all your things. 21 You will always think about the place where you keep your valuable things. You will want to be there in heaven.'

22 'Eyes are like lamps and your body is like a room. If your eyes are like a clean lamp, then your whole body will have light. 23 If your eyes are not good, then your whole body will be in the dark. If the light in your body has become dark, you will live in a very dark place.'

Jesus teaches the people about God and the things that we have

24 'A slave cannot work for two masters at the same time. He will not like one of the masters, but he will love the other master. He will always say good things about one of the masters and say bad things about the other master. You cannot have God as a master and have money also as your master.'

25 Jesus said to his disciples, 'What I say is true. Do not be anxious about food and drink to stay alive. Do not be anxious about clothes to wear either. Your life is more important than your food, and your body is more important than your clothes. 26 Think about the wild birds. They do not plant seeds in the ground. They do not cut down plants to eat. And they have no buildings to store food. God gives them food. And you are much more valuable than the birds. 27 Perhaps you are anxious about how long you will live. But you cannot live one hour longer, even if you are always thinking about it. No, you cannot do even a small thing like that. So do not be anxious about all these other things.

28 You should not be anxious about your clothes. Think about how the wild flowers grow. They do not work or make clothes for themselves. 29 But this is true. King Solomon wore very beautiful clothes. But even one wild flower is more beautiful than he was. 30 God gives beautiful clothes to the grass and to the wild flowers. They are alive in the field today, but tomorrow people will burn them. God will certainly give you clothes to wear. You should know that God will take care of you.'

31 Then Jesus said, 'Do not always be thinking about where you will find your food and drink and clothes. Do not be anxious. 32 People who do not know about God are always thinking about these things. God, your Father in heaven, knows that you need them. 33 Instead, think about the things that are important in the Kingdom of God. You should do everything that you can to obey God. Then God will also give you the other things that you need. 34 So do not be anxious about what might happen tomorrow. Tomorrow there will be enough problems for you to be anxious about. It is enough for you to be anxious each day about the problems of that day.'

Chapter 7

We should not judge other people

1 Jesus was still speaking to the people. 'Do not say to anybody, "You are a bad person." Then God will not say to you, "You are a bad person." 2 God will speak to you in the same way that you speak to other people. He will use the same rules for you as you use for other people.

3 Do not look at the small piece of wood dirt that is in your brother's eye. You should first see the big piece of wood that is in your own eye. 4 You should not say to your brother, "Please let me take the small piece of wood dirt out of your eye." But you yourself have not seen the big piece of wood that is in your own eye. 5 You think that you are better than your brother. But you are not. First, you must take the big piece of wood out of your own eye. Then your eyes will be clear and you will see well. After that, you can take the small piece of wood dirt out of your brother's eye.'

Jesus tells us to make our own mistakes right. After that, we can tell our friends about their mistakes. Jesus uses the word brother. This includes our friends.

6 'Do not give really good things that are for God to dogs. The dogs will turn round and attack you. Do not throw valuable things to pigs. The pigs will only stand on them and bury them in the dirt.'

Jesus teaches his disciples more about God

7 'Go on asking God for what you need. And then you will receive. Go on looking for what you need. And then you will find it. Go on knocking at the door. And then God will open it for you. 8 Everyone who asks for something will receive it. Everyone who looks for something will find it. God will open the door for everyone who knocks on it.

9 Some of you are fathers. You would not give your son a stone when he asks you for some bread. 10 You would not give your son a snake if he asks you for a fish. 11 Even if you are bad, you know how to give good things to your children. Your Father above knows much better than you do how to give good things. So he will give good things to those people who ask him.'

12 'In the same way that you want other people to do things to you, do things to other people. This is what the Law of Moses teaches us. It is also what the prophets wrote in their books.'

Jesus teaches people how to get true life

13 'You should go in through the narrow gate to get true life. The wide gate is easy to go through. The wide path is easy to travel on.

Many people find that wide gate, but it is the way to hell. 14 It is difficult to go through the small gate. It is difficult to walk on the narrow road. But when you do go that way, you will get true life. Not many people find that narrow gate.'

Jesus teaches the story about a tree and its fruit

15 'Watch out for prophets who tell you wrong things about God. These people seem to be like sheep that are not dangerous. But they are really like hungry wild dogs. What they teach will hurt you.

16 You will know these people by what they do. People do not pick good fruit from weeds. And they do not pick fruit to eat from wild plants.'

17 'Good fruit grows on a tree that is good. Bad fruit grows on a tree that is not good. 18 A good tree cannot make bad fruit. A bad tree cannot make good fruit. 19 The farmer will cut down any tree that does not make good fruit. He will burn that tree on a fire. 20 So you will know if a person is good or bad. Look at what they do. And look at what they say. A good person does good things. And a bad person does bad things.

21 Some people say to me, "Master, Master!" But not all of them will come into the Kingdom of Heaven. Only the people who obey God, my Father in heaven, will come in. They do what he wants them to do. 22 On the day when God judges, people will say, "Master, Master! We used your authority and we told people a message from you. We used your authority and we caused bad spirits to come out of people. We used your authority to do many powerful things." 23 Then I will say to these people, "I never knew you. You do not obey God; you are bad. So go away from me." '

Jesus tells a story about two men who each built a house

24 'I will tell you about a man. He hears my message and he obeys it. Now, this person understands my words. He is like a man who built his house on rock. 25 Then a storm came and brought a lot of water. The water hit the house and strong winds blew hard against that house. But the house did not fall down because the man had built it on rock. 26 Another man hears my message and he does not obey it. He is like a man who built his house on sand. 27 Then a storm came and brought a lot of water. The water hit the house and strong winds blew hard against it. The house fell down. The storm destroyed it completely.'

28 Jesus finished speaking. All the people were very surprised about the things that he taught them. 29 Jesus did not teach them in the same way as the teachers of the Law. Jesus had his own authority when he taught them.

Chapter 8

A man who had an illness of the skin comes to meet Jesus

1 A large crowd followed Jesus when he came down from the hill. 2 Then a man with an illness of the skin came to meet Jesus. The illness was called leprosy. The man went down on his knees in front of him. 'Sir, if you want', he said, 'you can make me well. Please do it.'

3 Jesus put out his hand towards him and touched him. 'I do want to help you. Be well', he said. Immediately, the illness left the man. 4 'You must not tell anyone about this', Jesus said to him. 'Instead, go and show yourself to the priest. Take him a gift for God, as Moses said. "Do this to thank God for what has happened. And this will also show everyone that you are now well." ' [Leviticus 14:1-32]

An officer in the army believes that Jesus can help him

5 When Jesus went into Capernaum, an officer in the army came to meet him. He asked Jesus to help him.

6 'Sir, my servant is lying in bed at home. He cannot move and he has a lot of pain.'

7 Jesus said to the officer, 'I will go with you to your house and I will make your servant well again.'

8 But the officer said to Jesus, 'Sir, you are too important to come into my house. You have authority. Instead, you can say that he will be well. And I know that my servant will be well again. 9 Someone has authority over me. I also have authority over other soldiers. I say to this soldier, "Go!" and he goes. I say to that soldier, "Come!" so, he comes. I say to one of my servants, "Do this!" so, he does it.'

10 Jesus heard what the officer said. And Jesus was very surprised. He spoke to the crowd that was following him. 'What I say is true. I have not found anybody like this man in Israel. Nobody else believes so well in me.'

11 'What I say is true. Many people will come from all over the world. They will take their place in the Kingdom of Heaven. They will sit down to eat with Abraham, Isaac and Jacob. 12 Some people were born to belong to the Kingdom. But God's angels will throw them into the dark places outside his kingdom. There the people will cry. And they will bite their teeth together because they are angry.'

13 Then Jesus said to the officer, 'Go home. You believed that I would make your servant well again. So I will do it for you.' And at that moment, Jesus made the servant well again.

Jesus makes many people well again

14 Jesus went into Peter's house. There, he saw the mother of Peter's wife. She was ill in bed and she felt very hot. 15 Jesus touched her hand and immediately she did not feel hot any longer. She got up and she prepared food and drink for Jesus.

16 That evening, some people brought other people to see Jesus. Bad spirits lived in many of these people. Jesus spoke a word and he caused the bad spirits to leave them. He made everybody who was ill well again. 17 Jesus did all this to cause the prophet Isaiah's words to become true:

'He took away all our weaknesses.

He took away everything that makes us sick.' [Isaiah 53:4]

18 One day, Jesus saw a large crowd round him. So he said to his disciples, 'Let us cross over to the other side of the lake.' 19 A teacher of the Law came to Jesus and said to him, 'Teacher, I want to become one of your disciples. I will go with you everywhere that you go.'

20 Jesus said to him, 'Wild dogs have a place to live. Wild birds also have their own places to live. But the Son of Man has no regular place to lie down and sleep.'

21 Another man who was already a disciple of Jesus spoke to him. 'Sir, I will come with you. But first, let me go home to bury my father. After that, I will come with you.'

22 Jesus said to him, 'Let those people who are dead bury their own dead people.'

Jesus stops a storm

23 Then Jesus climbed into a boat and his disciples followed him. 24 A great storm soon started on the lake. Water began to fill the boat, so that soon the boat was almost under the water. Jesus was sleeping. 25 The disciples went to him and they woke him. 'Save us, Master', they said. 'We will soon die in the water.'

26 'You should not be so frightened. You do not believe in me very much!' Jesus said. Then he stood up and he spoke to the wind and the water. 'Be quiet!' he said. 'Stop moving!' Then the wind stopped and the water became flat again.

27 The disciples were very surprised. 'What kind of man is this?' they asked each other. 'Even the wind and the water obey him!'

Jesus makes two men well again

28 Jesus arrived at the other side of Lake Galilee. He was in the part of the country called Gadara. The people who lived there were called Gadarenes. Jesus arrived near the place where they buried dead people. Two men came to meet Jesus. Bad spirits lived in these two men. The men were very dangerous. Everyone was too afraid to walk near this place because of them. 29 When the two men saw Jesus, they immediately shouted to him, 'What are you going to do with us? You are the Son of God. Have you come to punish us before the right time?'

30 A large group of pigs was feeding near to this place. 31 The bad spirits asked Jesus, 'If you cause us to leave these men, please send us to those pigs. Let us go into them.'

32 'Go!' said Jesus to the bad spirits. So the bad spirits came out of the men and went into the pigs. All the pigs rushed down the hill. They ran into the lake and they all died in the water. 33 There were some men there, who took care of the pigs. Those men ran away into the town, when this happened. They told people there everything that had happened to the men with bad spirits. 34 So everybody came out of the town to meet Jesus. And when they saw him, they said, 'Please leave our part of the country.'

Chapter 9

Jesus helps a man who cannot walk

1 Jesus then climbed back into the boat and he sailed across to the other side of the lake again. He returned to Capernaum, the town where he was living.

2 Some men from the town came to see Jesus. They brought another man with them who could not move his legs. He was lying on a flat piece of wood. Jesus saw the men. And he knew what they were thinking. They believed that Jesus could cause the man on the bed to be well again. Jesus said to the man who could not move, 'Do not be afraid, my friend. I forgive you for all the wrong things that you have done.'

3 Then some teachers of the Law began to speak to each other. 'This man should not have said this', they said to themselves. 'He is speaking as if he is God.'

4 Jesus knew what the teachers were thinking. So he said to them, 'You should not think these bad things. 5 I said to this man, "I forgive you for all the wrong things that you have done." I could have said to him, "Stand up and walk." 6 But I want you to know this. The Son of Man has authority on earth. He can forgive people for all the wrong things that they have done.' Then he said to the man who could not move his legs, 'Stand up. Pick up the bed where you are lying. And go home.' 7 So then the man stood up and he went home. 8 The people saw what had happened. They were very surprised and afraid. They saw that God had given much authority to men. So they said, 'God, how great and powerful you are.'

Jesus asks Matthew to come with him

9 Jesus walked away from that place. While he walked, he saw a man called Matthew. He was one of the men who received taxes for the government. He was sitting in his office. 'Come with me and be my disciple', Jesus said. So Matthew stood up and he went with Jesus.

10 Later, Jesus went into the house. Many other men who received money for the government came to the house. Jesus was eating a meal there. Many people who had done bad things also came. All these people came to eat a meal with Jesus and his disciples.

11 Some Pharisees saw all these people eating a meal with Jesus. They asked Jesus' disciples, 'Why does your teacher eat a meal with these people? They are people who have done bad things. And some of them take tax money.'

12 Jesus heard what the Pharisees were saying. 'People who are well do not need a doctor', he said to them. 'People who are ill need a doctor. 13 Go. And learn what the prophets wrote down in God's book. God says, "I want people to be kind to each other. I do not only want them to give me gifts in my house." Some people think that they have not done anything wrong. I do not ask such people to be my disciples. Many people know that they have done wrong things. It is these people that I am asking be my disciples.'

14 Then some of the disciples of John the Baptist came to meet Jesus. They asked him, 'We, and the disciples of the Pharisees, often stop eating so that we can pray. Why do your disciples never do that?'

15 Jesus answered them with a picture story. 'When the friends of a bridegroom are with him at his marriage, they do not stop eating. The time will come when people will take the bridegroom away from his friends. Then his friends will stop eating.'

16 Then Jesus said, 'Nobody uses a piece of new cloth to repair an old coat. If he did, the hole would grow bigger. When someone washed the coat, the new piece of cloth would become smaller. The new cloth would tear the old cloth again and it would make a bigger hole than before.

17 Nobody pours new wine into an old wineskin. If he does, then the new wine will tear the old wineskin. The wine will run out and he will lose it. And he will destroy the wineskin. Instead of this, you must put new wine into a new wineskin. Then there will be nothing to destroy the wine or the wineskin.'

Jesus causes a dead girl to become alive again

18 While Jesus was saying these things to the people, an important Jew came to him. The man went down on his knees in front of Jesus and said to him, 'My daughter has just died. Come to my house. Touch her with your hand and then she will be well again.' 19 So Jesus started to go along with the man. And his disciples also went along with them.

20 A woman was in the crowd near to Jesus. She had lost blood every day for 12 years. She came close behind Jesus and she touched the edge of his coat. 21 The woman thought, 'If I only touch his coat, Jesus will cause me to become well again.'

22 Jesus turned round and he saw the woman. 'Young woman, do not be afraid', he said. 'You are well again because you believed in me.' And immediately the woman became well again.

23 Then Jesus walked on until he arrived at the house of the important Jew. He went into the man's house. People there were making music with pipes made out of wood. The crowd in the house was also making a loud noise.

24 Jesus spoke to everybody in the house. 'Get out of here', he said. 'This girl is not dead. She is only sleeping.' The people laughed at Jesus. 25 But the family sent the crowd out of the house. Then Jesus went into the room where the girl was lying. He held her hand, and she stood up. 26 After that, people began to tell about what had happened. They told other people in all that part of the country.

Jesus causes two men to see again

27 Jesus left the house. While he walked along, two men began to follow him. They could not see. They were shouting out to him, 'Son of David, be kind to us and help us.'

King David was an ancestor of Jesus.

28 Jesus went into a house. And the men who could not see came to him. Jesus asked them, 'Do you believe that I can cause your eyes to become well?'

The men replied, 'Yes, Master, we believe that you can do this.'

29 So Jesus touched the men's eyes and he said, 'Because you believed in me, your eyes will become well again.' 30 Then immediately the men could see again. Jesus said to them, 'You must not tell anybody about this.' 31 So the men went away. But then they told everybody in that part of the country all about what Jesus had done for them.

Jesus causes a man to speak again

32 While those two men were leaving Jesus, some people brought another man to him. This man could not talk because a bad spirit was living inside him. 33 Jesus said to the bad spirit, 'Leave this man.' The spirit left him, and the man began to speak. Everybody there was very surprised. They said, 'Nobody has seen anything like this happen in Israel before.'

34 The Pharisees said, 'Because Satan makes him powerful, this man can send bad spirits out of people.' 35 Jesus went to visit many towns and villages in that part of the country. He taught the people in the places where they met to talk to God. He taught the good news about the Kingdom. He also caused sick people to become well again from all their illnesses.

Jesus wants God to send out more disciples

36 When Jesus saw the crowds, he felt sorry for them. The people were anxious. They had nobody to help them. Jesus thought, "These people are like sheep with nobody to take care of them." 37 Then Jesus said to his disciples, 'These people are like many good plants in the fields. The plants are ready for the workers to cut down. But there are not many workers. 38 You should ask the master of these fields to send out more workers. Then they can bring in all the plants.'

Chapter 10

Jesus chooses 12 men to be his apostles

1 One day, Jesus asked 12 of his disciples to come to him. He gave them authority over bad spirits that were living in people. These disciples could then cause the spirits to leave people. Jesus also gave them authority to cause sick people to become well again. They could remove all their illnesses.

2 These are the names of the 12 apostles:

The first apostle is Simon, who is also called Peter.

Then next is Simon's brother called Andrew.

There were James and his brother John, who were Zebedee's sons.

3 There were Philip and Bartholomew.

There were Thomas and Matthew. (Matthew received tax money before he became a disciple.)

And there was James who was the son of Alphaeus, and Thaddaeus.

4 Simon, who was called the Zealot, and Judas Iscariot.

Judas Iscariot helped the leaders of the Jews to take hold of Jesus.

Jesus sends out his 12 apostles

5 Jesus sent out these 12 men. Before they left, he said to them, 'Go only to places where Jews live. Do not go to any place where the people are not Jews. And you must not go to any towns where only Samaritans live.'

The Samaritan people and the Jews did not like each other. Some of the Samaritans' ancestor's were Jewish and some of them were not.

6 'Instead, you must go to the people of Israel', he said. 'They are like lost sheep with nobody to take care of them. 7 While you travel, you must tell people about the Kingdom of Heaven. You must tell them that it has become near. 8 Make sick people well again. Cause dead people to become alive again. And cause people with an illness of the skin to become well again. Say to bad spirits that are living in a person, "Come out of him." Then they will leave the person. I gave you the authority to do all these things. Now, go and do all these things for other people. This authority did not cost you anything. So do not ask them to pay you any money for what you do. 9 Do not take any money of any kind in your purse. 10 Do not take a bag with you, or an extra set of clothes. Do not take shoes or a stick. People should give a worker everything that he needs.'

11 'When you are travelling, go into towns and villages. Look for a good person who will take care of you. You should live in his house until you leave that town. 12 When you go into that man's house, say to the people inside, "I pray that you will be well." 13 If the master of the house accepts you, then everyone in the house will be well. But there may not be anybody in the house that accepts you. Then ask God not to cause them to be well. 14 Sometimes you will go into a home or a town and the people will not accept you. And they will not listen to your message. Then you should leave that home or that town. And say to the people, "There is dirt from your town on our feet. We will clean it off before we leave." 15 I am speaking what is true', Jesus said to his disciples. 'One day God will punish the people who refuse me. God will punish them more than he will punish the people from Sodom and Gomorrah.'

16 'Listen well. I am sending you to people who will want to kill you. Your journey will be dangerous. You will be like sheep among wild dogs. You must watch carefully, like a snake watches. But you must also be good and kind like a quiet bird.

17 Watch carefully! People will take hold of you and they will cause you to stand in front of the important Jews. They will take you into the places where they meet to talk to God. Then they will hit you with a whip. 18 People will cause you to stand in front of kings and rulers. This will happen because of me. This is the moment to tell them and those who are not Jews about me.

Tell them the Good News about me. 19 When the people because you stand in front of kings and rulers, do not be afraid. Do not think about what you should say. Do not be afraid about how you will say things. At that moment, God will tell you the right words to speak. 20 You will say words that do not come from you. God the Holy Spirit will tell you what to say.

21 Men will cause their own brothers to stand in front of kings and rulers. And these men will say, "Kill him because he believes in Jesus." Fathers will do the same to their own children. Some children will be against their parents. The children will cause their parents to stand in front of kings and rulers and they will say, "Kill my parents because they believe in Jesus."

22 Many people will not like you because you believe in me. But you should never stop believing in me. Then God will save you. 23 If people in one town hurt you because of me, you should leave that town immediately. You should go to another town. What I say is true. You will not have enough time to speak your message in all the towns of Israel. No, not before the Son of Man comes again.

24 A disciple is not more important than his teacher is. A servant is not more important than his master is. 25 A disciple should be happy if he knows as much as his teacher. A servant should be happy if he is as important as me, his master. Some people call the master of the house Beelzebub (that is "Satan"). These people will call the people in his house even worse names.

26 Do not be afraid of these people. God will remove the cover from everything that people have covered. He will tell everybody all the secrets. 27 I tell you secret things. But you must tell these things to the whole world. They must not be secret any longer. I have said things to you that other people did not hear. But now you must shout all these things from the tops of the houses.'

28 'Do not be afraid of those people who can only kill your body. These people cannot kill your soul. I say to you that you should be afraid of God. He can kill your body, and then he can also kill your soul in hell. 29 Think about this. People sell two small birds for a small coin of little value. One small bird may fall to the ground. But this can only happen if God lets it happen. 30 God even knows how many hairs there are on your head. 31 So do not be afraid of people. God thinks that you are more valuable than many small birds.

32 If a person says to everybody, "I believe in Jesus", then I will speak to God, my Father in heaven. I will say, "I know that person; he is one of my disciples." 33 If someone else says to everybody, "I do not believe in Jesus", I will then speak to God, my Father in heaven. I will say, "I do not know that person; he is not one of my disciples."

34 I will tell you why I have come into the world. I did not come so that everyone would agree with each other. I came to cause people to be in separate groups that fight against each other.

35   A man will fight against his father.

        A daughter will fight against her mother.

        A woman will fight against her husband's mother.

36   A man's family will fight against him.'

37 'A man must love his own father and mother less than he loves me', said Jesus. 'Then he can be my disciple. He must also love his own son or daughter less than he loves me. If he does not do this, then he cannot be my disciple.' 38 Jesus then spoke to the crowd and to his disciples. 'Perhaps some of you want to be my disciples', he said. 'If you do, then you cannot think first about yourself. And you cannot think about what you want to do. You must only do what God wants you to do. You must do this every day. You might even have to die. Then you can be one of my disciples. 39 If a person wants to keep himself safe, then he will never have true life. But instead, he may die because he believes in me. And then he will have true life for always.'

Jesus teaches the people about God's gifts

40 'If anyone accepts you in his home, then he also accepts me. Anyone who accepts me in his home also accepts God. 41 A person accepts a prophet into his home because the visitor is a prophet of God. God will give him the same gift that he gives to a prophet. A person accepts into his home a good man who obeys God. He only does this because the good man obeys God. God will give that person the same gift that he gives to the good man. 42 A person gives a drink of cold water to one of my least important disciples. He only does this because that person is one of my disciples. But it is also true that God will give that man good gifts.'

Chapter 11

Jesus talks about John the Baptist

1 When Jesus had finished telling all these things to his disciples, he went away from that place. And he went to teach people in their towns.

2 At that time, John the Baptist was in prison. But people told him about all the things that Jesus Christ was doing. So John sent some of his own disciples to ask Jesus some questions.

3 Then some of the disciples of John came to Jesus. They said to him, 'John the Baptist has sent us to you. He wants us to ask you a question. Are you the special person that God has sent to us? If you are not that person, should we wait for someone else?'

4 Jesus replied, 'Go back to John. Tell him what you have seen. Also, tell him what you have heard. 5 People who could not see can see again. People who could not walk can now walk again. Some people who were ill with an illness of the skin are now well again. Some people who could not hear can now hear again. Some people who were dead now live again. Poor people are hearing the good news. 6 If people are sure about me, they will be happy.'

7 John's disciples went away again. Then Jesus spoke to the crowd about John. 'You went out to the desert. You certainly did not go to see the wind blowing against a tall piece of grass. No, you did not go to see that. 8 You certainly did not go to see a man who was wearing expensive soft clothes. No, people like that have many beautiful things and they live in the houses of kings. 9 You went to see a man who receives messages from God's Holy Spirit. And John was even more important than that. 10 A long time ago, God said this about him:

"I will send someone before you.

He will tell you my message.

He will prepare the road in front of you." ' **[Malachi 3:1]**

11 Jesus said, 'John is a very important man. He is greater than any man who has ever lived. But a person who is not great in the Kingdom of Heaven, is more important than John.'

12 'From the time that John the Baptist began to teach until now', Jesus said, 'the Kingdom of Heaven is becoming very strong. Strong people who really believe God are taking hold of it. 13 All the prophets and the books of the Law spoke God's word. They spoke until the time that John the Baptist came. 14 The prophets wrote that Elijah would come back again. They were writing about John, if you can believe it. 15 Everyone who can hear must listen. They must listen to what I say.'

16 Jesus said, 'I will talk to you about the people who are alive today. They are like children who are sitting in the market place. They shout to each other,

17 "We played happy music on a pipe for you, but you did not dance.

We sang a sad song but you did not cry." '

People often play happy music with a pipe.

18 'John the Baptist often stopped eating for some time. He never drank wine. So you said that a bad spirit was living inside him.

19 And I, the Son of Man, both eat and drink. So you say about me, "He eats too much and he drinks too much. He is a friend of men who receive taxes and other bad people." God is good and he understands everything. People who understand my words know this. And they agree with God.'

20 Jesus had done many powerful things for the people to see. But some people in the cities did not believe in him. These people did not want to stop doing wrong things. And they did not want to start obeying God. 21 So Jesus said to them, 'Things will be bad for you, people in Chorazin. And things will be bad for you, people in Bethsaida. I have done great and powerful things in your cities. I did not do them a long time ago in the towns called Tyre and Sidon. If I had done them, the people there would have listened to me. They would then have put on clothes made out of goat's hair. They would also have put ash on their heads. This would have shown God that they were sorry. They would have stopped doing wrong things. And they would have started to obey God. 22 Yes, when God judges everyone, he will punish the people from Tyre and Sidon. But he will punish much more the people from Chorazin and Bethsaida. 23 I will tell you what will happen to the people in Capernaum. They try to lift themselves up to heaven. He will throw them down to hell. If I had done these powerful things in Sodom, Sodom would still be standing today. 24What I say is true. God will punish the people from Sodom. But he will not punish them as much as he will punish the people from Chorazin, Bethsaida and Capernaum.'

25 At this moment, Jesus said, 'Father, you rule over everything in the sky and on the earth! You have taught people who do not know many things. And so I thank you. But you have kept these things a secret from some other people. These people think that they know a lot. And they think that they understand everything. 26 Yes, Father, you chose everything to happen in this way.'

27 'My Father has given me all things. And only he knows who I am. Nobody else really knows that I am the Son. Only I know who my Father is. Nobody else knows him. But I choose to tell some people about him.

28 Come to me all of you who are tired. You are like people who have worked for a long time. You are like people who have carried heavy things. Come to me and you will find a place to rest.

29 Do what I teach you to do. Learn from me everything that is true. I am very kind and I obey God. Then you will have true life and you will not be anxious. 30 I will only ask you to do good things. I will not ask you to carry anything that is too heavy for you. And I will not ask you to do things that are too difficult.'

Chapter 12

The Pharisees watch what Jesus does on the Sabbath day

1 On one Sabbath day, Jesus was walking through some fields where wheat was growing. His disciples were hungry. So they began to pick some of the seeds of wheat and to eat them. 2 Some Pharisees were with them. And they saw Jesus' disciples eating the wheat seeds. 'Look at what your disciples are doing', they said to Jesus. 'It is against God's Law to do this on the day that we rest.'

3 Jesus said to the Pharisees, 'King David and his friends were hungry once. Remember what they did then. You have read about this. 4 David went into God's Great House. And he ate the special bread that was there. He also gave some of it to his friends. But it is against the Law for anyone except the priests to eat this bread.'

We can read about this in the book called 1 Samuel, chapter 21.

5 'Also, you should know what God's Law says. The priests are not obeying this Law when they work in God's Great House on the Sabbath day. But God's Law does not tell them that they are doing something wrong. 6 What I say is true. There is someone here more important than God's Great House. 7 A long time ago, a prophet wrote, "God wants people to be kind to each other. He does not only want you to give him gifts" **[Hosea 6:6]** . You do not understand what this really means. If you had understood this, then you would not have said to me, "Your disciples are doing something wrong." 8 The Son of Man has authority over the laws about the Sabbath day.'

9 Jesus left that place in the fields. He went into the place where the Jews met to pray. 10 A man was in there who had a small hand. It was very weak, so he could not use it. The Pharisees wanted to say to Jesus that he was doing wrong things. So they asked him, 'Is it right to make someone well again on the Sabbath?'

11 Jesus replied to them, 'One of you may have a sheep that falls into a deep hole on the Sabbath day. You will take hold of it and you will lift it out of the deep hole. 12 Now, a man is much more valuable than a sheep. So our Law says that we can do good things on the Sabbath day.'

13 Then Jesus said to the man with the weak hand, 'Hold out your hand.' So the man held out his hand. It was now the right size and it was strong. It was the same as his other hand. 14 Then the Pharisees went away from that building where they met. They began to talk to each other about how to kill Jesus.

God chose Jesus to do an important job

15 Jesus knew that the Pharisees wanted to kill him. So he went away from that place. Many people followed him and he caused all the sick people to become well again. 16 He said to all these people, 'You must not tell anyone about me.' 17 So what the prophet Isaiah said became true.

18 'Here is my servant.

I have chosen him to work for me.

I love him and he makes me very happy.

I will give him my Spirit so that he will be powerful.

He will tell people everywhere that I will judge them.

19 He will not argue or shout at people.

People will not hear him shouting in the streets.

20 He will not hurt weak people.

He will be kind to people who are not strong.

He will do this until there is justice everywhere.

21   And all people, everywhere, will believe that he can save them.' **[Isaiah 42:1-4]**

Jesus talks about Satan

22 After that, some people brought a man to Jesus. The man could not see and he could not speak because of a bad spirit in him. Jesus caused the man to become well again. So then the man could see and speak again. 23 All the people were very surprised about what Jesus did. They asked each other, 'Can Jesus really be the person that God sent to save us?'

24 The Pharisees also heard about what had happened. 'This man can cause bad spirits to come out of people', they said. 'Beelzebub is the ruler of all the bad spirits. So he is helping Jesus to do this.'

25 Jesus knew what the Pharisees were thinking. So he said to them, 'Maybe groups of people start fighting other groups of people in the same country. If they do this, then they will destroy their own country. Or perhaps the people in one city or one family start fighting each other. Then they will destroy their own city or family. 26 So, Satan would not fight against himself. If Satan fights against himself, he will soon destroy his own kingdom. 27 Some of you Jews can also send bad spirits out of people. Certainly you do not say that Beelzebub (Satan) helps them. So your own people show you that you are wrong about this. 28 I do send bad spirits out of people. I use the authority of the Spirit of God to do this. If I do this, then God is ruling among you. And certainly you must know that he is.

29 Nobody can go into the house of a strong man easily to rob him. To do this, he must first tie up the strong man. Then he can take away all that man's valuable things.'

30 Jesus then said, 'If someone is not working with me, then he is really working against me. If he is not helping me to bring the sheep together, he is against me. He is causing the sheep to run away in different directions. 31 God will forgive all the wrong things that people do against other people. Some people even say bad things against God. And he will forgive them. Some people say bad things against the Holy Spirit. But God will never forgive them for that. 32 God will forgive people who say bad things about me, the Son of Man. But God will not forgive, now or ever, people who say bad things against the Holy Spirit.'

Jesus talks about a tree and its fruit

33 Then Jesus said, 'To have good fruit you must have a good tree. If you have a bad tree, then you will get bad fruit from it. You can know all about every tree by the fruit that it makes. 34 You are like the children of dangerous snakes. You cannot say good things when your thoughts are bad. When you speak, your words show what is in your mind. 35 The good man says good things because he keeps good thoughts in his mind. The bad man says bad things because he keeps bad thoughts in his mind. 36 What I say is true. One day, God will judge everybody. On that day, you must tell God why you spoke each careless word.

37 God will then say to you, "The words that you spoke are good. I will not punish you." Or God may say to you, "The words that you spoke are bad. So I must punish you." '

The Pharisees want to see Jesus do something powerful

38 Then some teachers of the Law and some Pharisees spoke to Jesus, 'Teacher, we want to see you do something powerful. This will show us that God sent you.'

39 Jesus replied, 'The people who are alive today are very bad. They do not obey God, but they want him to show them something powerful.

But he will not do this. They will see only the same powerful thing that God did to Jonah. 40 Jonah stayed inside a big fish for three days and three nights. In the same way, the Son of Man will remain in the ground for three days and three nights. 41 On the day that God judges everyone, the people who lived in Nineveh will be there. They also will speak against you who are alive today. They will say that you are bad people. They stopped doing bad things when Jonah spoke to them. And then they obeyed God. Listen! Now there is someone here who is more important than Jonah.'

We can read about Jonah in the book called 'Jonah'. God sent Jonah to a city called Nineveh. Jonah said to the people in that city, 'You must stop doing bad things. You must show God that you are sorry. And you must start to obey him.'

42 Jesus then said, 'Many years ago, the queen of a country in the south travelled a long way to see King Solomon. She wanted to hear about everything that Solomon knew. So, when God judges all people, that queen will stand in front of him. And she will speak against you who are alive today. She will say that you are bad people. She listened to Solomon. But there is someone here today. And that person understands things much better than Solomon did. And you are not listening to that person.'

43 And Jesus said, 'When a bad spirit leaves a person, it travels through dry places. It is looking for somewhere new to live. But it does not find anywhere. So, it says to itself, "I will return to the person, to the place where I lived before." 44 Then it goes back to that person. It finds that the place is clean. Everything inside the place is good, but the place is empty. 45 So the bad spirit goes out and it brings back 7 worse spirits. They all go into the person and they live there. Now the person has more bad spirits than he had before. The same thing will happen to the bad people who are alive today.'

Jesus' mother and brothers come to see him

46 While he was still speaking to the crowds, Jesus' mother and brothers arrived. And they stood outside the house. They sent someone inside with a message. 'Tell Jesus that we want to speak to him', they said. 47 A crowd was sitting there with Jesus. Someone told him, 'Your mother and brothers are outside the house. They want to speak to you.'

48 Jesus replied, 'I will tell you who my mother and brothers are.' 49 Then Jesus pointed to his disciples. 'Look! Here are my mother and my brothers', he said. 50 'My brothers and sisters and mother are those people who obey God, my Father in heaven', said Jesus.

Chapter 13

Jesus tells a story about a farmer who planted seeds

1 Again Jesus left the house and he went down to the Lake Galilee. He sat down to teach. The crowd that came together was very large. So, he climbed into a boat and he sat down. The boat was in the water, and the people stood on the shore. 2 Jesus used stories to teach them many things. 3 'Listen to me', said Jesus. 'A farmer went out to plant seed in his field. 4 While he was throwing the seeds, some fell on the path. The wild birds came and they ate those seeds. 5 Some seeds fell on ground with rocks in it. There was not much soil. The seeds quickly began to grow, because the soil was not deep. 6 But when the sun rose, it burned the young plants. They soon dried up because the soil was not deep enough for them. 7 Some seeds fell among bushes with sharp branches. These weeds grew up with the young plants. The bushes stopped the seeds from growing into strong plants, so the plants did not make any new seeds. 8 Some seeds fell on good soil and good strong plants grew from those seeds. Some plants made 100 new seeds. Some plants made 60 new seeds and some plants made 30 new seeds.' 9 After Jesus had finished the story, he told the crowd, 'You have ears. So listen well to what I say!'

Jesus explains to his disciples why he teaches with stories

10 Then Jesus' disciples came to him. 'Why do you speak to the crowd with stories?' they asked.

11 'God has helped you to understand what the stories about the Kingdom of Heaven mean. But God has not helped these people to understand about these things.

12 Listen well. God will help the person who wants to understand my words. He will then really understand a lot more. Another person understands very little.

God will take away the little that he has. So then he will understand nothing at all. 13 The reason I use stories to talk to other people is this:

> "So these people look. But they do not see.

So they listen. But they do not hear or understand." ' **[Isaiah 6:9-10]**

14 'Isaiah, the prophet, wrote a message from God about this. And now that message has become true.

> "This people will listen and listen. But they will not understand.

> They will look and look. But they will not see anything.

15   The people do not really want to understand.

> > They are like people who have shut their ears.

> > They are like people who have shut their eyes.

> > If they did want to look, then they would see.

> > If they did want to listen, then they would hear.

> And then they would understand everything and they would turn back.

> And if they did turn back, then I would make them well." **[Isaiah 6:9-10]**

16 You should be happy because God has helped you to see. And he has helped you to hear. 17 What I say is true. Many prophets and good people from a long time ago wanted to see these things. But they did not see the things that you can see. They wanted to hear the things that you are hearing. But they did not hear them.'

Jesus explains the story about the farmer who planted his seeds

18 'Listen to me now. I will explain to you what this story about the farmer means. 19 Some seeds fell on the path. The path is like people who do not understand the message. They hear it but they do not understand it. Then the devil comes quickly to them. And he takes away what they have heard. 20 Some of the seeds fell on soil with rocks in it. This soil is like some people who hear the message from God. They are happy to believe it for a while. But it does not go into their lives and thoughts. 21 They believe in God for a while. But they are like plants that do not grow down in the soil. Because they obey God's words, other people give them problems. So when they meet trouble or difficulty, they stop believing.

22 Some seeds fell among weeds. This soil is like other people who hear the message from God. But they have many anxieties. They think that more money and other valuable things will cause them to be happy. These thoughts stop them obeying God. They are like plants that do not grow new seeds.

23 But some seeds fell on good soil. This soilis like other people who hear the message from God. They understand it and they obey God. These people are like good plants. From one seed, the good plants make 30 seeds. Other good plants make 60 new seeds, and some good plants make 100 new seeds.'

In this story, the seed that falls in different kinds of soil is the message of good news from God. The farmer is like a person who teaches people about that message.

Jesus tells a story about some weeds

24 Then Jesus told the people another story. 'This is what the Kingdom of Heaven is like', he said. 'A farmer planted some good wheat seeds into his field. 25 But one night, when everyone was sleeping, a bad person came to the farmer's field. He did not like the farmer. This bad person planted seeds from weeds among the good seeds. Then the bad person went away again. 26 The good seeds grew and the plants began to make seeds. But when this happened, the weeds also grew.

27 So the farmer's servants came to speak to him. "Master, many weeds are now growing in the ground where you planted the wheat seeds. How did this happen?" they asked him.

28 The farmer said to his servants, "A bad person who does not like me has done this."

"Do you want us to go and pull up the weeds?" the servants then asked the farmer.

29 "No", replied the farmer. "I do not want you to do that. If you pull up the weeds, you will also pull up some of the wheat plants. 30 Let the good plants and the weeds grow up together. After that, it will be time for the workers to cut the plants that have large seeds. They will bring them inside from the fields. I will ask the workers to cut the weeds down first. They can tie them together and burn them. Then they can cut the wheat and bring it into my building. I can store it there." '

Jesus tells a story about a small seed

31 Jesus told the people another story. 'I will tell you again what the Kingdom of Heaven is like', he said. 'It is like a very small seed. A man took this seed and he planted it in his field. 32 It is the smallest seed in the world. But when it starts to grow, it becomes bigger than the largest bush. It will become a tree. The wild birds will come and they will make places to live among the branches of that tree.'

Jesus tells a story about yeast

33 Jesus told the people another story. 'I will tell you another story about what the Kingdom of Heaven is like', he said. 'It is like some yeast and flour. A woman took the yeast and she mixed it in three large bowls of flour. The yeast grew and it caused all the bread to rise.'

34 Jesus told the crowd all these things. But he only used stories to teach them. 35 So what the prophet had said became true:

> 'I will use stories when I speak to them.

> And I will teach them secret things.

People have never learned these things before.' **[Psalm 78:2]**

36 Then Jesus went away from the place where the crowd was. He went into the house where he was staying. And his disciples also came into the house with him. 'Explain to us the story about the weeds in the soil', they said to Jesus.

Jesus explains the story about the weeds

37 Jesus replied to his disciples, 'The Son of Man is like the farmer who planted the wheat seed in the field.

38 The field is like the world. The good wheat seeds are like the people who belong to the Kingdom. The weeds are like the people who belong to Satan. 39 Satan is the bad person who planted the weed seeds in the field. The moment when the workers cut down all the plants is like the end of time. God's angels are the workers who cut the plants down.

40 The workers cut the weeds and they burn them in the fire. In the same way, the angels will do this at the end of time. They will do it to the people who belong to Satan. 41 The Son of Man will send his angels. They will take away all the people who are not really part of his Kingdom. They have caused other people not to obey God. And the angels will take away all the people who have not obeyed God. 42 The angels will throw the bad people into the great fire. There the people will cry. And they will bite their teeth together because they are angry. 43 The people who obeyed God will shine like the sun. They will be in the Kingdom of their Father. You have ears, so listen well to what I say.'

Jesus tells a story about a man who found valuable things in the ground

44 'I can tell you again what the Kingdom of Heaven is like', Jesus said. 'The Kingdom of Heaven is like something valuable that a man buried in a field. Another man found it, but then he covered it over again with dirt. Then that second man was very happy and he went away. He sold everything that he had. Then he went and bought the field with the valuable things in it.'

Jesus tells a story about some valuable stones

45 'I will tell you again what the Kingdom of Heaven is like', Jesus said. 'A man has a business. He looks for beautiful valuable stones that he can buy. 46 One day he found a very beautiful and very valuable stone that someone wanted to sell. So he went away. And he sold everything that he had. Then he went and he bought that very beautiful and very valuable stone.

47 I can tell you again what the Kingdom of Heaven is like', Jesus said. 'Some men had nets to catch fish in. They threw their nets into the lake and they caught many different kinds of fish. 48 When the net was full of fish, the men pulled it up on to the shore. Then they sat down. Some of the fish were good to eat, and they put these fish into baskets. Some of the fish were not good to eat, and they threw these fish away. 49 This is what will happen at the end of time. God will send his angels. They will put the people who did not obey God in one place. And they will put the people who obey God in another place. 50 The angels will throw the people who did not obey God into the great fire. There the people will cry. They will also bite their teeth together because they are angry.'

This story means the same as the story about the weeds in Matthew 13:37-43.

51 Then Jesus asked his disciples, 'Have you understood all these things?'

'Yes, we have', they replied.

52 'Some teachers of the Law have learned about the Kingdom of Heaven', Jesus said. 'These men are like the master of a house.

The master takes out some old things and also some new things from the place where he stores them.'

53 When Jesus had finished telling these stories, he went away from that place.

Jesus goes to Nazareth

54 Jesus went to the town called Nazareth. He had lived in Nazareth when he was a boy. He taught the people in the building where they met to pray.

The people were very surprised about the things that he was teaching them. 'Where did this man learn all these things?' they asked each other. 'How does he know so much? How does he do all these powerful things?' they said. 55 'We know who this man is. He is the son of a man who makes things out of wood. And Mary is his mother. We also know his brothers, James, Joseph, Simon and Judas. 56 All his sisters also live here in this town among us. So then, where did he learn to do all these things? Who caused him to be so powerful?' So the people were not happy with Jesus.

57 'People do not believe a prophet who comes from their own town', Jesus said to them. 'His own people and his own family do not believe that he receives messages from God. Only people in other places believe him.'

58 Jesus did not do many powerful things in Nazareth because the people

Chapter 14

Herod's soldiers kill John the Baptist

1 At that time, Herod the ruler heard reports about the things that Jesus was doing.

Herod was the ruler in one of the four parts of Israel at that time.

2 'That man Jesus is really John the Baptist', said Herod to his men. 'John was dead but he has become alive again. That is the reason that Jesus can do all these powerful things.'

3 Herod himself had said to his soldiers, 'Take hold of John. Tie his hands and feet and put him in prison.' Herod had done this because of his wife Herodias. Before Herod married her, she was the wife of Herod's brother Philip. 4 Because Herod had married her, John had said to him, 'Herodias was your brother's wife. So you did not do the right thing when you married her.'

5 Herod wanted to tell his soldiers that they must kill John. But the people thought that John was a prophet. So Herod was afraid to kill him.

6 But when it was Herod's birthday, he had a special meal. The daughter of Herodias danced in front of him and his visitors. Her dance caused Herod to become very happy. 7 'Ask me for anything that you want', Herod said. 'And I will give it to you. God is listening to me say this.' 8 Herodias suggested to her daughter, 'Ask Herod to give you John's head.' So her daughter asked Herod to give her the head of John the Baptist on a plate. 9 Then Herod was sad, but he had spoken a special promise in front of God. So he could not refuse her. And his visitors had heard him. So he sent his men to give Herodias's daughter what she had asked for. 10 He immediately said to a soldier, 'Cut off John's head and bring it here.' So, the soldier went to the prison and he cut off John's head. 11 Then he brought it back on a plate and he gave it to the girl. She then gave it to her mother. 12 John's disciples heard the news that John was dead. So, they went to the prison and they took away his body. And then they buried it. After that, they went to see Jesus. And they told him what had happened.

Jesus gives food to 5000 men and their families

13 Jesus heard about what had happened to John. After that, he went away from that place. He sailed in a boat to a quiet place where he could be alone. But the crowd heard where Jesus had gone. So they left their towns and they followed Jesus. They walked to the place where he was. 14 Jesus climbed out of the boat to the shore. He saw a large crowd there. He loved them and he felt sorry for them. He saw that there were sick people in the crowd. So he made them well again.

15 When it was almost evening, Jesus' disciples came to speak to him. They said to him, 'We are in a place where there are no houses. And it will soon be dark. So send the crowd away now, so that they can go to the villages near here. There they can buy some food for themselves to eat.'

16 'The people do not need to go away. You give them some food to eat', Jesus replied.

17 'But we only have 5 small loaves of bread and two fish', they said.

18 'Bring the bread and fish here to me', Jesus said. 19 Then Jesus said to the large crowd, 'Sit down on the grass.' Jesus received the 5 loaves of bread and two fish from his disciples. He looked up to the sky and he thanked God for the bread and the fish. Then he broke the bread into pieces. And he gave it to his disciples to give to the crowd.

20 Then everybody ate, and they all had enough. Then the disciples picked up all the food that the people had not eaten. And they filled 12 baskets with broken pieces of bread and fish. 21 About 5000 men ate the bread and fish. The women and children also ate it with them.

Jesus walks on the water

22 Immediately after this, Jesus said to his disciples, 'Get in the boat and sail across the lake. Go on in front of me while I send the crowd away.' 23 Then he sent the crowd away. After they had gone, he went up on a mountain alone to pray. And he was still there alone when it became dark. 24 Now, the boat was in the middle of the lake. The wind was blowing against the boat and the water was hitting it.

25 Then, when it was very early in the morning, Jesus walked across the water towards his disciples. 26 And the disciples saw him walking on top of the water. They were very frightened. 'It is a spirit', they said. And they shouted with loud voices because they were afraid.

27 But immediately, Jesus spoke to them. 'Be brave! Do not be afraid! It is I, Jesus', he said to them.

28 Peter replied, 'Sir', he said, 'are you really Jesus? Then say to me, "Come here! Walk on top of the water." '

29 'Come to me', said Jesus.

31 Immediately, Jesus put out his hand and he took hold of Peter. 'Why do you not really believe in me to help you?' he said to Peter. 'Why did you not believe that I could cause you to walk on the water?'

32 When Jesus and Peter climbed into the boat, the strong wind stopped blowing. 33 The disciples who were in the boat went down on their knees in front of Jesus. 'It is true. You are the person that God calls his son', they said.

34 When they had sailed across the lake to the shore, they climbed out of the boat. They were in the part of the country called Gennesaret.

35 The people who lived in that part of the country recognised Jesus. So they sent people to tell everyone in that part of the country that Jesus was there. They brought all their sick people to see him. 36 They asked Jesus to let them touch the edge of his clothes. And Jesus caused every sick person who touched his clothes to become well again.

Chapter 15

Jesus tells the Pharisees and teachers of the Law to obey God

1 After that, a group of Pharisees and teachers of the Law came from Jerusalem to talk to Jesus.

2 These men spoke to Jesus. 'Our ancestors taught us the right way to do everything. Why do your disciples not obey the things that our ancestors taught us? They do not wash their hands in the right way before they eat a meal.'

3 'Yes, God tells us the right way to obey him', Jesus replied. 'But you do not obey God. Instead, you do the things that you have taught the people to do. 4 Moses wrote in his law, "God says that you must love your father and mother. Do good things for them and only say good things about them." **[Exodus 20:12]**

God also said, "Someone should kill a person who says bad things about his own father or mother." **[Exodus 21:17]**

5 But instead of obeying this, you teach people something different. You let a person say to his father or mother, "I would have given these good gifts to you, but I cannot. Instead, I have given them to God." Then, you let him give nothing to his mother and father. 6 When you let a person do this, you have not obeyed God's Law. You have obeyed the laws of your ancestors instead. You do many other things like this. 7 You are hypocrites! What Isaiah said about you is true. He wrote down these words from God:

8   "These people say good things about me,

             but they do not really want to obey me.

9   They say that I am powerful and important.

             But what they say has no purpose.

They teach their own rules, which I did not give to them." **[Isaiah 29:13]** '

Jesus talks about the wrong things that people do

10 Jesus asked all the people to come together near him. 'Listen to me', he said, 'so that you can understand my words. 11 God will not say to a person, "I will not accept you because you ate a certain food." It is not the food that a person eats. Food does not cause God to say, "I cannot accept you." Instead, what comes out of his mouth is important. This can cause God to say, "I will not accept you." '

12 Jesus' disciples went near to him and they said, 'The Pharisees heard what you said to them. They are not happy with what you said. Do you know that?'

13 Jesus replied to his disciples, 'Those Pharisees are like plants that God, my Father in heaven, did not put in the soil. He will pull all these plants out of the soil. 14 Do not be anxious about them. They cannot see, but they are telling people which way to go.

A man who cannot see does not show another man like himself where to go. If he does this, then both men will fall into a deep hole in the road.'

15 Peter said to Jesus, 'Explain to us what you just said.'

16 'You still cannot understand what I am saying. You are like the Pharisees and the teachers of the Law', replied Jesus. 17 'The food that a person eats first goes into his mouth. Then it goes into his stomach, and then it goes out of his body. 18 The words that a person speaks come from their thoughts. So what a person says can cause God to say to him, "I will not accept you." 19 A person can think bad thoughts. These thoughts may cause him to kill somebody. Or they may cause him to have sex with another man's wife. He might rob somebody. He might say things that are not true about someone. Or he might say bad things about somebody.'

20 'All these bad things cause God to say to a person, "I cannot accept you." But perhaps a man does not wash his hands before he eats. This does not cause God to say, "I will not accept you." '

Jesus makes a girl well again

21 After that, Jesus left Gennesaret and he went to some places near to the cities called Tyre and Sidon.

22 A woman was living in this part of the country. She was one of the people from the group called the Canaanites. She went to see Jesus and she continued to shout with a loud voice to him. 'Son of David, help me, sir. A bad spirit is living inside my daughter. It is making her very ill.'

23 Jesus did not reply to the woman. So his disciples came to him. 'Please, please send this woman away', they said. 'She is following us and she is making a lot of noise.'

24 Jesus replied to his disciples, 'God sent me only to the people of Israel, because they are like lost sheep.'

25 The woman came to Jesus and she went down on her knees in front of him. 'Sir, please help me', she said.

26 Jesus did answer the woman this time. 'It is not right to take bread from the children and then to throw it to the dogs.'

27 The woman replied to Jesus. 'Yes sir, that is true. But even the dogs eat the small pieces of bread that fall from their master's table.'

28 'You are a woman who believes very well in me', said Jesus. 'So God will do what you asked.' And immediately, the woman's daughter became well again.

29 Jesus travelled on from that place and he walked along the shore of Lake Galilee. He climbed up a hill and he sat down there. 30 A large crowd came to him and they brought sick people with them. Some of these sick people could not walk very well, and some of them could not see. Some of the sick people had arms or legs that hurt. And some of them could not speak. There were also many other sick people who had different illnesses. Their friends put the sick people in front of Jesus. And Jesus caused them all to become well again. 31 The large crowd were very surprised about what they saw. People who could not speak could now speak again. Those people who could not walk very well could now walk well. The people who could not see could now see. They were all saying to God, 'God of Israel, you are powerful. You are great. You are very important. We thank you because you are so kind.'

Jesus feeds 4000 men and their families

32 Then Jesus spoke to his disciples, 'Come near to me. I feel sorry for this crowd', he said. 'They have stayed with me now for three days and they have no more food. I do not want to send them away while they are hungry. They may fall down on the way because they are weak and hungry.'

33 The disciples said to Jesus, 'We are in a place that is a long way from any town. Where can we find enough bread here to feed so many people?'

34 'How many loaves of bread do you have?' asked Jesus.

'We have 7 loaves of bread and a few small fish', they replied.

35 Jesus said to the crowd, 'Sit down on the ground.'

36 Then he held the 7 loaves and the fish in his hands and he thanked God for them. Then he broke the bread and the fish into pieces and he gave the food to his disciples. 'Give this food to the people', he said. 37 All the people ate and they all had enough. After the people had finished eating, there remained a lot of extra food. Jesus' disciples filled 7 baskets with the extra pieces of bread and fish. 38 4000 men ate the bread and fish. This number did not include the women and children who also ate. 39 Then Jesus spoke to the large crowd again. 'Now you should all go home', he said. After that, Jesus got into the boat. And they sailed away to the part of the country called Magadan.

Chapter 16

The Pharisees ask again to see something powerful

1 Some Pharisees and Sadducees went to see Jesus. They wanted to make Jesus do something wrong. 'Do something powerful for us to see', they asked him. 'Then we will know that God sent you.'

2 Jesus answered them. 'Sometimes the sky is red in the evening. Then you say that tomorrow the weather will be good. 3 Sometimes the sky is red in the morning and the sky has dark clouds in it. Then you say that today there will be a storm. You can look at the sky. And then you know what weather is coming. But special things are happening now. And you do not understand what they mean. 4 The people who are alive today are very bad. They do not obey God. They want God to show them something powerful. No! God will not show you anything. You will only see the same powerful thing that God did to Jonah.' So Jesus went away and left them.

Jesus talks about the yeast of the Pharisees and the Sadducees

5 Then Jesus and his disciples went over to the other side of the lake. His disciples forgot to take any bread with them. 6 'Be careful', Jesus said to them. 'You must be careful and watch for the yeast of the Pharisees and Sadducees.'

7 The disciples began to talk to each other about this. 'Jesus is saying this because we did not bring any bread with us', they said.

8 Jesus knew what they were talking about. So he said to them, 'You should not be talking about the fact that you did not bring any bread with you. You still do not believe very much in me. 9 You still do not understand. You should remember when I used 5 loaves of bread to give food to 5000 men and their families. You should remember how many baskets of bread you filled after the meal. 10 You should remember when I used 7 loaves of bread to give food to 4000 men and their families. You should remember how many baskets of bread you filled after the meal. 11 I spoke about the yeast of the Pharisees and the Sadducees. I said that you must be careful about it. You should have understood that this time I was not really speaking about bread.' 12 Then the disciples understood what Jesus was talking about. They did not need to be careful about the yeast that they used in their bread. They must be careful about what the Pharisees and Sadducees taught.

Peter says who Jesus is

13 Jesus went into the part of the country called Caesarea Philippi. While he was there, he asked his disciples a question. 'Tell me', he said. 'When people talk about the Son of Man, what do they say?'

14 'Some people say that you are John the Baptist', they replied. 'Other people say that you are Elijah. And some other people say that you are Jeremiah, or another prophet.'

15 'What do you think', he asked them. 'Who am I?'

16 Simon Peter answered him. 'You are the Christ. God sent you. You are the Son of the God who is alive.'

17 Jesus said to Simon Peter, 'Simon, son of Jonah, God has given help to you. No person on earth taught you that. God, my Father, who rules in heaven, taught you this. 18 What I say is true. You are called Peter, which means a rock. And I will build my Church on this rock. Not even the power of death can beat and destroy my Church. 19 I will give you the keys to the Kingdom where God rules in heaven. Perhaps you will say, "No, you cannot do that" to something that people want on earth. Then God will say "No" to it where he rules in heaven. Maybe you will say, "Yes, you can do that" to something that people want on earth. Then God will say "Yes" to it where he rules in heaven.'

20 Jesus spoke with authority to his disciples. 'Do not tell anyone that I am the Christ.'

Jesus tells his disciples how he would die

21 After this, Jesus began to explain everything to his disciples. 'I must go to Jerusalem', he told them. 'There, people will cause me to have great pain. The leaders of the Jews, the important priests, and the teachers of the Law will hurt me. And then people will kill me. But three days later, God will cause me to be alive again.'

22 Then Peter led Jesus away from the other disciples. Peter did not agree with what Jesus had said. He spoke with strong words to Jesus. 'No, Sir', he said. 'You must not say these things. I pray that God will never let this happen!'

23 Jesus turned towards Peter and said to him, 'Go away from me, Satan. I must obey God. But you are trying to stop me. Your thoughts do not come from God. Instead, you are thinking as men think.'

24 Then Jesus said to his disciples, 'Someone may want to come with me', he said. 'Then he must leave what he himself wants to do. He must carry a cross and he must be ready to die with me. 25 If a person wants to keep his life safe, he will lose it. But instead, he may die because he believes in me. And then he will have true life, which has no end. 26 A person could get the whole world for himself. This would not be good for him if he died as a result. There is nothing that a person can give to get back his life. 27 I tell you all this because I, the Son of Man, will come back here with God's angels. When I come, I will be powerful and important like God my Father. I will pay each person for what he has done on earth. 28 What I am saying now is true. I will tell you something about the people who are standing here. Some of them will not die until they see the Son of Man's kingdom begin.'

Chapter 17

God causes Jesus to become different to look at

1 Six days later, Jesus took Peter and the brothers James and John with him. He led them up a high mountain where they were alone together. 2 Peter, James and John watched Jesus and they saw him become different to look at. His face was bright and it shone like the sun. His clothes became very white and they shone. 3 Then Peter, James and John saw two men appear in front of them. These two men were Moses and Elijah and they were talking with Jesus.

4 Peter said to Jesus, 'Teacher, it is a good thing that we are here. Let us build three huts. One hut will be for you. One hut will be for Moses and one hut will be for Elijah.'

5 While Peter was still speaking, a bright cloud appeared. And it covered them all. They heard a voice, which came out from the cloud. 'This is my Son', it said. 'I love him and he makes me very happy. Listen to him.'

6 When the disciples heard the person speaking, they threw themselves down. And their faces touched the ground. They were very frightened. 7 But Jesus came to them and he touched them. 'Stand up again', he said. 'Do not be afraid.' 8 When they looked up, they could not see anyone else. Only Jesus was there.

9 While they were walking down the mountain again, Jesus spoke to Peter, James and John. 'You must not tell anyone about what you have just seen', he said. 'One day, the Son of Man will die and then become alive again. Then you can tell people about these things.'

10 Then the three disciples asked Jesus a question. 'The teachers of the Law say, "Elijah will return to earth first before anything else happens." Why do they say this?'

11 'Yes, Elijah does come first', said Jesus. 'He causes everything to be ready. 12 But I tell you that Elijah has already come. People did not recognise him. They did all the bad things to him that they wanted to do. In the same way, they will also hurt me, the Son of Man.' 13 Then the disciples understood that he was really talking about John the Baptist.

Jesus makes a boy well

14 Then Jesus, Peter, James and John returned to the place where the crowd was waiting for them. A man came to see Jesus. He went down on his knees in front of him. 15 'Teacher', he said. 'please be kind to my son. His mind is sick. Sometimes he does not know what he is doing. Often he falls into the fire, or he falls into water. 16 I brought the boy to your disciples. But they could not make him well.'

17 'You people today still do not believe in me', Jesus said. 'You have turned away from God. I have lived here among you for a long time. I cannot remain with you much longer. Now it is difficult for me to be patient with you.' Jesus then said to the man, 'Bring your son here to me.' 18 Jesus said to the bad spirit, 'Stop!' Then the bad spirit left the boy and immediately he became well.

19 When the disciples were alone with Jesus, they asked him, 'Why could we not cause the bad spirit to leave the boy?'

20 'You could not do it because you do not believe well in me', Jesus replied. 'What I say is true. If you believe in God even a little bit, then you can do great things. You can say to this mountain, "Move from this place to that other place." And it will move. You can do anything. 21 But you must pray and not eat for a time. That will cause this kind of spirit to leave a person', said Jesus.

22 When Jesus and his disciples all met together in Galilee, he said, 'Soon people will put the Son of Man into the hands of powerful men. 23 These men will kill him. But he will be alive again three days later.' The disciples were very sad.

24 After that, Jesus and his disciples arrived at Capernaum. Some men who received taxes went to talk to Peter. They asked him, 'Does your teacher pay the tax for God's Great House?'

25 'Yes', said Peter to them. 'My teacher does pay the tax.'

Then Peter returned to the house where Jesus was staying. He wanted to tell Jesus what had just happened. But Jesus spoke first. 'Here is a question for you to answer, Simon', he said. 'Who are the people who must pay taxes and money to the rulers of the world? Do the rulers take taxes from their own sons? Or do they take taxes from other people?'

26 'The kings take the taxes from other people', Simon replied.

Jesus said to him, 'This means that people from the ruler's own country do not need to pay anything. 27But we do not want to make these men who take the tax angry. So go to the lake and throw out a line to fish with. And pull up the first fish that you catch on your line. Open the mouth of the fish and you will find a gold coin inside it. Take the coin and give it to those who receive tax. This will be enough money for both my tax and yours.'

Chapter 18

Jesus says who is the most important person

1 Soon after this, the disciples came to Jesus and they asked him, 'Who is the most important person in the Kingdom of Heaven?'

2 There was a little child there. Jesus said to the child, 'Come here. Stand in front of everybody.' 3 'What I say is true', Jesus said. 'Unless you become like a child, you cannot come into the Kingdom of Heaven. 4This little child does not think that he is very important. You must also think as he does. A person who does this will be the most important person in the Kingdom of Heaven.

5 Any person who accepts a child because of me also accepts me.'

Jesus talks about causing people to do wrong things

6 'Maybe someone will cause a little person to stop believing in me', said Jesus. 'It would be better for this person if other people hung a big stone round his neck. Then they could throw that bad person into the deep sea together with the stone.

7 It is very bad that some things in the world cause people to do wrong things. You can be sure that bad things will come. But God will punish the person who makes these bad things happen.'

8 'Maybe your hand or your foot causes you to do wrong things. Then you should cut it off. And you should throw it away. It is better to have only one hand or one foot and to have God's true life. It is much worse to keep both hands and both feet and do wrong things. Then God will throw you into hell. 9 If your eye causes you to do wrong things, then you should take it out. You should throw it away. It is better to have only one of your eyes and have God's true life. It is much worse if God throws you with your two eyes into hell. There the fire does not ever stop burning.

10 Be careful that you do not think that these little people are not important. What I say is true. The angels who watch over them always remain with my Father in his home. And those angels speak to him.'

[11 The Son of Man has come to save that which was lost.]

12 'Think about a man who has 100 sheep.

He counts them. And he discovers that one of his sheep is not there. So he leaves all the other sheep on the hills. Then he goes to look for the lost sheep. 13 What I say is true. The man will be very happy if he finds that lost sheep. All the other sheep are safe on the hill. But they do not make him as happy as this sheep does. They were never lost. 14 God, who is my Father in heaven, is like this man. He does not want even one of these little people to be lost.'

A friend does wrong things against you

15 'If your brother has done wrong things against you, then you must go to him. You can talk about it together when you are alone with him. Then he may understand that you are right. If he does understand, then you can call him your friend again.'

16 'Maybe he does not want to listen to you. Then take one or two other people with you to him. These one or two people then know what wrong things your brother has done. They will know what you said to him. They will know that it is true. God's word said that we should do this. 17 If your brother will not listen to the two or three of you, go to the Church. Tell other people what has happened. Let those who obey me speak to your brother. If he is not sorry, stop being his friend. He is like somebody who refuses to obey God.'

18 'What I say is true. Maybe you will say, "No, you cannot do that" to something that people on earth want to do. God will say "No" to it where he rules in heaven. Maybe you will say, "Yes, you can do that" to something that people want on earth. God will then say "Yes" to it where he rules in heaven.

19 Two people may agree together to ask God for the same thing. Then my Father above will give them what they ask for.

20 Two or more people come together to speak to me because they believe in me. I am there with them.'

Jesus tells the people about the servant who did not forgive

21 Then Peter came to talk to Jesus. 'Teacher', he asked. 'If my brother does wrong things against me many times, how many times must I forgive him? Must I forgive him as many as 7 times for the wrong things that he has done against me?'

22 'I do not say 7 times', Jesus replied. 'I say, 7 times, and then again and again until you cannot count.'

Jesus is saying that we must continue to forgive people.

23 'I will tell you what the Kingdom of Heaven is like. A king wanted to check how much money his servants should give to him. 24 So the king began to check. Then his men led a servant to him who had a big debt. He must pay back 10 000 gold coins to the king.'

25 'The servant could not pay his debt to the king. So the king said to his men, "Sell the servant and his wife and children and all his things. Then I will keep the money to pay his debt."

26 Then the servant went down on his knees in front of the king. He said to him, "Please, please give me some more time, then I will pay you everything." 27 Then the king felt sorry for his servant and said to him, "You do not need to give me the money. You are free of the debt."

28 But then that same servant went away and he met another servant of the king. This other servant had to pay back a debt of 100 cheap coins to the first servant. The first servant took hold of the neck of the other servant. "Give me the money that is mine", he said.

29 The other servant went down on his knees in front of the first servant. "Please, please give me some more time", he said to the first servant. "Then I will give you the money."

30 But the first servant said, "I refuse to do that!" And he put the other servant in prison until he could pay his debt to him. 31 The other servants of the king saw what had happened. They were not happy about it. So they went to see the king. And they told him about everything that had happened.

32 So the king then sent a message to bring the first servant to him. "You are a very bad person", said the king to the servant. "I told you that you did not need to give me my money. I did this because you asked me. 33 You should be kind to the other servant in the same way that I was kind to you." 34 The king was very angry with the first servant. His men put the first servant in prison and they punished him. He would remain there until he could pay all his debt to the king.'

35 Then Jesus finished the story and he said, 'You must forgive your friend completely. If you do not forgive him completely, then, in the same way, my Father above will not forgive you.'

Chapter 19

Jesus teaches about when a man sends his own wife away

1 When Jesus had finished saying all these things, he went away from Galilee. He went to the part of Judea that is on the other side of the river Jordan. 2 Large crowds followed Jesus there. Jesus caused the sick people in the crowds to become well again.

3 Some Pharisees came to talk to Jesus. They tried to cause Jesus to give the wrong answers to their questions. They asked, 'Can a man send his own wife away and say to her, "You are no longer my wife." Does the Jewish Law let him do this for any reason he chooses?'

4 'You surely have read about this in God's book', Jesus replied. 'At the start of the world, God made men and he also made women.'

5 'Because of this, a man leaves his father and his mother. God joins him and his wife together. The man and the woman become like one person. 6 They are not two separate people any longer. They are like one person. God has joined them together to be husband and wife. So nobody must separate them.'

7 Then the Pharisees said to Jesus, 'Moses said that a man could give his own wife a paper. The paper shows that the man and woman are now separate. Then the man can send the woman away. Why did Moses say this?'

8 Jesus answered them. 'Moses said this because you people did not want to obey God. All these things were different at the start, when he made the world. 9 What I say is true. A man must not send his wife away unless she has had sex with another man. A man can only marry another woman if that has happened. If not, then he does a wrong thing if he marries another woman.'

10 Jesus' disciples replied, 'This is what it is like for a man and a woman to marry. Maybe it is better if a man does not marry.'

11 Jesus then answered, 'Not everyone can agree with this idea. God has not given it to everyone. 12 What I say is true. There are several different reasons why a man cannot marry. Some men cannot have sex. They were born like that. Some other men also cannot have sex. This is because men did something to them. And now they cannot have sex. Some men do not marry because they can work better for God without a wife. Anyone who can understand this can agree with it.'

Jesus wants children to come to him

13 Then some people brought their children to Jesus. They wanted him to put his hands on their children's heads. They wanted him to pray for their children. But the disciples did not like this. They said to them, 'Take your children away from here.'

14 But Jesus said, 'Do not stop the children. Let them come to me. People who are like these children can come into the Kingdom of Heaven.' 15 So Jesus put his hands on each of the children's heads and he prayed for them. Then, after that, he went away from that place.

Jesus meets a rich man

16 One day a man came to see Jesus. 'Teacher', he asked. 'What good thing must I do so that I can live for always?'

17 Jesus replied, 'You should not ask me about a good thing! Only God is good. If you want to live for always, then you must obey all God's laws.'

18 The man asked Jesus, 'Which laws must I obey?'

So Jesus replied, 'Do not kill anyone. Do not have sex with anyone who is not your wife. Do not rob anyone. Always say true things about people. 19 Love your father and your mother and only say good things about them. Love other people as much as you love yourself.'

20 'I have always obeyed these laws', the young man replied. 'What else must I do?' 21 'If you want to be completely good', Jesus said to him, 'then you must do this. You must sell everything that you have. Give the money to poor people and then you will have valuable things in heaven. Come back when you have done that. And then follow me.'

22 When the young man heard this, he was not happy. Then he went away. He was feeling sad because he was a very rich man.

23 Then Jesus said to his disciples, 'What I say is true. It is very difficult for a rich man to come into the Kingdom of Heaven. 24 Yes, it is difficult for a big animal to go through the hole in a needle. But it is much more difficult than that for a rich man to come into the Kingdom of Heaven.'

25 When the disciples heard this, they were even more surprised. 'Who then can God save?' they asked.

26 Jesus looked at them and he replied, 'Men cannot save themselves. But God can do it. God can do everything.'

27 'Listen!' Peter said to Jesus. 'We have left everything that we had. And now we are your disciples. What will we receive because we have done this?'

28 Jesus said to his disciples, 'What I say is true. The Son of Man will rule in the new world that will start one day. You who are my disciples will also rule. You will judge the 12 families of Israel. 29 Some people may leave their house or brothers or sisters or mother or father or children or fields. They leave them to go and tell other people the good news about me. Those people will receive 100 times more than they already have in this world. That is, they will receive many homes, many brothers and sisters, many mothers and children and fields. People will also hurt them because they are obeying God. But after they die, they will live with God for always. 30 But many people who are very important now will become the least important. Many who are now the least important people will become very important.'

Chapter 20

Jesus tells a story about some workers in a field

1 'I will tell you what the Kingdom of Heaven is like. The master of the house went out early in the morning. He wanted to find some people who would work in his field. He would pay these workers. 2 The master agreed with the workers that he would pay them one small silver coin a day. And he sent them to work in the field.'

3 'The master went out again about three hours later. He saw some other men standing in the market place. They had nothing to do. 4 So the master said to these men, "You also go and work in my field. I will pay you the right amount of money." 5 So the workers went to the master's field.

The master went out again at noon, and again he went out three hours after that. Both times he sent men to his field to work. 6 Two hours later, he went out again. And he still found men who were standing there. And they were doing nothing. The master asked them, "Why are you standing here all day and you are doing nothing?"

7 The men said to the master, "Nobody has asked us to work for him."

So the master said to them, "You also go and work in my field."

8 Then the evening came. And the master of the field went to see the man who watched the workers. "Tell the workers that they must come here", the master said to him. "And pay them their money. Begin with the workers who came last. Finish with the workers who came first."

9 The workers who had come last to work received one small silver coin each. 10 The workers who had come first to work also received a small silver coin. They thought that they would receive more than the other workers. 11 But when they received their money, they were not happy. And they told the master that they were not happy.

12 They said to him, "Some of these other workers came last and only worked for one hour. But you have paid them the same as you paid us. And we have worked all day in the hot sun."

13 Then the master said to one of the workers, "My friend, I am being fair to you. You did agree to work for one day and to receive one small silver coin. 14 Take your money and go home. I choose to give this last man the same amount of money as I gave to you. 15 It is my money. I can choose what to do with it. I want to be kind and give plenty of money to everyone. You should be happy about this." '

16 Jesus said, 'So, one day, those people who are the least important will be the most important. And those who are most important now will be least important.'

Jesus talks again about how he will die

17 Jesus was going to Jerusalem. They walked along. Then he led his 12 disciples to a quiet place where he could speak to them alone. 18 'Listen!' he said. "When we arrive in Jerusalem, someone will help people to take hold of me, the Son of Man. These people will take me to the leaders of the priests and the teachers of the Law. These important Jews will say that I must die. 19 Then these important Jews will take me. And they will give me to those who are not Jews. They will laugh at me and hit me with a whip. Then they will kill me on a cross. After three days, I will come back to life.'

The wife of Zebedee asks Jesus for something

20 Then Zebedee's wife came to see Jesus. She brought her two sons, James and John, with her. She went down on her knees in front of Jesus. She wanted to ask him to do something good for her.

21 'What do you want?' Jesus asked her.

'One day, you will be king and you will rule your kingdom', she said. 'Then I want one of my two sons to sit at your right side. I want the other son to sit at your left side. Please will you do this?'

22 Jesus replied to James and John. 'You do not understand what you are asking me to do', he said to them. 'Can you have pain and trouble in the same way that I will have pain and trouble?'

'Yes, we can do this', said James and John.

23 Jesus said to them, 'Yes, that is true. You will have pain and trouble in the same way that I will have pain and trouble. But I cannot promise that you will sit at my right side or at my left side. God has chosen who will sit there. He has prepared the places for them.'

24 When the other 10 disciples heard about this, they were angry with the two brothers. 25 But Jesus asked the 12 men to come near him. 'You know how the rulers of other countries rule', Jesus said. 'They have great power over the people. Their leaders have great authority over them. 26 I do not want you to be like that. The person who wants to be most important person among you must be a servant to the other disciples. 27 The person who wants to be the most important person must be like the least important servant to everyone. 28 The Son of Man himself came to earth to be a servant to other people. He did not come here to have servants who would work for him. He came to die so that many people can be free.'

Jesus causes two men to see again

29 When Jesus and his disciples left Jericho, a large crowd followed him.

30 Now, two men were sitting at the side of the road. These men could not see. But they heard that Jesus was walking along near them. So they shouted, 'Jesus, Son of David, please be kind to us.'

31 The people who were in the crowd were angry with them. And they tried to stop the men shouting. 'Be quiet!' they said. But the men shouted even louder, 'Son of David, please be kind to us.'

32 Jesus stopped walking and he spoke to the two men. 'What do you want me to do for you?' he asked.

33 'Sir', the men replied, 'we want to see again.'

34 Then Jesus felt sorry for the two men. He touched their eyes and immediately the men could see again. So they followed him along the road.

'Son of David' is another name for the special person, the Christ that God would send to save his people. It is another name for Jesus.

Chapter 21

Jesus goes into Jerusalem

1 Jesus and his 12 disciples were coming near to Jerusalem. They came first to the village called Bethphage. They were on the hill called the Hill of Olives.

2 'Go into the village that is in front of you', Jesus said to two of his disciples. 'As you go into the village, you will find a donkey tied there with her young donkey. Undo the ropes and bring them both here to me.'

3 'Someone may ask you, "Why are you taking the donkeys?" Say to him, "The Master needs them. He will send them back to you soon." '

4 This happened to cause the words that the prophet had spoken to become true,

5   'Say to the people in Jerusalem,

"Look, your king is coming.

He does not come like someone who thinks that he is important.

And he is riding on a donkey.

He is riding on the foal of a donkey." ' **[Zechariah 9:9]**.

6 So the two disciples went to the village. They did everything that Jesus had asked them to do. 7 They brought the donkey and the young donkey to Jesus. They put their coats on the donkeys. And then Jesus climbed up and he sat on one of them. 8 Many people in the crowd put their coats down on the road. Other people cut down some branches from the trees. And they put these branches down on the road.

9 Many people went in front of Jesus and many people followed him. All the people shouted,

'Welcome! We pray that God will be good to you, the Son of David!

Happy is the king who comes with God's authority

Let us say how good is our God in heaven.'

10 When Jesus rode into Jerusalem, everybody in the city was very happy. They were asking each other, 'Who is this man?'

11 The people in the crowd replied, 'This is Jesus. He comes from Nazareth in Galilee. He is the prophet that God promised to send.'

Jesus visits God's Great House

12 Jesus went to the place outside God's Great House. People were buying and selling things there. Jesus caused them all to leave. He pushed over the tables of the men who bought and sold money. He pushed over the seats of the men who sold birds.

13 Jesus spoke to them all. He said, 'The prophets wrote God's words in a book. "My House", God said, "will be a place where people can come to pray **[Isaiah 56:7]** ." But you have caused it to be a place where people rob other people.'

14 People who could not see went to meet Jesus at the place outside God's Great House. People who could not walk very well also went there. And Jesus caused them all to become well. 15 The important priests and teachers of the Law saw all the powerful things that Jesus did. They also saw children in the place outside God's Great House. The children were shouting, 'Welcome! We pray that God will be good to you, Son of David!' All these things caused the important Jews to become very angry.

16 They asked Jesus, 'Can you hear what these children are saying?'

'Yes', Jesus replied. 'I am sure that you have read this message from God,

"Babies and children say how important you are.

Their words will be completely beautiful and correct." ' **[Psalm 8:2]**

17 Then Jesus left everyone and he went out of Jerusalem. He stayed that night in Bethany.

Jesus causes a fruit tree to die

18 The next day, Jesus returned from Bethany to Jerusalem early in the morning. He was hungry. 19 And while he was walking along, he saw a fruit tree near to the road. He went to look for fruit on it. But there were only leaves on the tree, and no fruit. Jesus said to the tree, 'No fruit will ever grow on you again.' Then, immediately, the tree dried up and it died.

20 The disciples saw it happen and they were very surprised. And they asked Jesus, 'How did the tree dry up so quickly?' 21 'What I say to you is true', Jesus said to them. 'You must really believe in God. You must believe how powerful God really is. If you believe this, then you could do the same thing to this fruit tree. And also, you could say to this mountain, "Stand up and throw yourself into the sea." If you said that to the mountain, it would happen. 22 If you really believe, then pray. Ask him to give you something. And he will give you the thing that you ask him for.'

23 Then Jesus returned to the place outside God's Great House. While he was teaching the people, the leaders of the priests and important Jews went to him. 'What authority do you have to do these things?' they asked him. 'Tell us. Who gave you the authority to do them?'

24 'I also will ask you something', replied Jesus. 'If you tell me the right answer, then I will answer your question. I will tell you where my authority comes from. 25 John had authority to baptise people. Did this authority come from God or did a man tell him to do it?' Then all the Jewish leaders talked to each other about Jesus' question. 'We might say that John's authority came from God', they said. 'But then Jesus will ask us why we did not believe John. 26 We might say that a man gave John his authority. But the people all think that John was a prophet. We would be afraid that they might attack us.'

27 So the Jewish leaders answered Jesus. 'We do not know who gave John his authority.'

Jesus said to them, 'And I will not tell you who gave me authority to do these things.'

Jesus tells a story about two sons

28 Jesus said to the important Jews, 'Tell me what you think about this story. A man had two sons. He went to the older son and said, "Son, go and work in the field today."

29 The older son replied, "I do not want to go and work in the field today." But after he had said that, he decided to go to the field.

30 The man went to his other son and he said the same thing to him. The second son replied, "Yes father, I will go." But then he did not go to work in the field.

31 Now which of the man's sons did what his father wanted?' Jesus asked the important Jews.

They replied, 'The older son did what his father wanted.'

'What I say to you is true', said Jesus. 'The men who take taxes will go into the Kingdom of God before you. Also the women who have sex with men for money will go into the Kingdom of God before you. 32 I say this because of the way that John came to you. He explained to you the right way to obey God. You did not believe him. But those people who did really bad things believed John. You knew that these people believed him. But, even then, you would not believe John's message. You have done wrong things. But you would not tell God that you were sorry. And you would not obey him.'

Jesus tells a story about a farmer

33 Then Jesus spoke again to the important Jews. 'Listen to another story that I want to tell you. There was a man who had his own farm. He planted vines in his field, and then he built a wall round it. He dug a hole in the ground to put the grapes in. Later, he would make them into wine. He also made a tall building. From the top of the building, a servant would watch the field.' 'The man then found some farmers who would take care of his vines for him. He then went away to another country. 34 When it was time for the farmers to cut the grapes, the master sent his servants to them. The servants said to the farmers, "Please give us the fruit that is for our master."

35 Then the farmers took hold of the servants. They hit one servant with sticks. They killed another of the servants and they threw stones at the other servant.

36 So the master sent other servants to the field. He sent more servants than the first time. But the farmers did the same thing to these servants also. 37 After that, the master sent his own son to the farmers. He thought that the farmers would be kind to his son.

38 The farmers saw the master's son coming. "This is the master's own son", they said to each other. "When our master dies, his son will have this field. So, let us kill the master's son and then we can have the field." 39 Then the farmers took hold of the son. They pushed him out of the field and then they killed him.

40 One day, the master will return', said Jesus. 'What do you think he will do to those farmers?'

41 The important Jews said to Jesus, 'The master will ask someone to kill those bad people in a bad way. Then he will ask someone else to be the farmers in his field. Those new farmers will give the master the fruit that is for him.'

42 Jesus said to them, 'I am sure that you have read this. The prophets wrote,

"The people who built the house did not want to use one special stone.

They thought it had no value.

Now that stone is the most important stone.

It makes the corner of the wall strong.

God did this.

And we can see that he did something great." **[Psalm 118:22-23]**

43 I am telling you this because God will take his kingdom away from you. He will give it to people who will obey God.

44 When a person falls on to that stone, he will break his body. When that stone falls on top of someone, it will break him completely.'

Verse 44 is not in all copies of Matthew's book.

45 The leaders of the priests and the Pharisees heard what Jesus said. They understood that he was speaking against them in his stories. 46 They wanted to take hold of Jesus and put him in prison. But the people thought that Jesus was a prophet. So they did not try to do it because they were afraid of the people.

Chapter 22

Jesus tells a story about a meal at a marriage

1 Jesus continued to teach the people with stories. 2 'I will tell you again what the Kingdom of Heaven is like', he said. 'A king prepared to have a special meal for his son when he got married. He sent his servants to prepare a big meal for everyone to eat at the marriage. 3 He had asked many people to come. So he sent his servants out to tell them that the meal was ready. But many people refused to come.

4 So the king then sent out other servants. He said to them, "Please tell this message to all those people that I have asked to come. Say that the master says: 'My servants have prepared the meal. They have killed my large cow and some fat young cows. Everything is ready. Come to the meal at the marriage!' "

5 But none of the people was interested in the king's message. They went away to do their usual work. One man went to his farm and another man went to his business. 6 Other people took hold of the king's servants. They hurt them and then they killed them. 7 The king was very angry and he said to his soldiers, "Go out into the city where these people live. Kill those people who killed my servants. And burn down their city!"

8 Then the king said to his other servants, "The meal that my servants have prepared for the marriage is ready. But the people that I asked to come had no value. 9 Go out now to the wide streets in the town. Ask all the people that you meet there to come to the meal. The king has prepared it for his son." 10 Then those servants went out into the streets. And they brought to the king's house all the people that they met. Some were good people and some were bad people. Many people came so that the room for the marriage was full.

11 Then the king came into the room to see all the people. He saw one man who was not wearing the right clothes for a marriage. 12 The king said to the man, "So, how did you come in here, my friend? You are not wearing the right clothes for a marriage." The man did not answer.

13 The king said to his servants, "Tie him up so that he cannot move his hands or his feet. Throw him into the dark place outside. There, people will cry. They will also bite their teeth against each other because they are angry."

14 God asks many people to come under his rule. But he only chooses a few people.'

The Pharisees ask Jesus about paying taxes

15 After this, the Pharisees thought about what they could do. They wanted to ask Jesus difficult questions. They wanted to hear him say something bad about the Roman ruler. 16 So the Pharisees sent their own disciples to Jesus. And they also sent people who were in Herod's group. They all said to Jesus, 'Teacher, we know that you are an honest man. It really is true that you teach the right things about God. It does not matter to you what other people think. It does not matter to you if someone is an important person or not. 17 Here is a question for you, Jesus. Tell us what you think about this. Should we pay our taxes to the Roman ruler, called Caesar? Or should we not pay them?'

18 Jesus knew why they had asked him this question. It was because they wanted to do bad things to him. So he said to them, 'You are trying to cause me to say something wrong. You are hypocrites! 19 Show me the coin that you use for the tax.' They brought him a coin. 20 Then Jesus asked them, 'Whose picture and name are on the coin?'

21 They replied, 'It is Caesar's picture and Caesar's name.'

So Jesus said to them, 'Give to Caesar the things that are for Caesar. And give to God the things that are for God.'

22 When they heard Jesus' answer, they were very surprised. So they left him and they went away.

The Sadducees ask Jesus a question

23 On that day, some Sadducees also came to Jesus. These men did not believe that anyone will live again after his death. The Sadducees asked Jesus a question.

The Sadducees were a group of Jewish leaders.

24 'Teacher', they said to Jesus, 'Moses wrote these things for us in the Law. A woman marries a man. But the man dies before the woman has any children. That man's brother must then marry her. They can have children for the man who died. If they have children, the children will be called the children of the first husband. 25 Once, there were seven brothers who lived here. The oldest brother married a woman. Then he died before the woman had any children. 26 The next younger brother then married her. And then he also died. So a third brother married this woman. And the same thing happened to all the brothers down to the seventh brother. They all died before the woman had any children. 27 After this, the woman also died. 28 Now some people say that one day dead people will become alive again. On that day, whose wife will that woman be? She had married all seven of those brothers.'

29 Jesus said to the Sadducees, 'You are wrong. You do not know what God says in his book. You do not know how powerful God is. 30 One day, people who are dead will become alive again. But then men and women will not marry. They will be like the angels in heaven. They do not marry. 31 It is true that one day dead people will live again. You have read about what God said to you, 32 "I am the God of Abraham, the God of Isaac and the God of Jacob." **[Exodus 3:6]** God is not God of people who are dead. He is the God of people who are now alive.'

We can read about this in Exodus, chapter 3.

33 The crowd heard this. They were very surprised about what Jesus had told the Sadducees.

Jesus teaches the Pharisees about the most important Law

34 The Pharisees heard that Jesus had said these things to the Sadducees. Now the Sadducees had stopped asking Jesus any questions. So the Pharisees met together in one place.

35 One of the Pharisees was also a teacher of the Law. He asked Jesus a question. He wanted Jesus to say something wrong. 36 'Teacher', he said to Jesus, 'which of our Laws is the most important Law for us to obey?'

37 Jesus replied to the Pharisee, 'You must completely love the Lord your God. You should love him with all that you are. Love him in all that you think. Love him in all that you do. 38 This is the greatest Law and the most important of all the Laws. 39 The second Law is as important as the first. You must love other people as much as you love yourself. 40 All the Laws of Moses teach us that. And also all the things that the prophets teach about God are in these two Laws.'

Jesus teaches people about the Christ

41 While the Pharisees were together with Jesus, he asked them,

42 'What do you think about the Christ, the special person that God will send to us? Whose Son is he?'

The Pharisees replied, 'He will be from the family of King David.'

43 Jesus asked them, 'Can you explain this to me then? God's Holy Spirit told David that the special person from God was called Lord. David says, 44 "The Lord said to my Lord:

'Sit at the important place at my right side.

Remain there until I beat your enemies down to the ground.

I will put them down like a place to rest your feet.' " **[Psalm 110:1]**

45 So', Jesus said, 'we know that David calls this special person, "Lord". So how can he be a man from the family of King David?' 46 Nobody could answer the question that Jesus asked. After this, everyone was afraid to ask Jesus any more questions.

Chapter 23

Jesus talks about dangerous teachers

1 After that, Jesus spoke to the crowd and to his disciples. 2 'The teachers of the Law and the Pharisees have authority to explain the Law of Moses. 3 You must obey everything that they teach you. But you must not do the same things that they do. They teach you what the Law of Moses is. But then they themselves do not obey these rules. 4 The rules that they give you are hard to obey. They are like heavy luggage, which they tie on your shoulders. But they will not help you even a little bit to carry these heavy things.'

5 'They do everything so that the people will see them. They make their phylacteries very large and they make their tassels long.'

6 'But the teachers of the Law and the Pharisees like to sit in the important places at special meals. They also sit in the important places in the buildings where people meet to pray. 7 They like people to call them "My teacher." In the market place, they want many people to speak to them as people would speak to an important person.

8 You all believe in God. You have only one teacher. So nobody should call another person, "My teacher".'

Jesus alone is our master and teacher

9 'Do not call another person in the world "Father". You have only one Father, and he lives in heaven.'

Jesus was saying that God is their Father.

10 'Do not call each other "Leader". You have only one leader. And he is the Christ that God will send to you. 11 The person among you who is most important will be your servant. 12 Someone may think that he himself is very important. But God will cause that person to become the least important person. Someone may think that he is the least important person. But God will cause that person to become very important.'

Jesus tells the teachers of the Law and the Pharisees that they are hypocrites

13 Jesus spoke to the teachers of the Law and the Pharisees. 'Trouble will come to you', he said. 'You are hypocrites! You have taken away the key that opens a door. It is the door to where people learn about God. They want to go in and find out how God rules. You yourselves will not go into the Kingdom of Heaven. Nor will you let other people go in who want to.'

14 'Trouble will come to you, teachers of the Law and Pharisees. You are hypocrites! You take things away from women whose husbands have died. You want people to think good things about you, so you pray for a long time. God will punish you more than people who have not done these things.'

Verse 14 is not in all copies of Matthew's book.

15 'Trouble will come to you, teachers of the Law and Pharisees. You are hypocrites. You travel across land and across the sea. You do this to make one person believe what you believe.

Then when he does believe it, he is even worse than you. He does more bad things than you do. So you cause him to go to hell.

16 Trouble will come to you, teachers. You cannot see, but you are teaching people which way to go.' 'You say this to people. "Maybe you make a promise like this. 'I promise by the name of God's Great House'. Then you do not need to do what you promised to do. But then you make a different promise. You say, 'I promise by the gold on God's Great House.' Then you must do what you promised to do." 17 You are like a man who cannot see. And you are fools. I will tell you which of these two things is most important. The gold on God's Great House is not important. But God's Great House is really important and it makes the gold important. 18 You also teach the people this: "Maybe you make a promise like this. 'I promise by the name of the special table in God's House.' Then you do not need to do what you promised to do. But then you make a different promise. You say, 'I promise by the gift on the special table.' Then you should do what you promised to do.' 19 You are like people who cannot see. You are fools. I will tell you which of these two things is most important. The gift on the special table is not important. But the special table is really important and it makes the gift important. 20 Maybe a person makes a promise like this. He says, "I promise by the name of the special table in God's Great House". Then he is making a promise to God. It is God's table. All the gifts on it are for God. 21 Perhaps a person says this. "I promise by the name of God's Great House". Then he is making a promise to God. It is His House with everything in it. 22 Perhaps a person says, "I promise by the sky above". The sky is God's. It is the place where he sits. And he rules there.'

23 'Teachers of the Law and Pharisees, trouble is coming to you. You are hypocrites! You only obey the very small matters in the Law. You grow special small plants to use when you cook. You give to God one part out of ten parts of these plants. This is a small matter in the Law which you obey. But the more important parts of the Law you forget to obey.

It is important to be good and kind to other people. It is also important to believe and to obey God. You should do all these important things as well as the other things that are not so important. 24 You are like a man who cannot see, but you are showing other people the way. You take a small fly out of your cup so that you do not drink it. But you do not see the large animal that is swimming in it.'

25 'Teachers of the Law and Pharisees, trouble is coming to you. You are hypocrites! You are like someone who is careful to wash the outside of a cup and a plate. The inside of the cup and plate are also dirty. But you do not wash that. The dirt is like the things you do. You want more things than you should have. You hurt people to get what you want. 26 Pharisees, you are like men who cannot see. You must first clean the inside of the cup and plate. Then the outside will also be clean.

27 Teachers of the Law and Pharisees, trouble is coming to you. You are hypocrites! You bury dead people in holes in the rock. You put white paint outside the holes on the stones. You are like these white stones outside these holes. They look beautiful on the outside, but they are full of the bones of dead people and bad things. 28 You are the same as these holes. Other people look at you. They think that you obey God. But really, you are hypocrites and you do many very bad things.

29 Teachers of the Law and Pharisees, things will be bad for you. You are hypocrites! You build beautiful places. You bury the prophets in these places after they have died. You cause the places where you have buried good people to be beautiful. 30 You say, "Our ancestors killed God's prophets. If we had lived at that time, we would not have helped them to kill the prophets." 31 So you are speaking against yourselves. You are saying that you are the sons of these people. These people killed God's prophets. 32 Finish then the work that your ancestors began!

33 You are like snakes, and like a family of dangerous snakes. You will not be able to run away. I am sure that God will judge you. And he will send you to hell. 34 So I tell you this. I will send prophets to you. I will also send people who know many things. And I will send people to teach you. But you will kill some of these people.

You will kill some of them on a cross. In the places where you meet to pray, you will hit some of them with whips.

They will run from one town to another town, but you will follow them. 35 Let me tell you why I send these people to you. Because of the things that you will do, God will punish you. You will receive the punishment for the murder of Abel. He was a good man. You killed many other good men. You also murdered Zechariah, the son of Berechiah. He also was a good man, but your leaders killed him. He died between God's Great House and God's special table.'

36 'What I am saying is true. God will punish all you people who are alive today. He will do this because of all the bad things that your ancestors did.

37 Oh, you people who live in Jerusalem! Oh, you people who live in Jerusalem! When God sends prophets to you, you throw stones at them. And you kill them. Many times, I have wanted to bring all of you near to me. A bird brings all her little birds together and she covers them with her body. But you would not let me take care of you like that. 38 So listen! Soon nobody will remain here to live in this place. This is true. 39 One day you will say, "Happy is the man whom God sends here with his authority." But you will not see me again until you say that.' **[Psalm 118:26]**

Chapter 24

Jesus talks about things that would happen soon

1 Jesus left God's Great House, and his disciples came to him. They began to talk to Jesus about the buildings of God's Great House. 2 So Jesus said to them, 'Yes, you can see all these beautiful buildings now. But what I say is true. The day is coming soon when enemies will completely destroy them. They will not leave one stone on top of another stone. They will throw every stone down from the buildings.'

3 Jesus then sat on the hill called the Hill of Olives. While he was alone, his disciples came to him. 'Tell us when this will happen', they said to him. 'What will we see just before you return? What will show that God will soon end the world?'

4 Jesus said, 'Be careful and watch. Some people will tell you things that are not true. But do not believe them. 5 Many people will come and say, "I am the Christ." Many other people will believe that this is true. 6 You will hear the noise of wars near where you are. You will hear about people who are fighting wars in places a long way away. Do not be afraid. These things must happen first, but it is not yet the end of everything. 7 People in one country will attack the people in another country. Kings and their people will fight against other kings and their people. The ground will move in many different places. Some people will not have any food to eat because the plants for food will not grow. 8 These things will be like the first pains that start before a baby is born.

9 Then people will take hold of you because you believe in me. They will punish some of you and they will kill some of you. Some people in every country will hate you because you obey me. 10 At that time, many people who believe in me will stop believing. They will put some of those who follow me in the power of their rulers. And they will hate all those who still follow me.

11 Also at that time, many people will say that they are prophets. This will not be true, but many people will believe them. 12 More and more people everywhere will be doing very bad things. Because of this many people will no longer love each other in the way that they did. 13 But you must never stop believing in me. Then God will save you. 14 People will tell the good news about the Kingdom to people all over the world. People will know that the message is true. And they will tell it to other people in every country in the world. Only then will God cause the world to come to an end.

15 Long ago Daniel, the prophet, wrote in God's book. He said that one day people would put something very bad in God's Great House. They would put it in the special place for God. This will then happen. At that time, you must understand what Daniel wrote. 16 When you see this very bad thing, people in Judea must run to the hills. They must run so that their enemies do not catch them.

17 A man who is on the roof of his house must not go down into his house. He must not waste time to fetch anything in his home to take with him.'

At that time, people often sat on the roof of their house after they had finished their work. The roof was flat, and it was cool there. People told each other news across the roofs. There were steps outside the house up on to the roof.

18 'People who are outside the city in their fields must not go back home. They must not waste any time. So they must not even go to fetch their coats. 19 Those days will be bad for women who have a baby inside them! And those days will be bad for those women who have little babies! 20 You must pray to God and say, "Please do not let these things happen in winter. Please do not let them happen on the day when we rest." 21 People will have great troubles. From the time that God made the world, nothing so bad has ever happened. After this bad time has finished, it will never ever be so bad again. 22 God will make this time of great trouble shorter. If he did not do that, there would be nobody still alive. God will cause this time of trouble to be shorter to help the people that he has chosen. 23 Someone may say to you, "Look, here is the Christ." Or they may say, "Look, there is the Christ." When they say that, do not believe them. 24 Some people will say to you, "I am the special man. God has sent me." Other people will come and they will say, "I am a prophet of God." None of the things that these people say is true. They will do powerful things that people cannot usually do. They will be trying to cause people to believe that their words are true. They will even try to cause the people that God has chosen to believe in them. 25 So be careful and watch out! I have told you about all these things before they happen.

26 Some people may say to you, "Look, the Christ is out there in the desert." But you must not go out to see who is there. Some people may say to you, "Look, the Christ is in there in that secret room." You must not believe these people. 27 Lightning shines quickly and it lights up the whole of the sky. It will be like that when the Son of Man returns. 28 Big birds that eat meat arrive together. They all arrive where there is a dead body.'

29 'Then after all these bad things have happened,

"The sun will become dark.

The moon will stop shining.

Stars will fall down out of the sky,

and God will cause all the powerful things in the sky to move from their usual places." [Isaiah 13:10]

30 Then people will see something powerful in the sky. This will show them that the Son of Man is coming. All the people in the world will weep because they are very sad. Then people will see the Son of Man coming down in the clouds. He will be very powerful. He will be great and very beautiful. 31 The sound of a loud trumpet will go out. The Son of Man will send out God's angels in every direction. They will bring together all the people that God has chosen from every part of the world.'

Jesus tells a story about a fig tree

32 'I will tell you a story about a fig tree. You can learn something from what the tree does. When the new branches on the tree start to grow, the leaves appear. Then you know that the summer is coming soon. 33 In the same way, you will see all these things happen. Then you will know that the Son of Man is coming soon. He is like someone at the door who is ready to come in. 34 The things that I say to you are true. The people who are living then will see all these things. They will not die before all these things have happened. 35 One day, the earth and the sky will finish. But my words will never finish.'

Nobody will know when the Son of Man will return to the world

36 'Nobody knows the day or the time when all these things will happen. Even the angels in heaven do not know. Even God's Son does not know. Only God the Father knows when they will happen. 37 It was the same as this when Noah was alive. And it will be the same again when the Son of Man returns. 38 In the days before the rain came, people were eating. People were drinking. Men married women and women married men. They did all these things until the day that Noah climbed into his big boat. 39 The people did not know what would happen. Then rain fell for a long time and it killed these people died in the deep water. When the Son of Man returns, it will be the same. People will not know that it is going to happen at that moment. 40 At that time, it will be like this. Two men will be working in a field. God will take one man away, but he will leave the other man behind. 41 Two women will be working together in the same place. God will take one woman away, but he will leave the other woman behind.'

42 'Be careful and watch! You do not know the day or time when your Master will come. 43 You can be sure about this. The master of the house did not know at what time of night a man would come to rob him. If the master had known the time, he would have watched his house more carefully. Then the man would not have robbed his house. 44 So you must also be ready. It will be a surprise for you when the Son of Man returns.'

Jesus tells a story about two servants

45 Then Jesus finished teaching them. 'I will tell you about a good servant. His master knows that he will obey. He knows how to do everything well. The master chooses him to rule over all his other servants. He will give everyone the food that they need each day. 46 The master will come home. And he will see this servant obeying all that he told him to do. So the master will be kind to his servant. 47 What I say is true. The master will then ask the servant to rule over everything in his house. 48 But perhaps the servant is bad and he says to himself, "My master will not come yet." 49 So, he begins to hit the other servants. He hits both the men and the women. He eats too much. He also drinks with drunks.'

50 'Then the master of that servant will come home and he will surprise the servant. He did not think that his master would come home on that day or at that time. 51 Then the master will punish him a lot. He will put the servant with those people who do not obey him. The people in that place will cry. And they will bite their teeth together because they are angry.'

Chapter 25

Jesus tells a story about ten young women

1 'I will tell you again what the Kingdom of Heaven is like. There were ten young women who were going to a marriage. They took their lamps with them and they went to meet the bridegroom. 2 Five of these young women were silly. They were not careful about what they were doing. Five of these young women understood well. They were careful about what they were doing. 3 The silly young women took their lamps with them, but they did not take any extra oil with them. 4 The other five young women took jars of oil with them. These young women were careful about what they were doing. 5 The bridegroom did not come for a long time. So all the young women became tired, and they went to sleep.

6 In the middle of the night, someone shouted out, "The bridegroom is coming. Come out to meet him."

7 The ten young women woke up. Then they got up and they looked at their lamps. They tried to make their lamps work well. 8 The five young women who had not brought extra oil said to the other five young women, "Give us some of your oil, because our lamps are not burning well."

9 The careful young women who had extra oil replied, "If we did that, then there would not be enough oil for all of us. You must go instead to the people who sell oil. You must buy some oil for your lamps." '

10 'So these five women went to buy some oil. While they were away, the bridegroom arrived. He would soon marry. The five women who understood well were ready. They went with him into the house. Here the servants had prepared the meal for the marriage. Then the servants shut the door.

11 Later, the five silly women also came to the house. They said, "Sir, Sir, please open the door for us."

12 But he replied, "What I say is true. I do not know you." '

13 Then Jesus said, 'So you must watch well. You do not know on what day or at what time I will come.'

Jesus tells a story about three servants

14 'I will tell you again what the Kingdom of Heaven is like. A man was going on a journey. Before he went away, he asked his servants to come to him. He said to them, "Take care of all my money and all my things for me." 15 The master gave one servant 5000 gold coins. He gave another servant 2000 gold coins, and to another servant he gave 1000 gold coins. He gave to each servant what he would be able to use well. Then the master went away on his journey.'

16 'The servant who had received 5000 gold coins went out immediately. He bought and sold things with the money. This servant got 5000 more gold coins. 17 The servant who had received 2000 gold coins also went out immediately. He also bought and sold things with the money. This servant got 2000 more gold coins. 18 The servant who had received 1000 gold coins did something different. He went outside and he dug a hole in the ground. He buried the money that his master had given him.

19 After a long time, the master came home. He asked the servants to come to him. He wanted to know how much money they had now. 20 The servant who had received 5000 gold coins came to his master. The servant said to him, "Master, you gave me 5000 gold coins. And now I have another 5000 gold coins."

21 The master said to this servant, "You are a good servant; you have done really well. You were careful with a little money. I will give you much more money to use. I am really happy about this and I want you to be happy with me."

22 The servant who had received 2000 gold coins also came to his master. The servant said to him, "Master, you gave me 2000 gold coins. And now I have another two thousand gold coins."

23 The master said to his servant, "You are a good servant; you have done really well. You were careful with a little money. I will give you much more to use. I am really happy about this and I want you to be happy with me."

24 The servant who had received 1000 gold coins also came to his master. The servant said to him, "Master, I know what you are like. You ask people to do things all the time. You get seeds back from the ground, which you did not plant. You get fruit from trees that you did not plant. 25 I was afraid of you, so I buried your money in the ground. See, here it is. You can have it back again."

26 The master said to him, "You are a bad and lazy servant. You said that you know about me. I get seeds back that I did not plant. I get fruit from trees that I did not plant. And you knew all that. 27 You should have put the money into the bank. Then, when I came home, I could have received my money back from the bank again, with extra money also."

28 Then the master said to his other servants, "Take the 1000 gold coins from this man. Give them to the man who now has 10 thousand coins."

29 Then the master said, "What I say is true. I will give more to every person who already has something. He will have much more than he needs. Another person has almost nothing. I will take away even the small amount that he has. 30 This servant cannot work for me any longer. So you can throw him into a dark place outside. People will weep there. And they will bite their teeth together because they are angry." '

God judges everybody

31 'When I, the Son of Man return, I will be powerful and great and important and beautiful. All the angels will come with me. I will sit on my seat as king. 32 All the people in the world will be together in front of me. I will put them into two groups. I will do it in the same way that a shepherd puts his sheep and goats into two groups. 33 He puts the sheep on his right side and the goats on his left side.'

34 'The king will say to those people who are on his right side, "Come here. My Father has given you good things. He has prepared a place for you in his Kingdom. From the time that God made the world, he made a place ready for you." 35 Then the king said to them, "I was hungry and you gave me some food to eat. I needed to drink and you gave me some water. I was alone and you asked me to come to your home. 36 I did not have enough clothes and you gave me some more to wear. I was ill and you took care of me. I was in prison and you came to visit me there."

37 The people who did good things will speak to him. "Master, when did we see that you were hungry? And when did we give you some food? When did we see that you needed to drink? And when did we give you some water? 38 When did we see that you were alone? And when did we ask you to come to our home? When did we see that you did not have enough clothes? And when did we give you some more clothes? 39When did we see you that you were ill? And when did we take care of you? When did we know that you were in prison? And when did we come to visit you?"

40 The king will answer them, "What I say to you is true. You did all these things to help people. They were not important people, but they were my friends. If you helped them, then you also helped me."

41 Then the king will say to those people who are at his left side, "Go away from me. God has said that bad things will happen to you. God has prepared a fire that will burn for always. He has prepared it for Satan and those who help him. You will also go into that fire." 42 Then the king said to them, "I was hungry but you did not give me any food to eat. I needed to drink but you did not give me anything. 43 I was alone but you did not ask me to come to your home. I did not have enough clothes but you did not give me anything to wear. I was ill but you did not take care of me. I was in prison but you did not come to visit me."

44 Then these other people will speak to the king. "Master, when did we see you hungry, or needing something to drink? Or when did we see you alone, or without enough clothes? Or when did we see you ill, or in prison and we did not give you any help?"

45 Then the king will reply, "What I say to you is true. You did not do these things for people. They were not important people. But when you did not help them, you also did not help me."

46 These people who did not help other people will go away. God will punish them for always. But those good people who obey God will live for always.'

Chapter 26

Those who are against Jesus want to take hold of him

1 When Jesus finished saying these things, he said to his disciples. 2 'Now you know that after two days we will eat the Passover meal. Then those people who are against me will put me into the power of the rulers. They will fix me to a cross.'

3 Then the leaders of the priests and the important Jews met together in the house of Caiaphas. Caiaphas was the most important priest in Jerusalem. 4 They talked about the best way to take hold of Jesus. But they did not want other people to know about their idea. 5 They said to each other, 'We do not want to take hold of him during the Passover. The people may fight against us if we do that.'

A woman pours oil that has a beautiful smell on Jesus' head

6 Then Jesus went to Bethany and he visited Simon at his house. At one time, Simon had had an illness of the skin.

7 While Jesus was eating a meal, a woman came into the house. She brought a small stone jar with her. The jar contained very expensive oil. It had a very nice smell. She poured the oil over Jesus' head.

8 Jesus' disciples saw what the woman had done. They became angry and they said, 'This woman should not have wasted the oil. 9 She could have sold it for a lot of money. Then she could have given the money to poor people.'

10 Jesus knew what his disciples were saying. So he said to them, 'Do not be angry with her. Stop speaking to her like that. She has done a beautiful thing for me. 11 You will always have poor people with you. But I will not always be with you. 12 She poured oil over my body to prepare it. So, now my body is ready for people to bury me. 13 What I say to you is true. Everywhere people will tell this good news. They will also tell about what this woman did. Then other people will think about her because of what she did.'

Judas Iscariot promises to sell Jesus for money

14 Judas Iscariot was one of Jesus' 12 disciples. He went to see the important priests 15 and he asked them, 'How much money will you give me if I help you to take hold of Jesus?' The priests gave Judas 30 silver coins. 16 Judas then waited for the right moment to help them take hold of Jesus.

Jesus eats his last meal with his 12 disciples

17 It was now the first day of the Passover. On this day, people ate bread that they had made without yeast in it. Jesus disciples came to talk to him. 'Where do you want us to prepare the Passover meal for you to eat?' they said to him.

18 Jesus replied, 'Go to a certain man in the city and say to him, "The teacher says: This is the moment that God has prepared for me. I will eat the Passover meal with my disciples in your house." ' 19 So Jesus 'disciples did what he had asked them to do. And they prepared the Passover meal.

20 That evening, Jesus and the 12 disciples sat down to eat the Passover meal together. 21 While they were eating, Jesus said, 'What I say is true. One of you will help the Jewish rulers to take hold of me.'

22 They were very sad about what Jesus had said. Each one of them said to Jesus, 'Teacher, I am sure that you do not mean me.'

23 Jesus said to them 'It is the man who is putting the end of his bread into the same dish as me. That man will help the Jewish rulers to take hold of me.'

24 'The Son of Man will die in the way that God's prophets wrote. But trouble will come to the man who causes this to happen. He should not have helped the rulers to take hold of me. It would be better for that man if he had never come into this world.'

25 It was Judas who would help the Jewish rulers. But he said to Jesus, 'Teacher, it cannot be me who will do this.'

'Yes, it is you who will do this', Jesus replied to him.

26 While Jesus and his disciples were eating, he took a loaf of bread. He thanked God for it and then he broke the bread into pieces. He then gave it to each of them and he said, 'Take this bread and eat it. This bread is my body.'

27 Then Jesus took a cup. He thanked God for the wine in the cup. Then he gave it to them and each disciple drank from the cup. 28 'This wine is my blood', he said. 'This is the new promise between God and his people. When I die, my blood will come out. Then God can forgive people for all the wrong things that they have done. 29 I am telling you this. I will not drink wine again until I drink it with you again in my Father's kingdom.'

30 Then Jesus and his disciples sang a song to God. Then they all went out to the Hill of Olives.

Jesus tells Peter what will happen

31 Then Jesus spoke to his disciples. 'Tonight, you will all run away and you will stop believing in me. The prophets wrote this down:

"I will kill the man who takes care of the sheep.

Then all the sheep that he had will run away to different places." [Zechariah 13:7]

32 But after I die, God will cause me to become alive again. Then I will go before you to Galilee.'

33 Peter said to Jesus, 'Even if everyone else runs away, I will not leave you.'

34 Jesus replied to Peter, 'What I say is true. Tonight, you will say three times that you do not know me. This will happen before the rooster makes a noise for the first time in the morning.'

35 But Peter said, 'Jesus, I will never tell anyone that I do not know you. Even if that means that I must die with you.' All the other disciples said the same thing.

Jesus prays in the garden called Gethsemane on the Hill of Olives

36 Then they arrived at a large garden called Gethsemane. Jesus said to the disciples who were with him, 'Sit here while I go over there to pray.' 37 Jesus then took Peter and the two sons of Zebedee with him. He became very sad and troubled in his mind. 38 'I am very sad. I could die because I feel so sad. Please wait here and watch with me', Jesus said to them.

39 Jesus went a short way in front of them. He went down on his knees with his face on the ground. He prayed, 'Father, if it is possible, please save me from this time of great pain. But Father, do not give me what I want. But give me what you want for me.'

40 Jesus returned and he found the disciples. They were sleeping. He said to Peter, 'Simon, you are asleep! You could not stay awake with me for even one hour! 41 You must stay awake and pray. God can help you, so that you will not do the wrong thing. You really want to do the right thing, but you are too weak to stay awake.'

42 Jesus went away a second time and he prayed again. 'My Father, if you want, you can take away this pain. If it is not possible to save me from this time of great pain, then I want to obey you.'

43 Jesus returned again to them. He saw that they were sleeping. They could not keep their eyes open. 44 So Jesus went away again and he prayed a third time. He said the same words to God.

45 When he returned to them, he said, 'You should not be sleeping and resting. You have slept enough. The time has come for me to have much pain. Look! Someone will now help bad men to take hold of me. 46 Stand up now, because it is time to meet them. Look! Here is the man who will help them to take hold of me.'

The soldiers take hold of Jesus

47 While Jesus was still speaking, Judas arrived. He was one of Jesus' disciples. A crowd also appeared with him. They were all carrying long sharp knives and heavy sticks. The important priests, the teachers of the Law and the important Jews had sent these people with Judas. 48 Now, Judas would help the rulers of the Jews to take hold of Jesus. He had told the people, 'I will kiss one of the men. He is the man. Take hold of him.' 49 Judas went immediately to Jesus when they arrived. 'Teacher', he said to him. Then he kissed Jesus.

50 Jesus said to Judas, 'My friend, you must do what you have come here to do.'

Then the crowd of men came and they took hold of Jesus. 51 Then one of Jesus' disciples put out his hand and he took hold of his long sharp knife. He hit the servant of the most important priest with it and he cut off the servant's ear.

52 Then Jesus said to the man, 'Put your long sharp knife away in its place. Some people use a long sharp knife to kill. They will die. Someone will kill them with a long sharp knife. 53 You should know that I could ask my Father to help me. He would immediately send more than 12 large groups of angels to fight for me. 54 They would save me. But then everything that God said in his book would not happen. And the prophets have said how all these things must happen.'

55 Then Jesus spoke to the crowd. 'You have come out here with sharp knives and heavy sticks to take hold of me', he said. 'So you must believe that I am leading people to fight against the rulers. That is how you would take hold of a man like that. I was with you every day in the place outside God's Great House when I was teaching. But you did not take hold of me then. 56 The prophets wrote down that all this would happen to me. Now it has become true.' Then all of Jesus' disciples ran away and left him.

Jesus stands in front of all the important rulers

57 Then those men who had taken hold of Jesus took him to Caiaphas's house. Caiaphas was the most important priest. The teachers of the Law and the important Jews were meeting together there with Caiaphas.

58 Peter followed the men who were taking Jesus to the house of the most important priest. But he was not very near to them.

When everyone went into the place outside Caiaphas's house, Peter went in too. He sat down with the police who worked in God's Great House. He wanted to see what would happen.

59 The leaders of the priests and the important rulers wanted people to say things about Jesus that were not true. They wanted to kill Jesus. 60 Many people did come. And they said things about Jesus that were not true. But still they could not find a reason to kill Jesus. Then two men said, 61 'We heard this man say, "I can destroy God's Great House and in 3 days I can build it again." '

62 Then Caiaphas stood up in front of everybody and he said to Jesus, 'Will you not reply? These people have said that you have done many bad things. What do you say about this?' 63 But Jesus did not say anything.

And so Caiaphas said, 'I use God's authority to say to you, "Tell us what is true." Are you the Christ? Are you the Son of God?'

64 'I am', Jesus replied. 'And you will all see the Son of Man. He will be sitting at the right side of the Most Powerful God in the most important place. You will also see him coming to earth. And he will be riding on the clouds.' **[Daniel 7:13]**

65 Caiaphas tore his coat. 'Jesus spoke against God. We do not need anyone else to tell us about him', he said. 'You have heard him speak against God. 66 What have you decided to do with him?'

'Jesus must die because of the things that he has said', they replied.

Caiaphas tore his coat to show other people that he was very angry.

67 Then some of the men began to send water from their mouths into Jesus' face. They also hit him with their fists, 68 and they said, 'Tell us who hit you! If you were a prophet, you could certainly do that!' They also hit him with their open hands.

Peter says three times that he does not know Jesus

69 Now, while all these things were happening, Peter was still sitting outside the house. One of the girls who worked for most important priest went to talk to him. 'You were also with Jesus, the man from Galilee', she said.

70 Peter said in front of everyone who was there, 'That is not true. I do not know what you are talking about.'

71 Peter then walked to the gate, and another girl saw him. This girl said to the people who were standing there, 'This man was with Jesus, the man from Nazareth.'

72 Peter answered everyone again. 'I promise that I do not know that man from Nazareth. I will speak God's name to promise that.'

73 After a little while, other people who were standing at the gate spoke to Peter. 'We are sure that you are one of the friends of that man from Nazareth. We know this because you also speak like people who live in Galilee.'

74 Peter said to them, 'I do not know the man from Nazareth. If this is not true, then God should punish me!' Immediately after Peter said this, the rooster made a noise. 75 Then Peter remembered that Jesus had said to him, 'Tonight you will say three times that you do not know me. After that, the rooster will make a noise.' So Peter went outside the house alone. He had a very troubled mind and he began to weep a lot.

Chapter 27

The important Jews take Jesus to stand in front of Pilate

1 Early the next morning, all the leaders of the priests and the important Jews talked together. They decided to ask the Roman rulers to kill Jesus. 2 They tied Jesus' hands and feet and then they led him away to Pilate's house. The soldiers put Jesus under the authority of Pilate, the ruler.

Judas dies

3 Judas heard that the Jews had asked the Roman rulers to kill Jesus. Judas had told the Jews where Jesus was. Now he was very sorry about what he had done. So he took back the 30 valuable coins to the leaders of the priests and the important Jews. 4 Judas said to them, 'I have done the wrong thing. I helped you to take hold of a man who has done nothing wrong.'

They replied to Judas, 'That is not important to us. That is your problem.'

5 Judas threw the money down on the floor in God's Great House. Then he went away. He hung himself from a rope so that he died.

6 The leaders of the priests picked up the coins. They said, 'We used this money to catch and kill a man. So it is against our Law to now use this same money for God's Great House.' 7 They talked together. And they decided to use the money to buy a field. They would use this field to bury foreign people who died in the city. The man who once had this field had made pots and jars out of soil.

8 After this, the field was called 'The Field of Blood'. And it is still called that until today. 9 So the words of the prophet Jeremiah became true. He had said a long time before, 'Then they took the 30 silver coins. 10This was how much money the people of Israel had agreed to pay for him. They used this money to buy a field from a man who made pots. God said that I must do this.' **[Zechariah 11:12-13]** When the leaders of the priests bought the field, all these things happened.

Pilate asks Jesus some questions

11 At that time, Jesus stood in front of the Roman ruler. Pilate asked Jesus, 'Are you the king of the Jews?'

Jesus replied, 'Yes, it is as you say.'

12 The leaders of the priests and the important Jews told Pilate that Jesus had done many bad things. Jesus did not answer them. 13 So then, Pilate said to Jesus, 'These man say that you have done many bad things. You can hear what they are saying.' 14 But Jesus did not answer Pilate. He did not say anything about any of the bad things that the men were talking about. Pilate was very surprised about this.

15 Each year at the time for the Passover meal, Pilate let one person come out of the prison. The people could choose which person should be free. 16 At that time, there was a man called Barabbas in prison. Everyone knew about what he had done. 17 Then the crowd came together at Pilate's house. Pilate asked them, 'Do you want me to let Barabbas come out of the prison? Or do you want me to let Jesus out instead? Jesus is called the Christ.' 18 Pilate knew very well why the rulers of the Jews had given Jesus to him. They did not like the way that the people listened to Jesus. Many people listened to Jesus more than to their rulers.

19 Pilate was deciding what to do. Then his wife sent him a message. She said, 'Do not do anything to that man. He is a good man and he has done nothing wrong. Last night, when I was sleeping, I had a dream about him. The dream made me very anxious.'

20 But the leaders of the priests and the important Jews talked to the people. 'You must ask Pilate to let Barabbas come out of the prison', they said. 'Ask Pilate to kill Jesus.'

21 Pilate asked the people again, 'Which of these two men should come out of the prison?' The people answered, 'Barabbas.'

22 Then Pilate asked the people, 'What then should I do with Jesus, who is called the Christ?' The people all shouted, 'Kill him! Kill him on a cross.'

23 So Pilate said, 'Why should I kill him? What bad things has he done?'

24 Then Pilate knew that he could not do anything to make them quiet. He thought that the people would start to fight his soldiers. So, Pilate took a dish of water and he washed his hands in front of the people. He said, 'It is not because of me that this man will die. You have caused it to happen.'

25 All the people answered Pilate, 'We and our children will answer to God. He can punish us, if we have done the wrong thing.'

26 Then Pilate sent Barabbas out of the prison. Pilate said to the soldiers, 'Hit Jesus with a whip. Then fix him to a cross.'

27 Then Pilate's soldiers took Jesus into a large room in the ruler's house. All the other soldiers in their group were there. 28 They removed Jesus' clothes from him, and they put a dark red coat on him instead.29 They used plants with sharp branches and they made a crown for him. Then they put it on his head. And they put a long stick in his right hand. They went down on their knees in front of him. They laughed at him and they said, 'Welcome! You are the King of the Jews. We go down on our knees in front of you. We hope that you will live for a long time.'

30 Then the soldiers sent water from their mouths into Jesus' face. They took the stick and they hit Jesus on his head with it again and again. 31 After they had finished laughing at him, they removed the dark red coat. And they put Jesus' own clothes back on him. Then they led him to the place where they would kill him. They would fix him to a cross made out of wood.

The soldiers kill Jesus on a cross

32 On the way to that place, they took hold of a man called Simon. He was walking past Jesus and the soldiers. He came from the city called Cyrene. The Roman soldiers said to Simon, 'Carry this cross!' Then they pushed him to it. 33 The soldiers led Jesus to the place that is called Golgotha. (Golgotha means the place of a skull.)

A skull is the bone inside a person's head.

34 The soldiers tried to give Jesus some wine to drink. They had put something like medicine in it. Jesus tasted it, but he would not drink it. 35 Then the Roman soldiers fixed Jesus on to the cross and they took his clothes. They played a game among themselves. They did this to find out who would receive each piece of his clothes. 36 Then the soldiers sat down and they watched Jesus carefully. 37 Above his head they fixed a notice. They had written on it the reason why they were killing him. The words on the notice were, 'This man is Jesus, the king of the Jews.' 38 Then the soldiers also fixed two other men to crosses. Those men had robbed people. One man was at Jesus' right side, and one man was at his left side. 39 Those people who walked past Jesus said bad things to him. They moved their heads from one side to the other side while they looked at him. 40 And they said, 'You said that you could destroy God's Great House. You said that in three days you could build it again. If you really are the Son of God, save yourself. Come down from the cross.'

41 The leaders of the priests and the teachers of the Law and the important Jews were all laughing at him too. 42 'This man saved other people, but he cannot save himself.

He says that he is the king of Israel. If he came down from the cross now, then we would believe in him. 43 He believes in God. So if God wants him, let God save him now. He did say that he is the Son of God.' 44 Then the two men on crosses next to Jesus said the same bad things to him.

Jesus dies

45 It was now about noon. The whole country became dark for three hours. 46 About three hours after noon, Jesus shouted with a loud voice. He said, 'Eloi, Eloi, lama sabachthani?' That means, 'My God, my God, why have you left me alone?'

47 Some people were standing near to Jesus. They heard what he had shouted. And they said to each other, 'He is shouting to Elijah the prophet.'

48 One of these people ran quickly and he brought a piece of soft material. He poured wine that was not sweet on it. And then he put it on the end of a stick. He lifted it up to Jesus so that he could drink the wine from it. 49 The other people said, 'Wait a moment and watch. We will see if Elijah comes. He might save Jesus.'

50 Then Jesus shouted again with a loud voice. And after that, he died.

51 At that moment, something caused the curtain inside God's Great House to tear completely into two parts. It tore from the top to the other end. God caused the ground to move about and the rocks broke. 52 God opened up the places where people had buried dead bodies. Many of God's people who had died became alive again. 53 They came out of those places after Jesus became alive again. They went into Jerusalem city and many people saw them.

54 The officer and the soldiers were still watching Jesus. They all saw the ground moving. And they saw the rocks breaking. They were very frightened and they said, 'It is true that this man really was the Son of God.'

55 There were also many women there. They were watching a short way from the cross and they saw all these things happen. They had come from Galilee with Jesus to help prepare food for him. 56 Mary from Magdala was there. Mary, the mother of James and Joses, and Mary, the mother of Zebedee's sons, were also there.

Joseph from Arimathea buries Jesus' body

57 That evening a rich man who came from a town called Arimathea went to Pilate. The man's name was Joseph, and he had become a disciple of Jesus. 58 Joseph said to Pilate, 'I would like to take the dead body of Jesus.' Pilate said to his soldiers, 'Give the dead body of Jesus to Joseph.' 59 So Joseph took the body of Jesus. He put a clean piece of soft white cloth round it. 60 And he buried the body in a large hole in a rock. He had made the hole to bury his own body when he died. After he buried Jesus' body, he put a very big stone across the hole to shut it. Then he went away. 61 Mary from Magdala and Mary, the mother of James, were there and they were watching. They were sitting outside the hole in the rock where Joseph had buried Jesus.

Soldiers watch the place where Joseph had buried Jesus

62 The next day was the Sabbath day. The leaders of the priests and the Pharisees met together with Pilate. 63 'Sir,' they said, 'that man tried to cause people to believe things that are not true. He said, "I will come back three days after I die." He said that he would be alive again. We remember that. 64 Please would you put soldiers outside the rock where Joseph buried him? They should wait there for the next three days. Then his disciples cannot come to take his body away from the hole. If they took the body away, then they could say to the people, "God has caused Jesus to become alive again." This will be the second thing that is not true. And it will be worse than the first thing.'

65 Pilate said to them all, 'You can take a group of soldiers to watch the place. Let them fix the rock well, so that no person can open it.' 66 So the leaders of the priests and the Pharisees went to the rock.

They said to the group of soldiers, 'Watch this hole in the rock well. Do not let anyone go in.' Then they put a mark on the big stone. So, they would know if someone had moved it.

Chapter 28

Jesus becomes alive again

1 Early, on the first day of the week, Mary from Magdala and Mary the mother of James got up early. They went to the hole in the rock where Joseph had buried the dead body of Jesus.

2 At that moment, the ground moved about. One of God's angels came from heaven and he went to the rock. He rolled the big stone away from outside the hole and then he sat on top of the big stone. 3 His face shone like lightning. His clothes were very white like snow. 4 The soldiers who were watching the stone in front of the rock were very frightened. They fell down on the ground like dead men. They were so frightened that they could not move.

5 Then the angel said to the women, 'Do not be afraid. I know that you are looking for Jesus. The soldiers killed him on a cross. 6 But Jesus is not here. He has become alive again. He said that this would happen to him. Come here. You can see the place where he was lying. 7 After you have seen that, you must go quickly to his disciples. Tell them, "Jesus is alive again, and he is going to Galilee before you. You will see him there." That is the message that I have brought for you.'

8 So the women went away quickly from the hole in the rock. They were very frightened, but also very happy. They ran to tell the disciples the angel's message.

9 At that moment, Jesus met the two women. 'Hello', he said, and they went close to him. They held on to his feet and they said to him, 'You are so powerful. You are very important and beautiful.' 10 Then Jesus said to them, 'Do not be afraid. Go and speak to my disciples. Say to them, "Brothers, Jesus says to you, 'Go to Galilee. You will see me there.' " '

The soldiers tell the leaders of the priests what happened

11 The women went to tell the disciples Jesus' message. Some of the soldiers who had watched the rock also went into the city. These soldiers told the leaders of the priests everything that had happened at the rock. 12 The leaders of the priests and the important Jews met together. They talked about what they should do now. They decided to give the soldiers a lot of money so that they would obey them. 13 The leaders of the priests and the important Jews said to the soldiers, 'You must say this to the people. "Jesus disciples came in the night and they took his body away. We were asleep when they did this." 14 If Pilate hears about this, we will explain things to him. He will know that you did not do anything wrong.'

15 The soldiers took the money. And they told the people, 'Jesus' disciples took the body away from the hole.' The Jews still believe that this really happened. **Jesus appears to his apostles**

16 After this, the 11 disciples went to Galilee. They went to the mountain where Jesus had asked them to go. 17 When they arrived at the place, they saw Jesus. Then they went down on their knees. They told Jesus how powerful and beautiful and important he is. But some of his disciples were not sure that it really was Jesus. 18 Jesus went close to them and he said to them, 'God has given me all authority. I have authority over everyone and everything. I have all authority in heaven and in this world. 19 Go to the people in every country. Teach them how to become my disciples. Baptise them by the authority of God the Father, his Son and the Holy Spirit. 20 Teach them to obey everything that I have taught you. You can be sure that I will be with you always. I will be with you until the end of time.'

Mark tells us the Good News about Jesus

Mark

This is about the book that Mark wrote

Mark wrote this book while he was living in Rome. Rome is now the capital city of Italy. He wrote it at some time between AD 50 and AD 70. Mark was also called John Mark. He was a young man when Jesus was on earth. In the book called Acts, we can read some things about Mark. A group of Christians met together in the home of Mark's mother (Acts 12:12). Paul and Barnabas went to many different places to tell people about Jesus. And sometimes, Mark went with them.

Mark wrote his book for people who were not Jews. At that time, the Roman government, which ruled many countries in the world, was hurting Christians. Jesus had said that men would hurt his people. Mark wanted to tell everyone about the things that Jesus had done. He described how Jesus lived. He explained who Jesus was. Jesus was a man, but he was also God's son. Mark described how Jesus died on a cross. And he described how Jesus became alive again. He explained how people could let God rule in their lives. He wrote about the things that Jesus taught the people.

Mark was a friend of Peter. Peter was one of the 12 men that Jesus chose to be his disciples. He called them apostles. Mark often listened when Peter was talking about Jesus. He wrote down the things that Peter said. And he wrote about the things that he had seen himself.

This is a list of the different parts of Mark's book:

1   Jesus starts his work ~ 1:1-13

2   Jesus works in Galilee ~ 1:14–9:50

3   Jesus travels from Galilee to Jerusalem ~ 10:1–10:52

4   In Jerusalem, people kill Jesus and his friends bury him ~ 11:1–15:47

5   Jesus becomes alive again ~ 16:1-8

6   People see that Jesus is alive ~ 16:9-20

Jerusalem is now the capital city of Israel and Galilee is part of Israel.

Chapter 1

The start of the good news

1 This is the start of the good news about Jesus Christ. He is the Son of God. 2 Isaiah wrote this message from God in his book:

'I will send someone in front of you. He will speak my message.

He will prepare a way for you.'

3   'A voice is shouting in the wilderness:

"The Lord will come soon. So prepare a road for him to travel on.

Make the paths straight." '

4 So John came to a place in the wilderness with the message from God. 'You have done many wrong things', he taught everybody. 'You must change your minds. Then God will forgive you and I will baptise you.'

5 Many people who lived in Jerusalem city and in the country called Judea went to listen to John. The people told God about all the wrong things that they had done. Then John baptised the people in the river Jordan. 6 John wore clothes that he had made out of hair from a camel. He also wore a belt that he had made from the skin of an animal. His usual food was large insects and honey from the wilderness.

7 'A person will come soon', John said to the people. 'He is more important than I am. I should not even be the servant who undoes his shoes. 8 I have baptised you with water. But this other person will baptise you with the Holy Spirit.'

John baptises Jesus

9 Soon after this, Jesus came from the town called Nazareth in Galilee. John baptised him in the river Jordan. 10 While Jesus was coming up out of the water, the skies seemed to open. The Holy Spirit came down like a bird and he rested on Jesus. 11 A voice spoke from the sky. That voice said, 'You are my son and I love you. You make me very happy.'

Satan tries to cause Jesus to do wrong things

12 Immediately, the Holy Spirit sent Jesus out into the wilderness. 13 He was in the wilderness for 40 days. During this time, Satan tried to cause Jesus to do wrong things. There were wild animals near to Jesus in the wilderness. And God's angels were his servants.

Jesus asks some men to be his disciples

14 When John was in a prison, Jesus went to Galilee. He told people the good news about God. 15 'Now is the time when God will begin to rule his people', Jesus said. 'You have done many wrong things. You must change your minds. Believe the Good News.'

16 On one day, Jesus was walking along the shore of Lake Galilee. He saw two brothers called Simon and Andrew. Their job was to catch fish. They were throwing their nets into the lake to catch fish. 17 'Come with me', Jesus said to them. 'I will teach you how to catch people.' 18 Simon and Andrew immediately left their nets and they went with Jesus.

.19 Then Jesus continued to walk along the shore. Soon he saw two more men who were brothers. They were called James and John. They were the sons of Zebedee. They were in their boat and they were mending their nets. 20 Immediately, Jesus asked them to come with him. They left their father and his workers in the boat. And they went with Jesus.

Jesus causes a bad spirit to leave a man

21 Then Jesus and those disciples went into Capernaum. On the next Jewish day for rest, Jesus went into the meeting place. He began to teach the people there.

22 Jesus taught the people very well. He taught with authority and that surprised them. He was not like the teachers of God's rules, because they did not speak with authority.

23 In the meeting place, there was a man who had a bad spirit. The bad spirit caused the man to shout loudly. 24 'Jesus from Nazareth', it said, 'We have nothing in common! Do not kill us! I know who you are. You are holy and you have come from God.'

25 Jesus spoke to the bad spirit. 'Be quiet!' he said. 'Come out of the man!' 26 The bad spirit caused the man to fall. It shouted loudly and then it came out of the man.

27 All the people were very surprised, and they said to each other, 'This is very strange. Jesus is teaching us something new and he speaks with authority. He can say to bad spirits what they must do. And they obey him.' 28 Immediately, people began to tell the news about Jesus. Everywhere in Galilee, they were telling other people about him.

Jesus makes many people well

29 Then Jesus left the meeting place. He took James and John with him to the home of Simon and Andrew. 30 The mother of Simon's wife was ill in bed. Her body was very hot. Immediately, Simon and Andrew told Jesus about her. 31 So he went to her and he held her hand. Then he helped her to sit up and immediately she was well. Then she prepared food for Jesus and for his disciples.

32-33 That evening, when the sun had gone down, everybody in the town came. They brought to Jesus everyone who was ill. And they brought people with bad spirits. All these people were round the door of the house. 34 Jesus caused many sick people to become well. They had many different illnesses. He also caused many bad spirits to leave people. The spirits knew who he was. So Jesus did not let them speak.

Jesus prays alone in a quiet place

35 Jesus got up very early the next morning, while it was still dark. He went to a place where he could be alone. And there he prayed. 36 Simon and the other disciples had to look for him. 37 When they found him, they said, 'Everyone is looking for you.'

38 'We should go to some other place', Jesus replied. 'We will go to other towns near here, so that I can teach the people there also. I came here for that reason.' 39 So Jesus travelled everywhere in Galilee. He taught the people in their meeting places. He caused bad spirits to come out of people.

A man with an illness in his skin

40 On one day, a man who had an illness in his skin came to Jesus. He went down on his knees in front of Jesus. The man said. 'If you want to do it, you can make me well again.'

41 Jesus felt very sorry for the man. He moved his hand towards the man and he touched the man. 'I do want to help you', Jesus said. 'Be well!' 42 Immediately, the illness left the man and his skin was clean.

43 Jesus explained carefully to the man and he sent him away immediately. 44 'Listen. Do not tell anyone about this', Jesus said. 'But go and show yourself to the priest. Take a gift to him for God. Moses taught the people what gift to take to God after this kind of illness. This will show other people that you are now well.' 45 But instead, the man went away and he talked to everybody. He told them what had happened to him. Because he did this, it became too difficult for Jesus to go into the towns. Everybody knew him, and so Jesus stayed in places in the wilderness. And the people came from every direction to see him.

Chapter 2

Jesus helps a man who cannot walk

1 Jesus returned to Capernaum several days after that. People reported that he had come back to his home. 2 Many people came into the house. The house was so full that there was no room, even outside the door. Jesus was teaching the people. 3 Four men came. They were carrying another man, who could not walk. 4 They could not reach Jesus because of the crowd. So they made a hole in the roof above the place where Jesus was. They helped the man to go down through the hole. The man was still lying on his small carpet. 5 Jesus saw the man and his friends. And he knew that they believed. So he said to the man, 'My friend, I forgive you for the wrong things that you have done.'

6 But some teachers of God's rules were sitting there. They thought about the words that Jesus had spoken to the man. 7 'This man (Jesus) should not have said that', they thought. 'He is speaking as only God can speak. Only God can forgive people for the wrong things that they have done.'

8 Immediately, Jesus knew what the teachers were thinking. 'You should not think these things', he said to them. 9 'I said to this man, "I forgive you for the wrong things that you have done." Instead, I might have said to him, "Stand up! Pick up your small carpet and walk." You know which is easier to say. 10 But I want you to know this. I, the Son of Man, have authority on earth. I can forgive people for the wrong things that they have done.' Then he spoke to the man who could not walk. 11 'I am saying to you: Stand up! Pick up your small carpet and go to your home.' 12 The man stood up. Immediately, he picked up the small carpet. Everyone watched him walk out of the house. This surprised all the people very much. The people said that God had done this powerful thing. They said, 'We have never seen anything like this before.'

Jesus asks Levi to be his disciple

13 Jesus went back to the shore of Lake Galilee. A large crowd came to him, so he taught them. 14 While Jesus was walking along, he saw Levi. Levi was the son of Alphaeus. His job was to take money on behalf of the government. He was sitting in his office. 'Come with me', Jesus said to him. Levi stood up and he went with Jesus.

15 Then Jesus went to eat a meal at Levi's house. Many people followed Jesus and they ate there with him and with his disciples. Some of these people also took money on behalf of the government. Some of the people had done many wrong things. 16 Some teachers of God's rules saw Jesus while he was eating with all those people. They said to his disciples, 'Jesus should not eat with men who take money on behalf of the Roman government. And he should not eat with those other bad people.'

17 Jesus heard what the teachers of God's rules said. 'People who are well do not need a doctor', he answered them. 'People who are ill need a doctor. I did not come to help good people. I came to help bad people.'

18 At this time, the disciples of John the Baptist and the disciples of the Pharisees were not eating any food. Some people came to Jesus and they asked him this question. 'The disciples of John and the disciples of the Pharisees are not eating any food. So why are your disciples eating food?'

19 Jesus said to them, 'When a man marries, his friends cannot refuse to eat. They cannot refuse food while he is with them. 20 But there will be a time when people will take him away from them. Then his friends will refuse food.'

21 Jesus said, 'Nobody uses a piece of new cloth to mend an old coat. If he does, the new cloth will cause the old cloth to tear again. It will make a bigger hole than before. 22 And nobody pours new wine into old wineskins. If he does, the new wine will tear the old wineskins. He will lose the wine and the wineskins. Instead, you must put new wine into new wineskins.'

Jesus answers questions about the day when people should rest

23 On one Jewish day for rest, Jesus and his disciples were walking through the fields where wheat was growing. His disciples picked some wheat seeds. 24 Some Pharisees said to Jesus, 'Look at your disciples! They are doing what they should not do on the day for rest. It is against the rules.'

25 'Remember what David did', Jesus replied. 'He and the men with him were very hungry. You have read about this. 26 David went into God's Great House. He ate the special bread from there. And he gave it to the men who were with him. This happened during the life of Abiathar, who was the most important priest. It is against God's rules for anyone except the priests to eat this special bread.'

We can read about this in 1 Samuel, chapter 21.

27 Then Jesus said to the Pharisees, 'God wanted to help people. So he made the day when they should rest. He did not make people so that there would be a day to rest. 28 So, the Son of Man even has authority over the day when people should rest.'

Chapter 3

Jesus makes a man well

1 Again, Jesus went into the meeting place. A man was there. His hand was very small and weak and he could not use it. 2 Some Pharisees were watching Jesus carefully. They wanted to find a reason to say that Jesus was doing wrong things. It was the day when people should rest. So the Pharisees watched to see if Jesus would make the man well on this day. 3 Jesus said to the man, 'Stand here in front of everyone.'

4 Then Jesus said to the Pharisees, 'What can we do on our day for rest? What do the rules say? Do they say that we should do good things? Or do they say that we should do bad things? Should we save a person's life? Or should we kill?'

Nobody said anything.

5 Jesus looked round at everybody. He felt angry with them. He also felt sad because they did not want to change their minds. Then he said to the man, 'Lift your hand.' The man lifted it and his hand became well. 6 Then the Pharisees left the building immediately. They met a group of people who wanted to obey Herod. And they talked with them about how they could kill Jesus.

Crowds follow Jesus

7 Jesus left that place and he went away to Lake Galilee with his disciples. A large crowd from Galilee followed them. 8 Many people also came to him from Judea, Jerusalem and a part of Israel called Idumea. They came from places on the other side of the river Jordan. And they came from the towns called Tyre and Sidon. People were telling the news about the things that Jesus was doing. That is why all these people came. 9 The crowd was very large. So Jesus asked his disciples to prepare a small boat for him. They did this so that the people would not push against him. 10 Sick people pushed to the front, because they were trying to touch him. They knew that he had made many people well. 11 Often, a person with a bad spirit saw Jesus. Then, the spirit caused the person to fall down on the ground in front of Jesus. The spirit caused that person to shout out, 'You are the Son of God.' 12 Jesus often had to say to the bad spirits, 'You must not tell anyone who I am.'

Jesus chooses 12 apostles

13 Jesus went up a mountain.

He chose some men and he asked them to go there with him. So they met him there. 14 He chose a group of 12 men who would be his apostles. He wanted them to be with him. And he would send them to teach people about God. 15 He gave these men authority to cause bad spirits to leave people. 16 These are the names of the 12 apostles:

Simon, whom Jesus called Peter,

17   James and John who were the sons of Zebedee. Jesus called them 'Boanerges'. It means 'men who are like a loud noise in a storm',

18   Andrew,

Philip,

Bartholomew,

Matthew,

Thomas,

James, who was the son of Alphaeus,

Thaddaeus,

Simon the Zealot

19   and Judas Iscariot. He delivered Jesus to the people who were against him.

Jesus talks about Satan

20 Then Jesus went into a house. And again, a crowd came to the house. There were so many people that Jesus and his disciples were not even able to eat. 21 People told his family what was happening. So they went to take him away with them. They thought that Jesus was crazy.

22 Some teachers of God's rules came from Jerusalem. 'Jesus has a bad spirit called Beelzebul', they said. 'Satan rules all the bad spirits. So Satan has given authority to Jesus. That is how Jesus causes the bad spirits to come out of people.'

23 So Jesus spoke to the teachers of God's rules. 'Come here and listen', he said to them. He used stories to explain to them. 'Satan would not fight against himself! 24 If armies in the same country start to fight each other, then they will destroy their own country. 25 And if the people in one family start to fight against each other, they will destroy their own family. 26 So Satan would not fight against himself. If he did, he would destroy his own power. That would be his end. 27 Nobody can easily go into the house of a strong man to rob him. To do that, he must first tie up the strong man. Then he can take away all that man's valuable things. 28 What I say to you is true. God can forgive all the wrong things that people do. He can also forgive people who say bad things about him. 29 But God will never forgive people who say bad things about the Holy Spirit. They will always be guilty.'

30 Jesus said this to the teachers of God's rules, because they said, 'Jesus has a bad spirit.'

Jesus' mother and his brothers come to look for him

31 Then, Jesus' mother and his brothers arrived and they stood outside the house. They sent someone with a message. They wanted Jesus to come to them. 32 A crowd was sitting round Jesus. They said to him, 'Look! Your mother and brothers are outside. They are looking for you.'

33 Jesus answered, 'I will tell you who my mother and brothers really are.'

34 Then he looked at the people who were sitting round him in a circle. 'Look! Here are my mother and brothers! 35 My brothers and sisters and mother are those people who obey God', said Jesus.

Chapter 4

Jesus tells a story about a farmer's seeds

1 Again, Jesus began to teach by Lake Galilee. The crowd that came together was very large. So, he climbed into a boat and he sat down. The boat was in the water, and the people stayed on the shore. 2 Jesus used stories to teach them many things. 3 'Listen to me', said Jesus. 'A farmer went out to plant seeds. 4 While he was planting the seeds, some seeds fell on the path. The birds came and they ate those seeds. 5 Other seeds fell among the rocks. There was a little soil in that place. The seeds quickly began to grow, because the soil was not deep. 6 But when the sun rose, it burned the young plants. They soon died because they had not grown down into the soil. 7 Other seeds fell among bushes with sharp branches. Those bushes grew up with the young plants. The bushes were stronger than the farmer's plants. So the plants could not make any new seeds. 8 But some seeds fell on good soil. Good strong plants grew from these seeds. Some plants made 30 new seeds. Some plants made 60 new seeds. And some plants made 100 new seeds.'

9 Then Jesus said, 'You have heard my words. So do what I say.'

Jesus explains to his disciples why he uses stories

10 When Jesus was alone, his friends and the 12 disciples asked him about the story. 11 'God has let you understand how he rules his people', Jesus replied. 'But the other people listen to stories. 12 This is so that:

"They are looking and looking. But they do not see.

They are listening and listening. But they do not understand."

If they did understand, they would obey God. And if they did obey God, he would forgive them.'

Jesus explains the story about the seeds

13 Then Jesus answered the people who had asked him about the story. 'You should understand this story. If you do not understand it, you will not understand all the other stories. 14 The seeds mean the message from God. The farmer is like a person who teaches people about that message. 15 Some seeds fell on the path. The path is like some people who listen to the message. But then Satan comes quickly to them. And he takes the message away from their minds. 16 Some of the seeds fell among rocks. This is like some people who listen to the message from God. They are happy to believe it for a time.

17 But they are like plants that have not grown into the soil. So they will only believe for a short time. They may have problems. Or other people may do bad things to them because of God's message. The result is that those people stop believing. 18 Some seeds fell among bushes that had sharp branches. This is like some other people who listen to the message from God.

19 But they have many troubles in their minds. They think that more money and other valuable things will make them happy. So they do not let God's message change them. They are like plants that do not make new seeds. 20 But some seeds fell on good soil. This soil is like other people who listen to the message from God. They understand it and they obey God. These people are like good plants. From one seed, the good plants make 30 seeds. Other good plants make 60 new seeds, and some good plants make 100 new seeds.'

People put a light in a high place

21 Then Jesus said to his disciples, 'Nobody brings a lamp into a house and puts it under a jar or under a bed. You do not do that. You put it in a high place. 22 God hides some things now. But there will be a time when people will see them. God covers some things now because he does not want people to see them yet. But there will be a time when people will see all those things.' 23 Then Jesus said, 'You have heard my words. So do what I say.'

24 'You should be careful about how you listen', said Jesus. 'God will give to you in the way that you give to other people. And you will receive even more. 25 A person who has some things will receive more. Some people do not have those things. They will lose even the little bit that they do have.'

Jesus tells a story about seeds

26 Then Jesus said, 'I will explain how God rules his people. A man throws seeds in his field. 27 Then he sleeps each night and he wakes each day. The seeds start to grow into plants. They continue to grow, but the man does not know how. 28 The soil causes the plants to grow. The leaves of the plant grow first. Then the flower appears, and then the seeds appear. 29 When the plants have completely grown, the man will cut them down immediately. It is time for him to take the seeds to use for food.'

Jesus tells a story about a very small seed

30 'We should describe how God rules his people', said Jesus. 'I will explain it with another story. 31 It is like this. A man takes a seed of the plant called mustard. He puts it in the soil. It is smaller than any other seed that is in the soil. 32 But when it starts to grow, it becomes bigger than the largest bush. It will have big branches. And the birds will come from the sky and they will live there. They will build their homes in the shade of the branches.'

33 Jesus taught God's message to the people. He used many stories like these. He told the people as much as they could understand. 34 He always used stories to teach the people. Then he explained everything to his own disciples when he was alone with them.

Jesus stops a storm

35 On that same day, in the evening, Jesus spoke to his disciples. 'We should go across to the other side of the lake', he said. 36 So they left the crowd. Jesus was already in the boat. So the disciples took him across the lake. Some other boats also went with them. 37 Then a strong wind began to blow across the lake. Water began to fill the boat so that soon the boat was almost under the water. 38 Jesus was in a comfortable place at the back of the boat. He was asleep. The disciples woke Jesus, and they said to him, 'Teacher, it seems not to matter to you if we die!'

39 Jesus woke and he spoke to the wind and to the water. 'Be quiet!' he said. 'Stop!' Then the wind stopped and the water became flat again.

40 'You should not be afraid like that', Jesus said to his disciples. 'You should believe.'

41 Then they were very afraid. 'We do not know who Jesus really is', they said to each other. 'Even the wind and the water obey him.'

Chapter 5

Jesus meets a man who has many bad spirits inside him

1 Jesus and his disciples came to the other side of the lake. They came to a place near Gerasa.

2-4 Jesus came out of the boat. And immediately a man met him. A bad spirit was living inside this man. So the man lived in a place where there were many human bones. Nobody could hold him. Often people tried to put metal round his ankles. They wanted to keep him in a safe place. But they all failed. He broke the metal. 5 The man was always either by the bones or on the hills. During each day and each night, he screamed. And he used stones to cut himself.

6 He saw Jesus a long way away and he ran to meet him. He went down on his knees in front of Jesus. 7 He screamed loudly, 'Jesus, we have nothing in common. You are the Son of the powerful God above. Please promise God that you will not hurt me.' 8 He said that because Jesus had already said to the bad spirit, 'Come out of this man.'

9 Then Jesus asked the man, 'What is your name?'

The man replied, 'My name is Army because there are so many bad spirits in me.'

The word for 'Army' means a group of 6000 soldiers. People called him Army, because very many bad spirits lived in him. The bad spirits used the man's voice to speak to Jesus.

10 He said to Jesus many times, 'Please do not send these bad spirits out of this country.'

11 A large group of pigs was eating on the hill. 12 'Jesus, send us to the pigs. Let us go into them', said the bad spirits. 13 Jesus let them. So, the bad spirits came out of the man and they went into the pigs. All the pigs rushed together down the hill into the lake. About 2000 pigs died in the lake.

14 The men who were feeding these pigs ran away. They told the people in the town and in the farms. Those people came to see what had happened. 15 When they came to Jesus, they saw the man. The man was now sitting quietly. The bad spirits had gone out of him. He was wearing clothes and his mind was well again. This was the man that the army of bad spirits had ruled. All the people were afraid. 16 The men who saw these events spoke to them. They told the other people what had happened to the man with the bad spirits. And they explained about the pigs. 17 Then the people who lived there said to Jesus, 'Please leave our country.'

18 Jesus climbed back into the boat. But the man that the bad spirits had ruled spoke to him. He told Jesus that he very much wanted to be with him. 19 But Jesus did not let him. Instead, Jesus said to him, 'Go to your home and to your friends. Tell them what the Lord has done for you. Tell them how he has been kind to you.' 20 So the man went away. He began to speak to many people in the 10 cities there. He told them about the great things that Jesus had done for him. And all the people were very surprised.

Jesus makes a dead girl alive again

21 So Jesus returned in the boat. He came to the other side of the lake. A large crowd came to him there. And he was by the lake. 22 A man called Jairus came to Jesus. He was a leader at the meeting place. When he saw Jesus, he went down on his knees. 23 'Please, please come to my house and put your hands on my little daughter', he said to Jesus. 'She is very ill and she will soon die. But if you do this, she will live.' 24 So Jesus started to go with Jairus.

A large crowd followed Jesus. And the people were pushing against him. 25 There was a sick woman who had bled for 12 years. 26 She had paid many doctors to help her, but they could not do anything. They had caused her more pain instead. Now she had spent all her money and she had not become any better. Instead, she became worse. 27 People had told her about the things that Jesus did. So, she came in the crowd behind him and she touched his coat. 28 She said, 'Even if I can only touch his clothes, I will become well again.' 29 And immediately, the blood stopped. And she knew that she was well again.

30 Jesus knew immediately that something powerful had gone from him. So he turned round in the crowd and he asked, 'Who touched my clothes?'

31 'You can see that the crowd is pushing against you', said his disciples. 'You cannot ask who touched you!'

32 But Jesus looked round him. He wanted to see who had touched him. 33 The woman knew what had happened to her. And she felt very afraid. But she came to Jesus. And she went down on her knees. Then she told him everything that had happened to her. 34 'Young woman, do not have troubles in your mind', said Jesus. 'You are well again because you believed. Go now and be well.'

35 While Jesus was still speaking, some men arrived from Jairus's house. (Jairus was a leader at the meeting place.) 'Your daughter is dead', they said to Jairus. 'Do not ask any longer for the teacher to come.'

36 Jesus heard what the men said to Jairus. So Jesus said to him, 'Do not be afraid. Instead, believe.'

37 Jesus took only Peter, James and John (James's brother) with him. He would not let anyone else go with him. 38 Then they came to Jairus's house. And Jesus saw that there were many people there. They were all crying. They were making a loud noise. 39 Jesus went into the house and he said to the people, 'You should not be crying and making a loud noise. The child is not dead. She is asleep.' 40 The people laughed at him.

Then Jesus sent them all out. He went into the place where the child was lying. The child's father and mother were with him. He also took Peter, James and John with him. 41 Then Jesus held the little girl's hand. 'Talitha koum', he said to her. This means, 'Little girl, I ask you to stand up.' 42 The little girl stood up immediately and she walked about. She was 12 years old. They were very surprised. 43 'You must not tell anyone what has happened here', Jesus said to them. 'Now give the little girl something to eat.'

Chapter 6

Jesus goes to his own town

1 Jesus left there. He came to his own town. His disciples followed him.

2 When it was the Jewish day for rest, Jesus went to the meeting place. He began to teach the many people who were there. They were very surprised about the things that he was saying to them. 'We do not know how this man learned these things', they said to each other. 'We do not know how he knows so much. And we do not know how he does all these powerful things. 3 We know who this man is. He is the carpenter. He is the son of Mary. He is the brother of James, Joses, Simon and Judas. His sisters live here in the town among us.' This was the problem that they had with him.

4 'People everywhere may speak well about a servant of God. But the people in that man's own town will not do that', Jesus said to them. 'His own people and his own family will not speak well about him.'

5 Jesus could not do any powerful thing in that town. But he did put his hands on a few sick people and he made them well. 6 Jesus was very surprised because the people in that town would not believe.

Jesus sends the 12 disciples to tell God's message to people

7 Jesus asked his 12 disciples to come to him. He started to send pairs of them to tell God's message to people. And he gave them authority over bad spirits.

8 Jesus told the disciples that they must not take anything for the journey, except only a stick. They must not take bread, a bag or money in their pockets. 9 They should wear shoes. But they should not take extra clothes.

10 Jesus said to them, 'In each town, stay at the first house that you go into. Continue to stay there until you leave that town. 11 Perhaps you might go to a town where the people do not accept you. They will not listen to you. So you should leave that town. Clean that town's dirt off your feet. So then it will be clear that they have done something wrong.'

12 So they went out. They told the people that they must change their minds. 13 They caused many bad spirits to come out of people. They also put oil on many sick people; and the sick people became well.

Herod kills John the Baptist

14 People told King Herod about these things. People were talking about Jesus. Some people were saying that Jesus was John the Baptist. They also said that John had become alive again. 'That is why Jesus does these very powerful things', they said.

15 Other people said, 'Jesus is Elijah.' And other people said, 'He is a servant of God. He is like God's servants who lived a long time ago.'

16 But when someone told Herod, he said, 'This is John. I sent a soldier to cut off his head. But John has become alive again!'

17 Herod himself had sent his soldiers to take hold of John. He had said to his soldiers, 'Tie ropes round John's hands and feet and put him in a prison.' Herod had done that because of Herodias. She was the wife of Herod's brother Philip. But Herod had married her. 18 John had said to him, 'Herodias is your brother's wife. It is against the rules for you to have her as your wife.'

19 Herodias was very much against John. So she wanted to kill him. But she could not do that. 20 That was because Herod was afraid of John. Herod knew that John was a good man. And Herod knew that John was a servant of God. So Herod kept John safe. Herod liked to listen to what John said. But he did not know what to do about the things that John said.

21 Then, on one day, Herodias had her chance. It was Herod's birthday and he asked many people to come to a special meal. Important men and officers came. And the rulers from Galilee were also there. 22 The daughter of Herodias came in and she danced. Herod and his visitors were very happy when they saw her dance.

'Ask me for anything that you want', the king said to the young woman. 'I will give it to you.' 23 And he promised: 'What I say is completely true. I will give you anything that you ask me to give to you. I will even give you half of all that I rule over.'

24 The young woman went out and she said to her mother, 'What should I ask him for?' 'Ask for the head of John the Baptist', her mother replied.

25 The young woman returned quickly and she spoke immediately to Herod. 'I want the head of John the Baptist. Put it on a plate! Do it now!'

26 Then Herod felt very sad. But he did not want to disappoint her, because of his promise. All his visitors had heard it. 27 So, immediately, the king sent a soldier. The king told the soldier that he must bring John's head. So, the soldier went to the prison and he cut off John's head there. 28 Then he brought it back on a plate. He gave it to the young woman. And the young woman gave it to her mother. 29 People told John's disciples about it. So, they went to the prison and they took away John's dead body. And then they buried it.

Jesus gives food to 5000 men and to their families

30 The apostles all came to Jesus. They told him about all the things that they had done. And they told him what they had taught. 31 Many people were coming and going. Jesus and the disciples were too busy even to eat. So Jesus said to them, 'Come with me to a place where there are no other people. We should be alone together. Then we can rest for a short time.'

32 So they left the crowd. They went away in a boat together. They went into the wilderness. 33 But many people saw that they were leaving the town. Those people recognised them. So they ran out from all the towns. And they reached the place before Jesus and the disciples arrived. 34 Jesus climbed out of the boat and he saw a large crowd. Jesus felt sorry for them. He thought to himself, 'They are like sheep that have nobody to lead them.' So, he began to teach them many things.

35 When it was almost evening, Jesus' disciples came to speak to him. 'We are here in a place in the wilderness', they said. 'Soon it will be dark. 36 The people do not have anything to eat. So, send the crowd away now. Ask them to go to the farms and villages that are near here. There they can buy some food for themselves.'

37 'Give them some food to eat. You should do it', Jesus replied.

So the disciples said, 'We cannot go to buy bread for the people. A man must work for 8 months to get the 200 coins that we would need. We cannot give food to these people.'

38 Jesus asked them, 'How many loaves of bread do you have? Go and see.' When they had looked, they spoke to Jesus again. 'We have 5 loaves and 2 fishes', they said.

39 Jesus asked all the people to sit on the green grass. He wanted them to sit in large groups. 40 So the people sat down in groups. Each group had 50 or 100 people in it. 41 Then Jesus took the 5 loaves and the 2 fishes. He looked up to God's home, called heaven. And he thanked God for the food. Then he broke the bread into pieces. He gave the pieces of bread to the disciples. And they gave the bread to the people. Jesus also broke the two fishes into pieces for all the people. 42 Everyone ate and they all had enough food. 43 Jesus' disciples then picked up all the food that the people had not eaten. And they filled 12 baskets with pieces of bread and fish. 44 About 5000 men ate the loaves.

Women and children also ate the loaves and the fishes.

Jesus walks on water

45 Immediately, Jesus told his disciples that they must get into the boat. They should go to Bethsaida, which is on the other side of the lake. Jesus would go there after some time.

But first, he would send the crowd away. 46 So he said 'Goodbye' to the crowd. Then he went up a mountain to pray.

47 That evening, the boat was in the middle of the lake. Jesus was alone on the land.

48 But he could see his disciples. They were trying to cause the boat to move along. But it was very difficult for them because the wind was blowing in the opposite direction. Then, when it was very early in the morning, Jesus came towards them. He was walking on the water. He wanted to pass them. 49 But they saw that he was walking on the water. 'It is a spirit', they thought. And they screamed out. 50 They all saw him and they were afraid. But immediately, Jesus spoke with them. 'Be brave. It is I, Jesus. Do not be afraid', he said to them. 51 Then Jesus climbed into the boat with them. The strong wind stopped. They were completely surprised about what had happened. 52 They did not understand what had happened to the loaves. And they were not ready to learn.

Jesus makes many sick people well

53 They crossed the lake. They reached the shore at Gennesaret and they tied the boat there. 54 When they came out of the boat, the people recognised Jesus immediately. 55 They went to tell everyone who lived anywhere near there. They began to bring ill people to Jesus. They carried those ill people to him on small carpets. They brought those people to any place where he was. 56 Jesus went into villages, towns and fields. Everywhere that he went, they brought sick people into their market places to him. The sick people asked Jesus for help. They wanted to touch even the edge of his coat. And every sick person who touched him became well.

Chapter 7

Jesus speaks to Pharisees and to some teachers of God's rules

1 A group of Pharisees and some teachers of God's rules came from Jerusalem. They came to talk with Jesus. 2 They had watched Jesus' disciples. Some of the disciples did not wash their hands before a meal. Instead, they were eating their food as other people eat.

3 (The Pharisees and all the Jews do not eat until they have washed their hands carefully. They do this because of a rule that their leaders made many years ago. 4 When they come from the market place, they must always wash. Unless they do this, they cannot eat. Their leaders had also given them rules about how to do other things. For example, there are rules about how they should wash cups, pots and metal jars.)

5 The Pharisees and the teachers of God's rules said to Jesus, 'Your disciples do not obey the rules that our leaders made many years ago. Your disciples have not washed their hands. They are eating their food as other people eat.'

6 Jesus said to the Pharisees and to the teachers of God's rules, 'What Isaiah said about you is true. You are hypocrites. He wrote down these words from God.

"These people say good things about me,

but they do not really want to obey me.

7   They teach rules that men gave to them.

So they pray to me without any purpose." '

8 'You have stopped obeying God', Jesus said to them. 'Instead you obey the rules that men gave to people many years ago.'

9 He said to them, 'You are very careful to refuse God's rules, because then you can obey your own old rules! 10 For example, Moses wrote, "You must love your father and your mother and you must obey them." He also said, "A person should die if he says bad things against his father or against his mother." 11 But you teach that a person can say to his father or to his mother, "I would have given these gifts to you. But I cannot because I have given them to God instead." 12 Then, you let him do nothing for his father or for his mother. 13 So you have obeyed the rules that you received from your leaders many years ago. And you do not do what God wants. And you do many other things like that.'

14 Again, Jesus asked all the people to come near to him. 'Listen to me', he said, 'so that you can understand these things. 15 God's people are different from other people. But they are not different because of things from outside that go into their bodies. It is because of the things that come from their minds. 16 You have heard my words. So do what I say.'

Jesus explains to his disciples what he had taught

17 Jesus left the crowd and he went into a house. Then his disciples asked Jesus to explain what he had taught.

18 'I am surprised that you too are not able to understand', said Jesus. 'It should be clear that God's people are not different from other people because of their food. Food goes into a person's body from outside. 19 You know that food does not go into the mind of a person. First, it goes into his stomach and then it goes out of his body. So all foods are clean.'

20 And Jesus said, 'God's people are different from other people because of things that come from them. 21 So, bad thoughts come from a man's mind. And then that man does wrong things. He might have sex when he should not do it. He might rob somebody. He might kill somebody. He might have sex with another man's wife. 22 He might want other people's things. He might be cruel to other people. He might want other people to believe things that are not true. He wants whatever things he can get. He thinks whatever thoughts he wants to think about people. He speaks whatever wrong words he wants to say. He thinks that he is very important. He thinks very silly things.

23 All these wrong things begin inside people's minds. They come out of those people. But God's people must be different from those people.'

Jesus travels out of Israel

24 After that, Jesus went away. He was near the city called Tyre. He went into a house. He did not want anyone to know that he was there. But it was not possible to keep this a secret. 25 Immediately, someone told a certain woman about Jesus. This woman had a daughter who had a bad spirit. The woman came and she went down on her knees by Jesus' feet. 26 She was not a Jew; her family was from Syrophoenicia. She asked Jesus to cause the bad spirit to go out of her daughter.

27 Jesus said to the woman, 'First, the children must eat all that they want. It is not right to take bread from the children. You should not throw the children's food to the dogs.'

28 The woman replied. She said to him, 'Yes sir. But small pieces of bread drop while the children eat. And the dogs under the table eat those pieces.'

29 'Because you have said that, you can go to your home', Jesus replied. 'Now the bad spirit has left your daughter.'

30 The woman went to her home. She found the child, who was lying on the bed. The bad spirit had left the child.

31 Then Jesus went away from Tyre. He travelled through the city called Sidon. He went towards Lake Galilee. He was in the middle of the 10 cities there.

32 Some people brought a man to Jesus. This man could not hear and he could not speak clearly. The people asked Jesus to put his hand on the man.

33 Jesus led the man away from the crowd. Then he put his fingers into the man's ears. Then Jesus took water from his own mouth and he touched the man's tongue with it.

34 Jesus looked up towards the sky. He made a low, sad sound. Then he said to the man, 'Ephphatha!' That means, 'Become open!' 35 Then the man started to hear. And immediately, the man's tongue was able to move. And the man spoke clearly.

36 Jesus told the people that they must not tell anyone about this. But when Jesus asked them not to say anything, they spoke even more about it. 37 The people were very surprised about everything that Jesus did. 'Jesus has done everything well', they said. 'If people cannot hear, Jesus makes them able to hear. If people cannot speak, Jesus makes them able to speak.'

Chapter 8

Jesus gives food to 4000 people

1 At that time, another large crowd had come to hear Jesus. The people had nothing to eat. Jesus asked his disciples to come to him. Then he spoke to them. 2 'I feel sorry for this crowd. They have been with me now for three days and they do not have any food. 3 I do not want to send them back to their homes while they are hungry. They may fall down during their journey because of weakness. Some of them have travelled a long way.'

4 The disciples replied, 'We are in the wilderness. We cannot get enough bread to feed these people.'

5 'How many loaves of bread do you have?' Jesus asked. 'We have 7 loaves', they replied.

6 Jesus told the crowd that they should sit on the ground. Then he took the 7 loaves. He thanked God for them. Then he broke the bread and he gave the pieces to his disciples. The disciples gave the bread to the people. 7 The disciples also had a few small fishes, so Jesus thanked God for these. Then he told his disciples that they should give the fishes to the people too. 8 The people ate, and they all had enough food. After the people had eaten, there were still some pieces of bread and fish. Jesus' disciples filled 7 baskets with these pieces. 9 There were about 4000 people. And Jesus sent the people away. 10 Immediately, he got into the boat with his disciples. Then they all returned to the part of the country called Dalmanutha.

Dalmanutha is on the west shore of Lake Galilee. It is south of the flat part of the country called Gennesaret.

11 Some Pharisees came. They began to argue with Jesus. They wanted him to do something powerful. They wanted him to show them that God had sent him. 12 Jesus felt very sad. 'People today ask to see something powerful', he said. 'What I say is true. These people will not see the powerful thing that they want.' 13 Then Jesus left the Pharisees again. He got back into the boat to go to the other side of the lake.

Jesus talks about the yeast of the Pharisees and the yeast of Herod

14 Jesus' disciples had forgotten to bring bread with them. They only had one loaf in the boat. 15 'Be careful', Jesus said to them. 'You must watch for the yeast of the Pharisees and the yeast of Herod.'

16 The disciples began to talk to each other about this. 'Jesus is saying this because we do not have any bread', they said.

17 Jesus knew about this. So he said to them, 'You should not be talking about the fact that you do not have any bread. You still do not recognise or understand. You seem unable to learn. 18 You are like people who cannot see with their eyes. You are like people who cannot hear with their ears. Remember this! 19 I broke 5 loaves for 5000 men. How many baskets did you fill with pieces of bread?'

'There were 12 baskets', they replied.

20 'And then I broke 7 loaves for 4000 people. How many baskets did you fill with pieces of bread?' Jesus asked.

'There were 7 baskets', they replied.

21 'You should understand now', he said to them.

Jesus makes a blind man able to see

22 Jesus and his disciples came to a village called Bethsaida. Some people led a blind man to Jesus. They asked Jesus to touch the man. 23 Jesus took the blind man's hand and he led the man out of the village. Jesus put water from his own mouth on the man's eyes. And Jesus put his hands on the man. 'Can you see anything?' Jesus asked.

24 The man looked up. 'I can see people', he replied. 'But they seem like trees that are walking about.'

25 So Jesus put his hands on the man's eyes again. The man looked carefully and then his eyes were well. Now he could see everything clearly. 26 Jesus told the man that he must go back to his house. Jesus said, 'Do not even go into the village.'

Peter says who Jesus is

27 Then Jesus and his disciples went to visit some villages. They were near to the town called Caesarea that Philip built. On the way, Jesus asked his disciples, 'Who do people say that I am?'

28 'Some people say that you are John the Baptist', they replied. 'Other people say that you are Elijah. And some other people say that you are one of God's servants.'

29 'But what do you think?' Jesus asked them. 'Who do you say that I am?'

'You are the Messiah', Peter answered him.

30 Then Jesus spoke with authority to his disciples. He said that they must not tell anybody about him.

Jesus tells his disciples how he would die

31 Then Jesus began to teach his disciples about the things that must happen to the Son of Man. People would cause many troubles for him. Important people would be against him. They would include the important priests, the leaders and the teachers of God's rules. People would kill him. But after three days, he would become alive again.

32 What Jesus said was very clear. Then Peter took Jesus away from the other disciples. And Peter began to tell Jesus that he must not say those things.

33 But Jesus turned round and he saw his disciples. And he said that Peter was wrong. 'Satan, go away from me!' Jesus said to Peter. 'Your thoughts do not come from God. Instead, you are thinking like men think.'

34 Then Jesus asked the crowd and his disciples to come to him. He said to them, 'A person who wants to be my disciple must not think about himself. And he must not think about what he wants to do. He must decide that his own life is not important. And he must be like someone who carries his own cross. Then he should become my disciple. 35 The person who wants to save his life will die. But another person may die because of me and because of God's good news. Even if that person dies, he will save his life. 36 Think about a person who gets the whole world and everything in it. If he loses his life, he has not received anything. 37 A man can receive nothing that is better than his life. And all the money in the world cannot keep someone alive. 38 People today do not obey God. They are very bad. But you must not be ashamed of me or of my words. If you are, the Son of Man will be ashamed of you. He will be ashamed when he returns. On that day, the Son of Man will shine because his Father is so beautiful. And God's holy angels will be with him.'

Chapter 9

Three disciples see how great Jesus is

1 And Jesus said to them, 'What I am saying is true. Soon God will begin to rule his people with great power. And some of the people who are standing here will see it. They will certainly not die before this happens.'

2 Six days after that, Jesus asked Peter, James and John to go with him. Jesus led them up a high mountain, where they were alone together. And they saw Jesus as they had never seen him before. 3 His clothes became very white; they were shining. They were a brighter white than anyone on earth could wash them. 4 Then the three disciples saw Elijah with Moses, who appeared to them. Elijah and Moses were talking with Jesus.

5 So Peter said to Jesus, 'Teacher, it is good that we are here. Please let us build three huts. One hut will be for you. One hut will be for Moses. And one hut will be for Elijah.' 6 Peter did not really know what to say. That was because the three disciples had become very afraid.

7 Then a cloud came. It covered them all. A voice spoke from the cloud. That voice said, 'This is my son, and I love him. Listen to him.'

8 At that moment, the three disciples looked round. They saw that nobody else was there still. Only Jesus was with them.

9 While they were walking down the mountain again, Jesus said to the three disciples, 'You must not tell anyone about the things that you saw. Tell people only after the Son of Man has become alive after his death.' 10 These disciples kept these words secret. But they talked together about the words, 'alive after his death'. They wanted to understand those words.

11 Then the three disciples asked Jesus, 'Why do the teachers of God's rules say that Elijah must come first?'

12 Jesus said to them, 'Elijah does come first. He makes everything ready. But the Bible says that people will cause many troubles for the Son of Man. People will do the worst things to him. 13 But I tell you that Elijah has already come. People did to him whatever things they wanted to do. The Bible says that those things would happen to him.'

Jesus helps a boy who has a bad spirit

14 They reached the place where the other disciples were. They saw that there was a large crowd round the disciples. Some teachers of God's rules were arguing with them. 15 The people in the crowd saw Jesus. And immediately they were very surprised. They ran to say 'hello' to Jesus.

16 Jesus asked his disciples, 'What were you arguing about with the teachers of God's rules?'

17 A man in the crowd answered. He said to Jesus, 'Teacher, I brought my son to you. He is not able to speak because he has a bad spirit. 18 When the bad spirit takes hold of him, it throws him to the ground. Water comes out of his mouth and he bites his teeth together. Then his body seems dead. I asked your disciples to send the spirit out of him. But they were not able to do it.'

19 'You people today still do not believe', Jesus said to them. 'It is very difficult to be with you. I am always waiting for you to believe. Bring the boy to me.'

20 So the people brought the boy to Jesus. When the spirit saw Jesus, it immediately caused the boy to fall badly. The boy fell on to the ground and he rolled about. Water was coming from his mouth.

21 'How long has he been like this?' Jesus asked the boy's father.

'He has been like this since he was a small boy', the father replied. 22 'Often the spirit has caused him to fall into fire or into water. It is trying to kill him. But if you can do anything, be sorry for us. And help us!'

23 'You should not say, "If you can do anything" ', Jesus said to the father. 'Everything is possible for those people who believe.'

24 Immediately, the boy's father shouted, 'Oh! I believe! Help me to believe more!'

25 Jesus saw that a crowd was running together again. So he told the bad spirit that it must leave the boy. Jesus said to it, 'Spirit, I am telling you that you must leave this boy. He cannot hear or speak because of you. But you must come out of him and you must never go into him again.'

26 The spirit caused the boy to scream. It caused him to fall several times. Then it came out of him. The boy seemed to be dead. So, many people said, 'He is dead.' 27 But Jesus held the boy's hand and he helped the boy to stand up. So the boy stood up.

28 When Jesus went into a house, the disciples were alone with him. Then they asked him, 'Why could we not cause the bad spirit to leave the boy?'

29 'You must pray. No other thing can cause this kind of spirit to go out of a person', said Jesus.

30 Jesus and his disciples left that place. They passed through Galilee. Jesus did not want anyone to know where he was. 31 That was because he was teaching his disciples. He told them, 'Soon, someone will deliver the Son of Man to a group of men who will take him away. And they will kill him. And three days after that, he will become alive again.' 32 The disciples did not understand what Jesus meant. And they were afraid to ask him.

Jesus explains who will be the most important person

33 Jesus and his disciples arrived at Capernaum. When they were in the house, Jesus asked them, 'What were you arguing about on the way?' 34 But they did not say anything. They did not want to tell Jesus why they were arguing. On the way, they had argued about who was the most important disciple.

35 Jesus sat down. He asked the 12 disciples to come. Then he said to them, 'If you want to be the leader, make yourself less important than everyone else. Become the servant of everyone.'

36 Then he took a child. He put that child in the middle of the disciples. While Jesus hugged the child, he said to them,

37 'If someone accepts this child because of me, then he accepts me. If he accepts me, then he is not only accepting me. He is also accepting God, who sent me.'

38 'Teacher', John said to Jesus, 'we saw a man who is not in our group. He was causing bad spirits to go out of people. And he was using your authority to do it. He is not in our group. So we told him that he must not do it.'

39 'Do not tell him that', Jesus said. 'That man is using my authority to do something powerful. Someone who does that cannot soon say anything bad about me. 40 If someone is not against us, he is helping us. 41 Somebody may give you a cup of water because you are a servant of the Messiah. God will be good to that person; he will not disappoint that person. What I am saying is true.

42 A person who believes may not seem important. But you should never cause that person to do wrong things. It would be better if someone put a big stone round your neck. It would be better if someone then threw you into the sea!

43-44 If your hand causes you to do wrong things, you should cut it off. A person with only one hand can go to the place where God rules. That is better than to go to the place called hell. There, the fire always burns. 45-46 If your foot causes you to do wrong things, you should cut it off. A person with only one foot can go to the place where God rules. That is better than to go to the place called hell. 47 If your eye causes you to do wrong things, then you should take it out. A person with only one eye can go to the place where God rules. That is better than to go to the place called hell.

48 "In hell, the worms do not die,

and the fire never goes out." '

49 'God will put fire on everybody as people put salt on food.'

The fire will show what is good in everyone's lives.

50 'Salt is good. But it must be salty. If your salt is not salty, you cannot make it salty. Be like good salt and love each other. Do not cause trouble among yourselves.'

Chapter 10

Jesus teaches about men who send their wives away

1 Then Jesus left that place and he went to Judea. And he went to the east of the river Jordan. Large crowds came to him again. So he taught them as he had done before.

2 Some Pharisees came to Jesus. They wanted to see how Jesus would answer their question. They asked, 'Can a man send his wife away, so that she is no longer his wife?'

3 Jesus answered them with a question. 'What rules did Moses write about this for you?'

4 The Pharisees said, 'Moses said that a man could write a letter for his wife. The letter shows that the man and the woman are now separate. Then the man can send the woman away.'

5 'You did not want to obey God. That is why Moses made this rule for you', Jesus said to them. 6 'But at the start of the world, God made people male and female. 7 This is the reason that a man leaves his father and his mother. Then God joins him and his wife together. 8 Then the man and his wife become as one person. They are not separate; they are together as one person. 9 God has put them together to be husband and wife. So nobody should make them separate.'

Jesus was telling them about things that are in Genesis 2:24.

10 When Jesus went into the house, the disciples asked him about these things again. 11 So Jesus said to them, 'A man must not send his wife away and marry another woman. That is against God's rules. The man must not have sex with that other woman. 12 And a woman must not leave her husband and marry another man. That is also against God's rules. The woman must not have sex with the other man.'

Jesus prays for some children

13 People were bringing children to Jesus. They wanted him to put his hand on each child's head while he prayed for that child. The disciples told the people that they should not bring their children. 14 But when Jesus saw this, he was angry. 'Do not stop the children', Jesus said to them. 'Let them come to me. People must be like these children so that God can rule their lives. 15 What I say is true. A person must be like a child when that person asks God to rule his life. If he does not become like a child, God will not rule his life.' 16 And Jesus hugged the children. Then he put his hands on each of them and he prayed for them.

Jesus meets a rich man

17 While Jesus went on his way, a man ran to meet him. He went down on his knees in front of Jesus. 'Good Teacher', he said to Jesus, 'what must I do so that I can live always?'

18 'I would like to know why you are calling me good', Jesus said to him. 'Only God is good. 19 And you know God's rules.

> "Do not kill anyone.
>
> Do not have sex with a woman who is not your wife.
>
> Do not rob anyone.
>
> Do not say things that are not true.
>
> Do not take things that are not yours.
>
> Love and obey your father and your mother." '

20 'Teacher', the man replied, 'I have done all these things since I was a young boy.'

21 Jesus looked at the man and Jesus loved him. 'There is still something else that you must do', Jesus said to him. 'Go. You must sell everything that you have. Give the money to poor people. Then you will have valuable things in God's home called heaven. And come to me. Be my disciple.'

22 When the man heard that, he was sad. Because he was a very rich man, he went away sadly.

23 Jesus looked round and he said to his disciples, 'It is very difficult for rich people to let God rule their lives.'

24 They were very surprised about Jesus' words. Then Jesus spoke again to them. 'Young people, it is very difficult for anyone to let God rule his life or her life. 25 The hole in a needle is very small. The big animal called the camel cannot go through it. But it is even more difficult than that for a rich person to let God rule his life or her life.'

26 When his disciples heard Jesus, they were even more surprised. And they said to each other, 'So perhaps God will not save anyone!'

27 Jesus looked at them and he replied, 'It is impossible for people to do this. But God can do it. God can do everything.'

28 'Look!' Peter said to Jesus. 'We left everything to become your disciples.'

29 Jesus said, 'What I say is true. Some people have left their house. Or they have left their brothers or sisters. Or they have left their mother or their father. Or they have left their children or their fields. They have done that because of me. And they have done it because of God's good news. 30 But God will give those people many things instead. He will give them 100 things now, in this world, for each thing that they have left. They will receive houses and brothers and sisters. They will receive mothers and children and fields. But in this world, people will be against them. In the future world, they will live always. 31 But many people who are very important now will not be important then. And people who are not important now will be very important then.'

Jesus talks again about his death

32 Jesus and his disciples were walking along the road towards Jerusalem. Jesus was walking in front of them all, and the disciples were very surprised. The people who were following behind them were afraid. Jesus asked his 12 disciples to come close to him again. And he began to tell them what would happen to him soon. 33 'Look!' he said to them. 'We are going to Jerusalem. There, someone will deliver the Son of Man to the important priests and to the teachers of God's rules. These men will decide that he must die. Then they will deliver him to people who are not Jews. 34 They will laugh at him. They will spit on him. They will hit him with sticks. Then they will kill him. After three days, he will become alive again.'

James and John ask Jesus to do something for them

35 James and John, who were Zebedee's sons, came to Jesus. 'Teacher', they said, 'we want to ask for something. Please do it for us.'

36 'What do you want me to do?' Jesus asked them.

37 They said to him, 'When you are king, we want to sit on your right side and on your left side.'

38 'You do not understand what you are asking for', he said to them. 'People will cause troubles for me that are like a cup of very bad wine. Can you drink it too? They will be as bad as deep water that will cover me up to and over my head. Can you go to that place too?'

39 'Yes, we can do all that', said James and John. Jesus said to them, 'Your troubles will be like mine. They will be like a cup of bad wine that you must drink. They will be as bad as water that will cover you up to and over your head. 40 But I cannot give you the seats on my right side or on my left side. God has chosen who will sit there. He has prepared those seats for them.'

41 When the other 10 disciples knew about this, they were angry with James and John. 42 But Jesus asked the disciples to come. Jesus said, 'You know the things that rulers do. They think that they rule over countries. So they do the things that masters do. And important people use their authority over people. 43But you should not be like that. The person who wants to be great among you must be your servant. 44Anyone who wants to be the most important person must work for you all. 45 Even the Son of Man came to earth to be a servant. He did not come here to have servants who must work for him. He came to die so that many people can be free.'

Jesus causes a blind man to see

46 Then Jesus and his disciples arrived in Jericho. When they were leaving the city again, a large crowd followed them. A blind man called Bartimaeus was sitting by the side of the road. He was asking people to give him money. He was the son of Timaeus.

47 Somebody told Bartimaeus that Jesus from Nazareth was walking past him. So he began to shout. He said, 'Jesus, you are the Son of David. Please be kind to me!'

48 Many people told Bartimaeus that he should be quiet. But he shouted even louder than before, 'Jesus, Son of David, please be kind to me!'

49 Jesus stopped walking and he said to the people, 'Ask the man to come here.' So the people said to the blind man, 'Be brave. Stand up. Jesus is asking you to go to him.' 50 So Bartimaeus threw away his coat. He jumped up and he came to Jesus.

51 Because of this, Jesus said to Bartimaeus, 'What do you want me to do for you?'

The blind man said to Jesus, 'Teacher, I want to see.'

52 'Go', Jesus said to him. 'You are well because you believed.' Immediately, Bartimaeus could see and he followed Jesus along the road.

Chapter 11

Jesus rides into Jerusalem city

1 Jesus and his disciples were coming near to Jerusalem. They were almost at the villages called Bethphage and Bethany. They were on the hill called the Mount of Olives. Then Jesus sent two of his disciples.

2 'Go to the village that is in front of you', Jesus said to the two disciples. 'When you arrive at the village, you will immediately find a young donkey. Someone has tied it there. Nobody has ever yet ridden on it. Undo the rope and bring the donkey here. 3 Someone may ask you, "Why are you doing this?" Say to him, "The Master needs the donkey. He will send it back here soon." '

4 So the two disciples went. They found the young donkey in the street. Someone had tied it outside, by a door. So the disciples undid the rope. 5 Some people were standing there. They said to the two disciples, 'What are you doing? Why are you undoing the donkey's rope?' 6 The disciples answered them. They repeated what Jesus had asked them to say. The people then let them take the donkey away. 7 The two disciples brought the young donkey to Jesus. They put their coats on the back of the animal. Then Jesus sat on it. 8 Many people put their coats down on the road. Other people put down branches. They had cut those branches from the trees.

9 Many people went in front of Jesus, and other people followed him. All of them were shouting,

'We ask you to save us!

Great is the king who comes on behalf of the Lord!

10 Great will be the future government of our great King David!

We ask you to save us powerfully!'

11 Jesus arrived in Jerusalem. He went to God's Great House and he looked at everything there. It was late in the day, so he went out of the city to Bethany. And the 12 disciples went with him.

A tree without fruit

12 On the next day, they returned from Bethany. And Jesus was hungry. 13 He saw a fig tree, which was a long way away. There were leaves on it. So he went to see if it had fruit on it. When he reached it, he found nothing except leaves. That was because it was not the right season for fruit. 14 So Jesus said to the tree, 'Nobody will ever eat fruit from you again.' And his disciples heard this.

Jesus goes to God's Great House

15 When they arrived in Jerusalem, Jesus went to God's Great House. People were buying and selling things there. He caused them all to leave. Some people were supplying money there. He pushed over their tables. And he pushed over the seats of the men who sold birds.

16 Jesus would not let anyone carry things through there. 17 While he was teaching the people, Jesus said, 'The Bible says:

"My house will be a place where people from all countries pray.

But you have made it a place where robbers hide." '

18 The important priests and the teachers of God's rules heard this. And they thought about how they could kill him. They were afraid of him. That was because all the crowd were listening to him. And the things that he taught caused the crowd to be very surprised.

19 When it was evening, Jesus and his disciples went out of the city.

The fig tree is dead

20 The next morning, Jesus and his disciples passed the fig tree. They saw that it was completely dead. 21 Peter remembered what Jesus had said. So he said to Jesus, 'Teacher, look at that fig tree. You said that it should die. And it has died.'

22 So Jesus said to them, 'You must believe God. 23 What I say is true. A person could say to this mountain, "Move and throw yourself into the sea." He must not let other ideas come into his mind. He must believe that those things will happen. If he does believe it, those things will happen. 24 So I tell you this. When you pray to ask God for anything, believe. Believe that you have received that thing. If you do, you will have it. 25-26 When you stand to pray, forgive other people. If you have anything against anyone, forgive that person. If you do forgive them, your Father God, in his home called heaven, will forgive you. He will forgive you for the bad things that you have done.'

Jesus talks about his authority

27 Jesus and his disciples arrived again in Jerusalem. Jesus was walking about at God's Great House. The important priests, the teachers of God's rules and the important Jews came to Jesus. 28 'What authority do you have to do these things?' they asked him. 'Who gave you the authority to do these things?'

29 'I will ask you one question', Jesus replied. 'You should answer me. If you do that, I will answer you. And I will tell you what authority I have to do these things. 30 John baptised people. Was his authority from God, or was it from men? Tell me the answer.'

31 Then the Jewish leaders talked with each other. They said, 'We could say that God gave John his authority. But, if we say that, Jesus will say to us, "You should have believed him." 32 We do not want to say that men gave John his authority.' They did not want to say it because they were afraid of the crowd. All the people believed that John really was a special servant of God.

33 So the Jewish leaders answered Jesus and they said, 'We do not know who gave John his authority.'

And Jesus said to them, 'You will not tell me. So I will not tell you what authority I have to do these things.'

Chapter 12

Jesus tells a story about a garden

1 Then Jesus began to speak to the important Jews again. He told them stories. He said, 'There was a man who made a garden. He planted vines there and he planted strong bushes round them. He prepared a place where he could make the grapes into wine. He also made a tall building. Then the man found some men who would work for him. And he went away to another country.

2 When it was time to cut the grapes, the man sent a servant to the workers. The man wanted the workers to give him some fruit from the garden. 3 But the workers took the servant and they hit him with sticks. They sent him away with nothing. 4 So the man sent another servant to the workers. They hit this servant on the head. And they did other bad things to him. 5 The man then sent another servant, but the farmers killed this servant. He sent many other servants. The workers hit some servants with sticks. And the workers killed some servants.

6 The man had only one person that he could still send. This was his own son, and the man loved him very much. So, last of all, he sent his son to the workers. That was because he said, "The workers know that my son is important."

7 But those workers said to each other, "This son will receive the garden from his father. We should kill the son and then the garden will be ours." 8 The workers took the son and they killed him. Then they threw his dead body out of the garden.'

9 'I will tell you what the master of the garden will do', said Jesus. 'He will come and he will kill the workers. He will give the garden to other people.'

10 'I am sure that you have read these words in the Bible:

"The builders did not want to use a certain stone.

But that stone became the most important stone at the corner.

11   The Lord God did this.

And we can see that he did something great." '

12 The leaders wanted to put Jesus in a prison. They knew that he had told this story about them. But they were afraid of the crowd. So, they left him and they went away.

The Pharisees ask about the money that Caesar demanded

13 Then the leaders sent some Pharisees to Jesus. They also sent some men who wanted to obey King Herod. They tried to use Jesus' words to cause trouble for him. 14 These men came to Jesus. 'Teacher', they said, 'we know that you only say true things. It does not matter to you what other people think. You do not change your answers if someone is important. You really do teach us what God wants us to do. So should we pay money to Caesar (the Roman ruler), or should we not? 15 Should we give that money, or not?'

Jesus knew that those men were not honest. So he said, 'You should not ask that question to cause trouble for me. Bring me a coin. I want to see it.' 16 So they brought it. And Jesus said to them, 'Whose picture is on this coin? Whose name is on it?'

They replied, 'It is Caesar's picture, and Caesar's name.'

17 So Jesus said to them, 'So give to Caesar the things that are his. And give to God the things that are God's.'

They were very surprised.

The Sadducees ask Jesus a question

18 Also, some Sadducees came to Jesus. Sadducees do not believe that anyone can become alive again after death. They asked Jesus about this.

The Sadducees were a group of Jewish leaders. They taught that death was the end.

19 'Teacher', they said to Jesus, 'Moses wrote these things for us in our rules. If a man dies without children, his brother must marry the man's wife. And then their children will be called the children of the brother who died. 20 At one time, there were 7 brothers. The oldest brother married a woman. But he died without children. 21 So the second brother married her. He also died without children. Then the third brother married this woman. 22 And the same thing happened to all 7 brothers. They had no children. After this, the woman also died. 23 You teach that at some time dead people will live again. On that day, whose wife will that woman be? She married all 7 brothers.'

24 'You are very wrong', Jesus said to the Sadducees. 'This is because you do not know the Bible. And you do not know how powerful God is. 25 At some time, people who have died will become alive again. But then men and women will not marry. They will not have husbands or wives. Instead, they will be like the angels in God's home. 26 But God does make dead people alive again. You should have read what Moses wrote. See the chapter about the bush. There, God spoke to Moses and God said, "I am the God of Abraham. I am the God of Isaac. And I am the God of Jacob." 27 God is not the God of people who are dead. He is the God of people who are alive. So you are very wrong.'

Jesus teaches people about the most important rule

28 One of the teachers of God's rules came near. He heard Jesus' conversations with the leaders.

The teacher knew that Jesus had answered them well. So the teacher asked Jesus, 'Which rule is the most important among God's rules?'

29 'This rule is the most important rule', replied Jesus. 'Listen, everyone from Israel's families. The Lord, our God, is the only Lord. 30 And you must love the Lord, your God. Love him with all your mind. Love him with all your life. Love him with all your thoughts. Love him with all that you do. 31 The second most important rule is this: You must love other people as much as you love yourself. No other rules are as important as these two.'

32 The teacher of God's rules said to Jesus, 'Teacher, you answered well. You are right to say that the Lord is the only God. And there is no other God except him. 33 We must love him with all our mind. We must love him with all that we learn. We must love him with all that we do. We must also love other people as much as we love ourselves. This is more important than all the gifts or animals that we offer to God.'

34 Jesus heard that the man had answered well. So Jesus said to him, 'You are almost ready for God to rule your life.' After that, everybody was afraid to ask Jesus any more questions.

Jesus teaches the people about the Messiah

35 Jesus was teaching the people at God's Great House. He said, 'The teachers of God's rules talk about the Messiah.

And they say that he is King David's son. Think about this. 36 The Holy Spirit helped David himself to write:

"The Lord said to my Lord:

Sit at my right side until I win completely against your enemies.

You will even be able to put your feet on them."

37 David himself calls the Messiah "Lord". So we should not say that the Messiah is only David's son.'

Jesus explained a very important fact to the teachers of God's rules. Jesus is a man but he is also God. In verse 36, the first time that David says 'Lord' he is talking about God. The second time that he says 'Lord' he is talking about Jesus, the Messiah.

38 While Jesus was teaching the people, he said, 'Be careful about the teachers of God's rules. They want people to think that they are important. So they walk about in long clothes. They like it if people recognise them in the market place. 39 They want the best seats in the meeting places. They choose the most important places at special meals. 40 These men take everything away from women after their husbands have died, even their houses. Then they pray for a long time so that other people will hear them. God will punish those men very much because of these things.'

Jesus talks about people who give to God

41 The crowd were giving their gifts for God's Great House. They threw their coins into a box. Jesus sat near the box and he watched them. Many rich people put a lot of money into the box. 42 But then a woman came. Her husband had died and she was poor. She put in two coins that had very small value.

43 Jesus asked his disciples to come to him. 'What I say is true', he said to them. 'This poor woman has put a better gift into the box than all the other people have put in.

44 All those rich people only put a part of their money into the box. And they have plenty of money. This woman has nothing. But she put in all the money that she had. She has put in all the money that she needs to live.'

Chapter 13

Jesus talks about future events

1 Then Jesus left God's Great House. While he was leaving, one of his disciples said to him, 'Teacher, look at the large stones that are in the walls of God's House. The buildings are very strong!'

2 Jesus said to him, 'Look at all these large buildings! Enemies will completely destroy them. They will throw down every stone that is on top of another stone.'

3 After that, Jesus was sitting on the hill called the Mount of Olives. He could look across at God's Great House. Peter, James, John and Andrew went together to talk with him. The crowd was not there. 4 'Please tell us when these things will happen', they said. 'What will we see just before all these things happen?'

5 Jesus began to say to them, 'Be careful! Some people will tell you things that are not true. Do not believe those people. 6 Many people will say that they have come on my behalf. They will say, "I am here!" Many people will believe their false words.

7 People will tell you about wars. And there will be reports about wars. Do not be afraid. Those things must happen, but that is not yet the end. 8 People in one country will attack the people in another country. Kings and their armies will fight against other kings and their armies. The ground will move in many different places. Some people will be without food. These things are like the first pains before a baby is born.

9 So, be careful! People will take you to their rulers. People will hit you in the meeting places. People will bring you to stand in front of kings and in front of rulers. You will be there on my behalf. And you will tell them about me. 10 And you must first tell the good news to people in every country. 11 People will take you away and they will bring you to their leaders. But do not be afraid about the words that you should say. You should say the words that God puts into your mind at that time. You will not be speaking your own words. Those words will come into your mind from the Holy Spirit.

12 A man will send his own brother to die. A father will send his own child to die. Children will be against their parents and they will ask rulers to kill their parents. 13 All people will be cruel to you because you are mine. But God will save the person who waits patiently until the end.

14 There will be a time when you will see a very bad thing. It is the very bad thing that destroys. It will stand where it should not be. (When you read this, you must understand it.) When you see this thing, people in Judea must run to the hills to hide. 15 A person who is on his roof must not go down into his house. He must not stop to get anything from his home. 16 A person who is in a field must not go back to his home. He must not return to pick up his coat.

17 That time will be bad for women who are hoping to have a baby soon. And that time will be bad for those women who are trying to give milk to their babies. 18 You must pray to God that these troubles will not happen in winter. 19 Very bad troubles will happen to people. Nothing as bad as those troubles has ever happened since God made the world. Nothing as bad as those troubles will ever happen again after that time. 20 The Lord God will cause those days of very bad trouble to be less. If he did not do that, there would be nobody still alive. But God will cause those days to be less. He will do that to help the people that he has chosen. 21 Someone may say to you then, "Look, here is the Messiah!" Or they may say, "Look, he is there!" Do not believe them. 22 Some people will say to you, "I am the Messiah." Other people will say, "I am a special messenger from God." But their words are false. They will do powerful things. Those things will surprise everyone very much. If possible, they would even cause the people that God has chosen to believe them. 23 So be careful! I have told you about all these things before they happen.

The time when the Son of Man returns

24 Then, after all these bad things have happened, the sun will become dark. And the moon will not shine. 25 Stars will fall out of the sky. And the powerful things in the sky will leave their usual places.

26 Then people will see the Son of Man. He will come in the clouds. He will be very powerful and very beautiful. 27 Then he will send the angels. And they will bring together all the people that God has chosen. The angels will bring them from every direction. And God's people will come from every part of God's home and from every part of earth.

A lesson about the fig tree

28 Here is a lesson about the fig tree. When the new branches on the tree start to grow, the leaves appear. Then you know that the summer will begin soon. 29 So you will see that these things are happening. And then you will know that the Son of Man will come soon. He will be like someone at the door who is ready to come in. 30 What I say to you is true. The people who are alive will not all die first. Some of them will not die until all these things have happened. 31 The earth and the sky will have an end. But my words will never have an end.

Nobody knows when the Son of Man will return to the world

32 Nobody knows the day or the hour when all these things will happen. Even the angels who are in God's home do not know. Even the Son does not know. Only God the Father knows when they will happen. 33 Watch carefully! You do not know when all these things will happen. So keep yourselves ready. 34 It is like when a master begins a journey. Before he leaves his house, he gives authority to his servants. He tells each servant about the work that he should do. Then he tells the servant at the door to be ready for his master's return.

35 And you do not know when the master of the house will return. So keep yourselves ready and watch carefully. He might arrive in the evening, or in the middle of the night. Or he might arrive early in the morning, or just before the sun rises. 36 He may surprise you and he may find you asleep. 37 I am saying this to you. And I am also saying this to everyone else. Keep yourselves ready!'

Chapter 14

The important priests and the teachers of God's rules want to kill Jesus

1 It was now two days before the Passover and the days when the Jews eat flat bread. The important priests and the teachers of God's rules wanted to kill Jesus. But they wanted to take him away secretly. So they tried to decide how they could do that. 2 'We do not want to do it during the Passover', they said to each other. 'The people will be angry. And they may fight against us if we do that.'

A woman pours expensive oil on Jesus' head

3 While Jesus was in Bethany, he went to Simon's house. People called that man, 'Simon with the illness in his skin'. While Jesus was eating a meal, a woman came into the house. She brought a small stone jar that contained expensive oil with a lovely smell. The person who made that oil had used only one plant. It was the plant called nard. The woman broke the jar to open it. And then she poured the oil over Jesus' head.

4 But some people became angry. 'This woman should not have wasted the oil', they said to each other. 5 'she should have sold it and she should have given the money to poor people. She could have sold it for more than 300 coins. A man would have to work for a year to get that much money.' So, they spoke angrily to the woman.

6 But Jesus said, 'Do not speak to her like that! Do not cause trouble for her. She has done a good thing to me. 7 You will always have poor people with you. You can help them at any time that you want. But you will not always have me with you. 8 She did what she was able to do. She poured oil over my body to prepare it. So now, my body is ready for people to bury me. 9 What I say to you is true. Everywhere, people will tell other people about God's good news. At the same time, they will also tell those people about the thing that this woman did. And so they will remember her.'

Judas agrees to help the important priests

10 Then Judas Iscariot went to the important priests. He said that he would help them to catch Jesus. (Judas was one of the 12 disciples.) 11 The important priests were very happy about this. And they promised to give him money. Then Judas watched for the right moment for him to give Jesus to them.

Jesus eats his last meal with his 12 disciples

12 It was now the first day of the whole week when the Jews eat flat bread. On this day, each family would kill a young sheep for the Passover meal. Jesus' disciples said to him, 'We will go to prepare the Passover meal for you. Where do you want us to do that?'

13 So Jesus sent two disciples. 'Go into the city', he said to them. 'A man, who is carrying a jar of water, will meet you. Follow him. 14 He will go to a house. And you must say to the master of that house, "The Teacher sends this message to you: 'Where is the room for visitors where I can eat the Passover meal with my disciples?' " 15 Then the man will show you a large room upstairs. The room will have in it all the things that you will need. You should prepare the Passover meal for us there.'

16 Then the two disciples left and they went into the city. They found everything as Jesus had told them. So, they prepared the Passover meal there.

17 When it was evening, Jesus arrived with the 12 disciples. 18 While they were eating the meal, Jesus said, 'What I say to you is true. One of you will help the Jewish rulers to take me away. It is someone who is eating this meal with me.'

19 The disciples became very sad. Each one of them said to Jesus, 'I hope that you do not mean me!'

20 'It is one of the 12 disciples. That man is putting his bread into the same dish as I am', Jesus said to them.

There was a dish on the table with some food in it. They all put their bread into this dish and they ate the food with the bread.

21 'The Son of Man must go, as the Bible says', Jesus said. 'But it will be very bad for that man who helps to lead the Son of Man away. It would have been a better thing for that man if he had never been born.'

The Passover meal

22 While Jesus and his disciples were eating, he took a loaf. He thanked God for it. Then he broke the bread and he gave the pieces to them. 'Take this bread and eat it', he said to them. 'This is my body.'

23 Then Jesus took a cup. He thanked God. Then he gave the cup to them and they all drank from it.

24 'This is my blood', he said to them. 'It shows that there is a promise from God. When I die, my blood will leave my body. And so God will save many people.

25 What I say is true. I will not drink wine again until God begins to rule his people. And then I will drink the new wine.'

26 Then Jesus and his disciples sang a song to God. Then they went out. They went to the hill that people call the Mount of Olives.

Jesus tells the disciples what will happen

27 Then Jesus said to them, 'Tonight's events will cause you all to do wrong things. The Bible says:

"I will kill the man who leads the sheep.

And the sheep will run away in different directions."

28 But I will become alive again. Then I will go before you to Galilee.'

29 Peter said to Jesus, 'Even if everyone else does wrong things, I will not leave you.'

30 'What I say to you is true', Jesus replied to Peter. 'Tonight, you will say three times that you do not know me. You will do it before the cockerel makes its noise for the second time.'

31 But Peter answered Jesus strongly, 'If necessary, I will die with you. But I will never tell anyone that I do not know you.' All the other disciples said the same thing.

Jesus prays in the garden called Gethsemane

32 Then they arrived at a garden called Gethsemane. Jesus said to his disciples, 'Sit here while I pray.' 33Then Jesus took Peter, James and John with him. He started to feel that troubles were filling his mind. 34'I am very sad. I could die because I feel so sad. Wait here and keep awake', Jesus said to them.

35 Jesus went a short way in front of them. He went down on the ground. He prayed that, if possible, God would save him from the events of that time. 36 He said, 'Abba, (my Father), you can do anything. Please take this pain away from me. But I do not ask you to do what I want. I choose what you want.'

37 Jesus returned and he found Peter, James and John. They were sleeping. He said to Peter, 'Simon, you are asleep! You could not keep awake for even one hour! 38 You must keep awake and you must pray. If you do not do that, you might do the wrong thing. You really want to do the right thing, but it is too difficult for you.'

39 Jesus went away again and he prayed again. He said the same words to God. 40 Jesus returned again to Peter, James and John. He saw that they were sleeping. They could not keep their eyes open. They did not know what to say to him.

41 When Jesus returned the third time, he said to them, 'You should not be sleeping and resting. You have slept enough. This is the hour. Look! See the man who is helping bad men to take the Son of Man away. 42Stand up; we are going. Look! Here is the man who will help them to take me away.'

Judas leads the men who will take Jesus away

43 Jesus was still speaking when, immediately, Judas arrived.

He was one of Jesus' 12 disciples. A crowd came with him. They were carrying long sharp knives and heavy sticks. The important priests, the teachers of God's rules and the leaders had sent these men.

44 Before this, Judas had said to these men, 'I will kiss one of the men. That is the man that you must take away. Lead him away and do not let him go.' 45 When they arrived, Judas went immediately to Jesus. 'Teacher', he said to Jesus. Then he kissed Jesus in a friendly way. 46 So the men took hold of Jesus. 47 But a certain man who was standing there took his long sharp knife. And he used it against the servant of the most important priest. He cut off the servant's ear.

48 Then Jesus spoke to the crowd. 'You have come with long sharp knives and with heavy sticks to take me away', he said. 'That is how you would take a robber away. But you know that I am not a robber. 49 I was with you every day at God's Great House when I was teaching the people. You did not take me away then. But the things that are in the Bible must happen.' 50 Then all Jesus' disciples left him and they ran away.

51 A certain young man was following Jesus. He was only wearing one piece of cloth over his whole body. The men tried to take hold of this young man. 52 But the young man left the piece of cloth behind, and he ran away. When he ran away, he was not wearing anything.

We think that this young man was called Mark. Mark wrote this book.

The most important priest asks Jesus questions

53 The men took Jesus to the most important priest. All the important priests met, with the leaders and with the teachers of God's rules.

54 Peter followed Jesus. But he did not go near Jesus. So Peter went into the yard outside the house of the most important priest. He sat down with the guards. Peter kept himself warm by the fire.

55 The important priests and everyone at the meeting wanted Jesus to die. So they tried to find some men who could say things against Jesus. But they did not find anyone who could help them. 56 Many people said things about Jesus. But they were saying things that were not true. And they did not agree with each other.

57 Then some men stood up and they said something else about Jesus. But their words were also not true.58 They said, 'We heard Jesus say, "I will destroy God's Great House, which men have built. In three days, I will build another House for God. It will not be men who build this new house."' 59 Even then, these people who were speaking against Jesus did not say the same thing.

60 Then the most important priest stood up in the middle and he spoke to Jesus. 'You should reply now. These people have said that you have done many bad things. What do you say about this?' 61 But Jesus did not reply. He did not say anything.

So again, the most important priest asked Jesus, 'Are you the Messiah? Are you the Son of God?'

62 'I am', Jesus replied. 'And you will all see the Son of Man. He will be sitting at the right side of God, who is most powerful. And he will come with the clouds of God's home, which is called heaven.'

63 The most important priest tore his own clothes. 'We do not need anyone else to tell us about Jesus', he said. 64 'You have heard the bad words that he has spoken against God. What do you decide?'

Everyone agreed that Jesus should die.

Caiaphas tore his own clothes to show other people that he was very angry.

65 Then some of the men began to spit on Jesus. They covered his eyes and they hit him. They said, 'Speak God's words, if you can!' Then the guards slapped Jesus while they were taking him away.

Peter says three times that he does not know Jesus

66 Peter was still outside in the yard. One of the young women who worked for the most important priest came. 67 She saw Peter, who was making himself warm by the fire.

She looked at him and she said, 'You also were with Jesus, the man from Nazareth.'

68 'That is not true!' he replied. 'I do not know what you are talking about! I do not understand what you mean!' Then Peter walked to the gate of the house.

69 The young woman saw him, and again she began to say to the other people there, 'This man is one of the men who were with Jesus.' 70 But Peter again said that it was not true.

71 Peter began to speak strongly to them. 'I do not know this man that you are talking about', he said. And Peter asked God to punish him if his words were not true. 72 Immediately, the cockerel made its noise for a second time. Then Peter remembered what Jesus had said to him: 'You will say three times that you do not know me. You will do it before the cockerel makes its noise for the second time.'

When Peter thought about this, he wept.

Chapter 15

Pilate asks Jesus questions

1 Immediately in the morning, all the important people had a meeting. The important priests met with the leaders, the teachers of God's rules, and the other important people. They tied Jesus and they led him away. They brought him to Pilate.

Pilate ruled Jerusalem on behalf of the Roman government.

2 Pilate asked Jesus, 'Are you the king of the Jews?'

Jesus replied, 'Yes, it is as you say.'

3 Then the important priests said to Pilate that Jesus had done many bad things. 4 So Pilate asked him again, 'What is your answer? You should say something! Listen! They are saying that you have done many bad things.'

5 Jesus still did not answer him. And Pilate was very surprised about that.

6 Each year during the Passover, Pilate let one person go out of the prison. The people had to ask him for the person that they wanted. 7 A man called Barabbas was in the prison at that time. He and some other men had fought against the government. And they had killed someone when they were fighting. 8 The crowd came to Pilate. And they asked Pilate to do what he usually did.

9 Pilate answered the people, 'Do you want me to make the king of the Jews free for you?' 10 Pilate knew why the important priests had brought Jesus to him. The people seemed to like Jesus more than they liked the priests. And that had made the priests angry. 11 But the important priests talked strongly to the people. They told the people that they should ask Pilate to make Barabbas free instead.

12 So Pilate again asked the crowd, 'So what should I do to Jesus? He is the man that you call "the king of the Jews".'

13 The people shouted again. They shouted, 'Kill him on a cross!'

14 'Why should I kill him on a cross?' Pilate asked. 'What bad things has he done?'

But the people shouted even louder, 'Kill him on a cross!'

15 Pilate decided to do what the crowd wanted. So he made Barabbas free for them. He told his soldiers that they should take Jesus away. They should hit him many times with a whip. Then they should put him on a cross to die.

16 Then the soldiers took Jesus to the yard at the ruler's house. And they told all the soldiers in their group that they must come. 17 Then they put a dark red coat on Jesus. They made a crown out of sharp branches, and they put it on his head.

18 Then the soldiers began to shout to Jesus, 'Oh yes, King of the Jews!' 19 The soldiers took a stick and they hit Jesus on the head with it. They spat on him. Then they went down on their knees in front of him. They told him how great he was. 20 But they were laughing at him. Then they took off the dark red coat. They put Jesus' own clothes back on him. Then they led him towards the place where they would put him on the cross.

The soldiers put Jesus on a cross

21 A man called Simon was walking past Jesus and the soldiers. He was coming in from outside the city. The soldiers told Simon that he must carry Jesus' cross. Simon was from the city called Cyrene. He was the father of Alexander and Rufus. 22 The soldiers brought Jesus to the place that was called Golgotha. (Golgotha means 'the place of a skull'.)

23 They gave Jesus some wine to drink. They had put some medicine called myrrh into the wine. But Jesus would not drink the wine. 24 Then the soldiers put Jesus on the cross. They took his clothes for themselves. They played a game to decide which soldier would get each of his clothes.

25 It was 9 o'clock when the soldiers fixed Jesus to the cross. 26 Above his head, they put a notice to say why they were punishing him. The notice said, 'The King of the Jews'. 27 They also put two robbers' on crosses with Jesus. One robber was on the right side of Jesus. And the other robber was on his left side. 28(The Bible says that this would happen. And it did happen. The Bible says, 'People included him with people who did not obey God's rules.')

29 The people who walked by moved their heads from one side to the other side. And they said bad things to Jesus. They said to him, 'Oh! You said that you would destroy God's Great House. And you said that in three days you would build it again. 30 If you can really do that, save yourself. Come down from the cross!'

31 The important priests and the teachers of God's rules laughed about him to each other. 'This man saved other people. But he cannot save himself. 32 If he is the Messiah, the king of Israel, he should come down from the cross now. We would see it and then we would believe.' The two men who were on the crosses next to Jesus also said bad things to him.

Jesus dies

33 At midday, the whole country became dark. It continued to be dark until 3 o'clock. 34 At 3 o'clock, Jesus shouted loudly, 'Eloi, Eloi, lama sabachthani.' That means, 'My God, my God, I want to know why you have left me alone!'

35 Some people were standing near his cross and they heard him. They said, 'Look! He is asking Elijah to come.'

36 One man ran to get a soft cloth. He poured bad wine on it. And he put it on the end of a stick. Then he lifted it up to Jesus so that he could drink the wine from it. 'Wait!' he said. 'We will see if Elijah comes to take Jesus down from the cross.'

37 Then Jesus shouted loudly again and after that, he died.

38 And someone or something tore the curtain inside God's Great House completely into two parts from the top down.

39 The captain of the soldiers was standing in front of Jesus. He saw how Jesus died. 'It is true', he said. 'This man was the Son of God.'

40 Some women were also there. They were not very near the cross. But they were watching all these events. Mary, from the town called Magdala, was among the women. Another woman called Mary was also there. She was the mother of the younger James and Joses. Salome was also there. 41 These women had been Jesus' disciples when he was in Galilee. There, they had helped him. And many other women were there who had come to Jerusalem with him.

Joseph buries Jesus' dead body

42 It would soon be Friday evening. The Jews were preparing for Saturday, when they rested. 43 A man called Joseph went to see Pilate. Joseph was from a town called Arimathea. He was a good man and he was an important leader of the Jews. He was waiting for the time when God would start to rule his people. Joseph bravely asked Pilate for the dead body of Jesus. 44 Pilate was surprised that Jesus had already died. He asked the captain of the soldiers to come to him. Then he asked him when Jesus had died. 45 The captain told Pilate that Jesus was dead. So then Pilate let Joseph have Jesus' dead body. 46 Joseph bought a new piece of soft white cloth. He took Jesus down from the cross. He put the cloth round him. And he buried him in a large hole that Joseph's workers had cut into the rock. After this, he rolled a very big stone in front of the hole.

47 Mary from the town called Magdala, and Mary, the mother of Joses, were watching. They saw where Joseph had put Jesus' dead body.

Chapter 16

Jesus becomes alive again

1 After the day for rest had finished, the women bought some seeds with a beautiful smell. They wanted to put those seeds and some oil on Jesus' body. These women were Mary from Magdala, Salome, and Mary the mother of James. 2 They went out very early in the morning on the first day of the week (Sunday). The sun was just rising. They went to the hole in the rock where Joseph had buried Jesus' dead body.

3 The women asked each other, 'Who will roll the big stone away for us? It is in front of the hole in the rock where they buried Jesus.'

4 They looked and they saw the stone. It was a very big stone. But someone had already rolled it away from the hole.

5 When the women went into the hole in the rock, they saw a young man. He was sitting on the right side of the place. He wore long white clothes. They were very afraid.

This young man was an angel.

6 The young man said to them, 'Do not be afraid. You are looking for Jesus from Nazareth. The soldiers killed him on a cross, but he has become alive again. He is not here. Look! You can see the place where the men put him. 7 But you must go to tell his disciples and Peter about this. Tell them that Jesus is going before you to Galilee. There you will see him, as he told you.'

8 The women went out of the hole in the rock. They ran away from there. They felt afraid and confused. They did not say anything to anyone, because they were afraid.

9 Jesus became alive again early on the first day of the week, Sunday. He appeared first to Mary from Magdala. Jesus had caused 7 bad spirits to leave her. 10 She went to the people who had been with Jesus. They were all very sad and they were crying. Mary spoke to them. 11 She told them that Jesus was alive. And she told them that she had seen him. But they did not believe it.

12 After these things had happened, Jesus appeared to two other disciples. They were walking away from the town. He seemed to be different to them. 13 Those two disciples went and they told all the other disciples. But the other disciples also did not believe them.

14 After that, Jesus appeared to the 11 disciples while they were eating. He told them that they were wrong not to believe. They should have changed their minds. People had seen that he was alive. But the disciples did not believe them.

15 And Jesus said to them, 'Go to all people everywhere in the world. Tell God's good news to everyone. 16 If a person believes, then you should baptise that person. And God will save that person. But if a person does not believe, God will be that person's judge. And he will punish that person. 17 These powerful things will happen after people believe. On my behalf, they will send bad spirits out of people. They will speak new languages. 18 If they pick up a snake, it will not hurt them. If they drink poison, it will not hurt them. They will put their hands on ill people, and God will make those people well.'

Jesus goes up to God's home called heaven

19 So, after the Lord Jesus had spoken to them, God took him up into God's home. And Jesus sat down at the right side of God.

20 But the disciples went out everywhere. They told people God's good news. The Lord worked with them. And the Lord did powerful things to show that their message was true.   **Hear this Good News for Everybody!**

Luke 24

About this book

Luke obeyed what Jesus taught. He was also a doctor. People think that he was not a Jew. He wrote this book some time between the years AD 59 and AD 80. Some people think that he wrote it in the city called Rome. He wrote it for a man called Theophilus. He was an important Roman officer and he was a rich man.

Luke also wrote the book for other people that believed in Jesus. It would help them to know Jesus better. Then they could answer questions when people asked them about him. Many people had wrong ideas about Jesus. Luke wanted people to know what was true.

Luke writes about the Good News. The Good News is that God wants to rule in the lives of his people. God will rule in the lives of Jews and of those people that are not Jews. Luke tells us who Jesus is. And he tells us how Jesus was born. He also tells us about his life and death. Luke explains to us why Jesus came to earth. He also explains what he did during his life here. And he tells us how he went to live with God again. And, at the end, he explains to us about God's gift of the Holy Spirit.

Luke knew that Jesus had told people about the Good News. Jesus wanted his people to let everyone in the world know the message about himself. Luke wanted everyone to know what Jesus had said.

The book of Luke is in 4 parts:

1. What happened before Jesus started his work (1:1 - 4:13).

2. What happened when Jesus was working in the country called Galilee (4:14 - 9:50).

3. What happened when Jesus was working in the countries called Judea and Perea (9:51 - 19:27).

4. What happened in the city called Jerusalem in the last week of Jesus' life (19:28 - 24:53).

Chapter 1

1 Great things have happened in our country. Many people have tried to write about them. 2 Some people were present when these things started to happen. They saw everything that happened. They told us what they had seen. And they told us what they had heard. They are the people who told the Good News. 3 Most important Theophilus, I have checked all these facts. Now I also know about all the things that happened from the beginning. I am writing to tell them to you. It is good for you also to know all these facts. This is the reason for this letter. 4 You have already heard about all these things. Now you can be sure that they are true.

What happened before John the Baptist was born

5 There was a man whose name was Zechariah. He lived when Herod was king of Judea. Zechariah was apriest and he belonged to a group of priests from the family of Abijah. He had a wife called Elizabeth. And they were both from the family of the priest called Aaron.

6 Zechariah and Elizabeth obeyed God all the time. They did not do wrong things. God liked how they lived. 7 But they had no children. Elizabeth could not have a baby and they were both getting old.

8 One day, Zechariah's group was working at the Great House of God. And Zechariah had a special job to do. 9 The priests chose one of their group to go into a special room inside the Great House of God. Zechariah's job was to burn incense there.

10 While Zechariah was burning incense, many men were outside the special room. They were praying to God.

11 The incense was burning on a special table, when an angel from God appeared to Zechariah. The angelwas standing at the right hand side of the table.

12 When Zechariah saw the angel, he was very surprised. He was also very afraid. 13 'Zechariah, do not be afraid', the angel said to him. 'God has heard what you prayed. He will give you what you asked for. Your wife Elizabeth will have a baby boy. You will call him John. 14-15 He will be very important to the Lord. So, he will make you very happy. Many other people will also be very happy because he has been born. He must never drink anything with alcohol in it. From the time that he is born, the Holy Spirit will live inside him.

16 He will teach many people in Israel. Then they will turn their lives towards the Lord their God and they will obey God again. 17 John will prepare the people for the Lord. The Holy Spirit will lead John as he led Elijah. John will be as powerful as Elijah was. He will help fathers to love their children. He will teach people that do not obey God. Then they will think right things. And they will do right things that good people do. John will prepare Israel's people. Then they will be ready when the Lord comes.'

18 'How can I be sure about this?' Zechariah asked the angel. 'After all, I am an old man. My wife is also old.'

19 'I am called Gabriel', answered the angel. 'My place is in front of God. I am always ready to work for God. He has sent me to speak to you. He told me that I should tell you this good news.

20 Now listen to me. Because you did not believe my message, you will be quiet. You will not speak again until the time that your son is born. My message will become true at the right time.'

21 While this was happening, the people outside were waiting for Zechariah. They were thinking, 'Why has Zechariah stayed for such a long time in the special room? Why has he not come out yet?' 22 When he did come out, he tried to talk to them. But he could not speak. So they knew that he had seen something special in the room. He was moving his head and his hands about, to tell them what had happened. But he remained quiet.

23 When Zechariah had finished his work in the Great House of God, he returned home. 24 Soon, a baby was growing inside his wife Elizabeth. She stayed in her house for 5 months. 25 'The Lord has now given me a baby', she said. 'He has been kind to me. He has helped me to feel good about myself. Because of this, other people cannot say bad things about me any longer.'

What happened before Jesus was born

26 When Elizabeth's baby had grown inside her for nearly 6 months, God sent the angel Gabriel to Nazareth. Nazareth is a town in Galilee. 27 Gabriel went there to visit a young woman. Her name was Mary. She had never had sex with anyone. She had promised to marry a man called Joseph. He belonged to the family of King David.

28 Gabriel arrived. 'Hello, Mary', he said. 'God loves you very much. He is very near to you.'

29 Mary had a lot of problems in her mind about what Gabriel said. She did not understand why he said it. 30 'Do not be afraid, Mary', Gabriel went on to say. 'God has been kind to you. 31 Listen! A baby boy will grow inside you. When he is born, you will call him Jesus. 32 He will be great. The strong God above will call him his Son. The Lord God will make him king. He will rule as King David ruled. 33 He will rule over the family of Jacob for all time. He will be king for all time.'

34 'How can this happen?' Mary asked. 'I have never had sex with anyone.' 35 'The Holy Spirit will come to you', the angel answered. 'The power of God will cover you like a shadow. So, your child will be completely good. He will never do anything that is wrong. He will be called God's Son. 36 Another thing! Your cousin, Elizabeth, is very old. People said that she could not have a baby. Listen! She also will have a son. The baby has grown inside her now for nearly 6 months. 37 There is nothing that God cannot do.'

38 'I am the servant of the Lord', Mary answered. 'I have heard what you have said. I want the Lord to cause it to happen to me.' Then the angel left her.

Mary visits Elizabeth

39 After that, Mary prepared herself and she left on a journey. She hurried to a town in the hills of Judea. 40When she arrived at the home of Zechariah, she said, 'Hello' to Elizabeth. 41 When Elizabeth heard Mary speak, she felt her baby move quickly inside her. The Holy Spirit filled her. 42 Then she spoke to Mary in a loud voice, 'God has made you very happy. He has been more good and kind to you than to other women. He has also been good and kind to your baby. 43 I am not an important person and you are the mother of my Lord. So, it is a very good thing that you have visited me. 44 Listen! When I heard you say, "Hello" to me, the baby moved quickly inside me. He was very happy. 45 The Lord told you what would happen. And you believed what he told you. This makes you a very happy person.'

This is Mary's song

46 Then Mary said,

'All of me wants to say to the Lord, "How good and great you are!"

47 I am happy because of God. It is he who saves me.

48 I do not think that I am an important person.

God knows this, so he has looked at me with love.

Listen! From now on all people will say that

God has been very good and kind to me.

49 After all, God has done great things for me.

He is very powerful and strong.

He is good in everything.

50 He is kind to people that obey him.

He is also kind to all their children. He will do this for all time.

51 He has shown how strong he is.

Some people think that they are very important.

But he has sent them away alone in different directions.

52 Some people were ruling countries.

But he has taken their important jobs away from them.

He has given important work to people that do not feel important.

53 He has fed hungry people with good things.

He has sent rich people away with nothing.

54 He promised that he would never forget his people, Israel.

Now he has helped them.

55 He made a promise to Abraham and to our other fathers.

"I will be kind to you for all time", he said. Now he has done what he promised.'

56 Mary stayed with Elizabeth for about three months. Then she returned to her home.

John the Baptist is born

57 Then it was time for Elizabeth to have her baby. She had a son. 58 Her family and the people that lived near her heard about her baby. They knew that the Lord had been very kind to her. They saw that she was happy. So they were happy too. 59 When the child was 8 days old, they came to the house of Zechariah and Elizabeth. The child had to be circumcised on that day. The people wanted to call the child Zechariah. This was the same name that his father had.

60 'No', said Elizabeth. 'His name will be John.'

61 'You cannot really want his name to be John!' they said. 'You do not have anybody in your family called John.' 62 Then they moved their hands at his father. They wanted to know the boy's name.

63 So Zechariah asked for something to write on. He wrote, 'His name is John.' Everyone was very surprised at what he wrote. 64 Immediately, Zechariah could speak again. He could speak very well again. He began to tell God, 'You are very great!'

65 The people that lived near Zechariah and Elizabeth were surprised. They were surprised about what had happened. They saw how great God was. Many people that lived in the hills of Judea also talked about all these things. 66 Everyone that heard about these things thought about them. 'What will this child be?' they asked each other. After all, they could see that God really was with him.

This is Zechariah's song

67 The Holy Spirit filled John's father. Then he spoke well about God. The Holy Spirit helped him to speak this message.

68 'The Lord God of Israel is a great God.

He has come to save his people.

69 He has sent a very strong person that will save us.

This person is in the family of David. David was his servant.

70 Long ago, God gave his Spirit to good people so that they could tell us about this.

This is what they said:

71 "God will save us from our enemies.

He will save us from everyone that hates us.

72 He has promised to be kind to our fathers.

He will remember to do the things that he promised."

73 Yes, he will remember the promises that he said to Abraham.'

74 ' "I will keep you safe from your enemies.

Then you can work for me and not be afraid.

75 You can work for me in the right way.

You can do this all your lives." '

76 Zechariah then spoke to his child.

'You, child, will be called a servant of the great God above.

The Holy Spirit will give to you messages to speak.

You will go in front of the Lord to prepare a way for him.

77 You will tell his people how God can save them.

They have done wrong things but God will forgive them.

78 Our God will forgive us because he is very kind.

He will send someone from the highest place.

This person will be like the sunrise to us.

79 As the sun gives light to everybody, so he will shine on all people.

Some people are like people who are in the dark. They are living without God.

Some people are afraid to die.

But he will shine on everybody.

He will show us how to live so that we will not be afraid.'

80 Zechariah's child grew. God made him strong in his mind. He went and he lived in the desert for many years. Later, God sent him to Israel's people, to teach them.

Chapter 2

Jesus is born

1 While Mary's baby was growing inside her, Caesar Augustus was ruling the whole Roman world. He ordered his men, 'Count everyone who is in the Roman world.' 2 This was the first time that the Romans had counted everyone. Quirinius was the Roman ruler of Syria at this time.

3 So everyone went to his own home town for the Romans to count them. 4 Joseph also went to his home town. He was living in the town called Nazareth in Galilee. He went to the town called Bethlehem in Judea. King David had been born there, so Bethlehem was called the town of David. Joseph belonged to the family of David. That is why he went to Bethlehem.

5 Joseph took Mary with him so that the Romans could count them. She went because she had promised to marry him. She would soon have a baby.

6 While they were in Bethlehem, her baby was born. 7 This was her first baby, and it was a boy. She put cloths round him. Then she put him in an animal's feeding box. She did this because they could not stay in the hotel. There were no empty rooms for them.

Some people leave their sheep to go and see Jesus

8 That night some people were living in the fields near Bethlehem. They were keeping their sheep safe. 9 Then an angel of the Lord appeared to them. A bright light from God shone all round them. So that frightened them very much. 10 'Do not be afraid', the angel said. 'Listen! I bring you good news. This news will make everyone very happy. 11 Something happened today in the town of David. Someone special was born. It is he who will save you. He is the Messiah. He is the Lord. 12 I will tell you how you will know this baby. You will find him with cloths round him. He is lying in an animal's feeding box.'

13 Just then a lot more angels also appeared. They were speaking about God.

14 'God is beautiful and great and important', they said.

'He lives in the highest place.

He will be good to the people on earth that make him happy.

They will not have troubles in their minds or in their spirits.'

15 After that, the angels returned to God's home. Then these people said to each other, 'Perhaps we should leave the sheep and go to Bethlehem immediately! The Lord has sent angels to tell us what has happened. We want to see this baby.'

16 So they hurried to Bethlehem. There, they found Mary and Joseph with the baby. The baby really was lying in a feeding box. 17 After they had seen the baby, they told everybody about him. They told them what the angel had said to them. 18 Many people heard what the men said. They were very surprised. 19 Mary remembered all that the men from the fields had said. She thought about everything for a long time. 20 The men then returned to their sheep. 'How great you are!' they were saying to God. 'How good you are! Everything that the angel told us was true! We have heard good news. We have seen very special things!'

Mary and Joseph take Jesus to the Great House of God

21 When the baby was 8 days old, it was time for the priest to circumcise him. His parents called him Jesus. The angel had told Mary that she must call the baby, Jesus. He told her that before she had a baby inside her.

22 Long ago, the Lord gave Moses rules for his people to obey. One rule told how to become clean after a baby was born. Now the time had come for Mary and Joseph to obey this rule. So, they took the baby Jesus to the Great House of God in Jerusalem to show him to the Lord.

23 This is what the Lord had said: 'The first male baby born to a woman or to an animal is mine. So you must bring him to me. 24 When you do this, also bring two special birds for the priest to kill.' That is what Mary and Joseph did.

25 At this time, a man called Simeon was living in Jerusalem. He was good and he always obeyed God. He had waited a long time to see the special person that would save Israel. The Holy Spirit was with Simeon. 26 'You will not die yet', the Holy Spirit had told him. 'You know that God has promised to send the Messiah. You will see him before you die.' 27 Now the day had come. The Holy Spirit told Simeon that he should go to the Great House of God. Mary and Joseph were bringing the baby Jesus to do what the rule said. 28 Simeon went to them. He took Jesus from Mary and he held him in his arms. Then he thanked God.

29 'Master, you have done what you promised to your servant. Now, I can die with no trouble in my mind.

30 Now I really have seen the person that will save people.

31 You have sent him to earth so that everyone will know about him.

32 He will be like a light to people. He will show you to those that are not Jews. They will then know you. And they will know what you want from them. Then they will know what you want them to do. He will also show that your people of Israel are very special.'

33 That is what Simeon said about Jesus. His message surprised Mary and Joseph very much.

34 Then Simeon asked God to be good and kind to Mary and to Joseph. After that, he spoke just to Mary, the mother of Jesus. 'God has chosen this baby. Many people in Israel will become less important because of him. And many people will become alive again because of him. He will be like a sign that points to God. Many people will speak against him. 35 This will show their secret thoughts about God. This will make you very sad, too. It will seem that a sharp knife is cutting inside you. That is how sad you will be', Simeon said to her.

36 A very old lady called Anna was there in the Great House of God, too. She often spoke messages that the Holy Spirit gave to her. She was the daughter of Phanuel. She belonged to the family of Asher. She had lived with her husband for 7 years and then he had died.

37 After that, she had lived alone until she was 84 years old. Now she never left the Great House of God. She stayed there day and night to pray to God. Often she went without food so that she could pray better.

38 At that moment, Anna came to where Mary and Joseph were standing. When Anna saw the baby, she began to thank God for him. Then she began to speak about him to other people. Many people were waiting for God to make Jerusalem free. These were the people that she was speaking to.

39 When Mary and Joseph had finished obeying all the rules, they returned home. They went back to the town called Nazareth in Galilee. 40 There the child grew. God was good and kind to him and God made him strong. He could then understand many things.

The boy Jesus visits the Great House of God

41 Every year, Mary and Joseph went to Jerusalem for the Passover week.

42 When Jesus was 12 years old, his parents took him with them to Jerusalem. They went as usual for the Passover week. 43 When the week finished, everyone left to return home. The boy Jesus stayed behind in Jerusalem, but his parents did not know this. 44 They thought that he was with their group. So they travelled for a whole day. Then they began to look for him among their family and friends.

45 They could not find him, so they went back to Jerusalem. They looked for him for three days, 46 before they found him in the Great House of God. He was sitting among the teachers. He was listening to what they were saying. He was also asking them questions. 47 Everyone that was listening to Jesus was very surprised. He understood so many things and he could answer difficult questions. 48 When his parents saw him there, they were also very surprised. 'My son', said his mother, 'why have you done this to us? Your father and I have looked everywhere for you. We have had a lot of troubles in our mind.'

49 'You should not really have had to look for me', Jesus answered. 'I must be doing what my Father wants me to do. Really, you should have known that.' 50 But they did not really understand what he was saying to them.

51 Jesus returned to Nazareth with them and he obeyed them. Mary was careful to remember all the special things that had happened. She thought about them a lot. 52 Jesus grew into a man. He could understand more and more things. Everyone loved him and God also thought well of him.

Chapter 3

John the Baptist prepares people to welcome Jesus

1 This report about John, the son of Zechariah, began while Tiberius Caesar was ruling the Roman world. He had ruled for almost 15 years. Pontius Pilate was ruling the country called Judea. And Herod was ruling the land called Galilee. Philip was the brother of Herod. He was ruling the countries called Iturea and Traconitis. Lysanias was ruling Abilene. 2 While these men were ruling, the most important priests were Annas and Caiaphas. At that time John, the son of Zechariah, was living in the desert. He heard God speak to him.

3 John travelled to many places near to the river Jordan. 'You are doing many bad things', he taught everybody. 'Stop doing them. Be sorry for what you have done. If you are, I will baptise you with water. God will then forgive you.'

4 John was teaching as Isaiah had spoken a long time before. God gave him messages. Someone wrote down these messages in a book. Isaiah told people what would happen. He said:

'People will hear someone who is shouting in the desert:

"The Lord is coming. Make the road ready for him.

Make it straight.

5   Fill in every valley and make every mountain and hill flat.

Take away every curve so that the road is straight.

Take away all the rocks so that the road is flat.

6   Then you will see how God will save you." '

7 Crowds of people were coming out into the desert to hear John speak. They wanted John to baptise them. 'Yes', he said, 'God will soon punish people that do wrong things. But you are as dangerous as snakes. 8 You have to show that you are sorry. You have to show it by how you live. Stop doing things that God does not like. Do not begin to say to yourselves, "God will not punish us. After all, we are part of the family of Abraham." Listen! God can make children for Abraham out of these stones! 9 You are like trees that have bad fruit. People cut down bad trees and they throw them into the fire. In the same way, God will punish bad people. And he will do it very soon.'

10 'So, what should we do?' the crowd asked.

11 'If you have two shirts, give one away. Give it to a man that does not have a shirt. If you have some food, give some of it away. Give some to a man that has no food.'

12 In the crowd, there were people that took money on behalf of the government. These men also wanted John to baptise them. 'Teacher, what should we do?' they asked. 13 'You must take the right amount of money from the people. You must not take more than the rules say.'

14 Then some soldiers spoke. 'What about us? What should we do?'

'Do not rob people of their money', John replied. 'Do not say that a person has done something wrong, if he has not. It is wrong to get money by doing that. And you must be happy with the money that you get for your work.'

15 'Is John the Messiah?' the people were thinking. 'Is he the man that God will send to save Israel?' They were all hoping that he might be. 16 John knew what they were thinking. 'I have only baptised you with water', he said. 'But someone else is coming to baptise people. He is much greater and more important than I am. He is so important that I am not good enough even to undo his shoes. He will baptise some of you with the Holy Spirit and with fire. 17 Think about a farmer that brings the wheat home. Then he uses a tool to make the seeds separate from what remains. He stores all the seeds. But he burns all that remained. This person will be like that. He will come very soon. He will keep good people safe. But he willpunish bad people in the fire that nobody can put out.'

18 John said many more things to the people. He was telling them the good news about how God could change their lives. 19 But the ruler Herod stopped him. John had told Herod that it was wrong for him to marry Herodias. She was the wife of his brother. John had also told Herod that he had done many other bad things.

20 Then Herod did an even worse thing; he locked John up in prison.

John baptises Jesus

21 While John was baptising all the people, he also baptised Jesus. When Jesus was praying, the sky opened. 22 Then the Holy Spirit came down. He seemed like a bird. He came and he rested on Jesus. People heard a voice from the sky. 'You are my Son. I love you. You make me very happy.'

The family of Jesus

23 Jesus was about 30 years old when he started to tell the Good News. People thought that he was Joseph's son.

He was Heli's son.

24 Heli was Matthat's son.

Matthat was Levi's son.

Levi was Melki's son.

Melki was Jannai's son.

Jannai was Joseph's son.

25 Joseph was Mattathias' son.

Mattathias was Amos's son.

Amos was Nahum's son.

Nahum was Esli's son.

Esli was Naggai's son.

26 Naggai was Maath's son.

Maath was Mattathias's son.

Mattathias was Semein's son.

Semein was Josech's son.

Josech was Joda's son.

27 Joda was Joanan's son.

Joanan was Rhesa's son.

Rhesa was Zerubbabel's son.

Zerubbabel was Shealtiel's son.

Shealtiel was Neri's son.

28 Neri was Melki's son.

Melki was Addi's son.

Addi was Cosam's son.

Cosam was Elmadam's son.

Elmadam was Er's son.

29 Er was Joshua's son.

Joshua was Eliezer's son.

Eliezer was Jorim's son.

Jorim was Matthat's son.

Matthat was Levi's son.

30 Levi was Simeon's son.

Simeon was Judah's son.

Judah was Joseph's son.

Joseph was Jonam's son.

Jonam was Eliakim's son.

31 Eliakim was Melea's son.

Melea was Menna's son.

Menna was Mattatha's son.

Mattatha was Nathan's son.

Nathan was David's son.

32 David was Jesse's son.

Jesse was Obed's son.

Obed was Boaz's son.

Boaz was Salmon's son.

Salmon was Nahshon's son.

33 Nahshon was Amminadab's son.

Amminadab was Ram's son.

Ram was Hezron's son.

Hezron was Perez's son.

Perez was Judah's son.

34 Judah was Jacob's son.

Jacob was Isaac's son.

Isaac was Abraham's son.

Abraham was Terah's son.

Terah was Nahor's son.

35 Nahor was Serug's son.

Serug was Reu's son.

Reu was Peleg's son.

Peleg was Eber's son.

Eber was Shelah's son.

36 Shelah was Cainan's son.

Cainan was Arphaxad's son.

Arphaxad was Shem's son.

Shem was Noah's son.

Noah was Lamech's son.

37 Lamech was Methuselah's son.

Methuselah was Enoch's son.

Enoch was Jared's son.

Jared was Mahalaleel's son.

Mahalaleel was Kenan's son.

38 Kenan was Enosh's son.

Enosh was Seth's son.

Seth was Adam's son.

Adam was the son of God.

Chapter 4

The devil tries to cause Jesus to do wrong things

1 Jesus was now full of the Holy Spirit. When he returned from the river Jordan, the Holy Spirit led him into the desert. 2 He stayed there for 40 days and he did not eat anything. At the end of 40 days, he was very hungry. During this time the devil tried to cause Jesus to do wrong things. They were things that God did not want him to do.

3 'If you are the Son of God', the devil said, 'change this stone into food.'

4 'No!' Jesus replied, 'the book of God says that food alone cannot cause people to live.'

5 After that, the devil led Jesus up to a high place. In one moment, he showed him all the countries in the whole world. 6 'I will let you rule the whole world', the devil said, 'and I will give you power over everyone and over everything. It all belongs to me. So, I can give it to anyone that I choose. 7 Just bend your knee in front of me. And say that I am great and important. Then I will give you the whole world to rule over.'

8 'No!' Jesus replied. 'This is what God says in his book:

"Bend your knee in front of the Lord God. Tell him how great and important he is. Only obey him." '

9 The devil now took Jesus to Jerusalem. He led him to the highest part of the Great House of God. Then he said, 'If you are the Son of God, jump down from here to the ground. 10 After all, it says in God's book:

"God will order his angels to keep you safe."

11 It also says,

"They will hold you safe in their hands. They will not let you hurt your feet against a stone." '

12 'No!' replied Jesus. 'That is not what God wants. His book says,

"Do not do something dangerous just to cause God to save you." '

13 The devil tried to cause Jesus to do many things that God did not like. When the devil had finished, he left Jesus alone for a time.

Jesus goes to Nazareth

14 The Holy Spirit continued to make Jesus very powerful when he returned to Galilee. Everyone who lived in and near Galilee heard the news about him. 15 He taught in the Jewish meeting places and everyone said good things about him.

16 Jesus came to Nazareth, the town where he had grown up. On the Jewish day for rest, he went into the meeting place. He always did this. Then he stood up to read aloud from the Old Testament.

17 They gave him the book of messages that God had given to Isaiah. Jesus opened the book. He found the place where Isaiah wrote.

18 'The Spirit from the Lord God is upon me.

He has chosen me to tell good news to poor people.

He has sent me to tell people who are in prison, "You can go free!"

I must say to people that cannot see, "See again!"

I must cause people that are like slaves to be free.

19 I must tell everyone, "This is the year when God will save his people." '

20 Jesus closed the book and he gave it back to an officer of the meeting place. Then he sat down to teach the people. Everyone in the meeting place was looking at him.

21 'Today', Jesus said to them, 'this message has become true. It has happened while you were listening.'

22 Everyone was saying good things about Jesus. They were surprised. 'How well he spoke! And he is only the son of Joseph, is he not?' they were asking each other.

23 'Next', Jesus replied, 'you will be repeating the proverb, "Doctor, make people well in your own town." We have heard that you did many surprising things in Capernaum. This is your home town, so do the same things here! 24 People do not accept a person that comes from their home town. That really is true. They do not believe that he receives messages from God.

25 What I shall tell you now is true. Elijah received messages from God. Elijah said that it would stop raining. And it did not rain for three and a half years. So there was no food or water to drink in all the country. There were many widows in the country of Israel at that time. 26 But God did not send Elijah to stay with a widow in Israel. Instead, God sent Elijah to the country called Sidon. There Elijah stayed with a widow in a place called Zarephath.'

27 'Here is another example. There were many people in Israel with bad illnesses of the skin, when God's servant Elisha was alive. But God did not make any of them well. Instead, he made a man from the country called Syria well. The man was called Naaman.'

28 The people in the meeting place heard what Jesus said. They became very angry. 29 They stood up and they caused him to leave the town. The town was on the top of a hill. So, they took him to the top and they wanted to throw him down. 30 But Jesus walked through the middle of the crowd and he went away.

Jesus causes a bad spirit to leave a man

31 Jesus went down to a town in Galilee called Capernaum. On the Jewish day for rest, he began to teach in the meeting place. 32 They were really surprised because his words had authority. 33 In the meeting place was a sick man. He had a bad spirit that was living inside him. The spirit caused him to shout and to make a lot of noise. 34 'Jesus of Nazareth, what do you want to do to us? Have you come to destroy us? I know who you are. You are the Holy One. You come from God.'

35 'Be quiet!' Jesus replied. 'Come out of the man.' At this, the bad spirit caused the man to fall to the ground in front of the people. Then it came out without hurting him.

36 All the people were very surprised and they said to each other, 'How can this man speak in that way? He has power and authority. When he orders bad spirits to come out of people, they come out.' 37 Then they began to tell everyone about Jesus. As a result, people in all the places near Capernaum heard the news about Jesus.

Jesus makes many people well

38 Jesus then left the meeting place and he went into Simon's home. The mother of Simon's wife was sick with a very bad fever. So, they asked Jesus to make her well. 39 Jesus came and he stood near her. He then ordered the fever to go away and it left her. So, she got up immediately and she began to prepare food for her visitors.

40 When the sun began to go down, the people brought many sick people to see Jesus. They had many different illnesses. He put his hands on each person and they became well.

41 Bad spirits also came out of many people. The spirits knew that he was the Messiah. So, when they came out, they began to shout, 'Jesus, you are the Son of God.' But Jesus stopped them shouting. He would not let them speak.

42 Early the next morning, Jesus went alone to a quiet place. The people went to look for him. When they found him they said, 'Do not leave us! Please stay with us in Capernaum.' 43 'I cannot stay with you', Jesus replied. 'I must go to other towns to teach everyone the good news. I will tell them how God rules in the lives of his people. That is what God sent me to do.'

44 Then he left them. And he started to teach in other Jewish meeting places in the country called Judea.

Chapter 5

Jesus asks some men to follow him

1 One day, Jesus was standing on the shore of Lake Gennesaret. And a crowd was pushing to get near to him. They were listening to him. He was talking about the message of God.

2 Jesus saw two fishing boats at the edge of the lake. The fishermen had left the boats there and they were now washing their nets.

3 One of the boats was Simon's. So Jesus climbed into it. He then asked Simon to push it away a little from the shore. When Jesus had sat down in the boat, he started to teach the people again.

4 When he finished teaching them, he spoke to Simon. 'Now take the boat out into deep water', he said. 'Then put down the nets into the water to catch some fish.'

5 'Teacher', Simon replied, 'we worked all last night and we did not catch anything. But because you say it, I will put down the nets.' 6 So they went and they put the nets down into the water. When they did that, they caught many fish. There were so many fish that the nets began to break. 7 So Simon shouted to the other fishermen that always worked with him. 'Come', he said, 'we need you.' When they saw that, the men came in their boat. They filled both boats with the fish. There were so many that the boats began to go down. 8 When Simon saw all the fish, he went down on his knees in front of Jesus. He was afraid. 'Sir', he said, 'I am a bad man. So please leave me.'

9 Simon said this because he was very surprised. He was surprised because they had caught so many fish. His friends in the other boat were very surprised, too. 10 James and John were also very surprised. They were sons of Zebedee and they always worked with Simon. 'Do not be afraid of me', Jesus then said to Simon. 'From now on you will catch men!'

11 After that, they went and they pulled their boats up on the shore. Then they left everything and they went with Jesus.

This is about a man with an illness of his skin and bones

12 One day, Jesus was in a certain town. A man with an illness of his skin and bones that was called leprosy was there.

When the man saw Jesus, he threw himself down on his knees in front of him. 'Sir, if you want', he said, 'you can make me well. Please do it.'

13 Jesus touched him with his hand. 'I do want to', he said. 'Be well.' Immediately, the illness was gone. 14 'Do not tell anyone about this', Jesus said to him. 'Instead, go and show yourself to the priest. Take him a gift for God. Moses told people, "You must do this when you are better from this illness." So give this gift to God. This will show everyone that you are now well.'

15 After this, more and more people started to hear the news about Jesus. Crowds were coming to hear him teach. The sick ones also wanted him to make them well. 16 But he would go away from the crowd to pray in quiet places.

Jesus makes well a man that cannot walk

17 One day, while Jesus was teaching in a house, many people were sitting there. Some were Pharisees. Other people were teachers of God's rules. They had come from many villages in Galilee, and from Judea and Jerusalem. At that time, the power of the Lord was present for Jesus to make sick people well.

18 Then some men arrived. They were carrying a man on a small carpet. The man could not move his legs. They tried to get into the house, because they wanted to bring the man to Jesus. 19 But the house was full of people, and they could not get in. So, they carried the small carpet with the man on it to the flat roof of the house. Then they made a hole in the roof. After that, they put the small carpet down through the hole. The man was still lying on it. He came down in the middle of the crowd, in front of Jesus. 20 When Jesus saw this, he said to himself, 'These men really believe in me.' So, he spoke to the sick man. 'My friend', he said. 'I forgive you for all the bad things that you have done.'

21 The Pharisees and the teachers of God's rules were there. They heard what Jesus said. So, they began to talk to each other about it. 'What he says is wrong. He cannot forgive people for the things that they have done. Only God can do that. And he is only a man.' 22 Jesus knew what these men were saying. 'You should not be thinking these things', he told them. 23 'I said to this man, "I forgive you for all the bad things that you have done." But I could say to him, "Get up and walk." I want to show you that my words are true. Which is the best one to say? 24 Now I will show you that I, the Son of Man, have authority on earth. I can forgive people for the bad things that they have done. I will show you that I can forgive them.' Then he turned to the man that could not move his legs. 'I say to you', he said, 'stand up. Take up your carpet and go home!'

25 Immediately, the man stood up in front of them. He took the carpet that he had used to lie on. He went home. 'How great and powerful God is', he was saying. 26 What had happened surprised everyone. They were afraid. 'How great and powerful God is', they said to each other. 'We have seen very strange and special things happen today.'

Jesus asks Levi to come with him

27 After this happened, Jesus went for a walk. He saw a man that took money on behalf of the government. His name was Levi and he was working in his office. 'Follow me', Jesus said to him. 28 Levi got up and followed him. He left everything behind.

29 Soon after this, Levi made a large meal for Jesus at his house. A big crowd of people also came and they were eating with them. Many of these people also took money on behalf of the government. 30 SomePharisees and teachers of God's rules saw them. They did not like these people. So, they spoke to the men that followed Jesus. 'You eat and drink with these bad people. That is not right. Some of them even take money on behalf of the government.'

31 'People that are well do not need a doctor', Jesus answered them. 'It is sick people that need one. 32 I have not come for people that have not done wrong things. Some people know that they have done wrong things. I am asking those people to come to me. I want them to stop doing wrong things. I want them to start doing right things.'

33 When they heard this, they asked Jesus about something else. 'Some people obey what John the Baptist teaches. Those people often stop eating food to pray better. The people that obey the Pharisees do the same. Why do those that obey you never go without their meals?'

34 Jesus used a picture story to answer their question. 'When a man is marrying, he gives a big meal. His friends do not go without food then. 35 But the time will come when people will take him away from his friends. Then they will go without food.'

36 Then Jesus told them another picture story. 'You do not tear a piece of cloth from a new coat to mend an old one. If you do that, you will have torn the new coat. Also, the new piece of cloth will not seem the same as cloth from the old coat.

37 Bottles that people have made out of the skin of an animal teach us the same. Nobody pours new wine into an old skin bottle. If they do, the new wine will break the old bottle. The wine will run out and they will lose it. And they will have destroyed the bottle. 38 Instead, people must put new wine into a bottle that they have made out of new animal skin.

39 Also, after he has drunk old wine, nobody wants new wine. He says, "The old wine is much better." '

Chapter 6

What the Jews can do on their day for rest

1 On a Jewish day for rest, Jesus was walking through some fields where wheat was growing. Then the men that were following him began to pick some of the wheat. They were rubbing the seeds with their hands. Then they were eating the wheat that remained.

2 Some Pharisees were walking along with them. 'You should not be doing that', they said. 'You know that it is against God's rules to work on our day for rest.'

3 'Remember what David did. He did it when he and his men were hungry', Jesus replied. 'You have certainly read about it. 4 He went into the Great House of God. And he took the special bread that was there. It is against God's rules for anyone except the priests to eat that bread. But he ate some of it and he also gave some to his friends.

5 The Son of Man has authority to say what people can do on the day for rest', Jesus said.

Jesus makes a man well on their day for rest

6 On another Jewish day for rest, Jesus went into the meeting place and he taught. A man was there. His right hand was very small and weak. The man could not use this hand. 7 Some teachers of God's rules and some Pharisees were careful to watch Jesus. They wanted a reason to say that he was doing wrong things. If he made this man well, they would say, 'Jesus is not obeying the rules that God gave. He works on the day for rest.' 8 But Jesus knew what they were thinking. So he spoke to the man. 'Get up and stand in front of everyone.' The man got up and he stood there. 9 'Let me ask you something', Jesus then said to the people. 'What should we do on the day for rest? Do God's rules say that we should do good things? Or do they say that we should do bad things? Should we save the life of someone? Or should we destroy a life?' 10 Nobody replied. So Jesus looked round at everyone. 'Put out your hand', he said to the man. When he put it out, it became well. He could use it again.

11 Then the Pharisees and those that taught God's rules were very angry. They began to talk to each other. 'What can we do to Jesus?' they said.

Jesus chooses the 12 men

12 One day Jesus went up a hill to pray. He remained there all night and he was talking to God. 13 In the morning, he asked all those that were following him to come to him. Then he chose 12 of them that he would send out with his message. These 12 men were called apostles. These are their names:

14 Simon. Jesus called him Peter.

Andrew. He was the brother of Simon.

James,

John,

Philip,

Bartholomew,

15 Matthew,

Thomas,

James, the son of Alphaeus,

Simon the Zealot,

16 Judas, son of James,

Judas Iscariot. He sold Jesus to those who wanted to kill him.

Jesus tells a special message

17 After Jesus had chosen the 12 men, they all came down the hill. He stopped and he stood on a flat place. A large crowd of those that were following stood with him. There were also many people from Jerusalem and from the towns of Judea and the coast of Tyre and Sidon. 18 These people had all come to hear Jesus teach. Those that were ill wanted him to make them well. He was also making well those people that had bad spirits. 19 All the people were trying to touch him, because he was making each person well with his great power.

Jesus teaches those that follow him

20 Jesus looked at those that were following him. He spoke this message to them.

'Listen, you that are poor. You are children of God, so be happy.'

21 'Listen, you that are hungry now. God will feed you, so be happy.'

'Listen, you that are crying now. God will cause you to laugh, so be happy!'

22 'People may hate you, because you obey me, the Son of Man. They may say that you are very bad. They may cause you to go away. They may do other bad things to you. When that happens, be happy. 23 After all, God will give you many good things when you go to his home. So, be very happy! Jump up and down because you are so happy. Think about those that do bad things to you now. It was their fathers that also did the same bad things long ago. They did bad things to those that spoke messages from the Holy Spirit.

24 Listen, you that are rich now. And listen, you that have a comfortable life. Trouble will come to you.

25 Listen, you that are full now. You will be hungry.

Listen, you that are laughing now. You will be sad and you will cry.

26 Trouble will happen to you, if people always say good things about you. Your families long ago said the same good things about bad people. Those bad people said that they spoke messages from the Holy Spirit. But they did not.'

Love people that want to hurt you

27 'I say this to you who are listening carefully to me', Jesus said. 'Love people that want to hurt you. Do good things to people that hate you. 28 Say good things to people that say bad things to you. Pray for people that do bad things to you.

29 Someone may hit you on one side of your face. If he does, let him hit the other side of your face too. Someone may take away your coat. If he does, do not stop him from taking your shirt too. 30 Give to anyone that asks you for things. Someone may take things that are yours. If he does, let him keep them. Do not ask for them back again. 31 Do to other people the good things that you want them to do to you.

32 Do you only love people that love you? If you do, you are not doing anything special. Do not want people to speak well about you because you love like that. After all, even bad people love those who love them. 33 Do you only do good things to people that do good things to you? If you do, you are not doing anything special. Do not want people to speak well about you for that. After all, even bad people do the same. 34 Do you lend things only to people that will give your things back? If you do that, you are not doing anything special. After all, even bad people lend things to other people. They believe that they will get them back again. 35 No! I am telling you to love people that want to hurt you. Do good things to them. Lend things to them and do not want to get them back again. If you do this, the high God will give you a great gift. He is kind even to people that do not say "thank you". He is even kind to bad people. So you will really be his sons. 36 So be kind, as God your Father is kind.

37 Do not say to someone, "You are a bad person." If you do not, God will not say to you, "You are bad person." Do not say to people, "God should punish you because you are bad." If you do not, they will not say that to you. Forgive other people and God will forgive you. 38 Give to other people and God will give to you. He will give to you more than you gave. He will fill your pocket until no more will go in. It will be so full that it will come out over the top. How you give to other people, God will give to you.'

39 Jesus also used this picture story to teach the people. 'A blind man cannot lead another blind man. If he does, they both will fall into a hole in the ground.

40 A student is less important than his teacher is. But when the student has learned everything, he will be like his teacher.

41 Perhaps you want to tell your brother about his mistake. If you want to do that, first remember your own mistakes. 42 If you do not, you are like this: You are like a person that has a piece of wood in his eye. That person then says, "Brother, you have some dirt in your eye. Let me take it out for you."

Do not be like that person. You say one thing but you do something different yourselves. First, make right your own mistakes. Only then can you know how to tell another person about his mistake.'

A picture story about a tree and its fruit

43 'Good trees only make good fruit. Bad trees only make bad fruit. 44 So in this way you can know if a tree is good or bad. You can know by the fruit that it makes. You only pick good fruit from good fruit trees and bushes. Figs do not grow on thorn bushes. Grapes do not grow on briers.'

45 'People are the same. A good man brings good things out of his mind. His good thoughts are very valuable. A bad man brings bad thoughts out of his mind. He values the bad things inside his mind. So, when a person speaks, his words show something. They show whether his mind is full of good thoughts or bad thoughts.'

A picture story about men that are building a house

46 'Do not call me, "master, master", and then not obey me', said Jesus. 47 'Some people hear my message and they obey it. Let me tell you what those people are like. They are like a man who built a house. 48 This man dug down to the rocks. He put the first line of stones on the rock. After that, he built the house on top of the rock. Then a storm came and it brought a lot of water. The water hit the house but it could not move it. The water could not move the house because the man had built it very well.

49 Some other people hear my message but they do not obey it. Let me tell you about those people. They are like another man who built a house. This man did not dig down deep to the rock. Instead, he put the first line of stones on the ground and he built on them. Then a storm came and it brought a lot of water. It hit this house and it fell down immediately. The water completely destroyed it.'

Chapter 7

A Roman officer believes that Jesus can help him

1 After Jesus had finished speaking to the people, he went to Capernaum. 2 A Roman officer there had a servant that he loved. The servant was very ill and he was dying.

3 The officer heard about Jesus, so he sent some of the Jewish leaders to speak to him. 'Please go to Jesus', he said to them. 'I would like him to make my servant well. Ask him if he would come to do that.' 4 The Jewish leaders then went to Jesus. 'Please would you do something for this Roman officer', they were saying. 'Please would you go and make his servant well. 5 This man loves the Jewish people. He himself built a meeting place for us.'

6 So Jesus started to go with them. When he was not very far away from the house, the officer sent some friends to talk to him. He told them that they should say. 'Sir, I do not want to be a trouble to you. I am not as important as you are. So you should not come into my house. 7 I did not come to talk to you myself, because I am not good enough. Instead, just say a word and my servant will be well again. 8 After all, someone also has authority over me. And so I have authority over other soldiers. I say to one soldier, "Go!" and he goes. I say to another one, "Come!" and he comes. And I say to my servant, "Do this!" and he does it.'

9 When Jesus heard this message from the officer, he was very surprised. He turned towards the crowd that was following him. 'Listen!' he said. 'I have not found anyone like this man in all of Israel. Nobody else believes so well in me.'

10 The friends of the officer returned to his house. Then they saw that the servant was well again.

Jesus makes a dead man alive again

11 The next day, Jesus went to a town called Nain. Those that always followed him and a large group of other people went with him. 12 When he had almost reached the gate of the town, lots of people were coming out. They were carrying a dead man in a box to bury him. His mother had no other sons and her husband was also dead. A large crowd from the town was with her.

13 When the Lord Jesus saw her, he felt very sorry for her. 'Do not cry', he said. 14 He went to the box and he touched it. So the people that were carrying the box stopped. 'Young man', said Jesus, 'get up, I say to you!' 15 At this, the dead man sat up and he began to talk. Jesus then gave him back to his mother.

16 Everyone that saw this was afraid. 'How great and powerful God is', they said. 'An important servant of God has appeared among us. God has come to save his people.'

17 This news about Jesus went all through Judea. It also reached the people in the countries that were near there.

Jesus talks about John the Baptist

18 Then some men went to visit John the Baptist in prison. Those people obeyed what he taught them. They told him about Jesus and about all that he was doing. So, John chose two of them. 19 'I want you to go to the Lord Jesus for me', he said. 'Say to him, "John said that someone would come. John asks if you are that man. Are you the Messiah? Or should we still look for someone else?" '

20 So the two men came to Jesus. 'John the Baptist has sent us to you', they said. 'He wants us to ask you, "Are you the man that would come? Or should we still look for someone else to appear?" '

21 At that time, Jesus made many people well. They had many different illnesses. Some had bad spirits. Jesus also caused many that could not see to see again. 22 Then he replied to the two men that John had sent. 'Go back to John', he said. 'Tell him what you have seen. And tell him what you have heard. People that could not see can see now. People that could not walk can walk now. Some had illnesses of the skin; they are now well. Some could not hear, but now they can. Some people were dead; they now live again. Poor people are hearing the good news. 23 If anyone continues to believe in me, he will be happy.'

24 The two men that followed John left. Then Jesus began to speak to the crowd about him. 'You went out to see John in the desert. Think about what you went to see', he said to them. 'You certainly did not go to see a tall piece of grass. The wind blows grass about. John is not weak, as grass is. 25 If not that, think about what you went to see. You certainly did not go to see a man who was wearing expensive clothes. People like that have many beautiful things and they live in big houses. John is not like them. He lives in the desert. 26 So think about what you went out to see. You went out to see a man that receives messages from God. Yes, and John was even more important than that. 27 A long time ago, God spoke about him. "Listen! I will send someone with a message from me. He will arrive first to prepare your way." '

28 Jesus also said to the people, 'Yes, John is a very important person. He is greater than any man that has lived before. But there are people that are not great. But God rules in them. Any one of those people is more important than John.'

29 A lot of people heard what Jesus said. 'What God says about us is right', they said. So they asked John to baptise them. Some of these people took money on behalf of the government. 30 The Pharisees and the people that taught God's rules did not want John to baptise them. They did not believe the message that God was giving to them.

31 So Jesus continued to teach. 'I will talk to you about the people that are alive today. I will tell you what they are like', he said. 32 'They are like children who are sitting in the market place. They are playing. They shout out to other children, "We made happy music on a pipe for you, but you did not dance. We sang a sad song and you did not cry." 33 You are like those children. When John the Baptist came, he often went without food. He never drank wine. So you said that he had a bad spirit in him. 34 Then I, the Son of Man, came. I both eat and drink. So you say about me, "Look at this man! He eats and drinks too much. He is a friend of those people who take money on behalf of the government. He is a friend of other bad people." That is what you say about us. 35 But God is wise and good. Wise people understand and they agree with him.'

A woman pours expensive oil on Jesus

36 Then one of the Pharisees asked Jesus to eat a meal with him. So Jesus went to his house and sat down to eat. 37 In that town was a woman that did many wrong things. She heard that Jesus was eating a meal at the house of the Pharisee. So she took a small jar of oil and she went there. The oil was very expensive and it had a beautiful smell. Someone had made the small jar out of white stone. 38 When she went inside, she stood behind Jesus. She was crying and she made his feet wet with her tears. Then she dried them with her hair and she kissed them. She then poured all the oil out of the jar on to his feet. 39 When thePharisee saw this, he said to himself, 'This man cannot be someone that receives messages from God. If he were, he would know all about this woman. He would not let her touch him. He would know that she is a very bad person.'

40 'Simon', said Jesus to him, 'I want to tell you something.' 'Yes, Teacher, tell me', replied Simon. So he told him a picture story about two men.

41 'Someone had lent them money. He had lent one of them 500 silver coins. He had lent the other one 50 coins.'

42 'Neither of the men had the money to pay him back. Then the man that had lent them the moneyforgave them. "You do not need to pay back my money", he said to them both.

Which of these two men will love that man most?' Jesus asked.

43 'I think', replied Simon, 'that it is the first man. It is the man that needed to pay back the most money.'

'You are right', said Jesus. 44 Then he turned towards the woman. 'You see this woman', he said to Simon. 'When I came into your house, you did not give me water for my feet. But she has washed my feet with hertears and she has dried them with her hair. 45 You did not welcome me with a kiss', he went on to say. 'But this woman began to kiss my feet when she came in. And she has not stopped. 46 You did not put oilon my head. But she has brought expensive oil with a sweet smell to put on my feet.'

47 'So I tell you this. This woman has done many bad things. But I have forgiven them. She loves me a lot, because I have forgiven her a lot. If I only forgive a little, a person only loves me a little.'

48 'Woman', Jesus then said, 'I forgive you for all the bad things that you have done.'

49 The other people at the meal talked among themselves. 'Who is this man? Can he really forgive the bad things that people have done?'

50 'You believed that I could forgive you!' Jesus told the woman. 'You will not have troubles in your mind any longer. You can go now.'

Chapter 8

The women that helped Jesus

1 After this, Jesus started to travel from one place to another. In each town or village, he spoke the good news to the people. 'God wants to rule in your lives', he was telling them. The 12 men that always followed Jesus were going with him. 2 Some women were also travelling with them. These women had been ill, but Jesus had made them well again. One of the women was Mary Magdalene. Jesus had sent 7 bad spirits away from her. 3 Another of the women was Joanna, the wife of Chuza. Chuza had authority over all the people that worked in the house of King Herod. Another of the women was Susanna. These and other women were helping Jesus and the 12 men that he had chosen. They were using their own money to do this.

The picture story about a farmer that planted seeds

4 Large crowds of people were coming to Jesus from many towns. A large number were already together when Jesus told this story.

5 'A farmer went out to plant seeds in his field. While he was throwing the seeds, some fell on the path. Then people walked on them and the birds ate them. 6 Some seeds fell on ground with rocks in it. They started to grow, but the young plants had no roots. Because there was no water in the ground, they died. 7 Some seeds fell among weeds. Then the weeds grew up with the young plants. They stopped the young plants from becoming strong, so they soon died. 8 But some seeds fell on good ground. Good, strong plants grew up from them. Each of these plants made one hundred seeds.'

When Jesus finished the picture story, he said, 'You have ears. So listen well to what I say.'

Jesus explains why he tells picture stories

9 The men that always followed Jesus asked him about this story. They asked him what it meant. 10 'God helps you to understand what these stories mean', he replied. 'But they are a secret to other people. They do not understand how God rules in the lives of his people. So, I tell picture stories to teach them. They have their eyes wide open, but they do not really see. They hear the words, but they do not understand.'

Jesus explains the picture story about the seeds

11 'This is what the story means', he went on to say. 'The seed is like the message of God.

12 Some seeds fell on the path. Some people hear the message from God, but they do not think about it. They are like the path. The devil comes and he takes the message away from them. Because he takes it away, they cannot believe it. Because they do not believe it, God does not save them.

13 Some seeds fell on ground with rocks in it. People that are happy to hear the message of God are like this ground. But the message does not change their lives and their thoughts. They believe in God for a time. But when they have trouble or difficulty, they stop believing.

14 Some seeds fell among weeds. Some people hear the message and they believe for a time. They are like the ground with weeds. They start to think about the things of this world. They want to get money and things that make them happy in this life. These things push the message from God out from their lives, so they stop believing. They are like a plant that has no fruit.

15 Some seed fell on good ground. Some people that hear God's message are like this ground. They remember and they obey. They are good and honest. They continue to believe and they do many good things. They are like a plant that has lots of good fruit.'

16 'People do not light a lamp and then cover it', Jesus went on to say. 'Nor do they put the lamp in a jar or under a bed. Instead, they put it in a high place. Then other people that come into the room can see the light from the lamp.'

17 'The message of God is the same. It is a secret to some people. But one day everyone will see everything that has been a secret.

18 So you should be careful how you listen. The person that has really heard a message will hear more. Some have not listened to it, so they have nothing. They think that they have a little. But they will lose even that.'

The mother and brothers of Jesus come to see him

19 Then the mother and brothers of Jesus came to see him. But they could not reach him because of the large crowd. 20 'Your mother and brothers are standing outside', someone told Jesus. 'They want to see you.'

21 'I will tell you who my mother and brothers are', replied Jesus. 'Some people hear the message of God and they obey it. Those people are my mother and brothers.'

Jesus stops a storm

22 One day Jesus got into a boat with those that always followed him. 'I want us to go over to the other side of the lake', he said. So, they started to cross the lake. 23 While they sailed, Jesus began to sleep. Then a strong wind started to blow across the lake. Water began to fill the boat and they were in danger. 24 So those in the boat with Jesus woke him. 'Master, master, we shall die!' they said.

Then Jesus got up and he spoke to the wind and to the water. 'Stop', he said. 'Be quiet.' The wind stopped immediately and the water became flat. 25 'You do not believe in me and you should believe', Jesus said then.

The event frightened them and they were very surprised. 'So who is this man?' they asked each other. 'He even has authority over the wind and the water. He just speaks and they obey him.'

Jesus makes a man well

26 Jesus and the 12 men that always followed him arrived at Gadara. In Gadara, the people called Gerasenes lived. This place is across the lake from Galilee. 27 When Jesus got off the boat, a man from the town came towards him. He had many bad spirits and they were living inside him. He had not worn any clothes for a long time. He did not live in a house. Instead, he lived in a place where people buried dead bodies. 28 When he saw Jesus, he screamed. Then he fell to the ground in front of him. 'What do you want to do with me, Jesus?' he said in a loud voice. 'You are the Son of the powerful God above. Please do not hurt me.' 29 He said this because Jesus had spoken to the bad spirit. 'Come out of this man', he had ordered. People usually kept this man tied up. They tied his hands and feet with chains. But when the bad spirit took hold of him, he broke the chains. The spirit then caused him to go into the places where people do not live.

30 'What is your name?' Jesus then asked. 'My name is Legion', he replied. People called him this, because many bad spirits had gone into him.

31 The bad spirits asked Jesus again and again not to send them to hell.

32 There was a large group of pigs and they were eating their food on the side of the hill. 'Let us go into the pigs', they asked Jesus. 'You can go into them', he replied. 33 So the bad spirits came out of the man and they went into the pigs. All the pigs rushed together down the high hill. They ran into the lake and all of them died in the water.

34 The men that were taking care of the pigs saw this happen. They ran away to tell other people about the pigs. They went to all the towns and villages that were near. 35 So the people came out from all these places to see what had happened. When they arrived, they found the man. He was sitting at the feet of Jesus. The bad spirits had gone out of him. He was now quiet and his mind was well again. He was also wearing clothes. When the people saw this, they were afraid. 36 Some people had seen Jesus make the man well. They told the other people how he had done this. 37 Then all the people from the country of the people called Gerasenes spoke to Jesus. 'Please leave us', they said. They said this because they were very afraid. So, he got back into the boat. He was ready to return to the other side of the lake. 38 Then the man that had had the bad spirits spoke. 'Please let me come with you', he said to Jesus. 'No', he replied. 39 'You must return to your home. Go. And tell everyone all that God has done for you.'

So the man went away. He went everywhere in the town. He continued to tell all the people, 'Jesus has done very good things for me.'

Jesus makes Jairus's daughter well

40 When Jesus returned to the other side of the lake, the crowd was very happy to see him. They were all waiting for him to come back. 41 Then a man called Jairus came to see him. He was a ruler in the meeting place. He went down on his knees at the feet of Jesus. 'Please come to my house', he said. 42 'I have a daughter. She is 12 years old and she is very ill. She will die very soon. She is the only child that I have.'

So, Jesus started to go to see his daughter. A crowd of people went with him and they were pushing against him. 43 There was a woman in the crowd that had lost blood for 12 years. She had paid all her money to doctors and she had no money left. But nobody could stop her bleeding. 44 She came behind Jesus in the crowd. Then she touched the edge of his clothes. Immediately she stopped bleeding. 45 'Who touched me?' asked Jesus.

Everyone round him said, 'It was not me. I did not touch you.' 'Master', said Peter, 'the people are in a crowd round you. Many people are touching you.'

46 'Someone did touch me', said Jesus. 'I felt it when power went out from me.' 47 The woman knew that she could not hide it. So she was very afraid, when she came to Jesus. She went down on the ground in front of him. She spoke so that all the people could hear her. 'I wanted to be well', she told them, 'so I touched the edge of his clothes. As soon as I touched him, I became well.' 48 'Daughter', Jesus said to her, 'you are well again, because you believed in me. Do not have troubles in your mind any longer.'

49 While Jesus was still speaking to the woman, someone arrived from Jairus's house. 'Your daughter is dead', he told him. 'Do not ask the teacher to come now.'

50 Jesus heard what the man said. So he spoke to Jairus. 'Do not be afraid. Just believe that I can make her well.'

51 When they arrived at the house, Jesus would not let everyone go in. He only took Peter, James and John. He also let the mother and father of the girl go into the house. 52 Many people there were crying. They were hitting themselves because they were very sad. 'Do not cry', Jesus told them. 'She has not died. She is only asleep.'

53 They knew that she had died. So, they laughed at him. 54 But Jesus took hold of her hand. 'My child, get up', he then said to her in a loud voice. 55 She became alive again and she stood up immediately. 'Give her something to eat', he said to her parents. 56 They were very surprised. 'You must not tell anyone what has happened', he said to them.

Chapter 9

Jesus sends out the 12 men that always followed him

1 Jesus asked the 12 men that always followed him to come to him. Then he gave them power to make sick people well. He also gave them authority to send bad spirits out of people. 2 Then, he sent them out to tell other people about how God rules in the lives of his people. He told them also that they should make sick people well. 3 'When you go', he said, 'take nothing for your journey. Do not take a stick, a bag or food. Do not take any money or two sets of clothes.'

4 'Find a house where the people in it are happy to have you. Stay at that house all the time you are visiting people in that town. 5 In some towns, the people will not be happy to see you. They have not believed the message that God sent to them. When you are leaving them, clean the dirt of that town from your feet. This shows them that they have not believed the message.'

6 Then the 12 men that followed Jesus started out. While they were going from one village to another, they talked to all the people. They told them the good news about Jesus and they made many sick people well.

A ruler hears about Jesus

7 Herod the ruler heard reports about all that was happening. He was confused because people were saying different things about Jesus. Some were saying, 'John the Baptist has come back and he is alive again.' 8 Some were saying, 'It is Elijah that has come back.' Some other people were saying, 'This is one of God's servants that died a long time ago. He is alive again and he speaks messages from the Holy Spirit.'

9 'My soldiers killed John', Herod said. 'They cut off his head. So, who is this man? I hear strange stories about him.' So, he was trying to meet Jesus.

Jesus feeds 5000 men and their families

10 The 12 men that Jesus had sent out returned from their journeys. They told him what they had done. Then he took them away from the crowd, so that he could be alone with them. They went in the direction of a city called Bethsaida. 11 But the crowds found out where they were going. So they went to find Jesus. When he saw the crowds coming, he received them well. He told them how God rules in the lives of his people. Some sick people were there and he made them well.

12 When it was nearly evening, the 12 men that always followed Jesus came up to him. 'This is a place without houses', they said. 'Send the crowd away now, so that they can buy food. There are some villages and farms near here. Maybe they can sleep there.'

13 'You give them something to eat', said Jesus.

'But we only have 5 loaves of bread and 2 fish', they replied. 'Do you want us to go and buy food for all these people?' 14 There were about 5000 men in the crowd.

'Say to them that they should sit down on the ground in groups', Jesus replied. 'There should be about 50 people in each group.'

15 So they did this. When the people had sat down, 16 Jesus took the 5 loaves and the 2 fish. Then he looked up towards the sky and he thanked God for the food. He broke it into pieces. And he gave it to the 12 men that always followed him. 'Give it out to all the people', he said. 17 Everybody ate and they all had enough. Then they picked up all the food that remained. They filled 12 baskets with it.

Peter says who Jesus is

18 Jesus was alone and he was praying. The 12 men that always followed him came up to him. 'Who do the people say that I am?' he asked them.

19 'Many people say that you are John the Baptist', they replied. 'Some people say that you are Elijah. Other people say that you are one of the servants of God from long ago. They say that the servant has become alive again.'

20 'What do you think?' Jesus then asked them. 'Who do you say that I am?'

'You are the Messiah', replied Peter. 'God sent you.'

21 'Listen!' Jesus then said to them. 'You must not tell this to anyone, that I am the Messiah.' He said this very strongly.

22 'They will cause the Son of Man to have a lot of pain', he went on to say. 'The leaders of the Jews will be against him. The important priests and teachers of God's rules will also not accept him. They will kill him, but three days later God will cause him to be alive again.'

23 Then Jesus spoke to all the people that were there. 'Perhaps someone wants to obey me', he said to them. 'That person must say no to what he wants for himself in this life. He must live every day like a person that has only one day to live. He must obey me and he must become like me.

24 After all, whoever wants to keep his own life will lose it. But whoever gives up his life for me will save it. 25 Perhaps you want to get the whole world and all that is in it. You might do that but lose yourself. Then you will have nothing at all. You will have destroyed yourself in the end. 26 Perhaps you are now ashamed of me and of my words. If you are, I will be ashamed of you. I will be ashamed of you when I return. When I come back again, everyone will see me. I will look as great and beautiful as my Father God. The good angels of God will be with me, too. They will also look very great and beautiful.'

Jesus looks different and he meets Moses and Elijah

27 'Listen!' said Jesus. 'Some people that are standing here will soon see how God rules. They will see this before they die. They really will.'

28 About 8 days after Jesus had said these things, he went up a mountain to pray. And he took Peter, John and James with him. 29 While he was praying, his face began to look different. His clothes also became very white and shining. 30 Then two men appeared and they were talking with him. They were Moses and Elijah.

31 Moses and Elijah looked very great and beautiful. They talked with Jesus about how he would soon die in Jerusalem. This was how God wanted him to leave this world.

32 While this was happening, Peter was very, very tired. And those that were with him were very, very tired too. Then they really woke up and they saw Jesus. He looked very great and beautiful. They also saw the two men that were standing near to him. 33 Then the two men began to leave. So, Peter spoke to Jesus. 'Teacher', he said, 'it is very good that we are here. We should build three huts. One hut will be for you, one hut for Moses and one hut for Elijah.' He did not really know what he was saying.

34 While Peter was speaking, a cloud appeared. And it covered them all. When the shadow covered them, they were afraid. 35 Then they heard a voice from the cloud. 'This is my Son', the voice said. 'I have chosen him. So listen to him.'

36 The voice stopped speaking. Then the three men saw that they were alone with Jesus. They did not tell anyone at this time about what they had seen.

Jesus makes a boy well

37 The next day, Jesus and the three men that were with him came down from the mountain. A large crowd met him. 38 Then a man from the crowd shouted to him. 'Teacher, please, I ask you to be kind to my son. He is my only child. 39 Sometimes a bad spirit quickly takes hold of him and he screams. The spirit throws his body first one way then another and foam comes out of his mouth. When the spirit leaves him in the end, it has always hurt him. 40 I asked those that follow you to send the bad spirit out of him. But they could not do it.'

41 'You people today do not believe in God', Jesus said to the crowd. 'You have turned away from him. I have already been with you a long time. But you still do not believe in him. It is difficult to be patient with you.' Then he spoke to the man. 'Bring your son here.'

42 While the boy was coming, the bad spirit threw him to the ground. It pulled the boy first one way and then the other. 'Stop!' Jesus said to it. He then made the boy well and he gave him back to his father.

43 Everybody was very surprised at what they saw. They knew that God was very powerful.

Jesus speaks again about his death

The people were still thinking about everything that Jesus was doing. Then he began to talk to those that always followed him. 44 'Be careful. And do not forget what I am telling you. People will give the Son of Man to powerful men to kill them.' 45 But they did not understand what he had said. It was still a secret, so they could not understand his words. But they were afraid to ask him, 'What do you mean?'

Who will be the most important?

46 Then those that followed Jesus began to argue with each other. 'Which of us is the most important?' 'I am', they were each saying. 47 Jesus knew what they were thinking. So he picked up a small child. He made the child stand at one side of him. 48 'If someone accepts this child because of me', he said, 'he accepts me. And he also accepts him who sent me. After all, the person who makes himself the least important is really the greatest.'

49 'Teacher', John then said, 'we saw a man. He was speaking to people that had bad spirits in them. "Jesus says that you must come out", he was saying. We told the man that he must not do this. We said that because he is not in our group.'

50 'Do not try to stop him', Jesus said to him. 'If someone is not against you, he is working with you.'

People in a village in Samaria do not accept Jesus

51 Time was passing and soon Jesus would go back to God. He knew this, so he began to go to Jerusalem. 52 He arrived near a village in the country of Samaria. Then he sent some people to the village with a message. They went to ask for a place to stay for the night. 53 But the people in the village would not let him stay there. This was because he was going to Jerusalem.

54 Then James and John heard about what had happened. 'Jesus', they asked, 'do you want us to ask God to send fire down from the sky? Do you want us to kill these people?'

55 Jesus turned round. 'No!' he said, 'do not do that. That would be very wrong.' 56 Then they all went on to another village.

What it costs to obey Jesus

57 When they continued on their journey, a man spoke to Jesus. 'I will follow you. And I will go where you go.'

58 'Wild animals', he replied, 'have a place to sleep. Wild birds also have their own places to live. But I, the Son of Man, have no regular place to lie down and rest.'

59 'Come with me!' Jesus then said to another man. 'First', he replied, 'let me go home and bury my father. Then I will come with you.'

60 'No!' said Jesus, 'let dead people bury their own dead people. You go. And tell other people about how God rules.'

61 'Sir', said another man, 'I will come with you. But please let me first go to say goodbye to my family.'

62 'A man that ploughs a field must continue to look in front of him', replied Jesus. 'If he looks behind him, he cannot plough well. You are like a man that wants to look behind him. People like that cannot show other people how God really rules.'

Chapter 10

Jesus sends out 72 men that always followed him

1 After this, Jesus sent out another 72 men that always followed him. He sent them on in front of him in pairs. They went to every town and village that he would visit soon. 2 'Many people are wanting to believe God's message', he said to them before they went. 'They are like a field with many plants with ripe seeds. But there are very few workers to bring in the ripe seeds. So, you must pray to God to send out workers. They will go and tell his message.'

3 'I am sending you out', Jesus went on to say. 'So go! But listen! You will be like young sheep among wild animals. 4 Do not carry a purse or bag. Do not take extra shoes. When you meet other people on the road, do not waste time in long conversations.'

5 'When you go into a house, first say, "We pray that all will be well with you!" 6 Someone in the house may believe what you say. If he does, it will be well with him. But if nobody accepts your kind words, take them back. 7 While you are in the town, you should stay in the same house. Accept the food and drink that the people in the house give to you. This is for the work that you are doing. Do not go from one house to another to get food. 8 The people may accept you when you go into a town. Eat what those people give to you. 9 Make the sick people well in that town. Give this message to all the people there: "We bring the news that God wants to rule in your lives now." 10 Sometimes when you go into a town, the people will not accept you. You should then go into the streets of that town and you should say to the people, 11 "There is dirt from your town on our feet. We will clean it off to show that you have not accepted the message from God. Listen! God wants to rule in your lives, but you have refused him." 12 One day God will judge everyone. At that time, he really will punish the people from that town. Yes, he will punish them more than the people that lived in Sodom.'

Some towns where people did not believe

13 'It will be bad for you, people of Chorazin', Jesus went on to say. 'It will be bad for you, people of Bethsaida. I have done great things in your cities. If I had done such great things in Tyre and Sidon, the people there would have listened to me long ago. They would then have put on clothes made from the hair of a goat. They would also have put ash on their heads. This would show God that they were sorry. They would have stopped doing bad things and they would have started to obey him. 14 Yes, when God judges everyone, he will punish the people of Tyre and Sidon. But he will punish more the people of Chorazin and Bethsaida.

15 And the people in Capernaum, they try to lift themselves up to God's place. But he will throw them down to hell!'

16 'The person that listens to you, listens to me', Jesus told those that he was sending out. 'The person that does not accept you does not accept me. And the person that does not accept me also does not accept someone else. He does not accept him who sent me.'

The 72 men return

17 Later, the 72 men that Jesus sent out returned to him. They were very happy. 'Master', they said, 'even bad spirits obey us. We use your name and we say, "Leave!" Then they leave.'

18 'I was watching and I saw the devil fall', replied Jesus. 'He fell very fast, like lightning from the sky. 19 Listen! I have given authority and power to you. You will even stand on dangerous snakes and insects and you will have authority over all the power of the devil. Nothing will hurt you. 20 But do not be happy just because you have authority over bad spirits. Your names are in the book where God is. That is why you should be happy.'

Jesus is very happy

21 At this moment, the Holy Spirit made Jesus very happy. 'Father', he said, 'you rule all things above and on the earth! I thank you for this. You have taught people that do not know many things. Now they can understand this. But you have hidden all these things from other people. They think that they understand everything. And they think that they are wise. Yes, Father, this is how you chose it to happen.'

22 'My Father has given me all things', he then said. 'Only the Father knows who I am. Nobody else really knows that I am the Son of God. Only I know who the Father is. Nobody else knows, except those people that I choose to tell.'

23 Then he turned. And he spoke only to those that always followed him. 'Be happy! God has helped you to see the things that you see. 24 Listen! There have been many rulers. Many men have received messages from God. Those people all wanted to see the things that you are seeing. But they did not see them. They wanted to hear what you are hearing. But they did not hear it.'

This is a picture story about a good man from Samaria

25 A man that taught God's rules then stood up. He wanted to show that Jesus really did not know the rules well. So he asked a question. 'Teacher, what must I do to live for all time?'

26 'What do God's rules say?' Jesus asked. 'What do you understand from them?'

27 'It says that we should love the Lord our God', he replied. 'We should love him very much, with every part of our body and of our mind. We should also love people that live near to us. We should love them as much as we love ourselves.'

28 'You have told me the right answer', said Jesus. 'If you do this, you will live for all time.'

29 But the man wanted to show that he had been right to ask a question. So he asked, 'Who are the people near to me that I must love?'

30 Jesus answered by telling a picture story. 'A man was going down the road from Jerusalem to Jericho town. On the way, some men attacked him. They took away all his clothes and they hit him with sticks. He was almost dead when they left him. 31 But it happened that a priest was going down that road. He saw the man, who was lying there. But he walked past him on the other side of the road. 32 A Levite was also going down the road. He came to the place where the man was lying. He saw him. But he also walked past on the other side of the road.'

33 'But a man from Samaria was also travelling along the road. And he came to the place where the man was lying. When he saw him, he felt very sorry for him. 34 He went across to him. He poured oil and wineon the places where he was bleeding. Then he tied those places with clean cloths. After that, he put the man on his own animal. They arrived at a small hotel. He took him in and he was kind to him.'

35 'The next day, the man from Samaria took out two silver coins from his purse. He gave the money to the man that was taking care of the hotel. "Be kind to this man for me", he said. "I will return. This money may not be enough. I will pay you for any more that you have spent on him." '

36 Then Jesus asked the man that taught God's rules a question. 'Three men passed the man that was lying on the road. Which of them showed love to him?'

37 'It was the man that was kind to him', he answered.

Then Jesus said to him, 'Yes, you are right. So go and do the same for other people.'

Jesus visits the home of Martha and Mary

38 Jesus and those that always followed him continued their journey. They arrived at a certain village. There, a woman called Martha asked Jesus to come into her house. 39 This woman had a sister called Mary. Mary sat down near Jesus. She was listening to the things that he was teaching. 40 But Martha was thinking to herself, 'I cannot do all this work alone.' So she came to Jesus. 'Master', she said, 'my sister is not helping me with the work. She has left me to do it alone. You cannot really believe that this is right! Say to her that she must help me!'

41 'Martha, Martha', replied Jesus, 'you have troubles in your mind about very many things. 42 But only one thing is really important. And Mary has chosen it. Nobody will take it away from her.'

Chapter 11

Jesus teaches those that always followed him how to pray

1 One day, Jesus was praying in a certain place. He finished praying. Then, one of those that always followed him came to him. 'Master', he said, 'John taught those that followed him how to pray. Please teach us as he did.'

2 'When you pray', he replied, 'you should say this:

"Father, we want all people to know that you are good and important.

You will rule everyone one day. We pray that that day will come soon.

3   Please give us the food that we need each day.

4   Forgive us for all the wrong things that we have done.

After all, we also forgive everyone that has done wrong things to us.

Do not let us agree to do wrong things." '

5 He then told a picture story to teach them how to pray. 'Let me tell you about someone that goes to a friend at midnight. "My friend", he says, "please give me three loaves of bread. 6 Another friend of mine is on a journey and he has arrived at my house. But I have no food to give him." 7 But his friend answers from inside his house. "Do not cause problems for me! I have locked my door. My children and I have gone to bed. So, I cannot get up and give you any bread." 8 I will tell you what will happen. Perhaps the friend will not give him anything because they are good friends. But if he continues to knock, he will get up. If he continues to ask for bread, his friend will give him bread. He will give him everything that he asks for.

9 So I tell you this. Continue to ask for what you need. And you will receive it. Continue to look for what you need. And then you will find it. Continue to knock at the door and God will open it for you. 10 After all, everyone that asks for something will receive it. Everyone that looks for something will find it. God will open the door for everyone that knocks on it. 11 Some of you are fathers. You would not give your son a snake if he asks for fish! 12 If your son asks you for an egg, you would not give him an insect to hurt him.13 You are bad. But you know how to give good things to your children. And your Father above knows much better than you do how to give good things. So he will send the Holy Spirit to those people that ask him.'

Jesus teaches the people about the devil

14 One day, Jesus was ordering a bad spirit to come out of a man. Because of the bad spirit, the man could not speak. But after it had gone out of him, the man could speak. All the people that were watching were surprised at this. 15 But some people in the crowd were not happy with Jesus. 'Yes, this man can cause bad spirits to come out from people', they said. 'But the devil works with him, because the devilrules all the bad spirits.'

16 Some other people in the crowd did not believe in Jesus. They wanted to show that his power was not from God. 'Do something powerful', they were saying. 'If you do, we will believe. We will believe that God has sent you.'

17 But Jesus knew what those people were wanting. 'If groups of people in a country fight each other', he said to them, 'they will destroy their own country. If people in one family fight with each other, they will destroy their family. 18 The devil is the same. The people who obey him must not fight each other. If they do, he will soon not have anybody to rule. But you say that the devil helps me to send bad spirits out of people. If this were true, the devil would be fighting himself. He would soon not have anybody to rule. 19You say that the devil helps me to cause bad spirits to leave. But some men obey what you teach. And they also cause bad spirits to leave. So think about who helps them to do that. That shows that you are wrong. 20 So when I cause bad spirits to leave people, I use the power of God. This shows that God is ruling among you.

21 When a strong man has all his arms for war, he can take care of his own house. Nothing bad will happen to his things inside the house. 22 But someone may come that is stronger than he. Then the stronger man attacks him and beats him. The stronger person then takes away all his arms for war. These arms had made him feel safe. The stronger man will also give away all the things that he had taken.'

23 'If someone is not helping me, he is against me. If a person is not working with me to bring people together, he is causing them to run away from me.'

24 'When a bad spirit goes out of a person, it travels through dry places. It goes to look for a new place to live. If it does not find anywhere, it says to itself, "I will return to the house where I lived before." 25 It goes back to that house. But it finds that it is clean. Everything inside is in the right place. 26 So it goes out and it brings back 7 worse spirits. They all go into the house and they live there. Now the man is worse than he was at the beginning.'

27 While Jesus was saying this, a woman in the crowd shouted out. 'How happy is the woman that gave birth to you! How happy is the woman that fed you from her breasts!'

28 'How happy, rather', he replied, 'are the people that hear the message from God. That is if they obey it.'

Jesus talks about Jonah

29 The crowd round Jesus was growing larger, so he began to speak to them. 'The people that are alive today are very bad. They want God to show them some powerful work. But God will not show them anything. They will only see the same powerful thing that happened to Jonah. 30 Something happened to him. It showed the people in Nineveh that God had sent him. The same thing will happen to me, the Son of Man. I will be like Jonah to the people that are living today. Then they will know that God sent me.'

31 'Many years ago', Jesus then said, 'the queen of a country in the south travelled a long way to see King Solomon. She went to listen to the wise ideas that he taught. Listen! There is someone here today that is greater than Solomon. But you will not listen to him. So, when God judges all people, that queen will stand in front of him. And she will speak against the men that are alive today. After all, she travelled a long way to hear the wise ideas of Solomon.'

32 'Jonah is the same. When he spoke to the people in Nineveh, they stopped doing bad things. And they obeyed God. Listen! There is someone here today that is greater than Jonah. But you will not obey him. God will judge all people. Then those men that lived in Nineveh will stand in front of him. They will also speak against the people that are alive today. After all, when Jonah spoke to the people in Nineveh, they stopped doing bad things. And they obeyed God.'

Jesus talks about being full of light

33 'When someone lights a lamp, he does not hide it. Nor does he put a pot over it. Instead, he puts it in a high place, so that people will see the light. They will see it when they come in. 34 Your eyes are like a lamp, and your body is like a room. If a lamp is clean, the whole room has light. But if it is dirty, the whole room is in the dark. 35 So, be sure that your eyes are not like a dirty lamp. If they are, you will be bad, like a dark room. 36 So, your eyes should be like a clean lamp. There will be nothing bad in you. You will be like a room that is full of light.'

37 While Jesus was speaking, a Pharisee asked him to eat a meal with him. So, he went to his house and he sat down at the table. 38 Jesus did not wash his hands before he ate the meal. This surprised the Pharisee. 39 So the Lord Jesus spoke to him. 'You Pharisees are like someone that only cleans the outside of a cup and plate. You only clean the part that people can see. But inside, your mind is full of very bad thoughts. You think about taking valuable things from other people. 40 What fools you are! The God that made the outside of you also made the inside. He sees everything inside you. 41 So give to poor people with good thoughts. So then God will say that everything inside and outside of you is clean.'

42 'You Pharisees give to God one tenth of the little plants that have a nice smell. You also give him one tenth of the little plants that cause food to taste nice. You are right to give them.

But trouble will happen to you, because you do not also do the most important things. You do not love God. And you do not do what is right. You should do these. And you should also give him a tenth of what you grow.'

43 Trouble will happen to you Pharisees, because you like to have the best seats in the meeting place. And people speak to you in the market place as they speak to an important person. You like that too.

44 Yes, you want to seem good but you are not. So trouble will happen to you. Sometimes, when people bury a dead body, they do not put a mark there. Because of that, other people walk on that ground. You are like that ground. You seem good but, inside, you are not.'

45 Then one of those that taught God's rules spoke out. 'Teacher', he said, 'when you say these things, you are also saying bad things about us.'

46 'Trouble will also happen to you that teach God's rules', Jesus replied. 'You give rules to people to obey. They are like things that are too heavy to carry. You put them on their backs, but you do not help them to carry them. Not even with one finger do you help them!'

47 'Yes, trouble will happen to you that teach God's rules! A long time ago, your fathers killed the men that spoke for God. Now, you build up beautiful stones to remember the place where they buried them. 48 You know that your fathers killed these men. You build up these stones. So you show that you agree with your fathers. You agree with what they did. 49 God is wise. That is the reason that he said, "I will send men that I choose. I will also send other men that receive messages from me. They will speak my messages. But people will kill some of them. They will do bad things to some of them." 50 People have killed those that speak for God since the beginning of the world. But he will punish the people alive today for all those murders. 51 Abel was the first to die and Zechariah was the last. They killed him between the Great House of God and God's special table. The priests kill and burn animals as a gift to God on that special table. Yes, God will punish the people who are living today for all those murders.

52 Trouble will happen to you that teach God's rules. You have not taught other people to understand the messages from God. They wanted to find out what is true. You yourselves have not found out. And you have also stopped the people that wanted to know. So they could not find out.'

53 Then Jesus left that place. The Pharisees and those that taught God's rules started to be very much against him. They were asking him many difficult questions. 54 They were trying to cause him to say something wrong. They were waiting to take hold of him if he did.

Chapter 12

Jesus tells the people to be careful how they live

1 While all this was happening, many thousands of people were present. There were so many people that they were almost walking over each other. Jesus began to talk first to those that always followed him. 'Do not become like the Pharisees. They want other people to think that they are good. But they are not. They are like yeast that causes bread to grow.'

2 'People do things secretly, but everybody will know about those things. And people say things secretly, but everybody will know about those things. 3 You have said things in the dark of the night. But people will hear those things in the light of day. You have said things into someone's ear behind a door that you have shut. But people will shout out all those things from the tops of the houses.

4 You are my friends, so I tell you this. Do not be afraid of those people that can kill your body. After that, they can do nothing worse to you. 5 I tell you that you should be afraid of God. He has the power to kill and to throw people into hell. Once more I am telling you, be afraid of him.

6 People sell 5 small birds for 2 coins of little value. But each little bird is valuable to God. He takes care of them all. 7 He does the same for you. He even knows how many hairs there are on your head. So, do not be afraid of people. You are of more value to God than very many small birds.

8 I also say this to you. Say to other people, "I obey Jesus." If you do, I, the Son of Man, will say to the angels of God, "That person is someone that obeys me." 9 But another person who knows me will say, "I do not know Jesus. I do not obey him." If he does, I will say to the angels of God, "I do not know this person. He does not obey me."

10 Somebody may speak against the Son of Man, and God will forgive him. But somebody may speak against the Holy Spirit. And he may say that the Holy Spirit is bad. God will never forgive that person.'

11 'People will take you into places for meetings. They will cause you to stand in front of rulers and other people that have authority. These men will ask you questions. But do not be afraid of them. Do not think, "I do not know how to answer them." 12 When the time comes, the Holy Spirit will teach you. He will tell you what to say.'

Jesus tells a picture story about a rich fool

13 Someone in the crowd spoke to Jesus. 'Teacher', he said, 'I have a problem with my brother. Our father died. Tell my brother to give me my part of what our father left us.'

14 'It is not my job to say which of you is right or wrong', he replied. 'And it is not my job to say what each of you should have.' 15 Then he spoke to all the people. 'Think well and be very careful! Do not want more than you need. The life of a person is worth more than the things that he has. Even if he is very rich, that is still true.'

16 He then told them a picture story. 'A man had some very good ground, where he planted seeds. The plants grew very well. And he had much more than he planted. 17 He thought about how much he would soon have. "I have nowhere to store all the seeds from my plants", he said to himself. 18 But then he decided what to do. "I will pull down the building", he said to himself, "where I now store my seed. Then I will build a bigger building to store it all. There I will also keep everything else that is mine. 19 Then I will say to myself:

You have plenty of things stored away. These will be enough for you for many years. Now you can live an easy life. Eat and drink. Enjoy yourself."

20 But God said to the man, "You are a fool. Tonight you will die. You will have to leave everything behind. Think about all your things that you have stored away. Think about what will happen to them. Think about who will have them." '

21 'Some people think only about having many things for themselves', Jesus went on to say. 'That picture story is for those people. But God says about them, "They have nothing of value at all." '

Do not have troubles in your mind

22 'So I tell you that you should not be always thinking about things', Jesus then said to those that always followed him. 'Do not be always thinking about the food that you need to stay alive. Nor be always thinking about the clothes that you need to wear. 23 After all, your life is more important than your food. Your body is more important than your clothes.

24 Think about the birds. They do not plant seeds in the ground, nor cut down plants to eat. They have no buildings to store food. But they do not go hungry. God gives them food. You are of much more value than the birds.

25 Your life is the same. Even if you are always thinking about your life, you cannot make it any longer. 26 No, you cannot do a small thing like that. So, do not always be thinking about the things that you need. 27 Think about how the wild flowers grow. They do not work or make clothes for themselves. But I tell you this about them. It is true that King Solomon wore very beautiful clothes. But even one wild flower is more beautiful than he was. 28 It is God that gives beautiful clothes to wild flowers and grass. And they are alive in the field for a very short time. After that, people burn them. Yes, God gives clothes to those flowers, so he will do much more for you. He will give you all that you need. You do not yet believe in him very well.'

29 'Food and drink are the same. Do not always be thinking about the food and drink that you need. 30 People that do not know God are always thinking about these things. That is true. But your Father, God, knows that you need them. 31 Instead, always be thinking about the things that are important to him. Let him rule you. So then he will also give you the things that you need. 32 Yes, you are only a small group of people, but do not be afraid. After all, your Father, God, has chosen you to rule with him. 33 Sell what you have and give the money to poor people. Do good things. So you will have things of great value when you live in God's home. There your things will never become old. Their value will never decrease. Nor can anyone take them from you. No insect can destroy them there. 34 After all, you will want to be in the same place as the things that are of value to you.'

Be ready for Jesus to return

35 'Always be ready for my return. Be like those that are ready to start work. They have put on their clothes so that they are ready for work. And they have lit their lamps.

36 You must be like servants that are waiting for their master to arrive. When he returns home from the marriage party, he will knock on the door. His servants should be ready to open it for him immediately. 37 Those servants will be very happy if their master finds them awake. If he does, he will do this. He will tie his belt so that his clothes are short. He will say to them, "Sit at the table. I will come and I will give you some food." '

38 'The master may arrive in the middle of the night. He may even arrive just before the sun rises. But, if the master finds them awake and ready, the servants will be happy.

39 You must also understand this. The master of a house does not know when a robber will try to get in to his house. If he knew, he would keep awake. He would not let the robber come in and take away his things.

40 You also must be ready. The Son of Man will come at a time when you are not thinking, "He will come now." '

Be a good servant

41 Peter then asked Jesus. 'Master, are you only talking to us that follow you? Or is this picture story for everyone to hear?'

42 'Be wise. And be a man that the master can trust', said Jesus. 'The master will choose a man like that. He will say to him, "I want you to rule my house and the other servants. Give them food at the right time." 43 This servant will be very happy when his master comes home. His master sees that he has done everything well. So he is happy. 44 I will tell you what will happen. The master will let the servant rule over everything that he has. 45 But perhaps the servant says to himself, "My master will not come yet." So, he begins to hit the other servants. He hits both the men and the women. He eats too much. He also drinks too much and he becomes a drunk.

46 The master of that servant will come home and he will surprise the servant. He did not think that his master would come home on that day or at that time. Then the master will punish him a lot. He will put the servant with those people that do not obey him.

47 A servant may know what his master wants him to do. He should get ready and obey. If he does not, his master will punish him. He will hit him a lot. 48 But another servant perhaps did not know what his master wanted him to do. So he did the wrong things. The master will hit him because he did the wrong things. But he will not hit him as much. He did not know that those things were wrong. If masters give much to their servants, they will want a lot in return. And God wants much from the person to whom he has given much.

49 I came to start a fire on earth. I would be happy if that fire were already burning. 50 I have a baptism of pain to receive. I cannot rest until this has happened.'

51 'I did not come so that everyone will agree. Do not think that I came for that reason. No, that is not true. Instead, I came to make people into separate groups. 52 From now on, because of me, 5 people in a family will become 2 separate groups. 2 will be against the other 3. 3 of them will be against the other 2. 53 The father will be against his son and the son will be against his father. The mother will be against her daughter and the daughter will be against her mother. The mother will be against her son's wife. And the son's wife will be against his mother.'

54 'You see a cloud that is rising in the west', Jesus then said to the crowd. 'Immediately you say, "It will rain." And the rain does come. 55 Sometimes you know that the south wind is blowing. So you say, "It will be very hot weather." And the hot weather does come. 56 You want other people to think that you understand many things. So, you look at the earth and the sky. And you say what weather will come. Yes, you know how to do that. So look at the things that are happening near you now. They show you what will soon happen. But you do not understand what they are showing you. And you should know it.'

57 'Also, you should know what these things mean for you. You should do what is right. 58 After all, something like this may happen to you: Someone says, "You have a debt and you have done something wrong." So he takes you to the judge. Before you arrive at the office of the judge, try to agree with this man. If you do not agree together about the matter, it may be bad for you. He will say to the judge, "This man has not paid me back my money." So the judge will say to his officer that he should put you in prison. 59 I tell you what will happen then. You will not leave there until you have paid back all the debt.'

Chapter 13

Stop doing wrong things or die

1 At that time, some people were standing near to Jesus. They told him what happened to some people from Galilee. They were burning animals as a gift for God. Pilate sent some soldiers to kill them.

2 'So think about these people from Galilee', Jesus replied. 'Perhaps you think that they had done more bad things than other people from Galilee. And so that is why they had to die. 3 No, they were not worse than other people. All of you have also done many bad things. So, you must turn away from all bad things and you must turn to God. If you do not, I tell you this. You will also die as they did.

4 And you remember what happened to those 18 people in Siloam. A high building fell and it killed them. Perhaps you think that they had done more bad things than the other people in Jerusalem. 5 No, they had not. All of you have also done many bad things. So, you must turn away from all bad things and you must turn to God. If you do not, I tell you this. You will also die as they did.'

Jesus tells a picture story about a fig tree

6 Then he told this story. 'A man had a garden where he grew fruit. He had planted a fig tree there. But when he came to look for fruit, he could not find any.

7 "Look", he then said to his gardener, "For three years, I have come to look for fruit on this tree. But I have never found any. So cut the tree down! I do not think that it should be here. It is wasting the ground."

8 "Master", the gardener replied, "leave the tree in the ground for one more year. Let me dig round it and let me put some dirt from animals on it." '

9 ' "If I do that, next year, the fig tree may have some fruit on it. If it does not, I will cut it down for you." '

Jesus makes a sick woman well again

10 One day, Jesus was teaching in a meeting house. It was the Jewish day for rest.

11 There was a woman there that had a bad spirit inside her. It had lived there for 18 years and it had made her ill. She had to bend her back all the time. She could not stand up straight. 12 Jesus saw her. 'Woman, come here', he said. 'You are better from your illness.' 13 He put his hands on her and immediately she could stand up straight. 'How great you are!' she said to God. 'How good and powerful you are!'

14 But the leader of the meeting house was angry. He was angry because Jesus had made a sick person well on their day for rest. So he spoke to the people. 'There are 6 days each week when we should work', he said to them. 'Come on any of those days and get well. But you should not come on our rest day to get well.'

15 'You are wrong', the Lord Jesus said to him. 'You say one thing and you do something different yourselves. You each take your ox or your donkey outside on the day for rest. You then give them water to drink.'

16 'Look at this woman', he went on to say. 'She is in the family of Abraham. But it is like a bad spirit from the devil has kept her tied up for 18 years. So it is certainly right to make her free on our day for rest.' 17 These words caused the leaders of the meeting place to feel ashamed of themselves. But all the people there were very happy. They were happy because they had seen Jesus do many good and powerful things.

Jesus tells picture stories about seeds and yeast

18 Then he told them a story. 'I will tell you about the place where God rules. For example, 19 it is like a very small seed. A man takes it and he plants it. He puts it in his garden and it grows. It then grows into a tree. It is so big that birds can make a place to live among the branches.'

20 'Here is another example. The place where God rules is like this', he went on to say.

21 'It is like yeast. A woman takes some and she puts it in three large bowls of flour. Then the yeast grows and it goes through all the flour.'

This is a picture story about a narrow door

22 Jesus was continuing his journey to Jerusalem. On the way, he went through towns and villages. In each one, he taught the people. 23 One day, somebody asked him a question. 'Sir, will God only save a small number of people?'

24 'Do your best to go in by the narrow door', he said to the people. 'I tell you that many people will want to go in. But they will not be able to get in. 25 Soon the master of the house will get up and he will shut the door. And then you may still be standing outside the door. You will knock and you will say, "Master, open the door for us to come in."

"I do not know where you come from", he will reply. "I do not know you." 26 "But Master", you will begin to say, "we had meals with you. You taught us in the streets of our villages."

27 "No!" he will tell you, "I do not know you. All of you have done very bad things, so go away from me."

28 Then you will cry because you are outside. You will bite on your teeth because you are in pain. You will see Abraham and Isaac and Jacob in the place where God rules. You will also see all the people that brought messages from God there. But God will shut you outside. 29 At that time, people will come from the east and from the west. They will also come from the north and from the south. They will all come to the place where God rules. There they will sit down together to eat a special meal. 30 At that time, some people that are now last will be first. Some people that are now first will be last.'

31 At this moment, some Pharisees came to Jesus. 'Go away from here', they said to him. 'Go somewhere else because Herod wants to kill you.'

32 'Herod is a bad man', replied Jesus. 'Tell him that I am still causing bad spirits to come out of people. I am still making sick people well again. I will continue to do all these things for a little longer. Then I will have finished my work. 33 But I need to continue my journey for a little longer. After all, only in Jerusalem do people kill those that speak messages from God.

34 Oh, you poor people of Jerusalem! You kill those that speak God's messages to you. And you throw stones to kill those that God has sent to you. Many times, I have wanted to bring all of you near to me. A female bird brings all her babies together and she covers them with her body. But you would not let me keep you from danger, as she keeps her babies. 35 So listen! The place where you live will become like adesert. I tell you this. One day you will say, "Happy is the man that God sends here with his authority." But until you say that, you will not see me again.'

Chapter 14

Jesus goes to the house of a Pharisee

1 One Jewish day for rest, Jesus went into the house of a leader of the Pharisees. This man had asked him to come and to eat a meal with him. They were all watching him carefully. 2 A sick man came up to him. His arms and legs had become too large, because they were full of water. 3 So Jesus spoke to those that taught God's rules. He also spoke to the Pharisees. 'If we make someone well on our day for rest, are we obeying the message of God or not?'

4 But they would not say anything. So, he took the sick man and he made him well again. Then he let him go away. 5 'Think', said Jesus. 'You have a son or an animal that falls into a well on a day for rest. Think about what you do. You pull the animal out of the well immediately. Do you not do that even on a rest day?'

6 They had to agree. They could not say anything else.

7 Jesus then told a picture story to those that were sitting at the meal. He had watched how the people chose the best places to sit.

8 'When someone asks you to come to a meal', he said, 'do not sit in the best place. After all, a man that is more important than you may come later. 9 Then this might happen if you are sitting in the best seat. The man that asked you to the meal might say to you, "Give your place to this man." Then you will feel ashamed that you sat there. You will have to move to the lowest place and sit there. 10 Instead, when someone asks you to a meal, you should do this. Go and sit in the least important place. So the man that asked you will see you there. And he may say to you, "Friend, move up to a better place."

Everyone who is sitting at the table will see this happen to you. So they will know that you are an important person. 11 It will be the same where God rules. Some people may put themselves in an important place. God will send them all down lower. But he will send the man that puts himself in a low place to a higher one.'

12 Jesus also spoke to the man that had asked him to the meal. 'When you give a meal at midday or in the evening, do not ask your friends to come. Do not ask your brothers or your family. And do not ask the rich people that live near you. If you do, they will later ask you to eat at their house. This will pay you for the meal that you gave to them. 13 Instead, when you give a big meal, you should ask the poor people to come. Ask people that have lost an arm or a leg. And ask people that cannot walk very well. And ask people that cannot see. 14 Do this because they cannot later ask you to eat at their houses. So you will be happy because they cannot pay you for the meal. Instead, God will pay you. One day, people that have obeyed God will become alive again. On that day, God will pay you for what you did for those poor people.'

Jesus tells a picture story about a big meal

15 The men at the table heard what Jesus said. 'One day, there will be a big meal in the place where God rules. How happy are those people who will eat together at that big meal', one of the men said.

16 Jesus answered him by telling a story. 'One day an important man made a big meal. He asked many people to come to eat in his house. 17 When the meal was ready, he sent his servant out to tell them. So, the servant went to those that his master had asked. "Come now", he said. "The meal is ready for you." 18But each person gave a reason why he could not come to the meal. "I have bought a field", said the first man. "So I must go out and see it. Please say that I am sorry. Tell your master why I cannot come to his meal." 19 "I have bought 5 pairs of oxen", the next man said. "So I am just going to see if they work well together. Please say that I am sorry. Tell your master why I cannot come to his meal." 20 "I have just married", said the third man. "That is why I cannot come to the meal." '

21 'The servant went back to his master. He told him what everyone had said. Then the master of the house was very angry. "Go out quickly to every street in the town", he said to his servant. "Bring the poor people here. Bring those that have lost an arm or a leg. And bring those that cannot walk well. And bring those that cannot see." 22 The servant did that. Then he came back to his master. "Sir", he said, "I asked all these people to come to your meal. But there are still some empty places at the table." 23 The master spoke to his servant again. "Go out to the roads outside the town. Look for people by the side of the road.Order them all to come, so that my house is full. 24 But I tell you this. None of the people that I asked at the beginning will eat the meal." '

What it will be like to obey Jesus

25 Many people were travelling with Jesus on his journey. So he turned towards them. 26 'If someone wants to obey me', he said, 'he must live like this: He must love his own father and mother less than he loves me. He must love his wife and his children less than he loves me. He must love his brothers and sisters less than he loves me. He must even love himself less than he loves me. If he does not do that, he cannot obey me. 27 He must live like a person that will die very soon. Yes, if he is not ready to die for me, he cannot obey me. So think about what it will be like to obey me.'

28 'Here is an example. One of you wants to build a tall building. Before he starts to build, he will sit down. He will decide how much it will cost. He needs to know if he has enough money to finish the building. Think about it. 29 If he does not do this, he may not have enough money. He can put the lowest stones in the ground, but he cannot finish the building. If he then has to stop, other people will laugh at him. They will say to each other, 30 "That man is a fool. He started to build, but he could not finish." '

31 Then Jesus gave them another example. 'A king wants to fight a war against another king. But before he goes to fight, he sits down. He thinks to himself. "Can I win this war? My army is large, but the other king has twice as many soldiers in his army.

32 No, I cannot do it. I know I cannot beat the other king." So, while the stronger king is far away, he sends a man with a message. He tells the king that he does not want to fight. He wants to know what he can do to become a friend of the stronger king. 33 It is like that for all of you', Jesus then said. 'You must leave everything behind you. Only then, can you come and obey me.

34 So remember this. Salt is good. But if you mix the salt with something else, it is no longer any good. You cannot cause it to taste like salt again. 35 You would not put it on your field. It cannot make the ground good. You would throw it away. You have ears. So, listen well to what I am saying.'

Chapter 15

1 One day, all the people that had done many bad things were coming round Jesus. Some were people that took money on behalf of the government. They all wanted to hear what Jesus was saying. 2 The Pharisees and those that taught God's rules did not like this. They thought that it was wrong for him to be friendly to people like that. 'This man is friendly to people that have done bad things', they said. 'He even eats with them in their homes.'

Jesus tells a picture story about a sheep that a man has lost

3 So Jesus told them this story.

4 'Think about a man that has a hundred sheep', he said. 'He may lose one of them. Think about what he does. He leaves all the other sheep in the country where nobody lives. Then he goes. And he looks for the sheep that he has lost. He looks until he finds it. 5 When he finds the sheep, he is very happy. He lifts it up and he puts it across his shoulders. 6 Then he carries it back home. He speaks to all his friends and to the people that live near him. He asks them to come to his house. "I have found the sheep that I lost", he says. "So come here and we can all be happy together." 7 The same happens when one person turns away from doing wrong things. This makes those that live above with God very happy. They will be happier about him, than about the many people that already obey God.'

Jesus tells a picture story about a coin that a woman has lost

8 'Now think about a woman that has ten valuable coins. She may lose one of them. Think about what she does. She lights a lamp and she sweeps inside her house. She looks carefully until she finds the coin. 9 Then she speaks to all her friends and to those that live near to her. She asks them to come to her house. "I have found the coin that I lost", she says. "So come here and we can all be happy together."

10 The same happens when a person turns back to God. This makes the angels of God very happy.'

Jesus tells a picture story about two sons

11 Jesus then told another story. 'There was a man that had two sons. 12 The younger son went to his father. "Father, please give me now my part of your things", he said. So, the father gave both sons their part of his things. 13 After a few days, the younger son sold what his father had given to him. Then he left home. He took with him the money and everything that he had. He went on a long journey to a country far away. He wasted all his money there and he did many bad things. 14 Then after he had spent everything, something bad happened in that country. There was almost no food anywhere. So, the young man had nothing to eat. 15 He went to a man from that country and he asked for work. The man sent him into his fields to watch his pigs. 16 Nobody gave him anything to eat. So he even wanted to eat the food that the pigs were eating.

17 Then the son began to think about what he had done. "My father has many servants", he said to himself, "and they have plenty of food to eat. They even have extra food. But I shall die here because I do not have any food. 18 So I will go to my father. 'I have done bad things against God', I will tell him. 'And I have done them against you. 19 So I am not good enough for you to call me your son any longer. Instead, please accept me as one of your servants.' "

20 So he stood up and he returned to his father. But he was still a long way from the house when his father saw him. He felt very sorry for his son and he ran towards him. Then he put his arms round him and he kissed him. 21 "Father", the son said, "I have done bad things against God and against you. So I am not good enough for you to call me your son." 22 But the father shouted to his servants. "Hurry!" he said. "Fetch the most beautiful coat that we have. Put it on him and put a ring on one of his fingers. Put shoes on his feet. 23 Fetch the young cow that we keep ready to eat on a special day. It is already fat. Kill it and prepare it. We shall eat a big meal and we shall be happy together. 24 I thought that this son of mine was dead. But now he has returned to me alive. I thought that he had left me for all time. But now he has come home." Then they began to be happy together.

25 While these things were happening, the older son was working in the field. On his way back to the house, he heard music. He heard people who were dancing. 26 So he spoke to one of the servants. "What is happening?" he asked him. 27 "Your brother has returned", the servant replied. "Your father has killed the young fat cow for him. He did this because your brother is alive and well." 28 When he heard this, he was very angry. He would not go into the house, so his father came out. "Please come in", he said. 29 "Listen", replied the older son, "I have worked for you for many years. I have always obeyed you. But you never even killed a young goat for me. If you had done that, I could have been happy with my friends. We could have had a meal together. 30 But now this other son of yours has returned. He has wasted all the money that you gave to him. He has spent it on women of the streets. But you have killed the young fat cow just for him." 31 "My son", said his father, "you are always with me. All that I have is yours. 32 We thought that your brother was dead. But now he has returned to us alive. We thought that he had left us for all time. But now he has come home. So we must be happy together." '

Chapter 16

Jesus tells a picture story about a man that thought wisely

1 Jesus then told another story to those that followed him. 'A rich man had a servant who worked for him. The servant took care of the money that the man had. Then some people came to tell the rich man about his servant. They said that he was wasting his master's things. 2 So the master sent someone to fetch his servant. "I am hearing bad stories about you", he said. "So write down everything that you have done with my money and my things. After you have done this, you will stop working for me."

3 "I must think about what I can do", the servant said to himself. "My master will not let me work for him any longer. I am not strong enough to dig. And I would be ashamed to ask other people for money. 4 I must stop working for my master. I know what I can do then. If I do it, people will accept me into their homes."

5 Many people had a debt that they had not paid back to the master. So, the servant asked those people to come to him. "How big is your debt to my master?" he asked the first man. 6 "I have to give him 100 barrels of oil", he replied. "Here is the paper with your debt written down on it", said the servant. "Take the paper. Sit down and write quickly on the paper - 50 barrels." '

7 ' "And how big is your debt to my master?" he asked the next man. "I have to give him 100 baskets of wheat", he replied. "Here is the paper with your debt written down on it. Take the paper and write on it - 80 baskets." '

8 'The servant was not honest. But his master spoke well about what he had done. What he had done would help him later. People that do not obey God think carefully. They know how to do well with people like themselves. People that obey God often think less carefully.

9 I tell you this. People may get money in wrong ways. But you should use it to be good to those who need help. You will die, one day. Then those people will be happy to see you in that place where people live for all time.

10 If you can trust a person with a very small thing, you can also trust him with bigger things. And if you cannot trust a person with a very small thing, you cannot trust him with big things. 11 So if people cannot trust you with money in this world, nobody will trust you with really valuable things. 12 And if people cannot trust you with other people's things, nobody will give you things for yourself.

13 A slave cannot work for two masters. If he does, he will only like one of them. He will work well for one master and he will think bad things about the other one. God and money are like masters. You cannot work for both of them.'

14 The Pharisees heard all this. They loved money, so they laughed at him. 'You are wrong', they said to Jesus. 15 'You like it when people look at you', he replied. 'You want them to think that you are good people. But God sees inside you. He knows what you are thinking. People think that it is important for other people to think well of them. But God thinks that this is wrong.'

16 'Moses wrote down the rules that God gave to him. Other men wrote down messages that the Holy Spirit gave to them. Those books were the only authority until John the Baptist began to speak. From the time when John started to tell them about it, people have also heard the good news. The good news is about how God rules. Since then, everyone is really trying to get into where God rules.

17 But this does not mean that anyone can destroy God's rules. One day, God will destroy the earth and the sky. But everything that God's men have written in the book of rules must happen. 18 Sometimes, a man sends away his wife, and then he marries another woman. If he does this, he is very bad. And sometimes, a husband sends away his wife and she marries another man. This other man is also doing something wrong.'

Jesus tells a story about a rich man and a poor man

19 'At one time, there was a rich man that also had expensive clothes. Some of the clothes were purple. And some of them were soft and white. This man had large meals every day. 20 There was also a poor man called Lazarus. He had sores all over his skin. He lay at the gate of the rich man. 21 He was very hungry. He even wanted to eat the bits of food that the rich man threw away. And even the dogs came and they put their tongues on the sores on his body. 22 The poor man then died and angels carried him away. They put him at the side of Abraham. The rich man also died and his family buried him. 23 He went to a bad place called Hades. He was in a lot of pain there. He saw Abraham. He was far away from him. He also saw Lazarus at the side of Abraham. 24 So he shouted out, "Father Abraham, please be kind to me. Please send Lazarus to me. I am in great pain because I am in a fire. Let him put the end of his finger into some water. Let him use the water to make my mouth cool." 25 "My child", replied Abraham, "remember the time when you were alive on earth. Remember what happened then. You had lots of good things and Lazarus had lots of bad things. Now I am taking care of Lazarus, and you are in pain. 26 But that is not everything. Between you and us, there is a hole. It is wide and long and deep. There is a reason why this hole is there. Nobody can cross from here to where you are. And nobody can cross from where you are to come here." 27 "If that is true, Father Abraham", he said, "please send Lazarus to my family. 28 I have 5 brothers that are still alive. He can tell them not to do the same things as I did. So they will not also come here when they die. They will not be in great pain, as I am."

29 "They have the books that Moses wrote", said Abraham. "They have all the messages that other men wrote. The men that heard from God wrote them. Your family should listen to them." '

30 ' "No, Father Abraham", he said, "they will not listen to the messages that Moses and the other servants of God wrote. But if someone goes to them from among the dead people, they will listen. So then they will turn away from doing wrong things. And they will turn back to God."

31 "You say that they do not believe. They do not believe what Moses and the other servants of God said. So also they will not believe someone that comes back from among the dead people." '

Chapter 17

1 'Some people will try to cause other people to do wrong things. You can be sure about that', Jesus said to those that always followed him. 'But God will punish every person that tries to do that. 2 So he must stop doing it. If not, he should ask someone to hang a big stone round his neck. Then people should throw him into the sea with the stone. So he will not cause one of these little people to do wrong things.'

3 'Be careful how you think. If your brother does something wrong, talk to him about it. Your brother may say, "I am sorry for what I did. I will not do it again." If he says that, you must forgive him. 4 Your brother may do a bad thing to you many times in a day. He may turn to you many times and say, "I am sorry for what I did. I will not do it again." If he does that, you must forgive him.'

5 'Help us', said the 12 men that Jesus had chosen, 'to believe more and more in you.'

6 'The amount that you believe in me is not even as big as a small seed', the Lord replied. 'If it was as big as that, you could say to this tree, "Pull yourself out of the ground and plant yourself in the sea." And the tree would obey you.

7 Think about this. You have a servant that is ploughing. Or you have a servant that is taking care of your sheep. When he comes in from his work, you would not say to him, "Sit down and eat." 8 No, you would not say that. You would say to him, "Prepare the evening meal for me. Get yourself ready and bring the food to me. I will eat and drink first. You can eat when I have finished." 9 Servants should do what their masters order them to do. Their masters do not thank them when they do that. 10 It is the same with you. The Master tells you what you should do. And you do it. "We are not special servants", each of you should say to himself. "We have only done what we should do." '

The 10 men that had leprosy

11 On his journey to Jerusalem, Jesus was travelling along the border between Samaria and Galilee. 12When he was going into a village, 10 men came towards him. These men had an illness of the skin. They stopped some way away from Jesus 13 and they shouted, 'Jesus, Master, please be kind to us.'

14 Jesus saw them standing there. 'Go and show yourselves to the priests', he answered.

While they were going there, they became well again. 15 Then one of these 10 men saw that Jesus had made him well. He turned back and he started to shout out, 'God is very good. He has made me well.' 16He went down on his knees in front of Jesus. 'Thank you, Master', he said. This man was from Samaria.

17 'I made 10 men well again', Jesus said. 'There should be another 9 men! 18 Only this one man came back to thank God, and he is from Samaria. There should be other men that came from Israel.'

19 Then he spoke to the man. 'Stand up again and go on your way. You believed in me, so now you are really well.'

Jesus talks about the time when God will rule

20 Then some Pharisees asked Jesus a question. 'When will God begin to rule here?'

'You will not see anything different when God begins to rule here', Jesus replied. 'People will not see it happen. 21 Nobody will say, "Look everyone! God is ruling here", or "Look! God is ruling over there." No, it is not like that. God is already ruling in the lives of his people.

22 The days are coming when you will really want to see me return', he said to those that always followed him. 'But you will not see me. 23 At that time, people will say to you, "There he is!" or "Here he is!" But do not go out with them to look. 24 After all, when lightning shines, it makes the whole of the sky light. It will be like that when I return. Everyone will see me. 25 Before this happens, the people alive now will say, "We do not want Jesus to be our king. Kill him!" And I will feel much pain.'

26 'Remember the report about the time when Noah was alive. Remember what happened then. My return will happen quickly too. 27 While Noah was making his boat, people were eating food. And they were drinking. Men and women were marrying. They continued to do all this until the day when Noah went into his boat. Then it rained for a long time and the deep water killed all the people.'

28 'The same things happened when Lot was alive. People in the city called Sodom were eating. And they were drinking. They were buying and selling things. They were planting seeds and they were building houses. 29 But then, Lot went away from Sodom. On that same day, God caused it to rain fire and burning stones from the sky. This killed all the people in Sodom. 30 The same things will happen on the day when I show myself.

31 On that day, this is what people must do. If they are outside their house, they must not go back inside to get their things. In the same way, people that are working in the fields must not return to their house. They must not go back for the things that were in the house. No, they must just run away from Jerusalem. 32 Remember what happened to Lot's wife.'

33 'Whoever wants to save his life will lose it. But if he loses his life for me, he will save it. 34 I tell you this. At that time, two men will be sleeping in bed at night. The angels will take one of them and they will leave the other one behind. 35-36 Two women will be working together in the same place. The angels will take one of them and they will leave the other one behind.'

37 'Where will this happen?' those that followed Jesus asked him. 'If a dead body is lying somewhere, vultures will come together', he said to them.

Chapter 18

Jesus talks about how to pray

1 Then Jesus told those that always followed him a picture story. It taught them that they must not get tired. But they must go on praying. 2 'In a certain city', he said, 'there was a judge. He did not think that either God or people were important.'

3 'A woman lived in that same city. Her husband had died. She continued to come to the judge with a problem. "Please keep me safe from the person that is against me", she was saying. 4 For a time, the judge would not do anything for her. Later, he thought about himself. "I do not think that either God or people are important. 5 But this woman causes me trouble. If I do not do anything for her, she will continue to come to me again and again. She will make me very tired. So, I will help her. I will say that she is right." '

6 'This judge was not a good man', Jesus said. 'But you should think about what he said to himself. He will only help because the woman causes him trouble. 7 But God always helps those that he has chosen to be his children. When they continue to ask him for help, he will answer them immediately. He will not wait. 8 I tell you this. He will say that they are right. He will help them quickly. I shall return to earth. But I will not find many people that still believe in me then.'

Jesus tells a story about two men that were praying

9 Jesus also told another picture story to teach people. Some people thought that they were very good. They also thought that they were better than other men.

10 'One day, two men went into the Great House of God to pray. One man was a Pharisee. The other man received money on behalf of the government. 11 The Pharisee stood by himself. And he prayed where other people could see him. "Thank you, God, that I am different from all these other people. They rob. They are bad. They have sex with women that they have not married. Thank you also that I am different from this man. He receives money on behalf of the government. 12 I stop eating on two days of each week. I give to you one tenth of all that I receive."

13 But the other man stood very far away. He would not even look up to the sky.

He was hitting his body with his hands to show how sorry he was. "Please, God, be kind to me", he was saying. "I have done many bad things." '

14 'Let me tell you about these men when they went home', said Jesus. 'The man that received money on behalf of the government was now right with God. But the Pharisee had not made anything right with God. Some people say that they are good. God will say to them, "Go away from me. You are not good." Other people know that they are not good. God will say to them, "Come up here. I have made you good." '

Jesus is with little children

15 People were even bringing little children to Jesus. They were doing this so that he could touch the children. But those that always followed Jesus saw this. So they said to them, 'Stop bringing all these children here.'

16 Then Jesus shouted out to them. 'Let the children come to me. Do not try to stop them. God rules in the lives of people that are like these children. 17 Let me tell you something important. You must receive God as a child does. If you do not, God will never rule in your life.'

Jesus meets a rich ruler

18 A Jewish ruler came to Jesus. 'Good teacher', he asked, 'what should I do so that I can live for all time?'

19 'Why do you say that I am good?' said Jesus. 'Nobody is good, except God. 20 You know the rules of God. Do not have sex with anyone that is not your wife. Do not kill anyone. Do not rob anyone. Only say true things about people. Love your father and your mother.'

21 'I have obeyed all these rules since I was 12 years old', he replied.

22 Jesus heard what he said. 'You still need to do one thing', he said. 'You must sell everything that you have. Give the money to the poor people. So, then you will have many valuable things in the place above, where God lives. Then come back and obey me.'

23 When the ruler heard this, he became very sad. This was because he was very rich.

24 Jesus saw that the ruler had become sad. 'It is very difficult for rich people to ask God to rule in their lives', he said. 25 'After all, it is difficult for a big animal to pass through the hole in a needle. But it is even more difficult for a rich man to ask God to rule in his life.'

26 'So who will God save?' asked the people that were listening to Jesus.

27 'God can do things that no man can do', he replied.

28 'Listen!' said Peter, 'we have left everything to obey you.'

29 'Let me tell you something important', replied Jesus. 'Some people leave their home to obey God and to let him rule in their lives. They may leave their wife, their brothers, their parents and their children. 30These people will receive, in this life, very much more than they left. And after they die, they will have something else. They will have a life that does not have an end.'

31 Jesus took the 12 men that he had chosen away from the other people. 'Listen!' he said. 'We are going to Jerusalem. When we are there, many bad things will happen to me. A long time ago the servants of God wrote down messages from the Holy Spirit. Everything that he told them about the Son of Man will now happen to me. 32 This is what he said. The Jews will give me to those that are not Jews. They will laugh at me. They will do bad things to me. They will spit on me. 33 They will hit me with a whip and then they will kill me. But after three days, I will become alive again.'

34 The 12 men that Jesus had chosen did not understand any of these things. Something hid these things from them. So they did not know what Jesus was talking about.

Jesus makes a man well that cannot see

35 When Jesus was getting near to Jericho, a man was sitting by the side of the road. This man could not see and he was asking people to give him money. 36 Then he heard a large crowd of people who were passing by him. So, he asked the people near him what was happening.

37 'Jesus from Nazareth is passing by', they replied.

38 The man began to shout out. 'Jesus, Son of David, please be kind to me.' 39 The people that were walking in the front of the crowd tried to stop him. 'Be quiet!' they were saying to him.

But he started to shout even louder. 'Son of David, please be kind to me!'

40 Then Jesus stood still. 'Bring that man to me', he said. Then when the man came near, Jesus spoke to him.

41 'What do you want me to do for you?'

'Sir', he replied, 'please cause me to see again.'

42 'See again', said Jesus. 'You are well now because you believed in me.'

43 Immediately the man could see again. He started to follow Jesus. He was saying, 'God, you are very great and powerful.'

Many people saw what had happened. 'God, how great and important you are', they also said.

Chapter 19

Zacchaeus meets Jesus

1 Jesus went into Jericho and he was walking through the city. 2 There was an important man there called Zacchaeus. He took money on behalf of the government and he had become very rich. 3 He was trying to see who Jesus was. There was a big crowd there and he was a small man. So he could not see him. 4 So he ran on in front of the crowd and he climbed up a tree. He could see Jesus more easily from the tree, because he would walk along that way. 5 When Jesus came to the tree, he looked up. 'Zacchaeus, come down quickly', he said. 'Today I must stay in your home.'

6 So Zacchaeus came down quickly and took him into his home. He was very happy about this. 7 The people saw what had happened. And they were not happy. 'Jesus has gone to stay in the home of a man that does bad things', they were saying.

8 Zacchaeus then stood up in front of everyone and he spoke to the Master. 'Listen, Master', he said. 'I will give half of all that I have to poor people. I have taken too much money from some people. I will give them 4 times as much as I took from them wrongly.'

9-10 'Today', said Jesus to him, 'God's salvation has come to this home. After all, I came to look for people that God has lost. And I have come to save them. And Zacchaeus is also part of the family of Abraham.'

Jesus tells a picture story about 10 servants

11 While the people were still listening, he told them a story. He did this because he was getting near to Jerusalem. He knew that the people had wrong thoughts. They had wrong thoughts about what would happen there. They were thinking that God would begin to rule his people immediately after that.

12 'An important man left his home and he travelled a long way to another country', he told them. 'There he would receive authority to rule his own country. After that, he would return as king. 13 Before he left, he asked 10 of his servants to come to him. He gave each of them 10 pounds of silver. "Use this money to get more money for me while I am away", he said.'

14 'The people who were living in his country did not like the man. So, they sent a group of people after him with a message. That message was: "We do not want this man to rule over us."

15 When the king returned, he asked those 10 servants to come to him. He wanted to know how much more money they had made from his money. They should have bought things with it and then they should have sold those things again for more money.

16 The first servant came. "Master", he said, "your money has made 10 more pounds."

17 The master was happy. "You have done well. You are a good servant that I can trust. You have used a small amount of money well. So you will rule over 10 cities."

18 The second servant came. "Master, your money has made 5 more pounds."

19 "You will rule over 5 cities", the Master said to him.

20 Then another servant came. "Master", he said, "here is your money. I put it away in a piece of cloth. 21 I did this because I was afraid of you. After all, you tell people what they should do all the time. You take things that you did not work for. You do not put seeds in the ground, but you take the plants from the fields."

22 "You are a bad servant", the Master replied. "I will use your own words to show you that you have done the wrong thing. You said that you know about me. That I tell people what they should do all the time. That I take things that I did not work for. That I do not put seeds in the ground, but I take plants from the fields. 23 You should have put my money into the bank. When I came home, I might have had my money back again with extra." 24 Some other servants were standing near to their master. "Take the money from this servant", he said to them. "Give it to the servant that has 10 pounds."

25 "But, Master", they replied, "that servant has 10 pounds already."

26 "Let me tell you this", the Master said. "Some people have something. To them I give more. Other people have nothing. From them I take away even the small thing that they have. 27 Now I must punish these other people that did not want me to rule over them. Bring them here and kill them in front of me." '

Jesus goes into Jerusalem

28 When Jesus had said all this, he went on in front of them. He was going up to Jerusalem. 29 And he was getting near to two villages called Bethphage and Bethany. They were at the hill called the Mount of Olives. So, he sent two of those that always followed him into one of the villages.

30 'Go into the village that is in front of you. When you go in, you will find a young donkey. Someone has tied it up there. Nobody has ridden on it before. Remove the tie and bring the donkey here to me. 31 Someone may ask, "Why are you taking the donkey?" If they do, tell them: "The Master needs to use it." '

32 The two men that Jesus sent went into the village. They found everything there that Jesus had told them about. 33 While they were taking the young donkey, some men spoke to them. It was their donkey. They asked, 'Why are you taking the young donkey?' 34 'The Master needs to use it', they replied. 35 They brought it to Jesus, and they put their coats on top of it. Then they helped Jesus to get on to it. 36 While he was riding along, the people were putting their coats down on the road.

37 Jesus got near to the lowest part of the hill called the Mount of Olives. The whole crowd of those that followed him became very happy. 'God, how great and powerful you are', they were shouting out. 'You are very powerful. Thank you for all the great things that we have seen. 38 Happy is the King that comes with the authority of God. We want all to be well in the place above where God lives. We pray that it will be. He is beautiful. He has all power and authority.'

39 Some of the Pharisees in the crowd spoke to Jesus. 'Teacher', they said, 'stop those people that are following you from saying these things.'

40 'Let me tell you this', replied Jesus. 'If these people were quiet, the stones of the city would shout out instead!'

41 When Jesus got near to the city, he looked at it in front of him. He cried because he felt very sorry for the people in it. 42 'You need to know what you should do, to live without trouble', he said. 'You need to be well with God. But now, something is hiding these things from you. 43 As a result, bad days will come to you. Your enemies will build a wall round you. They will shut you in completely, and they will not let you leave. 44 You did not understand that God had come to save you. So your enemies will kill you and they will destroy your city. They will break down your walls and they will not leave one stone in the right place.'

Jesus teaches in the Great House of God

45 Jesus went into the Great House of God. Some people were selling things there. He began to cause them to leave. 46 'This is what God has said in his book', Jesus said. 'God has said, "My house will be a place where people come to pray." But you have made it into a place where people rob each other.'

47 Jesus was teaching every day in the Great House of God. The leaders of the priests and those that taught God's rules wanted to kill him. The leaders of the people also wanted to kill him. 48 But all the people were listening to him. They wanted to hear all that he was saying. So, the leaders did not know how to kill him.

Chapter 20

Jesus talks about his authority

1 One day, Jesus was teaching in the Great House of God. He was telling people the good news about how God rules. Then the leaders of the priests and the teachers of God's rules came to him. With them were some other Jewish leaders. 2 They all came to speak to him. 'Tell us what authority you have to do these things', they said. 'Who gave you this authority?'

3 'I also will ask you something', he answered them. 'Tell me this. 4 John had authority to baptise people. Did this authority come from God or did someone else give it to him?'

5 The Jewish leaders talked to each other about his question. 'We could say that God gave John authority. But if we say that, Jesus will say to us, "So why did you not believe him?" 6 Or we could say that someone else gave him that authority. Then all the people would throw stones at us to kill us. After all, they are sure that John received messages from the Holy Spirit.' 7 So they answered, 'We do not know who gave John authority to baptise.'

8 'So, I will not tell you who gave me authority to do these things', Jesus replied.

Jesus tells a picture story about farmers

9 Then Jesus began to tell this story to the people in the Great House of God.

'A man planted a field with vine plants. He let some farmers take care of the plants. Then he went away to another country and he stayed there for a long time.

10 When it was time to pick the fruit, the man sent a servant to the farmers. The servant said to them, "Please give me part of the fruit for my master."

But the farmers hit him with sticks and they sent him away with nothing.

11 The master then sent another servant to the field. They also hit him with sticks and they did other bad things to him. They also sent him away with nothing. 12 The master sent a third servant to the field. The farmers hurt him badly too and they threw him out of the field.

13 Then the master of the field said to himself, "I must think about what I should do. I know what I will do. I will send my son that I love very much. Perhaps they will be kind to him." 14 But the farmers saw him coming. "This is the son of our master", they said to each other. "When our master dies, he will have the field. We should kill him and then the field will be ours."

15 So they threw him out of the field and they killed him.'

'This is what the master will do to the farmers', said Jesus. 16 'He will come to those farmers. He will kill them and he will give the field to other farmers.'

'That must not happen!' replied the people when they heard this. 17 Jesus then looked at the people. 'You say that this must not happen. But this is what is in God's book.

> "The builders refused to use one special stone.

But that stone is now the one that makes the corner of the wall strong.

18 When a person falls on to that stone, it will break their body into pieces. But when that stone falls on top of someone, it will destroy him completely." '

The leaders ask Jesus a question

19 The teachers of God's rules and the priests wanted to take hold of Jesus immediately. They knew that Jesus was talking against them in the story. But they did not do it, because they were afraid of the people.

20 So this is what they did to catch Jesus. They gave money to people to ask him a difficult question. These people seemed to be good, but they were not honest. Instead, they wanted to hear Jesus say something wrong. Then they would take him to the ruler of the city for him to punish Jesus. 21 This is what these people asked: 'Teacher, everything that you say is right. And everything that you teach is right. We know that. You do not say something different to an important person to make him happy. Instead, you teach everyone the same message. And you say what God really wants them to do. 22 Should we pay money to the Roman leaders who rule us? Do God's rules let us do this or not?'

23 Jesus knew that the men wanted him to say the wrong thing. He knew that they only seemed to be good people. 24 'Show me a coin', he said to them. 'Whose picture and name are on it?'

25 'They are the picture and the name of the Roman ruler', they replied.

'So give to the Roman ruler the things that are his', said Jesus. 'And give to God the things that are his.'

26 So the Jewish leaders could not cause Jesus to say wrong things about the Roman ruler. They were very surprised at his answer to their question. This caused them to stop speaking.

The Sadducees ask Jesus a question

27 Then some of the Sadducees came to see Jesus. These men did not believe that any dead people will become alive again.

28 They asked him a question. 'Teacher', they said, 'Moses wrote this rule for us to obey. A man may die. If his wife has no children, the brother of her husband must marry her. We should call their children the children of the man that died. 29 But once there were 7 men that were brothers. One of the brothers married. Then he died but they had no children. 30 Another brother then married this woman, but he also died. 31 Then the third brother married the woman. The same thing happened to all 7 brothers. None of them had any children before they died. 32 After this, the woman also died. 33 People say this about those that have died. They say that one day they will live again. So, when that happens, whose wife will she be? After all, she had been wife to all 7 of them.'

34 'Men and women that are alive on earth get married', said Jesus to them. 35 'But dead people that live again do not marry. God has chosen some people to live again with him. He says that they are good. They do not marry 36 and they cannot die any more. This is because they live as the angels live. They are children of God. He has made them alive again.

37 It is true that dead people live again. Moses showed us this in the report about the burning bush. He told us that our God said this: "I am the God of Abraham, the God of Isaac and the God of Jacob."

38 But God is not a God of dead people. He is God of living people. Abraham, Isaac and Jacob are alive to him. Really, he sees all people as alive.'

39 Some of the teachers of God's rules agreed. 'Teacher', they said, 'that was a very good answer.' 40 They were afraid to ask him any more questions.

The Messiah is someone that David calls Master

41 Jesus said to them, 'Why do people say this, "The Messiah will be someone from the family of David"?42 After all, David himself said this in the book called Psalms:

"Our God said to my Master:

Sit at the place of importance, at my right side.

43 Remain there until I put your enemies under your feet.

You will rest your feet on them."

44 So David calls him Master. So how can he also be from the family of David?'

Be careful not to do the same as those that teach the rules

45 All the people were listening. Jesus then spoke to those that always followed him.

46 'Be careful not to do the same as the teachers of God's rules. They like to wear long clothes to show how important they are. They like people to speak to them in front of many people, as they would speak to an important person. They like to have the best seats at meetings. They like to sit in the most important places at special meals. 47 They cause women whose husbands have died to supply them with money. They use this for themselves. They pray in front of many people for a long time. This causes people to think that they are good. Because they do these things, God will punish these people a lot. It will be worse for them than for people that have not done these things.'

Chapter 21

Jesus talks about people who give things to God

1 Then Jesus looked at what was happening in the Great House of God. There was a box for money there. Many rich people were putting their gifts of money into it.

2 Then he saw a woman. Her husband had died. She was very poor. She put two very small coins of little value into the box. 3 'Let me tell you this', said Jesus. 'This poor woman has put more money into the box than everyone else. 4 The rich people put in money that they do not need. They have plenty more. This woman has less money than she needs. She needs money to buy bread to eat. But she put all of that money into the box.'

Jesus talks about things that will happen

5 Some of those that followed Jesus were talking about the Great House of God. They spoke about the many beautiful and valuable stones in the walls. They pointed out the many beautiful gifts to God that people had put on it. 6 'You can see all these beautiful things just now', Jesus said. 'But a day is coming when enemies will destroy it all. They will throw down every stone. Not one will remain on top of another.'

7 'Teacher', they asked, 'so when will this happen? What will we see just before this happens?'

8 'Be careful', he replied. 'Do not believe things that are not true. After all, many people will come and they will say, "I am Jesus." They will say that the right time for God is soon. Do not follow those people.

9 And when you hear about wars, do not be afraid. Also, do not be afraid when people are fighting against their governments. These things must happen first. But the end will not happen immediately.'

10 'Yes', he was saying, 'people from one country will fight people from another country. And kings will send their people to fight other kings and their people. 11 The ground will move so much that people will be afraid. In many different places, plants for food will not grow; so, many people will go hungry. Illnesses will go from one person to another; so, many people will die. Many things will also happen in the sky that will frighten people. 12 But before all those things happen, these things will happen: People that hate me will take hold of you. They will do bad things to you because you are obeying me. They will take you to their meeting places. They will bring you in front of kings and rulers. And they will ask them to put you in prison or to kill you. 13 This will be the moment to tell them the Good News about me. 14 So prepare your minds. Do not think about how to answer the questions of kings and rulers. 15 After all, I will give you the right words to speak so that nobody can argue with you. They will just be quiet. 16 Even your parents and other people in your family will bring you in front of kings and rulers. They will kill some of you. 17 Everybody will hate you, because you are obeying me. 18 But your life will be safe with me. You will not lose even one hair from your head. 19 Yes, you will really live, if you never stop obeying me.

20 One day you will see Jerusalem with armies all round it. Then you will know that enemies will soon destroy Jerusalem. 21 People in Judea must then run to the hills and hide. People that are inside the city must leave it. People that are outside the city must not go back into it. 22 This is when God will punish Israel's people. Then all the things will happen that his servants wrote about. 23 That time will be a very bad time for women that have a baby inside them! It will be very bad for those women that have little babies! Yes, very bad things will happen to all the people of this country. God will be very angry with them. 24 At that time, enemies will kill many people with sharp knives. They will take some people and they will cause them to leave their country. They will live in many other countries and they will not be free to return to this country. People that are not Jews will destroy Jerusalem. They will rule here until it is time for them to stop.'

25 'You will see strange things happen to the sun and moon and stars. On earth, the things that happen will make people in many countries very afraid. The sea will make a lot of noise and there will be big storms at sea. 26 This will cause trouble. And it will frighten people because they do not understand these things. The powerful things in the sky will move from their usual places. Then people will be afraid about what will happen next in the world. They will be so afraid that they will become very, very weak. 27 It is then that they will see the Son of Man. I will come in a cloud with a lot of power. I will look very important and very beautiful. 28 When these things begin to happen, stand up. And look up. God will soon save you.'

29 Jesus then explained to them what this time would be like. 'Think about the fig tree or any other tree. 30 You see new leaves on the tree. Then you know that summer will come soon. Nobody needs to tell you that. 31 It will be the same when you see all these things happening. You will then know that God will soon begin to rule.

32 Let me tell you this. Some of the people alive will not die until all this has happened. 33 The sky and the earth will go away. But my message will remain true. What I have said will happen.

34 But be careful. And watch how you live. Do not eat or drink too much. Do not waste your time like that. Do not waste time by having troubles in your mind about your life. If you do, that day will surprise you. It will come when you are not looking. 35 And it will surprise everyone who lives on earth. 36 So watch all the time! Continue to pray for power to get out of all these things! So then you will stand in front of me. And you will not be afraid of me.' 37 Jesus was teaching every day in the Great House of God. Each night he went out of the city and he stayed on the Mount of Olives. 38 He returned to the Great House of God each morning. All the people were going there early to hear him.

Chapter 22

Judas agrees to catch Jesus

1 The day was coming soon when the Jews would eat a special meal of bread without yeast. This time is called Passover.

2 The leaders of the priests and the teachers of God's rules wanted to kill Jesus. They were thinking about how they could do this. It was difficult because they were afraid of the people. They wanted to kill him secretly.

3 Then the devil began to live inside Judas Iscariot. He was one of the 12 men that Jesus had chosen. 4 Judas went away and he talked to the leaders of the priests. The police that worked at the Great House of God were also there. They talked about how Judas could give Jesus to them secretly. 5 They were very happy and they promised to give him money for this. 6 So Judas said that he would do it. He then began to watch for the right moment to catch Jesus. He wanted to do it when the crowd was not round Jesus.

Jesus eats his last meal with those that he had chosen

7 The day came for the meal of bread without yeast. The people had to kill the young sheep for the Passover meal on this day. 8 So Jesus sent Peter and John. 'Go and prepare the Passover meal', he said. 'Then we can all come and eat it.'

9 'Where would you like us to prepare the meal?' they asked him.

10 'Listen', he replied, 'When you start to go into the city, a man will meet you. He will be carrying a jar of water. Follow him until he goes into a house. 11 You must then say to the master of that house, "Our Teacher sends this message to you:

'Where is the room for visitors? I will eat the Passover meal there with those that always follow me.' "

12 The man will show you a large room upstairs. It will have all that you need in it. Prepare the Passover meal there for us all.'

13 So Peter and John went into the city. They found everything that Jesus had told them about. And they prepared the Passover meal.

14 When it was time to eat it, Jesus arrived. He sat down. The men that he had chosen sat down with him. 15 'I have wanted very much to eat this Passover meal with you', Jesus said to them. 'It has to happen before I die. 16 Yes, I will not eat another Passover meal after this one. I will not eat it again until God begins to rule.'

17 Then he took a cup and he thanked God for the wine. 'Take this cup', he said to them. 'Each of you drink some wine. 18 Let me tell you this. From now on, I will not drink wine until God begins to rule.'

19 Then he took a loaf of bread and he thanked God for it. He broke the bread into small bits and he gave it to each of them.

'This is my body. I am offering it up to God for each of you. When you do this from now on, remember me.'

20 Jesus did the same after the meal. He took a cup of wine and he gave it to them. 'This is about the new promise. It is between God and his people. I will let people kill me and pour out my blood. Then this promise can start to happen.'

21 'But look! The hand of the person that will give me to the rulers is on the table with me. 22 I shall die, as God wants me to. That is true. But it will be very bad for the man that causes it to happen.'

23 'Who is the man that would do this thing?' they asked each other.

Jesus tells who is most important

24 Then they began to argue among themselves. They were arguing about which of them was the most important. 25 'Kings of countries have great authority over their people', Jesus said to them. 'Kings want people to say good things about them. And kings want people to say that they are their friends. 26 You must be different. The most important person among you must become the same as the least important person. The person that is master must become the same as the servant. 27 After all, which person is the most important? Is it the person that sits at the table? Or is it the servant that puts out the meal? Yes, it is the person that sits at the table. But I am here to be your servant.

28 You have never left me. You have been by my side when I had difficult times. 29 And now, I say that you will rule with me. My Father has said that I will rule with him. So, I also say to you that you will rule with me. 30 You will be at my table where I rule. You will eat and drink with me. You will sit on rulers' chairs. You will judge the people of the 12 families of Israel.'

Jesus tells Peter what will happen

31 'Simon, Simon, be careful to listen to me! The devil has asked to have you all. He wants to cause all of you to stop obeying me. He will shake you as a farmer shakes seeds.'

32 'But I have prayed for you, Simon, that you will continue to believe in me. And you, when you have turned back to me, you must help your brothers to be strong again.'

33 'Master', said Simon, 'I am even ready to go to prison with you. I am ready to die with you!'

34 'Let me tell you this, Peter', Jesus replied. 'Three times tonight, you will say that you do not know me. You will say it before the cockerel makes a noise in the morning.'

35 Jesus then asked the men that he had chosen a question. 'When I sent you out without a purse, a bag or shoes, did you need anything?' 'No', they replied, 'nothing.'

36 'Now it is different', he said. 'If you have a purse or bag, take it with you. If you do not have a long sharp knife, sell your coat. Use the money to buy a knife. 37 Let me tell you why. In the book of God, people wrote down everything that will happen to me. It says, "People will include me with other bad men." And this must happen to me soon.'

38 'Master', they said, 'Look, we have two long sharp knives here.'

'It is enough', he replied.

Jesus prays on the hill called the Mount of Olives

39 Jesus left the city. And he went to the hill called the Mount of Olives. This is what he usually did. Those that always followed him went with him.

40 He arrived at the place where he wanted to go. Then he said to them. 'Ask God to keep you from wanting to do wrong things.'

41 He went away from them about as far as you can throw a stone. He bent his knees to the ground and he prayed. 42 'Father', he said, 'if you want, you can take away this time of pain from me. But do not let me do what I want. I want to do what you want.'

43 An angel then came to him from God. The angel made him stronger. 44 Jesus began to have troubles in his mind. He prayed again even more strongly. The sweat on his head became like large amounts of blood that fell to the ground.

45 He then stopped praying and he stood up again. He returned to the 11 men. And he found that they were sleeping. They were very tired because they were so sad. 46 'You should not be sleeping', he said. 'Get up and pray! Ask God to keep you from wanting to do wrong things.'

The soldiers catch Jesus

47 While Jesus was still speaking, a crowd of people and soldiers came towards him. Judas led the crowd. He was one of the 12 men that Jesus had chosen. He came near to Jesus to kiss him. 48 'Surely you will not kiss me, Judas', said Jesus, 'to show the soldiers which person to catch!'

49 Then those that followed Jesus saw what was happening. 'Should we use our long sharp knives, Master?' they asked him.

50 One of them hit the servant of the leader of the priests. He cut off his right ear. 51 'Enough!' said Jesus, 'Stop doing this!' He then touched the man and made his ear well again.

52 Then Jesus spoke to the people that had come to catch him. They were the leaders of the priests, and the leaders of the police in the Great House of God. Other important Jewish rulers were also there.

'You seem to have come out here with sharp knives and heavy sticks. You seem to have come to catch me as you would catch a dangerous robber. 53 I was with you every day in the Great House of God. You did not try to get hold of me then. Yes, this really is the time and the place for you to work. Now it is dark, and the devil rules in the dark.'

Peter says that he does not know Jesus

54 Then they took hold of Jesus. They took him away and they brought him to the house of the leader of the priests. Peter was following, but he did not get near them. 55 People lit a fire outside the house and they sat round it. Peter went and he sat among them. 56 A servant girl then saw Peter in the light from the fire. She looked carefully at him. 'This man was also one that followed Jesus', she said.

57 'Woman', Peter replied, 'I do not know him.'

58 After a short time, a man looked at him. 'You also are in their group', he said.

'Man', Peter replied, 'I am not one of them.'

59 After about an hour, someone else spoke. 'I am sure that this man was also with Jesus. He also is from Galilee.'

60 'Man', said Peter, 'I do not know what you are talking about.'

While Peter was still speaking, a cockerel made a noise. 61 Then the Master turned round and he looked at Peter. Peter remembered what the Master had said to him: 'Three times you will say tonight that you do not know me. You will say it three times before the cockerel makes a noise in the morning.'

62 Peter went away and he cried a lot.

The soldiers laugh at Jesus and they hit him

63 The men that were holding Jesus were laughing at him. They were hitting him.

64 They tied a cloth round his head so that he could not see. 'You say that you get messages from God!' they said. 'Tell us, who is hitting you now?' 65 And they were saying many other bad things to him.

The leaders of the Jews ask Jesus questions

66 When it was day, the leaders of the Jews met together. The leaders of the priests were at the meeting. The teachers of God's rules were also there. Then other men brought Jesus into the meeting. 67 'Are you the Messiah?' they asked. 'If you are, tell us.'

'If I do tell you', Jesus replied, 'you will not believe me. 68 I could ask you, "Who do you think that I am?" But you will not answer me, if I do that. 69 But from now on, I will be sitting in the most important place. I will be sitting at the right side of God. He is all powerful.'

70 'So, are you the Son of God?' they all said.

'You say that I am. And you are correct', he replied.

71 'We do not need anyone else to tell us what this man says. We ourselves have heard what he has said about himself', they said.

Chapter 23

Pilate asks Jesus questions

1 All the people at the meeting stood up, and they took Jesus to stand in front of Pilate.

2 Then they all started to tell him that Jesus had done bad things. 'We found this man when he was telling our people wrong things', they said. 'He said that we must not give money to the Roman government. He also said that he himself is the Messiah, a king.'

3 'Are you the king of the Jews?' Pilate asked Jesus.

'The words are yours', he replied. 'But you are correct.'

4 Pilate then spoke to the leaders of the priests and to all that were there. 'I cannot find anything that this man has done wrong.'

5 But they continued to speak strongly to him. 'He makes the people angry and ready to fight. He has taught these things everywhere in Judea. He started in Galilee and now he has come to Jerusalem.'

6 Pilate heard them say 'Galilee'. So, he asked if Jesus came from Galilee. 7 'Yes', they replied, 'he is from the country that Herod rules.' Herod was in Jerusalem at that time. So, Pilate sent Jesus to stand in front of him.

Herod asks Jesus questions

8 Herod was very happy to see Jesus. He had heard about him and he had wanted to meet him for a long time. He was hoping that he would see Jesus do some powerful work. 9 He asked him many questions, but Jesus did not answer any of them. 10 The rulers of the Jews stood there all the time. They were shouting out that Jesus had done many bad things. 11 Then Herod and his soldiers started to laugh at Jesus. They were saying things to make him feel bad. They put a beautiful coat on him. It was one that a ruler wears. Then they sent him back to Pilate. 12 Herod and Pilate became friends on that same day. Until then, they had not liked each other.

Pilate and the leaders of the Jews argue about Jesus

13 Pilate then said that all the leaders of the priests and leaders of the Jews must come back to him. 14 'You brought this man in front of me', he said to them. 'You said that he was causing the people to be against their rulers. Listen! I have asked him some questions in front of you. But I did not find that he has done anything wrong. 15 Herod also did not find that he had done anything wrong. After all, he has sent him back to me. So, you can see that this man has not done anything bad. There is no reason for me to say, "Kill him." 16 So I will order a soldier to whip him. Then I will let him go home.'

17 (Pilate had to let one person come out of the prison at Passover time.)

18 So the crowd shouted together, 'Take this man away and kill him. We want Barabbas to come out of prison.'

19 Barabbas had told the Jews that they should fight against the Roman rulers. He had also killed somebody in the fight. So, the rulers had put him in prison. 20 Pilate still wanted to let Jesus go. So, he again spoke to the crowd. 21 But they started to shout, 'Kill him on a cross, kill him on a cross.'

22 Pilate asked them the same question for the third time. 'Why do you want me to kill him on a cross? What wrong things has he done? You want me to say that he should die. I have not found anything wrong that would cause me to say that. So, I will order my soldiers to whip him. Then I will let him go.'

23 But they continued to shout at him. 'Kill him on a cross. Kill him on a cross.' They shouted very much. So, they got what they wanted. 24 Pilate said, 'Fix him on a cross, as they want.' 25 They had asked Pilate to let Barabbas out of the prison. He was the man that had caused Jews to be against the Roman rulers. He had also killed somebody while he was fighting the rulers. He was the man that Pilate let go free. As for Jesus, Pilate ordered his soldiers to take him away. And he ordered them to do what the crowd wanted.

26 So they started to take Jesus to the place where they would kill him. On the way, they took hold of a man called Simon. This man was from the town called Cyrene. He was coming in from outside the city. The soldiers took the cross that Jesus was carrying on his shoulders. They said to Simon, 'Carry this for Jesus.' So, Simon carried the cross and he walked behind Jesus.

Jesus tells what will happen to Jerusalem

27 A very large crowd of people were following Jesus. There were many women among them. They were crying with loud voices. They were hitting their own bodies because they were very sad. 28 So Jesus turned round and he spoke to them. 'You women that live in Jerusalem, do not cry for me. Cry for yourselves and for your children. 29 Listen! Days will come when people will say, "Happy are those women that could not have babies. Happy are those women that never had babies to feed." 30 Then people will begin to say, "It would be better if we were dead." They will ask the mountains to fall on top of them. They will ask the hills to cover them up.

31 I am like a living tree, but men are doing this to me. Much worse things will happen! Those events will be like a fire that burns dry wood!'

The soldiers fix Jesus to a cross

32 The soldiers led two other men out of the prison. These men had done some bad things. The soldiers would kill them when they killed Jesus. 33 They brought them to the place that is called 'The Skull'. There they fixed Jesus to a cross. They also fixed the two bad men to crosses. One of these men was on the right side of Jesus. The other was on the left side of Jesus.

34 'Father', Jesus was saying, 'they do not know what they are doing. So please forgive them.'

The soldiers then picked up the clothes that he had worn. Each soldier would have a part. So, they played a game among themselves, to know who won each piece. 35 The people stood there. They were watching, but the rulers of the people were laughing at Jesus. 'He saved other people, they say. He should save his own life! So then we will know that he is the Messiah. We will know that God has chosen him.'

36 The soldiers also laughed at him. They came up to him and they offered him cheap alcohol to drink. 37 'If you are the King of the Jews', they said, 'save your own life.'

38 There was also a notice at the top of the cross. 'This is the King of the Jews', it said.

39 One of the men on a cross at the side of Jesus started to speak badly to him.

'If you are the Messiah', he shouted, 'save your own life and our lives too.'

40 But the other bad man told him that he should be quiet. 'You should be more afraid of God. After all, all three of us will die. 41 Both of us have done very bad things. So, it is right that we die. But this man has not done anything wrong.' 42 Then the man spoke to Jesus. 'Remember me, Jesus', he said, 'when you become king.'

43 'I promise you', Jesus replied, 'today you will be with me in Paradise.'

Jesus dies

44 It was now about midday, but the sun stopped shining. So, the whole country was in the dark for three hours. 45 Then the curtain in the special room inside the Great House of God tore into two parts. 46 And Jesus shouted loudly, 'Father, I give my spirit to you.' After he shouted this, he died.

47 There was a captain there. He was watching the soldiers while they were doing their job. He saw what had happened. 'How great and powerful God is', he said. 'I am sure that this man had not done anything wrong.'

48 A very big crowd had come together to watch the men die. They saw what had happened. Then they began to go home. They were very sad, so they were hitting their own bodies with their hands. 49 The friends of Jesus were standing a long way away. The women that had followed him from Galilee were also there. All these people also saw what happened to him.

Joseph buries Jesus

50 A man called Joseph was also there. He was one of a special group of important Jewish leaders. He was a good man that wanted to do right things.

51 Joseph had not agreed with them that Jesus should die. He was from the Jewish town called Arimathea. He was waiting for God to begin to rule his people.

52 So he went to see Pilate. He asked to have the dead body of Jesus. Pilate agreed to this. 53 Joseph then went to the place where Jesus died. He took the dead body down from the cross. He covered it in a long piece of good cloth. He put the body into a large hole in the rock. He had caused someone dig this hole in the rock. It was a place to bury a dead body. It was the first time that anyone had used it.

54 This all happened on the day when people prepared meals for the Jewish day for rest. It was nearly time for the day for rest to begin.

Jesus becomes alive again

55 So the women that had come with Jesus from Galilee followed Joseph. They saw the place where the hole in the rock was. They also saw Joseph put Jesus' body into the empty hole. 56 Then they returned to the house where they were staying in Jerusalem. There they prepared seeds with a strong smell and expensive oil that had a beautiful smell. Then they stopped work because their day for rest was starting. They were obeying the rules in the book of God.

Chapter 24

1 Very early on Sunday morning, they went to the place where Joseph had buried Jesus. They took with them the oil and seeds that they had prepared. 2 They arrived there. And they found that someone had rolled the stone away from in front of the hole. 3 Then they went inside the hole in the rock, but they did not find the body of the Lord Jesus there. 4 They did not understand this at all. But, while they were thinking about it, two men in bright clothes appeared. 5 So the women became very afraid and they bent down towards the ground.

'You should not be looking here for someone that is alive', they said to the women. 'This is a place to bury dead people. 6 Jesus is not here. He has become alive again. Remember what he said to you. He said it while he was still in Galilee. 7 He said, "It is necessary that someone should give me to bad men. They will kill me on a cross. Three days later I will become alive again." '

8 Then the women remembered what Jesus had said. 9 They left the empty hole. They went to the 11 men that he had chosen. They then told them what had happened. They also told all the other people that had followed him. 10 It was Mary Magdalene and Joanna that told the news about Jesus. Mary, the mother of James, and other women were with them. They also told the news to the 11 men. 11 But they did not believe what the women said. They thought that it was just a silly story.

12 But Peter got up and he ran to the hole in the rock. He bent down and he looked inside. He saw only the cloth that they had put round Jesus' body. There was nothing else. So he went home again. He was thinking about what might have happened.

Jesus shows himself to two people that always followed Jesus

13 Later on that same day, two of those that had followed Jesus were going to a village. The village was called Emmaus. This village was about 7 miles from Jerusalem. 14 They were talking to each other about all the things that had happened. 15 While they were talking about everything, Jesus himself came near to them. He started to walk along with them. 16 They saw him, but for some reason they did not recognise him. 17 'What are you talking about while you walk along the road?' he asked them.

They stood still and they seemed sad. 18 Then one of them called Cleopas answered him. 'Many things have happened in Jerusalem in the last few days', he said. 'Are you the only visitor here that does not know about it?'

19 'What things have happened?' he asked.

'The things that happened to Jesus that was from Nazareth. The Holy Spirit gave him messages to speak. He did many very great things and he spoke powerful messages. God showed that his message was true. All the people believed him. 20 Then the leaders of the priests and our rulers caught him. They gave him to the Roman ruler. They told the ruler that Jesus had done wrong things. They said that he should die. So, they killed him by fixing him to a cross. 21 But we had hoped that God would use him to save Israel.

Yes, there are other things too. Today is the third day since he died. 22 After all this, some women in our group surprised us today. Early this morning, they were at the place where someone had buried him. 23 They did not find his body there. And they returned to us with a report. "Some angels appeared to us", they said. "They have told us that Jesus is alive." 24 So some people from our group went to the place where someone had buried him. They found everything the same as the women had said. But they did not see Jesus.'

25 Jesus then spoke to them. 'Oh, how silly you are! You do not understand much. You are so slow to believe everything that God spoke by his servants. 26 You should have known that the Messiah had to die. Only then would he start to show how great and powerful he really is.' 27 He then began to explain what Moses had taught. Then he talked about the other men that had received messages from the Holy Spirit. He explained to them everything that the other men had written about him.

28 They came near to the village that they were going to. It seemed that Jesus would continue his journey. 29 But they stopped him from going on. 'Please stay in our home with us', they said. 'It is getting late, and it will soon be night.'

So, Jesus went into their house to stay with them. 30 He sat down to eat with them. Then he took the bread and he thanked God for it. He broke it up and then he gave it to them. 31 Then, their eyes became clear and they recognised him. Then immediately they could no longer see him. 32 They spoke to each other. 'It was like a fire that was burning in us. We felt it while we were walking along the road. We also felt it when he was talking to us about God's book.'

33 They immediately got up and they returned to Jerusalem. There they found the 11 men that Jesus had chosen. Other people were together with them. 34 All the people gave them the news. 'It is true! The Master is alive again. He has appeared to Simon!'

35 Then the two that had seen Jesus spoke to the whole group. They told them what had happened to them on the road. They also told how they recognised Jesus. They recognised him when he broke the bread.

Jesus appears to the group

36 While they were still speaking, Jesus himself stood among them. 'Do not have troubles in your mind', he said to them.

37 But the whole group was very surprised and afraid. They thought that they were seeing a spirit. 38 'You should not be so afraid', he said to them. 'You seem to be not sure in your minds about what you can see. 39 But look at my hands and my feet. It is I, myself. Touch me. So you will know that I am not a spirit. A spirit does not have a body with skin and bones as I do. You can see that I have.'

40 When he had said this, he showed them his hands and his feet. 41 This was such good news that they could not believe it. They were very happy.

'Do you have anything that I could eat?' he asked. 42 So they gave him a piece of fish that they had cooked. 43 And while they were watching, he took it. And he ate it.

44 'I told you about these things while I was still with you', he then said. 'Moses wrote about me in his book of rules. Other servants of God received messages about me. They then wrote in books what they heard. The book called Psalms also tells about me. Everything that they wrote had to happen. And it has become true.'

45 Then he helped them to understand the messages in God's book. 46 'This is what it says. The Messiah had to die. Then, after three days, he had to become alive again. 47 Now you must start to tell everyone the good news about me. Begin in Jerusalem and go to the people in every country of the world. Tell them that they should turn away from wrong things. Tell them that they should turn to God. When they do this, God will forgive them. He will forgive all the bad things that they have done. 48 You must tell people about everything that you have seen. And tell people about everything that you have heard. 49 Now listen! I will send down to you the gift that God my Father has promised you. So, you must stay in the city until this happens. Then the power of God will cover you.'

Jesus goes up to where God lives above

50 Then he led the group out of the city. They all went to a place near Bethany. He held up his hands over them all. He asked God to be good and kind to them. 51 While he was praying for them, he went up away from them. God lifted him up to his home above. 52 They all bent down on their knees. 'How great and powerful you are', they all said to Jesus. 'How great is your power. You are very beautiful and important.' Then they returned to Jerusalem and they were all very happy. 53 They spent all their time in the Great House of God. They were thanking God. And they were telling him how good he is.

John's Good News

John

About this book

John's Gospel is one of the four Gospels. 'Gospel' means 'good news'. The Gospels are the books that tell us about Jesus' life on earth. John was one of the three disciples who knew the Lord Jesus Christ best. John called himself 'the disciple that Jesus loved'. We think that John wrote his Gospel in the city called Ephesus. He wrote it some years after Matthew, Mark and Luke wrote their Gospels. He wrote it about 70 years after Christ's birth.

John's Gospel is different from the other three Gospels. It does not describe many things that the Gospels of Matthew, Mark and Luke do describe. But it does include many things that are not in the other Gospels. John tells us much more about who Jesus was. John shows us Jesus as the Son of God – the only person who can cause us to live. John teaches us more about God's Spirit, too.

At the beginning of his Gospel, John calls Jesus 'the Word'.

Chapter 1

The Word became human

1 In the beginning, the Word was already there. The Word was with God. The Word was God.

2 He was with God in the beginning. 3 God made all things by the Word. God did not make anything without him. 4It is the Word who causes us to live. And because of this, he was the light to all people. 5 The light shines in the dark, and the dark cannot put out the light.

6 God sent a man. His name was John. 7 He came to tell people about the light. God wanted everyone to believe what John said. 8 John himself was not that light. God sent him to tell people about the light. 9 The true light, that gives light to every person, was coming into the world.

10 The Word was in the world. God made the world by him. But the world did not know who he was. 11 He came to what was his own. But his own people did not accept him. 12 But some people did accept him. Some people did believe who he was. So, he gave authority to those people so that they could become God's children. 13 These children were not born in the usual human way. They were not born because of what any people wanted. They were not born because of what any man decided. No! They were born from God. 14 The Word became human. He lived among us. We saw how great and how good he is. He is great and good as only the Father's one true Son can be. He is completely kind. He is full of what is true.

15 John told people about the Word. He shouted, 'This is the man that I told you about. He comes after me. But he is greater than I am. He was there before I was born.' 16 The Word is full of everything that we need. All of us have received from him. We have received one good thing after another good thing. 17 God gave his rules by Moses. But God has been kind to us by Jesus Christ. God has brought his true message to us by Jesus Christ. 18 No person has ever seen God. But God's only true Son, who is so very near to the Father, has shown God to us.

John the Baptist was not Christ

19 The Jews' leaders sent priests and Levites from Jerusalem to ask John, 'Who are you?' This is what he said. 20 John did not refuse to answer. He said, 'I am not the Christ.' 21 So they asked him, 'So who are you? Are you Elijah?' John said, 'No, I am not.' They asked, 'Are you the Prophet?' John answered, 'No.' 22Then they said, 'Tell us who you are. We must say something to the people who sent us. What do you say about yourself?' 23 He said, 'I am the voice that shouts in the wild places. I shout, "Make a straight path for the Lord to come." That is what the prophet Isaiah said.' 24 The men who came to ask these questions were Pharisees. 25 They said to John, 'Why do you baptise people, if you are neither the Christ nor Elijah nor the Prophet?'

26 John replied, 'I baptise people with water. But there is someone here among you that you do not know.27 It is he who comes after me. I am not good enough even to take off his shoes.' 28 All these things happened at a place east from the Jordan river. It was a village called Bethany. John was baptising people there.

29 The next day, John saw Jesus, who was coming towards him. John said, 'Look! Here is God's Lamb (young sheep), who takes away the world's sin. 30 This is the man that I told you about. I told you, "It is he who comes after me. But he is greater than I am. He was already there before I was born." 31 I did not know him. But I had to show Israel's people who he was. That is why I am baptising people with water.'

32John told them, 'I saw God's Spirit come down from the sky. He came like a dove (a kind of bird) and he stayed on Jesus. 33 I would not have known who Jesus was. But God had sent me to baptise people with water. And God told me, "You will see the Spirit come down. He will stay on someone. That is the person who will baptise people with my Holy (completely good) Spirit." 34 Now I have seen this. So, I can tell you that this is God's Son.'

Jesus' first disciples

35 John and two of his disciples were standing there the next day. 36 John saw Jesus, who was walking past them. John said, 'Look! There is God's Lamb (young sheep).' 37 When the two disciples heard this, they followed Jesus.

38 Then Jesus turned round. He saw that they were following him. He asked them, 'What do you want?' They said, 'Rabbi (which means Teacher), where are you staying?' 39 Jesus replied, 'Come, and you will see.' So, they went with him. And they saw where he was staying. It was about 10 in the morning. And they stayed with him that day.

40 Andrew was one of the two disciples who had followed Jesus. They had heard what John had said about Jesus. Andrew was Simon Peter's brother. 41 The first thing that Andrew did was to find his brother, Simon. Andrew said to Simon, 'We have found the Messiah.' (Messiah means Christ.) 42 Then he brought Simon to Jesus. Jesus looked at Simon and he said, 'You are Simon, John's son. Your name will be Cephas.' This name is the same as Peter, which means 'rock'.

43 The next day, Jesus decided to go to Galilee. He met Philip, and Jesus said to Philip, 'Follow me.' 44Philip, like Andrew and Peter, came from the town called Bethsaida. 45 Philip went to find Nathanael. He told Nathanael, 'We have found the man that Moses wrote about in the book of God's rules. The prophets wrote about him, too. He is Jesus, who is Joseph's son, from Nazareth.' 46 Nathanael said, 'I did not think that anything good could come from Nazareth!' Philip replied, 'Come and see.'

47 Jesus saw Nathanael, who was coming towards him. Jesus said, 'Here is a completely honest man. That is what a person from Israel should really be like.' 48 Nathanael asked, 'How do you know me?' Jesus answered, 'I saw you before Philip asked you to come. I saw you when you were under the fig (fruit) tree.'49 Nathanael said, 'Teacher, you are the Son of God. You are the King of Israel.' 50 Jesus said to him, 'I told you that I saw you under the fig (fruit) tree. And you believe me because I told you that. But you will see much greater things than that.' 51 And Jesus said to him, 'I am telling you what is true. You will see heaven (the sky) open. You will see God's angels. They will be going up and they will be coming down on the Son of Man.'

Chapter 2

The marriage at Cana

1 Two days after that, there was a marriage. It was in the town called Cana, in Galilee. Jesus' mother was there. 2 People had asked Jesus and his disciples to come to the party also. 3 When people had drunk all the wine, Jesus' mother said to him, 'They have no more wine.' 4 Jesus replied, 'Woman, why do you tell me this? It is not my time yet.' 5 His mother said to the servants, 'Do anything that he wants you to do.'

6 There were 6 big pots there, which people had made from stone. Each pot could contain 20 to 30 gallons of water. These pots contained water so that the Jews could wash themselves. The Jews had special rules about when they must wash themselves. 7 Jesus said to the servants, 'Fill the pots with water.' So they filled the pots to the top. 8 Then he said, 'Now take some of the water from the pots and give it to the master of the party.' So they took the water.

9 And the master of the party tasted the water. But the water had become wine. The master did not know where the wine had come from. But the servants who had given it to him knew. Then the master asked the bridegroom (the man who had just married) to come to him. 10 The master said to him, 'Everyone else brings out the best wine first. Then, when people have had plenty to drink, they give people cheaper wine. But you are different. You have kept the best wine until now.'

11 Jesus did this first miracle at Cana, in Galilee. In this way, Jesus showed how great and how powerful he was. Then his disciples believed him.

Jesus goes to God's Great House (the temple)

12 After this, Jesus went to Capernaum. His mother, his brothers and his disciples went with him. They stayed there for a few days.

13 It was almost time for the Jews' Passover. So, Jesus went to Jerusalem. 14 In God's Great House (the temple), he found people who were selling cows, sheep and doves (a kind of bird). Other people were sitting at tables. They were buying and selling coins there. 15 So Jesus made a whip from some pieces of rope. Then he caused all the people to run out of God's Great House, with the sheep and the cows. He threw all the money-changers' coins on to the ground and he turned their tables over. 16 He said to the people who sold birds, 'Take them out of here! Do not make my Father's house into a market!' 17 His disciples remembered what it says in the Old Testament: 'My love for your house burns inside me like a fire.'

18 Then the Jews asked Jesus, 'If you have authority to do this, show us a miracle. Then we will know that you really do have authority.' 19 Jesus answered them, 'If you destroy this house of God, I will build it up again in 3 days.' 20 The Jews replied, 'A lot of men worked for 46 years to build this house. And you say that you will build it in 3 days all by yourself!' 21 But the house that Jesus was speaking about was his own body. 22 The disciples remembered this when Jesus had become alive again after his death. They remembered that he had said this. Then they believed the Old Testament. And they believed the words that Jesus had spoken.

23 While Jesus was in Jerusalem for the Passover, he did many miracles. Many people saw these miracles. As a result, they believed who Jesus is. 24 But Jesus himself did not trust the people. He knew what all people are really like. 25 He did not need anyone to tell him what people are like. He knew already what was really in all people.

Chapter 3

Jesus and Nicodemus

1 There was a Pharisee called Nicodemus. He was one of the Jews' leaders. 2 He came to Jesus at night. He said to Jesus, 'Rabbi (teacher), we know that God has sent you to us. We have seen the miracles that you are doing. Nobody could do these things unless God was with him.' 3 Jesus replied, 'I am telling you what is true. Unless a person is born from above, they cannot see God's kingdom.' 4 Nicodemus asked, 'How can a man be born when he is old? He cannot return into his mother's body. He cannot be born a second time.' 5 Jesus explained, 'I am telling you what is true. Unless a person is born by water and by God's Spirit, he cannot go into God's kingdom. 6 Human people give birth to what is human. But God's Spirit gives birth to spirit. 7 I said to you, "You must be born from above." What I said should not surprise you. 8 Everyone who is born by God's Spirit is like the wind. The wind blows where it wants. You can hear it. But you cannot say where it came from. And you cannot say where it is going.'

9 Nicodemus asked, 'How can this happen?' 10 Jesus replied, 'You are a teacher in Israel. You ought to understand these things! 11 I am telling you what is true. We speak about things that we know. We tell you what we have seen. But even then, you people do not believe our words.

12 I have told you about things that happen in this world. And you do not believe me. But I am telling you about things that happen in heaven. So, I do not think that you will ever believe me about those things. 13 The Son of Man came down from heaven. Nobody else has gone up to heaven except him. 14 And people will lift up the Son of Man, as Moses lifted up the snake in the wild, dry place. Moses made a snake out of metal and he held it up to show it to Israel's people. In the same way, people will lift up the Son of Man for everyone to see.

15 As a result, everyone who believes him will be able to live always. 16 God loved the people in the world so much that he gave his one and only Son on their behalf. So, as a result, everyone who believes in the Son will not die. Instead, they will live always.'

17 God did not send his Son into the world because he wanted to punish people. No, God sent his Son to save the people in the world. 18 God will not decide to punish anyone who believes the Son. But God has already decided that he must punish some people. Some people refuse to believe who his one and only Son is. God must punish anyone who refuses to believe that.

19 This is why God has already decided to punish some people. It is because light has come into the world. But people did not love the light. They loved the dark instead. That was because they were doing bad things. 20 Everyone who does bad things hates the light. A person like that will not come to the light because he is afraid. He does not want everyone to see that he has done bad things. 21 But every person who obeys everything true comes to the light. So then the light will show that he was doing God's work. Everyone can see that he was obeying God.

Jesus and John the Baptist

22 After this, Jesus and his disciples went to the country places in Judea. Jesus stayed there with his disciples for some time, and they baptised people there. 23 John was baptising people too. He was at Aenon near Salim because there was a lot of water there. People were coming to him and John was baptising them. 24 (This was before the rulers put John in a prison.) 25 A certain Jew began to argue with John's disciples. They were arguing about some rules. Those rules told people when and how they should wash. 26 The disciples came to John. They said to him, 'Teacher, remember the man, Jesus that you spoke to us about. He was with you on the other side of the Jordan river. Now he is baptising people and everyone is going to him.'

27 John replied, 'A man can receive only what God gives to him. 28 You yourselves will remember what I said. I said, "I am not the Christ, but God sent me before the Christ." 29 The bride (woman who is marrying) is the bridegroom's (man who is marrying her). But the bridegroom's friend stands near him and he listens. That friend is very happy when he hears the bridegroom's voice. I am like that friend, so I am completely happy now. 30 He must become greater, but I must become less important.

31 He who comes from above is greater than all things. A person who comes from the earth belongs to the earth. A person like that speaks only about things that belong to the earth. He who comes from heaven is greater than all things. 32 He tells what he has seen. He tells what he has heard. But nobody believes what he is saying. 33 Anyone who does believe his message has said, "Yes, God is true." 34 He that God has sent speaks God's words. God fills him completely with God's Spirit. 35 The Father loves the Son. He has given the Son authority over all things. 36 Anyone who believes the Son is alive for always. But anyone who will not obey the Son will never really live. God will continue to be angry with a person who refuses to obey the Son.'

Chapter 4

Jesus talks to a woman from Samaria

1 The Pharisees heard the news that many people were joining Jesus' group of disciples. They heard that Jesus was baptising more disciples than John. 2 (But really Jesus himself did not baptise anyone. It was only Jesus' disciples who baptised people.) 3 So, when the Lord knew about this, he left Judea. He returned to Galilee. 4 On his way, Jesus had to go through Samaria.

5 He came to a town in Samaria called Sychar. It was near to the piece of land that Jacob had given to his son, Joseph, many years earlier. 6-8 Jacob's well was there. Jesus was tired after his journey. He sat down by the well. It was about 6 in the evening. His disciples had gone to buy food in the town. A woman from Samaria came to the well because she wanted to get some water. Jesus said to her, 'Give a drink to me.' 9 The woman from Samaria said to him, 'You are a Jew and I am a woman from Samaria. Why do you ask me for a drink?' (The Jews will not usually even talk to people who belong to Samaria.)

10 Jesus answered the woman, 'You do not know what God can give. I asked you to give a drink to me.

But you do not know who I am. If you did know, you would have asked me to give a drink to you. Then I would have given water to you that would cause you to live.' 11 The woman said, 'Sir, you have no bucket, and the well is deep. Where can you get this water that would cause me to live? 12 Jacob, our ancestor, gave this well to us. He, his sons, and his sheep and goats and cows all drank its water. Are you saying that you are greater than Jacob?'

13 Jesus answered, 'Everyone who drinks from this well will get thirsty again. 14 But I can give a different kind of water. Whoever drinks that kind of water will never get thirsty again. The water that I will give to him will become a well inside him. That well will continue to give fresh water that will cause him to live always.' 15 The woman said to him, 'Sir, give this water to me. Then I will never get thirsty again. And I will not have to continue to come here so that I can get water.'

16 Jesus said to her, 'Go, fetch your husband. Then return here.' 17 The woman replied, 'I have no husband.' Jesus said to her, 'You are right when you say, "I have no husband." 18 The fact is that you have had 5 husbands. And now you live with a man who is not your husband. What you have said is quite true.' 19 The woman said to him, 'Sir, I can see that you are a prophet. 20 Our ancestors worshipped on this mountain. But you Jews say that Jerusalem is the right place to worship God.'

21 Jesus spoke to her with authority, 'Believe me, woman. Soon you will not worship the Father either on this mountain or at Jerusalem. 22 You people from Samaria do not really know what you worship. But we Jews do know what we worship. The way that God has made to save people comes from the Jews. 23 But soon, people will really worship the Father. Really, it is that time already. Those people who really want to worship the Father will worship him from their spirits. The Father looks for people who will worship him like that. 24 God is spirit. Those people who worship him must worship from their spirits. They must really want to worship God.' 25 The woman said to Jesus, 'I know that the Messiah will come. He is called Christ. When he comes, he will explain everything to us.' 26 Then Jesus replied, 'I, who am speaking to you, am he.'

The disciples return

27 At this moment, his disciples returned. They were surprised to see that Jesus was talking to a woman. But none of them asked him, 'What do you want?' or, 'Why are you talking to her?' 28 Then the woman left her water-pot and she returned to the town. She said to the people there, 29 'Come! See a man who told me everything about myself. He told me all the things that I have ever done! He must be the Christ!' 30 So they left the town and they went to find Jesus.

31 While the woman was away, the disciples said to Jesus, 'Teacher, eat something.' 32 But he said to them, 'I have food that I can eat. But you do not know about it.' 33 So the disciples asked each other, 'Could someone have brought food to him?' 34 Jesus said to them, 'I must obey him who sent me. I must finish the work that he has given to me to do. That is my food. 35 You say, "The plants in the farmers' fields will be ready for the harvest after 4 more months." But I say that you should open your eyes. Look at the fields. The plants are ready for the harvest now. 36 God is paying the workers already. They are bringing in the fruit. They are bringing in people who will live always. The person who plants the seeds will be very happy. And the person who brings in the fruit will be very happy too. Both of them will be happy as a result of their work. 37 What people say is true. One person plants the seeds and another person brings in the fruit. 38 I sent you to fetch people like fruit that you have not worked for. Other people did the work. You have brought in the fruit (people) that they worked for.'

39 Many of the people who lived in that town in Samaria heard the woman's story. She had said to them, 'He told me all the things that I have ever done!' And because of this, they believed Jesus. 40 So when these people from Samaria came to Jesus, they asked him to stay with them. And he stayed there for two more days. 41 Many more people believed Jesus when they listened to his own words. 42 The people said to the woman, 'Now we believe him because we ourselves have heard him. Now we do not believe only because of what you said. This man really is the man who will save the world. We know that now.'

Jesus makes an officer's son well

43 After two days, Jesus left there and he went to Galilee. 44 (Jesus himself had said earlier, 'When a prophet visits places near his own home, the people there never believe him. The people there never think that a prophet from their place could be important.') 45 When he arrived in Galilee, the people there were happy to see him. They had been at the Passover also. And they had seen all the things that he had done at Jerusalem.

46 Jesus visited Cana, in Galilee, again. This was the town where he had changed the water into wine. A certain man who was one of the king's officers was there. This officer had a son who was at Capernaum. His son was very ill. 47 This man had heard the news that Jesus had arrived in Galilee from Judea. So, he went to Jesus. He asked Jesus to go to Capernaum, where the man's son was dying. He asked Jesus strongly to make his son well. 48 Then Jesus said to him, 'You people want me to do great miracles that will surprise you. Unless you see these great miracles, none of you will ever believe.' 49 The king's officer said to Jesus, 'Sir, come with me now before my child dies.' 50 Jesus replied, 'Go home. Your son will live.' The man believed what Jesus had said. And he started to go home. 51 While he was travelling home, his servants met him. They told him, 'Your boy will live.' 52 He asked them, 'At what time did he start to get well?' They told him, 'He stopped being ill yesterday, at 7 in the evening.' 53 Then the father remembered that time. It was the time when Jesus had spoken to him. It was when Jesus had said, 'Your son will live.' So, the man and all his family believed. 54 This was the second miracle that Jesus did after he returned from Judea to Galilee.

Chapter 5

Jesus makes a man able to walk

1 Sometime after that, Jesus went to Jerusalem, because it was time for one of the Jews' festivals.

2 There is a pool near the Sheep Gate in Jerusalem. Its name in the Jews' language is Bethesda. Round the pool, there is a building with 5 places that have a roof over them. 3 A large number of sick people were lying in these places. Some of them could not see. Some of them could not walk. Some of them could not move themselves properly. They were waiting for when the water started to move. 4 An angel went down into the pool at certain times and he moved the water. Then all the sick people tried to get into the pool. The first person who got into the water became well. That person became well, whatever his illness was.

5 One man there had been ill for 38 years. 6 Jesus saw this man, who was lying there. Jesus knew that the man had been ill like this for a very long time. So he asked the man, 'Do you want to get well?' 7 The sick man said, 'Sir, I do not have anyone who will help me. I need somebody who will put me into the pool. When the water starts to move, I try to get in. But someone else always gets in before me.' 8 Then Jesus said to him, 'Get up! Pick up your bed and walk.' 9 The man became well immediately. He picked up his bed and he walked. The day when this happened was a Sabbath day.

10 So, the Jews' leaders spoke to the man that Jesus had made well. They said to him, 'You must not carry your bed on the Sabbath day. You are not obeying the rules.' 11 He replied, 'A man made me well. That man said to me, "Pick up your bed and walk." ' 12 So they asked him, 'Who is this man? Who said to you, "Pick up your bed and walk"?' 13 The man that Jesus had made well did not know. He did not know who it was. Jesus had gone away into the crowd that was there.

14 Sometime after that, Jesus found the man in God's Great House (the temple). Jesus said to him, 'See, you have become well. Stop doing wrong things. If you do not stop, something worse may happen to you.' 15 Then the man went to the Jews' leaders. He told them that it was Jesus. It was Jesus who had made him well. 16 The Jews' leaders were angry because Jesus had made a man well on the Sabbath day. So, they began to cause a lot of trouble for Jesus. 17 But Jesus said to them, 'My Father is still working, and I am working too.' 18 So, because Jesus said this, the Jews' leaders got even angrier. They wanted even more to kill him. He not only worked on the Sabbath day. He was also calling God his own Father, so he was making himself equal with God.

19 So, Jesus answered them, 'I am telling you what is true. The Son can do nothing by himself. He sees what the Father does. And he can do only those same things. What the Father does, the Son does also. 20 The Father loves the Son. So, he shows the Son all the things that he himself does. And the Father will show the Son even greater things than these. These greater things will surprise you even more. 21 The Father raises dead people, to make them alive again. In the same way, the Son makes alive whoever he chooses.

22 More than that, the Father does not judge anyone. He has given authority to the Son completely so that the Son will judge all people. 23 So then all people will know how great the Son is. They know that the Father is very great. In the same way, they will know also that the Son is very great. Some people may refuse to think that the Son is great or important. But really, those people are thinking the same things about the Father, because he sent the Son. 24 I am telling you what is true. Everyone who hears my words should believe the Father. They should believe him who sent me. If they do believe, they are alive for always. God will not punish them because of the wrong things that they have done. They were dead, but now they have become alive.'

25 'I am telling you what is true. A time will happen soon when the dead people will hear the voice of the Son of God. Really, it is that time already. Those people who hear the Son's voice will live. 26 The Father himself can cause people to live. In the same way, he has made the Son able to do this also. The Son himself can cause people to live. 27 Also, the Father has given authority to the Son so that he judges people. The Son says what is right for each person. That is because he is the Son of Man. 28 Do not be surprised by this. There will be a time when all the dead people under the ground will hear the Son's voice. 29 They will come out from the ground. Those people who have done good things will rise. They will rise so that they can live with God always. Those people who have done bad things will rise. But they will rise so that God can punish them.'

Things that show who Jesus really is

30 'I can do nothing by myself. I hear what the Father says to me. Then, because of what he says, I judge. So, what I judge is right. I am not trying to do what I myself want. The Father sent me. And I want to do what he wants. 31 If I said great things about myself, my words would not be true. 32 But there is someone else who speaks about me. What he says about me is true. I know that. 33 You have sent your people to ask John about me. What he has told you about me is true. 34 I do not need any man to speak on my behalf. No, but I am telling you this only so that God will be able to save you. 35 John was like a light that shone brightly. And for a certain time, you enjoyed the light that he gave.'

36 'But other things show who I am. My Father has given work to me so that I could finish it. And these things that I do, they speak about me. They speak more strongly than John's words. They show that the Father has sent me. 37 Also, the Father himself, who sent me, has spoken about me. You have never heard his voice. And you have never seen his shape. 38 His word does not stay inside you. You do not believe the Person that he sent. That is why his word does not stay in you. 39 You study the Scriptures (Old Testament) carefully. You think that they will cause you to live. And the Scriptures (Old Testament) themselves tell you about me. 40 But you refuse to come to me so that you could really live! 41 'I am not wanting people to say great things about me. If people say great things about me, that is not important to me. 42 But I know what kind of people you are. I know that you do not really love God or other people. 43 I have come with my Father's authority, but you do not accept me. But if someone else comes with his own authority, you will accept him.

44 When you say good things about each other, it makes you happy. But you do not try to make God happy. You do not want the only God to say good things about you. That is why you cannot believe me. 45 But I will not tell the Father that you are wrong. Do not think that I will do that. No, because it is Moses who will do that. You hope that Moses will help you. But he will tell the Father that you are wrong. 46 If you had really believed Moses, you would have believed me. That is because Moses wrote about me. 47 But you do not believe what Moses wrote. So, you cannot believe what I say.'

Chapter 6

Jesus feeds 5000 men and their families

1 Sometime after that, Jesus went across Lake Galilee, which is also called Lake Tiberias. 2 A large crowd of people followed him, because of the mir3 Jesus went up a hill and he sat down there with his disciples. 4 It was nearly the time for the Jews' Passover Festival.

5 Jesus looked up. He saw a large crowd of people who were coming towards him. Then he said to Philip, 'Where can we buy enough bread to feed all these people?' 6 Jesus himself already knew what he would do. But he asked Philip this question for a reason. He wanted to know what Philip would say. 7 Philip answered, 'A man might work for 8 months. But, he still would not have enough money to buy bread for all these people. Still there would not be enough bread for each person here to have a little piece.' 8 Then Andrew, another one of Jesus' disciples, spoke. He was Simon Peter's brother. He said to Jesus, 9 'Here is a boy who has 5 small loaves and two small fish. But certainly, they will not be enough food for so many people.'

10 Jesus said, 'Cause the people to sit down.' There was plenty of grass in that place, so the people sat down. There were about 5000 men. 11 Jesus took the loaves and he thanked God for them. Then he broke the loaves into pieces. He passed them to all the people who were sitting there. Everyone had all the bread that they wanted to eat. Jesus did the same with the fish. 12 When all the people had eaten enough food, Jesus spoke. He said to his disciples, 'Do not waste anything. Pick up all the pieces that the people have not eaten.' 13 So the disciples picked up all the pieces. They filled 12 baskets with the pieces of bread that the people had not eaten.

14 The people had seen this miracle that Jesus had done. So, they began to talk about it. They said, 'Certainly, this man is the Prophet who must come into the world.' 15 The people wanted to take Jesus so that they could make him their king. But Jesus knew what they wanted to do. So, he went away alone to the hills again.

Jesus walks on the water

16 When it was evening, the disciples went down to the lake. 17 They got into a boat and they started to travel towards Capernaum. It was dark then and Jesus still had not come to them. 18 A very strong wind was blowing and so the water was moving powerfully. 19 The disciples were trying to pull the boat through the water with oars (special long, flat pieces of wood). When they had gone 3 or 4 miles (5-6 kilometres), they saw Jesus. He was coming near to the boat and he was walking on the water. And they were very afraid. 20 But he said to them, 'It is I. Do not be afraid.' 21 So, the disciples were happy to let Jesus get into the boat with them. Immediately, the boat came to the place where they wanted to be.

The crowd looks for Jesus

22 The crowd of people had stayed on the other side of the lake. The next day, they looked round. They saw that the only boat had gone. They knew that the disciples had taken it. And they knew that Jesus had not gone with his disciples.

23 (But other boats from Tiberias had arrived near to the place where all the people had eaten the bread. They had eaten that bread after the Lord had thanked God for it.) 24 The crowd saw that neither Jesus nor his disciples were there. So, they got into the boats and they went to Capernaum. They were looking for Jesus.

Jesus is the bread that causes us to live

25 The people found Jesus on the other side of the lake. So they asked him, 'Teacher, when did you arrive here?' 26 Jesus answered, 'I am telling you what is true. You saw me do miracles.

But you are not looking for me because of that. No, you are looking for me because you ate the loaves. You ate all the bread that you wanted to eat. So then you were full. 27 Do not work to get the food that does not continue. Instead, work to get the food that does continue.

Work to get the food that causes you to live always. God, the Father, has put his mark of authority upon the Son. That is why the Son of Man will give this food to you.'

28 Then the people asked him, 'How can we do the work that God wants us to do?' 29 Jesus answered, 'Believe him that God has sent to you. That is the work that God wants you to do.' 30 So then the people asked him, 'What miracle will you do? If we see a miracle, we will believe you. What will you do? 31 Our ancestors ate manna (special food from God) in the wild, dry places. As it says in the Old Testament, "God gave bread to them from heaven so that they could eat it." ' 32 Jesus said to them, 'I am telling you what is true. It was not Moses who gave that bread to you from heaven. No, but it is my Father who really gives to you the bread from heaven. 33 God's bread is he who comes down from heaven. He causes people in the world to live.' 34 So they said to him, 'Sir, give this bread to us now and always.'

35 Then Jesus said to them, 'I am the bread that causes people to live. Anyone who comes to me will never be hungry. Anyone who believes me will never be thirsty. 36 But you have seen me and still you do not believe me. I have told you that before. 37 Everyone that the Father gives to me will come to me. When anyone comes to me, I will never send that person away. 38 I have not come down from heaven to do what I myself choose to do. No, instead I have come to obey him who sent me. 39 He who sent me does not want me to lose anyone. He does not want me to lose even one of the people that he has given to me. He wants me to raise all of them up on the last day, so that they live with me always. 40 These are the people who will be alive for always: Everyone who sees the Son and believes him. And I will raise them up on the last day. That is what my Father wants.'

41 Jesus had said, 'I am the bread that came down from heaven.' When he said this, the Jews did not like it. So, they started to say bad things about Jesus. 42 They said, 'But this is Jesus, the son of Joseph. We know his father and his mother. So, he should not say that he came down from heaven.'

43 Jesus answered, 'Stop saying these bad things to each other. 44 The Father has sent me. Nobody can come to me unless the Father brings them to me. And I will raise that person up on the last day, so that they live with me always. 45 The prophets wrote in the Old Testament, "God will teach all the people." These are the people who come to me: Everyone who hears the Father and learns from him. 46 I do not mean that anyone has seen the Father. Nobody has seen the Father except the Person who has come from God. It is he who has seen the Father. 47 I am telling you what is true. The person who believes this is alive for always. 48 I am the bread that causes you to live. 49 Your ancestors ate the manna (special food from God) in the wild, dry places, but they died. 50 This bread that comes down from heaven is different. Anyone who eats this bread will not die. 51 I am the bread that is alive. This bread came down from heaven. If anyone eats this bread, he will live always. The bread that I will give is my body. I will give it so that all people in the world can live.'

52 Then the Jews became angry and they quarrelled with each other even more. They said, 'This man cannot give his body to us so that we can eat it!' 53 Jesus said to them, 'I tell you what is true. You must eat the body of the Son of Man and you must drink his blood. Unless you do those things, you are not really alive. 54 Every person needs to eat my body and they need to drink my blood. If they do those things, they are alive for always. And I will raise them up on the last day.

55 My body is proper food and my blood is proper drink.

56 Every person needs to eat my body and they need to drink my blood. If a person does that, that person lives in me. And I live in them. 57 The Father, who is alive, sent me. And I live because of him. In the same way, anyone who eats me will live because of me. 58 This is the bread that came down from heaven. It is not like the manna (special food from God) that your ancestors ate. They ate it but they died. But the person who eats this bread will live always.'

59 Jesus said these things while he was teaching in the synagogue at Capernaum.

Many disciples go away from Jesus

60 Many of Jesus' disciples did not like these words. They said, 'This thing that he teaches is too difficult. Nobody can agree with it!'

61 Jesus himself knew that the disciples were arguing. He did not need anyone to tell him. He said to them, 'This seems to make you surprised and angry. 62 So think about this. The Son of Man goes up again to the place where he was before. And you see him go up. Think about how you would feel then. 63 It is the Spirit that causes you to live. The body alone is worth nothing. The words that I have spoken to you are spirit. They cause you to live. 64 But some of you do not believe.' Jesus had known from the beginning which of them would not believe. Also, he had always known who would sell him to his enemies. 65 Then Jesus said these words: 'So I told you that only the Father can bring people to me. Nobody can come to me unless the Father makes them able to come.'

66 From that time, many of Jesus' disciples left him. They did not follow him any longer. 67 Then Jesus asked the 12 special disciples, 'Do you want to go away, too?' 68 Simon Peter answered him, 'Lord, we do not know whom we would go away to. You have the words that cause people to live always. 69 And we believe that you are the Holy One. We believe that you have come from God. We are sure about that.' 70 Jesus replied, 'I have chosen the 12 of you. But one of you is a devil (bad spirit from Satan)!' 71 He was speaking about Judas, the son of Simon Iscariot. Judas was one of the 12 special disciples. But after this time he would sell Jesus to Jesus' enemies.

Chapter 7

Jesus and his brothers

1 After this, Jesus visited many places in Galilee. He did not want to visit Judea because the Jews' leaders there wanted to kill him. 2 It was almost time for the Jews' Festival of Tabernacles. 3 So Jesus' brothers said to him, 'You should leave this place and you should go to Judea. Then your disciples can see the great things that you do. 4 Nobody does things secretly if he wants everyone to know him. You are doing these things, so you should show yourself to everybody.' 5 Even his own brothers did not believe about him.

6 So Jesus answered, 'It is not the right time for me yet. But any time is right for you. 7 People who belong to this world cannot hate you. But they hate me. The things that they do are wrong. And I show that those things are wrong. That is why they hate me. 8 You go to the festival. I will not go to it yet because it is not the right time for me yet.' 9 Jesus said this and then he stayed in Galilee.

Jesus goes to the Festival of Tabernacles

10 Sometime after his brothers had gone, Jesus went to the festival also. But he did not let everybody know that he was going. Instead, he went secretly. 11 The Jews' leaders were looking for him at the festival. They asked, 'Where is that man?' 12 Small groups in the crowd were talking quietly. Some people said, 'He is a good man.' But other people said, 'No, he is telling the people things that are not true.' 13 But nobody spoke loudly about him, because they were afraid of the Jews' leaders.

14 When about half of the time for the festival had finished, Jesus went to God's Great House (the temple). He started to teach there.

15 The Jews' leaders were very surprised. They asked, 'How does this man know so much? He has not learned in our schools.' 16 Jesus answered, 'What I teach does not come from me. No, it comes from him who sent me. 17 Anyone can choose to do what God wants. Those people will know about what I teach. They will know whether it comes from God. And they will know if it comes from my own thoughts.

18 A person who teaches his own ideas wants people to think great things about him. But a person who wants to show great things about someone else is different. A person like that wants people to think great things about him who sent him. A person like that is honest and there is nothing false in him. 19 Moses gave God's rules to you. But not one of you obeys those rules. Why are you trying to kill me?'

20 The crowd answered, 'You have a demon (bad spirit from Satan). Who is trying to kill you?' 21 Jesus replied, 'I have done one miracle on the Sabbath day, and all of you were surprised.

22 But you will circumcise a boy on the Sabbath day. Moses told you that you must circumcise your sons. That is why you will do it. Your ancestors did it even before Moses was born. 23 You will circumcise a boy on the Sabbath day so that you obey Moses' rules. So you should not be angry with me because I made a man completely well on the Sabbath day. 24 Do not judge about things because of what they may seem to be. Instead, judge about things because of what is right.'

The people talk about whether Jesus is the Messiah

25 Some of the people in Jerusalem began to say, 'This is the man that the leaders want to kill. 26 But look! He is speaking to the crowds. And the leaders are not saying anything to him! Perhaps they think that he is really the Christ! 27 But we know where this man came from. When the Christ comes, nobody will know that. Nobody will know where he has come from.'

28 Jesus was teaching in God's Great House (the temple). He shouted, 'Yes, you know me. And you know where I came from. I have not come because I myself decided to come. He who sent me is true. You do not know him. 29 But I know him because I have come from him. He sent me.' 30 When they heard this, they tried to take him to a prison. But nobody put their hands on him, because it was not the right time. It was not the right time for that to happen. 31 But many people in the crowd believed him. They said, 'This man has done so many miracles. Nobody could do more miracles. Surely he is the Christ!'

32 The Pharisees heard what the crowds were saying quietly about Jesus. Then the most important priests and the Pharisees sent some soldiers to take him away. 33 Jesus said, 'I will be with you for only a short time. Then I will go to him who sent me. 34 You will look for me, but you will not find me. You cannot go to the place where I will be.' 35 The Jews' leaders asked each other, 'What is he trying to tell us? Where can he go so that we cannot find him? Perhaps he will go to our people who live among the Greeks. Perhaps he will go to teach the Greeks. 36 He says, "You will look for me, but you will not find me." And he says, "You cannot go to the place where I will be." What does he mean?'

Streams of the water that causes people to live

37 The last day of the festival was the most important day. On that day, Jesus stood up and he spoke with a loud voice. He said, 'If anyone is thirsty, he should come to me. He should come to me and he should drink. 38 As it says in the Old Testament, "God will cause streams of water to pour out from anyone who believes me. Streams of the water that causes people to live will come out from inside that person." ' 39 Jesus was speaking about God's Spirit, who would come to people sometime after that. Those people who believed Jesus would receive God's Spirit then. But God had not given his Spirit yet, because he had not raised Jesus yet. He had not yet raised Jesus, so that Jesus could be in heaven with him again.

The people argue

40 Some of the people in the crowd heard Jesus say these words. Then they said, 'This man really is the Prophet that we were waiting for!' 41 Other people said, 'This man is the Christ.' But some people said, 'The Prophet will not come from Galilee!

42 The Old Testament says that the Christ will come from King David's family. He will come from Bethlehem, the town where David lived.' 43 So, the crowd of people could not agree about Jesus. 44 Some people wanted to take him to a prison. But nobody put their hands on him to take him away.

45 The soldiers returned to the most important priests and the Pharisees. They asked the soldiers, 'Why did you not bring him here?' 46 The soldiers answered, 'Nobody has ever spoken like this man speaks.' 47 The Pharisees replied, 'He seems to have caused you to believe these silly things!

48 None of the Pharisees or the leaders believes him. Surely, you know that! 49 But this crowd does not know Moses' rules. So, God will cause very bad things to happen to them.' 50 Nicodemus was one of the Pharisees. He was the man who had gone to see Jesus before. He said to the other people, 51 'Our rules say that we must listen to a man first. We must find out first what he has done. Only then can we judge him.' 52 They answered, 'Perhaps you come from Galilee, too! Study the Scriptures (Old Testament). You will learn from them that no prophet ever comes from Galilee.' 53 Then everyone went to his own home.

Chapter 8

The woman who was with a man who was not her husband

1 But Jesus went to the Mount (mountain) of Olives. 2 Early the next morning, he returned to God's Great House (the temple). All the people came to him. He sat down and he began to teach them.

3 The Pharisees and the scribes (men who taught God's rules) brought a woman to him. They had found her with another man. She was having sex with a man who was not her husband. They caused her to stand in front of all the people there. 4 They said to Jesus, 'Teacher, we found this woman. She was having sex with a man who was not her husband. 5 Moses' rules say that we should throw stones at this kind of woman, to kill her. What do you say about this?' 6 They asked this question for a reason. They wanted Jesus to say something that they could use against him. But Jesus bent himself down. He started to write on the ground with his finger.

7 They continued to ask him questions. Then he stood up. He said to them, 'If any one of you has never done anything wrong, he can throw the first stone at her.' 8 He bent himself down again and he wrote on the ground. 9 When they heard this, they began to leave. They went one at a time. The older ones went first. So then Jesus was alone with the woman. She was still standing there. 10 Jesus stood up. He said to her, 'Woman, where are they? There seems to be nobody still here who wants to punish you.' 11 She said, 'There is nobody, Sir.' So Jesus said, 'And I do not want to punish you. Go away and do not do wrong things again.'

Jesus is the light of the world

12 Jesus spoke to the people again. He said, 'I am the light of the world. Anyone who becomes my disciple will never walk in the dark. No, he will have the light that causes people to live.' 13 The Pharisees began to argue with him. They said, 'You are saying things about yourself. But you are only one man. So, what you say is not certainly true.'

14 Jesus answered, 'What I say is true. Even if I do speak on my own behalf, my words are true. I know where I came from. I know where I will go. But you do not know where I came from. You do not know where I will go. 15 You judge in a human way. I do not judge anyone. 16 But if I did judge anyone, I would judge correctly. That is because I am not alone. The Father, who sent me, is with me. 17 Your rules say, "There must be two people who agree about something. If there are two people, their words are true." 18 I speak on my own behalf. The Father, who sent me, speaks about me also.'

19 Then they asked him, 'Where is your Father?' Jesus answered, 'You do not know either me or my Father. If you knew me, you would know my Father also.' 20 Jesus said all these words while he taught in God's Great House (the temple). He was near the place where they kept the gifts of money. Nobody took him away to a prison, because it was not the right time for that yet.

Jesus says that he comes from above

21 Jesus said to them again, 'I will go away and you will look for me. But you are sinful and you will die sinful. You cannot go where I will go.' 22 So, the Jews' leaders said to each other, 'Perhaps he means that he will kill himself. He says, "You cannot go where I will go." Perhaps that is why he says this.'

23 Jesus answered, 'You belong to the things down here. But I come from above. You belong to this world, but I do not belong to this world. 24 That is why I told you this. I told you that you would die sinful. You must believe that "I am". If you will not believe, you will die sinful.'

25 Then they asked him, 'Who are you?' Jesus answered, 'I have told you who I am from the beginning. That is who I am. 26 I have many things to say about you. I must judge about many things that you do. But he who sent me is true. I tell the world only what I have heard from him.' 27 They did not understand that he was speaking to them about the Father. 28 So Jesus said, 'You will lift up the Son of Man. Then you will know that "I am". And you will know that I do nothing by myself. I say only what the Father has taught me to say. 29 He who sent me is with me. He has not caused me to be alone, because I obey him always. I do always the things that he wants me to do.' 30 Many people who heard Jesus say these things believed him.

What is true will make you free

31 Then Jesus spoke to the Jews who believed him. He said, 'Continue to obey the words that I have spoken to you. If you continue to do that, you are really my disciples. 32 And you will know what is true. And what is true will make you free.' 33 They answered him, 'We are Abraham's grandchildren. We have never been anyone's slaves. But you say to us, "You will become free." What do you mean?'

34 Jesus answered them, 'I am telling you what is true. Everyone who does sinful things is a slave to sin. 35 A slave does not belong to a family for always. But a son does belong to a family for always. 36 So, if the Son makes you free, you will really be free. 37 I know that you are Abraham's grandchildren. But you are trying to kill me, because you have no room in yourselves for my words. 38 I speak about what my Father has shown me. But you do what you have heard from your father.'

39 They answered, 'Abraham is our father!' Jesus replied, 'If you were really Abraham's children, you would be like him. You would do the same things that he did. 40 I am a man who has told you only true things. I have told you the true things that I have heard from God. But you want to kill me. Abraham did not do anything like that! 41 You do the same things that your father does.' They said to him, 'God himself is our only Father, and we are his proper sons!'

42 Jesus said to them, 'If God was really your Father, you would love me. I came from God and now I am here. I did not come because it was my own idea. No, but God sent me. 43 Why do you not understand what I say? It is because you cannot really hear my message. 44 You are the children of your father, the Devil. And you want to do the things that he wants. From the beginning, he was someone who killed people. He did not continue with what is true. There is nothing true in him. He says things that are not true. And then he is showing what he himself is like. He is the father of everything that is not true. 45 But I tell you what is true. And that is why you do not believe me. 46 None of you can show that I have done anything wrong. You should believe me, because I am telling you true things. 47 Someone who is God's hears God's words. But you are not God's. That is why you do not hear.'

48 The Jews answered him, 'What we say about you is right! You are from Samaria and you have a demon (bad spirit from Satan) in you!' 49 Jesus replied, 'There is no demon in me.

'But I want people to know how great and how good my Father is. And you want people to think bad things about me. 50 I myself am not wanting people to think great things about me. There is someone who does want people to think great things about me. And it is he who judges correctly about me.

51 I am telling you what is true. If anyone obeys my words, he will never die.' 52 The Jews shouted, 'Now we know that a demon (bad spirit) lives in you! Abraham and all the prophets died. But you say, "Anyone who obeys my words will never die!

53 You cannot be greater than our father Abraham, who died! You cannot be greater than all the prophets, who died! Who do you think that you are?'

54 Jesus replied, 'If I myself wanted people to think great things about me that would be worth nothing.

But it is my Father who wants that. And you say that he is your God. 55 You have never known him, but I know him. I might say, "I do not know him." But then I would be saying something that is not true. So, I would be like you. But I do know him, and I obey his words. 56 Your father Abraham knew that I would come. He knew that he would see that time. He knew that he would be very happy then. He did see that time, and he was very happy.'

57 The Jews said, 'You are not 50 years old yet. But you say that you have seen Abraham!' 58 Jesus said, 'I am telling you what is true. Before Abraham was even born, "I am".' 59 Then they picked up stones so that they could throw them at him. But Jesus hid himself, and he went out of God's Great House (the temple).

Chapter 9

Jesus makes a man able to see

1 While Jesus was walking along, he saw a certain man. This man had been unable to see since he was born. 2 Jesus' disciples asked him, 'Teacher, why was this man born unable to see? Was it because he himself did something wrong? Or was it because his parents did something wrong?' 3 Jesus answered, 'It was not because either this man or his parents did something wrong. It happened so that God could show his work in this man. 4 While it is still day, we must continue to work. We must do the work of him who sent me. We must work now because it will be night soon. Then nobody can work. 5 While I am in the world, I am the world's light.'

6 When Jesus had finished speaking, he spat (sent water from his mouth) on the ground. He mixed it on the ground so that he made mud. Then he put some of the mud on the eyes of the man who was unable to see. 7 Jesus said to him, 'Go and wash in the Siloam pool.' (The name Siloam means 'sent'.) So the man went there and he washed himself. When he returned, he could see.

8 Then people who knew the man began to talk about him. Also, people who had seen him before spoke to each other about him. They had seen him when he was asking for money. They asked, 'Is this the man who sat here? Is this the man who asked for money?' 9 Some people said, 'Yes, it is him.' But other people said, 'No, it is someone who is very like him.' So the man himself said, 'I am that man.' 10 Then they asked him, 'How did you become able to see?' 11 He answered, 'The man called Jesus made some mud. He put the mud on my eyes. Then he sent me to wash in the Siloam pool. So I went there and I washed. And then I could see.' 12 They asked him, 'Where is this man?' He replied, 'I do not know.'

The Pharisees talk to the man who had been unable to see

13 The people brought the man who had been unable to see to the Pharisees. 14 (Jesus had made the mud and then he had caused the man to see on a Sabbath day.)

5 So the Pharisees asked the man again, 'How did you become able to see?' The man replied, 'Jesus put mud on my eyes. Then I washed and now I can see.'

16 So some of the Pharisees said, 'This man (Jesus) cannot have come from God. He does not obey the rules about the Sabbath day.' But other Pharisees said, 'Nobody who is sinful could do great things like this!' So they did not agree with each other. 17 The Pharisees spoke again to the man who had been unable to see. They said, 'What do you yourself say about this man who has made you able to see?' The man replied, 'He is a prophet.'

18 The Jews' leaders did not want to believe that the man had really been unable to see. They did not want to believe that he had become able to see. So, they sent people to ask the man's parents to come to them. 19 They asked the parents, 'Is this your son? You say, "When he was born, he was unable to see." He now can see. How did this happen?' 20 The parents replied, 'We know that this is our son. And when he was born, he was unable to see. We know that, too.

21 But we do not know how he can see now. And we do not know who made him able to see. Ask him. He is old enough. He himself can answer!' 22 The man's parents said these things because they were afraid of the Jews' leaders. The Jews' leaders did not want anyone to say that Jesus was the Christ. They had already agreed to punish anyone who said that. The leaders would not let anyone like that belong to the synagogue. 23 That is why the man's parents said, 'Ask him. He is old enough.'

24 So the leaders asked again to speak to the man who had been unable to see. They said to him, 'Promise that you will speak only true things. Promise that in front of God. We know that this man is sinful.' 25 The man replied, 'I do not know whether he is sinful or not. But I do know one thing. I was unable to see and now I can see. I do know that.' 26 Then they asked him, 'What did he do to you? How did he make you able to see?' 27 He answered them, 'I have told you already and you would not listen. Why do you want to hear it again? Do you want to become his disciples too?' 28 Then they were very angry with him. They shouted at him, 'You are that man's disciple. But we are Moses' disciples. 29 We know that God spoke to Moses. But we do not even know where this man comes from.'

30 The man answered, 'That is a very strange thing! You do not know where Jesus comes from. But it was he who made me able to see. 31 We know that God does not listen to sinful people. But God does listen to some people:
People who believe how great he is.
People who do what he wants them to do.
He does listen to those people. We know that. 32 Nobody before has ever made a man able to see, who was born unable to see. Since the world began, nobody has ever done that! 33 Surely, this man who made me able to see has come from God. Unless he came from God, he could not do anything.' 34 The Jews' leaders answered, 'You have always been sinful, since the day that you were born. You cannot try to teach us!' And they threw him out.

Jesus came to cause people really to see

35 Jesus heard that the Jews' leaders had thrown the man out. So, he found the man. And Jesus asked him, 'Do you believe the Son of Man?' 36 The man answered, 'Sir, please tell me who he is. Then I can believe him.' 37 Jesus said to him, 'You have seen him. It is he who is talking to you now. I am he.' 38 Then the man said, 'Lord, I believe.' He bent down on his knees and he worshipped Jesus.

39 Then Jesus said, 'I came into this world to show what people are really like. So then, those people who do not see will be able to see. And those people who do see will become unable to see.' 40 Some of the Pharisees who were there with him heard this. They asked Jesus, 'Do you mean that we are unable to see also?' 41 Jesus said to them, 'If you were unable to see, you would not have done anything wrong. But you say that you can see. So, that means that you are still continuing to do something wrong.'

Chapter 10

The story about the shepherd

1 Jesus said, 'I am telling you what is true. A shepherd keeps his sheep in a safe place with a wall round it. There is a gate into that safe place. Anyone else who gets into that place by another way, not through the gate, is not the shepherd. That person is bad. He comes to take away the sheep that are not his. 2 The shepherd goes in through the gate.

3 The person who watches the gate opens it for the shepherd. The sheep recognise the shepherd's voice. He calls each of his own sheep by their name and he leads them out.

4 When he has brought all his own sheep out, he goes in front of them. And the sheep follow him because they know his voice. 5 They will not follow a stranger. They will run away from a stranger because they do not recognise his voice.'

6 Jesus told them this story that was like a picture. But they did not understand what he was saying to them.

Jesus is like the good shepherd

7 So Jesus spoke again. 'I am telling you what is true. I am like the gate for the sheep. 8 All other men who ever came to the sheep before me were bad. They wanted to take away the sheep that were not theirs. But the sheep did not listen to them. 9 I am like the gate. Anyone who comes in through me will be safe. He will come in and he will go out. And he will find plenty of food. 10 He who comes to take away my sheep comes only to kill them. He comes only to destroy. I have come so that they can live. And so they can have everything that they need.'

11 'I am like the good shepherd. The good shepherd would die so that he can save his sheep. 12 Another man may work with the sheep so that he gets money. But the sheep are not his own. A man like that is not the shepherd. A man like that runs away when he sees a wolf (a wild dog). The wolf comes to kill the sheep. But a man like that leaves the sheep and he runs away. So, the wolf attacks the sheep and it causes them to run in all directions. 13 That man runs away because the sheep are not his own. The sheep do not really matter to him.'

14 'I am like the good shepherd. I know my own sheep, and they know me. 15 I know them in the same way that my Father knows me. And they know me in the same way that I know the Father. And I will die on behalf of the sheep. 16 I have other sheep also, and I must bring them too. They do not belong to this group of sheep. But they will listen to my voice, and so all the sheep will become one group, with one shepherd. 17 The Father loves me because I will choose to die. I will choose to die so that then I can become alive again. 18 Nobody causes me to die. No, instead, I myself choose to die. I have authority so that I can choose to die. Also, I have authority so that I can become alive again. My Father has said that I must do that.'

19 Again, the Jews could not agree about these things that Jesus said. 20 Many of them said, 'He has a demon (bad spirit from Satan) and he is crazy. You should not listen to him!' 21 But other people said, 'A man with a demon (bad spirit) could not talk like this! A demon could not make people able to see!'

The Jews' leaders do not believe Jesus

22 It was the time for the Dedication Festival at Jerusalem.

23 It was winter. And Jesus was walking under a roof by the side of God's Great House (the temple). The place was called Solomon's porch. 24 The Jews' leaders stood round him. They said to him, 'We want to be sure about who you are. When will you tell us? If you are the Christ, tell us clearly.'

25 Jesus answered, 'I have told you, but you do not believe. The things that I do by my Father's authority show you about me. Those things show you who I am. 26 But you refuse to believe, because you do not belong to my sheep. 27 My sheep recognise my voice. I know them, and they follow me.

28 I cause them to live always. They will never die. Nobody can ever take them away from me. 29 My Father, who has given them to me, is greater than all things. Nobody can ever take my sheep out of my Father's hand. 30 My Father and I are one Person.' 31 Then the Jews' leaders picked up stones again to throw at Jesus so that they could kill him. 32 Jesus said to them, 'I have done many good things. The Father told me that I must do them. You have seen me do those good things. Which of those good things have caused you to throw stones at me?' 33 The Jews' leaders answered, 'We do not want to kill you with stones because of any good things that you have done. We want to kill you with stones because you are speaking against God. You are only a man. But you are saying that you are God.'

34 Jesus answered, 'It says in your own Scriptures (Old Testament) that God said, "You are gods." 35 God called the people to whom he spoke 'gods'. And the Scriptures are always true. 36 The Father chose me. And he sent me into the world. I said that I am God's Son. So you should not say, because of that, that I speak against God. 37 If I am not doing my Father's work, do not believe me. 38 But if I am doing his work, believe that work. Even if you do not believe me, believe my work. Believe the things that I do. Then you will know certainly that the Father is in me. And you will know that I am in the Father.'

39 Again, the Jews' leaders tried to catch Jesus. But he got away from them.

40 Jesus returned across the Jordan river again. He went to the place where John had baptised people. And Jesus stayed there. 41 Many people came to him. They said to each other, 'John did not do any miracles. But everything that John said about this man was true.' 42 And in that place, many people believed Jesus.

Chapter 11

Lazarus dies

1 A certain man, who was called Lazarus, became ill. Lazarus lived at Bethany, the village where Mary and her sister Martha lived too. 2 It was this Mary who had poured oil with a lovely smell over the Lord. Then she had cleaned his feet with her hair. It was her brother Lazarus who was ill. 3 So the two sisters sent a message to Jesus. The message said, 'Lord, the friend that you love is ill.'

4 Jesus heard the message. Then he said, 'This illness will not finish with Lazarus's death. No, its purpose is to show how great and how powerful God is. It will show how great God's Son is.' 5 Jesus loved Martha and her sister, and their brother Lazarus, too. 6 He heard the news that Lazarus was ill. But then he stayed in the place where he was for two more days.

7 After that, Jesus said to his disciples, 'We will return to Judea.' 8 The disciples said, 'Teacher, only a short time ago, the Jews there tried to kill you with stones. You should not return there!' 9 Jesus answered, 'You know that there are 12 hours in the day. Anyone who walks during the day will not fall down. He will not fall down because he sees this world's light. 10 But anyone who walks during the night will fall down. He will fall down because there is no light in him.'

11 Jesus said that. Then he said to them, 'Our friend Lazarus is sleeping. But I go there to wake him up.' 12 So the disciples said to him, 'If he is sleeping, Lord, he will get well.' 13 But Jesus meant that Lazarus had died. The disciples thought that Jesus was talking about sleep as rest. 14 So then, Jesus told them clearly, 'Lazarus is dead. 15 But I am happy that I was not with him. I am happy about that because now you will believe. We must go to him now.' 16 Thomas, who was called Didymus, spoke to the other disciples. He said, 'We will go with our Teacher, so that we can die with him!'

Jesus is able to make dead people alive

17 Jesus arrived at Bethany. Then he discovered that they had buried Lazarus 4 days earlier. 18 Bethany was less than 2 miles (about 3 kilometres) from Jerusalem. 19 Many Jews had come there to visit Martha and Mary. These Jews wanted to be kind to Martha and Mary because their brother had died.

20 Martha heard the news that Jesus was coming. So immediately, she went out to meet him. But Mary stayed at home. 21 Martha said to Jesus, 'Lord, if you had been here, my brother would not have died. 22 But I know that, even now, God will answer you. God will do whatever you ask him.' 23 Jesus told her, 'Your brother will rise, to become alive again.'

24 Martha replied, 'I know that he will rise, to become alive again, on the last day.' 25 Jesus said to her, 'It is I who raise dead people, to make them alive. I cause people to live. Anyone who believes me will live. Even if that person dies, he will live. 26 Some people will live and believe in me. Anyone who does that will never die. Do you believe that?' 27 She answered, 'Yes, Lord, I believe that you are the Christ, God's Son. You are the man that God promised to send into the world.'

Jesus weeps

28 After this, Martha went home and she spoke secretly to her sister, Mary. Martha said, 'The Teacher is here, and he is asking to meet you.' 29 When Mary heard this, she got up. She hurried out to meet Jesus. 30 Jesus had not arrived in the village yet. He was still in the place where Martha had met him. 31 The Jews in the house, who were being kind to Mary, saw her get up quickly. They saw her go out and so they followed her. They thought that she was going to the tomb to weep there.

32 Mary arrived at the place where Jesus was. When she saw Jesus, she fell at his feet. She said, 'Lord, if you had been here, my brother would not have died.' 33 Jesus saw that Mary was weeping. The Jews who had come with her were weeping, too. Jesus saw them and he felt very, very sad in his spirit. He was very sorry for them. 34 He asked them, 'Where have you put his dead body?' They answered, 'Come and see, Lord.' 35 Jesus wept. 36 Then the Jews said to each other, 'See how much he loved Lazarus!' 37 But some of them said, 'He opened the eyes of the man who could not see. So, surely he would have been able to stop Lazarus from dying.'

Jesus makes Lazarus alive again

38 Jesus felt very, very sad again while he was coming to the tomb. It was a big hole in the rock. A very big stone covered the way into it. 39 Jesus said, 'Take the stone away.' Martha, the dead man's sister, said to Jesus, 'But Lord, his dead body will have a bad smell. He has been dead for 4 days!' 40 Jesus said to her, 'I told you that you must believe. Then, as a result, you will see how great and how powerful God is. That is what I told you.' 41 So they took the stone away. Jesus looked up towards the sky. He said, 'Father, I thank you that you have listened to me. 42 I know that you listen to me always. But I said this because of all the people who are standing here. I want them to believe that you sent me.' 43 When Jesus had said this, he shouted with a loud voice, 'Lazarus, come out!' 44 The dead man came out. There were pieces of cloth round his hands and round his feet. Another piece of cloth was round his face. Jesus said to them, 'Undo the cloths and let him go.'

The Pharisees decide how to kill Jesus

45 Many of the Jews who had come to visit Mary saw this. They saw what Jesus did. So, they believed him. 46 But some of them went to the Pharisees. They told the Pharisees what Jesus had done. 47 Then the Pharisees and the most important priests had a meeting. They said to each other, 'What will we do? This man is doing so many miracles. 48 If we let him do more things like this, everyone will believe him. Then the Romans will come. And they will destroy our temple (God's Great House) and they will kill our people.'

49 One of them, who was called Caiaphas, was the priests' leader that year. He said, 'You do not understand the problem. 50 It is better that one man should die on behalf of the people. That is better than if all the people in our country died.' 51 Caiaphas did not say this because he had thought it by himself. No, he was speaking as a prophet because he was the priests' leader that year. He spoke as a prophet that Jesus would die on behalf of Israel's people. 52 And Jesus would die not only for Israel's people. Also, his death would bring together all God's people who lived in many different places. They would become like one big family.

53 From that day, the Jews' leaders decided together how they could kill Jesus. 54 So, Jesus stopped travelling about in Judea where everyone could see him. Instead, he went away secretly to a town called Ephraim. It was near to the wild place. He stayed there with the disciples.

55 It was almost time for the Jews' Passover Festival. Many people were going from their country places to Jerusalem. They were going to make themselves clean and ready for God before they went to the festival. 56 They were looking for Jesus. While they were standing in God's Great House (the temple), they spoke to each other about him. They asked each other, 'Do you think that he will come to the festival or not?' 57 The most important priests and the Pharisees had spoken to the people about Jesus. They had told them, 'Someone may know where Jesus is. If anyone does know that, you must tell us.' So then they could put him in a prison.

Chapter 12

Jesus at Bethany

1 Six days before the Passover, Jesus went to Bethany, the village where Lazarus lived. He was the man who had been dead. But Jesus had raised him, to make him alive again. 2 Some friends prepared a special meal there for Jesus. Martha gave out the food, and Lazarus sat among the visitors, with Jesus. 3 Then Mary brought a pound of very expensive oil that had a lovely smell. She poured it over Jesus' feet and then she cleaned his feet with her hair. The smell of the oil filled the whole house.

4 Then Judas Iscariot, one of Jesus' disciples, spoke. He was the man who would sell Jesus to Jesus' enemies. Judas said, 5 'She could have sold this expensive oil for as much money as someone would get for a year's work. And she could have given that money to poor people.' 6 He did not say this because he really wanted to help the poor people. No, he said it because he wanted the money himself. He kept the bag of money, and sometimes he took money from it for himself. 7 But Jesus said, 'Do not stop her! She has kept this oil for the day when they bury my dead body. 8 Poor people will always be with you, but I will not always be with you.'

9 By this time, a large crowd of Jews had heard the news that Jesus was at Bethany. So, they came there to see him. They came also to see Lazarus, because Jesus had made him alive again. 10 So the most important priests, who had already decided to kill Jesus, decided to kill Lazarus too. 11 They decided to do that because many Jews were refusing to obey them. Instead, these Jews were believing Jesus because of what he had done for Lazarus.

Jesus goes into Jerusalem as the Messiah

12 The next day, a large crowd of people were in Jerusalem for the festival. They heard the news that Jesus was on the way there. 13 So, they took branches from palm trees and they went out to meet Jesus. They were shouting, 'Save us now! God is good to the man who comes in the name of the Lord. God is good to the King of Israel!' 14 Jesus found a young donkey. And he sat on it, as it says in the Old Testament:

15 'Do not be afraid, people in Zion (Jerusalem).

Look! Your king is coming.

He is riding on a young donkey.'

16 Jesus' disciples did not understand all this at that time. They understood only after Jesus had returned to God in heaven. Then they remembered that the Old Testament said these things about him. And they remembered that these things had happened to him. 17 The crowd who had been with Jesus before, continued to tell people about Lazarus. Jesus had told Lazarus that he should come out of the tomb. Jesus had made Lazarus alive again after he had been dead. The crowd continued to tell people about this. 18That is why all the people came to meet Jesus. They had heard that he had done this miracle. 19 So, the Pharisees said to each other, 'This is not what we wanted. Look! All the people in the world are running after him!'

Jesus says that he will son die

20 There were some Greeks (people from Greece) among the people who had come to worship God at the festival. 21 These Greeks came to Philip, who was from Bethsaida city in Galilee. They said to him, 'Sir, we want to talk with Jesus.' 22 Philip went to Andrew and he told Andrew this. Then Philip and Andrew went to Jesus and they told him.

23 Jesus said to them, 'God will show how great and how good the Son of Man is. It is now time for that to happen.

24 I am telling you what is true. A seed of wheat continues to be only a single seed unless it dies. It must fall into the ground and then it must die. But if it dies, it grows to give a lot of seeds.'

25 'Anyone who loves his own life will lose it. But anyone who hates his life in this world will live always. 26Anyone who wants to be my servant must follow me. Then he will be with me, where I am. My Father will do great things for anyone who is my servant. 27 Now I feel very sad. And I have trouble in my mind. I might say, "Father, save me from this very difficult time!" But I came to the world for this purpose. I came so that I could go through this difficult time. 28 Father, show how great and how good you are.'

Then someone spoke from heaven, 'I have shown how great and how good I am. And I will do it again.' 29The crowd of people who were standing there heard the sound of this voice. And they said that it was like the noise of a storm. But other people said, 'An angel spoke to him!'

30 Jesus said, 'This voice did not speak so that it could help me. No, it spoke so that it could help you. 31 It is time now for God to judge the people in this world. Now he will throw out the ruler of this world. 32 But when people lift me up from the earth, then I will pull everyone towards myself.' 33 He said this to show how he would soon die.

34 The crowd said, 'The Scriptures (Old Testament) tell us that the Christ will continue always. So why do you say, "People must lift up the Son of Man"? Who is this Son of Man?' 35 Jesus answered, 'The light will be with you for only a short time longer. So, continue to walk while you still have the light. Then the dark will not come over you. Anyone who walks in the dark does not know the way. That person does not know where he is going. 36 Believe the light, while you have the light. So then you will become sons of light.' When Jesus had said this, he went away. And he hid himself from them.

The Jews still do not believe Jesus

37 Jesus had done so many miracles that the people themselves had seen. But even then, they still did not believe him. 38 This showed that the prophet Isaiah had spoken true words. Isaiah had said:

'Lord, nobody has believed our message.

Nobody has understood how powerful the Lord is.'

39 Isaiah spoke also about why the people could not believe. 40 He said:

'God has made their eyes unable to see.

He has closed their minds.

So they cannot see with their eyes and they cannot understand with their minds.

They will not turn to me, so that I can make them well.'

41 Isaiah had seen how great Christ is. That is why he said these things.

42 But many of the Jews' leaders did believe Jesus. But they did not tell people that they believed. They did not speak about it because they were afraid of the Pharisees. They were afraid that the Pharisees would send them away from the synagogue. 43 They wanted other people to think good things about them more than they wanted to make God happy.

Jesus' words will judge people

44 Jesus said in a loud voice, 'Anyone who believes me does not believe only me. That person believes also him who sent me. 45 Anyone who looks at me sees also him who sent me. 46 I have come into the world to be a light. Everyone who believes me will not remain in the dark. That is why I came. 47 Some people may hear my words but not obey them. I will not judge anyone who does that. I did not come to judge the people in the world. I came to save them. 48 Something else will judge anyone who refuses me. Something else will judge anyone who will not listen to my words. The message that I have spoken will judge him on the last day. 49 The words that I have spoken did not come from me myself. They came from the Father, who sent me. He told me what to say. And he told me how to say it. 50 What the Father says causes people to live always. I know that. So, I say only those things that the Father has said to me.'

Chapter 13

Jesus washes his disciples' feet

1 It was nearly time for the Passover Festival. Jesus knew that it was almost time for him to leave this world. It was almost time for him to go to the Father. He had always loved those people in the world who were his own. And he loved them to the end.

2 Jesus and his disciples were eating supper. The Devil had already put an idea into the mind of Judas Iscariot, Simon's son. The idea was to sell Jesus to his enemies. 3 Jesus knew that the Father had given him power over everything. He knew that he had come from God. And he knew that he would soon return to God. 4 So, during the meal, he stood up. He took off the coat that he wore over his other clothes. He tied a thick cloth round his body. 5 Then he poured water into a bowl (a wide pot) and he began to wash the disciples' feet. Jesus made their feet dry with the thick cloth that was round him.

6 Jesus came to Simon Peter. Peter asked him, 'Lord, will you wash my feet?' 7 Jesus answered him, 'You do not understand now what I am doing. But you will understand some time after this.' 8 Peter said, 'You will never, never wash my feet!' Jesus answered, 'If I do not wash you, you do not belong with me.' 9 Simon Peter replied, 'So Lord, do not wash my feet only! Wash my hands and my head too!' 10 Jesus said, 'A person who has had a bath is completely clean. He needs only to wash his feet. And all of you are clean, except one of you.' 11 Jesus knew already who would sell him to his enemies. That is why he said, 'All of you are clean, except one.'

12 When he had finished washing their feet, Jesus put on his coat. He returned to his place at the meal. He asked them, 'I want you to understand what I have just done to you. 13 You call me Teacher and Lord. And you are right when you say that. You are right, because I am your Teacher and Lord. 14 I am your Teacher and your Lord, and I have washed your feet. So, you should wash each other's feet also.

15 I have given you an example. So, you should do the same as I have done for you. 16 I am telling you what is true. No slave is more important than his master is. And no messenger is more important than the person who sent him. 17 Now you know these things. So, you will be happy if you do them.'

18 'I am not talking about all of you. I know the people that I have chosen. The Old Testament says, "Someone who ate food with me has become my enemy." So that is what must happen. 19 I am telling you this now, before it happens. So then, when it does happen, you will believe. You will believe that "I am".

20 I am telling you what is true. Some people will accept those that I send. And anyone who accepts them is accepting me also. And so some people will accept me. And anyone like that is accepting also him who sent me.'

Jesus tells the disciples that one of them will sell him to his enemies

21 After Jesus had said this, he felt very, very sad. And he had trouble in his mind. He said to them very seriously, 'I am telling you what is true. One of you will sell me to my enemies.' 22 The disciples looked at each other. They did not know which of them Jesus was speaking about.

23 One of them, the disciple that Jesus loved, was sitting very near to Jesus. 24 Simon Peter pointed at that disciple. Peter said, 'Ask Jesus whom he is speaking about.' 25 So that disciple moved even nearer to Jesus and he asked, 'Who is it, Lord?' 26 Jesus answered, 'I will put a piece of bread in the dish of food. Then I will give the bread to him. That is the man.' So he put a piece of bread in the dish. Then he gave it to Judas, the son of Simon Iscariot.

27 Then, when Judas had taken the bread, Satan came into him. Then Jesus said to Judas, 'Do quickly what you want to do.' 28 None of the other men who were sitting at the meal understood this. They did not know why Jesus said this to Judas. 29 Some of them thought that Jesus had asked Judas to buy some things. Judas was going out to buy what they needed for the festival. That was what some of them thought. Some of them thought that Jesus had asked Judas to give some money to the poor people. That was because Judas kept the bag of money on behalf of all of them.

30 Judas took the bread and then he went out immediately. And it was night.

The new rule

31 When Judas had left, Jesus said, 'Now people will see how great and how good the Son of Man is. And in him, they will see how great and how good God is. 32 The Son will show how great God is. Then God will take the Son to himself. And God will show how great the Son is. And he will do that immediately. 33 My children, I will be with you for only a short time. You will look for me. But I tell you now what I told the Jews. You cannot go where I go now. 34 I give a new rule to you. Love each other. You must love each other as I have loved you. 35 By this, everyone will know that you are my disciples. They will know it, if you really love each other.'

36 Simon Peter asked him, 'Where will you go, Lord?' Jesus replied, 'You cannot follow now where I will go. But you will follow sometime after this.' 37 Peter said, 'Lord, why can I not follow you now? I would die for you.' 38 Jesus answered, 'You say that you would die for me. But I am telling you what is true. You will say that you do not know me. Before the first bird sings, early in the morning, you will say it three times.'

Chapter 14

Jesus is the way to the Father

1 Then Jesus said to them, 'Do not let yourselves be sad and afraid. Believe God, and believe me also.

2 There are many rooms in my Father's house. I would not tell you this if it was not true. And I will go now so that I can prepare a place for you. 3 After I have prepared a place for you, I will return. I will take you so that you will be with me. So then you will be where I am. 4 You know the way to the place where I will go.'

5 Thomas said to him, 'Lord, we do not know where you will go. So how can we know the way to get there?' 6 Jesus answered, 'I am the way. I am what is true. And I am the life. Nobody comes to the Father except by me. 7 If you really know me, you will know my Father also. From this time, you do know him, and you have seen him.'

8 Philip said, 'Lord, show the Father to us. That is all that we need.' 9 Jesus answered, 'I have been with all of you for such a long time. But still you do not seem to know me, Philip! Anyone who has seen me has seen the Father. So why do you say, "Show the Father to us"? 10 I am in the Father and the Father is in me. You should believe that. The words that I say to you do not come from me myself. But the Father, who lives in me, is doing his work.

11 I am in the Father and the Father is in me. Believe me when I say that. Or, if you do not believe my words, believe because of my work. Believe because of the things that I have done. 12 I am telling you what is true. Anyone who believes me will do the same things as me. That person will do the same things that I have done. Yes, he will do even greater things than these, because I go to my Father. 13 Ask for things in my name (because you are mine). If you ask anything in my name, I will do it. So then the Son will show everyone how great and how good the Father is. 14 If you ask me for anything in my name, I will do it.'

Jesus promises God's Spirit

15 'If you love me, you will obey me. You will obey what I have asked you to do. 16 I will ask the Father. And he will give to you another Person who will help you. That Helper will stay with you always. 17 He is the Spirit, who shows you true things. The people who belong to this world cannot receive him. That is because they cannot see him. They cannot know him. But you know him because he stays with you. And he will be in you. 18 I will not let you remain alone, like children without parents. I will come to you.'

19 'After a short time, the people who belong to this world will not see me any longer. But you will see me. And because I live, you will live also. 20 On that day, you will know that I am in my Father. You will know that you are in me. And you will know that I am in you. 21 Some people will listen to what I have told them. And they will obey what I have said. It is those people who love me. My Father will love everyone who loves me. And I will love them and I will show myself to them.'

22 Then Judas (not Judas Iscariot) said, 'Lord, why will you show yourself only to us? Why will you not show yourself also to the people who belong to this world?'

23 Jesus replied, 'Anyone who loves me will obey my words. My Father will love him. And my Father and I will come to him and we will make our home with him. 24 Anyone who does not love me will not obey my words. And these words that you hear are not my own. No, these words come from the Father, who sent me. 25 I have said these things to you while I am still with you. 26 But the Father will send the Holy (completely good) Spirit. And it is he who will help you. He will come in my name. He will teach you all things. And he will cause you to remember everything that I have told you.'

27 'I will go away but I will cause a gift to stay with you. My gift is that I will give you power to be without trouble in your minds and in your hearts. In the same way that I myself have this power, I will cause you to have it also. My gift to you is not like what this world gives. Do not let yourselves be sad or afraid. 28 You heard me say to you, "I will go away, but I will return to you." If you loved me, you would be happy because of that. You would be happy because I go to the Father. And he is greater than I am. 29 I have told you this now, before it happens. So then, when it does happen, you will believe. 30 I will not talk with you much more, because the ruler of this world will come soon. He has no power over me. 31 But the people who belong to this world must learn about me. They must know that I love the Father. And I do everything that he asks me to do. I must show that to them. So get up, we must go.'

Chapter 15

The branches must stay in the vine

1 'I am the proper vine, and my Father is the gardener. 2 Some branches that are part of me ay have no fruit on them. So, my Father removes those branches.

And he cuts short every branch that does make fruit. He cleans all those branches, so that they will make more fruit. 3 The words that I have spoken to you have made you clean already. 4 Continue to live in me, and I will continue to live in you. A branch cannot make fruit by itself. It can make fruit only if it continues to be part of the vine. You are like that. You cannot make fruit unless you continue to live in me.'

5 'I am the vine, and you are the branches. You must remain in me and I must remain in you. Only if you do that will you make plenty of fruit. That is because you can do nothing without me. 6 If anyone does not remain in me, that person is like a dead branch. The gardener will throw that branch away and it will become dry. People take those dry branches and they throw them into the fire. So, those dry branches burn. 7 You must remain in me, and my words must remain in you. So then you can ask for anything that you want. And God will do it for you. 8 If you make plenty of fruit, you will be my disciples. You will show how great and how good my Father is.'

9 'I have loved you as the Father has loved me. Continue to know that I love you. 10 You must obey everything that I have taught you. So, as a result, you will continue to know that I love you. In the same way, I have obeyed everything that the Father has asked me to do. So, as a result, I continue to know that he loves me. 11 I have told you these things so that you can be really happy. You can be happy in the same way that I myself am happy. So you will be completely happy.'

12 'I tell you that you must do this: You must love each other, as I have loved you. 13 A person really loves his friends if he dies on behalf of them. Nobody could love anyone more than that. 14 And you are my friends, if you obey me. You must do what I ask you to do. 15 A servant does not know what his master is doing. So I do not call you servants any longer. But I have told you everything that I have heard from my Father. So, I call you friends. 16 You did not choose me, but I chose you. I chose you for a purpose. You must go and you must make fruit. You must make the kind of fruit that will continue. So, as a result, the Father will give you anything that you ask him. If you ask him in my name (because you are mine), he will give it to you. 17 This is what you must do: You must love each other.'

The world hates the disciples

18 'The people who belong to this world may hate you. But remember this: They hated me before they hated you. 19 If you belonged to this world, this world's people would love you. They would love you because you would belong with them. But I chose you so that you would be separate from this world's people. You do not belong with them, so they hate you. 20 Remember what I told you, "No slave is more important than his master." If they have caused trouble for me, they will cause trouble for you, too. But if they have obeyed my words, they will obey your words, too. 21 They will do all these things to you because of me. They do not know him who sent me. That is why they will do these things.'

22 'I have come and I have spoken to them. If I had not done that, they would not have done anything wrong. But now they cannot say, "We have not done anything wrong." 23 Anyone who hates me hates my Father also. 24 I did many great things when I was with them. Nobody else ever did things like that. If I had not done those things among them, they would not have done anything wrong. But they have seen what I did. And they have hated me. And they have hated my Father too. 25 But this had to happen. Their book of rules (the Old Testament) says, "They hated me without any good reason." And what it says had to happen.'

26 'But I will send the Helper to you from the Father. The Helper is the Spirit who speaks only true things. He comes from the Father. And he will speak about me. 27 You must speak about me, too, because you have been with me from the beginning.'

Chapter 16

1 'I have told you all this, so that nothing will cause you to stop believing me. 2 People will send you away from the synagogues. There will be a time when people will kill you. And they will even think that God has given them a duty to kill you.

3 They will do these things because they have never known either the Father or me. 4 But I have told you this so that you will remember. When they begin to do these things, you will remember. You will remember that I told you about them. I did not tell you this before, because I was with you.'

The work of God's Spirit

5 'Now I will go to him who sent me. But none of you asks me, "Where will you go?" 6 And now you are very sad, because of the things that I have told you. 7 But I am telling you what is true. I will go away because it will be better for you. Unless I go away, the Helper will not come to you. But if I do go away, I will send him to you. 8 When he comes, he will show things about this world's people. He will show that they are wrong. They are wrong about sin. They are wrong about how to be right with God. They are wrong about how God judges people.

9 They are wrong about sin, because they do not believe me. 10 They are wrong about how to be right with God, because I go to the Father. And you will not see me any longer. 11 They are wrong about how God judges people. They are wrong about that because God has already decided to punish the ruler of this world.'

12 'I have many more things to tell you. But you are not strong enough to know them now. 13 But the Spirit, who shows you true things, will come. And when he comes, he will be a guide to you. He will cause you to know everything that is true. He will tell you only what he hears. He will not speak his own words. He will tell you about things that will happen after this time. 14 He will receive what I have to say. And he will tell it to you. In that way, he will show how great and how good I am. 15 Everything that the Father has is mine. That is why I said, "The Spirit will receive what I have to say. And then he will tell it to you." '

The disciples will be sad first but after that they will be happy

16 'After a short time, you will not see me any longer. But soon after that, you will see me.' 17 Some of his disciples said to each other, 'What does he mean? He says, "After a short time, you will not see me any longer, but soon after that, you will see me." And he says, "because I go to the Father." 18 What does he mean by 'a short time'? We do not know what he is talking about!'

19 Jesus knew that they wanted to ask him about this. So, he said to them, 'I said, "After a short time, you will not see me any longer. But soon after that, you will see me." Perhaps you are asking each other about that. 20 I am telling you what is true. You will cry and you will be sad. But the people who belong to this world will be happy. First, you will be sad, but soon after that, you will become happy instead. 21 While a woman is giving birth to a baby, she is sad. She is sad at that time because it is painful. But after the baby is born, she is happy. She forgets the pain, because now she is so happy. She is so happy because a person has been born into the world.'

22 'It is like that for you. You are sad now. But I will see you again, and you will be happy. You will be so happy. And nobody will cause you to stop being happy. 23 On that day, you will not ask me for anything. I am telling you what is true. The Father will give you anything that you ask for in my name (because you are mine). 24 Until now, you have not asked for anything in my name. Ask, and you will receive. So then you will be completely happy.'

25 'I have spoken to you with words and stories that are like pictures. But there will be a time when I will not speak like that any longer. Instead, I will speak clearly to you about the Father. 26 On that day, you will ask in my name (because you are mine). I am not saying that I will ask the Father on your behalf.

27 No, because the Father himself loves you. He loves you because you love me. He loves you because you believe. You believe that I came from God. 28 I came from the Father, and I came into the world. And now I will leave the world, and I will return to the Father.'

29 His disciples said, 'Now you are speaking clearly. You are not speaking with words that are like pictures! 30 Now we are sure that you know everything. You do not need to ask people what they are thinking. Because of this, we believe that you came from God.' 31 Jesus answered them, 'You say that you believe now.

32 But it will happen very soon that all of you will run away to your own homes. Yes, it is that time already. You will leave me alone. But I am not really alone, because the Father is with me. 33 I have told you these things so that you will be without trouble in your minds and in your hearts. You will be like that because you are united with me. In this world, you will have trouble. But be strong! I have won! I have destroyed the power of this world.'

Chapter 17

Jesus prays for himself

1 After Jesus said this, he looked up to heaven. He said, 'Father, it is the time. Show how great and how good your Son is. So then I (the Son) can show how great and how good you are. 2 You gave to me (the Son) authority over all people. You did this so that I (the Son) could cause people to live always. I could cause all those people that you gave to me to live always. 3 And this is how they will live always. They will live because they will know you. They will know you. And only you really are God. And they will know Jesus Christ, whom you have sent. 4 I have finished the work that you gave to me to do. And so, I have shown on the earth how great and how good you are. 5 Now, Father, show how great and how good I am. Before the world began, I was with you. I was great and powerful with you. Show again that I am great like that.'

Jesus prays for his disciples

6 'You gave some men to me out of the world. I have shown them who you are. They were yours. You gave them to me, and they have obeyed your words. 7 Now they know about me. Everything that you have given to me really comes from you. They know that now. 8 I gave to them the words that you gave to me. And they accepted those words. They know certainly that I came from you. They believe that you sent me.'

9 'I pray for them. I am not praying for the people who belong to this world. No, but I am praying for those people that you have given to me. I am praying for them because they are yours. 10 Everything that is mine is yours. And everything that is yours is mine. And these people have shown how great and how good I am. 11 Now, I will not remain in the world any longer. I will come to you. But they are still in the world. Holy (completely good) Father, keep them safe in your name (by your own power), that you gave to me. So then they can be united in the same way that you and I are united. 12 While I was with them, I kept them safe. I kept them safe in your name (by your own power), that you gave to me. I kept them safe so that none of them went the wrong way, except one. That was the man who had to go the wrong way. What the Old Testament says had to happen.'

13 'Now, I will come to you. But I am saying these things while I am still in the world. I am saying them so that these men can be completely happy in their hearts. I want them to become completely happy in the same way that I am completely happy. 14 I have given your words to them. And the world's people have hated them because they do not belong to the world. They do not belong to the world, in the same way that I do not belong to the world. 15 I am not asking that you will take them out of the world. But I want you to keep them safe from him who is bad (the Devil). So I am asking you to do that. 16 They do not belong to the world, in the same way that I do not belong to the world. 17 Make them separate for yourself by your words, which are true. 18 I have sent them into the world, in the same way that you sent me into the world. 19 On behalf of them, I make myself separate, so that I obey only you. So then they can become separate for you also, by what is true.'

Jesus prays for everyone who will believe him

20 'I do not pray only for these people. I pray also for those people who will believe me because of their words. 21 I pray that all of them will be united. You, Father, are in me and I am in you. I pray that they also will be united in us. So then the world's people will believe that you sent me. 22 I have given to them the great and special gift that you gave to me. Now they can be united in the same way that you and I are united. 23 I will be in them, and you will be in me. So then they can be completely united. And, as a result, the world's people will know that you sent me. The world's people will know that you love them. You love them as you love me.'

24 'Father, you have given these people to me. And I want them to be with me where I am. You made me great and powerful because you loved me. You loved me before you made the world. And I want these people to see how great and how powerful I am. 25 Father, you always do what is right. The world's people do not know you, but I know you. And these disciples know that you have sent me. 26 I have shown them what you are like. And I will continue to show them who you are. So then they will love other people in the same way that you love me. And so I can be in them.'

Chapter 18

Soldiers take Jesus to the Chief Priest (priests' leader)

1 When Jesus had finished praying, he and his disciples went out. They went across the Kidron valley. On the other side, there was a garden. Jesus and his disciples went into it. 2 Judas, who sold Jesus to Jesus' enemies, knew the garden. He knew it because Jesus and his disciples had met there often. 3 The most important priests and the Pharisees had sent a group of soldiers and some officers to Judas. Judas led these soldiers and officers to the garden. The soldiers had long knives and they carried lights.

4 Jesus knew everything that would soon happen to him. So, he went towards them. He asked them, 'Whom are you looking for?' 5 They answered, 'Jesus, who comes from Nazareth.' Jesus said, 'I am.'

Judas, who sold Jesus to Jesus' enemies, was standing with the soldiers. 6 When Jesus said to them, 'I am', the soldiers moved away from him. They fell down to the ground. 7 So Jesus asked them again, 'Whom are you looking for?' And they said, 'Jesus, who comes from Nazareth.' 8 Jesus said, 'I have told you already that "I am" that person. So, if you are looking for me, let these other men go.' 9 Jesus said this for a reason. Earlier, he had said, 'I have lost none of those men that you gave to me.' And what he had spoken earlier had to happen.

10 Simon Peter had a long knife. He lifted the knife and he attacked the Chief Priest's (priest's leader's) servant. He cut off the servant's right ear. The servant's name was Malchus. 11 Then Jesus said to Peter, 'Put your knife into the thing that covers it! Let them take me. My Father has told me what must happen to me. And I will obey him completely.'

12 The group of soldiers, with their captain and the Jews' officers, took Jesus and they tied him. 13 They led him first to Annas, who was the father of Caiaphas's wife. Caiaphas was the Chief Priest (priests' leader) that year. 14 It was Caiaphas who had spoken to the Jews' leaders some time before. He had told them, 'It is better that one man should die on behalf of all the people.'

Peter says that he does not know Jesus

15 Simon Peter and another disciple followed Jesus. The Chief Priest (priests' leader) knew that other disciple. So, he went with Jesus into the yard of the Chief Priest's house. 16 But Peter stayed outside by the gate. Then the other disciple, whom the Chief Priest knew, went out again. He spoke to the girl who was at the gate. Then he brought Peter inside.

17 The girl who was at the gate spoke to Peter. She asked him, 'Are you another of this man's (Jesus') disciples?' Peter replied, 'No, I am not!' 18 It was cold. So the servants and the officers were standing round a fire that they had made. They were making themselves warm. Peter went to stand with them, so that he could make himself warm too.

The Priests' Leader asks Jesus some questions

19 The Chief Priest (priests' leader) asked Jesus about his disciples. He also asked Jesus about what Jesus taught. 20 Jesus answered him, 'I have spoken in public places so that everyone could hear.

I have always taught in synagogues, or in God's Great House (the temple), where all the Jews meet together. I have said nothing secretly. 21 So, you do not need to ask me these questions. Ask the people who heard me. Ask them what I said to them. They know what I said.' 22 When Jesus said this, one of the soldiers hit him on the face. The soldier said, 'You must never speak to the Chief Priest (priests' leader) like that!' 23 Jesus replied, 'If I said something wrong, tell everyone about it. But if I said something true, you should not have hit me.' 24 Then Annas sent Jesus, who still had ropes round his arms, to Caiaphas, the Chief Priest (priests' leader).

Peter says again that he does not know Jesus

25 Simon Peter was still standing there (by the fire) so that he could make himself warm. The other people there said to him, 'We think that you are one of that man's disciples.' But Peter said, 'No, I am not.'

26 A servant of the priests' leader belonged to the same family as the man whose ear Peter had cut off. This servant said to Peter, 'I am sure that I saw you in the garden with him (Jesus).' 27 Again, Peter said, 'No.' And immediately the first bird sang, early in the morning.

Pilate, the Roman ruler, asks Jesus some questions

28 The Jews led Jesus from Caiaphas's house to the Roman ruler's big house (called the Praetorium). It was early in the morning. The Jews' leaders themselves did not go into the house because they wanted to be 'clean'. They wanted to eat the Passover meal.

29 So Pilate went outside to meet them. He asked them, 'What do you say that this man has done wrong?' 30 They replied, 'We would not have brought him to you if he had done nothing wrong.' 31 So Pilate said to them, 'You yourselves take him away. You judge him by your own rules.' The Jews replied, 'We do not have authority to kill anyone.' 32 This happened because of what Jesus had said earlier. Jesus had told them how he would die. So, what he had said had to happen.

33 Pilate returned into his big house (the Praetorium). He told Jesus that he must come to him. Pilate asked Jesus, 'Are you the king of the Jews?' 34 Jesus said, 'Is that your own idea, or have other people spoken to you about me?' 35 Pilate replied, 'I am not a Jew! It was your own people and their most important priests who brought you to me. What have you done?' 36 Jesus said, 'My kingdom does not belong to this world. If it did, my people would have fought. They would have fought so that the Jews could not take me. No, my kingdom is from another place.' 37 Pilate said to him, 'So do you mean that you really are a king?' Jesus answered, 'It is you are using the word "king". I was born and I came into the world for only one purpose. I came to tell people what is true. Everyone who loves all true things hears my voice.' 38 Pilate said, 'I do not know if anything is really true.'

Then Pilate went out again to the Jews. He said to them, 'This man seems to have done nothing wrong. I have no reason to punish him. 39 But every year we do something for you Jews. We let one man go free from the prison at the time of your Passover. Do you want me to let the king of the Jews go free?' 40 They shouted their answer, 'No, we do not want him! We want Barabbas!' (Barabbas was a man who had robbed people.)

Chapter 19

1 Then Pilate told the soldiers that they should take Jesus outside. He told them that they should hit Jesus many times with a whip.

2 The soldiers took some branches that had sharp points all over them. They made the branches into a circle that they put on Jesus' head. Then they took a dark red coat (like a king's coat) and they put that on him. 3 The soldiers came to him and they hit him with their hands. While they were hitting him, they said to him, 'Hello, great King of the Jews!'

4 Pilate went outside once more. He said to the crowd, 'Look, I will bring him (Jesus) out here to you. So now you will know that I cannot find any reason to punish him.' 5 So Jesus came out, with the circle of branches on his head. He was wearing the dark red coat. Pilate said to them, 'Look. Here is the man!' 6When the most important priests and the officers saw Jesus, they shouted, 'Kill him! Kill him on a cross!' Pilate said to them, 'You take him yourselves, and you kill him on a cross. I find no reason why anyone should punish him.' 7 The Jews answered, 'We have a rule. That rule says that he must die. He must die because he said, "I am the Son of God".'

8 When Pilate heard that, he was even more afraid. 9 He returned into the big house (the Praetorium). He asked Jesus, 'Where are you from?' But Jesus did not answer. 10 Pilate said to him, 'Are you refusing to speak to me? Remember that I have authority. I can let you go free, or I can let them kill you on a cross.' 11Jesus answered, 'You could have no authority against me unless God had given it to you. So, the man who sent me to you has done a worse thing. That man has done a worse thing than you have done.' 12 From that moment, Pilate tried to let Jesus go free. But the Jews shouted back, 'If you let him go, you are not Caesar's friend. Nobody should say that he himself is a king. Anyone who says that is Caesar's enemy!'

13 When Pilate heard those words, he brought Jesus outside. Pilate sat down on a special seat, where he judged. The seat was in a place called 'Gabbatha' in the Jews' language. There were large flat stones there, which covered the ground. 14 It was about 6 in the morning on the day when they prepared the Passover meal. Pilate said to the Jews, 'Here is your king!' 15 But they shouted, 'Take him away! Take him away! Kill him on a cross!' Pilate asked them, 'Do you want me to kill your king on a cross?' The most important priests answered, 'Caesar is the only ruler that we call king.' 16 Then Pilate gave Jesus to them, so that they could kill him on a cross.

They fix Jesus to a cross

17 Jesus went out to the place called 'The Place of the Skull'. This place is called 'Golgotha' in the Jews' language. He was carrying his own cross.

18 They fixed him to the cross with nails (short, sharp pieces of metal) and then they lifted the cross up. They put two other men on crosses with him, one on each side of him. Jesus was between them.

19 Pilate wrote a notice, and then he put it on the cross. It said: 'Jesus from Nazareth, the King of the Jews'. 20 The place where they put Jesus on the cross was near to the city. So, many of the Jews read this notice. They could read it because Pilate had written the words three times. He had written it in the Jews' language and in the languages called Roman and Greek. 21 The Jews' most important priests said to Pilate, 'Do not write: the King of the Jews. Instead, write: This man said, "I am the King of the Jews".' 22Pilate answered, 'I will not change what I have written.'

23 After the soldiers had put Jesus on the cross, they took his clothes. They made them into 4 parts, one part for each soldier. Also, they took his coat, which somebody had made from one piece of cloth. It was not several pieces of cloth that somebody had put together. 24 So they said to each other, 'We will not tear it. Instead, we will play a game. The person who wins the game will have the coat.' This happened because the Old Testament says:

'Each of them took some of my clothes.

They played a game to win what I was wearing.'

So, that is what the soldiers did.

25 Some women stood near to Jesus while he was on the cross. They were his mother, his mother's sister - Mary the wife of Cleopas - and Mary Magdalene (Mary from Magdala).

26 Jesus saw his mother. Also he saw the disciple that he loved. That disciple was standing near Jesus' mother. So Jesus said to his mother, 'Woman, here is your son.' 27 Then he said to the disciple, 'Here is your mother.' From that time, the disciple took her to live in his own home.

Jesus dies

28 Now Jesus had done everything that God had sent him into the world to do. Jesus knew this. So, because of what it says in the Old Testament, he said, 'I want a drink.' What it says in the Old Testament had to happen.

29 There was a pot full of cheap wine there. So the soldiers put a cloth into the wine. They fixed the cloth to the end of a branch. The branch was from a plant called hyssop. Then they lifted the cloth up to Jesus' mouth. 30 Jesus drank the wine. Then he said, 'I have finished it.' Then he bent his head down and he let his spirit go.

A soldier puts a spear into Jesus

31 It was a Friday - the day when the Jews prepared themselves for the Sabbath day. And that Sabbath day was a very important one. The Jews did not want the dead bodies to stay on the cross on the Sabbath day. So they asked Pilate to speak to the soldiers. The soldiers would break the legs of the men who were on the crosses. Then they could take the dead bodies down from the crosses.

32 So the soldiers went there. And they broke the legs of the two other men who were on the crosses next to Jesus. 33 But when they came to Jesus, he was dead already. They saw that he was dead. So they did not break his legs. 34 But one of the soldiers put a spear into Jesus' side. Immediately, blood and water came out. 35 The man who saw this has spoken about it. What he says is true. He knows that it really happened. He says this so that you can believe. 36 This happened because of what the Old Testament says. It says:

'Nobody will break any of his bones.'

And what the Old Testament says must happen. 37 And, in another place, the Old Testament says:

'People will look at the man whose body they have made a hole in.'

Joseph buries Jesus

38 After that, a man asked Pilate if he could take Jesus' dead body away. The man was called Joseph. He came from the town called Arimathea. He was one of Jesus' disciples, but that was a secret. It was a secret because he was afraid of the Jews' leaders. Pilate told Joseph that he could take the dead body. So Joseph went there and he took it away. 39 Nicodemus, the man who, earlier, had visited Jesus at night, went with Joseph. Nicodemus brought about 100 pounds of spices called myrrh and aloes. 40 The two men covered Jesus' dead body with these spices. And they put long pieces of cloth round it again and again. That is how the Jews prepare a dead body before they bury it. 41 There was a garden at the place where they killed Jesus on the cross. In that garden there was a new tomb, where nobody had ever put a dead person. 42 The next day was the Jews' Sabbath, and this tomb was near. So, they put Jesus there.

Chapter 20

The tomb is empty

1 Early on the first day of the week, Mary from Magdala went to the tomb. It was still dark. She saw that someone had removed the big stone from the way into the tomb.

2 So she ran to where Simon Peter was. He was with the other disciple, the one that Jesus loved. She said to them, 'They have taken the Lord out of the tomb. And we do not know where they have put him!'

3 So Peter and the other disciple started to go to the tomb. 4 Both of them were running. But the other disciple ran faster than Peter ran. So he reached the tomb first. 5 He bent himself down and he looked inside the tomb. He saw the long pieces of cloth that were lying there. But he did not go in. 6 Simon Peter had run behind the other disciple. When Peter arrived, he went into the tomb. He saw the long pieces of cloth that were lying there. 7 Also, he saw the piece of cloth that had been round Jesus' head. This was not in the same place as the other pieces of cloth. Someone had put it carefully in a separate place. 8 Then the other disciple, who had reached the tomb first, went inside also. He saw and he believed. 9 They still did not understand what the Old Testament says. It says that Jesus had to become alive again. After he had died, he had to become alive again.

Jesus appears to Mary from Magdala

10 Then the disciples returned to their homes. 11 But Mary stood outside the tomb. She was crying. While she cried, she bent herself down to look inside the tomb. 12 She saw two angels who were wearing white clothes. They were sitting where Jesus' dead body had been. One angel was sitting where Jesus' head had been. The other angel was sitting where his feet had been.

13 They asked her, 'Woman, why are you crying?' 14 She replied, 'They have taken away my Lord. And I do not know where they have put him.' When she had said this, she turned round. And she saw a man who was standing there. It was Jesus, but she did not recognise him. 15 Jesus said to her, 'Woman, why are you crying? Whom are you looking for?' She thought that he was the gardener. So she said, 'Sir, if you have carried him away, please tell me. Tell me where you have put him. Then I will take him away.'

16 Jesus said to her, 'Mary.' She turned towards him and she said in the Jews' language, 'Rabboni!' (This means 'Teacher'.) 17 Jesus said, 'Do not hold on to me because I have not gone up to the Father yet. But go to my brothers (the disciples). Tell them, "I go up to my Father. And he is your Father. He is my God, and he is your God." ' 18 Mary from Magdala went to the disciples. She said to them, 'I have seen the Lord!' Then she told them what he had said to her.

Jesus appears to his disciples

19 On the evening of that same day, the first day of the week, the disciples were all together. They had locked the doors of the room because they were afraid of the Jews' leaders. Then Jesus came and he stood among them. He said to them, 'Be without trouble in your minds and in your hearts.' 20 After he had said this, he showed them his hands and his side. The disciples were very, very happy when they saw the Lord. 21 Jesus said again, 'Be without trouble in your minds and in your hearts. As the Father sent me, in the same way I am sending you.' 22 When he had said this, he caused air from his mouth to blow on them. And he said, 'Receive God's Spirit. 23 If you forgive a person's sins, God will forgive them too. If you do not forgive them, God will not forgive them.'

Jesus shows himself to Thomas

24 One of the 12 disciples was called Thomas. He was not with the other disciples when Jesus came. (Thomas was also called 'the Twin'.) 25 So the other disciples told him, 'We have seen the Lord.' But Thomas said to them, 'I will never believe that unless I myself see him. I want to see the marks of the nails in his hands. I want to put my finger where the nails were. I want to put my hand into the hole in his side. I will not believe unless I do those things.'

26 Eight days after that, the disciples were in the house again, and Thomas was with them. They had locked the door. But Jesus came and he stood among them. He said, 'Be without trouble in your minds and in your hearts.' 27 Then he said to Thomas, 'Put your finger in here. Look at my hands. Put your hand in my side. Do not refuse to believe, but instead, believe.' 28 Thomas answered him, 'My Lord, and my God!' 29 Jesus said to him, 'You believe because you have seen me. Other people have not seen, but they do believe. And God will be good to those people.'

The purpose of this book

30 Jesus did many other miracles while the disciples were with him. I have not written about them in this book. 31 But I have written about these things, so that you will be able to believe. You will be able to believe that Jesus is the Christ, the Son of God. And when you believe, you will be able to live. You will be able to live because of who he is.

Chapter 21

Jesus shows himself to the disciples again

1 After that, Jesus showed himself to the disciples again. They were by Lake Tiberias. This is how it happened. 2 Simon Peter, Thomas the Twin, and Nathanael (who came from Cana in Galilee) were together. They were with the sons of Zebedee (James and John) and two other disciples. 3 Simon Peter said to the other disciples, 'I am going to catch fish.' They replied, 'We will come with you.' So they went out and they got into the boat. But they caught nothing during that night.

4 Early in the morning, Jesus was standing on the shore. But the disciples did not know that it was Jesus. 5 Then Jesus asked them, 'Friends, have you caught any fish?' They answered, 'No!' 6 He said, 'Throw your net out on the right side of the boat. If you do that, you will catch some fish.' So they threw the net out. Then they caught so many fish that they could not pull the net into the boat.

7 The disciple that Jesus loved said to Peter, 'It is the Lord!' When Simon Peter heard him say, 'It is the Lord', he put on his coat. (He was wearing only a very few clothes.) Then Peter jumped into the water. 8 The other disciples followed him in the boat. They pulled the net that was full of fish behind them. They were not far from the shore. It was about 100 metres away. 9 When they came to the shore, they saw a red fire there. Some fish were lying on the fire. There was some bread there, too. 10 Jesus said to them, 'Bring some of the fish that you have just caught.'

11 Simon Peter got into the boat and he pulled the net on to the shore. It was full of big fish. There were 153 fish. There were so many fish, but the net did not tear. 12 Jesus said to them, 'Come and eat breakfast.' None of the disciples was brave enough to ask him, 'Who are you?' They knew that it was the Lord. 13 So Jesus went and he got the bread. Then he gave it to them. And he did the same with the fish.

14 This was the third time that Jesus showed himself to the disciples. After Jesus had died, he had become alive again. And this was the third time that he showed himself to them.

Jesus talks to Peter

15 When they had finished eating, Jesus spoke to Simon Peter. He said, 'Simon, son of John, do you love me more than these?' Peter answered, 'Yes Lord, you know that I love you.' Jesus said to him, 'Feed my lambs (young sheep).'

16 Jesus asked him a second time, 'Simon, son of John, do you love me?' Peter answered, 'Yes Lord, you know that I love you.' Jesus said to him, 'Look after my sheep.' 17 Jesus asked him a third time, 'Simon, son of John, do you love me?' Peter was sad because Jesus asked him a third time, 'Do you love me?' So he said to Jesus, 'Lord, you know everything. You know that I do love you!' Jesus said to him, 'Look after my sheep. 18 I am telling you what is true. When you were young, you got yourself ready. And you went to any place that you wanted to visit. But when you are old, it will be different. You will hold out your arms and someone else will tie you. Then they will take you where you do not want to go.' 19 Jesus was speaking about how Peter would die. It would show how great God is. Then Jesus said to Peter, 'Follow me.'

20 Peter turned round. He saw another disciple. It was the disciple that Jesus loved. This disciple was following them. He was the man who had been very near to Jesus at the supper. This disciple had asked Jesus, 'Lord, who will sell you to your enemies?' 21 When Peter saw this disciple, he asked Jesus, 'Lord, what will happen to him?' 22 Jesus answered him, 'Perhaps I might want him to live on the earth until I return. But it does not matter to you. You must follow me!'

23 Then people began to talk about these words that Jesus had said. People who believed Jesus began to have a wrong idea about this disciple. They thought that this disciple would not die. But Jesus did not say,

'He will not die.' Instead, he said, 'Perhaps I might want him to live until I return. But it does not matter to you.' 24 This is the disciple who spoke about these things. This is the disciple who wrote them down. And what he said is true. We know that.

25 Jesus did many other things also. If people wrote down all those things, there would be many, many books. I do not think that the whole world could contain all those books.

The work that Jesus' apostles did

Acts

This is about the book

Luke wrote this book in the year AD 63. He was not a Jew but he was a disciple of Jesus. He was a doctor. Luke was one of Paul's friends. Sometimes he went with Paul when Paul travelled from country to country. He went to Rome with Paul and he stayed there with him.

Luke wrote the book to send to Theophilus. Theophilus was an important Roman man. This is the second book that Luke wrote for him. The first book is called 'Luke'. In this second book, Luke tells us how God first gave his Holy Spirit to the apostles. He writes about the work of the apostles in Jerusalem and in cities in many other countries. He tells us how more and more people believed in Jesus. He also writes about problems between Christians. Some of these were Jews and some of them were not.

He also tells us that the leaders of the Jews did not believe in Jesus. They wanted the apostles to stop teaching the people about Jesus.

The book is in 5 parts:

A   How more people believed in Jesus in Judea and Jerusalem.

1   How the apostles took God's message about Jesus to the cities near Jerusalem.

2   How the apostles took God's message about Jesus to the cities in other countries. The other countries were near Judea.

B   How Paul travelled to many countries with the good news about Jesus. He also taught people who were not Jews about Jesus.

3   Where Paul went on his first journey to teach people about Jesus.

4   Where Paul went on his second journey to teach people about Jesus.

5   Paul's last big journey, when he went to Rome.

Chapter 1

Jesus tells the apostles that God will send the Holy Spirit to them

1 Jesus began to do many things when he was working on earth. He also began to teach people many things. I told you about all these things in the first book that I wrote for you, Theophilus.

That first book is called 'Luke'.

2 I told you about the things that Jesus did until God took Him up into heaven. Jesus had chosen some men to be his apostles. He had told them by the Holy Spirit what they must do. Then God took Jesus back to heaven. 3 Jesus had died and then he became alive again. During the 40 days after that, he showed himself many times to his apostles. He showed himself in different ways. They could then be sure that Jesus was really alive again. The apostles often saw Jesus, and he talked to them about the Kingdom of God.

4 While Jesus was still with his apostles, he spoke to them. He said, 'Do not leave Jerusalem yet. You must wait there for my Father's gift that I told you about. My Father promised to give it to you. 5 John baptised people with water, but after a few days God will baptise you with the Holy Spirit.'

God takes Jesus up to heaven

6 Jesus' apostles all met together with him. 'Lord', they said, 'will you at this time give the people of Israel their kingdom back? Will they now rule their own country again?'

7 'My Father decides when things will happen in the world', Jesus replied. 'He does not want you to know when this will happen. 8 But the Holy Spirit will come to you, and he will cause you to become powerful. The Holy Spirit will cause your spirit to be strong. Then you can tell other people about me. You will tell people about me in Jerusalem, in Judea, in Samaria and in all other countries.'

9 When Jesus had finished speaking to his apostles, God took him up into God's home. The apostles watched Jesus go. Then a cloud hid him and the apostles could not see him any longer.

10 The apostles were still looking carefully up into the sky when suddenly two men appeared. The men were wearing white clothes and they stood near the apostles.

11 Then they spoke to the apostles. 'You men from Galilee, you should not still be standing here', they said. 'You should not still look up into the sky. God has taken Jesus into heaven. You saw the way that Jesus went up to heaven. One day, he will return in the same way.'

The apostles choose Matthias to be an apostle

12 Then the apostles returned to Jerusalem from the hill called the Mount of Olives. The Mount of Olives was about one kilometre from the city. 13 When the apostles arrived in Jerusalem, they went upstairs. And they went into the room where they were staying. The names of the apostles were Peter, John, James and Andrew, Philip and Thomas, Bartholomew and Matthew. The other apostles, James the son of Alphaeus, Simon the Zealot, and Judas, the son of James, were also there.

14 The apostles often met together in a group to pray. They prayed together with Mary, Jesus' mother, other women and his brothers. 15 A few days after that, about 120 people met together. These people all believed in Jesus. Peter stood up and he spoke to them. 16 'My friends', he said, 'Long ago, the Holy Spirit spoke to King David and David wrote down this message. He wrote about the things that Judas would do.'

'These things had to happen and now they have happened. Judas showed the soldiers how to catch Jesus. Judas helped them to do it. 17 Judas was in our group, because Jesus chose him. He chose Judas to work together with us.'

18 The priests gave Judas some money because he had helped them. Judas bought a field with that money. But he then fell down in that field and he died. His body broke open and the inside of his body fell out. 19 All the people who lived in Jerusalem heard about the death of Judas. So the people called that field Akeldama in their own language. Akeldama means 'The Field of Blood'.

20 Peter continued, 'King David wrote in the book of Psalms,

"So the house that he had will be empty.

Nobody should live in it." '

'King David also wrote in the same book,

"So, another person must do his work." '

21 'Because of this, we need to choose another man', said Peter. 'This man must have been together with us from the beginning. He must have been in our group all the time that Jesus was with us. 22 The man must have been with us when John was baptising people. He must have stayed with us while Jesus was working. He must have been with us when Jesus went up to heaven. Then he can say to the people, "I know that our master died. I saw him after he became alive again." '

23 So the group said the names of two men. One of these men was Joseph, who had two other names. People also called him Barsabbas and sometimes people called him Justus. The other man was called Matthias. 24 Then the whole group prayed. 'Lord, you know what everybody is really thinking', they said. 'Please show us which man you have chosen. Which of these two men do you want to be an apostle? 25 Judas left his work as an apostle. He has gone to the right place for him.'

26 Then the group chose which of the men would do the work of an apostle. It happened that they chose Matthias. So Matthias took the place of Judas and he became the twelfth apostle, together with the other 11 men.

Chapter 2

The Holy Spirit comes

1 Then the day that the Jews called 'The Day of Pentecost' came. All the believers were meeting together in a house in Jerusalem.

2 Then, suddenly, as they were sitting together, they heard a noise. The sound came from the sky. It was like the sound of a strong wind. They could hear the noise everywhere in the house. 3 Then they saw something move, like many small separate fires. The small fires moved in the room and they touched every person. 4 God filled each person with the Holy Spirit. Then the believers began to speak in foreign languages that they had not learned. They spoke like that because the Holy Spirit helped them.

5 At that time, other Jews, who prayed to God every day, were living in Jerusalem. They came from many different countries in the world. 6 The believers made a loud noise when they spoke these other languages. When these other Jews heard this loud noise, they came together in a large crowd. Each person could hear the disciples speaking in their own language. This confused them. And so they did not know what to think. 7 But they were very surprised. 'These men who are speaking like this are from Galilee', they said. 8 'we do not know what is happening. We can all hear them speak in the language of our own home country.

9 Some of us are from Parthia, Media and Elam. Some of us are from Mesopotamia, Judea and Cappadocia. Some of us are from Pontus and Asia. 10 Some of us are from Phrygia and Pamphylia. Some of us are from Egypt. Some of us are from near the town called Cyrene. Cyrene is in the country called Libya. Some of us are from Rome. 11 Some of us are Jews. Some of us do not have Jewish parents, but now we believe in the God of the Jews. Some of us are from Crete and some of us are from Arabia. But we all hear these people speaking in our own languages. They are speaking about all the great things that God has done.' 12 All the people were very surprised. They did not understand what was happening. 'How can we explain all this?' they asked each other.

13 Other people laughed at the disciples. They said to each other, 'These people are drunk!'

Peter speaks to the crowd

14 Peter was with the other 11 apostles and he stood up. He began to speak to the crowd with a loud voice. He explained to them what was happening.

'You people, who are also Jews like us, listen to me. And all you people, who live here in Jerusalem, listen to me. I will explain to you everything that is happening. 15 Some of you think that my friends here are drunk. But they are not drunk, because it is only 9 o'clock in the morning.'

The Jewish day began at 6 o'clock in the morning. On the Day of Pentecost, the Jews prayed at 9 o'clock. Then they ate their first meal of the day at 10 o'clock. So at 9 o'clock they would not yet have had any food or drink that day. So they could not be drunk.

16 'Something different is happening here. Joel was a prophet and he spoke God's words about it a long time ago. He said that one day this would happen. This is what Joel said.'

We can read what Joel said in Joel 2:28-32.

17 '"This is what I will do in the last days", God says.

"I will give my Spirit to all people.

Your sons and daughters will speak my message to people

Your young men will see pictures from me in their minds.

> And your old men will see things in their dreams.

18 At that time, I will give my Spirit.

Yes, I will even give my Spirit to the men and women who are my servants.

> Then they will speak my message to people.

19 I will cause special things to appear in the sky.

I will also cause special things to appear on the earth. They will be powerful things that only I can do.

> There will be blood, fire and thick dark smoke.

20 And the sun will become dark, and it will not shine any longer.

The moon will become dark red like the colour of blood

These things will happen before the Lord God's very important day comes.

> On that day, my light will shine everywhere.

21 People will ask me to save them and I will give them new life", God said.'

We do many wrong things. The result is that we are separated from God. God's message is that only Jesus can save us from the result of these wrong things. Jesus can bring us close to God again. We must say sorry to God for all these wrong things that we have done. We must tell God that now we will obey him. Then God will welcome us into his kingdom. God will give us a new life.

22 'Now, people of Israel, listen to what I am saying!' Peter said. 'God sent Jesus of Nazareth to the earth to work for him. God worked by Jesus and did many powerful and special things. Because of this, people should know that God had sent Jesus. You know about all this. These things happened here, and you saw them. 23 God knew that the Romans would give Jesus to you. God had decided that this should happen. So you killed Jesus. You let bad men fix him to the cross. 24 And so Jesus died. But God caused him to become alive again. God saved Jesus from the power of death. It was impossible for Jesus to stay dead. 25 A long time ago, King David spoke about Jesus.

> "I saw the Lord in front of me all the time", he said.

> "He is next to me, so nothing will cause me trouble.

26 I am very happy because of this,

> so I must talk about it.

> I know that I am a man.

But I know that you have promised me these things. So they will certainly happen.

27 So you will not leave my soul with all the dead people.

> Your servant loves you.

> And so you will not let anything destroy his body when he dies.

28 You have shown me the good paths that lead me to true life.

> You are next to me, so I am completely happy." '

29 'People of Israel', Peter then said, 'I must speak clear words to you about King David. Long ago he was our ancestor and king. David died and people buried his body in the ground. The place where people buried him is still here today.

30 David spoke words from God. He knew what God had promised him. God promised David that a special man from his family would be a king. This man would be a king like David. 31 And David understood what God would do in future days. So David spoke about this special man that God would send to the world. When this person died, God would cause him to become alive again. David said that God would not let him remain dead among dead people. He said that nothing would destroy his body. 32 This man that David talked about was Jesus. Jesus died. But God caused him to become alive again. We ourselves saw this. 33 God took him back to his right side in heaven. So now Jesus is sitting in the most important place, next to his Father.'

'God is Jesus' Father, and he gave Jesus the Holy Spirit. God had promised Jesus that he would do this. Now Jesus has given us the Holy Spirit today as a gift. You are seeing and hearing the result of this. 34 David did not go up into heaven like Jesus did. But David said.

> "The Lord God said to my Lord:

> Sit here next to me at my right side.

35 While you sit here, I will beat your enemies.

> They will be under you, like a place to put your feet." '

36 'All you people of Israel must be sure to know this. You killed Jesus on a cross. But it is this same Jesus that God chose as that special person. God caused him to be Lord.'

37 The people heard what Peter said to them. Then they had much trouble in their minds. So they asked Peter and the other apostles for help. 'Friends, what must we do?' they said.

38 'Each of you has done wrong things', Peter told them. 'You must tell God that you are sorry about that. Then you must stop doing those wrong things. You must obey God and you must do right things. Then someone with the authority of Jesus Christ will baptise you. And God will forgive you for all the wrong things that you have done. Then God will give you his gift, which is the Holy Spirit. 39 God has promised to forgive you and your children. He has also promised to give the Holy Spirit to you and to your children. He has also promised this to people who live in other countries. God has chosen many people to believe in him. He includes all of them in his promise.'

40 So Peter told the people what they must do. He also told them many other things. He continued to speak with serious words to them. He said, 'Save yourselves from the punishment that God will send. God will send it to bad people who are alive now.'

41 Many of the people who listened to Peter believed his words. So the apostles baptised them. About three thousand joined the group that same day. They all believed in Jesus.

This is how the believers lived

42 These new believers stayed with the apostles so that they could learn more about Jesus. And they all became good friends with everyone else in the group. They prayed together and they ate meals together.

43 The Holy Spirit worked with the apostles. He caused them to be powerful, so that they could make sick people well. And they could do many other special things. All the people were very surprised and afraid because of these special things. 44 All the believers continued to be good friends with each other. They ate meals together, and they learned more about Jesus. They continued to pray together. They gave each other some of the things that they had. 45 They sold some of their own things. Then they gave that money to other believers who needed it.

46 The whole group of believers met together every day in the Great House of God. They ate their meals together in each other's homes and they were all very happy together. They thanked God for everything. 47 The believers often said how great and important God was. All the other people liked the believers. And they thought that the believers were very good people. Every day, more people asked the Lord to save them. So he was making the group of those who believed in him much bigger.

Chapter 3

This is what happened to the man with weak legs

1 One day, Peter and John went to the Great House of God in Jerusalem. It was 3 o'clock in the afternoon. This was the time that everyone went there to pray. 2 There was a man who could not walk. He had never been able to walk. Every day, his friends put him at the gate of the Great House of God. It was called the Beautiful Gate. As people were going through the gate into the Great House of God, the man asked them for money. His friends were carrying him to the gate when Peter and John came to the gate. 3 Then the man saw Peter and John come through the gate. So he asked them to give him some money. 4 Peter and John looked at the man's face. And Peter said to him, 'Look at us!' 5 So the man looked at Peter and John. He thought that they would give him some money.

6 Then Peter said to the man, 'I do not have any money. But I do have something else that I will give to you. Jesus Christ from Nazareth gave me authority to do this. So I order you to walk!' 7 Peter then held the man's right hand to help him stand up. Immediately the man's feet and ankles became strong. 8 So the man jumped up and he stood on his feet. Then he began to walk about and he went into the Great House of God with Peter and John. He was walking and jumping. And he was saying to God, 'You, God, are very powerful and good.' 9 A large crowd of people were with Peter and John. They saw the man walking. And they heard him saying good things about God. 10 'Look!' they said. 'We know this man. He usually sits at the Beautiful Gate. He used to have weak legs and he asked people for money. What has happened? He can now walk!' they said to each other. They were all very surprised.

Peter speaks to the crowd in the Great House of God

11 The man was still holding Peter and John as they went to Solomon's Porch. And the people were very surprised about what they were seeing. So they ran to them there. 12 Peter saw all the people. They were running towards him. So he said to them, 'People of Israel, you should not be so surprised about what you have seen. You should not look at us so much. Perhaps you think that we ourselves are powerful. Maybe you think that we are very good people. But we are not so powerful or so good that we could cause this man to walk. 13 Jesus was the special servant of God. Our ancestors Abraham, Isaac, Jacob and other people prayed to this same God long ago. God gave his authority to Jesus and caused him to be powerful. He showed people that Jesus was a very great and important person.'

'You gave Jesus to the rulers, and you told Pilate bad things about him. You wanted them to kill Jesus even after Pilate had spoken. "I do not believe that Jesus has done anything wrong", he said. "I have already decided that Jesus should leave the prison." 14 Jesus was completely good and he obeyed God all the time. But you did not accept him. There was also a bad man in the prison who had killed some people. You said to Pilate, "Please let the other man leave the prison. Do not let Jesus go out." 15 Then you asked Pilate to kill Jesus. But God caused Jesus to become alive again. He is the person who leads people to true life. We ourselves saw Jesus alive again after he had died. 16 Now, you know that this man here had weak legs. But Jesus is powerful. Jesus' authority caused this man's legs to become strong. This really happened because Jesus is powerful. You can see that. This man believed that Jesus could cause his legs to become strong. So Jesus made him well. And you yourselves can see that he is walking.

17 People, listen to what I say. You wanted Pilate's soldiers to kill Jesus. At that time, you and your leaders did not know what you were doing. 18 Jesus was the Christ, the special person that God would send to the world. A long time ago, many men spoke words from God about him. They told people what would happen to the Christ. "Bad people will hurt the Christ, and he will have a lot of pain", they said. God caused this to become true.

19 So you must say sorry to God for all the wrong things that you have done. You must say that you will obey God. Then God will forgive you for all the wrong things that you have done. 20 Then the Lord will be near to you and he will cause your spirit to be strong. God has already chosen Jesus for you. He is the Christ, God's special servant, and God will send him back to you again. 21 Jesus must stay in heaven until the day that he will make everything new. Those men who spoke words from God a long time ago told us about this. 22 "God sent me to you", Moses said to the people a long time ago. "He will also send another man later who will speak his words. This man will be one of your own people. You must listen to everything that he says to you. 23 God will take out from among his people everyone who does not obey this chosen man. God will then kill them." '

24 'God gave this same message to Samuel many years ago. God then gave it to many other men who came after Samuel. And they all told us what would happen at this time. 25 The men who spoke God's words told the people about God's promises. God promised these things to your ancestors, but you are also included in his promises. God said to Abraham. "By your family, I will do a good thing for all the people on the earth." '

26 'God chose Jesus to be his special servant. Then God sent him to you first. God wants you to say sorry to him for all the wrong things that you have done. Then you will obey God because he wants to do good things for you.'

Chapter 4

The priests put Peter and John in prison

1 Peter was still speaking to the crowd in Solomon's Porch and John was standing next to him. Then some priests, Sadducees and the leader of the policemen of the Great House of God came towards them. 2 These people were angry because of the things that Peter and John were saying to the crowd. They had said, 'Jesus became alive again after he had died.' This showed everyone that dead people could become alive again. 3 So the priests, Sadducees and the leader of the policemen took Peter and John away. And they put Peter and John in the prison, because by then it was late. They stayed in the prison all that night. 4 But many of the people in the crowd had believed Peter's message. Soon there were 5000 men who believed in Jesus.

Peter and John stand in front of the Sanhedrin

5 The next day, the leaders of the Jews met together in Jerusalem. The important priests and the teachers of the Law met together with them. 6 They met with Annas and Caiaphas who were the most important priests. John and Alexander were also there and they were part of their family. Other men from their family were with them.

7 The men in the Sanhedrin said to Peter and John, 'Stand in front of us!' They said to Peter and John, 'How did you cause that man's legs to become strong? Who gave you the power and the authority to do it?'

8 Then the Holy Spirit told Peter what to say to the men in the Sanhedrin. So Peter answered them. 'All you men are leaders of the people and you are the most important Jews. 9 Today you are asking us questions about the good thing that we did for this man. You are asking us how we caused his legs to become strong. 10 Now I need to tell you and all the people of Israel some things. Then you will all know how this happened. This man is standing with us in front of you. His legs are strong because Jesus Christ of Nazareth is powerful. Jesus has the authority to do this. You killed Jesus; you fixed him to a cross. He died, but after that, God caused him to become alive again. 11 Men who spoke God's words wrote this about Jesus a long time ago.

12 Then Peter said, 'Only Jesus can save people from the result of all the wrong things they have done. There has never been another person in the world that could do this. God has not given any other man the authority to save us.' 13 Then the men of the Sanhedrin saw that Peter and John were very brave. They also knew that Peter and John were not important people. They had not been to a special school. So the men were very surprised about how Peter and John spoke. They also understood that Peter and John had been with Jesus.

14 The men of the Sanhedrin could see the man who had had weak legs. And they could see that now his legs were strong. So they could not think of anything to say to Peter and John. 15 They ordered Peter and John to go out of the room. Then the men of the Sanhedrin talked to each other. 16 'What should we do with these men?' they said. 'Everyone who lives in Jerusalem knows about these things. They know that Peter and John did a very special thing for that man. So we cannot say that they did not do it. 17 But we want to stop more people from joining their group. So we must say to these men, "You must stop using the name of Jesus. You must stop speaking to people about Jesus." '

18 Then the men of the Sanhedrin asked Peter and John to come back into the room. They said to Peter and John, 'You must not speak or teach people again about Jesus. You do not have any authority.' 19 Then Peter and John replied to them. 'You must decide yourselves which of these things God wants us to do. Either we should obey you, or we should obey God. 20 We must continue to speak about these things. And we must tell people everything that we have seen and heard.'

21 The leaders of the Jews spoke in an angry way to them. 'Peter and John, you must not speak to the people again about Jesus. If you do not obey us, then we will punish you.' Then they let Peter and John go away into the street again. They could not punish Peter and John because they had helped the man to walk. All the people in Jerusalem were saying to God, 'You are great and good and powerful.' 22 The man whom God had caused to become well was more than 40 years old.

All the believers pray to God

23 So the leaders of the priests and the important Jews let Peter and John go out into the street again. Immediately, Peter and John went back to meet with all the other believers. They told them what the leaders of the priests and the important Jews had said. 24 And the believers listened to what Peter and John told them. Then they prayed together. 'You are God and you rule over everything', they prayed. 'You made the sky, the earth and the sea. You also made everything that is in them. 25 King David, our ancestor, was also your servant. You sent your Holy Spirit to help him. And your Spirit told King David to say, "People who were not Jews were very angry.

        The people made plans that would not happen.

26   The kings on the earth prepared to fight.

        The rulers of the world met together.

        They wanted to fight against the Lord.

They would also fight against the special servant that God chose." '

27 The believers continued to pray. 'Herod and Pontius Pilate met together with other people who are not Jews. They also met with the people of Israel who were here in Jerusalem. Together they spoke against Jesus. Jesus was your special servant and they all wanted to kill him. You had chosen him to be the Christ. 28 Yes, God, you are powerful. And you had already decided what these men would do to Jesus. So they met together. And they did what you wanted to happen to Jesus. 29 God, you know how the men of the Sanhedrin want to hurt Peter and John. You know what they said to your servants. So please help us to speak to the people again about you. And please cause us to become brave. 30 You are strong and you can cause sick people to become well. And you can also do other powerful things. The people will see these things happen when we speak Jesus' name. You gave your authority to Jesus. He is very good and he is your servant. So please do these things.'

31 The believers finished praying. Then, the house where they were meeting together moved about. God filled them all with his Holy Spirit. And the Holy Spirit caused them to be very brave and they spoke to the people about Jesus again.

The believers give their own things to each other

32 All the believers thought about everything in the same way. They did not keep any of their own things for themselves. They let all the other believers use them. 33 The words of the apostles were powerful and they told people about Jesus. 'After Jesus died, God caused him to live again', they said. They told them what they had seen. God helped the believers in many different ways. 34 They had everything that they needed. Some believers had land or houses, which they sold. They took the money that they received for these things. They brought it to the apostles and gave it to them. 35 Then the apostles gave the money to any of the believers who needed it.

36 There was a believer called Joseph. He was from the family of Levi. He was from the island called Cyprus. He helped the other believers to work well. So the apostles called him Barnabas. 37 Barnabas sold one of his fields. And he brought the money and he gave it all to the apostles.

Chapter 5

What happens to Ananias and Sapphira

1 But there was a man called Ananias and his wife who was called Sapphira. Together they sold one of their fields. 2 Ananias gave part of the money that he received to the apostles. But he also kept part of the money for himself. Sapphira knew all about what Ananias had done.

3 'Ananias, Satan wanted you to say something that was not true. And you obeyed him', Peter said to Ananias. 'You should not have listened to him. You should not tell the Holy Spirit something that is not true. You sold your field, but you did not give us all the money. You kept part of it for yourselves.'

The Holy Spirit had told Peter what Ananias had done. Ananias did not need to tell him.

4 'Before you sold the field, it was yours. And after you sold the field, the money was yours. You should not have decided to say that it was all the money. You did not only tell men something that was not true. You told God something that was not true.'

5 As soon as he had heard Peter say this, Ananias fell down immediately. And he died. This frightened everyone who heard about it. 6 Some young men came into the room. They put cloths round Ananias's dead body and they carried it outside. Then they buried it.

7 About three hours later, Ananias's wife, Sapphira, came into the room to see Peter. Sapphira did not know that Ananias was dead. 8 Peter asked Sapphira, 'Tell me about this money that you gave us. Was this all the money that you and your husband received for your field?' 'Yes', Sapphira answered. 'That was all the money that we received.'

9 'It was wrong for you and your husband to do this', Peter said to her. 'You should not have told God's Spirit something that was not true. You knew that this was wrong. The men who have just buried your husband are at the door again now. And they will also carry you out.'

10 Immediately, Sapphira fell down in front of Peter and she died. Then the young men came into the room. They saw that Sapphira was dead. So they carried her outside and they buried her next to her husband. 11 All the believers, and many other people, heard about what had happened to Ananias and Sapphira. They were all very afraid.

The apostles do some powerful things for the people to see

12 The apostles were doing many powerful things in front of the people. All the believers met together in a group.

They met outside the Great House of God in a place called Solomon's Porch. 13 Those people who were not believers did not sit with the group. They were afraid to do that. There were many people who said good things about the believers. 14 More and more people became believers and they joined the group. So now many men and women believed in Jesus. 15 People carried their sick friends into the streets and put them on beds and pieces of floor cloth. They did this because of all the special things that the apostles were doing. Some people only wanted Peter's shadow to pass over their sick friends.

16 Many people came into Jerusalem from the small towns near the city. They also brought their sick friends with them. They brought other people too. Bad spirits inside them were giving them trouble. And God caused all these people to become well again.

The most important priest puts the apostles in prison

17 All the people liked the apostles. And they liked what the apostles did. The most important priest, his friends, and some of the Sadducees, were not happy about this. So they decided to do something about the apostles. 18 These important men took hold of the apostles and they put them in the prison. 19 But during the night, one of God's angels opened the prison gates and he led the apostles out. The angel said to them, 20 'Go and stand in the Great House of God. Tell the people everything about this new way to live.'

21 The apostles heard the angel and they obeyed him. Early the next morning, the apostles went into the Great House of God. And then they began to teach the people. The most important priest and his friends ordered all the important Jews to meet with them. He wanted all the men of the Sanhedrin to meet together. Then the men of the Sanhedrin sent policemen with a message to the prison. They ordered the soldiers to bring the apostles to them. 22 But when the policemen arrived at the prison, they did not find the apostles there. So then the policemen returned to the men of the Sanhedrin. And they told them what they had seen at the prison. 23 'We arrived at the prison', they said. 'We saw that the soldiers had locked the gates. They were standing at the gates and they were guarding the prison. But when we opened the gates of the prison, we did not find any of the apostles inside.'

24 The leader of the policemen of the Great House of God and the leaders of the priests heard about this. 'We cannot understand what has happened to the apostles', they said.

25 Then a man came and he brought them a message. 'Listen to me!' he said. 'Those men that you put in the prison are now standing in the Great House of God. They are teaching the people.' 26 The leader of the policemen then took his policemen with him to the Great House of God.

He said to the apostles, 'Come back with us!' The policemen did not hurt the apostles or tie their arms and legs. They were afraid of the people. They thought that the people might throw stones at them.

27 The policemen brought the apostles into the room. They caused them to stand in front of the men of the Sanhedrin. The most important priest spoke to the apostles.

28 'We ordered that you must not teach the people again with the authority of Jesus. But now look at what you have done! Now people all over Jerusalem have heard you teaching. And you have taught the people that we ordered the death of Jesus.'

29 Peter and the other apostles answered. 'We must obey God', they said, 'rather than obey men. 30 The God of our ancestors caused Jesus to be alive again. You fixed Jesus to a cross and killed him. But then, God made him alive again. 31 God put Jesus next to him at his right side. Jesus is now the leader and the person who saves the people of Israel. Because of this, he helps those who believe in him. He helps them to say, "We are sorry" to God for all the wrong things that they have done. Then God forgives them and he helps them to do right things. 32 We tell people what we have seen and heard. He gives his Holy Spirit to people who obey him. And the Holy Spirit also tells people what God has done.'

33 The men of the Sanhedrin heard what the apostles said to them. They were so angry that they wanted to kill the apostles.

34 But one man did not agree. He stood up in front of the Sanhedrin. He was called Gamaliel and he was a Pharisee, a teacher of the Law. All the men of the Sanhedrin liked Gamaliel. And they thought that he was a good man. Gamaliel asked the policemen to take the apostles out of the room. 35 When they had gone, Gamaliel spoke to the Sanhedrin. 'Men of Israel!' he said. 'Be careful about what you want to do. Think again before you kill these men. 36 Remember what happened to Theudas a few years ago. That man told everyone, "I am a very important leader." Then about 400 men came to join his group. But then somebody killed Theudas, and his men all went away in different directions. Nobody hears about them now. 37 Remember what happened to Judas from Galilee. That man appeared when the Romans were counting the people. A crowd also came to help Judas, but somebody killed him. The men who followed Judas also went away in different directions. Nobody hears about them now either.'

38 'Now this same thing is happening again with these men. So I say that you must not do anything bad to them. Leave them alone. Perhaps these men are doing what some man told them to do. If that is true, then their work will fail. 39 But perhaps God has said that they must do this work. And if that is true, then you cannot stop them. You might even find that you are fighting against God!' So the men of the Sanhedrin did what Gamaliel said.

40 They ordered the apostles to return to the room. Then they said to the policemen, 'Hit these men with whips!' Then the men of the Sanhedrin said to the apostles, 'You must not teach the people again. Do not use the authority of Jesus.' After that, they let the apostles go out into the street again.

41 So the apostles walked away from the men of the Sanhedrin. They were very happy because they thought to themselves, 'God believes that we are good enough to receive punishment because of Jesus.' 42 So they continued to teach the people about Jesus. They spoke every day in people's homes and in the Great House of God. They told the people that Jesus was the Christ, the special servant of God. And so the apostles told people all the good news about Jesus.

Chapter 6

The believers choose 7 other men to do special work

1 At that time, more and more people every day became believers in Jesus. Some Jews in Jerusalem spoke the Greek language. Other Jews in Jerusalem spoke the Aramaic language. The Jews who spoke Greek had a problem with the other Jews.

Those who spoke Greek said to the other Jews, 'We have a problem with you. The husbands of some of your own women have died. They receive money from the apostles every day to buy food. The husbands of some of the women in our group have also died. But the apostles do not give these women money every day.'

2 The 12 apostles heard about the problem. So they asked all those who believed in Jesus to meet together with them. The apostles said, 'Our work is to teach people the message from God.

It is not right for us to stop doing this work. But we are giving out the money to those people who need things. That is not good.'3 So the apostles said to the believers, 'Our friends, please choose 7 men from among you. You must know that the Holy Spirit is living inside each of them. And they must know the things about God very well. We will ask these 7 men to do this work for us. 4 Then we will have more time to pray. We will also have more time to teach the people the good news about Jesus.'

5 The whole group was happy with the apostles' words. So first they chose a man called Stephen. Stephen believed God really well. The Holy Spirit lived inside him. The believers also chose 6 other men. These other men were called Philip, Prochorus, Nicanor, Timon, Parmenas and Nicolaus. Nicolaus was from Antioch. He was not born a Jew, but he had believed in the God of the Jews. 6 The group asked these 7 men to stand up in front of the apostles. Then the apostles put their hands on each man. They asked God to help the 7 men with their special work.

7 So more and more people heard the word of God. The number of believers in Jesus in Jerusalem continued to grow greater and greater. And many of the priests also believed in Jesus.

The important Jews take hold of Stephen

8 God helped Stephen in special ways and caused him to do powerful things. The people saw Stephen do many special things. 9 But some men did not like Stephen. They did not like what Stephen taught about Jesus. These men were from one of the synagogues in Jerusalem that was called the 'Synagogue of the Free Men'. The men from
this synagogue were Jews from the cities called Cyrene and Alexandria. And some of them were from towns in Cilicia and Asia. These men began to argue with Stephen.

10 The Holy Spirit gave Stephen great wisdom and caused him to speak in a very powerful way. So Stephen spoke to the men from this synagogue. And they could not say that he was wrong.

11 So the men from the synagogue gave money to some bad men. They paid them to say bad things about Stephen. But those things were not true. So the men who received the money said to the people, 'We heard this man, Stephen, say bad things about Moses and about God.'

12 People heard what these men said. And then the people became angry. The important Jews and the teachers of the Law also heard what these bad men were saying. They all became very angry. So they went up to Stephen and they took hold of him. Then they took him to stand in front of the men of the Sanhedrin. 13 The important Jews and the teachers of the Law brought in some men to say bad things about Stephen. The things that they said were not true. The men said, 'This man, Stephen, is always saying bad things about the Great House of God. He also says bad things about the Law that God gave to Moses. 14 We heard Stephen talk about Jesus, who comes from Nazareth. He said that Jesus will destroy the Great House of God. He said, "Jesus will change all that Moses taught the people." But Moses explained to us the right way to live.'

15 All the men of the Sanhedrin looked at Stephen. They saw that his face was very beautiful. And they thought that he was like an angel.

Chapter 7

Stephen speaks to the men of the Sanhedrin

1 The most important priest said to Stephen, 'These men are saying things about what you have taught. Are these things true?'

2 Stephen said, 'Men of Israel, listen to what I say. Our God is completely good and very powerful. He appeared to our ancestor, Abraham, when Abraham was still living in Mesopotamia.

This happened before he went to Haran. 3 God said to Abraham, "Leave your own country and your own family. Go to a different country that I will show you." '

4 'So Abraham left his country where people called Chaldeans also lived. Then he moved to Haran and he stayed there. But when Abraham's father died, God said to Abraham, "Leave this place." So God then sent him to live here, in Canaan. This is where we are now.'

5 'At that time, God did not give Abraham any part of Canaan for his own family. He did not even give Abraham a very small piece of ground. But at that time, God gave a promise to Abraham. "This land will become your own country", he said. "It will also be your children's country." When God said this to him, Abraham did not yet have any children.

6 This is what God said to him. "Your family will live in a country that other people rule. The people in that country will cause your family to be slaves for 400 years. They will not be kind to them. They will hit your family to cause them to work more." 7 Then God said, "I will punish those people who caused your family to work so much for them. After I have done that, your family will leave that country. They will come to this place. And here they will tell me how great and important I am." '

8 'Then God told the people of Israel that they would be his special people. So that they would remember this special promise, God said, "You must circumcise all your baby boys."

Abraham became the father of Isaac. And Abraham circumcised his son, Isaac, when the child was 8 days old. Isaac became the father of Jacob. Isaac also circumcised his son. Jacob had 12 sons. These sons were the 12 important ancestors of Israel. Jacob circumcised all of them.'

9 'One of Jacob's sons was called Joseph. Jacob loved Joseph more than he loved his other sons. For this reason, some of Jacob's sons did not like their brother, Joseph. So one day they took Joseph and they sold him as a slave. The men that bought Joseph took him to Egypt. There they sold him again and Joseph worked in Egypt as a slave. All this time, God stayed near to Joseph. 10 God helped him with all his troubles and God gave him great wisdom. At that time, Pharaoh was the king of Egypt. God helped Joseph so that Pharaoh liked him. He saw that Joseph was very wise, so he ordered Joseph to rule Egypt and everyone in Pharaoh's own house.

11 Then one year there was no rain. The food plants did not grow in Egypt or Canaan. So many people did not have enough food to eat. Our ancestors also had no food. 12 Jacob heard that Pharaoh had put a lot of wheat seeds in big huts. So he sent his sons to Egypt to buy food from Pharaoh. This was the first time that they went to Egypt.'

13 'Jacob then sent his sons back to Egypt for a second time. This time, Joseph told them that he was their brother. So then Pharaoh heard that Joseph's brothers had arrived. He heard about Joseph's family. 14After this, Joseph gave a message to his brothers. "Tell our father that I am here. Say that I want him to come. Say that he should bring all his family from Canaan to Egypt", he said to them. There were 75 people in Jacob's family.

15 So Jacob went to Egypt with all his family. And Jacob and his 12 sons lived there until they died.'

16 'When the people of Israel left Egypt, they carried with them the dead bodies of Joseph and his family. They took them back to Shechem and they buried them in a hole in a rocky hill. Abraham had bought this hole and rock from the family of a man called Hamor. He had paid money for it.'

17 'Now there were many people in Jacob's family and they all lived in Egypt. And soon God would cause his promise to Abraham to become true. 18 At this time, a different king ruled Egypt. This king did not know anything about the things that Joseph had done. 19 He told our ancestors things that were not true. He also did very bad things to them. He said that they must put their small babies out of their homes. He said that because he wanted the babies to die.

20 It was at this time that Moses was born. He was a very beautiful baby and his mother kept him safe for three months in her own home. 21 Then Moses' mother put him out of her home. But Pharaoh's daughter found Moses and she took him home with her. And he lived with her as her own son.'

22 'The Egyptians taught Moses all the things that they knew. He knew how to speak well. Moses said and did some very powerful things.

23 One day, Moses went to see how his own people lived. He was 40 years old when he did this.'

24 'Moses saw one of the Egyptians, who was hitting one of the Israelites. So Moses went to help the Israelite man and he killed the Egyptian man. He did this because the Egyptian had hurt one of Moses' own people. 25 Moses wanted to help the Israelites to get away from Egypt. He thought to himself, "The Israelites will know what I want to do. They will understand that God will use me to do this." But the people did not understand. 26 On the next day, Moses saw two Israelites, who were fighting each other. He wanted them to stop fighting. So he talked to them. "Men", he said, "please listen to me. You are in the same family. You should not hurt each other."

27 The man who was hurting the other man pushed Moses away. "You have no authority to rule us", he said to Moses. "You have no authority to be our judge. 28 Yesterday you killed an Egyptian man. Do you want to kill me also?" the man asked Moses.

29 Moses heard what the man said to him. So Moses ran away. He went to the country called Midian and he built a house there. He lived in it, and he and his wife had two sons.

30 Moses lived in Midian for 40 years. Then, one day, he was in the desert near the hill called Mount Sinai. He saw a bush there that was burning. An angel appeared to him in the fire.'

31 'Moses was very surprised by what he saw. He went near to the bush so that he could see it better. Then he heard God speak to him from the bush. 32 "I am the God of your ancestors", God said. "I am the God of Abraham, Isaac and Jacob." Moses was very frightened. He was too afraid to look at God, so he turned his face away from the bush.

33 God said to Moses, "Remove your shoes from your feet, because you are standing in a very special place. This is my own place. 34 I have seen all the bad things that the Egyptians are doing to my people. I have heard my people. They are crying. And I have come down here to save them. Come here

35 Stephen said, 'Moses is the man that the people of Israel would not accept. "You have no authority to rule us", they had said to him. "You have no authority to judge us." But God did send Moses to rule the people of Israel. And he did send Moses to save them from the Egyptians. God sent the angel that appeared to him. The angel spoke to him from a bush that was burning. 36 It was Moses who led the people of Israel out of Egypt. The people saw him do many special things. He did some powerful things before the people left Egypt. He did more special things by the Red Sea. Then he led the people through the desert for 40 years and he did some more special things there also.'

37 'It was Moses who said to the people of Israel, "God will send you a prophet. He will speak words from God. And he will be one of your own family, the same as I am one of your own family." 38 This is the same Moses that was with the people of Israel in the desert.

They were near the big hill called Mount Sinai. Moses was also there with our ancestors when the angel spoke to him on Mount Sinai. He also received the message from God to give to us. God's message was alive.

39 But our ancestors would not listen to Moses or obey him. They did not accept him and they wanted to go back to Egypt. 40 So the people said to Aaron, "Please make us some gods that we can carry in front of us. Moses brought us out of Egypt. But now we do not know what has happened to him." '

Aaron was the brother of Moses.

41 'It was then that the people made something. It would be their god. It was like a young male cow, and the people made it from gold. They killed some animals and they burned them as a gift for their god. The people then had a big meal together because they were very happy. They thought that they had made something beautiful and strong. And they thought that it was powerful.'

42 'So then God turned away from his people. He let them speak to the stars instead and he let them make gods of them. The people told the stars how great and beautiful they were. The people who spoke words from God wrote this: "God said,

'People of Israel, listen!

You did not kill and burn those animals as a gift for me.

When you were in the desert for 40 years,

43   you carried the house of the god called Moloch.

You also carried something else to put inside this house.

It was a smaller copy of another god of yours.

It was like the star of your god, Rephan.

You made these gods.

And you told them both how great and important they were.

So now I will send you away from your own country.

You will go to live in Babylon.' " '

44 'When our ancestors were in the desert, they carried a special tent with them. It contained God's Laws. It caused them to remember that God was there with them. God showed Moses how he wanted Moses and the people to make this special tent.'

45 'Our ancestors gave the special tent, which contained God's Law, to their families. They brought it with them when they came to this country. God gave this country to our people. And he caused the people that were already here to leave. At that time Joshua was their leader. The tent remained in Canaan until David became the king of Israel.'

46 'God helped King David very much, and King David caused God to be happy with him. So David said to God, "You are the God of our ancestor Jacob. Can I make a special house where you can live?"

47 But David did not build the house for God. Solomon built it.'

48 'But this also is true. Our God is of great importance. He does not live in a house that men have made. Isaiah spoke these words from God:

49   "The sky is like an important seat. I sit there to rule.

The earth is like a small seat. It is like a place to put my feet on.

        You could not build a better house for me to live in.

        You could not make a better place for me to sit down.

50   I have already made all these things myself", God said to his servant Isaiah.'

51 Then Stephen said to the people, 'You people do not want to understand about God. You are the same as the people that do not believe in the true God. And you do not want to listen to God's true message. So you are the same as your ancestors. They also did not want to obey the Holy Spirit. 52 Your ancestors did bad things to every person who spoke words from God to them. God's servants spoke about the completely good Man that God would send. But your ancestors killed those servants. Now you have given to an enemy this true and special servant that God sent. And you have killed him. 53 You received God's Law, which angels gave you. But you have not obeyed it.'

The men of the Sanhedrin kill Stephen

54 The men of the Sanhedrin listened to Stephen and they became more and more angry with him. They bit their teeth together because they were so angry. 55 Then the Holy Spirit filled Stephen with his authority. Stephen looked up to heaven and he saw how beautiful God is. God shone like a very bright light. Stephen also saw Jesus, who was standing at the right side of God. 56 'Look', Stephen said. 'I can see into heaven. It is open! I can see the Son of Man and he is standing at the right side of God!'

57 When the men of the Sanhedrin heard these things, they shouted very loudly at him. They put their hands over their ears. Then together they ran towards him. 58 They took hold of Stephen and they pulled him out of the city. They removed their coats. And they gave them to a young man to keep them safe. This young man was called Saul. Then they began to throw stones at Stephen. 59 While the men were throwing stones at him, Stephen prayed to the Lord. 'Lord Jesus', he said, 'please accept my spirit.' 60 Then Stephen fell down on his knees. He shouted loudly, 'Lord, please forgive these men because they are doing this to me.' After Stephen said this, he died.

Chapter 8

1 Saul was standing there. And he saw everything that happened. Saul said to the men of the Sanhedrin, 'It is good that you have killed Stephen.'

Saul puts some of the believers in prison

2 Some good men who obeyed God buried Stephen's dead body. They were very sad that the people had killed him. They cried with loud voices. 3 But Saul brought great troubles to the believers in Jerusalem. He wanted to stop people believing in Jesus. So Saul went from one house to other houses. He pulled the believers out of their homes and he put both the men and the women into prison.

Believers teach the people in Samaria the message about Jesus

4 The believers who had left Jerusalem went to many different towns. In each town, they told the people the message about Jesus. 5 Philip went to the city called Samaria. And there he told the people the message about Jesus Christ. He said, 'Jesus was the special person that God sent.'

6 Crowds of people came together in the city to hear Philip speak. They listened to him carefully. And they saw him do many special things. 7 Some people had bad spirits, which were living in them. Philip sent the bad spirits out of them. And as the bad spirits left them, they made a loud noise. Some other people had weak legs, and Philip caused their legs to become strong again. Some people could not move their arms and legs, but Philip caused them to become well again. 8 The people in that city were very happy.

The Holy Spirit lived inside Philip. And he helped Philip to speak in a powerful way. Because of this he could do these special things for the people. People who lived in Samaria were called Samaritans.

9 A man called Simon lived in Samaria. For a long time, he had used magic to do many things which surprised the people. The people who lived in Samaria had watched him. And they believed that Simon was a very important person.

10 The important people in the city had watched Simon carefully. And the people who were not important had also watched him carefully. Everyone had said, 'God has caused Simon to become powerful. He is a god himself.' 11 Simon had used his magic for a long time. The people watched him. He often surprised them with the things that he did. So they listened to him carefully. 12 But then Philip told them the message about how God rules as king. He told them all about Jesus. He said that Jesus was the Christ, God's special servant. Many men and women believed in Jesus, so Philip baptised them. 13 Simon also believed the message and so Philip baptised him. After this, Simon stayed close to Philip. Simon was very surprised at the many powerful and special things that Philip did.

14 The apostles were still living in Jerusalem. They heard that people in Samaria had believed God's word. So the apostles sent Peter and John to Samaria to talk to the people. 15 Philip had baptised those who believed. And when the two apostles arrived in Samaria, they prayed for these people. They asked God to give the new believers the Holy Spirit.

16 Until then, the Holy Spirit had not yet come down on these people. Philip had only baptised them. He used the name of the Lord Jesus when he did this. 17 When Peter and John put their hands on the head of each person, they received the Holy Spirit.

18 Simon saw that the Holy Spirit came when Peter and John put their hands on each person. So he said to Peter and John, 'Here is some money. I want to give it to you. 19 Please cause me also to be powerful. I want to do the same things as you. I want to put my hands on other people, so that they will receive the Holy Spirit.'

20 Peter answered Simon. 'I hope that you and your money go to the place of punishment. It is very wrong for you to think, "I can buy with money this gift which God gives." 21 No, you cannot work with us because you are not thinking the right things. And you are not obeying God. 22 Tell God that you are sorry about these bad thoughts. Stop thinking like that and think right thoughts. Say to God, "Please forgive me that I am thinking these bad things." 23 I can see that you think wrong thoughts. You do not have what the apostles have. And so you are angry. Satan is ruling you like a slave.'

24 Then Simon said to Peter and John, 'Please, will you pray to God for me? Then none of these bad things that you have spoken about will happen to me.'

25 Peter and John told the people what Jesus had done for them. After Peter and John had told the people a message from the Lord, Peter and John returned to Jerusalem. And on their way, they talked to people in the villages in Samaria. They taught the people the good news about the Kingdom of God.

Philip meets a man from Ethiopia

26 Then God sent an angel to speak to Philip. He said, 'Philip, prepare yourself and go south to the road between Jerusalem and Gaza. The road goes through the desert.'

27 So Philip went and he was walking along this road. And, while he was walking, he met an important man from Ethiopia. This man kept Candace's money safe. Candace was the queen of Ethiopia. The man was travelling home. He had been to Jerusalem to visit the Great House of God. He had thanked God that God was so good and great.

28 Now the man was travelling home again in his cart. And he was reading from the book that Isaiah the prophet wrote. 29 The Holy Spirit said to Philip, 'Go to that cart and walk at the side of it.'

30 So Philip ran to the cart and he walked close to it. He heard the man. He was reading aloud from the book called 'Isaiah'. So Philip asked the man, 'Do you understand the things that you are reading about?'

31 The man answered, 'I cannot understand it. First, I need someone to explain it to me.' The man said to Philip, 'Come up here and ride along in the cart with me.'

32 The man was reading this from the book of Isaiah,

'People led him like they lead a sheep. It is a sheep that they are going to kill.

    He did not make a noise.

    He was like a young sheep. It does not make a noise,

    when a man cuts the soft hair on its back.

    He was like that. He did not say anything.

33   People laughed at him.

They said bad things about him. They said things that were not true.

Nobody can talk about his children, because he did not have any.

    His life on earth has finished.'

34 The man from Ethiopia said to Philip, 'Please tell me who the prophet Isaiah wrote about. Was he writing about himself or about another person?' 35 Then Philip explained to the man the words that Isaiah had written. He told the man the good news about Jesus. 36 When they were travelling along the road, they came to some water. The man said to Philip, 'Look, here is a place where there is some water. Please will you baptise me? Is there anything to stop you?'

37 Philip said to him, 'I can baptise you if you really believe in Jesus.' The man said to Philip, 'I really do believe in Jesus. I believe that he is the Son of God.'

38 The man from Ethiopia said to the man who was driving the cart, 'Please stop the cart.' Then Philip and the man from Ethiopia went down into the water, and Philip baptised him. 39 They both walked out of the water again, and then the Holy Spirit quickly took Philip away from that place. The man did not see Philip again and the man continued his journey. He was very happy.

40 Philip saw that he was now in Azotus. So he walked towards the town called Caesarea. As he went through the towns on the way to Caesarea, he spoke to people. He told them the good news about the Kingdom of God.

Chapter 9

Saul knows that Jesus is his Lord

1 All this time, Saul was saying that he wanted to kill all the believers. So he went to see the most important priest. 2 'Please will you write some letters for me?' he said to the most important priest. 'I can give one of these letters to each leader of every synagogue in Damascus. Perhaps some people there believe what Jesus taught. And if I find any people like that, I can take hold of them. I can tie them with ropes. And I can bring all of them, men and women, back here to Jerusalem.'

3 Saul travelled towards Damascus. He was almost at the city when a very bright light suddenly appeared. The light came from the sky, and it shone all round him. 4 Saul fell to the ground. He heard someone say to him, 'Saul, Saul, you are fighting against me.'

5 Saul asked, 'Lord, who are you?' The voice said, 'I am Jesus. And you are fighting against me. 6 Now you should get up and you should go into Damascus. Someone will come to you when you arrive in the city. He will tell you what to do.'

7 The men who were with Saul stood still. They did not speak. They could hear that someone was talking. But they could not see anyone. 8 Saul stood up and he opened his eyes. But he could not see anything. The men who were with Saul held his hand. And they led him into Damascus. 9 For three days, Saul could not see anything. And for those three days he did not eat or drink anything.

10 Ananias was a believer who lived in Damascus. After Saul came to Damascus, Ananias had a dream. But Ananias was not asleep. In the dream, Jesus spoke to him. 'Ananias', Jesus said. Ananias answered him. He said, 'Master, I am here.'

11 'Prepare yourself and go to Straight Street', said Jesus, 'A man called Judas lives in that street. Go to his house. And ask for a man from Tarsus called Saul. He is praying to God.

12 Saul has also had a dream when he was not asleep. In his dream, Saul saw you, Ananias. You came to see him. You put your hands on Saul so that he could see again.'

13 'Lord, many people have told me about this man', Ananias said to the Lord Jesus. 'They told me about all the very bad things that he has done to your people in Jerusalem. 14 Now he has come to Damascus. And I know that he has brought letters with him from the leaders of the priests. They have given him authority over everyone who follows you. He will take them away and he will tie them with ropes.'

15 But the Lord said to Ananias, 'Go and do this for me. I have chosen Saul to work for me. He will tell those who are not Jews and their rulers about me. He will also tell the people of Israel about me. 16 Saul will have many troubles because he will work for me. I myself will tell him about these things.'

17 So Ananias went to Judas's house. He went into the house, and he put his hands on Saul. Then he said to him, 'Brother Saul, the Lord Jesus himself has sent me here to see you. It was Jesus that you saw on the road to Damascus. You saw him when you were coming here. He sent me to you so that you will be able to see again. God will also give his Holy Spirit to you.'

18 Then immediately something fell from Saul's eyes. It was like bits of fish skin. Then Saul could see again. So he stood up and Ananias baptised him. 19 Then Saul ate some food and he felt strong again.

Saul teaches the people in Damascus the good news about Jesus

Saul stayed with the believers in Damascus for a few days. 20 He immediately went to the synagogues. There, he taught the people about Jesus. 'Jesus is the son of God', he said to them. 21 Many people heard what Saul said. They were all very surprised and they said to each other, 'This is the same man who was in Jerusalem. We are sure about that. In Jerusalem, he killed people who believed in Jesus. Then he came here to Damascus to take hold of the believers. He wanted to take them back to Jerusalem. There they would stand in front of the leaders of the priests.' 22 But then Saul was even more powerful when he taught the people. He said, 'Jesus is the Christ, the special person that God sent to us.' Saul said all the right things about Jesus. So the Jews who lived in Damascus could not answer him. 23 After many days, the Jews met together. And they decided to kill Saul.

24 But someone told Saul about this. The Jews guarded the gates of the city all day and all night. They wanted to catch Saul and to kill him. 25 But one night, Saul's friends helped him to leave the city. They put Saul in a basket, and then they put the basket through a hole in the city wall. Then they let the basket go slowly down to the ground.

Saul returns to Jerusalem

26 When Saul returned to Jerusalem, he wanted to join the believers there. But they were afraid of him. They did not believe that he was now a disciple of Jesus. 27 A believer called Barnabas helped Saul. He took Saul to talk to the apostles. And Barnabas then explained to the apostles what had happened to Saul. Barnabas said to them, 'Saul saw the Lord when he was on the road to Damascus. And the Lord spoke to him. While Saul was in Damascus, he bravely spoke to the people with the authority of Jesus.' 28 So, after that, Saul stayed with the apostles. He went round all Jerusalem and taught the people in clear words, with the authority of Jesus. 29 Saul also talked with the Jews who spoke the Greek language. He argued with them about Jesus. So they tried to kill him.

30 The other believers heard about this. So they took Saul to Caesarea, and from there, Saul went away to Tarsus.

31 Now there were believers in Judea, Galilee and Samaria, and for some time they had no troubles. The Holy Spirit helped them to become strong. More people became believers. And they obeyed God in everything that they did.

Peter travels to Lydda and Joppa

32 Now Peter often travelled to different places and one day he travelled to Lydda. Some believers lived there, and Peter went to see them. 33 In Lydda, Peter met a man called Aeneas. Aeneas could not move his arms and legs, and so he lay on his bed all the time. He had done this for 8 years.

34 Peter said to Aeneas, 'Jesus will cause you to become well again. So stand up and pick up your things.' Immediately Aeneas stood up. 35 Many people who were living in Lydda and Sharon saw Aeneas. And they began to obey the Lord.

36 A woman called Tabitha lived in Joppa. She was a believer. Tabitha is a name in the Aramaic language. In Greek, her name was Dorcas. Dorcas is the word for a deer. Dorcas did good things and she helped poor people all the time.

37 Dorcas became very ill and then she died. Women washed her dead body and they put it in the room upstairs. 38 Joppa was not very far from Lydda. And the believers in Joppa heard that Peter was in Lydda. So they sent two men to him with a message. 'Please hurry and come to Joppa', they wrote in the message.

39 Peter prepared himself and he returned to Joppa with the two men. When he arrived at Dorcas's house, the women took him upstairs. Many other women were there. Their husbands had died. They were crying and they all came close to Peter. They showed him the shirts and coats that Dorcas had made. She made them while she was still with them.

40 Peter put all these women out of the room. He went down on his knees and he prayed to God. Then he turned his head towards the dead body. 'Tabitha', he said. 'Stand up!' She opened her eyes. And when she saw Peter, she sat up. 41 Peter took her by the hand and he helped her to stand up. Then he asked all the believers and the other women to come into the room. And he showed them that she was alive again. 42 The believers told other people what had happened. So then people all over Joppa heard what had happened. And many more people believed in the Lord Jesus. 43 Peter stayed in Joppa for many days. He stayed with a man called Simon. Simon was a tanner.

Chapter 10

Cornelius asks Peter to come to him

1 There was a man who lived in Caesarea. His name was Cornelius, and he was an officer and a leader of 100 men in the Roman army. His group in the army was called 'the group from Italy'. 2 Cornelius was a good man. He and all his family believed in God and they obeyed him. Cornelius prayed to God every day. And he gave a lot of money to help the poor Jews in Caesarea.

3 One afternoon, at about 3 o'clock, Cornelius had a special dream. But he was not really asleep. One of God's angels came in and spoke to him. 'Cornelius!' the angel said.

4 Cornelius looked at the angel and he was afraid. 'Master, what it is?' said Cornelius.

The angel said to Cornelius, 'God heard you when you prayed to him. And he has seen all the money that you give to the poor people. You make God very happy, and now he is answering you. 5 Send some men to Joppa. These men will find a man that is staying there. He is called Simon Peter. Your men must ask him to come here to Caesarea. 6 He is staying at the house of Simon the tanner. Simon's house is at the edge of the sea.'

7 Then the angel that spoke to Cornelius went away. Cornelius ordered two of his own servants, and one of his own soldiers, to come to him. The soldier was a good man who obeyed God. He helped Cornelius and he worked close to him. 8 Cornelius told these three men what had happened. And he told them what the angel had said to him. Then he sent them to Joppa.

9 The next day, at about noon, Cornelius's men were almost at Caesarea. At this same time, Peter went up on the roof of the house. He went there to pray to God.

10 Peter felt hungry, and he wanted to eat some food. While someone was preparing a meal for him, Peter had a special dream. But he was not really asleep.

11 Peter saw heaven open. He saw something like a large piece of cloth with 4 corners. An angel held it at each corner. Then they let the large piece of cloth come down to the ground next to Peter. 12 On the cloth there were many different animals. Some of these were farm animals, and some of them were wild animals. There were also some wild birds and things like snakes on the cloth. 13 Then Peter heard a voice that spoke to him. 'Peter, stand up and kill an animal. Then you can cook it and eat it.'

14 'No, Lord, I would certainly never do something like that', Peter answered. 'I have never eaten an animal that your law does not let me eat.'

15 Then the voice said to Peter, 'God has made these animals good to eat. You must not say that God will not accept you if you eat any of them.'

16 All this happened three times. And then immediately the cloth went back up into heaven.

17 Then Cornelius's men arrived from Joppa. They had found Simon's house. Peter was still thinking about his dream when the men stopped at the gate of the house. 18 The men shouted out, 'Is a man called Simon Peter staying here?'

19 Peter was still thinking about his dream. Then the Holy Spirit said to him, 'Simon Peter, there are three men downstairs. They are looking for you. 20 Get up and go downstairs to them. I have sent these men to see you. And it will be right for you to go with them.'

21 Peter went downstairs and said to the men, 'I am the person that you are looking for. Why have you come here?'

22 'We have come from the officer who is called Cornelius', the men answered. 'He is a good man. He prays to God and obeys him. And the Jews think good things about him. An angel from God said that he should send us here. The angel wanted you to return with us to Joppa. Cornelius wants to hear what you have to say.' 23 Then Peter said to the men, 'Please come into the house and stay here with us tonight.'

Peter goes to Cornelius's house

The next day, Peter travelled to Joppa with Cornelius's men. And some believers who lived in Joppa travelled with them. 24 Peter arrived in Caesarea the next day. Cornelius knew that they would be arriving. So he was waiting for Peter. The family and friends of Cornelius were also waiting with him. He had asked them to come to his house. 25 When Peter arrived, Cornelius went to the door to meet him. Then Cornelius went down on his knees in front of Peter. 26 But Peter said to him, 'Stand up. I also am only a man.'

27 Peter went into the house with Cornelius and he continued to talk to him. He then saw that many people were meeting together in the house. 28 He said to them, 'You people know that Jews do not usually come into the home of Gentiles. God's Law does not let a Jew have someone who is not a Jew as a friend. But God has now shown me something different. God has shown me that he accepts all men. And so I must accept everyone.'

29 Then Peter said, 'So when you asked me to come here, I was happy to come. I knew that it was right. But why did you ask me to come?'

30 Then Cornelius said, 'Three days ago, I was in my house. It was 3 o'clock in the afternoon, and I was praying to God. Suddenly, a man appeared in front of me. He was wearing white clothes that shone. 31"Cornelius", the man said to me. "You have prayed to God. You have done many good things for poor people. Now God wants to answer you. 32 So send some men to Joppa. These men will find a man called Simon Peter. He is staying there. Your men must ask him to come here to Caesarea. Simon Peter is staying at the house of Simon the tanner. His house is at the edge of the sea."

33 I sent the men immediately and they asked you to come. Thank you that you came. Now we are all here together, and God is here with us. We are waiting to hear what you have to say. Do you have a message from the Lord for us?'

Peter speaks to Cornelius and to his family and friends

34 Then Peter spoke to all the people in the room. 'Now I understand that God accepts all people in the same way', he said. 'And I now know that this is true. 35 God accepts all people who obey him. He accepts all people who do the right things. It is not important to God which country a person comes from. He accepts them all. 36 God sent this message to the people of Israel. He told them the good news about Jesus Christ. Jesus is the Lord of everything. Because of Jesus, we can be close to God again. 37 You know about the important things that have happened in Judea. These things began in Galilee after John talked to the people. And he baptised them. 38 You know about Jesus. He came from the town called Nazareth. God chose Jesus to do special work for him. He gave Jesus his Holy Spirit and helped him to do powerful things. Then Jesus went to many places. And he helped many people that the devil was holding. But Jesus did good things and caused all those people to become well again. He could do that because God was with him.

39 We all saw everything that Jesus did in Israel and in Jerusalem. Then the Jews fixed Jesus to a cross and they killed him. 40 But then, three days after that, God caused Jesus to become alive again. He caused him to appear to us. 41 Not everyone saw him. He appeared only to us because God has chosen us to work for him. So we are telling people about everything that we saw. We ate with him after he became alive again. And we drank with him, too. 42 Jesus said to us, "Go and tell people the good news about me. Tell them that God has given me authority to judge all people. I will judge those who are now alive. And I will judge those who have died." ' 43 Then Peter said, 'The prophets who spoke words from God a long time ago, spoke about Jesus. They said, "Everybody has done wrong things. But Jesus will forgive everyone who believes in him. He will do this by his powerful authority." '

Those who are not Jews receive the Holy Spirit

44 While Peter was still speaking, the Holy Spirit came down on all the people in the room. They were all listening to the message about Jesus. 45 The Jewish believers who had come from Joppa with Peter were very surprised. They saw that God had also given his Holy Spirit to Gentiles. 46 And the Jewish believers in the room heard them speaking in other languages. They were also saying, 'God, you are very great and powerful.'

Then Peter spoke. 47 'God has given his Holy Spirit to these people in the same way that he gave him to us', he said. 'So we should baptise them with water. That is the right thing to do.' 48 So Peter asked those who came with him to baptise the new believers. They spoke the name of Jesus Christ when they baptised them. And then Cornelius asked Peter to stay with them for a few days.

Chapter 11

Peter returns to Jerusalem

1 The apostles and the other believers in Judea heard about what had happened in Caesarea. They heard that Gentiles had also believed the message from God. 2 Peter then returned to Jerusalem. Some Jews there asked him questions to show that he had done something wrong. These Jews thought that the Gentiles must be circumcised. 3 So they said to Peter, 'You stayed in the house of men who were not circumcised. You even ate meals with them!'

4 Peter told these Jewish believers everything that had happened from the beginning. He explained to them, 5 'I was staying in a house in the city called Joppa', he said. 'One day, when I was praying, I had a special dream. I saw something that came down from heaven. It was like a large piece of cloth with 4 corners. An angel was holding it at each corner. The cloth came down to the ground next to me. 6 And I looked carefully at it. And I saw that there were farm animals, wild animals, things like snakes, and birds on it.

7 Then I heard the Lord speak to me. The voice said, "Peter, stand up and kill an animal. Then you can cook it and eat it."

8 I answered, "No, Lord, I would certainly never do something like that. I have never eaten an animal that your law does not let us eat."

9 Then the Lord said to me, "God has made these animals good to eat. So you must not say that God will not accept you if you eat any of them." 10 All this happened three times. Then immediately the cloth went back up into heaven.

11 At that moment, three men from Caesarea arrived at the house where I was staying. Someone had sent these men to find me. 12 The Holy Spirit said to me, "Get up and go downstairs. I have sent these men to see you. It is right for you to go with them." These 6 believers from Joppa also went with me to Caesarea. We all went into Cornelius's house.

13 Then Cornelius told us what had happened to him. He had seen an angel. The angel was standing in his house. And he had said to Cornelius, "Send someone to Joppa. They must find a man who is staying there. His name is Simon Peter. 14 He will come and speak to you. And his message will show you how God can save you. The message is for you and for your family and for your servants."

15 While I was telling Cornelius and his family the message, God gave them all his Holy Spirit. The Holy Spirit came to them in the same way as he first came to us. 16 Then I remembered what the Lord Jesus had said to us. "John baptised people with water, but God will baptise you with his Holy Spirit." 17 So we are sure about this. God gave those who are not Jews his gift of the Holy Spirit. He sent him to them in the same way that he gave him to us. He gave the Holy Spirit to us when we believed in the Lord Jesus Christ. And God also wanted to do this for those who are not Jews. I do not have the authority to be against God.'

18 The Jews heard what Peter said. And they told him that he had done the right things. So they said to God, 'You are very great and important. You helped those who are not Jews. So now they also can tell you that they are sorry. They also can stop doing bad things and they can start to obey you. They also can have true life.'

The believers go to Antioch

19 After the men of the Sanhedrin had killed Stephen, the believers went away to many different places. Some of them went away as far as Phoenicia, Cyprus and Antioch. They told people in those places God's message. But they only told the message to the Jews.

20 Some of the believers were from Cyprus and Cyrene. These men went to Antioch. There they told God's message to the Jews. But they also told it to those who were not Jews. They told everyone the good news about the Lord Jesus. 21 God helped these men and he caused them to become powerful. And many people believed the good news about Jesus. They asked Jesus to become their Lord.

22 The believers in Jerusalem heard about what had happened in Antioch. So they decided to send Barnabas there. 23 Barnabas arrived in Antioch. Then, he saw that God had done good things for the people. Barnabas was happy about this. So he said to the new believers, 'Continue to obey the Lord as you are doing. Obey him in everything that you do and say.' 24 Barnabas was a good man and God's Holy Spirit was living inside him. He believed God about everything all the time. Many people became believers.

25 Then Barnabas went to Tarsus to look for Saul. 26 And when Barnabas found him, Saul returned to Antioch with Barnabas. For one year, Barnabas and Saul met together with the believers at Antioch. And they taught a large group of believers all about Jesus. Antioch was the first place where the believers were called Christians.

27 At this time, some prophets travelled from Jerusalem to Antioch.

28 One of these men was called Agabus. He stood up and he told the people a message from God. The Holy Spirit told him what to say. 'Soon the food plants will not grow for a time all over the world', he said. And that happened when Caesar Claudius ruled the Roman world.

29 All those who believed in Jesus wanted to help the other believers in Judea. So they decided to send them some of their own money. 30 The believers in Antioch gave the money to Barnabas and Saul. So Barnabas and Saul took it and they gave it to the leaders of the believers in Judea.

Chapter 12

King Herod does bad things to the believers

1 At that time, King Herod began to do bad things to some of those who believed in Jesus. 2 Herod sent his soldiers to kill James with a big sharp knife. James was John's brother.

3 The Jews were happy because Herod's soldiers had killed James. Because the Jews were happy about it, Herod sent his soldiers to catch Peter. This happened during the week when the Jews made their bread without yeast.

4 After the soldiers caught Peter, they put him in prison. While he was in prison, 4 different groups of soldiers guarded him. There were 4 men in each group. Herod wanted Peter to stand in front of a judge. He could not do this until after this special Passover week had finished.

5 So Herod kept Peter in prison. But while he was in prison, the believers prayed to God about him.

Peter walks out of the prison

6 It was night and Peter was in the prison. Herod wanted him to stand in front of the judge the next morning. The soldiers had tied Peter with chains. And then they tied these chains to two other soldiers. So there was one soldier on each side of Peter while he was sleeping. Some soldiers were guarding the gate of the prison. 7 An angel from God suddenly appeared in the prison. He stood near to the place where Peter was sleeping. A bright light also shone in the prison. The angel touched Peter's shoulder. He caused Peter to wake up. 'Hurry, Peter! Stand up!' the angel said. And immediately the chains fell off Peter's hands.

8 Then the angel said, 'Tie your belt round your clothes and put on your shoes.' So Peter did what the angel asked him to do. Then the angel said, 'Put your coat on and follow after me.' 9 So Peter followed the angel out of the prison. Peter was not sure that all these things were really happening to him. He did not know if he was dreaming. 10 Peter and the angel walked past the first group of soldiers in the prison. Then they walked past the second group of soldiers. After that, they came to the big metal gate in the wall of the prison. The city was outside this gate. The gate opened by itself in front of them. So Peter and the angel walked out of the prison into the city. They walked together along one street and suddenly the angel went away.

11 Then Peter understood what had happened to him. 'Now I know that these things really have happened to me', he said to himself. 'The Lord sent one of his angels to me. The Jews wanted Herod to do bad things to me. And they thought that he would. But the angel saved me so that Herod could not hurt me.' 12When Peter understood all these things, he went to Mary's house. She was the mother of John Mark. Many people were meeting together in her house. They were praying.

13 Peter knocked on the outside door of the house. A servant girl called Rhoda came to the door. 14 She recognised Peter's voice and she was very happy. But she did not open the door. Instead, she ran back into the house and she spoke to all the people there. 'Peter is standing outside the door', she told them.

15 The people in the house said, 'You are crazy.' But she told them again that Peter really was there. So then they said, 'It is his angel.'

16 While all this was happening, Peter was still knocking at the door. Then someone opened the door. And they were all very surprised when they saw him there. 17 Peter put out his hand so that they would all be quiet. Then he explained to them how the Lord had brought him out of the prison. 'Tell James and all the other believers what has happened to me', he said. Then he left the house and he went away to another place.

18 When it was morning, there was a lot of trouble at the prison. The soldiers at the prison did not understand what had happened to Peter.

19 Herod said to the soldiers, 'Go and look for Peter!' But they could not find him. Herod asked the soldiers some questions about what they had done. And then he ordered other soldiers, 'Kill these men who let Peter go.'

After this happened, Herod went away from Judea. Then he stayed in Caesarea for some time.

King Herod dies

20 At that time, Herod was very angry with the people who lived in Tyre and Sidon. A group of men from these cities went together to speak to Herod about the problem. A man called Blastus was an important servant in King Herod's house.

The group spoke to Blastus and they said, 'Please help us when we speak to Herod.' Then the group went to speak to Herod. 'Please stop being angry with our people. We want to have you as a friend', they said to him. 'We must come to your country to buy our food.'

21 Herod decided on which day he would speak to the people. He put on his beautiful clothes and he sat in his special seat. And then he spoke to all the people. 22 They shouted, 'This is not a man who is speaking to us. He is a god!'

23 Herod liked what they said. He did not say that only God is very great and powerful. So immediately the angel of the Lord caused Herod to become ill. Worms ate Herod's body and he died.

Barnabas and Saul return to Antioch

24 Everywhere that the believers went, they told people the message from God about Jesus. So people in more and more places heard the message and they believed in Jesus.

25 Barnabas and Saul finished their work and they returned from Jerusalem. And John Mark came from Jerusalem with them.

Chapter 13

The believers in Antioch send Saul and Barnabas to Cyprus

1 There were some prophets among the believers in Antioch. And there were also teachers who taught the other believers more about Jesus. These men were called Barnabas and Simeon. People also called Simeon 'the Black'. There was also Lucius who had lived in Cyrene. Manaen and Saul were also among them. Manaen had lived together with Governor Herod when they were children.

2 One day, the believers were meeting together. They were praying. And they were saying how very great and powerful God is.

They were also fasting. While they were together that day, the Holy Spirit spoke to them. 'I have chosen Barnabas and Saul to do a special work', he said. 'Let them go now for me.'

3 The men finished talking to God and fasting. And then, they each put their hands on Barnabas and Saul. Then they sent them to start this new work.

What happened when Barnabas and Saul were in Cyprus

4 The Holy Spirit sent Barnabas and Saul away from Antioch. They travelled to the coast, to the town called Seleucia. Then they sailed on a boat from there to an island called Cyprus. 5 They arrived at a town called Salamis. Then they went into the Jewish synagogues and they told the people God's message about Jesus. John Mark went with Barnabas and Saul to help them with their work.

6 They travelled across the island to a town called Paphos. There they met a man called Bar-Jesus. He was a Jew and he did things by magic. He said that he spoke messages from God. But that was not true.

7 The ruler of Cyprus was called Sergius Paulus, and Bar-Jesus was his friend. Sergius Paulus understood things well. So he asked Barnabas and Saul to come to him. He wanted them to tell him the message about Jesus. 8 In the Greek language, Bar-Jesus was called Elymas. He did not like what Barnabas and Saul were saying. He did not want Sergius Paulus to believe in Jesus. So he tried to stop him. 9 Then God filled Saul again completely with his Holy Spirit. Saul was also called Paul. He looked straight at Elymas and he said,

10 'You are like a son of Satan. You do not like anything that is right. Your mind is full of all the bad things that you do. You are always trying to change the good things that the Lord says. You say that these things are not true. 11 The Lord will now touch your eyes and you will not see the light of day for some time.'

Immediately, something like a black cloud covered Elymas's eyes. When he walked about, he needed someone to lead him by the hand. 12 Then Sergius Paulus saw what had happened to Elymas. He was very surprised about all the things that Barnabas and Saul taught him about the Lord. And so he believed in Jesus.

Paul and Barnabas go to Antioch in Pisidia

13 Paul and Barnabas and John Mark sailed from Paphos. They came to the coast at the town called Perga. John left them there and he returned to Jerusalem. Perga was a town in the part of the country called Pamphylia. 14 Paul and Barnabas left there. And they went on to a town called Antioch in Pisidia. On the Sabbath day, they went into the synagogue and they sat down. 15 First someone read some of the words from the Law that God had given to Moses. And he also read some of the words that the prophets had written down. After this, the leaders of the synagogue sent a message to Paul and Barnabas. 'Friends', these men said to them, 'we want you to speak to the people. Do you have a message that will help them?'

16 So Paul stood up and he moved his hand towards them. Then he began to speak to them.

17 The God of the people of Israel chose our ancestors. While they were in Egypt, God caused Israel to become a large group of people. They were foreign people in Egypt. But because God was so powerful, he brought Israel out of Egypt.'

18 'They did not show God that they loved him. But God remained with the people of Israel in the desert for 40 years. 19 God destroyed 7 groups of people in the country called Canaan. And God gave Canaan to his people so that they could live there. 20 The people of Israel lived there for about 450 years.

After this time, God caused Israel to have leaders called judges. They ruled Israel until the time when Samuel was alive. Samuel was a prophet. 21 Then the people of Israel asked Samuel to choose a king for them. So God caused them to have Saul as their king. Saul was the son of Kish and he was from the family of Benjamin. And he ruled Israel for 40 years.'

22 'Then God caused Saul to stop ruling Israel. And God caused Israel to have David as their king instead. God said this about David: "I have watched David, the son of Jesse. He thinks like I think. So I know that he is the right kind of man. And he will do everything that I want."

23 Jesus was from the family of David. It is Jesus who saves the people of Israel. God had promised this to the ancestors of Israel. 24 Before Jesus began his work, John spoke to many of the people of Israel. He said, "You should stop doing wrong things. You should say sorry to God and then you should obey him. If you do that, I will baptise you then." '

25 'When John had almost finished his work, he said to the people, "Perhaps you think that I am God's special man. I am not that man. But listen! He is coming after me. And I am not good enough to remove his shoes." '

26 'I speak to you people here, who, like us, have Abraham as your ancestor. I also speak to you, who are not Jews. You also know that God is powerful and important. God gave us this message for all of you. He tells us how he will save us. 27 The people who live in Jerusalem, and their leaders, did not understand about Jesus. He came to save us. But the people in Jerusalem said that Jesus had done wrong things. And they said that he should die. So they caused the words of the prophets to become true. And someone reads these same words to you every Sabbath day.

28 They could not find any reason to kill Jesus. But they said to Pilate, "Your soldiers must kill him." 29 So the soldiers did everything that the prophets wrote about. Then some of Jesus' disciples took him down from the cross and they buried him. 30 But then God caused Jesus to live again. 31 So for many days after this, he appeared to his disciples. He showed himself to those people who had earlier travelled with him from Galilee to Jerusalem. They saw everything and now they can tell the people of Israel about it.'

32 'We have come here to tell you this good news. God promised our ancestors that he would do these things for us. 33 And now he has also done these things for everyone. He has caused Jesus to live again. We can read about this in the second Psalm. God says,

"You are my son.

Today, I have become your Father."

34 God caused Jesus to live again so that worms did not destroy his body. And he will not die again. This is what God said about it.

"I will also do the good things for you

that I promised to David."

35 God also says this in another Psalm.

"Your servant who loves you will not remain dead.

You will not let worms eat his body."

36 While David was king, he worked well for God. Then David died and men buried him next to his ancestors. Worms ate his body. 37 But God caused Jesus to become alive again. He did not die again and worms did not eat his body.

38 My friends, I want all of you to know this. We have all done many bad things. I am telling you this message about how God forgives us. God forgives us because of what Jesus did. 39 God can cause everyone to be right with him. Believe in Jesus. And then God will forgive all the bad things that you have done. The Law that God gave to Moses cannot do this for you. It cannot make you free. 40 Be careful then! The prophets spoke about what would happen. So do what I am saying. And then these things will not happen to you. This is what the prophets said:

41 "Listen to me! Many of you speak bad things about what God has said.

Be surprised at what I do. And then die.

I am working now, while you are still alive.

But still you will not believe what I am doing.

Even if someone explains everything to you, you will not believe." '

42 The people spoke to Paul and Barnabas while they were leaving the synagogue. 'Please return on the next Sabbath day', they said. 'Then you can tell us more about what you have already told us.'

43 When the meeting in the synagogue finished, many people followed Paul and Barnabas. These people were Jews and also some who believed in the God of the Jews. Paul and Barnabas spoke to them. 'You believe that God has done good things to help you', they said. 'You should continue to believe that God will help you.'

44 On the next Sabbath day, almost everyone in the town came to hear God's Message. 45 But there were some Jews who saw the crowd. All the people wanted to listen to Paul and Barnabas more than they listened to those Jews. So those Jews were angry with the people. And they said bad things about what Paul said. They also said bad things about Paul.

46 But Paul and Barnabas were not afraid of them. They said to the Jews, 'It was right, that we first tell you the message from God. But you say that the message is not true. You did not believe God's word. And you did not believe that God would give you true life. So we will leave you now. And we will give the message to those who are not Jews.

47 We will do that because the Lord has given us this message for you. He said to us,

"I have sent you out to be like a light to those who are not Jews.

You must tell people everywhere in the world how God saves people." '

48 The Gentiles were very happy when they heard this. And they thanked the Lord for the message about Jesus. The Lord had chosen some people to have true life. And those people believed his message.

49 Many people in that part of the country told each other the message about Jesus. 50 But the Jews spoke to the important men in the city. They also spoke to many rich women who were not Jewish. These women believed in the God of the Jews. But the Jews caused all these people to think bad thoughts against Paul. So these rulers started to say bad things about Paul and Barnabas. They caused Paul and Barnabas to leave that part of the country.

51 Paul and Barnabas cleaned the dirt off their feet. This showed to the people in that town that they had refused the message from God. And then they travelled to the town called Iconium. 52 Those who believed in Jesus in Antioch in Pisidia were very happy. The Holy Spirit completely filled them.

Chapter 14

Paul and Barnabas tell the good news about Jesus to the people in Iconium

1 Paul and Barnabas did the same in Iconium as they had done in Antioch in Pisidia. Paul and Barnabas went to the synagogue. They told the people their message about Jesus and many Jews and Gentiles believed it. And these people became disciples of Jesus. 2 But some of the Jews refused to believe their message. These Jews caused some of those who were not Jews to think bad thoughts against the believers. So they began to say bad things about them.

3 So Paul and Barnabas stayed in Iconium for a long time and they did many powerful things. They were not afraid to tell the people everything about Jesus. And the Lord showed the people that the message was true. He helped Paul and Barnabas to do powerful things. 4 The people in the city were in two groups. Some of them believed the message from Paul and Barnabas. But some of them joined the Jews who did not believe. 5 Then both the Jews and the Gentiles and all their leaders wanted to hurt Paul and Barnabas. They wanted to throw stones at them until they died. 6 Paul and Barnabas heard about what these people wanted to do to them. So they went away quickly to Lystra and Derbe, where they were safe. These places were cities in the part of the country called Lycaonia. They also went to other places near Lycaonia. 7 In all these places, they told people the good news about Jesus.

This is what happened in Lystra and in Derbe

8 There was a man who lived in Lystra. He could not walk because his feet were not strong. His feet had been weak since he was born. So he had never walked. 9 He was sitting near to Paul and he was listening to Paul's words. Paul could see that the man believed his message. Also the man believed that he could become well. And Paul knew that. 10 So Paul looked at the man and Paul said loudly, 'Stand up on your feet!' So the man jumped up and he began to walk about.

11 The crowd saw what Paul had done. So they began to shout in the language of the people who lived in Lycaonia. 'The gods have become like men and they have come down from the sky to us', they said. 12They called Barnabas by the name of their god Zeus. They called Paul by the name of their god Hermes because he usually spoke to the people.

13 The house where people prayed to Zeus was very near to the town. The priest who worked for Zeus brought animals to the gate of the house. He also brought some flowers. The priest and the crowd thought that Paul and Barnabas were their gods. And so they wanted to kill these animals as gifts to Paul and Barnabas.

14 Then Paul and Barnabas heard what the people were doing. They tore their own clothes and they ran into the middle of the crowd.

15 'Stop! You people should not do this', they shouted. 'We are only men like you. We are human; we are not gods. We came here to tell you the good news about Jesus. God wants you to stop doing this. Your gods have no value. Our God is alive. And he wants you to obey him. He made the sky, the earth and the sea, and everything else that is in them.

16 Before this time, God let all people do what they wanted to do. 17 But even then, God showed everybody that he was there. He has shown this by all the good things that he does for people. He causes the rain to fall from the sky. He causes the food plants to make their fruit and seeds at the right time. He gives you food and he causes you to be happy.' 18 Paul and Barnabas said this to stop the people. But they still wanted to kill the animals as gifts for Paul and Barnabas.

19 Some Jews had travelled from Antioch in Pisidia and from Iconium. And they caused the people to believe them instead of Paul. Then those Jews threw stones at Paul and they pulled him out of the town. They thought that he was dead. 20 But the believers came and they stood round him. Then Paul stood up and he went back into the town. The next day, he and Barnabas went to Derbe.

Paul and Barnabas return to Antioch in Syria.

21 Paul and Barnabas told the people in Derbe the good news about Jesus. Many people there believed what they taught. Then Paul and Barnabas returned to Lystra and from there they went back to Iconium. They also returned to Antioch in Pisidia. 22 They taught the believers in these towns more about Jesus. They said to them, 'Continue to believe in Jesus! All people who do believe will have difficult times in their lives. That will happen until God rules the earth.' 23 Paul and Barnabas chose leaders from each group of believers. Paul and Barnabas prayed and they fasted. And then they chose them. So, Paul and Barnabas asked Jesus to help these leaders and to keep them safe. That was because these leaders believed in him.

24 After Paul and Barnabas travelled through Pisidia, they arrived in Pamphylia. 25 There they taught the people in Perga the message about Jesus. Then they went down to the town called Attalia.

26 From there they sailed back to Antioch. It was in Antioch where they had begun their work. The believers in Antioch had asked God to keep Paul and Barnabas safe as they travelled. And now Paul and Barnabas had finished their work.

27 When they arrived, they sent a message to all the believers in Antioch. 'Come and meet together with us!' they said. So the believers all met together with them. Then Paul and Barnabas told them about their journey. They told the believers what God had done by them. They said, 'God has made it possible for people who are not Jews to believe in Jesus.' 28 Paul and Barnabas stayed with the believers in Antioch for a long time.

Chapter 15

Paul and Barnabas go to Jerusalem

1 Some men came from Judea to Antioch. And they began to teach the believers there. 'God cannot save you unless someone circumcises you', they said. 'This is in the Law that God gave to Moses.' 2 Paul and Barnabas argued with these men for a long time about this. So the believers in Antioch said, 'Let Paul, Barnabas and some of the other believers go to Jerusalem. They should meet with the apostles and leaders of the believers there. Then they can talk to them about circumcising new believers who are not Jews.' 3 The Christians at Antioch sent Paul and Barnabas to Jerusalem. They travelled through Phoenicia and Samaria. And they spoke to the believers in that part of the country. They said, 'People who are not Jews are also obeying God.' They were all very happy to hear this news. 4 When Paul and Barnabas arrived in Jerusalem they met with the Christians. And the apostles, all the believers and their leaders were happy to see them. Paul and Barnabas told them all about how God had worked by them.

5 Some of those who believed in Jesus were also part of a group of Pharisees. They stood up and spoke. They said, 'We must circumcise Gentiles when they become believers. They must also obey the Law that God gave to Moses.'

6 So the apostles and the leaders of the believers met to talk about this problem.

Peter talks to the apostles and the leaders of the believers in Jerusalem.

7 After they had all talked about this problem for a long time, Peter stood up. He said, 'My friends, you know that a long time ago, God chose me from among this group.

He wanted me to teach those who are not Jews the good news about Jesus. God wanted them to hear the message and to believe in Jesus. 8 God knows what people believe. He gave his Holy Spirit to those who are not Jews. He sent him to them in the same way as he sent him to us. So he accepted those who are not Jews. And he was showing that to us. 9 He saw no difference between them and us. He caused them to become right with himself because they believed in him.

10 God has shown us what to do. Let us not make God angry with us. We do not understand why you now want us to do something different. You will be causing problems for the Gentiles who believe God's message. All these same laws were too difficult for us and for our ancestors to obey. 11 It should not be like that for those who are not Jews. We are Jews. And we believed God's message and Jesus saved us. Jesus did this because he was kind to us. And he saves those who are not Jews in the same way.'

12 Now everybody in the group was quiet while Barnabas and Paul talked to them. They said, 'God worked by us. And he did many powerful things for those who are not Jews.' Then they told the group all about these powerful things.

13 When they had finished speaking, James spoke to the group. 'Listen to me, my friends!' he said. 14 'Simon Peter has just explained to us what happened first. He showed how God loved the Gentiles. God chose a group of people from among the Gentiles for himself.

15 These words that the prophets wrote agree completely with this. The Lord said,

16 "Later I will return.

People have destroyed the kingdom of David, but I will raise it up again.

I will make it strong again.

17 The other people in the world will then look for the Lord.

Also the Gentiles that are called by my name will look for me.

18 The Lord, who is doing all these things, says that." '

19 James then spoke again. 'This is what I think', he said. 'I think that we should do this: Many who are not Jews are now obeying God. We should not cause troubles for them and we should not make it difficult. 20 Instead of that, we should write a letter to them. We should say to them, "Someone may kill an animal and give it to his god. Then, do not eat the meat. The Lord says that it is not right for you to eat it. Also, do not have sex with anyone that is not your wife or husband. Someone may tie a rope round the neck of an animal to kill it. Do not eat that meat. The blood of the animal has remained in the meat. Do not eat blood." 21 I say this because, for many years, someone has read God's Law in the synagogues. On every Sabbath day, in every town, someone teaches the people the message from Moses.'

The believers in Jerusalem write a letter to the Gentiles

22 So then the apostles, the whole church and their leaders decided to choose some men. They chose them from their group. These men would go to Antioch with Paul and Barnabas. They chose Silas and Judas, who was also called Barsabbas. Everyone thought good things about both these men. 23 They sent this letter to Antioch with Judas, Silas, Barnabas and Paul.

24 'We have heard that some men from our group have confused your thoughts. The things that they said were not right. So you were not happy about it. But they did not have our authority to say those things to you.

25 So we all met together and we agreed about these things. We have chosen some men to bring this message to you. And they will travel with our good friends Barnabas and Paul. 26 These two men, Barnabas and Paul, have worked for the Lord Jesus Christ. Because of that, other people have nearly killed them. 27 So we are sending Judas and Silas to you. And they will tell you the same things that we have written in this letter. 28 We have agreed with the Holy Spirit about these rules. We do not want to cause problems for you. So these are the only things that we want you to do. 29 You should not eat any of the meat from animals that people killed as gifts to their gods. And you should not eat any blood. People sometimes tie a rope round the neck of an animal to kill it. You should not eat the meat from an animal like that. And you must not have sex with anyone that you are not married to. If you do not do any of these things, you will do well. Goodbye.'

30 So the apostles and other believers sent these 4 men to Antioch. When they arrived there, they said to the believers, 'Please come and meet together with us.' And when they all met together, Silas and Judas gave them the letter. 31 The believers in Antioch were very happy when they read the letter. They said, 'This message helps us to obey God.'

32 Judas and Silas were both prophets. They spoke a message from God to the believers in Antioch. They spoke to them for a long time. Their words helped them to obey God and not to be afraid. 33 They remained in Antioch for some time. Then the whole group of believers in Antioch sent Judas and Silas back to Jerusalem. The believers spoke kind words to them as they left. 34 (But Silas decided to stay there.)

35 Paul and Barnabas remained in Antioch for a longer time. And, together with many other believers, they told people the message about Jesus. They also taught the people more about Jesus.

36 After some time, Paul spoke to Barnabas. 'Let us go back and visit the believers in all those different cities. We can go to all the places where we taught people about Jesus. We can see how they are.' 37 Barnabas wanted to take John Mark with them. 38 But Paul said to Barnabas, 'John Mark did not remain with us until we had finished our work. So it is not a good thing to take him with us now.' John Mark had turned back and he had left Paul and Barnabas in Pamphylia. 39 Paul and Barnabas argued about whether they should take John Mark with them. They could not agree, so they went in different directions. Barnabas took John Mark with him and he sailed to Cyprus. 40 And Paul chose Silas to go with him. The believers in Antioch asked God to keep Paul and Silas safe. 41 They travelled together through Syria and Cilicia. And Paul taught the believers in those parts of the country. Then they would be strong in what they believed about Jesus.

Chapter 16

Timothy travels with Paul and Silas

1 So Paul travelled on to Derbe and Lystra. A man called Timothy lived in Lystra. He was a believer and Timothy's mother was also a believer. She was a Jew, but Timothy's father was a Greek. 2 All those who believed in Jesus in Lystra and Iconium said good things about Timothy. 3 Paul wanted Timothy to travel with him. All the Jews in Lystra and Iconium knew that Timothy's father was a Greek. So Paul circumcised Timothy.

4 Paul, Silas and Timothy travelled through many towns. And they read to the believers the letter from the apostles and other believers in Jesus in Jerusalem. They said, 'This letter tells you what you must not do. The apostles and leaders of the believers in Jerusalem agreed about these rules. You should obey these rules.' 5 So Paul helped the groups of believers in these towns to believe and to obey Jesus. More and more people began to believe in Jesus every day.

Paul has a dream

6 The Holy Spirit did not let Paul and his friends teach the people in Asia. So Paul, Silas and Timothy travelled through the country between the regions called Phrygia and Galatia. 7 They arrived at the region called Mysia. Then they wanted to go into the region called Bithynia. But the Holy Spirit did not let them go there.

8 So they did not stop travelling and they went through Mysia. They went down to the city called Troas. 9 Paul had a dream during the night when they arrived in Troas. In the dream, he saw a man from the country called Macedonia. The man was standing next to him. This man said, 'Please, please come across to Macedonia and help us.' 10 After Paul had dreamed this we prepared ourselves for the journey. We decided that God wanted us to go to Macedonia. He wanted us to tell the people there the good news about Jesus.

Lydia becomes a believer

11 We sailed from Troas. The boat took us across the sea to a town called Samothrace. And then, the next day, we went to a port called Neapolis. 12 We then walked away from the coast to Philippi. This city is the most important city in the country called Macedonia.
The Romans ruled the people who lived in Philippi. And we stayed a few days in that city.

13 On the Sabbath day, we went out of the city gate and we walked at the side of the river. We thought that the Jews would have a special place there. We thought that they would meet there to pray. We did see a group of women. So we sat down and we talked to them.

14 One of the women was called Lydia and she listened to us. She was from the city called Thyatira. And she sold expensive dark red cloth. Lydia knew that God was very powerful and important. The Lord helped her to understand Paul's message. So she believed the things that he said.

15 Then Paul and his friends baptised Lydia and all the people who lived in her house. After this, Lydia spoke to us. 'If you think', she said, and 'that I really believe in the Lord, then please stay in my house.' And so we went and we stayed there with her.

The Roman rulers put Paul and Silas in prison in Philippi

16 One day, we were going to the place where the Jews prayed to God. On the way there, a slave girl saw us. A bad spirit was living inside her. This bad spirit told her what would happen soon. People gave her masters a lot of money when she told them these future things. 17 She followed Paul and us, and she was shouting, 'These men are servants of the most important God! They are telling you how God can save you!' 18 The slave girl followed us and she shouted this for many days. But Paul was not happy about it. So he turned round and he spoke to the bad spirit. 'I am using the authority of Jesus to order you. Leave this woman.' The spirit left her immediately.

19 Her masters understood that the girl could not get money for them now. So they took hold of Paul and Silas and they pulled them to the centre of the city. They brought them in front of the men with authority in the city. 20 The masters brought them so that the Roman rulers would judge them. They said, 'These men are Jews and they are causing problems in our city. 21 They are teaching us to do wrong things. These things are against the rules of our city. We are Romans and so we cannot do them. And we cannot agree that these things are right.'

22 A crowd there also said bad things about Paul and Silas. So the men with authority said to their soldiers, 'Tear the clothes off Paul and Silas. Then hit them with sticks!' 23 The soldiers hit them many times and then they pushed them into the prison. The men with authority ordered the prison guard. 'Lock the door carefully', they said, 'so that these men cannot leave.'

24 The prison guard heard this. So he put Paul and Silas in a room deep inside the prison. And he put their feet between big heavy pieces of wood so that they could not move their legs.

25 In the middle of the night, Paul and Silas were praying and they were singing songs to God. The other people in the prison were listening to them. 26 The ground suddenly moved under them. The ground moved about under the prison. Immediately, all the prison doors opened and the chains fell off all the people in the prison. 27 The prison guard woke up. He saw that the prison doors were open. So he thought that all the people from the prison had gone outside. He decided that he should kill himself. So he pulled out his long sharp knife.

28 Paul shouted to him as loudly as he could. 'Do not hurt yourself! We are all still in here!'

29 The guard said, 'Bring me a light.' Then he ran into the room where Paul and Silas were. He was very frightened and he went down on his knees in front of them. 30 Then the guard led Paul and Silas out of the room. He said to them, 'What must I do so that God will save me?'

31 Paul and Silas said, 'Believe in the Lord Jesus and then God will save you. He will save you and your family.' 32 Then Paul and Silas spoke to the man and to all the people in his house. They told them all the good news about Jesus.

33 So that same hour of the night, the man took them. He led them into another room and he was kind to them. He washed the parts of their bodies that the soldiers had hurt. Then immediately after this, Paul and Silas baptised the man and his family. 34 The man took Paul and Silas into his house. Then he gave them some food. The man and his family were very happy because now they all believed in God.

35 The next morning, the men with authority sent their officers to the prison with a message. These officers said to the prison guard, 'Let those men go.' 36 The guard told Paul, 'The men with authority sent a message to me. They said, "Let Paul and Silas go out of the prison." So now you can leave the prison. Nobody will hurt you anymore.'

37 But Paul spoke to the officers who had brought the message. He said, 'The men with authority did not say that we had done anything wrong. But they ordered their soldiers to hit us with sticks. All the people were watching them when they did that to us.

We are special people of Rome but they pushed us into prison. Now they want us to leave the prison. They want this to be a secret. But we will not let that happen. The Roman officers have authority. They must come here to the prison themselves and they must let us out.'

38 So the officers returned to their masters with the message from Paul and Silas. The Roman officers heard that Paul and Silas were special people of Rome. And then they were afraid. 39 So they went to see Paul and Silas in the prison. 'We are sorry about what we did to you', they said to them. Then they led Paul and Silas out of the prison. The men with authority then said to them, 'Please leave the city now.' 40 Paul and Silas walked away from the prison and they went to Lydia's house. There they met many believers. Paul and Silas said good words to them. Then Paul and Silas left the city.

Chapter 17

What happened to Paul in Thessalonica

1 Paul, Silas and Timothy continued their journey. They went through the two cities called Amphipolis and Apollonia in the country called Greece. Then they arrived in a city called Thessalonica. There was a synagogue for the Jews in that city. 2 Paul went to this synagogue, as he usually did. On three Sabbath days, he talked to the people in the synagogue. He talked with them about all the things that the prophets had written down.

3 He explained to the people about all these things. 'I can show you that all these things are true', he said. 'God decided to send the Christ to you. And the prophets wrote that he would die. After that, God would cause him to live again. I have now told you all about Jesus Christ. He is the man whom God sent to you.' 4 Some people believed the message and they joined with Paul and Silas. A large number of Greeks also joined this group. These Greeks were not Jews. But they already knew that God was powerful and important. Many important women in the city also joined the group.

5 The Jews in the city were angry because many people joined the group with Paul and Silas. So the Jews found some people who often caused trouble in the city. They asked these bad people to come together in an angry crowd. The Jews and the crowd made a lot of noise in the streets of the city. They broke down the door of Jason's house because they wanted to find Paul and Silas. They wanted to bring them outside to the crowd. 6 But the Jews and the crowd did not find Paul and Silas. So they pulled Jason and some other believers to the men with authority in the city. The Jews shouted, 'These men have caused troubles everywhere. And now they have come to our city. 7 Jason has let them stay in his house. They speak against the laws that Caesar has given to us. And they say that there is another king. This other king is called Jesus.'

8 When the Jews shouted all this, the crowd shouted loudly. The men with authority in the city also became very angry. 9 The men with authority in the city said that Jason and the other believers must give them some money. And then they could all go. The men with authority let them go after they had paid the money.

Many people in Berea believe Paul's message

10 As soon as it was dark, the believers in Thessalonica sent Paul and Silas to Berea. When they arrived in that town, they went to the synagogue of the Jews. 11 The people at the synagogue were better people than those in Thessalonica. They were quick to listen to Paul's message. They wanted to understand the message more than the people in Thessalonica. They wanted to hear the message very much. Every day the people read the words in God's book. They wanted to see if Paul's message was really true. 12 Many of the people in the synagogue believed the good news about Jesus. Many Greek men and important Greek women also believed the message.

13 But then the Jews in Thessalonica heard that Paul was in Berea. And they heard that he was teaching the people about Jesus. So they came to Berea. They talked to some of the people there and they caused the people to become an angry crowd. 14 Immediately, the believers in Berea sent Paul with some other men to the coast. But Silas and Timothy stayed in Berea. 15 When Paul left Berea, some men went by boat with him. They went with him as far as the city called Athens. Before these men returned to Berea, Paul gave them a message for Silas and Timothy. He said, 'Please come quickly and meet me here in Athens.'

Paul visits Athens

16 While Paul was waiting in Athens for Silas and Timothy, he was sad and angry. He saw that the people in the city had many gods. 17 So Paul went to the synagogue every day and he talked together with the Jews there. And he also talked with those Gentiles who prayed to God. He also went to the market place in the city and he talked with the people there. 18 There were also some Epicurean and Stoic teachers in Athens who talked with Paul. 'Who is this man? He knows nothing', some of these teachers said. 'He thinks that he knows everything.' But some of these teachers said, 'We think that he is talking about the gods of foreign people.' They said this because Paul was talking about Jesus. He had also talked about the time when God will cause dead people to live again.

19 So these men asked Paul to go with them. They asked him to stand in front of the city's important men on the hill called Areopagus.

20 The important men said, 'We have never heard until now about the things that you are teaching us. Please explain them to us. Then we will understand them.' 21 (People who lived in Athens talked about many different things. They talked with people who visited the city. They were all telling and listening to the new ideas. They seemed to have time for nothing else.)

22 So Paul stood up in front of the important men of Athens. He said to them, 'I see that you have many gods. 23 I have walked through your city. And I have seen that you have built many special places out of stone for your gods. I saw one place where you had cut some words into the stone. These words were, "To the god that we do not know." So you already know that there is another god. You know that he is powerful and important. He is the true God, but you did not know this. So I am now teaching you about him.

24 The true God made the earth and all the plants and animals on it. He rules the earth and the sky. He does not live in the houses that men have built for him. 25 Men make things for God. But God does not need anything that men have made. God himself causes everything to live. He gives to living things everything that they need. 26 He made everybody in the world from one man. Then he caused people to live in different places on the earth. He decided all these things before he made the people. He decided where the people should live. And he also decided how long they should live. 27 God did all this so that people would look for him. They would try very hard to find him and then they would find him. God is close to all of us.'

28 'Someone said, "Because God is powerful, we are alive. We can move about. And we can be what we are." One of your writers has also said, "All of us are God's children."

29 And because we are God's children, we should also know this. Men are clever and they can cut stones. They can make valuable metals into different shapes. But God is not like these shapes.

30 At one time, men thought that God was in these stones and valuable metals. But God has decided to forget what men thought in the past. At that time people did not know the true things about God. But now, God says to people everywhere, "Stop doing bad things!" 31 God has decided on which day he will be the judge for everyone on the earth. He will judge so that nobody can say, "God is wrong." He will do this by a certain man that he has chosen. He has shown clearly to everyone that all this is true. He showed it like this: People killed that man. But God caused him to live again.'

32 Paul had said, 'God caused that man to live again.' When the people heard this, some of them laughed at him. But other people said to Paul, 'We want you to tell us more about this on another day.' 33 So Paul left the meeting of the important men of Athens. 34 And some people joined his group when he left. They believed the good news and they became believers. One of these people was a man called Dionysius. He was one of the important men of Athens. A woman called Damaris also became a believer. And some other people also believed Paul's message about Jesus.

Chapter 18

Paul visits Corinth

1 After Paul had spoken to the important men in Athens, he left the city. And from there, he then travelled to the city called Corinth.

2 In Corinth, he met a man called Aquila. Aquila was a Jew. And he had been born in the region called Pontus. He had just arrived in Corinth with his wife Priscilla. They had travelled from Italy to live in Corinth. At that time, Caesar Claudius had said that all Jews must leave Rome. Paul went to visit Aquila and Priscilla. 3 They knew how to make tents. They sold them so that they could use the money to buy food. Paul could do the same work. So he stayed with them and he worked with them.

4 Every Sabbath day, Paul taught both Jews and Greeks in the synagogue. He wanted them all to believe the good news about Jesus.

5 Then Silas and Timothy arrived from the country called Macedonia. After that, the only work that Paul did was to teach the people. He told the Jews the message about Jesus and he explained everything carefully to them. He said, 'God sent Jesus to be the Christ.'

6 The Jews did not agree with Paul and they said bad things about him. So he cleaned the dirt off his clothes and he said to them, 'If you are lost from God then it will not be because of me. It will be because of you. So I will now go to those who are not Jews.'

7 So Paul left the Jews and he went to stay in the house of Justus. He was not a Jew. But he was a man who prayed to the God of the Jews. His house was next to the synagogue. 8 A man called Crispus was the leader of the synagogue. He, and everyone else who lived in his house, believed in Jesus. Many other people heard Paul's message about Jesus. They also believed the message and someone baptised them.

9 One night, when Paul was staying in Corinth, the Lord appeared to him in a dream. 'Do not be afraid', he said. 'Continue to speak to the people here. Do not stop speaking to them. 10 I am here with you, so nobody will hurt you. There are many people in this city who will believe in me.'

11 So Paul stayed in Corinth for 18 months and he taught the people God's message about Jesus.

12 When Gallio became the leader of the government in Greece, the Jews met together. They held Paul and they brought him in front of

Gallio. He would judge Paul.

13 The Jews said to Gallio, 'This man is teaching people things that are against our law. He is asking us to believe some different things about God. But if we did these things we would go against our law.'

14 Paul was ready to speak, but Gallio spoke first to the Jews. 'If this man had done a very bad thing', he said, 'then I would do something about it. 15 But you are arguing about words and names in your own Law. So you yourselves must decide what to do about it. I will not be a judge for these things.' 16 Then Gallio said to his soldiers, 'Cause these men to go out of this room.' 17 Sosthenes was the leader of the synagogue. The Jews held him and they hit him with sticks in front of Gallio. But Gallio did nothing to stop them.

Paul travels from Corinth to Antioch

18 Paul remained in Corinth with the believers for many days. Then he said goodbye to them. And he sailed by boat to the country called Syria. Priscilla and Aquila also went with him. Before Paul sailed, he promised something to God. Because of this promise, he asked someone to cut off all the hair from his head.

19 Paul, Priscilla and Aquila arrived in the city called Ephesus. Paul left them there, and he went into the synagogue. And he talked with the Jews. 20 Some of them asked Paul to remain in Ephesus with them for a long time. But he did not agree to stay. 21 Paul said to them, 'If God wants me to come back, I will return to you.' So then Paul sailed from Ephesus to Caesarea. 22 When Paul arrived in Caesarea, he went on to Jerusalem. He said hello to all the believers there and then he travelled to Antioch in Syria.

23 He stayed in Antioch for some time. Then, after that, he left Antioch and he travelled through Galatia and Phrygia. He said to all the believers in these places, 'Continue to love and to obey God more strongly.'

These are some of the things that Apollos did

24 In Ephesus, there was a Jew called Apollos. He was born in Alexandria in Egypt. Now he had travelled from Alexandria to live in Ephesus. He could speak well. He knew all the words very well that were written in God's book.

25 Someone had taught him very well the message of the good news about Jesus. He was happy when he was speaking to people about Jesus. Everything that he said was true. But he only knew part of the message. He knew what John said. And he knew about how John baptised people. 26 Apollos was not afraid, so he began to teach the people in the synagogue. Priscilla and Aquila heard Apollos teach the people. So they said to him, 'Please come with us to our home. We can explain to you everything about Jesus. We can tell you all about how God wants us to live.' And so they did that.

27 After that, Apollos decided to go to Greece. So the believers in Ephesus helped him. They wrote a letter for him to give to the believers in Greece. They wrote, 'When Apollos arrives, please accept him.' When he did arrive in Greece, he helped the believers there very much. They had started to believe in Jesus because God helped them. 28 Apollos argued strongly with the Jews in front of the people. And he showed them from God's word that the Jews were wrong. He explained clearly. And he used the words of the prophets, to show that Jesus is the Christ.

Chapter 19

Paul speaks in Ephesus about Jesus

1 While Apollos was in Corinth, Paul travelled through Phrygia and Galatia. He then arrived in Ephesus and he found some believers there. 2 Paul asked them, 'When you believed the message about Jesus, did God give you his Holy Spirit?'

'We did not even know that there is a Holy Spirit', the believers answered.

3 So Paul asked them, 'When someone baptised you, what did you understand?'

'We received the baptism that John spoke about', they answered.

4 Then Paul said, 'John baptised people who listened to his message. These people knew that they had done wrong things. They wanted to stop doing these things and they wanted to obey God. John also said to the people of Israel, "You must believe in the person who will come soon." This person is Jesus.' 5 When these believers in Ephesus heard this, they said to Paul, 'Please baptise us, and use the name of the Lord Jesus.' 6 Then Paul touched each person with his hand. Then God gave them his Holy Spirit and they spoke in different languages. They also spoke messages from God. 7 There were 12 men there.

8 For three months, Paul often went to the synagogue in Ephesus. He was not afraid to speak to the people there. He argued with them. He wanted them to believe the true things about the Kingdom of God. 9 But some of them did not want to understand what Paul said.

They would not believe in Jesus. Some of them said bad things about the way of the Lord in front of the whole group. So Paul stopped speaking to these people. He took the other believers away from that group. And every day he talked with people in another place. It was in a large room, where a man with the name Tyrannus usually taught the people. 10 Paul taught the people in Ephesus for two years. In that time, all the people who lived in Asia heard the message about Jesus. Paul was teaching Jews and those who were not Jews.

The sons of Sceva order bad spirits to leave people

11 God was working by Paul and God was doing many powerful things. These were things that nobody had done before. 12 People took pieces of cloth and clothes that Paul gave to them. Paul had used these things. People took the cloths to those who were ill. After they received them, the sick people became well again. And bad spirits also left them.

13 There were some Jews who travelled about. They also caused bad spirits to leave people. Now they wanted to use the name of the Lord Jesus when they did this. These Jews said to the bad spirits, 'Paul has taught people about Jesus. So, we use the authority of Jesus to say to you, "Bad spirits, come out of these people." ' 14 Sceva was a most important Jewish priest in Ephesus. He had 7 sons who were ordering the bad spirit to come out of someone in this way. 15 But the bad spirit said to Sceva's sons, 'I know who Jesus is. And I also know about Paul. But I do not know who you are.' 16 A man had the bad spirit and it was living inside him. He fought strongly with the 7 sons and he won the fight. He had hurt the sons and he had torn their clothes off. So the sons ran away from the man's house.

17 All the Jews and Gentiles who lived in Ephesus heard about this. They were afraid and they said, 'This person called the Lord Jesus is very powerful. He is very much more powerful than we thought. He is a very important person.' 18 Many of the believers then told everyone about all the bad things that they had also done. 19 Those who had used powerful bad spirits brought all their books about magic. Then they burned the books so that everyone could see. They counted that these books had cost 50 000 valuable metal coins. 20 When these powerful things happened, more and more people heard the good news about Jesus. And they believed strongly everything about him.

Bad troubles happen in Ephesus.

21 After these things happened, Paul decided to travel through Macedonia and Greece. From there, he decided to travel to Jerusalem. He said, 'After I go there, I must go to see Rome.' 22 Timothy and Erastus were helping Paul with his work. Paul sent them to Macedonia while he stayed longer in the towns in Asia.

23 It was at this time that there were bad troubles in Ephesus. These troubles happened because of the things that Paul taught the people. He taught them how to follow Jesus. 24 In Ephesus there was a man called Demetrius. He made very small things. Those things looked like the house of the female god called Artemis. He made them out of valuable metal and he paid a lot of money to his workers. 25 So he asked all his workers to meet with him. And he also asked other men to come. These men all did the same kind of work that Demetrius did. He said to all these men, 'You know that our work has caused us to become rich.26 And you can see what this man Paul is doing. You yourselves can also hear what he is saying. Paul says, "Gods that men have made are not really gods." Here in Ephesus, and in all Asia, many people believe what he says. 27 It might happen that people will say bad things about our work. It might also happen that the house of Artemis will not continue to be important to people. And people will think that Artemis herself is not important. At this time, everyone in Asia and the Roman world thinks that Artemis is very great and important.'

28 When the crowd heard Demetrius, they became very angry. 'Artemis of Ephesus is really very great', they shouted. 29 More and more people through the whole city began to shout. Gaius and Aristarchus were from Macedonia and they were travelling with Paul. Some people from the crowd held these two men. They took the men quickly to the open place in the middle of the city where everyone met together.

30 Paul himself wanted to stand in front of the crowd. But the other believers would not let him. 31 Some important Roman men in Ephesus were Paul's friends and they sent a message to him. 'Do not stand in front of the crowd', they said.

32 The crowd was making even more noise. Some people were shouting one thing and other people were shouting something else. Not many of the people knew why they had all met together. 33 There was a man called Alexander in the crowd. The Jews caused him to stand in front of the crowd. Some of the people thought that he was the reason for all the noise. He raised his hands in front of him so that they would be quiet. He wanted to explain to the crowd that he and his friends had not caused this trouble. 34 But the crowd knew that Alexander was a Jew. So they continued to shout the same words for two hours. 'Artemis of Ephesus is really very great!' they shouted.

35 At the end of the two hours, an important man from the city caused the crowd to listen to him. 'People of Ephesus!' he said. 'The house of Artemis is here in Ephesus. The special stone that fell from the sky is also here in Ephesus.

The people know about both these things and they keep them safely. 36 Nobody can say that this is not true. So you must not do anything without first thinking about it carefully. 37 Gaius and Aristarchus did not take anything from the house of Artemis. They did not say anything bad about Artemis. But still you brought them here. 38 Perhaps Demetrius and his workers think that someone did a wrong thing. If they do, let them speak to a man with authority. The court is open on certain days for this. A Roman ruler will judge what he says. The ruler will say if it is correct or not correct. Demetrius and his workers can argue in front of him about what Paul is saying.'

39 'If you want to argue these problems more, go to the meeting of the important people of the city. These people rule in our city. 40 Today, the people here are shouting and fighting. Maybe the Roman rulers will hear about this. They will say that we have done wrong things. The people should not shout and fight each other. We could not explain it to them. There is no good reason for all this noise.' 41 When he had said those things, he said, 'All of you should go home now.'

Chapter 20

Paul visits Macedonia and Greece again

1 After that, the crowd went home. Then Paul asked all the believers to meet together with him. He said to them, 'Be strong! Continue to believe in Jesus. I am going away now.' Then Paul travelled on to Macedonia.

2 He travelled through Macedonia and he talked to the people in different places again. He talked to them about Jesus. Then he came to Greece.

3 When Paul arrived in Greece, he stayed there for three months. One day, he was preparing to travel on to Syria. But then he heard news that the Jews wanted to kill him. So he decided to return to Jerusalem through Macedonia.

4 Sopater, the son of Pyrrhus, from Berea, went with Paul. Aristarchus and Secundus from Thessalonica also went with him. Gaius from Derbe and Timothy, Tychicus and Trophimus from Asia also all went with him. 5 They all travelled in front of us and they waited for us in Troas.

6 We sailed by boat from Philippi after the special meal of bread without yeast.

Paul visits the believers in Troas for the last time

7 On the Saturday evening, we all met to break bread together. Paul was teaching the people. He was leaving Troas the next day and so he taught them until midnight.

8 Many lights were burning in the upstairs room where we met together. 9 A young man called Eutychus was at the meeting. He was sitting next to the window. Paul talked for a long time and Eutychus wanted to sleep. Then Eutychus really went to sleep. He fell out of the window past three rooms to the ground. The other believers lifted him up off the ground, but he was dead. 10 So Paul went down the stairs to them all. He lay on top of the young man and held him for a moment. Then Paul said, 'Do not be afraid. He is still alive.' 11 Then Paul went back upstairs and he ate with the believers. Paul talked to them until the sun rose. Then he left Troas.

12 The other believers led Eutychus to his home. He was alive and they were happy.

Paul travels from Troas to Miletus

13 We went on in front of Paul to the boat. And we sailed on it to Assos. Paul decided to meet us on the boat at Assos.

He was travelling to Assos across the land. He had told us that we should wait for him there. 14 When he met us at Assos, he came on the boat with us. Then we all sailed to Mitylene. 15 We sailed from there and we arrived the next day at the coast near Chios. The day after that, we came to Samos and, the next day, we arrived at Miletus. 16 Paul had decided to sail from there past Ephesus. He did not want to remain in Asia any longer. He wanted to travel to Jerusalem quickly, because he wanted to arrive there before the day called Pentecost.

Paul sends a message to the leaders of the believers in Ephesus

17 When Paul was in Miletus, he sent someone to Ephesus with a message. This message was for the leaders of the believers in Ephesus. Paul wrote, 'Please come to Miletus and meet together with me.' 18 Paul spoke to the believers from Ephesus when they arrived in Miletus. 'You know about everything that I did in Asia', he said. 'You saw me from the first day that I arrived in Asia. I was with you for the whole time. You knew all that I did. And you knew all that I said. 19 I did not say to people that I was an important man. I worked as a servant of God. And I often cried. My life was difficult because the Jews wanted to kill me. 20 I taught you in the streets and in your homes. You know that I told you all the important things. I told you everything that would help you. 21 I taught the same things both to the Jews and to the Gentiles. I was serious when I taught everybody. I said to them all, "You must stop doing wrong things. You must also say sorry to God because you have done those wrong things. Then you must obey God and you must believe in our Lord Jesus."

22 Now I am going to Jerusalem because the Holy Spirit is taking me there. I do not know what people will do to me there. 23 The Holy Spirit told me in every city about the dangers. He said to me, "People will put you in prison and they will cause many troubles for you." 24 I may live or I may die. But this is not important to me. The Lord Jesus gave me some work to do. So it is important that I finish this work. I must tell people the good news about how kind and good God is to them.

25 I have lived among you all and I have taught you all about the Kingdom of God. Now I know that none of you will see me again. 26 So I am being serious with you today. If any of you are lost to God, then it is not because of me. 27 I have told you everything that God wants you to know. 28 You should be careful about yourselves, and about what you are doing. Keep safe the people that the Holy Spirit has asked you to help. Lead all the groups of believers. Some men have their own sheep. They feed the sheep and they keep them safe. Be like that kind of man. All the believers belong to God because Jesus died for them. He gave his life blood for them. 29 I know what will happen. After I leave you, other people will come among you. They will be like dangerous wild animals that attack sheep. These men will cause trouble for the believers. 30 Men from your own group of believers will also teach you things that are not true. These men will want other believers to follow them. So the believers will no longer follow Jesus. So they will say things that are not true. 31 Be very careful! I often cried about my work when I stayed with you. I want you to remember this. I taught all of you for three years, in the day and in the night.

32 And now I ask God to keep you safe. He has been kind to us. I brought the message about this to you. You will be safe if you remember this message. God will cause your spirits to be strong. And at the end, he will give to you all the good things that he has for his special people. 33 I did not want to take money or clothes from people when I stayed with you.

34 You yourselves know that I worked a lot. Then my friends and I could have everything that we needed. 35 I have shown you how to live. And I have shown you how to work. Now you know how to be kind to sick or weak people. You should remember what Jesus himself said: "It may make you happy when you receive things. But it makes you more happy when you give things to someone." '

36 Then Paul finished speaking. He went down on his knees together with all the leaders of the believers from Ephesus. And they all prayed. 37 Then they each showed him great love. All the leaders were crying when they said goodbye to Paul. 38 Paul had said, 'I will never see you again.' And this made them sadder than anything else did. So then they walked with Paul to the ship.

Chapter 21

Paul goes to Jerusalem

1 We said goodbye to the leaders of the believers from Ephesus. Then we sailed straight across the sea, and we arrived at Cos. The next day, we arrived at Rhodes, and from there we went on to Patara.

2 At Patara, we found a boat that was going to Phoenicia. So we climbed on to the boat and we sailed on it.

3 We arrived at a place on the sea from where we could see Cyprus. We sailed south of Cyprus, and we arrived in Syria. We left the boat at Tyre and we went on to the land. The boat was carrying many things and, at Tyre, people took all these things off the ship. 4 We found some believers at Tyre and we stayed with them for a week. The Holy Spirit said by these believers, 'Paul, you should not to go to Jerusalem.' 5 We had stayed with them for a week. And then it was time for us to leave them. All the believers, together with their wives and children, went with us out of the city. At the beach, we all went down on our knees and we prayed together. 6 Then we said goodbye to each other and we went back on the boat. The believers and their families returned to their homes.

7 We continued our journey on the ship. We sailed from Tyre to Ptolemais. Here, we met some believers and we stayed with them for one day. 8 The next day, we left Ptolemais and we sailed to Caesarea. We visited Philip in Caesarea and we stayed with him. Philip taught people in Caesarea the good news about Jesus. Philip was one of the 7 men that the believers had chosen in Jerusalem.

9 Philip had 4 daughters and none of them was married. His daughters spoke messages from God.

10 We stayed with Philip for a few days. Then a man called Agabus came to the city from Judea. He was a prophet and he spoke messages from God. 11 Agabus visited us. He took Paul's belt and he tied it round his own feet and hands. He said, 'Listen to this message from the Holy Spirit. "The Jews in Jerusalem will tie the man who has this belt. They will tie him in the same way. And then they will give this man to those who are not Jews." '

12 When we heard this, we all said many times to Paul, 'Please do not go to Jerusalem.' 13 But Paul answered, 'Stop crying like this! You are making me very sad! I am ready for men in Jerusalem to tie me up. And I am also ready to die there. I am ready to do all this because I believe in the Lord Jesus.' 14 But we could not cause Paul to think in a different way. So we stopped saying to him, 'You should not go to Jerusalem.' And we said to him instead, 'We want what God wants to happen.'

15 We stayed in Caesarea for some time. Then we prepared ourselves and we travelled to Jerusalem. 16 Some of the believers from Caesarea also went with us. They took us to the house of a man called Mnason. We had decided to stay with him. His home town was on the island called Cyprus. He had been a believer for a long time.

Paul visits James in Jerusalem

17 Then we arrived in Jerusalem, where the believers were very happy to see us. 18 The next day, Paul went with us to see James. The leaders of the believers were also there. 19 Paul said hello to them and then he told them everything about his work. God had worked by him and God had done many good things for the Gentiles.

20 After they had heard Paul speak, they said, 'God is very good and powerful.' Then the leaders said, 'Brother Paul, you can see what has happened. There are now many thousands of Jews who have believed in Jesus. But they also really want to obey the Law of Moses.'

21 'These Jews have told us what you have taught people in other countries. They said that you teach the Jews, "You do not need to obey the Law of Moses any longer. You do not need to circumcise your children. Jews usually do certain things. But now you do not need to do all those things." 22 Those people will certainly hear that you are in Jerusalem. 23 You must do what we say. In the city, there are 4 men who have promised something to God. 24 Now they will go. And they will wash to make themselves clean in front of God. Go with them. And join with them when they do that. You pay the priest the money for them. Then the men can cut all the hair off their heads. When you do that, everyone will understand about you. People have said that you do not obey the Law of Moses. But they will see you do this. And then, they will know that it is not true. They will know that you yourself obey the Law of Moses. 25 But it is different for the Gentiles who believe in Jesus. We have sent a letter to them. We wrote, "You must not eat meat from animals that people have killed as a gift to their own gods. People tie a rope round the neck of some animals to kill them. You must not eat the meat from those animals because the blood did not run out of them. Also, you must not eat blood. And you must not have sex with someone who is not your husband or wife." '

26 So Paul went with the 4 men. He joined with them when they washed. They washed to make themselves clean in front of God. Then he went into the Great House of God. He told the priest for how long the 4 men must wait. And after that, each man would kill an animal as a gift for God.

27 After 7 days, some Jews from Asia saw Paul in the Great House of God. They said some things against Paul to the crowd. So the people became angry and they caught hold of Paul.

28 'People of Israel, come and help us!' the Jews from Asia shouted. 'This is the man who travels everywhere. He teaches everyone against the people of Israel. He also speaks against the Law of Moses and this Great House of God.

Now he has even led some men who are not Jews into this Great House of God. So now this Great House of God is not clean in front of God any longer.' 29 (The men said this because they had seen Paul with a man in the city. This man was called Trophimus and he came from Ephesus. He was not a Jew. And they thought that Paul had led Trophimus into the Great House of God.)

30 Many other people in the city heard what had happened. They also began to shout about these things. They all ran together and they held Paul. Then they pulled him out of the Great House of God and they closed the doors immediately.

31 The angry crowd was trying to kill Paul. Then someone sent a message to the leader of the Roman soldiers. The message was, 'People are fighting in the streets all over the city.'

32 Immediately, the leader of these soldiers went with an officer and some soldiers. And they ran down to the angry crowd. The people saw the leader with his soldiers. So then they stopped hitting Paul.

33 The leader of the Roman soldiers went to Paul and held him. Then the leader of the soldiers said, 'Tie two chains round the arms of this man.' Then he asked the people in the crowd, 'Who is this man and what has he done?'

34 Some people in the crowd shouted one thing and other people shouted something different. There was so much noise that the leader of the soldiers was not sure about the facts. He did not understand what had happened. So he said to his soldiers, 'Take this man up into the strong building!' 35 The soldiers then led Paul as far as the steps of the strong building. Then they carried him because the crowd was so angry. 36 The crowd ran after Paul and they were shouting, 'Kill him!'

37 While the soldiers were leading Paul into the strong building, he spoke to their leader. 'Please can I say something to you?' he said.

The leader of the soldiers answered, 'I understand now that you speak the Greek language. 38 Are you not the man who came from Egypt some time ago? This man caused the people to fight against the government. He led 4000 of his own soldiers, with arms, out into the desert. They wanted to kill the Roman soldiers.'

39 Paul answered, 'I am a Jew and I was born in Tarsus in Cilicia. I am a man from an important city. Please let me speak to this crowd.'

40 The leader of the soldiers said to Paul, 'Yes, you can speak to the people.' So Paul stood still on the steps of the strong building. He raised his hands so that the people became quiet. When the people were quiet, he spoke to them. He spoke in the language that the Jews used.

Chapter 22

Paul speaks to the crowd in Jerusalem

1 'Listen to me, you men who are also Jews. You, our leaders, listen to me! I want to explain to you all that I have done. I have not done anything wrong.'

2 The crowd heard Paul speaking to them in the Hebrew language. So they became even quieter.

Paul continued to speak. He said, 3 'I am a Jew. I was born in Tarsus in Cilicia. I lived here in Jerusalem when I was a boy. Gamaliel was my teacher. I learned how to obey the Laws of our ancestors. I tried as carefully as you do to obey God. I was like you who are here today.'

Gamaliel was a Pharisee. He taught boys and young men in the synagogue.

4 'I caused great trouble to the disciples of Jesus. I caused the death of some of them. And I held men and women and I put them in prison. 5 The most important priest and all the men in the Sanhedrin can tell you that this is true. The men in the Sanhedrin gave me letters for the Jews in Damascus. So I started my journey to Damascus to catch the believers in that city. I wanted to put chains on them and I wanted to bring them back to Jerusalem. The officers here in the city wanted to punish them.'

Paul tells the crowd how he began to believe in Jesus

6 'But as I was travelling along the road, I came near to Damascus. About midday, a bright light from the sky suddenly appeared round me. 7 I fell to the ground. Then I heard a voice that spoke to me. "Saul, Saul, why are you hurting me?" he said.

8 "Lord, who are you?" I asked.

"I am Jesus from Nazareth", he said to me. "You are hurting me." 9 The men with me saw the light, but they did not hear the voice. They did not hear what it said to me.

10 "Lord, what must I do?" I asked. He said to me, "Now you should get up and you should go into Damascus. When you arrive in the city, someone will come to you. He will tell you what God wants you to do." 11 The bright light hurt my eyes so that I could not see. So the men who were with me held my hand. Then they led me into Damascus.

12 In Damascus, there was a man called Ananias. He knew God and he obeyed God and our Law. All the Jews in Damascus said good things about him. 13 Ananias came to see me. He stood close to me and he said, "See again, Saul my friend!" And immediately I could see again, so I looked at him.

14 Then Ananias said to me, "The God that our ancestors obeyed has chosen you. He will tell you what he wants you to do. He wanted you to see God's special servant, who is completely good. And God wanted you to hear this servant's own voice. 15 You will work for Jesus. You will tell everybody everything that you have seen and heard. 16 And now you do not need to wait any longer. Stand up and I will baptise you. Believe in Jesus. Ask God. And he will remove from you the bad things that you have done." '

The people in the crowd become very angry with Paul

17 'So, after I returned to Jerusalem, I went into the Great House of God. I was praying. I was awake but I had a dream. 18 In the dream, I saw the Lord and he spoke to me. He said, "Hurry. Leave Jerusalem quickly. The people here will not believe what you say to them about me."

19 "Lord", I said, "The people here know me very well. They know that I went to the synagogues. And I caught people there who believed in you. I also hit them. 20 Stephen told people about you. I myself was there when the people killed him. I told the people that they were doing a good thing. And I held the coats of the people while they killed him."

21 "Go!" the Lord said to me. "I am sending you a long way away to the Gentiles." '

22 The people listened to Paul until he spoke about the Gentiles. But then they began to shout loudly, 'Take him away! Kill him! It is not right that he should live any longer!'

23 They were shouting. They were taking off their coats and they were throwing them about. They also threw dirt from the ground into the air.

24 The leader of the soldiers said to his men, 'Take this man into the strong building. Then hit him with a whip. We will then know what he has done. He will tell us why the Jews are shouting so loudly about him.'

25 So the soldiers tied ropes round Paul and they were ready to hit him. But Paul spoke to the officer who stood close to him. 'You will not be obeying your laws if you hit me', he said. 'I am a citizen of Rome. I have not yet stood in front of a judge. So no judge has said that I have done anything wrong.'

26 The officer heard what Paul said. So he went to the leader of the soldiers and he said, 'Do not do what you want to do! That man is a citizen of Rome!'

27 So the leader of the soldiers went to speak to Paul. 'Is this true that you are a citizen of Rome?' he asked Paul. 'Yes', he answered.

28 The leader of the soldiers said, 'I paid a lot of money to the government so that I could become a citizen of Rome.'

'But I am a citizen of Rome because my parents were', answered Paul.

29 Immediately, the men who would have asked Paul questions moved away from him. The leader of the soldiers was afraid because he had put chains on Paul's arms and legs. And he knew that he should not do that to a citizen of Rome.

30 The leader of the soldiers wanted to find the reason why the Jews had said bad things about Paul. He wanted to be sure about it. So the next day, he asked his soldiers to remove the chains from Paul. And he sent a message to the most important priest and to all the men of the Sanhedrin. 'Please come and meet together with me today', he said. Then he took Paul to them and he caused Paul to stand in front of them.

Chapter 23

Paul speaks to the men of the Sanhedrin

1 Paul looked at the men of the Sanhedrin and he spoke to them. 'My friends, who are also Israelites', he said. 'Today I have nothing to be ashamed about before God. I have always lived in a way that makes God happy with me.' 2 The most important priest was called Ananias. He said to the men who were near Paul, 'Hit that man on his mouth!' 3 Paul said to Ananias, 'It is certain that God will hit you. You are like a wall that someone has painted white.'

Paul said this to Ananias, because Ananias was doing one thing. But he was saying something else. Ananias wanted people to think that he was good. White paint would have covered dirt.

'You are sitting there and you are judging me. You are asking if I obey the Law of God. But you yourself are not obeying the Law because you said, "Hit that man!" ' 4 The men who were standing close to Paul answered him. 'You are saying bad things to the most important priest.'

5 'My brothers, I did not know that he was the most important priest.' Paul continued. 'I know that the prophets wrote, "Do not say bad things about the man who is ruling your people." '

6 Then Paul saw that there were some Sadducees and some Pharisees in the group. So he shouted out to all the men of the Sanhedrin, 'Men, I am a Pharisee and my father was a Pharisee. I believe that dead people will live again. God will cause this to happen.

And you are judging me today because I believe that.' 7 As soon as Paul said that, the Pharisees and Sadducees began to argue with each other. 8 (The Sadducees do not believe that dead people will live again. They do not believe that there are angels or spirits. But the Pharisees believe in all these things.)

9 The Sadducees and the Pharisees began to shout louder and louder. There were some teachers of the Law who were in the group of Pharisees. These teachers of the Law stood up. They were very angry about what was happening. 'We do not believe that this man has done anything wrong', they said. 'What he says may be true. A spirit or an angel may have spoken to him.' 10 The two groups argued more and more strongly. And the leader of the soldiers thought that someone might hurt Paul. They were pulling him in different directions. So he said to his soldiers, 'Go down into the group and take Paul away from them. Take him back into the strong building.'

11 That night, the Lord came and he stood close to Paul. He said to Paul, 'Continue to be brave! You have told people here in Jerusalem the true things about me. You must do the same thing in Rome.'

The Jews in Jerusalem decide to kill Paul

12 The next morning, some Jews talked together in a group about what they should do. And they decided to promise something to God. They would not eat or drink anything until they had killed Paul. 13 More than 40 Jews were in the group that decided this.

14 Then this group went to the leaders of the priests and the leaders of the Jews. They said, 'We have decided together to say a serious promise to God. We will not eat anything until after we have killed Paul. 15 Now we want you to send this message to the leader of the soldiers. "Please bring Paul down to the men of the Sanhedrin. We want to know more about what he has done." That is the message. We do not really want to ask him questions. We will wait for Paul and we will be ready to kill him. We will do this before he arrives in front of the Sanhedrin.'

16 But the son of Paul's sister heard what the Jews wanted to do. So he went into the strong building and he told Paul about it.

17 So Paul spoke to one of the officers who came to him. 'Please take this young man to the leader of the soldiers. He has something to tell him.' 18 Then the officer led the young man to the leader of the soldiers and said to him, 'Paul, who is in the prison, spoke to me. He asked me to bring this young man to you. He has something to tell you.'

19 The leader of the soldiers held the young man's hand. Then he led the young man to a room where there were no other people. Then he said to the young man, 'What do you want to tell me?'

20 The young man said, 'All the Jews with authority have agreed together to ask you to do something. They want you to take Paul down to the men of the Sanhedrin. They will say that they want to ask him more questions. But that is not true. 21 So do not listen to them. There are more than 40 men who will be hiding somewhere. They are waiting for Paul. They have said a serious promise to God. And they will not eat or drink anything until they have killed Paul. They are now ready to do this. And they are waiting to hear your answer.'

22 The leader of the soldiers said, 'Do not tell anybody that you told me about this.' Then he sent the young man away.

The leader of the soldiers sends Paul to Felix, the ruler

23 Then the leader of the soldiers asked two of his officers to come to him. He said to them, 'I want 200 soldiers to prepare themselves. I want them to go to Caesarea. I also want 70 men to ride on horses. Send with them 200 men. They should each carry a long piece of wood with a sharp point at the end. They should all be ready to leave at 9 o'clock tonight.

24 Have some horses ready for Paul to ride on. Keep him safely and lead him to Felix the ruler.'

25 Then the leader of the soldiers wrote a letter to Felix the ruler. In the letter he wrote,

26 'This letter is to Felix, our very important ruler. I, Claudius Lysias, am sending you this letter. Hello.

27 The Jews caught this man and they wanted to kill him. I learned that he is a citizen of Rome. So I went, together with my soldiers, and I saved him from them. 28 The Jews said that he had done some wrong things. I wanted to know more about him, so I took him to stand in front of their Sanhedrin. 29 I found out what he had done. But we could not put him in prison or kill him because of these things. The Jews said that he had not obeyed their own Law. 30 A group of Jews then decided to kill him. Someone told me about this, so I decided to send him to you. I have said to the Jews who say bad things about him, "You say that Paul has done something wrong. So, go and tell Felix the ruler about this." '

31 Then the soldiers did what their leader had asked them to do. They took Paul from the prison. That night, they took him as far as Antipatris. 32 The next day, the 200 soldiers who had walked with Paul returned to the strong building in Jerusalem. But the soldiers who rode horses travelled on with Paul.

33 They took Paul to Caesarea and they gave the letter to Felix, the ruler. Then they gave Paul to him. 34 Felix the ruler read the letter and he asked Paul, 'Which country are you from?' 'I am from Cilicia', Paul answered. 35 Felix said, 'When the Jews arrive, they will tell me everything about you. Then I will also listen to you and I will judge you.' Felix then said to his soldiers, 'Put this man in Herod's house and guard him carefully!'

Chapter 24

The Jews say bad things about Paul

1 Five days after that, Ananias, the most important priest, went to Caesarea. Some leaders of the Jews went with him. A man called Tertullus also went with them. Tertullus knew all about the law. All these people went to see Felix the ruler. Felix would judge Paul. So they told Felix what Paul had done. 2 Felix asked a soldier to fetch Paul. So Tertullus began first to speak against Paul. He said, 'Most important ruler, we know that you are a good leader. Because of you, our country has had no wars for a long time. You have also made new laws for us. These are all good for our country. 3 Everywhere, the people are happy about what you have done. And all the time they want to thank you very much for these things. 4 I do not want you to sit here for a long time. Please be kind to us and listen to me. I will speak for a short time, for all of us.

5 We know that this man is dangerous to the government. He causes bad problems among people everywhere. He causes Jews in every part of the world to fight each other. He is the leader of a group called the Nazarenes.'

Tertullus wanted Felix to think that Paul was a problem to the Roman authorities.

6 'He also did things in the Great House of God that are against our Law. So we held him. We wanted to judge him by what is in our own Law. 7 But Lysias, the leader of the soldiers, came to us. He attacked us and he took Paul away from us. 8 Then Lysias said to us, "Go to Felix. Some people think that this man has done wrong things. They should speak to Felix about it." You, Felix, can ask this man some questions. Then you will learn from him what wrong things he has done. And he will tell you about all the things that we are talking about.' 9 The Jews that were with Tertullus then said together, 'All these things that Tertullus has said are true.'

Paul tells Felix his own story

10 Then Felix the ruler raised his hands towards Paul. This showed Paul that he should speak. So he said to Felix, 'I know that you have judged the people in this country for many years. So now I am happy to tell you everything. 11 I went to Jerusalem about 12 days ago. You can check that that is true. I went there to thank God because he has helped me with my work. 12 And when the Jews saw me, I was not arguing with anybody in the Great House of God. I was not causing problems among the people in the synagogues. Nor did I cause problems in other places in the city. 13 So they cannot say that they have said true things about me. 14 I do agree that the next thing about me is true. I do obey the God of our ancestors, but I live in a different way. But these men say that this is not the right way. I also believe in all the Law of Moses. And I believe also in all the words in the books that the prophets wrote. 15 I also believe this. God will cause all men, both good and bad, to become alive again after they have died. These men here also believe this. 16 I always try not to cause trouble among people. And I always try to be right with God.

17 I had not been to Jerusalem for several years. And I went there this time to take some money as a gift for my own people. I also wanted to give some animals to the priest to kill. These were gifts to God. 18 I was giving these gifts to God in his house when these men found me. I had finished making myself clean in front of God. There was no crowd with me. Nobody was arguing or fighting. 19 But there were some Jews there who had come from Asia. They themselves should come here. They thought that I had done wrong things. So they should come and speak to you about it. 20 Or these men here should tell you what I have done wrong. Because of them, I stood in front of the men of the Sanhedrin. 21 But when I stood there, I did one thing. I shouted, "I believe this. God will cause people to become alive again after they have died." Because of that, you are judging me today.'

22 Felix knew all about God's new way that people should live. He told everyone that the meeting had finished. Then he said to Paul, 'Soon Lysias, the leader of the soldiers, will arrive here. And then I will decide what to do with you.' 23 Felix said to the officer who was guarding Paul, 'Put this man back into the prison, but continue to guard him. His friends can come and see him. They can help him and they can bring things for him.'

Felix and Drusilla listen to Paul

24 After some days, Felix came with Drusilla, his Jewish wife. He asked his soldiers to bring Paul to them. Paul talked to them.

And they listened to everything that he said. Paul spoke about how people believed in Jesus Christ. 25 Paul continued to speak. He talked about how people could be right with God. He also talked about people who did not stop themselves doing wrong things. And, he said, 'One day, God will judge all the good and bad things that people have done.' While Paul talked about these things, Felix became afraid. He said to Paul, 'You can leave us now. I will perhaps have some more time to listen to you. Then I will ask you to come here again.' 26 At the same time, Felix also hoped that Paul would give him some money. That was the reason that he met with Paul again. They often talked together.

27 This happened for two years. Then Porcius Festus became the ruler and Felix did not rule any longer. Felix wanted the Jews to say, 'Felix was a good ruler.' So he left Paul in the prison.

Chapter 25

Festus travels to Jerusalem to speak to the leaders of the Jews

1 Festus began to rule. Three days after that, he travelled from Caesarea to Jerusalem. 2 In Jerusalem, the leaders of the priests and the leaders of the Jews told him what Paul had done.

3 They said to Festus, 'Please hear us. We really want you to bring Paul to Jerusalem. Then we would be very happy.' They wanted to kill Paul while he was travelling to Jerusalem. 4 'Paul will remain in prison in Caesarea', Festus answered. 'I myself will return there soon. 5 Your leaders should go to Caesarea with me. Then if this man has done anything wrong, they can say that to him in front of me.'

6 Festus stayed for another 8 or 10 days with the leaders of the priests and the leaders of the Jews. Then he returned to Caesarea. On the next day, he sat down in the large room to judge people. He said to his soldiers, 'Bring Paul in here!' 7 When Paul arrived in the room, all the Jews from Jerusalem stood close to him. And they began to speak against Paul. They said that he had done very many bad things. But they could not show Festus that this was true.

8 Then Paul spoke about himself. 'I have obeyed the Law of the Jews', he said. 'I have not caused trouble in the Great House of God and I have not said anything bad about Caesar.'

9 Festus wanted the Jews to say, 'Festus is a good ruler.' So he asked Paul, 'The Jews here say that you have done bad things. Would you be happy to go to Jerusalem? I can decide there if this is true.'

10 'I am in the place where the officers of Caesar judge people', Paul answered. 'This is the correct place to decide if these things about me are true. I have never done any wrong thing against the Jews. And you yourself know that. 11 If I have not obeyed the Roman law, then I do not refuse to die. Have I done something bad that you can kill me for? If that is true, then I also agree to it. I should die. But the Jews are not speaking true words against me. You should not give me to them. So I ask you to send me to Caesar. I want him to listen to our words.'

12 Then Festus talked to his friends in the government about what Paul had said. And after that, Festus answered Paul. 'You have asked to go and talk to Caesar about yourself', he said. 'And it is right for you to go.'

King Agrippa and Bernice visit Festus

13 Several weeks after this, King Agrippa and Bernice came to Caesarea to visit Festus. They wanted to give him a welcome now that he had become the ruler.

14 After they had been in Caesarea for many days, Festus explained to Agrippa the problem about Paul. Festus said, 'There is a man here that Felix left in prison. 15 When I went to Jerusalem, the Jewish leaders and the leaders of their priests talked to me about him. "That man", they said, "has done some very bad things and you should kill him."

16 So I said to them, "Roman rulers do not usually give a man from prison to other people. Some of you are saying that this man has done wrong things. So he must first stand in front of the people who are speaking against him. Then he can answer them himself." 17 So the Jewish leaders and the leaders of their priests came here. I did not wait. On the next day I sat in the room to judge people. And I asked my soldiers to bring this man to me. 18 The men who had said bad things about him stood up. But they did not say what I had thought. They did not talk about any very bad things that he had done. 19 They were arguing with this man about what they believe about God. They were also arguing about a man called Jesus. They said that Jesus was dead. But Paul says that he is alive. 20 I could not decide how I could learn more about all these things. So I asked Paul, "Can I take you to Jerusalem? There you can answer these men before me. You can explain what they are saying against you." 21 But Paul did not want to go to Jerusalem. He said to me, "Please keep me here. I want the soldiers to continue to guard me. I want to go to Caesar. He can decide what to do with me." So I said to my soldiers, "Guard Paul until I send him to Caesar!" '

22 Agrippa said to Festus, 'I would like to hear this man myself.'

'You will hear him tomorrow', Festus answered.

23 The next day, Agrippa and Bernice came to the large room where Festus talked to people. They wore beautiful clothes and they had many servants with them. Roman officers and the important men in the city also went into the room with them. Festus said to his soldiers, 'Bring Paul here to us!' So they brought Paul into the room. 24 Festus said, 'King Agrippa, and everyone here now, listen. You see the man who is standing in front of you. Many Jews here have spoken to me about him. Also the Jews who are in Jerusalem have told me about him. They shout loudly, "This man has done wrong things. This man should not continue to live!" 25 But I could not find a reason to kill him. He has not done anything against our law. He himself has asked to speak to Caesar. So I have decided to send him to Caesar. 26 But I do not know what to write to Caesar about him. So I have brought him here to stand in front of you. King Agrippa, it is really for this reason that I have brought him here. Listen to what Paul says. Then I can write something about him for Caesar. 27 I can send a person from the prison to Caesar. But I must tell him what wrong things that person has done.'

Chapter 26

Paul speaks to Agrippa

1 Agrippa said to Paul, 'You can now speak about yourself.'

Paul raised his hand as he spoke. 2 'King Agrippa, please listen to me', he said. 'I am happy because I can speak to you today. The Jews say that I have done some wrong things. So I will explain to you all about the things that they say against me. 3 I can do this because you know all about the Jews. You know how we live. You also know very well what we argue about with each other. So please be patient and listen to me.

4 I have lived among the Jews and at Jerusalem since I was young. So all the Jews know how I have lived.

5 They have known me for a long time. And so they know that I was a Pharisee. I lived as a Pharisee.

I was very careful to obey God's Law, in the same way that they do. They could tell you that this is true. They could, if they wanted to tell you. 6 Now I stand here for men to judge me. I do this because I believe in God's promise to our ancestors.

7 He promised it to the 12 families of Israel. They speak to God by day and by night. And they say that he is very powerful and important. And so they hope to receive what he promised. I also hope to receive it. Powerful king, this is the reason that the Jews themselves say all these things about me. 8 God causes people to become alive again after they have died. You who hear me think that this is not possible. But I do not see why you should think that.

9 I myself thought that I should do many things against the authority of Jesus of Nazareth. 10 So that is what I did in Jerusalem. The leaders of the priests gave me authority to put many of God's people in prison. And I agreed with our leaders when they said, "These people must die." 11 Often, I said that my men should punish these people in the synagogues. I tried to cause them to say bad things about God. Because I was very angry with them, I travelled to other cities in other countries. Then I could also hurt those who believed in Jesus there.'

Paul tells Agrippa and Bernice about when he first believed in Jesus

12 'For that reason, I was travelling to Damascus. The leaders of the priests had given me a letter. They had written, "There are people in Damascus who believe in Jesus. And we have given Paul authority to catch them." 13 Powerful king, I was travelling along the road at midday. And I saw a light that was much brighter than the light from the sun. This very bright light shone all round me and round all the men who were with me. 14 All of us fell down to the ground. I heard a voice that spoke to me in the Hebrew language. "Saul, Saul, you are hurting me", he said. "You are like an ox that kicks against a sharp stick. And so you are hurting yourself." '

15 '"Lord, who are you?" I asked.

"I am Jesus", he said. "And you are hurting me. 16 Now you should get up. Stand on your feet. I have appeared to you because I have chosen you. I want you to work for me. You have seen me today. I want you to tell other people about this. After that, I will show you other things about me that you should tell people. 17 I will send you to speak to Jews and to those who are not Jews. Some of them will want to hurt you. But I will save you from them. 18 You will help them to understand who I am. They are like people who live in the dark. And so they cannot see. Teach them about me. Then they will be like people who live in the light. Now they are
in Satan's kingdom and he has power over them. Take them out and put them in God's kingdom. Because they believe in me, I will forgive them. I will forgive them for all the wrong things that they have done. I will give them a place among all the people that God has chosen." '

Paul tells Agrippa and Bernice about his work for God

19 'And so, King Agrippa, I obeyed the things that I heard
from heaven that day. 20 First, I taught the people in Damascus and in Jerusalem what they should do. I said to them, "You have done wrong things. You must tell God that you are sorry. And then you must obey God. You must show God that you are obeying him." I also taught this to both Jews and Gentiles in many different countries. 21 This is the reason that the Jews held me in the Great House of God. This is also the reason that they wanted to kill me. 22 But God has helped me every day. So now I can stand here. I can tell you what is true. I can speak to people who are very important. And I can also speak to people who are not important. Moses and God's other prophets told us that all these things would happen. And I am telling you these same things. 23 People would kill the Christ that God chose. The Christ would then first become alive again after death. In that way, he would show everyone that God saves Jews and Gentiles from death. That is what the prophets and Moses said.'

24 While Paul was telling Agrippa all these things, Festus shouted at Paul, 'Your mind is confused. You have learned many things. But all these things have caused your mind to be confused.'

25 'Important ruler, my mind is not confused', said Paul. 'Everything that I have said is true. And I am completely clear in my mind. 26 King Agrippa, I am not afraid to speak to you. I am sure that you already know about these things. I am sure that you have already heard everything. Nobody has hidden these things. 27 King Agrippa, do you believe what the prophets said? I am sure that you do believe them.'

28 Then Agrippa said to Paul, 'What do you think? Can you cause me to become a Christian in this short time?'

29 'It is not important if it takes a long time or a short time', Paul answered. 'I pray to God about you and about everyone who is listening to me today. I pray that you will all become like me. But I would not want you to wear these same chains!'

30 Then King Agrippa, Festus and Bernice and everyone else stood up. 31 After they left the room, they said to each other, 'This man has not done anything wrong. We should not kill him, or put him in prison.'

32 Agrippa said to Festus, 'We could let this man leave the prison. But he has asked to go to Caesar. So we cannot let him leave the prison.'

Chapter 27

Soldiers take Paul to Rome

1 Festus decided that we should sail to Italy. So he ordered a soldier called Julius to guard Paul. He also gave Julius authority over some other men who had been in the prison. Julius was an officer in the Roman army. He ruled a large group of soldiers that belonged to Caesar.

Luke was with Paul on this journey.

2 We went on to a boat that had come from Adramyttium. This ship was ready to leave. It would sail to the towns on the coast of Asia. We all sailed on this ship and Aristarchus also sailed with us. He was a man from Macedonia who had lived in Thessalonica.

3 The next day we arrived at Sidon. Julius was kind to Paul. He said, 'Paul, you can go and visit your friends here. They can give you anything that you need.' 4 Then we all sailed again from there. But the wind was blowing against the front of our ship. So we sailed round the island called Cyprus. We stayed on the side of the island where the wind was not strong. 5 When we were near to Cilicia and Pamphylia, we then sailed straight across the sea. We arrived at Myra, in the part of the country called Lycia. 6 The Roman officer found another ship there that had sailed from Alexandria. It would sail to Italy. So the officer took us off one ship and he put us on the other ship. 7 The ship sailed slowly for several days. It was difficult to sail. But in the end we arrived near the town called Cnidus. Because of the strong wind, we could not continue to sail in that direction. So we sailed down the side of the island called Crete. And the wind there was not strong. We passed the point of land called Salmone. 8 It was difficult to sail, so we stayed close to the coast. Then we came to another place called 'Safe Port'. Ships could stop here and be safe. This port was not far from the town called Lasea.

9 We remained there for many days. So then it had become dangerous to continue the journey. By then it was already after the Day of Atonement.

So Paul spoke to the army officer and to the men who sailed the boat. 10 'I understand that now our journey will be dangerous. The ship may break in pieces and you will lose the things in it. And all the people may also die in the water.' 11 But the army officer did not believe what Paul said. Instead, he believed what the owner of the ship and the captain said.

12 This port was not a good place for a ship to remain during the winter. Most of the men on the ship wanted to continue the journey. They wanted to sail as far as Phoenix, if they could get there. Phoenix was a better port to stay in for the winter. Phoenix was in Crete and it was open to the sea both to the southwest and to the northwest.

The ship is in a storm

13 The wind began to blow from the south, but it was not strong.

So the men thought, 'We can do what we wanted to do. We can sail to Phoenix.' So they pulled up the anchor. Then they sailed as close as they could to the coast. They went along the coast of Crete.

14 But soon a very strong wind began to blow. This wind was from the northeast (between north and east) and it blew down strongly across the island. 15 The wind blew against the ship. It was not possible for the men to sail the ship straight into the wind. So they did not try any longer. They let the wind blow the ship along. 16 We passed the south end of a small island called Cauda. Here we found a place where the strong wind did not blow as much. It was difficult, but we kept the ship's little boat safe. 17 They lifted it out of the water. Then they put it on the ship and they tied it there with ropes. Then they tied some more ropes under and round the ship so that it would not break. The men were afraid of what could happen. There were some places along the coast of Libya where the water was not very deep. The ship might sail on to one of these places and then it might break. So they took the ship's sails down. And they let the wind blow the ship along. 18 The big strong storm continued. The ship was carrying many things. So the next day, the men threw some of these things off the ship into the sea. 19 The day after that, the men themselves threw some of the sails and ropes off the ship into the sea. 20 For many days, we could not see the sun or the stars. The strong wind continued to blow. So then we thought, 'It is not possible for us to remain alive.'

21 The men had not eaten any food for a long time. Then Paul stood in front of them. 'Men, you should have listened to me!' he said. 'You should not have sailed from Crete. If we had not sailed, we would not have lost all these things from the ship. 22 Now I ask you, please be brave. The storm will completely destroy the ship, but not one of you will die. 23 I know this because last night one of God's angels came to me. He came from my God who is very great and powerful. 24 The angel said, "Paul, do not be afraid. You will stand in front of Caesar. God will be kind to you because he is good. So none of the men in the ship with you will die." 25 And so I say to you, "Men, be brave!" I believe in God. So everything will happen in the way that the angel told me. 26 But the wind will blow the ship on to an island.'

27 The storm had continued for 14 days and nights. The strong wind was blowing the ship across the Mediterranean Sea. About midnight, the sailors thought that we were close to the land. 28 So they tied a piece of metal to a thin rope. They held one end and they let the metal drop into the sea. They saw from the rope that the water was nearly 40 metres (120 feet) deep. A short time later they did this again. This time it was only 30 metres (90 feet) deep. 29 The sailors were afraid that the ship would hit some rocks. So from the back of the ship, they put 4 anchors on ropes into the sea.

After that, they wanted the morning to come soon. 30 Then the sailors tried to leave the ship. They put the little boat into the sea. 'We are going to the front of the ship', they said. 'We will put some more anchors on ropes down into the sea.' But that was not true. 31 Paul said to the army officer and soldiers, 'These sailors must stay on the ship. If they do not stay, you will not be safe.' 32 So the soldiers cut the ropes that held the small boat to the ship. The little boat fell into the water and the wind blew it away without the sailors.

33 Now it was almost morning and Paul said to everyone, 'Please come and eat some food. You have now waited for 14 days for the storm to stop. And you have not eaten anything during all that time. 34 You must eat some food. Then you will be strong enough to get to the shore. You will be safe. You will not even lose one hair from your head.' 35 After Paul said this, he took some bread. He prayed in front of them all and he thanked God for the bread. Then he broke the bread into small pieces and he began to eat it. 36 Everyone became less afraid and they all ate some of the bread. 37 There were 276 people on the ship. 38 After everyone had eaten enough, the sailors threw the wheat into the sea. Then the ship was not so heavy.

The sea completely destroys the ship

39 In the morning, the ship was close to some land. But the sailors did not know which island it was. But they saw a place on the shore with some sand on it. They wanted to put the ship on the sand. 40 So the sailors cut all the ropes with anchors on them. The anchors went down through the water to the ground. They also removed the ropes from the oars. Then they raised the sail at the front of the ship so that the wind would blow the ship along. Then the ship sailed straight towards the shore.

41 But there was a place where the water was not very deep. The ship sailed on to the sand and it stayed there. The front of the ship stayed on the sand and it could not move. The sea was very strong and it broke the back of the ship.

42 The soldiers wanted to kill the men who had been in the prison. They did not want these men to swim to the land and then to run away. 43 But the army officer wanted to save Paul. So he ordered the soldiers not to kill the men. Instead he said, 'Everyone who can swim, jump into the water first. Then swim to the shore. 44 You men, who cannot swim, follow them. Hold on to pieces of wood, or pieces of the ship.' This was the way that all of us arrived safely on the shore.

Chapter 28

What happened to Paul on the island called Malta

1 Then we were on the shore and we were all safe. The people there told us that the island was called Malta. 2 The people who lived on the island were very kind to us. Rain was falling and the weather was now cold. So the people who lived on the island lit a fire for us. And they welcomed us to their island. 3 Paul picked up some sticks to put on the fire. A dangerous snake came out from among the sticks. It had felt the heat from the fire. The snake bit Paul's hand and it remained fixed to his hand. 4 The people who lived on the island saw the snake. It was hanging from Paul's hand. So they said to each other, 'We know now that this man killed someone. He did not die in the sea but it is not right for him to live. The snake will kill him.' 5 Then Paul caused the snake to fall off his hand. It fell into the fire and it had not hurt Paul. 6 The people watched Paul carefully. They waited for his hand to become bigger. They thought that perhaps he would die immediately. They waited for a long time. But they did not see anything bad happen to Paul. So then they thought about this in a different way. They said, 'This man is a god.'

7 The leader of the people who lived on the island was called Publius. There were some of his fields not far from the shore. Publius said hello to us and he was kind to us. We stayed in his house for three days. 8 Publius's father was lying in bed because he was ill. He was sick and his body was hot. Paul went into his room and prayed for him. He put his hands on the head of Publius's father and he caused him to become well again. 9 After Paul did this, all the other sick people on the island came to him. And he caused them to become well again. 10 The people gave us many gifts. Later, they put everything that we needed on another ship for us. And then we left the island.

11 We had remained on Malta for three months. We then left the island on another ship. This ship was called 'The Twin Gods' and it had come from Alexandria. It had stayed in Malta during the winter.

The 'Twin Gods' were two Greek gods called Castor and Pollux. Twins are two children with the same mother who are born at about the same time. The people from Greece thought that these gods were very powerful.

12 We arrived at the port of the city called Syracuse. We stayed there for three days.

13 From Syracuse we sailed on. And we arrived at the city called Rhegium. The next day, the wind began to blow from the south. Two days after that, we arrived at the town called Puteoli. This was another port.

14 We found some people there who believed in Jesus. They asked us to stay with them for one week. After this we travelled on to Rome. 15 The believers in Rome had heard about us. So they came as far as the market of Appius and the Three Hotels to meet us. When Paul saw them, he thanked God for them. Paul was very happy that they had come to meet him.

16 When we arrived in Rome, the authorities said to Paul, 'You can live by yourself in your own house. But a soldier will guard you so that you cannot run away.'

17 After three days, Paul asked the leaders of the Jews in Rome to meet with him. When they met together, Paul said to them, 'Friends, you are Jews like I am. I want you to know that I have never done anything bad to our people. Our ancestors told us many things about how we should live. I always obeyed these rules. But the Jews put me in the prison in Jerusalem and then they gave me to the Roman rulers. 18 The Roman rulers asked me questions about what I had done. They found that I had not done anything wrong. There was no reason for which they could say, "He must die." So they did not want to keep me any longer. 19 But the Jews did not agree with the Roman rulers. So then I asked the Roman rulers if I could speak to Caesar. I had nothing bad to say about my own people. 20 Because of all that happened, I wanted to talk with you. I believe in the same promise that all the Jews believe in. And that is why I am in prison here.'

21 The leaders of the Jews in Rome said, 'We have not received any letters about you from Judea. No Jews have come here from Judea and told us news. And no Jews have said anything bad about you. 22 We do know that people everywhere say bad things about your group. So we would like you to tell us your ideas.'

23 So the Jews decided on a day on which they would meet again with Paul. And on that day, a large number of Jews arrived. They came to the house where Paul was staying. Paul talked to them about the Kingdom of God. He spoke from the morning until night and he explained his message to them. He spoke about everything written in the Law of Moses and the books of the prophets. And he showed the Jews that his message about Jesus was true. 24 Some of them believed that his message was true. But other Jews who were there would not believe him. 25 At the end of the day, all the Jews left his house. But they did not agree with each other about Paul's words. Before they left the house, Paul had said, 'The Holy Spirit spoke correctly by the prophet Isaiah. He spoke to your ancestors. The Holy Spirit said to Isaiah,

26 "Go and say to this people,

'You will listen and listen. But you will never understand anything.

You will look and look. But you will never see anything.'

27   This people do not want to understand anything with their minds.

    They still do not want to listen to anybody.

    If they wanted to look, they could see.

    If they wanted to listen, they could hear.

    Then they would also understand.

    And then they would obey me.

And I would forgive them and I would make them well." '

28 Paul then said, 'I want you to know that God has sent his message about Jesus to the Gentiles. And they will listen!' 29 After Paul had said these things, the Jews left. They were arguing with each other.

30 Paul lived for two years in Rome in his own house. He paid money to live in the house. Many people came to visit him and he was kind to them all. 31 He taught people about the Kingdom of God and about the Lord Jesus Christ. Paul spoke his message strongly. He could speak to everyone who visited him. Nobody tried to stop him.

Alive to God

Romans

About this book

The writer

Paul wrote this letter when he was staying at the city called Corinth. Corinth was in the south part of the country that we call Greece now.

The date

Paul wrote this letter about the year 57 AD. That was about 30 years after Jesus died.

The people that Paul was writing to

Paul wrote this letter to the Christians who were living at the city called Rome. Rome is the capital of the country that we call Italy now. At the time when he wrote this letter, Paul himself had never visited Rome. But he was hoping to visit it soon. Nobody knows how the church (group of Christians) at Rome started. Perhaps people who had travelled from Rome heard the good news about Jesus at Jerusalem city, the capital of Israel. (See Acts 2:10.) Then maybe they went home to Rome and they told the good news to people there.

Paul's message

Some of the Christians at Rome were Jews. That means that they belonged to Israel's people. Some of the Christians there were not Jews. These people were called Gentiles (1:13). There may have been problems between the Christian Jews and the Christian Gentiles because they thought about things differently. They may have been meeting in separate groups, in different places. So, Paul knew that he had to explain his message to both these groups of Christians.

Paul himself was a Jew. Many years before, God had given special rules to Israel's people by Moses. God gave those rules to them because he wanted them to be his own special people. He wanted them to obey him. God had not given those rules to the Gentiles. But some Christian Jews thought that Christian Gentiles should still obey those rules.

So, in this letter, Paul writes about the purpose of the rules that God gave to Moses. Those rules were very good and very important. They helped Israel's people to obey God. But Paul explains why those rules could not really save people.

In chapters 1-8, Paul explains that all people, both Jews and Gentiles, are born sinful. Our spirits are dead to God, and so we cannot really make him happy. All people need to become right with God. All of us need God to save us. But God accepts us as right with himself if we believe him. We must believe that Christ died on our behalf. And then, by God's powerful Spirit, we can become united with Christ. So, we can die to our old lives. And we can become new people, who can be God's friends.

In chapters 9-11, Paul writes about Israel's people. They are the people that God chose. Many of them have refused to believe Christ, but God has not turned away from them completely. And Paul knows that God will save them in the end.

The last part of Romans (chapters 12-16) describes how Christians should live their lives in this world. It is most important that Christians love each other, and other people. We should try always to help other people and to be kind to them.

Chapter 1

Paul and his message

1 This letter is from me, Paul. I am a servant of Christ Jesus. God chose me to be a special worker and teacher on his behalf. He sent me to tell his good news to people. 2 God promised this good news before by his prophets. They wrote about it in the Old Testament.

3-4 This good news is about God's Son, who is Jesus Christ, our Lord. He was born in the human way from David's family. But God showed clearly, by his completely good Spirit, that Jesus was his powerful Son. God showed that when he raised Jesus. God raised him, so that Jesus became alive again after his death. 5 It is because of Jesus Christ that God so kindly chose me to be a special worker on his behalf. God sent me so that people from all countries would believe and obey Christ. And I do this work to show how great Christ is. 6 And you people also are among those people that God has chosen to belong to Jesus Christ.

7 I am writing to all you Christians who are at Rome. God loves you and he has chosen you to be his own people. I pray that God, our Father, and the Lord Jesus Christ will continue to be very kind to you. I pray that they will cause you to be without trouble inside yourselves.

Paul wants to visit Rome

8 First, I thank my God, by Jesus Christ, because of all of you. Everywhere in the world, people are talking about how you believe Christ. 9 I obey God with my spirit while I tell people the good news about his Son. And God himself knows that I never stop praying on your behalf. 10 Every time that I pray, I remember you. I ask God that, after all this time, he will make it possible for me to visit you soon. That will happen if God wants it.

11 I want very much to visit you so that I can give some gift from God's Spirit to you. That will help you to believe Christ more strongly. 12 I mean that I want both you and I to help each other. You believe Christ, and I believe Christ. So we can help each other to believe Christ more strongly. 13 I want you to know, my friends that I have tried often to visit you. But until now, something has always stopped me. I want to do good work among you that will have good results. I want to work like that, as I have done among other Gentiles.

14 I must tell the good news about Christ to people, whether they speak the Greek language or not. I must tell it to people, whether they have studied much or not. 15 So then, I want very much to tell the good news also to you people who live at Rome.

The good news is powerful

16 I am not ashamed about the good news, because it is powerful. By the good news, God powerfully saves everyone who believes it. First, God saves the Jews who believe it. Then he saves the Gentiles who believe it. 17 The good news explains how God makes people right with himself. God accepts people as right with himself only when they believe Christ. It is as the Old Testament says:

'The person that I have accepted will live.

Those people will live because they believe me.'

God is angry with all people because they have not obeyed him

18 God is showing clearly, from heaven, that he is angry with people. He is angry with people who do not obey him. He is angry against all the wrong things that those people do. The wrong things that those people do stop other people from knowing the true things about God.

19 Everyone can know something clearly about God, because God himself has shown it to everyone. 20 Ever since God made the world, he has been showing people clearly about himself. We cannot see God. But the things that he has made show us what he is like. They show us that he will always be completely powerful. And they show us that only he is God. So nobody can say: 'We never knew about God.'

21 People knew what God is like. But they did not remember how great he is. They did not think that it was important to obey him. Nor did they thank him. Instead, they began to think silly thoughts. And they became unable to understand the things that God wanted them to know.

22 They said that they themselves were clever. They said that they understood many things. But really, they became fools. 23 They refused to worship the great and good God who can never die. Instead, they made and worshipped false gods. Their false gods were like human people, who must die. Also, their false gods were like birds, animals and snakes.

24 So God let those people become like slaves to bad, dirty things. They became unable to stop doing the dirty things that they wanted so much to do. And, as a result, they do bad, dirty things with each other's bodies. They do things that people should be ashamed to do. 25 They refused to believe the true things about God. Instead, they chose to believe something that is not true. They worshipped things that God has made. They became servants of those things. But they refused to worship God, who made all things. He is the God that everyone ought to worship. Everyone should say how very great he is always! This is true.

26 So, God let those people become like slaves to the bad things that they wanted very much to do. But people should be ashamed about those things. Even their women stopped having sex with their husbands, which is proper. And instead, they began to have sex with other women, which is not proper. 27 Also, the men stopped having sex with women. Instead, they wanted very, very much to have sex with other men. Men did very wrong things with other men. They did things that people should be ashamed about. As a result, God has punished those men themselves, as he ought to punish them. He ought to punish them because of the wrong things that they have done.

28 Those people decided that God was not worth anything to them. They thought that it was not important to know God. So God let them become unable to think right and proper thoughts. And, as a result, they do things that people ought not to do. 29 They are always wanting very much to do all kinds of wrong and bad things. They want things that belong to other people. They want to do bad things to other people. They hate people because they themselves want to be like those people. They kill people. They quarrel and fight with people. They are not honest or kind. They talk about people when they should not talk about them. 30They say bad things against people. They hate God. They are not polite to other people. They think that they themselves are very important. They say how important and clever they themselves are. They think of new ways to do bad things. They do not obey their parents.

31 They do not understand the difference between what is right or wrong. They do not do what they have promised to do. They do not even want to be kind to anyone. They do not want to help anyone. 32 These people know what God has said. People who do bad things like this ought to die. God has said that clearly. But still these people continue to do these kinds of bad things. Also, they are even happy when other people do these bad things.

Chapter 2

How and why God decides about Jews who do wrong things

1 So each one of you who decides about other people must be careful. You say that other people have done wrong things. You say that God should punish those people. But God will not excuse you yourself, because you do the same things too. So really you are saying that God should punish you also. 2 God is right and fair when he decides to punish people. We know that. He is right to punish people who do those kind of things.

3 You say that God should punish other people because of wrong things. But you yourself do the same things. So certainly, you should not think that you will get away from God. Certainly, he will punish you also. 4 God is very, very kind and patient with us. He waits a very long time before he punishes us. You should not forget how very kind he is. You should understand why he is being so kind to you. He is giving you a chance to change, so that you turn away from wrong things.

5 But you refuse to change. You refuse to be sorry about the wrong things that you have done. So, you are causing God to become even angrier with you. And he will punish you even more on that great day. On that day, he will show how angry he is. He will show what he has decided about each person. He decides fairly about all people. He decides what should happen to them. 6 God will give to each person what they ought to have. That will be because of the things that they have done.

7 Some people continue patiently to do good things, because they are thinking about God. They are wanting to live always with God, who is so great and so good. And God will cause those people to live with him always. 8 But other people think only about themselves. They refuse to obey the things that are true. Instead, they do things that are wrong. So, God will be very angry with those people and he will punish them. 9 God will cause very much trouble and pain for every person who does bad things. He will do that first to the Jews, and he will do it also to the Gentiles. 10 But God will be very good to every person who does good things. He will cause those people to live with him and he will make them great. He will do that first to the Jews, and he will do it also to the Gentiles. 11 God is always fair when he decides about people. He is never kinder to one person than he is to another person.

12 The Gentiles do not know Moses' rules (the rules that God gave to the Jews by Moses). If Gentiles do wrong things, they must be separate from God for always. But God will not use Moses' rules when he decides about the Gentiles. The Jews do know Moses' rules. So, if Jews do wrong things, God will use those rules to decide about them. 13 God does not accept people as right with himself because they know Moses' rules. No! God accepts only those people who obey those rules.

14 The Gentiles do not know Moses' rules. But they can still do the right things that those rules say. They do right things because of what they themselves think. So, they are showing that they themselves know certain rules. They do not know Moses' rules, but they do know some good rules in themselves. 15 The Gentiles know deep inside themselves the things that are right. The things that they do show this. And those are the same things that Moses' rules say. Also, each person is able to know the difference between what is right or wrong. Sometimes their thoughts say: 'You did what is wrong.' And sometimes their thoughts say: 'You did what is right.'

16 This is what will happen on that day. On that day, God will show what he has decided about people. He decides what should happen to them. And he will decide, by Christ Jesus, as a result of what people think secretly. This is part of the good news that I tell people.

The Jews and God's rules

17 Now I want to say this to each of you Jews. You say about yourself: 'I am a Jew.' You know the rules that God gave by Moses. And, as a result, you believe that God will be good to you. You say that you belong to God's own, special people. So you think that you are very important. 18 You know what God wants people to do.

You are able to know which things are good. You know that because you have learned Moses' rules. 19 You are sure that you yourself can show the true things about God to other people. You can show the right way to people who cannot see. You can be like a light to people who are in the dark. 20 You are sure that you can teach fools. You can teach people who still need to learn very much. You are sure that, because of Moses' rules, you know everything completely. You know everything that is true. That is what you think.

21 You teach other people, but you ought also to teach yourself. You tell other people: 'Do not rob anyone.' So, you yourself should never rob anyone. 22 You say: 'People should not have sex with anyone who is not their own wife or husband.' So, you yourself should never have sex with anyone who is not your wife or husband.

You say: 'I hate false gods. People should not worship false gods.' So, you yourself should never rob places where people worship false gods. 23 You know the rules that God gave by Moses. So, you say that you are very important. But you do not obey those rules. And, as a result, you cause other people to speak against God. 24 As it says in the Old Testament: 'Because of you Jews, the Gentiles say bad things about God.' **[Isaiah 52:5] [Ezekiel 36:22]**

God does not accept people only because of a mark on their bodies

25 You, who are a Jew, should obey Moses' rules. Then it is good that someone has circumcised you. But if you do not obey those rules, then it is worth nothing. Then it is worth nothing that someone has circumcised you. To God, you become like someone that nobody has ever circumcised. 26 But a Gentile, that nobody has ever circumcised, may obey what Moses' rules say. So then, to God, that Gentile will become like a person that someone has circumcised.

27 Nobody has circumcised the Gentiles. But if they obey God's rules, the Gentiles are showing something clearly about you Jews. They are showing that you are wrong. You Jews know Moses' rules because your people have written them down. Also, someone has circumcised you. But if you do not obey Moses' rules, God is still right to punish you. 28 Not everyone who seems to be a Jew is really a Jew. God does not accept a man because someone has circumcised that man's body. 29 No! A true Jew is someone who is a Jew inside himself. A true Jew is a person that God has circumcised deep inside, in their spirit. God's Spirit does that work in a person. Rules that people have written down cannot do that work in a person. Other people may not think that this kind of person is great or special. But God is very happy about a person that his Spirit has circumcised.

Chapter 3

1 So someone may ask: 'Does it help a person if they are a Jew rather than a Gentile?' Or: 'Does it help a person if someone has circumcised them?' 2 Yes, certainly it helps very much. The most important reason is that God chose to give his messages to the Jews. He wanted the Jews to believe and to obey his messages. 3 Some of the Jews did not believe or obey God's messages. They did not do what they had promised to do. That is true. So, you may ask: 'Will that stop God from doing what he promised to do?' 4 No, certainly it will not stop God! God always says what is true. Every person in this world may say things that are not true. But God will always do what he has promised to do. As it says in the Old Testament:

'Everything that you (God) say will show people about you.

Certainly, your words will show everyone that you are right.

People may say that you are wrong.

But you will win against what they say.

It will be clear that you are right.'

5 Maybe some people will say this: 'The wrong things that we do help to show something about God. They help to show more clearly to people how good and right God is. So, perhaps we could say that God is wrong to punish us.' 6 No, certainly he is not wrong! God always decides what is right and fair. That is why he will decide about all the people in the world. He will decide what should happen to them.

7 Someone might say: 'I do not always do the things that I have promised to do. But because I am like that, it shows something about God. God always does what he has promised to do. It shows that more clearly to people. And, as a result, people will say even more how great and good God is. So, God should not still decide to punish me. He should not punish me because of the wrong things that I do.'

8 It would be the same to say: 'We should do bad things so that they may cause this kind of good result.' Some people say that I teach this. So, they are saying things about me that are not true. And it is right that God should punish those people.

Nobody is right with God

9 So then, we cannot say that we Jews are any better than other people. No, certainly we cannot say that! I have said already that nobody, neither Jews nor Gentiles, can stop themselves being sinful. All of them are completely unable to stop being sinful. 10 As it says in the Old Testament:

> 'There is nobody who is right with God.
>
> There is not even one person who is like that.

11 There is nobody who understands.

> There is nobody who wants to know God.

12 All people have turned away from God.

> All people have become completely bad.
>
> Nobody does what is good.

There is not even one person who is like that.

13 They say very bad things that cause death.

They say things that are not true.

And they cause other people to believe those things.

> The things that they say are like snakes' poison.

14 They are always saying bad things because they want to cause trouble for people.

They say bad things against people because they hate people.

> 15 They hurry to kill people.
>
> 16 Everywhere they go, they destroy things.

Everywhere they go, they make people very sad.

17 They have never known how to be friends with God or with other people.

18 They are never afraid because of how great and powerful God is.

They never think that it is important to obey God.'

19 God told the Jews to obey everything that his rules said. We know that. So nobody, neither Jew nor Gentile, can say: 'There is a good reason why God should not punish me.' God has decided that he ought to punish everyone in the world. 20 Nobody can become completely right with God because they have obeyed Moses' rules. Those rules only cause people to know clearly how sinful they themselves are.

How God accepts people as right with himself

21 But now God has shown the way that he will accept people as right with himself. This way does not need Moses' rules. But Moses' rules, and the prophets' messages, told us about this new way. 22 God accepts people as right with himself because they believe Jesus Christ. God does this for every person who believes Christ. There is no difference between people. 23 All people are the same because all of them are sinful. They are not good and great, as God wanted them to be.

24 But because God is so very kind, he accepts people as right with himself. That is God's gift, which people do not have to pay for. God accepts us as right with himself by Christ Jesus, who bought us, to make us free. 25 God chose to offer Christ as a sacrifice so that he could forgive sinful people. God sent Christ to bleed and to die. And, as a result, God forgives people who believe Christ. God did this to show clearly that he is always completely right and fair. In past times, God did not punish people who were doing wrong things. 26 He did not punish them because he is so patient. But now God has given Christ, to show, at this time, that he is completely right and fair. God did this to show that he accepts people as right with himself. If any person believes Jesus, God accepts that person as right.

27 So then, nobody has any reason to say that they themselves are good enough to make God happy. Nobody becomes right with God because they have obeyed rules. No! God accepts a person only if that person believes Christ. 28 So, this is what we are saying. A person becomes right with God if that person believes Christ. God does not accept anyone because they obey Moses' rules.

29 God is not only the Jews' God. No! Certainly, he is the God of all other people also. 30 There is only one God. He will accept Jews as right with himself if they believe Christ. And he will accept other people as right with himself if they believe Christ.

31 So, people can only become right with God if they believe Christ. But we do not mean that Moses' rules have no purpose. No, we do not mean that! Instead, we are showing the true purpose of those rules.

Chapter 4

God accepted Abraham because Abraham believed him

1 Abraham was the grandfather of all of us who are Jews. Think about what Abraham discovered. 2 God did not accept Abraham because Abraham had done good things. If God had done that, then Abraham would have been able to say great things about himself. He would have been able to say how good he himself was. But Abraham had no reason to say that to God. 3 Remember what the Old Testament says. It says: 'Abraham believed God and, as a result, God accepted Abraham as right with himself.' **[Genesis 15:6]**

4 When a person works to get money, he ought to receive his money. Nobody thinks that the money is a gift. It is what that person ought to receive as a result of his work. 5 But nobody can do any work that will make himself right with God. Instead, he must believe God, who accepts bad people as right with himself. And because a person believes God, then God will accept that person as right. 6 David also wrote about the same thing. He described how happy God can cause people to be. God will accept people as right with himself even when they have not done good things. 7 David says:

'Those people that God has forgiven are really happy.

They have not always obeyed God, but he has forgiven them.

God has taken away the wrong things that those people have done.

8 A person is really happy when the Lord accepts him.

Because the Lord will not continue to remember the wrong things that the person has done.

9 All people can be really happy like this, whether they are Jews or not. God told only the Jews to circumcise each other. He did not tell the people who are not Jews to circumcise each other. But God will accept any person. God accepted Abraham as right with him because Abraham believed God. That is what we have been saying.

10 Think about the time when God accepted Abraham as right with him. It did not happen after someone had circumcised Abraham. No! God accepted Abraham before anyone had circumcised him. 11 At the time when nobody had circumcised Abraham, God accepted Abraham as right with him. God accepted Abraham because Abraham believed him. Then later, God told Abraham that someone should circumcise him. That was a mark, to show certainly that God had accepted Abraham as right with him. As a result, Abraham became the father of all people who believe God. God accepts all those people as right with him, even when nobody has circumcised them. 12 Also, Abraham is the father of all Jews who, like Abraham, believe God. Someone has circumcised those Jews, but they are also copying Abraham's example. They are believing God, as Abraham believed before anyone had circumcised him.

13 God promised to Abraham, and to all his children and grandchildren, that the world would be theirs. God did not promise that because Abraham obeyed rules. Instead, God promised it because Abraham believed him. And so, God accepted Abraham.

14 People cannot get what God promised because they obey rules. If they could get it like that, then it would be worth nothing to believe God. And what God promised would be worth nothing. 15 Moses' rules say that God will punish people. He will punish people who do not obey those rules. But without any rules, there is nothing to say which things are wrong.

16 So, people must believe God. Then they can receive what God has promised. God gives us what he has promised as a gift. He gives it because he is so very kind. He gives that gift to all of Abraham's people. God does not give it only to people who obey Moses' rules. Instead, God gives it to all people who believe him, as Abraham believed. Abraham is the father of all of us who believe God. 17 The Old Testament says that God spoke to Abraham. 'I have chosen that you will become the father of people from many countries', God said. **[Genesis 17:5]** God himself promised this to Abraham, who believed him. Abraham believed God, who causes dead people to become alive again. God speaks, and he causes things to be. He causes things to be that were not there before.

18 Abraham continued to believe God. He continued to hope for what God had promised. He continued to hope even when he had no good reason to hope. That is why he became the father of people from many countries. It happened as God had said. 'You will have many, many grandchildren,' God had said. **[Genesis 15:5]**

19 Abraham was about 100 years old. His body was already so old that it was nearly dead. Abraham knew that. Also, he knew that Sarah could not have children. But still Abraham did not stop believing God. 20 Abraham never stopped believing what God had promised. Instead, he believed God strongly. And he thanked God because of what God would do. 21 Abraham was completely sure about what God had promised. God is able to do what he has promised to do. Abraham was sure about that. 22 So, because Abraham believed God like this, 'God accepted Abraham as right with him.' **[Genesis 15:6]**

23 These words in the Old Testament, 'God accepted him as right' are not only speaking about Abraham. 24 They are speaking also about us. If we believe God, he will accept us as right with him. We must believe that God raised our Lord Jesus. God raised Jesus, so that he became alive again after his death. 25 God sent Jesus to die because of the wrong things that we have done. And God raised Jesus so that we could become right with God.

Chapter 5

We have become God's friends because of Jesus Christ

1 So now God has accepted us as right because we believe him. And, as a result, we are friends with God because of our Lord Jesus Christ. 2 Also, Jesus Christ has caused us to know how very good and kind God is. He has done that because we believe him. And we know that God is continuing to be very kind to us. Also, we are hoping certainly to live always with God, who is so very great and good. We are sure that we will live with him always. So, we are very happy.

3 Also, we are happy even when we have troubles and pain. Because we know that troubles and pain help us to become patient and brave. 4 And when we are patient and brave, we become stronger inside ourselves. We learn to know better what is the right thing to do. And so, God is happy about us. When we make God happy like this, it causes us to hope certainly. We hope for what God has promised. 5 And if we hope like this, we will never be sorry. God has given his Spirit to us. And God's Spirit has caused us to know, deep inside ourselves, how very much God loves us. So, we will never be sorry about what we hoped for.

6 While we were unable to help ourselves, Christ died on behalf of us. At the right time, Christ died on behalf of people who did not know God. 7 It is not often that someone will die on behalf of another person. Even if that other person always did right things, very few people would die on behalf of that person. Maybe someone might be brave enough to die on behalf of a person who is very good and kind. 8 But Christ died on behalf of us while we were still sinful. In that way, God has shown us how much he loves us.

9 So now, because Christ died, God accepts us as right with himself. And even more certainly, Christ will save us so that God will not punish us for always. 10 While we were still God's enemies, God's Son died. He died so that we could become God's friends. So, even more certainly, now that we are God's friends, his Son will save us. Christ will save us because he is alive. 11 But that is not everything! Also, we are very happy because of what God has done on our behalf by our Lord Jesus Christ. It is because of Christ that we have now become God's friends.

Adam and Christ

12 It was because of one man, Adam, that sin came into the world. And because Adam did not obey God, he died. So, as a result, all people died, because all of them failed to obey God. 13 Before God gave his rules to Moses, the people in the world were sinful. But at that time, there were no rules from God to say that certain things were right or wrong. So, God did not continue to remember the wrong things that people did during that time. 14 But still, from the time when Adam lived until the time when Moses lived, all people were dead to God. Adam died because he chose not to obey God's rule. Other people may have failed to obey God in different ways from Adam, but even those people died.

Adam was like a picture of that person who would come at a future time. Adam shows us something like the person who would come. 15 But God's free gift is not like the wrong thing that Adam did. Many people died because that one man did not obey God. But what God has done is much greater and more powerful than that! God has caused many people to know how very, very good and kind he is to them. Many people have received God's gift because of one man, Jesus Christ, who is so very kind.

16 Also, the result of God's gift is different from the result of the wrong thing that Adam did. Adam chose not to obey God once and, as a result, all people became sinful. So, God decided that he ought to punish all people. But the result of God's gift is that he accepts people as right with him. People have done many wrong things, not only one wrong thing, but still God accepts them as right with him. 17 One man did not obey God. And so, all people died because of that one man. But what that other man, Jesus Christ, did is much, much greater! Because of him, people can become right with God. They receive that great gift from God because he is so very, very good and kind. And, as a result, those people will live always and they will rule with Christ.

18 So, that wrong thing that one man, Adam, did caused all people to become sinful. And, as a result, God decided that he ought to punish all people. But that right thing that one man, Christ, did makes people free. It makes all those people who believe him free. People can become right with God, and so those people can really live. 19 One man did not obey God and, as a result, many people became sinful. But, because one man obeyed God, many people will become right with God.

20 As a result of Moses' rules, people saw that they were doing wrong things. But while people did more and more wrong things, God continued to be even kinder. 21 So then, all people became sinful and, as a result, they died. But all people can become right with God because he is so very kind. And, as a result, they will live always with God, because of our Lord Jesus Christ.

Chapter 6

We have died and become alive again with Christ

1 Someone might say: 'Perhaps we should continue to do wrong things. So then, God can continue to be even kinder to us.' 2 No! Certainly we should not do that! We have died to our old, sinful lives. So it is not right that we continue to do wrong things.

3 When God baptised us, to make us united with Christ Jesus, he baptised us into Christ's death. Certainly, you should know this. 4 So, because God baptised us into Christ's death, he buried us with Christ. And God, the Father, will also raise us, as he raised Christ. The Father is so great and powerful that he raised Christ, to make him alive again after his death. And he raises us too, so that we can live a new life.

5 We have become united with Christ in his death. So certainly, we will also become united with him in his new life. We will rise, to become alive again, as Christ rose. 6 We know that God has caused our old lives to die with Christ on the cross. This happened so that God could destroy our sinful nature that caused us not to obey him. So, as a result, we are not like slaves, who cannot stop doing wrong things, any more. 7 Sin has no authority over someone who has died. So, that person has become free.

8 So, we have died with Christ. And, as a result, we believe that we will live with him also. 9 God raised Christ, so that he became alive again after his death. And he will never die again. We know that. Death has no authority over him anymore. 10 When he died, he became dead to sin for always. And now that he is alive again, he lives only to make God happy. 11 So, you also should think about yourselves as people who are dead. You are dead to sin. And you live now to make God happy, because you are united with Christ Jesus.

12 So, do not let yourselves do wrong things. Do not let those things rule your bodies, which must certainly die. Do not obey the wrong things that your bodies may want to do. 13 Do not let any part of yourselves do wrong things. Do not use any part of yourselves for bad purposes. Instead, give yourselves completely to God, because you are alive to him. You were dead, but now you are alive. Give every part of yourselves to God, so that you can do right things. 14 Sin has no authority over you anymore. You are not trying any more to obey rules so that God will accept you. Instead, God has made you free to live for him, because he is so very good and kind.

God's people should be slaves to good things

15 But someone might say: 'We do not have to obey Moses' rules any more. Instead, God is saving us because he is so very kind. So, perhaps it does not matter if we do wrong things.' No! Certainly, that is not true! 16 When you give yourselves completely to someone as slaves, to obey him, then you will really become that person's slaves. You should know that. You are either slaves to sin, and, as a result, you will die. Or you are God's slaves, who obey him. And, as a result, God will accept you as right with him. 17 Before, you were slaves to sin. But then you really obeyed the true things about Christ that people taught you. So, we should thank God because of that! 18 God has made you free from sin. And you have become his slaves, who do right things.

19 It is difficult for people to understand these things. So, I am speaking about slaves to help you to understand. Before, you gave every part of yourselves completely to do wrong and dirty things. You were like slaves, who continued to do more and more wrong things. So now, you should give every part of yourselves to do right things. Then you will live only for God, as his own special people.

20 Before, you were slaves to sin. And you did not even think that you had to do right things. 21 You did things that you are ashamed about now. But those things did not help you. The result of those things will be that you must die. 22 But now God has made you free from sin. You have become God's slaves. That is helping you because God is making you completely good and clean. And the result will be that you will live with him always.

23 People who work receive money as a result of their work. In the same way, people who do not obey God have to die as a result. But those people who are united with Christ Jesus, our Lord have God's gift. God's gift to them is that he causes them to live with him always.

Chapter 7

Christians are free from Moses' rules

1 My friends, you are people who know about governments' rules. So certainly, you should understand what I am going to say. Rules have authority over a person only while that person is alive. 2 For example, a woman who has married a husband must obey certain rules. That woman must continue to be her husband's wife while her husband is alive. But if her husband dies, she becomes free from that rule about her husband. 3 So, that woman must not give herself to another man while her husband is still alive. She must not have sex with a man who is not her husband. If she does that, then people will call her a bad woman. But if her husband dies, she becomes free from that rule. So, as a result, if she marries another man then, she will not be doing anything wrong.

4 My friends, it is like that for you also. Moses' rules do not have authority over you anymore, because you have become dead to them. You have died with Christ's body. Now you are free to belong to someone else. You belong to Christ, whom God raised, to make him alive again after his death. And so, as a result, we can do good things that will make God happy. 5 When our sinful human nature was ruling us, we were wanting very much to do wrong things. Moses' rules said that certain things were wrong. But, in our bodies, we wanted to do those wrong things. And, as a result, we did bad things that lead to death. 6 But now we have become free from the rules that God gave to Moses. We have died to those rules, which were making us like people in prison. So now we are not still trying to obey rules that someone has written down. We are not trying to be God's servants in the old way like that. Instead, we are God's servants in a new way, because we obey his Spirit.

Moses' rules show us that we are sinful

7 Maybe someone might say: 'The rules that God gave to Moses are themselves bad.' No! Certainly, they are not bad! Without those rules, I would not have known which things were wrong. Moses' rules say: 'You must not want things that are other people's.' Without that rule, I would not have known that it is wrong to want other people's things. 8 But, because I was sinful, that rule gave me the chance to start wanting all kinds of wrong things. Rules tell us which things are wrong. So, without any rules, nobody can do anything wrong

9 There was a time when I did not know Moses' rules. During that time, I was living without any rules. But later, I learned what Moses' rules said. And, as a result, I began to want wrong things. 10 And so I died. God gave his rules so that people could live. But instead, those rules caused me to die. 11 Because I was sinful, Moses' rules gave me the chance to do something wrong. I died as a result of Moses' rules because I was sinful.

12 So then, the rules that God gave to Moses are completely good. Every rule that God gave is completely good and right. He gave every rule to help people. 13 So, maybe someone will say: 'This means that something good caused you to die.' No! Certainly, it did not do that! I died as a result of Moses' rules because I was sinful. I did not die because of those rules themselves. God's rules are good. They only showed what it is really like to be sinful. God's rules help to show clearly how very, very bad it is to be sinful.

We cannot obey God's rules

14 The rules that God gave to Moses are spiritual. We know that. But I am human. I am like a slave because sin has authority over me. 15 I do not understand what I do. I do not do the things that I want to do. Instead, I do the things that I hate. 16 I do not want to do the wrong things that I do. So, this shows something about me. I am agreeing that God's rules are good. It shows that. 17 So, it is not really I myself who am doing these wrong things. Instead, it is sin that lives in me. Sin makes me do wrong things.

18 There is nothing good in me, in the human person that I am. I know that. I want to do what is good. But I am unable to do it. 19 I do not do the good things that I want to do. Instead, I continue to do the bad things that I do not want to do. 20 I do not want to do the things that I do. So this shows something about me. It is not really I myself who am doing these bad things. Instead, it is sin that lives in me. Sin makes me do bad things.

21 So, it is clear that what always happens is this. When I want to do good things, I am able only to do bad things. 22 Deep inside myself, I really love God's rules and I want to obey them. 23 So, my mind tells me to obey God's rules. But I know also that something else always happens in me. Something in every part of me fights against what my mind tells me. It rules what my body does. It makes me like a slave, because I cannot stop being sinful. 24 This makes me so very sad! I need someone to make me free from this body, which is causing me to die. 25 I thank God that, because of Jesus Christ, our Lord, I can be free!

So then, with my mind I myself want to obey God's rules. But, at the same time, the human person that I am cannot stop being sinful.

Chapter 8

We can live by God's Spirit

1 So now God will never decide that Christ's people are not good enough. God will never say that about people who are united with Christ Jesus. He will never decide that he should punish them for always. 2 The reason is that God's Spirit has made me free. God's Spirit, who causes us to live because of Christ Jesus, has made me free. God's Spirit makes me free so that I can stop being sinful. He makes me free from the power of death.

3 The rules that God gave to Moses could not make us free like this. Those rules could not make us free because we human people were too weak to obey them. But God has done what those rules could not do. God sent his own Son as a human person like us. God sent his Son to be a sacrifice on behalf of us sinful people. God punished his Son instead of us, so that we do not have to be sinful any more. 4 God did this so that we could be right with him. The purpose of Moses' rules was that we should be right with God. And now we can be right, if we obey God's Spirit. We must live by the power that God's Spirit gives to us. We must not live by our own human power.

5 People who live by their own human power are always thinking about human things. They are always thinking about what they themselves understand. But people who obey God's Spirit are always thinking about God. They want to do the things that God's Spirit wants.

6 People who let their human thoughts rule them will die. But people who think about what God's Spirit wants will live. They will live because they are God's friends. And they will be without trouble inside themselves.

7 A person who always lets his own human thoughts rule him will be God's enemy. A person like that does not obey what God has said. A person who thinks like that is not even able to obey God. 8 People who live by their own human power cannot make God happy.

9 But you are not living by your own human power. Instead, you are obeying God's Spirit, if his Spirit is really living in you. If anyone does not have Christ's Spirit in them, that person does not belong to Christ. 10 But, if Christ is in you, your spirit is alive. Your spirit is alive because Christ has made you right with God. But your body must still die because you have been sinful. 11 The Spirit of God, who raised Jesus, to make him alive again after his death, lives in you. So God, who raised Christ from death, will also cause your human bodies to live. God will cause your bodies to live by his Spirit, who lives in you.

12 So, my friends, there is something that we have to do. We must be careful not to live by our own human power. 13 If you live by your own human power, you will die. Instead, you should live by the power of God's Spirit. Then you will continue to stop doing the wrong things that your bodies want to do. And, as a result, you will live.

14 All those people who let God's Spirit lead them are God's sons. 15 Because the Spirit that God has given to you does not make you like slaves again. He does not make you slaves who cannot stop being afraid. Instead, the Spirit that God has given to you causes you to become God's children. He makes us able to shout to God: 'You are my Father.' 16 God's Spirit himself causes us to know certainly what we know by our own spirits. We know that we are God's children.

17 And because we are God's children, we will also receive good things from him. We will receive the things that God has prepared for his children. Also, together with Christ, we will receive the things that God has kept for him. We will receive these things if we agree to have troubles and pain, as Christ did. So then, as a result, we will also live always with God, who is so great and so good.

God has prepared great things for his people

18 During this time now, we have troubles and pain. But I am sure that these troubles are not really very important. They are not really important because God has prepared much, much better things for us. He is keeping these great and good things for us. And when we think about these great things, our troubles now do not seem important. 19 All things that God has made are waiting for a future time. They want that time to come very much. At that time, God will show them who his sons really are.

20 God has caused the things that he made to become without real purpose. Those things are unable really to have any purpose. They did not choose to become like that. It was God who caused them to become like that. God did that because he was thinking about that future, better time. 21 At that time, God will also cause the things that he has made to become free. They will be free from the power that causes them to become old and to finish. They will be free to enjoy great things from God, as God's children are free.

22 All the things that God has made have been waiting until now. We know that. They have been waiting like a woman who is ready to have a baby. She cries because of her pain before she has her baby. 23 And it is not only those other things in the world that are waiting like that. But we ourselves, who have received God's Spirit as the first of his gifts to us, are also crying. We are crying deep inside ourselves, while we wait for God to finish making us his own children. We are waiting for God to make our bodies free.

24 Ever since God saved us, we have continued to hope certainly for this. One day, we will see what we have hoped for. And then we will not need to hope for it any more. Nobody continues to hope for something that he has already. 25 But we continue to hope for what we do not have yet. And so, we wait for it patiently.

26 God's Spirit also helps us, because we are weak. We do not know how we ought to pray. But God's Spirit himself prays on our behalf. He cries to God on our behalf in a way that nobody could say with words. 27 And God, who sees deep inside us, understands the Spirit. God sees completely what we are really like. And he understands what his Spirit is thinking. The Spirit prays on behalf of God's people as God wants him to pray.

28 God has good purposes for those people who love him. We know that. He uses everything that happens to them to bring good results on their behalf. He does this for those people that he has chosen. He has chosen his people to be what he wants them to be. 29 God had already chosen those people from the beginning. And he had decided that they should become like his Son. So then, as a result, his Son would be the first among many brothers. 30 God decided that those people would be like his Son. Also, he asked them to come to him. And after he had asked them to come to him, he made them right with himself. And when he had made them right with himself, he also caused them to become great. He made them great and good, in the same way that he himself is great and good.

Nothing can stop God and Christ from loving us

31 So, because of all these things, we can say this. If God is working on our behalf, nobody can really do anything against us, to beat us. 32 God did not even refuse to send his own Son. Instead, he gave his Son to die on behalf of all of us. So certainly, God will also be happy to give all things to us with his Son. 33 We are the people that God has chosen. Nobody can say that God's people have done anything wrong. God himself has said that we are right with him. 34 So, nobody can say that God should still punish us. Nobody can say that, because Christ Jesus himself died on our behalf. Also, God raised Christ so that he became alive again after his death. And now Christ is sitting at God's right side, and he himself is praying to God on our behalf.

35 Nothing can make us separate from Christ, who loves us. We may have troubles. Things may happen to us that cause us to be very sad or afraid. Enemies may do bad things to us and hurt us. We may have no food or no clothes. There may be danger, or people may try to kill us. But none of these things can stop Christ from loving us. 36 As it says in the Old Testament:

'Because we are your people, (God),

other people try to kill us all the time.

They think that we are worth no more than sheep.

Sheep that should go to the butcher so that he can kill them.'

37 But even if these troubles happen to us, we will always beat them completely. Christ has shown how much he loves us. And he makes us winners over every kind of trouble or problem. 38 Nothing can make us separate from God, who loves us. I am completely sure about that. Whether we are alive or dead, it does not matter. Neither angels nor bad spirits nor any other powerful spirits can stop God from loving us. Neither things that are now, nor future things, can stop him loving us. 39 Neither anything that is above the world, nor anything below the world, can stop him. There is nothing else in the whole world that can stop God from loving us. Christ Jesus, our Lord, causes us to know how much God loves us.

Chapter 9

Paul is sad because Israel's people have not believed Christ

1 What I am telling you now is true. I speak as someone who belongs to Christ. I am saying only what is true. I know the difference between what is right or wrong. And what I am saying is true. I know that. Also, God's Spirit is agreeing that these things are true. 2 I tell you that I am very, very sad deep inside myself. I am like someone who has a lot of pain all the time.

3 I am sad because of all those people who, like me, belong to Israel's people. They are my own people. They belong to the same big human family as I do. If it would help them, I would ask God to make me myself separate from Christ.

4 They are Israel's people that God chose. He chose them to be his own children. He wanted to make them great, as his people should be. He made his agreements with them and he gave his rules to them. He showed them how they should worship him. He promised many good things to them. 5 It was their grandfathers that God chose to make great many years ago. And Christ himself, as a human person, belonged to Israel's people. Christ is God over all things. Everyone should say always how very great he is! This is true!

6 God promised good things to Israel's people. But I am not saying that God has not done those things. No, because it is clear that not all of Israel's people are really God's people. 7 Neither are all of Abraham's children the people that God calls Abraham's children. No, because God told Abraham: 'Only Isaac's children and grandchildren will be the people that I call your children.' **[Genesis 21:12]**

8 This means that not all of Abraham's human children are really God's children. Instead, it is only those children who were born as a result of God's promise. Only they are the people that God calls Abraham's children. 9 God promised this to Abraham: 'At the right time I will come back, and Sarah, your wife, will have a son.'

10 And that is not everything. Later, Rebecca gave birth to two sons at the same time. Those children had the same father, who was our grandfather, Isaac.

11-12 And God spoke to Rebecca before her sons were born. God spoke before the boys had done anything either good or bad. God did this to show that he himself was choosing one child. He was choosing whoever he wanted to choose. God was not choosing someone because of what that person had done. God said to Rebecca: 'The older son will be a servant of the younger son.' **[Genesis 25:23]** 13 As the Old Testament says: 'I loved Jacob, but I hated Esau.' **[Malachi 1:2-3]**

14 So, perhaps we could say that God is not right and fair. No! Certainly, we should never say that! 15 God said to Moses: 'I will be kind to whoever I choose to be kind to. I will feel sorry for whoever I choose to feel sorry for.' **[Exodus 33:19]** 16 So then, God does not choose people because they want him to choose them. Nor does God choose people because they try very much to make him happy. Instead, God chooses people only because he himself wants to be kind.

17 The Old Testament says that God told Pharaoh (the king of Egypt): 'This is why I caused you to be king. It was so that I might use you to show how powerful I am. It was so that all people everywhere might know about me.' **[Exodus 9:16]** 18 So then, God is kind to whoever he chooses to be kind to. But he causes some people to refuse to listen to him. And he does that also to whoever he chooses.

God himself decides when he will be angry or kind

19 One of you may say to me: 'God always does what he wants to do. Nobody can change that. Nobody can refuse to do what God has caused them to do. So, God should not still say that people have done wrong things.' 20 But you are only a human person. You have no authority to say things like that about what God does. God has made you. And when somebody has made something, that thing has no authority over its maker. It has no authority to ask: 'Why did you make me like this?' 21 Somebody who makes pots has authority to make any kind of pots. He can make whatever kind of pots he chooses to make. He can use the same piece of clay to make different pots. He can make one pot for special, important purposes. And he can make another pot to use every day.

22 What God has done is like this also. God wants to show how angry he can be with people. And he wants people to know how powerful he is. But he was very, very patient, for a long time, with those people who caused him to be angry. Those are the people that God was ready to destroy.

23 God waited patiently so that he could show how very, very great and good he is. He wanted to show that to those people that he has chosen to be kind to. God has already prepared those people to live with him in that beautiful place where he lives. 24 We are the people that God has chosen to be his people. It is not only Jews that he has chosen. He has also chosen people who are not Jews. 25 As God says in the book of Hosea:

'I will say to the people who were not mine:

"You are my people."

I will say to the people that I did not love:

"I love you." '

26 And:

'In the same place where I said to them:

"You are not my people", it will happen like this.

In that same place, people will say:

"You are sons of God, who is alive." '

27 Also, Isaiah shouted this about Israel's people:

'There are so many of Israel's people,

that they are like the bits of sand at the edge of the sea.

But God will save only a few of them.

28 The Lord will not waste time

when he decides about the people on the earth.

He will finish that work quickly.

And he will punish people completely.'

29 It is as Isaiah said before:

'The Lord, who has authority over everything,

has let some of our children live.

If he had not done that,

then we would have become like the people in Sodom and Gomorrah.'

[Isaiah 1:9]

30 So, we must think about what all this means. The Gentiles were not trying to become right with God. But they have become right with God. God has accepted them as right with himself, because they have believed Christ. 31 But Israel's people were trying to become right with God. They were trying to obey God's rules. But they failed to become right with God. 32 They failed because they refused to believe Christ. Instead, they were trying to do certain things so that God would accept them. They fell down because of that 'stone which causes people to fall'. 33 As it says in the Old Testament:

'Look, I am putting a stone in Zion.

This stone will cause people to knock their feet against it,

so that they fall.

It is a rock that will make them fall down.

But any person who believes him will never be ashamed.

That person will never be sorry that they believed him.'

Chapter 10

1 My Christian friends, I want God to save Israel's people, who are my own people. I want that very, very much. I pray to God that he will save them. 2 I can say this about them, which is true. They really want to be God's servants. But they do not understand the correct way to make him happy. 3 They did not want to know the way that God accepts people as right with himself. But instead, they tried to make their own way to become right with God. And so they refused to obey God's way that would have made them right with him. 4 God gave his rules to Israel's people for a purpose. But Christ has finished that purpose. He has caused those rules to come to an end. So now, every person who believes Christ becomes right with God.

God wants to save everyone

5 Moses wrote about how God's rules could help people to be right with God. 'If a person obeys all those rules then, as a result, he will live', Moses said. **[Leviticus 18:5]** 6 But the Old Testament speaks also about how to become right with God because you believe him. It says: 'Do not say to yourself, "Someone will have to go up into heaven." ' **[Deuteronomy 30:12]** (That means: "Someone will have to bring Christ down.") 7 'Do not say to yourself either, "Someone will have to go down into the world below."**[Deuteronomy 30:13]** (That means: "Someone will have to bring Christ up from the place where dead people are.") 8 But instead, the Old Testament says: 'God's message is near you. You can speak about it. You can think about it and you can believe it.' **[Deuteronomy 30:14]** The message is this – that people must believe Christ. And it is this message that we are teaching to people.

9 This message explains how God will save you. It explains what you must do. You yourself must say very seriously to people: 'Jesus is Lord.' Also, you must believe deep inside yourself that God raised him, to make him alive again after his death. 10 We must believe this deep inside ourselves, and as a result, God will accept us as right with himself. We must tell people: 'Jesus is Lord', and as a result, God will save us.11 It says in the Old Testament:

'Any person who believes him will never be ashamed.

That person will never be sorry that they believed him.'

12 These words include everyone. There is no difference between Jews and people who are not Jews. The same Lord is the Lord of all of them. And he is very, very good to all people who ask him to help them. 13 As it says in the Old Testament: 'The Lord will save everyone who asks him to help them.' <r **[Joel 2:32]** </r

14 But certainly, people cannot ask Christ to help them if they have not believed him. Certainly, they cannot believe him if they have not known about him. Certainly, they cannot know about him unless somebody goes to tell the message to them. 15 And certainly, nobody can go to tell the message to people unless God sends them. As it says in the Old Testament: 'When people arrive to tell good news, it is beautiful.' **[Isaiah 52:7]**

16 But not every person who hears the good news obeys it. As Isaiah said: 'Lord, it seems that nobody has believed our message.' **[Isaiah 53:1]** 17 So then, people must hear the message before they can believe it. And someone must tell the message about Christ to people before they can hear it.

18 But I say this: 'Certainly, Israel's people have heard that message.' As the Old Testament says:

> 'Their sound has reached to all the earth.

People have heard their message in every part of the world.'

19 Also, I say this: 'Certainly, Israel's people did understand the message.' First, Moses wrote that God said this to them:

> 'I will be good to people who are nothing,
>
> so that you want very much to be like them.
>
> I will make you angry because of people who know nothing.'

20 Also, Isaiah is braver when he says:

'God says: Those people who were not looking for me have found me.

I showed myself to people who were not asking, "Where is God?" '

Verse 20 Isaiah is speaking about the Gentiles. They were not waiting for Christ, nor did they know anything about him. But God, because he is kind, sent his good news to them.

21 But Isaiah says this about Israel's people:

> 'God says: For a very long time,
>
> I have been asking my people to return to me.
>
> But they refused to obey me.

They continued to do the things that I had told them not to do.'

Verse 21 The Jews were waiting for Christ. The Old Testament told them that he would come. But when he came, they did not know him. See, for example, John 1:11.

Chapter 11

There are still some of Israel's people who have obeyed God's message

1 So, I ask this: 'Has God turned away completely from his people? Has he stopped wanting them to be his people?' No, certainly, he has not done that! I myself belong to Israel's people. I am a grandchild of Abraham and I belong to Benjamin's family group. 2 God has not stopped wanting his people that he chose from the beginning. Remember what the Old Testament says about Elijah. He was telling God how bad Israel's people were. Elijah said: 3 'Lord, they have killed your prophets. They have destroyed the places where people offered sacrifices to you. I am the only person alive who still believes you. And they are trying to kill me.' **[1 Kings 19:10] [1 Kings 19:14]** 4 Remember that God answered him like this: 'I have kept 7000 men for myself. Those men have not worshipped the false god Baal.' **[1 Kings 19:18]**

5 It is the same at this time also. There is a small number of Israel's people that God has chosen. He has chosen them because he is so very kind. 6 He has chosen them only because he himself is so very kind. He has not chosen them because of any good things that they have done. God does not choose people because of good things that they do. If he did, then the reason would not really be only because God is so very kind.

7 So, we can say this: Israel's people did not get what they were looking for. Instead, only those few people that God had chosen got it. And God caused all the other people of Israel to become unable to understand what he was saying. 8 As it says in the Old Testament:

'God caused them to be like people who are sleeping.

Even until this day, their eyes cannot really see, and their ears cannot really hear.'

9 And David says:

'I pray to God that he may catch those people at their meals together.

I pray that they will be like people who fall down

I want God to punish them because of what they have done.

10 I want their eyes to become dark so that they cannot see.

I want them to have many bad troubles always.

So then they will be like slaves who carry heavy things on their backs always.'

11 So, I ask this: 'When Israel's people failed to believe Christ, did they make themselves separate from God for always? No, certainly that did not happen! Instead, because they failed to believe, God is saving Gentiles. God began to save Gentiles so that Israel's people would want him to save them too. 12 Israel's people failed to believe Christ. So, as a result, God began to do very, very good things for the other people who live in the world. Israel's people failed to receive what God wanted to give them. So, as a result, the Gentiles received good things from God and they became rich. That was the result when Israel's people failed to obey God. And so, when enough of Israel's people do obey God completely, how much better the result will be!

Paul speaks to the Gentiles

13 Now I am speaking to you Gentiles. God has sent me to be a special worker and teacher on Christ's behalf. He has sent me to teach the good news about Christ to you Gentiles. And I thank him that he has given this important work to me. 14 I hope that maybe my work among you Gentiles will have good results also among my own people. Perhaps it will cause my own people to want God to save them too. So then, as a result, God will save some of them. 15 When God turned away from Israel's people, then he brought other people in the world back to himself. He caused those other people to become friends with him. So, when God does accept Israel's people, the result will be even better! It will be like he is causing dead people to become alive again!

16 If someone offers the first piece of bread to God, then, as a result, all the bread will be God's. If the roots of a tree belong to God, then, as a result, the branches are his also. 17 Israel's people are like a farmer's good olive tree. But God has broken off some of that tree's branches. Instead, he has taken a branch from a wild olive tree. And he has put that wild branch into the good tree, to become part of that tree. You Gentiles are like that wild branch. And now you receive good things from the good tree's root, to make you well and strong. 18 Israel's people are like the branches that God broke off. But you must not think that you are better than those proper branches. If you do begin to think like that, then you should remember something. Remember that you are only a branch. You do not hold the root up and you do not make it strong. No, instead the root holds you up and it makes you strong.

19 One of you might say: 'God broke off the branches so that he could make me part of the tree.' 20 That is true. God broke them off because they did not believe Christ. And you continue to be part of the good tree because you do believe Christ. So, do not think that you yourself are more important than anyone else. Instead, be afraid. 21 God was not sorry for the proper branches and he did not let them stay in the tree. So, do not think that he will let you stay either. He will not be sorry for you if you stop believing him.

22 So, you should understand this about God. He can be kind, but he can be quick to punish people also. He has punished Israel's people, who failed to believe Christ. But he is kind to you, if you continue to believe him. If you do not continue to believe him, then he will cut you off from his tree. 23 And if Israel's people will believe Christ, then God will accept them back again. God will put them back into the tree, because he is able to do that. 24 God cut you Gentiles from an olive tree that was wild. And he put you into the good olive tree, even when you did not belong to that tree before. So certainly, God will be even more ready to accept Israel's people back. He will put them back into that tree, where they did belong before.

God will save Israel's people

25 My Christian friends, I do not want you to think that you yourselves know everything. Instead, I want you to understand this secret that God has shown to us. Many of Israel's people have refused to believe Christ. And they will continue to refuse him until God has finished saving Gentiles. God will save the whole number of Gentiles who will believe him. 26 Then God will save all Israel's people. He will save them as it says in the Old Testament

'The one who makes his people free will come from Zion.

He will cause Jacob's people to obey God.

27 And I will make this agreement with them.

I will take away all the wrong things that they have done.'

28 Israel's people have become God's enemies because they have refused to believe the good news about Christ. But, as a result, this has helped you Gentiles. It has given you the chance for God to save you. But God did choose Israel's people. And he still loves them because of what he promised to their grandfathers.

29 God chose to give good things to Israel's people. He chose them to be his own people. And when God chooses people, that fact will not change. The fact that he has chosen them will never change.

30 In past times, you Gentiles did not obey God. But now, because Israel's people refused to obey him, God has been very kind to you. 31 Israel's people are not obeying God now, because God wanted to be very kind to you. But God will be very kind to them also. 32 God has caused all people to be like those who are in prison. They are in prison because they are not free to obey God. And, as a result, God will be very kind to all people.

33 How very great and rich God is! He knows and understands all things! The things that God decides are very great. They are greater than anyone can explain. No human person can understand how God does things. 34 As it says in the Old Testament:

'Nobody knows what the Lord thinks.

Nobody is able to tell him what he should do.'

35 'Nobody has ever given anything to him first,

so that he had a debt to pay to them.'

36 It is God who made all things. It is God who causes all things to continue. And the purpose of all things is to show how great God is. Everyone should say how very great God is always! This is true!

Chapter 12

We should live only to make God happy

1 My Christian friends, God has been so very good and kind to us. That is the reason why I am asking you very strongly to offer your bodies to him. Bring your bodies to him, as a sacrifice that is still alive. Give yourselves to him completely, so that he may be happy because of you. That is how you can really worship God. 2 Do not let yourselves be like the people who belong to this world. But instead, let God change how you think. Then you will become new people. You will be able to understand what God wants you to do. You will understand what is good. You will understand what makes God happy. And you will understand how to live completely as God wants you to live.

3 God has given authority to me because he is so very kind. So, as a result, I say this to every one of you. Do not think that you yourself are better or more important than you really are. But instead, think about yourself properly, as you ought to think. Remember that God has caused each of you to believe him. And he has made each of you able to do certain things well, because you believe him. 4 Each of us has one body, but that body has many different parts. And all those parts do different things to help the body. 5 In the same way, we are many people but we are united to Christ like one body. And we belong to each other, like the different parts of one body belong to each other.

6 God has given different gifts to each of us because he is so very kind to us. God gives a gift to some people so that they are able to speak his messages. So, those people should believe God when they speak his messages. And they should speak the messages that God has told to them. 7 God makes some people able to be like servants, who work for other people. So, those people should do that work. God makes another person able to teach. So, that person should teach.

8 Another person may be able to help other people to be brave and strong. So, that person should help people like that. Another person may be able to give gifts to people. So, that person should be happy to give what he is able to give. God may have given authority to another person so that he can be a leader. So, that leader should be careful to do his work well. Another person may be able to be kind to people who need help. So, that person should be happy to be kind to people.

Really love people and help them

9 You must not only seem to love people, but instead you should really love them. Hate anything that is bad. Continue to do only the things that are good. 10 Love each other like brothers and sisters who belong to the same family. Each of you should think about the other Christians as more important than you yourself are. 11 Do not be lazy, but instead want very much to work on the Lord's behalf. Continue to work on his behalf, as his servants, because you want very much to make him happy. 12 Be happy, because you can hope certainly for good things from God. Be patient when you have troubles. Whatever things may happen, always continue to pray. 13 If any of God's people need anything, then help them. Give to them what you can give. Be ready to say 'welcome' to visitors and be happy to let them stay in your home.

14 Ask God to be kind to people who cause trouble and pain for you. Yes, ask him to be kind; do not ask God to do bad things to those people. 15 If someone is happy, you be happy also. If someone is sad, you be sad also. 16 Be kind to each other, and try always to agree and to be friends with each other. Do not think that you yourselves are better or more important than other people. Instead, be happy to be friends with people who are not great or important. Do not think that you yourselves know everything.

17 If someone has done bad things to you, do not do bad things back to them. Try to do always what is good. So then all people will know that you do good things. 18 If it is possible, try always to be friends with other people. Try very much not to quarrel with other people. 19 My friends, if someone has done bad things to you, do not try to punish them yourselves. Instead, let God punish them, because it says in the Old Testament: '"I am the one who will punish people. I will punish people who do bad things to you", the Lord says.' **[Deuteronomy 32:35]** 20 But you should do this:

'If your enemy is hungry, feed him.

If he needs to drink, give him something to drink.

If you do these things, your enemy will become ashamed.

He will become sorry because of what he did to you.'

21 Other people may do bad things, but do not let those bad things beat you. Instead, do good things. So then, as a result, you will be the winner over those bad things.

Chapter 13

Obey the government

1 Everyone must obey the government. Nobody has authority to rule unless God has given it to them. It is God who has given authority to those people to rule now. 2 God has chosen to give authority to the government. So, if a person refuses to obey the government, he is also refusing to obey God. And anyone who does that will cause God to punish them.

3 People who do good things do not need to be afraid of the rulers. Only people who do bad things are afraid of the rulers. So, if you do not want to be afraid of a ruler, you must do good things. And then, as a result, the ruler will say that you are good.

4 Rulers are God's servants, who work to help you. But if you do bad things, then you should be afraid of them. You should be afraid because they really do have authority to punish people. They are God's servants, who punish people on God's behalf. They punish people who do bad things. 5 So, you must obey those people who rule. You must obey them not only so that they do not punish you. But you must obey them also because it is right to obey them. And you yourselves know that it is right.

6 This is also the reason why you should pay money to the government. You should pay because the rulers are God's servants. And they continue to do the duties that God has given to them. 7 So, you must pay to each person what you ought to pay. If you should pay money to the government for any reason, pay it. Always do what is proper to those people who have authority. Remember that they are important.

Christians have a duty always to love people

8 Always pay your debts to people. You should have one debt only, which is this. You must always love each other. Anyone who loves other people has obeyed all of God's rules.

9 God's rules say this: 'Do not have sex with anyone who is not your own wife or your own husband. Do not kill anyone. Do not rob anyone. Do not want things that are other people's.' **[Exodus 20:13-15] [Exodus 20:17] [Deuteronomy 5:17-21]** All these rules, and all the other rules, are really only one rule. That one rule is: 'Love every other person the same as you love yourself.' **[Leviticus 19:18]** 10 If you love other people, you will never do anything bad to them. So, anyone who loves other people has obeyed all God's rules.

11 Do these things that I have just told you. Do them, because you know about this time now. It is time now that you should stop being asleep. It is time to wake up. The time when God will finish saving us is near. That time is nearer than when we first believed him. 12 The night has nearly finished and the day is almost here. So, we must stop doing the things that belong to the dark. Instead, we must prepare ourselves like soldiers who are ready to fight in the light.

13 We must do what is right and good and honest. People who belong to the light ought to do those things. We must not go to bad parties and we must not be drunks. We must not have sex with anyone who is not our own wife or husband. We must not do wrong things with our bodies. We must not quarrel. We must not want to be like other people so much that we hate them. 14 But instead, you should put on the Lord Jesus Christ. And stop thinking about any wrong things that, as a human person, you may want to do sometimes.

Chapter 14

Do not think bad things about other Christians who are different from you

1 Some Christians may not be completely sure whether it is right for them to do certain things. You should still be happy to have people like that among you. But do not argue with them about what they ought to do. 2 Some people believe that they may eat all kinds of food. But other people, who are not so sure, may eat vegetables only. 3 People who eat all kinds of food must not think that they are better. They must not think bad things about people who do not eat all kinds of food. Also, people who do not eat all foods must not decide that other people are wrong. They must not decide like that about people who do eat all foods. Nobody should think bad things like that about other people, because God himself has accepted both kinds of people.

4 Nobody has any authority to decide about someone else's servants. Nobody should decide that someone else's servants are wrong. Only those servants' own master has authority to decide whether his servants are right or wrong. But the Lord will continue to accept his servants, because he is able to help them. The Lord can make them strong, so that they continue to believe him.

5 Some people think that certain days are special and more important than other days. Other people think that all days are the same. Each person should be completely sure himself about what seems right to him. 6 A person who makes a certain day special does that as the Lord's servant. That person chooses that day to show how great the Lord is. A person who eats all kinds of food also does that as the Lord's servant. He is thanking God for that food. A person who refuses to eat certain foods does that as the Lord's servant. And he is thanking God also.

7 None of us lives only to make himself happy. And none of us dies only to make himself happy. 8 While we live, our purpose is to make the Lord happy. And when we die, our purpose is to make the Lord happy. So, if we live, we are the Lord's. And if we die, we are the Lord's. 9 Christ died and then he rose, to become alive again, for this purpose. He did it so that he could be the Lord of all people. Whether people are dead or alive, Christ is their Lord.

10 So then, other Christians may not do the same things as you yourself do. But none of you should think that other Christians are wrong because of that. None of you should think that you are better than other Christians. No, because all of us will have to stand in front of God. And God will show what he has decided about us. God decides whether each of us has done what is right or wrong. 11 As it says in the Old Testament:

'"As certainly as the fact that I am alive,

this will happen", the Lord says.

"It will happen that every person will bend their knees in front of me.

And every person will say that I am God." '

12 So, each one of us will have to explain to God about the things that we have done.

Do not cause other Christians to do anything wrong

13 So, we should stop deciding that other Christians are wrong. Instead, you should decide never to do anything that might stop another Christian from obeying God. Never do anything that might cause someone else to do something wrong. 14 There is no kind of food that is itself wrong for a person to eat. I know that. I am completely sure about it, as someone who is united with the Lord Jesus. But a person may believe that it is wrong to eat certain food. And so, for that person, it would be wrong if he did eat that food.

15 You should not cause another Christian to be sad because of what you eat. If you do make him sad, then you are not really loving him. Do not let your food be a problem for another Christian, so that as a result he stops believing Christ. Remember that Christ died on behalf of that person. 16 You may think that something is good. But still you should not do it if it will cause people to say bad things about you. 17 We belong to God's people, the people that he rules over. But it does not really matter what we eat. Neither does it matter what we drink. Instead, these are the things that really matter to God's people. We should do what is right. We should be friends with God and with other people, and we should not cause trouble for other people. And we should be happy. God's Spirit makes us able to do these things. 18 Anyone who does these things is Christ's servant. And God will be happy with that person. Also, other people will say good things about that person.

19 So then, we should try always to do those things that will help people to agree and to be friends. We should try to help each other so that we become stronger as God's people. 20 Do not destroy what God has done, only because of your food. God lets us eat all kinds of food. But it is wrong to eat anything that will cause a problem for someone else. Do not cause anyone to do something that they believe to be wrong. 21 It is good not to do anything that might cause another person to become weaker as a Christian. If it does, it is good that you do not eat meat. And it is good that you do not drink wine.

22 What you believe about these things should be a secret between yourself and God. A person may know what is the right thing for him to do. Then, if he does it, he is happy as a result. He does not need to ask whether it is right. 23 But someone else may not be sure whether it is right to eat certain food. If that person does eat that food, then he is doing something wrong. He is not sure that it is right for him to eat it. Whatever things we do, we must be sure about them. We must be sure that they are right. If we are not sure about something, then it is wrong for us to do it.

Chapter 15

Stronger Christians should be patient and kind to weaker Christians

1 We who are sure and strong ought to help other people. We ought to help those people who are not strong. We ought to be patient with them, because they are not so sure. We should not do only those things that we ourselves would choose to do. 2 Instead, each of us should do the things that will help other Christians. We should try to help other Christians so that they believe God more strongly. 3 Even Christ did not do the things that he himself might have chosen to do. Instead, as it says in the Old Testament: 'People were angry with you (God), and they said bad things about you. But it was like they were also saying angry, bad things about me too.' **[Psalm 69:9]**

4 Everything that people wrote in the Old Testament in past times is there to teach us. Those words help us to continue being patient, brave and strong. So then, as a result, we can hope certainly for what God has promised to us.

5 It is God himself who makes us able to be patient, brave and strong. And I pray that God will help you to agree with each other and to be friends. That is how Christ Jesus wants you to live. 6 So then, all of you together will be united. You will think and say the same things. You will say how very great and good God, the Father of our Lord Jesus Christ, is.

Christ came to save both Jews and Gentiles

7 Christ has accepted you, so you must accept each other. So then, as a result, people will say how great God is. 8 I say to you that Christ became a servant of Israel's people. He came to show that God promises true things. God promised certain things to the grandfathers of Israel's people. And Christ caused those things to happen. 9 Also, Christ came so that the Gentiles could thank God. They could say how great and good God is. They could thank God because he has been so very kind to them. As it says in the Old Testament:

'For this reason I will say to everyone that you are God.

I will say that when I am among the Gentiles.

And I will sing to you, to show how great you are.'

10 It says also in the Old Testament:

'Be happy, you Gentiles, together with God's people.'

11 Again, it says also in the Old Testament:

'Say how great the Lord is, all you Gentiles.

All people, from every country, should say how great he is.'

12 Again, Isaiah says this:

'The root of Jesse will come.

He will come, to rule the Gentiles.

And the Gentiles will hope certainly because of him.

They will wait for him to do what he has promised to do.'

13 God is the one who causes us to hope certainly for good things. I pray that God will fill you. I pray that he will cause you to be completely happy and without trouble deep inside yourselves. He will do this because you believe him. Then, as a result, God's powerful Spirit will cause you to hope more and more certainly.

Paul speaks about the work that God has sent him to do

14 My Christian friends, I myself am quite sure that you are always good. You know completely all the things that God wants you to know. And you are able to teach each other when someone is wrong. I am quite sure about this. 15 But I have written to you strongly about certain things, so that you would remember those things. I have been brave enough to write like this because God has so kindly chosen me. 16 God has chosen me to work on behalf of Christ Jesus among the Gentiles. I tell God's good news to them. I work like a priest so that God will accept the Gentiles. He will accept them like a sacrifice, because God's Spirit has made them clean and ready for God.

17 So, because I am united with Christ Jesus, I can be happy about my work. I can be happy because of the things that I have done on God's behalf. 18 I will be brave enough to speak only about the work that Christ has made me able to do. He has made me able to lead the Gentiles to obey God.

They have obeyed God as a result of what I have said. They have obeyed him as a result also of what I have done. 19 God's powerful Spirit caused many great and powerful things to happen, that surprised people very much. So, as a result, I have told the whole good news about Christ to people. I have told it while I travelled all the way from Jerusalem city to Illyricum.

20 I always want very much to go to places where nobody has ever told the people about Christ before. I want to tell the good news to the people in those places. Then I will not be continuing someone else's work for God that they have started. I will not be continuing to build a house in a place where someone else has already begun to build. 21 Instead, I obey what it says in the Old Testament:

'People that nobody ever told about Christ will see.

Those people who never heard the message about him will understand.'

Paul hopes to visit Rome soon

22 That is why, many times, something has stopped me from visiting you. 23 But now I have finished my work in these places here. And for several years, I have been wanting to visit you. 24 I hope to visit you while I am travelling to Spain. I will stay with you for a short time and I will enjoy being with you. And I hope that you will help me on my journey.

25 But now, I am ready to go to Jerusalem so that I can help God's people there. 26 Some of God's people at Jerusalem are poor. And the Christians in Macedonia and Achaia wanted to help those people. So, they got some money to send to those poor people. 27 The Christians in Macedonia and Achaia were happy to do this. But really, they have a duty to help Christians who belong to Israel's people. It is because of Israel's people that the Gentiles have received good things from God. The Gentiles have received the spiritual good things that God promised to Israel's people. So, the Gentiles ought to help Israel's people with the things that they need in this world.

28 So, I must finish this job at Jerusalem. The Gentiles have given all this money to help the poor Christians there. And I must certainly take this money safely to those people. After that, I will leave Jerusalem. And I will visit you before I continue travelling to Spain. 29 When I visit you, Christ will be very, very good to us. I know that.

30 My Christian friends, I ask you very much to help me in my work. I ask you to pray to God on my behalf. Pray very strongly, together with me. I ask this because we belong to our Lord Jesus Christ. I ask it because God's Spirit causes us to love each other. 31 Pray that God will keep me safe. So then those people in Judea who refuse to believe Christ will not do anything to hurt me. Pray also that God's people at Jerusalem will accept this money. I want them to be happy because of this gift that I will bring to them.

32 After that, I will come to visit you, if God wants me to do that. I will be very happy when I come. And I will enjoy resting while I stay there with you. 33 God causes us to be without trouble inside ourselves. And I pray that he will be with all of you. This is what I pray.

Chapter 16

Paul says 'hello' to people at Rome

1 I want to tell you that Phoebe is a good person. She is like our sister because she belongs to Christ. And she is a special helper among the group of Christians at Cenchrea. 2 I want you to be kind to her because she is the Lord's. God's people ought to be kind to each other like that. Give to her whatever things she needs. Please help her, because she has helped many people. She has helped me myself also.

3 Say 'hello' on my behalf to Priscilla and Aquila, who worked together with me on behalf of Christ Jesus. 4 They were ready to die so that I could continue living. It is not only I myself who thank them. No! All the groups of Christian Gentiles thank them also. 5 Say 'hello' also to the group of Christians who meet in Priscilla and Aquila's house.

Say 'hello' to my friend Epaenetus that I love. He was the first person in Asia who believed Christ.

6 Say 'hello' to Mary, who worked very much on your behalf. 7 Say 'hello' to Andronicus and Junias. Like me, they belong to Israel's people. Also, they were in a prison together with me. God sent them to be special workers and teachers on Christ's behalf, and they do that work very, very well. They became Christians before I did.

8 Say 'hello' to Ampliatus on my behalf. I love him as someone who, like me, is the Lord's. 9 Say 'hello' to Urbanus, who works with us on Christ's behalf. And say 'hello' to my friend Stachys that I love. 10 Say 'hello' to Apelles. He has shown certainly how he really does believe Christ. Say 'hello' to those people who belong to Aristobulus's family. 11 Say 'hello' to Herodion, who, like me, belongs to Israel's people. Say 'hello' to those people in Narcissus' family who are the Lord's.

12 Say 'hello' to Tryphaena and Tryphosa, who work very much on the Lord's behalf. Say 'hello' to my friend Persis that I love. She has worked very much on the Lord's behalf. 13 Say 'hello' to Rufus, who is clearly the Lord's very good servant. Say 'hello' also to his mother, who has been like a mother to me, too.

14 Say 'hello' to Asyncritus, Phlegon, Hermes, Patrobas and Hermas. Say 'hello' also to all our Christian friends who are there with them. 15 Say 'hello' to Philologus and Julia, to Nereus and his sister, and to Olympas. Say 'hello' also to all God's people who are there with them.

16 When you meet each other, kiss each other as Christian brothers and sisters. All the groups of Christians here say 'hello' to you.

Paul tells the Christians at Rome to be careful about false teachers

17 My Christian friends, now I want to tell you something very strongly. Be very careful about those people who cause you to quarrel with each other. Be careful about people who cause other people to turn away from God.

They teach things that are different from God's true message. But you have learned the true message, and you must stay away from those people. 18 People who are like that are not servants of our Lord Christ. Instead, they are doing only the things that they themselves want to do. They say things that seem good and nice. But, as a result, they cause other people to believe false things. Those other people do not understand the difference between what is true or false.

19 Christians everywhere know how you obey God. So, for this reason, I am very happy because of you. But I want you always to understand clearly what things are good. And I want you never to do what is bad. 20Then God, who causes us to be without trouble inside ourselves, will make you winners over Satan soon. God will beat Satan so that he lies under your feet. I pray that our Lord Jesus will continue to be very kind to you.

Paul finishes his letter

21 Timothy, who is working together with me, says 'hello' to you. Lucius, Jason and Sosipater, who, like me, belong to Israel's people, say 'hello' to you also.

22 I am Tertius, and I have written down this letter. I say 'hello' to you as someone who, like you, is the Lord's.

23 Gaius says 'hello' to you also. He is letting me, Paul, stay in his house. The group of Christians here meet together in his house also.

Erastus, who keeps this city's money, says 'hello' to you. Our Christian friend Quartus says 'hello' to you too.

[24 I pray that our Lord Jesus Christ will continue to be very kind to all of you. This is what I pray.]

25 We should say how very great God is! He is able to make you strong, as I have told you. I told you when I taught the good news about Jesus Christ to you. That good news is the true message that God kept secret for a long, long time. But now he has shown this message to us. 26 Now all people can know this true message. We have told people what the prophets wrote about Christ. God, who lives always, has told us to tell it to people. God wants people from all countries to know this message. So then, as a result, they can believe God and they can obey him.

27 God is the only God. Only he himself knows and understands all things. Everyone should say always how very great he is! Everyone should say that always, because of Jesus Christ! This is true.

The greatest thing is love

1 Corinthians

About 1 Corinthians

Paul wrote this letter to the Christians at Corinth city. Corinth was a big, important, busy port in the country that we call Greece now. Most of the Christians there were Gentiles (not Israel's people). We think that Paul wrote this letter about the year AD 54. That was more than 20 years after Jesus died. Paul had stayed at Corinth for 18 months, to teach God's message to the people. (See Acts 18:11.)

After he had left Corinth, Paul heard news about some serious problems among the Christians there. Also, the Christians at Corinth had written a letter to Paul to ask him questions about certain things. (See 7:1.)

So, in this letter to Corinth, Paul tells them about the problems that he has heard about. He tries to tell them why they are wrong about some things.

Also, he answers the questions that the Christians at Corinth have asked him.

Chapter 1

1 This letter is from me, Paul, and from our Christian friend Sosthenes. God chose me to be a special worker and teacher on behalf of Christ Jesus. He sent me to tell the good news about Christ to people. God himself chose me for this purpose.

2 I am sending this letter to you Christians (the church) in the city called Corinth. God chose you for himself. He wanted you to be his special people, who belong to him. He has made you good and clean inside because he has made you join to Christ Jesus. Also, he has made you join to everyone everywhere who worships our Lord Jesus Christ. Jesus is their Lord, as he is our Lord.

3 We pray that God, our Father, and the Lord Jesus Christ, will continue to be very kind to you. We pray also that they will cause you to be without trouble inside yourselves.

Paul thanks God because of the Christians at Corinth

4 I thank God always because of you. I thank him because he has been so very kind to you. He has given such great things to you because he has made you join to Christ Jesus. 5 And, as a result, Christ has made you really like rich people in every way. You are like rich people because you can do many things. Christ has made you able to speak as he wants you to speak. And he has made you able to know everything that he wants you to know.

6 God has made our message about Christ clear in you who believe it. 7 You are not without any of God's gifts while you continue to wait for our Lord Jesus Christ's return. You want him to return very much. 8 God will cause you to continue believing him until the end. Then, on the day when our Lord Jesus Christ returns, nobody will be able to say bad things about you. Nobody will be able to say that you have done anything wrong. 9 God always does what he has promised to do. And God has chosen you to know Christ. He has made you join to his Son, Jesus Christ, who is our Lord.

Paul tells the Christians that they must not quarrel about who is their leader

10 My Christian friends, I speak to you with the authority of our Lord Jesus Christ. I ask you to agree with each other in what you say. Then there will not be differences between you. All of you will have the same mind always. That is, you will think about things in the same way. 11 Some people from Chloe's house have told me what is happening among you, my friends. They say that you are quarrelling among yourselves. 12I will explain: One of you says, 'Paul is my leader.' Another person says, 'Apollos is my leader.' Another person says, 'Peter is my leader.' And another person says, 'Christ is my leader.'

13 When you speak like that, it is bad. It is as if you are breaking Christ into several parts. Certainly, I, Paul, did not die on a cross on your behalf. Someone baptised you. But certainly, they did not use my name, as if you belonged to me. 14 I thank God that I did not baptise any of you except Crispus and Gaius.15 So, none of you can say, 'Paul is my leader because he baptised me.' 16 (Oh yes, I baptised Stephanas and his family also. I cannot remember that I baptised anyone else.) 17 Christ did not send me to baptise people. But he did send me to tell the good news to people. He does not want me to tell it with the same kind of clever words that clever people might say. That would destroy the power of the message about Jesus. The message is about how he died on a cross to save us.

The message about Christ's cross is powerful

18 People who are far from God cannot understand that message about Christ's death on the cross.

They think that it is silly. But that same message shows something to us whom God is saving. It shows us how powerful God is. 19 It says in the Old Testament:

'I will destroy all the words and thoughts of clever people.

I will put on one side the ideas of people who seem to understand a lot.'

20 So then, the clever people in this world are not great really. The clever students in this world are not great really. Some people know how to argue. But those people are not great really. No, because God has different ideas. He has shown that even the cleverest people in this world are fools. 21 God has his own great thoughts and ideas. And he has made it impossible for people to know him by their own thoughts and ideas. Instead, God uses that message about Jesus. He uses it to save everyone who believes it. And we tell that same message to everyone, even if it seems crazy.

22 Jews want to see God do something powerful so that they will believe. And people who are not Jews want to believe other people's clever ideas. 23 But as for us, we talk about how Christ died on a cross of wood. This is a message that the Jews refuse to believe. And the Gentiles (people who are not Jews) think that it is a silly message. 24 But all of us whom God has chosen, both Jews and the other people, we think different thoughts. To us, Christ is the power that comes from God. What Christ did is the result of God's great thoughts and ideas. 25 It seems to be a crazy thing for God to do. But it is better than the cleverest human thoughts and ideas. What seems to be God's weakness is stronger than any human power.

26 Christian friends, remember when God spoke to you. Remember what you were like then. Most of you were not clever or powerful. Most of you did not come from rich or important families. 27 People think that you are not great or important. But God chose you. He did this so that clever people would be ashamed. Yes, God chose the weak people in the world so that the powerful people would be ashamed. 28 God chose people who do not seem important in this world. He chose people who seem silly in this world. He chose people who seem to be worth nothing in this world. The people who do not know God think differently from him. They think that different kinds of people are great and important. But God destroys their ideas when he chooses his people.

29 So, because of all this, nobody can say in front of God: 'I am better than other people.' 30 It is God who has made you join to Christ Jesus. And, because of Christ, God causes us to know everything that he wants us to know. As a result of what Christ did, God makes us right with himself. Also he makes us his own special people. He makes us his free people that he has bought. 31 So now, as it says in the Old Testament:

'Anyone who wants to speak about great or important things should speak about the Lord.

That person should not speak about himself, nor about the things that he himself has done.

Instead, he should speak only about the great things that the Lord has done on his behalf.'

Chapter 2

We can understand God's secrets only by his Spirit

1 Christian friends, I came to tell you God's message, which is certainly true. I did not use clever words when I told it to you. I did not use great thoughts and ideas that were my own. 2 I decided to teach you only about Jesus Christ. I wanted to forget everything else while I was with you. So, I taught only about Jesus. I taught you about how he died on a cross of wood.

3 I was feeling very weak when I arrived. I was so afraid that I was trembling. 4 Neither clever words nor my own thoughts and ideas made you believe that my message was true. No, instead God's Spirit showed by my words how powerful God is. 5 So, you believe because of God's power. You do not believe because of human thoughts and ideas.

6 But we do speak about great ideas to those of you who really know Christ. We do not speak about clever human thoughts and ideas that belong to this world. The rulers of this world think thoughts and ideas like that, but they will stop being powerful soon. 7 No, the great ideas that we speak about are secret. They belong to God. He hid them from the people who belong to this world. But he decided to show these secrets to us so that we could live with him always. He decided this before he made the world. 8 None of the rulers of this world understood these great ideas. If they had understood, they would not have killed the Lord on a cross. They would not have killed the Lord, who is so very great and good. 9 It says in the Old Testament:

'Nobody ever saw or heard anything about this.

Nobody ever thought that it could happen.

But this is the thing that God has prepared for his people.

He has prepared it for those people who love him.'

10 But God has shown these secrets to us by his Spirit. God's Spirit looks at everything. He looks even at the things that are deep in God. 11 Only a person's own spirit, inside that person, can know everything about that person. And it is like that with God. Nobody can understand everything about God except God's Spirit. 12 We have not received the spirit that belongs to this world. No! We have received the Spirit who is from God. So, as a result, we can understand all the things that God has done on our behalf. We can know what God has given to us. 13 These are the things that we speak about. We do not use human ideas that other people have taught us. Instead, we use ideas that God's Spirit teaches us. That is why we can explain God's ideas to people. But we can explain only to people in whom God's Spirit is living.

14 If God's Spirit is not living inside people, they cannot receive anything from God. They cannot understand what God wants to teach them. They think that it is crazy. They think that it is worth nothing. 15 Only people with God's Spirit inside them can really understand and decide about all things. But people without God's Spirit cannot understand anything about God's people. 16 As it says in the Old Testament:

'Nobody can know what the Lord is thinking.

Nobody can teach him anything.'

But we can think as Christ thinks.

Chapter 3

You are God's house

1 Christian friends, in past times, I could not talk to you as I wanted to talk. I should have been able to talk to you as people who understand things by God's Spirit. But instead, I could only talk to you as people who understand things about this world. You were like babies because you did not understand very much about Christ. 2 I had to give milk to you, instead of proper food, because you were not ready to receive proper food. You are not ready for it even now! 3 You are still living like people who do not know God. You want things that other people have. And you quarrel with each other. This shows that you are not like God's people. You are still like people who do not know God. 4 One of you says, 'Paul is my leader.' And another person says, 'Apollos is my leader.' With words like these, you are talking like people who do not know God.

5 You should know that we, Apollos and Paul, are not important really. God used us as his servants, who could help you to believe Christ. The Lord has given a special job to each of us. 6 I was like a servant who planted seeds. Apollos was like the servant who gave water to the young plants. But it was God who caused the seeds and the plants to grow. 7 The servant who plants the seeds is not important really. The servant who gives water to the plants is not important really. The important person is God, because he causes the plants to grow. 8 The person who plants is doing God's work. The person who gives water is doing God's work also. We are equal servants. And God will give to each of us what is right because of our own work. 9 We work together with God. You are like God's field and you are like God's building.

10 God has made me able to work for him like a very good builder. So, I built the foundation for God's building. Now someone else is building on this foundation. But each person must be careful how he builds. 11 God has already put Jesus Christ as the only foundation of this building. So, nobody can put any other foundation there.

12 People may build on this foundation with gold, silver (another valuable metal) or valuable stones. Or instead, they may build on it with wood, grass or leaves. 13 But God will show how good each person's work is. He will show it on the day when Christ returns. There will be a fire on that day and God will put each person's work into the fire. The fire will show whether the work is good or not.

14 If the fire does not destroy the work, then the work is good. So, the person who did it will receive something good from God. 15 But if the fire destroys the work, then the work is not good. The person who did that work will lose it. God will still save that person. But that person will be like someone who must run through the fire to a safe place.

16 You ought to know that you yourselves are God's house. You ought to know that God's Spirit lives in you. 17 God's house belongs only to God. So, God will destroy anyone who destroys God's house. And you yourselves are God's house.

18 Nobody should think things about himself that are not really true. The people in this world who do not know God think differently from God. Maybe one of you thinks like them, that you are a very clever person. But instead, you should be ready for other people to think that you are a fool. Then you will really be clever. 19 The people in this world think that their ideas are very clever. But God thinks that they are crazy. It says in the Old Testament:

'People may try to show that they themselves are very clever.

But God causes those people to become confused.'

20 In another place the Old Testament says:

'The Lord knows that clever people's thoughts are worth nothing.'

21 So, nobody should think that clever or great people are important really. Do not think like that, because all things are yours. 22 Paul, Apollos and Peter, all of us are yours. All of this world is yours. While you live, all things are yours. And when you die, all things are yours. Both today and tomorrow are yours, because all things are yours. 23 And you are Christ's, and Christ is God's.

Chapter 4

Christ's servants

1 You should think about us, who are special workers and teachers on Christ's behalf, as Christ's servants. God has given a special job to us. He has shown his secrets to us and now we must explain them to other people.

2 A servant must remember all the things that his master wants him to do every day. He must do all those things, because his master wants him to do them.

3 But it is not important to me how you think about me. You may decide about how good I am. It does not matter to me what people decide about me. I do not even try to decide about myself. 4 I may think that I have not done any wrong things. But that does not make me right. Only the Lord can decide about me. 5 So, you should not decide about things before the right time comes. You must wait until the Lord comes again. He knows every secret. He knows everything that people are hiding in the dark. He will bring all those things out into the light. He will show to everyone the secret purposes that people have deep inside themselves. Then God will say good things about every person who has done good work.

6 Now, my Christian friends, I want to help you to understand better everything that I have said. I have used Apollos and myself as examples. So then you can learn by us what this means: 'Obey what it says in the Old Testament.' None of you should say that one person is more valuable than any other person.

7 You yourselves are no better than other people. God gave everything that you have to you. You know that. What you have was a gift. So, you should not think that you are more important than anyone else. You have no reason to think that.

8 You have plenty of everything already! You think that you are very rich already! So, you are ready to rule like kings, even while we are not rulers at all! I would really like you to be rulers, so that we could rule together with you! 9 God sent us, his special workers, to teach his message to people. But I think that he has given the least important place to us. We are like prisoners on our way to die in a place where everyone can see. Both people and angels are watching us. 10 People think that we are fools because of Christ. But you think that you yourselves understand so much! You think that, because you are united with Christ. You think that we are weak. And you think that you are strong! You think that we are not valuable. And you think that you yourselves are very valuable!

11 Until this day, we are often hungry, and we do not have any water to drink. Our clothes are very old. Sometimes people hit us, and we do not have a home. 12 We work very much, so that we are very tired. When people say bad things about us, we ask God to be good to them. When people are cruel to us, we are patient and brave. 13 When people say cruel words about us, we answer with kind words. Until this day, we are like the dirt of the whole world. We are like the dirty things that people throw away.

14 I do not write these things to make you ashamed. You are like my own children that I love. And I want to explain to you why you are wrong. I want you to understand correctly. 15 I told the good news to you, so I became like a father to you. You belong to Christ now. And even if you have ten thousand guides to help you, you do not have many fathers. 16 That is why I ask you to copy my example. 17 For this reason, I am sending Timothy to visit you. He is like a son to me, and I love him very much. He continues always to believe the Lord and to obey him. He will cause you to remember how I live as a Christian, united with Christ. I teach the same things to all groups of Christians everywhere.

18 Some of you think that I will never come to visit you. You think that you yourselves are very important and powerful. You think that you know everything. 19 But I will come to visit you soon, if the Lord sends me. Then I will discover more than only what you are saying about yourselves. I will discover what power you important people really have. 20 When people are really obeying God as their king, it shows. We can see it because God's people live by his power. We will not know it only by what they say. 21 Certainly, I will come to visit you. So, you must choose what I come to do. I might come to be angry with you and to punish you. Or, instead, I might come to speak kind words to you. I might show you that I love you. You must choose.

Chapter 5

Send the bad person away from you

1 We have heard very bad news about what is happening in your group. One of you is having sex with someone who is not his own wife. We have heard that he is having sex with his own father's wife! Even people who do not know God do not do things as bad as this! 2 But, you still think that you are important and good! Instead, you ought to be very ashamed and sad. You must put this man, who has done this bad thing, outside your meetings. You should not let him continue to belong to your group.

3 Even if I am far away from you, my spirit is present with you. It is quite the same as when I am with you. So, I have decided already about the man who has done this very bad thing. I have decided what you should do to this bad man. 4 When you meet together with the authority of the Lord Jesus, my spirit is with you. The power of our Lord Jesus is with you too. 5 When you meet like this, you must give this man to Satan. And Satan will destroy the man's body. So then God can save the man's spirit on the day when the Lord Jesus returns.

6 You should not think that you yourselves are so good and so important. You have no reason to think that. You should know about what yeast does in bread. A small amount of yeast makes the whole lot of dough become bigger.

This yeast in the dough is like one person among you who does wrong things. You must remove this old yeast from among you. Then you will be like new dough, with no yeast in it. You are like that really, because Christ died on our behalf. He is our lamb for the Passover. And that Passover is ready now, because he died. 8 So, we can have our Passover, but not with the old yeast. We must remove everything that is bad or wrong. Instead, we must be good and honest and true, so that we are like new bread, without any yeast.

9 I wrote a letter to you. In that letter, I told you that you must not be friends with bad people. You must stay away from people who have sex with anyone other than their own wife or husband. I told you that. 10But I did not mean people who do not know God. I did not mean that you must stay away from all those people. Some of those people often have sex with people who are not their own wife or husband. Some of them want more things than they need. Some of them take things that belong to other people. And some of them worship false gods. To stay away from all those people, you would have to leave this world.

11 What I meant was this: You should not be friends with any bad person among your group. That person may say that they are Christ's. But if they have sex with people other than their own wife or husband, do not be friends with those people. Some people want a lot more things than they need. Do not be friends with those people. If they worship false gods, do not be friends with them. If they say wrong things about other people, do not be friends with them. If they get drunk, do not be friends with them. If they take other people's things, do not be friends with them. Do not even eat a meal with anyone who does things like that. 12 It is not right for me to decide about the people outside – the people who do not believe Christ. But you should decide about the people inside – the people who meet together with you as Christians. It is right for you to decide whether they are right or wrong. 13 But God will decide about the people outside, who are not Christians. As the Old Testament says:

'You must send a bad person away from among yourselves.'

Chapter 6

People who do not believe Christ should not decide about your quarrels

1 Perhaps one of you does not agree with another Christian about something that matters. But you should not go for help to people who do not know God. No! Instead, you should go to God's people. And you should ask them to decide about this thing.

2 You should know that God's people will decide about all the people in the world one day. So, if you will decide about the world, certainly you should be able to decide about small things among yourselves. 3 You should know that we will even decide about the angels one day. So certainly, we should be able to decide about things that belong only to our lives here on earth.

4 Sometimes you may not agree among yourselves about things that belong to our lives here on earth. But when that happens, do not go to people outside the church (group of Christians). Do not choose to go to people who are nothing to the church. Do not choose those people to decide about these things. 5 I say this so that you will feel ashamed. Certainly, there should be one person in your group who understands enough to decide about things like this between believers. 6 But instead, you have let believers go to people in the government to argue against other believers! You stand in front of people who do not believe Christ! Then you let them decide what is right!

7 When you do this, you are completely wrong. You should not go to people in the government to argue with each other. It would be better to let other people do wrong things to you. Even if people rob you, that would be better. 8 Instead, you yourselves do wrong things, and you do those things to other believers! You even rob them.

9 God has prepared good things for his own people that he rules over. But he will never let any bad person receive those good things. You ought to know this. You can be very sure that no kind of bad person will receive those good things. People who have sex with anyone other than their own wife or husband will not receive them. People who worship false gods will not receive them. Men who have sex with men will not receive them. And women who have sex with women will not receive those good things either.

10 People who rob will not receive them. Some people want more than they need. Those people will not receive them. Drunks will not receive them. People who say wrong things about other people will not receive them. People who are not honest about other people's things will not receive those good things. God has prepared things for his own people that he rules over. But no bad people will ever receive those things.11 Some of you did bad things like this. But the Spirit of our God has washed you clean with the Lord Jesus Christ's authority. He has made you God's own people, who are separate from bad things. He has made you right with God, so that God can accept you now.

Use your bodies as God's servants should use them

12 One of you may say: 'I am free to do anything. I can do anything that I want to do.' But not everything will help you. I myself could say: 'I am free. I can do whatever thing I want to do.' Yes, but I will not let anything rule over me. 13 Someone else may say: 'Food is there for the stomach. So the stomach is there for me to fill it with food.' Yes, but God will destroy both the stomach and the food. The Lord gave our bodies to us. So, you should not have sex with anyone who is not your own wife or husband. You should not use your bodies like that. Instead, you should use your bodies as the Lord wants you to use them. 14God raised the Lord Jesus. God made him alive again after he had died. And God will use his own power to make us alive again also. 15 You ought to know that your bodies are parts of Christ's body. So, you must never take part of his body and make it part of a prostitute's body. Never let that happen! 16 Anyone who makes his own body join to a prostitute becomes one body with that prostitute. You should know that. It says in the Old Testament:

'The two people (the man and the woman) shall become one body.'

17 But everyone who is united to the Lord is one spirit with him. 18 So, do not have sex with anyone who is not your own wife or husband. Be careful never to do that. Any other bad thing that you do is outside your own body. But if you have sex with the wrong person, you do something wrong to your own body.

19 Your body is the home of God's Spirit, who is completely good and separate from everything bad. You should know that. God gave his Spirit to you and he lives in you. You do not belong to yourselves any longer. But you belong to God, 20 because God bought you. He paid the price for you. So, show how great and how good God is. Use your body to show that.

Chapter 7

Questions about marriage

1 You wrote to ask me about certain things. And now I will answer your questions. Yes, it is a good thing when a man does not marry. 2 Many people have sex with other people who are not their own wife or husband. But you must be careful never to do that. So, every man should have his own wife and every woman should have her own husband.

3 The husband should have sex with his wife to make her happy. He should do that because it is his duty. And the wife should do the same thing for her husband. 4 The wife does not rule over her own body, but her husband rules over it. In the same way, the husband does not rule over his own body, but his wife rules over it. 5 Do not refuse to have sex with each other, unless both of you agree to stop for a short time. So then you can use your time to pray. But you should come together again soon. You need each other so that Satan cannot cause you to have sex with other people. 6 I am not saying that you must do this. No, but I am saying that you can do it. You can stop like this for a short time if you want. 7 It would be good if all of you could be like me. But each person has his own gift from God. One person has a gift to do a certain thing. And another person has a different gift.

8 Now I want to say something to those of you who have not married yet.

Also, I am speaking to those of you whose husbands or wives have died. It is better for all of you to continue alone. That is what I do myself. 9 But if you cannot rule yourselves well, then you should marry. It is better for you to marry. That is better than to always want sex very much.

10 I speak now to people who have married. I tell you a rule that comes from the Lord himself, not from me. A wife must not leave her husband. 11 But if she does leave, she must continue to be alone. Or she must go back to stay with her husband. And a husband must not send his wife away.

12 To you other people, I myself say this. The Lord has not spoken about it. If a Christian man's wife does not believe Christ that man must not send his wife away. She may agree to continue living with him. Then he must not send her away. 13 If a Christian woman's husband does not believe Christ, she must not send him away. He may agree to continue living with her. Then she must not send him away. 14 God accepts a husband who does not believe Christ. God accepts him because of his Christian wife. Also, God accepts a wife who does not believe Christ. God accepts her because of her Christian husband. If this was not true, God would not accept your children. But God does accept them, because to him they are clean.

15 But the husband or wife who does not believe Christ may want to leave. If they want to do that, let them leave. Then the Christian man or woman does not have a duty to make them stay. God does not want us to fight with each other. 16 Perhaps, Christian wife, you will save your husband. Or perhaps, Christian husband, you will save your wife.

17 Each one of you has what the Lord has given to you. So, each of you should continue to live as God has chosen for you to live. I teach this rule to the churches (groups of Christians) in every place. 18 Some of you are Jews, so people circumcised you. That happened before you came to Christ. So, do not try to change it. Some of you are not Jews and nobody has ever circumcised you. So, continue like that and do not ask anyone to circumcise you. 19 It is not important whether someone has circumcised you or not. The important thing is this. Obey what God says.

20 At a certain time, God chose to speak to you so that you came to Christ. So, each of you should continue as you were then. 21 You may have been a slave when God spoke to you. That does not matter. But you may have the chance to become a free person. If you do, then use it. 22 Sometimes the Lord chooses a slave to belong to him. Then, that slave becomes the Lord's free person. In the same way, when a free person comes to Christ, he becomes Christ's slave.

23 God has bought you and he has paid the price for you. So, do not let anyone else make you their slave. 24 My friends, who are like brothers to me, each one of you should live for God. He put you where you were. Then he spoke to you. So, each of you should continue as you were then.

25 Now I want to answer your question about people who have not married. The Lord has not given any special rule about this. But I will tell you what I myself think about it. You can believe me. I speak as someone to whom the Lord has been very kind. He has made me able to be honest and true. 26 It is very difficult to live in the world today. So, it is better that each man continues as he is. That is what I think. 27 If you have a wife, you should continue like that. If you do not have a wife, do not look for one. 28 But if you do marry, that is not wrong. And if a young woman marries, that is not wrong. But those people who marry will have many troubles during their life together in this world. And I want to save you from that kind of trouble.

29 My friends, what I mean is this: The end of time will come soon. So, those men with wives should live as if they had none. 30 Some of you weep. But you should live as if you were not sad. Some of you laugh because you are happy. But you should live as if you were not happy. Some of you buy things. But you should live as if you did not have those things. 31 Some of you are busy with things in this world. But you should live as if these things were not important. This world, as it is now, will finish.

32 I want all of you to be free so that you are not thinking about problems and troubles. A Christian man who has not married thinks a lot about the Lord and his work. He wants to do what makes the Lord happy. 33 But a Christian man who has married is different. He thinks also about the things that belong to this world.

He thinks like that because he wants to make his wife happy too. 34 So, these things make him think in two opposite ways. Also, a Christian woman or young girl who has not married thinks a lot about the Lord and his work. She wants to belong to the Lord completely, both in her body and in her spirit. But a Christian woman who has married is different. She thinks also about the things that belong to this world. She thinks like that because she wants to make her husband happy too.

35 I am saying this because I want to help you. I am not trying to make rules that you have to obey. Instead, I want you to live in a right and proper way. I want you to be the Lord's servants, who listen to him. I do not want anything else to stop you thinking about the Lord.

36 Perhaps a man and a woman among you love each other but they have decided not to marry. They have agreed to wait. But, as they grow older, the man may begin to think differently. He may think that he cannot wait any longer. He may think that he needs to marry her. Then, if they want to marry, it is not wrong. 37 But another man among you may decide that he will never marry his young woman. He may be sure that he does not need to marry. He may be able to rule himself strongly, with authority. So, he need not marry her. He is doing the right thing also. 38 So, the man who marries does a good thing. But the man who does not marry does a better thing.

39 If a woman has married a man, he is her husband. She is not free to marry anyone else all the time that her husband is alive. But if he dies, then she is free. Then she can marry again. But she must marry someone who is the Lord's. 40 Even so, she would be happier if she continued without a husband. That is what I myself think. And I think that God's Spirit is my guide in all this.

Chapter 8

About food that people have offered to false gods

1 Now I want to answer your question about food that people have offered to false gods. We know that all of us know about many things. And when we know something that can make us think wrongly about ourselves and about other people. It can make us think that we are more important than other people. But when we love other people, it helps to make them strong.

2 Nobody should think that they really know about something. Some people might think that. But those people do not know anything yet as well as they should know it. 3 But God knows every person who loves him.

4 So, I will speak about the food that people have offered to false gods. I will speak about whether you should eat it. We know that a false god is not really a god at all. We know that there is only the one God. 5 Yes, people may have many false gods and many false lords. People do call other things gods, whether in heaven or on earth. 6 But for us there is only one God, who is the Father. All things come from him and we live for him. There is only one Lord, who is Jesus Christ. He made everything by his power. And he causes us to continue living by his power.

7 But some people do not understand these facts. Some people have worshipped false gods for many years. So now they cannot eat food that people have offered to a false god. They think that the food really belongs to that false god. So, they are doing something wrong if they eat that food. That is what they think. It makes them feel as if they are not clean. They cannot easily decide what is right or wrong. 8 But food does not bring us near to God. If we do not eat the food, that will not make us worse. If we do eat the food, it will not make us better.

9 But you must be very careful. You are free to do anything that is right. But some Christians are not so sure about what is right. So, you must not do anything that might cause them to do something wrong. 10 You may be eating food in a place where people worship false gods. Perhaps another Christian, who is not so sure about this, will see you. That Christian may think that you know more than they know. So then, they may think that they can eat that food too. They may think that it is right for them too. 11 Then you would destroy other Christians who are not so sure. What you know would be their guide. You must remember that Christ died on behalf of them too.

12 When other Christians do something wrong because of you, you do something wrong too. They are not sure what is right or wrong. So, when you hurt them like this, really you are hurting Christ. 13 I must not cause any other Christian, who is like a brother or a sister to me, to do anything wrong. So, I have decided this. I will never eat meat again, if my food causes another Christian to do anything wrong.

Chapter 9

Paul talks about himself as an example

1 You know that I am a free man. You know also that God has sent me to be a special worker and teacher on his behalf. You know that I have seen Jesus, our Lord. He chose me to work on his behalf. And you are the result of that work. You know that. 2 Other people may not accept me as a special worker whom the Lord has sent to them. But I am sure that you accept me like that. As a result of my work, you have become united with the Lord. And that fact shows that the Lord really sent me.

3 When people say bad things about me, this is my answer to them: 4 It is right that people give food and drink to me for my work. 5 It is right for each of us special workers to have a Christian wife. And it is right if we take our wives with us. We can take them with us to all the places where we go. The other men whom the Lord has sent to them, have their wives with them. So do the Lord's brothers and Peter. 6 Barnabas and I seem to be the only ones who must work with our hands. 7 Think about these examples, which are certainly true. A soldier never has to pay for his own food and clothes. A farmer will eat some of the fruit from the bushes that he has planted. A person who works with cows or sheep or goats will drink some of the milk from those animals.

8 I am not only saying what a man would say. The rules that God gave say the same thing. 9 God told Moses that he should write down these rules. And they say this:

'Your ox (strong male cow) works for you. It walks on your plants so that the seeds come out. Do not tie its mouth shut while it works. It is right for the ox to eat some of the seeds itself.'

God is not telling us only about oxen (cows) that work. 10 No, certainly he is speaking about us. God told Moses that he should write these words down. That was because God wanted to help us. A man ploughs the fields so that he can plant seeds. He is like us. The man who threshes the plants from the fields is like us too. Both of them hope to enjoy some of the food that has grown in the fields. 11 We have planted spiritual things in you. So, you can give to us the food and clothes that we need. That is not wrong. And that should not be too much for you to do.

12 Other people think that they should receive things like this from you. So, it is even more right for us to think like that. But we have not asked you to give anything to us. We do not want anyone to stop listening to the good news about Christ because of us. Instead, we would rather have any kind of trouble. So, we chose not to demand anything from you. 13 You know about the people who work in God's special house (the temple). They get their food there from that place. Also, you know about the people who work at the special table in God's house. On that table, they burn the gifts that other people bring to God. The people who work there at the table also get part of those gifts. 14 In the same way, the Lord has spoken about people who tell his good news. Those people need certain things so that they can live. Those people should receive those things as a result of their work. As a result of the good news, they should receive what they themselves need.

15 So, as a result of my work, I should receive everything that I need. That would be right. But I have not asked for anything. And I do not demand anything from you now, while I write to you. I would die, rather than demand anything for myself. This is the true reason that I can boast. And I do not want anyone to take it away. 16 I tell the good news to people. But I have no reason to boast because of that. No, because God has told me that I must tell it. If I did not tell the good news, I would be very sad. I would not be obeying God.

17 I was not the person who decided to tell the good news to people. If I myself had decided to do it, then I could demand money for this work. But it was God who decided. He has given a duty to me to tell the good news. 18 I do get something as a result of my work, but it is not money. Instead, it is this. It makes me very happy that I can tell the good news to people without any cost to them. It would be right if they did pay me for my work. But I do not ask them to pay, and that makes me very happy.

19 I am a free man. I am not anybody's slave. But I have made myself everybody's slave because I want to help as many people as possible. I want to bring them to Christ. 20 With Jews, I became like a Jew, because I wanted to bring Jews to Christ. The rules that God gave to Moses do not really have authority over me. But the Jews obey those rules. So, I chose to obey Moses' rules too. I became like the Jews, because I really wanted them to know Christ. 21 With people who are without Moses' rules, I became like someone without those rules too. (But this does not mean that I do not obey God's rules. No, I let Christ rule me.) I became like the people without Moses' rules because I really wanted them to know Christ. 22 With weak people, I became like someone who is weak too. I became weak like them because I really wanted them to know Christ. I have become all things to all people so that I could, by all possible ways, save some of them. 23 I do all these things because of the good news about Christ. I want other people, together with me, to enjoy the good things that the good news promises.

24 You should know that, in a race, all the runners run. But only one of them wins the race, and he receives the reward. You must run like that, to win the reward. 25 All people who do athletics make their own bodies practise. They want to make their bodies do what they want them to do. So they rule themselves in all things. They do this so that they will win a reward. But that reward continues for a short time only. But we rule ourselves in all things so that we will win God's reward. And that reward continues always.

26 So, I run in a straight line to the end of the race. Also, I fight like someone who hits well. I do not hit the air. 27 I rule my own body strongly and I make it my slave. I have taught other people about how to run this race. And I myself also want to win the reward from God. I do not want God to say to me: 'You yourself do not do the things that you teach. So, I am removing you from the race.'

Chapter 10

Stay away from false gods

1 My friends, I want you to remember something. Remember what happened to our grandfathers. They followed Moses many years ago. While they followed Moses, the cloud covered all of them. It covered them to keep them safe. And all of them walked through the Red Sea with dry feet. 2 God baptised all of them in the cloud and in the sea. He baptised them as those people who followed Moses. 3 All our grandfathers ate the same spiritual food. 4 All of them drank the same spiritual drink. They drank from the spiritual rock that went with them. And Christ was that rock. 5 But God was not happy with most of them. So, their dead bodies lay everywhere in that land, where there was no water.

6 These things that happened to our grandfathers are examples to us. Our grandfathers wanted bad things very much. But we must not be like them. We must not want bad things. 7 Nor must we worship false gods, as some of them did. The Old Testament says:

'The people sat down to eat and to drink. And they stood up to enjoy themselves. And they danced in front of their false god.'

8 Nor must we ever have sex with anyone who is not our own wife or husband. Some of our grandfathers did that, and so 23,000 of them died in one day. 9 Nor must we get angry with the Lord. We must not ask questions about what he is doing.

Some of our grandfathers did that. And so God sent snakes to bite them. And then they died. 10 Nor must you say that God is doing bad things. Some of our grandfathers spoke like that. And so God sent an angel to kill them.

11 All these things that happened to our grandfathers are examples to us. God caused people to write about these things so that we could learn from them. We ourselves must learn to be careful. We are alive today, but the end of all things will come soon. 12 Perhaps you think that you are standing strongly. But be very careful that you do not fall down! 13 Sometimes it will be difficult for you not to do something wrong. Or it will be difficult not to think something wrong. You will have difficulties like this. But they are the same kind of difficulties that every person has. God always does what he has promised to do. Remember this. He will not let any difficulty be too big for you. He does not want you to do anything wrong because of any difficulty. He will make you strong. He will show you a way out of the difficulty. So then you will be able to do what is right.

14 So then, my friends, whom I love, stay away from false gods. Do not worship them. 15 I am saying this to you because you are clever people. You can think clearly about things. You yourselves can decide about what I am saying. You can decide whether it is true. 16 At the Lord's Supper, we remember that Christ died on our behalf. We thank God when we drink the wine from the cup. We want to show that we belong to Christ by his blood. That is why we drink it. We break the bread and then we eat it. We want to show that we belong to Christ by his body. That is why we eat it. 17 We are many people, but all of us eat from one loaf of bread. All of us are one body because we eat from the same loaf.

18 Think about Israel's people. When they offer food to God in his special house, they are worshipping God. And all those people who eat any of that food are showing something about themselves. They are part of what is happening there in God's house. They are worshipping God too. 19 But I was speaking about false gods. I do not want you to think that false gods are important. I do not mean that you should think like that. The food that people offer to false gods is not important either. 20 But the people who offer food to false gods are worshipping demons (bad spirits). They are not worshipping God when they offer food to demons. I do not want you to be part of anything with demons. 21 You cannot drink from the Lord's cup and from the cup of demons. You cannot eat food from the Lord's Table and from the table of demons. 22 We will make the Lord angry if we do things like that. He will be angry because we should worship only him. And we are not stronger than the Lord is!

23 Some of you may say: 'We are free. We can do anything that we want to do!' But not everything is good for us to do. You may say: 'We are free to do anything!' But not everything helps to make us stronger. 24None of you should think only about the things that matter to you yourselves. Instead, each of you should think about what matters to other people.

25 You can eat anything that people sell in the meat market. You do not need to ask questions about whether that is right or wrong. 26 As it says in the Old Testament:

'The earth, and everything in it, is the Lord's.'

27 Perhaps people who do not believe Christ will ask you to eat a meal with them. And perhaps you will decide to go there. Then you should eat whatever food they give to you. You should not ask questions about the food. It does not matter where that food comes from. 28 But someone there may say to you: 'They offered this food to false gods.' If someone says that, do not eat the food. Do not eat it, because of the person who told you about it. He may not be sure that it is right to eat that food. And you would not want to cause a problem for that person. 29 It will not matter to you yourself. You are sure about what is right or wrong. But it will matter to a person who is not sure. Perhaps you will say: 'Why should another person decide what I ought to do?

30 I thank God for my food. So, when I eat that food, nobody else should say bad things about me. Nobody should say that it is wrong for me to eat it.' 31 But do everything to show how great and how good God is. Even when you eat and drink, do it like that. 32 Do not do anything that might cause difficulties for other people.

Do not cause difficulties either for Jews or for people who are not Jews. Do not cause difficulties for God's church (the people who belong to God). 33 Do what I do. All the time I try to do what everyone thinks is good. I am not doing that to help myself. No, but I am trying to help other people. I hope that God will save many people among them. That is why I live like this.

Chapter 11

1 Copy my example, because I copy Christ's example. I copy the example of how Christ lived.

Paul talks about men and women in Christian meetings

2 You make me very happy, because you always remember me. You remember everything that I taught you. And you are careful about what I taught you to do. 3 Now I want you to understand that Christ is the head (the leader) of every man. Also, the man is the head of the woman and God is the head of Christ.

4 So, when all of you meet together, you meet to worship God. When a man prays in your meeting, he should not cover his head. Or, when a man speaks a message from God in your meeting, he should not cover his head. If he covers his head, he is not showing the right thing about his leader. He is not showing that he respects Christ as his leader. 5 But when a woman prays in your meeting, she should cover her head. Or, when a woman speaks a message from God in your meeting, she should cover her head. If she does not cover her head, she is not showing the right thing about her leader. She is not showing that she respects the man as her leader. It looks very bad when someone cuts off all the hair from a woman's head. And it is bad in the same way when a woman does not cover her head in your meetings. 6 So, if a woman does not cover her head, she should cut off all her hair. But, if it is bad for a woman to cut off her hair, then she should cover her head.

7 A man should not cover his head, because God made the man like himself. God wanted to show how great and how good God himself is. That is why God made the man. But a woman shows how good and how beautiful people can be.

8 God made a man first. After that, God made a woman from that first man. God did not make the man from the woman. 9 Neither did God make the man to help the woman. No, God made the woman to help the man. 10 That is why a woman should cover her head. It shows that she has authority on her head. It shows that to the angels.

11 But we must live as the Lord's people. The women need the men. But the men need the women too. 12 It is true that God made the first woman from the first man. But it is also true that the mother of every man is a woman. But all things come from God.

13 Answer this question for yourselves: Perhaps a woman prays to God but she has not covered her head. Is that proper? 14 If a man has long hair, he should be ashamed. Everyone understands that. 15 But if a woman has long hair, it is beautiful. God gave long hair to her to cover her. 16 Some people may want to argue about this. But I have told you what we do. And all the churches (groups of Christians) do the same when they worship God.

The Lord's Supper

17 Now I must speak about something else. I am not happy about what happens at your meetings. Your meetings are more bad than good. 18 First, some people have told me that there are different groups among you. And these groups do not agree with each other when you meet together as God's people. I believe that some of this is true. 19 But perhaps these groups have some purpose. Perhaps you need to be in separate groups when you do not agree. Then, as a result, you can see clearly which people among you are right. You can see which people God is happy with.

20 You meet together so that you can worship the Lord. But you do not eat the Lord's Supper as you should eat it.

21 Each of you eats your own meal, and you do not wait for anyone else. So, as a result, one of you may be hungry, while another one drinks too much. 22 But certainly, you have your own homes where you can eat! You can drink there in your own homes too! You seem to think that God's church (the meeting of God's people) is not important. When you eat like this, you make the poor people feel ashamed. You cannot think that I will say good things about this. Certainly, I am not happy about these things that you do.

23 The Lord himself gave me this message, which I taught to you:

On the night when Judas sold the Lord Jesus to Jesus' enemies, Jesus had supper with his friends. Jesus took some bread at the supper. 24 He thanked God for the bread and then he broke it. He said: 'This is my body, which is for you. Eat this bread, so that you remember me.'

25 Then after supper, Jesus took a cup of wine. He said: 'Drink from this cup, because it is the new agreement. God has made this new agreement with my blood. Every time that you drink from the cup, do it to remember me.'

26 Every time that you eat bread together like this, you are telling about the Lord's death. You eat bread and you drink wine together. You are showing that he died on your behalf. You should continue to do this until he returns.

27 We want to show how great and how good the Lord is. So, we eat this bread and we drink from this cup together. But perhaps someone among us does not do it for that reason. Perhaps they do it in a way that they ought to be ashamed about. Then that person is doing something wrong. He should not be eating the Lord's Supper like that. He is doing something wrong against the Lord's body and the Lord's blood.

28 So, each of us needs to think very carefully about our own life. Then we will know whether everything is right. We need to be sure that everything in our life is right with God. We should do this first. Then we can eat this bread and we can drink from this cup. 29 Nobody should ever eat and drink at the Lord's Supper in a wrong way. Anyone who does that is not recognising the Lord's body. That person will cause God to be angry with them because they are doing something wrong. So, God will punish them. 30 That is why many of you are weak and sick. Some of you have died because of this. 31 But if we really think carefully about our own lives, we ourselves can recognise the wrong things. Then God will not need to decide about us because we are doing wrong things. He will not need to punish us. 32 The Lord decides to punish us now so that we will learn not to do wrong things any longer. At the end, he will punish all those people who do not believe Christ. But he does not want to punish us for always, together with them.

33 So, my Christian friends, you meet together to eat the Lord's Supper. Wait for each other when you meet like that. 34 If any of you are hungry, you should eat at home. Eat before you come. Then there will be nothing wrong. So then, when you meet together, the Lord will not need to punish you.

I will come to visit you. Then I will talk to you about all the other things.

Chapter 12

Gifts from God's Spirit

1 My friends, I want you to understand about those gifts that God's Spirit gives to us. 2 You know how you lived in past times. You lived as people who do not know Christ. Things made you, in whatever way, worship false gods that cannot speak. 3 I want you to understand me now. If God's Spirit is helping someone, they cannot say: 'Jesus is bad.' And, unless God's Spirit is helping them, nobody can really say: 'Jesus is Lord.'

4 There are different kinds of gifts. But it is the same Spirit who gives them. 5 We serve the Lord in many different ways, but all of us serve the same Lord. 6 Different people can do different things.

But the same God gives everything that we need to each of us. He makes us able to work for him as he wants us to do. 7 In each one of us, God shows in certain ways that his Spirit is present in us. He gives certain gifts to each of us so that we can help each other.

8 The Spirit gives to one person a message that causes people to understand something. And he gives to another person a message that causes people to know something. 9 The same Spirit causes another person to believe God strongly. And he gives to someone else gifts to make sick people well. 10 The same Spirit causes another person to do miracles. And he causes another person to speak messages from God. He causes someone else to recognise the differences between different spirits. He causes another person to speak in different kinds of languages. And the same Spirit causes someone else to explain what those languages mean. 11 It is the same Spirit who does all these things. He decides which gifts he will give to each person.

One body with many parts

12 Each person has only one body, but that body has many parts. All those different parts make only one body. And it is like that with Christ too. 13 God baptised all of us by his one Spirit into one body. It made no difference whether we were Jews or not. It made no difference whether we were slaves or free people. God gave his one Spirit to all of us to drink.

14 A person's body does not have only one part. No, it has many parts. 15 If the foot could speak, it might say: 'I am not a hand, so I do not belong to this body.' But what it says makes no difference. It is still a part of the body. 16 If the ear could speak, it might say: 'I am not an eye, so I do not belong to this body.' But what it says makes no difference. It does still belong to the body.

17 If the whole body was an eye, it could not hear. Or if the whole body was an ear, it could not know about different smells. 18 But God decided where he wanted to put each different part in our bodies.

19 A body is not a body if it has only one part. 20 But there are many parts, and there is one whole body. 21That is why the eye cannot say to the hand: 'I do not need you.' And the head cannot say to the feet: 'I do not need you.' 22 No. Even the parts of the body that seem to be weaker are really very necessary. 23 And we are most careful about the parts of our bodies that seem not to be worth very much. And we cover carefully those parts that we do not want people to see. 24 But we do not need to cover the beautiful parts of our bodies. God has put all the parts together in one body and some parts seem not to be worth very much. But God has made those parts more important. 25 So, the parts of the body do not quarrel. All the parts work together so that they help each other. 26 Then if one part of the body hurts, every other part hurts with it. Or perhaps people say that one part is doing well. Then every part is happy.

27 All of you are Christ's body. And each of you is a part of that body. 28 God has put different people in different places in his church (among his people). First, there are those people whom God sent to be special workers and leaders on his behalf. Second, there are those people whom God chose to speak his messages. Third, there are those people who are teachers. After that, there are people who do miracles. Then other people have gifts to make sick people well. There are those people who are able to help other people. There are those people who are guides to other people. And there are those people who can speak different kinds of languages.

29 God did not send all of you to be his special workers and leaders. Not all of you can speak his messages. Not all of you are teachers. Not all of you do miracles. 30 Not all of you have gifts to make sick people well. Not all of you can speak in different kinds of languages. Nor can all of you explain what they say in those languages. 31 But it is good if you really want the more important gifts.

Now I will show you a way that is better than any other way.

Chapter 13

The most important thing is to love

1 If I do not love, I am nothing. I may be able to speak different languages that people use. I may be able to speak languages that angels use. But that is worth nothing unless I love. It is only like someone who is making a loud noise. It is only like someone who is hitting a loud bell. 2 I may be able to speak messages from God. I may know all the facts and I may understand all the secret things. I may believe God enough so that I could move mountains. But I am nothing if I do not love. 3 I may give all the things that I have to poor people. I may even let other people burn my body so that I die. But that is worth nothing if I do not love.

4 If I love, I will be very patient. I will be kind. I will not want to be like other people so much that I get angry with them. I will not tell people how good I am. I will not think that I am better than other people. 5If I love, I will always be polite. I will think about what other people want. I will not think only about what I myself want. I will not get angry quickly. And I will not always be remembering the wrong things that other people have done to me. 6 If I love, I will not be happy about bad things. But instead, I will be happy about things that are right and true. 7 If I really love people, I will never stop loving them. It will not matter what happens. Whatever things may happen, I will still continue to live. If I love, then, during all things, I will still continue to believe. If I love, then, during all things, I will still continue to hope for good things. If I love then, during all things, I will still continue to be patient and strong.

8 If I love, that will never come to an end. But it is different for all those gifts that God has given to us. The time will come when we do not need them any longer. People will stop telling messages from God. They will stop speaking in special languages. The many things that people know will finish. 9 Now, at this time, we know only a small part of everything that is true. And we can tell other people only a small part of the messages that come from God. 10 Now, we have only a part of what God wants to give to us. But the time will come when he will give everything to us completely. Then we will not have only a part any longer.

11 When I was a child, I talked like a child. I thought like a child thinks. I understood only what a child understands. But now that I am a man, I have stopped being like a child. 12 Now we see things as if we were looking at them in a dark mirror. What we see is not clear. But the time will come when we will see everything clearly. Now we know some things, but then we will understand all things. God knows us and he understands us completely. And we will understand like that too, then.

13 So, there are three things that continue. We continue to believe God. We continue to hope for good things. We continue to love. But the greatest of these things is love.

Chapter 14

A language that people know is better than special languages

1 So, want to love more than you want anything else. Also, want very much to have gifts from God's Spirit. And want most to tell messages from God. Want that gift more than the other gifts. 2 Anyone who speaks in a special language speaks only to God. That person is not speaking to other people, because the other people do not understand him. The Spirit is causing him to speak about secret things, but other people do not understand. 3 But anyone who tells messages from God is speaking to other people. That person is helping other people to understand more, so that they become stronger. Also, he is helping people to be more sure and happier. He is helping them to be without trouble in their minds. 4 Anyone who speaks in a special language helps only himself. But a person who tells messages from God helps all the church (group of Christians) to be stronger.

5 I want all of you to speak in special languages. But even more, I want you to tell God's messages to people. Anyone who can tell messages from God is a very valuable person. That person is greater than someone who can speak in special languages. Anyone who speaks in special languages is less valuable to you.

That person is less valuable unless they themselves can explain their special words. Then everyone can understand those words, and so they will help the church (group of Christians).

6 My friends, if I come to visit you, perhaps I may speak in special languages to you. But that by itself will not help you. But I may tell you something that God has shown to me. Then, that will help you. I may tell you something that I know about God. Then, that will help you too. If I tell you a message from God, that will help you. Or if I teach you something, that will help you. 7 Think about music. The different kinds of instrument that we use to make music are not alive. We can use them to make clear, different sounds. If we do not use them like that, then nobody can recognise the music. 8 Soldiers will not prepare to fight the enemy unless they hear a clear sound from the trumpet.

9 It is the same for you. You must speak words that people can understand. Only then will your message be clear. If people do not understand your words, then you will only be speaking those words into the air.10 Certainly, there are many different languages in this world, and all of them mean something. 11 Perhaps a person will speak to me in a language that I do not know. But I will not understand what his words mean. So, I will be like a foreign person to him. And he will be like a foreign person to me also. 12 You yourselves really want the gifts that come from God's Spirit. That is good. But the best gifts are those that will help the church (group of Christians) to become stronger. So, want those gifts more than any other gifts.

13 So, anyone among you who speaks aloud in a special language should pray to God about it. Ask God to help you explain those words. 14 If I pray in a special language, only my spirit prays. But I do not use my mind while I pray like that. 15 So, the best way is this: I should pray both with my spirit and with my mind. Also, I should sing both with my spirit and with my mind. 16 If you thank God only with your spirit, other people cannot understand. They listen. But they do not understand what you are saying. So, they cannot agree with you and they cannot say 'Amen'. 17 You may be really thanking God, but your words do not help anyone else there.

18 I thank God that I speak in special languages more than all of you. 19 But when the church (group of Christians) meets together, I want you to understand my words. When we worship God together, I want you to learn more about him. So, I would rather say five words that you understand then. I would rather say five words like that than thousands of words in a special language.

20 My friends, do not think like children think. Babies do not know very much about bad things. So, with bad things, be like babies. But do not think and understand things like children. No, instead, think and understand like proper men and women. 21 It says in the Old Testament:

'I will cause foreign people to speak my messages to my people. These foreign people will speak to them in strange languages.

But my people will not listen to me, even if I speak to them by foreign people.' That is what the Lord said.

22 So then, the gift from God that causes people to speak in special languages is a sign. It shows something to people who do not believe God. But it is not a sign for those people who do believe God. Also, the other gift from God that causes people to speak his messages is a sign. It shows something to those people who believe God. But it is not a sign for those people who do not believe.

23 Think about when the whole church (group of Christians) meets together. Think about what might happen. All of you might be speaking in special languages, and then some strangers might come in. Those strangers might not know very much, or they might not believe God. Then certainly, they would say that you are crazy! 24 But if all of you are telling messages from God, it will be different. If a stranger comes in, then he will listen. He might not know very much, or he might not believe God. But still, he will understand that he is not right with God. The messages that all of you are telling will make him sure about that.

25 The messages from God will show every secret thought that the stranger thinks. And so, he will bend himself down and he will worship God. He will say with a loud voice: 'Certainly, God is here among you.'

How the church should worship properly

26 So, this is what you should do in your meetings, my friends. You meet together to worship God. And then, each person among you has something to bring. One of you can suggest a song that all of you can sing to God. Another person has something to teach you. Someone else has something that God has shown to him. Another person has words that he speaks aloud in a special language. So then someone else will explain what those words mean. Do all these things for one reason. Do them so that you help to make the church (group of Christians) stronger.

27 No more than two or three people should speak aloud in special languages. They should speak one person at a time. Then someone must explain what each person said. 28 But perhaps there is nobody there who can explain the special languages. Then, those people who can speak aloud in special languages must be quiet. They must speak only to themselves and to God.

29 Two or three people can tell messages from God. Then those of you who are listening must think carefully about each message. You should decide carefully whether each message is good. 30 Perhaps someone among you will receive a message from God during the meeting. Then, if another person is already telling a message at that time, that other person should stop. 31 Each person among you can tell a message from God, but you must speak one person at a time. Then everyone will learn something and it will help all of you to believe God more. 32 All of you who can tell messages from God have authority over your own spirits. 33 God does not want anyone to confuse his people. No, he wants us to do things properly. He wants us to be friends and to be without trouble among ourselves.

As in all the churches (groups) of God's people everywhere, 34 the women should be quiet in the meetings. They should not speak, because they should be under authority. That is what the Old Testament rules say also. 35 If a woman wants to ask about something, she should ask her husband at home. Women should be ashamed if they speak in the church. 36 Remember that the word of God certainly did not start from you! You are not the only people who have heard it, either.

37 Someone may think that he really tells messages from God well. He may think that he has received gifts from God's Spirit. So, that person should understand about what I am writing to you. He should recognise that it comes from the Lord himself. The Lord is telling his people that they must do it. 38 If that person refuses to recognise this, you should not believe his messages. Do not believe what he says.

39 So, my friends, you should really want to tell messages from God. And do not stop someone when they speak in a special language. 40 But you must do everything in a right and proper way.

Chapter 15

Christ certainly did become alive again after he died

1 Now, my friends, I want you to remember the good news that I taught you. You were happy to believe that message. And you still believe strongly that it is true. 2 You must continue to believe strongly that same good news. If you do, then it has saved you. If you do not, you have believed it for nothing.

3 I received the good news from Christ and then I told that same most important message to you. I told you that Christ died on our behalf. So then, as a result, God chooses not to remember all the wrong things that we have done. And the Old Testament told us that Christ would do this. 4 I told you that people buried Christ. Then God caused him to live again after three days. The Old Testament tells us about this too.

5 After that, Christ appeared to Peter. Then later he appeared to his 12 special workers that he sent to tell the good news. 6 And after that, he appeared to more than 500 believers at the same time. Most of those 500 people are still alive, but some of them have died. 7 Then Christ appeared to James. Later he appeared to all the special workers that he had sent to tell the good news.

8 After all these people had seen him, Christ appeared to me also. I was like someone who was born at the wrong time. 9 Christ sent other people to tell his message. And all of those other people are greater than I am. People should not really call me one of them, because I caused so much trouble for God's church (people). I hurt Christians and I killed them. 10 But God was very kind to me. He changed me. He has made me what I am today. And I have not wasted what he has done in me. No, because I have worked more than all the other people that Christ sent to tell his message. But it was not really I myself who did that work. No, it was God himself who made me able to do the work. 11 So then, all of us teach this same good news about Christ. I teach it. And all the other special workers that Christ sent teach it too. And this is the message that you have believed.

Dead people can live again in Christ

12 Our message is this: Christ died, but God raised him. God raised him, to make him alive again. So, some of you are wrong. You say that dead people do not live again. 13 But what you say cannot be true. It cannot be true, because then Christ would still be dead. You are saying, 'God did not raise him, to make him alive again.' 14 But if Christ is still dead, then our message to you is not true. There would be nothing for you to believe. 15 And even more important, we would have told you something false about God. We told you that God caused Christ to live again. But if dead people cannot live again, then that cannot be true. But it is true! 16 If God does not make dead people alive again, then Christ cannot be alive. But he is!

17 And if God did not make Christ alive again, then you have believed something false. There would be no reason for you to believe about Christ. God could not choose to forget all the wrong things that you have done. But he can! 18 Also, if God does not cause dead people to live again, then dead Christians would continue to be dead. They could not be alive with God. 19 And if Christ gives us a reason to hope during this life only, then we are the saddest people in the world! Then everybody should be more sorry for us than for any other people.

20 But it is true that God raised Christ. And he did make him alive again. Yes, Christ died. But he has become the first of all dead people to live again. 21 It was because of one man, Adam, that people died. And it is because of another man, Christ that people can rise. And people can live again. 22 All of us are in Adam's family, so all of us must die. But all people who are in Christ will live again. 23 It is like this: Christ died and then he became alive again. So, he shows us the way. When he returns, his people will live again too. 24 Then the end will come and Christ will destroy every other ruler and power and authority. Then he will give everything to God, the Father, and God will rule. 25 Christ must rule as king until God has put all enemies under Christ's feet (authority). 26 God will destroy the last enemy. And that enemy is death. 27 It says in the Old Testament:

> 'God has put all things under his feet (authority).'

But it is clear that the words 'all things' do not include God himself. No, because it is God who put all things under Christ's authority. 28 When God has put all things under Christ's authority, then Christ, the Son, will put himself under God's authority. So then God will be everything to everyone.

29 Some Christians have died before anyone could baptise them. Some of you have let people baptise you on their behalf. But if dead people do not live again, there is no reason to baptise anyone on their behalf.

30 Also, think about us! All the time we are in danger. 31 Christian friends, I say strongly to you that I die every day! That is as true as the fact that I am very happy because of you. It is a great thing that all of us are united with Christ Jesus our Lord. 32 At Ephesus city, I fought as a man fights wild animals. But that would be worth nothing if dead people do not live again. If dead people do not live again, then we could say:

> 'Tomorrow we will die.
>
> So let us eat and drink.'

33 Do not believe false words. But these words are true:

> 'Do not have friends who are bad. They will make you do the bad things that they do.'

34 Start thinking properly! Do what is right! Stop doing wrong things! Some of you do not really know God. So, I am saying all this to make you feel ashamed about that.

New bodies

35 One of you may ask: 'How does God raise dead people, to make them alive again? What kind of body will they have?' 36 You are a fool to ask those questions! When you plant a seed in the ground, it has to die first. It does not become alive again, unless it dies first. Then it can become alive again and grow into a new plant. 37 You put just a seed into the ground. It might be wheat or it might be another kind of seed. But you do not put into the ground the body of the plant that the seed will become. 38 But God makes that seed become a plant. He gives to it the special body that he has chosen for it. To each kind of seed, God gives its own body.

39 All things that are alive are not the same. They have different kinds of bodies. People have one kind of body. Animals have another, different kind of body. Birds have another kind of body and fish have another kind.

40 Also, there are bodies in the sky and there are bodies here on the earth. The bodies in the sky are beautiful. But they are beautiful in a different way from the bodies on the earth. 41 The sun is beautiful. The moon is beautiful also, but it is different from the sun. The stars are beautiful too, but again they are different from the sun and the moon. Also, among the stars, one star is brighter than another star.

42 So, when God makes a dead person alive again, it will be like this. The dead person's human body, which we bury in the ground, had to die. But when God makes it alive again, it will never die. 43 At the time that we bury a body, it is not beautiful any longer. It is weak. When God makes it alive again, that body will be beautiful and strong. 44 What we bury in the ground is only a human body. What God makes alive again is a spiritual body. There is a human body, so there has to be a spiritual body also.

45 It says in the Old Testament:

> 'The first man, Adam, became a human person who was alive.'

But the last Adam (Christ) is the spirit who makes people live.

46 The spiritual body does not come first. No, what is human comes first. Then, after that, what is spiritual comes. 47 God made the first man (Adam) out of the ground. But the second Adam came from heaven. 48 People who belong to the earth are like the first man. They are like the man who came from the ground. But people who belong to heaven are different. They are like the man who came from heaven.

49 Our human bodies are like the first man that God made out of the ground. But our spiritual bodies will be like the man who came from heaven. 50 I tell you this, Christian friends: Our human bodies cannot live always with God, in the place where he rules. The human body has to die. It cannot receive something that will continue always.

51 Listen to me while I tell you a secret. Not all of us will die, but God will change all of us. 52 It will happen when the last trumpet makes a sound. He will change us in a moment of time. There will not even be enough time to close our eyes, while he is changing us. When that trumpet makes its sound, God will make the dead people alive again. He will give them bodies that will never die. And he will change all of us.

53 All things that become old and weak must change. They must change into things that cannot become old and weak. Our bodies, that have to die, must change. They must become bodies that cannot die. 54 Our human bodies have to die. But they will become bodies that cannot die. And before this happens, God has told us about it in the Old Testament. It says:

> 'I have destroyed death. I have won completely!'

When he changes us, we will know this. We will know that it is true.

55 God says to believers:

> 'When you believers die, that is not the end.
>
> There is nothing to hurt you at that time.'

56 All of us have been wrong because we have not obeyed God's rules. So, without Jesus, we would be afraid to die, because then God would have to punish us. 57 But God causes us to win by our Lord Jesus Christ. So, we thank God! And we are not afraid to die.

58 So, my friends, that I love, continue to be strong. Continue holding on to God. Do not let anything move you from your place.

Continue always to work on the Lord's behalf. Work very much for him. Everything that you do for him will have good results. It will not be a waste of time. You know that this is true.

Chapter 16

The gift of money for God's people

1 Now, I want to speak about the money that you will give to God's people at Jerusalem. I told the churches (groups of Christians) in Galatia what they must do about that. You should do the same. 2 On the first day of every week, each of you should put some of your money in a special place. You should keep this money separate and safe. Then, when I come to you, your gift of money will be ready. Some of you have more money than other people, so you can give more. 3 Then you should choose people from your group who will take your gift to Jerusalem. I will visit you. And then, I will send those people to Jerusalem with letters from me. Those letters will tell the Christians at Jerusalem who is bringing your gift. 4 I may go myself also, if that seems the right thing for me to do. Then they can travel with me.

5 But I must go to Macedonia first. After I have travelled through Macedonia, then I will come to you. 6Perhaps I could remain with you for some time then. I may even stay for the whole winter.

Then you can help me to continue my journey to the next place. I am not sure yet where that may be. 7 I want to stay with you for more than a short time, so I will not come immediately. If the Lord says 'Yes' to this idea, then I hope to remain with you for many days. 8 But now, I will remain here at Ephesus city until Pentecost. 9 God has given me the chance to do a great and powerful work for him here. But there are many enemies here too.

Paul finishes his letter

10 If Timothy comes to you, then make him feel completely happy there with you. He is doing the Lord's work, the same as I am doing the Lord's work. 11 So, nobody should think that Timothy is not important. You must help him to be free from trouble. Then, send him on his way, so that he can return to me. I am waiting for him, with the other Christian friends, to return here.

12 Now I want to talk about our friend Apollos. I asked him very seriously to go, with the other Christians, so that he could visit you. But he does not think that this

13 Be awake. Watch what is happening. Never stop believing God. Be brave and strong. 14 Do everything because you love God and other people.

15 You know about Stephanas and his family. They were the first people in Achaia to become Christians. And they have given themselves to be servants of God's people always. So, my friends, I ask you this strongly. 16 I ask you to let people like these be your leaders. Also, be ready to obey everyone else who helps with the same work. 17 I was very happy when Stephanas, Fortunatus and Achaicus arrived here. You could not help me because you were far away. But they have given to me what you could not give. 18They have made my spirit strong and happy, the same as they made you strong and happy. People who are like that are very valuable. You ought to show them that you know that.

19 The churches (groups of Christians) here in Asia say 'Hello' to you. Aquila and Priscilla, and the group that meets in their house, want very much to say 'Hello' to you. They love you because you are also the Lord's people. 20 All the Christians here say 'Hello' to you. When you meet each other, kiss each other like brothers and sisters.

21 I myself am writing this now with my own hand: Hello from Paul. 22 If any of you do not really love the Lord, he will punish you. Come, Lord, we are waiting for you! 23 I ask the Lord Jesus Christ to be kind to all of you. 24 I love all of you, because Christ Jesus makes us join together.

When I am Weak, then I am Strong

2 Corinthians

About 2 Corinthians

Paul was working in Macedonia, which was north from the country called Greece now. Corinth was a city in Achaia (the south part of Greece). We think that Paul wrote this letter about AD 55. That was about 25 years after Jesus died. Something was wrong among the Christians at Corinth. Some people there had been doing very wrong things (see 2:5 and 12:21). Also, some of the Christians there had been listening to false teachers (see 11:4). Some of the Christians at Corinth were saying that Paul was not really Christ's servant (see 13:3).

Paul had written to the people at Corinth before and he had visited there twice. Before he wrote this letter, Paul had met his friend Titus again. Titus had just returned from a visit to the Christians at Corinth, and he told Paul good news about them. (See 7:5-7.) So, Paul wrote this letter to say how happy he was to hear this good news. He explains also that he really is working on Christ's behalf. And he says that he will visit Corinth again soon. He does not want to be angry with the Christians there. But he will be angry with anyone who is still not ready to put right any wrong things.

Chapter 1

1 This letter is from me, Paul, and from our friend Timothy, who is like a brother to us. God chose me to be a special worker and teacher on behalf of Christ Jesus. He sent me to tell people about Christ. I am sending this letter to you believers, who are God's church in Corinth city. I am sending it also to all of God's people who are in Achaia. 2 I pray that God, our Father, and the Lord Jesus Christ will continue to be very kind to you. I pray that they will cause you to be without trouble deep inside yourselves.

God himself comforts us

3 We thank God, the Father of our Lord Jesus Christ, because he is so good to us. He is such a very, very kind Father, and only he himself can really comfort us. 4 He comforts us during all things that cause trouble and pain for us. So then, as a result, we ourselves can comfort other people who have any kind of trouble or pain. We can comfort them because God himself has comforted us. 5 We have very much trouble and pain, as Christ did. We have very much trouble and pain because we are his. But, in the same way, we know also how very much Christ comforts us.

6 If we are sad because of troubles and pain, that helps you. It helps to comfort you, and it helps to save you. Or, if God comforts us, that helps to comfort you also. It helps you to be patient and strong during the same kind of troubles and pain as we have. 7 So, we continue to be completely sure about you. You have the same troubles and pain as we have. And, in the same way also, God will comfort you as he comforts us. We know this.

8 Friends, we want you to know about the great trouble that we had in Asia. It was very, very difficult, like a heavy weight that was much too heavy for us to carry. We ourselves were not strong enough to carry it. We thought that we were going to die.

9 Deep inside ourselves, we thought that we would certainly die. But these things happened so that we would learn not to believe in ourselves. No, but instead, we would learn to believe God, who causes dead people to live again. We would learn to believe that God would certainly help us. 10 And God did save us from such great danger that would have killed us. And he will save us. We believe strongly that he will continue to save us at future times. 11 Also, you help us because you join together to pray for us. Many people pray for us. And God will answer what they pray. He will be good to us. And so, many people will thank him on our behalf.

Paul explains why he did not visit Corinth earlier

12 We have lived in this world as God's people should live. We have been careful to be honest and good with everyone. And we have been like that very much with you. We ourselves are sure that this is true. And we are very happy about it. We have not tried to be clever as human people can be clever. But instead, we have done only what God has made us able to do. 13 We are writing to you only things that you yourselves can read and understand. And I hope that you will understand completely.

14 You do not understand us completely yet. But I hope that you will understand. On the day when our Lord Jesus will return, you will be very happy because of us. You will be as happy because of us as we will be happy because of you. I hope that you will understand this completely.

15-16 And because I was so sure about you, I decided to visit you first. I decided to visit you on my way to Macedonia. And then I would visit you again on my way back from Macedonia. So then you would see me twice and I could help you twice. And then you could help to send me on my journey to Judea. 17 When I decided this, I was serious about it. I do not decide to do things only because I myself want to do them. I am not ready to say 'Yes' and 'No' at the same time, like someone who does not know God.

18 As certainly as God is true, our message to you was not 'Yes' and 'No'. 19 Silas, Timothy and I told you about Jesus Christ, who is God's Son. He is not someone who is 'Yes' and 'No'. Instead, by him God was and is saying 'Yes' to us.

20 Everything that God has promised becomes 'Yes' because of Christ. That is why, by Christ, we can thank God. By him, we can agree that all God's promises are true. And we can say how very great and good God is.

21 God causes both us and you to be sure and strong because we are united with Christ. It is God himself who does this. And he has chosen us to be his own special servants. 22 God has also put his mark on us, to show that we are his. He has given his Spirit to us, to live deep inside us. And his Spirit causes us to be sure about what we will receive from God.

23 I decided not to come to Corinth at that time, for this reason. It was because I wanted to be kind to you. I did not want to be angry with you. God knows that this is true! 24 We are not trying to be like masters. Masters would tell you what to believe about everything. We are not trying to have authority over you like that. We know that you believed the right things. And you are strong because you believe those things. But instead, we are working with you so that you will be happy.

Chapter 2

1 So, I thought about what would be the best thing to do. And I decided not to visit you again at that time, because I did not want to make you sad. 2 If I make you sad, there will be nobody to make me happy. Only you, the people that I had made sad, could make me happy. 3 That is why I wrote that letter to you. I did not want you to make me sad when I visited you. But instead, you ought to make me happy. I felt sure about all of you. If I was happy, then all of you would be happy too. I was sure about that.

4 When I wrote that letter, I was very, very sad. I had very much trouble and pain deep inside myself, and I cried very much. I did not want to make you sad. Instead, I wanted you to know how very, very much I love you.

Forgive the person who did wrong things

5 Someone has done things that have made other people sad. And that person has made not only me sad. No, but really he has made all of you sad too. I do not want to say too much about the wrong things that he did. 6 Most of you have punished him, and that is enough for him.

7 Now, instead, you ought to forgive him and you ought to comfort him. So then, as a result, he will not become so very sad that he stops hoping to get better. 8 So, I ask you strongly to show him that you really do love him. 9 It was for this reason that I wrote to you. I wanted to know what you would do. I wanted to know whether you would obey me always. 10 When you forgive somebody for anything, I forgive that person also. Anything that I have forgiven, I have forgiven because of you, with Christ present. 11 I have done that so that Satan has no chance to be cleverer than us. We know very well the ways by which he tries to beat us.

God makes us winners in Christ

12 When I arrived at Troas city to tell the good news about Christ, the way was open for me. I discovered that the Lord had opened the way for my work there. 13 But in my spirit I could not rest, because I could not find my friend Titus. So, I said goodbye to the people there and I travelled on to Macedonia.

14 But I thank God, who leads us always as winners. He makes us winners because we are united with Christ. And by us, God shows people everywhere about Christ. In every place, like a lovely smell that comes to them, people come to know Christ. 15 Because, to God, we ourselves are the lovely smell that brings Christ. We are like that among those people that God is saving. And we are like it among those people who are dying. They are dying because they are far from God. 16 To the people that God is saving, we are like a lovely smell. We are like a lovely smell that causes them to live. To the people who are dying, far from God, we are like a bad smell from a dead thing. That bad smell leads them to death.

No person could think that he himself was able enough to do this work! 17 But we are not like so many other people, who sell God's message for money. No, God himself has sent us. And God sees what we are doing. So, we speak honestly because we really want people to know God's message. We speak as those who are united with Christ.

Chapter 3

God's new agreement is much greater than the old one

1 We are not trying again to make you think good things about us. We do not need letters, either to you or from you, that say good things about us. Some other people need letters like that, but we do not need them. 2 You yourselves are our letter that God has written deep inside us. Everybody can know and can read this letter. 3 It is clear that you are a letter from Christ. And he has given this letter to us to deliver. Nobody wrote this letter with a pen. Instead, the Spirit of God, who is alive, wrote it deep inside us. He did not write it on flat pieces of stone. Instead, he wrote it deep inside us.

4 We say these things only because, by Christ, we are sure about our work. We are sure that God makes us able to do it. 5 We are not able by ourselves even to think that we could do this work. No, but it is God who makes us able to do it. 6 God has made us able to be his servants, who tell people about his new agreement. This new agreement is not only rules. Rules tell people what to do. But this new agreement is not like that. No, instead it is something that happens by God's Spirit. Rules like that kill. But the Spirit causes us to live.

7 Moses wrote down on stones the words of the old agreement that caused people to die. But that agreement was still great and good, because it came from God. And Moses' face shone so brightly with God's light that Israel's people could not continue to look at it. The light on his face was becoming less bright, but still Israel's people could not look at it. That old agreement came by words that someone wrote on stones. 8 So certainly, the new agreement, which comes by God's Spirit, will be even greater and better. 9 As a result of the old agreement, God had to punish people. But still, that agreement was great and good. So, how very much greater and better must the new agreement be, that makes people right with God!

10 The old agreement was great and good once. But the new agreement is so very, very much greater and better than the old one. So, as a result, the old agreement does not seem to be anything now.

11 The old agreement, that had to come to an end, was great and good. So, how much greater and better must the new agreement be, that will continue always!

12 So, because we hope certainly for such great things, we speak bravely. 13 We are not like Moses. He covered his face with a cloth because the light from God was becoming less bright. So then Israel's people could not see that the light was coming to an end.

14 But those people could not understand anyway. Even until this day, they cannot understand the old agreement when they read it. They are like people who have a cloth over their minds. The cloth is still there because only Christ can remove it. He removes it when a person is united with him. 15 Even today, when they read Moses' rules, a cloth still covers their minds. 16 But when a person turns to the Lord, then the Lord takes the cloth away.

17 The Lord is the Spirit. And where the Lord's Spirit is, there people are free. 18 But all of us are like people who have no cloth over our faces. Like mirrors, we shine with God's bright light. And he is changing us so that we become more and more like him. We become brighter and brighter as the Lord's Spirit changes us.

Chapter 4

The good news brings light

1 God has given this work to us because he is so very kind. So, we do not let ourselves become sad about it.2 We have turned away completely from secret things that people should be ashamed to do. We refuse to do anything that is not honest. We refuse to say anything that is not true. We do not change God's message, to include things that are not really true. God is watching us. And we tell clearly only what is true. So, everyone should know that we are honest and good.

3 Not everyone can understand the good news that we tell. People who are dying because they are far from God cannot understand it. 4 Those people do not believe it, because the god of this world has kept their minds in the dark. He stops them from seeing the light. Christ is completely like God. And that light shines from the good news about how great Christ is.

5 We tell people about Christ Jesus because we want them to know him as Lord. We do not want anyone to think that we ourselves are Lord. We say only that we ourselves are your servants because of Jesus. 6God said: 'Let light shine in the dark.' And the same God has caused his light to shine deep inside us. He has given light to us because he has caused us to know him. He has caused us to know how great and good he is. And this light is in Christ's face. In Christ, we see how great and good God is.

We are like weak pots that contain something very valuable and powerful from God

7 But we, who have this very valuable gift in us, are quite like weak clay pots. And, as a result, it is clear that this very great power is from God, and not from ourselves. 8 We have every kind of bad trouble and pain, but those things do not beat us. Sometimes we do not understand what to do, but we never stop believing God. 9 We have many enemies, but we are never completely alone. People hurt us badly, but they never destroy us. 10 We carry Jesus' death in our bodies always. And so, we can show also in our bodies that Jesus is alive. 11 Yes, God is always sending us, who are alive, to death because of Jesus. So then, as a result, people can see in our weak, human bodies that Jesus is alive. 12 So, death is working in us but you are becoming more and more alive.

13 It says in the Old Testament: 'I believed, and so I spoke.' **[Psalm 116:10]** And we believe by the same Spirit. So, we also speak because we believe. 14 God, who raised the Lord Jesus, to become alive again after his death, will also raise us with Jesus. God will bring us, together with you, to the place where he is. We know that.

15 All this is helping you. God is showing to more and more people how very, very kind he is. And so, people will thank God more and more. They will show how very great and good God is.

16 That is why we do not let ourselves become sad about our work. The person that we are on the outside is getting older and less able. But the person that we are on the inside is becoming newer day by day. 17 We have these little troubles that continue only during this time now. But these troubles are preparing something much, much greater for us, which will continue always. As a result of them, we will enjoy something much better always with God, who is so great and so good.

18 So, we do not look at the things that we can see. But instead, we look at the things that we cannot see. The things that we can see are there for only a short time. But the things that we cannot see continue always.

Chapter 5

God has prepared a new body for us

1 Our body that we live in here on earth is like a tent. It is like a tent that God will tear down one day. But we have a building that God has made for us to live in. No human person made that house. It will always be there, in heaven. We know that. 2 Now, while we are in our body here, we cry inside ourselves. We want to put our house from heaven over us, like someone puts on new clothes. We want that very much. 3 We want to put on that new house, and then we will never be like people without clothes. 4 While we still live in our body here on earth, as in a tent, we cry inside ourselves. We do not really want to take off our old body. But instead, we want to put our new body over us, like new clothes. So then our new body, that will live always, will completely take the place of our old body. It will take the place of our old body, which had to die. 5 God is the one who has prepared us for this change. He has prepared us because he has given his Spirit to us. And his Spirit causes us to know that this change will certainly happen.

6 So, we are happy and brave because we are always sure. While we are at home in this body, we are away from the Lord. We know that.

7 We know it because we believe God. We believe him, and so we obey him. We do not live by the things that we can see. 8 I say again that we are always sure. It would be better if we could leave our home in this body. That is what we think. So then, we could be at home with the Lord. 9But, more than anything else, we want to make God happy. We want to do that, whether we are at home in our body here or away from it. 10 Because all of us must stand in front of Christ when he decides about us. He will decide about the things that we have done during our lives. So then, each person will receive from God as a result of the things that they have done. What each person has done while they lived in the body here may be either good or bad. And each person will receive from God what they ought to have as a result of those things.

God makes us new people in Christ

11 We know what it means to be afraid of the Lord. And so, because of this, we try to tell other people, so that they turn to him. But God himself knows what we really are. And I hope that, deep inside yourselves, you know us clearly also. 12 We are not trying again to make you think great things about us. No, but instead we want to give you the chance to show that you are happy about us. So then you will be able to answer those people who look at the outside of a person. To those people, the important thing is what somebody is like on the outside. But they do not think about what a person is like on the inside. 13 If we seem crazy, that is because we are God's. Or, if we are serious, and not crazy, that is to help you.

14 We want to obey only Christ, because he loves us so very much. And we are completely sure that one man died on behalf of all people. This means that all people died with him. 15 He died on behalf of all people, so that they should not live for themselves any more. But instead, all those people who live should live for him. They should live for him, who died on their behalf. He died and then he rose, to live again.

16 So, from now on, we do not know anyone only because they are human like us. We have even known Christ as a human person, but we do not know him like that any more. 17 When anyone is united with Christ, they become a new person. God makes them new. Old things have gone. See, they have become new! 18 All this is the work of God, who, because of Christ, has stopped being angry with us. By Christ, we have become God's friends instead of his enemies. And he wants us to bring other people to be his friends also. This is the job that he has given to us.

19 God wants us to tell people that, by Christ, he was bringing the world to himself. He was bringing all people in the world back to himself, to be his friends. God was not continuing to remember all the wrong things that people do. This is the message that God has given to us. He wants us to tell people that he has brought them back to himself.

20 So, we are speaking on behalf of Christ. It is quite as if God himself is asking you strongly by us. On behalf of Christ, we are asking you very strongly to become God's friends. 21 Christ never thought or did any wrong things. But God punished Christ as if, like us, he was wrong. God punished him on our behalf. So then, as a result, we become right with God when we are united with Christ.

Chapter 6

1 So we, who work together with God, ask you strongly to be careful. God is very good to us because he is so very kind. But be careful not to waste the good things that God has done for you. 2 In the Old Testament God says:

'I listened to you at the time when I was ready to be kind.

I helped you on the day when I was ready to save you.'

Listen! Now is the time when God is ready to be kind! Now is the day when he is ready to save you!

3 We do nothing that might cause anyone to be angry or sad because of us. We do not want anyone to think bad things about our work. 4 Instead, we want to show, by everything, that we are God's servants. We show that because we are very patient and brave during bad troubles and pain. Sometimes we have many difficulties and so we are very sad. 5 Sometimes people hit us. Sometimes they put us in prison. Sometimes people attack us. Sometimes we work very, very much. Sometimes we stay awake at night to watch. Sometimes we have no food. 6 But still we show that we are God's servants. We are good and clean inside ourselves and we have no bad purposes. We know what is true. We are patient and kind. We have God's Spirit, who is completely good. And we really love God and other people.

7 We speak only words that are true. We have God's power in us. We are right with God, and that makes us strong to fight on his behalf. It makes us strong, like people who fight with both their right hand and their left hand. 8 Sometimes people think that we are great and important. And sometimes they think that we are worth nothing. Sometimes people say bad things about us and sometimes they say good things. Sometimes people think that we are not honest about ourselves. But we are always honest and we say only true things. 9 People say that they do not know us. But really, everybody knows what we are. People think that we are dying. But see, we are still alive! People punish us but they do not kill us. 10 We seem sad, but we are always happy really. We seem poor, but we make many people rich. We seem to have nothing, but really we have everything.

11 Our friends at Corinth, we have spoken to you very honestly. We have hidden nothing from you. You know everything that we feel. 12 We have done nothing to stop you from being our friends that we know well. No, but you yourselves have not been completely honest with us. It is you yourselves who have not told us everything. 13 I am speaking to you as I would speak to my own children. Be fair to us! Be completely honest with us also. Tell us everything that you feel.

God's people are separate from people who do not believe God

14 Do not try to be united with people who do not believe Christ. God has made you right with himself. So, you cannot work together with people who are not right with him. Light and dark are completely different. 15 Christ and the Devil cannot agree. People who believe Christ have nothing in common with other people. Christ's people have nothing in common with people who do not believe Christ. 16 God's house has nothing in common with false gods. And we are the house of the God who is alive. As God has said:

'I will live with them and I will be among them.

I will be their God and they will be my people.'

17 And so, the Lord says:

'Come out from among them and be separate.

Touch nothing that is not good and clean.

And I will accept you.'

18 'I will be a Father to you,

and you will be my sons and my daughters.

This is what the Lord with all authority says.'

Chapter 7

1 So, my friends, that I love, God has promised these things to us. And so we must keep ourselves clean from everything that makes our bodies or our spirits dirty. We must remember always how very great and powerful God is. And, as a result, we should become more and more completely as God wants his own people to be.

2 Make room deep inside yourselves to love us. We have done nothing wrong to anyone. We have not hurt anyone. We have not used anyone for any wrong purposes of our own. 3 I am not saying this to show that you have done anything wrong. As I have told you before, you are very special to us. We love you so very much that, deep inside ourselves, you are always with us. And so, we live or die with you. 4 I am very sure about you. I am very happy because of you. God has comforted me very much. Even in all our troubles, I am still very, very happy.

5 When we arrived in Macedonia, our bodies did not rest at all. We had troubles everywhere. On the outside, other people were quarrelling with us. On the inside, we were afraid. 6 But God comforts people who are feeling sad and weak. And God comforted us because Titus arrived to be with us. 7 God comforted us not only because Titus came to us. He comforted us even more by what Titus told us about you. Titus said that you had comforted him. He told us how very much you want to see me. He told us how very sorry you are. He told us also how ready you are to help me. And so, I am even happier now.

8 But even if I made you sad by my letter, I am not sorry about that. I was sorry about it before. I saw that my letter made you sad for a short time. 9 But now I am happy, not because my letter made you sad. No, instead I am happy because it made you sad enough to turn away from wrong things. You became sad as God wanted you to be sad. So, as a result, we did not really hurt you or cause you loss in any way by our letter. 10 People need to become sad in the way that God wants. When they are sad like that, it causes them to turn away from wrong things. It causes them to turn to God, who saves them. And they will never be sorry that they did that! But this world makes people sad only because they have troubles or pain. It does not make them sad in a way that leads them to God. When the world makes people sad like that, it only causes them to die.

11 You became sad as God wanted you to be sad. And see what good results that has brought! It has made you think so seriously and so carefully. It has made you want so much to show that you have turned away from wrong things. It has made you so angry, so afraid, and so ready to change. It has made you want so very much to do better things. It has made you want to punish someone who was doing wrong things. You have shown that you yourselves have done everything possible to make things right.

12 I did not write that letter to you because of the person who had done something wrong. I did not write it to help that person. Neither did I write it to help the person that somebody had done something wrong to. Instead, I wrote the letter so that you could understand something. I wanted you to understand clearly how very much you yourselves love us. And God knows how much you love us. 13 That is what has comforted us.

Yes, that comforted us. And Titus made us even happier, because he himself was so happy. Titus was happy because all of you had helped him to feel stronger and braver. 14 I did say good things about you to Titus, and you have not disappointed me. We have always spoken only true things to you. And, in the same way, when we said good things about you to Titus, those things were true also. It has become clear that those things are true. 15 And Titus loves you even more when he thinks about you. He remembers how ready all of you were to obey. You were happy that he had come to visit you. But you were also very afraid. 16 I am happy because I am sure about you. I am completely sure that you will do only what is good and right.

Chapter 8

Paul wants the Christians at Corinth to give money for the poor people at Jerusalem

1 Friends, we want you to know how very good God has been to the groups of believers in Macedonia. 2 They have had very bad troubles. But those troubles caused them to show how much they really believed God. They were so very, very happy, and so they gave a lot of money to help other people. They themselves were very poor, but still they gave so much money. 3 I tell you this, which is certainly true. They gave as much money as they were able to give. They even gave more than they could. They themselves wanted to give that much money. 4 They asked us very strongly to receive their gift of money. They wanted very much to do something that would help God's people. 5 They did more than we had even hoped for! They gave themselves first to the Lord, and then they gave themselves to us also. They did that because God wanted them to do it.

6 So, because of this, we asked Titus if he would continue to help you. He is the person who started this good work. So, he will help you to finish it. He will help you to be kind in this way. 7 You have so very much of everything. You believe God very much. You speak well and you understand a lot. You want very much to help, and you love us. So, be ready also to give plenty so that you can be good and kind in this way.

8 I am not telling you that you must do this. But I have told you how very much other groups of believers want to help. And this is a way to show how much you really love other people. 9 You know how very, very kind our Lord Jesus Christ is. He was rich, but he made himself poor to help you. So then, because he became poor, as a result you could become rich.

10 Last year, you were the first people who wanted to give. And you were the first to begin that work. So, the best thing for you to do is to finish that work. That is what I think. 11 Now finish the work. When you started, you wanted very much to do it. Now be as ready to finish it. Give what you can give. 12 If you really want to give, then God will accept your gift. He will not want you to give more than you are able to give. But he will be happy because you have given. You have given as much as you can give.

13 You will make other people's lives easier because of your gift. But my purpose is not that your lives should become more difficult as a result. No, instead I want things to be equal. 14 At this time now, you yourselves have plenty. So, you should give to those people who do not have enough. Then, at a future time when they have plenty, they will be able to give to you. They will be able to help you when you do not have enough. So then, they will help you in the same way as you helped them. 15 As it says in the Old Testament:

'The person who brought back a lot did not have too much.

And the person who brought back a small amount still had enough.'

Paul is sending Titus and other Christian men to Corinth

16 God has caused Titus to love you so much that he really wants to help you. So, we thank God because of this. Titus wants to help you as much as we ourselves want to help you. 17 He was so happy when we asked him to help you. He already wanted so much to help you that he himself had decided to visit you. 18 We are sending another man, who is a believer like us, with Titus. All the groups of believers say very good things about this other man. He is famous among them because he tells the good news about Christ so very well. 19 And that is not everything. Also, the groups of believers have chosen this man to travel with us. They wanted him to help us when we take your gifts. They wanted him to help with this work that we do for God. We are doing it to show how great and good God is. We are doing it also because we want to help people.

20 We are being very careful about this large gift of money that we will take to people. We do not want anyone to say that we have done anything wrong. We want everyone to see that we are honest.

21 We want to do only what is right. We want the Lord to see that we are doing the right thing. Also, we want people to see that we are doing the right thing.

22 We are sending another man also, with these men. Many times, in many ways, this man has shown certainly that he wants very much to help. And now that he is so very sure about you, he wants to help even more. 23 If anyone asks about Titus, he works with me. He works together with me, to help you. If anyone asks about the other men, they are coming on behalf of the groups of believers. And those men are good servants of Christ. They show how great and good Christ is. 24 So, show these men certainly that you love them. Then all the groups of believers will be sure about you. They will be sure that we are right to say good things about you.

Chapter 9

1 I do not need to write to you about the money that we are sending to help God's people. 2 I know how much you want to help. I say good things about you to the people in Macedonia. I tell them that you people in Achaia have been ready to help since last year. And because you are so ready to help, most of them now want very much to help also. 3 But still, I am sending these men, who are believers like us. I am sending them to you so that you will really be ready to give your money. I have told people that you were ready. And now everyone will know that I spoke true words.

4 Perhaps some people from Macedonia might come with me. And I would not want them to find that you are not ready to help. Then I would be ashamed that I had been sure about you. And I am saying nothing about how ashamed you yourselves would be! 5 So, I thought that I must ask these men to visit you first. They will visit you before I myself come. They will help you to prepare the gift that you promised. Then it will be ready when I arrive. So, everyone will know that you really want to give this gift. You are not giving it because anyone is making you give it. Everyone will know that.

It is good to give plenty

6 Remember this: A farmer who plants only a few seeds will not get much as a result. But a farmer who plants plenty of seeds will bring plenty from his field as a result. 7 Each person should give as much as he himself has decided to give.

He should not give because he has to give. He should not give if he does not really want to give. God loves a giver who is really happy to give. 8 And God is able to give you more than you need of every good thing. You will always have everything that you need for yourselves. Also, you will have enough so that you can give plenty to every good work. 9 The Old Testament says this (about a person who lives for God):

'He has given very much to the poor people.

God will always remember how good and kind that person has been.'

10 It is God who supplies seeds for the farmer to plant. It is God who supplies bread for food. And God will make you like a farmer who plants good seeds. He will supply your seeds, and he will give more and more seeds to you. Also, he will cause those seeds to grow, to give more and more good results. You will have good results from all the good seeds that you plant. 11 God will make you rich always, so that you will always be able to give plenty to other people. Many people will thank God because of your gifts that they have received by us.

12 This good work that you are doing is helping God's people. It is helping to supply what God's people need. And it is not only doing that. It is also causing many people to thank God very, very much. 13 Your gift will show people what you are really like. You say that you believe the good news about Christ. And your gift will show how much you really want to obey God. You are happy to give so much to these people, and to everyone else. So, as a result, many people will say how good and great God is. 14 And they will pray on your behalf because they really love you very much. They will love you because God has caused you to be very, very kind. 15 We should thank God because of the very great gift that he has given to us. His gift is so great that no words could ever describe it!

Chapter 10

Paul speaks about his work as Christ's servant

1 I, Paul, myself am asking you something strongly. Some people say that, when I am present there with you, I am weak. They say that I am afraid to speak strong, angry words to you. But when I am away from you, I am brave enough to speak very strongly to you. That is what they say about me. But still, it is I who am asking you this. And I am asking it because Christ himself is so patient and so kind. 2 This is what I am asking. When I come to visit you, do not make me have to say angry words to you. Do not make me angry, as some people make me angry. Some people think that we live by our own human power. So, I am sure that I will have to speak angry words to them.

3 It is true that we are human. We live in human bodies. But we do not fight by our own human power. 4 We do not use human weapons to fight God's war. Instead, we use the weapons that come from God. These weapons are powerful enough to destroy the enemy's strong places. With these weapons, we destroy wrong ideas that people think.

5 We pull down every high thing that tries to stop people from knowing God. With these weapons, we take hold of every thought and we bring it to obey Christ. 6 You must obey completely everything that we have explained to you. And then we will be ready to punish anyone who will not obey God.

7 You are looking at things only as they seem to be on the outside. Anyone who is sure that he is Christ's should think again about himself. In the same way that he is Christ's, so we are Christ's. He should remember that we are Christ's also. 8 Maybe I say too many great things about the authority that the Lord has given to us. But I am not ashamed to say those things. He gave that authority to us so that we could help you to become stronger. He did not give it so that we could destroy you.

9 I do not want you to think that I am trying to frighten you by my letters. 10 Some people say: 'Paul's letters are very serious and strong, and his words are powerful. But when he is here with us, he is weak. And it is not worth listening to the words that he speaks.'

11 Anyone who says things like that should understand this. He should understand that there is no difference. We write certain things in our letters when we are away from you. And we will do certain things when we are present there with you. And those things are the same. There is no difference between them.

12 Some people say how very good and clever they themselves are. But we are not brave enough to include ourselves with them. We would not even want anyone to think that we were like those people. Those people are fools. They see what each other is like. Then, as a result, they decide how good they themselves are. They decide that only among themselves. So, they are fools. 13 But we will not say any good things about ourselves that are not proper. We will say good things only about the work that God has chosen to give to us. And that includes our work among you. 14 We are not trying to do anything more than what God has given to us to do. If we had not visited you, then we would be trying to do more. But we did come as far as where you are to tell the good news about Christ.

15 We do not say good things about ourselves as a result of other people's work. That would not be proper. Instead, we hope that you will continue to believe more and more strongly. Then, as a result, our proper work among you will become much greater. 16 We hope to tell the good news to people in places beyond where you are. But we will not say good things about ourselves as a result of work that other people have done already. That is their proper work; it is not ours. 17 But, as it says in the Old Testament:

'If a person says good and great things about anyone, they should speak only about the Lord.

That person should say how good and great the Lord is.'

18 If someone says good things about himself that does not really matter. But if the Lord says good things about a person that does really matter. That means that the person has really done well.

Chapter 11

Paul explains how dangerous false teachers are

1 Even if I seem to speak like a fool, please be patient with me. But you are being patient already! 2 I want you very much to continue being Christ's, as God himself wants that, too. I have brought you to one husband, who is Christ. And I want you to be only Christ's, like a good woman who has never had sex with any man.

3 But I am afraid that you might become like Eve. The snake told her things that were not true. And, because he was so clever, she believed him. And I am afraid that you might start to believe wrong ideas too. So then, as a result, you might stop believing and loving only Christ. 4 You are happy to listen to any other teachers who come to you. They might tell you about a different Jesus from the Jesus that we told you about. And you are happy to listen to them. You are happy to receive a different spirit from the one that you received by us. You are happy to believe a different 'good news' from the one that you first believed.

5 But I think that I am quite as good as those special teachers, I am not less able than those teachers that you enjoy listening to so much. 6 Perhaps I do not speak as well as they speak. But certainly, I do know what I am speaking about. We have made this very clear to you in every way and in all things.

7 When I told you the good news from God, I never asked you to pay me anything. I made myself less important so that you could be more important. I do not think that I was wrong to do that. 8 Other groups of believers gave money to me so that I could work among you. Perhaps I could say that I was robbing them. I was robbing them so that I could help you.

9 When I was present with you, I never asked anyone to give anything to me. Even when I needed something, I still did not ask you to give anything to me. Instead, the believers who came from Macedonia helped me. They supplied everything that I needed. I was very careful never to ask you for anything that I needed. And I will continue to be careful like that, so that I will never be any trouble to you. 10 As certainly as Christ's true message is in me, nothing will stop me saying these true things about myself. Nothing anywhere, in all of Achaia, will stop me. 11 I love you. That is the reason that nothing will stop me. And God knows that I love you.

12 I will continue to do the things that I am doing now. Then there will be no chance for those other teachers to say great things about themselves. They want a chance to say that they do the same work as us. They want everyone to think that they themselves are quite like us. 13 But those people are false teachers. They say things about their work that are not true. They want people to believe that they are really Christ's special workers and teachers. 14 And that should not surprise you!
Even Satan can make himself seem like an angel who belongs to the light. 15 So, it should not surprise you if Satan's servants make themselves seem good also. They can make themselves seem to be good and right, like God's servants. But God will punish them in the end as a result of the bad things that they do.

Paul describes all the troubles and pain that he has had as Christ's servant

16 I say again: nobody should think that I am a fool. But even if you do think that, still listen to me. Listen to me as you would listen to a fool. So then I may say a few good things about myself. 17 I am not saying what the Lord has told me to say. Instead, I am talking like a fool when I say these good things certainly about myself. 18 There are so many people who say good things about themselves. They speak about the reasons why they themselves are so important as human people. So, I will say things like that about myself too.

19 You think that you yourselves are so very clever! You think that you understand so very much! So, you are happy to listen to fools. 20 You listen to anyone who wants to make you like slaves. You listen to anyone who uses you for his own wrong purposes. You listen to anyone who makes you believe wrong things. You listen to anyone who makes himself seem much more important than you. You listen to anyone who hits you in your face. 21 I am ashamed to say that I was too weak to do things like that to you.

But if anyone else is brave enough to say good things about himself, I will be brave enough also. But now I am talking like a fool! 22 Those other teachers may say that they are Jews. And I am a Jew also. They may say that they belong to Israel's people. And I belong to Israel's people also. They may say that they belong to Abraham's family. And I belong to Abraham's family also. 23 They may say that they are Christ's servants. (I speak like a fool.) But I am a better servant than they are. I have worked much more than they have worked. I have been in prisons more often than they have been in prisons. I could not begin to count how many times people have hit me. I have nearly died many times.

24 At five different times, the Jews hit me with a stick 39 times. 25 Other people hit me with sticks three times. People threw stones at me to kill me once. Three times I have been on ships that broke in the sea. Once I was in the sea for a night and a day. 26 I have travelled very much. I have been in danger from rivers and from people who rob. I have been in danger from my own people and from other people, who do not know God. I have been in danger in cities and in country places. I have been in danger on the sea. And I have been in danger from people who said that they were Christ's. But those people were not really Christ's.

27 I have worked very much, so that I have been very, very tired. Many times I have not slept. Many times I have been hungry and I have had nothing to drink. Many times I have had no food and I have been cold and without clothes. 28 All these troubles have happened to me. But also, every day I think about all the groups of believers, because they matter so much to me. 29 When one of these believers is weak, then I feel weak too. When something causes one of them to do something wrong, then I am very sad and angry about it.

30 If I must say good things about myself, I will speak only about my own weakness. I will speak only about things that show my weakness.

31 I am saying only true things. And the God and Father of the Lord Jesus, whom everyone should thank always, knows that. 32 When I was in Damascus, the ruler of that city sent soldiers to look for me. The soldiers were round the city and they were trying to catch me. The ruler of the city was under the authority of Aretas, who was king. 33 But I got away from the ruler of the city. I got away in a basket. Some friends put the basket through a window and they let it go down the wall to the ground.

Chapter 12

God has shown Paul special things in heaven

1 I must say more things about myself, even if I am a fool to say them. But I will tell you about some of the special, secret things that the Lord has shown to me. 2 I know a man who is united with Christ. Fourteen (14) years ago, God took this man up to the highest heaven. I do not know whether this man was still in his body. I do not know whether he was out of his body. Only God knows. 3-4 I know that God took this man up to heaven. I do not know whether this man was still in his body or not. Only God knows. And when this man was in heaven, he heard special, secret things. He heard things that no words could ever describe. God will not let any human person speak about those things.

5 I will say good things about a man like that. But I will not say good things about myself. I will speak only about the things that show my own weakness. 6 If I did want to say good things about myself, I would not be a fool. No, because I would be saying true things. But I will not say good things about myself, because I want everyone to think properly about me. I do not want anyone to think better things about me than what they themselves see or hear.

God himself makes us strong when we are weak

7 God showed me so many things that were very great and special. But he did not want me to start thinking, as a result, that I myself was too great or special. So, he let me have something sharp and painful in my body, to stop me from thinking like that. This painful thing is an angel from Satan that he sent to hurt me. 8 I asked the Lord three times to take this painful thing away from me. 9 But he said to me: 'I myself will help you and I will make you strong. I am everything that you need. When you are weak, then I will be powerful in you. Then I will show more completely how powerful I myself am.'

So, I am very happy to speak about how weak I am. When I am weak, then Christ's power stays over me. 10 That is why I am very happy to be weak. I am happy when people say bad things about me. Sometimes I do not have things that I need. But I am happy then too. I am happy when people cause trouble and pain for me. I am happy when I am in difficulties. I am happy about these things because of Christ. Because when I am weak, then I am strong.

Paul is afraid about what the believers at Corinth might do

11 I am speaking like a fool but you have made me do it. You yourselves ought to be saying good things about me. You enjoy listening to those other special teachers. But even if I am nothing, I am quite as good as those teachers. 12 When I was there with you, I was very patient. I did many things to show certainly that God had sent me to be a special worker and teacher. I did powerful things that surprised you. You knew that only God could make me do things like that. 13 You were never less important to me than all the other groups of believers. I myself never asked you to give anything to me. That was because I did not want to be any trouble to you. But you should not feel less important because of that. You should not think that I did something wrong to you!

14 This is the third time now that I am ready to visit you. I will not ask you to give anything to me. I do not want the things that are yours. Instead, I want you yourselves. Children should not have to supply what their parents need. No, but instead, parents should supply what their children need.

15 I will be very happy to give everything that I have to you. I will be happy to give myself also, because I want so very much to help you. Perhaps I love you much more than I should love you. But I hope that you will not love me less because of that.

16 You must agree that I did not ask you for anything. But some of you say that I was not honest with you. I was clever and, like fools, you believed me. That is what some of you say. 17 I sent people to you. But I did not use any of them to get anything from you for myself. 18 I asked Titus to visit you, because I wanted him very much to do that. And I sent another friend, who is also a believer, with him. But certainly, you could not say that Titus used you to get anything for himself. And I had the same good purpose as Titus. We both wanted the same good things for you. The same Spirit led both of us.

19 Perhaps you think like this about us. All the time, we have been trying to show you how right we ourselves are. Perhaps this is what you think. But we are not doing that. We have been speaking as people who are united with Christ. And we know that God sees us always. Our friends that we love, we want only to help you. Everything that we do is to help you. That is so that you become stronger. 20 I am hoping to see good things when I come there to visit you. I know what kind of people I want you to be. But I am afraid that you might be different from that. You might not be as I wanted you to be. Also, I might be different from what you wanted me to be.

I am afraid that you might be quarrelling. Some of you might not be happy about what other people have got. You might be angry with each other. Some of you might be enemies because you want to be better than each other. You might be saying bad things about each other. Some of you might be thinking that you are more important than other people. You might not be agreeing, nor doing things properly. I am afraid that I might discover all these things about you.

21 I am afraid about something else also. The next time that I come to visit you, perhaps my God will cause me to feel ashamed about you. And so, I will be sad and I will weep. Many people among you did wrong things before. But still, those people are not sorry about those wrong things.

So, I will be sad because of those people. Many people among you have done bad, dirty things with their bodies. They have had sex with people who were not their own wife or husband. They have wanted very much to do wrong things like that. But they have not turned away from those things.

Chapter 13

Paul is ready to be angry with the Christians at Corinth

1 This is the third time that I will be coming to visit you. Remember this: 'There must be two or three people to say certainly that another person has done something wrong. Two or three people must agree about the facts.' **[Deuteronomy 19:15]** 2 I am speaking now to you people who did wrong things before. I am speaking also to all the other people. I said this before, when I visited you the second time. And I say it again now, while I am away from you. When I visit you again, I will make you feel sorry. I will make everyone who has done wrong things feel sorry. I will not try to be kind to anyone who has done wrong things.

3 You are demanding to know certainly that Christ speaks by me. So, I will cause you to know that certainly. When Christ works in you, he is not weak. No, but he does powerful things among you. 4 Certainly, Christ was weak when people killed him on the cross. But he lives by God's power. And, because we are united with him, we are weak too. But, by God's power, we will live with him so that we are strong to work among you.

5 Think carefully about how you yourselves are living. Ask yourselves whether you are really believing Christ. Decide certainly about yourselves. You ought to know that Jesus Christ is in you. You ought to know this, unless you do not really belong to him. 6 I hope that you will be sure about us. We do really belong to Jesus Christ. I hope that you will know that.

7 Now we pray to God that you will do nothing wrong. We do not pray this to show good things about ourselves. We only want you to do what is right. We want that, even if we seem to have failed. 8 We can only work on behalf of what is true. We cannot do anything against what is true. 9 We are happy when we are weak. If our weakness helps you to be strong, then we are happy. We want you to become completely as God wants you to be. We pray for that also.

10 I am writing these things to you while I am away from you. So then, when I arrive, I will not need to be angry with you. I will not have to use my authority to punish you. The Lord gave this authority to me so that I could help you to become stronger. He did not give it to me so that I could destroy you.

11 And now I say 'goodbye' to you, my friends. Try to do only good things. Listen to the things that I am asking you to do. Agree with each other. Do not quarrel, but instead try to be friends with everyone. Then the God who loves will be with you. The God who causes us to be without trouble inside ourselves will be with you. 12 Say 'hello' to each other with a friendly kiss because you are God's people. 13 All God's people here say 'hello' to you. 14 I pray that the Lord Jesus Christ will continue to be very kind to you. I pray that you will love God and each other as God loves you. And I pray that God's Spirit will cause you to be united.

Continue by God's Spirit

Galatians

About this book

Paul wrote this letter to the Christians who lived in Galatia. Galatia was part of the country that is called Turkey now. Paul had visited many towns in that part of the world. As a result of his visits, many people there had become Christians. Most of these Christians were Gentiles. That means that they were not Jews (Israel's people). But, at some time after Paul had left Galatia, certain Jews had visited these Christians. Those Jews had said to them: 'You cannot really be God's people unless you let someone circumcise you. Then you can be like Jews.'

Paul loved the Christians in Galatia as if they were his own children. He was angry that those Jews had tried to teach wrong ideas to them. He was sad that the Christians in Galatia had listened to these wrong ideas. So, Paul wrote this letter to explain more clearly why they did not need to let anyone circumcise them.

Chapter 1

1 This letter is from me, Paul. Jesus Christ and God the Father, who caused Jesus to become alive again after his death, have sent me. They have given authority to me to be a special worker and teacher on Christ's behalf. No human person sent me or gave that authority to me. 2 All the believers who are here with me also say 'hello' to you groups of believers in Galatia.

3 I pray that God, our Father, and the Lord Jesus Christ will continue to be very kind to you. I pray that they will cause you to be without trouble deep inside yourselves. 4 Jesus gave himself because of all the wrong things that we have done. He did that to save us from this bad world in which we live now. This is what our God and Father wanted him to do. 5 Everyone should say always how very good and great God is! This is true.

The believers in Galatia are listening to wrong ideas

6 I am very surprised about you! You are turning away so soon from God, who caused you to come to him by Christ. He caused you to live by Christ, because he is so very kind. But instead, you are listening now to a different 'good news'. 7 But really, there is no other 'good news'. Clearly, some people are confusing you. They are trying to change the good news about Christ.

8 Nobody should ever teach a different 'good news' from the one that we taught you. Neither we, nor even an angel from the sky, should ever teach a different message. I pray that God will punish always anyone who does that. 9 I will say again what I have just said. Someone may teach a different 'good news' from the one that you have believed. But God will punish always anyone who does that.

10 Certainly, I am not trying to make people happy by what I am saying. No, but I am trying to do what God wants. If I were still trying to make people happy, I would not be Christ's servant.

Paul's message is from God

11 The good news that I taught you did not come from any human person. I want you to know this, my friends. 12 No human person gave it to me or taught it to me. No, it was Jesus Christ himself who showed it to me.

13 You know about the things that I did before, as a Jew. At that time, I strongly believed the things that the Jews believe. And I caused very much trouble and pain for God's church (the Christians). I did my best to destroy it. 14 I was a better Jew than many other Jews who were about the same age as me. I wanted very, very much to obey and to teach the things that my grandfather's taught. 15 But God had chosen me even before I was born. He chose me to be his servant because he is so very kind. He decided 16to show his Son in me, so that I could tell the Gentiles about him. When God did that in me, I did not talk to any human person about it. 17 Nor did I go to Jerusalem to see Christ's special workers and teachers. Those men were Christ's special workers and teachers before I was. But I did not go to see them. No, instead, I went immediately to the place called Arabia, and later I went back to Damascus city.

18 Then, three years later, I went to Jerusalem to meet Peter. I stayed there with him for 15 days. 19 I did not see any of Christ's other special workers and teachers, except James, the Lord's brother. 20 What I am writing to you is true. And God knows that it is true! 21 Later I went to places in Syria and Cilicia. 22 The groups of believers in Judea had never met me. 23 They had only heard people say things about me. People said: 'This man caused bad trouble and pain for us before. He wanted to stop people believing Christ. He tried to destroy us. But now he himself is telling people to believe Christ.' 24 And so, the believers in Judea thanked God because of me. And they said how good and how great God is.

Chapter 2

The other special workers accept Paul

1 Then, 14 years later, I went to Jerusalem again. This time I went with Barnabas, and I took Titus with me also. 2 I went because God had shown me that I should go. I explained to the Christian leaders there the good news that I teach to the Gentiles. But I explained it only to those men who seemed to be the leaders. I wanted them to understand the message that I was teaching. I wanted them to agree that it was right. I was afraid that perhaps they might not agree. I was afraid that my work, both in past times and now, was not really worth anything.

3 Titus was with me then, and he is a Greek man (from the country called Greece). But the leaders at Jerusalem did not even say to me that anyone should circumcise Titus.

4 Some men, who had come into our meeting secretly, did want to circumcise Titus. Those men said that they were believers. But they were not really believers. They had come only to find out what we believe. They wanted to know how free we are from the Jews' rules because we are united to Christ. They wanted to make us slaves to those rules. 5 But we did not agree with what those men were saying, not even for a moment. We wanted you to continue believing the true good news.

6 Those people who seemed to be the leaders did not argue with me. It does not matter to me whether they were really important people or not. God does not look at what people seem to be on the outside. Those leaders did not say that I should teach anything more in my message.

7 No, instead they saw that God had given a special job to me, as he had to Peter. God wanted me to tell the good news about Christ to the Gentiles. And he had told Peter to tell the good news to the Jews. 8 God worked in Peter to make him a special teacher to the Jews. And God worked also in me to make me a special teacher to the Gentiles.

9 James, Peter and John, the important leaders in Jerusalem, understood that God had given this special job to me. So, they were happy to be friends with Barnabas and me, because all of us were Christ's special workers. They agreed that we should go to the Gentiles. And they themselves would go to the Jews. 10 The only thing that they asked us to remember was this: They wanted us to remember to help the poor people. And that was the same thing that I myself wanted very much to do.

Paul is angry with Peter at Antioch

11 But when Peter came to Antioch, I was angry with him. I stood in front of him. 'You are doing something that is wrong', I said to him. 12 Before certain men had arrived at Antioch, Peter had been eating meals with the Gentile believers there. Then James sent some men (Jews) from Jerusalem to Antioch. And after those men had arrived, Peter started to keep himself separate from the Gentiles. He stopped eating meals with them, because he was afraid. He was afraid of those Jews, who wanted to circumcise all the Gentiles. 13 All the other Jews at Antioch who were believers were afraid also. So, they did the same as Peter had done. And, as a result, even Barnabas copied their example.

14 But they were not doing what is really right. And I saw that it was not right. They were not obeying the true message that is the good news. Then I spoke to Peter in front of all of them. 'You are a Jew, but you have been living like a Gentile, and not like a Jew', I said. 'So you should not try to make Gentiles obey the same rules as the Jews.'

15 We were born Jews. We are not Gentiles, who are without the Law (the rules that God gave to the Jews). 16 But we know that those rules cannot make anyone right with God. A person only becomes right with God when that person really believes Jesus Christ. So we, too, have become believers in Christ Jesus so that we could be right with God. God accepts us as right with himself because we believe Christ. He does not accept us because we obey the Jews' rules. Nobody becomes right with God only because they obey the Jews' rules.

17 So then, we believe that we become right with God by Christ. But, at the same time, other people may see that we ourselves are doing some wrong things. But that does not mean that Christ causes people to do wrong things. Certainly, it does not mean that! 18 I could start to build again the things (the Jews' rules) that I tore down. But that would only show that I myself could not obey all those rules. 19 But, as a result of those rules, I have died to those rules. I died to them, so that now I can live for God. 20 Christ died on the cross, and I have died with him. I do not live any more, but Christ lives in me. The life that I live now, in my body, I live by the Son of God. I live because the Son of God causes me to believe him. He loves me and he gave himself on my behalf. 21 God has done so very much on our behalf because he is so very, very kind. And I refuse to say that God has done less than he has really done. If the Jews' rules could have made me right with God, then Christ died for no reason!

Chapter 3

We become right with God only because we believe him

1 You Christians in Galatia are fools! Someone has taught you to believe crazy ideas! I showed to you so very clearly how and why Jesus Christ died on the cross. 2 I want you to think about the reason why you received God's Spirit. You did not receive him because you were trying to obey the Jews' rules. No, instead you received him because you believed the good news.

You heard the good news, and you believed it. 3You have begun by God's Spirit. So, you should not try to continue by your own human power. You should not be such fools! You can never become completely as God wants you to be by human power. 4You have had so many difficulties and troubles that have taught you so very much. You should not throw away what you have learned as a result of all these troubles.

5 God gives his Spirit to you. And he does special things among you that surprise people. But he does not do these things because you obey the Jews' rules. No, he does them because you believe the good news. You believe the good news that you have heard.

6 Think about Abraham. 'Abraham believed God and, as a result, God accepted Abraham as right with himself' **[Genesis 15:6]** . 7 So, the people who believe God, they are Abraham's children. This is what you need to understand. 8 In the Old Testament it says that, at a future time, God would make the Gentiles right with himself. He would make them right with himself if they believed him. And so, the Old Testament told this future good news to Abraham. 'I will be good to people from all countries because of you', God said **[Genesis 12:3]** . 9 So then, God will be good to all those people who, like Abraham, believe him.

10 But God will punish all those people who believe only in the Jews' rules. Those people think that, by those rules, they can become right with God. But those people will have to be separate from God. It says in the Old Testament: 'God will punish everyone who does not always obey all the rules completely. Everyone must be careful always to do everything that is in the book of the Jews' rules' **[Deuteronomy 27:26]** . 11 It is clear that nobody can become right with God by the Jews' rules. It is clear because it says in the Old Testament: 'The person that I have accepted will live. Those people will live because they believe me.' **[Habakkuk 2:4]**

12 But the Jews' rules do not make it important to believe God. Those rules are not about that. No, instead it says in the Old Testament: 'The person who obeys all these rules completely will live by them' **[Leviticus 18:5]** . 13 As a result of the Jews' rules, God would have had to punish us. God would have had to make us separate from himself. But Christ bought us, to make us free, because God punished him on our behalf. It says in the Old Testament: 'When people hang someone on a tree to kill him, that person must be separate from God.' **[Deuteronomy 21:23]** 14 Christ did this so that the Gentiles could receive good things from God. They could receive, by Jesus Christ, what God had promised to Abraham. So then, if we believe Christ, we can receive God's Spirit. We can receive the Spirit that God promised.

The difference between the Jews' rules and what God promised

15 My friends, I will use an example from what people do. When two people make a proper agreement in the correct way, nobody else can change that agreement. Nobody can take away the power of that agreement, nor can anyone include any extra words in it.

16 In the same way, God promised things to Abraham and to Abraham's grandson. It does not say in the Old Testament 'to your grandsons'. That is, it does not mean 'to many people'. No, instead it says 'to your grandson'. That is, it means 'to one person only'. God promised those things to one person, and that person is Christ. 17 What I mean is this. God had made an agreement. He had promised to do what he had said. Then, 430 years later, God gave his rules to Israel's people. But those rules could not finish the power of God's agreement. Those rules could not stop what God had already promised. 18 We can receive what God gives to his children. But it is not as a result of the Jews' rules that we receive it. If that were true, then we would not receive it as a result of God's promise. But God gave it to Abraham because he had promised to give it.

19 So we could ask: Why did God give his rules to his people? He gave those rules to them to show them which things were wrong. God gave those rules until Abraham's one special grandson came. That was the grandson to whom God had given his promise. God used angels to give his rules to a man (Moses), who was there on behalf of all the people. That man was between God and the people. 20 But sometimes only one person is doing something by himself. And then it is not necessary to have a man in between like that. And God gave his promise by himself alone.

The purpose of the rules that God gave to Israel's people

21 So, perhaps someone could say that the Jews' rules are working against God's promises. No, certainly that is not true! If any rules could have made people alive to God, then God would have given those rules to people. Then those rules would really have made people right with God.

22 But it says in the Old Testament that all the people in the world are like people in prison. Sin keeps all people in prison. So then, we can only receive what God has promised by Jesus Christ. God gives what he has promised to every believer in Christ.

23 But before we believed Christ, the Jews' rules kept us safe. Those rules kept us safe, like people that someone had locked into a safe place. Those rules kept us safe until God showed Christ to us. God showed us that we must believe Christ. 24 So, the Jews' rules were like our teacher, who kept us safe. Those rules led us to Christ. So then we could become right with God because we believed Christ. 25 But now that we do believe Christ, the Jews' rules do not have authority as our teacher any more.

Sons of God

26 All of you are God's sons because you believe Christ Jesus. 27 All of you that God baptised into Christ have put on Christ. You have put on Christ, as someone puts on new clothes. 28 You are not different from each other anymore, because you are all united together in Christ Jesus. Whether you are Jews or Gentiles, men or women, slaves or free people, all of you are united in him. 29 And if you belong to Christ, then you are Abraham's grandchildren. So, you will receive everything that God promised to Abraham.

Chapter 4

Paul explains about sons

1 I will try to explain it like this. The oldest son in a family will receive what is his father's at the right age. But while he is a child, he is completely like a slave. One day he will be the master of all his father's things. But still he is completely like a slave now. 2 He has to obey teachers, and other people who have authority over him, until the right time. He must wait for the time that his father has chosen. 3 In the same way, we were like children also. We were slaves to the bad spirits that rule this world. 4 But when the time was completely right, God sent his own Son. He came as the son of a human mother. He was born a Jew, under the authority of the Jews' rules. 5 We were like slaves under the Jews' rules. But God's Son bought us, to make us free. So then we could become proper sons of God. 6 And because you are sons, God has sent his Son's Spirit to live deep inside us. His Spirit in us shouts to God: 'Father, my Father'. 7 So, you are not a slave any more, but you are a son. And because of that, you will receive everything that God gives to his sons.

Paul is afraid that the Christians in Galatia may stop believing Christ

8 Before, when you did not know God, you were slaves to other spirits. You were slaves to spirits that are not really gods. 9 But now you know God. Or really, I should say that God knows you. So, you should not turn back to those weak and poor spirits that rule this world. You should not want to become their slaves again! 10 You say that certain days, or months, or times, or years are special. 11 I am afraid about you. I worked so very much among you to help you. And I am afraid that I may have wasted my time.

12 My friends, I ask you very strongly to become like me, because I became like you. You have not done anything wrong to me. 13 I told the good news to you the first time because I was ill. You know that. 14 I caused trouble for you because I was ill. But still you were kind to me, and you did not say bad things to me. Instead, you said: 'Welcome!' You were as happy as if I were an angel from God, or even Christ Jesus himself. 15 But now I do not understand why you are not happy like that anymore. I can say certainly that you would have torn out your own eyes for me. If it had been possible, you would have given your own eyes to me. 16 And now I seem to have become your enemy because of what I am telling you! But I am telling you only what is true.

17 Those false teachers want very much to make you believe them. But they do not really want what is good for you. What they do want is to make you separate from me. They want you to think that they themselves are very clever and important. 18 It is good to want other people to believe certain things, if it is for a good purpose. It is always good to be like that, not only when I am there with you.

19 My children, I feel really like a mother who is giving birth to you again. I feel pain on your behalf until you become more completely like Christ. 20 I want very much to be present with you now. Then I could know better what I should say to you. Because I do not really know what to say.

Hagar and Sarah

21 So, you want the Jews' rules to have authority over you! Then you must know what those rules mean. 22 It says in the Old Testament that Abraham had two sons. He had one son by a woman, Hagar, who was a slave. And he had another son by Sarah, who was a free woman. 23 One woman was a slave. And her son was born as a result of what Abraham himself decided. But his son by the free woman was born as a result of what God had promised.

24 These two women are like pictures of the two agreements that God made with his people. Hagar is like the agreement that God made on Sinai mountain. That agreement causes people to become slaves. 25 Hagar is like a picture of Sinai mountain in Arabia. Also, she is like Jerusalem city here on earth now, because that city and its people are slaves. 26 But the Jerusalem that is above is free. And that Jerusalem is our mother. 27 It says in the Old Testament:

'Be happy, you woman who never had any children!

You are the woman who has never known the pain from a child's birth.

Shout loudly because you are so happy!

Because the sad and lonely woman has many more children

than the woman who has a husband.'

28 You, my friends, are children like Isaac. Like him, you were born as a

result of what God promised. 29 At that time, the son who was born as a result of what Abraham decided was not kind to Isaac. That first son, Ishmael, caused trouble and pain for Isaac, the son who was born because of God's Spirit. And it is the same now. 30 But it says in the Old Testament: 'Send away the woman who is a slave and her son. Because that woman's son will never receive what God has promised to the free woman's son.' **[Genesis 21:10]** 31 So then, my friends, we are not children of the woman who is a slave. No, we are children of the free woman.

Chapter 5

Continue to be free in Christ

1 Christ has made us free because he wants us to be free! So, be strong and continue to be free. Do not let yourselves become slaves again.

2 Listen carefully! I, Paul, tell you this. If you let someone circumcise you, then Christ will be worth nothing to you. 3 I say it again. Every man who lets someone circumcise him must then obey all of the Jews' rules. 4 You people who try to become right with God by the Jews' rules will make yourselves separate from Christ. You have stopped believing that only Christ can make you right with God. You have stopped believing how very kind God is to us. 5 But God's Spirit causes us to hope certainly that we will become right with God. We will be right with him because we believe him. We are waiting for this and we want it to happen very much. 6 We are united with Christ Jesus. And so, it does not matter whether anyone has circumcised us or not. The only thing that matters is that we believe God. And those who believe him must love God and other people. And then they will show that they believe him.

7 Like good runners, you were doing so well! You should not have let anyone stop you. You should not have stopped obeying what is true. 8 It is not God who has caused you to stop. No, because God asks you to come to him. 9 'Only a small amount of yeast can cause a whole lot of bread to rise', as people say. 10 But I still feel sure about you, because we are united in the Lord. I feel sure that you will not think differently from me. But God will punish the man who is confusing you. Whoever that man may be, God will punish him.

11 My friends, I do not still tell people that someone should circumcise them. If I did tell people that, then nobody would still cause trouble and pain for me. Then what I taught about Christ's cross would not cause anyone to become angry. 12 The people who are confusing you should cut their own bodies. That is what I want them to do!

Live by God's Spirit

13 My friends, God has asked you to come to him so that you can be free. But you must be free in the right way. You are not free to do everything that, as a human person, you may sometimes want to do. Instead, you must be like servants to each other because you love each other. 14 One rule brings together all the rules that God gave to the Jews. This one rule says: 'Love every other person the same as you love yourself.' 15 But do not be like wild animals. Wild animals fight and eat each other. If you are like that, be careful. Be careful that you do not destroy each other completely.

16 So, this is what I am saying to you. Live by the power that God's Spirit gives. And let him lead you. Then you will not do any wrong things that, as a human person, you may sometimes want to do. 17 Your own human power wants completely opposite things to what God's Spirit wants. It fights against what God's Spirit wants. And so, you cannot do the things that you really want to do. 18 But if God's Spirit leads you, then the Jews' rules have no authority over you.

19 Everyone knows the kinds of bad things that people can do by their own human power. They have sex with people who are not their own wife or husband. They think and they do dirty things. They do things that people ought to be very ashamed to do. 20 They worship false gods. They ask bad spirits to help them. They become enemies and they fight. They hate other people because they themselves want to be like those people. They become very angry without any good reason. They want to be more important than other people. They refuse to agree, and so they belong to separate groups. 21 They want things that are other people. They are drunks. They have parties where they do all kinds of bad things. I have told you before how dangerous it is to do these things. And now I am telling you again. People who do things like this will not be God's people. They will not belong to God's people that he rules over. Nor will they receive the things that God has prepared for his people.

22 But God's Spirit in us causes us to love God and other people. He causes us to be happy and without trouble deep inside ourselves. He causes us to be patient, kind and good. He causes us to believe that God will continue to help us. 23 He causes us not to think that we are better than other people. He causes us to rule ourselves properly. And there are no rules against these things that God's Spirit causes us to do.

24 Those people who belong to Christ Jesus have killed their own human power on his cross. They have killed it, so that it does not make them feel things any more. Nor does it make them want to do things any more. 25 We live by God's Spirit. So, we must obey God's Spirit and we must let him lead us. 26 We must not want people to think that we are better than anyone else. We must not make each other angry. We must not want each other's things so that, as a result, we hate each other.

Chapter 6

Be kind and good to each other

1 My friends, if anyone among you cannot stop doing a certain wrong thing, you must tell him to stop. Those people in your group who understand things by God's Spirit should tell him to stop. You should tell him what is the right thing to do.

But you must be careful to be kind when you tell him. Remember that you yourself might not always be able to stop yourself doing something wrong. 2 Like people who help to carry heavy things, you should help each other to be strong during troubles and problems. This is how you will obey Christ's rules. 3 None of you should think that you yourself are too important. If you are not that important really, then you would be believing something false. 4 Each person should think about the things that he himself has done. And he himself must decide whether those things are good. If they are good, then he can be happy. He can be happy because of what he himself has done. He does not need to think about whether he is better or worse than anyone else. 5 Each person must live his own life and do his own work.

6 Everyone who is learning God's message from a teacher should give good things to that teacher. Every learner should give some of all the good things that he has to his teacher.

7 Nobody can ever make God a fool. Do not let yourself think that anyone can ever do that! If someone puts a seed from a certain kind of plant into the ground, that seed will grow. And the result will be the same kind of plant. 8 A person may do the things that, as a human person, he himself wants to do. And the result will be that he will die. Or instead, a person may do the things that God's Spirit wants. And the result will be that God's Spirit will cause him to live always. 9 So, we should not stop doing what is good. We should not get tired of it. If we do not get tired, then we shall receive a good result at the proper time. 10 So then, every time that we have the chance, we must do good things for everyone. Certainly, we must do good things for those people who, like us, believe Christ. Those people belong to the same family as us because all of us believe Christ.

Paul finishes his letter

11 You can see what big letters I am making now! It is because I am writing to you now with my own hand!

12 Those people who want to seem clever and important are trying to confuse you. They are telling you that you should let someone circumcise you. They are doing that only for this reason. They do not want anyone to cause trouble and pain for them because of Christ's cross. 13 Even those men that someone has circumcised do not obey the Jews' rules. They want to circumcise you only to make themselves seem great. They want to say that they have authority over your bodies. 14 But I do not want to say any great things about myself. The only thing that makes me great is our Lord Jesus Christ's cross. By his cross, the world has become dead to me and I have become dead to the world. 15 It does not matter whether anyone has circumcised you or not. What matters is that God has made you a new person. 16 I pray that God will be kind to all those people who live by this rule. I pray that he will cause them to be without trouble deep inside themselves. I pray this for all those people who are really God's.

17 I want no more trouble from anyone after this. The marks on my body show that I am Jesus' servant.

18 My friends, I pray that our Lord Jesus Christ will continue to be very kind to you. I pray that he will be with your spirits. This is what I pray.

One Family in Christ

Ephesians

About Ephesians

Most students of the Bible think that Paul wrote this letter from Rome, about the year AD 62. That was more than 30 years after Jesus died. Paul was in prison at Rome. He wrote to the church (group of Christians) that was at Ephesus. Ephesus was a city in the south and west part of the country that we call Turkey now. But Paul may have sent this letter to other groups of Christians also.

In this letter, Paul explains the very great things that Jesus Christ has done on behalf of all people. Christ has taken away everything that caused people to be enemies to God and to each other. Now all people, both Jews and Gentiles, can be united in Christ. They can become God's people. All Christians belong to one family, and Christ is the head (the leader) of that family.

So, we must always try to agree and we must continue to love each other. We must live as God wants us to live. We must learn how to be strong as Christians. And we must always be ready to fight against the Devil when he attacks us in different ways.

Chapter 1

1 This letter is from me, Paul. God chose me to be a special worker and teacher on behalf of Christ Jesus. I am writing to you, God's people at Ephesus, who are continuing to believe and to obey Christ Jesus. 2 I pray that God, our Father, and the Lord Jesus Christ will continue to be very kind to you. I pray that they will cause you to be without trouble inside yourselves.

God has given so very much to us in Christ

3 We should thank the God and Father of our Lord Jesus Christ very, very much! He has been so very good to us! He has given to us every good spiritual thing in heaven because we are united with Christ! 4 This is true because he chose us to belong to Christ. God chose us in Christ before he made the world. He chose us in Christ to be completely good. So now, God thinks that there is nothing wrong with us. God loved us. 5 So he had already decided to bring us to himself to be his sons by Jesus Christ. He decided to do this because it made him very happy. 6 We should thank him so very much because he is so great and kind to us. God has been so kind to us by his son, whom he loves so much. 7 Christ bought us, by his blood, to make us free. In Christ, God has forgiven all the wrong things that we do. God has done these great things because he is so very kind to us.

8 He has done so very much on our behalf because he knew everything about us. He understood what we really needed. 9 God has shown to us the secret things that he himself wanted to do. He has shown his own secret purpose that makes him very happy. 10 God will finish his purpose when the time is completely right. Then he will bring everything together, the things in heaven, and the things on earth. God will bring everything together in Christ, with Christ as the head (the leader).

11 In Christ also, God chose us to be his own people. God had already decided that this was his purpose. And he does all things as a result of what he himself has decided to do. 12 God wanted us to show how very great and good he is. We show this after we have first hoped certainly because of Christ.

13 And you also became united with Christ after you heard the true message. You heard the good news about how God saves you. Then, when you believed, God gave his Spirit to you. He gave his own Spirit, as he had promised to do. He gave his Spirit to you to show certainly that you belong to him. 14 God's Spirit is the first part of what God will give to us. God has bought us to be his own people. God gives his Spirit to us until he makes us completely free. And then we will thank God. We will show how very great and good he is.

Christ is the head of his body

15 People have told me about how you continue to believe the Lord Jesus. They have told me that you love all God's people. So, since I have heard these things about you, 16 I never stop thanking God because of you. And when I pray, I remember to pray on your behalf. 17 I pray to the very great and good Father, who is the God of our Lord Jesus Christ. I pray that he will cause you to understand things by his Spirit. I ask God to show things to you by his Spirit, so that you can really know him. 18 I pray that God will open your minds. So then you will understand what he has chosen to give to you. You will know the good things that he has caused you to hope for certainly. You will know what very rich and great things he has prepared for his people. 19 And you will know how very, very powerful God is to us.

He is more powerful than anyone or anything else in us who believe him. God works in us by the same strong power 20 as he did in Christ. He worked powerfully to raise Christ, so that he became alive again after his death. God worked powerfully so that he caused Christ to sit at his right side in heaven. 21 There, Christ rules over every other ruler and over everything else that has any authority. Christ is much, much greater than any other power or any other master. He rules over every name that any person or spirit uses to have authority. Christ rules over them now, in this world. And he will rule over them in the world that will come. 22 God has put all things under Christ's feet (authority). God has made Christ the leader, the head over all things to his people, the church, 23 which is Christ's body. The church is full of Christ, who fills all things everywhere.

Chapter 2

God has made us alive with Christ

1 Before, your spirits were dead. You were doing wrong things and you were not obeying God. 2 You were doing the same kinds of wrong things as other people in this world do. You were like all the other people in the world who do not obey God. You were obeying the spirit who rules the spiritual powers in the air. That spirit is working now in everyone who refuses to obey God. 3 In past times, all of us were like those other people. We did whatever things our own bodies and minds caused us to want. God was angry with us, as he was angry with everyone else. And, as a result, he would have had to punish us.

4-5 But God is so very good and kind! Our spirits were dead and we were doing wrong things. But still God loved us so very much that he made us alive with Christ. God has saved you only because he himself is so very kind. 6 Also, God raised us up with Christ and he caused us to sit with Christ in heaven. God has done these things because he has joined us with Christ Jesus. 7 God did these things to show, for all future time, how very good he is to us. He wanted to show how very great and kind he is to us by Christ Jesus. 8 God has saved you only because he himself is so very kind. He has saved you because you believe him. You could not save yourselves, but it is God's gift to you. 9 He has not saved you as a result of any good thing that you yourselves have done. So, nobody has any reason to say how good they themselves are! 10 It is God who has worked in us. He himself has made us what we are. He had already prepared good things for us to do. And he has joined us with Christ Jesus so that we can do those good things.

Christ has brought Jews and Gentiles together

11 So, remember what you were before. You were born Gentiles, whom the Jews call 'those people that nobody has circumcised'. But
the Jews call themselves 'we whom somebody has circumcised'. They say that because of what men themselves do to their bodies.

12 Remember that, at that time, you were separate from Christ. You did not belong to Israel's people. You did not belong to the people that God had chosen. You were strangers. God had made no agreements with you, by which he promised certain things to you. You were living in this world with nothing good to hope for. You were living without God. 13 You were far away from God. But now, because you are united with Christ Jesus, God has brought you near to himself by Christ's blood.

14 It is Christ himself who has stopped us from being enemies. He himself has brought the two separate groups of people, the Jews and the Gentiles, to be one group. In his own body, he has broken down the wall between them that made them separate. He has taken away the thing that made them enemies. 15 He has brought to an end the Jews' rules. Those rules told them what they ought to do. In this way, he stopped the two groups of people from being enemies. 16 By his death on the cross, Christ stopped the Jews and the Gentiles from being enemies to each other. In one body, he brought both groups of people back to God, to be God's friends. 17 Christ came and he told people God's message. He told them about how they could be friends with God and with each other. He told it to you Gentiles, who were far away from God. He told it also to the Jews, who were near to God. 18 By Christ, all of us, both Jews and Gentiles, can come to the Father by the same Spirit.

19 So now, you Gentiles are not strangers any more. You are not foreign any more. But now, instead, you belong with God's people. You belong to God's family.

20 You belong to the building that is God's house. God's special workers, and the people who spoke his messages, are like strong stones under this building. They are like strong stones that hold the building up. And Jesus Christ himself is like the most important stone in the building. 21 He holds the whole building together. And he makes it grow into a house that belongs only to the Lord. 22 He himself is building you together also into a house where God lives by his Spirit.

Chapter 3

God has chosen Paul to help the Gentiles

1 I, Paul, am in prison because Christ Jesus has sent me to help you Gentiles. 2 Certainly, you must have heard that God has chosen me to help you. He has chosen me to work on your behalf because he is so very kind. 3 God has caused me to know his secret because he has shown it to me. I have written a few words about this already. 4 When you read these words, you will be able to understand that I know the secret about Christ. 5 God never showed this secret to the people who lived before this time. But now God's Spirit has shown it to the special workers and teachers that God has chosen. He has shown this secret also to the people who speak God's messages. 6 This secret is that the Gentiles, together with the Jews, will receive good things from God.
The Gentiles can belong to the same body as the Jews. By the good news, the Gentiles can receive what God promised in Christ Jesus.

7 I became a servant, to tell the good news, because God gave that special work to me. God himself worked powerfully in me because he is so kind. 8 I am the least important of all God's people. But still, God has given this special work to me because he is so kind. He has sent me to tell the Gentiles about the great things that are ours because of Christ. God gives such good things to us in Christ because Christ is so very rich. These things are more valuable than anyone could ever know.

9 God sent me also to make clear to everyone how he would cause his secret thing to happen. God, who made all things, hid this secret during past times. 10 His purpose was to show now, at this time, how completely he understands everything. He wanted the spiritual rulers that have authority in the heavens, to know this. They would know it by the church (God's people). 11 This had always been God's purpose. And he made it happen by Christ Jesus, our Lord. 12 Because we are united with Christ, we are sure enough to come near to God. We do not need to be afraid, but instead we can be sure. We can come to God because Christ himself has caused us to believe. 13 I have troubles and pain on your behalf. But I ask you not to let yourselves become afraid or weak because of that. No, but instead be happy, because my troubles and pain will help you.

Paul prays for the Christians at Ephesus to be strong

14 For this reason, then, I bend my knees to pray to the Father,

15 from whom every family gets its name. Every family, in heaven and on earth, receives its true name from him. 16 I pray that he will work powerfully by his Spirit to make you strong inside yourselves. I ask him to do this because he is so very great and rich. 17 I pray that Christ will live inside you, because you believe him. I pray that your roots will go down deep into God's love. So then you will be strong. 18 You will be strong to understand, with all God's people, how very much God loves. You will be able to understand how wide and long and high and deep God's love is. 19 You will know how very, very much Christ loves. He loves us more than anyone can ever really know. And then, because you know this, God will fill you completely with himself.

.20 God is able to do so much more than we could ever ask. He is able to do so very much more than we could even think. He does such great things because he works so powerfully in us. 21 So certainly, the church (God's people) should show always how very great and good God is. The church should show this, by Christ Jesus. They will never stop showing it.

Chapter 4

God's people must continue to be united

1 So I, who am in prison for the Lord, ask you something strongly. God has chosen you to be his own people. So, I ask you to live as God's own people should live. 2 Do not think that you are better or more important than other people. Always be kind and patient. Love each other, and do not become angry with each other quickly. 3 Do your best to let God's Spirit keep you united as friends, without any trouble between you. 4 There is one body and there is one Spirit. God has chosen you to be his own people, and all of us wait certainly for the same good things. 5 There is one Lord. There is one true message that we must believe. There is one baptism. 6 There is one God, who is the Father of all of us. He is over all. He works by all, and he is in all.

7 Christ has given special gifts to each one of us, as he has chosen. He has made each one of us able to do certain things well. 8 This is why it says in the Old Testament:

> 'When he went up to the highest place,
>
> he led many prisoners with him.
>
> And he gave gifts to men.'

9 It says: 'He went up.' So, it must mean that first Christ came down, to the lower parts of the earth. 10 So, the man who came down also went up. The same man went up, high above all the heavens, so that he would be able to fill all things.

11 It was Christ who gave some of his people the gift to be special workers and leaders on his behalf. He gave to some people the gift to speak messages from him. He gave to some people the gift to bring other people to himself. He gave to some people the gift to be pastors (leaders who help Christ's people to follow him) and teachers.

12 He gave all these gifts to prepare God's people, so that they could work together as his servants. So then, as a result, Christ's body would grow and it would become stronger. 13 In this way, all of us will become completely united by what we believe. All of us will become united because we really know God's Son. So, we will be like a man who has grown up properly and completely. We will be like a man who is as tall as Christ himself. We will be completely as God wants us to be.

14 So then we will not be children any more. Clever people may try to make us believe things that are not true. They may teach different kinds of ideas, to confuse us. But we will not be like children, who are easy to confuse. We will not let those different ideas change what we believe.

15 Instead, we must speak the true message because we love people. And, as a result, we will grow up in all things into Christ, who is the head. 16 He holds the whole body together. He joins every part together to make the body strong. So then each separate part can work as it should work. And, as a result, the whole body grows and makes itself stronger by love.

Live a new life in Christ

17 So, I say this to you. I am sure that the Lord wants me to say it. You must not live any longer like the people who do not know God. They do whatever their own silly thoughts cause them to do. 18 They cannot understand because their minds are in the dark. They are strangers to the life that God gives. They do not know him because, deep inside themselves, they are hard. So, they refuse God. 19 They have stopped knowing the difference between what is right or wrong. They have given themselves to do all kinds of bad and dirty things. And they want very much to do those things more and more.

20 But you have not learned anything like that from Christ! 21 And I am sure that you have heard about him. I am sure that people taught you the true message. They taught you the true message that is in Jesus. 22 So, you must put away the person that you were. That old person belongs to the way that you lived before. It wants to do things that are not really good. And those things are destroying it. 23 Let God's Spirit make you think in a completely new way. 24 You must put on the new person that God has made to be like him. That person only does what is right. That person is really and completely good, like God.

25 So, you must stop saying things that are not true. Everyone must speak only true things to every other person. This is because all of us are parts of the same body. 26 Even if you are angry, you must not let that cause you to do anything wrong. Do not let yourself continue to be angry after sunset. 27 Do not give any room to the Devil. 28 Any person who robbed people before must stop robbing. Instead, he should start to do honest work with his own hands. So then he will have something to give to anyone who needs anything.

29 Be careful not to say anything that is bad. Say only good things that will help people. Then you will help to make them strong. You will help to give them what they need. And so, your words will be good for those who hear them. 30 Do not make God's own, completely good Spirit sad. He is like a mark to show certainly that you belong to God. He shows that God will make you completely free, one day. 31 Do not become angry with people easily. Do not become so angry that you cannot be kind to them. Do not quarrel or fight. Do not shout at anyone or say bad things about them. Stop thinking bad things about anyone. 32 Instead, be kind to each other and try to understand each other. Forgive each other, quite as God has forgiven you. He has forgiven you because you are united with Christ.

Chapter 5

Live as God's children

1 You are God's children that he loves. So, you must try to be like him. 2 Continue always to love other people, as Christ loved you. He loved us so much that he gave himself on our behalf. He offered himself as a sacrifice to God. His sacrifice had a lovely smell that made God very happy.

3 So, you must never have sex with someone who is not your own wife or husband. You should not even want to do anything like that. Neither should you want too much of anything for yourselves. God's own people should never even want to think about anything that is bad or dirty. That is not how God's people should live. 4 Nor should you talk about bad or dirty or silly things, as fools do. It is not right or proper for God's people to talk like that. Instead, you should be thanking God. 5 Nobody who has sex with someone other than their own wife or husband can belong with God's people. Nobody who does bad, dirty things can belong with God's people. Nobody who wants too much of anything for themselves can belong with God's people. That person is really worshipping something else more than they are worshipping God. None of these kinds of people will ever receive what God has prepared for his own people. These kinds of people cannot belong with those people who accept Christ and God as their king. You can be sure about this.

6 Do not let anyone make you believe wrong ideas as a result of the false words that they speak. God will certainly be angry with people who do these bad things. He will punish people who do not obey him. 7 So, do not meet with those kinds of people. 8 Once you were dark. But now that you are the Lord's, you are light. So, live as people who belong to the light. 9 The light causes people to be good. It causes people to do what is right. And it causes them to say what is true. 10 Try to learn what the Lord thinks is right. 11 People who belong to the dark do wrong things. Never join in with wrong things like that. Those things have no good purpose. But instead, show how wrong those things really are. 12 People should be ashamed even to speak about the bad things that those people do secretly. 13 But when something comes out of the dark, God's light shines on it. 14 Anything that God's light shines on becomes light. That is why it says:

> 'Wake up, you who sleep.
>
> Get up from among the dead people,

and Christ will shine on you.'

15 So, you must be very careful how you live. Live like people who understand what is right and good. Do not live like people who do not understand anything. 16 These are bad times, so use every moment well. 17 Do not be fools. But instead, understand what the Lord wants. 18 Do not drink too much wine, because that will cause bad things. It will stop you ruling yourself properly. But instead, let God's Spirit fill you. 19 Speak to each other with all kinds of spiritual songs. Sing and make music to the Lord from inside yourselves. 20 Thank God, the Father, always for everything, by our Lord Jesus Christ's name.

Wives and husbands

21 Be servants to each other, because Christ is your master.

22 Wives, obey your own husbands as you obey the Lord. 23 Because a husband is the head of his wife, quite as Christ is the head of the church (his people). The church is Christ's body and he saves her. 24 As the church puts Christ first, so wives should put their husbands first in everything.

25 Husbands, love your wives as Christ loved the church (his people). Christ gave himself on behalf of the church, 26 so that he could make it completely good and clean. He washed it with water by his word. 27 So then he could bring it to himself as a beautiful church, without any bad or dirty mark on it. He could bring it to himself as a completely good church, with nothing wrong.

28 In the same way, husbands ought to love their wives quite as they love their own bodies. A man who loves his wife loves himself. 29 No man ever hates his own body. No, instead he feeds it and he cares for it. He cares for it as Christ cares for the church (his people). 30 Christ cares for us because we are parts of his own body.

31 As the Old Testament says: 'For this reason, a man will leave his father and his mother and he will become united with his wife. Then those two people will become one body.' **[Genesis 2:24]** 32 These words show us about important things that are difficult to understand. I am saying that they show us about Christ and the church. 33 But they are also important for you. Each one of you husbands should love your own wife as you love yourself. And each wife must be ready to obey her husband.

Chapter 6

Children and parents

1 Children, obey your parents. This is what the Lord wants. It is the right thing to do. 2 The first rule that God gave with a promise says: 'Always remember how important your father and your mother are. 3 Then, as a result, you will be happy and you will live for a long time on the earth.' **[Exodus 20:12] [Deuteronomy 5:16]**

4 Fathers, do not make your children angry. But instead, teach them as they grow up. Teach them about the right way in which the Lord wants them to live their lives.

Slaves and masters

5 Slaves, obey your human masters. Remember how important they are. And be afraid of them. Work well for them because you really want to make them happy. Work for them as if you were working for Christ. 6 Do not work well only when they can see you. Do not work well only to make people happy. But instead, always work well, as Christ's slaves. Work because you really want to obey God. 7 Be happy to work as well as you can for your human masters. Work as if you were working for the Lord, and not only for people. 8 Remember this: anyone who does any good thing will also receive something good from the Lord as a result. This will happen whether that person is a slave or a free person.

9 Masters, be good to your slaves in the same way. Do not say things that will frighten them. Do not say that you will punish them for no good reason. Remember that both you and your slaves have the same Master in heaven. And everyone is important to him. He is never kinder to one person than he is to another person.

God's soldiers

10 The last thing that I want to say to you is this. Be strong by the Lord's great power, because you are united with him. 11 Put on the whole armour that God gives to us. So then you will continue to be strong against all the clever ways by which the Devil attacks us. 12 You need to be strong because we are not fighting against human enemies. No, but instead we are fighting against the rulers and the powerful spirits that have authority over this dark world. We are fighting against powerful bad spirits who live in the heavens. 13 So, take the whole armour that God gives. Then you will be able to stand against the enemy when he attacks. And he will not be able to move you from your place. Then, after you have done everything, you will still be standing strongly in your place.

14 So stand. Always remember and obey God's true message. That will be like a belt round you. Always be right with God. That will be like a strong metal plate that you put over the front of your body. 15 Remember God's good news that makes you friends with God and with each other. That will be like shoes on your feet, to make you ready to fight. 16 Always continue to believe God. That will be like a shield that you hold in front of you. It will put out all the burning arrows that the Devil throws at you. 17 Remember that God has saved you. That will be like a strong metal hat on your head, to keep you safe. Also, remember what God has said. That will be like a strong knife that you can use, by God's Spirit, to fight.

18 To do all of this, pray all the time as God's Spirit leads you to pray. Pray about everything. Ask God for what you need. For this purpose, be careful to continue praying always for all God's people. 19 Pray for me, too. Pray that God will give me the right words to speak. Pray that I will not be afraid to tell people about the secret of the good news. 20 God sent me to tell the good news to people. And that is why I am in prison. So, pray that I will not be afraid to speak. I want to speak the good news bravely, as I ought to speak it.

Paul finishes his letter

21 Tychicus, a Christian friend that I love, will tell you all the news about me. He is the Lord's good servant, who continues to work well on the Lord's behalf. He will tell you what I am doing. So then you will know how I am. 22 This is the reason why I am sending him to you. I want him to tell you how we are. And I want him to help you so that you feel stronger and braver.

23 I pray that God, the Father, and our Lord Jesus Christ will be good to you believers. I pray that they will cause you to be without trouble inside yourselves. I pray that they will cause you to love God and other people, as you continue to believe. 24 I pray that God will be very kind to everyone who continues to love our Lord Jesus Christ.

Christ is Worth More than Everything

Philippians

About this letter

Paul wrote this letter while he was in a prison at Rome. Rome is the capital of the country called Italy now. At that time, the king of Rome was very powerful and he ruled many countries. We think that Paul wrote this letter about the year AD 62. That was more than 30 years after Jesus died. At that time, Philippi was an important city in Macedonia (the north part of Greece).

Paul visited Philippi about 12 years before he wrote this letter. He went there to teach the people about Jesus Christ.

Some people there became angry about the things that Paul was doing. So they put Paul in a prison. (See Acts 16:11-40.) We think that Paul visited Philippi again after that. He may have gone there several times. The Christians there were his special friends.

In his letter, Paul tells the Christians that they are very special to him. Like Paul, they are Christ's servants. So, because they also work for Christ, they help Paul to be stronger for Christ. Paul loves Christ. Christ is much, much more important to him than anything else is. The whole purpose of Paul's life is to tell people about Christ.

Christ obeyed God so completely that he died on our behalf. Paul wants the Christians at Philippi to obey God completely too. He wants them to be like Christ. Paul is afraid that they might listen to false teachers. The false teachers were teaching wrong ideas. Paul wants the Christians to do the things that make God happy. They must continue to believe God. They must continue to obey God, even when other people are not kind to them.

Also, Paul thanks the Christians at Philippi for the gifts that they had sent to him. He tells them that he will send Timothy and Epaphroditus to Philippi. These men will tell all the news about Paul to the Christians there.

Chapter 1

Paul and Timothy write a letter

1 Paul and Timothy, who are servants of Christ Jesus, are writing this letter. We are writing to you, God's people at Philippi, who are united to Christ Jesus. We are writing to all of you. This includes your leaders and those who help them.

Paul prays for the believers at Philippi

2 We pray that God our Father and the Lord Jesus Christ will continue to be very kind to you. We pray also that they will cause you to be without trouble inside yourselves.

3 Every time that I think about you, I thank my God because of you. 4 I am always praying for you. Every time that I pray for you, I feel very happy. 5 I am happy because you are helping people to know the good news about Christ. You have helped me with that work since the first day that someone told you about the good news. And you are still helping with that work. 6 I know that God has begun to do good things in you. And he will continue to work in you until the day when Jesus Christ returns. Then God will finish this work in you. I am sure about that.

7 It is right for me to feel like this about you, because I love you so much. You are very special friends to me. And, like me, all of you continue to know how very kind God is to us. You know it now, while I am in this prison. And you knew it before I was in a prison. Then I was free and could teach the good news. I explained to people why the good news is certainly true. And all of that is the reason that I love you. 8 God himself knows that I very much want to be with all of you. I love you in the same way that Christ Jesus himself loves you.

9 This is what I pray for you. I pray that you will continue to love each other more and more. I pray that you will continue to know God more and more. If you do that, you will understand things more completely. You will understand why things are right or wrong. 10 So then, you can choose to do what is best. So you can keep yourselves clean inside until the day when Christ returns. So, on that day, you will not have done anything wrong. 11 Jesus Christ will make you completely good and right with God. Jesus will help you also to do many good things. Then you will show everyone the great things that God has done in you. So people will say that God is very great.

God has done good things as a result of Paul's time in a prison

12 Friends, I want you to know this. The things that have happened to me have helped more people to know about God's good news. 13 I am in a prison because I am Christ's servant. All the soldiers in the king's house know that. And everyone else knows that too. 14 Also, because I am in a prison, almost all of the other Christians here are trusting in the Lord. So they have become much braver. The Lord has made them brave so that they are not afraid to speak God's message to people.

15 It is true that some of these Christians do not like me. So, they are telling people about Christ because they want to make me angry. These Christians want people to think great things about them. They want to be better than I am. But other Christians are friendly to me. They speak about Christ because they want to help me. 16 They speak about him because they love me. They know that God has put me here in this prison. And he wants me to explain to people why the good news is true. 17 Those other Christians, who do not like me, speak about Christ because of wrong reasons. They speak about him because they want to seem important. They do not really want people to know Christ. They want to cause trouble for me while I am here in this prison. 18 But it does not matter! All of them are telling people about Christ. That is the most important thing. Whether they speak because of wrong reasons or because of right reasons, they are speaking about Christ! So, because of that, I am happy.

Yes, and I will continue to be happy. 19 You are praying for me and Jesus Christ's Spirit is helping me. So, what has happened to me will have good results for me. God will save me. I know that, so I will continue to be happy. 20 I never want to do anything that will cause me to be ashamed. I hope very much that I will never do that. I hope that now, as always, I will be brave. In my body, I want to show that Christ is very great. I want to do that if I live. And I want to do that if I die.

21 Christ is everything that I live for. And if I die, that will be even better for me. 22 But if I continue to live in this body, I will be able to do more good work. That work will have good results. So perhaps I should continue to live. I do not know whether to live or to die. I do not know which to choose. 23 I want to do both things. I want to leave this world so that I can be with Christ. That is a much better thing. 24But you people need me to continue to live in my body. 25 I am sure that you need me. So I know that I will continue to live. I will continue to help all of you. I will help you to believe Christ more and more. So, you will become happier and happier. 26 And, when I am with you again, you will have an even better reason to thank Christ Jesus. You will say that he is very great. You will say that because of what he has done for me.

27 You have believed the good news about Christ. So, whatever things may happen, you must continue to live for Christ. You must do everything that Christ's people should do. So, whether I come to visit you or not, people will tell me good things about you. I will know that you are continuing to believe Christ strongly. You will be like one person with one spirit and one mind, because all of you have the same purpose. You will work together so that more people will believe the good news. 28 You will not be afraid of your enemies, but instead you will be brave. This will show your enemies that God will certainly destroy them. But it will show also that God will certainly save you from the results of sin. 29 God has given you special work to do as Christ's servants. He wants you to believe Christ. But also, he has chosen that you must have troubles and pain on behalf of Christ. 30 You are fighting the same fight that I am fighting. When I was with you, I was fighting that fight. You saw that. And now people are telling you that I am still fighting that fight.

Chapter 2

Be more like Christ

1 You are united with Christ, so he can make you strong and brave. He can help you not to be sad. You can know that he loves you very much. All of you can know his Spirit. So you can be kind to each other. You can love each other as Christ loves you. 2 So, make me completely happy because all of you agree. All of you should love each other in the same way. All of you should be like one person, because you have the same purpose. 3 You must not do only the things that you want. You should not do anything only for the reason that it makes you seem more important than other people. Instead, always think about what other people need. Do not think that you are better than other people. But think about other people as better than you. 4 Do not think only about the things that are important to you yourself. But each of you should think also about the things that are important to other people. 5 You should think in the same way as Christ Jesus thought:

6 Christ had completely the same nature as God.

He was as important as God.

But Christ did not demand that he should continue to be important like that.

7 Instead, he made himself much, much less important.

He took for himself a servant's nature.

He became like men.

8 And when he was a man,

he made himself even less important.

He obeyed God so completely that he died.

He even died on a cross!

9 That is why God raised Jesus Christ to the most important place.

God gave him the name that is greater than every other name.

10 So that, when they hear Jesus' name, everyone must bend down.

Everything that is alive in heaven must bend down.

Everything that is alive on earth, or under the earth, must bend down.

They must bend their knees to show that he is very great.

11 And everything that is alive must say aloud:

'Jesus Christ is Lord.'

That will show that God the Father is very great and very good.

Christians must be like lights in the world

12 So, my friends that I love, you too must obey God. When I was with you, you always obeyed. Now that I am not with you, that is even more important. You are people that God has worked to save from the results of sin. And you must live as people like that should live. You must be very careful to obey God always. You should be afraid not to do that. You must remember that he is very great and very powerful. 13 Obey God, because he is working in you. He is changing you so that you want to obey him. And he is making you able to do the things that make him happy.

14 When you do anything, do not become angry about it. And do not argue about it. 15 Then you will be clean inside yourselves. You will be without anything wrong in you, as God's children should be. And nobody will be able to say that you have done anything wrong. In this world, you are living with bad people all round you.

They have become very bad. And they want to do wrong things. But you must be like lights among them, like the bright stars that shine in the dark sky at night. 16 You will be like lights to these people while you tell Christ's message to them. That message can cause them to become really alive. If you are like this, I can be happy because of you. I will be happy on the day when Christ will return. Then I will know that all my work among you had good results. I will know that I did not waste my time.

17 You believe Christ, so you are his servants. You offer yourselves to God, like a sacrifice, to work for him. Perhaps I will have to die. Perhaps I must become like part of your sacrifice. Perhaps I must become like the drink that people pour on to their sacrifice. But if I die, I will be happy. And I want you to be happy also. 18 It is right that you should be happy too. You should be happy, as I will be happy.

Paul will send Timothy and Epaphroditus to Philippi

19 But I hope that the Lord Jesus will let me send Timothy to you soon. Then, when he returns to me, he can tell me news about you. And that will make me happy. 20 Timothy really loves you, as I do. He really has an interest in you. I have nobody else like him. 21 Everyone else thinks about the things that are important to themselves. They have no interest in the things that are important to Jesus Christ. 22 But you know that Timothy is a good man. He has worked with me like a son works with his father. You know that. He has helped me to tell people the good news. 23 That is why I hope to send him to you. I am waiting to discover what will happen to me. Then, when I know, I will send him. 24 But I believe that the Lord will let me come to you soon myself.

25 Epaphroditus is my Christian brother, who works with me. We are both like soldiers in Christ's army. When I needed help, you sent him to me. And he brought your message to me. But now I think that I must send him back to you. 26 He wants very much to meet all of you again. You knew that he was ill. So he has not been happy that you knew. He does not want you to be sad about him. 27 Certainly, he was very ill, and he almost died. But God was kind to him. God was also kind to me, so that I was not even more sad. 28 So I want even more to send him to you. When you see him, you can be happy. And I will not feel so sad.

29 Like you, he belongs to the Lord's people. So you must say 'welcome' to him. You should be very happy when he comes to visit you. People like Epaphroditus have done great things. So you should remember how important they are. 30 Epaphroditus nearly died because he worked for Christ. He would have died so that he could help me. He helped me because you could not help me yourselves.

Chapter 3

Christ is more important than anything

1 Now, friends, I want to say this to you. Be happy because you are united to the Lord. It is no trouble for me to write the same things to you again. And it will be safer for you. 2 Some people are teaching wrong things. They say that you must cut your bodies. They are like dangerous dogs. Be very careful that you do not believe them. 3 They are not really God's people. But we are God's people, because God himself has circumcised us. We are really his people, because we worship him by his Spirit. We thank God because of what Christ Jesus has done for us. We do not need to have marks on our bodies. We are sure that we cannot save ourselves from the results of sin.

4 I could think that I was good. I could think that I could save myself from the results of sin because of that. I have good reasons to think like that. I have better reasons to think like that than anyone else could have. 5 I belong to Israel's people, to Benjamin's family group. I am a Jew completely. They circumcised me when I was 8 days old. God's rules, that he gave to Israel's people, were very important to me. I was a Pharisee. 6 I wanted very much to be a good Jew. So I caused a lot of trouble and pain for the Christians. I obeyed all God's rules very carefully. I did everything right, as the rules said.

7 But all the things that were very important to me before are worth nothing to me now, because of Christ. 8 And it is not only those things that are worth nothing to me.

Now I think that all things are worth nothing, because of Christ. The only thing that is really important to me is to know Christ Jesus, my Lord. That is the most important thing. I have lost everything for him. But all the things that I have lost are only like dirt to me. I think about them like that, so that I can have Christ. 9 I can be united to him, so that I am completely right with God. If I obeyed all God's rules completely, I could never become right with God. Only God can make me right with himself, because I believe Christ.

10 The only thing that I want is to know Christ. He rose, to become alive again, after he had died. And I want to know in myself how powerful his new life is. Also, I want to have troubles and pain, as he did. I want to become like him in his death. 11 That is how I hope to rise from death myself. I hope to become alive again after death, so that I will live with God always.

Christians do not belong to this world

12 I am not saying that I have already got all those things. I have not yet become completely as God wants me to be. I am not saying that I have become like that already. But Christ Jesus has made me his own. And it is my whole purpose to become completely what he wants me to be. I am like someone who is running strongly to reach a certain point. 13 My friends, I do not think that I have reached that point yet. But this one thing is what I do. I forget past things, which are behind me. And I try very much to reach the things that are in front of me. 14 I run straight towards that point, so that I can win God's gift. God has chosen that I should live in heaven. Then I will be united to Christ Jesus. That is his gift to me.

15 So all of us who have learned to live properly for Christ should think like this. And if you think differently about anything, God will make it clear to you. 16 But we should continue to live as we have lived until now. I mean that we must continue to obey God. We must continue to do what God wants. As far as we understand it, we must do that.

17 My friends, all of you should try to do what I do. Also, watch everyone else who, like me, obeys God. And try to do what they do. Try to be like us. 18 Many people live like enemies of Christ's death on the cross. I have told you about these people many times before. And I am crying when I tell you about them now.

19 God must destroy them. Their god is their stomach. They do bad things that should make them ashamed. But they are not ashamed. Instead, they are happy because they do those bad things. They do bad things like that. And they think that they are clever because of it. They think only about the things that belong to this world. 20 But we belong to heaven. Our home is not really in this world. We are waiting for the Lord Jesus Christ, who saves us from the results of sin, to come from heaven. We very much want him to come. 21 He will change these poor bodies that we have now on this earth. He will make our bodies like his own beautiful body in heaven. Christ can do this because he is so powerful. He is so powerful that he can rule over everything.

Chapter 4

Paul is happy about the Christians at Philippi

1 My friends, I love you very much. And I want very much to meet you again. You make me very happy. You show that my work among you had good results. So I am very happy because of you. My good friends, please remember what I have told you. If you do remember it, you will continue to believe Christ strongly. You will continue to live for the Lord, because you are united to him.

Agree with each other

2 I say this to Euodia and I say it to Syntyche: 'You are like sisters because you are united to the Lord. So I ask very strongly that you agree with each other.'

3 I ask you too, my good friend, to help these women. You have worked with me to tell people the good news. And these women have worked with me too. They have worked very much so that people would believe the good news. They worked with Clement, and they worked with all my other workers. All those workers' names are in God's book. This book says who will live with him always.

Be happy and think good thoughts

4 Always be happy because you live united to the Lord. I will say it again, 'Be happy!' 5 Always be kind and patient. So everyone will see that you are very kind and good. Remember that the Lord is near. 6 Do not be afraid about anything. Do not let anything cause you trouble inside yourselves. Instead, tell everything to God. Pray to him. Ask him for everything that you need. And when you pray, always thank him. 7 If you do that, God will rule you. He will rule your minds by Christ Jesus. He will rule what you feel like. He will cause you to be without trouble inside yourselves. God is so great that he can do that for us. But we cannot understand how he does it.

8 Now friends, I want to say this to you. Think about the things that are true and honest. Think about the things that are right and good and lovely. Everyone can see that some things are completely good. Think about these things. 9 Do those things that you learned from me. Remember the things that I said. Remember the things that I did. You must do those things too. And so the God who causes us to be without trouble inside ourselves will be with you.

Paul thanks the believers at Philippi for their gifts to him

10 I am very happy that now you want to help me again. I thank the Lord that you want to help me. I know that you helped me before. But it is a long time since you had a chance to help me. 11 I am not saying this because I need anything. I have learned to be happy, whatever things may be happening to me. 12 I know what it is like to need things. I know what it is like to have plenty. I have learned to be happy at any time and during all things. I have learned this secret. I can be happy whether I have enough food or not. I can be happy whether I have plenty of things or nothing. 13 I can do everything because Christ makes me strong.

14 But certainly, you have been very kind to me. You have helped me at this time, when I am in trouble. 15 You helped me also earlier, when I was starting to tell people the good news. When I left Macedonia, you helped me.

You were the only group of Christians who helped me then. You people who live at Philippi know that yourselves. No other group of Christians gave gifts to me as you did. 16 Even when I was at Thessalonica, you helped me. More than once, you sent gifts to me because I needed things.

17 It is not your gifts themselves that I want. But instead, I want you to do good things so that God will be happy about you. So he will be good to you even more, because you have helped me. 18 Epaphroditus has brought the gifts that you sent to me. I have received those gifts, and now I do not need anything. You have sent me plenty. It is more than enough. Your gifts are like a sacrifice with a nice smell that people offer to God. God accepts a sacrifice like that, because it makes him happy. 19 My God, who has plenty of very good things for us because of Christ Jesus, will supply everything for you. By Christ, God will give to you everything that you need.

20 Everyone should always say that our God, our Father, is very great! They should never stop saying that! This is true.

21 On behalf of me, say 'hello' to everyone who belongs to Christ Jesus' people. The Christians who are here with me say 'hello' to you. 22 All God's people here say 'hello' to you. And those Christians who live in the king's house say a special 'hello' to you.

23 We pray that the Lord Jesus Christ will continue to be very kind to all of you.

Alive and New with Christ

Colossians

About this letter

Colossae was a city in Roman Asia. 'Asia' was the south and west part of the country that we call Turkey now. At that time, the Roman people were very powerful and they ruled many countries. (Rome is the capital of the country that we call Italy now.)

We think that Paul himself never visited Colossae. Instead, a man called Epaphras went there to tell the good news about Jesus Christ to the people. Epaphras had heard about the good news from Paul.

After that, when Paul was in a prison somewhere, Epaphras visited him. Epaphras told Paul the news about the Christians who lived at Colossae. Then Paul wrote this letter to them while he was still in the prison.

Epaphras had told Paul that false teachers were teaching wrong things to the Christians at Colossae. The false teachers were saying that the Christians must be more like the Jews. 'You must obey the same rules that God wanted the Jews to obey', they were saying. Also, they were teaching other wrong ideas and rules.

So, Paul tells the Christians that they should not believe the false teachers. Only Jesus Christ can save us from our old nature and from all the wrong things that we do. By 'old nature', we mean 'the kind of person that we are before we become a Christian'. Jesus made the world. And he wants to save the people who live in it. We only need to believe him. Then, in our spirits, we can die with Christ and we can become alive again with him. So, we can be new people, with a new nature. We must continue to believe Jesus. We must continue also to obey him. If we do that, we will be safe.

Chapter 1

1 We, Paul and our Christian friend, Timothy, are writing this letter. God has chosen me, Paul, to be a special worker and teacher on behalf of Christ Jesus. 2 We are writing to you, God's people who live at Colossae.

You are like brothers and sisters to us because you are united to Christ. And you are continuing to believe Christ. We pray that God, our Father, will continue to be very kind to you. We pray also that he will cause you to be without trouble inside yourselves.

Paul thanks God for the believers at Colossae

3 We always thank God, the Father of our Lord Jesus Christ, when we pray for you. 4 We thank God because people have told us good things about you. You are continuing to believe Christ Jesus and you are loving all God's people. 5 You are doing these things because you are hoping certainly for good things from God. God is keeping safe the things that you are hoping for. He is storing them in heaven for you. You learned about those things before, when people first told you the true message, the good news.

6 This good news has caused good results among you since the time when you heard it first. At that time, you understood clearly how very kind and good God really is. Also, people all over the world are hearing this good news. And it is causing more and more good results among them too. 7 You heard about this good news from Epaphras. Like us, he is Christ's servant. And we love Epaphras very much. He continues to work well for Christ on our behalf. 8 Epaphras has told us how God's Spirit has caused you to love other people.

Paul prays that they will know God more and more

9 It is because of these things that we have not stopped praying for you. We have prayed ever since the day that Epaphras told us news about you. We ask God that his Spirit will cause you to understand things properly. So you will know completely and clearly what God wants you to do. 10 So then you will be able to do those things that the Lord's people should do. And you will always do the things that make the Lord happy. As a result, you will do many kinds of good things during your lives. And you will know God more and more. 11 God will make you strong inside yourselves because he is so very great and powerful. So, whatever things may happen, you can be patient, brave and happy. 12 And you can thank the Father, who has made it possible for you to join his people. With them, you will receive what he has prepared for his people in the light. 13 God, our Father, has saved us from the authority of bad, dark powers. He loves his Son. And he has caused us to be his Son's people. And so now, his Son rules over us. 14 God's Son has made us free, so that God will not punish us. Because of his Son, God has forgiven us for the wrong things that we have done.

Who Christ is and what he has done for us

15 We cannot see God. But Jesus Christ is completely what God is. Even before God made anything, Jesus was already the Son of the Father. 16 God made everything that is on earth and in heaven by his Son. He made all the things that we can see. And he made those things that we cannot see. He made rulers; and he made leaders. He made them powerful; and he gave authority to them. God made them all by his Son. God made everything by his Son and for his Son. 17 Christ was there before anything else, and he holds all things together. 18 Think about Christ's people as his body. Christ is the head of that body. It is called the church. He is the beginning. And he is the Son of the Father. So he is the leader of everyone who will win the fight against death. As a result, Christ is first and most important in all things.

19 It really gave God pleasure that all of himself is in Christ. His whole nature is in Christ. 20 Also, it really gave God pleasure to bring all things back to himself. He did that by the cross. There Christ bled and died. His death brought God and all things together, whether things on earth or things in heaven. They are not still enemies.

21 At one time, you were far away from God. You were his enemies because you thought bad things. You were his enemies because you did bad things. 22 But now everything has changed. This happened because Christ died a human death. So God has decided to bring you back to himself. He has decided to make you completely good and clean inside. And nobody will ever be able to say that you have done anything wrong.

23 But you must continue to believe Christ strongly. You must not let anything cause you to stop. You must continue to hope strongly for everything that you have learned from the good news. People have told this good news to everyone in the world. And God has made me, Paul, a servant who tells people this good news.

Paul's work for Christ's people

24 At this time, I am having trouble and pain on your behalf, but I am happy. Christ had trouble and pain on behalf of his own people. And, while I live in my body, I am having trouble and pain also. I am helping to finish the full quantity of troubles and pain that Christ must still have. He must still have troubles and pain because of his body, which is his people.

25 God has made me a servant, who helps his people. He has chosen me to tell you his whole message. 26 This message is the secret that God hid from everyone before. He hid it from all the people who lived in past times. But now he is showing this secret to his people. 27 God wanted his people to know how very great this secret is. It is very, very good and it will help people from all countries very, very much. This secret is Christ in you. And because he is in you, you hope certainly for good things. You are sure that you will live with God always. You will be with him in the beautiful place where he lives. 28 That is why we tell everyone about Christ. We teach them everything that we know. We tell them what God wants them to do. We tell them what he does not want. Our purpose, for every person who is united to Christ, is this. We want every person to become completely what he or she should be. We want to bring each person to God like that. 29 That is why I work so very much. Christ makes me very strong for this difficult work. He works powerfully in me to make me strong.

Chapter 2

1 I want you to know how very much I am working for you and for the people at Laodicea. I am also working for all those people who have never met me. 2 I am working like this because I want all of you to become strong inside yourselves for Christ. I want you to be united because you love Christ and each other. So then you will really be rich, because you will really understand God's secret. You will be completely sure about it. You will know that secret, which is Christ. 3 Christ knows and understands everything. Only Christ can cause us to understand things properly. He can cause us to understand the really valuable things that we need to know.

4 I am telling you these things so that you will not listen to false teachers. Those teachers will try to teach you false things that may seem good. 5 My body is not there with you, but my spirit is with you. And I am happy about you. You are doing the things that Christ's people should do. Also, I am happy that you are continuing to believe Christ so strongly.

What Christ's people, who are united to Christ, should do

6 You have agreed that Christ Jesus should be your Lord. And you have become united to him. So, you must continue to do the things that Christ's people ought to do. 7 You must be like trees that have their roots deep in Christ. Continue to obey Christ, so that you become stronger and stronger as Christians. You must believe more and more strongly the things that we taught you. And you should always thank God very much for everything.

8 Some people may try to teach you false ideas. Be careful that you do not believe them. Those ideas may seem clever, but they will take you away from God. Those ideas are the result of things that people have taught for many years. But those ideas belong to this world. They do not come from Christ. 9 The whole of God himself lives in Christ, in his human body. 10 And because you are united to Christ, God has filled you. He has given you everything that you need in Christ. And Christ rules over all spirits that have authority.

11 Also, because you are united to Christ, God has circumcised you. No human person used his hands to circumcise you. But God has circumcised you, in the way that Christ has made possible. He has made you free from the power of your old nature (the kind of people that you were before you became Christians). He has taken away your old nature, which could never make God happy.

12 By baptism, God has buried you with Christ. And then he has raised you with Christ, so that you have become alive again with him. God raised you because you believe him. You believe that he is very powerful. And you believe that he raised Christ. He made him alive again after he had died.

13 At one time, you were like dead people because of all the wrong things that you did. Nobody had circumcised you in your spirits. But now God has caused you to become alive with Christ. God has forgiven us for all the wrong things that we have done. 14 He has chosen to forget that we have not obeyed all his rules. He has taken away the list of all the wrong things that we have done. He should have punished us because of that list. But instead, it is like he fixed that list to Christ's cross. So, he destroyed that list. 15 On the cross, Christ won the fight against all the bad spirits that have authority. He beat them completely. He took all their weapons away from them. He showed everyone that he is the ruler over all these other powerful spirits.

Christ's people should not obey men's ideas

16 So do not let anybody else say what is right for you to eat or to drink. Do not let anybody make rules about special days, new moons or Sabbaths (the Jews' seventh day of the week). 17 Rules like that are only like shadows. In past times, they showed people about the good things that would happen. But those good things really have happened now because of Christ.

18 Some people may say that God has shown them special things. They may tell you that you should do certain things to your bodies to become better people. They may tell you that you should worship angels. But you must not believe those false things. If you listen to them, you may lose something really important. People like that may think that they know a lot of things. But they are only thinking men's ideas. They do not understand how God thinks. 19 False teachers like that do not agree to be united to Christ. They do not obey Christ, who is the head of his body. His people are like a body. Christ holds the whole body together. Through the parts that join the body together, Christ supplies the body. He supplies what the body needs. And so, the body grows, because God causes it to grow.

20 You have died with Christ. So you do not have to obey the rules that belong to this world. You do not belong to this world now. So you should not still obey its rules! You do not need to obey rules like this: 21 'do not touch this thing! Do not taste that food! Keep away from that thing!' 22 Rules like that are only about things that will finish. Those things are like things that people use. But they are destroying those things while they are using them. Rules like that are only rules that people teach.

23 Rules like that may seem to be clever people's rules. They try to cause people to worship in certain ways. They cause people to hurt themselves, so that they can rule their bodies. So those people seem to be obeying God. But really, they are not obeying him. Those rules cannot really help people to rule what their bodies want. Those rules are not really worth anything. By those rules people can still do all the bad things that they want to do.

Chapter 3

The old life and the new life

1 God has raised you from death, so that you are alive with Christ. So, you should continue to look up. You should want more and more the things that are in heaven, with Christ. Christ is sitting next to God, at his right side. 2 Continue to think about things that are above. Do not think about things that are on the earth. 3 Think like that, because you have died. And now you are alive with Christ, who is united to God. God is keeping your life safe with Christ. 4 It is Christ who causes us to be alive. And when Christ shows himself clearly to everyone, then everyone will see you also with him. You will be like him and you will shine with him.

5 So you must refuse to do bad things that belong to this earth. So then those things will stop being part of your life. You must not have sex with someone who is not your husband or your wife. You must not think bad, dirty thoughts. You must not want to have sex with other people. You must not want to do bad things. You must not want to have more and more things for yourselves. People who want things strongly like that are making those things more important than God. They are really worshipping those things. 6 God will be very angry with people who do those bad things. And he will punish those people.

7 At one time, you were doing these kinds of bad things. These things were ruling your lives then. 8 But now you must refuse to do these kinds of things. You must not become angry easily. You must not continue to be angry with people. You must not want to do bad things to people. You must not say bad things that are not true about people. You must not speak bad and dirty words. 9 Stop saying things that are not true to each other. You should be like someone who has taken off old clothes. You have taken off the old nature. And, with that old nature, you have taken off all the bad things that you did before. That is why you should stop doing those things.

10 Instead, you have put on the new nature, which God has made. And God is continuing to make you more and more like him. So then you will know him more and more completely. 11 When people have this new nature, they are not different from each other. Jews are not different from people who are not Jews. It does not matter whether someone has circumcised you or not. It does not matter which country you come from. It does not matter whether you are a slave or a free person. But Christ is what matters. He is everything, and he is in everything.

12 God has chosen you to be his own special people. He loves you very much. So, you should choose to do good things, as God's people should do. You should be good and kind to other people.

You should want to help them. You should not think that you are better or more important than other people. But you should be patient with them. 13 Do not get angry with each other, but be patient. You may not be happy about something that someone else has done. But you should forgive that person. Forgive them as the Lord forgave you. 14 And you should love each other. That is the most important thing that you should do. Love is like clothes that go over all your other clothes. Love holds everything and everybody together. Love makes everything completely as it should be.

15 Let Christ rule what you think. Let him rule what you feel. If you do that, you will have no trouble inside yourselves or with other Christians. God wants you to be united like this, because all of you belong to one body really. And always thank God for everything.

16 Let Christ's message live in you. Let it work in you. It will do many good things in you. It will help you to teach each other. It will help you to understand things correctly. God's Spirit will cause you to sing different kinds of songs to each other, while you worship God. You will sing like this to thank him for everything that he has done. 17 Everything that you do should make the Lord Jesus happy. Everything that you say should make him happy. And whatever things you do, you should thank God the Father by the Lord Jesus' name.

Do what is right, at home and at work

18 Wives, obey your husbands. That is the right thing to do, because you are the Lord's.

19 Husbands, love your wives and be kind to them.

20 Children, you must obey your parents about everything. That is how you can make the Lord happy.

21 Fathers, do not make your children angry with you. They might think that they can never do anything to make you happy with them.

22 Slaves, always obey your human masters in everything. Do not work well only when they can see you. So then they will be happy with you. Instead, always do your work well, because you really love the Lord. So you want to make him happy. 23 Whatever things you do, do them for the Lord. Do them as well as you can for him. Do not work only for people. 24 So then the Lord will give to you all the good things that he has promised you. You know that. You are the Lord Christ's servants. 25 But the Lord will punish anyone who does wrong things. That is what ought to happen to people like that. God uses the same rules to decide what should happen to each person. It does not matter who that person is.

Chapter 4

1 Masters, give your servants what is right and fair. Remember that you have a Master also, in heaven.

Paul tells the believers that they should pray

2 Continue to pray. Do not let anything cause you to stop praying. Be like people who watch carefully. They watch carefully to see what is happening. And thank God when you pray. 3 Pray for us, too. Ask God to make it possible for us to tell people his message. We want to tell people the secret things about Christ that God has caused us to know. I am in a prison because I told people those things. 4 I want to tell people this message clearly, as I ought to do. Pray that I will be able to do that.

5 Sometimes you are with people who do not believe Christ. Be careful when you are with those people. Be careful about what you say. Be careful about what you do. Use your time with them as well as you can. Do everything that you can to help them to believe Christ.

6 Always speak words that are kind and proper. Speak words that will be good for those who hear you. When someone asks you a question, you should know what to say. You should know how you ought to answer each person.

Paul finishes his letter

7 Tychicus will tell you all the news about me. He is a Christian brother that we love. He continues to work well for the Lord. Like me, he is the Lord's servant. 8 I am sending him to you for this purpose. He will tell you all the news about us. And he will help you to be braver and stronger for Christ. 9 Onesimus, who belongs to your group, is travelling with him. Onesimus is another Christian brother that we love. He continues to believe and to obey Christ. These men will tell you everything that is happening here.

10 Aristarchus, who is with me in the prison, says 'hello' to you. Mark also says 'hello' to you. He is Barnabas's cousin. Mark may come to visit you. You should say 'welcome' to him if he comes. I have told you this already. I have told you that you should be kind to him. 11 Jesus, who is called Justus, also says 'hello' to you. These three men are the only Jews who are working with me. We work so that more people will believe Christ. So then they will belong to God's people, the people that he rules over. These men have helped me very much. And they have caused me to feel better.

12 Epaphras says 'hello' to you. He also belongs to your group, and he is Christ Jesus' servant. He is always praying strongly for you. He prays like someone who fights on behalf of you. He prays that you will continue to obey God. So you will always do everything that God wants. He asks God to make you completely as God wants you to be. 13 I tell you this about Epaphras, which is true. He is working very much for you, and for the people at Laodicea and at Hierapolis.

14 Our good friend Luke, the doctor, and Demas say 'hello' to you. 15 Say 'hello' for me to all the believers at Laodicea. Also say 'hello' for me to Nympha and to the Christians who meet in her house.

16 After someone has read this letter to all of you, send it to the church at Laodicea. Tell them that they must read it aloud too. And you must also read the letter that the Christians at Laodicea will send to you. 17 Say to Archippus, 'Remember the work that the Lord gave you to do. You must be careful to finish it completely.'

18 I, Paul, am writing these words here with my own hand. Remember that I am in a prison. I pray that God will continue to be very kind to you.

Be Ready for Jesus to Return

1 Thessalonians

About 1 Thessalonians

Thessalonica was a large city in Macedonia. Macedonia included the north part of the country that we call Greece. It included also the south part of the country that we call Yugoslavia. Thessalonica was an important port, and roads from several different directions joined there. So, people could travel easily to Thessalonica. It is still an important city today.

Paul was a great Christian teacher. He went to Thessalonica to teach the people there about Jesus Christ. He stayed there for only a short time, perhaps only a few weeks. Two other men, called Silas and Timothy, went there with him. As a result of what Paul taught them, some Jews at Thessalonica believed Christ. Many other people who were not Jews also believed. But the Jews who refused to believe Christ caused a lot of trouble for Paul and his friends. Paul had to leave the city at night. Paul and his friends went to Berea, which was a city about 50 miles west from Thessalonica. (See Acts 17:1-15.)

Paul taught the people at Berea too. Then he travelled to Athens, a city in the south of Greece. But Silas and Timothy stayed at Berea. Paul waited at Athens for them to come to him there (Acts 17:15-16). Paul was sorry that he had not had enough time at Thessalonica. He wanted to teach the new believers there a lot more about Christ. But he could not go himself (1 Thessalonians 2:17-18). So, he sent Timothy (chapter 3:1-3).

While Timothy went back to Thessalonica, Paul travelled to Corinth (Acts 18:1). The city called Corinth was also in the south part of Greece. After that, Silas and Timothy arrived in Corinth (Acts 18:5). Then Timothy told Paul the news about the Christians at Thessalonica. Paul was very happy to know that they were continuing to believe Christ. He wrote this letter to them from Corinth.

Paul, together with Silas and Timothy, wrote this letter in the year AD 50 or AD 51. That was about 20 years after Jesus died. So, this letter may be the first of Paul's letters that we have in the Bible. Paul wrote it only a few months after he had first taught the Christian message at Thessalonica. So, he was writing to people who had been Christians for only a short time.

Paul tells them that he always thinks about them. He wants very much to visit them again (chapters 2 and 3). Paul also teaches them about how they should do only good, right things, to make God happy. And in chapters 4 and 5, he teaches them about Jesus' return to the earth.

Chapter 1

Paul thanks God for the believers at Thessalonica

1 This letter is from Paul, Silas and Timothy to the Christians at Thessalonica. You are united to God the Father and to the Lord Jesus Christ. We pray that God will continue to be very kind to you. We pray also that he will cause you to be without trouble inside yourselves.

2 We thank God for all of you at all times. Every time that we pray, we always pray for you. 3 We speak about you to God, who is our Father. We remember the good things that you do. You do those things because you believe Christ. You work very much because you love Christ and other people. We remember also how you continue to hope strongly because of our Lord Jesus Christ.

4 You are like brothers and sisters to us, and God loves you. We know that God has chosen you to be his own. 5 We know that, because of us, our good news came to you not only with words. When we told it to you, the power of God's Spirit was there too. Also, we felt completely brave and strong when we spoke. You know how we lived among you. You know what kind of people we were. We were like good guides for you. 6 And you learned to live as we lived. So you learned also to live like the Lord. People caused you a lot of trouble and pain because you believed the message about Christ. But you did believe it, and God's Spirit caused you to be very happy. 7 And so you became like a guide to all the believers in Macedonia and in Achaia.

8 Because of you, people in many places have listened to the message about the Lord. It was not only the people in Macedonia and in Achaia who listened to these things. But people everywhere know how you believe God. So, we do not need to say anything. 9 Those people themselves speak about how you believed our message. They tell how you turned to God. They tell us how you stopped worshipping false gods. They themselves say that you are now God's servants. God is alive, and only he is really God. 10 Also, you are waiting for God's Son to come from heaven. God caused his Son, Jesus, to become alive again after he had died. And Jesus saves us so that God will not be angry with us at that future time.

Chapter 2

Paul's work in Thessalonica

1 Our friends, you yourselves know that our visit to you had good results. 2 Before we came to you, the people at Philippi had done bad things to hurt us. And they had spoken very bad words to us. You know that. But our God caused us to be brave so that we could tell you his good news. Many people tried to stop us, but we did tell you God's message.

3 We were telling you the good news so that you could believe God. We told you only true things. We had no wrong purpose. We did not want you to believe things that are not true. 4 Instead, we say what God wants us to say. He has chosen us to tell his good news. We do not speak so that we can make people happy. But we do want to make God happy. And God discovers what our purposes really are, deep inside ourselves. 5 We never tried to say nice things about you so that you would like us. You know that. We never demanded money or other things from you. We never had a secret purpose like that. God knows this. 6 We did not want people to say great things about us. We did not want you to do that. And we did not want anyone else to do that. We are Christ's special workers and teachers. So, we could have used our authority over you. We could have caused you to do things for us. We could have caused you to supply things for us.

7 But instead, we were kind when we were with you. We were kind like a mother who looks after her little children. 8 We were very fond of you. So, we wanted very much to tell you the good news from God. Also, we wanted to give ourselves completely to help you. We wanted to do these things because we loved you very much. 9 Our friends, you should certainly remember how we worked so very much. We worked during the day and at night. We worked so that we did not need to ask any of you for anything. So then, we did not cost you anything while we taught you God's good news.

10 When we were with you believers, we did nothing wrong. We did only what is completely good and right. You know that, and God knows it too. 11-12 You know that we helped each of you. We were like a father who helps his own children. We taught you and we helped you to be brave and strong as believers. And we told you very strongly what you must do. You must do what makes God happy. God has chosen you to belong to his own people, the people that he rules over. He wants you to be with him always, in the beautiful place where he lives.

13 There is also another reason why we continue to thank God always. When we told God's message to you, you believed it as words from God. You knew that it was not only a human message. You believed it as God's message, which it certainly is. And God's words do powerful things in you who believe him.

14 And now, my friends, you have become like the Christians who belong to God's people in Judea. People in your own country have caused trouble and pain for you. And that is what happened in Judea too to the believers in Christ Jesus there. People in their own country caused trouble and pain for them.

15 The people who caused that trouble even killed the Lord Jesus and the prophets. And they caused trouble for us so that they caused us to leave their country. God is not happy with those people. He is very angry with them. They are very much against people everywhere 16 because they do not want us to speak to people from other nations. They do not want God to save anyone from another nation. Those people always continue until they have done their last sin. But in the end, God has punished them.

Paul wants to visit the believers at Thessalonica again

17 But you are like brothers and sisters to us. We have had to go away from you for a short time. But it was only our bodies that left you. We did not stop thinking about you. We wanted very, very much to see your faces. And we tried very much to visit you again. 18 We wanted to return to you. Certainly, I, Paul, tried again and again to return, but Satan made it impossible. 19 We wanted so much to visit you because you cause us to hope so strongly! You make us sure that God will continue to work in you. You cause us to be very happy! To us, you are like a crown that a winner receives. The crown shows that the winner has done well. You show that our work among you had good results. So, you are our crown that makes us very happy. We will be very happy when we stand in front of our Lord Jesus. That will be when he comes again. 20 Yes, it is because of you that we are so happy. We are happy about the results of our work.

Chapter 3

Timothy has told good news to Paul about the believers at Thessalonica

1 When we could not wait any longer to know news about you, we decided to stay in Athens city alone. We thought that it was the best thing to do. 2 And we sent Timothy to visit you. He is like our brother. He works with us for God, to tell people the good news about Christ. We sent Timothy so that he could help you to believe Christ strongly and to be brave. 3 So then none of you will stop believing because of the troubles and pain that people cause you. You yourselves know that there must be troubles and pain for us. That is part of God's purpose for us.

4 Even when we were with you, we told you to be ready for future trouble. We told you that people would certainly cause you a lot of trouble and pain. And that did happen. You know that. 5 That is why I had to send Timothy. I could not wait any longer, so I sent him to you. I wanted to know whether you were continuing to believe Christ. I was afraid that Satan had caused you to turn away from Christ. So all our work among you would have no results.

6 But now Timothy has come back to us from you. And he has told us good news about you. He has told us how you are continuing to believe Christ. You are continuing, also, to love God and each other. And you are always happy when you think about us. You want very much to meet us again, as we want to meet you. Timothy has told us these things. 7 So, we have become stronger and braver because of you, who are like brothers and sisters to us. People have caused us very much trouble and pain. But we were very happy to know that you were continuing to believe Christ.

8 Now, because of you, we are like people who have become alive again. You are united to the Lord. And if you continue to believe him strongly, that makes us very happy. 9 Now we can thank God very much for you! We are very, very happy when we talk to God about you. And so we thank him for that. 10 We continue to ask God that we might visit you. We pray like that every day and every night. We want very, very much to visit you. We want to teach things to you that you still need to know. So then you can really believe Christ as you should believe him.

11 We pray this to God himself, who is our Father, and to our Lord Jesus. We pray that they will prepare the way for us to visit you. 12 We pray also that the Lord will cause you to love each other more and more. We love you. And we want you to go on loving all people more and more in the same way. 13 So, the Lord will cause you to become strong inside yourselves. You will be completely good and clean for God, who is our Father. So then nobody can ever say that you have done anything wrong. And you will stand in front of God when our Lord Jesus comes. Jesus will return to this earth, with all those who are his own.

Chapter 4

A life that makes God happy

1 Now, friends, we want to say this to you. We taught you how to live so that you make God happy. And certainly, you are living like that. Now we ask you very strongly to continue to live like that more and more. On behalf of the Lord Jesus, we ask you to do this. 2 You know what we told you. We told you what you must do. The Lord Jesus gave us authority to tell you those things.

3 What God wants is this: He wants you to be completely good, and separate from everything that is bad. So you must not have wrong sex. You must not have sex with anyone who is not your own wife or husband. 4 Each of you must learn how to rule his own body. So then you will always do what is right and proper. 5 You should not be like the people who do not know God. They are always wanting very much to have sex. They cannot stop themselves, because they want it so much. But you should not be like those people.

6 No man among you should ever have sex with a woman who is not his own wife. He would be taking something that is another man's. So, he would be doing a wrong thing to that man, who is like his brother. The Lord will punish everyone who does things like that. We have told you this very seriously before. 7 God did not choose us to do bad and dirty things. He chose us to be completely separate from everything that is bad. 8 So anyone who does not obey this rule is not refusing to obey a human person. Instead, he is refusing to do what God says. And God gives you his Spirit, who is completely good.

9 But I do not need to write to you about how you should love other believers. God himself has taught you to love each other. 10 Certainly, you do love all the believers in all Macedonia. But we ask you strongly, friends, to love each other more and more. 11 Try very much not to cause trouble for anyone. Be busy only with your own things, not with other people's things. And work with your hands. We told you before that you must do these things. 12 Then, if you do these things, other people will think good things about you. People who do not believe Christ will think good things about you. They will know that you are honest and good. Also, if you do these things, you will not need anyone else to supply anything for you.

Jesus' return and the believers who have died

13 Friends, we want you to understand properly about the people who have died. So you will not be sad about them, as other people are sad about their dead friends. Those other people are sad because they have nothing to hope for, after death. 14 But we believe that Jesus died. We believe that he became alive again after death. So, we also believe this about the people who have died united to Christ. We believe that God will bring those people back with Jesus.

15 We are now telling you something that the Lord has said. We tell you this about the day when the Lord will come. Those of us who are still alive on that day will not go to meet the Lord first. We will certainly not go before those people who have already died. 16 On that day, God will shout with authority. Also, people will hear the voice of an important angel. They will hear the sound of God's trumpet. And the Lord himself will come down from heaven. Then those people who have died united to Christ will become alive again. And they will rise first. 17 After that, those of us who are still alive at that time will go up. God will take us up to be together with them in the clouds. He will take us to meet the Lord in the air. And so we will be with the Lord always. 18 So tell these things to each other. So you will not need to continue being sad.

Chapter 5

We must be ready for Jesus to return

1 Friends, we do not need to write to you about the dates and times when these things will happen. 2 You know very well about how the day of the Lord's return will happen. That day will surprise people very much, as when someone comes to rob people at night. 3 At that time, people will say, 'We are safe and there is no trouble for us.' But then, when they are not ready for it, a lot of trouble and pain will happen to them. That trouble will happen to them like the pains of a woman who is giving birth to a baby. And it will be impossible for anyone to get free from that trouble.

4 But you people, who are like brothers and sisters to us, you know about these things. So, you are not like people who live in the dark. And so the day when the Lord returns should not surprise you. That day will not surprise you as when someone comes to rob people. 5 All of you are people who are the Lord's people. So, you belong to the light and to the day. We are not people who belong to the night or to the dark. 6 So, we should not be like other people. We should not be like people who are sleeping. Instead, we should be like people who continue to be awake. We should think clearly about what is happening.

7 It is at night that people sleep. It is at night that people are drunks. 8 But we belong to the day. So we should watch and we should think clearly. We must continue to believe God and to love him. So we will be like soldiers who put on breastplates. Also, we must continue to hope strongly that God will save us. So we will be like soldiers who put on metal hats to keep their heads safe.

9 God did not make us his people so that he could be angry with us. He has not chosen us so that he can punish us. Instead, he has chosen us so that he can save us. He saves us because of what our Lord Jesus Christ has done. 10 Jesus died for us so that we can live together with him. When he comes, we will live with him. Whether we are alive or dead at that time, there will not be any difference. We will all live with him. 11 So, tell these things to each other so that you do not feel sad or weak. Help each other to become stronger as believers, as you are doing already.

Paul's last words in this letter

12 Now we ask you, our friends, to remember how valuable your leaders are. They work among you and they look after you. They teach you how you should live as the Lord's people. They tell you when you do wrong things. 13 Show them how valuable they are to you. And love them very much because of the work that they do. Do not quarrel with each other.

14 Tell lazy people that they should work. Speak to those people who are afraid. Help them to be brave. Help those people who are weak. Be patient with everyone. Friends, we ask you strongly to do these things. 15 If a person has done something wrong to you, do not do something wrong back to them. Be careful that none of you does things like that. But always try to do good things to each other and to everyone else.

16 Always be happy. 17 Pray at all times. 18 Whatever things may happen to you, continue to thank God. God wants you to do this, because you are united to Christ Jesus. 19 Do not stop letting God's Spirit work in you as people might put out a fire. 20 Listen carefully when people speak messages on God's behalf. Remember that those messages are important. 21 But think carefully about everything, to see if it really is from God. Then be careful to remember and to obey everything that is good. 22 Refuse to have anything to do with any kind of bad or wrong thing.

23 God causes us to be without trouble inside ourselves. And I pray that God himself will make you completely good and clean. I pray that God will look after your spirits, your souls and your bodies. I pray that he will look after you completely. Then you will be completely good and clean when our Lord Jesus Christ returns. 24 God has chosen you to be his people. And he always does what he has promised to do. So, he will do this for you.

25 Our friends, please pray for us. 26 Say 'hello' to all the believers. Kiss them as you would kiss your brother.

27 I tell you very seriously, on behalf of the Lord, that you should read this letter to all the believers. 28 I pray that our Lord Jesus Christ will continue to be very kind to you.

Jesus Has Not Returned Yet

2 Thessalonians

About 2 Thessalonians

Thessalonica was a large city in Macedonia. Macedonia included the north part of the country that we call Greece. It also included the south part of the country that we call Yugoslavia. We think that Paul, together with Silas and Timothy, went to Thessalonica about the year AD 50. That was about 20 years after Jesus died. Paul went there for a short time, to tell the people about Jesus Christ. A few months after that, Paul wrote his first letter to the Christians who lived at Thessalonica. Paul wrote that first letter when he was in Corinth city. Corinth was about 300 kilometres (200 miles) south from Thessalonica.

While Paul was still at Corinth, people told him some news. The news was about the Christians who lived at Thessalonica. So, he wrote this second letter to them, only a short time after he had sent his first letter.

Paul knew that some people were still causing bad trouble for the Christians at Thessalonica. So he wrote to help them to be brave (chapter 1). He says that God knows about their troubles. God has a purpose in everything, and he will punish his people's enemies in the end.

Also, some people were teaching that Jesus had already returned to the earth. Other people were teaching that he would return very soon. Some of the Christians at Thessalonica may have believed what these people taught. We think that some of the Christians may even have stopped working as a result. So, Paul writes to explain that Jesus will not return yet. Certain things must happen before he returns (chapter 2). Paul also says that nobody should stop working (chapter 3). People should work so that they can get their own food.

Chapter 1

Paul starts his letter

1 This letter is from Paul, Silas and Timothy to God's people who live at Thessalonica. You are united to God our Father, and to the Lord Jesus Christ. 2 We pray that God the Father, and the Lord Jesus Christ will continue to be very kind to you. We pray also that they will cause you to be without trouble in your minds.

Paul thanks God because of the believers at Thessalonica

3 You are like brothers and sisters to us, and we ought to thank God because of you always. We should thank him, because you are learning to believe Christ more and more. And each of you is loving each of the other Christians more and more. 4 As a result, we speak about you to God's other groups of believers. We are so happy to tell them about you. You are showing how God's people should live. People often cause you bad trouble and pain because you are Christians. But you are continuing to believe Christ. You are continuing to be patient and brave.

5 All this shows us something clearly, about how God decides about people. God decides about people who die. He decides what should happen to those people. And he will always decide what is right for them.

People are causing great trouble for you now because God is your king. So it is right that, as a result, you should live always with God and his people. And God will cause this to happen to you.

6 God will do what is right. So he will punish those people who are causing trouble for you. He will cause trouble for them. 7 God will also do what is right for you. You have troubles now. But God will cause you to rest and to be without trouble. You will rest, together with us, when the Lord Jesus will come down from heaven. He will come with his powerful angels. 8 He will come with a very hot fire. And he will punish those people who refuse to know God. He will punish those people who do not obey the good news about our Lord Jesus. 9 To punish them, he will go on destroying them always. He will shut them out from where the Lord is present. So, they will never see how very powerful, great and beautiful he is. 10 All this will happen on that special day when Jesus will come. On that day, Jesus' own people will show what great things he has done for them. All those people who believe him will say great things about him. And you will be among them, because you believed our message. You believed what we told you.

Paul prays for the believers at Thessalonica

11 So we always pray for you. Our God has chosen you to be his own people. And you must continue to be the kind of people that he wants. So, we pray that he will be happy about you. We pray also that God will work powerfully in you. So then he will make it possible for you to do every good thing that you want to do. You want to do those good things because you believe Christ. 12 We pray this so that other people will say good things about our Lord Jesus because of you. They will see the great things that he has done for you. Also, Jesus will cause people to say good things about you. This will happen because our God and the Lord Jesus Christ are so very kind to you.

Chapter 2

Antichrist will come before Jesus returns

1 Our friends, we must explain something now about the time when our Lord Jesus Christ will return. You know that, at that time, he will bring us all together to be with him. But we ask you something very strongly. 2 You must not let yourselves become confused or afraid easily because of false messages about the Lord's return. Those messages say that the day of the Lord has already happened. Perhaps somebody might say that God's Spirit has shown him a message like that. Or somebody might report that we said it. Or they might say that we wrote it in a letter.

3 Do not let anyone cause you to believe something false in any way. That day will not happen until certain other things have happened first. Before that day, there will be a time when many people will turn against God completely. Also, before that day, people will see the man who completely refuses to obey God. He is the man that God will certainly kill. 4 This man will be God's enemy. He will be the enemy of everything that people call God. He will be the enemy of everything that people worship. He will think that he is much greater than any god. As a result, this man will even go into God's special house and he will sit down there. And he will tell people that he himself is God.

5 I told you these things when I was with you. I am sure that you remember that. 6 This man will come at the time that God has chosen. But something makes it impossible for him to come yet. And you know what it is. 7 Already Satan is working secretly to turn people against God and against God's rules. But there is someone who is making it impossible for Satan to work like that freely. And that someone will continue to make it impossible, until God takes that someone away. 8 Then people will see the man who completely refuses to obey God. But when the Lord Jesus will come, he will kill that man. Jesus will kill him with the words that Jesus speaks. Jesus will kill him with the very bright, powerful light that shines from Jesus himself.

.9 Satan will cause this very bad man to come. Also, Satan will cause this man to be very powerful. So, this very bad man will do all kinds of things that people cannot usually do. Those things will surprise people very much. Those things will cause people to believe this very bad man. They will cause people to believe things that are not true.

10 This very bad man will also do all kinds of bad things. He will cause bad people to believe what is not true. So, God will certainly kill those bad people. Those bad people will believe false things because they refused to love the true message. They refused to love the true message so that God could save them. 11 For this reason, God causes them to believe wrong things very easily and very strongly. So then they will believe what is not true. 12 The result is that God will decide to punish them. They refused to believe what is true. And instead, they enjoyed doing wrong things. So God will punish all of them.

The Christians at Thessalonica must continue to believe what Paul taught them

13 But you are like brothers and sisters to us, and the Lord loves you. We must thank God always because of you, because God has chosen you. God chose you to be among the first people that he would save. He saves you because his Spirit makes you God's special people. God's Spirit makes you separate from everything that is bad. God saves you because you believe him. You believe what is true. 14 God asked you strongly to become his special people. You heard him when we told you the good news. He wanted you to become special people who would live always with our Lord Jesus Christ. You will live in the beautiful place with Christ, who is so very great. 15 So, our friends, you must continue to believe Christ strongly. Continue to believe the true things that we taught you. God first taught those things to us. And we taught them to you when we spoke to you. We also taught them to you when we wrote our letter to you.

16 We pray about you to our Lord Jesus Christ himself, and to God, our Father. They have shown how much they love you and us. And they have promised to give good things to us all. So, we can continue to be brave and strong for all time. We can hope strongly for these good things. They will give these things to us because they are so very kind.

17 We pray that our Lord Jesus Christ and God, our Father, will make you brave. We pray that they will continue to make you strong in your minds. So you will always do what is good. And you will always say what is good.

Chapter 3

Paul asks the Christians to pray for him and for his friends

1 Now, friends, we ask you to pray for us. Pray that, because of us, more and more people will hear the Lord's message with pleasure soon. Pray that they will believe his message. So then they will thank God for it. That is what happened among you. 2 Pray also that God will not let very bad people cause bad trouble for us. Pray like that, because not everyone believes the message about our Lord. 3 But the Lord always does what he has promised. So, he will help you, so that you continue to believe him strongly. And he will keep you safe from Satan.

4 Also the Lord makes us sure about you. We told you things that you must do. You are doing those things. And you will continue to do those things. We are sure about that. 5 We pray that the Lord will help you to know him more and more. So then you will continue to understand more about how much God loves you. And he will cause you to be patient and strong, like Christ.

The Christians must not refuse to work

6 Our friends, we tell you this with the authority that the Lord Jesus Christ gives to us. You must stay away from every believer who is living in a lazy way. People like that are refusing to obey the things that we taught you. 7 You yourselves know that you ought to be like us. You ought to do the things that we did. We were not lazy when we were with you. 8 We always paid for all the food that we received from anyone. We worked very much, during the day and at night. We worked so that we did not need to ask any of you for anything. So, you did not have to supply anything for us. 9 We could have told you that you must supply things for us. We have authority to do that. But we wanted to show you ourselves what you should do. So then you could be like us. 10 Even when we were with you, we told you this rule. 'If anyone refuses to work, you should not let him eat', we said.

11 We say this because someone has told us news about you. They have told us that some people among you are living in a lazy way. Those people do not work themselves. But they talk very much about other people. They are busy with things that should not matter to them. 12 We speak strongly to those people who are lazy like that. We speak with the authority that the Lord Jesus Christ gives to us. We tell them strongly that it is their duty to work. They should work properly so that they may get their own food to eat.

13 But you other believers must never stop doing what is good. 14 We have written things in this letter to tell you what you should do. If anyone refuses to obey these things, tell everyone about him. And stay away from him, so that he may be ashamed. 15 But do not think about him or speak to him as your enemy. Instead, tell him seriously, like a brother, that he should obey our message.

Paul finishes his letter

16 The Lord causes us to be without trouble in our minds. And I pray that the Lord himself will do that for you at all times and in every way. I pray that the Lord will be with all of you.

17 I, Paul, am writing these words myself to say 'hello' to you. I write my name like this at the end of all my letters. This is how I write. 18 I pray that our Lord Jesus Christ will continue to be very kind to all of you.

Fight in the Good War

1 Timothy

About Paul's first letter to Timothy

Paul was a great Christian teacher. God sent him to many countries to tell the people about Jesus Christ. Timothy was a young man who had travelled with Paul on many of Paul's journeys. (See Acts 16:1-5.)

After Paul had taught in different places for many years, he went to prison at Rome. Rome is the capital of the country that we call Italy. The people who lived at Rome were called Romans. At that time, the Romans were powerful and they ruled many other countries. Paul stayed at Rome for two years (see Acts 28:30). We think that he stayed there at some time between AD 59 and AD 63. That was about 30-34 years after Jesus died. After those two years, we think that the Romans let Paul leave Rome. So, Paul started travelling. He started teaching the Christian message again. And Timothy went with him to Ephesus city. Ephesus was in the country that we call Turkey.

Paul made Timothy the leader of the Christians at Ephesus. When Paul wrote this first letter to Timothy, Paul had left Ephesus. But he had told Timothy to stay there. There was a dangerous problem among the Christians at Ephesus because some people were teaching wrong things. Paul had already told two men to leave the church (the group of Christians) because they were doing that. These wrong teachers had caused some of the Christians to obey the wrong ideas that they taught. So, Paul wrote to tell Timothy that he must stop those wrong teachers.

In this letter, Paul is teaching Timothy how to lead the Christians at Ephesus. Paul also describes how all Christian leaders should live. He says that they should be good examples to other people.

Chapter 1

Paul and Timothy

1 This letter is from me, Paul. God, who saves us, has sent me to be a special worker and teacher on Christ Jesus' behalf. Christ Jesus, who causes us to hope certainly for great things, has also sent me. 2 I am writing to you, Timothy. You are like my own child because, like me, you believe Christ. I pray that God the Father and Christ Jesus our Lord will be very kind and very good to you. I pray that they will cause you to be without trouble inside yourself.

Paul tells Timothy to stop the wrong teachers

3 When I was going to Macedonia, I asked you very strongly to stay in Ephesus. You must continue to stay there, because certain people there are teaching wrong things about God. You must tell them to stop doing that. 4 Neither should they listen to false stories. Nor should they always be studying long lists of their families' names from years ago. They should not believe that to study lists like that can help them. Those things only cause people to argue. Those things do not help God's work. To do God's work, people must believe him.

5 Here is the reason why I am telling you to do this. I want people really to love each other. Only people who are good and clean inside themselves can love like that. Those people know the difference between what is right and wrong. And they try to do only what is right. People love properly only when they really believe God. 6 But certain people have failed to do these things and they have turned away from them. They would rather talk about things that mean nothing. 7 They want to be teachers of God's rules. They seem very sure when they talk about things. They speak very strongly. But they do not understand what they are talking about.

The purpose of God's rules

8 We know that God's rules are good, if people use them properly. 9 We also know this. God did not make those rules for people who do right things. He made them for people who refuse to do right things. Those people refuse to obey good rules. God made his rules for people who like to do bad things. He made his rules for people who do not worship him. Those people do not want to obey God. God's rules are also for these people:

People who kill their fathers or their mothers

People who choose to kill other people

10   People who have sex with someone who is not their wife or their husband

Men who have sex with other men

People who catch other people and take them away to be slaves

People who say things that are not true

People who promise seriously to speak true things, but then they speak false things

People who do any other wrong things. Things like that are the opposite of the right things that God teaches us.

11 Those right things are part of the good news. This good news comes from God, who is so great and so good. God has chosen me to tell this good news to people.

Paul thanks Christ Jesus

12 I thank Christ Jesus our Lord, who chose me to work on his behalf. He believed that I would continue to obey him. And he has made me strong. 13 Before he chose me, I spoke bad things about him. I hurt his people and I caused great trouble for them. I said and did very bad things against Christ. But he was very kind and he chose not to remember those things. He chose not to punish me. He was kind because I did not believe him then. So, I did not know what I was doing. 14 Our Lord continued to be very, very good to me. He caused me to believe him. And he caused me to love other people as Christ Jesus loves them. These things happen to us when we are united to Christ Jesus.

15 Here are some words that everyone should believe. Everyone should agree that these words are true. 'Christ Jesus came into the world to save people who do wrong things.' And I am the worst of those people. 16 But, because I was the worst, God was kind to me. He wanted Christ Jesus to make me an example. Christ showed, by me, how completely patient he is. Christ made me an example to those people who would later believe him. Then, because they believed him, those people would live with God always. 17 God is the King who will rule always. He can never die. We cannot see him. He is the only God. Everyone should say always how very great he is! Everyone should do that always. This is true.

Timothy must fight against wrong things in the church

18 Timothy, you are like my own child. This is what I am telling you to do. People spoke words from God about you before, and you should remember those words. They will help you to fight well for what is true. You must be like someone who fights in a good war. 19 You must continue to believe God. And you must always do what you know to be right. Some people have known what is right. But they have refused to do it. As a result, they have completely stopped believing Christ. Their lives as believers are like ships that have sailed on to the rocks. 20 Hymenaeus and Alexander are like that. I have given them to Satan so that he has power over them. So then they can learn not to say bad things about God.

Chapter 2

Christians should pray when they meet together

1 So then, these are the most important things that I must ask you to do. Each of you should ask God to supply what others need. You must pray for everyone. You must ask God to help them. And you must thank God for what he has done for everyone. I strongly ask you to do these things. 2 You should pray for rulers and for everyone who has authority. You should pray for them, so that we may live our lives without trouble or danger. Then we can live for God. And we can always do what is right and proper in every way. 3It is good that we should pray like this. And it makes God, who saves us, happy. 4 It makes God happy because he wants to save all people. He wants everyone to know what is true.

5 There is only one God. And there is one person who brings God and people together. That person is the man Christ Jesus. 6 He gave himself on behalf of all people, to make them free. Jesus died at the time that God thought was best. As a result of Jesus' death, God showed that he wanted to save all people. 7 For this purpose, God chose me to be a special worker. He sent me to tell the message about Christ to those who do not belong to Israel's people. I must teach them the true things about Jesus. I must teach them what they should believe. (I am telling you only what is true!)

8 In every place where you meet together, then, I want the men to pray. They should live right lives for God and they should lift up their hands to pray. When they pray, they must not be angry. Nor must they quarrel with other people.

Paul teaches about Christian women

9 Also, I want the women to wear proper clothes. Women should wear clothes that do not show their bodies too much. A woman should not wear clothes that cause other people to be ashamed about her. Women should not do their hair in an expensive way that takes a lot of time. Nor should they wear gold or beautiful stones or expensive clothes. 10 Instead, women should do good things. Christian women say that they live for God. So, it is right for them to do good things. This is what makes them beautiful.

11 A woman should learn quietly when you meet together. She should obey the men who teach in the church. 12 I do not let a woman teach men. And I do not let a woman take authority over a man. Instead, she should be quiet when the men are teaching. 13 I say this because God made Adam first. Then he made Eve. 14 It was Eve, not Adam, who believed Satan. She believed the false things that Satan said. And so she was the first to do what was wrong.

15 But God will save women who give birth to children. He will do that if the women continue to believe him. Also, they must continue to love people. They must continue to live right lives because they are God's. And they must always do what is proper.

Chapter 3

Leaders of the church

1 These words are true: 'It is good work to lead a church. So, it is good if someone wants to become a leader of the church.' 2 A leader must live a good life. Then nobody can say anything bad about him. He must be the husband of one wife. He must think seriously and he must rule himself well. He must always do what is proper. He must be happy to have visitors in his home. He must be a good teacher. 3 He should not want to drink too much wine. He must not get angry quickly and fight people. But he should be kind. He should not be quick to quarrel with people. He must not want lots of money. 4 He must rule his own family well. He must cause his children to obey him. They should always respect people. 5 A man must know how to rule his own family. If he cannot do that, he certainly cannot look after God's church.

6 A leader should not be someone who has believed Christ for only a short time. Someone like that might think that he himself was more important than everyone else. Then God would have to punish him, as he had to punish the Devil. 7 Also, people outside the church should agree that the man is a good man. Then nobody can say anything to make him ashamed. And so, he will not come under the Devil's power.

Helpers in the church

8 Deacons (other special helpers in the church) must also be careful to live good lives. People must respect them. They must always speak what is true. They must not drink too much wine. They must not want money so much that they do wrong things to get it. 9 They must really believe the things that God has shown to us about Christ. Also, while they believe, they must always be careful to do nothing wrong. 10Deacons must first show the people in the church that they could do their work well. They must show everyone that they are good people. Then let them work as deacons. 11 Deacons' wives must also be careful to live good lives. They must not say bad things about people. They must think seriously and they must rule themselves well. Everyone should know that they are honest and good in every way.

12 A deacon must be the husband of one wife. He must rule his children well. He must also rule other people in his house well. 13 Those deacons who do their work well will cause everyone to think good things about them. And deacons like that will believe Christ Jesus more strongly. So, they will become braver. They will speak more strongly about what they believe.

14 I hope to come to you soon. But I am writing these things to you now. 15 So even if I cannot come soon, you will know about God's family. You will know how people in God's family should live. That family is the church of God, who is alive. God's church teaches people what is true. The church keeps those true things safe, just like strong parts of a building make that building strong and safe.

16 The things that God has shown us about Jesus Christ are very great. Nobody can argue about that.

Christ lived in a human body.

God's Spirit showed that he always did completely right things.

Angels saw him.

People taught about him in countries where the people do not know God.

People in the world believed him.

Chapter 4

Some people will stop believing Christ

1 But God's Spirit tells us clearly that, in later times, some people will stop believing Jesus Christ. Instead, they will listen to bad spirits who want them to believe wrong things. Those people will obey what these bad spirits teach. 2 The bad spirits teach through bad men. Those men seem to be good, but really, they are bad. They say things that are not true. Those teachers have stopped knowing the difference between what is good or bad. 3 Those bad teachers say that it is wrong to marry. They tell people not to eat certain kinds of food. But God made those foods for people who believe Christ. Those people know what is true. Believers should eat those foods, and they should thank God for them. 4 Everything that God has made is good. And we should refuse nothing that God has made. But we should thank God for everything when we receive it. 5 Then those things become good and clean for us to use. They become clean because we have prayed. And God's word also makes them good and clean.

How Timothy can be a good servant of Christ

6 You must teach the believers to remember these things that I have just said. Then you will be a good servant of Christ Jesus. You must continue to study the words of the Christian message. Continue to understand more of the true things about Christ that you have obeyed. Then you will become stronger for Christ. 7 But you must refuse to listen to silly stories that are not true. Stories like that are not from God. Continue to prepare yourself so that you live for God more and more completely. 8 A person may do sport to prepare his body to be strong and healthy. And that will help him a little. But if a person prepares himself to live for God more completely, that is even better. That will help him in everything. That person will live the kind of life that God has promised. This kind of life is not only for now, but also for always. 9These words are true. Everyone should agree that these words are true. Everyone should believe them. 10We work for God very much. We continue to work, through many difficulties, because we believe completely in God. We know that God is alive. And it is he who can save all people. Certainly, he saves everyone who believes him.

11 You must teach everyone to do these things. 12 You are still young. But let nobody think that they know better than you because of that. Be an example to the people who believe Christ. Be an example because of:

- What you say

- What you do

- How you love people

- How you believe God

- How you always do only what is right.

13 Until I come, be careful to continue doing these things. Read the Bible aloud to the people. Teach them to understand and to obey the message about Christ. 14 Do not stop using the gift that you have. God gave you that gift when people spoke messages from God about you. And the leaders of the church put their hands on you and they prayed for you.

15 Never stop doing these things. Do them all the time. So then, everyone will see that you are becoming better and stronger for Christ. 16 Think carefully about how you live. And think carefully about what you teach. You must continue to do all these things that I have said to you. Then God will save you yourself. And he will save those people who listen to you.

Chapter 5

Paul writes about different groups of people in the church

1 Do not tell an older man strongly what he should do. But tell him kindly what you think. Tell him as you would tell your father. And speak to younger men like they were your brothers. 2 Speak to older women as you would speak to your mother. And speak to younger women like they were your sisters. Always be completely right and proper when you are with these women.

Widows

3 Help widows. But only help those widows who are really alone. 4 If a widow has children or grandchildren, then they should help that widow. Those children or grandchildren should learn, before anything else, to do their duty to their own family. They should do this for God. In this way, they can give something back to their parents and their grandparents. That is what makes God happy.

5 A widow who is really alone has nobody to help her. So, she believes that God will be good to her. She continues to ask God to help her. She continues to pray, at night and during the day. 6 But a widow who lives only to enjoy herself is dead to God. Even while she lives, her spirit is dead. 7 Tell the people these things. So then, nobody can say that the believers are doing anything wrong.

8 A believer should supply what people in his own family need. Certainly, he should do that for the people who live with him. If anyone does not do that, then he has stopped really being a believer. That person is worse than someone who does not believe Christ.

9 Do not include a widow's name in the list of widows unless she is more than 60 years old. She must have been the wife of one husband. 10 People should know that she has done good things. She must have been a good mother to her children. She should have been happy to have visitors in her home. She should have helped God's people. She should have been like a servant who washes their feet. She should have helped people who had trouble. She must have continued to do all kinds of good things.

11 Refuse to include younger widows' names in the list, for this reason: When they want to have sex, they will want to marry again. They will want to marry more than they want to be Christ's servants. Then they will stop being Christ's servants. 12 So, they will not do what they had promised earlier to do for Christ. They will be wrong not to do that. And God will know that they are wrong.

13 They will also learn to be lazy. They will go about from house to house. And not only will they become lazy. They will also learn to talk too much. They will become busy talking wrongly about other people. And they will say things that they ought not to say. 14 So, I think that younger widows should marry. They should have children. And they should look after their homes. Then they will not give an enemy any chance to say bad things about them. 15 Some of the younger widows have already turned away from Christ, so that they can obey Satan.

16 A woman who believes Christ should help any widows in her own family. Then the church will not have to do that work. So then the church can help those widows who are really alone.

Leaders called elders

17 Leaders called elders who do their job well are very important to the church. So, the church should respect them and it should pay them properly. Certainly, the church must do these things for elders who speak God's message to you. The church should also do these things for elders who teach you. 18 The Bible says: 'You must not put anything over a cow's mouth when that cow is walking on the grain. You must not stop it eating some grain' (Deuteronomy 25:4). The Bible also says: 'You ought to pay a worker what he is worth' (Luke 10:7).

19 Somebody may say to you that an elder has done something wrong. But you must refuse to listen unless two or three people say the same thing. 20 If elders continue to do wrong things, you must tell them not to do those things. You must tell them when everyone in the church is present. So then, all the other people will be afraid to do things like that.

21 I tell you that it is your duty to obey these rules and to teach them. God and Christ Jesus agree with what I am saying. The angels that God has chosen also agree. You must not decide what to do about anyone before you know the facts about them. You must never be kinder to one person than to another. 22Do not hurry to put your hands on any man to make him a leader of the church. Perhaps that man has done something wrong. Then people might think that you agree with him. But have nothing to do with wrong things. Always do what is right and good. 23 Do not continue to drink only water, but drink a little wine. Do this to make your stomach well, because you are ill so often.

24 Some people do wrong things that everyone can see clearly. So everybody already knows that it is right to punish those people. But other people do wrong things secretly. Nobody knows about those wrong things until they discover about them later.

25 It is the same when people do good things. Many good things are clear for everyone to see. But even when people do good things secretly, nobody can continue to hide those things always.

Chapter 6

Slaves

1 All slaves should always respect their own masters properly. So then, other people will not say bad things about God's name. Neither will they say bad things about what believers teach. 2Some slaves have masters who believe Christ. So, as believers, their masters are like their brothers. But those slaves must not refuse to obey their masters properly because of that. Instead, those slaves should work even better for them because their masters believe Christ. And the slaves should work better because they love their masters. Those slaves can help their masters if they work well for them.

Teach these things and ask the believers very strongly to obey them.

Paul writes again about wrong teachers

3 Some people may teach things that are wrong. Those people do not agree with the true words that our Lord Jesus Christ taught. They do not agree with what believers teach about how to live for God.

4 A person like that who teaches wrong things thinks wrongly. He thinks that he knows a lot more than anyone else. But he knows nothing. His mind is sick, so that he always wants to argue. He wants to quarrel about words. And so, people begin to want what other people have. People become angry with each other and they do not agree. They say and believe bad things about each other. 5 People go on arguing with each other. They do these things because their minds have become confused and bad. They can no longer understand what is true. They want to believe God so that they can get lots of money. That is how they think.

How we can become really rich

6 But God's people should be happy with what they have. And they should really live for God. Then they are really rich. 7 When we were born, we brought nothing into this world. And when we die, we cannot take anything out of it.

8 So, if we have food and clothes, we should be happy. We should not want more things. 9 But if people want lots of money, Satan easily gets power over them. And he causes them to want all kinds of bad things. Those bad things are things that only fools want. Those bad things will hurt them. Those things completely destroy people. 10 When people really want money that causes all kinds of bad things to happen. Some people have stopped believing Christ because they want to get more and more money. But they have caused themselves to be sad because they have very many troubles.

Paul tells Timothy that he must continue to live for God

11 But you are a man who lives for God. So, you must have nothing to do with these bad things. Always try to do what is right. Live for God and believe him. Love other people. Continue to be brave and strong for Christ. And be kind to people. 12 You must be like someone who fights a good fight. You must fight against everything that could stop you living for Christ. Then you will certainly live with God always. God chose you to live with him. And you said that you believe the true things about Christ. You said that when many other people were present. Those people heard what you said.

13 God knows that I am telling you this. And it is God who causes all things to be alive. Christ Jesus also knows what I am telling you. Jesus spoke about these true things when Pontius Pilate was present.

14 So, I tell you this. It is your duty to obey what I have told you to do. Obey carefully and completely. Then nobody can say that you have done anything wrong. Continue to obey those things until our Lord Jesus Christ appears. 15 God will cause Christ to appear at the proper time. God is good, and he is the only ruler with all authority. He is the Greatest King and the Most Powerful Lord. 16 God is the only person who can never die. He lives in light that is very, very bright. It is so bright that people cannot go near it. No human person has ever seen God, and nobody can ever see him. Everyone should say always how great he is! He must rule always! This is true.

Rich people must be careful how they live

17 Say this strongly to people who are rich now, in this world. Tell them not to think that they are more important than other people. They must not believe that they will be safe because of all their money and their valuable things. They could easily lose all those things. Instead, they should believe God. He gives us so many things so that we can enjoy them. 18 Tell the rich people to do good things. They should do many good things. That is how they should be rich. They should be ready to give things to other people. They should be happy to let other people have some of their own things. 19 Then they will be storing really valuable things for themselves in heaven. And those things will be important for the life to come. Then they will certainly live with God always.

Timothy must continue to teach the Christian message

20 Timothy, God has chosen to give you his message to tell people. You must be like someone who keeps that message safe. Stay away from people who say a lot of wrong things.

Those things are not about God, and they mean nothing. Some people argue against what is true. They say that they know special, secret things. But they do not really know anything. 21 Some of the people who believe those secret things have stopped believing the true message about Christ.

I pray that God will continue to be very kind to you, Timothy, and to all those believers there with you.

Tell God's Message to People

2 Timothy

About Paul's second letter to Timothy

This is Paul's second letter to Timothy. Paul was a great Christian teacher. He wrote this second letter to Timothy from a prison in Rome. Rome is the capital of the country that we call Italy. At that time, the Romans were powerful and they ruled many other countries. They had made Paul go to prison because they did not like Christians. Timothy was a young man who had travelled with Paul on many of Paul's journeys. (See Acts 16:1-5.)

Some time earlier, Paul had made Timothy the leader of the Christians at Ephesus city. Ephesus was in the country that we call Turkey. When Paul wrote his first letter to Timothy, Timothy was in Ephesus (1 Timothy 1:3). And we think that Timothy was still in Ephesus when Paul wrote this letter to him.

We think that Paul wrote this letter at some time between AD 64 and AD 67. (That was more than 30 years after Jesus returned to God.)

Among the Christians at Ephesus, there were some people who were teaching wrong things. In his first letter to Timothy, Paul had told Timothy to stop those teachers. He told Timothy to teach the true Christian message. And in this letter, he tells Timothy to continue teaching it.

While he writes this letter, Paul knows that he will die soon. (See 4:6.) He wants to see Timothy again before he dies. (See 4:9.) Also, he wants Timothy to be ready for trouble. Timothy must remember that it is very important to obey Christ. He must be strong so that no troubles can stop him living for Christ.

We think that this is the last letter in the Bible from Paul. A short time after he wrote it, the Romans killed him.

Chapter 1

Paul thanks God for Timothy

1 This letter is from me, Paul. God chose me to be a special worker for Christ Jesus. God sent me to tell people about the life that he has promised us because of Christ Jesus. We can live like this when we are united to Christ. 2 I am writing to you, Timothy. You are like my own child, and I love you. I pray that God the Father and Christ Jesus our Lord will be very kind and very good to you. I pray that they will cause you to be without trouble inside yourself.

3 When I pray, at night and during the day, I always remember to pray for you. And I thank God for you. My grandfathers served God in the right way. They knew what was right or wrong. And they always tried to do what was right. And I serve God like that too. 4 I remember how you wept. I want to see you very much, so that I may be completely happy. 5 I remember how you really believe Christ. Your grandmother, Lois, and your mother, Eunice, believed Christ before you did. And I am sure that you really believe him also.

6 For this reason, I want you to remember the gift that God gave you. He gave you that gift inside yourself when I put my hands on you. You must use that gift. You must make it grow stronger, like when a wind blows on a very small fire. The wind makes that small fire grow into a big fire. 7 Do this, because God has given us his Spirit. And his Spirit does not cause us to be afraid of things. Instead, he causes us to be powerful. He causes us to love God and other people. And he causes us to rule ourselves properly.

Paul tells Timothy to be a brave teacher for Christ

8 So do not be ashamed of the message that we tell about our Lord. Neither be ashamed of me because I am in a prison. I am here because I serve Christ. Instead, be ready to have the same kind of trouble as I have. We have trouble because we tell people the good news about Christ. Let God make you strong when you have trouble. 9 God has saved us and he has chosen us to be his people. So, he wants us to be completely good and clean. He did not save us because of anything good that we have done. He did it because it was his own purpose. He did it because he is so very kind. He decided to be kind to us before time began. He decided to be kind by what Christ Jesus would do for us. 10 So now he has shown us how very kind he is. He has shown us because Christ Jesus has come. And it is Christ who saves us. He has destroyed death's power over us. And he has shown that we can live with God always. We can have bodies that never die. He has shown that also. He has shown this by the good news that he brought.

11 God has chosen me to tell this good news to people. He has sent me to be a special worker for Christ. He has chosen me to teach the Christian message to people. 12 That is why I have these troubles. But I am not ashamed, because I have believed Christ. I know him. He can keep safe what I have given him to keep safe. I am completely sure about that. He can keep it safe until that great day.

'That great day' means the day when Jesus will decide about everyone. He will decide what should happen to them after their death. He will decide that because of what they have done during their life on earth.

13 You have heard true words from me. Let those words be an example to you when you teach. And continue to believe God. Continue also to love God and other people. You can do these things because you are united to Christ.

14 God has given you a good thing (the true Christian message) to keep safe. You must not let anyone change it. God's Spirit, who lives in us, will help you to keep it safe.

15 You know that almost all the believers in Asia have turned against me. They include Phygelus and Hermogenes.

Onesiphorus

16 I pray that the Lord will be kind to Onesiphorus's family. He often helped me to be happier. He was not ashamed that I am in a prison. 17 But when he came to Rome, he looked for me. He looked carefully for me and he found me. 18 I pray that the Lord will choose to be kind to Onesiphorus on that great day. You know very well how much he did for me in Ephesus.

Chapter 2

A good soldier for Christ

1 So you, who are like my own child, must continue to be strong. You must let God make you strong. He will be kind to you like this because you are united to Christ Jesus. 2 You have heard the things that I have taught. Many other people were with us when you heard those things. You must tell the same things to other men, who can teach well. You must be sure that these men are good and honest. Then they can teach those things to other people also.

3 Be patient and brave through the troubles that we Christians have. Be like a good soldier for Christ Jesus. 4 A good soldier wants only to make his captain happy. So, that soldier does not let himself become busy with the things that other people do. He does only the things that soldiers do. 5 Also, someone who does athletics must obey the rules. He cannot win unless he does that. 6 A farmer works very much to grow plants for food. So, he should be the first person to get some of that food. 7 Think about what I am saying. The Lord will cause you to understand everything.

8 Remember Jesus Christ. After Jesus had died, God caused him to become alive again. Jesus came from David's family. These facts are part of the good news that I tell people. 9 And because I tell that good news, I have trouble. They have even tied me in a prison, like someone who has really done wrong things. But nobody can tie God's message in a prison. Other people will still teach God's message.

10 So I continue to be patient and brave during all these troubles. I do this because of all the people that God has chosen. I do this so that they may believe Christ also. I do it so that God will save them by Christ Jesus. And they will live with God always, in the beautiful place where he lives. 11 Here are some words that everyone can believe:

'If we have died with Christ,

we will also live with him.

12 If we continue to be patient and brave during troubles,

we will also rule with him.

But we must not say that we do not know Christ.

Because then he will also say that he does not know us.

13 If we turn away from him,

he will never turn away from us.

He cannot do anything that is against his own nature.'

A good worker for God

14 Continue to tell these things to your people, so that they remember them. Tell them that they must not quarrel about words. Tell them seriously, because God hears you. To quarrel about words does not help anyone. But it destroys those people who listen.

15 Always try to be the kind of person that God is happy about. Do everything that you can to be like that. Be a worker who has no reason to be ashamed of his work. Teach the true message correctly. 16 But stay away from people who talk about silly, wrong things. Those things do not help anyone and they do not come from God. Words like that cause people to do bad things. And those people will get worse all the time. 17 Words like that cause people who believe them to become like sick people. Those words cause people to get worse and worse. Hymenaeus and Philetus are people who talk like that. 18 They teach things that are different from the true message. They say that God has already caused all the dead people to become alive again. These men are confusing some Christians, so that those Christians do not know what to believe.

19 But what God has done can never change. His work is strong, like the strong stones that people use under a big building. Those stones do not move, and they hold the whole building up. And God's work has his mark on it. It is like a strong stone with these words on it:

'The Lord knows who his own people are' (Numbers 16:5). And: 'Everyone who calls himself the Lord's must stop doing wrong things' (Isaiah 26:13).

20 In a big house, there are different kinds of dishes. There are some dishes that people have made from gold or silver (another valuable metal). They use dishes like that only for special purposes. They do not let those dishes get dirty. There are also dishes that people have made from wood or clay (sticky material from the ground). They use those dishes for purposes that are not special. Those dishes may get very dirty. 21 It is like that with the Lord's people. If they make themselves completely separate from bad, dirty things, then they will be like dishes for special, clean purposes. They will be ready for God to use them. He is like the master of the house. They will be ready for him to use them for any good work.

22 Young people often want very much to do bad things. Have nothing to do with those bad things. Always try to do what is right. Continue to believe God. Love other people. And always try to be friendly to other people. Try not to argue with them. All those people who really love the Lord should do these things. Like you, those people pray to the Lord and they are really good inside themselves.

23 Stay away from people who want to talk about silly questions. They are fools. You know that those questions cause people to quarrel. 24 And the Lord's servant must not quarrel. Instead, he should be kind to everyone. He should be a good teacher. And he should be patient with people. 25 He should be kind to people who do not agree with him. He should teach them kindly what is correct. Maybe God will give them the chance to be sorry that they did not believe Christ. So then they may believe what is true. 26 And then they will start to think clearly. They will understand that Satan has been using them. He has caused them to do what he wanted. So then those people can get free from Satan's power.

Chapter 3

People will turn away from God in the last days

1 Understand this! During the last days (before Christ returns to earth), there will be times of great trouble.

2 People will love only themselves. They will want lots of money. They will think that they are much more important than other people. And they will talk about how great they are. They will say bad things about other people. They will not obey their parents. They will not thank anyone. They will not think that other people, or God, are important. They will not do what is proper to other people.

3 People will not even love their own families. They will refuse to agree with other people. They will say wrong things about other people, things that are not true. They will be unable to rule themselves properly. They will be cruel like wild animals. They will be enemies of everything that is good. 4 People will turn against their friends. They will not think carefully before they do things. They will be completely sure that they are very, very important. They will not love God, but instead they will want very much to enjoy themselves. 5Those people will seem to worship God. But really, they will refuse to let God work in them. You must stay away from people like that.

6 Among those people, there are some men who get into people's homes. They get power over silly women. These women have done many wrong things. They cannot stop themselves. They let themselves do wrong things because they want all kinds of things so much. 7 These women are always trying to learn new things. But they can never really understand God's true message. 8 Jannes and Jambres tried to stop Moses because they were his enemies. In the same way, these men are enemies of God's true message. Their minds have become confused and bad. They have failed to believe what is true. 9 But they will not continue to do many more bad things. Because everyone will see clearly that they are fools. That is just what happened to Jannes and Jambres.

Timothy must follow Paul's example

10 But you know everything about what I have taught. You know how I have lived. You know my purpose. You know how I believe God. You know how patient I have been.

You know that I love God and other people. I have continued to work for God, even during troubles. You know that. 11 You know how people caused all kinds of trouble for me in the cities called Antioch, Iconium and Lystra. They hurt me very much. I was brave when I had such bad troubles! But the Lord saved me from all these dangers.

12 People who are united to Christ Jesus want to live for God. But certainly, other people will cause trouble for them. 13 Some bad people will cause other people to believe things that are not true. These bad people, and all other bad people, will become worse and worse. And they themselves will also believe things that are not true.

It is important for us to know the Bible

14 But you must continue to believe the things that you have learned. You know that those things are true. Remember who taught you those things. 15 You have known the Bible from when you were a child. The Bible can cause you to understand how God can save us. He can save us when we really believe Christ Jesus. 16 Everything that the Bible says comes from God's Spirit. And we can use the Bible to teach what is true. We can use it to tell people when they are doing wrong things. It shows them what is right. Also, with the Bible, we can teach people how to live good lives. 17 As a result, a person who lives for God can know how to live properly. He will have everything that he needs to do every kind of good work.

Chapter 4

Timothy must continue to do his work for God

1 When Christ Jesus comes to rule as king, he will decide about all the people. He will decide about the people who are alive. He will decide also about the people who have died. He will decide what should happen to them.

He will decide that because of what each person has done during their life. Because of this, I am speaking very seriously to you. God and Christ know that I am telling you this. So, I tell you to do this, which is your duty. 2 You must tell God's message to people. Always be ready to tell it. Continue to tell it, whether people want to listen to you or not. Tell people when they are doing something wrong. Tell them that they must stop doing wrong things. Explain to them what they ought to do. Be very patient while you teach them.

3 A time will come when people will not listen to the true message about Christ. Instead, they will want to hear all kinds of different messages. So they will find more and more teachers for themselves. And those teachers will tell the people what they want to hear. 4 People will refuse to listen to the things that are true. Instead, they will want to listen to false stories. 5 But you yourself must continue to think seriously and clearly. Be patient and brave during troubles. Continue to tell the good news about Christ to people. As God's servant, do all the work that he has given you to do.

Paul says that he will die soon

6 Do this, because it is nearly time for me to die. It is time for me to be like an offering to God, like the drink offering that they pour out. Very soon, I will go to God.

7 I have served Christ properly, like someone who does athletics to win. I have finished everything that God wanted me to do. I have done everything, like a runner who has run to the end of the path. I have continued to believe God and I have obeyed him. 8 So now a gift is waiting for me, like the crown (a special hat) that a winner gets. The Lord will make me completely right and happy. This will be like a crown that the Lord will give me. The Lord is completely right when he decides about people. And he will give me the crown on that great day when he does decide. He will not give a crown to me only. He will give crowns also to all the people who want him to come very much.

Paul's last words to Timothy

9 Try very much to come to me soon. 10 Demas has left me. He wanted very much the things that he can enjoy now, in this world. And he has gone to Thessalonica city. Crescens has gone to Galatia. Titus has gone to Dalmatia.

11 Only Luke is with me. Fetch Mark and bring him with you. He can be a help to me with the work for God. 12 But I have sent Tychicus to Ephesus city.

13 I left my coat with Carpus at Troas city. Bring it when you come. Also bring the books. If you cannot bring all of them, then bring my special books only.

14 Alexander, the man who makes things from metal, caused a lot of trouble for me. The Lord will punish him because of the wrong things that he did. 15 You must also be careful that he does not cause trouble for you. He argued very strongly against our message.

16 I had to speak to the people with authority who put me in prison. I had to explain to them why I had done nothing wrong. And the first time that I had to speak to them, nobody came with me to help me. Everybody left me. I hope that God will not be angry with them because of that. 17 But the Lord stayed with me. He made me strong so that I could tell all his message. Then all the people from many countries could hear it. So the Lord saved me from great danger. 18 The Lord will save me from every bad thing. And he will bring me safely to his home above the earth, where he rules. Everyone should always say how very great he is! Everyone should do that always. This is true.

19 Say 'hello' to Priscilla and Aquila, and to Onesiphorus's family. 20 Erastus remained at Corinth city. I left Trophimus at Miletus city because he was sick.

Paul writes about Onesiphorus in 1:16.

21 Try very much to come before the winter. Eubulus, Pudens, Linus and Claudia say 'hello' to you. All the other believers here also say 'hello'.

22 I pray that the Lord will continue to make you strong in your spirit. I pray that he will be kind to all of you.

Show everyone how good God's Message is

Titus

About Paul's letter to Titus

Paul was a great Christian teacher. God sent him to many countries to tell the people about Jesus Christ. Titus was a young man who had travelled with Paul. He had been to Jerusalem with Paul. (See Galatians 2:1-3.) Sometime after that, Paul sent Titus to Corinth city. There were serious problems among the Christians at Corinth, and Paul sent Titus there to help them. (See, for example, 2 Corinthians 7:5-16; 8:16-24.)

We think that Paul wrote this letter at some time between AD 62 and AD 65. That was more than 30 years after Jesus died. Titus had travelled with Paul again. But Paul had asked him to stay on the island called Crete. Crete is in the Mediterranean Sea, south from the countries called Greece and Turkey. Paul left Crete and he travelled to other places. But Titus stayed on Crete, to help the Christians there.

The Christians who lived on Crete had believed Christ for only a short time. They needed good leaders. So, in this letter, Paul tells Titus what kind of people he should choose as leaders.

Also, there were some false teachers there. So, Paul tells Titus that he must not let the Christians believe those false teachers. Titus must teach only the true Christian message. The Christians must do good things that make God happy. And Titus must tell them that.

Chapter 1

Paul and Titus

1 This letter is from me, Paul. I am God's servant and I have to obey him completely. And I am a special worker and teacher on behalf of Jesus Christ. God has sent me to help the people that he has chosen. I help those people to believe God more completely. I help them so that they will understand the true message about Christ completely. So then they will know the things that they should do to make God happy. 2 As a result of this true message, those people will hope certainly that they will live with God always. God has promised that his people will live with him always. He promised that before the world began. And God always says only things that are true. 3 Then, at the proper time, God caused people to know what he had promised. God's servants started to tell his message to people. And God, our Saviour, has given this work to me also. He has said that I must tell his message to people.

4 I am writing to you, Titus. You are like my own child because we both believe the same things about Christ. I pray that God, the Father, and Christ Jesus, our Saviour, will be very kind to you. I pray that they will cause you to be without trouble inside yourself.

Titus's work on the island called Crete

5 I asked you to stay on Crete so that you could do certain things. Some things there are not as they should be. You must cause those things to become as they should be. Also, you must choose elders (leaders) for the Christians in every town, as I told you.

6 A leader must do what is good. So then, nobody can say anything bad about him. He must be the husband of only one wife. His children must be believers. They must always do what is right and proper. Everyone should know that a leader's children always obey him. 7 A leader has authority for God's work on God's behalf. So, nobody should ever be able to say anything bad about him. A leader must not think that he himself is very important. He must not always be causing other people to do what he wants. He must not become angry easily. He must not be a drunk. He must not be a person who likes to fight. He must not want money so much that he does wrong things to get it. 8 Instead, he must be happy to have visitors in his home. He must really want to do good things. He must rule himself well. He must do what is right. He must want always to make God happy. He must always do what is proper.

9 A leader must continue to believe strongly the true Christian message, as we taught it. So he will be able to teach true and right things to people. So then, he will help people to believe Christ more strongly. A leader like that will also be able to speak to people who argue against the Christian message. So, those people will know certainly that they are wrong.

Titus must not let the Christians on Crete believe false teachers

10 There are many people who refuse to obey anyone. They teach false things that are worth nothing. They want people to believe those false things. They certainly include the teachers who want to circumcise all Christian men.

The Jews circumcised men and boys to show that Israel's people were God's people. But the Bible does not say that Christians need to do that. We are God's people because Christ died for us. The Bible does not say that all Christian men should cut their bodies.

11 You must not let those people teach those false things. They are teaching things that they should not teach. So, they are causing whole families to stop believing the true message. Those false teachers' purpose is bad.

They are teaching only because they want people to give them money. 12 Many years ago, one great teacher who lived on Crete spoke like this about his own people. 'People who live on Crete are always doing bad things. They are always saying things that are not true. They are like dangerous wild animals. They are lazy and they eat too much food.'

13 What that man said is true. So, you must speak to those people who believe false things. Tell them very strongly that they are wrong. Tell them, so that they may believe the true Christian message. 14 They must stop listening to those Jewish stories that are not true. They must stop listening to people who have refused to believe the true message. They must stop obeying the human ideas that those people tell them.15 For people who have clean spirits and minds, everything is clean and good. But for people who have dirty spirits and minds, nothing is clean or good. The same thing is true about people who refuse to believe God's true message. Those people cannot think good thoughts. Even their consciences have become like something dirty. 16 Those bad people say that they know God. But they do bad things that God hates. So, everyone can see that those people do not really know God. They refuse to obey God and they are unable to do anything good.

Chapter 2

Titus must teach all the Christians to do right things

1 But you, Titus, you must teach right things that belong properly to God's message. 2 Tell the older men that they must rule themselves well. They must think seriously. They must always do what is proper. They must continue to believe Christ strongly. They must love other people and they must continue to be patient and brave.

3 Also, tell the older women what they must do. They must always do right and proper things, as God's people should do. They must never say bad things about people. They must not be drunks. They must teach what is good.

4 So then, they can teach the young women what they must do. The young women must love their own husbands and their own children. 5 The young women must always do what is proper. They must think clean thoughts and they must do good things. They must be good housewives. They must be kind and they must obey their own husbands. So then, nobody will be able to say bad things about God's message because of what the young women do.

6 Also, tell the young men strongly that they must always do right and proper things. 7 You yourself must always do good things. So you will show the young men what they should do. When you teach, be honest and serious. 8 Teach things that are correct. So, nobody will be able to say that you are wrong. And so our enemies will be ashamed, because they cannot say anything bad about us.

9 Tell the slaves that they must obey their masters always. They must make their masters happy. They must not argue with their masters. 10 Slaves must not rob their masters. Instead, slaves must always do properly what their masters have asked them to do. So people will see that those slaves are always good. So, as a result, everyone will like the message that we teach. They will like it because it has changed those servants. That message about God, our Saviour, is very good. And people will know that it is good.

We must do right things because Christ died to make us God's own people

11 God has shown us how very kind he is. He has shown us that, because he came to save all people. 12 And because God is so kind, he teaches us to do right things. We should stop doing bad things that do not make God happy. We should stop wanting strongly the things that belong to this world. Instead, God teaches us to rule ourselves properly. He teaches us to do what is right. He teaches us to do the things that make him happy. We should do these good things while we live in this world.

13 We should do these good things while we wait for Jesus to return.

This is our hope that makes us happy. On that good day, Jesus will certainly show everyone how very great he is. Jesus Christ is our great God and Saviour. 14 He gave himself for us. So he made us free from every bad thing, so that we could be completely good and clean inside ourselves. So then, we could become his own special people, who really want to do good things.

15 You should teach these things, with all authority. Tell the Christians strongly the things that they must do. Tell them the things that they must not do. Do not let anyone think that they know better than you.

Chapter 3

Christians must obey people who have authority

1 Your people must obey the rulers and the government. Tell them that they must remember that. They must obey everyone who has authority over them. They must be ready always to do what is good. 2 They should never say bad things about anyone. They should not quarrel with people, but instead they should be patient and friendly. They should always be polite and kind to everyone.

3 Before we believed Christ, we ourselves were fools too. We did not obey God or anyone. We believed things that are not true. We wanted to do many kinds of bad things. We could not stop ourselves. We were always bad. We were always angry about other people because we wanted to be like them. Other people hated us, and we hated each other. 4 But then God, our Saviour, did something to help us. He showed us how much he loves all people.

5 God did not save us because of any good things that we ourselves had done. Instead, he saved us because he himself is very kind. God has washed us so that we are completely clean in our spirits. His Spirit has caused us to be born again, so that we have become new people.

6 By Jesus Christ, our Saviour, God gave his Spirit to us, to fill us. 7 God did that because he is very kind. He did it so that he could make us right with him. So then, we could hope certainly that we will live with God always. That is what God has promised to his people. 8 These words are certainly true.

I want you to teach these things strongly. I want you to be sure that the people understand these things. So then, the people who have believed God will be careful to do good things. They should think always about good things that they can do. Those good things will help everyone.

9 But stay away from people who argue about silly questions and about lists of people's families' names from years ago. Refuse to quarrel. Refuse to argue about God's rules. Those kinds of things are not good and they do not help anyone. 10 Some people may teach things that are different from the true message. Anyone who teaches false things like that can cause the Christians not to agree with each other. So, you must tell him that he must stop. If he does not stop, you must tell him one more time. Then, if he still does not stop, stay away from him. 11 You know that a person like that has chosen not to believe the true message. He is doing what is wrong. And he knows that. But he continues to do what is wrong.

Paul hopes to meet Titus at Nicopolis

12 I will send either Artemas or Tychicus to you. After one of them has arrived, try very much to meet me at the city called Nicopolis. I have decided that I will stay at Nicopolis during the winter.

14 Our Christian people must learn to do good things always. They should help to supply the things that people really need. Then the Christians will not be lazy and they will not waste their time.

15 Everyone who is here with me says 'hello' to you. Say 'hello' on our behalf to those Christians there who love us. I pray that God will continue to be very kind to all of you.

The Slave Who Ran Away

Philemon

About this letter

Paul was a great Christian teacher. He was in prison, at either Rome or Ephesus, when he wrote this letter to Philemon. (Rome was a very important city at that time, because the king of Rome ruled many other countries. Ephesus was a city in the south and west part of the country that is called Turkey now.) Paul was in prison because he taught people about Jesus Christ. We think that Paul wrote this letter in the year AD 60 or 61. That was about 30 years after Jesus died.

Philemon was a Christian man who lived in the town called Colossae. Colossae was also in the south and west part of the country that is called Turkey now. Philemon had become a Christian because Paul had taught him about Christ. Philemon was a rich man who was the master of a house. A church (a group of Christians) met regularly in his house. A man called Onesimus was one of Philemon's slaves. We think that Onesimus had robbed Philemon. He may have taken some of Philemon's money or other things. Then Onesimus had run away from Colossae.

Paul was in prison in his own house. People came to visit him, and he taught them about Jesus. Onesimus met Paul and Paul taught him about Jesus. As a result, Onesimus believed Jesus and he became a Christian. After that, Paul wrote this letter and he gave it to Onesimus. Then he sent Onesimus back to Philemon at Colossae. Paul wanted Onesimus to give the letter to Philemon.

In his letter, Paul asks Philemon to forgive Onesimus. (To forgive means that you choose to forget the wrong things that someone has done.)

Paul asks Philemon to say 'welcome' to Onesimus, as another Christian, who is like his brother. This was very important for Onesimus. It was difficult for Onesimus to return to Philemon. He had taken some of Philemon's things and he was still one of Philemon's slaves. Philemon could have killed Onesimus because of what he had done.

Tychicus was a friend of Paul and he was also a Christian. Tychicus was taking a letter from Paul to the Christians at Colossae, so he travelled with Onesimus.

Chapter 1

1 I, Paul, am writing this letter. I am in prison because I am Christ Jesus's servant. Timothy, who is like our brother, is here with me also.

We are writing this letter to you, Philemon. You are our friend that we love. And you work on behalf of Christ, as we do. 2 We say 'hello' also to you, Apphia, who are like a sister to us. And we say 'hello' to you, Archippus. You work like a soldier on behalf of Christ, as we do. We say 'hello' also to the group of Christians who meet in your home.

3 We pray that God, our Father, and the Lord Jesus Christ will continue to be very kind to you. We pray that they will cause you to be without trouble inside yourselves.

Paul thanks God because of Philemon

4 When I pray for you, I thank my God because of you always. 5 I thank God because people tell me good things about you. You love and believe the Lord Jesus. And you love all God's people. 6 I pray that you may always be ready to talk to other people about Christ. Talk to them about what you believe. So then you will understand more completely every good thing that is ours because of Christ. 7 My friend, you have been kind to God's people. You have helped them and you have made them happy. I know that you love Jesus and all God's people. That makes me very happy. And it makes me feel much braver and stronger.

Paul asks Philemon to help Onesimus

8 There is something that you ought to do. I could tell you that you must do it. I could tell you that clearly, with the authority that comes from Christ. 9 But I am not telling you that you must do it. Instead, I am asking you to do it because you love people. I am Paul, and I am an old man. Also, I am in prison now because I am Christ Jesus's servant. 10 So I am asking you on behalf of Onesimus, who is like my own child. I taught him about Jesus while I was in prison. And now he has become really alive because he believes Jesus. So he is like my own child. 11 Before, Onesimus did not help you. But now he can help both you and me.

12 I love Onesimus so much that he is like part of me. But I am sending him back to you. 13 I wanted to keep him here with me while I am in prison. I am in prison because I taught people the good news about Jesus. If you were here, you would have helped me. I know that. And I wanted Onesimus to help me on your behalf. 14 But I wanted to ask you first. I did not want to do anything unless you agreed. I did not want you to think that you had to help me. I did not want you to help me because you thought like that. Instead, I wanted you to help me because you really want to help.

15 Perhaps God let Onesimus leave you for a short time so that you could have him back for always. 16 You can have him back again not only as your slave. Now he can be something much better than a slave. He can be like a brother that you love. I love Onesimus very much. But you will love him even more than I do. You will love him as a slave and you will love him also as a brother. He is like a brother to you because you and he are both the Lord's people.

17 I am your friend, who works with you. If you think about me as a friend like that, then please say 'welcome' to Onesimus. Be happy that he has come back to you. And be kind to him. If I came to meet you, you would say 'welcome' to me. And you would be happy to meet me. Be happy about him in the same way.

18 If Onesimus has done anything wrong to you, I will make it right again. If he ought to pay you some money, I will pay the money to you on his behalf. 19 I, Paul, am writing this with my own hand. I will pay the money back to you. But remember how very much you yourself have received from me. You have become really alive by Jesus Christ because I taught you about him.

20 So, my friend, I really want you to help me, because we are both the Lord's. Help me, so that I can feel stronger and happier. Help me because we are both united to Christ. 21 I write to you because I am sure about you. You will do what I ask. I am sure about that. Also, I know that you will do even more than this.

Paul finishes his letter

22 I want to ask you one more thing. Please prepare a room in your home where I can stay. I know that all of you are praying about me. I hope that, as a result, they will let me go out of prison. Then I will be able to visit you again.

23 Epaphras is also here in prison with me because he is Christ Jesus's servant. Epaphras says 'hello' to you. 24 Mark, Aristarchus, Demas and Luke, who work with me, say 'hello' to you also.

25 I pray that the Lord Jesus Christ will continue to be very kind to all of you.

Jesus is the Only Way to God

Hebrews

About the letter to the Hebrews

The Book of Hebrews is a letter to a group of Christians. We do not know who they were. 'Hebrews' is another name for Jews. So, many people think that they were Jews.

(That means that they belonged to Israel's people.) But the man who wrote this letter did not call it 'Hebrews'. Someone else gave it this name many years later. The letter says a lot about God's promises to the Jews. It talks about the Jews' special house for God (chapter 9) and how they worshipped him there. They killed animals to show that they were sorry. They were sorry for the wrong things that they had done.

We do not know where these Christians lived. Some people think that they lived at Rome. That is the capital city of the country that we call Italy. Other people think that they lived at Jerusalem, the capital of Israel. They may have lived somewhere else.

We do know that other people were causing a lot of trouble for these Christians. They still believed Jesus, but they were not strong. So, the writer is trying to make them stronger Christians. He says to them: 'Do not stop believing Christ, but go on, to believe him more and more strongly.'

He tells them to think about Jesus. He explains clearly who Jesus is. And he explains what Jesus has done for us. Jesus is God's great and powerful Son. He is much, much greater than the angels. He is much, much greater than Moses and Joshua, who were great leaders of Israel's people many years ago. He is a much, much greater priest (a special servant of God) than Israel's priests. They did wrong things sometimes, but Jesus never did anything wrong.

Jesus became a human person, like us. So he understands us completely. He offered himself to God as our sacrifice when he died for us. He was the only sacrifice that could really make us good and clean. He saves us completely. He has opened the way for us to come near to God. We can know God because of Jesus.

We must always continue to remember Jesus. He has gone in front of us, as our leader, and we must follow him. We must look beyond the troubles that we have sometimes during our lives on earth. Jesus had great trouble on our behalf. His Spirit will make us strong to go on living for him here. And after that, we will live with him and we will have no more troubles.

We must also remember all the other people who have believed God. Even before Jesus came to the earth, many people believed God. They often had great troubles, but they still believed. Chapter 11 of Hebrews tells us about some of these people.

We do not know who wrote the Book of Hebrews. Some people think that Paul wrote it. He wrote many of the other letters in the New Testament. (That is the part of the Bible that describes Jesus' life and work.) Most people agree that the writer wrote this letter about AD 60-70. That was about 30-40 years after Jesus died.

Chapter 1

God has spoken by his Son, Jesus

1 Many years ago, God spoke to our grandfathers (Israel's people) by the prophets (people who spoke God's messages). He spoke many times and in many different ways. 2 But in these last times, he has spoken to us by his Son. In the beginning, God made the whole world and everything that there is by his Son. And God has chosen that everything should be his Son's. 3 The Son shines with the bright light that comes from God. The Son's nature is a copy of God's nature. He shows us completely what God is like. The Son's powerful word causes everything in the world to continue. The Son himself made it possible for us to be clean from everything that we do wrong. After he had done that, he sat down in heaven. He sat at the right side of God, who is the greatest ruler, with all authority.

God's Son is greater than the angels

4 God has caused his Son to be much greater and much better than the angels. God has given him a much greater and much better name than the angels' names. 5 God never spoke like this to any angel:

'You are my Son.

Today I have given you the honour that goes with that name.'

Nor did God speak like this to any angel:

'I will be his Father,

and he will be my Son.'

6 But when God brings his first, greatest Son into the world, he says this about him:

'All God's angels must worship him.'

7 God speaks about the angels like this:

'God makes his angels like winds.

He makes his servants like fires that burn.'

8 But God speaks to his Son like this:

> 'You are God and you will never stop ruling!
>
> You rule as king.
>
> And you always do what is right and good.

9 You love what is right.

> And you hate what is wrong.
>
> That is why I have chosen you.
>
> I am your God and I have chosen you.

I have chosen you to be much greater and much happier

> than those who are with you.'

[Psalm 45:6-7]

10 God also speaks like this about the Son:

> 'Lord, you made the earth in the beginning.
>
> You yourself made the skies also.

11 The earth and the skies will come to an end,

> but you will continue always.
>
> They will all become old, just as clothes become old.

12 You will cause them to roll up,

> like someone rolls up an old coat to put it away.
>
> You will change them as people change clothes.
>
> But you will always be the same.
>
> Your life will never come to an end.'

13 God has never spoken like this to any of the angels:

> 'Sit at my right side
>
> until I make an end to your enemies.

I will make them like a place where you rest your feet.'

14 All the angels are spirits who are only God's servants. He sends them to help all the people that he will save.

Chapter 2

Jesus' message is greater than the angels' message

1 So we ought to be very careful. We must continue to remember the true words that we have heard. Then we will not go in the wrong direction, away from God. 2 The message that God spoke by angels was certainly powerful. God punished people when they did not obey his rules. It was right that he punished those people.

3 So we must think even more about how God saved us. He has done great things for us. If we forget those things, we cannot get away from God. He will certainly punish us. The Lord Jesus himself first told everyone that God would save people. And then the people who heard him told us. They showed us that this message was certainly true. 4 God also showed that this message was true. He did all kinds of great and powerful things that surprised people. He also gave people gifts by the Holy Spirit, as he chose.

Jesus became like us to save us

5 God did not choose angels to rule over the world that will come. And that world is what we are talking about. 6 But God has included in the Bible the words that follow. They are certainly true:

> 'Men and women do not seem very important, Lord,
>
> but you think about them.
>
> They are only human people,
>
> but they matter to you.

7 You made them less important than the angels

> for a short time.

But then you made them great and powerful, like kings.

8 You caused them to rule completely over everything.'

It says that God has caused people to rule over everything. So there is nothing that people do not have authority to rule over. We do not see people rule over everything yet. 9 But we do see Jesus! God made him less important than the angels for a short time. And now God has made him the great and powerful king because he died. God is so very kind, that he sent Jesus to die on behalf of all people.

10 God made all things for himself and he causes all things to continue. God's purpose was to bring many people to himself. He wanted them to live with him always as his children. Jesus leads us to God. He saves us from the results of everything that we do wrong. God had to let Jesus have trouble and pain in this world. He caused Jesus to become everything that was necessary to save us. 11 Jesus makes people completely good and clean inside themselves. Both Jesus and all the people that he makes good and clean have the same Father. So, Jesus is not ashamed to call all those people his brothers and sisters. 12 He says this to God about it:

> 'I will speak loudly about you to my brothers and sisters.
>
> When all your people meet together,
>
> I will sing songs to you.
>
> I will say how great you are.'

13 He also says this:

> 'I will believe that God will help me.'

He also says this:

> 'Here I am, with the children that God has given me.'

14 So Jesus speaks about people as his children. And because we all have human bodies, Jesus himself became human like us. So then he died to destroy the Devil and the Devil's power over death. 15 We were like slaves all our lives because we were so afraid of death. But Jesus has made us free. 16 It is clear that Jesus did not come to help the angels. He came to help all those people who are Abraham's family. Those people really believe God, like Abraham believed him.

17 For this reason, Jesus became completely like us, because we are his brothers and sisters. He became our kind, chief priest, who understands us. He always obeys God and he serves God on our behalf. Jesus died so that God could forgive us. God needs to forgive us for everything that we do wrong. So Jesus has brought us near to God. 18 The Devil (God's enemy) tried to make Jesus himself do wrong things. But Jesus did not do anything wrong because he never stopped obeying God. So now, he can help us not to do wrong things.

Chapter 3

Jesus is greater than Moses

1 You Christians are like my brothers and sisters because you are God's people too. God wants all of us to be with him in heaven. You must think seriously about Jesus. We Christians say that we believe Jesus. And God has sent him to be our chief priest. 2 Jesus did everything that God sent him to do, just like Moses. Moses obeyed God while he worked among all God's people many years ago. 3 But someone who has built a house is much more important than the house itself. And it is like that with Jesus. Jesus has done much greater things than Moses did. 4 Some person built every house, but God has built all things. 5 Moses obeyed everything that God told him. He was a servant to all God's people. He was like a servant in God's house. He spoke about the things that God would say in future times. 6 But Christ obeyed God because he is his Son. He is the master of God's house and we belong to his house. We are God's people if we continue to believe Jesus. So we must be brave. We must go on being sure about what we hope for, until the end.

A place where God's people can rest

7 God's Spirit, who is completely good, speaks to us like this:

> 'You must listen when you hear God speak today.

8 Do not refuse to listen to him.

Do not be like Israel's people many years ago, when they refused God.

They refused to believe him, in that dry, sandy place.

9 There your grandfathers tried to make God do what they wanted.

For 40 years, they saw the great things that God did for them.

But they refused to believe him.

They refused to wait for him.

10 So that is why God was angry with all those people.

"They always want to do what is wrong", he said.

"They refuse to obey me.

11 I am very angry with them.

So, I promise this and it will not change:

I prepared a place for them to rest.

But they will never arrive at the place that I prepared for them." '

12 So be careful, you Christians, who are like my brothers and sisters. Be careful that none of you refuses to believe God.

If anyone is really bad deep inside themselves, they will turn away. They will go away from God, who is alive. 13 So help each other every day to go on believing. Do that each day, because the word 'today' means 'now' for us. Then none of you will want to refuse God because of wrong things. We can tell ourselves that wrong things are not very bad. But if we do wrong things, we are fools. 14 When we became Christians, we believed strongly. We must go on being sure about Christ like that until the end. Then we will share in everything that is his. 15 We have seen what the Bible says:

> 'You must listen when you hear God speak today.
>
> Do not refuse to listen to him.

Do not be like Israel's people many years ago, when they refused to obey God.'

16 This speaks about all the people that Moses led away from Egypt. They heard God speak. But they refused to listen to him. 17 God was angry with those people for 40 years. They did what was wrong. So they died in that dry, sandy place. 18 God also spoke this serious promise:

> 'I prepared a place for them to rest.

But they will never arrive at the place that I prepared for them.'

He was speaking about those people who refused to obey him. 19 So we can see this. They could not go there because they refused to believe God.

Chapter 4

We can go in to rest if we believe

1 God promised his people a place where they could rest. And that promise is still true for us. So we should be very careful. We want all of you to arrive there. We do not want any of you to fail. 2 Certainly, we have heard the good news, just like the people with Moses heard it. But they failed to believe what they heard. So the message did not help them. 3 We who believe that message will arrive in that place. And then we will rest with God. It is as God said:

'I am very angry with them.

So, I promise this and it will not change:

I prepared a place for them to rest.

But they will never arrive at the place which I prepared for them.'

God said that. But he had finished his work when he made the world. 4 In the Bible God has spoken about the seventh day.

'God rested from all his work on the seventh day', the Bible says.

5 As we saw before, God also said later:

'I prepared a place for them to rest.

But they will never arrive at the place which I prepared for them.'

6 Those people who heard the good news first, refused to obey God. So they did not go to rest with him. But God's promise is still true for other people. Other people can go and rest with him. 7 So God chose another special time and he called it 'today'. He spoke by David a long time after Moses. As we have already seen, he said:

'You must listen when you hear God speak today.

Do not refuse to listen to him.'

8 Joshua did not bring the people to the place where they could rest. So God had to speak again later. He had to speak about another day. 9 There is still a place ready for God's people, where they can rest completely. They will rest like God rested on the seventh day. 10 God rested after he had finished his work. And it is the same for everyone who goes to rest with God. They will rest after they have finished their own work.

11 So we must do everything possible to receive that rest with God. Nobody should copy the example of those people who refused to obey God. Then none of us will fail to go in. 12 Every word that God speaks is alive and powerful. His word is sharper than any long knife that has two sharp edges. Just as that knife can cut deep, God's word goes very deep into us. His word can even cut between our human nature and our spirits. It is like a sharp knife that can cut between our bones, or even through our bones. God's word shows what we are really thinking. It shows what we really want. 13 There is nothing in the whole world that can hide from God. He can see everything completely and clearly. And we will have to explain to him everything that we have done during our lives.

Jesus is our great chief priest

14 We have a great chief priest, who has gone into heaven. He is Jesus, God's Son. We have said that we believe him. So we must continue to believe him strongly. 15 We have a chief priest who understands us. He knows how weak we are. The Devil tried to make him do all kinds of wrong things. So, Jesus understands all the wrong things that we might do. But he never did anything wrong himself. 16 So, when the Devil tries to make us do wrong things, we can ask God to help us. We can come bravely to God, who is our King. He will be very kind and very good to us. He will give us everything that we need.

Chapter 5

1 God has chosen each chief priest from among Israel's people. That priest's work is to serve God on behalf of all the other people. The chief priest offers gifts and sacrifices to God. The people give those gifts and sacrifices to him because they have done wrong things. 2 That priest himself may often make mistakes, because he is human. So, he can understand other people who make mistakes. He can be kind to people who do silly things. 3 The chief priest offers sacrifices to God for everything that people do wrong. But he must give sacrifices to God for himself too, because he can do wrong things also.

4 Nobody decides to be a chief priest by himself. God must choose him, just as God chose Aaron.

5 It is the same with Christ. He did not choose himself to do this important work. He did not choose to be a chief priest. God chose him. God said to him:

'You are my Son.

Today I have given you the honour that goes with that name.'

6 And in another place in the Bible God says this:

'You will always be a priest,

just like Melchizedek.'

7 When Jesus lived on earth as a man, he prayed loudly to God. He cried very much while he asked God to help him. He prayed strongly to God, who could save him from death. Jesus served and obeyed God. So God heard what Jesus said to him.

8 Jesus is God's Son. But he still learned what it is like to obey God. He learned because he had trouble and pain. 9 And as a result, Jesus is the only person who can save us. He saves us for all time from the results of what we do wrong. He saves all those people who obey him. 10 God has called Jesus the same kind of chief priest as Melchizedek.

We must be careful that we do not go away from Christ

11 We have a lot more to say to you about these things. But we can only explain things to you with difficulty because you understand so slowly. 12 After all this time, you ought to be teachers, but you are not teachers. Instead, you need someone to teach you the first lessons about God's message again. You have become like babies, who need milk instead of proper food.

13 Anyone who has to drink milk is still a baby. That person does not know what is right. They do not know when they are doing something wrong. 14 But people who have grown up properly eat proper food. As a result of practice, they have taught themselves. They have taught themselves to know the difference between what is right and wrong.

Chapter 6

1 So we must go on from the first lessons that we learned about Christ. We must learn more as Christians. Then we will understand everything that we should understand. We should not need to learn again about those first things. We already know that the beginning was important. We turned away from doing wrong things then. Those wrong things lead to death, but we believed God. 2 We have already learned about special ways to make things clean. We know that Christians put their hands on other Christians. They do that when they pray for them. We know that dead people will live again. And we have learned that God will decide about every person then. He will decide what is fair for them for all time. 3 So we must go on learning as Christians, if God helps us.

We must not turn away from Jesus

4 People who choose to turn away from Christ cannot come back to him. That is impossible. They once came into God's light. So they know what is true. They have really begun to know the good things that come from heaven. They have received the Holy Spirit. 5 They have learned how good God's message is. They have seen that the future world is very powerful. 6 But after all that, they turn against God! So it is impossible for them to come back to Christ again. Nobody can really help them to turn to Christ again. They are just like the people who fixed Jesus to a big cross. It is like they are killing the Son of God again themselves. They are ashamed of Christ in front of everyone.

7 Think about a field where God sends rain often. That ground can cause the plants in it to grow well for the farmer. Then the farmer can use those plants. 8 But a field where only weeds like thorns and thistles grow (plants with many sharp, hard points) is worth nothing. There is a danger that God will call that ground very bad. The farmer will burn that field.

9 We love you, good friends, and we are still sure about you. We speak like this, but we believe better things about you. God has saved you. And we are sure that you will continue with him. You will go on doing everything that Christians should do. 10 God is always right and fair. He will not forget how much you love him. He will remember how you helped his people. And you are still helping them.

11 But we want each one of you to continue to the end. You must show that you really want to go on. Then you will be sure about what you hope for at the end. 12 We do not want you to become lazy. You must copy the example of those people who continue believing God. They go on being very patient. And so, they receive what God has promised.

God's serious promise

13 For example, God spoke a promise to Abraham many years ago. And because there was nobody greater than God himself, God used his own name. His name caused the promise to be very serious. God would certainly do what he had said. 14 'I will certainly be good to you', God said. 'And I will give you many children and many, many grandchildren', God promised **[Genesis 22:17]** . 15 Abraham waited patiently for a long time. And then he received what God had promised.

16 When a person promises something very seriously, he uses the name of someone or something greater than himself. This shows that he will certainly obey his promise. Then nobody can argue about it. 17 God wanted to show even more certainly that he would never change his purpose. He wanted his people to know this clearly. They would certainly receive what he had promised. So, God spoke his promise and he used his own name. This showed that his promise would certainly happen. 18 These two facts cannot change. God can never say something that is not true. And these two facts cause us to feel strong and sure. We are like people who have run to God. We have run to God so that he can keep us safe. So, we must continue to hope strongly for what God has promised us.

19 We can be completely sure about what we hope for. God is like something really strong that does not move. When we hope, we fix our lives in God.

We fix our lives like an anchor stops a boat moving away. The anchor holds that boat safely in the same place. When we hope, we reach behind the special curtain in God's house in heaven. We reach into the Most Holy Room. 20 Jesus has already gone in there. He has gone before us, on our behalf. He has become our chief priest for always and he is a priest just like Melchizedek.

Chapter 7

Melchizedek, the king and priest

1 This Melchizedek was the King of Salem. And he was a priest of God himself, who is greater than everything. Melchizedek met Abraham when Abraham was returning from a fight. Abraham's men had just beaten 4 kings with their armies. And Melchizedek asked God to be good to Abraham. 2 Also, Abraham gave Melchizedek a tenth part of everything that he had won in the fight. The name 'Melchizedek' means 'King of everything that is right'. And his other name, 'King of Salem', means 'King of everything that is without trouble or war'. 3 Nobody wrote down that Melchizedek had a father or a mother. Nobody wrote down that he had any grandfathers. Nobody wrote about the beginning of his life and nobody wrote about the end. Melchizedek is like the Son of God. He continues to be a priest always.

4 Now think about how great this man, Melchizedek, was! Even Abraham, the grandfather of all Israel's people, gave gifts to Melchizedek. Abraham gave him a tenth part of everything that he had won in the fight. 5 Men from Levi's family group who become priests must take a tenth part from all their own people. The priests receive a tenth part of what the other people of Israel have. God's rules say that. But those priests and the other people are like brothers, because they all come from Abraham's family. 6Melchizedek did not come from Levi's family. But he received a tenth part of what Abraham had. Abraham had received God's promises. But Melchizedek asked God to be good to Abraham.

7 It is always the more important person who asks God to be good to a less important person. Everybody knows that this is true. 8 Israel's priests receive a tenth part of what their people have. But those priests die. Melchizedek received a tenth part from Abraham, but Melchizedek will always be alive. The Bible tells us that. 9 So, by the priests in his family, Levi gets the tenth part from the people. But we could say that, by Abraham, Levi also paid a tenth part to Melchizedek. 10 This is because Levi was Abraham's grandson. Levi was not yet born when Melchizedek met Abraham.

11 The priests from Levi's family were a necessary part of the rules that God gave to Israel's people. But those priests could not make the people completely right with God. So the people needed a different kind of priest to come. They needed a priest like Melchizedek, not someone else from Aaron's family. 12 And when there is a change in the kind of priest, there must also be a change in the rules. 13 The Bible speaks about our Lord as a priest (Psalm 110:4). But he belonged to a different family group from Levi's. Nobody else from our Lord's family group ever worked as a priest. 14 It is completely clear that our Lord came from Judah's family. Moses said nothing about men from Judah's family group being priests.

Jesus is a different kind of priest, like Melchizedek

15 What we have said becomes even clearer now. Another kind of priest has appeared, who is like Melchizedek. 16 Jesus did not become a priest because of rules about which family he came from. He became a priest because of his powerful life. Nothing can ever destroy that life. 17 The Bible speaks about him as a priest:

'You will always be a priest,

just like Melchizedek', the Bible says.

18 So the old rules have come to an end now. They could not really do anything good, so they were not really worth anything. 19 God's rules that he gave to Moses could not make anything completely right. But God has brought us something better to hope for. And because we hope for it, we can come near to God.

20 Also, God promised very seriously when he made Jesus a priest. He did not promise anything when other men became priests. 21 But Jesus received God's very serious promise because God spoke to him like this:

'The Lord has promised seriously,

and he will not change his mind.

You will always be a priest.'

22 So this means that Jesus shows us a much better agreement from God. God has promised us much better things than the old rules could give us. And Jesus makes us completely sure that we will receive these things.

23 There were many of those other priests, because each one died. Then they could not continue to work as priests. 24 But Jesus will always be alive, so he will never stop being a priest. 25 Jesus always lives to pray to God on our behalf. So, he can completely save everyone who comes to him. He will lead them to God.

26 Jesus is the kind of chief priest that we really need. He always obeys God. He has never done anything wrong. He is completely good and clean. He is separate from everyone who does wrong things. God has raised him to the most important place in heaven. 27 Jesus is not like any other chief priest. They need to offer sacrifices to God every day. First they offer sacrifices for the things that they themselves have done wrong. Then they offer sacrifices on behalf of the other people, for all the wrong things that the people have done. But Jesus offered one sacrifice for all time. He gave himself. 28 Moses' rules make men chief priests. And because those men are human, they can do wrong things. But God's very serious promise came after the rules that God gave to Moses. God promised his Son that he would be a chief priest always. And his Son has become everything that God wants him to be, completely and for always.

Chapter 8

Jesus is our chief priest who makes a better agreement from God possible

1 The most important thing that we are saying is this. We do have this kind of chief priest. He has sat down at the right side of where God sits as king in heaven. God is the greatest ruler, with all authority. 2 Our chief priest works in the Most Holy Room that is inside the true special tent. That tent is in heaven. The Lord himself made that special tent. No man built it.

3 It is the duty of every chief priest to offer gifts and sacrifices to God. So our chief priest must also have something to offer. 4 If he was living on earth, then he would not be a priest. There are already priests here who offer gifts to God. They obey the rules that God gave to Moses. 5 But the place where these priests work is only like a copy and a shadow of things in heaven. Many years ago, Moses was ready to make a special tent for God. So God spoke to him: 'Be careful to make everything just like the plan', God told him. 'I showed you the plan on the mountain', God said.

6 But now God has given Jesus much greater work as a priest. His work is greater than the work that those priests do on earth. Jesus has made it possible for God to agree a new and much better thing with his people. It is much better because it began with much better promises. 7 If there had been nothing wrong with that first agreement, then nobody would have needed a second agreement. 8 But God did find something wrong with it. So he spoke like this to the people:

'A new time is coming, the Lord says.

A time is coming when I will agree a new thing

with Israel's people and with Judah's people.

9 It will not be like the things

that I agreed with their grandfathers.

I led their grandfathers out of the country called Egypt.

I led them like someone who takes another person's hand.

But they did not continue to obey

the things that I had agreed with them.

So I turned away from them, the Lord says.

10 I will tell you what I will agree with Israel's people.

It will happen in the days that will come, the Lord says.

I will put my rules into their minds.

I will write my rules deep inside them.

I will be their God

and they will be my people.

11 None of them will ever have to teach their brothers how to know me.

None of them will need to say to anyone else, "You should know the Lord."

Everyone will know me, even the least important people.

And the most important people will know me too.

12 They have done wrong things,

but I will forgive them.

I will not continue to remember

what they have done wrong, the Lord says.'

13 God speaks about a 'new' thing that he will agree with his people. So he has caused the things that he agreed with his people a long time ago to become old. And nobody can go on using something that has become too old. It will soon come to an end.

Chapter 9

The old agreement and God's special tent on earth

1 The first agreement included rules about how people should worship God. It also included a special place for people to worship God on this earth. 2 Israel's people made a special tent for God. The first room in that special tent was called the Holy Room. The lampstand (where a light burned for God) was in this room. The special table where they offered bread to God was there too.

3 Behind the second curtain, there was a very special room called the Most Holy Room. 4 The special gold table where they burned incense was inside that room. And the special agreement box that had gold all over it was there too. This box contained the gold pot that had special food from God in it. The box also contained Aaron's stick that grew leaves. And it contained the two flat stones on which God had written the agreement. 5 The gold shapes of two special angels stood on the top of the agreement box. These special angels showed that God was present there. Under the angels' shadow, on top of the box, was a gold lid. That lid was the place where God forgave the people. But we cannot explain everything about these things now.

6 When they had prepared these things like this, the priests went into the first room every day. They went in there to do their duties. 7 But only the chief priest could go into the second room. He had to go in there alone, but he went in only once every year. He had to take blood from an animal, which he gave to God. He offered the blood because he was sorry. He was sorry for his own mistakes. And he was sorry for the mistakes that all the people had made.

8 God's Spirit, who is completely good, was showing something clearly by these things. He was showing that the Most Holy Room was not yet open to everyone. The first room in the special tent was still there while they worshipped God by these things. 9 This is like a picture that means something for us today. It shows us about the gifts and sacrifices that people brought to God. Those gifts and sacrifices could never make the person who worshipped God completely right with him. They could not make people stop thinking that they had done wrong things. 10 The old rules that God gave were only about foods and drinks and how to wash in special ways. Those rules were only about people's bodies. People had to use those rules only until the time when God would make things new and better.

Christ and the new agreement

11 But now Christ has appeared. He is the chief priest of the good things that have come. He works in a greater and much better tent. No man made that tent because it does not belong to this world. 12 Christ went into its Most Holy Room once, for all time. He did not offer the blood of goats and young cows when he went in there. He offered his own blood after he died. He made us free from everything that we do wrong. He has made us free always.

13 The people were not clean enough to worship God. The old rules said that the priest must make their bodies clean again. He must use the blood of goats and male cows. He must cause that blood to drop like rain on them. He must also burn a young cow and he must use the ashes on the people. And then those people's bodies became clean again.

14 But Christ's blood will do much, much more than this! God's Spirit, who lives always, made it possible for Christ to offer himself to God. Christ was a completely good sacrifice, without anything wrong. He offered his own blood to make us completely clean inside ourselves. The wrong things that we have done lead to death. But he will cause us to stop thinking about the wrong things that we have done. So then we can work for the God who is alive.

15 So Christ brings a new agreement from God. Christ's death made people free from the wrong things that they had done during the time of the first agreement. So now, the people that God chooses can receive from him. They can receive the good things that he has promised for always.

16 Before a person dies, he may make an agreement about all his own things. That agreement says who will get his things after his death. But nobody can get anything until that person has certainly died. 17 An agreement like that only means something after the death of the person who made it. It has no power while that person is still alive. 18 That is why even the first agreement with God needed blood from a death. The agreement could not work without that blood.

19 Moses read God's rules aloud to all Israel's people. He told them every rule that God had given them. Then Moses killed some young cows and goats. He took some of their blood and he mixed it with water. He used sheep's hair that people had made red. He used also some small branches of a plant called hyssop. He used the sheep's hair and the hyssop to throw the blood. He caused the blood to drop like rain. He caused some of the blood to drop on to the book of God's rules. And he caused some to drop on to all the people. 20 And Moses spoke to them. 'This is the blood of the agreement that God has told you to obey', he said. 21 In the same way, Moses put some of the blood on to God's special tent. He also caused blood to drop on to all the things that the priests used in their work there. 22 God's rules say that blood is necessary to make almost everything clean. And God will not forgive people unless a death gives the blood.

Christ's death is a better sacrifice

23 So animals' blood was necessary to make those things clean and right. They were copies of the true and proper things that are in heaven. But the proper things in heaven need better sacrifices than that to make them clean and right. 24 Christ did not go into a Most Holy Room that people had made on earth. A place like that is only a copy of the place in heaven. He went into heaven itself. And now he is present with God and he speaks to God on our behalf.

25 The chief priest here on earth goes into the Most Holy Room year after year. He takes an animal's blood to offer there each time, not his own blood. But Christ did not go into heaven to offer himself to God again and again. 26 He did not need to die again and again since the world began. Instead, he has appeared once, for all time. He has come now, when the world is near its end. He came to remove completely all the wrong things that we do. He died as a sacrifice for us. 27 God has chosen that every person must die once. After death, God will decide what is fair for that person. 28 So Christ also died and he offered himself once. He did this to take away wrong things for many people. And Christ will return to earth a second time, but not to take away wrong things. He will come to save those people who are waiting for him.

Chapter 10

1 Moses' rules are only like a shadow of the good things that will come. The rules do not show what those good things are really like. The rules say that the priest must continue to offer the same sacrifices for the people, year after year. The people bring their sacrifices when they come to worship God. So, people will never be completely good and clean because of those rules.

2 If the rules could do that, the priests would have stopped offering sacrifices. The people would have become completely good and clean once, for all time. They would have become clean like that when they came to worship God the first time. So they would not still think that they had done wrong things. 3 But those sacrifices cause people to remember, year after year, the wrong things that they have done. 4 It is impossible for the blood of male cows and of goats to take away wrong things. 5 So, when Christ came into the world, he spoke to God like this:

'You do not want gifts and sacrifices of animals,

but you have prepared a body for me.

6 The whole animals that they burn

do not make you happy.

The sacrifices for what people have done wrong

do not make you happy.

7 Then I spoke again: "Here I am, God.

I have come to do what you want.

That is what the book of your rules says about me." '

8 So Christ had said first: 'You do not want gifts and sacrifices of animals. You do not want the whole animals that they burn. You do not want sacrifices for what people have done wrong. These things do not make you happy.' But Moses' rules said that these sacrifices were necessary. 9 Then Christ spoke again: 'Here I am. I have come to do what you want', he said. So God takes away the old sacrifices and he puts Christ's sacrifice in their place. 10 God wants to make us completely good and clean. And he has done that because of Jesus Christ's sacrifice. Christ offered his own body once, for all time, when he died.

11 Every day, the priests stand and they do their work. They offer the same sacrifices to God again and again. But those sacrifices can never take away the wrong things that people have done. 12 This priest, Jesus Christ, offered one sacrifice for wrong things, for all time. Then he sat down at God's right side. 13 Since that time, he waits for God to make an end to his enemies. God will make Christ's enemies like a place for him to rest his feet. 14 As a result of one sacrifice, Christ has made his people completely right with God always. God is making those people completely separate from everything that is bad.

15 God's Spirit, who is completely good, also shows us about these things. He shows us that these things are true. He says this first:

16 'This is what I will agree with them

after that time, the Lord says.

I will put my rules deep inside them.

I will write my rules on their minds.'

17 Then he continues to speak:

'I will not continue to remember

the wrong things and the bad things

that they have don

18 So when God has forgiven these wrong things, no more sacrifices are necessary.

Christ made it possible that we can come near to God

19 So then, Christian friends, we are completely free to go into the Most Holy Room. We can be sure that we can go in there, because of Jesus' death. 20 Jesus has opened a new way to God for us. This way leads us through the curtain to God, where we will be alive. Jesus opened this way when he gave his own body. 21 And we have a great priest who is the master of God's house. 22 So when we come near to God, we must believe him completely. We must want only to obey him. He has made us clean deep inside ourselves so that we are free. We are free to stop thinking about the wrong things that we have done. We are really clean. It is like he has washed our bodies with clean water.

23 We say that we believe God's promises. And we must continue to be completely sure about what we hope for. God always does what he has promised. We can be sure because we know that. 24 We should think about how we can be kind to each other. Then other people will want to be kind too. They will really want to do good things, like us. 25 Some people have stopped going regularly to our Christian meetings, but we must not stop going there. Then we can help each other to be strong Christians. You should do this more and more, because the Lord's great day is coming. You know that the Lord will return soon.

We must not refuse to obey Christ

26 We have learned what is really true. We have believed it. So now, we must not decide to continue doing wrong things. There is no other sacrifice that will take away those wrong things. 27 There is only punishment that will make us very, very afraid. We must wait for God to decide about us. But the punishment would be the very hot fire that destroys people. That fire destroys everyone who refuses to obey God. 28 Anyone who refused to obey Moses' rules had to die. Two or three other people may have seen that person do something wrong. They had to say that the person certainly did something wrong. Then Israel's people had to kill that person. They could not be kind to a person like that.

29 So think about a person who refuses the Son of God. How much worse that person's punishment will be! He is like someone who has walked on God's Son. That person has made Christ's blood and God's agreement seem like something dirty. But it was Christ's death that made that person clean and right with God. That person has said very bad words against God's Spirit, who is so very kind. 30 We know God. And God said this: 'I will punish people for what they have done wrong. I will give them what they ought to have.' **[Deuteronomy 32:35]** He also said this: 'The Lord will decide what is fair for his people.'**[Deuteronomy 32:36]** 31 So anyone who refuses God should be very, very afraid. God, who is alive, will certainly punish that person.

32 Remember what happened to you in those early days when you first learned about Christ. Then you had a difficult fight against many troubles. But you continued to be strong. 33 Sometimes people made you ashamed in front of many other people.

They said bad words to you and they did bad things to you. And at other times, you chose to stay with other Christians who were receiving this kind of trouble. 34 You felt the trouble together with those who were in prison. When people took your own things away, you were still happy. You knew that you yourselves had something better. You had better things that will be yours always.

35 So do not stop being sure about what you believe as Christians. If you continue to be brave, you will receive great things. 36 You need to be patient and strong. Then you can do what God wants. As a result, you will receive what God has promised. 37 God promises this in the Bible:

'In a very short time,

the person who is coming will come.

He will not be late, the Lord said.

38 The person that I have accepted will live.

Those people will live because they believe me.

But if any of them turn back,

I will not be happy with them.'

39 But we are not among those people who turn back. If we were, God would destroy us. But we are people who believe God. And so, God will save us.

Chapter 11

We must believe God

1 If we believe God, we can be completely sure about things. We will be sure about the things that we hope for. We will be sure about things that we cannot see. 2 People who lived many years ago believed God. And so, God said good things about those people. 3 Because we believe God, we understand about the world. We understand that God made the whole world. He spoke and it happened. He made all the things that we can see. He made them from things that we cannot see.

4 Abel believed God. So he offered a better sacrifice to God than Cain offered. And because of that, God said that Abel was a good man. God said that he was happy with Abel's gifts. Abel is dead. But because he believed God, we can still learn from his example. So it is like Abel is speaking to us still.

5 Enoch believed God, so he did not die. Instead, God took him away. And nobody could find him, because God had taken him away. Before God took him away, Enoch had made God happy. The Bible tells us that.6 Unless we believe God, it is impossible for us to make God happy. Anyone who comes to God must believe him. That person must believe that God is really there. And they must believe that God is good to people. God gives good things to everyone who really wants to find him.

7 Noah believed God, and so he obeyed God. God told Noah about bad things that would happen. Nobody could yet see those events, but Noah believed God. So, Noah was careful to obey what God told him. He built a large boat to save his family. As a result, Noah showed that everyone else in the world was wrong. And Noah became one of those people that God accepted. They are right with God because they believe him.

8 After this, Abraham believed God, so he obeyed God. God told him to leave his home. God wanted him to go to another country. Abraham did not know where he was going. But God promised to give that other country to Abraham. He obeyed God and he started travelling. 9 Abraham believed God, so he went to live in that foreign country. He lived in the country that God had promised to him. He lived there in tents, like a stranger. Isaac and Jacob lived there in tents too. God had made the same promise to Abraham, to Isaac and to Jacob. 10 Abraham was waiting to live in the city that will always be there. He was completely sure that he would live in God's city. God made the plans for that city, and God built it.

11 Both Abraham and his wife, Sarah, were too old to have children. But they believed God's promise to Abraham about a child. God would always do what he had promised. They believed that. And so, God made it possible for even Sarah herself to have a baby. 12 Abraham was so old that he was almost like a dead man. But from this one man there came many, many grandchildren. After some years, there were so many of his people that nobody could count them. There were as many of Abraham's family as the stars in the sky. There were as many as the bits of sand on the sea's shore.

13 All these people continued to believe God until they died. But they did not receive all the things that God had promised to them. They understood that those things would come after a long time. They were like people who saw those things far away. All these people agreed that they were only strangers and travellers on the earth.

14 And people who say things like that are certainly looking for a country of their own. They are looking for a country where they will be at home. 15 None of these people continued to think about the country that they had left. If they had thought about it, they might have had the chance to return there. 16 Instead, they were wanting very much to go to a better country, in heaven. And for this reason, God is not ashamed to be called their God. He has prepared a city for them.

17 God wanted to see whether Abraham really believed him. So God told Abraham to offer his son, Isaac, as a sacrifice. And because Abraham did believe God, he obeyed. God had promised many grandchildren to Abraham. But Abraham was still ready to offer his only son as a sacrifice. 18 'It is through Isaac that your grandchildren will come', God had said to Abraham **[Genesis 21:12]** . 19 But Abraham was sure that God could cause Isaac to become alive again. So Isaac would live again, even after he had died. And we could say that it was like that for Abraham. It was like he did receive Isaac back from death.

20 Isaac believed God, so he promised good things to Jacob and Esau. He told them that God would be good to them in their future lives.

21 Jacob believed God. So he told Joseph's sons that God would be good to each of them. He did that when he was dying. He worshipped God while he used his stick to hold himself up.

22 Joseph believed God. So, when he was going to die, he spoke about all Israel's people. He spoke about the time when the people would leave Egypt. And he told them what to do with his bones.

23 Moses' parents believed God. So, when Moses was born, they hid him for three months. They saw that he was a very special child. So they did not obey the king, but they were not afraid.

24 Moses believed God. So, when he became a man, he refused to be called the son of the king's daughter.25 Moses chose to be with God's people. Egypt's people were doing bad things to them, but Moses still chose to be with them. He chose not to do what was wrong. Wrong things only make people happy for a short time. 26 Moses could have been very rich in Egypt. But instead, he let people do bad things to him. He let them make him ashamed because he believed about Christ. He thought that it was worth more than a lot of money. He thought only about what God would give him at a future time. 27 Moses believed God, so he left Egypt. The king was angry about that, but Moses was not afraid of him. Nobody can really see God. But Moses continued strongly with his purpose, like someone who could see God.

28 Moses believed God, so he prepared the first Passover. And he told Israel's people to put blood from the sacrifice round their doors. Then the angel who destroyed people came. He saw the blood and so he did not kill the oldest sons in the families of Israel's people.

29 Israel's people believed God, so they went through the Red Sea. They walked through just as they would cross dry land. But when the people from Egypt tried to cross that sea, they drowned.

30 Israel's people believed God, so they marched round Jericho city for 7 days. Then the city's walls fell down.

31 Some men from Israel had come to that city earlier. They wanted to discover how strong the people were. Rahab was friendly to those men and she gave help to them. She was a woman who had sold herself to men for sex. But then she believed God, so she did not die with all the other people in her city. Those other people did not believe God.

32 I could say a lot more, but there is not enough time. I could tell you about Gideon, Barak, Samson, Jephthah, David, Samuel and the prophets (people who spoke God's messages). 33 Because they believed God, some of them won wars against other countries. They did what is right and fair. And they received good things that God had promised. Some of them caused big wild cats called lions to shut their mouths.

34 Some of them put out fires that were burning very strongly. Some of them got away from people who wanted to kill them with long knives. After they had been weak, they became strong. They became very strong to fight wars. They beat foreign armies and they caused those armies to run away.

35 God caused some of these people who had died to become alive again. And the women in their families received them back. Other people refused to turn against God so that they could go free. So, their enemies did bad things to hurt them, which caused them to die. But these people were sure that they would have a better life after death. They were sure that they would live again with God.

36 Enemies said that these people were fools. The enemies said bad things to them and hit them with sticks. The enemies tied people with metal lines and put them in prison. 37 Enemies threw stones at them to kill them. They even cut them into two pieces to kill them. Enemies also killed some of them with long knives. Some of these people had to wear only the skins of sheep and goats while they walked about. They were very, very poor and they had a lot of trouble. Other people did very bad things to those who believed God. 38 These people who believed God were too good for this world. Some of them had to walk about in dry places where nobody lived. Some had to walk only in the mountains. Some had to live in holes in the rocks and in holes in the ground.

39 God said good things about all these people because they believed him. But they still did not receive everything that he had promised. 40 God had prepared something better for all of us. So, he did not make those people completely as he wanted them to be, without us.

Chapter 12

We must continue to follow Jesus

1 So then we ourselves know about all these people who believed God. They are our examples. They are like a very big crowd all round us. They show us how we can live for God. We must be like people who run in a race. We want to run fast in the race. So, we must throw away everything that would stop us. We want to live for God. So, we must refuse wrong things that stop us. Those wrong things can so easily hold us strongly. But we must continue to be brave and strong while we run the race. God has chosen the way that is in front of us.

2 We must always think about Jesus, like people who go on looking at him always. He is the example of someone who believes God completely. He leads us and he will cause us to believe completely. Jesus died on a cross that people had made from wood. He had a lot of pain and people were very ashamed of him. But he refused to think about that before he died. He knew that God had chosen the way for him. He knew that God had chosen to make him very, very happy later. And now he sits in the most important place next to where God sits as king. 3 Think carefully about Jesus. Bad people did such very bad things against him, but he continued to be brave and strong. Think about him, and then you will not become tired and weak as Christians.

We are really God's children

4 You are in the fight against everything that is wrong. But you have not yet had to continue fighting until someone killed you. 5 You have forgotten that someone wrote words to God's children. These words can make you brave and strong:

'My son, think seriously when the Lord punishes you.

He will sometimes show you that you are wrong.

You must not become sad and weak.

when he tells you that you are wrong.

6 Because the Lord does that to everyone that he loves.

He punishes everyone that he receives as a son.'

7 You must be patient and strong when life is difficult. Receive the trouble as punishment from God, who is your Father. God is teaching you as his children. There has never been any son whose father did not punish him. 8 God teaches all his children not to do wrong things. So if he does not punish you, then you are not really his children. Then you are like children who do not really belong to him. 9 Also, we have all had human fathers who punished us. And we thought that it was important to obey them. So it is much more important that we obey the Father of our spirits. If we obey him then we will live.

10 Our human fathers punished us for a short time, as they thought best. But God punishes us because that really is the best thing for us. Then we can become like him. We can become completely separate from everything that is bad. 11 No punishment makes us happy at the time when we receive it. It makes us sad then. But later we know that the punishment has taught us good things. It has made our lives more like God wants us to be. Then we are without trouble deep inside ourselves because we are right with God.

12 You have become tired as Christians, like people with hands that hang down. You are like people with weak knees. Lift up your hands and make your knees strong again! 13 Live for God, like people who walk on a straight, flat path. So then, people with weak legs, who cannot walk well, will not get worse. Their legs will not become unable to walk. But instead they will become well and strong.

We must not refuse to do what God says

14 Do everything that you can to live without trouble or quarrels between you and anyone else. Also, do everything that you can to live a completely good life for God. Nobody will see the Lord unless their life is good like that. 15 Be careful that nobody among you turns away from God. Nobody should refuse to receive from God, who is so very kind. Be careful that nobody becomes angry against God. A person like that can cause trouble among you, because they are like poison to other people's lives. A person like that can lead many other people away from God.

16 Be careful that nobody among you has sex with someone other than their wife or their husband. And watch that nobody is careless about God's rules, like Esau. He gave away everything that he would have received as his father's first son. He gave it all away so that he could get only one meal.

17 And later, as you know, he still wanted to receive those good things from his father. He wanted his father to ask God for good things for him. But that was impossible. Esau cried when he asked his father for those good things. But he could find no way to change things. Esau could not change what he had done.

The two mountains

18 You have not come to a place that you can touch, like the Sinai mountain. That mountain burned with fire. But where the people stood, it was very dark. It was so dark that it was black. There was a very strong wind and a storm. 19 There was the sound of a trumpet and a powerful voice that spoke to them. When the people heard that voice, they were very afraid. So they asked strongly that the voice would not speak to them anymore. 20 They remembered what God had already told them. So they were very afraid. 'If even an animal touches the mountain, you must kill it with stones', God had said **[Exodus 19:12-13]** . 21 Even Moses was very afraid. 'I am so afraid that my body cannot stop moving', Moses said **[Deuteronomy 9:19]** .

22 But you have come to Zion mountain and to the city of God, who is alive. You have come to the Jerusalem city that is in heaven. You have come to a place where there are thousands and thousands of happy angels all together.

23 All God's people, who are like his first and most important sons, meet here. God has written their names here in heaven, because they belong here. You have come to where God is. He will decide what is fair for all people. You have come to where people's spirits are. These are the spirits of all those people that God has made right. God has made those people be as he wants them to be. 24 You have come to Jesus, who brought the new agreement from God to his people. Remember also the blood that Jesus lost. He bled when he chose to die. That was how he made us clean. Jesus' blood shows us about better things than Abel's blood.

28 But we receive a place where we will rule with God. And nobody can ever move that place, so we should thank God. We should worship God in a way that makes him happy. We should worship him because he is so great and so powerful. 29 Our God is like a fire that can destroy everything.

Chapter 13

How we can live for God

1 Continue to love each other like brothers and sisters. 2 Always remember to be kind to strangers. Remember to let them stay in your homes. In this way, some people have received angels as visitors. But those people did not know that their visitors were angels. 3 Remember those people who are in prison. Think about what that would be like for you. Think like someone who is there with those people in prison. Remember those who have troubles because of other people. Other people are doing bad things to them. Trouble like that could also happen to you. Think about what that would be like for you yourselves.

4 When people have married each other, everyone should remember that. Everyone should remember that it is a very good and important thing. Husbands and wives must not have sex with anyone else. Nobody should have sex with someone who is not their own wife or their own husband. God will punish everyone who does not obey those rules.

5 Do not want lots of money. Do not live like that. Be happy with the things that you have. Be happy, because God has promised to be with you.

'I will never leave you;

I will never let you be completely alone', he said.

6 So we can bravely say this:

'The Lord comes to help me,

so I will not be afraid.

I will not be afraid of anything that people can do to me.'

7 Remember your leaders, who taught God's message to you. Continue to think about the result of how they lived. They really believed God; so copy their example. 8 Jesus Christ is the same today as he was yesterday. And he will be the same always.

9 Some people teach all kinds of strange things. Do not let them lead you the wrong way. God is very kind to us, so he will make us strong deep inside ourselves. It is good if we let him do that. Rules about what foods we eat do not make us strong like that. Those rules have never done anything good for the people who obey them.

10 Israel's priests worked for God in his special tent, and they ate there. But we have a sacrifice that they have no authority to eat from. 11 The chief priest brings the blood from the animal sacrifice into the Most Holy Room.

He offers that blood to God because Israel's people have done many wrong things. But they burn those animals' bodies outside the place where the people live. 12 For this reason Jesus also died outside the city's gate. And God saw the blood that he lost. Jesus died there as a sacrifice. He died there so that he could make people completely good and clean for God. 13 So we must go to him. We must be ready to go outside the place where everybody else lives. We must be ready for people to be ashamed of us, as they were ashamed of him. 14 Here on earth we do not have a home in a city that will always be there. But we are waiting for God's city that will come.

15 So we should always continue to thank God. We should say how great and how good he is. That is our sacrifice to him, because Jesus helps us. Then we will always be offering this gift to him while we speak his name. 16 Remember to be kind to other people. And remember to share what you have with other people. God is very happy with sacrifices like that.

17 Obey your leaders. Do what they tell you. They continue to watch over your lives on God's behalf. And they will have to explain to God how they have done that work. So, if you obey them, they will be happy with their work. Do not make them sad, because that would not help you.

18 Pray for us. We are completely sure that we have done nothing wrong. We always want to do only what is right. 19 I want you very much to pray that I may come back to you soon.

20 God can take away all difficulties and he can cause you to be without trouble inside yourselves. God caused our Lord Jesus to become alive again. He did not stay among the dead people. When Jesus died, the new agreement began. And it will continue always. Jesus is like a shepherd (someone who watches over his sheep). He is our great shepherd, and we are his sheep. 21 I pray that God will make you completely ready to serve him. He will give you every good thing that you need for that work. And then you can do everything that he wants. I pray that Jesus Christ will do these good things in us on God's behalf. Then we will make God happy. Everyone should say how great God is for all time and always. This is true.

22 Christian friends, I ask very much that you listen patiently to my message. I have written this to help you so that you can be brave and strong. And this letter is not very long. 23 I want you to know about Timothy, who is like a brother to us. They have let him go out of prison, so that he is free now. If he arrives soon, I will travel with him to meet you.

24 Say 'hello' on my behalf to your leaders and to all God's people. The Christians from the country called Italy say 'hello' to you too. 25 I pray that God will be very kind to all of you.

How to Live for Jesus

James

About James's letter

James wrote his letter to tell all Christians what they should do. He also told them what they should not do. The letter was in the Greek language. It is different from Paul's letters. It does not tell people what they must believe. James did not write it to tell them how to become Christians. He is writing to Christians. They know that Jesus died for them. He is writing to help them to live for Jesus. He is telling them how to become better Christians. After he had written his letter, he sent it to every Christian church. It is important to all Christians today. James was the brother of the Lord Jesus Christ. James was also a leader of the church in Jerusalem. (See Acts 12:17 and Acts 15:13-22.)

Chapter 1

1 This letter is from James, who is a servant of God and of the Lord Jesus Christ. I say 'hello' to the 12 tribes of the Jews, who live in many parts of the world.

2 My Christian brothers, be very happy when all kinds of tests happen to you. 3 You are continuing to fight these troubles. And you know that your faith will become stronger then. 4 Continue to be strong for the fight. So you will become completely mature and you will not need anything. 5 If any of you need wisdom, ask God for it. He is ready to give to everyone. And he never says that it is wrong to ask. God will give that wisdom to you. 6 But when you ask, you must believe. You must believe that God will give it to you. Some people are not sure whether God will give it to them. That kind of person is like the water that is in the sea. The wind blows it this way and that way. 7-8 A person who is like that never knows what to do. He is confused. He does not know what to think. He should not think that he will get anything from the Lord.

James is the brother of Jesus, but he describes himself as a servant of Jesus Christ. Christians should be servants too. In those days, servants were not free. They were like their master's things. They had to do everything that their master wanted. Some masters were bad and some were good. Christians are servants of God. And he is the best master that anyone could have.

9 The poor Christian in your group should be happy, because God will make him great. 10 And the rich Christian should be happy that God will make him small. He should remember that he will die like a wild flower. 11 The sun rises and hot winds dry the wild flowers. They fall and die. And they are no longer beautiful. In the same way, while the rich man is busy, he will die like a wild flower.

12 Some people do not stop believing even when troubles happen. God will bless a person who is like that. After he has won the fight, God will give a gift to him. That is the gift that God promised. This gift is eternal life. God will give this gift to all people who love him. 13 Trouble will happen to tempt us. But do not say that God is causing it to tempt you. Nothing bad can tempt God and God does not tempt anyone. 14 It is our own thoughts that tempt us sometimes. And then we want to do wrong things. We want what is bad. And that causes us to do wrong things. 15 Sometimes we do the bad things that we wanted to do. When we do that, we sin. In the end, the result of sin is death.

16 Do not make a mistake, my dear Christian brothers. 17 Every good gift and every perfect gift comes to us from God. He is the best Father. He is like a strong light that sends away all shadows. He does not change. 18 He chose to make us his children. He made us his children by his true word. The result is that we will be like the first part of his harvest.

It is not always easy to be a Christian. It is not easy to make God happy in all the things that we do. Life is sometimes very difficult. Sometimes we are sick or we feel pain. Or trouble happens to us. Sometimes other people hurt us because we are Christians. God does not cause these troubles to happen to us. But God loves us very much. He can use these troubles to help us to grow. Even pain can cause us to be more like God. If we ask him for help, he will hear us. He will help us to understand more. Sometimes life is difficult. But then we must not think that God has made it difficult. We must trust him to use difficult things. He can use them to make us stronger.

19 Understand this, my dear Christian brothers. We must all be careful to listen. We should not be too quick to speak. We should not get angry easily.

20 When a man is angry, he does not do the right things. He does not do what God wants. 21 So, stop doing and stop saying evil things. God has put his word in your minds, and it can save your souls. So, believe what it says.

22 But do not only listen to the word of God. Do what it says too. If you do not, you will be making a mistake. 23 You will be like a man who sees his face in a mirror. 24 This man looks at himself and then he goes away. And he immediately forgets what he is like. 25 But the person who continues to look into the good law of God will be free. That is, if he obeys it. That person will not forget what he hears. He will do what it says. And so God will bless that person in what he does.

26 We may want to do the things that make God happy. We may think that we are doing those things. But if we speak bad words, we are wrong. We are not making God happy. And what we think is not helping us.

27 Things that really make God our Father happy are good. For example, we should help children that have no parents. We should help women whose husbands have died. And we must keep away from all that is wrong in the world.

All God's servants must hear and remember his words. We must do what he wants. And we must obey his words. If we do those things, we will be happy. This is how we work for God. We may say that we are his servants. But we might not do what he wants. And so we are not saying what is true. To do good things cannot buy us a place that is near to God. We must not think that it can. But we should do the good things that God wants us to do. That will show our love for God. And so we will be good servants, and we will be God's good children.

Chapter 2

1 My Christian brothers, you trust the Lord Jesus Christ, who is full of glory. So, do not think that one person is more valuable than another person. 2 Two men may come into the place where you have your meetings. One of them is wearing good clothes and he has gold rings. The other man is poor, and he is wearing old clothes. 3 You look at the man who is wearing good clothes. You say to him, 'Please sit here in a good place.' But you say to the poor man, 'Stand there', or 'Sit at my feet.' 4 If you do that, you are not doing the right thing. You are thinking that each of them has a different value. You must not think that one of them is better than the other man. This is wrong and your thoughts are not correct.

5 My dear Christian brothers, listen to me. This is what God has done. He has chosen those that people of this world call poor. But those poor people believe in God, so he calls them rich. He will give to them a place in his kingdom. God has promised this to those who love him. 6 But you have done wrong things to the poor man. And so, you have caused him to feel ashamed. It is the rich people who cause trouble to happen to you. They ask judges to say without a good reason that you have done wrong things. 7 It is rich men who speak badly about the good name (Christ). But you are called his people (Christians).

Every Christian is important to God. Each Christian is valuable to him. Our money and good clothes are not important. God has chosen poor people to show us that his love is better than money or good clothes. We should be good to poor people and to rich people. God wants us to be good to people who are from every family and from every country. We may have more money than other people have. But that does not make us better than they are. God wants us to love other people. And he wants us to love him more than we love anyone else.

8 But God, who is king, has said in his word, 'Love other people as you love yourself.' If you really do that, you do well. 9 But perhaps you think that one man is better than another man. If you think that, you are sinning. God's law says that you are wrong. 10 That is because we must obey all of God's rules. We must obey every rule that the law tells us. If we fail to obey one small rule, we have failed to obey the whole law. 11 For example, God has said in his law, 'You must not have sex with another person who is not your husband or your wife.' But he has also said, 'Do not kill another person.' Perhaps you do not have wrong sex but you do murder. If you do that, you have not obeyed the law of God. 12 Speak as those whom God will judge by his law. And remember that, whatever you are doing. This law makes us free. By this law, God will say soon if our lives are good or bad. 13 God will not be kind to those who have not been kind. He will be kind to those who have been kind. And that is better than when he says, 'You are wrong.'

14 My Christian brothers, you say that you believe in God. But you show this when you do good things. But some people among you may not do any good things. What those people say is not worth anything. If your faith is like that, it cannot save you. 15 If a Christian brother or sister does not have enough clothes or enough food, he or she needs help. 16 It does not help them if you say to them, 'Go and be well. Keep yourself warm and eat well.' But you do not give to them what they need. That does not help them at all. 17 Perhaps you say that you believe. But you do not do good things. That is not worth anything. Christians must do good things. In that way, they show that they really believe in God.

18 Someone will say, 'You believe in God but I help people.' Show me that you believe in God. You cannot show me that if you are not doing any good things. But I will show you that I believe in God. I will show it to you when I help people.

19 You believe that there is one God. Good! The demons believe that, and it makes them very afraid. 20 You silly person, you should not need me to show you these facts. You may say that you believe. But, if you do not do good things, that is not worth anything. 21 Think about our father Abraham, who offered his son Isaac on an altar. God called him a good man because he did that. 22 Abraham did what God asked him to do. So you can see that he believed God. He obeyed God. So he showed that he really believed in God. 23 The Scriptures said that this would happen. They say, 'Abraham believed God, so God called him a good man.' God also called him his friend. 24 A person may say that he believes in God. But God does not call a person good only because he says that. God calls a person good when that person does good things too.

25 It was the same with Rahab. She was a person that men paid to have sex with her. But some Jews came to her. And then she did something that made God happy. They were enemies of her people and they had come to look at her city. To make God happy, she let them stay in her house. She kept them safe. Then she sent them back by a different way. So, because she did that, God called her good. 26 The body with no spirit is dead. In the same way, you may say that you believe in God. But perhaps you do not do good things. So, what you say is not worth anything.

If we do only one small wrong thing, God will be angry with us. Any wrong thing that we do makes God sad. He will punish us one day if we do bad things to other people. If we are kind to other people, God will be kind to us. But we must obey all his rules. We must do the things that make God happy. That is how we show our love to God. Words mean nothing if we do not do any good things. We must show that we are God's people. We must help other people. And we must do the things that make them happy. We show that we are God's people in that way. We should trust God as Abraham and Rahab trusted him. Rahab was a bad woman. But God forgave the bad things that she had done. She trusted God and he saved her whole family. (See Joshua 2:1-20; 6:22-23; James 2:25.) She became one of God's people, and she became an ancestor of his kings (Matthew 1:5, 6). She even became an ancestor of Jesus Christ.

Chapter 3

1 My Christian brothers, not many of you should be teachers. God will judge everybody. But at that time, he will demand more from teachers than he will demand from other people. 2 That is because we all make many mistakes. Perhaps one person never says anything that is wrong. That person is good in all that he does. He can cause his whole body to do what is right.

3 For example, think about what we do with a horse. We can cause it to obey us. We put a bit of iron in its mouth. After we have done that, we can turn it. And then we can cause its whole body to go where we want it to go. 4 Think about ships that sail on the sea. They are large, and strong winds push them over the water. But we fix a very small piece of wood under the back of the ship. With this piece of wood, a man can cause the ship to turn anywhere that he wants it to go. 5 The tongue is like that too. It is a very small part of the body but it talks about big things. A very small fire can cause a big forest to burn. 6 And the tongue is like a fire. It is like a whole world of evil things. The tongue is a small part of the body but it makes the whole person bad. It destroys all of his life. That fire is the fire that comes from hell. And that is what makes the tongue so dangerous.

7 Remember this: People can cause all kinds of animals, birds, snakes and fishes to do what they want them to do. 8 But no person can rule his tongue. No person can stop it from saying bad things. It is like a bad poison and it can cause death.

9 We use the tongue to praise our Lord and Father. We also use it to speak bad things against people. But God made people to be like himself. 10 So we use the same mouth to praise and to speak bad things. My Christian brothers, we should not do this. 11 Salt water and sweet water cannot come from the same well. 12 My Christian brothers, a fig tree cannot make olives. A plant that makes grapes cannot also make figs. And a well cannot have salt water and have sweet water too. In the same way, we should not use the tongue to praise God, and then to speak bad things.

If we choose to say only one wrong word, it can cause us to go away from God. One small wrong word can turn our minds away from God's way. Then we do or say more wrong things. This could take us a long way from God. We should let God help us with our minds and our words all the time.

Teachers must be careful to teach God's word correctly. They must teach all the words of the Bible. They must ask God to help them. And he will help them to understand the Bible. God wants teachers to teach by what they do. They should not only say the words. Teachers must show other Christians what they should do. The teachers should show them because the teachers do the right things themselves.

We must all be careful to speak only good words. The devil wants us to say bad things. We must not let him cause us to do that. God's people must not say things that are not true. And they should not say things that are not kind. God's people should say and do only good things.

13 Some of you may be wise. You will understand these things. So show that you are wise. Show it by what you do. Do things that are good and wise. 14 Perhaps you think bad things about other people. Some people may have what you want. And perhaps you feel bad because of that. Perhaps you want to make yourselves important and you do not think about anyone else. You may think these bad things. If you do, do not think, 'We are better than other people.' Do not say that you are wise. 15 Perhaps you think bad things about other people. But that is not how God would want you to think. People who do not know God may think like that. The bad parts of human nature cause you to think like that. It is like the way that demons think. 16 You may think bad things about other people. And you may think that you are better than those people. That will cause trouble among people and lots of bad things will happen. 17 If God makes you wise, you will first be clean and true. Then you will love to have peace with other people. You will be quiet. And you will not want to argue with people. You will be loving and kind. And you will do good things to all people. You will be honest. And you will be like that all the time.

18 Those who bring peace to other people help them to have peace with everyone. God will call those people good.

Chapter 4

1 You very often fight and quarrel among yourselves. You must know why that is. It is because you want to make yourselves happy. You have wrong thoughts. That is why you are doing this to each other.

2 You want something but you do not get it. You kill other people. And you try to take things that are not yours. But you cannot get them. You fight and you quarrel. But you do not get what you want. You do not get it because you do not ask God. 3 When you do ask, you do not receive anything. That is because you ask for the wrong reason. This is why you ask: You want to spend what you get to make yourselves happy. 4 You are like a wife who has sex with other men. Some people do not love God. Those people do the things that he does not like. If you want to do those things, you are against God. Some people choose to be friends of those who do wrong things. People who choose to do that are enemies of God. You should know that! 5 With good reason, the Scripture says to us: 'God has caused his Spirit to live in us. He wants very much to keep us for himself.' 6 But God gives more loving help to us. That is why the Scripture says, 'Some people think that they are very important. God is against those people. But some people know that they need God. He gives his loving help to those people.' 7 So give yourself only to God. Be strong against the devil and he will run away from you. 8 Come near to God and he will come near to you. Do not try to love sin and to love God at the same time. You cannot do that. So, start to love God only. Make your hearts and your minds clean. I am writing to those who want to go both ways. You cannot love sin and love God at the same time. 9 Be sorry and weep. Do not laugh but be sad. Do not be happy but be serious.

10 Think about yourselves as small in front of the Lord God. Then he will make you great.

11 My Christian brothers, do not say bad things against each other. Perhaps you speak against another Christian. If you do that, you are speaking against the law. If you make yourself another Christian's judge, you are speaking against the law too. When you say these things, you are not obeying the law. You are making yourself a judge instead. 12 God says what we should do. And he will be the judge. Only he can save us or kill us. So you must not try to be another person's judge.

Some people fight and argue. They are being like the devil. If we say bad things about God's word or about his people, we are being like the devil.

If we only want to make ourselves happy, God will not hear us. We must listen to God. We must be sorry about the wrong things that we have done. We must do good things. So God will give to us all that we need. As a result, we will be able to do the things that make him happy. Then we will be happy. We should fight the devil, and not fight other Christians. God will make us strong to fight. We must be strong against the devil. If we do that, he will run away. When we really trust God, the devil may attack us. But he cannot hurt us.

13 Listen to me, you who say, 'Today or tomorrow we will go to this city or to that city. We will stay there for a year. We will buy and sell. And we will get rich.' 14 You do not know what will happen tomorrow. Your life is like smoke. Smoke appears for a little while and then it is there no longer. 15 What you ought to say is, 'If the Lord wants it, we will live here or there. If he wants it, we will do this or that.' 16 But now you talk about what you will do. You speak as if you can cause it to happen. It is wrong to speak like that. 17 So, we all know the good things that we ought to do. If we do not do them, we sin.

We do not know what God will do tomorrow or the next day. We do know that he wants to do only the best things for his people. Troubles may happen to us sometimes. But we know that we can trust God, even at those times. We should obey what he teaches us every part of every day. If we do that, our lives will make him happy.

Chapter 5

1 So, you rich people, weep and cry aloud. Many troubles will soon happen to you. 2 Your money does not really have any value. Your beautiful clothes are as if moths had eaten them. 3 You have kept a lot of money for yourselves in these last days. Your money has mould on it. That mould will show how bad you are. And it will become like fire that is burning your bodies. 4 You have not paid the wages of those who worked in your fields. Listen! The Lord of all the angels heard the workers when they shouted for his help. The money that you have kept for yourselves shows God something. It shows him that you have done wrong things. 5 You have had all that you wanted. You have lived to make yourselves happy on this earth. You have made yourselves fat. Now you are like animals that are ready for men to kill. 6 You have said about the good man, 'He is bad. We should kill him.' He does not try to fight against you.

God and his word should be more important to us than anything else is. Our money and our good clothes do not make him happy. The good things that we do are important to him. And the kind words that we speak are important to him too. He wants us to be good to our workers. It makes God happy when rich people give money to help poor people.

7 So be patient my Christian brothers until the Lord comes. Think about this: The farmer is patient while he waits for the land to give food for him. He continues to wait for the rain to come in the autumn and in the spring. 8 You, too, be patient because the Lord will come soon. And be strong as you hope for that.

9 Do not say bad things about each other, my Christian brothers. If you do, God will judge you. He will come very soon to judge people.

10 Think about the prophets who brought messages from the Lord. They showed us how to be patient, my Christian brothers. They were patient even when much pain happened to them.

11 God blessed people who were like that. We know that he did. They were in trouble. But they continued to do what God wanted. For example, you have heard about Job. He continued to wait for God to help him. You have heard how, in the end, the Lord blessed him. The Lord was kind and the Lord did very many good things for him.

12 When you say a promise, never say, 'as sure as heaven is there' or 'as sure as earth is there' or anything like that. Your 'yes' should mean 'yes' and your 'no' should mean 'no'. If you say more than that, God may punish you.

13 If one of you is in trouble, talk to God about it. If one of you is happy, sing. And praise God. 14 If one of you is sick, he should ask the leaders of your church to come. They will put a little oil on him and they will say, 'In the name of the Lord Jesus we do this.' They will ask God to make him well. 15 Believe that God will answer. If you do, God will make the sick person well. He will become well again. And God will forgive any wrong things that he has done. 16 So, tell each other about any wrong things that you have done. God makes sick people well, so speak to him on behalf of each other. God really listens to a person who obeys God. God does powerful things when someone like that asks him to. 17 For example, Elijah was a man who was like us. He prayed that it would not rain. And he believed that God would answer him. And so it did not rain on the land for three years and six months. 18 After that, he asked God to send rain again. Rain came from the sky. And the seeds that were under the ground began to grow.

19 My Christian brothers, one of you may start to do or to think bad things. If he does, try to bring him back to God. 20 Whoever turns a person from sin will save that person's soul from death. You should know that. Then God will forgive that person for the many wrong things that he has done.

God always does everything that he has promised to do. He cannot say things that are not true. He can do more than we can understand. He will help us to be happy if we ask him. If we are ill, we should ask for his help. He can make us well again. We may have done something wrong. If another Christian prays for us, God will answer his prayer. We may turn away from what God wants us to do. If another Christian helps us to turn back to God, he will be saving us from death. God always listens to the prayers of people who are really obeying him.

Ready to live with God

1 Peter

About Peter's first letter

Peter was one of the 12 men that Jesus chose to be his special workers. (See Matthew 10:1-4; Mark 13:13-19; Luke 6:2-16.) Peter's name was Simon, but Jesus changed it to Peter. (See John 1:42.) 'Peter' means 'a rock' or 'a stone'.

Peter wrote this letter to groups of Christians in several different places. All of those places were in the country that we call Turkey now. We think that he wrote it about the year AD 65. That was about 35 years after Jesus died. Peter may have been in Rome city when he wrote it. (See chapter 5:13.)

At that time, enemies were causing a lot of trouble and pain for Christians. These enemies were killing many Christians. So it was not easy to be a Christian then, and many Christians were afraid. Peter wrote to them because he wanted to help them. He wanted them to be brave. He wanted them to continue believing Jesus strongly.

In his letter, Peter describes the great things that God has done on our behalf. He says that, as Christians, we will have trouble and pain during our lives on this earth. But we must remember that God knows about all our troubles.

And he lets us have troubles sometimes because he wants to make us like Jesus. Jesus had much trouble and pain on our behalf, but he never stopped obeying God. Also, Peter says that all Christians should obey people with authority. And Christians should always do what is right and good.

Chapter 1

God has given us a new life because of Christ

1 This letter is from me, Peter. Jesus Christ sent me to be a special worker and teacher on his behalf. I am writing to you, God's people, who are living in many different places. You are living in places in Pontus, Galatia, Cappadocia, Asia and Bithynia. You are living there as strangers because you are away from your true home. God has chosen you to be his people. 2 A long, long time ago, God, the Father, had already decided that you should be his people. By his Spirit, God has made you his own, separate people so that you would obey Jesus Christ. He made you his people so that Jesus Christ's blood could make you really clean inside yourselves.

I want you to know more and more how very kind God is to you. And I pray that he will cause you to be without trouble inside yourselves more and more.

3 We should thank God, who is the Father of our Lord Jesus Christ! We should say how very great he is! God is so very kind that he has caused us to be born again. He has given us a new life. This is possible because God raised Jesus Christ. God raised Jesus so that he became alive again after his death. And because of this new life, we continue to hope certainly for good things. We are sure that we will live with God always. 4 Also, we wait to receive all the good things that God has prepared for his children. Nobody can ever destroy those things. They will never become dirty. They will never become old or less beautiful. God is keeping those good things in heaven for you. 5 God is powerful and he is keeping you safe. He is keeping you safe because you believe him. He will keep you safe until the last day, when Christ will return. Then everyone will see that God has prepared to save you completely.

6 These things which God has done make you very happy. But now, for a short time, different kinds of troubles and difficulties may make you sad. 7 The purpose of these troubles is to show certainly whether you really believe God. It is very, very important that you continue to believe him. People put gold into a fire to make it completely clean. The fire burns everything that is not gold. So the fire shows certainly what is gold. But gold belongs only to this world, so it will come to an end. When you believe God, that is worth much more even than gold. If you continue to believe God, he will be very happy because of you. As a result, he will say very good things about you on the day when Jesus Christ comes again. And you will show everyone how very great God is.

8 You have never seen Jesus, but still you love him. You do not see him now, but you believe him. And so, you are very, very happy. There are no words to describe how happy you are. 9 You are happy now because you are sure. You are believing God. And God will give to you that which you hope for. He will save you from all the troubles and pain that you have now. You are sure about that.

10 Many years ago, the prophets (people who told God's messages) spoke about this. They spoke about how God would be so very kind to you. They wanted to know about how God would save people. They studied carefully. And they asked many questions because they wanted to understand about it. 11 Christ's Spirit was in those prophets and he was showing them about future events. The Spirit was showing them that Christ must have much trouble and pain. Then, after that trouble, great and good things would happen to him. The prophets were trying to discover when and how all these things would happen. 12 God showed the prophets that his messages about these things were not for themselves, but for you. Now you know the good news about Jesus Christ. God's Spirit, that he has sent from heaven, has helped people to tell the good news to you. Even the angels want very much to understand about these things.

Christians should do what is good

13 So, because of everything that God has done on your behalf, you must be ready to obey him. Get your mind ready to obey. Think seriously and clearly. Always continue to hope completely for the good things that you will receive from God. You will receive those things when Jesus Christ comes again. 14 Always obey God, like good children who obey their father. Before you knew Christ, you wanted to do bad things. Do not let yourselves do those bad things any more. Do not let them rule you. 15 God, who has chosen you to be his people, is completely good. So, whatever things you do, you must be completely good also. 16 The Bible says: 'Be completely good, because I (God) am completely good.'

17 When you pray to God, you call him Father. God decides about every person because of what that person has done. God decides what should happen to every person. And God is always fair when he decides about people. He is never kinder to one person than he is to another person. So always obey God, your Father, while you live as strangers here on earth. Always remember how great and powerful God is. 18 Your parents and the people who lived before you taught you to do certain things. Those things were worth nothing to God. But now God has saved you from doing things like that. You know that he has bought you for himself. He did not buy you with things like silver (a valuable metal) or gold, which will come to an end. 19 Instead, he bought you with Christ's own blood, which is worth very, very much to God. Christ was like a lamb (young sheep) that had nothing wrong with it.

20 Before God made the world, he had chosen Christ already. God had decided already that Christ would save us. But now, during these last days, God has shown Christ to the world so that he could help you. 21 It is because of Christ that you believe God. God raised Christ, so that he became alive again after his death. Then, God showed how very great and powerful Christ is. That is why you believe God. You are sure about him. He will do what he has promised. You are sure about that.

22 You have made yourselves really good and clean because you have obeyed God's true message. As a result, now you can really love other Christians, who are like brothers and sisters to you. So, continue to love each other very much. Love each other as much as you can. 23 God's message causes people to become alive. It will continue always and it will never change. You have been born again, into a new life, because of that message. It is not your human parents who caused you to be born into this new life. They must die. But it is God himself who has caused you to be born again. And he can never die. 24 The Bible says:

'All people are like grass.

Everything that is good or beautiful about people is only like the flowers in the fields.

The grass becomes dry and it dies.

Flowers fall off after a short time.

25   But the message that the Lord has spoken will continue always

That message is the good news, which people have taught you.

Chapter 2

1 So, you must refuse to do bad things. Always say only things that are true and right. Do not say one thing when really you mean something else. Do not want other people's things so much that you stop being kind to those people. Do not say bad things about people. 2 Instead, you should want always to know God more and more. New babies always want their mothers' milk, which makes them grow strong. Like them, you should want the true milk, which comes from God. Always want very much to know more about God's message. That message is like good food that will make you strong in your spirits. It will make you stronger and stronger, so that God will save you completely. 3 Already, you have begun to know how good the Lord is. So, you should want to know him more and more.

Jesus is like the most important stone in God's house

4 So come to the Lord Jesus. He is like a big stone that a builder uses to build a house. He is 'the stone that is alive'. People decided that he was worth nothing to them. So they refused him. But God chose him. To God, Jesus is like a stone that is worth very, very much. 5 You yourselves also are like stones that are alive, because of Jesus Christ. God is using you, like stones, to build his spiritual house. He has chosen you to work there as his priests (special servants who offer sacrifices). As priests you will offer spiritual sacrifices to God. And God will be happy with what you offer him, because of Jesus Christ.

6 In the Bible, God says this:

'Look, I have chosen a stone that is worth very, very much.

I have chosen this valuable stone as the most important stone,

> for the corner of my house.

> And I am putting that stone in Zion.

> Any person who believes him will never be ashamed.

That person will never be sorry that they believed him.'

7 This stone is worth very, very much to you who believe. But the Bible says this about the people who do not believe him:

'The stone that the builders refused has become the most important stone.

> It has become the stone at the corner of the house.'

8 The Bible says this also:

'This is a stone that will cause people to knock their feet against it so that they fall.

> It is a rock that will make them fall down.'

The reason why it causes people to fall is this. They fall because they refuse to obey God's message. A long, long time ago, God decided that this would happen to them.

9 But you are the people that God has chosen. You are a group of priests who are servants of God, the King. You are God's own special people, who obey only him. You belong to God. He has taken you out of the dark and he has brought you into his great light. He has chosen you so that you can tell people how great he is. 10 In past times, you were not God's people. But now you are God's people. In past times, you did not know how very kind God is. But now you know how very kind he is.

11 My friends, that I love, you live as strangers in this world. You are like visitors, who are staying in this world only for a short time. So I ask you strongly not to do those bad things that your bodies may want to do. Keep away from things like that, because they are like enemies to you. They fight against what is good for you. They stop you from doing good things. 12 You are living among people who do not know God. So be careful that you do good and right things always. Sometimes these people may say that you do bad things.

But you should continue to do good things. And then they will see that you are good. So, on the day when God visits us, they may thank God because of you. And they will say how great God is.

Obey people who have authority over you

13 Obey all people who have authority in this world. Obey them, because that will make the Lord happy. Obey the king, who rules everyone. 14 Also obey those officers of the government that the king has chosen to rule you. They punish people who do wrong things. And they say good words about people who do right things.

15 God wants you to do what is right. Then you will stop silly people, who do not know anything, from saying bad things about you. 16 You are people who are free. But do not think, because of that, that you have the chance to do bad things. Do not think that God will excuse you for bad things. Instead, do those things that God's servants should do. 17 Always do what is right and proper to all people. Love all those people who are like brothers and sisters to you. They are like your brothers and sisters because, like you, they believe Christ. Always remember how great and powerful God is. Always remember to obey the king.

18 You servants must obey your masters. You must always remember that they are important. You must obey not only masters who are good and kind. You must obey also masters who are cruel and not fair. 19 Sometimes a person may have trouble and pain when he has done nothing wrong. But if that person really wants to obey God, he should continue to be patient and brave. That is a good thing and it will make God happy. 20 If you do something wrong, then people ought to punish you. They might hit you. And you might be patient when they hit you. But that is no reason why anyone should say good things about you. But you may have trouble and pain because you have done good things. If you are patient during that trouble, then God will be happy about you. 21 God has chosen that you should be patient like this. Christ had trouble and pain on your behalf. And he is the person that you should copy. So you should do the same kind of things as Christ did. 22 The Bible says this:

> 'He never did anything that was wrong.

> He never said anything that was not true.'

23 People said bad things about Christ, but he did not say bad things back to them. People did bad things to him and they caused him trouble and pain. But he never said that he would do bad things to them. Instead, Christ continued to believe that God would help him. God always decides only what is right and fair. 24 Christ himself took away all the wrong things that we have done. He took them in his own body to the cross. He did this so that we should not continue to do wrong things. So we can be like people who are dead to wrong things. We are dead to them because those things do not rule us anymore. Instead, now we can do the right things that God wants us to do. People hurt Christ's body, but, because of that, you have become well. 25 Before, you were like sheep that were going the wrong way. But now you have returned to Christ, your Shepherd, who keeps all of you safe.

Chapter 3

Wives and husbands

1 You wives, each of you also should obey your own husband. There may be some husbands who do not believe God's message. But if their wives obey them, those husbands may turn to God. They may decide to believe God, even if their wives have said nothing to them about God's message. 2 Those husbands will see that you wives do only good things. They will see that you really obey God.

3 Do not be trying always to make your bodies beautiful. You do not need to prepare your hair in an expensive way. You do not need to wear gold or expensive clothes. 4 Instead, be beautiful because of what you are really like inside yourselves, in your spirits. Be patient and quiet, and do not become angry easily. Do not want to show everyone how important you are. Then you will never stop being beautiful. If you are beautiful in your spirits like this, it is worth very much to God.

5 This was how, many years ago, good women made themselves beautiful. They believed God. God would do what he had promised. They believed that. And so, because they were God's servants, they obeyed their own husbands. 6 They did the same as Sarah. She obeyed her husband, Abraham, and she called him, 'My master'. You wives also should do what is right. You should not let anything make you afraid. Then you will be like true daughters of Sarah.

7 Also, each of you husbands must live properly with your own wife. You should understand properly what she needs. She is not as strong as you are.

So, you should remember that and you should be kind to her. Remember that God has promised the same thing to both her and you together. He has promised that you will live with him always. So, you must be kind to your wife. And then nothing will stop God from answering what you pray.

Christians must be ready to have trouble, even when they do good things

8 Now I want to say this to you. All of you should agree with each other so that you do not argue. You should try to understand how other people are feeling. Love each other as brothers and sisters, because all of you belong to Christ. Be kind to each other. Do not want to be more important than anyone else. 9 If people do bad things to you, you must not do anything bad to them. If people say bad things against you, you must not say bad things back to them. Instead, you should pray that God will be good to those people. This is what God wants you to do. He has chosen you yourselves because he wants to be good to you. 10 The Bible says this:

'If a person wants to enjoy his life and to have good days,

    he must be careful not to say bad things.

    And he must stop saying things that are not true.

11   He must stop doing what is bad.

    Instead, he must do what is good.

He must try very much always to be friendly with people.

He must try always not to argue with them or to cause trouble.

12   Because the Lord is watching over those people who obey him.

    All the time, he is listening to what those people pray.

But the Lord turns away from people who do bad things.'

13 If you are trying always to do good things, then nobody can really hurt you. 14 People may cause you trouble and pain. But God will be good to you. So, do not let anyone make you afraid. 15 Instead, always remember that only Christ is your Lord. And always let him rule you, deep inside yourselves. People may ask you to explain why you hope certainly for good things because of Christ. Always be ready to answer anyone who asks you that.

16 Be kind and polite when you answer them. You know the difference between what is right or wrong. So, always do what is right. Then the people who say bad things about you Christians will be ashamed. They will see that you do good things. You do the good things that Christ's people should do. So, they will be ashamed.

17 Sometimes God may let you have trouble and pain even when you have done good things. But that is better than to have trouble and pain because you have done bad things. 18 Even Christ himself, who never did anything wrong, died on our behalf. He died to take away all the wrong things that we have done. He died once, for all time. He died to bring you to God. People killed his body, but God's Spirit made him alive again.

19 Then, as a spirit, he went to the spirits who were in prison. And he told his great news to them. 20 A long time ago, those spirits had refused to obey God.

God waited patiently for them at that time when Noah was building that big boat. But only a few people, only 8 people, went into that boat so that God could save them. God saved them when they went through the water. 21 That water is like a picture of baptism, which now saves you also. Baptism does not mean that the water washes dirt off a person's body. It means that a person has decided always to obey God. God has made that person really good and clean inside. And so that person is choosing always to do what is right. Baptism saves you because Jesus Christ rose, to become alive again after his death. 22 Jesus has gone into heaven now and he is sitting at God's right side. He rules over angels and over all other spirits that have authority or power.

Chapter 4

1 Christ had trouble and pain while he lived in his body. So, you should think like he thought. You should be ready to have trouble and pain while you live in your bodies too. If you think like that, you will make yourselves strong. Anyone who has had trouble and pain in his body has stopped wanting to do wrong things. 2 As a result, that person will obey God during all the time that he continues to live in his body. He will not want to do the bad things that people often want to do. He will not let those bad things rule him. Instead, that person will do what God wants him to do.

3 The people who do not know God want to do bad things. And, in past times, you did those bad things too. But now you have wasted enough time doing those bad things. You did wrong things that people should not do. The things that your bodies wanted to do ruled you. You had sex with people who were not your wife or your husband. You were drunks. You went to many bad parties and you drank too much alcohol. Also, you worshipped false gods, which is something that God hates.

4 The people who do not know God continue to do many, very wrong things. But now, you do not want to do wrong things any more as they do. So, those people are very surprised because of you, and they say bad things about you. 5 But those people will have to explain to God what they have done. He is ready to decide what should happen to every person. He will decide about all people, whether they are alive or dead. 6 This is why even the dead people heard the good news about Christ. Their bodies had to die, as all people must die. But they heard the good news so that their spirits could live. Their spirits could live as God wants them to live.

We must use God's gifts properly

7 The end of all things is near. So, think seriously and clearly. And rule yourselves properly so that you can pray. 8 Continue to love each other very much. This is more important than anything else. If you love people, then you will always want to be kind to them. You will always be ready to forgive (choose to forget) any wrong things that they have done. 9 Always be happy when other Christians visit your homes. Say 'welcome' to them and be kind to them.

10 God has been good to each of you in different ways. He has given a gift to each of you, so that you are able to do certain things well. So, each of you should use your gift so that you can help other people. Then you will be God's good servants because you will be using his gifts properly. 11 If you have a gift as a speaker, speak only God's messages. If you have a gift to help other people, let God make you strong to help them. Do everything so that people will thank God. They should say how great and good God is because of Jesus Christ. He will have all authority and power always. And everyone should always say how great he is! This is true!

Christians must be ready to have trouble and pain

12 My friends, that I love, do not be surprised by trouble and pain. People are causing you bad trouble and pain.

But these things are happening to show whether you really believe God. So, do not think that something strange is happening to you. 13 Instead, be happy that you have trouble and pain, like Christ. So then, you will also be very, very happy when Christ comes again. You will be happy when he comes to show everyone how very great and powerful he is. 14 People may say bad things about you because you are Christ's. But God will be good to you when that happens. It means that God's Spirit is with you. God's Spirit, who is so great and powerful, remains upon you.

15 But if you do wrong things, then people ought to punish you. They ought to cause you trouble and pain. So, be careful that none of you receives trouble and pain because of wrong things. You must not kill anyone. You must not rob anyone. You must not want to know more than you should know about other people's lives. None of you should ever have to receive trouble and pain because you have done those things. 16 But if you have trouble and pain because you are a Christian, do not be ashamed. Instead, thank God that people call you by Christ's name.

17 The time has come that God should begin to decide about people. He will decide what should happen to them. And he will decide first about the people who belong to him. God will decide even about us, who are his own people. Then he will decide about the people who do not obey his good news. So, very bad things must happen to those people in the end. 18 The Bible says:

'Even good people have many difficulties

before God finishes saving them.

So, think about the bad people who do not obey God.

Very bad things must happen to those people!

19 So then, people may cause you trouble and pain because God chooses that. But you should continue to believe God, who made you. God always does what he has promised. So, continue to believe that he will be good to you. And continue to do what is good.

Chapter 5

Peter writes to leaders and young men

1 Now I want to say something strongly to the elders (leaders) who belong to your group. I say this because I am an elder also. I saw the trouble and pain that people caused Christ. And, like you, I will live always with Christ, who is so very great and powerful. When he comes again, everyone will see how great he is. I say this strongly to you. 2 Watch over the group of God's people that God has given to you. Be like a shepherd to them. Do this work because you want to do it. That is how God wants you to be. Do not do it just because you have to do it. Do not do this work because you want to receive money. Instead, do it because you want to help people.

3 Do not try to rule over those people that God has given to you. Instead, do good things yourselves, so that they can copy you. Show them the right things that they should do. 4 As a result, Christ, who is the Shepherd of all of us, will give a gift to you. He will give that gift to you when he comes again. He will give you a beautiful crown that will never become old or less beautiful.

5 You younger men also must obey the elders (leaders). And all of you people must be ready to be like servants to each other. Because the Bible says:

'Some people think that they are better and more important than other people.

They think that they are always right.

God is an enemy to people who think like that.

But he is good to people who do not want to be very important.

He is good to people who are ready to be like servants to other people.

6 God is very powerful and strong to help you. So, be his servants, and let him rule you. Then he will cause you to be great and important at the right time. 7 Tell God about all the things that make you sad or afraid or angry. Give your thoughts about those things to him and let them remain with him. Do this, because you matter to him.

8 Think seriously and watch carefully. Be ready, because your enemy, the Devil, walks about like a lion (a big wild animal). He is like a lion that makes loud noises. He is looking for someone that he can eat. 9Refuse to obey the Devil. Instead, be strong against him because you choose to believe God strongly. Remember that, all over the world, Christians like you are having the same kind of troubles and pain.

10 You will have trouble and pain for a short time. But after that, God, who is so completely kind, will make everything right. God has caused you to be united to Christ, so that you will live with him always. You will live with him in the beautiful place where he lives. And God will make you completely as you should be. He will make you strong, so that nothing can ever stop you believing him. 11 God will rule always! This is true.

Peter finishes his letter

12 Silas, who is like our brother, has helped me to write this short letter to you. I know that he continues to believe Christ. And he continues to be Christ's good servant. I have written because I want you to be brave and strong. And I want you to know certainly that God has really been good to us. So, always remember how good God is. And then you will continue to be strong. 13 God has chosen the Christians who are in Babylon city, as he has chosen you. They say 'hello' to you. Mark, who is like my son, says 'hello' also. 14When you meet, kiss each other as Christian friends.

I pray on behalf of all of you who are united to Christ. I pray that God will cause you to be without trouble inside yourselves.

Be strong and watch for Jesus!

2 Peter

About Peter's second letter

Simon Peter was one of Jesus' special workers. He had lived and worked with Jesus himself. We can read a lot about Simon Peter in the books called Matthew, Mark, Luke, John and Acts.

This is the second letter that Peter wrote. Almost certainly, he wrote this letter between 35 and 38 years after Jesus returned to heaven (God's home). That was at some time between the years AD 65 and 68. Peter died soon after he wrote this letter.

Peter wrote this letter to Christians, who wanted to obey God. Some false teachers were teaching wrong ideas about Jesus and God. The false teachers wanted the Christians to believe those wrong ideas. So Peter wrote this letter to help the Christians. He wanted them to believe God, Christ and the Bible more strongly. He told them not to believe the false teachers. God would destroy the false teachers because they were so bad.

Also, Peter told the Christians to be like people who are watching carefully. They should be ready for Jesus, because he would certainly come back to the earth.

Chapter 1

God has given to us everything that we need to be his people

1 This letter is from me, Simon Peter. I am Jesus Christ's servant. He sent me to be a special worker and teacher on his behalf. I am writing this letter to you people who, like us, believe Christ. He has given the same valuable gift to all of us. He has caused us to believe him. He has done this because he is always completely right and fair. Jesus Christ is God. And he is the person who saves us.

2 I pray that God will be good to you more and more. I pray that he will cause you to be without trouble inside yourselves more and more. These things will happen because you know God and Jesus, our Lord.

3 God is very powerful because he is God. So he has given to us everything that we need to live always. We can do good things that make God happy. This is possible because we know him. God has chosen us to be his people because he is so very great and so very good. 4 Also, because of this, God has promised that he will do very great and valuable things on our behalf. As a result, you can become good like God. So, you can be free from wanting bad things that will destroy you. The people who belong to this world want to do bad things. And those bad things are destroying them.

5 God has done all this on your behalf. So you should not only believe Christ. You must also try very much to do always what is good. And you must try very much to know God more and more. 6 You must not only know God, but you must rule yourselves properly also. You must not only rule yourselves, but you must continue to be patient and brave also. And you must not only be patient and brave, but you must always make God happy. You must do what God wants. 7 You must not only make God happy, but you must be kind to each other also. You must love other Christians, as you would love your own brothers and sisters. And you must not only love other Christians, but you must love all people also.

8 You should do all of these things. You should continue to do those more and more. These things will show that you really know our Lord Jesus Christ. And, because you know him, you will work well on his behalf. And your work will have good results. 9 But some people do not do these things. They do not think that these things are important. They are like people who cannot see clearly. They cannot really see anything. They have forgotten that God made them clean inside themselves. God made them free from all the wrong things that they did before. But they have forgotten that.

10 So, my friends, try even more to do all these good things. Do them, because God has chosen you to be his own people. And these good things will show that you really are God's people. If you do these things, you will never turn away from God. 11 Also, God will be very happy. He will bring you into that place where Jesus Christ will rule always. You will live always with our Lord Jesus Christ, who saves us.

12 So, I will continue to tell you about these things again and again. You already know these things. And you are continuing to believe strongly that these things are true. But still, I will continue to tell you about them. 13 I will tell you about them while I am still alive on earth. I think that it is right to continue telling you. You should think about these things. So then you will not forget them. 14 I know that I will die soon. I know that because our Lord Jesus Christ has shown that to me. 15 So I will do everything that I can to tell you about these things now. So then, after I have died, you will be able to remember them always.

Peter himself saw how great Christ is

16 We told you that our Lord Jesus Christ is powerful. We told you that he will come to earth again. We were not telling you false stories that came from people's clever ideas. Instead, we were telling you what we ourselves had seen. We ourselves saw how very great Christ is. 17-18 We were with Jesus on the mountain that God visited. God, the Father, showed us how very great and powerful Jesus is. God, who is greater than everything, spoke about Jesus. God said: 'This is my son. I love him. He makes me very happy.' And we ourselves heard God's voice when he spoke from heaven.

God's messages in the Bible are very important

19 Also, we have the prophets' messages. They show us even more certainly that these things are true. It is good that you should remember those messages carefully. The prophets' words are like a light that shines in a dark place. That light continues to shine in the dark until the dawn comes. Then the morning star will rise and it will bring light deep inside you. 20 None of the prophets' messages in the Bible came just from the prophets' own ideas. It is most important that you should understand this. 21 None of the prophets' messages came from what a human person wanted to say. Instead, God's Spirit caused people to speak words that came from God.

Chapter 2

False teachers are bad and dangerous

1 Many years ago, there were false prophets (people who did not speak God's true messages) among God's people. In the same way, there will also be false teachers among you. They will teach wrong ideas that will destroy people. But they will say that those wrong ideas are true. Those false teachers will even refuse the Master, who bought them. And so they will cause God to destroy them quickly. 2 Many people will believe and copy the false teachers. So, those people will do very wrong things, like the false teachers. And, as a result, other people will say bad things about the true way that God wants us to live.

3 The false teachers only want your money. So, they will tell things to you that are not true. They will tell those false things to you so that you will give money to them. A long time ago, God decided that he must punish them. And he is ready to do that. Certainly, he will destroy them.

God punishes bad people but he helps good people

4 Remember that God did not let the bad angels go free. A long, long time ago, some angels refused to obey God. And God punished them because of what they had done. He threw them down into the deep hole where he sends all bad persons. And he will keep them in that dark prison until the day when he will decide about them. He will decide what should happen to them in the end.

5 Also, a long, long time ago, God punished all the bad people who lived in the world. God sent water over all the earth. So all those people who refused to obey him drowned in the water. But Noah was telling the people that they should do right things. He was telling them that they should obey God. So God saved Noah, and 7 other people.

6 Also, God punished the people who lived in the cities called Sodom and Gomorrah. God saw that the people there were doing very bad things. So, he decided that he must punish them. And he burned those cities completely, so that only ashes remained. And so God showed what will happen to all bad people. He will punish people who refuse to obey him. 7 Also, God saved Lot, who was a good man. Lot was very sad because the people in Sodom did not obey God's rules. They did many, very wrong things. 8 Lot lived among those bad people. Every day, he saw the bad things that they did. Every day, he heard the bad things that they said. As a result of all these bad things, Lot became very sad, because he was a good man.

9 We know that the Lord has done all these things in past times. And these things show us certainly that he knows how to save his people. He will help those people who obey him. He will save them from troubles and difficulties. But he will punish the bad people, who refuse to obey him. He will continue to punish them. And he will keep them until that day when he will decide about all people. He will decide what should happen to them. 10 God will punish very much those people who continue to have wrong sex. They do the wrong things that their bodies want to do. And those wrong things make those people even worse. Those bad people think that they do not have to obey anyone's authority.

The false teachers are like animals

These false teachers are not afraid to do what they want to do. They think that they themselves are very clever and important. They do not listen to what anyone else says. They are not afraid to say bad things about the beautiful beings. 11 The angels are stronger and more powerful than the false teachers are. But even angels will not say bad things against them when the Lord is present. 12 But these false teachers say bad things against anything that they do not understand. They are like wild animals that cannot think. They do what their nature causes them to do. Wild animals are born so that people can catch them and kill them. And, as people kill wild animals, God will destroy the false teachers.

13 The false teachers have done bad things to other people. So God will do bad things to them. They enjoy eating and drinking too much, even during the day. They enjoy doing the wrong things that they want to do. They enjoy those things while they are eating meals with you. So, like dirty marks on something that is clean, they cause people to be ashamed about you. 14 All the time, they are looking for women who will have sex with them. They never stop wanting to do bad things. They lead away people who do not believe Christ strongly. They cause those people to believe wrong things and to do wrong things. They have learned to want more and more money and other things for themselves. Certainly, God will punish these people, because they are so bad.

15 These false teachers have left the right way and they have gone the wrong way. They have done the same kind of wrong things that Balaam, Beor's son, did. Balaam wanted money so much that he did wrong things to get it. 16 But a donkey told Balaam that he was not obeying God. Donkeys cannot talk. But that donkey spoke as a human person speaks. So, the donkey stopped that prophet, Balaam, from doing any more crazy things.

God will punish the false teachers

17 These false teachers are like places in the ground where water should come up. But there is no water. They are like clouds in a storm. The strong wind blows those clouds away quickly so that they bring no rain. God has kept a completely black, dark place where these false teachers will have to stay.

18 The words that these teachers speak seem very important. But their words mean nothing. They tell people that it is not wrong to do bad things. People may do the bad things that their bodies strongly want to do. The false teachers say that it does not matter. So they lead people away from God. They lead away people who have only just stopped doing wrong things. Those people have just begun to be free from the wrong things that other people do. 19 The false teachers promise that these people will be free. But the false teachers themselves are not free. Instead, they are like slaves. They cannot stop doing the bad things that will destroy them. If anything has power over a person, then that person is its slave.

20 These false teachers knew our Lord Jesus Christ, who saves us. So they had become free from the power of the bad things that belong to this world. They had stopped doing those bad things, which make people even worse. But now they have started to do those bad things again, and those things have power over them. So, these false teachers are worse at the end than they were at the beginning. They are worse than before they knew the Lord.

21 It would have been better for them if they had never known God's right way. But they have known the right things that God wants us to do. So it is worse that they have stopped doing those things. They have stopped obeying God's rules, that people taught them. 22 People often say these true words: 'After a dog has been sick, it returns to that same place, to eat that food again.' And: 'A pig that someone has washed returns, to roll on the dirty, wet ground.' These words describe what has happened to these false teachers.

Chapter 3

Remember that the Lord will certainly come back to earth

1 My friends, this is the second letter that I have written to you. I have written both these letters so that I can help you to remember certain things. I want you to think correctly and honestly about these things. 2 I want you to remember the words that God's own prophets spoke a long time ago. Also, I want you to remember what our Lord told you to do. Our Lord, who saves us, taught you by his special workers. His special workers, that he sent to you, told you about these things.

3 The first thing that you should understand is this. In the last days, some people will think that God and God's rules are not important. They will say that you are silly. They will call you fools because you believe God. These people will do whatever bad things they want to do. 4 They will say: 'Christ promised that he would return! But he has not returned! Our early Christian leaders have died, but still all things continue. Since God made the world, all things continue in the same way.'

5 These people choose to forget the facts that they know. They forget that God made the sky and the earth a long, long time ago. God spoke his word, and so he made the sky. Also, by his word, God made the land separate from the water. He brought the land out through the water. 6 Also, it was water that God used to destroy that world a long time ago. 7 But, by God's same word, the sky and the earth that we see now are continuing. They will continue until that time when fire will burn them. God is keeping them until that time when he will decide about all people. He will decide what should happen to all people. And he will destroy the bad people who have not obeyed him.

8 But, my friends, there is one thing that you must not forget. The Lord thinks that one day is like 1000 years. And he thinks that 1000 years are like one day. 9 The Lord is not being slow to do what he has promised to do. Some people think that he is being slow to do it. But instead, he is being patient with you people. He does not want to destroy anyone. He wants all people to turn away from wrong things because they have decided to obey him.

10 But the day when the Lord will come back will surprise people. It will surprise people as when someone comes to rob them. The sky will go away with a very loud noise and it will not be there anymore. Fire will burn the sun, the moon and the stars and it will destroy them. The earth and everything that is on it will not be there anymore.

11 Certainly, God will destroy everything in this way. So, you ought to be the kind of people that God is happy about. You should give yourselves to God completely and you should obey him always. 12 You should obey God while you are waiting for Christ to return. God has chosen that day when he will return. You should be wanting that day to come very much. On that day, fire will burn the sky and the fire will destroy it. The heat will destroy the sun, the moon and the stars also. 13 But we are waiting for what God has promised. He has promised that there will be a new sky and a new earth. There, everything will always be good. And everyone will do only what is right.

14 So, my friends, because you are waiting for these things to happen, try very much to do only good things. Then God will see that you have done nothing wrong. He will see that there is no trouble between you yourselves, or between you and him. 15 Remember why our Lord is waiting before he will return. He is being patient because he wants to save people. Paul, whom we love like a brother, has written to you also about these things. He wrote about them because God caused him to understand them. 16 Paul writes like this about these things in all his letters. But some of the things that Paul has written in his letters are difficult to understand. And people who do not know much about God explain these things wrongly. Those people are not sure about what they believe. And they explain other things in the Bible wrongly also. As a result, those people themselves cause God to destroy them.

17 But you, my friends, know these things already. So, be very careful that you do not believe false teachers. They do not obey God's rules and they teach wrong things. Do not let those people lead you away from God. If you listen to them, you could stop being sure about the true things. So you will be like people who have moved away from a safe, strong place.

18 Instead, continue to do what is good. So then our Lord Jesus Christ, who saves us, will be good to you more and more. Also, continue to know him better and better. Everyone should say how very great and good he is! Everyone should say that, both now and always!

How Christians Should Love Each Other

1 John

About this letter

Most students believe that John wrote this letter. He was the apostle John, who also wrote the Gospel of John. And John also wrote the letters called 2 John and 3 John.

These three letters contain ideas very like those in John's Gospel. They have the same kinds of words. The Gospel tells people about Jesus, and how to know God. These letters are for people who know God. They tell those people how he wants them to live. The Gospel and these letters all speak about God's love and light. John wrote the Gospel to say that Jesus is the Son of God. He wanted them to know, and to believe that Jesus had died for them. He wanted them to become Christians. But these letters were for people who were already Christians. John wrote this letter against false teaching that some Christians had heard.

Chapter 1

1 We want to tell you about the person who is God's message to people. He is the person who gives people proper life. He was before the beginning of the world. We heard him speak. We saw him with our own eyes. We watched him and we touched him.

2 He showed himself on this earth. We saw him and we are telling you about it. We are telling you that he is the person who gives eternal life. From long ago he was together with God the Father, and he has shown himself to us. 3 We ourselves are united with God the Father, and Jesus Christ his Son. And we want you to be of the same mind as us, as you trust him. That is why we are telling you about the person whom we have seen and heard.

4 We are writing so that together we may be completely happy.

John is writing with authority. He is saying that he was with Jesus, the Word of God (God's message). He knows Jesus. And he knows what Jesus taught.

5 Jesus Christ gave us a message and this is the message: God is good and clean like light. There is nothing dark about him. 6 Now, someone may say that he is united to God. But he may still do things that do not please God. Then what he says is not true. He is living as if he were in the dark. What he does shows that he does not want to obey God's rules. 7 But when we do right things, it is like living in the light. God is always in the light. (He always does what is good and right.) When we live like this we are really united together. The death of Jesus, the Son of God makes us clean. He removes sin from us and he makes us clean in front of God. 8 We may say that we never do wrong things. But then, we are making a mistake. We may really believe that we never sin. Then we do not understand that God's words are true. 9 But if we tell God about our sins then he will forgive us. He will take away from us all our sins. God is true and fair. So, he will do what he promised. And he will do what is right. 10 God says that all people have sinned. But we may say that we have never sinned. Then we are saying that God is not telling the truth. We have not accepted his word at all.

Chapter 2

1 I am writing to you who are like dear children to me. I am writing this because I do not want you to sin. But if you do sin, tell him. Then God will forgive you.

God our Father forgives us. He does this because a completely good person asks him to do it. That person is Jesus Christ. 2 He died to take the punishment for our sin. He not only died to take the punishment for our sins. He died to take the punishment for the sins of all people everywhere.

3 We can be sure that we have become people who know Christ. And I want to tell you how we can be sure. It is when we obey his rules. 4 Someone may say, 'I know Christ.' If he does not obey Christ's rules, that person is lying. He does not know him. He has not obeyed the truth which he tells us in his rules. 5 But we should do the things that Christ said. Then we will show that we love God. By this we know that we live in him. 6 A person may say that he lives in God. Then he must live as Jesus did.

7 Dear Christian brothers, love each other. When I say this, I am not giving you a new rule. It is the old rule that you had for a long time. We gave it to you when you began to obey Christ. You have already heard this message. 8 But there is something new about it. The life of Christ shows us that this rule is new. Your lives also show that it is new. The life of Christ shows us the truth about God. And this truth is already shining in your lives. It is like a light that people can see. You did bad things before. They are like the dark, which is becoming less and less. 9 A person may say that he is in the light. He says that he obeys God. But, he may hate another Christian. Then he is still living as if he were in the dark. 10 Whoever loves other Christians is living in the light. He never causes other Christians to sin. 11 But a person may not love other Christians. He is like someone who is living in the dark. He does wrong things and he does not know God's rules. Because he does not know God's rules, he is like a blind person. He cannot see where he is going.

12 Dear children, I am writing to you because God has forgiven all your sins. God did this because of Christ. 13 I am writing to you who are like fathers. I am writing to you because you have known Christ for a long time. He was before the world began. I am writing to you who are like young men because you have beaten Satan. I write to you, my children. I am writing to you because you have become people who know God, our Father. 14 I write to you, fathers, because you know Jesus Christ. He was before the world began. I write to you young men because you are trusting Christ well. God's word is always in your minds and you have beaten Satan.

15 Whoever loves the wrong values of this world cannot also love God our Father. So I tell all of you, do not love the wrong values of this world. 16 When people only want to please themselves, this is wrong. Sometimes people want to have all the things that they see. This is wrong. Sometimes people want to tell other people what great things they have done. Sometimes they want to tell them how rich they are. This is also wrong. None of these ideas comes from the Father. They come from loving the wrong things in this world. 17 God has begun to destroy the wrong things in this world. Those who want bad things will die. But those who do what God wants will live forever.

18 Dear children, the world will soon end. You have heard that the enemy of Christ will appear. You now see that many enemies of Christ have already appeared. This shows us that the world really will soon end. 19 These enemies of Christ who used to be in our group no longer meet with us. They never really were Christians. If they had really been Christians, they would have remained with us. But they left. And so they showed that they were never really Christians. 20 But Christ has given you the Holy Spirit. Because of this, you all know what is true. 21 You do know that it is true. That is why I am writing this letter to you. Yes, you can be sure that the truth does not include anything false.

22 I will tell you who is the worst liar. It is the person who says that Jesus is not the Christ. When a person says that, he is refusing to believe in the Father of Jesus. He also refuses to believe that Jesus is the Son of God. Anyone who talks like this is the enemy of Christ. 23 Whoever believes that Jesus is the Son of God is united to God the Father. Whoever refuses to believe this is not united to the Father. 24 Always remember what you first heard about Christ. If you always remember that message you will remain united to God the Son and his Father. 25 Then he promises that we will receive eternal life.

26 Some people are trying to lead you away from what is true. I am writing these things to you about those people. 27 But the Holy Spirit, whom Christ gave, is still in you. So, you do not need anyone else to teach you what is true.

The same Holy Spirit shows you all the things that are true. There is nothing false in what he shows you. So, I say to you, remain united to Christ. Remain united to Christ as the Holy Spirit has told you to do.

28 Dear children, remain united to Christ. Then, when he comes back to this world, we will be brave. We will not be afraid to meet him. 29 Christ does what pleases God. You know that. So you should know that everyone who pleases God is his child.

Chapter 3

1 Think about how much God the Father loves us. He calls us his children. And we really have become children of God. The people of this world do not know God as Father. So they do not understand that we are his children. 2 Dear friends, we are already children of God. We do not know yet what we will become in the future. We do know that Christ will return to this world. Then we will see what he really is. And then we will become like him. 3 Christ does not sin. So every one of you who hopes to become like Christ ought to keep himself clean from sin.

4 If a person continues to sin, he is choosing not to obey God's rules. Sin is when we choose not to obey God. 5 You know that Jesus came into the world so that he might take away our sins. You know that he has never sinned. 6 A person who is united to Christ does not go on sinning. But if a person goes on sinning, he really does not know Christ at all. He does not understand who Christ is.

7 Dear children, be careful not to make this mistake. Do not let anyone lead you away from the truth. God sees as good only those people who do good things. People like that please God as Jesus Christ pleases God. 8 But some people go on doing what is wrong. Those people belong to the Devil. The Devil has been doing wrong things from the start. This is why the Son of God came. He came to destroy everything that the Devil had done.

9 No person who is a child of God should continue to sin. This is because God has given him a new life. He cannot continue to sin, because he is a child of God. 10 This is how we know who are the children of God. And this is how we know who are the children of the Devil. Some people do not do what is right. They are not his children. And people who do not love other Christians are not God's children.

11 Since you began to obey Christ, you have heard God's message. He says that we should love each other. 12 We should not be like Cain. He belonged to the Devil. He did things that were wrong. He even killed his brother. His brother did things that pleased God. That is why Cain killed him.

13 So, my Christian brothers, do not be surprised when people of this world hate you.

14 We know that we are no longer like dead people. We have become people who have life from God. We know this because we are now loving our Christian brothers. If someone does not love other Christians, he is still like a dead person. 15 Some people hate other people. Anyone like that is like someone who kills people. You know that a person like that does not have the eternal life.

16 This is how we know what love is. Christ gave his own life and he died for us. This shows us how we should really love other people. We ought to give our lives for other Christians. 17 Think about someone who has enough to buy all that he needs. That person knows another Christian. The other Christian does not have enough to buy all that he needs. He may refuse to help that poor Christian. Then he cannot say that he has God's love for that other Christian. 18 Dear children, let us not only show love for each other by what we say. Let us show love by really helping each other.

19 Then we will know that we really belong to God. We will be doing what is true. This will make us not afraid to come to God. 20 Our thoughts may say that we are bad. But God knows much more than we know in our thoughts. God knows everything.

21 Dear friends, our thoughts may not say that we are bad. Then we are not afraid to come to God. 22 And God gives us everything that we ask. He does this because we obey his rules. And we do what pleases him. 23 He said that we must do this. We must believe that Jesus Christ is his Son. And we should love each other, as he said. 24 Anyone who obeys God's rules is united to God. And God is united to him. God sent his Spirit to live in us. So we know that God is united to us.

Christians should love their Christian brothers and sisters. They should even be ready to die to save them. Their love will show the world that God lives in them. They have his Spirit. His Spirit helps us to do what God wants us to do. This pleases God.

Chapter 4

1 Dear friends, many people are travelling about who say that they have the Holy Spirit. But they are saying what is false. The messages that they give do not come from God. So, find out if the Holy Spirit gave them the message. If not, do not believe their message.

2 You can know that a person has the Spirit of God in him. This is how you can know it. Ask him if Jesus Christ came into the world as a human baby. If he says 'Yes', he has the Spirit of God. He belongs to God. 3 But some people say that Jesus did not come as a human baby. And anyone who says that does not have the Spirit of God. That person has a false spirit from the enemy of Christ. You have heard that this false spirit was coming to this world. And it is already in the world.

4 But, dear children, God has sent you. You have shown that these people are wrong. You have been able to do this because the Holy Spirit in you is powerful. He is more powerful than the spirit who rules the world. 5 Those wrong people do not know God. They are people of this world. So, they teach like other people who do not know God. So the people of this world believe what they teach. 6 But God has sent us. Everyone who knows God believes our message. But anyone whom God has not sent will not believe it. By this, we know if a person has the Spirit of God. A person may teach the truth that the Holy Spirit teaches. Then he believes our message. There is a different spirit, which teaches false things. Anyone with that spirit does not believe our message.

7 Dear friends, we should all continue to love each other. God makes us able to love other people. So, everyone who loves other people is a child of God. And he knows God. 8 Anyone who does not love other people does not know God. We know this because God shows his love in everything that he does. 9 This is how God showed his love for us. He sent his only Son into the world, so that we could have eternal life because of him. 10 We did not love God first. Rather, he loved us first. He sent his Son to die, to take away our sins. 11 This shows how much he loved us. So, dear friends, we should all love each other.

12 Nobody has ever seen God. But, if we love each other, he really lives in us. And he can love people completely in us. 13 God has given us his Holy Spirit. Because of this, we know that we are united to God. And we know that he is united to us. 14 We have seen that God the Father sent his Son to this world. Jesus saves the people of the world. We tell everybody that this is true. 15 Anyone who tells people that Jesus is the Son of God is united to God. God is also united to that person. 16 And we know well that God loves us. We also trust him to love us all the time. God always shows love. If a person continues to love God and people, he is united to God. And God is united to him.

17 This is how God loves people completely in us. Then, we will be safe on the day when God will judge all people. We can be sure about this. We have remained united to God, as Jesus did. So, we will not be afraid on that day. 18 Any person who knows that God loves him will not be afraid of God. This love causes us not to be afraid. Some people are afraid of God. They think that he will punish them. So, if someone is afraid of God, he is not completely trusting God. He is not completely trusting that God loves him.

19 We are able to love God and people because God first loved us. 20 Think about someone who hates other Christians. That person may say that he loves God. If he says that, he is telling a lie. He does not love the Christian that he can see.

So, he cannot love God that he has not seen. 21 So this is what God has told us to do. He has told us that anyone who loves God should also love other Christians.

Chapter 5

1 Whoever believes that Jesus is the Christ is a child of God. We may love someone who is a father. If we do, we will also love the child of that person. 2 This is how we know that we really love the children of God. We know it when we love God and obey his words. 3 Because, if we really love God, we will obey his words. And, it is not difficult for us to obey his words. 4 This is how we can refuse to live like people of this world. It is by believing in Jesus Christ. 5 Everyone who believes that Jesus is the Son of God can refuse to live like the people of this world. Nobody else can.

6 Jesus Christ is the person who came to this world from God's home. John baptised him in water. When Jesus died, his blood flowed out. He showed that he was human not only by his baptism in water. He showed it also when his blood flowed out. The Holy Spirit shows us that these things are true. He always says what is true. 7 So there are three signs. By these three signs, we know that Jesus was really human. 8 These signs are the Holy Spirit, the water and the blood. These signs all show us the same thing. 9 People tell us about things that they know. And we believe them. God is more important than man. And he has told us about things that he knows. He has told us about his Son. So we should believe his word.

10 Someone will believe that Jesus is the Son of God. Then he really will know that these things are true. But someone may not believe what God has said. So he is saying that God does not tell the truth. God is telling us about his own Son. But, this man still does not believe God. 11 God has given us life that never ends. He has given it by his Son. 12 So if anyone is united to the Son of God, he has this eternal life. But anyone who is not united to the Son of God does not have eternal life.

13 I have written these things to you who believe that Jesus is the Son of God. I wanted you to know that you have eternal life. 14 Also, we can be sure of this. We may ask God for something. Then we can be sure that he hears us. Yes, if we ask for something that he wants us to have, he will never refuse us. We can be sure about this. 15 We know that he hears us when we ask him. So, he will give us whatever we ask. We can be sure about that.

16 One Christian may know that another Christian is sinning. So he should pray to God about it. That person may not be doing something wrong that would cause him to die. Then God will answer your prayer. God will cause that person to live. I am only talking about a person who has done something that will not cause him to die. There is a sin that will cause a person to die. I am not saying that you should pray about that. 17 Any wrong thing that a person does is sin against God. But there are sins which do not cause people to die.

18 We know that no child of God continues to sin. Instead, the Son of God keeps him safe. The Devil cannot do something bad to a child of God. 19 We know that we are God's children. And we know that the Devil rules all those of this world. 20 We also know that the Son of God has come into the world. He gives us understanding so that we know the only true God. We are united to this true God, and to his Son, Jesus Christ. There is no other true God. He is the only person who can give people eternal life. 21 Dear children, be careful not to have anything to do with false gods.

The Truth about Jesus

2 John

About John's second letter

Most students believe that John wrote this letter. He was the apostle John, who also wrote the Gospel of John.

John calls himself a 'Church leader'. He has authority over churches. He was an old man, and he called the Christians 'his dear little children'. He wrote his letters for people to read out in church meetings. He called the churches that he was writing to, 'the lady and her children'. He is warning these churches against false teachers. Teachers like this do not teach the words of Jesus.

Chapter 1

1 I, the Church leader, am writing this letter to you, dear lady. God has chosen you and your children. I really love all of you. I am not the only person who really loves you. Everyone else who knows the true message about God also really loves you. 2 I love all of you because we know this true message. We will always know it. It remains with us forever. 3 As we know this truth and love each other, God will do good things for us. God our Father and his Son Jesus Christ will give us grace. God will be kind to us and he will help us to live in peace.

4 I was very happy to hear about some of your children. They are doing what God wants us to do. They really are doing what God our Father told us to do. 5 And now, dear lady, I will ask you to do something. It is that we should love one another. This is not a new rule. This is a rule that we had from the beginning. 6 We show our love for God when we obey his rules. So, love each other, as he told us from the beginning.

7 I say this because many false teachers are travelling about. They say many wrong things. They say that Jesus Christ did not come to this world as a human baby. If a person says that, he is a liar and an enemy of Christ. 8 So, watch and be careful. Then you will not believe what they teach. If you do, you will lose what you have worked for. Instead, make sure that you receive all that God has promised you. 9 Remember this. Perhaps a person is not happy with what Christ taught. And if he includes his own ideas, he does not have God. Other people continue to believe what Christ taught. Those people are united to both God the Father and his Son. 10 Someone may come to your house who does not teach the same things. Do not receive that person into your house. Do not receive him as a Christian. 11 If you receive a person like that as a Christian, you are helping him to do wrong. You also are doing wrong.

12 I would like to tell you many more things, but I do not want to write them in a letter. Instead, I hope to come and visit you. I want us to be together so that we can talk. Then we will be completely happy. 13 The children of your dear sister whom God has chosen send their love.

A Letter to a Christian Friend

3 John

About John's third letter

Most students believe that John wrote this letter. He was the apostle John, who also wrote the Gospel of John.

John wrote to a person called Gaius. John is sad, because Diotrephes is hurting Christian people. Diotrephes is not welcoming Christians. Also, he is saying bad things about John. He is telling lies. John is warning Gaius not to copy Diotrephes.

Chapter 1

1 I, the Church leader, am writing this letter to you, Gaius. I really love you. 2 My dear friend, I ask God to give you good health. Your spirit is well. I hope that you may do as well in everything. 3 I was very happy when I heard news about you. Some Christians arrived. And they told me that you are living as you should live. I know that you will continue to live like that. 4 It makes me really happy when I hear news like that about my children. I am happy when they are really living properly.

5 My dear friend, you have done many things to help other Christians. You help those who travel about and teach about Jesus Christ. You do this even when they are strangers to you. This shows that you really trust Christ. 6 These people that you helped have told the Christians here about your love. I say to you, 'Continue to help people who are like that.' Give them what they need to travel.

This pleases God. 7 Because these people are travelling about to tell about Jesus Christ. They do not take help from those that are not Christians. 8 So, we Christians ought to receive them. And we should give them what they need. So we will work together with them as they tell people the true message about Christ.

9 I wrote to the Christians in your town. But Diotrephes refuses to read to them what I wrote. He wants to be the only important person among them. 10 So, when I come, I will speak to the Christians there about this. Diotrephes is saying false and bad things about me to other people. He is doing something worse than that. He refuses to receive Christians from other places when you meet together. He will not let them teach the Christians in your town. And, if someone wants to receive those travelling Christians, he does not let them. He even sends away those who want to receive them.

11 My dear friend, do not copy bad people. Instead, you should copy what good people do. The person who does good things is a child of God. But the person who does bad things does not know God.

12 All Christians say that Demetrius is a good person. He really lives as God wants. And this shows that he is a good person. I also tell you that he is a good person. And whatever things I say about anyone are true. You know that.

13 I would like to tell you many more things. But I do not want to write them in a letter. 14 Instead, I hope to come and visit you soon. Then we can talk together.

I pray that God will give you peace. All your Christian friends here say hello to you. Say hello for me to each of my friends there.

Always Believe and Obey Only God's True Message

Jude

About Jude's letter

Verses 3-16 Jude's letter is a message to Christians about false teachers, who were teaching wrong things. Those teachers said that they themselves were Christians. But they were very dangerous, because they were stopping some people from obeying God. God is very angry with false teachers like that, and he will punish them.

Verses 17–23 So Jude tells the Christians that they must be very careful. They must continue to believe the right things that belong to God's true message. They must continue to love God and other people. They must try to help their friends who have believed the wrong things.

We do not know which Christians Jude was writing to. Nor do we know when he wrote his letter. But Jude's message is very important for all Christians at any time.

Chapter 1

False teachers are trying to turn people away from God

1 This letter is from me, Jude. I am Jesus Christ's servant and I am James's brother.

I am writing to you people that God, the Father, loves. God has chosen you to be his own people, and he is keeping you safe for Jesus Christ.

But, in his letter, Jude does not say that he was Jesus' brother. He thought about himself as Jesus' servant. Jesus became his Master. Jude wanted people to obey Jesus. He did not want people to think that he himself was very important.

2 I want you to know more and more how very kind God is to you. I pray that he will cause you to be without trouble inside yourselves more and more. And I want you to know more and more how much God loves you.

3 My friends that I love, I was wanting very much to write to you. I was wanting to write about how God has saved all of us. But instead, now I must write to you about something else. I must ask you very strongly to be like people who fight to keep God's true message safe. You must not let anyone stop you believing it. You must not let anyone stop you obeying it. God has given this true message to his people, and his message will never change.

4 I say this because certain bad men have come among you secretly. Those men do not want to obey God. Instead, they do whatever bad things they want to do. 'God lets us do these things because he is so very kind', they say. So they are trying to change God's true message. And, because they do these things, they are turning away from our only Master and Lord, Jesus Christ. Many years ago, people wrote that God would punish this kind of bad people.

Examples from the Old Testament to show that God punishes bad people

5 I want to tell you again about certain things. You know these facts already, but I want you to remember them. Remember how the Lord brought Israel's people out of the country called Egypt. At that time, he saved them. But later he destroyed all those people who did not believe him. 6 Also, remember the angels who refused to obey God. They took authority that God had not given to them. They left their own proper place in heaven. So God has tied them up for always. He has put them in the dark place below. He will keep them there until that great day when he will decide about everyone. He will decide what should happen to everyone in the world.

7 Also, remember the cities called Sodom and Gomorrah, and the other cities that were near them. The people who lived in those cities were doing bad things also, like those bad angels. They were having sex with people who were not their husbands or their wives. They were wanting very much to have sex in ways that are not right. God is punishing those people. He has put them into the fire that never stops burning. And that shows us what will happen to bad people like them.

8 These people who have come among you are doing the same kind of bad things. Because of their dreams, they do wrong things with their bodies. They refuse God's authority. And they say bad things about the beautiful, good angels. 9 Even Michael, who was one of the most important angels, did not speak bad words like that about the Devil. Many, many years ago, Michael was arguing with the Devil about who should have Moses' body. But Michael did not think that he himself was important enough to speak bad words to the Devil. Instead, Michael said only this: 'The Lord must tell you that you are wrong.' 10 But these men speak bad words against anything that they do not understand. They are like animals that cannot think. They do the things that their nature causes them to do. And those are the things that destroy them.

Three more examples from the Old Testament

11 Very bad things will happen to these false teachers. They have done the same kind of things as Cain did. Also, like Balaam, they wanted money so much that they have rushed to do wrong things. And, like Korah, they have refused to obey God, so God will destroy them.

The false teachers are very dangerous

12 When you Christians meet as friends to eat special meals together, these false teachers meet with you. But they come only because they want to eat and to drink. They do not think about God or about other people. They think about themselves only, and they are not ashamed about that.

They are like dangerous rocks in the sea that a ship must stay away from. They are like clouds that bring no rain. The wind just carries those clouds along. They are like trees that have no fruit, even at the right season for fruit. People pull trees like that out of the ground. So it is like those trees have died twice.

13 Those false teachers are like the water in the sea that moves very much during a storm. That water brings up a lot of dirt to the top of the sea. That dirt is like a picture of all the bad, dirty things that those people do. Those false teachers are like stars that have moved away from their proper places in the sky. So God has prepared a completely black, dark place for them, where they will have to stay always.

14 Enoch belonged to the seventh (number 7) family that was born after Adam. Enoch spoke about people like these false teachers also. He said: 'Look, the Lord will come with thousands and thousands of his completely good angels. 15 He will decide what should happen to all people. He will decide to punish all the bad people who have refused to obey him. He will punish them because of all the bad things that they have done against him. He will punish them because of all the bad words that they have spoken against him.'

16 These people are always saying that they themselves are not happy about things. They are always saying that other people have done things wrong. But they do whatever bad things they want to do. They speak great things about themselves, to show how important they are. But they say good things about other people only when they want something from those people.

Jude tells the Christians what they must do

17 But remember, my friends, what the Lord Jesus Christ's special teachers said before. They spoke about what would happen in future times. 18 They said this to you: 'In the last times, some people will think that God and God's rules are not important. They will say that it is silly to obey God. They will not want to obey him. Instead, they will do whatever bad things they want to do.' 19 It is these people who cause you Christians not to agree with each other. They cause you to belong to separate groups. These people let the things that belong to this world rule them. They do what they want to do. They do not have God's Spirit in them.

20 But you, my friends, have believed the message that comes from God himself. And you must do everything that you can to believe it more and more strongly. You must help each other to believe it. Let God's Spirit lead you when you pray. 21 Always remember that God loves you. So you should love and obey him always. And you should love other people. Love like this while you wait for our Lord Jesus Christ to come. He will cause you to live with him always, because he is so very kind.

22 Some people are not completely sure whether God's message is really true. You must be kind to those people and you must try to help them. 23 Some people are turning away from God and they are doing bad things. If they turn away completely, God will punish them in the fire. So you must try to stop those people. Then you will save them, because you will pull them out of the fire.

There are other people that you must try to help also. They are like people with very dirty clothes, because of all the bad, dirty things that they do. But you must be very careful, so that they do not lead you away from God. You must be careful like someone who will not even touch those people's dirty clothes.

Jude says how great and powerful God is

24 God is able to keep you safe so that you do not go the wrong way. He is able to make you completely good and clean inside yourselves. And so he can bring you near to himself.

You will come near to the beautiful light that shines from him. You will stand in front of God, who is so very great and good. And you will be very, very happy. 25 He is the only God. He saves us by our Lord Jesus Christ. So everyone should thank him always! Everyone should say how very great he is always! He has had all power and authority and he has ruled since time began, until now. And he will have all power and authority always! This is true.

Jesus Wins!

Revelation

About the Book of Revelation

Revelation is the last book in the Bible. It includes many ideas that we can find in other books in the Bible. It tells us about all the future events from John's time, until now, and until the end of this world. Revelation tells us that all Christians will have troubles during their lives on earth. So they will need to be patient and strong. We think that John wrote this book down about AD 95. That was more than 60 years after Jesus Christ lived on this earth. (But some people think that he wrote it before AD 70.)

It is a letter that Jesus told John to write to Christians. At that time, things were very difficult for Christians. The king of Rome ruled many countries and he was causing a lot of trouble for Christians. His soldiers were killing many of them. John was in a prison because he was a Christian. Rome is the capital of the country that we call Italy now.

Jesus appeared to John, as in a dream. Jesus also sent an angel (a being from God's home above the earth) to John. The angel showed John many future events that surprised him. These things made John afraid. Jesus told John to write down what he saw. Jesus wants us to know about things that will happen during the last days of the earth. He wants us to be ready.

John wrote Revelation to 7 churches (groups of Christians). These churches were in a place that people called 'Asia' at that time. This place is the south and west part of the country that we call Turkey now. In Chapters 2 and 3, there are separate messages from Jesus to each of these different churches. These messages tell us what is most important for Christians. We must continue to love and obey Jesus Christ. We must believe him, even when there is trouble.

'Revelation' means 'to show things that people could not see before'. This book describes many strange events. These events are difficult for us to understand. They are like pictures. They show us an idea of what will really happen. But Jesus wants us to think about these pictures. He wants us to understand as much as we can. He wants everyone to know what will happen, not only clever people.

One day God will destroy this earth and this sky. And he will make a new earth and a new sky. He will not let any bad people live there. But before that time, bad trouble will come to the whole world. Christians should be ready for things to be very difficult. Other people may do bad things to them. They will need to be strong. In many countries today, it is not easy to be a Christian.

But Jesus is the Lord and he will return to this earth. He will beat all his enemies in the end. He will make everything right that is wrong. And all those who love him will live with him always. Then nothing will ever hurt them or make them sad again. Revelation tells us to remember all this. It teaches us to wait patiently.

Chapter 1

John's message

1 This book describes the things that God showed to Jesus Christ. He wanted Jesus to show these things to his own servants.

These events must happen soon. Jesus sent his angel to show these things to his servant John.

2 John has told everything that he saw then. These things are a true message from God. Jesus Christ really said these things. 3 God will be good to the person who reads aloud the words of this prophecy. God will also be good to all those people who listen to these words. So, if they obey these words, all these people will be really happy. I, John, have written all that I saw. Those people who hear these words should remember them. These things are very important and they will happen soon.

John writes to the 7 churches

4 I am John, and I am writing to the 7 churches. You live in the country called Asia. I pray that God will continue to be very kind to you. I pray also that he will cause you to be without trouble inside yourselves. God will do these things for you. He is alive now and he has always been alive. And he will come.

The 7 spirits that are in front of God's throne will also do these things for you.

5 And Jesus Christ will also do these things for you. He always says and shows true things. He is the first person who became alive again after death for all time. He rules the rulers on the earth.

Jesus loves us. He bled and died for us. That is how he made us free. We are free from all the bad things that we have done. 6 He has made us belong to his family, who rule as kings. He has made us priests, to be servants of his God and Father. Jesus Christ will always be very great! All authority is his for all time. This is true.

7 Look, he will come on the clouds! Everyone will see him, even those who pierced him. People from all the countries on earth will be sad because of him. Yes, this is true.

But we think that 'those who pierced him' does not include only those soldiers. The leaders of Israel's people and of the Roman government in Israel decided to kill Jesus. And perhaps this verse also includes everyone else who does not want Jesus as their Lord. If they had been alive then, they would have wanted to kill him. All these people will see Jesus when he comes to the earth again. Then they will know that he is the Lord. They will know that they should have obeyed him. So they will be sad. (See also Zechariah 12:10.)

8 'I cause all things to begin and I cause the end of all things', says the Lord God. 'I have all authority. I am alive and I was always alive. And I will come.'

Jesus appears to John

9 I am John, and, like you, I believe Christ. So I am like a brother to you. Jesus is our king. And because we are his people, we are having trouble. So, like you, I need to be strong and patient. I was on Patmos Island because I had taught God's message. I told people what is true about Jesus.

10 On the Lord's Day, God's Spirit caused me to see and to hear things. It was like a dream as the Spirit showed me things. I heard somebody speak behind me. The sound was as loud as a trumpet. 11 The person said: 'Write what you see in a book. You must send the book to the 7 churches in these cities:

> Ephesus
> Smyrna
> Pergamum
> Thyatira
> Sardis

Philadelphia and Laodicea.'

12 I turned round to see who was speaking to me. When I turned, I saw 7 lights in gold lampstands. 13 In the middle of the lights, I saw someone like a man. He was wearing long clothes that reached down to his feet. And he wore a gold belt round the top half of his body. 14 His head and his hair were white like sheep's hair. They were very white, like snow. And his eyes were like fires that were burning. 15 His feet shone like yellow metal that shines brightly in a very hot fire. When he spoke, his voice was like the sound of many rivers. It was like many rivers that were moving very fast. 16 He held 7 stars in his right hand. And there was a sharp sword with two edges coming out of his mouth. His face was like the sun when it shines very brightly.

17 When I saw him, I fell down at his feet like a dead person. Then he put his right hand on me. 'Do not be afraid', he said to me. 'I am first and I am last. 18 I am God who is alive. I died once. But look, I am alive. And I will be alive always. And I have the keys to death and Hades. 19 So write down the things that you have seen. Write about what is happening now. And write about what will happen later.'

20 'You saw 7 stars in my right hand. You saw 7 lights, in gold lampstands. This is what they mean. The 7 stars mean the angels of you 7 churches. And the 7 lights in their lampstands mean you 7 churches.'

Chapter 2

Jesus' message to the believers at Ephesus

1 'Write this to the angel of the church at Ephesus:

This is the message from the one who holds the 7 stars. He holds them in his right hand. He also walks among the 7 lights in gold lampstands.

2 I know everything that you do. You have worked much for me. You have been patient through trouble. I know that you will not let bad men stay among you. Some men among you say that God has sent them to teach you. But he did not send them. You have thought carefully about what they say. And you have discovered that it is not true. 3 You have been patient and strong. You have had trouble because you are my servants. And still you have not become tired of obeying me.

4 But I have something to say against you. You loved me very much when you first believed in me. You do not love me as much now. 5 So remember how much you once loved me. Be sorry about the bad things that you do. Do again the good things that you did at the beginning. Unless you are sorry about the bad things, I will come to you. Then I will take away your lampstand from its place. 6 You hate what the Nicolaitans are doing. It is very good that you hate it. I also hate it.

7 God's Spirit is speaking to you in the churches. You should recognise that the Spirit is speaking. Everybody who recognises that should listen. They should listen to what he says. I will let everyone who wins against Satan eat my fruit. This fruit is from the tree that makes us alive. And this tree grows in God's garden.'

Jesus' message to the believers at Smyrna

8 'Write this to the angel of the church at Smyrna:

This is the message from the one who is first and last. He was dead, and he became alive again.

9 I know that bad people are hurting you very much. I know that you are poor. But really, you are rich. Some people there say that they are Jews. But I know that they say bad things about you. And I know that these things are not true. So they are not really my people, who obey me. They are really a group of Satan's people. 10 I know that trouble will soon come to you. But do not be afraid. Listen! The Devil will cause some of you to go to prison. He wants to see whether you will continue to believe me. And you will have trouble and pain for 10 days. But go on believing, even if you must die. You may have to die because you believe. But if you continue to believe, you can win against the Devil. And then I will give you a gift because you have won. I will cause you to live with me always. I will give you this gift, as they give a crown to a winner.

11 God's Spirit is speaking to you in the churches. You should recognise that the Spirit is speaking. Everybody who recognises that should listen. They should listen to what he says. The second death will not hurt anyone who wins against Satan.'

Jesus' message to the believers at Pergamum

12 'Write this to the angel of the church at Pergamum:

This is the message from the one who has the sharp sword. That sword has two edges.

13 I know where you live. It is the place where Satan sits as king. But still you go on serving me. You remember Antipas. He continued to speak about me. Some people who live in Pergamum killed him because of that. You saw it happen. But you continued to believe me and you told others about me. And you still do this, even there in that place where Satan lives.

14 But I have a few things to say against you. Some people among you do what Balaam taught. He taught Balak to do what was wrong. And Balak caused Israel's people to want to do wrong things. He caused them to eat food that people had given to false gods. And he caused them to have sex with people who were not their husbands or wives. 15 Also, some people among you do the bad things that the Nicolaitans teach. 16 So be sorry and stop doing all these bad things. If you are not sorry, I will come to you quickly. Then I will fight against those bad people with my sword. This sword comes out of my mouth.

17 God's Spirit is speaking to you in the churches. You should recognise that the Spirit is speaking. Everybody who recognises that should listen. They should listen to what he says. I will give my special food to everyone who wins against Satan. I will also give them a white stone. And I will write a new name on that stone. Nobody will know that name except the person who receives it.'

Jesus' message to the believers at Thyatira

18 'Write this to the angel of the church at Thyatira:

This is the message from the Son of God. He has eyes that burn like fires. His feet shine like bright yellow metal.

19 I know everything that you do. I know how much you love me. I know that you go on believing me. I know that you are my servants. I know that you are patient and strong. I know that you do more work now than you did before.

20 But I have something to say against you. You let that woman Jezebel teach you. She says that she speaks God's messages. But she leads my servants the wrong way. God's rules say that someone should have sex only with their wife or their husband. But she teaches my servants to have sex with other people. And she teaches them to eat food that people have given to false gods. 21 I have given her time to be sorry about these bad things. But she refuses to stop having sex with other men. 22 She has done bad things on a bed. So I will hurt her on a bed. I will cause a lot of trouble for those who loved her. They did bad things because of her. They will have very bad trouble unless they are sorry about those bad things. They must stop doing the bad things that she taught them to do. 23 And I will kill those who obey her. Then all the churches will know that I look deep inside people. I know what they really want. I know what they really think. And I will give each person among you what you ought to have. I will give you this because of what you have done.

24 But you other people in Thyatira, you have not done what Jezebel taught. You have not learned what they call 'Satan's deep secrets'. I say something else to you. I will not ask you to do anything that is too difficult. I do not want you to be like people who must carry something heavy. 25 Only be careful that you continue to believe in me. Believe me until I come.

26 Everyone who goes on doing what I say will win. They will win against Satan if they obey me until the end. I will give those people authority to rule all the countries on the earth. 27 They will rule those countries with an iron stick. They will rule like someone who breaks clay pots into pieces. I have received this authority from my Father. 28 I will also give those people the morning star. 29 God's Spirit is speaking to you in the churches. You should recognise that the Spirit is speaking. Everybody who recognises that should listen. They should listen to what he says.'

Chapter 3

Jesus' message to the believers at Sardis

1 'Write this to the angel of the church at Sardis:

This is the message from the one who holds the 7 spirits of God and the 7 stars.

I know everything that you do. I know what people think about you. They think that you are alive. But that is not true, because really you are dead. 2 Wake up! You still do a few things because you believe Christ. Make your lives as believers strong again, because they are ready to die. I have discovered that you have not done everything right. You have not done everything that God wanted. 3 So remember what you have heard. Remember what you have learned. Obey God, and turn away from wrong things. Be sorry for the wrong things that you have done. If you do not wake up, I will come to you. I will come secretly, like someone who robs. So, you will have no idea about what time I will come to you.

4 But you have a few people among you in Sardis who have not done anything bad. They are like people who have kept their clothes clean. They will walk with me and they will wear white clothes. The white clothes show that they are good. 5 Everyone who wins against Satan will wear white clothes. I will never remove their names from God's book. That book says who will live with me always. And I will tell my Father and his angels that those people are mine. 6 God's Spirit is speaking to you in the churches. You should recognise that the Spirit is speaking. Everybody who recognises that should listen. They should listen to what he says.'

Jesus' message to the believers at Philadelphia

7 'Write this to the angel of the church at Philadelphia:

This is the message from the one who is completely good. He is really God. He has David's key that shows his authority. What he opens, nobody can shut. And what he shuts, nobody can open.

8 I know everything that you do. Look, I have opened a door in front of you. Nobody can shut that door. I know that you are not very strong. But you have obeyed what I told you. And you have continued to believe me. 9 Some people there say that they themselves are Jews. But that is not true; they are not really God's people. They are a group of Satan's people. I will cause them to come and to bend down in front of you. Then they will know that I love you. 10 You have done what I told you. So you have continued to be very patient. So, I will keep you safe from the time of trouble that will come. It will come to the whole world. Trouble will come to everyone who lives on the earth. This difficult time will show me what each person will do.

11 I will come quickly. Be careful that you continue to believe me. Then nobody can take away your crown.

12 Everyone who wins against Satan will always remain in God's house. I will make them like the strong part of God's house that holds it up. They will never leave God's house again. I will write on them the name of my God and the name of my God's city. The name of that city is New Jerusalem. It will come down from my God. It will come from his home above the earth. I will also write my new name on those people. 13 God's Spirit is speaking to you in the churches. You should recognise that the Spirit is speaking. Everybody who recognises that should listen. They should listen to what he says.'

Jesus' message to the believers at Laodicea

14 'Write this to the angel of the church at Laodicea:

This is the message from the one whose name is Amen. That name means: 'God's promises and purposes will happen because of him'. He always obeys God. He says and shows only true things. Everything that God has made comes from him.

15 I, Jesus, know everything that you do. I know that you are neither cold nor hot. It would be better if you were either cold or hot. 16 But you are only warm. You are neither cold nor hot. So I am ready to throw you away completely.

17 "I am rich", you say. "I have done well and I do not need anything." But you do not know how very poor you are really! You are like people who cannot see. You are like people who are without clothes. So that really, other people should feel very sorry for you. 18 I tell you that you should buy gold from me. With my gold, you would be really rich. I have made my gold the very best, because it has been through fire. You should also buy white clothes from me to dress yourselves. Then you will not be ashamed because you have no clothes. You should also buy medicine from me to put on your eyes. Then you will see.

19 I explain things to everyone that I love. When they have done wrong things, I punish them. So choose only to obey me. Be sorry for what you have done. 20 Look! I am standing at the door of your house. I am knocking on your door. You can hear what I say. So, if you open the door, I will come in. Then we will eat a meal together.

21 I beat my enemies. Then I sat down with my Father on his throne. I will let everyone who wins against my enemies sit with me. They will sit on my throne with me. 22 God's Spirit is speaking to you in the churches. You should recognise that the Spirit is speaking. Everybody who recognises that should listen. They should listen to what he says.'

Chapter 4

God on his throne

1 After this I looked. And there in front of me was an open door in heaven. As before, I heard someone speak like a trumpet. 'Come up here', he said. 'I will show you what must happen after this.'

2 Immediately the Spirit caused me to see and to hear things. It was like a dream. I saw a throne in heaven, with someone sitting on it. 3 The one who sat there shone with bright red and white light, like beautiful stones. Round the throne there was a rainbow that shone with bright green light. 4 All round the throne there were 24 other thrones. And 24 leaders were sitting on these thrones. They were wearing white clothes and they had gold crowns on their heads. 5 It was like a storm as bright lights and loud noises came out from the throne. There were 7 lights of fire burning brightly in front of the throne. These lights are the 7 spirits of God. 6 Also in front of the throne there was something like a sea of glass. This sea shone with light like a mirror.

In the middle, round the throne, there were 4 other beings that were alive. They had eyes all over them, on their fronts and on their backs. 7 The first of these beings was like a lion and the second being was like a male cow. The next being had a face like a man's face. And the last being was like a big, strong bird called an eagle that was flying. 8 Each being had 6 wings. And they had eyes all over them, even under their wings. All day and all night they never stop saying:

'The Lord God is completely good and clean.

He is separate from everything that is bad. And he has all authority.

He was always alive and he is alive now.

And he will come.'

9 The 4 beings that are alive say how great and powerful God is. They thank God, who sits on the throne. He is alive always. 10 When the 4 beings do this, the 24 leaders bend down to the ground. They bend down in front of God, who sits on the throne. They bend down to worship him. He is alive always. They throw their crowns in front of the throne. And they say:

11 'Our Lord and our God, you are so great and so good!

Everyone should say how great and powerful you are!

Everyone should recognise your authority, because you made all things.

You wanted to make them.

And they are alive and they are here now.

That is only because you made them.'

Chapter 5

The book and the Lamb

1 Then I saw a book. God, who was sitting on the throne, was holding the book. He was holding it in his right hand. He had written inside the book and on the back of it. And he had locked the book with 7 locks. 2 And I saw a strong angel who spoke with a loud voice. 'Who is so good that they can break the locks?' he said. 'Who can open the book?' 3 But nobody in heaven could open the book. Neither could anyone on the earth nor anyone under the earth open it.

4 I wept much because there was nobody. Nobody was so good that they could open the book. So nobody could look inside it. 5 Then one of the leaders spoke to me. 'Do not weep', he said. 'Look! The one who is stronger than everyone else has won the fight.

His name is the Lion from Judah's family group. His name is also the Root of David. He belongs to David's family, but he is greater than David. He can break the 7 locks on the book so that he can open it.'

6 Then I saw a Lamb. He was standing in the middle of the throne. The 4 beings that were alive, and the leaders, were round him. He appeared to be the Lamb that someone had killed. This Lamb had 7 horns and 7 eyes. His eyes are the 7 spirits of God that God has sent into all parts of the world. 7 The Lamb came and took the book. He took it from the right hand of God, who was sitting on the throne. 8 And when he had taken the book, the 4 beings and the 24 leaders worshipped him. They bent down to the ground in front of the Lamb. Each leader had a harp to make music. And they were holding gold cups which were full of incense.
This incense makes a nice smell when it burns. These cups of incense are like a picture of everything that God's people pray to
him. 9 The beings and the leaders sang a new song. This is their song:

'You are so good!

You can take the book and break its locks.

You can do this because they killed you.

That is how you bought people for God with your blood.

You bought them from every family group,

from every language and every country.

10 You have caused them to belong to your family,

the family that rules over everything.

You have made them priests,

priests who are servants of our God.

And they will rule on the earth.'

11 Then I looked again, and I heard the sound of many angels. There were thousands and millions of them, and they were standing round the throne. They stood round the beings that were alive and round the leaders. 12 They sang like this with loud voices:

'The Lamb that they killed is very good!

He is so good that he must receive all authority.

He is rich and strong and he always knows everything.

Everyone must say how great and important he is.

Everyone must thank him!'

13 Then I heard everyone singing. Everything that God has made alive was singing. That included everything in God's home and everything on the earth. It also included everything under the earth and on the sea. They were singing:

'We thank you, who sit on the throne.

And we thank the Lamb.

You must have authority always!

Everyone must always recognise how great you are!

They must recognise how powerful you are!'

14 The 4 beings that were alive spoke then. 'Yes, this is true', they said. And the leaders bent down and they worshipped God and the Lamb.

Chapter 6

The Lamb opens the locks

1 Then I watched while the Lamb opened one of the 7 locks. And I heard one of the 4 beings say: 'Come!' It spoke very loudly. The noise was like a storm. 2 I looked, and there was a white horse. The person who was sitting on the horse was holding a bow. Someone gave him a crown. He had won many wars. Now he rode out to win many more wars.

3 Then the Lamb opened the second lock. And I heard another of the beings say: 'Come!' 4 Then another horse came out. This horse was bright red, like fire. The person who was sitting on the horse had authority. He could bring war on the earth, so that people killed each other. Someone gave him a large sword.

5 Then the Lamb opened the third lock. And I heard the next being say: 'Come!' I looked, and there was a black horse. The person who was sitting on the horse was holding something in his hand. He used it to weigh things. 6 Then I heard a sound like somebody speaking among the 4 beings. 'A litre of wheat is worth one day's work', it said. 'And 3 litres of barley is also worth one day's work. But do not hurt the olive oil and the wine.'

7 Then the Lamb opened the next (fourth) lock. And I heard the last being say: 'Come!' 8 I looked, and there was a grey horse. The name of the person who was sitting on the horse was Death. And Hades, the name of the place for dead people, was following, near to him. They had authority to kill people in a quarter of the earth. They could kill people in wars, or they could cause people to have no food. They could cause people to be very ill so that they died. They could also cause the wild animals on the earth to kill people.

9 Then the Lamb opened the next (fifth) lock. And I saw a special table where people offered gifts to God. I saw the spirits of some dead people under the table. These people had died because they had spoken about Jesus Christ. They had said that God's words are true. Other people had killed them because they had gone on speaking about Jesus. 10 These dead servants of Christ shouted loudly. 'Lord, you have all authority', they shouted. 'You are completely good. You always do what is right. When will you decide to do what is fair to people? You must decide about all the people who live on the earth. How much more time must pass before you decide? When will you punish the people who killed us?'

11 Then each dead servant of Christ received white clothes. And God told them to wait for a short time. They must wait until other servants of Christ have died too. God will still let the people on the earth kill a certain number of his servants.

12 I watched when the Lamb opened the next (sixth) lock. Then the ground moved and everything on the earth moved very much. The sun became black like thick black cloth. The whole moon became red like blood. 13 The stars in the sky fell to the earth. They fell like fruits fall from a tree when a strong wind blows.

14 The sky rolled up and went away. Every mountain and every island moved from its place. 15 Then everyone on the earth hid themselves. They hid in holes in the rocks. They hid among the rocks in the mountains. Even the rulers and the powerful people hid. Even the army rulers, the rich people and other people with authority, they all hid. Also all the other people hid, whether they were slaves or free people.

16 They shouted to the mountains and to the rocks: 'Fall on us. Hide us from God, who sits on the throne. Do not let him see us. Hide us, because the Lamb is very angry with us. 17 The great day has come. And God will show that he is angry. Nobody can do anything to stop him.'

Chapter 7

God marks his people from Israel

1 After this I saw 4 angels who were standing at the 4 corners of the earth. They were stopping the 4 winds of the earth. So, no wind could blow on the earth or on the sea or on any tree. 2 Then I saw another angel who was coming up from the east. He was carrying something to make a mark. It was the mark of the God who is alive. This angel shouted loudly to the 4 angels. They had received authority to destroy the land and the sea. 3 But he shouted to them: 'Do not destroy the land or the sea or the trees yet. Wait until we put a mark on our God's servants. We must put a mark on the front of their heads.'

4 Then I heard how many people received God's mark. The number was 144 000 from all the family groups of Israel's people. 5 There were 12 000 from each family group:

12 000 from Judah's family group
12 000 from Reuben's family group
12 000 from Gad's family group

6 12 000 from Asher's family group
12 000 from Naphtali's family group
12 000 from Manasseh's family group

7 12 000 from Simeon's family group
12 000 from Levi's family group
12 000 from Issachar's family group

8 12 000 from Zebulun's family group
12 000 from Joseph's family group
12 000 from Benjamin's family group

The large crowd who were wearing white clothes

9 After this, I looked, and I saw a very big crowd of people. There were so many people that nobody could count them. They came from every country, from every family group and from every language. They were standing in front of the throne and in front of the Lamb. They were wearing white clothes and they were holding branches of palm trees in their hands.

10 And they shouted loudly:

'It is our God and the Lamb who have saved us.

They saved us from trouble and danger.

Our God sits on the throne.'

11 All the angels were standing round the throne and round the leaders and round the 4 beings. They bent down so that their faces touched the ground in front of the throne. That was how they worshipped God. 12They said:

'This is true!

We want to worship our God.

We want to say how great and powerful he is.

Because he knows everything and we thank him.

He has authority and he will be strong always.

This is true!'

13 Then one of the leaders spoke to me. 'Who are these people in white clothes?' he asked. 'Where did they come from?' 14 'Only you know who they are, sir', I replied. 'They are the people who have come out of the time of bad trouble', he said to me. 'They have washed their clothes and they have made them white in the Lamb's blood.'

15 'That is why they are in front of God's throne. They are in his house all day and all night because they are his servants. And God, who sits on the throne, will live among them. He will keep them safe. 16 They will never again be hungry. They will never be without anything to drink. Neither the sun nor any other strong heat will burn them. 17 The Lamb is in the middle of the throne. He will supply everything that they need. He will lead them to water that comes up from the ground. It is the water that makes people alive. Their eyes were wet because they have cried. But God will make them happy. He will cause their eyes to be dry.'

Chapter 8

The Lamb opens the last lock

1 Then the Lamb opened the last (seventh) lock. And it was completely quiet in heaven for about half an hour. 2 Then I saw the 7 angels who stand in front of God. Someone gave them 7 trumpets.

3 Another angel came then. He stood at the special table where people offered gifts to God. He had a gold cup to burn incense. God gave him a lot of this incense which makes a nice smell. He offered it to God, with the words that all God's people prayed. He offered it all on the special gold table that was in front of the throne. 4 The smoke from the incense went up in front of God when the angel offered it. It went up with what God's people prayed. 5 Then the angel took the cup and he filled it with fire from the special table. He threw the cup down on to the earth. Then there were loud noises and bright lights, like a very bad storm. And everything on the earth moved.

The first 4 trumpets

6 Then the 7 angels who held the 7 trumpets prepared themselves. They were going to make a sound with their trumpets. 7 The first angel made a sound with his trumpet, and then hard rain like stones fell on the earth. It came down with fire and blood. It seemed that God was throwing it down. It burned a third (big part) of the earth. It burned a third of the trees, and all the green grass.

8 The second angel made a sound with his trumpet. Then I saw something like a very big mountain that was burning with fire. It seemed that God threw this mountain into the sea. And a third (big part) of the sea became blood. 9 A third of the animals in the sea died. It destroyed a third of the ships on the sea also.

10 The next (third) angel made a sound with his trumpet. And a very big star, which was burning with a bright light, fell from the sky. It fell on a third (many) of the rivers and on the places where water comes up from the ground. 11 The name of the star means 'It tastes bad'. So a third of the waters became bad. Many people died because they drank that bad water.

12 The next (fourth) angel made a sound with his trumpet. Then a third (big part) of the sun, a third of the moon and a third of the stars became dark. So there was no light for a third of the day and a third of the night.

13 Then I looked, and I saw a big bird called an eagle, with strong wings. It was flying high in the sky. I heard it say with a loud voice: 'Great trouble, great trouble, great trouble is coming to the people who live on the earth. When the other 3 angels make a sound with their trumpets, then very bad things will happen!'

Chapter 9

The next (fifth) trumpet

1 The next (fifth) angel made a sound with his trumpet. Then I saw a star that had fallen from the sky to the earth. Someone gave a key to that star. It was the key to the narrow way that goes into the deep hole. That hole is under the earth and it has no end. 2 The star opened the way into the deep hole. Smoke came up out of the hole, like the smoke from a very big fire. The sun and the sky became dark because of the smoke from the hole.

3 Locusts came out of the smoke and they came down upon the earth. They received authority to cause much pain. They were like scorpions, which are small animals with poison in their tails. 4 Someone told them that they must not do anything bad to the grass on the earth. They must not attack any plant or any tree. They could only attack people who did not have God's mark on the front of their heads. 5 The locusts did not have authority to kill those people. They could only cause them very bad pain for 5 months. The people's pain was like the pain from a scorpion. When a scorpion attacks someone, the poison from its tail can cause very bad pain. 6 During that sad time, people will want to kill themselves. They will want to die because of the pain. But God will not let them die.

7 The locusts were like horses that were ready to fight in a war. They wore what seemed to be gold crowns on their heads. And their faces were like human faces. 8 Their hair was like women's hair and their teeth were like lions' teeth. 9 They had something like large iron plates over the front of their bodies. And their wings made a great noise like many horses that are pulling carts. (The horses run with the carts to fight a war.) 10 They had tails, and they had poison in their tails like scorpions. They had authority to attack people with their tails and to cause them pain for 5 months. 11 The king that ruled them was the angel of the deep hole. His name is Abaddon in the Hebrew language, and Apollyon in the Greek language. (This name means: 'someone that destroys'.)

12 The first great trouble has finished. But there are two other great troubles still to come.

The next (sixth) trumpet

13 The next (sixth) angel made a sound with his trumpet. And I heard someone speak to him from the 4 corners of the special, gold table. (This was the table where they burned incense in front of God.) 14 'There are 4 angels at the great Euphrates river', the voice said. 'They cannot move. But now you must cause them to be free.' 15 God had kept those angels ready for that special time in that day, in that month and in that year. And the 4 angels became free to kill a third of (one out of every three) people everywhere. 16 I heard how many soldiers on horses there were in the army. They said that there were 200 million of them.

17 It was like a dream when I saw those soldiers and horses. They had something like big metal plates over the front of their bodies. These plates were bright red like fire, bright blue, and bright yellow like sulphur. The horses' heads were like lions' heads. And fire, smoke and sulphur came out of their mouths.

18 The fire, smoke and sulphur that came out of the horses' mouths killed people. These three bad things killed a third of (one out of every three) people everywhere. 19 The horses could kill people with their mouths and with their tails. Their tails were like snakes, with heads, and mouths that could bite people.

20 All the people that the fire, smoke and sulphur did not kill were still not sorry. They were not sorry for what they had done wrong. They had made false gods with their own hands. And they did not stop worshipping bad spirits or their false gods. They had made false gods out of gold, out of silver (a white metal) and out of bronze (a yellow metal). They had also made false gods out of stone and out of wood. Their false gods could neither see nor hear. Nor could their false gods walk. 21 The people were not sorry that they had done murders. They were not sorry that they used magic. They continued to have sex with people who were not their husbands or wives. They were not sorry about it at all. And they were not sorry that they robbed other people.

Chapter 10

The strong angel and the little book

1 Then I saw another strong angel who was coming down from heaven. He had a cloud all round him, like clothes. There was a rainbow over his head. His face was like the sun and his legs were like tall fires. 2 He had a little book, which was open, in his hand. He put his right foot on the sea and his left foot on the land. 3 Then he shouted with a loud voice like the sound that a lion makes. When he shouted, the 7 loud noises answered him. They were like the sounds of a storm. 4 When the 7 loud noises spoke, I was ready to write. But I heard someone speak to me from heaven. 'Keep secret what the 7 loud noises have said. Do not write it down', he said.

5 Then I looked again at the angel with one foot on the sea and the other foot on the land. He raised his right hand to heaven. 6 And he promised something by the name of God, who will always be alive. God made heaven and the earth and the sea and everything that is in them. The angel promised that nobody would have to wait any longer. 7 God will finish his secret purposes, just as he told his servants the prophets long ago. He will finish his purposes when the last (seventh) angel with a trumpet is ready. This angel will make a sound with his trumpet too.

8 Then I heard the same person speak to me from heaven again. 'Go to the angel who is standing with one foot on the sea and the other foot on the land', he said. 'Take the book that is open in his hand.' 9 So I went to the angel and I asked him for the little book. 'Take it and eat it', he said to me. 'It will be as sweet as sugar in your mouth. But it will hurt your stomach.' 10 So I took the little book from the angel's hand and I ate it. It was as sweet as sugar in my mouth. But when I had eaten the book, it hurt my stomach. 11 Then someone spoke to me. 'You must tell God's messages to people again', he said. 'You must tell about people from many countries, about people who speak many languages. And you must tell about many kings.'

Chapter 11

God's two witnesses

1 Someone gave me a long stick, like the sticks that people use to measure things. 'Go and measure God's house. And measure the special table where people offer gifts to God', he told me. 'You must count the people who are worshipping there. 2 But you must not include the yard outside God's house. Do not measure that yard, because God has given it to the other people. Those people are not Jews. They come from countries where nobody knows God. They will walk through the whole city where God's people live. They will destroy it for 42 months.

3 And I will give authority to my two witnesses. Then they will tell my messages during those 1260 days. They will wear cloth that people make from animals' hair. These clothes show that they are sad.'

4 These witnesses are the two olive trees and the two lampstands that stand in front of God. They stand in front of the Lord of the earth. 5 If anyone tries to do something bad to them, fire comes out of the witnesses' mouths. And this fire destroys their enemies. The fire will kill everyone who wants to do something bad to these witnesses. 6 These witnesses have authority. They can shut up the sky and then it will not rain. There will be no rain during the time that they tell their messages from God. They also have authority to cause the water on earth to become blood. And they can send many other troubles to the earth as often as they want.

7 When they finish speaking as God's witnesses, a strange animal will fight against them. This strange animal will come up out of the deep hole that has no end. And he will beat the witnesses and he will kill them. 8 Their dead bodies will lie in the street of the powerful city where people killed their Lord. They killed him on a cross. The name of this city might be Sodom or Egypt, because this city is as bad as those places.

9 People from every country, from every family group and from every language will look at the witnesses' dead bodies. The people will look at them for 3½ days. They will refuse to let anyone bury the bodies. 10 The people on the earth will be very happy because the witnesses are dead. They will be happy because these two prophets had caused bad trouble for them. They will send gifts to each other because they are very happy.

11 But after 3½ days, God's Spirit came into those dead bodies. He caused them to become alive again. So they stood up. And the people who saw them were very afraid. 12 Then the witnesses heard someone speak loudly to them from heaven. 'Come up here', he said. So they went up to heaven in a cloud, while their enemies watched them. 13 At the same time the ground moved. It moved so much that one in every ten of the buildings in the city fell down. And because the ground moved, 7000 people died there. Then the other people, who were still alive, were very afraid. And they said that the God of heaven is very great.

14 The second great trouble has finished. But the third great trouble will come soon.

The last (seventh) trumpet

15 The last (seventh) angel with a trumpet made a sound with it. Then there was the sound of loud voices in heaven. They shouted:

'Our Lord and his Christ now have all authority to rule the world!

God will rule always!'

16 The 24 leaders were sitting on their thrones in front of God. And they threw themselves down on their faces and they worshipped God. 17 They said this:

'We thank you, Lord God, because you have begun to rule!

You are alive now and you have always been alive.

You have all the power and you are using your great authority!

18 The countries that do not know you were very angry.

But now you are showing that you are very angry with them.

You will decide what is fair for all the people who have died.

You will give your servants what they ought to have.

Your servants include the prophets and everyone who really believes you.

Some of your servants are strong, important people,

and some are not.

Now you will destroy all those who destroy the earth.'

19 Then they opened God's house in heaven. And I saw God's special covenant box inside it. Then there were the bright lights and loud noises of a storm. The ground moved a lot and much hard rain fell from the sky. It was just like stones falling.

Chapter 12

The woman and the big red snake

1 A great surprise appeared in heaven. I saw a woman who was wearing the sun like clothes. The moon was under her feet and a crown of 12 stars was on her head. 2 She was going to have a baby. And she screamed because the pain hurt her very much.

3 Then another surprise appeared in heaven. It was a very big red animal like a snake. It had 7 heads and 10 horns, and there was a crown on each head. 4 His tail drew a third of the stars out of the sky and threw them down on the earth. Then the big snake stood in front of the woman who was giving birth to the baby. He was waiting to eat her child as soon as it was born. 5 She gave birth to a son, who will rule all the countries with an iron stick. But someone quickly took her child up to God and to his throne. 6 The woman ran away to a country place where nobody lives. God had prepared that place for her. He will feed her and keep her safe there for 1260 days.

7 And there was a war in heaven. Michael and his angels fought against the big snake. And the big snake and his angels fought back.

8 But the big snake and his army did not win. They lost their place in heaven. 9 Michael and his angels threw the big snake out of heaven. They threw him, and all his army of angels, down to the earth. The name of that snake has always been the Devil or Satan. He always says what is not true. So, he causes the whole world to believe what is wrong. 10 Then I heard someone in heaven say loudly:

'Now God has caused his people to be safe and free!

God has shown his authority and power as King.

And his Christ has shown his authority.

They have thrown the Devil out of heaven!

The Devil was the one who spoke against Christ's servants.

And they are like our brothers and sisters.

He continued to say bad things to God about them,

he continued all day and all night.

11 But our brothers and sisters beat him.

Because the Lamb died and his blood came out.

They beat the Devil because they spoke what is true.

They were ready to die.

They refused to stop saying what God has done for them.

12 So be happy, everyone who lives in heaven!

But you who live on the earth and the sea will have bad trouble.

The Devil has come down to you now,

and he is very angry.

He knows that he has only a short time.'

13 The big snake saw that they had thrown him down to the earth. So, he ran after the woman who had given birth to the baby boy. He wanted to cause trouble for her. 14 The woman received two wings, like the wings of a very big bird called an eagle. Then she could fly to her country place where she would be safe from the big snake. God will feed her and keep her safe there for a time, times and half a time.

15 Then the big snake sent water out of his mouth like a river. He was behind the woman. He wanted the water to carry her away. 16 But the ground was a help to the woman, so a big hole opened in the ground. Then the river that had come from the big snake's mouth went down into the hole. 17 The big snake was very angry with the woman. So he went away to fight a war against her other children and grandchildren. They are all the people who obey God's rules. They are the people who go on believing Jesus.

Chapter 13

The strange animal from the sea

1 And the big snake stood on the sea's shore.

Then I saw a strange animal that was coming up out of the sea. The animal had 10 horns and there was a crown on each horn. The animal also had 7 heads, and there was a bad name on each head. Those bad names were not polite to God. 2 The strange animal that I saw was like a leopard. But its feet were like a bear's feet and its mouth was like a lion's mouth. The big red snake made the strange animal king in his place. The snake gave his own power and great authority to the strange animal.

3 Someone had cut one of the strange animal's heads. They had cut the animal so badly that it seemed to have died. But the strange animal had become well again and it was alive. This surprised all the people who were living on the earth. As a result, they thought that the strange animal was very great. They were ready to obey what it said. 4 People worshipped the big snake because he had given his authority to the strange animal. They also worshipped the strange animal. 'Nobody is like the strange animal!' they said. 'Nobody can fight against him!'

5 The strange animal could use its authority for 42 months. It could say how important it was. Also, it could speak very bad words against God. God let it have this authority. 6 So the strange animal began to say many false things about God and about God's name. It spoke bad words about the place where God lives. And it spoke bad words about those who live in heaven. 7 It received authority to fight a war against God's own people. It had authority to beat them. It received authority against people from every family group, from every country and from every language. 8 Not every person who lives on earth has their name in God's book. All those without their names in God's book will worship the strange animal. That book says who will live with God always. It is the Lamb's own book. From the beginning of the world, the Lamb was ready to die and they killed him.

9 Everyone who can understand should listen to these words:

10 Anyone who must go to prison will go to prison.

If anyone kills another person with a sword,

someone will kill him like that too.

This means that God's people must go on being patient and strong. They must go on believing God.

The strange animal from the land

11 Then I saw another strange animal that was coming up out of the land. It had two horns like a lamb's horns, but it spoke like the big snake. 12 It used all the authority of the first strange animal, on that animal's behalf. It caused all the people on earth to worship the first strange animal. Someone had cut the first strange animal so much that it should have died. But it became well again.

13 The second strange animal did great things that surprised people. It even caused fire to come down from heaven to the earth. And everybody who was living on the earth saw the fire. 14 They believed what is not true. They believed because they saw these great things. The second animal had authority to do these things on behalf of the first strange animal. It spoke to the people who were living on the earth. It told them to make a god. They must worship this false god that was like the first strange animal. A sword had cut that animal, but it was alive. 15 The second strange animal received power. So, it caused the false god to seem to be alive. Then the false god could speak. 'Anyone who refuses to worship me must die!' it said.

16 The second strange animal also caused everyone to receive a mark. They put the mark on their right hands or on the front of their heads. They put the mark on the powerful, important people and on the people who were not powerful. They put it on people who were rich or poor, or slaves or free people.

17 Nobody could buy anything unless they had the mark. Nobody without the mark could sell anything. This mark is the first strange animal's name or its number, which means the same as its name.

18 Here is a problem that you must think about carefully. Anyone who is clever should try to understand the strange animal's number. It is a human number. The number is 666.

Chapter 14

The Lamb and the 144 000 people

1 Then I looked again and there was the Lamb. He was standing on Zion mountain and there were 144 000 people with him. Someone had written the Lamb's name and his Father's name on the front of those people's heads.

2 And I heard a sound from heaven like the sound of many rivers that were moving very fast. It was a very loud noise, as in a storm. The sound that I heard was like many people who were making music with harps. 3 The 144 000 people were singing a new song in front of the throne. They sang in front of the 4beings that were alive and in front of the leaders. Nobody could learn this song except these 144 000 people from the earth that God had saved.

4 These people have kept themselves clean in their spirits, like men who have not had sex with bad women. They are like people who have never had sex. These people follow the Lamb everywhere that he goes. They are those that God saved from among all people. They are the first people to offer themselves to God and to the Lamb. 5 These people never said anything that was not true. They have done nothing wrong.

The three angels with messages

6 Then I saw another angel who was flying high in the sky. He brought God's message of good news that is always true. He came to tell this news to everyone on the earth. He was telling it to people from every country, from every family group and from every language. 7 He spoke with a loud voice. 'Serve and obey God', he said. 'You should say how great God is. The time has come for him to decide about everyone on the earth. He will decide what is fair for them. Worship him because he made the heaven and the earth and the sea. He also made all the places where water comes up from the ground.'

8 A second angel followed the first one. 'God has destroyed that powerful city Babylon', he said. 'That city is like a bad woman and God has destroyed her. She caused every country to do the bad things that she did. So, they do things that are against God's rules. She enjoyed doing wrong things very much and all the countries have copied her. They are like people who all drink the same strong wine. They are drunks.'

9 A third angel followed them and he spoke another message with a loud voice. 'If anyone worships the strange animal and its false god, God will be angry', he said. 'If anyone receives that animal's mark on the front of their head or on their hand, God will be angry. 10 God will punish all those people. They will be like people who must drink God's wine. But God's wine cup is full of very strong wine. He has not mixed his wine with any water, because he is very angry. God will cause those people to have very bad pain. Fire and sulphur will burn them. God's angels and the Lamb will watch them while they burn. 11 And the smoke will never stop rising while they burn. Because they worship the strange animal and his false god, they will have no rest. They will have no rest during the day or during the night. Because they received the mark of the strange animal's name, they will always have trouble.'

12 This means that God's people must go on being patient and strong. They must go on obeying God's rules and they must go on believing in Jesus.

13 Then I heard someone else speak from heaven. 'Write this down', he said. 'From this time, the Lord's own people who die will be very happy. Those people really believe the Lord and they obey him', he said. 'Yes', the Spirit answers, 'they will rest from their work. And nobody will forget the good things that they have done.'

The earth's harvest

14 Then I looked, and there was a white cloud. Someone who was like a man was sitting on the cloud. He had a gold crown on his head and a sharp tool in his hand. People use those tools to cut down plants in the fields. They cut down the plants when their seeds are ready. 15 Then another angel came out from God's house. He shouted with a loud voice to the person who was sitting on the cloud. 'Use your sharp tool and start to work. It is time to bring in the harvest. It is time now. You must cut down the plants and bring them in. Your harvest on the earth is ready.'

16 Then the person who sat on the cloud moved his sharp tool over the earth. And he brought in the earth's harvest.

17 Another angel came out from God's house in heaven. He also had a sharp tool in his hand. 18 Yet another angel came from the special table where people offered gifts to God. This angel had authority for the fire on the special table. And he shouted with a loud voice to the angel with the sharp tool. 'Use your sharp tool and cut the grapes from off the earth's grapevine. The grapes are ready for you to bring in.'

A grapevine is a plant that climbs. It has small, sweet fruits that are called grapes.

19 So the angel moved his sharp tool over the earth and he cut the earth's grapes. He threw the grapes into a very big hole where they make wine. God was very angry with the harvest of grapes. 20 The grapes were in the big hole outside the city. The Lord Jesus walked on the grapes. Then blood came out of the hole. The blood rose as high as horses' necks for as far as 300 kilometres.

Chapter 15

The 7 angels with the last troubles

1 Then I saw another great surprise in heaven. I saw 7 angels with 7 troubles. They are the last troubles. And God will stop being angry when they have finished. 2 I saw what seemed to be a glass sea with fire in it. I also saw people who were standing at the edge of the glass sea. Those people had beaten the strange animal and its false god, and the number that means its name. They held harps, to make music. God had given them these harps. 3 And they sang the song of Moses, God's servant, and the Lamb's song. They sang:

'Lord God with all authority,

what you do is great and powerful!

You are King of all countries at all times.

Everything that you do is completely fair and honest.

4 Everyone will serve and obey you, Lord.

They will show how great your name is.

Only you are completely good and clean.

People from every country have seen what you do.

So they will come and worship you.

You always do what is right.'

5 After this I looked and God's house in heaven was open. That house is like God's tent, where he lived among his people Israel. 6 The 7 angels with the 7 troubles came out of God's house. They were wearing clean clothes that were shining. And they had gold belts round the top half of their bodies. 7 Then one of the 4 beings that were alive gave 7 gold cups to the 7 angels. The cups were full because God was very angry. He is the God who will always be alive. 8 And God's house became full of smoke because God is so great and so powerful. Nobody could go into God's house until the 7 troubles finished. The angels were bringing those last 7 troubles.

Chapter 16

The 7 cups with the 7 last troubles

1 Then I heard someone speak to the 7 angels. He was speaking loudly from God's house in heaven. 'Go and pour out your 7 cups on the earth', he said. 'The cups are full because God is very angry.'

2 The first angel went and poured out his cup on the land. Very bad and painful places appeared on people's skins because of what was in the angel's cup. These bad places appeared on everyone who had the strange animal's mark on them. They appeared on everyone who worshipped the animal's false god.

3 The second angel poured out what was in his cup on the sea. So, the sea became like the blood of a dead person. And everything that was alive in the sea died.

4 The next (third) angel poured out what was in his cup on the water. He poured it on the rivers and on the places where water comes up from the ground. And all the water became blood. 5 Then I heard the angel with authority for the waters say to God:

'Lord, you are alive now and you always have been alive.

You are completely good and clean.

You are right in everything that you decide.

6 These people have caused trouble for your people and your prophets.

They caused them to bleed and to die.

So you have given the people blood to drink.

That is what ought to happen to them.'

7 Then I heard someone agree from the special table in front of God. They said:

'Yes, Lord God, you have all authority.

And you decide what is right and fair!'

8 The next (fourth) angel poured out what was in his cup on the sun. And God gave great power to the sun so that it burned people with its fire. 9 The strong heat burned people and it hurt them very much. Then they said very bad things against God, because he caused these troubles. But they refused to be sorry for the bad things that they had done. They refused to stop doing those bad things. They refused to say how great God is.

10 The next (fifth) angel poured out what was in his cup on the strange animal's throne. Everywhere that the strange animal ruled became completely dark. And people even bit their mouths because of their great pain. 11 They shouted bad words against the God of heaven because of their pain and because their skins were hurting them. But they refused to be sorry for the bad things that they had done.

12 The next (sixth) angel poured out what was in his cup on the great Euphrates River. So the river became dry, to prepare a way. It was the way for the kings who come from the east. 13 Then I saw 3 bad spirits like frogs. One bad spirit came out of the big snake's mouth. Another bad spirit came out of the first strange animal's mouth. And the other bad spirit came out of the false prophet's (the second strange animal's) mouth. 14 They are the spirits of demons (bad spirits from the Devil). They also do things that surprise people. They go out to all the rulers in the whole world, to bring them together for the war. That war will happen on the great day of God, who has all authority.

15 The Lord says: 'Listen! I will come secretly, like someone who robs. Everyone who goes on watching for me will be happy. You must keep your clothes with you all the time. Then you will not have to walk about without clothes. So you will not be ashamed in front of other people.'

16 Then the bad spirits brought the rulers together. They came to the place called Armageddon in the Hebrew language.

17 The last (seventh) angel poured out what was in his cup into the air. And someone spoke loudly from the throne in God's house. 'It has finished,' he said. 18 There was a great storm, with bright lights and loud noises, and the ground moved very much. The ground has never moved so much during all the time that people have lived on the earth. 19 The powerful city broke into three parts. When the ground moved, it destroyed all the world's cities. And God did not forget to punish that powerful city Babylon. God was very angry with Babylon. It was like God had a cup of very bad wine. Then he caused that city to drink his wine. The people had to receive all the bad things that God did to them.

20 He made every island go away. There were no more mountains anywhere. 21 Very big stones of ice fell from the sky upon the people. The weight of each stone was about 50 kilos. The stones of ice caused very much trouble. And the people shouted bad words against God because of the trouble that the ice caused for them.

Chapter 17

The woman on the red strange animal

1 One of the 7 angels who had the 7 cups came to me. 'Come with me', he said. 'I will show you how God will punish the powerful bad woman. She sits upon many rivers. She is bad like a woman who sells herself to men for sex. 2 The rulers of countries on earth have done bad things because of that woman also. They are just like men who have sex with bad women. The people who live on the earth have done bad things. They have learned to enjoy what is bad. They have copied that woman's example. They are like drunks from the bad wine that she gave them.'

3 While God's Spirit was causing me to dream, the angel carried me away. He carried me to a country place where nobody lived. There I saw a woman who was sitting on a red strange animal. All over this strange animal, someone had written names that were not polite to God. The animal had 7 heads and 10 horns. 4 The woman was wearing purple and red clothes. She also shone with the gold, valuable stones and pearls that were all over her. She held a gold cup in her hand. The cup was full of the results of the very bad and dirty things that she had done. 5 Someone had written this secret name on the front of her head:

Powerful Babylon

Mother of all the bad women

and mother of everything that is bad on the earth.

6 I saw that the woman was a drunk. She was like someone who had drunk the blood of God's people. She had killed God's people, because they had told other people about Jesus. When I saw her, I was very surprised.

7 Then the angel spoke to me. 'Why does she surprise you?' he said. 'I will explain the secret of the woman to you, and the secret of the strange animal that she rides. The strange animal that you saw has 7 heads and 10 horns. 8 This animal was once alive, but it is not alive now. Soon it will come up out of the deep hole again and God will destroy it completely. This will surprise many people who live on the earth. They know that the animal was alive. And they know that it is not alive now. So, it will really surprise them when it appears again. They are the people whose names are not in God's book. That book says who will live with God always. God wrote people's names down in his book before he made the world.

9 Here is a problem that you need to think about carefully. The animal's 7 heads are like a picture of 7 hills where the woman sits. 10 They are also like a picture of 7 kings. Five of these kings have stopped ruling. They are dead and another king is ruling now. The last king has not yet come. When he does come, he must rule only for a short time. 11 The strange animal is another (eighth) king that belongs to this group of 7 kings. The animal was alive, but it is not alive now. And God will destroy it completely.

12 The 10 horns that you saw are like a picture of 10 kings. They have not yet received anywhere to rule. But they will receive authority as kings for one hour with the strange animal. 13 They all have the same purpose. They will give their authority to the strange animal and they will make him strong. 14 Together they will fight a war against the Lamb. But the Lamb will beat them because he is the most powerful Lord. He is the King who rules over all other kings. And the people who go on believing him will be with him. He has asked them to follow him. He has chosen them.'

15 Then the angel spoke to me again. 'You saw that the bad woman was sitting on many rivers', he said. 'Those rivers are like a picture of many countries and crowds of people from different family groups and languages. 16 The strange animal and the 10 horns that you saw will hate the bad woman. They will destroy her and they will take away her clothes. They will eat the meat on her body. Then they will burn what remains of her with fire. 17 God has given them their thoughts and he has caused them to agree. So, they will do what he wants. They will give all their authority as kings to the strange animal. The animal will continue to rule until everything has happened. Everything that God has said will certainly happen. 18 The woman that you saw is like a picture of the powerful city. That city rules the rulers on the earth.'

Chapter 18

The end of Babylon

1 After these things I saw another angel who was coming down from heaven. He had great authority. The bright light that shone from him made the whole world bright. 2 He shouted with a strong voice:

'It is the end!

It is the end for powerful Babylon!

She has become a place where bad spirits live.

She has become a home for every bad and dirty spirit.

She is a home for every bad bird.

God hates those birds because they are not clean.

3 The people of all countries have done very wrong things because of that city.

They have copied her people, like those who have drunk the same strong wine.

The rulers on the earth did wrong things because of her.

They were like those who have sex with other people.

They forget their husband or their wife.

And the people on earth who buy and sell things have become rich.

They have become rich because she bought so many expensive things from them.'

4 Then I heard God speak from heaven. He said:

'My people, come out of Babylon.

Then you will be separate from all the bad things that the people of that city have done.

Then you will not receive any of their troubles.

5 They have done so many bad things,

so many that they have reached as high as heaven.

And I have not forgotten what they have done wrong.

6 I will give her people what they ought to receive.

I will give it to her people because of the trouble that they have given.

I will punish them twice as badly as the bad things that they have done.

Her people caused trouble, like someone who mixes a bad drink for other people.

I will mix twice as much of a bad drink like that and I will give it to her people.

7 I will give her people as much pain as the pleasure that they gave to themselves.

I will cause her people to be as sad as they caused themselves to be rich and happy.

Her people say to themselves:

"Our city sits here like a queen.

We will never be sad like a woman whose husband has died."

8 But her people's troubles will come all together in one day.

> They will be sad.
>
> They will have no food.
>
> And death will come to them.
>
> Fire will destroy the city,
>
> because I, the Lord God, am strong.
>
> And I decide what is fair for everyone.'

9 The rulers on the earth will weep and they will be sad for the city. They will see the smoke while the city burns. They will cry because they did many bad things there. They enjoyed being rich in the city and forgetting God. 10 They will stand a long way from the city because they will be afraid. They will think that God will punish them too. And they will shout:

> 'It is bad! It is very bad for you!

You are the powerful, strong city that we called Babylon!

> In one hour God has punished you!'

11 The people on the earth who sell things will weep for the city also. They will be sad because nobody will buy their things any more. 12 The things that they sold included:

> Gold and other valuable metals
>
> Valuable stones and pearls
>
> Expensive cloth, including red and purple cloth
>
> Expensive wood
>
> Many different things that people had made out of horns, and out of expensive wood, metals and stone
>
> 13 Different materials that have a nice smell

Wine, olive oil, flour and wheat (the seeds that people make flour from)

> Cows, sheep, horses and carts
>
> Human slaves

14 The people who sold things will weep for the city. 'You have lost all the good things that you wanted so much', they will say. 'You have lost all those expensive and valuable things, and you will never have them again.'

15 The people who sold these things became rich because of the city. They will stand a long way from the city because they will be afraid. They will think that God will punish them too.

So they will weep and be sad. 16 They will shout:

> 'It is bad! It is very bad for you, powerful city!
>
> You wore beautiful purple and red clothes.
>
> You shone with gold, valuable stones and pearls.

17 But in one hour God has destroyed all those things,

> all the things that caused you to be so rich.'

All the people from the sea will stand a long way from the city. They include every ship's captain, everyone who travels on ships, and all the sailors. They also include all other people who get their money because they work at sea.

18 They will see the smoke while the city burns. Then they will shout: 'There was no other city like this powerful city!' 19 They will throw dirt from the ground on their heads because they are so sad. They will weep and they will shout:

> 'It is bad! It is bad for the powerful city!
>
> Everyone who had ships on the sea became rich.
>
> They were rich because she was so rich.
>
> But in one hour God has destroyed her.'

20 You who live in heaven, be happy!

> Be happy because God has destroyed Babylon

Be happy, God's people and his special workers and prophets!

God has punished the city because of what she did to you.

21 Then a strong angel lifted a very big, round stone. People use stones like that to make flour. The angel spoke while he threw the stone into the sea:

> 'God will throw you down, powerful Babylon city.

He will throw you down strongly, as I am throwing down this stone.

> Nobody will ever see you again.

22 Nobody will ever hear music in your streets again.

Nobody will hear the sound of people who are singing.

There will be nobody making music with harps, trumpets and other instruments.

> There will be no workers, nobody doing any work.
>
> Nobody will make flour ever again.
>
> So nobody can hear the sound of the stones that break seeds for the flour.

23 No light from people's homes will ever shine in your streets again.

> Nobody will ever hear the sound of men's and women's voices at their marriages again.
>
> Your people who sold things were the most powerful people on the earth.
>
> You caused all the countries to believe wrong things.
>
> They believed what is false because of your magic.

24 God punished you, Babylon, because he saw the blood of his people in your streets.

> Your people killed God's people and his prophets.

The blood of everyone on earth that other people have killed was in your streets!'

Chapter 19

The crowd in heaven thanks God

1 After these things I heard a sound like a very big crowd in heaven. They were shouting:

> 'How great our God is!
>
> He saves people.
>
> He is really great and powerful.
>
> He has all authority.

2 Everything that he decides is right and fair.

He has decided to punish the city, that powerful bad woman.

She made many people on the earth bad because of the bad things that she did.

She caused people to worship her false gods, like a bad woman who causes people to have sex with her.

God has punished her because she killed his servants.'

3 Then they shouted again:

> 'How great God is!

The smoke from the fire that burns her will continue to go up always.'

4 The 24 leaders and the 4 beings that were alive threw themselves down. And they worshipped God, who was sitting on the throne. They spoke with loud voices. 'It is true!' they said. God is very great!'

The Lamb's marriage

5 Then someone spoke from the throne. They said:

> 'All of you, who are God's servants,
>
> say how great our God is!

All of you who serve God and obey him must thank him.

You must thank him, whether you are powerful people or not.'

6 Again I heard a sound like a very big crowd, and they were shouting. The sound was like the noise of many rivers that were moving very fast. It was like loud noises in a storm. They shouted:

> 'How great God is!
>
> Our Lord God has all authority and he rules!

7 We will be very happy with him.

> We will say how great he is!
>
> The time for the Lamb's marriage has come
>
> and his wife has prepared herself.

8 God has given her bright, clean clothes to wear.'

9 Then the angel spoke to me. He said, 'Write down these words: "The people that God chooses will be very happy! He will ask them to come to the Lamb's special marriage meal." This is a true message from God.'

10 Then I bent down at his feet to worship him. 'You must not do that!' he said to me. 'I am God's servant, the same as you are. I am a servant, like all of you who go on believing Jesus. You are like brothers because you believe him. Worship God! Those who speak for Jesus know what to say because of his Spirit. His Spirit tells them what to say.'

The great king on a white horse

11 Then I saw heaven open, and there was a white horse. Someone was riding the horse. His name was this:

'He Always Obeys God and He is Completely Honest'. He is always right when he decides things. He is always fair. He is right when he fights a war. 12 His eyes burned like fires and many crowns were on his head. He had a name on him, but nobody knows that name except himself. 13 He was wearing clothes with blood all over them. His other name is: 'The Word of God'.

14 The armies in heaven were following him. They were riding white horses and they were wearing clean, white clothes. 15 A sharp sword was coming out of his mouth. He will beat all the countries with this sword. Then he will rule them with an iron stick so that they will obey him. He will punish people like someone who walks on grapes to make wine. This shows that God is very angry. God has all authority, and he will punish people. 16 This king had a name on his clothes and high on his leg. The name is: 'The King who Rules over All Other Kings; the Most Powerful Lord'.

17 Then I saw an angel who was standing in the sun. He shouted loudly to all the birds that were flying high in the sky. 'Come!' he shouted. 'Come together to God's big meal. 18 There you will eat the meat from the dead bodies. They will be the bodies of rulers, captains of armies and strong men. There will be bodies of horses and those who ride them. You can eat all the dead people, whether they are slaves or free people. There will be powerful people and those who are not powerful.'

19 Then I saw the first strange animal and the rulers of the earth and their armies all together. They had come together to fight a war. They fought against the person who rode the horse, and his army. 20 But the person on the horse and his army beat them. He and his army took and held the strange animal and the false prophet. That same false prophet who, on behalf of the strange animal, had done things that surprised people. The false prophet had caused people to believe him. He had told them what is not true. People believed him because of the things that he did. These were the same people who had the strange animal's mark on them. They worshipped his false god. The person on the horse threw the strange animal and the false prophet into the lake alive. It was the lake of fire that burns with sulphur. 21 The person who rode the horse killed all his enemies' armies. He killed them with the sword that came out of his mouth. And all the birds ate the meat from the dead bodies until they were completely full.

Chapter 20

The 1000 years

1 Then I saw an angel who was coming down from heaven. He held the key to the deep hole that has no end. In his hand, he also held a big metal chain. 2-3 He held the big red animal, that same old snake who is called the Devil and Satan. And he tied the snake up with the chain. Then he threw the snake into the deep hole. He closed the door to the deep hole, and he locked it over the snake. The snake must stay in the hole for 1000 years. During that time, he could not continue to work. He could not cause the people everywhere to believe false things. He could not work again until the 1000 years have passed. After that, the snake must be free for a short time.

4 Then I saw some thrones. The people who were sitting on the thrones had received authority. They had authority to decide what is fair. I also saw the spirits of those people who had died for Jesus. People had killed them because they had spoken to other people about Jesus. They had spoken God's messages, so other people had cut off their heads. The people who had died had not worshipped the strange animal nor his false god. They had not received his mark on the front of their heads nor on their hands. They became alive again and they ruled as kings with Christ for 1000 years. 5 This is the first time for this. It is the first time that God caused many people to become alive again. None of the other dead people became alive again until the 1000 years had finished. 6 The people who will become alive again during that first time will be very happy! They are God's own people. The second death has no power over them. They will be priests to serve God and Christ. And they will rule with Christ for 1000 years.

God sends Satan into the lake of fire

7 When the 1000 years have passed, God will let Satan go out of his prison.

8 Satan will go to people in countries all over the world, the countries that they call Gog and Magog. He will make them believe him. He will tell them what is not true. And Satan will bring them together to fight a war. There are very many of his people, as many as the bits of sand on the sea's shore. 9 They went across the whole earth. And they arrived at the city that God loves. Then they stood all-round the place where God's people were living. But fire came down from heaven and it destroyed them. 10 The Devil had caused them to believe him. He had told them what is not true. So God threw the Devil into that same lake of fire and sulphur. It was that same lake where the Lord had already thrown the strange animal and the false prophet. The fire there will cause them a lot of pain and trouble all day and all night. It will never finish.

God decides what is fair for the dead people

11 Then I saw a very big white throne. God was sitting on it. The earth and the sky rushed away from where he was. And I could not see them anymore. 12 Then I saw the dead people. They were standing in front of the throne. All the powerful and important people were there. And all those people who were not powerful were there too. Then someone opened the books. In these books, God had written all the things that the people had done. Then someone opened yet another book where God had written people's names. This book included the names of everyone who will live with God always. Then God decided what was fair for the dead people. He decided because of what they had done.

13 The sea brought up all the dead people who were in it. And death and Hades, that place for dead people, brought up all the dead people who were there. God decided what was fair for each person. He decided because of what they had done. 14 Then God threw death and Hades into that same lake of fire. The lake of fire is the second death. 15 God threw people into the lake of fire if he did not find their names in his book. Only those people with their names in his book will live with God.

Chapter 21

The new heaven and the new earth

1 Then I saw a new heaven and a new earth. The first heaven and the first earth had gone, and the sea was not there anymore. 2 I saw God's city, which is called New Jerusalem. It was coming down out of heaven from God. The city was ready, like a woman who is wearing beautiful clothes for her marriage. She is ready to meet the man that she is going to marry.

3 And then I heard someone speak loudly from the throne. 'Now God's home is with human beings!' he said. 'God will live among them and they will be his people. God himself will be with them and he will be their God. 4 Their eyes were wet because they have cried. But God will make them happy. He will cause their eyes to be dry. Nobody will ever die or be sad again. Nobody will ever cry. Nobody will ever have pain again. Everything bad has gone. Everything that belonged to the old world has gone.'

5 Then God, who was sitting on the throne, spoke. 'I am making everything new!' he said. 'Write this down, because these words are true. Everyone can believe them', he said to me. 6 Then he spoke again. 'It is finished!' he said. 'I am first and I am last. I cause all things to begin and I cause the end of all things. I will give water to everyone who needs to drink. My water comes up, like a stream comes up from the ground. My water causes people to be alive. And nobody will have to pay anything for it. 7 Everyone who goes on obeying Jesus will win the fight. They will receive all these things from me. And I will be their God and they will be my children. 8 But I will punish all the other people. They include:

- People who are not brave

- People who do not believe in Jesus

People who make themselves like very dirty people because they do very bad things

- People who do murders

People who have sex with someone who is not their husband or their wife

- People who do magic

- People who worship false gods

- People who say what is not true

All these people will go into the lake that burns with fire and sulphur. This lake is the second death.'

New Jerusalem city

9 Then one of the 7 angels with the 7 cups that were full of the 7 last troubles came to me. And he said: 'Come with me! I will show you the woman who will be the Lamb's wife.'

10 Then, while God's Spirit was causing me to dream, the angel carried me away. He took me to a very big, high mountain and he showed me God's city, Jerusalem. The city was coming down out of heaven from God. 11 It was shining with the very bright light that comes from God. The city shone like a very valuable stone. It shone with bright light, like a mirror. 12 It had a very big, high wall round it, with 12 gates. 12 angels stood at the gates, one angel at each gate. And someone had written a different name on each gate. They had written the names of the 12 family groups of Israel's people. 13 There were three gates on each side of the city:

- Three gates were on the east side

- Three gates were on the north side

- Three gates were on the south side, and

- Three gates were on the west side.

14 They had built the city's wall on top of 12 very big stones. They had written the name of one of the Lamb's 12 special workers on each big stone.

15 The angel who talked to me had a long gold stick. He used it to measure things. So he could measure the city and its gates and its wall. 16 The city was square. It was as long as it was wide.
The angel measured the city with his stick. It was 12 000 furlongs (2400 kilometres) long. And it was as wide and as high as it was long. 17 He also measured its wall. The wall was 144 cubits (66 metres) high (or thick). People use numbers like these to measure things. And the angel used the same numbers to measure with.

18 The wall was stone that shone with light, like a mirror. And the city was gold, of the very best kind. The light shone through it, as light shines through glass. 19 The big stones that were holding up the city's wall were very valuable stones. These valuable stones were different colours, so they were very beautiful. They were 12 different valuable stones:

- Yellow, brown and green jasper

- Blue sapphire

- Green agate

- Dark green emerald

20 Red onyx

- Dark red carnelian

- Yellow quartz

- Green beryl

- Yellow topaz

- Yellow-green chrysoprase

- Dark blue jacinth

- Blue-red amethyst

21 The 12 gates were 12 pearls. Each gate was from one separate pearl. The city's biggest street was gold, of the very best kind. The light shone through it, as light shines through glass.

22 The Lord God, who has all authority, and the Lamb, are there in the city. Nobody needs to go to a special house to worship them. So I saw no special house for people to worship God in the city. 23 Also, the city does not need either the sun or the moon to shine on it. The very bright light that comes from God gives it light. The Lamb is its light.

24 The people in all the world's countries will live in the city's light. And the earth's rulers will bring all their valuable things into the city. 25 Nobody will ever shut the city's gates because it will always be day. There will be no night there. 26 They will bring beautiful and valuable things into the city from every country. 27 But nothing that is bad or dirty can ever go into the city. Nobody who does what makes people ashamed can go in there. Nobody who says what is not true can go in. Only those people with their names in the Lamb's book can go in there. They will live with God always.

Chapter 22

The river and the tree in the city

1 Then the angel showed me a river that was bright, like a mirror. Its water causes people to be alive. The river started from God's throne, which is the Lamb's throne. 2 It came along the middle of the city's biggest street. The tree, with fruit that causes people to be alive, was growing on each side of the river. This tree has 12 different groups of fruit. It has new fruit every month. The tree's leaves are like medicine that makes people well in every country

3 No bad person, nor anything that God calls bad, will be in the city. But God's throne, which is the Lamb's throne, will be in the city. And God's servants will worship him there. 4 They will see his face, and his name will be on the front of their heads. 5 There will be no more night, so nobody will need a light. They will not need the sun's light, because the Lord God will be their light. And they will always rule as kings.

6 Then the angel spoke to me. 'All these words are true and everyone should believe them', he said. 'The Lord is God and he gives his Spirit to the prophets. He has sent his angel to his servants. The angel showed them what must happen soon.'

Jesus will come soon   Notes:

7 'Listen!' Jesus says. 'I will come quickly. Every person who obeys me will be happy! They must remember everything that this book describes.'

8 I am John. I myself heard and saw all these things. I finished hearing them and seeing them. Then I bent down at the angel's feet to worship him. I wanted to worship the angel because he had shown these things to me. 9 But he stopped me. 'You must not do that!' he said to me. 'I am God's servant, like you and the prophets, who are like your brothers. Yes, I am a servant like everyone who obeys God. God's servants do what this book says. So worship only God!'

10 Then he told me: 'Do not keep the words in this book secret, because these things will happen very soon. 11 Let everybody continue as they choose. Everyone who does wrong things must continue to do wrong things. Everyone who is bad and dirty must continue to be bad and dirty. Everyone who does right things must continue to do right things. Everyone who is God's is clean and good. They must continue to keep clean and to be good.'

12 'Listen! I will come quickly!' Jesus says to us. 'And I will give each person what they ought to have. They will receive this because of what they have done. 13 I am first and I am last. I cause all things to begin and I cause the end of all things. 14 Those people who believe me keep themselves clean. They are like people who always wash their clothes. They will be happy. I will let them eat the fruit from my tree. That fruit causes people to be alive. And I will let them go through the gates into the city. 15 But these people must stay outside the city:

- People who like to do what is bad

- People who do magic

People who have sex with someone who is not their husband or their wife

- People who do murders

- People who worship false gods

  Everyone who enjoys saying what is not true. And everyone who enjoys doing what is not honest.

16 I am Jesus. I have sent my angel to tell you these things. You must tell them to all the people in the churches. I caused David to be alive long ago, and I am David's grandson. I am the bright morning star.'

17 God's Spirit and all God's people tell Jesus: 'Come!' God's people are like a woman who waits to marry Jesus. Everyone who hears them should also say to Jesus: 'Come!' Anyone who needs to drink should come to Jesus. He will give water to anyone who wants it. They will not have to pay anything for it. This water causes people to be alive.

18 I am John, and I say this strongly. I am speaking to everyone who hears the words in this book. If anyone puts more words with the words in this book, God will punish them. The troubles that this book describes will happen to them. 19 And if anyone takes away from the words in this book, God will punish them. He will not let them eat the fruit from his tree. That fruit causes people to be alive. God will not let them live in his city either. This book describes all these things.

20 The person who tells us all these messages is Jesus. 'Yes, I will come quickly', he says. This must happen! Come, Lord Jesus!

21 I pray to the Lord Jesus for all God's people. I pray that he will continue to be very kind to you.

Made in United States
Troutdale, OR
05/22/2024